EUROPEAN REGISTERS
HANDBOOK 2000

Edited by David Partington

CONTENTS:

Cover Photo : A pair of Tiger Moths parked at Wevelgem, Belgium 23.8.99, on their way home from the Moth Club Rally at Woburn. In the background is D-EHHT c/n 85478 and in the foreground PH-CRO c/n 82018 which was reserved as D-ETHC in 7.99 and probably took up the marks in 12.99. (David Partington)

Rear Cover, Top : Scheibe Specht LN-GAD, built by the Jeloy Seilflyklubb in 1957, is now back with its original owners and still airworthy as seen at a vintage glider meeting at Jami, Finland on 21.7.98. (Eino Ritaranta)
Centre : A nice smile for the photographer as French Aerobatic Champion Catherine Maunoury manoeuvers herself into the cockpit of her CAP.232 F-GXCM for an engine run at Chartres-Champhol on 16.8.99. (David Partington)
Lower : Comco-built Ikarus C-42 Cyclone D-MREH seen at the Aero 99 Exhibition at Friedrichshafen in April 1999. (Chris Chatfield)

Published by	:	Air-Britain (Historians) Ltd
Registered Office	:	12, Lonsdale Gardens, Tunbridge Wells, Kent TN1 1PA, England
Sales Department	:	19 Kent Road, Grays, Essex RM17 6DE, England

Further information is available on our website: http://www.air-britain.com

ISBN O-85130-295-5   ISSN 0950-7477

Printed by Bell and Bain Ltd, Glasgow

EUROPEAN REGISTERS HANDBOOK 2000

INTRODUCTION

Welcome to the 2000 edition of European Registers Handbook, the fifteenth issue of this Air-Britain title, once again the largest edition so far.

The information incorporated into the Registers includes everything made available to the Editor by late March 2000, up to and including the contents of the " Air-Britain News" " Overseas Registers" section of April 2000 and with many of the additions scheduled for the May 2000 issue. Thanks to the regular contributors to that monthly publication, we are again able to include details of aircraft operating on permits, of registrations currently reserved, and often of microlight listings which do not appear in official publications. Yet again our efforts to supply complete coverage are frustrated by the lack of any updates to official data available from countries such as Portugal and Spain and thus we are most grateful for accurate reports of new sightings from these areas. Although our policy is generally to include aircraft still officially listed as current, we must point out that the Portuguese, Danish and Swedish registers also carry a lot of long-since expired aircraft which it is generally possible to identify as such in the lists and wherever possible we have noted these. This year we have continued to add a note next to German and French registrations which are Reservations or Permit aircraft and have extended this to other registers where the information is available. We have also continued our policy of cross-checking and standardising type names wherever possible, a task made necessary by the many variations between sources. In continuing to refine the main text we shall, from the 2001 issue, be including the full c/ns of all Cessna types!

In the field of microlights we are still in need of assistance from France and Italy in particular. In France, although we have added a lot more readers' records, we still need to break down the regional bureaucracy which administers the departmental allocations. It is pleasing to note that many more reports are reaching the Editor detailing microlights and even glider tail-codes - every little helps!. In Italy a few minor successes only serve to highlight the fact that we may still be a few thousand registrations short!

The introduction of Data Protection legislation in Germany has restricted some of our input but it is noticeable that other countries have stepped into the freedom of information arena offered by the Internet. A number of countries have clearly decided to abandon the use of the services of organisations such as Bureau Veritas which has again restricted our access to register information. Perhaps we could hope for European legislation making the publication of such official data mandatory, after all a major airline may easily be held to account but what would you be able to do if a microlight hit your house/car/tent/wife, and how would you be able to determine its legal status? In order to ensure the continued accuracy and topicality of this publication, we therefore repeat our request for readers to carefully record any information and sightings, compare them with our listings and pass on any new details or amendments without delay, either to Ian Burnett as Editor of " Overseas Registers" or to the ERH Editor at the address below - or preferably to both! Please send contributions as soon as possible, the updating process is ongoing.

As this Editor's main task has been to work with material provided for use in " Overseas Registers", which is of course pre-processed with a massive input from the incomparable Ian Burnett, I can only really repeat our joint thanks for the continued support of many contributors, without whom our work would be so much poorer. This year these include, in country order, Peter Gerhardt (Germany), José Manuel Santaner Bosch (Spain), Jacques Chillon and Justin Palmer (France), Anton Heumann (Switzerland), Kay Hagby (Norway), Jimmy Richardson (Austria), Eino Ritaranta (Finland), Bob Rongé/ASA (Belgium), Lars Finken, Hans Kofoed and Tavs Aas Mortensen (Denmark), Herman Dekker, Airnieuws and Scramble (Netherlands), Paul Compton, Fredric Lagerquist and Lars Lundin (Sweden), Graham Drabble, Steven and Beata May and Tony Morris (Poland), Robert Swan (Greece and Cyprus), Ole Nikolajsen (Turkey), Dan Willink (Iceland), Vojislav Jereb (Slovenia and Croatia), Barbu Nicolescu (Romania) and Bob Kent (Eastern Europe). In addition thanks are due for first-time, regular or specialist contributions from (alphabetically) John Beacom, Dave Beetham, David Buck, Chris Busby (aardvaark aviation.com), Richard Cawsey, Chris Chatfield, Barry Collman/Airclaims London, Ray Deerness, Phil Dunnington (Cameron Balloons), Paul Hewins, Nigel Hitchman, Pete Hughes, Geoff Jones, Stewart Lanham, Ken Parfitt, Jeremy Parkin, Tony Pither, Dave Richardson, Dominique Roosens, Bob Ruffle, Stephen Simms, Colin Smith, Barry Taylor, Bill Teasdale, Ken Tilley, Barrie Towey, Tony Wheeler, David Wright and the Air-Britain Travel participants. Grateful acknowledgement must also be made to AMCAR and BUCHair Publications and to other Air-Britain annual and periodical publications. To those not named here but who have provided data during the year, our thanks and apologies for omitting your names!

As many readers will know, additions to most of the Registers in this volume are published regularly in the " Overseas Registers" section of " Air-Britain News". Further details of Air-Britain membership and publications may be found at the back of this book, alternatively anyone who is not already a member is invited to write to Barry Collman at 1,Rose Cottages, 179 Penn Road, Hazlemere, Bucks HP15 7NE for additional information.

Any further comments, additions or amendments to this European Registers Handbook will as always be gratefully received by the Editor at the address below or by e-mail to: dave@abarchive.demon.co.uk.

David Partington,
"The Haven"
Nympsfield Road,
Nailsworth,
Gloucestershire GL6 0EA
United Kingdom

April, 2000

IMPORTANT NOTE

The publication of these Registers should not be taken to imply that access to Civil Airfields is always permissable,or that photography of civil aircraft is authorised. Visitors should check these points beforehand as many states do not allow open access to civil airfields.

CS - PORTUGAL

Regn.	Type	C/n	Prev.Id.

No official data has been published for several years. Aircraft still officially on the Register with CofAs which expired at least ten years ago or which are known to have been written-off have been removed. Others with expiry dates since 1990 and thought to be extant, or some earlier expiries which may be candidates for rebuild or restoration are indicated (*)

Regn.	Type	C/n	Prev.Id.
CS-AAQ	Piper J-3C-65 Cub	22021	G-AKBU
	(c/n suspect - 22021 was current as N77531 until 1977)		
CS-ABA(*)	Piper PA-12 Super Cruiser *(For rebuild)*	12-65	
CS-ABK	Piper J-3C-65 Cub	17674	
CS-ABO	Piper PA-25-150 Pawnee	25-646	N10F
CS-ABW	Piper J-3C-65 Cub	17242	
CS-ABY(*)	Piper J-3C-65 Cub *(Stored, Beja)*	17243	
CS-ACC	Piper PA-12 Super Cruiser	12-2907	
CS-ACE(*)	Piper PA-18 Super Cub 95 *(Exp 11.71)*	18-661	
CS-ACF	Piper PA-18A-150 Super Cub	18-5414	
CS-ACH	Piper PA-18 Super Cub 95	18-6863	
CS-ACY	Culver V	348	
CS-ADC(*)	Piper PA-20 Pacer 135 *(Exp 5.74)*	20-503	VP-KMV
			VR-SDU
			F-OAHU
CS-ADF	Cessna 150A	59232	N7132X
CS-ADT	Piper PA-25-150 Pawnee	25-146	
CS-ADU(*)	Piper PA-18A-150 Super Cub *(Exp 7.62)*	18-6715	
CS-ADX	Piper PA-28-180 Cherokee D	28-5389	N7972N
CS-AFF(*)	OGMA/ de Havilland DH.82 Tiger Moth	DHTM.18A	FAP1 ..
	(To Museo do Ar)		
CS-AFG	Beech A23-24 Musketeer Super	MA-350	
CS-AFI	Piper PA-28-180 Cherokee D	28-5463	N2110R
CS-AFP	SEEMS MS.892A Rallye Commodore 150	10503	F-BMVR
CS-AFQ(*)	Piper PA-28-180 Cherokee E *(Stored)*	28-5613	N11C
CS-AFR(*)	CEA Jodel DR.1050 Ambassadeur *(Stored)*	39	F-BJQP
CS-AFU	Piper PA-28R-200 Cherokee Arrow B	28R-35786	N5044S
CS-AGA	Rockwell S.2R-600 Thrush Commander	1484R	N8884Q
CS-AGB(*)	American AA-1 Yankee *(W/o 1988?)*	0377	N6177L
CS-AGI	SOCATA MS.893A Rallye Commodore 180	11782	
CS-AGK	SOCATA MS.894A Minerva 220 *(Stored)*	11833	
CS-AGP	Rockwell Commander 112A	0192	N1192J
CS-AGQ(*)	Rockwell Commander 112A *(Exp 1.82)*	0172	N1172J
CS-AGW	Piper PA-23-250 Aztec E	27-4665	N14054
CS-AGZ	SOCATA MS.894A Minerva 220	11940	
CS-AHC(*)	Reims/Cessna FR.172H Rocket *(W/o 8.96)*	0302	
CS-AHE	Reims/Cessna F.337F Skymaster	0037/01374	
CS-AHG(*)	Grumman G.44 Widgeon *(To Museo do Ar)*	1242	FAP120
CS-AHI	Reims/Cessna F.150L	0759	
CS-AHN	Reims/Cessna F.172H Rocket	0293	
CS-AHO	Rockwell S.2R Thrush Commander	1610R	CR-LNO
			CS-AHO
			N5510X
CS-AHQ	Reims/Cessna FR.172H Rocket	0318	
CS-AHS(*)	Cessna A.188B Agwagon *(Rebuilding)*	00873	N4473Q
CS-AHU	Wassmer WA.52 Europa	43	
CS-AHV	Reims/Cessna FR.172H Rocket	0333	
CS-AHW	Cessna 414	0280	N1565T
CS-AHX	Reims/Cessna FR.172H Rocket	0332	
CS-AIA	Piper PA-18 Super Cub 135	18-1295	CR-AKA
			FAP3206
			51-15295
CS-AIC	Piper PA-28-180 Cherokee C	28-4230	N4874L
CS-AID	SOCATA MS.893A Rallye Commodore 180	10920	
CS-AIG	Alon A-2 Aircoupe	B-280	N5480F
CS-AII	Piper PA-28-180 Cherokee D	28-4436	N5151L
CS-AIJ	SOCATA MS.893A Rallye Commodore 180	11000	F-BNGV
CS-AIP	Piper PA-22-160 Tri-Pacer	22-7615	CR-LEM
			G-ARGF
CS-AIQ	SOCATA MS.893A Rallye Commodore 180	11446	
CS-AIS(*)	Beech A23-24 Musketeer Super *(Exp 9.93)*	MA-106	HB-ENU
CS-AIT	SOCATA MS.880B Rallye Club	1538	
CS-AIW	SOCATA MS.880B Rallye Club	1348	
CS-AIY(*)	SOCATA MS.893A Rallye Commodore 180 *(W/o 1988?)*	11455	
CS-AJA	Wassmer Jodel D.120A Paris-Nice	338	
CS-AJB	SOCATA MS.893A Rallye Commodore 180	12034	

Regn.	Type	C/n	Prev.Id.
CS-AJC	Bellanca 7ECA Citabria	661	
CS-AJD	Cessna 421B Golden Eagle	0270	N3395Q
CS-AJE	Helio H-295 Courier	1404	
CS-AJG	Reims/Cessna FR.172J Rocket	0380	
CS-AJI (*)	Cessna A.188B Agtruck *(Exp 5.89, dism)*	01069T	N21840
CS-AJJ	Cessna 182P Skylane	61398	N21078
CS-AJN(*)	Slingsby T.66 Nipper Mk.III *(For rebuild)*	1620/S.114	
CS-AJS	Rockwell S.2R Thrush Commander	1504R	CR-LNN
			CS-AJS
			N8804Q
CS-AJW	Reims/Cessna FR.172J Rocket	0364	
CS-AJZ(*)	Reims/Cessna F.150L *(W/o by 8.91)*	0907	
CS-AKB	Reims/Cessna F.172H	0465	
CS-AKE	Reims/Cessna F.172H	0575	N14622
CS-AKF	Cessna 172C	49439	N1839Y
CS-AKH	Reims/Cessna F.172F	0153	OE-DLB
CS-AKI	Reims/Cessna F.172H	0504	
CS-AKJ	Cessna P.206 Super Skylane	0183	N2683X
CS-AKM	Cessna 182N Skylane	60359	N92796
CS-AKN(*)	Reims/Cessna F.172H *(W/o 5.96)*	0655	N10655
CS-AKS	Cessna 150B	59582	N1182Y
CS-AKV	Reims/Cessna F.172G	0303	
CS-AKX(*)	Cessna 182M Skylane *(Exp 12.74)*	59880	N91710
CS-AKY	Cessna U.206E Stationair	01678	N9478G
CS-AKZ	Reims/Cessna FR.172G Rocket	0168	D-ECFM
CS-ALA	Piper PA-22-108 Colt	22-9749	
CS-ALB	Paulistinha 56-C1	1162	PP-HME
CS-ALD(*)	Tipsy T.66 Nipper Mk.II *(Exp 2.80)*	41	(OY-ACR)
CS-ALE(*)	Helio H-250 Courier *(Exp 2.78)*	2502	(ET-ABN)
CS-ALF	Piper PA-32-260 Cherokee Six	32-631	N3718W
CS-ALI	Fournier RF-3	72	
CS-ALM	Piper PA-23-160 Apache *(For rebuild?)*	23-1252	N3302P
CS-ALO	Piper PA-28-180 Cherokee B	28-1542	
CS-ALP	Piper PA-22-108 Colt	22-9368	
CS-ALS	Mooney M.20E Super 21	554	
CS-ALT	Piper PA-24-180 Comanche	24-3404	N8197P
CS-ALV(*)	Beagle A.109 Airedale *(W/o 1996)*	B-529	
CS-ALX	Piper PA-32-300 Cherokee Six	32-40154	N4157W
CS-ALZ(*)	Piper PA-32-260 Cherokee Six	32-716	N3758W
	(Exp 12.74, stored .98)		
CS-AMB(*)	Auster D4/108 *(Exp 5.66)*	3603	
CS-AMG(*)	OGMA/Auster D5/160 *(Exp 5.73)*	10	
CS-AMJ(*)	OGMA/Auster D4/108 *(Exp 10.73)*	36	
CS-AMX(*)	OGMA/Auster D5/160 *(Exp 70s)*	81	
CS-AMY(*)	OGMA/Auster D5/160 *(Exp 9.71)*	95	
CS-AMZ	OGMA/Auster D5/160	99	
CS-ANB(*)	OGMA/Auster D5/160 *(Exp 10.82, displayed Faro)*	101	
CS-AND(*)	OGMA/Auster D5/160 *(Exp 12.81)*	108	
CS-ANF	OGMA/Auster D5/160	131	
CS-ANK(*)	OGMA/Auster D5/160 *(Exp 10.73)*	119	
CS-ANP(*)	OGMA/Auster D5/160 *(Exp 3.72)*	124	
CS-ANT(*)	OGMA/Auster D5/160 *(Stored)*	128	
CS-ANV(*)	OGMA/Auster D5/160 *(Exp 2.74)*	130	
CS-AOA(*)	Piper PA-34-200 Seneca *(W/o 9.10.94)*	34-7350126	N15998
CS-AOB(*)	Reims/Cessna FR.172J Rocket *(W/o .93)*	0367	
CS-AOD	Cessna 210L Centurion	59722	N22217
CS-AOE	Reims/Cessna F.150L	0915	
CS-AOJ	Piper PA-32-300 Cherokee Six	32-7340136	N55779
CS-AOO	Piper PA-28-180 Cherokee Challenger	28-7305192	N11C
CS-AOT	Reims/Cessna F.150L	0976	F-BRGV
			(CN-TBD)
CS-APA	Reims/Cessna F.150L	1068	F-BSGQ
			(F-BVBD)
CS-APC	Piper PA-34-200 Seneca	34-7450080	N56539
CS-APG(*)	Cessna 182P Skylane *(W/o 30.5.95)*	62625	N52461
CS-APN	Reims/Cessna F.172M	1158	F-BRGR
CS-APQ(*)	Rockwell S.2R Thrush Commander *(For rebuild)*	1823R	N5623X
CS-APT	Piper PA-28-180 Cherokee Archer	28-7405105	EC-YYT
			N9532N
CS-APU(*)	Piper PA-28-180 Cherokee Archer	28-7405109	EC-YYU
	(Impounded in Morocco)		N9542N
CS-APW	Grumman G.164A Agcat	1247	N9735
CS-APY	Grumman G.164A Agcat	1238	N9757
CS-AQD	Rockwell S.2R Thrush Commander	1865R	CR-AQJ
			N5665X

Regn.	Type	C/n	Prev.Id.
CS-AQH(*)	Dornier Do.27A-3 (W/o 1996)	384	FAP3462 / LC+161 / GA+381
CS-AQI (*)	Dornier Do.27A-3 (To Museo do Ar)	350	FAP3339 / QW+703 / PL+427
CS-AQM(*)	OGMA/DHC-1 Chipmunk T.20 (Stored)	OGMA-4	FAP1314
CS-AQN	Piper PA-18-150 Super Cub	18-7723	FAP ? / 61-2928 ?
CS-AQQ(*)	Piper PA-18 Super Cub 125 (Exp 7.85)	18-2561	FAP ? / 52-6243
CS-AQU	Cessna A.188B Agtruck	0029/03313T	N1978J
CS-AQW(*)	Reims/Cessna F.172N (Exp 4.90)	1914	
CS-AQX	Reims/Cessna F.172N	1903	
CS-AQY(*)	Piper PA-38-112 Tomahawk (W/o 1991)	38-79A0875	N25006 / N9676N
CS-ARA(*)	Aero Commander 100 (Exp 7.90)	084	
CS-ARB	Piper PA-28RT-201T Turbo Arrow IV	28R-8031171	N9602N / N82593
CS-ARC	Reims/Cessna F.152 (W/o 11.1.98)	1790	F-WZIM
CS-ARD	Piper PA-31-325 Navajo	31-7912102	N35379
CS-ARF(*)	Cessna A.188B Agtruck (Exp 12.92)	03512T	N2779J
CS-ARG	Cessna A.188B Agtruck	03531T	N2837J
CS-ARH(*)	Reims/Cessna F.152 (W/o 6.96)	1837	F-WZIY
CS-ARI	Robin HR.100/210 Safari	159	F-BUHV
CS-ARJ (*)	Cessna 402B (Exp 12.93)	0119	PJ-SAA / HP-717 / C9-ANL / CR-ANL / N7869Q
	(The tie-up on the PJ- identities for the three Cessna 402s is not confirmed)		
CS-ARK(*)	SOCATA MS.893A Rallye Commodore 180 (Wfu by 1.86)	11432	CS-AIL
CS-ARL	Cessna 402B	0318	PJ-SAB / HP-693 / C9-AOT / CR-AOT / ZS-IUO / N1559T
CS-ARM(*)	Piper PA-34-220T Seneca III (W/o 24.7.91)	34-8133112	N83934
CS-ARN(*)	Cessna 402B (Exp 7.83. Stored for spares)	0443	PJ-SAC / HP-718 / C9-AON / CR-AON / ZS-IVV / N69333
CS-ARO(*)	Rockwell Commander 680FLP (Exp 11.85, stored)	1651-32	I-ZANU / N4598E
CS-ARP	Cessna R.182 Skylane RG	01652	N6226S
CS-ARQ(*)	Piper PA-36-375 Pawnee Brave (W/o .92)	36-8102023	N6191A
CS-ART	Beech 58 Baron	TH-461	D-IFBF
CS-ARW(*)	Piper PA-36-375 Pawnee Brave (W/o .91)	36-8002001	N3773E
CS-ARY	Piaggio FWP.149D	038	D-ENTL / 90+26 / BF+403 / BF+703
CS-ARZ(*)	Cessna A.152 Aerobat (W/o 7.92)	1032	N758ZH
CS-ASB(*)	Grumman G.164A Agcat (W/o 7.97)	795B	
CS-ASC	PZL M-18A Dromader	1Z018-08	
CS-ASD	PZL M-18A Dromader	1Z018-09	
CS-ASF	Cessna A.188B Agtruck	01920T	G-BETS / SE-GGV / N70431
CS-ASG	Rockwell Commander 690B	11452	N115SB / N210EC / N119SA / (N81734)
CS-ASH	Mooney M.20J Model 201	24-0998	N3974H
CS-ASI	Piper PA-36-375 Pawnee Brave	36-8002031	N2456V
CS-ASJ	Hoffmann H-36 Dimona	36269	
CS-ASK	Piper PA-36-285 Pawnee Brave	36-7660050	N57732
CS-ASM	Grumman G.164B Agcat	811B	
CS-ASN	Grumman G.164B Agcat	812B	
CS-ASO	Cessna 152	82784	OY-CPN / N89553
CS-ASP	Cessna 152	82438	N69019
CS-ASQ	Cessna 152	81019	N48874
CS-ASR	Cessna 152	82999	N46113
CS-AST	Cessna 172N	72060	N6753E
CS-ASU	Cessna 172N	72821	N6470D
CS-ASV(*)	Reims/Cessna F.150L (W/o 1992/3)	0828	PH-CEY
CS-ASW	Piper PA-36-285 Pawnee Brave	36-7660003	N57604
CS-ASX	Reims/Cessna F.150M	1371	PH-BAR
CS-ASZ	Mooney M.20J Model 201	24-0958	G-BHRV / N3839H
CS-ATG	Dassault Falcon 20F	264	F-GJJS / (N86BL) / N773V / N777V / N373KC / N4428F / F-WJMN
CS-AUA	Piper PA-36-285 Pawnee Brave	36-7360027	N56070
CS-AUB	Piper PA-36-285 Pawnee Brave	36-7360045	N56444
CS-AUC	Piper PA-36-375 Pawnee Brave	36-8202001	N2321X
CS-AUD	Reims/Cessna F.172M	0983	D-EGJL
CS-AUE(*)	Piper PA-34-200T Seneca II (Stored)	34-7870101	N2936M
CS-AUF	Cessna TU.206G Turbo Stationair II	03577	D-EHLK(2) / N7240N
CS-AUG	Cessna 150L	74780	N10084
CS-AUH	Cessna 150L	72396	EC-ECY(2) / N6896G
CS-AUI	Cessna 152	83688	N4876B
CS-AUJ	Cessna 152	82656	N89162
CS-AUK	Cessna 152	80376	N24783
CS-AUL	Cessna 207A Skywagon	00367	D-EDOO / N1767U
CS-AUM	Beech F33A Bonanza	CE-763	N24162
CS-AUN	Cessna 152 (W/o)	80040	N757VP
CS-AUO	Cessna A.185F Skywagon	02324	N53028
CS-AUP	Cessna 172C	48845	N8345X
CS-AUR	Cessna 152	83659	N4826B
CS-AUS	Cessna 152	80296	N24507
CS-AUT	Reims/Cessna F.172H	0664	G-AXVX
CS-AUW	Cessna T.210L Turbo Centurion	60642	N1606X
CS-AUX	Reims/Cessna FTB.337G Skymaster (Sold to Spain .98)	0013	FAP-3712 / CS-APM
CS-AUY	Piper PA-28-236 Dakota	28-7911324	N80904
CS-AVA	Cessna 152	83295	G-BOBI / (G-BHJD) / N48172
CS-AVB	Cessna 152	79539	N714YN
CS-AVC	Cessna 152	79621	N757BY
CS-AVD	Cessna 152	79997	N757TS
CS-AVG	Maule MX7-180 Star Rocket	11055C	N61254
CS-AVH	Piper PA-28RT-201 Arrow IV	28R-7918069	G-BORU / N1015S / N9614N
CS-AVI	Reims/Cessna F.150L	0824	G-PAGE / PH-CEU
CS-AVJ (*)	Cessna 172N (W/o .95)	69875	N738CQ
CS-AVK	Mooney M.20J Model 201	24-1384	N5648U
CS-AVL	Beech 76 Duchess	ME-332	N6718D
CS-AVM	Piper PA-31-350 Navajo Chieftain	31-7752159	N503SC / G-BFDB / N27339
CS-AVN	Chincul/Piper PA-36-375 Pawnee Brave	AR36-8002016	
CS-AVO(*)	Chincul/Piper PA-36-375 Pawnee Brave (Stored)	AR36-8002025	
CS-AVP	PZL M-18A Dromader	1Z019-04	SP-FCG
CS-AVQ	PZL M-18A Dromader	1Z019-28	SP-FCA
CS-AVR	PZL M-18A Dromader	1Z019-29	SP-FCB
CS-AVS	Cessna 182J Skylane	57261	N3161F
CS-AVT	Cessna 172M	61830	N12132
CS-AVU	Piper PA-36-300 Pawnee Brave	36-8160009	N3107H / TG-BOM
CS-AVV	Piper PA-38-112 Tomahawk	38-79A0458	N2358K
CS-AYA	Reims/Cessna F.150J	0401	D-EABB
CS-AYC	Cessna R.172K Hawk XP	3056	N758FG
CS-AYG	Reims/Cessna F.152	1573	G-BGHK
CS-AYH	Reims/Cessna F.152	1612	G-BGOF

Regn.	Type	C/n	Prev.Id.
CS-AYI	Cessna T.310R	1408	N4943A
CS-AYJ	Reims/Cessna F.150L	0916	D-ECWL
CS-AYK	Cessna 152	82482	G-BPBH
			N69102
CS-AYL	Piper PA-28-140 Cherokee B	28-26315	N5585U
CS-AYM	Cessna A.152 Aerobat	0995	N761XR
CS-AYN	Cessna A.152 Aerobat	0990	N761VU
CS-AYQ	Partenavia P.68B	204	G-BNXN
			CN-TCD
			HB-LLV
CS-AYR	Cessna 152	81575	G-PACK
			N65477
CS-AYT	Dornier 228-200	8084	VP-FBK
			G-MAFS
			D-ILAB
			(D-CLAB)
CS-AYU	Cessna 152	82355	N68749
CS-AYV	Cessna 172N	73832	N5747J
CS-AYW	Cessna R.172K Hawk XP	3060	N758FL
CS-AYX	Cessna 152	84658	N6296M
CS-AYY	Cessna 501 Citation	0183/567	ZS-KPA
			N6777V
CS-AYZ	Cessna R.172K Hawk XP	3001	N758CZ
CS-AZA	Cessna 152	82210	N68249
CS-AZB	Cessna 152	81900	G-SACA
			G-HOSE
			N67538
CS-AZD	Cessna 172RG Cutlass	0979	G-RGII
			N9702B
CS-AZE	Aerotek Pitts S-2A	2147	N338BD
CS-AZF	SOCATA TB-9 Tampico	1454	F-OHDC
			F-WNGY
CS-AZG	SOCATA TB-9 Tampico	1455	F-OHDD
CS-AZH	SOCATA TB-20 Trinidad	1523	F-OHDE
CS-AZI	Beech F33A Bonanza	CE-312	N9777S
CS-AZJ	Cessna 172N	71535	N3410E
CS-AZK	Mooney M.20J Model 201	24-1525	N57881
CS-AZL	Douglas C-47B	14799/26244	9Q-CGW
			(9Q-CGC)
			ZS-DJZ
			VP-YSO
			ZS-DJZ
			G-AMSR
			KJ952
			43-48983
CS-AZM	OGMA/DHC-1 Chipmunk T.20	OGMA-07	FAP-1317
CS-AZN	OGMA/DHC-1 Chipmunk T.20	OGMA-14	FAP-1324
CS-AZO	OGMA/DHC-1 Chipmunk T.20	OGMA-48	FAP-1358
CS-AZQ	OGMA/DHC-1 Chipmunk T.20	OGMA-13	FAP-1323
CS-AZR	DHC-1 Chipmunk T.20	C1/0351	FAP-1309
CS-AZS	OGMA/DHC-1 Chipmunk T.20	OGMA-55	FAP-1365
CS-AZT	OGMA/DHC-1 Chipmunk T.20	OGMA-63	FAP-1373
CS-AZU	Piper PA-36-375 Pawnee Brave	36-8302015	VH-HSR
			N82678
CS-AZV	Piper PA-32R-301 Saratoga	32R-8013038	G-BHNN
			N3578C
CS-AZW	Cessna 402B	1231	N4185G
CS-AZX	OGMA/DHC-1 Chipmunk T.20	OGMA-24	FAP-1334
CS-AZY	OGMA/DHC-1 Chipmunk T.20	OGMA-40	FAP-1350
CS-DAA	SOCATA TB-9 Tampico	1553	F-OHDJ
CS-DAB	SOCATA TB-9 Tampico	1554	F-OHDK
CS-DAC	OGMA/DHC-1 Chipmunk T.20	OGMA-4	FAP-1353
CS-DAE	DHC-1 Chipmunk T.20	C1/0280	FAP-1304
CS-DAG	Cessna 172RG Cutlass	0003/0009	G-BHEP
			N4668R
CS-DAH(*)	Cessna TP.206A Turbo Skywagon *(W/o 28.5.96)*	0241	G-AYJU
			N176WM
			(N4641F)
CS-DAI	OGMA/DHC-1 Chipmunk T.20	OGMA-30	FAP-1340
CS-DAJ	OGMA/DHC-1 Chipmunk T.20	OGMA-32	FAP-1342
CS-DAK	Cessna 152	84563	N5363M
CS-DAL	Cessna R.172K Hawk XP	3296	N758RH
			V3-HEI
			N758RH
CS-DAM	SOCATA TB-20 Trinidad	1437	F-GLFJ
CS-DAN	Reims/Cessna F.172H	0611	D-EADA
			LX-IPH
CS-DAQ	OGMA/DHC-1 Chipmunk T.20	OGMA-57	FAP-1367
CS-DAS	Cessna 152	81047	N48916
CS-DAT	Cessna 152	83914	N6258B
CS-DAU	Cessna 172P	73917	N7572J
CS-DAV	Cessna 182M Skylane	59745	N71764
CS-DAX	Cessna R.182 Skylane RG	01716	N2885J
			(C-GRAV)
			N4603T
CS-DAY	Aviat Pitts S-2B	5282	
CS-DAZ	Cessna 152	83262	N47883
CS-DBA	Mooney M.20J Model 201	24-3100	G-MASL
			N1012U
CS-DBB	Mooney M.20K Model 252	25-1150	N252AB
			G-BREO
			N252BX
CS-DBC	Cessna 172N	71143	N205JA
			N2072E
CS-DBD	Reims/Cessna FTB.337G Super Skymaster	0032	FAP-3731
			CS-ABR
CS-DBE	SOCATA MS.893A Rallye Commodore 180	10663	F-BODH
CS-DBF	Cessna 172M	61139	N20263
CS-DBG	Piper PA-28-140 Cherokee F *(Stored)*	28-7325436	N55580
CS-DBH	Commander Aircraft 114B	14591	N6015K
CS-DBI	HOAC DV-20 Katana	20016	OE-COM
CS-DBJ	Beech A36 Bonanza	E-2513	N5539D
CS-DBK	Piper PA-28R-200 Cherokee Arrow II	28R-7235205	G-BAAP
			(G-AZYO)
CS-DBL	Piper PA-36-375 Pawnee Brave	36-8202016	EC-EJN
			N2376X
CS-DBM	Cessna 500 Citation	0200	N96EA
			N96G
			N250AA
			N200MW
			N520CC
CS-DBN	Cessna 172N	70051	N738LA
CS-DBO	Britten-Norman BN-2A-20 Islander	352	LN-FSK
			F-OGNV
			N352BN
			C-GCXB
			N24JA
			G-BBJC
CS-DBQ	Cessna 207A Skywagon	00424	N207TJ
CS-DBR	Piper PA-23-250 Aztec D	27-4021	G-BCPF
			N6748Y
CS-DBS	Reims/Cessna F.182Q	0052	D-EOTY
CS-DBU	Piper PA-36-375 Pawnee Brave	36-8302017	N90905
CS-DBV	Reims/Cessna FTB.337G Super Skymaster	0028	FAP-3727
			CS-ABL
CS-DBW	Beech C24R Sierra	MC-660	N6042V
CS-DBY	Short SD.3-30	SH.3030	(5N-OJU)
			G-BGNB
			N330MV
			G-BGNB
			G-14-3030
CS-DBZ	Grumman G.164A Agcat	797	EC-ECP
			G-WOLL
			G-AYTM
			N6555
CS-DCA	Cessna 500 Citation *(Reserved as EC-HFY)*	0157	N190AB
			PH-CTD
CS-DCB	Cessna 421B Golden Eagle	0548	G-OLDE
			G-BBSV
			(N69917)
CS-DCC	Grumman G.164A Agcat	1103	C-FJSH
			N4832
CS-DCD	SOCATA TB-9 Tampico	1127	F-GKUC
CS-DCE	Cessna S550 Citation S/II	0007	N30CX
			TC-SAM
			N573CC
			N51JH
			(N1256P)
CS-DCF	Piper PA-31-350 Chieftain	31-8052174	PH-ECO
			N4501Y

Regn.	Type	C/n	Prev.Id.
CS-DCI	Cessna 550 Citation II	0071	N404BF
			(N404BV)
			N404BF
			C-GDPD
			N4308G
CS-DCK	Dassault Falcon 20E	297	N297AG
			PK-TIR
			N121EU
			(N370EU)
			N4443F
			F-WMKF
CS-DCM	Dassault Falcon 2000	46	F-GMCK
			F-WWMN
			(N220JM)
			N2080
			F-WWMN
CS-DCP	Beech A90-1 King Air (U-21)	LM-22	N7034K
			66-18021
CS-DGA(*)	Douglas C-47A	19503	4X-AOC
	(Preserved as "CS-TDA" at Lisbon)		EI-ACK
			43-15037
CS-DGE	OGMA/Auster D5/180	132	
CS-DGF	OGMA/Auster D5/180	133	
CS-DGG(*)	OGMA/Auster D5/180 (Exp 11.79)	110	
CS-DGH	Beech 95-D55 Baron	TE-684	
CS-DGK	Rockwell Commander 114	14302	
CS-DGL	Beech P35 Bonanza	D-7230	N8605M
CS-DNA	Cessna S550 Citation SII	0032	N232QS
			N532CF
			N532CC
			(N1261A)
CS-DNB	Cessna S550 Citation SII	0051	N251QS
			N1270Y
CS-DNC	Cessna S550 Citation SII	0077	N277QS
			(N747GP)
			N747CP
			(N1273R)
CS-DNF	Cessna 650 Citation VII	7080	N780QS
CS-DNG	Cessna 650 Citation VII	7081	N781QS
CS-DNH	BAe.125-800A	258193/NA0457	N699EC
			N300PM
			N619BA
			G-5-677
CS-DNI	BAe.125-800A (Reservation)	258183/NA0451	N599EC
			N599PC
			N63PM
			N90PM
			N50PM
			N613BA
			G-5-666
CS-DNJ	Hawker 800XP (Reservation)	258399	N899QS
CS-DNK	Hawker 800XP	258430	N31590
CS-DNL	Hawker 800XP	258439	N31596
CS-DNM	Hawker 800XP	258422	N822QS
CS-DNN	Hawker 800XP	258435	N835QS
CS-DPB	Reims/Cessna FTB.337G Super Skymaster	0018	FAP-3717
			CS-AAT

Aircraft sold/delivered to Portugal for which no CS- marks are at present known:

Regn.	Type	C/n	Prev.Id.
CS-...	Air Tractor AT-400	400-0516	SE-IOE
			SU-JAF
			SE-IOE
CS-...	Cessna 172M	63470	N5256R
CS-...	Reims/Cessna FR.172F Rocket	0133	D-ECOR(2)
			F-WLIT
CS-...	Cessna T.210NTurbo Centurion II	63671	N4914C
CS-...	Cessna 650 Citation VII	7093	N793QS
CS-...	Dassault Falcon 900	175	F-WWFN
CS-...	Dornier Do.27H-2	2013	D-EFQK(2)
			HB-HAC
			V 606
CS-...	Piper PA-28-140 Cherokee E	28-7225536	C-FBLD
			CF-BLD
CS-...	Piper PA-36-285 Pawnee Brave	36-7460022	N44118
CS-...	Piper PA-36-285 Pawnee Brave	36-7560076	N9965P

Regn.	Type	C/n	Prev.Id.
CS-...	Piper PA-38-112 Tomahawk	38-79A0987	N8211P
			OE-CPB
CS-GAA(*)	Beagle-Wallis WA.116 Series 1	B.202	G-ARZA
	(Exp 7.93)		XR942
			G-ARZA
CS-GAB	Gyrocopter	unkn	
CS-HAA(*)	SO.1221-S Djinn (Exp 9.67)	1013/FR46	F-BHOU
			F-WHOU
CS-HAC(*)	SO.1221-S Djinn (Exp 6.67)	1044/FR94	F-BJON
CS-HAJ(*)	Bell 47G-2 (H-13E conversion)	738	N6398X
	(Exp 11.92)		CF-NXP
			N6398X
			51-13973
CS-HAM(*)	Bell 47D-1 (Barnes Conversion) (Exp 7.81)	SA2	N74090
CS-HAQ(*)	Bell 47G-2 (Exp 6.82)	2218	N6725D
CS-HAV	Hughes 269C	89-0826	G-HUSH
CS-HAX	Hughes 369D	1129D	D-HJUX
			(YV-542CP)
CS-HAZ	Hughes 269C	1084	SE-HMI
CS-HBL	Hughes 369E	0377E	
CS-HBM	Robinson R-22 Beta	0897	G-RCGI
CS-HBN	Hughes 369E	0333E	N500AH
CS-HBT	Bell UH-1E (204)	6167	N5010J
			BuA154945
CS-HBU(*)	Bell UH-1E (204) (Exp 6.93)	6203	N48SS
			BuA155348
CS-HBV	Bell TH-1L (204)	6426	N540GH
			N540AH
			N434RR
			BuA157831
CS-HCA	Bell 206B Jet Ranger II	2287	ZS-HHD
CS-HCC	Bell 205A-1	30013	F-GINO
			C-FHVX
CS-HCE	Hughes 369D	120-0856D	G-JIMI
			N1109T
CS-HCH	Robinson R-22 Beta	2038	
CS-HCL	Bell 206B Jet Ranger II	2587	N5014L
CS-HCM(*)	Robinson R-22 Beta (Dismantled .96)	2156	
CS-HCO	Agusta-Bell 206B Jet Ranger II	8678	I-BDPL
CS-HCP	Aérospatiale AS.350BA Ecureuil	2551	F-WYMX
CS-HCQ	Robinson R-22M Mariner	2281M	
CS-HCR	Robinson R-22 Beta	2209	N23466
CS-HCY	Aérospatiale AS.350B Ecureuil	1730	G-DSAM
			D-HHGG
CS-HDA	Bell 47G-3B2	6828	N8111J
CS-HDB	Robinson R-44 Astro	0183	
CS-HDD	Hughes 269B	16-0235	G-OHSD
			N9457F
CS-HDH	Bell 205A-1	30121	N25AL
CS-HDJ	Aérospatiale AS.355F1 Ecureuil 2	5092	I-ELDI
			G-BRUY
			N330E
			N330P
			N5788U
CS-HDK	Aérospatiale AS.350BA Ecureuil	1871	D-HHFZ
CS-HDL	Robinson R-22 Beta	1998	G-BUER
CS-HDM	Robinson R-44 Astro	183	
CS-HDO	Agusta-Bell 206B Jet Ranger II	8559	3A-MMM
			I-ELSI
CS-HDP	Aérospatiale AS.355N Ecureuil 2	5570	N888B
			N6097C
CS-HDS	Bell 222	47028	G-META
			N5733H
CS-HDT	Bell 222	47050	G-METC
			G-JAMC
CS-HDU	Bell 222	47055	G-METB
CS-HDV	Agusta-Bell 206B Jet Ranger II	8591	G-BWZB
			F-GCFS
CS-HDW	Robinson R-44 Astro	0359	G-OPHA
CS-HDX	Bell 222	47071	N307CK
			N8114X
CS-HDY	Bell 212	30591	N72383
			JA9518

Regn.	Type	C/n	Prev.Id.
CS-HDZ	Bell 205A-1	30293	C-FFHX
			N2008S
			LN-OTA
			N88HJ
			C-GWEA
			N88HJ
CS-HEA	Bell 205A-1	30091	C-GFHQ
			VH-HLH
			ZK-HUE
			N3009F
			HC-BDG
			N8168J
CS-HEB	Bell 205A-1	30100	C-GFHU
			EC-FZA
			EC-672
			C-GFHU
			VH-NST
			PK-HBU
CS-HEC	Aérospatiale AS.350BA Ecureuil	2245	EC-FGD
CS-HED	Aérospatiale AS.350B2 Ecureuil	2669	D-HJOE
			HB-XZY
			D-HWPL
CS-HEE	Aérospatiale AS.355F1 Ecureuil 2	5006	F-W . . .
CS-HEF	Robinson R-22B2 Beta	2802	
CS-HEG	Robinson R-22B2 Beta	2822	
CS-HEH	Robinson R-44 Clipper	0435	G-BXUN
CS-HEJ	Bell 212	30684	EC-GHO
			EC-FYC
			VH-NSU
			G-BOOY
			OY-HMA
			LN-OSQ
CS-HEK	Bell 206B Jet Ranger II	2914	N6280J
			(C- . . . .)
			N1078Q
CS-HEL	Aérospatiale AS.350B2 Ecureuil	2594	D-HEPB
			VH-HRK
			ZK-HLZ
CS-HFS	Aérospatiale AS.350B2 Ecureuil	2371	D-HFSB
CS-H . .	Bell 205A-1	30038	C-GFHC
			N70HJ
			C-GFHC
			VH-HHC
			C-GFHC
			VH-HHC
			C-GFHC
			VH-HHC
			C-GFHC
			PK-HBK
CS-H . .	Bell 206B Jet Ranger II	2800	N27785
CS-H . .	Bell 206B Jet Ranger II	2914	N6280J
CS-H . .	Robinson R-22 Beta	1932	G-BXMR
			N923FM
			N2306E
CS-H . .	Robinson R-44 Astro	0448	G-BXXM
CS-HM . }	These series were previously used for aircraft and helicopters registered in the		
CS-M . . }	Portuguese territory of Macau which reverted to Chinese rule on 19.12.99. All air-		
	craft should now have been re-registered in the B-M . . series and have therefore		
	been removed from this Register,		
CS-TEB	Lockheed L-1011 Tristar 500	1240	V2-LEO
			CS-TEB
CS-TEH	Airbus A.310-304	483	F-WWCS
CS-TEI	Airbus A.310-304	495	F-WWCO
CS-TEJ	Airbus A.310-304	494	F-WWCM
CS-TEW	Airbus A.310-304	541	F-WWCR
CS-TEX	Airbus A.310-304	565	F-WWCC
CS-TFC	Beech 58 Baron	TH-524	N8130R
CS-TGF(*)	Dornier 228-202 (Exp 11.93. Stored)	8159	D-COBE(2)
			D-CBDN(2)
CS-TGG	Dornier 228-202	8160	D-CORA(4)
			D-CBDQ(2)

Regn.	Type	C/n	Prev.Id.
CS-TGH(*)	Dornier 228-202 (Exp 11.93. Stored)	8152	D-CAOT(3)
			D-CBDO(3)
			TC-FBX
			D-CBDC(2)
CS-TGL	BAe. ATP	2019	G-BRTG
			G-11-19
CS-TGN	BAe. ATP	2031	G-11-31
CS-TGO	Dornier 228-202	8119	D-CMUC
			D-CIMC(2)
CS-TGP	Boeing 737-3Q8	24131	OO-LTX
			EC-FFC
			EC-592
			EC-EII
			EC-159
CS-TGQ	Boeing 737-36N	28570	
CS-TGR	Boeing 737-3Y0	24902	9V-TRB
CS-TGU	Airbus A.310-304	571	F-GJKQ
			TU-TAC
			F-WWYM
			F-GHYM
CS-TIB	Boeing 737-382	24365	
CS-TIG	Boeing 737-3K9	24213	
CS-TIH	Boeing 737-3K9	24214	
CS-TIK	Boeing 737-382	25161	
CS-TIN	Boeing 737-33A	23827	9H-ACS
			(LN-NOR)
			CS-TKD
			LN-NOR
			G-BNXW
			LN-NOR
			G-BNXW
			(LN-NOR)
CS-TIO	Boeing 737-33A	23830	9H-ACT
			(LN-NOS)
			CS-TKC
			LN-NOS
			G-BRXJ
			LN-NOS
			N5573K
CS-TMH	Short SD.3-60 Variant 100	SH.3694	G-BMNJ
			N694PC
			G-BMNJ
			G-14-3694
CS-TMJ	Dassault Falcon 50	190	I-CAFE
			F-WWHG
CS-TMK	Dassault Falcon 900	66	F-GJPM
			F-WWFE
CS-TML	Convair CV-440-54	484	N357SA
			N4402
CS-TMM	Convair CV-580	375	C-FHEN
			OO-EED
			N533SA
			N5828
CS-TMN	Short SD.3-60 Variant 100	SH.3638	G-ISLE
			G-BLEG
CS-TNA	Airbus A.320-211	0185	F-WWDB
CS-TNB	Airbus A.320-211	0191	F-WWDH
CS-TNC	Airbus A.320-211	0234	(N493GX)
			F-WWDF
CS-TND	Airbus A.320-211	0235	(N494GX)
			F-WWDM
CS-TNE	Airbus A.320-211	0395	F-WWBJ
CS-TNF	Airbus A.320-211	0407	F-WWDH
CS-TNG	Airbus A.320-214	0945	F-WWIX
CS-TNH	Airbus A.320-214	0960	F-WWBH
CS-TNI	Airbus A.320-214	0982	F-WWDF
CS-TOA	Airbus A.340-312	041	F-WWJB
CS-TOB	Airbus A.340-312	044	F-WWJN
CS-TOC	Airbus A.340-312	079	F-WWJS
CS-TOD	Airbus A.340-312	091	F-WWJA
CS-TPA	Fokker F.28-0100	11257	(N208BN)
			PH-LMF
			PH-EZA
CS-TPB	Fokker F.28-0100	11262	PH-EZE
CS-TPC	Fokker F.28-0100	11287	PH-LML

8

Regn.	Type	C/n	Prev.Id.
CS-TPD	Fokker F.28-0100	11317	PH-LNA
			PH-EZU
CS-TPE	Fokker F.28-0100	11342	PH-LNJ
CS-TPF	Fokker F.28-0100	11258	PH-FZD
			TR-LCR
			PH-EZD
CS-TPG	Embraer EMB-145	145-014	
CS-TPH	Embraer EMB-145	145-017	
CS-TPI	Embraer EMB-145	145-031	
CS-TPJ	Embraer EMB-145	145-037	
CS-TPL	Embraer EMB-145	145-051	
CS-TP .	Fokker F.28-0100	11341	PH-LNH
	(Reservation)		XA-RKM
			PH-LNH
			(N423PA)
			(N217BN)
CS-TTA	Airbus A.319-114	750	D-AVYO
CS-TTB	Airbus A.319-114	755	D-AVYJ
CS-TTC	Airbus A.319-114	763	D-AVYS
CS-TTE	Airbus A.319-111	821	D-AVYN
CS-TTF	Airbus A.319-111	837	D-AVYL
CS-TTG	Airbus A.319-111	906	D-AVYN
CS-TTH	Airbus A.319-111	917	D-AVYJ
CS-TTI	Airbus A.319-111	933	D-AVYP
CS-TTJ	Airbus A.319-111	979	D-AVYM
CS-TTM	Airbus A.319-111	1106	D-AVWR
CS-TTN	Airbus A.319-111	1120	D-AVYI
CS-TTO	Airbus A.319-111	1127	D-AVYH
CS-TTP	Airbus A.319-111	1165	D-AVWW
CS-...	Lockheed C-130A Hercules	3207	N207GM
	(Cancelled in USA 5.98 on sale to Portugal)		EL-AJM
			N22FV
			(HK-3017X)
			(N2267B)
			A97-207
			57-0500
CS-...	Lockheed C-130A Hercules	3216	N216CR
	(Cancelled in USA 5.98 on sale to Portugal)		N15FV
			(HK-3017X)
			(N2268W)
			A97-216
			57-0509
CS-XAA(*)	Evans VP-1 Volksplane *(Exp 4.87)*	V-1766	
CS-XAB	Taylor JT.1 Monoplane	ASVP/JT1/1/P	
CS-XAC	Aero Designs Pulsar XP	292	
CS-XAD	Ultravia Pelican PL	503	
CS-XAF	Rans S-10 Sakota	0194169	
CS-XAG	Zenair CH-601HDS Zodiac	unkn	
CS-X ..	Rand-Robinson KR-2	PFA/129-11068	G-BSKR
CS-XHA	Rotorway Exec 162F	unkn	N14897
CS-XHB	Rotorway Exec 162F	unkn	

BALLOONS

Regn.	Type	C/n	Prev.Id.
CS-BAB(*)	Cameron O-105 HAFB *(Exp 3.90)*	1963	
CS-BAC(*)	Cameron N-65 HAFB *(Exp 5.92)*	1284	LX-HII
CS-BAE	Colt 90A HAFB	2355	
CS-BAF	Colt 90A HAFB	2522	
CS-BAG	UltraMagic M-77 HAFB	77/108	
CS-BAH	Cameron N-77 HAFB	1491	LX-ISP
CS-BAI	Cameron N-65 HAFB	unkn	
CS-BAJ	Cameron C-80 HAFB	3834	
CS-BAK	Cameron N-77 HAFB	3841	
CS-BAL	UltraMagic M-105 HAFB	105/...	
CS-BAM	Cameron V-90 HAFB	unkn	
CS-BAN	Cameron C-80 HAFB	3966	
CS-BAO	Sky 77 HAFB	57	
CS-BAP	Sky Propane Cylinder SS HAFB	64	
CS-BAQ	Sky 65 HAFB	63	
CS-BAS	Cameron N-90 HAFB	4144	
CS-BAW	Cameron C-80 Concept HAFB	4414	
CS-BAY	Cameron N-77 HAFB	4356	
CS-BAZ	Cameron N-105 HAFB	4414	
CS-BBA	Cameron N-105 HAFB	4549	
CS-B ..	Lindstrand LBL-210A HAFB	068	G-BVXZ

GLIDERS AND MOTOR-GLIDERS

Regn.	Type	C/n	Prev.Id.
CS-PAD(*)	DFS 108-30 Kranich II *(Stored)*	983	
CS-PAF(*)	DFS Weihe A-3 *(Exp.)*	244	
CS-PAI(*)	Slingsby T-21B Sedbergh *(Stored)*	551	BGA619
CS-PAM(*)	EoN Baby 1 *(Exp 3.79)*	EON/B/035	
CS-PAO(*)	EoN Baby 1 *(Stored)*	EON/B/034	
CS-PAP(*)	Grunau Baby III *(Exp 9.81)*	31-53	
CS-PAQ	Schleicher Rhönlerche II	381	
CS-PAR(*)	Schleicher Rhönlerche II *(Exp 4.82)*	382	
CS-PAS(*)	Schleicher Rhönlerche II *(Stored)*	802	
CS-PAV(*)	Schleicher Rhönlerche II *(Exp 9.80)*	820	
CS-PAW(*)	LET L-13 Blanik *(Exp 4.80)*	173207	
CS-PAZ	SZD-22C Mucha Standard	F-770	
CS-PBA	Schleicher Rhönlerche II	3087	
CS-PBB(*)	Scheibe Bergfalke II *(Exp 12.86)*	341	
CS-PBC(*)	Schleicher Rhönlerche II *(Exp 5.89)*	3084/Br	
CS-PBD	LET L-13 Blanik	173350	
CS-PBE	Siebert SIE-3	3010	
CS-PBG	Scheibe SF-27M-A	6327	CS-AXC
			D-KHOE
CS-PBH	Grob G.103A Twin II Acro	3733-K-48	D-6188
CS-PBJ	"LAK-13" *(Type unknown: LAK-12 or L-13?)*	unkn	
CS-PBN	PZL PW-5 Smyk	17.09.021	
CS-PBR	PZL PW-5 Smyk	17.11.020	
CS-PBS	PZL PW-5 Smyk	17.12.004	SP-3640
CS-PBT	PZL PW-5 Smyk	17.12.009	SP-3645?
CS-PBY	LET L-13 Blanik	173220	
CS-PRP	LET L-13 Blanik	174222	DOSAAF
CS-P ..	LET L-13A Blanik	827421	OK-2730

MICROLIGHTS

Regn.	Type	C/n
CS-UAA	Eipper Quicksilver MX-II HP	1265
CS-UAB	Eipper Quicksilver MX-II HP	1266
CS-UAC	Cosmos Bidulm 53	B0032
CS-UAD	Eipper Quicksilver MXL-II	1267
CS-UAE	Eipper Quicksilver MX Sprint II	131
CS-UAF	Eipper Quicksilver MXL-II	1291
CS-UAH	Eipper Quicksilver MXL-II	1349
CS-UAI	Eipper Quicksilver GT-400	1343
CS-UAJ	Eipper Quicksilver MXL-II	1697
CS-UAK	Whittaker MW-5K Sorcerer	5K-0010-02
CS-UAL	Whittaker MW-5K Sorcerer	5K-0013-02
CS-UAO	Ferrari Tucano	0065
CS-UAP	Eipper Quicksilver GTS-400	1287
CS-UAQ	Alferrari Cormorano	1197
CS-UAT	Eipper Quicksilver MXL-II	1157
CS-UAU	Eipper Quicksilver MXL-II Sport	165
CS-UAW	Eipper Quicksilver MXL-II	1517
CS-UAX	Eipper Quicksilver MXL-II	1452
CS-UAY	Whittaker MW-5	5K-0016-02
CS-UAZ	Cosmos Hermes 15	B432
CS-UBA	Eipper Quicksilver MXL-II	191
CS-UBB	Type unknown	unkn
CS-UBF	Denney Kitfox	unkn
CS-UBG	Weedhopper JC-31 Premier AX3	0112856
CS-UBH	Weedhopper JC-31 Premier AX3	0112855
CS-UBI	Cobra AJS-2000	R644988
CS-UBJ	Eipper Quicksilver MX Sprint II	041

Regn.	Type	C/n	Prev.Id.
CS-UBK	Eipper Quicksilver GTS-500	0030	
CS-UBL	Eipper Quicksilver MXL-II	189	
CS-UBU	Eipper Quicksilver MXL-II Sport	190	
CS-UBV	Eipper Quicksilver GT-500	0094	
CS-UBW	Poari I	1	
CS-UBX	Eipper Quicksilver GTS-400	1242	
CS-UBY	Cosmos Turbo 6	675	
CS-UCA	Weedhopper AX3-503D	B1112965	
CS-UCB	Weedhopper AX-2	B1102953	
CS-UCC	Weedhopper JC-24S	1101149	
CS-UCD	Air Création Safari GT BI/SX16	91-252	
CS-UCE	Air Création Safari GT BI/SX16	unkn	
CS-UCF	Air Création Safari GT BI 503	8-91-282	
CS-UCG	Air Création Safari GT BI 503	8-91-288	
CS-UCI	Eipper Quicksilver MXL-II Sport	82	
CS-UCJ	Eipper Quicksilver MXL-II Sport	255	
CS-UCK	Eipper Quicksilver MXL-II Sport	165	
CS-UCL	Eipper Quicksilver MXL-II Sport	867	
CS-UCM	Air Création Safari GT BI 503/1	10-91-325	
CS-UCN	Air Création Safari GT BI 503/1	91-285	
CS-UCO	Air Création Safari GT BI 503/1	8-91-328	
CS-UCQ	Eipper Quicksilver GT-500	unkn	
CS-UCR	Cosmos Chronos	B-650	
CS-UCS	Cosmos Bidulm 53	unkn	
CS-UCT	Cosmos Bidulm 53	unkn	
CS-UCV	Cosmos Turbo 163	B-522	
CS-UCX	Weedhopper Europa II	302	
CS-UCY	Tango II GT Turbo 163	39142	
CS-UCZ	Ferrari Tucano	0055	
CS-UDA	Weedhopper Premier AX3	B1112965	
CS-UDB	Weedhopper AX2-503	B1112962	
CS-UDC	Weedhopper AX2-503	B1112963	
CS-UDD	Weedhopper AX2	B1112964	
CS-UDE	Cosmos Chronos 14	B-731	
CS-UDF	Cosmos Chronos	B-730	
CS-UDG	Cosmos Chronos 16	B-725	
CS-UDJ	Kolb Twin Star Mk.II	TS-III	
CS-UDK	Weedhopper AX-3	B2043007	
CS-UDL	Weedhopper AX-3	B2033000	
CS-UDM	Weedhopper JC-31 Premier AX3	B2032999	
CS-UDN	Rans S-4 Coyote 1	91162	
CS-UDO	Ferrari Tucano	199	
CS-UDR	Cosmos Chronos 14	B-784	
CS-UDS	Cosmos Chronos	7794	
CS-UDT	Cosmos Chronos	780	
CS-UDU	Cosmos Chronos 16	781	
CS-UDV	Cosmos Chronos 16	774	
CS-UDW	Epervier UL-582	6	
CS-UDX	Eipper Quicksilver MXL-II	unkn	
CS-UDY	Weedhopper AX-3	B2083504	
CS-UDZ	Daxiwings Falcon XP B2	01	
CS-UEB	Weedhopper AX-2	B3013091	
CS-UEC	Weedhopper AX-3	B3023092	
CS-UED	Air Création GT BI Q18	04-92-105	
CS-UEE	Air Création GT BI Q18	03-02-95	
CS-UEG	Air Création Safari GT-BI/SX-16	10 92-264	
CS-UEH	Eipper Quicksilver MXL-II Sport	342	
CS-UEJ	Comco Ikarus Fox-C22	9211-3479	
CS-UEL	Volero Volero	V4924	
CS-UEM	Eipper Quicksilver GT-500	207	
CS-UEN	Falcon B1	SMO 16	
CS-UEO	Eipper Quicksilver GT-500	200	
CS-UEP	Dynali Chickinox Kot Kot	2992-P4	
CS-UEQ	Dynali Chickinox Kot Kot	2992-P5	
CS-UES	Eipper Quicksilver MXL-II Sport	340	
CS-UET	Comco Ikarus Fox-C22	4100-5177	
CS-UEV	Eipper Quicksilver MXL-II Sport	384	
CS-UEW	Cosmos Hermes 16	B-670	
CS-UEZ	Eipper Quicksilver MXL-II Sport	303	
CS-UFA	Eipper Quicksilver MXL-II Sport	297	
CS-UFB	Quad City Challenger II	CH2-1092-894	
CS-UFC	Comco Ikarus Fox-C22	9306-3524	
CS-UFD	Comco Ikarus Fox-C22	4170-9983	
CS-UFE	Sunrise II	1	D-MXCL
CS-UFF	Synairgie Pelican 21	000125D	
CS-UFG	Cosmos Chronos	B-769	
CS-UFH	Tango II GT	7861	
CS-UFI	Synairgie Pelican 21	01	
CS-UFJ	Jose Figueira Probe I 43	CA-001E	
CS-UFK	Eipper Quicksilver MXL-II Sport	488	
CS-UFL	Eipper Quicksilver MXL-II Sport	489	
CS-UFM	Ferrari Tucano	0242	
CS-UFN	A.L.A. JF 91	35	
CS-UFO	Falcon DXW	3	
CS-UFP	Comco Ikarus Fox-C22	9311-3553	
CS-UFQ	Comco Ikarus Fox-C22	9311-3554	
CS-UFR	Eipper Quicksilver GT-500	232	
CS-UFS	Eipper Quicksilver GT-500	231	
CS-UFT	Ferrari ATAS-21	258	I- . . . .
CS-UFU	Rans S-6ES Coyote II	0792330	
CS-UFV	Cosmos Chronos 16	21012	
CS-UFW	Cosmos Chronos 16	unkn	
CS-UFX	Cosmos Chronos 16	865	
CS-UFY	Cosmos Chronos 16	21020	
CS-UFZ	Rans S-6ES Coyote II	0792331	
CS-UGA	Rans S-6ES Coyote II	0293448	
CS-UGB	Rans S-6ES Coyote II	0593501	
CS-UGC	Rans S-6ES Coyote II	0493479	
CS-UGD	Weedhopper AX-3	C3113178	
CS-UGE	Eipper Quicksilver MXL-II	527	
CS-UGF	Rans S-6ES Coyote II	0493478	
CS-UGG	Tecnam P.92 Echo	2	
CS-UGH	Albatros AE-209	54	
CS-UGI	Chickinox Kot-Kot	4091-P3	
CS-UGJ	Chickinox Kot-Kot	4692-P10	
CS-UGK	Chickinox Kot-Kot	4692-P15	
CS-UGL	Weedhopper AX-3	12595	
CS-UGM	Rans S-6ES Coyote II	0593506	
CS-UGN	Murphy Maverick	072M	
CS-UGO	Comco Ikarus Fox-C22	9408-31618	
CS-UGP	Skycraft AJS-2000	9040	
CS-UGQ	Chickinox Kot-Kot	4692-P12	
CS-UGR	Rans S-6ES Coyote II	0494608	
CS-UGS	Ferrari Tucano	P305	
CS-UGT	Rans S-6ES Coyote II	0195721	
CS-UGU	Eipper Quicksilver MXL-II	1351	
CS-UGV	Rans S-6ES Coyote II	0493476	
CS-UGW	SMAN Pétrel	11	
CS-UGX	Pegasus Quantum 15	6943	
CS-UGY	Tecnam P.92 Echo	98	
CS-UGZ	Rans S-6XL Coyote II	0195727	
CS-UHA	Air Création GT-BI/SX	3984635	
CS-UHB	Tecnam P.92 Echo	unkn	
CS-UHC	Tecnam P.92 Echo	unkn	
CS-UHE	Tecnam P.92 Echo	unkn	
CS-UHI	Rans S-6ES Coyote II	unkn	
CS-UHN	Rans S-6 Coyote II	unkn	
CS-UHO	Rans S-12XL Airaile	unkn	
CS-UHP	Rabs S-6ES Coyote II	unkn	
CS-UHT	Ikarus Fox C-22 floatplane	unkn	
CS-UIF	Jabiru SK	unkn	
CS-UIG	Jabiru SK	unkn	
CS-UII	Rans S-12 Airaile	unkn	
CS-U..	Light Aero Avid Flyer	329	G-BRNS
CS-U..	Light Aero Avid Flyer	908/PFA/189-12023	G-BTMS
CS-U . .	Dragon Fly	unkn	I-2692
CS-U..	Melvin Denney Kitfox II	615	N90EV
CS-U..	Solar Wings Pegasus XL-R	SW-WA-1551	G-MYCH

D - GERMANY

Regn.	Type	C/n	Prev.Id.
CLASS A : Aircraft of over 20 metric tonnes (20,000 kgs)			
D-AAAC	Fokker F.27 Friendship 500	10448	HB-ITY
			D-AAAC
			HB-ITY
			PH-JLN
			F-BSUN
			(PH-FPY)
D-AAAF	Fokker F.27 Friendship 500	10449	PH-JLN
			F-BSUO
D-AACI	Airbus A.319-115 (Reservation 10.99)	1157	
D-ABAB(2)	Boeing 737-4K5	24769	N11AB
D-ABAC(3)	Boeing 737-86J (Reservation 8.99)	30501	
D-ABAH(2)	Boeing 737-46J	27826	
D-ABAI	Boeing 737-46J	28038	
D-ABAK(3)	Boeing 737-46J	28271	
D-ABAL	Boeing 737-46J	28334	
D-ABAM(3)	Boeing 737-46J	28867	
D-ABAN(3)	Boeing 737-86J	28068	N35153
D-ABAO	Boeing 737-86J	28069	N5573B
D-ABAP(2)	Boeing 737-86J	28070	
D-ABAQ(2)	Boeing 737-86J	28071	
D-ABAR(2)	Boeing 737-86J	28072	N1786B
D-ABAS(4)	Boeing 737-86J	28073	N1795B
D-ABAT(2)	Boeing 737-46J	29120	N1786B
D-ABAU	Boeing 737-46J	29121	N1786B
D-ABAV(2)	Boeing 737-86J (Reservation 8.99)	30498	N1787B
D-ABAW(2)	Boeing 737-86J (Reservation 8.99)	30062	
D-ABAX(2)	Boeing 737-86J (Reservation 8.99)	30063	
D-ABAY(2)	Boeing 737-86J (Reservation 8.99)	30499	
D-ABAZ(2)	Boeing 737-86J (Reservation 8.99)	30500	
D-ABEA(2)	Boeing 737-330	24565	
D-ABEB(3)	Boeing 737-330	25148	
D-ABEC(2)	Boeing 737-330	25149	
D-ABED(2)	Boeing 737-330	25215	
D-ABEE	Boeing 737-330	25216	
D-ABEF(3)	Boeing 737-330	25217	
D-ABEH(2)	Boeing 737-330	25242	
D-ABEI(2)	Boeing 737-330	25359	(D-ABJK)
D-ABEK(2)	Boeing 737-330	25414	(D-ABJL)
D-ABEL(3)	Boeing 737-330	25415	(D-ABJM)
D-ABEM(2)	Boeing 737-330	25416	(D-ABJN)
D-ABEN(2)	Boeing 737-330	26428	(D-ABJP)
D-ABEO(2)	Boeing 737-330	26429	(D-ABJR)
D-ABEP(2)	Boeing 737-330	26430	(D-ABJS)
D-ABER(2)	Boeing 737-330	26431	(D-ABJT)
D-ABES(2)	Boeing 737-330	26432	(D-ABJU)
D-ABET(2)	Boeing 737-330	27903	(D-ABKM)
D-ABEU(2)	Boeing 737-330	27904	(D-ABKN)
D-ABEW(2)	Boeing 737-330	27905	(D-ABKP)
D-ABIA(2)	Boeing 737-530	24815	N3521N
D-ABIB(2)	Boeing 737-530	24816	
D-ABIC(2)	Boeing 737-530	24817	
D-ABID(2)	Boeing 737-530	24818	
D-ABIE(2)	Boeing 737-530	24819	
D-ABIF(2)	Boeing 737-530	24820	
D-ABIH(2)	Boeing 737-530	24821	
D-ABII(2)	Boeing 737-530	24822	
D-ABIK(2)	Boeing 737-530	24823	
D-ABIL(2)	Boeing 737-530	24824	
D-ABIM(2)	Boeing 737-530	24937	
D-ABIN(2)	Boeing 737-530	24938	
D-ABIO(2)	Boeing 737-530	24939	
D-ABIP(2)	Boeing 737-530	24940	
D-ABIR(3)	Boeing 737-530	24941	
D-ABIS(2)	Boeing 737-530	24942	
D-ABIT(2)	Boeing 737-530	24943	
D-ABIU(2)	Boeing 737-530	24944	
D-ABIW(2)	Boeing 737-530	24945	
D-ABIX(2)	Boeing 737-530	24946	
D-ABIY(2)	Boeing 737-530	25243	
D-ABIZ(2)	Boeing 737-530	25244	
D-ABJA	Boeing 737-530	25270	
D-ABJB	Boeing 737-530	25271	
D-ABJC	Boeing 737-530	25272	
D-ABJD	Boeing 737-530	25309	
D-ABJE	Boeing 737-530	25310	
D-ABJF	Boeing 737-530	25311	
D-ABJH	Boeing 737-530	25357	
D-ABJI	Boeing 737-530	25358	
D-ABKD	Boeing 737-430 (Reservation 10.99)	27003	9H-ADO
			EI-COK
			D-ABKD
D-ABNB	Boeing 757-230	24738	
D-ABNC	Boeing 757-230	24747	
D-ABND	Boeing 757-230	24748	
D-ABNE	Boeing 757-230	24749	N35153
D-ABNF	Boeing 757-230	25140	
D-ABNH	Boeing 757-230	25436	
D-ABNI(2)	Boeing 757-230	25437	
D-ABNK	Boeing 757-230	25438	
D-ABNL	Boeing 757-230	25439	
D-ABNM	Boeing 757-230	25440	
D-ABNN	Boeing 757-230	25441	
D-ABNO	Boeing 757-230	25901	
D-ABNP	Boeing 757-230	26433	
D-ABNR	Boeing 757-230	26434	
D-ABNS	Boeing 757-230	26435	
D-ABNT(2)	Boeing 757-230	26436	N1790B
			N3502P
D-ABOA	Boeing 757-330	29016	N757X
D-ABOB(2)	Boeing 757-330	29017	N6067B
D-ABOC(2)	Boeing 757-330	29015	N6069B
D-ABOE	Boeing 757-330	29012	N1012N
D-ABOF(2)	Boeing 757-330	29013	
D-ABOG(2)	Boeing 757-330	29014	N1786B
D-ABOH(2)	Boeing 757-330	30030	N1787B
D-ABOI	Boeing 757-330 (Reservation 4.99)	29018	N1002R
D-ABOJ	Boeing 757-330 (Reservation 4.99)	29019	
D-ABOK(2)	Boeing 757-330 (Reservation 4.99)	29020	
D-ABOL(2)	Boeing 757-330 (Reservation 4.99)	29021	
D-ABOM(2)	Boeing 757-330 (Reservation 4.99)	29022	
D-ABON(2)	Boeing 757-300 (Reservation 4.99)	29023	
D-ABTA	Boeing 747-430	24285	
D-ABTB	Boeing 747-430	24286	
D-ABTC	Boeing 747-430	24287	
D-ABTD	Boeing 747-430	24715	
D-ABTE	Boeing 747-430	24966	N6046P
D-ABTF	Boeing 747-430	24967	
D-ABTH	Boeing 747-430	25047	
D-ABUA(2)	Boeing 767-330ER	26991	
D-ABUB(2)	Boeing 767-330ER	26987	
D-ABUC(2)	Boeing 767-330ER	26992	
D-ABUD(2)	Boeing 767-330ER	26983	
D-ABUE(2)	Boeing 767-330ER	26984	N1788B
D-ABUF(2)	Boeing 767-330ER	26985	
D-ABUH(2)	Boeing 767-330ER	26986	
D-ABUI(2)	Boeing 767-330ER	26988	
D-ABVA	Boeing 747-430	23816	N6055X
D-ABVB	Boeing 747-430	23817	N5573S
D-ABVC	Boeing 747-430	24288	
D-ABVD	Boeing 747-430	24740	N60668
D-ABVE	Boeing 747-430	24741	
D-ABVF	Boeing 747-430	24761	N6018N
D-ABVG	Boeing 747-430 (Reservation)	29872	
D-ABVH	Boeing 747-430	25045	
D-ABVK	Boeing 747-430	25046	N6009F
D-ABVL	Boeing 747-430	26425	N60659
D-ABVM(2)	Boeing 747-430	29101	(V8-AC2)
D-ABVN	Boeing 747-430	26427	
D-ABVO	Boeing 747-430	28086	
D-ABVP	Boeing 747-430	28284	
D-ABVR	Boeing 747-430	28285	
D-ABVS	Boeing 747-430	28286	
D-ABVT	Boeing 747-430	28287	
D-ABVU	Boeing 747-430	29492	
D-ABVW	Boeing 747-430	29493	

Regn.	Type	C/n	Prev.Id.
D-ABVX	Boeing 747-430 (Reservation)	29868	
D-ABVY	Boeing 747-430 (Reservation)	29869	
D-ABVZ	Boeing 747-430 (Reservation)	29870	
D-ABWC	Boeing 737-330	23835	
D-ABWD	Boeing 737-330	23836	
D-ABWE	Boeing 737-330	23837	
D-ABWF	Boeing 737-330	24284	
D-ABXA	Boeing 737-330	23522	
D-ABXB	Boeing 737-330	23523	
D-ABXC	Boeing 737-330	23524	
D-ABXD	Boeing 737-330	23525	TF-ABL D-ABXD
D-ABXE	Boeing 737-330	23526	
D-ABXF	Boeing 737-330	23527	
D-ABXH	Boeing 737-330	23528	
D-ABXI	Boeing 737-330	23529	
D-ABXK	Boeing 737-330	23530	
D-ABXL	Boeing 737-330	23531	
D-ABXM	Boeing 737-330	23871	
D-ABXN	Boeing 737-330	23872	
D-ABXO	Boeing 737-330	23873	
D-ABXP	Boeing 737-330	23874	
D-ABXR	Boeing 737-330	23875	
D-ABXS	Boeing 737-330	24280	
D-ABXT	Boeing 737-330	24281	
D-ABXU	Boeing 737-330	24282	
D-ABXW	Boeing 737-330	24561	
D-ABXX	Boeing 737-330	24562	
D-ABXY	Boeing 737-330	24563	
D-ABXZ	Boeing 737-330	24564	
D-ABYA	Boeing 767-304ER	28039	G-OBYA D-AGYA G-OBYA
D-ABYM(2)	Boeing 747-230B Combi	21588	
D-ABYO	Boeing 747-230F	21592	
D-ABYP	Boeing 747-230B	21590	N8291V
D-ABYQ	Boeing 747-230B	21591	
D-ABYR	Boeing 747-230B Combi	21643	
D-ABYT	Boeing 747-230B Combi	22363	
D-ABYU	Boeing 747-230F	22668	N1785B
D-ABYX	Boeing 747-230B Combi	22670	
D-ABYY	Boeing 747-230B Combi	22671	
D-ABYZ	Boeing 747-230B	23286	I-DEMX D-ABYZ N6055X
D-ABZA	Boeing 747-230B Combi	23287	N6038E
D-ABZB	Boeing 747-230F	23348	N747MC D-ABZB N6005F
D-ABZC	Boeing 747-230B Combi	23393	N6046P
D-ABZD	Boeing 747-230B Combi	23407	N6005C
D-ABZE	Boeing 747-230B Combi	23509	N6038E
D-ABZF	Boeing 747-230B	23621	N6046P
D-ABZH	Boeing 747-230B	23622	N6046P
D-ABZI	Boeing 747-230F	24138	N6005C
D-ACAF	Airbus A.320-231	444	N444RX TC-ONF N444RX F-WWBY
D-ACCS	Fokker F.27 Friendship 500	10434	N981MA N271FA PH-EXF VH-EWN OY-STN PH-FPI
D-ACCT	Fokker F.27 Friendship 500	10639	G-JEAG D-ADAP G-JEAG VH-EWX PH-EXG
D-ACFA	BAe.146 Series 200	E-2200	G-BTVT G-6-200 (I-FLRZ)
D-ACIR(2)	Embraer EMB.145 (Reservation 11.99)	145-230	
D-ACJA	Canadair CL.600-2B19 Regional Jet	7122	C-FMKT
D-ACJB	Canadair CL.600-2B19 Regional Jet	7128	C-FMMQ(3)
D-ACJC	Canadair CL.600-2B19 Regional Jet	7130	C-FMMW(3)
D-ACJD	Canadair CL.600-2B19 Regional Jet	7135	C-FMNH(3)
D-ACJE	Canadair CL.600-2B19 Regional Jet	7165	C-FMNH(4)
D-ACJF	Canadair CL.600-2B19 Regional Jet	7200	
D-ACJG	Canadair CL.600-2B19 Regional Jet	7220	
D-ACJH	Canadair CL.600-2B19 Regional Jet	7266	
D-ACJI	Canadair CL.600-2B19 Regional Jet	7282	C-FNMY
D-ACJJ	Canadair CL.600-2B19 Regional Jet	7298	
D-ACLA	Canadair CL.600-2B19 Regional Jet	7004	C-GRJJ (D-ARJA)
D-ACLB	Canadair CL.600-2B19 Regional Jet	7005	C-GRJN (D-ARJB)
D-ACLC	Canadair CL.600-2B19 Regional Jet	7006	C-GRJO (D-ARJC)
D-ACLD(2)	Canadair CL.600-2B19 Regional Jet	7009	C-FMKW C-GRJQ
D-ACLE(2)	Canadair CL.600-2B19 Regional Jet	7010	C-GRJW
D-ACLF	Canadair CL.600-2B19 Regional Jet	7015	C-FMLQ (D-ARJF)
D-ACLG(2)	Canadair CL.600-2B19 Regional Jet	7016	C-FMLS
D-ACLH(2)	Canadair CL.600-2B19 Regional Jet	7007	C-FMKV
D-ACLI (2)	Canadair CL.600-2B19 Regional Jet	7019	C-FMLV
D-ACLJ(2)	Canadair CL.600-2B19 Regional Jet	7021	C-FMML
D-ACLK(2)	Canadair CL.600-2B19 Regional Jet	7023	C-FMMQ (D-ACLG) (D-ARJG)
D-ACLL(2)	Canadair CL.600-2B19 Regional Jet	7024	C-FMMT (D-ACLH) (D-ARJH)
D-ACLM(2)	Canadair CL.600-2B19 Regional Jet	7025	C-FMMW (D-ACLI) (D-ARJI)
D-ACLP	Canadair CL.600-2B19 Regional Jet	7064	C-FMNX
D-ACLQ	Canadair CL.600-2B19 Regional Jet	7073	C-FMKF
D-ACLR	Canadair CL.600-2B19 Regional Jet	7086	C-F . . .
D-ACLS	Canadair CL.600-2B19 Regional Jet	7090	C-F . . .
D-ACLT	Canadair CL.600-2B19 Regional Jet	7093	C-F . . .
D-ACLU	Canadair CL.600-2B19 Regional Jet	7104	C-FXPI
D-ACLV	Canadair CL.600-2B19 Regional Jet	7113	C-FMMQ
D-ACLW	Canadair CL.600-2B19 Regional Jet	7114	C-FMMT
D-ACLY	Canadair CL.600-2B19 Regional Jet	7119	C-FMND
D-ACLZ	Canadair CL.600-2B19 Regional Jet	7121	C-FMNQ
D-ACTU	Canadair CL.600-2B16 Challenger	5085	N618CC C-FJPI C-GLXD
D-ADAM(4)	VFW-614 (ATTAS Test Airframe)	G-017	D-BABP
D-ADBH	Boeing 737-3L9	27336	OY-MAO
D-ADBI	Boeing 737-3L9	27337	OY-MAP
D-ADBK	Boeing 737-31S	29055	
D-ADBL	Boeing 737-31S	29056	
D-ADBM	Boeing 737-31S	29057	
D-ADBN	Boeing 737-31S	29058	
D-ADBO(2)	Boeing 737-31S	29059	
D-ADBP	Boeing 737-31S	29060	
D-ADBQ	Boeing 737-31S	29099	
D-ADBR	Boeing 737-31S	29100	
D-ADBS	Boeing 737-31S	29116	
D-ADBT	Boeing 737-31S	29264	N1795B
D-ADBU	Boeing 737-31S	29265	N17878
D-ADBV	Boeing 737-31S	29266	N1786B
D-ADBW	Boeing 737-31S	29267	N60436 N1787B
D-ADEP	Fokker F.27 Friendship 600	10318	OY-CCK G-BLMM P2-ANS VH-FNS PH-FKN
D-ADIA(2)	Boeing 737-36Q	30333	
D-ADIB(3)	Boeing 737-36Q	30334	
D-ADIC(2)	Boeing 737-36Q	30335	N1786B
D-ADNA	Airbus A.319-133	1053	D-AVYN
D-ADND	Canadair CL.600-2B16 Challenger	5403	N604DC C-GLWW

Regn.	Type	C/n	Prev.Id.
D-ADNE	Canadair CL.600-2B16 Challenger	5422	N605DC
			C-GLXU
D-ADOP	Fokker F.27 Friendship 600	10316	OY-BVF
			PH-SFG
			A40-FN
			HL5262
			A40-FN
			G-AVDN
			PH-FKL
D-ADSO	McDonnell-Douglas DC-10-30 (F-GKZS res 9.99)	48252	
D-ADUP	Fokker F.27 Friendship 500	10686	OE-IPN
			N51OAW
			PH-EXF
D-AELC	Fokker F.27 Friendship 600	10438	OY-SLG
			S2-ABH
			PH-FPN
			(AP-AWN)
			PH-FPN
			PH-EXB
D-AELD	Fokker F.27 Friendship 600	10442	OY-SLF
			S2-ABP
			PH-FPR
			I-VANA
			PH-FPR
			PH-EXA
D-AELE	Fokker F.27 Friendship 600	10477	OY-SLE
			S2-ABO
			PH-FRB
			PH-EXC
			PH-EXB
D-AELF	Fokker F.27 Friendship 600	10323	PH-FKT
			(PH-XPA)
			A40-FD
			AP-BBJ
			A40-FD
			G-AZFD
			HB-AAW
			PH-FKT
D-AELG	Fokker F.27 Friendship 600	10338	VR-BLZ
			PH-XPS
			LX-LGD
			PH-FLI
D-AELH	Fokker F.27 Friendship 600	10340	VR-BLX
			PH-SFJ
			A2-AEC
			F-BYAA
			OO-SBP
			PH-FLL
D-AELI	Fokker F.27 Friendship 600	10514	N60AN
			OB-R-1082
			PH-EXF
D-AELJ	Fokker F.27 Friendship 600	10342	F-BYAB
			OO-HLN
			PH-FLN
			OY-DNF
			PH-FLN
D-AELK	Fokker F.27 Friendship 600	10361	F-GCJV
			EC-BOE
			PH-FMH
D-AELL	Fokker F.27 Friendship 200	10414	PH-FON
			VT-ETE
			PH-FON
			TF-FLO
			HL5209
			PH-FON
D-AELM	Fokker F.27 Friendship 600	10450	OY-CCL
			D-AARS
			OY-CCL
			EC-DSH
			9M-MCY
			PH-FTR
			I-ALML
			PH-FTR
			TU-TIA
			TU-VAJ

Regn.	Type	C/n	Prev.Id.
D-AERD	Airbus A.330-322	143	9M-MKY
			F-WWKY
D-AERF	Airbus A.330-322	082	F-WWKD
D-AERG	Airbus A.330-322	072	F-WWKY
D-AERH	Airbus A.330-322	087	F-WWKF
D-AERK	Airbus A.330-322	120	F-WWKN
D-AERQ	Airbus A.330-322	127	F-WWKO
D-AERS	Airbus A.330-322	171	F-WWKM
D-AETV	Canadair CL.600-2B16 Challenger	5417	N605MP
			C-GLYA
D-AEWA	BAe.146 Series 300	E-3163	G-BTJG
			HB-IXY
			G-BTJG
			G-3-163
			G-BTJG
			EC-FIU
			EC-876
			G-BTJG
			G-6-163
			N885DV
			G-6-163
D-AEWB	BAe.146 Series 300	E-3183	G-BUHB
			G-6-183
			G-BSYS
			G-6-183
D-AEWD	BAe.146 Series 200A	E-2069	OO-DJC
			G-UKLN
			OO-DJC
			(OO-DJY)
			G-BNKJ
			N407XV
			G-5-069
			G-BNKJ
			G-5-069
D-AEWE	BAe.146 Series 200A	E-2077	OO-DJD
			G-UKRH
			OO-DJD
			(OO-DJZ)
			G-BRNG
			N408XV
			G-5-077
D-AEWG	Aeritalia/SNIAS ATR-72-212	347	F-WWEC
D-AEWH	Aeritalia/SNIAS ATR-72-212	359	F-WWEV
D-AEWI	Aeritalia/SNIAS ATR-72-212	404	F-WWLO
D-AEWK	Aeritalia/SNIAS ATR-72-212	446	F-WWEA
D-AFFI	Fokker F.27-050	20272	PH-LXL
D-AFFX	Fokker F.27-050	20142	EC-GAF
			EC-781
			PH-FZC
			D-AFKG(2)
			PH-EXO
D-AFFY	Fokker F.27-050	20141	EC-GAE
			EC-780
			PH-FZB
			D-AFKF
			PH-EXN
D-AFFZ	Fokker F.27-050	20133	EC-GAD
			EC-771
			PH-FZA
			D-AFKE
			PH-EXG
D-AFKK	Fokker F.27-050	20205	PH EXN
D-AFKL	Fokker F.27-050	20213	PH-EXC
D-AFKM	Fokker F.27-050	20214	PH-EXD
D-AFKN	Fokker F.27-050	20223	PH-EXX
D-AFKO	Fokker F.27-050	20234	PH-JXO
D-AFKP	Fokker F.27-050	20235	PH-EXE
D-AFKU	Fokker F.27-050	20236	PH-JXL
D-AFRO(2)	Airbus A.320-231	230	G-BYFS
			(D-AFRO)
			A40-MA
			N230RX
			SX-BSJ
			N230RX
			F-WWDI

Regn.	Type	C/n	Prev.Id.
D-AFTI	Airbus A.320-231	338	N302ML
			N338RX
			F-WWIM
D-AGEL	Boeing 737-75B	28110	N1791B
D-AGEM	Boeing 737-75B	28099	N3502P
D-AGEN	Boeing 737-75B	28100	N1786B
D-AGEO	Boeing 737-75B	28101	N5573K
D-AGEP	Boeing 737-75B	28102	N5573B
D-AGEQ	Boeing 737-75B	28103	
D-AGER	Boeing 737-75B	28107	N1002R
D-AGES	Boeing 737-75B	28108	
D-AGET	Boeing 737-75B	28109	
D-AGEU	Boeing 737-75B	28104	
D-AGEV	Boeing 737-75B	28105	
D-AGEW	Boeing 737-75B	28106	
D-AGEY	Boeing 737-73S	29076	N102UN
D-AGEZ	Boeing 737-73S	29077	N103UN
D-AGWB	McDonnell-Douglas DC-9-83	49846	
D-AGYF	Boeing 767-304ER	28208	G-OBYF
D-AGYH	Boeing 767-304ER	28883	G-OBYH
D-AHFA	Boeing 737-8K5	27981	N737BX
D-AHFB	Boeing 737-8K5	27982	N35030
D-AHFC	Boeing 737-8K5	27977	N5573P
D-AHFD	Boeing 737-8K5	27978	N35161
D-AHFE	Boeing 737-8K5	27979	N3502P
D-AHFF	Boeing 737-8K5	27980	N3509J
D-AHFG	Boeing 737-8K5	27989	
D-AHFH	Boeing 737-8K5	27983	N1786B
D-AHFI	Boeing 737-8K5	27984	N1787B
D-AHJJ	Boeing 737-8K5	27990	
D-AHFK	Boeing 737-8K5	27991	N1786B
D-AHFL	Boeing 737-8K5	27985	N1786B
D-AHFM	Boeing 737-8K5 *(Reservation 3.99)*	27986	
D-AHFN	Boeing 737-8K5 *(Reservation 3.99)*	28228	N1786B
D-AHFO	Boeing 737-8K5 *(Reservation 3.99)*	27987	
D-AHFP	Boeing 737-8K5 *(Reservation 3.99)*	27988	
D-AHFQ	Boeing 737-8K5 *(Reservation 3.99)*	27992	N1786B
D-AHFR	Boeing 737-8K5 *(Reservation 11.99)*	30593	
D-AHFS	Boeing 737-8K5 *(Reservation 11.99)*	28623	
D-AHFT	Boeing 737-8K5 *(Reservation 11.99)*	30413	
D-AHFU	Boeing 737-8K5 *(Reservation 11.99)*	30414	
D-AHFV	Boeing 737-8K5 *(Reservation 11.99)*	30415	
D-AHLA(3)	Airbus A.310-304	520	F-WWCI
D-AHLB(4)	Airbus A.310-304	528	F-WWCE
D-AHLC(3)	Airbus A.310-304	620	F-WWCC
D-AHLF(3)	Boeing 737-5K5	24927	
D-AHLG(5)	Boeing 737-4K5	26316	
D-AHLI (2)	Boeing 737-5K5	25037	
D-AHLJ(2)	Boeing 737-4K5	24125	
D-AHLK(2)	Boeing 737-4K5	24126	
D-AHLL(2)	Boeing 737-4K5	24127	
D-AHLM(2)	Boeing 737-4K5	27102	
D-AHLO(2)	Boeing 737-4K5	24128	
D-AHLS(2)	Boeing 737-4K5	27074	(D-AHLG)
D-AHLT(2)	Boeing 737-4K5	27830	
D-AHLU(2)	Boeing 737-4K5	27831	
D-AHLV(2)	Airbus A.310-204	430	F-WWBL
D-AHLW	Airbus A.310-204	427	F-WWBK
D-AHLX	Airbus A.310-204	487	F-WWBO
D-AHLZ(2)	Airbus A.310-204	468	F-WWBM
D-AHOI (2)	BAe.146 Series 300A	E-3187	G-BSYT
			EC-FKF
			EC-899
			G-BSYT
			G-6-187
D-AIAH	Airbus A.300B4-603	380	F-WWAA
D-AIAI	Airbus A.300B4-603	391	F-WWAL
D-AIAK	Airbus A.300B4-603	401	F-WWAO
D-AIAL	Airbus A.300B4-603	405	F-WWAP
D-AIAM	Airbus A.300B4-603	408	F-WWAQ
D-AIAN	Airbus A.300B4-603	411	F-WWAR
D-AIAP	Airbus A.300B4-603	414	F-WWAS
D-AIAR	Airbus A.300B4-603	546	F-WWAP
D-AIAS	Airbus A.300B4-603	553	F-WWAX
D-AIAT	Airbus A.300B4-603	618	F-WWAM
D-AIAU	Airbus A.300B4-603	623	F-WWAT
D-AIAW	Airbus A.300B4-605R	764	F-WWAJ
D-AIAX	Airbus A.300B4-605R	773	F-WWAO
D-AIBA(2)	Airbus A.340-211	008	F-WWJA
D-AIBC(2)	Airbus A.340-211	011	F-WWJD
D-AIBD(2)	Airbus A.340-211	018	F-WWJI
D-AIBE	Airbus A.340-211	019	F-WWJJ
D-AIBF(2)	Airbus A.340-211	006	F-WWBE
D-AIBH	Airbus A.340-211	021	F-WWJL
D-AICA(2)	Airbus A.320-212	774	F-WWDN
D-AICB(2)	Airbus A.320-212	793	F-WWDU
D-AICC(2)	Airbus A.320-212	809	F-WWIE
D-AICD(2)	Airbus A.320-212	884	F-WWDE
D-AICE	Airbus A.320-212	894	F-WWDI
D-AICF(2)	Airbus A.320-212	905	F-WWDP
D-AICG	Airbus A.320-212	957	F-WWBE
D-AICH(2)	Airbus A.320-212	971	F-WWBY
D-AIDD	Airbus A.310-304	488	F-WWCE
D-AIDF	Airbus A.310-304	524	F-WWCA
D-AIDH	Airbus A.310-304	527	F-WWCD
D-AIDL	Airbus A.310-304	547	F-WWCU
D-AIDN	Airbus A.310-304	599	F-WWCZ
D-AIFA	Airbus A.340-313X *(Reservation 10.99)*	352	F-WW..
D-AIFB	Airbus A.340-313X *(Reservation 10.99)*	354	F-WW..
D-AIGA	Airbus A.340-311	020	F-WWJK
D-AIGB	Airbus A.340-311	024	F-WWJO
D-AIGC	Airbus A.340-311	027	F-WWJR
D-AIGD	Airbus A.340-311	028	F-WWJS
D-AIGF(2)	Airbus A.340-311	035	F-WWJV
D-AIGH(2)	Airbus A.340-311	052	F-WWJO
D-AIGI (2)	Airbus A.340-311	053	F-WWJJ
D-AIGK(2)	Airbus A.340-311	056	F-WWJK
D-AIGL	Airbus A.340-313X	135	F-WWJS
D-AIGM	Airbus A.340-313X	158	F-WWJN
D-AIGN	Airbus A.340-313X	213	F-WWJM
D-AIGO	Airbus A.340-313X	233	F-WWJJ
D-AIGP	Airbus A.340-313X	252	F-WWJM
D-AIGR	Airbus A.340-313X	274	F-WWJI
D-AIGS	Airbus A.340-313X	297	F-WWJK
D-AIGT	Airbus A.340-313X	304	F-WWJY
D-AIGU	Airbus A.340-313X *(Reservation 8.99)*	321	F-WWJM
D-AIGV	Airbus A.340-313X *(Reservation 8.99)*	325	F-WWJN
D-AIGW	Airbus A.340-313X *(Reservation 8.99)*	327	F-WW..
D-AIGX	Airbus A.340-313X *(Reservation 8.99)*	355	F-WW..
D-AIGY	Airbus A.340-313X *(Reservation 8.99)*	335	F-WW..
D-AIGZ	Airbus A.340-313X *(Reservation 8.99)*	347	F-WW..
D-AIHA to D-AIHF, H, I, K, L *Reservations for Airbus A.340-600s for Lufthansa*			
D-AILA	Airbus A.319-114	609	D-AVYF
D-AILB	Airbus A.319-114	610	D-AVYG
D-AILC	Airbus A.319-114	616	D-AVYI
D-AILD	Airbus A.319-114	623	D-AVYL
D-AILE	Airbus A.319-114	627	D-AVYO
D-AILF	Airbus A.319-114	636	D-AVYS
D-AILH	Airbus A.319-114	641	D-AVYV
D-AILI	Airbus A.319-114	651	D-AVYY
D-AILK	Airbus A.319-114	679	D-AVYG(2)
D-AILL	Airbus A.319-114	689	D-AVYL(2)
D-AILM	Airbus A.319-114	694	D-AVYR(2)
D-AILN	Airbus A.319-114	700	D-AVYU(2)
D-AILP	Airbus A.319-114	717	D-AVYA
D-AILR	Airbus A.319-114	723	D-AVYD(3)
D-AILS	Airbus A.319-114	729	D-AVYF(3)
D-AILT	Airbus A.319-114	738	D-AVYN(3)
D-AILU	Airbus A.319-114	744	D-AVYI (3)
D-AILW	Airbus A.319-114	853	D-AVYO(4)
D-AILX	Airbus A.319-114	860	D-AVYS(4)
D-AILY(2)	Airbus A.319-114	875	D-AVYC(5)
D-AIPA	Airbus A.320-211	069	F-WWII
D-AIPB	Airbus A.320-211	070	F-WWIJ
D-AIPC	Airbus A.320-211	071	F-WWIO
D-AIPD	Airbus A.320-211	072	F-WWIP
D-AIPE	Airbus A.320-211	078	F-WWIU
D-AIPF	Airbus A.320-211	083	F-WWDE
D-AIPH	Airbus A.320-211	086	F-WWDJ
D-AIPK	Airbus A.320-211	093	F-WWDQ

Regn.	Type	C/n	Prev.Id.
D-AIPL	Airbus A.320-211	094	F-WWDR
D-AIPM	Airbus A.320-211	104	F-WWIG
D-AIPP	Airbus A.320-211	110	F-WWID
D-AIPR	Airbus A.320-211	111	F-WWIE
D-AIPS	Airbus A.320-211	116	F-WWIK
D-AIPT	Airbus A.320-211	117	F-WWIL
D-AIPU	Airbus A.320-211	135	F-WWDB
D-AIPW	Airbus A.320-211	137	F-WWDD
D-AIPX	Airbus A.320-211	147	F-WWDN
D-AIPY	Airbus A.320-211	161	F-WWIA
D-AIPZ	Airbus A.320-211	162	F-WWDS
D-AIQA	Airbus A.320-211	172	F-WWIK
D-AIQB	Airbus A.320-211	200	F-WWDJ
D-AIQC	Airbus A.320-211	201	F-WWDL
D-AIQD	Airbus A.320-211	202	F-WWDM
D-AIQE	Airbus A.320-211	209	F-WWDY
D-AIQF	Airbus A.320-211	216	F-WWDR
D-AIQH	Airbus A.320-211	217	F-WWDS
D-AIQK	Airbus A.320-211	218	F-WWDX
D-AIQL	Airbus A.320-211	267	F-WWDY
D-AIQM	Airbus A.320-211	268	F-WWIB
D-AIQN	Airbus A.320-211	269	F-WWIC
D-AIQP	Airbus A.320-211	346	F-WWDX
D-AIQR	Airbus A.320-211	382	F-WWIZ
D-AIQS	Airbus A.320-211	401	F-WWBD
D-AIRA	Airbus A.321-131	458	F-WWIQ
D-AIRB	Airbus A.321-131	468	F-WWIS
D-AIRC	Airbus A.321-131	473	D-AVZC
D-AIRD	Airbus A.321-131	474	D-AVZD
D-AIRE	Airbus A.321-131	484	D-AVZF
D-AIRF	Airbus A.321-131	493	D-AVZH
D-AIRH	Airbus A.321-131	412	D-AVZA
			F-WWIC
D-AIRK	Airbus A.321-131	502	D-AVZL
D-AIRL	Airbus A.321-131	505	D-AVZM
D-AIRM	Airbus A.321-131	518	D-AVZT
D-AIRN	Airbus A.321-131	560	D-AVZK(2)
D-AIRO	Airbus A.321-131	563	D-AVZN(2)
D-AIRP	Airbus A.321-131	564	D-AVZL(2)
D-AIRR	Airbus A.321-131	567	D-AVZM(2)
D-AIRS	Airbus A.321-131	595	D-AVZX(2)
D-AIRT	Airbus A.321-131	652	D-AVZI (3)
D-AIRU	Airbus A.321-131	692	D-AVZT(3)
D-AIRW	Airbus A.321-131	699	D-AVZY(3)
D-AIRX	Airbus A.321-131	887	D-AVZI (5)
D-AIRY	Airbus A.321-131	901	D-AVZK(5)
D-AISC	Airbus A.321-231	1161	D-AVZG
D-AISD	Airbus A.321-231 *(Reservation 1.99)*	1188	D-AVZJ)
D-AISE	Airbus A.321-231 *(Reservation 1.99)*	1214	D-AV . .
D-AISF	Airbus A.321-231 *(Reservation 1.99)*	1273	D-AV . .
D-AISG	Airbus A.321-231 *(Reservation 1.99)*	1313	D-AV . .
D-AISY(2)	Fokker F.27 Friendship 600	10391	OY-CCR
			G-BNTB
			9Q-CLK
			PH-FNO
D-AJAB(3)	Canadair CL.600-2B16 Challenger	5327	HB-IKJ
			N609CC
			C-GLYK
D-AJET	BAe.146 Series 200	E-2201	G-6-201
D-AJWF	Airbus A.319-112	1002	D-AVYJ(6)
	(For Italian Air Force as MM62173)		
D-AKNF	Airbus A.319-112	646	D-AVYB
D-AKNG	Airbus A.319-112	654	D-AVYX
D-AKNH	Airbus A.319-112	794	D-AVYD
D-AKNI	Airbus A.319-112	1016	D-AVYK
D-AKNJ	Airbus A.319-112 *(Reservation 12.99)*	1172	D-AVWF
D-ALAA	Airbus A.320-232	565	F-WWDR
D-ALAB	Airbus A.320-232	575	F-WWDO
D-ALAC	Airbus A.320-232	580	F-WWDV
D-ALAD	Airbus A.320-232	661	F-WWDK
D-ALAE	Airbus A.320-232	659	F-WWIV
D-ALAF(2)	Airbus A.320-232	667	F-WWBC
D-ALAG	Airbus A.321-231	787	D-AVZL
D-ALAH	Airbus A.321-231	792	D-AVZM
D-ALAI	Airbus A.321-231	954	D-AVZD

Regn.	Type	C/n	Prev.Id.
D-ALAJ	Airbus A.320-232	990	F-WWBC
D-ALAK(2)	Airbus A.321-231	1004	D-AVZI
D-ALAL(2)	Airbus A.321-231 *(Reservation 6.99)*	1195	D-AVZK
D-ALAM(2)	Airbus A.321-231 *(Reservation 6.99)*	1199	D-AVZM
D-ALAN(2)	Airbus A.321-231 *(Reservation 6.99)*	1218	D-AV . .
D-ALCA	McDonnell-Douglas MD-11	48781	N9020Q
D-ALCB	McDonnell-Douglas MD-11F	48782	N9166N
D-ALCC	McDonnell-Douglas MD-11F	48783	
D-ALCD	McDonnell-Douglas MD-11F	48784	
D-ALCE	McDonnell-Douglas MD-11F	48785	
D-ALCF	McDonnell-Douglas MD-11F	48798	
D-ALCG	McDonnell-Douglas MD-11F	48799	
D-ALCH	McDonnell-Douglas MD-11F	48801	
D-ALCI	McDonnell-Douglas MD-11F	48800	
D-ALCJ	McDonnell-Douglas MD-11F *(Reservation)*	48802	
D-ALCK	McDonnell-Douglas MD-11F *(Reservation)*	48803	
D-ALCL	McDonnell-Douglas MD-11F *(Reservation)*	48804	
D-ALCM	McDonnell-Douglas MD-11F *(Reservation)*	48805	
D-ALCN	McDonnell-Douglas MD-11F *(Reservation)*	48806	
D-ALLE	McDonnell-Douglas DC-9-83	49449	
D-ALLF	McDonnell-Douglas DC-9-83	49602	
D-ALLO	McDonnell-Douglas DC-9-83	53012	
D-ALLQ	McDonnell-Douglas DC-9-83	53014	
D-ALLR	McDonnell-Douglas DC-9-83	53015	N13627
D-ALLV	McDonnell-Douglas DC-9-83	49620	EI-BTV
			EC-EZU
			EC-531
			EI-BTV
D-ALME	Dassault Falcon 900	101	N466FJ
			F-WWFO
D-ALOA(2)	BAe.146 Series 200	E-2066	N356BA
			XA-RTI
			N405XV
			C-FHNX
			N405XV
			G-5-066
			N405XV
D-ALTA	Airbus A.320-232	530	HC-BUM
			F-WWDP
D-AMIM	Canadair CL.600-2B16	5317	C-FYXC
D-AMUA	Boeing 757-2G5 *(Reservation 8.99)*	23118	EC-EFX
			D-AMUR
D-AMUB	Boeing 757-2G5 *(Reservation 8.99)*	23119	EC-EGH
			EC-116
			D-AMUS
D-AMUC(2)	Boeing 757-2G5 *(Reservation 8.99)*	23651	EC-ENQ
			EC-256
			D-AMUT
D-AMUG	Boeing 757-2G5	29488	
D-AMUH	Boeing 757-2G5	29489	
D-AMUI	Boeing 757-2G5	28112	
D-AMUJ	Boeing 767-3G5ER	28111	
D-AMUK	Boeing 757-225	22689	EC-ETZ
			EC-390
			N525EA
D-AMUM	Boeing 757-2G5	24451	
D-AMUN	Boeing 767-3G5	24259	
D-AMUO	Boeing 767-3G5ER	29435	
D-AMUP	Boeing 767-33A	25531	
D-AMUQ	Boeing 767-33A	26278	
D-AMUR(3)	Boeing 767-3G5	24257	N6046P
D-AMUS(2)	Boeing 767-3G5	24258	
D-AMUU	Boeing 757-225	22688	EC-FIY
			EC-896
			D-AMUU
			N524EA
D-AMUV	Boeing 757-2G5	23928	
D-AMUW	Boeing 757-2G5	23929	
D-AMUX	Boeing 757-2G5	23983	
D-AMUY	Boeing 757-2G5	24176	
D-AMUZ	Boeing 757-2G5	24497	
D-ANFA	Aeritalia/SNIAS ATR-72-202	224	F-WWEQ
D-ANFB	Aeritalia/SNIAS ATR-72-202	229	F-WWEX
D-ANFC	Aeritalia/SNIAS ATR-72-202	237	F-WWEG
D-ANFD	Aeritalia/SNIAS ATR-72-202	256	F-WWEE

Regn.	Type	C/n	Prev.Id.
D-ANFE	Aeritalia/SNIAS ATR-72-202	294	F-WWLS
D-ANFF	Aeritalia/SNIAS ATR-72-202	292	F-WWLT
D-AQUA	BAe.146 Series 300	E-3118	G-OAJF
			HB-IXZ
			G-6-118
			G-OAJF
'D-AQUI'	See D-CDLH		
D-ASAX	VFW-614 (Permit)	G-015	F-GATI
	(Advanced Technology Demonstrator)		D-BABN
D-ASKH	Boeing 737-73S	29082	N1787B
D-ASKY	Fokker F.27 Friendship 200 (Reservation)	10674	VT-SSB
			LN-AKC
			(SE-KXY)
			LN-AKC
			PH-EXG
D-ASRA	Airbus A.310-322	399	HB-IPF
			F-WWCC
D-ASTS(2)	Canadair CL.600-2B16 Challenger	5378	C-GDBZ
D-AUKE	Canadair CL.600-2B16 Challenger	5389	N604JE
			C-GLXM
D-AVRA	Avro 146-RJ85	E-2256	G-6-256
D-AVRB	Avro 146-RJ85	E-2253	G-BVWD
			G-6-253
D-AVRC	Avro 146-RJ85	E-2251	G-6-251
D-AVRD	Avro 146-RJ85	E-2257	G-6-257
D-AVRE	Avro 146-RJ85	E-2261	G-6-261
D-AVRF	Avro 146-RJ85	E-2269	G-JAYV
D-AVRG	Avro 146-RJ85	E-2266	G-6-266
D-AVRH	Avro 146-RJ85	E-2268	G-OCLH
			G-6-268
D-AVRI	Avro 146-RJ85	E-2270	G-CLHX
			G-6-270
D-AVRJ	Avro 146-RJ85	E-2277	G-BWKY
			G-6-277
D-AVRK	Avro 146-RJ85	E-2278	G-6-278
D-AVRL	Avro 146-RJ85	E-2285	G-6-285
D-AVRM	Avro 146-RJ85	E-2288	G-6-288
D-AVRN	Avro 146-RJ85	E-2293	G-6-293
D-AVRO	Avro 146-RJ85	E-2246	G-6-246
D-AVRP.	Avro 146-RJ85	E-2303	G-6-303
D-AVRQ	Avro 146-RJ85	E-2304	G-6-304
D-AVRR	Avro 146-RJ85	E-2317	G-6-317
D-AVYA to D-AVYZ	Reserved for Airbus A.319 Test Registrations		
D-AVZA to D-AVZZ	Reserved for Airbus A.321 Test Registrations		
D-AWDL	BAe.146 Series 100	E-1011	G-UKJF
			C-GNVY
			N803RW
			(N103RW)
			G-5-513
			PT-LEQ
D-AWOH	Boeing 737-73S	29083	
D-AWUE	BAe.146 Series 200	E-2050	PK-PJP
			G-5-517
			G-5-004
D-AYXA to D-AYXC	Reserved for Testzwecke TFTS		
D-AZUR	BAe.146 Series 200	E-2060	N352BA
			CP-2260
			N352BA
			XA-RMO
			N402XV
			G-5-060

Regn.	Type	C/n	Prev.Id.

CLASS B : Aircraft of between 14 and 20 Metric Tonnes

Regn.	Type	C/n	Prev.Id.
D-BAAA	Aeritalia/SNIAS ATR-42-310	092	N92BN
			9J-AFC
			F-WWER
D-BACH	DHC-8 Series 314	365	C-FWBB
D-BAGB	DHC-8 Series 103A	306	C-GFOD
D-BAKB	Fokker F.27 Friendship 600	10261	F-GHRC
			PH-FGC
			ST-ALF
			PH-FGC
			TG-TOA
			P2-ANF
			P2-BNF
			(F-BVTU)
			JA8636
			PH-FGC
D-BAKC	Fokker F.27 Friendship 600	10195	F-GFJS
			PT-ODM
			PH-FDK
			PK-PFR
			JA8605
			PH-FDK
D-BAKE(3)	Fokker F.27 Friendship 200	10263	PH-FGE
			TF-FLM
			TF-FIM
			JA8638
			PH-FGE
D-BAKF	Fokker F.27 Friendship 200	10249	PH-KFG
			I-ATIM
			PH-FFP
D-BAKG	Fokker F.27 Friendship 200	10240	PH-FFF
			TF-FLP
			OH-LKB
			TF-FLT
			HL5202
			PH-FFF
D-BAKH	Fokker F.27 Friendship 200	10233	PH-FEY
			TT-WAD
			PH-FEY
			TF-FLS
			G-BDVT
			S2-ABL
			PH-FEY
			9V-BAR
			9M-AMN
			PH-FEY
D-BAKJ	Fokker F.27 Friendship 200	10321	PH-FKR
			ST-AWB
			PH-FKR
			(PH-FJA)
			PT-BFZ
			(PH-LMP)
			PH-FKR
			LN-RNX
			I-ATIF
			PH-FKR
D-BAKK	Fokker F.27 Friendship 200	10229	G-BHMW
			F-BSIF
			F-OGIF
			F-BUTA
			JA8618
			PH-FEU
D-BALL	Dornier 328-300 (Permit)	3105	
D-BCRO	Aeritalia/SNIAS ATR-42-300	122	F-WWES
D-BCRP	Aeritalia/SNIAS ATR-42-300	158	F-WWEE
D-BCRQ	Aeritalia/SNIAS ATR-42-300	233	F-WWEO
D-BCRR	Aeritalia/SNIAS ATR-42-300	255	F-WWEC
D-BCRS	Aeritalia/SNIAS ATR-42-300	287	F-WWLL
D-BCRT	Aeritalia/SNIAS ATR-42-300	289	F-WWLN
D-BDTM	DHC-8 Series 314 (Reservation 8.99)	545	
D-BDUS	DHC-8 Series 106	253	OE-LLL
			C-GETI
D-BDXA to D-BDXZ	Test Registrations for Dornier 328 production		
D-BEEE	Aeritalia/SNIAS ATR-42-300	121	F-WWER

Regn.	Type	C/n	Prev.Id.
D-BEJR	Dornier 328-300 *(Permit)*	3102	
D-BERT(2)	Dassault Falcon 50	218	N218WA
			N50NK
			F-WWHA
D-BEST	Dassault Falcon 2000	50	F-WWME
D-BFAR	Dassault Falcon 50	16	D-BIRD
			F-WZHH
			(N50FM)
D-BGAB	Dornier 328-300 *(Reservation 11.99)*	3134	
D-BGAG	Dornier 328-300 *(Reservation 11.99)*	3133	D-BDXO(1)
D-BGAL	Dornier 328-300 *(Reservation 1.00)*	3131	D-BDXN(1)
D-BGAQ	Dornier 328-300 *(Reservation 11.99)*	3130	D-BGXM(1)
D-BHAL	DHC-8 Series 202	463	C-GFOD
D-BHAM	DHC-8 Series 311	313	OE-LEC
			(D-BSEE)
			OE-LEC
			C-GFOD
D-BHAS	DHC-8 Series 311	503	C-GDLD
D-BHAT	DHC-8 Series 311	505	C-GDFT
D-BHHH	Aeritalia/SNIAS ATR-42-300	173	F-WWED
D-BHOQ	DHC-8 Series 314 *(Reservation 8.99)*	544	
D-BIER	DHC-8 Series 102	310	OE-LEA
			C-GFCF
D-BIRD(2)	Dassault Falcon 2000	54	F-WWML
D-BIRT	DHC-8 Series 103A	260	
D-BJET	Dornier 328JET (Prototype) *(Permit)*	3002	D-CATI (3)
D-BJJJ	Aeritalia/SNIAS ATR-42-300	278	F-WWEC
D-BKIM	DHC-8 Series 311A	356	C-GFOD
D-BKKK	Aeritalia/SNIAS ATR-42-512	532	F-WWLP
D-BLEJ	DHC-8 Series 314	521	C-FDHU
D-BLLL	Aeritalia/SNIAS ATR-42-512	549	F-WWLB
D-BMAA	Dornier 328-300 *(Reservation 11.99)*	3141	
D-BMAB	Dornier 328-300 *(Reservation 11.99)*	3151	
D-BMAC	Dornier 328-300 *(Reservation 11.99)*	3158	
D-BMAD	Dornier 328-300 *(Reservation 11.99)*	3159	
D-BMAE	Dornier 328-300 *(Reservation 11.99)*	3173	
D-BMAF	Dornier 328-300 *(Reservation 11.99)*	3184	
D-BMAG	Dornier 328-300 *(Reservation 11.99)*	3192	
D-BMAH	Dornier 328-300 *(Reservation 11.99)*	3200	
D-BMAI	Dornier 328-300 *(Reservation 11.99)*	3204	
D-BMAJ	Dornier 328-300 *(Reservation 11.99)*	3212	
D-BMMM	Aeritalia/SNIAS ATR-42-512	546	F-WWLE
D-BMUC	DHC-8 Series 314	350	C-GUAY
D-BMYD	Dornier 328-300 *(Reservation 9.99)*	3121	D-BDXE(1)
D-BNNN	Aeritalia/SNIAS ATR-42-512	551	F-WWLL
D-BOBL	DHC-8 Series 102	225	C-GFQL
			D-BOBL
			C-GFQL
D-BOBO(2)	DHC-8 Series 102	153	C-GFOD
D-BOBU	DHC-8 Series 301A	252	C-GFCF
D-BOBY(4)	DHC-8 Series 102	177	C-GFQL
D-BOOK	Dassault Falcon 50	215	XA-SIM
			N297FJ
			F-WWHT
D-BOOO	Aeritalia/SNIAS ATR-42-512	559	F-WWLM
D-BPAD	DHC-8 Series 314	523	C-FDHW
D-BPPP	Aeritalia/SNIAS ATR-42-512	581	F-WWLE
D-BQQQ	Aeritalia/SNIAS ATR-42-512	584	F-WWEP
D-BRRR	Aeritalia/SNIAS ATR-42-512	601	F-WWEC
D-BSEE	DHC-8 Series 314	313	OE-LEC
			C-GFOD
D-BSNA	Canadair CL.600-1A11 Challenger	1066	N51TJ
			N701GA
			N701QS
			N721SW
			N67B
			C-GLXD
D-BSSS	Aeritalia/SNIAS ATR-42-512	602	F-WW..
D-BTTT	Aeritalia/SNIAS ATR-42-512	603	F-WW..
D-BUSY	Canadair CL.600-1A11 Challenger	1070	N670CL
			N24JK
			N70DJ
			HZ-MF1
			N3237S
			C-GLXO

Regn.	Type	C/n	Prev.Id.
D-BWAL	Dornier 328-300 *(Permit)*	3099	

CLASS C : *Aircraft of between 5.7 and 14 Metric Tonnes*

Regn.	Type	C/n	Prev.Id.
D-CAAA(2)	Beech B300 Super King Air	FL-116	N350EA
			(N350E)
			D-CAAA(2)
			N1552C
D-CAAM	Dornier 228-212	8205	D-CBDH(4)
D-CABE(2)	Fairchild-Swearingen SA.227AC Metro III	AC-523	N3109C
D-CACB	Beech 200T Super King Air	BT-27	N7244N
			AE-576
			N2854B
D-CADN	Beech B300 Super King Air	FL-101	N82311
D-CALL(3)	Cessna 550 Citation II	0834	N834CB
D-CALM(2)	Dornier 228-101	7051	
D-CALY	Dornier 228-212	8155	D-CAOS(2)
			D-CBDG(2)
D-CAMM	Beech 350 Super King Air	FL-64	
D-CAPA(2)	Beech 1900C	UB-72	OK-SEB
			D-CAPA(2)
			N3076N
D-CAPO(2)	Gates Learjet 35A	35A-159	N93CK
			N93C
D-CARA(2)	Beech 1900C	UB-59	N72391
D-CARL	Gates Learjet 35A	35A-387	
D-CASA(2)	Beech 300 Super King Air	FA-76	N7247Y
D-CATI (3)	Dornier 328-100	3002	
D-CATL	Gates Learjet 55	55-051	N55KD
			N55KS
			N22GH
			N22G
			N734
D-CATS(3)	Dornier 328-100	3009	
D-CAVE	Gates Learjet 35A	35A-423	(N335GA)
			N200TC
			N369XL
D-CAWI	Dornier 228-101	7014	D-IAWI
			(D-ICIO)
			(N1339U)
D-CAWU	Cessna 560 Citation V	0042	N42CV
			(N26648)
D-CBAD	Bombardier Learjet 60	60-129	N629LJ
D-CBBB(2)	Beech B300 Super King Air	FL-120	N1512H
D-CBDA to D-CBDZ *Test Registrations for Dornier 228 production*			
D-CBDQ(7)	Dornier 228-202	8157	G-BVTZ
			D-CTCB
			D-CBDV(4)
			TC-FBM
			D-CIRC
			(TC-FBM)
			D-CBDF(2)
D-CBEN	Cessna 560 Citation V	0282	N51055
D-CBMW(2)	Hawker 800XP	258345	D-CBMV
			N1135A
D-CBNA	Dassault Falcon 20C	63/411	PH-LPS
			F-WMKI
D-CBPL	Cessna 650 Citation III	0149	(CS-DNE)
			N139N
			N139M
			N649CC
			N1236B
D-CBSF	Beech 1900D	UE-8	N55778
D-CBST	Fairchild-Swearingen SA.227AC Merlin III	AC-470	C-FAFM
	(Reservation 2.99)		C-FJLX
			N470A
			(N470CA)
			N470A
			HB-LNB
			N30486

Regn.	Type	C/n	Prev.Id.
D-CCAA	Gates Learjet 35A	35A-315	N662AA
			N927GL
D-CCAB	Cessna 550 Citation II	0827	
D-CCAS	Short SD.3-60 Variant 300	SH.3737	G-OLBA
			G-BOFG
D-CCAT(3)	IAI-1125 Astra SP	059	N4341S
D-CCBW	Beech B300 Super King Air	FL-46	N81623
D-CCCA	Gates Learjet 35A	35A-160	
D-CCCB	Gates Learjet 35A	35A-663	N91480
D-CCCC(2)	Fairchild-Swearingen SA.227AT Merlin IVC	AT-511	N600N
			N600L
			N3108F
D-CCCF	Cessna 550 Citation II	0189	HB-VGP
			D-CAAT
			N98601
D-CCGN	Gates Learjet 55	55-017	N760AQ
D-CCHB	Gates Learjet 35A	35A-089	N3547F
D-CCON	Gates Learjet 55	55-098	N726L
D-CDBW	Cessna 560XL Citation Excel	5073	N5214K
D-CDEN	Gates Learjet 31	31-049	
D-CDHF	Dornier 328-100	3021	
D-CDLH	Junkers Ju 52/3mg8e	130714	N52JU
	(Painted as D-AQUI which was c/n 5489,		N130LW
	later LN-DAH and Luftwaffe - regd LN-KAF		HC-ABS
	in 5.46 this was rebuilt with fuselage of c/n		LN-KAF
	130714 (LN-KAL ntu) in 1947)		(LN-KAL)
			Luftwaffe
D-CDLR	Grob G.850 Strato 2C	30001	
D-CDNY	Bombardier Learjet 60	60-160	
D-CDNZ	Bombardier Learjet 60	60-161	
D-CDOL	Dornier 328-100	3003	
D-CDUW	Cessna 560 Citation V	0099	OE-GPA
			(N67905)
D-CDWN	Gates Learjet 35A	35A-175	
D-CDXA to D-CDXZ Test Registrations for Dornier 328 production			
D-CEIS	Beech 400 Beechjet	RK-10	N2842B
			(D-CLSG)
D-CESH	Bombardier Learjet 45	45-017	N417LJ
			(D-CWER)
D-CETV	Bombardier Learjet 60	60-148	N80701
D-CEWR(2)	Bombardier Learjet 45	45-013	N413LJ
D-CFAN(2)	BAe.125 Series 800B	258094	G-5-576
D-CFAO	Short SD.3-60 Variant 300	SH.3734	N164DD
			N134PC
			G-BOEL
			G-14-3734
D-CFCF(2)	Gates Learjet 35A	35A-413	N27KG
			N413MA
			F-GHAE
			N2637Z
			HB-VHE
D-CFDX	Short SD.3-60 Variant 300 (Reservation)	SH.3725	N162DD
			G-BNMV
			G-14-3725
D-CFFB	Bombardier Learjet 60	60-107	N107LJ
D-CFFU	Dornier 228-212	8180	
D-CFIS	IAI-1125 Astra	045	VH-FIS
			N91FD
D-CFLX	Short SD.3-60 Variant 300	SH.3735	VP-BKL
			VR-BKL
			G-BOEI
			G-14-3735
D-CFMA	Beech B300 Super King Air	FL-76	N8274U
D-CFMB	Beech B300 Super King Air	FL-97	N8297L
D-CFMC	Beech 300 Super King Air	FA-104	N310VE
			N215GA
			ZS-LSU
			N2660D
D-CFOX(2)	Cessna 560 Citation V	0277	
D-CFTG	Gates Learjet 35A	35A-204	(N277AM)
			N7PE
			N99ME
			N87MJ
			D-COSY
			N1466B

Regn.	Type	C/n	Prev.Id.
D-CFUX	Gates Learjet 55	55-061	N132L
			N222MC
			N117EL
D-CFXA	Short SD.3-60 Variant 300	SH.3754	N263GA
			N829BE
			N754CN
			G-BPKX
D-CFXB	Short SD.3-60 Variant 300	SH.3756	N264GA
			N830BE
			(B- . . . .)
			G-BPKZ
D-CFXC(2)	Short SD.3-60 Variant 300 (Reservation 11.99)	SH.3748	N478CC
			N748SA
			(G-BPFO)
			G-14-3748
D-CFXD	Short SD.3-60 Variant 300	SH.3749	N262GA
			N828BE
			G-BPFP
D-CFXE	Short SD.3-60 Variant 300	SH.3733	N163DD
			N133PC
			G-BOEG
			G-14-3733
D-CFXF	Short SD.3-60 Variant 300	SH.3740	(D-CSAO)
			N165DD
			G-BOFJ
			G-14-3740
D-CFXG	Short SD.3-60 Variant 300	SH.3753	N153CC
			N753CN
			G-BPKW
D-CFXH	Short SD.3-60 Variant 300	SH.3742	N742CC
			(G-BOWF)
			G-14-3742
D-CGAN	Dornier 328-110	3112	D-CDXE(4)
D-CGAO	Dornier 328-110	3113	D-CDXF(4)
D-CGAS	Cessna 550 Citation II	0443	OY-CYT
			N777FB
			N777FE
			N1220S
D-CGFA	Gates Learjet 35A	35A-179	N801PF
			C-FHLO
			N718SW
			(N696SC)
			N718SW
			D-CAPD
			(D-CCAR)
			N39412
D-CGFB	Gates Learjet 35A	35A-268	N2U
			N510SG
			(N286CP)
			N3857N
			YV-286CP
			N10870
D-CGFC	Gates Learjet 35A	35A-331	N435JW
			N700NW
			I-EJIB
			HB-VGU
			N1087D
D-CGFD	Gates Learjet 35A	35A-139	N15SC
D-CGFE	Gates Learjet 36A	36A-062	
D-CGFF	Gates Learjet 36A	36A-063	N1048X
D-CGGG	Gates Learjet 31A	31A-042	
D-CGPD	Gates Learjet 35A	35A-202	N499G
			VH-MIQ
D-CGRC	Gates Learjet 35A	35A-223	N215JW
D-CHAL	IAI-1124 Westwind	207	N666K
			N519ME
			N330PC
			N6053C
			N124P
			4X-CLE
D-CHAN	Cessna 550 Citation II	0874	N5194B

Regn.	Type	C/n	Prev.Id.
D-CHBL	IAI-1124 Westwind	226	N120S
			N124MB
			(N10BY)
			N100BC
			N300LS
			N500LS
			4X-CLX
D-CHCL	IAI-1124 Westwind	277	N504JC
			N288WW
			N2AJ
			4X-CNW
D-CHDE	Cessna 560 Citation V	0031	N1229F
D-CHDL	IAI-1124 Westwind	199	N999MS
			(N999)
			N111AG
			N1124P
			4X-CKW
D-CHIC(5)	Dornier 328-110	3021	D-CDXQ(2)
			D-CAOS(6)
			D-CDXN(2)
			VT-VIF
			D-CDXG(1)
			D-CDHF
D-CHOC	Dornier 328-110	3073	D-CDXG(4)
			F-GNPB
			D-CDXZ(2)
D-CHPD	Gates Learjet 35A	35A-309	N100MN
			N8216Z
			OE-GAR
			HB-VGT
D-CHSW	Beech 400A Beechjet	RK-84	N8138M
D-CHZF	Cessna 550 Citation Bravo	0866	N866CB
D-CICE	Dornier 228-101	7073	
D-CIFA(3)	Cessna 550 Citation II	0378	OH-CAT
			N3999H
			YV-299CP
			N27468
D-CINA(2)	Beech 350 Super King Air	FL-7	N5668F
D-CITI	Dornier 328-100	3004	
D-CITY(2)	Gates Learjet 35A	35A-177	N174CP
			N77CQ
			N77CP
			N1461B
D-CJPG	Gates Learjet 35A	35A-108	N86PC
			(N86PQ)
			N86PC
			F-GCLE
			D-COCO(2)
D-CKKK	Bombardier Learjet 60	60-144	N60144
D-CKWM	Beech B300 Super King Air	FL-124	N3198N
D-CLBA	Beech 400A Beechjet	RK-25	N81918
			(VR-CDA)
			N81918
D-CLBR	Dassault Falcon 20C	52	N825TC
			N85DB
			N72ET
			N881F
			F-WNGN
D-CLEO	Cessna 560 Citation V	0159	N68MA
			(N68854)
D-CLUE	Cessna 650 Citation III	0174	N674CC
			(N1782E)
D-CMAD	Gates Learjet 55C	55-143	N10871
D-CMAX(2)	Short SD.3-60 Variant 300	SH.3732	VP-BKM
			G-BOEF
			G-14-3732
D-CMEI	Cessna 560 Citation V	0117	N6804F
D-CMET	Dassault Falcon 20E	329/523	F-WRQV
D-CMIC(2)	Cessna 560XL Citation Excel	5021	N5244F
D-CMMM	Gates Learjet 24D	24D-328	D-IMMM
D-CMTM(4)	Dornier 328-110	3094	
D-CMUC(2)	Dornier 328-100	3098	D-CDXM(3)
D-CNAC	Fairchild-Swearingen SA.227DC Metro 23	DC-895B	N30384
D-CNAF	Fairchild-Swearingen SA.227AC Metro III	AC-505B	TF-BBG
			F-GHVC
			HB-LND
			EC-DXS
			HB-LND
			N31014
D-CNCI (2)	Cessna 560 Citation V	0061	N2701J
D-CNRX	BAe Jetstream 3103	616	G-BKUY
			G-31-616
D-CNRY	BAe Jetstream 3103	610	SE-KHC
			OY-EDB
			SE-KHC
			D-CONI (2)
			G-31-50
D-COCA(3)	Beech 1900D	UE-224	N224YV
D-CODE	Dornier 228-101	7083	(D-CEVA)
D-COEB	Beech B300 Super King Air (Permit 12.99)	FL-255	N3205M
D-COIL	Beech 300 Super King Air	FA-171	D-IKWM
			N15591
D-COKE	Gates Learjet 35A	35A-447	N300FN
			N127K
D-COLA	Beech B300 Super King Air	FL-75	HB-GJB
			N8097Y
D-COLB	Fairchild-Swearingen SA.227AC Metro III	AC-754B	N54NE
			N2746Z
D-COLC	Fairchild-Swearingen SA.227AC Metro III	AC-689	N706C
			N689NE
			N2705F
D-COLD	Fairchild-Swearingen SA.227AC Metro III	AC-421B	SE-LIM
			Fv.88003
			N5498M
D-COLE(2)	SAAB-Scania SF.340A	144	LV-WTF
			LV-PMG
			ZK-NSM
			SE-KRT
			D-CHBB
			SE-F44
D-COLT(2)	Fairchild-Swearingen SA.227AC Metro III	AC-690	N715C
			N690NE
			N2706B
D-COMM(3)	Bombardier Learjet 45	45-012	N412LJ
			N5009V
D-COOL(2)	Gates Learjet 55	55-052	N551DB
			N55GF
			YV-292CP
D-COSA(2)	Dornier 328-110	3085	D-CDXR(2)
D-COSY(2)	Gates Learjet 35A	35A-415	N415DJ
			N19GL
			N125AX
D-COWS	Bombardier Learjet 60	60-170	N50154
D-COXB	LET L-410-UVP Turbolet	820924	DDR-SXB
D-COXC	LET L-410-UVP Turbolet	820925	DDR-SXC
D-CPAS	BAe.125-800B	258130	G-ETOM
			G-BVFC
			G-TPHK
			G-FDSL
			G-5-620
D-CPRP	Dornier 328-110	3066	D-CDXL(2)
D-CPRR	Dornier 328-110 (Dbr 2.99)	3054	D-CDXV(2)
D-CPRS	Dornier 328-110	3046	D-CDXM
D-CPRT	Dornier 328-110	3042	D-CDXI
			(B-12281)
			D-CDXI
D-CPRU	Dornier 328-100	3091	
D-CPRV	Dornier 328-100	3093	D-CDXD(3)
D-CPRW	Dornier 328-100	3097	D-CDXY(3)
D-CPRX	Dornier 328-110	3101	D-CDXR(3)
D-CPRY	Dornier 328-110	3106	D-CDXC(4)
D-CRHR	Cessna 650 Citation III	0142	N20RD
			N142CC
			N1325L
D-CRIS	IAI-1125 Astra SPX	107	N997GA
D-CSAG(2)	Beech 1900D	UE-353	N23527

Regn.	Type	C/n	Prev.Id.
D-CSAL	Fairchild-Swearingen SA.227AC Metro III	AC-601	I-FSAH
			N90AG
			OY-BPJ
			N3117K
D-CSAP	Gates Learjet 31A	31A-057	N9147Q
D-CSFD	Cessna S550 Citation S/II	0148	N170RD
			ZS-IDC
			N1296Z
D-CSIX	Bombardier Learjet 60	60-120	N120LJ
D-CSKY	Beech B300 Super King Air	FL-130	
D-CTAN(2)	Hawker 800XP *(Reservation 6.99)*	258450	N41441
D-CUTT	Dornier 228-212	8200	D-CBDC(4)
D-CVHA	Cessna 560 Citation V	0275	(N275VP)
D-CVIP(2)	Gates Learjet 55	55-109	N348HM
D-CWAY	Gates Learjet 55	55-107	N304AT
			N155JT
			N760G
			N1466G
D-CWER	Bombardier Learjet 45	45-010	
D-CWOL	BAe.125-800B	258235	N258SA
			OY-RAA
			G-BWWA
			D-CBWW(3)
			G-5-774
D-CZAR	Cessna 560 Citation V	0114	OE-GPS
			N6803T

CLASS E : Single-Engined Aircraft under 2 Metric Tonnes

Regn.	Type	C/n	Prev.Id.
D-EAAA	Bölkow BO.209 Monsun 150F	161	
D-EAAC	Bölkow BO.209 Monsun 160RV	163	
D-EAAD(4)	Cessna 152	81564	N65459
D-EAAE(2)	Mooney M.20F Executive	22-1345	N6983V
D-EAAF(2)	Reims/Cessna F.182Q Skylane	0049	
D-EAAG	Bölkow B0.209 Monsun 160RV	167	
D-EAAH	Bölkow B0.209 Monsun 160RV	168	
D-EAAI	Bölkow B0.209 Monsun 160RV	169	
D-EAAJ(2)	Brditschka HB-207 Alfa *(Reservation 9.99)*	unkn	
D-EAAK	Bölkow B0.209 Monsun 150FF	171	
D-EAAL(2)	Reims/Cessna F.182Q Skylane	0059	
D-EAAM	Bölkow B0.209 Monsun 160RV	173	
D-EAAN	Bölkow B0.209 Monsun 160RV	174	
D-EAAO(2)	Reims/Cessna F.182Q Skylane	0063	(D-EAAD)
D-EAAP	Bölkow B0.209 Monsun 160RV	176	
D-EAAQ(3)	Schillen BMS.68 Comet-Sappho *(Permit 7.99)*	001-90	
D-EAAR(2)	Mooney M.20J Model 201	24-0964	(N3860H)
D-EAAS(3)	Cessna 152	83756	N5116B
D-EAAT	Bölkow BO.209 Monsun 150FF	179	
D-EAAU	Bölkow B0.209 Monsun 160FV	180	
D-EAAV	SOCATA MS.892A Rallye Commodore 150	11816	F-BSMT
D-EAAW	Bölkow BO.209 Monsun 160RV	181	
D-EAAY(3)	Cessna 172N	73474	N4927G
D-EAAZ(2)	Reims/Cessna F.172N	1660	
D-EABA	Reims/Cessna F.172H	0594	
D-EABB(2)	Piper PA-12 Super Cruiser	12-3115	N4219M
			NC4219M
D-EABC(2)	Mooney M.20F Executive	690058	
D-EABD	Cessna 172B	48613	N8113X
D-EABF(3)	SOCATA TB-9 Tampico	1066	
D-EABG(2)	Reims/Cessna FR.172F Rocket	0084	
D-EABH	Bölkow BO.208C Junior	694	
D-EABI (2)	Bölkow BO.208C Junior	699	D-EABM(1)
D-EABK	Bölkow BO.208C Junior	697	
D-EABL(2)	Piper PA-28R-200 Cherokee Arrow	28R-35131	N9419N
D-EABM(2)	SOCATA TB-10 Tobago	1043	
D-EABO	Reims/Cessna F.150J	0444	
D-EABP(2)	Reims/Cessna F.152	1575	
D-EABQ(2)	SIAI-Marchetti S.205/20R	4-242	
D-EABS(3)	Cessna 172P	76179	N97325

Regn.	Type	C/n	Prev.Id.
D-EABT(2)	CEA Jodel DR.1050 Ambassadeur	209	F-BJUI
D-EABU(3)	Wassmer Jodel D.120A Paris-Nice	205	F-BKCU
D-EABV(2)	Cessna 150H	68826	N23251
D-EABW(2)	Cessna 152	82703	N89289
D-EABX(3)	Cessna TR.182 Turbo Skylane RG	00871	(N737QD)
D-EABY(4)	SOCATA Rallye 235E-D Gabier	12705	F-BXYF
D-EABZ(3)	Cessna 152	79736	N757GU
D-EACA(2)	Fuji FA-200-160 Aero Subaru	89	
D-EACB(2)	Bölkow BO.209 Monsun	105A	HB-UEN
			D-EBOJ(1)
D-EACC	SOCATA MS.880B Rallye Club	1334	
D-EACD(2)	Fuji FA-200-180 Aero Subaru	133	
D-EACE	Fuji FA-200-160 Aero Subaru	131	
D-EACF(2)	Robin DR.300/180R Remorqueur	625	
D-EACG	CEA DR.360 Chevalier	626	
D-EACH	Piper PA-28-151 Warrior	28-7415065	N9610N
D-EACI	SAN Jodel D.117A Grand Tourisme	830	OE-ABI
D-EACJ	Reims/Cessna FR.172G Rocket	0183	(D-EFHL)
D-EACK(2)	Cessna 172P	76368	N98853
D-EACL(2)	CEA Jodel DR.1050 Ambassadeur	20	D-EOAB
			F-BJLN
D-EACM	Piper PA-24-260 Comanche C	24-4968	HB-OIW
			D-EACM
			N9460P
D-EACN	Piper PA-28-180 Cherokee F	28-7105041	N5187S
D-EACO(2)	Reims/Cessna FRA.150M Aerobat	0330	PH-BER
			N72567
			F-WZDC
			N81956
D-EACP	Wassmer WA.41 Baladou	155	F-BOYQ
D-EACQ	SOCATA TB-10 Tobago	722	
D-EACR(2)	SOCATA TB-10 Tobago	681	
D-EACS(4)	SOCATA TB-10 Tobago	689	
D-EACT	CEA DR.253B Régent	192	
D-EACU	CEA DR.253B Régent	193	
D-EACV	Robin DR.300/125	633	
D-EACW	SOCATA MS.883 Rallye 115	1511	F-BRYR
D-EACX	SOCATA TB-20 Trinidad	697	
D-EACZ	Champion 7GCBC Citabria	677-74	OE-AOA
D-EADA(2)	Diamond DA.20-A1 Katana	10265	
D-EADB(2)	Cessna P210N Pressurized Centurion II	00610	N2738C
			N734QE
D-EADC(2)	Piper PA-46-310P Malibu	46-8508005	N4376B
D-EADD	Reims/Cessna FR.172K Hawk XP	0607	
D-EADF(2)	Piper PA-28-235 Cherokee Pathfinder	28-7510048	N33580
D-EADH	Beech N35 Bonanza	D-6620	5Y-ADM
			3D-AAU
			5Y-ADM
			N9439Y
D-EADI	Robin DR.400/180R Remorqueur	791	
D-EADJ	Cessna 150M	78101	N9150U
D-EADK(2)	Cessna 172N	71544	N3428E
D-EADM	Cessna 182K Skylane	57960	N2760Q
D-EADN	Piper PA-28-140 Cherokee Cruiser	28-7325358	N11C
D-EADO	Reims/Cessna F.172H	0445	
D-EADP(2)	Piaggio FWP.149D	009	90+04
			BB+391
D-EADR	Cessna 210L Centurion	60579	OO-ADR
			N94276
D-EADS	Cessna 172N	71569	N3492E
D-EADU(2)	Cessna 152	83229	N47477
D-EADV	Cessna 152	79853	N757MR
D-EADW	Piper PA-28-180 Cherokee D	28-5308	N7861N
D-EADY	Cessna 172N	71568	N3491E
D-EAEA	Piper PA-28-151 Warrior	28-7415319	N9568N
D-EAEB	Piper PA-18 Super Cub 95	18-3085	OL-L11
			L-11
			53-4685
D-EAEC	Robin DR.300/180R Remorqueur	554	
D-EAED	Fuji FA-200-160 Aero Subaru	77	
D-EAEE	Fuji FA-200-180 Aero Subaru	91	
D-EAEF(3)	Cessna 152	85296	N67394
D-EAEG(2)	Cessna 152	83792	N5176B
D-EAEH(2)	Cessna 152	85703	N94514
D-EAEI (2)	Cessna 172N	73171	N6232F

Regn.	Type	C/n	Prev.Id.
D-EAEJ	Cessna 182K Skylane	57849	(D-EMAF)
			HB-CSN
			N2649Q
D-EAEK(2)	Reims/Cessna FR.182 Skylane RG	0012	PH-ABK
D-EAEL(3)	Reims/Cessna F.152	1495	HB-CXX
D-EAEM	CEA DR.253B Régent	180	
D-EAEN	Piper PA-28R-180 Cherokee Arrow	28R-30881	F-OCRF
			TR-LOA
			N7514J
D-EAEO(2)	Cessna 172P	76044	N90ER
			(N96223)
D-EAEP(2)	Robin DR.400/180S	1904	
D-EAER	Piper PA-18 Super Cub 95	18-1521	ALAT
			51-15521
D-EAES(2)	Cessna 172N	69365	N62LA
			N337ER
D-EAET	Piper PA-18 Super Cub 95	18-1571	ALAT
			51-15571
D-EAEU	Piper PA-18 Super Cub 95	18-1652	ALAT
			51-15652
D-EAEV	Robin DR.300/108	556	
D-EAEW(2)	Extra EA.300	V-1	
D-EAEX	Reims/Cessna F.172N	2027	HB-CFD
			(D-EIZT)
D-EAEZ	SOCATA MS.893A Rallye Commodore 180	11630	F-BSDY
D-EAFB(2)	Fischer Brause 35	001	
D-EAFC	SAN Jodel DR.1050 Ambassadeur	111	PH-ONE
			(PH-ONO)
D-EAFE(2)	Mooney M.20K Model 231	25-0854	N5791R
D-EAFF(2)	Piper PA-28-140 Cherokee C	28-26920	N5287S
D-EAFG	Macchi AL.60B-2	6255/75	
D-EAFH	SEEMS MS.892A Rallye Commodore 150	10480	F-BLSU
D-EAFI	Fuji FA-200-160 Aero Subaru	111	
D-EAFJ(2)	SOCATA TB-10 Tobago	894	
D-EAFK	Piper PA-28-180 Cherokee C	28-2509	N8329W
D-EAFM(2)	Piper PA-28-180 Cherokee F	28-7105168	D-EAPD
			N2148T
D-EAFN	Robin DR.300/180R Remorqueur	578	
D-EAFO(2)	Cessna 182Q Skylane	67187	N97772
D-EAFP	CEA DR.253B Régent	183	
D-EAFQ	CEA DR.253B Régent	186	
D-EAFR	Gyroflug SC-01 Speed Canard	S-21	
D-EAFS(2)	SOCATA TB-20 Trinidad	918	
D-EAFT	Reims/Cessna FRA.150L Aerobat	0187	HB-CEW
			D-ECWN
D-EAFU(2)	Cessna T.207A Turbo Stationair 8 (STOL)	00613	N73673
D-EAFV(2)	SOCATA TB-10 Tobago	922	
D-EAFW(2)	Piper PA-28RT-201T Turbo Arrow IV	28R-8331002	N8272B
D-EAFX(2)	Mooney M.20K Model 231	25-0865	N5807X
D-EAFY	Beech C33A Debonair 285	CE-176	OH-BDC
D-EAFZ	SOCATA TB-20 Trinidad	924	
D-EAGA	Gardan GY-80 Horizon 180	245	
D-EAGB(2)	Reims/Cessna F.172N	2007	PH-RAM
			PH-AYJ(3)
D-EAGC	Reims/Cessna F.172H	0637	(D-EBEB)
D-EAGD	Cessna 172D	50108	OE-DCB
			N2508U
D-EAGE(2)	Cessna 172N	71397	N2993E
D-EAGF(3)	Cessna 150F	63628	N7028F
D-EAGG(3)	SOCATA TB-10 Tobago	1077	
D-EAGH(2)	SOCATA TB-10 Tobago	1458	
D-EAGI	SOCATA MS.893A Rallye Commodore 180	11410	
D-EAGK	Reims/Cessna F.150J	0508	
D-EAGL(2)	Cessna P210N Pressurized Centurion II	00587	N732MS
D-EAGM(2)	Cessna 172N	73791	N5430J
D-EAGN	SOCATA MS.883 Rallye 115	1383	
D-EAGO	SOCATA MS.893A Rallye Commodore 180	11004	
D-EAGP(2)	Dornier Do.27B-1	206	55+66
			MD+385
			EC+385
			PH+205
			PE+109
D-EAGR	SOCATA MS.893A Rallye Commodore 180	11412	
D-EAGS(2)	Piper PA-28-181 Archer II	2890005	N9105V

Regn.	Type	C/n	Prev.Id.
D-EAGT(4)	American AG-5B Tiger	10131	OY-CKZ
			(SE-KVA)
			N502IT
D-EAGU(2)	SOCATA MS.880B Rallye Club	1611	F-BSFO
D-EAGV	Rockwell 114 Commander	14410	(D-EKCG)
D-EAGX	Cessna 182R Skylane	68571	N9635X
D-EAGY	SOCATA MS.883 Rallye 115	1365	
D-EAGZ	Robin DR.400/180 Régent	1414	I-SAGA
D-EAHA(2)	SOCATA MS.880B Rallye Club	1689	(D-EFHL)
D-EAHB	SOCATA MS.880B Rallye Club	1690	
D-EAHC	SOCATA MS.880B Rallye Club	1691	
D-EAHD	SOCATA MS.880B Rallye Club	1787	
D-EAHF	SOCATA MS.893A Rallye Commodore 180	11708	
D-EAHG(2)	Grumman AA-5B Tiger	0469	N6148A
D-EAHI (2)	Piper PA-28RT-201 Arrow IV	28R-7918222	N62TJ
			N2925L
D-EAHJ(2)	Cessna 152	84471	OH-CVN
			C-GRTC
			N4269M
D-EAHK(2)	Robin DR.400/180R Remorqueur	1314	
D-EAHL(2)	SOCATA MS.894A Minerva 220	11836	(G-AYVW)
D-EAHM	Fuji FA-200-180 Aero Subaru	106	
D-EAHN(2)	Cessna 172N	69925	N738ES
D-EAHO(2)	Cessna 172P	74783	N53590
D-EAHR	SAN Jodel DR.1050 Ambassadeur	372	
D-EAHS	SOCATA MS.893E Rallye 180GT Gaillard	12311	F-BUVC
D-EAHT	Cessna TU.206F Turbo Stationair	02201	HB-CDT
			N7431Q
D-EAHU(2)	Piper PA-28-181 Archer II	28-8190075	N82855
D-EAHW(2)	Robin DR.400/180 Régent	1373	
D-EAHX	Piper PA-18 Super Cub 95	18-3432	D-EAWK(1)
			96+12
			NL+109
			AC+520
			AA+520
			AS+520
			54-732
D-EAHZ	Piper PA-38-112 Tomahawk	38-81A0002	HB-PFN
D-EAIA(2)	Mooney M.20J Model 201	24-1301	
D-EAIB	Bölkow BO.209 Monsun 160FV	186	
D-EAIC(2)	Mooney M.20J Model 201	24-0399	
D-EAID(2)	Piper PA-28-181 Archer II	2890009	N9107J
D-EAIF(3)	Cessna 152	82287	N684Q
			N68412
D-EAIG	Bölkow BO.209 Monsun 160RV	191	
D-EAIH(2)	Reims/Cessna F.182P Skylane	0017	D-EATH
D-EAII (2)	Cessna 182P Skylane	63683	N4682K
D-EAIJ(3)	American AG-5B Tiger	10133	N1197J
D-EAIK(2)	SOCATA MS.880B Rallye Club	1904	F-BSZZ
D-EAIL(2)	Cessna 177 Cardinal	00868	N29408
D-EAIM(2)	Fuji FA-200-160 Aero Subaru	173	
D-EAIO	Robin DR.300/180R Remorqueur	549	
D-EAIP	Fuji FA-200-180 Aero Subaru	92	
D-EAIQ	Fuji FA-200-180 Aero Subaru	100	
D-EAIR(2)	Bölkow BO.209 Monsun 160RV	199	
D-EAIS(2)	Beech F33A Bonanza	CE-1243	N3083K
D-EAIT	Mooney M.20K Model 231	25-0771	
D-EAIU	Cessna 150B	59663	OE-AIU
			N1263Y
D-EAIV	Piper PA-28RT-201T Turbo Arrow IV	28R-7931062	N3072N
D-EAIX	Gyroflug SC-01B-160 Speed Canard	S-29	
D-EAJA	Gardan GY-80 Horizon 180	210	
D-EAJB(3)	SOCATA Rallye 100T	3042	OY-AJB
			F-ODIH
D-EAJC	Dornier Do.27B-1	292	56+24
			SE+534
			SC+712
D-EAJD(3)	Blair Denney Kitfox V Speedster	"V"	
D-EAJG	Robin DR.300/180R Remorqueur	712	
D-EAJH	Robin DR.300/180R Remorqueur	726	
D-EAJI	Robin DR.300/180R Remorqueur	722	
D-EAJK	Mooney M.20M TLS	27-0148	
D-EAJM	Cessna R.182 Skylane RG	00243	N3152C
D-EAJO	de Havilland DH.82A Tiger Moth	82360	VH-ALC
			N9259

Regn.	Type	C/n	Prev.Id.
D-EAJP(2)	Cessna TU.206G Turbo Stationair II	04485	N756YP
D-EAJR	Robin DR.400/180R Remorqueur	815	
D-EAJU	Kit aircraft, type unknown (Reservation 12.99)	unkn	
D-EAJW	SOCATA TB-10 Tobago	147	
D-EAJZ	Piper PA-38-112 Tomahawk	38-78A0563	N9654N
D-EAKA	Reims/Cessna F.150M	1157	
D-EAKB	Reims/Cessna F.150M	1158	
D-EAKC(2)	SOCATA TB-10 Tobago	1160	
D-EAKD(2)	SOCATA TB-10 Tobago	1161	
D-EAKE	Reims/Cessna F.177RG Cardinal RG	0124	
D-EAKF	SOCATA MS.893A Rallye Commodore 180	10813	F-BPQC
D-EAKG(2)	Piper PA-28-236 Dakota	28-7911115	N3066T
D-EAKH	Reims/Cessna FR.172J Rocket	0526	
D-EAKI (2)	Cessna 172R	80117	N9859F
D-EAKJ	SOCATA TB-10 Tobago	1162	
D-EAKK	Piper PA-28-181 Archer II	28-7990417	N2125G
D-EAKL(2)	Robin DR.400/180R Remorqueur	2228	
D-EAKM	SAN Jodel DR.1050 Ambassadeur	139	OE-AKM
D-EAKN(2)	Dornier Do.27H-2	2011	HB-HAA V-604
D-EAKO(3)	Piper PA-28RT-201T Turbo Arrow IV	28R-8131146	N8401A
D-EAKP(2)	Piper PA-28-181 Archer II	28-8590048	N69093
D-EAKT	Robin DR.400/180R Remorqueur	900	
D-EAKU(2)	Piper PA-28-181 Archer II	28-8590082	N2531X
D-EAKV	SOCATA TB-10 Tobago	1164	
D-EAKW(2)	Wohltmann (Hinz) BL2 Ara	1751	
D-EAKY(2)	Reims/Cessna F.177RG Cardinal RG	0035/00198	OE-DEE
D-EAKZ(2)	SOCATA TB-10 Tobago	1163	
D-EALA	Reims/Cessna F.152	1468	
D-EALB	Beech A23-24 Musketeer Super	MA-61	SE-EUW
D-EALC	Piper PA-28-180 Cherokee G	28-7205311	N11C
D-EALD	SOCATA ST-10 Diplomate	128	
D-EALE	Reims/Cessna F.172F	0178	
D-EALF	Robin DR.400/180 Régent	976	(D-EOKC)
D-EALG	Lake LA-4-200 Buccaneer	558	N9972F D-EALG OY-DVN N39794
D-EALH	Piper PA-28-181 Archer II	28-8090276	N8175N
D-EALI	Mooney M.20F Executive 21	680123	N3800N
D-EALK	Reims/Cessna F.152	1705	
D-EALL(2)	SOCATA TB-10 Tobago	786	
D-EALN	SOCATA MS.880B Rallye Club	2355	I-RALH
D-EALO(2)	Cessna 152	83822	N5270B
D-EALP	Reims/Cessna FRA.150M Aerobat	0298	(G-BEOE) (5Y-AZY)
D-EALR	Reims/Cessna FR.172J Rocket	0564	
D-EALS	Reims/Cessna FR.172J Rocket	0577	
D-EALT	Piper PA-28RT-201T Turbo Arrow IV	28R-7931130	N2149X
D-EALU	Piper PA-38-112 Tomahawk	38-79A0921	N9699N
D-EALW	SOCATA MS.894A Minerva 220	12002	F-BTPT
D-EALX(2)	Reims/Cessna F.150L	0766	OE-ALX
D-EALY(2)	Commander Aircraft 114B	14585	
D-EALZ	Cessna P.206D Super Skylane	0603	N5703J
D-EAMA	Fuji FA-200-160 Aero Subaru	73	
D-EAMB(2)	Bölkow BO.208C Junior	597	OE-AMB D-ECGE(1)
D-EAMC(3)	Cessna TR.182 Turbo Skylane RG	01555	N5369S
D-EAMD(2)	Piper PA-28RT-201T Turbo Arrow IV	28R-8331042	N4308Z
D-EAME	Cessna 182J Skylane	57363	N3363F
D-EAMF	Fuji FA-200-180 Aero Subaru	81	
D-EAMG(2)	Reims/Cessna F.182Q Skylane	0038	(D-EAMT) OE-DIP
D-EAMH(3)	SOCATA TB-10 Tobago	153	OE-DUZ
D-EAMI	Fuji FA-200-160 Aero Subaru	151	
D-EAMK	Cessna T.210F Turbo-System Centurion	0059	N6159R
D-EAML	Morane-Saulnier MS.500 Criquet	751	Fr.AF
D-EAMM	Wassmer WA.52 Europa	88	
D-EAMN(2)	Piper PA-28-181 Cherokee Archer II	28-7890515	N36428
D-EAMO	Fuji FA-200-180 Aero Subaru	148	
D-EAMR(2)	Cessna 182J Skylane	57493	N4786J D-EHKN N3493F
D-EAMS(2)	Piper PA-28-181 Archer II	28-8690046	N9085N N9512N
D-EAMU(2)	Cessna 172M	64783	N61762
D-EAMV	Fuji FA-200-160 Aero Subaru	177	
D-EAMW	Fuji FA-200-180 Aero Subaru	178	
D-EAMY	Piper PA-28-140 Cherokee Cruiser	28-7325212	N11C
D-EAMZ	Fuji FA-200-160 Aero Subaru	165	
D-EANA(2)	SOCATA TB-20 Trinidad	1308	N5555T
D-EAND(3)	Gyroflug SC-01B-160 Speed Canard	S-32	
D-EANE	Piper PA-28-151 Warrior	28-7415155	N9515N
D-EANF	Reims/Cessna F.172N	1684	
D-EANG(3)	SOCATA TB-10 Tobago	1112	
D-EANH(2)	SOCATA TB-10 Tobago	1626	
D-EANI (2)	Piper PA-28-161 Warrior II	28-8016369	N82401
D-EANJ(2)	Reims/Cessna F.172P	2110	D-EANH(1) (D-ECQY)
D-EANK(2)	Grob G.115A	8012	
D-EANL(3)	SOCATA TB-9 Tampico	879	
D-EANM	PZL-110 Koliber 150	038936	SP-ARY
D-EANO	Piper PA-28-181 Cherokee Archer II	28-7890433	N9648C
D-EANQ	Wassmer WA.51A Pacific	28	F-BSNQ
D-EANS	Mooney M.20G Statesman	680008	N586MA
D-EANT	Reims/Cessna FR.172G Rocket	0194	
D-EANW	Cessna 210L Centurion	60117	N59140
D-EAOA	Piper PA-28-181 Archer II	2890052	N9133X
D-EAOB	Piper PA-28-181 Archer II	2890082	N9147X
D-EAOD	Reims/Cessna F.152	1910	
D-EAOE	Cessna 172RG Cutlass	0380	N4795V
D-EAOF(2)	Commander Aircraft 114B (Reservation 4.99)	14672	
D-EAOJ	SOCATA TB-10 Tobago	995	
D EAOK	Piper PA-28-160 Cherokee B	28-681	OY-AOK N5577W
D-EAON	Piper PA-28R-200 Cherokee Arrow II	28R-7535273	N1408X
D-EAOO	Cessna T.210N Turbo Centurion II	63856	N6289C
D-EAOP	Beech K35 Bonanza	D-6028	D-ENOC
D-EAOR	Reims/Cessna FR.172F Rocket	0071	
D-EAOS	Beech F33A Bonanza	CE-951	
D-EAOU	SOCATA TB-20 Trinidad	999	
D-EAOV	Robin DR.400/180R Remorqueur	1959	
D-EAOY	SOCATA TB-20 Trinidad	998	
D-EAOZ	SOCATA TB-21 Trinidad TC	632	
D-EAPA	Grumman AA-5 Traveler	0752	(N1352R)
D-EAPB	Robin DR.400/180R Remorqueur	1629	
D-EAPD(2)	Mooney M.20J Model 201	24-0520	HB-DFE
D-EAPF	Robin DR.400/180R Remorqueur	1630	
D-EAPG	Mooney M.20K Model 252	25-1147	
D-EAPH	Zlin Z.526AFS Akrobat	1230	
D-EAPJ(2)	Reims/Cessna F.150M	1262	
D-EAPK	Reims/Cessna 182P Skylane	0026/63975	N9915E
D-EAPL(2)	Robin DR.400/180 Régent	1783	
D-EAPM(2)	Piel CP.301E Emeraude (Reservation)	065	OE-APR
D-EAPN(2)	Cessna 152	81272	N49444
D-EAPO	Piper PA-28RT-201 Arrow IV	28R-8018033	N8149D
D-EAPP	Piper PA-28-140 Cherokee Cruiser	28-7325261	N11C
D-EAPR	SOCATA TB-10 Tobago	739	
D-EAPS	Cessna 172L	59327	N7627G
D-EAPT(2)	Beech C23 Sundowner	M-2357	N6334X
D-EAPU	Cessna 172N	72551	SE-IYM N5376D
D-EAPW(3)	Piper PA-28-181 Archer II	28-8090298	N82018
D-EAPX	Piper PA-46-310P Malibu	46-8608051	N9092W
D-EAPY(2)	Piper PA-28RT-201T Turbo Arrow IV	28R-8431024	N43596
D-EAQH	Piper PA-28-161 Cadet	2841116	N91716 N9647N
D-EAQK	Piper PA-28-140 Cherokee Cruiser	28-7625065	N9639N
D-EAQL	Piper PA-28-181 Cherokee Archer II	28-7690212	N9542N
D-EAQM	Maule MX7-180 Star Rocket	11044C	N6116Q
D-EARB(2)	Mooney M.20F Executive	22-1259	HB-DWG
D-EARC	Rockwell Commander 112A	468	OY-PRD (SE-FLX) (N1468J)
D-EARE	Reims/Cessna F.150L	0792	
D-EARF	Robin DR.400/180R Remorqueur	1718	
D-EARI	Beech S35 Bonanza	D-7386	
D-EARK(2)	SIAT 223A-1 Flamingo	013	HB-EVH D-ENBJ(1)

Regn.	Type	C/n	Prev.Id.
D-EARL(2)	Cessna T.210M Turbo Centurion	61747	N8719J
			N732SW
D-EARM	Beech F35 Bonanza	D-4256	OO-JAO
			OO-JAC
D-EARN(2)	Piper PA-28-161 Cadet	2841113	N9645N
D-EARO	Cessna 182N Skylane	60106	N92237
D-EARP	SOCATA MS.880B Rallye Club	2054	F-BTRE
D-EARR	Beech C23 Sundowner 180	M-2275	
D-EARS(2)	Lake LA-4-200 Buccaneer	1106	N8543J
D-EART	Mooney M.20K Model 231	25-0376	
D-EARU(2)	Reims/Cessna F.172N	1817	(D-EOVV)
D-EARV	Grob G.115C	82039/C	
D-EARW	Piper PA-46-350P Malibu Mirage	4622068	N91811
D-EARY(3)	Piaggio FWP.149D	057	(D-EIJR)
			HB-EVU
			90+43
			SB+212
			SC+402
			AS+484
D-EARZ	Piper PA-28-180 Cherokee D	28-5345	OY-BKT
D-EASA	SOCATA MS.893A Rallye Commodore 180	10942	
D-EASB(3)	Cessna 172N	72535	N5347D
D-EASC(2)	Piper PA-28-181 Archer II	28-8090212	N81418
D-EASD	Fuji FA-200-160 Aero Subaru	87	
D-EASE	SOCATA MS.893A Rallye Commodore 180	11001	
D-EASF	Piper PA-28R-201 Cherokee Arrow III	28R-7737090	N38359
D-EASG(4)	Cessna 182S Skylane	80312	N2002X
D-EASH	Piper PA-28-180 Cherokee Archer	28-7505038	N9608N
D-EASI (2)	Piper PA-28-140 Cherokee Cruiser	28-7725095	N9542N
D-EASK	Sportavia-Pützer RF-6	6002	
D-EASL	Piper PA-28-180 Cherokee Archer	28-7505160	N9614N
D-EASM	Cessna 182M Skylane	59654	(N71534)
D-EASN	Mooney M.20J Model 201	24-1244	N1154Y
D-EASO	SOCATA MS.893A Rallye Commodore 180	10989	
D-EASP	SOCATA MS.880B Rallye Club	1609	F-BSDU
D-EASR(2)	SOCATA MS.892A Rallye Commodore 150	10528	D-EGGI (1)
D-EASS	Piper PA-28-235 Cherokee E	28-7110014	N8588N
D-EASU	SOCATA MS.893A Rallye Commodore 180	10988	
D-EASW	SAN Jodel DR.1050 Ambassadeur	131	F-BJJP
D-EASY	Reims/Cessna FR.172F Rocket	0064	
D-EATA(3)	Cessna TR.182 Turbo Skylane RG	01988	N6343T
D-EATB	SOCATA MS.892A Rallye Commodore 150	10953	OY-TRU
			SE-CIX
D-EATC	Cessna 150C	59805	N2005Z
D-EATE(2)	Cessna 172D	49983	N5099C
			N711RN
			N2383U
D-EATF	Reims/Cessna F.182P Skylane	0016	
D-EATG	Reims/Cessna F.182P Skylane	0013	
D-EATH(2)	Piper PA-28R-201T Turbo Arrow III	28R-7803346	
D-EATI (2)	Klink Europa (Permit 11.99)	EU-01	
D-EATJ	RFB Fantrainer 600	D1	98+30
D-EATK	SOCATA TB-10 Tobago	1114	
D-EATM	Piper PA-28R-200 Cherokee Arrow II	28R-7335100	N15883
D-EATN	SAN Jodel DR.1050 Ambassadeur	451	
D-EATO	Wassmer CE.43 Guepard	438	
D-EATP(2)	RFB Fantrainer 400 (Permit)	011	98+77
			D-EATP(2)
D-EATQ	Bellanca 7GCBC Citabria	835-75	OE-AOO
D-EATR	RFB Fantrainer 600	001	98+75
			D-EATR
D-EATS(3)	Piper PA-18-135 Super Cub	18-3351	N4282V
			EI-129
			I-EIHD
			53-7751
D-EATT	Piper PA-28R-200 Cherokee Arrow B	28R-7135095	N5095S
D-EATV(2)	Piper PA-28R-201T Turbo Cherokee Arrow III		
		28R-7703303	N40435
D-EATW(2)	Diamond DA.20-A1 Katana	10141	
D-EATX(2)	Gyroflug SC-01B-160 Speed Canard	S-48	
D-EAUA	SOCATA TB-10 Tobago	1097	
D-EAUB(4)	Cessna 172N	70150	N172TA
			N738QG
D-EAUF	SOCATA MS.893E Rallye 180GT Gaillard	12267	F-BUJE
D-EAUG	Bücker Bü.131/APM-150 Jungmann	75	HB-UUG
			A-62
			HB-USG
			A-62
D-EAUK	Bücker Bü.131/APM-150 Jungmann	27	HB-UUK
			A-18
D-EAUM	SOCATA TB-10 Tobago	1098	
D-EAUO	Robin DR.400/180R Remorqueur	2371	
D-EAUR	SOCATA TB-10 Tobago	1099	
D-EAUS(2)	Gyroflug SC-01B-160 Speed Canard	S-10	
D-EAUT(3)	Piper PA-18-150 Super Cub	18-7909190	N9754N
D-EAUU(2)	Bücker Bü.133C Jungmeister	10	OE-AUU
			D-EEEY(2)
			U-63
D-EAUW	Werner Rieseler R.III.22/K	1853	
D-EAUX(2)	Piper PA-28-180 Cherokee D	28-5423	N7996N
D-EAVA	Cessna 182M Skylane	59806	N91525
D-EAVB	Beech F33A Bonanza	CE-1127	
D-EAVC	Reims/Cessna F.172N	1728	N99OOA
D-EAVD	Piper PA-28R-201 Arrow III	28R-7837022	N47986
D-EAVE(2)	SOCATA TB-10 Tobago	930	
D-EAVG	Reims/Cessna F.172M	1362	(D-EDRO)
D-EAVI (3)	Nachson Velocity J-II	01	
D-EAVL	SAN Jodel DR.1050 Ambassadeur	360	
D-EAVM	AIAA/ Stampe SV-4C	1134	F-BALM
			Fr.Mil
D-EAVS	Robin DR.300/180R Remorqueur	706	
D-EAVV	Bücker Bü.131B Jungmann	12	HB-UUB
			A-5
D-EAWA	Gardan GY-80 Horizon 180	256	
D-EAWB	Cessna TP.206C Turbo Super Skylane	0451	N8651Z
D-EAWC	Mooney M.20E Chaparral	690036	N9172V
D-EAWD	Reims/Cessna F.150M	1259	
D-EAWF	Piper PA-32-300 Cherokee Six D	32-7140072	N2277T
D-EAWG	Reims/Cessna 182P Skylane	0055/64392	N1606M
D-EAWH	Robin DR.400/180R Remorqueur	1440	
D-EAWI(2)	Wegner Brändli BX-2 Cherry	AB-01	
D-EAWK(2)	Beech A36 Bonanza	E-2174	N184SB
D-EAWL(2)	Zlin Z.42M	0060	DDR-WNR
			DM-WNR
D-EAWM(3)	Piper PA-46-310P Malibu	46-8608021	N9232T
D-EAWN	Zlin Z.50LA	0026	HA-SIA
D-EAWP(3)	Mooney M.20K Model 231	25-0605	N1149E
D-EAWS(3)	Cessna T.210R Turbo Centurion II	64989	(N8518U)
D-EAWT	Robin HR.200/100 Club	18	
D-EAWU(2)	Cessna 172S	172S8148	N7267Q
D-EAWW(2)	Piper PA-28R-201 Arrow III	28R-7837199	N9469C
D-EAWZ	Reims/Cessna F.172M	1169	
D-EAXA	Grumman AA-5 Traveler	0497	(N7197L)
D-EAXB	Grumman AA-5 Traveler	0518	(N9518L)
D-EAXC	Grumman AA-5 Traveler	0544	N9544L
D-EAXD	Grumman AA-5 Traveler	0545	(N9545L)
D-EAXE	Grumman AA-5 Traveler	0553	(N9553L)
D-EAXG	Grumman AA-1B Trainer	0352	(N8852L)
D-EAXH	Grumman AA-1B Trainer	0356	(N8856L)
D-EAXP	Korte Aero Designs Pulsar XP	1809	
D-EAXT(2)	Piaggio FWP.149D	150	91+28
			AC+464
			AC+402
			AS+084
			KB+127
D-EAXU	SOCATA MS.893A Rallye Commodore 180	10935	F-BPAO
D-EAXX	SEEMS MS.885 Super Rallye	260	F-BKUI
D-EAXZ	Cessna 175C Skylark	57032	OE-DCH
			N8332T
D-EAYA	Cessna 150B	59377	OE-AYA
			N7277X
D-EAYB	Piper PA-28R-201 Cherokee Arrow III	28R-7737112	N38732
D-EAYD	Robin DR.400/180 Régent	847	
D-EAYO(2)	Beech A36 Bonanza	E-2651	
D-EAYP	Beech A36AT Bonanza	E-2656	
D-EAYQ	Beech A36AT Bonanza	E-2661	
D-EAYR	Piper PA-28R-200 Cherokee Arrow II	28R-7335191	N55187

Regn.	Type	C/n	Prev.Id.
D-EAYS	Cessna 172N	71029	N241FR / N241ER / N1509E
D-EAZA	Beech A36TC Bonanza	EA-249	
D-EAZE	Focke-Wulf FW.44J Stieglitz	2779	OH-SZI / SZ-20
D-EAZG(2)	Extra EA.200	02	
D-EAZO	Bücker Bü.131 Jungmann	52	HB-UTK / A-41
D-EAZT	SOCATA TB-10 Tobago	1113	
D-EAZW	Zech Neico Lancair 320	1700	
D-EAZZ(2)	Gardan GY-80 Horizon 180	136	HB-DCL / F-BMUU
D-EBAA(2)	Reims/Cessna F.182Q Skylane	0110	
D-EBAB(2)	Piper PA-28-151 Warrior	28-7415059	N9607N
D-EBAC(2)	Dornier Do.27A-4	381	56+76 / PA+323 / KD+... / PG+102
D-EBAD(6)	Bücker Bü.131 Jungmann	55	A-43
D-EBAE	CEA DR.253B Régent	147	(G-AXDG)
D-EBAF	Piper J-3C-65 Cub	13197	SL-AAR / F-BDTF / 45-4457
D-EBAG(2)	Reims/Cessna F.172N	1655	
D-EBAH(3)	Brditschka HB-207A	1858	
D-EBAI	CEA DR.253B Régent	144	F-BRFZ
D-EBAJ(3)	Robin R.3000/140	102	D-EHIA(1)
D-EBAK(3)	Piper PA-28R-201 Arrow III	28R-7837276	PH-TIF / N36359
D-EBAL(2)	Piper PA-18-150 Super Cub	18-5364	N5884 / ALAT
D-EBAM(2)	Cessna 210L Centurion II	61120	N210GV / N210GM
D-EBAN(2)	SOCATA MS.883 Rallye 115	1586	
D-EBAO	CEA DR.253B Régent	151	
D-EBAP(2)	SOCATA TB-10 Tobago	1069	
D-EBAR(3)	SOCATA TB-9 Tampico	933	
D-EBAS(3)	Piper PA-28RT-201T Turbo Arrow IV	28R-8231024	N8062L
D-EBAT(2)	Piaggio FWP.149D	030	90+20 / AC+416 / JA+392
D-EBAV(2)	Wassmer WA.52 Europa	19	F-WSQG
D-EBAW(3)	Piper PA-18-150 Super Cub	18-5389	ALAT
D-EBAX(3)	Grumman AA-5 Traveler	0751	(N1351R)
D-EBAY	Robin DR.300/180R Remorqueur	595	
D-EBAZ(6)	Baaz Neico Lancair 320	489/1697	
D-EBBA(3)	Aero Designs Pulsar XP (Reservation 10.99)	EB 432	
D-EBBB	Piper PA-18 Super Cub 95	18-3425	96+07 / PZ+901 / QZ+010 / AC+514 / AA+514 / AS+514 / 54-725
D-EBBD	Reims/Cessna FR.172F Rocket	0066	
D-EBBE(3)	SAN Jodel D.140C Mousquetaire III	119	F-BMBA
D-EBBF	Cessna 182M Skylane	59573	N71314
D-EBBG	Cessna 207 Super Skywagon	00108	(N91186)
D-EBBH	Reims/Cessna F.172G	0245	
D-EBBI(4)	Bartsch Van's RV-6	AB-000	
D-EBBJ	Reims/Cessna FR.172F Rocket	0119	
D-EBBK(2)	SOCATA TB-10 Tobago	399	F-OGKG
D-EBBM(3)	Cessna 172N	68151	N733AU
D-EBBN	Navion Rangemaster H	NAV-4-2530	(N2530T)
D-EBBO	Reims/Cessna F.172G	0266	
D-EBBP	Navion Rangemaster H	NAV-4-2531	(N2531T)
D-EBBR(2)	Piper PA-18-95 Super Cub (Reservation 1.99)	18-1586	(D-EHBR) / D-ELTQ / ALAT / 51-15586
D-EBBS(3)	Beech B36TC Bonanza	EA-457	N2749N
D-EBBT	Dornier Do.27A-1	185	55+53 / AC+911 / AS+911
D-EBBU	Cessna 182H Skylane	56627	N8527S
D-EBBV	Robin HR.100/285 Tiara	524	G-BGWD / F-BXRF
D-EBBW(2)	PZL-104 Wilga 35A	62167	DDR-WBW / DM-WBW
D-EBBX	Piper PA-28RT-201T Turbo Arrow IV	28R-8231024	N9147Y
D-EBBY(2)	Reims/Cessna F.172M	1337	
D-EBBZ	Beagle 121 Pup 150 (Permit)	142	G-AXSE / G-35-142
D-EBCA(2)	Reims/Cessna F.172H	0628	
D-EBCC	SAN Jodel DR.1050M Excellence	488	
D-EBCD	Piper PA-28-161 Warrior II	28-7816268	N9515N
D-EBCE(2)	Piper PA-28RT-201T Turbo Arrow IV	28R-8031093	N8190R
D-EBCG(2)	Winter LF-1 Zaunkönig	V-4	D-ECER
D-EBCH	Piper PA-28-180 Cherokee G	28-7205261	N11C
D-EBCI(2)	Piper PA-28-181 Cherokee Archer II	28-7690247	(D-EEEL) / N9556N
D-EBCK	Procaer F15B Picchio	35	OE-DGE
D-EBCL	Reims/Cessna F.150M	1405	
D-EBCM(2)	Beech 35 Bonanza	D-1497	N478B
D-EBCN	SNCAN/ Stampe SV.4C	543	F-BDCN / (OO-CDN) / F-BDCN
D-EBCP	Beech C23 Sundowner 180	M-1948	
D-EBCR(2)	Cessna 180H	51589	5N-ADL / N1789X
D-EBCS(3)	Robin DR.500 Super Régent	0005	
D-EBCT(2)	Cessna 152	80950	N48746
D-EBCU(2)	Reims/Cessna F.172H	0642	
D-EBCW	Cessna R.172K Hawk XP	2565	N736JN
D-EBDA(5)	Robin DR.400/180R Remorqueur	1298	SE-GSX
D-EBDB	Piper PA-28-140 Cherokee B	28-26026	OY-BDD
D-EBDC	Beech V35B Bonanza	D-10394	
D-EBDD(2)	Reims/Cessna F.182Q Skylane	0100	
D-EBDE	Piaggio FWP.149D	131	(91+10) / D-EBDE / KB+108
D-EBDI(2)	Cessna 152	81119	N49045
D-EBDK	Piper PA-32-300 Cherokee Six C	32-40963	N5257S
D-EBDL	Piper PA-46-310P Malibu	46-8608018	N9226M
D-EBDM	Cessna 172P	76375	N98897
D-EBDO(4)	Oberbach Van's RV-4	01	
D-EBDR(2)	Dornier Do.27A-1	272	56+05 / YA+014 ? / LC+158
D-EBDU(2)	Mooney M.20J Model 201	24-0880	(N4790H)
D-EBDW	HOAC DV-20 Katana	20050	
D-EBDY(3)	Cessna 172RG Cutlass	0745	N6518V
D-EBEA	Mudry CAP.10B	84	
D-EBEB(3)	Rösinger Denney Kitfox IV	1828	
D-EBED	SAAB S.91B Safir	91291	
D-EBEE	Reims/Cessna F.150K	0610	OO-HBE / (OO-WIE)
D-EBEF(2)	Beech C23 Sundowner 180	M-2195	
D-EBEG(2)	Piper PA-28R-201T Turbo Cherokee Arrow III	28R-7703064	N2401Q
D-EBEH(2)	Cessna 172C Skyhawk	9296	N1596Y
D-EBEI(2)	Messerschmitt Me.108D-1	2246	N108HP / N54208 / Luftwaffe
D-EBEK(2)	Piper PA-28-200 Cherokee Arrow II	28R-7335205	N55264
D-EBEL(4)	Grob G.115	8063	F-GGON / D-EIAU
D-EBEM(2)	Piper PA-28R-200 Cherokee Arrow II	28R-7335235	N55453
D-EBEN(2)	Mooney M.20L PFM	26-0013	
D-EBEO	Reims/Cessna F.182Q Skylane	0129	
D-EBEP(4)	Piper PA-28RT-201T Turbo Arrow IV	28R-7931150	N2195Y
D-EBES(2)	Piper PA-28R-201T Turbo Cherokee Arrow III	28R-7703063	N2295Q
D-EBET	SNCAN/ Stampe SV.4C	567	F-BDDM
D-EBEU	Piper PA-38-112 Tomahawk	38-79A0939	N9682N
D-EBEV(2)	Reims/Cessna F.172N	2023	(PH-AYE)
D-EBEW(5)	Extra EA.400 (Reservation)	05	
D-EBEX	Cessna 140	10300	N73084
D-EBEY	Piper PA-28-161 Warrior II	28-7916441	N2815S

Regn.	Type	C/n	Prev.Id.
D-EBEZ(2)	Piper PA-28RT-201 Arrow IV	28R-7918208	N2895Y
D-EBFA(2)	Piper PA-28-236 Dakota	28-7911253	N2940N
D-EBFB	Piper PA-18 Super Cub 95	18-3217	OL-L43
			L-143
			53-4817
D-EBFC	Piper PA-18 Super Cub 95	18-3161	OL-L83
			L-83
			53-4761
D-EBFE	SAN Jodel DR.1050 Ambassadeur	276	
D-EBFF	Piper PA-28R-200 Cherokee Arrow II	28R-7435139	N40898
	(Reserved as PH-DUB, 9.99)		
D-EBFG	SOCATA TB-10 Tobago	905	
D-EBFI (2)	Wassmer Jodel D.120 Paris-Nice	83	F-BIKN
D-EBFK(2)	Robin DR.400/180R Remorqueur	1960	
D-EBFL	RFB Fanliner FL-1	01	
D-EBFM	Maier Van's RV-4	AB-01	
D-EBFN	Cessna 172N	71227	N2306E
D-EBFO	Cessna 172A	47746	N6846X
D-EBFP	Cessna 172N	71283	N2438E
D-EBFR	Cessna 172M	63520	N5321R
D-EBFS	Robin DR.300/180R Remorqueur	667	
D-EBFT	Grob G.115B	8102	VH-AYB
			D-ERFI
			F-GGOR
			(HB-...)
D-EBFU	Piper PA-18 Super Cub 95	18-3126	L-52
			53-4726
D-EBFW(2)	Messerschmitt Me.108B Taifun	730253	D-EHAF
			PH-PBC
			Luftwaffe
D-EBFY	Pützer Elster C	022	
D-EBGB(2)	Piper PA-28-160 Cherokee	28-82	OO-RPC
			D-EBRO
			N11C
			(N5073W)
D-EBGC(2)	Piper PA-18-135 Super Cub	18-2549	PH-NYL
			ALAT
			52-6231
D-EBGD(2)	Reims/Cessna F.150J	0511	(HB-CTY)
D-EBGE(2)	Piper PA-38-112 Tomahawk	38-79A0986	N9710N
D-EBGG(2)	Reims/Cessna FR.172G Rocket	0151	
D-EBGH	Reims/Cessna F.150J	0528	HB-CUA
			F-BRBU
D-EBGK	SOCATA MS.887 Rallye 125	2117	F-BTVL
D-EBGL	Great Lakes 2T-1A-1	0504	N504GL
D-EBGN	Piper PA-28R-201T Turbo Cherokee Arrow III	28R-7703232	N38504
D-EBGO(2)	Cessna 182J Skylane	57497	N3497F
D-EBGR	Rösinger Murphy Renegade Spirit RG90	001	
D-EBGS	Robin DR.400/180R Remorqueur	1438	
D-EBGT	Reims/Cessna F.150J	0462	
D-EBGZ	Robin DR.400/180R Remorqueur	803	
D-EBHA(2)	Robin DR.400/RP Remorqueur	1784	
D-EBHB(3)	Robin DR.400/180 Régent	1311	
D-EBHC(2)	Dornier Do.27A-4	512	HB-HAI
			D-EFMG(2)
			57+58
			MB+904
			JC+904
			JC+390
			LB+163
D-EBHD(2)	Reims/Cessna F.172P	2198	
D-EBHE	Bölkow BO.207	232	
D-EBHF	Cessna 152	80844	N25902
D-EBHG	Bölkow BO.209 Monsun 160RV	160	(D-EBJT)
D-EBHI (2)	Piper PA-28-161 Warrior II	28-7916284	N9601N
D-EBHJ(2)	SNCAN/ Stampe SV.4C	165	F-BBPH
D-EBHK	Piper PA-28R-200 Cherokee Arrow II	28R-7235230	N5375T
D-EBHL(3)	SNCAN/ Stampe SV.4C	216	Fr.AF
			(F-BNGC)
			Fr.Navy
			Fr.AF
D-EBHM	Cessna 172M	61888	N12216
D-EBHN(2)	Mooney M.20K Model 231	25-0316	OE-KPS
			N231MX
D-EBHO(3)	Bellanca 7GCBC Citabria	759-74	OE-AOM
D-EBHP	Piper PA-22-150 Tri-Pacer	22-3141	HB-OPB
D-EBHR	AIAA/ Stampe SV.4A	1120	F-BAHE
			Fr.AF
D-EBHS	Mooney M.20J Model 201	24-0019	
D-EBHU	Cessna 175B Skylark	56978	N8278T
D-EBHV	Piper PA-18 Super Cub 95	18-2058	PH-JKB
			R-73
			52-2458
D-EBHW	Cessna 182M Skylane	59877	N91704
D-EBHY(2)	Piper PA-18 Super Cub 95	18-2099	D-EBHL(1)
			ALAT
			52-2499
D-EBHZ	Beech A36AT Bonanza	E-2717	
D-EBIA	Binder CP.301S Smaragd	100	
D-EBIB(2)	SAN Jodel DR.1050 Ambassadeur	184	
D-EBIC(2)	Cessna 175C Skylark	57119	N8519X
D-EBID	Piper PA-18 Super Cub 95	18-5660	
D-EBIF(2)	Piper PA-28R-200 Cherokee Arrow B	28R-7135194	N1973T
D-EBIG(3)	Diamond DA.20-A1 Katana	10033	N608F
D-EBIH(2)	Robin HR.100/210D Safari	199	
D-EBII	Robin HR.100/210D Safari	200	
D-EBIJ	Robin DR.400/180 Régent	969	
D-EBIL(2)	Piper PA-28-140 Cherokee Cruiser	28-7625104	N9507N
D-EBIM(2)	Piper PA-28R-200 Cherokee Arrow	28R-35089	9XR-BM
			D-EBIM(2)
			N9380N
D-EBIO	Reims/Cessna F.177RG Cardinal RG	0048	
D-EBIP(2)	Reims/Cessna F.150F	0048/63375	(N6775F)
D-EBIQ(2)	Cessna 175B	56814	OE-DCF
			N8114T
D-EBIS(2)	Piper J-3C-65 Cub	12513	(D-EDUS)
			(Norway)
			44-80217
D-EBIT	Piper PA-24-250 Comanche	24-393	
D-EBIV(4)	Piper PA-28-161 Warrior II	28-7916175	N9558N
D-EBIW(2)	Cessna U.206G Stationair II Soloy	03896	C-GBIW
			N7358C
	(Operates on skis/wheels or floats)		
D-EBIY	Piper PA-28RT-201T Arrow IV	28R-7931229	N2858D
D-EBJA(2)	Cessna 172N	70249	N738UN
D-EBJB(2)	Piper PA-18-135 Super Cub	18-3922	N4282R
			EI-226
			I-EIJW
			54-2522
D-EBJH(2)	Reims/Cessna F.172N	1567	
D-EBJL(2)	Cessna P210N Pressurized Centurion II	00042	N116RS
			G-IAIN
			N3623P
D-EBJN	Bölkow BO.209 Monsun 150FF	154	
D-EBJO	Bölkow BO.209 Monsun 150FF	155	
D-EBJP	Bölkow BO.209 Monsun 160RV	156	
D-EBJQ	Bölkow BO.209 Monsun 150FF	157	
D-EBJS(2)	Dornier Do.27A-1	604	57+65
			BD+398
D-EBJW	Dallach D4 Fascination	WD-003	
D-EBKA	Piper PA-22-108 Colt	22-8296	
D-EBKB	Mooney M.20J Model 201	24-0500	N201XP
D-EBKD	Morane-Saulnier MS.880B Rallye Club	115	F-BKKH
			(D-EMPY)
D-EBKF(2)	Cessna TR.182 Turbo Skylane RG	01898	N6093T
D-EBKH	Piper PA-24-260 Comanche C	24-5002	N9487P
D-EBKI (3)	Cessna 182S	unkn	
D-EBKK(2)	Piper PA-46-310P Malibu	4608120	N183WW
			N133WW
			N9136J
D-EBKL	Dornier Do.27B-1	363	56+68
			LC+160
			AS+942
D-EBKM	Cessna P210N Pressurized Centurion II	00177	N6416P
D-EBKN	Cessna 172M	61669	N3549Q
D-EBKO(2)	Cessna 172B	48348	PH-KKO
			N7848X
D-EBKP(2)	Reims/Cessna FR.172K Hawk XP	0661	N988PK
			HB-CNU
D-EBKR	Gyroflug SC-01B-1601 Speed Canard	S-13	

Regn.	Type	C/n	Prev.Id.
D-EBKS	SOCATA MS.893A Rallye Commodore 180	11454	F-BSCQ
D-EBKT	de Havilland DH.82A Tiger Moth	85223/ E-13	(D-EAPN)
			OY-DYJ
			D-EDOM(1)
			DE153
D-EBKU(2)	Piper PA-28-181 Archer II	28-7990543	N2903E
D-EBKW	Weiler Pottier P.180	155	
D-EBKY	Bölkow BO.207	234	
D-EBKZ	Robin DR.400/180 Régent	1055	
D-EBLA(2)	Mooney M.20K Model 231	25-0457	N4044H
D-EBLB	Reims/Cessna F.150J	0496	
D-EBLC	Reims/Cessna F.150J	0495	
D-EBLD(2)	Reims/Cessna F.172G	0189	OE-DLD
D-EBLE(2)	Beech 77 Skipper	WA-150	
D-EBLG	Reims/Cessna F.150J	0488	
D-EBLH(3)	Piper PA-28RT-201 Arrow IV	28R-7918059	N818PD
			N9610N
D-EBLI	Bölkow BO.207	223	
D-EBLJ	Reims/Cessna FR.172G Rocket	0148	
D-EBLK	Reims/Cessna F.150K	0542	
D-EBLL	Reims/Cessna F.172H	0663	
D-EBLN	Reims/Cessna FR.172G Rocket	0184	
D-EBLO	Bölkow BO.207	224	
D-EBLR	Reims/Cessna F.150K	0576	
D-EBLS	Reims/Cessna FR.172G Rocket	0207	
D-EBLT	Cessna 172B Skyhawk	48473	N7973X
D-EBLU(2)	Reims/Cessna FR.172G Rocket	0210	
D-EBLV	Reims/Cessna F.172H	0660	
D-EBLW(2)	Piper PA-28RT-201 Arrow IV	28R-8118056	PH-SDE
			OO-HKS
			N83364
D-EBLX	SEEMS MS.892A Rallye Commodore 150	10449	F-BLSX
D-EBLY(2)	Bölkow BO.207	288	D-EUXY
			HB-UXY
			D-ENWE(1)
D-EBMA	Bölkow BO.207	235	
D-EBMC	Reims/Cessna F.172H	0633	
D-EBMD	Reims/Cessna F.172H	0645	
D-EBME(2)	Reims/Cessna F.177RG Cardinal RG	0116	PH-OOG
D-EBMF	Reims/Cessna F.172H	0641	
D-EBMG	Reims/Cessna FR.172F Rocket	0063	
D-EBMH	Reims/Cessna FR.172F Rocket	0069	
D-EBMI	SAN Jodel DR.1050 Ambassadeur	353	
D-EBMK(2)	Beech B36C Bonanza	EA-422	N6844L
			N37PM
			N6844L
D-EBML(3)	Mooney M.20K Model 231	25-0009	N231HS
D-EBMM(3)	HOAC DV-20 Katana	20137	
D-EBMN	Piper PA-38-112 Tomahawk	38-78A0397	(D-EOMN)
			N9705N
D-EBMP	Reims/Cessna F.150J	0513	
D-EBMR	Reims/Cessna FR.172F Rocket	0123	(G-AXDA)
D-EBMS(2)	Maule MX7-235 Star Rocket	10067C	N6115Y
D-EBMT	Reims/Cessna FR.172F Rocket	0112	
D-EBMU(2)	Beech C23 Sundowner (Permit 11.99)	M-1467	OE-DMU
			D-ENNQ
D-EBMV	Gardan GY-80 Horizon 160	117	
D-EBMW(4)	Cessna 207 Skywagon	00088	OE-DEV
			(N91138)
D-EBMZ	Reims/Cessna FR.172F Rocket	0122	
D-EBNC	SOCATA MS.893E Rallye 180GT Gaillard	12632	F-BXDU
D-EBNE	Cessna 182E Skylane	53770	N9370X
D-EBNI	Cessna 182E Skylane	54109	N3109Y
D-EBNK	Beech B24R Sierra 200	MC-222	
D-EBNL	Beech B24R Sierra 200	MC-233	
D-EBNN	Beech B24R Sierra 200	MC-260	
D-EBNO(2)	Beech F33A Bonanza	CE-484	
D-EBNQ	Beech V35B Bonanza	D-9602	
D-EBNS	Piper PA-18A-150 Super Cub	18-6117	G-JELY
			PH-MAV
			N8182D
D-EBNY	Cessna 150D	60497	N4497U
D-EBOB(2)	Piper PA-18-150 Super Cub	18-7501	
D-EBOC(4)	Piper PA-28-181 Archer II	2890029	N9123N
D-EBOD(3)	Reims/Cessna F.152	1618	

Regn.	Type	C/n	Prev.Id.
D-EBOE	Bölkow BO.209 Monsun 160RV	102	
D-EBOF(3)	Piaggio FWP.149D	109	90+89
			AC+448
			JC+390
			AS+445
D-EBOG(2)	Kitplane, type unknown (Reservation)	01	
D-EBOI	Bölkow BO.209 Monsun 150FF	104	
D-EBOJ(2)	Bölkow BO.209 Monsun 160FV	"105"	
	(Built 1974 by R.Ficht using a new airframe and retaining		
	the documents and c/n of HB-UEN/ D-EBOJ(1). The latter		
	was rebuilt as D-EACB with c/n 105A)		
D-EBOK(2)	Mooney M.20K Model 231	25-0256	N231HD
D-EBOL(5)	Piper PA-38-112 Tomahawk	38-78A0267	N9669N
D-EBOM(2)	Beech F33A Bonanza	CE-1147	
D-EBON(2)	Cessna 172P	75093	PH-SCV
			N54961
D-EBOO(2)	Beech B24R Sierra 200	MC-229	OE-DMD
D-EBOP(3)	Reims/Cessna F.172N	1865	
D-EBOQ(2)	Bölkow BO.209 Monsun 150FV	109	
D-EBOR(3)	Reims/Cessna F.172G	0197	
D-EBOS	Bölkow BO.209 Monsun 150FV	110	
D-EBOV(2)	Cessna 172B	48526	D-ELIM
			N8026X
D-EBOW(2)	Bölkow BO.209 Monsun 160FV	112	
D-EBOX	Cessna 150	17179	N5679E
D-EBOY(3)	Fieseler Fi.156C-2 Storch	4389	N156SV
			D-EBOY(1)
			Fv.3808
D-EBOZ(2)	SNCAN/ Stampe SV.4C	297	F-BCGY
D-EBPC(2)	Reims/Cessna F.172P	2214	
D-EBPD	Bölkow BO.209 Monsun 150RV	115	
D-EBPE	Cessna 175C Skylark (Franklin)	57085	N8385T
D-EBPF(2)	Beech B36TC Bonanza	EA-478	
D-EBPG(2)	Robin DR.400/180R Remorqueur	1809	F-GGJN
D-EBPH	Bölkow BO.209 Monsun 150FF	118	
D-EBPI	Bölkow BO.207	237	
D-EBPJ	Bölkow BO.209S Monsun 130FF	119	
D-EBPK(2)	Sportavia-Pützer RS-180 Sportsman	6009	
D-EBPM	Sportavia-Pützer RS-180 Sportsman	6011	
D-EBPO(2)	Sportavia-Pützer RS-180 Sportsman	6013	
D-EBPP	CASA I-131E Jungmann	2091	E3B-489
D-EBPT	Bücker Bü.131 Jungmann	62	A-50
D-EBPY	Wassmer Jodel D.120 Paris-Nice	42	
D-EBQI	SEEMS MS.885 Super Rallye	5426	
D-EBQU	SEEMS MS.885 Super Rallye	5423	
D-EBRA	Erco 415CD Ercoupe	4833	OO-JDN
			NC94722
D-EBRC	Piper PA-28-181 Archer II	28-8190243	N83913
D-EBRD	SOCATA TB-20 Trinidad	467	
D-EBRE(2)	Piper PA-28-181 Archer II	28-8090017	N2972V
D-EBRF	Piper PA-28R-200 Cherokee Arrow B	28R-35658	N3034R
D-EBRG	Piper PA-18-150 Super Cub	18-7909189	N9750N
D-EBRH	Cessna P210N Pressurized Centurion II	00396	N6330K
D-EBRI (2)	Piper PA-28-181 Cherokee Archer II	28-7790055	N4680F
D-EBRK(2)	Tecnam P.92J Echo-VLA	005	
D-EBRM(2)	Cessna 172M	67348	4X-CGL
			N73291
D-EBRP	Wassmer WA.81 Piranha	816	F-GAIR
D-EBRS	Mooney M.20J Model 201	24-1469	
D-EBRT	Reims/Cessna FR.172K Hawk XP	0610	G-BFRT
			(LN-ALQ)
D-EBRU	Cessna 140	12604	OE-ABH
			HB-CAE
D-EBRV	Van's RV- ? (Reservation)	unkn	
D-EBRW(2)	Mooney M.20J Model 205	24-3280	
D-EBRY	Reims/Cessna F.172E	0052	
D-EBSA(2)	Piper PA-28-180 Cherokee D	28-5329	N7918N
D-EBSB	Piper PA-28-140 Cherokee C	28-26566	N5901U
D-EBSC	Robin DR.400/180R Remorqueur	1310	
D-EBSD(2)	Cessna T.207A Turbo Stationair 8	00644	N207PP
			N75798
D-EBSE	Cessna 172B	48088	N7588X
D-EBSF	Robin DR.400/180R Remorqueur	1041	
D-EBSG	SOCATA MS.894A Minerva 220	11828	F-BSMU
D-EBSH	Piper PA-28-235 Cherokee Pathfinder	28-7510016	N32281

Regn.	Type	C/n	Prev.Id.
D-EBSI	Cessna 172B	48089	N7589X
D-EBSJ	SOCATA Rallye 150ST-D	2614	F-BXDH
D-EBSK	Robin DR.400/180R Remorqueur	991	
D-EBSL	CEA DR.250/160 Capitaine	10	F-BMZI
D-EBSM	SOCATA MS.892A Rallye Commodore 150	11750	F-BSMF
D-EBSN(2)	Piper PA-28-181 Archer II	28-8190159	N8332K
D-EBSO	SOCATA MS.880B Rallye Club	1376	
D-EBSP	Cessna 182P Skylane	63620	N6061J
D-EBSQ	Robin DR.400/180R Remorqueur	1802	
D-EBSR	Robin DR.400/RP	1766	(D-ELRA(2))
D-EBST	Robin DR.400/180R Remorqueur	876	
D-EBSU	Cessna 175B	56862	N8162T
D-EBSV	Jodel D.11A Club	1021	HB-SVD
D-EBSW	Cessna 182J Skylane	56859	N2759F
D-EBSX	Reims/Cessna F.150M	1402	
D-EBSY(2)	Reims/Cessna F.172N	1598	
D-EBSZ	Robin DR.400/180R Remorqueur	1854	
D-EBTA	Bölkow BO.207	239	
D-EBTC	Piper PA-28-140 Cherokee B	28-25392	N8194N
D-EBTD	Piper PA-28R-200 Cherokee Arrow	28R-35065	N9358N
D-EBTH	Cessna 172P	76383	N98940
D-EBTK(2)	Thies Jurca MJ.5 Sirocco	023	
D-EBTM	Robin DR.400/180 Régent	1038	
D-EBTR	Reims/Cessna FR.172F Rocket	0141	
D-EBTT	Reims/Cessna F.172N	1877	
D-EBTU(3)	Grob G.115A	8028	D-EKVG
D-EBTV	Reims/Cessna FR.172F Rocket	0144	
D-EBTW	Cessna 210L Centurion II	1264	N2388S
D-EBTY	Cessna 150D	60459	N4459U
D-EBUA(3)	Reims/Cessna 182P Skylane	0004/63790	N6650M
D-EBUB	Cessna 170B	26934	HB-COX
			N2991D
D-EBUE	Reims/Cessna F.150J	0473	
D-EBUF(3)	Piper PA-28-161 Warrior II	28-7916570	OO-SUF
			N2942G
D-EBUG	Piper J-3C-90 Cub	12324	HB-OSB
			44-80028
D-EBUH(2)	Dornier Do.27Q-5	2063	
D-EBUL(2)	SOCATA MS.883 Rallye 115	1588	F-BTHL
D-EBUN(2)	Reims/Cessna T.210N Turbo Centurion II	0018/63136	N6660N
D-EBUO	Reims/Cessna F.172H	0634	
D-EBUR(2)	Piper J-3C-65 Cub	12408	HB-OEK
			44-80112
D-EBUS(2)	Piper PA-12 Super Cruiser	12-2857	N3973M
			NC3973M
D-EBUT(4)	SNCAN/ Stampe SV.4C	304	F-BCLD
D-EBUU	SOCATA MS.893A Rallye Commodore 180	10981	F-BRJI
D-EBUX(2)	Cessna 172RG Cutlass	0803	N9355B
D-EBUZ	Piper PA-18-150 Super Cub	18-6769	N3299P
D-EBVA(2)	Reims/Cessna F.172H	0419	(D-EDGE)
D-EBVB(2)	Beech B36TC Bonanza	EA-463	OE-KVB
			D-EBVB(2)
D-EBVF	Reims/Cessna A.185F AgCarryall	0006/03536	N2892Q
D-EBVG	SIAT 223A-1 Flamingo	012	HB-EVG
			D-EJDU(1)
D-EBVH	SOCATA MS.880B Rallye Club	1355	
D-EBVI	Reims/Cessna F.172E	0054	
D-EBVJ	Cessna 150F	63532	N6932F
D-EBVM(2)	Piper PA-28-161 Cadet	2841143	N9184Q
D-EBVO(2)	Reims/Cessna F.152	1767	
D-EBVP	SOCATA MS.894A Minerva 220	1056	
D-EBVR	Piper PA-28-161 Cadet	2841172	N9185N
D-EBVS(3)	Cessna A.185F Skywagon	03782	N102PM
			N9636Q
D-EBVT	Gardan GY-80 Horizon 160	69	F-BLVN
D-EBVU	Reims/Cessna F.172F	0112	
D-EBVY	Luscombe 8F Silvaire	6211	N1584B
D-EBVZ	Beech F33A Bonanza	CE-1078	
D-EBWA	Piper PA-28-140 Cherokee	28-20209	N6185W
D-EBWB	Piper PA-28-235 Cherokee	28-10611	N9037W
D-EBWC	SOCATA Rallye 100ST-D	2722	F-ODDA
D-EBWD	SOCATA MS.893E Rallye 180GT Gaillard	12682	F-ODDJ
D-EBWE	Piper PA-28-235 Cherokee	28-10431	N8874W
D-EBWF	Piper PA-28-140 Cherokee E	28-7225454	N11C
D-EBWG	SOCATA MS.893ED Rallye 180GT Gaillard	12683	F-ODDM

Regn.	Type	C/n	Prev.Id.
D-EBWI	Beech 35-C33 Debonair	CD-851	
D-EBWJ	SOCATA Rallye 150T-D	2660	F-ODDB
D-EBWL	SOCATA MS.894A Minerva 220	12094	F-BUVI
D-EBWM	SOCATA Rallye 235E-D Gabier	2707	F-ODDC
D-EBWO(2)	Robin DR.400/180R Remorqueur	1508	
D-EBWP	Piper PA-28R-200 Cherokee Arrow II	28R-7335224	N1776P
D-EBWQ	SOCATA MS.893E Rallye 180GT Gaillard	12723	F-ODDQ
D-EBWR	SOCATA Rallye 100S-D Sport	2298	F-BULP
D-EBWS(2)	Cessna T.210N Turbo Centurion II	64341	N6339Y
D-EBWT	SOCATA Rallye 100ST-D	2758	
D-EBWU	Piper PA-28-140 Cherokee	28-20377	N6321W
D-EBWV	SOCATA MS.893E Rallye 180GT Gaillard	12700	F-ODDT
D-EBWW	Piper PA-28-180 Cherokee D	28-4499	(D-EFWQ)
			N5208L
D-EBWX	SOCATA Rallye 235E-D Gabier	12771	
D-EBWY	Zlin Z.226T Trenér 6	870	F-BKRX
	(Third prototype converted from Z.126)		OO-AJT
			OK-JED
			OK-JEB
D-EBWZ(3)	SOCATA Rallye 235E-D Gabier	12765	F-BNGU
D-EBXA	Reims/Cessna FR.172E Rocket	0056	
D-EBXC	Reims/Cessna F.172M	1502	
D-EBXF	Piper PA-18 Super Cub 95	18-3456	96+32
			NL+110
			AC+528
			AS+528
			54-756
D-EBXG	Wallerkowski Hornisse	01	
D-EBXH	Reims/Cessna F.150M	1370	PH-AXK
D-EBXI	Reims/Cessna FR.172E Rocket	0053	
D-EBXM	Reims/Cessna F.172N	1525	
D-EBXN	Reims/Cessna F.172N	1548	
D-EBXO(2)	Kit Aircraft, type unknown (Reservation 12.99)	1599	
D-EBXP	Reims/Cessna F.182Q Skylane	0050	
D-EBXQ	Reims/Cessna F.172N	1759	
D-EBXR	Reims/Cessna FR.172K Hawk XP	0597	HB-CXO
D-EBXS	Reims/Cessna F.172N	1521	
D-EBXT	Cessna 210K Centurion	59455	OE-DSP
			N8155G
D-EBXU	Reims/Cessna FR.172E Rocket	0050	
D-EBXW	Reims/Cessna F.150M	1407	
D-EBXY(2)	SOCATA MS.880B Rallye Club	858	F-BODM
D-EBYA(2)	Mooney M.20J Model 201	24-1116	I-BYBY
			OO-JPM
D-EBYB	Piper PA-18 Super Cub 95	18-4648	
	(Has f/n 18-7841 - built 11.61)		
D-EBYC(2)	Beech V35B Bonanza	D-10033	
D-EBYE	Mooney M.20F Executive	670383	G-AYBF
			N3290F
D-EBYF(2)	Simon Piel CP.301E Emeraude	AB.416	
D-EBYG(3)	Cessna 182K Skylane	57946	OO-SIV
			(D-ENCY)
			N2746Q
D-EBYI	Reims/Cessna F.172N	1540	
D-EBYM(5)	Reims/Cessna F.152	1856	
D-EBYP(3)	Maule M6-235 Super Rocket	7402C	OH-MEN
			N5652V
D-EBYQ(3)	Reims/Cessna 182P Skylane	0009/63886	OO-ADI
			D-EEMK
			(SE-GKI)
			N6903M
D-EBYS(2)	Reims/Cessna F.172N	1579	
D-EBYT(2)	Reims/Cessna F.152	1487	
D-EBYU	Grumman AA-1 Yankee	0312	N2NZ
			D-ELXD
			N6112L
D-EBYV(2)	Piper PA-38-112 Tomahawk	38-78A0560	N9691N
D-EBYX(3)	Piper PA-18 Super Cub 95	18-3450	96+26
			NL+103
			AC+535
			AS+535
			54-750
D-EBYZ	Scheibe SF.23A Sperling	2017	
D-EBZA(2)	Piper PA-28RT-201T Turbo Arrow IV	28R-8131160	N8406J
D-EBZE	Reims/Cessna F.150G	0161	

Regn.	Type	C/n	Prev.Id.
D-EBZH	SOCATA TB-10 Tobago	213	
D-EBZI	Reims/Cessna F.150G	0172	
D-EBZK	Reims/Cessna F.172M	1458	
D-EBZL	SOCATA TB-10 Tobago	214	
D-EBZM	Cessna T.210L Turbo Centurion	61425	N732DC
D-EBZP	Robin DR.400/180R Remorqueur	1418	
D-EBZQ	SOCATA MS.893A Rallye Commodore 180	11771	F-BSZQ
D-EBZT	Mooney M.20J Model 201	24-0811	(N4700H)
D-EBZU	Reims/Cessna F.150G (W5/33 engine)	0186	
D-EBZW(2)	Mooney M.20K Model 231	25-0385	OE-DVU
			N3981H
D-ECAA	Reims/Cessna FA.150K Aerobat	0053	
D-ECAB(2)	Klemm Kl.107C	154	
D-ECAD(4)	SOCATA MS.893A Rallye Commodore 180	12066	F-BTPZ
D-ECAE	Reims/Cessna FA.150K Aerobat	0057	
D-ECAF(3)	Piper PA-18-135 Super Cub	18-3862	PH-KNO
			(PH-KNR)
			R-172
			54-2462
D-ECAG(3)	SOCATA TB-20 Trinidad	725	
D-ECAH	Klemm Kl.107B	126	
D-ECAI	Piper PA-18 Super Cub 95	18-1550	ALAT
			51-15550
D-ECAK(3)	Cessna R.172K Hawk XP	2868	
D-ECAL(2)	Cessna 210K Centurion	59255	N8255M
D-ECAM(2)	Piper PA-28-140 Cherokee Cruiser	28-7325421	N11C
D-ECAN(5)	Diamond DA.20-A1 Katana	10146	
D-ECAO(3)	Cessna 172R	80049	N9796F
D-ECAP(2)	Piper PA-28-180 Cherokee Challenger	28-7305172	N11C
D-ECAQ(2)	Bücker Bü.131 Jungmann	28	OE-AKW
			HB-URC
			A-19
D-ECAR(2)	Cessna 177A Cardinal	01245	N30419
D-ECAS(2)	Piper J-3C-65 Cub	12989	HB-OGR
	(c/n officially quoted as 12809 in error)		HB-ODF
			44-80693
D-ECAT(3)	Piper PA-28-161 Cadet	2841112	N9646N
			N9175Q
D-ECAU	Reims/Cessna FA.150K Aerobat	0080	(D-EHBL)
D-ECAW(3)	Gyroflug SC-01 Speed Canard	S-5	
D-ECAX(2)	Scheibe SF.23A-1 Sperling	2011	
D-ECAY(3)	Cessna 172R	80126	N9861F
D-ECAZ(4)	Cessna 182 (Reservation? Probably F.182P c/n 0001 ex D-EKMO)		
D-ECBA(2)	Piper PA-28R-200 Cherokee Arrow II	28R-7635398	N4294F
D-ECBB(2)	Mooney M.20K Model 252	25-1002	N252AX
D-ECBC(2)	Beech F33A Bonanza	CE-1240	
D-ECBD(2)	Bede BD-5B (Reservation 12.99)	01	
D-ECBF(2)	Reims/Cessna F.172N	1922	(F-GCHP)
D-ECBG(2)	Piper PA-28-181 Cherokee Archer II	28-7790393	N9621N
D-ECBH(2)	SOCATA MS.893E Rallye 180GT Gaillard	13231	F-GBSE
D-ECBJ (2)	Gyroflug SC-01B Speed Canard	S-11	
D-ECBK	Reims/Cessna F.172H	0685	
D-ECBL(2)	Beech A36 Bonanza	E-1541	OY-CBI
D-ECBM	Reims/Cessna F.150K	0564	
D-ECBN	Reims/Cessna F.172H	0699	
D-ECBO	Bölkow BO.207	228	
D-ECBP	Reims/Cessna F.150K	0609	
D-ECBQ	Reims/Cessna F.150K	0606	
D-ECBR	Cessna 210F Centurion	58747	HB-CBR
			N1847F
D-ECBS	Reims/Cessna F.150K	0608	
D-ECBT	Reims/Cessna F.150K	0605	
D-ECBU(2)	Reims/Cessna FA.150L Aerobat	0088	
D-ECBV	Reims/Cessna FR.172G Rocket	0175	
D-ECBW(2)	Piaggio P.149D	316	92+19
			AC+467
			AS+467
D-ECBX(4)	Reims/Cessna F.150L	0685	
D-ECBY(2)	Reims/Cessna F.172H	0717	
D-ECBZ	Reims/Cessna F.172H	0684	
D-ECCA(3)	Sondermann Christen Eagle II	0471	
D-ECCB	Reims/Cessna F.172H	0669	
D-ECCC(2)	CASA I-131E Jungmann	2230	E3B-630
	(Officially ex.E3B-619 but this is c/n 2219 / N72480)		
D-ECCD	Reims/Cessna F.150K	0547	

Regn.	Type	C/n	Prev.Id.
D-ECCE(2)	Grumman AA-5B Tiger	0652	
D-ECCF(3)	Cessna 152	85384	N93045
D-ECCG(2)	SOCATA MS.893A Rallye Commodore 180	11664	
D-ECCH	SOCATA MS.880B Rallye Club	1524	
D-ECCI	Klemm Kl.35D	1904	SE-BHX
			Fv5069
D-ECCK(2)	Reims/Cessna FR.172K Hawk XP	0668	
D-ECCL	SOCATA MS.880B Rallye Club	1561	
D-ECCM	SOCATA MS.880B Rallye Club	1581	
D-ECCN(3)	Piper PA-28-161 Cadet	2816093	N9183X
D-ECCO	Piper PA-28-140 Cherokee	28-20535	(N6462W)
D-ECCP	SOCATA MS.880B Rallye Club	1601	
D-ECCQ	SOCATA MS.893A Rallye Commodore 180	11456	
D-ECCS	SOCATA MS.893A Rallye Commodore 180	11466	F-BNGU
D-ECCT	SOCATA MS.893A Rallye Commodore 180	11469	
D-ECCU(3)	Heliopolis Gomhouria Mk.6	174	SU-337
D-ECCV	SOCATA MS.893A Rallye Commodore 180	11489	
D-ECCW(2)	Piper PA-18-150 Super Cub	18-7880	OE-ANE
			(N10F)
D-ECCX	SOCATA MS.893A Rallye Commodore 180	11497	
	(Reserved as SP-FRX 11.99)		
D-ECCY	Reims/Cessna F.172F	0136	
D-ECCZ	SOCATA MS.893A Rallye Commodore 180	11498	
D-ECDA(2)	Reims/Cessna F.150K	0619	
D-ECDB	Reims/Cessna F.150K	0623	
D-ECDC(3)	Claren Ente Ki 1 (Permit 5.99)	0018	
D-ECDD	Reims/Cessna FR.172G Rocket	0199	
D-ECDE(2)	Cessna 152	84281	N5245L
D-ECDF(2)	Cessna 182S	80008	N697SM
D-ECDH	SOCATA MS.880B Rallye Club	1607	
D-ECDJ	Cessna 207 Skywagon	00176	N1576U
D-ECDL	Navion Rangemaster H	NAV-4-2522	N2520T
D-ECDM	Reims/Cessna FA.150K Aerobat	0021	
D-ECDN	SEEMS MS.885 Super Rallye	5359	OE-CDN
			(D-EHDE)
D-ECDP	Reims/Cessna FA.150K Aerobat	023	
D-ECDQ(2)	Reims/Cessna F.172N	1646	
D-ECDT(2)	Piper PA-28R-201T Turbo Arrow III	28R-7803150	N2856M
D-ECDU(2)	Piper PA-38-112 Tomahawk	38-80A0036	N25140
D-ECDV	Reims/Cessna F.150K	0599	
D-ECDW	Aero Commander 200D	368	N5565M
D-ECEA	CEA Jodel DR.1050 Ambassadeur	620	
D-ECEB(2)	SAN Jodel DR.1050 Ambassadeur	174	
D-ECEC(2)	Reims/Cessna F.150L	0730	
D-ECED(2)	Mooney M.20F Executive	670121	N9544M
D-ECEE	Reims/Cessna F.150L	0729	
D-ECEF(2)	Reims/Cessna F.172N	1544	
D-ECEH	Klemm Kl.107C	127	
D-ECEI (2)	Reims/Cessna F.150L	0733	
D-ECEJ	Reims/Cessna F.172H	0693	
D-ECEL(2)	Cessna 182R Skylane	68466	N9892E
D-ECEM(3)	Mooney M.20F Executive	22-1262	
D-ECEP(2)	Reims/Cessna F.150K	0613	
	(Reserved as SP-FCE 10.99)		
D-ECEQ(2)	Reims/Cessna F.172N	0418	
D-ECER(3)	Robin DR.400/180 Régent	1294	
D-ECES(2)	Piper PA-16 Clipper (Reservation)	16-500	D-EIOG
			HB-OOG
D-ECEU	Reims/Cessna F.150K	0584	
D-ECEV(2)	Reims/Cessna F.150K	0585	
D-ECEW(2)	Reims/Cessna F.150K	0587	
D-ECEY(2)	Reims/Cessna F.150L	0666	
D-ECEZ(2)	Reims/Cessna F.172H	0702	
D-ECFA(2)	Cessna T.210K Turbo Centurion	59212	N8212M
D-ECFB	Reims/Cessna F.172H	0725	
D-ECFC(2)	Piper PA-28-181 Cherokee Archer II	28-7690103	N8124C
D-ECFD	Reims/Cessna F.150L	0737	
D-ECFE	Oberlerchner JOB 15-150	058	OE-CAO
D-ECFF	Reims/Cessna F.172L	0806	
D-ECFG	Piper PA-22-108 Colt	22-9591	OE-CFG
			N5781Z
D-ECFI	Oberlerchner JOB 15-150	060	OE-CAR
D-ECFK	Morane-Saulnier MS.880B Rallye Club	301	HB-EDS
D-ECFM(3)	Pützer Elster B	005	97+03
			D-EJIH

Regn.	Type	C/n	Prev.Id.
D-ECFN(2)	Reims/Cessna F.177RG Cardinal RG	0017/0136	(N8236G)
D-ECFP	Reims/Cessna F.150K	0588	
D-ECFR	Reims/Cessna F.150K	0596	
D-ECFS	Cessna 182N Skylane	60281	N92607
D-ECFT	Reims/Cessna FR.172G Rocket	0198	
D-ECFU	Bölkow BO.208C Junior	569	
D-ECFW	Reims/Cessna F.172H	0740	(G-AXUV)
D-ECFX	Reims/Cessna F.150L	0709	
D-ECFY	Cessna 182H Skylane	55948	N1848X
D-ECFZ	Reims/Cessna F.172K	0801	
D-ECGA(2)	Beech B36TC Bonanza	EA-392	N6749P
D-ECGC	Reims/Cessna F.150L	0670	
D-ECGD	Reims/Cessna FR.172H Rocket	0247	
D-ECGE(2)	Reims/Cessna F.172G	0251	
D-ECGG	Reims/Cessna F.150L	0736	
D-ECGH(2)	Piper PA-18 Super Cub 95	18-3449	96+25
			NL+115
			AC+534
			(D-EMDY)
			AC+534
			AA+534
			AS+534
			54-749
D-ECGI	Bölkow BO.208C Junior	598	
D-ECGK	Cessna 182N Skylane	60407	N92876
D-ECGL	Reims/Cessna F.150L	0680	
D-ECGM	Reims/Cessna FR.172H Rocket	0239	
D-ECGN	Reims/Cessna FA.150L Aerobat	0116	
D-ECGP	Reims/Cessna FA.150L Aerobat	0086	
D-ECGR	Reims/Cessna F.177RG Cardinal RG	00090/0004	(N8090G)
D-ECGS	Reims/Cessna F.177RG Cardinal RG	00094/0005	(N8094G)
D-ECGT(2)	Reims/Cessna FRA.150M Aerobat	0262	
D-ECGU(2)	Reims/Cessna FA.150K Aerobat	0068	
D-ECGW	Cessna 182N Skylane	60460	N8920G
D-ECGX	Reims/Cessna F.150L	0678	
D-ECGZ	Reims/Cessna FR.172H Rocket	0238	
D-ECHA(3)	Christen A-1 Husky	1058	N29732
D-ECHB	Reims/Cessna F.150K	0572	
D-ECHD	Reims/Cessna FR.172G Rocket	0173	
D-ECHE(2)	Reims/Cessna F.172H	0733	
D-ECHF	Reims/Cessna FR.172H Rocket	0252	
D-ECHG	Reims/Cessna F.150L	0705	
D-ECHH	Reims/Cessna F.150L	0664	
D-ECHI	Cessna 172A	47057	N7457T
D-ECHL(3)	Robin DR.400/180 Régent	497	
D-ECHM	Reims/Cessna FR.172G Rocket	0164	
D-ECHO	Cessna 172A	47343	N7743T
D-ECHP	Reims/Cessna F.150L	0662	
D-ECHQ	Piper PA-28-181 Cherokee Archer II	28-7890505	N36321
D-ECHR	Reims/Cessna F.177RG Cardinal RG	00106/0008	(N8206G)
D-ECHS	Reims/Cessna F.172K	0770	
D-ECHT(2)	Reims/Cessna FR.172H Rocket	0251	
D-ECHU(2)	Reims/Cessna F.150L	0681	
D-ECHW	Reims/Cessna F.150L	0699	
D-ECHY(3)	Piper PA-28R-201T Turbo-Arrow III	28R-7803070	N9853K
D-ECHZ(2)	Piper PA-38-112 Tomahawk	38-78A0554	N9690N
D-ECIA(3)	Robin DR.400/180S Régent	1995	
D-ECIB(2)	Wassmer Jodel D.120 Paris-Nice	186	
D-ECIC	Klemm Kl.35D-160	2013	SE-BHU
			Fv5064
D-ECIE	Reims/Cessna F.172K	0795	
D-ECIF(2)	SOCATA Rallye 180T-D Galérien	2974	
D-ECIH	Klemm Kl.107C	128	
D-ECII (3)	Reims/Cessna F.172N	1510	OO-LNC
	(Permit 8.99)		F-BUDU
D-ECIJ	Reims/Cessna F.172H	0708	(YU-BHJ)
D-ECIK(2)	Reims/Cessna FR.172H Rocket	0240	
D-ECIL	Auster Mk.5	1575	G-ANIL
			TJ527
D-ECIM(4)	Piper PA-28-140 Cherokee	28-7225596	C-FFQR
			CF-FQR
D-ECIO	Reims/Cessna F.177RG Cardinal RG	00125/0013	(N8225G)
D-ECIP(3)	Robin R.3000/160	152	
D-ECIQ(2)	Piper J-3C-65 Cub (Permit)	18167	N98024
D-ECIR(3)	Cessna 182N Skylane	60465	N8925G

Regn.	Type	C/n	Prev.Id.
D-ECIS(2)	Piper PA-28-181 Cherokee Archer II	28-7790207	N9548N
D-ECIV	Piper J-3C-85 Cub	11364	SL-AAK
			ALAT
			43-30073
D-ECIY	Reims/Cessna F.150L	0731	
D-ECJB(3)	Robin DR.400/180 Régent	2291	
D-ECJC	Reims/Cessna F.172H	0734	
D-ECJE	Reims/Cessna F.172H	0737	
D-ECJF	Reims/Cessna F.177RG Cardinal RG	00130/0015	(N8230G)
D-ECJG	Cessna 182N Skylane	60517	N8977G
D-ECJK	Reims/Cessna FR.172G Rocket	0212	
D-ECJL	Reims/Cessna F.172H	0742	
D-ECJM(2)	Reims/Cessna F.172P	2091	
D-ECJN	Reims/Cessna F.172H	0744	
D-ECJP(2)	SOCATA TB-20 Trinidad	292	
D-ECJR	Reims/Cessna F.177RG Cardinal RG	00186/0029	(N8286G)
D-ECJS	Reims/Cessna FR.172G Rocket	0176	
D-ECJT	Reims/Cessna F.172H	0736	
D-ECJU	Reims/Cessna F.172K	0804	
D-ECJV	Reims/Cessna FR.172H Rocket	0269	
D-ECJX(2)	Reims/Cessna FR.172H Rocket	0272	
D-ECJY(2)	Reims/Cessna F.150L	0727	
D-ECKA	Beech P35 Bonanza	D-7194	
D-ECKB(2)	Beech F33A Bonanza	CE-1614	N8240X
			(F-GIFM)
D-ECKC(2)	Aerotek Pitts S-2A	2127	N8073
D-ECKD	Reims/Cessna FR.172H Rocket	0243	
D-ECKE(2)	Piper PA-28-160 Cherokee	28-372	N5316W
D-ECKF	Reims/Cessna F.177RG Cardinal RG	00154/0021	"PH-LTU"
			(PH-LTT)
			D-ECKF
			(N8254G)
D-ECKH(2)	Holtz Neico Lancair 235 (Permit 5.99)	362B	
D-ECKI (3)	Rockwell Commander 112A	298	N1298J
D-ECKK	Reims/Cessna FR.172H Rocket	0259	
D-ECKL(2)	Robin DR.400/180R Remorqueur	1589	
D-ECKM	Reims/Cessna F.172K	0789	
D-ECKN	Reims/Cessna F.172K	0787	
D-ECKO(2)	Grumman AA-5 Traveler	0667	
D-ECKP	Reims/Cessna F.172K	0768	
D-ECKR	Reims/Cessna FR.172H Rocket	0249	
D-ECKS	Reims/Cessna F.172H	0750	
D-ECKT	Reims/Cessna FR.172G Rocket	0177	
D-ECKV	Reims/Cessna FR.172G Rocket	0166	
D-ECKW	Cessna 182N Skylane	60439	N92948
D-ECKY(3)	SOCATA MS.893E Rallye 180GT Gaillard	13010	
D-ECKZ	Reims/Cessna FR.172H Rocket	0231	
D-ECLB	Beech 35-C33 Debonair	CD-1010	
D-ECLC(2)	Mooney M.20K Model 252	25-1182	
D-ECLD	Beech 35-C33 Debonair	CD-1012	
D-ECLE(2)	Reims/Cessna F.172N	1563	
D-ECLF	Beech 35-C33 Debonair	CD-1014	
D-ECLG(2)	Cessna 172RG Cutlass	0767	N6544V
D-ECLH	Beech 35-C33 Debonair	CD-1016	
D-ECLI	Beech 35-C33 Debonair	CD-1017	
D-ECLK(2)	Piper PA-18-135 Super Cub	18-3321	EI-104
			I-EIKD
			53-7721
D-ECLL(2)	Cessna T.210N Turbo Centurion II	63807	OE-KKE
			N6113C
D-ECLM(2)	Piper PA-28RT-201T Turbo Arrow IV	28R-8331046	N4322N
			N9534N
			N4312V
D-ECLO(3)	Reims/Cessna F.182Q Skylane	0169	F-ODNO
D-ECLP(2)	Piper PA-28-180 Cherokee D	28-4404	N5121L
D-ECLQ(2)	Reims/Cessna F.150L	0734	
D-ECLR(2)	Piper PA-28-140 Cherokee	28-24130	N1718J
D-ECLS(2)	Cessna 182L Skylane	58917	N42235
D-ECLT(2)	Reims/Cessna 182P Skylane	0048/64355	N1504M
D-ECLW(2)	Reims/Cessna FR.172E Rocket	0052	
D-ECLX(2)	Reims/Cessna FR.172E Rocket	0054	
D ECLY(2)	Reims/Cessna FR.172E Rocket	0046	
D-ECMA(2)	Cessna 172M	66437	N80195
D-ECMB	Cessna 207 Skywagon	00195	(N1595U)
D-ECMC	Reims/Cessna F.172K	0780	(G-AYTI)

Regn.	Type	C/n	Prev.Id.
D-ECMD	Reims/Cessna FR.172H Rocket	0261	
D-ECMF(2)	Mooney M.20J Model 201	24-1011	(N4005H)
D-ECMG	Reims/Cessna F.177RG Cardinal RG	00110/0009	(N8210G)
D-ECMH(3)	Piper PA-28-181 Archer II	2890068	N9138Z
D-ECMI (2)	Robin DR.400/180R Remorqueur	2160	
D-ECMJ	Reims/Cessna F.177RG Cardinal RG	00156/0022	(N8256G)
D-ECML	Reims/Cessna F.150L	0717	
D-ECMM	SAN Jodel D.150 Rapid	17	
D-ECMN	Reims/Cessna F.172K	0784	
D-ECMP(2)	Cessna 172N	73915	N256FR
			N256ER
			N7557J
D-ECMQ	Reims/Cessna FR.172H Rocket	0232	
D-ECMR	Reims/Cessna FR.172H Rocket	0230	
D-ECMS	Reims/Cessna F.172K	0778	
D-ECMT	Reims/Cessna FR.172H Rocket	0237	
D-ECMV(2)	Cessna 172RG Cutlass	0549	N5514V
D-ECMW	Reims/Cessna F.150L	0697	
D-ECMX(2)	Cessna 207 Skywagon	00194	(N1594U)
D-ECMY	Beech 35-C33A Debonair	CE-59	
D-ECNA(2)	Cessna 172K Skyhawk	57639	N78493
D-ECNB(2)	Mooney M.20J Model 201	24-0059	
D-ECNC	Piper PA-28-180 Cherokee D	28-5029	N6575J
D-ECND	Bölkow B0.209 Monsun 160FV	128	(D-EFJF)
D-ECNE	Reims/Cessna F.172G	0234	HB-CBP
D-ECNG	Reims/Cessna F.177RG Cardinal RG	00182/0027	(N8282G)
D-ECNI	Cessna 150G	66209	N8309J
D-ECNJ	Reims/Cessna FR.172H Rocket	0226	
D-ECNK	Cessna 182N Skylane	60469	N8929G
D-ECNL	Cessna 150J Commuter	69649	N50927
D-ECNM	Reims/Cessna F.150L	0713	
D-ECNN	Reims/Cessna F.177RG Cardinal RG	00123/0012	(N8223G)
D-ECNO	Cessna 150G	66927	N3027S
D-ECNP(2)	Cessna T.210K Turbo Centurion	59456	N8156G
D-ECNQ	Reims/Cessna F.150L	0659	
D-ECNS(2)	Piper PA-32-300 Cherokee Six	32-7840153	N31908
D-ECNT	Reims/Cessna F.150L	0723	
D-ECNU	Reims/Cessna F.150H	0243	
D-ECNV	Reims/Cessna F.150L	0718	
D-ECNW(2)	SOCATA MS.893ED Rallye 180GT Gaillard	13009	
D-ECNX	Reims/Cessna F.177RG Cardinal RG	00202/0038	(N1802Q)
D-ECNZ	SIAI-Marchetti S.205-20/R	377	OO-JDC
D-ECOA(2)	Christen A-1 Husky	1142	
D-ECOB(2)	Reims/Cessna F.172K	0765	
D-ECOC(2)	Reims/Cessna F.172K	0766	
D-ECOE	Reims/Cessna F.172K	0769	
D-ECOF(3)	Piper PA-28-140 Cherokee Cruiser	28-7625139	N9526N
D-ECOG(2)	Piper PA-28R-200 Cherokee Arrow II	28R-7635266	N75116
D-ECOI	Reims/Cessna F.172K	0781	
D-ECOJ	Reims/Cessna F.150L	0714	F-WLIM
D-ECOK	Kreutzer Jodel D.9 Bébé	AB-10	
D-ECOL(3)	SOCATA TB-20 Trinidad	1749	
D-ECON	Piper PA-12 Super Cruiser	12-2918	N4034M
D-ECOO(2)	Cessna 172RG Cutlass (Reims-assembled)	0001/0060	N5464R
D-ECOP(2)	Reims/Cessna F.172K	0791	
D-ECOS(2)	Robin DR.400/180 Régent	1252	
D-ECOT(3)	Beech F33A Bonanza	CE-1716	N8146T
D-ECOU	Reims/Cessna F.172K	0797	
D-ECOV	Schwindt Jodel D.112 Club	278	SL-AAO
D-ECOW(2)	Reims/Cessna F.177RG Cardinal RG	00184/0028	(N8284G)
D-ECOX	Dornier Do.27Q-1	2018	
D-ECOY	Piaggio FWP.149D	020	90+11
			AC+443
			DB+394
D-ECOZ(4)	Reims/Cessna FR.172H Rocket	0274	
D-ECPB(2)	Christen A-1 Husky	1107	
D-ECPC	Reims/Cessna FA.150L Aerobat	0097	
D-ECPD(2)	Piper PA-28R-200 Cherokee Arrow II	28R-7535180	N33697
D-ECPE	Aeromere F8L Falco III	235	
D-ECPF	Reims/Cessna F.150L	0663	
D-ECPG(2)	SIAT 223A-1 Flamingo	017	HB-EVN
			D-ENBN(1)
D-ECPH(2)	Mooney M.20J Model 201	24-0966	N3865H
D-ECPI (3)	Sonntag Sequioa F.8L Falco	1649	
D-ECPJ	Reims/Cessna F.150L	0702	(D-ECMW)

Regn.	Type	C/n	Prev.Id.
D-ECPL(2)	Cessna 150	17858	D-EDOE(1)
			N6458T
D-ECPO	Reims/Cessna FA.150L Aerobat	0113	F-WLIP
D-ECPP	Reims/Cessna FA.150L Aerobat	0114	(OY-BYL)
			D-ECPP
			(G-AYUZ)
D-ECPQ	Reims/Cessna FA.150L Aerobat	0115	
D-ECPR	Reims/Cessna FA.150L Aerobat	0119	
D-ECPS(2)	SOCATA Rallye 180T-D Galérien	2975	
D-ECPT	Reims/Cessna FR.172H Rocket	0284	
D-ECPV	Reims/Cessna FR.172H Rocket	0288	
D-ECPW(2)	Robin DR.400/180 Régent	1664	(D-EEWP)
D-ECPX	Reims/Cessna F.172L	0820	
D-ECPY(2)	Orlican L-40 Meta-Sokol	150909	
D-ECPZ	Reims/Cessna FR.172H Rocket	0282	
D-ECQA	Piper PA-18 Super Cub 95	18-3182	R-84
			L-108
			53-4782
D-ECQC	Reims/Cessna FRA.150L Aerobat	0124	
D-ECQD	Reims/Cessna FR.172H Rocket	0286	
D-ECQE	Reims/Cessna FR.172E Rocket	0002	N20002
D-ECQF	Reims/Cessna F.150L	0762	
D-ECQG	Reims/Cessna F.172L	0816	
D-ECQH	Reims/Cessna FR.172H Rocket	0283	
D-ECQI	Reims/Cessna FR.172H Rocket	0285	
D-ECQL	Reims/Cessna F.150L	0764	
D-ECQO	Reims/Cessna F.172H	0347	
D-ECQP(2)	Grumman AA-5A Cheetah	0187	
D-ECQQ	Reims/Cessna F.150L	0768	
D-ECQV	Reims/Cessna F.172L	0824	
D-ECQW	Reims/Cessna F.172L	0826	
D-ECQX	Reims/Cessna F.172L	0827	
D-ECQZ	Reims/Cessna FR.172H Rocket	0294	
D-ECRA	Reims/Cessna FR.172H Rocket	0295	
D-ECRC	Reims/Cessna F.150L	0769	
D-ECRD	Beech V35B Bonanza	D-9181	
D-ECRE	Reims/Cessna F.150L	0770	
D-ECRF(2)	Beech B36TC Bonanza	EA-299	N24RF
			N6450A
D-ECRH	Reims/Cessna F.150M	1233	N67266
D-ECRI	Mooney M.20C Mark 21	2176	N6429U
D-ECRJ (2)	Reims/Cessna F.182P Skylane	0012	
D-ECRK(2)	Robin DR.400/180 Régent	2387	
D-ECRL	Reims/Cessna F.172L	0832	
D-ECRM	Reims/Cessna FR.172H Rocket	0296	
D-ECRO	SIAT 223 V-1 Flamingo	001	"D-EDON"
D-ECRP(2)	Reims/Cessna F.150L *(Reservation 7.99)*	0776	(OY-BYY)
			D-ECRF(1)
D-ECRQ	Reims/Cessna FR.172H Rocket	0299	
D-ECRR(2)	Aero Designs Pulsar XP *(Reservation)*	1881	
D-ECRS(2)	Cessna 182S	80021	N97SD
D-ECRU	Reims/Cessna F.172H	0499	
D-ECRV	Reims/Cessna F.150L	0758	
D-ECRW	Reims/Cessna FR.172H Rocket	0306	
D-ECRX	Reims/Cessna F.172L	0855	
D-ECRZ	Reims/Cessna F.172L	0854	
D-ECSA(2)	Mooney M.20J Model 201	24-0086	
D-ECSB(2)	Piper PA-28-140 Cherokee B	28-25086	N7233F
D-ECSC	Reims/Cessna FR.172H Rocket	0319	
D-ECSE(2)	Reims/Cessna FR.172H Rocket	0292	
D-ECSF	Piper PA-28-140 Cherokee	28-21121	HB-OYG
			(N6941W)
D-ECSG	Reims/Cessna F.172L	0813	
D-ECSH	Reims/Cessna F.150L	0779	
D-ECSI	Piper PA-28-180 Cherokee C	28-2325	N8197W
D-ECSJ	Reims/Cessna F.150L	0780	
D-ECSL	Reims/Cessna F.150L	0837	
D-ECSM(2)	Robin DR.400/180 Régent	1957	
D-ECSN	Reims/Cessna FR.172H Rocket	0305	
D-ECSQ(2)	Sportavia-Pützer RS-180 Sportsman	6003	
D-ECSR	Reims/Cessna FRA.150L Aerobat	0140	
D-ECSS	Reims/Cessna F.172L	0844	
D-ECST	Gardan GY-80 Horizon 180	131	
D-ECSU	Piper PA-28-140 Cherokee	28-20516	N11C
			N6444W

Regn.	Type	C/n	Prev.Id.
D-ECSW	Reims/Cessna F.172L	0846	
D-ECSX	Reims/Cessna F.172L	0847	
D-ECSY(2)	Cessna 210N Centurion	63434	N5432A
D-ECSZ	Reims/Cessna F.172L	0848	
D-ECTA	Reims/Cessna FR.172H Rocket	0313	
D-ECTC(2)	Reims/Cessna F.172P	2105	
D-ECTE	Reims/Cessna F.150H	0275	
D-ECTG(2)	Reims/Cessna FR.172E Rocket	0038	D-ENBS
			(HB-CTI)
D-ECTH	Piper PA-28-140 Cherokee C	28-26676	N5845U
D-ECTI	Reims/Cessna F.172H	0437	
D-ECTK	American AA-1 Yankee	0327	N6127L
D-ECTL	Reims/Cessna FR.172H Rocket	0315	
D-ECTN	CEA DR.340 Major	439	
D-ECTO(2)	Reims/Cessna F.150L	0746	
D-ECTQ	Cessna 182P Skylane	61034	(D-EIWI)
			(D-EECD)
			N7394Q
D-ECTR	Reims/Cessna F.150L	0742	
D-ECTS(2)	Beech F33A Bonanza	CE-1186	N3113T
D-ECTT	Reims/Cessna F.150L	0884	
D-ECTV	Piper PA-22-108 Colt	22-8861	HB-OTV
D-ECTW(2)	Zlin Z.143L	0024	
D-ECTX	Reims/Cessna F.150L	0896	
D-ECTY	Reims/Cessna F.150H	0235	
D-ECTZ	Reims/Cessna F.150L	0897	
D-ECUB(2)	Reims/Cessna F.172N	1823	
D-ECUC(2)	Aeronca 7DC Champion (7AC convn)	7AC-3889	OO-SPA
D-ECUE	Reims/Cessna F.150L	0901	
D-ECUF(2)	Piper PA-28R-200 Cherokee Arrow	28R-7535169	N19EC
D-ECUJ	Reims/Cessna FRA.150L Aerobat	0184	
D-ECUK	Jodel D.9 Bébé	AB-07	
D-ECUL(2)	Piper PA-28-161 Warrior II	28-8316010	N8292R
D-ECUM	Piper PA-12 Super Cruiser	12-276	N98924
D-ECUN(2)	Ambrosini F.7 Rondone II	010	
D-ECUO	Reims/Cessna F.172M	0921	
D-ECUP(2)	Alpavia Jodel D.117A Grand Tourisme	1061/05	
D-ECUQ(2)	Reims/Cessna F.172M	0925	
D-ECUS(4)	Piper PA-28R-200 Cherokee Arrow II	28R-7435118	N40742
D-ECUT(2)	Reims/Cessna F.172M	0930	
D-ECUU	Reims/Cessna F.172M	0932	
D-ECUV(2)	Reims/Cessna F.172M	0934	
D-ECUW	Wassmer Jodel D.120R Paris-Nice	157	
D-ECUY	Reims/Cessna F.172M	0935	
D-ECUZ	Auster Mk.5 Alpha	3414	G-APUL
D-ECVA	GEMS MS.892A Rallye Commodore 150	10529	
D-ECVB	Reims/Cessna F.172M	0937	
D-ECVC	Reims/Cessna FR.172J Rocket	0361	
D-ECVE	GEMS MS.892A Rallye Commodore 150	10536	
D-ECVF	Reims/Cessna FR.172J Rocket	0378	
D-ECVH	Reims/Cessna FR.172J Rocket	0381	
D-ECVI	GEMS MS.892A Rallye Commodore 150	10537	
D-ECVJ	Reims/Cessna FR.172J Rocket	0382	
D-ECVK(2)	Reims/Cessna F.172N	1397	
D-ECVL	Cessna 182P Skylane	61603	(N21389)
D-ECVO	GEMS MS.892A Rallye Commodore 150	10543	
D-ECVQ	Reims/Cessna F.150L	0899	
D-ECVS	Reims/Cessna F.150L	0902	
D-ECVT	Reims/Cessna F.150L	0904	
D-ECVU	Reims/Cessna F.172G	0182	
D-ECVX	Reims/Cessna F.150L	0910	
D-ECVY	Champion 7GCB Challenger	152	N9948Y
D-ECVZ(2)	Reims/Cessna F.177RG Cardinal RG	074	
D-ECWA	Piper PA-24-260 Comanche	24-4104	N8698P
D-ECWB	Reims/Cessna F.172M	0940	
D-ECWC(2)	SOCATA MS.893E Rallye 180GT Gaillard	12639	F-BVNY
D-ECWE(2)	Eggert Stoddard-Hamilton Glasair II RG-S	2010	
D-ECWF	Reims/Cessna F.172M	0943	
D-ECWG	Reims/Cessna FR.172J Rocket	0384	
D-ECWM	Cessna 182H Skylane	56192	N2092X
D-ECWJ	Reims/Cessna FR.172J Rocket	0387	
D-ECWK	Reims/Cessna F.150L	0912	
D-ECWM	Reims/Cessna F.150L	0917	
D-ECWN(2)	Robin DR.400/180 Régent	2145	
D-ECWO(2)	Piper PA-28-181 Archer II	2890121	N9183Z

Regn.	Type	C/n	Prev.Id.
D-ECWP	Reims/Cessna F.172M	0948	
D-ECWQ	Reims/Cessna F.172M	0950	
D-ECWR	Reims/Cessna F.172M	0951	
D-ECWS	Reims/Cessna F.172M	0952	
D-ECWT	SOCATA MS.893E Rallye 180GT Gaillard	12641	F-BXMJ
D-ECWV	Cessna 182P Skylane	61627	N21418
D-ECWX	Cessna 182P Skylane	61823	N79461
D-ECWY	Beech V35 Bonanza	D-8079	
D-ECXC	Cessna 182P Skylane	61618	N21407
D-ECXD	Cessna 182P Skylane	61583	N21356
D-ECXF	Reims/Cessna FR.172J Rocket	0397	(OE-DTG)
D-ECXG	Reims/Cessna FR.172J Rocket	0399	
D-ECXI (2)	Reims/Cessna F.150M	1249	HB-CXI
			N31056
D-ECXJ	Reims/Cessna F.172M	0974	
D-ECXK	Reims/Cessna F.172M	0975	
D-ECXM	Reims/Cessna FR.172J Rocket	0407	
D-ECXN	Reims/Cessna FR.172J Rocket	0410	
D-ECXO	Piper PA-18 Super Cub 95	18-1596	ALAT
			51-15596
D-ECXR	Reims/Cessna F.177RG Cardinal RG	0076	
D-ECXS	Cessna 182P Skylane	61750	N78101
D-ECXT	Cessna 182P Skylane	61848	N79935
D-ECXU	Piper PA-18 Super Cub 95	18-1484	ALAT
			51-15484
D-ECYC(2)	Cessna 182P Skylane	61833	(N79555)
D-ECYD(2)	Piper PA-38-112 Tomahawk	38-78A0417	N9669N
D-ECYF(2)	Cessna T.210L Turbo Centurion	59915	N30370
D-ECYG(2)	Reims/Cessna F.150L	0918	
D-ECYM(3)	Cessna 182P Skylane	62593	N52417
D-ECYO	Reims/Cessna F.150L	0934	
D-ECYR(3)	SOCATA Rallye 180T-D Galérien	2976	
D-ECYS(2)	Scheibe SF-23C Sperling	3500	
D-ECYV	Bücker Bü.181B-1 Bestmann	331381	SL-AAS
			Luftwaffe
D-ECYY	Wassmer WA.54 Atlantic	143	
D-ECZA	Procaer F.15B Picchio	24	
D-ECZB	Reims/Cessna FR.172F Rocket	0107	
D-ECZC	CEA Jodel DR.1050 Ambassadeur	28	F-BJOY
D-ECZD	Piper PA-18-100 Super Cub	18-3196	OL-L22
			L-122
			53-4796
D-ECZH	Reims/Cessna FR.172K Hawk XP	0672	I-ECZH
			D-ECZH
D-ECZI	Piper J-3C-65 Cub	20488	N7224H
			NC7224H
D-ECZJ	Reims/Cessna F.172M	0967	
D-ECZK	Reims/Cessna F.172M	0968	
D-ECZL(3)	Mooney M.20J Model 205	24-3333	
D-ECZN	Reims/Cessna FR.172J Rocket	0388	
D-ECZO(2)	Reims/Cessna FR.172J Rocket	0389	
D-ECZR	Reims/Cessna FR.172J Rocket	0391	
D-ECZS	Reims/Cessna FR.172J Rocket	0394	
D-ECZT	Reims/Cessna FR.172J Rocket	0395	
D-ECZU	GEMS MS.893A Rallye Commodore 150	10504	
D-ECZV	Reims/Cessna F.172M	1410	
D-EDAB(2)	Piper PA-28R-180 Cherokee Arrow	28R-30279	N3937T
D-EDAD(3)	Piper PA-28-180 Cherokee Archer	28-7405196	N43520
			N9638N
D-EDAE(2)	Reims/Cessna F.150L	0908	D-EDEA(1)
D-EDAF(2)	Piper PA-22-160 Tri-Pacer	22-6869	OY-AEY
D-EDAG(2)	Piper PA-38-112 Tomahawk	38-80A0034	N25137
D-EDAH(4)	Beech 35-C33 Debonair	CD-918	N19J
			N462KK
			D-EMYU
D-EDAI	Cessna 182N Skylane	60236	N92504
D-EDAJ	Cessna 172M	61886	N12214
D-EDAK(3)	Cessna 172N	68783	N734DW
D-EDAL(2)	Reims/Cessna FR.172J Rocket	0366	
D-EDAN(2)	Cessna 150J	70110	N60156
D-EDAO	Cessna 172N	68025	N75900
D-EDAP(2)	Cessna 150L	75118	N10898
D-EDAQ(2)	Bellanca 17-31ATC Turbo Viking	74-31100	N44313
			D-EDAQ
			N1HE

Regn.	Type	C/n	Prev.Id.
D-EDAR(3)	Cessna 150J	71060	N5560G
D-EDAS(4)	Diamond DA.20-A1 Katana	10239	
D-EDAU	Piper PA-28-181 Cherokee Archer II	28-7890363	N6342C
D-EDAV(3)	Robin DR.400/180R Remorqueur	1743	F-GEKR
D-EDAW(4)	Wördemann Pottier P.230S Panda	465	
D-EDAX(3)	Cessna 172M	65372	N5199H
D-EDAY(2)	Cessna T.210N Turbo Centurion II	64305	N6240Y
D-EDAZ(3)	Reims/Cessna F.172M	0959	
D-EDBA	Cessna 182D Skylane	53449	N9049X
D-EDBB(2)	Robin HR.100/210D Safari	213	
D-EDBC(2)	Reims/Cessna F.182Q Skylane	0149	HB-CIK
			D-EFPV
			(D-EFQF)
D-EDBD	SOCATA MS.880B Rallye Club	2372	F-BUXF
D-EDBE(4)	Reims/Cessna 182P Skylane	0053/64362	N1520M
D-EDBF(3)	Robin DR.400/180RP Remorqueur	1857	
D-EDBG(3)	Piper PA-28-181 Archer II	2890150	N92104
D-EDBH(2)	Reims/Cessna FR.182 Skylane RG	0007	
D-EDBI (2)	CASA I-131E Jungmann	2085	E3B-374
D-EDBK	Reims/Cessna F.182Q Skylane	0085	
D-EDBL(2)	Reims/Cessna FR.182 Skylane RG	0006	
D-EDBM(2)	PZL-104 Wilga 35	61118	DDR-WBM
			DM-WBM(2)
D-EDBN	Reims/Cessna F.182Q Skylane	0070	
D-EDBP(2)	Robin DR.400/180R Remorqueur	2178	
D-EDBQ	Reims/Cessna F.172N	1569	PH-AXL
			F-WZDD
D-EDBR	Reims/Cessna F.172P	2082	
D-EDBS(2)	Beech F33A Bonanza	CE-1615	
D-EDBT(2)	CASA I-131E Jungmann	2083	E3B-479
D-EDBU(3)	Piper PA-46-310P Malibu	4608013	SE-IUM
			N9084N
D-EDBV(2)	Piper PA-28-236 Dakota	28-8011131	N8247T
D-EDBW(3)	Piaggio FWP.149D	107	90+88
			AC+438
			CA+012
			AS+426
D-EDBX	Cessna 182P Skylane	63175	OY-RPN
			D-EOQQ
			N7392N
D-EDBY	Linzenkirchner Piel CP.301A Emeraude	AB.423	
D-EDBZ	Reims/Cessna F.182Q Skylane	0090	
D-EDCA(2)	Beech V35B Bonanza	D-9131	N4262A
D-EDCB(2)	Piper PA-22-108 Colt	22-8719	D-EDCA
D-EDCC(5)	Piper PA-32-300 Cherokee Six	32-7840193	N22408
D-EDCD(3)	Cessna 182P Skylane	62697	OY-BFF
			(N52596)
D-EDCE	Piper PA-22-108 Colt	22-8665	
D-EDCF	Wassmer WA.41 Baladou	157	F-BPTZ
D-EDCG	Dornier Do.27B-1	245	55+87
			PA+316
			PA+109
			PG+107
D-EDCI	Piper PA-18 Super Cub 95	18-1976	L-5
			52-2376
D-EDCJ	SOCATA MS.894A Minerva 220	11939	
D-EDCK(2)	SNCAN/ Stampe SV.4C	540	F-BDCK
D-EDCL	SIAT 223 A-1 Flamingo	052	EC-52A
D-EDCM(3)	Piper PA-28RT-201 Arrow IV	28R-8018103	N8259X
D-EDCN	Cessna TR.182 Turbo Skylane RG	00742	N736MU
D-EDCO	Cessna 175B Skylark	56812	OE-DCE
			N8112T
D-EDCP	Reims/Cessna F.152	1507	
D-EDCQ	Reims/Cessna F.172N	1736	
D-EDCR(2)	Cessna TR.182 Turbo Skylane RG	01099	(N756KY)
D-EDCS	Dornier Do.27A-1	268	56+01
			SA+115
			SA+723
			D-ELMU
			GB+ . . .
D-EDCU	Cessna 182G Skylane	55342	(N2142R)
D-EDCV	Dornier Do.27A-4	390	56+82
			PE+220
			PP+104
			PL+424

Regn.	Type	C/n	Prev.Id.
D-EDCW	Reims/Cessna F.172N	1776	
D-EDCZ	Piaggio FWP.149D	019	90+10
			AC+442
			ND+107
			DB+393
D-EDDA	Piper PA-18-150 Super Cub	18-7583	
D-EDDB(2)	Cessna 172P	74499	N52352
D-EDDC(2)	Piper PA-28R-200 Cherokee Arrow II	28R-7535186	N33749
D-EDDD	CASA I-131E Jungmann	2223	E3B-604
D-EDDE	Wassmer Jodel D.120R Paris-Nice	20	F-BHTT
D-EDDI (2)	CASA I-131E Jungmann	2172	E3B-552
D-EDDK	Piper PA-28R-200 Cherokee Arrow II	28R-7535189	N33760
D-EDDL(3)	Cessna R.182 Skylane RG	01887	N5534T
D-EDDM(2)	PZL-104 Wilga 35A	118413	
D-EDDN	Mooney M.20C Mark 21	2595	(N6891U)
D-EDDO(2)	Grumman AA-5B Tiger	0005	N6144A
D-EDDP	Cessna 182L Skylane	58765	(N3465R)
D-EDDR(2)	SOCATA TB-10 Tobago	1642	
D-EDDT	Mooney M.20C Ranger	680103	N6802N
D-EDDU(5)	Piper PA-28-201T Turbo Arrow III	28R-7803065	OY-BTK
D-EDDV(3)	Cessna 172S	172S8165	N7256C
D-EDDW	Piper PA-22-108 Colt	22-8879	D-EDDI
D-EDDY	Dornier Do.27Q-5	2096	
D-EDDZ	PZL-104 Wilga 35A	129453	
D-EDEA(2)	Reims/Cessna FR.172K Hawk XP	0640	I-BZEA
D-EDEB(4)	Reims/Cessna FR.172J Rocket	0418	
D-EDED(3)	Mooney M.20J Model 201	24-1149	N1138Z
D-EDEE(2)	Aerotek Pitts S-2A	2188	G-FREE
			LN-NAC
D-EDEF	Bücker Bü.131 Lerche R-180	63	HB-ESA
			A-87
			HB-ESA
D-EDEG(4)	Beech B36TC Bonanza	EA-447	N7243E
D-EDEH(3)	Robin DR.400/180R Remorqueur	1429	
D-EDEK(3)	Piper PA-28-236 Dakota	28-8011082	N8143H
D-EDEL(3)	Piper PA-32-300 Cherokee Six D	32-7140009	N8617N
D-EDEM(3)	Cessna 172RG Cutlass	1142	ZS-LED
			N9376D
D-EDEO	Reims/Cessna F.150L	0925	
D-EDEQ(2)	Beech B24R Sierra 200	MC-239	
D-EDER(3)	Beech B24R Sierra 200	MC-250	
D-EDEU	Reims/Cessna F.172M	0958	
D-EDEW(3)	Piper J-3C-65 Cub	"49215"	D-EDET
	(Uses paperwork of 43-29215 c/n 10506 which		(Norway)
	actually became D-EBUS/ OE-AAN)		44-. . . . . .
D-EDEX	Klemm Kl.35D Special	1916	SE-BPI
			Fv5027
D-EDEY	Reims/Cessna F.172M	0973	F-WLIL
D-EDFA(2)	Robin DR.400/RP Remorqueur	1803	
D-EDFB(3)	Piper PA-28-181 Archer II	28-8190131	N8318S
D-EDFC	Reims/Cessna F.150H	0246	
D-EDFD(2)	Piper PA-28-181 Archer II	2890145	N649CT
			N9203D
D-EDFE(2)	Cessna 172R	80109	
D-EDFF	Reims/Cessna F.172H	0463	
D-EDFG	Reims/Cessna F.172H	0481	
D-EDFH(3)	Zlin Z.142	0217	HA-SFH
D-EDFJ(2)	Cessna 150G (Reservation 1.99)	66503	N8603J
D-EDFK	SOCATA MS.893A Rallye Commodore 180	11775	F-BSXX
D-EDFL	Dornier Do.27B-3	392	56+84
			YA+913
			D-EDFL
			D-EBIV
D-EDFM	Robin DR.400/180 Régent	1326	
D-EDFN(3)	Cessna 210LCenturion	60673	OE-DFN
			N1637X
D-EDFO(3)	Reims/Cessna F.172N	1558	
D-EDFP	SIAI-Marchetti S.205-22/R	4-127	D-EDPF
			OO-RAS
D-EDFR	Robin DR.400/180R Remorqueur	1334	
D-EDFS	Dornier Do.27H-2	2006	
D-EDFT	Piper PA-18 Super Cub 95	18-3452	96+28
			NL+119
			AC+527
			AS+527, 54-752

Regn.	Type	C/n	Prev.Id.
D-EDFU	Piper PA-22-108 Colt	22-8904	
D-EDFY	Cessna 182H Skylane	56023	N1923X
D-EDFZ	Piper PA-18 Super Cub 95	18-3427	96+09
			NL+1 ..
			AC+516
			AA+516
			AS+516
			54-727
D-EDGA(4)	Piper PA-28-161 Warrior II	28-8516024	N9512N
D-EDGC(3)	Piper PA-18 Super Cub 95	18-1522	ALAT
			51-15522
D-EDGD	Piper PA-18 Super Cub 95	18-1387	ALAT
			51-15387
D-EDGE(3)	Extra EA330/L (Permit)	03	
D-EDGF	SIAI-Marchetti SF.260	2-38	OH-SRB
			(OO-HEW)
D-EDGG	Reims/Cessna F.152	1932	
D-EDGH	Gyroflug SC-01 Speed Canard	S-17	
D-EDGI (2)	Mooney M.20K Model 231	25-0193	N231CE
D-EDGK	Cessna TR.182 Turbo Skylane RG	00941	PH-AYM
			N738MD
D-EDGL	Reims/Cessna F.150M	1235	
D-EDGM	Robin DR.400/180 Major	2384	
D-EDGR	SOCATA Rallye 235ED Gabier	13154	
D-EDGT	Rockwell Commander 114A	14521	N5904N
D-EDGU	Reims/Cessna F.150H	0232	
D-EDGV	Rockwell Commander 114A	14531	
D-EDGW	SOCATA MS.880B Rallye Club	2509	F-BVLS
D-EDGY	Reims/Cessna F.172H	0451	
D-EDGZ	Horstmann Jurca MJ.5-D2 Sirocco	025D	
D-EDHA	Pützer Elster C	040	
D-EDHB(3)	Piper PA-28-181 Archer II	28-8690038	N9091B
			(N173AV)
			N9500N
D-EDHC	Beech 23 Musketeer	M-454	OE-DRK
			SE-EEP
			D-ENXI
D-EDHD	Reims/Cessna F.172H	0321	N17012
D-EDHE	Pützer Elster C	041	
D-EDHF(2)	Mooney M.20J Model 201	24-0199	
D-EDHG	Robin DR.400/180 Régent	873	
D-EDHH	Piper PA-28R-200 Cherokee Arrow B	28R-7135063	N2118T
D-EDHI	Piper PA-28-180 Cherokee C	28-3149	N9107J
D-EDHK(2)	Beech F33A Bonanza	CE-1319	
D-EDHM	Robin DR.400/180 Régent	1574	
D-EDHN(2)	Cessna 172R	80183	
D-EDHO	Piper PA-28-180 Cherokee C	28-3324	N9249J
D-EDHP	Beech V35 Bonanza	D-8568	HB-EHC
			N6207V
D-EDHQ	SOCATA MS.893A Rallye Commodore 180	11928	F-BTIY
D-EDHR	Gardan GY-80 Horizon 180	197	
D-EDHS(2)	SOCATA TB-20 Trinidad	1456	F-GLFT
D-EDHT	Winter D.31 Turbulent KWSA	D31-01	ZS-UHT
D-EDHU	Reims/Cessna F.150H	0236	
D-EDHV	Piper PA-18 Super Cub 95	18-1514	(D-EEMV)
			ALAT
			51-15514
D-EDHW	Beech A36 Bonanza	E-1044	
D-EDHZ(2)	Piper PA-18 Super Cub 95	18-3129	(OO-HBV)
			D-EHTR
			OL-L55
			L-55
			53-4729
D-EDIA(2)	Reims/Cessna F.172P	2131	
D-EDIC(2)	Reims/Cessna F.150L	1264	
D-EDIE(2)	Cessna 172RG Cutlass	1058	N9856B
D-EDIF(3)	Robin DR.400/180 Régent	925	
D-EDIG(2)	SOCATA MS.893A Rallye Commodore 180	11971	F-BTJC
D-EDIH(2)	Reims/Cessna F.172P	2156	
D-EDII (2)	Aviat Pitts S-2B	5209	
D-EDIJ	Reims/Cessna F.172P	2174	
D-EDIK(2)	Piper PA-28R-200 Cherokee Arrow B	28R-7135202	N1974T
D-EDIL(2)	Reims/Cessna F.172M	1418	
D-EDIM(3)	Robin DR.400/160 Chevalier	1009	
D-EDIN(2)	Reims/Cessna F.150M	1267	

Regn.	Type	C/n	Prev.Id.
D-EDIO	SOCATA TB-10 Tobago	229	
D-EDIQ	Pützer Elster C	009	
D-EDIR(3)	Piper PA-28-140 Cherokee	28-21275	N6602W
D-EDIS(3)	Piper PA-28RT-201T Turbo Arrow IV	28R-8031102	N8211C
D-EDIT	Piper J-3C-65 Cub	12722	44-80426
	(Officially quoted with fuselage number 12552 as c/n)		
D-EDIU	Bölkow BO.208C Junior	701	
D-EDIW(3)	Mooney M.20K Model 252	25-1173	
D-EDIX(2)	Cessna 175 Skylark	55114	N9314B
D-EDIZ(2)	Reims/Cessna F.172G	0219	
D-EDJA	Reims/Cessna F.150L	1100	
D-EDJC	Reims/Cessna F.172M	1178	
D-EDJD	Reims/Cessna F.150M	1146	
D-EDJE	Reims/Cessna F.177RG Cardinal RG	0108	
D-EDJF(2)	Mooney M.20K Model 231	25-0442	D-EKDW
			(N3666H)
D-EDJG	Reims/Cessna F.150L	1112	
D-EDJH	Reims/Cessna FRA.150L Aerobat	0241	
D-EDJI	Reims/Cessna FRA.150L Aerobat	0242	
D-EDJJ (2)	Cessna 172N	73723	N5786J
D-EDJK	Reims/Cessna F.172M	1161	
D-EDJL	Reims/Cessna F.172M	1162	
D-EDJN(2)	Piper PA-28R-200 Cherokee Arrow B	28R-7635264	HB-PAS
			N75086
D-EDJP(2)	SOCATA Rallye 235E Gabier	13339	
D-EDJR	Reims/Cessna F.172M	1176	
D-EDJT	Cessna 182P Skylane	62781	N52700
D-EDJW	Cessna 182P Skylane	63107	N7323N
D-EDJY	Reims/Cessna FR.172J Rocket	0503	
D-EDJZ	Cessna T.210L Turbo Centurion	60200	N59300
D-EDKA(2)	Reims/Cessna F.172G	0270	
D-EDKB	Piper PA-28-235 Cherokee C	28-11230	N9490W
D-EDKC	SOCATA MS.892A Rallye Commodore 150	10609	OY-DKB
D-EDKD	SOCATA TB-10 Tobago	230	
D-EDKE(2)	SOCATA TB-9 Tampico	231	
D-EDKH	Morane-Saulnier MS.880B Rallye Club	21	F-BKDJ
D-EDKI	Cessna 182F Skylane	54573	N3173U
D-EDKK	SOCATA MS.893A Rallye Commodore 180	10934	F-BPYY
D-EDKL(2)	Robin DR.400/RP Remorqueur	1845	
D-EDKM	Piper PA-18-135 Super Cub	18-4027	EI-283
			MM542627
			I-EIVJ
			54-2627
D-EDKN	Beech A36 Bonanza	E-1697	
D-EDKO	Cessna 172D	49967	N2367U
D-EDKP(2)	Beech V35 Bonanza	D-8217	N9595Q
D-EDKR(2)	Piaggio FWP.149D	093	90+75
			BF+406
			AS+412
D-EDKS(2)	Mooney M.20K Model 252	25-1223	
D-EDKT(2)	Reims/Cessna U.206G Stationair	0012/04816	PH-ALH
			PH-AYI
			N734AJ
D-EDKU(2)	Piper PA-28-180 Cherokee Challenger	28-7305115	
D-EDKV	Piper PA-28R-200 Cherokee Arrow B	28R-35709	N4969S
D-EDKX	SOCATA TB-10 Tobago	215	
D-EDLC(2)	Cessna P210N Pressurized Centurion II	00608	N734NX
D-EDLD(3)	Beech 77 Skipper	WA-173	N806Y
D-EDLE(3)	Piper PA-28RT-201T Turbo Arrow IV	28R-8131027	N8298H
D-EDLF(3)	Robin DR.400/180 Régent	2115	
D-EDLG	Beech V35B Bonanza	D-10338	
D-EDLH	Cessna 172	28871	N6771A
D-EDLI (2)	Robin DR.400/180R Remorqueur	1991	
D-EDLK	Reims/Cessna FR.172E Rocket	0007	
D-EDLL(2)	Boeing Stearman A75N1	75-2764	C-FUCB
			CF-UCB
			N49948
			41-25275
D-EDLM(2)	Gyroflug SC-01B-160 Speed Canard	S-36	F-GGCA
D-EDLN(2)	Cessna 152	80618	N25367
D-EDLO(3)	Robin DR 400/180 Régent	2308	
D-EDLP	Reims/Cessna FR.172E Rocket	0018	(G-AVYI)
D-EDLR	Reims/Cessna F.172H	0516	
D-EDLS	Reims/Cessna F.150H	0324	
D-EDLT(2)	Piper PA-28R-201 Arrow III	28R-7837093	N2574M

Regn.	Type	C/n	Prev.Id.
D-EDLV	Reims/Cessna FR.172E Rocket	0009	
D-EDLW	Reims/Cessna F.172H	0502	
D-EDLX	SOCATA Rallye 180T-D Galérien	3088	OE-DHL
D-EDLY	Reims/Cessna F.172F	0126	
D-EDMA(4)	Dornier Do.27A-4	396	56+88
			PS+716
			QW+720
			PL+426
D-EDMB(2)	SOCATA MS.880B Rallye Club	2510	F-BVLT
D-EDMC(2)	Schmidl Light Aero Avid Flyer Magnum *(Permit)*	1815	
D-EDMD	SOCATA TB-9 Tampico	232	
D-EDME	Bölkow BO.208C Junior	571	
D-EDMG(2)	Cessna 152	85279	N64830
D-EDMH	DDMH Homebuilt *(Permit 10.99)*	1951	
D-EDMI (3)	Commander Aircraft 114B	14645	
D-EDMJ	General Avia F.22BV Pinguino	013	
D-EDMK(2)	Oberlerchner JOB 15-150	052	OE-CAM
D-EDML	SOCATA MS.893E Rallye 180GT Gaillard	12183	F-BUCS
D-EDMM	Robin DR.400/180R Remorqueur	707	
D-EDMN	Piper PA-28R-200 Cherokee Arrow B II	28R-7235240	N1218T
D-EDMP(3)	General Avia F.22B Pinguino *(Reservation)*	022	
D-EDMR(2)	SOCATA TB-21 Trinidad TC	793	I-GLMC
			F-ODSD
D-EDMS	Cessna 172RG Cutlass	0560	PH-AXE
			N5534V
			(N5434K)
D-EDMT	Reims/Cessna F.172N	1570	
D-EDMU	Piper J-3C-85 Cub	5082	N30744
			NC30744
D-EDMV	SOCATA TB-10 Tobago	328	
D-EDMW	Piper PA-18 Super Cub 95	18-3426	96+08
			SA+120
			AC+515
			AS+515
			54-726
D-EDMZ	SOCATA TB-10 Tobago	787	
D-EDNA	Bölkow BO.208C Junior	578	
D-EDNC	Wassmer WA.51 Pacific	08	
D-EDNE	Bölkow BO.208C Junior	579	
D-EDNF	CEA Jodel DR.1050 Ambassadeur	34	F-BJYC
D-EDNG	SOCATA TB-9 Tampico	38	
D-EDNK	Cessna 182J Skylane	57422	SU-AOO
			D-EKDY
			N3422F
D-EDNL(2)	Piper PA-28R-200 Cherokee Arrow II	28R-7435240	OE-DRI
			N42850
D-EDNM	Reims/Cessna F.150M	1166	
D-EDNN(2)	Piaggio FWP.149D	173	91+51
			EB+391
			DA+385
			KB+149
D-EDNO(3)	Pützer Elster B	044	97+21
			D-ELBF
D-EDNP	Zlin Z.43	0059	
D-EDNR	SOCATA TB-9 Tampico	211	
D-EDNS	Mooney M.20E Chaparral	700041	N9482V
D-EDNT	Beech G35 Bonanza	D-4481	N174B
D-EDNU	Dornier Do.27B-3	401	56+92
			MC+901
			JB+901
			AC+959
D-EDNW(2)	Dornier Do.27B-1	176	55+46
			AS+902
			AC+906
			AS+906
D-EDNY(2)	Grumman AA-5B Tiger	1096	EC-DGF
			N4527C
D-EDNZ	CEA DR.253B Régent	139	OY-DNZ
D-EDOA	Piper PA-28R-201 Arrow III	28R-7837298	N39474
D-EDOB(2)	SOCATA TB-10 Tobago	242	
D-EDOC(3)	Cessna T.210M Turbo Centurion (Reims-assembled)	0005/61910	PH-DOC
			(PH-MDA)
			G-DAWN
			(N732ZS)
D-EDOD(2)	SOCATA TB-9 Tampico	239	

Regn.	Type	C/n	Prev.Id.
D-EDOE(2)	Schmidt Denney Kitfox IV	1691	
D-EDOF(3)	Robin DR.400/180R Remorqueur	965	
D-EDOG(2)	Reims/Cessna F.182Q Skylane	0128	
D-EDOH	Piper J-3C-65 Cub	unkn	SL-AAZ
	(C/n unknown - officially registered as "43-79321")		F-BGQV
			43-.....
D-EDOK(2)	Robin DR.400/180 Régent	1898	F-GGXL
D-EDOL(2)	Wassmer Jodel D.120A Paris-Nice	179	
D-EDOM(2)	Robin HR.200/120B Super Club	61	(D-EHKW)
D-EDON(3)	Beech A36 Bonanza	E-2071	
D-EDOP(3)	Opp Brändli BX-2 Cherry	01	
D-EDOR(2)	Reims/Cessna F.182P Skylane	0025/63993	N9933E
D-EDOS(2)	Reims/Cessna F.172P	2223	
D-EDOT(2)	Piper J-3C-65 Cub	11843	(D-EBOR(1))
	(Officially regd.with f/n 11671)		44-79547
D-EDOV(2)	Reims/Cessna F.172G	0227	
D-EDOW(2)	Schlör Stern ST-87 Europlane 1 *(Permit)*	1830	
D-EDOZ(2)	Reims/Cessna F.172G	0236	
D-EDPA(2)	Piper PA-28-181 Archer II	28-8690051	N9125Y
D-EDPB(2)	Bunte Van's RV-4	1632	
D-EDPC	Reims/Cessna F.172M	253	
D-EDPD	Piper PA-28R-200 Cherokee Arrow B II	28R-7235056	N4456T
D-EDPE	Piper PA-18-150 Super Cub	18-7736	N10F
D-EDPF(2)	Piper PA-18 Super Cub 95	18-3423	96+05
			NL+111
			AC+503
			AS+502
			54-723
D-EDPG	SOCATA TB-10 Tobago	243	
D-EDPH	Reims/Cessna TR.182 Turbo Skylane RG II	0006/01030	N756BG
D-EDPI	Morane-Saulnier MS.885 Super Rallye	133	OY-AFY
D-EDPK	Robin DR.400/180R Remorqueur	994	
D-EDPL	Robin DR.400/180R Remorqueur	1004	
D-EDPO(2)	Piaggio FWP.149D	168	91+46
			JD+393
			JE+393
D-EDPR	Dornier Do.27B-3	398	56+90
			PX+221
			PP+106
			PC+224
D-EDPS(2)	Cessna 172RG Cutlass	0114	N6204R
D-EDPT	Reims/Cessna F.172M	1272	
D-EDPU	Aeromere F.8L Falco America	234	(D-ENSO)
D-EDPV	Cessna 172RG Cutlass	0557	(F-GCQJ)
			N5531V
D-EDPX	Reims/Cessna F.152	1933	
D-EDPY	Weihermuller Binder CP.301S Smaragd	AB.701	
D-EDPZ	Dornier Do.27A-3	367	56+69
			YA+908
			AC+957
D-EDQC	Reims/Cessna F.182Q Skylane	0026	
D-EDQE(2)	Robin DR.400/180R Remorqueur	2193	
D-EDQF(2)	Robin DR.400/180R Remorqueur	1670	
D-EDQI	Reims/Cessna F.172H	0520	
D-EDQK	Reims/Cessna F.172M	1338	
D-EDQL	Reims/Cessna FR.172J Rocket	0555	
D-EDQP	Reims/Cessna 182P Skylane	0011/63869	N6869M
D-EDQQ	Reims/Cessna 182P Skylane	0013/63892	N6929M
D-EDQR	Robin DR.400/180R Remorqueur	1047	
D-EDQT(2)	Piper PA-28-236 Dakota	28-8011005	N8099X
D-EDQU	Reims/Cessna FR.172E Rocket	0060	
D-EDQV	CEA DR.315 Petit Prince	477	
D-EDQW	Cessna 210D Centurion	58342	HB-CMX
			(D-ECMX)
			HB-CMX
			N3842Y
D-EDRA	CEA DR.250/160 Capitaine	50	
D-EDRB(3)	Cessna 177B Cardinal	01422	N30720
D-EDRD	SOCATA MS.893ED Rallye 180GT Gaillard	12701	
D-EDRF(2)	Reims/Cessna F.172P	2183	
D-EDRG	SOCATA Rallye 235E-D Gabier	12714	
D-EDRH	Piper PA-28-151 Warrior	28-7415359	N9580N
D-EDRI (5)	Piper PA-28R-201T Turbo Cherokee Arrow III		
		28R-7703247	N38592
D-EDRJ	Cessna 182S	80514	N7282D

Regn.	Type	C/n	Prev.Id.
D-EDRK(3)	Dieth Stephens Acro Sport II	1654	
D-EDRL(2)	Robin DR.400/180R Remorqueur *(Reservn 12.99)*	1391	OE-DRP
D-EDRM	Cessna P210N Pressurized Centurion II	00448	OE-DUK
			N731EV
D-EDRN	Reims/Cessna F.172M	1249	
D-EDRO(4)	Piper PA-28RT-201 Arrow IV	28R-8118021	N8287U
D-EDRP(2)	Reims/Cessna F.172P	2179	
D-EDRQ	SOCATA Rallye 100ST-D	2910	
D-EDRR	Cessna 210B	57992	OE-DKM
			N9692X
D-EDRS	Dornier Do.27B-1	306	56+31
			PF+220
			PF+110
			PL+413
D-EDRT	SOCATA MS.893ED Rallye 180GT Gaillard	12755	
D-EDRU	Cessna 180D Skywagon	50956	N6456X
D-EDRW	Cessna 182P (Reims-assembled)	0032/64059	N6002F
D-EDRX	SOCATA Rallye 100ST-D	2911	
D-EDRY	Piper PA-18 Super Cub 95	18-7194	N3196Z
D-EDRZ	Piper PA-28R-200 Cherokee Arrow II	28R-7335230	N55422
D-EDSA	Cessna 180F Skywagon	51308	N4608U
D-EDSB(2)	Seger Pottier P.50P	01	
D-EDSC	Reims/Cessna F.172H	0688	
D-EDSD	Robin DR.400/180R Remorqueur	1299	
D-EDSE	Cessna 210-5	0399	N8399Z
D-EDSF	Piaggio P.149D	276	OE-DSF
			91+91
			AC+427
			AS+427
D-EDSG(2)	Reims/Cessna FR.172K Hawk XP	0665	
D-EDSH	Cessna 210A	57733	OE-DSH
			N9433X
D-EDSI	Cessna 210C	58135	N3635Y
D-EDSJ	Reims/Cessna F.152	1493	
D-EDSK	Reims/Cessna F.172M	1269	
D-EDSL	Piper PA-18 Super Cub 95	18-3438	96+17
			AC+506
			AS+505
			54-738
D-EDSM	Dornier Do.27A-1	279	56+11
			DB+901
			GD+159
			LB+159
			CC+. . .
D-EDSN(2)	HOAC DV-20 Katana	20146	
D-EDSO	Reims/Cessna F.172D	0002/49996	F-WLIP
			(N2396U)
D-EDSP	Dornier Do.27A-3	465	57+36
			MB+902
			JC+902
			AA+934 ?
D-EDSR(2)	Cessna 172P	75353	N62896
D-EDSS	CEA DR.315 Petit Prince	407	
D-EDST	Mooney M.20F Executive	22-1296	
D-EDSU	Cessna 182F Skylane	54714	N3314U
D-EDSW(2)	Stoddard-Hamilton Glasair IIS-RG *(Reservn 12.99)*	2179	
D-EDSX	HOAC DV-20 Katana	20062	
D-EDSY(3)	HOAC DV-20 Katana	20053	
D-EDSZ	Reims/Cessna F.152	1518	
D-EDTA	Piper PA-28-180 Cherokee C	28-3631	N9510J
D-EDTB	Reims/Cessna F.172H	0415	
D-EDTC(2)	Reims/Cessna F.172M	1323	(SE-GKG)
D-EDTE	Piper PA-18-150 Super Cub	18-7662	
D-EDTF(2)	Cessna 182P Skylane	61139	(N7499Q)
D-EDTG(2)	Piper PA-28-180 Cherokee D	28-4842	TF-VON
			N6424J
D-EDTH(2)	HOAC DV-20 Katana	20052	
D-EDTI	Morane-Saulnier MS.885 Super Rallye	257	HB-EDW
D-EDTJ	Reims/Cessna F.172H	0474	
D-EDTK	SAN Jodel D.117 Grand Tourisme	420	F-BHNE
D-EDTL(2)	Cessna A.152 Aerobat	1033	N758ZJ
D-EDTM	Piper PA-28R-180 Cherokee Arrow	28R-30644	N4923J
D-EDTN(2)	Cessna 177B Cardinal	02068	OE-DTR
D-EDTO	Cessna 150D	60482	N4482U
D-EDTP	Zlin Z.526 Trenér Master	1048	

Regn.	Type	C/n	Prev.Id.
D-EDTQ	Reims/Cessna FR.172F Rocket	0090	
D-EDTR	Cessna T.210L Turbo Centurion	60162	N59211
D-EDTS	Piper PA-28-181 Archer II	28-8090010	N8229E
			N9611N
D-EDTT(2)	Cessna P210N Pressurized Centurion II	00462	OE-DUD
			(N73IHM)
D-EDTU(2)	Cessna 172N	74459	N52249
D-EDTW	Gyroflug SC-01B-160 Speed Canard	S-6	
D-EDTX	Piper PA-28-181 Archer II	28-8290065	N8467E
D-EDTY(2)	Robin DR.400/120D Petit Prince	1876	
D-EDUA	CEA DR.253B Régent	173	
D-EDUB	Bücker Bü.181 Bestmann	25071	Fv25071
D-EDUC(3)	Piper PA-28-181 Archer II	2890170	N92327
D-EDUD(2)	Piper PA-28-181 Archer II	28-8090148	N81219
D-EDUE	CEA DR.253 Régent	174	
D-EDUF(3)	Cessna 172N	72224	N9320E
D-EDUG	SAN Jodel DR.1050 Ambassadeur	186	
D-EDUH(2)	Pützer Elster B	020	97+13
			D-EDYM
D-EDUK(2)	Reims/Cessna F.172M	1214	
D-EDUM(2)	Piper PA-28-181 Archer II	2890055	N9134R
D-EDUN(3)	Piper PA-18 Super Cub 95	18-1602	(D-ENCG)
	(Has f/n 18-1515 ex.51-15540 changed when		ALAT
	in ALAT service)		51-15602
D-EDUO	CEA DR.315 Petit Prince	481	
D-EDUP(2)	Piper PA-28-181 Archer II	28-8190081	N8289Y
D-EDUQ(2)	Piper PA-32-260 Cherokee Six	32-637	N11C
D-EDUR(2)	SIAI-Marchetti SF-260	1-10	OO-RUR
			F-BRUR
			OO-HAP
D-EDUS(3)	Cessna 172N	70580	N739JM
D-EDUT	Piper J-3C-90 Cub	8962	HB-ODM
			42-38393
D-EDUU(2)	Piper PA-28-181 Archer II	2890100	N9158D
D-EDUV(2)	SAN Jodel DR.1050 Ambassadeur	187	
D-EDUW(2)	Piper PA-28-140 Cherokee	28-23243	N9759W
			(G-AVKV)
			N9759W
D-EDUX(3)	Pitts S-1S Special	AB-K-025 (502)	
D-EDUY	Robin DR.300/180R Remorqueur	490	F-BSBU
D-EDUZ(2)	Reims/Cessna FR.172E Rocket	0035	
D-EDVA(2)	SOCATA MS.880B Rallye-Club	2335	OO-LVA
			F-BUVM
D-EDVB	Reims/Cessna F.172M	1439	
D-EDVC	Reims/Cessna F.172M	1442	
D-EDVD	Reims/Cessna F.172M	1452	
D-EDVE(3)	Robin DR.400/RP Remorqueur	1826	
D-EDVG	Reims/Cessna F.172N	1604	
D-EDVH(2)	Christen A-1 Husky	1106	
D-EDVI (2)	Reims/Cessna F.172N	1594	
D-EDVJ	Piper PA-28-140 Cherokee E	28-7225453	N11C
D-EDVK	Piper PA-28-180 Cherokee G	28-7205304	N11C
D-EDVM	SOCATA MS.893E Rallye 180GT Gaillard	12788	
D-EDVN	SOCATA MS.893E Rallye 180GT Gaillard	12789	
D-EDVP	SOCATA Rallye 150T-D	2776	
D-EDVR	Reims/Cessna F.150M	1363	
D-EDVS	Mooney M.20F Executive	670359	HB-DVS
D-EDVT(2)	Mooney M.20E Chaparral	690038	HB-DVT
D-EDVW	Beech V35B Bonanza	D-10381	N1847M
D-EDVX	Mooney M.20E Chaparral	21-0017	HB-DVX
D-EDVZ	Reims/Cessna F.150L	1003	F-BUMR
D-EDWA	Pützer Elster C	034	
D-EDWB(2)	Cessna P210N Pressurized Centurion II	00571	N732AC
D-EDWD	CASA I-131E Jungmann	196	
D-EDWH(2)	Piper PA-28R-201T Turbo Cherokee Arrow III		
		28R-7703266	N38722
D-EDWI	Pützer Elster C	036	
D-EDWJ (2)	CASA I-131E Jungmann	2136	E3B-453
	(c/n is as officially quoted - possibly 2054)		
D-EDWK	CASA I-131E Jungmann	2080	E3B-470
D-EDWL(2)	CASA I-131E Jungmann	2082	E3B-486
	(officially quoted as c/n 2062 - this is D-EGBM)		
D-EDWN(2)	Robin DR.400/180R Remorqueur	1927	
D-EDWO(2)	Westermann Polliwagen	002	
D-EDWP	Beech F33A Bonanza	CE-654	

Regn.	Type	C/n	Prev.Id.
D-EDWQ	Cessna 172R	80536	N9552W
D-EDWR(2)	SIAI-Marchetti SF.260C	725	
D-EDWS(2)	Reims/Cessna F.182Q Skylane	0034	
D-EDWW(2)	Piper PA-28R-200 Cherokee Arrow II	28R-7335436	N56438
D-EDWZ	CASA I-131E Jungmann	2015	E3B-411
D-EDXA	Reims/Cessna FA.150K Aerobat	0032	
D-EDXB	Reims/Cessna F.172H	0712	
D-EDXC	Reims/Cessna F.172N (Reservation 11.99)	1944	
D-EDXD	Reims/Cessna FR.172G Rocket	0211	
D-EDXE	Reims/Cessna F.172H	0726	
D EDXF	Reims/Cessna FR.172G Rocket	0169	
D-EDXG(3)	Drescher Skystar Kitfox V (Permit 11.99)	S 9508-0142	
D-EDXL	Reims/Cessna F.172M	1098	
D-EDXM	Reims/Cessna F.172M	1100	
D-EDXN	Reims/Cessna F.172M	1101	
D-EDXO	Reims/Cessna F.172M	1105	
D-EDXP	Reims/Cessna F.172M	1106	
D-EDXQ	Reims/Cessna F.172M	1112	
D-EDXR	Reims/Cessna F.172M	1034	F-BUMA
D-EDXT	Grumman AA-5A Cheetah	0085	OY-GAK
D-EDXV	SOCATA TB-10 Tobago	455	
D-EDXW	SOCATA TB-10 Tobago	462	
D-EDXX	SOCATA TB-10 Tobago	461	
D-EDYA	Bölkow BO.207	286	HB-UYA
			D-ENVY
D-EDYC(2)	Piper PA-28RT-201T Turbo Arrow IV	28R-7931165	N2174Z
D-EDYH	Piper PA-12 Super Cruiser	12-3480	SL-ABE
			F-BEGP
			NC4052H
D-EDYK	Piper PA-18-150 Super Cub	18-6300	
D-EDYL(2)	Pützer Elster B	019	97+12
			D-EDYL
D-EDYP(2)	Piper PA-28-181 Cherokee Archer II	28-7890545	N39625
D-EDYQ(2)	Piper PA-32-260 Cherokee Six	32-415	
D-EDYS(2)	Cessna 150F	63806	YN-BBH
			AN-BBH
			N7706F
D-EDYT	Piper J-3C-65 Cub	11771	HB-OEG
			43-30480
D-EDYV	Focke-Wulf FW.44J Stieglitz	2549	Fv667
	(Quoted identity suspect - believed ex Fv5771 or 5772)		
D-EDZE	Cessna 210	57160	N7460E
D-EDZG	Reims/Cessna FR.172J Rocket	0540	PH-RPF
			F-BJDY
D-EDZI	Reims/Cessna F.172E	0023/50578	OE-DEO
			(N2978U)
D-EDZL	Cessna 182P (Reims-assembled)	0001/63772	N6598M
D-EDZM	Cessna 182P (Reims-assembled)	0002/63788	N6644M
D-EDZN	Reims/Cessna F.150M	1168	
D-EDZO(2)	Cessna 182P Skylane	63549	N5811J
D-EDZQ	Piper PA-28R-180 Cherokee Arrow	28R-31120	N3172R
D-EDZU	Cessna 182H Skylane	56163	N2063X
D-EDZW	Piper PA-38-112 Tomahawk	38-81A0103	N26022
D-EDZY	Cessna 182H Skylane	56392	N2492X
D-EEAA	Reims/Cessna FR.172K Hawk XP	0639	
D-EEAB	Bölkow BO.208C Junior	681	
D-EEAC	Bölkow BO.208C Junior	682	
D-EEAD	Stark Piel CP.301A Emeraude	101-052	OY-EAD
D-EEAF(3)	Dornier Do.27B-1	274	HB-HAF
			D-EATA(1)
			56+07
			AC+926
			AS+926
D-EEAG(2)	Oberlerchner JOB 15-150	053	OE-CAG
D-EEAH	Bölkow BO.208C Junior	658	(D-EJMH)
D-EEAI	Bölkow BO.208C Junior	686	
D-EEAJ (2)	de Havilland DH.82A Tiger Moth	86450	F-BGCA
			Fr.AF
			NM130
D-EEAK(2)	Reims/Cessna F.150J	0466	
D-EEAL(2)	Piper PA-28-180 Cherokee D	28-4734	N6326J
D-EEAM(2)	Cessna 170B	25080	HB-COM
			N8228A
D-EEAN(2)	Piper PA-28-181 Archer II	28-8390025	N8322X
D-EEAO(2)	Cessna P210R Pressurized Centurion II	00646	N5289A

Regn.	Type	C/n	Prev.Id.
D-EEAP	Reims/Cessna FR.172F Rocket	0067	
D-EEAR	SAN Jodel D.140C Mousquetaire III	143	
D-EEAS(3)	Cessna P210N Pressurized Centurion II	00328	N4809K
D-EEAT	Reims/Cessna FR.172F Rocket	0062	(G-AXBT)
D-EEAU(3)	Robin HR.200/120B	274	
D-EEAW	Robin HR.200/100 Club	48	
D-EEAY	Ruschmeyer R90-230RG	017	
D-EEAZ	Piaggio P.149D	323	92+25
			AS+403
			AS+473
D-EEBA(2)	Reims/Cessna F.150L	0787	PH-VSE
D-EEBB	Reims/Cessna F.150J	0507	
D-EEBC(2)	Reims/Cessna F.150M	1270	
D-EEBD	Reims/Cessna F.172H	0640	
D-EEBE(2)	Piper PA-38-112 Tomahawk	38-80A0112	N24817
D-EEBF(2)	Maule M-6-235 Super Rocket	7490C	N5671T
D-EEBG	Reims/Cessna F.152	1437	
D-EEBI	Robin DR.400/180R Remorqueur	1462	
D-EEBK	Piper PA-28R-200 Cherokee Arrow II	28R-7435014	N56574
D-EEBL	Piper PA-28R-201T Turbo Arrow IV	28R-8031065	N8158B
D-EEBM	Robin DR.400/180 Régent	929	
D-EEBN(2)	Beech F33A Bonanza	CE-1280	N3217M
D-EEBO(2)	Reims/Cessna F.150M	1273	
D-EEBP	Reims/Cessna F.182Q Skylane	0041	
D-EEBS(2)	Zlin Z.526F Trenér Master	1151	(D-EJLL)
			SP-CDM
D-EEBT(2)	Beech F33A Bonanza	CE-1479	N44LR
D-EEBU	Piper PA-28-235 Cherokee B	28-10848	N9190W
D-EEBV	Ruschmeyer R90-230RG	011	
D-EEBW	Mooney M.20J Model 201	24-0424	
D-EEBZ	SOCATA TB-10 Tobago	983	
D-EECA	Beech V35B Bonanza	D-9120	
D-EECB	Reims/Cessna FR.172J Rocket	0487	
D-EECE	Reims/Cessna FR.172J Rocket	0495	
D-EECF	Cessna 182P Skylane	62784	N52706
D-EECH	Cessna 182P Skylane	62850	N52794
D-EECI (2)	Piper PA-46-350P Malibu	4622123	N312CC
			JA4194
			N111K
			JA4194
			N9208Z
			(N444JM)
			N9208Z
D-EECK	Wassmer WA.52 Europa	56	
D-EECL(3)	Rockwell Commander 112TC	13039	N112FH
D-EECM(2)	Reims/Cessna F.172M	1444	
D-EECN	Piper PA-28-235 Cherokee Charger	28-7310156	N55766
D-EECO	Beech V35B Bonanza	D-9229	
D-EECP(2)	Piper PA-28-161 Warrior II	28-8116242	N9543N
D-EECQ	Reims/Cessna F.172M	1280	
D-EECR(2)	Ruschmeyer R90-230FG	001	
D-EECU(2)	Robin DR.400/180R Remorqueur	1215	
D-EECV	Reims/Cessna F.172N	1634	(SU-...)
D-EECW(2)	Heliopolis Gomhouria Mk.6	186	SU-345
			EAF-345
D-EEDB(2)	Bartling Cozy-Canard	01	
D-EEDD(2)	Diamond DA.20-A1 Katana	10315	N315DA
D-EEDE	SOCATA MS.883 Rallye 115	1573	F-BTHJ
D-EEDF(2)	Cessna 172N	69683	N737UJ
D-EEDG	Reims/Cessna F.172M	0906	
D-EEDH	Reims/Cessna F.172M	0913	
D-EEDI (2)	Sebald Monnett Sonerai IVS	VS-1	
D-EEDJ	Reims/Cessna FR.172J Rocket	0355	
D-EEDK(2)	Reims/Cessna F.150L	0941	(D-EGKD)
D-EEDL	Reims/Cessna FR.172J Rocket	0359	
D-EEDM(2)	Piper PA-28R-200 Cherokee Arrow II	28R-7435266	N43391
D-EEDN	Reims/Cessna F.150L	0874	
D-EEDP	Reims/Cessna F.150L	0878	
D-EEDR	Reims/Cessna F.172M	0917	
D-EEDS(2)	Beech A36AT Bonanza	E-2714	
D-EEDT	Reims/Cessna F.172M	0919	
D-EEDU	Cessna 182P Skylane	61537	N21284
D-EEDV	Cessna 182P Skylane	61524	N21262
D-EEDW(2)	SNCAN/ Stampe SV.4C	245	F-BCKD
D-EEDX	Cessna 182P Skylane	61530	N21272

Regn.	Type	C/n	Prev.Id.
D-EEDY	Cessna 182P Skylane	61544	N21295
D-EEEA	SOCATA TB-10 Tobago	116	
D-EEEB	SOCATA TB-10 Tobago	117	
D-EEEC	SOCATA TB-10 Tobago	118	
D-EEED	Piper PA-28RT-201 Arrow IV	28R-7918253	N2591U
D-EEEE(2)	SOCATA TB-20 Trinidad	300	
D-EEEF	Robin DR.400/160 Chevalier	883	
D-EEEG(2)	Gyroflug SC-01 Speed Canard	S-15	
D-EEEH	SOCATA Rallye 180TS Galérien	3322	
D-EEEI	SOCATA Rallye 180TS Galérien	3321	
D-EEEJ	SOCATA TB-10 Tobago	148	
D-EEEK	CASA I-131E Jungmann	2056	E3B-455
D-EEEL(2)	Piper PA-28RT-201 Arrow IV	28R-8018055	N8178A
D-EEEM	SOCATA Rallye 235E-D Gabier	13155	
D-EEEN	Mooney M.20J Model 201	24-0975	N3882H
D-EEEO(2)	CASA I-131E Jungmann	2042	E3B-436
D-EEEP	SOCATA TB-9 Tampico	140	
D-EEEQ	SOCATA TB-200 Tobago XL	1760	
D-EEER	SOCATA TB-10 Tobago	137	
D-EEES	Reims/Cessna FR.172E Rocket	0049	D-EBXO
D-EEET	SOCATA TB-10 Tobago	136	
D-EEEU	Morane-Saulnier MS.885 Super Rallye	136	F-BKLL
D-EEEW	Gyroflug SC-01B Speed Canard	A-3	
D-EEEX	Gyroflug SC-01B Speed Canard	A1-80	
D-EEEY(3)	Piper PA-46-350P Malibu Mirage	4622005	N9148V
D-EEEZ	Krauss Vari-eze VW-VP	A-0329	
D-EEFA	Piper PA-28-140 Cherokee C	28-26658	N5827U
D-EEFC	Piper PA-24-260 Comanche C	24-4932	N9425P
D-EEFD	Piper PA-28-140 Cherokee C	28-26598	N5774U
D-EEFE	Reims/Cessna F.172P	2168	
D-EEFF	Ficht Bölkow BO.209 Monsun 160RV *(from parts)*	301	
D-EEFG(3)	Beech F33A Bonanza	CE-1626	N82689
D-EEFH	Piper PA-28-140 Cherokee C	28-26736	N5885U
D-EEFJ	Piper PA-28R-200 Cherokee Arrow B	28R-35660	N3036R
D-EEFK(2)	Mooney M.20K Model 252	25-1175	
D-EEFL(2)	Beech F33A Bonanza	CE-1752	
D-EEFM	Piper PA-28R-200 Cherokee Arrow B	28R-35674	N4902S
D-EEFN(2)	Mooney M.20J Model 205	24-3215	
D-EEFO	Piper PA-28R-200 Cherokee Arrow B	28R-35679	N4907S
D-EEFP	Reims/Cessna F.172M	1238	
D-EEFQ	Cessna 172R	80342	
D-EEFR	Reims/Cessna F.172M	1246	
D-EEFS	Reims/Cessna F.172P	2186	
D-EEFU(2)	Rallye 235ED Gabier	13329	
D-EEFV	Piper PA-28-180 Cherokee E	28-5757	N3655R
D-EEFW	SOCATA MS.893A Rallye Commodore 180	11461	F-BSAU
D-EEFY(2)	Reims/Cessna F.172P	2229	
D-EEFZ	Cessna 172R	80341	N9491Z
D-EEGA	Beech B24R Sierra 200	MC-275	
D-EEGB	Beech B24R Sierra 200	MC-262	
D-EEGC	Robin DR.400/180R Remorqueur	1357	
D-EEGD	Piaggio P.149D	315	92+18 CA+478 AC+466 AS+466
D-EEGE(2)	Cessna T.210N Turbo Centurion II	63674	N4920C
D-EEGF	Robin DR.400/180 Régent	1013	
D-EEGG(2)	Mooney M.20J Model 205	24-3015	
D-EEGH(2)	Commander Aircraft 114B	14632	
D-EEGI	Piper PA-28-181 Cherokee Archer II	28-7790403	N2539Q
D-EEGJ	Piper PA-28-181 Archer II	2890066	N9137X
D-EEGK(2)	Cessna 182J Skylane	56742	N2642F
D-EEGL	Reims/Cessna F.172M	1335	
D-EEGM	Reims/Cessna T.210M Turbo Centurion	0010/62433	PH-ADK D-EGSD PH-LTM (PH-AYM) N761QL
D-EEGN(2)	CASA I-131E Jungmann	2095	E3B-351
D-EEGO	Piper PA-28-140 Cherokee Cruiser	28-7725210	N9632N
D-EEGP	Reims/Cessna F.172N	1981	
D-EEGR(2)	Piper PA-28R-201T Turbo Arrow	2831037	N4363P
D-EEGT	Robin DR.400/180 Régent	1061	
D-EEGU	Piper PA-28-161 Warrior II	28-7916457	N2831A
D-EEGV	Piper PA-28-140 Cherokee Cruiser	28-7325009	OO-TGB N15167
D-EEGZ	Reims/Cessna F.177RG Cardinal RG	0121	
D-EEHA	American AA-5 Traveler	0031	(N5831L)
D-EEHB	American AA-5 Traveler	0032	(N5832L)
D-EEHC	American AA-5 Traveler	0117	(N6017L)
D-EEHD	American AA-5 Traveler	0118	(N6018L)
D-EEHE(2)	Ruschmeyer R90-MF-85P-RG	V-001	(D-EJHR)
D-EEHF	American AA-5 Traveler	0136	(N6036L)
D-EEHG(2)	Cessna 182Q Skylane	67235	N97871
D-EEHH(2)	Ruschmeyer R90-230RG	007	
D-EEHK	American AA-5 Traveler	0288	(N7288L)
D-EEHL(2)	Mooney M.20J Model 201	24-1612	
D-EEHM	American AA-5 Traveler	0318	(N5418L)
D-EEHN	American AA-5 Traveler	0345	(N5445L)
D-EEHO	Piper PA-28-140 Cherokee	28-20779	CF-RWL
D-EEHP(2)	Reims/Cessna F.182Q Skylane	0165	OE-DOV
D-EEHR	Cessna 182P Skylane	61008	N7368Q
D-EEHS	American AA-5 Traveler	0411	
D-EEHT	American AA-5 Traveler	0412	
D-EEHU	PZL-104 Wilga 35A	86269	DDR-WHU DM-WHU
D-EEHV	Bücker Bü.181B-1 Bestmann	25008	OE-ABK Fv.25008
D-EEHW	Cessna P210N Pressurized Centurion II	00455	N731FX
D-EEHX	Ruschmeyer R90-230RG	008	
D-EEHZ(2)	Ruschmeyer R90-230RG	009	
D-EEIA(3)	Robin DR.400/180R Remorqueur	1692	
D-EEIC	Reims/Cessna FR.172J Rocket	0510	
D-EEID	Reims/Cessna FR.172J Rocket	0512	
D-EEIE	Reims/Cessna F.177RG Cardinal RG	0117	
D-EEIF	Reims/Cessna F.172M	1375	
D-EEII (2)	Piper PA-46-310P Malibu	4608036	N9106D
D-EEIK	Robin DR.400/180 Régent	890	
D-EEIL(3)	Piper PA-18-150 Super Cub	18-7909091	N82295
D-EEIM	Robin DR.400/180R Remorqueur	849	
D-EEIN (3)	Robin DR.400/180R Remorqueur	1938	
D-EEIP(2)	Bölkow BO.209 Monsun 160RV	152	HB-UEP D-EBJL
D-EEIR	Beech V35B Bonanza	D-9802	
D-EEIS(2)	Cessna 150L	75235	N11165
D-EEIT	SOCATA TB-200 Tobago XL	1625	
D-EEIU	Reims/Cessna F.172H	0512	PH-AAC
D-EEIV	Reims/Cessna F.172M	1372	
D-EEIW	Reims/Cessna F.172M	1371	
D-EEJA(2)	Yakovlev YAK-50	80-1705	DDR-WQO
D-EEJB	Robin DR.400/180R Remorqueur	968	
D-EEJC	Robin HR.200/100 Club	40	
D-EEJD	Robin HR.200/100 Club	42	
D-EEJE	Robin DR.400/180S	1894	
D-EEJF	Piper PA-46-310P Malibu	4608135	OE-KEF N67JB
D-EEJG	Cessna 172N	72269	N9455E
D-EEJH	Mooney M.20J Model 201	24-0586	
D-EEJI	Reims/Cessna F.152	1517	
D-EEJJ(2)	Beech A36AT Bonanza	E-2862	N3122D
D-EEJK	Reims/Cessna F.172P	2117	
D-EEJL	Reims/Cessna F.152	1545	
D-EEJM(2)	Cessna 172N	70216	N7381C
D-EEJN	Piper PA-28RT-201 Arrow IV	28R-7918074	HB-PDM N3048U
D-EEJO	Robin HR.100/210D Safari	202	
D-EEJP(2)	Reims/Cessna F.150G	0175	OE-CMU D-EFMU (D-EHER)
D-EEJQ	Cessna 152	83155	N46978
D-EEJR(2)	Ruschmeyer R90-230RG	020	
D-EEJS(2)	Beech B36TC Bonanza	EA-312	N170HP N6498U
D-EEJT(2)	Timmermann Denney Kitfox II	01/248	
D-EEKA	Zlin Z.226T Trenér 6	195	OE-CKA OK-MGW
D-EEKB(2)	Cessna 182S	80334	N9510P
D-EEKC	Wassmer CE.43 Guepard	469	

Regn.	Type	C/n	Prev.Id.
D-EEKD	Piper PA-28-180 Cherokee C	28-1999	N7952W
			6Y-JGM
			N7952W
D-EEKE	Beech F33A Bonanza	CE-1145	N500TK
			N500TL
D-EEKF	Reims/Cessna F.172M	1260	
D-EEKG	Reims/Cessna F.150M	1230	
D-EEKH	Gardan GY-80 Horizon 160	16	D-EGZB
			HB-DVA
D-EEKI	Wassmer WA.54 Atlantic	123	
D-EEKK	Jodel D.119OS Compostela	E.99	EC-BAC
D-EEKM	MS.885 Super Rallye	48	HB-EDQ
			OO-TEL
			F-BKEU
D-EEKO	Cessna 150F	62773	N8673G
D-EEKP	SOCATA TB-20 Trinidad	324	
D-EEKR	Robin DR.400/180R Remorqueur	746	F-BTZA
D-EEKT	Robin DR.400/180 Régent	1181	
D-EEKU	Piper PA-18-150 Super Cub	18-5380	ALAT
D-EEKW	Mraz M.1C Sokol	211	HB-TAD
D-EELA	Grumman AA-5 Traveler	0724	N5140A
			(N1324R)
D-EELB	Robin DR.300/180R Remorqueur	534	LX-FIZ
			F-BSLI
D-EELC(3)	Beech F33A Bonanza	CE-1589	N33PN
			F-GIFJ
D-EELD	Droge Jurca MJ.5-D2 Sirocco	030	
D-EELE	CASA I-131E Jungmann	2195	E3B-589
D-EELF	Gardan GY-80 Horizon 180	149	
D-EELH(2)	Cessna 172N	71463	N3192E
D-EELI	CEA DR.250/160 Capitaine	69	F-BNVG
D-EELK	Cessna 210L Centurion	60104	N59120
D-EELM	Grumman AA-5B Tiger	0151	
D-EELN	SOCATA Rallye 180TS Galérien	3359	
D-EELO	Robin DR.400/180R Remorqueur	951	
D-EELQ	Robin DR.400/180R Remorqueur	944	
D-EELR	Robin DR.400/180R Remorqueur	950	
D-EELS	Robin HR.100/210D Safari	191	
D-EELT	Cessna 172C Skyhawk	48963	N8463X
D-EELU(2)	Mooney M.20E Chaparral	700002	N9332V
D-EELV	Cessna 172N	73031	N1941F
D-EELW(2)	Beech F33A Bonanza	CE-1180	N3121A
D-EELY	Piper PA-28-161 Archer II	28-8216121	N9636N
D-EELZ(2)	Gyroflug SC01B-160 Speed Canard	S-4	(D-EBDA)
D-EEMA	SOCATA MS.892A Rallye Commodore 150	11440	F-BRYH
D-EEMB(2)	Piper PA-28-181 Archer II	28-8690047	N9096U
			N9513N
			N109IU
D-EEMC	Cessna 172M	66840	
D-EEMD	Cessna T.210L Turbo Centurion	60911	N5331V
D-EEME	Cessna T.210N Turbo Centurion II	64262	N6135Y
D-EEMG	Cessna 210C Centurion	58150	HB-CMG
			N3650Y
D-EEMI	Piper PA-28-151 Warrior	28-7415223	N9535N
D-EEML	Robin HR.200/100 Club	101	
D-EEMM(2)	Sondermann Christen Eagle II	S-0470	
D-EEMN	Cessna FR.182 Skylane RG	0040	PH-AXB
D-EEMO	SOCATA MS.892E Rallye 150GT	12377	F-BVNO
D-EEMP	Reims/Cessna F.150M	1247	
D-EEMR	Reims/Cessna F.172M	1356	(F-BXZV)
			(D-EJTA)
D-EEMS	Piper PA-18 Super Cub 95	18-3229	OL-L52
			L-155
			53-4829
D-EEMU	Robin DR.400/180 Régent	1036	
D-EEMV(2)	Cessna 172N	70839	N739VK
D-EEMW	Beech A36TC Bonanza	EA-190	
D-EEMX	Gyroflug SC-01B-160 Speed Canard	XM-49	
D-EEMY	Piper PA-32R-300 Lance	32R-7780248	N2489Q
D-EENA(2)	SOCATA TB-21 Trinidad TC	1378	HB-KDU
			D-ERHP
D-EENB	Cessna 182P Skylane	62476	N52239
D-EENC	Cessna 182P Skylane	62616	N52449
D-EEND	Cessna 182P Skylane	62622	N52457
D-EENE	Reims/Cessna F.150L	1073	
D-EENF	Reims/Cessna F.150L	1075	

Regn.	Type	C/n	Prev.Id.
D-EENG	Reims/Cessna F.150L	1076	
D-EENI	Reims/Cessna F.150L	1086	
D-EENK	Reims/Cessna F.172M	1119	
D-EENL	Reims/Cessna F.172M	1121	
D-EENO(2)	Cessna T.210N Turbo Centurion II	64162	N5321Y
D-EENP	Reims/Cessna FR.172J Rocket	0482	
D-EENQ	Reims/Cessna FR.172J Rocket	0484	
D-EENR	Reims/Cessna F.172M	1152	
D-EENT	Reims/Cessna FR.172J Rocket	0473	
D-EENU	Reims/Cessna FR.172J Rocket	0474	
D-EENW	Reims/Cessna F.150L	1089	
D-EENX	Reims/Cessna F.150L	1059	
D-EEOC	Reims/Cessna 182P Skylane	0024/63948	N9887E
D-EEOE(2)	Beech F33A Bonanza	CE-1647	N82627
D-EEOF	Robin DR.400/180 Régent	1435	
D-EEOI	Reims/Cessna F.150M	1279	
D-EEOK	Reims/Cessna F.172M	1286	
D-EEOL	Beech V35B Bonanza	D-10294	N66696
D-EEOM	Reims/Cessna F.172M	1295	
D-EEOO	Reims/Cessna 210M Centurion II	0013/62648	F-WZJE
			N761ZL
D-EEOP	Robin DR.400/180R Remorqueur	1434	
D-EEOR(2)	Reims/Cessna FR.172K Hawk XP	0624	PH-JET
D-EEOS	Reims/Cessna F.172P	2078	
D-EEOT	Piper PA-28-180 Cherokee Archer	28-7405193	N43408
D-EEOV	Robin DR.400/180 Régent	1427	F-GCAP
D-EEOW	SOCATA MS.894A Minerva 220	11024	F-BRDD
D-EEPA(2)	Piper PA-28-181 Archer II	28-8690045	
D-EEPB	Wassmer WA.40A Super IV	78	PH-TAK
			SE-CWI
D-EEPC	Reims/Cessna F.182P Skylane	0005	
D-EEPD	Piper PA-28R-200 Cherokee Arrow II	28R-7335013	N15072
D-EEPE	Robin DR.400/180R Remorqueur	1222	
D-EEPF(2)	Robin DR.400/180S	1958	
D-EEPG(2)	Robin R.2160D (Reservation 10.99)	160	HB-EQH
			F-ODIK
D-EEPH	Reims/Cessna F.172M	1216	(D-EOFY)
D-EEPI	Wassmer WA.54 Atlantic	151	
D-EEPJ	Dornier Do.27A-1	173	55+43
			AC+923
			AS+923
D-EEPK(2)	CASA I-131E Jungmann	2101	E3B-303
D-EEPL	Reims/Cessna F.172N	1539	
D-EEPM	Piper PA-28R-200 Cherokee Arrow II	28R-7435283	N43613
D-EEPN	Dornier Do.27A-4	395	56+87
			QA+101
			QW+709
			PL+435
			D-EJIG
D-EEPO	Cessna 182P Skylane	63418	N9652G
D-EEPP	Beech B24R Sierra 200	MC-378	OE-DFP
D-EEPQ	Robin DR.400/180 Régent	1234	
D-EEPR	Piper PA-38-112 Tomahawk	38-78A0292	N9676N
D-EEPS(3)	Cessna 172M	65632	N172WM
			N6893H
D-EEPU	Reims/Cessna F.150M	1286	
D-EEPW	Reims/Cessna F.182P Skylane	0003	
D-EEPY	Cessna TR.182 Turbo Skylane RG	01431	N4796S
D-EEQA(2)	Reims/Cessna F.172N	1697	
D-EEQH(2)	Reims/Cessna F.182Q Skylane	0078	
D-EEQI (2)	Piper PA-38-112 Tomahawk	38-79A0747	N9679N
D-EEQN(2)	Beech C24R Sierra 200	MC-663	
D-EEQP	CASA I-131E Jungmann	2100	E3B-493
D-EEQS	Reims/Cessna F.172N	1909	(LN-HOJ)
D-EEQT	Reims/Cessna F.172N	1920	
D-EEQW	Piper PA-18 Super Cub 95	18-3421	96+03
			NL+106
			AC+512
			AA+512
			AS+512
			54-721
D-EERA	Wassmer CE.43 Guepard	467	
D-EERB(2)	Piper PA-28-181 Archer II	28-8090366	N82408
D-EERC	Wassmer WA.54 Atlantic	154	
D-EERD	Piper PA-28-181 Cherokee Archer II	28-7790240	N9564N

Regn.	Type	C/n	Prev.Id.
D-EERE	Piper PA-28-235 Cherokee	28-10419	N8864W
D-EERF(2)	Wassmer WA.54 Atlantic	135	
D-EERG(2)	Beech F33A Bonanza	CE-1266	
D-EERH(2)	Ruschmeyer R90-230RG	003	
D-EERI(3)	Piper PA-28R-201T Turbo Arrow III	28R-7803273	N9691C
D-EERK(2)	Reims/Cessna FR.182 Skylane RG	0063	
D-EERL	Wassmer CE.43 Guepard	470	
D-EERM	Piper PA-28-180 Cherokee Archer	28-7405206	N9512N
D-EERN(2)	SOCATA TB-20 Trinidad	643	F-GENX
D-EERP	Piaggio P.149D	259	91+77
			AC+410
			AS+410
D-EERQ	Wassmer WA.81 Piranha	818	
D-EERS(2)	SOCATA TB-20 Trinidad	334	
D-EERT(2)	Reims/Cessna F.172M	1416	
D-EERU	Reims/Cessna F.152	1662	N1659C
D-EERV	Wassmer WA.81 Piranha	823	
D-EERZ	Piper PA-24-260 Comanche C	24-4920	N9415P
D-EESA	Reims/Cessna F.172M	1244	
D-EESB(2)	Cessna 172P	75461	N63648
D-EESC	Reims/Cessna F.172M	1289	
D-EESD	Beech V35B Bonanza	D-9786	
D-EESE	Reims/Cessna F.172M	1297	
D-EESF	Reims/Cessna F.172M	1309	
D-EESG(2)	Reims/Cessna F.172M	1315	
D-EESH	Reims/Cessna F.172M	1318	
D-EESI	Reims/Cessna F.172M	1322	
D-EESJ	Reims/Cessna F.172M	1325	
D-EESL	Reims/Cessna FR.172J Rocket	0549	
D-EESM	Reims/Cessna F.172N	1547	
D-EESN	SOCATA TB-10 Tobago	268	
D-EESO	Piper PA-28R-200 Cherokee Arrow II	28R-7435189	N41478
D-EESP	SOCATA TB-10 Tobago	269	
D-EESR	Piper PA-38-112 Tomahawk	38-79A0751	N9680N
D-EESS	Cessna P.210N Pressurized Centurion II (Robertson STOL version)	00648	N5169W
D-EEST	Piper PA-28R-200 Cherokee Arrow B	28R-35749	N5017S
D-EESX	SOCATA TB-9 Tampico	299	
D-EESY	Brand Rutan Vari-eze	1523/01E	
D-EETC	Reims/Cessna F.172H	0625	
D-EETD	Reims/Cessna F.150J	0456	
D-EETE	Piper PA-28R-200 Cherokee Arrow	28R-35179	N9463N
D-EETF(2)	Reims/Cessna F.177RG Cardinal RG	0137	OE-DRD
			D-EHRD
D-EETH	Beagle B.121 Pup 100	081	G-35-081
D-EETI	SOCATA MS.893A Rallye Commodore 180	11417	
D-EETK(2)	Reims/Cessna F.152	1513	F-GBJC
D-EETL(3)	Diamond DA.20-A1 Katana	10321	
D-EETM(2)	Robin DR.400/180R Remorqueur	1230	
D-EETN(2)	Robin DR.400/180R Remorqueur	1293	
D-EETO	Reims/Cessna F.172H	0646	
D-EETP	Reims/Cessna F.150J	0433	
D-EETQ	Reims/Cessna F.150J	0435	
D-EETR	Piper PA-28-140 Cherokee B	28-25767	N5598F
D-EETS(2)	Cessna 172P	75904	N65836
D-EETT(2)	Piper PA-18-150 Super Cub	18-850	R-201
			51-15685
D-EETU(3)	Haubold Aero Designs Pulsar XP	1810	
D-EETW(2)	Diamond DA.20-A1 Katana	10253	
D-EETX	Cessna 182K Skylane	58070	OE-DEB
			N3070Q
D-EETY	Piaggio FWP.149D	139	91+18
			ND+208
			DF+390
			AS+476
			KB+116
D-EEUA	SOCATA MS.893ED Rallye 180GT Gaillard	13110	
D-EEUB	SOCATA MS.893ED Rallye 180GT Gaillard	13111	
D-EEUD(2)	SOCATA TB-20 Trinidad	275	
D-EEUE	SOCATA Rallye 180TS Galérien	3193	
D-EEUF	SOCATA Rallye 180T-D Galérien	3194	
D-EEUH	SOCATA Rallye 180T-D Galérien	3195	
D-EEUI	SOCATA Rallye 180T-D Galérien	3196	
D-EEUJ	SOCATA Rallye 180TS Galérien	3197	
D-EEUK(2)	SOCATA Rallye 150T-D	2971	F-GBCC
D-EEUL	SOCATA Rallye 180TS Galérien	3136	
D-EEUM(2)	SOCATA TB-10 Tobago	270	
D-EEUO	SOCATA Rallye 180TS Galérien	3245	
D-EEUP	SOCATA Rallye 180TS Galérien	3246	
D-EEUQ	SOCATA Rallye 180TS Galérien	3247	
D-EEUR	SOCATA Rallye 180TS Galérien	3248	
D-EEUS	SOCATA Rallye 180TS Galérien	3249	
D-EEUT	Piper PA-18-150 Super Cub	18-8726	N4395Z
D-EEUU(2)	Cessna 172P	74551	N52538
D-EEUV	SOCATA Rallye 180TS Galérien	3251	
D-EEUW	SOCATA Rallye 180TS Galérien	3252	
D-EEUX	Huss Denney Kitfox 4-1200	1758	
D-EEVA(3)	Robin DR.400/160D Major 80	1576	
D-EEVB	Reims/Cessna F.172M	1209	
D-EEVD	Reims/Cessna F.172M	1202	
D-EEVE(2)	Cessna 172M	66168	N9467H
D-EEVG	Reims/Cessna F.150M	1180	
D-EEVH	Reims/Cessna F.150M	1190	
D-EEVI(3)	Mooney M.20J Model 201	24-1648	
D-EEVJ	Reims/Cessna F.172M	1270	
D-EEVK(2)	SIAT 223A-1 Flamingo	014	HB-EVK
			D-ENBK(1)
D-EEVM	Reims/Cessna F.172M	1291	
D-EEVN	Reims/Cessna F.172M	1293	
D-EEVO(2)	Mooney M.20J Model 201	24-0829	N4735H
D-EEVQ(2)	Reims/Cessna F.152	1655	N1662Q
D-EEVV	CASA I-131E Jungmann	2218	E3B-618
D-EEVX	American AG-5B Tiger	10144	
D-EEVY	Cessna 170A	19537	D-ELYC
			N5503C
D-EEVZ	SOCATA TB-9 Tampico	895	
D-EEWB	Reims/Cessna F.172L	0880	
D-EEWC	Cessna P210N Pressurized Centurion II	00542	N2108J
			(N731SA)
D-EEWD	Beech F33A Bonanza	CE-905	
D-EEWE(2)	Robin DR.400/180R Remorqueur	1973	
D-EEWF(3)	Cessna 172P	75316	N62632
D-EEWG(2)	Cessna 172P	74944	(D-EEAS)
			N54282
D-EEWH	Reims/Cessna F.172H	0603	D-EETM
D-EEWI	Beech F33A Bonanza	CE-509	
D-EEWK	Robin HR.100/210D Safari	195	
D-EEWL	Piper PA-18 Super Cub 95	18-3448	96+24
			NL+114
			AC+533
			AS+533
			54-748
D-EEWM	SOCATA MS.893ED Rallye 180GT Gaillard	13181	
D-EEWN	Beech A36 Bonanza	E-1823	
D-EEWO	Piper PA-18-150 Super Cub	18-554	R-202
	(Dismantled, 9.99, f/n 18-486)		51-15668
			N7183K
D-EEWP(3)	Ruschmeyer R90-230G	013	D-EEBY
D-EEWS	SOCATA MS.880B Rallye Club	2112	F-BTVT
D-EEWT	SOCATA MS.893E Rallye 180GT Gaillard	12214	F-BUCU
D-EEWW	Bölkow BO.208C Junior	645	(D-EGNU)
D-EEWX	Beech F33A Bonanza	CE-947	HB-EWX
D-EEWY	Reims/Cessna F.172M	0956	
D-EEXA	Reims/Cessna F.177RG Cardinal RG	0061	
D-EEXC	Reims/Cessna FR.172H Rocket	0330	
D-EEXE(2)	Heliopolis Gomhouria Mk.6	148	SU-325
			EAF-325
D-EEXG	Cessna T.210L Turbo Centurion	59508	N4608Q
D-EEXH	Reims/Cessna F.150L	0795	
D-EEXJ	Reims/Cessna F.150L	0797	
D-EEXK	Reims/Cessna F.150L	0803	
D-EEXL(2)	Piper PA-28-161 Warrior II	28-8116115	F-GFIG
			N8316D
D-EEXM	Reims/Cessna F.172L	0851	
D-EEXN	Reims/Cessna F.172L	0858	
D-EEXQ	Reims/Cessna FR.172H Rocket	0323	
D-EEXS	Reims/Cessna F.172L	0840	
D-EEXT	Cessna 182P Skylane	61164	(N20734)
D-EEXX	Reims/Cessna F.177RG Cardinal RG	0044	
D-EEXZ	Cessna 182P Skylane	61174	(N20745)

Regn.	Type	C/n	Prev.Id.
D-EEYC	Reims/Cessna F.150L	0773	
D-EEYD	Reims/Cessna F.150L	0799	
D-EEYE	Reims/Cessna F.150L	0805	
D-EEYG	Reims/Cessna F.172L	0869	
D-EEYI	Reims/Cessna F.172L	0872	
D-EEYJ	Reims/Cessna FR.172H Rocket	0322	
D-EEYM	Reims/Cessna FR.172H Rocket	0328	
D-EEYN	Reims/Cessna FR.172H Rocket	0329	
D-EEYO	Reims/Cessna F.150L	0808	
D-EEYP	Reims/Cessna F.150L	0811	
D-EEYQ	Reims/Cessna F.150L	0812	
D-EEYU(2)	Cessna TU.206F Turbo Stationair	02001	N51404
D-EEYY	Reims/Cessna F.172L	0876	
D-EEYZ	Reims/Cessna F.177RG Cardinal RG	0045	N4939
D-EEZA	Reims/Cessna F.177RG Cardinal RG	0062	
D-EEZB	Reims/Cessna F.177RG Cardinal RG	0060	
D-EEZC	Reims/Cessna FRA.150L Aerobat	0149	
D-EEZD	Reims/Cessna FRA.150L Aerobat	0159	
D-EEZE	Reims/Cessna F.172L	0875	
D-EEZF	Cessna 182P Skylane	61171	(N20742)
D-EEZH	Reims/Cessna F.172L	0871	
D-EEZJ	Cessna 182P Skylane	61450	(N21154)
D-EEZK	Cessna 182P Skylane	61493	(N21214)
D-EEZL	Cessna 182P Skylane	61713	(N21555)
D-EEZM	Reims/Cessna F.150L	0804	(G-AZKY)
D-EEZP(2)	Zuckschwerdt Vari-eze	1005	
D-EEZQ	Reims/Cessna F.150L	0865	
D-EEZR	Reims/Cessna F.150L	0868	
D-EEZT	Reims/Cessna F.172L	0867	
D-EEZU	Reims/Cessna FR.172H Rocket	0310	
D-EEZV	Reims/Cessna FR.172H Rocket	0338	
D-EEZW	Reims/Cessna F.172L	0884	
D-EEZX	Reims/Cessna FR.172H Rocket	0339	
D-EEZY	Reims/Cessna FR.172H Rocket	0340	
D-EEZZ	Reims/Cessna FR.172H Rocket	0341	
D-EFAA	SOCATA MS.894A Minerva 220	11625	F-BSFA
D-EFAB(2)	CEA DR.360 Major	576	
D-EFAC(4)	Robin DR.400/180R Remorqueur	2333	
D-EFAD(3)	Mooney M.20K Model 252	25-1157	N2528W
D-EFAE	Robin DR.400/180R Remorqueur	798	
D-EFAF	Stark Turbulent D-1	111	
D-EFAG(3)	Piper PA-18 Super Cub 95	18-1543	D-EFTG(1)
			ALAT
			51-15543
D-EFAH	Klemm Kl.107C	136	
D-EFAI	Zlin Z.326 Trenér Master	876	SE-CWK
			D-EFAI
			(D-ENQE)
D-EFAJ	Dornier Do.27B-1	104	55+01
			AC+901
			AS+901
D-EFAL(3)	Grob G.115A	8013	
D-EFAM(5)	Cessna 182S	80442	N7269H
D-EFAN(5)	Piper PA-28-161 Warrior II	28-7716163	N9647N
D-EFAO	Piper PA-18-150 Super Cub	18-5362	ALAT
D-EFAP(2)	Cessna P210N Pressurized Centurion II	00680	N5382W
D-EFAQ	Scintex CP.301C Emeraude	540	
D-EFAS	Cessna 140	10463	N76069
D-EFAT(3)	SOCATA MS.883 Rallye 115	1566	F-BTHI
D-EFAV(2)	SOCATA TB-9 Tampico	244	
D-EFAW(2)	Mooney M.20K Model 252	25-1184	
D-EFAX(3)	Reims/Cessna F.182Q Skylane	0137	PH-AXO
D-EFAY	Piper PA-28-161 Warrior II	28-8516070	N2495X
D-EFAZ(2)	Dornier Do.27A-1	285	56+17
			SE+527
			SC+705
			D-EKYB
D-EFBA(2)	Reims/Cessna F.152	1845	PH-MJE
			PH-AXH
D-EFBB	Beech 23 Musketeer	M-106	HB-ENB
D-EFBC	Robin DR.400/140 Major	884	
D-EFBE	Piper PA-18 Super Cub 95	18-6278	N8674D
D-EFBF	Sportavia RS-180 Sportsman	6014	
D-EFBG	Reims/Cessna F.182Q Skylane	0032	(F-GAGU)
D-EFBH	Sportavia RS-180 Sportsman	6015	

Regn.	Type	C/n	Prev.Id.
D-EFBI (2)	Sportavia RS-180 Sportsman	6016	
D-EFBJ(2)	SOCATA TB-9 Tampico	1041	
D-EFBK(2)	Robin DR.400/180R Remorqueur	1535	
D-EFBL	Piper PA-28-180 Cherokee G	28-7205282	N11C
D-EFBM	Sportavia RS-180 Sportsman	6019	
D-EFBN	Sportavia RS-180 Sportsman	6020	
D-EFBO(2)	Dornier Do.27A-1	338	56+52
			BD+399
			AB+399
D-EFBP(2)	Reims/Cessna FR.172K Hawk XP	0664	PH-AXF
D-EFBQ	Sportavia RS-180 Sportsman	6021	
D-EFBR	Piper PA-18 Super Cub 95	18-3457	96+33
			NL+112
			AC+539
			AS+539
			54-757
D-EFBS(2)	Sportavia RS-180 Sportsman	6022	
D-EFBT(2)	Reims/Cessna F.172N	1751	(D-EILW)
			PH-AXI
			(D-EMSP)
D-EFBU	Piper PA-18-150 Super Cub	18-8062	N4068Z
D-EFBV	Beech 77 Skipper	WA-250	
D-EFBW	Robin R.2160D Acrobin	117	F-OCSK
D-EFBZ	SOCATA TB-200 Tobago XL	1530	
D-EFCA	Cessna 172C	49056	N1356Y
D-EFCB(2)	CASA I-131E Jungmann	2225	E3B-606
D-EFCC	Reims/Cessna FR.172F Rocket	0089	
D-EFCE	Cessna 172C Skyhawk	49065	N1365Y
D-EFCH(2)	Piper PA-46-310P Malibu	46-8608037	N9082E
D-EFCI (2)	Gulfstream American AA-5B Tiger	1170	
D-EFCJ	Piper PA-28-180 Cherokee F	28-7105040	N5186S
D-EFCK	Piper PA-18 Super Cub 95	18-3436	96+15
			NL+101
			AC+504
			AS+503
			54-736
D-EFCL(2)	Robin DR.400/180R Remorqueur	751	F-BTZD
D-EFCM(3)	Cessna 182Q Skylane	67597	N5248N
D-EFCN	Piper PA-18 Super Cub 95	18-3439	96+18
			NL+117
			AC+524
			AS+524
			54-739
D-EFCO(2)	Wassmer WA.54 Atlantic	147	HB-DCO
D-EFCP	Piper PA-28-140 Cherokee F	28-7325302	N11C
D-EFCR(2)	Piper PA-28-181 Archer II	2890013	N9108Q
D-EFCU	SOCATA MS.893E Rallye 180GT Gaillard	12604	TL-HCU
D-EFCV	Piper PA-28RT-201 Arrow IV	28R-8018048	N81677
D-EFDA	Piper PA-24-250 Comanche	24-2977	N7850P
D-EFDB	Piper PA-18-135 Super Cub	18-3923	EI-227
			I-EIJX
			54-2523
D-EFDC(2)	SOCATA MS.893A Rallye Commodore 180	11776	F-BSMJ
D-EFDD	SAN Jodel DR.1050 Sicile	486	
D-EFDE(2)	Cessna 177A Cardinal	01273	N30466
D-EFDF(3)	Robin DR.400/RP	1787	
D-EFDG	Reims/Cessna F.152	1696	
D-EFDH	SOCATA TB-10 Tobago	716	
D-EFDI (3)	Piper PA-28-181 Archer II	28-8290111	N8180U
D-EFDK	Grumman AA-5 Traveler	0646	
D-EFDL	Grumman AA-5 Traveler	0645	
D-EFDN	Reims/Cessna F.152	1721	
D-EFDP	Dornier Do.27A-4	463	57+34
			PZ+222
			PG+105
			QM+019
			KD+113
			(D-ENLC)
D-EFDQ	Reims/Cessna F.172M	1298	
D-EFDR(2)	Piper PA-46-310P Malibu	4608061	N9124B
D-EFDS	Reims/Cessna F.172M	1312	
D-EFDT(2)	Cessna 172N	70544	N739GZ
D-EFDU(2)	Reims/Cessna F.152	1738	
D-EFEA(3)	Piper PA-28-181 Archer II	2890163	HB-PHF
			(HB-PHC)

Regn.	Type	C/n	Prev.Id.
D-EFEB(2)	Reims/Cessna F.172N	1737	
D-EFEC(2)	Cessna 140	14812	HB-CAM
			N3540V
D-EFED(2)	Robin DR.400/180 Régent	1203	
D-EFEE(2)	Cessna 172M	60996	G-BSAY
			N20086
D-EFEF	Stark Turbulent D	112	
D-EFEG(2)	Reims/Cessna F.172N	1734	
D-EFEH(2)	Reims/Cessna F.172N	1647	
D-EFEJ	Piper PA-28-181 Cherokee Archer II	28-7790329	HB-PBL
			N167OH
D-EFEK(2)	Reims/Cessna F.152	1522	
D-EFEL	Aeronca 65CA	C1868	HB-URU
D-EFEM(3)	Mooney M.20J Model 201	24-1589	
D-EFEN(2)	Reims/Cessna F.152	1526	
D-EFEO(2)	Christen A-1 Husky	1130	
D-EFEP(2)	Cessna 172	36481	N8781B
D-EFER(2)	Reims/Cessna F.172N	1702	
D-EFES(2)	Piper PA-28-161 Warrior II	28-8316037	N9627N
D-EFET(2)	SOCATA MS.894E Minerva 220GT	12132	F-BTVA
D-EFEU	Aero-Jodel D.11A Club	AB.6	
D-EFEV(3)	Reims/Cessna F.172P	2176	
D-EFEW(3)	Reims/Cessna F.172N	1710	
D-EFEX	Piper PA-22-150 Tri-Pacer	22-4892	
D-EFEY	Piper PA-28R-200 Cherokee Arrow B	28R-35718	N4993S
D-EFEZ	Klemm Kl.107B	111	
D-EFFA(4)	Ruschmeyer R.90-230RG	018	D-ELVY(2)
			(D-EEBY(2))
D-EFFC	Jodel DR.250/160 Capitaine	49	
D-EFFD	Robin DR.400/125 Petit Prince	716	
D-EFFE(2)	Reims/Cessna F.172M	1394	
D-EFFF	Robin DR.400/180 Régent	721	
D-EFFG	CEA DR.253B Régent	171	
D-EFFH	Cessna T.210L Turbo Centurion	60616	N8128L
D-EFFI (3)	Hankers Van's RV-4	1588/V-1	
D-EFFK	Piper PA-28R-200 Cherokee Arrow II	28R-7235273	N1384T
D-EFFL(3)	Piper PA-28R-201 Arrow IV	2837034	N9187X
D-EFFM	SAN Jodel D.150 Rapid	59	
D-EFFN	Piper PA-28-180 Cherokee G	28-7205309	N1497T
D-EFFO(2)	Reims/Cessna F.150M	1319	
D-EFFP	Piper PA-32-300 Cherokee Six	32-7440042	N57317
D-EFFR	Piper PA-28-181 Cherokee Archer II	28-7690190	N8885E
			N953ON
D-EFFS	Mooney M.20F Executive	680149	N3902N
D-EFFT	Reims/Cessna F.150M	1251	
D-EFFU	Berger Piel CP.301A Emeraude	AB-420	
D-EFFV	Piper PA-28-181 Cherokee Archer II	28-7790327	N9597N
D-EFFW	Gardan GY-80 Horizon 160	43	OO-JON
D-EFFX(2)	Grob G.115A	8048	
D-EFFY(4)	Grob G.115A	8041	
D-EFGB	Reims/Cessna F.150H	0248	
D-EFGD	Mooney M.20C Mark 21	3393	HB-DWE
			N3410X
D-EFGF(2)	Cessna 150M	78657	N704JW
D-EFGG(2)	Robin HR.200/120B	276	
D-EFGH(2)	Robin DR.400/200R Remo 200 (Reservn 12.99)	2433	
D-EFGK(2)	Piper PA-28RT-201T Turbo Arrow IV	28R-8231035	N8144R
D-EFGL(2)	Reims/Cessna FR.182 Skylane RG	0032	
D-EFGM	Reims/Cessna F.172P	2102	PH-AXJ
D-EFGO	Cessna 150	17640	N7840E
D-EFGS(2)	Göbel Brändli BX-2 Cherry	21	
D-EFGT	Reims/Cessna F.172N	1774	
D-EFGV	Robin DR.400/140 Major	816	
D-EFGX	Reims/Cessna F.172N	1793	
D-EFGY(2)	Reims/Cessna F.172E	0069	
D-EFHA	Piper PA-28-160 Cherokee B	28-1293	
D-EFHB(4)	Robin R.3000/160	161	
D-EFHC	Reims/Cessna F.172H	0596	
D-EFHE(2)	Reims/Cessna F.150G	0093	
D-EFHF	Morane-Saulnier MS.885 Super Rallye	59	F-BKER
D-EFHG(2)	Robin HR.200/120B	264	
D-EFHH(2)	SOCATA MS.893A Rallye Commodore 180	11667	
D-EFHI (2)	Beech A36 Bonanza	E-1092	
D-EFHJ	Piper J-3C-65 Cub	18970	N98739
			NC98739

Regn.	Type	C/n	Prev.Id.
D-EFHK(2)	SOCATA MS.893A Rallye Commodore 180	11668	
D-EFHL(3)	Piper PA-28R-200 Cherokee Arrow II	28R-7435246	N43084
D-EFHM(2)	SOCATA TB-200 Tobago XL	1748	
D-EFHN(2)	Robin DR.400/180 Régent	1512	
D-EFHO(3)	Reims/Cessna F.172N	1907	OE-DHO
			LN-HOI
D-EFHP	Piper PA-28-151 Warrior	28-7615428	N9634N
D-EFHQ	Robin DR.400/180R Remorqueur	1513	
D-EFHR	Piper PA-28-180 Cherokee D	28-4509	N5216L
D-EFHS	Beech F33A Bonanza	CE-812	OE-DUB
D-EFHT	Reims/Cessna F.172M	1411	(D-EOVO)
D-EFHV	Robin DR.400/180R Remorqueur	1452	
D-EFHW	Rockwell Commander 112A	402	N1402J
D-EFHZ	Zlin Z.526F Trenér	1153	SP-CDO
D-EFIA	Reims/Cessna F.152	1755	
D-EFIC	Cessna 182J Skylane	57150	N3050F
D-EFID(2)	Reims/Cessna F.172H	0537	
D-EFIE	Keller Jodel D11A Club	"Liz.639"	OE-ACX
D-EFIG	Cessna 182J Skylane	57180	N3080F
D-EFIH(2)	SOCATA TB-10 Tobago	470	
D-EFII	Piper PA-28-140 Cherokee E	28-7225106	N11C
D-EFIK	CEA Jodel DR.1050 Ambassadeur	553	F-BLZU
D-EFIL(2)	Piper PA-38-112 Tomahawk	38-80A0100	D-EEIL(2)
			N9702N
D-EFIM(2)	Cessna 172M	63568	N1423V
D-EFIN(2)	Reims/Cessna F.172M	1229	
D-EFIO	Grumman AA-5B Tiger	108	
D-EFIP(3)	SOCATA ST-10 Diplomate	129	LX-VIP
			D-EHAX(2)
D-EFIQ	Reims/Cessna F.172G	0271	
D-EFIS(2)	Reims/Cessna FR.172F Rocket	0108	
D-EFIV(2)	Reims/Cessna F.152	1769	
D-EFIW(2)	Piper PA-12 Super Cruiser	12-545	N7665H
D-EFIX(2)	CASA I-131E Jungmann	2063	E3B-471
D-EFIY	SNCAN/ Stampe SV.4C	136	F-BBIY
			F-BBHY
D-EFJA(2)	Reims/Cessna F.152	1778	
D-EFJB(2)	Böhm Starlite SL-1/B	001/1678	
D-EFJC	Bölkow BO.209 Monsun 160RV	125	
D-EFJD	Bölkow BO.209 Monsun 160FV	126	
D-EFJG	Bölkow BO.209 Monsun 160RV	129	
D-EFJH	Bölkow BO.209 Monsun 160RV	130	
D-EFJI	Bölkow BO.209 Monsun 160RV	131	(D-ELIE)
D-EFJJ	Bölkow BO.209 Monsun 160RV	132	
D-EFJK	Bölkow BO.209 Monsun 160RV	133	(D-EDAK(2))
D-EFJL	Bölkow BO.209 Monsun 160RV	134	
D-EFJM	Bölkow BO.209 Monsun 150FF	135	
D-EFJN	Bölkow BO.209 Monsun 150FF	136	I-SUDB
			D-EFJN
D-EFJP	Bölkow BO.209 Monsun 150FF	138	(D-EFSG)
D-EFJQ(2)	Reims/Cessna F.172N	1919	
D-EFJR(2)	CASA I-131E Jungmann	2072	E3B-465
D-EFJS(2)	Reims/Cessna F.182Q Skylane	0116	
D-EFJV	Reims/Cessna F.172N	1937	
D-EFJX	Reims/Cessna F.172N	1962	
D-EFJZ	Reims/Cessna F.172N	1967	
D-EFKA(3)	Piper PA-28R-201T Turbo Arrow III	28R-7803337	N36726
D-EFKB	Piper PA-18-180 Super Cub	18-5390	ALAT
D-EFKD	Reims/Cessna F.172N	2000	
D-EFKE(2)	Maule M-5-210C Strata Rocket	6055C	
D-EFKF	Robin DR.400/180R Remorqueur	1550	
D-EFKG	Beech V35B Bonanza	D-9759	
D-EFKK	Mooney M.20F Executive	22-1202	
D-EFKM	Reims/Cessna F.172N	2004	
D-EFKN	Reims/Cessna F.152	1713	
D-EFKO(2)	Piper PA-28-140 Cherokee	24-24639	N7288J
D-EFKP(2)	Piper PA-28-181 Cherokee Archer II	28-7890477	N31733
D-EFKR	Reims/Cessna FR.172K Hawk XP	0635	PH-AXT
D-EFKS(2)	Mooney M.20K Model 252	25-1164	N252MM
			D-EFKS(2)
D-EFKT(2)	Cessna 177RG Cardinal RG	1341	N53081
D-EFKV	Robin DR.400/180 Régent	1549	
D-EFKW(2)	Reims/Cessna F.172P	2151	
D-EFKZ	Robin HR.200/120B	260	
D-EFLA(2)	SOCATA TB-10 Tobago	679	

Regn.	Type	C/n	Prev.Id.
D-EFLB	Cessna 172N	71629	N4555E
D-EFLC	Piper PA-18 Super Cub 95	18-3422	96+04
			NL+105
			AC+513
			AA+513
			AS+513
			54-722
D-EFLD	Piper PA-28-181 Archer II	28-7990106	N2125A
D-EFLE(2)	Piper PA-28-180 Cherokee Challenger	28-7305370	N55326
D-EFLF	Cessna 172N	72217	N9303E
D-EFLH	Cessna 172RG Cutlass	0351	N4660V
D-EFLI (3)	Piper PA-28-181 Archer II	28-8190082	N82891
D-EFLJ	Reims/Cessna F.172F	0139	
D-EFLK	Cessna 152	84190	N4601L
D-EFLL	Cessna 172P	75489	N63841
D-EFLM	Piaggio FWP.149D	082	90+64
			GA+402
			AS+491
D-EFLO(2)	SOCATA TB-10 Tobago	633	
D-EFLP	Piper PA-28-151 Warrior	28-7415195	N9520N
D-EFLQ	Piper PA-28-140 Cherokee D	28-7125370	N8589N
D-EFLR	Reims/Cessna F.177RG Cardinal RG	0055	
D-EFLS(2)	Piper PA-28RT-201T Turbo Arrow IV	28R-7931022	N2129K
D-EFLT(2)	SOCATA TB-10 Tobago	678	
D-EFLU(2)	Robin DR.300/180R Remoqueur	525	
D-EFLV	Piper PA-28-140 Cherokee D	28-7125248	N5082S
D-EFLW(2)	Cessna 182R Skylane	67929	OY-JRE
			N9307H
D-EFLX	Cauxen Denney Kitfox V	S 94030004B	
D-EFLY(2)	Robin DR.300/108 2+2	519	
D-EFLZ	SOCATA TB-10 Tobago	1067	
D-EFMA(2)	Maule MX.7-235 Star Rocket	10070C	N61245
D-EFMB	Bölkow BO.208C Junior	632	
D-EFMC	Bölkow BO.208C Junior	633	
D-EFMD(2)	Robin DR.400/180 Régent	1477	
D-EFME	Bölkow BO.208C Junior	635	
D-EFMF(2)	Piper PA-28R-180 Cherokee Arrow	28R-30184	N3861T
D-EFMG(3)	Piper PA-28-181 Archer II	28-8590022	N4385C
D-EFMH(2)	CASA I.131E Jungmann (Lycoming)	2066	E3B-473
D-EFMI (2)	Gyroflug SC-01B-160 Speed Canard	S-28	(D-EAMT)
D-EFMJ(2)	Piper PA-28-140 Cherokee C	28-26832	N5933U
D-EFMK	CEA DR.253B Régent	123	
D-EFML	Fairchild F.24R-46A Argus III	947	HB-EIR
			HB709
			43-14983
D-EFMM	SOCATA MS.894A Minerva 220	11023	
D-EFMN(2)	Robin DR.400/180R Remorqueur	1460	
D-EFMO(2)	Cessna 152	81868	N67498
D-EFMP	Reims/Cessna F.172N	2018	
D-EFMR	Reims/Cessna F.172M	1378	
D-EFMS(3)	Maule MX-7-235 Star Rocket	4058C	N6119V
			(D-EJSO)
D-EFMT	Beech B36TC Bonanza	EA-317	
D-EFMU(2)	Cessna 152	83254	N47809
D-EFMY	Piper PA-28-140 Cherokee	28-20703	N6609W
D-EFMZ	Aviat A-1 Husky	1280	
D-EFNA	Oberlerchner JOB 15-180/2	063	OE-CAX
D-EFNB	SOCATA TB-10 Tobago	820	
D-EFNC	Cessna 172RG Cutlass	0310	N5263U
D-EFND	Reims/Cessna F.152	1659	N1664Q
D-EFNE	Aerotek Pitts S-2B	5024	N20NE
			(N5316C)
D-EFNH	Reims/Cessna FR.182 Skylane RG	0058	
D-EFNI (2)	Oberlerchner JOB 15-150/2	067	OE-CAT
D-EFNK(3)	Cessna 172N	71263	N2392E
D-EFNL	Robin DR.400/180R Remorqueur	1551	
D-EFNN	Mooney M.20E Chaparral	21-1178	N6844V
D-EFNP(2)	Piper PA-28RT-201 Arrow IV	28R-7918018	N2125K
D-EFNR	Piaggio FWP.149D	115	90+95
			SB+215
			SB+421
			AS+074
			AS+440
D-EFNS(2)	Piper PA-28-181 Archer II	28-8090282	N44WK
			N8187Z

Regn.	Type	C/n	Prev.Id.
D-EFNT	Cessna TR.182 Turbo Skylane RG	00772	OE-DNT
			N736UQ
D-EFNW	Reims/Cessna FR.182 Skylane RG	0015	(D-EDBV)
D-EFNX	Reims/Cessna F.152	1563	
D-EFNY	Bölkow BO.208C Junior	606	
D-EFOB(2)	Dornier Do.27A-4	389	56+81
			QW+111
			QW+715
			QM+615
			PL+423
D-EFOC(2)	Piper PA-18-150 Super Cub	18-3084	
	(Quoted c/n is incorrect - this was D-ECBE. Thought		
	to be c/n 18-3127 ex.L-53 /53-4727)		
D-EFOD(2)	Piper PA-28-140 Cherokee	28-7325043	OY-DLZ
			N15341
D-EFOE	SOCATA TB-9 Tampico	106	
D-EFOF(2)	SOCATA TB-9 Tampico	108	
D-EFOG(2)	Piper PA-28-180 Cherokee Challenger	28-7305300	N11C
D-EFOH	Klemm Kl.107C	139	
D-EFOJ	Robin DR.400/120D Petit Prince	1565	
D-EFOK(2)	Piper PA-28-140 Cherokee F	28-7325289	N11C
D-EFOL(2)	Piper PA-28-140 Cherokee F	28-7325316	N11C
D-EFOM	DHC-1 Chipmunk 22 (Franklin)	C1/0248	G-AOJN
			WD306
D-EFOO	Cessna T.210N Turbo Centurion II	64296	N6208Y
D-EFOP(2)	Reims/Cessna F.172E	50580/0025	OE-DCO
			(N2980U)
D-EFOQ	Scintex CP.301C Emeraude	542	
D-EFOR(2)	Binder CP.301S Smaragd	107	
D-EFOS(2)	Mooney M.20K Model 252	25-1090	N252YV
D-EFOT(2)	Cessna 172P	75595	N64622
D-EFOV(2)	Robin DR.400/180R Remorqueur	1571	
D-EFOW(2)	Cessna T.210L Turbo Centurion	61148	PH-PLX
			OO-ADI
			D-EATX
			N2187S
D-EFOX(4)	Piaggio FWP.149D	126	91+05
			BF+414
			AS+013
			KB+103
D-EFPA(3)	Piper PA-28-181 Archer II	2890077	N9143X
D-EFPB(3)	Cessna 172R	80365	
D-EFPC	Mooney M.20J Model 201	24-0131	
D-EFPD	Piper PA-28-180 Cherokee Challenger	28-7305121	(N15696)
			N11C
D-EFPE(2)	Reims/Cessna F.172P	2119	
D-EFPF(2)	Cessna 172RG Cutlass	0484	N5248V
D-EFPH(2)	Philips Denney Kitfox IV Speedster	1313	
D-EFPJ	SOCATA TB-9 Tampico	107	
D-EFPK	SOCATA TB-10 Tobago	104	
D-EFPL	Piper PA-28-161 Warrior II	28-7916424	N29259
D-EFPM	Cessna 182G Skylane	55416	HB-CMP
			N2316R
D-EFPN	Piper PA-28RT-201 Arrow IV	28R-7918143	N29699
D-EFPO	Bölkow BO.207	262	
D-EFPP	Cessna TR.182 Turbo Skylane RG	01436	N4846S
D-EFPQ	Robin DR.400/180 Régent	1322	
D-EFPR	Pützer Elster C	042	97+19
			D-ELBC
D-EFPS	SNCAN/ Stampe SV-4C	415	F-BCQY
D-EFPZ	Robin DR.400/180R Remorqueur	1597	
D-EFQA	Bölkow BO.207	265	
D-EFQB	Robin DR.400/180R Remorqueur	1367	
D-EFQC	Piper PA-28-140 Cherokee E	28-7225313	F-BTQC
			N11C
D-EFQD	SOCATA TB-20 Trinidad	623	F-GHSA
			N20EN
D-EFQE	Bölkow BO.207	266	
D-EFQF(2)	Grob G.115A (Permit 12.99)	8053	F-GGOF
			F-WGOF
			(PH-SBD)
D-EFQG	Grob G.115A	8017	F-GGOA
			F-WGOA
D-EFQH	Grob G.115A (Reservation 6.99)	8080	F-GGOG
D-EFQI	Piper PA-22-108 Colt	22-9365	

Regn.	Type	C/n	Prev.Id.
D-EFQN(2)	Robin DR.400/180 Régent *(Permit 6.99)*	1744	(F-GNBJ)
			D-EFQN(2)
			F-GEKS
D-EFQP	CASA I-131E Jungmann	2046	E3B-442
D-EFQR	Robin DR.400/180 Régent	1369	
D-EFQS	SOCATA TB-9 Tampico	765	F-GFQS
D-EFQT	Dornier Do.27A-3	437	57+11
			BF+950
			KD+101
D-EFQU	Reims/Cessna F.172E	0053	
D-EFQV	Dornier Do.27B-1	175	55+45
			CC+053
			AC+925 ?
			AS+925 ?
D-EFRA	Reims/Cessna F.172D	50071/0005	(N2471U)
D-EFRB(3)	Cessna 152	85120	N445MW
			N5542Q
D-EFRC	Reims/Cessna F.172H	0651	
D-EFRD	Reims/Cessna F.172H	0654	
D-EFRE	Reims/Cessna F.172D	50111/0007	F-WLIT
			(N2511U)
D-EFRF	Reims/Cessna FR.172F Rocket	0088	
D-EFRG	Cessna 172RG Cutlass	0554	N5527V
D-EFRH(3)	Cessna P210N Pressurized Centurion II	00771	N6410W
D-EFRK	Mooney M.20J Model 201	24-0730	(N4433H)
D-EFRL	Mooney M.20K Model 231	25-0153	
D-EFRM	SOCATA Rallye 180TS Galérien	3334	
D-EFRN	SOCATA Rallye 180TS Galérien	3335	
D-EFRP	Cessna 172P	74657	N53001
D-EFRQ	SOCATA Rallye 110ST Galopin	3332	
D-EFRR(2)	American AG-5B Tiger	10161	N1198N
D-EFRS	Robin DR.400/120D Petit Prince	1714	
D-EFRT	Cessna P210N Pressurized Centurion II	00401	N7360K
D-EFRV	Reims/Cessna F.172P	2096	
D-EFRW	Reims/Cessna F.172P	2090	
D-EFRX	SOCATA Rallye110ST Galopin	3333	
D-EFSA(2)	Cessna 182J Skylane	57009	N2909F
D-EFSB(2)	Cessna 172N	70400	N739AY
D-EFSC(4)	Dornier Do.27A-4	2109	MAAW-16
			D-EGVQ
			D-12/OT-AMK
			OL-D12
			D-12
D-EFSE(3)	Cessna P210N Pressurized Centurion II	00814	N4680A
D-EFSF(2)	Reims/Cessna FR.172K Hawk XP	0658	PH-PWH
			PH-AXT(3)
D-EFSG(2)	Cessna 180J Skywagon	52662	D-EFJO
			N9967N
D-EFSH(2)	Piper PA-28RT-201T Turbo Arrow IV	28R-8031127	N99IOD
			N9569N
D-EFSI	Bölkow BO.207	213	HB-UXM
			D-EFSI
D-EFSL	Cessna 182Q Skylane	65374	N735EV
D-EFSM(2)	Cessna 150L	72950	N1650Q
D-EFSN	Cessna 172RG Cutlass	1026	N9772B
D-EFSO(2)	Piper PA-28-140 Cherokee F	28-7325365	N11C
D-EFSR	Piper PA-28-181 Archer II	28-8190003	N8247E
D-EFSS(2)	Mooney M.20M TLS	27-0129	N888JS
			N230M
D-EFSU(3)	Beech F33A Bonanza	CE-1519	
D-EFSV(2)	Cessna 182Q Skylane	67470	N4945N
D-EFSW(2)	Piper PA-18 Super Cub 105	18-3437	96+16
			PX+901
			QZ+030
			AC+505
			AS+504
			54-737
D-EFSY	Bölkow BO.207	216	
D-EFSZ	Mooney M.20K Model 231	25-0467	N277TA
			N4090H
D-EFTA(3)	Beech A36 Bonanza	E-840	
D-EFTB(2)	Piper PA-18 Super Cub 95	18-3455	96+31
			NL+...
			AC+537
			AS+537, 54-755

Regn.	Type	C/n	Prev.Id.
D-EFTC	Bölkow BO.209 Monsun 150FF	172	G-AZTC
			D-EAAL
D-EFTD	Piper PA-32R-301T Saratoga SP	32R-8129055	N83595
D-EFTE(3)	Klemm L 25-1A *(Permit)*	152	G-AAHW
			D-ELFK
			G-AAHW
D-EFTH(2)	Cessna 195B	16087	N195MB
			N2102C
D-EFTI	Bölkow BO.207	219	
D-EFTK	Reims/Cessna F.172M	1265	
D-EFTL	Reims/Cessna F.172M	1273	
D-EFTN(2)	de Havilland DH.82A Tiger Moth	unkn	G-ANIX
	(Reservation 5.99. Composite rebuild using identity		D-EFTF(2)
	of c/n 84764, ex T6390, D-ELOM, dbf 12.63)		
D-EFTO(3)	Reims/Cessna F.152	1958	
D-EFTP	Reims/Cessna FR.172H Rocket	0276	
D-EFTQ	Robin DR.400/180R Remorqueur	1472	
D-EFTR(2)	SOCATA TB-10 Tobago	206	
D-EFTS	SAN Jodel DR.1050 Ambassadeur	397	
D-EFTT(2)	Cessna P210N Pressurized Centurion II	00580	N732HP
D-EFTU(2)	Piaggio FWP.149D	091	90+73
			AS+404
D-EFTW(2)	Robin DR.400/180 Régent	1274	
D-EFTX	Boeing Stearman A75N1 Kaydet	75-3475	G-BHUW
			N474
			N64639
			BuA30038
D-EFTY(3)	Klemm Kl.35D *(Permit 6.99)*	1462	G-BWRD
	(Painted as Luftwaffe '7')		D-EFTG(2)
			D-EHUX(2)
			SE-AIP
			Fv5081
			SE-AIP
D-EFTZ	Cessna 172RG Cutlass	0814	N9403B
D-EFUB	Klemm Kl.35D	1810	HB-UXC
			SE-BGH
			Fv5011
D-EFUE	Reims/Cessna F.152	1533	
D-EFUF	Stark Turbulent D-1M	115	
D-EFUG(3)	Reims/Cessna F.152	1554	
D-EFUI	Reims/Cessna F.152	1550	
D-EFUJ	Reims/Cessna F.172N	1843	
D-EFUK(2)	Reims/Cessna F.172N	1841	
D-EFUL	Piper J-3C-65 Cub	11313	HB-OAI
			43-30022
D-EFUM(2)	Piper PA-28-140 Cherokee Cruiser	28-7725080	N9530N
D-EFUN(3)	Reims/Cessna FR.172E Rocket	0043	
D-EFUO	Reims/Cessna F.172N	1840	(D-EJCU)
D-EFUP	Fischer RW3-P75 Multoplan	005	
D-EFUS(2)	SOCATA MS.880B Rallye Club	2149	F-BUCA
D-EFUT(3)	Beech A36 Bonanza	E-2983	N3263U
D-EFUV(2)	Cessna 140	10385	N81091
D-EFUX(2)	Beech F33A Bonanza	CE-1150	
D-EFVA	FVA-18/3 Krähe V-1	01	
D-EFVB	Reims/Cessna FR.172K Hawk	0636	
D-EFVD	Reims/Cessna T.210M Turbo Centurion	0012/62650	N761ZN
D-EFVE	Reims/Cessna F.172E	0076	
D-EFVF	Robin DR.400/180 Régent	1343	
D-EFVH(2)	Beech F33A Bonanza	CE-1770	N15229
			N1529L
			(D-EEJJ)
D-EFVI	Piaggio P.149D	254	(91+72)
			D-EFVI
			AC+405
			AS+405
D-EFVL	Reims/Cessna F.150F	63485/0057	(G-ATOF)
			(N6885F)
D-EFVM(2)	Ludwig Stark Turbulent D	AB-501	D-EGSU
D-EFVO(2)	Reims/Cessna F.150G	0159	
D-EFVQ	Reims/Cessna F.172P	2085	
D-EFVS	Wassmer WA.52 Europa	22	
D-EFVU	Cessna 182H Skylane	56080	N1980X
D-EFVZ	Zendler Hina BL2-ARA	1777	
D-EFWA(2)	SOCATA Rallye 100ST-D	3043	OY-ARG
			F-ODII

Regn.	Type	C/n	Prev.Id.
D-EFWB	Reims/Cessna F.150M	1151	
D-EFWC(2)	Piper PA-24-250 Comanche	24-3294	OE-DST / N8139P / N10F
D-EFWD	Beech V35B Bonanza	D-10347	
D-EFWE	Piper PA-28-140 Cherokee	28-20715	N6682W
D-EFWF	Piper PA-28R-200 Cherokee Arrow II	28R-7535170	(D-ILAX) / N33651
D-EFWJ	Wassmer WA.54 Atlantic	109	(D-EAIJ)
D-EFWK	Cessna 150F	63679	N7079F
D-EFWL	Wassmer WA.54 Atlantic	107	
D-EFWM	Piper PA-28-181 Cherokee Archer II	28-7790419	N2917Q
D-EFWO(2)	Robin DR.400/180R Remorqueur	1546	
D-EFWP(2)	Piaggio FWP.149D	118	90+98 / D-EKLI / AS+459
D-EFWR	Piper PA-28R-201T Turbo Cherokee Arrow III	28R-7703140	N5655V
D-EFWS(2)	Cessna 172R	80615	N95520
D-EFWT	SOCATA TB-10 Tobago	291	
D-EFWU	Bölkow BO.208 Junior	573	
D-EFWW	Piper PA-28-180 Cherokee Archer	28-7405075	N9648N
D-EFWX	Folz WAR FW.190	001-EB	
D-EFWY	Reims/Cessna F.172F	0154	
D-EFWZ	Piper PA-28-235 Cherokee	28-10207	N8676W
D-EFXA	SOCATA MS.880B Rallye Club	1220	
D-EFXC(2)	Piper PA-28-161 Cadet	2841051	N9632N / N9163K
D-EFXD(2)	Piper PA-28-161 Cadet	2841070	N91642
D-EFXE(2)	Piper PA-28-161 Cadet	2841069	N9164Z
D-EFXF(2)	Piper PA-28-161 Cadet	2841082	N9504N / N9167H
D-EFXG	Piper PA-28-161 Cadet	2841087	N9170H
D-EFXI (2)	Piper PA-28-161 Cadet	2841118	N9649N
D-EFXK	Piper PA-28-161 Cadet	2841124	N9510N / N9180X
D-EFXL	Piper PA-28-161 Cadet	2841126	N9181G
D-EFXM	Piper PA-28-161 Cadet	2841128	N9181J
D-EFXO	Robin DR.300/108 2+2	496	
D-EFXP(2)	Piper PA-28-161 Cadet	2841163	N9514N
D-EFXQ	Piper PA-28-161 Cadet	2841168	N9515N
D-EFXR	Piper PA-28-161 Cadet	2841201	N9189W
D-EFXS	Piper PA-28-161 Cadet	2841243	N9192P
D-EFXT	Piper PA-28-161 Cadet	2841244	N9192X
D-EFXU	Robin DR.300/180R Remorqueur	497	
D-EFXY	Piper PA-18-150 Super Cub	nil	(RBAF)
	(Built from spare fuselage no.18-4963)		
D-EFXZ	Piper PA-28-161 Cadet	2841286	N92032
D-EFYA	Reims/Cessna F.182Q Skylane	0142	PH-AXZ
D-EFYB(2)	Piper PA-32-300 Cherokee Six	32-7340188	OY-DLK / CS-AOU / N56526
D-EFYC	Reims/Cessna F.172G	0223	
D-EFYD	Cessna 170B	20628	N2476D
D-EFYF(2)	Piper PA-28RT-201 Arrow IV	28R-8118063	N83691
D-EFYH(2)	Cessna 152	83107	N46802
D-EFYK(2)	Piper PA-18 Super Cub 95	18-3424	96+06 / SE+540 / CA+511 / D-9503 / (D-EMEV) / CA+511 / AC+511 / AS+511 / 54-724
D-EFYL(2)	Pützer Elster B	014	97+07 / D-EFYL
D-EFYN(3)	Reims/Cessna F.172P	2089	
D-EFYP	Pützer Elster C	002	
D-EFYQ	Reims/Cessna F.172G	0259	
D-EFYW(2)	Dornier Do.27B-1	221	55+75 / CA+045 / GB+386 / CA+927 / (AS+927)

Regn.	Type	C/n	Prev.Id.
D-EFYX(2)	Ryan Navion A	NAV-4-1385	N4385K
D-EFYZ(2)	Piaggio FWP.149D	101	90+82 / ND+103 / D-EHUW / AS+403
D-EFZA	Cessna 182H Skylane	56343	N2443X
D-EFZB(2)	Piper PA-28-161 Warrior II	28-8016233	N9608N
D-EFZC	SIAI-Marchetti S.208	2-18	
D-EFZE	Cessna 182H Skylane	56346	N2446X
D-EFZF	Cessna 172N	71249	N2360E
D-EFZG	Cessna 172RG Cutlass	0559	N5533V
D-EFZH	Cessna 182H Skylane	68307	N733HM
D-EFZI	Piper PA-18 Super Cub 95	18-6109	OE-AEE
D-EFZJ	Cessna 172RG Cutlass	0046	N5204R
D-EFZK	Cessna R.172K Hawk XP	2496	N736FR
D-EFZM	Dornier Do.27A-4	483	57+48 / GA+376 / KD+141 ?
D-EFZO	Reims/Cessna F.172F	0156	
D-EFZQ	Cessna 172P	74510	N52414
D-EFZR	Cessna 172N	72920	N7398D
D-EFZS	Cessna 172P	75531	N64189
D-EFZT	Cessna 182K Skylane	58476	N2876R
D-EFZV	CEA DR.253B Régent	106	6V-ABU / F-OCKM
D-EFZW(2)	HOAC DV-20 Katana	20061	
D-EGAA(2)	Reims/Cessna F.150H	0359	
D-EGAB(2)	Cessna 182J Skylane	56709	N2609F
D-EGAD(2)	Fuji FA-200-160 Aero Subaru	121	
D-EGAE	Fuji FA-200-180 Aero Subaru	114	
D-EGAF	Piper J-3C-65 Cub	12943	HB-ONI / 44-80647
D-EGAG(3)	SOCATA TB-20 Trinidad	1675	
D-EGAI	Fuji FA-200-160 Aero Subaru	122	
D-EGAJ	Fuji FA-200-160 Aero Subaru	123	
D-EGAK(3)	Piper PA-28R-200 Cherokee Arrow II	28R-7635091	N7035C
D-EGAL(3)	Bölkow BO.208C Junior	641	
D-EGAM(3)	Fuji FA-200-180 Aero Subaru	117	
D-EGAN(2)	Piper PA-28-181 Archer II	28-8590023	N9514N
D-EGAO	Dornier Do.27B-3	2200	(D-EFKP)
D-EGAP(3)	Dornier Do.27Q-5	2045	D-EKYC
D-EGAQ(2)	Piper PA-18-150 Super Cub	18-8344	N4163Z
D-EGAR(2)	Piper PA-28-151 Warrior	28-7615131	N9525N
D-EGAS(4)	Mooney M.20J Model 205	24-3164	
D-EGAT(2)	Piper PA-28-151 Warrior	28-7415083	N9623N
D-EGAU	Piper PA-28-181 Archer II	28-8090215	N8145Y
D-EGAV	Wassmer Jodel D.120	141	
D-EGAW(2)	Robin HR.100/200B	117	
D-EGAX(3)	Piper PA-28RT-201T Turbo Arrow IV	28R-7931187	N28529
D-EGAY(2)	Christen A-1 Husky	1113	
D-EGAZ(4)	Cessna 172RG Cutlass	0531	OY-BNN / (D-EBNM) / OY-BNN / N5435V
D-EGBA(2)	Heliopolis Gomhouria Mk.6	184	SU-346 / EAF-346
D-EGBB(2)	Robin HR.200/120B	268	
D-EGBD	Reims/Cessna F.150L	0947	
D-EGBE(2)	Reims/Cessna F.172M	0977	
D-EGBF	Reims/Cessna F.172M	0978	
D-EGBG	Reims/Cessna F.172M	0979	
D-EGBH(2)	Robin DR.400/180R Remorqueur	1742	
D-EGBI (2)	PZL-104 Wilga 35	61113	DDR-WBH / DM-WBH(2)
D-EGBJ	Reims/Cessna F.172M	0980	
D-EGBK	Reims/Cessna F.172M	0981	
D-EGBM(3)	CASA I-131E Jungmann	2062	E3B-415
D-EGBN	Reims/Cessna FRA.150L Aerobat	0192	(OO-FCF)
D-EGBO	SAN Jodel DR.1050 Ambassadeur	367	(D-EDRO)
D-EGBP	Reims/Cessna FR.172J Rocket	0417	
D-EGBQ	Reims/Cessna FR.172J Rocket	0419	
D-EGBR(2)	Focke-Wulf FW.44J Stieglitz	2906	OH-SZK / SZ-9 / OH-SZK / SZ-5

Regn.	Type	C/n	Prev.Id.
D-EGBS(2)	Beech A36AT Bonanza	E-2719	
D-EGBV	Reims/Cessna F.172M *(on rebuild)*	0986	
D-EGBW	Reims/Cessna F.172M	0987	
D-EGBX(2)	Cessna 182P Skylane	62656	N52523
D-EGBY	Bölkow BO.208 Junior	533	D-EGQA(1)
D-EGBZ	Cessna 182P Skylane	62261	N58728
D-EGCA	Reims/Cessna F.172H	0425	
D-EGCB	Reims/Cessna F.150L	0965	
D-EGCC	CEA DR.253B Régent	178	
D-EGCD	Cessna 172N	68311	N733HR
D-EGCE	Reims/Cessna F.172H	0408	
D-EGCF	Piper PA-18-150 Super Cub	18-8547	SE-GCE / Fv51238
D-EGCG	Robin DR.400/180R Remorqueur	1413	
D-EGCH	Bellanca 7GCBC Citabria	733-74	OE-AOH
D-EGCI (2)	Grob G.115A	8015	(D-EGRN(2))
D-EGCJ	Reims/Cessna F.150L	0968	
D-EGCM	Reims/Cessna F.150L	0972	
D-EGCN	Reims/Cessna FRA.150L Aerobat *(Permit 10.99)*	0211	
D-EGCO(2)	Reims/Cessna F.172M	0988	
D-EGCP	Reims/Cessna F.172M	0989	
D-EGCQ	Reims/Cessna F.172M	0993	
D-EGCS	Reims/Cessna F.172M	1001	
D-EGCT(2)	Reims/Cessna F.152	1692	
D-EGCU	Reims/Cessna F.172H	0401	
D-EGCW(2)	Reims/Cessna F.152	1691	
D-EGDA(2)	Robin DR.400/180 Régent	2293	
D-EGDB(2)	Grumman AA-5A Cheetah	0551	
D-EGDC	Grumman AA-5B Tiger	0728	
D-EGDD	Grumman AA-5B Tiger	0827	
D-EGDE	Reims/Cessna F.150G	0114	
D-EGDF	Grumman AA-5B Tiger	0776	
D-EGDG	Grumman AA-5A Cheetah	0656	
D-EGDH	Grumman AA-5B Tiger	0932	
D-EGDI	SOCATA MS.892A Rallye Commodore 150	10550	
D-EGDK	SOCATA MS.893E Rallye 180GT Gaillard	12209	F-BUXL
D-EGDL	Grumman AA-5B Tiger	0779	
D-EGDM(2)	Cessna 150M	77827	N7730U
D-EGDN	Grumman AA-5B Tiger	0750	
D-EGDO(2)	Reims/Cessna F.172H	0334	
D-EGDR	Grumman AA-5B Tiger	1132	(N4527C)
D-EGDS(2)	Bücker Bü.133C Jungmeister	11	G-AXIH / HB-MIP / U-64
D-EGDV(2)	Robin DR.400/180R Remorqueur	1578	
D-EGDX	Robin DR.400/180R Remorqueur	1588	
D-EGDY	Reims/Cessna F.150G	0086	
D-EGEA(2)	Dornier Do.27A-4	377	56+74 / PD+338 / PD+112 / PK+103
D-EGEB(2)	Cessna 172M	63918	N21262
D-EGEC(2)	Piaggio FWP.149D	153	91+31 / ND+104 / KB+130
D-EGEE	SIAI-Marchetti S.205-22/R	4-130	
D-EGEF(2)	SOCATA MS.893ED Rallye 180GT Gaillard	13301	
D-EGEG(2)	Cessna 172B	48683	N8183X
D-EGEH(3)	SOCATA TB-10 Tobago	105	
D-EGEI	Piaggio FWP.149D	121	91+01 / D-ELHU / AS+410
D-EGEL(4)	SOCATA Rallye 180TS Galérien	3239	PH-AFE
D-EGEM(3)	Blume Bl 502 V-2 *(Reservation 1.99)*	03	D-EGEM(1)
D-EGEN(2)	Maier Piel CP.301A Emeraude	AB.402	
D-EGEP(2)	Wassmer CE.43 Guepard	435	
D-EGER(2)	Piper PA-28-235 Cherokee E	28-7110002	N8582N
D-EGES(2)	Reims/Cessna F.150G	0160	
D-EGET(2)	SOCATA MS.893ED Rallye 180GT Gaillard	13300	
D-EGEU	Piper PA-22-108 Colt	22-9055	EL-AEU / 5N-AEH
D-EGEV(2)	Fuji FA-200-180 Aero Subaru	204	
D-EGEW(3)	Extra EA.300	016	
D-EGEX(2)	Robin DR.400/RP Remorqueur	1847	
D-EGEY	Cessna P210N Pressurized Centurion II	00403	N7511K
D-EGEZ(2)	SOCATA Rallye 235ED Gabier	12873	F-GAKI
D-EGFA(3)	Reims/Cessna F.150M	1228	
D-EGFC(2)	Piper PA-28-181 Archer II	28-8590016	N4382M
D-EGFD	Reims/Cessna F.152	1630	OE-CFD
D-EGFE(2)	SOCATA MS.880B Rallye Club	867	F-BONS
D-EGFF	Piper PA-28-161 Warrior II	28-7716104	N9624N
D-EGFG	Piper PA-18 Super Cub 95	18-3420	96+02 / NL+107 / AC+501 / AS+509 / 54-720
D-EGFH	Pützer Elster B	043	97+20 / D-ELBD
D-EGFI	Bölkow BO.208C Junior	638	
D-EGFK	Cessna 182M Skylane	59666	(N71566)
D-EGFL(2)	Piper PA-28-181 Archer II	28-8190239	N8389X
D-EGFM	Reims/Cessna FR.172H Rocket	0277	
D-EGFN	Robin DR.400/180R Remorqueur	1586	
D-EGFO	Bölkow BO.208C Junior	639	
D-EGFR	Dornier Do.27A-1	160	55+36 / BD+9 .. / SE+521 / SC+718 / QM+606 / PC+113
D-EGFS	Piper PA-18-150 Super Cub	18-7709056	HB-PBM / N83524
D-EGFT	Piper PA-28-181 Archer II	28-7990296	N2223P
D-EGFU	Bölkow BO.208C Junior	640	
D-EGFV	Robin R.3000/120D	116	
D-EGFW	Piper PA-38-112 Tomahawk	38-81A0005	N25460
D-EGFY	Cessna 182P Skylane	62266	N58737
D-EGGA(2)	Reims/Cessna F.172N	1832	
D-EGGB	Rockwell Commander 114A	14517	
D-EGGC	Cessna 172P	74492	N52303
D-EGGD	SOCATA MS.893A Rallye Commodore 180	11669	F-BSXQ
D-EGGF	Cessna 172RG Cutlass	0301	N107JB / N5250U
D-EGGG(2)	Beech C24R Sierra 200	MC-626	N60137
D-EGGH	SOCATA MS.893A Rallye Commodore 180	11633	F-BSFV
D-EGGI (2)	Piper PA-28-235 Cherokee Pathfinder	28-7610074	N8361C
D-EGGJ	Cessna 172P	74402	N52053
D-EGGK	Cessna 172N	69306	N737CC
D-EGGL	Cessna 172M	61484	N20677
D-EGGM	Piper PA-18-150 Super Cub	18-5401	ALAT
D-EGGN	Gardan GY-80 Horizon 150	1	F-BLIB
D-EGGO(3)	Cessna T.210J Turbo-System Centurion	0404	N4207P / D-EBSS(1) / N2254R
D-EGGR	Beech F33A Bonanza	CE-393	
D-EGGS	Bölkow BO.209 Monsun 160RV	175	HB-UEO / D-EAAO(1)
D-EGGU	Reims/Cessna F.172H	0459	
D-EGGV	Cessna 182P Skylane	62176	N58615
D-EGGW(2)	SOCATA TB-9 Tampico	261	
D-EGGX	Cessna 172RG Cutlass	0307	N5260U
D-EGGY	Reims/Cessna F.150H	0237	
D-EGGZ	Cessna R.182 Skylane RG	00175	N2390C
D-EGHA(3)	Piper PA-28R-201T Turbo Arrow III	28R-7803264	N9540C
D-EGHB	SAN Jodel D.140C Mousquetaire III	136	F-BMBU
D-EGHE	Piper PA-24-260 Comanche B	24-4473	N9012P
D-EGHG(2)	Grässer Neico Lancair 235	002	
D-EGHH(2)	Piper PA-28RT-201T Turbo Arrow IV	28R-8131003	N8271N
D-EGHI	CEA DR.253B Régent	154	
D-EGHJ	CEA DR.315 Petit Prince	419	
D-EGHK(2)	Beech F33A Bonanza	CE-1135	
D-EGHL	Cessna 182J Skylane	56806	N2706F
D-EGHM	Reims/Cessna F.150J	0480	F-BRBT
D-EGHN	Reims/Cessna F.172H	0629	
D-EGHO(2)	Cessna 182P Skylane	63484	N5667J
D-EGHP	Cessna 172RG Cutlass	1155	N9423D
D-EGHQ	Robin DR.400/180R Remorqueur	1570	
D-EGHR	Rohn Doppelraab IV	EB.1	D-5412
D-EGHS	Robin DR.400/180R Remorqueur	893	
D-EGHT(2)	Beech F33A Bonanza	CE-1732	N80617

Regn.	Type	C/n	Prev.Id.
D-EGHV	Piper PA-28-181 Archer II	28-8090278	N8182D
D-EGHW(2)	Bölkow BO.209 Monsun 150FV	170	HB-UER
			D-EAAJ
D-EGHY	Piper PA-28-180 Cherokee D	28-5473	N2158R
D-EGHZ	Beech V35B Bonanza	D-10024	
D-EGIA(2)	Robin DR.400/180R Remorqueur	1545	
D-EGIB(2)	Piper PA-28-181 Archer II	28-8190017	N8257E
D-EGIC(2)	Bölkow BO.208C Junior	642	
D-EGID(2)	Wassmer WA.52 Europa	64	
D-EGIF(3)	Brditschka HB-207 Alfa *(Reservation)*	207-018	
D-EGIG	Luscombe 8A Silvaire	4252	OO-GMA
			N1525K
D-EGIH(3)	Cessna 172RG Cutlass	0021	N4745R
D-EGII	Huschle Stephens Acro Sport II	388	
D-EGIK(2)	Piper PA-28-140 Cherokee	28-21605	N11C
D-EGIL(2)	Piper PA-28R-200 Cherokee Arrow II	28R-7535218	N1018X
D-EGIM(2)	Piper PA-28R-200 Cherokee Arrow B	28R-7235304	N11C
D-EGIN	Piper PA-18 Super Cub 95	18-5652	
D-EGIP(3)	Cessna P210R Pressurized Centurion II	00849	N5361A
D-EGIR(2)	Reims/Cessna F.172M	1360	
D-EGIS(2)	Piper PA-38-112 Tomahawk	38-78A0264	N9725N
D-EGIT(2)	Piaggio P.149D	260	91+78
			AC+411
			AS+411
D-EGIV(2)	Piper PA-28-181 Archer II	28-7990568	N2936A
D-EGIW(2)	Wassmer WA.52 Europa	63	
D-EGIZ(2)	Robin DR.400/180R Remorqueur	1039	
D-EGJA	Reims/Cessna F.172M	1003	
D-EGJC	Reims/Cessna F.172M	1006	
D-EGJD	Reims/Cessna FR.172J Rocket	0420	
D-EGJE	Reims/Cessna FR.172J Rocket	0421	
D-EGJF	Reims/Cessna FR.172J Rocket	0422	
D-EGJG(2)	SOCATA TB-20 Trinidad	873	
D-EGJH(2)	Reims/Cessna F.172N	1930	
D-EGJJ	Reims/Cessna F.177RG Cardinal RG	0086	
D-EGJK	Cessna 182P Skylane	62660	N52535
D-EGJM(2)	Robin DR.400/180 Régent	2296	
D-EGJN	Piper PA-18-150 Super Cub	18-564	R-210
			51-15678
			N7193K
D-EGJP	Cessna U.206F Stationair	01972	N51014
D-EGJQ	Reims/Cessna FR.172J Rocket	0426	
D-EGJS	Reims/Cessna F.150L	1046	
D-EGJT(2)	Robin HR.200/120B Club	306	
D-EGJU	Cessna 182P Skylane	62275	N58752
D-EGJX	Reims/Cessna F.150L	0974	
D-EGKA	Cessna 182H Skylane	56265	N2365X
D-EGKB	Reims/Cessna FR.172E Rocket	0008	
D-EGKC	Reims/Cessna F.150L	0978	
D-EGKD(2)	Reims/Cessna F.150L	0980	
D-EGKE(2)	SOCATA Rallye 180TS Galérien	3325	
D-EGKF(2)	SOCATA TB-10 Tobago	166	
D-EGKG(2)	SOCATA TB-10 Tobago	167	
D-EGKH(3)	SOCATA TB-10 Tobago	168	
D-EGKJ(2)	SOCATA TB-10 Tobago	170	
D-EGKK	Piper PA-28R-200 Cherokee Arrow II	28R-7335442	N56472
D-EGKL	Cessna 182J Skylane	57059	N2959F
D-EGKM	Piper PA-28-181 Archer II	28-8090223	N8146Y
D-EGKN	SOCATA TB-10 Tobago	189	
D-EGKP	SOCATA TB-9 Tampico	195	
D-EGKQ	SOCATA TB-9 Tampico	196	
D-EGKR(2)	Cessna T.210M Turbo Centurion	0006/61914	OO-BVC
			D-EBVC
			HB-CXR
			(N732ZW)
D-EGKS	Cessna 152	80891	N25978
D-EGKT	Reims/Cessna F.172P	2058	
D-EGKU	Bölkow BO.207	252	
D-EGKV	Piper PA-38-112 Tomahawk	38-78A0123	N9519T
D-EGKW(2)	Klinke K1	001	
D-EGKY(2)	Reims/Cessna F.150L	1051	
D-EGLB	Reims/Cessna F.172N	1810	
D-EGLE	Bölkow BO.207	254	
D-EGLF	Reims/Cessna FR.182 Skylane RG	0034	
D-EGLG(2)	Reims/Cessna F.152	1600	

Regn.	Type	C/n	Prev.Id.
D-EGLH	Reims/Cessna F.152	1602	
D-EGLI	Bölkow BO.207 *(Reservation)*	255	
D-EGLJ	Cessna 172P	76144	N97005
D-EGLK(2)	Schwämmle HS-3 Motorlerche	844	
D-EGLL(3)	Cessna 172R	80332	N95216
D-EGLM	Cessna 172N	71780	N5224E
D-EGLN	Cessna 172P	76274	N98291
D-EGLO	Bölkow BO.207	256	(G-ASCW)
			D-EGLO
D-EGLP	Reims/Cessna FRA.150M Aerobat	0319	
D-EGLQ	Robin DR.400/140 Major	858	
D-EGLR	Robin DR.400/180 Régent	857	
D-EGLS	Reims/Cessna F.152	1605	
D-EGLT(2)	Cessna 172M	62963	N13716
D-EGLU	Bölkow BO.207	257	G-ASAY
			D-EGLU
D-EGLV	Piper PA-18-150 Super Cub	18-8009036	N6102A
			N9760N
D-EGLW	Piper PA-38-112 Tomahawk	38-80A0105	N9694N
D-EGLX	Cessna 172N	71099	N1697E
D-EGLY(2)	Cessna 172N	72917	N7370D
D-EGLZ	Cessna TR.182 Turbo Skylane RG	01011	N739VX
D-EGMA(2)	Beech F33A Bonanza	CE-903	N6746L
D-EGMB	Reims/Cessna F.172P	2121	
D-EGMC	CEA DR.253B Régent *(Permit)*	155	
D-EGMD	CEA DR.315 Petit Prince	422	
D-EGME(3)	Piaggio FWP.149D	183	91+61
			BF+420
			AS+022
			KB+145
D-EGMF	Reims/Cessna FR.172K Hawk XP	0592	
D-EGMH	SOCATA MS.893E Rallye 180GT Gaillard	12318	F-BUZF
D-EGMK	Piper PA-28R-200 Cherokee Arrow II	28R-7335424	N56370
D-EGMM	SOCATA MS.894A Minerva 220	11831	F-BSMM
D-EGMN	Gyroflug SC-01B-160 Speed Canard	S-42	
D-EGMO(3)	Piper PA-18 Super Cub 95	18-3195	OL-L21
			L-121
			53-4795
D-EGMQ	SOCATA MS.894A Minerva 220	11037	D-EAGF
D-EGMR	SIAI-Marchetti SF.260	2-55	OY-BEA
D-EGMS	Robin DR.400/180 Régent	1836	
D-EGMT	Reims/Cessna F.182Q (Porsche)	0057	
D-EGMV	Reims/Cessna F.152	1762	
D-EGMW	Reims/Cessna F.177RG Cardinal RG	0133	(D-EGWM)
D-EGMX	Reims/Cessna F.152	1601	PH-AYL
D-EGMY(2)	Bölkow BO.208C Junior	644	
D-EGNA(2)	Wassmer WA.54 Atlantic	128	
D-EGNB	SOCATA Rallye 150TD	2805	
D-EGNC	SOCATA MS.893ED Rallye 180GT Gaillard	12847	
D-EGND	SOCATA Rallye 150TD	2804	
D-EGNE	Bölkow BO.208 Junior	526	
D-EGNF	SOCATA Rallye 150TD	2968	
D-EGNG	SOCATA MS.893ED Rallye 180GT Gaillard	12825	
D-EGNH	SOCATA MS.893ED Rallye 180GT Gaillard	12826	
D-EGNI (2)	Piper PA-28-140 Cherokee C	28-26712	N5936U
D-EGNJ	SOCATA Rallye 150TD	2806	
D-EGNK	SOCATA MS.893ED Rallye 180GT Gaillard	12827	
D-EGNL	SOCATA Rallye 235ED Gabier	12833	
D-EGNM(2)	Piper PA-28-181 Archer II	28-8290010	N8438L
D-EGNN	SOCATA Rallye 150TD	2807	
D-EGNO(2)	Cessna 172P	75546	N64331
D-EGNP(2)	Diamond DA.40-180 Star *(Reservation 7.99)*	"00"	
D-EGNR	Reims/Cessna F.172P	2116	
D-EGNS	SOCATA MS.893ED Rallye 180GT Gaillard	12866	
D-EGNU(3)	Reims/Cessna F.172N	0379	
D-EGNY	Bölkow BO.208 Junior	530	
D-EGOA	Piper PA-28-181 Archer II	28-8190020	N8257V
D-EGOB(2)	Robin DR.300/125 Petit Prince	662	
D-EGOC(2)	Bölkow BO.208C Junior	646	
D-EGOD(2)	Robin HR.100/210D Safari	160	F-BUPY
D-EGOE	Robin HR.100/210D Safari	166	F-BUPV
D-EGOF(3)	Piper PA-28-161 Warrior II	28-8216122	N9637N
D-EGOG(3)	Grözinger Viking Dragonfly	293	
D-EGOH(2)	SOCATA MS.893A Rallye Commodore 180	11779	F-BSZC
D-EGOI	Reims/Cessna F.172N	2013	

Regn.	Type	C/n	Prev.Id.
D-EGOJ	Reims/Cessna F.152	1647	
D-EGOK(3)	Piper PA-28-140 Cherokee	28-21724	N11C
D-EGOL(3)	Piper PA-28RT-201T Turbo Arrow IV	28R-7931197	N29322
D-EGOM(2)	Cessna 182P Skylane	62263	CS-AOQ
			N58733
D-EGON	Fieseler Fi.156C-3 Trop Storch	5987	PH-NEL
			(PH-NDF)
			(PH-PBD)
			VN266
			Luftwaffe
D-EGOO(2)	Cessna P210N Pressurized Centurion II	00147	N6156P
D-EGOP(4)	Cessna TU.206G Turbo Stationair II	06109	N5411Z
D-EGOR(2)	Reims/Cessna F.152	1595	
D-EGOS	Piaggio FWP.149D	061	90+47
			AC+406
			DA+389
D-EGOT(2)	Grumman AA-5A Cheetah	0032	PH-GOL
			OO-HAH
D-EGOV(2)	Beech F33A Bonanza	CE-1576	N81863
D-EGOW(2)	Reims/Cessna T.210M Turbo Centurion	0014/62673	PH-AXP
			N6065B
D-EGOZ	Beech F33A Bonanza	CE-959	OE-KEK
			N1814D
D-EGPA(2)	Piper PA-28-181 Cherokee Archer II	28-7690189	N9529N
D-EGPC	Champion 7GCBC Citabria	0156	
D-EGPD(2)	Piper PA-28-181 Cherokee Archer II	28-7790471	N4575Q
D-EGPE(3)	CASA I-131E Jungmann	2092	D-EGRF
			E3B-441
D-EGPF(2)	Reims/Cessna FA.150L Aerobat	0094	D-ECHQ
D-EGPG(2)	Robin DR.400/120D Petit Prince	1544	
D-EGPH	Bellanca 7GCBC Citabria	798-75	N8586V
D-EGPI (3)	Reims/Cessna F.150G	0169	
D-EGPK	Cessna TR.182 Turbo Skylane RG	00804	N123CC
			(N736ZM)
D-EGPL(2)	Piper PA-28-236 Dakota	28-8011103	N8197L
D-EGPM	Piper PA-28-140 Cherokee E	28-7225452	N11C
D-EGPO	Orlican L-40 Meta-Sokol	150703	
D-EGPP	Mooney M.20J Model 201	24-1644	
D-EGPR(2)	Piper PA-28-181 Archer II	28-8190292	N84196
D-EGPS(2)	Cessna 172RG Cutlass	0542	OE-DVS
			N5478V
D-EGPT	SOCATA MS.893A Rallye Commodore 180	10793	F-BPGT
D-EGPW	Great Lakes 2T-1A-1	0505	N505GL
D-EGPX	Reims/Cessna FR.182 Skylane RG II	0060	
D-EGQA(2)	Bölkow BO.208C Junior	647	
D-EGQB	Reims/Cessna F.172N	1638	
D-EGQC	Reims/Cessna F.172N	1618	
D-EGQD	Reims/Cessna F.172N	1523	
D-EGQF	Reims/Cessna F.172N	1593	
D-EGQR	Cessna 172RG Cutlass	0544	(N5480V)
D-EGQU(2)	Reims/Cessna F.150G	0183	
D-EGRA(4)	SOCATA MS.894A Minerva 220	11835	F-BSMV
D-EGRC	SOCATA TB-10 Tobago	15	F-ODKD
D-EGRD	SOCATA TB-10 Tobago	46	F-ODMD
D-EGRE(4)	SOCATA TB-10 Tobago	119	
D-EGRG	Reims/Cessna FR.172F Rocket	0120	
D-EGRK	Piper PA-28R-200 Cherokee Arrow II	28R-7235299	N11C
D-EGRM	CASA I-131E Jungmann	2143	E3B-543
D-EGRO(3)	Grobholz G-2000 Symphonie	EB-01	
D-EGRP(3)	Piper PA-28-161 Cadet	2841207	N158ER
D-EGRQ	SOCATA TB-10 Tobago	115	
D-EGRS	SOCATA TB-10 Tobago	43	F-ODME
D-EGRT(2)	Beech C23 Sundowner	M-2358	N18355
D-EGRU	Oberlerchner JOB 15-180/2	055	OE-CAI
D-EGRV	SOCATA TB-10 Tobago	64	
D-EGRW	Piper PA-28-235 Cherokee C	28-11251	N8508N
D-EGRX	SOCATA TB-10 Tobago	47	F-ODMF
D-EGRY(2)	Robin DR.400/180R Remorqueur	1206	SE-GRY
D-EGRZ	SOCATA TB-10 Tobago	65	
D-EGSB	Reims/Cessna F.172L	0896	F-BTUT
D-EGSC	Reims/Cessna F.172N	1898	(PH-AXD)
D-EGSD(3)	Mooney M.20R Ovation	29-0073	
D-EGSE(2)	Piper PA-28R-200 Cherokee Arrow II	28R-7635272	N75170
D-EGSF	Reims/Cessna F.172N	1711	

Regn.	Type	C/n	Prev.Id.
D-EGSG	Piaggio P.149D	282	91+96
			AC+433
			AS+433
D-EGSH	Grumman AA-5A Cheetah	0563	N26399
D-EGSI (2)	Cessna T.210L Turbo Centurion	60057	N59058
D-EGSJ	CEA DR.253B Régent	199	
D-EGSK	Robin DR.300/180R Remorqueur	653	
D-EGSL(3)	Cessna R.182 Skylane RG	01364	N4641S
D-EGSM(2)	Piper PA-28-180 Cherokee Challenger	28-7305506	D-EBFH
			N55944
D-EGSO	SOCATA MS.893A Rallye Commodore 180	10818	F-BPSA
D-EGSP(2)	Piper PA-28R-200 Cherokee Arrow II	28R-7535299	N1493X
D-EGSR	Reims/Cessna F.172N	1857	
D-EGST	Reims/Cessna F.172F	0141	
D-EGSU(2)	CEA Jodel DR.1050M Ambassadeur	21	F-BJLQ
D-EGSW	Cessna 180J Skywagon	52645	N999ON
D-EGSX	SOCATA TB-9 Tampico	929	
D-EGSY(2)	SOCATA TB-10 Tobago	1078	
D-EGTA(2)	Grob G.115TA	8501	
D-EGTB(2)	Bek Me.109R3	1727	
D-EGTD	Reims/Cessna FR.182 Skylane RG	0003	
D-EGTE(2)	Robin DR.400/180 Régent	1953	F-GJQD
D-EGTF	Reims/Cessna FR.172K Hawk XP	0614	
D-EGTG	Reims/Cessna FR.182 Skylane RG	0005	
D-EGTH	Reims/Cessna F.172N	1516	F-WLIP
D-EGTJ	Cessna TR.182 Turbo Skylane RG	01437	N4847S
D-EGTL	Grumman AA-5 Traveler	0602	
D-EGTM	Reims/Cessna F.172N	1698	
D-EGTN(3)	Cessna 152	80509	N25036
D-EGTP	Robin DR.400/180 Régent	1261	
D-EGTQ	Robin DR.400/180R Remorqueur	1264	
D-EGTR(2)	SOCATA TB-20 Trinidad	706	
D-EGTS	Piper PA-38-112 Tomahawk	38-79A1059	N23871
D-EGTT	SOCATA MS.893E Rallye 180GT Gaillard	13084	SE-GTT
D-EGTU(2)	SOCATA MS.880B Rallye Club	1164	F-BPGE
D-EGTV	Piper PA-38-112 Tomahawk	38-78A0545	N9716N
D-EGTW(2)	Robin DR.400/180R Remorqueur	1260	
D-EGTY(2)	Morane-Saulnier MS.505 Criquet (Permit)	73	G-BWRF
			D-EFTY(2)
			F-BAUV
			Fr.AF
D-EGUB(3)	HOAC DV-20 Katana	20157	
D-EGUC(3)	Morane-Saulnier MS.880B Rallye Club	176	F-BKTB
D-EGUE	Reims/Cessna F.152	1578	
D-EGUG	Cessna 170B	26213	N2569C
D-EGUH(2)	Reims/Cessna F.152	1590	
D-EGUI	Bellanca 8GCBC Scout	200-76	SE-GUE
			OE-AOU
D-EGUJ	Cessna 172N	71599	N3591E
D-EGUK(2)	Cessna 172N	69403	N737GH
D-EGUL(2)	Cessna T.210N Turbo Centurion II	63924	OE-DUL
			(N6588C)
D-EGUM	Piper J-3C-65 Cub	12859	HB-OAF
			44-80563
			(PH-AXU)
D-EGUP(2)	Reims/Cessna F.172N	1946	
D-EGUQ(2)	Piper PA-28-140 Cherokee	28-21577	N11C
D-EGUR(2)	SAN Jodel D.140B Mousquetaire II	52	
D-EGUS(2)	SOCATA TB-10 Tobago	714	
D-EGUT(3)	Cessna TR.182 Turbo Skylane RG	00668	N9204D
D-EGUV(2)	Piper PA-28-140 Cherokee	28-21619	N11C
D-EGUW(2)	Beech V35B Bonanza	D-9505	
D-EGUX(2)	Reims/Cessna F.152	1615	
D-EGUY	Gyroflug SC-01B-160i Speed Canard	S-7	
D-EGVA(2)	Piper PA-28R-200 Cherokee Arrow II	28R-7635229	N9255K
D-EGVC	Dornier Do.27A-4	2059	OL-D03/
			OT-AMC
			D-3/D-9506
D-EGVE	Bölkow BO.208C Junior	661	
D-EGVF(2)	Reims/Cessna F.172N	1924	(PH-AXJ)
D-EGVG(2)	Reims/Cessna F.172N	1933	(PH-AXK)
D-EGVH(2)	Robin R.2160D Acrobin	199	
D-EGVI	Bölkow BO.208C Junior	662	
D-EGVK	Wassmer WA.54 Atlantic	127	
D-EGVL	Wassmer WA.54 Atlantic	129	

Regn.	Type	C/n	Prev.Id.
D-EGVM	SNCAN/ Stampe SV.4C	218	F-BCNZ
			Fr.AF
D-EGVN	Dornier Do.27A-4	2106	HC-...
			G-BNVX
			7P-AAX
			D-EGVN
			D-O9/OT-AMH
			OL-DO9
			D-9
D-EGVS	Piper J-3L Cub	12769	D-EGYS
			HB-OAA
			44-80473
D-EGVT	Beech C24R Sierra 200	MC-605	N2012Z
D-EGVU	Bölkow BO.208C Junior	664	
	(Converted to Sauer ST2500 engine)		
D-EGVV	Test registration for Grob G.115 production		
D-EGVW	Reims/Cessna F.172G	0209	D-EDOF
D-EGVZ	Robin DR.400/180R Remorqueur	1593	
D-EGWA(2)	Gardan GY-80 Horizon 180	203	OY-DTJ
D-EGWB	SOCATA MS.893E Rallye 180GT Gaillard	12330	F-BUXO
D-EGWC	Piper J-3C-65 Cub	6679	D-ECWC
			N37900
D-EGWD	Pützer Elster B	030	97+18
			D-ELBY
D-EGWE	Piper PA-28-180 Cherokee C	28-2043	
D-EGWF(2)	Reims/Cessna F.182Q Skylane	0140	PH-AXX
D-EGWG(2)	Robin DR.400/180R Remorqueur	1214	
D-EGWH	Piper J-3C-90/SGAC Marabout	EN.1	F-BGKF
D-EGWJ(2)	Cessna 172N	71517	N3362E
D-EGWK	Piaggio FWP.149D	174	91+52
			SC+336
			AS+415
			KB+139
D-EGWL(2)	SOCATA Rallye 235E-D Gabier	12797	F-GALE
D-EGWM(2)	Beth Pitts S-1S Special	AB-K-098	
D-EGWN	Fuji FA-200-160 Aero Subaru	227	
D-EGWO	Beech A-23 Musketeer II	M-771	
D-EGWR	Piper PA-28-161 Warrior II	28-7816670	N9630N
D-EGWS(2)	Mooney M.20J Model 201	24-0240	(N201HU)
D-EGWT	Robin R.2160D Acrobin	174	
D-EGWY	Bölkow BO.208C Junior	666	
D-EGWZ(3)	Gyroflug SC.01B-160 Speed Canard	S-38	
D-EGXA	Bölkow BO.208C Junior	667	
D-EGXE	Cessna 182J Skylane	56983	N2883F
D-EGXI (2)	Grob G.115A	8029	
D-EGXO	Bölkow BO.208C Junior	669	
D-EGXP	Mannebeck Aero Designs Pulsar XP	XP-002	
D-EGXY(2)	SNCAN/ Stampe SV.4C	651	F-BDMU
D-EGYA	Beech C23 Sundowner 180	M-1923	
D-EGYC(2)	Reims/Cessna F.172H	0328	
D-EGYD(2)	Beech C24R Sierra 200	MC-479	
D-EGYF(2)	SOCATA TB-10 Tobago	433	
D-EGYH(2)	SOCATA MS.893ED Rallye 180GT Gaillard	12990	
D-EGYI	SOCATA Rallye 100ST-D	2956	
D-EGYJ	SOCATA MS.893ED Rallye 180GT Gaillard	12992	
D-EGYK(2)	SOCATA MS.893ED Rallye 180GT Gaillard	12991	
D-EGYM(2)	Reims/Cessna F.172M	1344	
D-EGYN(2)	Reims/Cessna F.172M	1241	
D-EGYP(2)	SOCATA MS.893ED Rallye 180GT Gaillard	13012	
D-EGYQ	Cessna 182C Skylane	52862	N8962T
D-EGYR(2)	Reims/Cessna F.172M	1248	
D-EGYS(2)	SOCATA Rallye 180TD Galérien	3023	
D-EGYT(3)	SOCATA Rallye 180TD Galérien	3025	
D-EGYU	SOCATA Rallye 180TD Galérien	3024	
D-EGYW(2)	SOCATA Rallye 180TD Galérien	3026	
D-EGYX(4)	SOCATA MS.893A Rallye Commodore 180	10625	
D-EGYZ	SOCATA MS.893A Rallye Commodore 180	10615	
D-EGZA	Piper J-3C-90 Cub	10086	OE-AEW
			NC60443
			43-1225
D-EGZB(3)	Cessna 172M	65568	N444DA
			N6754H
D-EGZC(3)	Cessna 172P	74803	N53701
D-EGZE	Reims/Cessna F.172F	0120	
D-EGZG(2)	Piper J-3C-65 Cub	11295	N9829F
			G-AIYV
			43-30004
D-EGZH	Bölkow BO.208C Junior	675	
D-EGZJ(3)	Reims/Cessna F.172H	0553	
D-EGZL	Bölkow BO.208C Junior	678	
D-EGZM	Bölkow BO.208C Junior	679	
D-EGZN(2)	SEEMS MS.885 Super Rallye	270	F-BKUX
D-EGZO	Bölkow BO.208C Junior	575	
D-EGZP	Bayer Leverkusen Binder CP.301S Smaragd	AB.708	
D-EGZR	Heliopolis Gomhouria Mk.6	185	SU-347
D-EGZT	Reims/Cessna F.172N	1891	(PH-AXG)
D-EGZU(2)	Cessna 210B	57970	OE-DED
			N9670X
D-EGZW	Piper PA-38-112 Tomahawk	38-81A0104	N26024
D-EGZY	Cessna 182H Skylane	56276	N2376X
D-EHAA	Robin DR.400/180R Remorqueur	1541	
D-EHAB(2)	Piper PA-28-181 Cherokee Archer II	28-7790293	N9587N
D-EHAC(2)	Bölkow BO.208C Junior	709	(D-ENVD)
D-EHAD	Cessna 172	29059	N6959A
D-EHAE(2)	Robin DR.400/180R Remorqueur	1211	
D-EHAF(2)	Cessna P210N Pressurized Centurion	00188	N6539P
D-EHAG(2)	Cessna 182G Skylane	55275	N2075R
D-EHAH(3)	Piper PA-28-181 Archer II	28-8190109	N8308D
D-EHAI (2)	Robin DR.400/180R Remorqueur	1547	
D-EHAJ	Fuji FA-200-160 Aero Subaru	88	
D-EHAK(2)	Piper PA-32R-300 Lance	32R-7680154	(D-EFAN)
			N8616E
D-EHAL(3)	Piper PA-28RT-201 Arrow IV	28R-8118006	N8275Y
D-EHAM(2)	Cessna 172B	48415	N7915X
D-EHAN(3)	Mooney M.20C Mark 21	3314	N200EK
			D-EHAH
D-EHAO(2)	Piper PA-28-151 Warrior	28-7515278	OY-CBE
			N32942
D-EHAP(3)	Piper PA-18 Super Cub 95	18-1530	D-EOCF
			ALAT
			51-15530
D-EHAQ(2)	Robin DR.400/RP Remorqueur	1812	
D-EHAR(4)	Heier Neico Lancair 235	229	
D-EHAS	Piper PA-22-150 Tri-Pacer	22-5510	
D-EHAU(2)	Hauser Neico Lancair 235	1645	
D-EHAV(2)	Aviat Pitts S-2B	5302	N98AV
D-EHAW(2)	Fuji FA-200-160 Aero Subaru	120	
D-EHAY	CEA DR.253B Régent	190	
D-EHAZ(4)	Hötzel Brändli BX-2 Cherry	1694	
D-EHBA(2)	Reims/Cessna F.172G	0319	
D-EHBB	SOCATA MS.893A Rallye Commodore 180	11777	F-BSXY
D-EHBC(2)	SIAI-Marchetti SF.260	2-59	OO-HOC
D-EHBE(2)	Reims/Cessna F.150G	0116	
D-EHBF(2)	Piper PA-28RT-201T Turbo Arrow IV	28R-8231046	N8196U
D-EHBH	Piper PA-28-180 Cherokee Challenger	28-7305466	N55782
D-EHBI (3)	Reims/Cessna F.152	1534	
D-EHBK	Reims/Cessna FA.150K Aerobat	0075	
D-EHBL(2)	Reims/Cessna F.172G	0194	OO-HBF
			OO-WMF
			OO-SIF
D-EHBM(2)	Mooney M.20J Model 205 (Reservation 6.99)	24-3404	N68AG
			OE-KST
D-EHBN	Reims/Cessna F.172N	1755	
D-EHBO	Piel CP.301A Emeraude	263	F-BISA
D-EHBR(4)	Piper PA-18 Super Cub 95	18-1586	D-ELTQ
	(Reserved as D-EBBR(2) , 1.99)		ALAT
			51-15586
D-EHBT(2)	Tennant Europa	SB193, formerly 1796	
D-EHBU	Wassmer Jodel D.112 Club	1114	F-BKCX
D-EHBY	SAN Jodel D.140 Mousquetaire	32	F-BIZQ
D-EHCA	Cessna 210J Centurion	59179	N3379S
D-EHCC(3)	Grob G.115A	8056	
D-EHCD	Piper PA-18 Super Cub 95	18-3137	OL-L63
			L-63
			53-4737
D-EHCE(2)	Christen A-1 Husky	1148	
D-EHCF	Piper PA-18 Super Cub 95	18-3190	OL-L16
			L-116
			53-4790

Regn.	Type	C/n	Prev.Id.
D-EHCG	Erco 415D Ercoupe	4697	N3996H
			NC3996H
D-EHCH(2)	Mooney M.20M TLS	27-0077	
D-EHCK	Piper PA-18 Super Cub 95	18-1491	ALAT
			51-15491
D-EHCL	Piper PA-18 Super Cub 95	18-1436	ALAT
			51-15436
D-EHCM(2)	SOCATA MS.893A Rallye Commodore 180	11501	F-BSCR
D-EHCN(3)	Piper PA-28-161 Cadet	2841202	N91891
D-EHCO	Piper PA-18 Super Cub 95	18-1529	ALAT
			51-15529
D-EHCP(2)	Reims/Cessna F.172N	1760	
D-EHCR	Reims/Cessna F.172N	1762	
D-EHCS	Robin DR.400/180 Régent	1628	
D-EHCU	Piper PA-18 Super Cub 95	18-1447	N1156R
			ALAT
			51-15447
D-EHCW(2)	Beech B36TC Bonanza	EA-412	N72319
			N6866W
D-EHDA(2)	Laverda F.8L Falco IV	406	
D-EHDB	Cessna T.210L Turbo Centurion	59719	HB-CDI
			N22205
D-EHDC	Robin R.2160D Acrobin	165	
D-EHDE(3)	Commander Aircraft 114B	14545	N132A
D-EHDF	Piaggio FWP.149D	170	91+48
			EB+389
			DA+387
			KB+146
D-EHDG(2)	Robin HR.100/210D Safari	175	F-OCTY
D-EHDJ	Wassmer WA.52 Europa	68	
D-EHDL(2)	Piper PA-32R-301T Saratoga	32R-8229035	N8147H
D-EHDM(3)	Piper PA-28-181 Archer II	28-8490072	N4359U
D-EHDO(3)	AIAA/ Stampe SV.4A	1080	F-BCDO
			Fr.Navy
D-EHDQ(2)	Robin DR.400/180 Régent	1647	
D-EHDR(2)	Robin DR.400/180R Remorqueur	1646	
D-EHDT(2)	CASA I-131E Jungmann 180	2181	E3B-564
D-EHDU	Cessna 172C	49360	D-EHPI
			N1660Y
D-EHDW(3)	Hawickhorst Pitts S-1S Special	AB-K-O99	
D-EHDZ(2)	Piper PA-28RT-201T Turbo Arrow IV	28R-7931142	N2081Y
D-EHEA	Piper PA-28-235 Cherokee D	28-11305	N8563N
D-EHEB(4)	Busse Jodel D.92	AB18	D-EKYH
D-EHED(3)	Piper PA-18-150 Super Cub	18-5993	OE-AED
			(XB-ZUU)
D-EHEE	Mooney M.20F Executive	680180	
D-EHEF(2)	Reims/Cessna F.150G	0154	
D-EHEG(2)	Robin DR.400/180R Remorqueur	1078	
D-EHEI	Piper PA-28R-200 Cherokee Arrow II	28R-7235040	N4415T
D-EHEL(3)	Piper PA-28-180 Cherokee Challenger	28-7305160	N11C
D-EHEM(5)	HOAC DV-20 Katana	20065	
D-EHEN(2)	Aerotek Pitts S-2A	2088	G-BCXD
			N80044
D-EHEO	Robin DR.400/180 Régent	747	
D-EHEP(2)	CASA I-131E Jungmann (Lyco 0-360)	2013	D-EDEE(1)
			E3B-409
D-EHEQ	Focke-Wulf FW.44J Stieglitz	unkn	SE-BZI
			Fv664
D-EHER(5)	Piper PA-28-181 Archer II	28-8390008	N8293L
D-EHES(2)	Robin DR.400/180R Remorqueur	1049	
D-EHET(6)	SOCATA MS.893A Rallye Commodore 180	11491	OO-ACM
D-EHEU(3)	Cessna 182S	80155	
D-EHEV(2)	Robin DR.400/180R Remorqueur	1079	
D-EHEW	Eheim Piel CP.301A Emeraude	AB.401	(D-EMYV)
D-EHEY	Beech C23 Sundowner 180	M-2078	
D-EHEZ(2)	Robin DR.400/180 Régent	1080	
D-EHFA(2)	Piper PA-28-181 Cherokee Archer II	28-7790485	N5616V
D-EHFB	Gardan GY-80 Horizon 160	116	
D-EHFC(2)	Piper PA-28-140 Cherokee	28-7725172	N9609N
D-EHFD	Piper PA-28-140 Cherokee D	28-7125045	N1730T
D-EHFE(2)	Piper PA-28-180 Cherokee E	28-5658	(D-EKSY)
			N3322R
D-EHFF	Piper PA-28R-200 Cherokee Arrow II	28R-7335084	(D-EEPD)
			N11C
D-EHFG(2)	Beech F-33A Bonanza	CE-730	

Regn.	Type	C/n	Prev.Id.
D-EHFH(2)	Robin DR.400/180R Remorqueur	1886	
D-EHFI	Reims/Cessna F.172G	0220	
D-EHFK	Piper PA-28-140 Cherokee B	28-26086	N98174
D-EHFL	Piper PA-28R-200 Cherokee Arrow	28R-35245	N2674R
D-EHFM	Piper PA-28-180 Cherokee E	28-5610	N3687R
D-EHFN(3)	Robin DR.400/180R Remorqueur	1936	
D-EHFO	Piper PA-28-140 Cherokee E	28-7225136	N4313T
			N11C
D-EHFP	Piper PA-28-140 Cherokee B	28-25596	N98007
D-EHFR(2)	Cessna 172M	65729	N9645Q
D-EHFS	Piper PA-28-140 Cherokee C	28-26460	N5663U
D-EHFT(2)	Piper PA-24-250 Comanche	24-3558	N8308P
D-EHFU	Reims/Cessna F.172F	0164	
D-EHFW	Piper PA-28R-180 Cherokee Arrow	28R-30405	N4544J
D-EHFY	Reims/Cessna F.172G	0184	
D-EHFZ	Piper PA-28R-200 Cherokee Arrow II	28R-7235279	N1405T
D-EHGA(2)	Grumman AA-5B Tiger	0009	N1509R
D-EHGB	SIAI-Marchetti SF.260	2-42	
D-EHGC(2)	Piper PA-28-180 Cherokee E	28-5727	N3688R
D-EHGD	Robin DR.400/180 Régent	2159	
D-EHGE(2)	Rockwell Commander 114	14385	
D-EHGF	Piper PA-28-181 Cherokee Archer II	28-7790188	N9534N
D-EHGH	Beech F33A Bonanza	CE-1438	N5516K
D-EHGI (2)	Piper PA-28RT-201T Turbo Arrow IV	28R-8031056	N8152Q
D-EHGK	Piper PA-28-180 Cherokee Challenger	28-7305428	N15689
D-EHGL	Piper PA-28-140 Cherokee Fliteliner	28-7125194	OE-DFB
			N415FL
D-EHGM(3)	Piper PA-28-161 Cadet	2841084	N9169E
D-EHGN	Reims/Cessna F.172N	1554	
D-EHGO(2)	Rockwell Commander 114	14389	
D-EHGQ	Robin R.2160D	270	
D-EHGR	Piper PA-28RT-201T Turbo Arrow IV	28R-8231015	N80039
D-EHGS	Reims/Cessna F.150L	0735	PH-TGS
D-EHGT	Beech F33A Bonanza	CE-1148	
D-EHGV	Robin DR.400/180 Régent	2248	
D-EHGX	Cessna 182R Skylane	68476	N9972E
D-EHGY(2)	Reims/Cessna F.172N	1704	
D-EHGZ	Horstmann Jodel D.18	115	
D-EHHC	Fuji FA-200-160 Aero Subaru	112	
D-EHHD	Fuji FA-200-160 Aero Subaru	113	
D-EHHE	Aeromere F.8L Falco III America	227	HB-UOI
			D-EHHE
D-EHHF(3)	Piper PA-28RT-201 Arrow IV	28R-7918064	N3004T
D-EHHG(2)	Robin DR.400/180R Remorqueur	1972	
D-EHHH(2)	Steen Skybolt (Reservation)	1729	
D-EHHI (2)	Christen A-1 Husky	1080	N9594F
D-EHHJ	Beech 35-E33 Bonanza	CD-1165	N8384N
D-EHHK	CEA Jodel DR.1050 Ambassadeur	47	HB-EBP
D-EHHL	Mooney M.20F Executive	670325	N2931L
			(D-ECTJ)
			N2931L
D-EHHM	Reims/Cessna F.172H	0352	
D-EHHN	Jodel D.112 Club	886	D-EJCS(1)
			F-PJCS
D-EHHO	Piper PA-24-250 Comanche	24-3211	N7974P
D-EHHP	Robin R.1180TD Aiglon	231	
D-EHHS	Cessna 177A Cardinal	01294	N30509
D-EHHT(2)	de Havilland DH.82A Tiger Moth	85478/E-3	D-EDAM(2)
	(Identity officially quoted as T6746)		D-EDAN
			DE482
D-EHHU	Reims/Cessna F.172F	0129	
D-EHHV	Piper PA-28-181 Archer II	28-8490064	N9580N
D-EHHW(2)	Piper PA-28-160 Cherokee	28-546	TJ-ADK
			TU-TDG
			D-EMBA
			(N5465W)
D-EHHX	Cessna P210N Pressurized Centurion II	00679	N5379W
D-EHHY	CEA DR.220A 2+2	103	F-BPKA
D-EHHZ	Piaggio FWP.149D	063	90+49
			DB+389
D-EHIA(2)	Robin R.3000/160	172	
D-EHIC(2)	SAN Jodel D.140B Mousquetaire II	53	
D-EHIE	CEA Jodel DR.1050 Ambassadeur	291	
D-EHIF(2)	Reims/Cessna F.172G	0299	
D-EHIG(3)	Piper PA-28RT-201T Turbo Arrow IV	28R-7931114	N2153V

Regn.	Type	C/n	Prev.Id.
D-EHIH	Stark Turbulent D	119	
D-EHIK(3)	Piper PA-28RT-201T Turbo Arrow IV	28R-8531013	N91082
D-EHIM	Beech 35 Bonanza	D-499	OO-NDH
			D-EHIM
			OO-ECI
			HB-ECI
			NC90580
D-EHIN(2)	Reims/Cessna F.172H	0342	
D-EHIO	Robin DR.400/RP Remorqueur	1765	
D-EHIP(2)	Robin R.3000/160	138	
D-EHIQ	Ernst Piel CP.301 Emeraude	AB.408	
D-EHIR	Erco 415C Ercoupe	2650	N2027H
D-EHIS	Stark Turbulent D (V-4)	104	
D-EHIX(2)	Cessna 182J Skylane	57185	N3085F
D-EHIY	Robin DR.400/180 Régent	1221	EC-EQS
			D-EEIY
D-EHIZ	Bücker Bü.181B-1 Bestmann	FR.20	SL-ABI
			F-BBLX
			Luftwaffe
D-EHJB(2)	Cessna 172N	73633	N9682G
D-EHJC	Piper PA-18-150 Super Cub	18-5334	(D-EDBH)
			N5883
			ALAT
D-EHJD	Piper PA-28-180 Cherokee F	28-7105090	N3986R
D-EHJF(3)	Piper PA-28-236 Dakota	28-7911074	HB-PDE
			N2153H
D-EHJG(2)	SOCATA TB-9 Tampico	751	
D-EHJH	SOCATA TB-9 Tampico	756	
D-EHJI	SOCATA TB-9 Tampico	757	
D-EHJJ	SOCATA TB-10 Tobago	768	
D-EHJK	Piaggio FWP.149D	031	90+21
			AC+421
D-EHJL	Piaggio FWP.149D	045	90+31
			AC+441
			AS+441
			GA+394
			D-EGEW
			GA+394
D-EHJM	Mooney M.20J Model 201	24-0190	N201RM
D-EHJN	Piper PA-28-235 Cherokee Pathfinder	28-7410011	N56575
D-EHJO	SOCATA TB-10 Tobago	767	
D-EHJP(2)	Robin DR.400/180 Régent	2181	
D-EHJS	SAN Jodel DR.1050 Ambassadeur	358	
D-EHJT	SOCATA MS.880B Rallye Club	1178	F-BPGD
D-EHJV	Wassmer WA.51A Pacific	74	
D-EHKA	SAN Jodel DR.1050 Ambassadeur	476	
D-EHKB	Robin R.1180TD Aiglon	262	
D-EHKC(2)	Piper PA-28R-201T Turbo Cherokee Arrow III	28R-7703408	N47607
D-EHKD	Cessna 182K Skylane	58418	PH-WIT
			D-EGGO
			N2818R
D-EHKE(2)	Robin DR.400/180 Régent	2285	
D-EHKF(2)	Heigl Denney Kitfox III	908	
D-EHKG	Piper PA-28R-200 Cherokee Arrow II	28R-7235267	N1353T
D-EHKH	Piper PA-28R-200 Cherokee Arrow	28R-35119	D-EHGM
			N9407N
D-EHKK(3)	Reims/Cessna FR.172K Hawk XP	0630	PH-RAS
			(PH-RAF)
D-EHKL	Robin DR.400/180R Remorqueur	1209	
D-EHKM	Piper PA-32R-300 Lance	32R-7780071	N7648F
D-EHKO(2)	Klemm Kl.35D	1854	D-EBIB
			SE-BHR
			Fv5020
D-EHKP	Piper PA-28-151 Warrior	28-7715088	N9508N
D-EHKR	CEA DR.340 Major	425	F-BRVF
D-EHKS	Piper PA-32-300 Cherokee Six E	32-7240038	N8691N
D-EHKT	Mooney M.20J Model 201	24-1550	N5808Y
D-EHKU(2)	Beech F33A Bonanza	CE-1474	OY-GEE
D-EHKW(2)	Cessna TR.182 Turbo Skylane RG	00751	N736PX
D-EHKY	Bölkow BO.207	272	
D-EHLA	Bölkow BO.207	273	
D-EHLB	Cessna 182L Skylane	58691	N3391R
D-EHLC	Cessna 182L Skylane	58771	N3471R

Regn.	Type	C/n	Prev.Id.
D-EHLD(3)	Piper PA-28-161 Cadet	2841050	N9631N
			N9162Z
D-EHLE(4)	Piper PA-28-161 Cadet	2841081	N91663
D-EHLF	Reims/Cessna F.172H	0515	
D-EHLG(3)	Cessna 150L	73550	N16217
D-EHLH	Cessna 182K Skylane	58475	N2875R
D-EHLI(2)	Piper PA-28R-200 Cherokee Arrow II	28R-7435260	N43310
D-EHLJ	Piper PA-18 Super Cub 95	18-3440	QZ+020
			AC+531
			AS+531
			54-740
D-EHLL	Reims/Cessna FR.172E Rocket	0023	
D-EHLM(2)	Diamond DA.20-A1 Katana	10229	
D-EHLN	Morane-Saulnier MS.885 Super Rallye	236	F-BKUE
D-EHLO(2)	Diamond DA.20-A1 Katana	10233	
D-EHLP	Darter Commander 100	10A-085	N5554M
D-EHLR	Robin DR.400/180R Remorqueur	1162	
D-EHLS	Piper PA-28R-200 Cherokee Arrow II	28R-7235052	N4451T
D-EHLT	Cessna 172N	70921	N739YV
D-EHLU	Bölkow BO.207	277	
D-EHLV	SOCATA MS.893E Rallye 180GT Gaillard	12523	F-BVNP
D-EHLW	Beech C23 Sundowner 180	M-2205	
D-EHLY(2)	Piper PA-28-181 Cherokee Archer II	28-7790224	N9557N
D-EHLZ	Cessna TU.206G Turbo Stationair II	05318	N5552U
	(Now HL1004 but still not cancelled)		
D-EHMA(2)	Dornier Do.27A-4	388	56+80
			QW+110
			QW+701
			QM+614
			PL+422
D-EHMB(2)	Reims/Cessna F.172P	2237	LN-AFD
			OY-BHD
			(G-BLZO)
D-EHMC	Reims/Cessna F.150J	0529	
D-EHMD	Reims/Cessna F.150J	0515	
D-EHME(2)	Robin DR.400/140 Major	879	
D-EHMF(2)	Cessna P210N Pressurized Centurion II	00426	N7784K
D-EHMH	Piper PA-28-180 Cherokee F	28-7105180	N5143S
D-EHMI	Piper PA-18-150 Super Cub	18-6242	N8584D
D-EHMK	Piper PA-28-160 Cherokee	28-560	D-EMMJ
D-EHMM(2)	Great Lakes 2T-1A-2	0762	N3767F
D-EHMN	Piper PA-28RT-201T Turbo Arrow IV	28R-7931158	N2128Z
D-EHMO(2)	Mönke Hummel	1623/002	
D-EHMP	Piper PA-28-161 Warrior II	28-8616021	N9097E
			(N157AV)
			N9635N
D-EHMQ	Cessna 172N	73091	N4863F
D-EHMS(3)	Zlin Z.143L	0023	
D-EHMT	CASA I-131E Jungmann	2017	E3B-413
D-EHMU	Beech 35-33 Debonair	CD-82	N662V
D-EHMV	Piper PA-28-151 Warrior	28-7415190	N9512N
D-EHMW(2)	Mooney M.20J Model 201	24-1394	
D-EHMZ	SAN Jodel DR.1050 Ambassadeur	485	
D-EHNA	Piper PA-22-108 Colt	22-9112	SE-CZX
D-EHNB	Piper PA-28-140 Cherokee	28-22717	N4341J
D-EHND	Reims/Cessna F.152	1576	
D-EHNE	Cessna 150D	60367	N4367U
D-EHNF	Reims/Cessna F.152	1584	
D-EHNG	Reims/Cessna F.152	1585	
D-EHNH	Reims/Cessna F.152	1608	
D-EHNI (3)	Laverda F.8L Falco IV	417	D-EFEV(2)
D-EHNJ	Mooney M.20E Super 21	1151	OY-DDR
			N3475X
D-EHNL(2)	Christen A-1 Husky	1178	
D-EHNM	SOCATA Rallye 235E-D Gabier	13324	LN-BIE
D-EHNN	Reims/Cessna F.152	1619	
D-EHNQ	SOCATA MS.893E Rallye 180GT Gaillard	12524	F-BVNQ
D-EHNS	SOCATA TB-21 Trinidad TC	554	
D-EHNW	Cessna T.210L Turbo Centurion	60771	N1750X
D-EHNY	Reims/Cessna F.172F	0173	
D-EHOA	Rockwell Commander 114A	14537	
D-EHOB(2)	Piper PA-28-180 Cherokee C	28-2941	N8931J
D-EHOD(3)	Beech V35B Bonanza	D-10149	
D-EHOF(4)	Reims/Cessna F.172P	2250	
D-EHOG(2)	Commander Aircraft 114B	14592	N60132

Regn.	Type	C/n	Prev.Id.
D-EHOI	Cessna 152	79589	N757AQ
D-EHOK(2)	Piper PA-28-180 Cherokee C	28-2997	N8974J
D-EHOL(3)	Reims/Cessna F.172M	1328	PH-JDB
			D-EDZJ
D-EHOM(2)	Robin DR.400/180R Remorqueur	1204	
D-EHON(2)	Robin DR.400/180R Remorqueur	1205	
D-EHOP(2)	Bölkow BO.207	206	
D-EHOR(2)	Piper PA-28-180 Cherokee C	28-2965	N8947J
D-EHOS	Beech F-33A Bonanza	CE-847	
D-EHOT	Cessna 172	28683	N6083A
D-EHOU	SOCATA MS.880B Rallye Club	1852	F-BSMY
D-EHOV	Piper PA-28-180 Cherokee C	28-2765	N8813J
D-EHOW(2)	Rockwell Commander 114A	14536	
D-EHOZ(2)	Reims/Cessna F.152	1636	
D-EHPA(2)	Piper PA-46-350P Malibu	4622057	N9167H
D-EHPB	Piper PA-28RT-201T Turbo Arrow IV	28R-8131001	N8268T
D-EHPC	Reims/Cessna F.182Q Skylane	0067	N70846
D-EHPD	Piper PA-28-180 Cherokee G	28-7205318	N11C
D-EHPE	S.A.I. KZ-III	69	OY-DSY
D-EHPF	Cessna 150M	76751	N45140
D-EHPG	Cessna T.210L Turbo Centurion	61020	N2053S
D-EHPH	Champion 7GCBC Citabria	734-74	OE-AOI
D-EHPI (2)	Piper PA-28-140 Cherokee B	28-25752	N8887N
D-EHPK	Mooney M.20J Model 201	24-0137	HB-DWK
D-EHPL(2)	Robin HR.100/210D Safari	194	
D-EHPM	Haubs Polliwagen	001	
D-EHPN	Cessna 172N	72748	N6362D
D-EHPO	Cessna 172C	49362	N1662Y
D-EHPP(2)	Timmermann Christen Eagle II	229	
D-EHPR	Piper PA-32R-301T Turbo Saratoga SP	32R-8129073	N959CJ
			N326SP
			N4446M
			XB-CTR
			N8393T
D-EHPS	Piper PA-28-180 Cherokee Challenger	28-7305424	N55609
D-EHPW(2)	Beech A36 Bonanza	E-1181	OY-ATN
D-EHPY(2)	Reims/Cessna F.172N	1799	
D-EHPZ	Piper PA-32R-301 Saratoga	32R-8013078	N81751
			N9535N
D-EHQI	SIAT 223 V-3 Flamingo	003	
D-EHQO	Cessna 182H Skylane	55989	OE-DDP
			N1889X
D-EHQT(2)	Reims/Cessna FR.182 Skylane RG	0011	HB-CHH
			OE-DNG
D-EHRA(3)	Robin DR.400/180R Remorqueur	1990	
D-EHRB(3)	Piper PA-46-350P Malibu Mirage	4622043	OY-JEJ
			N9175P
D-EHRC	Reims/Cessna F.177RG Cardinal RG	0135	
D-EHRD(2)	SOCATA TB-21 Trinidad TC	698	
D-EHRE	Piper PA-22-160 Tri-Pacer	22-7011	N3056Z
D-EHRF(2)	Cessna 172N	72487	N5272D
D-EHRG	Doppelraab RE2 (Stored)	516	D-1824
			D-KOBA
			D-1824
D-EHRH(2)	Hoffmann Aero Designs Pulsar XP	333/1805	
D-EHRI	Cessna 172A	47693	N9893T
D-EHRK	SIAI-Marchetti SF.260	2-51	
D-EHRL(2)	Kotschi Pitts S-1S Special	AB-K-024 (501)	
D-EHRM	Mooney M.20F Executive	700044	N9476V
D-EHRN(2)	Cessna 210L Centurion	60326	(F-BVVT)
			N93264
D-EHRO(2)	Piper PA-28-181 Cherokee Archer II	28-7790546	N38378
D-EHRP	SOCATA MS.893A Rallye Commodore 180	11778	F-BSXZ
D-EHRS(2)	Reims/Cessna FR.172K Hawk XP II	0622	N70788
D-EHRT	Reims/Cessna FR.172H Rocket	0270	(D-ECJX)
D-EHRU	Cessna 175 Skylark	55620	N7320M
D-EHRV	Cessna 172RG Cutlass	1048	N98238
D-EHRW	Piper PA-28-181 Archer II	28-8590060	N6917C
D-EHSA	Cessna 182F Skylane	54655	N3255U
D-EHSC	Cessna 140	14442	N2211V
D-EHSF(2)	Wassmer WA.40 Super IV	25	F-BKAY
D-EHSG(2)	Piper PA-28R-200 Cherokee Arrow II	28R-7535346	N1505X
D-EHSH	SOCATA MS.893A Rallye Commodore 180	10811	
D-EHSI (2)	Piper PA-28R-200 Cherokee Arrow II	28R-7235092	N4564T
D-EHSJ (2)	Reims/Cessna F.150H	0267	
D-EHSL	SOCATA MS.880B Rallye Club	1207	
D-EHSM	Maule M-4-210C Rocket	1045C	
D-EHSN	SOCATA MS.880B Rallye Club	1256	
D-EHSO(2)	Piper PA-28-140 Cherokee Cruiser	28-7625189	N9562N
D-EHSP	SOCATA MS.893A Rallye Commodore 180	10915	
D-EHSQ	SOCATA MS.893A Rallye Commodore 180	10828	
D-EHSR	SOCATA MS.893A Rallye Commodore 180	10823	
D-EHST(2)	Cessna 210L Centurion	61066	N2100S
D-EHSW	SOCATA MS.880B Rallye Club	1240	
D-EHSX	SOCATA MS.893A Rallye Commodore 180	10829	
D-EHSY	Reims/Cessna F.172E	0078	
D-EHSZ	Cessna 182P Skylane	63106	PH-IFL
			N7322N
D-EHTB	CEA DR.360 Major	517	
D-EHTC	Robin R.2100A Club	139	
D-EHTE	Piper PA-28-160 Cherokee	28-617	N5526W
D-EHTI (2)	Cessna 172K	58446	N5132G
			N84372
D-EHTK	Gyroflug SC-01B Speed Canard	S-9	
D-EHTL(2)	Langér Cozy BL	001	
D-EHTN(2)	Cessna 172N	72699	N6293D
D-EHTP	Robin DR.400/180R Remorqueur	1342	
D-EHTS(2)	Robin DR.400/180R Remorqueur	1631	
D-EHTT(2)	Cessna 172N	70049	N738KY
D-EHTU	Piper J-3C-65 Cub	12602	OE-ADV
			Czech.AF
			44-80306
D-EHTW(3)	Cessna 172R	80003	N172NU
D-EHUA	Reims/Cessna 182P Skylane	0031/64046	N9986E
D-EHUB(2)	Commander Aircraft 114B	14556	N6007S
D-EHUC	Aero-Jodel D.11A Club	V-2	
D-EHUD(2)	Reims/Cessna FR.172K Hawk XP	0642	N1019Z
D-EHUE(2)	Cessna 152	82964	N45966
D-EHUF(2)	Cessna 175A Skylark	56285	(D-EHUQ)
			N6785E
D-EHUG(4)	Hirsch Aero Designs Pulsar XP	1840	
D-EHUH(2)	SAN Jodel DR.1050 Ambassadeur	285	D-EHPA(1)
D-EHUI	Cessna 182P (Reims-assembled)	0030/64041	N9981E
D-EHUL(3)	Piper PA-28-181 Archer II	28-8290007	N84363
D-EHUM(4)	Reims/Cessna F.152	1502	
D-EHUN(2)	Auster J/1 Autocrat	2119	OY-DPE
D-EHUP(2)	Reims/Cessna F.152	1645	
D-EHUQ(2)	Bölkow BO.207	207	
D-EHUR(2)	Robin DR.300/108 2+2	529	
D-EHUS(2)	Reims/Cessna FR.172F Rocket	0138	F-WLIT
D-EHUT(2)	Piper PA-28-181 Archer III	2890226	N9253X
D-EHUU	Robin DR.400/160 Chevalier	705	
D-EHUV(2)	Robin DR.400/180 Régent	1596	
D-EHUW(3)	Staub Binder CP.301S Smaragd	AB.703	
D-EHUX(3)	SOCATA TB-20 Trinidad	453	
D-EHUY	Piper PA-28-140 Cherokee Cruiser	28-7725073	N9527N
D-EHUZ(2)	Reims/Cessna F.172N	1881	"D-EOSJ"
D-EHVA	Piper PA-22-108 Colt	22-9622	
D-EHVC	Beech V35B Bonanza	D-10241	
D-EHVD(2)	SIAT 223K-1 Flamingo	20	HB-EVD
			D-ENBR(1)
D-EHVG	Robin DR.400/180R Remorqueur	1633	
D-EHVH	Piaggio P.149D	345	92+27
			AC+451
			AS+451
D-EHVI	Piper PA-22-108 Colt	22-9510	
D-EHVL	Cessna 172C	49517	N2017Y
D-EHVM(2)	Beech B36TC Bonanza	EA-315	N724T
			N6511X
D-EHVO(2)	Piaggio FWP.149D	081	90+63
			JA+391
			AS+490
D-EHVP(2)	Piaggio FWP.149D	080	90+62
			AC+466
			AS+489
D-EHVR	Piaggio FWP.149D	054	90+40
			SC+331
			AS+481
D-EHVS	Reims/Cessna F.172N	1693	
D-EHVT	Reims/Cessna F.172N	1706	

Regn.	Type	C/n	Prev.Id.
D-EHVY	Mooney M.20D Master	165	N6739U
D-EHWA	Cessna 182G Skylane	55467	N2367R
D-EHWB(2)	Beech C23 Sundowner 180	M-2233	
D-EHWC(2)	Wolfrum Stoddard-Hamilton Glasair IIRG	1039	
D-EHWD	Beech F33A Bonanza	CE-440	
D-EHWE(3)	Ehringhaus Denney Kitfox II	472	
D-EHWF	Robin DR.400RP Remo 212	1800	
D-EHWG(2)	Robin DR.400/180S Régent	2026	
D-EHWH(2)	Zlin Z.50LS	0040/03	OK-PRH
D-EHWI (2)	Mooney M.20K Model 231	25-0221	N231FL
D-EHWJ	Beech C23 Sundowner 180	M-1479	
D-EHWK	Cessna 182G Skylane	55475	N2375R
D-EHWM	Beech B24R Sierra 200	MC-175	
D-EHWN(3)	Piper PA-28-181 Archer II	28-8590008	N144AV
D-EHWP(2)	Cessna 140	13721	N4250N
			NC4250N
D-EHWR	Reims/Cessna FR.182 Skylane RG	0020	(G-BGAR)
D-EHWS(2)	Robin DR.400/180 Régent	1985	
D-EHWT	Gardan GY-80 Horizon 180	223	
D-EHWW(2)	Piper PA-28R-201T Turbo Arrow III	28R-7803259	N9441C
D-EHWY	Beech A23 Musketeer Custom	M-678	
D-EHWZ(2)	Reims/Cessna FR.182 Skylane RG	0022	(PH-ADM)
			PH-AXW
D-EHXG	Rockwell Commander 112	53	N1053J
D-EHXH(2)	de Havilland DH.82A Tiger Moth	85652	G-AIXH
			N5445
			VR-HFH
			VR-HEL
			G-AIXH
			DE722
D-EHXI	Rockwell Commander 112	119	N1175J
			(N1119J)
D-EHXJ	Rockwell Commander 112 (Permit 11.99)	122	N1171J
			(N1122J)
D-EHXK	Rockwell Commander 112	121	N1005J
			(N1121J)
D-EHXL	Rockwell Commander 112A	129	N1176J
			(N1129J)
D-EHXM	Rockwell Commander 112A	191	N1149J
			(N1191J)
D-EHXN	Rockwell Commander 112A	209	N1209J
D-EHXO	Rockwell Commander 112A	214	N1214J
D-EHXR	Rockwell Commander 112A	324	N1324J
D-EHXS	Rockwell Commander 112A	357	N1357J
D-EHXU	Rockwell Commander 112A	467	N1467J
D-EHXV	Rockwell Commander 112A	472	(D-EIFB)
			N1472J
D-EHXW	Rockwell Commander 112A	475	(N1475J)
D-EHXX	Rockwell Commander 112A	279	N1279J
D-EHXY	Rockwell Commander 112A	489	(N1489J)
D-EHXZ	Bölkow BO.207	289	HB-UXZ
			(D-ENWI)
D-EHYD	Aeronca 7AC Champion	3957	N85224
D-EHYF	Erco Ercoupe 415E de luxe	4907	N94794
D-EHYG	Piper J-4A Cub Coupé	4-880	N26758
D-EHYH	Ranz Jodel D.9 Bébé	AB.14 (Liz.225)	
D-EHYM	Piper J-3C-85 Cub	10776	D-EDIF
			PH-NFI
			PH-NAE
			43-29485
D-EHYS(2)	Cessna 172F	52400	N8500U
D-EHYX	Bölkow BO.207	209	
D-EHZA	Cessna 175C Skylark	57048	N8348T
D-EHZK	Beech C24R Sierra 200	MC-648	N60181
D-EHZW	Piper PA-28RT-201T Turbo Arrow IV	28R-8231043	N81852
D-EIAA	Reims/Cessna F.152	1537	
D-EIAD	Morane-Saulnier MS.885 Super Rallye	252	F-BKUF
	(Reserved as SP-FRV 11.99)		
D-EIAE	CEA DR.220 2+2	42	F-BOKM
D-EIAG(2)	Cessna 152	85163	N6140Q
D-EIAH(2)	Piper PA-46-310P Malibu	46-8508060	N4391V
D-EIAI	Piper PA-28-181 Archer II	28-8090365	N8240T
D-EIAK(2)	Reims/Cessna FA.152 Aerobat	0424	
D-EIAL	Piper PA-28-161 Warrior II	28-8116076	N8291D
D-EIAM	Piper PA-28-180 Cherokee F	28-7105141	N1687T

Regn.	Type	C/n	Prev.Id.
D-EIAN	Grob G.115A	8062	
D-EIAO	SOCATA MS.893E Rallye 180GT Gaillard	12310	F-BUVB
D-EIAP	SAN Jodel DR.1050 Ambassadeur	356	
D-EIAR	CEA DR.250/160 Capitaine	98	
D-EIAS	Cessna TU.206F Turbo Stationair	03187	N8326Q
D-EIAT	Piper PA-28R-200 Cherokee Arrow B	28R-7135210	N1975T
D-EIAV	Robin DR.400/180R Remorqueur	1658	
D-EIAW(3)	Beech V35B Bonanza	D-10289	N66648
D-EIAX	Cessna TR.182 Turbo Skylane RG	01462	N4923S
D-EIAY	Grob G.115A	8050	
D-EIAZ	Rockwell Commander 112A	314	N1314J
D EIBA	Piper PA-28-181 Cherokee Archer II	28-7690150	N9518N
D-EIBB	SOCATA MS.892A Rallye Commodore 150	10801	F-BPHQ
D-EIBD	Rockwell Commander 114B	14400	
D-EIBE	Dornier Do.27A-1	310	56+34
			GD+154
			LB+154
			CC+...
			CB+002
D-EIBF	Reims/Cessna F.152	1566	
D-EIBG	Reims/Cessna F.152	1574	
D-EIBH	Piper PA-28R-200 Cherokee Arrow II	28R-7235255	N11C
D-EIBI	Reims/Cessna F.182Q Skylane	0062	
D-EIBJ	Diamond DA.20-A1 Katana	10270	
D-EIBK	Piper PA-28-161 Warrior II	28-8116197	N83658
D-EIBL	Piper PA-18A-150 Super Cub	18-8009024	N63928
D-EIBO(2)	Cessna P210N Pressurized Centurion II	00714	N6100W
D-EIBR	Piper PA-38-112 Tomahawk	38-81A0117	N23137
D-EIBS	Reims/Cessna F.152	1772	
D-EIBV(2)	Piper PA-28-161 Warrior II	28-8216115	N9630N
D-EIBW	Piper PA-28RT-201T Turbo Arrow IV	28R-8131162	N8406V
D-EIBY	Robin HR.100/200B	126	F-BTBY
D-EICA	Mooney M.20F Executive	700035	N9446V
D-EICB	Cessna 172RG Cutlass	0543	N5479V
D-EICC	Robin DR.300/180R Remorqueur	727	
D-EICD	Piaggio FWP.149D	182	91+60
			BF+419
			AS+021
			KB+144
D-EICE	Piper PA-28R-201T Turbo Arrow III	28R-7803330	N36620
D-EICF	Cherdron Christen Eagle II	0162	
D-EICG	Piper PA-28-200 Cherokee Arrow II	28R-7535128	N33162
D-EICH(4)	Beech F33A Bonanza	CE-1162	N3144W
D-EICI (2)	Aviat A-1 Husky	1296	
D-EICK	Piper PA-28-200 Cherokee Arrow B	28R-35601	N3046R
D-EICL	Reims/Cessna F.172N	1769	PH-AXR
D-EICM	Piper PA-28-181 Archer II	2890146	N9203P
D-EICN(2)	Piper PA-28R-201T Turbo Arrow IV	28R-8431025	N4356X
D-EICP	Reims/Cessna F.172N	1722	
D-EICR	Piper PA-28-181 Archer II	28-8490075	N4359T
			(D-EFZN)
D-EICS	Cessna U.206F Stationair II	03118	N8257Q
D-EICT	Piper PA-28RT-201T Turbo Arrow IV	28R-8231055	N8216J
D-EICY	Reims/Cessna F.177RG Cardinal RG	0167	(D-EIMP)
D-EIDA	Fuji FA-200-160 Aero Subaru	164	
D-EIDC	Fuji FA-200-180 Aero Subaru	223	
D-EIDE	Fuji FA-200-180 Aero Subaru	214	
D-EIDF	Fuji FA-200-180 Aero Subaru	205	
D-EIDG	Fuji FA-200-180AO Aero Subaru	270	
D-EIDH(2)	Fuji FA-200-180 Aero Subaru	279	
D-EIDJ	Fuji FA-200-160 Aero Subaru	267	
D-EIDK	Fuji FA-200-180 Aero Subaru	203	
D-EIDL	Fuji FA-200-180 Aero Subaru	206	
D-EIDM	Fuji FA-200-160 Aero Subaru	221	
D-EIDO	Fuji FA-200-180AO Aero Subaru	248	
D-EIDP(2)	Beech F33A Bonanza	CE-1482	
D-EIDQ	Fuji FA-200-160 Aero Subaru	266	
D-EIDR	Fuji FA-200-160 Aero Subaru	180	
D-EIDS	Fuji FA-200-180 Aero Subaru	273	
D-EIDU	Fuji FA-200-180AO Aero Subaru	274	
D-EIDV	Fuji FA-200-180 Aero Subaru	162	N73542
D-EIDW	Fuji FA-200-180 Aero Subaru	208	
D-EIDX	Fuji FA-200-180AO Aero Subaru	264	
D-EIDY	Fuji FA-200-180AO Aero Subaru	275	
D-EIDZ	Fuji FA-200-180AO Aero Subaru	276	

Regn.	Type	C/n	Prev.Id.
D-EIEA	Reims/Cessna F.152	1598	
D-EIEB	Reims/Cessna F.152	1613	
D-EIED	Reims/Cessna F.172N	1852	
D-EIEE	Reims/Cessna F.172N	1875	
D-EIEG(3)	Cessna 180K Skywagon	53147	N2983K
D-EIEH	Robin DR.400/180R Remorqueur	1405	
D-EIEI (2)	Piper PA-18 Super Cub 95	18-1374	(D-EKQJ)
	(See D-EKRG)		ALAT
			51-15374
D-EIEK	Piper PA-28-180 Cherokee C	28-2821	N8852J
D-EIEL	Zlin Z.526 Trenér Master	1011	D-EIFL
			OK-VRF
D-EIEM	SOCATA TB-20 Trinidad	311	
D-EIEN	SOCATA TB-9 Tampico	313	
D-EIEO	SOCATA TB-10 Tobago	314	
D-EIEP(2)	Grob G.115A	8031	
D-EIER(2)	Robin DR.400/180R Remorqueur	1198	
D-EIET	Robin DR.400/180R Remorqueur	2114	
D-EIEW	Extra Pitts S-1E Special	8-9043	
D-EIFA(2)	Piper PA-46-350P Malibu Mirage	4622099	OY-FFA
			SE-KMC
D-EIFB(2)	SOCATA TB-21 Trinidad TC	717	
D-EIFC	Reims/Cessna FR.182 Skylane	0002	
D-EIFE	Piaggio FWP.149D	129	91+08
			BF+417
			AS+016
			KB+106
D-EIFF	Rhein-West-Flug RW3P-75 Multoplan	009	(D-ELOL)
D-EIFG	Piper PA-28R-200 Cherokee Arrow II	28R-7635161	N8442C
D-EIFH	Piper PA-38-112 Tomahawk	38-78A0414	N9679N
D-EIFJ	Mooney M.20K Model 231	25-0118	N231JJ
D-EIFK	Fuji FA-200-180 Aero Subaru	185	
D-EIFL(3)	Hergarten Neico Lancair 320	736-320-579	
D-EIFM	Reims/Cessna F.152	1709	
D-EIFN	Piper PA-28-181 Archer III	2890229	N9255F
D-EIFO	Piper PA-28-181 Cherokee Archer	28-7890548	N39645
D-EIFR(2)	Piper PA-28-236 Dakota	2811026	N91727
D-EIFS	Andres Binder CP.301S Passat	AB.01	
D-EIFT	Robin DR.400/180R Remorqueur	1014	
D-EIFW(2)	Heuer FW190 (Half-scale)	333AB	
D-EIFY(2)	Reims/Cessna F.152	1723	
D-EIGA	Reims/Cessna F.172N	1846	(D-ELFS)
D-EIGB	Mooney M.20E Chapparral	700031	N30PK
			D-EIGB
			N9443V
D-EIGC	Piper PA-28-236 Dakota	2811033	N92139
D-EIGD	Gardan GY-80-160D Horizon	247	
D-EIGE	Reims/Cessna F.172N	1808	
D-EIGF	Gardan GY-80 Horizon 160D	248	
D-EIGH(2)	Piper PA-28-181 Archer II	2890127	N9185K
D-EIGI	Piper PA-28-181 Archer II	28-8090279	
D-EIGK	Mudry CAP.10B	74	F-BXHM
D-EIGL	Piper PA-28-181 Archer II	28-8690009	N2608Y
D-EIGN	Reims/Cessna F.150L	0672	SE-FXD
D-EIGO(2)	Beech F33A Bonanza	CE-1720	OE-KSB
D-EIGP	Piper PA-28-180 Cherokee Challenger	28-7305460	N55647
D-EIGT	Piper PA-28-181 Archer II	28-8190218	N8379Z
D-EIGY	Cessna 182N Skylane	60464	N8924G
D-EIGZ	SOCATA TB-21 Trinidad TC	1478	
D-EIHA	Piper PA-28-161 Warrior II	28-7916296	N9609N
D-EIHB	SOCATA MS.883 Rallye 115	1647	F-BTHP
D-EIHD	Stampe & Renard/ Stampe SV.4B	1169	G-AZUL
			V-27
D-EIHE	Cessna 182G Skylane	55081	HB-CMM
			N3681U
D-EIHG(2)	Reims/Cessna FA.150K Aerobat	0064	D-ECAN(2)
D-EIHH(2)	SOCATA Rallye 235E-D Gabier	12795	OO-ADN
			F-GACT
D-EIHI	Reims/Cessna F.152	1591	
D-EIHK(2)	Piper PA-28-161 Warrior II	2816002	N9089K
D-EIHL(2)	Piper PA-28-140 Cherokee F	28-7325400	D-EHWW(1)
			N11C
D-EIHM	Piper PA-28-181 Archer II	28-8290052	N8358F
D-EIHN	SOCATA MS.883 Rallye 115	1645	F-BTHN

Regn.	Type	C/n	Prev.Id.
D-EIHO	Piper PA-38-112 Tomahawk	38-79A0256	(SX-ALW)
			D-EIHO
D-EIHP	Cessna TR.182 Turbo Skylane RG	01982	N6326T
D-EIHQ	HOAC DV-20 Katana	20084	
D-EIHS	SOCATA MS.880B Rallye Club	2044	F-BTPO
D-EIHV	Robin DR.400/180R Remorqueur	1908	
D-EIHW	Cessna TU.206G Turbo Stationair II	06114	(N5443Z)
D-EIHY	Piper PA-28RT-201 Arrow IV	28R-8018068	
D-EIIA(3)	Robin R.3000/160	164	
D-EIIB	Piper PA-28RT-201T Turbo Arrow IV	28R-7931275	N2957D
D-EIIC(3)	Klemm Kl.35D (Permit)	3171	(D-EHDY(3))
			D-EBBW
			OE-ABW
D-EIID	Piper PA-28-181 Archer II	28-8090361	N8237Z
D-EIIE	Piper PA-28-235 Cherokee	28-10224	N8691W
D-EIIF(3)	Christen Pitts S-2A	5139	N15PF
D-EIIG	Reims/Cessna F.182Q Skylane	0069	
D-EIII (3)	Bücker Bü.133D Jungmeister	1069	E1-...
D-EIIJ	Mooney M.20K Model 231	25-0830	N5764N
D-EIIK	Robin HR.200/100 Club	31	
D-EIIL	Robin HR.200/100 Club	34	
D-EIIM	Robin DR.400/180R Remorqueur	956	
D-EIIN	Robin DR.400/180 Régent	946	
D-EIIO(2)	Robin DR.400/180 Régent (Permit 12.99)	2441	
D-EIIP	Reims/Cessna F.182Q Skylane	0091	
D-EIIT(2)	Piper PA-28-161 Warrior II	2816011	N9118X
D-EIIV(2)	Piper PA-28RT-201T Turbo Arrow IV	28R-8031091	LX-FRL
			N8190B
D-EIIX	Aviat Pitts S-2A	5210	
D-EIIY	Mooney M.20J Model 201	24-1152	N1139L
D-EIJA	SOCATA MS.880B Rallye Club	2516	F-BVNN
D-EIJB	Robin DR.400/180 Régent	2232	
D-EIJF	Coopavia Piel CP.301A Emeraude	206	F-BIJF
D-EIJH	Piper PA-28-181 Archer II	28-7990552	N2914N
D-EIJI	Robin DR.400/180 Régent	1029	
D-EIJJ	Cessna 152	85216	N6273Q
D-EIJK(2)	Kurz Rieseler Ma.III	N01/1848	
D-EIJL	CASA I-131E Jungmann	2088	E3B-392
D-EIJN	Piper PA-28-181 Archer II	28-8190019	N8257H
D-EIJT	Piaggio P.149D	303	92+07
			AC+454
			AS+454
D-EIJW	Wilkenloh Bede BD-5W	01-AB	
D-EIKA(2)	Mooney M.20J Model 201	24-1645	
D-EIKB	Morane-Saulnier MS.885 Super Rallye (Res 3.99)	51	
D-EIKC(2)	Cessna P210N Pressurized Centurion II	00554	N731XF
D-EIKD	Reims/Cessna F.172P	2107	
D-EIKE(2)	Mooney M.20J Model 205	24-3209	
D-EIKF	Reims/Cessna FR.172K Hawk XP	0675	
D-EIKH(2)	Grob G.115A	8077	
D-EIKI	SOCATA MS.893E Rallye 180GT Gaillard	12182	F-BUCR
D-EIKL	CEA DR.220 2+2	22	F-BOCP
D-EIKM	Beech V35B Bonanza	D-9919	N4KM
D-EIKN(2)	Cessna 172S	172S8126	N866SP
D-EIKO	Robin DR.400/180R Remorqueur	1130	(F-GABH)
D-EIKP(2)	Cessna 172RG Cutlass	0645	N6382V
D-EIKR(2)	Robin DR.400/180 Régent	1839	F-ODSI
D-EIKS(2)	Reims/Cessna F.182Q Skylane	0075	
D-EIKT	Reims/Cessna F.172N	2012	
D-EIKV(2)	Reims/Cessna FR.172K Hawk XP	0667	
D-EIKW(2)	Piper PA-28-236 Dakota	28-8211013	G-BOJE
			N84600
D-EIKY	Bücker Bü.133D-1 Jungmeister	2005	OE-AKE
D-EIKZ	Cessna 172RG Cutlass	0546	N5491V
D-EILA(2)	Cessna T.210L Turbo Centurion	61046	OE-DFT
			D-ECCC
			N2079S
D-EILB	PZL-104 Wilga 35A	62177	(D-EWBO)
			DDR-WBO
			DM-WBO
D-EILD	Cessna 172RG Cutlass	0508	(N5337V)
D-EILE	Reims/Cessna F.172H	0548	
D-EILF(2)	Piper PA-28-160 Cherokee	28-368	C-GBBE
			SLN-...
			D-EJPI (1), N11C

Regn.	Type	C/n	Prev.Id.
D-EILG	Piper PA-28-181 Archer II	28-7990495	N2852N
D-EILH(2)	Robin DR.400/RP Remorqueur	1837	OE-KLH
			D-ELSR
D-EILI (2)	Cessna 182R Skylane	68449	N9810E
D-EILJ	SOCATA TB-9 Tampico	920	
D-EILK	Piper PA-28-181 Archer III	2843144	N4123Q
D-EILL	Cessna P210N Pressurized Centurion II	00544	N731TG
D-EILM	SOCATA MS.887 Rallye 125	2178	F-BVLN
D-EILO(2)	Piper PA-28-181 Archer II	28-7990379	N2163Y
D-EILP	Reims/Cessna F.152	1922	
D-EILQ	Reims/Cessna F.152	1893	N90740
D-EILR	Reims/Cessna F.172P	2165	
D-EILS	Piper PA-28RT-201 Arrow IV	28R-7918126	N28409
D-EILT(2)	Mooney M.20F Executive	22-1343	
D-EILU	Piper PA-38-112 Tomahawk	38-79A0673	N9659N
D-EILW(2)	Beech 77 Skipper	WA-95	
D-EILX	Cessna 172RG Cutlass	0817	D-EOCD
			(N9417B)
D-EILY	Wassmer WA.52 Europa	49	
D-EILZ	Cessna TR.182 Turbo Skylane RG	1490	N4952S
D-EIMA(2)	Mooney M.20K Model 231	25-0805	N5733H
D-EIMB	Beech C24R Sierra 200	MC-603	
D-EIMC	Reims/Cessna F.172N	1859	
D-EIMD	Reims/Cessna F.172P	2054	
D-EIMF	Beech V35B Bonanza	D-9245	N9245Q
D-EIMG	Piper PA-28-181 Archer II	28-8090040	N4513L
D-EIMH	Reims/Cessna F.172P	2147	
D-EIMI	Reims/Cessna F.172N	1906	
D-EIMK	Krause Super Acro Sport	1	
D-EIML(2)	Reims/Cessna F.172P	2252	
D-EIMM(2)	Cessna P210N Pressurized Centurion	00225	HB-CJT
			N9FV
			(N4588K)
D-EIMN	Reims/Cessna F.172P	2171	F-WZDT
			(D-EGLK)
D-EIMO	Cessna T.210G Turbo-System Centurion	0276	N6876R
D-EIMP(2)	Cessna 182R Skylane	67947	PH-AXP
			N9434H
D-EIMR	Reims/Cessna F.172P	2136	(D-EODZ)
D-EIMS	Reims/Cessna F.150M	1312	
D-EIMT	Reims/Cessna F.152	1941	
D-EIMU	Bellanca 7ECA Citabria	956-73	
D-EIMV	Reims/Cessna F.172P	2143	
D-EIMW	Reims/Cessna F.150K	0531	PH-ALF
D-EIMY	Reims/Cessna F.172N	1908	
D-EIMZ	Reims/Cessna F.172P	2226	F-WZIB
D-EINB	Navion Rangemaster H	NAV-4-2543	(N2543T)
D-EINC(2)	Cessna 172R	80001	N172KS
D-EINE(2)	CASA I-131E Jungmann	2202	E3B-582
D-EINF	Navion Rangemaster H	NAV-4-2546	(N2546T)
D-EING	Navion Rangemaster H	NAV-4-2547	(N2547T)
D-EINH(2)	Robin DR.300/108 2+2	530	
D-EINI	SAN Jodel D.150 Mascaret (Rotax 914)	32	
D-EINK(2)	Piper PA-28RT-201T Turbo Arrow IV	28R-8331034	N4301K
D-EINL	Navion Rangemaster H	NAV-4-2544	D-EINC
			(N2544T)
D-EINS	Piper PA-24 Comanche 250	24-1492	N6382P
D-EINT	Reims/Cessna FR.172K Hawk XP	0663	
D-EINU	Stark Turbulent D	132	HB-SVF
			D-EKEV
D-EINW	Cessna 172RG Cutlass	0407	(N4877V)
D-EINY	Wassmer WA.54 Atlantic	111	
D-EINZ	Piper PA-18-150 Super Cub	18-8310	N7443Z
D-EIOF	Hoffmann H-40	40001	
D-EIOI	Mooney M.20K Model 231	25-0315	SE-IEI
			N231MV
D-EIOL	Piper PA-28-181 Archer II	2890167	N9091U
			N92043
D-EIOO	CASA I-131E Jungmann	2215	D-EDNN(1)
			E3B-615
D-EIOR	Mooney M.20J Model 201	24-0622	N102CK
			N4106H
D-EIOS(2)	Reims/Cessna F.152	1934	
D-EIOU(2)	Piper PA-28RT-201T Turbo Arrow IV	28R-7931270	N2510U
			N9597N
D-EIPA	Piper PA-28RT-201T Turbo Arrow IV	28R-7931242	N2874W
D-EIPB	Beech B24R Sierra 200	MC-427	
D-EIPC	Beech C23 Sundowner 180	M-1835	
D-EIPD	Beech V35B Bonanza	D-9899	
D-EIPE	Reims/Cessna FR.172K Hawk XP	0613	
D-EIPF	Reims/Cessna F.177RG Cardinal RG	0176	
D-EIPG	Mooney M.20E Chaparral	690017	N9089V
D-EIPH	Beech A23A Musketeer Custom	M-967	
D-EIPK	Mooney M.20F Executive	700036	N9451V
D-EIPL	Piaggio P.149D	279	OE-DKK
			91+93
			AC+430
			AS+430
D-EIPM	Reims/Cessna F.152	1515	
D-EIPO	Reims/Cessna F.152	1500	
D-EIPP	Christen A-1 Husky	1081	N9594P
D-EIPT	Reims/Cessna F.172N	1721	
D-EIPU	Robin DR.400/180R Remorqueur	1622	
D-EIPV	SOCATA TB-20 Trinidad	443	
D-EIPX	Cessna TR.182 Turbo Skylane RG	00981	OY-BNI
			(N739BG)
D-EIQC	Reims/Cessna F.150L	1064	
D-EIQD	Reims/Cessna FRA.150L Aerobat	0216	
D-EIQI	Reims/Cessna F.150L	1067	
D-EIQK	Reims/Cessna F.172M	1052	
D-EIQO	Reims/Cessna FR.172J Rocket	0447	
D-EIQP	Reims/Cessna FR.172J Rocket	0455	
D-EIQQ	Reims/Cessna FR.172J Rocket	0462	
D-EIQR	Reims/Cessna FR.172J Rocket	0463	
D-EIQS	Reims/Cessna F.177RG Cardinal RG	0093	
D-EIQU	Reims/Cessna F.172M	1081	
D-EIQV	Reims/Cessna F.150L	1054	
D-EIQY	Cessna 210L Centurion	60194	N59290
D-EIRA	Piper PA-28-180 Cherokee Archer	28-7505174	N9623N
D-EIRB	Reims/Cessna FR.182 Skylane RG	0023	PH-AXX
D-EIRC(2)	American AG-5B Tiger	10006	N1190N
D-EIRD	Reims/Cessna F.172N	1935	
D-EIRE	Beech V35B Bonanza	D-9201	
D-EIRF(4)	SOCATA TB-20 Trinidad	583	F-GLPG
			N102U
D-EIRH	Reims/Cessna F.172N	2022	
D-EIRJ	Cessna 172RG Cutlass	0551	N5519V
D-EIRL(2)	Robin DR.400/180 Régent	2191	
D-EIRM	Reims/Cessna F.172N	1571	
D-EIRN	Reims/Cessna F.172P	2038	
D-EIRR(2)	Ressel Neico Lancair 360	311	
D-EIRS	Cessna 180K Skywagon	53164	
D-EIRT(2)	Robin DR.400/180 Régent	2412	
D-EIRV	Cessna 182Q Skylane	67338	N4751N
D-EIRW(2)	Piper PA-32-300 Cherokee Six	32-40074	HB-OMC
			N4052W
D-EIRX	Reims/Cessna F.172P	2109	
D-EIRZ	Reims/Cessna F.152	1844	
D-EISA	SAN Jodel D.140B Mousquetaire II	67	OE-DOP
D-EISB	Reims/Cessna F.172P	2243	LN-RAV
D-EISC	Gyroflug SC-01B-160 Speed Canard	S-14	
D-EISD	Robin DR.400/180R Remorqueur	1903	
D-EISF	Robin DR.400/180R Remorqueur	1115	
D-EISG	Robin DR.400/180R Remorqueur	1116	
D-EISH	Robin DR.400/180R Remorqueur	1117	
D-EISI	Robin DR.400/180R Remorqueur	1129	
D-EISK(2)	Cessna 172R	80165	
D-EISL	PiperPA-28-181 Archer II	28-8190116	PH-SDC
			N8312H
D-EISM	Cessna 182Q Skylane	65651	N735SQ
D-EISO	SOCATA MS.892A Rallye Commodore 150	10563	F-BNSO
D-EISP	Reims/Cessna FR.172K Hawk XP	0633	
D-EISQ	Cessna TU.206F Turbo Stationair	02990	N2715Q
			(D-ECBS)
			N2715Q
D-EISR	Robin DR.400/180R Remorqueur	1650	
D-EISS	Piper PA-28R-200 Cherokee Arrow B	28R-7135079	N5077S
D-EIST	Piper PA-28-181 Archer II	28-8090041	N2317U
D-EISU	Piper PA-28-161 Warrior II	28-7916540	N2916Y
D-EISW	Piper PA-28-181 Archer II	28-8290100	N9639N

Regn.	Type	C/n	Prev.Id.
D-EISY	Piper PA-22-150 Tri-Pacer	22-3369	D-EFIT
D-EITA(2)	Piper PA-28RT-201T Turbo Arrow IV	28R-8031086	N81837
D-EITC	Reims/Cessna F.152	1819	
D-EITD	Reims/Cessna F.152	1759	
D-EITE(2)	Reims/Cessna F.172P	2245	
D-EITF(2)	Cessna 152	79850	N757MN
D-EITG	Reims/Cessna F.172N	2002	
D-EITH(2)	Piper PA-28RT-201T Turbo Arrow IV	28R-7931038	N2222L
D-EITI (2)	Piper PA-28-181 Archer II	28-7990554	N2917X
D-EITK	Reims/Cessna F.152	1896	
D-EITL	Piper PA-28-200 Cherokee Arrow II	28R-7335018	N15085
D-EITM	Reims/Cessna FR.172K Hawk XP II	0662	
D-EITN	Cessna 172E	51442	D-EFGY
			N5542T
D-EITO	SOCATA MS.893E Rallye 180GT Gaillard	12128	F-BTVV
D-EITP(2)	Reims/Cessna F.172P	2249	
D-EITR	Robin DR.400/180R Remorqueur	1651	
D-EITS	Cessna T.210N Turbo Centurion II	64392	N6462Y
D-EITT(2)	Fuji FA-200-180 Aero Subaru	189	
D-EITU	Piper PA-28RT-201 Arrow IV	28R-7918241	N2967A
D-EITY	Piper PA-28RT-201T Turbo Arrow IV	28R-8031063	N8156U
D-EITZ	Reims/Cessna F.172F	0092	D-EMQU
D-EIUA	SOCATA MS.893E Rallye 180GT Gaillard	12496	F-BVNL
D-EIUB	SOCATA MS.880B Rallye Club	2541	F-BVZE
D-EIUH	Piper PA-18 Super Cub 95	18-3125	D-EETU
			OL-L51
			L-51
			53-4725
D-EIUL	Piper PA-28R-201 Arrow III	28R-7837250	PH-SRV
			OO-HCO
			N31755
D-EIUW	Reims/Cessna FA.152	0421	
D-EIVA	Piper PA-28RT-201T Turbo Arrow IV	28R-7931301	N8083N
D-EIVB	PZL-110 Koliber 150	03920049	
D-EIVC	Reims/Cessna F.182Q Skylane	0162	
D-EIVD	PZL-110 Koliber 150	03920050	
D-EIVE	Dornier Do.27A-1	328	56+46
			LC+161
			JA+382
D-EIVF	PZL-110 Koliber 150	03930051	
D-EIVG	PZL-110 Koliber 150	03930052	
D-EIVH	PZL-110 Koliber 150	03930053	
D-EIVI (3)	Cessna 172N	71061	N1601E
D-EIVJ	PZL-110 Koliber 150	03940054	
D-EIVK	PZL-110 Koliber 150	03940055	
D-EIVL	SOCATA MS.894A Minerva 220	11881	F-BTHE
D-EIVM	Reims/Cessna F.150M	1404	
D-EIVN	Reims/Cessna F.150M	1392	
D-EIVO	Reims/Cessna F.172M	1482	
D-EIVP	Reims/Cessna F.172M	1493	
D-EIVQ	Reims/Cessna F.172M	1504	
D-EIVR(3)	PZL-110 Koliber 150	03900043	
D-EIVS	PZL-110 Koliber 150	03900044	
D-EIVT(2)	PZL-110 Koliber 150	04950079	
D-EIVU(2)	PZL-110 Koliber 150	03920046	
D-EIVV	PZL-110 Koliber 150	03920047	
D-EIWA	Reims/Cessna F.150M	1173	
D-EIWB(2)	Piper PA-28-181 Archer II	2890119	N9179Z
D-EIWE(2)	Zlin Z.143L	0007	
D-EIWF	Beech K35 Bonanza	D-5969	HB-EGX
D-EIWJ	Yakovlev YAK-50	80-1704	DDR-WQN
D-EIWK(2)	Piper PA-28-236 Dakota	28-8011100	N81879
D-EIWL	Piper PA-28-181 Archer II	2890073	N9140Z
D-EIWM(2)	Piper PA-46-350PMalibu	4636202	N41346
D-EIWN	Robin DR.400/200R Remorqueur	2268	
D-EIWO	Piper PA-28R-180 Cherokee Arrow	28R-30424	N4562J
D-EIWP(2)	Robin DR.400/180RP Remo 212	1806	
D-EIWR	Robin R.2160D	177	
D-EIWS(2)	Piper PA-28RT-201 Arrow IV	28R-8118048	N8320A
D-EIWW(2)	CASA I-131E Jungmann	2028	D-ENHD
			E3B-432
D-EIWZ	RFB Fantrainer 600 (Permit)	005	98+76
			D-EIWZ
D-EIXB	Rockwell Commander 114	14102	N4709W
D-EIXE	Rockwell Commander 114B	14200	(N4870W)

Regn.	Type	C/n	Prev.Id.
D-EIXF	Rockwell Commander 114B	14213	N4883W
D-EIXI	Rockwell Commander 114B	14277	(N4957W)
D-EIXK	Rockwell Commander 112TC	13030	N1841J
D-EIXN	Rockwell Commander 112TC	13090	N4585W
D-EIXR	Rockwell Commander 114B	14299	(N4979W)
D-EIXS	Rockwell Commander 114B	14248	
D-EIXT	Rockwell Commander 114B	14261	(N4939W)
D-EIXX	Aviat A-1 Husky	1295	
D-EIYA	Reims/Cessna F.172N	1792	
D-EIYB	Reims/Cessna F.152	1592	
D-EIYC	Reims/Cessna F.172N	1831	
D-EIYD	Reims/Cessna F.152	1562	
D-EIYE	Reims/Cessna F.152	1583	
D-EIYF	Reims/Cessna F.152	1594	
D-EIYH	Reims/Cessna TR.182 Turbo Skylane RG	0005/00987	N739CP
D-EIYJ	Reims/Cessna F.172N	1869	
D-EIYL(2)	Cessna 172RG Cutlass	0886	N9567B
D-EIYN	Reims/Cessna F.172N	1855	
D-EIYQ	Reims/Cessna F.172N	1882	
D-EIYR	Reims/Cessna F.172N	1838	
D-EIYS	Reims/Cessna F.182Q Skylane	0123	
D-EIYT	Reims/Cessna F.172N	1926	
D-EIYV	Reims/Cessna F.152	1726	
D-EIYW	Reims/Cessna F.172N	1943	
D-EIYY	Reims/Cessna F.172N	1961	
D-EIZB	Reims/Cessna F.172P	2079	
D-EIZC(2)	Reims/Cessna F.172P	2154	
D-EIZD(2)	Beech F33A Bonanza	CE-1359	OY-GEY
D-EIZE	Beech F33A Bonanza	CE-774	
D-EIZF	Beech F33A Bonanza	CE-775	
D-EIZG	Beech F33A Bonanza	CE-779	
D-EIZH	Beech F33A Bonanza	CE-784	
D-EIZJ	Beech F33A Bonanza	CE-788	
D-EIZK	Beech F33A Bonanza	CE-789	
D-EIZL	Beech F33A Bonanza	CE-791	
D-EIZM	Reims/Cessna F.182Q Skylane	0138	
D-EIZN	Reims/Cessna FR.182 Skylane RG	0055	
D-EIZP(2)	Reims/Cessna F.152	1811	
D-EIZQ(2)	Beech F33A Bonanza	CE-1093	
D-EIZR(2)	Beech F33A Bonanza	CE-1094	
D-EIZS	Reims/Cessna F.172N	2011	
D-EIZT(2)	Beech F33A Bonanza	CE-1095	
D-EIZV	Cessna TR.182 Turbo Skylane RG	01480	N4941S
D-EIZW	Reims/Cessna F.152	1814	
D-EIZY	Cessna 172RG Cutlass	0562	N5537V
D-EJAA	SOCATA MS.894A Minerva 220	11977	F-BTJH
D-EJAB(5)	Zlin Z.526S Trenér Master	1033	OO-YGO
			(OO-UGO)
			YU-DIK
			JRV41108
			OK-XRC
D-EJAD(2)	Reims/Cessna F.182Q Skylane	0163	
D-EJAE(3)	Wassmer WA.40 Super IV	30	D-EJAE(1)
D-EJAF(2)	Cessna 172R	80182	
D-EJAG(3)	Acro II (Reservation)	20724	
D-EJAH(2)	SOCATA TB-10 Tobago	600	
D-EJAI (2)	Piaggio FWP.149D	094	90+76
			BF+407
			AS+421
D-EJAK(2)	Piper PA-28-236 Dakota	28-7911242	N2909W
D-EJAL(2)	Reims/Cessna F.150F	63307/0045	(N6707F)
D-EJAM(2)	Reims/Cessna F.172M	1497	
D-EJAN(3)	SOCATA TB-10 Tobago	580	
D-EJAP	Cessna 172	28916	N6816A
D-EJAS(4)	Robin DR.400/180R Remorqueur	1266	
D-EJAT	Piper PA-22-150 Tri-Pacer	22-1067	N1269C
D-EJAW(2)	Reims/Cessna F.150F	63124/0035	(N6524F)
D-EJAY(2)	SOCATA TB-20 Trinidad	1611	
D-EJAZ(2)	Rockwell Commander 114A	14507	(N5894N)
	(Rebuilt from 114B airframe c/n 14439/ D-ENPL(1))		
D-EJBA(2)	Robin DR.300/180R Remorqueur	589	
D-EJBB	Robin DR.300/180R Remorqueur	590	
D-EJBC	Robin DR.300/180R Remorqueur	594	
D-EJBD	CEA DR.253B Régent	187	
D-EJBE(2)	CEA DR.360 Major	597	

Regn.	Type	C/n	Prev.Id.
D-EJBF	CEA DR.360 Major	598	
D-EJBG	Robin DR.300/108 2+2	592	
D-EJBH	Robin DR.300/108 2+2	593	
D-EJBI	Bölkow BO.207	242	
D-EJBK	Cessna 172N	70466	N739DS
D-EJBR	Mooney M.20J Model 201	24-1660	
D-EJBS	Cessna 150F	64510	N3110X
D-EJBT	Reims/Cessna F.172H	0534	D-ELNM
D-EJBY	Bölkow BO.207	245	
D-EJCA(3)	Commander Aircraft 114B	14544	N6007S
D-EJCB	Grumman AA-5B Tiger	0291	HB-UCB
D-EJCC	Piper PA-46-310P Malibu	46-8508055	OE-KKM
			N530DP
			N4391H
D-EJCD	Cessna 182P (Reims-assembled)	0063/64442	OE-DIF
			N1782M
D-EJCE(3)	SOCATA MS.893A Rallye Commodore 180	10666	
D-EJCF	Reims/Cessna F.182P Skylane	0011	
D-EJCH(2)	Macchi MB.308 (Reservation)	71/5844	D-EJUP(1)
			I-NCOM
D-EJCI (2)	Reims/Cessna F.182P Skylane	0019	
D-EJCK	Reims/Cessna F.182P Skylane	0015	
D-EJCM	Cessna T.210L Turbo Centurion	61215	N2272S
D-EJCO(2)	Cessna 177B Cardinal	02193	N35079
D-EJCP	Reims/Cessna F.152	1632	
D-EJCR	Robin DR.400/180 Régent	2381	
D-EJCS(2)	SIAT 223A-1 Flamingo	016	HB-EVM
D-EJDC	Gyroflug SC-01B-160 Speed Canard	S-47	
D-EJDE(2)	Gyroflug SC-01B-160 Speed Canard	S-51	
D-EJDF	Drees Star-Lite SL-1	001	
D-EJDI	Cessna 150F	61588	N6288R
D-EJDK	Cessna P210N Pressurized Centurion II	00808	N4598A
D-EJDZ	FFT Eurotrainer 2000A(Permit)	A-1	
D-EJEB(2)	Mooney M.20A	1676	OE-DOM
			N6080X
D-EJEC(2)	Piper PA-28-181 Archer II	28-8090369	N8241F
D-EJED(2)	Robin DR.400/180R Remorqueur	1317	
D-EJEE	SAN Jodel DR.1050M Excellence	487	
D-EJEF(4)	Feldmann Denney Kitfox IV	01/1745	
D-EJEG(2)	Beech F33A Bonanza	CE-723	
D-EJEK(2)	Robin DR.400/180R Remorqueur	1141	F-GABX
D-EJEL(3)	Cessna 182P Skylane	62613	HB-CEB
			N52444
D-EJEM(2)	Reims/Cessna F.172G	0261	
D-EJEN(2)	Piper PA-18 Super Cub 95	18-5644	OE-AEN
			2A-AS
			(N9365D)
D-EJEP	Piper PA-18-150 Super Cub	18-6629	
D-EJER	Aeronca 11AC Chief	1609	OO-KER
			OO-LUC
D-EJET(2)	Piper PA-28R-200 Cherokee Arrow II	28R-7535325	N1559X
D-EJEV(2)	Reims/Cessna F.150G	0190	
D-EJEX	Dornier Do.27Q-1	2021	
D-EJFA(2)	Piper J-5A Cub Cruiser	5-529	N35021
			NC35021
D-EJFD	Gyroflug SC-01B-160 Speed Canard	S-19	
D-EJFF	Piper PA-28R-200 Cherokee Arrow II	28R-7435285	N43642
D-EJFG	Piper PA-28RT-201T Turbo Arrow IV	28R-8531008	N43846
D-EJFH	Robin DR.400/180R Remorqueur	1939	
D-EJFK	Piper PA-28-181 Archer II	2890140	N9196Z
D-EJFL(2)	Beech V35B Bonanza	D-9717	(D-EANG(2))
			ZS-JFI
			N9377S
D-EJFN	Neumayer Stoddard-Hamilton Glasair II-FT	1057AB	
D-EJFO	Bölkow BO.207	248	
D-EJFP	Piper PA-32R-301T Turbo Saratoga	32R-8129048	N8341L
D-EJFR	CEA Jodel DR.1050 Ambassadeur	406	F-BLAG
D-EJFS	SIAI-Marchetti SF.260	2-34	LX-FZB
			D-EFZB
D-EJFU(3)	Mooney M.20J Model 201	24-1617	
D-EJFW	Schöneseifen FW.190 (Permit 4.99)	E-01/293	
D-EJGA	Cessna 172C	49395	N1695Y
D-EJGB	Mooney M.20K Model 231	25-0711	(N1172G)
D-EJGD	Mooney M.20K Model 231	25-0703	(D-EJGO(3))
			N231AV
			(N1170X)
D-EJGF	Yakovlev YAK-18A (Permit)	0527	DM-WGI
			LSK-...
D-EJGI	Piper J-3C-65 Cub	13204	(D-EIJG)
			D-EJGI
			OE-ABD
			HB-OVO
			45-4464
D-EJGL	Cessna 172RG Cutlass	0247	N5120U
D-EJGM	Dornier Do.27A-1	281	56+13
			SE+523
			SC+701
D-EJGO(4)	Goldbrunner Marco J-5	001	
D-EJGR	Piper PA-18 Super Cub 95	18-3454	96+30
			NL+116
			AC+536
			AS+536
			54-754
D-EJGS	Yakovlev YAK-50	791505	DDR-WQP
			DM-WQP
D-EJGT	Cessna 172N	71416	N3046E
D-EJGZ	Cessna 172N	68340	N733JX
D-EJHA	Holzäpfel Rutan Vari-eze	1	
D-EJHB(2)	Beech A36 Bonanza	E-2286	N7205C
D-EJHC	Commander Aircraft 114B	14646	
D-EJHD	Dinkl Jurca MJ.5 Sirocco	D-29	
D-EJHE	Mooney M.20F Executive	670388	N3295F
D-EJHF(2)	Piper PA-46-310P Malibu	4608081	OE-KEG
			D-EIIA
			N9119N
D-EJHG	Gold Aero Designs Pulsar XP (Permit 9.99)	P 001	
D-EJHH	SAN Jodel D.150 Mascaret	54	
D-EJHK	Wassmer WA.51 Pacific	05	
D-EJHL	Cessna 172N	73730	N5204J
D-EJHM	Rockwell 114B Commander	14366	PH-CGY
			(PH-CHI)
			OO-TRL
			N5788N
D-EJHO	Oberlerchner JOB 15-150/2	062	OE-CAY
D-EJHP	Cessna 172M	64376	N9574V
D-EJHS	Beech F33A Bonanza	CE-1661	N8051H
D-EJHW(2)	Robin DR.400/200R Remorqueur 200	2389	
D-EJIA	Robin R.3000/160	157	
D-EJIB(2)	Piper PA-46-310P Malibu	4608095	N9122D
D-EJIC	SAN Jodel DR.1050 Ambassadeur	199	
D-EJII	Cessna P210N Pressurized Centurion II	00823	N4801A
			(D-EVAL)
			N4801A
			C-GEWN
			N480IA
			(N828VG)
			N4801A
D-EJIM(3)	Piper PA-18 Super Cub 95	18-1531	OO-BLV
			OO-HNC
			ALAT
			51-15531
D-EJIP(2)	Iser Kelly Hatz CB-1	273	
D-EJIR(2)	Reims/Cessna F.150M	1260	
D-EJIV	Orlican L-40 Meta-Sokol	150405	OK-NMK
D-EJIW	Orlican L-40 Meta-Sokol	150408	
D-EJIX	Piper J-3C-65 Cub	11714	OK-ZKK
			43-30423
D-EJJG	Gralfs Europa	1781	
D-EJJJ	Dornier Do.27B-1	192	55+59
			PF+219
			PF+106
			PD+107
D-EJJM	Robin DR.400/180R Remorqueur	2346	
D-EJJO	SAN Jodel DR.1050 Ambassadeur	123	F-BJJO
D-EJKA(2)	SNCAN/ Stampe SV.4A (Permit 7.99) (Flies in green camouflage Fr.AF c/s)	396	G-BWRE
			D-EJKA(2)
			F-BDOT
			Fr.AF
D-EJKB	Bäuerle Neico Lancair 4B	IV-00-20	
D-EJKF	Sauter Denney Kitfox III	1641	
D-EJKG	Seufert Sisler Cygnet SF-2A	001	

Regn.	Type	C/n	Prev.Id.
D-EJKH	Erco Ercoupe 415D	2249	N99626
D-EJKK	Piper PA-28RT-201T Turbo Arrow IV	28R-8031106	N8219N
D-EJKL	Cessna 172N	70102	N738NF
D-EJKM	Piper PA-28-140 Cherokee E	28-7225449	N11C
D-EJKO	Reims/Cessna F.172G	0268	
D-EJKR	Rehmann RE-3 Steen Skybolt	001	
D-EJKS(3)	Extra EA.300/S	010	
D-EJKT	Zlin Z.526F Trenér Master	1109	DDR-WKT
			DM-WKT
D-EJKW	Piper PA-28RT-201 Arrow IV	28R-7918049	N2187P
D-EJLA	Bölkow BO.208C Junior	581	
D-EJLD	Piper PA-28-161 Cadet	2841345	N92155
			N623FT
			(F-GJOT)
			(F-GIEU)
D-EJLE	Bölkow BO.208C Junior	582	
D-EJLF	Cessna 150M	78648	N704JM
D-EJLG(2)	Robin DR.400/180 Régent	2391	
D-EJLH	Piper PA-28RT-201 Arrow IV	28R-7918146	N29566
D-EJLI	Bölkow BO.208C Junior	583	
D-EJLK	Piper PA-38-112 Tomahawk	38-78A0651	PH-SRS
			N9703N
D-EJLL(2)	Zlin Z.526F Trenér Master	1113	SP-CDK
D-EJLM	Piper PA-28-235 Cherokee Charger	28-7310117	N55141
D-EJLR	Robin DR.400/180 Régent	1762	
D-EJLT	Rockwell Commander 114B	14195	PH-VON
			N4865W
D-EJLU	Bölkow BO.208 Junior	550	
D-EJLW	Beech F33A Bonanza	CE-1497	
D-EJLY	Cessna 182K Skylane	57879	N2679Q
D-EJMA	Bölkow BO.208C Junior	651	
D-EJMB	Bölkow BO.208C Junior	652	
D-EJMC(2)	Donnerhack Master Crow	1	
D-EJME(2)	Cessna 182K Skylane	58194	N3194Q
D-EJMF	Bölkow BO.208C Junior	656	
D-EJMH(2)	Cessna 172RG Cutlass	0249	N5128U
D-EJMM	Zlin Z.526F Trenér Master	1280	SP-EMM
D-EJMO(3)	American AG-5B Tiger	10149	N1197Y
D-EJMP(2)	Cessna 182Q Skylane	66213	N759SB
D-EJMR	Reims/Cessna F.172N	1749	PH-JMR
			PH-AYN
D-EJMS(2)	Neico Neico Lancair 360 (Reservation)	1804	
D-EJMT(2)	Cessna 172N	73182	N6290F
D-EJMU	Bölkow BO.208C Junior	585	
D-EJMV	Piper PA-46-310P Malibu	4608085	N69074
D-EJMW	Klemm Denney Kitfox III	1/1109	
D-EJNA	Bölkow BO.208C Junior	587	
D-EJNB	Cessna U206G Stationair 6	06560	PH-JNB
			OY-SUV
			(SE-...)
			OY-SUV
			N9597Z
D-EJNC	Extra EA.230	002	
D-EJNG	Cessna R.182 Skylane RG	00337	N4182C
D-EJNI	Bölkow BO.208C Junior	589	
D-EJNO	SEEMS MS.880B Rallye Club	304	OE-CGW
D-EJNY	Reims/Cessna F.172H	0558	
D-EJNZ	SAN Jodel DR.1050 Ambassadeur	169	F-BJNZ
D-EJOA	Bücker Bü.133C Jungmeister	48	HB-MIK
			U-49
D-EJOB(2)	Oberlerchner JOB 15-150/2	070	OE-DOB
			(D-EKEM)
D-EJOD(3)	Pützer Elster B	V-1	D-EJOB(1)
D-EJOE	Piper PA-28-161 Warrior II	28-7916468	N2845N
D-EJOF(4)	Piper PA-28RT-201T Turbo Arrow IV	28R-7931257	N2920F
D-EJOG	Orlican L-40 Meta-Sokol	150402	OK-NMB
D-EJOH(4)	SOCATA TB-20 Trinidad	1627	
D-EJOI	Focke-Wulf FW.44J Stieglitz	2929	(D-EHDW)
			OH-SZA
			SZ-26
D-EJOK(3)	Mooney M.20K Model 231	25-0377	N231RH
D-EJON(4)	Commander Aircraft 114B	14547	
D-EJOO	Piper PA-28-181 Archer II	2890072	HB-PLS
D-EJOP(2)	Reims/Cessna F.182Q Skylane	0164	
D-EJOR	Erco 415CD Ercoupe	4737	N9963F
			HB-ERD
			OO-EXE
			(NC94630)
D-EJOS(2)	Cessna T.210N Turbo Centurion II	63980	N4675Y
D-EJOY	Piper PA-28R-200 Cherokee Arrow B	28R-35616	N3054R
D-EJPA(2)	Reims/Cessna F.172G	0302	
D-EJPB	Piper PA-28-235 Cherokee Charger	28-7310007	N11C
D-EJPC	Reims/Cessna 182P Skylane	0037/64106	N6091F
D-EJPD(2)	Commander Aircraft 114B	14599	
D-EJPE(2)	Reims/Cessna F.152	1577	(F-GBQC)
D-EJPF(2)	Cessna 152	79420	C-GTVJ
			N714TM
D-EJPG	SOCATA TB-10 Tobago	394	
D-EJPH	SOCATA TB-10 Tobago	396	
D-EJPI (3)	Cessna 172N	69682	C-GZLA
			(N737UH)
D-EJPJ	SOCATA TB-10 Tobago	398	
D-EJPK	SOCATA TB-10 Tobago	407	
D-EJPL	SOCATA TB-20 Trinidad	408	
D-EJPM	Marschall Denney Kitfox II	512	
D-EJPO	Piper PA-22-108 Colt	22-9330	
D-EJPP	Jentsch Prescott Pusher	055	
D-EJPQ	SOCATA TB-10 Tobago	430	
D-EJPR	SOCATA TB-20 Trinidad	424	
D-EJPS	Cessna 172N	72803	C-GSRF
			N6443D
D-EJPT	Grumman AA-5B Tiger	0416	
D-EJPU	Beech 35-B33 Debonair	CD-499	SE-CPP
			D-EJPU
D-EJQF	Robin DR.400/180R Remorqueur	1617	
D-EJQO(2)	Piper PA-18 Super Cub 95	18-3206	OL-L32
			L-132
			53-4806
D-EJRA	Reims/Cessna F.150G	0082	
D-EJRC	SOCATA TB-10 Tobago	362	HB-KAA
D-EJRD	Robin DR.400/180R Remorqueur	1660	F-WZZU
D-EJRE(2)	Reims/Cessna F.172M	1334	D-EFCM(2)
			HB-CWW
			(OE-DTU)
D-EJRG	Piper PA-28R-201 Arrow III	28R-7837229	N30489
D-EJRK	Piper PA-38-112 Tomahawk	38-79A0894	N9672N
D-EJRL(2)	Limbacher Rand-Robinson KR-2	01/1688	
D-EJRM	Reims/Cessna F.150M	1145	N94276
D-EJRP	Bellanca 17-30A Viking	76-30818	C-GBDT
D-EJRR	Piper PA-18 Super Cub 95	18-3429	96+10
			SB+220
			AC+518
			AS+518
			54-729
D-EJRS	Piper PA-28-161 Cadet	2841115	N9175X
D-EJRU	Reims/Cessna F.150G	0166	
D-EJRV	SOCATA TB-9 Tampico	921	
D-EJRW	Cessna 172R	80198	
D-EJSB	Piper PA-28-180 Cherokee G	28-7205086	N11C
D-EJSC	Robin R.3000/160	171	
D-EJSD	Robin DR.400/180R Remorqueur	2011	
D-EJSG	Cessna 182Q Skylane	65989	N759GT
D-EJSH	Robin DR.400/180R Remorqueur	2348	
D-EJSM(3)	Piper PA-28RT-201T Turbo Arrow IV	28R-8031050	N8167B
			N9618N
D-EJSP(2)	Mooney M.20M TLS	27-0055	
D-EJSR(2)	Robin DR.400/180S Régent	2085	
D-EJST	Piper PA-28R-201 Arrow III	28R-7837243	N31675
D-EJSU	Reims/Cessna F.172H	0449	
D-EJSW	Champion 7GCBC Citabria	110	N1845G
D-EJSY	Piper PA-28R-201T Turbo Cherokee Arrow III	28R-7703099	N106WC
			N9643N
D-EJTA(2)	Robin DR.400/180 Régent	2184	
D-EJTB(3)	Commander Aircraft 114B	14577	
D-EJTC	Cessna 182P Skylane	63630	N6090J
D-EJTD	Reims/Cessna 182P Skylane	0003/63779	N6615M
D-EJTF	Piper PA-32R-301 Saratoga SP	3213034	N9195X

Regn.	Type	C/n	Prev.Id.
D-EJTG	Piper PA-28-161 Cadet	2841306	N9263N N9207Z
D-EJTH	Thümmler Brändli BX-2 Cherry	1607	
D-EJTI	Piper PA-28-161 Cadet	2841308	N9265N N9208X
D-EJTK	Piper PA-28-161 Cadet	2841305	N9262N N9206B
D-EJTL	Piper PA-28-161 Cadet	2841313	N9270N N9210N
D-EJTN	Piper PA-28-161 Cadet	2841312	N9269N N9210F
D-EJTP	Robin DR.400/180R Remorqueur	1918	
D-EJTR	Bücker Bü.131 Jungmann	49	HB-UTR A-38
D-EJTU	Beech F33A Bonanza	CE-1381	N133EK N5579Z
D-EJTW	Cessna T.210N Turbo Centurion II	62965	(D-ELBT) N6194N
D-EJUB(3)	Reims/Cessna F.172G	0265	
D-EJUD(2)	Kitplane, type unknown (Reservation 5.99)	M212/M202/98	
D-EJUF(2)	Beech F33A Bonanza	CE-1247	
D-EJUG(2)	Däumer Van's RV-4	3394	
D-EJUI	Aeronca 65CA	C13661	N33798 NC33798
D-EJUK	Klemm Kl.107B	124	
D-EJUM(3)	Piper J-3C-65 Cub	1165	(D-EDIX) G-AFFJ
D-EJUP(2)	Piper PA-32-300 Lance	32R-7780153	OY-BTC
D-EJUR(2)	Robin R.1180TD Aiglon	267	OE-DRX
D-EJUS(2)	Reims/Cessna F.172G	0317	
D-EJUT(3)	Piper PA-28-180 Cherokee B	28-904	HB-OVV N7174W
D-EJUW	Orlican L-40 Meta-Sokol	150409	
D-EJVA(2)	Piper PA-28RT-201T Turbo Arrow IV	28R-8031002	N81042
D-EJVC	Christen Pitts S-2B	5141	SE-KOD N6052U
D-EJVL	Mooney M.20E Super 21	670018	HB-DVL N3225F
D-EJVR	Cessna 182P (Reims assembled)	0059/64420	PH-PCN D-EBYP(2) (PH-DIK) G-BDVE N1733M
D-EJVU	Beech A23-24 Musketeer Super	MA-355	
D-EJVY	Beech A23-24 Musketeer Super	MA-354	
D-EJWB(2)	Piper PA-28-161 Cadet	2841083	N9169B
D-EJWD	Europa Aviation Europa (Permit)	1854	
D-EJWE	Piper PA-28-235 Cherokee B	28-10896	N9228W
D-EJWF	Piper PA-28-181 Archer II	2890148	SE-KMV
D-EJWG	Mooney M.20K Model 231	25-0400	(N4047H)
D-EJWH(3)	Cessna U.206G Stationair II	04376	N756UW
D-EJWK	Robin DR.400/180 Régent	744	
D-EJWM	Reims/Cessna F.172N	1874	
D-EJWO	Reims/Cessna F.172H	0411	
D-EJWP	SOCATA TB-20 Trinidad	1100	N2805V
D-EJWR	Cessna 172N	73829	N5733J
D-EJWS(3)	Grumman AA-5 Traveler	0355	N5455L
D-EJWU	Reims/Cessna F.172H	0417	
D-EJWW	Piper PA-28R-201T Turbo Arrow III	28R-7803224	N6387C
D-EJWY	CEA Jodel DR.1050 Ambassadeur	208	F-BJZE
D-EJXB	Reims/Cessna F.172M	1016	
D-EJXC	Reims/Cessna F.172M	1007	
D-EJXD	Reims/Cessna F.172M	1017	
D-EJXH	Reims/Cessna F.150L	0985	
D-EJXI	Reims/Cessna F.150L	0988	
D-EJXM	Reims/Cessna F.172M	1012	
D-EJXN	Reims/Cessna F.172M	1013	
D-EJXO(2)	Reims/Cessna F.172M	1174	
D-EJXP	Reims/Cessna F.150L	1014	
D-EJXQ	Reims/Cessna F.172M	1020	
D-EJXR	Reims/Cessna F.150L	1018	
D-EJXS	Reims/Cessna F.172M	1022	
D-EJXT	Reims/Cessna F.172M	1023	
D-EJXW(2)	Reims/Cessna F.172M	1157	
D-EJXY(2)	Reims/Cessna F.150L	1091	
D-EJYB	Globe GC-1B Swift	1320	N3327K
D-EJYC(2)	SIAI-Marchetti S.205-18/R	219	
D-EJYD	Piper J-3C-65 Cub	11658	G-AJDS 43-30367
D-EJYF	Aero-Jodel D.11A Club	AB.5 (Liz.228/625)	
D-EJYR(3)	SOCATA MS.880B Rallye Club	1105	
D-EJYT(2)	SAN Jodel DR.1050 Ambassadeur	200	(D-ELFI)
D-EJYW	RFB RW3-P75	022	
D-EJYX(2)	Bölkow BO.207	292	
D-EJYZ	Cessna 175A Skylark	56267	N6767E
D-EKAA	Reims/Cessna FR.172K Hawk XP	0631	
D-EKAB(2)	Piper PA-18A-135 Super Cub	18-2810	HB-OOW
D-EKAC	Cessna 150	17835	N6435T
D-EKAD(4)	Cessna P210N Pressurized Centurion II	00644	N27AM N5139W
D-EKAE	Piper PA-28R-201 Arrow III	28R-7837253	N31882
D-EKAG(3)	Reims/Cessna FR.172K Hawk XP	0634	
D-EKAH(2)	Beech F33A Bonanza	CE-757	N23791
D-EKAI (2)	Robin DR.400/180 Régent	1127	
D-EKAJ(2)	Reims/Cessna 182P Skylane	0050/64327	N1429M
D-EKAK(2)	Beagle B.121 Pup 150	135	G-AXSB G-35-135
D-EKAL(2)	Piper PA-28R-200 Cherokee Arrow II	28R-7635198	N8726E
D-EKAM(2)	Piper PA-28-181 Archer II	2890129	N9187Q
D-EKAN(2)	Piper PA-28R-200 Cherokee Arrow B	28R-35672	N3062R
D-EKAO	Piper PA-28R-201 Arrow III	28R-7837212	N9632C
D-EKAP(3)	Piper PA-28R-200 Cherokee Arrow II	28R-7435178	N41403
D-EKAR(3)	Piper PA-28-140 Cherokee Cruiser	28-7325451	N11C
D-EKAS(2)	Schneider TC-1 Dragonfly	X-01	
D-EKAT(3)	Piper PA-28RT-201T Turbo Arrow IV	28R-7931185	N28518
D-EKAU(2)	Piper PA-46-350P Malibu Mirage	4622100	N558RS N9193V
D-EKAV(3)	American AA-1A Trainer	0448	OY-AYH (N6248L)
D-EKAW	Beech 35-33 Debonair	CD-27	
D-EKAX(3)	Boeing Stearman A75N1	75-8360	LN-KAX N65951 BuA43266
D-EKAY	Piper PA-18 Super Cub 95	18-1340	D-ENLG ALAT 51-15340
D-EKAZ(2)	Piper PA-28-181 Archer III	2843141	N9293N
D-EKBA(2)	SOCATA TB-200 Tobago XL	1798	
D-EKBB(3)	Fuji FA-200-180 Aero Subaru	99	OY-FRI LX-JFY LX-MDM D-EMYY
D-EKBC	Reims/Cessna FR.172G Rocket	0205	
D-EKBD	Reims/Cessna FR.172G Rocket	0174	
D-EKBE(2)	Jodel D.9 Bébé	Liz.301	(D-EGBM(2))
D-EKBF(2)	Piper PA-28R-200 Cherokee Arrow II	28R-7235310	N1517T
D-EKBG	Reims/Cessna FA.150K Aerobat	0052	
D-EKBI (2)	SOCATA TB-20 Trinidad	355	HB-EZY
D-EKBJ	Robin R.3000/120D	129	HB-KBT
D-EKBK	Cessna P210N Pressurized Centurion II (STOL)	00661	N5244W
D-EKBL(2)	SOCATA TB-10 Tobago	732	
D-EKBM(2)	Piper PA-28-201T Turbo Dakota	28-7921068	N2855A
D-EKBO(2)	Piper PA-18 Super Cub 95	18-3453	96+29 NL+120 AC+509 AS+508 54-753
D-EKBR	Piper PA-28R-201T Turbo Cherokee Arrow III	28R-7703241	N38753
D-EKBS	Reims/Cessna F.172N	1546	
D-EKBT	Beech B36TC Bonanza	EA-514	
D-EKBW	Mooney M.20F Executive	670340	N2981L
D-EKBY	Reims/Cessna FP.172D	57166/0002	(N8566X)
D-EKCA	Gardan GY-80 Horizon 160	96	
D-EKCB	Reims/Cessna F.172N	1739	
D-EKCD	SOCATA MS.893A Rallye Commodore 180	11434	F-BSAT
D-EKCE(2)	Cessna 172M	63000	N13762
D-EKCG(2)	Commander Aircraft 114B	14548	N162A
D-EKCH	Christen A-1 Husky	1087	N9596G
D-EKCI	Oberlerchner JOB 15-180/2	065	OE-CAV

Regn.	Type	C/n	Prev.Id.
D-EKCL	Reims/Cessna F.172N	1676	
D-EKCM(2)	Driessen Pottier P.220S Koala	1835	
D-EKCN	Piper PA-38-112 Tomahawk	38-78A0408	N9700N
D-EKCO(2)	Cessna 152	85240	N6386Q
D-EKCP	Reims/Cessna F.150M	1395	
D-EKCR	Beech 35 Bonanza	D-686	HB-ECR NC90573
D-EKCT	Robin DR.400/180R Remorqueur	1331	
D-EKCW	Piper PA-28-181 Archer II	28-8190018	N8257G
D-EKDB	Mooney M.20K Model 231	25-0565	N231BW
D-EKDE(3)	Piper PA-28-235 Cherokee B	28-10961	N9285W
D-EKDF(2)	Akaflieg München Mü.30 Schlacro (Permit 12.99)	001	
D-EKDG	Robin DR.400/180R Remorqueur	1638	
D-EKDH	Robin DR.400/120D Petit Prince	1644	
D-EKDI	Bölkow BO.208C Junior	593	
D-EKDL	Piper PA-28-161 Warrior II	28-7916562	N2941F
D-EKDN	Beech A36 Bonanza	E-2353	N7241Y
D-EKDO(3)	Cessna P210N Pressurized Centurion	00781	LX-FLC D-EMRR N6444W
D-EKDP	Robin DR.400/180R Remorqueur	1645	
D-EKDR	Zlin Z.226T Trenér 6	156	OE-CMW OK-MFL
D-EKDS	Rockwell Commander 114	14206	N4876W
D-EKDT	Bähr Aero Designs Pulsar XP (Permit 11.99)	EB 00	
D-EKDU	Bölkow BO.208C Junior	595	(HB-UXW)
D-EKDV	HOAC DV-20 Katana	20075	
D-EKDY(2)	Reims/Cessna F.172N	1939	
D-EKEA	Hinz BL1-KEA	1	
D-EKEB(2)	Mooney M.20J Model 205	24-3364	
D-EKEC(2)	Reims/Cessna F.172N	1960	
D-EKEG(3)	Reims/Cessna FR.172K Hawk XP	0666	N8495B
D-EKEH(2)	Piper PA-28-181 Archer II	2890080	SE-KEH
D-EKEI	Piper PA-38-112 Tomahawk	38-80A0096	N9700N
D-EKEK	Klemm Kl.107C	132	
D-EKEL(3)	SOCATA MS.893E Rallye 180GT Gaillard	12633	
D-EKEM(3)	Piper PA-38-112 Tomahawk	38-80A0097	N9701N
D-EKEN(2)	Reims/Cessna F.172N	1991	
D-EKEP(3)	Reims/Cessna F.150J	0424	
D-EKET(3)	Reims/Cessna F.150J	0395	
D-EKEZ	Aeromere F.8L Falco	210	
D-EKFA	Champion 7GCB Challenger	7GCB-159	
D-EKFB(2)	Piper PA-28RT-201T Turbo Arrow IV	28R-8131062	N83245
D-EKFC	Mooney M.20J Model 205	24-3083	
D-EKFD(3)	Piper PA-46-350P Malibu Mirage	4622008	OE-KFD D-ENII (2) N9151X
D-EKFF	Piper PA-28RT-201T Turbo Arrow IV	28R-8131022	N8296P
D-EKFG	Dornier Do.27A-4	471	57+40 XB+901 GA+374 KD+129
D-EKFH	Robin R.2160D Acrobin	122	
D-EKFI	Piper PA-12 Super Cruiser	12-1528	(D-EMCO) N2413M
D-EKFJ	Beech A36 Bonanza	E-2444	
D-EKFL	Piper PA-28-181 Archer II	28-8190110	N8309H
D-EKFN	CEA DR.250/160 Capitaine	36	PH-REN
D-EKFR	Cessna 172N	71154	N2093E
D-EKFS(2)	Stuttgart FS-28 Avispa	V-1/1832	D-EAFS(1)
D-EKFT	Mooney M.20J Model 201	24-0834	(N4748H)
D-EKFW	Piper PA-28-181 Cherokee Archer II	28-7690339	N6108J N9582N
D-EKFY	Piper PA-18-150 Super Cub	18-8123	N4113Z
D-EKGA(2)	Cessna 152	79906	N757PX
D-EKGB	Reims/Cessna F.150G	0088	OE-AVK
D-EKGC	Zlin Z.43	0017	LSK-22
D-EKGD(3)	Rockwell Commander 114	14397	OE-KGD D-EIBC
D-EKGE	SIAI-Marchetti S.205-18/R	358	
D-EKGF	Zlin Z.43	0020	LSK-26
D-EKGG	SAN Jodel D.140E Mousquetaire IV	193	
D-EKGI	SIAI-Marchetti S.205-18/R	365	
D-EKGK	Kitplane, type unknown (Reservation 1199)	262	
D-EKGL	Mooney M.20J Model 205	24-3232	N91ZL
D-EKGM	Piper PA-18-100 Super Cub	18-1527	F-BOMR ALAT 51-15527
D-EKGN	Zlin Z.43	0022	LSK-16
D-EKGO	SIAI-Marchetti S.205-20/R	4-110	
D-EKGR(2)	Cessna 172N	68212	SE-GUM N733DJ
D-EKGS	Robin DR.400/180R Remorqueur	1092	
D-EKHA(4)	Aero Designs Pulsar XP (Reservation)	1930	
D-EKHB(2)	Mooney M.20E Super 21	1202	HB-DWA N9255M
D-EKHD(2)	Focke-Wulf FW.44J Stieglitz	"648"	LX-OOI HB-EBO D-EBOB(1) SE-AYY Fv648
D-EKHE(2)	SOCATA MS.880B Rallye Club	2288	F-BULE
D-EKHF(2)	Fahr Jurca MJ.2 Tempête	AB-01	
D-EKHG(2)	SOCATA MS.887 Rallye 125	2161	(D-EAPW) F-BUCF
D-EKHI (2)	SOCATA MS.887 Rallye 125	2177	F-BVLO
D-EKHJ	Cessna 210K Centurion	59285	N8285M
D-EKHK	SOCATA MS.894E Minerva 220GT	12204	F-BULC
D-EKHL(2)	SOCATA MS.893E Rallye 180GT Gaillard	12207	F-BUXJ
D-EKHM(2)	SOCATA MS.893E Rallye 180GT Gaillard	12525	F-BVNS
D-EKHN(2)	SOCATA MS.893E Rallye 180GT Gaillard	12526	F-BVNT
D-EKHO(2)	Piper PA-18 Super Cub 95	18-1009	RHAF115312 51-15312
D-EKHP	SOCATA MS.893E Rallye 180GT Gaillard	12205	F-BUVF
D-EKHQ	SOCATA MS.894E Minerva 220GT	12147	F-BUVE
D-EKHR	Reims/Cessna F.172F	0094	
D-EKHS(2)	Piper PA-32RT-300T Turbo Lance	32R-7887160	N39755
D-EKHT	SOCATA MS.894E Minerva 220GT	12146	F-BUNY
D-EKHU	Laverda F.8L Falco IV	405	
D-EKHV	SOCATA MS.894E Minerva 220GT	12203	F-BULB
D-EKHW(2)	Piper PA-28RT-201T Turbo Arrow IV	28R-8031094	
D-EKHY(2)	SOCATA MS.893A Rallye Commodore 180	10723	
D-EKHZ	Cessna 182Q	66466	OE-KHZ N94628
D-EKIA	Robin DR.400/180S Régent	1893	
D-EKIB(2)	Piper PA-18-150 Super Cub	18-8321	N5736Y
D-EKIC	Nord 1203 Norécrin II	309	HB-DAK
D-EKIE	Dornier Do.27A-1	172	55+42 AC+922 AS+922
D-EKIF	de Havilland DH.82A Tiger Moth	83091	G-AOED R5216
D-EKIG	SAN Jodel DR.1050 Ambassadeur	108	
D-EKIK(2)	Piper PA-28-181 Archer III	2843067	N9279N
D-EKIL(2)	SOCATA MS.893A Rallye Commodore 180	10724	
D-EKIM(2)	Piper PA-28RT-201T Turbo Arrow IV	28R-7931243	N2888Y
D-EKIN(3)	Piper PA-28-181 Archer II	2890141	SE-KIZ
D-EKIO	Piper PA-28-161 Cadet	2841171	SE-KIO
D-EKIP	Piper J-3C-65 Cub	9086	N42033 NC42033
D-EKIQ	Reims/Cessna F.150F	62944/0024	(N8844G)
D-EKIR	Piper PA-18-150 Super Cub	18-3698	HB-OOY
D-EKIS(2)	Piper J-3C-65 Cub	20791	D-ECIS(1) N2024M NC2024M
D-EKIT(2)	Reims/Cessna F.172N	1994	
D-EKIW	Beech 35-33 Debonair	CD-180	
D-EKIX(2)	Beech A36 Bonanza	E-1319	
D-EKIZ(2)	Bellanca 8GCBC Scout 180	92-74	OE-AOG
D-EKJA	SOCATA MS.893E Rallye 180GT Gaillard	12379	F-BVAG
D-EKJB	Robin DR.400/180R Remorqueur	1001	
D-EKJD	Reims/Cessna FR.172J Rocket	0582	
D-EKJH(2)	Beech F33A Bonanza	CE-1125	N517RM
D-EKJK	Piper PA-46-310P Malibu	4608089	N100JW N9129F
D-EKJL(2)	Cessna R.182 Skylane RG	00529	N1712R
D-EKJM	Montjoie Denney Kitfox II	1625/528	
D-EKKA	Piper J-3C-65 Cub	6298	HB-OXB NC35331
D-EKKB	Reims/Cessna F.150K	0545	

Regn.	Type	C/n	Prev.Id.
D-EKKC	Reims/Cessna FR.172F Rocket	0130	
D-EKKD	Reims/Cessna F.172H	665	(D-EKKR)
D-EKKE	Piper PA-24-250 Comanche	24-469	N5415P
D-EKKF(3)	Piper PA-18 Super Cub 95	18-1418	ALAT
			51-15418
D-EKKG	Reims/Cessna F.150K	0616	
D-EKKI	Cessna 182F Skylane	54908	N3508U
D-EKKJ(2)	Piper PA-28-140 Cherokee C	28-26874	N98386
D-EKKK(2)	Mooney M.20K Model 252	25-1142	N252HW
D-EKKM	Reims/Cessna FR.172G Rocket	0158	
D-EKKN	Reims/Cessna FR.172G Rocket	0149	
D-EKKO(2)	Reims/Cessna FR.172G Rocket	0185	
D-EKKR(2)	Aeronca 65C	C.1738	D-EKON(1)
			HB-UPI
D-EKKS(3)	Cessna 172N	72162	N8275E
D-EKKT	Cessna 210J Centurion	59153	N3353S
D-EKKU(2)	CEA DR.253B Régent	159	
D-EKKV(2)	Piper PA-28RT-201T Turbo Arrow IV	28R-8031042	N600KR
			N9585N
D-EKKW(2)	SOCATA MS.892E Rallye 150GT	12238	(D-EARU)
			F-BULY
D-EKKZ	Piper PA-28-180 Cherokee Challenger	28-7305446	N55690
D-EKLA(2)	Wassmer WA.51 Pacific	96	F-BUKH
D-EKLB	Lemberger Grade Monoplan Replica V-1	7	
D-EKLC	Extra EA400 (Reservation)	04	
D-EKLE(2)	Grob G.115A	8069	
D-EKLF(2)	Reims/Cessna F.152	1812	HB-CFU
D-EKLG(3)	Robin DR.400/180 Régent (Reserved for rebuild)	2281	
D-EKLH	Piper PA-28-161 Cadet	2841125	N9511N
			N9181D
D-EKLL	Piper PA-38-112 Tomahawk	38-79A0512	N2391G
D-EKLM	Cessna T.210M Turbo Centurion	61592	(N732LG)
D-EKLN	Reims/Cessna F.172N	1998	
D-EKLS	Cessna 150F	62405	PH-ALS
			N8305G
D-EKLT	Piper PA-28-181 Archer II	28-7990427	N28901
D-EKLW	Beech V35B Bonanza	D-9714	N7258R
D-EKLX	Morane-Saulnier MS.885 Super Rallye	160	F-BKLY
D-EKLY	Piaggio FWP.149D	119	(90+99)
			D-EKLY
			AS+461
D-EKMA	SAN Jodel DR.1050 Ambassadeur	380	F-BKHT
D-EKMB(5)	SOCATA TB-10 Tobago	1133	OE-KMB
D-EKMC	Cessna TP.206E Turbo Super Skylane	00611	N5711J
D-EKME(2)	SOCATA TB-200 Tobago XL	1446	
D-EKMF	Mooney M.20J Model 201	24-0429	
D-EKMG	Cessna 172N Skyhawk	70868	N739WQ
D-EKMJ	Zlin Z.43	0027	LSK-21
D-EKMK	Aeromere F.8L Falco	232	
D-EKMN	Zlin Z.43	0018	LSK-23
D-EKMO(3)	Zlin Z.43	0012	LSK-25
D-EKMP(2)	Zlin Z.43	0024	LSK-18
D-EKMQ	Zlin Z.43	0026	LSK-20
D-EKMR(2)	SOCATA TB-20 Trinidad	617	F-GENV
D-EKMS(2)	Cessna TR.182 Turbo Skylane RG	00623	N4903R
D-EKMT	Reims/Cessna F.152	1734	
D-EKMU(2)	Reims/Cessna FR.182 Skylane RG	0028	
D-EKMV	SOCATA TB-20 Trinidad	724	
D-EKMW(2)	Mooney M.20J Model 205	24-3213	
D-EKMX	Zlin Z.43	0025	LSK-19
D-EKMY	Bölkow BO.208C Junior	514	G-ASAS
			D-ENCY(1)
D-EKMZ	Zlin Z.43	0021	LSK-27
D-EKNA	Mooney M.20F Executive	670297	N9737M
D-EKNB	Reims/Cessna F.172H	0541	
D-EKNE(3)	Cessna TR.182 Turbo Skylane RG	00854	N737MR
D-EKNF	Reims/Cessna F.172N	2001	PH-AYK
D-EKNI	SOCATA MS.892A Rallye Commodore 150	10551	
D-EKNK	Cessna 172RG Cutlass	0568	N5550V
D-EKNM	Cessna R.182 Skylane RG	00568	N1809R
D-EKNO(2)	Mooney M.20J Model 201	24-0045	
D-EKNR	Piper PA-28RT-201 Arrow IV	28R-7918187	I-NALD
			N2873D
D-EKNS(2)	Cessna 177RG Cardinal RG	1103	N45313
D-EKNW	Piper PA-32-260 Cherokee Six	32-714	N3789W

Regn.	Type	C/n	Prev.Id.
D-EKOA	Piper PA-28RT-201T Turbo Arrow IV	28R-8131112	N8364Z
D-EKOB(2)	Piper PA-28R-201 Cherokee Arrow III	28R-7737170	N47499
D-EKOC(3)	Mooney M.20J Model 205	24-3064	N5684D
			(N205BG)
			N5684D
D-EKOF	S.A.I. KZ-VII Laerke	192	(F-AZGK)
			D-EKOF
			HB-EPV
D-EKOG(2)	Reims/Cessna F.172N	1975	(D-EOOX)
D-EKOH(2)	Piper PA-18-150 Super Cub	18-3224	OL-L50
			L-150
			53-4824
D-EKOK	Klemm Kl.107C	133	
D-EKOL	Piper PA-18-150 Super Cub	18-5612	
D-EKOM(3)	Piper PA-28RT-201T Turbo Arrow IV	28R-8031034	N3563X
D-EKON(2)	Reims/Cessna F.172N	927	
D-EKOO	HOAC DV-20 Katana	20015	
D-EKOP(2)	Cessna P210N Pressurized Centurion II	00069	N3890P
D-EKOQ	Cessna 172A	47504	N9704T
D-EKOR(2)	Piper PA-28R-201T Turbo Cherokee Arrow III		
		28R-7703054	N1146Q
D-EKOT(2)	Reims/Cessna F.172G	0274	
D-EKOW	Beech 35-33 Debonair	CD-207	
D-EKOX(2)	Reims/Cessna F.172N	1685	
D-EKPA	Reims/Cessna F.172E	0084	
D-EKPC(2)	Mooney M.20J Model 201	24-1625	
D-EKPD	Beech B36TC Bonanza	EA-492	N15519
D-EKPE(3)	Reims/Cessna F.152	1956	
D-EKPH(2)	Aero Designs Pulsar XP (Reservation)	1836	
D-EKPI	Piper PA-28-160 Cherokee B	28-1138	N5704W
D-EKPL(2)	Cessna 172N	73995	N5163K
D-EKPM	Reims/Cessna F.172M	1480	
D-EKPO(2)	Cessna 182J Skylane	57303	N3303F
D-EKPP	Mooney M.20J Model 201	24-0268	
D-EKPR	Piper PA-28-181 Archer II	28-8190114	N8311A
D-EKPS	Reims/Cessna F.182Q Skylane	0077	
D-EKPT(2)	Robin DR.400/180S Régent	1889	
D-EKPU	Reims/Cessna F.172F	0088	
D-EKPW	Piper PA-32R-300 Lance	32R-7680100	HB-PBG
			(D-EANC)
			N8363C
D-EKPY	Reims/Cessna F.172F	0169	
D-EKQC	Piper PA-18 Super Cub 95	18-1461	ALAT
			51-15461
D-EKQD	Piper PA-18 Super Cub 95	18-1508	ALAT
			51-15508
D-EKQF	Piper PA-18 Super Cub 95	18-1621	ALAT
			51-15621
D-EKQG	Piper PA-18 Super Cub 95	18-3141	OL-L67
			L-67
			53-4741
D-EKQI (2)	Reims/Cessna F.150K	0600	
D-EKQO	Cessna 182N Skylane	60102	N92228
D-EKRA	Reims/Cessna F.172G	0286	
D-EKRC	Reims/Cessna F.172F	0174	
D-EKRD	Piper PA-38-112 Tomahawk	38-79A0920	N9697N
D-EKRE(2)	Bücker Bü.133C Jungmeister	5	HB-MKF
			U-58
D-EKRF	Robin HR.100/250TR Safari	551	
D-EKRG	Piper PA-18-100 Super Cub	"18-2546"	
	(C/n as officially quoted however its f/n is 18-1302 which should be c/n 18-1374, but this is D-EIEI)		
D-EKRI	Beech 35-E33 Debonair	CD-1160	N8354N
D-EKRM	Mooney M.20K Model 252	25-1230	
D-EKRS	Cessna T.210L Turbo Centurion	59569	N4669Q
D-EKRU	Beech E33C Bonanza	CJ-25	
D-EKSA(2)	Piper PA-28RT-201T Turbo Arrow IV	28R-8031096	N81981
D-EKSB	Beech 35-B33 Debonair	CD-702	HB-EKL
D-EKSC	Gyroflug SC-01B-160 Speed Canard (Res 8.99)	S-20	
D-EKSD	Cessna 152	83480	N49604
D-EKSE(2)	Robin DR.400/180R Remorqueur	1396	OE-KSE
			D-EISE(2)
D-EKSF	Cessna P210N Pressurized Centurion II	00503	N731NF
D-EKSG(2)	Piper PA-28-181 Archer II	28-8290075	N8020K
D-EKSH	Piper PA-28-161 Cadet	2841319	N9213Q

Regn.	Type	C/n	Prev.Id.
D-EKSI (2)	Robin DR.400/180R Remorqueur	1380	
D-EKSL	Cessna T.210N Turbo Centurion II	64855	(N5254U)
D-EKSP	Cessna 182H Skylane	56425	N8325S
D-EKSR	Robin DR.400/180S Régent	2035	
D-EKSS	Mooney M.20J Model 205	24-3278	
D-EKST	Reims/Cessna F.172G	0267	OO-RPA
			PH-RPA
D-EKSU	Cessna 150D	60091	N7991Z
D-EKSW	Robin DR.400/180R Remorqueur	844	
D-EKSY(2)	Piper PA-28-180 Cherokee C	28-3535	F-OCJU
			N9424J
D-EKTB	SOCATA TB-10 Tobago	371	
D-EKTC	Piper PA-28R-201T Turbo Arrow III	28R-7803364	N21431
D-EKTD	SOCATA TB-10 Tobago	374	
D-EKTF	SOCATA TB-10 Tobago	375	
D-EKTG	SOCATA TB-10 Tobago	376	
D-EKTH	SOCATA TB-9 Tampico	387	
D-EKTI (2)	Beech A-36 Bonanza	E-1646	
D-EKTJ	SOCATA Rallye 180TS Galérien	3374	
D-EKTK	SOCATA TB-10 Tobago	366	
D-EKTM	SOCATA TB-10 Tobago	367	
D-EKTN	SOCATA TB-20 Trinidad	386	
D-EKTO	Reims/Cessna F.172G	0180	
D-EKTY(2)	Dornier Do.27A-1	322	56+41
			D-9500
D-EKUC(2)	Piper PA-28-180 Cherokee Challenger	28-7305470	N55791
D-EKUF	Beech G35 Bonanza	D-4713	N12B
D-EKUG	Cessna 150	17818	N6418T
D-EKUH(2)	Luscombe 8F Silvaire	6295	HB-DUC
			NC1868B
D-EKUI	Dornier Do.27A-4	230	D-EKUT(2)
			D-EBAJ
			55+83
			YA+907
			D-EHYL
D-EKUK(2)	Rockwell Commander 114A	14533	
D-EKUL(2)	Piper PA-28-181 Archer II	28-8090042	N2322U
D-EKUM	Rhein RW-3-V2 Multoplan	2	
D-EKUN(3)	SOCATA MS.893E Rallye 180GT Gaillard	12180	F-BUCN
D-EKUO	Morane-Saulnier MS.885 Super Rallye	245	F-BKUO
D-EKUP(2)	Cessna 182E Skylane	53847	HB-CBB
			OE-DDB
			(N2847Y)
D-EKUQ	Piper PA-18-100 Super Cub	18-6413	N8974D
D-EKUR(2)	Mooney M.20K Model 231	25-0437	(N3655H)
D-EKUT(3)	Dornier Do.27Q-4	2024	HB-FAA
D-EKUW(2)	Piper PA-28RT-201T Turbo Arrow IV	28R-8031167	N82557
D-EKVA(2)	Beech A36 Bonanza	E-2328	N2644M
D-EKVB	Cessna 150L	73720	N18002
D-EKVE	Beech 35-C33 Debonair	CD-860	
D-EKVF	Robin DR.400/180 Régent	1697	G-BLYS
D-EKVH	Piper PA-46-310P Malibu	46-8408041	HB-PKB
			(D-EIDN(2))
			HB-PKB
			D-ERAS
			HB-PKB
			(D-ERAS)
			HB-PKB
			D-ELBU(3)
			N43467
D-EKVL	Robin DR.400/180R Remorqueur	1196	
D-EKVM(2)	Cessna U.206G Stationair II	05474	HB-CLK
			N6394U
D-EKVU	Beech 35-C33 Debonair	CD-1036	
D-EKVW	Cessna P.210N Pressurized Centurion	00579	N732GV
	(Robertson STOL conversion)		
D-EKWA(4)	Reims/Cessna 182P Skylane	0041/64136	N6234F
D-EKWB(2)	Mooney M.20K Model 252	25-1104	
D-EKWF	Piper PA-28-140 Cherokee E	28-7225456	N11C
D-EKWG(2)	Mooney M.20K Model 252	25-1091	N252YW
D-EKWH(2)	Piper PA-38-112 Tomahawk	38-78A0173	N9718N
D-EKWJ	Beech V35B Bonanza	D-9763	
D-EKWL	Maule MX.7-235 Star Rocket	10064C	N6109Q
D-EKWM	Cessna 182E Skylane	54307	OE-DDE
			N3307Y

Regn.	Type	C/n	Prev.Id.
D-EKWO	Cessna P210N Pressurized Centurion II	00657	N5227W
D-EKWR(2)	Robin DR.400/180 Régent	2327	
D-EKWS(2)	Robin DR.400/180RP Remorqueur	1790	
D-EKWT	Piper PA-24-260 Comanche C	24-4937	N9429P
D-EKWW	Piper PA-38-112 Tomahawk	38-78A0420	N9727N
D-EKXA	Beech F33C Bonanza	CJ-29	
D-EKXB	CEA DR.253B Régent	162	
D-EKXC	CEA DR.253B Régent	164	
D-EKXD	CEA DR.253B Régent	166	
D-EKXE	Beech F33A Bonanza	CE-298	
D-EKXF	CEA DR.315 Petit Prince	460	
D-EKXO	Beech A23-24 Musketeer Super	MA-363	
D-EKXY	Beech A24R Musketeer Super R	MC-11	N8014R
D-EKYL	Piper PA-18 Super Cub 95	18-4462	N2872P
D-EKYM(2)	Scheibe SF.23A Sperling	2019	
D-EKYN(3)	SEEMS MS.880B Rallye Club	314	F-BKYN
D-EKYP	Scheibe SF.23A Sperling	2008	
D-EKYS(2)	Mooney M.20J Model 201	24-1095	
D-EKYT(3)	Piper PA-28-140 Cherokee C	28-26868	N5967U
D-EKYV(2)	Piper PA-28R-200 Cherokee Arrow B	28R-35750	N5018S
D-EKYW(2)	Robin DR.400/180 Régent	1702	
D-EKYX	Scintex CP.301C Emeraude	523	
D-EKZA	Piper PA-28-140 Cherokee	28-20970	N6830W
D-EKZI	Piper PA-28-140 Cherokee	28-21427	N11C
D-EKZK	SEEMS MS.880B Rallye Club	371	F-BKZK
D-EKZO	Piper PA-28-140 Cherokee	28-21443	N11C
D-EKZU	Piper PA-28-140 Cherokee	28-21395	N11C
D-EKZY	Piper PA-28-140 Cherokee	28-21419	N11C
D-ELAA	Reims/Cessna F.182Q Skylane	0108	
D-ELAB(2)	Cessna 152	80850	N25908
D-ELAC(2)	Bölkow BO.208C Junior	626	
D-ELAD(2)	Reims/Cessna F.172P	2232	
D-ELAG(2)	Cessna TU.206G Turbo Stationair II	03740	N9964N
D-ELAH(2)	Gardan GY-80 Horizon 180	141	
D-ELAI	Bellanca 17-31 ATC Viking 260	73-31059	
D-ELAJ	Piper PA-28-140 Cherokee E	28-7225471	N11C
D-ELAK(2)	Piper PA-28-140 Cherokee E	28-7225094	N4210T
D-ELAL(4)	Piper PA-32RT-300T Turbo Lance	32R-7887012	
D-ELAM(2)	Piper PA-28RT-201 Arrow IV	28R-7918175	N2853L
D-ELAN(2)	Bramsche Piel CP.301 Emeraude	AB.419	
D-ELAO(2)	Piper PA-46-310P Malibu	46-8608019	HB-POA
			I-GHIO
			G-BMMT
			N9230T
D-ELAP(2)	Cessna 182Q Skylane	65228	N7579S
D-ELAQ(2)	Piper PA-28-181 Cherokee Archer II	28-7890432	N9567N
D-ELAR(3)	Robin DR.400/RP Remorqueur	1793	
D-ELAS(2)	Zlin Z.126 Trenér 2	865	OE-AES
			2A-AN
D-ELAT(2)	Wullenweber Jurca MJ.5 Sirocco	021D	
D-ELAU	Piper PA-28-140 Cherokee Cruiser	28-7325296	N11C
D-ELAV(3)	Piper PA-28-181 Archer II	28-8190151	N8326B
D-ELAW(2)	Bölkow BO.208C Junior	627	
D-ELAX	Cessna 172	29817	N8017B
D-ELAY	Bellanca 17-31 ATC Turbo-Viking	72-31034	
D-ELAZ(2)	Robin DR.300/108 2+2	542	
D-ELBB	SAN Jodel D.150 Mascaret	30	
D-ELBC(2)	Robin R.2160D Acrobin	121	(F-ODHO)
D-ELBD(3)	Piper PA-28-181 Archer III	2843079	N9273N
D-ELBE(4)	Cessna 182R Skylane	68208	(N2499E)
D-ELBF(2)	Reims/Cessna F.152	1561	
D-ELBG	Reims/Cessna F.172H	0439	
D-ELBH(2)	SOCATA MS.880B Rallye Club	1372	F-BRRB
D-ELBM	Cessna P210N Pressurized Centurion II	00171	N6335P
D-ELBO(2)	Piper PA-28-235 Cherokee D	28-11375	N8573N
D-ELBS(2)	Piper PA-28-181 Cherokee Archer II	28-7890317	OY-CBS
			(N3614M)
			(D-EIIW)
			OY-CBS
			N3614M
D-ELBT(2)	Robin DR.400/RP Remorqueur	1798	
D-ELBW	Reims/Cessna F.172N	1557	
D-ELBY(4)	SOCATA Rallye 235A	13331	F-GDRB
D-ELCA	Göbel Binder CP.301S Smaragd	AB.434	
D-ELCB	Fuji FA-200-180 Aero Subaru	272	

Regn.	Type	C/n	Prev.id.
D-ELCC	Piper PA-38-112 Tomahawk	38-79A0672	N9697N
D-ELCD	Piper PA-38-112 Tomahawk	38-80A0095	N9689N
D-ELCE(2)	Piper PA-28-181 Cherokee Archer II	28-7790043	N4550F
D-ELCG	Reims/Cessna F.172N	1947	
D-ELCH(3)	Commander Aircraft 114B	14566	
D-ELCI (2)	Piper PA-28-181 Cherokee Archer II	28-7690293	N75097
D-ELCL	Piper PA-28RT-201T Turbo Arrow IV	2831016	N9135Z
D-ELCM	Piper PA-28-181 Archer II	28-8690043	N565DH
			N9202C
			N9274Y
D-ELCN	Piper PA-18 Super Cub 95	18-3446	96+22
			NL+102
			AC+532
			AS+532
			54-746
D-ELCO(3)	Cessna 172RG Cutlass	0130	N6268R
D-ELCP	Mooney M.20G Statesman	680070	N3969N
D-ELCQ	Piper PA-28-140 Cherokee	28-24206	N1783J
D-ELCR	SNCAN/ Stampe SV-4C	20	F-BLCO
			Fr.AF
D-ELCS(2)	Cessna 182Q Skylane	67140	N97586
			D-ELCS
			N97586
D-ELCT	Piper PA-28-181 Archer II	2890049	N9130X
D-ELCU	Piper PA-18 Super Cub 95	18-3114	L-40
			53-4714
D-ELCV	Piper PA-28-161 Warrior II	28-8216045	N9591N
D-ELCW	Piper PA-28R-201T Arrow IV	2803010	N9185X
D-ELCX	Piper PA-28-181 Archer II	28-8690031	N165AV
D-ELCY	CEA DR.250/160 Capitaine	93	
D-ELDA	Wassmer WA.52 Europa	61	"D-EFDA"
D-ELDB	Piper PA-28RT-201 Arrow IV	28R-8018067	N8198Z
D-ELDC(2)	Piper PA-28-181 Archer III *(Permit 11.99)*	2890208	SE-KXF
D-ELDD	Beech F33A Bonanza	CE-869	
D-ELDH	Piper PA-32R-300 Lance	32R-7680047	N7538C
D-ELDI (2)	Piper PA-28-236 Dakota	28-7911065	N2151J
D-ELDK(2)	Mooney M.20M TLS	27-0027	
D-ELDM(2)	SOCATA TB-20 Trinidad	860	OY-CDM
D-ELDO(3)	Piper PA-28-161 Cadet	2841340	N9215Q
			N128ND
			(OH-PFI)
			(OH-PFA)
D-ELDP	Robin DR.400/180R Remorqueur	1461	
D-ELDW	Piper PA-28RT-201T Turbo Arrow IV	28R-8031164	N8253C
			N9595N
D-ELEA	Reims/Cessna F.172H	0394	
D-ELEB(2)	CASA I-131E Jungmann	2145	E3B-528
D-ELEC	Piper PA-22-160 Tri-Pacer	22-6321	N9310D
D-ELED(2)	HOAC DV-20 Katana	20026	
D-ELEF(3)	Robin DR.400/RP Remorqueur	1818	
D-ELEG(2)	Piper PA-18-150 Super Cub	18-6421	N8979D
D-ELEH	Cessna 175 Skylark	56117	N6617E
D-ELEI	Cessna 172F	52236	(D-ENAG(3))
			N8336U
D-ELEK(3)	SOCATA TB-10 Tobago	143	F-GCOH
D-ELEL(3)	Reims/Cessna F.172G	0258	(D-ELIG)
D-ELEM(2)	Beech V35B Bonanza	D-9885	
D-ELEN(2)	Piper PA-28-140 Cherokee D	28-7125103	N1788T
D-ELEO	Reims/Cessna FR.172H Rocket	0228	N9448
D-ELEP	Diemer Piel CP.301A Emeraude	AB.404	
D-ELEQ	Klemm Kl.107C	148	
D-ELES(2)	Beech C24R Sierra 200	MC-669	
D-ELET(4)	Piper PA-32R-301T Saratoga II TC	3257056	N41257
			91+22
			GA+405
			AS+079
			(KB+121)
D-ELEV(2)	Piaggio FWP.149D	144	
D-ELEX(3)	Piper PA-46-350P Malibu	4636105	N92832
D-ELEY(2)	Mooney M.20J Model 201	24-0231	PH-IHD
			N201HD
D-ELFC	Piper PA-28R-180 Cherokee Arrow	28R-30398	N4539J
D-ELFE(2)	Piper J-3C-65 Cub	12261	D-EJAX
			OK-ANO
			44-79965
	(Quoted officially with f/n 12089 as c/n)		
D-ELFF(2)	Piper PA-28-181 Archer II	28-8090068	N8077M
D-ELFG	Piper PA-28R-200 Cherokee Arrow II	28R-7335196	N55221
D-ELFH	Cessna 172E	50984	C-GLHE
			D-EDTH
			N3784S
D-ELFI (3)	Piper PA-28-140 Cherokee E	28-7225112	N11C
D-ELFN	Reims/Cessna F.172N	1499	
D-ELFP	Cessna 182N Skylane	60301	N92663
D-ELFR	Robin DR.400/180R Régent	1341	
D-ELFS(2)	Robin DR.400/180R Remorqueur	1875	
D-ELFT(2)	Piper PA-28-161 Cadet	2841287	N9526N
			N92043
D-ELFU(2)	LFU 205	V-1	
D-ELFW	Brandl Jurca FW190 A5	0001	
D-ELFY(2)	SOCATA MS.894A Minerva 220	11626	
D-ELGA(2)	PZL-104 Wilga 35	21930951	
D-ELGB(2)	Piaggio FWP.149D	112	90+92
			MB+383
			JC+393
			AS+422
D-ELGC	Piper PA-18 Super Cub 95	18-6456	N9084D
D-ELGD	Piper PA-12 Super Cruiser	12-3395	N4443M
D-ELGE(2)	Piper PA-38-112 Tomahawk	38-79A0447	N9729N
D-ELGH(2)	Piper PA-28R-200 Cherokee Arrow II	28R-7535150	N33426
D-ELGI (2)	Piper PA-28-151 Warrior	28-7415150	N9513N
D-ELGK	Piper PA-12 Super Cruiser	12-2345	N3501M
D-ELGL(2)	Cessna 172N	71825	N5297E
D-ELGM	Piper PA-24-250 Comanche	24-782	N5708P
D-ELGN	Reims/Cessna F.172F	0107	
D-ELGO(2)	Piper PA-38-112 Tomahawk	38-78A0142	N9666N
D-ELGP	Reims/Cessna F.172F	0111	
D-ELGR(2)	Cessna 172N	71094	N1687E
D-ELGS	Cessna 182K Skylane	57993	N2793Q
D-ELGT(2)	Cessna 182R Skylane	68360	N6349E
D-ELGU(2)	Piaggio FWP.149D	111	90+91
			MB+382
			JC+392
			AS+419
D-ELGV	CEA DR.315 Petit Prince	448	
D-ELGW	CEA DR.253B Régent	160	
D-ELHB(2)	Piper PA-46-310P Malibu	46-8608038	LX-ADC
			D-ESMK
			N921BC
			N9082F
D-ELHE(2)	SOCATA MS.894A Minerva 220	11996	F-BTPU
D-ELHF(2)	Mooney M.20J Model 201	24-1610	N5752E
D-ELHG(3)	Robin DR.400/180 Régent	1600	
D-ELHI (2)	Robin DR.400/180 Régent	1208	
D-ELHK	Beech V35B Bonanza	D-10020	
D-ELHL(2)	Piper PA-32R-301T Turbo Saratoga	32R-8429013	N4360H
D-ELHM	Piper PA-18 Super Cub 95	18-1336	ALAT
			51-15336
D-ELHN	Reims/Cessna F.172M	1141	HB-CEG
D-ELHO(2)	Robin DR.400/180R Remorqueur	1210	
D-ELHP	Piper PA-18-150 Super Cub	nil	(RBAF)
	(Built from spare fuselage no.18-4908)		
D-ELHQ	CEA DR.300/180R (Convtd.from DR.315)	479	
D-ELHR	Fuji FA-200-160 Aero Subaru	78	
D-ELHS	Fuji FA-200-180 Aero Subaru	80	
D-ELHT	Piper PA-18 Super Cub 95	18-1015	ALAT
			51-15318
D-ELHV	Fuji FA-200-180 Aero Subaru	82	
D-ELHW	Mooney M.20J Model 201	24-0421	N201AX
D-ELHY(2)	Grumman AA-5B Tiger	0975	G-BLHP
			OO-RTH
			(OO-HRR)
D-ELIA	SAN Jodel D.150 Mascaret	57	
D-ELIB(2)	Reims/Cessna F.150M	1419	
D-ELIC(2)	Piper PA-28-140 Cherokee	28-20515	N6443W
D-ELIF(2)	Gardan GY-80 Horizon 160	3	F-BLIF
D-ELIG(3)	Piper PA-28-140 Cherokee Cruiser	28-7325309	N11C
D-ELIH	Piper PA-18-150 Super Cub	18-7031	
D-ELII	Piper PA-28-140 Cherokee C	28-26664	N5833U
D-ELIK	Klemm Kl.107B	104	
D-ELIL(4)	Piper PA-28-181 Archer II	28-7990114	N3020A
D-ELIM(2)	Wassmer WA.54 Atlantic	119	

Regn.	Type	C/n	Prev.Id.
D-ELIN(2)	Piper PA-28-181 Cherokee Archer II	28-7890345	N6446C
			N9540N
D-ELIO	CEA DR.253B Régent	172	
D-ELIP(3)	Lipp Denney Kitfox III (Permit)	1036	
D-ELIS(2)	Piper PA-46-310P Malibu	46-8508038	N385R
			N4386L
D-ELIT(2)	Piper PA-28R-201T Turbo Arrow III	28R-7803363	N21349
D-ELIW(3)	Mooney M.20J Model 201	24-1005	(N3996H)
D-ELIX	Erco Ercoupe 415C	1079	N93757
D-ELIZ(2)	SOCATA ST-10 Diplomate	120	
D-ELJA(2)	Gruber Neico Lancair 235	1705	
D-ELJH	Hirt Starlite SL-1	1	
D-ELJK	Mooney M.20J Model 205	24-3230	
D-ELJR	SAN Jodel DR.1050M-1 Excellence	468	(D-EHPL)
			F-BLJR
D-ELJS	Bücker Bü.131 Jungmann (Lycoming)	70	(D-EEJS)
			A-57
D-ELKA(3)	Piper PA-28R-201T Turbo Cherokee Arrow III		
		28R-7703174	N5982V
D-ELKC	Piper PA-28-181 Archer III	2843246	N4135Z
D-ELKD	Piper PA-28-236 Dakota	28-8211001	N8438A
D-ELKE(2)	Piper PA-28-161 Warrior II	2816062	N9138N
D-ELKF(2)	Zlin Z.526 Trenér Master	1071	OO-PKG
			OK-YR .
D-ELKG	Piper PA-18-150 Super Cub	18-2540	ALAT
			52-6222
D-ELKH	Morane-Saulnier MS.500 Criquet	699	F-BEJE
			Fr.AF
D-ELKI (2)	Reims/Cessna F.172N	1918	
D-ELKK	Krause Steen Skybolt	3	
D-ELKM	Cessna T.210L Turbo Centurion	60946	N5433V
D-ELKR(2)	Leverkusen Rand-Robinson KR-2/B	1808/002	
D-ELKS	Piaggio P.149D	256	91+74
			D-EBCI
			AC+407
			AS+407
D-ELKU(2)	Reims/Cessna FR.172K Hawk XP	0656	
D-ELKW	Wirth Rutan LongEz	1083	
D-ELKY	Pützer Elster B	032	
D-ELLA(2)	SOCATA MS.894E Minerva 220GT	12198	F-BVZB
D-ELLB(2)	Piper PA-28-236 Dakota	2811024	N91637
D-ELLC	Piper PA-28-161 Warrior II	28-8116178	(N83514)
D-ELLD	Piper PA-28RT-201T Turbo Arrow IV	28R-7931303	N8090P
D-ELLE(2)	Reims/Cessna F.182P Skylane	0002	
D-ELLG	Beech A36 Bonanza	E-2423	
D-ELLH	Piper PA-28-181 Archer II	2890134	N919OV
D-ELLI	Cessna 210	57339	N9539T
D-ELLJ	Piper PA-24-250 Comanche	24-1907	I-ELLI
			N6776P
D-ELLK	Piper PA-28-161 Cadet	2841288	N9527N
			N92067
D-ELLL(2)	Robin HR.200/120B	44	HB-EXK
D-ELLM(2)	Piper PA-28-181 Archer II	2890144	N91739
D-ELLN	Piper PA-28-161 Warrior II	2816058	N9132Z
D-ELLO(2)	Reims/Cessna F.172M	1319	
D-ELLP	SOCATA MS.893A Rallye Commodore 180	11823	
D-ELLQ(2)	SOCATA MS.893A Rallye Commodore 180	11839	
D-ELLR	SOCATA MS.893A Rallye Commodore 180	11840	
D-ELLS	SOCATA MS.883 Rallye 115	1587	F-BTHK
D-ELLU(2)	Piper PA-28-181 Archer II	28-8190271	N8408T
D-ELLV	Piper PA-28-181 Archer II	2890123	N9144Z
D-ELLX	Piper PA-28-181 Archer II	2890101	N9158Z
D-ELLY(2)	Cessna 150F	64526	(D-ECJH)
			C-FUTL
			CF-UTL
			N3126X
D-ELLZ	Cessna 182R Skylane	67974	(PH-AXO)
			N9650H
D-ELMA(2)	Piper PA-28-235 Cherokee Pathfinder	28-7510110	N1589X
			N9584N
D-ELMB(2)	Mooney M.20J Model 201	24-1634	
D-ELMC(2)	Mooney M.20K Model 252	25-1116	
D-ELMG	Reims/Cessna F.150M	1299	LX-AVD
			LX-AIO
			(F-GAAA)

Regn.	Type	C/n	Prev.Id.
D-ELMH	Grumman AA-5B Tiger	0107	
D-ELMI (3)	Cessna 182J Skylane	57426	N3426F
D-ELMK	Beech A36 Bonanza	E-1544	
D-ELMM(2)	Robin DR.400/180R Remorqueur	2006	
D-ELMN	CEA Jodel DR.1050 Sicile	437	F-BLMN
D-ELMO	CEA Jodel DR.1050 Ambassadeur	210	
D-ELMR	Bareiss Brändli BX-2 Cherry (Damaged 5.99)	Eb 001/83	
D-ELMS(2)	Piper PA-28RT-201T Turbo Arrow IV	28R-8031133	N82377
D-ELMT	Cessna T.210N Turbo Centurion II	64530	N9507Y
	(Cr 18.3.96, repaired using parts of D-EPAS c/n		
	61019 but dbr on ground 16.10.98)		
D-ELMU(2)	Bölkow BO.208C Junior	705	(D-ENYO)
D-ELMW	Cessna T.210L Turbo Centurion	60912	N5338V
D-ELMY(3)	Aviat A-1 Husky	1325	
D-ELMZ	Piper PA-28-180 Cherokee D	28-5156	LN-LMZ
D-ELNA(2)	Reims/Cessna F.172G	0238	
D-ELNB	Reims/Cessna F.172H	0530	
D-ELNC	Reims/Cessna F.15 H	0357	
D-ELNF	Reims/Cessna F.172H	0540	
D-ELNI (2)	Piper PA-18 Super Cub 95	18-456	Greek AF
			50-1800
D-ELNN(2)	SOCATA Rallye 110ST Galopin	3383	F-GENN
			F-OGMB
D-ELNP	Reims/Cessna F.15 H	0355	
D-ELNQ	Reims/Cessna F.172H	0547	
D-ELNY(2)	Beech F33A Bonanza	CE-787	
D-ELOA	Piper PA-28-161 Warrior II	28-8016239	N9613N
D-ELOB(3)	Reims/Cessna F.172M	1103	
D-ELOC	Piper PA-18-150 Super Cub	18-6635	(N9370D)
D-ELOD(2)	Reims/Cessna F.172G	0203	
D-ELOE	Piper PA-28-181 Archer II	28-8490038	N9570N
			N4334L
D-ELOF	Piper PA-18-135 Super Cub	18-2490	HB-OEC
D-ELOG(2)	Reims/Cessna F.150G	0096	
D-ELOI	Mooney M.20F Executive	680130	N3849N
D-ELOK(2)	Piper PA-18-150 Super Cub	18-8797	N4450Z
D-ELOL(3)	Reims/Cessna F.172G	0207	
D-ELOO	Reims/Cessna F.172G	0290	
D-ELOR(2)	Reims/Cessna F.172G	0210	
D-ELOS(2)	Reims/Cessna F.150L	1127	(D-EOQB)
D-ELOT(3)	Reims/Cessna F.152	1637	OY-BNC
D-ELOU	Beech A23A Musketeer	M-937	N2338W
D-ELOV(3)	Piper PA-32RT-300T Turbo Lance II	32R-7887155	N39728
D-ELOW	Piper PA-18-150 Super Cub	18-7095	
D-ELOX	Klemm Kl.35D	1959	LN-TAI
			Fv5040
D-ELOY	Reims/Cessna F.182Q Skylane	0073	
D-ELOZ(2)	Robin DR.300/108 2+2	526	
D-ELPA(2)	Beech V35B Bonanza	D-10251	
D-ELPC	Piper PA-28-181 Cherokee Archer II	28-7790292	N9586N
D-ELPD	Reims/Cessna F.172N	1825	
D-ELPH	Reims/Cessna F.172N	1833	
D-ELPI (2)	Zlin Z.126 Trenér 2	808	OE-AEU
			2A-AK
			OK-KMH
D-ELPK	Mooney M.20C Ranger	20-1255	
D-ELPL	Cessna P210N Pressurized Centurion II	00535	N46932
			D-ELPL
			(N731QW)
D-ELPM(2)	Piper PA-28-161 Warrior II	28-8116298	N8427H
D-ELPN	HOAC DV-20 Katana	20023	
D-ELPP(2)	HOAC DV-20 Katana (Permit 10.99)	20094	N144DV
D-ELPR	Homebuilt (Reservation)	190SB	
D-ELPS(2)	Styrsky Neico Lancair 235 Pegasos	001/475	
D-ELPT	Fuji FA-200-180AO Aero Subaru	261	
D-ELPU(2)	Reims/Cessna F.172P	2149	
D-ELPY(2)	SOCATA MS.893E Rallye 180GT Gaillard	12315	F-GFVX
			HB-ETG
			F-BUZC
D-ELQE	SEEMS MS.885 Super Rallye	5412	
D-ELQI	Cessna 172E	51424	N5524T
D-ELQU	Mooney M.20A	1597	N6009X
D-ELQY	Piper PA-18 Super Cub 95	18-3083	L-9
			53-4683
D-ELRB	Reims/Cessna FR.172F Rocket	0096	

Regn.	Type	C/n	Prev.Id.
D-ELRC	Reims/Cessna FR.172F Rocket	0092	
D-ELRD	Reims/Cessna FR.172F Rocket	0095	
D-ELRE(2)	Reims/Cessna F.152	1763	
D-ELRF(2)	Piper PA-28-140 Cherokee C	28-26670	N5839U
D-ELRG	Cessna T.210J Turbo-System Centurion	0408	(N2258R)
D-ELRI (3)	Hartz Piel CP.301E Emeraude	AB.405	D-ECAG(2)
D-ELRK	Reims/Cessna F.150J	0493	
D-ELRO(2)	Beech B36TC Bonanza	EA-377	N67269
D-ELRP	Reims/Cessna F.182Q Skylane	0056	
D-ELRS	Robin DR.400/180R Remorqueur	1231	
D-ELRT	Robin DR.400/180R Remorqueur	1236	
D-ELRY	Gardan GY-80 Horizon 160	64	
D-ELSA(3)	Piper PA-28-200 Cherokee Arrow II	28R-7535039	N9614N
D-ELSB	Robin DR.400/180R Remorqueur	1145	
D-ELSC(2)	Robin DR.400/180R Remorqueur	1108	LN-SAT
			SE-GRH
D-ELSD	Cessna 152	81427	N49987
D-ELSE	Cessna 182G Skylane	55547	N2447R
D-ELSF	Dornier Do.27B-1	273	56+06
			AS+901
D-ELSG	Piper PA-18 Super Cub 95	18-3200	(D-EETT)
			OL-L26
			L-126
			53-4800
D-ELSH	Cessna R.182 Skylane RG	01871	N5457T
D-ELSI (2)	Piper PA-28-181 Cherokee Archer II	28-7790206	N9547N
D-ELSK	CASA I-131E Jungmann	2120	E3B-417
D-ELSM	SAN Jodel D.117A Grand Tourisme	839	F-BITL
D-ELSN	Cessna 172R	80158	
D-ELSO	SAN Jodel DR.1050 Ambassadeur	396	
D-ELSP	Grob G.115A	8016	
D-ELSR(2)	Robin DR.400/180R Remorqueur	2012	
D-ELST(2)	Cessna 172N	73727	(D-EGPB(2))
			N5196J
D-ELSU(3)	Piper PA-32RT-301 Saratoga SP	32R-8013088	N8188M
D-ELSV(2)	Reims/Cessna F.172P	2242	
D-ELSW	Cessna 180K Skywagon	52975	N2533K
D-ELTA	Beech K35 Bonanza	D-5968	
D-ELTB(2)	Reims/Cessna F.182Q Skylane	0082	
D-ELTC(2)	Reims/Cessna F.182Q Skylane	0139	
D-ELTD	Piper PA-18-150 Super Cub	18-1460	ALAT
			51-15460
D-ELTE(2)	Piper PA-12 Super Cruiser	12-1874	N3204M
D-ELTG(2)	HOAC DV-20 Katana	20022	
D-ELTH	Piper PA-18-150 Super Cub	18-1580	ALAT
			51-15580
D-ELTI (3)	Piper PA-12 Super Cruiser	12-3462	D-ELQB
			D-ELOB
			N4036H
			NC4036H
D-ELTM	Mooney M.20F Executive	680147	
D-ELTO(2)	TEAM Minimax 1600 (Reservation)	1883	
D-ELTP	Piper PA-18 Super Cub 95	18-1567	ALAT
			51-15567
D-ELTT	Dornier Do.27B-3	430	57+04
			CB+003
			LC+156 ?
D-ELTU(2)	SOCATA MS.893E Rallye 180GT Gaillard	12326	F-BUVH
D-ELTY(2)	Pützer Elster B	008	97+06
			D-EDEQ
D-ELTZ	Cessna T.210N Turbo Centurion II	64486	ZS-LTU
			N9364Y
D-ELUB	Piper PA-18 Super Cub 95	18-5989	
D-ELUC(2)	Piper PA-28-201T Turbo Cherokee Arrow III	28R-7703370	N47401
D-ELUD	Zlin Z.126 Trenér 2	841	
D-ELUE(2)	Piper PA-28-161 Warrior II	28-7916484	N2856Y
D-ELUF(2)	Piper PA-18-180 Super Cub	18-2046	PH-LUF
			PH-JWK
			R-50
			52-2446
D-ELUH(2)	Piper PA-28R-201T Turbo Cherokee Arrow III	28R-7703324	N43986
D-ELUI	Reims/Cessna F.172N	1719	
D-ELUK(2)	Piper PA-18-150 Super Cub	18-7446	N6813P

Regn.	Type	C/n	Prev.Id.
D-ELUM	Piper J-3C-65 Cub	11005	HB-OFG
	(C/n officially listed as 13249 which is		43-29714
	HB-OCK. D-ELUM has f/n 10830)		
D-ELUN(3)	Robin DR.400/180R Remorqueur	1102	I-ALSA
D-ELUP(3)	Reims/Cessna F.172N	1528	PH-SRO
			OO-LWC
			PH-SRO
D-ELUS(3)	Reims/Cessna F.150G	0106	
D-ELUT(2)	Piper PA-28R-200 Cherokee Arrow II	28R-7435009	N56514
D-ELUV(2)	Cessna 170B	20471	D-ELIL
			OO-SPA
			N2319D
D-ELUW(2)	Aeromere F.8L Falco III	226	
D-ELUX(2)	Huber Monnett Moni H1	1	
D-ELVA	Reims/Cessna F.172E	0067	
D-ELVD	Reims/Cessna FR.172F Rocket	0085	
D-ELVE(2)	Piper PA-28R-200 Cherokee Arrow II	28R-7635327	N6255J
D-ELVF	Reims/Cessna FR.172F Rocket	0070	
D-ELVG(2)	Robin DR.400/180R Remorqueur	2383	
D-ELVH	Reims/Cessna FR.172F Rocket	0117	
D-ELVI	Piper PA-28-180 Cherokee B	28-720	N7037W
D-ELVJ	Reims/Cessna FR.172F Rocket	0118	
D-ELVK	Dornier Do.27A-1	329	56+47
			GC+377
			AS+943
D-ELVM	SOCATA MS.894A Minerva 220	11675	F-BSVM
D-ELVO(2)	Reims/Cessna F.172H	0325	(D-EGDO)
D-ELVP	Gardan GY-80 Horizon 160	75	F-BLVP
D-ELVS	PZL-104 Wilga 35	19880863	SP-FWA
D-ELVY(3)	Mooney M.20M TLS	27-0205	G-BWIS
D-ELWA(2)	SIAI-Marchetti SF.260	2-44	HB-EMK
D-ELWD	Robin R.3000/160	145	
D-ELWE	Piper J-3C-65 Cub	15081	OE-AAZ
			N42770
D-ELWF	Grob G.115A	8049	
D-ELWG	Reims/Cessna F.150M	1308	
D-ELWH	Mooney M.20K Model 231	25-0123	N3702H
			N231BW
D-ELWI	Cessna 170B	26722	N4378B
D-ELWK(2)	Mooney M.20K Model 231	25-0378	N231RN
D-ELWL	Cessna 182M Skylane	59566	N71294
D-ELWM	Robin DR.400/180 Régent	1599	
D-ELWN	HOAC DV-20 Katana	20156	
D-ELWO	Piper PA-28-180 Cherokee B	28-1706	N7748W
D-ELWP	Hirt Denney Kitfox IV-1200 (Permit)	1733	
	(C/n now quoted as DCU-025)		
D-ELWS	Air Products F-1A Aircoupe	5752	G-AROR
			N25B
D-ELWU	Cessna 150	17833	OE-ADW
			N6433T
D-ELWW	Piper PA-28-140 Cherokee Cruiser	28-7525259	N9640N
D-ELWZ(2)	Grob G.115A	8065	
D-ELXC	American AA-1 Yankee	0385	(N6185L)
D-ELXI	Reims/Cessna F.172H	0431	
D-ELXP	Cessna 172N	71831	N5305E
D-ELYA	Maule MX.7-180 Star Rocket	11042C	N6116E
D-ELYD	Auster Mk.5	1790	G-ANKI
			TW446
D-ELYH	Piper PA-18 Super Cub 95	18-7069	
D-ELYK	Cessna TU.206G Turbo Stationair II	06285	N6466Z
D-ELYP(2)	Robin R.2100A	138	
D-ELYQ	Klemm Kl.107C	152	
D-ELYR	Uetz Jodel D.11/85	400/3	HB-SUE
D-ELYS	Cessna 172	29353	N7253A
D-ELYW	Piper PA-18A-125 Super Cub	18-7096	
D-ELZA(2)	Piper PA-28-161 Cadet	2841185	N9188B
D-ELZH	Grob G.115C	82020	
D-ELZI (2)	Piper PA-28-161 Cadet	2841242	N9192J
D-ELZO(2)	Linke Brditschka HB-207 Alpha (Permit)	207-022	
D-ELZU	Reims/Cessna F.172E	0051	
D-EMAA	Piper PA-28-180 Cherokee Archer	28-7405073	N9645N
D-EMAB(2)	Reims/Cessna F.172P	2236	
D-EMAC(3)	Cessna T.210N Turbo Centurion II	64213	N5460Y
			(N500EL)
			N5460Y

Regn.	Type	C/n	Prev.Id.
D-EMAD(2)	Piper PA-18-100 Super Cub	18-2030	R-33
			52-2430
D-EMAE(2)	Mooney M.20F Executive	22-1211	
D-EMAF(3)	SOCATA MS.893A Rallye Commodore 180	10721	F-BPBU
D-EMAG(2)	Cessna 170B	27036	OE-DBO
			HB-CPC
			N3493D
D-EMAH	Orlican L-40 Meta-Sokol	150503	OK-NMF
D-EMAI	Piper PA-18-135 Super Cub	18-7180	N3185Z
D-EMAJ	Piper PA-28-181 Archer II	28-8190165	N83353
D-EMAK(3)	Beech F33A Bonanza	CE-1506	
D-EMAL(3)	Piper PA-18-150 Super Cub	1809023	OY-JEH
D-EMAM(2)	Piper PA-18 Super Cub 95	18-2037	R-39
			52-2437
D-EMAN(2)	CEA Jodel DR.1050 Ambassadeur	44	F-BJUC
D-EMAO(2)	Piper PA-28RT-201T Turbo Arrow IV	28R-8031085	N8182R
D-EMAP(2)	Piper PA-28-181 Cherokee Archer II	28-7790453	N3345Q
D-EMAR(2)	Piper PA-28R-200 Cherokee Arrow II	28R-7635372	N6990J
D-EMAS	Bücker Bü.181B-1 Bestmann	120518/FR.33	SL-AAL
			F-BCSX
			F-BBLA
			VM772
			Luftwaffe
D-EMAT(2)	Timmermann Christen Eagle II	02/1602-348	
D-EMAU	Cessna T.210H Turbo-System Centurion	0385	(N2235R)
D-EMAV(2)	Mraz K-65 Cap	741	D-EKUS
	(Officially regd.as a Fieseler Fi.156 Storch)		HB-IKA
			OK-DF .
D-EMAW	Scheibe SF.23A-1 Sperling	2500	
D-EMAX(3)	Focke-Wulf FW.44J Stieglitz	83	(D-EMIQ(2))
			D-EMIL(3)
			D-EFUD
			SE-AWT
			Fv.631
D-EMAY	Bellanca 17-31ATC Turbo-Viking	75-131113	
D-EMAZ(3)	Cessna P210N Pressurized Centurion II	00629	N4896W
D-EMBA(3)	Piaggio FWP.149D	055	90+41
			ND+206
			AS+482
D-EMBB	Dornier Do.27B-1	307	56+32
			PA+319
			PF+111
			PL+414
D-EMBC	Reims/Cessna F.150J	0501	
D-EMBD(2)	Piper PA-28-180 Cherokee G	28-7205314	N11C
D-EMBE	Cessna 182E Skylane	54349	N3349Y
D-EMBF	Fuji FA-200-160 Aero Subaru	152	
D-EMBG	Fuji FA-200-180 Aero Subaru	157	
D-EMBI (2)	Beech A36AT Bonanza	E-2710	N55764
D-EMBL	Piper PA-28-180 Cherokee D	28-5315	N7950N
D-EMBM	Piper PA-28RT-201 Arrow IV	28R-7918173	N2845G
D-EMBO(2)	Gardan GY-80 Horizon 180	157	
D-EMBR	Cessna TU.206F Turbo Stationair	01761	(N9561G)
D-EMBS	Reims/Cessna FR.172H Rocket	0275	
D-EMBU(2)	Piper PA-28RT-201T Turbo Arrow IV	28R-7931252	N2909N
D-EMBV	Fuji FA-200-180 Aero Subaru	242	
D-EMBW	Piper PA-28R-201T Turbo Cherokee Arrow III		
		28R-7703394	N47533
D-EMBY(2)	Cessna 172M	65860	N9916Q
D-EMCA(4)	Commander Aircraft 114B	14661	
D-EMCB	Piper PA-28-140 Cherokee D	28-7125520	N1849T
D-EMCC	Piper PA-28R-200 Cherokee Arrow II	28R-7235219	N5294T
D-EMCD	Piper PA-28R-200 Cherokee Arrow II	28R-7235150	N2872T
D-EMCG(2)	Reims/Cessna F.172P	2206	
D-EMCH	Piper PA-28-180 Cherokee Challenger	28-7305375	N55404
D-EMCI	Piper PA-18A-150 Super Cub	18-5549	N6968D
D-EMCL	Piper PA-28-151 Warrior	28-7415086	N9626N
D-EMCM	Gardan GY-80 Horizon 160D	166	F-BPAF
D-EMCN	Piper PA-38-112 Tomahawk	38-78A0324	N9693N
D-EMCO(2)	Piper PA-28-235 Cherokee	28-10365	N8817W
D-EMCP	Reims/Cessna F.172N	1678	
D-EMCR	Cessna TR.182 Turbo Skylane RG	00/94	OO-ADM
			PH-ADM
			"PH-NEL"
			PH-ADM, PH-AYC, N736YX

Regn.	Type	C/n	Prev.Id.
D-EMCS	Piper PA-28-151 Warrior	28-7415298	N9561N
D-EMCT	Cessna 182M Skylane	59492	N71089
D-EMCU	Piper PA-28-235 Cherokee	28-10366	N8818W
D-EMCW	Piper PA-28RT-201T Turbo Arrow IV	28R-7931285	N2967C
D-EMDA	Cessna 172E Skyhawk	50594	N2994U
D-EMDB(2)	Piper PA-46-350P Malibu	4622004	N9140F
D-EMDD	Reims/Cessna F.150K	0603	
D-EMDE	Cessna 172E	50596	N2996U
D-EMDF	Reims/Cessna F.172H	0715	
D-EMDG	Reims/Cessna FR.172G Rocket	0201	
D-EMDH	Reims/Cessna F.150K	0617	
D-EMDI	Reims/Cessna F.172E	50577/0022	(N2977U)
D-EMDK	Reims/Cessna F.172H	0713	
D-EMDL	Reims/Cessna FR.172G Rocket	0200	
D-EMDM	Piper PA-28R-200 Cherokee Arrow II	28R-7335225	N55384
D-EMDN(2)	SOCATA TB-9 Tampico	907	
D-EMDO	Cessna 172E Skyhawk	50595	N2995U
D-EMDP	Piper PA-28R-200 Cherokee Arrow B	28R-7135075	N5071S
D-EMDS	Reims/Cessna FR.172H Rocket	0290	
D-EMDW	Wassmer WA.52 Europa	26	
D-EMDY(2)	Cessna 172B	48053	D-ELGB
			N7553X
D-EMEC(3)	Piaggio FWP.149D	181	91+59
			D-ECEM
D-EMED(3)	Reims/Cessna F.152	1508	
D-EMEE(2)	Cessna 172N	71788	N5236E
D-EMEF(2)	Beech K35 Bonanza	D-5897	
D-EMEG(2)	Beech V35B Bonanza	D-10270	
D-EMEH(3)	Cessna 150A	59081	N6681T
D-EMEI	Zlin Z.526L Trenér Master	1155	OE-AGA
D-EMEJ	Dornier Do.27A-3	429	57+03
			GB+901
			LC+155
D-EMEK(2)	Piper PA-18 Super Cub 95	18-3433	96+13
			SC+340
			AC+521
			AA+521
			AS+521
			54-733
D-EMEL(3)	Pützer Elster B	016	97+09
			D-EDIF
D-EMEM(3)	Piper PA-28-181 Archer II	28-8290157	N82469
			N9530N
D-EMEP(3)	Piper PA-38-112 Tomahawk	38-78A0620	N4469E
D-EMER	Piper J-3C-85 Cub	13210	HB-OCB
			45-4470
D-EMES(2)	Piper PA-28R-201T Turbo Arrow III	28R-7803214	N6258C
D-EMEV(2)	Gardan GY-80 Horizon 160D	221	F-BRLS
D-EMEX(2)	SOCATA MS.880B Rallye-Club	1921	F-BTIJ
D-EMEY	Piper PA-28-161 Warrior II	28-7716186	N5612V
D-EMFA	Morane-Saulnier MS.885 Super Rallye	5135	
D-EMFB	Robin HR.100/210D Safari	190	
D-EMFE	Beech V35B Bonanza	D-10263	
D-EMFF	SOCATA MS.893E Rallye 180GT Gaillard	12739	F-GAFL
D-EMFG(3)	Cessna P210N Pressurized Centurion II	00458	N731GW
D-EMFJ	Piper PA-28-236 Dakota	28-8011027	N81170
D-EMFK	Piper PA-28-181 Cherokee Archer II	28-7890428	N9566N
D-EMFL	Reims/Cessna F.150M	1298	
D-EMFM(2)	Cessna 152	79655	N757DK
D-EMFN	Diamond DA.20-A1 Katana	10165	
D-EMFP	Piper PA-28RT-201 Arrow IV	28R-8118058	N8354A
D-EMFR	Cessna 172P	74651	N52980
D-EMFS	Reims/Cessna F.150G	0174	(OH-CER)
D-EMFU	Bölkow BO.208C Junior	574	
D-EMFX	SOCATA TB-9 Tampico Club	932	
D-EMFY(2)	Reims/Cessna F.172N	1606	
D-EMGA	SAN Jodel D.140C Mousquetaire III	114	F-BKSZ
D-EMGB	Piper PA-18A-150 Super Cub	18-4466	PH-AAS
	(Rebuilt using spare fuselage no.18-8017)		G-APYR
			N2999P
D-EMGC	Mooney M 20K Model 231	25-0409	
D-EMGG	Piper PA-28-181 Archer II	28-7990387	N2245Y
D-EMGH	SAN Jodel DR.1050 Sicile	480	
D-EMGI(2)	Mooney M.20M TLS	27-0256	N2156F
D-EMGK	HOAC DV-20 Katana	20140	

Regn.	Type	C/n	Prev.Id.
D-EMGL	Cessna 182S	80385	
D-EMGM	Wassmer WA.52 Europa	32	
D-EMGO	Reims/Cessna F.172H	0440	
D-EMGR	Cessna 182J Skylane	57058	N2958F
D-EMGS	Piper PA-28R-200 Cherokee Arrow II	28R-7335421	N56365
D-EMGW	Reims/Cessna FR.182 Skylane RG	0024	
D-EMGY	Piper PA-28-140 Cherokee	28-20948	N6812W
D-EMHA(2)	Cessna 182Q Skylane	67287	(D-ESAH)
			YV-180P
			N4665N
D-EMHB	Reims/Cessna F.172F	0152	N5054T
			D-EMHB
D-EMHC	Piper PA-18 Super Cub 95	18-3430	96+11
			AC+519
			AA+519
			AS+519
			54-730
D-EMHD	Bücker Bü.131 Jungmann	23	N131BJ
			HB-USL
			A-14
D-EMHE	Mooney M.20E Super 21	719	
D-EMHF	Mooney M.20E Super 21	670004	
D-EMHG	Grässer Viking Dragonfly	001	
D-EMHH(2)	Cessna 172RG Cutlass	0198	G-OIFR
			G-BHJG
			N6529R
D-EMHI	Piper PA-18-180 Super Cub	18-8245	N5995Z
D-EMHJ	Cessna T.210N Turbo Centurion II	63564	N7346A
D-EMHL	Rockwell Commander 114B	14151	N4821W
D-EMHM	Cessna T.210M Turbo Centurion	62746	N6331B
D-EMHN	Klemm Kl.35D	1842	SE-BPL
			Fv5065
D-EMHO(2)	Mooney M.20J Model 201	24-1002	(N3991H)
D-EMHP	Robin R.1180TD Aiglon	238	
D-EMHR	Rockwell Commander 114	14082	N1205J
D-EMHS(3)	Cessna 177B Cardinal	01687	N34169
D-EMHW	Piper PA-28R-201 Cherokee Arrow III	28R-7737125	N38975
D-EMIA	Morane-Saulnier MS.885 Super Rallye	53	F-BKEV
D-EMIB(2)	Beech A36 Bonanza	E-1578	
D-EMIE(2)	Piper PA-46-310P Malibu	46-8508057	N4391S
D-EMIF(2)	Reims/Cessna F.150H	0125	
D-EMIG	Focke-Wulf FW.44J Stieglitz	2293	SE-BXO
			Fv625
D-EMIH	Dornier Do.27Q-5	2027	
D-EMIK(2)	Robin DR.400/140B Major	1107	
D-EMIL(4)	Focke-Wulf FW.44J Stieglitz	unkn	D-EMIL(2)
			(D-EKNE)
			(D-EKXG)
			SE-BXG
			Fv662
D-EMIM(2)	Extra EA.300	03	G-OHIM
			D-EBTS
			G-OHIM
			D-EBTS
D-EMIO(3)	Champion 7FC Tri-Traveler	455	D-EMIO(1)
			N9923Y
D-EMIP(2)	Robin DR.400/180R Remorqueur	1375	
D-EMIR(2)	Piper PA-28-180 Cherokee F	28-7105060	N3955R
D-EMIS(2)	Reims/Cessna F.172H	0335	
D-EMIT(2)	Cessna 182P Skylane	62063	N58439
D-EMIU	Cessna 182L Skylane	59133	N42675
D-EMIW	Piper PA-24-250 Comanche	24-1917	N6892P
D-EMIX(2)	Piper PA-32-300 Lance	32R-7780225	N1137Q
D-EMIY	Ströhle Aero Designs Pulsar XP *(Permit 4.99)*	AB431	
	(C/n formerly quoted as 1839)		
D-EMIZ(3)	Aerotek Pitts S-1S	1-0028	YV-24P
			YV-TAPA
D-EMJB(2)	Cessna 172N	69627	N737RY
D-EMJF	SOCATA MS.893A Rallye Commodore 180	12069	(D-ENMC)
D-EMJH(2)	Robin DR.400/180 Régent	2324	
D-EMJI	SOCATA MS.893A Rallye Commodore 180	12061	
D-EMJK	SOCATA MS.893A Rallye Commodore 180	12071	F-BUGB
			(D-ENME(2))
D-EMJN(2)	HOAC DV-20 Katana	20155	

Regn.	Type	C/n	Prev.Id.
D-EMJP	Piper PA-18 Super Cub 95	18-3199	D-EABS(2)
			OL-L03
			L-125
			53-4799
D-EMJR	Great Lakes 2T-1A-2	0786	N3818F
D-EMJT	SOCATA TB-20 Trinidad	711	
D-EMKA(3)	Dornier Do.27B-1	152	55+32
			PG+216
			PF+108
			PD+103
D-EMKB	Hirth Hi-27 Akrostar Mk.II	4001	
D-EMKC	Piper PA-28R-201T Turbo Cherokee Arrow III		
		28R-7703247	N47696
D-EMKD	Cessna T.210L Turbo Centurion	61110	N2149S
D-EMKE(3)	Reims/Cessna F.182Q Skylane	0115	PH-AYN
D-EMKG	SOCATA TB-20 Trinidad	705	
D-EMKH(2)	Beech F33A Bonanza	CE-1341	
D-EMKI (2)	Beech 77 Skipper	WA-94	
D-EMKJ	Mooney M.20C Mark 21	2550	HB-DEC
			N6845U
D-EMKK(2)	Reims/Cessna F.150M	1380	
D-EMKL	Robin DR.400/180R Remorqueur	2187	F-WZZX
D-EMKO(3)	Cessna 172P	75371	N62985
D-EMKP(2)	Krause Light Aero Avid Flyer	682-AB	
D-EMKR	Wassmer WA.52 Europa	59	
D-EMKS	Reims/Cessna F.182Q Skylane II	0054	
D-EMKU	Binder CP.301S Smaragd	103	
D-EMKV	Reims/Cessna F.172N	1559	
D-EMKW	Piper PA-32-300 Cherokee Six B	32-40683	N4246R
D-EMKY	Binder CP.301S Smaragd	104	
D-EMLA	Kibler Piel CP.301E Emeraude	AB.425	
D-EMLB	Reims/Cessna F.172N	1580	
D-EMLD	Robin DR.400/180R Remorqueur	1494	
D-EMLE(2)	Piper PA-18-150 Super Cub	nil	(RBAF)
	(Built from spare fuselage no.18-4912)		
D-EMLG	Reims/Cessna F.172H	0565	D-EBCG
			OY-AGJ
D-EMLH	Piper PA-28-181 Archer II	28-8090015	N2971Q
D-EMLI	Cessna 182S	80645	
D-EMLL	Mooney M.20K Model 231	25-0699	N1169D
D-EMLO	Cessna 172C	48744	N8244X
D-EMLR	Pilatus P.2-05	25	U-105
			A-105
D-EMLS	Cessna T.210L Turbo Centurion	60094	(G-BCCJ)
			N59107
D-EMLT	Cessna R.172K Hawk XP	2495	N736FQ
D-EMLW	Beech A24R Sierra	MC-81	OY-AJD
			N9729Q
D-EMLY	Piper PA-18 Super Cub 95	18-7235	N3295Z
D-EMLZ	Zeddies Skystar Kitfox V *(Reservation 3.99)*	S9502-0105	(D-ESLZ)
D-EMMA	Piper PA-18-150 Super Cub	18-6466	
D-EMMB(2)	Piper PA-28-181 Archer II	2890051	N9133N
D-EMMC	SOCATA MS.880B Rallye Club	1254	
D-EMMD	SOCATA MS.893A Rallye Commodore 180	10930	
D-EMME	Piper PA-18-150 Super Cub	18-5107	N6985B
D-EMMF(2)	Piper PA-46-350P Malibu	4622103	OY-JEU
			N9197F
D-EMMG	SAN Jodel DR.1050 Ambassadeur	371	
D-EMMH	Reims/Cessna F.172N	0528	
D-EMMI (3)	Focke-Wulf FW.44J Stieglitz	unkn	D-ECAN
			SE-BWN
			Fv667
D-EMMJ(2)	Piper PA-28R-180 Cherokee Arrow	28R-30580	D-ELRF
			N4680J
D-EMMK(2)	Mooney M.20J Model 201	24-1260	N1157S
D-EMML(3)	Mooney M.20K Model 252	25-1153	HB-DHC
D-EMMM	Fuji FA-200-160 Aero Subaru	154	
D-EMMN	Cessna 210H	59001	(G-AWGI)
			N6101F
D-EMMO(3)	Cessna 182R Skylane	67964	N9565H
D-EMMP	Morane-Saulnier MS.880B Rallye Club	72	F-BKDZ
D-EMMQ	Laverda F.8L Falco IV	415	
D-EMMR	Laverda F.8L Falco IV	420	

Regn.	Type	C/n	Prev.Id.
D-EMMS	Cessna 185 Skywagon	0163	TJ-ADG
			TR-LKK
			F-OBVB
			N9963X
D-EMMT	Reims/Cessna F.172F	0148	
D-EMMU(2)	Piper PA-28-180 Cherokee F	28-7105056	N5196S
D-EMMV	Piper J-3C-90 Cub	12837	D-EHAC
			HB-OGU
			44-80541
D-EMMW	Piper PA-32-300 Cherokee Six C	32-40922	N5225S
D-EMMX(2)	Maule MX.7-235 Star Rocket	10057C	N5GF
D-EMMY	Piper PA-18-150 Super Cub	18-7403	
D-EMMZ(2)	Mooney M.20J Model 205	24-3367	
D-EMNA(2)	Heier Rutan LongEz	448	D-EFAR(3)
D-EMNC	Tecnam P.92J Echo-VLA	004	
D-EMNH	Piper PA-38-112 Tomahawk	38-78A0355	N6249A
D-EMNL	SIAI-Marchetti SF.260	2-37	OO-ADF
			OO-HAQ
			I-SJAQ
D-EMNQ	Dornier Do.27B-1	305	56+30
			EA+384
			QM+613
			PL+412
D-EMNU	Beech A23-24 Musketeer Super	MA-36	
D-EMOA	Mooney M.20J Model 201	24-1652	
D-EMOB(2)	Cessna 172RG Cutlass	0523	HB-CNW
			(N5406V)
D-EMOC(3)	Mooney M.20J Model 205	24-3071	N205YY
D-EMOD(3)	Rockwell Commander 114	14421	(N5876N)
D-EMOE	Reims/Cessna F.172N	1984	
D-EMOF	Focke-Wulf FW.44J Stieglitz	ASJA-82	SE-CBE
			Fv630
D-EMOG(2)	Piper PA-32R-300 Lance	32R-7780247	N2429Q
D-EMOH(3)	Mooney M.20J Model 201	24-1599	
D-EMOI	Robin DR.400/180R Remorqueur	1392	
D-EMOJ	Mooney M.20J Model 205	24-3042	
D-EMOK	Höxter Aero-Jodel D.11A Club	AB.14	
D-EMOL(3)	Reims/Cessna FR.172F Rocket	0079	
D-EMOM(2)	Mooney M.20J Model 201	24-0990	(N3947H)
D-EMOO(3)	Dallach/Stevens Akro Diabolo 2	EB-002	
D-EMOP	Piper PA-22-125 Tri-Pacer	22-329	D-EMOL
			N1416A
D-EMOQ	Cessna 182 Skylane	33406	HB-CPI
			N5406B
D-EMOR(3)	Mooney M.20J Model 205	24-3058	
D-EMOS(2)	Piper PA-32-300 Cherokee Six D	32-7240103	OE-DRZ
			N5284T
D-EMOT	Piper J-3C-65 Cub	16842	N92380
D-EMOU(2)	Mooney M.20J Model 205	24-3172	
D-EMOV(2)	Reims/Cessna FR.172K Hawk XP	0660	
D-EMOW	Piper PA-18 Super Cub 105	18-7353	
D-EMOX(2)	Beech F33A Bonanza	CE-875	
D-EMOY	Piper PA-28-161 Warrior II	28-8016365	N8240G
D-EMOZ(2)	Niederdellmann Binder CP.301S Smaragd	AB.22	
D-EMPB	Robin DR.400/180R Remorqueur	825	
D-EMPC	Reims/Cessna F.152	1466	
D-EMPD	Rockwell Commander 114B	14431	
D-EMPE(3)	Mooney M.20J Model 205	24-3186	N9118X
D-EMPF(2)	Cessna 177RG Cardinal RG	1344	OO-RAD
			N53096
D-EMPG	Reims/Cessna F.172N	1692	
D-EMPH	Cessna 180K Skywagon	52979	N2537K
D-EMPI	Morane-Saulnier MS.885 Super Rallye	85	
D-EMPK(2)	Piper PA-46-350P Malibu Mirage	4636093	N92862
D-EMPL(3)	HOAC DV-20 Katana	20041	
D-EMPM	SNCAN/ Stampe SV.4C	159	F-BMKM
			CEV
			F-BFLH
			CEV
			F-BDKY
D-EMPN	Piper PA-28RT-201T Turbo Arrow IV	28R-7931254	N2915A
D-EMPO	Morane-Saulnier MS.885 Super Rallye	5143	(D-EMTO)
D-EMPR	Piper PA-28-181 Archer II	28-7990579	N2952N
D-EMPS	Piper PA-28R-200 Cherokee Arrow II	28R-7335180	N55103
D-EMPT	Reims/Cessna FR.172K Hawk XP	0629	

Regn.	Type	C/n	Prev.Id.
D-EMPV	Piper PA-32-301 Saratoga	32-8006041	N8200K
D-EMPW	Piper PA-28RT-201 Arrow IV	28R-7918114	N2164Z
D-EMQA	Reims/Cessna F.172E	50707/0037	(N3507S)
D-EMQE	Reims/Cessna F.172E	0056	
D-EMQI	Cessna 182G Skylane	55129	(OY-BJI)
			D-EMQI
			N3729U
D-EMQO	Cessna 210D Centurion	58369	N3869Y
D-EMRA(2)	Mooney M.20J Model 205	24-3195	
D-EMRB	Piper PA-38-112 Tomahawk	38-80A0008	
D-EMRD	Beech V35B Bonanza	D-10138	
D-EMRE	Piper PA-18-150 Super Cub	18-6237	N8579D
D-EMRF	Robin DR.400/180R Remorqueur	2071	
D-EMRG	Mooney M.20A	1444	OE-DMC
			N8173E
D-EMRH	SOCATA TB-10 Tobago	14	HB-EYU
			F-ODKC
D-EMRI	Cessna 172A	47638	N9838T
D-EMRK(3)	Cessna 172RG Cutlass	0780	N6610V
D-EMRM	Piper PA-28-181 Cherokee Archer II	28-7790030	N9643N
D-EMRO	Scintex Piel CP.301C Emeraude	518	
D-EMRP	Cessna 177B Cardinal	02363	N11736
D-EMRS	Reims/Cessna F.152	1511	
D-EMRT	SOCATA TB-20 Trinidad	452	
D-EMRU	Cessna 172	29004	OE-DBF
			N6904A
D-EMRW	Piper PA-28R-200 Cherokee Arrow II	28R-7235213	N5275T
D-EMRY(2)	Piper PA-28R-201 Cherokee Arrow III	28R-7737066	N5617V
D-EMRZ	Robin DR.400/180 Régent	718	
D-EMSA	Morane-Saulnier MS.880B Rallye Club	79	
D-EMSB	Cessna 152	81418	N49969
D-EMSC	Cessna 152	81440	N64829
D-EMSD	Reims/Cessna FR.182 Skylane RG	0053	(PH-AXP)
D-EMSE(2)	Cessna 172P	76280	N98346
D-EMSF	Zlin Z.142	0001	OK-078
D-EMSG(2)	Reims/Cessna F.152	1795	PH-CBE
D-EMSH(2)	Reims/Cessna F.152	1935	
D-EMSI	Morane-Saulnier MS.885 Super Rallye	129	
D-EMSJ	Reims/Cessna F.152	1787	PH-CBC
D-EMSK	Reims/Cessna F.172M	1340	(SE-GKH)
D-EMSL	Robin DR.300/180R Remorqueur	464	F-BRZR
D-EMSM	Cessna 150M	77389	N63551
D-EMSN	Cessna 150M	77564	N6164K
D-EMSO	Morane-Saulnier MS.885 Super Rallye	5127	
D-EMSP(2)	Reims/Cessna F.172N	1743	
D-EMSQ	Reims/Cessna F.152	1808	PH-CBH
D-EMSS	Cessna 172N	69915	N738EG
D-EMST	Piper PA-28-140 Cherokee D	28-7125141	N5587U
D-EMSU	Morane-Saulnier MS.885 Super Rallye	5170	
D-EMSW	Mooney M.20F Aerostar 220	22-0010	(D-EHTW)
			N9619V
D-EMSX	Cessna 172P	74630	N52893
D-EMSY	Morane-Saulnier MS.885 Super Rallye	165	(D-EMTU)
D-EMSZ	Cessna 172P	75049	N54759
D-EMTA(2)	Grob G.115A	8057	
D-EMTB	Reims/Cessna F.150H (Rotax engine)	0329	
D-EMTD(2)	Mooney M.20J Model 205	24-3279	
D-EMTH	Piper PA-18 Super Cub 95	18-1569	ALAT
			51-15569
D-EMTI (2)	SOCATA TB-10 Tobago	1608	
D-EMTJ(2)	Piper PA-28-161 Warrior II	28-8016061	N47TX
			N8082Y
D-EMTK(2)	Piper PA-28RT-201T Turbo Arrow IV	28R-8131039	SE-KGI
			N8305D
D-EMTM	Reims/Cessna F.150K	0535	
D-EMTN	Reims/Cessna FR.172G Rocket	0147	
D-EMTO(2)	Piper PA-28-181 Cherokee Archer II	28-7890547	N39635
D-EMTP	Robin DR.400/180R Remorqueur	1328	F-GBII
D-EMTT	Fuji FA-200-180 Aero Subaru	190	(D-EITT(1))
D-EMTU	Morane-Saulnier MS.885 Super Rallye	168	
D-EMTW	Piper PA-38-112 Tomahawk	38-78A0583	ZS-KHS
			N4381E
D-EMTX	Piper PA-28R-201 Arrow III	28R-7837173	ZS-KYV
			N6555C
D-EMTY	Morane-Saulnier MS.885 Super Rallye	5169	

Regn.	Type	C/n	Prev.Id.
D-EMUA	CEA Jodel DR.1050M-1 Sicile Record	630	
D-EMUE	SAN Jodel DR.1050 Ambassadeur	359	
D-EMUF	Eichelsdörfer Piel CP.301A Emeraude	AB.412	
D-EMUG(2)	Gardan GY-80 Horizon 160	91	F-BMUG
D-EMUH	Bölkow BO.208C Junior	623	
D-EMUK(2)	Beech V35B Bonanza	D-9986	
D-EMUL(2)	Cessna 120	11226	N76794 NC76794
D-EMUM(2)	Piper PA-18-150 Super Cub	18-7709158	N82464
D-EMUN	Cessna 175 Skylark	55239	N9439B
D-EMUP(2)	Piper PA-28-140 Cherokee D	28-7125047	N1731T
D-EMUR(2)	Sportavia-Pützer RS-180 Sportsman	6008	
D-EMUS(2)	Gardan GY-80 Horizon 160D	126	F-BMUS
D-EMUT(4)	Cessna 172R	80524	N9574D
D-EMUX(2)	Piper J-3C-90 Cub	11496	OO-DAA 43-30205
D-EMVB	Pützer Elster B	029	97+17 D-ELBU
D-EMVE	Morane-Saulnier MS.880B Rallye Club	5219	
D-EMVF(2)	Piper PA-46-350P Malibu Mirage	4622148	N1221K N9235X
D-EMVG	Gliczinski Neico Lancair 320 (Permit 11.99)	1852	
D-EMVI	SEEMS MS.880B Rallye Club	5312	
D-EMVP	"OMF-100" Homebuilt (Permit 9.99)	0001	
D-EMVR	Cessna 182Q Skylane	67132	N97560
D-EMVT	Arado Ar.79B	0047	D-ECUV(1) SL-AAP VA+HP
D-EMVZ	SOCATA TB-9 Tampico	1793	
D-EMWA(2)	Mooney M.20M TLS	27-0167	
D-EMWB(2)	Reims/Cessna 182P Skylane	0047/64338	N1463M
D-EMWC	Piper PA-28R-180 Cherokee Arrow	28R-30532	N4642J
D-EMWE(2)	Cessna 172M	66864	N1135U
D-EMWF(2)	Reims/Cessna F.172N	1587	
D-EMWH	Piper PA-28R-200 Cherokee Arrow	28R-35355	N3018R
D-EMWI	Reims/Cessna F.172E	50643/0033	(N3043U)
D-EMWJ(2)	Cessna 182S	80571	N7276Y
D-EMWK(2)	Cessna TR.182 Skylane RG	00703	N9407R
D-EMWL	Piper PA-28R-200 Cherokee Arrow B	28R-35706	N4986S
D-EMWM(2)	Mooney M.20J Model 201	24-0993	N3960H
D-EMWO	Oberlerchner JOB 15-150	056	OE-CAA
D-EMWP	Piper PA-28-140 Cherokee C	28-26820	N11C
D-EMWQ	Piper PA-28-140 Cherokee C	28-26819	N5992U
D-EMWR(2)	Beech F33A Bonanza	CE-1554	N8105X
D-EMWS	Piper PA-28-140 Cherokee D	28-7125170	N11C
D-EMWT(2)	Beech F33A Bonanza	CE-1529	
D-EMWU	Reims/Cessna F.172E	0043	
D-EMWW	Piper PA-28R-200 Cherokee Arrow B	28R-7135166	N2203T
D-EMWX	Piper PA-28-140 Cherokee D	28-7125389	N8590N
D-EMWY	Reims/Cessna F.172E	50739/0038	(N3539S)
D-EMWZ	Piper PA-28-235 Cherokee D	28-11377	N8574N
D-EMXB	Reims/Cessna F.172H	0623	
D-EMXD	CEA DR.253B Régent	158	
D-EMXE	Cessna 177 Cardinal	01149	N30249
D-EMXG	Reims/Cessna F.172H	0630	
D-EMXI	SIAT 223A-1 Flamingo	015	HB-EVL D-ENBL
D-EMXS	Maule MX-7-180 Star Rocket	11040C	N6115K
D-EMXX	Piper PA-32RT-300T Turbo Lance II	32R-7987091	N3051K
D-EMYC	Brillinger Jodel D.9 Bébé	AB.1	
D-EMYE	Beech 35-C33 Debonair	CD-913	
D-EMYF	Mraz M.1C Sokol	175	OK-UHE
D-EMYJ	Fuji FA-200-160 Aero Subaru	72	
D-EMYL	Piper J-3C-65 Cub	11740	HB-OSR 43-30449
D-EMYM(2)	Mylius My 102 Tornado (Permit) (Second prototype, formerly c/n V-2)	102	
D-EMYN(2)	SOCATA MS.893A Rallye Commodore 180	10619	
D-EMYP(2)	SOCATA MS.893A Rallye Commodore 180	10620	
D-EMYR(2)	Mooney M.20J Model 201	24-0527	
D-EMYS(3)	Mylius My.102 Tornado	V-1	
D-EMYT(2)	Beech 35-C33 Debonair	CD-1008	
D-EMYX(2)	SOCATA MS.893A Rallye Commodore 180	10624	
D-EMYZ(2)	SAN Jodel DR.1050M Excellence	191	F-BJNX
D-EMZB	Reims/Cessna F.172H	0618	
D-EMZC	Reims/Cessna FR.172G Rocket	0154	
D-EMZD	Reims/Cessna FR.172G Rocket	0157	
D-EMZF	Reims/Cessna F.172H	0667	
D-EMZG	Reims/Cessna F.150K	0537	
D-EMZH	Reims/Cessna F.150K	0579	
D-EMZI	Reims/Cessna F.172F	0166	
D-EMZO	SOCATA MS.893A Rallye Commodore 180	10569	
D-EMZY(2)	Piper PA-28-161 Warrior II	28-7816011	N40069
D-ENAB(2)	SOCATA MS.893A Rallye Commodore 180	11460	F-BSZE OY-DJW F-BNGV
D-ENAC(2)	SOCATA MS.880B Rallye Club	1699	OE-DHC D-EOVK F-BSVK
D-ENAD	Wassmer Jodel D.120 Paris-Nice	138	
D-ENAF(2)	Piper PA-32R-300 Lance	32R-7780304	N3314Q
D-ENAG(4)	Mooney M.20J Model 201	24-0234	N201HN
D-ENAI	Reims/Cessna F.152	1737	
D-ENAK(2)	Piper PA-28RT-201T Turbo Arrow IV	28R-7931097	N385A N9615N
D-ENAL(2)	Reims/Cessna F.152	1768	
D-ENAM(2)	Rockwell Commander 114	14008	N1908J
D-ENAN(2)	Piper PA-18 Super Cub 95	18-2072	R-61 52-2472
D-ENAP	Mraz M.1D Sokol	274	OK-DHO
D-ENAQ	Piper PA-18 Super Cub 95	18-7397	
D-ENAR(2)	Cessna TR.182 Turbo Skylane RG	01433	C-GTSN N4825S
D-ENAT(5)	Reims/Cessna F.152	1753	
D-ENAV(2)	Piper PA-28-161 Warrior II	28-7716106	(OO-FVP) D-ENAV(2) N9625N
D-ENAW(3)	Piper PA-28R-201 Arrow III	28R-7837143	N3947M
D-ENAY	Focke-Wulf FW.44J Stieglitz	unkn	D-EGAM SE-BWH Fv663
D-ENAZ	Stark Turbulent D-1	125	
D-ENBA	Cessna 210-5	205-0075	N1875Z
D-ENBB(3)	Piper PA-38-112 Tomahawk	38-82A0035	N91461
D-ENBC	Reims/Cessna F.172H	0373	
D-ENBF	Reims/Cessna F.172H	0524	
D-ENBG	Piper PA-28R-180 Cherokee Arrow	28R-30548	N4654J
D-ENBH	Piper PA-28R-180 Cherokee Arrow	28R-30556	N4660J
D-ENBI	Piper PA-18-150 Super Cub	18-7868	
D-ENBJ(2)	Piper PA-28R-180 Cherokee Arrow	28R-30675	N4939J
D-ENBL(2)	Piper PA-28R-200 Cherokee Arrow II	28R-7235235	N5494T
D-ENBM(2)	Piper PA-28R-180 Cherokee Arrow	28R-30678	N4941J
D-ENBO(2)	Piper PA-28RT-201 Turbo Arrow IV	28R-8031048	N3579K
D-ENBP(2)	Reims/Cessna FR.172F Rocket	0068	
D-ENBR(3)	Ruschmeyer R.90-230RG	021	
D-ENBU(2)	Piper PA-28-181 Archer II	28-8390034	N9630N
D-ENBW	Robin DR.400/180R Remorqueur	1715	
D-ENBY(2)	Champion 7GCB Challenger	7GCB-100	OE-ADN
D-ENBZ	Reims/Cessna F.150J	0429	
D-ENCA(3)	Beech V35B Bonanza	D-10134	
D-ENCB(3)	Reims/Cessna F.172N	1797	
D-ENCC(2)	Piper PA-18-150 Super Cub	18-1483	ALAT 51-15483
D-ENCD(3)	Reims/Cessna F.172N	1795	
D-ENCG(3)	Reims/Cessna FR.172K Hawk XP II	0637	
D-ENCH(3)	Piper PA-28-181 Archer II	28-8190164	N8295H N9518N
D-ENCI	Bölkow BO.208 Junior	511	(CS-ALX)
D-ENCL	Reims/Cessna F.172P	2227	
D-ENCM	Reims/Cessna F.182Q Skylane	0048	
D-ENCO(2)	Piper PA-28-140 Cherokee D	28-7125097	N1782T
D-ENCU(2)	Reims/Cessna F.172G	0307	
D-ENCW	Piper PA-28-140 Cherokee E	28-7225455	N11C
D-ENCY(4)	Cessna 177RG Cardinal RG	0069	N8069G
D-ENDC	Langer Brändli BX-2 Cherry	Eb 001	
D-ENDE(3)	Reims/Cessna F.182Q Skylane	0146	
D-ENDI (3)	de Havilland DH.82A Tiger Moth	82335	G-ANDI N40DH G-ANDI (G-ANDM), N9240

Regn.	Type	C/n	Prev.Id.
D-ENDK	Robin DR.400/180 Régent	1318	
D-ENDO(2)	Reims/Cessna F.172G	289	
D-ENDR	Cessna 172N	68804	N734EU
D-ENDS	Grob G.115A	8040	I-GROD
			D-EGVV
D-ENDT	Reims/Cessna F.150M	1171	
D-ENDY	Bölkow BO.208C Junior	520	
D-ENEA(2)	Cessna 182P Skylane	60895	N9355G
D-ENEB	Aeromere F.8L Falco III	201	
D-ENEC(2)	Piper PA-32R-301T Turbo Saratoga SP	32R-8129056	N8360A
D-ENED	Wassmer Jodel D.120R Paris-Nice	139	
D-ENEE(2)	Piper PA-28-181 Archer II	2890070	N4311Z
D-ENEF	Piper J-3C-90 Cub	6347	N35441
D-ENEG	Cessna 180 Skywagon	31463	N4564B
D-ENEH(5)	SOCATA TB-10 Tobago	1136	
D-ENEI	SOCATA MS.880B Rallye Club	1655	
D-ENEJ	SOCATA MS.880B Rallye Club	1660	
D-ENEL(2)	Cessna T.210N Turbo Centurion II	64002	N4755Y
D-ENEM(2)	Mooney M.20J Model 201	24-0492	
D-ENEN(2)	Robin R.3000/160	148	
D-ENEP(2)	Bölkow BO.208C Junior	619	
D-ENER(4)	Piper PA-28-160 Cherokee C	28-2392	VH-NER
			D-EMGU
			N5877W
D-ENET(2)	Piper PA-28RT-201T Turbo Arrow IV	28R-8131076	N8333A
D-ENEU(2)	Piper PA-28-161 Cadet	2841114	N9175Q
			N9646N
D-ENEW(2)	Cessna 182P Skylane	62589	N52412
D-ENEY	SAN Jodel DR.1050 Ambassadeur	145	F-BJNH
D-ENEZ(3)	Piper PA-28-161 Warrior II	28-8116207	N3998P
			D-ENEZ(3)
			(N8378B)
D-ENFA(3)	Reims/Cessna F.172H	0489	
D-ENFB(2)	Piper PA-46-310P Malibu	4608105	N9132B
D-ENFC	Piper PA-18-135 Super Cub	18-3830	R-140
			54-2430
D-ENFD	Reims/Cessna F.172N	1819	PH-AYE
D-ENFE	SAN Jodel DR.1050 Ambassadeur	381	
D-ENFF	Piper PA-28-161 Warrior II	28-8116075	N8291B
D-ENFH	SOCATA MS.893E Rallye 180GT Gaillard	12988	
D-ENFI (2)	Mooney M.20K Model 231	25-0217	N231FJ
D-ENFL	Grumman AA-5B Tiger	0310	
D-ENFM	Grob G.115A	8066	G-BRUR
			D-EHTA(3)
D-ENFO	Piper PA-18-150 Super Cub	18-7611	N3852Z
D-ENFP	Piper PA-28-181 Archer II	28-8190173	N8342U
D-ENFR	Cessna 172P	75499	N6286A
			(N694)
			N63937
D-ENFS	Cessna 172M	66396	N30MX
			N30MP
			(N80136)
D-ENFU	Piper PA-18-150 Super Cub	18-6588	N9282D
D-ENFY	Reims/Cessna F.172D	50303/0018	(N2703U)
D-ENGA(3)	Cessna 172RG Cutlass	0432	N4964V
D-ENGB	Robin DR.400/180R Remorqueur	1735	
D-ENGD	Grob G.115D Acro	82018	
D-ENGI (2)	Reims/Cessna F.150M	1314	
D-ENGK	Kälberer Viking Dragonfly Mk.II	01	
D-ENGM	Piper PA-28R-201T Turbo Arrow III	28R-7803327	N36515
D-ENGN	Cessna 152	80160	N24225
D-ENGO(2)	SOCATA TB-10 Tobago	934	
D-ENGR	Robin DR.400/180 Régent	1251	
D-ENGW	SOCATA MS.880B Rallye Club	1127	F-BPBI
D-ENGY(2)	Piper PA-28-181 Cherokee Archer II	28-7690338	N6107J
			N9581N
D-ENHB	Robin HR.100/210D Safari	212	
D-ENHF(2)	Mooney M.20J Model 205	24-3290	
D-ENHG	Robin DR.400/180 Régent	2004	
D-ENHK(2)	Piper PA-28-181 Archer II	28-8290135	N8209B
D-ENHL	Reims/Cessna F.150M	1258	
D-ENHR	Robin HR.200/100 Club	98	
D-ENHS(2)	Piper PA-28-181 Archer II	28-8490032	N4332D
D-ENHU	Cessna 182G Skylane	55099	N3699U
D-ENHV	Robin DR.400/180 Régent	2200	

Regn.	Type	C/n	Prev.Id.
D-ENIA	Cessna 150	17844	OE-AIP
			N6444T
D-ENIB	Aeromere F.8L Falco III	203	
D-ENID	Champion 7FC Tri-Traveller	105	HB-UAG
D-ENIE	Cessna 172N	71889	N5557E
D-ENIH(3)	Stinson 108-1 Voyager *(Reservation 4.99)*	108-1-1341	LV-NJH
			NC8341K
D-ENIK	Piper PA-12 Super Cruiser	12-1221	N2728M
D-ENIL(2)	Cessna 210L Centurion	60320	(N93256)
D-ENIM(2)	Robin DR.400/RP Remorqueur	1827	
D-ENIN	Stark Turbulent D	122	
D-ENIP	Mraz M.1C Sokol	267	OK-DHH
D-ENIS	Auster Mk.5	1812	TW473
D-ENIX(3)	Piper PA-28-140 Cherokee C	28-26640	N5811U
D-ENIY	Piper PA-28-161 Warrior II	28-8616026	N9095V
			(N162AV)
			N9640N
D-ENJA	Piaggio FWP.149D	024	90+14
			AC+434
			DD+394
D-ENJB	Wassmer WA.52 Europa	45	
D-ENJC	Wassmer WA.52 Europa	44	
D-ENJD	Robin HR.100/200B	128	
D-ENJH	Piaggio FWP.149D	077	90+59
			MC+381
			JB+392
D-ENJK	CEA DR.360 Major	641	
D-ENJL	Wassmer WA.52 Europa	46	
D-ENJM	SOCATA MS.892A Rallye Commodore 150	11877	F-BTJB
D-ENJN	Robin DR.300/180R Remorqueur	708	
D-ENJQ	Piaggio FWP.149D	042	90+29
			EA+391
			GA+391
D-ENJR	Piper PA-18A-135 Super Cub	18-3345	EI-125
	(Quoted officially with f/n 18-3300 as c/n)		I-EIKX
			MM537745
			53-7745
D-ENJU	SOCATA MS.893A Rallye Commodore 180	11970	F-BTJE
D-ENJW	Piaggio FWP.149D	069	90+52
			JA+389
D-ENJZ	SEEMS MS.885 Super Rallye	5361	OE-CDM
D-ENKA	GEMS MS.892A Rallye Commodore 150	10465	
D-ENKB	Piper PA-18 Super Cub 95	18-3193	OL-L19
			L-119
			54-4793
D-ENKC(2)	Cessna 152	83246	N47770
D-ENKF	Robin DR.400/180 Régent	693	D-EFEE(1)
D-ENKM	Heliopolis Gomhouria Mk.6	177	SU-341
D-ENKO	Cessna 150E	61021	OE-AYU
			N252IJ
D-ENKS	Cessna 172R	80136	
D-ENKT	Reims/Cessna F.150M Commuter	1357	PH-ENK
			D-EFAX
			PH-AYF
D-ENKU	Aero Commander 100	10A-128	
D-ENKW	Piper PA-28R-201 Cherokee Arrow III	28R-7737074	SE-GPV
D-ENKY(2)	Sportavia-Pützer RS-180 Sportsman	6007	
D-ENLA	Reims/Cessna F.150K	0575	
D-ENLC(2)	Piper PA-18 Super Cub 95	18-2033	R-36
			52-2433
D-ENLD	Reims/Cessna F.172H	0686	
D-ENLE	Reims/Cessna FR.172G Rocket	0152	
D-ENLF	Piper PA-18 Super Cub 95	18-1337	(G-BERU)
			D-ENLF
			ALAT
			51-15337
D-ENLH	Piper PA-18 Super Cub 95	18-1394	ALAT
			51-15394
D-ENLK(2)	Piper PA-18 Super Cub 95	18-1556	ALAT
			51-15556
D-ENLL	Piper PA-18 Super Cub 95	18-1578	ALAT
			51-15578
D-ENLM	Piper PA-18 Super Cub 95	18-1592	ALAT
			51-15592
D-ENLS	Robin DR.400/180 Régent	724	

Regn.	Type	C/n	Prev.Id.
D-ENLT	Robin DR.400/180R Remorqueur	725	
D-ENLU	Reims/Cessna F.150H	0220	N20220
D-ENLW	Cessna U.206G Stationair II	06858	N9418R
D-ENLY	Piper PA-28R-201 Arrow III	28R-7837211	N9608C
D-ENMC(2)	Mooney M.20K Model 252	25-1195	
D-ENMD(2)	SOCATA MS.893A Rallye Commodore 180	12073	F-BUGD (D-ENMG)
D-ENMI	Cessna 182F Skylane	54782	N3382U
D-ENMK(2)	Kempf Denney Kitfox IV-1200	1788	
D-ENMM(2)	Zlin Z.50LA	0027	HA-SIB
D-ENMR	SOCATA MS.893A Rallye Commodore 180	12072	F-BUGC (D-ENMF)
D-ENMT	Cessna 172P	75060	N54831
D-ENNA(3)	Reims/Cessna F.172G	0305	
D-ENNC	SOCATA MS.893A Rallye Commodore 180	10566	F-BNNC
D-ENNE(3)	SOCATA TB-9 Tampico Club	1132	
D-ENNF	SOCATA TB-9 Tampico Club	1134	
D-ENNN	CASA I-131E Jungmann	2026	D-EOII E3B-426
D-ENNO(2)	Piper PA-28R-201 Arrow III	28R-7837056	N6188H
D-ENNP	Piper PA-28-180 Cherokee Challenger	28-7305483	N55851
D-ENNR	Beech F33A Bonanza	CE-428	
D-ENNS(2)	Piper PA-28R-201T Arrow III	28R-7803013	N47762
D-ENNU(2)	Piper PA-28-161 Cadet	2841085	N9505N N9169Z
D-ENNY(2)	Piper PA-28-161 Warrior II	28-7716179	N9503N
D-ENOB	Aeromere F.8L Falco	206	
D-ENOC(2)	Reims/Cessna F.172N	1872	
D-ENOD	Cessna 172	36382	N8682B
D-ENOG	Menavia Piel CP.301A Emeraude	290	
D-ENOH(2)	Bölkow BO.209 Monsun 150FF	158	(D-EBJR)
D-ENOL(3)	Diamond DA.20-A1 Katana	10238	
D-ENOM	Aero-Jodel D.11A Club	AB.13	
D-ENON(2)	HOAC DV-20 Katana	20153	
D-ENOO	Cessna 182R Skylane	67733	N5462N
D-ENOP(3)	Mooney M.20K Model 231	25-0017	N4563H
D-ENOQ	Piper PA-24-250 Comanche	24-1557	N6893P (G-APZH)
D-ENOR	Cessna 140	11087	N76647
D-ENOS(2)	Piper PA-18 Super Cub 95	18-3156	OL-L78 L-78 53-4756
D-ENOT(3)	SOCATA MS.883 Rallye 115	1390	F-BRYC
D-ENOU	Neico Lancair	369	
D-ENOV(2)	Cessna 150M	78295	N9346U
D-ENOX(2)	Piper PA-28R-201T Turbo Cherokee Arrow III	28R-7703141	N5656V
D-ENPA(2)	Piper PA-28-161 Warrior II	2816005	N9107R
D-ENPB	Reims/Cessna F.172H	0598	
D-ENPC	Reims/Cessna F.172H	0600	
D-ENPE(2)	Robin DR.400/180 Régent	1590	(D-EFDX)
D-ENPF	Piper PA-28-181 Archer II	28-8290049	N8454E
D-ENPH	Pfeiffer Neico Lancair 320	1711	
D-ENPK	SOCATA MS.886 Rallye 160	1683	F-BTHQ
D-ENPL(2)	Rockwell Commander 114A	14509	
	(Built from Commander 114B airframe c/n 14441 ex N5896N)		
D-ENPR	Piper PA-28-181 Archer II	28-8090016	N2972G
D-ENPS	Piper PA-28-151 Warrior	28-7415324	N9571N
D-ENPW	Piper PA-28R-201T Arrow IV	2803008	N91832
D-ENPY	Piper PA-28-180 Cherokee B	28-1088	N11C
D-ENQA	Reims/Cessna F.172D	50227/0014	(N2627U)
D-ENQE	Reims/Cessna F.172F	0109	
D-ENQO	Piper PA-18-150 Super Cub	18-8202	N4135Z
D-ENQY	Piper PA-28R-180 Cherokee Arrow	28R-30677	N4940J
D-ENRA	Cessna 170B	26989	OE-DBB HB-COY N3446D
D-ENRB	Beech A36TC Bonanza	EA-74	
D-ENRD	SOCATA TB-20 Trinidad	1253	
D-ENRE(2)	Piper PA-46-310P Malibu	46-8608004	N9104P N9103M
D-ENRG	Piper PA-32R-301 Turbo Saratoga SP	32R-8129088	N8416T
D-ENRH	Aermacchi AL.60B-2	6243/63	
D-ENRI	Schriek Piel CP.301A Emeraude	AB.410	
D-ENRK	Piper PA-28-161 Warrior II	28-8016234	N9609N
D-ENRO(3)	Röllinghoff Dallach D4-ERI Fascination	D4-001	
D-ENRP	Cessna 172R	80076	N9850F
D-ENRS	Reims/Cessna FRA.150M Aerobat	0312	PH-YET (PH-AYL) D-EKDM N96069
D-ENRW	Cessna TU.206G Turbo Stationair II	04072	N756GD
D-ENRY	Piper PA-18-150 Super Cub	18-7323	N3487Z
D-ENSA(2)	Mooney M.20M TLS	27-0010	
D-ENSC	Gyroflug SC-01B Speed Canard	S-26	
D-ENSE(2)	Reims/Cessna F.172G	0296	
D-ENSG	LET Z-37A Cmelák	17-25	DDR-SSG DM-SSG
D-ENSO(2)	Reims/Cessna F.172G	0312	
D-ENSP	Cessna 172N	73602	N6506G
D-ENSR	Mayer Stoddard-Hamilton Glasair II-SRG (Permit)	2317	
D-ENST	Piper PA-28-140 Cherokee Cruiser	28-7725164	N9603N
D-ENSW	Piper PA-32R-301T Turbo Saratoga SP	32R-8129045	N8341A
D-ENSX	Piper PA-28-181 Archer III	2890220	N9250J
D-ENSY(2)	Piper PA-28-181 Cherokee Archer II	28-7790450	N3335Q
D-ENTB(2)	Piper PA-28R-201T Turbo Arrow III	28R-7803188	N3707M
D-ENTD(2)	Mooney M.20J Model 205	24-3048	
D-ENTE(5)	Reims/Cessna F.172N	1553	
D-ENTI (2)	Pallaske Denney Kitfox 4-1200 Speedster	KCS-142/1029	
D-ENTM	Piaggio FWP.149D	060	90+46 GA+401 AS+487
D-ENTO(2)	American AG-5B Tiger	10166	N1198T
D-ENTP	Piaggio FWP.149D	027	90+17 AC+403 DE+393
D-ENTS(2)	Piper PA-28R-201 Cherokee Arrow III	28R-7737124	G-BPDN N38959
D-ENUB(2)	Reims/Cessna F.172M	1379	
D-ENUC(2)	Ercoupe 415D	4718	OO-PTE OO-FIL OO-LXG PH-NCG NC94617
D-ENUF(2)	Cessna 172R	80002	N172SE
D-ENUI	Piper PA-18 Super Cub 95	18-2084	ALAT 52-2484 HB-CPF N5694A
D-ENUK	Cessna 172	28294	
D-ENUQ	Piper PA-18 Super Cub 95	18-7376	
D-ENUR(2)	Mattleuer PUL 10	1793	
D-ENUS(2)	Reims/Cessna F.172P	2160	
D-ENUT	Piper PA-18 Super Cub 95	18-7260	N3379Z
D-ENVA(2)	Zlin Z.43 (Reservation)	0023	D-ENDB(2) LSK-17
D-ENVI	Bölkow BO.207	283	
D-ENVM	CEA DR.250/160 Capitaine	73	F-BNVM
D-ENVO	Bölkow BO.207	284	
D-ENVR	CEA DR.250/160 Capitaine	77	F-BNVR
D-ENVU	Bölkow BO.207	285	
D-ENWA	Bölkow BO.207	287	
D-ENWB	Piper PA-24-260 Comanche C	24-4926	N9420P
D-ENWE(2)	Cessna 182J Skylane	57197	N3097F
D-ENWH	Cessna U.206F Stationair	02788	N35898
D-ENWK	Cessna U.206D Super Skywagon	1384	SE-FKZ N72374
D-ENWO(2)	Piper PA-18-150 Super Cub	18-2032	R-35 52-2432
D-ENWP	Robin DR.400/180 Régent	2339	
D-ENWS	Airconcept Vowi 10	76001 (002)	
D-ENWU(2)	Mooney M.20J Model 205	24-3099	
D-ENWW	SAN Jodel DR.1050 Ambassadeur	491	
D-ENXB	Piper PA-28-161 Warrior II	28-7716035	N1658H
D-ENXF	Piper PA-28-161 Cadet	2841299	N9205Z
D-ENXI (2)	Piper PA-28-161 Cadet	2841013	N9153X
D-ENXM	Piper PA-28-161 Cadet	2841295	N9204X
D-ENXN	Piper PA-28-161 Cadet	2841261	N9194N
D-ENYE	Bölkow BO.208C Junior	703	
D-ENYP(3)	SOCATA MS.880B Rallye Club	1121	

Regn.	Type	C/n	Prev.Id.
D-ENYR(2)	Cessna 172C	49253	SE-EAB
			N1553Y
D-ENYS	Aeronca 11BC Chief	1608	OO-TWM
D-ENYZ(2)	Gardan GY-80 Horizon 160D	151	F-BNQH
D-ENZA	Cessna 150C	59757	N1957Z
D-ENZE	Scheibe SF.23C Sperling	3501	
D-ENZI	Beech 23 Musketeer I	M-129	
D-ENZL	Piper PA-28-140 Cherokee Cruiser	28-7625216	N9577N
D-ENZM	Grob G.115B (Reserved as F-GNBI)	8010	
D-ENZO(2)	SOCATA TB-10 Tobago	1060	
D-ENZU	Piper PA-22-108 Colt	22-9524	
D-ENZY(2)	SOCATA TB-20 Trinidad	1184	
D-EOAB(3)	Piper PA-28-181 Cherokee Archer II	28-7790152	N5950F
D-EOAC	Dornier Do.27A-4	452	57+24
			PG+218
			PG+108
			QM+008
			KD+...?
D-EOAD	Dornier Do.27A-4	459	57+30
			PK+222
			PL+105
			QM+015
			KD+...?
D-EOAF	Wassmer WA.51A Pacific	36	
D-EOAG	Robin DR.300/180R Remorqueur	669	
D-EOAH	SOCATA MS.880B Rallye Club	1518	F-BRYI
D-EOAJ	Piaggio FWP.149D	028	90+18
			AC+409
			DE+394
D-EOAK(2)	Dornier Do.27A-4	481	57+47
			BF+951
			GB+374
			KD+139
D-EOAL(2)	Beech B36TC Bonanza	EA-301	N117FM
			N6454L
D-EOAO	Piaggio FWP.149D	003	90+03
	(Built from Piaggio c/n 327)		AC+426
			DC+393
			BA+393
			AS+478
D-EOAP	SOCATA ST-10 Diplomate	146	F-BTIQ
D-EOAR(2)	Piper PA-18A-150 Super Cub	18-3875	PH-WAR
	(officially quoted with c/n 18-3892 as c/n)		R-185
			54-2475
D-EOAT	Dornier Do.27A-1	319	56+39
			YA+903
			YA+003
D-EOBA	SOCATA MS.893A Rallye Commodore 180	10817	F-BPHV
D-EOBB(2)	Robin DR.400/RP Remorqueur	1810	
D-EOBC(3)	Reims/Cessna F.172N	1828	OY-BNJ
D-EOBD	Fuji FA-200-180 Aero Subaru	119	
D-EOBE	SOCATA MS.880B Rallye Club	1865	
D-EOBF	SOCATA MS.880B Rallye Club	1866	
D-EOBH	SOCATA MS.893A Rallye Commodore 180	11820	
D-EOBI	SOCATA MS.893A Rallye Commodore 180	11821	
D-EOBK	Reims/Cessna F.177RG Cardinal RG	00200/0036	(N.....)
D-EOBL(2)	Cessna 172N	73840	N5809J
D-EOBN	Fuji FA-200-180 Aero Subaru	125	
D-EOBO(2)	Reims/Cessna F.182Q Skylane	0092	OY-CBO
			PH-AXF
D-EOBP	Fuji FA-200-160 Aero Subaru	128	
D-EOBQ	Fuji FA-200-160 Aero Subaru	129	
D-EOBR	Robin DR.300/108 2+2	602	
D-EOBS	Robin DR.300/180R Remorqueur	606	
D-EOBU	Piaggio FWP.149D	138	91+17
			BB+395
			KB+115
D-EOBV(2)	Piper PA-46-310P Malibu	46-8508095	OE-KTA
			(D-ELUZ)
			N9127Y
			(SE-IOP)
D-EOBW	Piaggio FWP.149D	158	91+36
			AS+402
			AS+O90
			KB+135

Regn.	Type	C/n	Prev.Id.
D-EOCA	Piper PA-18 Super Cub 95	18-1481	D-EHCN
			ALAT
			51-15481
D-EOCB(2)	Cessna 152	84798	N4673P
D-EOCC(2)	Cessna 172N	70077	N738MD
D-EOCG(2)	Reims/Cessna F.172P	2205	
D-EOCH	Fuji FA-200-180 Aero Subaru	140	
D-EOCK	Fuji FA-200-160 Aero Subaru	142	
D-EOCL	Fuji FA-200-160 Aero Subaru	149	
D-EOCM(2)	Piper PA-28-181 Archer II	2890118	N9176P
D-EOCN(2)	Beech C24R Sierra	MC-770	N6188A
D-EOCO	SOCATA MS.893A Rallye Commodore 180	11843	F-BSZV
D-EOCP	Robin DR.300/180R Remorqueur	631	
D-EOCQ	SIAI-Marchetti S.208	2-24	
D-EOCR(2)	Cessna 172RG Cutlass	0115	N6207R
D-EOCS	Aero Z.131 (C-104)	213	HB-USY
D-EOCT(3)	Cessna 177RG Cardinal RG	1339	N53078
D-EOCU	American AA-5 Traveler	0018	(N5818L)
D-EOCW	Robin DR.300/180R Remorqueur	639	
D-EOCX	Robin DR.300/180R Remorqueur	643	
D-EOCZ	CEA DR.253B Régent	194	
D-EODA	Piper PA-18-150 Super Cub	18-5388	ALAT
D-EODB	SOCATA MS.892A Rallye Commodore 150	11845	F-BSZY
D-EODC	SOCATA MS.892A Rallye Commodore 150	10714	F-BOVF
D-EODE	SOCATA MS.883 Rallye 115	1565	F-BTHH
D-EODG	SIAI-Marchetti SF.260	111	OO-HID
			OY-DND
D-EODH	SOCATA MS.880B Rallye Club	1920	
D-EODI	SOCATA MS.880B Rallye Club	1910	
D-EODK	SOCATA MS.893A Rallye Commodore 180	11889	
D-EODL	SOCATA MS.893A Rallye Commodore 180	11890	
D-EODM(2)	Robin DR.300/180R Remorqueur	547	
D-EODN	SNCAN/ Stampe SV.4C	113	F-BCFY
D-EODO	Robin DR.300/180R Remorqueur	645	
D-EODR	CEA DR.360 Chevalier	652	
D-EODS	Wassmer WA.52 Europa	35	
D-EODT	CEA DR.253B Régent	198	
D-EODU	Robin DR.300/108 2+2	650	
D-EODV(2)	Reims/Cessna FR.182 Skylane RG	0069	
D-EODW(2)	Reims/Cessna FR.182 Skylane RG	0070	
D-EODY	Reims/Cessna FR.172H Rocket	0308	
D-EOEB	Morane-Saulnier MS.885 Super Rallye	12	F-BKEB
D-EOEC	Bölkow BO.209 Monsun 150FV	201	
D-EOED	Piper PA-28-140 Cherokee E	28-7225451	N11C
D-EOEG	Piper PA-28-235 Cherokee	28-10411	HB-OLG
			N8857W
D-EOEM	Reims/Cessna F.172N	1581	SE-GZL
D-EOEN	CEA Jodel DR.1050M-1 Sicile Record	623	PH-PEN
D-EOEO	Piper PA-28R-201 Arrow III	28R-7837079	N2281M
D-EOER	Reims/Cessna F.172N	1986	
D-EOES	SOCATA MS.894A Minerva 220	11873	F-BSXF
D-EOEU	Cessna 172R	80200	N9949F
D-EOEV	Cessna 172N	71153	N2091E
D-EOEW	Robin DR.400/180R Remorqueur	1465	
D-EOFA	Reims/Cessna F.150L	1005	F-BURC
D-EOFB(2)	SOCATA MS.880B Rallye Club	2481	F-BVLX
D-EOFC	Piper PA-28-180 Cherokee Challenger	28-7305332	N11C
D-EOFF	Cessna TU.206G Turbo Stationair II	03838	N4621C
D-EOFG	Cessna 210D	58225	OE-DFG
			N3725Y
D-EOFH	Reims/Cessna F.172P	2071	
D-EOFK	Reims/Cessna F.172N	1993	(D-EDFJ)
D-EOFL	Piper PA-28-181 Cherokee Archer II	28-7690376	N9595N
D-EOFM	Reims/Cessna F.172N	1988	
D-EOFO	Reims/Cessna F.150M	1210	
D-EOFP	Reims/Cessna F.172P	2095	
D-EOFR	Reims/Cessna F.172P	2101	
D-EOFS(2)	Grob G.115A	8039	
D-EOFU(2)	Reims/Cessna F.172N	1575	
D-EOFW	Piper PA-28-181 Archer II	2890096	N9154R
D-EOFY	Reims/Cessna F.172M	1051	
D-EOGA	Reims/Cessna F.172M	1317	
D-EOGB(2)	Piper PA-46-310P Malibu	4608070	N9131B
			N9593N
D-EOGC	Grob G.115A	8051	

Regn.	Type	C/n	Prev.Id.
D-EOGE(2)	Piaggio FWP.149D	125	91+04
			BF+413
			AS+012
			KB+102
D-EOGG	CASA I.131E Jungmann	unkn	E3B-576
D-EOGI	Dornier Do.27A-4	473	57+42
			EA+385
			KD+131 ?
D-EOGK	Cessna 172N	71511	N3338E
D-EOGN	Grumman-American AA-5 Cheetah (Permit 12.99)	0349	HB-UCI
D-EOGO	Reims/Cessna F.172M	1348	
D-EOGP	Cessna 172RG Cutlass	0545	N5481V
D-EOGS	Robin DR.400/RP Remorqueur	1808	
D-EOGU	Reims/Cessna F.172M	1346	
D-EOHA	Reims/Cessna F.172M	1420	
D-EOHB(2)	Maule MX7-235 Star Rocket	10065C	N6111S
D-EOHC	Reims/Cessna F.150M	1292	
D-EOHD	Piper PA-28-181 Archer II	2890116	N9152Q
D-EOHF	Robin DR.400/180 Régent	1397	
D-EOHG	Robin DR.400/180 Régent	1402	
D-EOHH	Reims/Cessna F.172N	1804	
D-EOHK	Mooney M.20C Ranger	20-1230	
D-EOHM	Cessna 172N	70905	N739YD
D-EOHO	Reims/Cessna F.172N	1519	
D-EOHP	SAN Jodel DR.1050 Ambassadeur	297	F-BKHB
D-EOHR	Cessna 152 Commuter	81123	N49051
D-EOHU	Reims/Cessna F.172N	1614	
D-EOHW	Beech F33A Bonanza	CE-1155	D-EBMB(2)
D-EOIA(2)	Robin DR.400/180R Remorqueur	2061	
D-EOIC(3)	Piper PA-28-181 Archer III	2843049	N9272N
D-EOII (2)	Piper J-3C-65 Cub	13113	HB-OII
			F-BFBC
			44-80817
D-EOIL(2)	Beech F35 Bonanza Reservation)	D-4305	N6606C
			C-GJRF
			D-EJRF
			C-GJRF
D-EOIR	Piper PA-18-150 Super Cub	18-8734	N4401Z
D-EOIT	Piper PA-28-180 Cherokee E	28-5647	N2556R
D-EOJA	Reims/Cessna F.172N	1534	
D-EOJC	Cessna 172P	74457	SE-IPO
			N52247
D-EOJE	Reims/Cessna F.172N	1537	(F-GASO)
D-EOJI	Reims/Cessna F.172N	1628	
D-EOJK	Kurz Klemm 25D	AB-1	
D-EOJM	Piper J-3C-90 Cub	22633	N4494M
			NC4494M
D-EOJN	Piper PA-38-112 Tomahawk	38-79A0528	SE-ICD
D-EOJO	Reims/Cessna F.172N	1551	
D-EOJT	Cessna 150L	75013	N10759
D-EOJU	Reims/Cessna F.172N	1635	
D-EOJX	Reims/Cessna F.150L	0738	
D-EOKA	Robin HR.200/100 Club	49	
D-EOKB(2)	Mooney M.20R Ovation	29-0122	
D-EOKC(2)	Cessna P210N Pressurized Centurion II	0134	N6005P
D-EOKG	Mooney M.20K Model 252	25-1213	OE-KMO
			D-EOWK
D-EOKI	Reims/Cessna FR.172F Rocket	0131	
D-EOKK	Cessna 152	81132	N49068
D-EOKL	Gardan GY-80 Horizon 180	246	
D-EOKM	Cessna 210N Centurion II	63426	N5422A
D-EOKO(3)	Reims/Cessna F.172N	1895	
D-EOKS	Christen A-1 Husky	1103	
D-EOKT(2)	Cessna 177RG Cardinal RG	1325	N53022
D-EOKU	Reims/Cessna F.150M	1389	
D-EOLA	CEA DR.315 Petit Prince	317	F-BPRD
D-EOLB	Cessna 172N	70813	N739UH
D-EOLC	Cessna 172RG Cutlass	0208	N6606R
D-EOLD(2)	Piper PA-28-161 Warrior II	28-8516030	N4390F
			N9531N
D-EOLE	Reims/Cessna 182P Skylane	0008/63838	(F-BOFU)
			N6790M
D-EOLF	Piper PA-28-235 Cherokee Pathfinder	28-7410010	N56564
D-EOLG	Cessna 182L Skylane	58630	N3330R
D-EOLH	Cessna 210N Centurion II	64220	N5479Y
D-EOLI (2)	Reims/Cessna F.182Q Skylane	0081	
D-EOLK	Robin DR.400/180 Régent (Permit 12.99)	2434	
D-EOLL(2)	Cessna 177RG Cardinal RG	1318	(D-EOKT)
			N52948
D-EOLM(3)	Cessna 172R	80125	
D-EOLO	Reims/Cessna 182P Skylane	0035/64092	N6077F
D-EOLP	Reims/Cessna F.182Q Skylane	0160	(OY-BNT)
D-EOLS	Robin DR.300/180R Remorqueur	555	
D-EOLT(2)	Beech B36TC Bonanza	EA-470	N2844B
D-EOLU	Reims/Cessna F.182Q Skylane	0086	
D-EOLV	Cessna 172RG Cutlass	0691	N6430V
D-EOLW(2)	Maule MX.7-180 Star Rocket	11050C	N6118L
D-EOLY(2)	Reims/Cessna F.182Q Skylane	0079	
D-EOLZ	Cessna 172RG Cutlass	0552	N5524V
D-EOMA(2)	Diamond DA.20-A1 Katana	10314	N644DA
D-EOMB	Reims/Cessna F.172P	2222	
D-EOMC	Reims/Cessna F.172L	0900	F-BTUX
D-EOME(2)	Reims/Cessna F.172N	1679	
D-EOMF(3)	Cessna 172N	68877	N734HY
D-EOMG(2)	Cessna 172N	70151	N738QH
D-EOMH	Cessna 172N	71876	N5472E
D-EOMI	Navion Rangemaster G	NAV-4-2479	HB-ESN
			(D-EBMY)
			N2479T
D-EOMK	Robin DR.400/180 Régent	1267	
D-EOMM	CASA I-131E Jungmann	2001	E3B-404
D-EOMN(2)	Cessna 172P	76594	N9638L
D-EOMO	Reims/Cessna F.150H	0375	
D-EOMP	Piper PA-28-181 Cherokee Archer II	28-7890124	N47721
D-EOMQ	Piaggio FWP.149D	051	90+37
			SB+211
			SC+401
			AS+478
D-EOMR	Reims/Cessna F.172P	2241	
D-EOMT	Cessna 152	83960	N6617B
D-EOMU	Reims/Cessna F.150H	0386	
D-EOMV	Cessna 152	84293	N5310L
D-EOMW	Cessna 172N	68110	N76064
D-EOMX	Cessna 172P	75304	N62587
D-EOMZ	Cessna 172RG Cutlass	1074	N9905B
D-EONA(2)	Piaggio P.149D	312	92+16
			AC+463
			AS+463
D-EONC	Piper PA-28-181 Archer II	2890122	SE-KIS
D-EONE	Reims/Cessna F.150J	0393	
D-EONH	Stinson L-5C Sentinel	76-3615 ?	(G-BNUM)
	(C/n unconfirmed, serial quoted as c/n)		N8035H
			N63485
			44-17328
D-EONI	Reims/Cessna F.172H	0590	
D-EONN	Reims/Cessna F.172N	1805	
D-EONT(2)	Cessna 152	81309	N49493
D-EONU	Reims/Cessna F.172H	0583	
D-EONW	Reims/Cessna F.182Q Skylane	0051	
D-EONX	Cessna U.206G Stationair II (Soloy)	05584	N5150X
D-EOOB	Reims/Cessna F.172N	1956	
D-EOOC	Reims/Cessna F.172N	1957	
D-EOOD	Reims/Cessna F.172N	1958	
D-EOOE	CEA DR.250/160 Capitaine	84	F-BOCE
D-EOOF(2)	Piper PA-18 Super Cub 95	18-1500	D-EOCE
			ALAT
			51-15500
D-EOOG	Reims/Cessna F.172N	1952	
D-EOOL(2)	Piper PA-28-236 Dakota	28-8311004	N8290Z
D-EOOM(2)	Cessna 172D (Permit 9.99)	49978	OO-MET
			N2378U
D-EOOO(2)	Cessna P210N Soloy	00439	N731CM
D-EOOP	Reims/Cessna F.152	1588	D-EOOO(1)
D-EOOR	Reims/Cessna F.172N	1973	
D-EOOS	SNCAN/ Stampe SV.4A	336	F-BCGC
D-EOOV	Reims/Cessna F.172N	1970	
D-EOOW	Reims/Cessna F.172N	1971	
D-EOOX(2)	Reims/Cessna F.152	1794	
D-EOOY(2)	HOAC DV-20 Katana	20064	

Regn.	Type	C/n	Prev.Id.
D-EOPA	Piper PA-18 Super Cub 95	18-1523	N8944
			D-ECEI
			ALAT
			51-15523
D-EOPC	Reims/Cessna F.182Q Skylane	0159	
D-EOPD	Reims/Cessna F.172N	1955	
D-EOPE	SOCATA ST-10 Diplomate	107	F-OCPE
D-EOPF	Piper PA-32R-300 Lance	32R-7780098	N8443F
D-EOPH	Cessna 172RG Cutlass	0652	N6389V
D-EOPI	Erco 415D Ercoupe	541	(D-EBUY)
			D-EBUP
			N87368
D-EOPK	Reims/Cessna F.182Q Skylane	0044	OY-BUW
D-EOPL(2)	Beech B36TC Bonanza	EA-517	N8217W
D-EOPM	Piper PA-28-181 Cherokee Archer II	28-7790104	N5944F
			N9516N
D-EOPO	Reims/Cessna F.172N	1609	
D-EOPR(2)	Cessna 182Q Skylane (Porsche)	66605	N95709
D-EOPS	Reims/Cessna F.152	1670	
D-EOPY	Reims/Cessna F.150M	1424	
D-EOPZ	Murphy Rebel (Reservation)	1926	
D-EOQA	Reims/Cessna F.150L	1124	
D-EOQC(4)	Cessna TR.182 Turbo Skylane RG	01656	
D-EOQE	Reims/Cessna F.172M	1188	
D-EOQF	Reims/Cessna F.172M	1189	
D-EOQG	Reims/Cessna F.172M	1191	
D-EOQH	Reims/Cessna F.172M	1192	
D-EOQK	Reims/Cessna F.172M	1199	
D-EOQL	Reims/Cessna F.172M	1203	
D-EOQM	Reims/Cessna F.172M	1211	
D-EOQP	Cessna 182P Skylane	63114	N7330N
D-EOQY	SNCAN/ Stampe SV.4A	468	F-GCCY
			EC-AYL
			F-BDBE
D-EORA	Reims/Cessna F.172M	1374	
D-EORC(2)	Piper PA-28-181 Archer II	2890132	SE-KIY
D-EORD	Reims/Cessna F.172N	1959	(D-EOOF)
D-EORE(2)	Reims/Cessna F.177RG Cardinal RG	0174	
D-EORF	Reims/Cessna F.172N	1954	"D-EOCY"
D-EORH	Morane-Saulnier MS.885 Super Rallye	47	D-EBRR(2)
			D-EMPU(2)
			(D-EMPI)
			(N2625S)
D-EORI	Cessna 210L Centurion	61343	
D-EORK(2)	Piper PA-28RT-201T Turbo Arrow IV	28R-8131017	N8284H
D-EORM	Beech A24R Musketeer Super	MC-65	HB-EWK
D-EORO	Piper PA-28R-200 Cherokee Arrow II	28R-7335306	N55894
D-EORP	SOCATA TB-9 Tampico	286	HB-EQO
D-EORR	Reims/Cessna F.172N	1814	
D-EORT	Cessna 172N	70994	N1426E
D-EORZ	CEA DR.250/160 Capitaine	100	
D-EOSA	Piper PA-28-181 Cherokee Archer II	28-7790189	N9535N
D-EOSC(2)	Kurz Udet U12K Flamingo Replica	01	
D-EOSD	Mooney M.20J Model 201	24-0598	N7201K
D-EOSE	Cessna U.206F Stationair	03293	N8434Q
D-EOSI	Wassmer WA.40 Super IV	27	HB-DCH
			F-BKCC
D-EOSJ	Reims/Cessna F.172N	1873	
D-EOSK	SOCATA ST-10 Diplomate	135	F-BTHA
D-EOSO	Reims/Cessna F.182Q Skylane	0064	
D-EOSR	Robin DR.400/180R Remorqueur	1575	
D-EOST	SOCATA MS.893A Rallye Commodore 180	12070	F-BUGA
			(D-ENMD)
D-EOSU	Cessna TU.206F Turbo Stationair	03298	N8439Q
D-EOSY	Cessna 182P Skylane	63184	OY-BIT
			SE-GGD
			N7403N
D-EOTA(2)	Grob G.115A	8047	
D-EOTB	Robin DR.400/180 Régent	1607	
D-EOTC	SOCATA TB-10 Tobago	1115	
D-EOTE	Reims/Cessna F.172N	1627	
D-EOTI	Reims/Cessna F.172N	1538	
D-EOTK	Piper PA-22-150 Tri-Pacer	22-2752	HB-OTK
			D-EFYV
			N2341P
D-EOTO	Reims/Cessna F.172N	1629	
D-EOTR	Piper PA-28-236 Dakota	2811022	N9156W
D-EOTT	Reims/Cessna F.172N	1816	
D-EOTU	Reims/Cessna F.150M	1383	
D-EOTW	Reims/Cessna F.172P	2088	
D-EOUC	Cessna 172R	80197	
D-EOUH	Cessna 182M Skylane	59392	OE-DUH
			OE-BUM
			N70848
D-EOUI	LET Z-37A-2 Cmelák	20-02	DDR-SWI
			DM-SWI
D-EOUK	Cessna 207 Skywagon	0008	HB-CUK
			N91009
D-EOUT	CASA I-131E Jungmann	2138	E3B-523
D-EOUV	Becker Binder CP.301S Mistral	AB.01	
D-EOVA	Reims/Cessna F.172N	1625	
D-EOVC	Cessna 182Q Skylane	66760	OH-CVC
			N96564
D-EOVE	Reims/Cessna F.172N	1636	
D-EOVI	Reims/Cessna F.172N	1701	
D-EOVL	SOCATA MS.893A Rallye Commodore 180	10717	F-BOVL
D-EOVO(2)	Reims/Cessna F.150M	1411	
D-EOVU	Reims/Cessna F.172N	1624	
D-EOVV(2)	Reims/Cessna F.172N	1940	
D-EOVY	Reims/Cessna F.172N	1520	
D-EOWA	Reims/Cessna F.172N	1724	
D-EOWB	Reims/Cessna F.172P	2164	
D-EOWC	Piper PA-28RT-201T Turbo Arrow IV	28R-8231008	N8454T
D-EOWE	Reims/Cessna F.172N	1729	
D-EOWF	Cessna 182P Skylane	61091	HB-CWF
			N7451Q
D-EOWH	Piper PA-22-108 Colt	22-9426	(D-EHVH)
			HB-OWH
			D-ENSY
			N5643Z
D-EOWI (2)	Reims/Cessna F.172N	1733	
D-EOWJ	SOCATA Rallye 180TD Galerien	3135	F-GBCO
D-EOWM(2)	Maule MX.7-180 Star Rocket	11047C	N6121Q
D-EOWN	Cessna 172RG Cutlass	0704	D-EIKP
			N6443V
D-EOWO	Reims/Cessna F.172M	1218	(SE-GKM)
D-EOWP	Piper PA-38-112 Tomahawk	38-79A0336	OY-BRR
D-EOWR	Cessna 210N Centurion II	64234	N5516Y
D-EOWS(2)	Mooney M.20J Model 201	24-1227	N1151L
D-EOWU	Cessna 172RG Cutlass	0675	N6413V
D-EOWY	Reims/Cessna F.172N	1696	
D-EOXA	Reims/Cessna F.172N	1705	
D-EOXC	Piper PA-28-181 Archer II	2890083	N9148N
D-EOXE(2)	LET Z-37A-2 Cmelák	16-01	DDR-SRE
			DM-SRE
D-EOXG	Dätwyler/Piper J-3C-100-D1 Cub	MDC-1036	HB-OXG
D-EOXI	Reims/Cessna F.172M	1419	
D-EOXO	Reims/Cessna F.172N	1708	
D-EOXQ	PZL-104 Wilga 35	107336	DDR-WRK
			DM-WRK
D-EOXR	PZL-104 Wilga 35	96324	DDR-WRA
			DM-WRA
D-EOXS	PZL-104 Wilga 35	96330	DDR-WRG
			DM-WRG
D-EOXT	Bölkow BO.208C Junior	570	HB-UXT
			D-EDMA(1)
D-EOXU	Reims/Cessna F.172N	1714	
D-EOXX	Bölkow BO.207	291	HB-UXX
			(D-EJYR)
D-EOXY(2)	LET Z-37A-2 Cmelák	19-03	DDR-SRY
			DM-SRY
D-EOYC	Piper PA-28-181 Archer II	2890210	PH-AEB
D-EOYE	Reims/Cessna F.172N	1752	
D-EOYH	SOCATA TB-9 Tampico	272	OE-DYH
D-EOYO	Reims/Cessna F.182Q Skylane	0087	
D-EOYS	Cessna 172N	69857	N214FR
			N214ER
			N738BV
D-EOYU	Reims/Cessna F.172N	1803	
D-EOYW	LET Z-37A-2 Cmelák	19-01	DDR-SRW
			DM-SRW

Regn.	Type	C/n	Prev.Id.
D-EOYX	LET Z-37A-2 Cmelák	19-04	DDR-SRZ
			DM-SRZ
D-EOYY	Cessna 172N Skyhawk	70143	N738PZ
D-EOYZ	LET Z-37-2 Cmelák	06-29	DDR-SNZ
			DM-SNZ
D-EOZA	SEEMS MS.880B Rallye Club	326	F-BKZA
D-EOZC	SOCATA TB-21 Trinidad TC	806	SE-KBB
D-EOZD	SOCATA MS.893E Rallye 180GT Gaillard	12529	F-BVZD
D-EOZE	Reims/Cessna F.172N	1716	
D-EOZH	Piper PA-28R-180 Cherokee Arrow	28R-30695	HB-OZH
			N4948J
D-EOZI	Reims/Cessna FRA.150M Aerobat	0335	
D-EOZL	LET Z-37A-2 Cmelák	12-21	DDR-SLL
			DM-SLL(2)
D-EOZN	Piper PA-28-140 Cherokee	28-25146	HB-OZN
			N7234F
D-EOZU	Reims/Cessna F.172N	1717	
D-EOZW	Aermacchi AL.60B-2	6267/87	
D-EOZX	LET Z-37A-2 Cmelák	19-02	DDR-SRX
			DM-SRX
D-EOZY	Dornier Do.27B-1	224	55+77
			PD+334
			PD+109
			PF+106
D-EOZZ	Binder CP.301S Smaragd	AB.25	
D-EPAA	Piper PA-28-181 Archer II	28-8490074	PH-JVT
			N43573
D-EPAB	Reiss Brändli BX-2 Cherry	002	
D-EPAC	Cessna TU.206F Turbo Stationair	03131	N8270Q
D-EPAD	Cessna 172N	69018	N734PY
D-EPAI	Piper PA-46-350P Malibu Mirage	4622122	N50MP
			(N48CK)
			N9227R
D-EPAK	DHC-1 Chipmunk 22	C1/0328	G-BDIC
			WD388
D-EPAL	Piper PA-28-181 Cherokee Archer II	28-7890054	N47335
D-EPAO	Piper PA-28-151 Warrior	28-7615121	SE-GLX
D-EPAP	Piper PA-28RT-201T Turbo Arrow IV	28R-8231004	N214CD
			N8448E
D-EPAS(2)	Piper PA-28-181 Archer III	2843080	N92854
D-EPAW	Zlin Z.42M	0065	DDR-WNW
			DM-WNW
D-EPBB	Cessna 150K	71458	N5958G
D-EPBC	HOAC DV-20 Katana	20005	OE-CDI
D-EPBM	Miny Aero Designs Pulsar XP (Reservation 2.99)	1850	
D-EPCD	Aviat A-1 Husky	1324	
D-EPCG	Güthoff Brditschka HB-207 VRG Alfa	207013	
D-EPCH	Schneider Zenith CH-601 HD Zodiac	6-1724	
D-EPCL	DHC-1 Chipmunk 22	C1/0137	OO-NCL
			G-AOUN
			WB689
D-EPCM	Piper PA-28-161 Cadet	2841335	N92043
			(N125ND)
D-EPCN	Piper PA-28-161 Warrior II	2816102	N9196X
			(HB-PNN)
D-EPCO	Cessna R.172K Hawk XP	2439	N736DF
D-EPDA	Diamond DA.20-A1 Katana	10255	
D-EPDB	Diamond DA.20-A1 Katana	10166	
D-EPDH	Grob G.115A	8022	LV-RTA
			LV-DML
D-EPDK	Extra EA.400	7	
D-EPDR	HOAC DV-20 Katana	20091	
D-EPEB	Beech A36 Bonanza	E-2731	TC-SMS
			N80287
D-EPEE	Cessna 182Q Skylane	67637	N5308N
D-EPEG	Slepcev Storch Mk.IV (Permit 9.99)	SS 51	
D-EPEP	Piper PA-28-181 Archer III	2890217	N92263
D-EPET(2)	Extra EA330/L (Permit)	02	
D-EPEW	Mooney M.20K Model 231	25-0170	N231DN
D-EPFS	Piper PA-28-161 Warrior II	28-8216051	N84570
D-EPFW	Reims/Cessna F.150G	0151	D-ENYQ(2)
D-EPGC	Cessna TR.182 Turbo Skylane RG	02018	OE-KEE
			D-EFIB(3)
			N6423T
D-EPGH	Piper PA-32R-301T SaratogAII TC	3257036	N41277

Regn.	Type	C/n	Prev.Id.
D-EPGS	Robin DR.400/180R Remorqueur	2167	
D-EPHB	Cessna TR.182 Turbo Skylane RG	00858	(D-EVAS)
			N737NC
D-EPHC	Beech A36 Bonanza	E-1773	PH-ASB
			C-FGYI
			N979P
			YV-1979P
D-EPHD	Pitts S-2A Special	K-0009	
D-EPHL	Piper PA-28-201T Turbo Arrow IV	28R-8631004	N9129Z
D-EPHM(2)	Stoddard-Hamilton Glasair II RG-S (Reservation)	1919	
D-EPHN	Robin DR.500 Super Régent	007	
D-EPHP	Robin DR.400/180 Régent	2244	
D-EPHS	Hell Denney Kitfox V	1839	
D-EPHW	Piper PA-28RT-201 Arrow IV	28R-7918005	N3066K
D-EPHZ	Piper PA-28R-201T Arrow III	28R-7803277	D-EGLA(2)
			N9766C
D-EPIA	Cessna 152	80580	N25299
D-EPIC	Cessna 172N	67785	N75530
D-EPIE	Piper PA-28RT-201T Turbo Arrow IV	28R-7931119	N2102V
D-EPIH	Bölkow BO.208C Junior	674	F-BPIH
			D-EGZG(1)
D-EPIK	Piper PA-32R-300 Lance	32R-7680107	N8352C
D-EPIM	SOCATA TB-20 Trinidad	1116	N200DB
			D-EALJ
D-EPIP	Cessna 177RG Cardinal RG	0362	N1962Q
D-EPIT	Aerotek Pitts S-2A	2015	N80007
D-EPIZ	Christen Pitts S-2B	5159	OH-TOM
D-EPJD	Sky Arrow 650TC	C006	N271SA
D-EPJH	Holland Aero Designs Pulsar XP (Permit 11.99)	1799	
D-EPJM	Cessna 172R	80336	D-EPRP
			N9525
D-EPJS	Beech A36 Bonanza Soloy	E-2997	N1067Z
D-EPKF	Holmholz Denney Kitfox IV	00001	
D-EPKH	Gieffers/Murphy Renegade Spirit 912	1636	(D-ERGB)
D-EPKN	SOCATA Rallye 235ED Gabier	13019	EL-WHS
			EL-AHS
			EL-SPC
			F-ODMB
D-EPKO	Piper PA-46-310P Malibu	4608017	N9101Z
D-EPLA	Wassmer WA.52 Europa (Permit 8.99)	62	OE-KLA
			HB-DCG
			(D-EGRJ)
D-EPLH	Cessna R.182 Skylane RG	00063	N757ZW
			N84W
			N757ZW
D-EPLK	Piper PA-46-310P Malibu	46-8608030	N68JT
			N62JT
			N9515N
			N9294A
D-EPLZ	Cessna 182S	80344	N2624L
D-EPMA	Mooney M.20M TLS	27-0147	N133PR
D-EPMB	Piper PA-18 Super Cub	unkn	
D-EPMC	Pitzer Aero Designs Pulsar XP (Permit)	1301	(D-EPMY)
D-EPMH	Beech F33A Bonanza	CE-1480	N55440
D-EPMI	Robin HR.200/120B	262	
D-EPMK	Cessna TU.206G Turbo Stationair II	05119	N4827U
D-EPMM	Piper PA-24-260 Comanche B	24-4456	N8995P
D-EPMS	Cessna TU.206F Turbo Stationair	02695	N33254
D-EPNR	SOCATA Rallye 235ED Gabier	12906	HB-EYR
			(YV-1444P)
D-EPOE	Piper PA-46-350P Malibu Mirage	4622180	N92581
			D-EPOE
			N9251R
D-EPOI	Extra EA.300	024	LN-ACN
			D-EDCM
D-EPOL	Cessna TR.182 Turbo Skylane RG	00990	N739CX
D-EPOS	American AG-5B Tiger	10078	N1194G
D-EPOT	Piper PA-28-236 Dakota	28-7911108	(SE-LDT)
			OH-POT
			N70WH
			N2089R
D-EPPA	Robin DR.400/180 Régent	2282	
D-EPPE	Piper PA-32-300 Cherokee Six	32-7640116	HB-PPE
			OE-DIT
			N4487F

Regn.	Type	C/n	Prev.Id.
D-EPPL	Piper PA-28-181 Archer III	2843044	N9268L
D-EPPM	Schulze Denney Kitfox Speedster	1686	
D-EPPN	Neumann Denney Kitfox IV-1200	KBS-081	
D-EPPP	Mooney M.20J Model 205	24-3292	
D-EPPR	Beech C23 Sundowner	M-2075	N2074K
D-EPPW	Mooney M.20K Model 231	25-0624	N1150Z
D-EPRA	Piper PA-36-310P Malibu (Permit 10.99)	4608055	N777PG
			N9580N
			N9119N
D-EPRE	Cessna P210N Pressurized Centurion II	00570	N731ZT
D-EPRK	Kehl Aero Designs Pulsar XP	01	
D-EPRL	Leveringhaus Capella XLS-TR	1746	
D-EPRO	Cessna 150M	76080	(D-ERLE)
			N66493
D-EPRW	Beech B36TC Bonanza	EA-521	
D-EPSA	Diamond DA.20-A1 Katana	10148	
D-EPSB	Cessna T.210L Turbo Centurion	60262	N31622
			YS-15C
			TG-JKH
			N93098
D-EPSC	Diamond DA.20-A1 Katana	10150	
D-EPSE	Lake LA-4-200 Buccaneer	919	SE-IUT
			D-EMAZ(2)
			N2804P
D-EPST	Grob G.115C2	82058	
D-EPTA	Röckeisen Avid Flyer Speedwing Mk.IV	313/1721	
D-EPTB	Maule MX-7-235 Star Rocket	10004C	N39TB
D-EPTC	Piper PA-46-350P Malibu Mirage	4636012	N92575
D-EPTL	Cessna 152	83947	N6547B
D-EPTP	American AG-5B Tiger	10173	N11986
D-EPTU	Cessna 150M	76423	N3214V
D-EPUD	Bölkow BO.209 Monsun 160FV (Reservation 10.99)	196	HB-UED
			D-EAIL(1)
D-EPUK	SOCATA TB-20 Trinidad	325	OO-RDL
			(D-EEKX)
D-EPUL	Robin DR.300/180R Remorqueur	513	F-BSJO
D-EPUT	Cessna 172M (Reservation 11.99)	62514	N13124
D-EPVA	Piper PA-28-180 Cherokee Challenger	28-7305352	N222MM
			N35286
D-EPWB	Binder Europa	1/149	
D-EPWC	Piper PA-28R-201T Turbo Cherokee Arrow III		
		28R-7703323	N43975
D-EPWE	Cessna 172N	72533	N5345D
D-EPWF	Cessna TU.206G Turbo Stationair II	03901	I- IPAE
			N7363C
D-EPWH	Homebuilt, type unknown (Reservation)	V-1	
D-EPWL	Beech F33A Bonanza	CE-1587	N8187Z
D-EPWM	Beech F33A Bonanza	CE-1712	
D-EPWP	Beech F33A Bonanza	CE-1654	
D-EPXP	Baumgartner Aero Designs Pulsar XP	1776	
D-EPZL	PZL-104 Wilga 35A	21960957	
D-EQAP	Cessna TR.182 Turbo Skylane RG	01179	SE-IXZ
			N756WL
D-EQAS	Beech V35 Bonanza	D-8390	N3750Q
D-EQAX(2)	Focke-Wulf FW.44J Stieglitz	1899	ZS-WRI
			D-EFUR
			Fv617
D-EQCA	Commander Aircraft 114B	14565	
D-EQCO	Cessna 172N	70723	N739QP
D-EQCT	Schneider Denney Kitfox Vixen 1200	FCV 008	
D-EQFA	Robin DR.400/180R Remorqueur	1470	HB-EQF
D-EQHB	Boeing Stearman A75N1 (Reservation 6.99)	75-5659	SE-AMT
			G-BAVN
			4X-AMT
			42-17496
D-EQIA	Robin DR.500 Super Régent	0003	
D-EQMF	Cessna 182Q Skylane	67051	HB-CCX
			N97302
D-EQMI	Robin HR.200/120B Super Club	273	
D-EQMS	Homebuilt, type unknown (Reservation)	007	
D-EQQQ	Cessna 172N	73670	N4725J
D-EQTT	SOCATA ST-10 Diplomate	116	HB-EQT
			D-ELEZ(2)
D-EQUI	Aquila A.210 (Reservation 3.99)	210-100	

Regn.	Type	C/n	Prev.Id.
D-EQUS	Luscombe 8E Silvaire	5651	G-BSHJ
			N2924K
			NC2924K
D-EQVA	Mudry CAP.10B (Reservation 6.99)	02	F-GNVA
			Fr.AF F-TFVA
			F-TFVQ
			F-ZWRM
D-EQWM	Maier FW.190 (Half-scale replica)	S-001	
D-ERAB	Piper PA-28RT-201T Turbo Arrow IV	28R-7931277	N2963A
D-ERAC	Piper PA-28-161 Warrior II	28-8116103	N83079
D-ERAD	Robin DR.400/180 Régent	2217	
D-ERAF(2)	Grob G.115E (Development a/c, Permit 1.99)	82085	
D-ERAG	Dallach D4/E Fascination (Permit 7.99)	EB010	
D-ERAL	Cessna 172N	71122	N2024E
D-ERAM	Mooney M.20M TLS	27-0097	N712D
D-ERAN	Zlin Z.143L	0014	
D-ERAP(2)	Piper PA-28-161 Cadet	2841311	SE-KEO
			N9268N
			(N9209B)
D-ERAS(2)	Piper PA-28-151 Warrior	28-7415284	N41584
D-ERAT	SIAI-Marchetti S.208	2-25	I- LARS
D-ERAW	Mooney M.20M TLS	27-0092	
D-ERAZ	Cessna 172N	72506	N5306D
D-ERBB	CASA I-131E Jungmann	unkn	E3B-347
D-ERBC	Kleitz Druine D.5 Turbi	85	
D-ERBE	Cessna P210N Pressurized Centurion II	00769	N6408W
D-ERBF	Reims/Cessna F.172N	1904	G-MOGG
			G-BHDY
			(LN-HOH)
D-ERBI	SOCATA TB-9 Tampico Club	1596	
D-ERBK	Cessna 172R	80393	
D-ERBM	Jodel D.117 (Built as D.11A) (Permit 8.99)	615	OE-ABM
D-ERBT	Mudry CAP.10B	15	Fr.AF: F-TFVI
			F-TESM
D-ERBW	Piper PA-28-180 Cherokee E	28-4761	N6351J
D-ERBY	Robin DR.400/180S Régent	2067	
D-ERCA	Rockwell Commander 114A	14500	N114BK
			N5884N
D-ERCC	Piper PA-38-112 Tomahawk	38-82A0013	N91358
D-ERCF	SOCATA TB-20 Trinidad (Reservation 10.99)	1924	
D-ERCH	Mooney M.20M TLS	27-0210	
D-ERCL	Steen Skybolt (Reservation 6.99)	unkn, see D-ERFK	
D-ERCM	Diamond DA.20-A1 Katana	10243	
D-ERCO	HOAC DV-20 Katana	20116	
D-ERDA	SNCAN/ Stampe SV.4C	599	D-EOWS(1)
			F-BDET
D-ERDB	Piper PA-28-180 Cherokee Challenger	28-7305284	N16563
D-ERDE	American AG-5B Tiger	10158	N1198E
			PH-MLE
D-ERDF	Beech F33A Bonanza	CE-1572	N8120N
D-ERDG	HOAC DV-20 Katana	20020	OE-V. .
D-ERDL	Cessna 150M	78768	N704PP
D-ERDZ	American AG-5B Tiger	10159	N1198G
D-ERED	SOCATA TB-9 Tampico Club	1609	
D-EREE	Cessna 172P	74041	N5281K
D-EREH	SOCATA TB-200 Tobago XL	1632	
D-EREK(2)	SAAB S.91B Safir	91343	SE-ITF
			(LN-HAI)
			RNoAF 57343
D-EREN	Cessna TR.182 Turbo Skylane RG	01019	N182RH
			N739ZJ
D-ERER	Remmers Acro Sport II	1506	
D-EREV	HOAC DV-20 Katana	20144	
D-EREW	Cessna P210N Pressurized Centurion II / Soloy	00669	HB-CQG
			N5284W
D-ERFB	Piper PA-28-181 Archer II	28-8490001	N4317M
D-ERFD	Beech G35 Bonanza	D-4776	HB-EFD
			F-DAFB
D-ERFK	Kopsieker Steen Skybolt	K 01	
	(Quoted with same Type No. L.1869 as D-ERCL, same acft?)		
D-ERFL	Mooney M.20J Model 205	24-3206	N91VR
			N12WA
			D-EKJH(1)
			N12WA
D-ERFS	Mooney M.20J Model 201	24-1176	N1142U

Regn.	Type	C/n	Prev.Id.
D-ERFU	Mooney M.20M TLS	27-0089	
D-ERGO	Robin DR.400/160D Chevalier	2024	
D-ERGR	CASA I-131E Jungmann	2010	E3B-406
D-ERGS	Beech F33A Bonanza	CE-1758	N80639
D-ERHA	Mooney M.20R Ovation	29-0054	
D-ERHE	SOCATA TB-20 Trinidad	432	F-GDQK
			F-ODQK
D-ERHG	Beech F33A Bonanza	CE-1507	N67HG
			D-EARY(2)
D-ERHH	Piper J-3F-50 Cub	1997	OY-AIS
			(SE-AIS)
D-ERHK	Beech F33A Bonanza	CE-1608	N8235W
D-ERHM	SOCATA TB-10 Tobago	1747	
D-ERHN	Piper PA-28RT-201 Arrow IV	28R-8218007	N84571
D-ERHS	SOCATA TB-20 Trinidad	584	F-GJAL
			N103J
D-ERHV	Hassler Denney Kitfox III	758	
D-ERIA	Robin DR.400/200R Remo 200	2205	
D-ERIC	Piper PA-28-140 Cherokee	28-21907	C-GEXM
			N7193R
D-ERIF	Piper PA-28RT-201T Turbo Arrow IV	28R-8131163	N8411Y
D-ERIK	Jodel D.119	1243	OE-ACZ
D-ERIM	Mooney M.20M TLS	27-0198	
D-ERJA	Beech C23 Sundowner	M-2136	N6015W
D-ERJC	SOCATA TB-200 Tobago XL	1630	
D-ERJM	SOCATA TB-10 Tobago	1731	
D-ERKA	Reims/Cessna F.172N	1870	N5189D
			D-EFOS(1)
D-ERKB	Piper PA-28-181 Archer II	28-8190293	OH-PDN
			SE-ILC
D-ERKF	Dudeck Denney Kitfox 4-1200	1757	
D-ERKH	Heumann Aero Designs Pulsar XP (Permit)	001	
D-ERKK	Murphy Rebel (Reservation)	1908	
D-ERKM	Zlin Z.142	0526	OK-VNG
D-ERKP	Reims/Cessna F.150G	0140	OE-AVO
D-ERKR	Roth Van's RV-4	3614	
D-ERKW	Aero Designs Pulsar XP (Permit 10.99)	1907	
D-ERKY	Piper PA-28RT-201T Turbo Arrow IV	28R-8031068	LX-SKY
			N81623
D-ERLA	SNCAN/ Stampe SV.4C	101	D-EBHL(2)
			F-BBVA
D-ERLB	Cessna T.182 Turbo Skylane	67773	(D-EGRR)
			SE-IHU
			N5531N
D-ERLE(2)	Diamond DA.20-A1 Katana	10231	
D-ERLH	Grob G.115C2	82058/C2	(D-EPST)
D-ERLO	Oberbach Van's RV-6	002	
	(C/n formerly quoted as 1871)		
D-ERLP	Funke Denney Kitfox III	1028	
D-ERLR	Beech F33A Bonanza	CE-1565	N8233X
D-ERMA	Beech V35B Bonanza	D-10053	N235Y
			N18389
D-ERMB	Beech F33A Bonanza	CE-1500	N150RM
D-ERMH	Zlin Z.42MU	0019	DDR-WMH
			DM-WMH
D-ERMI	Piper PA-28RT-201T Turbo Arrow III	28R-7803247	N9264C
D-ERML	Langer MX1 Solitär (Permit)	1/1998	
D-ERMO	Diamond DA.20-A1 Katana	10099	C-FDVK
D-ERMR	Cessna 172P	74404	N52066
D-ERNA	SOCATA TB-200 Tobago XL	1612	
D-ERNI (2)	SOCATA TB-9 Tampico Club	1647	
D-EROB	SNCAN/ Stampe SV.4C	151	D-ECDI (2)
			F-BNDI
			Fr.AF/CEV
D-EROC	HOAC DV-20 Katana	20090	
D-EROG	American AG-5B Tiger	10115	N1196Z
D-EROH	Cessna 182R Skylane	68155	OH-CTR
			G-BOPF
			N9984H
D-EROK	Diamond DA.20-A1 Katana	10155	
D-EROL	Zlin Z.143L	0026	
D-EROM	Cessna T.182 Turbo Skylane	68517	G-BRFV
			N9418X
D-ERON	SOCATA TB-20 Trinidad	1441	F-GLFN
D-EROP	Amann Europa	240.0	

Regn.	Type	C/n	Prev.Id.
D-EROS	Piper PA-28-161 Warrior II	28-8116181	N8352P
D-EROW	Cessna 172R	80328	
D-EROY	Mooney M.20M TLS	27-0154	
D-ERPA(2)	Beech F33A Bonanza	CE-1452	HB-KCU
D-ERPC	Cessna 152	80733	N25565
D-ERPE	Reims/Cessna F.172N	1979	D-EIYZ
D-ERPH	Cessna 172N	71171	N2159E
D-ERPI	Cessna U.206G Stationair II (Reservation)	03596	SE-GUF
			N7272N
D-ERPL	Cessna 172P	74722	N53328
D-ERPS	Poth Pottier P.220S	1849	
D-ERPW	Cessna 182Q Skylane	67212	N61PG
			N97827
D-ERRA	Cessna 182Q Skylane	67254	N97957
D-ERRE	Rengers Aero Designs Pulsar XP (Permit 10.99)	402	
D-ERRI	American AG-5B Tiger	10092	N1195D
D-ERRK	Beech A36 Bonanza	E-2913	N1565F
D-ERRN	Aero Designs Pulsar XP (Permit 12.99)	007	
D-ERRO	Piper PA-28R-201 Arrow IV	2844005	N92698
D-ERRR	Cessna P210N Pressurized Centurion II	00227	N4590K
D-ERRS	Neico Lancair 320	1795	
D-ERRV	Van's (Reservation - Type unconfirmed)	2293	
D-ERSA	Piper PA-28-161 Warrior II	28-7816189	N9736K
D-ERSB	Piper PA-28-161 Warrior II	28-8016122	N8115V
D-ERSE	Cessna 172P	75559	OH-COB
			N64422
D-ERSO	Mooney M.20J Model 201	24-1672	N224DM
D-ERSS	Piper PA-28-181 Archer II	2890076	OH-PSS
D-ERST	SOCATA TB-9 Tampico Club	1295	
D-ERTB	Cessna 177RG Cardinal RG	0962	N303RN
D-ERTI	Cessna 182Q Skylane	66337	N759XH
D-ERTY(2)	DHC-1 Chipmunk 22	C1/0718	G-BDCB
			(D-E . . .)
			G-BDCB
			WP835
D-ERUG	PZL-150 Koliber 150	3900042	SE-KUG
			(SE-KUO)
			(G- . . . .)
			PH-BIJ
D-ERUV	Focke-Wulf FW.44J Stieglitz (Reservation 9.99)	"666"	Fv666
	(Swedish serial quoted as c/n, true c/n unknown)		
D-ERVB	Zlin Z.143L	0012	
D-ERWA	Piper PA-28-181 Archer II	28-8590078	N2491Y
D-ERWB	Piper PA-46-350P Malibu Mirage	4622125	N192PM
			N9223R
D-ERWE	Mooney M.20R Ovation	29-0011	
D-ERWF	Commander Aircraft 114B	14580	
D-ERWH	Homebuilt, type unknown (Reservation)	000	
D-ERWK	HOAC DV-20 Katana	20051	
D-ERWM	Cessna 172M	64449	N9669V
D-ERWW	Mooney M.20K Model 231	25-0676	N1164A
D-ERXP	Aero Designs Pulsar XP	425	
D-ERYS	Cessna 170B	25390	D-EMEE(1)
			N3148B
D-ESAB	Lake LA-4-200 Buccaneer	975	EI-BSR
			N3076P
D-ESAC	Cessna 177RG Cardinal RG	0066	N8066G
D-ESAD	Cessna 172R	80149	
D-ESAE	Cessna 172SP	172S08118	
D-ESAH(2)	Piper PA-28-181 Archer II	2890120	OH-PBM
			OY-JEG
D-ESAL	Cessna 172N	72082	N7307E
D-ESAN(2)	Piper PA-28-181 Archer III	2843028	N9181J
D-ESAP	Cessna 182Q Skylane	67138	N97582
D-ESAR	Springer Neico Lancair 235	007	
D-ESAS	Robin DR.400/180R Remorqueur	1680	HB-KAS
D-ESAT	Commander Aircraft 114B	14551	N6000Z
D-ESBA	Cessna 150M	77114	N63116
D-ESBB	Cessna 152	80052	N532CA
			N757WB
D-ESBC	Cessna 152	84684	N6344M
D-ESBD	Cessna 172N	72765	N6379D
D-ESBE	Cessna 152	85576	N93952

Regn.	Type	C/n	Prev.Id.
D-ESBH	Messerschmitt Bf.108B	3701-14	HB-ESM
			G-AFZO
			AW167
			D-IJHW
D-ESBM	Cessna 172R	80327	
D-ESBO	Reims/Cessna F.172P	2254	LN-RAW
D-ESBR	Robin R.2160D	275	
D-ESBW	Piper PA-28RT-201T Turbo Arrow IV	28R-7931251	OE-KBT
			OY-PEE
			N2904G
D-ESCA	Commander Aircraft 114B	14569	
D-ESCH	Piper PA-28RT-201 Arrow IV	28R-7918093	N2147X
D-ESCM	Robin DR.400/180 Major	2365	
D-ESCN	Beech F33A Bonanza	CE-1466	N33VW
			G-TERI
			N5664X
D-ESCO	Cessna 172N	73735	N5214J
D-ESCR	Cessna P210N Pressurized Centurion II	00207	N4517K
D-ESDA	Cessna 152	80868	N25937
D-ESDB	American AG-5B Tiger	10147	N1198A
D-ESDF	Piper PA-28R-201 Arrow III	28R-7837182	OE-DRT
			N9237C
D-ESDH	Piper PA-28-181 Archer II	28-8490076	N129AV
D-ESDK	Piper PA-28-180 Cherokee B	28-1710	D-ECKC(1)
			5U-BAA
			(F-OCDX)
			N7749W
D-ESEL	Piper PA-28RT-201T Turbo Arrow IV	28R-8131010	G-BSZR
			N8281B
D-ESEO(2)	Stoddard-Hamilton Glasair III *(Reservation 10.99)*	01	
D-ESER	Mraz M.1C Sokol	220	D-EHSO(1)
			F-BESZ
			OK-...
			N4686S
D-ESES	Cessna TR.182 Turbo Skylane RG	01379	
D-ESEW(3)	Extra EA.300/L	091	
	(Converted from EA.330 D-ESEW(2) c/n 01)		
D-ESEX(2)	SAN Jodel D.117A Grand Tourisme	837	OE-ATI
D-ESFC	Robin DR.400/180 Régent	2305	
D-ESFD	Reims/Cessna F.152	1467	OO-CPP
D-ESFF	Piper PA-32R-301T Turbo Saratoga	32R-8029071	N363CC
			N1025N
			N81754
D-ESFL	Christen A-1 Husky	1351	
D-ESFR	Beech F33A Bonanza	CE-1535	N81562
			N4341J
			(SE-KTL)
			N81562
			N76108
D-ESFS	Cessna 172N	68127	
D-ESFW	HOAC DV-20 Katana	20056	
D-ESGB	Kitplane *(Reservation - Type unknown)*	313	
D-ESGI	Cessna 172N	73033	N1943F
D-ESGJ	Cessna 172N	71222	N2289E
D-ESGK	HOAC DV-20 Katana	20079	
D-ESGR	Gyroflug SC-01B Speed Canard	S-23	D-ECEX(2)
D-ESGW	Cessna 172N	73058	N1969F
D-ESHA	Schmaderer Aero Designs Pulsar XP	EB-001	
D-ESHB	Commander Aircraft 114B	14572	
D-ESHD	Drache Piel CP.301A Emeraude	AB-407	HB-SPC
			D-ENUR
D-ESHG	SOCATA TB-21 Trinidad TC	690	HB-KBG
D-ESHH(2)	Cessna R.182 Skylane RG	01624	N6144S
			(D-ESTE)
			N6144S
D-ESHK	Robin R.3000/160	162	
D-ESHO	Robin DR.400/180R Remorqueur	2245	
D-ESHP	Aeromere F.8L Falco III	205	LX-AIW
			D-ENUB(1)
D-ESHS	Commander Aircraft 114B	14582	N582CA
D-ESHW	Commander Aircraft 114B	14558	
D-ESIA	Robin DR.400/200R Remo 200	2246	
D-ESIG	Cessna 182Q Skylane	65410	SE-KOF
			N735GJ
D-ESIL	Cessna 150L	75403	N11415
D-ESIS	Cessna 182S	80486	
D-ESJD	Drumm Van's RV-6A	1689	
D-ESJK	Kurz Messerschmitt Me.163 Replica	1788	
	(Now reserved as D-1634 10.99)		
D-ESJO	Piper J-3C-65 Cub	13260	D-EKQE
			PH-UCX
			45-4520
D-ESJP	SOCATA TB-20 Trinidad	870	D-EAFA(3)
D-ESKA	Diamond DA.20-A1 Katana	10093	N195DA
			C-GKAC
D-ESKF	Cessna 172P	75390	N63097
D-ESKG	Cessna 172P	75228	SE-KKH
			N62202
D-ESKH	SOCATA Rallye 180T-D Galérien	3213	OE-DKH
D-ESKI	Cessna TU.206G Stationair II /Soloy	04873	HB-CKN
			(D-EMRK(2))
			N28SC
			N734TZ
D-ESKK	SIAI-Marchetti S.205-20/R	221	PH-RYK
			(PH-NOW)
D-ESKL	Cessna 172D	50189	N2589U
D-ESKM	Beech F33A Bonanza	CE-1736	N80990
D-ESKS	Piper PA-18 Super Cub 95	18-1427	OY-EFO
			D-EECY
			ALAT
			51-15427
D-ESKW	Cessna 172R	80329	
D-ESKY	Cessna R.182 Skylane RG	00477	SE-KRY
			N9874C
D-ESLB	Biesinger Velocity RG	001	
D-ESLF	Ruschmeyer R90-230G	05	(D-EEHQ)
D-ESLL	Cessna 177RG Cardinal RG	0020	N8020G
D-ESLR(2)	Mooney M.20R Ovation *(Reservation 1.99)*	29-0118	N10822
D-ESLX	SOCATA TB-10 Tobago	350	LX-EUR
D-ESLZ(3)	Zeddies Denney Kitfox V	S 9502-0105	
	(Reserved as D-EMLZ, 3.99)		
D-ESMA	Bölkow BO.207	259	D-EGMA(1)
D-ESMB	Jensen Druine D.31 Turbulent	1	OY-AMB
	(Originally Stark Turbulent D c/n 133)		OY-EAB
			D-EKIV(1)
D-ESMG	Gess Van's RV-6	1692	
D-ESMH	Piper PA-28RT-201T Turbo Arrow IV	28R-8131006	N8277S
D-ESMI	Robin DR.400/180R Remorqueur	2080	
D-ESMM	Piper PA-28-181 Cherokee Archer II	28-7790091	N5336F
D-ESMN	Cessna 172N	67781	N888TJ
			N75526
D-ESMP	Reims/Cessna F.172N	1633	G-BFKA
D-ESMR	Robin R.1180TD Aiglon	281	PH-RBA
D-ESMS	Cessna TR.182 Turbo Skylane RG	01407	N4739S
D-ESMW(2)	Cessna 172N	73212	N6380F
D-ESNB	Mooney M.20J Model 201	24-0426	OE-KFC
			HB-DFC
D-ESND	Kitplane, type unknown *(Reservation 10.99)*	1	
D-ESOC	SOCATA TB-10 Tobago	1794	
D-ESOK	Mraz M.1D Sokol	281	D-ENEV
			OK-DHU
D-ESON	Piper PA-28-236 Dakota	28-8611002	HB-POT
			N9203M
D-ESOR	Piper PA-28R-201T Turbo Cherokee Arrow III		
		28R-7703254	N38637
D-ESPA	Piper PA-28-181 Archer II	28-8490041	N4334Z
D-ESPC	Cessna T.210L Turbo Centurion	60632	N8145L
D-ESPE	Piper PA-46-350P Malibu Mirage	4622063	N186DM
			N9179P
D-ESPH	Van's RV-6 *(Permit 11.99)*	1937	
D-ESPK	Mudry CAP.10B	136	F-GNPK
			Fr.AF
D-ESPR	Piper PA-28-151 Warrior	28-7715284	OE-DKA
			N9574N
D-ESPW	Cessna R.172K Hawk XP	2690	N736YH
D-ESQE	LET Z-37 Cmelák	08-29	DDR-SQE
			DM-SQE
D-ESRA	SOCATA TB-10 Tobago	1369	
D-ESRE	Ehmann RE-4 Grasmücke	01	
D-ESRG(2)	Cessna 150M	77275	N63385
			(D-ECDR)
			N63385

Regn.	Type	C/n	Prev.Id.
D-ESRK	Kitplane, type unknown *(Reservation 7.99)*	001	
D-ESRL(2)	Mooney M.20R Ovation	29-0064	
D-ESRP(2)	Cessna 172R	80360	N443ES
D-ESRR	Cessna 172R	80212	
D-ESSB(2)	Cessna 172R	80133	
D-ESSI (2)	Mooney M.20K Model 231	25-0105	(N164GT)
			N683AA
			YV-1683P
D-ESSK	Piper PA-28-151 Warrior	28-7515397	N1174X
D-ESSN	LET Z-37A Cmelák	18-02	DDR-SSN
			DM-SSN
D-ESSO(2)	Mooney M.20M TLS	27-0204	
D-ESST	Cessna 172N	71634	N4769E
D-ESSV(2)	Beech A36 Bonanza	E-2587	N58JM
			N8094K
D-ESTA	SOCATA TB-20 Trinidad	1362	
D-ESTB	Piper PA-28-161 Cadet	2841333	N9216N
D-ESTD	Piper PA-28-161 Cadet	2841341	N9184X
			N62IFT
			(OH-PFB)
D-ESTE	Stemme S-15	15-001	
D-ESTI	Piper PA-28-161 Cadet	2841350	N9233N
D-ESTL	Markett Neico Lancair 320	FB145AB	
D-ESTN	Piper PA-28-161 Warrior II	2816101	N92333
D-ESTO	Piper PA-28-161 Cadet	2841304	N9261N
			N9196X
D-ESTR	HOAC DV-20 Katana	20029	
D-ESTU	SOCATA TB-20 Trinidad	654	F-GFQR
			N20GN
D-ESTW	Commander Aircraft 114B	14612	N6026V
D-ESUK	LET Z-37A Cmelák	18-29	DDR-SUK
			DM-SUK
D-ESUM	Maiss Denney Kitfox IV	1 02	
D-ESUN	Zlin Z.226T	357	DM-WIE
D-ESUV(2)	Piper PA-32R-301T Turbo Saratoga II TC	3257024	N9295X
D-ESUX	LET Z-37A Cmelák	19-21	DDR-SUX
			DM-SUX
D-ESVH	LET Z-37A Cmelák	20-11	DDR-SVH
			DM-SVH
D-ESVJ	LET Z-37A Cmelák	20-13	DDR-SVJ
			DM-SVJ
D-ESVL	LET Z-37A Cmelák	20-15	DDR-SVL
			DM-SVL
D-ESVO	LET Z-37A Cmelák	20-18	DDR-SVO
			DM-SVO
D-ESVU	LET Z-37A Cmelák	20-24	DDR-SVU
			DM-SVU
D-ESVW	LET Z-37A Cmelák	20-26	DDR-SVW
			DM-SVW
D-ESWA(2)	SOCATA MS.893A Rallye Commodore 180	11712	F-BSVC
D-ESWE	LET Z-37A Cmelák	21-04	DDR-SWE
			DM-SWE
D-ESWH	LET Z-37A Cmelák	21-07	DDR-SWH
			DM-SWH
D-ESWK	Kunert Buddy Baby	001	
D-ESWM	LET Z-37A Cmelák	22-04	DDR-SWM
			DM-SWM
D-ESWO	LET Z-37A Cmelák	17-05	DDR-SWO
			DM-SWO
			SP-GDA
D-ESWP	Piper PA-20-135 Pacer	20-1053	N10339
			N791
D-ESWS	Wegscheider Neico Lancair 320	1586	
D-ESWW	Cessna 182D Skylane	53201	OE-DDA
			N8801X
D-ESYL	Gyroflug SC-01B-160 Speed Canard	S-53	
D-ETAA	Piper PA-38-112 Tomahawk	38-79A0582	N2341K
D-ETAB	Piper PA-38-112 Tomahawk	38-78A0243	N9913T
D-ETAC	Piper PA-38-112 Tomahawk	38-79A0298	N2408D
D-ETAD	Piper PA-38-112 Tomahawk	38-79A0220	N2534C
D-ETAE	Cessna 172N	7614	N73701
D-ETAF	Piper PA-28-181 Archer II	2890156	N92115
D-ETAG	Cessna 182R Skylane	67994	N9749H
			(N182PW)
			N9749H

Regn.	Type	C/n	Prev.Id.
D-ETAI	Piper PA-28RT-201T Turbo.Arrow IV	28R-8131147	N8402H
D-ETAJ	Piper PA-28-181 Archer II	2890161	N9117Q
			(F-GJOD)
D-ETAK	Piper PA-28-181 Archer II	2890162	N9212N
			(SE-KME)
D-ETAL	Ohlrogge Rand-Robinson KR-2	1	
D-ETAN(2)	HOAC DV-20 Katana	20122	
D-ETAR	Cessna 182Q Skylane	66456	N94597
D-ETAS(2)	Piper PA-28-181 Archer III	2843231	N4129P
			(ZS-OJP)
			N4129P
			N9512N
D-ETAU	Cessna 210L Centurion	59676	(D-EAJT)
			F-BYBC
			TR-LQQ
			N1176Q
D-ETAV	Piper PA-38-112 Tomahawk	38-79A1002	HB-PED
			N9715N
D-ETAX	Mooney M.20J Model 201	24-1006	HB-DGA
			N3997H
D-ETAY	SOCATA TB-9 Tampico	1300	SE-KBK
D-ETAZ	Piper PA-38-112 Tomahawk	38-78A0640	HB-PCR
			N9695N
D-ETBA	Mooney M.20M TLS	27-0006	N1036M
D-ETBB	Cessna 172M	61629	N92818
D-ETBD	SOCATA TB-20 Trinidad	989	HB-KCP
D-ETBE	Cessna U.206G Stationair II /Soloy	03989	N16737
			HB-CKX
			N250ST
			N638HM
			(N756CS)
			OH-TBA
D-ETBH	SOCATA TB-10 Tobago	029	F-GBHQ
			(F-ODKM)
D-ETBK	Cessna 152	82677	G-BTBK
			N89218
D-ETBL	Piper PA-46-310P Malibu	4608001	N181CA
			OY-CEL
D-ETBR	Bek Me 109R4	002	
D-ETBT	Piper PA-38-112 Tomahawk	38-79A0299	N2409D
D-ETBW	Wams Aero Designs Pulsar XP	413	
D-ETBX	Beck Aero Designs Pulsar XP	1814	
D-ETCB	Piper PA-28-181 Archer II	2890179	N9145B
D-ETCC	Piper PA-28-181 Archer II	2890180	N9145H
D-ETCE	Piper PA-28-181 Archer II	2890176	N9149G
			(F-GJOE)
D-ETCH	Piper PA-28-181 Archer II	2890016	N9111F
D-ETCI	Cessna 172N	70556	N739HM
D-ETCK	Piper PA-28-181 Archer II	2890187	N9179P
D-ETCL	Piper PA-28-181 Archer II	2890188	N9180W
D-ETCM	Piper PA-28-181 Archer II	2890184	N9177J
D-ETCN	Piper PA-28-181 Archer II	2890186	N9178B
D-ETCO	Cessna 172N	68595	N733VZ
D-ETCP	Piper PA-28-181 Archer II	2890193	N9226Z
D-ETCR	Cessna 152	79929	N757QW
D-ETCV	Piper PA-28-181 Archer II	2890194	N9227K
D-ETCW	White Stoddard-Hamilton Glastar GS-1 *(Permit 2.99)*	5627	
D-ETCX	Piper PA-28-181 Archer II	2890195	N9234D
D-ETDA	Schroeder Jodel D.18 *(Permit)*	375	
D-ETDB	Bartling Cozy BL *(Permit 4.99)*	01, formerly 1608	(D-EEDB)
D-ETDF	Evers/Brditschka HB-207 Alpha *(Reservn.)*	207-004	(PH-STP)
D-ETDI	Robin R.3000/160	159	
D-ETDP	Piper PA-28-181 Cherokee Archer II	28-7890043	G-BIDP
			N44956
D-ETEB	Diamond DA.20-A1 Katana	10240	
D-ETEC(2)	SOCATA MS.880B Rallye-Club	1521	OY-DJL
D-ETED	Robin DR.400/180R	2347	
D-ETEE	Marthiens Stoddard-Hamilton Glasair IIRG-S	V-1/2038	
D-ETEG	Beech F33A Bonanza	CE-1440	N5541L
D-ETEL(2)	Diamond DA.20-A1 Katana	10241	
D-ETEN	SOCATA TB-21 Trinidad TC	1377	
D-ETER	Cessna 172N	70770	N739SN
D-ETES	SOCATA TB-10 Tobago	1667	
D-ETET	Cessna 150L	73183	N5283Q
D-ETEW(2)	Extra EA.300/L *(Permit .99)*	084	

Regn.	Type	C/n	Prev.Id.
D-ETEX	Diamond DA.20-A1 Katana	10242	
D-ETFA	Piper PA-32RT-300 Lance	32R-7985033	N2218D
D-ETFD	Beech F33A Bonanza	CE-1492	N15482
D-ETFK	Cessna 182J Skylane	57115	N3015F
D-ETFL	Piper PA-28-181 Cherokee Archer II	28-7690058	N7145C
D-ETFS	Reims/Cessna F.150L	0821	D-EEWA
D-ETFW	HOAC DV-20 Katana	20059	
D-ETGE	Cessna 180H	52249	ZP-TGE
			ZP-PGE
			N9749G
D-ETGJ	Thiel Denney Kitfox III	982	
D-ETHB	Bücker Brändli BX-2 Cherry	101	
D-ETHC	de Havilland DH.82A Tiger Moth	82018	PH-CRO
	(Reservation 7.99)		G-AISY
			VT-CZV
			G-AISY
			N6740
D-ETHE	Aviat Pitts S-2B	5164	N5KE
D-ETHH	Meier Rutan LongEz	1082	
D-ETHK	HK Aircraft Technology Wega Ex *(Permit)*	426	
	(Formerly regd as Keller Pulsar XP with c/n 426/1831)		
D-ETHL	Mooney M.20M TLS	27-0133	
D-ETHM	Beech A36 Bonanza	E-3023	N3267Q
D-ETHN	Pilatus P.2-05 *(Permit 10.99)*	27	HB-RAT
			U-107
			A-107
D-ETHP	Pfeiffer Denney Kitfox IV-1200	JCU 113	
D-ETHS	Mooney M.20K Model 252	25-1123	HB-DGU
D-ETHW	Cessna TU206G Soloy Stationair II	03923	N103CS
			C-GDCF
			N7596C
D-ETIA	Mooney M.20K Model 231	25-0835	N231WF
D-ETIB	Mooney M.20K Model 231	25-0397	N4042H
D-ETIC	Cessna 172N	72428	N5121D
D-ETID	Mooney M.20J Model 201	24-1213	N309FW
D-ETIF	Piper PA-28R-201T Turbo Arrow IV	28R-8131021	N8290K
D-ETIG	American AG-5B Tiger	10139	N1197T
D-ETIH	Mooney M.20K Model 231	25-0741	HB-DGH
D-ETII	Lake LA-4-200 Buccaneer	921	N2820P
D-ETIK	Piper PA-28-161 Warrior II	2816116	N9254N
D-ETIN	HOAC DV-20 Katana	20110	
D-ETIP	Cessna 150M	78962	N704XT
D-ETIS	Piper PA-28-181 Archer III	2843133	N41237
D-ETIT	Tittl Denney Kitfox	1684	
D-ETIX	Piper PA-28-161 Warrior III	2842001	N9217N
D-ETIZ	Mooney M.20K Model 231	25-0479	N9404P
D-ETJA	Piper PA-28-181 Archer II	28-8690044	N9178Y
D-ETJG	Piper PA-46-350P Malibu Mirage	4622121	N91947
			(N555PS)
			N9215Q
D-ETJK	Cessna 140	8216	G-BSYE
			D-ESYE
			(D-ETDS)
			G-BSYE
			N89196
			NC89196
D-ETJR	Kit Aircraft (Type unknown)	2	
D-ETKA	Piper PA-28RT-201T Turbo Arrow IV	28R-8031173	OO-JJA
			N82623
D-ETKB	Cessna 172N	70174	N738RG
D-ETKC	Cessna 172N	72983	N1279F
D-ETKD	Cessna 152	85609	N94150
D-ETKE	Cessna 172N	73452	N4905G
D-ETKG	Reims/Cessna F.172H *(Permit 7.99)*	0429	N5002X
			D-ELXY
D-ETKH	Aviat A-1 Husky	1281	
D-ETKM	Cessna 172N	72198	N8425E
D-ETKO	Cessna 150M	76275	N66782
D-ETKP	Cessna 150L	73727	(OY- . . .)
			G-BPWO
			N18010
D-ETKR	Cessna 150M	78318	(OY- . . .)
			G-BPUZ
			N9369U

Regn.	Type	C/n	Prev.Id.
D-ETKS	Cessna TR.182 Turbo Skylane RG	0937	G-GARY
			N738KV
D-ETLA	Piper PA-28-181 Archer III	2843015	N9260J
D-ETLI	Hoffmann Denney Kitfox IV	1749/KBS-077	
D-ETLK	Piper PA-28-161 Warrior II	28-7916396	HB-PDY
			N3016Z
D-ETLL	Cessna 150M	77050	N123WT
			N63032
D-ETLX	Piper PA-28-181 Archer III	2890212	N92509
D-ETMA	SOCATA TB-9 Tampico	128	HB-EZO
			(D-ETMC)
			HB-EZO
D-ETMB	Stark Turbulent D-1	135	HB-SVG
			D-EKUV
D-ETMG	HOAC DV-20 Katana	20080	
D-ETMH	Cessna 172M	66298	N9661H
D-ETMI	Robin DR.400/180R Remorqueur	2144	
D-ETMJ	Mylius My 104 *(Reservation)*	unkn	
D-ETMM	Cessna P210N Pressurized Centurion II	00780	N6443W
D-ETMS	Stehr Denney Kitfox	681/1690	
D-ETMT	Beech F33A Bonanza	CE-1669	N8061P
D-ETMU	Fuji FA.200-160 Aero Subaru *(Permit 9.99)*	145	HB-ESZ
D-ETMV	Cessna 152	83134	N46890
D-ETMY	Mylius My-103 Mistral *(Permit)*	01	
D-ETNA	SOCATA TB-200 Tobago XL	1656	
D-ETNT	Cessna TR.182 Turbo Skylane RG	01812	N4979T
D-ETOF	Mooney M.20E Super 21	693	HB-DEI
			N5674Q
D-ETOG	Cessna 172N	73228	SE-KGL
			N6473F
D-ETOI	SAN Jodel DR.1050 Ambassadeur	483	D-EARL(1)
D-ETOL	Cessna 182Q Skylane	67591	N5237N
D-ETOM	Cessna 152	84787	N4629P
D-ETON	SOCATA TB-10 Tobago	1190	N55391
D-ETOR	Beech F33A Bonanza	CE-1050	N7214Z
D-ETOW	Morane-Saulnier MS.885 Super Rallye	5254	PH-TOW
			D-EHQA
			OH-MRD
D-ETOY	CASA I-131E Jungmann	2151	(D-EDWW)
			E3B-535
D-ETPC	Piper PA-28-181 Archer II	28-7990269	N2101N
D-ETPE	Piper PA-28-181 Archer III	2843003	N9256N
D-ETPL	Piper PA-28-161 Cadet	2841362	N92494
			(N628FT)
			(N9234Q)
D-ETPM	Piper PA-28-161 Cadet	2841363	N9234Q
			(N629FT)
			(N9235D)
D-ETPS	Piper PA-28-161 Cadet	2841364	N9237Q
			(N630FT)
			(N9236J)
D-ETPW	Piper PA-46-310P Malibu	46-8608002	D-ENHP
			N9094T
			(N193M)
			N9094T
D-ETPY	Piper PA-28-161 Cadet	2841365	N9250G
			(N631FT)
			(N9228J)
D-ETRA	Beech C24R Sierra	MC-547	N22PZ
			N22PS
D-ETRG	Cessna 152	85109	N5410Q
D-ETRI	Etrich Taube Replica *(Reservation 2.99)*	1913	
D-ETRS	Robin DR.400/180S Régent	2095	
D-ETRV	Cessna 175C Skylark	57046	HB-CRV
			(N8346T)
D-ETRY	Diamond DA.20-A1 Katana	10323	
D-ETSA	Bölkow BO.209 Monsun	197	HB-UEI
			D-EAIM(1)
D-ETSB	Beyer Denney Kitfox III	810	
D-ETSI	Piper PA-46-310P Malibu	46-8508012	HB-PKY
			D-EKLG(1)
			N4379M
D-ETSM	Piper PA-28RT-201T Turbo Arrow IV	28R-7931200	N29580
D-ETSR	Robin DR.400/200R Remorqueur	2243	
D-ETSW	Piper PA-32R-301 Saratoga	3213077	N9238Q

Regn.	Type	C/n	Prev.ld.
D-ETSY	Aviat A-1 Husky	1377	
D-ETTA	SOCATA TB-9 Tampico Club	1400	
D-ETTB	Borgwardt Neico Lancair 320	1644	
D-ETTC	Commander 114TC	20006	
D-ETTE	Beech F33A Bonanza	CE-1611	N209P
D-ETTG	Piper PA-46-310P Malibu	46-8508079	N6915P
			(N88PL)
			N6915P
D-ETTT(2)	Cessna 172R	80331	N9511W
D-ETUI	Aeronca 65CA Super Chief	17951	N36894
			NC36894
D-ETUS	Robin DR.400/180R Remorqueur	2188	
D-ETUV	Cessna 182Q Skylane	66403	N94108
D-ETVH	Robin DR.400/180R Remorqueur	2157	F-GLVH
D-ETVS	PZL-104 Wilga 35A	74205	SP-FWV
			PLW-205
D-ETWA	Piper PA-46-310P Malibu	46-8408014	N4320E
D-ETWB	Cessna 172M	64568	N9950V
D-ETWF	Frank Denney Kitfox II	597	
D-ETWH	Mooney M.20M TLS	27-0140	
D-ETWK	Küster Denney Kitfox III	809/1765	
D-ETWO	Dallach D4/E Fascination (Permit)	E-006	
D-ETWW	Cessna 172N	70981	N1383E
D-ETZE	Extra EA.300/L	024	
D-ETZX	Extra EA.300/L	039	
D-EUAL	Laue/Andreasson EBA-1	01/1842	
D-EUAP	Piper PA-28RT-201T Turbo Arrow IV	28R-8131166	N8412H
D-EUBA	SIAI-Marchetti S.205-18/F	352	D-EKGA(1)
D-EUCA	Commander Aircraft 114B	14571	
D-EUCE(2)	Cessna 172RG Cutlass	0475	I-TYPE
			N5219V
D-EUCH	HOAC DV-20 Katana	20083	
D-EUCO	Cessna 172N	73373	N4825G
D-EUDA	Diamond DA.20-A1 Katana	10268	
D-EUDO	Piper PA-28-236 Dakota	28-7911111	N333WE
			N3022R
D-EUDR	Piper PA-46-310P Malibu	4608040	N54FM
			N9111Z
D-EUEU	Piper PA-32-301 Saratoga	32-8106068	I-CONT
			N8392W
D-EUFR	Beech A36 Bonanza	E-3021	
D-EUGS	HOAC DV-20 Katana	20034	
D-EUGW	Cessna 172N	73946	N9877J
D-EUHB	Cessna P210R Pressurized Centurion II	00843	N5277A
D-EUHF	Mooney M.20J Model 205	24-3360	
D-EUHP	Cessna T.207A Turbo Stationair 7 /Soloy	00553	N70549
D-EUHS	Reims/Cessna F.172P	2197	SE-IHS
D-EUHU	SOCATA TB-20 Trinidad	1521	
D-EUHW	Beech A36 Bonanza	E-2990	N3218G
D-EUIB	Cessna P210N Pressurized Centurion II	00162	N6292P
D-EUIR	Piper PA-18-150 Super Cub	1809038	N4153D
D-EUJF	Aero Designs Pulsar XP (Permit)	1874	
D-EUJL	Lenhard Stoddard-Hamilton Glasair III	"00"	
D-EUKA	Europa Aviation Europa (Permit)	1782	
D-EUKD	Grob G.115C	82071/C1	
D-EULE	Linkohr Brändli BX-2 Cherry	132	
D-EULF	Cessna 150L	74244	N19216
D-EULI	Bronner Rutan LongEz	1044	
D-EUMI	Robin R.2160D Acrobin	304	
D-EUML	Löffler Murphy Rebel	1798	
D-EUMM	Diamond DA.20-A1 Katana	10250	
D-EUOS	Cessna P210N Pressurized Centurion II	00368	N4918K
D-EUPA	Kitplane, type unkn - Europa? (Reservation 3.99)	1843	
D-EUPC	Reims/Cessna FR.172G Rocket	0192	OE-DUC
			HB-CUC
D-EURA	Jodel D.92 Bébé	216	D-ENIC
			SL-AAM
D-EURE	SOCATA TB-9 Tampico Club	1319	
D-EURO	SOCATA TB-9 Tampico Club	1399	
D-EURR	Hinz BL2-ARA (Reservation)	1909	
D-EURS	Piper PA-46-310P Malibu	4608093	N9121N
D-EUSA	Cessna 150H	68758	N23154
D-EUTE	American AG-5B Tiger	10080	N1194L
D-EUTT	Diamond DA.20-A1 Katana	10246	
D-EUTZ	Mooney M.20K Model 252	25-1056	N252DW
D-EUUL	Piper PA-28-161 Warrior II	2816070	N9144D
D-EUUU	Champion 7EC Traveler	7FC-404	D-EBMQ
	(converted from 7FC Tri-Traveler)		N9829Y
D-EUVM	Piper PA-28-161 Warrior II	28-7916119	N21619
D-EUVT	Kitplane (Reservation - Type unknown)	XS 01	
D-EUWE	Hinz BL 2-2ARA	1716	
D-EUWH	Extra EA.300/L	01	
D-EUWM	Beech F33A Bonanza	CE-1635	N82689
D-EUWN	Kitplane (Reservation - Type unknown)	OGS-1	
D-EUWR	Beech A36AT Bonanza	E-2788	N82404
D-EUWW	Robin DR.400/180 Régent	2249	
D-EUXY	Bölkow BO.207	288	HB-UXY
			D-ENWE(1)
D-EVAB	HOAC DV-20 Katana	20025	
D-EVAC	Robin DR.400/180 Régent	2418	
D-EVAF	Cessna 150L	73798	N18118
D-EVAG	Piper PA-28RT-201T Turbo Arrow IV	28R-8131187	N82001
			N9569N
			N84209
D-EVAH	Piper PA-28RT-201T Turbo Arrow IV	28R-8031016	N8116B
D-EVAL(2)	Grob G.115D2	82044/D2	
D-EVAM(2)	Cessna 172R	80083	N382ES
D-EVAN	Cessna 152	84234	N4826L
D-EVAO	Cessna 172R	80395	
D-EVAR	Beech F33A Bonanza	CE-1651	N55389
D-EVAS(2)	Cessna 152	84799	N4680P
D-EVAT	Piper PA-28-181 Archer II	28-8590057	N6915R
D-EVAU	SOCATA TB-20 Trinidad	1569	
D-EVBA	Beech F33A Bonanza	CE-908	N36641
D-EVBB	Cessna 172M	66228	N9557H
D-EVBE	Cessna U.206G Stationair II /Soloy	06381	N7595Z
D-EVBI	Beech F33A Bonanza	CE-909	N36667
D-EVCA	Commander Aircraft 114B	14568	
D-EVCO	Cessna 152	81216	N49275
D-EVDA	Diamond DA.20-A1 Katana	10235	N237DA
D-EVDI	Reims/Cessna F.172M	1320	OE-DTU
D-EVEB	Beech F33A Bonanza	CE-1380	N725MA
			N1569F
D-EVEE	Beech F33A Bonanza	CE-1354	N5583R
D-EVEI	Beech A36 Bonanza	E-2722	TC-ARZ
			TC-ARI
			N80225
D-EVEL	Cessna 172N	73253	N333WB
			N7364F
D-EVEM	Robin DR.400/140B Major	1398	PH-SRW
D-EVEN	SOCATA TB-9 Tampico Club	1320	
D-EVER	Cessna 182Q Skylane	66424	N94393
D-EVET	Resch Acro Sport II	1652	
D-EVEW	Beech C24R Sierra	MC-651	N6014Y
D-EVEZ	Resch Jodel D.18	104	
D-EVFH	Cessna 172N	68918	N734KR
D-EVFM	Piper PA-28-181 Archer II	28-8290063	N8466W
D-EVFR	Cessna 150J	70974	N61337
D-EVGH	Piper PA-28RT-201T Turbo Arrow IV	28R-7931002	N44DY
			N2079B
D-EVGM	Robin DR.400/180R Remorqueur	2143	
D-EVGR	Beech F33A Bonanza	CE-1494	N334MW
D-EVHB	Piper PA-38-112 Tomahawk	38-80A0012	N24849
D-EVHM(2)	SOCATA TB-20 Trinidad	1837	
D-EVHN(2)	SOCATA TB-200 Tobago XL (Reservation 9.99)	2000	
D-EVHP	Piper PA-28-181 Archer II (Permit)	28-8290131	N8208Q
D-EVHS	Piper PA-28-181 Archer II	28-8390061	HB-PHS
D-EVIA	Robin R.2160D Acrobin	289	
D-EVIB(2)	Piper PA-28-181 Archer III	2843043	N9274L
D-EVIC	Piper PA-28-181 Archer III	2843071	N9285N
D-EVID	Piper PA-28RT-201T Turbo Arrow IV	28R-8331045	N43081
D-EVII (2)	Aviat A-1 Husky	1241	
D-EVIK	Beech A36 Bonanza	E-2347	N900TT
			N2611L
D-EVIL	Cessna 172N	70159	N781MB
D-EVIM	HOAC DV-20 Katana	20033	
D-EVIN	SOCATA TB-10 Tobago	1476	
D-EVIO(2)	Piper PA-32RT-300 Lance II	32R-7885144	G-WOZA
			G-BYBB
			N31957

Regn.	Type	C/n	Prev.Id.
D-EVIP(2)	Cessna 172N	72002	N6283E
D-EVIS	SOCATA TB-200 Tobago XL	1474	
D-EVIT	Cessna TU.206F Turbo Stationair	02246	N1538U
D-EVJO	Cessna 172P	74591	N52715
D-EVKB	Piper PA-28-181 Archer II	28-8390054	N4300Z
D-EVKG	Piper PA-46-310P Malibu	4608022	N9094Z
			N9103Q
D-EVLB	Reims/Cessna FR.172K Hawk XP	0659	OE-DSX
D-EVLF	HOAC DV-20 Katana	20117	
D-EVLS	Diamond DA.20-A1	10244	
D-EVMC	Cessna 182P Skylane	64653	N9034M
D-EVMH	SOCATA TB-200 Tobago XL	1629	
D-EVMI	Piper PA-28R-200 Cherokee Arrow II	28R-7535099	I-KIMI
			N32914
D-EVNM	SOCATA TB-200 Tobago XL	1439	D-EVHM
			F-OHDA
D-EVNO	Extra EA.200	018	
D-EVOB	Cessna 172N	73543	N5094G
D-EVOC	Cessna 172N	71387	N2961E
D-EVOI	HOAC DV-20 Katana	20130	
D-EVOM	Cessna 150M	79122	N714EP
D-EVON	SOCATA TB-200 Tobago XL	1475	F-WNGZ
D-EVOO	HOAC DV-20 Katana	20042	
D-EVOP(2)	SIAT 223V-2 Flamingo (Permit)	002	HB-EVO
			D-EHQE
			HB-EVO
			D-EHQE
D-EVOR	HOAC DV-20 Katana	20017	
D-EVOS	Cessna 182Q Skylane	66835	N96740
D-EVOT	Krieger Zenith CH-601 HD/S Zodiac	6-3102	
D-EVOX	HOAC DV-20 Katana	20038	
D-EVPA	Piper PA-46-350P Malibu Mirage	4622138	N9210P
			(N9234Z)
D-EVPI	Cessna 172N	68881	N734JC
D-EVPW	Diamond DA.20-A1 Katana	10144	
D-EVRA	Robin DR.400/180R Remorqueur	2207	
D-EVSA	Grob G.115D2 Bavarian	82002/D2	
D-EVSC	Cessna 172P	76141	N96997
			C-GSIU
D-EVSM	Piper PA-46-350P Malibu Mirage	4622072	HB-PMO
D-EVSR	Robin DR.400/180 Régent	2066	
D-EVTA	Piper PA-28-181 Archer II	2843033	N92703
D-EVTE	Robin R.3000/160	168	
D-EVTO	Piper PA-28-161 Warrior II	28-8016271	N81615
D-EVTZ	SOCATA TB-20 Trinidad	1767	
D-EVUG	Grünig Neico Lancair 360 (Permit)	1762	
D-EVUJ	Piper PA-28RT-201T Turbo Arrow IV	28R-7931134	N2124N
			N2152X
D-EVVA	Mooney M.20M TLS	27-0002	N1002K
D-EVVV	Extra EA.300/S	006	
D-EVWM	Beech A36 Bonanza	E-3012	N10575
D-EWAA(2)	Cessna 172R	80406	N9518Z
D-EWAB	Cessna 150M	78509	N704CQ
D-EWAD	Reims/Cessna F.150L	0919	D-EGBC
D-EWAE	Cessna 172R	80045	
D-EWAF	Cessna 182Q Skylane	65548	LN-VIM
			N735NE
D-EWAG	Diamond DA.20-A1 Katana	10163	
D-EWAH	SOCATA MS.883 Rallye 115	1366	OO-CBL
			F-BRMQ
D-EWAI	Diamond DA.20-A1 Katana	10162	
D-EWAK	Kirchhof Denney Kitfox 4-1200 (Permit)	1687/1744	
D-EWAL	Striedieck Denney Kitfox III	808 AB	
D-EWAM	Robin DR.400/180R Remorqueur	2225	
D-EWAO	HOAC DV-20 Katana	20085	
D-EWAP	Extra EA.300	034	D-EKFD(1)
D-EWAR	Piper PA-28-161 Warrior II	28-8616053	N9082X
D-EWAS	Schulze Denney Kitfox III	1160	
D-EWAT	Commander Aircraft 114B	14564	
D-EWAU	Cessna 172R	80329	N9502R
			(D-ESKW)
D-EWAV	Diamond DA.20-A1 Katana	10164	
D-EWAW	Cessna 172P	75329	N6270R
D-EWAX	HOAC DV-20 Katana	20068	
D-EWAY	HOAC DV-20 Katana	20069	

Regn.	Type	C/n	Prev.Id.
D-EWAZ	SOCATA TB-200 Tobago XL	1628	
D-EWBA	PZL-104 Wilga 35A	61106	DDR-WBA
			DM-WBA(2)
D-EWBB	PZL-104 Wilga 35A	61107	DDR-WBB
			DM-WBB(2)
D-EWBC	Cessna R.182 Skylane RG	00442	N9199C
D-EWBE	Cessna 172N	68608	N733WN
D-EWBF	PZL-104 Wilga 35A	61111	DDR-WBF
			DM-WBF(2)
D-EWBG	PZL-104 Wilga 35A	61112	DDR-WBG
			DM-WBG(2)
D-EWBJ	PZL-104 Wilga 35A	61115	DDR-WBJ
			DM-WBJ(2)
D-EWBM	Mooney M.20M TLS	27-0225	
D-EWBN	PZL-104 Wilga 35A	62175	DDR-WBN
			DM-WBN(2)
D-EWBQ	PZL-104 Wilga 35A	62179	DDR-WBQ
			DM-WBQ(2)
D-EWBS	PZL-104 Wilga 35A	62181	DDR-WBS
			DM-WBS(2)
D-EWBT	PZL-104 Wilga 35A	62182	DDR-WBT
			DM-WBT (2)
D-EWBU	PZL-104 Wilga 35A	62183	DDR-WBU
			DM-WBU(2)
D-EWBV	PZL-104 Wilga 35A	62166	DDR-WBV
			DM-WBV(2)
D-EWBX	PZL-104 Wilga 35A	62162	DDR-WBX
			DM-WBX(2)
D-EWBY	PZL-104 Wilga 35A	62163	DDR-WBY
			DM-WBY(2)
D-EWBZ	PZL-104 Wilga 35A	140537	DDR-WBZ
			DM-WBZ(2)
D-EWCA	Commander Aircraft 114B	14562	
D-EWCB	Cessna 182Q Skylane	65707	N735UZ
D-EWCE	Cessna 210D Centurion	58403	D-EMWJ
			N3903Y
D-EWCN	Orlican L-40 Meta-Sokol	150511	DM-WCN
D-EWCO(3)	Extra EA400 (Permit)	03	
D-EWCR	Maule M-6-235 Super Rocket	7443C	N600AB
D-EWDA	Diamond DA.20-A1 Katana	10271	
D-EWDB	Cessna 172N	70622	N739LF
D-EWDC	Diamond DA.20-A1 Katana	10316	N646DA
D-EWDR	Cessna 172P	75322	PH-ASZ
			N62676
D-EWDZ	Cessna 210N Centurion II (Reservation)	60761	D-EDMI (1)
			N1740X
D-EWEB	Cessna P210N Pressurized Centurion II	00597	N732XW
D-EWED	Cessna 182Q Skylane	66805	N96676
D-EWEI	Cessna 182S	80190	
D-EWEJ	Zlin Z.226T Trenér 6	243	DM-WEJ
D-EWEK	Piper PA-22-108 Colt (Permit)	22-9654	D-EKCE
			N5830Z
D-EWES	SOCATA TB-21 Trinidad TC	963	HB-KDJ
			D-EPRD
			OE-KHG
D-EWEZ	Piper PA-28R-201 Cherokee Arrow III	28R-7737096	N38534
D-EWFA	Zlin Z.43	0038	DDR-WFA
			DM-WFA(3)
D-EWFB	Zlin Z.43	0039/01	DDR-WFB
			DM-WFB(2)
D-EWFC	Zlin Z.43	0040/01	DDR-WFC
			DM-WFC(2)
D-EWFD	Zlin Z.43	0041/02	DDR-WFD
			DM-WFD(2)
D-EWFE	Zlin Z.43	0042/02	DDR-WFE
			DM-WFE(2)
D-EWFF	Van's RV-4 (Permit)	2107B	
D-EWFG	Zlin Z.43	0043/02	DDR-WFG
			DM-WFG(2)
D-EWFH	Zlin Z.43	0044/02	DDR-WFH
			DM-WFH(2)
D-EWFI	Zlin Z.43	0074	DDR-WFI
			DM-WFI (2)
D-EWGA	Cessna R182	01281	N5131T

Regn.	Type	C/n	Prev.Id.
D-EWGB	Piper PA-18-150 Super Cub	18-7442	D-EMFI (1)
			N4346P
D-EWGN	Cessna 172N	72343	SE-INU
			N4732D
D-EWGO	Goldbrunner G8UL	1847	
D-EWGS	Diamond DA.20-A1 Katana	10171	C-FYVM
D-EWHA	PZL-104 Wilga 35A	74213	DDR-WHA
			DM-WHA(2)
D-EWHB	Cessna 172P	75482	N63775
D-EWHC	PZL-104 Wilga 35A	74215	DDR-WHC
			DM-WHC(2)
D-EWHD	PZL-104 Wilga 35A	74216	DDR-WHD
			DM-WHD(2)
D-EWHE	PZL-104 Wilga 35A	86226	DDR-WHE
			DM-WHE(2)
D-EWHF	PZL-104 Wilga 35A	86227	DDR-WHF
			DM-WHF(2)
D-EWHI	PZL-104 Wilga 35A	86229	DDR-WHI
			DM-WHI (2)
D-EWHJ	Zlin Z.526 Trenér Master	1006	SE-XFE
			D-EGED(2)
			OK-V . .
D-EWHK	PZL-104 Wilga 35A	86230	DDR-WHK
			DM-WHK
D-EWHL	PZL-104 Wilga 35A	86231	DDR-WHL
			DM-WHL
D-EWHM	PZL-104 Wilga 35A	86232	DDR-WHM
			DM-WHM
D-EWHN	PZL-104 Wilga 35A	86233	DDR-WHN
			DM-WHN
D-EWHO	Beech A36AT Bonanza	E-2707	
D-EWHP	PZL-104 Wilga 35A	86264	DDR-WHP
			DM-WHP
D-EWHR	PZL-104 Wilga 35A	86266	DDR-WHR
			DM-WHR
D-EWHS	PZL-104 Wilga 35A	86267	DDR-WHS
			DM-WHS
D-EWHT	PZL-104 Wilga 35A	86268	DDR-WHT
			DM-WHT
D-EWHV	PZL-104 Wilga 35A	96319	DDR-WHV
			DM-WHV
D-EWHW	PZL-104 Wilga 35A	96320	DDR-WHW
			DM-WHW
D-EWHY	PZL-104 Wilga 35A	96322	DDR-WHY
			DM-WHY
D-EWHZ	PZL-104 Wilga 35A	96323	DDR-WHZ
			DM-WHZ
D-EWIA	Zlin Z.226T Trenér 6	353	DDR-WIA
			DM-WIA
D-EWIH	Rockwell Commander 114B	14153	N4823W
D-EWIK	Cessna 177B Cardinal	02091	OE-DTS
			(N34922)
D-EWIL	Zlin Z.526F Trenér Master	1260	YR-ZAG
D-EWIM	Beech F33A Bonanza	CE-1388	N5584N
D-EWIP	Robin DR.400/180R Remorqueur	2229	
D-EWKA	Cessna 152	81131	N47064
D-EWKE	Keiper Denney Kitfox III	1074	
D-EWKH	Buchs Neico Lancair 320	1737	
D-EWKI	Zlin Z.143L	0025	
D-EWKK	Cessna 152	80245	N129SC
			(N24380)
D-EWKL	Extra EA.300/L	064	
D-EWKO	Beech F33A Bonanza	CE-1617	N8243J
D-EWMA	Zlin Z.42MU	0012	DDR-WMA
			DM-WMA
D-EWMB	Diamond DA.20-A1 Katana	10248	
D-EWMC	Zlin Z.42MU	0014	DDR-WMC
			DM-WMC
D-EWMD	Zlin Z.42MU	0015	DDR-WMD
			DM-WMD
D-EWME	Zlin Z.42MU	0069	DDR-WME
			DM-WME
D-EWMF	Zlin Z.42MU	0017	DDR-WMF
			DM-WMF
D-EWMG	Dallach D4/E Fascination (Permit)	EB011, formerly 1905	
D-EWMH	Cessna 182S	80293	N2385N
D-EWMI	Aviat A-1 Husky	1376	
D-EWMK	Zlin Z.42MU	0021	DDR-WMK
			DM-WMK
D-EWML	Zlin Z.42MU	0022	DDR-WML
			DM-WML
D-EWMM	Zlin Z.42MU	0023	DDR-WMM
			DM-WMM
D-EWMN	Zlin Z.42MU	0024	DDR-WMN
			DM-WMN
D-EWMO	Zlin Z.42MU	0025	DDR-WMO
			DM-WMO
D-EWMP	Zlin Z.42MU	0026	DDR-WMP
			DM-WMP
D-EWMQ	Zlin Z.42MU	0028	DDR-WMQ
			DM-WMQ
D-EWMR	Zlin Z.42MU	0029	DDR-WMR
			DM-WMR
D-EWMS	Zlin Z.42MU	0030	DDR-WMS
			DM-WMS
D-EWMT	Zlin Z.42MU	0031	DDR-WMT
			DM-WMT
D-EWMU	Zlin Z.42MU	0032	DDR-WMU
			DM-WMU
D-EWMV	Zlin Z.42MU	0033	DDR-WMV
			DM-WMV
D-EWMW	Zlin Z.42MU	0034	DDR-WMW
			DM-WMW
D-EWMX	Zlin Z.42MU	0035	DDR-WMX
			DM-WMX
D-EWMY	Zlin Z.42MU	0036	DDR-WMY
			DM-WMY
D-EWMZ	Zlin Z.42MU	0037	DDR-WMZ
			DM-WMZ
D-EWNA	Zlin Z.42MU	0038	DDR-WNA
			DM-WNA
D-EWNC	Zlin Z.42MU	0040	DDR-WNC
			DM-WNC
D-EWND	Zlin Z.42MU	0041	DDR-WND
			DM-WND
D-EWNE	Zlin Z.42MU	0042	DDR-WNE
			DM-WNE
D-EWNG	Zlin Z.526F Trenér Master	1076	OK-YRC
D-EWNK	Zlin Z.42MU	0047	DDR-WNK
			DM-WNK
D-EWNL	Zlin Z.42MU	0049	DDR-WNL
			DM-WNL
D-EWNO	Zlin Z.42MU	0051/02	DDR-WNO
			DM-WNO
D-EWNP	Zlin Z.42MU	0052/02	DDR-WNP
			DM-WNP
D-EWNQ	Zlin Z.42MU	0053/02	DDR-WNQ
			DM-WNQ
D-EWNT	Zlin Z.42M	0062	DDR-WNT
			DM-WNT
D-EWNU	Zlin Z.42M	0063	DDR-WNU
			DM-WNU
D-EWNX	Zlin Z.42M	0066	DDR-WNX
			DM-WNX
D-EWNY	Zlin Z.42M	0067	DDR-WNY
			DM-WNY
D-EWOB	Zlin Z.42M	0084	DDR-WOB
			DM-WOB
D-EWOC	Zlin Z.42M	0085	DDR-WOC
			DM-WOC
D-EWOD	Zlin Z.42M	0086	DDR-WOD
			DM-WOD
D-EWOE	Zlin Z.42M	0087	DDR-WOE
			DM-WOE
D-EWOF	Zlin Z.42M	0111	DDR-WOF
			DM-WOF
D-EWOG	Zlin Z.42M	0112/04	DDR-WOG
			DM-WOG
D-EWOH	Zlin Z.42M	0113	DDR-WOH
			DM-WOH

Regn.	Type	C/n	Prev.Id.
D-EWOI	Zlin Z.42M	0114/04	DDR-WOI
			DM-WOI
D-EWOK	Zlin Z.42M	0115	DDR-WOK
			DM-WOK
D-EWOL	Zlin Z.42M	0130/05	DDR-WOL
			DM-WOL
D-EWOM	Zlin Z.42M	0131	DDR-WOM
			DM-WOM
D-EWON	Zlin Z.42M	0132	DDR-WON
			DM-WON
D-EWOP	Zlin Z.42M	0133/05	DDR-WOP
			DM-WOP
D-EWOQ	Zlin Z.42MU	0157	DDR-WOQ
			DM-WOQ
D-EWOR(2)	Röhl Brändli BX-2 Cherry *(Permit)*	313/38	
D-EWOS	Cessna P210N Pressurized Centurion II	00190	N6571P
D-EWOW	Kitplane, type unknown *(Reservation 4.99)*	1548	
D-EWPA	PZL-104 Wilga 35A	118411	DDR-WPA
			DM-WPA
D-EWPB	Zlin Z.50LS	0064	
D-EWPE	Beech F33A Bonanza	CE-1391	N5586M
D-EWPG	Robin R.3000/160	166	
D-EWPH	Brditschka HB-207 Alfa *(Reservation)*	1882	
D-EWPM	Beech F33A Bonanza	CE-1774	N1551N
D-EWPR	Cessna 172N	72032	N6539E
D-EWPW	Beech A36AT Bonanza	E-2950	(N820V)
			N10PW
D-EWQA	Zlin Z.526AFS Akrobat	1205	DDR-WQA
			DM-WQA
D-EWQC	Zlin Z.526AFS Akrobat	1207	DDR-WQC
			DM-WQC
D-EWQH	Zlin Z.526AFS Akrobat	1212	DDR-WQH
			DM-WQH
D-EWQL	Zlin Z.526AFS Akrobat	1217	DDR-WQL
			DM-WQL
D-EWRA	Joerges Wright Flyer Model A Replica	1770	
D-EWRB	PZL-104 Wilga 35A	96325	DDR-WRB
			DM-WRB
D-EWRC	PZL-104 Wilga 35A	96326	DDR-WRC
			DM-WRC
D-EWRD	HOAC DV-20 Katana	20085	
D-EWRE	PZL-104 Wilga 35A	96328	DDR-WRE
			DM-WRE
D-EWRF	PZL-104 Wilga 35A	96329	DDR-WRF
			DM-WRF
D-EWRG	Dornier Do.27B-1	276	HB-HAG
			D-EMAE(1)
			56+09
			BD+928
			AC+928
			AS+928
D-EWRH	PZL-104 Wilga 35A	96331	DDR-WRH
			DM-WRH
D-EWRI	PZL-104 Wilga 35A	107337	DDR-WRI
			DM-WRI
D-EWRJ	PZL-104 Wilga 35A	107338	DDR-WRJ
			DM-WRJ
D-EWRK	Zlin Z.50LS	0065	OK-WRK
D-EWRL	PZL-104 Wilga 35A	118391	DDR-WRL
			DM-WRL
D-EWRM	PZL-104 Wilga 35A	18392	DDR-WRM
			DM-WRM
D-EWRN	PZL-104 Wilga 35A	118393	DDR-WRN
			DM-WRN
D-EWRO	PZL-104 Wilga 35A	118394	DDR-WRO
			DM-WRO
D-EWRP	PZL-104 Wilga 35A	118395	DDR-WRP
			DM-WRP
D-EWRQ	PZL-104 Wilga 35A	118396	DDR-WRQ
			DM-WRQ
D-EWRR	Pottier P.220S Koala *(Reservation)*	313	
D-EWRT	PZL-104 Wilga 35A	118398	DDR-WRT
			DM-WRT
D-EWRU	PZL-104 Wilga 35A	118399	DDR-WRU
			DM-WRU

Regn.	Type	C/n	Prev.Id.
D-EWRV	PZL-104 Wilga 35A	118400	DDR-WRV
			DM-WRV
D-EWRX	PZL-104 Wilga 35A	118408	DDR-WRX
			DM-WRX
D-EWRY	PZL-104 Wilga 35A	118409	DDR-WRY
			DM-WRY
D-EWRZ	PZL-104 Wilga 35A	118410	DDR-WRZ
			DM-WRZ
D-EWSB	Homebuilt, type unknown *(Reservation)*	E1D4	
D-EWSG	Reims/Cessna F.172M	1008	OE-KSG
			D-EJXE
D-EWSH	Huber Colomban MC-100 Banbi *(Permit)*	02	
D-EWSM	HOAC DV-20 Katana	20043	
D-EWSP	Piper PA-24-260 Comanche B	24-4514	OE-KGW
			G-AVGN
			N9049P
D-EWSR	Robin DR.400/180 Régent	2196	
D-EWSS	Robin DR.400/180 Régent	2079	
D-EWST	Cessna TR.182 Turbo Skylane RG	01091	N756KE
D-EWTC	Commander 114TC	20010	
D-EWTE	Cessna 182Q Skylane	67125	N97536
D-EWTM	Van's RV-6 *(Reservation)*	1845	
D-EWTR	Zlin Z.326A Akrobat *(Permit 5.99)*	555	DM-WKA
D-EWWZ	SOCATA TB-20 Trinidad	1711	
D-EWWE	Ruschmeyer R.90-230RG	024	(D-EECY)
D-EWWF	HOAC DV-20 Katana	20057	
D-EWWH	Hohmann Neico Lancair 320	001	
D-EWWM	Piper PA-28-181 Archer III	2890223	N9227R
D-EWYY	Cessna TR.182 Turbo Skylane RG	00659	N9042R
D-EXAI	Piper PA-18 Super Cub 95	18-3184	OE-ADM
			D-EDVO
			R-86
			(OL-L110)
			53-4784
D-EXAL	SOCATA TB-20 Trinidad *(Reservation 9.99)*	1917	
D-EXAM	Mooney M.20R Ovation	29-0042	
D-EXAP(2)	Cessna TR.182 Turbo Skylane RG *(Reservation 12.99)*	01948	RA-01558
			D-EXAP(2)
			F-GGLT
			N6253T
D-EXAS	Piper PA-38-112 Tomahawk	38-80A0071	HB-PFI
			N9698N
D-EXCA	Commander Aircraft 114B	14557	
D-EXCC	Piper PA-46-350P Malibu Mirage	4622085	N9188D
D-EXDA	Diamond DA.20-A1 Katana	10275	
D-EXDB	Aero Designs Pulsar XP *(Permit)*	410	
D-EXEL(2)	Cessna 172R	80195	N9943F
D-EXER	Grob G.115C	82040/C	
D-EXEW	Extra EA.300/L	05	
D-EXFT	Extra EA.200	025	
D-EXGC	Extra EA.200	027	
D-EXGV	Robin HR.100/250TR Président *(Reservation)*	547	F-BXGV
D-EXGW	Kitplane, type unknown *(Reservation 4.99)*	3256	
D-EXHB	Cessna 182P Skylane	62472	N8505Z
			N1279M
			D-EENA
			N52233
D-EXHG	Extra EA.300/L	03	
D-EXIB	Extra EA.300/L *(Reservation 11.99)*	101	
D-EXIH	Extra EA.300/L *(Reservation 11.99)*	102	
D-EXIL	SOCATA TB-20 Trinidad	1298	
D-EXIT	SOCATA TB-20 Trinidad	1299	
D-EXJM	SOCATA TB-20 Trinidad	1297	
D-EXKA	Piper PA-28-161 Warrior II	28-7816601	N31967
D-EXKB	Aviat A-1 Husky	1244	
D-EXKJ	Kitplane, type unknown *(Reservation 10.99)*	D4	
D-EXMB	Mooney M.20K Model 231	25-0813	N5744N
D-EXME	Maule MX-7-180 Star Rocket	11037C	N5671N
D-EXMI	Robin DR.400/180R Remorqueur	2078	
D-EXMM	de Havilland DH.82A Tiger Moth	82814	G-ERTY
			D-EFYZ(1)
			LX-JON
			G-ANDC
			R4897

Regn.	Type	C/n	Prev.Id.
D-EXOT	Piper PA-46-310P Malibu	46-8508010	N4378T
			(N55BT)
			N4378T
D-EXPD	Piper PA-46-350P Malibu Mirage	4636100	OY-JAM
D-EXPK	Van's RV-6A *(Permit 10.99)*	1301	
D-EXPO	Piper PA-28-181 Archer III	2843083	N92876
D-EXPS	Extra EA.300/L	090	
D-EXRB	Extra EA.230 *(Reservation 2.99)*	001	N230X
			D-EKEW(2)
D-EXRT	Piper PA-28-181 Archer II	28-8090353	N8233A
D-EXRV	Hühn Van's RV-4	2849	
D-EXSL	Extra EA.300/L	08	
D-EXTA	Piper PA-46-350P Malibu Mirage	4636026	N9264Q
D-EXTC	Fürle Denney Kitfox IV-1200 *(Permit)*	003	
D-EXTR/S/T	*Test Registrations for Extra EA.200/300 production*		
D-EXVR	Aviat Pitts S-2B	5272	
D-EXWE	Extra EA.200	014	
D-EXWL	Focke-Wulf FW.44J Stieglitz	2776	D-EXEK
			OH-XEK
			FinAF:SZ-14
			RNorAF:3
			D-EXWL
D-EXWM	Aviat A-1 Husky	1350	
D-EXWS	Aerotek Pitts S-2A	2269	OE-AHH
			D-ELUP(2)
			N255CA
D-EXXA	Piper PA-28R-201 Arrow IV	2837033	N9185Z
D-EXXB	Piper PA-28R-201 Arrow IV	2837036	N91871
D-EXXC	Piper PA-28R-201 Arrow IV	2837037	N91886
D-EXXD	Piper PA-28R-201 Arrow IV	2837054	N9235F
D-EXXE	SOCATA TB-200 Tobago XL	1447	
D-EXXI	SOCATA TB-20 Trinidad	1481	
D-EXXO	SOCATA TB-20 Trinidad	1710	
D-EXXP	Aero Designs Pulsar XP	1887	
D-EXXX	Mudry CAP.10B	259	
D-EXXY	Mudry CAP.10B	275	
D-EXYY	HOAC DV-20 Katana	20037	
D-EXYX	Alpavia Jodel D.117A Grand Tourisme	1038	D-ENTI (1)
D-EXYZ	Christen A-1 Husky	1059	HB-KIR
			D-ECHX(2)
			N2974C
D-EXZY	Kitplane, type unknown *(Reservation 6.99)*	122	
D-EYAA	Robin DR.400/180R Remorqueur	1386	HB-EYA
D-EYAK	Nanchang CJ-6	132007	PLAAFoC
D-EYAS	Siebenritt Jodel DR.1050M	AB 834-M	
D-EYCM	Cessna 152	80506	N25029
D-EYDT	Piper PA-38-112 Tomahawk *(Permit)*	38-82A0108	N9158A
D-EYES	Diamond DA.20-A1 Katana	10137	
D-EYEY	Piper PA-28RT-201T Turbo Arrow IV	28R-8031007	N8105Z
D-EYGA	Gabbe Europa	1784	
D-EYHB	Brditschka HB-207 Alfa *(Permit 8.99)*	207-025	
D-EYKL	Dallach D4-EB016 Fascination *(Reservation)*	1932	
D-EYLE	PZL-104 Wilga 35A	20890888	SP-FWI
D-EYMH	Grob G.115B	8109	VH-AYE(3)
			D-ELCF(2)
D-EYML	Mooney M.20J Model 205	24-3249	SE-KUM
D-EYMR	Cessna 150F	62325	N3525L
D-EYON	HOAC DV-20 Katana	20152	
D-EYPA	Piper PA-28-181 Archer III	2843035	N9268B
D-EYPC	Cessna R.182 Skylane RG	01822	N4407F
			(C-GPGH)
			(N5138T)
D-EYRM	Maule M-6-235 Super Rocket	7472C	N5665K
D-EYTT	Zlin Z.226 Trenér 6	171-15	HB-TRT
			D-EHSE(1)
			OK-MFZ
D-EYWM	American AG-5B Tiger	10026	N1192G
D-EYXA	Beech F33A Bonanza	CE-1740	N82903
D-EYYY	Piper PA-28RT-201 Arrow IV	28R-8018104	N8262V
D-EZAA	Homebuilt, type unknown *(Reservation)*	0	
D-EZAC	Diamond DA.20-A1 Katana	10089	D-EDAS(3)
D-EZAG	Piper PA-28RT-201T Turbo Arrow IV	28R-8131058	N8320J
D-EZAI	HOAC DV-20 Katana	20121	
D-EZAK	Morane-Saulnier MS.505 Criquet	700	F-BDQT
D-EZAP	Cessna 152	83078	N46598

Regn.	Type	C/n	Prev.Id.
D-EZAR	Aviat A-1 Husky	1235	
D-EZAS(2)	Piper PA-28-181 Archer III	2843253	N4127N
D-EZBA	Reims/Cessna F.152	1884	N3953A
D-EZBC	Clemens Aero Designs Pulsar XP	1861	
D-EZBG	Cessna 152	85775	N94736
D-EZDA	Diamond DA.20-A1 Katana	10266	
D-EZDB	Diamond DA.20-A1 Katana	10267	D-EQDA
D-EZEB	Piper PA-28-181 Archer III	2843007	N9255N
D-EZEE	Fehrling Rutan Vari-eze	1	
D-EZEI (2)	Piper PA-28-181 Archer III	2843091	N92885
			(N971PA)
D-EZEL	Robin DR.400/180R Remorqueur	2345	
D-EZET	Piper PA-28-181 Archer III	2843008	N9258E
D-EZEW	Piper PA-28-181 Archer III	2890228	N9251R
D-EZFF	Robin DR.400/180R Remorqueur	2113	
D-EZFW	Hanusa Jurca MJ.8/FW.190A Replica	1656	
D-EZGA	Cessna 152	85178	N6164Q
D-EZHB	Robin DR.400/180 Régent	1450	F-GCID
D-EZIC	Diamond DA.20-A1 Katana	10054	N228P
D-EZII	Erco 415D Ercoupe *(Reservation 12.99)*	1769	N99146
			NC99146
D-EZIP	Piper PA-28-181 Archer III	2843013	N92580
			D-ESAN(1)
D-EZIS	Piper PA-28-181 Archer III	2843056	N9278N
D-EZKK	Mooney M.20K Model 231	25-0128	N231KK
D-EZLA	Mooney M.20J Model 205	24-3389	
D-EZLN	Zlin Z.143L	0004	
D-EZMA	Aviat A-1 Husky	1245	HB-KDZ
			D-EXKL
D-EZMC	Beech C24R Sierra	MC-477	N24013
D-EZMH	Heeren Denney Kitfox Vixen 1200	JCV 021	
D-EZOE	Cessna R.182 Skylane RG	00540	N1734R
			(D-EASG)
			N1734R
D-EZOF	Piper PA-28-181 Archer II	28-7990236	N2121K
D-EZOZ	Extra EA.300/L	029	D-ETZJ
D-EZPA	Piper PA-46-350P Malibu Mirage	4622184	N9251K
D-EZRL	Zenair CH-601 Zodiac *(Reservation 6.99)*	6-3666	
D-EZRS	Robin DR.400/180 Régent	2309	
D-EZSB	Reims/Cessna F.172N	1607	N289YY
			D-EOHI
D-EZTT	Zlin Z.526AFS Akrobat	1211	DDR-WQG
			DM-WQG
D-EZUG	Christen Pitts S-2B	5129	N6032R
D-EZUP	HOAC DV-20 Katana	20008	
D-EZWF	Robin R.3000/160	132	
D-EZWM	CASA I-131E Jungmann *(Permit 8.99)*	unkn	E3B-568
D-EZWZ	Morane-Saulnier MS.885 Super Rallye	82	HB-EDL
D-EZZZ	Fieseler Fi.156C-3 Storch	4370	D-EBGY(2)
			(D-EAXY)
			Fv3805
			CK+KI

CLASS F : Single-Engined Aircraft of between 2 and 5.7 Metric Tonnes

Regn.	Type	C/n	Prev.Id.
D-FABE	CCF/North American Harvard IV	CCF4-499	AA+624
			52-8578
D-FAIR	Antonov AN-2	17205	LSK-450
D-FALB	Cessna 208B Grand Caravan	0744	
D-FALF	SOCATA TBM-700 (Reservation 8.99)	157	
D-FALK	Cessna 208 Caravan	00023	N9354F
D-FALL	Pilatus PC-6/B2-H4 Turbo Porter	860	
D-FAME(2)	CCF/North American Harvard IV	CCF4-77	G-BKCK
			N13631
			G-BKCK
			N13631
			RCAF20286
D-FAMT	Pilatus PC-9/B	164	HB-HQK(2)
D-FASS	North American AT-6D Harvard III	88-13483	SAAF7429
			EX847
D-FAST(2)	Cessna 208 Caravan	00207	N208MC
			N208MT
D-FAXI	Pilatus PC-6/B2-H4 Turbo Porter	862	(F-GPGA)
			G-ITPS
D-FBAW	Antonov AN-2T	1G160-01	LSK-804
D-FBFS	SOCATA TBM-700A	74	F-OHBK
			(D-FASC)
D-FBJU	Antonov AN-2	1G63-29	DOSAAF-04
D-FBMT	Pilatus PC-9/B	165	HB-HQL(2)
D-FCJA	Pilatus PC-12	177	HB-FSM
D-FCLG	Pilatus PC-6/B2-H2 Turbo-Porter	636	F-BOSZ
D-FCMT	Pilatus PC-9/B	166	
D-FDFF	Pilatus PC-6/B1-H2 Turbo Porter	629	HB-FDF
			5Y-AHR
			HB-FDF
			HB-FEG
D-FDHM	Pilatus PC-6/C1-H2 Turbo Porter	688	HB-FEG
D-FDLR	Cessna 208B Grand Caravan	0708	
D-FDME	Messerschmitt Bf.109G-10	151591	ZK-CIX
			D-FEHD(2)
			Luftwaffe
D-FDMT	Pilatus PC-9/B	167	HB-HPI
D-FEIN	SOCATA TBM-700A	89	N930SU
D-FELI	Pilatus PC-6/B2-H4 Turbo Porter	845	JA8223
			HB-FAB
D-FEMT	Pilatus PC-9/B	168	
D-FFBU	SOCATA TBM-700A	22	F-GLBM
			F-OHBF
D-FFBZ(2)	Pilatus PC-6/B2-H4 Turbo Porter	869	
D-FFMT	Pilatus PC-9/B	169	
D-FGEE	Grob G.500 Egrett	10002	
D-FGGG	Antonov AN-2T	113901	LSK-469
			DM-WCX
D-FGMT	Pilatus PC-9/B	170	
D-FGRO	Grob G.500 Egrett Strato I	10005	
D-FGYY(2)	SOCATA TBM-700 (Reservation 12.99)	162	
D-FHEW	Cessna 208B Grand Caravan	0401	N401MC
			N1214Z
D-FHGK	Noorduyn/North American AT-16 Harvard IIb	14-324	G-AXCR
			U-322
			FE590
			42-787
D-FHGL	North American SNJ-5 Texan	88-14713	N2965S
	(Regd with "c/n" 51-819, see USN serial)		(D-FIII)
			C.6-162/793-15
			N7804B
			BuA51819
D-FHMT	Pilatus PC-9/B	171	HB-HQD
D-FIJL	Antonov AN-2T	1G157-04	DDR-WJL
			DM-WJL
D-FIMT	Pilatus PC-9/B	172	
D-FIRE	SOCATA TBM-700A	137	
D-FJJF	Antonov AN-2T	1G108-70	DDR-WJF
			DM-WJF
			DDR-WJP
			LSK-839
D-FJKA	Antonov AN-2T	19318	

Regn.	Type	C/n	Prev.Id.
D-FJMO	Pilatus PC-6/B1-H2 Turbo Porter	561	F-GOMO
			N1421Z
D-FJMT	Pilatus PC-9/B	173	
D-FKMA	Antonov AN-2T	117411	LSK-440
D-FKMB	Antonov AN-2T	17308	LSK-451
D-FKMC	Antonov AN-2T	17612	LSK-454
D-FKMD	Antonov AN-2T	17812	LSK-456
D-FKME	Antonov AN-2T	17805	LSK-457
D-FKMG	Antonov AN-2T	12801	LSK-801
D-FKMI	Antonov AN-2T	17207	LSK-845
			DM-SKA
D-FLAX	Cessna 208B Grand Caravan	0604	
D-FLOH	Cessna 208B Grand Caravan	0576	N1041F
D-FMBB(2)	Messerschmitt Me.109G-6	156	C4K-...
	(Constructed from a Hispano HA.1112-MIL		
	airframe and parts from D-FMBB(1))		
D-FMOR	SOCATA TBM-700 (Reservation 1.99)	148	
D-FNRE	SOCATA TBM-700A	142	
D-FNVA	Antonov AN-2T	19320	(D-FORK)
			LSK-817
D-FOAA	PZL-106A Kruk (Reservation 11.98, believed	48039	DDR-TAA
	still at Finow Museum. Permit issued 11.99)		DM-TAA
D-FOAB	PZL-106A Kruk (2-seat conversion)	48040	DDR-TAB
			DM-TAB
D-FODS	PZL-106BR Kruk (Reservation 8.99)	09870206	DDR-TDS
D-FODW	PZL-106BR Kruk (Reservation 8.99)	09870198	DDR-TDW
			SP-WBF
D-FODZ	PZL-106BR Kruk (Reservation 8.99)	09870208	DDR-TDZ
D-FOEB	PZL-106BR Kruk (Reservation 8.99)	10880210	DDR-TEB
D-FOEG	PZL-106BR Kruk (Reservation 8.99)	10880215	DDR-TEG
D-FOEH	PZL-106BR Kruk (Reservation 8.99)	10880216	DDR-TEH
D-FOEL	PZL-106BR Kruk (Reservation 8.99)	10880225	DDR-TEL
D-FOEM	PZL-106BR Kruk (Reservation 8.99)	10880226	N117RA
			D-FOEM
			DDR-TEM
D-FOEN	PZL-106BR Kruk (Reservation 8.99)	10880227	DDR-TEN
D-FOEQ	PZL-106BR Kruk (Reservation 8.99)	10890235	DDR-TEQ
D-FOFM	Antonov AN-2T	12802	LSK-802
D-FOJB	Antonov AN-2T	1G86-42	DDR-WJB
			DM-WJB
D-FOJN	Antonov AN-2T	1G166-39	DDR-WJN
			DM-WJN
D-FOKK	Antonov AN-2T	19504	DDR-SKK
			DM-SKK
D-FOKY	Antonov AN-2T	1G86-49	DDR-SKY
			DM-SKY
D-FOLE(2)	Cessna 208B Grand Caravan	0523	
D-FOMD	PZL M-18A Dromader	1Z021-10	DDR-TMD
D-FOME	PZL M-18A Dromader	1Z021-11	DDR-TME
D-FOMG	PZL M-18A Dromader	1Z021-13	DDR-TMG
D-FOMH	PZL M-18A Dromader	1Z021-14	DDR-TMH
D-FOMI	PZL M-18A Dromader	1Z021-15	DDR-TMI
D-FOMK	PZL M-18A Dromader	1Z021-17	DDR-TMK
D-FONC	Antonov AN-2TD (Wfu, stored)	1G180-42	DDR-SKC(2)
			LSK-800
D-FOND	Antonov AN-2P	19508	DDR-SKD(2)
			LSK-815
D-FONE	Antonov AN-2T	18118	DDR-SKE(2)
			LSK-459
D-FONF	Antonov AN-2P	117419	DDR-SKF(2)
			LSK-811
D-FONJ	Antonov AN-2T	19317	DDR-SKJ(2)
			LSK-866
D-FONL	Antonov AN-2T	17802	DDR-SKL(2)
			LSK-888
D-FOTO(2)	Cessna 208 Caravan 1	00192	N9773F
D-FOXY	EKW C-3605	315	N7129V
			C-535
D-FPET	Antonov AN-2R (Reservation, damaged 7.97)	1G186-23	OK-JII
D-FREE	Pilatus PC-6/B1-H2 Turbo-Porter	731	HB-F..
			C-GZCZ
			VH-ZCZ
			A14-705
			A14-731
			HB-FFS

Regn.	Type	C/n	Prev.Id.
D-FROG	Cessna 208A Caravan *(Reservation)*	00124	N203CA
			A2-AHL
			N65570
			C-FKAL
			(N9681F)
D-FSCB	Pilatus PC-6/B1-H2 Turbo-Porter	634	C-FPZB
			ZK-FZB
			VH-FZB
			LN-BIJ
			HB-FCU
D-FSKY	Pilatus PC-6/B2-H4 Turbo-Porter	878	
D-FSTN	Grob G.520 Egrett II	10003	D-FEGR
			N27ES
			D-FGEO
D-FTBM	SOCATA TBM-700A	1	F-GLBE
			N300PW
			F-OHBM
D-FUKK	CCF/North American Harvard IV	CCF4-46	N305GS
			RCAF20255
D-FUKM	Antonov AN-2T	17710	(D-FKMF)
			LSK-455
D-FUMP	Cessna 208B Grand Caravan	0743	
D-FUNY	Pilatus PC-6/B2-H4 Turbo-Porter	894	
D-FVIP	DHC-2 Beaver Mk 1 Floatplane	1512	N6246X
			ZK-CCY
			VH-XIX
			ZK-CCY
D-FWCK	Flug Werke FW.190A-8/N	990002	
D-FWGJ	SOCATA TBM-700A	19	N79Z
D-FWJA	Antonov AN-2T	1G86-41	(D-FAJA)
			DDR-WJA
			DM-WJA
D-FWJC	Antonov AN-2T	1G86-50	DDR-WJC
			DM-WJC
D-FWJD	Antonov AN-2T	1G98-51	(D-FCJD)
			DDR-WJD
			DM-WJD
D-FWJE	Antonov AN-2T	1G108-69	(D-FCJE)
			DDR-WJE
			DM-WJE
D-FWJG	Antonov AN-2T	1G142-32	(D-FCJG)
			DDR-WJG
			DM-WJG
D-FWJH	Antonov AN-2T	1G142-33	(D-FIJH)
			DDR-WJH
			DM-WJH
D-FWJK	Antonov AN-2T	1G142-34	(D-FCJK)
			DDR-WJK
			DM-WJK
D-FWJM	Antonov AN-2T	1G166-38	DDR-WJM
			DM-WJM
D-FWJO	Antonov AN-2T	1G174-26	DDR-WJO
			DM-WJO
D-FWME	Hispano HA.1112-ML *(Reservation)*	139	N3109G
	(For conversion to Bf 109G-6 standard)		G-AWHG
			C4K-75
D-FWUB	Focke-Wulf FW 190 *(Reservation)*	1876	
D-FWWC	Colling Focke-Wulf FW 190A-8 Replica	990001	
D-F . . .	Yakovlev YAK-11	171314	F-AZSF
			EAF: . . .

CLASS G : *Twin-Engined Aircraft of below 2 Metric Tonnes*

Regn.	Type	C/n	Prev.Id.
D-GAAA	Piper PA-44-180 Seminole	44-7995174	N3001H
D-GAAB	Piper PA-34-200T Seneca II	34-7670050	N139RJ
			N4463X
D-GABE(2)	Piper PA-34-220T Seneca III	34-8133181	N2913A
D-GABO	LET Aero 145	19-020	OK-NHL?
D-GABS	Partenavia P.68C-TC	399-47-TC	
D-GABT	Piper PA-34-220T Seneca III	34-8333098	N8210L
			N9511N
D-GABY(2)	Piper PA-30-160 Twin Comanche B	30-1405	OE-FPG
			N8397Y
D-GACH	Piper PA-44-180 Seminole	44-7995292	OE-FBN
			D-GFBN
			N2186Z
D-GACI	Piper PA-34-200T Seneca II	34-7770197	D-IACI
			N2796Q
D-GACR	Piper PA-34-220T Seneca III	34-8133215	N8429L
D-GACW	Piper PA-34-220T Seneca III	3433152	N91678
D-GADA	LET Aero 145	15-018	OK-NHC
D-GADE	Cessna 336 Skymaster	0058	N1758Z
D-GADN	Piper PA-34-200 Seneca	34-7250161	OK-CKK
			D-GADN
			N4545T
D-GADS	Piper PA-39 Twin Comanche C/R	39-67	PH-GAD
			G-AYFI
			N8922Y
			N9705N
D-GADY	Cessna 336 Skymaster *(Wfu)*	0158	N3858U
D-GAFC	Piper PA-44-180 Seminole	44-7995048	N21399
D-GAFI (2)	Piper PA-30-160 Twin Comanche B	30-1194	N10240
			D-GAFI (2)
			TJ-ADY
			F-OCHU
			(N8080Y)
D-GAFU	Piper PA-34-200T Seneca II	34-7970290	N2848S
D-GAFY	Cessna 337A Super Skymaster	0389	(N6389F)
D-GAGA	Piper PA-30-160 Twin Comanche	30-331	(PH-TPL)
			D-GAGA
			N7352Y
D-GAGE	Piper PA-30-160 Twin Comanche	30-804	N7715Y
D-GAGI	Piper PA-34-200 Seneca	34-7350223	N55496
D-GAHB(2)	Piper PA-34-220T Seneca III	34-8233005	N84556
D-GAHS	Piper PA-30-160 Twin Comanche C	30-1929	PH-ATV
			N8773Y
D-GAIR	Piper PA-34-200T Seneca II	34-8070003	N81008
D-GAJP	Piper PA-34-220T Seneca III	3433161	N9182D
D-GAKI	Piper PA-34-220T Seneca III	34-8233187	N8218Y
D-GAKK	Piper PA-34-200T Seneca II	34-7770097	D-IKKD
			OE-FDZ
			D-IHNI
			N9008F
D-GAKS	Piper PA-34-220T Seneca III	34-8133276	PH-HDG
			N8449W
D-GALA	Cessna 337D Super Skymaster	1014	N85894
D-GALE	LET L-200A Morava	170712	DDR-WLB
			DM-WLB
			OE-FTU
			OK-PHA
D-GALF	Piper PA-30-160 Twin Comanche C	30-1966	HB-LFH
			N8809Y
D-GAMA	Piper PA-44-180T Turbo Seminole	44-8207017	N8246S
D-GAMB	Piper PA-34-200T Seneca II	34-8070110	C-FSHC
			N81404
			N32DD
			N81404
D-GAME	Piper PA-34-200 Seneca	34-7350289	OE-FKA
			N56144
D-GAMI	Piper PA-34-200T Seneca II	34-7970286	C-GMDJ
			N285ON
D-GAMM	Piper PA-34-200T Seneca II	34-7870037	D-IDMM
			N9777K
D-GAMO	Piper PA-34-220T Seneca III	34-8233072	N8064M

Regn.	Type	C/n	Prev.Id.
D-GAMU	Piper PA-44-180T Turbo Seminole	44-8107034	N8153H / ZP-PTV
D-GAMW	Piper PA-34-200T Seneca II	34-7870468	OY-PEO / N30699
D-GANA	Partenavia P.68B	117	
D-GANI	Piper PA-34-200T Seneca II	34-7870021	HB-LKR / N47963
D-GANS(2)	Piper PA-44-180 Seminole	44-7995207	G-BOFV / N2198K
D-GANU	Piper PA-34-200T Seneca IV	3448079	N9255Q
D-GAPA	Piper PA-34-220T Seneca III	34-8633014	N9297Y
D-GAPP	Piper PA-44-180 Seminole	4496001	N9256R
D-GARE(2)	Piper PA-34-200T Seneca II	34-7870205	SE-GVN
D-GASA(2)	LET Aero 145	19-014	G-AROE / (D-GONE) / G-AROE / OK-NHF
D-GASB	Piper PA-34-200T Seneca II	34-8070032	N75TT / N70TT / N8123J
D-GASM	Piper PA-34-200T Seneca II	34-7970163	D-IASM / N3067U
D-GAST	Piper PA-30-160 Twin Comanche	30-379	N7362Y
D-GATA	Partenavia P.68B	82	
D-GATB	Piper PA-34-200T Seneca II	34-7570013	N32273
D-GATE(2)	Piper PA-34-220T Seneca III	3449007	N9285D
D-GAVA(2)	Piper PA-34-200T Seneca II	34-7870112	N3426M
D-GAWF(2)	Piper PA-34-200T Seneca II	34-7570025	D-IAWF / N32485
D-GAWO	Piper PA-34-220T Seneca III	3433038	N9121K
D-GAWP	Piper PA-34-200 Seneca	34-7250354	N15049
D-GAZE	Piper PA-30-160 Twin Comanche	30-681	N7646Y
D-GBAV	Piper PA-44-180T Turbo Seminole	44-8107051	N83709
D-GBCW	Piper PA-34-220T Seneca III	34-8233044	N8472E
D-GBFM	Piper PA-34-200 Seneca	34-7350259	N55602
D-GBFW	Piper PA-34-200 Seneca	34-7350116	N15992
D-GBGK	Partenavia P.68C-TC	267-18-TC	N2958W
D-GBIE	Beech B-95A Travel Air	TD-517	
D-GBIG	Piper PA-34-200T Seneca II	34-8070018	N8110J
D-GBPN	Piper PA-34-200T Seneca II	34-7770167	D-ILAC / N1066Q
D-GBRD	Partenavia P.68B	14	OY-DZR
D-GBRS	Partenavia P.68B	34	HB-LHN
D-GBSK	Piper PA-44-180T Turbo Seminole	44-8107050	N8363D
D-GBSL	Beech E95 Travel Air	TD-715	OY-BSL / D-GECA
D-GBTA	Beech 76 Duchess	ME-220	
D-GBTF	Beech 76 Duchess	ME-341	
D-GBWA	Piper PA-34-200T Seneca II	34-7670245	D-IAWA / N75375
D-GCCC	Piper PA-34-220T Seneca III	34-8233108	N8161C
D-GCCF	Piper PA-34-200T Seneca II	34-8070001	N45123
D-GCMH	Piper PA-44-180 Seminole	44-7995306	N2916N
D-GCPA(2)	Colomban MC-15 Cri-Cri (Reservn 12.99)	473-001 CS.PA	
D-GCRI	Grünenthal Colomban MC-12 Cri-Cri	1537	
D-GCWB	Piper PA-34-220T Seneca IV	3448070	N9251H
D-GDCO	Piper PA-23-160 Apache	23-1800	SE-EDG / D-GABA / N4369P
D-GDDC	Piper PA-34-200T Seneca II	34-7770016	D-IMGU / N5401F
D-GDEC	Piper PA-34-200T Seneca II	34-7870272	D-IDEC / PH-KAM / N31890
D-GDEF	Klein Rutan Defiant KII	161-AB	
D-GDMF	Piper PA-34-200T Seneca II	34-8133113	N122RM / N8396L
D-GDMW	Beech 76 Duchess	ME-316	LX-DRS / F-GCGB
D-GDTP	Piper PA-34-200T Seneca II	34-7970122	SE-IAZ
D-GDWL	Piper PA-34-220T Seneca III	3448025	N9121G
D-GDWR	Piper PA-34-200T Seneca II	34-7970448	OY-CBJ / N2499U
D-GEAB	Piper PA-30-160 Twin Comanche B	30-1373	N8247Y
D-GEAS	Piper PA-34-200T Seneca II	34-8070186	LN-MTS / SE-IDH
D-GEBD	Piper PA-44-180T Turbo Seminole	44-8207018	N92PA / N9588N
D-GEBE	Piper PA-34-220T Seneca III	34-8133228	N8435A
D-GEDM	Piper PA-44-180 Seminole	44-7995232	N3042N
D-GEDU	Piper PA-34-220T Seneca III	34-8133176	N8417G / D-GERN / N8417G
D-GEHB	Piper PA-30-160 Twin Comanche B	30-1417	N8283Y
D-GEIS	Piper PA-34-200T Seneca II	34-7870302	D-INIS / N36203
D-GEJJ	Piper PA-34-220T Seneca III	3433123	N9143Z
D-GEJL	Piper PA-34-200T Seneca II	34-7870265	N31744
D-GEJT	Piper PA-34-200T Seneca II	34-7970197	D-IEJT / N3058Y
D-GEKW	Piper PA-34-220T Seneca III	34-8133140	D-IILY / N8403L
D-GELA	Partenavia P.68B	137	
D-GELB	PZL M-20-03 Mewa	1AH003-07	
D-GELI	Partenavia P.68B	108	
D-GELX	Piper PA-34-220T Seneca V	3449059	N41184
D-GELY	Piper PA-44-180 Seminole	44-7995036	N20957
D-GEMA(2)	Partenavia P.68B	175	(YV-1834P)
D-GEMB	Partenavia P.68B	188	
D-GEMC	Partenavia P.68B	200	
D-GEMF	Partenavia P.68C-TC	237-03-TC	
D-GEMI	Partenavia P.68C-TC	247-09-TC	
D-GEMK	Partenavia P.68C-TC	258-16-TC	
D-GEPA	Piper PA-34-220T Seneca III	3433041	N9120D
D-GERA	Partenavia P.68B	101	CS-AYB / D-GERA
D-GERB	Partenavia P.68 Observer	173	
D-GERI	Partenavia P.68C	367	
D-GERM	Meinhardt Colomban MC-15 Cri-Cri	256	(Reserved as D-GNSL, 5.99)
D-GERT	Partenavia P.68B	47	
D-GERY	Partenavia P.68B	49	
D-GEST	Grumman GA-7 Cougar	0102	
D-GETT	Piper PA-34-200T Seneca II	34-7770376	D-IETT / N44924
D-GEUH	Piper PA-34-220T Seneca III	34-8133161	N8413K / ZP-TVM / N8413K
D-GEVA	Piper PA-34-200 Seneca	34-7250165	N4894T
D-GEWO	Piper PA-34-200 Seneca	34-7450077	HB-LEX / 4X-CAD / D-GAEN / N40773
D-GEWU	Beech 76 Duchess	ME-398	
D-GEXA	Beech 76 Duchess	ME-170	N6021L
D-GFCM	Piper PA-44-180 Seminole	44-7995027	N39705
D-GFEY	Piper PA-34-200T Seneca II	34-7870343	D-IFEY / N36599
D-GFGH	Piper PA-34-220T Seneca III	3447018	N9271L
D-GFGP	PZL M20-03 Mewa	1AH003-06	
D-GFIT	Piper PA-34-200T Seneca II	34-7870221	N215RW / N9775C
D-GFKH	Piper PA-34-220T Seneca III	3448028	N9155H
D-GFPE	Piper PA-30-160 Twin Comanche C	30-1962	OE-FPE / N8846Y
D-GFPG	Partenavia P.68B	170	
D-GFPI	Partenavia P.68B	158	N146BK / (N2084J) / D-GFPI
D-GFTL	Piper PA-39 Twin Comanche C/R	39-124	N228MF / N9659N
D-GGAB	Piper PA-34-220T Seneca IV	3447020	N9275C
D-GGDH	Heuer Colomban MC-15 Cri-Cri	164	
D-GGFB	Bulmahn Colomban MC-15 Cri-Cri	365	
D-GGGA	Piper PA-34-220T Seneca III	34-8533034	N2477Y / N9547N
D-GGOD	Piper PA-44-180 Seminole	44-7995322	N4509L
D-GGOH	Piper PA-34-200T Seneca V	3449074	N41238
D-GGOW	Piper PA-34-200 Seneca	34-7350225	N55521

Regn.	Type	C/n	Prev.Id.
D-GGRO	Piper PA-34-200T Seneca II	34-7570322	N4354X / N9600N
D-GGRT	Piper PA-34-220T Seneca III	34-8333003	N8230S
D-GGRZ	Piper PA-34-200T Seneca II	34-7770373	N7714M / C-GRHW / N7714M / N9599N
D-GGTT	Piper PA-34-220T Seneca III	34-8333115	N43129 / N9535N / N43129 / N9522N
D-GHBN	Aero 45 (Reservation)	51159	
	(Possible identity c/n 51195 ex HB-EKC ?)		
D-GHCH	PZL M20-03 Mewa	1AH002-17	
D-GHEB	Piper PA-34-200T Seneca II	34-7870168	N9367C / N9550N
D-GHFW(2)	Piper PA-30-160 Twin Comanche B	30-1326	N8228Y
D-GHGM	Piper PA-34-200 Seneca	34-7250157	N4502T
D-GHHZ	Zeiler Colomban MC-15 Cri-Cri	Z-01	
D-GHIK	Piper PA-39 Twin Comanche C/R	39-130	D-GHSH / G-AZNM / N8967Y
D-GHPA	Piper PA-34-220T Seneca III	3433131	D-IHPA(2) / D-GHPA / N9150Z
D-GHWB	Huber Colomban MC-15 Cri-Cri	H/EB-01/149	
D-GHWW	Piper PA-23-160 Apache (Reservation 6.99)	23-1816	N4315P
D-GIBA	Piper PA-23-160 Apache	23-1579	
D-GIFK	Piper PA-34-220T Seneca III	34-8333028	N8291D / N9540N / N823IA
	(Formerly c/n 34-8233170)		
D-GIFR	Partenvia P.68B	57	LN-LMS
D-GIFT	Piper PA-34-200 Seneca	34-7350290	N56156
D-GIGI (3)	Piper PA-34-220T Seneca III	34-8233117	HB-LNF
D-GIGY	Beech 76 Duchess	ME-80	
D-GIHZ	Beech 76 Duchess	ME-4	HB-GGT / N18876
D-GILA	Partenavia P.68B	52	
D-GILD	Piper PA-34-200T Seneca II	34-7570164	N33805
D-GIMR	Piper PA-34-220T Seneca V	3449070	N41278
D-GIMY	Piper PA-34-220T Seneca III	3433139	N9163N
D-GINA(2)	Partenavia P.68B	59	
D-GIOR	Piper PA-34-200T Seneca II	34-7570119	D-ICOR / N33430
D-GIOW	Piper PA-34-200T Seneca II	34-7570270	D-IKOW / N1520X
D-GIPA	Piper PA-34-220T Seneca III	3433159	N9178E
D-GIPC	Piper PA-34-220T Seneca IV	3448057	N92485
D-GIRL(2)	Piper PA-30-160 Twin Comanche	30-63	HB-LAG / N7052Y
D-GIRO	Partenavia P.68B	69	
D-GISE	Piper PA-34-200T Seneca II	34-7870193	D-IHSE / N9508C
D-GISO	Piper PA-44-180T Turbo Seminole	44-8107065	N82112 / N9602N
D-GITA	Partenavia P.68B	92	
D-GITY(2)	Partenavia P.68C-TC	360-41-TC	HB-LRK / D-GAHI / N360TC
D-GIVB	Piper PA-34-220T Seneca III	34-8633001	D-IHVB(3) / D-GHVB / N9247M
D-GIWA	Piper PA-34-200T Seneca II	34-8070145	D-IEWA / N8166B
D-GIWL	Piper PA-34-200T Seneca II	34-7570307	D-IFWL / N3903X
D-GIWO	Piper PA-34-200T Seneca II	34-7670076	OE-FRS / N4579X
D-GIXB	Piper PA-34-220T Seneca III	34-8233151	SE-IXB / OY-CGR / N8210K
D-GJBA	Piper PA-34-200T Seneca II	34-8070116	N8149H
D-GJET	Piper PA-44-180T Turbo Seminole	44-8107003	N8196U
D-GJFN	Piper PA-34-220T Seneca III	34-8133061	SE-IYR / OY-CGI / N8371J
D-GJTL	Piper PA-34-220T Seneca III	34-8233147	N8207J
D-GJVM	Piper PA-34-200T Seneca II	34-7970225	(D-GFOX) / OE-FOX / N28598
D-GKFE	Cessna 337A Super Skymaster	0358	N958TM / N6358F
D-GKHF	Piper PA-34-200T Seneca II	34-7970255	D-IKHF / N29545
D-GKIM	Piper PA-34-200T Seneca II	34-7970228	N28710
D-GKKD(2)	Piper PA-44-180T Turbo Seminole	44-8207016	N94PA / N81419 / N9550N / N82525
D-GKMI	Piper PA-34-200T Seneca II	34-8070290	I-ARMT / N8252D / N963PG
D-GLAD	Piper PA-34-200T Seneca II	34-7970427	LX-YES / N2967X
D-GLAN	Piper PA-34-200 Seneca	34-7350110	N15932
D-GLIN(2)	Linkohr Colomban MC-15 Cri-Cri	312	
D-GLIV	Piper PA-34-200T Seneca II	34-7870203	PH-FEJ / OO-FEJ / PH-FEJ / N9620C
D-GLPE	Piper PA-34-200T Seneca III	3447014	N9267L
D-GLUT	Piper PA-44-180T Turbo Seminole	44-8107019	N82556
D-GMAB	Piper PA-34-220T Seneca III	3433168	N9220J / N9180W
D-GMAI	Piper PA-39 Twin Comanche C/R	39-50	N8892Y
D-GMBE	Piper PA-34-200T Seneca II	34-7870209	D-IMBE / N9679C
D-GMBK	Piper PA-34-220T Seneca III	34-8233035	OE-FEK / N8467Z
D-GMCW	Piper PA-34-200T Seneca II	34-7770163	N999LF
D-GMFB	Piper PA-34-220T Seneca III	34-8433036	EC-FNE / LN-KLV / N4348P
D-GMMR	Piper PA-34-220T Seneca III	34-8133225	N8434Z
D-GMOF	Piper PA-34-200T Seneca II	34-7870301	D-IMOF / N36184
D-GMOH	Piper PA-34-200T Seneca II	34-7870281	D-IMOH
D-GMUT	Piper PA-34-220T Seneca III	3433091	N9136P
D-GMWA	Piper PA-30-160 Twin Comanche B	30-1178	N8064Y
D-GMWF	Piper PA-34-200 Seneca	34-7250105	N4471T
D-GMYU	Beech 76 Duchess	ME-330	OE-FEW / D-GBTE
D-GMZE	Piper PA-34-200T Seneca II	34-7870452	OO-CFA / N21901
D-GNAT	Piper PA-34-220T Seneca III	34-8133223	N8434P
D-GNFJ	Piper PA-44-180 Seminole	44-7995084	PH-SYB / N2118A
D-GNNN	Piper PA-34-220T Seneca III	3447017	N9272L
D-GNOM	Piper PA-34-220T Seneca III	34-8233022	N8460K
D-GNSL	Meinhardt/Colomban MC-15 Cri-Cri	256AB	
	(Reservation 5.99)		
D-GOAC	Piper PA-34-200T Seneca II	34-7770007	N5329F
D-GOBB	Piper PA-34-200 Seneca	34-7350253	N55871
D-GOBN	Piper PA-34-220T Seneca III	34-8133023	N8344M
D-GOFW	Piper PA-44-180 Seminole	44-7995123	N3011C
D-GOFY(3)	Piper PA-34-200T Seneca II	34-8170041	N8297L
D-GOGO(2)	Partenavia P.68C-TC	343-31-TC	
D-GOJR	Piper PA-34-220T Seneca III	34-8233036	N84671
D-GOKI	Piper PA-44-180T Turbo Seminole	44-8107005	N8226A
D-GOLD(2)	Piper PA-34-220T Seneca V	3449054	N9293W
D-GOLF	Piper PA-23-160 Apache	23-1361	N3398P / (D-GEKL) / N3398P
D-GOMM	Piper PA-34-220T Seneca III	34-8433020	SE-KOT / N4324K
D-GONG	Piper PA-34-200T Seneca II	34-7570047	D-IJSK / N44007

Regn.	Type	C/n	Prev.Id.
D-GOOO	Piper PA-34-200T Seneca II	34-7970360	OE-FBP
			N19499
			N9591N
D-GOPS	Piper PA-34-200T Seneca II	34-7970028	D-GOBC
			N2169D
D-GORC	Piper PA-34-200T Seneca II	34-8170068	N8310H
D-GOSR	Piper PA-34-220T Seneca III	34-8133017	N8340S
D-GOVA	Piper PA-34-200T Seneca II	34-8070209	PH-SYC
			N81922
D-GPEZ	Piper PA-30-160 Twin Comanche C	30-1871	N8798Y
			N9703N
D-GPJB	Piper PA-34-220T Seneca III	34-8133173	N84131
D-GPTT	Piper PA-34-220T Seneca IV	3448043	N9245J
D-GRHZ	Hermle Colomban MC-15 Cri-Cri	469	
D-GRRR	Piper PA-44-180T Turbo Seminole	44-8107038	N8332A
D-GSKY	Piper PA-34-220T Seneca V	3449102	N41225
D-GSMH	Hagensieker Colomban MC-15 Cri-Cri	2175	
D-GULL	LET L.200D Morava	171407	OK-UHA
D-GUTE	Piper PA-34-200T Seneca II	34-7770382	N44989
D-GVST	Piper PA-34-200T Seneca II	34-7870263	N31725
D-GWPL	Piper PA-34-220T Seneca III	34-8433005	N4323Y
			N9509N
D-GWWW	Piper PA-34-220T Seneca V	3449021	N92882

CLASS H : All Rotary-winged Aircraft without Weight Limit

Regn.	Type	C/n	Prev.Id.
D-HAAA(3)	Westland-Bell 47G-3B1 /Soloy	WA/386	G-BHKB
			XT227
D-HAAD(2)	Agusta A.109A	7122	VR-CCO
			ZK-HBC(2)
			N91969
			XC-CAL
D-HAAE	Hiller UH-12E Soloy	2039	C-GMTF
			N9060F
			CF-OKC
			CF-MHI
D-HAAF	Aérospatiale SA.341G Gazelle	1111	
D-HAAG	Agusta A.109A-II	7274	I-DACC
D-HAAH(2)	Aérospatiale SA.360C Dauphin	1005	N47287
D-HAAK(2)	Aérospatiale SA.365C3 Dauphin 2	5039	YR-DFD
D-HAAL	Aérospatiale SA.360C Dauphin	1030	
D-HAAM	Aérospatiale AS.350B Ecureuil	1910	
D-HAAN	Helibras HB.350B Esquilo	HB1038/1580	PT-HMB
D-HAAP	Agusta A.109C	7617	JA9989
D-HAAR(2)	Enstrom 280C Shark	1189	(D-HAAH)
			D-HGBX
			SE-HKX
D-HAAS	Enstrom F-28A-D	086	
D-HAAZ	Agusta A.109A	7230	SX-HCA
			D-HORN(2)
			N24PT
			N12FU
			I-VDMC
D-HABA(3)	Bell 206B Jet Ranger II	4259	
D-HABB	Bell 206L Long Ranger	45783	N102RD
D-HABN	Hughes 269A (TH-55A)	105-0394	N62468
			64-18082
D-HABY(2)	Westland-Bell 47G-3B1/Soloy	WA/610	G-BHKD
			XT848
D-HACC(3)	Bell 407	53322	N322RT
D-HACK	Agusta-Bell 47J-2A	2071	5B-CAF
			CR-1
D-HACM	Helicraft Ultrasport 496 (Permit 5.99)	496001	
D-HADG	Westland-Bell 47G-3B1	WA/508	OE-CXA
			D-HHRW
			XT801
D-HADO(3)	Bölkow BO.105S	S-544	(D-HDNS)

Regn.	Type	C/n	Prev.Id.
D-HAEW	Enstrom F-28A-D	095	
D-HAFA(4)	Bell 206B Jet Ranger II	124	G-HELO
			G-BAZN
			9J-RIN
			ZS-HCJ
D-HAFB(2)	Westland-Bell 47G-3B1	WA/426	D-HAFW
			(D-HAFN)
			XT514
D-HAFC(2)	Agusta-Bell 206B Jet Ranger II	8323	OE-BXR
D-HAFD(5)	Agusta-Bell 206B Jet Ranger II	8534	G-BMCH
			SE-HGR
D-HAFG(3)	Agusta-Bell 212 (Permit 11.99)	5522	RSAF1413
D-HAFH(2)	Bell 205A-1	30291	SE-HVT
			LN-OPS
			N5019N
D-HAFI (2)	Agusta-Bell 206B Jet Ranger II	8492	OE-BXT
D-HAFJ	Westland-Bell 47G-3B1	WA/701	XW181
D-HAFK	Westland-Bell 47G-3B1	WA/331	XT172
D-HAFL(2)	Bell 205A-1	30056	LN-ORY
			SE-HLU
			AMDB-102
D-HAFM(3)	Bell 205A-1	30101	VR-BFW
			VH-BHW
			N7036J
D-HAFN(2)	Bell 206B Jet Ranger II	1957	N9909K
D-HAFR(2)	Bell 205A-1	30318	N8227H
			LN-OLM
			C-GFHN
D-HAFS(2)	Bell 212	30655	ZK-HNK
		·	EI-BAM
			G-BCPY
D-HAFT	Aérospatiale AS.350B Ecureuil	1457	
D-HAFU(3)	Aérospatiale AS.350B Ecureuil	1788	
D-HAFV(2)	Agusta-Bell AB.212	5504	I-AGUV
D-HAFY(2)	Agusta-Bell 206B Jet Ranger III	8654	
D-HAFZ	Westland-Bell 47G-3B1	WA/702	XW182
D-HAGA	Aérospatiale SA.318C Alouette Astazou	1933	
D-HAGE	Aérospatiale SA.318C Alouette Astazou	1943	
D-HAGI	Aérospatiale SA.318C Alouette Astazou	1944	
D-HAGR	Hiller UH-12E (Soloy)	5184	N4033J
D-HAHA	Hiller UH-12B	613	Fr.AF
D-HAHN(4)	Aérospatiale AS.350B2 Ecureuil	9003	
D-HAHY	Aérospatiale SA.318C Alouette Astazou	1972	
D-HAJO(2)	Bell 212	30573	
D-HAKG	Hughes 269C	59-0798	
D-HAKN	Agusta-Bell 47G-2	268	74+26
			AS+380
			LA+110
			AS+068
D-HAKW	Küffner KH92 Rotorway Exec 90	92001	
	(Permit expired, to Sinsheim Museum)		
D-HAKY(2)	Bell 206B Jet Ranger II	2687	OE-DXU
			D-HAKY(2)
			N2755C
D-HALA	Bell UH-1D (205)	8051	(70+21)
D-HALB(2)	Schweizer 269C	S-1465	
D-HALD(2)	Robinson R-44 Astro	0538	
D-HALE	Bell UH-1D (205)	8052	(70+22)
D-HALF(2)	Robinson R-44 Astro	0543	
D-HALI	Bell UH-1D (205)	8053	(70+23)
D-HALJ	Robinson R-44 Astro	0544	
D-HALL(3)	Robinson R-44 Astro	0578	
D-HALM(2)	Schweizer 269C	S-1379	N7507X
D-HALN	Robinson R-44 Astro	0609	
D-HALO	Bell UH-1D (205)	8054	(70+24)
D-HALP	Robinson R-44 Astro	0614	
D-HALS	Bell 212	30575	
D-HALT(3)	Bell 206L-3 Long Ranger III	51578	C-FNLC
D-HALY	Bell UH-1D (205)	8055	(70+25)
D-HAMA	Aérospatiale SA.318C Alouette Astazou	1984	
D-HAMB	Bölkow BO.105S	S-205	HB-XFN
			D-HDFT(2)
D-HAMF	Agusta A.109A	7217	N77HG
			C-GDDA
			N9046U

Regn.	Type	C/n	Prev.Id.	Regn.	Type	C/n	Prev.Id.
D-HAMS(3)	Agusta-Bell 47G-4A *(Reservation 10.99)*	2530	G-BYCI	D-HAVI	Agusta-Bell 206A Jet Ranger II	8234	
			EC-BSC	D-HAVM	Robinson R-22 Beta	1592	
D-HAMY(2)	Bölkow BO.105S	S-426	D-HDMY	D-HAWA(2)	Enstrom F-28A-D	255	
D-HAND	Bell 212	30568		D-HAWB	Hemberger Skorpion	unkn	
D-HANE	Bell 206B Jet Ranger II	3601	N206PW	D-HAWK(2)	MBB-Kawasaki BK.117B-2	7225	D-HFDP
			N911SE	D-HAWY	Bölkow BO.105S	S-594	(D-HDQQ)
			N911SL	D-HAXA	Aérospatiale SA.330J Puma	1201	
			N2262F	D-HAXC	Aérospatiale SA.330J Puma	1241	
D-HANO(2)	Robinson R-22A Alpha	0486	N85611	D-HAXD	Aérospatiale SA.330J Puma	1285	
D-HANS(3)	MBB-Kawasaki BK.117B-2 *(Reservation 4.99)*	7001	D-HIFR(2)	D-HAXE	Aérospatiale SA.330J Puma	1289	
			D-HMBF(4)	D-HAXF	Aérospatiale SA.330J Puma	1291	
			D-HBKC	D-HAXG	Aérospatiale SA.330J Puma	1332	
D-HAPI (2)	Aérospatiale AS.350B Ecureuil	1184	F-WZF .	D-HAXH	Aérospatiale SA.330J Puma	1410	
D-HAPL	Eurocopter EC.120B Colibri	1026		D-HAXI	Aérospatiale SA.330J Puma	1429	
D-HAPP	Bell 47G-4A	7736	C-GUKW	D-HAXJ	Aérospatiale SA.330J Puma	1434	
D-HAPY(2)	Bell 206L-3 Long Ranger III	51040		D-HAXK	Aérospatiale SA.330J Puma	1442	
D-HAQA	Bell UH-1D (205)	8056	(70+26)	D-HAXL	Aérospatiale SA.330J Puma	1454	
D-HAQE	Bell UH-1D (205)	8057	(70+27)	D-HAXM	Aérospatiale SA.330J Puma	1496	F-WZCE
D-HAQI	Bell UH-1D (205)	8058	(70+28)	D-HAXN	Aérospatiale SA.330J Puma	1499	
D-HARD(2)	Bell 206A Jet Ranger	486	N2288W	D-HAXO	Aérospatiale SA.330J Puma	1537	
D-HARE	Aérospatiale SA.318C Alouette Astazou	2075		D-HAXP	Aérospatiale SA.330J Puma	1545	
D-HARI (3)	Agusta A.109C	7619	TC-HHI	D-HAXQ	Aérospatiale SA.330J Puma	1549	
			D-HAAX	D-HAXR	Aérospatiale SA.330J Puma	1553	
			JA6608	D-HAXS	Aérospatiale SA.330J Puma	1573	
D-HARO(2)	Bölkow BO.105S	S-831	OE-XFS	D-HAXT	Aérospatiale SA.330J Puma	1577	
			HB-XXK	D-HAXU	Aérospatiale SA.330J Puma	1596	
			D-HFCO	D-HAXV	Aérospatiale SA.330J Puma	1592	
D-HARS	Schönherr GMS-3	001		D-HAXW	Aérospatiale SA.330J Puma	1594	
D-HART	Hughes 269C	100-0058		D-HAYA	Bölkow BO.105C	S-126	D-HDDS
D-HARU(2)	Bölkow BO.105S	S-425	D-HDMX	D-HAYE	Bölkow BO.105C	S-140	(D-HDEH)
D-HARZ	Bell 212	30598		D-HAYI	Bölkow BO.105S	S-368	(D-HDLD)
D-HASA(4)	Bell 206L-3 Long Ranger III	51278	G-SEAN	D-HAZI	Agusta A.109A-II	7303	N109MB
			N7061H				N212BT
D-HASB	Bell 47G-2	1466	N2816B				N109PD
D-HASC	Bell 47G-5	7843	N1393X	D-HAZY(2)	Bölkow BO.105S	S-832	D-HAIY(2)
D-HASI (4)	Bell 407	53062					D-HFCP
D-HASP	Hughes 369E *(Reserved as F-GYCC 11.99)*	0325E	I-BNAR	D-HBAD(4)	Bell 206B Jet Ranger II	3819	N3203Z
D-HASW	Westland-Bell 47G-3B-1	WA/521	XT814	D-HBAP	Bell 407	53208	
D-HASY	Bölkow BO.105S	S-427	D-HDMZ	D-HBAS	Aérospatiale AS.350B1 Ecureuil	2204	F-GHFL
D-HATE	Bell UH-1D (205)	8063	(70+33)		*(Reserved as F-GMBZ & F-GUPF .99)*		N607S
D-HATI	Bell UH-1D (205)	8064	(70+34)	D-HBAT(2)	Schneider Sch-2	AB 1	
D-HATO	Bell UH-1D (205)	8065	(70+35)	D-HBAY(3)	MBB-Kawasaki BK.117B-2	7205	LN-OSY
D-HATS(2)	Westland-Bell 47G3B1 /Soloy	WA/709	HB-XMM				D-HIMV
			XW189	D-HBBA	Hughes 369HS	34-0574S	N5197Y
D-HATU	Bell UH-1D (205)	8066	(70+36)				G-NUNK
D-HAUA	Bell 206L-3 Long Ranger III	51328	N21AH				G-BMSP
			N21830				C-GOEA
D-HAUC(2)	Agusta-Bell 47G-3B-1	1585	XT121	D-HBBB(2)	MBB-Kawasaki BK.117B-2	7220	LN-OSV
D-HAUD(2)	Aérospatiale AS.355N Ecureuil 2	5538	F-WYMA				D-HFDK
			F-WZKL	D-HBBH	Blunck Invader Gyrocopter	BB1-3509	
D-HAUE(2)	Bell 206B Jet Ranger II	4195		D-HBEE	Schweizer 269C	S-1597	N41S
D-HAUF(2)	Agusta-Bell 206B Jet Ranger II	8190	OE-BXN	D-HBEL(2)	Bell 407	53236	(N6375S)
D-HAUG	Sikorsky S-58C	58-836	R.Belg.AF	D-HBEN(2)	Bell 407	53153	
			B-15/OT-ZKP	D-HBER(2)	Schweizer 269C	S-1522	N69A
			OO-SHP	D-HBFJ	Hughes 269C	100-0980	N1112P
			N869	D-HBGF	Elisport CH-7 Angel *(Reservation 11.99)*	136	
D-HAUH	Westland-Bell 47G-3B1	WA/441	(D-HOBZ)	D-HBGR	Sikorsky S-76B	760320	
			XT552	D-HBGS	Bölkow BO.105C	S-11	(D-HBAY)
D-HAUI	Westland-Bell 47G-3B1	WA/368	XT209	D-HBHG	MBB-Kawasaki BK.117B-2	7164	Abu Dhabi
D-HAUK	Aérospatiale AS.350BA Ecureuil	1750	D-HFFG				D-HBHG
D-HAUL	Aérospatiale SA.360C Dauphin	1009	F-GCMG	D-HBIN	Schweizer 269C	S-1639	N86G
D-HAUM(2)	Aérospatiale AS.350B1 Ecureuil	1939	D-HAUX	D-HBIV	Bölkow BO.105S	S-891	D-HMB .
	(Rebuild using parts of D-HAUM(1) c/n 1359		D-HAHG				(D-HFNW)
	and identity of D-HAUX)			D-HBJA	Aérospatiale SA.318C Alouette Astazou	2017	77+28
D-HAUN	Aérospatiale AS.350B Ecureuil	2056		D-HBJB	Aérospatiale SA.318C Alouette Astazou	2027	77+29
D-HAUP	Aérospatiale SA.360C Dauphin	1018	JA9244	D-HBJC	Aérospatiale SA.318C Alouette Astazou	2031	77+30
D-HAUQ	Aérospatiale AS.350B Ecureuil *(Reservation)*	1850	F-GFBC	D-HBJE	Aérospatiale SA.318C Alouette Astazou	2046	77+34
D-HAUR	Aérospatiale AS.350B2 Ecureuil	2394	HB-XUY	D-HBJF	Aérospatiale SA.318C Alouette Astazou	2047	77+35
D-HAUS(3)	Aérospatiale SA.360C Dauphin	1022	JA9277	D-HBJG	Aérospatiale SA.318C Alouette Astazou	2107	77+57
D-HAUT(2)	Robinson R-44 Astro	0504		D-HBJH	Aérospatiale SA.318C Alouette Astazou	2108	77+58
D-HAUU	Aérospatiale AS.350B1 Ecureuil	2072	D-HAUZ	D-HBJI	Aérospatiale SA.318C Alouette Astazou	2113	77+59
			HB-XUK	D-HBJJ	Aérospatiale SA.318C Alouette Astazou	2116	77+62
			I-ORTA	D-HBJK	Aérospatiale SA.318C Alouette Astazou	2248	77+78
D-HAUV	Eurocopter EC.120B Colibri	1010		D-HBJL	Aérospatiale SA.318C Alouette Astazou	2086	77+48
D-HAUW	Aérospatiale AS.350B3 Ecureuil	3170		D-HBJM	Aérospatiale SA.318C Alouette Astazou	2091	77+49

Regn.	Type	C/n	Prev.Id.
D-HBJN	Aérospatiale SA.318C Alouette Astazou	2100	77+53
D-HBJO	Aérospatiale SA.318C Alouette Astazou	2101	77+54
D-HBJP	Aérospatiale SA.318C Alouette Astazou	2105	77+55
D-HBJQ	Aérospatiale SA.318C Alouette Astazou	2106	77+56
D-HBJR	Aérospatiale SA.318C Alouette Astazou	2130	77+71
D-HBJS	Aérospatiale SA.318C Alouette Astazou	2131	77+72
D-HBJT	Aérospatiale SA.318C Alouette Astazou	2132	77+73
D-HBJU	Aérospatiale SA.318C Alouette Astazou	2134	77+74
D-HBJV	Aérospatiale SA.318C Alouette Astazou	2016	77+27
D-HBJW	Aérospatiale SA.318C Alouette Astazou	2092	77+50
D-HBJX	Aérospatiale SA.318C Alouette Astazou	2114	77+60
D-HBJY	Aérospatiale SA.318C Alouette Astazou	2061	77+39
D-HBJZ	Aérospatiale SA.318C Alouette Astazou	2032	77+31
D-HBKK	MBB-Kawasaki BK.117B-2	7009	
D-HBKX(2)	MBB-Kawasaki BK.117C-1 (Reservation, for Italy)	7525	
D-HBLE	Westland-Bell 47G-3B1/Soloy	WA450	HB-XLE
			XT561
D-HBLK	Agusta-Bell 206B Jet Ranger II	8379	
D-HBND	MBB-Kawasaki BK.117B-2	7056	OO-XCY
			D-HBND
			OO-VCY
			OO-XCY
			(OO-VCY)
			(N156BK)
			D-HBND
			(N157BK)
D-HBNE	MBB-Kawasaki BK.117A-4	7057	
D-HBOA(2)	Bölkow BO.105C	S-929	
D-HBOB	Bölkow BO.105C	S-175	(D-HDFM)
D-HBOC	Bölkow BO.105C	S-325	(D-HDJC)
D-HBOD	Bölkow BO.105C	S-326	(D-HDJD)
D-HBOE	Bölkow BO.105C	S-415	(D-HDMN)
D-HBRE	MBB-Kawasaki BK.117B-2	7184	G-HMBB
			D-HIMA
			(N5405K)
D-HBRO(2)	Robinson R-22B2 Beta	unkn	
D-HBSF	Schweizer 269C	S-1582	N86G
D-HBSI	Bölkow BO.105C	S-9	(D-HMTU)
D-HBUR	Bell 206L-3 Long Ranger III	51329	N21837
D-HBWF(2)	MBB-Kawasaki BK.117B-2	7247	D-HFIL
D-HBWG	MBB-Kawasaki BK.117B-2	7250	D-HFIO
D-HBWP	Bell 212	30645	N59586
D-HBXL	Robinson R-22 Beta	2185	N2342N
D-HBYA	Eurocopter EC.135P1	0057	
D-HBYB	Eurocopter EC.135P1	0059	
D-HBYD	Eurocopter EC.135P1	0061	
D-HBYE	Eurocopter EC.135P1	0075	
D-HBYF	Eurocopter EC.135P1	0078	
D-HBYG(2)	Eurocopter EC.135P1	0080	
D-HBYH(2)	Eurocopter EC.135P1	0100	
D-HBYI (2)	Eurocopter EC.135P1	0096	
D-HBZS	Bell 212	30879	
D-HBZT	Bell 212	30943	
D-HCAN	Bell 222UT	47548	N222HW
			SE-HOU
D-HCAP	Hughes 269B	116-0290	D-HDUR
			LN-ORL
D-HCAT(2)	Robinson R-44 Astro	0180	
D-HCCC(3)	Hiller UH-12E /Soloy	HA-3035	N135HA
D-HCCS	Schweizer 269C	S-1741	
D-HCFE	Robinson R-44 Astro	0233	
D-HCGA	Robinson R-44 Astro	0108	
D-HCHS(2)	Hughes 369E	0230E	OE-XXL
			N1602N
D-HCKV	Agusta A.109A-II	7345	N109HC
			N2GN
D-HCOL	Aérospatiale AS.350B2 Ecureuil	2814	F-WYMI
D-HCOR	Aérospatiale AS.350B Ecureuil	1601	
D-HCWB	Schweizer 269C	S-1772	N69A
D-HCWK	Schweizer 269C	S-1740	
D-HDAC(2)	MBB-Kawasaki BK.117B-2	7005	D-HBKG
D-HDAN(4)	Aérospatiale AS.350B3 Ecureuil	3124	
D-HDCS(3)	Agusta-Bell 206B Jet Ranger II	8364	HB-XPA
			D-HHRT
D-HDDD(4)	MBB-Kawasaki BK.117C-1	7507	N6096U
			D-HMBG(2)

Regn.	Type	C/n	Prev.Id.
D-HDDP	Bölkow BO.105C	S-123	
D-HDEL(3)	Hughes 269C	71-1071	N5045J
D-HDFU(2)	Bölkow BO.105S	S-206	
D-HDKW	Agusta-Bell 47G-2	238	74+07
			AS+397
D-HDLW(2)	Robinson R-44 Astro	0106	
D-HDMA(2)	Bölkow BO.105S	S-414	(D-HDMM)
D-HDML(2)	Bölkow BO.105S	S-438	
D-HDNM	Bölkow BO.105LS	S-459	
D-HDOR	Hughes 369D	29-0450D	LY-HAS
			D-HDOR
			CS-H..
			D-HDOR
			C-GRYV
D-HDPB	Bell 206B Jet Ranger II	4151	OH-HTS
D-HDPS(2)	Bölkow BO.105S	S-570	
D-HDRA(3)	Bölkow BO.105S	S-391	D-HBBB
			D-HDLG
D-HDWM	Hughes 369HS	73-0498S	F-GBGR
			D-HDWM
D-HEAA	Bölkow BO.105S	S-904	
D-HEAS(3)	Bell 206B Jet Ranger II	4163	LN-OBE
			C-FKDT
D-HEBA(2)	Bell 47G-3B1 Soloy	3575	N51SP
			66-8075
D-HEBB(3)	Bell 407 (Permit 1.99)	53336	
D-HEBE	Brantly B-2	40	N4998C
D-HEBI (2)	Bell 206B Jet Ranger II	3662	G-BSBJ
			N3171P
			N678LD
D-HEBM	Bell 206B Jet Ranger II	3533	I-MIBA
			N2300H
D-HEBS	Bell 47J-2 Ranger	2855	N73291
D-HECA to HECZ Test registrations for Eurocopter Deutschland for EC.135 production			
D-HECD	MBB-Kawasaki BK.117C-1	7500	
D-HECE(2)	MBB-Kawasaki BK.117B-2	7244	D-HDDD(3)
			D-HECE(2)
			(D-HFII)
D-HECI (2)	Westland-Bell 47G-3B-1	WA591	XT829
D-HECS	Aérospatiale AS.350B Ecureuil	2361	F-GGPY
D-HECX	Eurocopter EC-135B-1	S-01	D-HBOX
D-HECY(3)	Eurocopter EC-135D-1	S-02	
D-HECZ	Eurocopter EC-135B-1	S-03	
D-HEDI (2)	Aérospatiale SA.318C Alouette Astazou	2026	
D-HEEC	Aérospatiale AS.350B Ecureuil	1934	
D-HEED	Agusta A.109A	7201	N3983N
			HB-XNF
			I-PATZ
D-HEEE(2)	Bölkow BO.105S	S-713	LX-HAR
			D-HEEE(2)
			(N713XY)
			D-HDRA
D-HEEH	Aérospatiale AS.350B2 Ecureuil	1598	N65452
			N5804T
D-HEER(2)	Enstrom 280F	1501	N966D
			N9660
			N8617Z
D-HEES	Schäfer KW-1 Rotorway Executive 90	3510	
D-HEGA(2)	Aérospatiale AS.332L1 Super Puma	2234	
D-HEGB	Aérospatiale AS.332L1 Super Puma	2265	F-WYML
D-HEGC	Aérospatiale AS.332L1 Super Puma	2268	
D-HEHB	Bell 206L Long Ranger	45011	
D-HEHE	Schweizer 269C	S-1416	N919FH
			N7508D
D-HEHR	Ehringhaus Revolution Mini-500 (Permit)	100	
D-HEIA(2)	Bell 47G3B1 /Soloy	3433	N54SP
			64-17867
D-HEIM(2)	Bölkow BO.105S	S-672	N4573T
			D-HDUN
			N4573T
			D-HDUN
D-HEKW	Bell 206B Jet Ranger II	2101	
D-HELB	Bell 222B	47154	JA9691
			N32064
D-HELC	Popp HP-1 Gyrocopter	01	

Regn.	Type	C/n	Prev.Id.
D-HELF(2)	Bell 206L Long Ranger	45029	N9954K
D-HELI (2)	Aérospatiale AS.350BA Ecureuil	1241	F-WZFL
D-HELK(2)	Hughes 269C	40-0912	N1094A
D-HELM(2)	Bölkow BO.105S	S-851	(D-HFHS)
D-HELO(2)	Agusta-Bell 47G-2 (Permit)	228	D-HAUS(1)
			74+04
			AS+395
D-HELP(2)	Aérospatiale AS.350B Ecureuil	1826	
D-HELT	Agusta-Bell 47J	1058	G-APTH
			5N-ACP
			G-APTH
D-HEMB	Hernberger TH-II		TH-II-01
D-HEMD(4)	Schweizer 269C-1	0060	
D-HEMM	Robinson R-22 Beta	2248	
D-HEMS	Bölkow BO.105S	S-615	(D-HDSK)
D-HENA	Aérospatiale AS.350B Ecureuil	1781	OE-KXC
			D-HENA
D-HEND	Aérospatiale AS.350B1 Ecureuil	1707	F-OJJJ
			F-WQDO(4)
			F-GIZC
			F-WYMZ
			CS-HBP
			JA9355
D-HENG	Hughes 369D	27-0088D	CS-H ..
			D-HLUD
			LY-H ..
			D-HLUD
			CS-HCS
			D-HLUD
			C-GYTZ
D-HEOP	Robinson R-44 Astro	0008	N2361V
D-HEOY	Eurocopter EC.135T1 (Reservation 7.99)	0035	I-HEMS
			D-HEC .
D-HEPP	Bell 212	30650	
D-HEPT	Aérospatiale AS.350BA Ecureuil	1237	F-WYMG
			N36062
D-HEPY(2)	Bell 206L-3 Long Ranger III	51260	C-FDFM
D-HERA	Bell 47G-4A	3368	ZS-HDH
			5R-MDM
			N1194W
D-HERD	Hughes 369D	79-0543D	SE-HNO
			N779FA
D-HERI (2)	Aérospatiale AS.350B2 Ecureuil	2827	N60972
D-HERO	Agusta-Bell 47G-4A	2543	
D-HERR(2)	Bell 47G-4A	6685	F-GEDY
			C-FXFX
			CF-XFX
D-HERZ	Bell 47G-2	1992	74+36
			AS+395
			YA+031
			PA+120
D-HESA	Agusta-Bell 206B Jet Ranger II	8373	
D-HESI	Robinson R-22 Beta	0643	
D-HESK	Robinson R-22B2 Beta (Permit)	2844	
D-HEST	Schweizer 269C-1	0031	
D-HETZ	Eurocopter EC.135P1 (Permit)	0030	
D-HEUH	Aérospatiale AS.355F2 Ecureuil 2	5155	F- ....
			(G-BPRK)
			N361E
D-HEUR(2)	Eurocopter EC.135T1	0042	
D-HEVE	Bell 206L-1/Soloy Gemini	45494	N206SE
			(N600TH)
			D-HEVE
D-HEWR	Aérospatiale AS.350B Ecureuil	1789	(F-GJPS)
			D-HEWR
D-HEXE(5)	Bölkow BO.105C	S-125	D-HBOA(1)
			D-HDDU
			(D-HDDR)
D-HEXI (4)	Schweizer 269C (Reservation 10.99)	S-1737	D-HCDK
D-HFAB	Schweizer 269C	S-1516	N6042K
D-HFAI (2)	Aérospatiale AS.355F1 Ecureuil 2	5009	N5774M
			HC-BFC
			N5774M
D-HFAN	Robinson R-22 Beta	1810	
D-HFBO	Bell 206B Jet Ranger II	1105	

Regn.	Type	C/n	Prev.Id.
D-HFBR	Enstrom 280FX Shark	2075	
D-HFCB(2)	Robinson R-44 Astro	0135	
D-HFER	Robinson R-22 Beta	2250	N2349X
D-HFFF(2)	Bölkow BO.105S	S-811	D-HDZU
D-HFGD	Aérospatiale AS.350B Ecureuil	1846	
D-HFGH	Robinson R-22 Beta	2448	N83117
D-HFHL	Bölkow BO.105S	S-854	
D-HFIN	MBB-Kawasaki BK.117B	7249	
D-HFIX	Aérospatiale AS.350B2 Ecureuil	9010	
D-HFJS	Aérospatiale AS.350B Ecureuil	2014	CS-HBF
D-HFKB	Bell 206L-1 Long Ranger II	45374	HB-XBB
			D-HHJJ
D-HFLI	Hughes 269C	110-0988	N1108W
D-HFLO(2)	Robinson R-22 Beta	1772	
D-HFLY	Hughes 369E	0312E	HA-MSK
D-HFMW(2)	Agusta A.109A-II	7307	G-JLCY
			N109AB
D-HFNH	Robinson R-22B2 Beta	2800	
D-HFNU	Bölkow BO.105S	S-889	
D-HFOX	Hughes 369D	38-0289D	ZK-HLP
D-HFRD(2)	Enstrom F-28F	707	N86201
D-HFRH	Robinson R-22 Beta	2661	
D-HFSB	Aérospatiale AS.350B2 Ecureuil	2371	
D-HFSC(2)	Aérospatiale AS.350B Ecureuil	1737	SE-HNF
D-HFSE	Robinson R-22 Beta	2492	
D-HFSF(2)	Aérospatiale AS.350B Ecureuil	1690	D-HALL(2)
D-HFSJ	Aérospatiale SA.316B Alouette III	2244	OE-OXW
			N224E
			TG-TEJ
D-HFUX	Robinson R-22 Beta	1058	N8045X
D-HFZA	Kaman K-1200 K-Max	A94-0018	
D-HGAB(2)	Bölkow BO.105S	S-848	D-HFHF
D-HGAP	Aérospatiale SA.315B Lama	2625	N27387
D-HGGG	Westland-Bell 47G-3B-1	WA/364	XT205
D-HGIG	Hiller UH-12B	733	N8505
			0-5
			54-2939
D-HGMS	Bell 206B Jet Ranger II	4373	
D-HGPP	Bell 212	30807	
D-HGSA	Bölkow BO.105C	S-12	(D-HMDI)
D-HGSB	Bölkow BO.105C	S-13	
D-HGSC	Bölkow BO.105C	S-14	
D-HGSD	Bölkow BO.105C	S-15	
D-HGSE	Bölkow BO.105S	S-908	
D-HGSF	Bölkow BO.105S	S-913	
D-HGSG	Bölkow BO.105S	S-914	
D-HGSH	Bölkow BO.105S	S-915	
D-HGSI	Bölkow BO.105S	S-916	
D-HGSJ	Bölkow BO.105S	S-917	
D-HGSK	Bölkow BO.105S	S-918	
D-HGSL	Bölkow BO.105S	S-919	
D-HGSM	Bölkow BO.105S	S-920	
D-HGSN	Bölkow BO.105S	S-921	
D-HGSO	Bölkow BO.105S	S-922	
D-HGSP	Bölkow BO.105S	S-923	
D-HGSQ	Bölkow BO.105S	S-924	
D-HGSR	Bölkow BO.105S	S-925	
D-HGSS	Bölkow BO.105S	S-926	
D-HGST	Bölkow BO.105S	S-927	
D-HGSU	Bölkow BO.105S	S-928	
D-HGUN	Schweizer 269C	S-1563	F-GLRT
			N41S
D-HGYN	Bölkow BO.105S	S-661	(D-HDUC)
D-HGYR	Schuffenhauer Gyrocopter	SG-3	
D-HHAA(3)	MBB-Kawasaki BK.117C-1 (Reservation 4.99)	7540	
D-HHAI (2)	Robinson R-22 Beta	0988	G-HTRF
D-HHBB(4)	Bell 407 (Permit 1.99)	53311	N82317
D-HHBG	Bölkow BO.105S	S-625	D-HDSU
			VH-PHO
			VH-NSL
			D-HDSU
			9V-BNP
			(N4572M)
			D-HDSU
D-HHBI (2)	Bell 206B Jet Ranger II	4210	

Regn.	Type	C/n	Prev.Id.
D-HHBP	Aérospatiale AS.350B1 Ecureuil	1973	
D-HHBW	Bölkow BO.105S	S-346	N6170K
			XC-CAR
			N46981
			D-HDJX
D-HHCC(2)	Bell 412	36066	N6227S
D-HHCW(3)	Bell 407	53058	
D-HHDD	Aérospatiale AS.350B Ecureuil	1825	
D-HHEX	Schweizer 269C	S-1596	OO-FEE
			D-HHEX
			N41S
D-HHEY	Robinson R-44 Astro	0254	
D-HHFB	Hughes 269C	90-0971	OE-CXD
			D-HLUX
			N1104U
D-HHFS(2)	Bell 206B Jet Ranger II	2757	G-SHJJ
			N220PJ
			N27676
D-HHFW	Bell 206B Jet Ranger II	4257	
D-HHGB	Aérospatiale AS.350B Ecureuil	1708	
D-HHHH	Westland-Bell 47G-3B-1	WA417	XT505
D-HHHL	Robinson R-22B2 Beta	2838	
D-HHHS(2)	Bell 206L-3 Long Ranger III	51454	SE-HVG
			OY-HVG
			SE-HVG
			C-FJYL
D-HHIT	MBB-Bölkow BO.105S	S-872	N5096Y
			D-HMBN
			(D-HFND)
D-HHJR	Rotorway Exec 90	3519	
D-HHKK(2)	Schweizer 269C	S-1524	N41S
D-HHKW	Bell 206B Jet Ranger II	3651	(N206AJ)
			N202VW
			N2289T
D-HHLA	Robinson R-44 Astro	0079	
D-HHMC	McDonnell-Douglas 369E	0473E	(F-GHTX)
D-HHMM(2)	Bell 206L-3 Long Ranger III	51247	C-FBYX
D-HHMP(2)	Bell 206B Jet Ranger II	3823	
D-HHMS(2)	Robinson R-22B2 Beta	2843	
D-HHOL	Schweizer 269C	S-1452	
D-HHOT	Schweizer 269C	S-1450	
D-HHOY	Schweizer 269C	S-1469	
D-HHPO	Schweizer 269C	S-1594	N86G
D-HHPP	Bell 212	30801	
D-HHRB	Elisport CH-7 Angel	3522	
D-HHRF	Robinson R-22 Beta	2355	N8008Q
D-HHRR	Aérospatiale AS.355F1 Ecureuil 2	5086	YV-05CP
			N5781P
D-HHRW(2)	Bell 206L Long Ranger	45082	N17EA
			N16762
D-HHSB(3)	Enstrom F-28C Turbo	431	OE-XAM
			G-SHDD
			G-BNBS
			SE-HIL
D-HHSC	Bell 222	47080	N131GS
			N20461
D-HHSH	Bell 222SP	47063	N82NR
			N2220P
			N86NR
			N2220P
D-HHSJ	Bell 206L-4 Long Ranger IV	52022	N6227Q
D-HHSM(3)	Bell 222B	47139	N91GC
			N878TX
D-HHSP	Enstrom F-28A-D	087	
D-HHSW	Bell 206L-1 Long Ranger II	45193	G-DWMI
			N18092
D-HHTA	MBB-Kawasaki BK.117A-3 *(Reservation 8.99)*	7028	HB-XSG
			C-GALI
			N3926D
			D-HBMC(1)
D-HHTC	Bell 206B Jet Ranger II *(Reservation 6.99)*	3814	OE-XKH
			N3189T
D-HHTF	HTM FJ-Sky-Trac	14	
D-HHTP	Agusta-Bell 206B Jet Ranger II	8549	SE-HGK
D-HHTT	MBB-Kawasaki BK.117C-1 *(Reservation 4.99)*	7541	

Regn.	Type	C/n	Prev.Id.
D-HHUB	Aérospatiale AS.350B2 Ecureuil	2406	HB-XVD
D-HHUD	Bell 206B Jet Ranger II	2327	N65CW
			N700WD
D-HHUU	Bell 412	36057	N6162A
D-HHVV(2)	Bell 412	36059	N6173A
D-HHWE	Ewig Elisport CH-7 Angel	035/3514	
D-HHWF	Bell 206B Jet Ranger II	2530	N5008Z
D-HHWS	Hughes 269C	80-0028	
D-HHWW	Aérospatiale AS.350B2 Ecureuil	2437	
D-HHXX	Bell 412	36076	OE-XMM
			(D-HHXX)
			N2038G
D-HHYY	Bell 412	36051	N4382A
D-HHZZ(3)	Bell 412	36065	OE-XNN
			D-HHFF(3)
			N6227V
D-HIAR	Robinson R-44 Astro	0432	
D-HIBY(3)	Bölkow BO.105D	S-75	HB-XLV
			G-BCRG
			D-HDBZ
D-HICA(3)	Bell 47G-4A	7637	N14SP
D-HICE(2)	Westland-Bell 47G-3B-1	WA327	XT168
D-HIEV	Bell 206B Jet Ranger II	2967	N2JC
			N5734M
D-HIFA(4)	Bölkow BO.105S	S-550	LN-OSQ
			N378RL
			N42010
			D-HDNY
D-HIFR(2)	MBB-Kawasaki BK.117B-2	7001	D-HMBF(4)
	(Reserved as D-HANS(3) 4.99)		D-HBKC
D-HIGH(2)	Robinson R-22 Beta	2171	N23399
D-HIHI (2)	Robinson R-44 Astro	0155	
D-HIIH	Robinson R-22 Mariner	0661M	VH-HII
			N661FR
D-HIII (2)	Bölkow BO.105S	S-874	N3203L
			D-HMBN(3)
			(D-HFNF)
D-HIIX	Aérospatiale AS.350B2 Ecureuil	9005	
D-HIKE	Hughes 369E	0148E	VH-JBE
			N5229J
D-HIKK	Robinson R-44 Astro	0376	
D-HIKO	Robinson R-22 Beta	1406	
D-HIKS(2)	Robinson R-22 Beta	2219	
D-HILE	Robinson R-22 Beta	1355	
D-HILL(2)	Robinson R-44 Astro	0018	N2363A
D-HILV(2)	Hughes 369E	0323E	HB-XVF
			N16030
			JY-ACC
D-HIMB	MBB-Kawasaki BK.117B-1	7185	D-HIMB
			(N5406V)
			D-HIMB
D-HIMM(4)	Robinson R-44 Astro	0505	
D-HIMP(2)	Robinson R-44 Astro	0335	
D-HIMT	MBB-Kawasaki BK.117B-2	7203	
D-HIMU	MBB-Kawasaki BK.117B-2	7204	
D-HINA(2)	Schweizer 269C	S-1383	N41S
D-HING	Hughes 369D	47-0120D	CS-HCT
			D-HING
			C-GTWQ
			SU-BAY
			N4248A
			C-GJWG
			N8604F
D-HINN	Robinson R-44 Astro	0092	
D-HINS(2)	Schweizer 269C	S-1587	N41S
D-HIOU	Bell 47G-4	3347	N1217W
			CF-SCF
D-HIPA	Robinson R-22 Beta	2344	N81687
D-HIPO(2)	Bell 47G-4A	7661	G-OIBC
			G-FORE
			N1415W
D-HIPP(2)	Bell 212	30661	
D-HIPT	Eurocopter EC.135P1	0109	
D-HIPY(2)	Bell 206B Jet Ranger II	4186	
D-HIRO	Robinson R-22 Beta	2336	

Regn.	Type	C/n	Prev.Id.
D-HIRR(2)	Robinson R-44 Astro	0459	
D-HISA	Schweizer 269C	S-1425	F-GKJM
D-HISF	Bell 407	53039	C-FZIY
			N97PM
			N1164Z
D-HISW	Hughes 269C	31-0105	
D-HITA(2)	Hughes 369E	0281E	I-HENO
			HB-XTH
D-HITH	McDonnell-Douglas MD-900	00029	N9125N
D-HITT	Bell 47G-4A	7746	N7914J
D-HIZZ	Robinson R-44 Astro	0109	
D-HJAN	Henseleit Elisport CH-7 Angel	"007"	
D-HJAR	Eurocopter EC.135T1	0044	
D-HJET(2)	Bell 206B Jet Ranger II	3777	HB-XSB
			N3181G
D-HJIM	Aérospatiale AS.350BA Ecureuil	1302	F-W...
			F-GCVD
			LV-ATX
			F-GCVD
			(G-BHYH)
			(D-HDXC)
D-HJJJ	Bölkow BO.105S	S-741	
D-HJOE(2)	Aérospatiale AS.350BA Ecureuil	9013	
D-HJOH	Schweizer 269C	S-1500	F-GFEK(2)
D-HJOS	Hughes 369D	29-0449D	C-GRYU
D-HJPH	Robinson R-44 Astro	0196	
D-HJUS	Hughes 369HS	109-0207S	N4259K
			JA9040
D-HJUX(2)	Hughes 369D	89-0583D	ZK-HNS
D-HKAZ	Robinson R-44 Astro	0114	(ES-...)
	(Reserved as F-GJKD 12.99)		D-HKAZ
D-HKEL	Schweizer 269C	S-1679	N86G
D-HKEM(2)	Bell 47G-4A /Soloy	7635	N605
D-HKIT	Hughes 269C	77-0615	OY-HDR
			D-HKIT
			SE-HHK
D-HKKK	Westland-Bell 47G-3B-1	WA/708	XW188
D-HKLW(2)	Bell 206L-3 Long Ranger III	51206	N3205J
D-HKMC	Aérospatiale AS.350B3 Ecureuil	3222	
D-HKMG	Aérospatiale AS.350BA Ecureuil	2650	
D-HKMW	Robinson R-44 Astro	0121	
D-HKSL	Bell 222	47079	N66UT
			N2291W
D-HKUG	Eurocopter EC.135P1	0090	
D-HLAT	Agusta A.109C	7612	3A-MIS
D-HLEA	Aérospatiale AS.350BA Ecureuil	2532	VR-HJF
			F-OHEL
D-HLEU	Eurocopter EC-135T1	0007	
D-HLFB	Bölkow BO.105C	S-868	N3203K
			D-HMBM(1)
			(D-HFHZ)
D-HLFM	Schweizer 269C	S-1748	
D-HLHL	Robinson R-22 Beta	2301	N80074
D-HLIA	Hughes 369D	50-0717D	N1099Z
D-HLIX	Aérospatiale AS.350BA Ecureuil	1525	F-GBMR
D-HLKB	Bell 206B Jet Ranger II	4209	
D-HLLL(2)	Bölkow BO.105S	S-875	N4345F
			D-HMBM(2)
			(D-HSNG)
D-HLPY	Bell 206L-4 Long Ranger IV	52185	
D-HLRG	Bölkow BO.105S	S-603	D-HDQZ
D-HLRZ	Aérospatiale AS.365N4 / Eurocopter EC.155B	6545	
D-HLTA	Aérospatiale AS.365N4 / Eurocopter EC.155B	6546	
D-HLTB	MBB-Kawasaki BK.117B-1	7224	(N8196H)
			D-HFDO
D-HLTH(2)	Aérospatiale AS.365N4 / Eurocopter EC.155B	6544	
D-HLUX(3)	Hughes 369D	29-0450D	CS-H..
			D-HDOR
			LY-HAS
			D-HDOR
			CS-H..
			D-HDOR
			C-GRYV
D-HMAC(3)	Schweizer 269C	S-1636	N69A
D-HMAS	Bell 206B Jet Ranger II	4351	
D-HMBA to HMBZ	*Test registrations for Eurocopter Deutschland for BK-117 production*		

Regn.	Type	C/n	Prev.Id.
D-HMCB	Bell 206B Jet Ranger II	4120	
D-HMCP	Schweizer 269C	S-1518	N146DM
D-HMDX(2)	McDonnell-Douglas MD.900 Explorer	00036	N9198Y
D-HMEI	Bell 206B Jet Ranger II	2550	
D-HMIC	Hughes 369E	0362E	OE-XKK
			D-HMIC
D-HMIK	Hughes 369D	127-0251D	CS-HCX
			D-HMIK
			C-GSZV
D-HMIM	Schweizer 269C	S-1637	N86G
D-HMIT	Agusta-Bell 206A Jet Ranger II	8256	F-GBRE
			3A-MCC
			F-BSEG
D-HMLY	Enstrom 480	5009	G-BWHL
D-HMMF	Enstrom F-28A-D	093	
D-HMMM(2)	MBB-Kawasaki BK.117B-2	7228	SE-JBC
			D-HMBN(7)
			(D-HFDS)
D-HMMW	Aérospatiale AS.350B2 Ecureuil	2727	F-WYMT
D-HMOD	Agusta A.109A	7139	SE-HGM
			I-CAMA
			SE-HGM
D-HMOE	Hughes 369D	91-1077D	N5284C
D-HMOL(2)	Schweizer 269C	S-1680	N41S
D-HMON(2)	Bell 407	53001	N407BT
			C-FWQY
D-HMOT(2)	Bell 206B Jet Ranger II	3947	
D-HMRG	Hughes 369HS	70-0241S	
D-HMRS	Robinson R-22A Alpha	0443	N8543P
D-HMUC(2)	Bölkow BO.105C	S-680	(D-HDUV)
D-HMUF	MBB-Kawasaki BK.117A-4	7105	D-HBPZ
D-HMUM(2)	MBB-Kawasaki BK.117A-4	7080	(D-HBPA)
D-HMUS	MBB-Kawasaki BK.117A-4	7031	(D-HBMF)
D-HMUZ(4)	MBB-Kawasaki BK.117A-4	7100	D-HBPU
D-HMVA	Eurocopter EC.135P1	0046	
D-HMWP	Robinson R-22B Beta	0686	
D-HMXB	Hughes 269B	116-0281	SE-HCT
			OY-HAS
			SE-HCT
D-HMXI	Bölkow BO.105S	S-911	
D-HNAH(2)	Robinson R-44 Astro	0244	
D-HNEU(2)	Schweizer 269C	S-1530	OY-HDP
			D-HBAL
D-HNIC	Bell 222B	47142	N811CE
			N31904
D-HNIK	Schweizer 269C	S-1638	N41S
D-HNIN	Schweizer 269C	S-1381	
D-HNNN(2)	Bölkow BO.105S	S-662	D-HDUD
D-HNOF	Fröhlich Elisport CH-7 Angel	3512	
D-HNSL	Elisport CH-7 Angel (Reservation)	022	
D-HNWA	Bölkow BO.105S	S-398	D-HDLN
D-HNWB	Bölkow BO.105S	S-399	D-HDLO
D-HNWD	Bölkow BO.105S	S-431	D-HDME
D-HNWE	Bölkow BO.105S	S-456	D-HDNJ
D-HNWF	Bölkow BO.105S	S-626	(D-HDSV)
D-HNWG	Bölkow BO.105S	S-684	D-HDUZ
			(N4573S)
D-HNWH	Bölkow BO.105S	S-714	(N714XY)
			D-HDRB
D-HNWJ	Bölkow BO.105S	S-777	D-HDYM
D-HNWK	MBB-Kawasaki BK.117B-2	7200	(D-HIMQ)
D-HNWL	MBB-Kawasaki BK.117B-2	7212	(D-HFDC)
D-HOBB(3)	Bell 206B Jet Ranger II (Reservation)	"007"	
D-HOBM	Agusta A.109E	11007	HB-XQH
D-HOBR	Aerospatial AS.355N Ecureuil 2	5647	(F-OHVE)
D-HOBY(2)	Hughes 369D	107-0215D	VH-HRJ
			N8689F
D-HOCH(3)	Agusta-Bell 206B Jet Ranger II	8405	G-BHSM
			EI-BHE
			OO-MHS
			F-BVEM
D-HOCY(2)	Robinson R-44 Astro	0587	
D-HOED	Agusta-Bell 47G-2	259	74+17
			AS+059
D-HOFF	Bölkow BO.105S	S-612	D-HDSH

Regn.	Type	C/n	Prev.Id.
D-HOFP	Agusta A.109C	7636	I-SEIN
D-HOFY	Aérospatiale SA.318C Alouette Astazou	1883	
D-HOHO(2)	McDonnell-Douglas 369E	0240E	N1603L
D-HOLA	Enstrom F-28A-D	184	
D-HOLD	Enstrom F-28A-D	185	
D-HOLF	Hughes 269C	76-0519	SE-HHC
D-HOLL	Schweizer 269C	S-1203	N41S
D-HOLM	Robinson R-22 Beta	2337	
D-HOLO	Robinson R-22 Beta	2220	
D-HOLY(2)	Bell 206L-4 Long Ranger IV	52039	N206RT
D-HOME(2)	Robinson R-44 Astro	0532	
D-HOMF	Bell 206B Jet Ranger II	1987	N9932K
D-HOMM(2)	Robinson R-22 Beta	2347	
D-HONI	Robinson R-22 Beta	1405	
D-HONY(2)	Bell 206B Jet Ranger II	2433	N5002U
D-HOOD	Agusta-Bell 47G-4A	2544	
D-HOOK(3)	Bell 205A-1	30206	N205AH
			N49641
D-HOON	Agusta-Bell 206B Jet Ranger II	8597	
D-HOOO	Enstrom F-28A-D	256	
D-HOPA(2)	Hughes 269B	19-0410	
D-HOPE	Aérospatiale SA.365C2 Dauphin 2	5009	F-WXFD
D-HOPL	Aérospatiale SA.342J Gazelle	1095	
D-HOPN	Aérospatiale SA.342J Gazelle	1601	
D-HOPO	Aérospatiale SA.342J Gazelle	1708	
D-HOPP(2)	Aérospatiale SA.342J Gazelle	1695	
D-HOPQ	Aérospatiale SA.365C2 Dauphin 2	5062	
D-HOPS(2)	Agusta-Bell 47G-2	282	HB-XCH
			TR-LLY
			F-OBVK
D-HOPY(2)	Bell 206L-3 Long Ranger III	51287	
D-HORF	Enstrom 280D Shark	1002	N9262
D-HORG	Agusta-Bell 206B Jet Ranger II	8375	G-BBXN
			HP-634
			G-BBXN
D-HOSA(2)	Sikorsky S-76A	760093	G-BVCW
			D-HOSA(2)
D-HOSB(2	Sikorsky S-76A	760191	
D-HOSC	Sikorsky S-76A	760032	N4937M
			VR-MHB
			N4937M
D-HOSD(2)	Sikorsky S-76A	760150	N75GY
			(N75GX)
			N75GY
			N5415N
D-HOSE(4)	Schweizer 269C-1	0047	
D-HOSF	Sikorsky S-76B	760413	N5006B
D-HOSI	Hiller UH-12E-3 /Soloy	5025	G-HILR
			N525HA
D-HOSS(2)	Schweizer 269C	S-1512	N150DM
D-HOST(2)	Schweizer 269C	S-1531	N41S
D-HOTO(2)	Robinson R-22 Beta	2251	
D-HOTT(2)	Bell 206L-3 Long Ranger III	51587	C-FNOQ
D-HOUV	Huschle Elisport CH-7 Angel	3511	
D-HOWA	Mil Mi-8T	10535	94+02
			LSK-906
D-HOWB	Mil Mi-8T	10536	94+03
			LSK-907
D-HOXC	Mil Mi-8T	10583	DDR-SPC
			DM-SPC
D-HOXP	Mil Mi-8T	105102	DDR-SPP
D-HOXQ	Mil Mi-8T	105103	DDR-SJA
D-HOYG	Hughes 269C	48-0678	
D-HOZH	Mil Mi-8T	10534	94+24
			D-HOZH
			DDR-VHK
			LSK-985
D-HOZI	Mil Mi-8T	0826	94+15
			D-HOZI
			DDR-VHL
			LSK-397
D-HOZJ	Mil Mi-8T	10520	94+16
			D-HOZJ
			DDR-VHM
			LSK-971

Regn.	Type	C/n	Prev.Id.
D-HPAP	Schweizer 269C	S-1459	HB-XNQ
			D-HHOR
			N99DM
D-HPEP	Robinson R-22 Beta	2327	
D-HPET	Hughes 369D	37-0095D	OE-KXL
			D-HMOL(1)
			C-GYUA
D-HPFA	Robinson R-44 Astro	0096	
D-HPIP	Robinson R-22 Beta	2352	
D-HPLA	Aérospatiale SA.315B Lama	2439	HB-XYT
			D-HBRA
			G-BMUB
			N47276
D-HPMA	Agusta A.109C	7671	N1TV
D-HPNA	McDonnell-Douglas MD-900	900-0059	N9223K
D-HPNB	McDonnell-Douglas MD-900	900-0061	N92139
D-HPNC	McDonnell-Douglas MD-900	900-0062	N3064K
D-HPOL	Aérospatiale AS.350B2 Ecureuil	2637	HB-XYS
D-HPPP	Bölkow BO.105S	S-734	C-GJDA
			N734MB
			D-HDRV
D-HPRO	Bell 407	53196	
D-HQQQ(2)	MBB-Kawasaki BK.117B-2	7071	PT-YMD
			D-HECC
			SE-JBG
			D-HMBG(1)
			N117VB
			N117VU
			N953MB
			D-HBNS
D-HRAM	Aérospatiale AS.350B Ecureuil	2591	
D-HRBW	Robinson R-22 Beta	1826	N4064S
D-HRET	Eurocopter EC.135T1	0045	
D-HRFB	Bell 206B Jet Ranger II	3665	G-OPWL
			G-BPCZ
			N17EA
			HI-405
			N3172A
D-HRHM	Eurocopter EC.135T1	0027	
D-HRMM	Bell 206B Jet Ranger II	4339	
D-HRNL	Robinson R-22 Beta	2098	N2324V
D-HROY	Robinson R-44 Astro	0487	
D-HRPS	Robinson R-22 Beta	2200	N2345W
D-HRRR	Robinson R-22 Beta	0754	G-MUSI
D-HRST	Robinson R-22 Beta	2116	
D-HRUT	Schweizer 269C	S-1533	N69A
D-HRWI	Elisport CH-7 Angel	CH-042	
D-HSAB	MBB Bölkow BO.105S	S-873	(D-HFNE)
			N3176Q
D-HSAS	MBB-Kawasaki BK.117B-2	7241	D-HMBO(2)
			D-HFIF
D-HSAT	MBB-Kawasaki BK.117B-2	7233	(D-HFDX)
D-HSAV	Agusta-Bell 206B Jet Ranger II	8733	TC-HKJ
			D-HSAV
			I-GPFP
			I-PIEF
D-HSBA	Bell 206B Jet Ranger II	3640	G-IMLH
			N18096
D-HSDA	Bell 206L-4 Long Ranger IV	52057	C-GLZW
D-HSDD	McDonnell-Douglas MD-900	00026	N9094T
			(D-HMDX)
			(D-HMCD)
D-HSEA	Schweizer 269C	S-1681	N69A
D-HSEP	Schweizer 269C	S-1451	F-GKAI
			D-HLEX
			N41S
D-HSFB	MBB-Kawasaki BK.117B-2	7240	D-HFIE
D-HSGD	Bell 206B Jet Ranger II	3119	N5754J
D-HSKY	Bell 407	53109	
D-HSML	MBB-Kawasaki BK.117C-1	7514	N40027
			D-HMB .
D-HSMS	Stromberg Revolution Mini-500 (Permit)	0216	
D-HSNA	PZL W-3A Sokol	370503	
D-HSNB	PZL W-3A Sokol	370708	SP-SYM
D-HSNC(2)	Eurocopter EC.135T1	0092	

Regn.	Type	C/n	Prev.Id.
D-HSND	PZL W-3A Sokol (Reservation)	unkn	
D-HSNE	PZL W-3A Sokol (Reservation)	unkn	
D-HSNF	PZL W-3A Sokol (Reservation)	unkn	
D-HSNG	PZL W-3A Sokol (Reservation)	unkn	
D-HSOL	Schweizer 269C	S-1461	N128DM
D-HSOS	Eurocopter EC.135P1	0071	
D-HSPH	Schweizer 269C	S-1526	
D-HSPO	McDonnell-Douglas 369E	0207E	HA-MSF
D-HSSS	MBB-Kawasaki BK.117B-2	7245	D-HFIJ
D-HSTP	Bölkow BO.105C (Reservation)	S-416	D-HDMO
D-HSUS	Robinson R-44 Astro	0105	
D-HSYG	Gebel Rotorway Exec 90 (Permit)	3508	
D-HTAC(2)	Robinson R-44 Astro	0405	
D-HTEN	Bell 222U	47549	JA9628
D-HTHA	Bölkow BO.105S	S-858	(D-HFHP)
D-HTHB	Bölkow BO.105S	S-866	N3202Y, D-HMBK(1), (D-HFHX)
D-HTIB(2)	MBB-Kawasaki BK.117A-3	7022	EC-EZT, N117UV, N39281, D-HBKX
D-HTIK	Robinson R-22 Beta	2135	
D-HTIM(2)	Bell 222B	47153	JA9668
D-HTME	McDonnell-Douglas 369E	0479E	
D-HTOM	Bell 206B Jet Ranger II	2434	N4811E, PT-HPJ, N5002K
D-HTRI (2)	Bell 206B Jet Ranger II	4331	
D-HTTT	MBB-Kawasaki BK.117B-2	7246	D-HFIK
D-HUAB	Bölkow BO.105C (Reservation)	S-203	D-HDFH(2)
D-HUAC	Bölkow BO.105C (Reservation)	S-204	D-HDFS(2)
D-HUAD	Aérospatiale SA.315B Lama (Reservation 10.99)	2486	N315LG, D-HURA, F-GEHK, I-MADO
D-HUAH	Robinson R-44 Astro	0279	
D-HUBE	Bölkow BO.105S	S-883	D-HMBT(2), D-HFNO
D-HUBI	Robinson R-22 Beta	1877	
D-HUBU	Revolution Mini-500 (Permit 10.99)	340	
D-HUBW	Aérospatiale AS.350B2 Ecureuil	2105	G-PLME, G-BONN
D-HUBY	Robinson R-22 Beta	0555	N555GH, (D-HEMD), D-HOSE(3)
D-HUFE	Robinson R-22 Beta	0866	G-BPAP
D-HUGH	Schweizer 269C	S-1432	N433MS
D-HUGI	Robinson R-22 Beta	1878	
D-HUHN	Bölkow BO.105S	S-867	N32022, D-HMBL(2), (D-HFHY)
D-HUHU	Robinson R-22 Beta	2237	N2351X
D-HUKI	Robinson R-22 Beta (Reservation)	2183	N2342W
D-HUKM	Bell 222UT	47501	N222AD, PH-HBP, N3179U
D-HULF	Hughes 369E	0150E	G-BMFW
D-HULI	Robinson R-22 Beta	1879	
D-HUML(2)	Robinson R-44 Astro	0103	
D-HUND	Robinson R-44 Astro	0126	
D-HUPE	Bölkow BO.105S	S-871	N4346G, D-HMBL(3), (D-HFNC)
D-HUSA	Schweizer 269C-1	0046	
D-HUTA	Bell 407	53158	
D-HUTE(2)	McDonnell-Douglas 369E	0203E	HA-MSB
D-HUUU	MBB-Kawasaki BK.117B-2	7242	(D-HFIG), N3202U, D-HMBN
D-HUWE	Schweizer 269C	S-1534	N41S
D-HVHM	Enstrom F-28F	784	JA7858
D-HVIP(2)	Eurocopter EC.120B Colibri	1024	
D-HVST	McDonnell-Douglas MD.520N	LN-076	N52319
D-HVVV	Bell 47G-4A /Soloy	7608	HB-XKY, N52OPA
D-HWAL	Westland-Bell 47G-4A (Reservation 10.99)	WA/719	G-AXKN, EC-EDF, G-AXKN, G-17-4
D-HWFW	Bell 206B Jet Ranger II	4159	HB-XYF
D-HWHD	Bölkow BO.105LSA-3	2003	N ....., XA-STZ, N6148U, XA-RTJ, N911LS, N9733N, D-HLSC
D-HWIT	Robinson R-44 Astro	0147	
D-HWJW	Wilkenloh Rotorway Exec 162F	96-01/16214	
D-HWKW	McDonnell-Douglas 369E	0537E	N9237X
D-HWLL	Bell 206B Jet Ranger II	2359	N119AJ
D-HWMO	Elisport CH-7 Angel	3516	
D-HWPP	Bell 206L-3 Long Ranger III	51480	C-FKKE
D-HWPY	Bell 206L-3 Long Ranger III	51491	N600TH, N4309M
D-HWWW	MBB-Kawasaki BK.117B-2	7248	D-HFIM
D-HXGA	Hughes 369HE	59-0102E	HB-XGA, D-HCAB, G-AYNK, EI-AUA, N9012F
D-HXXH(2)	Bell 206B Jet Ranger II (Reservation)	2631	(N4380A), I-GRAO, N5016V
D-HXXX	McDonnell-Douglas 369E	0322E	G-TUBE
D-HYES	Robinson R-22 Beta	2167	
D-HYNO	Robinson R-22 Beta	1707	N1707R, (D-H . . .), OY-HFH
D-HYYY	Eurocopter EC.135T1	0006	(D-HSML)
D-HZAK	Robinson R-22B2 Beta	2862	
D-HZIK	Robinson R-22B2 Beta	2853	
D-HZPA	Mil Mi-2	538117033	DDR-VPE
D-HZPD	Mil Mi-2	538840114	(D-HOIM), DDR-VPH
D-HZPF	Mil Mi-2	563402034	(DDR-VGA), LSK-302
D-HZPI	Mil Mi-2	568837104	DDR-VGD, LSK-311
D-HZPJ	Mil Mi-2	568838104	DDR-VGE, LSK-312
D-HZPK	Mil Mi-2	569341085	DDR-VGF, LSK-314
D-HZPL	Mil Mi-2	569342085	DDR-VGH, LSK-322
D-HZPN	Mil Mi-2	562817043	(DDR-VGJ), LSK-420
D-HZPO	Mil Mi-2	543048083	DDR-VGK, LSK-500
D-HZZZ	Robinson R-22 Beta	2040	N2322B

CLASS I : Twin-Engined Aircraft of 2 to 5.7 Metric Tonnes

Regn.	Type	C/n	Prev.Id.
D-IAAA(2)	Piper PA-60 Aerostar 601P	62P-0924-8165048	N6896X
D-IAAC	Cessna 441 Conquest	0073	N88834
D-IAAD(2)	Cessna F.406 Caravan II	0047	N6589A, (PH-ALN), F-WZDV
D-IAAE(2)	Dornier Do.28D-2 Skyservant (Reservn 12.99)	4199	59+24
D-IAAH(2)	Beech C90A King Air	LJ-1247	N5651J

Regn.	Type	C/n	Prev.id.
D-IAAI (2)	Pilatus Britten-Norman BN-2B-26 Islander	2167	N405RM / I-LILY / G-BKOD
D-IAAM	Reims/Cessna FT.337GP Super Skymaster II	0020/0270	D-GAAM / F-WZDY / (N1ZN) ?
D-IAAP	Cessna T.310R	1348	(N3999A)
D-IAAQ	Cessna 414A Chancellor II	0420	(N2692Y)
D-IAAR	Cessna 310R	1304	(N6159X)
D-IAAT	Cessna 421C Golden Eagle	0496	N8482N
D-IAAV	Cessna 441 Conquest	0160	(N2630B)
D-IAAZ	Cessna 404 Titan	0416	N8805K
D-IABB(3)	Beech C90A King Air	LJ-235	N1569N
D-IABS	Piper PA-31-310 Navajo B	31-540	N6610L
D-IACC	Beech 95-B55 Baron	TC-1737	OE-FME
D-IACL	Cessna 340A	0459	(N6275N)
D-IADF	Cessna 421C Golden Eagle	1402	N1204B
D-IADR(2)	Cessna 340A	0441	(N555HL) / N6245X
D-IAEB	Britten-Norman BN-2A-8 Islander	218	OH-BNB / G-51-218
D-IAED	Cessna 414	0808	N1251G
D-IAFC(3)	Cessna T.303 Crusader	00244	N9959C
D-IAFF(2)	Beech 65-C90A King Air	LJ-229	N422TW / N422RJ / N5547Y
D-IAFL	Cessna 414A Chancellor II	0256	N37222
D-IAFM	Cessna 414	0354	N1574T
D-IAFS	Beech 95-B55 Baron	TC-1796	N8773R
D-IAGA(2)	Cessna 441 Conquest	0362	LX-ETB / G-BMOA / (N1283F)
D-IAGC	Cessna 340/RAM	0109	N222BQ / N222BG / N222BC / N500TM / (N4559L)
D-IAGL	Cessna 421B Golden Eagle	0006	N8006Q
D-IAHB	Cessna 414	0547	N1990G
D-IAHW	Cessna 340A	0355	N6LR / N37337
D-IAIN	Cessna 340A	0921	N2741N / (N200MR) / N2741N
D-IAJJ	Cessna 500 Citation (Reservation 11.99)	0245	N245BC / (N245MG) / 9M-FAZ / XC-BUR / TI-AHH / (TI-AHE) / N5245J / N550TF / N55OTP / N29979
D-IAKK	Beech B200 Super King Air	BB-1265	
D-IAKM	Beech 58 Baron	TH-1625	
D-IALL(2)	Cessna 525 CitationJet	0143	D-IOMP
D-IAMA	Piper PA-23-250 Aztec E	27-7305204	N40485
D-IAMB(2)	Beech 200 Super King Air	BB-790	F-GIAX / N3814B
D-IAME(2)	Cessna 525 CitationJet	0315	(D-IIRR(2))
D-IAMM(2)	Cessna 525 CitationJet	0041	HB-VJQ / N525GG
D-IAMU	Cessna 421B Golden Eagle	0528	EC-CHK / N69894
D-IANA(3)	Beech B200 Super King Air	BB-1517	N3217V
D-IANI	Cessna 340A	0101	N3929S / C-GFWZ / (N1545G)
D-IAPA	Piper PA-31T1 Cheyenne	31T-8104032	(N5SS) / N5SL / N821CM
D-IAPD(3)	Cessna 404 Titan	0679	N679R / N6762R / (N3336K) / N6762R
D-IAPS	Cessna 310	35250	(D-IBBJ) / (D-IABO) / ZS-DNV / N3050D
D-IARC	Cessna 404 Titan	0020	OO-GIS / SE-GZA / Fv87002/872 / N3985C
D-IARF	Beech 65-C90 King Air	LJ-1034	(D-IFOC)
D-IARP	Cessna 340	0326	N69484
D-IARZ	Cessna 421A Golden Eagle	0136	(N4046L)
D-IAST	Beech 95-E55 Baron	TE-905	OE-FPD / (D-INAD)
D-IASW	Piper PA-31T1 Cheyenne I	31T-8104101	N104MC / N711UP / N136CC / EC-CJH / N116CC
D-IATC	Cessna 500 Citation	0116	
D-IATH	Cessna 414	0914	N4646G
D-IAWA(2)	Cessna 551 Citation II	0422	N550RD / OE-GES / SE-DEF / OO-RJE / (N421CJ) / N1217V / (N64735)
D-IBAB(6)	Beech 300LW Super King Air	FA-225	N82396
D-IBAD(4)	Beech B200 Super King Air	BB-1229	
D-IBAG(4)	Rockwell Commander 690A	11211	
D-IBAM(2)	Cessna 340A	0091	(N1392G)
D-IBAR(4)	Beech B200 Super King Air	BB-1280	
D-IBAU	Cessna 401A	0101	(N6175Q)
D-IBAZ	Piper PA-23-250 Aztec B	27-2221	N5193Y
D-IBBB(5)	Mitsubishi MU-2B-40	452SA	N388NC / N230MA
D-IBBH(3)	Cessna 414A Chancellor	0238	(N8846K)
D-IBBK	Cessna 340A	0338	LX-RST / F-GEJL / D-ILAK / N37310
D-IBDH	Beech C90A King Air	LJ-1307	N8053U
D-IBEL(2)	Cessna 340A	1814	G-ENAM / N1232G
D-IBER(4)	Beech 300LW Super King Air	FA-184	
D-IBFS	Beech B200 Super King Air	BB-1349	N200KG / N200KA
D-IBFT	Beech B200 Super King Air	BB-1535	N1135Z
D-IBGF	Cessna 402B	0802	C-GGUZ / N3794C
D-IBHE	Cessna 310R	0066	N3370Q
D-IBHK	Beech 200 Super King Air	BB-366	N1230
D-IBHM	Cessna 414	0487	N7855Q
D-IBHN	Cessna 337F Super Skymaster	01340	N1740M
D-IBHS	Cessna T.337C Super Skymaster	0820	N2520S
D-IBIE	Cessna 340A	0715	(PH-AXG) / N98954
D-IBIJ	Cessna 402B	0327	YU-BIJ / N3189K
D-IBIS(4)	Cessna T.310Q (Reservation 10.99)	0929	OE-FEX / D-IKAW / N69702
D-IBIT(2)	Cessna 525 CitationJet (Reservation 9.99)	0393	
D-IBIW(2)	Piper PA-31T1 Cheyenne I	31T-8004011	N76TG / (N803AW) / N76TG / N707CM / N208SW
D-IBJH	Cessna T.303 Crusader	00297	N5433V
D-IBMC(2)	Beech C90 King Air	LJ-931	HB-GIE / I-FIRS / N931KA / HB-GHB
D-IBMJ	Cessna 310Q	0903	(G-BBNP) / N69613
D-IBMM	Cessna 310Q	0905	N69638

Regn.	Type	C/n	Prev.Id.
D-IBMP(2)	Beech B200 Super King Air	BB-1284	N6321V
			ZS-LWE
			N72410
D-IBMS(3)	Cessna 525 CitationJet	0309	
D-IBNF	Pilatus Britten-Norman BN-2B-26 Islander	2205	G-BOMG
D-IBNK	Beech 300LW Super King Air	FA-204	N5662T
D-IBON(3)	Cessna 340A	0603	N8612K
D-IBOS(5)	Cessna 404 Titan	0809	SE-IRB
			D-IBUB(2)
			N67659
D-IBOV(2)	Piper PA-23-250 Aztec C	27-2591	SE-EMA
D-IBPN	Beech 58P Baron	TJ-424	N6526S
D-IBPW	Cessna 340A	0924	N39983
			XB-BHW
			(N2742A)
D-IBRH	Piper PA-23-250 Aztec E	27-7305137	N40374
D-IBRO(2)	Cessna T.303 Crusader	00215	HB-LRP
			N9824C
D-IBSA	Piper PA-31T-620 Cheyenne II	31T-8120033	N42TW
D-IBSD	Piper PA-23-250 Aztec F	27-7754027	N62811
D-IBTS	Cessna 340A	1804	D-IIKB
			N123OR
D-IBUF(3)	Dornier Do.28D-6 Turbo Skyservant (Model 128-6)	4302	
D-IBUR(4)	Cessna T.303 Crusader	00079	N2255C
D-IBWA	Cessna 340A	1510	N6870T
D-IBWF	Cessna 402B	0221	(N7893Q)
D-IBYH(2)	Piper PA-23-250 Aztec C	27-2812	OE-FMA
			N5692Y
D-ICAC(2)	Cessna 414A Chancellor	0811	D-IFKR
			OE-FRD
			N2743N
D-ICBC	Beech 300LW Super King Air	FA-227	N81418
D-ICBH	Piper PA-31T Cheyenne	31T-8120008	N812SW
D-ICCC	Cessna 500 Citation	0269	N5269J
D-ICDE	Cessna T.303 Crusader	00057	N1297C
D-ICDO	Dornier Do.228-200 (Permit)	4359	
D-ICDS(2)	Claudius Dornier CD-2 Seastar	1001	
D-ICDU	Piper PA-31T2 Cheyenne IIXL	31T-1166003	N2604R
			(N68TW)
			N2604R
D-ICDY	Dornier Do.28D-2 Skyservant	4164	58+89
D-ICEE(2)	Cessna 525 CitationJet	0096	N5153X
D-ICEN(2)	Cessna 340A	0555	OE-FUA
			N340GT
			N340HB
			N4584N
D-ICER	Cessna 340A	0508	(PH-AXN)
			N6339X
D-ICEY	Cessna 525 CitationJet	0286	N51666
D-ICFG	Cessna 340A	0537	N4345C
D-ICGA	Piper PA-31T2 Cheyenne IIXL	31T-8166056	N550TL
			N550T
			N9165Y
			(N715CA)
D-ICGB	Piper PA-42-720 Cheyenne IIIA	42-5501007	N834CM
			N142TW
			N142PC
D-ICHG	Beech B200 Super King Air	BB-1400	N8085D
D-ICHO	Cessna T.337GP Super Skymaster	0288	N2QR
D-ICHS(2)	Cessna 425 Conquest I	0233	N80938
			N1262H
D-ICHT	Beech 300LW Super King Air	FA-214	N5666S
D-ICIM	Beech 95-58TC Baron	TK-48	
D-ICIR	Beech B200 Super King Air	BB-1051	N6912T
			(G-BJWG)
D-ICJL	Cessna T.303 Crusader	00109	N7SX
			N3681C
D-ICKC	Cessna 414	0472	OE-FKH
			N1679T
D-ICKK	Cessna 421C Golden Eagle	0214	N421TS
			N5467G
			YV-175CP
			N5467G
D-ICKM	Beech B200 Super King Air	BB-1005	OE-FKW
			D-ICOH
D-ICKS(2)	Claudius Dornier CD-2 Seastar	1002	
D-ICKY	Beech B-60 Duke	P-342	
D-ICLY	Cessna T.303 Crusader	00159	N6588C
D-ICMF(2)	Cessna 425 Conquest I	0102	N151GA
			YV-2246P
			YV-414CP
			(N68493)
D-ICOB	Cessna 414	0352	N1572T
D-ICOL(2)	Cessna 525 CitationJet (Reservation)	0353	
D-ICRF	Cessna 404 Titan Courier	0406	N8776K
D-ICRK	Fairchild-Swearingen SA.226TC Metro II	TC-333	4X-CSD
			N1007A
D-ICSB	Reims/Cessna FT.337GP Super Skymaster	0003/0047	G-BAGP
D-ICSS	Cessna 525 CitationJet (Reservation 12.99)	0121	TC-EMA
			N5264S
D-ICTA	Cessna 551 Citation 2/SP	0051	(D-IHAT)
			N6863C
D-ICUR	Cessna 550 Citation II	0379	N500ER
			N551PL
			N168CB
			N26369
D-ICUS	Cessna 340A	1012	N4350C
D-ICVA	Beech 58P Baron	TJ-422	N6587M
D-ICVW(3)	Cessna 421C Golden Eagle	0260	N6146G
D-ICVY	Beech 95-58P Baron	TJ-46	N1546L
D-ICWB	Cessna 525 CitationJet	0349	
D-ICWM	Beech B200CSuper King Air	BL-49	N51CV
			Z-TAM
			N17KK
			(EI-BME)
			N3836E
			(XA-...)
D-ICWS	Reims/Cessna FT.337GP Super Skymaster	0014/0195	
D-IDAC(2)	Cessna 421C Golden Eagle II	0024	N421TF
			N421WT
			N98409
D-IDAG(2)	Cessna 525 CitationJet	0144	
D-IDAK(4)	Beech C90 King Air	LJ-647	LX-DAK
			N9075S
D-IDAS(2)	Cessna 421C Golden Eagle	0855	OY-SUI
			N266RW
			N2660T
D-IDBB(2)	Dornier Do.28D-2 Skyservant	4080	58+05
			D-9571
D-IDBH(2)	Dornier Do.28D-2 Skyservant	4167	58+92
D-IDBU	Piper PA-42-720 Cheyenne III	42-5501029	N700CC
			(N800DG)
			N41OLD
			G-BLSA
D-IDBW	Cessna 525 CitationJet	0044	N55DG
			XA-SKW
			N2617K
D-IDCA(2)	Beech 95-B55 Baron	TC-1942	
D-IDDD(3)	Cessna 421C Golden Eagle II	1094	S5-CAD
			SL-CAD
			YU-BPS
			N6868B
D-IDEA(3)	Fairchild-Swearingen SA.226T Merlin III	T-322	N312AC
			N70312
			D-IOKG
			OO-HSA
			N1006K
D-IDEE(3)	Piper PA-60 Aerostar 602P	60-8365012	I-TOLA
			N64716
			N5403U
D-IDEK(2)	Beech B60 Duke	P-306	YV-35CP
			YV-TAKJ
D-IDEL(2)	Cessna 421C Golden Eagle	1079	N422TM
			LN-VID
			N68660
D-IDEN	Cessna 414	0431	(N64735)
			I-SANQ
			(N1651T)
D-IDES(2)	Dornier Do.28D-2 Skyservant	4187	59+12
D-IDEY	Beech 65-88 Queen Air	LP-5	N881E

Regn.	Type	C/n	Prev.Id.
D-IDHC(3)	DHC-6 Twin Otter 100	71	C- FCIJ / CF-CIJ / VH-EWM / N16430
D-IDHG(2)	Cessna 421C Golden Eagle	1007	N6340X / N215MC / HC-BNZ / N6340X
D-IDIA	Piper PA-42-720 Cheyenne IIIA (Permit 11.99)	42-5501055	N955TA / (OY-...) / JA8724 / N9198F / D-IOSG(2)
D-IDIT(2)	Cessna 414	0953	N9KJ / (N11FX) / N9KJ / N9KT / (N5401G)
D-IDOS(2)	Cessna 404 Titan	0665	N5375C
D-IDOZ	Dornier Do.28D-2 Skyservant (Permit)	4200	59+25
D-IDPA	Reims/Cessna FT.337GP Super Skymaster	0017/0231	
D-IDPW(2)	Cessna 421C Golden Eagle	1201	N26517
D-IDRB(2)	Cessna 421C Golden Eagle	unkn	
D-IDRH	Dornier Do.28D-2 Skyservant	4127	58+52
D-IDRM	Piper PA-23-250 Aztec E	27-7305183	N40466
D-IDRP	Dornier Do.28D-2 Skyservant	4178	59+03
D-IDRR	Dornier Do.28D-2 Skyservant	4129	58+54
D-IDSM	Beech B200 Super King Air	BB-1259	N734P
D-IDTH	Cessna 421C Golden Eagle	1062	N6865D
D-IDUX	Cessna 340A	0934	(N2743B)
D-IDVL	Beech 65 Queen Air	LC-148	
D-IDXQ	Piper PA-31-310 Navajo	31-294	N9227Y
D-IEAA	Cessna 414A Chancellor	0635	
D-IEAH	Beech 65-C90A King Air	LJ-1216	D-IHAH / N1562Z
D-IEAR	Cessna 551 Citation II	0018	N387MA / LN-AAD / N556CC / N666AJ / N455DM / N2663F
D-IEBE(2)	Beech C90A King Air	LJ-1267	A6-FAE / HB-GIM
D-IECS	Cessna 414	0023	OE-FMB / N8123Q
D-IEDI (3)	Beech B200 Super King Air	BB-1633	N2345M
D-IEEG	Cessna T.303 Crusader	0211	N9748C
D-IEFB	Beech B200 Super King Air	BB-897	N200TM / N1837S
D-IEGA	Cessna 441 Conquest	0193	OE-FRZ / D-IBAA(1) / (N2725X)
D-IEHB(2)	Beech 95-B55 Baron	TC-1961	OE-FMF
D-IEHP	Cessna 340A	0242	HB-LIO / N3953G
D-IEIR	Cessna 501 Citation I/SP	0259	N501MS / VR-BJW / N261WD / N26IWR / (N261WB) / (N77111) / N1758E / (N1783M)
D-IEJB	Reims/Cessna F.337F Super Skymaster	0043/01383	HB-GIH / D-IIIS / (D-IFOM)
D-IEKG	Beech 65-C90 King Air	LJ-867	
D-IEPE	Pilatus Britten-Norman BN-2B-20 Islander	2253	G-BTLY
D-IERI	Beech B100 King Air	BE-29	N7729B / N333NB / N888RK / N18429
D-IERS	Cessna T303 Crusader	00134	N5409C
D-IESE	Piper PA-31-310 Navajo C	31-7812102	N27712
D-IESG	Beech B60 Duke	P-341	
D-IESK	Cessna 340	0231	SE-GOC / G-BBAA / N7852Q
D-IESS	Fairchild-Swearingen SA.226TC Metro II	TC-338	N90141 / H4-SIA / N1008K
D-IETL	Beech 95-A55 Baron	TC-259	OH-ABD
D-IETW	Cessna 414A Chancellor	0418	N2692S
D-IEVE	Aero Commander 680FP	1431-150	N600EJ / N600BR / (OO-TCA) / N600BR / N357CK / KAF-301 / N6350U
D-IEWR	Piper PA-23-250 Aztec D	27-4451	N13806
D-IEWS	Cessna 525 CitationJet	0217	N5202D
D-IEXB	Beech 99	U-70	G-NUIT / C-GESP / N8013R / N1191C
D-IEXF	Beech 99	U-62	LN-SAZ / OO-WAZ / F-BSUJ / N1178C
D-IFAN(2)	Cessna 525 CitationJet	0214	
D-IFAO	Cessna 340A	0021	(D-IFFL) / OE-FFL / N3KP / N98531
D-IFBB	Beech 95-E55 Baron	TE-978	
D-IFBN	Pilatus Britten-Norman BN-2B-26 Islander	2185	G-BLNF
D-IFBU	Piper PA-31-310 Navajo C	31-8012050	N3557W
D-IFCC	Fouga CM.170R Magister	079	93+02 / SB+202 / SC+603 / (AA+179)
D-IFDK	Cessna 421C Golden Eagle	0445	SE-IHO / LN-VIL / N6708C
D-IFES	Beech 200 Super King Air	BB-827	
D-IFFB	Beech 300LW Super King Air	FA-224	N56449
D-IFFF	Piper PA-60 Aerostar 602P	62P-0897-8165027	N602CP / D-IFFF / N6893X
D-IFFM	Cessna 414	0801	N1221G / (N15CT) / N1221G
D-IFFW	Cessna 340A (RAM Srs.IV conv)	0763	N2676N
D-IFHI	Beech C90 King Air	LJ-977	N1813P
D-IFHS(2)	Cessna 411	0138	N4938T
D-IFHZ	Piper PA-31T1 Cheyenne IA	31T-1104016	N91201
D-IFIG	Ted Smith Aerostar 601	61P-0183-012	OE-FIG / N246HG / N7467S
D-IFIK	Cessna 421C Golden Eagle	1115	N2652Y
D-IFJM	Cessna 421C Golden Eagle	1244	N2734N
D-IFKL	Cessna T.303 Crusader	00261	N1220V
D-IFKU	Pilatus Britten-Norman BN-2B-20 Islander	2290	G-BVXY
D-IFLC	Cessna 421A Golden Eagle	0033	N2933Q
D-IFLN(2)	Pilatus Britten-Norman BN-2B-20 Islander	2241	G-BSPU
D-IFLY(5)	DHC-6 Twin Otter 300	628	LN-BNT
D-IFME	Cessna 414A Chancellor	0120	N5645C
D-IFMI	Beech C90A King Air	LJ-1101	N17EL / N17FL / N72206
D-IFOX	Pilatus Britten-Norman BN-2B-26 Islander	2186	G-BLNG
D-IFPS	Cessna 340A	0540	OE-FCF / (N4374A)
D-IFSA	de Havilland DH.104 Dove 7XC	04531	
D-IFSB(2)	Cessna 421B Golden Eagle	0561	N421SB / N8216Q
D-IFUN	Beech C90 King Air	LJ-874	N44486 / G-SPTS / G-BHAP

Regn.	Type	C/n	Prev.Id.
D-IFWA	Cessna 340A	0094	PH-AIC
			D-IFDF
			(N1395G)
D-IFZH	Piper PA-23-250 Aztec C	27-3124	N5955Y
D-IGAH(2)	Beech C90AKing Air	LJ-1539	(D-IUWM)
			N2217Q
D-IGAS(4)	Cessna 525 CitationJet	0223	
D-IGBB	Beech 58P Baron	TJ-193	N6030Q
D-IGBH	Beech 58P Baron	TJ-188	N770JC
			N80AJ
			N96487
			G-BIYS
			G-UBKP
D-IGCA	Piper PA-23-250 Aztec C	27-2924	N696JA
			N5794Y
D-IGCW	Cessna T.303 Crusader	00177	N9457C
D-IGEL(4)	Cessna 340A	1231	OE-FSA
			N6828Z
D-IGEO	Cessna 402C	0409	N6785Z
D-IGKN	Beech C90A King Air	LJ-1077	N4B
			N4CH
			N69297
D-IGLB	Rockwell Commander 690B	11456	(N81750)
D-IGME(2)	Cessna 525 CitationJet	0279	
D-IGOB	Piaggio P.180 Avanti	1016	I-PJAT
D-IGOS	Cessna 421C Golden Eagle	0883	N5875C
D-IGPS	Cessna T.303 Crusader	00308	N303PK
			N303ER
			N6332V
D-IGZA	Cessna 525 CitationJet	0260	N5197A
D-IHAH(2)	Beech C90B King Air	LJ-1370	N1570C
D-IHAK(2)	Cessna 421C Golden Eagle	0128	N3876C
			G-FIHL
			N3876C
D-IHAM(2)	Cessna 411A	0272	N2620
			(N3272R)
D-IHAN(3)	Beech B200 Super King Air	BB-1478	N8150N
D-IHAS	Aero Commander 680FP	1290-133	
D-IHBB(2)	Cessna 340A	0217	I-CCTT
			N3880G
D-IHBL	Fairchild-Swearingen SA.227TT Fairchild 300	TT-512A	N123GM
			N927DC
			N13JV
			N3108G
			N3252J
D-IHBP	Beech C90B King Air *(Crashed 4.99)*	LJ-1424	
D-IHCC	Beech 95-B55 Baron	TC-2215	
D-IHDE	Beech C90 King Air	LJ-725	
D-IHDS	Cessna T.310R	0658 98242	
D-IHDT	Cessna T.303 Crusader	00068	N3869C
			C-GPDW
			(N2217C)
D-IHEB(4)	Cessna 525 CitationJet	0064	
D-IHEF	Cessna 414	0456	N1663T
D-IHFW(2)	Piper PA-23-250 Aztec D	27-4189	N6845Y
D-IHGB(2)	Piper PA-23-250 Aztec D	27-4281	LX-KRL
			D-IHGF
			N6925Y
			N8227P
D-IHHE	Beech C90A King Air	LJ-1327	
D-IHHH(3)	Piper PA-42-1000 Cheyenne 400LS *(Reservation)*	42-5527038	HK-3459P
			HK-3459
			HK-3459X
			(N518B)
			N9127N
D-IHHS(2)	Cessna 525 CitationJet	0082	N5090Y
D-IHJK	Piper PA-31T1 Cheyenne I	31T-8104057	N62BW
			N134CC
			(N169KD)
			N134CC
D-IHKH(2)	Rockwell Commander 690B	11541	N9177N
			N821MC
			N321MC
			(N31MG)
			N81689
			G-NATS
			N81689
D-IHKL	Cessna T.303 Crusader	00135	N5423C
D-IHKM	Beech C90A King Air	LJ-1158	N38H
			N793PA
D-IHLA(2)	Piper PA-42-720 Cheyenne IIIA	42-8301001	N842PC
			JA8869
			N842PC
D-IHLB(3)	Cessna 402B	1340	N6377X
D-IHLK	Cessna 421B Golden Eagle	0451	(N41101)
D-IHML	Cessna 421C Golden Eagle	1080	N25M
			N68561
D-IHMM	Piper PA-31T1 Cheyenne	31T-8104066	N82LC
			N32LC
			N600DR
			N2590Y
			(N259PC)
			N2590Y
D-IHMO	Piaggio P.180 Avanti	1009	I-RAIH
D-IHMS	Piper PA-31T Cheyenne	31T-8120009	N97MA
			(N2198T)
			N97MA
			N466WP
			N2385X
D-IHMV	Beech C90A King Air	LJ-1325	N8135M
D-IHOL(2)	Cessna 525 CitationJet	0229	
D-IHOS(2)	Cessna 421C Golden Eagle	0478	N6845C
D-IHPS	Cessna 340A	0262	(N4025G)
D-IHRA	Piaggio P.180 Avanti	1019	
D-IHSI	Rockwell Commander 695	95039	N9790S
D-IHST	Cessna 414	0072	HB-LGN
			N8172Q
D-IHSW	Beech C90B King Air	LJ-1315	N8103E
D-IHUT	Beech B200 Super King Air	BB-1590	
D-IHVA(2)	Piper PA-42-720 Cheyenne IIIA	42-5501025	
D-IHWA	Beech 95-E55 Baron	TE-925	
D-IHWE	Beech 95-E55 Baron	TE-923	
D-IIAS	Cessna 421C Golden Eagle	1055	HB-LQH
			N67979
D-IIFB	Piper PA-23-250 Aztec F	27-8054044	N2528Z
D-IIGI	Rockwell 690A Commander	11172	N60B
			TF-ERR(3)
			C-GERR
			TF-ERR(3)
			N9164N
D-IIHA	Beech C90 King Air	LJ-562	N137B
			(N333FJ)
			N137B
D-IIHS	Beech 58P Baron	TJ-345	N3839B
D-IIJS	Cessna 525 CitationJet	0310	(D-IVBG)
D-IIKB(2)	Cessna 340A	0906	TC-OTK
			N2701X
			VH-JLT
			ZK-JLT
			N2701X
D-IIKM	Beech C90A King Air	LJ-1120	N7237K
D-IILG	Beech 300LW Super King Air	FA-63	D-ILLG
			N985GA
			ZK-MGP
			N7235Z
D-IIPW	Beech 58P Baron	TJ-97	5N-ASG
D-IIRR(2)	Cessna 525 CitationJet *(Reservation)*	0315	
D-IITR	Cessna 421B Golden Eagle	0234	D-IHJF
			OE-FGH
			N5991M
D-IIUK	Beech 95-B55 Baron	TC-1885	HB-GDY
D-IIVK	Cessna T.303 Crusader	00287	N5096V
D-IIVT	Beech 58 Baron	TH-373	N678
D-IIWA	Piper PA-60 Aerostar 602P	62P-0903-8165032	N666BC
			N68936
D-IIWB(2)	Beech C90A King Air	LJ-1340	N10799
			LV-WCW
			LV-PGL
			OE-FAL
D-IIWE	Aero Commander 500B	1301-116	N14P
D-IJCL	Piaggio P.180 Avanti	1017	N180AV
			N180TP

Regn.	Type	C/n	Prev.Id.
D-IJET(2)	Piper PA-31T1 Cheyenne 1	31T-8104042	N2590X
D-IJGW	Cessna 425 Conquest I	0193	N1221X
D-IJJJ	Cessna 421C Golden Eagle	1012	G-FROZ
			LN-VIR
			N6792D
D-IJOY	Cessna 425 Conquest I	0164	N6887F
			(N425RJ)
			N6887F
D-IJYP	Cessna 525 CitationJet	0165	
D-IKAF(2)	Cessna 421B Golden Eagle	0377	OE-FLD
			N8065Q
D-IKAI	Piaggio P.180 Avanti	1014	I-ACTC
D-IKAT	Cessna 401B	0027	N7927Q
D-IKBA	Dornier 228-201	8066	D-CBDR(5)
			D-CANA(3)
			HB-LPC
			D-IAHG
			D-CECK
D-IKBJ	Beech B200 Super King Air	BB-1209	N46GA
			D-ICID
D-IKEO	Cessna 340	0527	N41045
D-IKES	Beech C90 King Air	LJ-942	
D-IKET	Piper PA-31T Cheyenne	31T-8020017	N154CA
			(N802SW)
			I-APIT
			N802SW
			(N100ES)
			N802SW
			(N2359W)
D-IKEW	Piper PA-31T Cheyenne	31T-7820066	N6108A
D-IKHS	Piper PA-61P Aerostar 601P	61P-0542-231	(N8059J)
D-IKIM	Beech C90A King Air	LJ-1324	N82430
D-IKIW	Beech C90 King Air	LJ-641	N7128H
			G-BMEF
			N7338R
			(N27CG)
			N7338R
D-IKJH	Cessna T.303 Crusader	00209	N9741C
D-IKKE	Cessna T.337G Turbo Skymaster	0015	N19MC
			N8649M
			(N22143)
D-IKKK	Piper PA-31T Cheyenne II	31T-8120004	N811SW
D-IKKY	Mitsubishi MU-2B-40 Solitaire	420SA	I-SOLT
			N5KD
			N154MA
D-IKMA(2)	Cessna T.303 Crusader	00024	N9545T
D-IKOB(2)	Beech B200 Super King Air	BB-921	N244JB
			N76MP
D-IKOM(2)	Cessna 340A	0680	N74RL
D-IKOP	Cessna 525 CitationJet	0016	N216CJ
			(N1328M)
D-IKPM	Ted Smith Aerostar 601P	61P-0183-012	OE-FIG
			(D-IFIG)
			OE-FIG
			N246HG
			N7467S
D-IKRP	Cessna 421C Golden Eagle II	0214	C-FWQK
			D-IKRP
			TC-DBH
			(D-ICKK)
			N42ITS
			N5467G
			YV-175CP
			N5467G
D-IKST(2)	Cessna 421C Golden Eagle II	1024	N432SW
			ZK-FYY
			NZ7941
			(NZ7924)
			N6793X
D-IKSW	Cessna T.337GP Super Skymaster	0124	N60E
			N6CE
D-IKUB	Beech 95-55 Baron	TC-145	N55AW
			D-IKUB

Regn.	Type	C/n	Prev.Id.
D-IKUL(2)	Cessna 421C Golden Eagle	0613	N88621
			TG-SIR
			N88621
D-IKUR	de Havilland DH.104 Dove 2B	04296	HB-LAR
			G-AMEI
D-ILAN(3)	Cessna 551 Citation II/SP	0614	
D-ILAS(4)	Cessna T.303 Crusader	00087	N2282C
D-ILAT(2)	Cessna 525 CitationJet	0209	
D-ILAY(2)	Cessna 414	0360	N1580T
D-ILBB	Cessna 340	0510	D-ILBA(2)
			(N1599G)
D-ILCA(3)	Piper PA-31-310 Navajo C	31-7912035	N27923
D-ILCB	Cessna 525 CitationJet	0193	N193CJ
D-ILCC(3)	Cessna 551 Citation	0335/0298	N431DS
			N74KV
			N68873
D-ILCE(2)	Piper PA-31T1 Cheyenne 1	31T-8004053	
D-ILCY	Beech A60 Duke	P-150	(OH-BDE)
D-ILDK	Cessna 340A	0972	HB-LMZ
			OE-FCH
			(N5703C)
D-ILEI	Cessna T.303 Crusader	00102	N3141C
D-ILEN	Cessna T.303 Crusader	00301	N5526V
D-ILEO	Cessna T.303 Crusader	00052	N114TM
			D-ILEO
			N9894T
D-ILEV	Cessna 421B Golden Eagle (Stored)	0655	N1559G
D-ILEW	Piper PA-23-250 Aztec E	27-7405306	HB-LEW
			N40564
D-ILFA(2)	Pilatus Britten-Norman BN-2B-26 Islander	2243	G-BSWO
D-ILFB	Pilatus Britten-Norman BN-2B-26 Islander	2271	G-BUBO
D-ILFH(2)	Pilatus Britten-Norman BN-2B-26 Islander	2212	G-BPXS
D-ILGA(4)	Piper PA-31T1 Cheyenne 1	31T-1104014	N3382T
D-ILGI (2)	Beech C90A King Air	LJ-1090	N7210H
D-ILHW(3)	Piper PA-34-220T Seneca III	34-8433055	G-GISY
			N4356G
D-ILIA(2)	Piper PA-60 Aerostar 602P	62P-0917-8165042	N6895X
D-ILIN	Beech 200 Super King Air	BB-545	OY-CBY
D-ILIT	de Havilland DH.89A Dragon Rapide (Permit 12.99)	6879	G-AMAI
			D-ILIT
			"G-RCYR"
			EC-AGP
			G-AMAI
			NR803
D-ILKA(2)	Dornier 228-100 (Reservation 12.99)	7005	LN-HTB
			D-IDOM(2)
D-ILKC	Beech A90 King Air	LJ-211	N9OJR
			N76CV
			N76CB
			N553Z
			N550Z
			N867K
D-ILKY	Beech 95-B55 Baron	TC-1048	
D-ILLF	Beech B200 Super King Air	BB-1568	N1067V
D-ILLI (2)	Beech B60 Duke	P-537	(D-ILAH)
D-ILLL(2)	Cessna 414A Chancellor	1212	G-CHDI
			N12464
D-ILMC	Cessna 414	0906	N4635G
			D-ILMC
			N4635G
D-ILMS(3)	Cessna 421C Golden Eagle	0891	N919PW
			N6120C
D-ILMW	Cessna 340A	0224	OE-FLV
			N3894G
D-ILOS(2)	Cessna 421C Golden Eagle	0859	N421WM
			(N26600)
D-ILOT	Cessna 414	0040	N414BT
			C-GCIC
			N414JB
			C-GCIC
			(N12DT)
			C-GCIC
			N8140Q
D-ILPA	Beech 95-B55 Baron	TC-616	

Regn.	Type	C/n	Prev.Id.
D-ILPB	Dornier Do.28A-1	3015	TF-DOV / (OO-MAI) / D-ILPB / 15+01 / ND+108 / CA+041 / D-IBAK
D-ILPT	Cessna 414	0817	N281DM / N1520G
D-ILPY	Beech 95-D55 Baron	TE-746	
D-ILSA(2)	Piper PA-23-250 Aztec E	27-7305215	N40490
D-ILUB	Cessna 340	0076	N4090L
D-ILWA	Cessna 340A (Robertson STOL)	0502	N6333X
D-ILWB	Dornier 228-201	8035	D-CDIZ / D-IASX / (D-IDBF)
D-ILWD	Dornier 228-200	8069	D-CHOF
D-ILWS	Dornier 228-200	8002	D-CBDU(6) / OY-CHJ / 9M-AXB / D-IDCO / 9M-AXB / D-IDCO
D-IMAP	Cessna 404 Titan	0427	N89DS / C-GNWF / N80DS / (N26771) / N8832K
D-IMAY(2)	Piper PA-42-1000 Cheyenne 400LS	42-5527024	N41126 / (N400TM)
D-IMCB	Rockwell Commander 700	70007	N700GA
D-IMCM	Reims/Cessna F.337F Super Skymaster	0047/01401	(D-GMCC) / OO-GCM / N5443
D-IMEI	Beech A60 Duke	P-145	HB-GEO
D-IMEL	Beech 95-E55 Baron	TE-855	N9443Q
D-IMFL	Cessna 421C Golden Eagle	1243	N2734D
D-IMGL	Beech B200 Super King Air	BB-1228	N69VC / N6LD / N90PR / N7237J
D-IMHH	Piper PA-60 Aerostar 602P	60-8365010	N6901D
D-IMHW(2)	Cessna 340A	1518	N6871C
D-IMIC	Cessna 340A	1223	HB-LNW / N68279
D-IMIK(2)	Dornier 228-200	8058	D-CMIC / VH-NSX / D-IHKB / G-SJAD / VH-NSC / D-IERA / (D-CERA)
D-IMKL	Cessna 340A	1279	N68692
D-IMKU	Piper PA-23-250 Aztec B	27-2095	N5077Y
D-IMLP	Piaggio P.180 Avanti	1032	
D-IMMA	Cessna 340A	1205	I-AFSA / N6825C
D-IMMD	Cessna 525 CitationJet	0211	
D-IMME(3)	Cessna 551 Citation II/SP	0400	N280JS / N95CT / N550WR / (N67983)
D-IMMF	Beech 300LW Super King Air	FA-164	N1524H
D-IMMI (3)	Cessna 525 CitationJet	0303	N51612
D-IMMM(2)	Beech B200 Super King Air	BB-1201	N6815X
D-IMMO(3)	Piper PA-60 Aerostar 700P	60-8423002	N700ET / N700AH / N9564N
D-IMOK	Cessna 414	0057	OY-AKW / N8157Q
D-IMON(2)	Beech 200 Super King Air	BB-276	TF-ELT(5) / N198SC / EC-FQQ / N130LP / N205X
D-IMPL(2)	Cessna T.310R	1375	OE-FCD / N4155A
D-IMRT	Cessna T.303 Crusader	00097	N2679C
D-IMRX	Cessna 501 Citation 1/SP	0688	
D-IMTM	Cessna 551 Citation 2/SP	0009	N1959E
D-IMTT(2)	Messerschmitt Me.262	501241	US Navy / Luftwaffe
D-IMUB	Cessna 414A Chancellor	0233	(N8834K)
D-IMUK	Cessna 414	0847	N3844C
D-IMWK(2)	Fairchild-Swearingen SA.227TT Merlin IIIC	TT-529A	N3109S
D-IMWM	Cessna 340	0095	N4507Q
D-IMWW	Beech 95-E55 Baron	TE-930	(OH-BBW)
D-INAB(2)	Cessna 402B	0921	N87116
D-INAG	Beech 95-B55 Baron	TC-1550	
D-INAL	Cessna 414A Chancellor	0500	(N36984)
D-INAT(2)	Cessna 421C Golden Eagle	0457	N6774C / D-INAT(2) / N6774C
D-INAV	Piper PA-31-325 Navajo	31-7612069	N59868
D-INBK	Beech B60 Duke	P-478	N555BK / D-ILMS(2)
D-INDI (2)	Cessna 421B Golden Eagle	0317	D-JCZ / I-CLAA / N5945M
D-INDY	Cessna 340/RAM	0103	OE-FES / N4547Q
D-INEC	Beech B60 Duke	P-549	N614EC / N610PG / N742RH / N570U
D-INEW	Ted Smith Aerostar 601P	61P-0167-006	N7535S
D-INGA(3)	Cessna 425 Conquest I	0003	N98751
D-INGE(3)	Cessna 340A	1258	N8841N / (N777TG) / N8841N
D-INGI	Cessna 340A	0037	N98569
D-INGO(2)	Cessna 340A	1025	N340MM / N4756A
D-INGU	Piper PA-61 Aerostar 601P	61P-0613-7963276	N8211J
D-INKA(7)	Cessna T.303 Crusader	00245	N9960C
D-INNN	Piper PA-31T Cheyenne II	31T-8120102	N822SW
D-INOS	Cessna 421C Golden Eagle	1252	N6787L
D-INPA	Cessna 421B Golden Eagle	0647	OE-FVW
D-INRR	Cessna 414A Chancellor	0097	PH-LTO / N4828A
D-INSP	Beech B60 Duke	P-554	N120SP / N3699R
D-INTA	Cessna 421B Golden Eagle	0246	HB-LHP / D-JUM / N300RX / N300PX / (N33362Q)
D-INUS	Reims/Cessna F.406 Caravan II	0043	
D-INWG(2)	Beech B60 Duke	P-446	N7860X
D-INWK	Swearingen SA.226T Merlin IIIA	T-255	N5349M
D-IOAA	Cessna 421C Golden Eagle	0861	OE-FBL / (N26602)
D-IOAN	Beech 200 Super King Air	BB-872	F-GHMN / N1850T / (YV-429CP)
D-IOBO	Cessna 525 CitationJet	0025	N9LR / (N1330D)
D-IOEB(2)	Beech 300LW Super King Air	FA-220	
D-IOFA	Cessna T.303 Crusader	00038	N9690T
D-IOHL	Cessna 441 Conquest	0357	PH-BMP / N1214B
D-IOKP	Piper PA-42-720 Cheyenne IIIA	42-5501043	D-IOSC
D-IOLA(2)	Pilatus Britten-Norman BN-2B-26 Islander	2187	G-BLNH
D-IOLB	Cessna 404 Titan	0691	SE-IVG / VH-PVG / N67632
D-IOLT(2)	Cessna T.303 Crusader	00294	N5357V
D-IOMG	Beech C90A King Air	LJ-1321	N8232L

Regn.	Type	C/n	Prev.Id.
D-IONE	Piper PA-42-1000 Cheyenne IIIA	42-5527036	N . . . . .
			TC-EEE
			TC-SCM
			N742TW
			N9095N
			N9548N
D-IOOO(3)	Beech 58P Baron	TJ-300	N3687X
D-IORE	Cessna 404 Titan	0604	I-NARA
			OY-BNZ
			N2683F
D-IORF	Britten-Norman BN-2A-26 Islander	2020	N100DA
			N60PA
			G-BEXJ
			N412JA
			G-51-2020
			G-BEXJ
D-IOSA	Piper PA-42-720 Cheyenne IIIA	42-5501041	N9578N
D-IOSB	Piper PA-42-720 Cheyenne IIIA	42-5501042	
D-IOSD	Piper PA-42-720 Cheyenne IIIA	42-5501044	
D-IOSH	Piper PA-34-220T Seneca V	3449044	
D-IOSI (2)	Piper PA-34-220T Seneca V	3449045	
D-IOSJ	Piper PA-34-220T Seneca V	3449047	
D-IOSK(2)	Piper PA-34-220T Seneca V	3449048	
D-IOTA	Beech 58P Baron	TJ-312	N3693L
D-IOTT(2)	Piper PA-31T Cheyenne II	31T-7920010	N6196A
D-IOVB	Cessna 421C Golden Eagle II	1061	N6798X
D-IPEI	Cessna 421C Golden Eagle II	0863	N611FC
			N6117C
			N26604
D-IPEL	Beech C90A King Air	LJ-1236	N5598L
D-IPIA	Piaggio P.180 Avanti	1021	
D-IPMG	Cessna T.303 Crusader	00222	N121JH
			N9858C
D-IPOS	Cessna 425 Conquest I	0120	N425R
			N68817
D-IPRC	Cessna 340A	1248	TC- . . .
			N87453
			- ? -
			(N87453)
D-IPSY	Beech B200 Super King Air	BB-1591	N1819H
D-IPWA	Cessna 421B Golden Eagle	0632	N4939M
			D-ILYR
			(N1536G)
			(N322KW)
D-IQAS	Piper PA-42-1000 Cheyenne	42-5527022	N551AC
			N41187
D-IQQQ	Cessna 421C Golden Eagle	1227	N616WC
			N616JC
			N2712X
D-IRAS	Cessna T.303 Crusader	00143	PH-JAF
			OY-BHC
			SE-IHZ
			(N5524C)
D-IRES	Dornier Do.28D-2 Skyservant	4186	59+11
D-IRIS	Beech F90 King Air	LA-229	N7209Z
D-IRKE	Cessna 525 CitationJet	0123	
D-IRMA	Cessna 525 CitationJet (Reservation 10.99)	0366	
D-IRON	Cessna 525 CitationJet	0168	
D-IRTY	Cessna 340A	0707	N8603G
			F-GFYP
			N8603G
D-IRVA(2)	Cessna T.303 Crusader	00050	N2181W
			D-INAA
			(N9883T)
D-IRWP	Beech B60 Duke	P-581	D-IUTE
			N39JT
			N850YR
D-IRWR	Cessna 525 CitationJet	0118	N118AZ
			(N61TF)
			N52178
D-ISAR	Cessna 425 Conquest I	0214	N425JM
			N475JM
			(N12249)
D-ISAZ	Beech B200 Super King Air	BB-983	(N983AJ)
			D-ISAZ
			N983EB
			D-ILT0
			N87FE
			N6JE
			(D-IKFC)
			N6JE
			N6JL
D-ISCA	Cessna T.303 Crusader	00175	N9382C
D-ISEE	Cessna T.330 Crusader	00205	N988PK
			G-BTLN
			N9688C
D-ISGW	Cessna 525 CitationJet	0070	N70HW
D-ISHW	Cessna 525 CitationJet	0289	
D-ISHY	Reims/Cessna F.406 Caravan II	0027	PH-FWH
			F-WZDX
D-ISIG	Piper PA-31T1 Cheyenne	31T 8104055	N123AT
			N48TW
			(N880WW)
			N48TW
D-ISIX	Beech C90A King Air	LJ-1355	N995PA
			D-ISIX
			N8105D
D-ISJP	Beech 200 Super King Air	BB-575	VT-SLS
			OY-PAL
			N307P
			N580
			N6656W
D-ISKY	DHC-6-300 Twin Otter	462	C-GGVX
D-ISLA(2)	Cessna T.303 Crusader	00226	F-GFTP
			N510TF
			N9868C
D-ISSI	Piper PA-31-310 Navajo (Reservation)	31-635	F-BRNN
			N6729L
D-ISSS(2)	Cessna 500 Citation I	0392	I-FLYB
			N26461
D-ISTA	Cessna 340	0323	OY-BYG
			D-IKEB
D-ISTB	Beech F90 King Air	LA-227	N330VP
			N7206Z
D-ISWA	Cessna 525 CitationJet	0236	
D-ITAB	Beech B200 Super King Air	BB-1166	N717RM
			N10HE
			N6693D
D-ITLL	Beech F90 King Air	LA 192	N17TS
			N6331Q
D-ITMS	Beech E50 Twin Bonanza	EH-56	N211EL
			A-711
			HB-HOU
D-ITOL	Cessna T.303 Crusader	00048	G-BTDJ
			I-BELT
			N377CB
			(N377GS)
			N377CB
			N9839T
D-ITPV	Piaggio P.180 Avanti	1012	N180TE
D-ITSV	Cessna 525 CitationJet	0084	
D-ITTT(2)	Cessna 421C Golden Eagle	0803	HB-LQD
			N4266P
			N805WW
			N26561
D-IUAK	Piper PA-60 Aerostar 602P	62P-0920-8165044	N602PM
			D-INFW
			N6896D
D-IUDE	Beech C90A King Air	LJ-1323	N9OKA
D-IUHD	Cessna 421C Golden Eagle II	1233	N2722S
D-IURH	Cessna 525 CitationJet	0196	
D-IURS	Cessna 525 CitationJet	0343	N5244F
D-IUSA	Beech B60 Duke	P-565	N3828L
D-IUTA(2)	Rockwell 690C Jetprop 840	11639	HB-LOL
			N63RB
			(N5891K)
D-IUTE	Beech B60 Duke (Permit 9.99)	P-593	N593HP
			N821BE

Regn.	Type	C/n	Prev.Id.
D-IUTI	Beech B60 Duke	P-582	N578D
D-IUWM	Beech C90 King Air (Reservation)	LJ-1539	N2217Q
D-IVBG	Cessna 525 CitationJet (Reservation)	0310	
D-IVER	DHC-6-300 Twin Otter	411	SE-IYP
			LN-FKG
			CS-TFF
			LN-FKC
			C-FHBR
			HK-2950X
			C-FHBR
D-IVHN	Beech B200 King Air	BB-1124	N678EB
			ZS-MMO
			N200JW
			N800RD
			N30SL
			N301D
D-IVIN	Cessna 525 CitationJet	0188	
D-IWAL	Beech F90 King Air	LA-100	HB-GHP
			G-BIED
D-IWET	Cessna 421C Golden Eagle II	1257	TC-BKT
			N421WF
			HB-LPB
			N1200L
			N13308
D-IWHL	Cessna 525 CitationJet	0029	
D-IWIL	Cessna 525 CitationJet	0221	
D-IWKA(2)	Beech B200 Super King Air	BB-1406	D-IWKB
			N274NA
			JA8880
			N81536
D-IWMS	Hispano HA.200 Saeta (Permit)	20/73	EC-FVU
			EC-648
			A10B-67
			C10B-67
			E14B-67
D-IWSH	Beech B200 Super King Air	BB-1462	N82425
D-IWWW	Cessna 421C Golden Eagle II	0042	N421BS
			(D-IWWW)
			N421BS
			N98441
D-IXEB	Cessna 340A	0097	N1530G
D-IXIE	Beech F90 King Air	LA-96	N932G
			N37390
			N3739C
D-IXXI	Cessna 340A	1543	N1228K
D-IYES	Piper PA-42-720 Cheyenne III	42-8001043	OY-YES
			N809AA
			HB-LRI
			N48WA
D-IYYY	Cessna 421C Golden Eagle II	1082	N68664
D-IZZI	Cessna 421C Golden Eagle II	1256	N398EP
			(N398EB)
			N1200K
D-IZZY	Cessna 421C Golden Eagle II	0804	N26563

CLASS K : Self-Launching and Winch-Launched Powered Gliders

Regn.	Type	C/n	Prev.Id.
D-KAAA	Scheibe SF-25B Falke	4851	
D-KAAB	Scheibe SF-25B Falke	4852	
D-KAAC	Scheibe SF-25B Falke	4853	
D-KAAE	Scheibe SF-25B Falke	4855	
D-KAAF	Scheibe SF-25B Falke	4856	
D-KAAG	Scheibe SF-25B Falke	4857	
D-KAAH(2)	Glaser-Dirks DG-600M	6-72M23	
D-KAAI	Scheibe SF-25B Falke	4859	

Regn.	Type	C/n	Prev.Id.
D-KAAJ	Scheibe SF-25B Falke	4860	
D-KAAK	Scheibe SF-25C Falke 1700	4402	
D-KAAL(4)	Sportavia-Pützer RF-5B Sperber	51075	PH-741
			D-KAIT
D-KAAO(3)	Fournier RF-4D	4040	OE-9055
			D-KIRO
D-KAAP	Scheibe SF-25D Falke 1700	46212D	
D-KAAS(2)	Scheibe SF-25C Falke 2000	44454	
D-KAAT(3)	Scheibe SF-25B Falke	46257	
D-KAAV	Scheibe SF-25B Falke	46220	
D-KAAW	Scheibe SF-25C Falke 1700	4406	
D-KAAY(2)	Scheibe SF-25C Falke 1700	4408	
D-KAAZ(2)	Scheibe SF-25C Falke 1700	44249	
D-KABA(3)	Scheibe SF-25C Falke 2000	44311	
D-KABB(2)	Grob G.102 Astir CS/TOP	1024	D-5873
D-KABC	Scheibe SF-25B Falke	4656	
D-KABE	Scheibe SF-24A/KM29	4002	
D-KABF(2)	HOAC HK-36R Super Dimona	36321	OE-9371
D-KABG(2)	Fournier RF-5	5072	
D-KABH	Fournier RF-4D	4152	
D-KABI (2)	Fournier RF-5	5083	HB-2012
D-KABJ(2)	Brditschka HB-23/2400SP	23046	PH-1032
			(D-KSCV)
			OE-9332
D-KABK(2)	Glaser-Dirks DG-400	4-254	
D-KABL(3)	Scheibe SF-25C Falke 2000	44505	
D-KABM	Scheibe SFS-31 Milan	6603	
D-KABO(2)	Schempp-Hirth Janus CM	10	
D-KABP	Scheibe SF-25B Falke	46117	
D-KABR(2)	Scheibe SF-25C Falke 2000	44444	
D-KABS(2)	ABS RF-9	9021	
D-KABU(2)	Scheibe SF-25C Falke 1700	44128	(D-KLDE)
D-KABV(2)	Schempp-Hirth Nimbus 4DM (Reservation 10.99)	39/55	
D-KABW	Scheibe SF-25B Falke	46123	
D-KABX	Scheibe SF-25D Falke	46124D	
D-KABY(2)	Schleicher ASW-22BLE	22044	
D-KACB	Scheibe SF-25B Falke	4661	
D-KACC	Scheibe SF-25B Falke	4660	
D-KACD	Scheibe SF-25B Falke	4662	
D-KACF	Scheibe SF-25B Falke	4663	
D-KACI	Blessing Raab Krähe III V-6	5	
	(Quoted c/n is that of the builder - Raab c/n is 8)		
D-KACJ(3)	Scheibe SF-25C Rotax-Falke	44604	
D-KACN(2)	Glaser-Dirks DG-500M	5E-126M53	
D-KACO(3)	AVO 68v Samburo	008	OE-9118
D-KACS(2)	Scheibe SF-28A Tandem-Falke	5766	
D-KACW(2)	LET L-13SL Vivat	930506	
D-KACY(2)	Hoffmann H-36 Dimona	3634	
D-KADA(2)	Hoffmann H-36 Dimona	36231	
D-KADC	Scheibe SF-25B Falke	46127	
D-KADF	Scheibe SF-25D Falke	46129D	
D-KADG(6)	Glaser-Dirks DG-800	8-2A2	
D-KADH	Scheibe SF-25B Falke	46131	
D-KADI (4)	Glaser-Dirks DG-400	4-28	(F-WFVA)
D-KADK	Scheibe SF-25B Falke	46133	
D-KADL	Scheibe SF-25B Falke	46134	
D-KADO(4)	Schempp-Hirth Ventus 2cM	36/64	
D-KADT	Technoflug Piccolo	007	
D-KADU(2)	Scheibe SF-25C Falke 1700	44193	
D-KADW	HOAC HK-36TTC Super Dimona	36537	
D-KADY(3)	Technoflug Piccolo B	083	
D-KAEA	Scheibe SF-25D Falke	4862D	
D-KAEB(2)	Schempp-Hirth Discus bT	153/547	
D-KAED	Scheibe SF-25B Falke	4865	
D-KAEE	Scheibe SF-25B Falke	4866	
D-KAEI	Doppelraab VII M (ACOG 1)	1	(D-KAMG)
			D-1577
D-KAEJ(2)	Glaser-Dirks DG-400	4-171	
D-KAEK	Scheibe SFS-31 Milan	6610	
D-KAEL(2)	LET L-13M Blanik	026055	D-3720
D-KAER	Scheibe SF-25B Falke	46229	
D-KAES	Scheibe SF-25C Falke 1700	4410	
D-KAET	Scheibe SF-25C Falke 1700	4411	
D-KAEW	Scheibe SF-25C Falke 1700	4414	
D-KAEX	Scheibe SF-25C Falke	46231C	

Regn.	Type	C/n	Prev.Id.
D-KAEZ	Scheibe SF-25C Falke 2000	46233C	
D-KAFF	Technoflug Piccolo B	111	
D-KAFG-PV	Schempp-Hirth Standard Cirrus B/TOP	681	D-2285
D-KAFI (3)	Brditschka AVO-68R Samburo	018	D-KEGN
			OE-9152
D-KAFM	Hoffmann H-36 Dimona	3693	
D-KAFO(2)	Fournier RF-5	5090	
D-KAFR	Glaser-Dirks DG-400	4-105	(ZK-GPL)
D-KAFU(2)	Fournier RF-5	5091	
D-KAFV	Grob G.102 Astir CS77/TOP	1656	D-4824
D-KAFW	Hoffmann H-36 Dimona	3632	
D-KAFZ	Schleicher ASH-26E	26080	
D-KAGA(2)	Scheibe SF-25C Rotax-Falke	44632	
D-KAGB(2)	Grob G.109B	6440	
D-KAGC	Scheibe SF-25C Rotax-Falke	44646	
D-KAGD	Schleicher ASH-26E	26100	
D-KAGE	Scheibe SF-25A Motorfalke	4508	(D-KAME)
D-KAGF	Scheibe SF-25C Falke (Reservation 12.99)	44658	
D-KAGH	Grob G.102 Astir CS Jeans/TOP	2213	D-3827
D-KAGI	Scheibe SF-25A Motorfalke	4509	
D-KAGJ	Scheibe SF-25B Falke	46175	
D-KAGL(2)	Hoffmann HK-36R Super Dimona	36332	
D-KAGN	Scheibe SF-25B Falke	46180	
D-KAGO(4)	Hoffmann H-36 Dimona	3617	
D-KAGQ	Scheibe SF-25B Falke	46183	
D-KAGR	Scheibe SF-25C Falke 1700	46184	
D-KAGS(2)	Schleicher ASH-26E	26089	
D-KAGU	Scheibe SF-25A Motorfalke	4511	
D-KAGV	Schempp-Hirth Ventus cM	29/462	
D-KAGW	Schleicher ASW-20L/TOP	20242	D-3182
D-KAGY(2)	Schleicher ASH-25E	25112	
D-KAHB(2)	Grob G.109B	6378	
D-KAHC	Fournier RF-5	5018	
D-KAHD	Fournier RF-5	5020	
D-KAHE(2)	Schempp-Hirth Ventus cT	120/394	OH-781
D-KAHF(2)	Schempp-Hirth Discus bM	4/447	
D-KAHG(3)	Schempp-Hirth Nimbus 4 DM	17/26	
D-KAHI (3)	Grob G.109	6103	
D-KAHL	Scheibe SF-25D Falke	4817D	
D-KAHN	Scheibe SF-25B Falke	4807	
D-KAHQ	Scheibe SF-25B Falke	4809	
D-KAHR	Scheibe SF-25B Falke	4810	
D-KAHS	Schleicher ASW-20/TOP	20247	D-3376
D-KAHT	Technoflug Piccolo B	092	
D-KAHW	Schempp-Hirth Ventus cM	34/466	
D-KAIA(2)	Technoflug Piccolo	011	5H-MTF
			D-KAIA(2)
D-KAID(2)	Hoffmann H-36 Dimona	3687	
D-KAIG	Fournier RF-4D	4157	(PT-DVX)
D-KAIH	Scheibe SF-25C Falke 1700	4206	
D-KAII	Scheibe SF-25C Falke 1700	4207	
D-KAIL	Scheibe SF-25C Falke 1700	4210	
D-KAIN(2)	Scheibe SF-25C Falke 1700	44270	
D-KAIR	Glaser-Dirks DG-400	4-60	G-BLAB
D-KAIS(2)	Grob G.109B	6510	
D-KAIX(2)	Technoflug Piccolo B	105	
D-KAIZ	Glaser-Dirks DG-400	4-44	
D-KAJA(3)	Schleicher ASH-26E	26134	
D-KAJB(2)	Glaser-Dirks DG-400 (Reservation)	4-35	
D-KAJC	Scheibe SF-25C Falke 1700	4241	
D-KAJE(2)	Scheibe SF-25C Falke 1700	4243	
D-KAJH(2)	Glaser-Dirks DG-400	4-232	
D-KAJK(2)	Glaser-Dirks DG-400	4-158	
D-KAJP	Valentin Taifun 17E-II	1135	
D-KAJR	Schempp-Hirth Ventus cT	113/384	
D-KAJS-S6	Schleicher ASH-25E	25068	
D-KAJU(2)	Grob G.109B	6261	
D-KAJW	Schempp-Hirth Discus bT	116/470	
D KAKA	Scheibe SF-25A Motorfalke	4526	
D-KAKE	Scheibe SF-25A Motorfalke	4525	
D-KAKG	Schleicher ASW-24E	24856	
D-KAKI	Scheibe SF-25A Motorfalke	4533	
D-KAKK	Grob G.109B	6327	
D-KAKO(4)	Schleicher ASH-25M	25166	D-2715
D-KAKS	Grob G.109B	6250	

Regn.	Type	C/n	Prev.Id.
D-KAKU	Scheibe SF-25A Motorfalke	4536	
D-KALB(2)	Fournier RF-4D	4146	
D-KALC	Fournier RF-4D	4102	
D-KALD(2)	Hoffmann HK-36R Super Dimona	36311	
D-KALF(2)	LF-820E (Permit 10.99)	1	
D-KALG	Fournier RF-4D	4108	
D-KALH(2)	Schleicher ASH-26E	26047	OO-LAU
D-KALI	Scheibe SF-25A Motorfalke (Reservation 7.99)	4539	
D-KALJ(2)	Scheibe SF-25B Falke	4632	
D-KALL(2)	Scheibe SF-25B Falke	4634	
D-KALM(2)	Scheibe SF-25B Falke	4644	
D-KALN	Scheibe SF-25B Falke	4637	
D-KALO	AVO 68v Samburo	029	
D-KALP	DoppelraabBIV/V-M	1021/542	D-4688
D-KALR	Ruppert Rhönlerche II	01	
	(Constructed from Rhönlerche II c/n 3026 ex.D-5301)		
D-KALT-LT	Schempp-Hirth Nimbus 3DT	22	
D-KALZ	Schempp-Hirth Ventus 2cM	10/27	
D-KAMA	Scheibe SF-25A Motorfalke	4527	
D-KAMB(2)	Grob G.109/2400	6010	
D-KAMC	Schleicher ASW-20C/TOP	20843	D-3365
D-KAME(3)	Grob G.103C Twin IIISL	35007	
D-KAMG(2)	Scheibe SF-27M-A	6319	OE-9034
			D-KECJ(2)
D-KAMI (2)	Hoffmann H-36 Dimona II	36259	OE-9300
D-KAMK	Sportavia-Pützer RF-5B	51056	N55JR
			D-KAEK(3)
D-KAML(2)	Glaser-Dirks DG-400	4-186	
D-KAMM	Scheibe SF-25C Falke 1700	44205	(D-KDFI)
D-KAMN	Scheibe SF-25C Rotax-Falke	44519	
D-KAMO(2)	Scheibe SF-25C Rotax-Falke	44621	
D-KAMR	Schempp-Hirth Discus bT	42/355	
D-KAMT	Aeromot AMT-200 Super Ximango	200-060	
D-KAMU(2)	Grob G.109/2400	6138	
D-KAMV	Grob G.103C Twin IIISL	35026	
D-KAMW	Glaser-Dirks DG-500M	5E-15M9	
D-KAMX	Grob G.103C Twin IIISL	35034	
D-KAMY(3)	Scheibe SF-25C Rotax-Falke	44547	
D-KANA(3)	Eiriavion PIK-20E	20204	OY-XJN
			(OH-554)
D-KANC(3)	Grob G.109	6039	
D-KAND(2)	Glaser-Dirks DG-800LA	8-25A22	
D-KANE	Scheibe SF-27M-B	6330	
D-KANF(2)	Technoflug Piccolo	014	
D-KANI	Scheibe SF-25A Motorfalke	4543	
D-KANN	Scheibe SF-27M-A (Reservation 6.99)	6306	G-AWSX
			D-KIMK
D-KANO(4)	Hoffmann H-36 Dimona	3622	
D-KANT(2)	Fournier RF-4D	4086	F-BOXO
D-KANU(2)	Schleicher ASK-16	16023	
D-KANZ(2)	Scheibe SF-25C Falke 2000	44165	(D-KEFQ)
D-KAOA(2)	Scheibe SF-25C Falke 1700	4231	
D-KAOC	Scheibe SF-25B Falke	4868	
D-KAOD(2)	Scheibe SF-25C Falke 1700	4229	
D-KAOE(2)	Scheibe SF-25C Falke 1700	4230	
D-KAOH	Scheibe SF-25C Falke 2000	4203	
D-KAOJ	Scheibe SF-25C Falke 1700	4205	
D-KAOL	Scheibe SF-25C Falke 2000	4416	
D-KAON	Scheibe SF-25C Falke 1700	4418	
D-KAOO	Scheibe SF-25C Falke 1700	4419	
D-KAOR	Scheibe SF-25B Falke	AB.46306	
D-KAOS	Scheibe SF-28A Tandem-Falke	5703	
D-KAOU	Scheibe SF-25C Falke 1700	4234	
D-KAOV	Scheibe SF-25C Falke 1700	4235	
D-KAOW	Scheibe SF-25C Falke 1700	4237	
D-KAOX	Scheibe SF-25C Falke 1700	4239	
D-KAPA(2)	Sportavia Fournier RF-4D	4052	C-FAZO
			CF-AZO
			N2187
			D-KAQE
D-KAPC	Scheibe SF-25B Falke	4667	
D-KAPF	Scheibe SF-25B Falke	4669	
D-KAPG(2)	Hoffmann HK-36R Super Dimona	36389	
D-KAPI (2)	Grob G.109/2400	6072	(VH-...)
D-KAPM	Schempp-Hirth Ventus cT	164/535	

Regn.	Type	C/n	Prev.Id.
D-KAPP	Scheibe SF-25C Falke 1700	4252	
D-KAPR	Glaser-Dirks DG-400	4-228	
D-KAPS(2)	Glaser-Dirks DG-800LA	8-62A37	
D-KAPT	Fournier RF-4D	4083	PH-DYL
			OO-WAD
D-KAPU(2)	Hoffmann H-36 Dimona	3602	
D-KAPV	Schempp-Hirth Ventus 2cM	72/148	
D-KAQA	Fournier RF-4D	4038	
D-KAQI	Fournier RF-4D	4053	
D-KAQY(2)	Schleicher ASK-14	14022	HB-2002
D-KARA(4)	Scheibe SF-25C Rotax-Falke	44607	
D-KARE	Scheibe SF-25A Motorfalke	4556	
D-KARF	Scheibe SF-25C Falke 2000	44268	
D-KARG	Hoffmann H-36 Dimona	36104	
D-KARH	Schempp-Hirth Ventus bT	13/148	D-KADR
D-KARJ	AVO-68S Samburo	012	HB-2039
			OE-9140
			OE-9117
D-KARK	Grob G.109B	6243	LN-GMS
D-KARL(2)	Fournier RF-4D	4155	
D-KARO	Scheibe SF-25D Falke	4607D	
D-KARP	Grob G.109	6146	OY-XMP
D-KARR(2)	Schempp-Hirth Discus bT	91/429	
D-KARS	ICA/Brasov I S.28M2/G	69	
D-KART	Scheibe SF-25A Motorfalke	4523	OE-9019
	(Rotax engine conversion)		(D-KAJU)
D-KARU	Scheibe SF-25D Falke	4608D	
D-KARW	Glaser Dirks DG-400	4-53	
D-KARZ	Glaser Dirks DG-400	4-26	
D-KASA	Scheibe SF-25B Falke	46186	
D-KASB	Scheibe SF-25B Falke (Reservation 9.99)	46187	
D-KASD(3)	Hoffmann HK-36R Super Dimona	36387	
D-KASE(4)	Schempp-Hirth Ventus bT	90/337	
D-KASH(2)	Scheibe SF-25C Falke 2000	44411	
D-KASI	Scheibe SF-25B Falke	46194	
D-KASK	Scheibe SF-25B Falke	46196	
D-KASL	Scheibe SF-25B Falke	46197	
D-KASM	Scheibe SF-25B Falke	46198	
D-KASN	Scheibe SF-25B Falke	46199	
D-KASO	Scheibe SF-25B Falke	46200	
D-KASP(2)	Scheibe SF-25C Rotax-Falke	44539	
D-KASR	Scheibe SF-25C Falke 2000	46203C	
D KASS(2)	Schleicher ASH-25M	25122	
D-KAST(2)	Scheibe SF-25C Falke 1700	46213C	
D-KASU(2)	Scheibe SF-25B Falke	46224	
D-KASV	Scheibe SF-25D Falke	46215D	
D-KASW(2)	Schleicher ASH-26E (Reservation 9.99)	26172	
D-KASX(2)	Schempp-Hirth Standard Cirrus B/TOP	685	D-6602
D-KASY(2)	Scheibe SF-25B Falke	46230	
D-KASZ	Scheibe SF-25C Falke 1700	44395	
D-KATA(2)	LET L-13SL Vivat (Reservation 12.99)	920419	OK-2102
D-KATB	Scheibe SF-25B Falke	4673	
D-KATC	Scheibe SF-25B Falke	4674	
D-KATD(2)	Technoflug Piccolo	009	
D-KATE(2)	Technoflug Piccolo B	091	
D-KATF	Fournier RF-5	5050	
D-KATG	Glaser-Dirks DG-500M	5E-9OM38	(D-KCGM)
D-KATH	Technoflug Piccolo	017	
D-KATI (2)	Fournier RF-5	5016	
D-KATK(2)	Valentin Taifun 17E	1114	HB-2137
			D-KHVA(34)
D-KATL(2)	Grob G.103C Twin IIISL	35005	
D-KATM(2)	Sportavia-Pützer RF-5B Sperber	51077	(VH-...)
D-KATO	Fournier RF-5	5093	
D-KATP	Schleicher ASH-26E	26032	
D-KATR	Valentin Taifun 17E	1085	
D-KATS	Glaser Dirks DG-400	4-22	
D-KATT	Technoflug Piccolo	006	
D-KATW	Grob G.109B	6313	G-BLMY
D-KATY(2)	Scheibe SF-25C Falke 2000	4446	OE-9084
			D-KDAF
D-KATZ(2)	Fournier RF-5	5122	
D-KAUB(2)	AVO 68s Samburo 2000	010	OE-9119
D-KAUC	Hoffmann H-36 Dimona	36256	
D-KAUF(2)	Grob G.109B	6287	

Regn.	Type	C/n	Prev.Id.
D-KAUH	Schempp-Hirth Ventus cT	155/502	
D-KAUM(2)	LET L-13SEH Vivat	920427	OK-2104
D-KAUP	Fournier RF-5	5118	
D-KAUW	Glaser-Dirks DG-600M	6-70M17	
D-KAUZ	Scheibe SF-25C Falke 1700	4455	(D-KOAB)
D-KAVA	Scheibe SF-25B Falke	46241	
D-KAVC	Scheibe SF-25C Falke 1700	46243C	
D-KAVD	Scheibe SF-25B Falke	46244	
D-KAVF(2)	Glaser-Dirks DG-800B	8-107B41	
D-KAVH	Scheibe SF-25B Falke	46248	
D-KAVI (2)	Böcker Doppelraab V (Bömora)	AB-03	
D-KAVL	Scheibe SF-25C Falke 1700	4422	
D-KAVR	Schleicher ASK-16	16009	
D-KAVS	Schleicher ASK-16	16010	
D-KAVT	Schleicher ASK-16	16011	
D-KAVU	Schleicher ASK-16	16003	
D-KAVV	Lo 170-2M	V-1	D-0117
D-KAWA(2)	Scheibe SF-25C Falke	44650	
D-KAWB(2)	Schleicher ASH-26E	26003	D-6161
D-KAWC(2)	Scheibe SF-25E Super-Falke (Reservation 12.99)	4307	OE-9163
			D-KMTF
			(D-KDDB)
D-KAWD	Scheibe SF-25C Falke 1700	4215	
D-KAWE(2)	Schempp-Hirth Ventus bT	8/133	
D-KAWG	Hoffmann H-36 Dimona	3520	
D-KAWI	Grob G.109B	6343	
D-KAWJ	Glaser-Dirks DG-800	8-21A18	
D-KAWL	Scheibe SF-25B Falke	AB.46304	
D-KAWM	Schleicher ASH-26E	26099	
D-KAWN	Schleicher ASW-20L/TOP	20258	D-7647
D-KAWO	Hoffmann H-36 Dimona	3698	
D-KAWR	Technoflug Piccolo B	079	
D-KAWS	Hoffmann HK-36R Super Dimona	36336	
D-KAWT	Grob G.109B	6254	
D-KAWW	Schempp-Hirth Nimbus 4T	19	
D-KAXA	Schleicher ASK-16	16032	
D-KAXC	Schleicher ASK-16	16041	
D-KAXD(2)	Schleicher ASW-24/TOP	24822	
D-KAXE	Schleicher ASK-16	16044	
D-KAXG(2)	Scheibe SF-25C Rotax-Falke	44550	
D-KAXI	Schleicher ASW-24E	24823	
D-KAXK	Schleicher ASW-24E	24817	
D-KAXL-M4	Schleicher ASW-24E	25109	
D-KAXN	Schleicher ASW-22BE	22052	D-4942
D-KAXO	Schleicher ASW-24E	24839	
D-KAXP	Schleicher ASW-24E	24842	
D-KAXQ	Schleicher ASW-24/TOP	24847	
D-KAXR	Schleicher ASW-24E	24849	
D-KAXS(2)	Schleicher ASW-24/TOP	24853	
D-KAXU	Schleicher ASH-25E	25142	
D-KAXV	Schleicher ASW-24E	24855	
D-KAXW	Schleicher ASW-22BE	22066	
D-KAXX	Schleicher ASW-24E	24829	
D-KAXY(2)	Schelicher ASW-22BLE	22062	
D-KAYV	Schempp-Hirth Ventus bT	16/154	
D-KAYX	HOAC HK-36TTC Super Dimona (Reservn 9.99)	36692	
D-KAYY(2)	Schempp-Hirth Ventus 2cM	21/39	
D-KAZF	SZD-41AT Jantar Standard Turbo	B-749	D-4200
D-KAZW	LET L-13SL Vivat	930514	
D-KAZX-ZX	Glaser-Dirks DG-400	4-9	D-KAML
D-KBAA	Schempp-Hirth Nimbus 4M	22/6	
D-KBAB	Scheibe SF-25B Falke	4676	
D-KBAF	Scheibe SF-25B Falke	4680	
D-KBAH(2)	Scheibe SF-25B Falke	4686	(D-KBIT)
D-KBAI	Scheibe SF-25B Falke	4683	
D-KBAJ(2)	Schleicher ASH-26E	26152	
D-KBAK(2)	Hoffmann H-36 Dimona	3501	OE-9199
D-KBAM	Fournier RF-5	5063	
D-KBAN	Fournier RF-5	5064	
D-KBAP	Scheibe SF-25B Falke	4802	
D-KBAR	Scheibe SF-25D Falke	4804D	
D-KBAS	Scheibe SF-25B Falke	4805	
D-KBAU(2)	Schleicher ASH-26E	26130	
D-KBAZ	Scheibe SF-25D Falke	4818D	
D-KBBA	Schleicher ASH-25E	25077	

Regn.	Type	C/n	Prev.Id.
D-KBBB	Grob G.109B	6301	
D-KBBK	Schempp-Hirth Discus bT	161/567	
D-KBBO	Schleicher ASW-22M	22041M	OY-XOI
			D-KBBO
			OY-XOI
			D-KBBO
D-KBBS	Hoffmann HK-36R Super Dimona	36306	
D-KBBT	Schempp-Hirth Ventus bT	1/96	
D-KBBU	HOAC HK-36TTC Super Dimona	36534	OE-9434
D-KBBW	Grob G.109B	6337	
D-KBBY	Schleicher ASW-22M	22023M	
D-KBCA	Scheibe SF-25C Falke 2000	44410	
D-KBCB	Scheibe SF-25C Falke 2000	44579	
D-KBCC	Schempp-Hirth Ventus cT	105/367	
D-KBCD	Technoflug Piccolo	033	
D-KBCE	Technoflug Piccolo	034	
D-KBCF	Scheibe SF-25C Falke 2000	44556	
D-KBCG	Scheibe SF-25C Falke 2000	44524	
D-KBCH	Schempp-Hirth Ventus cM	26/459	
D-KBCM	Scheibe SF-25C Falke 2000	44603	
D-KBCN	Scheibe SF-25C Falke 2000	44633	
D-KBCP	Valentin Taifun 17E2	1109	
D-KBCR	Valentin Taifun 17E	1021	
D-KBCS	Schempp-Hirth Ventus 2cM	76/159	
D-KBCW	Glaser-Dirks DG-600M/18M	6-73M21	
D-KBDA	Fournier RF-4D	4158	
D-KBDB	Glaser-Dirks DG-600M/18M	6-87M33	
D-KBDC	Glaser-Dirks DG-600M	6-62M13	
D-KBDF	Hoffmann HK-36R Super Dimona	36397	
D-KBDP	Schleicher ASH-26E	26147	
D-KBDS	Technoflug Piccolo B	071	
D-KBDV	Schempp-Hirth Ventus cM	110/611	
D-KBEE	Schleicher ASW-22M	22028M	
D-KBEH	Stemme S-10	10-4	
D-KBEJ	Schleicher ASH-26E	26126	
D-KBEL	Technoflug Piccolo B	087	
D-KBEM	Glaser-Dirks DG-400	4-175	
D-KBER	Grob G.109	6058	
D-KBES	Hoffman H-36 Dimona	3646	
D-KBEU	Grob G.109B	6550	
D-KBEW	Schempp-Hirth Discus bT	107/454	
D-KBFG	Schempp-Hirth Nimbus 3DT	43	
D-KBFH	Schleicher ASH-25E	25059	
D-KBFL(2)	Schleicher ASH-26E	26052	
D-KBFM	Scheibe SF-25C Rotax-Falke	44542	
D-KBFO	Schempp-Hirth Nimbus 4T	15	
D-KBFR	Grob G.109B	6334	
D-KBFU	Schleicher ASH-25E	25168	
D-KBFW	AVO 68v Samburo 2000	007	OE-9120
D-KBFX	Schempp-Hirth Ventus cT *(Reservation 8.99)*	94/345	RAFGSA16
D-KBGH	Valentin Kiwi	3004	
D-KBGM	Valentin Taifun 17E	1023	
D-KBGN	Grob G.109B	6209	
D-KBGR	Scheibe SF-25C Falke 2000	44363	
D-KBGV	Schempp-Hirth Discus bT	47/363	
D-KBHD	Schleicher ASW-22BLE	22058	
D-KBHE	Schleicher ASH-26E	26112	
D-KBHF	Schleicher ASH-26E	26029	
D-KBHG	Schempp-Hirth Ventus cM	13/437	
D-KBHH	Schempp-Hirth Ventus T	115/386	D-5888
D-KBHI	LET L-13SEH Vivat	940516	D-KOLB
D-KBHJ	Valentin Taifun 17E	1062	
D-KBHK(2)	Schempp-Hirth Discus bT	21/311	
D-KBHL	Glaser-Dirks DG-400	4-182	
D-KBHS	Schleicher ASW-22BE	22061	
D-KBHW	Schleicher ASW-20/TOP	20006	D-7552
D-KBIA	Scheibe SF-25B Falke	46156	
D-KBIC	Scheibe SF-25B Falke	46158	
D-KBID	Scheibe SF-25D Falke	46159D	
D-KBIE	Scheibe SF-25D Falke	46160D	
D-KBIG	Scheibe SF-25D Falke	46162D	
D-KBIH	Scheibe SF-25B Falke	46163	
D-KBII (2)	Schempp-Hirth Ventus cM	3/403	
D-KBIK	Scheibe SF-25C Falke 1700	4401	
D-KBIL	Scheibe SF-25B Falke	46166	

Regn.	Type	C/n	Prev.Id.
D-KBIM	Scheibe SF-25B Falke	46167	
D-KBIO(2)	Glaser-Dirks DG-500M	5E-51M23	OY-XTW
D-KBIP	Scheibe SF-25B Falke	46170	
D-KBIQ	Scheibe SF-25B Falke	46171	
D-KBIR	Scheibe SF-25B Falke	46172	
D-KBIT(2)	Fournier RF-5	5046	
D-KBIU	Scheibe SF-25D Falke	46174D	
D-KBIX(2)	Schempp-Hirth Ventus cM	88/571	
D-KBJF	Schempp-Hirth Ventus cT	178/583	
D-KBJL	Schleicher ASW-22BLE	22065	
D-KBKA	Schempp-Hirth Discus bT	49/366	
D-KBKB	Hoffmann HK-36R Super Dimona	36323	
D-KBKD	Schempp-Hirth Discus bT	162/570	
D-KBKJ	Schleicher ASH-26E	26067	
D-KBKL	Schleicher ASH-25EB	25190	
D-KBKM	Schleicher ASH-26E	26087	
D-KBLA	Schleicher ASK-16	16031	
D-KBLB	Valentin Taifun 17E	1104	
D-KBLI	Schempp-Hirth Ventus cT	85/330	
D-KBLL	Glaser-Dirks DG-600M/18M	6-105M47	HB-2216
D-KBLN	HOACHK-36TTC Super Dimona	36601	
D-KBLO	Grob G.109B	6572	
D-KBLS	HOAC HK-36TTC Super Dimona	36553	
D-KBLV	AVO 68v Samburo 2000	011	
D-KBLW	Glaser-Dirks DG-600/18M	6-53M7	D-5807
D-KBMH	Hoffmann H-36 Dimona	36232	OE-9276
D-KBML	Schleicher ASH-26E	26013	D-0962
			(D-KWML(1))
			D-0962
D-KBNA	Grob G.109B	6441	
D-KBNG	Schleicher ASH-25M	25098M	OE-9347
D-KBNO	Glaser-Dirks DG-500M	5E-68M29	
D-KBNT	Schempp-Hirth Ventus cT	122/396	
D-KBOB	Hoffmann H-36 Dimona	3620	
D-KBOE	Hoffmann H-36 Dimona	3628	
D-KBON	HOAC HK-36TC Super Dimona	36521	
D-KBOV	Schleicher ASW-24E	24825	
D-KBOY	Technoflug Piccolo B	066	
D-KBPB	Glaser-Dirks DG-400	4-265	
D-KBPC	Schleicher ASH-25M	25200	(OO-WZW)
D-KBPK	Hoffmann HK-36R Super Dimona	36391	
D-KBPT	Schleicher ASH-25M	25184	
D-KBPV	Eiriavion PIK-20E	20209	
D-KBRC	Schempp-Hirth Ventus cT	78/317	
D-KBRD	Schempp-Hirth Discus bT	103/445	
D-KBRE	Stemme S-10	10-3	
D-KBRU	Grob G.109B	6575	
D-KBSD	Glaser-Dirks DG-800LA	8-16A13	
D-KBSJ	Glaser-Dirks DG-600M	6-68M18	
D-KBSM	Scheibe SF-25B Falke	46105	D-KECS
D-KBSR	Schleicher ASH-26E	26114	
D-KBST	Schempp-Hirth Ventus bT	26/191	
D-KBSX	Schempp-Hirth Ventus cM	108/607	
D-KBTB	Schempp-Hirth Nimbus 4 DM	26/37	
D-KBTL-TL	Schempp-Hirth Ventus 2cM	3/17	
D-KBTS	Schempp-Hirth Discus bM	5/456	
D-KBTT	Hoffmann HK-36R Super Dimona	36357	OE-9375
D-KBUA	Scheibe SF-25C Falke 2000	44478	
D-KBUB	Scheibe SF-25C Falke 2000	44462	
D-KBUC	Scheibe SF-25C Falke 2000	44476	
D-KBUD	Scheibe SF-25C Falke 2000	44517	
D-KBUE	Scheibe SF-25C Rotax-Falke	44545	
D-KBUF	Scheibe SF-25C Rotax-Falke	44557	
D-KBUG	Scheibe SF-25C Falke 2000	44420	
D-KBUH	Scheibe SF-25C Falke	44640	
D-KBUI	Scheibe SF-25C Falke 2000	44490	
D-KBUK	Scheibe SF-25C Rotax-Falke	44587	
D-KBUL	Scheibe SF-25C Rotax-Falke	44611	
D-KBUM	Scheibe SF-25C Rotax-Falke	44558	
D-KBUO	Scheibe SF-25C Rotax-Falke	44642	
D-KBUP	Scheibe SF-25C Rotax-Falke	44586	
D-KBUQ	Scheibe SF-25C Rotax-Falke	44625	
D-KBUR	Scheibe SF-25C Rotax-Falke	44631	
D-KBUS(2)	Scheibe SF-25C Rotax-Falke	44622	
D-KBUT	Scheibe SF-25C Rotax-Falke	44565	

Regn.	Type	C/n	Prev.ld.
D-KBUV	Scheibe SF-25C Rotax-Falke	44623	
D-KBUW	Scheibe SF-25C Rotax-Falke	44627	
D-KBUX	Scheibe SF-25C Rotax-Falke	44626	
D-KBUZ	Scheibe SF-25C Falke 2000	44616	
D-KBVB	Schempp-Hirth Ventus 2cM	39/69	
D-KBVF	Glaser-Dirks DG-800B *(Reservation 11.99)*	8-191B113	
D-KBVG	Schempp-Hirth Ventus 2cM *(Res. 2.99)*	64/132	D-3543
	(Originally built as Ventus 2c c/n 46/132 and res as D-KBVM)		
D-KBVH	Schempp-Hirth Discus bT	125/483	
D-KBWB	Glaser-Dirks DG-400	4-62	
D-KBWG	Schempp-Hirth Ventus cM	35/471	
D-KBWH	Schleicher ASH-25E	25106	
D-KBWK	Schleicher ASH-26E	26075	
D-KBWL	Schempp-Hirth Nimbus 4 DM	3/9	
D-KBWM	Schleicher ASW-20L/TOP	20409	OE-9368
			OE-5368
D-KBWS(2)	Schleicher ASH-26E	26051	
D-KBWW	Hoffmann HK-36R Super Dimona	36310	
D-KBXH	Schempp-Hirth Ventus cM	72/537	
D-KBYT	Grob G.109	6025	
D-KCAA(2)	Scheibe SF-25C Rotax-Falke	44620	
D-KCAD(2)	Grob G.109B	6418	
D-KCAE(2)	Schempp-Hirth Standard Cirrus/TOP	381	D-9226
D-KCAG	Scheibe SF-25D Falke	46140D	
D-KCAJ(2)	Scheibe SF-25B Falke	46207	(D-KASD)
D-KCAK(2)	Schempp-Hirth Ventus 2cM	63/125	
D-KCAM	Scheibe SF-25B Falke	46146	
D-KCAN(2)	SZD-45A Ogar	B-652	DDR-3504
			DM-3504
D-KCAO	Scheibe SF-25D Falke	46149D	
D-KCAQ	Scheibe SF-25D Falke	46151D	
D-KCAR(2)	HOAC HK-36R Super Dimona	36396	
D-KCAX	Sportavia-Pützer RF-5B Sperber	51023	
D-KCBB	Eiriavion PIK-20E	20268	
D-KCBC	Schempp-Hirth Ventus cM	27/460	(OE-9340)
D-KCBN	Hoffmann HK-36R Super Dimona	36339	
D-KCBO	Schleicher ASW-24E	24824	
D-KCBT	Hoffmann H-36 Dimona	3635	
D-KCCA	Hoffmann H-36 Dimona	3606	
D-KCCB	Valentin Taifun 17E	1028	
D-KCCH(2)	Schleicher ASH-26E	26060	
D-KCCN	Schleicher ASH-26E	26144	
D-KCCO	KOAC HK-36TTC Super Dimona	36563	
D-KCCP	Hoffmann H-36 Dimona	3521	
D-KCDG(2)	Glaser-Dirks DG-800B	8-88B24	(D-KEIS(2))
D-KCDW	Schleicher ASH-26E	26125	
D-KCEE	Schempp-Hirth Ventus cM	42/481	
D-KCEH	Schempp-Hirth Discus bT	36/347	
D-KCEK	SchempOp-Hirth Ventus bT	24/182	
D-KCEL	Schempp-Hirth Discus bT	45/359	
D-KCFB	Technoflug Piccolo	025	
D-KCFD	Technoflug Piccolo	027	
D-KCFF	Technoflug Piccolo	029	
D-KCFI	Technoflug Piccolo	032	
D-KCFL	Schempp-Hirth Discus bT	94/433	
D-KCGA-GA	Schempp-Hirth Ventus cM	62/519	
D-KCGB	Stemme S-10	10-13	
D-KCHA	Scheibe SF-24A Motorspatz *(Wfu)*	4016	D-KACE
D-KCHB	Schempp-Hirth Ventus cT	128/402	
D-KCHD	Glaser-Dirks DG-800B	8-84B21	
D-KCHE	Glaser-Dirks DG-400	4-46	
D-KCHF	Eiriavion PIK-20E	20205	
D-KCHG-S5	Schempp-Hirth Ventus cT	87/332	
D-KCHH	Glaser-Dirks DG-400	4-164	
D-KCHL	Schempp-Hirth Ventus cM	54/501	
D-KCHM	Schleicher ASW-22BLE	22073	
D-KCHO	Technoflug Piccolo B	078	
D-KCHS(2)	Schempp-Hirth Ventus 2cT	40/131	
D-KCHT	Hoffmann HK-36R Super Dimona	36341	
D-KCIB(2)	Fournier RF-5	5105	
D-KCID(2)	Fournier RF-5	5115	
D-KCIE	Fournier RF-5	5103	
D-KCIF(2)	Glaser-Dirks DG-400	4-213	
D-KCIH	Sportavia-Pützer RF-5B Sperber	51007	
D-KCII	Sportavia-Pützer RF-5B Sperber	51008	

Regn.	Type	C/n	Prev.ld.
D-KCIJ	Sportavia-Pützer RF-5B Sperber	51011	
D-KCIK	Sportavia-Pützer RF-5B Sperber	51003	
D-KCIL(2)	Technoflug Piccolo B	104	
D-KCIN	Sportavia-Pützer RF-5B Sperber	51015	
D-KCJT	Schempp-Hirth Ventus 2cM	52/106	
D-KCLB(2)	Schleicher ASW-20CL/TOP	20738	D-3838
D-KCLD	Scheibe SF-28A Tandem-Falke	5774	
D-KCLI	Scheibe SF-28A Tandem-Falke	5779	
D-KCLO	Grob G.109B	6346	
D-KCLS	Technoflug Piccolo	012	
D-KCMH	Schleicher ASH-26E	26024	
D-KCMM-MM	Schempp-Hirth Nimbus 3DM	2/14	
D-KCOA	SZD-45A Ogar	B-661	
D-KCOC	SZD-45A Ogar	B-752	
D-KCOD	SZD-45A Ogar	B-754	
D-KCOE	HOAC H-36VT Dimona *(Permit 12.99)*	36275	OE-9318
D-KCOK	Hoffmann H-36 Dimona	3623	
D-KCOL	AVO 68v Samburo	025	
D-KCPC	Fournier RF-5	5124	
D-KCPE(2)	Glaser-Dirks DG-800B	8-128B57	
D-KCPF(2)	Glaser-Dirks DG-500M	5E-32M16	
D-KCPI	SZD-45A Ogar	B-763	DDR-3510
			DM-3510
D-KCPR	Scheibe SF-25C Falke 2000	44512	
D-KCPS	Schempp-Hirth Ventus cM	52/498	
D-KCRA	Grob G.109B	6520	
D-KCRE-RE	Glaser-Dirks DG-400	4-194	
D-KCRM	Schempp-Hirth Ventus 2cT	41/134	
D-KCRO	Schempp-Hirth Ventus cT	139/427	
D-KCRT	Schempp-Hirth Janus CT	14/273	
D-KCSA(2)	LET L-13SL Vivat	930511	
D-KCSG	Schleicher ASW-24E	24835	
D-KCTF	Technoflug TFK-2 Carat	001	
D-KCTT	Schempp-Hirth Ventus cM	53/500	
D-KCTO	Schempp-Hirth Ventus cM	8-59B8	
D-KCWB	Glaser-Dirks DG-400	4-267	
D-KCWD	Schleicher ASH-26E	26108	
D-KCWE	Schempp-Hirth Discus bT	48/364	
D-KCWH	Schempp-Hirth Janus CM	16/196	D-4109
D-KCWM	Grob G.103C Twin IIISL	35029	
D-KCWS	Schempp-Hirth Discus bT	63/387	
D-KCWW	Schleicher ASH-26E	26104	
D-KCYI	Schleicher ASK-16	16030	G-BCYI
			D-KIWE(1)
D-KDAA	Scheibe SF-25C Falke 1700	4441	(D-KATZ)
D-KDAB	Scheibe SF-25C Falke 1700	4442	
D-KDAC(2)	Scheibe SF-25C Falke 2000	44265	(D-KDBX)
D-KDAD(2)	Scheibe SF-25C Falke 1700	4451	
D-KDAF(2)	Scheibe SF-25C Falke 1700	44195	
D-KDAG	Scheibe SF-25C Falke 1700	4447	
D-KDAI	Scheibe SF-25C Falke 1700	4449	
D-KDAJ	Scheibe SF-25C Falke 1700	4450	
D-KDAN(2)	Hoffmann HK-36R Super Dimona	36337	
D-KDA0	Scheibe SF-28A Tandem-Falke	5715	
D-KDAP	Komwestheim DoppelraaBIV/017	01	D-1642
D-KDAR(2)	Technoflug Piccolo	047	
D-KDAS(2)	Schempp-Hirth Ventus cT	159/513	
D-KDBA	Scheibe SF-25C Falke 1700	44247	
D-KDBB	Scheibe SF-25C Falke 1700	44246	
D-KDBC	Scheibe SF-25C Falke 1700	44248	
D-KDBD	Scheibe SF-25E Super-Falke	4343	
D-KDBI (2)	Scheibe SF-25C Falke 1700	44258	
D-KDBJ	Scheibe SF-25C Falke 1700	44255	
D-KDBK	Scheibe SF-25K Falke 1700	4901	
D-KDBL(2)	Scheibe SF-25C Falke 1700	44266	
D-KDBM(2)	Scheibe SF-25C Falke 1700	44271	
D-KDBN(2)	Scheibe SF-25C Falke 1700	44263	
D-KDB0(2)	Scheibe SF-25C Falke 1700	44269	
D-KDBQ(2)	Scheibe SF-25C Falke 2000	44273	
D-KDBR(2)	Scheibe SF-25C Falke 1700	44277	
D-KDBS(2)	Scheibe SF-25E Super-Falke	4347	
D-KDBU(3)	Scheibe SF-25C Falke 1700	44279	
D-KDBV	Scheibe SF-25C Falke 1700	44264	
D-KDBW	Scheibe SF-25C Falke 1700	44261	
D-KDBX(3)	Scheibe SF-25C Falke 1700	44276	

Regn.	Type	C/n	Prev.Id.
D-KDBY(2)	Scheibe SF-25C Falke 2000	44272	
D-KDBZ	Scheibe SF-25E Super-Falke	4345	
D-KDCB(2)	Rollanden-Schneider LS-9 (Reservation 10.99)	9007	
D-KDCE(2)	Scheibe SF-25C Falke 1700	44235	
D-KDCG	Scheibe SF-25C Falke 2000	44389	HB-2115 D-KNIE(2)
D-KDCH	Scheibe SF-25E Super-Falke	4337	
D-KDCI	Scheibe SF-25C Falke 1700	44234	
D-KDCJ(2)	Scheibe SF-25C Falke 1700	44239	
D-KDCK(2)	Scheibe SF-25C Falke 1700	44243	
D-KDCM	Scheibe SF-25C Falke 1700	44236	
D-KDCN(2)	Scheibe SF-25C Falke 1700	44242	
D-KDCO	Scheibe SF-25C Falke 1700	44237	
D-KDCS	Scheibe SF-25C Falke 1700	44245	
D-KDCT	Scheibe SF-25C Falke 1700	44240	
D-KDDA(2)	Scheibe SF-25E Super-Falke	4311	
D-KDDC	Scheibe SF-25E Super-Falke	4308	
D-KDDD	Scheibe SF-25E Super-Falke	4309	
D-KDDF	Scheibe SF-25C Falke 1700	44131	
D-KDDG	Scheibe SF-25C Falke 1700	44132	
D-KDDK	Scheibe SF-25C Falke 1700	44136	
D-KDDP	Scheibe Bergfalke IVM	5901	
D-KDDW	Glaser-Dirks DG-600M	6-91M37	
D-KDEB	Scheibe SF 25C Falke 1700	44144	
D-KDEG	Scheibe SF 25C Falke 1700	44149	
D-KDEJ	Scheibe SF-25C Falke 1700	44177	
D-KDEK	Scheibe SF-25C Falke 1700	44180	
D-KDEN	Scheibe SF-25C Falke 1700	44184	
D-KDEO	Scheibe SF-25C Falke 1700	44185	
D-KDEP	Scheibe SF-25C Falke 1700	44186	
D-KDES	Scheibe SF-25C Falke 1700	44188	
D-KDET	Scheibe SF-25C Falke 1700	44190	
D-KDEU	Scheibe SF-25C Falke 1700	44194	
D-KDEW	Scheibe SF-25C Falke 1700	44202	
D-KDEZ	Scheibe SF-25C Falke 1700	44199	
D-KDFA	Scheibe SF-25C Falke 1700	44200	
D-KDFB(2)	Scheibe SF-25C Falke 1700	44214	
D-KDFC	Scheibe SF-25C Falke 1700	44201	
D-KDFE(2)	Scheibe SF-25C Falke 1700	44211	
D-KDFF(4)	Stemme S-10VT	11-029	
D-KDFG	Scheibe SF-25C Falke 1700	44207	
D-KDFI (2)	Scheibe SF-25C Falke 1700	44217	
D-KDFJ(3)	Scheibe SF-25C Falke 1700	44222	
D-KDFK(2)	Schleicher ASH-26E	26018	
D-KDFL	Scheibe SF-25B Falke	46118	OE-9035 (D-KABQ)
D-KDFM(2)	Scheibe SF-25C Falke 1700	44218	
D-KDFN(4)	Scheibe SF-25E Super-Falke	4335	
D-KDFP	Scheibe SF-25C Falke 1700	46236C	HB-2019 (D-KAEP)
D-KDFQ(2)	Scheibe SF-25C Falke 1700	44220	
D-KDFS	Scheibe SF-25C Falke 1700	44208	
D-KDFT	Scheibe SF-25C Falke 1700	44216	
D-KDFU(2)	Scheibe SF-25C Falke 1700	44221	
D-KDGB	Scheibe SF-25C Falke 2000	44280	
D-KDGD	Scheibe SF-25C Falke 2000	44284	
D-KDGE	Scheibe SF-25C Falke 1700	44285	
D-KDGF	Scheibe SF-25E Super-Falke	4350	
D-KDGH(2)	Scheibe SF-25C Falke 1700	44288	
D-KDGI (2)	Scheibe SF-25C Falke 1700	44289	
D-KDGL	Scheibe SF-25C Falke 2000	44282	
D-KDGM	Scheibe SF-35	4701	
D-KDGN(2)	Scheibe SF-25C Falke 1700	44293	
D-KDGP(2)	Scheibe SF-25C Falke 1700	44295	
D-KDGQ(3)	Scheibe SF-25C Falke 1700 (Code "G")	44299	
D-KDGT(2)	Scheibe SF-25K Falke 1700	4904	
D-KDGU(3)	Scheibe SF-25C Falke 2000	4356C	
D-KDGW(3)	Scheibe SF-25C Falke 2000	44303	
D-KDGX	Scheibe SF-25K Falke 1700	4906	
D-KDHF	Schempp-Hirth Discus bT	58/380	
D-KDHH-IHH	Schempp-Hirth Ventus cM	50/494	
D-KDHL	Glaser-Dirks DG-600/18M	6-99M45	OO-IVC
D-KDIE	Schempp-Hirth Ventus bT	59/271	
D-KDIM	Hoffmann H-36 Dimona	3601	
D-KDIT	Grob G.109B	6385	
D-KDJG	Schleicher ASH-26E	26138	
D-KDJK	AVO-68R Samburo	028	OE-9165
D-KDJR	Schempp-Hirth Ventus 2cM	65/133	
D-KDKD	Hoffmann HK-36R Super Dimona	36328	
D-KDLA	Grob G.109B	6219	OY-XMG
D-KDLB	Schleicher ASH-26E	26118	
D-KDLS	Technoflug Piccolo B	116	
D-KDMA	Brditschka HB-23/2400SP	23042	OE-9325
D-KDMB	Schempp-Hirth Ventus cM	95/585	I-IMBG
D-KDMG	Grob G.109	6047	
D-KDMS	Grob G.109	6059	
D-KDOA(2)	Schempp-Hirth Janus CT	11/270	
D-KDOM	Hoffmann HK-36R Super Dimona	36313	
D-KDON	Glaser-Dirks DG-400	4-41	
D-KDOS-OS	Schempp-Hirth Discus bT	46/362	
D-KDOT	HOAC HK-36TTC Super Dimona	36603	
D-KDOV	Schleicher ASH-25M	25143	D-7062
D-KDPB	Hoffmann HK-36R Super Dimona	36348	
D-KDPC	Grob G.102 Astir CS/TOP	1263	D-7358
D-KDPR	Hoffmann HK-36R Super Dimona	36340	
D-KDPS	Hoffmann HK-36R Super Dimona	36361	
D-KDPT	Hoffmann HK-36R Super Dimona	36362	
D-KDPV	Hoffmann HK-36R Super Dimona	36364	
D-KDPZ-PZ	Schempp-Hirth Ventus cT	156/503	
D-KDRA	Hoffmann HK-36R Super Dimona	36334	
D-KDSA(2)	Glaser-Dirks DG-400	4-256	
D-KDST(2)	Glaser-Dirks DG-800B (Reservation 4.99)	8-175B99	
D-KDSV	Scheibe SF-25B Falke	46259	
D-KDSY	Schleicher ASH-26E	26084	
D-KDTA	Grob G.109	6090	
D-KDTB	Grob G.109	6089	
D-KDTH	Grob G.109B	6415	N721DL
D-KDTZ	Hoffmann H-36 Dimona	3666	
D-KDUG	Schleicher ASH-26E	26040	
D-KDUL	Glaser-Dirks DG-50 M	5E-19M11	
D-KDUT	Schempp-Hirth Discus bT	8/271	
D-KDWD	Glaser-Dirks DG-800B (Reservation 7.99)	8-126B55	N98NL
D-KDWN	Grob G.109B	6221	
D-KDWR	Glaser-Dirks DG-400	4-97	
D-KDWS	Valentin Kiwi	K-3012	
D-KEAA	Fournier RF-5	5092	
D-KEAB	Hirth Doppelraab V	523/57-2/53	D-4663
D-KEAC	Scheibe SF-25C Falke 2000	4222	
D-KEAF	Scheibe SF-25C Falke 1700	4225	
D-KEAG	Scheibe SF-25C Falke 1700	4226	
D-KEAH	Fournier RF-5	5110	
D-KEAL	Sportavia-Pützer RF-5B Sperber	51028	
D-KEAM(2)	Schleicher ASH-26E	26116	
D-KEAN(3)	Grob G.109	6041	
D-KEAS(2)	Schempp-Hirth Ventus cT	165/540	
D-KEAT	Scheibe SF-25B Falke	46253	
D-KEAZ(2)	Scheibe SF-25C Rotax-Falke	44578	
D-KEBA(2)	Hoffmann H-36 Dimona	3 67	
D-KEBE(2)	Grob G.109	6043	
D-KEBF	Scheibe SF-25B Falke	4647	
D-KEBG(2)	Schempp-Hirth Discus bT	28/324	
D-KEBH(3)	HOAC HK-36TC Super Dimona	36519	
D-KEBL	Scheibe SFS-31 Milan	6602	D-KEBK
D-KEBM(2)	Glaser-Dirks DG-400	4-5	(D-KGGJ)
D-KEBP	Glaser-Dirks DG-400	4-19	
D-KEBR	Schempp-Hirth Discus bT	152/544	(D-KEBS)
D-KEBT(2)	Eiriavion PIK-20E	20210	
D-KEBU(2)	Scheibe SF-25B Falke	4808	D-KETT(1) (D-KAHP)
D-KEBV	Schempp-Hirth Nimbus 3DM	16/39	
D-KEBW	Glaser-Dirks DG-400	4-79	
D-KEBY	Mü.23 Saurier	V-1	
D-KECA(2)	Eiriavion PIK-20E	20246	
D-KECB	Schleicher ASK-14	14014	
D-KECD(2)	Schempp-Hirth Ventus cT	111/379	
D-KECF	Scheibe SF-27M-A	6315	
D-KECK(2)	Scheibe SF-25B Falke	4697	
D-KECM	Scheibe SF-25B Falke	46100	
D-KECN	Scheibe SF-25B Falke	46101	
D-KECO(2)	Grob G.109/2400	6042	

Regn.	Type	C/n	Prev.Id.
D-KECP(2)	Glaser-Dirks DG-400	4-10	
D-KECQ	Scheibe SF-25D Falke	46103D	
D-KECT	Scheibe SF-27M-A	6318	
D-KECU	Scheibe SF-24B Motorspatz	4030	
D-KECW(2)	Schempp-Hirth Ventus cT	79/319	
D-KEDA(2)	SZD-45A Ogar	B-663	
D-KEDB(2)	Scheibe SF-25B Falke	4638	
D-KEDC(3)	Scheibe SF-27M-A	6311	
D-KEDE(3)	Schleicher ASK-14	14016	
D-KEDG(2)	Scheibe SF-25B Falke	4642	
D-KEDI(3)	Glaser-Dirks DG-800B *(Reservation 7.99)*	8-181B105	
D-KEDJ(2)	Schempp-Hirth Ventus cM	43/483	
D-KEDU	Raab Krähe IV *(Permit 9.99)*	05	
D-KEDV	Schempp-Hirth Ventus cM	70/534	
D-KEEB	Scheibe SF-25C Rotax-Falke	44535	
D-KEEE	Fournier RF-4D	4039	OE-9020
D-KEEG	Scheibe SF-25C Rotax-Falke	44592	
D-KEEI	Schempp-Hirth Ventus 2cT	25/93	
D-KEEN	Glaser-Dirks DG-800B	8-164B88	
D-KEEP	Scheibe SF-28A Tandem-Falke	5730	(D-KOAS)
D-KEEY	Hoffmann H-36 Dimona	3643	
D-KEFC	Scheibe SF-25C Falke 1700	44153	
D-KEFD	Scheibe SF-25C Falke 1700	44154	
D-KEFF	Scheibe SF-25C Falke 1700	44156	
D-KEFG	Scheibe SF-25C Falke 1700	44157	
D-KEFH	Scheibe SF-25C Falke 1700	44158	
D-KEFI(2)	Scheibe SF-25C Falke 1700	44159	
D-KEFJ	Scheibe SF-25C Falke 1700	44162	
D-KEFK	Scheibe SF-25E Super-Falke	4318	
D-KEFN	Scheibe SF-25C Falke 1700	44161	
D-KEFO	Scheibe SF-25C Falke 1700 *(Wfu)*	44163	
D-KEFR(2)	Scheibe SF-25E Super-Falke	4324	
D-KEFS	Scheibe SF-25C Falke 1700	44167	
D-KEFT	Scheibe SF-25C Falke 1700	44170	
D-KEFW	Scheibe SF-25C Falke 1700	44168	
D-KEFY(2)	Scheibe SF-25C Falke 1700	44174	
D-KEFZ	Scheibe SF-25C Falke 1700	44172	
D-KEGB	Scheibe SF-25C Falke 2000	44466	
D-KEGF	Schleicher ASH-26E	26046	D-8771
D-KEGL(2)	Scheibe SF-25C Rotax-Falke	44525	
D-KEGM	Schleicher ASH-25E	25047	
D-KEGO(2)	Hoffmann H-36 Dimona	36261	OE-9308
D-KEGR	Glaser-Dirks DG-400	4-261	
D-KEGS	Grob G.109	6140	N426BG
D-KEGU(2)	Schleicher ASK-14	14013	
D-KEGV	Hoffmann H-36 Dimona	3673	
D-KEHA	Eiriavion PIK-20E	20239	
D-KEHC	Glaser Dirks DG-400	4-34	
D-KEHE	Schleicher ASK-14	14017	
D-KEHF	Glaser-Dirks DG-400	4-163	I-KEHF
			D-KEHF
D-KEHG	Schleicher ASH-25E	25070	
D-KEHH-IHH	Schempp-Hirth Ventus bT	20/170	D-4110
D-KEHM	Technoflug Piccolo	004	
D-KEHO(2)	Grob G.109	6022	
D-KEHR(2)	Schempp-Hirth Ventus cT *(Reservation 11.99)*	92/340	D-KEHB
D-KEHU(2)	Hoffmann HK-36R Super Dimona	36315	
D-KEHY(2)	Hoyer Marco J-5/Ho	01	
D-KEIA(2)	Scheibe SF-25C Falke 1700	4491	
D-KEIE(2)	Scheibe SF-25C Falke 1700	4494	
D-KEIF	Scheibe SF-25C Falke 1700	4486	
D-KEIH	Scheibe SF-25C Falke 1700	4488	
D-KEIJ	Scheibe SF-25C Falke 1700	4490	
D-KEIK	Schleicher ASK-16	16019	
D-KEIL	Fournier RF-5	5066	F-BPLY
D-KEIM(2)	Hoffmann H-36 Dimona	36142	
D-KEIN(2)	Schempp-Hirth Discus bT	25/318	
D-KEIR	Scheibe SF-25C Falke 1700	44100	
D-KEIT	Glaser-Dirks DG-400	4-224	
D-KEIZ(2)	Schleicher ASW-24E	24850	
D-KEJA-JA	Schempp-Hirth Ventus cM	24/457	
D-KEJC-JC	Schempp-Hirth Janus CT	1/167	
D-KEJD	Glaser-Dirks DG-00	4-131	
D-KEJE-JE	Glaser-Dirks DG-400	4-73	
D-KEJK	Schempp-Hirth Nimbus 3DM	11/29	

Regn.	Type	C/n	Prev.Id.
D-KEKB	Schempp-Hirth Ventus cT	97/350	
D-KEKE	Stemme S-10VT	11-009	D-KSTE(9)
D-KEKF	Glaser-Dirks DG-400	4-18	
D-KEKH	Scheibe SF-25C Falke 1700	44244	(D-KDCU)
D-KEKK	Hoffmann H-36 Dimona	36248	
D-KEKM	Grob G.109B	6427	
D-KEKO(3)	Grob G.109B	6252	
D-KEKS	Scheibe SF-25C Falke 2000	44391	
D-KELA(2)	Scheibe SF-25C Falke 2000	44479	
D-KELE	Schleicher ASW-24E	24834	OE-9355
D-KELF	Schleicher ASW-24E	24816	
D-KELG	Hoffmann H-36 Dimona	36257	
D-KELH-IHB	Schempp-Hirth Ventus cM	30/463	
D-KELI	Grob G.109	6013	
D-KELL	Sportavia-Pützer RF-5B Sperber	51079	
D-KELM	Hoffmann H-36 Dimona	3633	
D-KELN	Hoffmann H-36 Dimona	3697	
D-KELO	Eiriavion PIK-20E	20243	
D-KELR	Technoflug Piccolo	042	
D-KELS	Eiriavion PIK-20E	20261	
D-KELY	Hoffmann H-36 Dimona	3625	
D-KELZ(3)	Scheibe SF-25C Falke 2000	44451	
D-KEMA(2)	Glaser-Dirks DG-400	4-170	
D-KEME	Schempp-Hirth Ventus bT	44/234	D-8898
D-KEMH	Schempp-Hirth Nimbus 3DM	12/34	
D-KEMI	Schleicher ASK-16	16040	
D-KEMK	Schempp-Hirth Discus bT	139/515	
D-KEMO	Schleicher ASK-16B	16039	N16KS
			HB-2039
D-KEMP	Fournier RF-5	5096	
D-KEMS	Hoffmann H-36 Dimona	3641	
D-KEMW	Schleicher ASH-26E	26050	
D-KEMY	Schleicher ASW-24E	24810	
D-KENC	Valentin Taifun 17E *(Reservation 12.99)*	1014	
D-KENI	Hoffmann H-36 Dimona	3603	
D-KENJ	Technoflug Piccolo B	094	
D-KENN	Schleicher ASW-20L/TOP	20333	D-7544
D-KEOA	Grob G.109B	6281	
D-KEOB	Grob G.109B	6283	
D-KEOC	Grob G.109B	6288	
D-KEOD	Grob G.109B	6294	
D-KEOE	Grob G.109B	6297	
D-KEOF	Grob G.109B	6305	
D-KEOH	Grob G.109B	6312	
D-KEOI	Grob G.109B	6309	
D-KEOJ	Grob G.109B	6324	
D-KEOK	Grob G.109B	6328	
D-KEOM	Grob G.109B	6298	
D-KEOP	Grob G.109B	6314	
D-KEOW	Grob G.109B	6306	
D-KEPA	Schleicher ASH-25E	25031	
D-KEPB	Grob G.109B	6347	
D-KEPC	Glaser-Dirks DG-400	4-66	
D-KEPE(3)	Schempp-Hirth Nimbus 3DT ("PE")	25	
D-KEPI	Grob G.109	6023	
D-KEPM	Scheibe SF-28A Tandem-Falke	5718	HB-2034
			D-KAZE(1)
			(D-KOAJ)
D-KEPO	Hoffmann H-36 Dimona *(Cld 3.95, Permit 6.99)*	3689	
D-KEPP	Hoffmann H-36 Dimona	3618	
D-KEPS	Schempp-Hirth Discus bT	23/316	
D-KERA(2)	Glaser-Dirks DG-400	4-159	
D-KERB-2i	Schleicher ASH-25E	25083	
D-KERC	Grob G.109	6102	
D-KERD	Glaser-Dirks DG-400	4-166	
D-KERF-RF	Schempp-Hirth Nimbus IIIMR	1	
D-KERG(2)	Glaser-Dirks DG-800B *(Reservation 6.99)*	8-187B111	
D-KERJ	Grob G.109B	6372	
D-KERK	Grob G.109B	6428	G-BMLY
D-KERL(2)	Fournier RF-4D	4046	OY-DXW
D-KERN	Technoflug Piccolo B	080	
D-KERW	Schleicher ASH-26E	26078	
D-KESD	HOAC HK-36TTC Super Dimona	36556	
D-KESE	Fournier RF-5	5008	(D-KIGY)
D-KESP(2)	Schempp-Hirth Ventus 2cM ("ES")	71/146	

Regn.	Type	C/n	Prev.Id.
D-KESS(2)	Scheibe SF-25C Falke 1700	44110	
D-KEST	Glaser-Dirks DG-400	4-20	
D-KESU	Schempp-Hirth Ventus 2cM(Permit)	56/110	
D-KETB	Grob G.109B	6503	
D-KETL-4H	Grob G.102 Astir CS 77/TOP	1662	D-3873
D-KETU	Schempp-Hirth Ventus 2cM	68/140	
D-KETY	Scheibe SF-25C Falke 1700	4227	
D-KETZ	Grob G.109B	6361	HB-2110 (EAF-672)
D-KEUL	Karlsruhe AK 1	01	
D-KEUN	Valentin Taifun 17E	1063	G-OFUN D-KHVA(5)
D-KEUP	Glaser-Dirks DG-600M	6-52M6	D-5808
D-KEUX	Fournier RF-9	10	
D-KEVA(2)	Glaser-Dirks DG-800B	8-99B34	
D-KEVE	Grob G.109B	6397	G-LIVE
D-KEVI	Pfeifer C 10/85	1	
D-KEV V	Schempp-Hirth Ventus bT	22/178	
D-KEWA	Hoffmann H-36 Dimona	3532	
D-KEWB	Glaser-Dirks DG-400	4-93	
D-KEWD	Grob G.109B	6431	
D-KEWE	Schempp-Hirth Ventus cT	109/372	
D-KEWG	Hoffmann H-36 Dimona	36243	
D-KEWI (3)	Schleicher ASH-26E	26044	
D-KEWL	Hoffmann H-36 Dimona	3657	
D-KEWR	Glaser-Dirks DG-800	8-49A33	
D-KEWS	Schempp-Hirth Ventus bT	2/101	
D-KEWW	Scheibe SF-25C Rotax-Falke	44608	
D-KEXI	Technoflug Piccolo	016	
D-KEXO	Hoffmann H-36 Dimona	36238	
D-KEXX	Schempp-Hirth Nimbus 3DT	2	
D-KEXY(2)	Technoflug Piccolo	048	D-KIBI (3)
D-KEYY-YY	Schempp-Hirth Ventus cM	7/423	
D-KEZA	Grob G.109B	6259	
D-KEZL	Scheibe SF-25C Falke 2000	44485	
D-KFAA	Schempp-Hirth Ventus 2cM	23/44	
D-KFAB	Schempp-Hirth Ventus 2cM (Reservation 8.99)	80/167	
D-KFAF	Schempp-Hirth Nimbus 4 DM	5/12	
D-KFAG(2)	Scheibe SF-25C Rotax-Falke	44618	
D-KFAI	Valentin Taifun 17E	1055	OO-TAI D-KHVA(2)
D-KFAL	DoppelraaBIV MSR	EB-2	D-6207
D-KFAR	Grob G.109B	6211	HB-2080
D-KFAT	Scheibe SF-25C Rotax-Falke	44569	
D-KFBA	Valentin Taifun 17E	1084	
D-KFBB	Hoffmann HK-36R Super Dimona	36356	
D-KFBE	Scheibe SF-25C Falke 1700	44210	
D-KFBG	Eiriavion PIK-20E	20223	
D-KFBO	Schleicher ASH-26E	26137	
D-KFBW	Aeromot AMT-200 Super Ximango	200-070	
D-KFBZ	Hoffmann H-36F Dimona (Modified by Frisch Engineering to Rotax 912)	3669	
D-KFCD	Hoffmann HK-36R Super Dimona	36350	
D-KFCE	Scheibe SF-25C Rotax-Falke	44533	
D-KFCH	Technoflug Piccolo B	098	
D-KFCK	SZD-45A Ogar	B-649	DDR-3503 DM-3503
D-KFCM	Hoffmann H-36 Dimona	3681	
D-KFCO	Grob G.109	6120	OE-9259 F-WAQL
D-KFCP	Glaser-Dirks DG-400	4-263	HB-2158
D-KFCW	Grob G.109B	6249	
D-KFDI	Valentin Taifun 17E-II	1127	F-CGAI F-WGAI (D-KHVA)
D-KFDW	Schleicher ASW-20CL/TOP	20742	D-5358
D-KFEB	Grob G.109B	6430	
D-KFEC	Scheibe SF-25C Rotax-Falke	44571	
D-KFEE	Hoffmann H-36 Dimona	36273	
D-KFEL	Scheibe SF-25C Falke 2000	44495	
D-KFFA(2)	Glaser-Dirks DG-400	4-220	D-KAHM(2)
D-KFFB(2)	Schempp-Hirth Discus bT	3/252	
D-KFFF	Scheibe SF-25C Falke 2000	44385	(D-KFFA)
D-KFFG	Scheibe SF-25C Falke 2000	44457	
D-KFFK	Glaser-Dirks DG-800B	8-158B82	
D-KFFR	Glaser-Dirks DG-500M	5E-18M10	
D-KFGE	Eiriavion PIK-20E	20278	
D-KFGG	Schempp-Hirth Discus bT	134/508	
D-KFGH	Schempp-Hirth Janus CT	8/252	
D-KFGM	Scheibe SF-25C Falke 2000	44400	
D-KFGN	Nitsche AVO-68R Samburo	024R	OE-9166
D-KFGP	Hoffmann HK-36 Dimona	36304	HB-2186
D-KFGS	Schempp-Hirth Ventus 2cM	49/101	
D-KFGT(2)	HOAC HK-36TTC Super Dimona	36572	
D-KFGW	Schempp-Hirth Ventus 2cT	6/14	
D-KFHA(2)	Schempp-Hirth Nimbus 4 DM	7/15	(D-9153)
D-KFHD	Schleicher ASH-26E (Reservation 9.99)	26165	
D-KFHI	Fournier RF-4D	4090	SE-TGY
D-KFIF	Schleicher ASW-22BE	22056	
D-KFIH	Valentin Taifun 17E	1057	SE-UBA D-KHVA(4)
D-KFIT	Glaser-Dirks DG-400	4-23	OO-FIT (OO-ZUD) (OO-PUD)
D-KFKA	Schempp-Hirth Ventus bT	4/120	D-1137
D-KFKF	Hoffmann H-36 Dimona	3511	
D-KFKS	Eiri PIK-20E	20217	LN-GME G-LYDE
D-KFLA	Glaser-Dirks DG-800	8-48B3	
D-KFLO	Glaser-Dirks DG-400	4-138	
D-KFLY	Valentin Kiwi	3007	
D-KFMA	Glaser-Dirks DG-800B	8-87B23	
D-KFMF	Schempp-Hirth Discus bT	110/460	
D-KFMH	Schleicher ASH-26E	26035	
D-KFMO	Hoffmann H-36 Dimona	36227	OE-9269
D-KFNT	Schempp-Hirth Discus bT	2/250	D-5070
D-KFNW	Grob G.103C Twin IIISL	35045	
D-KFOR	Scheibe SF-25C Rotax-Falke	44563	
D-KFOW-OW	Schleicher ASH-25E	25025	
D-KFPS	LET L-13SDM Vivat	950607	
D-KFRA	Scheibe SF-25C Falke 2000	44441	
D-KFRK	Hoffmann H-36 Dimona	36253	
D-KFSG	SFS-31 Milan	6612	(D-KAUT)
D-KFSK	HOAC HK-36TTC Super Dimona	36577	
D-KFSL	Grob G.102 Astir CS77/TOP	1703	D-7632
D-KFSM	Glaser-Dirks DG-400	4-245	
D-KFSN	AVO 68s Samburo 2000	019	
D-KFSO	Hoffmann HK-36TC Super Dimona	36505	OE-9406
D-KFSP	Brditschka HB-21	21017	OE-9168
D-KFSS	Schleicher ASH-26E	26002	
D-KFST	Fournier RF-4D	4151	OO-YES PH-JFE
D-KFSU	Schempp-Hirth Ventus bT	23/181	D-2928
D-KFSV	Hoffmann HK-36R Super Dimona	36314	
D-KFTA	HOAC HK-36TS Super Dimona	36512	
D-KFTT	Schempp-Hirth Ventus 2cM (Reservation 11.99)	82/172	
D-KFUN	Valentin Taifun 17E	1101	
D-KFUW	Scheibe SF-25C Falke 2000	44491	
D-KFVA	Fournier RF-5	5099	
D-KFVS	Scheibe SF-25C Falke 2000	44515	
D-KFWC	Hoffmann H-36 Dimona	3613	
D-KFWD	Glaser-Dirks DG-800B (Reservation 3.99)	8-160B84	
D-KFWE	Schleicher ASW-22BLE	22055	
D-KFWH(2)	Schempp-Hirth Ventus 2cT	29/100	
D-KFWM	Hoffmann HK-36R Super Dimona	36344	
D-KFWJ	Scheibe SF-25C Falke 2000	44267	
D-KFWP	Schleicher ASK-16	16036	
D-KFWS	Schempp-Hirth Ventus 2cM	66/135	
D-KFZA	Technoflug Piccolo B	097	
D-KFZW	Hoffmann HK-36R Super Dimona	36395	
D-KGAA	Scheibe SF-25C Falke 1700	4217	
D-KGAB	Scheibe SF-25C Falke 1700	4218	
D-KGAD	Scheibe SF-25C Falke 2000	4220	
D-KGAE	Scheibe SF-25C Falke 1700	4221	
D-KGAF	Hoffmann H-36 Dimona	3503	
D-KGAH	Scheibe SF-25C Falke 2000	44296	
D-KGAI	Scheibe SF-25C Falke 1700	44460	
D-KGAJ	Scheibe SF-25C Rotax-Falke	44606	
D-KGAK	Scheibe SF-25C Falke 1700	44346	
D-KGAL	Scheibe SF-25C Falke 1700	44310	

Regn.	Type	C/n	Prev.Id.
D-KGAM	Scheibe SF-25C Falke 1700	44322	
D-KGAN	Valentin Taifun 17E	1052	D-ECAN(3) D-KGAN
D-KGAO	Scheibe SF-25C Falke 1700	44437	
D-KGAP	Scheibe SF-25C Falke 1700	44326	
D-KGAQ	Scheibe SF-25C Rotax-Falke	44617	
D-KGAR	Scheibe SF-25C Falke 1700	44340	
D-KGAS	Scheibe SF-25C Falke 2000	44367	
D-KGAT(2)	Scheibe SF-25C Falke 1700	44483	
D-KGAU	Scheibe SF-25C Falke 1700	44527	
D-KGAV	Scheibe SF-25C Falke 1700	44567	
D-KGAW	Scheibe SF-25C Falke 1700	44506	
D-KGAX	Scheibe SF-25C Falke 1700	44585	
D-KGAY	Scheibe SF-25C Falke 1700	44548	
D-KGAZ(2)	Scheibe SF-25C Falke 1700	44415	
D-KGBA	Valentin Taifun 17E-II	1108	
D-KGBB	Schempp-Hirth Ventus cT	101/360	
D-KGBI	Stemme S-10VT	11-030	
D-KGBL	ICA/Brasov I S.28M2/G	70	
D-KGBN	Scheibe SF-25C Rotax-Falke	44628	
D-KGBS	Schempp-Hirth Ventus 2cM	28/50	
D-KGBT	Schempp-Hirth Discus bT	136/511	
D-KGCA	Stemme S-10V	14-019M	
D-KGCB	Stemme S-10V	10-47M	
D-KGCC	Scheibe SF-25B Falke	AB46307	
D-KGCD(5)	Stemme S-10	10-50	
D-KGCF	Stemme S-10V	14-018M	
D-KGCG-MO	Stemme S-10	10-22	
D-KGCH(3)	Stemme S-10	10-52	
D-KGCI (6)	Stemme S10V (Formerly c/n 14-003)	14-056M	OO-VCN D-KGCI (4)
D-KGCL(2)	Stemme S-10V	14-007	
D-KGCN	Stemme S-10	10-31	
D-KGCO(2)	Stemme S-10	10-35	
D-KGCP	Stemme S-10	10-36	
D-KGCQ	Stemme S-10V	14-038M	(D-KSTE)
D-KGCR(2)	Stemme S-10VT	11-001	
D-KGCV	Stemme S-10	10-45	
D-KGCW	Stemme S-10	10-40	
D-KGCY(3)	Stemme S-10V (Formerly c/n 14-004)	14-057M	
D-KGCZ(3)	Stemme S-10V	14-017	
D-KGDA(3)	Stemme S-10V	14-024	
D-KGDB(3)	Stemme S-10V	14-025	
D-KGDC(3)	Stemme S-10V	14-028	
D-KGDD(3)	Stemme S-10V	14-026	
D-KGDS	Schleicher ASW-24E	24841	
D-KGEB	Schempp-Hirth Ventus bT	45/237	
D-KGEM	Hoffman HK-36 Super Dimona	36304	(D-KFGP) HB-2186
D-KGER	Glaser-Dirks DG-800B	8-65B9	(D-KKER)
D-KGFA	Grob G.109B	6201	
D-KGFC	Grob G.109B	6207	
D-KGFD	Grob G.109B	6212	G-BNZF D-KGFD
D-KGFH	Grob G.109	6080	F-WAQK
D-KGFI	Grob G.109B	6218	
D-KGFL	Fournier RF-5	5038	
D-KGFM	Grob G.109B	6205	
D-KGFP	Grob G.109B	6251	
D-KGFQ	Grob G.109B	6245	
D-KGFR	Grob G.109B	6253	
D-KGFS	Grob G.109B	6226	
D-KGFT	Grob G.109B	6206	
D-KGFU	Grob G.109B	6264	
D-KGFV	Grob G.109B	6263	
D-KGFW	Grob G.109B	6238	
D-KGFX	Grob G.109B	6247	
D-KGFY	Grob G.109B	6256	
D-KGFZ	Grob G.109B	6282	
D-KGGL	Schleicher ASH-26E	26034	
D-KGGO(2)	Schleicher ASH-25M (Reservation 10.99)	25216	
D-KGHH	Grob G.103C Twin IIISL	35020	
D-KGHP	Schleicher ASH-25M	25203	
D-KGHS	Glaser-Dirks DG-400	4-236	OY-PVX
D-KGHW-HW	Schleicher ASH-25E	25014	
D-KGIB	Grob G.109	6044	
D-KGIN(2)	Glaser-Dirks DG-500M	5E-92M39	
D-KGKB	Schleicher ASH-26E (Reservation)	26148	
D-KGKG	Schleicher ASW-22BE	22060	
D-KGKS	Schleicher ASH-26E	26014	D-5599
D-KGLG	Glaser-Dirks DG-600M	6-111M52	
D-KGLM	Grob G.109B	6237	
D-KGMD	Schleicher ASH-26E	26121	
D-KGMR	Hoffmann H-36 Dimona	36254	
D-KGMW	Schempp-Hirth Nimbus 4 DM	18/27	
D-KGMY	Schempp-Hirth Ventus bT	3/116	
D-KGND	Stemme S-10V	14-026M	
	(Formerly S-10 c/n 10-26)		
D-KGOD(2)	Schempp-Hirth Ventus cT	171/561	
D-KGOM	Hoffmann H-36 Dimona	3644	
D-KGOR	Schleicher ASK-16	16020	I-AGOR D-KGOR
D-KGOS	Valentin Taifun 17E	1024	
D-KGPA	Hoffmann HK-36R Super Dimona	36343	
D-KGPB	HOAC HK-36TS Super Dimona	36586	
D-KGPG	Glaser-Dirks DG-500M	5E-72M30	(D-KGPL)
D-KGPI (2)	Glaser-Dirks DG-800	8-53B6	
D-KGPR	LET L-13SEH Vivat	940522	OK-4101
D-KGRA(2)	Scheibe SF-25B Falke (Reservation 12.99)	4035	D-KAHH (D-KIBU)
D-KGRB	Scheibe SF-24A Motorspatz (Reservation 12.99)	4011	D-KADA(1)
D-KGRM	Hoffmann H-36 Dimona	36193	OE-9245
D-KGRP	Grob G.103C Twin IIISL	35042	
D-KGRS	Fournier RF-5	5068	OE-9033
D-KGRU	Fournier RF-4D	4132	OY-XBA SE-TGU
D-KGSE	Schempp-Hirth Ventus cT	107/370	D-KBEK
D-KGSF	Schempp-Hirth Duo Discus (Reservation 10.99)	3/232	
D-KGST	Hoffmann H-36 Dimona	36100	
D-KGSW	Schempp-Hirth Ventus cM	59/514	
D-KGTA(2)	HOAC HK-36R Super Dimona	36410	
D-KGTB	HOAC HK-36R Super Dimona	36411	
D-KGTC	HOAC HK-36R Super Dimona	36414	
D-KGTD	HOAC HK-36TS Super Dimona	36508	
D-KGTE	HOAC HK-36TS Super Dimona	36510	
D-KGTF	HOAC HK-36TC Super Dimona	36605	
D-KGUA	Hoffmann HK-36R Super Dimona	36381	
D-KGUB	Hoffmann HK-36R Super Dimona	36382	
D-KGVS	Schempp-Hirth Ventus cM	40/478	
D-KGWB	Glaser-Dirks DG-400	4-95	
D-KGWG	Fournier RF-4D	4020	F-BORG
D-KGWH	Grob G.109B	6511	
D-KGWS	Schempp-Hirth Ventus 2cM	13/30	
D-KGWW	Stemme S-10	10-37	
D-KGZT-99	Schempp-Hirth Nimbus 3DT	5	
D-KHAA(2)	Technoflug Piccolo B	081	
D-KHAC	Hoffmann HK-36R Super Dimona	36359	
D-KHAI	Borowski AN-20K Piccolo	001	
D-KHAL	Schleicher ASK-16B	16043	OE-9132 (D-KAXD)
D-KHAM	Schempp-Hirth Nimbus 4 DM	19/28	
D-KHAN	Technoflug Piccolo	046	
D-KHAS	Schleicher ASK-16	16038	
D-KHBA	Grob G.109B	6370	
D-KHBB(2)	Schleicher ASH-26E	26095	
D-KHBC	Schleicher ASW-24/TOP	24804	
D-KHBE(2)	Glaser-Dirks DG-400	4-279	
D-KHBM	Hoffmann H-36 Dimona	3629	
D-KHBS	Glaser-Dirks DG-400	4-290	
D-KHCC	Schempp-Hirth Ventus bT	34/215	
D-KHCD-CD	Schempp-Hirth Discus bT	17/303	
D-KHCE	Schempp-Hirth Ventus cM	84/563	
D-KHCO	Valentin Taifun 17E-II	1110	
D-KHDF	Hoffmann H-36 Dimona	3656	
D-KHDG	Schleicher ASH-25E	25163	
D-KHDK	Schempp-Hirth Discus bT	30/327	
D-KHDV	Glaser-Dirks DG-400	4-280	
D-KHEA	Scheibe SF-25B Falke	4821	
D-KHEB	Scheibe SF-25B Falke	4822	
D-KHEC(2)	Scheibe SF-25C Falke 2000	44494	

Regn.	Type	C/n	Prev.Id.
D-KHED	Scheibe SF-25B Falke	4824	
D-KHEE(2)	Grob G.103C Twin IIISL	35030	(D-KSOL)
D-KHEF(2)	Scheibe SF-25C Falke 1700	4244	(D-KAJF)
D-KHEH(2)	Grob G.109B	6436	
D-KHEK	Sportavia RF-5B Sperber	51001	
D-KHEM(2)	Schempp-Hirth Ventus cT	135/415	
D-KHEN(2)	Scheibe SF-25C Rotax-Falke	44634	
D-KHEP	Scheibe SF-25B Falke	4833	
D-KHER	Scheibe SF-25B Falke	4835	
D-KHEV	Scheibe SF-25B Falke	4839	
D-KHEW	Scheibe SF-25B Falke	4840	
D-KHEX	Scheibe SF-25B Falke	4841	
D-KHEY	Scheibe SF-25B Falke	4842	
D-KHEZ(2)	Valentin Taifun 17E	1072	F-WGAE
			D-KHVA
D-KHFA	Scheibe SF-25B Falke	4843	
D-KHFB(2)	Hoffmann HK-36R Super Dimona	36346	
D-KHFC	Scheibe SF-25D Falke	4845D	
D-KHFD	Scheibe SF-25D Falke	4846D	
D-KHFE	Scheibe SF-25B Falke	4847	
D-KHFF	Scheibe SF-25B Falke	4848	
D-KHFG	Scheibe SF-25B Falke	4849	
D-KHFH	Scheibe SF-25B Falke	4850	
D-KHFL	Schleicher ASW-20/TOP	20002	D-3860
D-KHFP	Schleicher ASH-26E	26026	G-MORE
D-KHFR	Franke Doppelraab 7M (Hankur 1)	001	D-5626(1)
D-KHGA	Scheibe SF-25C Falke 2000	44358	
D-KHGB	Schempp-Hirth Standard Cirrus/TOP	477	D-3719
D-KHGG	Schleicher ASH-22BLE	22050	
D-KHGH	Scheibe SF-28A Tandem-Falke	5710	
D-KHGO	Gomolzig RF-9-ABS	9021	(D-KABS)
D-KHGR	Schleicher ASH-25E	25149	D-0825
D-KHGS	Schempp-Hirth Ventus bT	27/194	
D-KHGT	Grob G.109	6087	
D-KHHA	Valentin Taifun 17E-II	1126	
D-KHHD	Technoflug Piccolo	054	
D-KHHG(2)	Schleicher ASH-25M	25174	D-5763
D-KHHI	Schleicher ASH-26E	26036	
D-KHHL	Technoflug Piccolo	050	
D-KHHO	Schleicher ASH-25M	25188	
D-KHHS	Technoflug Piccolo	039	
D-KHHT	Scheibe SF-25C Falke 2000	44354	
D-KHIG-3	Schempp-Hirth Janus CM	14/190	
D-KHIK	Schempp-Hirth Janus CM	18/202	
D-KHIM	Valentin Taifun 17E	1032	
D-KHIO	Schempp-Hirth Nimbus 4T	8	
D-KHIR	Hoffmann H-36 Dimona	3619	
D-KHIS	Valentin Kiwi	3005	
D-KHJB	Glaser-Dirks DG-500M	5E-14M8	
D-KHJC	Schempp-Hirth Discus bT	146/525	
D-KHJG	Fournier RF-4D	4129	F-BPLM
D-KHJM	Glaser-Dirks DG-800B	8-125B54	
D-KHJO	Schleicher ASK- 4	AB14061	(D-KICH)
D-KHJR	Eiri PIK-20E	20228	G-BHFR
D-KHJT	Technoflug Piccolo	013	
D-KHKA-LO	Schempp-Hirth Nimbus IIM V-2	02	
D-KHKG	Grob G.103C Twin IIISL	35036	
D-KHKI	Technoflug Piccolo B	089	
D-KHKW	Glaser-Dirks DG-400	4-217	
D-KHLL	Grob G.103C Twin IIISL	35033	
D-KHMA	Grob G.109B	6257	
D-KHMB	Schleicher ASH-26E	26007	
D-KHMG	Hoffmann HK-36R Super Dimona	36318	
D-KHML	Rolladen-Schneider LS-9 (Reservation)	9003	
D-KHMM	Scheibe SF-25C Falke 2000	44384	
D-KHMS	Glaser-Dirks DG-400	4-132	
D-KHMW	Glaser-Dirks DG-600M	6-50M5	
D-KHMY	Schleicher ASH-25M	25201	
D-KHMZ	Glaser-Dirks DG-400	4-77	
D-KHNO	Valentin Taifun 17E	1007	(D-KEKO(2))
D-KHOA	Scheibe SF-27M-A	6323	
D-KHOB(3)	Schempp-Hirth Ventus cM ("9A")	80/553	
D-KHOC	Scheibe SF-27M-A	6325	
D-KHOE(2)	HOAC HK-36TTC Super Dimona	36575	
D-KHOF	Scheibe SF-25D Falke	4639D	

Regn.	Type	C/n	Prev.Id.
D-KHOI	Scheibe SF-25C Falke 1700	4425	
D-KHOJ	Scheibe SF-25C Falke 1700	4426	
D-KHOL(2)	Schleicher ASH-25E	25135	
D-KHOM	Scheibe SF-25C Falke 1700	4429	
D-KHOO(2)	Rolladen-Schneider LS-9 (Permit 10.99)	9005	
D-KHOP(2)	Scheibe SF-28A Tandem-Falke	5706	
D-KHOT	Scheibe SF-28A Tandem-Falke	5710	
D-KHOX	Hoffmann HK-36R Super Dimona	36402	
D-KHOY	Technoflug Piccolo	002	
D-KHPC	Schempp-Hirth Ventus cM	48/489	
D-KHPE	Glaser-Dirks DG-600M	6-55M9	
D-KHPH	Valentin Taifun 17E	1036	
D-KHPR	HOAC HK-36TTS Super Dimona	36587	
D-KHPS	Grob G.109B	6296	
D-KHRA	Hoffmann HK-36R Super Dimona	36380	
D-KHRB	Hoffmann HK-36R Super Dimona	36376	
D-KHRC	Hoffmann HK-36R Super Dimona	36377	
D-KHRL	Schleicher ASH-25M (Permit 1.00)	25214	
D-KHRO	SZD-45A Ogar	B-764	DDR-3511
			DM-3511
D-KHRW	Schleicher ASW-22BE	22051	D-4753
D-KHSC	Schempp-Hirth Nimbus 2M	06	
D-KHSS-SS	Schempp-Hirth Nimbus 3T	90/24	
D-KHSW	Valentin Mistral CM	MC-071/85	
D-KHTA	Grob G.109B	6501	
D-KHTB	Grob G.109B	6543	
D-KHUB	Glaser-Dirks DG-800B	8-162B86	
D-KHUH	Schleicher ASW-22BLE	22071	
D-KHUK(2)	Hoffmann H-36 Dimona	3638	
D-KHUL	Hoffmann H-36 Dimona	3699	
D-KHVI	Grob G.102 Astir CS77/TOP	1797	D-7773
D-KHVL	Scheibe SF-25C Rotax-Falke	44554	
D-KHWA	Glaser-Dirks DG-400	4-229	
D-KHWC	Schempp-Hirth Nimbus IIM V-1	01	
D-KHWD	Fournier RF-4D	4060	F-BOXH
D-KHWE	Brditschka HB-23/2400SP	23029-U	OE-9304
D-KHWG	AVO 68R Samburo	009R	OE-9121
	(Converted from AVO 68v c/n 009, 6.99)		
D-KHWH	Grob G.109B	6321	G-KIAM
D-KHWK	Glaser-Dirks DG-600M	6-78M25	
D-KHWM	Glaser-Dirks DG-400	4-255	
D-KHWS	Schempp-Hirth Discus bT	77/406	
D-KHXX(2)	Schempp-Hirth Nimbus 4M ("XX")	1/5	
D-KHXY	Schempp-Hirth Ventus cM	107/606	
D-KHYN	Schempp-Hirth Discus bT	117/473	
D-KHZZ	Grob G.103C Twin IIISL	35037	
D-KIAA(2)	Scheibe SF-25C Falke 2000	44438	
D-KIAB(2)	Scheibe SF-25C Falke 2000	44439	
D-KIAC(2)	Scheibe SF-25C Falke 2100	44440	
D-KIAD	Scheibe SF-25C Falke 2000	44443	
D-KIAE	Scheibe SF-25C Falke 2000	44455	
D-KIAF	Scheibe SF-25C Falke 2000	44445	
D-KIAG	Scheibe SF-25C Falke 2000	44442	
D-KIAH(2)	Scheibe SF-25C Falke 2000	44456	
D-KIAI (2)	Scheibe SF-25C Falke 2000	44467	
D-KIAK(2)	Scheibe SF-25C Falke 2000	44463	
D-KIAL	Scheibe SF-25C Falke 2000	44450	
D-KIAM	Scheibe SF-25C Falke 2000	44446	
D-KIAN	Scheibe SF-25C Falke 2000	44468	
D-KIAP	Scheibe SF-25C Falke 2000	44465	
D-KIAR	Scheibe SF-25C Falke 2000	44458	
D-KIAS	Scheibe SF-25C Falke 2000	44470	
D-KIAT	Scheibe SF-25C Falke 2000	44472	
D-KIAU	Scheibe SF-25C Falke 2000	44461	
D-KIAV(2)	Scheibe SF-25E Super Falke	4334	G-BFHN
			D-KDFW
D-KIAW	Scheibe SF-25C Falke 2000	44473	
D-KIAX	Scheibe SF-25C Falke 2000	44475	
D-KIAY(3)	Scheibe SF-25C Falke 2000	44482	
D-KIAZ	Scheibe SF-25C Falke 2000	44474	
D-KIBA(2)	Eiriavion PIK-20E	20207	
D-KIBC(2)	HOAC HK-36R Super Dimona	36360	
D-KIBN	Eiriavion PIK-20E	20251	OE-9255
			D-KERH
D-KIBO(3)	Schempp-Hirth Janus BM	1/56	

Regn.	Type	C/n	Prev.Id.
D-KIBS	Hoffmann H-36 Dimona	36242	
D-KIBT	Schempp-Hirth Discus bT	142/520	
D-KIBU(2)	Glaser-Dirks DG-800B	8-82B19	
D-KIBY	Schempp-Hirth Janus CM	3	(D-KJMB)
D-KICB(2)	Glaser-Dirks DG-800B	8-125B53	
D-KICC(3)	Schempp-Hirth Ventus 2cM	79/162	
D-KICE(3)	Schleicher ASK-14	14058	
D-KICF(2)	Schleicher ASK-14	14059	
D-KICG(3)	Schleicher ASK-14/KM29	14055	
D-KICH(3)	Schleicher ASK-16	16002	
D-KICI (3)	Hoffmann H-36 Dimona	3604	
D-KICK(2)	Schleicher ASH-26E	26085	
D-KICM	Schempp-Hirth Ventus cM	55/504	
D-KICO(2)	Valentin Taifun 17E-II	1121	
D-KICP	Schleicher ASW-24E	24860	
D-KICR	Schempp-Hirth Discus bT	101/443	
D-KICS	Glaser-Dirks DG-800B	8-151B75	
D-KICY	Scheibe SF-25A Motorfalke	4534	(D-KAKO)
D-KIDA(2)	Hoffmann H-36 Dimona	3614	
D-KIDB	Eiri PIK-20E	20269	
D-KIDD(2)	Schempp-Hirth Discus bT	144/522	
D-KIDF	Schleicher ASH-26E	26153	
D-KIDH	Schleicher ASH-26E	26031	D-1349
D-KIDI (2)	FBW Valentin Kiwi	K-3011	
D-KIDK	Schempp-Hirth Discus bT	6/264	
D-KIDL	Glaser-Dirks DG-500M	5E-31M15	
D-KIDM(2)	Schleicher ASH-25M	25199	
D-KIDO(2)	Schleicher ASH-26E	26107	
D-KIDS	Glaser-Dirks DG-400	4-208	
D-KIEA	Scheibe SF-25C Falke (Permit 5.99)	44648	
D-KIEB-E4	Schempp-Hirth Ventus cT	112/381	
D-KIEC	Scheibe SF-25C Falke	44647	
D-KIED	Hoffmann H-36 Dimona	3651	
D-KIEE	Scheibe SF-25C Falke	44644	
D-KIEF	Schempp-Hirth Janus CT	7/244	
D-KIEG	Glaser-Dirks DG-600M	6-84M30	
D-KIEH	Glaser-Dirks DG-600M	6-85M31	
D-KIEJ	Scheibe SF-25C Falke	44651	
D-KIEK	Scheibe SF-25C Rotax-Falke	44638	
	(Permit, Rotax 912 test aircraft)		
D-KIEL(3)	Valentin Taifun 17E	1002	OY-XYA
	(w/o 4.1.92 ?)		D-KINC(2)
			(D-KLFM)
D-KIEM	Schempp-Hirth Ventus bT	29/198	
D-KIEN	Scheibe SF-25C Falke	44653	
D-KIEO	Scheibe SF-25C Falke	44654	
D-KIEP	Scheibe SF-25C Falke	44652	
D-KIER	Scheibe SF-25C Rotax-Falke	44637	
D-KIES	Glaser-Dirks DG-400	4-106	
D-KIEU	Schleicher ASW-24E	24840	
D-KIEW	Scheibe SF-25C Rotax-Falke	44629	
D-KIEX	Scheibe SF-25C Rotax-Falke	44643	
D-KIEZ	Scheibe SF-25C Rotax-Falke	44639	
D-KIFA(3)	Eiriavion PIK-20E	20247	
D-KIFB(2)	Glaser-Dirks DG-400	4-205	
D-KIFF	SFS-31 Milan	6604	
D-KIFH	Schleicher ASH-26E	26016	
D-KIFI	Scheibe SF-25 Motorfalke	4505	
D-KIFL(2)	Schempp-Hirth Ventus cT ("MA")	121/395	
D-KIFP	Fournier RF-5	5088	
D-KIFR	Valentin Taifun 17E	1006	
D-KIFW	Glaser-Dirks DG-400	4-76	D-KOBI (3)
D-KIFZ	Schempp-Hirth Discus bT	59/381	
D-KIGB	Technoflug Piccolo B	082	
D-KIGE(2)	Grob G.109B	6246	
D-KIGH	Schleicher ASH-25M	25189	
D-KIGI	Fournier RF-5	5004	
D-KIGM-GM	Schempp-Hirth Discus bT	7/269	
D-KIGP	Schleicher ASH-26E	26038	
D-KIGR-GR	Schleicher ASH-25E	25035	
D-KIGS	Grob G.102 Astir CS77/TOP	1717	D-2535
D-KIGT	Fournier RF-4D	4154	OE-9029
D-KIGU	Fournier RF-5	5006	
D-KIGV-GV	Schempp-Hirth Ventus bT	7/131	
D-KIGW	Grob G.109B	6573	

Regn.	Type	C/n	Prev.Id.
D-KIHA	Fournier RF-5	5009	
D-KIHB(2)	Schempp-Hirth Ventus cM	104/600	
D-KIHD(2)	Schempp-Hirth Ventus cM	39/477	
D-KIHE	Fournier RF-5	5010	
D-KIHG	Grob G.102 Astir CS/TOP	1305	D-7347
D-KIHH	Glaser-Dirks DG-400	4-55	
D-KIHI (3)	Glaser-Dirks DG-800B (Reservation .99)	8-168B92	
D-KIHK	Glaser-Dirks DG-400	4-80	
D-KIHM	Hoffmann H-36 Dimona	3649	
D-KIHN	Schempp-Hirth Discus bT	4/257	
D-KIHO	Fournier RF-5	5012	
D-KIHP(2)	Schempp-Hirth Ventus cT ("HP")	133/412	
D-KIHR	Glaser-Dirks DG-600/18M	6-110M51	(D-KCWC)
D-KIHW	Schleicher ASH-25E	25110	VH-YBE
			VH-ZHW
			D-KIHW
D-KIII (2)	Schempp-Hirth Ventus cM	14/441	HB-2166
			D-KCPA
D-KIIK-7K	Schempp-Hirth Ventus bT	25/89	
D-KIIL	Schempp-Hirth Discus bT	132/502	
D-KIIN	Schempp-Hirth Ventus cM	69/533	
D-KIIV-TB	Schempp-Hirth Ventus AM	1/48	
D-KIIX- I I	Schempp-Hirth Ventus cT	66/286	
D-KIJC	Glaser-Dirks DG-600M	6-77M24	
D-KIJH	Schempp-Hirth Ventus 2cM	8/25	
D-KIJO	Glaser-Dirks DG-600/18M	6-97M43	
D-KIKA(2)	Schleicher ASW-20L/TOP ("IKT")	20395	D-2694
D-KIKD	Hoffmann HK-36R Super Dimona	36303	
D-KIKE	Fournier RF-3	42	
D-KIKI	Fournier RF-3	38	
D-KIKK	Schempp-Hirth Ventus cT	146/452	
D-KIKL	Schleicher ASH-25M	25176	
D-KIKO(2)	Grob G.109	6017	
D-KIKR-KR	Schempp-Hirth Ventus cT	132/410	
D-KIKS	Glaser-Dirks DG-800B	8-169B93	
D-KIKT	Glaser-Dirks DG-400	4-167	
D-KIKW	Schempp-Hirth Discus bT	149/539	
D-KILD	Hoffmann HK-36R Super Dimona	36329	
D-KILE(2)	Glaser-Dirks DG-600/18M	6-90M36	(PH-939)
D-KILG	Hoffmann H-36 Dimona	3636	
D-KILH	Schempp-Hirth Ventus 2cM	12/29	
D-KILI (2)	IAR I S.28M2/G	68	YR-1995
D-KILK	Schleicher ASH-25E	25072	
D-KILL(2)	HOAC HK-36R Super Dimona	36325	OE-9361
D-KILM	Glaser-Dirks DG-600M	6-57M11	
D-KILO	Schempp-Hirth Nimbus 4M (Permit 12.99)	14/35	
D-KILS	Rolladen-Schneider LS-9 (Permit)	9000	
D-KILT	Fournier RF-4D	4027	
D-KILU(2)	Berlin B-13 ("CD")	001	
D-KILY	Schleicher ASK-14 (Reserved as F-CIPH .99)	14015	
D-KIMA(2)	Schempp-Hirth Ventus bT	39/229	
D-KIMB	Glaser-Dirks DG-400	4-201	
D-KIMC	Grob G.109	6093	
D-KIMD	Technoflug Piccolo	040	(D-KEXY)
D-KIME(2)	Technoflug Piccolo B	058	
D-KIMG(2)	Technoflug Piccolo B	056	
D-KIMH-MH	Schleicher ASW-24E	24805	
D-KIMI	Scheibe SF-25B Falke	4628	
D-KIMJ(2)	Schempp-Hirth Discus bT	27/321	
D-KIMK(2)	Schleicher ASW-24E	24845	
D-KIMM(2)	Scheibe SF-25C Falke 1700	4456	OY-VTX
			(D-KOAC)
D-KIMP	Fournier RF-5	5070	
D-KIMR(2)	Glaser-Dirks DG-400	4-231	
D-KIMS	Hoffmann H-36 Dimona	3665	
D-KIMU	Schempp-Hirth Discus bT	62/386	
D-KIMW(3)	Schempp-Hirth Ventus 2cM	70/142	
D-KINA(2)	Scheibe SF-25C Falke 2000	44464	
D-KIND	Fournier RF-5	5056	
D-KINE(2)	Grob G.109B	6423	
D-KING	Schempp-Hirth Standard Cirrus M (Permit)	G-54M	
D-KINI (2)	Grob G.109	6029	
D-KINK	Grob G.109B	6366	(EAF675)
D-KINN-DG	Glaser-Dirks DG-800	8-19A16	
D-KINO	Fournier RF-3	75	

Regn.	Type	C/n	Prev.Id.
D-KINS	Glaser-Dirks DG-400 (Reserved as F-CHHY 9.99)	4-6	
D-KINT	Scheibe SF-25C Falke 2000	44412	
D-KINY	Grob G.109	6060	
D-KINZ	Schempp-Hirth Discus bT	18/304	
D-KIOA(2)	Scheibe SF-25C Falke 2000	44486	
D-KIOB(2)	Scheibe SF-25C Falke 2000	44488	
D-KIOC(2)	Scheibe SF-25C Falke 2000	44489	
D-KIOD(3)	Scheibe SF-25C Falke 2000	44496	
D-KIOE(2)	Scheibe SF-25C Falke 2000	44498	
D-KIOF(2)	Scheibe SF-25C Falke 2000	44493	
D-KIOG(3)	Scheibe SF-25C Falke 2000	44504	
D-KIOH(2)	Schleicher ASW-20/TOP	20038	D-7948
D-KIOI (2)	Scheibe SF-25C Falke 2000	44516	
D-KIOK(3)	Scheibe SF-25C Falke 2000	44522	
D-KIOL	Scheibe SF-25C Falke 2000	44511	
D-KIOM	Scheibe SF-25C Falke 2100	44521	
D-KION	Scheibe SF-25C Rotax-Falke	44526	
D-KIOO	Scheibe SF-25C Falke 2000	44528	
D-KIOP	Scheibe SF-25C Falke 2000	44523	
D-KIOQ	Scheibe SF-25C Rotax-Falke	44529	
D-KIOR	Scheibe SF-25C Falke 2000	44530	
D-KIOS	Scheibe SF-25C Rotax-Falke	44538	
D-KIOT	Scheibe SF-25C Falke 2000	44514	
D-KIOU(2)	Scheibe SF-25C Rotax-Falke	44551	
D-KIOV	Scheibe SF-25C Rotax-Falke	44541	
D-KIOW	Scheibe SF-25C Rotax-Falke	44537	
D-KIOX	Scheibe SF-25C Falke 2000	44507	
D-KIOY	Scheibe SF-25C Falke	44596	
D-KIOZ	Scheibe SF-25C Rotax-Falke	44544	
D-KIPA	Scheibe SF-25C Falke 1700	44111	
D-KIPB(2)	Glaser-Dirks DG-800B	8-47B2	
D-KIPC	Scheibe SF-25C Falke 1700	44113	
D-KIPD	Scheibe SF-25C Falke 1700	44114	
D-KIPE	Scheibe SF-25C Falke 1700	44115	
D-KIPF	Stemme S-10	10-10	
D-KIPH	Schempp-Hirth Ventus cT	116/390	
D-KIPI	Grob G.109	6068	
D-KIPL	Technoflug Piccolo	036	
D-KIPM	Scheibe SF-25C Falke	44318	HB-2060 (D-KOOI)
D-KIPP	Schleicher ASK-16	16025	
D-KIPS	Hoffmann H-36 Dimona	36204	N89PS OE-9264
D-KIPW	Schleicher ASH-26E	26143	
D-KIPZ	Schempp-Hirth Ventus 2cT	20/82	
D-KIRA	Fournier RF-4	02	
D-KIRC(2)	Schleicher ASW-22BLE	22072	
D-KIRE	Fournier RF-4D	4011	
D-KIRF	Glaser-Dirks DG-400	4-94	
D-KIRG	Schempp-Hirth Discus bT	29/326	
D-KIRI	Darmstadt D-39b	40	
D-KIRK	Sportavia-Pützer RF-5B Sperber	51063	
D-KIRL(2)	Schleicher ASH-25E	25034	OH-800
D-KIRN	Scheibe SF-25B Falke	4606	(D-KODO)
D-KIRO(2)	Grob G.109B	6200	
D-KIRR	Glaser-Dirks DG-500M	5E-30M14	
D-KIRW	Roth Moroe WR-II	364-58-2-89	D-4363
D-KISA(5)	Glaser-Dirks DG-400	4-192	D-KBJA
D-KISB	Hoffmann HK-36R Super Dimona	36345	
D-KISF	Technoflug Piccolo B	075	
D-KISG	Schleicher ASH-25E	25084	
D-KISH	Schempp-Hirth Ventus cT	70/293	
D-KISI (4)	Grob G.109B	6408	
D-KISJ	Schempp-Hirth Janus CT	16/277	
D-KISK(2)	Schempp-Hirth Ventus 2cT	44/143	
D-KISL	Schleicher ASK-14	14053	
D-KISM-SM	Schempp-Hirth Discus bT	9272	
D-KISN	Schleicher ASW-22BLE	22057	D-KIWW F-WGKS
D-KISO(3)	Schleicher ASK-16 V-1	16001	
D-KISR-SR	Glaser-Dirks DG-400	4-74	(D-KOSP)
D-KISS	Schleicher ASK-14	14049	
D-KISW	Glaser-Dirks DG-400	4-197	
D-KISY(3)	Schleicher ASH-25E	25145	
D-KITA	Fournier RF-3	58	

Regn.	Type	C/n	Prev.Id.
D-KITB	Fournier RF-5	5069	
D-KITE	Fournier RF-3	65	
D-KITF	Technoflug Piccolo (Exhibited 4.99)	unkn	
D-KITH	Schempp-Hirth Discus bT	44/358	
D-KITI	Fournier RF-3	57	
D-KITL-TL	Schempp-Hirth Ventus cT	86/331	
D-KITT(4)	Schempp-Hirth Ventus 2cM (Reservation 7.99)	95/...	
D-KITY	Schleicher ASK-16	16028	
D-KITZ(2)	Grob G.109B	6403	(F-WAQS)
D-KIVA	Scheibe SF-25A Motorfalke	4503	
D-KIVE	Schleicher ASK-16	16013	
D-KIVI (2)	Valentin Kiwi	3002	
D-KIVO	Kaiser K 16X	002	
D-KIVP	Schempp-Hirth Ventus cM	102/595	
D-KIVU(2)	Valentin Taifun 17E	1019	
D-KIVW-VW	Schleicher ASW-24E	24803	
D-KIVY	Schleicher ASK-16	16015	
D-KIWB	Schleicher ASW-15B/KM27	15001M	
	(Converted from ASW-15 airframe c/n 15440)		
D-KIWC	Scheibe SF-25C Rotax-Falke	44589	
D-KIWE(2)	Schempp-Hirth Nimbus 3T	27/93	
D-KIWF	Schempp-Hirth Ventus cM	9/424	
D-KIWG	Glaser-Dirks DG-600/18M	6-94M40	OE-9340
D-KIWK-WK	Schleicher ASH-25E	25079	
D-KIWM	Schempp-Hirth Ventus cT	154/497	
D-KIWO(2)	Grob G.109	6112	OE-9203
D-KIWP	Schleicher ASK-16B	16042	
D-KIWR	Schleicher ASW-24E	24808	
D-KIWS	Glaser-Dirks DG-400	4-65	
D-KIWY	AVO 68v Samburo	015	
D-KIXI	Fournier RF-4D	4153	OE-9028
D-KIXT	Schleicher ASH-25E	25040	D-4920
D-KIXX	Schempp-Hirth Nimbus T	19/70	BGA3100/FAE D-KHIC(2)
D-KIYY	Schempp-Hirth Ventus bT	42/232	
D-KIZY	Glaser-Dirks DG-800B	8-94B29	
D-KJAA(2)	Schleicher ASH-25M	25192	
D-KJAD	Hoffmann HK-36R Super Dimona	36358	
D-KJAK	Grob G.103C Twin IIISL	35040	
D-KJAN(2)	Glaser-Dirks DG-800B	8-130B59	
D-KJAS	Schleicher ASH-26E	26162	
D-KJBA	Scheibe SF-25C Falke 2000	44399	
D-KJBW	Glaser-Dirks DG-600M	6-81M27	
D-KJBY	Schempp-Hirth Ventus cM	82/557	
D-KJCB	Schempp-Hirth Nimbus 3T	14/71	BGA3648/FZE D-KAHA(2)
D-KJCT	Schleicher ASH-26E	26132	
D-KJET	Grob G.109	6015	(D-KISA)
D-KJFS-CH	Schempp-Hirth Discus bT	20/307	
D-KJHE	Glaser-Dirks DG-400	4-154	HB-2112
D-KJHK	Schempp-Hirth Ventus bT	5/124	
D-KJHL	Schempp-Hirth Discus 2T (Reservation 12.99)	1/64	
D-KJHM	Scheibe SF-25B Falke	46144	OE-9138 D-KCAK
D-KJJI	Schempp-Hirth Ventus cM	92/580	
D-KJJP	Schleicher ASW-24E	24809	
D-KJMA-MA	Schempp-Hirth Janus CM	2	
D-KJMM	Schempp-Hirth Nimbus 4 DM	29/43	
D-KJNN	Fournier RF-4D	4135	F-BPLP
D-KJOS	Glaser-Dirks DG-800B	8-165B89	
D-KJOY	Schempp-Hirth Ventus 2cM	16/34	D-0575
D-KJPJ	Glaser-Dirks DG-600M	6-45M3	
D-KJPM	Scheibe SF-25C Falke 1700	44120	(D-KNOY)
D-KJQA	Sportavia RF-5B Sperber	51067	
D-KJRA	Schempp-Hirth Ventus cT	185/610	
D-KJRW	Schempp-Hirth Discus bT	60/382	
D-KJTN	Valentin Taifun 17E	1074	
D-KJUL	Grob G.109	6018	
D-KJUN-V5	Schempp-Hirth Nimbus 3T	18/81	
D-KJWD	Schempp-Hirth Janus CM	25/223	D-KCGE
D-KJWL	Eiri PIK-20E	20249	LX-CAF
D-KJWT	Glaser-Dirks DG-800B	8-74B15	
D-KKAA	Hoffmann HK-36R Super Dimona	36309	
D-KKAC	Schempp-Hirth Ventus cM	74/541	N144AB D-KKAB

Regn.	Type	C/n	Prev.Id.
D-KKAD	Scheibe SF-25C Falke 2000	44373	
D-KKAE	Schempp-Hirth Ventus 2cT	5/13	
D-KKAG	Schempp-Hirth Ventus 2cM	20/38	
D-KKAI	Grob G.102 Astir CS/TOP	1303	D-7325
D-KKAS-25	Schleicher ASH-25E	25066	
D-KKBA	Glaser-Dirks DG-400	4-281	(D-KODM)
D-KKBB-4T	Schempp-Hirth Janus CT	22/300	
D-KKBM	Schleicher ASW-24E	24858	
D-KKBS	Schempp-Hirth Ventus cM	10/426	
D-KKCC	HOAC HK-36TTS Super Dimona	36588	
D-KKCO	Schleicher ASH-25E	25117	
D-KKDD	Schleicher ASW-20L/TOP	20090	D-0604 PH-604
D-KKDV	Schempp-Hirth Ventus cM (Reservation 11.99)	12/434	OE-9334
D-KKEC	Scheibe SF-25C Falke 1700	44368	
D-KKEJ	Glaser-Dirks DG-600M	6-96M42	
D-KKEK	Schleicher ASH-26E	26068	
D-KKEM	Schempp-Hirth Ventus cM	76/547	
D-KKFL	Sportavia RF-5B Sperber	51021	
D-KKFM(2)	Glaser-Dirks DG-800B	8-159B83	
D-KKFW	Glaser-Dirks DG-800B	8-127B56	
D-KKGD	Schempp-Hirth Discus bT	135/510	
D-KKGG	Valentin Taifun 17E	1008	HB-2076 D-KIHB(1)
D-KKGH	Schempp-Hirth Discus bT	80/412	
D-KKGS	Schempp-Hirth Ventus cM	78/551	
D-KKHF	Grob G.103 Twin IIISL	35010	N103SL D-KOID(2)
D-KKHG	Schempp-Hirth Discus bT	98/440	
D-KKHR	Schleicher ASH-26E	26045	
D-KKHW	Darmstadt D-39HKW	01	
D-KKII	Schempp-Hirth Ventus 2cM	2/16	
D-KKIK-IK	Schempp-Hirth Ventus 2cT	1/1	
D-KKIL	Schempp-Hirth Ventus cM	75/544	
D-KKIS	Glaser-Dirks DG-800B	8-106B40	
D-KKJB	Schempp-Hirth Ventus 2cM	18/36	
D-KKJP	Schleicher ASW-22BE	22042	
D-KKKB	Schleicher ASH-26E	26065	
D-KKKK	Doppelraab/Hankur 1	1051	D-6210 (D-KBOP) D-6210
D-KKKL(2)	Schleicher ASW-22BLE (Permit)	22076	
D-KKLB	Schleicher ASH-26E	26093	
D-KKLD	LET L-13SDM Vivat	970615	
D-KKLH	Schempp-Hirth Ventus cM	77/548	
D-KKLL	Grob G.109B	6271	
D-KKLS	Schempp-Hirth Discus bT	82/415	
D-KKLW	Schleicher ASH-25M	25206	
D-KKMA	Hoffmann H-36 Dimona	36222	SE-UBR
D-KKMM	Schempp-Hirth Janus CM	24/220	G-LIME
D-KKNA	Brditschka HB-21 (Permit)	21020	OE-9172 D-KKNA OE-9172
D-KKPA	Technoflug Piccolo	044	
D-KKPC	Schleicher ASH-25M (Permit 9.99)	25218	
D-KKPE	Schempp-Hirth Nimbus 4 DM	31/45	
D-KKPO	Schempp-Hirth Discus bT	15/300	
D-KKPP	Schempp-Hirth Ventus cM	106/603	
D-KKPT	Scheibe SF-25B Falke	46240	G-BTLI RAFGSA560 D-KAIF
D-KKRH	Schempp-Hirth Ventus 2cT	16/63	
D-KKRM	Glaser-Dirks DG-800LA	8-86A42	
D-KKSA	Schleicher ASW-24E	24819	
D-KKSC	Valentin Taifun 17E	1013	
D-KKSG	Rolladen-Schneider LS-9 (Permit)	9002	
D-KKSK	Schleicher ASW-24E	24889	
D-KKTB	Schempp-Hirth Ventus cM	79/552	
D-KKTE	Glaser-Dirks DG-400	4-4	
D-KKTH	Schleicher ASH-25M (Permit .99)	25212	
D-KKTK	Fournier RF-3	68	OE-9159 D-KITO
D-KKTT	Schleicher ASW-24E	24806	
D-KKUP-KV	Schleicher ASW-22BE	22043	
D-KKVB	Schempp-Hirth Nimbus 4 DM	16/25	
D-KKVF	Schempp-Hirth Ventus cM	68/532	
D-KKWE	Schempp-Hirth Ventus 2cM	4/18	
D-KKWW	Schempp-Hirth Discus bT	137/512	
D-KKXL	Schempp-Hirth Ventus 2cM	44/83	
D-KKYB	Schleicher ASH-25E	25029	(D-KEJB) D-3125
D-KKYD	Schleicher ASH-25M	25197	
D-KKYY	Schempp-Hirth Nimbus 3DT	9	D-4444
D-KLAB	Scheibe SF-25B Falke	46206	(D-KASC)
D-KLAC(2)	Schempp-Hirth Ventus2cT	30/102	
D-KLAD(2)	Schempp-Hirth Nimbus 4M ("AD")	4/17	
D-KLAG	Valentin Taifun 17E	1042	
D-KLAH-AH	Schempp-Hirth Ventus cT	106/369	
D-KLAI	HOAC HK-36TTC Super Dimona	36567	
D-KLAK(2)	Fournier RF-3	12	F-BLXD
D-KLAM	Fournier RF-5	5123	
D-KLAN	Glaser-Dirks DG-400	4-234	
D-KLAP(2)	Glaser-Dirks DG-500M ("AP")	5E-4M3	
D-KLAR	Schleicher ASK-14	14038	
D-KLAS(2)	Technoflug Piccolo	020	
D-KLAT	Hoffmann H-36 Dimona	36246	
D-KLAU	Scheibe SF-25C Falke 2000	44481	
D-KLAX	Scheibe SF-25C Falke 2000	44428	
D-KLBA	Scheibe SF-25B Falke	4621	OE-9341 D-KEGI
D-KLBB	Schleicher ASW-24E	24801	
D-KLBE	Technoflug Piccolo B	106	
D-KLBG	Schempp-Hirth Ventus cT	158/511	
D-KLBI	Technoflug Piccolo	053	
D-KLBP	Schleicher ASH-25M	25186	
D-KLBR	Glaser-Dirks DG-600/18M	6-104M38	OH-843
D-KLBW	Grob G.109B	6368	
D-KLBY	Klotz Moka 1	1	
D-KLCW	Grob G.109B	6574	(D-KMBG)
D-KLDA	Scheibe SF-25C Falke 1700	44124	
D-KLDB(2)	SZD-45A Ogar	B-762	DDR-3509 DM-3509
D-KLDD	Scheibe SF-25C Falke 1700	44127	
D-KLDH(2)	Schempp-Hirth Discus bT ("DH")	1/245	
D-KLDS	Hoffmann H-36 Dimona	36234	
D-KLDT	Scheibe SF-25C Rotax-Falke	44636	
D-KLEB	Schempp-Hirth Ventus cT	177/581	
D-KLEC	Scheibe SF-25C Rotax-Falke	44546	
D-KLEE	Fournier RF-5	5076	
D-KLEH(2)	Hoffmann H-36 Dimona	36213	SU-184 OE-9316 D-KFLB
D-KLEI	Fournier RF-5	5077	
D-KLEM(2)	HOAC HK-36TTC Super Dimona (Reservn 12.99)	36657	
D-KLER	Fournier RF-5	5051	
D-KLES	Schempp-Hirth Nimbus 3DM	13/36	F-CFUK D-KFUK
D-KLET(2)	Glaser-Dirks DG-400	4-174	OY-XOO
D-KLEU	Glaser-Dirks DG-400	4-180	
D-KLEX	Scheibe SF-25C Falke 1700	44431	
D-KLFA	Grob G.109B	6210	HB-2079
D-KLFV	Schempp-Hirth Discus bM	9/542	
D-KLFW	Hoffmann H-36 Dimona	36249	OE-9290
D-KLGA	Schleicher ASH-26E	26058	
D-KLGH(2)	HOAC HK-36TTS Super Dimona	36621	
D-KLGR	Glaser-Dirks DG-400	4-129	G-BUXG D-KEHJ
D-KLGS	Schleicher ASH-26E	26077	
D-KLHA	Schempp-Hirth Discus bT	79/411	
D-KLHB	Schleicher ASH-26E	26049	
D-KLHG	Schleicher ASW-24/TOP	24821	
D-KLHH	Technoflug Piccolo	043	
D-KLHL-HL	Schleicher ASW-22BLE	22070	
D-KLHM	Schempp-Hirth Nimbus 4 DM	21/31	
D-KLHS	Schleicher ASH-26E	26066	
D-KLHW	Schleicher ASH-25EB	25172	
D-KLHZ	Glaser-Dirks DG-800	8-72A40	
D-KLIA	Schleicher ASH-26E	26081	
D-KLID	LET L-13SDM Vivat	970613	

Regn.	Type	C/n	Prev.Id.
D-KLII	Schleicher ASW-24/TOP	24807	HB-2227
			D-KCCL
D-KLIK	Fournier RF-5	5125	
D-KLIL	Eiriavion PIK-20E	20224	
D-KLIM	Technoflug Piccolo	049	
D-KLIN(3)	Hoffmann H-36 Dimona	3616	HB-2066
D-KLIO	Scheibe SF-25A Motorfalke	4520	OE-9015
			D-KAJE(1)
D-KLIP	Glaser-Dirks DG-400	4-153	OO-NIN
D-KLIR	Fournier RF-5	5052	
D-KLIS	Schempp-Hirth Ventus 2cT	36/124	
D-KLIX(2)	SZD-45A Ogar	B-767	DDR-3514
			DM-3514
D-KLJC	Glaser-Dirks DG-400	4-114	
D-KLJP	Schleicher ASH-25E	25082	
D-KLKA	Schempp-Hirth Ventus cT	169/556	
D-KLKG	Schleicher ASH-26E	26135	(D-KLUF)
D-KLKL	Schleicher ASH-25E	25053	
D-KLKM	Eiri PIK-20E	20258	HB-2050
D-KLKW	Schleicher ASH-25M (Reservation 9.99)	25215	
D-KLLI (2)	Schleicher ASH-25E	25153	
D-KLLW	Schempp-Hirth Ventus cM	58/508	
D-KLLX	Schempp-Hirth Ventus 2cM	17/35	
D-KLMC	Glaser-Dirks DG-600/18M	6-106M48	
D-KLMI	Hoffmann HK-36R Super Dimona	36365	
D-KLMJ	Hoffmann HK-36R Super Dimona	36366	
D-KLMK	Hoffmann HK-36R Super Dimona	36367	
D-KLML	Hoffmann HK-36R Super Dimona	36368	
D-KLMM	Hoffmann HK-36R Super Dimona	36369	
D-KLMN	Hoffmann HK-36R Super Dimona	36370	
D-KLMT	Glaser-Dirks DG-800B	8-108B42	
D-KLOA	Schleicher ASW-24E	24859	
D-KLOC	Glaser-Dirks DG-500MB (Reservation)	5E-190MB5	
D-KLOE	Schempp-Hirth Ventus bT	49/247	
D-KLOF	Rolladen-Schneider LS-9 (Permit 11.99)	9004	
D-KLOR	Fournier RF-5	5053	
D-KLOU(2)	Scheibe SF-25C Falke 2000	44508	
D-KLPC	Glaser-Dirks DG-400	4-190	
D-KLPH	Hoffmann HK-36R Super Dimona	36383	PH-1030
			D-KMDD
D-KLPN	Glaser-Dirks DG-400	4-251	
D-KLPP	Glaser-Dirks DG-400	4-179	
D-KLPR	Glaser-Dirks DG-800B	8-85B22	
D-KLPW	Schleicher ASH-26E	26113	
D-KLPY	Schleicher ASH-26E	26079	
D-KLRD	SZD-45A Ogar	B-648	DDR-3502
			DM-3502
D-KLRK	Hoffmann H-36 Dimona	3626	PH-724
D-KLRS(2)	Glaser-Dirks DG-400	4-81	
D-KLSB	Scheibe SF-25C Falke 2000	44503	
D-KLSC	Schleicher ASK-14	AB14066	
D-KLSG	Scheibe SF-25C Falke 2000	44336	
D-KLSH	Schempp-Hirth Ventus 2cM	31/55	
D-KLSI	Grob G.103C Twin IIISL	35044	
D-KLSW(2)	Scheibe SF-25C Rotax-Falke	44580	
D-KLTE	Valentin Taifun 17E	1077	(D-KLET)
D-KLTS	Schleicher ASW-24E	24802	
D-KLUB(2)	Scheibe SF-25C Rotax-Falke	44543	
D-KLUG(2)	Hoffmann H-36 Dimona	36271	
D-KLUW	Valentin Taifun 17E	1035	
D-KLUX(2)	Schempp-Hirth Ventus 2cM	58/114	
D-KLUZ	SZD-45A Ogar	B-659	DDR-3506
			DM-3506
			(SP-0020)
D-KLVD	IAR I S.28M2/GR	78	
D-KLVE	HOAC HK-36TS Super Dimona	36506	
D-KLVG	AVO 68v Samburo 2000	023	
D-KLVI	Grob G.109B	6559	
D-KLVO	Schleicher ASK-14	14019	(D-KEHO)
D-KLVS	AVO 68s Samburo	020	
D-KLWA	Glaser-Dirks DG-800B	8-96B31	
D-KLWE	Schleicher ASH-25M	25202	
D-KLWG	HOAC HK-36TTS Super Dimona	36584	
D-KLWM	Glaser-Dirks DG-400	4-72	HB-2095
D-KLWS	Schempp-Hirth Ventus cM	91/578	
D-KLWW	ICA/Brasov I S.28M2/G	71	
D-KLYY	Schempp-Hirth Ventus cM	28/461	D-2444
D-KLZM	Rolladen-Schneider LS-9 (Permit)	9001	
D-KMAA	Scheibe SF-25B Falke	46106	
D-KMAB	Scheibe SF-25D Falke	46107D	
D-KMAC(2)	Valentin Kiwi	3019	
D-KMAD	Scheibe SF-25B Falke	46109	
D-KMAG	Scheibe SF-25B Falke	46112	
D-KMAI	Scheibe SF-25B Falke	46114	
D-KMAK(2)	Scheibe SF-25D Falke	46147D	OE-9182
			D-KMAK
D-KMAL(2)	HOAC KH-36TTS Super Dimona	36585	
D-KMAM	Stemme S-10V	14-020	F-CGYO
			(D-KGDC(2))
D-KMAN	Bergfalke IVSM	5902	
D-KMAR	Scheibe SF-25C Falke 2000	4415	
D-KMAS	Schleicher ASH-26E	26102	
D-KMAX	Scheibe SF-25C Falke 2000	44381	
D-KMBB	Scheibe SF-25D Falke	46182D	
D-KMBG(2)	Grob G.109B	6558	
D-KMBL	HOAC HK-36TTC Super Dimona	36574	
D-KMBP	Schleicher ASW-22BE	22045	VH-...
D-KMCA	Scheibe SF-25C Rotax-Falke	44605	
D-KMCB	Stemme S-10	10-6	
D-KMCL	Technoflug Piccolo B	120	
D-KMCO	Glaser-Dirks DG-600M	6-54M8	F-CGRQ
			D-KBDG(2)
D-KMCW	Glaser-Dirks DG-800B	8-149B73	
D-KMDB	Hoffmann HK-36R Super Dimona	36385	
D-KMDC	Hoffmann HK-36R Super Dimona	36384	
D-KMDG(2)	Glaser-Dirks DG-600/18M	6-38M1	
D-KMDK	Schleicher ASH-25M	25182	
D-KMDP	Fournier RF-3	37	F-BMDP
D-KMDS	Schempp-Hirth Discus bT	72/400	
D-KMDZ	Fournier RF-3	50	F-BMDZ
D-KMED	Grob G.109B	6291	
D-KMEI	Technoflug Piccolo B	063	
D-KMEJ	Glaser-Dirks DG.800B	8-134B63	
D-KMEM	Fournier RF-4D	4037	G-BMEM
			CN-TZZ
D-KMER	Valentin Taifun 17E	1018	
D-KMES	Schleicher ASK-16	16034	
D-KMET	Schleicher ASK-16	16007	
D-KMEY	Scheibe SF-25C Falke 2000	44484	
D-KMFE	Schempp-Hirth Discus bT	26/319	
D-KMFN	Schempp-Hirth Ventus 2cT	33/115	
D-KMFS	Scheibe SF-25C Falke	44215	OO-VZA
			D-KDFV(1)
D-KMGB	Scheibe SF-28A Tandem-Falke	5752	
D-KMGC	Scheibe SF-28A Tandem-Falke	5753	
D-KMGD(2)	Schempp-Hirth Nimbus 3DT ("GD")	11	
D-KMGI	Scheibe SF-28A Tandem-Falke	5759	
D-KMGO	HOAC HK-36TTC Super Dimona	36568	
D-KMGR	Schempp-Hirth Ventus 2cT	18/76	
D-KMGS	Schleicher ASH-26E	26117	
D-KMHA	Valentin Taifun 17E	1061	HB-2113
	(Repaired using new fuselage c/n 1105)		D-KMHA
D-KMHB	Valentin Kiwi	3006	
D-KMHF	Schempp-Hirth Nimbus 3T	23/89	
D-KMHG	Schleicher ASH-25M	25175	
D-KMHK	Technoflug Piccolo	052	
D-KMHS	Schempp-Hirth Ventus 2cM	11/28	
D-KMHW	Glaser-Dirks DG-800LA	8-58A35	
D-KMIF	Schleicher ASK-16	16033	
D-KMIG -IG	Schempp-Hirth Nimbus 3T	21/85	
D-KMII	Schempp-Hirth Ventus bT	33/208	
D-KMIJ-WJ	Schempp-Hirth Ventus bT	280/65	
D-KMIL(2)	Schempp-Hirth Ventus bT	11/146	
D-KMIM	Schempp-Hirth Janus CT	5/200	
D-KMIN	Schempp-Hirth Ventus bT	17/80	
D-KMJE	Scheibe SF-25C Falke 1700	44105	
D-KMJF	Scheibe SF-25C Falke 1700	44106	
D-KMJH	Scheibe SF-25C Falke 1700	44108	
D-KMJI	Scheibe SF-25C Falke 1700	44109	

Regn.	Type	C/n	Prev.Id.
D-KMKA	Valentin Taifun 17E-II	1134	HB-2162
			D-KHVA
D-KMKM	Schleicher ASW-24E	24818	
D-KMKN	Schempp-Hirth Discus bT	166/579	
D-KMKR	Hoffmann H-36 Dimona	36255	
D-KMKS	Hoffmann HK-36R Super Dimona	36409	
D-KMKW-AX	Schleicher ASH-25E	25151	D-6925
D-KMLH-LH	Schempp-Hirth Ventus bT	40/230	
D-KMLL	Scheibe SF-25C Falke 2100	44510	
D-KMLN	Schempp-Hirth Ventus 2cM	7/24	F-CGLU
			D-8137
D-KMLR	Glaser-Dirks DG-400	4-152	
D-KMLT	Schempp-Hirth Nimbus 4 DM	12/21	
D-KMLV	Grob G.109B	6260	
D-KMMA	Schempp-Hirth Ventus 2cM	14/31	
D-KMMC	Schempp-Hirth Discus bT	118/474	
D-KMMG	Scheibe SF-36A	4105	G-BKAH
			(D-KOGF)
D-KMML(3)	HOAC HK-36TTC Super Dimona	36573	
D-KMMM	Scheibe SF-25C Falke 2000	44502	
D-KMMO	Schleicher ASH-26E (Reservation 7.99)	26173	
D-KMMR	Schempp-Hirth Discus bT	64/389	
D-KMMW	Schempp-Hirth Ventus cM	31/464	
D-KMNC	Grob G.103C Twin IIISL	35023	
D-KMNW	Glaser-Dirks DG-400	4-249	
D-KMOA	Glaser-Dirks DG-400	4-96	HB-2234
			OO-DGI
D-KMOB	Grob G.103C Twin IIISL	35031	
D-KMOD	Scheibe SF-25C Rotax-Falke	44610	
D-KMOE	Schempp-Hirth Ventus cT	129/406	
D-KMOR	Scheibe SF-25C Falke 2000	44532	
D-KMPA	Scheibe SF-25C Falke 1700	4248	(D-KAJK)
D-KMPB(2)	Schempp-Hirth Ventus 2cM	46/95	
D-KMPC(2)	Hoffmann HK-36R Super Dimona	36322	
D-KMPD	Sportavia-Pützer RF-5B Sperber	51070	
D-KMPE	Scheibe SF-25C Falke 1700	4253	
D-KMPF	Sportavia-Pützer RF-5B Sperber	51071	
D-KMPK	Schempp-Hirth Ventus 2cM	34/60	
D-KMPP	Schleicher ASH-25M	25191	
D-KMPR	Schleicher ASH-26E	26056	
D-KMPS	Scheibe SF-25C Falke 1700	4255	
D-KMRA	Glaser-Dirks DG-400	4-92	HB-2085
D-KMRD	Schleicher ASH-26E	26083	
D-KMRH	Scheibe SF-25C Rotax-Falke	44540	(D-KIOU)
D-KMRM	Grob G.109	6076	(D-KIRC)
D-KMRV-RV	Schempp-Hirth Ventus 2cM	54/108	
D-KMRW	Sportavia-Pützer RF-5B Sperber	1010	EAF-6
D-KMSA	Technoflug Piccolo B	090	
D-KMSC	Scheibe SF-25C Rotax-Falke	44577	
D-KMSE	Reichelt Erpel	V-1	
D-KMSF-SF	Schempp-Hirth Ventus cT	100/357	
D-KMSG	Scheibe SF-25C Falke 1700	4424	
D-KMSH	Schleicher ASW-24E	24837	
D-KMSL	Hoffmann H-36 Dimona	36250	
D-KMSN(2)	Grob G.109B	6571	
D-KMSP	Scheibe SF-25C Falke 1700	4433	
D-KMSQ	Scheibe SF-25C Falke 2000	4435	
D-KMSR	Scheibe SF-25C Falke 1700	4436	
D-KMSS	Scheibe SF-25C Falke 1700	4437	
D-KMSU	Scheibe SF-25C Falke 1700	4439	
D-KMSV	Scheibe SF-25C Falke 1700	4440	
D-KMSW	Scheibe SF-25C Falke 1700	4434	
D-KMSY	Schempp-Hirth Ventus 2cM	61/121	
D-KMTB	Glaser-Dirks DG-800	8-20A17	
D-KMTE	Stemme S-10VT	11-006	D-KSTF(2)
D-KMTL(2)	Schempp-Hirth Ventus cM	5/413	D-KLAZ
D-KMTO	Glaser-Dirks DG-800LA	8-17A14	
D-KMTT	Hoffmann H-36 Dimona	3630	
D-KMUE	Stemme S-10	10-12	
D-KMVB	Technoflug Piccolo B	107	
D-KMWD	Schempp-Hirth Discus bT	86/421	
D-KMWF	Schempp-Hirth Ventus 2cM (Reservation 9.99)	81/171	
D-KMWM	Glaser-Dirks DG-800B (Reservation 8.99)	8-193B115	
D-KMWP	Schleicher ASH-26E	26115	
D-KMWS	Glaser-Dirks DG-600M	6-43M2	

Regn.	Type	C/n	Prev.Id.
D-KMWW	Glaser-Dirks DG-400	4-250	
D-KMZX	Schleicher ASW-22BE	22059	
D-KNAA	Scheibe SF-25C Falke 1700	44335	
D-KNAB	Scheibe SF-25C Falke 2000	44338	
D-KNAC	Scheibe SF-25C Falke 2000	44341	
D-KNAD	Scheibe SF-25C Falke 2000	44337	
D-KNAE(2)	Scheibe SF-25C Falke 2000	44345	
D-KNAG(2)	Scheibe SF-25C Falke 2000	44419	
D-KNAH	Scheibe SF-25C Falke 2000	44349	
D-KNAJ	Scheibe SF-25C Falke 2000	44352	
D-KNAK(5)	Fournier RF-3	88	OE-9102
			D-KILE(1)
D-KNAL	Scheibe SF-25C Falke 2000	44178	
D-KNAM(2)	Scheibe SF-25C Falke 2000	44356	
D-KNAN	Scheibe SF-25C Falke 2000	44357	
D-KNAO	Scheibe SF-25C Falke 2000	44361	
D-KNAP	Scheibe SF-25C Falke 2000	44353	
D-KNAQ(2)	Scheibe SF-25C Falke 2000	44366	
D-KNAR	Scheibe SF-25C Falke 2000	44359	
D-KNAS	Scheibe SF-25C Falke 2000	44365	
D-KNAT	Scheibe SF-25C Falke 2000	44364	
D-KNAU(2)	Scheibe SF-25E Super Falke	4363	
D-KNAV	Scheibe SF-25C Falke 2000	44369	
D-KNAW	Scheibe SF-25C Falke 2000	44372	
D-KNAX	Scheibe SF-25C Falke 2000	44362	
D-KNAY	Scheibe SF-25C Falke 2000	44374	
D-KNAZ	Scheibe SF-25C Falke 2000	44371	
D-KNBE	Schempp-Hirth Ventus cT	141/435	D-5092
D-KNBY	Schleicher ASH-25E	25111	
D-KNCM	Schempp-Hirth Ventus cM	98/589	
D-KNEB	Grob G.109B	6340	
D-KNEC	Grob G.109B	6350	
D-KNED	Grob G.109B	6354	
D-KNEE	Grob G.109B	6351	
D-KNEF	Grob G.109B	6358	
D-KNEG	Grob G.109B	6359	
D-KNEH	Grob G.109B	6380	
D-KNEI	Grob G.109B	6379	
D-KNEK	Grob G.109B	6437	
D-KNEL	Grob G.109B	6426	
D-KNEM	Grob G.109B	6422	
D-KNEN	Grob G.109B	6438	
D-KNEO	Grob G.109B	6439	
D-KNER	Grob G.109B	6551	
D-KNES	Grob G.109B	6421	
D-KNEU	LET L-13SL Vivat	920423	
D-KNEW	Grob G.109B	6360	(EAF-671)
D-KNEX	Grob G.109B	6402	
D-KNFA	Schempp-Hirth Discus bT	150/541	
D-KNFN	Schempp-Hirth Discus bT	88/425	
D-KNFU	Schempp-Hirth Discus bT	151/543	
D-KNGD	Schleicher ASH-25M (Reservation 10.99)	25217	
D-KNGS	Schempp-Hirth Ventus cM	57/507	
D-KNHB	Schleicher ASH-26E	26048	
D-KNHC	Schempp-Hirth Ventus 2cM	16/37	D-3241
D-KNHD	Schempp-Hirth Ventus cT	136/418	
D-KNIA	Scheibe SF-25C Falke 2000	44377	
D-KNIB	Scheibe SF-25C Falke 2000	44378	
D-KNIC	Scheibe SF-25C Falke 2000	44379	
D-KNID	Scheibe SF-25C Falke 2000	44380	
D-KNIF(2)	Scheibe SF-25C Falke 2000	44390	
D-KNIG(2)	Scheibe SF-25C Falke 2000	44397	
D-KNIH(2)	Scheibe SF-25C Falke 2000	44398	
D-KNII (2)	Scheibe SF-25C Falke 2000	44402	
D-KNIJ(2)	Scheibe SF-25C Falke 2000	44404	
D-KNIK	Scheibe SF-25C Falke 2000	44405	
D-KNIL(2)	Scheibe SF-25C Falke 2000	44417	
D-KNIM(2)	Scheibe SF-25C Falke 2000	44418	
D-KNIN(2)	Scheibe SF-25C Falke 2000	44421	
D-KNIO(2)	Scheibe SF-25C Falke 2000	44423	
D-KNIP	Scheibe SF-25C Falke 2000	44416	
D-KNIQ	Scheibe SF-25C Falke 2000	44403	
D-KNIR	Scheibe SF-25C Falke 2000	44426	
D-KNIS	Scheibe SF-25C Falke 2000	44424	
D-KNIT	Scheibe SF-25C Falke 2000	44427	

Regn.	Type	C/n	Prev.Id.
D-KNIU(2)	Scheibe SF-25C Falke 2000	44429	
D-KNIV	Scheibe SF-25C Falke 2000	44432	
D-KNIW	Scheibe SF-25C Falke 2000	44409	
D-KNIX	Scheibe SF-25C Falke 2000	44196	HB-2041
			(D-KDAM)
D-KNIZ	Scheibe SF-25C Falke 2000	44430	
D-KNJA	Technoflug Piccolo B	022	OE-9307
			D-KCTC
D-KNKK	Glaser-Dirks DG-400	4-141	(ZS-...)
D-KNKN	Scheibe SF-25K Falke	4902	
D-KNLH	Schempp-Hirth Nimbus 4 DM	4/10	
D-KNMB(2)	Glaser-Dirks DG-800B	8-54B7	
D-KNNN	Grob G.109B	6202	OY-XNN
			D-KGFB
D-KNOM	Glaser-Dirks DG-800B	8-167B91	
D-KNOP	Scheibe SF-25C Falke 2000	44116	
D-KNOR	Scheibe SF-25C Falke 1700	44118	
D-KNOT(2)	Scheibe SF-25C Falke 2000	44375	HB-2106
			D-KNBA(1)
			N713BR
D-KNOW	Grob G.109B	6267	N53553
D-KNOX(2)	Valentin Taifun 17E	1010	
D-KNPF	Knechtel KN-1	V-1	
D-KNPS	Grob G.109B	6535	
D-KNSN	HOAC HK-36TC Super Dimona	36576	
D-KNUE	Technoflug Piccolo B	062	D-MNUE
			D-KNUE
D-KNUM	Valentin Taifun 17E-2	1115	
D-KNUS	Schleicher ASK-16	16027	
D-KNUT(2)	Hoffmann H-36 Dimona	3677	
D-KNWF	Hoffmann H-36 Dimona	36247	OE-9383
			D-KITT(2)
D-KNWN	Schleicher Rhönlerche II-Storch	1	
D-KNWS	Schempp-Hirth Discus bT	56/377	
D-KNZZ	Schempp-Hirth Discus bT	112/464	
D-KOAA	Scheibe SF-25C Falke 1700	4454	
D-KOAB	*Test Registration for Schleicher production*		
D-KOAC(2)	Glaser-Dirks DG-600/18M	6-98M44	(D-KJAG)
D-KOAD	Scheibe SF-25C Falke 1700	4457	
D-KOAF	Scheibe SF-25C Falke 1700	4459	
D-KOAG	Scheibe SF-25C Falke 2000	4460	
D-KOAH	Scheibe SF-28A Tandem-Falke	5716	
D-KOAK(2)	Schempp-Hirth Ventus cM	73/539	
D-KOAM(2)	Schempp-Hirth Ventus cM	81/555	
D-KOAP	Scheibe SF-28A Tandem-Falke	5727	
D-KOAS(2)	Grob G.109	6113	
D-KOAU	Scheibe SF-25C Falke 1700	4463	
D-KOAW	Scheibe SF-25C Falke 1700	4464	
D-KOAZ	Scheibe SF-25C Falke 1700	4467	
D-KOBA(3)	Grob G.102 Astir CS/TOP	1025	D-5874
D-KOBB(2)	HOAC HK-36TTC Super Dimona	36560	
D-KOBD(2)	Glaser-Dirks DG-600M	6-48M4	
D-KOBE(3)	Glaser-Dirks DG-400	4-69	
D-KOBF	Scheibe SF-27M-A	6309	
D-KOBG(2)	Schempp-Hirth Nimbus 3DT	7	
D-KOBH(2)	Schempp-Hirth Discus bT	154/549	
D-KOBI (4)	Glaser-Dirks DG-400	4-161	
D-KOBJ	Scheibe SF-25C Falke 1700	4468	
D-KOBK	Scheibe SF-25C Falke 1700	4469	
D-KOBL(2)	Grob G.109B	6579	
D-KOBM	Glaser-Dirks DG-600M	6-56M10	(D-KEJB(2))
D-KOBN	Scheibe SF-25C Rotax-Falke	44609	
D-KOBO	Raab Krähe IV	102	
D-KOBR	Glaser-Dirks DG-600M	6-71M20	
D-KOBT	Schempp-Hirth Discus bT	109/458	
D-KOBY(2)	Scheibe SF-25B Falke	4616	
D-KOCA(2)	Technoflug Piccolo B	088	
D-KOCC	Grob G.109	6012	
D-KOCD	Scheibe SF-25C Falke 2000	44492	
D-KOCI (2)	Sportavia-Pützer RF-5	5127	G-BJCG
			(D-KOCI)
D-KOCK	Scheibe SF-25C Rotax-Falke	44534	
D-KOCO(2)	Valentin Taifun 17E	1045	
D-KOCP	Glaser-Dirks DG-800B	8-104B38	(G-BXFA)
D-KODA(2)	Scheibe SF-25C Falke 2000	44422	

Regn.	Type	C/n	Prev.Id.
D-KODC	Scheibe SF-25D Falke	4613D	
D-KODD	Scheibe SF-25B Falke	4615	
D-KODE(2)	Scheibe SF-25B Falke	4604	
D-KODG	Scheibe SF-25D Falke	4618D	
D-KODI	Scheibe SF-25B Falke	4605	
D-KODO(2)	Scheibe SF-25B Falke	4614	
D-KODU	Scheibe SF-25D Falke	4623D	(D-KEGU)
D-KOEA	Scheibe SF-28A Tandem-Falke	5731	
D-KOEB(4)	Schempp-Hirth Ventus cT	142/439	
D-KOEF	Scheibe SF-28A Tandem-Falke	5736	
D-KOEI (2)	Scheibe SF-28A Tandem-Falke	5744	
D-KOEJ	Scheibe SF-28A Tandem-Falke	5740	
D-KOEL(2)	Valentin Taifun 17E	1020	
D-KOEM	Scheibe SF-25C Falke 1700	4472	
D-KOEN	Scheibe SF-25C Falke 1700	4473	
D-KOEP	Scheibe SF-25C Falke 1700	4475	
D-KOEQ	Scheibe SF-25C Falke 2000	4476	
D-KOER	Scheibe SF-25C Falke 1700	4477	
D-KOES	Fournier RF-5	5047	
D-KOET	Scheibe SF-25C Falke 1700	4478	
D-KOEU	Scheibe SF-25C Falke 2000	4479	
D-KOEV	Scheibe SF-25C Falke 1700	4480	
D-KOEX	Scheibe SF-28A Tandem-Falke	5746	
D-KOFC(2)	Glaser-Dirks DG-400	4-278	
D-KOFI (2)	Scheibe SF-25B Falke	4625	
D-KOFN	Glaser-Dirks DG-600M	6-74M22	
D-KOFO(2)	Detmold K.8B/Lloyd	8724M	
D-KOFU	Scheibe SF-25A Motorfalke	4551	
D-KOFY(3)	Valentin Taifun 17E-II	1103	
D-KOGA	Kaiser K 12	12001M	
D-KOGB	Schleicher ASH-26E	26015	
D-KOGE(2)	SZD-45A Ogar	B-647	DDR-3501
			DM-3501(2)
D-KOGH	Schleicher ASH-25E	25061	
D-KOGI (2)	Scheibe SF-25E Super-Falke	4302	
D-KOGM	Schempp-Hirth Nimbus 3DT	27	
D-KOGN	Scheibe SF-25C Falke 2000	44531	
D-KOGO(3)	Sportavia RF-5B Sperber	51057	
D-KOGR	SZD-45A Ogar	B-662	DDR-3507
			DM-3507
D-KOGS	AVO 68v Samburo	027	
D-KOGY(2)	Valentin Taifun 17E *(Reservation 11.99)*	1058	(D-KBHA)
			F-CGAH
			F-WGAH
			D-KBHA
D-KOHA	Fournier RF-4D	4072	
D-KOHE	Fournier RF-4D	4073	
D-KOHF	Schleicher ASK-14	14033	
D-KOHG	Schleicher ASK-14	14036	
D-KOHI (2)	Fournier RF-4D	4081	
D-KOHK(2)	Schempp-Hirth Ventus 2cT	24/92	
D-KOHL	Schleicher ASK-14	14046	
D-KOHO	Fournier RF-4D	4079	
D-KOHS	Glaser-Dirks DG-400	4-287	
D-KOHU	Fournier RF-4D	4091	
D-KOIL	Schleicher ASH-26E	26131	
D-KOIS	Hoffmann HK-36R Super Dimona	36333	
D-KOIW	Schempp-Hirth Discus bT	104/449	
D-KOJB	Scheibe SF-25C Rotax-Falke	44591	
D-KOJO	Schempp-Hirth Nimbus 4M	9/26	
D-KOKA(2)	Valentin Taifun 17E	1003	(D-KJMS)
D-KOKG	Glaser-Dirks DG-400	4-24	
D-KOKI (2)	Scheibe SF-25A Motorfalke	4553	D-KOGI (1)
D-KOKK	Glaser-Dirks DG-500M	5E-87M37	
D-KOKO(2)	Fournier RF-5	5 42	
D-KOLA(3)	Schleicher ASH-25E	25067	
D-KOLC	Schempp-Hirth Discus bM	3/438	
D-KOLD	RF-5B Sperber	51061	
D-KOLE-48	Scheibe SF-27M-B	6302	
D-KOLG	Schleicher ASH-26E	26091	
D-KOLH	Grob G.109B	6295	
D-KOLI	AVO 68v Samburo	013	
D-KOLK	Technoflug Piccolo	038	
D-KOLL	Glaser-Dirks DG-400	4-1	G-KOLL
			D-KOLL

Regn.	Type	C/n	Prev.Id.
D-KOLN	Schempp-Hirth Nimbus 2M	05	
D-KOLT	Scheibe SF-25C Falke 2000	44449	
D-KOMA	Schleicher ASK-14	14025	
D-KOMB	Brditschka HB-23/2400SP	23039-U	OE-9324
D-KOME	Schleicher ASK-14	14027	
D-KOMH	HOAC HK-36TTC Super Dimona	36593	
D-KOMI (2)	Scheibe SF-25C Falke 1700	4254	
D-KOMM	Scheibe SF-25B Falke	4 58	
D-KOMO(2)	Glaser-Dirks DG-400	4-71	LN-GMW G-BLCX
D-KOMS	Grob G.109	6101	
D-KOMU	Schleicher ASK-14	14029	
D-KOMY(2)	Schempp-Hirth Ventus 2cM ("9A")	9/26	
D-KONA	Schleicher ASK-14	14039	
D-KONB(2)	Schleicher ASK-14	14043	
D-KOND	Schleicher ASK-14	14042	
D-KONE	Schleicher ASK-14	14044	
D-KONF	Fournier RF-5	5057	
D-KONG	Fournier RF-5	5058	
D-KONH	Fournier RF-5	5059	
D-KONI (2)	Schleicher ASH-25M	25179	
D-KONK(2)	Fedrau Aquila	001	
D-KONO(2)	Röhrdanz JR1 Tinetta 17R/70	01	
	(Rebuild from Taifun 17E D-KONO(1) c/n 01)		
D-KONX-NX	Schleicher ASW-22BLE	22048	
D-KONY(2)	Hoffmann H-36 Dimona	36131	OE-9234
D-KONZ	Scheibe SF-25C Falke 2000	44477	
D-KOOB(2)	Scheibe SF-25C Falke 1700	44312	
D-KOOC(2)	Scheibe SF-25C Falke 2000	44314	
D-KOOD(2)	Scheibe SF-25C Falke 2000	44313	
D-KOOE(2)	Scheibe SF-25C Falke 2000	44315	
D-KOOF	Scheibe SF-25C Falke 1700	44305	
D-KOOG(2)	Scheibe SF-25C Falke 2000	44316	
D-KOOH(3)	Scheibe SF-25C Falke 2000	44319	
D-KOOI (2)	Scheibe SF-36A	4103	
D-KOOJ	Scheibe SF-25C Falke 2000	AB44321	
D-KOOK	Scheibe SF-25C Falke 2000	44320	
D-KOOL	Scheibe SF-25C Falke 2000	44323	
D-KOOM	Scheibe SF-25C Falke 1700	4484	HB-2028 (D-KEID)
D-KOOO	Scheibe SF-36A	4106	
D-KOOP	Scheibe SF-36A	4101	
D-KOOR	Scheibe SF-25C Falke 1700	4443	OE-9198 OE-9060 (D-KDAC)
D-KOOS	Scheibe SF-25C Falke 1700	44329	
D-KOOT	Scheibe SF-25C Falke 2000	44330	
D-KOOU	Scheibe SF-25C Falke 2000	44331	
D-KOOV(2)	Scheibe SF-25C Falke 2000	44332	VH-HDM D-KOOV(2)
D-KOOW(2)	Scheibe SF-25C Falke 2000	44333	
D-KOOX	Scheibe SF-25C Falke 2000	44327	
D-KOPA	Hoffman H-36 Dimona	36267	
D-KOPC	Glaser-Dirks DG-400	4-237	
D-KOPF(2)	Fournier RF-5	5082	JA2127 D-KIEL(1)
D-KOPP	Hoffmann H-36 Dimona	3654	
D-KOPR	Hoffmann HK-36R Super Dimona	36347	
D-KOPY	Glaser-Dirks DG-800LA	8-40A30	HB-2267
D-KOQY	Scheibe SF-25C Falke 2000	44206	(D-KDFH)
D-KORA	Fournier RF-5	5025	
D-KORB	Fournier RF-5	5029	
D-KORC	Fournier RF-5	5030	
D-KORD	Valentin Taifun 17E	1016	
D-KORE	Scheibe SFS-31 Milan (Permit 9.99)	6601	OE-9083 D-KORO(1)
D-KORF-WG	Schempp-Hirth Nimbus 2M	07	(D-KOKI)
D-KORG	Glaser-Dirks DG-400	4-145	OY-XYW
D-KORI	Grob G.109	6099	
D-KORK(2)	Scheibe SF-25C Falke 1700	44328	
D-KORL	Raab Krähe IV	14	D-KODL (D-KOPD) D-KEDI (1)
D-KORM	Fournier RF-4D	4035	F-BORM
D-KORO(2)	Schempp-Hirth Ventus cT	103/364	

Regn.	Type	C/n	Prev.Id.
D-KORR	Schleicher ASH-26E	26061	
D-KORT	Kortenbach Kora I	V-2	
D-KORU	Stemme S-10	10-11	
D-KOSA	Scheibe SF-25C Falke 1700	4250	(D-KOJA)
D-KOSD	Scheibe SF-25B Falke	4690	
D-KOSG	Scheibe SF-25D Falke	4693D	
D-KOSI	Scheibe SF-25B Falke	4695	
D-KOSJ-SJ	Schleicher ASW-20L/TOP	20573	D-1646
D-KOSK	Scheibe SF-25B Falke	4687	
D-KOSL	Scheibe SF-27M-A	6316	(D-KHIL)
D-KOSM	Scheibe SF-27M-A	6317	
D-KOSO(2)	Hoffmann H-36 Dimona	3647	HB-2065
D-KOSR	Schempp-Hirth Ventus bT	52/254	
D-KOST(2)	Scheibe SF-25C Falke 2000	44286	(D-KDGN)
D-KOSY	Schempp-Hirth Ventus cT	99/354	
D-KOTO	Hoffmann H-36 Dimona	3660	
D-KOTZ	Glaser-Dirks DG-400	4-21	
D-KOWB-WB	Schleicher ASH25M	25901	
D-KOWC	Scheibe SF-25C Falke 1700	44302	HB-2054 (D-KDGY)
D-KOWE(2)	Schempp-Hirth Nimbus 4M	2/11	
D-KOWF	Glaser-Dirks DG-400	4-70	
D-KOWI	Brditschka HB-23/2400SP	23044	
D-KOWO	Valentin Taifun 17E	1087	
D-KOWW	Scheibe SF-36R	4102	
D-KOYY	Schempp-Hirth Nimbus 4T	9	
D-KOZY	Scheibe SF-25C Falke 1700	4453	(D-KMST)
D-KOZZ	Test Registration for Rolladen-Schneider LS-9 production		
D-KPAA	Hoffmann HK-36R Super Dimona	36378	
D-KPAB	Hoffmann HK-36R Super Dimona	36379	
D-KPAC	Schempp-Hirth Discus bT	124/482	
D-KPAF	Scheibe SF-25C Falke 2000	44513	
D-KPAK	Schempp-Hirth Ventus 2cM	50/104	
D-KPDG	Glaser-Dirks DG-800B (Exhibited 4.99)	8-174B98	
D-KPIB	Schempp-Hirth Ventus cM	96/587	
D-KPIN	Schempp-Hirth Ventus cM	65/527	F-CGLR
D-KPJS	Schempp-Hirth Nimbus 4M	23/7	
D-KPLH	Schempp-Hirth Ventus 2cM (Reservation 12.99)	85/1 ..	
D-KPMS	Schempp-Hirth Ventus 2cT	23/88	
D-KPMW	Grob G.102 Astir CS/TOP	1008	D-6504
D-KPOL	Scheibe SF-25C Falke 2000	44536	
D-KPPP	Glaser-Dirks DG-400	4-188	OE-9273
D-KPRW	Schleicher ASH-25M	25164	D-5547
D-KPSN	Scheibe SF-25C Falke 2000	44518	
D-KPTL	Grob G.109B	6216	OO-DPC
D-KPTZ	Schempp-Hirth Nimbus 4 DM	25/35	
D-KPUA	Glaser-Dirks DG-800LA	8-22A19	
D-KPUK	LET L-13SL Vivat	940521	OK-4100
D-KPUR	Schleicher ASH-25M (Permit 7.99)	25213	
D-KPWD	Glaser-Dirks DG-600M	6-88M34	
D-KPZZ	Schempp-Hirth Nimbus 4DT	4/7	
D-KRAA	Hoffmann HK-36R Super Dimona	36335	
D-KRAI	Schempp-Hirth Discus bT	74/402	
D-KRAK-AK	Schempp-Hirth Discus bM	6/463	
D-KRAM	Scheibe SF-25C Rotax-Falke	44582	
D-KRAP	Schempp-Hirth Discus bT	102/444	
D-KRAS	Schleicher ASH-25M	25183	
D-KRAW	Schleicher ASH-26E	26103	
D-KRBH	Schempp-Hirth Ventus2cT	31/103	
D-KRBP	Schleicher ASH-25M	25177	
D-KRDG	Glaser-Dirks DG-500MB Elan (Res 3.99)	5E-193MB8	
D-KREB	Schempp-Hirth Ventus cM	93/582	
D-KREH-4D	Schempp-Hirth Nimbus 4 DM	1/4	
D-KREM	Schleicher ASH-25EB	25178	
D-KRES	HOAC HK-36TTC Super Dimona	36602	
D-KRGW	Schempp-Hirth Ventus cM	100/591	
D-KRHA	Grob G.109B	6406	G-BNAY N920BG
D-KRHG	Schleicher ASH-25M (Reservation .99)	25211	
D-KRHL	Rolladen-Schneider LS-9 (Permit 12.99)	9005	
D-KRHT	Schleicher ASH-26E (Formerly ASH-26)	26071	D-9426
D-KRII	Glaser-Dirks DG-800B	8-172B96	
D-KRIM	Glaser-Dirks DG-800LA	8-6A5	
D-KRJS	Schleicher ASH-26E	26025	
D-KRLH	Schleicher ASH-26E	26119	

Regn.	Type	C/n	Prev.Id.
D-KRMA	Schleicher ASH-26E	26017	
D-KROG	Schempp-Hirth Discus bT	126/484	
D-KROP	Grob G.109	6124	PH-948
			N3837S
D-KRRK(2)	Valentin Taifun 17E-2/2400	1128	OE-9330
			D-KHVA
D-KRRR	Glaser-Dirks DG-800B	8-132NB61	
D-KRSH	Glaser-Dirks DG-800	8-63B10	
D-KRTS	Schempp-Hirth Ventus 2cT	19/81	
D-KRUG-OK	Schleicher ASH-26E	26006	
D-KRUM	Scheibe SF-25C Rotax Falke	44566	
D-KRWA	Aeromot AMT-200 Super Ximango	200-093	
D-KRWR	Glaser-Dirks DG-600M	6-95M41	
D-KSAG	Schleicher ASH-25M (Reservation)	25220	
D-KSAK	Scheibe SF-25C Rotax-Falke	44619	
D-KSAM	Nitzsche AVO 68-R115 Samburo Turbo (Permit 6.99)	001	
D-KSAS	Schleicher ASW-22BLE	22071	D-KKUH
D-KSAV	Glaser-Dirks DG-400	4-235	I-ASAV
D-KSBC	Grob G.103C Twin IIISL	35038	
D-KSBD	HOAC HK-36TTC Super Dimona	36522	OE-9422
D-KSBS	Schleicher ASH-26E	26145	
D-KSCF	Glaser-Dirks DG-500M	5E-59M24	
D-KSCH	HOAC HK-36R Super Dimona	36327	OE-9365
D-KSDB	Grob G.103C Twin IIISL	35004	
D-KSDF	HOAC HK-36TTC Super Dimona	36579	
D-KSDL	LET L-13SDL Vivat	910428	OK-....
D-KSDM	LET L-13SDM Vivat	930509	OK-3905
D-KSEF	Schempp-Hirth Duo Discus T (Permit 12.99)	1/187	
D-KSEP	Schempp-Hirth Ventus cT	162/526	
D-KSFC	Hoffmann HK-36R Super Dimona	36342	
D-KSFM	Glaser-Dirks DG-500M	5E-98M44	OE-9388
D-KSFU	HOAC HK-36TC Super Dimona	36648	
D-KSGF	Glaser-Dirks DG-500MB (Permit)	5E-185MB2	
D-KSGS	Schempp-Hirth Ventus 2cM	22/40	
D-KSHA	Schempp-Hirth Nimbus 4 DM	13/22	
D-KSHB	Hoffmann HK-36R Super Dimona	36403	OE-9403
			(D-KAIB(2))
D-KSHL	LET L-13SL Vivat	920426	
D-KSHS	Schempp-Hirth Discus bT	130/495	
D-KSHW	Schleicher ASW-24E	24838	HB-2195
D-KSIE	Pussycat	1	
D-KSIG	Glaser-Dirks DG-800LA	8-15A12	
D-KSJM	Schempp-Hirth Ventus 2cM	47/97	
D-KSKI (2)	Schempp-Hirth Discus 2T (Reservation 10.99)	2/66	
D-KSKS	Glaser-Dirks DG-800B	8-89B25	
D-KSLA	Glaser-Dirks DG-800B	8-91B27	
D-KSLG	Grob G.103C Twin IIISL	35002	
D-KSMC	Schleicher ASH-26E	26023	
D-KSMH	Schleicher ASH-25M	25160	D-0541
D-KSMO	HOAC HK-36TTC Super Dimona (Reservn 10.99)	36663	
D-KSMU	Grob G.109B (Vigilant T.1)	6556	ZH210
D-KSOL(2)	Grob G.103C Twin IIISL	35039	
D-KSOP	Schempp-Hirth Discus bT	121/477	
D-KSPK	Scheibe SF-25C Rotax-Falke	44635	
D-KSPL(2)	Glaser-Dirks DG-400	4-286	
D-KSPM	Glaser-Dirks DG-800B	8-157B81	
D-KSPR	Glaser-Dirks DG-500M	5E-80M33	
D-KSPT	Schempp-Hirth Ventus bT	3/233	HB-2104
D-KSRV	Schempp-Hirth Discus bT	138/514	
D-KSRW	Schleicher ASH-26E	26101	
D-KSSW	Schempp-Hirth Ventus cM	61/523	
D-KSTE to D-KSTI Test Registrations for Stemme S-10VT production			
D-KSTS	Schleicher ASH-26E	26005	
D-KSTY	Studeny STY-1	1	
D-KSUB	Hoffmann HK-36R Super Dimona	36390	
D-KSUT	Schleicher ASH-26E	26120	
D-KSVB	Schleicher ASW-22BLE (Reservation 10.99)	22082	
D-KSWG	SZD-45A Ogar (Permit 11.99)	B-753	D-KLHP
			DDR-3508
			DM-3508
D-KSWH	Schempp-Hirth Ventus cM	97/587	OH-861
D-KSWJ	Schleicher ASH-26E	26098	
D-KSWS	Technoflug Piccolo B	096	
D-KSXR	Schleicher ASH-26E	26154	

Regn.	Type	C/n	Prev.Id.
D-KTAS	Schempp-Hirth Ventus 2cT	21/85	
D-KTAW	Technoflug Piccolo B	073	
D-KTBB	Glaser-Dirks DG-800	8-67B12	
D-KTBC	Glaser-Dirks DG-400	4-67	(D-KXCB)
			OE-9225
D-KTBT	Schempp-Hirth Discus bT	141/516	
D-KTCB	Schleicher ASH-26E	26128	(D-5222)
D-KTCC	Schempp-Hirth Ventus 2cM	33/57	
D-KTCH	Technoflug Piccolo B	099	
D-KTCW	Glaser-Dirks DG-800LA	8-46A32	
D-KTDD	Glaser-Dirks DG-800A	8-52A34	
D-KTDG(2)	Glaser-Dirks DG-500MB Elan (Permit 7.99)	5E-150MB1	
D-KTDM	Schempp-Hirth Ventus 2cM	15/32	D-4486
D-KTEG	Schleicher ASH-26E	26129	
D-KTEN	Glaser-Dirks DG-800B	8-155B79	
D-KTFP	Schempp-Hirth Nimbus 3T (Reservation 5.99)	4/51	HB-2147
			D-KAPE
			VH-GAA
D-KTFW	Glaser-Dirks DG-600M	6-89M35	(D-KGBD)
			EC-FJC
			D-1245
D-KTGG	Schempp-Hirth Ventus cM	99/592	
D-KTGR	Technoflug Piccolo B	074	
D-KTHA	Schempp-Hirth Ventus 2cM	35/62	
D-KTHB	Schempp-Hirth Ventus 2cM	38/68	
D-KTHK	Schleicher ASH-26E	26086	
D-KTHN	Schempp-Hirth Discus bT	160/564	
D-KTHT	HOACHK-36TTS Super Dimona	36513	
D-KTIA	Scheibe SF-25C Rotax-Falke	44560	
D-KTIB	Scheibe SF-25C Rotax-Falke	44572	
D-KTIC	Scheibe SF-25C Rotax-Falke	44555	
D-KTID	Scheibe SF-25C Rotax-Falke	44575	
D-KTIE	Scheibe SF-25C Rotax-Falke	44568	
D-KTIF	Scheibe SF-25C Rotax-Falke	44549	
D-KTIG	Scheibe SF-25C Rotax-Falke	44552	
D-KTIH(2)	Scheibe SF-25C Rotax-Falke	44593	
D-KTII	Scheibe SF-25C Rotax-Falke	44573	
D-KTIK	Scheibe SF-25C Rotax-Falke	44588	
D-KTIL	Scheibe SF-25C Rotax-Falke	44562	
D-KTIM	Scheibe SF-25C Rotax-Falke	44564	
D-KTIN	Scheibe SF-25C Rotax-Falke	44574	
D-KTIO	Scheibe SF-25C Rotax-Falke	44559	
D-KTIP	Scheibe SF-36R	4107	
D-KTIQ	Scheibe SF-25C Rotax-Falke	44597	
D-KTIR	Scheibe SF-25C Rotax-Falke	44590	
D-KTIS	Scheibe SF-25C Rotax-Falke	44584	
D-KTIT(2)	Scheibe SF-25C Rotax-Falke	44599	
D-KTIU(3)	Scheibe SF-25C Falke 1700	44225	OE-9142
			D-KDFN(3)
D-KTIV(2)	Scheibe SF-25C Rotax-Falke	44614	
D-KTIW(2)	Scheibe SF-25C Rotax-Falke	44615	
D-KTIX	Scheibe SF-25C Rotax-Falke	44624	
D-KTIZ	Scheibe SF-25C Falke 1700	44300	OE-9176
			D-KDGU(2)
D-KTKM	Glaser-Dirks DG-600M	6-103M46	
D-KTLL(2)	Glaser-Dirks DG-800B	8-152B76	
D-KTME	Schempp-Hirth Ventus 2cT	47/147	
D-KTMW	Glaser-Dirks DG-800B	8-69B14	
D-KTOA, B, C Test registrations for Glaser-Dirks production			
D-KTOL	HOAC HK-36TTC Super Dimona	36600	
D-KTPR	Technoflug Piccolo B	072	
D-KTRB	Glaser-Dirks DG-800B	8-119B48	
D-KTSG	Schempp-Hirth Discus bT	100/442	
D-KTVS	Schleicher ASH-26E	26069	
D-KTWI	Valentin Taifun 17E-II	T-1136	(D-KAJP)
D-KTWG	Glaser-Dirks DG-800B	8-146B70	
D-KTWR	Glaser-Dirks DG-800	8-80A41	
D-KTWS	Schleicher ASH-26E	26140	
D-KUAS	Schleicher ASH-25M (Permit)	25204	
D-KUBA	Scheibe SF-24B Motorspatz (Reservation 2.99)	4031	OE-9007
			D-KIBE(1)
D-KUBE	Glaser-Dirks DG-800B	8-103B37	
D-KUBO	Schempp-Hirth Discus bT	131/498	
D-KUDL	Hoffmann HK-36R Super Dimona	36398	
D-KUEM	Schleicher ASW-22BLE	22068	

Regn.	Type	C/n	Prev.Id.
D-KUEP	Fournier RF-3	82	F-BMTQ
D-KUFP	HOAC HK-36R Super Dimona	36331	F-CGAY
D-KUHE	Glaser-Dirks DG-800B	8-103B37	
D-KUHL	Schempp-Hirth Ventus cM	90/575	
D-KUHR	Schempp-Hirth Discus bM	2/423	
D-KUKI	Glaser-Dirks DG-400 (Reservation 11.99)	4-156	I-KFAP / D-KFAP
D-KULA	Schleicher ASH-25M (Reservation 11.99)	25180	D-KGGO(1)
D-KULE	Glaser-Dirks DG-800LA	8-7A6	
D-KULM	Technoflug Piccolo B	085	
D-KUNK(2)	Schempp-Hirth Duo Discus T (Permit 12.99)	2/229	
D-KUNT	IAR I S.28M2/GR (Cr 27.7.99, Permit expired)	79	
D-KURA	Technoflug Piccolo B	060	
D-KURT(2)	Valentin Taifun 17E	1009	F-WGAA
D-KURZ	Scheibe SF-25C Falke	44612	
D-KUSS	Glaser-Dirks DG-500M	5E-147M59	
D-KUSU	Scheibe SF-25C Falke	44645	
D-KUYH	Schempp-Hirth Janus CM	23/216	JA2360
D-KVAS-26	Schleicher ASH-26E	26001	
D-KVFL	Scheibe SF-25C Rotax-Falke	44613	
D-KVIN	Stemme S-10VT	11-002	
D-KVKA	Schempp-Hirth Discus bT	159/561	
D-KVMC	Grob G.109B	6352	N109KC
D-KVOK	HOAC HK-36TTC Super Dimona	36566	
D-KVRS	Glaser-Dirks DG-500M	5E-61M26	
D-KVVJ-VJ	Schempp-Hirth Discus bT	90/427	
D-KVZC	Glaser-Dirks DG-800B	8-68B13	
D-KWAG	Glaser-Dirks DG-800LA	8-5A4	
D-KWAK	Scheibe SF-25C Rotax-Falke	44581	
D-KWAL	Schleicher ASH-26E	26106	
D-KWAT	Watzlawek M76	001	(D-KFHR)
D-KWAX	HOAC HK-36TS Super Dimona	36501	
D-KWAZ	HOAC HK-36TTS Super Dimona	36509	
D-KWBM	Schempp-Hirth Discus bM	1/384	
D-KWDG(2)	Glaser-Dirks DG-800B	8-148B72	
D-KWDO	IAR I S.28M2/GR (Permit)	75	YR-1997
D-KWEN	Nitzsche AVO 68-R100 Samburo (Permit 12.99)	002	
D-KWER	HOAC HK-36TTC Super Dimona	36578	
D-KWES	Schleicher ASW-22BLE	22069	D-6822
D-KWFG	Scheibe SF-25C Rotax-Falke	44576	
D-KWGB	Scheibe SF-25C Rotax-Falke	44561	
D-KWHB	Schleicher ASH-26E	26030	
D-KWHJ	Technoflug Piccolo B	115	
D-KWII	Glaser-Dirks DG-800LA	8-18A15	
D-KWIL	Schleicher ASH-26E	26004	
D-KWML(2)	Schleicher ASH-26E	26054	
D-KWNW	Schempp-Hirth Discus bT	71/398	
D-KWOB	HOAC HK-36TS Super Dimona	36415	OE-9415 / (D-KLHT)
D-KWPG-PG	Schempp-Hirth Discus bT	113/466	
D-KWRR	Schempp-Hirth Ventus cM	109/608	
D-KWRT	Schleicher ASH-26E	26109	
D-KWSC	Hoffmann H-36 Dimona	36233	OE-9286
D-KWSE	Glaser-Dirks DG-600/18M	6-114M54	
D-KWSF	Grob G.109B	6224	HB-2209 / D-KGFK
D-KWSJ	LET L-13SL Vivat	930510	
D-KWSL	Grob G.103C Twin IIISL	35046	
D-KWST	Schleicher ASH-26E	26063	
D-KWTI	Gyroflug	1136	
D-KWTT	Eiri PIK-20E	20232	LX-CWC / D-KEHI (2)
D-KWVE	Scheibe SF-25C Rotax-Falke	44553	
D-KWVE-2E	Schempp-Hirth Ventus 2cM	1/5	
D-KWWF	HOAC HK-336TTS Super Dimona	36622	
D-KWWM	Schleicher ASH-26E	26020	
D-KWWS	Grob G.109B	6363	G-BMCM / (EAF-674)
D-KWWW	HOAC HK-36TTC Super Dimona	36569	
D-KWYS	Glaser-Dirks DG-800A	8-4A3	
D-KXAS	Schleicher ASH-26E	26	
D-KXCB	Glaser-Dirks DG-400	4-67	OE-9225
D-KXCM	Schempp-Hirth Ventus 2cM	67/138	
D-KXCP	Glaser-Dirks DG-400	4-178	HB-2118
D-KXLH	Schempp-Hirth Ventus 2cM	53/107	

Regn.	Type	C/n	Prev.Id.
D-KXXL	Akaflieg Stuttgart Icaré (Damaged 15.7.98)	2	
D-KXYA	LET L-13SEH Vivat	940520	
D-KYBD	Technoflug Piccolo B	077	D-MYBD
D-KYBL	Scheibe SF-25C Rotax-Falke	44413	D-KEGL(1)
D-KYGI	Scheibe SF-25C Falke 2000	44408	OY-XYG / (D-KNIN)
D-KYGL	Scheibe SF-25C Rotax-Falke	44641	
D-KYHF	Schempp-Hirth Nimbus 4M	5/20	
D-KYHL	Scheibe SF-25C Falke (Reservation 10.99)	44655	
D-KYHN	Scheibe SF-25C Rotax-Falke	44630	
D-KYNT	Scheibe SF-25C Rotax-Falke	44583	
D-KYSA	Glaser-Dirks DG-800B	8-114B43	
D-KYTT	Schempp-Hirth Ventus 2cT	28/98	
D-KYXL	Schempp-Hirth Nimbus 4 DM	24/34	D-KCGG
D-KYYY	Schempp-Hirth Janus CM	27/227	OY-XYY
D-KZAR	Schleicher ASH-26E	26155	
D-KZGO	Schleicher ASH-25E	25132	
D-KZSE	Grob G.103C Twin IIISL	35047	
D-KZSF	Glaser-Dirks DG-400	4-284	
D-KZZZ	Schleicher ASH-26E	26151	

CLASS L : Airships

Regn.	Type	C/n	Prev.Id.
D-LDFO	WDL-1 (PL4360A) Airship	101A	JA1002 / D-LDFN
D-LDFQ	WDL-1B Airship	106	JA1007 / D-LDFQ
D-LDFR	WDL-1B Airship	107	JA1008 / D-LDFR
D-LION	Zeppelin LZ NO7 Airship (Reservation)	W3	
D-LJOE	Cargo-Lifter Joey B (Permit 10.99)	1	
D-LZFN	Zeppelin LZ N07-100 Airship (Permit)	001	

CLASS M : Microlights

Regn.	Type	C/n	Prev.Id.
D-MAAA	Flight Team Spider D	049	
D-MAAB	Fresh Breeze 110 AL2F	326	
D-MAAC	NST Minimum Nimbus 62	M527	
D-MAAD	Platzer Kiebitz-B	144	
D-MAAF(1)	Ultra-Vector F 610	1399	
D-MAAG	Behlen Power-Trike Euro III	8400100	
D-MAAH	UPM Funplane	19002	
D-MAAK	Ultraleichtverbund Bi 90	963	
D-MAAQ	UPM Funplane	86006	
D-MAAS	Fresh Breeze 110 AL2F	356	
D-MABC(2)	Ultraleichtverbund Bi 90	21226	
D-MABD	Aviasud Mistral BA-53	003	
D-MABK	UPM Funplane	86007	
D-MABL	Fresh Breeze 110 AL4H	27	
D-MABN	Albatros	109	
D-MABO	Comco Fox D	8505-FD27	
D-MABT	Ultra-Vector H	1758	
D-MABY	Warnke Euro III Trike	SI 030	
D-MABZ	Fisher FP-202 Koala	2183	
D-MACB	UPM Funplane Trike	86010	
D-MACC	NST Minimum	46/85-1501	
D-MACD	AJS-2000	033	
D-MACE	Behlen Power-Trike Vampir II	85013	
D-MACG	NST Minimum Focus 18	M184	
D-MACI	Klüver Kaiman Trike	080706	

Regn.	Type	C/n	Prev.Id.
D-MACL	Comco Fox-C22	8705-3059	
D-MACO	Ultraleichtverbund Bi 90	993	
D-MACP	Sky-Walker II	202	
D-MACQ	Platzer kiebitz II	052	
D-MACR	NST Minimum Saphir 16	M307	
D-MACX	Comco Fox-C22	8901-3163	
D-MACY	Comco Fox-C22	8904-3171	
D-MACZ	Albatros 52	121	
D-MADC	Ultraleichtverbund Bi 90	21002	
D-MADD	Fair Fax Euro III Trike	026	
D-MADE	Schmidtler Ranger M	M1817	
D-MADG	NST Minimum	M576	
D-MADH	Sky-Walker II	211	
D-MADL	NST Schwarze Mimimum	462	
D-MADM	Take Off Maximum Lotus 16	027020	
D-MADN	Sky-Walker II	208	
D-MADP	Klüver Racer SX 12	371903	
D-MADR	Fair Fax Euro III Trike	022	
D-MADS	Wisch Star-Trike Hazard 15M	127.04.898	
D-MADU	Comco Ikarus Fox II Doppel	8604-3013	
D-MADV	Fair Fax Trike	27	
D-MADW	Fisher FP-202 Koala	001	
D-MADZ	Ultraleichtverbund Bi 90	21003	
D-MAEB	ASO Viper 15 Trike	15/16791	
D-MAEC	Schönleber DS Enduro Trike Lotus 18	03/0489	
D-MAED	Fair Fax Euro III Trike	029	
D-MAEE	Ultraleichtverbund Bi 90	21043	
D-MAEG	ASO Viper 15M Trike	15/18290	
D-MAEH	Mosquito IB	004	
D-MAEI	Sky-Walker II	235	
D-MAEJ	Fisher FP-404 Classic	Schmidt 1	
D-MAEK	Comco Ikarus Fox-C22	9003-3222	
D-MAEL	Comco Ikarus Fox D	014	
D-MAEM	Comco Ikarus Fox-C22	9003-3224	
D-MAEP(2)	Kümmerle Mini-Fly-Set	44465	
D-MAER	Ultraleichtverbund Bi 90	21000	
D-MAES(2)	Kümmerle Mini-Fly-Set	73085-3	
D-MAET	Behlen Power-Trike	90026	
D-MAEU	Sky-Walker II	246	
D-MAEV	Fair Fax DR Hazard Trike	D009	
D-MAEW	HFL Stratos 300K	300-019K	
D-MAEX	Schmidtler Enduro Focus 18	010885	
D-MAFB	Sky-Walker II	248	
D-MAFC	Sky-Walker II	243	
D-MAFD	Ultraleichtverbund Bi 90	21010	
D-MAFE	UPM Cobra Raven Trike	910113	
D-MAFH	Fisher FP-202 Koala	002 Wachter	
D-MAFI	Dallach Sunrise IIA	027	
D-MAFJ	Ultraleichtverbund Bi 90	3957004	
D-MAFK	Sky-Walker II	253	
D-MAFM	Klüver Twin Racer Quartz SX 16	834910	
D-MAFN	Klüver Twin Racer Quartz SX 16	835910	
D-MAFO	NST Minimum	M525	
D-MAFP	Comco Ikarus Fox-C22	8911-3247	
D-MAFQ	Ultraleichtverbund Bi 90	21049	
D-MAFS	Pioneer Flightstar	672	
D-MAFT	Aviasud Mistral 53	006	
D-MAFU(1)	Sky-Walker II	250	
D-MAFU(2)	UPM Funplane	unkn	
D-MAFW	NST Minimum	M324	
D-MAFX	Dallach Sunrise II	028	
D-MAFZ	Behlen Power-Trike	90016	
D-MAGA	Behlen Power-Trike Vampir II	89040	
D-MAGB	Ultraleichtverbund Bi 90	21093	
D-MAGC	Ultraleichtverbund Bi 90	21080	
D-MAGE	Comco Ikarus Fox-C22	042	
D-MAGG	Dallach Sunrise II	018	
D-MAGI	UPM Cobra Trike	920119	
D-MAGK(2)	Tandem Air Sunny Sport	045-93	
D-MAGL	TVS 700 Tandem Air Sunny Sport	08.91	
D-MAHA	Behlen Power Trike Vampir II	85/029	
D-MAHB	Fair Fax DR Trike	D026	
D-MAHF	Enduro DS	20KS20	
D-MAHL	Fresh Breeze 110 AL4H	24	
D-MAHN	Comco Ikarus Fox II Doppel	8605-3016	
D-MAHW	Behlen Power-Trike	92002	
D-MAHZ	Solid Air Twin Diamant Trike	T-011	
D-MAID	Behlen Power-Trike	830025	
D-MAIE	Ultraleichtverbund Bi 90	4105552	
D-MAIH	Tandem Air Sunny Sport	13.91	
D-MAII	Take Off Maximum Trike	75109	
D-MAIS	Tandem Air Sunny Sport	42.92	
D-MAIW	Klüver Twin Racer SX 16	542008	
D-MAJA	Drachenstudio Piccolo	01/92	
D-MAJB	Klüver Racer SX 12	443904	
D-MAJH	Fair Fax Euro III Trike	005	
D-MAJJ	FUL Graffiti Trike	022/0082	
D-MAJS	Scheibe Uli 1	5208	
D-MAJU	Junkers Profly JUL Trike	94/1061	
D-MAKE	Comco Ikarus Fox II Doppel	8607-3024	
D-MAKJ	Kümmerle Mini-Fly-Set	1279 91-5	
D-MAKK	Albatros	165	
D-MAKL	NST Minimum	M319	
D-MAKM	Schmidtler Enduro Trike	02-014	
D-MAKN	Tandem Air Sunny Targa	TA 009.93	
D-MAKP	UPM Cobra BF 52UL Trike	940126	
D-MAKZ	ASO Viper	VI22048308	
D-MALA	ASO Viper Hazard 15 Trike	11039208	
D-MALB	Comco Ikarus Sherpa II	8407-1072	
D-MALD	Fair Fax DR Hazard 15	D029	
D-MALE	FUL Graffiti Trike	031/0097	
D-MALG	Fair Fax Trike	021	
D-MALL	Fresh Breeze 110 AL 4B	107	
D-MALM	Platzer Kiebitz-B8	115	
D-MALN	Comco Ikarus Fox-C22	002	
D-MALO	Take Off Maximum Hazard 15M	T055051	
D-MALS	Light Aero Avid Flyer	618	
D-MALU	NST Minimum Saphir 17	M163	
D-MALV	Fair Fax AH Trike	25	
D-MALW	Flight Team Spider D	D022	
D-MAME	Comco Ikarus Fox-C22	9103-3323	
D-MAMG	Schönleber Enduro KS Speed 14	3585491	
D-MAMI	Comco Ikarus Fox-C22	021	
D-MAMR	Steinbach Austro-Trike	108/85	
D-MAMT	Albatros	105	
D-MAND	ASO Viper 15 Trike	15/17791	
D-MANE	Fresh Breeze 110 AL 2F	57	
D-MANI	ASO Viper 15 Trike	15/12291	
D-MANJ	Behlen Power-Trike	86017	
D-MANN	Scheibe Ultra	3404	
D-MANO	Fair Fax DR Hazard 15M	D022	
D-MANR	Pago Jet M4	951102	
D-MANY	Klüver Bison II Trike	247901	
D-MANZ	Schmidtler Enduro Trike	02-005	
D-MAOC	Pago Jet M4	RB97002	
D-MAOE	NST Minimum Nimbus	M295	
D-MAOR(2)	Comco Ikarus Fox II Doppel	8605-3017	
D-MAOS	Flight Team Twister	D-002	
D-MAPA	Pioneer Flightstar	383	
D-MAPB	UPM Cobra Raven Trike	900101	
D-MAPC	AJS Sky-Craft	2000-37	
D-MAPG	Light Aero Avid Mk.IV	1305	
D-MAPH	NST Minimum Saphir 16	M621	
D-MAPI	Schmidtler Enduro	18/40	
D-MAPK	Drachenstudio Royal Karat 13	01-9307	
D-MAPO	NST Minimum Saphir	M86	
D-MAPP	NST Minimum	M548	
D-MAPT	Ultraleichtverbund Bi 90	553	
D-MAQB	NST Minimum Saphir 17	128850	
D-MARB	Ultralight Flight Phantom	0311-041001	
D-MARD	Steinbach Austro Trike Euro III	134	
D-MARF(2)	Comco Ikarus Sherpa II	8503-1093	
D-MARH	Flight Team Spider Hazard 13M	D005	
D-MARI	FUL Graffiti Trike	0340/0106	
D-MARJ	Klüver Racer SX 12	444904	
D-MARK(2)	Schmidtler Enduro	unkn	
D-MARL	Sky-Walker II	322	
D-MARN	Comco Ikarus Fox-C22	9004-3262	
D-MARR(2)	ARCO Spacer L	665	
D-MART	Fresh Breeze 110 AL 2F	36	

Regn.	Type	C/n	Prev.Id.
D-MARU	Behlen Power-Trike	91025	
D-MARW	Ultraleichtverbund Bi 90	21216	
D-MARX	Flight Team Spider	5	
D-MARZ	Comco Ikarus Fox-C22	9110-3369	
D-MASA	Comco Ikarus Fox D	012	
D-MASC	Comco Ikarus Fox-C22	9205-3375	
D-MASE	Behlen Power-Trike /Rotax 582	980014	
D-MASF	Warnke Skylight Trike	031	
D-MASH	Eipper Quicksilver MX	4180	
D-MASI	Fresh Breeze 122 AL 2F	377	
D-MASJ	Flight Team Twister	D003	
D-MASM	Schmidtler Ranger M	1813	
D-MASS	Scheibe Ultra	3401	
D-MASR	Comco Ikarus Fox-C22	9009-3293	
D-MAST	Flight Team Twister	1	
D-MASW	Sky-Walker II	167	
D-MASX	Comco Ikarus Fox-C22	9106-3327	
D-MATB	Krampen Ikarus S	53	
D-MATE	Sky-Walker II	314	
D-MATK	Schönleber DS Lotus Trike	01/0190	
D-MATL	ARCO Spacer L	11812	
D-MATP	Klüver Racer Quartz SX 12	080303	
D-MATT	NST Minimum	M416	
D-MATW	Albatros	116	
D-MATZ	Scheibe Uli 1	5207	
D-MAUI	Aériane Sirocco II	131	
D-MAUM	Drachenstudio Royal Trike	03-9612	
D-MAUS	Flight Team Spider	D045	
D-MAVB	Comco Ikarus Fox-C22	9109-3335	
D-MAVH	Löbenstein Racer SX 12	001	
D-MAVI	Light Aero Avid Flyer	441	
D-MAVK	Rans S-6 Coyote II	0792329	
D-MAVS	Kümmerle Mini-Fly-Set	1270/91-5	
D-MAWE	UL-F Jochum Eagle III	970502	
	(Possibly re-regd, same c/n quoted for D-MKME)		
D-MAWH	ASO Viper 15/582 Trike	12033206	
D-MAWI	Comco Ikarus Fox-C22	8807-3140	
D-MAWL	Sky-Walker II	391	
D-MAWO	Comco Ikarus Fox-C22	8907-3198	
D-MAWS	Fresh Breeze 110 AL2F	152	
D-MAWT	NST Minimum SierrAllM	151	
D-MAWW	Behlen Power-Trike /Rotax 582	9800015	
D-MAXE	Ultraleichtverbund Bi 90	21313	
D-MAXS	Comco Ikarus Fox-C22	9303-3496	
D-MAXT	WDFL Sunwheel R	003	
D-MAXW	Behlen Power-Trike	85012	
D-MAXX	Comco Ikarus Sherpa II	8311-1047	
D-MAXY	Comco Ikarus Fox-C22	034	
D-MAYA	Kümmerle Mini-Fly-Set Saphir 17	258/86-4	
D-MAYT	Junkers L582 Trike	094002/II	
D-MAZA	Comco Ikarus Fox-C22	9208-3386	
D-MAZD	UPM Funplane Lotus 18	003	
D-MAZT	Kümmerle Mini-Fly-Set	1312/91-6	
D-MAZZ	Schmidtler Enduro Lotus 18	02-008	
D-MBAC	Sky-Walker II	205	
D-MBAD	Behlen Power-Trike	89000109	
D-MBAE	Klüver Racer SX 12	834012	
D-MBAK	Bek ME 109R	001	
D-MBAL	Comco Ikarus Fox-C22	9110-3384	
D-MBAN	Dallach Sunrise II	010	
D-MBAO	Behlen Trike Vampir II	87027	
D-MBAR	Ultralight Flight Phantom	410	
D-MBAS	HFL Stratos 300K	300-009K	
D-MBAT	UPM Funplane	900085	
D-MBAU	Büttner Crazyplane III	003	
D-MBAW	Platzer Kiebitz-B	033	
D-MBBA	Comco Ikarus Fox-C22	9202-3377	
D-MBBC	Platzer Kiebitz-B	100	
D-MBBE	LO-120	EB 001	
D-MBBH	Krampen Ikarus S	65	
D-MBBI	Fresh Breeze 110 AL 2F	40	
D-MBBL	Take Off Merlin Karat 13	21193	
D-MBBM	Platzer Kiebitz-B6	023	
D-MBBN	HFL Stratos IIe	002	
D-MBBO	Fresh Breeze 110 AL2F	96	

Regn.	Type	C/n	Prev.Id.
D-MBBR(1)	Scheibe Uli 1	5205	
D-MBBR(2)	Drachenstudio Royal	190598	
D-MBBS	Comco Ikarus Fox-C22	920 .-3412	
D-MBBT	FUL Graffiti Trike	036/0102	
D-MBBW	Comco Ikarus Fox-C22	9201-3372	
D-MBCA(2)	Schmidtler Enduro	02-015	
D-MBCB	Albatros 64	166	
D-MBCD(2)	Dallach Sunrise IIA	030	
D-MBCH	Scheibe Ultra	3408	
D-MBCN	Take Off Merlin Trike	205093	
D-MBCT	Behlen Power-Trike	89014	
D-MBDB	Comco Ikarus Fox D	005	
D-MBDD	Kümmerle Mini-Fly-Set	1084-1	
D-MBDE	NST Minimum Saphir 17	34765	
D-MBDS	Rans S-6 Coyote II	0293446	
D-MBEA	MKB Ranger M	0100785	
D-MBEC	Light Aero Avid Flyer	808	
D-MBEE	Behlen Power-Trike /Rotax 582	980022	
D-MBEF	HFL Stratos 300	300-002	
D-MBEI	Schönleber DS Trike	10293	
D-MBEK(2)	Behlen Power-Trike /Rotax 582	980022	
D-MBEL	Ultraleichtverbund Bi 90	21298	
D-MBEN	Fresh Breeze 122 AL 2F	241	
D-MBEO	Platzer Kiebitz-B	048	
D-MBES	Fisher FP-202 Koala	1988/1/1	
D-MBET	Tandem Air Sunny Sport	22.91	
D-MBEW	Behlen Power-Trike	877947/900/12	
D-MBFA	UPM Cobra Raven Trike	91108	
	(Correct c/n may be 910108)		
D-MBFC	Ultraleichtverbund Bi 90	21312	
D-MBFF	Mosquito IB	016	
D-MBFK	Comco Ikarus Fox-C22	9208-3437	
D-MBFM	Rans S-10 Sakota	0189040	
D-MBFR	Light Aero Avid Flyer	1103	
D-MBFW	Light Aero Avid Flyer	1102	
D-MBGH	Behlen Power-Trike /Rotax 582	950002	
D-MBGR	FUL Graffiti Trike	027/0093	
D-MBHG	Aériane Sirocco	140	
D-MBHH	Pioneer Flightstar	384	
D-MBHJ	Comco Ikarus Fox-C22	9309-3508	
D-MBHM	UPM Funplane	850001	
D-MBHO	Flight Team Spider Hazard 13	D016	
D-MBHR	Air Création XP GT 582S	0494	
D-MBHT	Fresh Breeze 110 AL 2F	158	
D-MBHW	Fresh Breeze 122 AL 2F	420	
D-MBIA	Comco Ikarus Fox-C22	9202-3385	
D-MBIC	Fresh Breeze 110 AL 2F	151	
D-MBIL	Platzer Kiebitz-B4	082	
D-MBIR	Fresh Breeze 110 AL 2F	361	
D-MBJH	ASO Viper Trike	12059404	
D-MBJK	Klüver Bison Trike	089706	
D-MBJR	Take Off Maximum Karat 13	083121	
D-MBJU	Junkers Profly JUL Trike	4339	
D-MBKE	Air Création GTE 582S	7954557569	
D-MBKG	Ultraleichtverbund Bi 90	21090	
D-MBKK	Ghostbuster	95001	
D-MBLC	LO-120S	006	
D-MBLF	Sky-Service Pago Jet M4	95302	
D-MBLI	Behlen Power-Trike	94001	
D-MBLN	Platzer Motte B2	32	
D-MBLP	Ultraleichtverbund Bi 90	21239	
D-MBLS	ASO Viper Trike	VIII 22071503	
D-MBLW	NST Minimum Zephir	M440	
D-MBMA	Ultraleichtverbund Bi 90	7894016045	
D-MBMB	NST Minimum	0474	
D-MBMG	Behlen Power-Trike Vampir II	89023	
D-MBMH	Ultraleichtverbund Bi 90	927	
D-MBMI	Rans S-12 Airaile	1092298	
D-MBMW	Schmidtler Enduro Focus 18	M868086	
D-MBNS	Büttner Crazyplane III	7	
D-MBNY	Light Aero Avid Flyer IV	1228	
D-MBOC	HFL Stratos 300	300-007	
D-MBOD	NST Minimum Saphir	M159	
D-MBOL	Sky-Walker II	263	
D-MBOP	Schönleber DS Speed KS 14	L04/0489	

Regn.	Type	C/n	Prev.Id.
D-MBOS	J-3 Kitten	8610-3	
D-MBOY	UPM Cobra Raven Trike	900092	
	(Same c/n also quoted for D-MULB)		
D-MBPQ	Fresh Breeze 122 AL 2F	463	
D-MBPR	Behlen Power-Trike	88017	
D-MBPV	MKB Enduro Focus 18M	00187	
D-MBPW	Tandem Air Sunny	006	
D-MBRB	Ultralight Flight Phantom T-44	328	
D-MBRE	Flight Team Spider	D041	
D-MBRH	Kiggen/Heiland Air Création GTE	54173187195	
D-MBRK	Rans S-6 Coyote II	0992357	
D-MBRP	Fresh Breeze 110 AL4H	21	
D-MBRT	Drachenstudio Royal Trike	01-9610	
D-MBSE	ARCO Spacer L	1178	
D-MBSF	Behlen Power-Trike /Rotax 582	97006	
D-MBSJ	UL-F Jochum Eagle III	980907	
D-MBSK	Comco Ikarus Fox-C22	9105-3325	
D-MBSM	Dallach Sunrise II	005	
D-MBSO	NST Minimum	M551	
D-MBSR	NST Minimum Zephir	421	
D-MBST	Comco Ikarus Fox-C22	9308-3516	
D-MBSU	FUL Graffiti Trike	024/0090	
D-MBSV	Drachenstudio Royal Trike	150996	
D-MBSW	Sky Walker II	161	
D-MBSX	Albatros SX	200	
D-MBTB	Drachenstudio Royal Karat 13	02-9308	
D-MBTL	NST Minimum	M221	
D-MBTS	Solid Air Diamant Twin	T-009	
D-MBTT	Tandem Air Sunny Targa	TA 008.93	
D-MBTX	Warnke Trike	SI 033	
D-MBUF	Schmidtler Enduro Lotus 16	020993	
D-MBUM	Bäumer Racer (Homebuilt)	01/90	
D-MBUR	Flight Team Spider	D042	
D-MBUT	Solid Air Diamant Sierra Trike	014	
D-MBVB	Comco Ikarus Fox-C22	9108-3337	
D-MBVO	Take Off Merlin Karat 13	22344	
D-MBWB	Seiffert Mini II	10	
D-MBWG	Pago Jet M4	96701	
D-MBWO	Drachenstudio Royal Trike	170/879	
D-MBWP	Behlen Trike	83/1	
D-MBWS	Light Aero Avid Flyer	939	
D-MBXX	UL-F Jochum Eagle III	970803	
D-MBYE	Klüver Twin Racer SX 16	950103891	
D-MBYS	Light Aero Avid Flyer	443C	
D-MBYV	Light Aero Avid Flyer	1101D	
D-MBYZ	Flight Team Spider Trike	D032	
D-MBZZ	Tandem Air Sunny Sport	25.91	
D-MCAA	UPM Cobra Trike	91107	
	(Correct c/n may be 910107)		
D-MCAB	Fair Fax DR Hazard 15	D015	
D-MCAC	Klüver Twin Racer SX 16	616205	
D-MCAD	Fresh Breeze 110 AL2F	30	
D-MCAE	Comco Ikarus Fox	004	
D-MCAH	Comco Ikarus Fox-C22	9009-3272	
D-MCAK	Fresh Breeze 122 AL 2F	341	
D-MCAL	Ultraleichtverband Bi 90	B21152	
D-MCAM	Sky Walker II	387	
D-MCAN	ARCO Spacer L	689	
D-MCAS	Solid Air Diamant Euro III	016	
D-MCAT	Behlen Power Trike II	980020	
D-MCAW	Behlen Power-Trike /Rotax 582	93003	
D-MCAX	NST Minimum Saphir	M530	
D-MCBB	Schönleber DS Trike	5153	
D-MCBC	UL-F Jochum Eagle III	980405	
D-MCBQ	Fresh Breeze 110 AL 2F	105	
D-MCBS	ASO Viper Trike	V III 22071807	
D-MCCE	Sky-Walker II	237	
D-MCCI	Büttner Crazyplane III	86	
D-MCCL	Comco Ikarus Fox-C22	9107-3368	
D-MCCP	Behlen Power-Trike	95003	
D-MCCR	Platzer Kiebitz B	084	
D-MCCS	Ultraleichtverbund Bi 90	985	
D-MCCX	Kümmerle Mini-Fly-Set	1281/91-5	
D-MCDC	UL-F Jochum Eagle III	970501	
D-MCDF	Take Off Merlin Trike	23135	
D-MCDI	Sky-Service Pago Jet	95201	
D-MCDK	NST Minimum	M541	
D-MCDP(2)	Büttner Crazyplane III	82	
D-MCDR	Kilb Air Création GTE 5	AC 004	
D-MCDV	Comco Ikarus Fox-C22	9109-3356	
D-MCDW	Ultraleichtverbund Bi 90	21053	
D-MCDX	Schönleber Trike	TK 01/0395	
D-MCEC	NST Minimum	M569	
D-MCEH	Ultraleichtverbund Bi 90	21297	
D-MCEK	Comco Ikarus Fox-C22	9106-3331	
D-MCES(2)	HFL Stratos 300K	300-028K	
D-MCET	Flight Team Spider Hazard 15	002	
D-MCFA	Light Aero Avid Flyer SW	1304D	
D-MCFK	Funk FK-9	013	
D-MCFR	Light Aero Avid Flyer	418	
D-MCGB	Drachenstudio Royal Trike	03-03039	
D-MCGE	Ultraleichtverbund Bi 90	690	
D-MCHA	Fisher FP-404 Koala	001	
D-MCHB	NST Minimum	120623	
D-MCHF	Rans S-10 Sakota	0491128	
D-MCHK	Dallach Sunrise IIA	032	
D-MCHM	ASO Viper Trike	VIII 122070503	
D-MCHP	Albatros 52	131	
D-MCHR	NST Minimum	M577	
D-MCHS	ASO Viper Trike	VII 2049309	
D-MCHW	NST Minimum	M567	
D-MCIB	NST Minimum Saphir 17	M297	
D-MCII	Schmidtler Enduro Trike	865186	
D-MCIL	UPM Cobra BF 52 UL Trike	950134	
D-MCIN	Schönleber DS Trike	11290	
D-MCJA	Fresh Breeze 110 AL 2F	38	
D-MCJJ	Behlen Power-Trike /Rotax 582	980016	
D-MCJN	Behlen Power Trike II	97010	
D-MCJW	FUL Graffiti Trike	037/0103	
D-MCKT	Comco Ikarus Fox-C22	9207-3428	
D-MCLA	Fresh Breeze 110 AL 2F	213	
D-MCLU	Albatros Milan	08085	
D-MCMA	NST Minimum Zephir CX	M524	
D-MCMC	Tandem Air Sunny Sport	2-91	
D-MCMK	FUL Graffiti Trike	001/0045	
D-MCMP	Ultraleichtverbund Bi 90	21060	
D-MCNO	Fresh Breeze 122 AL 2F	212	
D-MCOB	Tandem Air Sunny Sport	1-91	
D-MCOG	Fresh Breeze 110 AL 4H	25	
D-MCOL	Kümmerle Mini-Fly-Set	73185-3	
D-MCOM	Comco Ikarus Fox D	8406-001	
D-MCON	Sky-Walker II	264	
D-MCOQ	Warnke Trike	51/009	
D-MCOR	Fresh Breeze 122 AL 2F	389	
D-MCOW	Sky-Walker II	236	
D-MCOY	Rans S-6ES Coyote II	0392280	
D-MCPI	Büttner Crazyplane I	103	
D-MCPM(2)	Büttner Easy Plane	8	
D-MCRB	Ultralight Flight Phantom	402	
D-MCRC	Light Aero Avid Flyer	870	
D-MCRH	NST Schwarze Trike	MT66	
D-MCSA	Light Aero Avid Flyer	1154D	
D-MCSB	Schmidtler Enduro Trike	01-002	
D-MCSW	Sky-Walker II	162	
D-MCTO	Warnke Trike	034	
D-MCTR	Fresh Breeze 110 AL 2F	42	
D-MCTS	Warnke Skylight Trike	2	
D-MCUL	Ultraleichtverbund Bi 90	21178	
D-MCWA	Albatros 64	130	
D-MCWE	Ultraleichtverbund Bi 90	21036	
D-MCWM	FUL Graffiti Trike	38/0104	
D-MCWW	Fair Fax DR Trike	1022	
D-MCYZ	Fresh Breeze 110 AL 2F	93	
D-MDAA	Klüver Twin Racer SX 16	555203	
D-MDAB	Schönleber DS Lotus 18 Trike	020490	
D-MDAL	Dallach Sunrise IIA	033	
D-MDAM	ASO Viper Trike	12059404	
D-MDAN	Sky-Walker II	232	
D-MDAS	Tandem Air Sunny Targa	TA 07.93	
D-MDAT	Take Off Merlin 1100	28368	

Regn.	Type	C/n	Prev.Id.
D-MDAV	Behlen Power Trike II	89044	
D-MDBB	Dallach Sunrise IIA	020	
D-MDBG	Fresh Breeze 110 AL2F	33	
D-MDBH	WDFL Sunwheel	008	
D-MDBI	Flight Team Spider	D038	
D-MDBK	Pago Jet M4	961201	
D-MDBL	Take Off Merlin Trike	22114	
D-MDBS	Mantel Mono-Dragster	2248410002	
D-MDBX(2)	HFL Stratos IIe	11e/005	
D-MDCL	Behlen Power-Trike	88023	
D-MDCM	NST Minimum Sierra	SN 105	
D-MDCS	Schmidtler Enduro Trike	02-003	
D-MDCW	NST Minimum	M323	
D-MDDB	Funk FK-9	022	
D-MDDD	Aviasud Mistral BRD	085	
D-MDDP	Sky-Walker II	392	
D-MDDT	Behlen Power Trike II	98011	
D-MDEA	Wisch Star-Trike	12601	
D-MDEB	Behlen Power-Trike	95001	
D-MDEC(2)	Fresh Breeze 110 AL 2F	421	
D-MDEE	Fresh Breeze 110 AL 2F	411	
D-MDEF	Behlen Power-Trike	94003	
D-MDEG	Comco Ikarus Fox-C22	9104-3334	
D-MDEI	Take Off Merlin Trike	25125	
D-MDEL	Seiffert Mini-Speed Trike	unkn	
D-MDET	NST Minimum Pamir	M523	
D-MDEW	Fresh Breeze 110 AL 2F	12	
D-MDFC	Ultraleichtverbund Bi 90	976-4105546	
D-MDFD	Fresh Breeze 110 AL2F	35	
D-MDFG	NST Minimum	MT81	
D-MDFI	Ultraleichtverbund Bi 90	B21122	
D-MDGS	UPM Cobra Trike	900099	
D-MDHE	Comco Ikarus Fox-C22	9303-3481	
D-MDHF	Tandem Air Sunny	46.93	
D-MDHG	Behlen Power-Trike	97011	
D-MDHH	Kümmerle Mini-Fly-Set	1278/91-5	
D-MDHP	Ultralight Flight Phantom	327	
D-MDHX	Büttner Crazyplane IV	14	
D-MDII	FUL Graffiti Trike	030/0096	
D-MDIN	Dallach Sunrise IIA	026	
D-MDIS	MKB Ranger M	01/006/85	
D-MDKE	Drachenstudio Piccolo II Trike	099306	
D-MDKH	Comco Ikarus Fox-C22	8705-3062	
D-MDKL	NST Minimum SierrAII	558	
D-MDKM	Behlen Power-Trike Hazard 15M	91034	
D-MDKR	Comco Ikarus Fox II Doppel	8608-3029	
D-MDKT	Comco Ikarus Fox-C22	9103-3315	PH-2G8
D-MDKU	Light Aero Avid Flyer	1155C	
D-MDLT	Sky-Service Pago Jet M4	95303	
D-MDLW	Comco Ikarus Fox-C22	9111-3357	
D-MDMA	Behlen Power-Trike	86027	
D-MDMC	Behlen Power-Trike	M878502	
D-MDMJ	Behlen Power-Trike Vampir II	88018	
D-MDMK	Behlen Power-Trike	7017	
D-MDMR	Behlen Power-Trike Vampir II	M876642	
D-MDMT	Comco Ikarus Fox-C22	8905-3201	
D-MDMV	Fresh Breeze 110 AL 2F	413	
D-MDMY	Comco Ikarus Fox-C22	9008-3292	
D-MDNK	Pago Jet M4	960501	
D-MDOB	Behlen Power-Trike	93002	
D-MDOC	Tandem Air Sunny	30.92	
D-MDOG(2)	Funk FK-9	006	
D-MDOL	Junkers Profly JUL Trike	00594	
D-MDOX	Steinbach Austro Trike Spot IIM	1915	
D-MDPA	Schmidtler Ranger M	18-24	
D-MDPG	Take Off Merlin Karat 13	20573	
D-MDPW	Drachenstudio Royal Trike	13-0696	
D-MDRB	Ultralight Flight Phantom T44	0293	
D-MDRM	Take Off Merlin Trike	25516	
D-MDRP	WDFL Sunwheel	002	
D-MDRT	Platzer Kiebitz-B4	099	
D-MDSB	Take Off Merlin Trike	26356	
D-MDSC	UPM Funplane	860016	
D-MDSF	Behlen Power-Trike Vampir II	89014	
D-MDSG	Take Off Merlin Trike	21393	
D-MDSK	Flight Team Spider Hazard 13	D013	
D-MDSL	Comco Ikarus Fox-C22B	9202-3389	
D-MDSM	Kilb Air Création GTE 5	AC 005	
D-MDSO	Ultraleichtverbund Bi 90	529	
D-MDSR	Flight Team Spider Trike	D023	
D-MDSS	HFL Stratos IIe	IIe-008	
D-MDSW	Flight Team Spider Trike	D039	
D-MDTA	FUL Graffiti Trike	002/0049	
D-MDTG	Fresh Breeze 110 AL 2A	140	
D-MDTL	Seiffert Mini II	774	
D-MDTW	Behlen Power-Trike /Rotax 582	980017	
D-MDUD	Fresh Breeze 110 AL 2F	200	
D-MDUG	Wildente	109	
D-MDUO	Comco Ikarus Fox II Doppel	001/85	
D-MDUP	Ultraleichtverbund Bi 90	623	
D-MDUS	Sky-Walker II	350	
	(Same c/n quoted for D-MHRF)		
D-MDVK	Behlen Power-Trike	91021	
D-MDWW	Comco Ikarus Fox-C22	9305-3501	
D-MDZR	Fresh Breeze 122 AL 2F	170	
D-MDZZ	Sky-Service Pago Jet	95308	
D-MEAA	Sky-Service Pago Jet	95301	
D-MEAB	Solid Air Diamant Trike	18	
D-MEAC	Behlen Power-Trike /Rotax 582	980023	
D-MEAF	Klüver Racer SX 12	14007	
D-MEAL	FUL Graffiti Trike	014/0074	
D-MEAS	Ultraleichtverbund Bi 90	609	
D-MEAT	Warnke Puma Sprint DS	D003	
D-MEBA	Behlen Power-Trike	86026	
D-MEBE	Flight Team Spider Trike	D011	
D-MEBI	Flight Team Spider Trike	D029	
D-MEBL	Take Off Merlin Karat 13	22544	
D-MEBR	Ultraleichtverbund Bi 90	21065	
D-MEBS	Comco Ikarus Fox D	8410-FD21	
D-MEBY	Sky-Walker II	257	
D-MECA	Solid Air Diamant SierrAI	003	
D-MECC	NST Minimum Zephir	M353	
D-MEDD	NST Minimum	1449	
D-MEDE	Comco Ikarus Fox-C22	9107-3365	
D-MEDI	Ultralight Flight Phantom T-44	420	
D-MEDO	NST Minimum	M535	
D-MEDP	NST Minimum	M521	
D-MEDS	Behlen Power-Trike	002583	
D-MEDT	Kümmerle Mini-Fly-Set	1273/91-5	
D-MEEC	Ultraleichtverbund Bi 90	168308471	
D-MEEL	Comco Ikarus Fox-C22	9207-3440	
D-MEEM	Fresh Breeze 110 AL 2F	113	
D-MEEV	Sky-Walker II	283	
D-MEFA	Schönleber DS Speed KS 14 Trike	KS01/0192	
D-MEFB	Flight Team Spider Trike	D033	
D-MEFE	Ultraleichtverbund Bi 90	6480	
D-MEFG	Fair Fax Trike	024	
D-MEFH	Schmidtler Enduro Trike	01-003	
D-MEFK	Fresh Breeze 110 AL 2F	163	
D-MEFL	Ultraleichtverbund Bi 90	552	
D-MEFW	NST Minimum Zephir	M520/23670	
D-MEGG	Tandem Air Sunny Sport	33.92	
D-MEGI (2)	Funk FK-9	005	
D-MEGW	Platzer Kiebitz-B	074	
D-MEHC	Fresh Breeze 110 AL2F	39	
D-MEHE	Behlen Power-Trike	92001	
D-MEHF	Comco Ikarus Fox-C22	8906-3197	
D-MEHG	HFL Stratos 300K	300-011K	
D-MEHK	Fresh Breeze 110 AL 2F	156	
D-MEHL (2)	Pago Jet M4	970401	
D-MEHR	Scheibe Uli-2	3304	
D-MEHU	Fisher FP-202 Koala	2322	
D-MEHV	Behlen Power-Trike	875022	
D-MEHW	Behlen Power-Trike II Hazard 15M	910604	
D-MEIA	Flight Team Spider Hazard 13	D021	
D-MEII	Fisher FP-202 Koala	JE 001	
D-MEIN	Büttner Crazyplane I	118	
D-MEIR	UPM Funplane Trike	870027	
D-MEIS	Behlen Power-Trike	1000683	
D-MEIT	Wisch Star-Trike Vampir II	12603895	

Regn.	Type	C/n	Prev.Id.
D-MEJK	Behlen Power-Trike Vampir II	88020	
D-MEJR	Comco Ikarus Fox II Doppel	8607-3027	
D-MEKA	Comco Ikarus Fox I	054	
D-MEKE	Flight Team Spider	D047	
D-MEKI	Platzer Kiebitz-B8	031	
D-MEKU	Platzer Motte B	047	
D-MEKW	Comco Ikarus Fox D	8505-FD20	
D-MELE	Klüver Bison Trike	982704	
D-MELF(2)	Schmidtler Enduro Trike	M3557747	
D-MELG	Take Off Maximum Karat 13 Trike	035100	
D-MELL	LO-120S	010-A	
D-MELM	Behlen Power-Trike Falcon	1718	
D-MELS	Schmidtler Ranger M	14/49	
D-MELX	Fresh Breeze 122 AL 2F	410	
D-MELY	Light Aero Avid Flyer	936	
D-MEMB	Take Off Merlin Trike	25726	
D-MEMJ	Fresh Breeze 110 AL 2F	201	
D-MEMK	ASO Viper Hazard 15 Trike	11290	
D-MEMO	Ultra	3409	
D-MEMR	Schmidtler Enduro Trike	02-007	
D-MEND	Sky-Walker II	358	
D-MENG	Sky-Walker II	234	
D-MENO	UPM Cobra BF 52UL Trike	950133	
D-MENU	Behlen Power-Trike II Hazard 15	90020	
D-MEPA	ASO Viper 13/582 Hazard 13 Trike	122020108	
D-MEPG	Albatros AN-22	8332	
D-MEPI	Fair Fax DR Trike	D012	
D-MEPS	ASO Viper Trike	22038208	
D-MEPU	Pioneer Flightstar	678	
D-MEPW	Comco Ikarus Fox-C22	8906-3204	
D-MERA	Kiggen/Heiland Air Création GTE 582S	9954557785	
D-MERB	Ultralight Flight Phantom	0294	
D-MERC	Enduro Trike (Homebuilt)	12/92	
D-MERD	UPM Omega Focus 20	880032	
D-MERF	Comco Ikarus Fox D	8710-FD41	
D-MERG	Dallach Sunrise IIA	038	
D-MERH	NST Minimum	24598	
D-MERK	Fresh Breeze 110 AL2F	7439	
D-MERL	Behlen Trike	86023	
D-MERO	Scheibe UL-1 Coach IIS	003	
D-MERS	Comco Ikarus Fox-C22	9204-3395	
D-MERT	Albatros SX	503	
D-MERZ	Scheibe Uli 1	5216	
D-MESA	ASO Viper Hazard 15 Trike	11024201	
D-MESB	Comco Ikarus Fox II Doppel	8606-3023	
D-MESG	Behlen Power-Trike	87028	
D-MESL	Comco Ikarus Fox-C22	9203-3392	
D-MESP	UPM Cobra Trike	900105	
D-MESR	FUL Graffiti Trike	018/0076	
D-MEST	Ultraleichtverbund Bi 90	4926438690	
D-MESW	Sky-Walker II	169	
D-METE	Comco Ikarus Fox-C22	9207-3417	
D-METH	Platzer Kiebitz-B4	019	
D-METL	Schmidtler Enduro Trike	01001	
D-METT	Light Aero Avid Flyer D	1153	
D-METU	Aériane Sirocco II	116	
D-METY	Drachenstudio Royal Trike	14-0896	
D-METZ	Schmidtler Enduro Trike	02-018	
D-MEUB	Junkers Profly JUL Trike	0001	
D-MEUL	FUL Graffiti Trike	034/0100	
D-MEUR	Flight Team Spider Hazard 15	D011	
D-MEVA	HFL Stratos IIe	IIe-OO9	
D-MEVC	Büttner Crazyplane III	5	
D-MEVI	Light Aero Avid Flyer	972	
D-MEVT	Kümmerle Mini-Fly-Set	251864	
D-MEWE	Albatros 52	115	
D-MEWL	Flight Team Spider Trike	D030	
D-MEWO	NST Minimum SierrAll	231	
D-MEWU	Klüver Kaiman Trike	701612	
D-MEZE	UPM Cobra BF 52UL Trike	950132	
D-MFAA	Comco Ikarus Fox-C22	8703-3036	
D-MFAB	Comco Ikarus Fox II Doppel	8612-3051	
D-MFAC	Comco Ikarus Fox II Doppel	8609-3033	
D-MFAD	Comco Ikarus Fox II Doppel	8611-3034	
D-MFAN	Comco Ikarus Fox-C22	8703-3039	
D-MFAO	Comco Ikarus Fox II Doppel	8703-3037	
D-MFAP	Comco Ikarus Fox II Doppel	8706-3040	
D-MFAQ	Comco Ikarus Fox II Doppel	8703-3038	
D-MFAS	Solid Air Twin Diamant Trike	T-010	
D-MFAT	Comco Ikarus Fox II Doppel	8706-3041	
D-MFAU	Comco Ikarus Fox-C22	8707-3091	
D-MFAX	Comco Ikarus Fox D	8512-FD37	
D-MFBA	Comco Ikarus Fox-C22	8907-3175	
D-MFBC	Comco Ikarus Fox-C22	8907-3176	
D-MFBD	Comco Ikarus Fox-C22	8905-3178	
D-MFBE	Comco Ikarus Fox-C22	8907-3177	
D-MFBL	MKB Enduro Focus 18	0300185	
D-MFBM	Platzer Kiebitz-B8	121	
D-MFBP	ASO Viper 15 Hazard Trike	15/ 2690	
D-MFBW	Ultraleichtverbund Bi 90	994	
D-MFBT	Fresh Breeze 110 AL2F	103	
D-MFCA	Comco Ikarus Fox-C22	9308-3525	
D-MFDH	Behlen Power-Trike	92012	
D-MFDK	Fresh Breeze 110 AL2F	72	
D-MFEA	Comco Ikarus Fox-C22	8711-3098	
D-MFEC	Comco Ikarus Fox-C22	8709-3093	
D-MFED	Comco Ikarus Fox-C22	8709-3094	
D-MFEE	Comco Ikarus Fox II Doppel	035-063	
D-MFEH	Tandem Air Sunny Sport	29.92	
D-MFEI (2)	Comco Ikarus Fox-C22	8709-3095	
D-MFEL	Comco Ikarus Fox-C22	8710-3097	
D-MFEM	Comco Ikarus Fox II Doppel	8604-3014	
D-MFEN	Comco Ikarus Fox-C22	8711-3099	
D-MFEP	Firebird M-1	59092	
D-MFEQ	Comco Ikarus Fox-C22	8805-3100	
D-MFER	Comco Ikarus Fox-C22	8804-3103	
D-MFES	Comco Ikarus Fox-C22	8808-3102	
D-MFET	Comco Ikarus Fox-C22	8807-3101	
D-MFFA	Rans S-6 Coyote II	0193422	
D-MFFD	Fair Fax Trike	011	
D-MFFK	Fair-Fax Euro III Trike	045	
D-MFFM	Fair Fax Trike	042	
D-MFFN	Fair Fax DR Trike	D028	
D-MFFT	Comco Ikarus Fox-C22	8809-3152	
D-MFFW	Fair Fax DR Hazard 15M Trike	D017	
D-MFGG	Albatros 52	141	
D-MFGH	Albatros 64	302	
D-MFGI	Fresh Breeze 110AL2F	55	
D-MFGL	Fresh Breeze 110 AL 2F	343	
D-MFGM	ASO Viper Trike	12044 503	
D-MFGT	Albatros SX	502	
D-MFHG	Comco Ikarus Fox-C22	9010-3295	
D-MFHJ	NST Minimum	M540	
D-MFIB	Comco Ikarus Fox-C22	8809-3161	
D-MFID	Comco Ikarus Fox-C22	8811-3162	
D-MFIG	Comco Ikarus Fox-C22	8903-3164	
D-MFIH	Comco Ikarus Fox-C22	8903-3165	
D-MFIM	Comco Ikarus Fox-C22	8903-3167	
D-MFIN	Comco Ikarus Fox-C22	8904-3168	
D-MFIP	Comco Ikarus Fox II Doppel	8706-3042	
D-MFIR	Comco Ikarus Fox-C22	8905-3169	
D-MFIS	Comco Ikarus Fox-C22	8905-3170	
D-MFIV	Comco Ikarus Fox-C22	8904-3172	
D-MFIW	Comco Ikarus Fox-C22	8906-3173	
D-MFIX	Dallach Sunrise IIA	004	
D-MFIZ	Comco Ikarus Fox-C22	8908-3174	
D-MFJS	Fair Fax DR Trike	D019	
D-MFKA	Klüver Bison Trike	883806	
D-MFKE	Comco Ikarus Fox-C22	8805-3109	
D-MFKH	J-3 Kitten	01	
D-MFKK	Platzer Kiebitz-B2	102	
D-MFKL	Seiffert Mini II	0101/89-1	
D-MFKO	Sky-Walker 1+1	26122	
D-MFKW	Comco Ikarus Fox II Doppel	8603-3012	
D-MFLA	Light Aero Avid Flyer C	1325C	
D-MFLB	ASO Viper Trike	15181090	
D-MFLE	Comco Ikarus Fox-C22B	8809-3110	
D-MFLH	Comco Ikarus Fox II Doppel	8606-3020	
D-MFLI	Aviasud Mistral BRD	151	
D-MFLO	Take Off Maximum Trike	109013	

Regn.	Type	C/n	Prev.Id.
D-MFLS	ASO Viper Hazard 15 Trike	15I 6990	
D-MFLU	Albatros 64	303	
D-MFLY	Behlen Power-Trike /Rotax 582	88027	
D-MFMA	Comco Ikarus Fox-C22	8701-3031	
D-MFMF	Tandem Air Sunny	15.91	
D-MFMN	Fresh Breeze 110 AL 2F	10	
D-MFMV	Schönleber Trike	V070198	
D-MFMW	ARCO Spacer L	966	
D-MFOB	Krampen Ikarus S	59	
D-MFOQ	Klüver Twin Racer Quartz SX 16	236004	
D-MFOS	Comco Ikarus Fox-C22	8707-3044	
D-MFOX	Comco Ikarus Fox D	023	
D-MFPB	NST Minimum	M430	
D-MFPF	FUL Graffiti Trike	028/0094	
D-MFPK	Platzer Kiebitz-B2	103	
D-MFRA	Fresh Breeze 110 AL 2F	63	
D-MFRC	FULMaverick Trike	unkn	
D-MFRD	Schönleber DS Lotus KS 16 Trike	KS01/0191	
D-MFRE	NST Minimum	M231	
D-MFRG	Fair Fax DR Trike	001	
D-MFRI	Comco Ikarus Sherpa 1	8306-1029	
D-MFRK	Light Aero Avid Flyer	809	
D-MFRW	T2	N33931534	
D-MFRZ	Platzer Kiebitz-B8	135	
D-MFSA	Comco Ikarus Fox-C22	8805-3108	
D-MFSG	ASO Viper Trike	VI 12037207	
D-MFSI	Fresh Breeze 110 AL2F	87	
D-MFSS	Schmidtler Ranger M Trike	1832	
D-MFST	Platzer Motte B-2	039	
D-MFTA	Comco Ikarus Fox-C22	8808-3104	
D-MFTE	Comco Ikarus Fox-C22	8808-3105	
D-MFTI	Comco Ikarus Fox-C22	8808-3107	
D-MFTN	NST Minimum	10873	
D-MFTO	Comco Ikarus Fox-C22	8808-3106	
D-MFUA	ASO Viper Trike	V 15 I 14491	
D-MFUE	Klüver Twin Racer SX 16	554203	
D-MFUF	Klüver Twin Racer SX 16	773209	
D-MFUI	T2	4	
D-MFUL	FUL Graffiti Trike	042/0142	
D-MFUN	UPM Funplane	86009	
D-MFUS	Comco Ikarus Fox-C22	9211-3483	
D-MFUX	Comco Ikarus Fox-C22	8705-3043	
D-MFWD	Dallach Sunrise II	009	
D-MFWH	Light Aero Avid Flyer	1295	
D-MGAD	Sky-Walker II	209	
D-MGAF	Pioneer Flightstar	373	
D-MGAH	Behlen Power Trike II	96007	
D-MGAI	Flight Team Spider	D019	
D-MGAK	Tandem Air Sunny Sport	13.91	
D-MGAP	Comco Ikarus Fox-C22	9108-3355	
D-MGAR	Light Aero Avid Flyer	811	
D-MGAT	Flight Team Spider Trike	D008	
D-MGAY	ARCO Spacer L	361	
D-MGBB	Klüver Racer SX 12	094002	
D-MGBC	Büttner Crazyplane III	106	
D-MGBK	Klüver Twin Racer Quartz SX	838910	
D-MGBL (1)	Scheibe Ultra	3412	
D-MGBL (2)	Type unknown	27197	
D-MGBP	Fresh Breeze 110 AL 2F	240	
D-MGBW	Flight Team Spider Hazard 13M	D007	
D-MGBY	NST Minimum Saphir	1128	
D-MGCB	Sky-Walker II	261	
D-MGCC	Light Aero Avid Flyer C	942C	
D-MGED	Comco Ikarus Fox II Doppel	8607-3030	
D-MGEG	Ultraleichtverbund Bi 90	6363951644	
D-MGEH	Kümmerle Mini-Fly-Set	483/86-4	
D-MGEO	Warnke Skylight Trike	SI 035	
D-MGER	Rans S-12 Airaile	1292339	
D-MGET	Comco Ikarus Fox-C22	9205-3402	
D-MGFA	Schönleber DS Lotus KS 18 Trike	KS02/0389	
D-MGFC	Ultraleichtverbund Bi 90	21296	
D-MGFE	Schmidtler Ranger M Trike	1821	
D-MGFH	Seiffert Mini II	M-SC88646	
D-MGFL	Light Aero Avid Flyer	683	
D-MGFR	NST Minimum	M562	
D-MGFU	Behlen Power-Trike	88025	
D-MGFX	Swift	SA020	
D-MGFY	Swift	SA034	
D-MGGB	Tandem Air Sunny Sport	14.91	
D-MGGF	Behlen Power Trike II	878188	
D-MGGG	Platzer Kiebitz-B2	035	
D-MGGK	Ultraleichtverbund Bi 90	96974171166	
D-MGGM	Platzer Kiebitz-B9	021	
D-MGGP	FUL Graffiti Trike	011/0072	
D-MGHA	NST Minimum Zephir	2378	
D-MGHB	Pioneer Flightstar	682	
D-MGHD	Behlen Power-Trike	463	
D-MGHE	Comco Ikarus Fox II Doppel	8606-3021	
D-MGHF	Ultraleichtverbund Bi 90	21278	
D-MGHH	Albatros 64	301	
D-MGHI	Klüver Twin Racer SX 16	543008	
D-MGHK	Büttner Crazyplane II	51	
D-MGHL	Ultraleichetverbund Bi 90	635	
D-MGHM	Dallach Sunrise IIA	036	
D-MGHS	Light Aero Avid Flyer	810	
D-MGHT	Take Off Merlin Trike	24565	
D-MGIN	Ultraleichtverbund Bi 90	595	
D-MGIS	Kümmerle Mini-Fly-Set	12897-8	
D-MGJB	NST Minimum Santana	M503	
D-MGJH	Fresh Breeze 122 AL 2F	357	
D-MGJT	Klüver Bison Trike	427711	
D-MGKK	Behlen Trike	90028	
D-MGKL	Sky-Walker II	238	
D-MGKP	Ultraleichtverbund Bi 90	21199	
D-MGLK	Ghostbuster	199651	
D-MGKU	LO-120	007A	
D-MGLM	Rans S-6 Coyote II	0293436	
D-MGLR	Seiffert Mini II	100	
D-MGLU	Klüver Bison Trike	645802	
D-MGMB	Sky-Walker II	181	
D-MGMC	Schmidtler Enduro Trike	02-017	
D-MGMM	Comco Ikarus Fox-C22	9307-3528	
D-MGMP	Comco Ikarus Fox-C22	9206-3404	
D-MGNI	ARCO Spacer L	877	
D-MGOD	Solid Air Diamant 55db(A) Trike	023	
D-MGOH	ASO Viper Trike	12022001	
D-MGPC	Kiggen/Hieland Air Création GTE 582 S	4317124295	
D-MGPD	Fresh Breeze 110 AL 2F	471	
D-MGPG	Take Off Maximum Trike	016/0077	
D-MGPP	Büttner Crazyplane II	97	
D-MGPR	UL Flugservice Bod Quasar II .TC	SW-WQT-0551/SW-TQD-0111	
D-MGPS	Krampen Ikarus S	62	
D-MGRC	Blankert (Homebuilt)	E25	
D-MGRD	Comco Ikarus Fox II Doppel	9008-3291	
D-MGRE	Ultraleichtverbund Bi 90	999	
D-MGRG	FUL Graffiti Trike	003/0053	
D-MGRI	FUL Graffiti Trike	0055	
D-MGRJ	FUL Graffiti Trike	0046	
D-MGRK	FUL Graffiti Trike	010/0048	
D-MGRL	FUL Graffiti Trike	019/0079	
D-MGRM	Schönleber DS Lotus KS 16 Trike	KS01/1190	
D-MGRO	Ultraleichtverbund Bi 90	21018	
D-MGRP	NST Minimum	M539	
D-MGRR	FUL Graffiti Trike	200080	
D-MGRS	Ultraleichtverbund Bi 90	794	
D-MGRT	Comco Ikarus Fox-C22	9211-3422	
D-MGRU	ASO Viper Hazard 15 Trike	15791	
D-MGRV	Comco Ikarus Fox-C22	9108-3350	
D-MGRW	Sky-Walker II	278	
D-MGRX	ASO Viper Trike	12052402	
D-MGRY	FUL Graffiti Trike	009/0047	
D-MGRZ	FUL Graffiti Trike	0050	
D-MGSA	NST Schwarze Trike	M564	
D-MGSC	Behlen Power-Trike	91029	
D-MGSH	Seiffert Mini-Speed Trike	1000000	
D-MGSL	NST Minimum	010205	
D-MGSM	HFL Stratos IIe	IIe-011	
D-MGSO	Behlen Power-Trike II	91022	
D-MGSP	Büttner Crazyplane I	105	
D-MGSR	Pago Jet M4	RB 98008	

Regn.	Type	C/n	Prev.Id.
D-MGSS	Behlen Power-Trike	1715	
D-MGST	HFL Stratos 300	300-006	
D-MGSY	Schönleber Trike 4	TK01/0296	
D-MGTE	UPM Cobra Trike	920114	
D-MGTF	Take Off Maximum Trike	13079	
D-MGTJ	Comco Ikarus Fox-C22	9106-3339	
D-MGTL	Comco Ikarus Fox-C22	9106-3338	
D-MGTR	Ultraleichtverbund Bi 90	3762057	
D-MGTW	NST Minimum	M1454	
D-MGUD	ASO Viper Trike	VIII 22072506	
D-MGUE	Albatros SX	501	
D-MGUI	Warnke Skylight Trike	SI 037	
D-MGUL	Kiggen/Heiland Air Création GTE 5	4954433118	
D-MGUS	Flight Team Spider Trike	D031	
D-MGUT	Flight Team Spider Trike	D036	
D-MGUZ	Klüver Twin Racer SX 16	235004	
D-MGVA	Platzer Kiebitz-B8	055	
D-MGVH	Moskito Ib	020	
D-MGVL	Ultraleichtverbund Bi 90	21041	
D-MGWM	Platzer Motte B-2	11	
D-MGWR	Behlen Power-Trike /Rotax 582	98010	
D-MGZI	Kümmerle Mini-Fly-Set	67986-4	
D-MHAC	Sky-Walker II	390	
D-MHAD	ASO Viper Hazard 13 Trike	22053403	
D-MHAF	ASO Viper Trike	10504	
D-MHAG	Comco Ikarus Fox II Doppel	8603-3011	
D-MHAH	Kümmerle Mini-Fly-Set Thalhofer GT	1304/91-6	
D-MHAI	ASO Viper Trike	12060405	
D-MHAJ	FUL Graffiti Trike	033/0099	
D-MHAL	Comco Ikarus Fox-C22	9008-3280	
D-MHAN	ASO Viper Trike	VIII 22064408	
D-MHAO	Kiggen/Hieland Air Création GTE 582 S	5954173091	
D-MHAP	Kiggen/Hieland Air Création GTE 582 S	3954317120	
D-MHAQ	Kiggen/Hieland Air Création GTE 582 S	5954173195	
D-MHAS	Comco Ikarus Sherpa II	8505-1098	
D-MHAZ	NST Minimum	1147	
D-MHBJ	Sky-Walker II	328	
D-MHBK	Comco Ikarus Fox-C22	9304-3498	
D-MHBO	Ultraleichtverbund Bi 90	21123	
D-MHBP	Sky-Walker II	272	
D-MHBW	Klüver Racer Quartz SX 16	247004	
D-MHCP	Büttner Crazyplane III	90	
D-MHCR	Platzer Kiebitz-B9	065	
D-MHDE	Skystar S34	002	
D-MHDH	Solid Air Diamant Trike	017	
D-MHDO	Solid Air Diamant 55dB(A) Trike	019	
D-MHDS	Flight Team Spider Hazard 15	D024	
D-MHDV	Klüver Twin Racer Quartz SX 16	720208	
D-MHDW	FUL Graffiti Trike	95	
D-MHDZ	Pegasus Quasar II	6637	
D-MHED	Comco Ikarus Fox-C22	8809-3154	
D-MHEL	Flight Team Spider Trike	D015	
D-MHEM	WDFL Sunwheel	007	
D-MHEN	Fresh Breeze 110 AL2F	88	
D-MHET (1)	Platzer Kiebitz-B3	004	
D-MHET (2)	Flight Team Spider	D052	
D-MHFB	Junkers Profly JUL Trike	94/1062	
D-MHFG	Ultraleichtverbund Bi 90	21052	
D-MHFK	Behlen Power-Trike	90011	
D-MHFL	HFL Stratos IIe	004	
D-MHFM	NST Minimum Zephir	438	
D-MHFW	Kümmerle Mini-Fly-Set	1284/91-5	
D-MHGA	Sky-Service Pago Jet	95602	
D-MHGD	Ultraleichtverbund Bi 90	21231	
D-MHGE	Fresh Breeze 122 AL 2F	354	
D-MHGK	Ultraleichtverbund Bi 90	5323804244	
D-MHGP	Comco Ikarus Fox-C22	9102-3317	
D-MHGR	UL-F Jochum Eagle III	980506	
D-MHGS	T2	2	
D-MHGT	Comco Ikarus Fox-C22	9204-3405	
D-MHGW	Sky-Walker II	199	
D-MHHB	Comco Ikarus Fox-C22	9305-3507	
D-MHHD	Take Off Maximum Trike	095052	
D-MHHG	Kümmerle Mini-Fly-Set	1275/91-5	
D-MHHK	Light Aero Avid Flyer Speedwing	1229	
D-MHHO	Kiggen/Hieland Air Création GTE 582 S	7954557566	
D-MHHS	MKB Ranger M Trike	1835	
D-MHHT	Comco Ikarus Fox-C22	9301-3423	
D-MHHZ	Schönleber Trike Speed 14	010893	
D-MHIB	Kilb Air Création GTE 582 S Trike	AC 006	
D-MHIE	Büttner Crazyplane II	96	
D-MHII	Fisher FP-404 Super Koala	JE-02	
D-MHIN	Take Off Merlin Trike	23955	
D-MHIT	Ultraleichtverbund Bi 90	21237	
D-MHJE	NST Minimum	031205	
D-MHJF	Schönleber DS Speed KS 14 Trike	14010992	
D-MHJI	Warnke Skylight Trike	026	
D-MHJS	Ultraleichtverbund Bi 90	21054	
D-MHJV	Fresh Breeze 110 AL2F	92	
D-MHKA	Air Création GTE 582 S	5964559925	
D-MHKB	Dallach Sunrise IIA	021	
D-MHKE	Behlen Power-Trike	91024	
D-MHKF	Rans S-6 Coyote II	1292404	
D-MHKH	Sky-Walker II	216	
D-MHKJ	WDFL Sunwheel	005	
D-MHKK	Kümmerle Mini-Fly-Set Windfex II	9841	
D-MHKL	Kiggen/Hieland Air Création GTE 5	4954433120	
D-MHKM	Sky-Walker II	316	
D-MHKP	Air Création GTE 582 S	3984890749	
D-MHKS	Fair Fax Euro II Trike	012	
D-MHKV	Schönleber DS Speed KS 14 Trike TK	02/0893	
D-MHLA	FUL Graffiti Trike	170078	
D-MHLB	Fair Fax DR Trike	D014	
D-MHLC	Take Off Merlin Trike	10564	
D-MHLK	Fair Fax DR Trike	D027	
D-MHLL	Fair Fax DR Trike	D024	
D-MHLM	Behlen Trike	830037	
D-MHLR	Take Off Merlin Trike	26146	
D-MHLS	Behlen Power Trike II	96004	
D-MHLX	Take Off Merlin Trike	26957	
D-MHMA	UPM Cobra Raven Trike	900096	
D-MHMJ	Büttner Crazyplane IV	4	
D-MHMM	Sky-Walker II	249	
D-MHMS	Fair Fax DR Trike	D025	
D-MHNG	Comco Ikarus Fox-C22	9304-3500	
D-MHNP	FUL Graffiti Trike	005/0052	
D-MHNW	Seiffert Mini-Speed Trike	73	
D-MHOB	Dallach Sunrise II	017	
D-MHOF	WDFL Sunwheel	004	
D-MHOH	Take Off Maximum Trike	039110	
D-MHOR	Fresh Breeze 110 AL2F	49	
D-MHOS	NST Minimum	M301	
D-MHOT	Fair Fax DR Hazard 15M Trike	D020	
D-MHOW	Klüver Twin Racer SX 16 Trike	541008	
D-MHPA	Behlen Power-Trike	08/020	
D-MHPE	WDFL Sunwheel	006	
D-MHPF	Comco Ikarus Fox-C22	9104-3324	
D-MHRA	Solid Air Diamant Trike	006	
D-MHRB	Comco Ikarus Fox-C22	8512-FD36	
D-MHRF	Sky-Walker II	350	
	(Same c/n quoted for D-MDUS)		
D-MHRG	Fisher FP-202 Koala	St-004	
D-MHRL	UL Flugservice Bod Quasar II.TC	SW-WQT-0585/SW-TQD-0125	
D-MHRS	Schönleber DS Trike	16020692	
D-MHRT	Ultraleichtverbund Bi 90	21108	
D-MHRW	Ultraleichtverbund Bi 90	21099	
D-MHSB	ASO Viper Hazard Trike	VI 22027202	
D-MHSC	J-3 Kitten	01033	
D-MHSD	Behlen Trike	850026	
D-MHSH	Dallach Sunrise II	002	
D-MHSI	Ultraleichtverbund Bi 90	21287	
D-MHSK	Take Off Maximum Trike	T079191	
D-MHSO	Take Off Merlin 1100	27958	
D-MHSP	FUL Graffiti Trike	012/0073	
D-MHSS	Behlen Power-Trike II Hazard 15M	90025	
D-MHST	Behlen Power-Trike /Rotax 582	980012	
D-MHSV	Schönleber Trike Speed	14020993	
D-MHTC	Kiggen/Heiland Air Création GTE 582 S	9954559387	
D-MHTE	Kiggen/Heiland Air Création GTE 582 S	3964655068	
D-MHTG	MKB Enduro Trike	04/003/85	

Regn.	Type	C/n	Prev.Id.
D-MHTL	ASO Viper Trike	22034206	
D-MHUB	Fresh Breeze 122 AL 2F	112	
D-MHUE	Platzer Motte B-2	002	
D-MHUG	Scarma Libre II LO-120	002A	
D-MHUM	Sky-Service Pago Jet	94003	
D-MHUS	Platzer Kiebitz-B	037	
D-MHUU	Ultraleichtverbund Bi 90	21036	
D-MHVK	Fresh Breeze 110 AL2F	37	
D-MHVL	HFL Stratos 300	300-010K	
D-MHVV	Flight Team Spider	D 18	
D-MHWA	Albatros Milan	07085	
D-MHWE	Comco Ikarus Fox-C22	9202-3374	
D-MHWH	Comco Ikarus Fox-C22	9211-3448	
D-MHWK	Platzer Kiebitz-B2	040	
D-MHWL	Warnke Skylight Trike	027	
D-MHWS	Comco Ikarus Fox	043	
D-MHYF	Behlen Power-Trike	88041	
D-MHZH	Solid Air Twin Diamant Trike	T005	
D-MHZI	Pegasus Quasar II	6717	
D-MHZT	UPM Omega Trike	88006	
D-MIAA	Flight Team Spider	D 048	
D-MIAB	NST Minimum	M549	
D-MIAC	Comco Ikarus Fox-C22	9006-3281	
D-MIAD	Platzer Kiebitz-B9	143	
D-MIAE	Firebird Tri CX	288	
D-MIAL(2)	Flight Team Spider	51	
D-MIAM	Light Aero Avid Flyer	1011	
D-MIAN	Comco Ikarus Fox D	022	
D-MIAR	Take Off Maximum Trike	070591	
D-MIAS	Ultra-Vector H	1424	
D-MIAU	Platzer Kiebitz-B	072	
D-MIAW	Krampen Ikarus S	63	
D-MIBA	Kümmerle Mini-Fly-Set	127591-5	
D-MIBC	Comco Ikarus Fox-C22	9009-3282	
D-MIBE	Fair Fax Trike Euro III	040	
D-MIBI	Fresh Breeze 110 AL 2F	153	
D-MIBJ	Comco Ikarus Fox-C22	9301-3463	
D-MIBL	Air Création Buggy XP	unkn	
D-MICA	Comco Ikarus Fox-C22	8907-3216	
D-MICB	Comco Ikarus Fox-C22	8907-3217	
D-MICC	Dallach Sunrise II	022	
D-MICD	Comco Ikarus Fox-C22	8907-3220	
D-MICE	Comco Ikarus Fox-C22	8909-3219	
D-MICG	Comco Ikarus Fox-C22	9003-3221	
D-MICH	Schmidtler Enduro Trike	180485	
D-MICK	Comco Ikarus Sherpa I	8306-1026	
D-MICL	Comco Ikarus Fox-C22	9003-3225	
D-MICM	Comco Ikarus Fox-C22	9003-3226	
D-MICN	Comco Ikarus Fox-C22	9004-3227	
D-MIC0	Comco Ikarus Fox-C22	8908-3228	
D-MICP	Comco Ikarus Fox-C22	9005-3229	
D-MICQ	Comco Ikarus Fox-C22	9004-3230	
D-MICR	Comco Ikarus Fox-C22	9004-3231	
D-MICS	Comco Ikarus Fox-C2	9008-3232	
D-MICT	Comco Ikarus Fox-C22	9004-3233	
D-MICU	Comco Ikarus Fox-C22	9002-3234	
D-MICW	Comco Ikarus Fox-C22	9005-3235	
D-MICV	Comco Ikarus Fox D	8410-FD15	
D-MICX	Comco Ikarus Fox-C22	9103-3314	
D-MICZ	Comco Ikarus Fox-C22	9104-3313	
D-MIDC	Comco Ikarus Fox-C22	9009-3285	
D-MID0	Pioneer Flightstar	617	
D-MIEC	Comco Ikarus Fox-C22	9008-3283	
D-MIEF	Tandem Air Sunny Sport	21-91	
D-MIEG	UPM Cobra Trike	900090	
D-MIEH	Comco Ikarus Fox-C22	9209-3424	
D-MIEK	ASO Viper Hazard 15 Trike	041302	
D-MIES	Behlen Power-Trike	90014	
D-MIEZ	Scheibe Uli 1	5201	
D-MIFC	Comco Ikarus Fox-C22	9009-3284	
D-MIFD	Behlen Power-Trike Focus 20	89012	
D-MIFL	Ultraleichtverbund Bi 90	B21154	
D-MIFT	Comco Ikarus Fox-C22	8902-3188	
D-MIFU	Schmidtler Enduro Trike	02-019	
D-MIGH	Ultraleichtverbund Bi 90	941	

Regn.	Type	C/n	Prev.Id.
D-MIGT	Eipper Quicksilver GT	1032	
D-MIHA	Comco Ikarus Fox-C22	9302-3491	
D-MIHB	Comco Ikarus Fox-C22	8807-3138	
D-MIHC	Comco Ikarus Fox-C22	9009-3286	
D-MIHG	Behlen Power Trike II	615205	
D-MIHI	Kümmerle Mini-Fly-Set	67886-4	
D-MIHK	Comco Ikarus Sherpa I	8308-1038	
D-MIHV	Fresh Breeze 122 AL 2F	382	
D-MIHY	Platzer Motte B-3	43	
D-MIII	Comco Ikarus Fox-C22	8908-3215	
D-MIIW	NST Minimum	M572/92	
D-MIJF	FUL Graffiti Trike	043/0149	
D-MIJI	NST Minimum	M555	
D-MIJR	Take Off Merlin Trike	24155	
D-MIJT	NST Minimum Santana	M532	
D-MIKC	Comco Ikarus Fox-C22	9010-3287	
D-MIKE	Ultraleichtverbund Bi 90	21227	
D-MIKG	Take Off Maximum Trike	001049	
D-MIKI	Schmidtler Enduro Trike	02-013	
D-MIKL	Platzer Motte B2	60	
D-MIKR	Behlen Trike	84012	
D-MIKS	Ultraleichtverbund Bi 90	530380431167	
D-MIKY	MKB Ranger M	0100284	
D-MILA(2)	Pago Jet M4	RB 97000	
D-MILC	Comco Ikarus Fox-C22	9010-3288	
D-MILD	Aviasud Mistral BRD	088	
D-MILE	Scheibe Uli 1	5226	
D-MILF	Schönleber Trike	010794	
D-MILJ	Behlen Power-Trike II	90024	
D-MILM	Comco Ikarus Fox-C22	9005-3265	
D-MILO	Dallach Sunrise IIB	031	
D-MILT	Seiffert Mini-Speed Trike	001	
D-MILU	Ultraleichtverbund Bi 90	21151	
D-MILZ	Klüver Racer SX 12 Trike	652907	
D-MIMB	Comco Ikarus Fox-C22	9103-3321	
D-MIMC	Comco Ikarus Fox-C22	9009-3289	
D-MIMI	Comco Ikarus Fox-C22	9209-3441	
D-MIMM	Comco Ikarus Fox-C22	9208-3416	
D-MIMN	Ultraleichtverbund Bi 90	21074	
D-MINE	Fresh Breeze 110 AL2A	352	
D-MING	Platzer Motte-B2	013	
D-MINI	Scheibe Uli 1	5209	
D-MINK	NST Minimum	M447	
D-MINU	HFL Stratos 300	300-004	
D-MINZ	Scheibe UL-1 Coach	3202	
D-MIOA	Comco Ikarus Fox-C22	9101-3302	
D-MIOC	Comco Ikarus Fox-C22	9009-3290	
D-MIOD	Comco Ikarus Fox D	8806-FD43	
D-MIOG	Fresh Breeze 110 AL 2F	332	
D-MIOO	Light Aero Avid Flyer D	1230	
D-MIPC	Comco Ikarus Fox-C22	9012-3303	
D-MIPS	Light Aero Avid Flyer C	943	
D-MIPV	Comco Ikarus Fox-C22	9106-3362	
D-MIPW	Schmidtler Enduro Trike	02-016	
D-MIQC	Comco Ikarus Fox-C22	9101-3304	
D-MIRB	Comco Ikarus Fox-C22	9106-3305	
D-MIRC	Albatros 52	129	
D-MIRI	Behlen Power-Trike	97003	
D-MIRJ	Comco Fox	045	
D-MIRT	Schönleber DS Trike	030492	
D-MISA	Schmidtler Ranger M	18/37	
D-MISC	Comco Ikarus Fox-C22	9102-3306	
D-MISE	Light Aero Avid Flyer D	1231	
D-MISI	Comco Ikarus Fox-C22	8612-3054	
D-MISL	Comco Ikarus Sherpa I	8305-1017	
D-MIST	Comco Ikarus Fox	008	
D-MITB	Seiffert Mini II	4392	
D-MITC	Comco Ikarus Fox-C22	9102-3307	
D-MITF	Rans S-12 Airaile	0192168	
D-MITG	Comco Ikarus Fox-C22	9207-3388	
D-MITI	NST Minimum	unkn	
D-MITL	Schönleber DS Trike	020794	
D-MITT	Fresh Breeze 110 AL 2F	160	
D-MITV	Platzer Kiebitz B6-450	12	
D-MIUB	Ultraleichtverbund Bi 90	B21155	

Regn.	Type	C/n	Prev.Id.
D-MIUC	Comco Ikarus Fox-C22	9102-3308	
D-MIUS	Pioneer Flightstar	539	
D-MIVC	Comco Ikarus Fox-C22	9104-3309	
D-MIVK	Behlen Power-Trike Vampir II	85-027	
D-MIWC	Comco Ikarus Fox-C22	9105-3310	
D-MIWW	Flight Team Spider	D050	
D-MIWW	Flight Team Spider	D043	
D-MIXC	Comco Ikarus Fox-C22	9102-3311	
D-MIZA	Pioneer Flightstar	377	
D-MIZC	Comco Ikarus Fox-C22	9102-3312	
D-MIZE	MKB Ranger M Trike	01/009/86	
D-MIZG	NST Minimum Pamir	443	
D-MIZP	Comco Ikarus Fox-C22	9009-3316	
D-MIZZ	Flight Team Spider	D044	
D-MJAE	Klüver Twin Racer Quartz SX 16	228004	
D-MJAG(2)	Funk FK-9	007	
D-MJAI	Kümmerle Mini-Fly-Set	1305916	
D-MJAL	Fair Fax DR Trike	D016	
D-MJAM	Platzer Kiebitz-B6	20	
D-MJAN	Behlen Power-Trike II	90027	
D-MJAS	Ultraleichtverbund Bi 90	736	
D-MJAT	TVS 700 Tandem Air Sunny	991	
D-MJAU	Light Aero Avid Flyer	491	
D-MJBH	NST Minimum Saphir 17	976	
D-MJBL	J.Blank Trike (Homebuilt)	unkn	
D-MJBU	Comco Ikarus Fox-C22	9002-3253	
D-MJCE	Behlen Power-Trike /Rotax 582	980019	
D-MJCT	Ultraleichtverbund Bi 90	1055508906	
D-MJDO	Schmidtler Ranger M Trike	1812	
D-MJEH	Take Off Maximum Trike	T057061	
D-MJET	TVS 700 Tandem Air Sunny	006	
D-MJEW	Flight Team Spider Trike	D037	
D-MJFC	UPM Cobra BF 52UL Trike	930123	
D-MJFE	Sky Walker	240	
D-MJFO	Take Off Maximum Trike	107013	
D-MJHB	Behlen Power-Trike II	90022	
D-MJHH	Moskito Ib	012	PH-2D5
D-MJHM	Take Off Maximum Trike	063071	
D-MJHS	Platzer Kiebitz-B2	068	
D-MJIY	Dallach Sunrise II	006	
D-MJJA	TVS 700 Tandem Air Sunny	004	
D-MJJC	Behlen Power-Trike	960002	
D-MJJJ	Solid Air Twin Diamant	7	
D-MJJY	TVS 700 Tandem Air Sunny	003	
D-MJJZ	TVS 700 Tandem Air Sunny	002	
D-MJKB	Fair Fax AH Euro III Trike	32	
D-MJKE	Büttner Crazyplane III	2	
D-MJKG	Fresh Breeze 110 AL2F	98	
D-MJKH	Comco Ikarus Fox-C22	9006-3271	
D-MJKI	UPM Funplane	870.023	
D-MJKO	Behlen Power Trike II	89038	
D-MJKP	Behlen Power-Trike /Rotax 582	97002	
D-MJKW	Fair Fax DR Trike	D005	
D-MJLC	Solid Air Diamant 55dB(A) Trike	011	
D-MJLP	J-3 Kitten	12-8-88	
D-MJLS	Kiggen/Heiland Air Création GTE 582 S	6954556835	
D-MJMA	Skywalker 1+1	26127	
D-MJMB	Behlen Power-Trike	91027	
D-MJMJ	UPM Cobra BF 52UL Trike	940128	
D-MJMK	Fresh Breeze 110 AL 2F	332	
D-MJMO	UPM Cobra Trike	900094	
D-MJNA	ARCO Spacer L	463	
D-MJND	Drachenstudio Piccolo II	089-94/04	
D-MJNN	Kilb Air Création GTE 5	AC 009	
D-MJOA	Behlen Power-Trike	87019	
D-MJOB	Behlen Power-Trike	92002	
D-MJOE	NST Minimum Pamir	503	
D-MJOH	Klüver Twin Racer SX 16 Trike	449007	
D-MJPA	NST Minimum	M542	
D-MJPC	Fresh Breeze 110 AL 2F	222	
D-MJPG(2)	Rans S-12 Airaile	1091138	
D-MJPK	Light Aero Avid Flyer	868	
D-MJPW	Seiffert Mini-Speed Trike	7	
D-MJRB	Fresh Breeze 110 AL 2F	951105	
D-MJRN	Fresh Breeze 110 AL 2F	951103	

Regn.	Type	C/n	Prev.Id.
D-MJRR	Mantel Mono-Dragster	M508	
D-MJSH	Fisher FP-202 Koala	2302	
D-MJSJ	FUL Graffiti Trike	015/0075	
D-MJSL	Air Création XP GT 582 ES	17/511994	
D-MJSN	Platzer Kiebitz-B6	034	
D-MJSS	Platzer Motte D	01	
D-MJST	Tandem Air Sunny Sport	032-92	
D-MJSW	Comco Ikarus Fox-C22	9010-3301	
D-MJTR	UPM Funplane	950050	
D-MJUA	Steinbach Austro-Trike	101	
D-MJUG	LO-120	003A	
D-MJUH	Behlen Power-Trike /Rotax 582	98009	
D-MJUK	Take Off Maximum Trike	47041	
D-MJUN	Junkers Profly JUL Trike	094/003	
D-MJUR	Comco Ikarus Fox-C22	910 .-3326	
D-MJUT	NST Minimum	M547	
D-MJUV	Junkers Profly JUL Trike	58294003	
D-MJVS	J.van Stappen (Homebuilt)	SC 89746	
D-MJWB	HFL HFL Stratos IIe	007	
D-MJWD	Ultraleichtverbund Bi 90	6118903	
D-MJWS	NST Minimum	M537	
	(Also listed, probably in error, as a UPM Funplane with this c/n)		
D-MJWW	Flight Team Spider Trike	D028	
D-MJYY	Sky Walker 1+1	26129	
D-MKAA	Ultraleichtverbund Bi 90	21064	
D-MKAC	Air Création SX GT 582ES Quartz SX 16	AC 001	
D-MKAE(2)	Sky Walker II	193	
D-MKAF	Take Off Maximum Trike	87022	
D-MKAH	Büttner Crazyplane III	106	
D-MKAP	Drachenstudio Royal Trike	180997	
D-MKAS	Behlen Power-Trike	91033	
D-MKBA	Behlen Power-Trike /Rotax 582	980018	
D-MKBB	Platzer Kiebitz-B6	154	
D-MKBE	Comco Ikarus Sherpa I	8306-1028	
D-MKBG	Ultraleichtverbund Bi 90	701	
D-MKBK	HFL Stratos 300	300-012K	
D-MKBM	Behlen Power-Trike II	95005	
D-MKBR	NST Minimum	M531	
D-MKCH	Sky-Walker II	383	
D-MKCM	Point Avn/Albatros AN-22	01	
D-MKDI	Behlen Power-Trike II	90021	
D-MKDL	NST Minimum	C2483	
D-MKDM	Behlen Power-Trike	91028	
D-MKEA	Behlen Power-Trike	89042	
D-MKEH	UPM Funplane	870026	
D-MKEJ	Behlen Power-Trike	90009	
D-MKER	Fisher FP-202 Koala	ST-005	
D-MKES	Tandem Air Sunny Sport	26-91	
D-MKFA	Ultraleichtverbund Bi 90	6613917738	
D-MKFH	Take Off Maximum Karat 13 Trike	081111	
D-MKFS	Fresh Breeze 122 AL 2F	349	
D-MKFW	Behlen Power-Trike	94002	
D-MKGA(2)	Ultraleichtverband 90	331-7740	
D-MKGB	Ultraleichtverbund Bi 90	908	
D-MKGC	Ultraleichtverbund Bi 90	3950478	
D-MKGH	Kilb Air Création GTE 5	AC 007	
D-MKGI	Comco Ikarus Fox II Doppel	8607-3025	
D-MKGR	Comco Ikarus Fox-C22	9205-3432	
D-MKHA	Flight Team Spider	D046	
D-MKHB	Behlen Power-Trike	89015	
D-MKHE	Comco Ikarus Fox-C22	9102-3318	
D-MKHG	Behlen Power-Trike	92015	
D-MKHH	NST Minimum	M590	
D-MKHK	HFL Stratos 300	300-018K	
D-MKHL	Comco Ikarus Fox-C22	8706-3071	
D-MKHM	Sky-Walker II	329	
D-MKHP	Tandem Air Sunny	007	
D-MKHR	Behlen Power-Trike /Rotax 582	86013	
D-MKHS(2)	Rans S-6 Coyote II	0192263	
D-MKHT	Schmidtler Enduro Trike	02-012	
D-MKHW	Behlen Power-Trike	84229	
D-MKID	Ultraleichtverbund Bi 90	79282054016042	
D-MKIK	Platzer Kiebitz-B	119	
D-MKIS	Ultraleichtverbund Bi 90	9604171161	
D-MKIT	Denney Kitfox II	1839	

Regn.	Type	C/n	Prev.Id.
D-MKJA	Fresh Breeze 110 AL 2F	51	
D-MKJB	Platzer Kiebitz-B	079	
D-MKJC	Fresh Breeze 110 AL 2F	66	
D-MKJD	Fresh Breeze 110 AL 2F	65	
D-MKJE	Fresh Breeze 110 AL 2F	64	
D-MKJF	Fresh Breeze 110 AL 2F	195	
D-MKJG	Fresh Breeze 110 AL 2F	56	
D-MKJH	Fresh Breeze 110 AL 2F	203	
D-MKKC	Kilb Air Création GTE 582 S Trike	AC 008	
D-MKKH	Tandem Air Sunny Sport	48.93	
D-MKKO	Take Off Merlin Trike	24705	
D-MKKW	Behlen Ladas M Trike	M041120200	
D-MKLA	Klüver Kaiman Profil 17 Trike	269916703	
D-MKLC	Klüver Bison Trike	917703	
D-MKLE	Solid Air Diamant Trike	9	
D-MKLI	ASO Viper Hazard 13 Trike	22047307	
D-MKLK	Light Aero Avid Flyer D	1271D	
D-MKLN	Comco Ikarus Fox-C22	9007-3278	
D-MKLS	Take Off Maximum Trike	093052	
D-MKLV	Ultralight Flight Phantom	312	
D-MKME	UL-F Jochum Eagle III	970502	
	(Possibly ex D-MAWE, same c/n quoted)		
D-MKMG	Fresh Breeze 110 AL 2F	211	
D-MKMI	Comco Ikarus Fox D	8410-FD16	
D-MKMS	Platzer Kiebitz B	026	
D-MKNE	Kümmerle Mini-Fly-Set	1265/91-4	
D-MKNU	Light Aero Avid Flyer C	938	
D-MKOA	Fisher FP-202 Koala	001	
D-MKOB	Take Off Maximum Chronos 14	101072	
D-MKOC	Comco Ikarus Fox-C22	9304-3467	
D-MKOF	Comco Ikarus Fox-C22	9308-3477	
D-MKOG	Comco Ikarus Fox-C22	9307-3476	
D-MKOI	Comco Ikarus Fox-C22	9308-3474	
D-MKOK	Comco Ikarus Fox-C22	9307-3473	
D-MKOL	Platzer Kiebitz-B2	076	
D-MKOM	Comco Ikarus Fox-C22	8909-3240	
D-MKOO	Comco Ikarus Fox-C22	9307-3472	
D-MKOP	Comco Ikarus Fox-C22	9303-3471	
D-MKOQ	Comco Ikarus Fox-C22	9307-3470	
D-MKOS	Comco Ikarus Fox-C22	9304-3469	
D-MKOX	Air Création GTE 582 S	7974656039	
D-MKPB	Behlen Power-Trike	85010	
D-MKPC	UPM Cobra BF 52UL Trike	950135	
D-MKPF	Eipper Quicksilver	4603	
D-MKPG	Flight Team Spider Trike	D027	
D-MKPI	Flight Team Spider Trike	D035	
D-MKPP	Comco Ikarus Fox-C22	9305-3421	
D-MKPT	Flight Team Spider Trike	D034	
D-MKPW	Backes Mini-Speed Trike (Homebuilt)	15/94	
D-MKRA	Comco Ikarus Fox-C22	9306-3460	
D-MKRB(1)	Comco Ikarus Fox-C22	9305-3459	
D-MKRB(2)	Behlen Power-Trike /Rotax 582	97012	
D-MKRC	Comco Ikarus Fox-C22	9304-3458	
D-MKRD	Comco Ikarus Fox-C22	9308-3457	
D-MKRE	Comco Ikarus Fox-C22	9305-3456	
D-MKRF	Comco Ikarus Fox-C22	9305-3455	
D-MKRG	Comco Ikarus Fox-C22	9305-3454	
D-MKRH	Comco Ikarus Fox-C22	9305-3453	
D-MKRI	Comco Ikarus Fox-C22	9210-3452	
D-MKRJ	Comco Ikarus Fox-C22	9303-3451	
D-MKRK	Comco Ikarus Fox-C22	9304-3450	
D-MKRL	Comco Ikarus Fox-C22	9303-3449	
D-MKRM	Comco Ikarus Fox-C22	9303-3497	
D-MKRN	Comco Ikarus Fox-C22	9210-3447	
D-MKRP	Comco Ikarus Fox-C22	9210-3445	
D-MKRQ	Comco Ikarus Fox-C22	9210-3444	
D-MKRR	Comco Ikarus Fox-C22	9209-3443	
D-MKRS	Comco Ikarus Fox-C22	9209-3442	
D-MKRT	Ultraleichtverbund Bi 90	21204	
D-MKRU	Comco Ikarus Fox D	8810-FD44	
D-MKRW	Sky-Walker II	252	
D-MKSA	Klüver Bison	16807002	
D-MKSE	Take Off Merlin 1100	28568	
D-MKSM	Comco Ikarus Fox-C22	9207-3426	
D-MKST	ASO Viper Trike	VIII 12063408	
D-MKTG	Fresh Breeze 122 AL 2F	400	
D-MKTM	Comco Ikarus Fox-C22	9107-3346	
D-MKTO	NST Minimum	M331	
D-MKTS	Fresh Breeze 110 AL 2F	195	
D-MKTZ	MKB Enduro Trike	08/85	
D-MKUE	NST Minimum	M194	
D-MKUK	Tandem Air Sunny Targa	TA-015	
D-MKUL	Ultraleichtverbund Bi 90	601	
D-MKUM	Dallach Sunrise IIA	031	
D-MKUR	Schönleber Trike Speed 14	01/1293	
D-MKUS	Flight Team Spider Hazard 15 Trike	D025	
D-MKWM	FUL Graffiti Trike	024/0081	
D-MKWP	Solid Air Twin Diamant	T006	
D-MKWR	Flight Team Spider	D020	
D-MKWS	Comco Ikarus Fox-C22	9008-3279	
D-MLAA	Klüver Racer SX 12 Trike	624009	
D-MLAB	Rans S-12 Airaile (Believed w/o 30.5.98)	0892256	
D-MLAD	Platzer Kiebitz-B	059	
D-MLAU	NST Minimum	M283	
D-MLBB	ASO-Storch 503	11002206	
D-MLBC	Rans S-6 Coyote II	0791209	
D-MLBH	Comco Ikarus Fox-C22	9208-3461	
D-MLBK	Comco Ikarus Fox-C22	9311-3522	
D-MLCB	Take Off Merlin Trike	22744	
D-MLCH	Sky-Walker II	395	
D-MLDK	NST Minimum	M544	
D-MLEA	ASO Viper Hazard 15	13451	
D-MLEE	Rans S-6 Coyote II	0992351	
D-MLEF	Ultraleichtverbund Bi 90	4559418	
D-MLEI	Behlen Power Trike Vampir II	88018	
D-MLEK	Ultraleichtverbund Bi 90	21167	
D-MLES	Comco Ikarus Fox-C22	9204-3391	
D-MLEV	Sky-Walker 1 + 1	26139	
D-MLFE	Ultraleichtverbund Bi 90	703	
D-MLFI	Ultraleichtverbund Bi 90	21048	
D-MLFL	Dallach Sunrise IIA	039	
D-MLGG	Schmidtler Ranger M	18-25	
D-MLHJ	Drachenstudio Royal Trike	05-9506	
D-MLHM	UPM Cobra BF 52UL Raven	930121	
D-MLIA	Behlen Power-Trike II	95006	
D-MLII	Ultraleichtverbund Bi 90	41055519681	
D-MLIM	Fresh Breeze 110 AL2F	69	
D-MLIN	Tandem Air Sunny Sport	10-91	
D-MLIP	Comco Ikarus Fox-C22	9105-3336	
D-MLIS	Klüver Bison II Quartz SX 16	567801	
D-MLIU	NST Minimum	M313	
D-MLIY	Platzer Kiebitz-B	153	
D-MLIZ	Comco Ikarus Fox-C22	9306-3510	
D-MLJA	Klüver Bison	982704	
D-MLJP	Kümmerle Mini-Fly-Set	1274/91-5	
D-MLKF	Air Création Mild GT 582 ES	2	
D-MLKH	Comco Ikarus Sherpa II Doppel	8501-1087	
D-MLKK	Klüver Racer SX 12	442904	
D-MLKS	Comco Ikarus Fox-C22	9202-3390	
D-MLKW	Comco Ikarus Fox-C22	9104-3333	
D-MLLA	Tandem Air Sunny Sport	035-92	
D-MLLB	Take Off Maximum	027040	
D-MLLC(1)	Tandem Air Sunny Sport	032-92	
D-MLLC(2)	Behlen Power Trike Vampir II	M877829	
D-MLLM	Büttner Crazyplane IV	2	
D-MLMK	Schönleber DS Speed 14	9010891	
D-MLML	Enduro Trike	1004	
D-MLMM	Eipper Quicksilver GT	1250	
D-MLMT	Sky-Walker 1+1	26123	
D-MLOE	Platzer Kiebitz-B	094	
D-MLOP	UPM Funplane Trike	870019	
D-MLOR	Kümmerle Mini-Fly-Set	1306/91-6	
D-MLOT	Aviasud Mistral 53	011	
D-MLOZ	Fresh Breeze 110 AL 2F	333	
D-MLPW	Schönleber Trike Speed KS 14	TK 01/0395	
D-MLPX	Fresh Breeze 110 AL 2F	112	
D-MLRG	Pago Jet M4	960503	
D-MLRL	NST Minimum Zephir CX	M436	
D-MLSD	Comco Ikarus Fox-C22	9106-3340	
D-MLSE	Comco Ikarus Fox-C22	9107-3343	

Regn.	Type	C/n	Prev.Id.	Regn.	Type	C/n	Prev.Id.
D-MLSJ	Air Création GTE 582 S	2974656186		D-MMKU	Fresh Breeze 110 AL 2F	61	
D-MLST	NST Minimum Zephir	M528		D-MMLA	Comco Ikarus Fox-C22	9209-3430	
D-MLSW	UPM Cobra Raven Trike	90007		D-MMLB	UPM Cobra BF 52 UL Trike	930122	
D-MLSZ	Comco Ikarus Fox-C22	9010-3294		D-MMLH	Flight Team Spider Trike	D014	
D-MLTG	Comco Ikarus Fox-C22	9208-3387		D-MMLI	Behlen Power-Trike /Rotax 582	980025	
D-MLTI	Kümmerle Mini-Fly-Set	734 85-3		D-MMLL	Sky-Walker II	274	
D-MLTR	Comco Ikarus Fox-C22	9206-3397		D-MMLO	Comco Ikarus Fox-C22	9205-3403	
D-MLTU	FUL Graffiti Trike	023/0083		D-MMLU	Take Off Maximum	097062	
D-MLUA	Platzer Kiebitz-B	049		D-MMMB	Albatros 64	304	
D-MLUI	Behlen Power-Trike	92/014		D-MMMD	Ultraleichtverbund Bi 90	702	
D-MLUP	Behlen Ladas M Trike	04-001-82		D-MMMI	Comco Ikarus Fox-C22	9306-3506	
D-MLUW	Fresh Breeze 110 AL2F	77		D-MMMM	T2	5	
D-MLUX	Comco Ikarus Fox-C22	9308-3509			*(Regn worn by a WDFL Fascination, Friedrichshafen 4.99)*		
D-MLVA	Fresh Breeze 122 AL 2F	242		D-MMMT	Behlen Power-Trike II	95008	
D-MLVE	Sky-Walker II	310		D-MMMW	Kiebitx-B-450	128	
D-MLVT	Tandem Air Sunny Sport	11-91		D-MMND	Fresh Breeze 122 AL 2F	233	
D-MLWB	ASO Viper Trike	3690		D-MMNS	Comco Ikarus Fox-C22	8812-3184	
D-MLWM	NST Minimum	M563		D-MMOC	Ultraleichtverbund Bi 90	21079	
D-MLWS	Krampen Ikarus S	52		D-MMPA	Fresh Breeze 110 AL 2F	951104	
D-MLZV	Solid Air Twin Diamant Trike	T004		D-MMPE	NST Minimum	M441	
D-MMAA	Moskito	005		D-MMPG	Fresh Breeze 110 AL 2F	54	
D-MMAB	Kümmerle Mini-Fly-Set	1276/91-5		D-MMPK	ASO Viper Trike	VIII 12069502	
D-MMAG	Sky-Walker II	357		D-MMPL	Sky-Walker II	267	
D-MMAI	Warnke Puma Sprint	D002		D-MMPR	NST Schwarze-Trike	010	
D-MMAJ	Sky-Service Pago Jet	941001		D-MMPS	Pegasus Quantum 15	6738	
D-MMAL	Ultraleichtverbund Bi 90	21205		D-MMRA	Ultraleichtverbund Bi 90	4017031	
D-MMAN	Fresh Breeze 110 AL 2F	234		D-MMRB(1)	Ultralight Flight Phantom	403	
D-MMAR	Behlen Power Trike II	97005		D-MMRB(2)	NST Minimum	M556	
D-MMAS	Solid-Air Diamant	013		D-MMRH	Ultraleichtverbund Bi 90	21254	
D-MMAT	Kümmerle Mini-Fly-Set	1278/91-5		D-MMRL	Behlen Power-Trike /Rotax 582	91026	
D-MMAU	Solid Air Twin Diamant Hazard	T008		D-MMRP	Kümmerle Mini-Fly-Set	67686-4	
D-MMAW	Kümmerle Mini-Fly-Set	1285/91-5		D-MMRR	Enduro Lotus/Air Création XP	02/003	
D-MMAX	Fresh Breeze 110 AL 2F	43		D-MMRS	Fresh Breeze 122 AL 2F	391	
D-MMAY	Pegasus Quantum Super Sport	7444		D-MMSB	Rans S-12 Airaile	1292359	
D-MMBB	Ultraleichtverbund Bi 90	977		D-MMSG	Comco Ikarus Fox-C22	9110-3361	
D-MMBJ	NST Minimum	M580		D-MMSL	Take Off Merlin Trike	G20363	
D-MMBN	Behlen Power Trike Vampir II	86017		D-MMSM(1)	Moskito 1b	019	
D-MMBR	Pegasus Quantum 15	6683		D-MMSM(2)	NST Minimum	M462	
D-MMBT	Behlen Power Trike II	97001		D-MMSP	Großklaus Silent Racer	3	
D-MMBV	ASO Viper Hazard 15	18991		D-MMSR	NST Minimum	M517	
D-MMBW	Seiffert Mini II	F020890		D-MMST	Klüver Bison	0168	
D-MMCI	Fisher FP-202 Koala	003		D-MMSU	Platzer Kiebitz-B	111	
D-MMCO	FUL Graffiti Trike	032/0098		D-MMSW	Kümmerle Mini-Fly-Set	67786-4	
D-MMDH(2)	Funk FK-9	010		D-MMSY	ASO Viper Trike	VIII 12068501	
D-MMDR	Schmidtler Enduro Trike	02-006		D-MMTC	Comco Ikarus Fox-C22	9205-3396	
D-MMDW	Funk FK-9	011		D-MMTI	Fresh Breeze 110 AL2F	102	
D-MMFK	Funk FK-9	012		D-MMTK	Behlen Trike Vampir II 18M	9002A785	
D-MMGB	Comco Ikarus Fox-C22	9208-3436		D-MMTT	Pegasus Quasar II	6738	
D-MMGD	ASO Viper Trike	4590		D-MMTW(1)	Comco Ikarus Sherpa II Doppel	8505-1099	
D-MMGH	Platzer Kiebitz-B9-450	125		D-MMTW(2)	Fresh Breeze 110 AL 2F	159	
D-MMGM	Take Off Maximum	17099		D-MMUM	NST Minimum	M508	
D-MMGR	Fresh Breeze 110 AL2F	31		D-MMUR	Fresh Breeze 110 AL 2F	338	
D-MMGZ	NST Minimum	M464		D-MMUW	NST Minimum	M554	
D-MMHB	Behlen Power-Trike	87001		D-MMVB	Comco Ikarus Fox-C22	8808-3149	
D-MMHE	Fresh Breeze 110 AL 2F	71		D-MMWA	Dallach Sunrise II	034	
D-MMHF	Denney Kitfox	1841		D-MMWB	ASO Viper Trike	12061405	
D-MMHH	Comco Ikarus Fox-C22	8905-3200		D-MMWC	NST Minimum	M560	
D-MMHI	Comco Ikarus Fox D	8410-FD17		D-MMWD	Funk FK-9	009	
D-MMHK	Behlen Trike	85024		D-MMWE	ASO Viper Trike	12066408	
D-MMHM	Schönleber Trike 40kw	TK 02/0198		D-MMWG	UL-F Jochum Eagle III	970804	
D-MMHZ	Behlen Trike	83033		D-MMWL	Fresh Breeze 110 AL 2F	443	
D-MMIB	NST Minimum	M545		D-MMWN	Take Off Merlin Karat 13	20993	
D-MMIG	Tandem Air Sunny Sport	24.91		D-MMWS	Fresh Breeze 110 AL 2F	76	
D-MMII	Klüver Bison	646802		D-MMWW(1)	Platzer Kiebitz-B2	105	
D-MMIK	Bobcat	146 EB		D-MMWW(2)	Ultraleichtverbund Bi 90	21238	
D-MMIL	Behlen Power Trike Vampir II	89016		D-MMYY	Schmidtler Enduro Trike	02-011	
D-MMIS	Behlen Power Trike Vampir II	89011		D-MMYZ	Kiggen/Heiland Air Création GTE 582 S	7954557567	
D-MMIX	Light Aero Avid Flyer C	1104		D-MMZY	Kiggen/Heiland Air Création GTE 582 S	9954557782	
D-MMJA	ASO Viper Trike	VIII 12067501		D-MMZZ	Kiggen/Heiland Air Création GTE 582 S	7954557571	
D-MMJS	FUL Graffiti Trike	025/0091		D-MNAA	Rans S-6 Coyote II	0693514	
D-MMJT	Sky-Service Pago Jet M4	94002		D-MNAB	Rans S-6ES Coyote II	0391168	
D-MMJV	FUL Graffiti Trike	026/0092		D-MNAC	Rans S-6 Coyote II	0393460	
D-MMKB	MKB Ranger	028841		D-MNAD	Comco Ikarus Fox-C22	9309-3530	
D-MMKG	MKB Ranger M	01/005/85		D-MNAF	Comco Ikarus Fox-C22	9310-3532	
D-MMKT	Flight Team Spider Trike	D040		D-MNAG	Comco Ikarus Fox-C22	93. .-3535	

Regn.	Type	C/n	Prev.id.
D-MNAH	Comco Ikarus Fox-C22	93 . .-3537	
D-MNAI	Klüver Bison Profil 19	557801	
D-MNAJ (1)	Comco Ikarus Fox-C22	9101-3299/3538	
D-MNAJ (2)	Fisher FP-202 Koala	HO.001.1	
D-MNAK(2)	Rans S-6 Coyote II	0596990	
D-MNAL	Comco Ikarus C-42 Cyclone	9807-6107	
D-MNAM	Behlen Power-Trike	84009	
D-MNAO	Comco Ikarus Fox-C22	9107-3365	
D-MNAP	Light Aero Avid Flyer IV	1273D	
D-MNAQ	Rans S-6 Coyote II	0192261	OO-A52 / 59-MO
D-MNAR	Rans S-6 Coyote II	0992352	
D-MNAS	Aviasud Mistral BRD	191	
D-MNAT	Aviasud Mistral BRD	195	
	(Same c/n given for OO-C22, presumably sold to Belgium?)		
D-MNAU	Rans S-6 Coyote II	0593493	
D-MNAV	Rans S-6 Coyote II	0393464	
D-MNAW	Platzer Kiebitz-B	148	
D-MNAX	Fisher FP-404 Classic	4169	
D-MNAY	Albatros	306	
D-MNAZ	Albatros	305	
D-MNBA(2)	Remos Gemini Ultra	023	
D-MNBC	Funk FK-9	024	
D-MNBD	Klüver Bison	202708	
D-MNBE	Tandem Air Sunny Targa	TA-017	
D-MNBG	Comco Ikarus Fox-C22	9310-3541	
D-MNBH	Scheibe Uli 1	5223	
D-MNBI	Rans S-12 Airaile	1292356	
	(Also registered as 68-GH in France)		
D-MNBJ	Rans S-6 Coyote II	0693515	
D-MNBK	Rans S-6 Coyote II	0593508	
D-MNBL	Comco Ikarus Fox-C22	940 .-3546	
D-MNBM(2)	WDFL Fascination	015	
D-MNBN	Rans S-12 Airaile	1092299	
D-MNBO	Klüver Kaiman Trike	945703	
D-MNBP	Bek ME.109R Replica	003	
D-MNBQ	Tandem Air Sunny Targa	TA-003	
D-MNBT	Comco Ikarus Fox-C22	9208-3434	
D-MNBU	Comco Ikarus Fox-C22	9409-3597	
D-MNBV	Murphy Renegade	530	
D-MNBW	WDFL Sunwheel	028	
D-MNBX	Tandem Air Sunny	58.94	
D-MNBY	Light Aero Avid Flyer	499	
D-MNBZ	Platzer Kiebitz-B9	155	
D-MNCA	Comco Ikarus C-42 Cyclone	9702-6024	
D-MNCB	Tandem Air Sunny s.b.s.	11.94	
D-MNCC	Rans S-6 Coyote II	0994-676	
D-MNCD	Murphy Renegade	521	
D-MNCE	Jet Fox	D-0017	
D-MNCF	Jet Fox	D-0016	
D-MNCH	Comco Ikarus Fox-C22	8909-3219	
D-MNCJ	Fisher Super Koala	001	
D-MNCL	Light Aero Avid Flyer	947	
D-MNCM	Eipper Quicksilver MX	1133	D-MASB
D-MNCO	Light Aero Avid Flyer	1427	
D-MNDB	Funk FK-9	034	
D-MNDD	Comco Ikarus Fox-C22B	9408-3619	
D-MNDE	Comco Ikarus Fox-C22B	3686	
D-MNDG	Dyn'Aero MCR-01 Banbi	73	
D-MNDM	Comco Ikarus C-42 Cyclone	9803-6085	
D-MNDP	Comco Ikarus C-42 Cyclone	9809-6122	
D-MNDR	Comco Ikarus Fox-C22B	9509-3671	
D-MNDS	Rans S-12 Airaile	1292347	
D-MNDT	Comco Ikarus Fox-C22	9206-3410	
D-MNEA	Fisher FP-404 Classic	4128	
D-MNEB	Light Aero Avid Flyer	975	
D-MNEC	Comco Ikarus Fox-C22	9502-3653	
D-MNED	Murphy Renegade II	409	
D-MNEE	ASO-Storch	11015506	
D-MNEF	Comco Ikarus C-42 Cyclone	9806-6104	
D-MNEH	Rans S-6 Coyote II	0293449	
D-MNEK	Comco Ikarus Fox-C22	9201-3360	
D-MNEL	Behlen Power-Trike	86022	
D-MNEP	Airbike	002	
D-MNER	Scheibe SF-40B	3105	

Regn.	Type	C/n	Prev.id.
D-MNES	Scout	D 012-84	
D-MNEV	Evektor EV.97 Eurostar	98 01 01	
D-MNEW	Schönleber DS Lotus KS 16	010790	
D-MNEZ	III Sky Arrow 450TG	058	
D-MNFB	Comco Ikarus C-42 Cyclone	9901-6105	
D-MNFC	Comco Ikarus Fox-C22C	9807-3740	
D-MNFH	Sky-Service Pago Jet	95603	
D-MNFJ	Comco Ikarus Fox II Doppel	8605-3019	
D-MNFK	Funk FK-9	025	
D-MNFL	Fisher FP-202 Koala	Ho 001	
D-MNFM	Platzer Kiebitz-B9	003	
D-MNFR	III Sky Arrow 450TG	047	
D-MNFT	Rans S-6 Coyote II	1092363	N7010L
D-MNFW	WDFL Sunwheel	026	
D-MNFZ	Tecnam P.92 Echo	245	
D-MNGB	Jaguar	1001	
D-MNGD	LO-120S	012A	
D-MNGE	Pioneer Flightstar	546	
D-MNGF	HFL Stratos 300	300-005	
D-MNGH	Tecnam P.92 Echo	167	
D-MNGI	Funk FK-9	058	
D-MNGK	WDFL Fascination	020	
D-MNGM	Comco Ikarus C-42 Cyclone	9804-6125	
D-MNGS	Murphy Renegade Spirit	32004	
D-MNGT	Albatros	104	
D-MNHA	Scheibe SF-40	3102	
D-MNHB	Kümmerle Mini-Fly-Set	1269/91-51 66	
D-MNHD	WDFL Fascination	035	
D-MNHE	Comco Ikarus C-42 Cyclone	9710-6036	
D-MNHF	Rans S-12 Airaile	0691098	
D-MNHG	Pioneer Flightstar	950501	
D-MNHH	Rans S-6 Coyote II	1293572	
D-MNHK	LO-120S	014A	
D-MNHL	Funk FK-12 Comet	016	
D-MNHO	Tandem Air Sunny s.b.s.	SuS 01.96	
D-MNHR	Rans S-6 Coyote II	0594626	
D-MNHS	Rans S-6TD Coyote II	0994672	
D-MNHZ	Zenair CH-601D Zodiac	6-3413/015 0097	
D-MNIC	Aviasud BA-83 Mistral	004	
D-MNIE	ASO Viper Trike	15 I7990	
D-MNII	Tandem Air Sunny Targa	005/92	
D-MNIJ	Tandem Air Sunny s.b.s.	SuS 02.94	
D-MNIK	NST Minimum	503	
D-MNIR	NST Minimum	081593	
D-MNIS	Tandem Air Sunny s.b.s.	036/92	
D-MNIT	Tecnam P.92 Echo	185	
D-MNIU	Funk FK-9	065	
D-MNIV	Dallach Sunrise II	003	
D-MNIW	Dallach Sunrise II	007	
D-MNIZ	Zenair CH-601D Zodiac	6-8027/009 0397	
D-MNJB	Jet Fox	004	
D-MNJC	Tecnam P.92 Echo	294	
D-MNJJ	Tecnam P.92 Echo	180	
D-MNJS	WDFL Sunwheel	014	
D-MNJU	Junkers Profly Ultima	JU 001 97	
D-MNKA	NST Minimum	M515	
D-MNKB	Comco Ikarus Fox-C22C	9704-3725	
D-MNKC	Comco Ikarus C-42 Cyclone	9803-6084	
D-MNKD	Comco Ikarus C-42 Cyclone	9901-6146	
D-MNKE	Funk FK-9TG	091	
D-MNKF	Comco Ikarus C-42 Cyclone	9709-6048	
D-MNKG	Flight Design CT	97.06.01.00	
D-MNKH	Tecnam P.92 Echo	126	
D-MNKI	Comco Ikarus C-42 Cyclone	9804-6081	
D-MNKJ	Rans S-6 Coyote II	"4172285"	
	(Quoted c/n is actually Rotax engine number)		
D-MNKK	Ikarusflug Eurofox	040097	
D-MNKL	Flight Design CT	97.07.01.00	
D-MNKM	Light Aero Avid Flyer	1458	
D-MNKR	Albatros SX	504	
D-MNKS	Rans S-12 Airaile	1092341	
D-MNKU	Ultravia Pelican	unkn	
D-MNLC	Comco Ikarus Fox-C22B	9407-3606	
D-MNLE	Light Aero Avid Flyer	1493	
D-MNLF	Jet Fox	014	

Regn.	Type	C/n	Prev.Id.
D-MNLG	Funk FK-9 TG	077	
D-MNLK	Comco Ikarus Fox-C22	9108-3349	
D-MNLL	Zenair CH-601D Zodiac	6-3648	
D-MNLR	Air-Light Wild Thing	004	
D-MNLT	Rans S-6 Coyote II XL	1294712	
D-MNMF	Tandem Air Sunny Sport	64.96	
D-MNMP	Comco Ikarus Fox-C22	3636	
D-MNMS	Air-Light Wild Thing	036	
D-MNNA	Albatros 64	311	
D-MNNB	Albatros 64	501	
D-MNNM	Behlen Power-Trike	023	
D-MNNN	Comco Ikarus Fox-C22	9002-3254	
D-MNNO	Light Aero Avid Flyer STOL	1401C	
D-MNNP	Funk FK-9	043	
D-MNNQ	Funk FK-9	042	
D-MNNZ	Comco Ikarus C-42 Cyclone	9701-6023	
D-MNOB	Comco Ikarus Fox-C22	9706-3731	
D-MNOC	Comco Ikarus Fox-C22B	9602-3693	
D-MNOD	Kümmerle Mini-Fly-Set	25986-4	
D-MNOE	Comco Ikarus C-42 Cyclone	9804-6078	
D-MNOF	Light Aero Avid Flyer	501	
D-MNOK	Kappa KP.2V Sova	unkn	
D-MNOM	Funk FK-9	057	
D-MNON	Funk FK-9	056	
D-MNOP	Mosquito IB	011	
D-MNOR	NST Minimum	1783	
D-MNOX	Rans S-10 Sakota	0488010	
D-MNPC	Eipper Quicksilver MXL	1148	
D-MNPE	Comco Ikarus C-42 Cyclone	9810-6144	
D-MNPF	PC Flight Pretty Flight	01	
D-MNPR	Remos Gemini Ultra	031	
D-MNPS	Tecnam P.92 Echo	321	
D-MNPU	Remos Gemini 3 Mirage	044	
	(Same c/n quoted for D-MRIM)		
D-MNPZ	Comco Ikarus C-42 Cyclone	9708-6034	
D-MNRA	Ikarusflug Eurofox	051098	
D-MNRB	Tecnam P.92 Echo	182	
D-MNRD	Tecnam P.92 Echo	198	
D-MNRF	Ferrari Tucano	308	
D-MNRH	Comco Ikarus Fox-C22	3572	
D-MNRL	WDFL Sunwheel R	025	
D-MNRM	Funk FK-9	028	
D-MNRO	Funk FK-9	033	
D-MNRS	Jet Fox	007	
D-MNRU	Comco Ikarus C-42 Cyclone	9804-6132	
D-MNRV	Tecnam P.92 Echo	338	
D-MNRW	Comco Ikarus Fox-C22B	9602-3692	
D-MNSB	Zenair CH-601D Zodiac	003	
D-MNSH	Tandem Air Sunny Sport	56.93	
D-MNSI	Rans S-6 "Trike" (?)	1294714F	
D-MNSJ	Comco Ikarus C-42 Cyclone	9807-6106	
D-MNSK	Albatros 64	308	
D-MNSM	Comco Ikarus Fox-C22B	940.-3595	
D-MNSR	Jet Fox	005	
D-MNSS	Jet Fox	006	
D-MNST	Jet Fox	008	
D-MNTB	Comco Ikarus Fox-C22B	9407-3596	
D-MNTE	WDFL Fascination	014	
D-MNTH	Zenair CH-601D Zodiac	6-3457	
D-MNTM	Comco Ikarus C-42 Cyclone	9...-6017	
D-MNTS	Remos Gemini 3 Mirage	051	
D-MNTT	Funk FK-9	047	
D-MNTW	Tecnam P.92 Echo	187	
D-MNUM	Comco Ikarus Fox-C22	9207-3414	
D-MNUN	Rans S-6 Coyote II	0193420	
D-MNVB	Murphy Renegade	414	
D-MNVF	Vagabund	004	
D-MNVH	ASO Storch	11017508	
D-MNVM	Light Aero Avid Flyer	1294D	
D-MNWC	Light Aero Avid Flyer	1354	
D-MNWE	Tecnam P.92 Echo	324	
D-MNWH	Funk FK-9	021	
D-MNWI	Comco Ikarus C-42 Cyclone	9609-6006	
D-MNWJ	Platzer Kiebitz-B9	060	
D-MNWL	Comco Ikarus C-42 Cyclone	9803-6089	
D-MNWN	NST Minimum	04911	
D-MNWS	TL-232 Condor	98 C 09	
D-MNWT	Air-Light Wild Thing	028	
D-MNWW	Air-Light Wild Thing	002	
D-MNWZ	Comco Ikarus C-42 Cyclone	9804-6126	
D-MNXU	Rotorcraft CH-7 Angel	unkn	
D-MNYT	Skystar S-34	012	
D-MNZB	Air-Light Wild Thing	027	
D-MNZZ	Comco Ikarus C-42 Cyclone	9806-6119	
D-MOAB	Tandem Air Sunny Sport	17.91	
D-MOAC	Technoflug Piccolo BM	109	
D-MOAE	Technoflug Piccolo BM	110	
D-MOAF	Tecnam P.92 Echo	226	
D-MOAG	WDFL Fascination	025	
D-MOAI	Tecnam P.96 Golf	10	
D-MOAK	Rans S-6 Coyote II	1294713	
D-MOAL	Comco Ikarus C-42 Cyclone	9704-6029	
D-MOAM	Tecnam P.96 Golf	13	
D-MOAN	Platzer Kiebitz-B-450	187	
D-MOAO	Air-Light Wild Thing	040	
D-MOAP	Tandem Air Sunny Sport	38.92	
D-MOAS	Jet Fox	012	
D-MOAW	Tecnam P.92 Echo	300	
D-MOAZ	Moskito 1b	015	
D-MOBA	Tecnam P.96 Golf	031	
D-MOBF	Funk FK-9	038	
D-MOBH	Pretty Flight	003	
D-MOBI (2)	Funk FK-9	075	
D-MOBK	Funk FK-9 TG	046	
D-MOBL	Fisher FP-404 Classic	AB 001	
D-MOBS	UPM Cobra Raven Trike	900102	
D-MOBT	Light Aero Avid Flyer	617	
D-MOBY(1)	Take Off Maximum Karat 13	005059	
D-MOBY(2)	Rans S-6 Coyote II	0893532	
D-MOCA	Warnke Skylight Trike	038	
D-MOCB	WDFL Sunwheel	036	
D-MOCC	Comco Ikarus C-42 Cyclone	9707-6016	
D-MOCF	Comco Ikarus Fox-C22C	9606-3710	
D-MOCO	Flight Design CT	97.08.02.06	
D-MOCT	Flight Design CT	CT 006/97	
D-MOCV	NST Minimum	1781	
D-MODD	Schönleber DS Trike	04/0989	
D-MODE(2)	Tandem Air Sunny	47.93	
D-MODF	MAI 890-1	142	
D-MODG	WDFL Sunwheel R	023	
D-MODI	Comco Ikarus C-42 Cyclone	9704-6018	
D-MODL	NST Minimum Zephir CX	M456	
D-MODM	WDFL Fascination	038	
D-MOEC	Comco Ikarus C-42 Cyclone	9611-6030	
D-MOEE	Flight Design CT	97.12.01.16	
D-MOEN	Comco Ikarus Fox-C22	9403-3579	
D-MOES	Jet Fox	003	
D-MOET	Comco Ikarus Fox-C22	94083608	
D-MOEU	Tecnam P.92 Echo	083	
D-MOEZ	AMF Chevvron 2-32	037	
D-MOFF	Comco Ikarus Fox-C22B	9506-3670	
D-MOFK	Funk FK-9	061	
D-MOFT	Platzer Kiebitz-B6	171	
D-MOFU	Rans S-10 Sakota	0697184	
D-MOGA	WDFL Sunwheel R	021	
D-MOGH	ASO 26 Storch	160	
D-MOGK	Zenair CH-601 Zodiac	6-2008	
D-MOGL	Murphy Renegade Spirit	518	
D-MOGS	WDFL Fascination	016	
D-MOHA	Rans S-12 Airaile	1292346	
D-MOHB	Remos Gemini 3 Mirage	047	
D-MOHD	Evektor EV.97 Eurostar	98 03 06	
D-MOHE	TL-232 Condor	98 C 08	
D-MOHF	Denney Kitfox	1876	
D-MOHG	Pioneer Flightstar	960701	
D-MOHI	Ikarusflug Eurofox	026096	
D-MOHK	HK 12	001	
D-MOHM	Comco Ikarus C-42 Cyclone	9809-6131	
D-MOHN	Scheibe Uli 1	5222	
D-MOHR	Sky-Walker II	147	

Regn.	Type	C/n	Prev.Id.
D-MOHS	Weedhopper	0998	
D-MOHT	Tecnam P.92 Echo	258	
D-MOHW	Behlen Power-Trike /Rotax 582	92028	
D-MOHY	Jet Fox 91D	00122	
D-MOIC	ASO Viper Hazard 15	11031204	
D-MOIK	WDFL Fascination	010	
D-MOIL	Comco Ikarus C-42 Cyclone	9804-6101	
D-MOIN	Warnke Skylight Trike	S2005	
D-MOIS	Pretty Flight	02	
D-MOJB	Jet Fox	D 0013	
D-MOJE	Funk FK-12 Comet	004	
D-MOJH	Tandem Air Sunny Targa	TA 014	
D-MOJS	Comco Ikarus C-42 Cyclone	9811-6152	
D-MOKA	Scheibe Ultra	3411	
D-MOKE	Racer (Homebuilt)	004/90	
D-MOKF	Funk FK-9 Mk3	098	
D-MOKG	Rans S-6ES Coyote II	0496966	
D-MOKI	Zephir CX	unkn	
D-MOKK	Comco Ikarus C-42 Cyclone	9712-6072	
D-MOKL	Rans S-6 Coyote II	10961045	
D-MOKM	Tecnam P.92 Echo	225	
D-MOKN	Platzer Kiebitz-B6	195	
D-MOKO	Moskito	006	
D-MOKS	Tecnam P.92 Echo	135	
D-MOKT	Tandem Air Sunny Sport	57.94	
D-MOLA(1)	Fair Fax Trike	21	
D-MOLA(2)	Solair II	unkn	
D-MOLB	Flight Team Spider Trike	DOO9	
D-MOLC	Comco Ikarus Fox-C22B	9405-3603	
D-MOLD	Moskito	002	
D-MOLE	NST Minimum Santana	100378	
D-MOLG	Flight Design CT	98.04.05.32	
D-MOLI	Pioneer Flightstar	545	
D-MOLL	Scheibe UL-1 Coach	3201	
D-MOLM	Comco Ikarus Fox-C22	9108-3352	
D-MOLO	LO-120S	021	
D-MOLS	Tecnam P.92 Echo	252	
D-MOLT	ASO Viper Hazard 15	12023103	
D-MOLV	Funk FK-9 Mk3	09-03-101	
D-MOLW	Platzer Kiebitz-B	066	
D-MOLY	Light Aero Avid Flyer	867	
D-MOMC	Funk FK-9 Mk3	107	
D-MOMD	Comco Ikarus C-42 Cyclone	9803-6087	
D-MOMF	WDFL Fascination	042	
D-MOMN	Comco Ikarus C-42 Cyclone	9703-6032	
D-MOMO	Scheibe Ultra	3414	
D-MOMP	Klüver Racer Quartz SX 12	309005	
D-MOMS	Ikarusflug Eurofox	024096	
D-MONA	Ultra-Vector H	1401	
D-MONB	Comco Ikarus Fox-C22	9407-3574	
D-MONC	Rans S-6 Coyote II	0494609	
D-MOND	Warnke Puma Sprint	D001	
D-MONE	Comco Ikarus Fox	015	
D-MONG	Albatros 64	502	
D-MONI	Power Power-Trike Euro III	84018	
D-MONJ	UPM Omega Trike	880045	
D-MONL	Comco Ikarus Fox-C22	940 .-3575	
D-MONM	Platzer Kiebitz	016	
D-MONO	Scheibe Uli 1	5211	
D-MONW	Comco Ikarus Fox-C22B	95 . .-3678	
D-MOOB	Kümmerle Mini Fly Set Bullet C	73285-4	
D-MOOF	Comco Ikarus Fox-C22C	9605-3708	
D-MOOI	Pretty Flight	001	
D-MOOL	SG Storm 400	unkn	
D-MOOQ	Rans S-6 Coyote II	0295739XL	
D-MOOS	SG Storm 280	508G	
D-MOOT	Tandem Air Sunny s.b.s.	SuS 03.96	
D-MOOY	Aero Style Breezer	unkn	
D-MOPC	UPM Omega Lotus 18	069/883	
D-MOPE	Scheibe SF-40	3101	
D-MOPF	Rans S-6 Coyote II	0895864	
D-MOPG	Comco Ikarus C-42 Cyclone	9611-6026	
D-MOPH	Tecnam P.92 Echo	214	
D-MOPI	Funk FK-9	060	
D-MOPL	Comco Ikarus Fox-C22	9502-3657	

Regn.	Type	C/n	Prev.Id.
D-MOPO	Funk FK-9 TG	044	
D-MOPP	Take Off Maximum	7069	
D-MOPT	Zenair CH-601D Zodiac	6-3530/013	0897
D-MOPU	Rans S-6 Coyote II	0396956	
D-MOPV	Funk FK-9 Mk3	092	
D-MOPZ	Comco Ikarus Fox-C22B	9505-3677	
D-MORD	Seiffert Mini II	296	
D-MORE	Warnke Skylight Trike	028	
D-MORJ	WDFL Sunwheel	030	
D-MORK	Platzer Kiebitz-B9	129	
D-MORL	Tecnam P.92 Echo	136	
D-MORO	Light Aero Avid Flyer	1495	
D-MORS	Ultra-Vector F 610	1402	
D-MORW	WDFL Fascination	008	
D-MORY	Fair Fax DR Trike	004	
D-MORZ	Dallach Sunrise IIA	035	
D-MOSA	Air-Light Wild Thing	033	
D-MOSG	Comco Ikarus C-42 Cyclone	9902-6155	
D-MOSH	Funk FK-9	078	
D-MOSK	NST Minimum Saphir 17	345	
D-MOSM	Comco Ikarus Fox-C22B	940 .-3605	
D-MOSS	Rans S-6 Coyote II XL	1095886	
D-MOST	Scheibe Ultra	3407	
D-MOSW	Sky-Walker 1+1	26118	
D-MOTA	Platzer Motte B2	04	
D-MOTB	Light Aero Avid Flyer	1522	
D-MOTI	Albatros AN-22	8327	
D-MOTO	Behlen Trike	87011	
D-MOTP	Tecnam P.92 Echo	319	
D-MOTR	Fisher FP-404 Classic	001	
D-MOTT	Funk FK-9 Mk3	113	
D-MOTU	Capella FW1 C50	691055	
D-MOTV	Comco Ikarus C-42 Cyclone	9706-6070	
D-MOTY	Capella FW2 BR	061941	
D-MOTZ	ASO Viper Hazard 15	11026202	
D-MOUG	Funk FK-9	018	
D-MOUL	Tandem Air Sunny s.b.s.	SuS-05.94	
D-MOUS	Pioneer Flightstar	370	
D-MOUZ	Platzer Motte B2/B3	48	
D-MOVA	Zenair CH-601D Zodiac	6-8061/008	0297
D-MOVG	Zenair CH-601D Zodiac	6-3406/017	0097
D-MOVI	Comco Ikarus Fox-C22	9210-3429	
D-MOVO	Remos Gemini Ultra	015	
D-MOVW	Air-Light Wild Thing	030	
D-MOVY	Rans S-12 Airaile	0794508	
D-MOWB	Rans S-6 Coyote II	10971168	
D-MOWE	Schmidtler Ranger M	18/22	
D-MOWI (3)	Drifter	001	
D-MOWK	Comco Ikarus C-42 Cyclone	9812-6139	
D-MOWL	Platzer Kiebitz B	077	
D-MOWO	Comco Ikarus Fox-C22B	9604-3699	
D-MOWR	Platzer Motte BR	18	
D-MOWS	Funk FK-9	085	
D-MOWZ	Aerotechnik Cobra S1	unkn	
D-MOXE	Comco Ikarus Fox-C22	9404-3560	
D-MOYO	WDFL Sunwheel	035	
D-MOYS	Platzer Kiebitz-B	053	
D-MOYZ	Air-Light Wild Thing	016	
D-MOZI	Funk FK-9	039	
D-MOZO	Comco Ikarus Fox-C22	9503-3646	
D-MOZR	Comco Ikarus Fox-C22	940 .-3551	
D-MOZZ	Klüver Twin Racer Quartz SX 16	229004	
D-MPAA	Remos Gemini Ultra	E11.12	
D-MPAC	Comco Ikarus Fox-C22C	9310-3542	
D-MPAD	Mantel Mono-Dragster	857	
D-MPAE	Bobcat	Bü-02	
D-MPAH(2)	Behlen Power Trike II	91125	
D-MPAJ	Mantel Mono-Dragster	874225	
D-MPAM	Comco Ikarus Fox-C22B	9404-3556	
D-MPAN	NST Minimum Zephir CX	M467	
D-MPAP	Comco Ikarus Fox-C22	9209-3406	
D-MPAQ	Comco Ikarus Fox-C22B	9407-3598	
D-MPAR	Comco Ikarus Fox-C22	9403-3578	
D-MPAW	Kolb Twinstar Mk.III	M3-100	
D-MPBA	EEL ULF-2	002	

Regn.	Type	C/n	Prev.Id.
D-MPBB	Light Aero Avid Flyer	1290	
D-MPBF	Funk FK-9	040	
D-MPBH	Platzer Kiebitz-B	173	
D-MPBK	Funk FK-9 Mk3	105	
D-MPBL	Ultrastar	018	
D-MPBO	Funk FK-9 Classic	066	
D-MPBS	Dallach Sunrise II	012	
D-MPBT	Fair Fax DR Trike	34	
D-MPCB	Albatros	114	
D-MPCC	Rans S-6 Coyote II	0495805	
D-MPCF	Rans S-6 Coyote II	0396963	
D-MBCH	Fisher Super Koala	B291248	
D-MPCM	Funk FK-9 Mk3	094	
D-MPCN	Comco Ikarus C-42 Cyclone	9704-6025	
D-MPCR	Platzer Kiebitz-B2	007	
D-MPCT	Flight Design CT	97.10.01.10	
D-MPDG	Platzer Kiebitz-B2	041	
D-MPDH	Tandem Air Sunny Sport	31.92	
D-MPEA	Schönleber DS Lotus KS 18	010490	
D-MPEB	UPM Funplane	890059	
D-MPEC	Homebuilt, possibly Enduro	8/90	
D-MPEE	Comco Ikarus Fox-C22B	9501-3642	
D-MPEG	Scheibe Uli 1	5217	
D-MPEJ	Comco Ikarus C-42 Cyclone	9807-6116	
D-MPEP	Comco Ikarus Fox-C22B	9603-3697	
D-MPER	Scheibe Uli 1	5225	
D-MPES	Jet Fox	010	
D-MPEU	Comco Ikarus Fox-C22	9...-3544	
D-MPEV	Evektor EV.97 Eurostar	98 03 01	
D-MPEW	Funk FK-9	064	
D-MPEZ	Comco Ikarus Fox-C22	9311-3545	
D-MPFA	ASO Viper Trike	22035206	
D-MPFF	Rans S-6 Coyote II	04981223	
D-MPFI	Sky-Walker II	504	
D-MPFK	J-3 Kitten	001	
D-MPGA	Firebird Sierra Trike	unkn	
D-MPGH	Tecnam P.92 Echo	243	
D-MPGI	Dallach Sunrise II	011	
D-MPGK	Ikarusflug Eurofox Pro	039097	
D-MPGN	Comco Ikarus Fox-C22	8707-3045	
D-MPHA	Jet Fox Einzel	00134	
D-MPHC	Platzer Kiebitz	unkn	
D-MPHD	Skystar S.34	013	
D-MPHE	Comco Ikarus Fox-C22B	9511-3679	
D-MPHF	Comco Ikarus C-42 Cyclone	9803-6088	
D-MPHI	Behlen Power-Trike	830002	
D-MPHM	Funk FK-12 Comet	020	
D-MPHR	Capella FW2 C80	1011	
D-MPHS	WDFL Sunwheel R	042	
D-MPHW	WDFL Fascination	023	
D-MPIE	Comco Ikarus Fox-C22E	9507-3669	
D-MPIL	Comco Ikarus Fox-C22	9208-3418	
D-MPIR	Comco Ikarus Fox-C22	9208-3427	
D-MPIW	Flight Design CT	97.11.03.15	
D-MPJF	Platzer Kiebitz-B	038	
D-MPJK	Light Aero Avid Flyer	5115	
D-MPJL	Ikarusflug Eurofox	029097	
D-MPKG	Flight Design CT	98.05.01.33	
D-MPKI	LO-120S	016-A	
D-MPKM	Funk FK-9 TG	063	
D-MPKP	Aviasud Mistral BRD	182/92	
D-MPKS	Comco Ikarus C-42 Cyclone	9707-6050	
D-MPKW	Comco Ikarus Fox-C22 Seaplane	9303-3344	
D-MPLA	Rans S-6S Coyote II	0196922	
D-MPLE	Take Off Maximum Hazard 15 Trike	019109	
D-MPLH	WDFL Fascination	027	
D-MPLI	Funk FK.12 Comet	001	
D-MPLL	ASO Storch	11014503	
D-MPLO	Comco Ikarus C-42 Cyclone	9801-6077	
D-MPLR	Light Aero Avid Flyer	1435D	
D-MPLV	Comco Ikarus Fox-C22	9203-3401	
D-MPLW	Sky Craft 2000	2000-39	
D-MPMA	Behlen Power-Trike II	91030	
D-MPMB	Comco Ikarus C-42 Cyclone	9707-6066	
D-MPMN	Comco Ikarus C-42 Cyclone	9803-6086	
D-MPNR	Tecnam P.92 Echo	325	
D-MPOE	NST Minimum	M347	
D-MPOJ	Tandem Air Sunny s.b.s.	0496	
D-MPOL	Schmidtler Ranger M Trike	1819	
D-MPOP	Tecnam P.92 Echo	165	
D-MPOW	Remos Gemini 3 Mirage	050	
D-MPOZ	Comco Ikarus Sherpa II	8512-1112	
D-MPPB	Air-Light Wild Thing	021	
D-MPPC	Remos Gemini 3 Mirage	046	
D-MPPH	WDFL Sunwheel	019	
D-MPPR	Comco Ikarus Fox-C22	9201-3382	
D-MPPS	Comco Ikarus C-42 Cyclone	9809-6129	
D-MPPW	Klüver Twin Racer Trike	574008	
D-MPQR	Comco Ikarus Fox-C22	9407-3581	
D-MPRA	TL-96 Star	unkn	
D-MPRE	Comco Ikarus Fox-C22	9104-3345	
D-MPRG	Comco Ikarus C-42 Cyclone	9702-6068	
D-MPRH	Flight Design CT	98.02.04.24	
D-MPRK	Comco Ikarus Fox-C22	9307-3520	
D-MPRM	Comco Fox	037	
D-MPRO	Albatros	102	
D-MPRP	Comco Ikarus Fox-C22	9705-3726	
D-MPRS	Jet Fox	015	
D-MPRU	Comco Ikarus C-42 Cyclone	9704-6015	
D-MPRW	Comco Ikarus Fox-C22C	9608-3716	
D-MPSA	Air-Light Wild Thing	023	
D-MPSB	Air-Light Wild Thing	010	
D-MPSC	Comco Ikarus Fox	039	
D-MPSG	Zenair CH-601 Zodiac	6-3209/012 0097	
D-MPSH	Comco Ikarus C-42 Cyclone	9812-6110	
D-MPSK	Tulak	unkn	
D-MPSN	Comco Ikarus Fox-C22	9404-3518	
D-MPSR	Light Aero Avid Flyer	941	
D-MPSS	Comco Ikarus C-42 Cyclone	9806-6124	
D-MPSW	Comco Ikarus C-42 Cyclone	9809-6123	
D-MPTC	Ultraleichtverbund Bi 90	942	
D-MPTS	Comco Ikarus Fox-C22	9307-3515	
D-MPTU	Comco Ikarus C-42 Cyclone	9611-6019	
D-MPUK	Comco Ikarus Fox-C22B	9503-3643	
D-MPUL	Comco Ikarus Sherpa	8403-1059	
D-MPUR	Comco Ikarus Fox-C22	9111-3381	
D-MPVM	Platzer Kiebitz-B6	11/2	
D-MPVP	Tecnam P.92 Echo	158	
D-MPWE	Funk FK-9	030	
D-MPWK	Tecnam P.92 Echo	157	
D-MPWP	Tandem Air Sunny Sport	60.95	
D-MPWS	Flight Design CT	98.04.04.31	
D-MPYA	Platzer Kiebitz-B6	008	
D-MPYT	Comco Ikarus Fox-C22	8612-3055	
D-MQAK	Schmidtler Enduro XP-15	01-005	
D-MQBF	Funk FK-9	036	
D-MQBK	Light Aero Avid Flyer	1293	
D-MQBT	HFL Stratos 300K	300-014K	D-MJBT(1)
D-MQCC	Flight Design CT	97.08.03	
D-MQFK	Comco Ikarus C-42 Cyclone	9708-6064	
D-MQHG	Pioneer Flightstar II SL	970501	
D-MQII	WDFL Sunwheel	46	
D-MQIK	Flight Design CT	98.06.01.34	
D-MQJB	Albatros AE 209	121	
D-MQQQ	Rans S-12 Airaile	1292340	N7082C
D-MQRF	EEL ULF-2 Prototype	001	
D-MQRS	Tecnam P.92 Echo	096	
D-MQXZ	Tecnam P.92 Echo	127	
D-MQYJ	Platzer Kiebitz-B	010	
D-MQYV	WDFL Sunwheel R	020	
D-MRAB	Fisher FP-202 Koala	2183-1	
D-MRAC(3)	Platzer Kiebitz-B2	142	
D-MRAD	Comco Ikarus C-42 Cyclone	9606-6008	
D-MRAH	Platzer Kiebitz-B2	178	
D-MRAI	Denney Kitfox IV-1200	JCU-114	
D-MRAJ	SG Storm 280	D002	
D-MRAK	Comco Ikarus Fox-C22	8812-3185	
D-MRAL	Sky-Walker II	321	
D-MRAM	Light Aero Avid Flyer	1274	
D-MRAO	Comco Ikarus Fox-C22	9...-3609	

Regn.	Type	C/n	Prev.Id.
D-MRAP	Platzer Kiebitz-B9	090	
D-MRAQ	Comco Ikarus Fox-C22	9407-3549	
D-MRAS	Sky-Walker II	323	
D-MRAU	Comco Ikarus Fox-C22	8808-3139	
D-MRAW	Funk FK-12 Comet	012-006	
D-MRAX	Funk FK-9 Mk3	102	
D-MRAY	Comco Ikarus C-42 Cyclone	9709-6035	
D-MRAZ	Light Aero Avid Flyer	"989952-199" or "9999"	
D-MRBB	Flight Design CT	97.06.02.00	
D-MRBC	Rans S-6 Coyote II	0293435	
D-MRBD	Comco Ikarus C-42 Cyclone	9801-6037	
D-MRBF	Air-Light Wild Thing	012	
D-MRBG	Flight Design CT	97.11.02.14	
D-MRBH	WDFL Fascination	004	
D-MRBI	Comco Ikarus C-42 Cyclone	9609-6012	
D-MRBL	Eipper Quicksilver GT	GT-280-1193	
D-MRBP	Remos Gemini 3 Mirage	049	
D-MRBZ	Cora CT	unkn	
D-MRCB	Rans S-6 Coyote II	0295738	
D-MRCD	Comco Ikarus Fox-C22	8702-3048	
D-MRCF	Moskito 1b	013	
D-MRCI	Remos Gemini 3 Mirage	unkn	
D-MRCM	Albatros 52	133	
D-MRCT	Flight Design CT	98.01.03.20	
D-MRCU	Comco Ikarus Fox-C22B	9407-3602	
D-MRDC	Comco Ikarus Fox-C22	9502-3656	
D-MRDF	WDFL Fascination	018	
D-MRDG	Funk FK-9	037	
D-MRDK	Platzer Kiebitz-B2	132	
D-MRDL	Rans S-6 Coyote II	1193560	
D-MRDM	Funk FK-9	059	
	(C/n 059 alternatively listed as FK-9 TG D-MRMD)		
D-MRDW	Ultraleichtverbund Bi 90	704	
D-MRED	Remos Gemini Ultra	16.17/032	
D-MREE	Rans S-6 Coyote II	594630	
D-MREH	Comco Ikarus C-42 Cyclone	9708-6046	
D-MREI	Platzer Kiebitz-B2	039	
D-MREM	Remos Gemini Ultra	E15.16/016	
D-MRES	Rans S-6 Coyote II	0494611	
D-MREV	Comco Ikarus C-42 Cyclone	9609-6011	
D-MREU	Tandem Air Sunny	55.93	
D-MRFB	Delda-S/A Delta Dart II	002	
D-MRFC	Ferrari Tucano-A	303	
D-MRFF	Comco Ikarus Fox-C22C	9705-37..	
D-MRFG	Ultra-Vector H	1383	
D-MRFK	Funk FK-9 Mk 3	089	
D-MRFS	Rans S-12 Airaile	1292360	
D-MRGA	Platzer Motte B-3	033	
D-MRGB	Murphy Renegade	387	
D-MRGD	III Sky Arrow 450TG	018	
D-MRGE	Ultraleichtverbund Bi 90	935	
D-MRGH	Murphy Renegade II	458	
D-MRGL	Jet Fox 91D	009	
D-MRGO	Comco Ikarus C-42 Cyclone	9805-6056	
D-MRGW	Sky-Walker II	221	
D-MRHA	Funk FK-9 Mk3	110	
D-MRHB	Comco Ikarus Fox-C22	940 .-3571	
D-MRHE	Flight Design CT	007/97	
D-MRHF	Behlen Power-Trike	88011	
D-MRHH	Tecnam P.92 Echo	194	
D-MRHK	Tecnam P.92 Echo	266	
D-MRHL	Remos Gemini 3 Mirage	041	
D-MRHM	Rans S-6ES Coyote II	0895880	
D-MRHN	Comco Ikarus Fox-C22	9208-3420	D- MIAL(1)
D-MRHO	Ultraleichtverbund Bi 90	3957005	
D-MRHP	Ultraleichtverbund Bi 90	970	
D-MRHR	Comco Ikarus Fox-C22	9309-3539	
D-MRHU	Funk FK-9 Mk3	097	
D-MRHW	Schönleber DS Speed KS 14 Trike KS	01/0391	
D-MRHZ	Zenair CH-601D Zodiac	6-3521/006 0997	
D-MRID	Comco Ikarus Fox-C22	9404-3555	
D-MRIE	Seiffert Mini II	F0111/88	
D-MRIF	Aviasud Mistral 53	010	
D-MRIK	Tecnam P.92 Echo	265	

Regn.	Type	C/n	Prev.Id.
D-MRIM	Remos Gemini 3 Mirage	044	
	(Same c/n quoted as D-MNPU)		
D-MRIS	Tecnam P.96 Golf	16	
D-MRIT	Albatros Av.Sud	037	
D-MRIW	WDFL Fascination	043	
D-MRIX	Scheibe Uli 1	5204	
D-MRIY	Scheibe Uli 1	5210	
D-MRIZ	Remos Gemini 3 Mirage	040	
D-MRJA	Seiffert Mini II	F0209/87	
D-MRJF	Comco Ikarus Fox-C22B	9510-3700	
D-MRJH	Comco Ikarus C-42 Cyclone	9710-6074	
D-MRJL	Funk FK-9 Mk3	108	
D-MRJR	Flight Design CT	98.11.01.40	
D-MRKA	Moskito	003	
D-MRKB	Comco Ikarus Fox-C22	9308-3519	
D-MRKD	Tecnam P.96 Golf	020	
D-MRKE	Comco Ikarus C-42 Cyclone	9612-6027	
D-MRKF	Rans S-6TD Coyote II	1294703	
D-MRKJ	Comco Ikarus C-42 Cyclone	9903-6164	
D-MRKM	Air Light Wild Thing	9702018	
D-MRKO	Comco Ikarus C-42 Cyclone	9709-6055	
D-MRKP	Comco Ikarus C-42 Cyclone	9707-6069	
D-MRKR	Funk FK-9 TG	053	
D-MRKW	Light Aero Avid Flyer D	1156D	
D-MRLA	Behlen Power-Trike	877353	
D-MRLD	Tecnam P.92 Echo	278	
D-MRLM	Sky-Walker II	393	
D-MRLW	Comco Ikarus Fox-C22B	9606-3703	
D-MRMA	Funk FK-9 Mk3	09-03-100	
D-MRMC	Sky-Walker II	265	
D-MRMD	Funk FK-9 TG (see D-MRDM entry)	059	
D-MRMF	Comco Ikarus Fox-C22B	9...-3681	
D-MRMG	Remos Gemini Ultra	010	
D-MRMI	Remos Gemini 3 Mirage	038	
D-MRMK	Comco Ikarus Fox-C22	9109-3353	
D-MRMM	Funk FK-9	084	
D-MRMN	Comco Ikarus Fox-C22C	9705-3715	
D-MRMS	Comco Ikarus C-42 Cyclone	9801-6075	
D-MRMU	Warnke Trike Euro III	183001	
D-MRMZ	Comco Ikarus C-42 Cyclone	9707-6045	
D-MRNG	Murphy Renegade	412	
D-MROD	Rans S-10 Sakota	0194170	
D-MROE	Comco Ikarus Fox-C22	9406-3573	
D-MROH	Rans S-6 Coyote II	0794652	
D-MROK	NST Minimum	157	
D-MROM	Platzer Kiebitz-B4	109	
D-MROS	Tandem Air Sunny	23.91	
D-MROT	NST Minimum	M431	
D-MROU	Comco Ikarus Fox-C22	9206-3409	
D-MROY	Comco Ikarus Fox-C22	9112-3298	
D-MRPD	Rans S-6 Coyote II XL	08971150	
D-MRPK	Comco Ikarus Fox-C22	9310-3521	
D-MRPM	Sky Craft 2000	2000-31	
D-MRPS	Behlen Power-Trike	unkn	
D-MRPW	Funk FK-9	049	
D-MRRG	WDFL Fascination	049	
D-MRRH	UPM Funplane	870024	
D-MRRK	Tecnam P.92 Echo	296	
D-MRRL	Tecnam P.96 Golf	16	
D-MRRM	Sky Craft 2000	2000-38	
D-MRRP	Funk FK-9	050	
D-MRRR	WDFL Sunwheel	009	
D-MRRS	Comco Ikarus Sherpa II	8310-1044	PH-1M2
D-MRRZ	Kümmerle Mini-Fly-Set	1268/91-5	
D-MRSA	WDFL Sunwheel R	032	
D-MRSB	Sky Craft AJS	2000-32	
D-MRSE	Rans S-6 Coyote II	12961078	
D-MRSH	Murphy Renegade Spirit	410	
D-MRSK	Comco Ikarus C-42 Cyclone	9806-6091	
D-MRSM	Comco Ikarus Fox-C22	9406-3593	
D-MRSN	Rans S-12 Airaile	1090028	
D-MRSO	Fair Fax DR Trike	002	
D-MRSR	Tecnam P.96 Golf	002	
D-MRSS	Ultraleichtverbund Bi 90	555395	
D-MRST(1)	Schmidtler Ranger M Trike	unkn	

Regn.	Type	C/n	Prev.Id.
D-MRST(2)	Platzer Kiebitz-B6	141	
D-MRSU	NST Minimum Zephir	M497	
D-MRTA	Schmidtler Ranger M Trike	18-23	
D-MRTB	Funk FK-9	026	
D-MRTF	Rans S-10 Sakota	0190084	
D-MRTH	Zenair CH-601D Zodiac	6-3485/021 0897	
D-MRTL	Comco Ikarus Fox-C22	9107-3347	
D-MRTN	Tecnam P.92 Echo	188	
D-MRTR	Rans S-12 Airaile	0491064	
D-MRTS	Ferrari Tucano-A	305	
D-MRTT	Comco Ikarus C-42 Cyclone	9802-6044	
D-MRTV	Comco Ikarus Fox-C22	9206-3415	
D-MRUK	Comco Ikarus Fox-C22B	9508-3668	
D-MRUL	Rans S-12 Airaile	0291054	
D-MRUT	Comco Ikarus Fox-C22	9212-3425	
D-MRUW	UW-8 Rebell	001	
D-MRVE	Platzer Kiebitz-B1	002	
D-MRVH	Tandem Air Sunny s.b.s.	SuS 05.95	
D-MRWB	Comco Ikarus Fox-C22	9211-3482	
D-MRWD	Warnke Puma Sprint Trike	D007	
D-MRWE	WDFL Fascination	006	
D-MRWG	Comco Ikarus C-42 Cyclone	9803-6095	
D-MRWH	WDFL Fascination	002	
D-MRWI	Fresh Breeze 110 AL2F	50	
D-MRWK	Klüver Racer Quartz SX 12 Trike	445904	
D-MRZJ	Comco Ikarus Fox-C22	94 . .-3590	
D-MSAD	Schönleber DS Trike	502/0991	
D-MSAE	NST Minimum	M63	
D-MSAF	Light Aero Avid Flyer C	869	
D-MSAG	Tandem Air Sunny Sport	62.95	
D-MSAH	Ultraleichtverbund Bi 90	493	
D-MSAI	Tandem Air Sunny Targa	TA-013	
D-MSAK	Tandem Air Sunny Sport	39.92	
D-MSAL	Schmidtler Enduro Trike	0401086	
D-MSAO	Light Aero Avid Flyer	1520	
D-MSAT	Comco Ikarus Fox-C22C	9107-3348	
D-MSAU	Tandem Air Sunny s.b.s.	SuS-10.94	
D-MSAV	Comco Ikarus Fox-C22B	9403-3577	
D-MSAW	WDFL Sunwheel R	039	
D-MSBB	Comco Ikarus Fox-C22	9106-3330	
D-MSBG	Remos Gemini 3 Mirage	unkn	
D-MSBH	Tecnam P.92 Echo	257	
D-MSBI	SF-45SA Spirit	unkn	
D-MSBK	Take Off Merlin Karat 13 Trike	21904	
D-MSBM	Comco Ikarus C-42 Cyclone	960 .-6002	
D-MSBN	Tandem Air Sunny s.b.s.	01-95	
D-MSBP	Comco Ikarus Fox-C22	9304-3499	
D-MSBT	Funk FK-9TG	062	
D-MSBZ	Comco Ikarus C-42 Cyclone	9902-6163	
D-MSCB	Tecnam P.92 Echo	179	
D-MSCC	Rans S-6ES Coyote II	1195900	
D-MSCF	Comco Ikarus Fox-C22C	9706-3723	
D-MSCL	Comco Ikarus Fox-C22	9106-3341	
D-MSCN	WDFL Fascination	028	
D-MSDS	Kümmerle Mini-Fly-Set	1303/91-6	
D-MSCT	Flight Design CT	97.09.03.09	
D-MSCU	Comco Ikarus C-42 Cyclone	9711-6071	
D-MSCW	Brack Denney Kitfox	613	D-ERPB
D-MSCY	Urban Air Lambada UFM-13	unkn	
D-MSDB	ASO 26 Storch	160.1	
D-MSDW	SDW Maximum Trike	1	
D-MSEC	Tecnam P.92 Echo	173	
D-MSED	Tecnam P.92 Echo	174	
D-MSEI	Behlen Power-Trike Vampir II	88012	
D-MSEJ	Rans S-6 Coyote II	0593509	
D-MSEL	Comco Ikarus Fox-C22	9107-3342	
D-MSEM	Light Aero Avid Flyer	619	
D-MSEN	Kümmerle Mini-Fly-Set Zephir CX	1272/91-5	
D-MSEO	Comco Ikarus C-42 Cyclone	9804-6097	
D-MSER	Scheibe SF-40	3106	
D-MSET	Platzer Motte B2	35	
D-MSEU	Murphy Renegade	411	
D-MSEV	Evektor EV.97 Eurostar	unkn	
D-MSEX	Behlen Trike	830014	
D-MSFA	Warnke Trike	M869530	
D-MSFB	Rans S-6 Coyote II	0393462	
D-MSFC	Warnke Europlane Euro III Trike	M867935	
D-MSFE	Warnke Trike	1028	
D-MSFF	Comco Ikarus C-42 Cyclone	9807-6115	
D-MSFG	UPM Funplane	86011	
D-MSFO	Steinbach Austro-Trike Euro IIIM	1200	
D-MSFS	Comco Ikarus Fox-C22	9401-3543	
D-MSFU	Tecnam P.96 Golf	11	
D-MSFV	Comco Ikarus C-42 Cyclone	9802-6080	
D-MSGA	Moskito	007	
D-MSGE	Comco Ikarus C-42 Cyclone	9902-6175	
D-MSGF	Comco Fox	unkn	
D-MSGG	Comco Ikarus C-42 Cyclone	9801-6057	
D-MSGH	Comco Ikarus C-42 Cyclone	9709-6059	
D-MSGK	Comco Ikarus Fox-C22	9001-3250	
D-MSGL	Behlen Power-Trike	86-015	
D-MSGM	Comco Ikarus C-42 Cyclone	9806-6120	
D-MSGO	Remos Gemini Ultra	036R	
D-MSGS	Tandem Air Sunny Sport	44.93	
D-MSGU	Tandem Air Sunny Targa	TA-018	
D-MSGV	Klüver Twin Racer	407112	
D-MSGW	Light Aero Avid Flyer	1011	
D-MSHE	Comco Ikarus Sherpa	8305-1019	
D-MSHG	Comco Ikarus Sherpa I	8304-1021	
D-MSHH	WDFL Fascination	044	
D-MSHJ	Comco Ikarus C-42 Cyclone	9807-6111	
D-MSHM	Tecnam P.92 Echo	232	
D-MSHN	Comco Ikarus Sherpa I	8307-1032	
D-MSHR	Comco Ikarus Sherpa I	8311-02	
D-MSHS	Comco Ikarus C-42 Cyclone	9810-6137	
D-MSIA	Comco Ikarus Sherpa II	8408-1079	
D-MSIB	Comco Ikarus Sherpa II	8410-1083	
D-MSIC	Comco Ikarus Sherpa II	8501-1088	
D-MSID	Comco Ikarus Sherpa II	850 .-1089	
D-MSIF	Comco Fox D	8507-FD30	
D-MSIG(2)	TL-232 Condor	97 C 04	
D-MSIH	Comco Fox D	8409-FD12	
D-MSIL	Comco Fox D	8507-FD31	
D-MSIM	Comco Fox D	8508-FD32	
D-MSIP	Comco Fox D	8503-FD24	
D-MSIR	Comco Ikarus Sherpa II	850 .-1090	
D-MSIS	Comco Fox II	8605-3018	
D-MSIT	WDFL Fascination	022	
D-MSIV	Comco Ikarus Sherpa II	8412-1075	
D-MSIW	Comco Ikarus Sherpa II	8503-1092	
D-MSIX	Comco Ikarus Sherpa II	850 .-1091	
D-MSIZ	Comco Ikarus Sherpa II	8504-1094	
D-MSJA	Funk FK-9	073	
D-MSJR	NST Minimum Trike Profil 17M	206	
D-MSJS	Comco Ikarus C-42 Cyclone	9802-6054	
D-MSKA	Comco Ikarus C-42 Cyclone	9807-6121	
D-MSKB	Comco Ikarus C-42 Cyclone	9710-6062	
D-MSKC	Comco Ikarus Sherpa I	8307-1037	
D-MSKD	Comco Ikarus Sherpa II	8406-1070	
D-MSKE	Comco Ikarus Sherpa II	8402-1051	
D-MSKF	Funk FK-9	055	
D-MSKI	Flight Design CT	97.07.02.04	
D-MSKJ	Comco Ikarus Sherpa II	8406-1068	
D-MSKL	Comco Ikarus Sherpa II	8410-1082	
D-MSKM	Comco Ikarus Sherpa II	8409-10 . .	
D-MSKN(2)	Albatros 64	309	
D-MSKP	Comco Ikarus Fox-C22B	9403-3558	
D-MSKQ	Comco Ikarus Fox-C22	9 . . . .-3585	
D-MSKR	Comco Ikarus Sherpa II	8311-1048	
D-MSKS	Comco Ikarus Sherpa II	8403-1054	
D-MSKT	Comco Ikarus Sherpa II	8408-1077	
D-MSKV	Comco Ikarus Sherpa II	8407-1071	
D-MSKW	Comco Ikarus Sherpa II	8405-1066	
D-MSKX	Comco Ikarus Sherpa II	8407-1074	
D-MSKZ	Comco Ikarus Sherpa II	8407-1073	
D-MSLA	Comco Ikarus Sherpa II	8506-1102	
D-MSLC	Comco Ikarus Sherpa II D	8507-1104	
D-MSLD	Comco Ikarus Sherpa II D	8511-1109	
D-MSLE	Comco Ikarus Sherpa II D	8606-1122	
D-MSLG	Comco Fox	038	

Regn.	Type	C/n	Prev.Id.
D-MSLI	Comco Ikarus Fox-C22	8607-3026	
D-MSLJ	Tandem Air Sunny s.b.s.	SuS-08.94	
D-MSLL(2)	Tecnam P.92 Echo	215	
D-MSLM	WDFL Sunwheel R	038	
D-MSLN	Mosquito Ib	021	
D-MSLO	Funk FK-12 Comet	015	
D-MSLP	Funk FK-12 Comet	005	
D-MSLS	Zenair CH-601D Zodiac	6-3650	
D-MSLU	Comco Ikarus Fox-C22B	940 .-3600	
D-MSMB	WDFL Sunwheel R	047	
D-MSMH	WDFL Sunwheel	017	
D-MSMI	Comco Ikarus Fox-C22C	9602-3682	
D-MSML(2)	Albatros 64	310	
D-MSMM	Rans S-12 Airaile	1292357	
D-MSMS	Rans S-12 Airaile	0493406	
D-MSMT	Tandem Air Sunny Sport	53.93	
D-MSMV	WDFL Fascination	011	
D-MSNR	NST Minimum Saphir 17	M471	
D-MSNW	Comco Ikarus Fox-C22C	9608-3711	
D-MSOB	Steinbach Austro-Trike Euro IIIM	1129	
D-MSOC	ASO Storch	11010408	
D-MSOD	Comco Ikarus Fox-C22B	9403-3547	
D-MSOE	Tandem Air Sunny s.b.s.	SuS-04.94	
D-MSOF	ASO Storch	11011408	
D-MSOG	ASO Storch	11012409	
D-MSOH	NST Minimum	218	
D-MSOI	Comco Ikarus Fox-C22B	9507-3667	
D-MSOL(2)	Comco Ikarus C-42 Cyclone	9702-6039	
D-MSOM	Comco Ikarus C-42 Cyclone	9604-6004	
D-MSOO	Flight Design CT	98.02.01.21	
D-MSOP	Comco Ikarus C-42 Cyclone	9604-6005	
D-MSOQ	Zenair CH-601 Zodiac	6-3523	
D-MSOR	Comco Ikarus Fox-C22B	9208-3413	
D-MSOS	Schmidtler Ranger M Trike	M 868066	
D-MSOT	Mantel Mono-Dragster	M 873089	
D-MSOV	Comco Ikarus C-42 Cyclone	95-7-0001	
D-MSOW	Solid Air Diamant 55dB(A) Trike	018	
D-MSPC	Rans S-6 Coyote II	0795856	
D-MSPE	Tandem Air Sunny s.b.s.	SuS-01.94	
D-MSPK	Funk FK-11 (Prototype)	11912	
D-MSPO	Flight Design CT	98.03.01.25	
D-MSPP	Albatros 52	128	
D-MSPR	Ultraleichtverbund Bi 90	7373917708	
D-MSPS	NST Minimum Saphir 17	465	
D-MSPW	Schmidtler Enduro Trike	02001	
D-MSPY	Fair Fax Trike Euro III	043	
D-MSRB	Zenair CH-601D Zodiac	6-3404/023 0697	
D-MSRG	Dallach Sunrise II	025	D-MLOH
D-MSRH	Zenair CH-701 STOL	001	
D-MSRJ	Tecnam P.92 Echo	233	
D-MSRL	Tecnam P.96 Golf	027	
D-MSRO	Ultraleichtverbund Bi 90	674	
D-MSRP	Tecnam P.92 Echo	131	
D-MSRR	Tandem Air Sunny Targa	TA-001	
D-MSRS	Aviasud Mistral 53	008	
D-MSRU	Platzer Kiebitz-B2	087	
D-MSRW	Tecnam P.96 Golf	025	
D-MSSB	Behlen Power-Trike Vampir	87023	
D-MSSC	Eipper Quicksilver GT-400	GT 2801326	
D-MSSG	Klüver Twin Racer SX 16 Trike	503202	
D-MSSK	Tecnam P.96 Golf	034	
D-MSSL	Comco Ikarus Fox-C22C	9606-3717	
D-MSSO	Tecnam P.92 Echo	227	
D-MSSR	Jet Fox 91D	0011	
D-MSSW	WDFL Sunwheel DZ	044	
D-MSSZ	TL-232 Condor	97 C 03	
D-MSTB	HFL Stratos 300K	300-024K	
D-MSTC	HFL Stratos 300K	300-025K	
D-MSTD	HFL Stratos 300K	300-026K	
D-MSTE	Warnke Skylight Trike	1010	
D-MSTG	Funk FK-9 TG	083	
D-MSTI	Comco Ikarus Fox-C22	9309-3517	
D-MSTK	Ultraleichtverbund Bi 90	B987	
D-MSTO	NST Schwarze Trike	T285	
D-MSTT	NST Minimum	M250	
D-MSTU	Comco Ikarus Fox-C22	9504-3644	
D-MSTW	Fisher FP-404 Classic	C084	
D-MSTZ	Sport Parasol	002	
D-MSUB(2)	Comco Ikarus Fox-C22C	9901-3741	
D-MSUE	Kümmerle Mini-Fly-Set	1309/91-6	
D-MSUF	Funk FK-12 Comet	012-007	
D-MSUN	Dallach Sunrise II	016	
D-MSUR	Rans S-6 Coyote II	0391171	G-MWUM
D-MSUW	Comco Ikarus Fox-C22C	9804-3738	
D-MSVS(2)	Air Création GTE 582 S	7974656042	
D-MSWC	Sky-Walker	102	
D-MSWD	Sky-Walker 1+1	26134	
D-MSWE	Sky-Walker 1+1	26135	
D-MSWF	Sky-Walker 1+1	26136	
D-MSWG	Sky-Walker 1+1	26137	
D-MSWI	Sky-Walker 1+1	26138	
D-MSWJ	Comco Fox D	8506-FD28	
D-MSWK	Tecnam P.96 Golf	026	
D-MSWL	HFL Stratos 300K	300-016K	
D-MSWN	Sky-Walker 1+1	26141	
D-MSWO	Sky-Walker 1+1	26130	
D-MSWP	Sky-Walker II	144	
D-MSWQ	Sky-Walker II	145	
D-MSWR	Sky-Walker 1+1	26146	
D-MSWT	Sky-Walker II	157	
D-MSWU	Sky-Walker II	212	
D-MSWV	Sky-Walker II	159	
D-MSWW	Sky-Walker II	160	
D-MSWX	Sky-Walker 1+1	26124	
D-MSWY	Sky-Walker 1+1	26125	
D-MSWZ	Sky-Walker 1+1	26126	
D-MSYK	Platzer Kiebitz-B6	162	
D-MSYW	Sky-Walker II	185	
D-MSYY	Albatros 64	127	
D-MSYZ	Lohle Mustang 5151	001	
D-MSZW	UPM Cobra Trike	920116	
D-MTAA(2)	Comco Ikarus Fox-C22	9706-3728	
D-MTAB	Pioneer Flightstar	535	
D-MTAC(2)	WDFL Sunwheel R	043	
D-MTAD(2)	Comco Ikarus Fox-C22C	97 . .-3730	
D-MTAE	Pioneer Flightstar	538	
D-MTAG	Pioneer Flightstar	540	
D-MTAH(2)	Comco Ikarus Fox-C22	9205-3398	
D-MTAJ	Tandem Air Sunny s.b.s.	03.94	
D-MTAK	Pioneer Flightstar	544	
D-MTAL	Comco Ikarus C-42 Cyclone	9706-6038	
D-MTAN	Pioneer Flightstar	553	
D-MTAR	Pioneer Flightstar	550	
D-MTAS	Pioneer Flightstar	551	
D-MTAU	Pioneer Flightstar	543	
D-MTAV	Tandem Air Sunny Targa	002	
D-MTAX	Klüver Racer SX 12 Trike	078809	
D-MTAY	Comco Ikarus Fox-C22B	9404-3576	
D-MTAZ	Klüver Twin Racer Trike	233109	
D-MTBA(2)	Comco Ikarus Fox-C22C	9705-3727	
D-MTBC	Warnke Skylight Trike	043	
D-MTBD	Comco Ikarus Fox-C22	3616	
D-MTBE	Comco Ikarus Fox-C22B	9409-3617	
D-MTBF	Comco Ikarus Fox-C22C	9607-3712	
D-MTBG	LO-120S	022	
D-MTBJ	NST Minimum	M536	
D-MTBK	Comco Ikarus Fox-C22	9306-3523	
D-MTBQ	Behlen Trike	87020	
D-MTBS	LO-120	008A	
D-MTBW	Comco Ikarus C-42 Cyclone	9809-6134	
D-MTCA	Comco Ikarus Fox-C22C	9411-3615	
D-MTCC	Flight Design CT	98.04.03.30	
D-MTCH	Behlen Power Trike Vampir II	0025/83	
D-MTCI	Air-Light Wild Thing	97 02 009	
D-MTCT	Flight Design CT	98.09.01.37	
D-MTDC	Comco Ikarus C-42 Cyclone	9801-6060	
D-MTDD	Funk FK-10	001	
D-MTDN	Comco Ikarus Fox-C22B	9110-3359	
D-MTDP	Rans S-6S Coyote II	0795860	
D-MTDX	Comco Ikarus Fox-C22B	940 .-3583	

Regn.	Type	C/n	Prev.Id.
D-MTEA	Comco Ikarus Fox-C22C	9. . .-3680	
D-MTEB	Comco Ikarus Fox-C22B	9601-3698	
D-MTEC	Light Aero Avid Flyer D	1358	
D-MTED	Sky-Walker II	262	
D-MTEF	Ikarusflug Eurofox	048098	
D-MTEG	Comco Ikarus Fox-C22C	9804-3737	
D-MTEI	Rans S-6 Coyote II	895879	
D-MTEK	Comco Ikarus C-42 Cyclone	9705-6028	
D-MTES	Air-Light Wild Thing	024	
D-MTEV	Klüver Twin Racer SX 16 Trike	836910	
D-MTFC	Comco Ikarus Fox-C22B	9403-3557	
D-MTFF	Comco Ikarus C-42 Cyclone	9711-6092	
D-MTFJ	Warnke Skylight Trike	SI 032	
D-MTFL	Comco Ikarus Fox-C22C	9. . .-3720	
D-MTFT	Rans S-12 XL Airaile	06950613	
D-MTFZ	Tecnam P.96 Golf	021	
D-MTGA	Comco Ikarus Fox-C22	9109-3354	
D-MTGB	Funk FK-9TG	041	
D-MTGE	Tecnam P.92 Echo	118	
D-MTGM	Seiffert Mini II	FO 10189	
D-MTHA	Platzer Kiebitz B	086	
D-MTHE	Dallach Sunrise IIa	024	
D-MTHG	Bek Me 109R	007	
D-MTHH	Albatros SX	506	
D-MTHI	Eipper Quicksilver MX	4315	
D-MTHL	Comco Ikarus C-42 Cyclone	9709-6040	
D-MTHM	Comco Ikarus C-42 Cyclone	9805-6083	
D-MTHR	Zenair CH-601RD Zodiac	6-8052	
D-MTHS	WDFL Sunwheel R	040	
D-MTHU	Albatros SX	505	
D-MTHW	Ultraleichtverbund Bi 90	21001	
D-MTIC	WDFL Fascination	046	
D-MTIG	Tecnam P.92 Echo	216	
D-MTII	Schönleber Trike Speed 14	011093	
D-MTIL	Comco Ikarus Fox-C22B	940 .-3599	
D-MTIP	Klüver Kaiman Trike	076809	
D-MTIS	Tecnam P.92 Echo	288	
D-MTIT	Platzer Kiebitz-B2	080	
D-MTIY	WDFL Sunwheel R	012	
D-MTJG	Behlen Power-Trike II Hazard 15	93001	
D-MTKB	Flight Design CT	98.03.02.26	
D-MTKF	Pioneer Flightstar I	980316	
D-MTKM	WDFL Fascination	033	
D-MTKN	Funk FK-9	008	
D-MTKR	Comco Ikarus Fox-C22	9209-3431	
D-MTLD	Schönleber DS Lotus KS 16 Trike	030589	
D-MTLF	Tecnam P.92 Echo	205	
D-MTLI	HFL Stratos 300	300-029	
D-MTLM	Tandem Air Sunny	27-92	
D-MTLU	TST-232 Condor	98 C 07	
D-MTMA	NST Minimum	M312	
D-MTMM	Behlen Power-Trike	840012	
D-MTMT	Zenair CH-601D Zodiac	6-8047/004 0097	
D-MTNT	Comco Ikarus Fox-C22	950 .-3645	
D-MTOF	Take Off Maximum Hazard 15M	T033080	
D-MTOG	Tecnam P.92 Echo	117	
D-MTOH	Technoflug Piccolo BM	103	
D-MTOP	Funk FK-9	082	
D-MTOS	Tandem Air Sunny Sport	18.91	
D-MTOY	Evektor EV.97 Eurostar	98 02 06	
D-MTPA	Sky-Walker 1+1	26117	
D-MTPC	Tecnam P.92 Echo	175	
D-MTPK	Funk FK-9 Mk3	106	
D-MTPS	Comco Ikarus Fox-C22	9501-3655	
D-MTRH	Comco Ikarus C-42 Cyclone	9809-6128	
D-MTRI	Ikarusflug Eurofox Pro	027096	
D-MTRL	Comco Ikarus C-42 Cyclone	9607-6003	
D-MTRS	Eipper Quicksilver	3898	
D-MTRT	Comco Ikarus Fox-C22	9407-3586	
D-MTRW	Funk FK-9	014	
D-MTSA	Solid Air Twin Diamant Trike	002	
D-MTSB	Funk FK-9	035	
D-MTSD	Murphy Renegade	483	
D-MTSM	Comco Ikarus Fox-C22B	9406-3594	
D-MTSS	Rans S-6 Coyote II	0395782	

Regn.	Type	C/n	Prev.Id.
D-MTST	Behlen Power-Trike	84003	
D-MTTA	Pioneer Flightstar	385	
D-MTTF	Pioneer Flightstar	379	
D-MTTP(2)	Rans S-6ES Coyote II	019811991 ES	
D-MTTR	Ultraleichtverbund Bi 90	3916759	
D-MTTV	Comco Ikarus Fox-C22	9208-3419	
D-MTUD	Funk FK-6	002	
D-MTUI	Tecnam P.92 Echo	261	
D-MTUS	Comco Ikarus Fox-C22B	9507-3666	
D-MTVM	WDFL Sunwheel R	016	
D-MTVV	Comco Ikarus C-42 Cyclone	"9705-028"	
D-MTWD	Ikarusflug Eurofox Pro	054098	
D-MTWE	Sky-Walker II	396	
D-MTWL	Comco Ikarus Fox-C22B	9404-3561	
D-MTWO	WDFL Sunwheel	022	
D-MTWT	Air-Light Wild Thing	001	
D-MTWZ(2)	Drachenstudio Piccolo	003	
D-MUAB	Sky-Walker II	500	
D-MUAC	Fisher FP-404 Classic	4065	
D-MUAE	Comco Ikarus Fox-C22	8812-3183	
D-MUAG	Comco Ikarus C-42 Cyclone	9803-6138	
D-MUAZ	Behlen Power Trike II	91023	
D-MUBB	Warnke Skylight Trike	036	
D-MUBF	Rans S-10 Sakota	1189068	
D-MUBK	Comco Ikarus Fox-C22	9403-3548	
D-MUBS	Air-Light Wild Thing	015	
D-MUBT	Comco Ikarus Fox-C22B	9404-3563	
D-MUCB	Sky-Walker II	309	
D-MUCE	Air-Light Wild Thing	022	
D-MUCH	Comco Ikarus Fox-C22	9508-3687	
D-MUCI	WDFL Sunwheel R	018	
D-MUCK	Scheibe Uli 1	5215	
D-MUCZ	Bek Me 109 R	004	
D-MUDD	Fair Fax Trike Euro III	1712	
D-MUDI	Klüver Bison Profil 19 Trike	M3485733	
D-MUDM	UPM-Trike	880051	
D-MUDO	Platzer Motte B-2	49	
D-MUDP	Comco Ikarus Fox-C22	8905-3196	
D-MUED	Funk FK-9 Mk3	111	
D-MUEF	Ikarusflug Eurofox Pro	050098	
D-MUEK	Ikarusflug Eurofox Bugrad	045098	
D-MUEN	Sky-Walker 1+1	156	
D-MUES	NST Minimum Santana Trike	M329	
D-MUFD	Comco Ikarus Fox-C22	9503-3631	
D-MUFE	Comco Ikarus Fox-C22	9303-3495	
D-MUFG	Comco Ikarus C-42 Cyclone	97-4-6013	
D-MUFK	Funk FK-9TG Mk3	096	
D-MUFL	Light Aero Avid Flyer	1457D	
D-MUFM	Tecnam P.92 Echo	320	
D-MUFO	Comco Ikarus Fox-C22	8709-3083	
D-MUFS	Funk FK-9 Mk3	09-03-099	
D-MUGK	Platzer Kiebitz-B2	117	
D-MUGS	WDFL Sunwheel R	041	
D-MUHF	Comco Ikarus Fox-C22	9403-3584	
D-MUHG	Remos Gemini 3 Mirage	048	
D-MUHI	Ultraleichtverbund Bi 90	21000	
D-MUHK	Light Aero Avid Flyer STOL	1521D	
D-MUHL(2)	Mitchell Wing B	AB-01	
D-MUHR	Air-Light Wild Thing	003	
D-MUHS	Rans S-10 Sakota	0790109	
D-MUID	Comco Ikarus C-42 Cyclone	9612-6014	
D-MUIF(2)	Ikarusflug Eurofox Basic	033097	
D-MUKD	Comco Ikarus Fox-C22B	9702-3704	
D-MUKE	Fair Fax Trike	015	
D-MUKI	Schmidtler Ranger M Trike	18-33	
D-MUKK	Warnke Puma Sprint Trike	D006	
D-MUKL	Scheibe Uli 1	5212	
D-MUKU	Micro Star	01	
D-MUKW	Rans S-6 Coyote II	1294702	N8046U
D-MUKY	Moskito Ib	018	
D-MULA	Scheibe Uli 1	5214	
D-MULB	UPM Cobra Trike	900092	
	(Same c/n also quoted for D-MBOY)		
D-MULE	Light Aero Avid Flyer D	1402	
D-MULI	Scheibe Uli 1	5203	

Regn.	Type	C/n	Prev.Id.
D-MULJ	Platzer Kiebitz-B4	108	
D-MULK	Comco Ikarus C-42 Cyclone	9706-6043	
D-MULN	Klüver Twin Racer Trike	232109	
D-MULO	LO-120S	015A	
D-MULP	Comco Ikarus C-42 Cyclone	9 . . . -6052	
D-MULR	Ultraleichtverbund Bi 90	940	
D-MULT	NST Minimum	359	
D-MUMA	Klüver Twin Racer SX 16 Trike	117106	
D-MUMD	Comco Ikarus C-42 Cyclone	9809-6143	
D-MUMI	Tecnam P.92 Echo	295	
D-MUMO	Lohle Mustang 5151	006	
D-MUMS	Platzer Kiebitz-B8	107	
D-MUMU	Funk FK-9	019	
D-MUMY	Behlen Power-Trike II Focus 20	85029	
D-MUNA	Schönleber DS Speed KS 14	L01039093	
D-MUND	Platzer Motte B3	55	
D-MUNI	Bobcat	09AD91	
D-MUNK	Comco Ikarus C-42 Cyclone	9702-6031	
D-MUNO	Comco Ikarus Fox-C22B	9507-3665	
D-MUON	Klüver Twin Racer Quartz SX 16	504202	
D-MUPA	Tandem Air Sunny s.b.s.	SuS-V-4.95	
D-MUPF	WDFL Sunwheel R	031	
D-MUPW	Funk FK-9	088	
D-MUPZ	Tecnam P.96 Golf	022	
D-MUQI	Evektor EV.97 Eurostar	98 03 05	
D-MURA	Warnke Skylight Trike	S 1019	
D-MURB	Scout	013	
D-MURD	Platzer Kiebitz-B9	160	
D-MURE	Scheibe Uli 1	5218	
D-MURI	Scheibe Uli 1	5213	
D-MURJ	Comco Ikarus C-42 Cyclone	9803-6103	
D-MURK	Comco Ikarus Fox-C22	9304-3494	
D-MURR	Sky-Walker 1+1	26116	
D-MURT	Comco Ikarus Fox-C22	9202-3 . . .	
D-MURX	Scheibe Uli 1	5220	
D-MUSA	Rans S-12 Airaile	0294479	
D-MUSC	Comco Ikarus Fox-C22	9006-3270	
D-MUSE	Scheibe Uli 1	3303	
D-MUSI	Tecnam P.92 Echo	339	
D-MUSJ	ASO Viper Hazard 15M Trike	1102502	
D-MUSL	Comco Ikarus Fox-C22	9209-3464	
D-MUSM	Comco Ikarus Fox-C22	9502-3632	
D-MUSS	Behlen Power-Trike Vampir II	85031	
D-MUST	Behlen Power-Trike	88026	
D-MUSW	Schmidtler Enduro Trike	F03/86	
D-MUTA	Platzer Kiebitz-B8	042	
D-MUTF	Tandem Air Sunny s.b.s.	SuS 04.96	
D-MUTS	Schmidtler Ranger M Trike	0021	
D-MUTT	Air-Light Wild Thing	013	
D-MUTV	Platzer Kiebitz-B8	110	
D-MUUU(2)	Comco Ikarus C-42 Cyclone	9810-6156	
D-MUVI	Tecnam P.92 Echo	210	
D-MUVO	Bobcat	KA-1	
D-MUWH	Comco Ikarus C-42 Cyclone	unkn	
D-MUXI	Remos Gemini Ultra	029	
D-MUXS	Comco Ikarus Fox-C22	940 . -3589	
D-MUXX	WDFL Fascination	050	
D-MUZE	Schmidtler Enduro Trike	02002	
D-MVAB	Comco Ikarus Fox-C22B	940 . -3601	
D-MVAC	Comco Ikarus Fox-C22	9 . . . -3614	
D-MVAD	Platzer Kiebitz-B9	161	
D-MVAE	Tecnam P.92 Echo	234	
D-MVAG	Saurier Flug Vagabond	unkn	
D-MVAL	Rans S-6S Coyote II	1195897 S	
D-MVBB	WDFL Fascination	032	
D-MVBD	ASO Viper Trike	22028202	
D-MVBF(2)	Platzer Kiebitz-B2	101	
D-MVBG	Albatros Av.Sud	940550812	
D-MVBL	Klüver Bison Trike	112706	
D-MVBM	WDFL Fascination	041	
D-MVBP	Sky Walker II	384	
D-MVBS	Scheibe SF-40	3104	
D-MVBU	Comco Ikarus Fox-C22	9407-3588	
D-MVCT	Flight Design CT	CT 005	
D-MVCY	Tandem Air Sunny Targa	TA-011.93	

Regn.	Type	C/n	Prev.Id.
D-MVDC	Comco Ikarus Fox-C22	9205-3407	
D-MVDO	Funk FK-9 TG	045	
D-MVEB	Comco Ikarus C-42 Cyclone	9811-6148	
D-MVEF	Ikarusflug Eurofox	unkn	
D-MVEL	Air-Light Wild Thing	026	
D-MVER	Comco Ikarus Fox-C22	9101-3300/3511	
D-MVET	Comco Ikarus C-42 Cyclone	9610-6053	
D-MVFB	Comco Ikarus Fox-C22	9105-3332	
D-MVFF	Comco Ikarus Sherpa	8403-1053	
D-MVFK	Funk FK-14 Polaris	unkn	
D-MVFL	Comco Ikarus Fox-C22B	9506-3664	
D-MVFP	Rans S-6 Coyote II	0994675	
D-MVGS	Air-Light Wild Thing	029	
D-MVGW	Vagabund	002	
D-MVHB	WDFL Fascination	021	
D-MVHE	WDFL Fascination	026	
D-MVHP	Funk FK-9	090	
D-MVHR	Comco Ikarus C-42 Cyclone	9804-6133	
D-MVIC	Platzer Kiebitz-B6	165	
D-MVIL	Rans S-6 Coyote II	1295914	
D-MVIP	Klüver Racer SX 12 Trike	641907	
D-MVIR	Comco Ikarus Fox-C22B	9405-3564	
D-MVIS	Comco Ikarus Fox-C22	9501-3633	
D-MVJB	Comco Ikarus C-42 Cyclone	9708-6049	
D-MVKA	Comco Ikarus C-42 Cyclone	9712-6041	
D-MVKB	Platzer Motte B2	58	
D-MVKM	Remos Gemini 3 Mirage	052	
D-MVKO	Sky-Walker II	382	
D-MVKR	Sky-Walker II	268	
D-MVKV	Tecnam P.92 Echo	164	
D-MVLL	Comco Ikarus Fox-C22	950 . -3647	
D-MVLP	Comco Ikarus Fox-C22	9109-3351	
D-MVNE	Light Aero Avid Mk.IV	1496	
D-MVNO	Comco Ikarus Fox-C22C	9607-3713	
D-MVOE	WDFL Fascination	003	
D-MVOG	Wisch Star-Trike Profil 17M	09870020	
D-MVOI	Comco Ikarus C-42 Cyclone	9706-6033	
D-MVOK	Rans S-12 Airaile	0593416	
D-MVOL	Rans S-7 Courier	0597219	
D-MVOM	Scheibe SF-40	3103	
D-MVRA	Comco Ikarus C-42 Cyclone	9808-6114	
D-MVRS	Tecnam P.92 Echo	155	
D-MVSE	WDFL Fascination	017	
D-MVSK	ASO Viper Hazard 15 Trike	15I17791	
D-MVST	Tandem Air Sunny s.b.s.	SuS 06.96	
D-MVVA	Klüver Racer Quartz SX 12 Trike	734011	
D-MVVB	AGREX	001	
D-MVVH	Comco Ikarus Fox-C22B	9 . . . -3702	
D-MVVR	Flight Design CT	CT 008/97	
D-MVVV	Aviasud Mistral BRD	125	
D-MVVX	Schmidtler Enduro Focus 18M Trike	040385	
D-MVXY	NST Minimum	460	
D-MVYY	Ikarusflug Eurofox	022096	
D-MWAA	Remos Gemini 3 Mirage	035	
D-MWAC	Remos Gemini Ultra	004	
D-MWAD	Behlen Power-Trike Hazard 15	92031	
D-MWAE	Platzer Kiebitz-B2	133	
D-MWAF	Take Off Maximum Trike	3059	
D-MWAG	Platzer Kiebitz-B2	030	
D-MWAH	Fisher FP-404 Classic	C087	
D-MWAI	Comco Ikarus Fox-C22C	9708-3732	
D-MWAK	Funk FK-9	052	
D-MWAL	Ultraleichtverbund Bi 90	9234016831	
D-MWAM	Comco Ikarus C-42 Cyclone	9807-6130	
D-MWAN	Rans S-12XL Airaile	08950641	
D-MWAR	Air-Light Wild Thing	017	
D-MWAV	NST Minimum	M472	
D-MWAW	Comco Ikarus Fox-C22	9502-3613	
D-MWBA	Weedhopper	1006	D-MDJK?
	(Same c/n quoted but D-MDJK no longer current)		
D-MWBB	Ikarusflug Eurofox	030097	
D-MWBC	Weedhopper	0999	
D-MWBE	Funbird	1005/84	
D-MWBH	Funbird	0143/82	
D-MWBK	Comco Fox	040	

Regn.	Type	C/n	Prev.Id.
D-MWBM	Comco Ikarus Fox-C22C	9710-3733	
D-MWBS	Air-Light Wild Thing	unkn	
D-MWBV	Rans S-7 Courier	0193103	
D-MWBW	Comco Ikarus Fox-C22	9...-3612	
D-MWCA	Fair Fax DR Hazard 15M Trike	D007	
D-MWCB	Comco Ikarus Fox-C22	9...-3611	
D-MWCC	Comco Ikarus Fox-C22B	9506-3675	
D-MWCO	WDFL Fascination	039	
D-MWDA	WDFL Sunwheel R	001	
D-MWDG	Rans S-6 Coyote II XL	1294707	
D-MWDH	WDFL Fascination	005	
D-MWDI	Platzer Kiebitz-B4	175	
D-MWDK	Remos Gemini Ultra	E12.013	
D-MWDL	Zenair CH-601D Zodiac	6-3653	
D-MWDR	Tecnam P.92 Echo	277	
D-MWEA	Rans S-6 Coyote II	0895876	
D-MWEC	Comco Ikarus C-42 Cyclone	9806-6098	
D-MWEF	Hummer	15184	
D-MWEH	Fisher Super Koala	Ei-10	
D-MWEI	Schönleber DS Trike 40kw	030389	
D-MWEP	Comco Ikarus Fox-C22B	9...-3683	
D-MWER	Comco Ikarus Fox-C22	9010-3296	
D-MWES	Funk FK-9 Mk3	109	
D-MWEW	Funk FK-12 Comet	014	
D-MWFG	Comco Ikarus C-42 Cyclone	9805-6096	
D-MWFP	Flight Design CT	98.02.04.24	
D-MWFR	WDFL Fascination	040	
D-MWFS	Comco Ikarus C-42 Cyclone	9811-6099	
D-MWFT	Zenair CH-601D Zodiac	6-3529/014 0097	
D-MWFZ	Loehle Sport Parasol	001	
D-MWGB(2)	Comco Ikarus C-42 Cyclone	9801-6063	
D-MWGE	Funk FK-9	069	
D-MWGF	Platzer Kiebitz-B9	202	
D-MWGH	Funk FK-9	054	
D-MWGJ	Comco Ikarus C-42 Cyclone	9810-6140	
D-MWGN	Platzer Kiebitz-B9	140	
D-MWGS	Remos Gemini Ultra	009	
D-MWGT	Platzer Kiebitz-B6	182	
D-MWHA	Remos Gemini Ultra	030	
D-MWHB	Take Off Maximum Lotus 18	021129	
D-MWHC	Comco Ikarus C-42 Cyclone	9810-6136	
D-MWHD	UPM Cobra Trike	920117	
D-MWHF	ATEC Zephyr	unkn	
D-MWHG	MKB Enduro Focus 18 Trike	030886	
D-MWHH	NST Minimum	M245	
D-MWHI	Sky-Walker II	271	
D-MWHJ	Remos Gemini Ultra	008	
D-MWHM	ASO 26 Storch 582	160.2	
D-MWHO	Ultraleichtverbund Bi 90	662	
D-MWHR	Tandem Air Sunny Sport	49.93	
D-MWHU	Denney Kitfox IV	1860	
D-MWHW	Comco Ikarus Fox-C22	9203-3373	
D-MWIE	Platzer Kiebitz-B2	032	
D-MWIF	Ikarusflug Eurofox	95017	
D-MWII	WDFL Fascination	024	
D-MWIK	Fair Fax Trike	016	
D-MWIR	Behlen Power-Trike II	95007	
D-MWIT	Ultraleichtverbund Bi 90	4017032	
D-MWIW	Take Off Maximum Hazard 15	037110	
D-MWJA	Zenair CH-601D Zodiac	6-3520	
D-MWJB	Remos Gemini Ultra	E13.014	
D-MWJN	Ultraleichtverbund Bi 90	735	
D-MWJO	WDFL Sunwheel	029	
D-MWKA	Comco Ikarus Fox-C22B	9504-3659	
D-MWKB	HFL Stratos IIe	IIe-010	D-MMDH?
D-MWKD	Platzer Kiebitz-B8	027	
D-MWKE	Comco Ikarus Fox-C22	9204-3393	
D-MWKF	Platzer Kiebitz-B8	130	
D-MWKG	Comco Ikarus Fox-C22B	9504-3660	
D-MWKH	Dallach Sunrise II	019	
D-MWKJ	WDFL Fascination	007	
D-MWKL	Comco Ikarus C-42 Cyclone	9804-6093	
D-MWKN	Murphy Renegade	517	
D-MWKO	Comco Ikarus Fox-C22	9501-3610	
D-MWKS	ASO Viper Hazard 15 Trike	1234	

Regn.	Type	C/n	Prev.Id.
D-MWKT	Comco Ikarus Fox-C22	9...-3626	
D-MWKU	Comco Ikarus Fox-C22	9...-3649	
D-MWKV	Platzer Kiebitz-B6	46	
D-MWKW	Platzer Kiebitz-B4	126	
D-MWLA	Pioneer Flightstar	683	
D-MWLB	Zenair CH-601D Zodiac	6-3451/019 0097	
D-MWLC	Comco Ikarus Fox-C22	9501-3627	
D-MWLD	Comco Ikarus Fox-C22	9205-3408	
D-MWLF	Comco Ikarus Fox-C22	9505-3651	
D-MWLM	Comco Ikarus Fox-C22	9501-3628	
D-MWLR	Comco Ikarus Fox-C22	9...-3650	
D-MWLT	Klüver Bison Trike	22/708	
D-MWLZ	Comco Ikarus Fox-C22	9310-3533	
D-MWMA	Flight Design CT	97.11.03.13	
D-MWMF	Rans S-12 Airaile	1292358	
D-MWMG	Lohle Mustang 5151	008	
D-MWMH	Sky-Walker II	511	
D-MWMI	Platzer Kiebitz-B8	122	
D-MWML	Platzer Kiebitz-B9	098	
D-MWMN	Mantel Mono-Dragster	M870226	
D-MWMS	NST Minimum	M504	
D-MWMZ	Light Aero Avid Flyer	877	
D-MWNN	Rans S-6ES Coyote II	1292414	
D-MWOB	Comco Ikarus Fox-C22	9...-3531	
D-MWOC	Comco Ikarus Fox-C22	9...-3329	
D-MWOL	WDFL Fascination	001	
D-MWOP	Behlen Power-Trike	87013	
D-MWOR	Comco Ikarus Fox-C22	9110-3358	
D-MWOT	Comco Ikarus C-42 Cyclone	9806-6109	
D-MWPB	Comco Ikarus Fox II Doppel	8606-3022	
D-MWPG	Comco Ikarus C-42 Cyclone	9711-6065	
D-MWPL	Murphy Renegade II	549	
D-MWPM	TL-232 Condor	unkn	
D-MWPN	Flight Design CT	98.02.02.22	
D-MWPP	Sky-Walker II	254	
D-MWPW	Albatros Av.Sud	940550802	
D-MWRA	Rans S-6ES Coyote II	595817ES	
D-MWRB	Klüver Twin Racer Quartz SX 16	695010	
D-MWRC	Comco Ikarus C-42 Cyclone	9810-6182	
D-MWRD	Tecnam P.92 Echo	204	
D-MWRF	Comco Ikarus C-42 Cyclone	9902-6160	
D-MWRG	Murphy Renegade	592	
D-MWRH	Evektor EV.97 Eurostar	98 02 02	
D-MWRO	Tecnam P.92 Echo	210	
D-MWRS	Remos Gemini Ultra	007	
D-MWRW	NST Minimum	unkn	
D-MWRX	Platzer Kiebitz-B2	043	
D-MWSA	ASO Viper Trike	15I1690	
D-MWSB	Sky-Walker II	269	
D-MWSD	Remos Gemini Ultra	011	
D-MWSE	Rans S-6 Coyote II	0694636	
D-MWSH	Platzer Kiebitz-B-450	177	
D-MWSI (1)	Dallach Sunrise II	015	
D-MWSI (2)	Schmidtler Enduro DS Trike	010987	
D-MWSK(1)	ASO Viper Trike	3101	
D-MWSK(2)	Comco Ikarus Fox-C22	9509-3688	
D-MWSM	Steinbach Austro-Trike	unkn	
D-MWSP	Behlen Power-Trike	374	
D-MWSS	Comco Ikarus C-42 Cyclone	9901-6135	
D-MWSW	Take Off Maximum Trike	045021	
D-MWSY	Tandem Air Sunny Targa	010	
D-MWSZ	Zenair CH-601 Zodiac	6-3412/007 0597	
D-MWTC	Air-Light Wild Thing	007	
D-MWTD	ULF Moskito	01B	
D-MWTL	TL-232 Condor Plus	96C01	
D-MWTS	Comco Ikarus Fox-C22	940.-3552	
D-MWTT	Fair Fax Trike	028	
D-MWTV	Albatros 52	124	
D-MWTW	Comco Ikarus Fox-C22	9503-3648	
D-MWUD	Albatros 64	307	
D-MWUM	Light Aero Avid Flyer	1465	
D-MWUT	Comco Ikarus Fox-C22B	9506-3663	
D-MWWA	Klüver Bison Trike	253708	
D-MWWH	Albatros	113	
D-MWWR	Ultraleichtverbund Bi 90	3957007	

Regn.	Type	C/n	Prev.Id.
D-MWWV	Schönleber Minimum	LO 1/0288	
D-MWWZ	Schmidtler Enduro Trike	01-002	
D-MWWR(2)	Sky-Walker II	148	
D-MWWT	Air-Light Wild Thing	032	
D-MWWW	Sky-Walker 1+1	26143	
D-MWXB	Comco Ikarus Fox-C22	9309-3529	
D-MWXW	Comco Ikarus Fox-C22	9501-3630	
D-MWYC	Albatros	125	
D-MWYY	Funk FK-9	017	
D-MWZL	Comco Ikarus Fox-C22	9...-3536	
D-MXAC	Platzer Motte B Rumpf	VO 001	
D-MXAF	Platzer Kiebitz A	001	
D-MXAQ	Aériane Sirocco	042	
D-MXAY	Funk FK-9 TG	068	
D-MXAZ	Götz 50	001	
D-MXBA(2)	ASO 26 Storch 503	FT460	
D-MXBC	Comco Ikarus Sherpa	8309-001	
D-MXBD	Aviasud Mistral 53	002	
D-MXBE(2)	Comco Ikarus Fox-C22B	9404-3562	
D-MXBM	Aviasud Mistral 53	001	
D-MXBV	Funk FK-9 Mk.3	116	
D-MXBW	Homebuilt, type unknown	1	
D-MXBX	Rans S-12 Airaile	0594493	
D-MXBY	ASO 26 Storch	FT240	
D-MXBZ	ASO 26 Storch 503	FT234	
D-MXCC	Light Aero Avid Flyer	261	
D-MXCH	Chinook	02817	
D-MXCM	Bobcat	001	
D-MXDE	ASO Storch/503	11001202	
D-MXDI	Solid Air Diamant Twin Hazard 13	T003	
D-MXEG	Dallach Sunrise II	014	
D-MXET	Flight Team Spider Trike	D017	
D-MXFK	Funk FK-9	001	
D-MXFO	Snoopy II	001	
D-MXFT	Rans S-6 Coyote II	0889060	
D-MXGI	Comco Ikarus C-42 Cyclone	9804-6090	
D-MXHE	LO-120	001	
D-MXHL	Weedhopper	2214	
D-MXHM	Eipper Quicksilver	1100	
D-MXHT	HFL Stratos 300	300-001	
D-MXHW	Air-Light Wild Thing	014	
D-MXIM	Bobcat	AB-RM 001	
D-MXIS	ME.13B	003	
D-MXIW	Fisher FP-202 Koala	001	
D-MXKA	NST Minimum	M249	
D-MXKD	J-3 Kitten	AF 131285L	
D-MXKK	Eipper Quicksilver Sprint II	215	
D-MXKW	S.T.A.B. Trike XP-15	unkn	
D-MXLR	Scheibe UL-1 Coach IIb	001	
D-MXMD	Light Aero Avid Flyer	498	
D-MXMM	Mitchell Wing	P-808	
D-MXNA	Eipper Quicksilver Sprint II	216	
D-MXNO	Bobcat	EI-01	
D-MXNP	Light Aero Avid Flyer	616	
D-MXNV	Eipper Quicksilver	1393	
D-MXOF	Funk FK-6	003	
D-MXPC	Rans S-6 Coyote II	0994677	
D-MXPG	Flight Team Spider Trike	0031169213	
D-MXPJ	Bobcat	PAU-1	
D-MXPK	Funk FK-9	031	
D-MXPL	UltraviaPelican Super Sport	98-001	C-IFTP
D-MXPM	Platzer Motte B2/B3	05	
D-MXRS	Tecnam P.92 Echo	200	
D-MXSB	Schmidtler Enduro Trike	01-002	
D-MXSP	Sky Pup	01	
D-MXSS	Tecnam P.92 Echo	197	
D-MXSX	Zenair CH-701D STOL	unkn	
D-MXTH	Comco Ikarus Fox-C22	9...-3550	
D-MXTN	J-3 Kitten	A001	
D-MXTO	Comco Fox II Doppel Prototype	02	
D-MXTV	J-3 Kitten	001	
D-MXUI	Solid Air Diamant	022	
D-MXUR	Light Aero Avid Flyer	262	
D-MXVW	Klüver Twin Racer	423201	
D-MXWO	Eipper Quicksilver	3962	

Regn.	Type	C/n	Prev.Id.
D-MXWJ	Ferrari Tucano	076	
D-MXWX	Comco Ikarus Fox-C22B	9604-3701	
D-MXXW	Bobcat	WI-1	
D-MXXX	Fresh Breeze 110 AL 4B	46464	
D-MXXZ	Tecnam P.92 Echo	253	
D-MXYZ(2)	Murphy Renegade II	584	
D-MYAA	Sky-Walker II	325	
D-MYAB	Sky-Walker II	327	
D-MYAC	Scheibe UL-1 Coach IIb	002	
D-MYAF	Moskito Ib	014	
D-MYAK	Funk FK-9	016	
D-MYAL	Tandem Air Sunny Sport	2-91	
D-MYAN	Rans S-6 Coyote II	1291243	
D-MYAQ	ASO Storch	11005305	
D-MYAR	Denney Kitfox	546	
D-MYAS	Tandem Air Sunny	010	
D-MYAU	Rans S-12 Airaile	0192170	
D-MYAV	AMF Chevvron 2-32	035	
D-MYAW	LO-120S	005A	
D-MYAX	Technoflug Piccolo BM	068	
D-MYAY	Technoflug Piccolo BM	069	
D-MYBA	Funk FK-9	015	
D-MYBC	Funk FK-9	002	
D-MYBF	ASO Storch	11006306	
D-MYBG	Fisher FP-404 Classic	01	
D-MYBI	Jet Fox	001	
D-MYBJ	ASO Storch	11008307	
D-MYBK	Moskito Ib	017	
D-MYBL	Jet Fox	002	
D-MYBM	Fisher FP-404 Classic	TM-01	
D-MYBN	ASO Storch	11007307	
D-MYBO	Funk FK-9	020	
D-MYDM	UPM Conra Trike	910113	
D-MYEK	Tecnam P.92 Echo	244	
D-MYET	Comco Ikarus Fox-C22	9310-3514	
D-MYFB	Platzer Kiebitz-B2	047	
D-MYGH	Funk FK-9 TG	086	
D-MYGK	Comco Ikarus C-42 Cyclone	9612-6067	
D-MYGL	Comco Ikarus C-42 Cyclone	9701-6021	
D-MYHA	ASO Storch	11009408	
D-MYHE	Light Aero Avid Flyer	937	
D-MYHG	Pioneer Flightstar CL	950101	
D-MYHH	WDFL Fascination	034	
D-MYHL	Air-Light Wild Thing	025	
D-MYIF	Ikarusflug Eurofox	038097	
D-MYKA	Comco Ikarus C-42 Cyclone	9710-6058	
D-MYKB	Air-Light Wild Thing	020	
D-MYKD	Comco Ikarus Fox-C22C	9...-3658	
D-MYKE	Fisher Super Koala	SK 028	
D-MYKF	Zenair CH-601D Zodiac	6-3791	
D-MYKI	Comco Ikarus Fox-C22C	9605-3707	
D-MYKL	Ikarusflug Eurofox Pro	042097	
D-MYKO	Comco Ikarus Fox-C22	9305-3512	
D-MYLI	Technoflug Piccolo BM	026	D-KCFC
D-MYMS	Ultraleichtverbund Bi 90	922	
D-MYOB	Flight Design CT	98.04.02.29	
D-MYPL	Funk FK-9	023	
D-MYRE	Zenair CH-601D Zodiac	6-3574/002 1097	
D-MYRI	Comco Ikarus Fox-C22	9402-3567	
D-MYRS	Tandem Air Sunny	32	
D-MYSB	Flight Design CT	98.10.01.39	
D-MYST	Klüver Twin Racer Quartz SX 16	419201	
D-MYTH	Funk FK-9	072	
D-MYTR	Air-Light Wild Thing	006	
D-MYTW	Flight Design CT	97.09.02.08	
D-MYUL	Rans S-6 Coyote II XL	0895877	
D-MYXA	WDFL Sunwheel R	024	
D-MYXZ	Tecnam P.92 Echo	166	
D-MYYY	Platzer Kiebitz-B4	036	
D-MYYZ	Flight Design CT	97.10.02.011	
D-MZAC	Remos Gemini 3 Mirage	039	
D-MZAD	WDFL Sunwheel R	045	
D-MZAE	Air Energy AE-1 Silent	001	
D-MZAG	J-3 Kitten	AL-1	
D-MZAH	Comco Ikarus C-42 Cyclone	9805-6100	

Regn.	Type	C/n	Prev.Id.
D-MZAM	Comco Ikarus Fox-C22	9405-3587	
D-MZAN	Comco Ikarus Fox-C22B	9507-3662	
D-MZAR	Racer (Homebuilt)	02/90	
D-MZAS	Comco Ikarus Fox-C22	9405-3582	
D-MZAT	Comco Ikarus Fox-C22	9503-3635	
D-MZAY	Aviasud Mistral BA-83	009	
D-MZBA	JK-1	001	
D-MZBG	Comco Ikarus Fox-C22C	9...-3685	
D-MZCH	Comco Ikarus C-42 Cyclone	9805-6127	
D-MZCW	UPM-Trike	880057	
D-MZDF(2)	Comco Fox	009	
D-MZEN	Light Aero Avid Flyer	1292	
D-MZES	Flight Design CT	97.10.03.12	
D-MZFG	Behlen Power-Trike	89011	
D-MZFT	Remos Gemini 3 Mirage	055	
D-MZHT	UPM-Trike	88058	
D-MZIH	Pioneer Flightstar CL	950302	
D-MZII	Platzer Kiebitz-B8	139	
D-MZIN	Comco Ikarus Fox-C22B	9404-3559	
D-MZIO	Comco Ikarus Fox-C22	9...-3634	
D-MZIP	Air-Light Wild Thing	005	
D-MZIS	Evektor EV.97 Eurostar	98 03 08	
D-MZIW	Tandem Air Sunny Sport	61.94	
D-MZKS	Remos Gemini 3 Mirage	053	
D-MZLW	Comco Ikarus Fox-C22	9312-3534	
D-MZMN	Comco Ikarus C-42 Cyclone	9707-6042	
D-MZMZ	Comco Ikarus Fox-C22	9108-3364	
D-MZNF	WDFL Sunwheel R	037	
D-MZNN	Light Aero Avid Flyer	1291	
D-MZOH	Typhoon Trike (Homebuilt)	T1282667L	
D-MZON	Comco Ikarus Fox-C22C	9703-3714	
D-MZOO	Murphy Renegade	221	
D-MZRH	Zenair CH-601D Zodiac	001	
D-MZRK	Racer (Homebuilt)	10/91	
D-MZRS	Tecnam P.96 Golf	042	
D-MZRX	Point Avn/Albatros AN-22M	001	
D-MZRZ	Zenair CH-601D Zodiac	002	
D-MZTA	Comco Ikarus Fox-C22B	3684	
D-MZTF	Comco Ikarus Fox-C22C	9807-3739	
D-MZTS	Remos Gemini 3 Mirage	042	
D-MZWT	UPM-Trike	880059	
D-MZXX	Air-Light Wild Thing	008	
D-MZYA	Kümmerle Mini-Fly-Set	1261/91-4	

The following registrations were also listed as current 2.99 by the DULV although no types are identified - any further details would therefore be welcome:

MAAE	MABI	MACT	MAGV	MAHC	MAIQ	MAKH
MALT	MAMP	MAMX	MANC	MAPS	MAPW	MARO
MASL	MATA	MATI	MAWD	MAYE	MBAG	MBBP
MBDW	MBER	MBFT	MBKA	MBKR	MBLA	MBMK
MBRC	MBRR	MBRW	MBSS	MBUL	MBWF	MCDG
MCKR	MCPG	MCRS	MDGH	MDMD	MDPT	MDTM
MEAG	MEBW	MEIQ	MEKB	MEUE	MFFF	MFHK
MFRY	MFSV	MFSW	MFUC	MFVK	MGBA	MGBR
MGMG	MGPW	MGRA	MGRB	MGSW	MGTA	MGTB
MHBB	MHBR	MHJH	MHJO	MHKC	MHKO	MHKW
MHMO	MHND	MHRU	MHTB	MHWR	MHWZ	MIAF
MIDI	MIFF	MIGK	MIIL	MIKA	MILL	MIMA
MIMF	MIML	MINA	MIWE	MJUC	MJZP	MKAL
MKGP	MKIE	MKLP	MKMU	MKNN	MKNP	MKWW
MLHB	MLMA	MLMO	MLPS	MLTV	MLWH	MMCD
MMCS	MMDD	MMDJ	MMFR	MMKS	MMLW	MMMH
MMMR	MMOA	MMOB	MMSS	MMWF	MMWK	MRBS
MSMA	MXAH	MXAS	MXOP	MXTT	MXVY	MXWI
MXWL	MXXL	MXYW	MYOL			

CLASS N : Unpowered Microlights

The D-N . . . series is used for unpowered Microlight Gliders and hang gliders.

CLASS O : Balloons

Regn.	Type	C/n	Prev.Id.
D-OAAA	Thunder AX8-105 SI HAFB	1984	
D-OAAL	Schroeder Fire Balloons G HAFB	330	
D-OAAO	Cameron N-77 HAFB	793	D-Felsenkeller(1)
D-OAAR	Raven Europe S-60A HAFB	E-343	
D-OABA	Cameron O-84 HAFB	2372	D-Saxonia(1)
D-OABC	Cameron N-105 HAFB (Reservation)	2636	
D-OABD(2)	Schroeder Fire Balloons G HAFB (Res 12.99)	3116	
D-OABG	Lindstrand LBL-120A HAFB (Res 12.99)	655	
D-OABI	Schroeder Fire Balloons G HAFB	266	
D-OABK	Cameron A-105 HAFB	3117	
D-OABL	Colt 105A HAFB	3572	
D-OABO	Wörner NL-1000/STU Gas Balloon	1060	
D-OABP	Cameron A-105 HAFB	3118	
D-OABR	Cameron N-105 HAFB	3247	
D-OABS	Schroeder Fire Balloons G HAFB	572	
D-OABT	Cameron N-105 HAFB	2146	D-Vagabund(2)
D-OACL	Schroeder Fire Balloons G HAFB	420	
D-OACT	Schroeder Fire Balloons G HAFB	214	
D-OADI	Schroeder Fire Balloons GHAFB	753	
D-OADL	Cameron A-210 HAFB	4403	
D-OAEB	Cameron N-105 HAFB	3148	
D-OAEC	Thunder AX8-9O SII HAFB	2478	
D-OAFC	Thunder AX8-105 SII HAFB	3802	
D-OAGA	Cameron N-77 HAFB (Reservation 12.99)	1179	D-AGFA(3)
D-OAGB	Cameron O-105 HAFB	974	D-Papage I
D-OAGF	Schroeder Fire Balloons G HAFB	260	
D-OAGG	Schroeder Fire Balloons G HAFB	634	
D-OAHG	Schroeder Fire Balloons G HAFB	235	D-Fireballoon(2)
D-OAHM	Schroeder Fire Balloons G HAFB	650	
D-OAHO	Thunder AX8-9O SI HAFB	2545	
D-OAHR	Thunder AX8-105 SII HAFB	2552	
D-OAHW	Thunder AX9-120 SII HAFB (Res 12.99)	2253	
D-OAIB	Thunder AX9-120 SII HAFB	4626	
D-OAIR	UltraMagic S-160 HAFB	160/18	
D-OAIX	Sky 220-24 HAFB (Reservation)	096	G-BXPH
D-OAJG	Schroeder Fire Balloons G HAFB	389	
D-OAKB	Lindstrand LBL-105A HAFB	462	
D-OAKE	Schroeder Fire Balloons G HAFB	467	
D-OAKF	Colt 160A HAFB	1731	D-Sachsen G-BSJD
D-OAKK	Schroeder Fire Balloons G HAFB	493	
D-OAKL	Schroeder Fire Balloons G HAFB	655	
D-OAKO	Schroeder Fire Balloons G HAFB	610	
D-OAKS	Schroeder Fire Balloons G HAFB	410	
D-OAKT	Cameron A-210 HAFB (Reservation 11.99)	4737	
D-OALF	Wörner K-1000/3-STU Gas Balloon (Res 8.99)	0277	D-Halfeneis
D-OALG	Cameron N-105 HAFB	2890	D-Allgau(2)
D-OALI (3)	Cameron O-105 HAFB	4311	
D-OALK	UltraMagic M-145 HAFB	145/04	
D-OALP	Thunder AX8-84 SI HAFB	1037	D-Sonthofen
D-OALS	Schroeder Fire Balloons G HAFB	529	
D-OALZ	Schroeder Fire Balloons G HAFB	546	
D-OAMB	Cameron O-90 HAFB	2225	D-Wegener
D-OAMD	Cameron N-90 HAFB	2478	D-Radio
D-OAME	Cameron O-90 HAFB	2510	D-Marburg(2)
D-OAMF	Cameron N-90 HAFB	2637	D-Marburg(3)
D-OAMG	Cameron N-105 HAFB	3250	
D-OAMH	Cameron A-105 HAFB (Reservation)	4579	
D-OAMS	Schroeder Fire Balloons G HAFB	402	
D-OAMW	Schroeder Fire Balloons G HAFB	515	
D-OAMY	Cameron A-250 HAFB	3788	
D-OANA	Raven Europe S-66A HAFB	E-321	
D-OANS	Schroeder Fire Balloons G HAFB	345	D-OHOT
D-OANT	Lindstrand LBL-90A	498	
D-OAOA	Schroeder Fire Balloons G HAFB	263	
D-OAOB	Cameron O-120 HAFB (Reservation 5.99)	1670	G-BOHE
D-OAOC	Cameron A-105 HAFB	3690	
D-OAOD	Cameron A-210 HAFB	3689	
D-OAOE	Sky 180 HAFB	021	
D-OAOF	Sky 105 HAFB	026	
D-OAOG	Cameron N-160 HAFB	4592	
D-OAOH	Cameron N-145 HAFB (Reservation 10.99)	3554	

Regn.	Type	C/n	Prev.Id.
D-OAPP	Thunder AX9-120 SII HAFB	4057	
D-OAPS	Cameron N-105 HAFB	3781	
D-OARA	Thunder AX8-105 SII HAFB	2226	
D-OARC	Schroeder Fire Balloons G HAFB	37	D-Arcobrau
D-OARD	Cameron A-375 HAFB (Reservation 11.99)	3682	
D-OARE	Augsburg K-780/2-RI Gas Balloon	10147	D-Ergee VI
D-OARG	Augsburg K-1050/3-RI Gas Balloon	10120	D-Ergee V
D-OARS	Thunder AX8-105 SII HAFB	2626	
D-OART	Raven-Europe S-60A HAFB (Reservation)	E-282	
D-OARW	Cameron N-120 HAFB	3153	
D-OASA	Schroeder Fire Balloons G HAFB	262	
D-OASB	Thunder AX8-105 SII HAFB	2169	
D-OASE(2)	Schroeder Fire Balloons G HAFB	688	
D-OASH(2)	Wörner K-1050/S-STU Gas Balloon (Res.)	1053	
D-OASI	Colt 77A HAFB (Reservation 10.99)	3818	
D-OASP	Cameron N-120 HAFB	2599	
D-OAST	Cameron N-105 HAFB	4675	
	(Replaced envelope c/n 2638)		
D-OASU	Thunder AX9-120 SII HAFB	4193	
D-OASW	Schroeder Fire Balloons G HAFB	369	
D-OATC	Schroeder Fire Balloons G HAFB	600	
D-OATD	Cameron O-84 HAFB	2549	D-Bauknecht(2)
D-OATF	Schroeder Fire Balloons G HAFB	668	
D-OATM	Schroeder Fire Balloons G HAFB	212	
D-OATS	Schroeder Fire Balloons G HAFB (Res 11.99)	205	
D-OAUN	Cameron A-140 HAFB	2680	D-OFUN(1) G-BTVZ
	(Reservation 11.99)		
D-OAWD	Schroeder Fire Balloons G HAFB	497	
D-OAWF	Raven-Europe FS-57A HAFB	E-284	
D-OAWS	Sky 105 HAFB	069	
D-OAWU	Schroeder Fire Balloons G HAFB	612	
D-OAWW	Schroeder Fire Balloons G HAFB	665	
D-OBAC	Schroeder Fire Balloons G HAFB	582	
D-OBAD(2)	Lindstrand LBL-150A HAFB	402	
D-OBAF	Cameron A-120 HAFB	4452	
D-OBAH	Colt 105A HAFB	3861	
D-OBAL	Schroeder Fire Balloons G HAFB	382	
D-OBAM	Lindstrand LBL-310A HAFB	190	
D-OBAR	Schroeder Fire Balloons G HAFB	479	
D-OBAS	Colt 105A HAFB	3498	
D-OBAU	Thunder AX9-120 SII HAFB	2264	
D-OBAV	Cameron O-84 HAFB	2915	
D-OBAY	Schroeder Fire Balloons G HAFB	216	
D-OBAZ	Raven Europe S-66A HAFB	E-283	D-Russberger(2)
D-OBBB	Schroeder Fire Balloons G HAFB	191	
D-OBBC	Colt 105A HAFB	4349	
D-OBBE	Schroeder Fire Balloons G HAFB	270	
D-OBBI	Colt 120A HAFB (Reservation)	1732	D-Potsdam G-BSJE
D-OBBL(2)	Cameron A-120 HAFB (Reservation)	4774	
D-OBBM(2)	Schroeder Fire Balloons G HAFB	667	
D-OBBO	Thunder AX8-105 SII HAFB	4055	
D-OBBR	Schroeder Fire Balloons G HAFB (Res 10.99)	349	
D-OBBS	Cameron O-105 HAFB	2854	
D-OBBT(2)	Cameron Brandenburger Tor SS HAFB	2742	PH-BBT
D-OBBW(2)	Wörner NL-510/STU Gas Balloon	1042	
D-OBBY	Balloon Works Firefly F9 HAFB (Res 8.99)	F9-051	
D-OBCC	Raven-Europe S-60A HAFB	E-253	
D-OBCD	Lindstrand LBL-120A HAFB	424	
D-OBCE	Schroeder Fire Balloons G HAFB	578	
D-OBCG	Thunder AX9-120 SII HAFB	2177	G-BUGK
D-OBCH	Schroeder Fire Balloons G HAFB	296	
D-OBCI	Schroeder Fire Balloons G HAFB	509	
D-OBCW	Wörner NL-1000/STU Gas Balloon	1059	
	(Previously listed as c/n 1051, 1996-9)		
D-OBDB	Schroeder Fire Balloons G HAFB (Res 12.99)	794	
D-OBDF	Cameron A-210 HAFB	4126	
D-OBDM	Schroeder Fire Balloons G HAFB (Reservation)	195	D-Melitta
D-OBDW	Thunder AX8-105 SII HAFB	3530	
D-OBEB	Thunder AX8-105 SII HAFB	2606	
D-OBEC	Cameron N-133 HAFB	3926	
D-OBED	Lindstrand LBL-150A HAFB	264	
D-OBEE	Lindstrand LBL-105A HAFB	559	
D-OBEG	Thunder AX9-120 SII HAFB	4136	
D-OBEI (2)	Thunder AX9-120 SII HAFB (Reservation)	4622	

Regn.	Type	C/n	Prev.Id.
D-OBEK	Sky 120 HAFB	080	
D-OBEN	Sky 105 HAFB	100	
D-OBEO	Cameron O-120 HAFB (Reservation 11.99)	3126	
D-OBER	Colt 105A HAFB	1985	D-Oberstauffen(2)
D-OBET	Cameron N-105 HAFB	3457	
D-OBEX(2)	Thunder AX9-140 SII HAFB	4416	
D-OBFA	Augsburg K-1050/3-RI Gas Balloon	67465	
D-OBFB	Schroeder Fire Balloons G HAFB	494	
D-OBFE	Sky 120 HAFB	167	
D-OBGH	Sky 120 HAFB	162	
D-OBGN	Schroeder Fire Balloons G HAFB	165	D-Bellevue(2)
D-OBHC	UltraMagic M-105 HAFB	105/34	
D-OBHG	Schroeder Fire Balloons G HAFB	528	
D-OBHH	Colt 180A HAFB (Reservation)	2360	
D-OBHM	Schroeder Fire Balloons G HAFB	710	
D-OBHR	Cameron O-105 HAFB (Reservation)	1928	D-Valerie
D-OBHS	Thunder AX8-105 SII HAFB	2551	
D-OBHT	Schroeder Fire Balloons G HAFB	252	D-Brandkasse(2)
D-OBHW	Schroeder Fire Balloons G HAFB	681	
D-OBIB	Schroeder Fire Balloons G HAFB	438	
D-OBIG(3)	Cameron A-210 HAFB (Reservation 11.99)	4796	
	(Replaced D-OBIG(2) c/n 3322 ex D-OERT)		
D-OBII	Schroeder Fire Balloons G HAFB	368	D-OBIG
D-OBIL	Wörner K-1000/3-STU Gas Balloon	0285/2	D-Mobil IV
D-OBIM	Colt 300A HAFB	2416	
D-OBIO	Schroeder Fire Balloons G HAFB	247	D-OBIC
D-OBIP	Thunder AX8-105 SII HAFB	4225	
D-OBIS	Cameron N-77 HAFB	961	D-Kurbis(2)
D-OBIT	Schroeder Fire Balloons G HAFB	116	D-Rheinbau
D-OBIX	Schroeder Fire Balloons G HAFB	387	
D-OBJW	Lindstrand LBL-180A HAFB	499	
D-OBKA	Thunder AX8-105 SII HAFB	3886	
D-OBKB	Cameron A-210 HAFB (Reservation 11.99)	3896	
D-OBKD	Thunder AX9-140 HAFB	4435	
D-OBKL	Schroeder Fire Balloons G HAFB	630	
D-OBKM	Schroeder Fire Balloons G HAFB (Reservation)	337	
D-OBKO	Schroeder Fire Balloons G HAFB	557	
D-OBKS	Schroeder Fire Balloons G HAFB (Res 11.99)	250	
D-OBLA	Cameron N-105 HAFB	3804	
D-OBLB(2)	Cameron N-120 HAFB	4265	
D-OBLC(2)	Thunder AX8-105 SII HAFB	4240	
D-OBLW	Schroeder Fire Balloons G HAFB	338	
D-OBLX	Cameron V-90 HAFB	3178	
D-OBMB	Thunder AX8-105 SII HAFB	2532	
D-OBMG	Schroeder Fire Balloons G HAFB	539	
D-OBMI	Schroeder Fire Balloons G HAFB	699	
D-OBNG	Cameron N-105 HAFB	3047	
D-OBNL	Schroeder Fire Balloons G HAFB	347	
D-OBNR	Schroeder Fire Balloons G HAFB	272	
D-OBNW	Thunder AX8-105 SII HAFB (Res 10.99)	2164	
D-OBOB	Schroeder Fire Balloons G HAFB	219	
D-OBOC	Schroeder Fire Balloons G HAFB	367	
D-OBOL	Schroeder Fire Balloons G HAFB	185	D-Bolberg(2)
D-OBOM	Lindstrand LBL-105A HAFB (Reservation)	545	
D-OBOR	Schroeder Fire Balloons G HAFB	274	
D-OBOX	Thunder AX8-105 SII HAFB	1749	HB-BWO D-Gemini
D-OBOY	Lindstrand LBL-310A HAFB (Res 11.99)	070	
D-OBPP(2)	Thunder AX8-105 SII HAFB	4593	
D-OBPZ	Colt 120A HAFB	1618	HB-BPZ
D-OBRG	Thunder AX9-140 SII HAFB	3659	
D-OBRI	Schroeder Fire Balloons G HAFB	541	
D-OBRS	Schroeder Fire Balloons G HAFB	395	
D-OBRT	Schroeder Fire Balloons G HAFB	309	
D-OBRW	Cameron N-180 HAFB	3154	
D-OBSA	Colt 120A HAFB	4175	
D-OBSB	Cameron O-105 HAFB (Reservation)	1948	PH-BSP
D-OBSH	Schroeder Fire Balloons G HAFB	162	D-Luftschloss
D-OBSK	Schroeder Fire Balloons G HAFB (Reservation)	28	D-Schlossbau
D-OBSM	Cameron V-90 HAFB	2754	
D-OBSN	Cameron O-77 HAFB	894	D-Noris
D-OBSP	Schroeder Fire Balloons G HAFB	84	D-Schmitt(3)
D-OBSS	Schroeder Fire Balloons G HAFB	418	
D-OBST	Cameron N-133 HAFB	2875	
D-OBTH	Schroeder Fire Balloons G HAFB	101	D-Alpinist

Regn.	Type	C/n	Prev.Id.
D-OBTK	Schroeder Fire Balloons G HAFB	411	
D-OBTR	Thunder AX10-150 SII HAFB *(Res 12.99)*	4755	
D-OBTS	Schroeder Fire Balloons G HAFB	383	
D-OBUM	Colt 300A HAFB	2411	
D-OBUS	Schroeder Fire Balloons G HAFB	527	
D-OBVB	Lindstrand LBL-180A HAFB	041	
D-OBVG	Cameron N-133 HAFB	3613	
D-OBVL	Thunder AX8-105 SII HAFB	2335	
D-OBWE	Cameron A-210 HAFB *(Reservation 12.99)*	3492	
D-OBWF	Cameron A-105 HAFB *(Reservation 11.99)*	1540	D-Hammonia(1)
D-OBWG	Cameron N-145 HAFB *(Reservation 12.99)*	3491	
D-OBWI	Cameron A-250 HAFB *(Reservation 12.99)*	3708	
D-OBWJ	Lindstrand LBL-210A HAFB *(Reservation 12.99)*	334	
D-OBWK	Cameron A-160 HAFB *(Reservation 11.99)*	4201	
D-OBWL	Cameron A-160 HAFB *(Reservation 11.99)*	4273	
D-OBWM	Cameron A-160 HAFB *(Reservation 12.99)*	4274	
D-OBWN	Cameron N-160 HAFB *(Reservation 12.99)*	4578	
D-OBWO	Sky 120 HAFB *(Reservation 12.99)*	035	
D-OBWW	Schroeder Fire Balloons G HAFB	404	
D-OBXX	Schroeder Fire Balloons G HAFB	462	
D-OBXZ	Colt 180A HAFB	1894	HB-BXZ G-BTFI
D-OBZA	Colt 105A HAFB	4412	
D-OCAA	Schroeder Fire Balloons G HAFB *(Res 11.99)*	765	
D-OCAC	AS.105GD HAFB *(Permit)*	0006	
D-OCAI	Schroeder Fire Balloons G HAFB	342	
D-OCAL	Schroeder Fire Balloons G HAFB	339	
D-OCAM	Thunder AX8-105 SII HAFB	2359	
D-OCAN	Schroeder Fire Balloons G HAFB *(Res 11.99)*	579	
D-OCAR	Schroeder Fire Balloons G HAFB *(Reservation)*	336	
D-OCAT(2)	Colt 105A HAFB	3749	
D-OCBM	Thunder AX9-120 SII HAFB *(Res 12.99)*	2598	
D-OCBS	Lindstrand LBL-210A HAFB *(Res 4.99)*	602	
D-OCCC(2)	Cameron O-105 HAFB	4448	
D-OCCG	Cameron O-105 HAFB	2379	D-OCCC(1) D-Commerzbank (2)
D-OCCM	Cameron A-140 HAFB	3545	
D-OCCO	Schroeder Fire Balloons G HAFB	361	
D-OCDM	Lindstrand LBL-180A HAFB *(Res 9.99)*	500	
D-OCDZ	Thunder AX9-120 SII HAFB	3794	
D-OCEL	Raven Europe FS-57A HAFB	E-153	D-Celle
D-OCEM	Sky 140 HAFB *(Reservation 10.99)*	156	
D-OCES	Colt 90A HAFB	2368	
D-OCFM	Sky 140 HAFB *(Reservation 10.99)*	175	
D-OCFT	Wörner N-1000/STU Gas Balloon	1041	
D-OCGI	Thunder AX8-105SII HAFB	2356	
D-OCGM	Sky 120 HAFB *(Reservation 12.99)*	181	
D-OCHA	Schroeder Fire Balloons G HAFB	639	
D-OCHR	Schroeder Fire Balloons G HAFB	227	
D-OCHT	Cameron A-180 HAFB	3766	
D-OCHY	Cameron A-105 HAFB	2985	
D-OCIO(2)	Schroeder Fire Balloons G HAFB	"750"	
D-OCIX	Schroeder Fire Balloons G HAFB	692	
D-OCKI	Aerostar RX-8 HAFB	3241	
D-OCKL	Cameron N-105 HAFB	3615	
D-OCKM	Wörner K-780/2-STU Gas Balloon	1040	
D-OCLD	Cameron O-105 HAFB	1241	D-Nurnberg
D-OCMA	Schroeder Fire Balloons G HAFB	259	
D-OCMC	Aerostar S-60A HAFB	3208	
D-OCME	Schroeder Fire Balloons G HAFB	469	
D-OCMF	Schroeder Fire Balloons G HAFB	685	
D-OCOC(2)	Schroeder Fire Balloons G HAFB	757	
D-OCOE(2)	Schroeder Fire Balloons G HAFB	459	
D-OCOL	Wörner NL-1000/STU Gas Balloon	1039	D-OBBW(1)
D-OCOM	Cameron A-105 HAFB	1793	D-Fuggerstadt
D-OCON	Cameron O-84 HAFB	2707	
D-OCOX	Wörner NL-1000/STU Gas Balloon	1054	
D-OCPW	Schroeder Fire Balloons G HAFB	474	
D-OCRF	Cameron N-105 HAFB	4089	
D-OCRI	Lindstrand LBL-150A HAFB	524	
D-OCST	Cameron O-120 HAFB	3090	
D-OCTA	Raven-Europe RX-7 HAFB	E-202	D-Octanorm
D-OCTO	Thunder AX8-105 SII HAFB *(Reservation)*	1639	D-Jonathan
D-OCUB	Schroeder Fire Balloons G HAFB	207	
D-OCVL	Schroeder Fire Balloons G HAFB	617	
D-OCZL	Schroeder Fire Balloons G HAFB	696	
D-ODAC	Thunder AX9-140 SII HAFB	2594	
D-ODAN	Thunder AX8-105 SI HAFB	2530	
D-ODAR	Raven-Europe RX-8 HAFB	E-199	PH-VFM
D-ODAS	UltraMagic M-105 HAFB	105/50	
D-ODAT	AS.105GD Hot Air Airship	0009	
	(Reservation 7.99. Presumably a Geva Flug or Colt example)		
D-ODAU	Schroeder Fire Balloons G HAFB	585	
D-ODBW	Schroeder Fire Balloons G HAFB *(Res 2.99)*	287	
D-ODCW	UltraMagic M-105 HAFB	105/31	
D-ODDH	Wörner K-1000/3-STU Gas Balloon	0274	D-Dusseldorf
D-ODEG	Schroeder Fire Balloons G HAFB	640	
D-ODEL	Thunder AX8-9O SI HAFB	unkn	
D-ODEM	Wörner K-1260/3-STU Gas Balloon	0310	
D-ODER	Raven S-60A HAFB *(Reservation)*	337	N4397D
D-ODHB	Colt 105A HAFB	2621	
D-ODHM	Schroeder Fire Balloons G HAFB *(Res 10.99)*	752	
D-ODHT	Schroeder Fire Balloons G HAFB	581	
D-ODIE	Schroeder Fire Balloons G HAFB	535	
D-ODIN	Cameron O-84 HAFB	2652	
D-ODJL	Thunder AX7-77 SI HAFB *(Reservation)*	2510	
D-ODKD	Colt 105A HAFB	4106	
D-ODKV	Schroeder Fire Balloons G HAFB	703	
D-ODLW	Schroeder Fire Balloons G HAFB	713	
D-ODMA	Cameron N-105 HAFB	3629	
D-ODMI	Schroeder Fire Balloons GHAFB	765	
D-ODMW	Schroeder Fire Balloons G HAFB	290	
D-ODNI	Thunder AX8-105 SII HAFB	2236	
D-ODOC	Raven-Europe FS-57A HAFB	E-327	
D-ODON	Raven-Europe S-60A HAFB	E-444	
D-ODOR	Thunder AX10-150 SII HAFB	4554	
D-ODPM	Schroeder Fire Balloons G HAFB *(Reservation)*	412	
D-ODRA	Raven-Europe FS-57A HAFB	E-292	
D-ODRH	Raven Europe S-60A HAFB	E-344	
D-ODRV	Aerostar S-60A HAFB	3207	
D-ODST	Schroeder Fire Balloons G HAFB	547	
D-ODUB	Lindstrand LBL-105AHAFB	593	
D-ODUC	Schroeder Fire Balloons G HAFB	746	
D-ODUD	Cameron A-180 HAFB	4163	
D-ODUE	Lindstrand LBL-120A	521	
D-ODUR	Schroeder Fire Balloons G HAFB	649	
D-ODUS	Wörner K-1000/3-STU Gas Balloon *(Res 11.99)*	1034	
D-ODWS	Schroeder Fire Balloons G HAFB	451	
D-ODYN	Schroeder Fire Balloons G HAFB	613	
D-OEAR	Raven-Europe FS-57A HAFB	E-217	D-Aerostar
D-OEAS	Schroeder Fire Balloons G HAFB	626	
D-OEBM(2)	Colt 105A HAFB	3940	
D-OECO	Schroeder Fire Balloons G HAFB	393	
D-OEDL	Cameron A-250 HAFB	3898	
D-OEDM(2)	Colt 105A HAFB	3940	
D-OEDO	Lindstrand LBL-240A HAFB *(Reservation)*	431	
D-OEDR	Schroeder Fire Balloons G HAFB	524	
D-OEEE	Thunder AX8-105 SII HAFB	4569	
D-OEEJ	Schroeder Fire Balloons G HAFB	460	
D-OEEU	Cameron A-400 HAFB	4508	
D-OEFC	Thunder AX8-105 SII	4038	
D-OEGP	Wörner NL-840/STU Gas Balloon	1057	
D-OEHD	Cameron A-160 HAFB	4521	
D-OEIC	Schroeder Fire Balloons G HAFB	392	
D-OEII	Schroeder Fire Balloons G HAFB	279	
D-OEIM	Wörner NL-510/STU Gas Balloon	1056	
D-OEKB	Thunder AX8-105 SI HAFB	3753	
D-OEKD	Thunder AX8-105 SI HAFB	3757	
D-OEKO	Aerostar S-60A HAFB *(Res 12.99)*	3259	
D-OELD	Cameron Lager Bottle SS HAFB *(Res 3.99)*	4571	
D-OELE(3)	Schroeder Fire Balloons G HAFB	750	
	(Formerly used by c/ns 79 and 234)		
D-OELG	Cameron A-160 HAFB	4253	
D-OELH	Schroeder Fire Balloons GHAFB	768	
D-OELK	Schroeder Fire Balloons G HAFB	380	
D-OEMB	Schroeder Fire Balloons G HAFB	315	
D-OEMD	Schroeder Fire Balloons G HAFB	658	
D-OEMS	Lindstrand LBL-150A HAFB	365	
D-OEMU	Cameron N-105 HAFB	2790	D-Rheingas(4)
D-OEON	Schroeder Fire Balloons G HAFB *(Reservation)*	2002	

Regn.	Type	C/n	Prev.Id.
D-OEPA	Thunder AX8-105 SII HAFB	4290	
D-OERD	Lindstrand LBL-150A HAFB	592	
D-OERE	Schroeder Fire Balloons G HAFB	256	
D-OERR	Cameron A-105 HAFB	2289	D-Dorr
D-OERT	Cameron A-210 HAFB	3322	(D-OBIG(2))
			D-OERT
D-OESA	Schroeder Fire Balloons G HAFB	726	
D-OESE	Cameron N-120 HAFB	4453	
D-OESI	Cameron N-120 HAFB	3809	
D-OESL	Colt 105A HAFB	3608	
D-OESM	Thunder AX8-9O SI HAFB	2501	
D-OETS	Schroeder Fire Balloons G HAFB	690	
D-OEUF	Schroeder Fire Balloons G HAFB	565	
D-OEUR	Schroeder Fire Balloons G HAFB	302	
D-OEUX	Thunder AX8-105 SII HAFB	2192	D-OLUX(2)
D-OEVA	Cameron O-140 HAFB	2927	
D-OEVE	Thunder AX8-9O SII HAFB	1320	D-Oeventrop
D-OEVN	Lindstrand LBL-105A HAFB	145	
D-OEWA	Cameron A-140 HAFB	4444	
D-OEWB(2)	Schroeder Fire Balloons G HAFB	694	
D-OEWP	Schroeder Fire Balloons G HAFB	52-2	D-OEWB(1)
			D-Cirrus
D-OEWS	Cameron O-105 HAFB	4111	
D-OEXC	Schroeder Fire Balloons G HAFB (Res 11.99)	288	
D-OFAL	Thunder AX8-105 SII HAFB	3882	
D-OFAR	Schroeder Fire Balloons G HAFB	629	
D-OFAS	Aerostar S-60A HAFB	3227	
D-OFAT(2)	Cameron A-180 HAFB	3641	
D-OFAX	Schroeder Fire Balloons Lefax SS HAFB	615	
D-OFAZ	Schroeder Fire Balloons G HAFB	490	
D-OFBH	Schroeder Fire Balloons G HAFB	385	
D-OFBI	Schroeder Fire Balloons G HAFB	131	
D-OFBK	Aerostar RXS-8 HAFB	3070	
D-OFBT	Schroeder Fire Balloons G HAFB	646	
D-OFCS	Cameron N-105 HAFB (Reservation 11.99)	957	D-Europa(1)
D-OFEH	Colt 90A HAFB	4212	
D-OFEL	Sky 105 HAFB	145	
D-OFEN	Schroeder Fire Balloons G HAFB	11	D-Feuertute
D-OFER	Schroeder Fire Balloons G HAFB	202	
D-OFES	Cameron N-105 HAFB (Reservation)	2697	D-Feldschlossen
D-OFFB	Cameron N-105 HAFB	3571	
D-OFFN	Lindstrand LBL-210A HAFB (Res 9.99)	483	
D-OFGR	Thunder AX8-105 SII HAFB	4037	
D-OFHF	Schroeder Fire Balloons g HAFB	621	
D-OFHG	Lindstrand LBL-120A HAFB (Res 12.99)	290	
D-OFID	Schroeder Fire Balloons G HAFB	759	
D-OFII	Schroeder Fire Balloons GHAFB	760	
D-OFIL(2)	Schroeder Fire Balloons G HAFB	660	
D-OFIN	Schroeder Fire Balloons G HAFB	173	D-Finanzgruppe
D-OFIR	Cameron A-120 HAFB	4458	
D-OFJH	Lindstrand LBL-105A HAFB	136	
D-OFJS	Cameron N-105 HAFB	1531	D-Felsenkeller(2)
D-OFLO	Schroeder Fire Balloons G HAFB	210	
D-OFLS	Cameron V-77 HAFB (Reservation 5.99)	1050	D-Otto
D-OFMA(2)	Thunder AX10-210 SII HAFB	4316	
D-OFMG	Aerostar S-60A HAFB	3226	
D-OFNY	Cameron A-105 HAFB (Res 11.99)	2409	D-Eichbaum
D-OFOR	Schroeder Fire Balloons G HAFB	589	
D-OFOS	Colt 180A HAFB (Reservation)	2525	
D-OFOX	Cameron Fox Head SSHAFB	3270	D-Fuchs(2)
D-OFPP	Schroeder Fire Balloons GHAFB	754	
D-OFRA	Schroeder Fire Balloons G HAFB	294	
D-OFRB(2)	Cameron O-105 HAFB	1397	D-Zollernalb
D-OFRI	Schroeder Fire Balloons G HAFB	308	
D-OFSA	Schroeder Fire Balloons G HAFB	468	
D-OFSV	Colt 105A HAFB	4287	
D-OFTL	Schroeder Fire Balloons G HAFB	691	
D-OFTM	Lindstrand LBL-105A HAFB	544	
D-OFTR	Cameron A-105 HAFB	3879	
D-OFUN(2)	Cameron A-140 HAFB	3401	
D-OFUS	Schroeder Fire Balloons G HAFB	483	
D-OFUX	Thunder AX8-105 SII	4301	
D-OFVA	Augsburg K-1050/3-RI Gas Balloon (Res.)	44217	
D-OFVB	Lindstrand LBL-210A HAFB	427	
D-OFVV	Schroeder Fire Balloons G HAFB	464	

Regn.	Type	C/n	Prev.Id.
D-OFZB	Thunder AX10-150 SIIHAFB	4616	
D-OGAB	Raven Europe S-60A HAFB	E-275	
D-OGAL	Raven Europe S-60A HAFB	E-374	
D-OGAS	Schroeder Fire Balloons G HAFB (Res 10.99)	790	
D-OGAV	Cameron N-133 HAFB	2920	
D-OGBA	Thunder AX9-140 SII HAFB (Res 11.99)	4044	
D-OGBB	Thunder AX9-140 SII HAFB	4531	
D-OGBC	Thunder AX10-150 SII HAFB (Reservation)	4664	
D-OGBK	Cameron A-340 HAFB	4491	
D-OGBO	Colt 120A HAFB	2240	
D-OGBS	Schroeder Fire Balloons G HAFB	444	
D-OGBW	Cameron A-105 HAFB	3114	
D-OGDP	Schroeder Fire Balloons G HAFB	466	
D-OGEG	Cameron N-77 HAFB	4070	
D-OGEK	Lindstrand LBL-150AHAFB	596	
D-OGEN	Schroeder Fire Balloons G HAFB	554	
D-OGEO	Aerostar RXS-8 HAFB	3065	
D-OGER	Raven Europe FS-57A HAFB	E-187	
D-OGFA	Schroeder Fire Balloons GHAFB	745	
D-OGFB	Schroeder Fire Balloons G HAFB	374	
D-OGGE	Schroeder Fire Balloons G HAFB	419	
D-OGGG(2)	Cameron O-105 HAFB	3392	
D-OGIB	Schroeder Fire Balloons G HAFB (Reservation)	333	
D-OGIE	Thunder AX7-77 SI HAFB	1571	D-Merkur
D-OGIL	Cameron N-133 HAFB	3308	
D-OGIN	Balloon Works Firefly 9 HAFB	F9-056	N25532
D-OGIS	Schroeder Fire Balloons G HAFB	568	
D-OGKW	Cameron O-84 HAFB	779	D-Bunte Kuh(1)
D-OGMA	Cameron A-120 HAFB (Res 10.99)	2445	D-Horizont
D-OGMW(2)	Thunder AX8-105 SII HAFB	3833	
D-OGMZ	Cameron N-105 HAFB	3196	
D-OGNI	UltraMagic M-160 HAFB (Reservation)	160/17	
D-OGOG	Schroeder Fire Balloons G HAFB	716	
D-OGOT	Schroeder Fire Balloons G HAFB	194	D-Bitburger
D-OGOU	Cameron N-120 HAFB	3648	
D-OGPK	Schroeder Fire Balloons G HAFB	489	
D-OGQU	Cameron N-105 HAFB	3070	
D-OGRA	Raven Europe S-60A HAFB	E-350	
D-OGRE	Lindstrand LBL-210A HAFB	603	
D-OGRM	Schroeder Fire Balloons G HAFB	543	
D-OGRO	Cameron O-105 HAFB	2833	
D-OGRU	Cameron A-160 HAFB	3957	PH-GRU
			(D-OGRU)
D-OGSC	Thunder AX8-105 SII HAFB	4029	
D-OGSE	Schroeder Fire Balloons Schwartau SS HAFB	731	
D-OGST	Colt 105AHAFB (Reservation 12.99)	4753	
D-OGTS	Schroeder Fire Balloons G HAFB	620	
D-OGUG	Raven Europe FS-57A HAFB	E-318	
D-OGUT	Schroeder Fire Balloons G HAFB	322	
D-OGVE	Schroeder Fire Balloons G HAFB	446	
D-OGVF	Schroeder Fire Balloons G HAFB	149	D-Erdgas(2)
D-OGVU	Colt 140A HAFB (Reservation 10.99)	4463	
D-OHAC	Cameron N-105 HAFB	3373	
D-OHAD	Head AX8-88 HAFB	187	N45244
D-OHAG	Schroeder Fire Balloons G HAFB	381	
D-OHAH	Thunder AX9-140SII HAFB	3795	
D-OHAI	Colt 105A HAFB	3891	
D-OHAL	Raven Europe FS-57A HAFB	E-046	D-Halberg
D-OHAM	Cameron N-105 HAFB (Reservation 11.99)	2683	D-Hammonia(2)
D-OHAN	Cameron O-105 HAFB (Reservation)	2538	D-Hannover
D-OHAS	Schroeder Fire Balloons G HAFB	641	
D-OHAW	Raven RX-7 HAFB	3187	D-Bruchhausen(1)
D-OHAX	Aerostar RX-7 HAFB	3320	
D-OHBA	Thunder AX9-140 SII HAFB	2315	
D-OHBB	Thunder AX9-140 SII HAFB	2316	
D-OHBC	Thunder AX9-140 SII HAFB	2585	
D-OHBD	Thunder AX9-140 SII HAFB	1825	D-Condor(2)
D-OHBE(2)	Thunder AX10-160 SII HAFB	3784	
D-OHBF	Thunder AX9-140 SII HAFB	1726	D-Lowentor(2)
D-OHBG(2)	Colt 210A HAFB	3487	
D-OHBH	Thunder AX9-140 SII HAFB	1490	D-Stadt-Calw(2)
D-OHBI	Thunder AX9-140 SII HAFB	3486	
D-OHBJ	Colt 210A HAFB	3610	
D-OHBK	Thunder AX10-160 SII HAFB	4589	
D-OHBL	Cameron V-90 HAFB	3229	

Regn.	Type	C/n	Prev.Id.
D-OHBM	Colt 240A HAFB	4094	
D-OHCC	Aerostar S-60A HAFB	3222	
D-OHCD	Cameron N-90 HAFB	1708	D-IBEXCO
D-OHDE	Cameron O-105 HAFB	2874	D-Wolkenhopper(2)
D-OHDG	Thunder AX8-105 SII HAFB	2336	
D-OHDH	Cameron N-120 HAFB	4049	
D-OHDI	Cameron A-105 HAFB	3162	
D-OHDM	Lindstrand LBL-105A HAFB	137	
D-OHDR	Raven Europe S-60A HAFB	E-...	
D-OHDV	Schroeder Fire Balloons G HAFB	659	
D-OHEB	Cameron A-105 HAFB	3434	
D-OHED	Cameron O-90 HAFB	3170	
D-OHEI	Cameron O-77 HAFB	1635	D-Heilbronn(3)
D-OHEL	Cameron A-105 HAFB	2662	D-Hellenstein(2)
D-OHES	Thunder AX10-160 SII HAFB	4559	
D-OHET	Thunder AX8-105 SII HAFB (Res 11.99)	2168	
D-OHEX	Lindstrand LBL-150A HAFB	457	
D-OHFA	Colt 105A HAFB	1849	D-Hagdorn(1)
D-OHFM	Schroeder Fire Balloons G HAFB	243	
D-OHFU	Cameron O-105 HAFB	3923	
D-OHGL	Schroeder Fire Balloons G HAFB	470	
D-OHGT	Cameron A-105 HAFB	4025	
D-OHHH	Schroeder Fire Balloons G HAFB	25	D-Super
D-OHIO	Schroeder Fire Balloons G HAFB	356	
D-OHIW	Thunder AX8-105 SII HAFB (Res 11.99)	4370	
D-OHJE	Lindstrand LBL-400A HAFB	422	
D-OHJM	Schroeder Fire Balloons G HAFB	204	
D-OHJO	Lindstrand LBL-400A HAFB	423	
D-OHJW	Aerostar RXS-8 HAFB	3088	
D-OHKH	Schroeder Fire Balloons G HAFB	363	
D-OHKP	Raven-Europe S-60A HAFB	E-280	
D-OHLE	Thunder AX8-105 SII HAFB	2128	
D-OHLM	Schroeder Fire Balloons G HAFB	730	
D-OHMA	Colt 180A HAFB	3580	
D-OHMG	Schroeder Fire Balloons G HAFB	644	
D-OHMM	Raven Europe S-60A HAFB	E-338	
D-OHMS	Raven-Europe S-60A HAFB	E-322	
D-OHNE	Thunder AX8-105 SII HAFB	2262	
D-OHOF	Raven-Euorpe FS-57A HAFB	E-281	
D-OHOH	Raven-Europe FS-57A HAFB	E-...	
D-OHOI	Schroeder Fire Balloons G HAFB	443	
D-OHOL	Thunder AX8-105 SII HAFB (Reservation)	1896	D-Holsten
D-OHOM	Schroeder Fire Balloons G HAFB	384	
D-OHOR	Schroeder Fire Balloons G HAFB	407	
D-OHOT	Schroeder Fire Balloons G HAFB	463	
D-OHPH	Raven Europe S-60A HAFB	E-399	
D-OHPL	Schroeder Fire Balloons G HAFB	738	
D-OHPS	Cameron A-140 HAFB	3565	
D-OHRA	Schroeder Fire Balloons G HAFB	365	
D-OHRB	Cameron V-65 HAFB	1985	D-Helios
D-OHRF	Schroeder Fire Balloons G HAFB	434	
D-OHRM	Schroeder Fire Balloons G HAFB	697	
D-OHRN	Cameron N-105 HAFB	3184	
D-OHSD	Colt 105A HAFB	4026	
D-OHSI	Thunder AX8-90 SII HAFB	3632	
D-OHSS	Schroeder Fire Balloons G HAFB	672	
D-OHTB	Schroeder Fire Balloons G HAFB	492	
D-OHUH	Thunder AX9-140 SII HAFB	3696	
D-OHUP	Colt 140A HAFB	4053	
D-OHVR	Cameron V-90 HAFB (Reservation)	2910	
D-OHVW	Cameron N-90 HAFB	1175	SE-ZBO
D-OHWK	Cameron N-105 HAFB	5881	N194DR
D-OHWW	Cameron N-105 HAFB	2816	
D-OHXH	Raven-Europe RX-7 HAFB	E-342	
D-OIAH	Thunder AX10-150 SIIHAFB	4599	
D-OIAR	Raven Europe S-60A HAFB	E-386	
D-OIAT	Cameron A-120 HAFB	2817	D-OURS(1)
D-OIBB	Wörner NL-840/STU Gas Balloon	1048	
D-OIBF	Thunder AX8-105 SII HAFB	4040	
D-OIBM	Cameron N-105 HAFB	4302	
D-OIBP	Cameron Bierkrug 90 SS HAFB (Reservation)	4133	(G-BXFY)
D-OICF	Lindstrand LBL-240A HAFB	482	
D-OIDA	Balloon Works Firefly 8 HAFB	F8-412	
D-OIDE	Thunder AX9-120 SII HAFB	2420	
D-OIGB	Thunder AX8-90 SII HAFB	2091	
D-OIGM	Thunder AX8-105 SII HAFB (Reservation)	2514	
D-OIGR	Lindstrand LBL-240A HAFB	307	
D-OIII	Cameron O-90 HAFB	1995	D-Drachengas(1) D-Hessen(2)
D-OIKF	Colt 180A HAFB	4447	
D-OILB	Thunder AX8-105 SIIHAFB	4618	
D-OILX	Cameron A-180 HAFB	2975	
D-OILY	Cameron O-105 HAFB	2595	G-SMAX G-MADM
D-OILZ	Cameron O-140 HAFB	2887	
D-OIMM	Schroeder Fire Balloons G HAFB	500	
D-OINA	Cameron N-120SV HAFB	3875	
D-OING	Schroeder Fire Balloons G HAFB	718	
D-OINN	Schroeder Fire Balloons G HAFB	508	
D-OIOO	Balloon Works Firefly 8 HAFB	F8-418	
D-OIPA	Colt 105A HAFB	4315	
D-OIRO	Schroeder Fire Balloons GHAFB	739	
D-OISA	Colt 105 HAFB (Reservation)	1686	D-Schlossquell
D-OISO	Cameron A-105 HAFB	3276	
D-OITB	Lindstrand LBL-120A HAFB (Res 11.99)	511	
D-OIZI	Thunder AX8-105 SI HAFB	2546	
D-OJAH	Thunder AX9-120 SII HAFB	2387	
D-OJAM	Cameron A-250 HAFB (Reservation 12.99)	4504	
D-OJAT	Thunder AX10-210 SII HAFB (Res 12.99)	3932	
D-OJCA	Cameron A-140 HAFB (Reservation 11.99)	3482	
D-OJCB(2)	Cameron A-120 HAFB	3592	
D-OJFK	Schroeder Fire Balloons G HAFB	625	
D-OJIL	Thunder AX10-150 SII HAFB (Res 6.99)	4646	
D-OJJJ	Thunder AX9-120 SII HAFB (Res 3.99)	2613	
D-OJLW	Schroeder Fire Balloons G HAFB	373	
D-OJMC	Aerostar S-60A HAFB	3218	
D-OJMN	Thunder AX8-105 SII HAFB	2090	
D-OJOE	Colt 210A HAFB (Reservation)	2425	
D-OJOR	Schroeder Fire Balloons G HAFB	642	
D-OJPI	Thunder AX8-105 SII HAFB	3797	
D-OJRW	Lindstrand LBL-150A HAFB	576	
D-OJSB	Cameron A-105 HAFB	unkn	
D-OJUC	Colt 105A HAFB	2556	
D-OJUH	Colt 77A HAFB	4437	
D-OJUL	Schroeder Fire Balloons G HAFB	unkn	
D-OJUP	Wörner NL-1000/STU Gas Balloon	1052	
D-OJWC	Schroeder Fire Balloons G HAFB (Res 11.99)	495	
D-OJWO	Schroeder Fire Balloons G HAFB	447	
D-OKAB	Cameron A-250 HAFB	4289	
D-OKAE	Lindstrand LBL-150A HAFB	494	
D-OKAF	Cameron A-105 HAFB	2974	
D-OKAI	Raven-Europe RX-7 HAFB	E-289	
D-OKAL	Schroeder Fire Balloons G HAFB	399	
D-OKAM	Schroeder Fire Balloons G HAFB	334	
D-OKAS	Thunder AX8-105 SII HAFB (Reservation)	4707	
D-OKAT	Schroeder Fire Balloons G HAFB	320	
D-OKAY	Aerostar RXS-8 HAFB	3082	
D-OKBB	Schroeder Fire Balloons G HAFB	249	
D-OKBC	Thunder AX8-105 SII HAFB	4488	
D-OKBD	Thunder AX8-105 SII HAFB	3649	
D-OKBE	Thunder AX8-105 SII HAFB	3650	
D-OKBF	Thunder AX8-105 SII HAFB	3511	
D-OKBG	Thunder AX8-105 SII HAFB	3651	
D-OKBH	Thunder AX8-105 SII HAFB	3887	
D-OKBK	Thunder AX8-105 SIIHAFB	2557	
D-OKBL	Thunder AX8-105 SII HAFB	3779	
D-OKBM	Thunder AX8-105 SII HAFB	4489	
D-OKBU	Thunder AX8-105 SII HAFB	4581	
D-OKBV	Thunder AX8-105 SII HAFB (Res 11.99)	4735	
D-OKBW	Thunder AX8-105 SII HAFB	4068	
D-OKBX	Thunder AX8-105 SII HAFB	4582	
D-OKBZ	Thunder AX8-105 SIIHAFB	4583	
D-OKCF	Thunder AX8-9O SII HAFB	2607	
D-OKCG	Schroeder Fire Balloons G HAFB (Res 11.99)	286	
D-OKEH	Balloon Works Firefly F8B-15 HAFB	F8B-464	
D-OKEL	Lindstrand LBL-105A	463	
D-OKEV	Thunder AX9-140 SII HAFB (Res 11.99)	2497	
D-OKEY	Schroeder Fire Balloons G HAFB	636	
D-OKFR	Cameron Tiger 90 SS HAFB	4288	
D-OKGB	UltraMagic N-250 HAFB	250/04	

Regn.	Type	C/n	Prev.Id.
D-OKGF	Schroeder Fire Balloons G HAFB	217	
D-OKGH	UltraMagic S-105 HAFB	105/58	
D-OKHG	Schroeder Fire Balloons G HAFB	32	D-Sonnenbuhl
D-OKHP	UltraMagic M-145 HAFB	145/07	
D-OKHW	Schroeder Fire Balloons G HAFB	426	
D-OKIA	Colt 90A HAFB	2269	
D-OKIB	Colt 90A HAFB	2329	
D-OKIC(2)	Thunder AX8-105 SI HAFB	4478	
D-OKID	Colt 105A HAFB	2681	
D-OKIE	Thunder AX8-9O SII HAFB	3853	
D-OKII	Thunder AX8-105 SII HAFB	2059	D-Karriere(2)
D-OKIT	Cameron O-84 HAFB	2172	G-BROS
D-OKIZ	Schroeder Fire Balloons G HAFB	473	
D-OKKK	Cameron N-105 HAFB	2317	D-Schafer(2)
D-OKLD	Cameron N-133 HAFB *(Reservation 12.99)*	4722	
D-OKLE	Cameron N-90 HAFB	3448	
D-OKMF	Raven-Europe S-60A HAFB	E-245	
D-OKMS	Schroeder Fire Balloons G HAFB	588	
D-OKOK	Thunder AX8-90 SII HAFB	2053USA	N224TC
D-OKOM	Colt 105A HAFB	3860	
D-OKON	Schroeder Fire Balloons G HAFB	558	
D-OKPB	Schroeder Fire Balloons G HAFB	532	
D-OKPC	Cameron A-180 HAFB	2562	G-BTKO
D-OKPG	Schroeder Fire Balloons G HAFB	352	
D-OKPH	Cameron A-120 HAFB *(Reservation)*	4686	
D-OKRE	Cameron O-105 HAFB	2776	
D-OKRI	Cameron A-140 HAFB	2861	
D-OKRS	Cameron O-90 HAFB	3397	
D-OKSA	Balloon Works Firefly F8-24 HAFB	F8-393	
D-OKSB	Colt 120A HAFB	2130	G-BUCD
D-OKSC	Balloon Works Firefly F9 HAFB	F9-061	
D-OKSK	Schroeder Fire Balloons G HAFB	536	
D-OKSR	Cameron 90SS Coffee Jug HAFB	3789	
D-OKSW	Thunder AX8-9O SII HAFB	2358	
D-OKSY	Cameron N-120 HAFB	2864	
D-OKTO(2)	Lindstrand LBL-150A HAFB	526	
D-OKUE	Raven Europe S-60A HAFB	E-345	
D-OKUH	Cameron A-105 HAFB *(Res 9.99)*	2918	
D-OKUR	Schroeder Fire Balloons G HAFB	138	D-Wittgensteiner(3)
D-OKVR	Colt 105A HAFB	2431	
D-OKWE	Thunder AX9-120 SII HAFB	3761	
D-OKXC	Cameron V-77 HAFB	973	G-BKXC
D-OLAA	Lindstrand LBL-150A HAFB *(Res 12.99)*	654	
D-OLAB	Thunder AX9-120 SII HAFB	4462	
D-OLAC	Schroeder Fire Balloons G HAFB	729	
D-OLAF	Raven Europe S-60A HAFB	E-313	
D-OLAG	Aerostar S-57A	3197	
D-OLAM(2)	Cameron A-210 HAFB *(Reservation)*	3800	
D-OLAN	Schroeder Fire Balloons G HAFB	85	D-Landshut(2)
D-OLAP	Thunder AX8-105 SII HAFB	4276	
D-OLAR	Lindstrand LBL-9OA HAFB	193	
D-OLAT	Lindstrand LBL-105A HAFB	523	
D-OLAU	Raven-Europe FS-57A HAFB	E-274	
D-OLAV	Thunder AX8-105SII HAFB	3518	
D-OLBB	Schroeder Fire Balloons G HAFB	455	
D-OLBC	Schroeder Fire Balloons G HAFB	403	
D-OLBF	Lindstrand LBL-105A	477	
D-OLBI	Cameron O-84 HAFB	1465	G-GWIT
D-OLBK	Schroeder Fire Balloons G HAFB	181	D-LBS(4)
D-OLBL	Lindstrand LBL-105A	254	G-LBLB
D-OLBM	Cameron N-105 HAFB	3679	
D-OLBS(3)	Cameron A-105 HAFB *(Res 11.99)*	4736	
D-OLBY	Cameron A-105 HAFB	2955	
D-OLCE	Cameron N-105 HAFB	3097	
D-OLCI	Raven Europe S-60A HAFB	E-393	
D-OLDD	Schroeder Fire Balloons G HAFB	312	
D-OLDY	Raven-Europe FS-57A HAFB	E-088	D-Stella
D-OLEA	Colt 120A HAFB	4036	
D-OLEE	Cameron O-120 HAFB*(Reservation)*	3066	
D-OLEF(2)	Schroeder Fire Balloons G HAFB	673	
D-OLEG	Cameron O-105 HAFB	3027	
D-OLEH	Colt 105A HAFB	2612	D-Hagdorn(2)
D-OLEN	Cameron N-105 HAFB *(Res 3.99)*	3251	
D-OLEV(2)	Schroeder Fire Balloons G HAFB	728	
	(Formerly Schroeder Fire Balloons G c/n 200)		
D-OLEX	Cameron O-90 HAFB	3356	
D-OLFI	Schroeder Fire Balloons G HAFB	86	D-Marabu
D-OLGL	Thunder AX8-9O SI HAFB	2249	
D-OLGP	Thunder AX8-105 SII HAFB	678	
D-OLHM	Schroeder Fire Balloons G HAFB	507	
D-OLIA	Thunder AX9-140 SII HAFB *(Res 5.99)*	4627	
D-OLIB	Wörner NL-1000/STU Gas Balloon	1049	
D-OLIE	Schroeder Fire Balloons G HAFB *(Res 11.99)*	285	
D-OLIM	Raven Europe S-60A HAFB	E-319	
D-OLIP(2)	Schroeder Fire Balloons G HAFB	531	
D-OLIS	Schroeder Fire Balloons G HAFB	599	
D-OLIV(2)	Aerostar S-60A HAFB	3241	
	(Formerly Raven S-60A c/n 380)		
D-OLIX	Schroeder Fire Balloons G HAFB	22	D-Achalm(1)
D-OLLA(3)	Thunder AX10-150 SII HAFB	4514	
D-OLLB	Colt 105A HAFB*(Reservation)*	1943	D-Wellenreiter
D-OLLD	Thunder AX8-105 SII HAFB	1987	D-Bothfeld(2)
D-OLLE(2)	Schroeder Fire Balloons GHAFB	747	
D-OLLG	Thunder AX9-120 SII HAFB *(Res 9.99)*	4012	
D-OLLH	Thunder AX8-105 SII HAFB *(Reservation)*	2201	
D-OLLI	Schroeder Fire Balloons G HAFB	228	
D-OLLL(2)	Cameron A-105 HAFB *(Reservation 8.99)*	4744	
	(Formerly A-105 c/n 2119 ex D-Lesespass)		
D-OLMA	Raven Europe FS-57A HAFB	E-085	D-Almandin
D-OLMH	Schroeder Fire Balloons G HAFB	522	
D-OLOR	Lindstrand LBL-105A HAFB	490	
D-OLOT	Cameron O-105 HAFB	2570	D-Heilbronn/4
D-OLOW(2)	Schroeder Fire Balloons G HAFB	707	
D-OLPB	Cameron N-90 HAFB	2601	D-Light
D-OLPE	Cameron N-120 HAFB	2311	D-Dresden G-BSRE
D-OLPP(2)	Wörner NL-840/STU Gas Balloon	1044	
D-OLTB	Lindstrand LBL-120A HAFB	354	
D-OLTS	UltraMagic N-210 HAFB	210/10	
D-OLTT	Raven Europe S-60A HAFB	E-367	
D-OLUD	Schroeder Fire Balloons G HAFB	549	
D-OLUG	Sky 140 HAFB	086	
D-OLUM	Schroeder Fire Balloons G HAFB	533	
D-OLUS	Thunder AX8-9O SI HAFB	2488	
D-OLWM	Schroeder Fire Balloons G HAFB	657	
D-OMAC	Cameron N-90 HAFB	3062	
D-OMAD	Schroeder Fire Balloons G HAFB	562	
D-OMAG	Cameron V-77 HAFB	2167	D-OSEH G-BSEH
D-OMAL	Raven Europe S-60A HAFB	E-339	
D-OMAM	Schroeder Fire Balloons G HAFB *(Res 10.99)*	400	
D-OMAN(2)	Cameron A-300 HAFB *(Res 11.99)*	4115	
D-OMAR	Schroeder Fire Balloons G HAFB	258	
D-OMAS	Cameron N-120 HAFB	3566	
D-OMAW	Schroeder Fire Balloons G HAFB	499	
D-OMAX	Lindstrand LBL-240A HAFB	589	
D-OMBB	Thunder AX8-105 SI HAFB	4189	
D-OMBF	Cameron A-105 HAFB	3032	
D-OMBG	Schroeder Fire Balloons G HAFB	477	
D-OMBL	Schroeder Fire Balloons G HAFB	705	
D-OMBO(2)	Thunder AX9-120 SII HAFB	4368	
D-OMBS	Colt 120A HAFB	3609	
D-OMBZ	Lindstrand LBL-150A HAFB	398	
D-OMCB	Cameron N-105 HAFB	3108	
D-OMCD	Cameron N-105 HAFB	3431	
D-OMCG	Schroeder Fire Balloons G HAFB *(Res 11.99)*	48	D-Germany(2)
D-OMDR	Schroeder Fire Balloons G HAFB	386	
D-OMEB	Cameron O-140 HAFB *(Reservation 10.99)*	3031	
D-OMEC(2)	Cameron N-120 HAFB	4267	
D-OMEK	Schroeder Fire Balloons G HAFB	608	
D-OMEN	Schroeder Fire Balloons G HAFB	234	D-OELE
D-OMES	Schroeder Fire Balloons GHAFB	709	
D-OMET	Thunder AX7-77 SI HAFB	1572	D-Meteor D-Jever(2)
D-OMEW	Schroeder Fire Balloons G HAFB	664	
D-OMEY(2)	Schroeder Fire Balloons G HAFB	563	
D-OMFM	Raven Europe S-60A HAFB	E-351	
D-OMFX	Cameron N-105 HAFB	3443	PH-OMF
D-OMFY	Cameron N-90 HAFB	2275	D-Somfy D-Mondi(2)

Regn.	Type	C/n	Prev.Id.
D-OMGL	Thunder AX10-180 SII HAFB *(Res 10.99)*	2423	F-GMGL
			G-BVCH
D-OMGM	Schroeder Fire Balloons G HAFB	417	
D-OMGV	Raven-Europe S-60A HAFB	E-270	
D-OMHM	Schroeder Fire Balloons G HAFB	512	
D-OMHN	Thunder AX9-140 SII HAFB	2339	
D-OMHS	Schroeder Fire Balloons G HAFB	445	
D-OMIC	Schroeder Fire Balloons G HAFB	725	
D-OMIK	Schroeder Fire Balloons SS Cat HAFB	305	
D-OMIL	Cameron N-105 HAFB	3819	
D-OMIS	Lindstrand LBL-150A HAFB	540	
D-OMIT	Thunder AX9-140 SII HAFB	2312	
D-OMIX	Schroeder Fire Balloons G HAFB	390	
D-OMJS	Schroeder Fire Balloons G HAFB	548	
D-OMKA	Cameron N-90 HAFB	2737	
D-OMKC	Schroeder Fire Balloons G HAFB	637	
D-OMKE	Schroeder Fire Balloons G HAFB	619	
D-OMKL	Schroeder Fire Balloons GHAFB	764	
D-OMKV	Schroeder Fire Balloons G HAFB	569	
D-OMLE	Lindstrand LBL-150A HAFB	533	
D-OMLW	Thunder AX8-105 SII HAFB	2570	
D-OMMA(2)	Colt 105A HAFB	2639	
D-OMMB	Cameron O-120 HAFB	3965	
D-OMME	Schroeder Fire Balloons G HAFB	677	
D-OMMF	Schroeder Fire Balloons G HAFB	609	
D-OMMG	Cameron O-105 HAFB	2806	
D-OMMH	Thunder AX8-105 SII HAFB	3528	
D-OMML	Schroeder Fire Balloons G HAFB	198	
D-OMMM	Cameron O-105 HAFB *(Res 4.99)*	1199	
D-OMMN	Thunder AX8-105 SII HAFB	783	G-BMMN
D-OMMO	Cameron N-105 HAFB	2908	
D-OMMW	Schroeder Fire Balloons G HAFB	737	
D-OMMY	Balloon Works Firefly 9 HAFB	F9-070	
D-OMNA	Schroeder Fire Balloons G HAFB *(Res 12.99)*	114	
D-OMNB	Thunder AX8-105 SII HAFB	3531	
D-OMNG	Schroeder Fire Balloons G HAFB	606	
D-OMNI	Cameron A-180 HAFB *(Reservation 6.99)*	3425	
D-OMNK	Schroeder Fire Balloons G HAFB	523	
D-OMOG	Aerostar S-57A HAFB	3191	
D-OMOM	Schroeder Fire Balloons G HAFB	670	
D-OMON	Schroeder Fire Balloons G HAFB	391	
D-OMOR	Raven Europe S-60A HAFB	E-302	
D-OMOS	Cameron N-105 HAFB	3008	
D-OMOZ	Aerostar S-60A HAFB	3236	
D-OMPA	Schroeder Fire Balloons G HAFB	518	
D-OMPD	Colt 105A HAFB	2131	
D-OMPH	Cameron N-105 HAFB	4270	
D-OMPS	Lindstrand LBL-310A HAFB	558	
D-OMRB	Schroeder Fire Balloons G HAFB	722	
D-OMRL	Schroeder Fire Balloons G HAFB	501	
D-OMRV	Schroeder Fire Balloons G HAFB	505	
D-OMSA	Schroeder Fire Balloons G HAFB	537	
D-OMSF	Schroeder Fire Balloons G HAFB	734	
D-OMST	Colt 105A HAFB	2153	PH-IAK
D-OMTI	Schroeder Fire Balloons G HAFB	647	
D-OMUC	Wörner NL-840/STU Gas Balloon *(Res 6.99)*	1062	
D-OMUH	Schroeder Fire Balloons G HAFB	435	
D-OMUM	Cameron O-105 HAFB	4192	
D-OMUT	Raven-Europe S-60A HAFB	E-272	
D-OMUU	Schroeder Fire Balloons G HAFB	458	
D-OMWA	Thunder AX9-120 SII HAFB	4393	
D-OMWH	Lindstrand LBL-150A HAFB	597	
D-OMWY	Schroeder Fire Balloons G HAFB	530	
D-OMZF	Thunder AX8-105 SII HAFB	4398	
D-ONAA	Stuttgart K-780/2-STU Gas Balloon	0102	D-Sony
D-ONAM	UltraMagic N-210 HAFB	210/07	
D-ONAR	Lindstrand LBL-120A HAFB	519	
D-ONAT	Schroeder Fire Balloons G HAFB	55	D-Natreen
D-ONAU	Cameron O-105 HAFB	2836	
D-ONBC	Thunder AX9-140 SIIHAFB	4563	
D-ONBG(2)	Schroeder Fire Balloons G HAFB	651	
D-ONBM	Colt 90A HAFB	912	G-BNBM
D-ONBY	Thunder AX9-120 SII HAFB	2017	G-BUFS
D-ONCC	Cameron N-105 HAFB	3427	
D-ONCH	Cameron N-105 HAFB	3602	
D-ONCK	Cameron N-133 HAFB	3084	
D-ONDI	Cameron N-105 HAFB *(Reservation)*	1725	D-Mondi(1)
D-ONDO	Cameron N-105 HAFB	2851	
D-ONDY	Cameron N-105 HAFB	4630	
D-ONEE	Schroeder Fire Balloons Maus SS HAFB	614	
D-ONEK	Thunder AX9-140 SII	2333	
D-ONEO	Schroeder Fire Balloons G HAFB *(Reservn)*	2001	
D-ONER	Raven S-60A HAFB	242	
D-ONES(2)	Cameron N-133 HAFB *(Reservation)*	4647	
D-ONET(2)	Cameron N-105 HAFB	3669	
D-ONEU	Raven Europe S-60A HAFB	E-341	
D-ONEW	Lindstrand LBL-105A HAFB	116	
D-ONGO	Cameron N-133 HAFB	3751	
D-ONIG	Cameron V-90 HAFB	3653	
D-ONIK	Schroeder Fire Balloons G HAFB	295	
D-ONIL	Thunder AX8-90 SII HAFB	3534	D-ODIL
D-ONIS	Schroeder Fire Balloons G HAFB	346	
D-ONIX	Lindstrand LBL-120A HAFB	349	
D-ONJA	Cameron N-105 HAFB	3252	
D-ONKA	Cameron O-120 HAFB	2596	D-ONKY
			G-BTME
D-ONKE	Lindstrand LBL-105A HAFB	126	
D-ONKH	Cameron N-105 HAFB	3113	
D-ONKI	Lindstrand LBL-180A HAFB *(Res 9.99)*	090	
D-ONKJ	Lindstrand LBL-210A HAFB *(Res 11.99)*	336	
D-ONKL	Cameron N-133 HAFB	4419	
D-ONKO	Lindstrand LBL-105A HAFB *(Res 11.99)*	604	
D-ONLB	Schroeder Fire Balloons G HAFB	645	
D-ONLY	Cameron A-105 HAFB	2900	
D-ONMB	Thunder AX8-105 SII HAFB	4308	
D-ONMR	Colt 105A HAFB	2120	D-ORAC
D-ONNA	Cameron A-210 HAFB	3014	
D-ONNI	Cameron N-120 HAFB	3765	
D-ONNN	Cameron A-210 HAFB *(Reservation 11.99)*	3284	
D-ONOE	Cameron O-90 HAFB	2799	D-Nordlicht(2)
D-ONOW	Thunder AX8-9O SI HAFB	2268	
D-ONPM	Aerostar S-60A HAFB	3223	
D-ONRA	Colt 77A HAFB	074	LN-CBC
			SE-ZVX
D-ONRJ	Lindstrand LBL-210A HAFB	555	
D-ONRW	Schroeder Fire Balloons G HAFB	126	D-Sportland
D-ONSB	Colt 105A HAFB	3750	
D-ONUE	Cameron N-105 HAFB *(Reservation)*	4676	
D-ONUP	UltraMagic M-105 HAFB	105/40	
D-ONUT	Colt 240A HAFB *(Reservation 11.99)*	2320	
D-ONUV	Schroeder Fire Balloons G HAFB	590	
D-OOAM	Schroeder Fire Balloons G HAFB *(Res 11.99)*	542	
D-OOAS	UltraMagic S-90 HAFB	90/11	
D-OOBI	Cameron A-105 HAFB	2893	
D-OOBU(2)	Thunder AX9-140SII HAFB	3948	
D-OOBW	Schroeder Fire Balloons G HAFB	472	
D-OOCA	Thunder AX8-105 SII HAFB *(Res 11.99)*	4746	
D-OODI	Schroeder Fire Balloons G HAFB	534	
D-OODL	Schroeder Fire Balloons G HAFB	683	
D-OODM	Schroeder Fire Balloons GHAFB	344	
D-OOEG	Schroeder Fire Balloons G HAFB	654	
D-OOEH	Schroeder Fire Balloons G HAFB	550	
D-OOEL(2)	Schroeder Fire Balloons G HAFB	628	
D-OOEN	Raven Europe S-60A HAFB	E-197	
D-OOES	Colt 180A HAFB *(Reservation)*	2578	
D-OOFB	Schroeder Fire Balloons G HAFB	652	
D-OOFI	Schroeder Fire Balloons G HAFB	616	
D-OOFW	Schroeder Fire Balloons G HAFB	756	
D-OOGB	Schroeder Fire Balloons G HAFB	594	
D-OOGE	Colt 105A HAFB	2553	
D-OOGS	Schroeder Fire Balloons G HAFB	720	
D-OOHD	Aerostar S-60A HAFB	3238	
D-OOHF	Schroeder Fire Balloons G HAFB	676	
D-OOHK	Schroeder Fire Balloons G HAFB	635	
D-OOHO	Raven Europe S-60A HAFB	E-304	
D-OOHP	UltraMagic M-65 HAFB *(Reservation)*	65/70	HB-QDY
D-OOHR	Schroeder Fire Balloons G HAFB	611	
D-OOIL	Schroeder Fire Balloons G HAFB	454	
D-OOJA	Schroeder Fire Balloons G HAFB	682	
D-OOKW	Schroeder Fire Balloons G HAFB	567	

Regn.	Type	C/n	Prev.Id.
D-OOLD	Cameron O-105 HAFB	2444	D-Goldmarie
D-OOLE	Schroeder Fire Balloons G HAFB	592	
D-OOLK	Cameron O-105 HAFB	1865	D-Wokenkratzer
D-OOLS	Schroeder Fire Balloons G HAFB	351	
D-OOMA	Cameron O-105 HAFB	unkn	
D-OOMG	Schroeder Fire Balloons G HAFB	736	
D-OOMP	Cameron N-105 HAFB (Reservation 12.99)	2223	
D-OONE	Cameron N-105 HAFB	3064	
D-OOOA	Cameron N-133 HAFB (Reservation)	3455	
D-OOOH(2)	Colt 140A HAFB (Reservation)	4665	
D-OOOI	Cameron N-105 HAFB	3496	
D-OOOL	Schroeder Fire Balloons G HAFB	303	
D-OOOM	Colt 105A HAFB (Reservation)	2575	
D-OOOO	Cameron N-105 HAFB	3110	
D-OOOR	Colt 120A HAFB	1863	G-BTLO
D-OOOS	Thunder AX8-105 SII HAFB	2132	G-BUBV
D-OOOT	Colt 120A HAFB (Reservation)	2270	
D-OOPA	Cameron O-105 HAFB	1562	D-Lloyd(1)
D-OOPH	UltraMagic M-105 HAFB	105/28	
D-OOPS	Cameron V-56 HAFB	3260	
D-OOPT	Schroeder Fire Balloons G HAFB	605	
D-OOPW	Schroeder Fire Balloons G HAFB	513	
D-OORH	Schroeder Fire Balloons G HAFB	140	
D-OORJ	Schroeder Fire Balloons G HAFB	354	
D-OORL	Schroeder Fire Balloons G HAFB	unkn	
D-OORO	Thunder AX9-140 SII HAFB	2332	
D-OORT	Cameron O-105 HAFB	2775	
D-OOSM	Thunder AX8-90 SI HAFB	2620	
D-OOTS	Schroeder Fire Balloons G HAFB	416	
D-OOTW	Schroeder Fire Balloons G HAFB	744	
D-OOUM	UltraMagic H-42 HAFB	42/04	
D-OOVW	Schroeder Fire Balloons G HAFB	406	
D-OOWE	Wörner NL-1000/STU Gas Balloon	1055	
D-OOWL(2)	Schroeder Fire Balloons G HAFB	762	
D-OOZI	Thunder AX8-105 SII HAFB	2363	
D-OPAA(2)	Thunder AX9-140 SII HAFB	4530	
D-OPAB	Thunder AX10-210 SII HAFB (Res 12.99)	3925	
D-OPAC	Cameron O-120 HAFB	4474	
D-OPAH	Schroeder Fire Balloons G HAFB	56	D-Lichtenstein
D-OPAK	Schroeder Fire Balloons G HAFB	160	D-Arjomari
D-OPAL	Balloon Works Firefly 8B-15 HAFB	F8B-486	
D-OPAP(2)	Schroeder Fire Balloons G HAFB	475	
D-OPAS	Cameron O-105 HAFB	2653	
D-OPBL	Cameron N-105 HAFB	4203	
D-OPBP	Wörner FK-5550/STU Gas Balloon (Res.)	6004	
D-OPCM	Schroeder Fire Balloons G HAFB (Res 10.99)	424	
D-OPDS	Thunder AX10-150 SII HAFB	4558	
D-OPEB	Thunder AX7-77A SIII HAFB	325	
D-OPEC	Thunder AX7-77 SI HAFB	1970	
D-OPEL	Schroeder Fire Balloons G HAFB	503	
D-OPEN	Schroeder Fire Balloons G HAFB	273	
D-OPEP	Schroeder Fire Balloons G HAFB	661	
D-OPHC	Cameron N-105 HAFB	2871	
D-OPIE	Schroeder Fire Balloons Pinguin SS HAFB	341	
D-OPIF	Cameron N-105 HAFB	505	D-Pfiffikus
			HB-BAW
D-OPIH	Aerostar S-66A HAFB	3062	
D-OPIP	Schroeder Fire Balloons G HAFB	421	
D-OPIT	Cameron N-133 HAFB	3992	
D-OPKW	Schroeder Fire Balloons G HAFB	427	
D-OPLA	Schroeder Fire Balloons G HAFB (Res 10.99)	278	
D-OPLB	Schroeder Fire Balloons G HAFB (Res 10.99)	201	D-Arolsen
	(Now quoted as c/n 201/278 - new envelope?)		
D-OPLK	Schroeder Fire Balloons G HAFB (Res 10.99)	791	
D-OPMB	Wörner NL-1000/STU Gas Balloon	1045	
D-OPMD	Thunder AX8-90 SII HAFB	2481	
D-OPMF	Schroeder Fire Balloons G HAFB	430	
D-OPMI	Cameron O-120 HAFB	2686	
D-OPMN	Colt 105A HAFB	4147	
D-OPMS	Schroeder Fire Balloons G HAFB (Res 11.99)	638	
D-OPON	Schroeder Fire Balloons G HAFB	314	
D-OPOR	Thunder AX7-77 SI HAFB (Reservation)	1846	
D-OPPA	Cameron A-105 HAFB	1569	D-Lloyd(2)
D-OPPE	Lindstrand LBL-150A HAFB	364	
D-OPPO	Thunder AX8-90 SII HAFB	905	D-Parkbrau

Regn.	Type	C/n	Prev.Id.
D-OPPP(3)	Schroeder Fire Balloons G HAFB (Res 11.99)	809	
D-OPPT	Schroeder Fire Balloons G HAFB	331	
D-OPPY	Schroeder Fire Balloons G HAFB	297	
D-OPRI	Schroeder Fire Balloons G HAFB	359	
D-OPRO	Cameron N-90 HAFB	2906	
D-OPSD	Thunder AX8-90 SI HAFB	4625	
D-OPSI	Raven-Europe FS-57A HAFB	E-159	D-Mopsi
D-OPTJ	Thunder AX7-77 SI HAFB	800	D-Optimist
D-OPUM	Cameron A-120 HAFB	3483	
D-OPUN	Cameron A-120 HAFB	3203	
D-OPUP	Schroeder Fire Balloons G HAFB	564	
D-OPUS	Schroeder Fire Balloons G HAFB	224	
D-OPWC	UltraMagic S-90 HAFB	90/34	
D-OPYT	Schroeder Fire Balloons G HAFB	471	
D-OQCL(2)	Lindstrand LBL-240A HAFB	588	
D-OQEL	Colt 180A HAFB	2330	
D-OQIN	Balloon Works Firefly 8 HAFB	F8-1048	
D-OQQQ	Sky 90 HAFB	005	G-BWLU
D-ORAC(2)	Colt 180A HAFB	3497	
D-ORAE	Lindstrand LBL-120A HAFB (Reservation)	346	
D-ORAM	Cameron N-105 HAFB	3294	
D-ORAN	Cameron O-105 HAFB	2688	
D-ORAR	Sky 180 HAFB (Reservation 12.99)	042	
D-ORAS	Lindstrand LBL-150A HAFB	536	
D-ORAU	Thunder AX8-90 SII HAFB	2369	
D-ORCA(2)	Thunder AX8-105 SII HAFB	4438	
D-ORCC	Cameron A-140 HAFB	4485	
D-ORCK	Thunder AX9-140 SII HAFB	4312	
D-ORDO	Schroeder Fire Balloons G HAFB	429	
D-ORDU	Cameron A-120 HAFB (Reservation)	2902	
D-OREC	Schroeder Fire Balloons G HAFB	663	
D-ORED(2)	Lindstrand LBL-120A HAFB	464	
D-OREE	Cameron N-105 HAFB	4123	
D-OREG	Cameron V-77 HAFB	2679	
D-OREH	Cameron O-140 HAFB	2997	
D-OREI	Cameron N-105 HAFB	3245	
D-OREL	Lindstrand LBL-210A HAFB	135	
D-OREM	Cameron A-250 HAFB (Reservation 10.99)	3224	
D-OREN	Schroeder Fire Balloons G HAFB (Res 11.99)	440	
D-OREV	Cameron N-105 HAFB	3109	
D-OREW	Schroeder Fire Balloons G HAFB	597	
D-OREX	Cameron A-105 HAFB (Reservation)	2859	
D-ORFA	Cameron O-105 HAFB	1209	D-OATC
			D-Albstadt(2)
			D-Bauknecht(1)
D-ORFW	Raven Europe S-60A HAFB	E-361	
D-ORGA	Cameron N-105 HAFB	2716	
D-ORGL	Schroeder Fire Balloons G HAFB	684	
D-ORGS	Stuttgart K-1260/3-STU Gas Balloon (Res)	0309	D-Ruhrgas
D-ORHA	Raven Europe FS-57A HAFB	E-207	
D-ORHB	Schroeder Fire Balloons G HAFB	283	D-Hessen(3)
D-ORHE	Schroeder Fire Balloons G HAFB	360	
D-ORHT	Lindstrand LBL-150A HAFB	561	G-BWJJ
D-ORHV	Colt 180A HAFB (Reservation 7.99)	1563	G-BRHV
D-ORHW	Schroeder Fire Balloons G HAFB	675	
D-ORIA	Cameron A-105 HAFB	2844	
D-ORIB	Cameron A-105 HAFB	3894	
D-ORIC	Lindstrand LBL-150A HAFB	529	
D-ORIE	Schroeder Fire Balloons G HAFB	307	
D-ORIF	Thunder AX8-105 SII HAFB	4528	
D-ORIH	Cameron N-105 HAFB (Reservation)	3704	
D-ORIS	Thunder AX8-90 SI HAFB	2406	
D-ORIT(2)	Schroeder Fire Balloons G HAFB	526	
D-ORIZ	Colt 105A HAFB	4465	
D-ORJB	Schroeder Fire Balloons G HAFB	544	
D-ORJL	Colt 105A HAFB	3488	
D-ORKA(2)	Wörner FK-5500/STU Gas Balloon (Res 10.99)	6016	
D-ORLI	Cameron A-105 HAFB	2544	D-Rosenberg
D-ORMA	Schroeder Fire Balloons G HAFB	425	
D-ORMD	Schroeder Fire Balloons G HAFB	763	
D-ORNI	Thunder AX8-105 SII HAFB	2179	
D-OROL	Colt 105A HAFB	3835	
D-OROM	Cameron A-105 HAFB	2261	D-Krombach
D-ORON	Raven RX-7 HAFB	362	HB-BFK
D-OROP	Thunder AX8-105 SII HAFB	4352	

Regn.	Type	C/n	Prev.Id.
D-OROS	Schroeder Fire Balloons G HAFB	409	
D-OROT	Colt 105A HAFB	2289	
D-ORPR	Schroeder Fire Balloons G HAFB	484	
D-ORRJ	Schroeder Fire Balloons G HAFB	712	
D-ORRT	Cameron N-120 HAFB	3729	
D-ORRU	Schroeder Fire Balloons G HAFB	570	
D-ORRZ	Schroeder Fire Balloons G HAFB	478	
D-ORSB	Lindstrand LBL-150A HAFB	568	
D-ORSD	Cameron N-105 HAFB (Reservation)	1568	G-BSRD
D-ORSE	Head AX8-105 HAFB	257	
D-ORSI	Schroeder Fire Balloons G HAFB	561	
D-ORSS	Cameron N-105 HAFB	3193	
D-ORST	Cameron A-210 HAFB (Reservation 11.99)	3263	
D-ORSW	Schroeder Fire Balloons G HAFB	379	
D-ORSY	Schroeder Fire Balloons G HAFB	442	
D-ORTA	Cameron O-90 HAFB	3104	
D-ORTL	Cameron A-140 HAFB	4468	
D-ORTS	Cameron A-105 HAFB	3202	
D-ORUE	Schroeder Fire Balloons G HAFB (Reservation)	242	
D-ORUI	Schroeder Fire Balloons G HAFB	248	D-Metabo
D-ORUL(2)	Schroeder Fire Balloons GHAFB	735	
D-ORUM(2)	Cameron N-105 HAFB	"5001"	
D-ORUP	Schroeder Fire Balloons G HAFB	648	
D-ORUT(2)	Cameron O-105 HAFB	4484	
D-ORUV	Raven Europe S-60A HAFB	E-268	
D-ORVS	Cameron O-105 HAFB	4600	
D-ORWL	Thunder AX8-105SII HAFB (Reservation)	3825	
D-ORWM	Schroeder Fire Balloons G HAFB (Res 11.99)	251	
D-OSAA	Cameron A-105 HAFB	3803	
D-OSAE	Colt 105A HAFB	4033	
D-OSAL	Schroeder Fire Balloons G HAFB	603	
D-OSAM	Wörner FK-280/STU Gas Balloon	6001	
D-OSAP	Colt 210A HAFB (Reservation 10.99)	4724	
D-OSAR	Schroeder Fire Balloons G HAFB	271	
D-OSAT	Schroeder Fire Balloons G HAFB	721	
D-OSAU	Wörner K-1000/3-STU Gas Balloon (Res 5.99)	0292	
	(Now shown as c/n 0229/0292)		
D-OSAV	Colt 240A HAFB	2176	
D-OSBA	Thunder AX9-120 SII HAFB	2306	
D-OSBB	Colt 105A HAFB	4046	
D-OSBD	Thunder AX9-120 SII HAFB	2337	
D-OSBJ	Thunder AX8-1065 SII HAFB	3798	
D-OSBL	Thunder AX8-90 SII HAFB (Res 5.99)	1425	
D-OSBM	Thunder AX9-120 SII HAFB	4556	
D-OSBT	Cameron A-140 HAFB (Res 9.99)	3187	
D-OSBZ	Colt 69A HAFB	2334	
D-OSCA(2)	Schroeder Fire Balloons G HAFB (Res 12.99)	860	
D-OSCB	Raven Europe S-60A HAFB	E-358	
D-OSCC	Lindstrand LBL-150AHAFB	584	
D-OSCH	Schroeder Fire Balloons G HAFB	601	
D-OSEC	Cameron N-105 HAFB	3306	
D-OSED(2)	UltraMagic M-105 HAFB	105/39	
D-OSEE(2)	Cameron A-105 HAFB	3691	
D-OSEN	Schroeder Fire Balloons G HAFB	482	
D-OSEP	UltraMagic Z-90 HAFB	90/14	
D-OSFB	Schroeder Fire Balloons G HAFB	465	
D-OSFD	Aerostar S-60A HAFB	3228	
D-OSFE	Thunder AX8-105 SII HAFB (Res 11.99)	2527	
D-OSHA	Schroeder Fire Balloons G HAFB	218	
D-OSHB	Cameron N-105 HAFB	3590	
D-OSHG	UltraMagic M-145 HAFB	145/06	
D-OSHI	Cameron N-105 HAFB	4303	
D-OSHR	Cameron A-210SV HAFB	3897	
D-OSIB	Cameron O-77 HAFB	861	D-Bamberg
D-OSIG	Schroeder Fire Balloons G HAFB	150	
D-OSIL	Stuttgart K-630/1-STU Gas Balloon (Res)	0120	D-Silentium
D-OSIN	Colt 105A HAFB	2057	
D-OSIS	Cameron N-105 HAFB	2957	
D-OSKA	Colt 105A HAFB	unkn	
D-OSKB	Schroeder Fire Balloons G HAFB	687	
D-OSKF	Schroeder Fire Balloons G HAFB	698	
D-OSKU	Schroeder Fire Balloons G HAFB	552	
D-OSKW	Schroeder Fire Balloons G HAFB	727	
D-OSLO	Cameron N-120 HAFB (Reservation 10.99)	2350	D-Hammer
			G-BSSU
D-OSLS	Cameron O-84 HAFB	1551	D-Telge II
D-OSMB	Schroeder Fire Balloons GHAFB	751	
D-OSMC(2)	Cameron N-105 HAFB	4721	
	(Reservation - replacement for c/n 3663)		
D-OSMP	Thunder AX10-160 SI HAFB (Reservation)	1419	D-OAXL
			D-Jupiter
			G-BPXP
D-OSMS	Schroeder Fire Balloons G HAFB	674	
D-OSNA(2)	Thunder AX10-180 SII HAFB (Reservation)	3521	
D-OSOM	Raven Europe RX-7 HAFB	E-121	D-Sommer Traum
D-OSPB	Cameron O-105 HAFB	958	D-Sparkasse(2)
D-OSPD	Cameron O-84 HAFB	2916	
D-OSPE	Cameron A-105 HAFB	3871	
D-OSPM(2)	Colt 210A HAFB (Reservation)	4724	
	(Replacement for c/n 3523)		
D-OSPN	Lindstrand LBL-180A HAFB	421	
D-OSPS	Balloon Works Firefly 7-15 HAFB (Res.)	F7-834-3	
D-OSRP	Schroeder Fire Balloons G HAFB	415	
D-OSSH	Schroeder Fire Balloons G HAFB	353	
D-OSSI	Cameron V-77 HAFB	2664	
D-OSSR	Schroeder Fire Balloons G HAFB	761	
D-OSST	Cameron A-300 HAFB (Res 11.99)	4668	
D-OSSW	Cameron O-120 HAFB	4157	
D-OSTA(2)	Schroeder Fire Balloons G HAFB	215	
D-OSTB	Schroeder Fire Balloons G HAFB	633	
D-OSTD	Schroeder Fire Balloons G HAFB	1.96-2	
D-OSTL	Schroeder Fire Balloons G HAFB	264	
D-OSTM	Schroeder Fire Balloons G HAFB	436	
D-OSTY	Wörner NL-840/STU Gas Balloon (Res 12.99)	1063	
D-OSTZ	Wörner K-1000/3-STU Gas Balloon	1035	
D-OSUB	Schroeder Fire Balloons G HAFB	519	
D-OSUD	Schroeder Fire Balloons G HAFB	607	
D-OSUL	Cameron V-90 HAFB	2807	PH-JME
D-OSUN	Schroeder Fire Balloons G HAFB	571	
D-OSUS(2)	Schroeder Fire Balloons G HAFB	456	
D-OSUV	Schroeder Fire Balloons G HAFB (Res 8.99)	370	
D-OSWA	Colt 105A HAFB	2142	
D-OSWB	Cameron N-120 HAFB	3927	
D-OSWH	Cameron N-105 HAFB	3919	
D-OSWN	Lindstrand LBL-120A	541	
D-OSWR	Cameron O-90 HAFB	4284	
D-OSWT	Cameron O-120 HAFB	4285	
D-OSWW	Schroeder Fire Balloons G HAFB	559	
D-OSZB	Wörner K-780/2-STU Gas Balloon	1033	
D-OSZO(2)	Schroeder Fire Balloons G HAFB (Res 12.99)	808	
	(Replacement for c/n 174 ex OE-SZO)		
D-OTAB	Schroeder Fire Balloons G HAFB (Res 9.99)	792	
D-OTAK	Aerostar RXS-8 HAFB	3077	
D-OTAM	Thunder AX8-84 SI HAFB	4516	
D-OTBL	Schroeder Fire Balloons G HAFB	321	
D-OTCA	Colt 90A HAFB	2524	
D-OTCC	Schroeder Fire Balloons G HAFB	496	
D-OTDI	Schroeder Fire Balloons G HAFB	540	
D-OTEC	Colt 120A HAFB	2391	
D-OTED	Schroeder Fire Balloons G HAFB	553	
D-OTEN	Thunder AX7-77 SI HAFB	1804	G-BTEN
D-OTEO	Schroeder Fire Balloons G HAFB	355	
D-OTGV	Cameron N-105 HAFB	3786	
D-OTHA	Schroeder Fire Balloons G HAFB	632	
D-OTHI	UltraMagic V-90 HAFB	90/24	
D-OTHL	Schroeder Fire Balloons G HAFB	74	D-Reutlingen
D-OTHT	Schroeder Fire Balloons G HAFB	631	
D-OTIG	Cameron A-210 HAFB (Reservation 12.99)	3045	
D-OTIL	Cameron O-84 HAFB	1321	D-Johannes
D-OTIM(2)	Schroeder Fire Balloons G HAFB (Res 11.99)	799	
	(Replacement for c/n 313)		
D-OTIS	Schroeder Fire Balloons G HAFB	209	D-OWPG
D-OTIW	Schroeder Fire Balloons G HAFB	686	
D-OTKU	Cameron A-105 HAFB	2574	G-BTKU
D-OTLN	Schroeder Fire Balloons G HAFB	487	
D-OTMA	Raven Europe S-60A HAFB	E-193	
D-OTMF	Lindstrand LBL-120A HAFB (Res 11.99)	648	
D-OTML	Schroeder Fire Balloons G HAFB	327	
D-OTMU	Thunder AX8-105 SII HAFB	1977	G-BTMU
D-OTOA	Colt 240A HAFB	2518	

Regn.	Type	C/n	Prev.Id.
D-OTOB(2)	Colt 180A HAFB	3468	
D-OTOC	Thunder AX9-140 SII HAFB	2293	
D-OTOE	Colt 120A HAFB	4019	
D-OTOM	Schroeder Fire Balloons G HAFB	206	
D-OTON(2)	Cameron N-77 HAFB	3830	
D-OTOP	Thunder AX8-105 SII HAFB (Reservation)	2225	
D-OTOR	Colt 105A HAFB	2537	
D-OTOS	Schroeder Fire Balloons G HAFB	618	
D-OTPA	Colt 105A HAFB	4128	
D-OTPU	Cameron N-105 HAFB	2591	G-BTPU
D-OTPW	Cameron N-105 HAFB	2580	D-Provital / G-BTPW
D-OTRA	Cameron A-210 HAFB	3283	
D-OTRE	Schroeder Fire Balloons G HAFB	602	
D-OTRI	Cameron N-105 HAFB	3368	
D-OTSS	Thunder AX8-105 SII HAFB	2636	
D-OTTI	Schroeder Fire Balloons Ottifant SS Balloon	33	D-Ottifant
D-OTTO(2)	Cameron N-120SV HAFB	3870	
D-OTTP	Lindstrand LBL-210A HAFB	358	
D-OTTS	Schroeder Fire Balloons G HAFB	525	
D-OTTT(2)	Cameron O-90 HAFB	4095	
D-OTTU	Cameron V-90 HAFB	2646	G-BTTU
D-OTUA	Schroeder Fire Balloons G HAFB	457	
D-OTUI	Cameron N-90 HAFB	4443	
D-OTUL	Schroeder Fire Balloons G HAFB	577	
D-OTUT	Cameron A-210 HAFB	3557	
D-OTUV	Schroeder Fire Balloons G HAFB	538	
D-OTWD	Lindstrand LBL-105A HAFB (Res 12.99)	659	
D-OTWG	Thunder AX10-160 SII HAFB	2062	G-BTWG
D-OTWO	Cameron A-120 HAFB	3271	
D-OTYM	Cameron O-84 HAFB	3211	
D-OTZC	Colt 90A HAFB (Reservation 11.99)	1876	G-BTZC
D-OTZE	Schroeder Fire Balloons G HAFB	284	D-Wikinger(2)
D-OUAE	Thunder AX8-105 SII HAFB	2032	G-BUAE
D-OUAK	Thunder AX8-105 SII HAFB	2080	G-BUAK
D-OUAM	Schroeder Fire Balloons G HAFB	701	
D-OUAT	Schroeder Fire Balloons G HAFB (Res 11.99)	292	
D-OUCH	Cameron A-210 HAFB (Reservation 7.99)	3352	G-BWAX
D-OUDO(2)	Colt 90A HAFB	2496	G-BVEI
D-OUDP	Thunder AX8-105 SII HAFB	2178	D-Reineburg(2)
D-OUDR	Thunder AX9-140 SII HAFB	4553	
D-OUDQ	Thunder AX9-120 SII HAFB	3748	
D-OUEE	Wörner K-1000/3-STU Gas Balloon	0325	D-Queen
D-OULI	Schroeder Fire Balloons G HAFB	304	
D-OULM	Cameron O-84 HAFB	1817	D-Wurttfeuer(3)
D-OULP	Thunder AX9-120 SII HAFB (Res 5.99)	2266	G-BULP
D-OUNG	Schroeder Fire Balloons G HAFB	394	
D-OUNS	Cameron A-120 HAFB	4127	
D-OUOG	Colt 90A HAFB	2224	G-BUOG
D-OUPD	Schroeder Fire Balloons G HAFB	622	
D-OURS(3)	Cameron A-210 HAFB	4568	
D-OUSA	Raven Europe S-60A HAFB	E-311	
D-OUSB(2)	Thunder AX10-210 SII HAFB	4334	
D-OUTA	Lindstrand LBL-105A HAFB	379	
D-OUUU	Cameron A-315SV HAFB (Reservation 11.99)	3399	
D-OUVM	Schroeder Fire Balloons G HAFB	241	
D-OUWE	Cameron N-90 HAFB (Res 6.99)	2602	D-Fresh
D-OUWI	Schroeder Fire Balloons G HAFB	604	
D-OUYO	Thunder AX7-77 SI HAFB	953	G-BOGL
D-OUZO	Cameron O-120 HAFB	3298	
D-OUZR	Thunder AX8-90 SII HAFB	4445	
D-OVAI (2)	UltraMagic M-130 HAFB	130/21	
D-OVAL	Schroeder Fire Balloons G HAFB	275	
D-OVAT	Schroeder Fire Balloons G HAFB	291	
D-OVBG	Schroeder Fire Balloons G HAFB	627	
D-OVBW	Lindstrand LBL-120A HAFB	047	G-BVBW
D-OVDT	Thunder AX8-105 SII HAFB	3524	
D-OVEC	Colt 105A HAFB	3855	
D-OVEG	Cameron N-105 HAFB	2077	D-Grevenstein(2)
D-OVEL	Cameron N-105 HAFB	3951	
D-OVER	Schroeder Fire Balloons G HAFB	325	
D-OVES	Lindstrand LBL-120A HAFB	510	
D-OVEX	Lindstrand LBL-105A HAFB	56	
D-OVFL	Thunder AX9-140 SII	4084	
D-OVHM	Cameron A-140 HAFB	3343	
D-OVHS	Schroeder Fire Balloons G HAFB	408	
D-OVID	Cameron N-105 HAFB	2687	
D-OVIT	Aerostar S-60A HAFB	3255	
D-OVMH	Schroeder Fire Balloons G HAFB	510	
D-OVNT	Thunder AX9-120 SII HAFB (Res 11.99)	2520	G-BVNT
D-OVOL(2)	Lindstrand LBL-150A HAFB	256	
D-OVOM	Schroeder Fire Balloons G HAFB	715	
D-OVON	Schroeder Fire Balloons G HAFB	362	
D-OVOR	Aerostar RXS-8 HAFB	3066	
D-OVRR	Schroeder Fire Balloons G HAFB	340	
D-OVSH	Cameron O-84 HAFB	1280	D-Ostsee
D-OVSS	Thunder AX8-105 SII HAFB (Res 10.99)	3533	
D-OVUS	Schroeder Fire Balloons G HAFB (Res 11.99)	485	
D-OVVV(2)	Lindstrand LBL-400A HAFB	396	
D-OVWW	Thunder AX7-77 SI HAFB	4338	
D-OWAA	Schroeder Fire Balloons G HAFB (Reservation)	239	
D-OWAB	Schroeder Fire Balloons G HAFB	240	
D-OWAC	Cameron O-77 HAFB	2721	
D-OWAD	Thunder AX7-65 SI HAFB	2107	
D-OWAE	Thunder AX7-65 SI HAFB	2108	
D-OWAF(2)	Raven-Europe FS-57A HAFB	E-284	
D-OWAG	Schroeder Fire Balloons G HAFB	267	D-Propanunion(2)
D-OWAH	Thunder AX7-65 SI HAFB	2562	
D-OWAI	Thunder AX7-65 SI HAFB	3796	
D-OWAK	Raven-Europe S-60A HAFB	E-297	
D-OWAM	Thunder AX8-84 SI HAFB	2565	
D-OWAR	Thunder AX7-65 SI HAFB	2564	
D-OWAS	Colt 69A HAFB	2566	
D-OWAT	Schroeder Fire Balloons G HAFB	666	
D-OWAU	Cameron N-77 HAFB	unkn	
D-OWAW	Thunder AX8-84 SI HAFB	2563	
D-OWAX	UltraMagic M65C HAFB	65/72	
D-OWAY	Thunder AX9-120 SII HAFB	4108	
D-OWBB	Schroeder Fire Balloons G HAFB	587	
D-OWBF	Wörner NL-1000/STU Gas Balloon	1058	
D-OWBS	Colt 105A HAFB	2127	
D-OWBT	Schroeder Fire Balloons G HAFB	141	D-Happy
D-OWBZ	UltraMagic M-65C HAFB	65/77	
D-OWCD	Cameron A-120 HAFB (Reservation)	2399	G-BWCD / G-OCBC
D-OWCW(2)	Cameron N-105 HAFB	3924	
D-OWDR	Schroeder Fire Balloons G HAFB	583	
D-OWEB	Schroeder Fire Balloons G HAFB	521	
D-OWED	Cameron N-105 HAFB (Reservation)	4670	
D-OWEF	Schroeder Fire Balloons G HAFB	317	
D-OWEG	Schroeder Fire Balloons G HAFB	289	
D-OWEI	Cameron A-105 HAFB	3846	
D-OWEW	Schroeder Fire Balloons G HAFB	551	
D-OWFA	Cameron N-90 HAFB	3096	
D-OWFO	Colt 105A HAFB	1697	D-Schatz
D-OWGM	Schroeder Fire Balloons G HAFB	711	
D-OWGU	Cameron A-105 HAFB	4050	
D-OWHC	Schroeder Fire Balloons G HAFB	517	
D-OWIE	Schroeder Fire Balloons G HAFB	556	
D-OWIL	Cameron O-105 HAFB	2774	
D-OWIM	Schroeder Fire Balloons G HAFB	439	
D-OWIN	Schroeder Fire Balloons G HAFB	575	
D-OWIS	Colt 140A HAFB	2637	G-BVTI
D-OWKA	Schroeder Fire Balloons G HAFB	506	
D-OWKM	Schroeder Fire Balloons G HAFB	01	D-Trier(2)
D-OWML	Wörner NL-1000/STU Gas Balloon	1050	
D-OWMP	Schroeder Fire Balloons G HAFB	574	
D-OWOB	Raven-Europe FS-57A HAFB	E-279	
D-OWOF	Schroeder Fire Balloons G HAFB	378	
D-OWOL	Schroeder Fire Balloons G HAFB	598	
D-OWOT	Cameron A-105 HAFB	1790	D-? / OE-PZM
D-OWOW	Schroeder Fire Balloons G HAFB	733	
D-OWPG	Lindstrand LBL-105A HAFB (Res 11.99)	450	
D-OWPM(2)	UltraMagic H-77 HAFB	77/167	
D-OWPT	Schroeder Fire Balloons G HAFB	714	
D-OWPZ	Schroeder Fire Balloons G HAFB	281	
D-OWSA	Schroeder Fire Balloons G HAFB	433	
D-OWSH(2)	Cameron N-105 HAFB	4584	
D-OWSI	Schroeder Fire Balloons G HAFB	511	

Regn.	Type	C/n	Prev.Id.
D-OWSW(2)	Cameron N-105 HAFB	3292	
D-OWTB	Cameron O-120 HAFB	2973	
D-OWTC	Cameron N-105 HAFB	4256	
D-OWTM	Lindstrand LBL-120A HAFB	271	
D-OWUE	Schroeder Fire Balloons G HAFB	520	
D-OWUN	Sky 120 HAFB	051	
D-OWWD	Schroeder Fire Balloons GHAFB	758	
D-OWWE	Colt 105A HAFB	2583	D-OWWL(1)
D-OWWL(2)	Schroeder Fire Balloons G HAFB	516	
D-OWYZ	Cameron V-90 HAFB	2983	
D-OXFT	Cameron N-105 HAFB	3018	
D-OXID	Lindstrand LBL-105A HAFB	397	
D-OXTT	Cameron A-120 HAFB	3267	
D-OXUS	Schroeder Fire Balloons G HAFB	157	D-Limes
D-OXXL	Lindstrand LBL-400A HAFB	587	
D-OXXX	Schroeder Fire Balloons G HAFB	397	
D-OYCT	Cameron N-105 HAFB	3626	(D-OXTC)
D-OYEG	Specon S90 HAFB	001	
D-OYOT	Schroeder Fire Balloons G HAFB	593	
D-OYPO	Wörner K-1000/3-STU Gas Balloon	1038	
D-OYPQ	Colt 180A HAFB	1569	G-HYPO
D-OYTO	Raven Europe S-60A HAFB	E-347	
D-OYYY	Cameron N-77 HAFB	535	D-Kurbis(1)
			G-BHCS
D-OZAK	Cameron N-105 HAFB	3307	(D-OBRE)
D-OZAM	Wörner NL-1000/STU Gas Balloon	1043	
D-OZAN	Lindstrand LBL-105A HAFB	395	
D-OZDF	Schroeder Fire Balloons G HAFB	623	
D-OZEL	Raven Europe S-60A HAFB	E-355	F-GMNU
D-OZEP	Schroeder Fire Balloons G HAFB	441	
D-OZIN	Cameron A-105 HAFB	2476	D-Württfeuer(4)
D-OZLM	Schroeder Fire Balloons G HAFB	724	
D-OZOG(2)	Cameron N-105 HAFB	3142	
D-OZON	Cameron V-90 HAFB	2661	
D-OZOO	Lindstrand LBL-120A HAFB	221	
D-OZRL	Cameron N-105 HAFB	2630	
D-OZUG	Schroeder Fire Balloons G HAFB	432	
D-OZZZ	Thunder AX7-77 SI HAFB	2338	

The following Balloons were identified in the former system by name only. Many of those older balloons below will probably no longer be currently active. Some have already appeared in the D-O... registration sequence but the tie-ups are not known. All those remaining active must be re-registered in the D-O... sequence by 1.3.2000.

GAS BALLOONS

Regn.	Type	C/n	Prev.Id.
D-Alb	Augsburg K-780/2-STU	0234	
D-Albatross	Stuttgart K-1260/3-STU	0252	
D-Arag	Type unknown	unkn	
D-Augsburg	Bronschofen K-1050/3-RI	10406	
D-Bavaria	Stuttgart K-1000/3-STU	0280	
D-Beldrive	Stuttgart K-1000/3-STU	0307	
D-Bitterfeld	Bronschofen K-1050/3-RI	10523	
D-Clouth IX	Augsburg K-1260/3-RI	8763	
D-Columbus	Stuttgart K-1000/3-STU	0320	
D-Continentale	Stuttgart K-1000/3-STU	0314	
D-Dehner	Augsburg K-630	unkn	
D-Die Arag	Bronschofen K-1050/3-RI	41764	
D-DKV Aktiv	Bronschofen K-1260/3-RI	10570	
D-Ergee II	Augsburg K-780/2/RI	10431	
D-Euregio	Stuttgart K-1000/3-STU	0316	
D-Europa	Augsburg K-630/I-STU	0134	
D-Ferdinand Eimermacher	Augsburg K-1680	unkn	
D-Frau Antje	Bronschofen K-1260/3-STU	10421	
D-Gatzweiler II	Stuttgart K-1000/3-STU	0229	
D-Germania	Stuttgart K-1000/3-STU	0270	
D-Gerolsteiner	Augsburg K-1000/3-STU	unkn	
D-Graf Zeppelin	Augsburg K-1050	unkn	
D-Hicom	Stuttgart K-1000/3-STU	0306	
D-Hoechst II	Stuttgart K-1000/3-STU	0253	
D-Hopfenblute	Stuttgart K-1000/3-STU	0312	
D-Huels	Type unknown (K-1050)	unkn	
D-Humana	Stuttgart K-1000/3-STU	0298	
D-Ibbenbüren	Augsburg K-1000/3-STU	0225	

Regn.	Type	C/n	Prev.Id.
D-Jan Wellem	Augsburg K-1000/3-STU	1028	
D-Kabel	Stuttgart K-1000/3-STU	0311	
D-Karstadt	Stuttgart K-1000/3-STU	0321	
D-Kiepenkerl II	Stuttgart K-780/2-STU	0279	
D-Kneipp	Augsburg K-780	unkn	
D-Köln I	Type unknown (K-1050)	unkn	
D-Königin	Stuttgart K-1260/3-STU	0278	
D-Lodenfrei III	Augsburg K-780	unkn	
D-MAN	Augsburg K-1260	unkn	
D-Mausi	Bronschofen K-630/I-RI	49242	
D-Monte Carlo	Bronschofen K-1350/4-RI	44134	
D-Münster- F.E.	Stuttgart K-780/2-STU	0267	
D-Münsterland II	Augsburg K-1000/3-STU	0297	
D-Munte	Augsburg K-1050/3-RI	45778	
D-Musketier	Type unknown (K-1050)	unkn	
D-Pirat	Stuttgart K-1000/3-STU	1030	
D-Posthorn	Bronschofen K-1050/3-RI	10498	
D-Premium	Stuttgart K-1260/3-STU	0296	
D-Ratio	Type unknown (K-945)	unkn	
D-Rolinck II	Augsburg K-945/2-STU	02688458	
D-Rosie	Stuttgart K-780/2-STU	0305	
D-Ruhrgas	Stuttgart K-1260/3-STU	0309	
	(Reserved as D-ORGS 12.98)		
D-Ruhrpott	Stuttgart K-1000/3-STU	1031	
D-Sandemann	Type unknown (K-1200)	9250	PH-HBC(1)
D-Schneider Von Ulm	Bronschofen B-800/2-RI	10497	
D-Silentium	Stuttgart K-630/1-STU	0120	
	(Reserved as D-OSIL 11.98)		
D-Spar	Stuttgart K-945/2-STU	0269	
D-Stadt Essen	Type unknown (K-1050)	unkn	
D-Stadt Münster	Stuttgart K-1000/3-STU	0286	
D-Stadt Wuppertal	Bronschofen K-945/2-RI	4890	
D-Stern-Pils	Type unknown (K-1050)	unkn	
D-Stuttgart	Type unknown (K-780)	unkn	
D-SZ	Stuttgart K-780/2-STU	0291	
D-Tarkett	Stuttgart K-1000/3-STU	0257	
D-Tecklenburger Land	Augsburg K-1000/3-STU	0232	
D-Trevira	Bronschofen K-780/2-RI	10110	
D-Veltins	Augsburg K-1000/3-STU	0274	
D-Warsteiner	Stuttgart K-1000/3-STU	0265	
D-Warsteiner I	Type unknown (K-1050)	unkn	
D-Warsteiner II	Type unknown (K-1050)	unkn	
D-Westmilch	Type unknown (K-1050)	unkn	
D-Wicküler	Type unknown (K-945)	unkn	
D-Zeppelin	Stuttgart K-1000/3-STU	0248	

Many of the Stuttgart balloons above fall into the c/n range shown elsewhere as built by Ballonbau Wörner.

HOT-AIR BALLOONS

Regn.	Type	C/n	Prev.Id.
D-Achalm (2)	Schroeder Fire Balloons G	170	
D-Adler	Cameron O-84(Reservation)	531	
D-Adlerbrauerei	Cameron A-105	1572	
D-Agfa II	Cameron N-77	1178	
D-Agfa III	Cameron N-77	642	D-Agfa I (I)
D-Aggergas (2)	Cameron N-105	3426	
D-Aktiva	Cameron N-105	1138	
D-Albstadt (3)	Cameron O-105	1276	
D-Albuch	Cameron A-105	1855	
D-Aloisius	Cameron O-84	1469	
D-Alpha	Thunder AX7-77SI	1605	
D-Alztal	Cameron O-84	1227	D-Alz III
			D-Warstein(2)
D-Ariel	Cameron N-105	2610	G-BTTC
D-Arizona	Thunder AX7-77Z	450	
D-Arosa	Colt 105A	1789	
D-Aspirin (1)	Cameron N-77	421	
D-Aspirin (3)	Cameron N-77	1027	
D-Assekuranz	Cameron N-105	1527	
D-Astra	Thunder AX7-77	858	D-Quo Vadis(2)
D-Augustus	Schroeder Fire Balloons G	042	
D-Autoradio	Schroeder Fire Balloons G	058	
D-Barbel	Schroeder Fire Balloons G	026	

Regn.	Type	C/n	Prev.Id.
D-BarmeniAl	Cameron O-84	1026	
D-Bayernland	Cameron N-90	1744	
D-Becker Pils	Raven Balloon	unkn	
D-Becker II	Cameron N-90	1168	
D-Becks	Cameron N-105	2412	
D-Belair	Cameron O-84	1118	
D-Bellevue (1)	Cameron O-84	1223 (or 1221?)	
D-Berlin	Raven Europe FS-57A	E-093	
D-Berson	Cameron O-77	2302	
D-Biberach	Cameron A-120	2673	
D-Bielefeld	Cameron O-105	2529	G-BTKR
D-Bitt	Thunder AX8-105	268	
D-Bitburg	Colt 77A	661	D-Bitt II
D-Blue Bell	Thunder AX7-77A	114	D-Bruijn I
D-Bones	Cameron V-77	1688	
D-Borken (2)	Thunder AX8-105	2587	
D-Brandenburg	Colt 120A	1733	G-BSJF
D-Brandkasse (1)	Cameron N-90	1344	
D-Braunbaer (2)	Cameron N-105	2114	G-BSDF
D-Break	Thunder AX7-77 SI	641	
D-Bremen (2)	Cameron N-105	1578	
D-Breuninger (2)	Schroeder Fire Balloons G	051	
D-Bruchhausen (2)	Aerostar RX-7	3107	N64894
D-Bunte Kuh (2)	Cameron O-84	1327	
D-Buntspecht	Cameron O-105	1710	
D-Catsan	Thunder AX8-90 SII	1712	
D-Cesar	Thunder AX8-90 SII	1714	
D-Chappi	Thunder AX8-90	1717	
D-Chemnitz	Thunder AX8-105 SI	1833	
D-Chiemsee	Cameron A-105	1902	
D-Classic	Thunder AX7-77Z	239	
D-Cliff	Schroeder Fire Balloons G	40	
D-Coca Cola	Cameron N-105	1953	
D-Colgate (2)	Cameron N-105	2429	
D-Colonia	Cameron N-105	2145	
D-Computer	Cameron N-105	2223	
D-Cumulus	Thunder AX7-77	980	
D-Daimler	Cameron N-90	2375	
D-Deutschland	Thunder AX7-65 SI	1767	
D-Dithmarschen	Thunder AX8-105 SII	4063	
D-Dora	Colt 105A	520	
D-Dortmund	Schroeder Fire Balloons G	020	
D-Drachen	Schroeder Fire Balloons G	166	
D-Drachengas (2)	Cameron A-105	3893	
D-Draco	Schroeder Fire Balloons G	018	
D-Eifel	Schroeder Fire Balloons G	004	
D-Eimermacher	Cameron O-105	2615	G-BTUI
D-Eismann (2)	Cameron N-105	3185	
D-Eisvogel	Cameron O-105	2022	
D-Elias (3)	Cameron A-105 (Reservation)	1858	
D-Emmerich	Thunder AX7-77 SI	1783	
D-Energie	Cameron O-90	232	
D-Enterprise	Cameron O-84	1279	
D-Epson (2)	Schroeder Fire Balloons G	035	
D-Erbsloh	Cameron O-65	2298	
D-Erdnuss	Cameron N-105	1699	
D-Erftkreis	Cameron O-120	2207	D-DKSK
D-Ergee III (2)	Thunder AX8-90	202	
D-Erzgebirge	Schroeder Fire Balloons G	177	
D-Erzquell (1)	Cameron N-77	797	
D-Erzquell (2)	Cameron N-77	1004	
D-Erzquell (3)	Cameron N-90	1672	
D-EuropAl (2)	Cameron N-105	1814	
D-Felina	Thunder AX8-105 SII	1835	
D-Feuervogel (3)	Schroeder Fire Balloons G	211	
D-Filstal(1)	Cameron O-77	678	D-Lenor II
D-Fire Balloon (2)	Schroeder Fire Balloons G	045	
D-Firstl	Cameron A-120	2374	
D-Fliegender Teppich	Type unknown	unkn	
D-Flips	Colt 77A	1310	
D-Florian	Raven Europe S-60A	E-126	
D-Franken (2)	Cameron O-84	1092	
D-Frankenland	Cameron O-120	2286	
D-Frankenbrunnen	Cameron N-105	2236	
D-Frankfurt (2)	Schroeder Fire Balloons G	151	

Regn.	Type	C/n	Prev.Id.
D-Frolic	Thunder AX8-90	1713	
D-Fuggerstad	Cameron N-77	1352	D-Hitachi
D-Fürstenburg (2)	Cameron N-90	1954	
D-Gabriele	Thunder AX7-77SI	1902	
D-Gefaflug	GEFA-FLUG AS.80GD	01	G-BSLY
	(Colt AS.80 Hot Air Airship c/n 1641 modified)		
D-Gericke	Cameron O-77	2299	
D-Gloria	Fire Balloon	23	
D-Goliath	Cameron N-90	2324	
D-Grand Raid	Thunder AX7-77	271	
D-Greven	Cameron A-120	2319	G-BSGX
D-Gruenfink	Cameron O-105	1698	
D-Gutfried	Fire Balloon SS	64	
D-Gutsel	Raven Europe S-60A	E-072	
D-Halbergbrebh	Raven S-55A	0239	
D-Hamburg	Cameron V-77 (Reservation)	1228	
D-Hannen	Cameron N-77	568	
D-Hansano	Cameron N-105	2218	
D-Hanseat (2)	Cameron N-105	1342	
D-Hans Cramer	Thunder AX8-105	496	
D-Hanxheim (2)	Raven Europe RX-7	E-214	
D-Hause	Type unknown	unkn	
D-Hemden	Cameron N-90	1539	
D-Herforder Pils	Cameron N-90	1049	
D-Hippo	Colt 77A	600	D-Westfalen I (2)
D-Hof	Type unknown	unkn	
D-Höfler	Cameron N-90	2351	
D-Hohner (2)	Raven Europe S-60A	E-042	
D-Huckebein (2)	Cameron O-105	2058	
D-IBIS Hotel	Cameron N-77	543	F-GBZZ
D-Ikarus (2)	Schroeder Fire Balloons G	225	
D-Instand	Schroeder Fire Balloons G	19	
D-Jever (1)	Thunder AX8-90 SII (Reservation)	1425	
D-Kellogg	Thunder AX8-90	1236	
D-Kinzig (4)	Colt 105A	1422	
D-Kitekat	Thunder AX8-90 SII	1709	
D-Klima	Schroeder Fire Balloons G	003	
D-Kloster Alt (3)	Cameron N-90	1530	
D-Klosterbräu	Type unknown	unkn	
D-Köln	Cameron O-105	898	
D-Kranich	Schroeder Fire Balloons G (Reservation)	46	
D-Kreissparkasse	Cameron O-90	3693	
D-Krokodil	Colt 90A	4043	
D-Krombacher	Thunder AX8-105	521	
D-Landesbank	Colt 105A	1886	
D-Landessbaus Parkasse	Colt 90A	1257	
D-Landgraf	Cameron N-90	1231	
D-Lange Gas (2)	Cameron O-84	1037	
D-Langkorn (2)	Thunder AX8-90 SII	1810	
D-LBS Bayern	Cameron O-84	1033	
D-Leipzig	Schroeder Fire Balloons G	115	
D-Leonardo da Vinci	Colt 105A (Reservation)	774	
D-Leverkusen (2)	Cameron N-105	1379	
D-Licher I	Cameron N-90	1043	
D-Limit	Colt 77A	1574	
D-Linde	Schroeder Fire Balloons G	167	
D-Lizzy	Cameron A-105	2259	
D-Löwenbräu	Cameron A-105	1557	
D-Löwentor	Thunder AX9-140 SII (Reservation)	1491	
D-Lufthansa	Thunder AX9-140 SII	1915	
D-Luftikus	Cameron N-90	1185	
D-Magnus	Cameron V-90	2524	G-BTKM
D-Mainz	Raven-Europe	E-87	
D-Manna	Schroeder Fire Balloons G (Reservation)	114	
D-Marburg (1)	Cameron O-77	245	PH-CEA
D-Marburg II	Thunder AX7-77 Series 1	651	G-BLXZ
D-Maschal	Cameron N-105	1990	
D-Medica (2)	Thunder AX8-90 SII	2432	
D-Meisterpreis	Cameron N-105	2477	
D-Mercedes-Benz (2)	Thunder AX9-140 SII	2113	
D-Messer-Griesheim(2)	Thunder AX8-90	699	
D-Mona Lisa	Schroeder Fire Balloons G	069	
D-Monasterium	Cameron O-84	1329	
D-Montgolfiere	Cameron O-105	2394	
D-Monti	Thunder AX8-105 SII	1629	

Regn.	Type	C/n	Prev.Id.
D-Mosel (2)	Colt 77A	662	
D-Mosella (2)	Schroeder Fire Balloons G	34	
D-Münster	Cameron O-84	1776	
D-Münsterland	Cameron N-77	702	
D-Mutlangen	Aerostar S-55A	3002	
D-Oberberg	Cameron N-105	933	
D-Ochsenfrosch	Cameron O-105	2640	
D-Oelde	Colt SS Bottle	1705	G-BSMW
D-Orion	Cameron O-105	2917	
D-Pan (2)	Schroeder Fire Balloons G	78	
D-Paulaner	Cameron N-105	1215	
D-Peter	Cameron O-105	1955	
D-Petzi	Schroeder Fire Balloons G	95-2	D-Feuerzahn(1)
D-Peugeot (2)	Schroeder Fire Balloons G	41	
D-Phoenix	Cameron N-105	1647	
D-Pilskrone III	Thunder AX7-77A	157	
D-Pinguin	Cameron N-90	2589	
D-Poroton (2)	Cameron N-77 (Reservation)	3120	
D-Preussen	Cameron V-77	1528	D-Bremen(1)
D-Primagas	Schroeder Fire Balloons G	197	
D-Profi	Cameron O-90	2528	
D-Profilzylinder	Colt 77A	1083	
D-Propan (3)	Colt 90A	1702	
D-Provinzial (3)	Colt 105A	2610	
D-Provinzial II	Cameron O-77	1002	
D-Provinzial Munster	Cameron O-84	1173	
D-Puma	Cameron N-77	1023	
D-Quatro (3)	Schroeder Fire Balloons G	292	
D-Quelle	Cameron A-105	2268	
D-Quieta	Cameron N-105	1440	
D-Range Rover	Type unknown	unkn	
D-Ratiopharm (2)	Thunder AX9-140 SII	1728	
D-Raumdekor	Thunder AX7-77A	140	
D-Regenbauen	Aerostar RX-7	3188	
D-Reichenstein	Cameron A-105	2616	
D-Renaissance	Aerostar RX-7	3199	
D-Rentschler	Cameron A-105	2059	
D-Rheinprovinz	Cameron N-90	1964	
D-Rhenag	Cameron A-105	1740	
D-Reichshof (2)	Cameron O-105	1484	
D-Rheingas II	Cameron N-90	1100	D-Bruhl
D-Rheinland	Cameron N-105	2545	
D-Rheinprovinz	Cameron N-90	4399	
D-Riegele	Cameron N-90	1036	
D-Rittersport	Colt 105A	1913	
D-Robbi	Colt 120A	1899	
D-Roland (2)	Cameron N-90	1343	
D-Ronneburg	Cameron O-84	1629	D-Propan(2)
D-Rosalie	Cameron N-77	1201	
D-Rothenburger	Schroeder Fire Balloons G	065	
D-Rugen	Colt 120A	1735	G-BSJH
D-SAG	Type unknown	unkn	
D-Saarland	Thunder AX8-90	195	D-Landesgirokasse
D-Sachsen	Colt 160A	1731	G-BSJD
D-Sakret	Colt 77A	592	
D-Salzach II (3)	Cameron O-105	1769	
D-Sanssouci	Schroeder Fire Balloons G	159	
D-Sauerland (2)	Thunder AX7-77Z	503	
D-Schärf	Cameron N-105	2489	
D-Schauinsland	Cameron O-105	1586	
D-Scheidegger	Colt 77A	312	G-BIOL
D-Schinderhannes	Schroeder Fire Balloons G	02	
D-Schlossbau	Schroeder Fire Balloons G	28	
D-Schmackos	Thunder AX8-9O SII	1707	
D-Schmitt (4)	Schroeder Fire Balloons G	265	
D-Schultheiss	Cameron N-105	2804	
D-Schwaben	Thunder AX6-56Z	222	G-BGTM
D-Schwarzkopf	Cameron O-105	1709	
D-Schwarzwald (2)	Raven-Europe S-55A	E-052	
D-Schweinfurt	Cameron A-105	1669	
D-Securitas (2)	Cameron N-105	2434	
D-Seidenschnitt	Cameron N-105 (Reservation)	1893	
D-Seidensticker	Cameron N-77	749	
D-Selzen	Raven Europe FS-57A	E-212	
D-Senator	Cameron N-90	1104	

Regn.	Type	C/n	Prev.Id.
D-Sheba	Thunder AX8-9OSII	1716	
D-Sicherheit	Cameron O-77	227	PH-OLM
D-Siggi	Cameron A-105	2539	
D-Skipper	Schroeder Fire Balloons G	91	
D-Sparkasse II (1)	Cameron O-84	177	
D-Sparkasse IV	Cameron O-84	778	
D-Speldorf	Cameron N-105	1935	
D-Spezi	Cameron A-105	2210	
D-Sport (2)	Schroeder Fire Balloons G	293	
D-Stadt Telgte	Cameron O-84	1010	
D-Star Micronics	Raven-Europe S-60A	E-022	
D-Steiff	Thunder AX8-105	502	
D-Steinlach	Cameron N-105	1108	
D-Stern Pils II	Colt 105A	787	
D-Storch (2)	Schroeder Fire Balloons G	132	
D-Stuhr (1)	Cameron A-105	2568	
D-Stuttgart IV	Thunder AX8-90	411	D-Vogt
D-Stuttgart VI	Thunder AX8-90	773	D-Raab Karcher
D-Süring	Cameron O-77	2301	
D-Tassilo (2)	Cameron O-84 (Reservation)	1749	
D-Teefix	Schroeder Fire Balloons Theepot SS	31	
D-Telefon	Cameron Telephone Kiosk SS	1918	
D-Telekom	Colt 105A	1934	
D-Telgte (2)	Colt 105A	2609	
D-Tiger	Cameron SS-90 Tiger	2290	G-BSRW
D-Toshiba	Cameron N-105	2435	
D-Touring	Cameron A-105	1656	
D-Tradition (2)	Cameron N-90	1091	
D-Treveris	Schroeder Fire Balloons G	077	
D-Trill	Thunder AX8-90 SII	1708	
D-Tübingen (2)	Cameron A-120	2475	
D-Tucher (4)	Cameron N-77	772	D-Lünen
D-Union Gas	Cameron O-77	509	
D-Urlaub	Cameron O-90	2304	
D-Vagabund (1)	Cameron O-105	1362	
D-Valeo	Schroeder Fire Balloons G	62	
D-Veba(2)	Colt 77A (Reservation)	1190	
D-Vobis	Colt 77A	1567	
D-Warsteiner-Land (2)	Thunder AX7-77Z	495	
D-Wefah (2)	Thunder AX8-105 SII (Reservation)	1907	
D-Welde (2)	Raven-Europe S-60A	E-236	
D-Werne	Thunder AX8-90 SII	1689	
D-Westfalen Gas	Colt 77A	1084	
D-Westfalia (2)	Cameron O-84	804	
D-Westspiel (2)	Cameron N-90	1693	
D-Wetterau	Thunder AX8-105 SII	1903	
D-Wetzel	Cameron O-105	1409	
D-Whiskas	Thunder AX8-90 SII	1715	
D-Wiedenbrück (2)	Cameron N-105	1679	
D-Wiehl	Cameron N-105	1598	
D-Wikinger	Cameron N-105	2438	
D-Windspiel	Cameron N-105	1642	
D-Winergy	Colt 120A	1837	
D-Wurn II	Thunder AX7-77	138	
D-Wurn	Thunder AX7-77	850	
D-Wurst	Cameron N-105	1404	
D-Württemberg	Thunder AX7-77	606	
D-Würzburg	Cameron O-84	1424	
D-Zunft (2)	Cameron N-77	2294	

CLASS U : Unmanned aircraft

D-UISD	Universität Stuttgart Lotte (Remote-controlled airship)	unkn	

Regn.	Type	C/n	Prev.Id.

GLIDERS

Regn.	Type	C/n	Prev.Id.
D-0001	Test registration for Schleicher ASH-25, 26 production		
D-0002	Bölkow Phoebus A-1 *(Reservation)*	820	
D-0003	Schleicher Ka.2B Rhönschwalbe	262	
D-0004	Scheibe Bergfalke II/55	239	
D-0005	Scheibe Zugvogel IIIA	1061	
D-0006	Schleicher Ka.6E	4132	
D-0007	Schleicher ASW-2	12003	
D-0008	Scheibe L-Spatz 55	622	
D-0009	Schleicher ASK-21	21463	
D-0010	Schleicher K.8B	AB8750	
D-0011	Schleicher ASW-19	19011	
D-0012	Marganski MDM-1 Fox	217	
D-0013	Schleicher K.8B	AB8759	
D-0014	Scheibe L-Spatz 55 *(Reservation 12.99)*	566	
D-0015	Test Registration for Glaser-Dirks DG-800S production		
D-0016	Schempp-Hirth Discus CS	233CS	
D-0018	Schempp-Hirth Duo Discus	86	
D-0019	Schleicher ASK-13	13665AB	
D-0020	Glasflügel H201 Standard Libelle	11	
D-0021	Schempp-Hirth Nimbus 2C	224	HB-1534
D-0022	AFH 22 *(Permit 6.99)*	V-1	
D-0023	Glaser-Dirks DG-100G Elan	E119-G88	OE-5307
D-0024	AFH 24 *(Permit)*	1	
D-0025	Grunau Baby IIb *(Reservation 7.99)*	4	
D-0026	Glasflügel H303 Mosquito	99	
D-0027	Schleicher ASK-13	13666AB	
D-0028	Glaser-Dirks DG-300 Elan	3E-268	
D-0029	Grob Standard Cirrus	496G	F-CEFY
D-0030	Schleicher K.8B *(Reservation - dd?)*	8260	
D-0032	Rolladen-Schneider LC-8-18 *(Permit 10.99)*	8291	
D-0033	Glaser-Dirks DG-100 Elan	E-33	HB-1535
D-0034	Schleicher K.8B	8203	
D-0035	Schleicher K.8B	8666	
D-0036	Scheibe L-Spatz 55	617	
D-0037	Göppingen Gö III Minimoa *(Reservation 4.99)*	AB-001M	
D-0038	Scheibe Bergfalke III	5626	
D-0039	Schleicher K7 Rhönadler	7175	
D-0040	Schleicher K.8B	8850/AB	
D-0041	Scheibe L-Spatz 55	603	
D-0042	SG-38 Schulgleiter	1	
D-0043	Glaser-Dirks DG-300 Elan	3E-138	
D-0044	Glaser-Dirks DG-100 Elan	E219-G185	
D-0045	Rolladen-Schneider LS-6C	6278	
D-0046	Schleicher ASW-12	12005	OO-ZBE
D-0047	Schleicher K7 Rhönadler	269	
D-0048	Rolladen-Schneider LS-8-18 *(Permit 12.99)*	8296	
D-0049	Glasflügel H301B Libelle	88	
D-0050	Schleicher K.8B	8039	
D-0051	Rolladen-Schneider LS-8-18 *(Permit 12.99)*	8293	
D-0052	Rolladen-Schneider LS-4	4605	
D-0053	Schempp-Hirth Cirrus	26	
D-0054	Scheibe SF-27B	6201	
D-0055	Schleicher K.8B	8762	
D-0056	Schempp-Hirth Janus C	116	
D-0057	Rolladen-Schneider LS-4A	4677	
D-0058	Schleicher Ka.6E	4180	
D-0059	Schleicher Ka.6E	4213	
D-0060	PZL PW-5 Smyk	17.06.018	
D-0061	Glaser-Dirks DG-300 Elan	3E-263	
D-0062	Scheibe Bergfalke III	5628	
D-0063	Glasflügel H201B Standard Libelle	13	
D-0064	Akaflieg Braunschweig SB-5B Sperber	5045/A	
D-0065	Grunau Baby IIB *(Permit 4.99)*	94	
D-0066	Scheibe SF-27A	6108	
D-0067	Scheibe Spatz B	533	
D-0068	Schempp-Hirth Cirrus	31	
D-0069	Schleicher ASK-13	13088	
D-0070	Rolladen-Schneider LS-1-0	4	
D-0071	Glaser-Dirks DG-300 Elan	3E-326	
D-0072	Schleicher Ka.6E	4214	
D-0073	Schempp-Hirth Duo Discus	26	
D-0075	Schleicher Ka.6E	4216	
D-0076	Schleicher Ka.6E	4218	
D-0077	Schleicher K.8B	8745	
D-0078	Schleicher ASK-13	13111	
D-0079	Schleicher Ka.6E	4232	
D-0080	Schleicher ASK-13	13116	
D-0081	Schleicher ASK-13	13122	
D-0082	Standard Libelle	14	
D-0083	Schleicher K.8B *(Reservation - dd?)*	8576/A	
D-0084	Focke-Wulf Weihe 50	8	
D-0086	Schleicher Ka.6E	4233	
D-0087	Glaser-Dirks DG-100	14-G168	HB-1285
D-0088	Bölkow Phoebus C	845	
D-0089	Rolladen-Schneider LS-8-18 *(Permit 10.99)*	8289	
D-0091	Schleicher Ka.6E	4249	
D-0092	Schleicher Ka.6E	4238	
D-0093	Schleicher K.8B	8669	
D-0094	Schempp-Hirth Discus b	446	
D-0095	Schleicher ASK-13	13126	
D-0096	Schleicher ASK-13	13129	
D-0097	Schleicher ASK-13	13133	
D-0098	Schleicher Ka.6E	4253	
D-0099	Schleicher Ka.6E	4254	
D-0100	Vogt LO-100 Zwergreiher *(Reservation 11.99)*	27A	
D-0101	Schempp-Hirth Cirrus	30	
D-0102	Schleicher K.8B	8668	
D-0103	Schleicher K.8B	8671	
D-0104	Schempp-Hirth Discus CS	045CS	
D-0105	Akaflieg Braunschweig SB-5B Sperber	5036/A	
D-0106	Schleicher ASW-24	24122	
D-0107	Glasflügel H304	211	
D-0108	Schempp-Hirth Discus CS	059CS	
D-0109	Schempp-Hirth Standard Cirrus	122	
D-0110	Schleicher K.8B	8327	D-KIFA
D-0111	Glasflügel H401 Kestrel	3	
D-0113	Schleicher Ka.6E	4154	
D-0114	Glasflügel H201B Standard Libelle	211	
D-0115	Rolladen-Schneider LS-4	4546	
D-0117	Grunau Baby IIB	117	
D-0118	Glaser-Dirks DG-300 Elan	3E-417	
D-0119	Rolladen-Schneider LS-4	4544	
D-0120	Schleicher ASK-13	13681AB	
D-0121	Rolladen-Schneider LS-1-0	6	
D-0122	Schleicher K.8B	8788/AB	
D-0123	Bölkow Phoebus C	870	
D-0125	Dittmar Condor IV *(Reservation - dd?)*	18	
D-0126	Schleicher K.8B	219/61	
D-0127	Kranich III	87	
D-0128	Bölkow Phoebus B-1	875	
D-0129	Schleicher K.8B	8115/SH	
D-0131	Glaser-Dirks DG-300 Club Elan	3E-351C40	
D-0132	Akaflieg Braunschweig SB-5E Sperber	AB5004	
D-0133	Schempp-Hirth Ventus c	305	
D-0134	Rolladen-Schneider LS-4A	4675	
D-0135	Bölkow Phoebus C	860	
D-0136	Rolladen-Schneider LS-1-10 *(Reservation - dd?)*	11	
D-0137	Rolladen-Schneider LS-4	4607	
D-0138-IYB	Schempp-Hirth Discus CS	027CS	
D-0139	Glasflügel H201B Standard Libelle	222	
D-0140	Glasflügel H201 Standard Libelle	236	
D-0141	Glasflügel H201B Standard Libelle	237	
D-0142	Rolladen-Schneider LS-1B	25	
D-0143	Schleicher Ka.6E	4256	
D-0144	Schleicher ASK-13	13096	
D-0145	Schleicher ASK-13	13134	
D-0146	Schempp-Hirth Discus CS	064CS	
D-0147	Grob G.102 Astir CS Jeans	2106	
D-0148	Schleicher ASK-13	13135	
D-0149	Schleicher ASK-13	13138	
D-0150	LO-150 Zwergreiher	AB.1	
D-0151	Schleicher ASK-13	13141	
D-0152	Glaser-Dirks DG-200/17	2-136/1734	
D-0153	Glaser-Dirks DG-200/17	2-137/1735	
D-0154	Schempp-Hirth Cirrus *(Reservation)*	40	
D-0155	Bölkow Phoebus C	868	
D-0156	Rolladen-Schneider LS-1C	10	

Regn.	Type	C/n	Prev.Id.
D-0157	Rollarden-Schneider LS-4B	4761	
D-0158	Rollarden-Schneider LS-4	4378	
D-0159-IMW	Glasflügel H304	212	
D-0160	Schleicher Ka.6E	4262	
D-0161	Schleicher ASW-15	15004	
D-0162	Schleicher K.8B	8786	
D-0163	Schleicher Ka.6E	4266	
D-0164	Schleicher Ka.6E	4274	
D-0165	Rollarden-Schneider LS-4	4608	
D-0166	Glaser-Dirks DG-500 Elan Orion	5E169X24	
D-0167	Schleicher Ka.6E	4269	
D-0168	Glaser-Dirks DG-500 Elan Orion	5E-168X23	
D-0170	Glasflügel H201 Standard Libelle	223	
D-0171	Rollarden-Schneider LS-4	4609	
D-0172	Schleicher Ka.6CR Rhönsegler	6656/Si	
D-0173	Rollarden-Schneider LS-4	4610	
D-0174	Glasflügel H201 Standard Libelle	185	
D-0175	Bölkow Phoebus C	878	
D-0176	Glasflügel H201 Standard Libelle	51	
D-0177	Standard Austria SH-1	74	
D-0178	Akaflieg Braunschweig SB-5E Sperber (Reservn)	5038/A	
D-0179	Schempp-Hirth Duo Discus	28	
D-0180	Rollarden-Schneider LS-1-0	19	
D-0181	Rollarden-Schneider LS-1-0	18	
D-0182	Rollarden-Schneider LS-1-0	9	
D-0183	Rollarden-Schneider LS-4	4611	
D-0184	Schempp-Hirth Cirrus	43	
D-0185	Scheibe SF-27A	6109	
D-0187	Schempp-Hirth Cirrus	56	
D-0188	Schempp-Hirth Mini-Nimbus HS-7	06	HB-1391 D-3791
D-0189	Rollarden-Schneider LS-8-18 (Permit 5.99)	8261	
D-0190	Schempp-Hirth Standard Cirrus	128	
D-0191	Rollarden-Schneider LS-4	4583	
D-0192	Schleicher Ka.6CR Rhönsegler (Res 11.99)	6535/3/A	
D-0193	Glaser-Dirks DG-300 Club Elan	3E-427C72	
D-0194	Akaflieg Braunschweig SB-5B Sperber	5048/A	
D-0195	Schleicher Ka.6E	4281	
D-0196	Schleicher Ka.6E (Permit - old?)	4265	
D-0197	Schleicher ASW-24	24205	
D-0198	Schleicher Ka.6E	4273	
D-0199	Schleicher ASK-13	13157	
D-0200	Schleicher ASW-15	15179	
D-0201	Schleicher Ka. E	4271	
D-0202	Schleicher K.8B	8779	
D-0203	Schleicher Ka.6E	4275	
D-0204	Glasflügel H401 Kestrel	52	
D-0205	Rollarden-Schneider LS-6C	6311	
D-0206	Schleicher K7 Rhönadler	AB/7281	
D-0207	Rollarden-Schneider LS-8-18 (Permit 7.99)	8266	
D-0208	Schleicher ASK-13	13071/A	
D-0209	Schleicher K.8B	05	D-KAMB D-8877
D-0210	Schempp-Hirth Duo Discus	30	
D-0212	Schleicher K.8B	8740	
D-0213	Glaser-Dirks DG-500T Elan Trainer	5E-21T3	
D-0214	Schleicher Rhönlerche II (Reservation - old?)	3088/Br	
D-0215	Bölkow Phoebus B-1	877	
D-0216	Bölkow Phoebus B-2	873	
D-0217	Schleicher K.8B	8288 EI	
D-0218	Schleicher ASW-24	24186	
D-0219	Glaser-Dirks DG-300 Elan Acro	3E-445A8	
D-0220	Schleicher ASK-13	13292	
D-0221	Rollarden-Schneider LS-4A	4671	
D-0222	Rollarden-Schneider LS-1-0	28	
D-0223	Schleicher Ka.6E	4282	
D-0224	Schleicher ASW-15	15006	
D-0225	Schleicher ASW-15	15007	
D-0226	Glaser-Dirks DG-500/22 Elan	5E-16S5	
D-0227	Schleicher ASK-13	13152	
D-0228	Schleicher ASK-13	13156	
D-0229	Schleicher Ka.6E	4288	
D-0230	Schleicher Ka. E	4280	
D-0231	Schempp-Hirth Discus CS	056CS	
D-0232	Schleicher ASK-13	13161	
D-0233	Schleicher Ka.6E	4270	
D-0234	Schempp-Hirth Duo Discus	98	
D-0235	Schleicher ASK-13	13165	
D-0236	Schleicher K.8B	8782	
D-0237	Schleicher Ka.6E	4283	
D-0238	Schleicher ASK-13	13162	
D-0239	Schleicher ASK-13	13163	
D-0240	Schleicher ASK-13	13164	
D-0242	Schleicher ASK-13	13300/AB	
D-0243	Glasflügel H201 Standard Libelle	56	
D-0244	Schleicher ASK-21	21667	
D-0245	Glaser-Dirks DG-500T Elan Trainer	5E-26T6	
D-0246	Bölkow Phoebus C	881	
D-0247	Schleicher K.8B	8667	
D-0248	Akaflieg Braunschweig SB-5E Sperber	5033A	
D-0249	Schempp-Hirth Duo Discus	124	
D-0250	Schempp-Hirth Cirrus	63	
D-0251	Rollarden-Schneider LS-1-0	8	
D-0252	Schempp-Hirth Discus CS	058CS	
D-0253	Schempp-Hirth Standard Cirrus	132	
D-0254-31	Rollarden-Schneider LS-6B	6164	
D-0255	Schempp-Hirth Duo Discus	31	
D-0256	SZD-32A Foka 5	W-519	DDR-2256 DM-2256
D-0257	Schleicher ASK-13	13167	
D-0258	Schleicher ASK-21	21403	
D-0260	Schleicher ASK-13	13168	
D-0261	Glaser-Dirks DG-500T Elan Trainer	5E-57T24	
D-0263	Schempp-Hirth Discus CS	087CS	
D-0265	Schleicher ASK-13 (Reserved as F-CHSE)	13175	
D-0266	Schleicher ASK-13	13174	
D-0267	Schleicher ASK-13	13176	
D-0269	Schleicher ASK-13	13179	
D-0270	Schleicher ASK-13	13180	
D-0271	Schleicher ASK-13	13181	
D-0272	Rollarden-Schneider LS-4A	4679	
D-0273	Schleicher K.8B	8798	
D-0274	Schempp-Hirth Ventus 2b	41	
D-0275	Rollarden-Schneider LS-4	4101	
D-0276	Schleicher Ka.2B Rhönschwalbe	937/61	
D-0277	Glasflügel H401 Kestrel	41	
D-0278	Glasflügel H401 Kestrel	39	
D-0280	Rollarden-Schneider LS-8-18 (Permit .98)	8198	
D-0281	Glasflügel H401 Kestrel	43	
D-0282	Glaser-Dirks DG-500/22 Elan	5E-8S2	
D-0283	Rollarden-Schneider LS-4	4100	
D-0284	Schleicher ASK-13	13151	
D-0285	Rollarden-Schneider LS-8-18 (Permit 11.99)	8270	
D-0286	Schleicher K.8B	8771/AB	
D-0287	Rollarden-Schneider LS-8A	8182	
D-0288	PIK-16C Vasama	06	OH-288 OH-VAF
D-0290	Schempp-Hirth Cirrus	66	
D-0291	VFW Fokker FK-3	0002	
D-0292	VFW Fokker FK-3	0003	
D-0293	VFW Fokker FK-3	0004	
D-0294	Rollarden-Schneider LS-4B	4751	
D-0295	Akaflieg Braunschweig SB-5E Sperber	5041/A	
D-0296	Schleicher ASW-24	24130	
D-0298	Schempp-Hirth Discus CS	091CS	
D-0299	Schempp-Hirth Ventus c	590	
D-0300	Glasflügel H304	256	
D-0301	Focke-Wulf Weihe 50	SB.01	
D-0302	Glaser-Dirks DG-300 Club Elan	3E-423C71	
D-0303	Schleicher K.8B	8684/A	
D-0304	Glasflügel H201B Standard Libelle	57	
D-0305	Glaser-Dirks DG-300 Elan	3E-425	
D-0306	Schleicher K.8B	8668 EI	
D-0307	Glaser-Dirks DG-500 Elan Trainer	5E-81T35	
D-0308	Scheibe Bergfalke IV	5811	
D-0309-WS	Rollarden-Schneider LS-6B	6175	
D-0310	Schempp-Hirth Cirrus	72	
D-0311	Scheibe SF-27A	6112	
D-0312	Glasflügel H401 Kestrel	47	
D-0313	Glasflügel H101 Salto	3	

Regn.	Type	C/n	Prev.Id.
D-0314	Rolladen-Schneider LS-4B	4907	
D-0315	Schempp-Hirth Standard Cirrus	108	
D-0316	Schempp-Hirth Standard Cirrus	109	
D-0317	Schleicher ASK-21	21592	
D-0318	Schempp-Hirth Standard Cirrus	111	
D-0319	Schempp-Hirth Standard Cirrus	112	
D-0320	Rolladen-Schneider LS-4	4160	
D-0321	Schempp-Hirth Standard Cirrus	115	
D-0322	Rolladen-Schneider LS-6	6177	
D-0323	Rolladen-Schneider LS-3A	3130	OO-ZWS
D-0324	Schempp-Hirth Discus CS	029CS	
D-0325	Scheibe Bergfalke III	5635	
D-0326	Schempp-Hirth Discus CS	170CS	
D-0327-PV	Glaser-Dirks DG-500 Elan Trainer	5E-119T50	
D-0328	Schempp-Hirth Standard Cirrus	135	
D-0330	Schempp-Hirth Standard Cirrus	138	
D-0331	Rolladen-Schneider LS- A	3142	PH-629
D-0332	Schleicher K.8B	8791AB	
D-0333	Glasflügel H201 Standard Libelle	69	
D-0334	Bölkow Phoebus B-1	896	F-CDOE
D-0335	Schleicher ASK-13	13184	
D-0336	Schleicher Ka.6E	4309	
D-0337	Glaser-Dirks DG-300 Elan	3E-277	
D-0338	Schleicher ASK-13	13185	
D-0339	Schleicher Ka.6E (Reservation 7.99)	4306	
D-0340	Glasflügel H304 (Reservation 12.99)	259	
D-0341	Schempp-Hirth Duo Discus	32	
D-0342	Schleicher Ka.6E	4310	
D-0343	Schleicher ASK-13	13192	
D-0344	Glaser-Dirks DG-300 Club Elan	3E-279/C5	
D-0345	Schleicher ASK-13	13193	
D-0346	Schleicher ASK-13	13197	
D-0347	Schleicher ASK-13	13191	
D-0348	Rolladen-Schneider LS-4	4246	
D-0349	Schleicher Ka.6E	4313	
D-0350	Schleicher K.8B	8807	
D-0351	Schleicher Ka.6E	4318	
D-0352	Schleicher ASK-13	13204	
D-0353	Rolladen-Schneider LS-4B	4947	
D-0354	Schleicher ASK-13	13206	
D-0355	Glasflügel H201B Standard Libelle	277	
D-0356	Schleicher Rhönlerche II	AB 94/59	
D-0357	Glaser-Dirks DG-300 Club Elan	3E-282/C7	
D-0358	Glasflügel H401 Kestrel	11	
D-0359	Glaser-Dirks DG-300 Club Elan	3E-283/C8	
D-0360	Scheibe L-Spatz 55	507/614	
D-0361	Glaser-Dirks DG-300 Elan	3E-22	
D-0362	Schempp-Hirth Standard Cirrus	174	
D-0363	Grob Standard Cirrus	154G	
D-0364	Grob Standard Cirrus	155G	
D-0365	Grunau Baby IIB	33	
D-0366	Schleicher ASK-21	21671	
D-0367	Schleicher ASK-13	13186	
D-0368	Glasflügel H201B Standard Libelle	77	
D-0369	Glasflügel H201 Standard Libelle	289	
D-0370	Glasflügel H201 Standard Libelle	291	
D-0371	Glasflügel H201 Standard Libelle	291	
D-0372	SZD-9bis Bocian IE	P-562	DDR-3372
			DM-3372
D-0373	Vogt LO-100 Zwergreiher	01	
D-0374	Schempp-Hirth Discus CS	065CS	
D-0375	Scheibe Bergfalke IV	5814	("D-KAAO")
D-0376	Scheibe Bergfalke IV	5818	("D-KAAQ")
D-0377	SZD-24-4A Foka 4	W-237	OY-XEB
D-0378	Rolladen-Schneider LS-8	unkn	
D-0379	Rolladen-Schneider LS-1C	95	
D-0381	Schempp-Hirth Janus CE	301	
D-0382	Rolladen-Schneider LS-1C	30	
D-0383	Rolladen-Schneider LS-1C	31	
D-0384	Rolladen-Schneider LS-1C	32	
D-0386	Scheibe SF-27A	6093	
D-0387	Rolladen-Schneider LS-4B	4961	
D-0388	Schempp-Hirth Standard Cirrus	3	
D-0389	Schempp-Hirth Cirrus	85	
D-0390	Rolladen-Schneider LS-4	4115	
D-0391	Schleicher Ka.6CR Rhönsegler	6399	

Regn.	Type	C/n	Prev.Id.
D-0392	Glasflügel H-101 Salto	2	
D-0393	Rolladen-Schneider LS-4	4379	
D-0394	Rolladen-Schneider LS-4B	4962	
D-0395	Rolladen-Schneider LS-6	6183	
D-0397	Glasflügel H401 Kestrel	16	
D-0398	Glasflügel H401 Kestrel	17	
D-0399	Rolladen-Schneider LS-1E	92	
D-0400	Schempp-Hirth Duo Discus (Reservation 10.99)	239	
D-0401	Rolladen-Schneider LS-4	4388	
D-0402	Rolladen-Schneider LS-1D (Reservation 10.99)	34	
D-0403	Glaser-Dirks DG-500/22 Elan	5E-17S6	
D-0404	Rolladen-Schneider LS-4A	4681	
D-0405	Rolladen-Schneider LS-4B	4682	
D-0406	Rolladen-Schneider LS-4A	4683	
D-0407	VFW Fokker FK-3	0006	
D-0408	VFW Fokker FK-3	0007	
D-0409	Schempp-Hirth Duo Discus	127	
D-0410	Schempp-Hirth Discus b	504	
D-0411	Rolladen-Schneider LS-4B	4684	
D-0412	Rolladen-Schneider LS-4A	4697	
D-0413	Schleicher ASK-13	13207	
D-0414	Schleicher ASW-27	27042	
D-0415	Rolladen-Schneider LS-4B	4685	
D-0416	Schleicher K.8B	8812	
D-0417	Schempp-Hirth Ventus 2A (Reservation 12.99)	100	
D-0418	Schleicher ASW-15	15035	
D-0419	Schleicher ASK-13	13217	
D-0420	Glaser Dirks DG-500 Elan Orion	5E-164X19	
D-0421	Schleicher K.8B	8813	
D-0422	Schleicher ASK-13	13218	
D-0423	Rolladen-Schneider LS-1D	42	
D-0424	Glaser-Dirks DG-200/17	2-139/1736	
D-0425	Glaser-Dirks DG-200/17	2-140/1737	
D-0426	Schempp-Hirth Standard Cirrus	4	
D-0427	Schempp-Hirth Standard Cirrus	5	
D-0428	Schempp-Hirth Standard Cirrus	6	
D-0429	Schempp-Hirth Standard Cirrus	7	
D-0430	Glaser-Dirks DG-300 Club Elan	3E-286/C10	
D-0431	Schleicher ASW-15	15183	
D-0432	Rolladen-Schneider LS-1D	44	
D-0433	Glasflügel H401 Kestrel	57	
D-0434	Glasflügel H401 Kestrel	59	
D-0435	Schleicher K.8B	8578/A	
D-0436	SZD-48-3 Jantar Standard 3	B-1946	DDR-2436
D-0437	Rolladen-Schneider LS-1D	41	
D-0438	Glasflügel H201 Standard Libelle	91	
D-0439	Rolladen-Schneider LS-1D	48	
D-0440	Rolladen-Schneider LS-1D	38	
D-0441	Rolladen-Schneider LS-4A	4698	
D-0442	Rolladen-Schneider LS-1C	45	
D-0443	Glasflügel H201B Standard Libelle	92	
D-0444	Schempp-Hirth Discus 2b (Permit)	14	
D-0445	Glasflügel H201 Standard Libelle	285	
D-0446	Schleicher Ka.6E	4326	
D-0447	Bölkow Phoebus C	920	
D-0448	Schleicher K.8B	8601/A	
D-0449	Rolladen-Schneider LS-1C	96	
D-0450	Rolladen-Schneider LS-1C	90	
D-0451	Glasflügel H401 Kestrel	51	
D-0452	Schempp-Hirth Duo Discus	141	
D-0453	Schempp-Hirth Standard Cirrus	13	
D-0454	SZD-9bis Bocian 1D (Reservation 10.99)	P-350	OE-0451
D-0455	Schempp-Hirth Standard Cirrus G	16	
D-0457	Schleicher K.8B	8847/AB	
D-0458	Rolladen-Schneider LS-1C	109	
D-0459	Bölkow Phoebus C	922	
D-0460	Schleicher ASW-15	15036	
D-0461	Schleicher ASK-13	13219	
D-0463	Schleicher Ka.6E	4327	
D-0464	Rolladen-Schneider LS-4	4052	
D-0465	Schleicher ASK-13	13221	
D-0466	Schleicher ASK-13	13223	
D-0467	Schleicher ASW-15	15040	
D-0468	Schleicher ASK-13	13225	
D-0469	Schleicher ASK-13	13226	

Regn.	Type	C/n	Prev.Id.
D-0470	Rolladen-Schneider LS-1C	100	
D-0471	Schempp-Hirth Cirrus	104	
D-0472	Schleicher Ka.6E	4308	
D-0473	Rolladen-Schneider LS-4A	4699	
D-0474	Glasflügel H401 Kestrel	56	
D-0475	Glasflügel H401 Kestrel	25	
D-0476	Rolladen-Schneider LS-1C	103	
D-0477	Rolladen-Schneider LS-4	4103	
D-0478	Schleicher ASK-13	13017	OO-ZXQ
			PL-61 (Belgian
			Air Cadets)
D-0479	Schempp-Hirth Cirrus	90	
D-0480	Rolladen-Schneider LS-4A	4700	
D-0481	Schempp-Hirth Cirrus	92	
D-0482	Glasflügel H201B Standard Libelle	115	
D-0483	Rolladen-Schneider LS-4A	4701	
D-0484	Schempp-Hirth Standard Cirrus	26	
D-0485	Schempp-Hirth Duo Discus	33	
D-0486	Rolladen-Schneider LS-4B	4946	
D-0487	Schempp-Hirth Standard Cirrus	29	
D-0488	Schleicher ASK-13	13215	
D-0489	Rolladen-Schneider LS-1C	56	
D-0491	Schleicher ASK-13	13227	
D-0492	Schleicher ASK-13	13228	
D-0494	Rolladen-Schneider LS-4A	4702	
D-0495	Schleicher ASW-15	15045	
D-0496	Glasflügel H401 Kestrel	50	
D-0497	Rolladen-Schneider LS-4A	4703	
D-0498	Schleicher ASK-13	13230	
D-0499	Schleicher ASK-13	13231	
D-0500	Glasflügel H201B Standard Libelle	95	
D-0501	Glasflügel H201 Standard Libelle	207	
D-0502	Glaser-Dirks DG-300 Elan	3E-248	HB-1914
D-0503	Rolladen-Schneider LS-4A	4704	
D-0504	VTC-75 Standard Cirrus	115Y	
D-0505	VTC-75 Standard Cirrus	116Y	
D-0506	VTC-75 Standard Cirrus	117Y	
D-0507	Schleicher ASW-15	15047	
D-0508	Schleicher ASW-15	15057	
D-0509	Schleicher Ka.6E	4334	
D-0510	Glaser-Dirks DG-300 Elan	3E-290	
D-0511	Glaser-Dirks DG-300 Club Elan	3E-292C13	
D-0513	Schleicher ASK-13	13233	
D-0514	Schleicher ASK-13	13234	
D-0515	Schleicher ASK-13	13235	
D-0516	Schleicher ASW-15	15051	
D-0517	Glasflügel H401 Kestrel	20	
D-0519	Rolladen-Schneider LS-1C	104	
D-0520	Glasflügel H304	251	
D-0521	Glasflügel H401 Kestrel	45	
D-0522	Glasflügel H201 Standard Libelle	120	
D-0523	Scheibe Bergfalke IV	5803	
D-0524	Scheibe Bergfalke IV	5804	
D-0525	Scheibe Bergfalke IV	5805	
D-0526	Rolladen-Schneider LS-4A	4705	
D-0527	Schleicher ASW-27	27019	
D-0528	Glasflügel H201B Standard Libelle	260	
D-0529	Schempp-Hirth Standard Cirrus	37	
D-0530	Schempp-Hirth Standard Cirrus	38	
D-0531	Rolladen-Schneider LS-6-18W	6351	
D-0532	Scheibe L-Spatz 55	716	OE-0521
D-0533	Glasflügel H401 Kestrel	38	
D-0534	Schleicher K.8B	8819	
D-0535	Schleicher ASK-13	13236	
D-0536	Schleicher ASW-15	15052	
D-0537	Schleicher ASK-13	13237	
D-0538	Schleicher ASK-13	13240	
D-0539	Schleicher Ka.6E	4340	
D-0540	Schleicher ASW-15	15055	
D-0543	Rolladen-Schneider LS-8-18 (Reservation 12.99)	8297	
D-0544	Schempp-Hirth Ventus 2b	3	
D-0545	Schleicher Ka.6E	4339	
D-0546	Vogt LO-100 Zwergreiher	204	OE-0446
D-0547	Schleicher Ka.6E	4342	
D-0548	Schleicher K.8B	8828	
D-0549	Schleicher K.8B	8829	
D-0550	Schleicher ASK-13	13248	
D-0551	Schleicher ASK-13	13249	
D-0552	Schleicher ASK-13	13250	
D-0554	Glasflügel H201 Standard Libelle	171	
D-0555	Schleicher ASK-13	13072/1	
D-0556	Schempp-Hirth Cirrus	93	
D-0557	Schempp-Hirth Standard Cirrus	117	
D-0558	Schempp-Hirth Duo Discus	204	
D-0559	Bölkow Phoebus C	935	
D-0560	Schleicher K.8B	225/61	
D-0561	Schleicher K.8B	8687/AB	
D-0562	Schempp-Hirth Discus CS	066CS	
D-0563	Schempp-Hirth Cirrus	95	
D-0564	Schempp-Hirth Janus CE	294	
D-0565	Rolladen-Schneider LS-1C	99	
D-0566	Schempp-Hirth Nimbus 2	42	ZS-GJB
			D-2154
D-0567	Rolladen-Schneider LS-4B	4796	
D-0568	Rolladen-Schneider LS-4B	4797	
D-0569	Schempp-Hirth Standard Cirrus	50	
D-0570	Rolladen-Schneider LS-4B	4798	
D-0571	Bölkow Phoebus C	938	
D-0572	Siebert SIE-3 (Reservation 7.99)	3021	
D-0573	Rolladen-Schneider LS-4B	4799	
D-0574	HBV Diamant 16.5	067	
D-0576	Schleicher K7 Rhönadler	7191/A	
D-0577	Scheibe Bergfalke III	5643	
D-0579	Rolladen-Schneider LS-4B	4926	
D-0580	Glaser-Dirks DG-100G Elan	E145-G113	
D-0581	Schempp-Hirth Standard Cirrus	54	
D-0582	Schempp-Hirth Standard Cirrus	55	
D-0583	Siebert SIE-3	3004	
D-0584	Bölkow Phoebus C	953	
D-0585	Schempp-Hirth Discus CS	030CS	
D-0586	Schempp-Hirth Cirrus	98	
D-0587	Rolladen-Schneider LS-8-18 (Reservation 11.99)	8292	
D-0588	Schempp-Hirth Standard Cirrus	185	
D-0589	Schleicher ASK-13	13645AB	JA2357
D-0590	Schempp-Hirth Standard Cirrus	191	
D-0591	Grob G.103C Twin III	36004	
D-0592	Bölkow Phoebus A-1	711	
D-0593	Schempp-Hirth Standard Cirrus	58	
D-0594	Schempp-Hirth Standard Cirrus	64	
D-0595	Schempp-Hirth Standard Cirrus	69	
D-0597	Schleicher Ka.6CR Rhönsegler	1114	
D-0598	Glasflügel H401 Kestrel	26	
D-0599	Glasflügel H201 Standard Libelle	154	
D-0600	Rolladen-Schneider LS-1C	102	
D-0601	Siebert SIE-3	3017	
D-0602	Schempp-Hirth Ventus 2c	28	
D-0603	Glasflügel H203 Standard Libelle	1	
D-0606	Schleicher Ka.6E	4346	
D-0607	Schleicher K.8B	8831	
D-0608	Schleicher ASW-15	15020	
D-0609	Schempp-Hirth Ventus c	378	
D-0610	SZD-50-3 Puchacz	B-1327	DDR-3610
D-0611	Glaser-Dirks DG-100G Elan	E144-G112	
D-0612	Schleicher Ka.6E	4347	
D-0613	Schleicher ASK-13 (Reservation)	13255	
D-0614	Schleicher K.8B	8833	
D-0615	Schleicher ASW-15	15066	
D-0616	Rolladen-Schneider LS-6	6100	HB-1889
D-0617	Schleicher K.8B	8835	
D-0618	Schleicher ASK-13	13258	
D-0619	Schleicher ASK-13	13259	
D-0620	Schleicher ASW-15	15087	
D-0621	Schleicher ASK-13	13262	
D-0622	Schleicher K.8B	8837	
D-0623	Rolladen-Schneider LS-4	4564	D-3392
D-0624	Schleicher ASK-13	13267	
D-0625	Schempp-Hirth Standard Cirrus G	56	
D-0626	Schleicher ASK-21	21559	
D-0627	Schleicher ASW-15	15078	
D-0628	Schleicher K.8B	8840	

Regn.	Type	C/n	Prev.Id.	Regn.	Type	C/n	Prev.Id.
D-0629	Schleicher K.8B	8842		D-0708	Schleicher ASW-15	15107	
D-0630	Schleicher ASK-13	13269		D-0709	Schleicher Ka.6E	4363	
D-0631	Schleicher ASK-13	13270		D-0710	Schempp-Hirth Duo Discus	18	
D-0632	Schleicher K.8B	8844		D-0711	Schempp-Hirth Discus CS	166CS	
D-0633	Schleicher ASW-15	15081		D-0713	Schleicher ASW-15 (Reservation 7.99)	15112	
D-0634	Scheibe SF-34	5102	4X-GGM	D-0714	Schleicher K.8B	8857	
			D-3336	D-0715	Schleicher ASW-15B	15114	
D-0635	Schleicher ASK-13	13272		D-0716	Schleicher ASW-15	15115	
D-0636	Schleicher ASW-15	15083		D-0717	SZD-30 Pirat	S-07.25	DDR-1717
D-0637	Schleicher K.8B	8845					DM-1717
D-0638	SZD-50-3 Puchacz	B-1403	DDR-3637	D-0718	Schleicher Ka.2 Rhönschwalbe	40	
D-0639	Schleicher ASK-13	13276		D-0719	Schempp-Hirth Standard Cirrus	107	
D-0640	Glaser-Dirks DG100G	88-G9	HB-1339	D-0720	Grob G.102 Club Astir IIIB	5567CB	
D-0641	Schleicher ASK-21	21566		D-0721	Schleicher ASK-21	21350	
D-0642	Schleicher ASW-15	15088		D-0722	SZD-42-2 Jantar 2B	B-939	HB-1522
D-0643	Schleicher ASK-13	13277		D-0723	Rolladen-Schneider LS-4B	4802	
D-0644	Schleicher ASK-13	13278		D-0724	Rolladen-Schneider LS-4B	4803	
D-0645	Schleicher ASK-13	13288		D-0725	Rolladen-Schneider LS-1D	153	
D-0646	Schleicher ASK-13	13282		D-0726	Schleicher ASH-26	26010	
D-0647	Glasflügel H201B Standard Libelle (Res 10.99)	157		D-0727	Rolladen-Schneider LS-1C	55	
D-0648	Schempp-Hirth Cirrus	100		D-0728	Rolladen-Schneider LS-1D	67	
D-0649	Rolladen-Schneider LS-6	6125		D-0729	SZD-30 Pirat	B-319	DDR-1729
D-0650	Schleicher ASK-21	21567					DM-1729
D-0651	Grob G.102 Standard Astir III	5637S	N102FK	D-0730	SZD-30 Pirat	B-314	DDR-1731
D-0652	Schempp-Hirth Standard Cirrus	76					DM-1731
D-0653	Siebert SIE-3	3005		D-0731	HBV Diamant 18	080	
D-0654	Schleicher ASW-15	15095		D-0732	Schempp-Hirth Standard Cirrus	95	
D-0655	Schleicher Ka.6E	4357		D-0733	SZD-30 Pirat	B-316	DDR-1733
D-0656	Rolladen-Schneider LS-1D	112					DM-1733
D-0657	Schleicher ASW-15	15101		D-0735	Schleicher ASK-21	21557	
D-0658	Schleicher ASK-13	13289		D-0736	Schempp-Hirth Standard Cirrus	104	
D-0660	Schleicher ASW-15	15100		D-0737	Schempp-Hirth Standard Cirrus	105	
D-0661	Rolladen-Schneider LS-6C	6257		D-0738	Schleicher ASK-21	21575	
D-0662-6F	Rolladen-Schneider LS-6	6000		D-0739	VTC-75 Standard Cirrus	137Y	OE-0970
D-0663	Schleicher ASK-13	13291		D-0740	LSD Ornith (Permit 3.99)	V-1	
D-0664	Rolladen-Schneider LS-1D	73		D-0741	Schempp-Hirth Standard Cirrus	100	
D-0665	Glaser-Dirks DG-300 Club Elan Acro	3E-355C79A13		D-0742	Glasflügel H201B Standard Libelle	204	
D-0666	Glasflügel H201B Standard Libelle	167		D-0743	Glasflügel H201 Standard Libelle	205	
D-0667	Rolladen-Schneider LS-1C	57		D-0744	Schleicher ASK-21	21570	
D-0668	Rolladen-Schneider LS-1D	63		D-0745	Schleicher ASK-13	13302	
D-0669	Rolladen-Schneider LS-1D	62		D-0746	Schleicher ASK-13	13303	
D-0670	Rolladen-Schneider LS-1D	64		D-0747	Schleicher ASW-15	15120	
D-0671	Glasflügel H201 Standard Libelle	172		D-0749	Schleicher K.8B	8861	
D-0672	Rolladen-Schneider LS-1C	69		D-0750	Rolladen-Schneider LS-4	4546	D-0115
D-0674	Rolladen-Schneider LS-1C	58		D-0751	SZD-30 Pirat	B-345	DDR-1751
D-0675	Schleicher ASK-21	21569					DM-1751
D-0676	Rolladen-Schneider LS-1C	76		D-0752	Schleicher ASK-13	13309	
D-0677	Schempp-Hirth Standard Cirrus	82		D-0753	Schleicher ASK-15	15124	
D-0678	Schempp-Hirth Standard Cirrus (Reservation)	83		D-0754	Schleicher ASK-13	13304	
D-0679	Rolladen-Schneider LS-1C	116		D-0755	Schleicher ASK-13	13310	
D-0680	Schleicher ASK-21	21555		D-0756	Schleicher ASW-15	15125	
D-0681	Rolladen-Schneider LS-1C	71		D-0757	Schleicher ASK-13	13311	
D-0682	Kranich III	55		D-0758	Schleicher ASW-15	15126	
D-0683	Rolladen-Schneider LS-1C	74		D-0759	Schleicher ASW-27	27044	
D-0684	Rolladen-Schneider LS-1D	68		D-0760	Schleicher Ka.6E	4374	
D-0685	Rolladen-Schneider LS-1C	60		D-0761	Schleicher ASK-13	13318	
D-0686	Rolladen-Schneider LS-1C	66		D-0762	Schleicher ASK-13	13321	
D-0687	Schempp-Hirth Standard Cirrus	86		D-0764	Rolladen-Schneider LS-1D	85	
D-0688	Schempp-Hirth Standard Cirrus	536		D-0765	Rolladen-Schneider LS-1C	78	
D-0689	Schempp-Hirth Standard Cirrus	88		D-0766	Schleicher ASH-25	25013	
D-0690	Schempp-Hirth Standard Cirrus	89		D-0767	Scheibe L-Spatz	577	
D-0691	Schempp-Hirth Standard Cirrus	92		D-0769	Glasflügel H201B Standard Libelle	298	
D-0692	Rolladen-Schneider LS-4B	4853		D-0770	Glasflügel H201 Standard Libelle	299	
D-0693	Siebert SIE-3	3007		D-0771	Glasflügel H201B Standard Libelle	300	
D-0694	Rolladen-Schneider LS-1D	65		D-0772	Schempp-Hirth Standard Cirrus	159	
D-0698	Schleicher ASK-21	21556		D-0773	Schleicher ASW-20	20500	
D-0699-VS	Rolladen-Schneider LS-4B	4963		D-0774	Schleicher ASK-21	21096	
D-0700	Focke-Wulf Weihe 50	01		D-0775	Schleicher ASW-20L	20555	
D-0701	Glasflügel H201B Standard Libelle	184		D-0776	Schleicher ASW-20	20556	
D-0702	Schempp-Hirth Standard Cirrus	180		D-0777	Glasflügel H401 Kestrel	36	
D-0703	Schempp-Hirth Standard Cirrus	181		D-0778	Schempp-Hirth Discus CS	077CS	
D-0704	Schempp-Hirth Standard Cirrus	555		D-0779	Schempp-Hirth Standard Cirrus	164	
D-0705	Schempp-Hirth Standard Cirrus	183		D-0780	Rolladen-Schneider LS-1C	107	
D-0706	Schempp-Hirth Standard Cirrus	184		D-0781	Rolladen-Schneider LS-1D	98	
D-0707	Schleicher ASK-13	13287		D-0783	Schempp-Hirth Standard Cirrus	192	

Regn.	Type	C/n	Prev.Id.
D-0784	Schempp-Hirth Standard Cirrus	193	
D-0786	Grob Standard Cirrus	200G	
D-0787	Rolladen-Schneider LS-1D	121	
D-0788	Slingsby T.59D Kestrel *(Permit 10.99)*	1847	
D-0789	Schempp-Hirth Discus b	162	
D-0790	SZD-48-1 Jantar Standard 2	B-1004	SP-3176
D-0791	Schleicher ASW-15	15147	
D-0792	Schleicher ASW-15	15142	
D-0793	Schleicher ASW-15	15144	
D-0795	Glasflügel H301 Libelle	36	OE-0796
D-0796	Schleicher ASW-15	15148	
D-0797	SZD-30 Pirat	B-440	DDR-1797
			DM-1797
D-0798	Schleicher K.8B	8871	
D-0799	Schleicher ASW-15	15150	
D-0800	Rolladen-Schneider LS-4B	4820	
D-0801	SZD-30 Pirat	B-444	DDR-1801
			DM-1801
D-0802	Schleicher ASW-15	15154	
D-0803	Schleicher ASW-15	15155	
D-0804	Schleicher ASW-15B	15158	
D-0805	Schleicher K.8B	8874	
D-0806	Schleicher ASK-13	13346	
D-0807	SZD-51-1 Junior	B-1924	DDR-2807
D-0808	Schleicher ASW-20L	20417	
D-0809	Rolladen-Schneider LS-1C	101	
D-0810	Schleicher ASW-17	17018	N15UF
D-0811	Grunau Baby IIB	29	
D-0812	Rolladen-Schneider LS-1D	120	
D-0814	Grob Standard Cirrus	157G	
D-0815	Glasflügel H401 Kestrel	62	
D-0816	Schleicher K.8B	923	
D-0817	Rolladen-Schneider LS-1C	118	
D-0819	Grob G.103A Twin II Acro	3756-K-51	
D-0821	Schleicher Ka.6CR Rhönsegler	6201	
D-0822	Schleicher ASW-15	15159	
D-0824	Schleicher ASK-13	13351	
D-0825	Bölkow Phoebus C	924	OE-0820
D-0826	Schleicher ASK-13	13352	
D-0827	Schleicher ASW-27	27011	
D-0828	Schleicher ASW-15	15165	
D-0829	Schleicher ASK-13	13345	
D-0830	Schleicher K.8B	8877	
D-0831	SZD-30 Pirat	B-509	DDR-1831
			DM-1831
D-0832	Glasflügel H401 Kestrel	48	
D-0833	Rolladen-Schneider LS-1C	114	
D-0834	Rolladen-Schneider LS-1D	125	
D-0835	Grunau Baby IIB	3	
D-0836	Schempp-Hirth Standard Cirrus	226	
D-0837	Rolladen-Schneider LS-1EF	106	
D-0838	Glasflügel H-101 Salto	8	
D-0839	Glaser-Dirks DG-500 Elan Trainer	5E-IOOT40	
D-0840	LET L-13 Blanik	175107	
D-0841	Rolladen-Schneider LS-4B	4948	
D-0843	Schleicher ASW-15	15138	
D-0844	Schempp-Hirth Discus CS	169CS	
D-0845	Glasflügel H201B Standard Libelle	305	
D-0846	Schleicher K.8B *(Permit 12.99)*	8881/AB	
D-0847	Glasflügel H401 Kestrel	46	
D-0848	Schleicher K.8B	8878	
D-0849	Schleicher ASK-13	13358	
D-0850	Schleicher K.8B	8875	
D-0851	Schleicher ASW-15	15172	
D-0852	Schleicher ASK-13	13360	
D-0853	Schleicher ASK-13	13361	
D-0854	Schleicher ASW-15	15173	
D-0855	Schleicher ASK-13	13362	
D-0856	Schleicher ASW-15	15175	
D-0858	Schleicher ASK-13	13341	
D-0859	Schleicher ASW-15	15176	
D-0860	Schleicher ASW-15	15177	
D-0861	Schleicher ASW-15	15178	
D-0862	Schempp-Hirth Discus CS	179CS	

Regn.	Type	C/n	Prev.Id.
D-0863	SZD-30 Pirat	B-585	DDR-1863
			DM-1863
D-0864	Schleicher ASW-15	15181	
D-0865	Schleicher ASK-13	13368	
D-0866	Bölkow Phoebus C *(Reservation 8.99)*	808	
D-0867	Schleicher ASK-13	13369	
D-0868	Schleicher ASW-15B	15184	
D-0869	Schleicher K.8B	8887	
D-0870	Schleicher ASW-15B	15185	
D-0871	Schleicher K.8B	8889	
D-0872	Glaser-Dirks DG-500 Elan Orion	5E-183X34	
D-0873	LET L-13 Blanik	175130	
D-0874	Rolladen-Schneider LS-1C	127	
D-0875	SZD-30 Pirat	S-01.05	DDR-1875
			DM-1875
D-0876	Schleicher ASW-15B	15192	
D-0877	Schleicher ASK-21	21561	
D-0878	Schempp-Hirth SHK-1 *(Permit 12.99)*	16	
D-0879	SZD-30 Pirat	S-01.25	DDR-1879
			DM-1879
D-0880	Schleicher ASW-15B	15194	
D-0881	Schempp-Hirth Discus CS	178CS	
D-0882	SZD-30 Pirat	S-01.28	DDR-1882
			DM-1882
D-0883	Schleicher ASW-20	20559	
D-0884	Schleicher ASW-20	20557	
D-0885	Schleicher ASW-20	20561	
D-0887	Schempp-Hirth Discus b	193	
D-0888	Glasflügel H201 Standard Libelle	278	
D-0889	Schempp-Hirth Discus b	201	
D-0890	Schempp-Hirth Standard Cirrus	210	
D-0891	Glasflügel H201B Standard Libelle	313	
D-0892	Rolladen-Schneider LS-1C	122	
D-0893	Schempp-Hirth Discus b	203	
D-0894	Rolladen-Schneider LS-4	4387	
D-0895	Schleicher ASW-15B	15197	
D-0896	Schleicher ASW-15B	15199	
D-0897	Schleicher ASW-15B	15200	
D-0898	Rolladen-Schneider LS-4B	4794	
D-0899	Rolladen-Schneider LS-8A *(Reservation 9.99)*	8284	
D-0900	Schleicher ASW-15B	15204	
D-0901	Schleicher K.8B	8895	
D-0903	Schleicher K.8B	8896	
D-0904	Schleicher K.8B	8897	
D-0905	Schleicher ASK-13	13391	
D-0906	Schleicher ASW-15B	15209	
D-0907	Schleicher ASW-15B	15210	
D-0908	Schleicher ASK-13	13392	
D-0909	Schempp-Hirth Discus b	188	
D-0910	LET L-13 Blanik	173461	HB-910
D-0911	Glasflügel H201B Standard Libelle	306	
D-0912	Rolladen-Schneider LS-1C	129	
D-0913	Glasflügel H201B Standard Libelle	250	
D-0914	Schempp-Hirth Janus C	239	
D-0915	Glasflügel H401 Kestrel	65	
D-0916	Schleicher ASK-13	13286AB	
D-0918	Siebert SIE-3	3019	
D-0920	Glasflügel H201 Standard Libelle	315	
D-0921-EP	Schempp-Hirth Discus b	215	
D-0922	Rolladen-Schneider LS-1D	119	
D-0923	Rolladen-Schneider LS-1C	132	
D-0924	Start & Flug H-101 Salto	10	
D-0925	Schempp-Hirth Standard Cirrus	212	
D-0926	Schempp-Hirth Standard Cirrus	213	
D-0927	Schempp-Hirth Standard Cirrus	218	
D-0928	Grob Standard Cirrus	405G	F-CEFJ
D-0930	Schempp-Hirth Discus b	196	
D-0931	Schleicher Ka.6CR Rhönsegler	897	
D-0932	Schleicher ASK-13	13393	
D-0933	Schempp-Hirth Discus b	209	
D-0934	Schleicher K.8B	8898	
D-0935	Rolladen-Schneider LS-8-18 *(Permit 9.99)*	8271	
D-0936	Glaser-Dirks DG-800S	8-26S3	
D-0937	Schempp-Hirth Ventus c	382	
D-0938	Darmstadt D-38	39	

Regn.	Type	C/n	Prev.Id.
D-0939	Schleicher ASW-15B	15203	OE-0937
D-0941	Schleicher ASW-15B	15206	OE-0941
D-0942	Schleicher K.8B	8899	
D-0943	Schleicher K.8B	8901	
D-0944	Schleicher ASK-13	13395	
D-0945	Schleicher ASW-15B	15219	
D-0946	Schleicher K.8B	8902	
D-0947	Glaser-Dirks DG-300 Elan Acro	3E-460A16	
D-0948	Schleicher ASK-13	13397	
D-0949	Schleicher ASW-15B	15221	
D-0950	Glasflügel H304	262	
D-0951	Schleicher ASW-15B	15222	
D-0952	Glasflügel H401 Kestrel	60	
D-0953	Grob Standard Cirrus	224G	
D-0954	Grob Standard Cirrus	230G	
D-0955	Avialsa-Scheibe A.60 Fauconnet	131K	F-CDLI
D-0956	Grob Standard Cirrus	232G	
D-0957	Glasflügel H401 Kestrel 17	69	OE-0950
D-0958	Start & Flug H-101 Salto	11	
D-0959	Vogt LO-100 Zwergreiher	04	
D-0961	Schleicher ASK-13	13246AB	
D-0963	Rolladen-Schneider LS-1C	134	
D-0965	Rolladen-Schneider LS-6-18W	6340	
D-0966	Glasflügel H201B Standard Libelle	330	
D-0967	Grob Standard Cirrus	240G	
D-0968	Grob Standard Cirrus	241G	
D-0969	Grob Standard Cirrus	242G	
D-0971	Schempp-Hirth Discus b	224	
D-0972	Rolladen-Schneider LS-6C	6341	
D-0973	Rolladen-Schneider LS-4B	4805	
D-0975	Schempp-Hirth Standard Cirrus	227	
D-0976	Schempp-Hirth Standard Cirrus	229	
D-0977	LET L-13 Blanik (Reservation)	174921	
D-0979	Glasflügel H401 Kestrel	66	
D-0980	Schempp-Hirth Discus CS	031CS	
D-0981	Schleicher K.8B	8903	
D-0982	Schleicher ASK-13	13398	
D-0983	Schempp-Hirth Ventus c	515	
D-0984	Schleicher ASW-15B	15223	
D-0985	Schleicher ASK-21	21576	
D-0986	Schleicher Ka.6E	4390	
D-0987	Schleicher ASW-15B	15227	
D-0988	Schleicher ASK-13	13400	
D-0989	Schleicher K.8B	8910	
D-0990	Schleicher ASK-21	21456	
D-0991	Rolladen-Schneider LS-6C-18	6348	
D-0992	Rolladen-Schneider LS-1C	139	
D-0993	Glaser-Dirks DG-300 Elan	3E-173	HB-1869
D-0994	Schleicher K.8B	8915	
D-0995	Schleicher ASW-15B	15239	
D-0996	Schleicher K.8B	8914	
D-0997	Schleicher ASW-15B	15240	
D-0998	Schleicher ASW-17	17011	
D-0999	Glasflügel H401 Kestrel	54	
D-1000	Grob G.103 Twin Astir	3136	
D-1002	Scheibe SF-27A	6046	
D-1003	Rolladen-Schneider LS-8A	6260	
D-1004	Schempp-Hirth Discus b	220	
D-1005	SZD-9bis Bocian 1E	P-717	DDR-3005
			DM-3005
D-1006	Schleicher ASK-13	13170	
D-1007	Glasflügel H401 Kestrel	24	HB-1001
D-1008	Schleicher Ka.6E	4008	
D-1009	Glasflügel H304B	323	
D-1010	Glasflügel H304B	324	
D-1011	Schleicher K.8B	8742	
D-1012	Scheibe SF-27A	6033	
D-1013	Grunau Baby III (Reservation 1.99)	76	
D-1014	Scheibe Bergfalke III	5569	
D-1015	Schempp-Hirth Discus b	189	
D-1016	Schempp-Hirth Ventus b/16.6	115	HB-1742
D-1017	Glaser-Dirks DG-300 Elan	3E-92	OY-XLU
D-1018	Grunau Baby IIB (Reservation)	05	
D-1020	Schleicher Ka.6CR Rhönsegler	6589	
D-1021	Glasflügel H304B	326	

Regn.	Type	C/n	Prev.Id.
D-1022	Rolladen-Schneider LS-1C	133	
D-1023	Glaser-Dirks DG-300 Club Elan	3E-391C59	
D-1024	Schleicher Ka.2 Rhönschwalbe	80	
D-1025	Schleicher ASH-25	25001	
D-1026	Schleicher K.8B	8385/A	
D-1027	Glaser-Dirks DG-600	6-27	
D-1028	Schempp-Hirth Discus b	198	
D-1029	SZD-55-1	551192047	I-NTRE
D-1030	Rolladen-Schneider LS-1C	123	
D-1031	Rolladen-Schneider LS-1D	135	
D-1032	Schempp-Hirth Nimbus 3D	1/3	D-KAYY
D-1033	Glasflügel H-101 Salto	18	
D-1034	Schleicher ASW-24	24141	
D-1035	Schempp-Hirth Ventus 2c	44/130	
D-1036	Scheibe Spatz A	V-1	
D-1037	Schleicher Ka.6CR Rhönsegler	6312	
D-1038	SZD-9bis Bocian 1E	P-459	DDR-3038
			DM-3038
D-1039	Rolladen-Schneider LS-6	6101	I-FAMF
			D-1094
D-1040	Schempp-Hirth Ventus c	348	
D-1041	HBV Diamant	007	OE-0821
			HB-890
D-1042	LET L-13 Blanik	173046	
D-1043	Schempp-Hirth Duo Discus	121	
D-1044	Schleicher ASW-19B	19004	D-3751
D-1045	Neukom Elfe S4	28	HB-1035
D-1046	Neukom Elfe S4A	75	HB-1040
D-1048	Schempp-Hirth Discus b	237	
D-1049	Rolladen-Schneider LS-6-18W	6365	
D-1050	Schleicher Ka.6CR Rhönsegler	948	
D-1051	Glasflügel H.201B Standard Libelle	293	HB-1054
D-1052	Grunau Baby III	E-2	
D-1053	Schleicher K.8B	1000	
D-1054	Rolladen-Schneider LS-6C-18	6331	
D-1055	Rolladen-Schneider LS-4A	4696	
D-1056	Glaser-Dirks DG-300 Club Elan	3E-404C63	
D-1057	Rolladen-Schneider LS-4	4584	
D-1058	Rolladen-Schneider LS-4	4585	
D-1059	Olympia-Meise	0240	OE-0052
D-1060	Vogt LO-100 Zwergreiher	AB-34	
D-1061	Rolladen-Schneider LS-4B	4952	
D-1062	Schmepp-Hirth Duo Discus	54	
D-1063	Glasflügel H401 Kestrel	68	
D-1064	Schleicher K.8B (Reservation 11.99)	8410	
D-1065	Rolladen-Schneider LS-1C	153	F-CDAZ
			F-CBAZ
D-1066	Schleicher ASK-13	13671AB	
D-1068	Schempp-Hirth Duo Discus	52	
D-1069	Schempp-Hirth Standard Cirrus	228	
D-1070	Glaser-Dirks DG-300 Elan	3E-5	
D-1071	Schempp-Hirth Nimbus 2	16	
D-1072	Neukom S4 Elfe	57	HB-1073
D-1073	Grunau Baby IIB	101	
D-1074	Schempp-Hirth Standard Cirrus	239	
D-1075	Schempp-Hirth Standard Cirrus	246	
D-1076	Rolladen-Schneider LS-4	4602	
D-1077	Schleicher Ka.6CR Rhönsegler	6340/SIE	
D-1078	Musger Mg.19 Steinadler	026	OE-0373
D-1079	SZD-9bis Bocian 1D	P-364	OE-0499
D-1080	Göppingen Gö. IV Gövier II	1	
D-1081	Slingsby T.31B Cadet III	704	PH-797
			WT909
D-1082	Neukom S4 Elfe	4/X	HB-1084
D-1083	Schleicher Ka.6CR Rhönsegler	6285	
D-1084	Rolladen-Schneider LS-4	4603	
D-1085	Glaser-Dirks DG-200/17C	2-141/CL-11	
D-1086	Glaser-Dirks DG-200/17	2-143/1738	
D-1087	Schempp-Hirth Duo Discus	58	
D-1088	Schleicher Ka.6CR Rhönsegler	6526	
D-1089	Rolladen-Schneider LS-4	4604	
D-1090	Glasflügel H301 Libelle	57	
D-1091	Schempp-Hirth Discus b	227	
D-1092	Schleicher ASH-25 (Museum)(Reservation 3.95)	unkn	
D-1093	Scheibe Bergfalke IV	5825	

Regn.	Type	C/n	Prev.Id.
D-1094	Schempp-Hirth Duo Discus	140	
D-1095	Glasflügel H201B Standard Libelle	348	
D-1096	Glasflügel H201B Standard Libelle	349	
D-1097	Glasflügel H201B Standard Libelle	350	
D-1098	Akaflieg Braunschweig SB-5E Sperber	5027/1	
D-1099	Schleicher K7 Rhönadler	367	
D-1100	Grunau Baby III (Reservation 7.99)	001	
D-1101	Schleicher ASW-19B	19055	
D-1102	Rolladen-Schneider LS-1C	142	
D-1103	Schleicher K.8B	8437/A	
D-1104	Pilatus B4-PC11AF	005	HB-1104
D-1105	Akaflieg Braunschweig SB-5B Sperber	5005	
D-1106	Schempp-Hirth Nimbus 3/24.5	17	
D-1107	SZD-50-3 Puchacz	B-2046	
D-1108	Rolladen-Schneider LS-4B	4953	
D-1109	Glasflügel H201B Standard Libelle	358	
D-1110	Schleicher ASW-20L	20150	
D-1111	Schleicher K.8B	8667/AB	
D-1112	SZD-55-1	551198104	
D-1113	SB-13 (Permit 8.99)	1	
D-1114	LET L-13 Blanik	175017	
D-1115	Pilatus B4-PC11AF	043	HB-1119
D-1116	Grunau Baby III	01	
D-1118	Rolladen-Schneider LS-3	3195	N9TE
D-1119	Schleicher Ka.6CR Rhönsegler	6606	
D-1120	Scheibe Spatz A (Reservation)	3	
D-1121	Schleicher K.8B	3	
D-1122	Rolladen-Schneider LS-4	4430	
D-1123	Rolladen-Schneider LS-4B	41029	
D-1124	Schleicher ASW-24	24001	
D-1125	Grob Standard Cirrus	263G	
D-1127	Schleicher K7 Rhönadler	7026	
D-1128	Akaflieg München Mü.28 (Permit 9.99)	V-4	
D-1129	Schempp-Hirth Nimbus 2	38	HB-1159
D-1130	Schleicher ASK-21	21606	
D-1131	Akaflieg Stuttgart FS.31 (Permit 4.99)	V-1	
D-1132	Scheibe Bergfalke II	162	
D-1133	Scheibe L-Spatz III	816	
D-1134	Schempp-Hirth Discus 2b (Reservation 12.99)	59	
D-1135	Glaser-Dirks DG-100G Elan	E213-G179	
D-1136	Scheibe Bergfalke II (Reservation -dd?)	163	
D-1137	Rolladen-Schneider LS-4B	4806	
D-1138	Rolladen-Schneider LS-4B	4807	
D-1139	Grob Standard Cirrus	259G	
D-1140	Schempp-Hirth Standard Cirrus	270	
D-1141	Grunau Baby IIB	9	
D-1142	Schleicher ASK-21	21274	
D-1144	Rolladen-Schneider LS-1D	144	
D-1145	Scheibe Bergfalke II	147/U	
D-1146	Dittmar Condor IV/3	28/53	OE-0869 D-1147
D-1148	Scheibe Bergfalke III	5566	
D-1149	Grob Standard Cirrus	253G	
D-1150	Rolladen-Schneider LS-4	4508	
D-1151	Mü.13E Bergfalke	310	
D-1152	Rolladen-Schneider LS-8A	8014	
D-1153	Rolladen-Schneider LS-4B	4875	
D-1154	Schleicher ASK-21	21194	N174KS
D-1156	Fauvel AV.36C	37	
D-1157	Schleicher K.8B	8577	
D-1158	SZD-36A Cobra 15	W-621	HB-1153
D-1159	Schempp-Hirth Duo Discus	168	
D-1160	Schempp-Hirth Duo Discus	166	
D-1161	Rolladen-Schneider LS-8A	8251	
D-1162	Rolladen-Schneider LS-1C	147	
D-1163	Rolladen-Schneider LS-8A	8204	
D-1164	Scheibe Bergfalke III	5545	
D-1165	Schleicher ASK-21	21510	
D-1166	Scheibe Specht (Reservation - dd?)	808	
D-1167	Mü.13E Bergfalke II	176	
D-1168	Glaser-Dirks DG-100G Elan	F-160/G-127	
D-1169	Glasflügel H401 Kestrel	72	
D-1170	Glasflügel H401 Kestrel	75	
D-1171	Glasflügel H205 Club Libelle	144	OE-5065
D-1172	Glaser-Dirks DG-800S	8-70S18	
D-1173	Glaser-Dirks DG-500T Elan Trainer	5E-39T13	
D-1174	Schempp-Hirth Discus CS	063CS	
D-1175	Schleicher K.8B	8930Br	
D-1176	Scheibe SF-27A	6027	
D-1177	Akaflieg Braunschweig SB.11	01	
D-1178	Glasflügel H201B Standard Libelle (Formerly Aeberli 201M Libelle)	133	HB-2056 HB-1007
D-1179	Rolladen-Schneider LS-6C	6213	
D-1180	Rolladen-Schneider LS-4B	41011	
D-1181	Schleicher Ka.6CR Rhönsegler	60/03	
D-1182	SZD-48-3 Jantar Standard 3	B-1364	
D-1183	Scheibe Specht	01	
D-1184	Glaser-Dirks DG-300 Elan	3E-222	
D-1185	Glaser-Dirks DG-300 Elan	3E-8	OH-789 D-1300
D-1186	Scheibe Bergfalke II	319	
D-1187	Marganski MDM-1 Fox	219	
D-1188	Kranich III	85	
D-1189	Glaser-Dirks DG-300 Elan	3E-225	
D-1190	Grob Standard Cirrus	255G	
D-1191	Grob Standard Cirrus	262G	
D-1192	Akaflieg München Mü.13E Bergfalke	1	
D-1193	Schleicher Ka.6CR Rhönsegler	6445	
D-1194	Valentin Mistral C	MC 069/86	
D-1195	Schleicher K7 Rhönadler	7258	
D-1196	Scheibe SF-27A	6091	
D-1197	Grunau Baby IIB	3	
D-1198	Schleicher K.8B	8487	
D-1199	Glaser-Dirks DG-300 Club Elan	3E-368/C49	OE-5523
D-1200	Scheibe SF-26A Standard	5007	
D-1201	Fauvel AV-36CR	86	
D-1202	Schempp-Hirth Nimbus 2	68	HB-1202
D-1203	SZD-30 Pirat	B-446	DDR-1803 DM-1803
D-1204	Scheibe Spatz A	1	
D-1205	Neukom S-4 Elfe (Reservation - dd?)	53	
D-1206	Schempp-Hirth Ventus 2b	17	
D-1207	Schempp-Hirth Nimbus 2	19	
D-1208	Schempp-Hirth Duo Discus	91	
D-1209	LET L-13 Blanik	175303	
D-1210	Rolladen-Schneider LS-1E	155	
D-1211	Schempp-Hirth Nimbus 4D	1/3	
D-1212	Schleicher Ka.6CR Rhönsegler	6483	
D-1213	Glasflügel H201B Standard Libelle	538	HB-1210
D-1214	Scheibe Bergfalke III	5555	
D-1215	Glaser-Dirks DG-300 Elan	3E-226	
D-1217	SZD-9bis Bocian 1E	P-494	DDR-3217 DM-3217
D-1218	Neukom Elfe S-4A	81	HB-3079
D-1219	Schleicher Ka.6CR Rhönsegler	6458	
D-1220	Schleicher K.8B	8906/AB	
D-1221	Schleicher ASW-12BV	12014	N12AJ
D-1222	Scheibe SF-27A	6004	
D-1223	Glasflügel H401 Kestrel	13	N19GW CF-YAW
D-1224	Scheibe L-Spatz	531	
D-1225	SB-12	1 AB	
D-1226	SZD-32A Foka 5	W-471	DDR-2226 DM-2226
D-1227	Neukom Elfe S-4A	51	HB-1228
D-1228	Schleicher K7 Rhönadler	303	
D-1229	Grob G.103A Twin II Acro	3757-K-52	
D-1230	Grob G.103A Twin II Acro	3767-K-53	
D-1231	Schleicher Ka.6CR Rhönsegler	6025	
D-1232	Rolladen-Schneider LS-4B	4967	
D-1233	Glaser-Dirks DG-500 Elan Trainer	5E-76T32	
D-1234	Scheibe Bergfalke II	326	
D-1235	Rolladen-Schneider LS-4	4622	
D-1236	Schleicher ASK-21	21514	
D-1237	Scheibe Bergfalke III	5562	
D-1238	Pilatus B4-PC11	074	
D-1239	Schleicher Ka.6CR Rhönsegler	6496	
D-1240	Schleicher K.8B	8611	D-KOSV D-1240
D-1241	Glaser-Dirks DG-100G Elan	E148-G115	

Regn.	Type	C/n	Prev.Id.
D-1242	Schempp-Hirth Ventus c	366	
D-1243	SZD-32A Foka 5	W-472	DDR-2243
			DM-2243
D-1244	Schleicher K7 Rhönadler	7217	
D-1245	Rolladen-Schneider LS-6-18W	6324	
D-1247	Rolladen-Schneider LS-4A	4624	
D-1248	Schleicher ASH-25	25131	
D-1249	Rolladen-Schneider LS-6	6128	
D-1250	Scheibe L-Spatz 55	545	
D-1251	Scheibe Bergfalke II	367	
D-1252	Schleicher ASK-21	21469	
D-1253	Rolladen-Schneider LS-4B	4968	
D-1254	Rolladen-Schneider LS-4B	4969	
D-1255	Scheibe Bergfalke II	333	
D-1256	Schleicher ASW-24	24099	
D-1257	Schleicher ASH-25	25102	
D-1258	Schleicher ASK-21	21471	
D-1259	Scheibe L-Spatz 55	548	EC-DGL
			LX-CBE
D-1260	Schleicher ASK-21	21472	
D-1261	Grunau Baby IIB	2	
D-1262	Glaser-Dirks DG-300 Elan	3E-103	
D-1263	Glaser-Dirks DG-100G Elan	E182-G148	
D-1264	Schleicher ASW-24	24105	
D-1265	Schleicher ASW-24	24108	
D-1266	Schleicher K.8B	8247/A	
D-1267	Schleicher K.8B	8510/A	
D-1268	Bölkow Phoebus A-1	759	
D-1269	Schleicher ASW-19B	19361	
D-1270	Schleicher ASW-20L	20562	
D-1271	Schempp-Hirth Nimbus 4	7	
D-1272	Schleicher ASW-15B	15246	OE-0956
D-1274	Scheibe Bergfalke II	4	
D-1275	Schleicher ASH-25	25108	
D-1278	Schleicher ASW-24	24104	
D-1279	Grob G.103A Twin II Acro	3768-K-54	
D-1280	Grob G.103A Twin II Acro	3769-K-55	
D-1281	Rolladen-Schneider LS-4B	4909	
D-1282	Schleicher Ka.6CR Rhönsegler	6522/Si	
D-1283	Schleicher Ka.6CR Rhönsegler	6012	D-8866
D-1284	Scheibe SF-27A	6041	
D-1285	Schleicher ASW-24	24110	
D-1286	Rolladen-Schneider LS-4A	4661	
D-1287	Akaflieg Braunschweig SB-5B Sperber	5044	
D-1288	Neukom Elfe S4A	74	HB-1280
D-1290	Rolladen-Schneider LS-4	4590	
D-1291	Rolladen-Schneider LS-4B	4753	
D-1292	Schleicher ASK-23B	23124	
D-1293	Rolladen-Schneider LS-6B	6131	
D-1294	Scheibe L-Spatz 55	552	
D-1295	Neukom Elfe S4A	64	HB-1297
D-1296	Scheibe SF-27A	6080	
D-1297	Rolladen-Schneider LS-4A	4755	
D-1298	Rolladen-Schneider LS-4B	4756	
D-1299	Rolladen-Schneider LS-4A	4757	
D-1301	LET L-23 Super Blanik	917913	
D-1302	Bölkow Phoebus C	825	
D-1303	Glasflügel Mosquito	01	
D-1304	Sche be Bergfalke III	5608	
D-1305	Akaflieg München Mü.13D	N 3	
D-1306	Start & Flug H101 Salto	55	
D-1307	Schleicher K.8B	8594	
D-1308	Bölkow Phoebus B-1	736	
D-1309	Rolladen-Schneider LS-7	7030	
D-1310	Grob G.103 Twin II	3763	
D-1311	LET L-13 Blanik (Reservation 11.99)	026835	DOSAAF
D-1312	Neukom Elfe S4A	77	HB-1312
D-1313	Schleicher ASK-13	13686AB	
D-1314	Neukom Elfe S4A	76	HB-1311
D-1315	Scheibe Bergfalke III	5581	
D-1316	LET L-13 Blanik	173332	D-1313
D-1317	Scheibe Bergfalke II	E-1	
D-1318	Schleicher K.8B	8112	
D-1319	SZD-30 Pirat	B-318	DDR-1719
			DM-1719
D-1320	Schleicher ASW-20L	20560	
D-1321	Rolladen-Schneider LS-4B	4954	
D-1322	Schleicher ASW-19B	19360	
D-1323	Rolladen-Schneider LS-7	7026	
D-1324	Scheibe Bergfalke III	5619	
D-1325	Scheibe L-Spatz III	805	
D-1327	Grob G.102 Club Astir IIIB	5596CB	
D-1328	Rolladen-Schneider LS-7	7024	
D-1329	Rolladen-Schneider LS-7	7023	
D-1330	Schleicher Ka.6CR Rhönsegler	6528	
D-1331	Scheibe Bergfalke III	5582	
D-1332	Grob G.103 Twin II	3749	
D-1333	Grunau Baby IIB	1	
D-1334	Grob G.103 Twin II	3761	
D-1335	Schleicher ASK-13	13687AB	
D-1336	Schleicher Ka.6CR Rhönsegler	6595	
D-1337	Schleicher K7 Rhönadler	7011	
D-1338	Schleicher ASK-21	21571	
D-1339	Grob G.103A Twin II Acro	3771-K-57	
D-1340	Rolladen-Schneider LS-6B	6135	
D-1341	Scheibe SF-27A	6063	
D-1342	Rolladen-Schneider LS-4A	4662	
D-1343	Scheibe Bergfalke III	5620	
D-1344	Grunau Baby IIB	001	
D-1345	SZD-30 Pirat	B-529	DDR-1845
			DM-1845
D-1346	Schleicher Ka.6CR Rhönsegler	6632	
D-1347	Schempp-Hirth Ventus c	613	
D-1348	Olympia-Meise	1	
D-1350	SZD-30 Pirat	B-569	DDR-1850
			DM-1850
D-1351	Bölkow Phoebus C	817	
D-1352	Schempp-Hirth Discus CS	032CS	D-1321
D-1353	Scheibe Bergfalke III	5615	
D-1354	Eiri PIK-20D	20528	HB-1350
D-1355	Schleicher ASK-13	13659AB	
D-1356	Rolladen-Schneider LS-3	3001	HB-1352
D-1357	Glaser-Dirks DG-300 Elan	3E-227	
D-1358	Rolladen-Schneider LS-4	4642	
D-1359	SZD-9bis Bocian 1E	P-546	DDR-3359
			DM-3359
D-1360	Rolladen-Schneider LS-4A	4737	
D-1361	Schleicher ASK-13	13691AB	
D-1362	Scheibe SF-27A	6077	
D-1363	Glaser-Dirks DG-300	3E-18	
D-1364	Scheibe L-Spatz 55	579	
D-1365	Rolladen-Schneider LS-4A	4663	
D-1366	Schleicher ASK-13	13019	
D-1367	Rolladen-Schneider LS-4	4591	
D-1368	Rolladen-Schneider LS-3	3057	HB-1368
D-1369	Rolladen-Schneider LS-4A	4735	
D-1370	Rolladen-Schneider LS-4A	4734	
D-1371	Rolladen-Schneider LS-4	4594	
D-1372	Glaser-Dirks DG-300 Elan	3E-174	
D-1373	Glaser-Dirks DG-300 Elan	3E-178	
D-1374	Rolladen-Schneider LS-8A	8046	
D-1376	SZD-30 Pirat	S-01.22	DDR-1876
			DM-1876
D-1377	Schempp-Hirth Duo Discus	153	
D-1378	Schleicher ASK-13	13041	
D-1379	Schleicher Ka.2B Rhönschwalbe (Reservation - dd?)	3	
D-1380	DFS Olympia Meise (Reservation 1.99)	3	
D-1381	Rolladen-Schneider LS-4A	4730	
D-1382	Rolladen-Schneider LS-4A	4729	
D-1384	Akaflieg Braunschweig SB.5B	5006	
D-1385	Schempp-Hirth Ventus b/16.6	255	
D-1386	Scheibe L-Spatz III	13	
D-1387	Rolladen-Schneider LS-4A	4647	
D-1388	Glaser-Dirks DG-100G	87-G8	HB-1338
D-1389	Rolladen-Schneider LS-4B	4758	
D-1390	Schleicher ASK-13	13653AB	
	(C/n same as BGA4683, ex RAFGGA509, thus probably sold & dd)		
D-1391	Schleicher ASK-21	21126	
D-1392	Rolladen-Schneider LS-4B	4759	
D-1393	Schleicher ASK-13	13683AB	

Regn.	Type	C/n	Prev.Id.
D-1394	Schempp-Hirth Standard Cirrus	67	OE-0867
D-1395	Schleicher K.8B	876	
D-1396	Scheibe SF-27A	6059	
D-1397	Rolladen-Schneider LS-3A	3239	HB-1397
D-1398	Schleicher ASH-26 (Museum) (Reservation -dd?)	unkn	
D-1399	Schempp-Hirth Ventus 2c	27	
D-1400	Schempp-Hirth Discus b	280	
D-1401	Grunau Baby IIB (Reservation 5.99)	001	
D-1402	Schleicher ASK-21	21162	
D-1403	Schleicher ASW-19B	19387	
D-1404	Schleicher ASW-19B	19388	
D-1405	Glasflügel H-301 Libelle	79	
D-1406	SZD-30 Pirat (Reservation 11.99)	S-03.49	DDR-1909 DM-1909
D-1407	Schleicher K.8B	8317/A	
D-1408	Glasflügel H201 Standard Libelle	18	
D-1409	Schleicher Ka.2B Rhönschwalbe	243	
D-1410	Scheibe Bergfalke III	5547	
D-1411	SZD-30 Pirat	B-474	DDR-1811 DM-1811
D-1413	Scheibe L-Spatz	002	
D-1414	Rolladen-Schneider LS-1C	105	
D-1415	Scheibe L-Spatz 55	524	
D-1416	Glaser-Dirks DG-200	2-30	HB-1415
D-1417	Schempp-Hirth Ventus b/16.6	183	
D-1418	Schempp-Hirth Discus CS	067CS	
D-1419	Schempp-Hirth Ventus b/16.6	189	
D-1420	DFS Olympia-Meise	unkn	
D-1421	Scheibe L-Spatz 55	3	
D-1422	SZD-36A Cobra 15 (Reservation - dd?)	W-673	HB-1223
D-1423	Scheibe Specht	848	
D-1424	Glasflügel H.201B Standard Libelle	10	OE-0906
D-1425	Rolladen-Schneider LS-4A	4651	
D-1426	Scheibe SF-27A	6007	
D-1427	Scheibe Bergfalke II/55	229	
D-1428	Schleicher K.8B	8550	
D-1429	Rolladen-Schneider LS-8A	8183	
D-1430	Schleicher ASW-20CL	20810	ZK-GRZ D-3430
D-1431	Schleicher ASK-21	21574	
D-1432	Schleicher ASW-20L	20240	
D-1433	Schleicher ASW-19B	19213	
D-1434	Bölkow Phoebus A-1	710	
D-1435	Rolladen-Schneider LS-4B	4931	
D-1436	Grob G.103 Twin Astir	3159	HB-1436
D-1437	Rolladen-Schneider LS-8-18 (Permit 12.99)	8205	
D-1438	Scheibe Bergfalke III	4/5609	
D-1439	Grob G.102 Astir CS 77	1748	HB-1435
D-1440	LET L-23 Super Blanik	917901	
D-1441	Scheibe Bergfalke III (Reservation -dd?)	5531	
D-1442	Rolladen-Schneider LS-4A	4666	
D-1443	Schempp-Hirth Ventus 2b	19	
D-1444	Glaser-Dirks DG-300 Elan	3E-172	OY-XOE
D-1445	Rolladen-Schneider LS-4A	4667	
D-1446	Schempp-Hirth Mini-Nimbus B	43	HB-1404
D-1447	Scheibe L-Spatz 55	931	
D-1448	Schleicher ASW-27	27083	
D-1449	Scheibe L-Spatz 55	01	
D-1450	Schleicher Ka.6E	4184	
D-1451	Scheibe L-Spatz 55	618	
D-1452	Scheibe Bergfalke II	334	
D-1453-CM	Schleicher ASH-25	25015	
D-1454	Scheibe L-Spatz 55	57	
D-1456	Schleicher ASK-21	21341	
D-1457	Schleicher Ka.6 Rhönsegler	306	
D-1458	Rolladen-Schneider LS-6C-18	6272	
D-1459	Grunau Baby III	EB-02	
D-1460	SZD-30 Pirat	B-582	DDR-1860 DM-1860
D-1461	Scheibe L-Spatz 55	64	
D-1462	Rolladen-Schneider LS-6-18W	6279	
D-1463	Schleicher ASK-21	21342	
D-1464	Schleicher K7 Rhönadler	366	
D-1465	Scheibe Bergfalke III	5607	
D-1466	Scheibe Zugvogel IIIA	1031	
D-1467	Rolladen-Schneider LS-3A	3228	HB-1461
D-1468	Scheibe L-Spatz 55	536	
D-1469	Glaser-Dirks DG-100G Elan	E-2	HB-1465
D-1470	Schleicher K.8	351/57	
D-1471	Scheibe Bergfalke III	5614	
D-1472	Rolladen-Schneider LS-4B	4929	
D-1473	Schleicher ASK-21	21165	
D-1474	Schleicher ASK-21	21166	
D-1475	Schleicher ASK-21	21167	
D-1477	SZD-30 Pirat	B-406	DDR-1777 DM-1777
D-1478	Schleicher Ka.6CR Rhönsegler	6586/Si	
D-1479	Rolladen-Schneider LS-4B	4930	
D-1480	SZD-51-1 Junior	B-2137	
D-1481	Schleicher ASK-21	21343	
D-1482	Schleicher K.8B	8631	
D-1483	Schleicher ASK-21	21127	
D-1484	Kaiser KA-1	1	
D-1485	Glaser-Dirks DG-100G Elan	E181-G147	
D-1486	Glaser-Dirks DG-500 Elan Orion	5E-152X9	
D-1487	Schleicher ASK-21	21128	
D-1488	Rolladen-Schneider LS-4B	4970	
D-1489	Schleicher ASK-21	21345	
D-1491	Glaser-Dirks DG-500 Elan Orion	5E-153X10	
D-1492	Rolladen-Schneider LS-7	7057	
D-1493	Schleicher ASK-23B	23097	
D-1494	Rolladen-Schneider LS-4A	4808	
D-1495	Rolladen-Schneider LS-4B	4809	
D-1496	Rolladen-Schneider LS-4	4547	
D-1497	Rolladen-Schneider LS-4B	4971	
D-1498	SZD-30 Pirat	B-441	DDR-1798 DM-1798
D-1499	Scheibe L-Spatz 55	003	
D-1500	Scheibe Bergfalke II/55	255	
D-1501	Glaser-Dirks DG-100G Elan	E149-G116	
D-1502	Neukom Elfe S4A	60	HB-1205
D-1504	Schempp-Hirth Discus b	524	
D-1505	SZD-30 Pirat	S-03.45	DDR-1905 DM-1905
D-1506	LET L-23 Super Blanik	917909	
D-1507	Rolladen-Schneider LS-8A	8008	
D-1508	Rolladen-Schneider LS-8A	8009	
D-1509	Rolladen-Schneider LS-4B	4932	
D-1510	Rolladen-Schneider LS-8A	8107	
D-1511	SG-38 Schulgleiter	0011	DDR-551
D-1512	Scheibe Bergfalke II	01/53	
D-1513	Schleicher ASK-21	21288	LN-GIA
D-1514	Scheibe L-Spatz 55	750	
D-1515	Bölkow Phoebus C	839	
D-1516	Schleicher ASK-21	21358	
D-1517	Scheibe L-Spatz 55	2/A	
D-1518	Rolladen-Schneider LS-4A	4668	
D-1519	Scheibe Bergfalke III	5584	
D-1520	Scheibe Spatz B (Reservation - dd?)	3	
D-1521	Schleicher ASK-21	21221	
D-1522	Olympia-Meise	E-002	
D-1523	SZD-55-1	551195065	
D-1524	Schempp-Hirth Duo Discus	10	
D-1525	Scheibe L-Spatz 55	556	
D-1526AG	Schempp-Hirth Discus b	493	
D-1528	Scheibe L-Spatz III	829	
D-1529	Schleicher ASH-25	25027	
D-1530	Grunau Baby IIb	536	
D-1532	SZD-55-1	551195074	
D-1533	Schleicher ASK-21	21355	
D-1534	Schempp-Hirth Discus 2A (Reservation - dd?)	25	
D-1535	Schleicher K.8B	584	
D-1536	Schleicher K7 Rhönadler	537	
D-1537	Bölkow Phoebus A-1	753	
D-1538	SG-38 Schulgleiter	013 AB	
D-1539	SZD-30 Pirat	B-519	DDR-1839 DM-1839
D-1540	Schleicher ASK-21	21359	
D-1541	Schleicher ASK-23B	23101	
D-1542	Schleicher K.8B	582	

Regn.	Type	C/n	Prev.Id.
D-1543	Scheibe L-Spatz 55	87	
D-1544	Schleicher ASK-21	21613	
D-1545	Schleicher ASK-21	21360	
D-1546	Schempp-Hirth Discus CS	068CS	
D-1547	Schleicher ASK-23B	23099	
D-1548	SZD-55-1	551195075	
D-1549	Scheibe SF-27A	6085	
D-1550	Schleicher ASK-23B	23102	
D-1551	Schleicher Ka.6CR Rhönsegler	571	
D-1552	Glaser-Dirks DG-100G Elan	E110-G80	HB-1652
D-1553	SZD-30 Pirat	B-357	DDR-1753 DM-1753
D-1554	Grob G.103A Twin II Acro	3803-K-70	
D-1555	Grob G.103A Twin II Acro	3808-K-71	
D-1556	Grob G.102 Standard Astir III	5604S	
D-1557	Bölkow Phoebus A-1	754	
D-1559	Schleicher ASW-27	27101	
D-1560	Rolladen-Schneider LS-4A	4669	
D-1561	Scheibe Zugvogel IIIA	1045	
D-1562	Scheibe Zugvogel IIIB	1072	
D-1563	Schleicher K7 Rhönadler	564	
D-1564	Scheibe Zugvogel IVA	1509	
D-1565	Schempp-Hirth Discus CS	082CS	
D-1566	Glaser-Dirks DG-300 Elan	3E-76	
D-1567	Schempp-Hirth Discus CS	079CS	
D-1568	Schleicher Ka.6BR Rhönsegler	482	
D-1569	Schleicher K7 Rhönadler	479	
D-1570	Glasflügel Hornet C	99	
D-1571	Scheibe L-Spatz 55	3/809	
D-1572	Glaser-Dirks DG-300 Club Elan	3E-307C20	
D-1573	Schleicher K.8B	8391/A	
D-1574	Schleicher ASW-20L	20570	
D-1575	Schleicher ASW-20	20571	
D-1576	Schleicher ASK-21	21107	
D-1577	Schleicher ASW-19B	19364	
D-1578	Schleicher ASW-24	24062	
D-1579	Schleicher ASK-21	21422	
D-1580	Schleicher ASW-24	24048	
D-1581	Scheibe L-Spatz 55	684	
D-1582	Schleicher ASW-24	24049	
D-1583	Schleicher ASK-21	21423	
D-1584	Schleicher ASW-24	24050	
D-1585	Schleicher ASK-21	21615	(JA2538)
D-1586	Schleicher ASW-24	24051	
D-1587	Schempp-Hirth Discus CS	172CS	
D-1588	SZD-30 Pirat	B-431	DDR-1788 DM-1788
D-1589	Schleicher Ka.6CR Rhönsegler	622	
D-1590	Schempp-Hirth Discus CS	168CS	
D-1591	Scheibe Zugvogel IVA	1511	
D-1592	Rolladen-Schneider LS-4B	4773	
D-1593	Rolladen-Schneider LS-4B	4774	
D-1596	Schempp-Hirth Duo Discus	61	
D-1597	Rolladen-Schneider LS-4B	4940	
D-1598	Rolladen-Schneider LS-4B	4777	
D-1599	Rolladen-Schneider LS-4B	4778	
D-1600	Scheibe Bergfalke III	5550	
D-1601	Scheibe Bergfalke III	5527	
D-1602	Glaser-Dirks DG-300 Club Elan	3E-374C53	
D-1603	Scheibe Bergfalke III	5606	
D-1604	Rolladen-Schneider LS-4	4069	HB-1603
D-1605	Scheibe L-Spatz 55	004	
D-1606	Schleicher ASW-24	24052	
D-1607	Schleicher ASK-21	21425	
D-1608	Rolladen-Schneider LS-4B	41012	
D-1609	Schleicher ASW-24	24065	
D-1610	Schleicher ASK-21	21435	
D-1611	Schleicher ASH-25	25078	
D-1612	Schleicher K.8B	AB 4/95	
D-1613	Schleicher Ka.6CR Rhönsegler	6635/Si	
D-1614	Schleicher K.8B	745	
D-1616	Glasflügel H303 Mosquito B	187	OE-5243
D-1618	Schempp-Hirth Discus 2b (Reservation 11.99)	70	
D-1619	Schleicher ASH-26	26149	
D-1620	SZD-50-3 Puchacz	B-1337	DDR-3620

Regn.	Type	C/n	Prev.Id.
D-1621	Scheibe L-Spatz 55	850 K	
D-1622	Scheibe Bergfalke II/55	309	
D-1623	SZD-48-3 Jantar Standard 3	B-1966	
D-1624	SZD-48-3 Jantar Standard 3	B-1970	
D-1625	Scheibe Spatz B	696	
D-1627	Grunau Baby IIb	621	
D-1628	Schleicher K7 Rhönadler	769	
D-1629	Scheibe L-Spatz 55	712	
D-1630	Schleicher Ka.6CR Rhönsegler	6444	
D-1631	LET L-13 Blanik	173353	
D-1632	FS-32 (Permit 6.99)	V-1	
D-1633	Glaser-Dirks DG-300 Elan (Permit 7.99)	3E-61/17	
D-1634	Kurz Me 163B replica (Reservation 10.99)	1	D-ESJK
D-1635	Schleicher Ka.6CR Rhönsegler	6159	OE-0635
D-1636	Rolladen-Schneider LS-8	8002	
D-1637	Schleicher ASW-20	20602	
D-1638	Schleicher ASK-21	21136	
D-1639-I HZ	Schleicher ASW-20L	20601	
D-1640	Scheibe L-Spatz 55	855 K	
D-1641	Schleicher K.8B	8514	
D-1642	SZD-30 Pirat	B-563	DDR-1842 DM-1842
D-1643	LET L-23 Super Blanik	948120	
D-1644	Rolladen-Schneider LS-4B	4781	
D-1645	Schempp-Hirth Ventus 2a	20	
D-1646	Rolladen-Schneider LS-8A	8010	
D-1647	Schleicher ASK-21	21110	
D-1648	Schleicher ASW-20	20575	
D-1649	Schleicher ASW-20L	20577	
D-1650	Schleicher ASK-21	21112	
D-1651	Scheibe Bergfalke III	5601	
D-1652	Schleicher ASK-21	21134	
D-1654	SZD-50-3 Puchacz	B-1538	DDR-3654
D-1655	Schleicher Ka.3 (Reservation)	01	
D-1657	Schleicher ASW-20C	20822	
D-1658	Grunau Baby IIB	01A	
D-1659	SZD-50-3 Puchacz	B-1543	DDR-3659
D-1660	Rolladen-Schneider LS-4	4122	
D-1661	Schempp-Hirth Discus b	135	
D-1662	Schleicher Ka.6CR Rhönsegler	896	
D-1663	Schleicher K.8B	816	
D-1664	SZD-30 Pirat	B-588	DDR-1864 DM-1864
D-1665	Schleicher Ka.6CR Rhönsegler	852	
D-1666	SZD-30 Pirat	W-411	D-6710 DDR-1710 DM-1710
D-1667	Glasflügel H101 Salto	67	
D-1668	Scheibe L-Spatz 55	657	OE-0668
D-1669	SZD-32A Foka 5	W-429	OE-0892 SP-2533
D-1671	SZD-30 Pirat	B-400	DDR-1771 DM-1771
D-1672	SZD-30 Pirat	B-401	DDR-1772 DM-1772
D-1673	Scheibe SF-26A Standard	5048	
D-1674	Rolladen-Schneider LS-7	7036	
D-1675	Rolladen-Schneider LS-7	7037	
D-1677	Rolladen-Schneider LS-4	4418	
D-1678	Rolladen-Schneider LS-7	7038	
D-1679	Schleicher K.8B	909	
D-1680	Schleicher K7 Rhönadler	982	
D-1681	Rolladen-Schneider LS-8A	8085	
D-1683	Rolladen-Schneider LS-8A	8059	
D-1684	Rolladen-Schneider LS-7	7039	
D-1685	Grob G.102 Club Astir IIIB	5520CB	
D-1686	Scheibe L-Spatz 55	851 K	
D-1687	Scheibe L-Spatz 55	820 K	
D-1688	Rolladen-Schneider LS-8	8011	
D-1689	Rolladen-Schneider LS-4B	4928	
D-1690	SZD-30 Pirat	B-433	DDR-1790 DM-1790
D-1693	SZD-30 Pirat	B-436	DDR-1793 DM-1793
D-1694	Scheibe SF-27A	6018	

Regn.	Type	C/n	Prev.Id.
D-1695	SZD-30 Pirat	B-438	DDR-1795
			DM-1795
D-1696	Grob Standard Cirrus	G54M	
D 1697	Schleicher ASK-21	21580	
D-1698	Rolladen-Schneider LS-8A *(Permit 3.99)*	8206	
D-1699	SZD-41A Jantar Standard	B-802	OE-5143
D-1700	Glaser-Dirks DG-100G Elan	E65-G40	
D-1701	Glaser-Dirks DG-100G Elan	E67-G42	
D-1702-AF	SZD-30 Pirat *(Permit 5.99)*	W-403	DDR-1706
			DM-1706
D-1703	Glaser-Dirks DG-300 Elan	3E-23	
D-1704	Scheibe SF-26A Standard	5009	
D-1706	Bölkow Phoebus C	823	
D-1707	Glaser-Dirks DG-300 Elan	3E-325	
D-1708	Scheibe L-Spatz 55	748	(D-8397)
			D-1708
D-1709	SZD-30 Pirat	W-405	DDR-1708
			DM-1708
D-1710	SZD-30 Pirat	W-416	DDR-1715
			DM-1715
D-1711	Scheibe SF-34	5118	
D-1712	SZD-30 Pirat	W-412	DDR-1711
			DM-1711
D-1713	Rolladen-Schneider LS-7	7051	
D-1714	Rolladen-Schneider LS-7	7052	
D-1715	Schleicher K.8B	130	
D-1716	Scheibe L-Spatz 55	689	
D-1717	Akaflieg München Mü.17 *(Reservation)*	03	
D-1718	SZD-30 Pirat	W-413	DDR-1712
			DM-1712
D-1720	Schleicher Ka.6 Rhönsegler	267	
D-1721	SZD-30 Pirat	B-302	DDR-1720
			DM-1720
D-1722-FA	Schleicher ASW-20L	20481	HB-1728
D-1723-6C	SZD-30 Pirat	B-305	DDR-1722
			DM-1722
D-1724	Schleicher ASH-25	25173	
D-1725	Schempp-Hirth Discus b	343	
D-1726	SZD-30 Pirat	B-307	DDR-1726
			DM-1726
D-1727	Glasflügel H304 *(Built from spares)*	9265	
D-1728	SZD-30 Pirat	B-397	DDR-1768
			DM-1768
D-1729-IYY	Schleicher ASW-20C	20713	
D-1730	Schleicher ASW-20C	20714	
D-1731	Schleicher ASW-20CL	20728	
D-1732	Schleicher K.8B	13/117	
D-1733	SZD-30 Pirat *(Reservation - old?)*	W-414	DDR-1713
			DM-1713
D-1734	SZD-30 Pirat *(Reservation)*	B-298	DDR-1724
			DM-1724
			SP-2531
D-1735	Scheibe Bergfalke II/55	314	
D-1736	SZD-30 Pirat *(Reservation 2.99)*	W-417	DDR-1716
			DM-1716
D-1737	Scheibe Bergfalke III	5554	
D-1738	Scheibe L-Spatz 55	766	
D-1739	SZD-30 Pirat	B-432	DDR-1789
			DM-1789
D-1740	Akaflieg München Mü.17	02	
D-1741	Schleicher K7 Rhönadler	1030	
D-1742	Schleicher K7 Rhönadler	1031	
D-1743	SZD-30 Pirat	B-331	DDR-1742
			DM-1742
D-1744	Schempp-Hirth Duo Discus	74	
D-1745	Schleicher K7 Rhönadler	1032	
D-1747	Rolladen-Schneider LS-4	4445	
D-1748	Schleicher Ka.6CR Rhönsegler	1069	
D-1749	Schleicher K.8B	136	
D-1750	Schempp-Hirth Ventus c (M)	33/467	
D-1751	Schempp-Hirth Discus b	312	
D-1752	Schempp-Hirth Discus b	322	
D-1753	Fauvel AV-36C1	V-1/250	
D-1754	Schempp-Hirth Janus C	263	
D-1755	Rolladen-Schneider LS-8A	8015	
D-1756	Schleicher Ka.6BR Rhönsegler	362	
D-1757	Schleicher K.8B	8034	D-KIBO
			D-1757
D-1758	Schleicher Ka.6CR Rhönsegler	6003	
D-1759	Schempp-Hirth Discus b	330	
D-1760	Schempp-Hirth Discus b	338	
D-1762	Schempp-Hirth Duo Discus	147	
D-1763	Schleicher ASH-25	25021	
D-1764	SZD-30 Pirat	B-395	DDR-1766
			DM-1766
D-1765	Schleicher K.8B	8040	
D-1766	Scheibe Bergfalke II	181	
D-1767	SZD-30 Pirat *(Permit 5.99)*	B-356	DDR-1761
			DM-1761
D-1768	SZD-30 Pirat	B-367	DDR-1764
			DM-1764
D-1769	Schleicher Ka.6CR Rhönsegler	6035	
D-1770	Schempp-Hirth Ventus 2b	58	
D-1771	Grunau Baby III	01	
D-1772	Schempp-Hirth Duo Discus	122	
D-1773	SZD-48-3 Jantar Standard 3	B-1447	HB-1772
D-1774	Schleicher K.8B	8038	
D-1775	Glaser-Dirks DG-500 Elan Orion	5E-149X7	
D-1776	SZD-30 Pirat	B-402	DDR-1773
			DM-1773
D-1777	Akaflieg Braunschweig SB-5B Sperber	5047	
D-1778	SZD-30 Pirat	B-407	DDR-1778
			DM-1778
D-1779	Schleicher K.8B	8572	
D-1780	Glaser-Dirks DG-800S	8-41S10	
D-1781	Schleicher K7 Rhönadler	1095	
D-1782	SZD-30 Pirat	B-410	DDR-1781
			DM-1781
D-1783	Schleicher ASK-13	13220AB	
D-1784	Scheibe L-Spatz 55	653	
D-1785	Schempp-Hirth Duo Discus	92	
D-1786	Schempp-Hirth Duo Discus	158	
D-1787	Rolladen-Schneider LS-8A	8156	
D-1788	Schempp-Hirth Ventus b/16.6 *(Reservation)*	196	HB-1743
D-1789	Schempp-Hirth Ventus 2b	25	
D-1790	Scheibe SF-27A	6054	
D-1791	Rolladen-Schneider LS-4A	4399	
D-1792	Rolladen-Schneider LS-4	4400	
D-1793	Rolladen-Schneider LS-4	4401	
D-1794	Rolladen-Schneider LS-1C	146	
D-1795	Akaflieg Braunschweig SB-5B Sperber	AB5054	
D-1796	LET L-13 Blanik	175230	
D-1797	Glasflügel H201B Standard Libelle	377	
D-1798	Rolladen-Schneider LS-1C	130	
D-1799	SZD-30 Pirat	B-435	DDR-1792
			DM-1792
D-1800	Schleicher ASK-13	13674AB	
D-1801	SZD-30 Pirat	S-01.27	DDR-1881
			DM-1881
D-1802	Schleicher ASK-21	21130	
D-1803	Schleicher ASW-20	20605	
D-1804	Schleicher ASK-21	21145	
D-1805	Rolladen-Schneider LS-1C	145	
D-1806	Scheibe Bergfalke II/55	364	
D-1807	Schleicher ASH-26	26019	
D-1808	Schleicher Ka.6E	4204	OH-652
D-1809	SZD-30 Pirat	B-461	DDR-1805
			DM-1805
D-1810	Bölkow Phoebus A1	853	
D-1811	Schleicher ASH-25	25058	
D-1812	Glaser Dirks DG-300 Elan	3E-115	HB-1817
D-1813	Glaser-Dirks DG-100G Elan	E118-G87	
D-1814	Schleicher K7 Rhönadler	7207	
D-1815	SZD-55-1	551194068	
D-1816	Schempp-Hirth Discus b	339	
D-1817	Schempp-Hirth Discus b (T)	37/348	
D-1818	Schleicher ASK-18	18017	F-CERC
D-1819	SZD-30 Pirat	B-479	DDR-1815
			DM-1815

Regn.	Type	C/n	Prev.Id.
D-1820	SZD-30 Pirat	B-471	DDR-1810
			DM-1810
D-1821	SZD-30 Pirat	S-01.09	DDR-1871
			DM-1871
D-1822	Schleicher ASK-21	21169	
D-1823	Schleicher ASK-21	21170	
D-1824	Schleicher ASW-19B	19391	
D-1825	Schempp-Hirth Standard Cirrus	217	SE-TKU
D-1826	Schleicher K.8B	8165/03	
D-1827	SZD-30 Pirat	B-517	DDR-1837
			DM-1837
D-1828	Schempp-Hirth Janus C	240	
D-1829	Schleicher Ka.6CR Rhönsegler	6228	
D-1830	Grob G.103C Twin III Acro	34128	
D-1831	Schempp-Hirth Duo Discus	55	
D-1832	Rolladen-Schneider LS-8A	8019	
D-1833	Glaser-Dirks DG-600	6-18	PH-833
D-1834	SZD-30 Pirat	B-516	DDR-1836
			DM-1836
D-1835	Schleicher Ka.6CR Rhönsegler	6242	
D-1836	Schleicher Ka.6CR Rhönsegler	6187	
D-1837	Schleicher K.8B	189/60	
D-1838	Schleicher K.8B (Reservation - old?)	8223	
D-1839	Scheibe Spatz B	01/517	
D-1840	Schleicher K.8B	8334/A	
D-1841	SZD-30 Pirat	B-561	DDR-1841
			DM-1841
D-1842	Rolladen-Schneider LS-4A	4744	
D-1843	Scheibe L-Spatz	773	
D-1844	Rolladen-Schneider LS-4A	4743	
D-1845	Rolladen-Schneider LS-4A	4742	
D-1846	Rolladen-Schneider LS-4A	4741	
D-1847	SZD-30 Pirat	B-531	DDR-1847
			DM-1847
D-1848-2F	Akaflieg München Mü.22B	V-3	
D-1849	SZD-30 Pirat	B-530	DDR-1846
			DM-1846
D-1850	Schleicher ASK-13	13684AB	
D-1851	Scheibe SF-27A	6001	
D-1852	Grob G.103C Twin III Acro	34111	
D-1853	Grob G.103C Twin III Acro	34124	
D-1854	Schleicher Ka.6CR Rhönsegler	6225	
D-1855	Schleicher Ka.6CR Rhönsegler	6338Si	
D-1857	Scheibe L-Spatz III	801	
D-1858	Schleicher Ka.6CR Rhönsegler	6316	
D-1859	Schleicher Ka.6CR Rhönsegler	6355	
D-1860	Scheibe SF-27A	6005	
D-1861	SZD-30 Pirat (Reservation 3.99)	B-584	DDR-1862
			DM-1862
D-1862	Grob G.103A Twin II Acro	3809-K-72	
D-1863	Grob G.103A Twin II Acro	3810-K-73	
D-1865	Scheibe L-Spatz 55	765	
D-1866	Scheibe Bergfalke II/55	387	
D-1867	SZD-30 Pirat	B-577	DDR-1857
			DM-1857
D-1868	Rolladen-Schneider LS-6-18W	6366	
D-1869	SZD-30 Pirat	S-01.06	DDR-1868
			DM-1868
D-1870	Grob G.103C Twin III Acro	34112	
D-1871	Rolladen-Schneider LS-8A	8184	
D-1872	Glaser-Dirks DG-300 Elan	3E-24	
D-1873	SZD-30 Pirat	S-01.08	DDR-1870
			DM-1870
D-1874	SZD-30 Pirat	S-01.23	DDR-1877
			DM-1877
D-1875	Schleicher K7 Rhönadler	7109	
D-1876	Schempp-Hirth Ventus 2a	82	
D-1877	Grob G.103C Twin III Acro	34126	
D-1879	Schempp-Hirth Discus CS	008CS	
D-1880	Schempp-Hirth Janus C	262	
D-1881	Schleicher K.8B	995	
D-1882	Schleicher K.8B	8452	
D-1885	Schleicher K.8B	8456	
D-1886	Scheibe L-Spatz	201	
D-1887	Schleicher K7 Rhönadler	7028	

Regn.	Type	C/n	Prev.Id.
D-1888	Glasflügel H-101 Salto	66	
D-1889	Scheibe SF-26A Standard	5001/V-2	
D-1890	Schleicher K.8B	8133	
D-1891	Schleicher Ka.2B Rhönschwalbe	2007	
D-1892	SZD-30 Pirat	S-03.07	DDR-1892
			DM-1892
D-1893	Scheibe SF-26A Standard	5014	
D-1894	SZD-30 Pirat	B-513	DDR-1834
			DM-1834
D-1895	SZD-30 Pirat	S-03.08	DDR-1893
			DM-1893
D-1896	Rolladen-Schneider LS-8A	8108	
D-1897	SZD-30 Pirat	S-03.21	DDR-1896
			DM-1896
D-1898	SZD-30 Pirat	S-03.22	DDR-1897
			DM-1897
D-1899	SZD-30 Pirat	B-544	DDR-1849
			DM-1849
D-1900	Schleicher ASK-13	13678AB	
D-1901	Schleicher Ka.6CR Rhönsegler	6173	
D-1902	Schleicher K.8B	8031	
D-1903	Scheibe Zugvogel IIIB	1078	
D-1904	SZD-30 Pirat	S-03.25	DDR-1900
			DM-1900
D-1905	Schleicher K7 Rhönadler	7131	
D-1906-3F	Schleicher K.8B	8273/A	
D-1908-K3	Schempp-Hirth Discus CS	128CS	
D-1909	SZD-30 Pirat	S-03.46	DDR-1906
			DM-1906
D-1910	Rolladen-Schneider LS-6	6123	HB-1911
D-1912	Schleicher ASK-13	13641AB	
D-1913	Glaser-Dirks DG-600	6-21	
D-1914	Glaser-Dirks DG-600	6-22	
D-1915	SZD-30 Pirat	S-04.21	DDR-1914
			DM-1914
D-1916	SZD-30C Pirat	P-809	DDR-1916
			DM-1916
D-1917	Schleicher Ka.6E	4189	
D-1918	Schleicher Ka.6BR Rhönsegler	439	ZS-GPK
			D-1918
			HB-918
D-1920	Schleicher Ka.6CR Rhönsegler	6069	
D-1921	Schempp-Hirth Ventus 2a (Reservation 11.99)	99	
D-1923	Rolladen-Schneider LS-8-18 (Permit 3.99)	8157	
D-1924	Schleicher ASK-21	21325	
D-1925	Schleicher K7 Rhönadler	296	
D-1926	SZD-30 Pirat (Reservation)	S-04.20	DDR-1913
			DM-1913
D-1927	Grunau Baby III	1	
D-1928	Schleicher ASK-21	21464	
D-1929	Scheibe Bergfalke II/55	385	
D-1930	Glaser-Dirks DG-300 Club Elan	3E-313C22	
D-1931	Schempp-Hirth Discus CS	040CS	
D-1932	Schempp-Hirth Duo Discus	162	
D-1933	Rolladen-Schneider LS-6-18W	6369	
D-1934	SZD-30 Pirat	S-03.44	DDR-1904
			DM-1904
D-1935	Schleicher Ka.6CR Rhönsegler	6278	
D-1936	DFS Olympia Meise	1 Burg Feuerstein	
D-1937	Schleicher Ka.6E	4193	
D-1938	Schleicher Ka.6CR Rhönsegler	6307	
D-1939	Grunau Baby IIB	0123	
D-1940	Schleicher ASK-21	21698	
D-1941	Schleicher Ka.6CR Rhönsegler	6224/A	
D-1942	Schempp-Hirth Discus b	222	HB-1968
D-1943-20	Schleicher Ka.6E	4170	
D-1944	Scheibe Specht	862	
D-1945	Schleicher K7 Rhönadler	7211	
D-1946	SZD-30 Pirat	S-03.43	DDR-1903
			DM-1903
D-1947	Schleicher ASK-21	21363	
D-1948	DFS Olympia Meise (Reservation)	09	
D-1949	Schleicher Ka.6CR Rhönsegler	6219	
D-1950	Glasflügel H201B Standard Libelle	429	F-CEBO
D-1951	Akaflieg Braunschweig SB-5E Sperber	5037	

Regn.	Type	C/n	Prev.Id.
D-1952	Schleicher K7 Rhönadler *(Reservation)*	7110	
D-1954	Schleicher Ka.6CR Rhönsegler	6277	
D-1955	Pilatus B4-PC11	019	
D-1956	Glaser-Dirks DG100G Elan	E56-G32	
D-1957	Vogt LO-100 Zwergreiher	1	
D-1959	Schleicher Ka.2B Rhönschwalbe	245	
D-1960	Schleicher K.10A	10004	
D-1961	Rolladen-Schneider LS-8A	8185	
D-1962	Schleicher K.8B	8067	
D-1963	Schleicher K.8B	8080/5	
D-1964	Scheibe L-Spatz 55	776	
D-1965	Schleicher K7 Rhönadler	7051	
D-1966	Glaser-Dirks DG-300 Club Elan	3E-356/C43	
D-1967	Glaser-Dirks DG-300 Club Elan	3E-357/C44	
D-1969	Glaser-Dirks DG-300 Elan	3E-359	
D-1970	Scheibe SF-27A	6064	
D-1971	Schempp-Hirth Discus CS	041CS	
D-1972	Grunau Baby III	1	
D-1973	Schleicher ASW-24	24134	
D 1974	Schleicher K.8B	8388/A	
D-1975	SZD-51-1 Junior	B-2133	
D-1976	SZD-51-1 Junior	unkn	
D-1977	Grunau Baby III	04	
D-1978	SZD-30 Pirat	S-01.24	DDR-1878 DM-1878
D-1979	Glaser-Dirks DG-200	2-77	
D-1980	Scheibe L-Spatz	535	
D-1981	Schempp-Hirth Standard Cirrus	268	OO-ZLK
D-1982	Grunau Baby IIB	16	
D-1983	Schempp-Hirth Standard Cirrus	419	
D-1984	Grob Standard Cirrus	278G	
D-1985	SZD-30 Pirat	S-02.41	DDR-1885 DM-1885
D-1986	Grob Standard Cirrus	285G	
D-1987	VTC-75 Standard Cirrus	131Y	
D-1988	Schempp-Hirth Nimbus 2	21	
D-1989	Rolladen-Schneider LS-1C	152	
D-1990	Grob Standard Cirrus	275G	
D-1991	Grob Standard Cirrus	286G	
D-1992	Schempp-Hirth Standard Cirrus	382	
D-1993	Rolladen-Schneider LS-4B	4852	
D-1994	Grob Standard Cirrus	287G	
D-1995	Marganski MDM-1 Fox	208	OE-5625
D-1996	Grob Standard Cirrus	307G	
D-1997	Glasflügel H201 Standard Libelle	194	HB-1006
D-1998	Glasflügel H401 Kestrel	82	
D-1999	Schleicher ASK-21	21440	
D-2001	Schleicher ASK-13	13359	
D-2002	Schleicher ASK-21	21604	
D-2003	Rolladen-Schneider LS-8	8012	
D-2004	Schleicher Ka.6BR Rhönsegler	529	
D-2005	Vogt LO-100 Zwergreiher *(Reservation - old?)*	AB 103	
D-2006	SZD-9bis Bocian 1E	P-718	DDR-3006 DM-3006
D-2007	Schleicher ASW-15B	15414	
D-2008	Schleicher K.8B	001AB	
D-2009	Schempp-Hirth Discus 2b *(Reservation 9.99)*	47	
D-2010	Schleicher K.8B	8490	
D-2011	Kranich III	66	
D-2012	Akaflieg Braunschweig SB-5B	5022/13A	
D-2013	Akaflieg Braunschweig SB-5E Sperber	13	
D-2014	Schleicher K.8B	03	
D-2015	Glaser-Dirks DG-100G Elan	E163-G129	
D-2016	Schempp-Hirth Nimbus 2B	116	D-7258
D-2017	SZD-41A Jantar Standard	B-748	DDR-2417 DM-2417
D-2018	Rolladen-Schneider LS-8-18 *(Reservation 9.99)*	8287	
D-2019	Schleicher Ka.6CR Rhönsegler	566	
D-2020	Schleicher ASW-20	20327	
D-2021	Schleicher K.8B	687	
D-2022	Scheibe L-Spatz 55	12	
D-2023	Schleicher ASK-23B	23138	
D-2024	Glasflügel H303 Mosquito	192	
D-2025	Schleicher ASW-15B	15389	
D-2027	Vogt LO-100 Zwergreiher	12	
D-2028	Schempp-Hirth Discus b	342	
D-2030	Schleicher Ka.6CR Rhönsegler	1115	
D-2031	Schleicher K7 Rhönadler	7010	
D-2032	Start & Flug H101 Salto	9	OY-MZX
D-2033	Schempp-Hirth Cirrus	071	
D-2034	Schleicher ASW-20C	20715	
D-2035	Schempp-Hirth Standard Cirrus	315	I-LETJ
D-2036	Schleicher ASW-20C	20722	
D-2037	Scheibe SF-27A	6309	D-KOBF
D-2038	Schleicher Ka.6E	4148	OO-ZBJ
D-2039	Schleicher ASK-13	13319AB	
D-2040	Start & Flug H-101 Salto	V-1	
D-2041	Rolladen-Schneider LS-1C	51	
D-2042	Bölkow Phoebus C *(Permit 4.99)*	940	
D-2043	Schempp-Hirth Discus CS	242CS	
D-2044	Glasflügel H204 Standard Libelle	1	
D-2045	Rolladen-Schneider LS-1D	173	
D-2046	Rolladen-Schneider LS-1C	160	
D-2047	Schleicher K.8B	8907/AB	
D-2048	Glasflügel H401 Kestrel	37	
D-2049	SZD-30 Pirat	B-343	DDR-1749 DM-1749
D-2050	Pilatus B4-PC11	042	
D-2051	Grob Standard Cirrus	283G	
D-2052	Schempp-Hirth Standard Cirrus	291	
D-2053	Schempp-Hirth Standard Cirrus	292	
D-2054	Schempp-Hirth Standard Cirrus	293	
D-2055	Schempp-Hirth Janus C	261	
D-2056	Schempp-Hirth Janus C	284	
D-2057	Grob Standard Cirrus	299G	
D-2058	Schempp-Hirth Standard Cirrus	300	
D-2059	Schempp-Hirth Standard Cirrus	303	
D-2060	SZD-48-3 Jantar Standard 3	B-1663	DOSAAF
D-2061	Schempp-Hirth Discus 2A *(Permit - old?)*	7	
D-2062	SZD-24C Foka	W-148	DDR-2036 DM-2036
D-2063	Schempp-Hirth Standard Cirrus	311	
D-2064	Schempp-Hirth Duo Discus	62	
D-2065	Schleicher ASW-15B	15241	
D-2066	Schleicher ASK-13	13408	
D-2067	Schleicher ASW-15B	15237	
D-2068	Schempp-Hirth Duo Discus	123	
D-2069-WU	Schleicher ASW-15B	15245	
D-2070	Schleicher ASW-15B	15247	
D-2071	Schleicher ASW-15B	15248	
D-2072	Schleicher ASW-15B	15235	
D-2073	Schleicher ASW-15B	15251	
D-2074	Schleicher ASK-13	13418	
D-2075	Schleicher K.8B	8920	
D-2076	Schleicher ASW-15B *(Reservation)*	15252	
D-2077	Schleicher K.8B	8921	
D-2078	Schleicher ASK-13	13415	
D-2079	Schleicher ASW-15B	15254	
D-2081	Rolladen-Schneider LS-1C	167	
D-2082	Schempp-Hirth Duo Discus	209	
D-2083	Start & Flug H101 Salto	19	
D-2084	Schempp-Hirth Ventus 2b	46	
D-2085	Glasflügel 604	9	
D-2086	Glasflügel H401 Kestrel	83	
D-2087	Glasflügel H401 Kestrel	85	
D-2088	Rolladen-Schneider LS-6C	6280	
D-2089	Rolladen-Schneider LS-1C	149	
D-2090	Rolladen-Schneider LS-1D	182	
D-2092	Schempp-Hirth Janus B	83	HB-1488
D-2093	LET L-13 Blanik	025412	
D-2094	Schleicher Ka.6CR Rhönsegler	6659AB	
D-2095	SZD-24-4A Foka 4	W-306	DDR-2045 DM-2045
D-2096	Rolladen-Schneider LS-1D	169	
D-2097	Rolladen-Schneider LS-8-18 *(Reservation 11.99)*	8288	
D-2098	Glasflügel H201B Standard Libelle	404	
D-2099	Schleicher Ka.6E	4097	
D-2100	Bölkow Phoebus B-1	929	
D-2101	Schempp-Hirth Standard Cirrus	351	
D-2102	Schempp-Hirth Standard Cirrus	274	

Regn.	Type	C/n	Prev.Id.
D-2103	Schempp-Hirth Standard Cirrus	290	
D-2104	Schempp-Hirth Standard Cirrus	301	
D-2105	SZD-51-1 Junior	B-1922	DDR-2805
D-2106	Rolladen-Schneider LS-6C	6265	SE-URR
D-2108	Rolladen-Schneider LS-4	4419	
D-2109	Rolladen-Schneider LS-8-18 (Reservation 9.99)	8274	
D-2110	Caproni Vizzola A.21S Calif	224	
D-2111	Schempp-Hirth Ventus 2a	1	
D-2112	Rolladen-Schneider LS-8-18 (Permit 12.99)	8207	
D-2113	Rolladen-Schneider LS-4B	41028	
D-2114	Schempp-Hirth Duo Discus	38	
D-2115	Schleicher ASK-13	13420	
D-2116	Schleicher K.8B	8922	
D-2117	Schleicher ASW-15B	15257	
D-2118	SZD-41A Jantar Standard	B-854	DDR-2418
			DM-2418
D-2119-7	Glasflügel H201B Standard Libelle	244	OE-0919
D-2120	Schleicher ASK-13	13421	
D-2121	Schleicher ASW-15B	15261	
D-2122	Schleicher ASK-13	13422	
D-2123	Glasflügel H201 Standard Libelle	196	HB-1009
D-2124	Schempp-Hirth Discus 2b (Reservation 11.99)	65	
D-2125	SZD-24-4A Foka 4	W-337	DDR-2225
			DM-2225
D-2126	Schleicher ASW-15B	15263	
D-2127	Schleicher K.8B	8924	
D-2128	Schempp-Hirth Duo Discus	65	
D-2129	Schleicher K.8B	8925	
D-2130	Schleicher ASW-15B	15265	
D-2131	Schleicher ASW-17	17015	
D-2132	Glaser-Dirks DG-300 Elan	3E-415	
D-2133	SZD-48-3 Jantar Standard 3	B-1943	DDR-2433
D-2134	Rolladen-Schneider LS-6C-18 (Reservation - old?)	6379	
D-2135	Schleicher ASK-13	13428	
D-2136	Schleicher K.8B	8928	
D-2137	Schleicher ASK-13	13429	
D-2138	Glaser-Dirks DG-100G Elan	E166-G132	
D-2139	Schleicher ASK-13	13430	
D-2140	Schempp-Hirth Discus 2A (Permit - old?)	9	
D-2141	Schleicher ASW-15B	15275	
D-2142	Schleicher Ka.6CR Rhönsegler	6139	OO-ZHT
D-2143	Schempp-Hirth Discus b	536	
D-2144	Rolladen-Schneider LS-4B	4884	
D-2145	Scheibe Bergfalke IV	5828	
D-2146	SZD-32A Foka 5	W-485	DDR-2246
			DM-2246
D-2147	Siebert SIE-3 (Reservation - old?)	3023	
D-2148	Rolladen-Schneider LS-4B	4885	
D-2149	Schempp-Hirth Duo Discus	34	
D-2150	Schempp-Hirth Standard Cirrus	354	
D-2151	Schempp-Hirth Standard Cirrus	355	
D-2153	Schempp-Hirth Duo Discus	35	
D-2154	Rolladen-Schneider LS-6C	6295	
D-2155	Rolladen-Schneider LS-4B	4886	
D-2156	Schempp-Hirth Ventus 2b	83	
D-2157	Scheibe Bergfalke IV	5829	
D-2158	Scheibe Bergfalke IV (Reservation - old?)	5831	
D-2159	Glasflügel H201B Standard Libelle	435	
D-2160	Glasflügel H201B Standard Libelle	436	
D-2161	Rolladen-Schneider LS-4B	4887	
D-2163	Glasflügel H401 Kestrel	88	
D-2164	Glasflügel H401 Kestrel	89	
D-2165	Glasflügel H401 Kestrel	90	
D-2166	Glasflügel H401 Kestrel	91	
D-2167	Schleicher ASW-24	24209	
D-2168	Schempp-Hirth Duo Discus	36	
D-2169	Pilatus B4-PC11AF	121	HB-1137
D-2170	Glasflügel H201B Standard Libelle	442	
D-2171	Rolladen-Schneider LS-4B	41013	
D-2173	Grob Standard Cirrus	360G	
D-2174	Scheibe Bergfalke III	5647	
D-2175	LET L-13 Blanik	025430	
D-2176	Schempp-Hirth Discus CS	047CS	
D-2177	Schleicher K.8B	8941	
D-2178	Schleicher ASK-13	13447	

Regn.	Type	C/n	Prev.Id.
D-2179	Schleicher ASW-15B	15201	D-0899
D-2180	Schleicher ASW-15B	15300	
D-2181	Schleicher ASW-15B	15301	
D-2182	Schleicher ASK-13	13452	
D-2183	Schleicher ASW-15B	15302	
D-2184	Schleicher K.8B	8945	
D-2185	Schleicher ASW-15B	15303	
D-2186	Schleicher ASW-15B	15304	
D-2187	Schleicher ASK-13	13453	
D-2188	Schleicher ASK-13	13454	
D-2189	Schleicher ASK-13	13455	
D-2190	Schleicher ASK-13	13456	
D-2192	Start & Flug H-101 Salto	28	
D-2193	Start & Flug H-101 Salto	29	
D-2194	Start & Flug H-101 Salto	32	
D-2195	Rolladen-Schneider LS-4B	4904	
D-2196	Glasflügel H401 Kestrel	92	
D-2197	Glasflügel H401 Kestrel	93	
D-2198	Rolladen-Schneider LS-4B	4904	
D-2199	Glasflügel H401 Kestrel	96	
D-2200	Glaser-Dirks DG-500/22 Elan	5E-11S3	
D-2202	SZD-38A Jantar 1	B-642	DDR-2402
			DM-2402
D-2203	Schleicher ASW-22	22003	
D-2204-1E	Schleicher ASW-22 (Permit 5.99)	22011	
D-2205	SZD-32A Foka 5	W-518	DDR-2255
			DM-2255
D-2206	SZD-59 Acro (Permit 4.99)	B-2176	SP-3629
D-2207	SZD-32A Foka 5	W-520	DDR-2257
			DM-2257
D-2208	Glasflügel H401 Kestrel	97	
D-2209	Rolladen-Schneider LS-8 (Permit 3.99)	8005	
D-2210	Glasflügel H401 Kestrel	100	
D-2211	Start & Flug H101 Salto	31	
D-2212	Pilatus B4-PC11A	130	
D-2213	Start & Flug H101 Salto	22	
D-2214	Glasflügel H201B Standard Libelle	477	
D-2215	Glasflügel H201B Standard Libelle	478	
D-2216	Glasflügel H201B Standard Libelle	479	
D-2217	Pilatus B4-PC11	89	
D-2218	Start & Flug H101 Salto	33	
D-2219	LET L-13 Blanik	025428	
D-2220	Start & Flug H101 Salto	35	
D-2221	Start & Flug H101 Salto	36	
D-2222	Schleicher Ka.6CR Rhönsegler	6366/BI	
D-2223	Rolladen-Schneider LS-1C	170	
D-2224	Start & Flug H101 Salto	37	
D-2225	Rolladen-Schneider LS-1F	251	
D-2227	Rolladen-Schneider LS-1C	252	
D-2228	LET L-13 Blanik	173335	
D-2229	SZD-32A Foka 5	W-445	DDR-2206
			DM-2206
D-2230	SZD-24-4A Foka 4	W-354	DDR-2230
			DM-2230
D-2231	SZD-24-4A Foka 4	W-383	DDR-2232
			DM-2232
D-2232	SZD-24-4A Foka 4	W-344	DDR-2233
			DM-2233
D-2234	Rolladen-Schneider LS-1F	195	
D-2235	Schleicher ASW-22	22033	
D-2236	Schleicher Ka.6CR Rhönsegler	6502	
D-2237	Schempp-Hirth Standard Cirrus	600	
D-2238	Grob Standard Cirrus	422G	
D-2240	Rolladen-Schneider LS-1C	184	
D-2241	Rolladen-Schneider LS-1C	267	
D-2242	Rolladen-Schneider LS-1F	185	
D-2243	SZD-32A Foka 5	W-526	DDR-2263
			DM-2263
D-2244	Rolladen-Schneider LS-1F	259	
D-2245	Rolladen-Schneider LS-1F	255	
D-2246	Rolladen-Schneider LS-1F	263	
D-2247	Rolladen-Schneider LS-1F	275	
D-2248	Rolladen-Schneider LS-1F	318	
D-2250	Rolladen-Schneider LS-1F	283	
D-2251	Rolladen-Schneider LS-1F	308	

Regn.	Type	C/n	Prev.Id.
D-2252	Rolladen-Schneider LS-1F	289	
D-2253	Rolladen-Schneider LS-1F	355	
D-2254	Rolladen-Schneider LS-1F	374	
D-2255	Schleicher ASW-22BL *(Permit 7.99)*	22081	
D-2256	Rolladen-Schneider LS-1F	314	
D-2257	SZD-32A Foka 5	W-513	DDR-2252 DM-2252
D-2258	Rolladen-Schneider LS-4	4538	
D-2259	Schleicher Ka.6E	4291	I-BZJR
D-2261	Rolladen-Schneider LS-1F	350	
D-2262	Rolladen-Schneider LS-4	4540	
D-2263	Glasflügel H401 Kestrel	87	D-KOWA D-2263
D-2264	Glasflügel H401 Kestrel	127	
D-2265	Glasflügel H401 Kestrel	128	
D-2266	Glasflügel H401 Kestrel	129	
D-2267	Caproni-Vizzola A-21S Calif	230	
D-2268	Scheibe Bergfalke III	5655	
D-2269	Schleicher ASK-13	13601AB	
D-2270	SZD-51-1 Junior	B-2149	
D-2271	SZD-24-4A Foka 4	W-338	DDR-2227 DM-2227
D-2272	SZD-32A Foka 5	W-525	DDR-2262 DM-2262
D-2273	Grob G.102 Speed Astir IIB	4086	
D-2274	Grob G.102 Speed Astir IIB	4090	
D-2275	Grob G.102 Speed Astir II	4006	BGA2484/DYK
D-2276	Grob G.103 Twin Astir	3203	
D-2277	Rolladen-Schneider LS-4B	4896	
D-2278	Darmstadt D-37	38	D-KEDD
D-2279	Rolladen-Schneider LS-4	4541	
D-2280	Schleicher K.8B	8715	OY-BXW
D-2281	Schleicher K.8B	8981/AB	
D-2282	Schleicher ASW-22	22021	
D-2283	Schleicher ASW-22	22018	
D-2284	Schleicher ASW-22	22019	
D-2285	Glaser-Dirks DG-300 Elan	3E-476	
D-2286	Glaser-Dirks DG-100G Elan	E138-G106	S5-3024 YU-4346
D-2287	Schempp-Hirth Standard Cirrus	664	
D-2288	Schempp-Hirth Standard Cirrus	665	
D-2289	Schempp-Hirth Standard Cirrus	502	
D-2290	SZD-32A Foka 5	W-425	DDR-2200 DM-2200
D-2291	Schempp-Hirth Discus CS	198CS	
D-2292	Grob Standard Cirrus	386G	
D-2293	Rolladen-Schneider LS-4B	4888	
D-2294	Grob Standard Cirrus	402G	
D-2295	Bölkow Phoebus C	1001	
D-2296	Rolladen-Schneider LS-4B	4889	
D-2297	SZD-32A Foka 5	W-486	DDR-2247 DM-2247
D-2298	Schempp-Hirth Ventus 2c	43/127	
D-2299	Rolladen-Schneider LS-1C	244	
D-2300	Pilatus B4-PC11AF	097	
D-2301	Pilatus B4-PC11AF	238	
D-2302	Schleicher ASK-13	13457	
D-2303	Schleicher ASW-15B	15315	
D-2304	Schleicher K.8B	8951	
D-2305	Schempp-Hirth Duo Discus	144	
D-2306	SZD-36A Cobra 15	W-646	DDR-2309 DM-2309
D-2307	Schleicher ASW-15B	15319	
D-2308	Schleicher ASW-15B	15320	
D-2309	Schleicher K.8B	8954	
D-2310	Schleicher ASW-15B	15321	
D-2311	Schleicher ASW-15B	15322	
D-2313	Schleicher ASW-15B	15324	
D-2314	Schleicher ASW-15B	15325	
D-2315	Rolladen-Schneider LS-4B	41020	
D-2316	Schleicher K.8B	8961	
D-2317	Schleicher ASK-13	13463	
D-2318	Schleicher ASK-15B	15328	
D-2319	Schleicher K.8B	8960	
D-2320	Schleicher K.8B	8963	
D-2321	Schleicher K.8B	8959	
D-2322	Schleicher ASW-22BL *(Permit - old?)*	22040	
D-2323	LET L-23 Super Blanik	938101	
D-2324	Schleicher K.8B	8965	
D-2326	Schleicher ASK-13	13464	
D-2327	Schleicher ASW-15B	15333	
D-2328	LET L-23 Super Blanik	928004	D-8064
D-2329	Schleicher ASW-15B	15334	
D-2330	Schleicher ASW-15B	15335	
D-2331	Schleicher ASW-17	17027	
D-2332	Schleicher ASK-13	13466	
D-2333	Schleicher K.8B	8967	
D-2334	Schleicher ASW-15B	15331	
D-2335	Schleicher ASW-15B	15332	
D-2336	Schleicher ASW-15B	15338	
D-2337	Schleicher ASW-15B	15339	
D-2338	Schleicher ASK-13	13468	
D-2339	Schleicher ASW-15B	15341	
D-2340	Schleicher ASW-15B	15336	
D-2341	Schleicher ASW-15B	15342	
D-2342	Schleicher ASK-13	13469	
D-2343	Rolladen-Schneider LS-6-18W	6343	
D-2344	Schleicher K.8C	81001	
D-2345	LET L-23 Super Blanik	938104	
D-2346	Schleicher ASW-15B	15357	
D-2347	Schleicher ASK-13	13470	
D-2349	Schleicher ASW-15B	15345	
D-2350	Schleicher ASW-17	17029	
D-2351	Schleicher K.8B *(Reservation 8.99)*	8964	
D-2352	Schempp-Hirth Duo Discus	42	
D-2353	Schleicher ASK-13	13473	
D-2354	Schleicher ASK-13	13465	
D-2355	Schleicher ASW-15B	15343	
D-2356	Schleicher ASW-15B	15351	
D-2357	Schleicher ASW-15B	15352	
D-2358	Rolladen-Schneider LS-4B	4890	
D-2359	Schleicher K.8B	8561/A	D-KOBE D-5359
D-2361	Schleicher ASW-15B	15354	
D-2362	Schleicher K.8B	8969	
D-2363	Schleicher ASW-15B	15355	
D-2364	Schleicher ASK-13	13477	
D-2365	Rolladen-Schneider LS-8A	8024	
D-2366	Rolladen-Schneider LS-8A *(Reservation 9.99)*	8283	
D-2367	Schleicher ASW-15B	15359	
D-2368	Schleicher ASW-15B	15360	
D-2369	Rolladen-Schneider LS-8A	8158	
D-2370	Schleicher ASW-15B	15362	
D-2371	Schleicher ASW-15B	15363	
D-2372	Schleicher ASW-15B	15364	
D-2373	Schleicher ASK-13	13481	
D-2374	Rolladen-Schneider LS-4B	4891	
D-2375	Schleicher ASW-15B	15365	
D-2376	Schempp-Hirth Duo Discus	53	
D-2377	Schleicher ASK-13	13483	
D-2378	SZD-9bis Bocian 1E	P-568	DDR-3378 DM-3378
D-2379	Schleicher ASW-15B	15368	
D-2380	Schleicher ASW-15B	15369	
D-2381	SZD-36A Cobra 15	W-651	DDR-2312 DM-2312
D-2382	Schleicher ASW-15B	15372	
D-2383	Schleicher K.8B	8971	
D-2384	Schleicher ASW-17	17034	
D-2385	Schleicher ASW-15B	15373	
D-2386	Schleicher ASW-15B	15216	
D-2387	Grob G.103 Twin Astir	3251	
D-2388	Grob G.103 Twin Astir Trainer	3252-T-29	
D-2389	Schempp-Hirth Ventus 2c	6/9	
D-2390	Grob G.103 Twin Astir	3257	
D-2391	Grob G.102 Astir CS Jeans	2246	
D-2392	Grob G.102 Astir CS 77	1833	
D-2393	Grob G.102 Astir CS 77	1834	
D-2394	Grob G.103 Twin Astir Trainer	3265-T-32	
D-2395	Grob G.102 Club Astir II	5001C	

Regn.	Type	C/n	Prev.Id.
D-2396	LET L-23 Super Blanik	938103	
D-2399	Scheibe Spatz B	502	
D-2400	Glasflügel H201B Standard Libelle	493	
D-2401	Glasflügel H201B Standard Libelle	494	
D-2402	Glasflügel H401 Kestrel	105	
D-2403	Glasflügel H201B Standard Libelle	499	
D-2404	Glasflügel H201B Standard Libelle	500	
D-2405	Glasflügel H201B Standard Libelle	501	
D-2407	Glasflügel H201B Standard Libelle	507	
D-2408	Schleicher ASK-21	21172	
D-2409	Schleicher ASK-21	21191	
D-2410	Schempp-Hirth Duo Discus	199	
D-2411	Rolladen-Schneider LS-8A	8159	
D-2412	Glasflügel H201B Standard Libelle	518	
D-2413	Glasflügel H201B Standard Libelle	521	
D-2414	Slingsby T-59D Kestrel 19 *(Permit 5.99)*	1852	
D-2415	Glasflügel H401 Kestrel	106	
D-2416	Glasflügel H201B Standard Libelle	497	
D-2417	Glasflügel H401 Kestrel	107	
D-2418	Schempp-Hirth Discus CS	150CS	
D-2419	Glasflügel H201B Standard Libelle	532	
D-2420	Glasflügel H201B Standard Libelle	533	
D-2421	Glasflügel H201B Standard Libelle	534	
D-2422	Glasflügel H201B Standard Libelle	535	
D-2423	Rolladen-Schneider LS-4B	4979	
D-2424	Glasflügel H201B Standard Libelle	537	
D-2425	Glasflügel H401 Kestrel	108	
D-2427	SZD-42-2 Jantar 2B	B-937	DDR-2428 DM-2428
D-2428	IAR IS.29D *(Reservation - dd?)*	23	
D-2429	SZD-42-2 Jantar 2B	B-951	DDR-2429 DM-2429
D-2430	Rolladen-Schneider LS-1F	297	
D-2431	Rolladen-Schneider LS-8-18 *(Permit 5.99)*	8252	
D-2432	Rolladen-Schneider LS-1F	280	
D-2434	Glasflügel H205 Club Libelle	36	
D-2435	Rolladen-Schneider LS-8-18 *(Permit 3.99)*	8025	
D-2436	Glasflügel H205 Club Libelle	38	
D-2437	Glasflügel H205 Club Libelle	39	
D-2438	Glasflügel H205 Club Libelle	40	
D-2439	Pilatus B4-PC11	153	
D-2440	Glasflügel H205 Club Libelle	64	
D-2441	Glasflügel H205 Club Libelle	65	
D-2442	Schleicher ASW-24	24004	
D-2443	Schempp-Hirth Duo Discus	171	
D-2444	Glasflügel H205 Club Libelle	68	
D-2445	Glasflügel H205 Club Libelle	69	
D-2447	Glasflügel H205 Club Libelle	77	
D-2448	Glasflügel H205 Club Libelle	78	
D-2449	Glasflügel H205 Club Libelle	79	
D-2450	Glasflügel H205 Club Libelle	141	
D-2451	Glasflügel H205 Club Libelle	86	
D-2452	Glasflügel H205 Club Libelle	87	
D-2453	Glasflügel H205 Club Libelle	90	
D-2454	SZD-38A Jantar 1	B-640	DDR-2404 DM-2404
D-2455	Glasflügel H205 Club Libelle	92	
D-2456	Glasflügel H205 Club Libelle	93	
D-2457	Glasflügel H205 Club Libelle	94	
D-2458	Glasflügel H205 Club Libelle	95	
D-2459	Glasflügel H205 Club Libelle	96	
D-2460	Glasflügel H205 Club Libelle	124	
D-2462	Glasflügel H205 Club Libelle	100	
D-2463	Glasflügel H205 Club Libelle	101	
D-2464	Glasflügel H205 Club Libelle	102	
D-2465	Rolladen-Schneider LS-8A	8026	
D-2467	Glasflügel H205 Club Libelle	113	
D-2468	Glasflügel H205 Club Libelle	114	
D-2469	Glasflügel H205 Club Libelle	115	
D-2471	Glasflügel H205 Club Libelle	117	
D-2472	Glasflügel H205 Club Libelle	118	
D-2473	Glasflügel H205 Club Libelle	119	
D-2474	Glasflügel H205 Club Libelle	120	
D-2475	Glasflügel H205 Club Libelle	121	
D-2476	Rolladen-Schneider LS-4B	4893	
D-2477	Schempp-Hirth Janus	12	
D-2478	Glasflügel H205 Club Libelle	137	
D-2479	Schempp-Hirth Nimbus 2	110	
D-2480	Schempp-Hirth Janus	55	
D-2481	Rolladen-Schneider LS-6	6061	
D-2482	Schleicher ASW-24	24066	
D-2483	Schleicher ASW-24	24067	
D-2484	SZD-48-3 Jantar Standard 3	B-1944	DDR-2434
D-2485	Schleicher ASW-24	24068	
D-2486	Schleicher ASW-20L	20413	
D-2487	Schleicher ASK-21	21049	
D-2488	Schleicher ASK-21	21050	
D-2489	Schleicher ASK-21	21051	
D-2490	Schleicher ASW-20L	20424	
D-2491	Schleicher ASW-20L	20425	
D-2492	Schleicher ASK-21	21055	
D-2493	Schleicher ASW-19B	19337	
D-2494	Schleicher ASW-19B	19338	
D-2495	Schleicher ASK-21	21057	
D-2496	Rolladen-Schneider LS-8A	8027	
D-2497	Schleicher ASK-21	21058	
D-2499	Schleicher ASW-20L	20414	
D-2500	Glasflügel H401 Kestrel	104	PH-477
D-2501	Vogt LO-100 Zwergreiher	1/2	
D-2502	M.2	1	
D-2503	Rolladen-Schneider LS-6	6062	
D-2504	Glaser-Dirks DG-100 Elan	E-83	
D-2505	Glaser-Dirks DG-100G Elan	E80-G55	
D-2506	Glaser-Dirks DG-100G Elan	E82-G57	
D-2507	Glaser-Dirks DG-100G Elan	E73-G48	
D-2508	Glaser-Dirks DG-100G Elan	E84-G58	
D-2509	Rolladen-Schneider LS-4B	41016	
D-2510	Schleicher ASW-20C	20749	
D-2511	Schleicher ASW-20C	20737	
D-2512	Scheibe Bergfalke IV	5815	
D-2513	Schleicher ASK-21	21441	
D-2514	Schleicher ASW-24	24071	
D-2515	Rolladen-Schneider LS-4	4252	
D-2516	Schleicher ASK-21	21442	
D-2517	Neukom Elfe S-4D	413AB	
D-2518	Schempp-Hirth Duo Discus	45	
D-2519	Schempp-Hirth Discus CS	244CS	
D-2520	Schempp-Hirth Janus C	178	
D-2521	Schempp-Hirth Discus CS	086CS	
D-2523	Schempp-Hirth Ventus A/16.6	16	
D-2524	Schleicher ASH-25	25169	
D-2525	Glaser-Dirks DG-300 Elan	3E-111	
D-2526	Rolladen-Schneider LS-4	4348	
D-2527	Schempp-Hirth Discus CS	110CS	
D-2528	Rolladen-Schneider LS-4	4373	
D-2529	Rolladen-Schneider LS-4B	4910	
D-2530	Schleicher ASH-25	25003	
D-2531	Grob G.102 Astir CS Jeans	2121	
D-2532	Grob G.102 Astir CS Jeans	2122	
D-2533	Grob G.102 Astir CS Jeans	2124	
D-2534	Grob G.102 Astir CS Jeans	2125	
D-2535	Rolladen-Schneider LS-4B	4980	
D-2536	Schempp-Hirth Ventus 2c	41/120	
D-2537	Grob G.102 Astir CS Jeans	2129	
D-2538	SG-38 Schulgleiter	44	
D-2539	Grob G.102 Astir CS Jeans	2132	
D-2540	Grob G.102 Astir CS Jeans	2133	
D-2541	Grob G.102 Astir CS Jeans	2134	
D-2542	Rolladen-Schneider LS-6C	6249	
D-2543	SZD-24-4A Foka 4	W-304	DDR-2043 DM-2043
D-2544	Grob G.102 Astir CS Jeans	2139	
D-2545	Grob G.102 Astir CS 77	1732	
D-2546	Grob G.102 Astir CS 77	1737	
D-2547	Grob G.102 Astir CS Jeans	2146	
D-2548	Grob G.102 Astir CS Jeans	2147	
D-2549	Grob G.102 Astir CS Jeans	2148	
D-2550	Schempp-Hirth Discus CS	108CS	
D-2551	Rolladen-Schneider LS-1D	194	OO-ZMV
D-2552	*Test Registration for Grob G.103 Twin Astir*		

Regn.	Type	C/n	Prev.Id.
D-2553	SZD-41A Jantar Standard	B-803	
D-2554	Glasflügel H303 Mosquito B	193	
D-2556	Neukom Elfe S-4D	418AB	
D-2557	Glasflügel Hornet C	94	
D-2558	Schempp-Hirth Ventus 2b	11	
D-2559	Glasflügel H303 Mosquito B	190	
D-2560	Glasflügel H303 Mosquito B	147	
D-2561	LET L-13 Blanik	026017	
D-2562	Rolladen-Schneider LS-8-18 *(Permit 3.99)*	8249	
D-2563	Rolladen-Schneider LS-3A	3242	
D-2564	Rolladen-Schneider LS-3A	3207	
D-2565	Rolladen-Schneider LS-3A	3144	
D-2566	Rolladen-Schneider LS-3A	3127	
D-2568	Rolladen-Schneider LS-3A	3134	
D-2569-VK	Rolladen-Schneider LS-6	6065	
D-2570	Rolladen-Schneider LS-3A	3101	
D-2571	Rolladen-Schneider LS-6-18W	6371	
D-2572	Schempp-Hirth Discus b	489	
D-2573	Glaser-Dirks DG-200/17	2-97/1725	
D-2574	Schempp-Hirth Discus CS	151CS	
D-2575	Schempp-Hirth Duo Discus	66	
D-2576	Glaser-Dirks DG-100	25	
D-2577	Glaser-Dirks DG-100	26	
D-2578	Glaser-Dirks DG-100	39	
D-2579	Rolladen-Schneider LS-8A	8132	
D-2580	Glaser-Dirks DG-100	41	
D-2581	Schempp-Hirth Discus CS	107CS	
D-2582	Glaser-Dirks DG-100	54	
D-2583	Glaser-Dirks DG-100	56	
D-2584	Rolladen-Schneider LS-6C	6262	
D-2585	Glaser-Dirks DG-100	62	
D-2586	Schleicher ASW-24	24076	
D-2587	Glaser-Dirks DG-100	65	
D-2588	Schempp-Hirth Duo Discus	19	
D-2589	Glaser-Dirks DG-100	67	
D-2590	Schleicher ASK-21	21448	
D-2591	Glaser-Dirks DG-100	78	
D-2592	Glaser-Dirks DG-100G	80G4	
D-2594	Glaser-Dirks DG-100G Elan	E8-G2	
D-2595	Glaser-Dirks DG-100 Elan	E-6	
D-2596	Glaser-Dirks DG-200/17	2-65/1704	
D-2597	Glaser-Dirks DG-200	2-66	
D-2598	VEB LOM 58/1 *(Reservation)*	090	
D-2599	Grob G.103A Twin II Acro	3656-K-25	
D-2600	Schempp-Hirth Discus 2b *(Permit 3.99)*	34	
D-2601	Grob G.102 Standard Astir III	5538S	
D-2602	Rolladen-Schneider LS-3	3142	PH-629
			D-0331
D-2603	Schleicher ASH-26	26008	
D-2604	Schempp-Hirth Ventus 2a	12	
D-2605	Schleicher ASW-20L	20438	
D-2607	Schleicher ASW-20	20439	
D-2608	Schleicher ASW-20L	20442	
D-2609	Rolladen-Schneider LS-3A	3067	
D-2610	Rolladen-Schneider LS-3A	3068	
D-2611	SZD-36A Cobra 15	W-650	DDR-2311
			DM-2311
D-2612	Schleicher ASK-21	21404	
D-2613	SZD-50-3 Puchacz	B-1330	DDR-3613
D-2614	Schleicher ASW-24	24034	
D-2615	Schempp-Hirth Ventus 2a	53	
D-2616	Schleicher ASK-21	21407	
D-2617	Schleicher ASK-21	21408	
D-2618	Rolladen-Schneider LS-3	3074	
D-2619	Rolladen-Schneider LS-3A	3158	
D-2620	Glaser-Dirks DG-100G Elan	E142-G110	
D-2621	Rolladen-Schneider LS-3	3093	
D-2622	Rolladen-Schneider LS-3	3173	
D-2623	Schempp-Hirth Discus CS	152CS	
D-2624	Rolladen-Schneider LS-3A	3463	
D-2625	Rolladen-Schneider LS-4	4003	
D-2626	Rolladen-Schneider LS-3A	3464	
D-2627	Rolladen-Schneider LS-3-17	3334	
D-2628	SZD-50-3 Puchacz	B-1389	DDR-3628
D-2629	Schleicher ASK-21	21411	
D-2630	Schempp-Hirth Ventus 2a	48	
D-2631	Schleicher ASK-21	21412	
D-2632	Rolladen-Schneider LS-3	3237	
D-2633-KM	Schleicher ASH-25	25063	
D-2634	Rolladen-Schneider LS-3	3236	
D-2635	Rolladen-Schneider LS-3	3316	
D-2636	Rolladen-Schneider LS-3	3317	
D-2637	Rolladen-Schneider LS-3A	3318	
D-2638	Rolladen-Schneider LS-8A	8028	
D-2639	Schleicher ASW-24	24040	
D-2640	Rolladen-Schneider LS-4	4429	
D-2641	Schempp-Hirth Discus CS	157CS	
D-2642	Schleicher ASW-20L	20126	
D-2643	Schleicher ASW-19B	19232	
D-2645	Schleicher ASW-19B	19238	
D-2646	Schleicher ASW-19B	19235	
D-2647	Schleicher ASK-13	13600	
D-2648	Schleicher ASW-19B	19236	
D-2649	Schleicher ASW-20	20119	
D-2650	Schleicher ASW-20L	20123	
D-2651	Schleicher ASW-20L	20128	
D-2652	Schleicher ASK-13	13603	
D-2653	Schleicher ASW-19B	19244	
D-2654	Schleicher ASW-20	20133	
D-2655	SZD-50-3 Puchacz	B-1539	DDR-3655
D-2656	Schleicher ASW-19B	19249	
D-2657	Schleicher ASW-20	20127	
D-2658	Schleicher ASW-20L	20137	
D-2659	Schempp-Hirth Ventus 2a	90	
D-2660	Glaser-Dirks DG-600	6-75	
D-2661	Schleicher ASW-20	20140	
D-2662	Glasflügel H303 Mosquito	98	
D-2663	Schleicher ASK-13	13476	
D-2665	Rolladen-Schneider LS-3	3120	
D-2666	Lanaverre CS-11/75L Standard Cirrus	25	
D-2667	Grob G.103 Twin II	3562	
D-2668	Grob G.103 Twin II	3563	
D-2669	Rolladen-Schneider LS-4B	4981	
D-2670	Grob G.103A Twin II Acro	3653-K-22	
D-2671	Schempp-Hirth Duo Discus	69	
D-2672	Schleicher ASW-19	19206	
D-2673	Schleicher ASW-19	19207	
D-2674	Schleicher ASW-20	20084	
D-2675	Schleicher ASW-20	20085	
D-2676	Schleicher ASW-19B	19211	
D-2677	Schleicher ASK-13	13595	
D-2678	Rolladen-Schneider LS-8A	8029	
D-2680	Schleicher ASW-19	19216	
D-2681	Schempp-Hirth Discus CS	155CS	
D-2682	Schleicher ASW-19	19217	
D-2683	Schleicher ASW-20	20096	
D-2684	Schempp-Hirth Discus CS	062CS	
D-2685	Schleicher ASW-20	20097	
D-2686	Schleicher ASW-20	20098	
D-2687	Schleicher ASW-19B	19223	
D-2688	Schleicher ASW-19	19225	
D-2689	Schleicher ASW-20	20107	
D-2690	Schempp-Hirth Ventus 2b	13	
D-2691	Schleicher ASW-20	20103	
D-2692	Schleicher ASW-20	20393	
D-2693	Schleicher ASW-20L	20394	
D-2694	Glaser-Dirks DG-100G Elan	E135-G103	HB-1694
D-2695	Schleicher ASW-20	20399	
D-2696	Schleicher ASW-20L	20498	HB-2168
			HB-1613
D-2697	Schleicher ASW-24	24157	
D-2698	Rolladen-Schneider LS-4	4240	
D-2699	Rolladen-Schneider LS-4	4157	
D-2700	Rolladen-Schneider LS-4	4165	
D-2701	Neukom S4D Elfe	410AB	
D-2702	SZD-32A Foka 5	W-427	DDR-2202
			DM-2202
D-2703	SZD-30 Pirat	W-398	DDR-1703
			DM-1703

Regn.	Type	C/n	Prev.Id.
D-2704	SZD-36A Cobra 15	W-611	DDR-2304
			DM-2304
D-2705	SZD-30 Pirat	W-402	DDR-1705
			DM-1705
D-2706	Rolladen-Schneider LS-4	4265	
D-2707	Rolladen-Schneider LS-4	4297	
D-2708	Glaser-Dirks DG-300 Club Elan	3E-336/C31	
D-2709	Glaser-Dirks DG-300 Club Elan	3E-342/C34	
D-2710	Schleicher Ka.6CR Rhönsegler	6372/Si	D-5428
D-2711	Rolladen-Schneider LS-4	4218	
D-2712	Schleicher ASK-18	18049	
D-2714	Schleicher ASW-20	20109	
D-2716	Schleicher ASW-19	19219	
D-2717	Rolladen-Schneider LS-3A	3077	
D-2718	Schleicher ASW-19B	19327	
D-2719	Schleicher ASK-21	21043	
D-2720	Schleicher ASW-20L	20400	
D-2721	SZD-30 Pirat	B-303	DDR-1721
			DM-1721
D-2722	Schleicher ASW-24	24140	
D-2723	Grob G.103 Twin II	3528	
D-2724	Schleicher ASK-21	21651	
D-2725	Schleicher ASW-19B	19344	
D-2726	Schleicher ASW-20	20445	
D-2727	Schempp-Hirth Janus B	64	
D-2728	Glasflügel H303 Mosquito B	179	
D-2729	Glasflügel H303 Mosquito B	174	
D-2730	Glasflügel H303 Mosquito B	127	
D-2731	Glasflügel H303 Mosquito B	151	
D-2732	Rolladen-Schneider LS-1F	444	
D-2733	Rolladen-Schneider LS-1F	445	
D-2735	Glaser-Dirks DG-300 Elan	3E-77	
D-2736	Glaser-Dirks DG-300 Elan	3E-78	
D-2737	Rolladen-Schneider LS-1F	316	
D-2738	Rolladen-Schneider LS-8A	8083	
D-2739	Rolladen-Schneider LS-1F	332	
D-2740	Glaser-Dirks DG-300 Elan	3E-79	
D-2741	Rolladen-Schneider LS-1F	345	
D-2742	Rolladen-Schneider LS-1F	346	
D-2743	Glaser-Dirks DG-300 Elan	3E-83	
D-2744	Schleicher ASK-21	21599	
D-2745	Rolladen-Schneider LS-1F	356	
D-2746	Glaser-Dirks DG-300 Elan	3E-104	
D-2747	SZD-30 Pirat	B-341	DDR-1747
			DM-1747
D-2748	Rolladen-Schneider LS-1F	414	
D-2749	Glaser-Dirks DG-300 Elan	3E-84	
D-2750	Glaser-Dirks DG-300 Elan	3E-86	
D-2751	Glaser-Dirks DG-300 Elan	3E-87	
D-2752	SZD-30 Pirat	B-352	DDR-1752
			DM-1752
D-2753	Schleicher ASW-27	27053	
D-2754	SZD-30 Pirat	B-358	DDR-1754
			DM-1754
D-2755	Rolladen-Schneider LS-4	4018	
D-2756	Rolladen-Schneider LS-3-17	3449	
D-2757	Schempp-Hirth Discus b	388	
D-2758	Rolladen-Schneider LS-3-17	3418	
D-2759	Rolladen-Schneider LS-1F	348	
D-2760	Rolladen-Schneider LS-1F	347	
D-2761	Schempp-Hirth Discus CS	035CS	
D-2762	Rolladen-Schneider LS-1F	323	
D-2763	Rolladen-Schneider LS-1F	336	
D-2764	Rolladen-Schneider LS-4B	4784	
D-2765	Rolladen-Schneider LS-6C	6323	
D-2766	Rolladen-Schneider LS-1F	339	
D-2767	Rolladen-Schneider LS-1F	340	
D-2768	Rolladen-Schneider LS-1F	341	
D-2770	Glaser-Dirks DG-100G Elan	E143-G111	
D-2771	Rolladen-Schneider LS-1F	315	
D-2772	Rolladen-Schneider LS-1F	304	
D-2773	Rolladen-Schneider LS-1F	305	
D-2774	Rolladen-Schneider LS-4A	4786	
D-2775	Rolladen-Schneider LS-4A	4787	
D-2776	Rolladen-Schneider LS-1F	301	

Regn.	Type	C/n	Prev.Id.
D-2777	Schempp-Hirth Standard Cirrus	238	CF-DMW
D-2779	Schempp-Hirth Standard Cirrus	480	
D-2780	SZD-30 Pirat	B-412	DDR-1783
			DM-1783
D-2781	Schempp-Hirth Standard Cirrus	500	
D-2782	Schempp-Hirth Duo Discus	64	
D-2783	Schempp-Hirth Nimbus 2	77	
D-2785	Schempp-Hirth Discus b	465	
D-2786	Rolladen-Schneider LS-8A	8208	
D-2787	SZD-30 Pirat	B-430	DDR-1787
			DM-1787
D-2788	SZD-51-1 Junior	B-2190	
D-2789	Schempp-Hirth Nimbus 2	118	
D-2790	Schempp-Hirth Nimbus 2	119	
D-2791-GI	Rolladen-Schneider LS-8A	8235	
D-2792	Schempp-Hirth Nimbus 2B	164	
D-2793	Schempp-Hirth HS-7 Mini-Nimbus	55	
D-2794	Schempp-Hirth HS-7 Mini-Nimbus	56	
D-2795	Rolladen-Schneider LS-4B	4996	
D-2796	Schempp-Hirth Nimbus 2C	205	
D-2797	Rolladen-Schneider LS-4B	4983	
D-2798	Schempp-Hirth Nimbus 2C	217	
D-2799	Schempp-Hirth Nimbus 2C	218	
D-2800	Glaser-Dirks DG-600/17	6-32	
D-2801	Glaser-Dirks DG-300 Elan	3E-93	
D-2802	SZD-51-1 Junior	B-1844	DDR-2801
D-2804	Rolladen-Schneider LS-3	3038	
D-2805	Rolladen-Schneider LS-3	3039	
D-2806	SZD-51-1 Junior	B-1923	DDR-2806
D-2807	SZD-51-1 Junior	B-1919	DDR-2802
D-2808	Rolladen-Schneider LS-3	3042	
D-2809	SZD-51-1 Junior	W-961	DDR-2800
D-2810	Rolladen-Schneider LS-3	3044	
D-2811	Rolladen-Schneider LS-3	3045	
D-2812	SZD-30 Pirat	B-475	DDR-1812
			DM-1812
D-2813	Rolladen-Schneider LS-3	3047	
D-2814	Schempp-Hirth Nimbus 3/24.5	42	OY-XPR
D-2815	Schempp-Hirth Janus C	182	
D-2816	Schempp-Hirth Ventus b/16.6	179	
D-2817	Rolladen-Schneider LS-3	3053	
D-2818	Rolladen-Schneider LS-3	3054	
D-2819	Rolladen-Schneider LS-4B	4941	
D-2820	Rolladen-Schneider LS-4B	4789	
D-2821	Rolladen-Schneider LS-3	3073	
D-2822	Rolladen-Schneider LS-4B	4790	
D-2823	Rolladen-Schneider LS-4B	4791	
D-2824	Rolladen-Schneider LS-3	3061	
D-2825	Rolladen-Schneider LS-3	3117	
D-2827	Akaflieg München Mü.27 *(Permit 4.99)*	V1	
D-2828	Glaser-Dirks DG-300 Elan	3E-81	HB-1791
D-2829	Schempp-Hirth Nimbus 2B	173	
D-2830	Rolladen-Schneider LS-4B	41017	
D-2831	Schempp-Hirth Nimbus 2B	184	
D-2832	Schempp-Hirth Nimbus 2C	185	
D-2833	Rolladen-Schneider LS-4	4040	
D-2834	Rolladen-Schneider LS-8A	8033	
D-2837	SZD-30 Pirat	B-323	DDR-1737
			DM-1737
D-2838	ICA/Brasov IS.28B2	237	
D-2839	Rolladen-Schneider LS-6C	6269	
D-2840	ICA/Brasov IS.28B2	310	
D-2841	ICA/Brasov IS.28B2	318	
D-2842	Rolladen-Schneider LS-8A	8160	
D-2843	SZD-51-1 Junior	B-1918	DDR-2803
D-2844	Rolladen-Schneider LS-3A	3266	
D-2845	ICA/Brasov IS.28B2	312	
D-2846	Rolladen-Schneider LS-3A	3258	
D-2847	Rolladen-Schneider LS-3A	3209	
D-2848	Rolladen-Schneider LS-3-17	3146	
D-2849	Rolladen-Schneider LS-3A	3171	
D-2850	Rolladen-Schneider LS-4A	4792	
D-2851	Rolladen-Schneider LS-4A	4793	
D-2852	Bölkow Phoebus B-1	815	OE-0852
D-2853	Schleicher ASW-19B	19318	

Regn.	Type	C/n	Prev.Id.
D-2854	Schleicher ASK-21	21021	
D-2855	Schleicher ASK-21	21025	
D-2856	Schleicher ASW-19B	19319	
D-2857	Rolladen-Schneider LS-8A	8161	
D-2858	Glaser-Dirks DG-300 Elan	3E-129	
D-2859	SZD-30 Pirat	B-581	DDR-1859
			DM-1859
D-2860	Rolladen-Schneider LS-3A	3107	
D-2861	Glasflügel Hornet C	96	
D-2862	Rolladen-Schneider LS-3A	3424	
D-2863	Rolladen-Schneider LS-3A	3285	
D-2864	Rolladen-Schneider LS-3A	3168	
D-2865	Rolladen-Schneider LS-3A	3333	
D-2866	SZD-30 Pirat	S-01.03	DDR-1866
			DM-1866
D-2869	Rolladen-Schneider LS-3-17	3340	
D-2870	Glaser-Dirks DG-300 Elan	3E-132	
D-2871	Glaser-Dirks DG-300 Elan	3E-136	
D-2872	Glaser-Dirks DG-300 Elan	3E-453	
D-2873	Schleicher ASW-20L	20446	
D-2874	Schleicher ASW-20	20447	
D-2875	Schleicher ASW-20	20449	
D-2876	Schempp-Hirth Discus b	557	
D-2877	Glasflügel Hornet C	100	OY-XKN
D-2879	Schempp-Hirth Nimbus 2C	204	
D-2880	Glaser-Dirks DG-800S	8-28S5	
D-2881	Schempp-Hirth Mini-Nimbus C	142	
D-2882	Schleicher ASW-19B	19308	
D-2883	Schleicher ASW-20	20318	
D-2884	Schleicher Ka.6E	4093	HB-885
D-2885	Schleicher ASK-21	21014	
D-2886	Schleicher ASW-20L	20320	
D-2887	Schmepp-Hirth Discus CS	199CS	
D-2888	Eiri PIK-20D	20570	
D-2889	Rolladen-Schneider LS-3-17	3369	
D-2890	Grob G.103 Twin II	3792	
D-2891	Grob G.103A Twin II Acro	3811-K-74	
D-2892	Grob G.103A Twin II Acro	3819-K-80	
D-2893	Rolladen-Schneider LS-3-17	3397	
D-2894	Rolladen-Schneider LS-3A	3257	
D-2895	Rolladen-Schneider LS-3-17	3409	
D-2896	Rolladen-Schneider LS-4	4284	
D-2897	Rolladen-Schneider LS-7	7091	
D-2898	SZD-30 Pirat	S-03.23	DDR-1898
			DM-1898
D-2899	Rolladen-Schneider LS-4	4300	
D-2900	Glaser-Dirks DG-300 Club Elan	3E-354/C42	
D-2901	Grob G.102 Astir CS 77	1839	
D-2902	Grob G.102 Astir CS 77	1840	
D-2903	Schempp-Hirth Duo Discus	195	
D-2904	Rolladen-Schneider LS-7	7094	
D-2905	Grob G.102 Speed Astir IIB	4063	
D-2906	Schleicher ASK-21	21512	
D-2907	Grob G.102 Speed Astir IIB	4065	
D-2908	Schempp-Hirth Ventus 2a	10	
D-2909	Grob G.102 Speed Astir IIB	4067	
D-2910	SZD-30 Pirat	S-04.11	DDR-1910
			DM-1910
D-2911	Pilatus B4-PC11AF	235	
D-2912	Grob G.103 Twin II	3541	
D-2913	Grob G.103A Twin II Acro	3544-K-1	
D-2914	Grob G.103 Twin II	3545	
D-2915	Grob G.103A Twin II Acro	3546-K-3	
D-2916	Grob G.103 Twin II	3548	
D-2917	Grob G.102 Standard Astir II	5050S	
D-2918	Grob G.102 Club Astir II	5060C	
D-2919	Grob G.102 Club Astir II	5056C	
D-2920	Grob G.102 Standard Astir II	5051S	
D-2921	Schleicher ASK-21	21668	
D-2923	Schempp-Hirth Ventus b/16.6	187	
D-2924	Schempp-Hirth Ventus b/16.6	185	
D-2925	Schempp-Hirth Duo Discus	75	
D-2926	Schempp-Hirth Duo Discus	216	
D-2927	Schempp-Hirth Ventus b/16.6	200	
D-2928	Rolladen-Schneider LS-7	7095	
D-2929	FS.29	V-1	
D-2930	Scheibe SF-30A Club-Spatz	6805	
D-2931	Rolladen-Schneider LS-4B	4911	
D-2932	Schempp-Hirth Standard Cirrus	384	
D-2934	Schleicher K.8B	AB8962	
D-2935	Schempp-Hirth Duo Discus	97	
D-2936	Grob G.103C Twin III	36007	
D-2937	LET L-13 Blanik	025901	
D-2939	Rolladen-Schneider LS-1F	268	
D-2940	Rolladen-Schneider LS-8A	8034	
D-2941	Grob G.103C Twin III Acro	34173	
D-2942	Rolladen-Schneider LS-4	4131	
D-2943	Rolladen-Schneider LS-8A	8186	
D-2944	Schempp-Hirth Discus b	100	
D-2947	Schempp-Hirth Standard Cirrus	313	
D-2948	Schempp-Hirth Standard Cirrus	314	
D-2951	Glasflügel H201B Standard Libelle	413	
D-2953	Rolladen-Schneider LS-1C	197	
D-2954	Grob Standard Cirrus	309G	
D-2955	Grob Standard Cirrus	316G	
D-2956	Grob Standard Cirrus	317G	
D-2957	Grob Standard Cirrus	325G	
D-2958	Grob Standard Cirrus	328G	
D-2959	Grob Standard Cirrus	329G	
D-2960	Schleicher K.8B	8927AB	
D-2961	Glaser-Dirks DG-500 Elan Trainer	5E-9T39	
D-2962	Glasflügel H201B Standard Libelle	410	
D-2963	Glasflügel H201B Standard Libelle	393	
D-2964	Glaser-Dirks DG-100G Elan	E99-G69	
D-2965	Schempp-Hirth Standard Cirrus	321	
D-2967	Schempp-Hirth Nimbus 2	33	
D-2968	Schempp-Hirth Duo Discus	94	
D-2969	LET L-13 Blanik	025308	D-KOPI
D-2970	Glaser-Dirks DG-100G Elan	E212-G178	
D-2971	Rolladen-Schneider LS-2 (Permit 3.99)	243	
D-2972	Glasflügel H201B Standard Libelle	415	
D-2973	Glasflügel H201B Standard Libelle	417	
D-2974	Glasflügel H201B Standard Libelle	418	
D-2975	Rolladen-Schneider LS-1D	126	
D-2976	Schempp-Hirth Ventus c	290	
D-2977	Rolladen-Schneider LS-1C	166	
D-2978	Schleicher ASK-13	13434	
D-2979	Schleicher ASK-13	13435	
D-2980	Schleicher ASW-15B	15277	
D-2981	Schleicher ASW-15B	15278	
D-2982	Schleicher ASW-15B	15279	
D-2983	Schleicher ASK-13	13432	
D-2985	Schempp-Hirth Discus b	101	
D-2986	Schleicher ASW-15B	15284	
D-2987	Schleicher ASW-15B	15285	
D-2988	Schempp-Hirth Janus C	232	HB-1897
D-2989	Schleicher ASK-13	13443	
D-2990	Schleicher ASK-13	13444	
D-2991	Schleicher ASK-21	21676	
D-2992	Schleicher ASK-13	13446	
D-2993	Rolladen-Schneider LS-8A	8109	
D-2994	Glaser-Dirks DG-300 Elan Acro	3E-431A2	
D-2995	Start & Flug H-101 Salto	25	
D-2996	Start & Flug H-101 Salto	26	
D-2997	Start & Flug H-101 Salto	27	
D-2998	Rolladen-Schneider LS-1C	165	
D-2999	Grob Standard Cirrus	343G	
D-3000	Grob Standard Cirrus	235G	
D-3001	Rolladen-Schneider LS-1C	154	
D-3002	Schempp-Hirth Standard Cirrus	332	
D-3003	Schempp-Hirth Standard Cirrus	334	
D-3004	Schempp-Hirth Standard Cirrus	336	
D-3005	Grob Standard Cirrus	347G	
D-3007	Schempp-Hirth Standard Cirrus	350	
D-3008	SZD-9bis Bocian 1E	P-720	DDR-3008
			DM-3008
D-3009	Schempp-Hirth Nimbus 2	37	
D-3010	Test Registration for Glaser-Dirks production		
D-3011	VTC-75 Standard Cirrus	138Y	
D-3012	VTC-75 Standard Cirrus	140Y	

Regn.	Type	C/n	Prev.Id.
D-3013	Schempp-Hirth Discus b	104	
D-3014	Vogt LO-100 Zwergreiher	EB 01	
D-3015	Schleicher Ka.6BR-PE Rhönsegler	342	
D-3016	Siebert SIE-3	3022	
D-3017	Glasflügel H203 Standard Libelle	2	
D-3018	SZD-9bis Bocian 1E	P-727	DDR-3014
			DM-3014
D-3019	Glasflügel H201B Standard Libelle	424	
D-3020	Glasflügel H201B Standard Libelle	425	
D-3021	Schleicher Rhönlerche II (Reservation)	557	
D-3022	Schleicher K.8B	587	
D-3023	Rolladen-Schneider LS-1C	150	
D-3024	Schempp-Hirth Discus b	105	
D-3025	Kaiser KA-1	0101	
D-3026	Schleicher K7 Rhönadler	7005	
D-3027	Schleicher K.8B	8222	
D-3028	Schleicher K.8B	8418	
D-3029	Glasflügel H304	263	
D-3030	Schempp-Hirth Nimbus 2	60	
D-3031	Glaser-Dirks DG-100G Elan	E211-G157	
D-3032	Glasflügel H304	255	
D-3033	Start & Flug H101 Salto	21	
D-3034	Schleicher K.8B	8530	
D-3035	Schleicher K7 Rhönadler	7251	
D-3036	Schleicher K.8B	8716	
D-3037	Schleicher Ka.6CR Rhönsegler	6540	
D-3038	Grob G.102 Astir CS	1178	
D-3039	Schleicher Ka.6CR Rhönsegler	6627	
D-3040	Schleicher Ka.6CR Rhönsegler	6660AB	
D-3041	Glaser-Dirks DG-300 Elan	3E-119	
D-3042	Schempp-Hirth Nimbus 2	46	
D-3043	Glaser-Dirks DG-100G Elan	E209-G175	
D-3044	Schempp-Hirth Duo Discus	222	
D-3045	Bölkow Phoebus C	1002	
D-3046	Rolladen-Schneider LS-1F	188	
D-3047	SZD-9bis Bocian 1D	F-802	OH-292
			OH-KBW
D-3048	SZD-9bis Bocian 1E	P-469	DDR-3046
			DM-3046
D-3049	Schempp-Hirth Ventus b/16.6	69	
D-3050	Akaflieg Braunschweig SB-5E Sperber	AB5053	
D-3051	Schempp-Hirth Nimbus 3/24.5	12	
D-3052	Glaser-Dirks DG-300 Elan	3E-142	
D-3053	Grunau Baby IIB	1	
D-3054	Bölkow Phoebus B-1	949	
D-3056	Grob G.103 Twin II	3510	
D-3057	SZD-9bis Bocian 1E	P-475	DDR-3054
			DM-3054
D-3058	Grob G.102 Standard Astir II	5046S	
D-3059	SZD-9bis Bocian 1E	P-444	DDR-3019
			DM-3019
D-3060	Glasflügel H210B Standard Libelle	295	
D-3061	Glaser-Dirks DG-300 Elan	3E-152	
D-3062	Glaser-Dirks DG-100G Elan	E208-G174	
D-3063	SZD-9bis Bocian 1E	P-480	DDR-3067
			DM-3067
D-3064	LET L-13 Blanik	026442	DOSAAF
D-3065	SZD-9bis Bocian 1E	P-479	DDR-3063
			DM-3063
D-3066	Grob G.103 Twin II	3516	
D-3067	Grob G.102 Standard Astir II	5049S	
D-3068	Grob G.103 Twin II	3518	
D-3069	Grob G.103 Twin II	3519	
D-3070	Rolladen-Schneider LS-1D	193	
D-3071	Schempp-Hirth Duo Discus	72	
D-3073	Grob G.103A Twin II Acro	3626-K-13	
D-3074	Grob G.103A Twin II Acro	3632-K-14	
D-3076	Grob G.103A Twin II Acro	3636-K-17	
D-3077	Rolladen-Schneider LS-1F	306	
D-3078	Grob G.103A Twin II Acro	3637-K-18	
D-3079	SZD-9bis Bocian 1E	P-756	DDR-3070
			DM-3070
D-3081	Schleicher ASW-20C (Permit 3.99)	20838	
D-3082	Schleicher ASK-23	23045	
D-3083	Schleicher ASK-23	23046	
D-3084	SZD-9bis Bocian 1E	P-481	DDR-3084
			DM-3084
			OO-ZCJ (1)
D-3085	Schempp-Hirth Standard Cirrus B	598	
D-3086	Rolladen-Schneider LS-8A	8016	
D-3087	Schempp-Hirth Standard Cirrus	691	
D-3088	Schempp-Hirth Standard Cirrus	548	
D-3089	Schempp-Hirth Nimbus 3	11	
D-3090	Schempp-Hirth Janus B	146	
D-3091	Glaser-Dirks DG-100G Elan	E178-G144	
D-3092	Schempp-Hirth Standard Cirrus (Permit 4.99)	623	
D-3093	Schempp-Hirth Standard Cirrus	504	
D-3094	Schempp-Hirth Ventus 2c	49/150	
D-3095	Schempp-Hirth Standard Cirrus	557	
D-3096	Grob Standard Cirrus	558G	
D-3097	Glaser-Dirks DG-100G Elan	E125-G93	
D-3098	Schempp-Hirth Standard Cirrus	503	
D-3099	Grob Standard Cirrus	407G	I-ACOB
D-3100	Vogt LO-100 Zwergreiher	AB/117	
D-3101	Grob Standard Cirrus	435G	
D-3102	Schempp-Hirth Nimbus 2	64	
D-3103	Neukom S-4D Elfe	419AB	
D-3104	Schempp-Hirth Standard Cirrus	427	
D-3105	Schempp-Hirth Standard Cirrus	428	
D-3106	Grob Standard Cirrus	441G	
D-3107	Grob Standard Cirrus	442G	
D-3108	Schempp-Hirth Ventus b/16.6	302	
D-3109	Glasflügel H201B Standard Libelle	570	
D-3110	Rolladen-Schneider LS-4	4745	OE-5459
			D-1841
D-3111	SZD-50-3 Puchacz	B-1085	DDR-3601
D-3112	Schempp-Hirth Janus	02	
D-3113	Rolladen-Schneider LS-1F	438	N40MH
D-3114	Rolladen-Schneider LS-4B	41023	
D-3115	Glaser-Dirks DG-100G Elan	E146-G114	
D-3116	Schleicher ASW-20L	20220	D-KGPF
			D-3156
D-3117	Schempp-Hirth Ventus c	531	
D-3118	Rolladen-Schneider LS-8A	8133	
D-3119	SZD-9bis Bocian 1E	P-499	DDR-3219
			DM-3219
D-3121	Schempp-Hirth Janus B	145	
D-3122	Schempp-Hirth Standard Cirrus	547	
D-3123	Schempp-Hirth Duo Discus	71	
D-3124-BG	Rolladen-Schneider LS-4	4422	
D-3125	Schleicher ASH-25	25017	HB-1920
D-3126	Rolladen-Schneider LS-1F	325	
D-3127	SZD-9bis Bocian 1E	P-509	DDR-3227
			DM-3227
D-3128-19	Rolladen-Schneider LS-1F	423	
D-3129	Rolladen-Schneider LS-1F	424	
D-3130	Rolladen-Schneider LS-1F	425	
D-3131-DV	Rolladen-Schneider LS-1F	426	
D-3132	Rolladen-Schneider LS-1F	427	
D-3133	Rolladen-Schneider LS-1F	299	
D-3134	Rolladen-Schneider LS-1F	354	
D-3135	Rolladen-Schneider LS-1F	357	
D-3136	Rolladen-Schneider LS-1F	370	
D-3138	Glaser-Dirks DG-100G Elan	E114-G83	
D-3139	Glaser-Dirks DG-100G Elan	E113-G82	
D-3140	Glaser-Dirks DG-100G Elan	E117-G86	
D-3141	Schleicher ASK-21	21284	
D-3142	Schleicher ASK-23B	23055	
D-3143	Schempp-Hirth Ventus b/16.6	147	SE-TYY
D-3144	Rolladen-Schneider LS-4B	4991	
D-3146	Schleicher ASK-21	21628	
D-3148	Schempp-Hirth Ventus b/16.6	111	
D-3149	Rolladen-Schneider LS-1F	441	
D-3150	Schleicher ASW-20CL	20839	
D-3151	Schempp-Hirth Nimbus 3/24.5	30	
D-3152	Schempp-Hirth Ventus b/16.6	117	
D-3153	Rolladen-Schneider LS-4B	4992	
D-3154	Schleicher ASW-20	20218	
D-3155	Schleicher ASW-20L	20219	
D-3156	Glaser-Dirks DG-800S	8-78S21	
D-3157	Schleicher ASW-20	20226	

Regn.	Type	C/n	Prev.Id.
D-3158	Schleicher ASW-20	20227	
D-3159	Schempp-Hirth Duo Discus	164	
D-3160	Rolladen-Schneider LS-4B	4993	
D-3161	Schleicher ASW-19B	19278	
D-3162	Schleicher ASW-20	20229	
D-3163	Schleicher ASW-20	20230	
D-3164	Schempp-Hirth Janus B	113	
D-3165	Schempp-Hirth Nimbus 2C	219	
D-3166	Schempp-Hirth Nimbus 2C	228	
D-3167	Schempp-Hirth Nimbus 2B *(Permit 11.99)*	168	
D-3168	Schempp-Hirth Mini-Nimbus B	71	
D-3169	Schleicher Ka.2B Rhönschwalbe *(Reservn - old?)*	118	
D-3170	SZD-42-2 Jantar 2B	B-875	
D-3171	Schleicher ASW-20CL	20840	
D-3172	Schleicher ASK-21	21280	
D-3173	Glaser-Dirks DG-300 Elan	3E-151	
D-3174	Schempp-Hirth Standard Cirrus G	702	
D-3175	Glaser-Dirks DG-300 Elan	3E-470	
D-3176	Schempp-Hirth Nimbus 3/24.5	37	
D-3177	Glaser-Dirks DG-300 Elan	3E-149	
D-3178	Schleicher ASW-20L	20237	
D-3179	Rolladen-Schneider LS-4B	4994	
D-3180	PZL PW-5 Smyk	17.08.011	
D-3181	Schleicher ASW-20	20241	
D-3182	SZD-9bis Bocian 1E	P-588	DDR-3382
			DM-3382
D-3183	Glaser-Dirks DG-300 Elan	3E-148	
D-3184	Rolladen-Schneider LS-3A	3243	
D-3185	Schleicher ASW-24B	24235	
D-3186	Rolladen-Schneider LS-3-17	3251	
D-3187	Rolladen-Schneider LS-6C	6281	
D-3188	Schempp-Hirth Ventus b/16.6	127	
D-3189	Rolladen-Schneider LS-8A	8237	
D-3190	Schempp-Hirth Nimbus 3/24.5	40	
D-3191	Schempp-Hirth Ventus b	128	
D-3192	Schempp-Hirth Ventus b	130	
D-3193	Schempp-Hirth Mini-Nimbus C	133	
D-3194	Schempp-Hirth Mini-Nimbus C	134	
D-3195	Schempp-Hirth Mini-Nimbus C	135	
D-3196	Glaser-Dirks DG-500/22 Elan	5E-94S14	
D-3197	Schempp-Hirth Janus B	90	
D-3198	Rolladen-Schneider LS-4B	4995	
D-3199	Neukom S-4D Elfe	407AB	
D-3200	LET L-13 Blanik	027068	DDR-3201
			DM-3201
D-3201	Schleicher ASK-13	13091	
D-3203	LET L-13 Blanik	027361	DDR-3203
			DM-3203
D-3204	Glaser-Dirks DG-100	27	
D-3205	Focke-Wulf Kranich III	70	
D-3206	SZD-9bis Bocian 1E	P-508	DDR-3226
			DM-3226
D-3207	Scheibe Bergfalke III	5629	
D-3208	FES 530/II Lehrmeister *(Reservation 9.99)*	0152	DM-3152
D-3209	Schleicher ASK-13	13090	
D-3210	Schleicher Ka.6CR Rhönsegler	6005	
D-3211	Schleicher Ka.6CR Rhönsegler	6253/Si	
D-3212	Glaser-Dirks DG-300 Elan	3E-147	
D-3213	Glaser-Dirks DG-300 Elan	3E-145	
D-3214	Scheibe Spatz A	02	
D-3215	Schleicher K.8B	992	
D-3216	Scheibe L-Spatz 55	564	
D-3217	Schleicher Ka.6CR Rhönsegler	998	
D-3218	Scheibe L-Spatz 55	736	
D-3219	Schleicher Ka.6 Rhönsegler	221	
D-3220	Schleicher Ka.6CR Rhönsegler	6012	
D-3221	Scheibe Bergfalke II/55	273	
D-3222	Scheibe SF-27A	6023	
D-3223	Schempp-Hirth Duo Discus	205	
D-3224	Schleicher ASK-23	23021	
D-3225	Scheibe L-Spatz 55 *(Reservation - old?)*	628	
D-3226	SZD-9bis Bocian 1E	P-507	DDR-3225
			DM-3225
D-3227	Schleicher Ka.6BR Rhönsegler	414	
D-3228	Glaser-Dirks DG-300 Elan	3E-144	

Regn.	Type	C/n	Prev.Id.
D-3231	SZD-9bis Bocian 1E	P-517	DDR-3235
			DM-3235
D-3232	Schleicher K.8B	635	
D-3233	SZD-9bis Bocian 1E	P-525	DDR-3238
			DM-3238
D-3234	Schleicher K.8B	736	
D-3235-JP	Schempp-Hirth Nimbus 3/24.5	24	
D-3236	Schleicher Ka.6CR Rhönsegler	10	
D-3237	Schleicher ASK-21	21091	
D-3238	Schleicher ASK-21	21072	
D-3239	SZD-24-4A Foka 4	W-352	DDR-2239
			DM-2239
D-3240	Glasflügel H301 Libelle	3	
D-3242	Schleicher Ka.6CR Rhönsegler	6341/Si	
D-3243	SZD-9bis Bocian 1E	P-529	DDR-3242
			DM-3242
D-3244	Rolladen-Schneider LS-4A	4733	
D-3245	Schleicher Ka.6CR-PE Rhönsegler	6293/Bi	
D-3246	Glasflügel H201B Standard Libelle	472	
D-3247	Schleicher ASK-21	21074	
D-3248	SZD-9bis Bocian 1E	P-533	DDR-3246
			DM-3246
D-3249	Schleicher ASW-20L	20456	
D-3250	Schleicher ASK-13	13022	
D-3251	SZD-9bis Bocian 1E	P-537	DDR-3250
			DM-3250
D 3252	Rolladen-Schneider LS-1F	279	
D-3253	Rolladen-Schneider LS-1F	273	
D-3254	Schleicher ASK-21 *(Reservation 12.99)*	21707	
D-3255	Grob Standard Cirrus	456G	
D-3256	Glasflügel H201B Standard Libelle	543	
D-3257	Glasflügel H201B Standard Libelle	544	
D-3258	Rolladen-Schneider LS-1F	272	
D-3259	Scheibe Bergfalke III	5657	
D-3260	Rolladen-Schneider LS-1F *(Permit - old?)*	265	
D-3261	Schempp-Hirth Standard Cirrus B	398	
D-3262	Schempp-Hirth Standard Cirrus	420	
D-3263	Schempp-Hirth Standard Cirrus	445	
D-3264	Grob Standard Cirrus *(Permit - old?)*	533G	
D-3265	Schempp-Hirth Standard Cirrus	527	
D-3266	SZD-9bis Bocian 1E	P-493	DDR-3216
			DM-3216
D-3267	Schempp-Hirth Standard Cirrus	526	
D-3268	Schempp-Hirth Ventus 2a	54	
D-3269	Grob Standard Cirrus	517G	
D-3271	Schempp-Hirth Standard Cirrus	575	
D-3272	Schempp-Hirth Standard Cirrus	578	
D-3273	Grob G.102 Astir CS	1033	
D-3274	Grob G.102 Astir CS	1034	
D-3275	Grob G.102 Astir CS	1035	
D-3276	Grob G.102 Astir CS	1036	
D-3277-IY	Grob G.102 Astir CS	1037	
D-3278	Schleicher ASK-21	21292	
D-3279	Grob G.102 Astir CS	1039	
D-3280	Grob G.102 Astir CS	1040	
D-3281	SZD-9bis Bocian 1E	P-577	DDR-3381
			DM-3381
D-3282	Grob G.102 Astir CS	1042	
D-3283	Grob G.102 Astir CS	1056	
D-3284	Grob G.102 Astir CS	1057	
D-3285	SZD-9bis Bocian 1E	P-492	DDR-3215
			DM-3215
D-3286	Grob G.102 Astir CS	1062	
D-3288	Grob G.102 Astir CS	1064	
D-3289	Grob G.102 Astir CS	1065	
D-3290	Glaser-Dirks DG-300 Elan	3E-141	
D-3291	Grob G.102 Astir CS	1067	
D-3292	Grob G.102 Astir CS	1068	
D-3293	Schleicher ASW-20	20404	
D-3294	Schleicher ASK-21	21044	
D-3295	Schleicher ASW-20L	20402	OY-XXF
			D-3295
D-3296	Schleicher ASK-21	21045	
D-3297	Schleicher ASW-20L	20406	
D-3298	Glasflügel H303 Mosquito B	143	

Regn.	Type	C/n	Prev.Id.
D-3299	Glasflügel H303 Mosquito B	107	
D-3300	Glaser-Dirks DG-300 Club Elan	3E-269/C1	
D-3301	Grob G.102 Astir CS	1069	
D-3302	Grob G.102 Astir CS	1070	
D-3303	Grob G.102 Astir CS	1071	
D-3304	SZD-55-1	551196086	
D-3305	Grob G.102 Astir CS	1073	
D-3306	Grob G.102 Astir CS	1074	
D-3307	Grob G.102 Astir CS	1075	
D-3308	SZD-9bis Bocian 1E	P-558	DDR-3368
			DM-3368
D-3309-C7	Schempp-Hirth Discus b	548	
D-3310	Schleicher ASK-23B	23061	
D-3312	Grob G.102 Astir CS	1082	
D-3313	Glaser-Dirks DG-100G	90G10	
D-3314	Glaser-Dirks DG-100	92	
D-3315	Glaser-Dirks DG-100	94	
D-3316	Glaser-Dirks DG-100	23	
D-3317	Glaser-Dirks DG-200/17C	2-129/CL06	
D-3318	Glaser-Dirks DG-200/17C	2-131/CL08	
D-3319	Schleicher ASW-19B	19286	
D-3320	Glaser-Dirks DG-100G Elan	E90-G62	
D-3321	Glaser-Dirks DG-500 Elan Trainer	5E-77T33	
D-3322	Grob G.103 Twin II	3606	
D-3323	Schleicher ASW-20L	20138	
D-3324	Glaser-Dirks DG-300 Elan	3E-69	
D-3325	Glaser-Dirks DG-300 Elan	3E-70	
D-3326	Glaser-Dirks DG-500 Elan Trainer	5E-84T36	
D-3327	Schleicher ASW-19B	19254	
D-3328	SZD-9bis Bocian 1E	P-510	DDR-3228
			DM-3228
D-3329	Schleicher ASW-19B	19256	
D-3330	Schleicher ASW-20	20124	
D-3331	SZD-9bis Bocian 1E	P-600	DDR-3391
			DM-3391
D-3333	Start & Flug H101 Salto	51	
D-3334	Scheibe SF-34	5101	
D-3335	Pilatus B4-PC11AF	308	
D-3336	Schleicher ASW-24B	24239	
D-3339	Scheibe SF-34	5106	
D-3340	Schempp-Hirth Duo Discus	70	
D-3341	Scheibe SF-34	5107	
D-3342	Scheibe SF-34	5108	
D-3343	SZD-9bis Bocian 1E	P-589	DDR-3383
			DM-3383
D-3344	LET L-13 Blanik	026344	
D-3345	LET L-13 Blanik	025605	OY-VXH
D-3346	LET L-13 Blanik	026807	
D-3347	Glaser-Dirks DG-300 Elan	3E-71	
D-3348	LET L-13 Blanik	026527	
D-3349	SZD-9bis Bocian 1E	P-596	DDR-3389
			DM-3389
D-3350	Rolladen-Schneider LS-8A	8162	
D-3351	Glaser-Dirks DG-300 Elan	3E-73	
D-3353	LET L-13 Blanik	026858	
D-3354	Schleicher ASK-21	21285	
D-3355	Rolladen-Schneider LS-4	4035	
D-3356	SZD-9bis Bocian 1E	P-542	DDR-3355
			DM-3355
D-3357	Rolladen-Schneider LS-8A	8187	
D-3358	Rolladen-Schneider LS-4	4031	
D-3359	Rolladen-Schneider LS-4	4036	
D-3360	Rolladen-Schneider LS-4	4046	
D-3361	Rolladen-Schneider LS-8A	8238	
D-3362	LET L-13 Blanik	026841	
D-3363	Schempp-Hirth Mini-Nimbus C	112	
D-3364	Schempp-Hirth Duo Discus	154	
D-3365	SZD-9bis Bocian 1E	P-550	DDR-3363
			DM-3363
D-3366	Rolladen-Schneider LS-4B	4998	
D-3367	SZD-9bis Bocian 1E	P-547	DDR-3360
			DM-3360
D-3368	Schempp-Hirth Mini-Nimbus C	115	
D-3369	Schempp-Hirth Duo Discus	73	
D-3370	Schleicher ASK-21	21295	
D-3371	Schempp-Hirth Nimbus 2C	193	
D-3372	Schleicher ASK-21	21296	
D-3373	Schempp-Hirth Ventus 2c	35/91	
D-3374	Schleicher ASW-20L	20244	
D-3375	Schleicher ASW-19B	19283	
D-3376	SZD-9bis Bocian 1E	P-564	DDR-3374
			DM-3374
D-3377	Schleicher ASW-19B	19274	
D-3378	Schleicher ASW-20L	20250	
D-3379	Schleicher ASW-20	20252	
D-3380	Schleicher ASW-19B	19292	
D-3381	Schleicher Ka.6E	4034	OH-338
			OH-RSX
D-3383	Schleicher ASW-20	20295	
D-3384	Schleicher ASW-19B	19299	
D-3385	Glaser-Dirks DG-300 Elan	3E-188	
D-3386	Schleicher ASW-20	20298	
D-3387	Schleicher ASW-19B	19301	
D-3388	Glasflügel H303 Mosquito	84	
D-3389	Glasflügel H303 Mosquito	85	
D-3390	SZD-9bis Bocian 1E	P-609	DDR-3392
			DM-3392
D-3391	Rolladen-Schneider LS-4	4563	
D-3392	Rolladen-Schneider LS-4B	4895	
D-3393	SZD-9bis Bocian 1E	P-634	DDR-3397
			DM-3397
D-3394	Rolladen-Schneider LS-7	7065	
D-3395	Rolladen-Schneider LS-7	7066	
D-3396	Rolladen-Schneider LS-4B	4810	
D-3397	Rolladen-Schneider LS-4A	4811	
D-3398	Glaser-Dirks DG-300 Club Elan	3E454C78	
D-3399	Schleicher ASW-19	19095	
D-3401	Schleicher Ka.6CR Rhönsegler	6208	HB-774
D-3402	Schleicher K.8B	8481SH	HB-819
D-3403	Glasflügel H304	245	F-CEBR
D-3404	Glaser-Dirks DG-600	6-34	
D-3405	Rolladen-Schneider LS-6	6080	
D-3406	Rolladen-Schneider LS-4	4565	
D-3407	SZD-9bis Bocian 1E	P-719	DDR-3007
			DM-3007
D-3408	Rolladen-Schneider LS-4	4567	
D-3409	SZD-9bis Bocian 1E	P-486	DDR-3209
			DM-3209
D-3410	Schleicher ASW-20CL	20768	
D-3411	Schleicher ASK-23B	23003	
D-3412	Schleicher ASW-20C	20769	
D-3413	Schleicher ASW-20C	20770	
D-3414	Schleicher ASK-21	21230	
D-3415	Schleicher ASK-21	21229	
D-3416	Schleicher ASW-20CL	20773	
D-3417	Schleicher ASK-21	21233	
D-3418	Schleicher ASW-20C	20784	
D-3419	Schleicher ASW-20C	20777	
D-3420	Schleicher ASW-20CL	20783	
D-3421	Schleicher ASW-20CL	20788	
D-3422	Schleicher ASW-22	22037	
D-3423	Schleicher ASW-20C	20789	
D-3424	Schempp-Hirth Duo Discus	174	
D-3425	Schleicher ASK-23	23013	
D-3426	Schleicher ASW-20CL	20794	
D-3427	Schleicher ASK-23 (Permit - old?)	23017	
D-3428	Schleicher ASW-20C	20796	
D-3429	Schleicher ASK-21	21247	
D-3430	SZD-9bis Bocian 1E	P-512	DDR-3230
			DM-3230
D-3431	Schleicher ASW-20C	20811	
D-3432	SZD-48-3 Jantar Standard 3	B-1942	DDR-2432
D-3433	Schleicher ASK-21	21257	
D-3434	Schleicher ASK-23B	23025	
D-3435	SZD-48-3 Jantar Standard 3	B-1945	DDR-2435
D-3436	Rolladen-Schneider LS-4	4442	
D-3437	Rolladen-Schneider LS-4	4443	
D-3438	Rolladen-Schneider LS-4	4444	
D-3439	SZD-9bis Bocian 1E	P-526	DDR-3239
			DM-3239

Regn.	Type	C/n	Prev.Id.
D-3440	Rolladen-Schneider LS-4	4447	
D-3441	Rolladen-Schneider LS-8A	8163	
D-3442	Rolladen-Schneider LS-4	4455	
D-3443	Rolladen-Schneider LS-4	4454	
D-3444	Rolladen-Schneider LS-4	4449	
D-3445	Rolladen-Schneider LS-4	4457	
D-3446	Rolladen-Schneider LS-4B	4813	
D-3447-L4	Rolladen-Schneider LS-4A	4814	
D-3448	Glaser-Dirks DG-500/20 Elan	5E-127W2	
D-3449	Rolladen-Schneider LS-4	4495	
D-3450	Rolladen-Schneider LS-4	4463	
D-3451	Schleicher ASK-21	21548	
D-3452	Rolladen-Schneider LS-4	4464	
D-3453	Rolladen-Schneider LS-4B	4816	
D-3454	Rolladen-Schneider LS-4A	4817	
D-3455	Rolladen-Schneider LS-4	4475	
D-3456	Glaser-Dirks DG-100G Elan	E130-G98	LX-CDE(1)
D-3457	Schempp-Hirth Standard Cirrus	622	HB-1284
D-3458	Schempp-Hirth Ventus 2c *(Reservation 10.99)*	58/169	
D-3459	Rolladen-Schneider LS-4	4480	
D-3460	Glaser-Dirks DG-500 Elan Trainer	5E-130T56	
D-3461	Schleicher ASK-21	21386	
D-3462	Schleicher ASK-21	21387	
D-3463	Schleicher ASK-21	21550	
D-3464	Schleicher ASK-21	21388	
D-3465	Schleicher ASW-24	24017	
D-3466	Schleicher ASW-24	24018	
D-3467	Schleicher ASK-21	21389	
D-3468	Schleicher ASK-21	21390	
D-3469	Schleicher ASK-21	21391	
D-3470	Rolladen-Schneider LS-4	4503	
D-3471	Schempp-Hirth Discus CS *(Reservation 12.99)*	270CS	
D-3472	Schempp-Hirth Duo Discus	112	
D-3473	Schleicher ASW-24	24021	
D-3474	Schleicher ASH-25	25054	
D-3475	Schleicher ASK-21	21393	
D-3476	Schleicher ASK-21	21396	
D-3477	Schleicher ASH-25	25049	
D-3478	Rolladen-Schneider LS-4	4512	
D-3479	Rolladen-Schneider LS-4	4513	
D-3480	Schempp-Hirth Ventus c	546	
D-3481	Schleicher ASW-24	24214	
D-3482	Schleicher ASK-21	21584	
D-3483	Rolladen-Schneider LS-6C	6197	
D-3484	Rolladen-Schneider LS-4	4531	
D-3485	Rolladen-Schneider LS-4	4530	
D-3486	Rolladen-Schneider LS-8A	8135	
D-3487	Rolladen-Schneider LS-4	4528	
D-3488	Schempp-Hirth Discus CS	127CS	
D-3489	Rolladen-Schneider LS-4	4526	
D-3490	Schleicher ASK-21	21260	
D-3491	Schleicher ASW-20BL	20677	
D-3492	Schleicher ASK-23	23027	
D-3493	Schleicher ASW-20C	20824	
D-3494	Schleicher ASW-19B	19418	
D-3495	Schleicher ASW-20CL	20820	
D-3496	Schleicher ASK-23	23033	
D-3497	Schleicher ASK-23	23040	
D-3498	Schleicher ASK-23	23044	
D-3499	Schempp-Hirth Ventus 2c	34/90	
D-3500	Grob G.102 Speed Astir IIB	4082	
D-3501	Rolladen-Schneider LS-4	4268	
D-3502	Rolladen-Schneider LS-4B	4821	
D-3503	Rolladen-Schneider LS-4B	4822	
D-3504	Rolladen-Schneider LS-4	4178	
D-3505	Schleicher ASW-20CL	20736	
D-3506	Schleicher ASW-20C	20723	
D-3507	Schleicher ASW-20C *(Permit 4.99)*	20724	
D-3508	Rolladen-Schneider LS-4	4213	
D-3509	Rolladen-Schneider LS-4B	4823	
D-3510	Grob G.103A Twin II Acro	3657-K-26	
D-3511	Grob G.102 Club Astir IIIB	5571CB	
D-3512	Grob G.102 Club Astir IIIB	5572CB	
D-3513	SZD-9bis Bocian 1E	P-726	DDR-3013 DM-3013
D-3514	Rolladen-Schneider LS-3-17	3154	
D-3515	Rolladen-Schneider LS-4	4524	
D-3516	Rolladen-Schneider LS-4	4521	
D-3517	Rolladen-Schneider LS-3-17	3289	
D-3518	Schempp-Hirth Discus b	448	
D-3519	Schempp-Hirth Janus C	48	OO-ZCE
D-3521	Schempp-Hirth Duo Discus	78	
D-3522	Schleicher ASW-22	22035	
D-3523	Rolladen-Schneider LS-3-17	3330	
D-3524	Schleicher ASW-19B	19379	
D-3525	Schleicher ASW-19B	19380	
D-3526	Rolladen-Schneider LS-4B	4824	
D-3527	Rolladen-Schneider LS-4B	4912	
D-3528	Rolladen-Schneider LS-4A	4826	
D-3529	Schempp-Hirth Discus b	471	
D-3530	Rolladen-Schneider LS-3-17	3322	
D-3531	Schempp-Hirth Nimbus 3/24.5	41	
D-3532	SZD-9bis Bocian 1E	P-514	DDR-3232 DM-3232
D-3533	Schempp-Hirth Ventus b/16.6	145	
D-3534	SG-38 Schulgleiter	8	
D-3535	Glasflügel H201B Standard Libelle	142	
D-3536	Schleicher ASK-13	AB13433	RAFGGA535 D-3535
D-3537	Rolladen-Schneider LS-3A	3433	
D-3538	Rolladen-Schneider LS-3A	3434	
D-3539	Rolladen-Schneider LS-4B	4841	
D-3540	SZD-9bis Bocian 1E	P-461	DDR-3040 DM-3040
D-3541	Rolladen-Schneider LS-4	4570	
D-3542	Rolladen-Schneider LS-4	4571	
D-3543	Schempp-Hirth Ventus 2c *(For conversion to Ventus 2cM c/n 64/132 as D-KBVG)*	46/132	
D-3544	Schleicher ASK-21	21297	
D-3545	Rolladen-Schneider LS-3-17	3282	
D-3546	Schleicher ASW-20C	20805	
D-3547	Rolladen-Schneider LS-8A	8071	
D-3548	SZD-9bis Bocian 1E	P-527	DDR-3240 DM-3240
D-3549	Schleicher Ka.6 Rhönsegler	198	
D-3550	Glasflügel H303 Mosquito B	194	
D-3551	Schempp-Hirth Ventus b/16.6	76	
D-3552	Schempp-Hirth Ventus A	1	
D-3553	Rolladen-Schneider LS-4	4071	
D-3554	Vogt LO-100 Zwergreiher	101AB	
D-3555	Schleicher Ka.6CR Rhönsegler	788	
D-3556	Rolladen-Schneider LS-4	4360	
D-3557	Rolladen-Schneider LS-4	4408	
D-3558	Schleicher ASK-13	13209	RAFGGA554
D-3559	Rolladen-Schneider LS-4	4104	
D-3560	Schleicher Ka.6BR Rhönsegler	360	
D-3561	Rolladen-Schneider LS-4	4078	
D-3562	Schleicher ASW-20C	20750	
D 3563	Schleicher ASW-19B	19405	
D-3564	Rolladen-Schneider LS-4B	4877	
D-3565	Schleicher K.8B	480	D-KAMP D-3565
D-3566	Grob G.103A Twin II Acro	3814-K-75	
D-3567	Grob G.103A Twin II Acro	3827-K-84	
D-3568	SZD-9bis Bocian 1E	P-753	DDR-3068 DM-3068
D-3569	Grob G.103A Twin II Acro	3826-K-83	
D-3570	Schleicher K.8	519	
D-3571	Rolladen-Schneider LS-8A	8086	
D-3572	Bölkow Phoebus B-1	721	
D-3573	Schleicher ASW-20C	20848	
D-3574	Rolladen-Schneider LS-4	4070	
D-3575	Rolladen-Schneider LS-4	4105	
D-3576	Rolladen-Schneider LS-4	4111	
D-3577	Rolladen-Schneider LS-4	4109	
D-3578	Rolladen-Schneider LS-4	4110	
D-3579	Grunau Baby IIB *(Reservation 4.99)*	11	
D-3580	Glaser-Dirks DG-300 Elan Acro	3E-479A22	
D-3581	Rolladen-Schneider LS-4	4331	
D-3582	Rolladen-Schneider LS-4A	4818	

Regn.	Type	C/n	Prev.Id.
D-3583	Rolladen-Schneider LS-4B	4819	
D-3584	Schleicher Rhönlerche II	55	
D-3585	Glaser-Dirks DG-300 Elan	3E-44	
D-3586	Glaser-Dirks DG-300 Elan	3E-45	
D-3587	Schleicher ASW-24	24210	
D-3588	SZD-50-3 Puchacz	B-2112	
D-3589	Schleicher ASK-21	21299	
D-3590	SZD-9bis Bocian 1E	P-599	DDR-3390
			DM-3390
D-3591	Schleicher K7 Rhönadler	1034	
D-3592	Rolladen-Schneider LS-4B	4844	
D-3593	Schleicher K.8B	8030	
D-3594	Schleicher K.8B	8008	
D-3595	Schleicher Rhönlerche II	2	
D-3596	Rolladen-Schneider LS-8A	8048	
D-3597	Schleicher K7 Rhönadler	7041	
D-3598	Rolladen-Schneider LS-8A	8042	
D-3599	Grob G.103C Twin III Acro	34149	D-KGSL
D-3600	Schempp-Hirth Janus C	189	
D-3601	Schleicher K7 Rhönadler	7043	
D-3602	Schleicher K.8B	8070	
D-3603	SZD-50-3 Puchacz	B-1087	DDR-3603
D-3604	Schempp-Hirth Discus 2b (Reservation - old?)	16	
D-3605	Rolladen-Schneider LS-8A	8049	
D-3606	Schleicher K.8B	8726	
D-3607	Schleicher Rhönlerche II	1/62	
D-3608	Rolladen-Schneider LS-4B	41024	
D-3609	Rolladen-Schneider LS-4B	4828	
D-3610	Schleicher K7 Rhönadler	7111	
D-3611	SZD-50-3 Puchacz	B-1328	DDR-3611
D-3612	Rolladen-Schneider LS-4A	4829	
D-3613	Rolladen-Schneider LS-4B	4830	
D-3614	Schleicher K.8B	8310	
D-3615	Schleicher Ka.6CR Rhönsegler	6238	
D-3616	Rolladen-Schneider LS-4	4580	
D-3617	SZD-50-3 Puchacz	B-1388	DDR-3627
D-3618	Schleicher Ka.6CR Rhönsegler	6254Si	
D-3619	Schleicher K-10A	10002	
D-3620	SZD-50-3 Puchacz	B-1344	DDR-3625
D-3621	Schleicher Ka.3	102	
D-3622	Schleicher K.8B	8398	
D-3623	Schleicher K.8B	8408	
D-3624	Schleicher ASW-24	24035	
D-3626	Rolladen-Schneider LS-8A	8087	
D-3628	Rolladen-Schneider LS-4	4582	
D-3629	Schleicher K-10A	10012	
D-3630	SZD-50-3 Puchacz	B-1465	DDR-3639
D-3631	SZD-50-3 Puchacz	B-1400	DDR-3634
D-3632	Scheibe L-Spatz III	812	
D-3633	Schleicher K.8B	8532	
D-3634	Schleicher K.8B	8531	
D-3635	SZD-24-4A Foka 4	W-294	
D-3636	Schleicher K-10A	10009	
D-3637	Grunau Baby IIB	04304	
D-3638	Schleicher ASK-21	21282	
D-3639	SZD-24-4A Foka 4	W-239	
D-3640	Schempp-Hirth Duo Discus (Reservation 11.99)	242	
D-3641	Schleicher ASW-20CL	20752	
D-3643	Schleicher K7 Rhönadler	7274	
D-3644	SZD-50-3 Puchacz	B-1474	DDR-3644
D-3645	Schleicher K.8B	8635	
D-3646	Bölkow Phoebus A-1	764	
D-3647	Schleicher K.8B	8633	
D-3648	Schleicher Ka.6CR Rhönsegler	6567	
D-3649	SZD-50-3 Puchacz	B-1480	DDR-3648
D-3650	Rolladen-Schneider LS-6	6036	
D-3651	SZD-50-3 Puchacz	B-1535	DDR-3651
D-3652	SZD-50-3 Puchacz	B-1542	DDR-3658
D-3653	Rolladen-Schneider LS-6	6039	
D-3654	Focke-Wulf Weihe 50	3	
D-3655	SZD-50-3 Puchacz	B-1540	DDR-3656
D-3657	Schleicher Ka.6E	4084	
D-3658	Schleicher K.8B	8711	
D-3659	Rolladen-Schneider LS-4	4389	
D-3661	SZD-30 Pirat	W-318	
D-3662	Fauvel AV-36C	573	
D-3663	Glaser-Dirks DG-100	74	HB-1327
D-3664	Schleicher Ka.6CR Rhönsegler	6621Si	
D-3665	SZD-50-3 Puchacz	B-1552	DDR-3661
D-3666	Schempp-Hirth Janus CE	283	
D-3667	Scheibe L-Spatz III (Reservation)	241	
D-3668	Rolladen-Schneider LS-4	4572	
D-3670	Schleicher ASK-13	13082	
D-3671	SZD-50-3 Puchacz	B-1394	DDR-3631
D-3672	Rolladen-Schneider LS-4	4574	
D-3673	Rolladen-Schneider LS-7	7137	
D-3674	Grob G.103C Twin III Acro	34186	
D-3675	LET L-13 Blanik	026506	
D-3676	SZD-50-3 Puchacz	B-1387	DDR-3626
D-3677	LET L-13 Blanik	026057	
D-3678	Rolladen-Schneider LS-4	4166	
D-3679	Schleicher ASK-21	21588	
D-3680	Rolladen-Schneider LS-8A	8110	
D-3681	Rolladen-Schneider LS-4	4241	
D-3682	Rolladen-Schneider LS-6C	6328	
D-3683	Grob Standard Cirrus	465G	
D-3684	SZD-50-3 Puchacz	B-1331	DDR-3614
D-3685	SZD-9bis Bocian 1E	P-522	DDR-3385
			DM-3385
D-3686	Rolladen-Schneider LS-1F	198	
D-3687	SZD-50-3 Puchacz	B-1479	DDR-3647
D-3688	Schempp-Hirth Standard Cirrus	447	
D-3689	Schempp-Hirth Standard Cirrus	457	
D-3691	Grob Standard Cirrus	464G	
D-3692	Grob Standard Cirrus	467G	
D-3693	Schleicher ASW-15B	15268	HB-1093
D-3694	Glasflügel H401 Kestrel	109	
D-3695	Grob G.103C Twin III Acro	34133	
D-3696	Grob G.103C Twin III Acro	34131	
D-3697	Grob G.103C Twin III Acro	34127	
D-3698	Rolladen-Schneider LS-8A	8136	
D-3699	Scheibe Bergfalke IV	5841	
D-3700	Scheibe Bergfalke IV	5842	
D-3701	Scheibe Bergfalke IV	5843	
D-3702	Schempp-Hirth Discus CS	226CS	
D-3703	Glasflügel H401 Kestrel	110	
D-3704	Glasflügel H201B Standard Libelle	552	
D-3705	Grob Standard Cirrus	471G	
D-3706	Grob Standard Cirrus	472G	
D-3707	Glasflügel H201B Standard Libelle	561	
D-3708	Rolladen-Schneider LS-4B	4846	
D-3709	Pilatus B4-PC11	115	
D-3710	LET L-13 Blanik	026018	
D-3711	Rolladen-Schneider LS-6C	6201	
D-3712	Glasflügel H401 Kestrel	112	
D-3713	Rolladen-Schneider LS-3A	3283	
D-3714	Glasflügel H401 Kestrel	114	
D-3715	Glasflügel H201B Standard Libelle	568	
D-3716	Glasflügel H201B Standard Libelle	565	
D-3717	Rolladen-Schneider LS-1F	295	
D-3718	Grob Standard Cirrus	470G	
D-3719	Rolladen-Schneider LS-1F	375	F-CEHZ
D-3720	Schleicher ASW-20	20346	
D-3722	Glaser-Dirks DG-300 Elan	3E-232	
D-3723	Rolladen-Schneider LS-4B	4848	
D-3724	Glaser-Dirks DG-100	6	
D-3725-PW	Rolladen-Schneider LS-8A	8053	
D-3726	Rolladen-Schneider LS-4B	4849	
D-3727	Glaser-Dirks DG-100	9	
D-3728	Glaser-Dirks DG-100	10	
D-3729	Pilatus B4-PC11	137	
D-3730	Rolladen-Schneider LS-4B	4850	
D-3732	Glaser-Dirks DG-100	19	
D-3733	Glaser-Dirks DG-300 Elan	3E-116	
D-3734	Glaser-Dirks DG-100	21	
D-3736	Glaser-Dirks DG-100	28	
D-3737	Glaser-Dirks DG-100	29	
D-3738	Schleicher ASW-20BL	20695	
D-3739	Glaser-Dirks DG-100	32	
D-3740	Glaser-Dirks DG-100	38	

Regn.	Type	C/n	Prev.Id.
D-3741	Glaser-Dirks DG100G Elan	E39-G21	
D-3742	SZD-50-3 Puchacz	B-1472	DDR-3642
D-3743	Schleicher ASK-18	18016	
D-3744	Schleicher ASK-13	13524	
D-3745	Schleicher ASK-18	18018	
D-3746	Schleicher ASK-13	13525	
D-3747	Schleicher ASK-18	18019	
D-3748	Schleicher ASK-18	18020	
D-3749	Schleicher ASW-19	19002	
D-3750	Schleicher ASW-19	19003	
D-3751	Rolladen-Schneider LS-8A	8054	
D-3752	Schleicher ASW-15B	15451	
D-3753	Schleicher ASK-13	13533	
D-3754	Schleicher ASW-19	19005	
D-3755	Schleicher ASW-19	19006	
D-3756	Schleicher ASK-13	13534	
D-3757-B-10	Rolladen-Schneider LS-4B	4854	
D-3758	Schleicher ASW-15B	15453	
D-3759	SZD-30 Pirat	B-363	DDR-1759
			DM-1759
D-3760	Schleicher ASK-13	13535	
D-3761	Schleicher ASW-19	19008	
D-3762	Schleicher ASW-19	19009	
D-3763	Schleicher ASK-13	13536	
D-3764	Rolladen-Schneider LS-8A	8055	
D-3765-ICH	Schleicher ASW-24	24081	
D-3766	Schleicher ASK-21	21453	
D-3767	Schleicher ASW-19	19013	
D-3768	Glaser-Dirks DG-100G Elan	E32-G17	
D-3769	Glaser-Dirks DG-100 Elan	E-29	
D-3770	SZD-30 Pirat *(Reservation 10.99)*	B-398	DDR-1769
			DM1769
D-3771	Glaser-Dirks DG-100 Elan	E-25	
D-3772	Schempp-Hirth Ventus 2b *(Permit 3.99)*	84	
D-3773	Glaser-Dirks DG-100 Elan	E-23	
D-3774	Glaser-Dirks DG-100G Elan	E21-G11	
D-3775	Glaser-Dirks DG-100G Elan	E22-G12	
D-3776	Rolladen-Schneider LS-4B	4855	
D-3777	Glasflügel H205 Club Libelle	80	
D-3778	Grob G.102 Club Astir III	5550C	
D-3779	Grob G.103 Twin II	3668	
D-3780	Grob G.103A Twin II Acro	3677-K-28	
D-3781	Grob G.103 Twin II	3659	
D-3782	Schempp-Hirth Janus B	86	
D-3783	Schempp-Hirth Nimbus 2B	144	
D-3784	Schempp-Hirth Nimbus 2B	146	
D-3785	Schempp-Hirth Janus	39	
D-3786	SZD-30 Pirat	B-429	DDR-1786
			DM-1786
D-3787	Schempp-Hirth Janus	35	
D-3788	Schempp-Hirth Janus	09	
D-3790	Grob G.102 Club Astir III	5577C	
D-3791	Schleicher ASK-21	21454	
D-3792	Schleicher ASW-24	24085	
D-3793	Schleicher ASK-21	21457	
D-3794	Schleicher ASK-21	21458	
D-3795	Schempp-Hirth HS-7 Mini-Nimbus	23	
D-3796	Glaser-Dirks DG-200/17C	2-111/CL03	
D-3797	Glaser-Dirks DG-200/17	2-110/1718	
D-3798	Glaser-Dirks DG-200/17C	2-108/CL01	
D-3799	Schempp-Hirth Discus 2A *(Reservation - old?)*	33	
D-3800	*Test Registration for Glaser-Dirks production*		
D-3801	Glaser-Dirks DG-100	103	
D-3802	Glaser-Dirks DG-100G	98G14	
D-3803	Glaser-Dirks DG-100G	97G13	
D-3804	Glaser-Dirks DG-200/17	2-124/1720	
D-3805	SZD-50-3 Puchacz	B-1089	DDR-3605
D-3806	Glaser-Dirks DG-100G	101G15	
D-3807	SZD-50-3 Puchacz	B-1093	DDR-3607
D-3808	Glaser-Dirks DG-200/17	2-100/1712	
D-3809	Glaser-Dirks DG-200/17	2-102/1713	
D-3810	Glaser-Dirks DG-200/17	2-103/1714	
D-3811	Glaser-Dirks DG-200/17	2-107/1717	
D-3812	Rolladen-Schneider LS-4B	4856	
D-3813	Grob G.102 Astir CS Jeans	2190	

Regn.	Type	C/n	Prev.Id.
D-3814	Grob G.102 Astir CS Jeans	2191	
D-3815	Grob G.102 Astir CS Jeans	2192	
D-3816	Rolladen-Schneider LS-4B	41018	
D-3817	Grob G.102 Astir CS Jeans	2195	
D-3818	SZD-30 Pirat	B-492	DDR-1818
			DM-1818
D-3819	Grob G.102 Astir CS Jeans	2199	
D-3820	Grob G.102 Speed Astir II	4002	
D-3821	Schleicher ASK-21	21646	
D-3822	Grob G.102 Astir CS Jeans	2203	
D-3823	Rolladen-Schneider LS-8A	8056	
D-3824	Grob G.102 Astir CS Jeans	2208	
D-3826	Grob G.102 Astir CS Jeans	2212	
D-3827	SZD-30 Pirat	B-506	DDR-1827
			DM-1827
D-3828	Grob G.102 Astir CS Jeans	2215	
D-3830	Grob G.102 Astir CS Jeans	2217	
D-3831	Grob G.102 Astir CS Jeans	2218	
D-3832-SK	Rolladen-Schneider LS-8A	8089	
D-3833	Grob G.102 Speed Astir II	4003	
D-3834	Schempp-Hirth Janus CE	279	
D-3835	Grob G.102 Speed Astir II	4007	
D-3836-AV	Schempp-Hirth Duo Discus	177	
D-3837	Rolladen-Schneider LS-1F	337	HB-1237
D-3839	Grob G.102 Speed Astir II	4013	
D-3840	Schempp-Hirth Ventus 2c	22/58	
D-3841	Schleicher ASW-19	19092	
D-3842	Schleicher ASW-19	19093	
D-3843	Schleicher ASK-13	13565	
D-3844	Schleicher ASW-19	19096	
D-3845	Schleicher ASK-21	21447	
D-3846	Schleicher ASW-24	24087	
D-3847	Schleicher ASW-19	19098	
D-3848	Schleicher ASW-19	19099	
D-3849	Schleicher ASW-19	19100	
D-3850	Schleicher ASW-17	17052	
D-3851	Schleicher ASK-21	21459	
D-3852	Schleicher ASW-24	24093	
D-3853	Schleicher ASW-19	19102	
D-3854	Schleicher ASK-13	13570	
D-3855	Schleicher ASW-19	19103	
D-3856	Grunau Baby IIB	03	
D-3857	Schleicher ASK-21	21047	D-8807
D-3858	Schleicher ASK-13	13571	
D-3859	Glaser-Dirks DG-8A	8188	
D-3860	Schempp-Hirth Duo Discus	46	
D-3861	Schleicher ASW-20	20005	
D-3863	Schleicher ASW-19	19107	
D-3864	Schleicher ASK-13	13572	
D-3865	Rolladen-Schneider LS-4	4022	
D-3866	Schleicher ASK-21	21173	
D-3867	Schleicher ASK-21	21178	
D-3868	Schleicher ASK-21	21177	
D-3869	Rolladen-Schneider LS-4	4045	
D-3870	Bölkow Phoebus C	939	
D-3871	Bölkow Phoebus C-2 *(Permit 5.99)*	954	
D-3872	Rolladen-Schneider LS-7	7145	
D-3873	Rolladen-Schneider LS-7	7146	
D-3874	Grob G.102 Astir CS Jeans	2011	
D-3875	Rolladen-Schneider LS-7	7147	
D-3876	Grob G.102 Astir CS Jeans	2027	
D-3877	Glaser-Dirks DG-500 Elan Orion	5E-162X17	
D-3878	Grob G.102 Astir CS Jeans	2032	
D-3879	SZD-9bis Bocian 1E	P-575	DDR-3379
			DM-3379
D-3880	Rolladen-Schneider LS-4B	4858	
D-3881	Grob G.102 Astir CS Jeans	2035	
D-3882	Glaser-Dirks DG-300 Club Elan Acro	3E-477C85A21	
D-3883-83	Schempp-Hirth Discus b	92	
D-3884	Grob G.102 Astir CS Jeans	2039	
D-3885	Grob G.102 Astir CS Jeans	2041	
D-3886	Grob G.102 Astir CS Jeans	2042	
D-3888	Grob G.102 Astir CS Jeans	2049	
D-3889	Grob G.102 Astir CS Jeans	2050	
D-3890	Grob G.102 Astir CS Jeans	2052	

Regn.	Type	C/n	Prev.Id.
D-3891	Grob G.102 Astir CS Jeans	2063	
D-3892	Grob G.102 Astir CS Jeans	2054	
D-3893	Rolladen-Schneider LS-3A	3153	
D-3894	SZD-30 Pirat	S-03.09	DDR-1894
			DM-1894
D-3895	Rolladen-Schneider LS-3	3104	
D-3896	Rolladen-Schneider LS-3 (Permit 3.99)	3078	
D-3897	Rolladen-Schneider LS-7	7149	
D-3898	Rolladen-Schneider LS-3	3164	
D-3899	Glaser-Dirks DG-800S	8-79S22	
D-3900	Rolladen-Schneider LS-3	3106	
D-3901	SZD-9bis Bocian 1E	P-706	DDR-3001
			DM-3001
D-3903	Rolladen-Schneider LS-7	7150	
D-3904	Glaser-Dirks DG-500 Elan Orion	5E-158X15	
D-3905	Schempp-Hirth Standard Cirrus	518	
D-3906	Schempp-Hirth Discus b	146	PH-777
D-3907	SZD-30 Pirat	S-03.47	DDR-1907
			DM-1907
D-3908	Rolladen-Schneider LS-4	4279	
D-3909	Rolladen-Schneider LS-4	4283	
D-3910	Rolladen-Schneider LS-4	4289	
D-3911	Rolladen-Schneider LS-4	4302	
D-3912	Rolladen-Schneider LS-3	3208	
D-3913	Schleicher ASK-21	21465	
D-3914	Schleicher ASK-21	21462	
D-3915	SZD-9bis Bocian 1E	P-728	DDR-3015
			DM-3015
D-3916	Rolladen-Schneider LS-3-AKE (Permit 7.99)	3341	
D-3917	Rolladen-Schneider LS-3-AKE (Permit 2.99)	3342	
D-3918	Schempp-Hirth Discus CS	069CS	
D-3919	Rolladen-Schneider LS-7	7152	
D-3920	Rolladen-Schneider LS-3A	3156	
D-3921	Rolladen-Schneider LS-3A	3296	
D-3922	Rolladen-Schneider LS-3A	3188	
D-3923	Grob G.102 Club Astir IIIB	5652CB	
D-3924	Rolladen-Schneider LS-3A	3152	
D-3925	Rolladen-Schneider LS-3A	3151	
D-3926	Rolladen-Schneider LS-3A	3155	
D-3927	Rolladen-Schneider LS-3A	3161	
D-3928	Schleicher ASK-21	21397	
D-3929	Schleicher ASK-21	21398	
D-3930	Schleicher ASK-21	21399	
D-3931	Schleicher ASK-21	21401	
D-3932	Schleicher ASK-21	21402	
D-3933	Rolladen-Schneider LS-3-17	3294	
D-3934	Rolladen-Schneider LS-8-18 (Permit 11.99)	8286	
D-3935	Rolladen-Schneider LS-3A	3408	
D-3936	Rolladen-Schneider LS-3A	3407	
D-3937	Rolladen-Schneider LS-3-17	3268	
D-3938	Glaser-Dirks DG-200/17	2-191/1764	
D-3939	Schleicher ASW-22	22020	
D-3940	Darmstadt D-40 (Permit 4.99)	41	
D-3941	SZD-9bis Bocian 1E	P-464	DDR-3041
			DM-3041
D-3942	Rolladen-Schneider LS-3A	3202	
D-3943	SZD-9bis Bocian 1E	P-530	DDR-3243
			DM-3243
D-3944	Grob G.103 Twin Astir	3081	
D-3945	Grob G.103 Twin Astir	3083	
D-3946	Grob G.103 Twin Astir	3085	
D-3947	Grob G.103 Twin Astir	3086	
D-3948	Schempp-Hirth Ventus 2a	38	
D-3949	Schempp-Hirth Duo Discus	220	
D-3950	Schempp-Hirth Duo Discus	51	
D-3951	Grob G.103 Twin Astir Trainer	3095	
D-3952	Glaser-Dirks DG-300 Elan	3E-468	
D-3953	Grob G.103 Twin Astir	3097	
D-3954	Grob G.103 Twin Astir	3084	
D-3955	Rolladen-Schneider LS-4B	4859	
D-3956	Grob G.103 Twin Astir	3099	
D-3957	Grob G.103 Twin Astir	3100	
D-3958	Schempp-Hirth Duo Discus	224	
D-3959	Schleicher ASH-25	25018	
D-3960	Schempp-Hirth Discus CS	072CS	
D-3962	Rolladen-Schneider LS-8A	8189	
D-3963	Rolladen-Schneider LS-8A	8090	
D-3964	Grob G.103 Twin II	3597	
D-3965	Grob G.103 Twin II	3598	
D-3966	Grob G.103 Twin II	3599	
D-3967	Schleicher ASK-13	13268AB	
D-3969	Schleicher ASW-15B	15421	
D-3970	Schleicher ASW-15B	15422	
D-3971	Schleicher ASK-13	13503	
D-3972	Schleicher ASW-15B	15423	
D-3973	Schleicher ASW-15B	15424	
D-3974	Schleicher ASW-15B	15425	
D-3975	Schleicher ASW-17	17041	
D-3976	Rolladen-Schneider LS-8A	8239	
D-3977	Schleicher ASK-13	13504	
D-3978	Schleicher ASK-13	13154	
D-3979	Schleicher ASW-15	15084	
D-3980	Schleicher ASW-15B	15426	
D-3981	Schleicher ASW-15B	15434	
D-3982	Schleicher ASK-13	13505	
D-3983	Schleicher ASW-15B	15431	
D-3984	Schleicher ASW-15B	15432	
D-3985	Schleicher ASW-15B	15433	
D-3986	Schleicher ASK-13	13507	
D-3987	Schleicher ASK-13	13508	
D-3988	SZD-50-3 Puchacz	B-2110	
D-3989	Schleicher ASK-21	21508	
D-3990	Schleicher ASW-15B	15435	
D-3991	Schleicher ASK-18	18006	
D-3992	Schempp-Hirth Duo Discus	176	
D-3993	Pilatus B4-PC11AF	310	
D-3994	Schleicher ASK-21	21509	
D-3995	Grob G.102 Club Astir IIIB	5546CB	
D-3996	Grob G.102 Club Astir IIIB	5549CB	
D-3997	Grob G.102 Club Astir III	5555C	
D-3998	Rolladen-Schneider LS-1F	262	
D-3999	Schleicher K.8B	8968AB	
D-4000	Scheibe SF-27A	6022	
D-4001	Glasflügel H401 Kestrel	64	PH-400
			D-0972
D-4003	Schleicher Rhönlerche II	1119	
D-4004	Schleicher ASW-19B	19112	
D-4005	Glaser-Dirks DG-300 Elan Acro	3E-451A11	S5-3333
D-4006	Glasflügel H205 Club Libelle	5	
D-4007	Focke-Wulf Kranich III	56	
D-4009	Glaser-Dirks DG-300 Elan Acro	3E-446A9	
D-4010	Schempp-Hirth Duo Discus	100	
D-4011	Schleicher K.8B	126	
D-4012	Glasflügel H401 Kestrel	15	I-JOJO
D-4013	Schempp-Hirth Ventus b/16.6	270	
D-4014	Schempp-Hirth Discus b	57	
D-4015	Schempp-Hirth Janus B	212	
D-4016	Start & Flug H-101 Salto	49	
D-4018	Rolladen-Schneider LS-4B	4972	
D-4019	Schempp-Hirth Discus b	66	
D-4020	Schempp-Hirth Duo Discus	183	
D-4021	Schempp-Hirth Duo Discus	202	
D-4022	Schleicher Ka.6CR Rhönsegler	6409	
D-4023	SZD-9bis Bocian 1E	P-448	DDR-3023
			DM-3023
D-4024	Schleicher Rhönlerche II	3037	
D-4025	Schleicher ASW-15	15145	HB-1025
D-4026	Scheibe SF-27A	6030	
D-4027	SZD-9bis Bocian 1E	P-452	DDR-3027
			DM-3027
D-4028	Schempp-Hirth Ventus 2b	52	
D-4029	Rolladen-Schneider LS-4B	4860	
D-4030	Rolladen-Schneider LS-4B	4973	
D-4031	Schleicher K7 Rhönadler	890	
D-4032	Schleicher Rhönlerche II	112	
D-4033	SZD-9bis Bocian 1E	P-457	DDR-3033
			DM-3033
D-4035	Grob G.103C Twin III Acro	34148	
D-4036	Schleicher Ka.6CR Rhönsegler	1110	
D-4037	Scheibe SF-27A	6016	

Regn.	Type	C/n	Prev.Id.
D-4038	Schleicher Ka.2 Rhönschwalbe	125	
D-4039	Schleicher K7 Rhönadler	7083	
D-4040	Glaser-Dirks DG-500 Elan Trainer	5E-112T46	
D-4041	Schleicher Ka.6BR Rhönsegler	358	
D-4042	SZD-9bis Bocian 1E	P-465	DDR-3042
			DM-3042
D-4043	Rolladen-Schneider LS-4	4616	
D-4044	Rolladen-Schneider LS-4	4274	
D-4045	Schleicher Rhönlerche II	132	
D-4046	Rolladen-Schneider LS-4	4617	
D-4047	SZD-9bis Bocian 1E	P-470	DDR-3047
			DM-3047
D-4048	Schempp-Hirth Discus b	18	
D-4049	Schleicher Ka.6 Rhönsegler	280	
D-4050	Glasflügel Mosquito B	181	OH-569
D-4051	Schleicher ASK-21	21491	
D-4052	Schempp-Hirth Duo Discus	81	
D-4053	Scheibe SF-27A	6107	
D-4054	Schleicher Ka.6BR Rhönsegler	525	
D-4055	Rolladen-Schneider LS-4	4619	
D-4056	Rolladen-Schneider LS-4	4620	
D-4058	Rolladen-Schneider LS-6C	6218	
D-4059	Glasflügel H201B Standard Libelle	286	HB-1059
D-4061	Schempp-Hirth Ventus b/16.6	35	
D-4062	Schleicher K.8B	8417	
D-4063	Rolladen-Schneider LS-6C	6237	
D-4064	Rolladen-Schneider LS-8-18 *(Permit 3.99)*	8240	
D-4065	Siebert SIE-3 *(Permit 11.99)*	3013	
D-4066	Schleicher Ka.6CR Rhönsegler *(Reservation)*	959	
D-4067	Schleicher Ka.6CR Rhönsegler	6226Si	
D-4068	Schleicher K.8B	755	
D-4069	Schleicher K7 Rhönadler	Liz.172/60	
D-4070	Scheibe L-Spatz 55	718	
D-4071	Schleicher Ka.6CR Rhönsegler *(Reservation - old?)*	1043	
D-4072	Schleicher K.8B	8256	
D-4073	Rolladen-Schneider LS-8A	8017	
D-4074	Grob G.103C Twin III Acro	34139	
D-4075	Schleicher Ka.6E	4140	
D-4076	Schleicher K7 Rhönadler	833	
D-4077	Schleicher Ka.6CR Rhönsegler	1070	
D-4078	Schleicher K.8B	1146	
D-4079	Schleicher Ka.6E	4036	
D-4080	Schleicher ASK-23B	23145	
D-4081	Schleicher K.8B	Liz.182/60	
D-4082	Grob G.103C Twin III Acro	34137	
D-4083	Schleicher Ka.6CR Rhönsegler	1074	
D-4084	Rolladen-Schneider LS-6C	6238	
D-4085	SZD-48-1 Jantar Standard 2	B-1221	OE-5303
D-4086	Rolladen-Schneider LS-6C	6239	
D-4087	Schleicher ASW-20L	20359	
D-4088	Schleicher ASK-21	21029	
D-4089	Schleicher ASK-21	21060	
D-4090	Schleicher ASW-20	20360	
D-4091-91	Schempp-Hirth Discus b	562	
D-4092	Rolladen-Schneider LS-6C	6219	
D-4093	Schempp-Hirth Discus 2b *(Permit 4.99)*	29	
D-4094	Schempp-Hirth Duo Discus	107	
D-4095	Rolladen-Schneider LS-6C	6240	
D-4097	Schleicher Ka.6CR Rhönsegler	6272	
D-4099	SZD-48-3 Jantar Standard 3 *(Permit 10.99)*	B-1448	
D-4100	Schleicher Ka.6CR Rhönsegler	6369Si	
D-4101	Glaser-Dirks DG100G Elan	E164-G130	
D-4102	Glaser-Dirks DG100G Elan	E165-G131	
D-4103	Rolladen-Schneider LS-4B	4862	
D-4104	Rolladen-Schneider LS-4B	4974	
D-4105	Rolladen-Schneider LS-4	4351	
D-4106	Rolladen-Schneider LS-4A	4352	
D-4107	Rolladen-Schneider LS-6C	6241	
D-4108	Schempp-Hirth Duo Discus	143	
D-4109	Schempp-Hirth Duo Discus	194	
D-4110	Rolladen-Schneider LS-4B	4863	
D-4111	Schempp-Hirth Ventus 2a	27	
D-4112	Schleicher K7 Rhönadler	285/A	
D-4113	Darmstadt D-41 *(Permit - old?)*	42	
D-4114	Schleicher ASW-19B	19350	
D-4117	Schleicher K.8B	8583	
D-4118	Schleicher K.8B	8606	
D-4119	Rolladen-Schneider LS-8A *(Permit 6.99)*	8164	
D-4120	Schleicher Ka.6CR Rhönsegler	6566	
D-4121	Schleicher Ka.6CR Rhönsegler	6593	
D-4122	Schleicher Ka.6CR Rhönsegler	6582	
D-4123	Scheibe SF-34B	5122	
D-4124	Rolladen-Schneider LS-4B	4942	
D-4125	Schleicher Ka.6CR Rhönsegler	6612	
D-4126	Schleicher Ka.6CR Rhönsegler	6610	
D-4127	Schleicher Ka.6E	4107	
D-4128	Schleicher Ka.6E	4100	
D-4129	Schleicher Ka.6CR Rhönsegler	6654	
D-4130	Glaser-Dirks DG-100G Elan	E189-G155	
D-4131	Schempp-Hirth Standard Austria S	16	D-8437
D-4132	Schleicher Ka.6CR Rhönsegler	6509Si	
D-4133	Schleicher ASK-13	13067	
D-4134	Schleicher ASK-13	13066	
D-4135	Schleicher ASK-13	13075	
D-4136	Schleicher K.8B	8746	
D-4137	Scheibe Bergfalke III	5510	
D-4138	Scheibe Zugvogel IIIA	1056	
D-4139	Schempp-Hirth Discus CS	112CS	
D-4140	Schleicher ASK-13	13620AB	
D-4141	Schleicher ASW-19B	19085	
D-4142	Schleicher ASK-13	13621AB	
D-4143	Glaser-Dirks DG-500 Elan Trainer	5E-106T42	
D-4144	Pilatus B4-PC11AF	231	
D-4145	Pilatus B4-PC11AF	197	
D-4146	Pilatus B4-PC11AF	202	
D-4147	Schempp-Hirth Ventus b/16.6	285	
D-4148	Rolladen-Schneider LS-4B	41025	
D-4149	Schempp-Hirth Discus CS	247CS	
D-4150	Schempp-Hirth Janus C	176	
D-4151	SZD-41A Jantar Standard	B-739	
D-4152	Schempp-Hirth HS-7 Mini-Nimbus C	152	
D-4153	Schempp-Hirth Duo Discus	85	
D-4156	Rolladen-Schneider LS-4B	4925	
	(Also listed as S-H Discus, coded '3S' in 7.99)		
D-4157	SZD-41A Jantar Standard	B-879	
D-4158	Glaser-Dirks DG-100G Elan	EI90-G156	
D-4159	Glaser-Dirks DG-100G Elan	EI91-G157	
D-4160	Schempp-Hirth Discus b	416	
D-4161	Schleicher Ka.6CR Rhönsegler	6299	
D-4162	SZD-41A Jantar Standard	B-857	
D-4163	Grob G.102 Astir CS	1103	
D-4164	Grob G.102 Astir CS	1104	
D-4165	Grob G.102 Astir CS	1105	
D-4166	Grob G.102 Astir CS	1106	
D-4167	Grob Standard Cirrus	295G	HB-1096
D-4168	Grob G.102 Astir CS	1108	
D-4169	Schempp-Hirth Duo Discus	179	
D-4170	Grob G.102 Astir CS	1110	
D-4171	Grob G.102 Astir CS	1111	
D-4172	Scheibe SF-34B	5137	
D-4173	Glaser-Dirks DG-100G Elan	E173-G139	
D-4174	Rolladen-Schneider LS-4B	4975	
D-4175	Scheibe SF-34B	5135	
D-4176	Glaser-Dirks DG-500/20 Elan	5E-159W7	
D-4177	Glaser-Dirks DG-300 Club Elan Acro	3E-463C83A18	
	(C/n conflicts with HB-3190, one is probably -A17)		
D-4178	Glaser-Dirks DG-100G Elan	EI99-G165	
D-4179	Grob G.102 Astir CS	1135	
D-4180	Grob G.102 Astir CS	1136	
D-4181	Grob G.102 Astir CS	1134	
D-4182	Glaser-Dirks DG-500 Elan Orion	5E-177X29	
D-4183	Schleicher ASK-21	21531	
D-4184	Rolladen-Schneider LS-4	4184	N29798
D-4185	Glasflügel H304	243	
D-4186	Glasflügel H304	244	
D-4187	Grob G.102 Astir CS	1166	
D-4188	Rolladen-Schneider LS-4	4034	
D-4189	Rolladen-Schneider LS-4B	41014	
D-4190	Rolladen-Schneider LS-4	4041	
D-4191	Grob Standard Cirrus	408G	HB-1191

Regn.	Type	C/n	Prev.Id.		Regn.	Type	C/n	Prev.Id.
D-4192	Schleicher ASK-21	21532			D-4267	Grob G.102 Astir CS	1401	
D-4193	Grob G.102 Astir CS	1183			D-4268	Grob G .102 Astir CS	1402	
D-4194	Schleicher ASK-21	21533			D-4269	Grob G.102 Astir CS	1403	
D-4195	Schleicher ASK-21	21534			D-4270	Grob G.102 Astir CS	1404	
D-4196	Grob G.102 Astir CS	1222			D-4271	Grob G.102 Astir CS	1405	
D-4197	Grob G.102 Astir CS	1223			D-4273	Grob G.102 Astir CS	1417	
D-4198	Grob G.102 Astir CS	1224			D-4274	Grob G.102 Astir CS	1420	
D-4199	Marganski MDM-1 Fox (Reservation ?)	unkn			D-4275	Grob G.102 Astir CS	1421	
D-4200	SZD-55-1	551197097			D-4276	Grob G.102 Astir CS	1422	
D-4201	Scheibe SF-34B	5123			D-4277	Grob G.102 Astir CS	1423	
D-4202	Scheibe SF-34B	5124			D-4278	Schleicher ASK-23B	23131	
D-4203	Scheibe SF-34B	5128			D-4279	Grob G.103C Twin III Acro	34101-K-331	
D-4204	Grob G.102 Astir CS	1230			D-4280	Grob G.103A Twin II Acro	34077-K-307	
D-4205	Schleicher ASK-21	21536			D-4281	Grob G.103A Twin II Acro	34078-K-308	
D-4206	Grob G.102 Astir CS	1232			D-4282	Rolladen-Schneider LS-8A	8018	
D-4208	Schleicher ASK-21	21537			D-4284	Rolladen-Schneider LS-4B	4831	
D-4210	Grob G.102 Astir CS	1241			D-4285	Schleicher ASK-21	21539	
D-4211	Grob G.102 Astir CS	1242			D-4286	Rolladen-Schneider LS-3A	3183	
D-4212	Schempp-Hirth Duo Discus	12			D-4287	Rolladen-Schneider LS-4	4323	
D-4213	Schempp-Hirth Duo Discus	105			D-4288	Schempp-Hirth Nimbus 2B	141	HB-1657
D-4214	Grob G.102 Astir CS	1245						D-7851
D-4215	Grob G.102 Astir CS	1315			D-4289	Rolladen-Schneider LS-4B	4833	
D-4216	Schempp-Hirth Standard Cirrus	429	HB-1217		D-4290	Schleicher ASK-21	21647	
D-4217	Grob G.102 Astir CS	1317			D-4291	Rolladen-Schneider LS-3A	3256	
D-4218	Schempp-Hirth Duo Discus	169			D-4292	Rolladen-Schneider LS-3-17	3371	
D-4219	Grob G.102 Astir CS	1319			D-4293	Rolladen-Schneider LS-4	4275	
D-4220	Schleicher ASK-21	21525			D-4294	Rolladen-Schneider LS-4	4273	
D-4221	Grob G.102 Astir CS	1322			D-4295	Schempp-Hirth Nimbus 4 (Permit 5.99)	12/33	
D-4222	Grob G.104 Speed Astir IIC	4501				(Intended for conversion to Nimbus 4M as c/n 11/33)		
D-4223	Schleicher ASW-20L	20302			D-4296	Rolladen-Schneider LS-4B	4835	
D-4224	Schleicher ASW-20	20297			D-4297	Rolladen-Schneider LS-4B	4836	
D-4225	Schleicher ASW-20L	20321			D-4298	Rolladen-Schneider LS-4B	4837	
D-4226	Schleicher ASW-20	20303			D-4299	SZD-48-1 Jantar Standard 2	B-1222	
D-4228	Schleicher ASW-20L	20306			D-4301	Schleicher Rhönlerche II (Reservation 10.99)	407	
D-4229	SZD-24-4A Foka 4	W-345	DDR-2229		D-4302	Glaser-Dirks DG-300 Elan	3E-97	
			DM-2229		D-4303	Glaser-Dirks DG-300 Elan	3E-395	
D-4230	Rolladen-Schneider LS-4B	4976			D-4304	Glasflügel H304	203	
D-4231	Schempp-Hirth Duo Discus	82			D-4305	Grob G.103C Twin III	36011	
D-4232	Schleicher ASK-21	21527			D-4306	Schleicher K.8	481	
D-4233	Scheibe SF-34B	5130			D-4307	Glaser-Dirks DG-300 Elan	3E-380	
D-4234	Scheibe SF-34B	5129			D-4308	Grunau Baby IIB	1	
D-4235	Rolladen-Schneider LS-4	4019			D-4309	Rolladen-Schneider LS-6C-18	6367	
D-4236	Akaflieg Braunschweig SB-5B Sperber	5024A			D-4310	Schleicher ASW-20	20610	
D-4237	SZD-24-4A Foka 4	W-350	DDR-2237		D-4311	Schleicher ASK-21	21137	
			DM-2237		D-4312	Schleicher Rhönlerche II	1021	
D-4238	Rolladen-Schneider LS-4	4125			D-4313	Glaser-Dirks DG-300 Elan	3E-175	
D-4239	Rolladen-Schneider LS-4	4123			D-4315	Schleicher K.8B	1019	
D-4241	SZD-9bis Bocian 1E	P-528	DDR-3241		D-4316	Pilatus B4-PC11	234	HB-1316
			DM-3241		D-4317	Schempp-Hirth Discus CS	142CS	
D-4242	Schleicher ASW-17	17042			D-4318	Schleicher K7 Rhönadler	7152	
D-4243	Rolladen-Schneider LS-4	4132			D-4319	Schleicher K.8	472	
D-4244	Rolladen-Schneider LS-4	4167			D-4320	Grob G.103C Twin III Acro	34203	
D-4245	Rolladen-Schneider LS-4	4127			D-4321	Schempp-Hirth Discus CS	149CS	
D-4246	Rolladen-Schneider LS-4	4144			D-4322	Schleicher Rhönlerche II	3025	
D-4247	Rolladen-Schneider LS-4	4135			D-4323	Schleicher K7 Rhönadler	7117	
D-4248	Rolladen-Schneider LS-4	4130			D-4324	Schleicher K7 Rhönadler	7189	
D-4249	Grunau Baby III	83			D-4325	Schempp-Hirth Ventus 2a	32	
D-4250	Rolladen-Schneider LS-4	4322			D-4326	Schleicher ASW-20	20611	
D-4251	Schleicher ASK-21	21528			D-4327	Grunau Baby III	1	
D-4252	Rolladen-Schneider LS-4	4179			D-4328	Scheibe L-Spatz 55	634	
D-4253	Grob G.102 Astir CS	1246			D-4329	Schleicher K.8B	920	
D-4254	SZD-32A Foka 5	W-515	DDR-2254		D-4330	Schleicher ASW-24	24211	
			DM-2254		D-4331	Rolladen-Schneider LS-4B	4839	
D-4255	Grob G.102 Ast r CS	1249			D-4332	Glaser-Dirks DG-500 Elan Orion	5E-156X13	S5-7505
D-4256	Grob G.102 Astir CS	1250			D-4333	Steinlehner/Huber SH-2H (Permit 6.99)	01	
D-4257	Schempp-Hirth Ventus 2b	81			D-4334	LET L-33 Solo	940210	
D-4258	Grob G.102 Astir CS	1252			D-4335	Schleicher K.8B	8376	
D-4259	Schleicher ASK-21	21530			D-4336	Schleicher K7 Rhönadler	500	
D-4260	Grob G.102 Astir CS	1254			D-4337	Schleicher ASK-21	21542	
D-4261	SZD-32A Foka 5	W-524	DDR-2261		D-4338	Schleicher Ka.6CR Rhönsegler	6447	
			DM-2261		D-4339	Schleicher ASK-21	21543	
D-4262	Grob G.102 Astir CS	1385			D-4340	Glaser-Dirks DG-100G Elan	E106-G75	
D-4264	Grob G.102 Astir CS	1390			D-4342	Schempp-Hirth Ventus 2b	77	
D-4265	Grob G.102 Astir CS	1391			D-4343	LET L-33 Solo (Reservation 1.99)	990317	
D-4266	Rolladen-Schneider LS-4	4201	N42RL		D-4344	Rolladen-Schneider LS-8-18 (Permit 6.99)	8247	

Regn.	Type	C/n	Prev.Id.
D-4345	Schleicher K.8B	8444	D-KOBC
			D-4345
D-4346	Schempp-Hirth Discus CS	254CS	
D-4347	Schleicher Ka.6CR Rhönsegler	6389	
D-4348	Schempp-Hirth Discus CS	111CS	
D-4349	Schleicher Ka.6 Rhönsegler	187	
D-4350	Schempp-Hirth Discus CS	116CS	
D-4351	Schleicher Ka.6 Rhönsegler	130	
D-4352	Schleicher K.8B	8670	
D-4353	Schleicher K.8B	8690	
D-4354	Schempp-Hirth Discus b	141	
D-4355	Glaser-Dirks DG-100G Elan	E222-G188	
	(C/n also quoted for I-LYNO)		
D-4356	SZD-30 Pirat	B-576	DDR-1856
			DM-1856
D-4357	Schleicher K7 Rhönadler	7212	
D-4358	Schempp-Hirth Janus C	230	
D-4359	Schempp-Hirth Discus b	155	
D-4360	Schempp-Hirth Discus b	143	
D-4361	Schleicher K.8	P1	
D-4362	Schempp-Hirth Discus b	161	
D-4363	Schempp-Hirth Ventus 2c	4/7	
D-4364	Schleicher ASK-13	13060	
D-4365	Schleicher Ka.6CR Rhönsegler	618	
D-4366	Bölkow Phoebus A-1	765	
D-4367	Rolladen-Schneider LS-8A	8155	N98YG
D-4368	Schleicher Ka.6E	4114	
D-4369	Schleicher K.8B	740	
D-4370	Schleicher Ka.6CR Rhönsegler	6414Si	
D-4372	Schleicher Ka.6E	4155	
D-4373	Schleicher K.8B	738	
D-4374	Rolladen-Schneider LS-6C	6282	
D-4375	SZD-9bis Bocian 1E	P-565	DDR-3375
			DM-3375
D-4376	Rolladen-Schneider LS-8A	8241	
D-4377	SZD-9bis Bocian 1E	P-567	DDR-3377
			DM-3377
D-4378	Schleicher Rhönlerche II	804	
D-4379	Schleicher K.8B	817	
D-4381	Schleicher K.8B	918	
D-4382	Schleicher K.8B	8696	
D-4383	Schleicher K.8B	972	
D-4384	Schleicher Ka.6CR Rhönsegler	967	
D-4385	Schleicher Rhönlerche II	940	
D-4386	Schleicher ASK-13	13016	
D-4387	Rolladen-Schneider LS-4B	4878	
D-4388	Schleicher Ka.6CR Rhönsegler	1066	
D-4389	Scheibe SF-27A	6047	
D-4391	Schleicher K7 Rhönadler	7001	
D-4392	Schleicher K.8B	8002	
D-4393	Schempp-Hirth Discus b	164	
D-4394	Schleicher K.8B	8009	
D-4395	Schempp-Hirth Discus b	174	
D-4396	Pilatus B4-PC11AF	241	
D-4397	Schleicher K7 Rhönadler	7023	
D-4398	Rolladen-Schneider LS-4B	4913	
D-4399	Schleicher Ka.6CR Rhönsegler	6221/B	
D-4400	Schleicher Ka.6E	4157	
D-4401	SZD-48-3 Jantar Standard 3	B-1967	
D-4402	Schempp-Hirth Discus b	173	
D-4403	Schleicher K7 Rhönadler	7249	
D-4404	SZD-48-3 Jantar Standard 3	B-1349	SP-3249
D-4405	Schleicher Ka.6CR Rhönsegler	6508	
D-4406	Rolladen-Schneider LS-1D	257	
D-4408	Rolladen-Schneider LS-8-18 *(Permit 12.99)*	8298	
D-4409	Schleicher K.8B	114	
D-4410	Grunau Baby IIB	AB-1	
D-4411	Schleicher K.8B	8313	
D-4412	Rolladen-Schneider LS-4B	4851	
D-4413	Glasflügel H206 Hornet C	97	
D-4414	LET L-23 Super Blanik	917811	
D-4415	HBV Diamant 18	057	
D-4416	SZD-41A Jantar Standard	B-747	DDR-2416
			DM-2416
D-4417	Schleicher Ka.6E	4188	
D-4418	Schempp-Hirth Discus CS	113CS	
D-4419	Grob G.103 Twin III	36012	D-5291
D-4420	Schleicher K.8B	8616	
D-4421	Schleicher ASK-13	13081	
D-4422	Schleicher Ka.6CR Rhönsegler	6643	
D-4423	Schleicher ASK-13	13076	
D-4424	SZD-42-2 Jantar 2B	B-865	DDR-2423
			DM-2423
D-4425	Schleicher ASW-15	15001	
D-4426	Schleicher K.8B	8414	
D-4427	Schleicher ASW-27	27069	
D-4428	Grob G.103C Twin III Acro	34158	
D-4429	Schempp-Hirth Discus CS	024CS	
D-4430	Glasflügel H303 Mosquito	31	
D-4431	Glasflügel H303 Mosquito	30	
D-4432	Glasflügel H303 Mosquito	29	
D-4433	Vogt LO-100 Zwergreiher	AB 33	
D-4434	Glasflügel H303 Mosquito B	116	
D-4435	Glasflügel H303 Mosquito B	117	
D-4436	Schleicher ASK-21	21594	
D-4438	Glasflügel H303 Mosquito B	124	
D-4439	Glasflügel H303 Mosquito B	144	
D-4440	Schempp-Hirth Discus 2A *(Permit 10.99)*	3	
D-4441	WM-1	V-1	
D-4442	Rolladen-Schneider LS-4	4116	
D-4443	Akaflieg Braunschweig SB-5E Sperber	AB5059	
D-4444	Schempp-Hirth Duo Discus *(Reservation 6.99)*	"9999"	
D-4445	Rolladen-Schneider LS-6E *(Permit 1.99)*	6364	
D-4446	Glasflügel H303 Mosquito	13	
D-4447	Glasflügel H303 Mosquito	23	
D-4448	Glasflügel H206 Hornet	88	
D-4449	Glasflügel H206 Hornet	89	
D-4450	Rolladen-Schneider LS-4B	4876	
D-4451	Rolladen-Schneider LS-4A	4676	
D-4453	Glasflügel H303 Mosquito	78	
D-4454	SG-38 Schulgleiter *(Reservation 12.99)*	1310/691	
D-4455	Glasflügel H303 Mosquito	100	
D-4456	Glaser-Dirks DG-300 Elan	3E-196	
D-4457	Glaser-Dirks DG-300 Elan	3E-198	
D-4458	Glasflügel H206 Hornet	83	
D-4459	Glasflügel H206 Hornet	69	
D-4460	Glasflügel H303 Mosquito B	131	
D-4461	Glasflügel H206 Hornet	60	
D-4462	Glasflügel H206 Hornet	61	
D-4463	Schleicher ASK-21	21071	
D-4464	Schleicher ASK-21	21076	
D-4465	Schleicher ASK-21	21077	
D-4466	Grob G.102 Astir CS	1167	
D-4467	Schleicher ASK-13	13554	
D-4468	Schleicher ASK-13	13555	
D-4469	Schleicher ASW-19	19063	
D-4470	Schempp-Hirth Discus b	23	
D-4471	Schleicher ASK-13	13557	
D-4472	Schleicher ASW-19	19071	
D-4473	Schleicher ASW-19B	19072	
D-4474	Schleicher ASW-19	19073	
D-4475	Schleicher ASK-13	13558	
D-4476	Schleicher ASW-19B	19074	
D-4477	Rolladen-Schneider LS-8A *(Reservation 9.99)*	8282	
D-4478	Schleicher ASW-19	19076	
D-4479	Schleicher ASK-13	13560	
D-4480	Schleicher ASK-13	13564	
D-4481	Schleicher ASW-19	19077	
D-4482	Schleicher ASW-19	19078	
D-4483	Schleicher ASK-13	13561	
D-4484	Schleicher ASW-19B	19079	
D-4485	Schleicher ASW-19	19080	
D-4487	Rolladen-Schneider LS-4B	4943	
D-4488	Schempp-Hirth Duo Discus	50	
D-4490	Schleicher ASK-13 *(Reservation 4.99)*	13563	
D-4491	Schleicher ASK-21	21061	
D-4492	Schleicher ASK-21	21063	
D-4493	Schleicher ASW-19B	19352	
D-4494	Schleicher ASW-19	19087	
D-4495	Schempp-Hirth Duo Discus	96	

Regn.	Type	C/n	Prev.Id.
D-4496	Grob G.102 Speed Astir II	4016	
D-4497	Grob G.102 Speed Astir II	4015	
D-4498	Schempp-Hirth Discus 2b *(Permit - old?)*	17	
D-4499(2)	Schempp-Hirth Discus 2a *(Permit 7.99)*	18	
D-4500	Grob G.102 Speed Astir IIB	4029	
D-4501	Grob G.102 Speed Astir II	4008	
D-4502	Schempp-Hirth Janus CT	13/272	
D-4503	Schempp-Hirth Discus CS	014CS	
D-4504	Grob G.104 Speed Astir IIB *(Permit 4.99)*	4045	HB-1502
D-4505	Grob G.102 Speed Astir II	4024	
D-4506	Schleicher ASW-19	19136	
D-4507	Schempp-Hirth Duo Discus *(Reservation 10.99)*	245	
D-4508	Schempp-Hirth Discus CS	022CS	
D-4509	Schempp-Hirth Discus CS	013CS	
D-4510	Glaser-Dirks DG-200	2-39	
D-4511	Glaser-Dirks DG-200	2-80	
D-4512	Schleicher ASK-21	21497	
D-4513	Schleicher ASK-21	21498	
D-4514	Schleicher ASK-21	21496	
D-4515	SZD-48-1 Jantar Standard 2	B-996	
D-4516	Schempp-Hirth Duo Discus	108	
D-4517	Schempp-Hirth Discus CS	025CS	
D-4518	Rolladen-Schneider LS-8A	8111	
D-4519	SZD-42-2 Jantar 2B	B-1668	DOSAAF
D-4520	Glaser-Dirks DG-500 Elan Trainer	3E-54T21	
D-4521	Schleicher ASK-21	21204	
D-4522	Schleicher ASW-20CL	20729	
D-4523	Schleicher ASW-20CL	20726	
D-4524	Schleicher ASK-13	13540	
D-4525	Schleicher ASW-19B	19025	
D-4526	Schleicher ASW-19	19018	
D-4527	Schleicher K.8C	81012	
D-4528	Schleicher ASW-19	19028	
D-4529	Schempp-Hirth Discus CS	055CS	
D-4530	Schempp-Hirth Janus CT	15/276	
D-4532	Schleicher ASW-19	19029	
D-4533	Schleicher ASK-18	18031	
D-4534	Schleicher ASK-13	13543	
D-4535	Schleicher ASW-24B	24234	
D-4536	Schleicher ASW-19	19037	
D-4537	Schleicher ASW-19	19035	
D-4538	Schleicher ASK-13	13546	
D-4539	Schempp-Hirth Ventus 2c	48/149	
	(Intended for conversion to Ventus 2cT c/n 48/149 later)		
D-4540	Glasflügel H303 Mosquito B	196	
D-4543	Rolladen-Schneider LS-4	4247	
D-4544	Rolladen-Schneider LS-4	4478	
D-4545	Rolladen-Schneider LS-4	4350	
D-4546	Grob G.103A Twin II Acro	3730-K-46	
D-4547	Schempp-Hirth Ventus 2a	55	
D-4548	LET L-23 Super Blanik	948125	
D-4549	Grob G.102 Club Astir IIIB	5580CB	
D-4550	Grob G.102 Standard Astir II	5002S	
D-4551	Grob G.103 Twin II	3731	
D-4552	Grob G.102 Club Astir IIIB	5584CB	
D-4553	Rolladen-Schneider LS-8A	8112	
D-4554	Schempp-Hirth Discus CS	101CS	
D-4557	Grob G.102 Astir CS Jeans	2162	
D-4558	Grob G.102 Astir CS 77	1741	
D-4559	Grob G.102 Astir CS 77	1746	
D-4560	Grob G.102 Astir CS 77	1747	
D-4561	Grob G.102 Astir CS Jeans	2165	
D-4562	Grob G.102 Astir CS Jeans	2166	
D-4563	Grob G.102 Astir CS 77	1756	
D-4564	Grob G.102 Astir CS Jeans	2167	
D-4565	Grob G.102 Astir CS 77	1750	
D-4566	Glaser-Dirks DG-500 Elan Orion	5E-137X3	
D-4567	Grob G.102 Astir CS Jeans	2168	
D-4568	Glaser-Dirks DG-800S	8-77S20	
D-4570	SZD-59 Acro	X-150	SP-3570
			SP-P570
D-4571	SZD-55-1	551196087	
D-4572-NA	Rolladen-Schneider LS-8A	8113	
D-4574	Schempp-Hirth Discus CS	126CS	
D-4575	Rolladen-Schneider LS-3A	3252	
D-4576	Schleicher ASK-21	21538	
D-4577	Glaser-Dirks DG-300 Club Elan	3E-296/C14	
D-4578	Glaser-Dirks DG-300 Club Elan	3E-297/C15	
D-4579	Rolladen-Schneider LS-3A	3417	
D-4580	Rolladen-Schneider LS-3-17	3381	
D-4581	Glaser-Dirks DG-300 Club Elan	3E-298/C16	
D-4582	Schleicher ASK-23B	23126	
D-4585	Rolladen-Schneider LS-3A	3432	
D-4586	Rolladen-Schneider LS-7	7021	
D-4587	Rolladen-Schneider LS-8-18 *(Reservation 5.99)*	8253	
D-4588	Rolladen-Schneider LS-3-17	3331	
D-4589	Schempp-Hirth Janus B	184	
D-4590	Schempp-Hirth Janus C	191	
D-4591-KS	Schempp-Hirth Nimbus 3/24.5	61	
D-4592	Rolladen-Schneider LS-3A	3370	
D-4593	Glaser-Dirks DG-300 Elan	3E-214	
D-4594	Rolladen-Schneider LS-8A	8254	
D-4595	Glaser-Dirks DG-300 Elan	3E-216	
D-4596	Schleicher ASK-21	21499	
D-4597	Neukom S-4D Elfe	408AB	
D-4598	Neukom S-4D Elfe	411AB	
D-4599	Schleicher ASK-21	21607	HB-3159
D-4600	Neukom S-4 Elfe	50	
D-4601	Scheibe L-Spatz 55	656/56	
D-4602	Schleicher Ka.6CR Rhönsegler	6503	
D-4603	Schleicher K.8	391	
D-4604	Rolladen-Schneider LS-8A	8114	
D-4605	Schleicher K.8B	8235	
D-4606	Glaser-Dirks DG-300 Elan	3E-241	
D-4607	Schleicher Ka.6CR Rhönsegler	6523Si	
D-4608	Schleicher K.8B	107	
D-4610	Schleicher Ka.6CR Rhönsegler	1040	
D-4611	Schleicher ASK-21	21502	
D-4612	Schleicher K7 Rhönadler	7177	
D-4613	Rolladen-Schneider LS-4B	4944	
D-4614	Schleicher Ka.6CR Rhönsegler	6056	
D-4615	Scheibe Bergfalke II/55	386	
D-4616	Glaser-Dirks DG-300 Elan Acro	3E-441A6	
D-4617	Rolladen-Schneider LS-8-18 *(Reservation 6.99)*	8255	
D-4618	Schleicher K.8B	8722	
D-4619	Schleicher Ka.6E	4033	
D-4620	Schleicher K7 Rhönadler	1097	
D-4621	Akaflieg Braunschweig SB-5E Sperber	5011A	
D-4622	SZD-50-3 Puchacz *(Reservation 2.99)*	B-1341	DDR-3622
D-4623	Schleicher K7 Rhönadler	7275	
D-4625	Schleicher ASK-21	21500	
D-4626	Schleicher K7 Rhönadler	7033	
D-4627	Schleicher ASW-24	24125	
D-4628	Schleicher K.8B	154/59	
D-4630	Scheibe Bergfalke II/55	SF-230	
D-4631	Schleicher ASK-13	13663AB	
D-4632	Schleicher ASK-13	13664AB	
D-4633	Glaser-Dirks DG-100G Elan	E215-G181	
D-4634	Schleicher K7 Rhönadler	7214	
D-4635	SZD-50-3 Puchacz	B-1401	DDR-3635
D-4636	SZD-50-2 Puchacz	B-1402	DDR-3636
D-4637	Glaser-Dirks DG-300 Elan	3E-239	
D-4638	Schleicher ASH-25	25115	
D-4639	Schleicher ASK-21	21493	
D-4640	Schleicher K7 Rhönadler	981	
D-4641	Schleicher K7 Rhönadler	7034	
D-4642	Grunau Baby III	AB 01	
D-4643	Rolladen-Schneider LS-1F	468	SE-TRL
D-4644	Rolladen-Schneider LS-4	4067	SE-TXB
D-4645	Glaser-Dirks DG-100G Elan	E201-G167	
D-4646	Schleicher Rhönlerche II *(Reservation - old?)*	66/57	
D-4648	Schleicher ASK-21	21495	
D-4649	Schleicher ASW-12BV *(Permit 4.99)*	12007	D-0074
D-4650	Schempp-Hirth Nimbus 2C	177	ZS-GKT
			D-6564
D-4652	Schleicher Ka.6E	4083	
D-4653	SZD-50-3 Puchacz	B-1537	DDR-3653
D-4654	Scheibe L-Spatz 55	613	
D-4655	Schleicher K.8B	8270	
D-4656	Schleicher ASW-15	15098S	

Regn.	Type	C/n	Prev.Id.
D-4657	Rolladen-Schneider LS-8-18 *(Permit 6.99)*	8264	
D-4658	Schleicher ASK-21	21494	
D-4659	Schleicher Ka.6E	4030	
D-4660	Schleicher K.8B	907	
D-4661	Rolladen-Schneider LS-8A	8013	
D-4662	Glaser-Dirks DG-300 Elan	3E-327	
D-4663	Schempp-Hirth Discus b	131	
D-4664-YY	Schempp-Hirth Ventus b/16.6	309	
D-4665	Schleicher Ka.6E	4145	
D-4666	Grob G.103 Twin Astir	3129	HB-1426
D-4667	Glaser-Dirks DG-300 Club Elan	3E-323/C26	
D-4668	Schleicher ASK-13	13101	
D-4669	Scheibe L-Spatz 55	752	
D-4670	Rolladen-Schneider LS-4A	4670	D-6796
D-4671	Rolladen-Schneider LS-8-18 *(Permit 6.99)*	8265	
D-4672	Schleicher K.8B	8137	
D-4673	Schempp-Hirth Discus b	133	
D-4674	Scheibe L-Spatz 55	761	
D-4676	Schempp-Hirth Duo Discus	212	
D-4677	Schleicher K7 Rhönadler	7256	
D-4679	Schleicher ASK-18 (Museum) *(Reservation - old?)*	unkn	
D-4680	Schleicher ASK-21	21626	
D-4681	Schleicher ASK-13	13025	
D-4682	Schempp-Hirth Discus CS	195CS	
D-4683	Schleicher Ka.6CR Rhönsegler	6212	
D-4685	Schleicher ASK-21	21506	
D-4686	Darmstadt D-36 *(Permit 3.99)*	V-2	
D-4687	Schleicher ASW-20L	20579	
D-4688	Schleicher ASW-20L	20569	
D-4690	Schempp-Hirth Discus CS	196CS	
D-4691	Schleicher ASW-20L	20581	
D-4692	Schleicher Ka.6CR Rhönsegler	6297	
D-4693	Rolladen-Schneider LS-8A	8190	
D-4695	Schleicher ASH-25	25125	
D-4696	Akaflieg Braunschweig SB-5B Sperber	5007	
D-4697	Scheibe L-Spatz 55	4	D-KONK
D-4698	Schleicher Ka.6E	4150	
D-4699	Schleicher Ka.6E	4144	
D-4700	Schleicher K7 Rhönadler	7208	
D-4701	Glaser-Dirks DG-100G Elan	E194-G160	
D-4702	Glaser-Dirks DG-100G Elan	E195-G161	
D-4703	Glaser-Dirks DG-300 Club Elan	3E-273/C4	
D-4704	Schleicher Ka.6CR Rhönsegler	6435	
D-4705	Schleicher ASW-24	24203	
D-4706	Schleicher Ka.6CR Rhönsegler	6437	
D-4707	Schempp-Hirth Duo Discus	41	
D-4708	Schleicher ASK-21	21361	
D-4710	Schleicher K.8B	8614	
D-4711	Grob Standard Cirrus	466G	
D-4712	Schleicher K.8B	8756	
D-4713	Glaser-Dirks DG-300 Elan	3E-154	
D-4714	Schleicher K.8B	8632	
D-4715	Schleicher ASK-21	21364	
D-4716	Schleicher Ka.6E	4060	
D-4717	Schleicher ASK-13	13011	
D-4719	Scheibe SF-27A	6071	
D-4721	Schleicher ASK-21	21156	
D-4722	Schleicher Ka.6CR Rhönsegler	6604	
D-4724	Schleicher K.8B	987	
D-4725	Akaflieg Braunschweig SB-5B Sperber	5031A	
D-4728	Schleicher ASK-21	21674	
D-4729	Schleicher Ka.6CR Rhönsegler	6052Si	
D-4730	Bölkow Phoebus C	806	
D-4731	Schleicher Ka.6E	4185	
D-4732	Schleicher ASK-21	21365	
D-4733	Schempp-Hirth Discus b	469	
D-4734	Glaser-Dirks DG-100G Elan	E197-G163	
D-4735	Rolladen-Schneider LS-8A	8073	
D-4736	VTC-75 Standard Cirrus	150Y	
D-4737	VTC-75 Standard Cirrus	151Y	
D-4738	Schleicher ASK-21	21367	
D-4739	Schempp-Hirth Standard Cirrus	385	
D-4740	Schempp-Hirth Standard Cirrus	395	
D-4741	Scheibe Zugvogel IIIA	1098A	D-1896
D-4742	Grob Standard Cirrus	410G	
D-4743	Schempp-Hirth Standard Cirrus	400	
D-4744	Schempp-Hirth Standard Cirrus	411	
D-4745	Schleicher ASK-21	21329	
D-4746	Grob Standard Cirrus	433G	
D-4747	Grob Standard Cirrus K *(Permit 6.99)*	437G	
D-4748	Schempp-Hirth Standard Cirrus	397	
D-4749	Schempp-Hirth Standard Cirrus	415	
D-4750	Schleicher ASK-21	21339	
D-4751	VTC-75 Standard Cirrus	160Y	
D-4752	Grob Standard Cirrus	560G	
D-4753	Start & Flug H-101 Salto	72	I-FIUR
D-4754	Rolladen-Schneider LS-4B	41004	
D-4755	Grob Standard Cirrus	561G	
D-4756	SZD-30 Pirat	B-360	DDR-1756
			DM-1756
D-4757	Glaser-Dirks DG-300 Elan	3E-169	
D-4758	Grob G.104 Speed Astir II	4025	OE-5408
			D-4503
D-4759	Scheibe Bergfalke IV	5852	
D-4760	Scheibe Bergfalke IV	5853	
D-4761	Scheibe Bergfalke IV	5854	
D-4762	Schleicher ASK-21	21330	
D-4763	Scheibe Bergfalke III	AB5653	
D-4764	LET L-13 Blanik	026842	
D-4765	Eiri PIK-20D	20534	
D-4766	Eiri PIK-20D	20556	
D-4767	Eiri PIK-20D	20555	
D-4768	Eiri PIK-20D	20557	
D-4769	Schleicher ASK-21	21371	
D-4770	Grob G.103 Twin II	3520	
D-4771	Grob G.103 Twin II	3521	
D-4772	Schempp-Hirth Duo Discus	150	
D-4773	Grob G.103 Twin II	3524	
D-4774	LET L-23 Super Blanik	917808	
D-4775	SZD-30 Pirat	B-404	DDR-1775
			DM-1775
D-4776	Eiri PIK-20D	20623	
D-4777	Schleicher Ka.6CR Rhönsegler	6426Si	
D-4778	Schleicher ASK-21	21331	
D-4779	Eiri PIK-20D	20522	
D-4780	Schleicher ASK-21	21332	
D-4781	Eiri PIK-20D	20503	
D-4782	Eiri PIK-20D	20535	
D-4783	Grob G.102 Astir CS	1470	
D-4784	Grob G.102 Astir CS	1477	
D-4785	Schleicher ASK-21	21372	
D-4786	Schleicher ASK-21	21286	
D-4787	Grob G.102 Astir CS	1481	
D-4788	Schempp-Hirth Discus b	21	
D-4789	Schempp-Hirth Nimbus 4 *(Permit 6.99)*	14/34	
	(Intended for conversion to Nimbus 4M c/n 12/34 as OO-XXL)		
D-4790	Valentin Kiwi S	001	D-KELT
D-4791	Schempp-Hirth Duo Discus	79	
D-4792	Grob G.102 Astir CS	1489	
D-4793	Schleicher ASK-23	23056	
D-4795	Grob G.102 Astir CS	1493	
D-4796	Grob G.102 Astir CS	1495	
D-4797	Grob G.102 Astir CS	1497	
D-4798	Schleicher ASK-21	21287	
D-4799	Schempp-Hirth Duo Discus	93	
D-4800	Grob G.102 Astir CS 77	1624	
D-4801	Grob G.102 Astir CS 77	1623	
D-4802	Grob G.102 Astir CS 77	1601	
D-4803	Grob G.102 Astir CS 77	1602	
D-4804	Grob G.102 Astir CS 77	1603	
D-4805	Grob G.102 Astir CS 77	1604	
D-4806	Grob G.102 Astir CS	1520	
D-4807	SZD-30 Pirat	B-463	DDR-1807
			DM-1807
D-4808	Grob G.102 Astir CS 77	1622	
D-4809	Grob G.102 Astir CS 77	1608	
D-4811	Grob G.102 Astir CS 77	1610	
D-4812	Schempp-Hirth Duo Discus	149	
D-4813	Grob G.102 Astir CS 77	1642	
D-4814	Rolladen-Schneider LS-8A	8091	

Regn.	Type	C/n	Prev.Id.	Regn.	Type	C/n	Prev.Id.
D-4815	Grob G.102 Astir CS 77	1619		D-4895	Grob G.102 Astir CS Jeans	2149	
D-4816	Schleicher ASK-21	21333		D-4896	Grob G.102 Astir CS 77	1733	
D-4817	Schempp-Hirth Janus	44		D-4897	Grob G.102 Astir CS 77	1738	
D-4818	Schempp-Hirth HS-7 Mini-Nimbus	13		D-4898	Schleicher ASK-21	21385	
D-4819	Schempp-Hirth HS-7 Mini-Nimbus	15		D-4899	Grob G.102 Astir CS 77	1740	
D-4820	SZD-30 Pirat	B-498	DDR-1821	D-4902	Schempp-Hirth Mini-Nimbus C	128	
			DM-1821	D-4903	Schempp-Hirth Mini-Nimbus C	129	
D-4821	Schleicher ASW-20CL	20857		D-4904	Schleicher ASH-25	25141	
D-4822	Grob G.102 Astir CS 77	1644		D-4905	Valentin Mistral C	MC 002/77	
D-4823	SZD-30 Pirat	B-500	DDR-1823	D-4906	Valentin Mistral C	MC 003/77	
			DM-1823	D-4908	SZD-30 Pirat	S-03.48	DDR-1908
D-4824	Schempp-Hirth Duo Discus	89					DM-1908
D-4825	Grob G.102 Astir CS 77	1655		D-4909	Glaser-Dirks DG-100G Elan	E180-G146	
D-4826	Schleicher ASK-21	21334		D-4910	Valentin Mistral C	MC 010/77	
D-4827	Schleicher ASW-20CL	20858		D-4912	Glaser-Dirks DG-300 Elan	3E-234	
D-4828-CD	Rolladen-Schneider LS-8A	8092		D-4913	Glaser-Dirks DG-300 Elan	3E-120	
D-4829	Grob G.102 Astir CS Jeans	2022		D-4914	Glaser-Dirks DG-300 Elan	3E-236	
D-4830	Grob G.102 Astir CS Jeans	2021		D-4915	Valentin Mistral C	MC 015/78	
D-4831	Glaser-Dirks DG-300 Elan	3E-131		D-4916	Valentin Mistral C	MC 016/78	
D-4832	Grob G.102 Astir CS Jeans	2019		D-4917	Rolladen-Schneider LS-6C	6294	
D-4833	Schleicher ASK-21	21337		D-4918	Schleicher ASK-21	21376	
D-4834	Grob G.102 Astir CS Jeans	2017		D-4919	Valentin Mistral C	MC 019/79	
D-4835	Grob G.102 Astir CS Jeans	2016		D-4922	Valentin Mistral C	MC 023/79	
D-4836	Schleicher ASK-21	21336		D-4923	Schleicher ASK-23B	23106	
D-4837	Schempp-Hirth Discus CS	222CS		D-4924	Schleicher ASW-24	24003	
D-4838	Schempp-Hirth Discus CS	224CS		D-4925	Valentin Mistral C	MC 025/81	
D-4839	Grob G.103 Twin Astir	3043		D-4926	Valentin Mistral C	MC 026/80	
D-4840	Grob G.103 Twin Astir	3045		D-4928	Valentin Mistral C	MC 028/81	
D-4841	Grob G.103 Twin Astir	3047		D-4929	Valentin Mistral C	MC 029/81	
D-4842	Grob G.103 Twin Astir	3048		D-4930	Valentin Mistral C	MC 030/81	
D-4844	Grob G.103 Twin Astir	3053		D-4931	Valentin Mistral C	MC 031/81	
D-4845	Grob G.103 Twin Astir	3054		D-4932	Valentin Mistral C	MC 032/81	
D-4847	Schempp-Hirth Janus B	194		D-4933	Rolladen-Schneider LS-6-18W	6370	
D-4849	Rolladen-Schneider LS-3A	3227	HB-1462	D-4934	Valentin Mistral C	MC 034/81	
D-4850	Grob G.103 Twin Astir	3060		D-4935	Schleicher ASK-21	21383	
D-4851	Grob G.103 Twin Astir	3065		D-4936	Schempp-Hirth Discus CS	219CS	
D-4852	Grob G.103 Twin Astir	3066		D-4937	Valentin Mistral C	MC 037/81	
D-4854	Grob G.103 Twin Astir	3068		D-4938	Valentin Mistral C	MC 038/81	
D-4855	SZD-55-1	551195079		D-4939	Valentin Mistral C	MC 039/81	
D-4856	Grob G.103 Twin Astir	3071		D-4940	Schleicher ASK-21	21378	
D-4857	SZD-51-1 Junior	511199243		D-4941	Valentin Mistral C	MC 041/81	
D-4858	Grob G.103 Twin Astir	3073		D-4942	Rolladen-Schneider LS-6-18W	6363	
D-4859	Schleicher ASW-20CL	20859		D-4943	Valentin Mistral C	MC 043/81	
D-4860	Grob G.103 Twin Astir	3075		D-4944	Valentin Mistral C	MC 044/81	
D-4861	Grob G.103 Twin Astir	3076		D-4945	Valentin Mistral C	MC 045/82	
D-4862	Schleicher ASK-21	21374		D-4946	Valentin Mistral C	MC 046/82	
D-4863	Schleicher ASW-19B	19420		D-4947	Valentin Mistral C (Reservation)	MC 047/82	
D-4865	Schleicher ASK-21	21265		D-4949	Valentin Mistral C	MC 049/82	
D-4866	Grob G.103 Twin II	3593		D-4950	Schempp-Hirth Duo Discus	80	
D-4867	Schempp-Hirth Discus CS	216CS		D-4951	Valentin Mistral C	MC 051/83	
D-4868	Grob G.103 Twin II	3595		D-4952	Glaser-Dirks DG-100G Elan	E177-G143	
D-4869	Grob G.102 Speed Astir IIB	4102		D-4953	Valentin Mistral C	MC 055/85	
D-4870	Schleicher ASH-25	25010		D-4955	Schleicher ASK-21	21242	
D-4871	Grob G.102 Speed Astir IIB	4036		D-4956	Valentin Mistral C	MC 056/86	
D-4872	Rolladen-Schneider LS-8A	8115		D-4957	Schempp-Hirth Discus b	394	
D-4873	Grob G.102 Speed Astir IIB	4038		D-4958	Valentin Mistral C	MC 058/85	
D-4874	Grob G.102 Speed Astir IIB	4046		D-4960	Valentin Mistral C	MC 060/85	
D-4875	Grob G.102 Speed Astir IIB	4071		D-4961	Glaser-Dirks DG-500 Elan Orion	5E-165X20	
D-4876	Grob G.102 Speed Astir IIB	4030		D-4962	Valentin Mistral C	MC 062/85	
D-4877	Grob G.102 Speed Astir IIB	4039		D-4963	Valentin Mistral C	MC 063/83	
D-4878	Grob G.102 Speed Astir IIB	4048		D-4964	Valentin Mistral C	MC 064/85	
D-4879	Grob G.102 Speed Astir IIB	4047		D-4965	Valentin Mistral C	MC 065/83	
D-4880	Akaflieg Braunschweig SB-5E Sperber	5039A		D-4966	Rolladen-Schneider LS-4	4490	
D-4881	Grob G.103 Twin II	3501		D-4967	Rolladen-Schneider LS-4	4491	
D-4883	Grob G.102 Standard Astir II	5005S		D-4968	Rolladen-Schneider LS-4	4492	
D-4884	Schempp-Hirth Ventus 2c	33/87		D-4969	Rolladen-Schneider LS-4	4493	
D-4885	Grob G.102 Standard Astir II	5006S		D-4970	Rolladen-Schneider LS-4	4494	
D-4886	Grob G.102 Club Astir II	5008C		D-4971	Rolladen-Schneider LS-4	4496	
D-4887	Grob G.102 Club Astir II	5009C		D-4972	Rolladen-Schneider LS-4	4497	
D-4888	Grob G.102 Astir CS Jeans	2068		D-4973	Test Registration for Rolladen-Schneider LS-4A		
D-4889	Schleicher ASK-21	21338		D-4974	Schleicher ASK-21	21381	
D-4890	Grob G.102 Astir CS Jeans	2154		D-4975	Test Registration for Rolladen-Schneider LS-4B		
D-4891	Grob G.102 Astir CS Jeans	2152		D-4977	Schempp-Hirth Discus b	27	
D-4892	Glaser-Dirks DG-300 Elan	3E-113	OE-5371	D-4978	Grunau Baby III	004A	
D-4894	Grob G.102 Astir CS Jeans	2155		D-4979	Glaser-Dirks DG-100G Elan	E187-G153	

Regn.	Type	C/n	Prev.Id.
D-4980	Glasflügel Mosquito	89	N302C
			N39JH
D-4981	Schempp-Hirth Nimbus 2B	152	
D-4982	Rolladen-Schneider LS-4A	4686	
D-4983	Schempp-Hirth HS-7 Mini-Nimbus	20	
D-4984	Schempp-Hirth HS-7 Mini-Nimbus	21	
D-4985	Grob G.103C Twin III Acro	34151	
D-4986	Schempp-Hirth HS-7 Mini-Nimbus	57	
D-4987	Schempp-Hirth Nimbus 2C	166	
D-4988	Schempp-Hirth HS-7 Mini-Nimbus	65	
D-4989	Rolladen-Schneider LS-4A	4687	
D-4990	Schempp-Hirth Mini-Nimbus B	75	
D-4991	Schempp-Hirth Mini-Nimbus B	76	
D-4992	Schempp-Hirth Mini-Nimbus B	77	
D-4993	Rolladen-Schneider LS-4A	4688	
D-4994	Valentin Mistral C	MC 007/77	
D-4995	Schempp-Hirth Discus CS	218CS	
D-4996	Valentin Mistral C	MC 066/85	
D-4997	Schleicher K.8B	8868AB	
D-4998	Valentin Mistral A	V-1	
D-4999	Rolladen-Schneider LS-4A	4689	
D-5000	Schmetz Condor IV/2	005	
D-5001	Rolladen-Schneider LS-4A	4690	
D-5002	Neukom S-4D Elfe	414AB	
D-5004	Rolladen-Schneider LS-4A	4692	
D-5005	Glaser-Dirks DG-500 Elan Trainer	5E-48T18	
D-5006	Rolladen-Schneider LS-4A	4693	
D-5008	Rolladen-Schneider LS-4A	4695	
D-5009	Schleicher K7 Rhönadler	7239	
D-5010	Schleicher ASK-13	13672AB	
D-5011	LET L-13A Blanik	978503	
D-5012	Schempp-Hirth HS.7 Mini-Nimbus	12	HB-1386
D-5013	Schleicher K.8B	185/60	
D-5014	Schleicher K7 Rhönadler	887	
D-5015	Neukom Elfe S-4A	58	HB-1097
D-5016	Schleicher Ka.6CR Rhönsegler	6067	
D-5017	SZD-9bis Bocian 1E	P-734	DDR-3017
			DM-3017
D-5018	Schleicher Ka.6CR Rhönsegler	904	
D-5019	Schleicher K.8B	215/61	
D-5020	Grob G.103C Twin III	36013	
D-5021	Grob G.102 Club Astir IIIB	5542CB	OH-640
D-5022	Glaser-Dirks DG-100G Elan	E121-G9O	
D-5023	Schleicher K.8B	198/60	D-KIFU
			D-5023
D-5024	SZD-9bis Bocian 1E	P-449	DDR-3024
			DM-3024
D-5025	Rolladen-Schneider LS-4	4281	
D-5026	LET L-13 Blanik	026227	OH-491
D-5027	Schleicher K.8B	1145	
D-5028	Rolladen-Schneider LS-6C	6283	
D-5029	Schleicher K7 Rhönadler	7027/A	
D-5030	Glaser-Dirks DG-100G Elan *(Res 8.99)*	E161-G128	
D-5031	Schleicher Ka.6CR Rhönsegler	905	
D-5032	SZD-24A-4A Foka 4	W-248	
D-5033	Glaser-Dirks DG-500 Elan Trainer	5E-55T22	
D-5034	Schempp-Hirth Discus CS	220CS	
D-5035	Glaser-Dirks DG-500 Elan Trainer	5E-117T49	
D-5036-36	Schempp-Hirth Discus b	494	
D-5037	Schleicher ASK-21 *(Reservation 11.99)*	21706	
D-5038	Rolladen-Schneider LS-6	6194	
D-5039	Glaser-Dirks DG-300 Elan	3E-295	
D-5040	Rolladen-Schneider LS-7	7053	
D-5041	Schleicher K.8B	8445	HB-754
D-5042	Schleicher K.8B	199/60	
D-5044	Schempp-Hirth Discus b	246	
D-5045	Schleicher K.8B	913	
D-5046	LET L-13 Blanik	173033	OE-5044
D-5047	Glaser-Dirks DG-500 Elan Orion	5E-134X1	
D-5048	Schempp-Hirth Ventus 2c	53/160	
	(Intended for conversion to Ventus 2cM c/n 77/160 later)		
D-5049	Schleicher K7 Rhönadler	935	
D-5050	Schleicher ASK-23B	23150	
D-5051	Schleicher Rhönlerche II	3020	
D-5052	Schempp-Hirth Ventus c	138/422	
D-5053	Schleicher K7 Rhönadler	7144	
D-5054	Schleicher K7 Rhönadler	983	
D-5055	Schempp-Hirth Ventus c	389	
D-5056	Schleicher K.8B	921	
D-5057	Schempp-Hirth Discus b	273	
D-5058	Glaser-Dirks DG-500 Elaan Orion	5E-188X37	
D-5059	Schempp-Hirth Ventus c	336	
D-5060	Schleicher Ka.6CR Rhönsegler	966	
D-5061	Scheibe Bergfalke III	5502	
D-5062	Glaser-Dirks DG-500 Elan Orion	5E-195X39	
D-5063	Schempp-Hirth Ventus A/16.6	82	
D-5064	Schempp-Hirth Discus b	286	
D-5065	Schempp-Hirth Discus b	283	
D-5066	Glasflügel H401 Kestrel	2	
D-5067	Schleicher K.8B *(Reservation)*	8520	
D-5068-B4	Schempp-Hirth Janus C	255	
D-5069	Glasflügel H206 Hornet	29	OE-5060
D-5071	SZD-24-4A Foka 4	W-250	
D-5072	Schleicher ASK-21	21248	
D-5073	Schleicher ASK-23	23018	
D-5074	Schleicher ASK-21	21249	
D-5075	Schempp-Hirth Discus b	289	
D-5077	Glaser-Dirks DG-100	83	
D-5078	Schempp-Hirth Discus b	284	
D-5079	Schleicher Ka.2B Rhönschwalbe	2001	
D-5080	Schempp-Hirth Janus C	249	
D-5081	Schleicher K.8B	8509SH	
D-5082	Schempp-Hirth Discus b	285	
D-5083	Schleicher K.8B	193/60	
D-5084	Schempp-Hirth Janus C	251	
D-5086	Schleicher Ka.6CR Rhönsegler	1156	
D-5087	Dittmar Condor IV	21/53	
D-5088	Schempp-Hirth Janus C	248	
D-5089	Rolladen-Schneider LS-6C	6274	
D-5090	Schleicher K.8B	8425	
D-5091	Schleicher K.8B *(Wfu: Reservation ?)*	8524	
D-5092	Schempp-Hirth Duo Discus *(Reservation 11.99)*	249	
D-5093	Glaser-Dirks DG-300 Elan	3E-139	OE-5379
D-5094	Scheibe L-Spatz 55	620	
D-5095	Schempp-Hirth Discus b	288	
D-5096	Schleicher K.8B	1014	
D-5097	Schempp-Hirth Discus b	260	
D-5098	Schempp-Hirth Discus b	239	
D-5099	Schleicher Ka.6CR Rhönsegler	6454	
D-5100	Schempp-Hirth Discus 2b *(Reservation 7.99)*	56	
D-5101	Schempp-Hirth Discus b	501	
D-5102	Rolladen-Schneider LS-4A	4708	
D-5103	Schleicher K7 Rhönadler	1141	
D-5104	Rolladen-Schneider LS-4B	4709	
D-5105	Schleicher K.8B	131	
D-5106	Schleicher K.8B	8591	
D-5107	Rolladen-Schneider LS-4A	4710	
D-5108	Schleicher K.8	217/61	
D-5109	Rolladen-Schneider LS-4A	4711	
D-5110	Schleicher Ka.6E	4035	
D-5111	Schleicher K.8B	8336/A	
D-5112	Glaser-Dirks DG-100G Elan	E134-G102	
D-5113	SZD-51-1 Junior	B-1781	
D-5114	Rolladen-Schneider LS-4A	4712	
D-5115	Rolladen-Schneider LS-4A	4713	
D-5116	Schleicher K7 Rhönadler	174/60	
D-5117	Rolladen-Schneider LS-4B	4879	
D-5118	Schleicher K7 Rhönadler	1036	
D-5119	Rolladen-Schneider LS-4A	4714	
D-5120	Glaser-Dirks DG-300 Elan	3E-364	
D-5121	Schleicher Ka.6CR Rhönsegler	993	
D-5122	Rolladen-Schneider LS-4A	4716	
D-5123	Schleicher ASK-21	21513	
D-5124-9G	Schleicher ASW-24	24114	
D-5125	Schleicher Ka.6E	4021	
D-5126	Schleicher ASH 26	26072	
D-5127	Schleicher K.8B	1057	
D-5128	Schempp-Hirth Duo Discus *(Reservation 10.99)*	251	
D-5129	Schleicher ASK-21	21501	
D-5130	Schleicher K7 Rhönadler	7252	

Regn.	Type	C/n	Prev.Id.
D-5131	Schleicher K.8B	1061	
D-5132	Schleicher K7 Rhönadler	1090	
D-5133	Schleicher ASK-21	21492	
D-5134	Schleicher ASW-24	24119	
D-5135	Schleicher K.8B	8564	
D-5136	Eiri PIK-20D	20569	OE-5132
D-5137	Schleicher ASK-21	21490	
D-5138	Schleicher K.8B *(Reservation)*	8066	
D-5139	Schleicher ASW-24	24112	
D-5140	Grob G.103A Twin II Acro	3844-K-9O	
D-5141	Grob G.103A Twin II Acro	3856-K-102	
D-5142	Schleicher Ka.6E	4116	
D-5143	Glaser-Dirks DG-300 Elan	3E-199	
D-5144	Glaser-Dirks DG-300 Elan	3E-200	
D-5145	Schleicher Ka.6CR Rhönsegler	6009	
D-5146	Schleicher K.8B *(Reservation)*	221/61	
D-5147	Schleicher Ka.6CR Rhönsegler	6460	
D-5148	Glaser-Dirks DG-300 Elan	3E-201	
D-5149	Grunau Baby IIB	5	
D-5150	Glaser-Dirks DG-300 Elan	3E-302	
D-5151	Schleicher ASW-20	20609	
D-5152	Schleicher K.8B	8097	
D-5154	Schleicher ASK-21	21595	
D-5155	Schleicher K.8B	8107	
D-5156	Schempp-Hirth Mini-Nimbus HS-7	38	OE-5157
D-5157	Glaser-Dirks DG-100	99	OE-5128
D-5161	Rolladen-Schneider LS-7	7044	
D-5163	Rolladen-Schneider LS-7	7046	
D-5164	Rolladen-Schneider LS-4	4466	
D-5165	Schleicher Ka.6CR Rhönsegler	1117	
D-5166	Schempp-Hirth Janus CE	285	
D-5167	Rolladen-Schneider LS-4	4468	
D-5169	Schleicher K.8B	8312	
D-5170	Rolladen-Schneider LS-4	4469	
D-5171	Schleicher K7 Rhönadler	1143	
D-5172	Rolladen-Schneider LS-4A	4750	
D-5173	Rolladen-Schneider LS-4A	4749	
D-5174	Rolladen-Schneider LS-4A	4748	
D-5176	SZD-24-4A Foka 4	W-249	
D-5177	Schleicher Ka.2B Rhönschwalbe	1134	
D-5178	Schempp-Hirth Discus CS	103CS	
D-5179	Schleicher Ka.6CR Rhönsegler	1127	
D-5180	Rolladen-Schneider LS-4	4595	
D-5181	Schleicher Ka.6CR Rhönsegler	1129	
D-5182	Schleicher K7 Rhönadler	7030	
D-5183	Schleicher K.8B	191/60	
D-5185	Rolladen-Schneider LS-4A	4747	
D-5186	Scheibe Zugvogel IIIA	1064	
D-5187	Rolladen-Schneider LS-4A	4746	
D-5188	Schleicher Ka.6CR Rhönsegler	6467Si	
D-5189	Schempp-Hirth Discus CS	104CS	
D-5190	Schleicher K.8B	8001	
D-5191	Schleicher K.8B	8028	D-KEBT D-5191
D-5192	Schleicher Ka.6CR Rhönsegler	6107	
D-5193	Scheibe SF-27A	6048	
D-5194	Glaser-Dirks DG-100G Elan	E131-G99	
D-5197	Schleicher Ka.6CR Rhönsegler	552	
D-5198	Grob G.103C Twin III Acro	34113	
D-5199	Grob G.103C Twin III Acro	34102	
D-5200	Grob G.103C Twin III Acro	34109	
D-5201	Schleicher K7 Rhönadler	7012	
D-5202	SZD-36A Cobra 15	W-563	DDR-2302 DM-2302
D-5203	Schempp-Hirth Cirrus	61	
D-5206	Schempp-Hirth Ventus 2c	10	
D-5207	Schleicher K.8B	8096/A	
D-5208	Grob G.103C Twin III	36009	
D-5210	SZD-9bis Bocian 1E	P-487	DDR-3210 DM-3210
D-5211	Schleicher K.8B	8092	
D-5212	Glaser-Dirks DG-500 Elan Trainer	5E-45T15	
D-5213	Schleicher Ka.2B Rhönschwalbe	2002	
D-5215	Grob G.103C Twin III Acro	34104	
D-5216	Schleicher K.8B	8087/A	
D-5217	Schleicher ASW-17	17004	OE-0939
D-5218	Scheibe SF-27A	6076	
D-5220	Schleicher K.8B	8378	
D-5221	Grunau Baby IIB	6	
D-5222	Schleicher ASW-27	27071	
D-5223	Schleicher ASK-23B	23141	
D-5224	Schleicher ASW-20L	20246	OE-5224
D-5225	Schleicher ASH-25	25011	
D-5226	Schleicher Ka.6CR Rhönsegler	6158	
D-5227	Schempp-Hirth Standard Cirrus	683	OE-5227
D-5228	Schempp-Hirth Discus b	72	
D-5229	Schleicher K.8B	8061	D-KARB D-5229
D-5230	Schempp-Hirth Discus b	81	
D-5231	Schempp-Hirth Ventus c	296	
D-5232	LET L-23 Super Blanik	917904	
D-5233	Grob G.103C Twin III Acro	34116	
D-5234	Schleicher K.8B	8062	
D-5236	Schempp-Hirth Ventus b/16.6	223	
D-5238	Schleicher K7 Rhönadler	7260	
D-5240	Scheibe Bergfalke II/55	362	
D-5241	Schleicher ASW-24	24091	
D-5242	Schleicher ASH-25	25113	
D-5244	Schleicher K7 Rhönadler	7035	
D-5245	Schleicher Ka.6CR Rhönsegler	6090Si	
D-5246	Rolladen-Schneider LS-4A	4727	
D-5247	Rolladen-Schneider LS-4A	4726	
D-5248	Rolladen-Schneider LS-4B	4783	
D-5249	Rolladen-Schneider LS-4A	4724	
D-5250	Schleicher K7 Rhönadler	7063	
D-5251	Schleicher K.8B	8237	
D-5252	Glaser-Dirks DG-500/22 Elan	5E-5S1	
D-5253	Rolladen-Schneider LS-4	4589	
D-5254	Rolladen-Schneider LS-4A	4723	
D-5255	Rolladen-Schneider LS-4A	4739	
D-5256	Rolladen-Schneider LS-4A	4596	
D-5257	Rolladen-Schneider LS-4A	4721	
D-5258	Rolladen-Schneider LS-4	4597	
D-5260	Schempp-Hirth Nimbus 2C *(Reservation - old?)*	230	OE-5260
D-5262	Grob G.103C Twin III Acro	34108	
D-5263	Rolladen-Schneider LS-4	4598	
D-5264	Rolladen-Schneider LS-4A	4719	
D-5265	Rolladen-Schneider LS-4A	4718	
D-5266	Schleicher Rhönlerche II	3027	
D-5267	Schleicher Ka.6CR Rhönsegler	6127Si	
D-5268	Grob G.103A Twin II Acro	3624-K-11	OE-5269
D-5269	Bölkow Phoebus A-1	719	
D-5270	Glaser-Dirks DG-800S	8-60S17	
D-5272	Schleicher Ka.6CR Rhönsegler	6125Si	
D-5274	Schempp-Hirth Duo Discus	132	
D-5275-MH	Rolladen-Schneider LS-7	7101	
D-5276	Schleicher K.8B	8148	
D-5277	Schempp-Hirth Ventus b/16.6	197	
D-5280	Glaser-Dirks DG-300 Elan	3E-249	
D-5281	Schleicher Ka.6CR Rhönsegler	6135	
D-5282	Schleicher ASK-13	13085	
D-5283	Schleicher Ka.6CR Rhönsegler	6137	
D-5284	Glaser-Dirks DG-300 Club Elan	3E-352/C41	
D-5285	Rolladen-Schneider LS-4	4414	
D-5286	Rolladen-Schneider LS-4	4412	
D-5287	Glaser-Dirks DG-100G Elan *(Reservation 10.99)*	E35-G19	
D-5288	Glaser-Dirks DG-300 Elan	3E-367	
D-5289	Schleicher Ka.6CR Rhönsegler	6375Si	
D-5290	Glaser-Dirks DG-300 Elan	3E-250	
D-5291	Grob G.103C Twin III	36012	
D-5293	Schleicher K.8B	8192/A	
D-5294	Grob G.103C Twin III	36003	
D-5295	Schleicher ASW-27	27023	
D-5296	Schleicher K.8B	8171/EI	
D-5297	Schleicher ASK-21	21643	
D-5298	Schleicher ASW-24B	24246	
D-5300	Schleicher Ka.6CR Rhönsegler	6170	
D-5301	Glasflügel H401 Kestrel	123	OE-5311
D-5302	Glaser-Dirks DG-100G Elan	E220-G186	
D-5303	Schleicher K7 Rhönadler	7272	

Regn.	Type	C/n	Prev.Id.
D-5304	Glasflügel H304CZ *(Reservation 10.99)*	21	
D-5305	Schleicher K.8B	8177	
D-5307	Schleicher Ka.6CR Rhönsegler	6128Si	
D-5308	Schleicher K.8B	8181	
D-5309	Rolladen-Schneider LS-7	7104	
D-5310	SZD-36A Cobra 15	W-647	DDR-2310
			DM-2310
D-5311	Schleicher ASK-13	13040	
D-5312	Schleicher K.8B	8466	
D-5313	Schleicher Ka.6E	4134	
D-5314	Schempp-Hirth Discus CS	042CS	
D-5315	Schleicher K7 Rhönadler	7279	
D-5316	Schempp-Hirth Duo Discus *(Reservation - old?)*	250	
D-5318	Schleicher Ka.6CR Rhönsegler	6553	
D-5319	Schleicher Ka.6CR Rhönsegler	6152Si	
D-5320	Schleicher ASW-24	24005	
D-5321	Schleicher ASK-21	21309	
D-5322	Bölkow Phoebus A-1	724	
D-5323	Grob G.103C Twin III Acro	34130	
D-5324	Scheibe SF-34B	5141	
D-5325	Grob G.103C Twin III Acro	34115	
D-5327	Schempp-Hirth Nimbus 3/24.5	56	
D-5328	Schempp-Hirth Ventus b/16.6	180	
D-5329	Schleicher K.8B	8211	
D-5331	Rolladen-Schneider LS-7	7107	
D-5332	Schleicher Ka.6BR Rhönsegler *(Reservation - old?)*	369	D-0409
D-5333	Schleicher Ka.6CR Rhönsegler	6376	
D-5334	Schleicher ASW-20CL	20850	
D-5335	Schempp-Hirth Ventus b/16.6	8	
D-5336	Schleicher ASK-23B	23080	
D-5337	Rolladen-Schneider LS-7	7109	
D-5338	Schleicher K.8B	8292	
D-5339	Schleicher K.8B	8085/2	(D-KABL)
			D-5339
D-5340	Schleicher ASK-13	13055	
D-5341	Schleicher K.8B	8492	
D-5343	Schleicher K.8B	8218/EI	
D-5344	Schleicher K7 Rhönadler	7100	
D-5345	Schleicher ASW-20CL	20851	
D-5346	Schleicher K.8B	8219	
D-5347	Schleicher ASW-24	24142	
D-5348	Schleicher K.8B	8191/A/SH	
D-5349	Schleicher ASK-21	21312	
D-5350	Schleicher ASK-23B	23082	
D-5351	Glaser-Dirks DG-300 Elan	3E-394	
D-5352	Glaser-Dirks DG-300 Club Elan	3E-397/C61	
D-5353	SZD-48-3 Jantar Standard 3	B-1354	
D-5355	Scheibe L-Spatz III	803	
D-5356	Schleicher K.8B	8242	
D-5357	SZD-9bis Bocian 1E	P-544	DDR-3357
			DM-3357
D-5359	Schleicher ASK-21	21208	
D-5360	Schleicher ASW-20CL	20727	
D-5361	Schleicher K7 Rhönadler	7119	
D-5363	Scheibe L-Spatz	1	
D-5364	Schleicher Ka.6CR Rhönsegler	6176	
D-5365	SZD-9bis Bocian 1E	P-521	DDR-3365
			DM-3365
D-5366	Schleicher ASK-13	13119	I-UFFA
D-5367	Schleicher ASK-21	21313	
D-5368	Schleicher Ka.6CR Rhönsegler	6191Si	
D-5369	Schleicher K7 Rhönadler	7113	
D-5370	Schleicher K.8B	8761/AB	
D-5371	Schleicher ASK-21	21214	
D-5372	Schleicher ASW-19B	19403	
D-5375	Schleicher K.8B	8244	D-KANT
			D-5375
D-5380	Vogt LO-100 Zwergreiher	1	
D-5383	Schleicher ASK-21	21317	
D-5384	Schempp-Hirth Discus CS	051CS	
D-5385	Schleicher ASK-13	13095	
D-5386	Glaser-Dirks DG-500 Elan Trainer	5E-58T25	
D-5388	Schleicher K7 Rhönadler *(Reservation 10.99)*	7126	
D-5389	Schleicher K.8	8282/A	
D-5390	Rolladen-Schneider LS-6C	6275	

Regn.	Type	C/n	Prev.Id.
D-5391	Doppelraab 7	2	RAFGGA589
D-5392	Schleicher K.8B	8460	D-5100
D-5393	SZD-9bis Bocian 1E	P-610	DDR-3393
			DM-3393
D-5394	Schleicher ASK-21	21322	
D-5396	Schleicher ASK-21	21577	
D-5398	Rolladen-Schneider LS-4B	4880	
D-5399	Glaser-Dirks DG-300 Club Elan	3E-402/C62	
D-5400	Schleicher ASK-23B	23074	
D-5401	Schleicher ASK-21	21335	
D-5402	Schleicher Ka.2B Rhönschwalbe	272	
D-5403	Schleicher ASW-20BL	20699	
D-5404	Schleicher K7 Rhönadler	7124/A	
D-5405	Kranich III	82	
D-5406	Vogt LO-100 Zwergreiher	17	
D-5407	Scheibe L-Spatz 55	253	
D-5410	SZD-36A Cobra 15	W-582	OH-419
D-5411	Schleicher K.8B	8245/A	
D-5412	Doppelraab IV	EB-1	
D-5413	Glaser-Dirks DG-100G Elan	E205-G171	OE-5404
D-5414	Schleicher K7 Rhönadler	7130	
D-5416	Schleicher K.8B	8757	
D-5417	Schleicher ASK-21	21637	
D-5418	Schleicher ASK-21	21324	
D-5419	Schleicher K.8B	8285	
D-5420	Schempp-Hirth Nimbus 2B	148	OO-ZYZ
D-5421	Schleicher ASK-21 *(Reservation 12.99)*	21709	
D-5422	Schleicher ASK-21	21291	
D-5423	Grunau Baby IIB	2	
D-5424	Schleicher Ka.6CR Rhönsegler	6436	
D-5425	Schleicher K.8B	8362	
D-5427	Schleicher ASK-21	21340	
D-5428	PZL PW-5 Smyk	17.04.014	OE-5628
D-5429	Schleicher ASK-21	21328	
D-5430	Glasflügel H304	232	
D-5431	Schleicher K.8B	8470	
D-5432	Schleicher ASK-23B	23092	
D-5434	Schleicher Ka.2 Rhönschwalbe	126	
D-5435	Schleicher K.8B	8276	
D-5436	Doppelraab V	1	
D-5437	Schleicher K.8B	8302	
D-5438	SZD-24-4A Foka 4	W-305	(D-2444)
			DDR-2044
			DM-2044
D-5439	Schleicher ASK-21	21321	
D-5441	Scheibe Bergfalke III	5539	
D-5442	Grob G.103C Twin III	36001	
D-5443	Grob G.103C Twin III	36002	
D-5444	Glasflügel H201B Standard Libelle	519	HB-1195
D-5445	Schempp-Hirth SHK-1	27	
D-5446	Schempp-Hirth HS-7 Mini-Nimbus	07	OE-5442
			HB-1392
D-5447	Scheibe L-Spatz III	825	
D-5448	Glaser-Dirks DG-500 Elan Trainer	5E-67T28	
D-5449	Schleicher Ka.6CR Rhönsegler	6633Si	
D-5450	SZD-38A Jantar 1	B-611	DDR-2400
			DM-2400
D-5451	Rolladen-Schneider LS-3	3006	PH-545
D-5452	Schleicher K.8B	8212	
D-5453	Schleicher K7 Rhönadler	7149	
D-5454	Schleicher Ka.6CR Rhönsegler	6261	
D-5455	Schleicher Ka.2B Rhönschwalbe	189	
D-5456	Schleicher K.8B	8448	
D-5457	Grunau Baby IIB	54	
D-5458	Grunau Baby IIB	030888	
D-5459	Scheibe SF-27A	6086	
D-5460	Glaser-Dirks DG-500 Elan Trainer	5E-108T44	
D-5461	Schempp-Hirth Discus b	10/275	
D-5464	Schleicher K7 Rhönadler	7154	
D-5465	Schleicher K7 Rhönadler	7257	
D-5466	Schempp-Hirth Ventus 2b	66	
D-5467	Schempp-Hirth Nimbus 2B	158	OE-5467
			D-2828
D-5468	Schleicher Ka.6 Rhönsegler	176	
D-5471	Schempp-Hirth Ventus 2b	51	

Regn.	Type	C/n	Prev.Id.
D-5474	Schempp-Hirth Janus CE	275	
D-5475	Schempp-Hirth Discus b	390	
D-5476	Schempp-Hirth Discus bT	66/392	
D-5477	Scheibe L-Spatz 55	588	
D-5480	Akaflieg Braunschweig SB-5B Sperber	5013/A	
D-5481	Schleicher Ka.2B Rhönschwalbe	213	
D-5483	Schleicher Ka.2B Rhönschwalbe	197	
D-5485	Schleicher Ka.6CR Rhönsegler	6368Si	
D-5486	Scheibe L-Spatz 55	02	
D-5487	Schleicher K.8B	8321/A	D-KANC
			D-5487
D-5488	Glaser-Dirks DG-500 Elan Trainer	5E-120T51	
D-5489	Schleicher Ka.6BR Rhönsegler	531	
D-5491	Schleicher ASK-21	21652	
D-5493	Schempp-Hirth Discus CS	184CS	
D-5494	Schempp-Hirth Discus CS	182CS	
D-5495	LET L-13 Blanik	026808	
D-5499	Rolladen-Schneider LS-4B	4934	
D-5500	Ahrens LY-542K Stoesser	V-1	D-7128
			D-0026
			D-5440
D-5501	LET L-23 Super Blanik	938110	OK-3201
D-5502	Schleicher K7 Rhönadler	7159	
D-5503	Schleicher Ka.2B Rhönschwalbe	224	
D-5504	Schleicher K.8B	8337/A	
D-5506	Scheibe L-Spatz 55	854K	
D-5507	Glaser-Dirks DG-300 Club Elan	3E-383/C55	
D-5508	Glaser-Dirks DG-300 Club Elan	3E-388/C57	
D-5509	Neukom S-4D Elfe	422AB	
D-5510	Rolladen-Schneider LS-4B	4881	
D-5511	Schleicher ASK-13	13028	
D-5513	SZD-55-1	551193051	PH-993
D-5514	Schleicher ASK-13	13205	D-0353
D-5515	Grunau Baby III	1	
D-5516	SZD-48-1 Jantar Standard 2	W-897	OE-5216
D-5518	SZD-55-1	X-144	SP-3501
			SP-P501
D-5519	Schleicher Ka.6CR Rhönsegler	6419	
D-5520	Schleicher Ka.6CR Rhönsegler	6515	
D-5521	Schleicher K7 Rhönadler	7122	
D-5522	Schleicher Ka.6 Rhönsegler	277	
D-5523	Schleicher ASK-23B	23140	
D-5524	Schleicher Ka.6E	4147	
D-5525	LET L-23 Super Blanik	917823	
D-5526	AFH-26	1	
D-5528	Grob G.103C Twin III Acro	34177	
D-5529	Rolladen-Schneider LS-4	4117	
D-5530	Schleicher ASK-23B	23146	
D-5531	SZD-41A Jantar Standard	B-933	OE-5231
D-5532	Grob G.103C Twin III Acro	34147	
D-5533	Schleicher Ka.2B Rhönschwalbe	253	
D-5534	Schleicher Ka.1 (Reservation - old?)	001	
D-5535	Schleicher Ka.6CR Rhönsegler	6505	
D-5536	Schempp-Hirth Ventus 2b	35	
D-5537	Schleicher Ka.6CR Rhönsegler	6257Si	
D-5539	Musger Mg 19a Steinadler (Reservation - old?)	16	OE-5339
D-5541	Scheibe L-Spatz 55 (Reservation)	4/58	
D-5542	Schleicher K.8B	8515SH	
D-5544	Rolladen-Schneider LS-4B	4978	
D-5545	Schleicher Ka.6 Rhönsegler	292	
D-5548	Schempp-Hirth Duo Discus	117	
D-5550	SG-38 Schulgleiter	0010	
D-5551	Scheibe Specht (Reservation)	02/55	OE-0319
D-5552	Schempp-Hirth Discus b	492	
D-5553	Rolladen-Schneider LS-6B	6138	
D-5554	Schleicher Ka.6BR Rhönsegler	355	
D-5555	LET L-13 Blanik	026053	
D-5557	Schleicher Ka.6E	4130	
D-5558	Scheibe L-Spatz 55 (Reservation - old?)	304	
D-5559	Glaser-Dirks DG-800S	8-30S7	
D-5560	Scheibe L-Spatz 55	721	
D-5563	Schleicher K.8B	8372	
D-5564	Glaser-Dirks DG-300 Club Elan (See HB-1984)	3E-316C25	
D-5565	Glaser-Dirks DG-500 Elan Orion	5E-140X5	
D-5566	Glaser-Dirks DG-300 Elan	3E-398	
D-5569	Schleicher K.8B	8566	
D-5570	Schleicher Ka.6E	4006	
D-5571	Rolladen-Schneider LS-6B	6143	
D-5574	Schleicher K.8B	8569	
D-5575	Schleicher Ka.6CR Rhönsegler	6588	
D-5576	Schleicher Ka.6CR Rhönsegler	6313	
D-5577	Schleicher K7 Rhönadler	7172	
D-5578	Glasflügel H301B Libelle	42	
D-5579	Schempp-Hirth Discus b	167	
D-5580	Schempp-Hirth Janus CT	17/280	
D-5582	Schempp-Hirth Discus b	178	
D-5583	Schleicher K7 Rhönadler	7176	
D-5584	Schempp-Hirth Discus b	186	
D-5585	Schempp-Hirth Standard Austria SH	48	
D-5587	Schleicher ASK-21	21158	
D-5588	Rolladen-Schneider LS-4B	4914	
D-5589	Schleicher ASK-21	21159	
D-5590	Schleicher Ka.6BR Rhönsegler	202	
D-5591	Schleicher Ka.6BR Rhönsegler	325	
D-5592	Scheibe SF-27A	6100	
D-5593	Schleicher K.8B	8394SH	
D-5594	Schleicher K.8B	8375	
D-5596	Schleicher Ka.2B Rhönschwalbe	403	
D-5598	Schleicher K7 Rhönadler	7170	
D-5599	Schleicher ASW-27	27015	
D-5600	Ahrens Delphin (Reservation - old?)	V-1	
D-5601	Schleicher Ka.6CR Rhönsegler	6428Si	
D-5602	Scheibe SF-27A	6074	
D-5603	Glaser-Dirks DG-300 Elan	3E-376	
D-5604	Glaser-Dirks DG-300 Club Elan	3E-381/C54	
D-5605	Schleicher ASK-21	21689	
D-5606	Schleicher K7 Rhönadler (Reservation - old?)	7179	
D-5607	Schleicher K7 Rhönadler	7183	
D-5608	Schempp-Hirth Duo Discus (Reservation 10.99)	246	
D-5609	Schleicher K.8B	8435/A	
D-5610	Scheibe SF-27A	6050	
D-5611	Bölkow Phoebus A-1	733	
D-5612	SZD-50-3 Puchacz	B-1329	DDR-3612
D-5613	Schleicher K7 Rhönadler	2	
D-5614	Glaser-Dirks DG-200	2-164	HB-1614
D-5616	LET L-13 Blanik	026060	OE-5016
D-5617	Schleicher K.8B	8416	
D-5619-JB	Glaser-Dirks DG-200/17	2-182/1760	
D-5620	Schleicher ASK-13	13680AB	
D-5621	Schleicher K.8B	8665	D-KLSV
D-5622	Schleicher ASK-13	13679AB	
D-5623	Schleicher Ka.6CR Rhönsegler	6323	
D-5624	Schleicher ASK-13	13689AB	
D-5625	Schleicher ASK-21	21081	
D-5626	Schleicher ASK-21	21082	
D-5627	Schleicher ASW-19B	19354	
D-5628	Schleicher ASK-21	21083	
D-5629	Schleicher ASK-21	21084	
D-5630	Schleicher K7 Rhönadler	413	
D-5631	Schleicher Ka.6BR Rhönsegler	416	
D-5632	SZD-50-3 Puchacz	B-1396	DDR-3632
D-5635	LET L-13 Blanik	026925	OE-5130
D-5636	LET L-13 Blanik	025913	OE-0991
D-5637	Schleicher Ka.6BR Rhönsegler	397	
D-5638	Schleicher K.8B	8472	
D-5639	Schleicher K7 Rhönadler	7178/A	
D-5640	Schleicher Ka.6BR Rhönsegler	383	
D-5642	Glaser-Dirks DG-100G Elan	E167-G133	
D-5643	Scheibe L-Spatz 55	1/59	
D-5644	Schleicher Ka.6CR Rhönsegler	6347Si	
D-5645	Schleicher K.8	451	
D-5646	Schleicher Ka.6E	4039	
D-5647	SZD-48-3 Jantar Standard 3	B-1947	DOSAAF
D-5649	Scheibe L-Spatz 55	3	
D-5650	Rolladen-Schneider LS-1F	312	
D-5651	Schleicher Ka.6CR Rhönsegler	1071	
D-5652	Schleicher Ka.6CR Rhönsegler	6360	
D-5654	Schleicher Ka.6CR Rhönsegler	6352	
D-5655	Schleicher Ka.6BR Rhönsegler	532	
D-5656	Schleicher ASK-13	13618	

Regn.	Type	C/n	Prev.Id.
D-5657	Schempp-Hirth Discus CS	097CS	
D-5658	Schleicher ASK-21	21593	
D-5659	Schleicher K7 Rhönadler	502	
D-5660	SZD-50-3 Puchacz	B-1551	DDR-3660
D-5661	Glaser-Dirks DG-500 Elan Trainer	5E-116T48	
D-5662	Schleicher Ka.6CR Rhönsegler	6424	
D-5663	Schleicher ASK-21	21125	HB-1663
D-5665	Schleicher K.8B (Reservation)	216	OE-5295
D-5666	Schempp-Hirth Discus CS	156CS	
D-5670	Schempp-Hirth Discus 2b	39	
D-5671	Schleicher K.8	8436	
D-5673	Rolladen-Schneider LS-6	6144	
D-5674	Schleicher K.8	508	
D-5676	Schleicher ASK-23B	23135	
D-5677	Schleicher K.8	514	
D-5680	Schleicher Ka.6CR Rhönsegler	6381	
D-5682	Schleicher K.8B	8432H	
D-5684	Schleicher Ka.6BR Rhönsegler	483	
D-5686	Schleicher K.8	512	
D-5688	Schleicher K7 Rhönadler	548	
D-5692	Schleicher K.8B	545	
D-5694	Rolladen-Schneider LS-4	4427	
D-5695	Bölkow Pheobus A-1	749	
D-5696	Rolladen-Schneider LS-4	4428	
D-5698	Schleicher K7 Rhönadler	7202	
D-5699	Schleicher K7 Rhönadler	577	
D-5700	Schempp-Hirth Ventus c	334	OO-PPC
D-5701	Schleicher ASK-13	13001	
D-5702	Glaser-Dirks DG-600	6-30	
D-5703	Grunau Baby IIB	120	
D-5704	Schleicher K.8B	134/59	
D-5705	Schleicher Ka.6CR Rhönsegler	6439Si	
D-5709	Schleicher K7 Rhönadler	578	
D-5710	Glaser-Dirks DG-300 Elan	3E-180	
D-5713	Schleicher ASW-19B	19395	
D-5714	Schleicher ASK-21	21206	
D-5715	Schleicher K.8B	107/58	
D-5716	Glaser-Dirks DG-300 Elan	3E-185	
D-5717	Schleicher K7 Rhönadler	605	
D-5719	Schmepp-Hirth Janus C	151	PH-719
D-5720	Glasflügel 604	6	I-ETAB
D-5722	Glaser-Dirks DG-100G Elan	E192-G158	
D-5725	Glaser-Dirks DG-300 Elan	3E-163	
D-5727	Schleicher K.8B	153/59	
D-5728	Schleicher K.8B	685	
D-5729	Glaser-Dirks DG-300 Elan	3E-186	
D-5731	Schleicher K.8B	138/59	
D-5732	Schleicher K.8B	8023/SH/A	
D-5733	Glaser-Dirks DG-300 Elan	3E-189	
D-5734	Schempp-Hirth Duo Discus	109	
D-5736	Schleicher K7 Rhönadler	701	
D-5737	Schleicher Ka.6CR Rhönsegler	6562	
D-5738	Schleicher K.8B	8465	
D-5739	Glaser-Dirks DG-300 Elan	3E-190	
D-5741	Rolladen-Schneider LS-4	4625	
D-5743	Rolladen-Schneider LS-4	4626	
D-5744	Schempp-Hirth Duo Discus	200	
D-5747	BS.1	13	
D-5748	Schleicher K.8B (Reservation - old?)	737	
D-5749	Schleicher K7 Rhönadler	774	
D-5750	Grob G.103C Twin III	36010	
D-5751	Rolladen-Schneider LS-4	4629	
D-5752	Schleicher ASK-21	21683	
D-5755	SZD-30 Pirat	B-359	DDR-1755
			DM-1755
D-5756	Schleicher Ka.6 Rhönsegler	247	
D-5757	Schleicher Ka.6CR Rhönsegler	718	
D-5758	Rolladen-Schneider LS-4	4630	
D-5760	Schleicher K.8B	850	
D-5761	Akaflieg Braunschweig SB-5E Sperber	5016	
D-5762	SZD-30 Pirat	B-365	DDR-1762
			DM-1762
D-5764	Schleicher K.8B	163/60	
D-5765	Schleicher K.8	110/58	
D-5766	Schleicher ASW-20	20603	OH-666
D-5767	Rolladen-Schneider LS-4	4631	
D-5769	SZD-30 Pirat (Reservation - old?)	B-398	DDR-1769
			DM-1769
D-5770	Schempp-Hirth Discus CS	043CS	
D-5771	Schleicher ASH-26	26021	
D-5772	Schleicher K.8	158/59	
D-5773	Schleicher K7 Rhönadler	77/57	
D-5774	Rolladen-Schneider LS-8-18 (Reservation 9.99)	8285	
D-5776	Schempp-Hirth Duo Discus	133	
D-5777	Schleicher K.8B	640	D-KOBU
			D-5747
D-5778	Schleicher K7 Rhönadler	778	
D-5779	Schleicher K7 Rhönadler	7218	
D-5780	Scheibe SF-27A	6087	
D-5781	Schleicher K7 Rhönadler	832	
D-5782	Schleicher K.8	170/60	
D-5783	Rolladen-Schneider LS-7	7061	
D-5784	Rolladen-Schneider LS-7	7062	
D-5787	Start & Flug H-101 Salto	68	
D-5789	Schleicher Rhönlerche II	805	
D-5790	Schempp-Hirth Ventus c	579	OY-XSS
D-5791	SZD-30 Pirat (old 1.93 ?)	B-434	DDR-1791
			DM-1791
D-5792	Rolladen-Schneider LS-7	7064	
D-5793	Vogt LO-100 Zwergreiher	21	D-4093
D-5794	Schleicher Ka.6CR Rhönsegler	848	
D-5796	Schleicher K7 Rhönadler	866	
D-5797	Rolladen-Schneider LS-6-18W	6358	
D-5798	Schleicher K.8	168/60	
D-5799	Schleicher ASK-13	13032	
D-5800	Schleicher ASK-13 (Reserved as F-CHSB)	13670AB	
D-5802	Schleicher K.8B (Reservation)	841	
D-5803	Schleicher K.8B	842	
D-5804	SZD-51-1 Junior	B-1920	DDR-2804
D-5805	Glaser-Dirks DG-300 Elan	3E-106	
D-5806	Schleicher K.8B	877	
D-5808	Rolladen-Schneider LS-8-18 (Permit 11.99)	8290	
D-5809	Schleicher K.8B	186/60	
D-5810	Schleicher ASK-21	21696	
D-5811	Schleicher ASW-24	24213	
D-5813	VEB LOM 57 Libelle	015	
D-5814	Schleicher K.8B	8428/A	
D-5815	Glaser-Dirks DG-500 Elan Trainer	5E-86T37	
D-5817	SZD-30 Pirat	B-485	DDR-1817
			DM-1817
D-5818	Schleicher Ka.6CR Rhönsegler	6650	
D-5820	Schleicher K7 Rhönadler	7220	
D-5821	Schleicher Ka.6CR Rhönsegler	6425	
D-5822	SZD-30 Pirat	B-499	DDR-1822
			DM-1822
D-5823	Schleicher K.8B	8501	
D-5824	Schleicher K.8B	AB8980	
D-5828	Rock Geier IIB	03	
D-5831	Glaser-Dirks DG-100G Elan	E93-G64	
D-5832	Schleicher ASK-13	13012	
D-5833	SZD-30 Pirat	B-512	DDR-1833
			DM-1833
D-5834	Schleicher ASW-24B	24227	
D-5835	Schleicher K.8B	8429SH	
D-5836	Schleicher Ka.6CR Rhönsegler	6579	
D-5837	Scheibe SF-27A	6067	
D-5838	Glaser-Dirks DG-100G Elan	E92-G63	
D-5839	SZD-55-1	551196092	
D-5840	Rolladen-Schneider LS-6	6108	
D-5841	Schleicher Ka.6CR Rhönsegler	6577	
D-5842	Glaser-Dirks DG-100G Elan	E89-G61	
D-5843	Scheibe SF-27A	6068	
D-5844	Schleicher K7 Rhönadler	7265	
D-5845	Scheibe SF-27A	6069	
D-5846	Glasflügel H304	224	
D-5847	Glasflügel H304	225	
D-5849	Schleicher Ka.6E	4139	
D-5850	BS.1	6	
D-5851	Schleicher K.8B	8739/A	
D-5852	Schleicher K.8B	8737/A	

Regn.	Type	C/n	Prev.Id.
D-5854	Schleicher Ka.6CR Rhönsegler	6637	
D-5855	Scheibe Zugvogel IIIA	1055	
D-5856	Schleicher Ka.6CR Rhönsegler (Reservation)	6290	
D-5857	Schleicher ASK-13	13068	
D-5858	Schleicher K.8B	8748	
D-5859	Neukom S-4D Elfe	415AB	
D-5860	Rolladen-Schneider LS-6B	6110	
D-5861	Glaser-Dirks DG-100G Elan	E88-G60	
D-5862	Focke-Wulf Weihe 50 (Museum) (Reservation - dd?)	unkn	
D-5863	Schleicher Ka.6CR Rhönsegler	6378	
D-5865	Glasflügel H304	258	
D-5866	Grob G.103C Twin III Acro	34195	
D-5867	Glaser-Dirks DG-100G Elan	E98-G68	
D-5869	Glasflügel H301 Libelle	15	HB-794
D-5870	Grob G.102 Astir CS	1021	
D-5871	Grob G.102 Astir CS	1022	
D-5872	Glaser-Dirks DG-100G Elan	E96-G66	
D-5875	Grob G.102 Astir CS (Reservation)	1026	
D-5876	Grob G.102 Astir CS	1027	
D-5877	Glaser-Dirks DG-200	2-169	
D-5878	Grob G.102 Astir CS	1029	
D-5879	Grob G.102 Astir CS	1030	
D-5880	Grob G.102 Astir CS	1031	
D-5881	Grob G.102 Astir CS	1032	
D-5882	Scheibe SF-27A	6002	
D-5883	SZD-30 Pirat	S-01.29	DDR-1883 DM-1883
D-5884	Glaser-Dirks DG-200/17C	2-170/CL16	
D-5885	Schempp-Hirth Ventus 2a	56	
D-5886	Rolladen-Schneider LS-1F	256	
D-5887	Rolladen-Schneider LS-1F	285	
D-5888	SZD-30 Pirat	S-02.44	DDR-1888 DM-1888
D-5889	HBV Diamant	008	HB-889
D-5890	Rolladen-Schneider LS-6B	6111	
D-5891	Glasflügel H201B Standard Libelle	503/A	
D-5895	Schempp-Hirth Janus B	157	
D-5896	Schempp-Hirth Nimbus 3/24.5	25	
D-5898	Rolladen-Schneider LS-3A	3284	
D-5900	Grob G.103C Twin III Acro	34185	
D-5901	Rolladen-Schneider LS-3A	3160	
D-5902	Rolladen-Schneider LS-4	4137	
D-5903	Rolladen-Schneider LS-4	4153	
D-5904-BG	Rolladen-Schneider LS-4	4118	
D-5905	Glaser-Dirks DG-300 Elan	3E-233	
D-5906	Rolladen-Schneider LS-6C	6276	
D-5907	Glasflügel H303 Mosquito B	152	
D-5909	Schleicher ASW-19B	19330	
D-5910	Grob G.103 Twin II	3640	
D-5911	Grob G.103 Twin II	3641	
D-5913	Grob G.102 Astir CS 77	1822	
D-5914	Grob G.102 Astir CS 77	1823	
D-5915	Grob G.102 Astir CS Jeans	2232	
D-5916	Grob G.102 Astir CS Jeans	2236	
D-5918	Grob G.102 Astir CS Jeans	2238	
D-5919	Grob G.102 Astir CS 77	1824	
D-5920	Grob G.102 Speed Astir IIB	4028	
D-5921	Grob G.102 Astir CS 77	1832	
D-5923	Schleicher ASK-21	21108	
D-5924	Glaser-Dirks DG-100G Elan	E122-G91	
D-5926	Glaser-Dirks DG-100G Elan	E124-G92	
D-5927	Glasflügel H304	239	
D-5928	Glasflügel H304	240	
D-5929	Glasflügel H304	242	
D-5931	Glasflügel H304	236	
D-5932	Schleicher ASW-20CL	20754	
D-5933	Schleicher ASW-20CL	20756	
D-5934	Schleicher ASW-19B	19407	
D-5935	Schleicher ASW-20 L	20759	
D-5936	Schleicher ASW-20BL	20647	
D-5940	Scheibe Bergfalke IV	5863	
D-5942	Schleicher ASK-21	21587	
D-5944	Grob G.102 Astir CS 77	1827	
D-5945	Grob G.102 Astir CS 77	1828	
D-5947	Grob G.102 Astir CS Jeans	2242	
D-5948	Grob G.102 Astir CS Jeans	2243	
D-5950	Grob G.102 Astir CS 77	1825	
D-5952	SZD-48-3 Jantar Standard 3	B-1952	
D-5954	Grob G.103 Twin Astir	3194	
D-5955	SZD-55-1	551193059	SP-3602
D-5956	Grob G.103 Twin Astir	3196	
D-5957	PZL PW-5 Smyk (del. to Russia?)	17.04.022	
D-5959	FFA Diamant 18	75	OO-ZDI
D-5960	Grob G.103 Twin Astir	3207	
D-5961	Schleicher ASH-26	26009	
D-5963	Grob G.103 Twin Astir Trainer	3211-T-24	
D-5964	Grob G.103 Twin Astir	3213	
D-5967	Grob G.103 Twin Astir	3225	
D-5968	Grob G.103 Twin Astir	3227	
D-5969	Grob G.103 Twin Astir	3230	
D-5970	Rolladen-Schneider LS-6C-18	6359	
D-5971	Grob G.103 Twin Astir	3246	
D-5974	Schleicher ASW-19B	19257	
D-5975	Schleicher ASW-20L	20145	
D-5976	Schleicher ASW-19B	19258	
D-5977	Schleicher ASW-19B	19260	
D-5978	Schleicher ASW-19B	19261	
D-5983	Schleicher ASW-24	24223	ZK-GRC
D-5986	Rolladen-Schneider LS-4	4288	
D-5988	Rolladen-Schneider LS-4	4341	
D-5990	Eiri PIK-20D	20523	
D-5991	Schempp-Hirth Janus C	133	
D-5992	Schempp-Hirth Ventus A	30	
D-5994	Schleicher ASH-25	25159	
D-5995	Rolladen-Schneider LS-4	4042	
D-5997	Rolladen-Schneider LS-4	4030	
D-5998	Rolladen-Schneider LS-4	4214	
D-5999	Glaser-Dirks DG-200/17	2-168/1754	D-1532 HB-1634
D-6000	Glaser-Dirks DG-200/17	2-161/1752	
D-6001	Schempp-Hirth HS-7 Mini-Nimbus B	70	
D-6002	Schleicher K.8B	8145/A	
D-6003	Schleicher Rhönlerche II	10	
D-6004	Grunau Baby III	02	
D-6006	SZD-9bis Bocian 1E	P-716	DDR-3004 DM-3004
D-6007	Glasflügel H304	249	
D-6008	Glaser-Dirks DG-300 Elan	3E-26	
D-6009	Glaser-Dirks DG-300 Elan	3E-29	
D-6010	Schleicher K7 Rhönadler	7167/AB	
D-6011	Schempp-Hirth Discus b	308	
D-6012	SZD-9bis Bocian 1E	P-725	DDR-3012 DM-3012
D-6013	Focke-Wulf Kranich III	54	
D-6014	Eiri PIK-20D	20654	OH-600
D-6015	Akaflieg Braunschweig SB-8	V-1	
D-6017	Schleicher K.8B	8287	
D-6018	Focke-Wulf Kranich III	53	
D-6019	Schleicher ASW-19B	19389	
D-6020	Glaser-Dirks DG-500/20 Elan	5E-171W9	
D-6021	Schleicher K.8B	8248/2	
D-6022	Schleicher Ka.6CR Rhönsegler	6057	
D-6023	Glaser-Dirks DG-500/22 Elan	5E-63S10	
D-6025	Schleicher Ka.6CR Rhönsegler	6557Si	
D-6026	Cumulus CU-II F	01	
D-6027	Schleicher K.8B (Reservation - dd?)	8169	
D-6028	Schleicher K.8B	8224	
D-6030	Schleicher K.8B	1	
D-6031-X4	Schempp-Hirth Discus A	50	
D-6033	Schleicher Rhönlerche II	84	
D-6034	Schempp-Hirth Ventus c	289	
D-6036	Schleicher K.8B	8215	
D-6037	Schleicher ASK-21	21634	
D-6038	Schleicher K.8B	8397	
D-6041	Rolladen-Schneider LS-4	4627	
D-6042	Rolladen-Schneider LS-7	7157	
D-6043	Dittmar Condor IV	13	LV-EHB
D-6044	Focke-Wulf Kranich III	64	
D-6045	Schleicher K.8B	8663	

Regn.	Type	C/n	Prev.Id.
D-6046	Olympia-Meise	1/95	BGA2080 D-6220
D-6047	Rolladen-Schneider LS-6	6116	
D-6049	Rolladen-Schneider LS-7	7160	
D-6050	Schleicher K7 Rhönadler	7064/A	
D-6051	Grunau Baby IIB	06	
D-6052	Schleicher ASK-13	13020	
D-6053	Schleicher Ka.6CR Rhönsegler	6590	
D-6054	Grunau Baby III (Reservation 1.99)	unkn	
D-6055	Schempp-Hirth Ventus b/16.6	250	
D-6056	Schleicher ASK-13	13027	
D-6057	Grob G.102 Club Astir IIIB	5515CB	
D-6058	Grob G.102 Club Astir III	5518C	
D-6059	Cumulus CU-III F	02	
D-6060	Schleicher ASK-13	13506AB	
D-6061	Doppelraab V	532	
D-6062	Rolladen-Schneider LS-6	6118	
D-6063	Schleicher ASK-13	13021	
D-6064	Doppelraab V (Permit 8.99)	534	
D-6065	Schempp-Hirth Ventus b/16.6	249	
D-6066	Schleicher K.8B	8700	
D-6067	Schleicher K7 Rhönadler	02/62	
D-6070	Schleicher K7 Rhönadler	7074	
D-6071	Focke-Wulf Kranich III	68	
D-6072	Schleicher Ka.6CR Rhönsegler	6292	
D-6073	Focke-Wulf Kranich III	71	
D-6074	Schleicher ASK-21	21467	
D-6075	Schleicher ASW-24	24094	
D-6076	Schleicher ASW-24	24097	
D-6077	Glaser-Dirks DG-300 Elan	3E-335	
D-6080	Schleicher K7 Rhönadler	7229	
D-6083	Schleicher K.8B	8720	
D-6084	Rolladen-Schneider LS-7	7164	
D-6085	Akaflieg Braunschweig SB-10	01	
D-6086	Rolladen-Schneider LS-4	4301	
D-6087	Schleicher ASW-24	24098	
D-6088	Schleicher ASH-25	25089	
D-6089	Schleicher Ka.6CR Rhönsegler	6484Si	
D-6090	Glaser-Dirks DG-200/17	2-173/1756	
D-6092	Schleicher ASW-24	24100	
D-6093	Schleicher ASH-25	25101	
D-6094	Schempp-Hirth Nimbus 3/24.5	72	
D-6096	SZD-9bis Bocian 1E (Permit 10.99)	P-484	DDR-3096 DM-3096
D-6098	SZD-9bis Bocian 1E	P-485	DDR-3098 DM-3098
D-6099	Schleicher K.8B	8071	
D-6100	Glaser-Dirks DG-100G	86G7	
D-6101	Start & Flug H-101 Salto	70	
D-6102	Grob G.102 Astir CS (Reservation - old?)	1001	
D-6103	Akaflieg Braunschweig SB-7B (Reservation 11.99)	1	
D-6104	Schleicher Ka.6CR Rhönsegler (Reservn - old?)	6109Si	
D-6105	Grob G.102 Standard Astir III	5535S	
D-6106	Grob G.103 Twin II	3642	
D-6107	Scheibe Bergfalke III	5570	
D-6110	Grob G.103C Twin III Acro	34179	
D-6111	Schempp-Hirth Discus 2b (Permit 12.99)	1	
D-6112	Scheibe Spatz A	1	
D-6113	Schleicher ASK-13	13619AB	
D-6115	Schleicher Ka.6E	4166	
D-6118	Schleicher Ka.6CR Rhönsegler	6636	
D-6120	Schleicher ASW-20CL	20865	
D-6121	Schleicher ASK-21	21616	(JA2539)
D-6122	Schempp-Hirth Duo Discus	68	
D-6123	Schleicher Ka.6CR Rhönsegler	6162	
D-6124	Schleicher K.8B	8331SH	
D-6125	Schleicher Ka.2 Rhönschwalbe	105	
D-6126	Schleicher ASH-26	26059	
D-6127	Schempp-Hirth Cirrus	14	
D-6128	Schleicher ASK-21	21085	
D-6129	Schleicher ASK-21	21086	
D-6130	Schleicher K.8B	8183	
D-6132	Schleicher ASW-24	24128	
D-6133-JU	Schleicher K.8B	18/8132	D-3033
D-6135	Schleicher Ka.6E	4164	
D-6136	Schleicher ASK-21	21623	
D-6138	Schleicher ASW-24	24156	
D-6139	Schleicher ASW-24	24158	
D-6140	Schleicher ASW-24	24159	
D-6141	Schleicher Ka.2 Rhönschwalbe (Reservation)	79	
D-6142	Schleicher ASW-24	24161	
D-6143	Scheibe L-Spatz 55	03	
D-6144	Schleicher ASK-21	21426	
D-6145	Schleicher ASW-24	24055	
D-6146-J6	Schleicher ASK-21	21428	
D-6147	Scheibe Bergfalke III	5522	
D-6148	Doppelraab 7	01	
D-6149	Schleicher ASW-24	24163	
D-6150	Doppelraab 7	0110	
D-6151	Schleicher ASW-24	24164	
D-6153	Schleicher ASK-21	21461	
D-6154	Scheibe Bergfalke III	5563	
D-6155	Schleicher ASK-21	21633	
D-6156	Scheibe Zugvogel IIIB	1106	
D-6157	Schleicher ASW-24	24169	
D-6158	Grob G.102 Standard Astir III	5522S	
D-6159	Schempp-Hirth Discus b	80	I-AYEZ D-5241
D-6160	Scheibe L-Spatz	01	
D-6162	Grunau Baby IIB	1	
D-6163	Schleicher Ka.6CR Rhönsegler	6026	D-KODY D-6163
D-6164	Schleicher Rhönlerche II	3080Br	
D-6165	Glaser-Dirks DG-300 Elan	3E-401	
D-6166	Rolladen-Schneider LS-4B	4955	
D-6167	Schleicher Ka.3 (Reservation 12.99)	06	
D-6168	Grunau Baby III (Reservation 11.99)	4	
D-6169	SZD-50-3 Puchacz	B-2053	
D-6170	Schleicher Ka.6CR Rhönsegler (Reservation)	6163	
D-6171	Schempp-Hirth Discus b	42	
D-6172	Schleicher ASW-24	24170	
D-6173	Schleicher Ka.2B Rhönschwalbe	195	
D-6174	Schleicher K-10A	10001	
D-6175	Rolladen-Schneider LS-6C	6235	
D-6176	Grunau Baby IIB	03	
D-6178	Schleicher K.8B	8046	
D-6179-M6	Schleicher ASK-21	21429	
D-6180	Schleicher ASW-24	24059	
D-6181	Bölkow Phoebus A-1	788	
D-6182	Schleicher ASW-24	24060	
D-6183	Schleicher ASH-25	25076	
D-6184	Schleicher ASK-21	21432	
D-6185	Schleicher ASK-21	21433	
D-6186	Schleicher ASW-24	24064	
D-6188	Grob G.103C Twin III Acro	34143	
D-6190	Grob G.103 Twin II	3734	
D-6191	Rolladen-Schneider LS-6	6119	
D-6192	Rolladen-Schneider LS-7	7142	
D-6193	Rolladen-Schneider LS-7	7143	
D-6194	Schleicher K.8B	8065	D-6121
D-6196	Focke-Wulf Kranich III	76	
D-6198	Schleicher Ka.2B Rhönschwalbe	274	
D-6199	Rolladen-Schneider LS-4B	4915	
D-6200	Fauvel AV-36	222	
D-6201	Schleicher K7 Rhönadler	7216	
D-6202	SZD-48-1 Jantar Standard	B-1209	OE-5302
D-6203	Glasflügel H304	233	
D-6205	Schempp-Hirth Janus C	208	
D-6206	Schleicher K7 Rhönadler	304	
D-6207	SZD-9bis Bocian 1D	P-362	DDR-3207 DM-3207
D-6208	Schleicher K7 Rhönadler	286	
D-6210	Rolladen-Schneider LS-6C	6204	
D-6211	Test Registration for Schempp-Hirth Discus b		
D-6212	Vogt LO-100 Zwergreiher	14	
D-6213	Schleicher Rhönlerche II	311	
D-6214	SZD-36A Cobra 15	W-668	HB-1214
D-6215	Schleicher ASW-24	24181	
D-6216	Rolladen-Schneider LS-6C	6207	
D-6217	Glaser-Dirks DG-200/17	2-91/1708	

Regn.	Type	C/n	Prev.Id.
D-6218	Glaser-Dirks DG-200	2-76	
D-6219	Schleicher K7 Rhönadler	5	
D-6220	Glaser-Dirks DG-200/17	2-81/1702	
D-6221	Glaser-Dirks DG-200	2-78	
D-6222	Schleicher Ka.6BR Rhönsegler	395	
D-6223	Glaser-Dirks DG-200	2-79	
D-6224	Grunau Baby III	1	
D-6225	Grunau Baby IIb	0001	
D-6226	Schleicher Ka.6BR Rhönsegler	418	
D-6227	Focke-Wulf Kranich III (Reservation)	88	
D-6228	Focke-Wulf Kranich III	90	
D-6229	Scheibe L-Spatz 55	01	
D-6230	Glaser-Dirks DG-300 Elan	3E-53	
D-6231	Schleicher ASW-24	24185	
D-6232	Schleicher Ka.6CR Rhönsegler	6185	
D-6234	Schleicher ASK-21	21437	
D-6235	Schleicher ASK-21	21449	
D-6236	Schleicher ASK-21	21450	
D-6237	Schleicher K7 Rhönadler (Reservation - old?)	394	
D-6238	Schleicher Ka.6CR Rhönsegler	6574	
D-6240	Schleicher K.8	510	
D-6241	Schleicher ASW-24	24191	
D-6242	Schleicher K.8	04	
D-6243	Schleicher K.8B (Reservation - old?)	515	
D-6245	Schleicher ASW-24	24198	
D-6248	Schleicher K.8B	1016	
D-6249	SZD-9bis Bocian 1E (Reservation 2.99)	P-536	DDR-3249 DM-3249
D-6250	Schleicher Ka.6 Rhönsegler	600	
D-6251	Schleicher K.8	03	
D-6253	Schleicher ASW-24	24042	
D-6254	Schleicher ASK-21	21415	
D-6255	Schleicher ASK-21	21416	
D-6256	Schleicher K7 Rhönadler	7098	
D-6257	Schleicher K7 Rhönadler	536	
D-6260	Glaser-Dirks DG-600	6-16	
D-6261	Schleicher K.8B	589	
D-6262	Rolladen-Schneider LS-6	6043	
D-6263-71	Rolladen-Schneider LS-6	6044	
D-6264	Grob G.102 Standard Astir III	5528S	
D-6266	Scheibe SF-34B	5133	
D-6267	Schleicher Rhönlerche II	615	
D-6268	Schleicher Ka.6CR Rhönsegler (Reservation - old?)	601	
D-6269	Schleicher Ka.6E	4020	
D-6270	Schleicher ASW-24	24197	
D-6271	Schleicher K.8B	8415	
D-6272	SZD-55-1	551196088	
D-6273	Schleicher K.8B	734	
D-6274	Focke-Wulf Kranich III	62	
D-6276	Grob G.103C Twin III Acro	34170	
D-6277	Grob G.103C Twin III Acro	34106	
D-6278	Scheibe Zugvogel IVA	1512	
D-6280	Schleicher Ka.6CR Rhönsegler	783	
D-6282	Grob G.103C Twin III Acro	34153	
D-6283	Grob G.103C Twin III Acro	34145	
D-6284	Grob G.103C Twin III Acro	34142	
D-6285-LS	Grob G.103C Twin III Acro	34144	
D-6286	Grob G.103C Twin III Acro	34150	
D-6287	Schleicher ASK-21	21069	
D-6288	Schleicher Ka.6CR Rhönsegler	825	
D-6290	Schleicher Ka.6CR Rhönsegler	809	
D-6291	Schleicher K7 Rhönadler	792	
D-6292	Lanaverre Standard Cirrus CS11/75L	14	F-CEVO
D-6295	Scheibe L-Spatz 55	554	
D-6296	Schleicher K.8B	1	
D-6297	Schempp-Hirth Discus 2b	42	
D-6298	Schempp-Hirth Duo Discus	126	
D-6299	Akaflieg Braunschweig SB-5C (Reservation 11.99)	V-1	
D-6300	Akaflieg Braunschweig SB-5E	6	
D-6301	Neukom S-4D Elfe	402AB	
D-6302	Schleicher ASW-20L	20101	
D-6304	Schleicher K7 Rhönadler	888	
D-6305	Schleicher K.8B	5/142/59	
D-6307	SZD-36A Cobra 15	W-628	DDR-2307 DM-2307

Regn.	Type	C/n	Prev.Id.
D-6308	SZD-36A Cobra 15	W-617	DDR-2308 DM-2308
D-6309	Glaser-Dirks DG-300 Elan Acro	3E-429A1	HB-3072
D-6311	Schleicher Ka.6E	4191	
D-6312	Schempp-Hirth Nimbus 3D	12	
D-6313	Rolladen-Schneider LS-4	4313	
D-6314	Rolladen-Schneider LS-8A	8141	
D-6315	Rolladen-Schneider LS-8A	8142	
D-6316	Schleicher Rhönlerche II	1046	
D-6317	Schleicher Ka.6CR Rhönsegler	1068	
D-6318	Schempp-Hirth Nimbus 4	9/28	
D-6319	Schleicher Ka.6CR Rhönsegler	1044	
D-6321	Schleicher ASK-21	21586	
D-6322	Schleicher Rhönlerche II (Reservation - old?)	1048	
D-6323	LET L-23 Super Blanik	948126	
D-6324	Schleicher K.8B	1103	
D-6326	Schleicher K7 Rhönadler	1135	
D-6327	Schleicher ASW-27	27012	
D-6328	IAR IS.29D	30	HB-1328
D-6330	SZD-51-1 Junior	B-2152	
D-6331	Schleicher Rhönlerche II	3007	
D-6333	Schleicher K.8B	8090El	
D-6334	LET L-33 Solo	940304	
D-6335	Rolladen-Schneider LS-4	4486	
D-6336-MY	Rolladen-Schneider LS-6	6027	
D-6337	LET L-23 Super Blanik	907627	
D-6338	LET L-23 Super Blanik	907628	
D-6340	Grunau Baby III	75	
D-6341	Schleicher K.8B	8294	
D-6342	Schleicher Ka.6CR Rhönsegler	6487Si	
D-6343	LET L-13 Blanik	172729	
D-6344	Grunau Baby III	1/53	
D-6345	Glasflügel H201B Standard Libelle	128	I-AVSC
D-6346	Schleicher K.8B	8359	
D-6347	Schleicher Ka.6CR Rhönsegler	6600	
D-6348	Schleicher K.8B	223/61	
D-6350	Bölkow Phoebus B-1	800	
D-6351	SZD-9bis Bocian 1E	P-538	DDR-3351 DM-3351
D-6352	Schleicher Ka.6CR Rhönsegler (Reservation 8.99)	6306	
D-6353	Rolladen-Schneider LS-8 (Permit 11.99)	8001	BGA4109 D-6353
D-6354	Scheibe L-Spatz 55 (Reservation)	E-2	
D-6355	Schleicher K.8B	8381	
D-6357	Schleicher K7 Rhönadler	7188	
D-6358	Schleicher K7 Rhönadler	7203	
D-6359	Glaser-Dirks DG-500 Elan Orion	5E-135X2	
D-6360	Schleicher K.8B	8453	
D-6361	Schleicher K.8B	8547	
D-6362	Schleicher K.8B (Reservation)	8454	
D-6363	Schleicher Ka.6CR Rhönsegler	6497	
D-6364	Schempp-Hirth Discus b	517	
D-6366	Rolladen-Schneider LS-6-18W	6356	
D-6367	Grunau Baby III	2	
D-6368	Schleicher K.8B	8455	
D-6370	Rolladen-Schneider LS-6	6088	
D-6371	Rolladen-Schneider LS-6	6089	
D-6373	SZD-24-4A Foka 4	W-241	
D-6374	Schleicher K.8B	8584	
D-6375	Rolladen-Schneider LS-4B	4964	
D-6376	Rolladen-Schneider LS-4B	4965	
D-6377	Schleicher Ka.6CR Rhönsegler	6533Si	
D-6378	Rolladen-Schneider LS-6A	6092	
D-6380	Schleicher Ka.6CR Rhönsegler	857	
D-6381	Schleicher Ka.6CR Rhönsegler	6547	
D-6383	Schleicher Ka.6CR Rhönsegler	6490Si	
D-6385	Scheibe SF-27A	6062	
D-6386	Schleicher K7 Rhönadler	979	
D-6390	Schleicher ASK-23B	23139	
D-6392	Schleicher ASK-21	21090	
D-6394	Schempp-Hirth Standard Cirrus	593	
D-6395	Schempp-Hirth Standard Cirrus	596	
D-6396	Scheibe Bergfalke IV/55	307	
D-6397	Grob G.103A Twin II Acro	34041-K-272	
D-6398	Grob G.103A Twin II Acro	34039-K-270	

Regn.	Type	C/n	Prev.Id.
D-6399	Schleicher Ka.6CR Rhönsegler	1005	
D-6400	Bölkow Phoebus B-1	715	
D-6401	Glaser-Dirks DG-500/20 Elan	5E-178W11	
D-6402	Schempp-Hirth Ventus b/16.6	47	
D-6403	Glaser-Dirks DG-200/17	2-188/1762	
D-6404	Schleicher Ka.6BR Rhönsegler	357	
D-6406	Rolladen-Schneider LS-7	7125	
D-6407	Rolladen-Schneider LS-7	7126	
D-6408	Schleicher Ka.6CR Rhönsegler	6124Si	D-4671
D-6409	Glaser-Dirks DG-100G Elan *(Reservation - old?)*	105G16	LX-CCW
			D-6101
D-6410	Rolladen-Schneider LS-7	7129	
D-6411	Rolladen-Schneider LS-4	4173	
D-6412	Grob G.103A Twin II Acro	34059-K-289	
D-6413	Scheibe Bergfalke II/55	244	OE-0413
D-6414	Rolladen-Schneider LS-7	7131	
D-6415	Rolladen-Schneider LS-4	4043	
D-6416	Schelicher ASW-24	24180	
D-6417	Rolladen-Schneider LS-6C	6236	
D-6418	Grob Standard Cirrus *(Reservation 3.99)*	308G	D-2062
D-6419	Schleicher ASK-21 *(Reservation)*	21392	HB-1964
D-6420	Schempp-Hirth Janus CE	298	
D-6421	Grob G.103A Twin II Acro	34064-K-294	
D-6423	Rolladen-Schneider LS-6C	6224	
D-6424	Schleicher ASW-24B	24237	
D-6425	Rolladen-Schneider LS-6C	6226	
D-6427	Schempp-Hirth Standard Cirrus	19	
D-6428	Rolladen-Schneider LS-4	4023	
D-6429	Grob G.103A Twin II Acro	34065-K-295	
D-6430	Glaser-Dirks DG-100G Elan	E141-G109	
D-6432	Rolladen-Schneider LS-4	4028	
D-6433	Glasflügel H205 Club Libelle	44	
D-6435	Grob G.103 Twin II	3574	
D-6437	Grob G.103 Twin II	3610	
D-6438	Grob G.103 Twin II	3611	
D-6441	Schempp-Hirth Nimbus 2B	171	
D-6443	Schempp-Hirth Mini-Nimbus B	68	
D-6444	Glasflügel H205 Club Libelle	45	HB-1244
D-6445	Grob G.103A Twin II Acro	34066-K-296	
D-6446	Grob G.103A Twin II Acro *(Reservation)*	34067-K-297	
D-6447	Schleicher K.8B	8290/EI	
D-6448	Schleicher ASK-21	21682	
D-6449	Schleicher ASK-21	21418	
D-6450	Schleicher ASW-24	24043	
D-6451	Schleicher ASW-24	24046	
D-6452	Schleicher ASK-21	21421	
D-6453	Schleicher Ka.6CR Rhönsegler	6155	
D-6454	Schleicher K.8B	134/04	
D-6455	SZD-55-1	551195067	
D-6456	Glasflügel H401 Kestrel	122	
D-6457	Schleicher ASW-27	27052	
D-6458	Grob G.103A Twin II Acro	34073-K-303	
D-6459	Grob G.103A Twin II Acro	34074-K-304	
D-6460	Rolladen-Schneider LS-6	6001	
D-6461	Rolladen-Schneider LS-4	4436	
D-6462	Caproni Vizzola A-21S Calif	217	I-VIZP
D-6464	SZD-55-1	551194072	
D-6465	Schempp-Hirth Standard Austria S	15	OO-ZLI
D-6466	Scheibe LCF-2	1	
D-6467	Grob G.102 Club Astir IIIB	5503CB	
D-6468	Grob G.103A Twin II Acro	3638-K-19	
D-6469	Grob G.103A Twin II Acro	3639-K-20	
D-6471	Schleicher Ka.6CR Rhönsegler	6517Si	
D-6472	Rolladen-Schneider LS-6C	6228	
D-6473	Schempp-Hirth Duo Discus	203	
D-6474	Rolladen-Schneider LS-1F	364	
D-6476	Rolladen-Schneider LS-1F	288	
D-6477	Rolladen-Schneider LS-1F	368	
D-6478	Rolladen-Schneider LS-1F	287	
D-6479	Rolladen-Schneider LS-1F	369	
D-6480	Rolladen-Schneider LS-1F	373	
D-6481	Schleicher ASW-27	27017	
D-6482	Rolladen-Schneider LS-1F	407	
D-6485	Schleicher ASK-13	13489	
D-6486	Glaser-Dirks DG-100 Elan	E-5	

Regn.	Type	C/n	Prev.Id.
D-6488	Rolladen-Schneider LS-8-18 *(Reservation 11.99)*	8294	
D-6489	Schleicher ASK-13	13648AB	
D-6490	Schempp-Hirth Duo Discus	101	
D-6491	Schempp-Hirth Standard Cirrus	586	
D-6492	Schempp-Hirth Standard Cirrus	597	
D-6493	Schempp-Hirth Standard Cirrus	599	
D-6495	Schempp-Hirth Nimbus 2	99	
D-6497	Rolladen-Schneider LS-1F	386	
D-6498	Glasflügel H206 Hornet	40	
D-6499	Schleicher ASW-20CL	20735	
D-6500	Schleicher K.8B	8086	D-KOCE
			D-4047
D-6501	Rolladen-Schneider LS-6C	6232	
D-6502	Rolladen-Schneider LS-6C	6233	
D-6503	Grob G.102 Astir CS	1006	
D-6504	Glasflügel H201B Standard Libelle	559	PH-504
D-6505	Glaser-Dirks DG-500 Elan Orion *(Reservn)*	5E-197X41	
D-6506	Grob G.102 Astir CS	1010	
D-6507	Schleicher ASK-21	21579	
D-6508	Schempp-Hirth Duo Discus *(Reservation 9.99)*	235	
D-6509	Grob G.102 Astir CS	1013	
D-6510	Grob G.102 Astir CS	1014	
D-6511	Schempp-Hirth Ventus b/16.6	244	
D-6512	Glasflügel H205 Club Libelle	107	
D-6513	Schleicher ASW-19B	19414	
D-6515	Schleicher ASK-23	23020	
D-6516	Schleicher ASK-21	1250	
D-6517	Schleicher ASK-23	23019	
D-6518	Schleicher ASW-20C	20803	
D-6519	Schleicher ASW-20CL	20804	
D-6520	Schleicher ASW-20L	20552	D-KHHG
			OE-9394
			OE-5294
D-6521	Rolladen-Schneider LS-1F	479	
D-6522	Schempp-Hirth Ventus 2c	24/65	
D-6523	Rolladen-Schneider LS-1F	481	
D-6524	Schleicher ASW-19B	19300	
D-6525	Schleicher ASW-20	20305	
D-6526	Schleicher ASW-19B	19303	
D-6528	Schleicher ASK-21	21012	
D-6529	Schleicher ASW-19B	19306	
D-6530	Schleicher ASK-21	21013	
D-6531	Schleicher ASW-19B	19307	
D-6533-UP	Schleicher ASW-20L	20307	
D-6534	Schleicher ASW-20	20283	
D-6535	Schleicher ASW-20L	20281	
D-6536	Schleicher ASK-21	21004	
D-6537	Schleicher ASK-21	21005	
D-6538	Schleicher ASW-20L	20285	
D-6539	Schleicher ASK-21	21006	
D-6541	Schleicher ASK-13	13617	
D-6542	Schleicher ASW-20L	20287	
D-6543	Schleicher ASW-20L	20290	
D-6544	SZD-9bis Bocian 1E	P-531	DDR-3244
			DM-3244
D-6546	Glaser-Dirks DG-200/17	2-135/1733	
D-6547	Glaser-Dirks DG-100G Elan	E48-G27	
D-6549	Schleicher ASW-19B	19298	
D-6550	Schleicher ASW-20	20231	
D-6551	Schleicher ASW-20	20291	
D-6552	Schleicher ASK-21	21011	
D-6553	Schleicher ASW-20CL	20808	
D-6556	Schleicher ASK-21	21122	HB-1656
D-6560	Rolladen-Schneider LS-3-17	3386	
D-6561	Rolladen-Schneider LS-6-18W	6360	
D-6562	Rolladen-Schneider LS-3-17	3425	
D-6563	SZD-48-3 Jantar Standard 3	B-1753	DOSAAF
D-6564	Schleicher ASW-20L	20125	PH-648
D-6565	Rolladen-Schneider LS-7	7134	
D-6566	Rolladen-Schneider LS-6A	6140	HB-1922
D-6567	Glaser-Dirks DG-100G Elan	E52-G30	
D-6568	Schempp-Hirth Ventus c	505	
D-6569	Schempp-Hirth Discus b	370	
D-6570	Schleicher K7 Rhönadler	283	
D-6571	Schempp-Hirth Janus CE	274	

Regn.	Type	C/n	Prev.Id.
D-6572	Rolladen-Schneider LS-4	4029	
D-6573	Rolladen-Schneider LS-4	4044	
D-6574	Schempp-Hirth Discus CS	019CS	
D-6575	Schempp-Hirth Discus CS	020CS	
D-6576	Rolladen-Schneider LS-4	4032	
D-6577	Schleicher ASW-20	20276	N320CF
D-6578	Schempp-Hirth Ventus 2a	78	
D-6580	Glaser-Dirks DG-800S	8-42S11	
D-6581	Rolladen-Schneider LS-4	4021	
D-6582	Scheibe L-Spatz 55	302	
D-6583	Schempp-Hirth Discus CS	129CS	
D-6585	Rolladen-Schneider LS-4	4432	
D-6586	Rolladen-Schneider LS-4A	4433	
D-6587	Eiri PIK-20D	20600	
D-6588	Rolladen-Schneider LS-6	6021	
D-6589	Rolladen-Schneider LS-6	6008	
D-6590	Schempp-Hirth Ventus c	491	
D-6592	Rolladen-Schneider LS-4	4507	
D-6593-WX	Rolladen-Schneider LS-6	6018	
D-6594	Rolladen-Schneider LS-6	6019	
D-6595	Glaser-Dirks DG-500 Elan Trainer	5E-139X4	
D-6596	Rolladen-Schneider LS-6	6020	
D-6597	Rolladen-Schneider LS-8-18 *(Permit 4.99)*	8257	
D-6598	Rolladen-Schneider LS-8-18 *(Permit 4.99)*	8258	
D-6599	Glasflügel H206 Hornet	86	LX-CHF
			OO-ZAD
D-6600	Caproni-Vizzola A.21S Calif	238	F-CEUD
D-6601	Schempp-Hirth Janus B	69	D-4989
D-6602	Schleicher ASW-24	24220	
D-6603	Schempp-Hirth Standard Cirrus B	687	
D-6605	Glaser-Dirks DG-300 Club Elan	3E-414/C68	
D-6606	Schempp-Hirth Mini-Nimbus B	72	
D-6607	Schempp-Hirth Standard Cirrus	633	OE-5062
D-6608	SZD-50-3 Puchacz	B-1094	DDR-3608
D-6609	Glaser-Dirks DG-300 Club Elan	3E-406/C65	
D-6610	Schleicher Ka.6BR Rhönsegler	368	
D-6611	Schleicher Ka.6E	4183	
D-6612	Schempp-Hirth Discus b	197	OO-ZPX
D-6613	Schleicher ASW-15B *(Permit -dd?)*	15450	HB-1300
D-6614	Caproni-Vizzola A-21S Calif	231	
D-6615	Caproni-Vizzola A-21S Calif	239	
D-6616	Caproni-Vizzola A-21S Calif	246	
D-6617	Caproni-Vizzola A-21S Calif	248	
D-6618	SZD-50-3 Puchacz	B-1335	DDR-3618
D-6619	SZD-50-3 Puchacz	B-1336	DDR-3619
D-6620	Schleicher K7 Rhönadler	7115	
D-6621	Schleicher ASK-21	21151	BGA3712/GBW
			ZD651
			BGA2891/ERM
D-6622	Glasflügel H303 Mosquito B	162	
D-6623	Glaser-Dirks DG-800S *(Reservation 11.99)*	8-190S36	
D-6624	Schleicher ASW-20C	20763	
D-6625	Schleicher ASW-20CL	20755	
D-6626	Schleicher ASW-20	20337	
D-6627	Grob G.102 Club Astir IIIB	5505CB	
D-6628	Grob G.102 Club Astir IIIB	5506CB	
D-6629	Grob G.102 Club Astir IIIB	5507CB	
D-6630	SZD-50-3 Puchacz	B-1392	DDR-3630
D-6631	Gomolzig A.21S Calif	255GO	
D-6632	Schleicher K.8B	97	
D-6633	Schempp-Hirth Mini-Nimbus C	114	D-3392
D-6634	Schleicher Ka.6CR Rhönsegler	826	
D-6635	Gomolzig A.21S Calif	257GO	
D-6636	SZD-50-3 Puchacz	B-1092	DDR-3606
D-6637	Glasflügel H101 Salto	58	
D-6642	Schleicher ASW-27	27008	
D-6643	Grob G.103 Twin II	3614	
D-6644	Grob G.102 Astir CS Jeans	2143	
D-6645	Glaser-Dirks DG-200	2-40	
D-6646	Glaser-Dirks DG-200	2-44	
D-6647	Glaser-Dirks DG-200	2-45	
D-6648	Gomolzig A.21S Calif	258GO	
D-6649	Rolladen-Schneider LS-4B	4949	
D-6651	Rolladen-Schneider LS-3	3096	
D-6652	Rolladen-Schneider LS-3	3088	

Regn.	Type	C/n	Prev.Id.
D-6653	Rolladen-Schneider LS-3	3092	
D-6655	Rolladen-Schneider LS-3	3121	
D-6656	Schleicher ASK-21	21318	
D-6657	Rolladen-Schneider LS-3	3049	
D-6658	Rolladen-Schneider LS-3	3056	
D-6659	Rolladen-Schneider LS-3	3184	
D-6660	Glaser-Dirks DG-200 *(Reservation - dd?)*	2-42	
D-6661	Rolladen-Schneider LS-6-18W	6377	
D-6662	Glaser-Dirks DG-200	2-47	
D-6663	Glaser-Dirks DG-200	2-49	
D-6664	Schleicher ASW-24	24204	
D-6665	Glaser-Dirks DG-200	2-51	
D-6666	Rolladen-Schneider LS-4B	41019	
D-6667	Schempp-Hirth Ventus b/16.6	125	
D-6668	Neukom S-4D Elfe *(Reservation - dd?)*	403AB	
D-6669	Neukom S-4D Elfe	404AB	
D-6670	Schleicher K.8	517	
D-6671	Scheibe Zugvogel II	1022	OE-0493
D-6672	Schempp-Hirth Mini-Nimbus C	122	
D-6673	Rolladen-Schneider LS-4	4079	
D-6674	Rolladen-Schneider LS-4	4244	
D-6675	Rolladen-Schneider LS-4	4272	
D-6676	Rolladen-Schneider LS-4	4164	
D-6677	Grob G.102 Astir CS	1187	
D-6678	Grob G.103C Twin III Acro	34197	
D-6679	Grob G.103C Twin III Acro	34202	
D-6680	Rolladen-Schneider LS-4	4000	
D-6681	Gomolzig A.21S Calif	259GO	
D-6682	Gomolzig A.21S Calif	260GO	
D-6685	Rolladen-Schneider LS-4	4403	
D-6686	Rolladen-Schneider LS-6A	6029	D-6556
D-6688	Grob Standard Cirrus	388G	D-9230
D-6690	Glasflügel H303 Mosquito B	105	
D-6691	Schempp-Hirth Nimbus 2C	196	
D-6692	Schempp-Hirth Janus C	87	
D-6693	Schempp-Hirth Mini-Nimbus C	127	
D-6695	Eiri PIK-20D	20590	
D-6696	Eiri PIK-20D	20583	
D-6697	Eiri PIK-20D	20604	
D-6698	Eiri PIK-20D	20596	
D-6700	Eiri PIK-20D	20560	
D-6704	Eiri PIK-20D	20574	
D-6705	Schleicher Ka.6CR Rhönsegler	964	
D-6706	Schleicher ASW-24B	24233	
D-6707	SZD-32A Foka 5	W-440	DDR-2204
			DM-2204
D-6708	Eiri PIK-20D	20578	
D-6709	Schleicher ASK-21	21688	
D-6711	Schleicher ASW-19	19040	
D-6712	Schleicher ASW-19	19043	
D-6713	Schleicher ASW-19	19044	
D-6714	Schleicher ASW-19B	19045	
D-6715	Schleicher ASW-19	19046	
D-6716	Schleicher ASW-19	19047	
D-6719	Schempp-Hirth Ventus b/16.6	71	
D-6720	Schempp-Hirth Ventus b/16.6	72	
D-6721	Schleicher ASW-19	19049	
D-6722	Schleicher ASW-19	19050	
D-6723	Schleicher ASW-13	13551	
D-6724	Schleicher ASW-19	19051	
D-6725	Schleicher ASW-19B	19027	
D-6726	Schleicher ASK-18	18041	
D-6727	Schleicher ASW-13	13552	
D-6728	SZD-30 Pirat	B-309	DDR-1728
			DM-1728
D-6729	Schleicher ASW-19	19057	
D-6730	SZD-30 Pirat	S-03.29	
D-6731	Glasflügel H303 Mosquito	81	
D-6732	Glasflügel H303 Mosquito	86	
D-6733	Schempp-Hirth HS-7 Mini-Nimbus	51	
D-6735	Schempp-Hirth Nimbus 2B	163	
D-6737	Schempp-Hirth Mini-Nimbus B	89	
D-6739	Schempp-Hirth Janus B	78	
D-6740	Schempp-Hirth Mini-Nimbus C	98	
D-6742	Schempp-Hirth Mini-Nimbus C	100	

Regn.	Type	C/n	Prev.Id.
D-6743	Schempp-Hirth Mini-Nimbus C	101	
D-6744	Schleicher ASW-20	20407	
D-6746	Schleicher ASK-21	21048	
D-6748	Schleicher ASW-20L	20411	
D-6749	Schleicher ASW-20	20412	
D-6750	Schleicher Ka.6CR Rhönsegler	898	
D-6751	Grob G.103 Twin Astir Trainer	3248-T-28	
D-6752	Grob G.102 Astir CS 77	1816	
D-6753	Schleicher ASK-21	21600	
D-6756	Grob G.102 Astir CS Jeans	2224	
D-6757	Grob G.102 Astir CS Jeans	2225	
D-6758	SZD-30 Pirat	B-362	DDR-1758
			DM-1758
D-6760	Rolladen-Schneider LS-3-17	3346	OO-ZLD
D-6761	Rolladen-Schneider LS-4	4632	
D-6762	Grob G.102 Astir CS Jeans	2228	
D-6763	Schempp-Hirth Nimbus 2C	206	
D-6764	Schempp-Hirth Mini-Nimbus C	151	
D-6765	Schempp-Hirth Janus C	127	
D-6766	Schempp-Hirth Ventus A	24	
D-6767	Schempp-Hirth Ventus b/16.6	21	ZS-GPI
			D-KERA
			D-6767
D-6768	SZD-55-1	551195077	
D-6769	Schempp-Hirth Duo Discus	4	
D-6770	Rolladen-Schneider LS-4	4634	
D-6771	Schleicher K.8	2/60	
D-6772	Rolladen-Schneider LS-4	4635	
D-6773	Rolladen-Schneider LS-4	4636	
D-6774	Rolladen-Schneider LS-3-17	3293	
D-6776	Rolladen-Schneider LS-3A	3400	
D-6781	Glaser-Dirks DG-200	2-24	
D-6783	Glaser-Dirks DG-200	2-28	
D-6784	SZD-30 Pirat	B-413	DDR-1784
			DM-1784
D-6785	Glaser-Dirks DG-200	2-32	
D-6786	Rolladen-Schneider LS-4	4637	
D-6787	Glaser-Dirks DG-200	2-41	
D-6788	Glaser-Dirks DG-100 Elan	E-14	
D-6789	Glaser-Dirks DG-100 Elan	E10-G4	
D-6790	Schempp-Hirth Discus 2b	35	
D-6791	Glaser-Dirks DG-200	2-71	
D-6792	Glaser-Dirks DG-200	2-72	
D-6793	Glaser-Dirks DG-200	2-70	
D-6794	Glaser-Dirks DG-100G Elan	E42-G23	
D-6795	Schleicher Ka.6CR Rhönsegler	6530	OE-0795
D-6799	SZD-30 Pirat	B-442	DDR-1799
			DM-1799
D-6800	Glaser-Dirks DG-300 Club Elan	3E-337/C32	
D-6801	Pilatus B4-PC11	170	
D-6802	Rolladen-Schneider LS-4	4640	
D-6803	Rolladen-Schneider LS-4	4641	
D-6804	Schleicher ASW-20	20206	
D-6805	Schleicher ASW-20L	20203	
D-6806	SZD-30 Pirat	B-462	DDR-1806
			DM-1806
D-6807	Schleicher ASW-20	20209	
D-6808	Schleicher ASW-20L	20210	
D-6809	Schleicher ASW-19B	19270	
D-6810	Schempp-Hirth Duo Discus (Reservation 10.99)	247	
D-6811	Schempp-Hirth Discus CS	176CS	
D-6812	Schleicher ASW-19B	19273	
D-6813	Schleicher ASW-20	20216	
D-6816	Schleicher K.7 Rhönadler (Reservation 11.99)	7069	
D-6817	Schleicher ASW-27	27080	
D-6818	Grob G.102 Speed Astir IIB	4104	
D-6820	Grob G.102 Speed Astir IIB	4105	
D-6821	Grob G.102 Speed Astir IIB	4107	
D-6823	Grob G.102 Standard Astir II	5032S	
D-6824	Schempp-Hirth Nimbus 2	113	OO-ZBT
D-6825	Schleicher Ka.6CR Rhönsegler	6116	
D-6826	Schleicher ASH-26	26097	
D-6827	Rolladen-Schneider LS-3A	3114	
D-6828	Rolladen-Schneider LS-3A	3125	
D-6829	Grob G.102 Standard Astir	5526S	HB-1580

Regn.	Type	C/n	Prev.Id.
D-6830	Rolladen-Schneider LS-3	3335	
D-6831	Rolladen-Schneider LS-3A	3116	
D-6832	Rolladen-Schneider LS-3	3337	
D-6833	Rolladen-Schneider LS-3	3338	
D-6835	Rolladen-Schneider LS-3A	3143	
D-6836	Glasflügel H304	206	
D-6837	Glasflügel H304	207	
D-6838	Glasflügel H304	213	D-KBOO
D-6840	Schleicher ASW-27	27054	
D-6841	Schleicher ASW-27	27056	
D-6842	Schempp-Hirth Duo Discus	191	
D-6844	Glaser-Dirks DG-200/17	2-90/1707	
D-6845	Glaser-Dirks DG-100 Elan	E-62	
D-6847	Glaser-Dirks DG-100G Elan	E63-G38	
D-6849	Schempp-Hirth Janus C	123	
D-6850	Eiri PIK-20D	20598	
D-6852	SZD-30 Pirat	B-572	DDR-1852
			DM-1852
D-6853	Schleicher ASW-20	20582	
D-6854	Schleicher ASK-21	21116	
D-6855	Schleicher ASK-21	21117	
D-6856	Schleicher ASW-22	22010	
D-6857	Schleicher ASK-21	21118	
D-6858	Schleicher ASW-20L	20590	
D-6859	Schleicher ASW-20	20586	
D-6861	Schleicher K.8B	140	
D-6863	Glasflügel H304/17	214	
D-6864	Schleicher ASK-13	13511	
D-6865	SZD-30 Pirat	S-01.02	DDR-1865
			DM-1865
D-6866	Schleicher ASW-15B	15438	
D-6867	Schleicher ASW-15B	15439	
D-6869	Schleicher ASW-15B	15436	
D-6870	Schleicher ASK-18	18008	
D-6872	SZD-30 Pirat	S-01.10	DDR-1872
			DM-1872
D-6874	Schleicher ASK-13	13514	
D-6875	Schleicher ASK-13	13515	
D-6876	Schleicher ASK-13	13516	
D-6877	Schleicher ASW-15B	15444	
D-6878	Schleicher ASK-18	18012	
D-6879	Schleicher ASK-13	13517	
D-6880	Schleicher ASW-15B	15445	
D-6881	Schleicher ASK-18	18013	
D-6882	Schleicher ASK-13	13518	
D-6883	Schempp-Hirth Ventus b/16.6	164	PH-883
			BGA3208/FET
			ZS-GOT
D-6884	Schleicher K.8C	81007	
D-6885	Schleicher ASW-15B	15446	
D-6886	Schleicher ASK-13	13519	
D-6888	Schleicher ASK-18	18015	
D-6890	Schempp-Hirth Janus B	92	
D-6891	Schempp-Hirth Janus B	93	
D-6892	Schleicher K.8B	8182	
D-6893	Schleicher ASK-13	13630AB	
D-6896	Rolladen-Schneider LS-6	6006	OH-689
D-6897	Schleicher ASW-27	27036	
D-6899	Schleicher ASW-15B	15346	OE-O999
D-6900	Glasflügel H201B Standard Libelle	38	
D-6901	Rolladen-Schneider LS-8-18 (Permit 12.99)	8299	
D-6902	SZD-30 Pirat	S-03.42	DDR-1902
			DM-1902
D-6903	HBV Diamant 18	076	
D-6904	Schempp-Hirth Ventus A	3	
D-6905	Grob G.103A Twin II Acro	3857-K-103	
D-6906	Grob G.103 Twin II	3862	
D-6908	Grob G.103 Twin II	3864	
D-6909	Grob G.103A Twin II Acro	3859-K-105	
D-6911	Schleicher ASW-20C	20786	
D-6912	Schleicher AS-22-2 (Permit 5.99)	22201	
D-6913	Schleicher ASW-20C	20780	
D-6914	Schleicher ASW-20C	20781	
D-6915	SZD-30C Pirat	P-808	DDR-1915
			DM-1915

Regn.	Type	C/n	Prev.Id.
D-6916	Rolladen-Schneider LS-1F	367	
D-6917	Rolladen-Schneider LS-1F	428	
D-6918	Rolladen-Schneider LS-1F	429	
D-6919	Rolladen-Schneider LS-1F	430	
D-6920	Rolladen-Schneider LS-1F	431	
D-6921	Rolladen-Schneider LS-1F	432	
D-6922	Rolladen-Schneider LS-3-17	3359	
D-6924	Rolladen-Schneider LS-4B	41022	
D-6927	Rolladen-Schneider LS-4	4361	
D-6931	Rolladen-Schneider LS-3-17	3329	
D-6933	Rolladen-Schneider LS-3-17	3302	
D-6934	DFS Olympia Meise	01	
D-6937	Rolladen-Schneider LS-3A	3175	
D-6938	Rolladen-Schneider LS-3A	3165	
D-6939	Grob G.103A Twin II Acro	3772-K-58	
D-6940	Grob G.103A Twin II Acro	3691-K-42	OH-645
D-6941	Grob G.103A Twin II Acro	3775-K-61	
D-6942	Rolladen-Schneider LS-3A	3169	
D-6943	Rolladen-Schneider LS-3A	3174	
D-6944	Glasflügel H201B Standard Libelle	43	HB-944
D-6945	Schempp-Hirth Discus CS	119CS	
D-6947	Schempp-Hirth Discus CS	123CS	
D-6948	Schempp-Hirth Discus CS	124CS	
D-6949	Rolladen-Schneider LS-3A	3181	
D-6950	Grob G.102 Club Astir IIIB	5597CB	
D-6951	Grob G.102 Standard Astir III	5600S	
D-6952	Grob G.103 Twin II	3765	
D-6954	Schempp-Hirth Discus CS	125CS	
D-6955	Schempp-Hirth Cirrus	46	HB-955
D-6956	Schleicher ASW-20	20280	
D-6957	Schleicher ASW-21	21002	
D-6958	Schleicher ASW-20	20289	
D-6959	Schleicher ASW-20	20282	
D-6960	Schleicher ASW-20	20293	
D-6963	Schempp-Hirth Discus CS	255CS	
D-6965	Schempp-Hirth Ventus 2c (Reservation 11.99)	32	
D-6966	Schleicher Ka.6CR Rhönsegler	6544	
D-6968	Schleicher Ka.6CR Rhönsegler	6580	
D-6969	Schleicher ASK-21	21503	
D-6970	Grob G.102 Astir CS	1116	
D-6972	Grob G.102 Astir CS	1118	
D-6973	Grob G.102 Astir CS	1119	
D-6974-VA	Schempp-Hirth Duo Discus	178	
D-6975	Grob G.102 Astir CS	1121	
D-6977	Schempp-Hirth Discus a (Permit 5.99)	41	
D-6978	Grob G.102 Astir CS	1124	
D-6979	Grob G.102 Astir CS	1125	
D-6980	Grob G.102 Astir CS	1127	
D-6981	Grob G.102 Astir CS	1128	
D-6983	Grob G.102 Astir CS	1102	
D-6987	Schleicher ASK-23B	23028	OH-698
D-6988	Schleicher ASW-20BL	20667	OE-5363
D-6989	Grob G.102 Astir CS	1089	
D-6990	Grob G.102 Astir CS	1091	
D-6992	Grob G.102 Astir CS	1093	
D-6993	Grob G.102 Astir CS	1099	
D-6995	Grob G.102 Astir CS	1016	
D-6996	Schempp-Hirth Ventus A	57	N101AG
D-6998	Grob G.102 Astir CS	1019	
D-6999	Grob G.102 Astir CS	1020	
D-7000	Rolladen-Schneider LS-6C	6310	D-7900
D-7001	SZD-9bis Bocian 1E	P-713	DDR-3002 DM-3002
D-7002	DFS Kranich III (Reservation 3.99)	57	
D-7003	SZD-9bis Bocian 1E	P-714	DDR-3003 DM-3003
D-7005	Schempp-Hirth Ventus A	5	
D-7006	Schleicher ASH-25	25158	
D-7007	Schempp-Hirth Mini-Nimbus C	126	
D-7008	Rolladen-Schneider LS-4A	4728	
D-7009	Schleicher K.8B	1108	
D-7010	SZD-9bis Bocian 1E	P-722	DDR-3010 DM-3010
D-7011	SZD-9bis Bocian 1E	P-723	DDR-3011 DM-3011
D-7012	Schempp-Hirth Janus C	111	
D-7013	SZD-9bis Bocian 1E	P-489	DDR-3212 DM-3212
D-7014	Greif II	V-2	
D-7015	Schleicher K.8B	8291/EI	
D-7016	Schleicher K.8B	925	
D-7017	Glasflügel H304	254	
D-7019	Schleicher ASK-21	21573	
D-7020	Schleicher K.8B	8271SH	
D-7021	Schleicher ASK-21	21562	
D-7022	Schleicher K.8	442	
D-7023	Rolladen-Schneider LS-4B	4898	
D-7024	Schleicher ASK-21	21015	
D-7025	Schleicher ASK-21	21016	
D-7026	Rolladen-Schneider LS-4B	4899	
D-7027	Schleicher ASK-21	21018	
D-7028	Schleicher ASW-19B	19310	
D-7029	Rolladen-Schneider LS-4B	4900	
D-7030	SZD-9bis Bocian 1E	P-454	DDR-3030 DM-3030
D-7031	Schempp-Hirth Ventus b	41	
D-7032	Schempp-Hirth Nimbus 3/24.5	4	
D-7034	Schempp-Hirth Discus CS	050CS	
D-7035	Schempp-Hirth Nimbus 4T	4	
D-7036	Schleicher Ka.6CR Rhönsegler	806	
D-7037	Glasflügel H201B Standard Libelle	23	OE-5037
D-7038	SG-38 Schulgleiter	AB-002S	
D-7039	Schleicher Ka.2B Rhönschwalbe	229	
D-7040	Rolladen-Schneider LS-4B	4901	
D-7042	Schleicher Ka.2B Rhönschwalbe	2008/A	
D-7043	VFW Fokker FK-3 V-1	0001	
D-7044	Rolladen-Schneider LS-4B	4902	
D-7045	Schleicher Ka.6E	4201	
D-7046	Schleicher ASK-21	21215	
D-7047	Schleicher ASW-19B	19404	
D-7048	Schleicher ASK-21	21216	
D-7049	Rolladen-Schneider LS-4B	4903	
D-7050	Glasflügel H303 Mosquito	57	
D-7051	SG-38 Schulgleiter	ABX/OSC	
D-7053	Schleicher ASH-25	25133	
D-7054	Schleicher ASK-21	21518	
D-7055	SG-38 Schulgleiter	AB001/OSC	
D-7056	Schleicher K.8B	583	
D-7057	SZD-9bis Bocian 1E	P-477	DDR-3057 DM-3057
D-7058	Schempp-Hirth Discus CS	044CS	
D-7059	Schleicher Rhönbussard	485	BGA395/AGX G-ALKY (RAF) BGA395
D-7060	Schleicher K7 Rhönadler	7139	
D-7061	Göppingen Gövier III	411	OE-0891 D-9009
D-7063	Schleicher ASH-25	25144	
D-7064	Schleicher ASH-25	25146	
D-7065	Schleicher K7 Rhönadler	375	
D-7066	Schleicher ASK-23B	23132	
D-7067	Rolladen-Schneider LS-4	4461	
D-7069	Rolladen-Schneider LS-4	4485	
D-7070	Schleicher ASK-21	21654	
D-7071	SZD-9bis Bocian 1E	P-757	DDR-3071 DM-3071
D-7073	Schempp-Hirth Ventus A/16.6	23	
D-7074	SZD-9bis Bocian 1E	P-763	DDR-3074 DM-3074
D-7076	SZD-9bis Bocian 1E	P-765	DDR-3076 DM-3076
D-7077	BS.1 (Permit)	20	
D-7078	Grunau Baby II b	AB-04	
D-7079	Schleicher Rhönlerche II (Permit - old?)	220	
D-7080	Focke-Wulf Weihe 50	1/A	
D-7081	Schleicher ASK-21	21031	
D-7082	Schleicher ASW-20	20370	
D-7084	Schleicher ASW-20L	20371	
D-7086	Schleicher K.8	5	

Regn.	Type	C/n	Prev.Id.
D-7087	Schleicher ASK-21	21583	
D-7088	Schleicher K.8	94	
D-7089	Schleicher K.8B	563	
D-7090	Schleicher Ka.6CR Rhönsegler	6548	
D-7091	Doppelraab VI	02	
D-7092	Grob G.103C Twin III	36014	
D-7093	SZD-9bis Bocian 1E	P-483	DDR-3093 DM-3093
D-7094	Grob G.103C Twin III Acro	34193	
D-7095	Schleicher K7 Rhönadler	604	
D-7096	Rollanden-Schneider LS-4	4518	
D-7097	Rollanden-Schneider LS-4	4519	
D-7098	Rollanden-Schneider LS-4	4520	
D-7099	Glaser-Dirks DG-100G Elan	E104-G77	
D-7100	Glaser-Dirks DG-100	1	
D-7101	Glasflügel H301B Libelle	43	OE-0952
D-7103	Schempp-Hirth Janus B	62	
D-7104	Schleicher K.8B	8401	
D-7105	Rollanden-Schneider LS-1D	253	
D-7106	Rollanden-Schneider LS-1C	254	
D-7107	Glaser-Dirks DG-100	51	
D-7108	Schleicher K.8B	220/61	
D-7109	Schleicher ASK-21	21649	
D-7110	Cumulus Cu-II F	3/54	
D-7111	Rollanden-Schneider LS-1D	227	F-CEHN
D-7112	Glaser-Dirks DG-100	42	
D-7113	Glaser-Dirks DG-100	47	
D-7115	Schleicher K7 Rhönadler	501	
D-7116	SZD-50-3 Puchacz	B-1333	DDR-3616
D-7117	Schempp-Hirth Janus B	58	
D-7118	Schleicher K7 Rhönadler	744	
D-7119	Schleicher ASK-21	21686	
D-7121	Schleicher ASK-21	21603	
D-7122	Schleicher ASW-22	22001	
D-7124	Akaflieg Braunschweig SB-5E Sperber	5019/A	
D-7126	Schleicher K.8B	8229/A	
D-7127	Schleicher K.8B	8525	
D-7128	Schempp-Hirth Mini-Nimbus B	66	
D-7129	SZD-51-1 Junior	B-2151	
D-7130	Schleicher K.8B	8662	
D-7131	Schleicher ASK-23B	23147	
D-7132	Schleicher K.8B	688	
D-7134	Vogt LO-100 Zwergreiher	01	
D-7135	Schleicher ASK-21	21672	
D-7138	Scheibe L-Spatz 55	549	
D-7139	Schleicher K.8B	813	
D-7140	Schleicher K.8B	8426/A	
D-7141	Schleicher Rhönlerche II *(Reservation)*	3015	
D-7142	Glasflügel H201B Standard Libelle	529	OY-VXR
D-7143	Schleicher Ka.6CR Rhönsegler	1158	
D-7144	Schleicher Rhönlerche II	3002	
D-7146	Schleicher K7 Rhönadler	7016	
D-7147	Schleicher ASK-13	13652AB	
D-7149	Schleicher Ka.6E	4181	
D-7150	Schleicher K7 Rhönadler	7088	
D-7153	Schleicher Ka.6CR Rhönsegler	6500	
D-7154	Schleicher Ka.6CR Rhönsegler	6193Si	
D-7155	Schleicher Ka.6CR Rhönsegler	6126Si	
D-7156	Grunau Baby IIB	01	
D-7158	Schleicher Ka.6CR-PE Rhönsegler	717	
D-7159	Schempp-Hirth Discus CS	092CS	
D-7161	Schleicher ASW-24B	24244	
D-7162	Schempp-Hirth Mini-Nimbus B	64	
D-7163	Vogt LO-100 Zwergreiher	07	
D-7164	Schempp-Hirth Discus CS	095CS	
D-7165	Schleicher Ka.6CR Rhönsegler	6478	
D-7166	Schempp-Hirth Discus CS	096CS	
D-7167	Schempp-Hirth Discus CS	201CS	
D-7168	Schempp-Hirth Discus CS	204CS	
D-7169	Schmepp-Hirth Discus CS	203CS	
D-7170	Scheibe L-Spatz 55	709	
D-7171	Schleicher Ka.6E	4225	
D-7172	Scheibe SF-27A	6088	
D-7173	SZD-51-1 Junior	B-2144	
D-7174	Schempp-Hirth Ventus 2b	47	
D-7175	Schempp-Hirth Discus b	94	
D-7176-XD	Schempp-Hirth Discus b	71	
D-7177	Glasflügel H401 Kestrel	61	OO-ZPC
D-7178	Schempp-Hirth Discus b	85	
D-7179	Schempp-Hirth Discus b	84	
D-7181	Schleicher Ka.6CR Rhönsegler	6117	
D-7184	Schleicher Ka.6CR Rhönsegler	6361	
D-7185	Schleicher Ka.6CR Rhönsegler	6374/Si	
D-7186	Scheibe Bergfalke II	327	
D-7187	Glasflügel H401 Kestrel	99	HB-1181
D-7189	Schleicher K7 Rhönadler	7225	
D-7190	Schleicher Ka.6CR Rhönsegler	6434	
D-7191	Rollanden-Schneider LS-6C	6344	
D-7192	Schleicher K.8B	8228/A/SH	
D-7193	Schleicher K.8B	8522	
D-7194	Glaser-Dirks DG-300 Elan	3E-220	
D-7195	Schempp-Hirth Discus 2b *(Permit - old?)*	19	
D-7196	Schleicher Rhönlerche II	65/57	
D-7197	Schleicher Ka.6CR Rhönsegler	6466	
D-7198	Glaser-Dirks DG-300 Elan	3E-221	
D-7199	Schleicher K7 Rhönadler	690	
D-7200	Schempp-Hirth Cirrus	19	
D-7201	Schempp-Hirth Discus b	459	D-0299
D-7202	Glaser-Dirks DG-200/17C	2-133/CL-09	
D-7206	Schempp-Hirth Duo Discus	6	
D-7207	Schempp-Hirth Duo Discus	7	
D-7208	Bölkow Phoebus A-1 *(Reservation 3.99)*	767	
D-7209	Scheibe L-Spatz 55	714	
D-7210	Schleicher ASK-13	13014	
D-7211	Schleicher Ka.6CR Rhönsegler	859	
D-7212	Schleicher K.8B	8717	
D-7213	SZD-9bis Bocian 1E	P-490	DDR-3213 DM-3213
D-7214	Schleicher Ka.6E	4195	
D-7215	Grunau Baby IIB *(Reservation - old?)*	94	PH-215
D-7216	Schleicher ASK-21	21578	
D-7218	Glaser-Dirks DG-200	2-11	
D-7219	Glaser-Dirks DG-200	2-17	
D-7220	Schleicher Ka.6E	4119	
D-7221	Schempp-Hirth Ventus b	97	
D-7222	Schleicher Ka.6CR Rhönsegler	6617	
D-7223	Grob G.102 Astir CS	1138	
D-7224	Grob G.102 Astir CS	1139	
D-7225	Grob G.102 Astir CS	1140	
D-7226	Grob G.102 Astir CS	1137	
D-7227	Grob G.102 Astir CS	1143	
D-7228	Grob G.102 Astir CS	1144	
D-7230	Grob G.102 Astir CS	1043	
D-7231	Grob G.102 Astir CS	1046	
D-7232	Grob G.102 Astir CS	1047	
D-7233	SZD-9bis Bocian 1E	P-515	DDR-3233 DM-3233
D-7234	Grob G.102 Astir CS	1050	
D-7235	Grob G.102 Astir CS	1051	
D-7237	Grob G.102 Astir CS	1053	
D-7239	Grob G.102 Astir CS	1055	
D-7240	Schempp-Hirth Standard Cirrus	628	
D-7241	Schempp-Hirth Standard Cirrus	629	
D-7242	Schempp-Hirth Standard Cirrus	630	
D-7243	Schempp-Hirth Standard Cirrus B	631	
D-7244	Schempp-Hirth Standard Cirrus B	636	
D-7245	Schleicher ASW-19B	19370	D-1390
D-7246	Schempp-Hirth Janus B	104	
D-7249	Schempp-Hirth Janus C	18	
D-7250	Schempp-Hirth Janus	20	
D-7251	Grob G.102 Astir CS	1155	
D-7252	Grob G.102 Astir CS	1157	
D-7253	Grob G.102 Astir CS	1159	
D-7254	Grob G.102 Astir CS	1153	
D-7255	Rollanden-Schneider LS-4B	4722	
D-7256	Grob G.102 Astir CS	1158	
D-7257	Schempp-Hirth Janus	19	
D-7258	SZD-32A Foka 5	W-521	DDR-2258 DM-2258
D-7259	Glasflügel H206 Hornet	56	

Regn.	Type	C/n	Prev.Id.
D-7261	Glaser-Dirks DG-100	55	
D-7262	Schempp-Hirth Standard Cirrus	651	
D-7264	Glaser-Dirks DG-100 (Reservation 9.99)	60	
D-7265	Glaser-Dirks DG-100	61	
D-7266	Schleicher ASW-24	24144	
D-7267	Glaser-Dirks DG-200/17C	2-118/CL-04	
D-7268	Schleicher ASW-24	24151	
D-7269	Schleicher ASW-24	24154	
D-7270	Grob G.102 Astir CS	1146	
D-7271	Grob G.102 Astir CS	1147	
D-7272	Grob G.102 Astir CS	1148	
D-7273	Grob G.102 Astir CS	1149	
D-7275	Grob G.102 Astir CS	1202	
D-7276	Grob G.102 Astir CS	1203	
D-7277	Grob G.102 Astir CS	1204	
D-7278	Grob G.102 Astir CS	1205	
D-7279	Grob G.102 Astir CS	1206	
D-7280-HSN	Schleicher ASH-25	25138	
D-7281	Grob G.102 Astir CS	1208	
D-7282	Glaser-Dirks DG-500 Elan Orion	5E-154X11	
D-7283	Grob G.102 Astir CS	1210	
D-7286	Grob G.102 Astir CS	1213	
D-7287	Grob G.102 Astir CS	1214	
D-7288	Schleicher K.8C	81011	OY-XME D-3765
D-7289	Grob G.102 Astir CS	1216	
D-7290	Grob G.102 Astir CS	1217	
D-7291	Grob G.102 Astir CS	1218	
D-7293	Grob G.102 Astir CS	1168	
D-7295	Glaser-Dirks DG-500/20 Elan	5E-173W10	
D-7296	Grob G.102 Astir CS	1175	
D-7297	Schleicher K.8B	8885AB	
D-7298	Rolladen-Schneider LS-8-18 (Permit 3.99)	8228	
D-7299	Grob G.102 Astir CS	1179	
D-7300	Grob G.102 Astir CS	1180	
D-7301	Grob G.102 Astir CS	1184	
D-7303	Grob G.102 Astir CS	1176	
D-7304	Grob G.102 Astir CS	1177	
D-7305	Grob G.102 Astir CS	1188	
D-7306	Glasflügel H206 Hornet	63	HB-1306
D-7309	Marganski MDM-1 Fox	210	OE-5624
D-7310	Grob G.102 Astir CS	1193	
D-7311	Schempp-Hirth Duo Discus	184	
D-7313	Grob G.102 Astir CS	1196	
D-7314	Grob G.102 Astir CS	1197	
D-7315	Glasflügel H205 Club Libelle	164	
D-7319	Grob G.102 Astir CS	1238	
D-7322	Schleicher ASW-22	22036	
D-7324	Glaser-Dirks DG-100 (Reservation)	70	HB-1324
D-7326	Grob G.102 Astir CS	1304	
D-7327	Schleicher ASW-19B	19355	
D-7328	Schleicher ASW-20	20497	
D-7329	Schleicher ASW-19B	19358	
D-7330	Glasflügel H206 Hornet	66	
D-7331	Rolladen-Schneider LS-1F	482	
D-7332	Rolladen-Schneider LS-1F	483	
D-7333	Rolladen-Schneider LS-1F	484	
D-7334	Rolladen-Schneider LS-1F	485	
D-7336	Schempp-Hirth Janus	23	
D-7339	Rolladen-Schneider LS-6C	6254	
D-7340	Schempp-Hirth Standard Cirrus	671	
D-7341	LET L-13 Blanik	026649	
D-7343	Schleicher Ka.6CR Rhönsegler	6661AB	
D-7344	Schempp-Hirth Standard Cirrus B	659	
D-7345	Schempp-Hirth Standard Cirrus B	604	
D-7346	Grunau Baby V (Permit - old?)	530	LX-CAC
D-7347	Schempp-Hirth Ventus c	308	OH-734
D-7351-LD	Rolladen-Schneider LS-6C	6256	
D-7353	Schempp-Hirth Janus B	61	
D-7354	Rolladen-Schneider LS-4B	4916	
D-7355	Grob G.102 Astir CS	1314	
D-7356	Grob G.102 Astir CS	1261	
D-7357	Grob G.102 Astir CS	1262	
D-7359	Grob G.102 Astir CS	1264	
D-7360	Schempp-Hirth Ventus 2b	36	
D-7361	SZD-9bis Bocian 1E	P-548	DDR-3361 DM-3361
D-7362	SZD-9bis Bocian 1E	P-549	DDR-3362 DM-3362
D-7363	Grob G.102 Astir CS	1268	
D-7364	Grob G.102 Astir CS	1269	
D-7365	Grob G.102 Astir CS	1270	
D-7366	Grob G.102 Astir CS	1271	
D-7368	Grob G.102 Astir CS	1273	
D-7369	Grob G.102 Astir CS	1274	
D-7372	Grob G.102 Astir CS	1278	
D-7373	Grob G.102 Astir CS	1280	
D-7374	Glaser-Dirks DG-800S	8-113S29	
D-7375	Grob G.102 Astir CS	1275	
D-7379	Grob G.102 Astir CS	1293	
D-7380	Grob G.102 Astir CS	1333	
D-7381	Grob G.102 Astir CS	1335	
D-7383	LET L-13 Blanik	978504	
D-7384	Grob G.102 Astir CS	1346	
D-7385	Grob G.102 Astir CS	1347	
D-7387	Grob G.102 Astir CS	1358	
D-7388	Grob G.102 Astir CS	1359	
D-7389	Grob G.102 Astir CS	1360	
D-7390	Rolladen-Schneider LS-6C	6285	
D-7391	Grob G.102 Astir CS	1364	
D-7393	Grob G.102 Astir CS	1366	
D-7395	SZD-9bis Bocian 1E	P-612	DDR-3395 DM -3395
D-7396	Schempp-Hirth Nimbus 2B	134	
D-7397	Bölkow Phoebus B3 (Permit 3.99)	1003	
D-7398	Schleicher ASW-15	15060	OH-398 OH-RWB
D-7399	Schempp-Hirth Janus	30	
D-7401	Pilatus B4-PC11AF	228	
D-7404	Grob G.102 Astir CS	1375	
D-7405	Schleicher ASW-27	27047	
D-7406	Grob G .102 Astir CS	1378	
D-7407	Grob G.102 Astir CS	1398	
D-7409	Grob G.102 Astir CS	1382	
D-7410	Grob G.102 Astir CS	1388	
D-7411	Grob G.102 Astir CS	1389	
D-7412	Grob G.102 Astir CS	1392	
D-7413	Schempp-Hirth Discus CS	130CS	
D-7414	Rolladen-Schneider LS-1C	46	OE-0819
D-7415	Glasflügel H206 Hornet	81	
D-7416	Glasflügel H206 Hornet	82	
D-7418	Glaser-Dirks DG-200	2-26	
D-7419	Glaser-Dirks DG-200	2-83	
D-7420	Glaser-Dirks DG-200/17	2-84/1703	
D-7421	SZD-42-2 Jantar 2B	B-866	DDR-2422 DM-2422
D-7422	Neukom S-4D Elfe	417AB	
D-7423	Glasflügel H401 Kestrel	79	
D-7424	Grob G.102 Club Astir IIIB	5645CB	
D-7426	Grob G.102 Astir CS	1436	
D-7427	Grob G.102 Astir CS	1437	
D-7428	Grob G.102 Astir CS	1438	
D-7430	Grob G.102 Astir CS	1441	
D-7432	Schleicher ASK-23B	23161	
D-7433	Grob G.102 Astir CS	1452	
D-7436	Grob G.102 Astir CS	1464	
D-7437	Rolladen-Schneider LS-8A	8068	
D-7439	Grob G.102 Astir CS	1468	
D-7440	Grob G.102 Astir CS	1469	
D-7441	Grob G.102 Astir CS	1453	
D-7442	Grob G.102 Astir CS	1419	
D-7443	Grob G.102 Astir CS	1425	
D-7444	Glasflügel H303 Mosquito B	191	
D-7445	Grob G.102 Astir CS	1454	
D-7446	Grob G.102 Astir CS	1455	
D-7448	Grob G.102 Astir CS	1457	
D-7449	Grob G.102 Astir CS	1458	
D-7451	Grob G.102 Astir CS	1461	
D-7452	Grob G.102 Astir CS 77	1611	
D-7453	Schempp-Hirth Ventus 2c	38/112	

Regn.	Type	C/n	Prev.Id.
D-7456	Schleicher ASW-27	27028	
D-7457	Grob G.102 Astir CS	1516	
D-7458	Schempp-Hirth Duo Discus	2	
D-7459	Schempp-Hirth Duo Discus	3	
D-7462	Grob G.102 Astir CS	1504	
D-7463	Grob G.102 Astir CS	1528	
D-7464	Grob G.102 Astir CS	1529	
D-7465	Grob G.102 Astir CS	1530	
D-7466	Schempp-Hirth Mini-Nimbus C	116	HB-1466
D-7470	Grob G.102 Astir CS 77	1639	
D-7471	Schleicher ASK-21	21639	
D-7472	Grob G.102 Astir CS 77	1645	
D-7473	Glasflügel H303 Mosquito	19	PH-566
D-7474	Schempp-Hirth Ventus2B	62	
D-7475	Grob G.103 Twin Astir	3002	
D-7477	Rolladen-Schneider LS-4B	4956	
D-7480	Grob G.103 Twin Astir	3026	
D-7481	Schleicher ASK-21	21521	
D-7482	Schleicher ASK-21	21522	
D-7483	Schleicher ASK-21	21523	
D-7484	Grob G.103 Twin Astir	3011	
D-7485	Glasflügel H303 Mosquito	102	
D-7489	Glasflügel H303 Mosquito	44	
D-7490	Glasflügel H303 Mosquito	45	
D-7493	Grob G.102 Astir CS Jeans	2003	
D-7494	Grob G.102 Astir CS Jeans	2002	
D-7496	Grob G.102 Astir CS Jeans	2005	
D-7497	Grob G.102 Astir CS Jeans	2004	
D-7498	Grob G.102 Astir CS 77	1661	
D-7499	Grob G.104 Speed Astir IIB	4061	HB-1499
D-7500	Pilatus B4-PC11AF	181	
D-7501	Schleicher Ka.6CR Rhönsegler	6356	
D-7502	Schleicher ASH-25	25152	
D-7503	Scheibe L-Spatz 55	670	
D-7504	Schleicher ASK-21	21677	
D-7505	Schleicher K.8B	8593	
D-7507	Schleicher ASK-13	AB13693	
D-7508	Schempp-Hirth HS-7 Mini-Nimbus	22	
D-7510	Pilatus B4-PC11	185	
D-7511	Grob G.102 Astir CS Jeans	2007	
D-7512	Grob G.102 Astir CS Jeans	2008	
D-7514	Schempp-Hirth Nimbus 2C	190	F-CEDN
			F-WEDN
D-7516	Grob G.102 Astir CS Jeans	2012	
D-7517	Grob G.102 Astir CS Jeans	2013	
D-7519	Grob G.102 Astir CS Jeans	2015	
D-7520	Glasflügel H303 Mosquito B	164	
D-7522	Schleicher ASK-21	13692AB	
D-7523	Grob G.103 Twin Astir	3017	
D-7525	Grob G.103 Twin Astir	3019	
D-7527	Schleicher ASW-27	27021	
D-7528	Grob G.103 Twin Astir	3033	
D-7529	Grob G.102 Astir CS Jeans	2087	
D-7530	Grob G.102 Astir CS Jeans	2088	
D-7533	Grob G.102 Astir CS Jeans	2091	
D-7536	Grob G.102 Astir CS Jeans	2095	
D-7537	Grob G.102 Astir CS Jeans	2096	
D-7538	Grob G.102 Astir CS Jeans	2097	
D-7540	Schleicher ASW-20L	20329	
D-7541	Schleicher ASW-20L	20330	
D-7542	Schleicher ASW-20L	20331	
D-7543	Schleicher ASW-20	20332	
D-7545	Schleicher ASW-19	19108	
D-7546	Schleicher ASW-19	19109	
D-7547	Schleicher ASW-20	20004	
D-7548	Schleicher ASW-19	19111	
D-7550	Schleicher ASW-19	19113	
D-7551	Eiri PIK-20D	20649	OH-551
D-7553	Schleicher ASK-13	13575	
D-7554	Schleicher ASK-13	13576	
D-7558	Schleicher ASK-13	13578	
D-7559	Schleicher ASW-19	9127	
D-7561	Schleicher ASK-13	13580	
D-7564	Schleicher ASW-19	19132	
D-7565	Schleicher ASW-19	19133	
D-7566	Schleicher ASK-13	13581	
D-7567	Schleicher ASW-19	19134	
D-7569	Schleicher ASW-20	20021	
D-7570	Schleicher ASW-19B	19114	
D-7571	Schleicher ASW-19	19143	
D-7572	Schleicher ASW-20	20022	
D-7573	Schleicher ASW-19	19145	
D-7575	Rolladen-Schneider LS-7	7032	
D-7576	SZD-48-3 Jantar Standard 3	B-1716	DOSAAF
D-7577	Grob G.102 Astir CS Jeans	2057	
D-7578	Grob G.102 Astir CS Jeans	2058	
D-7580	Grob G.102 Astir CS Jeans	2064	
D-7581	Grob G.102 Astir CS Jeans	2065	
D-7582	Grob G.102 Astir CS Jeans	2067	
D-7583	Grob G.102 Astir CS Jeans	2069	
D-7585	Grob G.102 Astir CS Jeans	2072	
D-7588	Grob G.102 Astir CS Jeans	2075	
D-7590	Grob G.102 Astir CS Jeans	2077	
D-7592	Grob G.102 Astir CS Jeans	2082	
D-7593	Grob G.102 Astir CS Jeans	2083	
D-7594	Grob G.102 Astir CS Jeans	2085	
D-7595	Grob G.102 Astir CS Jeans	2086	
D-7597	Glasflügel H206 Hornet C	93	
D-7598	Glasflügel H303 Mosquito B	161	
D-7599	Glasflügel H303 Mosquito B	163	
D-7600	Grob G.103A Twin II Acro	3867-K-108	
D-7601	Grob G.103 Twin II	3866	
D-7602	SZD-50-3 Puchacz	B-1086	DDR-3602
D-7604	Schempp-Hirth Duo Discus *(Reservation 11.99)*	248	
D-7606	Rolladen-Schneider LS-4	4315	
D-7607	Rolladen-Schneider LS-4	4316	
D-7608	Rolladen-Schneider LS-4	4317	
D-7611	Glaser-Dirks DG-200/17	2-87/1705	
D-7612	Akaflieg Berlin B-12T *(Permit 4.99)*	001	
D-7613	Schempp-Hirth Duo Discus	148	
D-7614	Rolladen-Schneider LS-8A	8203	
D-7615	Schleicher ASW-20C	20778	
D-7616	Schleicher ASW-20	20334	
D-7617	Schleicher ASW-19B	19313	
D-7618	Schleicher ASW-20L	20335	
D-7619	Schleicher ASW-19B	19311	
D-7620	Schempp-Hirth Mini-Nimbus B	73	
D-7621	SZD-50-3 Puchacz	B-1340	DDR-3621
D-7622	Glaser-Dirks DG-600	6-76	
D-7623	SZD-50-3 Puchacz *(Reservation 2.99)*	B-1342	DDR-3623
D-7624	Schempp-Hirth Duo Discus	192	
D-7626	Grob G.102 Astir CS 77	1700	
D-7627- 27	Schleicher ASW-27	27105	
D-7628	Grob G.102 Astir CS Jeans	2100	
D-7629	Grob G.102 Astir CS Jeans	2101	
D-7635	Grob G.102 Astir CS Jeans	2105	
D-7636	Schleicher ASK-21	21591	
D-7637	Grob G.102 Astir CS Jeans	2109	
D-7639	Grob G.102 Astir CS Jeans	2112	
D-7640	Grob G.102 Astir CS Jeans	2114	
D-7641	Grob G.102 Astir CS Jeans	2127	
D-7642	Grob G.102 Astir CS Jeans	2116	
D-7643	SZD-50-3 Puchacz	B-1478	DDR-3646
D-7644	SZD-55-1	551195066	
D-7646	Schleicher ASW-20L	20217	
D-7648	Schleicher ASW-20	20259	
D-7649	Schleicher ASW-20L	20260	
D-7653	Schleicher ASK-21	21650	
D-7655	Schleicher ASW-19	19183	
D-7657	Schleicher ASW-20	20067	
D-7658	Schleicher ASW-20L	20050	
D-7659	Schleicher ASW-20	20071	
D-7660	Schleicher ASW-19	19196	
D-7662	Schleicher ASW-20	20075	
D-7663	Schleicher ASW-20	20077	
D-7664	Schleicher ASK-13	13592	
D-7667	Schleicher ASW-20	20080	
D-7668	Schleicher ASW-19B	19201	
D-7669	Schleicher ASW-20	20081	
D-7670	Schleicher ASW-20	20070	

Regn.	Type	C/n	Prev.Id.	Regn.	Type	C/n	Prev.Id.
D-7671	Schleicher ASK-13	13593		D-7751	Rolladen-Schneider LS-4	4303	
D-7672	Schleicher ASK-13	13589		D-7752	Rolladen-Schneider LS-4	4183	
D-7673	Schleicher ASW-17	17054		D-7753	Rolladen-Schneider LS-4	4304	
D-7674	Schleicher ASW-20	20087		D-7754	Rolladen-Schneider LS-4	4305	
D-7675	Schleicher ASW-20 (Reservation)	20069		D-7756	Grob G.102 Astir CS Jeans	2176	
D-7676	Schleicher ASW-20	20074		D-7757	Grob G.102 Astir CS Jeans	2181	
D-7677	Grob G.102 Astir CS 77	1844	HB-1506	D-7758	Grob G.102 Astir CS Jeans	2183	
D-7678	Schleicher ASW-19B	19205		D-7759	Grob G.102 Astir CS Jeans	2184	
D-7679	Schleicher ASW-20	20094		D-7761	Grob G.102 Astir CS Jeans	2186	
D-7680	Glasflügel H206 Hornet C	90		D-7762	Grob G.102 Astir CS Jeans	2187	
D-7681	Schleicher ASW-24	24218		D-7763	Grob G.102 Astir CS Jeans	2188	
D-7682	Glasflügel H303 Mosquito B	158		D-7765	Grob G.102 Astir CS Jeans	2220	
D-7683	Glasflügel H206 Hornet C	92		D-7766	Grob G.102 Astir CS Jeans	2221	
D-7684	Schleicher ASW-20	20051		D-7767	Grob G.102 Astir CS Jeans	2222	
D-7685	Grob G.102 Astir CS 77	1752		D-7768	Scheibe SF-27A	6020	OE-0768
D-7686	Grob G.102 Astir CS 77	1760		D-7769	Grob G.102 Astir CS Jeans	2223	
D-7690	Grob G.102 Astir CS 77	1784		D-7770	Schleicher ASW-27	27072	
D-7691	Grob G.102 Astir CS 77	1785		D-7771	Akaflieg Braunschweig SB-5E	AB5043	
D-7692	Grob G.102 Astir CS 77	1792		D-7772	Grob G.102 Astir CS 77	1796	
D-7693	Grob G.102 Astir CS 77	1793		D-7773-JU	Glasfaser Albatros (Reservation 3.99)	1	
D-7694	Grob G.102 Astir CS 77	1799		D-7774	Grob G.102 Astir CS 77	1806	
D-7696	Schempp-Hirth Discus b	182		D-7775	Streifeneder Falcon	1	
D-7697	Schempp-Hirth Discus b	194		D-7776	Glasflügel H303 Mosquito B	140	C-GDFZ
D-7698	Schleicher ASK-21	21589		D-7777-HL	Glasflügel H201B Standard Libelle	547	
D-7699	Schempp-Hirth Discus b	181		D-7778	Grob G.103 Twin Astir Trainer	3106	
D-7700	Schleicher ASH-25 (Formerly ASH-25E)	25170	D-KKEW	D-7779	Schempp-Hirth Discus b (Permit 3.99)	574	
D-7701	Neukom S-4D Elfe	406AB		D-7780	Grob G.103 Twin Astir	3109	
D-7702	Glaser-Dirks DG-200	2-8		D-7781	Grob G.103 Twin Astir Trainer	3112-T-9	
D-7703	Glaser-Dirks DG-200	2-10		D-7782	Grob G.103 Twin Astir Trainer	3115	
D-7704	Schempp-Hirth Discus CS (Reservation 9.99)	269CS		D-7784	SZD-30 Pirat	B-403	DDR-1774
D-7705	SZD-48-3 Jantar Standard 3	B-1573	SP-3341				DM-1774
D-7706	Rolladen-Schneider LS-3	3210		D-7785	Grob G.102 Astir CS 77	1651	HB-1385
D-7707	Schleicher ASW-20L	20584		D-7786	Grob G.103 Twin Astir	3138	
D-7708	Schleicher ASK-21	21160		D-7788	Rolladen-Schneider LS-4B	4917	
D-7709	Focke-Wulf Weihe 50 (Reservation 9.99)	290		D-7790	Grob G.103 Twin Astir Trainer	3139	
D-7710	Schleicher ASW-19B	19378		D-7791	Grob G.103 Twin Astir	3148	
D-7711	Scheibe Bergfalke IV	5816		D-7792	Grob G.103 Twin Astir	3149	
D-7712	Schleicher Ka.3	E1		D-7794	SZD-30 Pirat	B-437	DDR-1794
D-7713	SZD-30 Pirat	W-415	DDR-1714				DM-1794
			DM-1714	D-7795	Grob G.103 Twin Astir	3150	
D-7715	Schempp-Hirth Ventus b/16.6	176		D-7797	Grob G.103 Twin Astir	3167	
D-7716	Schempp-Hirth Ventus b/16.6	177		D-7798	Rolladen-Schneider LS-6	6072	
D-7717	Glasflügel H304	215	D-6862	D-7799	Pilatus B4-PC11AF	322	
D-7718	Rolladen-Schneider LS-8A	8057		D-7800	Rolladen-Schneider LS-6	073	
D-7719	Schleicher ASW-19B (Reservation 11.99)	19340	OH-626	D-7801	Rolladen-Schneider LS-3A	3206	
D-7720	Schempp-Hirth Ventus b/16.6	174		D-7802	Rolladen-Schneider LS-6	6074	
D-7721	Schleicher ASW-24	24184		D-7803	Rolladen-Schneider LS-6A	6075	
D-7722	Rolladen-Schneider LS-3	3003		D-7806	Schleicher ASK-23B	23143	
D-7723	Rolladen-Schneider LS-3	3004		D-7807	Grob G.103 Twin Astir	3170	
D-7725	Schleicher ASH-25	25032		D-7808	SZD-55-1	551196080	
D-7726	Rolladen-Schneider LS-3	3007		D-7810	Grob G.103 Twin Astir Trainer	3174-T-17	
D-7727	Neukom Elfe S4A	87		D-7811-EZ	Rolladen-Schneider LS-6	6121	
D-7728	Schempp-Hirth Duo Discus	189		D-7812	Schleicher ASK-21	21582	
D-7730	FFA Diamant 18	077	HB-202	D-7813	Grob G.103 Twin Astir	3178	
			HB-2020	D-7815	Schempp-Hirth Ventus c	355	
D-7731	Rolladen-Schneider LS-3	3064		D-7816	Schempp-Hirth Discus b	184	
D-7732	Rolladen-Schneider LS-3 (Reservation)	3091		D-7817	Glasflügel H206 Hornet	51	
D-7733	Rolladen-Schneider LS-3A	3110		D-7818	Glasflügel H206 Hornet	44	
D-7734	Rolladen-Schneider LS-3	3105		D-7819	Glasflügel H206 Hornet	43	
D-7735	Rolladen-Schneider LS-3	3108		D-7820	Glasflügel H206 Hornet	42	
D-7736	Schleicher ASK-21	21658		D-7821	Glasflügel H206 Hornet	45	
D-7737	Rolladen-Schneider LS-7	7000		D-7822	Glasflügel H206 Hornet	41	
D-7738	SG-38 Schulgleiter	1310/585		D-7823	Glasflügel H206 Hornet	5	
D-7739	Rolladen-Schneider LS-3	3126		D-7824	SZD-30 Pirat	B-501	DDR-1824
D-7740	Neukom S-4D Elfe	405AB					DM-1824
D-7741	Rolladen-Schneider LS-1F	443		D-7825	Rolladen-Schneider LS-4	4364	
D-7742	Rolladen-Schneider LS-5 (Permit 3.99)	5001		D-7826	Rolladen-Schneider LS-4	4365	
D-7743	SZD-30 Pirat	B-332	DDR-1743	D-7828	Rolladen-Schneider LS-4	4366	
			DM-1743	D-7829	Rolladen-Schneider LS-4	4367	
D-7744	Schempp-Hirth Standard Cirrus	177		D-7830	SZD-30 Pirat	B-508	DDR-1830
D-7745	Rolladen-Schneider LS-3A	3404	OO-ZLS				DM-1830
D-7747	Rolladen-Schneider LS-3	3122		D-7832	SZD-30 Pirat	B-510	DDR-1832
D-7748	Rolladen-Schneider LS-6C	6248	SE-UKK				DM-1832
D-7749	Rolladen-Schneider LS-3A	3123		D-7833	Glasflügel H206 Hornet	26	
D-7750	Rolladen-Schneider LS-3A	3075		D-7834	Glasflügel H206 Hornet	35	

Regn.	Type	C/n	Prev.Id.
D-7835	Glasflügel H206 Hornet	36	
D-7836	Glasflügel H206 Hornet	37	
D-7837	Glasflügel H206 Hornet	34	
D-7838	Schleicher ASK-21	21238	
D-7839	Schleicher ASW-19B	19412	
D-7840	Schleicher ASW-20BL	20661	
D-7841	Glasflügel H206 Hornet	55	
D-7844	Scheibe Bergfalke III	5654	
D-7845	Glasflügel H206 Hornet	84	
D-7848	Schempp-Hirth Janus	36	
D-7851	SZD-30 Pirat	B-573	DDR-1853
			DM-1853
D-7852	Schempp-Hirth Standard Cirrus	700	
D-7853	Schempp-Hirth Standard Cirrus B	697	
D-7854	Schempp-Hirth Standard Cirrus B	701	
D-7855	Grob G.102 Astir CS	1532	
D-7856	Glasflügel H303 Mosquito	28	
D-7857	Glasflügel H303 Mosquito	35	
D-7858	SZD-30 Pirat	B-578	DDR-1858
			DM-1858
D-7859	Glasflügel H303 Mosquito B	104	
D-7861	Schleicher ASW-27	27063	
D-7865	Schempp-Hirth Mini-Nimbus C	125	
D-7866	Rolladen-Schneider LS-8A (Reservation 9.99)	8280	
D-7867	Glaser-Dirks DG-200	2-36	
D-7868	Glaser-Dirks DG-200	2-38	
D-7869	Glasflügel H303 Mosquito	93	
D-7870	Schempp-Hirth Discus b	457	
D-7871	Rolladen-Schneider LS-4	4548	
D-7872	Rolladen-Schneider LS-3A	3109	
D-7873	Schleicher ASW-22	22039	
D-7874	SZD-30 Pirat (Reservation - old?)	S-01.12	DDR-1874
			DM-1874
D-7875	Rolladen-Schneider LS-4B	4882	
D-7876	Schleicher ASK-21	21198	
D-7877	Rolladen-Schneider LS-3	3217	
D-7878	Rolladen-Schneider LS-3	3111	
D-7879	Rolladen-Schneider LS-3A	3084	
D-7880-JT	Rolladen-Schneider LS-4	4549	
D-7881	Rolladen-Schneider LS-3A	3097	
D-7882	Rolladen-Schneider LS-4	4550	
D-7883	Schleicher ASW-27	27006	
D-7884	Rolladen-Schneider LS-3A	3112	
D-7885	Rolladen-Schneider LS-3A	3113	
D-7886	Glasflügel H303 Mosquito B	114	
D-7887	Focke-Wulf Weihe 50	02	
D-7888	Schleicher K.8B	8931	OE-0972
D-7890	Rolladen-Schneider LS-3A	3304	
D-7891	SZD-30 Pirat	S-03.06	DDR-1891
			DM-1891
D-7892	Rolladen-Schneider LS-3-17	3115	
D-7894	Grob G.103A Twin II Acro	3773-K-59	
D-7895	Grob G.103 Twin II	3778	
D-7896	Grob G.102 Club Astir IIIB	5603CB	
D-7898	Rolladen-Schneider LS-4	4552	
D-7899	Rolladen-Schneider LS-3A	3060	
D-7901	Rolladen-Schneider LS-3	3011	
D-7902	Rolladen-Schneider LS-3	3012	
D-7903	Rolladen-Schneider LS-4	4553	
D-7904	Rolladen-Schneider LS-4	4554	
D-7905	Rolladen-Schneider LS-3	3015	
D-7906	Rolladen-Schneider LS-3	3016	
D-7907	Rolladen-Schneider LS-3	3017	
D-7908	Rolladen-Schneider LS-3	3018	
D-7909	Rolladen-Schneider LS-3	3019	
D-7910	Rolladen-Schneider LS-3	3020	
D-7911	SZD-48-3 Jantar Standard 3	B-1951	
D-7912	Schempp-Hirth Discus 2b (Reservation 11.99)	61	
D-7913	Grob G.103A Twin II Acro	3786-K-64	
D-7914	Grob G.103 Twin II	3789	
D-7915	Grob G.102 Club Astir IIIB	5602CB	
D-7917	Rolladen-Schneider LS-3	3027	
D-7918	Rolladen-Schneider LS-4	4555	
D-7919	Rolladen-Schneider LS-4	4556	
D-7920	Rolladen-Schneider LS-3	3030	

Regn.	Type	C/n	Prev.Id.
D-7921	Rolladen-Schneider LS-3	3031	
D-7922	Schleicher ASK-23B	23136	
D-7923	Schleicher ASK-21	21635	
D-7924	Grob G.103A Twin II Acro	3801-K-68	
D-7926	Schempp-Hirth HS-7 Mini-Nimbus	45	
D-7929	Schempp-Hirth Nimbus 2B	159	
D-7930	Neukom S-4D Elfe	420AB	
D-7931	Bölkow Phoebus C	931	
D-7932	Schleicher ASW-19B	19146	
D-7933	Schleicher ASW-19	19148	
D-7934	Schleicher ASW-20	20031	
D-7935	Schleicher ASW-20	20057	
D-7936	Schleicher ASW-19	19149	
D-7942	LET L-23 Super Blanik	917810	
D-7945	Schleicher ASW-20	20036	
D-7946	Schleicher ASW-19	19155	
D-7949	Schleicher ASK-13	13584	
D-7950	Rolladen-Schneider LS-4B	4950	
D-7951	Schleicher ASW-20	20039	
D-7952	Schleicher ASW-20	20043	
D-7953	Schleicher ASW-19B	19165	
D-7956	Schleicher ASW-19	19167	
D-7957	Schleicher ASK-13	13585	
D-7959	Schleicher ASW-19	19170	
D-7960	Schleicher ASW-19	19169	
D-7961	Schleicher ASK-13	13587	
D-7962	Schleicher ASK-13	13588	
D-7963	Schleicher ASW-19	19181	
D-7964	Schleicher ASW-20	20052	
D-7966	Schleicher ASW-19	19172	
D-7967	Schleicher ASW-19	19171	
D-7970	Schleicher ASW-19B	19175	
D-7971	Schleicher ASW-19	19176	
D-7972	Schleicher ASW-19B	19195	
D-7975	Schleicher ASW-19	19177	
D-7976	Schleicher ASW-20	20066	
D-7977	Schleicher ASW-20	20055	
D-7979	Schleicher ASW-20	20023	
D-7980	Schleicher ASW-19B	19180	
D-7981	Schleicher ASW-19	19182	
D-7982	Glasflügel H303 Mosquito B	122	
D-7984	Schleicher ASW-19	19197	
D-7985	Grob G.103A Twin II Acro	3623-K-10	
D-7986	Grob G.102 Club Astir IIIB	5508CB	
D-7987	Schleicher ASK-23B	23057	
D-7988	Glasflügel H303 Mosquito B	132	
D-7989	Schleicher ASK-21	21289	
D-7990	Schleicher ASW-19B	19150	
D-7991	Akaflieg Braunschweig SB-5E Sperber	5050AB	
D-7992	Schempp-Hirth Mini-Nimbus C	154	
D-7993	Schempp-Hirth Nimbus 2C	213	
D-7994	Schempp-Hirth Nimbus 2C	215	
D-7995	Schempp-Hirth Nimbus 2C	214	
D-7996	Schempp-Hirth Mini-Nimbus 2C	156	
D-7997	Schempp-Hirth Ventus c	576	
D-7998	Schleicher ASK-23B	23051	
D-7999	Grob G.102 Astir CS Jeans	2104	
D-8000	Vogt LO-100 Zwergreiher	AB 38	
D-8001	SZD-9bis Bocian 1E	P-705	DDR-3000
			DM-3000
D-8002	Habicht E	ABH 1/OSC	
D-8003-800	Glaser-Dirks DG-800S	8-3S1	
D-8004	Glasflügel H304	208	
D-8005	Focke-Wulf Weihe 50	164	
D-8006	Rolladen-Schneider LS-3A	3170	
D-8007	Glaser-Dirks DG-600	6-39	
D-8008	SZD-9bis Bocian 1E	P-721	DDR-3009
			DM-3009
D-8009	Glasflügel H304	221	
D-8010	Glaser-Dirks DG-300 Elan	3E-62	
D-8011	Glaser-Dirks DG-300 Elan	3E-57	
D-8012	Glaser-Dirks DG-500 Elan Trainer	5E-107T43	
D-8013	Schleicher K.8B	10	
D-8015	Glaser-Dirks DG-100G Elan	E171-G137	
D-8016	Rolladen-Schneider LS-4A	4652	

Regn.	Type	C/n	Prev.Id.
D-8018	SZD-9bis Bocian 1E	P-443	DDR-3018
			DM-3018
D-8019	Glaser-Dirks DG-100G Elan	E170-G136	
D-8020	Schleicher ASW-20	20001	
D-8021	Schleicher Ka.6CR Rhönsegler	6284	
D-8022	Scheibe Bergfalke II/55	238	
D-8023	Rolladen-Schneider LS-8 *(Reservation - old?)*	8003	
D-8024	Rolladen-Schneider LS-4A	4653	
D-8026	Akaflieg Braunschweig SB-5B Sperber	5012/A	
D-8028	Schleicher ASW-28 *(Reservation 12.99)*	28001	
D-8030	Rolladen-Schneider LS-4A	4655	
D-8031	Rolladen-Schneider LS-4A	4656	
D-8032	Schleicher Ka.6CR Rhönsegler	556	
D-8033	Schleicher Ka.6E	4152	
D-8034	Rolladen-Schneider LS-4A	4657	
D-8035	Schleicher ASK-21	21657	
D-8036	Rolladen-Schneider LS-8 *(Permit 12.99)*	8006	
D-8037	Rolladen-Schneider LS-6-18W	6345	
D-8038	Focke-Wulf Kranich III	60	
D-8039	SZD-9bis Bocian 1E	P-460	DDR-3039
			DM-3039
D-8040	Glaser-Dirks DG-500 Elan Trainer	5E-IIT45	
D-8041	Schleicher Ka.6CR Rhönsegler	150/59	
D-8042	Rolladen-Schneider LS-4A	4658	
D-8043	Schleicher Ka.6CR Rhönsegler	6190Si	
D-8044	SZD-9bis Bocian 1E	P-467	DDR-3044
			DM-3044
D-8045	SZD-9bis Bocian 1E	P-468	DDR-3045
			DM-3045
D-8046	Schleicher ASW-27	27061	
D-8047	Rolladen-Schneider LS-8A	8035	
D-8048	Glaser-Dirks DG-800S	8-27S4	
D-8049	Scheibe L-Spatz 55 *(Reservation - old?)*	624	
D-8050	Schempp-Hirth Duo Discus	5	
D-8051	Schleicher Ka.6E	4120	
D-8053	Rolladen-Schneider LS-6B	6148	
D-8055	Glaser-Dirks DG-500 Elan Trainer	5E-125T54	
D-8058	SZD-9bis Bocian 1E	P-478	DDR-3058
			DM-3058
D-8060	Schempp-Hirth Discus b	480	
D-8062	Grob G.103A Twin II Acro	33966-K-199	
D-8063	Grunau Baby II b *(Reservation 8.99)*	AB-002	
D-8064	Göppingen Gö.III Minimoa	184	N2664B
			HB-626
			D-8064
D-8066	Glaser-Dirks DG-300 Elan	3E-182	ZK-GSS
D-8068	SZD-42-2 Jantar 2B	B-871	DOSAAF
D-8069	Grob G.103A Twin II Acro	34013-K-246	
D-8070	Vogt LO-100 Zwergreiher	AB-36	
D-8071	Schempp-Hirth Discus b	565	
D-8072	Grob G.103A Twin II Acro	33967-K-200	
D-8073	SZD-9bis Bocian 1E	P-762	DDR-3073
			DM-3073
D-8077	SZD-9bis Bocian 1E	P-766	DDR-3077
			DM-3077
D-8078	Glasflügel H201 Standard Libelle	2	
D-8079	Doppelraab IV	AB-01	
D-8080	Glasflügel H201B Standard Libelle	1	
D-8081	Schleicher ASW-24	24077	HB-3030
D-8085	Schleicher Ka.6CR Rhönsegler	6148	
D-8086	Schempp-Hirth Duo Discus	110	
D-8087	Grob G.103A Twin II Acro	33973-K-206	
D-8088	Schempp-Hirth Janus CE	292	
D-8091	Rolladen-Schneider LS-4B	4864	
D-8092	Rolladen-Schneider LS-4B	4865	
D-8093	Rolladen-Schneider LS-4B	4866	
D-8094	Rolladen-Schneider LS-4B	4867	
D-8095	Rolladen-Schneider LS-4B	4868	
D-8097	Grob G.103A Twin II Acro	33974-K-207	
D-8098	Rolladen-Schneider LS-4B	4869	
D-8099	Rolladen-Schneider LS-4B	4870	
D-8100	Schleicher ASK-13	13058	
D-8101	Scheibe Bergfalke III	5509	
D-8102	Vogt LO-100 Zwergreiher	AB-37	
D-8103	Eiri PIK-20D	20520	OE-5103
D-8104	Rolladen-Schneider LS-4B	4872	
D-8105	Rolladen-Schneider LS-4B	4873	
D-8106	Schempp-Hirth Nimbus 2B	138	OE-5106
D-8108	Schempp-Hirth Duo Discus	8	
D-8109	Scheibe Bergfalke II	172	
D-8110	Rolladen-Schneider LS-6B	6156	
D-8111	Schempp-Hirth Duo Discus	1	
D-8112	Grob G.102 Club Astir IIIB	5634CB	
D-8113	Neukom S-4D Elfe	425AB	
D-8115	Schleicher ASW-27	27051	
D-8117	Rolladen-Schneider LS-6B	6158	
D-8118	Vogt LO-100 Zwergreiher	11	
D-8120	Scheibe L-Spatz 55	737	
D-8122	Schleicher ASH-25	25162	OH-854
			D-7021
D-8123	Schleicher ASW-20C	20758	
D-8124	Schleicher ASK-21	21227	
D-8125	Schempp-Hirth Discus CS	144CS	
D-8126	Schempp-Hirth Discus CS	145CS	
D-8127	Schempp-Hirth Discus CS	140CS	
D-8128	Scheibe Spatz A	AB 01	
D-8129	Schempp-Hirth Duo Discus	196	
D-8133	Schleicher Ka.6E	4182	
D-8134	Schleicher Ka.2B Rhönschwalbe	199	
D-8136	Schempp-Hirth Duo Discus	83	
D-8137	Schempp-Hirth Ventus 2c	11/24	
D-8138	Schempp-Hirth Duo Discus	90	
D-8140	Schempp-Hirth Discus 2b *(Permit - old?)*	5	
D-8141	Akaflieg Stuttgart FS.25	V-1	
D-8148	Scheibe Bergfalke II	174	
D-8150	Grob G.103A Twin II Acro	33989-K-222	
D-8151	Schleicher ASW-27	27093	
D-8153	Schleicher ASK-21	21473	
D-8155	Grob G.103A Twin II Acro	34000-K-233	
D-8159	Scheibe Bergfalke II	4	
D-8160	Scheibe L-Spatz 55	583	
D-8161	Rolladen-Schneider LS-4	4395	D-5499
D-8163	Standard Austria Series 1	12	OE-0663
D-8164	Schleicher Ka.6CR Rhönsegler	716	
D-8165	Bölkow Phoebus C	783	
D-8166	Schempp-Hirth Ventus 2a	86	
D-8170	Glasflügel H301B Libelle	82	
D-8171	Pilatus B4-PC11AF	90	HB-1129
D-8176	Rolladen-Schneider LS-7	7084	
D-8177	Schleicher K.8B	8049/1	
D-8178	Rolladen-Schneider LS-7	7085	
D-8179	Rolladen-Schneider LS-7	7086	
D-8180	Glaser-Dirks DG-800S	8-37S8	
D-8181	Rolladen-Schneider LS-7	7088	
D-8182	Rolladen-Schneider LS-7	7089	
D-8183	Schleicher ASW-24B	24242	
D-8184	Göppingen Gö IV Göevier III	409	OO-ZHW
			D-5946
			D-6041
			D8102
D-8187	Grunau Baby III *(Reservation)*	"XYZ"	
D-8188	Schempp-Hirth Ventus 2a *(Reservation ?)*	unkn	
D-8189	Rolladen-Schneider LS-4	4290	
D-8191	Schleicher ASK-21	21627	
D-8192	Rolladen-Schneider LS-7	7114	
D-8193	Rolladen-Schneider LS-7	7115	
D-8194	Schleicher ASW-27	27088	
D-8196	Glaser-Dirks DG-100G Elan	E132-G100	
D-8197	Rolladen-Schneider LS-7	7118	
D-8198	Scheibe Bergfalke II/55	212	
D-8199	Grob G.103A Twin II Acro	34001-K-234	
D-8200	Glaser-Dirks DG-200	2-1	
D-8201	SG-38 Schulgleiter	1A	
D-8202	Scheibe Bergfalke II	3	
D-8203	Grob G.103A Twin II Acro	34008-K-241	
D-8204	SZD-48-1 Jantar Standard	W-893	
D-8205	Glasflügel H205 Club Libelle	66	F-CEQA
D-8206	Rolladen-Schneider LS-7	7122	
D-8207	Schempp-Hirth Duo Discus	49	
D-8208	Rolladen-Schneider LS-7	7124	

Regn.	Type	C/n	Prev.Id.
D-8209	Scheibe L-Spatz 55	695	
D-8210	Schleicher K.8B	975	
D-8211	Scheibe L-Spatz	570	
D-8212	Rolladen-Schneider LS-6C	6286	
D-8214	Schleicher Ka.6E	4199	
D-8215	Schempp-Hirth Duo Discus	165	
D-8216	Schleicher K.8B	8567	
D-8217	Rolladen-Schneider LS-8-18 *(Permit 1.99)*	8232	
D-8218	Rolladen-Schneider LS-8-18 *(Permit 1.99)*	8236	
D-8219	Schleicher ASW-19B	19218	
D-8220	Schleicher ASH-25	25155	
D-8221	SZD-32A Foka 5	W-469	DDR-2221
			DM-2221
D-8222	SZD-9bis Bocian 1E	P-502	DDR-3222
			DM-3222
D-8223	Scheibe L-Spatz	AB.03	
D-8224	Schempp-Hirth Discus CS	007CS	
D-8225	Schempp-Hirth Discus b	345	
D-8226	Schempp-Hirth Discus b	356	
D-8227	Schempp-Hirth Ventus c	482	
D-8228	Schempp-Hirth Discus b	24/317	
D-8229	Schempp-Hirth Discus CS	015CS	
D-8230	Schempp-Hirth Discus b	329	
D-8231	SZD-9bis Bocian 1E	P-513	DDR-3231
			DM-3231
D-8232	SZD-24-4A Foka 4	W-347	DDR-2234
			DM-2234
D-8233	Grunau Baby IIB	"AB xyz"	
D-8234	SZD-9bis Bocian 1E	P-516	DDR-3234
			DM-3234
D-8235	Schleicher ASK-21	21598	
D-8236	Akaflieg Braunschweig SB-5E Sperber	5008	
D-8237	SZD-9bis Bocian 1E	P-524	DDR-3237
			DM-3237
D-8238	Schleicher ASK-21	21602	
D-8239	Focke-Wulf Weihe 50	266	
D-8240	Scheibe Bergfalke II/55	251	
D-8241	Schleicher Rhönlerche II	232	
D-8242	SZD-9bis Bocian 1E	P-534	DDR-3247
			DM-3247
D-8244	Schleicher Ka.6 Rhönsegler	246	
D-8245	SZD-9bis Bocian 1E	P-532	DDR-3245
			DM-3245
D-8246	Scheibe L-Spatz 55	598	
D-8248	SZD-9bis Bocian 1E	P-535	DDR-3248
			DM-3248
D-8249	SZD-32A Foka 5	W-499	DDR-2249
			DM-2249
D-8250	Rolladen-Schneider LS-4B	41005	
D-8251	Rolladen-Schneider LS-4B	41006	
D-8252	Rolladen-Schneider LS-4B	41007	
D-8253	Schleicher ASW-20CL	20785	
D-8254	Schleicher ASW-20BL	20666	
D-8255	Vogt LO-100 Zwergreiher	AB 01	
D-8256	Vogt LO-100 Zwergreiher	05A	
D-8257	Schempp-Hirth Discus b	551	
D-8258	Schempp-Hirth Discus b	552	
D-8259	Schempp-Hirth Discus b	553	
D-8260	Schempp-Hirth Discus b	554	
D-8261	Schempp-Hirth Discus b	555	
	(C/n 155/555 is also quoted for LN-GPS)		
D-8262	Scheibe L-Spatz 55	595	
D-8263	Scheibe Spatz B	AB-01	
D-8264	SZD-32A Foka 5	W-527	DDR-2264
			DM-2264
D-8265	LET L-23 Super Blanik	978402	
D-8266	Scheibe Specht *(Reservation 1.99)*	816	
D-8268	Valentin Mistral C	MC 068/86	
D-8269	Scheibe Specht	AB-01	
D-8271	Scheibe L-Spatz 55	1	
D-8275	Schleicher ASW-20CL	20846	
D-8277	SZD-48-1 Jantar Standard	B-1166	OE-5277
D-8280	Schleicher Rhönlerche II	363	
D-8281	Schleicher Ka.6BR Rhönsegler	346	
D-8282	Schempp-Hirth Discus CS	049CS	

Regn.	Type	C/n	Prev.Id.
D-8283	Schempp-Hirth Discus CS	159CS	
D-8284	Schempp-Hirth Discus CS	163CS	
D-8285	Schleicher Rhönlerche II	AB-08	
D-8286	Rolladen-Schneider LS-4B	4883	
D-8288	Schempp-Hirth Janus CE	291	
D-8290	Schempp-Hirth Ventus b/16.6	33	
D-8291	Schempp-Hirth Duo Discus	136	
D-8295	Schleicher K7 Rhönadler	434	
D-8296	Glaser-Dirks DG-300 Elan Acro	3E-469A19	
D-8297	Glaser-Dirks DG-300 Elan	3E-472	
D-8299	Glaser-Dirks DG-600	6-13	HB-1957
D-8300	SZD-36A Cobra 15	W-558	DDR-2300
			DM-2300
D-8301	Schleicher Rhönlerche II	04	
D-8302	Schempp-Hirth Nimbus 4D	2/8	
D-8303	Glaser-Dirks DG-300 Club Elan	3E-462C82	
D-8305	SZD-51-1 Junior	B-2148	
D-8306	Dittmar Condor IV/3	47	
D-8308	Glaser-Dirks DG-800S	8-100S24	
D-8310	Scheibe L-Spatz 55	545	
D-8311	Schleicher ASK-21	21155	
D-8312	Schleicher Ka.6BR Rhönsegler	496	
D-8313	SZD-36A Cobra 15	W-638	DDR-2313
			DM-2313
D-8314	Scheibe L-Spatz 55	666	
D-8316	Schleicher K.8B	516	
D-8317	Scheibe L-Spatz 55	677	
D-8318	Schleicher ASW-19B	19424	
D-8320	Schleicher ASK-21 *(Reservation 12.99)*	"25221"	
D-8321	Schleicher ASK-21	21135	HB-1677
D-8322	Glaser-Dirks DG-500/20 Elan	5E-144W6	
D-8325	Schleicher ASK-23B	23144	
D-8326	Schleicher ASH-26	26110	
D-8327	Schleicher Ka.6CR Rhönsegler	6479	
D-8328	Schleicher ASW-27	27025	
D-8329	Schleicher ASW-27	27026	
D-8330	Schleicher Rhönlerche II	469	
D-8332	Scheibe Zugvogel III	1038	
D-8333-38	Schempp-Hirth Ventus b/16.6	190	
D-8334	Schleicher K.8B	639	
D-8336	Glaser-Dirks DG-100	79	HB-1336
D-8338	Scheibe L-Spatz 55	AB 04	
D-8340	Schleicher K7 Rhönadler	E 3	
D-8342	Schleicher Ka.6CR-PE Rhönsegler	679	
D-8345	Schleicher ASW-15B *(Permit 9.99)*	15376	I-FLIK
D-8347	Sperber	2	
D-8348	Glasflügel H304	220	
D-8350	SZD-55-1	551196083	
D 8351	Scheibe Zugvogel IIIA	1052	
D-8353	SZD-9bis Bocian 1E	P-540	DDR-3353
			DM-3353
D-8356	Scheibe Zugvogel IIIA	1051	
D-8357	Scheibe L-Spatz 55	717	
D-8358	Doppelraab IV *(Reservation 4.99)*	02	
D-8360	Schleicher ASW-27	27014	
D-8361	Schleicher K.8B	840	
D-8363	Schempp-Hirth Duo Discus	104	
D-8364	Scheibe SF-27A	6066	
D-8365	Musterle H2 PL *(Permit 8.99)*	AB-001S	
D-8367	Schempp-Hirth Discus CS	003CS	OK-0367
D-8368	Scheibe L-Spatz	E-1	
D-8369	Nabern FS-24 Phönix T	405	
D-8370	SZD-9bis Bocian 1E	P-560	DDR-3370
			DM-3370
D-8371	SZD-9bis Bocian 1E	P-561	DDR-3371
			DM-3371
D-8373	Schleicher ASK-23 (Museum) *(Reservation - old?)*	unkn	
D-8374	Schleicher Ka.6CR Rhönsegler	965	
D-8376	SZD-9bis Bocian 1E	P-566	DDR-3376
			DM-3376
D-8377	Schempp-Hirth Discus CS	214CS	
D-8381	Schleicher Ka.6CR Rhönsegler	999	
D-8383	Scheibe SF-27A *(Reservation 11.99)*	6092	
D-8384	Glaser-Dirks DG-800S	8-109S25	
D-8385	Schleicher ASK-23B	23067	

Regn.	Type	C/n	Prev.Id.
D-8386	Schleicher K7 Rhönadler	1006	
D-8387	Schleicher Ka.6CR Rhönsegler	AB-04/201	
D-8388	SZD-9bis Bocian 1E	P-595	DDR-3388
			DM-3388
D-8392	Schleicher K.8B	1060	
D-8393	Schleicher Ka.6CR Rhönsegler	1109	
D-8394	Scheibe Bergfalke II/55	344	
D-8395	Schleicher K.8B	133	
D-8399	Schleicher ASK-21	21301	
D-8400	Schleicher Ka.6CR Rhönsegler	1116	
D-8401	Schleicher K.8B	1101	
D-8403	Schleicher ASK-21	21302	
D-8404	Scheibe L-Spatz 55	751	
D-8405	Schleicher ASK-23B	23073	
D-8406	SZD-41A Jantar Standard	B-697	DDR-2406
			DM-2406
D-8407	Grob G.102 Standard Astir II	5017S	HB-1528
D-8408	Schleicher Ka.6CR Rhönsegler	6011	
D-8409	Schleicher Ka.6CR Rhönsegler	6031Si	
D-8410	Schleicher K.8	1107	
D-8411	Glaser-Dirks DG-300 Elan	3E-259	OE-5420
D-8412	Schleicher K.8B	8007	
D-8414	Schleicher ASW-24B	24248	
D-8415	Hütter H-30 GFK	1	
D-8417	Schleicher K.8B	8041	
D-8418	Schleicher ASK-21	21678	
D-8419	Scheibe L-Spatz 55	585	
D-8420	SZD-41A Jantar Standard	B-856	DDR-2420
			DM-2420
D-8421	Schleicher K.8B	8421	D-KOCA
D-8424	Schleicher Ka.6CR Rhönsegler	6045	
D-8426	SZD-48-1 Jantar Standard 2	W-847	DDR-2426
			DM-2426
			SP-3118
D-8427	SZD-48-1 Jantar Standard 2	W-855	DDR-2427
			DM-2427
			(SP-3083)
D-8428	Schleicher K.8B	E 4	
D-8434	Scheibe Bergfalke III	5507	
D-8435	Schempp-Hirth Duo Discus	197	
D-8437	Schleicher ASW-20C	20841	
D-8438	Schleicher K.8B	8011	
D-8439	Schleicher K.8B	281/A/3	
D-8440	SZD-48-1 Jantar Standard 2	B-1052	DDR-2430
			DM-2430
D-8441	Rolladen-Schneider LS-4	4536	
D-8443	Scheibe Bergfalke II/55	366	
D-8444	Schleicher Ka.6CR Rhönsegler	6063	
D-8445	Vogt LO-100 Zwergreiher (Reservation)	203	BGA3378/FMV
			OE-0445
D-8446	Schleicher K.8B	103/98	
D-8447	Vogt LO-100 Zwergreiher	205	
D-8448	Nabern FS-24 Phönix T (Reservation - old?)	407	
D-8449	Schleicher K.8B	8443	D-KMAL
			D-4034
D-8450	Schleicher K.8B	8168	
D-8451	Schleicher Ka.6CR Rhönsegler	6113	
D-8455	Grob G.102 Astir CS	1290	PH-551
D-8459	Schleicher Ka.6CR Rhönsegler	6136	
D-8460	Schleicher ASK-21	21303	
D-8461	Schleicher K.8B	1054	
D-8462	Schleicher ASK-21	21305	
D-8463	Schleicher K7 Rhönadler	7087	
D-8464	Schleicher ASK-21	21306	
D-8466	Schleicher ASK-23B	23076	
D-8467	Rock Geier IIB	E 1	
D-8468	Schempp-Hirth Janus C	193	
D-8469	Test Registration for Schempp-Hirth Discus a		
D-8471	Schleicher K.8B	8262	
D-8474	Schleicher K.8B	122	
D-8475	Doppelraab VI	03	
D-8476	Schleicher K.8B	8257	
D-8477	Schleicher Ka.6CR Rhönsegler	6181	
D-8480	Scheibe SF-26A Standard	5025	
D-8481	Schleicher Ka.6CR Rhönsegler	6196	
D-8482	Scheibe Zugvogel IIIB	1086	
D-8483	Schleicher Ka.6CR Rhönsegler	6227Si	
D-8485	Schleicher Ka.6CR Rhönsegler	6234	
D-8487	Schleicher Ka.6CR Rhönsegler	6245	
D-8488	Grob G.102 Speed Astir IIB	4043	
D-8489	Scheibe Zugvogel IIIB	1090	
D-8490	Rolladen-Schneider LS-4	4534	
D-8491	Bölkow Phoebus B-1 (Permit 6.99)	701	
D-8494	Rolladen-Schneider LS-4	4047	
D-8495	Scheibe Bergfalke III	5516	
D-8496	Schleicher Ka.6CR-PE Rhönsegler	6223Bi	
D-8497	Schleicher K7 Rhönadler	7162	
D-8498	Neukom S-4D Elfe	424AB	
D-8499	Schleicher Ka.6CR Rhönsegler	6300	
D-8500	Scheibe Bergfalke III	5612	
D-8501	Scheibe Bergfalke IV/55	339	
D-8502	Schempp-Hirth Ventus 2b	5	
D-8504	Kranich II	24	
D-8505	Rolladen-Schneider LS-6	6060	
D-8506	Focke-Wulf Kranich III	74	
D-8507	Focke-Wulf Kranich III	84	F-CCBR
D-8508	Schleicher K7 Rhönadler	7076	
D-8509	Rolladen-Schneider LS-6	6059	
D-8510	Scheibe L-Spatz 55	69	
D-8511	Grunau Baby III	03	
D-8512	Schleicher K.8B	997	
D-8513	Glasflügel H201B Standard Libelle	12	
D-8514	Schempp-Hirth Discus CS	205CS	
D-8515	Schempp-Hirth Discus CS	207CS	
D-8516	Schempp-Hirth Discus CS	213CS	
D-8518	Schleicher ASW-27	27082	
D-8521	Scheibe SF-27A	6078	
D-8522	Schleicher K.8B	8019	
D-8523	Schleicher K.8B	8072	
D-8525	Schleicher K.8B	8236	
D-8526	Rolladen-Schneider LS-8-18 (Permit 8.99)	8272	
D-8527	Rolladen-Schneider LS-8-18 (Permit 8.99)	8273	
D-8528	Rolladen-Schneider LS-4	4474	
D-8529	Schleicher K.8B	8340/A	
D-8530	Schleicher K.8B	919	
D-8531	Schleicher Rhönlerche II (Reservation - old?)	3	
D-8532	Glaser-Dirks DG-500 Elan Trainer	5E-69T29	
D-8533	Schleicher Rhönlerche II	01	
D-8534	Schleicher K.8B	8360	
D-8535	Schleicher Ka.6BR Rhönsegler	387	
D-8537	Schempp-Hirth Nimbus 2B	117	PH-537
D-8540	Schleicher Ka.6CR Rhönsegler	6638	
D-8541	Schleicher K.8B	8585	
D-8543	Kranich III	59	
D-8545	Schleicher ASW-24	24207	
D-8548	Rolladen-Schneider LS-4	4431	
D-8551	Grob G.102 Astir CS Jeans	2196	OO-ZJS
D-8552	Schleicher Ka.2B Rhönschwalbe	1012	
D-8554	Scheibe Bergfalke IV/55	363	
D-8555	Grob G.103C Twin III Acro	34198	
D-8556	Glasflügel H304	228	
D-8557-FI	Glasflügel H304	229	
D-8558	Schempp-Hirth Ventus 2b	6	
D-8559	Schempp-Hirth Ventus 2a	7	
D-8560	Schempp-Hirth Ventus 2a	8	
D-8561	Schleicher Rhönlerche II	34/55	
D-8563	Schempp-Hirth Nimbus 4D	3/11	
D-8564	L-10 Libelle	1	
D-8565	Schleicher Ka.6E	4051	
D-8566	Schleicher Ka.6 Rhönsegler	278	
D-8567	Schleicher K.8B	8059	
D-8568	Schleicher Ka.6CR Rhönsegler	6291	
D-8569	Olympia-Meise	3	
D-8570	Bölkow Phoebus C	802	
D-8572	Schempp-Hirth Discus A	533	
D-8574	Schleicher K.8B	120/58	
D-8575	SZD-48-3 Jantar Standard	B-1890	SP-3541
D-8576	Scheibe Bergfalke IV/55	338	
D-8577	Schempp-Hirth Ventus 2a	34	
D-8578	Schleicher K.8	115/58	

Regn.	Type	C/n	Prev.Id.
D-8579	Schleicher Ka.6CR Rhönsegler	002 AB	
D-8580	Glaser-Dirks DG-800S	8-92S23	
D-8581	Schleicher ASW-20C	20766	
D-8582	Schleicher ASW-20CL	20767	
D-8584	Neukom Elfe S4	15	
D-8585	Grunau Baby III	AB 1	
D-8586	SZD-51-1 Junior	B-2019	SP-3583
D-8587	Doppelraab V	533	D-8080
D-8590	Scheibe L-Spatz (Wfu)	508B	
D-8591	Schleicher Rhönlerche II	3065A	
D-8593	Schleicher Ka.6CR Rhönsegler	6061	
D-8595	Schleicher ASK-23B	23134	
D-8598	Schleicher K.8B	01	
D-8599	Schleicher Ka.6CR-PE Rhönsegler	858	
D-8600-1E	Glaser-Dirks DG-600	6-7	
D-8601	Schleicher Ka.6CR Rhönsegler	946	
D-8602	Schleicher K.8B	8275	
D-8603	Glaser-Dirks DG-600	6-35	
D-8604	SZD-50-3 Puchacz	B-1088	DDR-3604
D-8606	Schleicher Ka.6 Rhönsegler	248	
D-8607	Schleicher Ka.6CR-PE Rhönsegler	6229Bi	
D-8608	Schleicher Ka.6CR Rhönsegler	6432Si	
D-8610	Schleicher K.8B	8488	
D-8611	Schleicher ASK-13	13056	
D-8612	Schleicher Ka.2B Rhönschwalbe	003	
D-8616	Schleicher K.8B	1055	
D-8618	Schleicher K.8B	8511	
D-8619	Schleicher Ka.6CR Rhönsegler	6470Si	
D-8620	Schleicher Ka.6CR Rhönsegler	6494	
D-8621	Schempp-Hirth SHK-1	47	HB-862
D-8622	Schleicher Ka.6BR Rhönsegler	386	
D-8623	Schleicher K.8B	8588Gö	
D-8624	SZD-50-3 Puchacz	B-1343	DDR-3624
D-8626	Schleicher Ka.6CR Rhönsegler	6644	
D-8627	Schleicher K.8B	8570	
D-8628	Schleicher ASK-21	21120	
D-8629	Schleicher ASK-21	21121	
D-8630	Schleicher ASW-19B	19367	
D-8631	Schleicher ASW-20	20585	
D-8632	Schleicher ASW-20	20591	
D-8633	Bölkow Phoebus A-1	731	
D-8634	Scheibe SF-27A	6043	
D-8637	Schleicher Ka.6CR Rhönsegler	6546	
D-8640	SZD-50-3 Puchacz	B-1470	DDR-3640
D-8641	Schleicher ASW-15B	15397	
D-8642	Schleicher ASW-15B	15398	
D-8643	Schleicher ASK-13	13494	
D-8644	Schleicher ASW-15B	15409	
D-8645	Schleicher ASW-15B	15400	
D-8646	Schleicher ASW-15B	15402	
D-8647	Schleicher ASW-15B	15401	
D-8648	Schleicher ASK-13	13501	
D-8649	Rolladen-Schneider LS-4B	4918	
D-8650	Schleicher ASW-15B	15403	
D-8652	Schleicher K.8C	81004	
D-8653	Schleicher ASW-15B	15410	
D-8654	Schleicher ASW-17	17040	
D-8655	Schleicher ASW-15B	15412	
D-8656	Schleicher ASW-15B	15408	
D-8657	Schleicher K.8B	8973	
D-8658	Schleicher ASW-15B	15411	
D-8659	Schleicher ASK-13	13500	
D-8660	Schleicher ASW-15B	15415	
D-8661	Schleicher ASW-15B	15416	
D-8662	Schleicher ASW-15B	15417	
D-8665	Schleicher ASW-15B	15420	
D-8666	Rolladen-Schneider LS-1F	378	
D-8667	Rolladen-Schneider LS-1F	334	
D-8668	Rolladen-Schneider LS-1F	330	
D-8669	Rolladen-Schneider LS-1F	327	
D-8670	Schempp-Hirth Standard Cirrus	522	OE-5360 PH-509
D-8671	Rolladen-Schneider LS-1F	298	
D-8672	Rolladen-Schneider LS-1F	277	
D-8676	Glaser-Dirks DG-100	13	
D-8677	LET L-23 Super Blanik	948119	
D-8678	LET L-33 Solo	940309	
D-8679	Rolladen-Schneider LS-1F	381	
D-8681	Grob G.102 Astir CS	1003	
D-8682	Grob G.102 Astir CS	1004	
D-8684	Glasflügel H205 Club Libelle	72	
D-8685	Glasflügel H205 Club Libelle	73	
D-8686	Glasflügel H205 Club Libelle	74	
D-8688	Scheibe Bergfalke III	5651	
D-8690	Glasflügel H401 Kestrel	125	
D-8691	Glasflügel H401 Kestrel	126	
D-8692	Grob G.103 Twin II	3670	
D-8694	Grob G.103A Twin II Acro	3689-K-40	
D-8695	Grob G.102 Club Astir IIIB	5554CB	
D-8698	Grob G.103A Twin II Acro	3690-K-41	
D-8700	Grob G.102 Speed Astir IIB	4094	
D-8701	Grob Standard Cirrus	566G	
D-8702	LET L-13 Blanik	026356	
D-8704	Grob G.102 Club Astir IIIB	5566CB	
D-8706	LET L-23 Super Blanik	907610	
D-8707	Schempp-Hirth Duo Discus	22	
D-8709	Schleicher ASW-20CL	20719	
D-8711	Rolladen-Schneider LS-4	4014	
D-8712	Rolladen-Schneider LS-4	4015	
D-8713	Rolladen-Schneider LS-4	4557	
D-8714	Rolladen-Schneider LS-1F	453	
D-8716	Grob G.102 Speed Astir IIB	4050	
D-8717	Grob G.102 Speed Astir IIB	4052	
D-8718	Grob G.102 Speed Astir IIB	4053	
D-8719	Grob G.102 Speed Astir IIB	4054	
D-8720	Grob G.102 Speed Astir IIB	4055	
D-8721	Grob G.102 Speed Astir IIB	4056	
D-8722	Grob G.102 Speed Astir IIB	4072	
D-8724	Schleicher ASW-24	24150	I-GLID
D-8725	SZD-30 Pirat	B-306	DDR-1725 DM-1725
D-8726	Akaflieg München Mü.26	V-1	
D-8728	Grob G.102 Club Astir II	5058C	
D-8729	Grob G.103 Twin II	3535	
D-8730	Grob G.103 Twin II	3536	
D-8731	Grob G.103 Twin II	3538	
D-8732	SZD-30 Pirat	B-315	DDR-1732 DM-1732
D-8733	Schempp-Hirth Duo Discus	156	
D-8735	Schleicher Ka.6E	4156	
D-8736	Grob G.103 Twin Astir	3275	
D-8737	Grob G.102 Speed Astir IIB	4092	
D-8738	Grob G.102 Speed Astir IIB	4093	
D-8739	Grob G.102 Speed Astir IIB	4095	
D-8741	Grob G.102 Standard Astir II	5003S	
D-8742	Grob G.102 Club Astir II	5012C	
D-8743	Grob G.102 Club Astir II	5018C	
D-8745	Grob G.102 Speed Astir IIB	4099	
D-8746	Schempp-Hirth Nimbus 2C	221	
D-8747	Schempp-Hirth Nimbus 2C	222	
D-8748	Grob G.103 Twin II	3549	
D-8749	Grob G.103A Twin II Acro	3558-K-4	
D-8750	Grob G.103 Twin II	3525	
D-8751	Grob G.103 Twin II	3526	
D-8752	Grob G.103 Twin II	3527	
D-8754	Schleicher K.8B	8419	
D-8755	Grob G.103A Twin II Acro	3559-K-5	
D-8756	Grob G.103 Twin II	3532	
D-8757	Schleicher ASK-23B	23066	OH-757
D-8759	Grob G.102 Club Astir II	5061C	
D-8760	Schleicher Ka.2 Rhönschwalbe	72	
D-8761	Grob G.103 Twin II	3554	
D-8762	Grob G.103 Twin II	3555	
D-8766	Grob G.103 Twin II	3560	
D-8767	PIK-16C Vasama	26	
D-8770	Schleicher Ka.6CR Rhönsegler	6281	
D-8773	Scheibe Zugvogel 1	1002	
D-8774	Schleicher K.8B (Reservation 2.99)	02	
D-8775	Schleicher ASW-20L	20372	
D-8776	Schleicher Ka.2 Rhönschwalbe	106	

Regn.	Type	C/n	Prev.Id.
D-8777	Scheibe L-Spatz 55	553	
D-8778	Schleicher K.8B	8332SH	
D-8780	SZD-30 Pirat	B-409	DDR-1780
			DM-1780
D-8781	Schleicher ASW-20L	20377	
D-8782	Schleicher K.8B	8338/A	
D-8783	Schleicher K.8B	8356	
D-8784	Schleicher ASK-21	21640	
D-8785	Scheibe L-Spatz 55	550	LN-GAH
D-8787	Scheibe Zugvogel IIIB	1093	
D-8788	Schleicher Rhönlerche II	115	
D-8790	Glasflügel H201B Standard Libelle	4	
D-8791	Schleicher K.8B	8389/A	
D-8792	Schleicher ASW-20L	20368	
D-8793	Schleicher Ka.6CR Rhönsegler	6324	
D-8794	Grob G.103 Twin II	3529	
D-8795	Grob G.103 Twin II	3561	
D-8796	SZD-30 Pirat	B-439	DDR-1796
			DM-1796
D-8797	Grob G.103 Twin II	3534	
D-8798	Schleicher ASK-21	21032	
D-8800	Schempp-Hirth Nimbus 2B	175	
D-8801	Schleicher ASK-21	21036	
D-8802	SZD-24-4A Foka 4	W-370	DDR-2231
			DM-2231
D-8803	SZD-24-4A Foka 4	W-353	DDR-2240
			DM-2240
D-8804	Schempp-Hirth SHK-1	4	OY-XEV
			D-6265
D-8805	Schleicher K.8B	8278	
D-8806	Scheibe L-Spatz 55	1	
D-8808	Schleicher Ka.6CR Rhönsegler	313	
D-8809	Schleicher ASW-19B	19324	
D-8810	Schleicher ASW-20L	20383	
D-8811	Rolladen-Schneider LS-8A (Reservation 9.99)	8278	
D-8812	Scheibe Bergfalke II	167	
D-8813	Scheibe Spatz A	4	
D-8816	Scheibe Bergfalke III	5585	
D-8817	Rolladen-Schneider LS-6-18W	6374	
D-8818	SZD-9bis Bocian 1E	P-563	DDR-3373
			DM-3373
D-8819	Schleicher K7 Rhönadler	7253	
D-8820	Scheibe Zugvogel IIIB	1103	
D-8821	Scheibe L-Spatz 55	640	
D-8822	Schleicher ASW-20L	20389	
D-8823	Schleicher Ka.6CR Rhönsegler	6370Si	
D-8824	Scheibe Zugvogel IIIB	1028	
D-8825	Schleicher ASK-21	21037	
D-8827	Schleicher ASW-20L	20390	
D-8828	Schleicher K.8B	454	
D-8829	SZD-30 Pirat	B-507	DDR-1829
			DM-1829
D-8830	Grob G.103C Twin III Acro	34196	
D-8831	Schleicher ASW-19B	19347	
D-8832	Schleicher ASW-20	20391	
D-8833	Rolladen-Schneider LS-4B	4906	
D-8834	Schleicher ASW-20	20429	
D-8836	Schleicher K7 Rhönadler	694	
D-8837	SZD-48-3 Jantar Standard 3	B-1363	SP-3266
D-8838	Schleicher K.8B	8634	
D-8840	Schleicher Ka.6CR Rhönsegler	6100	D-6215
D-8841	Schleicher Ka.6CR Rhönsegler	1073	OO-ZMZ
			OO-ZMS
			D-5367
D-8842	Scheibe L-Spatz 55	700	
D-8843	PZL PW-5 Smyk	17.07.016	
D-8844	Glaser-Dirks DG-300 Club Elan	3E-288C12	
D-8845	Grob G.102 Club Astir IIIB	5510CB	
D-8846	Grob G.102 Club Astir IIIB	5511CB	
D-8847	Grob G.102 Club Astir IIIB	5512CB	
D-8849	Vogt LO-100/150 Zwergreiher	13	
D-8850	SZD-42-2 Jantar 2B	B-1491	
D-8851	SZD-30 Pirat	B-575	DDR-1855
			DM-1855
D-8852	Schleicher K.8B	03	

Regn.	Type	C/n	Prev.Id.
D-8853	Schleicher K.8B	977	
D-8854	Scheibe Bergfalke III	5617	
D-8855	Schleicher ASW-20L	20565	
D-8856	Schleicher K.8B	AB8856	
D-8858	Scheibe L-Spatz 55	741	
D-8860	Schleicher Ka.6CR Rhönsegler	1075	
D-8861	SZD-30 Pirat	S-01.04	DDR-1867
			DM-1867
D-8862	Glaser-Dirks DG-300 Elan	3E-265	
D-8863	Rolladen-Schneider LS-4	4371	
D-8864	Rolladen-Schneider LS-4	4372	
D-8865	Rolladen-Schneider LS-4	4381	
D-8869	Schleicher ASK-21	21641	
D-8872	Rolladen-Schneider LS-4	4450	
D-8873	Rolladen-Schneider LS-4	4451	
D-8874	Rolladen-Schneider LS-4	4452	
D-8875	Rolladen-Schneider LS-4	4453	
D-8876	Akaflieg München Mü.13D	1	
D-8877	Schempp-Hirth Nimbus 2B	161	
D-8878	Glaser-Dirks DG-300 Elan	3E-164	
D-8879	Schleicher Ka.6CR Rhönsegler	6095Si	
D-8880	Grunau Baby III (Reservation 11.99)	1-52	
D-8882	Schleicher Ka.6CR Rhönsegler	6543	
D-8883	SZD-30 Pirat	S-01.26	DDR-1880
			DM-1880
D-8884	SZD-30 Pirat	S-01.30	DDR-1884
			DM-1884
D-8885	Scheibe L-Spatz 55	781	
D-8886	Schleicher K7 Rhönadler	7114	
D-8887	SZD-30 Pirat	S-02.43	DDR-1887
			DM-1887
D-8888	Schleicher ASK-21	21406	
D-8889	Scheibe Bergfalke III	5543	
D-8890	Schempp-Hirth Discus b	37	
D-8892	Schleicher Ka.6CR Rhönsegler	6427Si	(D-KAI A)
			D-8892
D-8893	Schleicher Ka.2 Rhönschwalbe (Reservation)	25	
D-8894	Scheibe L-Spatz 55	701	
D-8895	Schleicher Ka.6E	4005	
D-8896	Schleicher ASW-27	27005	
D-8897	Schleicher ASW-20L	20204	HB-1477
D-8898	Schleicher ASW-20	20589	HB-1659
D-8899	Schleicher Ka.1	33	
D-8900	Bölkow Phoebus C	854	
D-8901	Scheibe L-Spatz 55	575	
D-8902	Schleicher Ka.6CR Rhönsegler	6482	
D-8903	Schleicher ASW-27	27033	
D-8904	Schleicher K7 Rhönadler	7264	
D-8905	AK-5 (Permit 5.99)	501	
D-8906	Schleicher Ka.6CR Rhönsegler	6597	
D-8907	Bölkow Phoebus C (Reservation 2.99)	890	
D-8908	Schleicher K.8	108/58/A	
D-8909	Schleicher ASW-24B	24238	
D-8910	Schleicher Ka.2 Rhönschwalbe	02	
D-8911	SZD-30 Pirat	S-04.12	DDR-1911
			DM-1911
D-8912	Schleicher Ka.6CR Rhönsegler	6410	
D-8913	Scheibe L-Spatz 55	675	
D-8915	Schempp-Hirth Standard Cirrus	538	
D-8917	Grob Standard Cirrus	543G	
D-8918	Schempp-Hirth Standard Cirrus	549	
D-8920	Rolladen-Schneider LS-1F	281	
D-8921	Rolladen-Schneider LS-1F	286	
D-8923	Rolladen-Schneider LS-1F	300	
D-8924	LET L-13 Blanik	026360	
D-8925	Rolladen-Schneider LS-4	4559	
D-8926	Glasflügel H205 Club Libelle	81	
D-8927	Glasflügel H205 Club Libelle	82	
D-8928	Glasflügel H205 Club Libelle	83	
D-8932	SZD-30 Pirat	S-04.19	DDR-1912
			DM-1912
D-8933	Rolladen-Schneider LS-1F	359	
D-8934	Rolladen-Schneider LS-1F	417	
D-8935	Rolladen-Schneider LS-1F	307	
D-8936	Rolladen-Schneider LS-1F	418	

Regn.	Type	C/n	Prev.Id.
D-8939	Rolladen-Schneider LS-1F	421	
D-8941	Rolladen-Schneider LS-1	454	
D-8943	Glasflügel H206 Hornet	38	
D-8946	Akaflieg Braunschweig SB-5E Sperber	AB5057	
D-8947	Akaflieg Braunschweig SB-5E Sperber	AB5058	
D-8948	Glasflügel H304	222	
D-8949	Glasflügel H304 *(Reservation - cld?)*	223	
D-8950	Grob G.103C Twin III Acro	34175	
D-8951	Schleicher Ka.6CR Rhönsegler	328	
D-8952	Schleicher K.8B	8912/AB	
D-8954	Schleicher ASW-20L	20416	
D-8955	Schleicher ASK-21	21061	
D-8956	Glaser-Dirks DG-300 Elan	3E-206	
D-8958	Rolladen-Schneider LS-4	4560	
D-8960	Rolladen-Schneider LS-4	4562	
D-8961	Rolladen-Schneider LS-1F	460	
D-8962	Rolladen-Schneider LS-1F	461	
D-8963	Schleicher ASK-13	AB13644	
D-8964	Schleicher ASK-13	AB13649	
D-8965	Glaser-Dirks DG-300 Elan	3E-208	
D-8966	Rolladen-Schneider LS-4	4250	
D-8967	Glaser-Dirks DG-300 Elan *(Reservation)*	3E-209	
D-8968	Glaser-Dirks DG-300 Elan	3E-210	
D-8969	Glaser-Dirks DG-300 Elan	3E-218	
D-8970	Glaser-Dirks DG-300 Elan	3E-213	
D-8971	Rolladen-Schneider LS-1F	470	
D-8972	Rolladen-Schneider LS-1F	471	
D-8973	Rolladen-Schneider LS-4	4522	
D-8974	Grob G.103C Twin III Acro	34199	
D-8975	Grob G.103 Twin II	3647	
D-8976	Grob G.103 Twin II	3667	
D-8977	Schempp-Hirth Discus b	70	
D-8978	Schleicher ASK-23B	23116	
D-8979	Schleicher ASK-21	21451	
D-8980	Rolladen-Schneider LS-1F	487	
D-8982	Rolladen-Schneider LS-1F	489	
D-8984	Schleicher ASK-13	13399	
D-8985	SG-38 Schulgleiter	E-1	
D-8987	Glaser-Dirks DG-200/17	2-73/CL-24	
D-8988	Grob G.103A Twin II Acro	3687-K-38	
D-8989	Grob G.102 Club Astir IIIB	5541CB	
D-8992	Rolladen-Schneider LS-4	4294	
D-8993	Rolladen-Schneider LS-6	6052	
D-8994	Rolladen-Schneider LS-IF	442	
D-8995	Schempp-Hirth Nimbus 2B	154	I-AKOB
D-8996	Glasflügel H318 Mosquito	15	OO-ZDD
D-8997	Rolladen-Schneider LS-6	6051	
D-8998	Rolladen-Schneider LS-6	6050	
D-8999	LET L-13 Blanik	026345	
D-9000	Rolladen-Schneider LS-4B	4752	
D-9001	SZD-24C Foka	W-144	I-FOKA
			HB-715
D-9002	Glasflügel H303 Mosquito	40	OY-XHO
D-9003	Scheibe Spatz A	505	
D-9005	Schleicher Ka.6CR Rhönsegler	6476	
D-9006	Glaser-Dirks DG-300 Elan	3E-257	OY-XYI
D-9007	Grob G.102 Astir CS	1443	D-9000
D-9008	Glasflügel H201B Standard Libelle	426	PH-467
D-9009	Grob G.102 Club Astir IIIB	5501CB	
D-9010	Rolladen-Schneider LS-6C	6198	
D-9011	Rolladen-Schneider LS-6C	6199	
D-9012	Schleicher K.8B	8099	
D-9013	Rolladen-Schneider LS-6C	6200	
D-9014	Rolladen-Schneider LS-4B	4763	
D-9015	Rolladen-Schneider LS-4B	4772	
D-9016	Rolladen-Schneider LS-4B	4764	
D-9017	Rolladen-Schneider LS-4B	4765	
D-9018	Rolladen-Schneider LS-4B	4766	
D-9019	Rolladen-Schneider LS-4B	4767	
D-9020	Rolladen-Schneider LS-4A	4768	
D-9025	Schleicher Rhönsperber *(Reservation)*	AB-02	
D-9026	Göppingen Gö.1 Wolf	AB-1	
D-9028	Schleicher Ka.6E	4187	
D-9030	Schleicher Ka.6CR Rhönsegler	6038	

Regn.	Type	C/n	Prev.Id.
D-9031	SZD-9bis Bocian 1E	P-455	DDR-3031
			DM-3031
D-9032	SZD-9bis Bocian 1E	P-456	DDR-3032
			DM-3032
D-9033	Schempp-Hirth Discus b	505	
D-9034	Scheibe Bergfalke II/55	379	
D-9035	Schleicher K.8B	8491	
D-9036	Schleicher K.8B	8753	
D-9037	Schleicher Ka.6CR Rhönsegler	6450	
D-9039	Schleicher Ka.6CR Rhönsegler	6039Si	
D-9041	Schempp-Hirth Duo Discus	135	
D-9042	SZD-24-4A Foka 4	W-299	DDR-2042
			DM-2042
D-9044	Schleicher K7 Rhönadler	7142	
D-9046	Rolladen-Schneider LS-4	4188	
D-9048	Schleicher K.8B	8104	
D-9051	Schleicher Ka.2 Rhönschwalbe	88	
D-9055	SZD-55-1XM	551198105XM	
D-9057	Schleicher Ka.6CR Rhönsegler	6093Si	
D-9060	Schleicher K.8B	116	
D-9061	SZD-9bis Bocian 1E	P-754	DDR-3069
			DM-3069
D-9062	SG-38 Schulgleiter	BWLV-15	
D-9063	Schleicher K.8B	113	
D-9064	Schleicher ASK-13	13098	
D-9065	Schleicher ASK-21	21638	
D-9067	SZD-30 Pirat	B-396	DDR-1767
			DM-1767
D-9070	Schempp-Hirth Discus b	500	
D-9071	Schleicher K.8B	8487	D-KOPF
	(Same c/n quoted as D-1198)		D-1071
D-9072	Scheibe L-Spatz 55	512	
D-9073	Bölkow Phoebus A-1	713	
D-9074	Scheibe L-Spatz 55	567	(D-KOHN(2))
D-9075	Schleicher Ka.6 Rhönsegler	194	
D-9076	Schleicher Ka.6CR Rhönsegler	6359	
D-9077	Schempp-Hirth Ventus c	432	
D-9079	Scheibe Bergfalke II/55	224	
D-9080	Schleicher ASK-21	21590	
D-9082	Schleicher K.8B	8042	
D-9083	Doppelraab IV	E-1	
D-9084	Schleicher Ka.2B Rhönschwalbe	190	
D-9088	Schempp-Hirth Duo Discus	17	
D-9090	Schleicher K.8B	8010	
D-9091	Scheibe Spatz A	001 TAB	
D-9092	Schleicher Ka.6CR Rhönsegler	1027	
D-9093	Schleicher ASW-27	27024	
D-9095	Schempp-Hirth Duo Discus	63	
D-9097	Schleicher K.8	3	
D-9098	Scheibe Bergfalke II/55	357	
D-9099	Rolladen-Schneider LS-7	7054	
D-9100	SZD-30 Pirat	B-443	DDR-1800
			DM-1800
D-9101	Start & Flug H-101 Salto	71	
D-9102	Rolladen-Schneider LS-4	4376	
D-9103	Schempp-Hirth Ventus c	568	HB-3103
D-9104	Rolladen-Schneider LS-4	4156	
D-9106	Rolladen-Schneider LS-4	4195	
D-9109	Schleicher K.8	455	
D-9115	Scheibe L-Spatz 55	678	
D-9116	Schleicher Ka.6BR Rhönsegler	530	
D-9117	Schleicher Ka.6CR Rhönsegler	553	
D-9119	Schleicher ASK-21	21124	
D-9120	Bölkow Phoebus A-1	709	
D-9121	Schempp-Hirth Discus CS	132CS	
D-9122	Schempp-Hirth Discus CS	135CS	
D-9123	Schempp-Hirth Discus CS	136CS	(PH-1000)
D-9124	Schempp-Hirth Discus CS	133CS	
D-9125	Schempp-Hirth Discus CS	137CS	
D-9126	Glaser-Dirks DG-100	35	
D-9127	Schempp-Hirth Discus b	12	
D-9129	Rock Geier II	1	
D-9130	Glasflügel H303 Mosquito B	106	
D-9131	Schleicher Ka.6CR Rhönsegler	6564	
D-9132	Glasflügel H301 Libelle	19	

Regn.	Type	C/n	Prev.Id.
D-9133	Schleicher K.8B	714	
D-9134	Scheibe Bergfalke II/55	AB 350	
D-9135	Schleicher Rhönlerche II	885/1/58	
D-9140	Scheibe Spatz A	V-1	
D-9141	SZD-24-4A Foka 4	W-225	
D-9142	Schempp-Hirth Duo Discus	125	
D-9143	Rolladen-Schneider LS-4	4405	
D-9145	Rolladen-Schneider LS-4	4407	
D-9146	Schleicher K.8B	882	
D-9147	Schleicher K.8B	111	
D-9148	Schempp-Hirth Duo Discus	37	
D-9149	Schempp-Hirth Duo Discus	39	
D-9152	Schempp-Hirth Discus b	540	
D-9153	Schempp-Hirth Nimbus 4D	4/15	(D-KFHA)
D-9154	Schempp-Hirth Ventus 2b	9	
D-9155	Schleicher K.8B	233/1	
D-9156	Schleicher K7 Rhönadler	7032	
D-9157	Schleicher K.8B	AB.05	
D-9158	Schleicher Ka.6CR Rhönsegler	6184	
D-9159	Scheibe Bergfalke II/55	346	
D-9160	Scheibe Bergfalke II/55	380	
D-9161	Schleicher K.8B	3/8196	
D-9163	Schleicher Ka.2B Rhönschwalbe	E 1	
D-9165	Schleicher Ka.6CR Rhönsegler	6220	
D-9167	Schleicher Ka.6CR Rhönsegler	6318Si	
D-9169	SZD-9bis Bocian 1E	P-559	DDR-3369
			DM-3369
D-9173	Schleicher K.8B	8358	
D-9174	Schleicher K.8B	8374	
D-9176	Focke-Wulf Kranich III	58	
D-9177	Scheibe Bergfalke III	5524	
D-9180	Schleicher Ka.6E	4028	
D-9181	Schleicher ASK-21	21622	
D-9182	Schleicher Ka.6CR Rhönsegler	6504	
D-9184	Schleicher Ka.6CR Rhönsegler	6507	
D-9185	Scheibe SF-27A	6038	
D-9186	Schleicher Ka.6CR Rhönsegler	6489Si	
D-9188	Schleicher Ka.6CR Rhönsegler	6514	
D-9189	Scheibe Bergfalke III	5528	
D-9190	Neukom S-4A Elfe	66	HB-1229
D-9191	Schleicher Ka.6E	4040	
D-9192	Rock Geier II	V-2	
D-9193	Schleicher Ka.6CR Rhönsegler	6304	
D-9194	Schempp-Hirth Duo Discus	15	
D-9195	SZD-30 Pirat	W-397	OY-DXH
D-9196	LET L-13 Blanik	173343	
D-9199	Bölkow Phoebus A-1	752	
D-9201	Schleicher Ka.6CR Rhönsegler	6578	
D-9202	Schempp-Hirth Janus CE	286	
D-9204	Schempp-Hirth Duo Discus	172	
D-9205	Bölkow Phoebus A-1	768	
D-9206	Schleicher Ka.6CR Rhönsegler	6123Si	
D-9207	Schleicher Ka.6CR Rhönsegler (Reservation - dd?)	6599	
D-9208	LET L-13 Blanik	170718	DDR-3208
			DM-3208
			OK-0901
D-9209	Schempp-Hirth Duo Discus	159	
D-9211	Schleicher K.8B	8644/A	
D-9212	Schempp-Hirth Discus 2A (Permit 10.99)	4	
D-9213	Glasflügel H201B Standard Libelle	412	
D-9214	Bölkow Phoebus C	784	
D-9216	Schleicher K.8B	8732	
D-9217	Nabern FS-24 Phönix T	406	
D-9218	Schleicher K.8B	8300/A	
D-9219	Scheibe SF-27A	6099	
D-9220	Schleicher ASK-13	13092	
D-9221	Rolladen-Schneider LS-1D	181	
D-9222	Schempp-Hirth Ventus 2a	2	
D-9223	SZD-41A Jantar Standard	B-815	LX-CRP
D-9224	Schempp-Hirth Standard Cirrus	368	
D-9225	SZD-9bis Bocian 1E	P-506	DDR-3224
			DM-3224
D-9227	Scheibe Bergfalke IV	5832	
D-9228	Grob Standard Cirrus	375G	

Regn.	Type	C/n	Prev.Id.
D-9229	SZD-9bis Bocian 1E	P-511	DDR-3229
			DM-3229
D-9230	SZD-41A Jantar Standard	B-932	OE-5230
D-9231	Rolladen-Schneider LS-1D	246	
D-9233	Glasflügel H401 Kestrel	101	
D-9234	Glasflügel H201B Standard Libelle	491	
D-9235	Grob Standard Cirrus	374G	
D-9236	Glasflügel H201B Standard Libelle	484	
D-9238	Glasflügel H201B Standard Libelle	486	
D-9240	Start & Flug H101 Salto	40	
D-9241	Start & Flug H101 Salto	41	
D-9242	Schleicher ASW-27	27040	HB-3242
D-9243	Start & Flug H101 Salto	38	
D-9244	Rolladen-Schneider LS-1D	260	
D-9245	Schempp-Hirth Standard Cirrus	412	
D-9246	Schempp-Hirth Standard Cirrus	413	
D-9247	Rolladen-Schneider LS-1D	3	OE-5247
D-9249	Schempp-Hirth Nimbus 2	59	
D-9250-HI	Glasflügel H201B Standard Libelle	513	
D-9251	Glasflügel H201B Standard Libelle	515	
D-9252	Glasflügel H201B Standard Libelle	516	
D-9253	SZD-32A Foka 5	W-514	DDR-2253
			DM-2253
D-9254	Schempp-Hirth Cirrus	17	HB-925
D-9255	Schleicher K.8B	8949/A	
D-9256	VTC-75 Standard Cirrus	154Y	
D-9257	VTC-75 Standard Cirrus	155Y	
D-9259	Start & Flug H101 Salto	46	
D-9260	Start & Flug H101 Salto	47	
D-9261	Schleicher Ka.6CR Rhönsegler	6486Si	D-KOFA
			D-4637
D-9262	Rolladen-Schneider LS-1F	274	
D-9264	Glasflügel H201B Standard Libelle	569	
D-9265	Schleicher ASK-13	13479	
D-9266	Schleicher ASW-15B	5374	
D-9267	Schleicher ASW-15B	15375	
D-9268	Schleicher ASW-15B	15377	
D-9269	Schleicher ASW-15B	15378	
D-9270	Schleicher ASW-15B	15387	
D-9271	Schempp-Hirth Nimbus 4	6	
D-9272	Schleicher ASK-13	13480	
D-9273	Schleicher ASW-15B	15381	
D-9274	Schleicher ASW-17	17036	
D-9275	Schleicher ASK-13	13490	
D-9276	Schleicher ASW-15B	15386	
D-9277	Schleicher ASK-13	13491	
D-9278	Schleicher ASW-15B	15379	
D-9280	Schleicher ASK-18	18001	
D-9281	Schleicher ASW-15B	15390	
D-9283	Schleicher ASW-15B	15392	
D-9284	Schleicher ASW-17	17035	
D-9285	Schleicher ASW-15B	15395	
D-9286	Schleicher ASW-15B	15396	
D-9287	Rolladen-Schneider LS-6	6049	
D-9288	Schleicher ASW-15B	15393	
D-9290	Rolladen-Schneider LS-1F	321	
D-9291	Rolladen-Schneider LS-1F	326	
D-9292	Rolladen-Schneider LS-6	6048	
D-9293	Rolladen-Schneider LS-1F	176	
D-9294	Schempp-Hirth Ventus 2a	4	
D-9296	Rolladen-Schneider LS-1F	296	
D-9297	Grunau Baby III	1	
D-9298	Glasflügel H401 Kestrel	115	
D-9299	Glasflügel H401 Kestrel	116	
D-9300	SZD-50-3 Puchacz	B-1082	DDR-3600
D-9301	SZD-50-3 Puchacz	B-1634	SP-3402
D-9302	Schleicher Ka.6CR Rhönsegler	6398	
D-9303	Glaser-Dirks DG-300 Elan Acro	3E-452A12	
D-9304	Glasflügel H304	201	
D-9305	Glaser-Dirks DG-300 Club Elan	3E-284C9	
D-9306	Glaser-Dirks DG-300 Club Elan	3E-287C11	
D-9307	Scheibe Bergfalke III	5538	
D-9309	Akaflieg Braunschweig SB-5B Sperber	5015	
D-9311	Schleicher Ka.6CR Rhönsegler	6397	
D-9312	Schleicher K.8B	8226	

214

Regn.	Type	C/n	Prev.Id.
D-9313	Schleicher Ka.6CR Rhönsegler	6401	
D-9314	Schleicher K.8B	8392/SH	
D-9315	Bölkow Phoebus A-1	702	
D-9316	Schleicher ASW-27	27076	
D-9317	Schleicher Rhönlerche II (Reservation)	102	
D-9320	Bölkow Phoebus B-1	707	
D-9321	Scheibe Bergfalke III	5533	
D-9322	Schleicher K.8B	8617/SH	
D-9323	Glasflügel H301 Libelle	9	
D-9325	Schleicher K7 Rhönadler	7204	
D-9328	Schleicher K.8B	8174/A	
D-9330	Schleicher ASK-21	21551	
D-9331	Schleicher ASH-25	25057	
D-9333	Schleicher K.8C	AB81008	
D-9334	Scheibe SF-27A	6011	
D-9336	BS-1	14	
D-9338	Schempp-Hirth SHK-1	21	
D-9340	Schleicher Ka.6CR Rhönsegler	953	
D-9343	Scheibe SF-27A (Reservation 8.99)	6072	
D-9348	Schleicher Ka.6CR Rhönsegler	6443	
D-9349	Glasflügel H304	204	
D-9350	Rolladen-Schneider LS-3A	3233	PH-638
D-9352	Glaser-Dirks DG-300 Elan	3E-134	
D-9355	Schleicher Ka.6E	4012	
D-9357	SZD-24-4A Foka 4	W-251	
D-9359	Akaflieg Braunschweig SB-5B Sperber	5014	
D-9360	Scheibe Bergfalke III	5557	
D-9361	Scheibe Bergfalke III	5556	
D-9363	Schempp-Hirth Discus b	38	
D-9365	Schleicher Ka.6E	4001	
D-9366	Schempp-Hirth SHK-1	06	
D-9367	SZD-9bis Bocian 1E	P-554	DDR-3367 DM-3367
D-9369	Schleicher Ka.6CR Rhönsegler	6488Si	
D-9370	Scheibe L-Spatz 55	511	
D-9371	Bölkow Phoebus B-1	720	
D-9372	Schleicher Ka.6CR Rhönsegler	6499	
D-9373	Glaser-Dirks DG-300 Elan	3E-181	
D-9375	Glasflügel H304B	349	
D-9378	Glasflügel H301 Libelle	20	
D-9380	SZD-9bis Bocian 1E	P-576	DDR-3380 DM-3380
D-9381	Schleicher K.8B	8541/SH	
D-9382	Scheibe L-Spatz III	818	
D-9383	Akaflieg Braunschweig SB-5B Sperber	5029	
D-9384	SZD-9bis Bocian 1E	P-590	DDR-3384 DM-3384
D-9385	Scheibe Bergfalke III	5575	
D-9386	Schleicher K.8B	8225/A	
D-9387	Schempp-Hirth Discus CS	227CS	
D-9388	Schempp-Hirth Discus CS	228CS	
D-9389-AF	Schempp-Hirth Discus CS	232CS	
D-9390	Schempp-Hirth Discus CS	231CS	
D-9391	Schleicher ASW-20CL	20720	
D-9392	Schleicher ASK-21	21193	
D-9393	Schleicher ASW-20CL	20721	
D-9395	Schempp-Hirth Janus CE	303	
D-9396	Schempp-Hirth Discus CS	234CS	
D-9397	Schleicher Ka.6CR Rhönsegler	6550	
D-9398	Scheibe SF-27A	6052	
D-9399	Schleicher Ka.6CR Rhönsegler	6563	
D-9401	Schleicher Ka.6CR Rhönsegler	6561	
D-9402	Scheibe Bergfalke II/55	208	
D-9403	Schleicher ASK-13	13006	
D-9404	Schleicher K.8B	8691	
D-9405	Schleicher Ka.6CR Rhönsegler	6576	
D-9406	SZD-38A Jantar 1	B-639	DDR-2403 DM-2403
D-9407	SZD-41A Jantar Standard	B-696	DDR-2407 DM-2407
D-9408	Schleicher Ka.6CR Rhönsegler	6592	
D-9409	Schleicher K.8B	8698	
D-9411	Scheibe SF-27A	6081	
D-9412	Glasflügel H301 Libelle	45	
D-9413	Rolladen-Schneider LS-1F	311	

Regn.	Type	C/n	Prev.Id.
D-9414	Schleicher ASK-13	13039	
D-9415	BS.1	10	
D-9416	BS.1	11	
D-9417	Scheibe Bergfalke III	5611	
D-9418	Scheibe SF-27A	6104	
D-9419	Scheibe L-Spatz III	830	
D-9420	Schempp-Hirth Discus 2b (Reservation 11.99)	69	
D-9421	SZD-42-1 Jantar 2	B-778	DDR-2421 DM-2421
D-9422	Schempp-Hirth Cirrus	16	
D-9424	Scheibe Bergfalke III	5610	
D-9425	SZD-41A Jantar Standard	B-899	DDR-2425 DM-2425
D-9427 -Y	Glaser-Dirks DG-200/17C	2-157/CL-13	
D-9428	Glasflügel H201B Standard Libelle	110	SE-TIT
D-9429	Glaser-Dirks DG-100G Elan	E81-G56	
D-9430	Scheibe Bergfalke III	5618	
D-9431	Glasflügel H304	234	
D-9432	Glasflügel H206 Hornet	1	
D-9433	Grob Standard Cirrus	487G	
D-9434	Grob Standard Cirrus	494G	
D-9435	Rolladen-Schneider LS-1F	162	
D-9436	SZD-48-3 Jantar Standard 3	B-1969	
D-9438	Schempp-Hirth Ventus c	347	PH-943 D-5470 D-KBHK(1)
D-9439	Rolladen-Schneider LS-1F	319	
D-9440	Schempp-Hirth Duo Discus	160	
D-9442	Glasflügel H401 Kestrel	118	
D-9443	Schempp-Hirth Standard Cirrus	479	
D-9444	Glasflügel H205 Club Libelle	6	
D-9445	Glasflügel H205 Club Libelle	7	
D-9446	LET L-13 Blanik (Permit 9.99)	026056	
D-9447	Glasflügel H201B Standard Libelle	592	
D-9448	Glasflügel H201B Standard Libelle	593	
D-9449	Glasflügel H201B Standard Libelle	594	
D-9450	Rolladen-Schneider LS-1F	186	
D-9451	Glasflügel H205 Club Libelle	8	
D-9452	Glasflügel H205 Club Libelle	9	
D-9453	Rolladen-Schneider LS-1F	302	
D-9454	Start & Flug H101 Salto	59	
D-9455	Schempp-Hirth Duo Discus	95	
D-9456	Rolladen-Schneider LS-1F	174	
D-9457	Grob Standard Cirrus	519G	
D-9458	Grob Standard Cirrus	534G	
D-9459	Rolladen-Schneider LS-1F	317	
D-9460	LET L-13 Blanik	026114	
D-9461	Schleicher ASH-26	26092	
D-9463	Glasflügel H205 Club Libelle	10	
D-9464	Glasflügel H205 Club Libelle	11	
D-9465	Glasflügel H205 Club Libelle	12	
D-9466	Glasflügel H205 Club Libelle	13	
D-9467	Glasflügel H205 Club Libelle	14	
D-9468	Rolladen-Schneider LS-1F	282	
D-9469	Glasflügel H205 Club Libelle	15	
D-9470	Glasflügel H205 Club Libelle	16	
D-9471	Glasflügel H205 Club Libelle	17	
D-9473	Glasflügel H205 Club Libelle	19	
D-9474	Glasflügel H205 Club Libelle	20	
D-9475	Glasflügel H205 Club Libelle	21	
D-9477	Glasflügel H205 Club Libelle	23	
D-9478	Glasflügel H205 Club Libelle	24	
D-9479	Rolladen-Schneider LS-1F	249	
D-9480	Schempp-Hirth Nimbus 2	90	
D-9481	Glasflügel H205 Club Libelle	25	
D-9482	Glasflügel H205 Club Libelle	26	
D-9483	Rolladen-Schneider LS-1F	335	
D-9484	Rolladen-Schneider LS-1F	360	
D-9485	Rolladen-Schneider LS-1F	361	
D-9486	Rolladen-Schneider LS-1F	362	
D-9487	Glasflügel H205 Club Libelle	27	
D-9488	Rolladen-Schneider LS-1F	372	
D-9489	Schempp-Hirth Standard Cirrus	523	
D-9490	Schleicher ASK-21	21684	
D-9491	Schleicher ASW-17	17038	

Regn.	Type	C/n	Prev.Id.
D-9492	Schempp-Hirth Discus CS	002CS	D-0866
			OK-0366 ?
D-9493	Glasflügel H205 Club Libelle	32	
D-9494	Glasflügel H205 Club Libelle	33	
D-9495	Glasflügel H205 Club Libelle	34	
D-9496	Schleicher ASW-20CL	20779	D-KAWH
			D-8786
D-9497	Grob Standard Cirrus	540G	
D-9498	Rolladen-Schneider LS-1F	328	
D-9499	Schleicher ASW-24	24074	
D-9500	Start & Flug H101 Salto	64	
D-9510	Marganski MDM-1 Fox	214	
D-9512	Grob G.104 Speed Astir IIB	4076	HB-1512
D-9520	Grob G.104 Speed Astir IIB	4098	HB-1520
D-9521	Schleicher ASK-21	21630	
D-9522	Schleicher ASK-21	21653	
D-9525	Schleicher ASH-25	25140	OE-5525
D-9555	Marganski MDM-1 Fox	209	OE-5626
D-9571	Glasflügel H304	238	HB-1571
D-9595-AD	Schempp-Hirth Ventus 2a	49	
D-9605	AK-5B (Permit 5.99)	502 (formerly 1)	
D-9621	Schempp-Hirth Ventus b/16.6 (Reservation 11.99)	74	
D-9664	Rolladen-Schneider LS-3-17 (Reservation 12.99)	3461	
D-9666	Schempp-Hirth Nimbus 2	83	OE-5019
D-9669	Rolladen-Schneider LS-8A	8074	
D-9676	LET L-13 Blanik (Reservation 6.99)	026249	
D-9680	Schleicher ASW-27	27077	
D-9696	Schempp-Hirth Ventus 2b	50	
D-9727 - K	Schleicher ASW-27	27050	
D-9733	FS-33 (Permit 10.99)	33-1	
D-9760	Schempp-Hirth Discus b	9	HB-1760
D-9777	Schleicher ASW-17 (Reservation 12.99)	17006	OO-VAT
			PL-69
			OO-ZUU
D-9800	Glaser-Dirks DG-800S (Reservation - old?)	8-140S33	
D-9801	Rolladen-Schneider LS-8A	8099	
D-9802	Schleicher ASK-21	21680	
D-9821	Schempp-Hirth ASK-21	21673	
D-9827	Schleicher ASW-27	27073	
D-9888	Rolladen-Schneider LS-8A	8123	
D-9901	Rolladen-Schneider LS-6C-18	6382	
D-9913	Grob G.102 Astir CS (Reservation 8.99)	1117	OY-XIY
			D-6971
D-9950	SZD-50-3 Puchacz	B-1534	DDR-3650
D-9959	SZD-59 Acro	B-2179	
D-9966	Glaser-Dirks DG-800S	8-56S15	
D-9970	B-5 (Permit 6.99)	01	
D-9977	Schleicher ASW-27	27075	
D-9988	Rolladen-Schneider LS-8A (Permit - old?)	8181	
D-9999	Schempp-Hirth Duo Discus	129	

EC - SPAIN

Regn.	Type	C/n	Prev.Id.

Another country which has not published an official register for several years, as demonstrated by the large number of unidentified registrations and the growing list of aircraft imported for which no marks are known. It appears to be current practice to allocate new marks to aircraft which leave the Spanish register and then return, and even to those which change ownership, hence the growing number of previous identities.

Regn.	Type	C/n	Prev.Id.
EC-AAP	Piper L-14	5-3007	CU-P18
			NC41594
			(45-55531)
EC-ACA	de Havilland DH.87A Hornet Moth (Stored)	8039	EC-CAI
			EC-EBE
			EC-W51
EC-ACB	Miles M.3 Falcon (Museum)	197	EC-CAO
			EC-BDD
EC-ACJ	Auster J/1 Autocrat (Stored)	1960	EC-DAZ
			G-AHCF
EC-ACU	Miles M.38 Messenger 2A (Stored)	6360	EC-UAU
			(EC-EAL)
			G-AJEZ
EC-ADA	Piper PA-12 Super Cruiser	12-3535	
EC-ADG	Auster J/1 Autocrat (Stored)	2216	G-AJAL
EC-ADS	Piper J-3C-65 Cub (Damaged 22.2.97)	22467	
EC-ADU	Stinson 108-3 Voyager	4386	N6386M
EC-ADY	Stinson 108-3 Voyager	4344	N6344M
EC-AEE	Stinson 108-3 Voyager	4394	N6394M
EC-AFB	Cessna 170	19169	F-OAGF
			N11B
			N9708A
EC-AFC	Piper PA-12 Super Cruiser	12-1641	
EC-AFF	Stinson 108-3 Voyager	5183	N4183C
EC-AFG	Stinson 108-3 Voyager	4366	N6366M
EC-AGH	Piper PA-20 Pacer 125	20-648	
EC-AGJ	North American Navion 4	4-1519	F-OAIP
			N4519K
EC-AGM	Macchi MB.308	5807/34	I-MACC
EC-AGZ	Slingsby T-45 Swallow	1614	
EC-AHB	Percival P.34A Proctor 3	H.463	G-AMCO
			LZ681
EC-AHD	Piper J-3C-65 Cub	22468	
EC-AHG	Piper PA-12 Super Cruiser	12-2451	OO-XAZ
			NC2290M
EC-AHL	CASA I-131L Jungmann (Rebuild)	unkn	EE3-205
EC-AIA	Slingsby T-45 Swallow	1656	
EC-AIF	Boeing Stearman E75 (Museum)	75-5513	N4657V
			42-17350
EC-AIJ	Piper PA-18-135 Super Cub	18-2479	
EC-AIQ	Piper PA-18-150 Super Cub	18-4615	F-BHAB
EC-AIS	Auster J/1 Autocrat	2190	G-AIGH
EC-AIU	de Havilland DH.82A Tiger Moth (Rebuild)	3657	MM30-116
			F-AQJX
EC-AJE	Piper PA-18A-135 Super Cub	18-2935	
EC-AJF	Piper PA-18A-135 Super Cub	18-2883	
EC-AJM	Boeing Stearman E75	75-5498	N4889V
	(Reserved as N126SE)		42-17335
EC-AJR	Auster Mk.5	1505	EC-WJR
			TJ517
EC-AJU	Grumman G.44A Widgeon	734	N41971
EC-AJY	Piper J-3C-65 Cub (Museum)	12965	HB-OCM
			44-80669
EC-AJZ	Fairchild F.24W-41A Argus II	663	HB-EAP
	(Believed WFU and stored)		FZ723
			43-14697
EC-AKD	Piper J-3C-65 Cub	11691	G-AISP
			43-30400
EC-AKE	Auster Mk.5	1526	HB-EOB
			TJ479
EC-AKK	AISA I-11B Peque	005	
EC-AKL	AISA I-11B Peque	006	
EC-AKO	de Havilland DH.89A Dragon Rapide (Dismantled)	6345	G-AERN
EC-AKQ	Piper J-3C-65 Cub	11190	HB-ONR
			43-29899
EC-AKU	Auster Mk.4	865	G-ALVV
			MT143

Regn.	Type	C/n	Prev.Id.
EC-AKX	Auster Mk.5	668	HB-EUA
			G-AJTN
			NJ668
EC-ALD	Auster J/1 Autocrat	1967	G-AGXS
EC-ALK	Piper PA-18A-150 Super Cub	18-3791	
EC-ALP	CASA I-133C Jungmeister (Museum)	041/1023	ES-1-17
EC-ALS	Aerodiffusion Jodel D.112	E.5	
EC-ALU	Aerodiffusion Jodel D.112	E.8	
EC-AMK	Piper PA-18A-150 Super Cub	18-4859	
EC-ANB	Aerodiffusion Jodel D.112	E.17	
EC-AND	Aerodiffusion Jodel D.112	E.19	
EC-ANF	Aerodiffusion Jodel D.112	E.21	
EC-ANH	Piper PA-20 Pacer 135	20-847	F-OAKO
EC-ANI	Auster Mk.5	1262	HB-EOG
			RT635
EC-ANM	North American Navion D-16	4-753	EC-WNM
			N8753H
EC-AOM	Aerodiffusion Jodel D.112	E.32	
EC-AOR	Aerodiffusion Jodel D.112	E.37	
EC-AOU	Aerodiffusion Jodel D.112	E.41	
EC-AOV	Aerodiffusion Jodel D.112	E.42	
EC-APB	Beech 35-C33A Debonair	CE-70	D-ECMO
EC-APH	Omnipol Super Aero 45	04-005	
EC-API	Cessna 182 Skylane	33615	N5615B
EC-APJ	PZL-101-G2 Gawron	101701	SP-PBK
			SP-PAG
EC-APK	Aerodiffusion Jodel D.112	E.45	
EC-APO	Aerodiffusion Jodel D.112	E.54	
EC-APR	Schleicher Ka.6CR Rhönsegler (Museum)	784	
EC-APS	Schleicher Ka.6CR Rhönsegler	727	
EC-AQA	AISA I-11B Peque	54	L8C-54
EC-AQB	Douglas C-47A-20-DK	12844	EC-WQB
			N54705
			42-92983
EC-AQJ	PZL-101-G2 Gawron	30019	SP-CED
EC-AQO	Piper PA-25-150 Pawnee	25-350	TG-DIR-F
EC-AQS	Piper PA-25-150 Pawnee	25-430	
EC-AQV	Piper PA-25-150 Pawnee	25-432	
EC-ARD	Piper PA-25-150 Pawnee	25-446	
EC-ARG	Piper PA-25-150 Pawnee (2-seater)	25-464	N6351Z
EC-ARX	Piper PA-25-150 Pawnee	25-629	N10F
EC-ARY	Piper PA-25-150 Pawnee	25-645	N10F
EC-ASA	Piper PA-25-150 Pawnee	25-491	
EC-ASB	Piper PA-25-150 Pawnee	25-651	
EC-ASJ	Beech C-45H (Museum)	AF-752	N9962Z
			52-10822
EC-ASO	Edgar Percival EP-9 Prospector	25	G-APCT
			G-43-4
EC-ASU	Piper PA-18A-150 Super Cub	18-4607	CN-TEH
	(Badly damaged 3.7.94)		F-DAEN
EC-ASV	Piper PA-18A-150 Super Cub	18-5408	CN-TEC
			F-DAFC
EC-ASY	Piper PA-18A-135 Super Cub	18-2937	CN-TEB
	(Crashed 7.79)		F-DABP
EC-ATJ	Aerodiffusion Jodel D.112	E.50	
EC-ATK	Piper PA-25-150 Pawnee	25-707	
EC-ATS	Aerodiffusion Jodel D.1190-S	E.58	
EC-AUD	Agusta-Bell 47G-3B	1520	
EC-AUE	Agusta-Bell 47G-3B	1521	
EC-AUF	Beech H35 Bonanza	D-5105	HB-EBA
			D-EJIN
			N12B
EC-AUI	Piper PA-25-235 Pawnee	25-2179	N6617Z
EC-AUK	Mooney M.20C Mark 21	2395	N6668U
EC-AUL	Aerodiffusion Jodel D.1190-S	E.59	
EC-AUO	Piper PA-25-235 Pawnee	25-2315	
EC-AUQ	CEA Jodel DR.1050 Ambassadeur	421	EC-WUQ
EC-AUT	Piper PA-25-235 Pawnee	25-2327	
EC-AUU	Piper PA-25-235 Pawnee	25-2330	
EC-AVB	Piper PA-25-150 Pawnee	25-725	
EC-AVC	Piper PA-25-150 Pawnee	25-726	
EC-AVE	Aerodiffusion Jodel D.1190-S	E.60	
EC-AVF	Cessna 182F Skylane	54594	N3194U
EC-AVG	Aerodiffusion Jodel D.1190-S	E.62	
EC-AVH	Tipsy T.66 Nipper Mk.2	63	OO-FOL
EC-AVI	Hughes 269A	43-0201	
EC-AVJ	Cessna 170B	20573	N2421D
EC-AVK	Cessna 182F Skylane	54426	N3526Y
EC-AVL	Reims/Cessna F.172E	0027/50582	
EC-AVM	Dornier Do.27Q-5	2038	OE-DCA
			OE-VAK
EC-AVO	Piper PA-25-235 Pawnee	25-2428	N6829Z
EC-AVQ	Aerodiffusion Jodel D.1190-S	E.68	
EC-AVR	Aerodiffusion Jodel D.1190-S	E.65	
EC-AVU	Aerodiffusion Jodel D.1190-S	E.66	
EC-AVX	Aero Commander 520	10	EC-WVX
			F-BBDY
			N4109B
EC-AXA	Zlin Z.326A Akrobat	861	EC-WXA
EC-AXD	Zlin Z.326A Akrobat	898	EC-WXD
EC-AXG	Aerodiffusion Jodel D.1190-S	E.67	
EC-AXL	Zlin Z.326A Akrobat	899	
EC-AXO	Piper PA-25-235 Pawnee	25-2582	N6886Z
EC-AXQ	Piper PA-28-180 Cherokee B	28-1732	N7725W
EC-AXT	Aerodiffusion Jodel D.1190-S	E.73	
EC-AXV	Beech 95-B55 Baron	TC-730	
EC-AXY	LET L-13 Blanik	173109	
EC-AYM	Piper PA-25-235 Pawnee B	25-3068	
EC-AYU	L-Spatz 55	735	
EC-AYV	Piper PA-25-235 Pawnee B	25-3065	
EC-AYX	Aerodiffusion Jodel D.1190-S	E.78	
EC-AZE	Piper PA-25-235 Pawnee B	25-3103	
EC-AZF	Piper PA-25-235 Pawnee B	25-3114	
EC-AZI	Agusta-Bell 47G-4	2509	MM80412
EC-AZJ	Piper PA-25-235 Pawnee B	25-3130	
EC-AZL	Piper PA-25-235 Pawnee B	25-3123	
EC-AZM	Piper PA-25-235 Pawnee B	25-3113	
EC-AZQ	Stinson 108-3 Voyager	unkn	L2-17
EC-AZV	Piper PA-23-250 Aztec C	27-2846	N5762Y
EC-AZY	Reims/Cessna F.172F	0161	EC-WZY
EC-BAH	Aerodiffusion Jodel D.1190-S	E.86	
EC-BAI	Aerodiffusion Jodel D.1190-S	E.87	
EC-BAK	Piper PA-22-150 Tri-Pacer	22-5427	SE-CDB
			N7747D
EC-BAL	Piper PA-25-235 Pawnee B	25-3102	
EC-BAM	Piper PA-28-180 Cherokee C	28-2206	N11C
			N8107W
EC-BAN	Grumman G.164 Agcat	334	N605U
EC-BAP	Gardan GY-80 Horizon 160	95	
EC-BAS	Aerodiffusion Jodel D.1190-S	E.101	(D-ELCO)
EC-BAT	Aerodiffusion Jodel D.1190-S	E.102	
EC-BAY	LET L-13 Blanik	173308	
EC-BBB	Reims/Cessna F.172F	0175	EC-WBB
EC-BBE	Piper PA-23-250 Aztec C	27-2914	N5784Y
EC-BBF	Piper PA-30-160 Twin Comanche	30-814	N7725Y
EC-BBG	Bölkow BO.208C Junior	512	D-ENCO
EC-BBI	Piper PA-25-235 Pawnee B	25-3280	
EC-BBJ	Reims/Cessna F.172G	0193	EC-WBJ
EC-BBL	MS.886 Rallye 150	440	
EC-BBM	Aerodiffusion Jodel D.1190-S	E.83	
EC-BBO	Aerodiffusion Jodel D.1190-S	E.85	
EC-BBS	Piper PA-18-150 Super Cub	18-8264	N7147Z
EC-BBU	Mooney M.20E Super 21	720	
EC-BBX	Piper PA-30-160 Twin Comanche	30-642	N7576Y
EC-BBZ	Piper PA-23-250 Aztec C	27-2938	N5805Y
EC-BCA	Reims/Cessna F.172G	0215	EC-WCA
EC-BCB	Beech D95A Travel Air	TD-635	D-GARE
EC-BCC	Agusta-Bell 47G-4	2510	
EC-BCG	Piper PA-25-235 Pawnee B	25-3454	N7458Z
EC-BCL	Aerodiffusion Jodel D.1190-S	E.92	
EC-BCN	Slingsby T-45 Swallow	1488	
EC-BCO	Slingsby T-45 Swallow	1490	
EC-BCP	Piper PA-25-235 Pawnee B	25-3398	N7423Z
EC-BCR	Piper PA-25-235 Pawnee B	25-0487	N7479Z
EC-BCS	Piper PA-25-235 Pawnee B	25-3432	N7442Z
EC-BCT	Beech A23 Musketeer	M-765	D-EMNE
EC-BCV	Agusta-Bell 47G-4	2513	
EC-BCX	Piper PA-25-235 Pawnee B	25-3493	N7483Z
EC-BDA	Piper PA-25-235 Pawnee B	25-3640	N7574Z
EC-BDB	Piper PA-25-235 Pawnee B	25-3414	N7431Z

Regn.	Type	C/n	Prev.Id.
EC-BDJ	SOCATA MS.893A Rallye Commodore 180	10571	
EC-BDN	Piper PA-28-180 Cherokee C	28-2816	
EC-BDO	Cessna 172E	51687	N5787T
EC-BDP	Aerodiffusion Jodel D.1190-S	E.90	
EC-BDQ	Aerodiffusion Jodel D.1190-S	E.93	
EC-BDR	Aerodiffusion Jodel D.1190-S	E.94	
EC-BDS	Zlin Z.526A Akrobat	1001	EC-WDS
EC-BDV	Zlin Z.526A Akrobat (Dismantled)	1004	EC-WDV
EC-BEI	Cessna 182J Skylane	56945	N2845F
EC-BEK	Aerodiffusion Jodel D.1190-S	E.103	
EC-BEL	Aerodiffusion Jodel D.1190-S	E.109	
EC-BEM	Mooney M.20E Super 21	1081	
EC-BEP	Beech A23-19 Musketeer	MB-161	HB-ENY
EC-BEQ	Piper PA-28-180 Cherokee C	28-4008	N11C
EC-BEU	Scheibe Bergfalke III	5568	
EC-BEZ	Scheibe Bergfalke III	5559	
EC-BFD	Scheibe L-Spatz 55	808	
EC-BFE	Scheibe L-Spatz 55	809	
EC-BFF	Scheibe L-Spatz 55 (Stored)	810	
EC-BFG	Scheibe L-Spatz 55	811	
EC-BFN	Grumman G.164 Agcat	399	N663U
EC-BFO	Piper PA-28-180 Cherokee C	28-3077	N9046J
EC-BFU	Hughes 269B	116-0275	
EC-BFX	Hughes 269B	106-0268	
EC-BFY	Hughes 269B	106-0269	
EC-BFZ	Aerodiffusion Jodel D.1190-S	E.104	
EC-BGA	Reims/Cessna F.150G	0104	
EC-BGC	Piper PA-28-180 Cherokee C	28-3254	N9186J
EC-BGD	Piper PA-25-235 Pawnee B	25-4009	N4498Y
EC-BGG	Cessna A.188 Agwagon	00172	N9722V
EC-BGH	Piper PA-28-140 Cherokee	28-22148	N11C
EC-BGI	Piper PA-25-235 Pawnee B	25-3761	N7791Z
EC-BGJ	Piper PA-25-235 Pawnee B	25-3762	N7792Z
EC-BGK	Piper PA-25-235 Pawnee B	25-3842	N4459Y
EC-BGM	Piper PA-25-235 Pawnee B	25-3926	N7747Z
EC-BGN	Piper PA-25-235 Pawnee B	25-3759	N7790Z
EC-BGO	Reims/Cessna F.150G	0105	
EC-BGP	Piper PA-25-235 Pawnee B	25-3924	N7744Z
EC-BGQ	Piper PA-25-235 Pawnee B	25-3775	N7793Z
EC-BGS	Piper PA-25-235 Pawnee B	25-3779	N7795Z
EC-BGT	Piper PA-25-235 Pawnee B	25-4012	N4499Y
EC-BGU	Piper PA-25-235 Pawnee B	25-4017	N4501Y
EC-BGV	Piper PA-25-235 Pawnee B	25-4015	N4500Y
EC-BGX	Piper PA-14 Family Cruiser	14-177	F-BLXZ OO-ARY
EC-BGZ	Aerodiffusion Jodel D.1190-S	E.105	
EC-BHF	Slingsby T-45 Swallow	1540	
EC-BHG	Slingsby T-45 Swallow (Stored)	1541	
EC-BHI	Slingsby T-45 Swallow (Stored)	1544	
EC-BHK	Slingsby T-45 Swallow	1546	
EC-BHM	Slingsby T-45 Swallow	1547	
EC-BHN	Slingsby T-45 Swallow	1549	
EC-BHO	Slingsby T-45 Swallow (Museum)	1548	
EC-BHR	Slingsby T-45 Swallow	1552	
EC-BHS	Slingsby T-45 Swallow	1553	
EC-BHU	Slingsby T-45 Swallow	1555	
EC-BHV	Slingsby T-45 Swallow	1556	
EC-BHZ	Slingsby T-45 Swallow	1559	
EC-BIH	McDonnell-Douglas DC-9-32	47076	
EC-BIK	McDonnell-Douglas DC-9-32	47080	
EC-BIM	McDonnell-Douglas DC-9-32	47088	
EC-BIO	McDonnell-Douglas DC-9-32	47090	
EC-BIP	McDonnell-Douglas DC-9-32	47091	
EC-BIR	McDonnell-Douglas DC-9-32	47093	
EC-BIY	LET L-13 Blanik	173320	
EC-BIZ	LET L-13 Blanik	173321	
EC-BJA	LET L-13 Blanik	173338	
EC-BJB	LET L-13 Blanik	173339	
EC-BJE	Beech A23-24 Musketeer Super	MA-75	D-EKWA
EC-BJJ	Reims/Cessna F.172H	0338	
EC-BJL	Cessna A.188 Agwagon	00224	N9774V
EC-BJM	Scheibe Bergfalke III	5534	
EC-BJN	Scheibe Bergfalke III	5546	
EC-BJO	Scheibe Bergfalke III	5548	
EC-BJP	Beech A23-19 Musketeer Sport	MB-117	D-EJVA

Regn.	Type	C/n	Prev.Id.
EC-BJR	Piper PA-30-160 Twin Comanche B	30-1266	N8153Y
EC-BJS	Piper PA-25-235 Pawnee C (W/o 7.94)	25-4215	N4557Y
EC-BJU	Piper PA-23-250 Aztec C (Wfu)	27-3603	N6339Y
EC-BJX	Beech D95A Travel Air	TD-696	D-GARU
EC-BJY	SIAI-Marchetti S.205-20/R	362	EC-WJY
EC-BKA	CASA I-131H Jungmann (Sold in Brazil)	1081	E3B-370
EC-BKB	AISA I-11B Peque	unkn	L8C-4
EC-BKC	AISA I-11B Peque	unkn	L8C-5
EC-BKF	AISA I-11B Peque	unkn	L8C-14
EC-BKG	Beech D95A Travel Air	TD-689	D-GARO
EC-BKH	AISA I-11B Peque (Museum)	unkn	L8C-16
EC-BKK	AISA I-11B Peque	unkn	L8C-21
EC-BKN	Piper PA-18-150 Super Cub	18-4061	54-2661
EC-BKT	AISA I-11B Peque	unkn	L8C-40
EC-BKY	AISA I-11B Peque	unkn	L8C-51
EC-BLJ	Grumman G.164A Agcat	536	
EC-BLS	AISA I-11B Peque	unkn	L8C-108
EC-BLX	AISA I-11B Peque (W/o 2.9.94)	unkn	L8C-123
EC-BLY	AISA I-11B Peque	unkn	L8C-132
EC-BLZ	Aerodiffusion Jodel D.1190-S	E.110	
EC-BMA	Beech A23-24 Musketeer Super	MA-218	D-EJVE
EC-BMC	Agusta-Bell 47G-4	2520	
EC-BMF	Piper PA-25-235 Pawnee C	25-4365	(N4645Y)
EC-BMG	SIAI-Marchetti S.205-20/R	4-107	EC-WMG
EC-BMH	SIAI-Marchetti S.205-20/R	4-115	EC-WMH
EC-BMK	Piper PA-28-180 Cherokee C	28-3973	N9774J
EC-BMN	Piper PA-25-235 Pawnee C	25-4323	
EC-BMO	Piper PA-32-300 Cherokee Six	32-40132	N4136W
EC-BMP	Bölkow Phoebus A-1	708	D-1206
EC-BMR	Cessna 182K Skylane	58034	N3034Q
EC-BNB	Piper PA-25-235 Pawnee C	25-4369	N4649Y
EC-BND	Piper PA-32-260 Cherokee Six	32-927	N5509J
EC-BNE	Reims/Cessna F.172H	0460	EC-WNE (G-AVIS)
EC-BNI	Piper PA-30-160 Twin Comanche B	30-1462	N8394Y
EC-BNK	Piper PA-28R-180 Cherokee Arrow	28R-30056	N11C
EC-BNO	Beech A23-24 Musketeer Super	MA-219	D-EJVI
EC-BNP	Piper PA-23-250 Aztec C	7-2963	YV-T-HTH
EC-BNT	SA.3180 Alouette Astazou	2001	F-BPFE
EC-BNV	Cessna 182L Skylane	58852	N42099
EC-BNY	Piper PA-28R-180 Cherokee Arrow	28R-30302	N11C
EC-BOF	Piper PA-28-140 Cherokee	28-24125	N11C
EC-BOG	Piper PA-25-235 Pawnee C	25-4449	N4714Y
EC-BOH	Piper PA-28R-180 Cherokee Arrow (Stored)	28R-30440	N11C
EC-BOI	DHC-1 Chipmunk 22	C1/0147	D-EJAN G-AOJV WB699
EC-BOJ	Aerodiffusion Jodel D. 1190 -S	E.115	
EC-BOK	SOCATA MS.893A Rallye Commodore 180 (Damaged 23.3.97)	10749	
EC-BOL	Slingsby HP-14C	1637	BGA1402
EC-BOM	SZD-24A Foka 4 (Stored)	W-366	
EC-BON	SZD-24A Foka 4 (Museum)	W-367	
EC-BOR	SIAI-Marchetti S.205-20/R	4-200	
EC-BOS	Piper PA-25-260 Pawnee C	25-4524	N4764Y
EC-BOT	Piper PA-25-260 Pawnee C	25-4514	N4756Y
EC-BOU	Piper PA-25-260 Pawnee C	25-4489	N4751Y
EC-BOX	Bölkow Phoebus C	841	
EC-BOY	Fournier RF-4D	4067	
EC-BPD	Piper PA-28R-180 Cherokee Arrow	28R-30672	N11C
EC-BPI	Brockmeier/Schleicher Rhönlerche II	3081/Br	
EC-BPN	AISA I-11B Peque	unkn	L8C-11
EC-BPR	AISA I-11B Peque	unkn	L8C-87
EC-BPT	AISA I-11B Peque	unkn	L8C-129
EC-BPV	Brockmeier/Schleicher Rhönlerche II (Wreck noted at Cuatro Vientos 1994)	3082/Br	
EC-BPX	Brockmeier/Schleicher Rhönlerche II	3083/Br	
EC-BPY	AISA I-11B Peque	unkn	L8C-134
EC-BPZ	Aerodiffusion Jodel D.1190-S	E.117	
EC-BQC	Piper PA-30-160 Twin Comanche B	30-1723	N8571Y
EC-BQD	Piper PA-28R-180 Cherokee Arrow	28R-30709	N4960J
EC-BQE	Piper PA-28-140 Cherokee	28-24604	N7260J
EC-BQN	SIAI-Marchetti S.205-20/R	4-162	
EC-BQO	SIAI-Marchetti S.205-20/F	4-163	
EC-BQP	SIAI-Marchetti S.205-20/R	4-160	

Regn.	Type	C/n	Prev.Id.
EC-BQR	Aerodiffusion Jodel D.1190-S	E.118	
EC-BQY	McDonnell-Douglas DC-9-32	47455	
EC-BQZ	McDonnell-Douglas DC-9-32	47456	
EC-BRA	Piper PA-23-250 Aztec D	27-4127	N6849Y
EC-BRB	Aerodiffusion Jodel D.1190-S	E.119	
EC-BRD	Beech 95-D55 Baron	TE-689	N7856R
EC-BRE	Piper PA-23-250 Aztec D	27-4120	N6784Y
EC-BRF	Piper PA-28-140 Cherokee B	28-25164	
EC-BRI	Hughes 269C	30-0015	
EC-BRK	Aerodiffusion Jodel D.1190-S	E.125	
EC-BRM	Beech 95-B55 Baron	TC-1290	
EC-BRT	Reims/Cessna FR.172F Rocket	0109	
EC-BRV	Piper PA-25-260 Pawnee C	25-4969	
EC-BRZ	Aerodiffusion Jodel D.1190-S	E.120	
EC-BSF	SAN Jodel D.140E Mousquetaire IV	214	
EC-BSG	Piper PA-30-160 Twin Comanche C *(Damaged 2.3.97)*	30-1919	N8763Y
EC-BSH	SIAI-Marchetti S.205-20/F	4-273	
EC-BSI	Piper PA-28R-200 Cherokee Arrow	28R-35215	N9494N
EC-BSJ	Piper PA-25-260 Pawnee C	25-4861	
EC-BSM	Piper PA-25-260 Pawnee C	25-4972	N8552L
EC-BSN	Piper PA-23-250 Aztec D	27-4289	N6932Y
EC-BSO	Piper PA-30-160 Twin Comanche C	30-1945	N8787Y
EC-BSR	Piper PA-23-250 Aztec D	27-4301	N6997Y
EC-BSS	Aerodiffusion Jodel D.1190-S	E.121	
EC-BST	Aerodiffusion Jodel D.1190-S	E.122	
EC-BSU	Aerodiffusion Jodel D.1190-S	E.123	
EC-BSV	Piper PA-28R-200 Cherokee Arrow	28R-35343	N11C
EC-BSX	Dornier Do.27Q-5	2094	D-EFKA
EC-BSZ	Piper PA-23-250 Aztec D	27-4364	N6993Y
EC-BTA	Cessna T.337D Turbo Skymaster	1090	N86129
EC-BTD	Piper PA-28R-200 Cherokee Arrow	28R-35271	N2727R
EC-BTH(2)	Schleicher ASK-21	21323	
EC-BTI (2)	Robin DR.400/180R Remorqueur *(W/o 10.5.97)*	1758	
EC-BTK(2)	Stinson 108-3 Voyager *(Museum)*	4226	N6226M NC6226M
EC-BTM	AISA I-11B Peque	106	L8C-106
EC-BTN(2)	Robin DR.400/180R Remorqueur	1759	
EC-BTQ(2)	Robin DR.400/180R Remorqueur	1760	
EC-BTX	AISA I-11B Peque	unkn	L8C-67
EC-BTY	AISA I-11B Peque	unkn	L8C-68
EC-BUB	AISA I-11B Peque	unkn	L8C-77
EC-BUC(2)	Schleicher ASK-21	21352	
EC-BUD	AISA I-11B Peque	unkn	L8C-84
EC-BUF(2)	Schleicher ASK-21	21351	
EC-BUI (2)	Schleicher ASK-21	21348	
EC-BUK(2)	Schleicher ASK-21	21353	
EC-BUO(2)	Schleicher ASK-21	21347	
EC-BUP	AISA I-11B Peque	unkn	L8C-117
EC-BUR	AISA I-11B Peque	unkn	L8C-?
EC-BUT	AISA I-11B Peque	unkn	L8C-121
EC-BUV	AISA I-11B Peque	unkn	L8C-127
EC-BUY	AISA I-11B Peque	206	L8C-128
EC-BUZ	AISA I-11B Peque	207	L8C-?
EC-BVE	Agusta-Bell 47G-4A	2532	
EC-BVG	Dornier Do.27Q-5	2060	D-EANL (D-ENAH) F-OCLX
EC-BVH	Reims/Cessna F.172H	0480	
EC-BVI	Piper PA-25-260 Pawnee C	25-5154	
EC-BVJ	Zlin Z.526F Trenér Master	1122	
EC-BVK	Zlin Z.526F Trenér Master *(Stored)*	1123	
EC-BVL	Reims/Cessna F.337E Skymaster	0007/01236	
EC-BVM	Reims/Cessna FA.150K Aerobat	0039	
EC-BVO	Aerodiffusion Jodel D. 1190-S	E.126	
EC-BVQ	Piper PA-28-140 Cherokee B	28-26212	N11C
EC-BVS	Piper PA-25-260 Pawnee C	25-5248	
EC-BVU	SIAI-Marchetti S.205-20/R	4-274	
EC-BVY	Piper PA-28R-200 Cherokee Arrow	28R-35711	N11C
EC-BXA	Cessna 177B Cardinal	01478	N30813
EC-BXB	Piper PA-23-250 Aztec D	27-4530	N13896
EC-BXD	Piper PA-18-150 Super Cub	18-8829	N4499Z
EC-BXH	Macchi AL.60B-2	30/6210	D-EIRF I-MACW
EC-BXO	Piper PA-22-160 Tri-Pacer	22-4987	N7127D

Regn.	Type	C/n	Prev.Id.
EC-BXS	Reims/Cessna F.150K	0644	F-BSIH
EC-BXT	Piper PA-25-260 Pawnee C	25-5283	N8796L
EC-BXU	Fournier RF-5	5081	
EC-BXX	Piper PA-25-260 Pawnee C	25-5259	N8774L
EC-BXY	Piper PA-28-180 Cherokee F	28-7105044	N11C
EC-BXZ	Piper PA-25-260 Pawnee C	25-5256	N8771L
EC-BYA	Beech C23 Sundowner	M-1291	N9237Q
EC-BYE	McDonnell-Douglas DC-9-32	47504	
EC-BYF	McDonnell-Douglas DC-9-32	47542	
EC-BYI	McDonnell-Douglas DC-9-32	47452	
EC-BYJ	McDonnell-Douglas DC-9-32	47461	
EC-BYO	Cessna A.188 Agwagon	00443	(CN-TEM) N8193V
EC-BYP	Piper PA-28-180 Cherokee F	28-7105047	N11C
EC-BYQ	Cessna 207 Skywagon *(Wfu)*	00198	N1598U
EC-BYR	LET L-13 Blanik	174802	
EC-BYS	LET L-13 Blanik	174803	
EC-BYT	Reims/Cessna F.177RG Cardinal RG	0030/00193	
EC-BYU	SZD-30 Pirat	B-311	
EC-BYX	Piper PA-25-260 Pawnee C	25-5344	N8833L
EC-BYY	Piper PA-25-260 Pawnee C	25-5305	
EC-BYZ	Piper PA-25-260 Pawnee C	25-5333	
EC-BZA	Piper PA-25-260 Pawnee C	25-5340	(PT-DVD)
EC-BZB	Piper PA-28-140 Cherokee E	28-7225217	
EC-BZC	LET L-13 Blanik	174825	
EC-BZE	LET L-13 Blanik	174827	
EC-BZF	Bell OH-13H Sioux	1880	56-2168
EC-BZG	Bell OH-13H Sioux	1934	56-2222
EC-BZH	Bell OH-13H Sioux	1955	56-2243
EC-BZI	Bell OH-13H Sioux	2052	57-1814
EC-BZK	Piper PA-28-140 Cherokee D	28-7125534	N11C
EC-BZM	Piper PA-25-260 Pawnee C	25-5387	N8925L
EC-BZT	Brockmeier /Schleicher Rhönlerche II *(Wreck noted at Cuatro Vientos 1994)*	3090/Br	
EC-BZX	Reims/Cessna F.177RG Cardinal RG	0042/00206	
EC-CAA	SA.319B Alouette III	1904	
EC-CAB	Cessna A.188A Agwagon	00661	N1561M
EC-CAC	Piper PA-23-250 Aztec E	27-4770	N14212
EC-CAF	Hughes 369HS	12-0366S	
EC-CAG	Reims/Cessna F.177RG Cardinal RG	0041/00205	
EC-CAH	Reims/Cessna F.150L *(Wreck)*	0774	F-WLIQ
EC-CAL	Reims/Cessna F.150L *(Wreck)*	0765	F-WLIP
EC-CAN	SAAB-Scania MFI-10B Vipan	02	SE-CPH Fv54381
EC-CAQ	Piper PA-25-260 Pawnee C	25-5461	
EC-CAS	LET L-13 Blanik	174824	
EC-CAV	Piper PA-28-140 Cherokee E	28-7225329	N11C
EC-CAY	Piper PA-28R-200 Arrow	28R-7235284	N11C
EC-CAZ	Piper PA-28-140 Cherokee E	28-7225526	
EC-CBA	Boeing 727-256	20595	N1787B N1788B
EC-CBF	Boeing 727-256	20600	N1789B
EC-CBR	Beech A24R Sierra	MC-126	N9786L
EC-CBS	Hirth Hi.27 Akrostar Mk.II	4008	D-EMBD
EC-CBT	Piper PA-28-235 Cherokee Charger	28-7310012	N11C
EC-CBU	Piper PA-28-180 Cherokee Challenger	28-7305015	N11C
EC-CBV	LET L-13 Blanik	175201	
EC-CBY	SA.319B Alouette III	2021	
EC-CCB	LET L-13 Blanik	175225	
EC-CCD	Beech 65-80 Queen Air	LD-91	D-ILDO SE-EXU D-ILDO
EC-CCE	Cessna 414	0391	N1611T
EC-CCI	Reims/Cessna F.150L	0987	
EC-CCJ	LET L-13 Blanik	025305	
EC-CCK	LET L-13 Blanik	025306	
EC-CCL	Enstrom F-28A	101	
EC-CCM	Piper PA-28-140 Cherokee E	28-7225568	N11C
EC-CCN	McDonnell-Douglas DC-8-33 *(Wfu)*	45569	F-BIUY TU-TCE F-BIUY
EC-CCO	Reims/Cessna F.337E Skymaster	0005/01218	G-AXWN
EC-CCQ	Cessna A.188B Agwagon	01088	N21870
EC-CCR	Beech 58 Baron	TH-280	

Regn.	Type	C/n	Prev.Id.
EC-CCT	Beech 65-80 Queen Air	LD-47	SE-EWU / D-ILDA
EC-CCU	LET L-13 Blanik	175209	
EC-CCV	Piper PA-28-140 Cherokee	28-7325270	N11C
EC-CCZ	Reims/Cessna FR.172J Rocket	0405	
EC-CDC	McDonnell-Douglas DC-8-53	45567	F-BJLA / N9601Z
	(Wfu)		
EC-CDD	Cessna 421B Golden Eagle	0348	N7563Q
EC-CDE	Beech 95-B55 Baron (Also SpAF: E20-10)	TC-1554	
EC-CDF	Beech 95-B55 Baron (Also SpAF: E20-11)	TC-1555	
EC-CDH	Beech 95-B55 Baron (Also SpAF: E20-13)	TC-1582	
EC-CDI	Beech 65-C90 King Air (Also SpAF: E22-1)	LJ-603	
EC-CDJ	Beech 65-C90 King Air (Also SpAF: E22-2)	LJ-605	
EC-CDK	Beech 65-C90 King Air (Also SpAF: E22-3)	LJ-608	
EC-CDL	Cessna A.188B Agwagon	00872	N4472Q
EC-CDM	Rockwell S.2R Thrush Commander	1729R	N5529X
EC-CDP	Reims/Cessna F.150L	0906	
EC-CDS	Piper PA-31-310 Navajo	31-7300951	N7561L
EC-CDU	Scheibe L-Spatz 55	674	
EC-CDX	Bell 47G-5A	25108	
EC-CDZ	Piper PA-23-250 Aztec E	27-7305111	N40296
EC-CEB	SOCATA MS.894E Minerva 220GT	12135	F-OCTF
EC-CED	Piper PA-28-140 Cherokee	28-7325505	N11C
EC-CEE	LET L-13 Blanik	025509	
EC-CEG	Bell 47G-5A	25120	
EC-CEI	Cessna TU.206D Turbo Stationair	1311	G-AZVU / 4X-ALK / N72180
EC-CEJ	LET L-13 Blanik	025510	
EC-CEK	SOCATA MS.893E Rallye 180GT Gaillard	12307	F-OCUI
EC-CEL	SOCATA Rallye 100S Sport	2336	F-OCUF
EC-CEM	Piper PA-28-140 Cherokee	28-7325498	
EC-CEO	Piper PA-28-140 Cherokee	28-7325547	N9503N
EC-CEQ	Piper PA-36-285 Pawnee Brave	36-7360016	N9542N
EC-CES	Piper PA-28-180 Cherokee Challenger	28-7305498	N9510N
EC-CET	SZD-30 Pirat	B-550	
EC-CEU	SZD-30 Pirat	B-551	
EC-CEY	Piper PA-34-200 Seneca	34-7350311	N56279
EC-CEZ	McDonnell-Douglas DC-10-30	47980	
EC-CFA	Boeing 727-256	20811	
EC-CFB	Boeing 727-256	20812	
EC-CFC	Boeing 727-256	20813	
EC-CFD	Boeing 727-256	20814	
EC-CFE	Boeing 727-256	20815	
EC-CFF	Boeing 727-256	20816	
EC-CFG	Boeing 727-256	20817	
EC-CFH	Boeing 727-256	20818	
EC-CFI	Boeing 727-256	20819	
EC-CFK	Boeing 727-256	20821	
EC-CFM	Dornier Do.27A-5	122	L9-59 / 55+15 / AC+916 / AS+916 / PA+114
EC-CFN	Dornier Do.27B-1 (Museum)	129	L9-60 / 55+21 / MA+391 / DE+391 / PB+108 / PB+105
EC-CFO	Dornier Do.27B-1	149	L9-61 / 55+30 / SA+114 / SA+721 / PL+112 / PC+106
EC-CFP	Dornier Do.27A-1	166	L9-62 / 55+39 / AC+920 / AS+920
EC-CFQ	Dornier Do.27B-1	244	L9-63 / 55+86 / GB+387 / PG+106
EC-CFS	Dornier Do.27B-1	193	L9-65 / 55+60 / MD+386 / EC+386 / QB+403
EC-CFU	Dornier Do.27A-1D	359	L9-67 / 56+65 / ND+106 / AC+932 / AC+938 / AS+938
EC-CFV	Piper PA-28-180 Cherokee Challenger	28-7305502	N9511N
EC-CFZ	Beech 58 Baron	TH-353	N2867W
EC-CGC	LET L-13 Blanik	025521	
EC-CGD	LET L-13 Blanik	025522	
EC-CGE	Piper PA-34-200 Seneca	34-7350324	N56378
EC-CGH	Piper PA-34-200 Seneca	34-7450013	N56644
EC-CGI	Piper PA-28-180 Cherokee Challenger	28-7305599	N9556N
EC-CGJ	CASA/SIAT 223-A1 Flamingo	056	
EC-CGK	CASA/SIAT 223-A1 Flamingo	057	
EC-CGL	CASA/SIAT 223-A1 Flamingo	058	
EC-CGM	CASA/SIAT 223-A1 Flamingo	059	
EC-CGN	McDonnell-Douglas DC-9-32	47637	
EC-CGO	McDonnell-Douglas DC-9-32	47640	
EC-CGP	McDonnell-Douglas DC-9-32	47642	
EC-CGQ	McDonnell-Douglas DC-9-32	47643	
EC-CGR	McDonnell-Douglas DC-9-32	47644	
EC-CGT	Piper PA-28-180 Cherokee Challenger	28-7305598	N9555N
EC-CGU	Piper PA-28-180 Cherokee Challenger	28-7305576	N9549N
EC-CGV	Piper PA-28-180 Cherokee Challenger	28-7305583	N9552N
EC-CGX	VTC-75 Cirrus	145	
EC-CHA	Beech 65-C90 King Air (Also SpAF: E22-4)	LJ-621	
EC-CHC	Beech 65-C90 King Air (Also SpAF: E22-6)	LJ-624	
EC-CHE	Beech A100 King Air (Also SpAF: E23-2)	B-195	
EC-CHF	Piper PA-28-140 Cherokee	28-7425011	N9583N
EC-CHG	LET L-13 Blanik	025629	
EC-CHH	SEMCO TC-4A HAFB	SEM-88	
EC-CHJ	Reims/Cessna FRA.150L Aerobat	0210	F-BUUA / F-WLIQ
EC-CHM	SOCATA Rallye 100S Sport	2418	F-OCVQ
EC-CHN	Dornier Do.27A-5	408	L9-68 / 56+94 / PB+221
EC-CHO	Dornier Do.27A-5	428	L9-69 / 57+02 / PK+220
EC-CHQ	Dornier Do.27A-5	445	L9-71 / 57+17 / PC+221 / PC+106
EC-CIA	Glasflügel H201B Standard Libelle	488	
EC-CIB	SOCATA MS.893E Rallye 180GT Gaillard	12383	F-OCVX
EC-CIC	Piper PA-31-350 Navajo Chieftain	31-7405412	N66901
EC-CID	Boeing 727-256	20974	
EC-CIE	Boeing 727-256	20975	
EC-CIF	Piper PA-18-150 Super Cub	18-7409029	
EC-CIG	Piper PA-23-250 Aztec E	27-7405309	N40568
EC-CIK	Cessna A.188B Agtruck	01393T	N9149G
EC-CIL	VTC-75 Cirrus	149	
EC-CIN	SZD-30 Pirat	S-01.13	
EC-CIO	SZD-30 Pirat	B-549	
EC-CIP	SZD-30 Pirat	S-01.19	
EC-CIQ	SOCATA MS.880B Rallye Club	2413	F-OCVO
EC-CIR	LET L-13 Blanik	025602	
EC-CIS	LET L-13 Blanik	025601	
EC-CIT	LET L-13 Blanik	025628	
EC-CIU	LET L-13 Blanik	025613	
EC-CIV	LET L-13 Blanik	025612	
EC-CIX	SOCATA MS.893E Rallye 180GT Gaillard	12382	F-OCVU
EC-CIY	Piper PA-31-350 Navajo Chieftain	31-7405181	N66875
EC-CJB	SOCATA Rallye 100S Sport	2417	F-OCVP
EC-CJC	SOCATA MS.880B Rallye Club	2412	F-OCVN
EC-CJF	Reims/Cessna F.337G Skymaster	0063/01513	F-BSIH / F-WLIQ
EC-CJJ	SOCATA Rallye 100S Sport	2420	F-OCYC

Regn.	Type	C/n	Prev.Id.
EC-CJK	SOCATA Rallye 100S Sport	2419	F-OCYB
EC-CJL	Piper PA-31-350 Navajo Chieftain	31-7405198	N66907
EC-CJM	Scheibe L-Spatz 55	671	
EC-CJN	SOCATA MS.880B Rallye Club	2427	F-OCVV
EC-CJO	SOCATA MS.880B Rallye Club	2459	F-OCYF
EC-CJQ	SOCATA MS.893E Rallye 180GT Gaillard	12434	F-OCYE
EC-CJR	Emmert Rehaz U.L-Spatz	6	
EC-CJS	Piper PA-28-180 Cherokee Archer	28-7405089	N9516N
EC-CJT	Piper PA-28-151 Cherokee Warrior	28-7415101	N9640N
EC-CJV	Piper PA-28-140 Cherokee	28-7425246	N9538N
EC-CJZ	SZD-30 Pirat	S-01.36	
EC-CKA	SZD-30 Pirat	S-01.41	
EC-CKC	Piper PA-18-150 Super Cub	18-7409057	
EC-CKE	LET L-13 Blanik	026005	
EC-CKF	LET L-13 Blanik	025912	
EC-CKJ	Glasflügel H201B Standard Libelle	571	
EC-CKK	Britten-Norman BN-2A-27 Islander	714	G-BBZX
EC-CKL	Britten-Norman BN-2A-27 Islander	715	G-BBZY
EC-CKM	Rockwell S.2R Thrush Commander	1920R	
EC-CKN	Piper PA-23-250 Aztec E	27-7405420	N54120
EC-CKO	VTC-75 Cirrus	153	
EC-CKP	SAN Jodel D.140E Mousquetaire IV	194	F-BOPJ
EC-CKQ	SOCATA Rallye 100S Sport	2394	F-OCYZ
			F-BUZU
EC-CKS	SOCATA MS.894A Minerva 220	11998	F-OCZD
EC-CKT	Schleicher ASW-17	17003	
EC-CKU	Piper PA-28-180 Archer	28-7405086	EC-YYS
			N9509N
EC-CKY	Piper PA-36-285 Pawnee Brave	36-7460025	N9532N
EC-CKZ	Cessna 182P Skylane	62820	N52752
EC-CLA	Piper PA-28-140 Cherokee	28-7425165	N9624N
EC-CLC	Piper PA-36-285 Pawnee Brave	36-7460027	N9535N
EC-CLD	McDonnell-Douglas DC-9-32	47675	
EC-CLF	SOCATA MS.893E Rallye 180GT Gaillard	12491	F-OCSZ
EC-CLG	Beech F33A Bonanza (Also SpAF: E24B-30)	CE-517	
EC-CLK	Beech F33A Bonanza (Also SpAF: E24B-34)	CE-529	
EC-CLM	Beech F33A Bonanza (Also SpAF: E24B-36)	CE-531	
EC-CLT	Piper PA-28-151 Cherokee Warrior	28-7415213	N9528N
			N41435
EC-CLU	Piper PA-28-140 Cherokee	28-7425418	N9543N
EC-CLX	Piper PA-28-140 Cherokee C	28-25530	N8886N
EC-CLY	SOCATA Rallye 100S Sport	2362	F-OCYU
			F-BUVY
EC-CLZ	Reims/Cessna FR.172J Rocket	0464	F-BSGV
EC-CMA	Piper PA-28-180 Cherokee Archer	28-7405135	N9569N
EC-CMB	Aérospatiale SA.341G Gazelle	1166	F-WXFQ
EC-CMC	Reims/Cessna F.150L	1137	F-BSGR
			(HB-CEE)
EC-CMD	SOCATA Rallye 100S Sport	2363	F-OCYV
			F-BUVZ
EC-CME	SZD-30 Pirat	S.02-47	
EC-CMF	Cessna A.188B Agtruck	01772T	N53335
EC-CMJ	Piper PA-28-140 Cherokee	28-7525053	N9621N
EC-CMK	SOCATA Rallye 100S Sport	2367	F-OCYY
			F-BUXD
EC-CML	SOCATA Rallye 100S.Sport	2365	F-OCYX
			F-BUXB
EC-CMM	Piper PA-28-180 Cherokee Archer	28-7405141	N9572N
EC-CMN	Rockwell S.2R Thrush Commander	2088R	
EC-CMO	Piper PA-28-151 Cherokee Warrior	28-7515125	N9620N
			N32320
EC-CMP	Reims/Cessna FR.172J Rocket	0521	F-BSGN
EC-CMQ	Rockwell Commander 112A	183	N1066J
EC-CMR	Piper PA-28R-180 Cherokee Arrow	28R-30686	PH-ATU
			N4944J
EC-CMX	Cessna 182P Skylane	63181	N7398N
EC-CNC	Cessna 310Q	1123	N1272G
EC-CNE	Piper J-3C-65 Cub	11680	HB-OCS
			D-EBYK
			HB-OCS
			43-30389
EC-CNI	Reims/Cessna FRA.150L Aerobat	0257	F-BJDD
EC-CNL	SZD-30 Pirat	S-02.39	
EC-CNM	LET L-13 Blanik	026108	
EC-CNN	LET L-13 Blanik	026109	
EC-CNO	LET L-13 Blanik	026119	
EC-CNP	LET L-13 Blanik	026120	
EC-CNQ	SZD-30 Pirat	S-01.18	
EC-CNR	SZD-30 Pirat	S-01.20	
EC-CNS	SZD-30 Pirat	S-01.38	
EC-CNU	SZD-30 Pirat	S-02.06	
EC-CNV	SZD-30 Pirat	S-02.37	
EC-CNY	SZD-30 Pirat	S-02.46	
EC-CNZ	LET L-13 Blanik	025829	
EC-COA	Beech 95-B55 Baron (Also SpAF: E20-12)	TC-1808	
EC-COC	Beech 95-B55 Baron (Also SpAF: E20-14)	TC-1814	
EC-COD	Beech 95-B55 Baron (Also SpAF: E20-15)	TC-1834	
EC-COF	Beech 95-B55 Baron (Also SpAF: E20-17)	TC-1855	
EC-COG	Beech 95-B55 Baron (Also SpAF: E20-18)	TC-1844	
EC-COH	Beech 95-B55 Baron (Also SpAF: E20-19)	TC-1856	
EC-COI	Beech 65-C90 King Air (Also SpAF: E22-7) (Wfu)	LJ-663	
EC-COL	Beech 65-C90 King Air (Also SpAF: E22-10)	LJ-666	
EC-COO	Beech F33A Bonanza (Also SpAF: E24B-44)	CE-579	
EC-COQ	Beech F33A Bonanza (Also SpAF: E24B-46)	CE-584	
EC-COS	Beech F33A Bonanza (Also SpAF: E24B-48)	CE-588	
EC-COT	Beech F33A Bonanza (Also SpAF: E24B-49)	CE-590	
EC-COU	Beech F33A Bonanza (Also SpAF: E24B-50)	CE-593	
EC-COV	Beech F33A Bonanza (Also SpAF: E24B-51)	CE-586	
EC-COX	Beech F33A Bonanza (Also SpAF: E24B-52)	CE-587	
EC-COY	Beech F33A Bonanza (Also SpAF: E24B-53)	CE-589	
EC-CPA	LET L-13 Blanik	025911	
EC-CPB	LET L-13 Blanik	026006	
EC-CPC	LET L-13 Blanik	026019	
EC-CPD	LET L-13 Blanik	026020	
EC-CPE	LET L-13 Blanik	026034	
EC-CPG	Reims/Cessna F.337G Skymaster	0071/01592	F-BJDG
EC-CPJ	LET L-13 Blanik	026033	
EC-CPK	LET L-13 Blanik	026045	
EC-CPN	LET L-13 Blanik	026059	
EC-CPO	Douglas C-47D	17094/34361 T.3-50	
			N86442
			45-1091
EC-CPP	Dornier Do.28A-1	3002	D-IHIL
EC-CPQ	Reims/Cessna F.150L	1139	F-BSGO
EC-CPR	Piper PA-36-285 Pawnee Brave	36-7560008	
EC-CPS	Reims/Cessna FRA.150L Aerobat	0255	F-BJDC
EC-CPT	Reims/Cessna FRA.150L Aerobat	0259	F-BJDE
			(TR-LTP)
EC-CPU	Reims/Cessna FRA.150L Aerobat	0252	F-BJDA
			(I-AFAE)
EC-CPV	Reims/Cessna F.150M	1181	F-BPPY
EC-CPX	Piper PA-36-285 Pawnee Brave	36-7560016	
EC-CQB	Cessna 182P Skylane	63609	N6026J
EC-CQC	SZD-30 Pirat	S-03.33	
EC-CQE	SZD-30 Pirat	S-03.39	
EC-CQG	SZD-30 Pirat (Also SpAF: UE.15-1)	S-02.07	
EC-CQJ	SZD-30 Pirat	S-03.18	
EC-CQN	LET L-13 Blanik	026131	
EC-CQU	Piper PA-36-285 Pawnee Brave	36-7560015	N9745N
EC-CQX	Piper PA-28-180 Cherokee Archer	28-7505183	N9627N
EC-CRI	AISA I-115	54	E9-54
EC-CRK	Cessna 207 Skywagon	00230	N1630U
EC-CRL	Reims/Cessna F.177RG Cardinal RG	0096	N14499
			(N14491)
EC-CRM	LET L-13 Blanik	026132	
EC-CRO	Piper PA-36-285 Pawnee Brave	36-7560026	N9736N
EC-CRP	Piper PA-28-140 Cherokee	28-7525267	N9648N
EC-CRQ	Piper PA-28-151 Cherokee Warrior	28-7515094	N9619N
EC-CRT	AISA I-115	197	E9-197
EC-CRU	Piper PA-36-285 Pawnee Brave	36-7560038	N9654N
EC-CRY	Piper PA-23-250 Aztec E	27-7554041	N54249
EC-CRZ	Reims/Cessna FR.172J Rocket	0446	CS-APE
	(Damaged 3.5.94)		F-BSGZ
EC-CSA	AISA I-115	9	E9-9
EC-CSD	AISA I-115	132	E9-132
EC-CSF	AISA I-115	165	E9-165
EC-CSI	Cessna 310Q	1043	CS-APP
			N69956
EC-CSM	SZD-30 Pirat	S-02.40	
EC-CSN	SZD-30 Pirat	S-04.27	

Regn.	Type	C/n	Prev.Id.
EC-CSO	SZD-30 Pirat	S-04.07	
EC-CSP	SOCATA Rallye 100S Sport	2559	F-ODAR
EC-CSQ	Piper PA-28R-200 Arrow	28R-7535058	N32451
EC-CSR	LET L-13 Blanik	026153	
EC-CSS	LET L-13 Blanik	026152	
EC-CST	Piper PA-28R-200 Arrow	28R-7535319	N9580N
EC-CSU	Piper PA-28-180 Cherokee Archer	28-7505236	N9576N
EC-CSX	Piper PA-28-140 Cherokee	28-7525251	N9633N
EC-CSY	Reims/Cessna F.172M	1111	CS-APF
	(Damaged 27.11.94)		F-BSGP
EC-CTB	Reims/Cessna FRA.150L Aerobat	0212	N14492
EC-CTC	Reims/Cessna FR.172J Rocket	0544	F-BPQQ
EC-CTF	Reims/Cessna FR.172J Rocket	0448	EC-535
			CS-APR
			F-BSGR
EC-CTG	Piper PA-31P-425 Pressurized Navajo	31P-7530017	N54946
EC-CTH	Reims/Cessna F.150L	1048	CS-APH
			F-BSGN
EC-CTI	Cessna 210L Centurion	60139	EC-532
			N59169
EC-CTK	Piper PA-34-200T Seneca II	34-7670055	N4493X
EC-CTL	Cessna TU.206F Turbo Stationair	02629	PH-AOD
			N1596F
			N59182
EC-CTM	Reims/Cessna FR.172J Rocket	0538	F-BJDT
EC-CTN	Piper PA-28-140 Cherokee *(Crashed 5.99)*	28-7625035	N9615N
EC-CTO	Aero Commander 680F	1195-100	OE-FAI
EC-CTP	Piper PA-28-140 Cherokee	28-7625036	N9619N
EC-CTR	McDonnell-Douglas DC-9-34CF	47702	N19B
EC-CTS	McDonnell-Douglas DC-9-34CF	47704	
EC-CTT	McDonnell-Douglas DC-9-34CF	47706	
EC-CTU	McDonnell-Douglas DC-9-34CF	47707	
EC-CTX	Eiri PIK-20	20089	
EC-CTY	Piper PA-28-151 Cherokee Warrior	28-7515448	N9612N
EC-CUB	Piper PA-28-151 Cherokee Warrior	28-7415218	EC-YYR
			N9530N
EC-CUC	Reims/Cessna F.150M	1237	F-BJDK
EC-CUD	Piper PA-36-285 Pawnee Brave	36-7560127	
EC-CUE	Piper PA-28-151 Cherokee Warrior	28-7515449	N9613N
EC-CUG	Cessna 421B Golden Eagle	0936	EC-5310
			N5386J
EC-CUI	Schempp-Hirth Standard Cirrus B	652	
EC-CUJ	Schempp-Hirth Nimbus II	104	
EC-CUK	SOCATA MS.893E Rallye 180GT Gaillard	12640	F-ODAY
EC-CUL	Reims/Cessna FA.150K Aerobat	0069	D-ECHK
EC-CUN	Cessna A.188B Agtruck	02427T	N4909R
EC-CUO	SIAI-Marchetti S.205-18/F	216	F-BNLM
EC-CUR	Piper PA-28R-200 Arrow	28R-7535243	N9618N
			N3995X
			YV-TAST
			N9521N
EC-CUT	Cessna 340	0303	ECT-538
			N69449
EC-CUU	Piper PA-36-285 Pawnee Brave	36-7660007	
EC-CUV	Piper PA-36-285 Pawnee Brave	36-7660012	
EC-CUX	Piper PA-36-285 Pawnee Brave	36-7560065	N9954P
EC-CVB	AISA I-115	124	E9-124
EC-CVC	AISA I-115	136	E9-136
EC-CVD	Piper PA-25-260 Pawnee D	25-7405725	N9598P
EC-CVE	Piper PA-32R-300 Lance	32R-7680079	N8148C
EC-CVF	Cessna 210L Centurion	60563	N94254
EC-CVG	Reims/Cessna F.177RG Cardinal RG	0126	F-BJDH
			F-WLIQ
EC-CVI	Schempp-Hirth Standard Cirrus	658	
EC-CVK	SA.318C Alouette Astazou	2415	
EC-CVL	Piper PA-36-285 Pawnee Brave	36-7560011	N9906P
EC-CVN	Reims/Cessna FR.172J Rocket	0533	N94722
EC-CVO	Dornier Do.27B-1	151	OO-PAN
	(Derelict at Cuatro Vientos 1996)		D-EKOV
			55+31
			ND+205
			PF+107
			PD+102
EC-CVP	Reims/Cessna FRA.150M Aerobat	0271	F-BJDF
EC-CVQ	Reims/Cessna FRA.150M Aerobat	0277	F-BJDG
EC-CVR	Piper PA-34-200T Seneca II	34-7570312	N7623C
			N9594N
EC-CVS	SOCATA Rallye 100S Sport	2542	F-ODAV
EC-CVT	PZL-104 Wilga 35A	86282	SP-WFG
	(Remains reported at Cordoba In 1991)		
EC-CVU	PZL-104 Wilga 35A	86278	SP-WFF
	(Remains reported at Oviedo in 1983)		
EC-CVV	Cessna 414	0631	ECT-555
			N69816
EC-CVX	Reims/Cessna FR.172G Rocket	0218	CS-AKW
EC-CVY	Reims/Cessna FR.172J Rocket	0385	CS-AJT
EC-CXA	Piper PA-28-181 Cherokee Archer II	28-7690191	N9531N
EC-CXB	Cessna 310R	0010	ECT-552
			ECT-5310
			N1326G
EC-CXC	Reims/Cessna F.337F Skymaster	0042/01381	CS-AHH
EC-CXD	Piper PA-18-150 Super Cub	18-7609036	N54107
EC-CXE	Piper PA-25-260 Pawnee D	25-7405621	N9535P
EC-CXG	Cessna A.118B Agtruck	02553T	N4816Q
EC-CXH	Cessna A.188B Agtruck	02510T	N4758Q
EC-CXI	Cessna A.188B Agtruck	02507T	N4749Q
EC-CXJ	Piper PA-31P-425 Pressurized Navajo	31P-7630012	N57547
EC-CXK	Piper PA-28-140 Cherokee	28-7625157	N9537N
EC-CXL	Piper PA-25-260 Pawnee D	25-7405614	N9528P
EC-CXM	Piper PA-28R-200 Arrow	28R-7335117	CS-AOL
			N11C
EC-CXN	Piper PA-28-140 Cherokee	28-7625131	N9523N
EC-CXO	Piper PA-25-260 Pawnee D	25-7405723	N9588P
EC-CXP	Reims/Cessna F.172H	0367	CS-AKU
EC-CXQ	Cessna 172C	49438	CS-AKO
			N1838Y
EC-CXR	Piper PA-28-151 Cherokee Warrior	28-7615301	N9583N
EC-CXT	LET L-13 Blanik	026305	
EC-CXU	LET L-13 Blanik	026308	
EC-CXZ	SOCATA Rallye 150T	2655	F-ODAX
EC-CYA	SOCATA Rallye 235E Gabier	12796	F-ODDY
EC-CYB	Cessna 207 Skywagon *(W/o 13.10.96)*	00271	N1671U
EC-CYC	Bellanca 7GCBC Citabria	832-75	OE-AOV
EC-CYD	Beech A36 Bonanza	E-788	ECT-012
			N6787S
EC-CYE	Piper PA-28-151 Cherokee Warrior	28-7615281	N9573N
			N75288
EC-CYF	Piper PA-31P-425 Pressurized Navajo	31P-7630017	N57554
EC-CYG	Reims/Cessna FR.172J Rocket	0537	F-BJDE
EC-CYH	Rockwell Commander 112A	296	N1296J
EC-CYL	SOCATA Rallye 100S Sport	2813	F-ODDV
EC-CYO	SOCATA Rallye 235E Gabier	12801	F-ODDU
EC-CYP	LET L-13 Blanik	026245	
EC-CYR	Cessna A.188B Agtruck	02769T	N731BN
EC-CYS	Cessna A.188B Agtruck	02355T	N4836R
EC-CYT	LET L-13 Blanik	026646	
EC-CYV	SZD-30 Pirat	S-07.20	
EC-CYX	SZD-30 Pirat	S-07.24	
EC-CYY	SZD-30 Pirat	S-07.21	
EC-CYZ	SZD-30 Pirat	S-07.22	
EC-CZA	SZD-30 Pirat	S-07.23	
EC-CZB	SOCATA MS.893E Rallye 180GT Gaillard	12741	F-ODEH
EC-CZC	Grumman G.164A Agcat	1294	
EC-CZD	Piper PA-25-260 Pawnee D	25-7756029	N82486
EC-CZF	Reims/Cessna F.177RG Cardinal RG	0067	CS-AJH
EC-CZG	Reims/Cessna FR.172J Rocket	0558	F-BOFC
			(D-EOGV)
EC-CZH	Piper PA-28R-200 Arrow	28R-7635077	N9627N
EC-CZI	Cessna 310R	0638	N98895
EC-CZJ	Piper PA-28R-200 Arrow	28R-7635318	N9592N
EC-CZL	Piper PA-18-150 Super Cub	18-7709055	N83522
EC-CZM	Piper PA-36-300 Pawnee Brave	36-7760023	N9559N
EC-CZN	Piper PA-28-140 Cherokee	28-7625225	N9588N
EC-CZO	Piper PA-28-181 Cherokee Archer II	28-7790353	N9605N
EC-CZP	Piper PA-28-140 Cherokee *(Stored)*	28-7725099	N9551N
EC-CZQ	Piper PA-34-200T Seneca II	34-7670162	N8617E
EC-CZR	Reims/Cessna FR.172J Rocket	0534	F-BJDD
EC-CZS	Cessna A.188B Agtruck	02882T	N731GJ
EC-CZT	Cessna 182P (Reims-assembled)	0023/63956	N9895E
EC-CZU	Zlin Z.526L *(Wfu)*	1160	

Regn.	Type	C/n	Prev.Id.
EC-CZV	Aerotek Pitts S-2A	2135	
EC-CZX	Reims/Cessna F.150M	1345	F-BJDH
EC-CZY	Grumman G.164A Agcat	240	N670Y
EC-CZZ	Reims/Cessna FR.172J Rocket	0550	F-BOFB
			(D-EEVQ)
EC-DAA	Cessna 310R	0618	N98855
EC-DAB	Grumman AA-5A Cheetah	0346	
EC-DAC	Grumman AA-5A Cheetah	0347	
EC-DAD	Piper PA-28-140 Cherokee	28-7725181	N9615N
EC-DAE	Reims/Cessna FR.172J Rocket	0539	F-BJDJ
EC-DAF	Piper PA-28-161 Cherokee Warrior II	28-7716229	N9537N
EC-DAG	SOCATA Rallye 100ST	2944	F-ODHD
EC-DAH	CASA I-131E Jungmann	2041	E3B-273
EC-DAI	CASA I-131E Jungmann	1067	E3B-421
EC-DAJ	CASA I-131E Jungmann	2061	E3B-457
EC-DAK	CASA I-131E Jungmann *(Damaged 12.94)*	2022	E3B-463
EC-DAL	CASA I-131E Jungmann	2065	E3B-472
EC-DAM	CASA I-131E Jungmann	2160	E3B-488
EC-DAO	CASA I-131E Jungmann	2107	E3B-511
EC-DAP	CASA I-131E Jungmann *(Cr. 23.1.97)*	2147	E3B-547
EC-DAQ	CASA I-131E Jungmann	2183	E3B-578
EC-DAR	CASA I-131E Jungmann	2174	E3B-581
EC-DAS	CASA I-131E Jungmann	2186	E3B-583
EC-DAU	CASA I-131E Jungmann	2103	E3B-608
EC-DAV	CASA I-131E Jungmann	2217	E3B-617
EC-DAX	CASA I-131E Jungmann	unkn	E3B-567
EC-DAY	Reims/Cessna FR.172J Rocket	0545	F-BJDZ
			(D-EESK)
EC-DAZ	Piper PA-28-140 Cherokee	28-7725276	N9544N
EC-DBA	Piper PA-28-140 Cherokee	28-7725277	N9545N
EC-DBF	SOCATA MS.893E Rallye 180GT Gaillard	12980	F-ODHG
EC-DBG	SOCATA MS.893E Rallye 180GT Gaillard	12981	F-ODHH
EC-DBH	Piper PA-28-140 Cherokee	28-7725281	N9547N
EC-DBI	SOCATA Rallye 235E Gabier	12802	F-ODEG
EC-DBJ	Piper PA-28-140 Cherokee	28-7725280	N9546N
EC-DBL	Reims/Cessna F.172N	1562	ECT-537
			F-BJDJ
EC-DBP	Piper PA-28-140 Cherokee	28-7725100	N9552N
EC-DBQ	Piper PA-25-260 Pawnee D	25-7756026	N82479
EC-DBR	Piper PA-36-300 Pawnee Brave	36-7760139	N82667
EC-DBS	Reims/Cessna F.150M	1369	
EC-DBT	Reims/Cessna F.150M	1362	
EC-DBU	Piper PA-28-181 Cherokee Archer II	28-7890126	N9629N
EC-DBX	SOCATA Rallye 150T	2970	F-ODHF
EC-DBZ	Reims/Cessna F.337F Skymaster	0031/01353	G-BDVK
			F-OCZZ
			F-BSIZ
EC-DCA	Piper PA-28-161 Cherokee Warrior II	28-7816149	N9635N
EC-DCC	Boeing 727-256	21609	
EC-DCD	Boeing 727-256	21610	
EC-DCE	Boeing 727-256	21611	
EC-DCF	Piper PA-36-300 Pawnee Brave	36-7860015	N9666N
EC-DCG	SOCATA Rallye 180T Galérien	3091	
EC-DCH	SOCATA Rallye 180T Galérien	3027	
EC-DCI	Cessna A.188B Agtruck	0001/03082T	N731QX
EC-DCJ	SOCATA Rallye 235E Gabier	12870	
EC-DCM	SOCATA Rallye 235E Gabier	12871	
EC-DCO	Reims/Cessna FR.172K Hawk XP	0604	F-BNGX
			(F-GAQF)
EC-DCP	Reims/Cessna FR.172K Hawk XP	0598	F-GAST
EC-DCR	Reims/Cessna F.172N	1595	F-BNGY
	(W/o 14.6.90)		(F-GAQJ)
EC-DCS	SOCATA Rallye 100ST	3002	
EC-DCU	Piper PA-36-285 Pawnee Brave	36-7660062	N57753
EC-DCV	SOCATA MS.893E Rallye 180GT Gaillard	13052	
EC-DCX	Piper PA-25-260 Pawnee D	25-7856050	N4154E
EC-DCY	Thunder AX7-77A HAFB	145	
EC-DCZ	Thunder AX7-77A HAFB	149	
EC-DDA	Piper PA-25-260 Pawnee D	25-7856051	N4157E
EC-DDB	Piper PA-28-161 Cherokee Warrior II	28-7816589	N9586N
EC-DDC	SOCATA MS.883 Rallye 115	1360	F-BRMN
EC-DDD	Morane-Saulnier MS.885 Super Rallye	153	F-BMHL
			HB-EDT
EC-DDE	Piper PA-28-161 Cherokee Warrior II	28-7816588	N9585N
EC-DDF	Thunder AX7-77A HAFB	035	G-BDAZ

Regn.	Type	C/n	Prev.Id.
EC-DDG	Rockwell S.2R Thrush Commander	2456R	N8846Q
EC-DDI	SOCATA Rallye 150ST	3139	
EC-DDJ	Piper PA-28-181 Cherokee Archer II	28-7890506	N9594N
EC-DDK	Reims/Cessna F.182Q Skylane II	0047	F-BNGT
			F-BJDK
EC-DDL	Piper PA-32R-300 Lance	32R-7780238	N2267Q
EC-DDM	SOCATA MS.893E Rallye 180GT Gaillard	13131	
EC-DDN	AISA I-115 *(Museum)*	196	E9-196
EC-DDO	Grumman AA-5B Tiger	0705	N28892
EC-DDP	Grumman AA-5A Cheetah	0550	N26704
EC-DDT	Piper PA-28R-201T Turbo Arrow III	28R-7703345	N11C
			N44942
EC-DDY	Boeing 727-256	21780	
EC-DDZ	Boeing 727-256	21781	
EC-DEA	McDonnell-Douglas DC-10-30	47982	
EC-DEC	Reims/Cessna F.150M	1360	F-BNGV
EC-DED	Reims/Cessna FR.172J Rocket	0567	F-BSGV
			F-BJDH
			F-BLIK
EC-DEE	Reims/Cessna F.172N	1517	N96092
EC-DEF	Cessna 337D Skymaster	0987	N2687S
EC-DEH	Piper PA-38-112 Tomahawk	38-78A0457	N9676N
EC-DEI	AISA I-115	53	E9-53
EC-DEJ	AISA I-115	123	E9-123
EC-DEK	Agusta-Bell 206B Jet Ranger	8568	
EC-DEL	Reims/Cessna F.177RG Cardinal RG	0173	ECT-012
			F-BPQQ
EC-DEN	Piper PA-38-112 Tomahawk	38-78A0452	N9673N
EC-DEO	AISA I-115	194	E9-194
EC-DEQ	Cessna 401B	0115	D-IEPC
	(Damaged 3.7.94)		N7975Q
EC-DER	Grumman AA-5A Cheetah	0629	N26756
EC-DET	Cessna T.310R	0644	N98907
EC-DEU	Piper PA-38-112 Tomahawk	38-78A0589	N9664N
EC-DEV	Piper PA-36-375 Pawnee Brave	36-7802017	N9727N
EC-DEX	Reims/Cessna F.182Q Skylane	0088	F-BNGR
EC-DEY	Aérospatiale SA.315B Lama	2398	F-BXAX
EC-DEZ	Thunder AX7-77A HAFB	177	
EC-DFB	Robin R.1180T Aiglon	216	F-GBMR
EC-DFD	Cessna A.188B Agtruck	0017/03306T	N1962J
EC-DFE	Piper PA-28-161 Warrior II	28-7916042	N9507N
EC-DFF	Piper PA-25-260 Pawnee D	25-7856056	(AN-BUW)
EC-DFG	Schleicher ASW-17	17055	
EC-DFH	Cameron V-77 HAFB	470	
EC-DFI	SOCATA Rallye 180T Galérien *(Dam.18.12.94)*	3203	
EC-DFJ	Cessna A.188B Agtruck	0016/03305T	N1961J
EC-DFK	Piper PA-28-161 Warrior II	28-7916041	N9506N
EC-DFM	SOCATA MS.893E Rallye 180GT Gaillard	13130	
EC-DFN	Piper PA-25-260 Pawnee D	25-7956005	N9771N
EC-DFQ	Piper PA-25-260 Pawnee D	25-7856054	(AN-BUV)
			N4169E
EC-DFT	SZD-45A Ogar	B-820	
EC-DFU	Piper PA-38-112 Tomahawk	38-78A0597	N9671N
EC-DFV	Schempp-Hirth Standard Cirrus	197	BGA1679
EC-DFX	Rolladen-Schneider LS-3A	3182	
EC-DFZ	Thunder AX7-77 HAFB	191	
EC-DGA	Piper PA-38-112 Tomahawk	38-78A0767	N9686N
EC-DGB	McDonnell-Douglas DC-9-34	48103	
EC-DGC	McDonnell-Douglas DC-9-34	48104	
EC-DGD	McDonnell-Douglas DC-9-34	48105	
EC-DGE	McDonnell-Douglas DC-9-34	48106	
EC-DGG	Piper PA-34-200T Seneca II	34-7670161	HB-LHU
			N8567E
EC-DGH	Piper PA-28RT-201T Turbo Arrow IV	28R-7931124	N9632N
EC-DGI	Piper PA-36-375 Pawnee Brave	36-7902007	N9737N
EC-DGJ	Piper PA-28-181 Archer II	28-7990034	N9647N
EC-DGK	Agusta-Bell 47G-2	210	(F-BTSR)
			ALAT
			Fr.AF
EC-DGM	Robin R.2100A	168	F-BXQY
EC-DGN	Cessna T.188C Husky	03334T	N2029J
EC-DGO	Piper PA-44-180 Seminole	44-7995213	N3064K
EC-DGP	Piper PA-25-235 Pawnee D	25-7856029	N9179T
EC-DGQ	Piper PA-28RT-201 Arrow IV	28R-7918056	N3050R
EC-DGR	Reims/Cessna FRA.150M Aerobat	0316	F-BXXK

Regn.	Type	C/n	Prev.Id.
EC-DGS	SOCATA Rallye 180T Galérien *(Crashed 7.99)*	3204	
EC-DGT	Scheibe SF-25C Falke	44123	D-KACK
EC-DGV	Piper PA-38-112 Tomahawk	38-79A0015	N9664N
EC-DGX	Piper PA-28-181 Archer II	28-7990344	N9626N
EC-DGY	Thunder AX6-56 Bolt HAFB	188	
EC-DHA	SA.316B Alouette III	2207	HB-XKI
			FAP9406
EC-DHB	Grumman GA-7 Cougar	0086	N796GA
EC-DHC	Cameron V-56 HAFB	271	(EP-FHK)
EC-DHD	Piper PA-34-200T Seneca II	34-7770218	N3130Q
EC-DHF	Piper PA-31T Cheyenne	31T-7920073	N23699
EC-DHG	Piper PA-28-161 Warrior II	28-7916450	N9539N
EC-DHH	Piper PA-38-112 Tomahawk	38-78A0593	N9666N
EC-DHJ	Lake LA-4-200 Buccaneer	948	N2964P
EC-DHK	Piper PA-38-112 Tomahawk	38-79A0237	N9709N
EC-DHL	Piper PA-32-300 Cherokee Six	32-7940214	N2838A
			N9592N
EC-DHN	Piper PA-28-161 Warrior II	28-7916506	N9576N
EC-DHP	SOCATA Rallye 100ST *(Stored)*	3038	
EC-DHR	SOCATA TB-10 Tobago	25	F-ODKJ
EC-DHS	Scheibe SF-28A Tandem-Falke	57106	D-KDGG
EC-DHT	Hiller UH-12E	5108	(SE-HVD)
			EC-DHT
EC-DHU	Aerotek Pitts S-2A *(Museum)*	2181	
EC-DHV	Cameron V-56 HAFB	545	
EC-DHX	Cameron V-56 HAFB	546	
EC-DHZ	McDonnell-Douglas DC-10-30	47834	
EC-DIA	Boeing 747-256B	22238	
EC-DIB	Boeing 747-256B	22239	
EC-DID	CASA I-131E Jungmann	2119	E3B-319
EC-DIE	Schempp-Hirth Nimbus IIC	223	
EC-DIF	Grob G.102 Astir CS	1086	
EC-DIG	Scheibe Bergfalke II	164	
EC-DII	SOCATA Rallye 100ST	3039	
EC-DIJ	SOCATA Rallye 150ST	3138	(D-EEUM)
EC-DIK	Schempp-Hirth Mini-Nimbus HS-7	58	PH-606
EC-DIL	Piper PA-28-181 Archer II	28-7990486	N9621N
			N2841V
EC-DIM	Thunder AX7-77 HAFB	204	
EC-DIN	Cessna 337G Super Skymaster	01788	N53693
EC-DIO	Piper PA-28-181 Archer II	28-7990515	N9620N
			N2876P
EC-DIP	Thunder AX7-77 HAFB	201	
EC-DIQ	SA.318C Alouette Astazou	2416	
EC-DIS	Piper PA-25-235 Pawnee D	25-8056002	N9769N
EC-DIT	Piper PA-25-235 Pawnee D	25-8056003	N9770N
EC-DIU	Piper PA-28RT-201 Arrow IV	28R-7918266	N8111Q
			N9642N
EC-DIV	Piper PA-25-260 Pawnee D	25-7956035	N9772N
EC-DIY	Piper PA-38-112 Tomahawk	38-79A1010	N9729N
EC-DIZ	Thunder AX8-105 HAFB	237	
EC-DJA	Schleicher ASW-20	20294	
EC-DJB	Cameron N-77 HAFB	572	
EC-DJD	Piper PA-38-112 Tomahawk	38-79A1011	N9716N
EC-DJE	Cessna 210N Centurion	63385	N5355A
EC-DJF	Piper PA-25-260 Pawnee D	25-7956037	N9775N
EC-DJG	Piper PA-36-375 Pawnee Brave	36-7902047	N9742N
EC-DJH	Piper PA-25-260 Pawnee D	25-8056010	N2407Q
EC-DJJ	Piper PA-28-161 Warrior II	28-8016183	N9536N
EC-DJK	Piper PA-28-161 Warrior II	28-8016184	N9537N
EC-DJL	CASA I-131E Jungmann	unkn	E3B-534
EC-DJP	Piper PA-25-260 Pawnee D	25-8056012	N9772N
EC-DJQ	Reims/Cessna FR.172K Hawk XP	0648	F-WZIA
EC-DJT	Scheibe SF-28A Tandem-Falke	57110	D-KDGV
EC-DJU	Scheibe SF-28A Tandem-Falke	57111	D-KDGW
EC-DJV	Piper PA-38-112 Tomahawk *(W/o 28.6.97)*	38-79A1176	N9724N
EC-DJX	Piper PA-28RT-201T Turbo Arrow IV	28R-7931194	N9523N
EC-DJY	Cessna T.188C AgHusky	03461T	N2425J
EC-DJZ	Piper PA-28-161 Warrior II	28-8016267	N9645N
EC-DKA	Piper PA-18-150 Super Cub	18-8009013	N9174T
EC-DKB	Piper PA-28-181 Archer II	28-8090248	N9504N
EC-DKC	Piper PA-28-181 Archer II	28-8090249	N9512N
EC-DKD	Cessna 337G Super Skymaster	01797	N53706
EC-DKE	Bölkow Phoebus A-1	717	
EC-DKF	Scheibe SF-27A	6058	

Regn.	Type	C/n	Prev.Id.
EC-DKG	Schleicher K.8B	8396SH	
EC-DKJ	Scheibe SF-28A Tandem-Falke	57114	D-KDGV
EC-DKK	SAN Jodel D.140E1 Mousquetaire IV	38	F-BIZR
EC-DKL	Cameron N-77 HAFB	653	
EC-DKM	ICA/Brasov IS-28M2	28	
EC-DKN	Reims/Cessna F.152	1686	N1660C
EC-DKP	Cessna 402C	0275	N2757A
EC-DKR	Piper PA-28RT-201 Arrow IV	28R-8018056	N9542N
EC-DKX	CASAI-131E Jungmann	2016	E3B-412
EC-DKZ	Cessna 210N Centurion	63653	(N4868C)
EC-DLA	Piper PA-28RT-201T Turbo Arrow IV	28R-8031113	N82377
			N9564N
EC-DLB	Piper PA-38-112 Tomahawk	38-79A1174	N24702
EC-DLC	Boeing 747-256B	22454	
EC-DLD	Boeing 747-256B	22455	
EC-DLE	Airbus A.300B4-120 *(Wfu)*	130	F-WZEI
EC-DLF	Airbus A.300B4-120	133	F-WZEB
EC-DLG	Airbus A.300B4-120	135	F-WZEA
EC-DLH	Airbus A.300B4-120	136	F-WZEN
EC-DLK	Westland-Bell 47G3B1 (Soloy)	WA/329	G-BHBU
			XT170
EC-DLL	Piper PA-38-112 Tomahawk	38-79A1179	N9650N
EC-DLM	Piper PA-18-150 Super Cub	18-2546	D-EMMX
			ALAT
			52-6228
EC-DLO	Cessna R.172K Hawk XP	3324	N758SM
EC-DLP	Cameron N-77 HAFB	534	
EC-DLQ	Thunder-Colt 56A HAFB	065	
EC-DLR	Reims/Cessna FR.172K Hawk XP	0593	F-ODHP
			F-GAGP
EC-DLS	Reims/Cessna F.337G Super Skymaster	0078	N65327
			F-BRGQ
EC-DLT	Piper PA-28-161 Warrior II	28-8016330	N9557N
EC-DLV	Zlin Z.50L	0022	
EC-DLX	Zlin Z.50L	0023	
EC-DLZ	Cameron D-50 Hot Air Airship	752	
EC-DMB	Scheibe L-Spatz 105	1	OO-ZMG
EC-DMC	Reims/Cessna F.152	1783	F-WZII
EC-DMD	Scheibe SF-25E Super Falke	4319	ECT-029
			OY-XGX
			D-KECV
EC-DME	Reims/Cessna F.152	1784	F-WZIJ
EC-DMF	Piper PA-25-235 Pawnee D	25-8056036	N9770N
EC-DMI	Scheibe L-Spatz 55	797	
EC-DMJ	CASA I-131E Jungmann	2062	E3B-464
EC-DMK	CASA I-131E Jungmann	2049	E3B-344
EC-DMM	Cameron D-96 Hot Air Airship	675	
EC-DMO	Piper PA-36-375 Pawnee Brave	36-7802058	N3921E
EC-DMQ	Grob G.103 Twin Astir	3553	
EC-DMR	Cessna 172RG Cutlass	0547	(N5496V)
EC-DMU	Scheibe SF-25E Super Falke	4358	D-KOOA
EC-DMV	Piper PA-38-112 Tomahawk	38-79A0448	N2444F
EC-DMX	SOCATA Rallye 235E Gabier *(W/o 25.6.97)*	13148	F-ODNF
			N357RA
EC-DMY	SOCATA Rallye 235E Gabier	294	
EC-DNA	Thunder AX7-77 HAFB	309	
EC-DND	Reims/Cessna FR.182 Skylane RG	0021	N9012F
EC-DNG	Cessna 172RG Cutlass	0526	(N5417V)
EC-DNI	Schleicher ASW-20L	20408	
EC-DNJ	Piper PA-28-161 Warrior II	28-8116142	N9512N
EC-DNL	Agusta A.109A Hirundo	7182	N4210P
EC-DNM	Agusta A.109A Hirundo	7222	N4210X
EC-DNN	Cessna 152-II	84203	N4645L
EC-DNO	SOCATA TB-10 Tobago	171	ECT-040
			F-ODNM
EC-DNP	Boeing 747-256B	22764	N8296V
EC-DNQ	Airbus A.300B4-120	156	F-WZMF
EC-DNR	Airbus A.300B4-120	170	F-WZMQ
EC-DNS	Thunder AX6-56 HAFB	291	
EC-DNT	Reims/Cessna F.172G	0293	D-ENDI
EC-DNU	Aérospatiale AS.350B Ecureuil	1475	F-WZFH
EC-DNV	Cessna R.172K Hawk	3401	N758VT
EC-DNX	Reims/Cessna F.172N	1987	N1660C
			(D-EOCT)
EC-DOA	Piper PA-36-300 Pawnee Brave	36-8060006	N9740N

Regn.	Type	C/n	Prev.Id.
EC-DOB	Fournier RF-9	6	F-BZCX
			F-ODNP
EC-DOD	Thunder AX7-77 HAFB	346	
EC-DOF	Thunder AX3-17/5C Sky Chariot HAFB	296	G-BILC
EC-DOG	Cessna 152-II	84365	N6151L
EC-DOI (2)	Cessna TU.206G Turbo Stationair II	06369	D-EHTT
			N7566Z
EC-DOJ	Piper PA-32RT-300T Turbo Lance	32R-7887284	N30693
EC-DOK	Piper PA-38-112 Tomahawk	38-81A0020	N25621
EC-DOL	Agusta-Bell 206B Jet Ranger III	8615	
EC-DOM	Piper PA-25-260 Pawnee D	25-8156002	N90831
EC-DON	AISA I-115	138	E9-138
EC-DOP	Piper PA-38-112 Tomahawk	38-81A0109	N26030
EC-DOT	Piper PA-28RT-201 Arrow IV	28R-8118020	N9610N
EC-DOU	SZD-42-2 Jantar 2B	B-1074	
EC-DOV	Thunder AX8-90 HAFB	336	SE-ZYC(2)
EC-DOX	Piper PA-28-181 Archer II	28-8190194	N9525N
EC-DOY	Scheibe SF-25C Falke	4129	D-KLDF
EC-DOZ	Thunder AX6-56Z HAFB	232	G-BGYO
EC-DPA	Grob G.103A Twin II Acro	3679-K-30	
EC-DPB	Grob G.103A Twin II Acro	3680-K-31	
EC-DPC	Grob G.103A Twin II Acro	3681-K-32	
EC-DPD	Grob G.103A Twin II Acro	3682-K-33	
EC-DPE	Grob G.103A Twin II Acro	3683-K-34	
EC-DPF	Grob G.103A Twin II Acro	3684-K-35	
EC-DPG	Grob G.103A Twin II Acro	3685-K-36	
EC-DPH	Grob G.103A Twin II Acro	3686-K-37	
EC-DPI	SOCATA Rallye 180T Galérien	3349	F-OGLA
EC-DPJ	SOCATA Rallye 180T Galérien	3350	F-OGLB
EC-DPK	SOCATA Rallye 180T Galérien	3351	F-OGLC
EC-DPL	SOCATA Rallye 180T Galérien	3352	F-OGLD
EC-DPM	SOCATA Rallye 235C	13353	F-OGLE
EC-DPN	SOCATA Rallye 235C	13354	F-OGLF
EC-DPO	SOCATA Rallye 235C	13355	F-OGLG
	(Fuselage replaced with c/n "13365" which is probably incorrect)		
EC-DPP	SOCATA Rallye 235C	13356	F-OGLH
EC-DPQ	Piper PA-28-181 Archer II	28-8190059	N9605N
EC-DPR	Cameron V-56 HAFB	750	
EC-DPS	Cameron D-38/50 Hot Air Airship	751	
EC-DPT	Avialsa-Scheibe A.60	27	F-CCQE
EC-DPU	ICA/Brasov IS-29-D2	150	
EC-DPV	ICA/Brasov IS-28-B2	260	
EC-DPX	ICA/Brasov IS-28-M2	36	
EC-DPY	Piper PA-25-260 Pawnee D	25-8156001	N90829
EC-DQA	Hughes 369D	61-0995D	N1108N
EC-DQB	SOCATA TB-10 Tobago	157	F-ODNX
			F-GCOP
EC-DQG	Aérospatiale SN.601 Corvette	27	N26674
	(Derelict, Madrid)		F-BVPH
EC-DQH	Schleicher ASW-19	19007	
EC-DQI (2)	Cessna TU.206G Turbo Stationair II	06010	N4743Z
EC-DQM	Cameron V-77 HAFB	789	
EC-DQN	Raven S-55A HAFB	835	
EC-DQS	SOCATA MS.880B Rallye Club	1954	F-BTJK
EC-DQU	Cessna L-19A Bird Dog (O-1A)	unkn	U12-11
			51-12688
EC-DQV	Beech 95-B55 Baron	TC-2338	
EC-DQX	Cessna L-19A Bird Dog (O-1A)	unkn	U12-5
			51-11931
EC-DQY	Cessna L-19A Bird Dog (O-1A)	unkn	U12-6
			51-11929
EC-DQZ	Cessna L-19A Bird Dog (O-1A)	unkn	U12-13
			51-4720
EC-DRC	SOCATA MS.893E Rallye 180GT Gaillard	13128	F-GBXB
			D-EEUD
EC-DRD	SOCATA Rallye 110ST Galopin	3357	F-OGLM
EC-DRE	SOCATA Rallye 110ST Galopin	3358	F-OGLO
EC-DRF	SOCATA TB-9 Tampico	262	F-OGLI
EC-DRG	Aérospatiale AS.350B Ecureuil	1597	
EC-DRJ	Robinson R-22	0259	N9076H
EC-DRK	Robinson R-22	0236	N9074F
EC-DRL	Piper PA-38-112 Tomahawk	38-81A0021	N25622
EC-DRM	SOCATA MS.893E Rallye 180GT Gaillard	13198	F-GBKO
EC-DRN	CASA C.212 Aviocar	247	
EC-DRP	Grob G.109	6106	D-KHAA
EC-DRQ	SOCATA MS.880B Rallye Club	1662	F-BSKU
EC-DRS	SOCATA Rallye 235C	13317	F-GCEG
EC-DRT	Cameron O-77 HAFB	784	
EC-DRV	Reims/Cessna F.152	1916	F-WZNC
EC-DRX	SOCATA TB-10 Tobago	295	F-OGLP
EC-DRZ	Reims/Cessna F.172H	0424	D-ELGT
EC-DSA	Aero Commander 680T	1564-20	I-ARBO
			N1199Z
EC-DSB	Cessna 152	80888	N25974
EC-DSD	Piper PA-28-161 Warrior II	28-8116182	N9522N
EC-DSG	Cessna T.188C Husky	03923T	N9994J
EC-DSJ	Hughes 369D	1169D	
EC-DSK	SOCATA TB-10 Tobago	308	F-OGLQ
EC-DSL	Piper PA-38-112 Tomahawk	38-82A0088	N9659N
EC-DSM	Piper PA-28-161 Warrior II	28-8116183	N9523N
EC-DSN	Thunder AX7-77A HAFB	454	
EC-DSQ	Agusta-Bell 47G-2	271	F-BIND
			F-OBND
			I-ELIT
EC-DSR	Cameron D-50 Hot Air Airship	892	
EC-DSU	MBB Bölkow BO.105S (Catalunya "02")	S-623	D-HDSS
EC-DSY	Reims/Cessna F.152	1789	F-WZIL
EC-DSZ	Grob G.109	6122	D-KCVO
EC-DTA	Piper PA-28RT-201 Arrow IV	28R-8118038	N8315H
			N9624N
EC-DTB	SOCATA Rallye 235E Gabier	13018	F-GBXD
EC-DTD	Hughes 369D (Damaged 30.6.94)	1172D	
EC-DTE	MBB Bölkow BO.105C	S-576	D-HDPY
EC-DTF	MBB Bölkow BO.105C	S-599	D-HDQV
EC-DTG	Piper PA-23-250 Aztec C	27-3180	D-IDAX
			LN-KAG
EC-DTH	Colt AS-90 Hot Air Airship	451	
EC-DTJ	Piper PA-36-375 Pawnee Brave	36-8102014	N6172A
	(Damaged 4.1.97)		
EC-DTK	Cameron D-50 Hot Air Airship	854	
EC-DTM	PADC/MBB Bölkow BO.105C	S.9-402	D-HDNS(3)
			RP-C214
			(D-HDMA)
EC-DTN	SOCATA Rallye 180T Galérien	3373	F-ODQB
EC-DTQ	Piper PA-28R-201T Turbo Arrow IV	28R-8331051	N9546N
EC-DTS	Partenavia P.68 Observer	324-17-OB	
EC-DTT	Grob G.102 Astir IIIB	5583CB	
EC-DTX	Schleicher ASW-20	20711	
EC-DTY	Piper PA-25-260 Pawnee C	25-4509	SE-FCY
EC-DTZ	Piper PA-25-260 Pawnee C	25-5301	SE-FYA
EC-DUA	Agusta-Bell 206B Jet Ranger	8665	
EC-DUC	Reims/Cessna F.172N	1818	D-EJCA(2)
EC-DUD	Grumman G.164B Agcat	733B	
EC-DUH	Bell 47G-2	1969	F-BUYV
			74+32
			AS+387
EC-DUI	Hoffmann H-36 Dimona	3608	OE-9202
			(D-KAHG)
EC-DUJ	CASA C.101CC	98	
	(On display at CASA factory at Getafe)		
EC-DUK	Agusta-Bell 47G-2	205	D-HIPO
			IDFAF
			FrAF
EC-DUN	North American T.6G Harvard	unkn	E16-201
	(Museum, painted as E16-201)		FrAF
			52-8216
EC-DUP	MBB Bölkow BO.105C	S-614	D-HDSJ
EC-DUS	Agusta-Bell 206B Jet Ranger III	8633	OE-DXE
EC-DUU(2)	Schleicher ASK-21	21346	
EC-DUX	Piper PA-32-300 Cherokee Six	32-7340074	F-BSGY
			5T-TJR
			N11C
EC-DUY	MBB Bölkow BO.105C	S-628	D-HDSX
EC-DUZ	MBB Bölkow BO.105C	S-629	D-HDSY
EC-DVA	Hoffmann H-36 Dimona (Damaged)	3536	OE-9237
EC-DVF	Schleicher Ka.6CR Rhönsegler	6302	D-....
			OO-ZME
EC-DVG	Cameron O-65 HAFB	1076	
EC-DVI	SOCATA MS.893E Rallye 180GT Gaillard	12122	F-BTVE
EC-DVJ	Hoffmann H-36 Dimona (Stored)	3671	D-KCED

Regn.	Type	C/n	Prev.Id.
EC-DVK	MBB Bölkow BO.105C	S-630	(N5489A)
			D-HDSZ
EC-DVL	MBB Bölkow BO.105C	S-631	(N5489C)
			D-HDTA
EC-DVP	Cameron 0-65 HAFB	1124	
EC-DVQ	CASA C.101CC	107	
EC-DVR	Agusta A.109A	7231	
EC-DVS	Robin DR.400/180R Remorqueur	1682	
EC-DVU	Grob G.103A Twin II Acro	33919-K-154	
EC-DVV	Grob G.103A Twin II Acro	33918-K-153	
EC-DVX	Grob G.103A Twin II Acro	33920-K-155	
EC-DXA	Rockwell Commander 690A	11328	D-IHVB
			N81449
EC-DXC	MBB Bölkow BO.105C	S-690	D-HDVD
EC-DXD	MBB Bölkow BO.105C	S-697	D-HDVK
EC-DXG	Aero Commander 680V (Stored)	1711-86	N535SM
EC-DXH	MBB Bölkow BO.105C	S-698	D-HDVL
EC-DXI	MBB Bölkow BO.105C	S-699	D-HDVM
EC-DXJ	Hispano HA.220D Super Saeta	22/119	A10C-114
			C.10C-114
EC-DXL	Wassmer WA.421-250	409	F-BPTL
EC-DXM	Aérospatiale SA.365C2 Dauphin 2	5007	PH-SSL
			G-BKXV
			PH-SSL
			F-WIPF
			N90045
EC-DXN	Aérospatiale AS.350B Ecureuil	1387	
EC-DXO	UltraMagic V-65 HAFB	65/04	
EC-DXP	UltraMagic V-65 HAFB	65/07	
EC-DXQ	UltraMagic V-77 HAFB	77/04	
EC-DXR	Hispano HA.200 Super Saeta (Museum)	20/56	A.10B-50
			C.10C-50
EC-DXU	Vickers V.806 Viscount (Wfu)	264	G-AOYO
EC-DXX	Reims/Cessna F.152 (W/o 5.97)	1674	N8062P
			(G-BGLR)
EC-DXY	Reims/Cessna F.152	1793	F-WZIU
EC-DXZ	Bell 206B Jet Ranger II	1051	HB-XFH
			F-BVUE
			HP-1533-71
			N58156
EC-DYD	Bell 47G-2	1620	D-HKBM
			74+29
			AS+389
			YA+028
			PA+118
			AS+383
EC-DYI	UltraMagic H-77 HAFB	77/13	
EC-DYJ	UltraMagic V-65 HAFB	65/06	
EC-DYK	Aérospatiale AS.350B Ecureuil	1863	
EC-DYL	Piper PA-28-140 Cherokee E	28-7225250	G-AZVZ
EC-DYM	MBB Bölkow BO.105C	S-700	D-HDVN
EC-DYN	MBB Bölkow BO.105C	S-707	D-HDVU
EC-DYQ	Agusta-Bell 206B Jet Ranger III	8677	HB-XML
EC-DYR	Continental El Tomcat 6B (Bell OH-13H)	CCI-74-8	CS-HAS
			N9026T
EC-DYS	SOCATA MS.893E Rallye 180GT Gaillard	12313	F-BUNZ
EC-DYT	Cessna 340A	0687	G-VELT
			HB-LLZ
			N5462G
EC-DYU	Aérospatiale SA.365C-1 Dauphin 2	5053	PH-SSC
			LV-APO
			PH-SSC
			N3610B
EC-DYV	UltraMagic V-77 HAFB	77/06	
EC-DZD	UltraMagic AX-6 HAFB	56/F1	
EC-DZE	Agusta-Bell 47G-4A	2535	I-CRIT
EC-DZF	Reims/Cessna F.172M	1210	LN-NFE
			SE-GKB
			(OE-DTP)
EC-DZI	Agusta-Bell 47G-4A (W/o 6.3.94)	2536	I-ITOX
EC-DZJ	Bell 47G-3B (OH-13S)	3905	FAMET/
			HE.7B-29
			65-13009
EC-DZK	Agusta-Bell 47G-3B-1	1614	FAMET/
			HE.7B-32

Regn.	Type	C/n	Prev.Id.
EC-DZL	Agusta-Bell 47G-3B-1	1613	FAMET/
			HE.7B-31
EC-DZM	Agusta-Bell 47G-3B-1	1509	FAMET
			Z.7B-18
EC-DZN	UltraMagic H-65 HAFB	65/05	
EC-DZO	UltraMagic V-65 HAFB	65/11	
EC-DZP	UltraMagic V-77 HAFB	77/07	
EC-DZR	Piper PA-32-300 Cherokee Six D	32-7140028	CS-AFV
	(W/o 22.10.95)		N8635N
EC-DZS	UltraMagic V-77 HAFB	77/10	
EC-DZT	Agusta A.109A	7159	HB-XIU
EC-DZU	Valentin Taifun 17E	1060	D-KFHA
EC-DZV	Cessna 310Q	OO39	D-ICAA
			PH-PLW
			(PH-ADZ)
			D-ICAA
			N7539Q
EC-DZX	Aérospatiale AS.355F1 Ecureuil 2	5243	F-WYMT
EC-DZY	Aérospatiale SA.315B Lama	2381	F-BVUD
EC-DZZ	Piper PA-36-375 Pawnee Brave	36-7802048	N3912E
EC-EAA	Piper PA-36-375 Pawnee Brave	36-7802020	HP-1060
			YS-666A
			N9741N
EC-EAB	Cessna 402	0167	G-BAWZ
			N99JH
			G-BAWZ
			5Y-ANJ
			OY-AHP
			N4067Q
EC-EAE	Piper PA-38-112 Tomahawk	38-82AOO90	N9661N
EC-EAG	Aero Commander 680W	1776-14	N680W
			N121AB
			N13TV
			N4988E
EC-EAH	Cessna T.310R	1271	N6104C
EC-EAI	Reims/Cessna F.150K	0532	N8892
EC-EAJ	UltraMagic V-77 HAFB	77/09	
EC-EAL	Westland-Bell 47G-3B-1	WA/431	D-HAFH
			XT542
EC-EAR	UltraMagic V-65 HAFB	65/13	
EC-EAT	UltraMagic H-77 HAFB	77/08	
EC-EAX	Agusta-Bell 47G-3B	1510	HE.7B-19
			751-9
			Z.7B-19
EC-EAY	Agusta-Bell 47G-3B	1511	HE.7B-20
			751-10
			Z.7B-20
EC-EBB	Aérospatiale SA.365C Dauphin 2	5013	F-GBOU
EC-EBD	Grumman G.164D Turbo-Agcat	15D	G-BIVO
			N8311K
EC-EBE	Grumman G.164D Turbo-Agcat	07D	G-TCAT
			N816 IK
EC-EBF	Agusta-Bell 206B Jet Ranger II	8704	
EC-EBH	SA.316B Alouette III	1783	Zimbabwe/
			Rh.AF
			N3048
EC-EBI	SA.316B Alouette III	1498	RJAF-314
EC-EBK	Colt 56A HAFB	930	
EC-EBL	Ultramagic H-77 HAFB	77/14	
EC-EBP	Schempp-Hirth Nimbus 3/24.5	1	D-2111
EC-EBQ	Piper PA-36-375 Pawnee Brave	36-7802031	N3863E
EC-EBS	Ultramagic V-65 HAFB	65/9	
EC-EBT	Ultramagic H-77 HAFB	77/11	
EC-EBU	Piper PA-36-300 Pawnee Brave	36-8160012	N2346Y
EC-EBC	Ultramagic H-65 HAFB	65/17	
EC-ECE	Cessna T.188C AgHusky	03935T	N9348K
EC-ECF	Grumman G.164A Agcat	1426	N8597H
EC-ECG	UltraMagic H-65 HAFB	65/15	
EC-ECH	MBB-Bölkow BO.105CB	S-667	N . . . . .
			(D-HDUI)
EC-ECI	MBB-Bölkow BO.105CB	S-720	D-HDRH(2)
EC-ECJ	Aérospatiale AS.350B Ecureuil (W/o 13.8.94)	2031	
EC-ECK	Cessna 402	0284	D-IFAK
			N8436F
EC-ECL	Hoffmann H-36 Dimona	36218	

Regn.	Type	C/n	Prev.Id.
EC-ECT	Bell 206B Jet Ranger II	2237	D-HIPI (2) N16824
EC-ECV	Valentin Taifun 17E	1079	D-KLPA
EC-ECX	Piper PA-36-300 Pawnee Brave *(Damaged 31.8.94)*	36-7902046	N999NA N3658E
EC-ECZ	Grumman G.164B Agcat	686B	N8401K
EC-EDA	Grumman G.164B Agcat	695B	N695GA
EC-EDB	Reims/Cessna F.337G Super Skymaster	0067/01564	OO-EDU F-BVSX
EC-EDC	Dassault Falcon 20	6	N750SS N497 N65311 C-GOQG (N21DT) N21JM N20JM N805F F-BMKH F-WMKH
EC-EDD	Grumman G.164B Agcat	116B	G-BEIJ N48685
EC-EDH	Robinson R-22	0071	N90348
EC-EDJ	Grumman G.164C Agcat	36C	N2734A
EC-EDN	Cessna 501 Citation	0010	VH-POZ (N500MD) N7WF EP-PBC N7WF N36859
EC-EDP	Grumman G.164B Agcat	318B	G-BFJO N6814Q
EC-EDQ	Eiri PIK-30	726	
EC-EDR	Grumman G.164B Agcat	343B	N6504K
EC-EDS	Grumman G.164B Agcat	262B	N25CD
EC-EDU	Grumman G.164C Agcat	7C	N6597K
EC-EDV	Grumman G.164 Agcat	214	N403Y
EC-EDX	Grumman G.164B Agcat	782B	N3633Z
EC-EDY	Grumman G.164B Agcat	790B	
EC-EDZ	Grumman G.164C Agcat	43C	N8085K
EC-EEA	Robin ATL	47	F-GFOX
EC-EED	SOCATA MS.894A Minerva 220	11718	CS-AGV
EC-EEH	MBB-Kawasaki BK.117A-3	7091	D-HBPL
EC-EEI	Bell 206L-3 Long Ranger III	51161	N3198T
EC-EEJ	Westland-Bell 47G-3B1	WA/314	D-HFFF XT155 EC-136 N6005C
EC-EEK	Boeing 747-256B Combi	24071	
EC-EEL	Ultramagic V-77 HAFB	77/12	
EC-EEN	Agusta-Bell 204B	3002	HB-XCG I-AGUG
EC-EEO(2)	Cessna 150M	77601	N6233K
EC-EEQ	Bell 212	30612	D-HOBB(2) EC-DYP D-HOBB(2) LN-OSM
EC-EER	Piper PA-36-375 Pawnee Brave	36-8002029	N2453V
EC-EES	Bell 206L Long Ranger	45153	N16942
EC-EEV	Valentin Taifun 17E	1102	D-KFAC
EC-EEX	Piper PA-36-375 Pawnee Brave *(Damaged 2.5.97)*	36-7902028	N3983E
EC-EEZ	Bell 47G-5	7802	G-BLDF N8558F
EC-EFA	MBB-Kawasaki BK.117A-3	7116	D-HBCK (N90186)
EC-EFC	MBB-Kawasaki BK.117A-3	7120	D-HBCO (N9019V)
EC-EFF	Hoffmann H-36 Dimona II	36230	OE-9289
EC-EFG	Rockwell Commander 690A	11130	N11VS N294BC N570H
EC-EFI (2)	Ultramagic M-160 HAFB	160/01	
EC-EFL(2)	Piper PA-34-200T Seneca II	34-7970246	N29691
EC-EFM	Piper PA-28RT-201T Turbo Arrow IV	28R-7931292	N46008 XB-BKM N9627N
EC-EFN	Cessna 210M Centurion	62158	N8866A
EC-EFO	Piper PA-34-200T Seneca II	34-7770092	N549BR N73GH N8584F
EC-EFP	Hoffmann H-36 Dimona	36214	OE-9270
EC-EFQ	Lanaverre Standard Cirrus CS-11/75	667	F-CEMV
EC-EFS	Rockwell Commander 690	11034	N400JJ N9234N
EC-EFT	CASA I-131E Jungmann *(Museum)*	2226	E3B-607
EC-EFV	Cameron N-77 HAFB	1064	
EC-EFX	Boeing 757-2G5 *(Reserved as D-AMUA 8.99)*	23118	D-AMUR(2)
EC-EFY	SAN Jodel D.140C Mousquetaire III	162	F-BMFY
EC-EFZ	Ultramagic H-56 HAFB	56/2	
EC-EGA	Ultramagic V-65 HAFB	65/12	
EC-EGB	Ultramagic V-77 HAFB	77/15	
EC-EGC	Ultramagic H-56 HAFB	56/3	
EC-EGD	Cessna TU.206G Turbo Stationair II	06043	G-HCHU HB-CHU G-BKKJ N4890Z
EC-EGE	Ultramagic V-65 HAFB	65/16	
EC-EGG	Ultramagic H-56 HAFB	56/4	
EC-EGH	Boeing 757-2G5 *(Reserved as D-AMUB 8.99)*	23119	EC-116 D-AMUS
EC-EGJ	Brditschka HB23/2400	23023-S-5	
EC-EGK	Brditschka HB23/2400	23021-S-4	
EC-EGN	Cessna T.210M Turbo Centurion	62448	N761RB
EC-EGP	CASA I-131E Jungmann	2222	E3B-603
EC-EGS	HS.125 Series 600A	256034	EC-115 N600SB N600FL N90BL N90B N39BH
EC-EGT	HS.125 Series 1A-522	25080	N23KL C-GLEO EI-BGW G-BDYE 3D-AAB VQ-ZIL
EC-EGU	Cessna T.188C AgHusky	03437T	N2200J
EC-EGV	Aérospatiale SA.365C Dauphin 2	5032	F-GBTB
EC-EGX	Piper PA-28RT-201T Turbo Arrow IV	28R-7931102	N2165U
EC-EGY	Gates Learjet 25D	25D-373	N29EW
EC-EGZ	Aérospatiale SA.316B Alouette III	2319	HB-XRY N9005D
EC-EHB	Piper PA-36-375 Pawnee Brave	36-8102001	N2364Y
EC-EHC	Dassault Falcon 20DC	46	N46VG (N144FE) N7FE N23555 CF-ESO F-WMKG
EC-EHE	Beech A36 Bonanza	E-115	OO-KRZ D-EKRZ
EC-EHF	BAe.125 Series 600A	256011	N81D N42622 VR-BGS N555GB N555CB N6001H N24BH
EC-EHI	Cessna T.210M Turbo Centurion	61956	N1749M
EC-EHK	Cessna TU.206G Turbo Stationair II	06260	N6386Z
EC-EHL	Cessna T.310R	0101	N134SW G-BMHE ZS-JCF N69593
EC-EHN	Piper PA-36-375 Pawnee Brave	36-7802022	N3830E
EC-EHO	SA.316B Alouette III	1585	F-GEPJ F-ODTF FAP9306
EC-EHP	Cessna 402B	1232	N720J N4186G

Regn.	Type	C/n	Prev.Id.
EC-EHV	Bell UH-1B (204)	953	N88389
			63-8728
EC-EIB	Piper PA-36-285 Pawnee Brave	36-7360029	N56123
EC-EIE	Grumman G.164B Agcat	768B	N3632D
EC-EIF	Grumman G.164B Agcat	740B	N3629B
EC-EIH	Rockwell Commander 690A	11212	N690BT
			C-GIAA
			N9165N
EC-EIJ	Maule MX-7-180 Star Rocket	11033C	N5672A
EC-EIL	Rockwell Commander 690	11007	N171TT
			N71ITT
			N9207N
			ZS-NHG
			N9207N
EC-EIM	Piper PA-31T1 Cheyenne	31T-7904026	N458SC
			XC-CUA
			(TG-...)
			N23447
EC-EIN	Air Tractor AT-502	502-0021	
EC-EIO	Air Tractor AT-502	502-0019	
EC-EIP	Piper PA-36-375 Pawnee Brave	36-8002008	N2322Y
			ZK-EQJ
EC-EIQ	Reims/Cessna F.150L	0900	D-ECUD(2)
EC-EIS	Douglas C-47B	16066/32814	(N519GL)
	(Damaged 7.6.89, believed restored)		N3176Q
			CA+017
			GR+114
			0-476482
			KN393
			44-76482
EC-EIT	Ultramagic M-65 HAFB	65/23	
EC-EIU	Ultramagic V-65 HAFB (Also quoted as c/n 65/33)	65/26	
EC-EIX	Rockwell S.2R Thrush Commander	2171R	N4963X
EC-EIY	Air Tractor AT-501	501-0016	N10018
EC-EIZ	Air Tractor AT-401	401-0679	N73173
EC-EJA	Piper PA-36-375 Pawnee Brave	36-8160022	N2393Y
EC-EJB	Douglas C-47	4479	EC-177
			(N514GL)
			N330
			(5N-ARC)
			N330
			F-OART
			N2077A
			HK-1201
			C-1201
			41-18417
EC-EJC	Ayres S.2R-T34 Turbo Thrush	6017	N4009W
EC-EJD	Cessna T.188C AgHusky	03686T	N3898J
EC-EJF	Air Tractor AT-401	401-0685	
EC-EJG	Cessna 172N	73863	N6324J
EC-EJH	Cessna TU.206G Turbo Stationair II	04172	N756LH
EC-EJI	Piper PA-28RT-201T Turbo Arrow IV	28R-8131192	N8425D
EC-EJJ	Ayres S.2R-T15 Turbo Thrush (W/o 10.7.94)	T15-006	N40184
EC-EJL	Glasflügel H205 Libelle	165	F-CEQP
EC-EJO	Bell 206B Jet Ranger II	2864	HB-XLD
EC-EJP	Air Tractor AT-301	301-0665	N73120
EC-EJR	Piper PA-36-375 Pawnee Brave	36-8002041	N2318Y
EC-EJS	Ultramagic V-65 HAFB	65/14	
EC-EJT	Ultramagic V-65 HAFB	65/08	
EC-EJV	Piper PA-34-200T Seneca II (Dam. 22.2.97)	34-7970030	N2215D
EC-EJX	Piper PA-36-375 Pawnee Brave	36-7902039	N3992E
EC-EJY	Piper PA-36-375 Pawnee Brave	36-7902010	N3972E
EC-EKA	Bell UH-1B (204)	313	N9050Q
			61-733
EC-EKB	Bell UH-1B (204)	345	N4991D
			61-765
EC-EKC	Bell UH-1B (204)	684	N394HP
			62-12533
EC-EKD	Cessna 172N	70671	G-BNSK
			N739NJ
EC-EKE	Schempp-Hirth Discus b	232	
EC-EKF	Reims/Cessna F.172P (Damaged 11.5.97)	2189	HB-CGP
EC-EKG	Cessna 402B Utililiner II	1209	N321RF
			N321PC
			(N4163G)

Regn.	Type	C/n	Prev.Id.
EC-EKH	Piper PA-28RT-201T Turbo Arrow IV	28R-8131008	N8277Y
EC-EKI	Cessna 150J	69733	N51055
EC-EKJ	Cessna 172N	70334	N738YD
EC-EKK	Dassault Falcon 20C	106	N31V
			N9300M
			F-GBPG
			N987F
			F-WJMM
EC-EKL	Ultramagic V-77 HAFB	77/16	
EC-EKN	Cessna U.206F Stationair	03721	N7952N
EC-EKO	Bell 206B Jet Ranger II	2406	N50006
EC-EKP	Grob G.102 Astir CS	1517	
EC-EKR	Piper PA-36-285 Pawnee Brave	36-7660049	N57728
EC-EKS	Ultramagic M-77 HAFB	77/23	
EC-EKU	Grob G.103 Twin Astir Trainer	3103	
EC-EKV	Cessna T.210N Turbo Centurion II	63817	N6166C
EC-EKX	Reims/Cessna F.172M	1180	D-EDJO
EC-EKY	Maule M-5-180C	8012C	N5642T
EC-EKZ	Maule M-5-210C Strata Rocket	6007C	N51467
EC-ELB	Bell 47G-5A	25103	CS-HAG
EC-ELD	Piper PA-36-375 Pawnee Brave	36-7802037	N3896E
EC-ELH	Mooney M.20J Model 201 (Damaged 22.8.94)	24-1322	N1171U
EC-ELI	Cessna 152-II	85289	G-BNSJ
			N65576
EC-ELK	BAe.125 Series 800B	258022	EC-193
			HZ-KSA
			G-5-569
			G-JJCB
			G-5-16
EC-ELL	Piper PA-36-375 Pawnee Brave	36-8202011	N2351X
EC-ELO	Aérospatiale AS.350B1 Ecureuil	2129	
EC-ELP	Cessna 172N	68568	C-GSOG
			N733UW
EC-ELQ	Cessna 150M	78731	C-GYEE
			(N704MY)
EC-ELR	Ultramagic H-56 HAFB	56/05	
EC-ELT	BAe.146 Series 200QT	E-2102	EC-198
			G-5-102
			G-BOKZ
			G-5-102
EC-ELU	Piper PA-36-375 Pawnee Brave	36-8002017	TI-APF
			N9734N
EC-ELX	Piper PA-36-375 Pawnee Brave	36-8002021	C-GJEB
			N2410V
EC-ELY	Boeing 737-3K9	24211	EC-188
EC-ELZ	Piper PA-38-112 Tomahawk	38-78A0299	N9257T
EC-EMB	Piper PA-34-200T Seneca II	34-7870034	N9052K
EC-EMC	Piper PA-36-375 Pawnee Brave	36-8002022	C-GJFZ
			N2411V
EC-EMD	McDonnell-Douglas DC-8-62F	46023	EC-217
			N731PL
			JA8035
EC-EME	Cessna 172N	71082	D-EGGQ
			N1653E
EC-EMF	Agusta-Bell 206B Jet Ranger II	8715	
EC-EMH	Cessna 402B	0534	N101GP
EC-EML	Piper PA-36-375 Pawnee Brave	36-8202008	N2346X
EC-EMM	Cessna 172N	68338	D-EGGO(2)
			N733JV
EC-EMO	CASA-Nurtanio CN-235 Tetuko	C-006	EC-011
EC-EMP	Cessna 172M	62854	D-EGGP
			N13569
EC-EMQ	UltraMagic M-77 HAFB	77/26	
EC-EMR	UltraMagic S-105 HAFB	105/02	
EC-EMS	UltraMagic S-90 HAFB	90/01	
EC-EMX	McDonnell-Douglas DC-8-62	45921	EC-230
			N729PL
			N756UA
			SE-DBG
EC-EMZ	Pilatus PC-6/B1-H2 Turbo-Porter	672	F-GHAS
			C-GXIK
			N62149
			XW-PEF
			HB-FEI
EC-ENA	Ayres S.2R-R1820	001DC	N40225

Regn.	Type	C/n	Prev.Id.
EC-ENB	Ayres S.2R-R1820	015DC	N3086L
EC-ENC	Cessna T.188C Husky	03697T	N3933J
EC-END	Air Tractor AT-401	401-0698	N1007G
EC-ENE	Cessna 172N	68844	N734GN
EC-ENF	Cessna T.188C Husky	03942T	N9414K
EC-ENG	Piper PA-28-161 Cadet	2841027	N9619N
EC-ENH	Cessna T.310R	1309	N6171X
EC-ENI	Schempp-Hirth Ventus b/16.6	172	D-7717
EC-ENJ	Bell 47G-5	7938	N1477W
EC-ENK	Thunder AX7-77 HAFB	1174	
EC-ENL	Air Tractor AT-401	401-0700	N1005A
EC-ENM	Air Tractor AT-503	503-0001	N7309X
EC-ENN	Air Tractor AT-502	502-0007	N7315N
EC-ENO	Rockwell S.2R Thrush Commander	2101R	N4911X
EC-ENP	Cessna 152	84480	N4709M
EC-ENQ	Boeing 757-2G5 (Reserved as D-AMUC(2) 8.99)	23651	EC-256 D-AMUT
EC-ENR	Piper PA-28RT-201T Turbo Arrow IV	28R-8131137	N8385A
EC-ENV	Maule M-5-235C Lunar Rocket	7164C	N6129M
EC-ENX	Bell UH-1B (204)	977	N5598G 63-12916
EC-ENY	Piper PA-36-375 Pawnee Brave	36-8202009	N2349X
EC-EOA	Cessna 172P (Dbr 10.2.94, dumped)	75892	N65794
EC-EOB	Maule M-5-180C	8005C	N5635U
EC-EOC	UltraMagic H-77 HAFB	77/27	
EC-EOD	Cessna 177RG Cardinal RG	0912	N7857V
EC-EOE	Robinson R-22 Beta	0695	HB-XSF
EC-EOF	Aérospatiale SA.315B Lama	2261	F-GEJS N13583 (N515HA) N13583
EC-EOI	Bell UH-1B (204)	408	N5023U 62-1888
EC-EON	Airbus A.300B4-203	076	EC-273 G-BMZK D-AIBD F-WZEI
EC-EOO	Airbus A.300B4-203 (Wfu)	077	EC-274 G-BMZL D-AIBF F-WZEJ
EC-EOP	Schleicher ASW-20	20020	D-7568
EC-EOR	UltraMagic S-105 HAFB	105/05	
EC-EOS	Piper PA-28-161 Cadet	2841064	N9629N
EC-EOT	Cessna 172N	73765	N5367J
EC-EOU	SOCATA TB-10 Tobago	634	F-GFFE N20FD
EC-EOV	Cessna 337G Super Skymaster	01779	N53681
EC-EOX	Bell UH-1B (204)	1214	N90632 64-14090
EC-EPA	BAe.146 Series 200QT	E-2089	EC-281 G-TNTH (F-GTNT) G-BNYC G-5-089
EC-EPC	UltraMagic M-77 HAFB	77/33	
EC-EPD	Wassmer WA.26P	09	F-CDQB
EC-EPE	UltraMagic M-77 HAFB	77/34	
EC-EPG	Robin ATL	76	F-GFSA
EC-EPH	Maule MX.7-180 Star Rocket	11039C	N6114M
EC-EPI	UltraMagic M-65 HAFB	65/29	
EC-EPJ	Cessna 152	84583	N5408M
EC-EPK	Cessna 402B (Wfo 12.2.97)	1036	N98666
EC-EPO	Glaser-Dirks DG-400	4-223	(D-KIDG)
EC-EPP	Cessna T.337H Turbo Skymaster	01837	N1345L
EC-EPQ	Piper PA-36-375 Pawnee Brave	36-8102012	C-GJFT N6167A
EC-EPR	Piper PA-34-200T Seneca II	34-7870191	N9479C
EC-EPS	Cessna 172M	61304	N20458
EC-EPT	Cessna 172N	67611	N73685 N739QB
EC-EPU	Grob G.103 Astir Trainer	3237	F-CFHC
EC-EPV	UltraMagic F2 HAFB (Pegaso Truck SS)	F2/01	EC-197
EC-EPX	Piper PA-34-220T Seneca III	34-8233029	D-GBON N8464B
EC-EPY	Mooney M.20J Model 205	24-3112	N1010H
EC-EPZ	Piper PA-32-301T Turbo Saratoga	32-8024001	N9326C
EC-EQA	Cessna 150J	70498	N60683
EC-EQB	Cessna 150M (Damaged 9.9.94)	78829	N704SC
EC-EQC	Bell 47G-5A	25054	FAP-647 N2972W
EC-EQD	Bell 47G-5A	25057	FAP-650 N2975W
EC-EQE	Bell 47G-5A	25063	FAP-652 N2977W
EC-EQF	Bell 47G-5A	25065	FAP-654 N2981W
EC-EQG	Reims/Cessna F.172N	2008	G-WAGY
EC-EQJ	Cessna 411	0198	YV-455CP
EC-EQK	Cessna 310R	1610	N36873
EC-EQL	Bell 47G-3B1	6524	FAP-621 66-621
EC-EQM	Cessna 152	81103	N49017
EC-EQN	Cessna 152	80727	D-EMBP N152LK (N25544)
EC-EQO	Cessna 152	82262	D-EMFO(2) N68330
EC-EQP	Dassault Falcon 20	149	EC-263 N568Q (N4359F) N1818S N4359F F-WNGO
EC-EQR	Robinson R-22M Mariner	1043M	
EC-EQT	Cessna 172M	61170	N20297
EC-EQU	Aérospatiale SA.342J Gazelle	1057	C-GEJE N341NA N9042U C-FGCE CF-GCE
EC-EQV	Piper PA-34-200T Seneca II	34-7770006	N5266F
EC-EQY	MBB-Bölkow BO.105CBS	S-810	D-HDZT
EC-EQZ	SOCATA TB-10 Tobago	926	
EC-ERA	Piper PA-18-150 Super Cub	18-8929	N4508Y
EC-ERB	Grumman G.164B Agcat	814B	
EC-ERC	Piper PA-28-181 Cherokee Archer	28-7790257	N8539F
EC-ERD	Aérospatiale AS.350B Ecureuil	1530	G-JORR G-BJMY
EC-ERE	Aérospatiale AS.350B Ecureuil	1865	D-HGBA
EC-ERF	Bell 47G-2A1	2870	N510J
EC-ERG	Cessna 152	79558	N714ZH
EC-ERH	Cessna 402B	1086	N543GB N543GA (N1927G)
EC-ERI	Piper PA-36-285 Pawnee Brave (Damaged 5.2.97)	36-7360035	N56297
EC-ERK	Bell UH-1E (204)	6069	N151LC BuA151875
EC-ERL	Beech F33A Bonanza	CE-1245	N3084D
EC-ERM	Cessna U.206F Stationair	02291	N987CA
EC-ERN	Piper PA-38-112 Tomahawk	38-78A0719	N2501A
EC-ERO	CASA I-131E Jungmann	2012	E3B-408
EC-ERP	CASA I-131E Jungmann	unkn	E3B-321
EC-ERQ	Beech 200 Super King Air (W/o 9.10.97)	BB-218	EC-351 N575HA N575HW N9209Q
EC-ERR	Aérospatiale AS.350B Ecureuil	2271	
EC-ERS	Cessna 340A	0524	N4277C
EC-ERT	Cessna 172N	71250	N2362E
EC-ERU	Cessna 172N	73475	N4928G
EC-ERV	Cessna 152	81959	N67647
EC-ERY	Sikorsky S-76 Arriel 1S	760037	EC-364 F-GHUI N9007F PH-NZM N4254S
EC-ERZ	Aérospatiale AS.350B Ecureuil	2261	
EC-ESA	Aérospatiale AS.350B Ecureuil	2260	F-WYMF

Regn.	Type	C/n	Prev.Id.
EC-ESB	Hoffmann H-36 Dimona	36209	OE-9268
EC-ESD	Cessna 150M	79292	N714MY
EC-ESH	Reims/Cessna FA.150L Aerobat	0099	D-ECPK
EC-ESI	Scheibe SF-25E Super Falke	4341	D-KDCR
EC-ESK	SOCATA TB-20 Trinidad	747	F-GFQN
EC-ESL	Piper PA-36-285 Pawnee Brave	36-7660087	C-GJIK
			N57774
EC-ESM	Cessna U.206F Stationair	01902	D-EGJR
			N50045
EC-ESN	Piper PA-36-285 Pawnee Brave	36-7560066	C-GUAR
			N9955P
EC-ESO	Cessna 152	81549	N65433
EC-ESP	Piper PA-38-112 Tomahawk	38-79A0460	N2463F
EC-ESQ	Piper PA-38-112 Tomahawk II (W/o 30.5.97)	38-82A0084	N91595
EC-ESS	Aeritalia/SNIAS ATR-72-202	154	EC-383
			F-WWEK
EC-ESU	Beech F33A Bonanza	CE-1410	N56620
EC-ESX	MBB-Kawasaki BK.117B-1	7176	D-HBHS
EC-ESY	Grob G.102 Speed Astir IIB	4106	D-6819
EC-ESZ	Piper PA-23-250 Aztec E	27-7305201	D-IGAU
			N40483
EC-ETA	PZL M-18A Dromader	1Z021-05	SP-DCB
EC-ETC	Cessna 172N	69216	D-EFZN(2)
			N734YG
EC-ETE	Piper PA-28-181 Cherokee Archer II	28-7790459	N3461Q
EC-ETF	Agusta A.109C	7605	3A-MOR
EC-ETG	Soloy-Hiller UH-12J3	5067	N4027K
EC-ETH	Cessna 425 Conquest I	0151	N81798
EC-ETJ	UltraMagic M-160 HAFB	160/02	
EC-ETK	UltraMagic M-77 HAFB	77/39	
EC-ETN	Glaser-Dirks DG-200	2-86	F-CAYB
			F-WAQA
EC-ETO	Grob G.102 Astir CS	1486	D-4790
EC-ETP	UltraMagic H-65 HAFB	65/27	
EC-ETQ	UltraMagic V-77 HAFB	77/35	
EC-ETR	UltraMagic M-77 HAFB	77/37	
EC-ETS	Cessna T.188C AgHusky	03872T	N9937J
EC-ETT	CASA I-131E Jungmann	unkn	E3B-397
EC-ETU	Cessna 337G Super Skymaster	01573	N6AX
EC-ETV	SOCATA TB-20 Trinidad	743	F-GFQK
EC-ETX	Cessna 182P Skylane	64317	N1404M
EC-ETY	Thunder AX7-77 HAFB	1360	
EC-EUA	UltraMagic S-105 HAFB	105/08	
EC-EUB	Lanaverre CS-11/75L Standard Cirrus	10	F-CEVK
EC-EUG	Air Tractor AT-501 (Damaged 10.9.94)	501-0083	
EC-EUH	Air Tractor AT-501	501-0082	
EC-EUI	UltraMagic H-65 HAFB	65/25	
EC-EUJ	Aeritalia/SNIAS ATR-72-202	157	EC-384
			F-WWEL
EC-EUK	Cessna 172N	71869	N5441E
EC-EUM	Piper PA-36-285 Pawnee Brave	36-7660033	N57709
EC-EUN	Piper PA-34-200T Seneca II	34-7970213	N2193Z
EC-EUO	Cessna T.210M Turbo Centurion	62810	N6660B
EC-EUP	Reims/Cessna F.150M	1192	D-EIWD
EC-EUQ	Thunder AX8-105 HAFB	1644	
EC-EUR	Wassmer WA.26P	23	F-CDSB
EC-EUS	SOCATA TB-9 Tampico	1028	
EC-EUT	Bell 206L-3 Long Ranger III	51337	N8212U
EC-EUV	Cessna 172N (Damaged 21.6.97)	72980	N1237F
EC-EUX	Cessna 172M	64726	N61682
EC-EUY	Cessna 152	83383	N48864
EC-EVA	Aérospatiale AS.350B Ecureuil	1345	HB-XMA
			D-HLTH
EC-EVF	UltraMagic M-77 HAFB	77/49	
	(Quoted officially as 77/79, new canopy?)		
EC-EVG	PZL M-18A Dromader	1Z020-21	N21MX
EC-EVH	PZL M-18A Dromader	1Z020-10	N81695
EC-EVI	PZL M-18A Dromader	1Z020-09	N8169Q
EC-EVJ	Grumman G-159 Gulfstream 1	39	EC-376
			N39TG
			N40Y
EC-EVK	Consolidated PBY-5A Catalina	2008	EC-359
	(Stored, Madrid)		C-GFFH
			N6458C
			BuA46644
EC-EVL	PZL M-18A Dromader	1Z012-27	N46831
EC-EVM	Aérospatiale AS.350B Ecureuil	2312	
EC-EVN	Robinson R-22 Beta	0854	OY-HFA
EC-EVO	PZL M-18A Dromader (Damaged 23.7.94)	1Z020-16	N81702
EC-EVP	PZL M-18A Dromader	1Z020-12	N8170Q
EC-EVQ	PZL M-18A Dromader	1Z019-08	N8085K
			SP-DBR
EC-EVS	Bell 204	893	EC-463
			N400SD
			N9378A
			63-8668
EC-EVT	MBB-Kawasaki BK.117A-4 (Catalunya "03")	7074	D-HBNV
EC-EVV	ICA-Brasov IS.28B2	339	
EC-EVX	SOCATA TB-10 Tobago	649	F-GENZ
EC-EVZ	Hughes 369HS	125-0785S	G-WHYZ
			5B-CGZ
			N9265F
EC-EXA	UltraMagic M-77 HAFB	77/52	
EC-EXB	Grumman G-159 Gulfstream 1	153	EC-433
			N153TG
			N80AC
			N733NM
			N733G
EC-EXC	Bell 206B Jet Ranger II	1457	HB-XVO
			N59573
EC-EXE	Bell 206B Jet Ranger II	1073	HB-XXA
			G-BKDD
			C-FDVB
			CF-DVB
			N83159
EC-EXF	McDonnell-Douglas DC-9-87	49832	EC-295
EC-EXG	McDonnell-Douglas DC-9-87	49833	EC-296
EC-EXI	UltraMagic S-105 HAFB	105/09	
EC-EXJ	Mooney M.20J Model 201	24-1689	EC-447
			N10882
EC-EXK	Mooney M.20J Model 201	24-1690	EC-448
			N10898
EC-EXL	Cessna 152	84055	N4980H
EC-EXM	McDonnell-Douglas DC-9-87	49835	EC-298
EC-EXN	McDonnell-Douglas DC-9-87	49836	EC-299
EC-EXO	Bell 204	202	EC-436
			N18SX
			N18SP
			N3145F
			60-3556
EC-EXP	Cessna U.206F Stationair	02398	N206CT
EC-EXQ	Grumman G-159 Gulfstream 1	142	EC-461
	(Wfu ?)		N142TG
			N10ZA
			N764G
EC-EXR	McDonnell-Douglas DC-9-87	49834	EC-297
EC-EXS	Grumman G-159 Gulfstream 1	64	EC-460
	(Wfu ?)		N64TG
			N49401
			CF-COL
			N4466P
			N764G
EC-EXT	McDonnell-Douglas DC-9-87	49837	EC-300
EC-EXU	Cessna T.210N Turbo Centurion II	63389	N5360A
EC-EXZ	PZL M-18A Dromader	1Z021-06	EC-450
			SP-DCC
EC-EYA	Cameron V-56 HAFB	2216	
EC-EYB	McDonnell-Douglas DC-9-87	49838	EC-301
EC-EYD	Fleet 2 (Museum)	324	EC-500
			LV-ZCD
EC-EYE	PZL M-18A Dromader	1Z022-02	SP-DCR
EC-EYF	PZL M-18A Dromader	1Z021-03	EC-453
			SP-DBZ
EC-EYG	PZL M-18A Dromader	1Z021-04	SP-DCA
EC-EYH	PZL M-18A Dromader	1Z022-01	SP-DCP
EC-EYI	PZL M-18A Dromader	1Z021-23	SP-DCG
EC-EYJ	PZL M-18A Dromader (W/o 6.8.94)	1Z021-29	SP-DCN
EC-EYK	Aeritalia/SNIAS ATR-72-202	183	EC-515
			F-WWES
EC-EYL	Cessna 150L (Damaged 2.1.94)	75347	N11355

Regn.	Type	C/n	Prev.Id.
EC-EYN	Piper PA-38-112 Tomahawk	38-79A0184	N2435C
EC-EYO	Piper PA-36-375 Pawnee Brave (Damaged 4.5.97)	36-8202006	N2337X
EC-EYQ	Piper PA-36-375 Pawnee Brave	36-8102021	N99NA
			N6186A
EC-EYT	Cessna 210L Centurion	60803	D-EOGY
			N1783X
EC-EYU	CASA I-131E Jungmann	unkn	E3B-340
EC-EYV	Piper PA-34-220T Seneca III	34-8233109	OE-FYB
			N8161K
EC-EYX	McDonnell-Douglas DC-9-87	49839	EC-302
EC-EYY	McDonnell-Douglas DC-9-87	49840	EC-303
EC-EYZ	McDonnell-Douglas DC-9-87	49841	EC-304
EC-EZA	McDonnell-Douglas DC-9-87	49842	EC-305
EC-EZB	Avialsa-Scheibe A.60	58	F-CCVK
EC-EZC	Schempp-Hirth Discus b	344	
EC-EZD	Fairchild-Swearingen SA.226TC Metro II	TC-314	EC-488
			N232AM
EC-EZE	Fairchild-Swearingen SA.226TC Metro II	TC-319	EC-487
			N233AM
EC-EZF	UltraMagic M-77 HAFB	77/43	
EC-EZH	UltraMagic V-65 HAFB	65/35	
EC-EZI	UltraMagic M-77 HAFB	77/42	
EC-EZK	UltraMagic S-130 HAFB	130/02	
EC-EZL	Piper PA-32-300 Cherokee Six	32-7840113	N9709C
EC-EZM	Valentin Taifun 17E	1086	G-BMXF
			D-KHVA
EC-EZN	Beech 65-A80 Queen Air	LD-205	EC-EEO(1)
			G-ASXV
			OO-ATO
			G-ASXV
EC-EZO	Grumman G.159 Gulfstream 1 (Wfu ?)	41	EC-494
			N41TG
			N9ZA
			N7PG
EC-EZP	Aérospatiale AS.350B Ecureuil	2413	EC-562
			F-WYMC
EC-EZQ	Piper PA-38-112 Tomahawk	38-79A0754	N2539L
EC-EZS	McDonnell-Douglas DC-9-87	49843	EC-306
EC-EZV	Piper PA-38-112 Tomahawk	38-78A0310	N9273T
EC-EZX	Piper PA-28-181 Archer II	28-7990301	N2138R
EC-EZY	Piper PA-28RT-201T Turbo Arrow IV	28R-8231002	N8448B
EC-EZZ	Piper PA-28-181 Archer II	28-8190295	EC-572
			N8420F
EC-FAA	SOCATA MS.893E Rallye 180GT Gaillard	12605	F-BXDY
EC-FAB	Piper PA-28R-201T Arrow III	28R-7703139	N5650V
EC-FAC	CASA/Nurtanio CN.235-100	029	EC-OO9
EC-FAD	CASA/Nurtanio CN.235-100	018	
EC-FAG	Cessna 310R	1255	N6056X
EC-FAH	Douglas C-47A	9336	EC-530
			F-BVJH
			F-OCKH
			F-BRGO
			Fr.AF
			F-BFGA
			42-23740
EC-FAI	Robinson R-22 Alpha	0427	G-GAZE
			N8522K
EC-FAJ	Maule MX.7-180 Star Rocket	11074C	EC-599
EC-FAK	Piper PA-38-112 Tomahawk	38-78A0465	N2441E
EC-FAL	Aérospatiale SA.316C Alouette III	2146	EC-555
			F-GIFF
			N62248
EC-FAN	Cessna T.210M Turbo Centurion	62564	N761VY
EC-FAO	Bell 206L-3 Long Ranger III	51289	N206WC
			C-FFCE
EC-FAR	Cessna 172N (Damaged 29.3.94)	72445	N5202D
EC-FAT	PZL M-18A Dromader	1Z022-03	EC-471
			SP-DCS
EC-FAU	PZL M-18A Dromader	1Z022-04	EC-4..
			SP-DCT
EC-FAV	PZL M-18A Dromader	1Z021-27	EC-458
			SP-DCL
EC-FAX	PZL M-18A Dromader	1Z021-24	EC-4..
			SP-DCH
EC-FAY	PZL M-18A Dromader	1Z022-05	EC-470
			SP-DCU
EC-FAZ	Piper PA-36-375 Pawnee Brave	36-7802007	N102RS
			SE-GVM
EC-FBA	Piper PA-36-375 Pawnee Brave	36-7802045	N3873E
EC-FBB	UltraMagic F4 Bird SS HAFB	F4/01	
EC-FBC	CASA/Nurtanio CN.235-100	033	
EC-FBE	Piper PA-36-375 Pawnee Brave (Damaged 18.6.97)	36-8202002	N2323X
EC-FBF	PZL M-18A Dromader	1Z021-28	EC-4..
			SP-DCM
EC-FBG	PZL M-18A Dromader	1Z021-30	EC-4..
			SP-DCO
EC-FBH	PZL M-18A Dromader (Damaged 21.7.94)	1Z021-22	EC-4..
			SP-DCF
EC-FBI	PZL M-18A Dromader	1Z021-26	EC-4..
			SP-DCK
EC-FBJ	PZL M-18A Dromader (Damaged 26.8.94)	1Z021-25	EC-4..
			SP-DCI
EC-FBK	Piper PA-36-375 Pawnee Brave	36-7802071	N3959E
EC-FBL	Bell 212	30558	EC-553
			LN-OQZ
			(G-BGFE)
			LN-OQZ
			N83079
EC-FBM	Bell 212	30574	EC-552
			LN-ORG
			(LN-OQV)
			N58025
EC-FBN	PZL M-18A Dromader	1Z021-20	SP-DCD
EC-FBO	PZL M-18A Dromader	1Z021-21	SP-DCE
EC-FBT	Robinson R-22 Beta	1593	
EC-FBU	UltraMagic S-105 HAFB	105/15	
EC-FBV	PZL M-18A Dromader	1Z020-27	N2178Q
EC-FBY	Mooney M.20K Model 231	25-0290	N231KU
EC-FBZ	Robinson R-22 Beta	1496	EC-557
EC-FCA	UltraMagic N-77 HAFB	77/54	
EC-FCB	Airbus A.320-211	158	EC-579
			F-WWIC
EC-FCC	Cessna 402B	1013	N113JG
			N87184
EC-FCD	Rolladen-Schneider LS-1D	205	F-CDVI
EC-FCF	SOCATA TB-20 Trinidad	957	F-GKUJ
EC-FCG	Cessna 172M (W/o 9.1.99)	62924	N13665
EC-FCH	Cessna 152	82310	N864WC
			N68474
EC-FCJ	UltraMagic N-77 HAFB	77/44	
EC-FCK	UltraMagic N-77 HAFB	77/62	
EC-FCL	Pitts Aerobatics S-2B (Damaged 20.7.94)	5037	N5353G
EC-FCM	Agusta-Bell 47G-2	267	D-HAVO
			74+25
			AS+067
EC-FCN	Piper PA-38-112 Tomahawk	38-78A0703	EC-FBW
			N2472A
EC-FCO	Bell 206L-3 Long Ranger III	51179	N52CH
EC-FCP	Agusta-Bell 206B Jet Ranger II	8006	G-BPIB
			D-HABI
			SX-HAA
EC-FCR	Cessna 150E	60906	G-AWPX
			5N-AFR
			N11B
			N6206T
EC-FCS	Colt 77A HAFB	1788	
EC-FCT	Continental El Tomcat 6C	CC7.77.7	N9098T
EC-FCU	Boeing 767-3YOER	24999	EC-547
EC-FCV	UltraMagic N-65 HAFB	65/36	
EC-FCX	PZL M-18A Dromader	1Z020-08	N2178F
EC-FCY	Piper PA-28R-201T Turbo Arrow III	28R-7803166	N3329M
EC-FCZ	Grob G.102 Astir CS	1355	D-7394
EC-FDA	Airbus A.320-211	176	EC-581
			F-WWIO
EC-FDB	Airbus A.320-211	173	EC-580
			F-WWIL
EC-FDC	Schleicher ASW-15B	15330	D-2323
EC-FDD	Beech F33A Bonanza	CE-1571	N81728

Regn.	Type	C/n	Prev.Id.
EC-FDE	Piper PA-34-200T Seneca II	34-7970421	N2958Y
EC-FDF	Piper PA-28-181 Archer II	28-8090122	N21AG
			N81038
EC-FDI	Wassmer WA.26P	59	F-CDXR
EC-FDJ	UltraMagic V-65 HAFB	65/38	
EC-FDK	Piper PA-28RT-201 Arrow IV	28R-7918200	N2887W
EC-FDM	PZL M-18A Dromader	1Z022-16	SP-DBV
EC-FDN	PZL M-18A Dromader	1Z022-18	SP-DCY
EC-FDO	PZL M-18A Dromader (W/o 3.2.97)	1Z022-20	SP-DCX
EC-FDP	PZL M-18A Dromader	1Z022-17	SP-DCZ
EC-FDQ	PZL M-18A Dromader	1Z022-21	SP-DCV
EC-FDR	PZL M-18A Dromader	1Z022-22	SP-DAA
EC-FDS	PZL M-18A Dromader	1Z022-23	SP-DAB
EC-FDT	PZL M-18A Dromader	1Z022-24	SP-DAC
EC-FDU	PZL M-18A Dromader	1Z022-25	SP-DAD
EC-FDV	PZL M-18A Dromader	1Z022-26	SP-DAE
EC-FDX	Thunder AX7-77 HAFB	1822	
EC-FDY	Thunder AX7-77 HAFB	1893	
EC-FEA	Piper PA-28R-200 Cherokee Arrow	28R-7435239	N42682
EC-FEC	Cessna 150H	68793	N23208
EC-FED	Cessna 152	83528	N53272
EC-FEE	Boeing 757-236	25053	EC-667
			(G-BSNA)
EC-FEG	Cessna T.210N Turbo Centurion II	64713	N1639U
			N17CD
			N1639U
EC-FEH	Cessna 150L	73157	N92AV
			N5257Q
EC-FEI	Cessna 340	0113	EC-644
			N888CW
			N4569Q
EC-FEJ	Cessna 152	83173	N47118
EC-FEK	Cessna 172RG Cutlass (Damaged 19.2.94)	1088	N9939B
EC-FEL	Agusta-Bell AB.412	25576	EC-607
EC-FES	Cessna 550 Citation II	0678	EC-777
EC-FEU	Robin ATL	109	F-GGHC
EC-FEV	Bell 206B Jet Ranger II	1162	C-GZPX
			N59388
EC-FEX	Robinson R-22 Beta	1293	C-GZAR
EC-FEY	McDonnell-Douglas DC-9-87	53208	EC-634
EC-FEZ	McDonnell-Douglas DC-9-87	53207	EC-633
EC-FFA	McDonnell-Douglas DC-9-87	53209	EC-635
EC-FFD	Cessna 421B Golden Eagle	0485	N421CC
			(N41159)
EC-FFE	Rockwell Commander 690A	11344	N900FT
			N81500
EC-FFF	McDonnell-Douglas DC-9-83	49792	EC-733
			XA-RPH
EC-FFG	Cessna 152	84573	N5384M
EC-FFH	McDonnell-Douglas DC-9-87	53211	EC-637
EC-FFI	McDonnell-Douglas DC-9-87	53210	EC-636
EC-FFJ	Mooney M.20J Model 205	24-3217	EC-665
			N9133N
EC-FFK	Boeing 757-236	24122	EC-744
			G-BNSF
			(D-AOEB)
			G-BNSF
			EC-ELS
			EC-203
			G-BNSF
EC-FFP	Piper PA-28RT-201T Turbo Arrow IV	28R-8131043	N83093
EC-FFQ	Bell 206L-3 Long Ranger III	51463	N6635Y
EC-FFR	UltraMagic N-77 HAFB	77/66	
EC-FFS	UltraMagic V-65 HAFB	65/22	
EC-FFT	UltraMagic V-65 HAFB	65/39	
EC-FFU	UltraMagic N-77 HAFB	77/67	
EC-FFV	Bölkow BO.105S	S-852	D-HFHJ
EC-FFX	Cessna 411	0085	N7385U
EC-FFY	BAe.146 Series 300QT	E-3154	EC-712
			G-TNTF
			G-BRXI
			G-6-154
EC-FFZ	Pilatus Britten-Norman BN-2B-26 Islander	2224	EC-750
			G-BRPD
EC-FGA	UltraMagic V-65 HAFB	65/40	

Regn.	Type	C/n	Prev.Id.
EC-FGB	UltraMagic 180 HAFB	180/03	
EC-FGC	Aérospatiale AS.350B Ecureuil	2250	
EC-FGD	Aérospatiale AS.350B Ecureuil	2245	
EC-FGE	SOCATA TB-10 Tobago (Stored)	1239	F-GKVF
EC-FGF	Cessna 172N	71103	N1708E
EC-FGH	Airbus A.320-211	223	EC-585
			F-WWIA
EC-FGI	Cessna 172N	71255	N2374E
EC-FGJ	Cessna T.210N Turbo Centurion II	64334	N6317Y
EC-FGK	Piper PA-38-112 Tomahawk	38-78A0040	N9329T
EC-FGL	Bell 206L-3 Long Ranger III	51379	N65108
			C-FIPJ
EC-FGM	McDonnell Douglas DC-9-88	53193	EC-751
			N19B
EC-FGO	Piper PA-28-161 Warrior II	28-8216212	N363FT
			N9600N
EC-FGP	Cessna 152	81421	N49972
EC-FGR	Airbus A.320-211	224	EC-586
			F-WWIM
EC-FGS	Aérospatiale AS.350B2 Ecureuil	2537	
EC-FGU	Airbus A.320-211	199	EC-583
			F-WWDI
EC-FGV	Airbus A.320-211	207	EC-584
			F-WWDQ
EC-FGX	Lockheed L.1329 Jetstar 731	5062/12	EC-697
			VR-BHF
			N9739B
			VR-BHF
			N111G
			RP-57
			N2200M
			N679RW
EC-FGY	Colt 180A HAFB	1701	
EC-FHA	Boeing 767-3YOER	25000	EC-548
EC-FHC	Piper PA-32R-300T Turbo Lance (Derelict, noted 12.99)	32R-7887193	N21156
EC-FHD	McDonnell-Douglas DC-9-87	53212	EC-638
EC-FHE	Reims/Cessna F.177RG Cardinal RG	0163	OO-DFV
			PH-AXS
EC-FHF	SOCATA TB-9 Tampico	1317	F-GKVL
EC-FHG	McDonnell Douglas DC-9-88	53194	EC-752
EC-FHH	Piper PA-28R-180 Cherokee Arrow	28R-30537	N505FP
			N4644J
EC-FHI	Aérospatiale SA.319B Alouette III	2369	Chile AF
			N49542
EC-FHJ	Aérospatiale SA.319B Alouette III	2322	Chile:H-60
			N49519
EC-FHK	McDonnell-Douglas DC-9-87	53213	EC-639
EC-FHL	SZD-50-3 Puchacz	B-2042	
EC-FHM	SZD-48-3 Jantar Standard 3	B-1960	
EC-FHO	SZD-51-1 Junior	B-1998	
EC-FHP	SZD-48-3 Jantar Standard 3	B-1962	
EC-FHQ	SZD-51-1 Junior	B-1999	
EC-FHT	Grob G.103 Twin II	3573	D-0651
			D-6434
EC-FHV	Piper PA-28-161 Cherokee Warrior II	28-7816361	N3610M
EC-FHX	Bell 206B Jet Ranger II	3786	G-OCAP
			G-OACS
			G-OCAP
			N18096
EC-FHY	Piper PA-34-200T Seneca II	34-7870184	N9365C
EC-FHZ	Piper PA-28R-200 Arrow	28R-7135127	EC-757
			N8591N
EC-FIA	Airbus A.320-211	240	EC-587
			F-WWIP
EC-FIB	Aérospatiale AS.350B2 Ecureuil	2558	EC-853
EC-FIC	Airbus A.320-211	241	EC-588
			F-WWDD
EC-FID	Piper PA-34-200T Seneca II	34-7970269	N2832Y
EC-FIE	Robinson R-22 Beta	1594	
EC-FIF	Piper PA-34-220T Seneca III	34-8333072	OY-CEJ
			N4300D
			N9639N
EC-FIG	McDonnell Douglas DC-9-88	53195	EC-753
EC-FIH	McDonnell Douglas DC-9-88	53196	EC-754

Regn.	Type	C/n	Prev.Id.
EC-FII	Colt 69A HAFB	1930	
EC-FIJ	Piper PA-18A Super Cub	18-1729	EC-820
			N136AA
			XB-PUU
			N1897A
EC-FIM	SOCATA TB-9 Tampico Club (Stored)	1338	F-GKVN
EC-FIO	Grumman G-159 Gulfstream 1	40	EC-494
			N40AG
			N8ZA
			N6PG
EC-FIP	Britten-Norman BN-2A-26 Islander	623	EC-844
			G-AYJE
			CR-CAS
			G-AYJE
			(EI-AVE)
			G-AYJE
EC-FIR	UltraMagic H-77 HAFB	77/58	
EC-FIS	UltraMagic H-77 HAFB	77/64	
EC-FIT	SZD-51-1 Junior	B-1921	
EC-FIV	Aeritalia/SNIAS ATR-72-201	260	EC-873
			F-WWEH
EC-FIZ	Glaser-Dirks DG-600	6-80S54	
EC-FJA	Aérospatiale SA.319B Alouette III	2297	EC-746
			Chile AF
			N49517
EC-FJB	Beech 95-B55 Baron	TC-1689	EC-741
EC-FJD	UltraMagic V-77 HAFB	77/71	
EC-FJE	McDonnell Douglas DC-9-88	53197	EC-755
EC-FJF	Cessna 414 Chancellor	0523	N4212C
EC-FJG	Piper PA-36-300 Pawnee Brave	36-7660118	TG-SAN
EC-FJH	Rolladen-Schneider LS-7	7159	
EC-FJI	Piper PA-28-181 Cherokee Archer II	28-7890342	N3943M
EC-FJJ	Sikorsky S-61N	61299	EC-862
			LN-ORE
EC-FJL	PZL M-18A Dromader	1Z022-29	SP-DEC
EC-FJM	PZL M-18A Dromader	1Z022-27	SP-DEA
EC-FJN	Beech B95A Travel Air	TD-516	EC-828
			N1570S
EC-FJO	PZL M-18A Dromader	1Z022-28	SP-DEB
EC-FJS	Cessna 172P	74320	N51564
EC-FJT	Cessna 414 Chancellor	0174	N3LS
			N8244Q
EC-FJU	Sportavia-Pützer RF-5B Sperber	1008	EC-650
			D-KILL
			EAF:660
EC-FJV	Aérospatiale AS.350B2 Ecureuil	2580	
EC-FJX	Aeritalia/SNIAS ATR-72-201	267	EC-874
			F-WWEM
EC-FJY	Schempp-Hirth Standard Cirrus	unkn	
EC-FKA	Piper PA-28R-201 Arrow III	28R-7837054	N6136H
EC-FKD	Airbus A.320-211	264	EC-880
			F-WWBN
EC-FKE	UltraMagic S-105 HAFB	105/19	
EC-FKG	Cessna 414A Chancellor	0406	N2690L
			(YV-2123P)
			N2690L
EC-FKK	Cessna 401	0279	EC-EXH(1)
			HI-517
			N32CM
			N2777
			N8431F
EC-FKL	Piaggio P.180 Avanti	1008	EC-619
			I-RAIP
EC-FKM	Piper PA-28RT-201T Turbo Arrow IV	28R-7931094	N2132U
EC-FKN	Piper PA-36-375 Pawnee Brave	36-7802012	N3812E
EC-FKO	Piper PA-28R-180 Arrow	28R-30658	N4936J
EC-FKQ	Aeritalia/SNIAS ATR-72-201	276	EC-935
			F-WWLB
EC-FKR	Piper PA-28R-200 Arrow II	28R-7535254	N1429S
EC-FKU	Air Tractor AT-502	502-0125	N4548Y
EC-FKV	Air Tractor AT-502	502-0162	N1529N
EC-FKX	Air Tractor AT-502	502-0168	N15337
EC-FKY	Thunder AX7-77 HAFB	1806	
EC-FKZ	Ayres S.2R-T34 Turbo Thrush	6032	N4012S
			C-GDHB
			N4012S
EC-FLA	Ayres S.2R-T34 Turbo Thrush	T34-005	N40172
EC-FLB	Robin R.3000/160	154	
EC-FLC	Wassmer WA.28 Espadon	108	F-CEOC
EC-FLF	Boeing 737-36E	25263	EC-705
EC-FLH	American AG-5B Tiger	10091	EC-928
			N1195F
EC-FLI	Piper PA-36-300 Pawnee Brave	36-7760080	N59670
EC-FLJ	Piper PA-36-375 Pawnee Brave	36-7902014	N3979E
EC-FLK	McDonnell-Douglas DC-9-88	53304	EC-946
EC-FLL	SOCATA MS.880B Rallye Club	2556	F-BVZY
EC-FLM	Piper PA-30-160 Twin Comanche	30-657	LV-IMD
			LV-PCK
EC-FLN	McDonnell-Douglas DC-9-88	53303	EC-945
EC-FLO	Reims/Cessna FR.172J Rocket	0402	EC-963
			F-BUMN
EC-FLP	Airbus A.320-211	266	EC-881
			F-WWBO
EC-FLQ	Airbus A.320-211	274	EC-882
			F-WWBR
EC-FLR	Robinson R-22 Beta	2032	EC-951
EC-FLS	UltraMagic V-65 HAFB	65/46	
EC-FLU	Piper PA-28RT-201T Turbo Arrow IV	28R-7931159	EC-969
			N2138Z
EC-FMA	SA.316B Alouette III	2341	HB-XVQ
			5N-ALE
EC-FMB	Robinson R-22 Beta	2045	
EC-FMC	Consolidated PBY-5A Catalina (Coded '72';, stored, Madrid)	2134	EC-940
			C-FIZZ
			CF-IZZ
			F-ZBAZ
			CF-IZZ
			F-ZBAZ
			CF-IZZ
			BuA64064
EC-FMD	SOCATA MS.894E Minerva 220GT	12148	F-BUVD
EC-FME	Aérospatiale AS.350B2 Ecureuil	2448	F-GKLR
EC-FMF	Grob G.102 Astir CS	1479	D-....
			PH-571
EC-FMG	Cameron A-120 HAFB	2645	
EC-FMH	Piper PA-28RT-201T Turbo Arrow IV	28R-7931054	N3003N
EC-FMI	Centrair ASW-20F	20529	OO-ZYT
			BGA3313/FKC
			OO-ZMA
EC-FMK	UltraMagic H-77 HAFB	77/75	
EC-FML	Airbus A.320-211	303	EC-883
			F-WWDT
EC-FMN	Airbus A.320-211	312	EC-884
			F-WWIS
EC-FMR	Robinson R-22 Beta	2047	
EC-FMT	Maule MXT-7-180 Star Rocket	14007C	EC-707
EC-FMU	PZL M-18A Dromader	1Z021-07	SP-FCM
			SP-DCW
EC-FMV	PZL M-18A Dromader	1Z022-30	SP-FCN
EC-FMX	Piper PA-34-200T Seneca II	34-7970396	N606RH
			N50MF
			N9605N
EC-FMZ	Sikorsky S-61N	61361	LN-ORH
EC-FNA	Fournier RF-5-AJI (W/o 28.3.93)	E-001	
EC-FNB	Fournier RF-5-AJI	E-003	
EC-FNC	Fournier RF-5-AJI	E-002	
EC-FND	McDonnell-Douglas DC-9-88	53305	EC-964
EC-FNG	UltraMagic S-130 HAFB	130/03	
EC-FNH	SOCATA MS.893A Rallye Commodore 180	11875	F-BTID
EC-FNJ	UltraMagic V-77 HAFB	77/81	
EC-FNK	UltraMagic S-160 HAFB	160/06	
EC-FNL	UltraMagic F8 Church SS HAFB	F8/01	
EC-FNM	Boeing Stearman PT-17 (Museum)	75-8089	EC-973
			(LV-HDT)
			LQ-HDT
			LV-HDT
			Navy 0325/1-E-74
			BuA38468

Regn.	Type	C/n	Prev.Id.
EC-FNN	MBB-Bölkow BO.105S	S-869	D-HMBL (D-HFNA)
EC-FNO	MBB-Bölkow BO.105S	S-870	D-HMBM (D-HFNB)
EC-FNQ	Hughes 269C	128-0743	G-OSHE N58204
EC-FNR	Airbus A.320-211	323	EC-885 F-WWBM
EC-FNT	Piper PA-28-161 Warrior II	28-7916153	N2243D
EC-FNV	Colt 77A HAFB	1738	
EC-FNY	Grob G.103 Twin Astir (Damaged 9.7.94)	3036	D-4838
EC-FNZ	Grob G.102 Speed Astir	4037	D-4872
EC-FOA	Aérospatiale AS.350B1 Ecureuil	2626	F-WYMK
EC-FOB	UltraMagic M-77 HAFB	77/78	
EC-FOD	Piper PA-36-300 Pawnee Brave	36-7760069	N59660 CF-JLO N69897
EC-FOE	Piper PA-36-375 Pawnee Brave	36-8202015	N2370X
EC-FOF	McDonnell-Douglas DC-9-88	53307	EC-966
EC-FOG	McDonnell-Douglas DC-9-88	53306	EC-965
EC-FOI	Fournier RF-5-AJI	E-0004	
EC-FOJ	Fournier RF-5-AJI	E-0005	
EC-FOK	Beech 35-33 Debonair	CD-617	N260LB N9780Y
EC-FOL	Bell 206L-3 Long Ranger III	51417	N6605R
EC-FOM	UltraMagic M-77 HAFB	77/77	
EC-FON	Mooney M.20J Model 205	24-3260	EC-980
EC-FOO	Cessna 172N	71847	N5409E
EC-FOP	Cessna 152 (Damaged 31.1.94)	84679	N4276R XB-CFH (N6338M)
EC-FOQ	Aérospatiale AS.350B2 Ecureuil	2639	
EC-FOR	American AG-5B Tiger	10099	N100AG
EC-FOS	UltraMagic V-65 HAFB	65/44	
EC-FOV	Cessna 177B Cardinal	02476	N13908
EC-FOX	Aérospatiale SA.365C2 Dauphin 2	5024	EC-136 CC-CGV
EC-FOZ	McDonnell-Douglas DC-9-88	53308	EC-987
EC-FPA	Cessna 421B Golden Eagle	0530	EC-138 N69897 CF-JLO N69897
EC-FPB	Piper PA-38-112 Tomahawk	38-78A0728	N801DV N2519A
EC-FPC	Fairchild-Swearingen SA.226TC Metro IV	TC-408	EC-243 N252AM N1013F
EC-FPD	McDonnell-Douglas DC-9-88	53309	EC-988
EC-FPE	Cessna 152	84717	N4276M XB-CFJ (N6416M)
EC-FPF	SOCATA TBM-700	12	F-OHBD
EC-FPI	Dassault Falcon 900	115	EC-235 F-WWFL
EC-FPJ	McDonnell-Douglas DC-9-88	53310	EC-989
EC-FPK	SOCATA TB-10 Tobago (Damaged 26.1.94)	1482	
EC-FPL	SOCATA TB-10 Tobago	1483	
EC-FPM	SOCATA TB-10 Tobago	1484	
EC-FPN	SOCATA TB-10 Tobago	1485	
EC-FPO	SOCATA TB-10 Tobago	1486	
EC-FPP	SOCATA TB-10 Tobago	1492	
EC-FPQ	Cessna 150L	74733	N7838G
EC-FPR	Piper PA-38-112 Tomahawk	38-79A0811	N2365N
EC-FPS	Aérospatiale SA.315B Lama	2402	HB-XVN N62338
EC-FPT	UltraMagic H-42 HAFB	42/01	
EC-FPU	UltraMagic H-42 HAFB	"245"	
EC-FPV	UltraMagic N-250 HAFB	250/01	
EC-FPX	Grob G.102 Astir CS 77	1620	D-7461
EC-FPY	UltraMagic M-77 HAFB	77/84	
EC-FQA	Cessna 337G Super Skymaster	01713	N53575
EC-FQC	Mudry CAP.10B (W/o 22.3.97)	205	F-GDTL
EC-FQD	Cessna 172P	75140	N55239
EC-FQE	Cessna 172N (Possibly wfu)	73515	N4968G
EC-FQF	UltraMagic M-65 HAFB	65/43	
EC-FQG	UltraMagic N-180 HAFB	180/04	
EC-FQH	Aérospatiale AS.350B2 Ecureuil	2674	
EC-FQI	Aerostatiale SA.316B Alouette III	1926	I-BYCS F-BYCS RAN-12
EC-FQJ	Agusta A.109C	7664	N1YU
EC-FQK	Cessna 177B Cardinal	02738	N1496C
EC-FQL	Cessna 177RG Cardinal RG	0515	EC-157 N2115Q
EC-FQM	Robinson R-22 Beta	2206	EC-259
EC-FQN	American AG-5B Tiger	10132	EC-278
EC-FQO	Bell 205A	30011	EC-554 N43162 IDFAF N4007G
EC-FQR	Cessna R.172K Hawk XP	3167	N758KX
EC-FQS	Cessna 150L	74851	N10421 (N45RG) N10421
EC-FQT	Grob G.103 Twin Astir	3116	D-7783
EC-FQU	Bölkow Phoebus C	912	F-CDOH
EC-FQV	Hughes 269C	35-0406	N7401F
EC-FQX	Lockheed L.1329-25 Jetstar II	5202	EC-232 N20GB N333KN N717X N717 N5528L
EC-FQY	Airbus A.320-211	356	EC-886 F-WWIH
EC-FQZ	UltraMagic S-160 HAFB	160/10	
EC-FRA	Westland-Bell 47G3B1	WA/396	D-HAFL XT237
EC-FRB	Aviat Pitts S-2B	5263	N473
EC-FRC	UltraMagic M-105 HAFB	105/23	
EC-FRD	Robinson R-22 Beta	0675	G-BNVF
EC-FRE	Piper PA-38-112 Tomahawk	38-79A0223	N2544C
EC-FRF	Schempp-Hirth Standard Cirrus	661	D-2286
EC-FRH	UltraMagic V-65 HAFB	65/41	
EC-FRI	UltraMagic S-160 HAFB	160/11	
EC-FRJ	Piper PA-28-140 Cherokee	28-7325592	EC-289 N56255
EC-FRK	Piper PA-28-140 Cherokee	28-7125264	EC-291 N464FL
EC-FRL	Piper PA-28R-180 Cherokee Arrow (Damaged 23.3.97)	28R-31044	N7643J
EC-FRM	PZL M-18 Dromader	1Z013-02	YN-BZJ
EC-FRN	PZL M-18 Dromader	1Z012-19	YN-CAE
EC-FRO	Robinson R-22 Beta	2234	N2351P
EC-FRQ	Piper PA-28-140 Cherokee	28-26659	EC-302 N5828U
EC-FRS	Bell 206L-1 Long Ranger II	45412	HK-3166X C-GMFQ N1081Y
EC-FRT	Colt 77A HAFB	2302	
EC-FRU	Bell 206B Jet Ranger II	4268	
EC-FRV	Grumman G.1159 Gulfstream II	237	EC-363 XA-SDM XA-BAL XA-MIX N25BH N816GA
EC-FRX	Hughes 369D	116-0029D	EC-316 N4320K G-BESS
EC-FRY	Bell 206L-3 Long Ranger III	51330	N43904 JA9859
EC-FSD	Cessna TR.182 Turbo Skylane RG	01004	N739TV
EC-FSE	Robinson R-22 Beta	0963	G-BPOF
EC-FSF	Piper PA-31P-425 Pressurized Navajo	31P-7730012	N821BJ N277BW N82608
EC-FSG	CASA I-131E Jungmann	2124	E3B-544
EC-FSH	CASA I-131E Jungmann	2220	E3B-601
EC-FSI	CASA I-131E Jungmann	2164	E3B-548

Regn.	Type	C/n	Prev.Id.
EC-FSK	SOCATA TB-10 Tobago	1555	
EC-FSL	SOCATA TB-10 Tobago	1556	
EC-FSM	SOCATA TB-10 Tobago	1557	
EC-FSN	SOCATA TB-10 Tobago	1559	
EC-FSO	SOCATA TB-10 Tobago	1560	
EC-FSP	SOCATA TB-10 Tobago	1561	
EC-FSQ	Robinson R-22 Beta	2097	EC-986
EC-FSR	Cessna 172M	62684	N13341
EC-FSS	CASA I-131E Jungmann	2231	E3B-319
EC-FSU	Cessna T.210N Turbo Centurion II	63741	N5404C
EC-FSV	Fairchild-Swearingen SA.227AC Metro IV	AC-461B	EC-437
			N120FA
			F-GGLF
			OY-CHB
			N222JC
			N109TA
EC-FTA	Cessna 414 Chancellor	0647	N414TJ
	(Damaged 14.2.97)		N69976
EC-FTB	Sikorsky S-61N	61741	LN-OSY
			OY-HDS
			LN-OSY
EC-FTC	American AG-5B Tiger	10148	EC-311
EC-FTD	SOCATA TB-10 Tobago *(W/o 20.5.97)*	1565	
EC-FTE	SOCATA TB-10 Tobago	1566	
EC-FTF	SOCATA TB-10 Tobago *(Dam. 13.2.97)*	1567	EC-395
EC-FTG	SOCATA TB-10 Tobago	1570	
EC-FTH	SOCATA TB-10 Tobago	1571	
EC-FTI	SOCATA TB-10 Tobago	1572	
EC-FTJ	SOCATA TB-10 Tobago	1573	
EC-FTK	SOCATA TB-10 Tobago	1574	
EC-FTM	Bell 206L-4 Long Ranger IV	52024	
EC-FTN	Bell 412	36006	EC-329
			C-GOPP
EC-FTO	UltraMagic F9 HAFB	F9/01	
EC-FTP	PZL M-18A Dromader	1Z023-27	SP-DDG
EC-FTQ	PZL M-18A Dromader	1Z023-28	SP-DDH
EC-FTR	Boeing 757-256	26239	EC-420
EC-FTS	McDonnell-Douglas DC-9-83	49621	EC-479
			EC-EJU
			EC-149
EC-FTU	McDonnell-Douglas DC-9-83	49672	EC-487
			EC-EJQ
			EC-150
EC-FTX	Aérospatiale AS.355N Ecureuil 2	5550	F-WYMU
EC-FTY	Robin HR.200/120B	251	
EC-FTZ	CASA I-131E Jungmann	2170	E3B-556
EC-FUC	American AG-5B Tiger	10169	EC-488
EC-FUD	UltraMagic N-180 HAFB	180/06	
EC-FUE	UltraMagic S-90 HAFB	90/07	
EC-FUF	Aérospatiale AS.350B Ecureuil	2596	EC-427
			(D-HFSC)
EC-FUG	Piper PA-28-140 Cherokee	28-21412	N4657R
EC-FUH	Aérospatiale AS.355N Ecureuil 2	5554	F-WYMB
EC-FUI	UltraMagic M-77 HAFB	77/89	
EC-FUJ	Beech 65-B80 Queen Air	LD-408	EC-508
			N5130Q
			CF-CGV
EC-FUK	UltraMagic S-160 HAFB	160/12	
EC-FUN	UltraMagic M-105 HAFB	105/24	
EC-FUO	UltraMagic M-65 HAFB	65/52	
EC-FUP	UltraMagic M-65 HAFB	65/47	
EC-FUQ	UltraMagic M-77 HAFB	77/92	
EC-FUR	Rockwell Commander 112TC	13085	N4593W
EC-FUS	Cameron DP-70 Hot Air Airship	1130	G-BMEZ
EC-FUU	CASA I-131E Jungmann	2167	E3B-554
EC-FUX	Fairchild-Swearingen SA.226AT Merlin IVA	AT-038	EC-509
			OO-JPN
			N5FJ
			SAAF-12
			N5360M
EC-FUY	Agusta A.109C	7670	EC-453
			N1TV
EC-FUZ	Piper PA-28-140 Cherokee	28-22772	G-AVGB
			N11C
EC-FVD	UltraMagic S-130 HAFB	130/04	

Regn.	Type	C/n	Prev.Id.
EC-FVE	UltraMagic M-77 HAFB	77/93	
EC-FVF	UltraMagic M-77 HAFB	77/94	
EC-FVG	SOCATA MS.893A Rallye Commodore 180	11636	F-BSFI
EC-FVH	Thunder AX7-77A HAFB	2519	
EC-FVI	Rolladen-Schneider LS-6C	6319	
EC-FVK	Mudry CAP.10B	264	EC-391
EC-FVL	UltraMagic M-77 HAFB	77/97	
EC-FVN	Robinson R-22 Beta	0606	EC-562
			G-DLTI
			N2540J
EC-FVO	Sikorsky S-61N	61756	EC-575
			LN-OSX
EC-FVP	Cessna 172N	70627	N739LL
EC-FVQ	UltraMagic S-105 HAFB	105/25	
EC-FVR	McDonnell-Douglas DC-9-83	49574	EC-591
			N574PJ
			EC-EFU
			EC-348
			EC-EFU
EC-FVS	Bell 206B Jet Ranger II	4012	N323BH
			C-FDBJ
EC-FVY	BAe.146 Series 200QT	E-2117	EC-615
			G-TNTO
			F-GTNT
			G-BPBS
EC-FVZ	SZD-50-3 Puchacz	B-2087	
EC-FXA	McDonnell-Douglas DC-9-83	49938	EC-592
			SE-DPU
			VH-LNH
			XA-RTK
EC-FXB	Airbus A.310-324	638	EC-640
			VR-BOU
			EC-FNI
			EC-117
			F-WWCK
EC-FXC	UltraMagic S-160 HAFB	160/13	
EC-FXE	Schleicher K7 Rhönadler	930	D-6310
EC-FXF	UltraMagic M-77 HAFB	77/57	
EC-FXG	Zlin Z.50LS	0031	D-EMUJ
EC-FXH	Aérospatiale AS.350B2 Ecureuil	2638	(OY-HDO)
EC-FXI	McDonnell-Douglas DC-9-83	49630	EC-638
			EC-EPL
			EC-216
EC-FXK	UltraMagic F-10 HAFB	F-10/01	
EC-FXL	Robinson R-22 Beta	0938	EC-570
			I-HNTA
EC-FXM	UltraMagic M-77 HAFB	77/86	
EC-FXN	Consolidated PBY-6A Catalina	2029	CC-CNP
			CC-CNG
			N9555C
			BuA46665
EC-FXO	SA.319B Alouette III	2227	HD.16-5
			HA.16-5
			Z.16-5/ET352
EC-FXP	Boeing 737-4Y0	24706	EC-644
			9M-MJD
EC-FXQ	Boeing 737-4Y0	24707	EC-645
			9M-MJE
EC-FXR	Cessna 152	85137	EC-519
			N6112Q
EC-FXS	Piper PA-28-161 Warrior II	28-8316003	EC-518
			N82811
EC-FXT	Cessna 152	79718	EC-....
	(Badly damaged 3.4.97)		N757GA
EC-FXU	Boeing 757-256	26240	EC-616
			EC-FUA
			EC-421
EC-FXV	Boeing 757-256	26241	EC-617
			EC-FUB
			EC-422
EC-FXY	McDonnell-Douglas DC-9-83	49627	EC-646
			EC-EOZ
			EC-215

Regn.	Type	C/n	Prev.Id.
EC-FXZ	Beech F33A Bonanza	CE-521	EC-683 ?
			E.24B-32
			EC-CLI
EC-FYA	Agusta-Bell 206B Jet Ranger II	8647	I-DACF
EC-FYD	UltraMagic S-90 HAFB	90/90	
EC-FYH	UltraMagic M-105 HAFB	105/27	
EC-FYI	SA.319B Alouette III	2256	HD.16-7
			Z.16-7
			EC-STO
EC-FYJ	Boeing 757-256	26242	EC-608
			N35030
EC-FYK	Boeing 757-256	26243	EC-609
EC-FYM	Boeing 757-256	26245	EC-611
EC-FYN	Boeing 757-256	26246	EC-612
EC-FYO	Beech F33A Bonanza	CE-532	EC-688 ?
			E.24B-37
			EC-CLN
EC-FYP	Cessna 172RG Cutlass	0770	F-GIHS
			N6547V
EC-FYQ	UltraMagic N-180 HAFB	180/07	
EC-FYR	UltraMagic S-105 HAFB	105/26	
EC-FYS	UltraMagic M-77 HAFB	77/96	
EC-FYT	Robin ATL	35	EC-568
			F-GFOK
			F-WFOK
EC-FYU	Cessna 172N	68333	N733JQ
EC-FYV	MBB-Bölkow BO.105CBS-5 (Catalunya "01")	S-896	D-HMBT(5)
EC-FYX	Thunder AX7-77A HAFB	2590	
EC-FZB	Fairchild-Swearingen SA.226TC Metro	TC-221	EC-666
			OO-JPI
EC-FZC	McDonnell-Douglas DC-9-83	49790	EC-742
			EC-ESJ
			EC-307
EC-FZD	Cessna 172RG Cutlass	0187	N6498R
EC-FZE	BAe.146 Series 200QT	E-2105	EC-719
			G-TNTP
			HA-TAB
			G-BOMI
			G-5-105
EC-FZF	PZL M-18A Dromader	1Z015-14	EC-684
			D-FOHY
			DDR-TKY
EC-FZG	PZL M-18A Dromader	1Z019-26	EC-...
			D-FOLR
			DDR-TLR
EC-FZI	Cessna 172N	71135	N2056E
EC-FZJ	Sikorsky S-61N	61758	EC-717
			LN-OQE(2)
EC-FZK	Fournier RF-5-AJI	E-007	
EC-FZL	Fournier RF-5-AJI	E-008	
EC-FZM	Fournier RF-5-AJI	E-009	
EC-FZN	Colt 120A HAFB	2560	
EC-FZO	Cessna 152	82427	N69005
EC-FZP	Cessna 525 CitationJet	0065	EC-704
			N2649Y
EC-FZR	UltraMagic V-77 HAFB	77/80	
EC-FZS	Beech F33A Bonanza	CE-525	EC-621
			EC-CLJ
			E24B-33
EC-FZU	Tango II	3901	
EC-FZV	Rans S-12 Airaile	S-12-119	
EC-FZY	Rolladen-Schneider LS-3A	3230	D-4290
EC-FZZ	Boeing 737-4Y0	24686	EC-772
			9M-MJH
			(G-OOAA)
EC-GAA	Bell 205A-1	30134	EC-756
			D-HOEB
			N58087
EC-GAB	PZL M-18A Dromader	1Z024-02	SP-DDL
EC-GAC	UltraMagic M-77 HAFB	77/106	
EC-GAG	Boeing 747-256	20137	EC-765
			EC-BRQ
			EC-287
			F-GHPC
			EC-BRQ

Regn.	Type	C/n	Prev.Id.
EC-GAH	PZL M-18A Dromader	1Z020-01	D-FOLU
			DDR-TLU
EC-GAI	PZL M-18A Dromader	1Z021-16	D-FOMJ
	(Identity officially quoted as "3599")		DDR-TMJ
EC-GAJ	SA.319B Alouette III	2212	HD.16-4
			HA.16-4
			Z.16-4
EC-GAK	Cessna 172N	69089	N734SZ
EC-GAL	Colt 69A HAFB	1867	
EC-GAM	Glasflügel H201B Standard Libelle	430	F-CEBP
EC-GAN	Fairchild-Swearingen SA.226TC Metro II	TC-203	EC-701
			OY-BYH
			N5303M
EC-GAO	Aérospatiale SA.316B Alouette III	2324	EC-801
			F-WQDG
			Rwanda:10K04
EC-GAQ	PZL M-18A Dromader	1Z021-08	D-FOMB
			DDR-TMB
EC-GAR	PZL M-18A Dromader	1Z019-27	D-FOLS
			DDR-TLS
EC-GAS	Bell 205A-1	30081	EC-844
			F-GKCD
			VH-NGN
			C-GFHQ
			VH-NSN
			C-GFHQ
			VH-UHN
EC-GAT	McDonnell-Douglas DC-9-83	49709	EC-835
			F-GGMC
			N6203D
EC-GAU	Robinson R-22	0015	EC-824
			N9017K
EC-GAV	Piper PA-31-310 Navajo	31-579	EC-411
			E.18-1
			N6641L
EC-GAX	Cessna 177RG Cardinal RG	0038	N8038G
EC-GAY	Cessna 172N	70738	N739RE
EC-GAZ	Boeing 737-4Y0	24906	EC-850
			9M-MJO
EC-GBA	McDonnell-Douglas DC-9-83	49626	EC-805
			EI-CGS
			EC-EMG
			EC-223
			N2606Z
EC-GBB	Beech 200 Super King Air	BB-182	EC-727
			N922JB
			N155BT
			N155PT
EC-GBC	Fournier RF-5-AJI	E-010	
EC-GBD	SE.3130 Alouette II	1916	F-GJLN
			V-64
EC-GBE	Agusta-Bell AB.412	25503	EC-757
			Fv.11339
			I-MGPE
EC-GBF	Convair CV-580	458	EC-830
			OO-DHB
			(OO-VGB)
			N537SA
			N583PL
			N5829
			N8421H
			VH-BZH
EC-GBG	Fokker F.27-050	20109	EC-868
			D-AFKH
			(VH-FND)
			PH-EXR
			(PH-WDL)
			PH-EXR
EC-GBH	Fokker F.27-050	20159	EC-869
			D-AFKI
			PH-LBT
			(ST-ALP)
			PH-EXC

Regn.	Type	C/n	Prev.Id.
EC-GBI	Fairchild-Swearingen SA.226AT Merlin IV	AT-041	EC-867 / OO-JPA / N6FJ / SAAF-14 / N5362M
EC-GBL	Piper PA-28-161 Warrior II	2816113	N9252N
EC-GBM	Piper PA-28-161 Warrior II	2816114	N92516
EC-GBN	Boeing 737-4Y0	24912	EC-851 / 9M-MJQ / N1786B
EC-GBO	Piper PA-28-161 Warrior II	2816115	N9252K
EC-GBP	Canadair CL.215-1A10	1031	EC-957 / UD.13-3
EC-GBQ	Canadair CL.215-1A10	1033	EC-958 / UD.13-5
EC-GBR	Canadair CL.215-1A10	1051	EC-983 / UD.13-11
EC-GBS	Canadair CL.215-1A10	1052	EC-984 / UD.13-12
EC-GBT	Canadair CL.215-1A10	1054	EC-985 / UD.13-14
EC-GBX	Boeing 757-236	25597	EC-897 / D-AMUL / EC-FLY / EC-957
EC-GBZ	Thunder AX7-77 HAFB	3464	
EC-GCA	Boeing 757-236	22185	EC-845 / N27OAE / YV-78C / G-BPGW / EC-EOK / EC-265 / G-BPGW / N8294V / (G-BNEP) / (G-BIKO)
EC-GCB	Boeing 757-236	23227	EC-847 / N271AE / YV-77C / G-BLVH / (G-BNHG) / (G-CJIG)
EC-GCC	UltraMagic V-77 HAFB	77/87	
EC-GCD	UltraMagic M-77 HAFB	77/110	
EC-GCE	CASA I-131E Jungmann	2161	E3B-545
EC-GCF	SOCATA MS.892A Rallye Commodore 150	10591	(D-EAGW) / OO-ADY / F-BOVB
EC-GCI	Boeing 727-256	20598	EC-CBD / N1788B
EC-GCJ	Boeing 727-256	20602	EC-CBH
EC-GCK	Boeing 727-256	20603	EC-CBI / N1788B
EC-GCL	Boeing 727-256	20604	EC-CBJ
EC-GCM	Boeing 727-256	20606	EC-CBL / EC-326 / LV-VFL / EC-CBL / N1788B
EC-GCN	Bell 206B Jet Ranger II	2545	G-WOSP / N18096
EC-GCO	PZL-104 Wilga 80	CF21940948	EC-803
EC-GCP	Beech F33A Bonanza	CE-530	EC-CLL / E.24B-35
EC-GCQ	Agusta A.109C	7665	EC-895 / N1ZL
EC-GCU	Bell 206L-LT Twin Ranger	52105	EC-843 / N4261U
EC-GCV	McDonnell-Douglas DC-9-82	53165	EC-894 / N834AI
EC-GCX	Cessna 177RG Cardinal RG	0567	N2167Q

Regn.	Type	C/n	Prev.Id.
EC-GCZ	Aérospatiale SA.365C2 Dauphin 2	5037	EC-887 / PH-SSH / EC-DVZ / PH-SSH / G-BLFN / PH-SSH / 5N-ALI / PH-SSH / (PH-BOL) / F-WXFG
EC-GDB	Agusta-Bell 206B Jet Ranger II	8095	F-GJAU / F-OGUL / F-GAJL / G-AWRV
EC-GDC	Piper PA-28-140 Cherokee	28-7125346	EC-718 / N521FL
EC-GDD	Fokker F.27-050	20160	EC-871 / D-AFKJ / PH-EXD / (PH-LBV) / (ST-ALR) / PH-EXD
EC-GDE	Agusta-Bell AB.412	25502	EC-863 / VR-BQC / G-BVYN / I-INGO
EC-GDF	Piper PA-28R-201T Arrow IV	28R-7803097	YV-1431P
EC-GDG	Fairchild-Swearingen SA.226TC Metro III (W/o 18.2.98)	TC-220	EC-930 / N220AT / C-GFAP / N443JA / N5370M
EC-GDH	Piper PA-28-151 Cherokee Warrior	28-7415142	EC-913 / N41227
EC-GDI	Air Tractor AT-802 (W/o 18.5.97)	802-0019	EC-882 ? / N61254
EC-GDJ	Bell UH-1H (205)	5320	N82818 / 66-00837
EC-GDK	Bell UH-1H (205)	5639	N82814 / 66-01156
EC-GDL	Aérospatiale AS.350B2 Ecureuil	2879	
EC-GDM	Bell UH-1H (205)	5398	N205UD / 66-00915
EC-GDN	Bell UH-1H (205)	5721	N6190P / 66-16027
EC-GDO	Bell UH-1H (205)	8800	N205UE / 66-16606
EC-GDP	Aérospatiale AS.350B2 Ecureuil	2886	
EC-GDQ	UltraMagic V-90 HAFB	90/13	
EC-GDR	Fairchild-Swearingen SA.226AT Merlin IV	AT-074	EC-702 / OY-CHA / N1006Y / C-GDEF / N1006Y
EC-GDS	Air Tractor AT-802	802-0018	EC-881 ? / N61246
EC-GDT	Robinson R-22 Beta	2056	G-BWMR
EC-GDU	Beech F33A Bonanza	CE-574	EC-COW / E.24B-42
EC-GDV	Fairchild-Swearingen SA.226AT Merlin IV	AT-043	EC-975 / F-GGAF / N814MM / N5371M / ZS-LID / SAAF-15 / N5371M
EC-GDX	Eipper Quicksilver MXL-II	1691	
EC-GDY	Convair CV-580	25	EC-943 / OO-DHG / N73117
EC-GDZ	Cessna 337G Skymaster (W/o 6.96)	01687	EC-852 / N53532
EC-GEB	Cessna 152	83355	EC-914 / N48642
EC-GEC	Cessna 152	80337	N24720

Regn.	Type	C/n	Prev.Id.
EC-GED	Cessna 152 *(W/o 6.99)*	83461	N625CA
EC-GEG	Piper PA-28-161 Warrior II	28-8516003	N4377F
			(EC-...)
			N4377F
EC-GEH	Bell 206B Jet Ranger II	2201	EC-972
			VH-HJG
			N995KP
			N2276K
			N77AH
EC-GEI	UltraMagic V-77 HAFB	77/112	
EC-GEJ	CASA/Nurtanio CN.235-200QC	C-041	EC-996
			N235CA
EC-GEK	UltraMagic S-90 HAFB	90/10	
EC-GEL	UltraMagic M-77 HAFB	77/101	
EC-GEM	Cameron Beer-Mug SS Balloon	2739	
EC-GEN	Fairchild-Swearingen SA.227AC Metro III	AC-688	EC-126
			N727C
			N688NE
			N2701X
EC-GEQ	Boeing 737-3Y0	23750	EC-135
			PT-TED
EC-GER	Wassmer WA.26P Squale	74	F-CDZI
EC-GES	Cessna 172RG Cutlass RG	0008	N4650R
EC-GET	Mainair Gemini/Flash IIA	78302907 W5	
EC-GEU	Boeing 737-3Y0	23808	EC-136
			PT-TEE
			(C-....)
EC-GEV	Tango II	6871	
EC-GEX	UltraMagic N-180 HAFB	180/04	
EC-GEY	Hispano HA.200 Saeta	20/79	E14A-...
EC-GEZ	Eipper Quicksilver MX-Sprint IIR	447	
EC-GFA	UltraMagic S-130 HAFB	130/08	
EC-GFB	UltraMagic M-77 HAFB	77/115	
EC-GFC	UltraMagic M-105 HAFB	105/32	EC-025
EC-GFD	Rolladen-Schneider LS-6C	6251	SE-UKM
EC-GFF	UltraMagic F-13 HAFB	F13/01	
EC-GFG	Cessna 172K	58536	G-BVBC
			N84587
EC-GFH	Piper PA-28-161 Cherokee Warrior II	28-7716101	G-MERV
			N2364Q
EC-GFI	UltraMagic H-77 HAFB	77/113	
EC-GFK	Fairchild-Swearingen SA.226AT Merlin IV	AT-062	EC-125
			OY-FFD
			N548SM
			OY-FFD
			(OY-NPB)
			(OO-VGD)
			YU-ALF
			D-IFAD
			(F-GBBB)
			D-IFAD
			N5456M
			OY-HFN
EC-GFL	Robinson R-22 Beta	1949	
EC-GFM	SAAB-Scania 340B	315	EC-158
			F-GMVQ
			SE-KXB
			SE-C15
EC-GFN	Schleicher ASH-26E	26070	
EC-GFO	Robin HR.200/120B	296	F-WZZZ
EC-GFP	Fokker F.27-050	20239	EC-152
			PH-JXN
			D-AFKW
			PH-JXN
EC-GFQ	PZL M-18A Dromader	1Z025-25	N9279F
EC-GFR	PZL M-18A Dromader	1Z025-26	N81458
EC-GFS	Reims/Cessna F.172H	0635	D-EFHD
EC-GFT	Piper PA-28-140 Cherokee	28-24823	N1899J
EC-GFU	Boeing 737-3Y0	24256	EC-204
	(Intended for France as F-GNFU .00)		EC-FVJ
			EC-542
			G-MONM
EC-GFV	UltraMagic F-12 HAFB	F12/01	
EC-GFX	Air Tractor AT-802	802-0027	N6065G
EC-GFZ	UltraMagic N-180 HAFB	180/11	
EC-GGA	Eipper Quicksilver MX-Sprint II	238	
EC-GGB	Douglas DC-7C	45112	EC-888
			N90802
			G-AOIB
EC-GGC	Douglas DC-7C	45215	EC-889
			N9734Z
			SE-CCF
EC-GGD	Stemme S-10V	14-023	D-KGDF(2)
EC-GGF	Piper PA-23-250 Aztec E	27-4810	E.19-4
			N14240
EC-GGG	Rans S-6ES Coyote II	S-6A-106	
EC-GGH	UltraMagic H-77 HAFB	77/121	
EC-GGI	Robinson R-44 Astro	0209	G-BWIF
EC-GGJ	Colt 69A HAFB	3767	EC-191
EC-GGL	Glaser-Dirks DG-200/17C	2-109CL02	D-3799
EC-GGM	Reims/Cessna F.150L	1107	F-BVSH
EC-GGO	Boeing 737-3M8	24376	EC-238
			N681MA
			OO-LTD
			(F-GKTF)
			OO-LTD
			(OO-LTF)
EC-GGP	UltraMagic M-77 HAFB	77/88	
EC-GGQ	Air Tractor AT-802	802-0028	N60660
EC-GGR	UltraMagic N-180 HAFB	180/09	
EC-GGS	Airbus A.340-313	125	EC-154
			F-WWJB
EC-GGT	Mooney M.20J Model 205	24-3076	G-BPGA
EC-GGU	Air Création Safari GT BI Mild 16	9506084	
EC-GGV	McDonnell-Douglas DC-9-83	49791	EC-166
			EC-FVX
			EC-546
			VR-BMJ
			F-ODTN
EC-GGY	Air Tractor AT-802	802-0031	N6097U
EC-GHA	Piper PA-44-180T Turbo Seminole	44-8107006	N9153D
			EC-720
			N83SM
			N8231L
EC-GHB	Fokker F.27-050	20257	EC-282
			PH-KXY
			D-AFFA
			PH-KXY
EC-GHC	Fokker F.27-050	20262	EC-287
			PH-KXX
			D-AFFD
			PH-KXX
EC-GHD	Boeing 737-3M8	25071	EC-262
			N682MA
			OO-LTN
EC-GHE	McDonnell-Douglas DC-9-83	49398	EC-245
			HB-IUK
			SE-DPS
			EI-CBE
			EC-EXX
			EC-479
			EI-CBE
			G-PATA
			(G-LOGI)
EC-GHG	UltraMagic M-105 HAFB	105/35	
EC-GHH	McDonnell-Douglas DC-9-83	49578	EC-291
			EC-FSZ
			EC-390
			SE-DHD
EC-GHI	Air Tractor AT-502B	502B-0360	N6095Z
EC-GHL	Air Tractor AT-802	802-0032	N61289
EC-GHM	Boeing 767-204	24457	EC-276
			G-BPFV
EC-GHN	Convair CV-580	186	EC-255
			OO-DHH
			N73156
EC-GHP	Bell 212	30557	EC-FYB
			N83079
			VH-HVX
			ZK-HBK
			LN-OQY, (G-BHAG), LN-OQY, N83072

Regn.	Type	C/n	Prev.Id.
EC-GHQ	UltraMagic M-77 HAFB	77/117	
EC-GHR	Robinson R-22B2 Beta	2598	
EC-GHS	Partenavia P.68 Observer	329-20-OB	G-OBSV
EC-GHU	Aero Commander 680	483-153	EC-252
			D-IDIH
EC-GHV	Christen Pitts S-2B	5048	N5326C
EC-GHX	Airbus A.340-313	134	EC-155
			F-WWJR
EC-GHY	Aérospatiale AS.355F1 Ecureuil 2	5089	N866MP
EC-GHZ	Beech 200 Super King Air	BB-555	D-IFOR
EC-GIC	Bell 212	30775	LN-OQD
EC-GID	Bell 212	31155	OY-HCU
EC-GIE	Cessna 525 CitationJet	0133	EC-261
			N52038
EC-GIF	Bell 212	30887	C-GZII
EC-GIG	Robinson R-22 Beta	1200	N3176S
			JA7785
			N8054U
EC-GIH	UltraMagic S-90 HAFB	90/19	
EC-GII	Robinson R-22 Beta	2348	HA-MIP
			N83090
EC-GIJ	Beech 65-B90 King Air	LJ-382	F-WQCC
			F-GLED
			EC-860
			N25DC
			N922K
EC-GIK	Piper PA-38-112 Tomahawk	38-81A0166	N91331
	(Damaged 17.3.97)		
EC-GIM	Tango II-GT	8861	
EC-GIN	CASA I-131E Jungmann	2208	E38-591
EC-GIO	CASA I-131E Jungmann	2153	E38-542
EC-GIP	CASA I-131E Jungmann	2171	E38-557 ?
EC-GIQ	CASA I-131E Jungmann	2192	E38-573
EC-GIR	CASA I-131E Jungmann	2239	E38-620
EC-GIS	CASA I-131E Jungmann	2229	E38-610
EC-GIT	CASA I-131E Jungmann	2245	E38-626
EC-GIU	Bell UH-1H (205)	5265	N12UH
			66-00782
EC-GIV	Bell UH-1H (205)	12481	N11UH
			70-15871
EC-GIX	Cameron C-80 HAFB	3573	
EC-GIY	Aérospatiale AS.350B Ecureuil	2175	OY-HEP
EC-GIZ	Bell UH-1H (205)	5631	N6738B
			66-01148
EC-GJA	Bell UH-1H (205)	5387	N205UD
			N8154L
			66-904
EC-GJB	Bell UH-1H (205)	9262	N8154S
			66-17068
EC-GJE	Aérospatiale SA.365N1 Dauphin 2	6308	LX-HUM
			F-GLHU
			EC-EKQ
			EC-194
			G-BOKC
EC-GJG	Robin R.1180TD Aiglon	246	F-GCRB
EC-GJH	Robin R.1180TD Aiglon	255	F-GCRK
EC-GJI	Fokker F.27-050	20258	EC-284
			PH-KXU
			D-AFFB
			PH-KXU
EC-GJL	Bell UH-1H(205)	unkn	"66-4010"
EC-GJJ	Reims/Cessna F.172L	0823	D-ECQM
EC-GJL	Agusta-Bell 205A	4010	HD.10A-5
			Z.10-5
			EC-SSH
			EC-BDF-R
EC-GJM	Fairchild-Swearingen SA.227BC Metro	BC-772B	EC-307
			N702AM
			XA-RWK
			N2756T
EC-GJN	Tango II-GT	2883	
EC-GJO	Tango II-GT	2895	
EC-GJP	Robinson R-44 Astro	0244	
EC-GJQ	Air Création Safari GT BI XP15	494003	
EC-GJR	Rans S-12XL Airaile	S-12-155	

Regn.	Type	C/n	Prev.Id.
EC-GJS	Beech F33A Bonanza	CE-576	E24B-43
			EC-CON
EC-GJT	Airbus A.340-313	145	EC-156
			F-WWJF
EC-GJX	Fairchild-Swearingen SA.227DC Metro IV	DC-855B	N454LA
			N3026U
EC-GJY	Fokker F.27-050	20265	D-AFFH
			PH-LXF
			(9M-MGL)
EC-GJZ	Swearingen SA.26AT Merlin IIB	T26-149	N829HS
			N329HS
			N642PB
			N642RB
			N193G
			N25AC
EC-GKA	Piper PA-23-250 Aztec	27-48..	Sp.AF E.18-?
	(Either c/n 27-4801 ex E.18-1 or c/n 27-4807 ex E.18-2)		
EC-GKB	Schempp-Hirth Nimbus 3DM	17/40	F-CFUL
			D-KFUL
EC-GKC	Tango II	5894	
EC-GKD	Cessna 210M Centurion	61892	N732YY
EC-GKE	Fokker F.27-050	20263	D-AFFG
			PH-LXE
EC-GKF	McDonnell-Douglas DC-9-87	49389	SE-DHG
			SX-BAW
			SE-DHG
			N287MD
EC-GKG	McDonnell-Douglas DC-9-87	49706	SE-DHI
			SX-BAV
			SE-DHI
EC-GKH	Convair CV-580	135	OO-DHD
			N536SA
			N582PL
			N5812
			N7600
			CF-ECS
			PH-CGK
			PJ-CVB
EC-GKK	Fairchild-Swearingen SA.227AC Metro IV	unkn	
EC-GKN	UltraMagic M-77 HAFB	77/122	
EC-GKO	UltraMagic H-77 HAFB	77/124	
EC-GKP	Schleicher ASW-20C/TOP	20748	D-KCAS(3)
			D-8859
EC-GKQ	UltraMagic H-77 HAFB	77/61	
EC-GKR	Fairchild-Swearingen SA.227AC Metro IV	AC-620	N174SW
EC-GKS	McDonnell-Douglas DC-9-83	49708	EC-440
			EC-FVV
			EC-607
			TC-RTU
			XA-TUR
			N6203U
EC-GKT	Tango II-GT	T1922	
EC-GKU	Fokker F.27-050	20273	D-AFFJ
			PH-LXM
EC-GKV	Fokker F.27-050	20274	D-AFFK
			PH-LXN
EC-GKX	Fokker F.27-050	20275	D-AFFL
			PH-LXO
EC-GKY	Bell UH-1H (205)	13274	HE.10B-37
			72-21575
EC-GKZ	Bell UH-1H (205)	13275	HE.10B-38
			72-21576
EC-GLA	Piper PA-23-250 Aztec E	27-4811	E.19-5
			N14241
EC-GLB	UltraMagic M-65 HAFB	65/63	
EC-GLE	Airbus A.340-313	146	EC-157
			F-WWJD
EC-GLF	Cessna 172N	70201	N7388M
EC-GLG	Cessna 150M	78171	N9221U
EC-GLJ	Piper PA-23-250 Aztec E	27-4812	E.19-6
			N14242
EC-GLK	Aerotek Pitts S-2A	2009	N9WK
EC-GLL	Cessna 172N	68321	N733JB
EC-GLN	Glasflügel H201B Standard Libelle	203	OY-MGX
EC-GLO	Cessna 172	unkn	

Regn.	Type	C/n	Prev.Id.
EC-GLP	Piper PA-28-161 Warrior II	28-8116163	G-BOPL
			N8342J
EC-GLQ	PZL PW-5 Smyk	17.03.014	
EC-GLS	Bell 212	31155	OY-HCU
EC-GLZ	Colt 77A HAFB	3942	
EC-GMA	Hispano HA-200 Saeta	unkn	Sp.AF E.14A-?
EC-GME	Piper PA-28-	unkn	
EC-GMF	Piper PA-28-161 Warrior II *(W/o 12.10.97)*	28-7916386	N2208Z
EC-GMG	Fairchild-Swearingen SA.226TC Metro III	TC-371	OY-BJT
			SE-IMD
			OY-BJT
			N1010B
EC-GMH	PZL-104 Wilga 80	CF20890880	ZK-PZP
	(Identity not yet confirmed)		SP-FWP
EC-GMJ	Cessna 172	unkn	
EC-GMK	Cameron C-80 Concept HAFB	3717	
EC-GMO	Dassault Falcon 900EX	6	F-OIBL
			F-WWFK
EC-GMM	Peterson 260SE STOL *(Cessna 182 convn ?)*	unkn	N6745M
EC-GMS	Cameron A-120 HAFB	4011	
EC-GMU	Airbus A.310-304	451	N571SW
			C-GCIV
			N815PA
			F-WWCY
EC-GMX	Air Tractor AT-802A	802A-0039	N5001X
EC-GMY	Boeing 737-36Q	28658	
EC-GMZ	Eurocopter EC-135T1	0016	D-HECG
EC-GNA	Eurocopter EC-135T1	0017	D-HECH
EC-GNG	McDonnell-Douglas DC-10-30	46953	YV-139C
			EC-CSK
EC-GNK	Dassault Falcon 2000	37	F-WWMH
EC-GNL	Schempp-Hirth Nimbus 4 DM	unkn	
EC-GNO	Bell 206B Jet Ranger II	3091	HB-XSI
			N604PA
			N604PD
EC-GNR	Bell 206-LT Twin Ranger	52051	N41060
EC-GNS	Cessna 172	unkn	
EC-GNT	Air Tractor AT-802	802-0046	N5007H
EC-GNU	Boeing 737-36Q	28660	
EC-GNV	Cessna 172	unkn	
EC-GNX	HAFB	unkn	
EC-GNY	McDonnell-Douglas DC-9-83	49396	(SE-DHB)
			N396GE
			SX-BFO
			SE-DHB
			EC-FIX
			EC-389
			SE-DHB
EC-GNZ	Boeing 737-4Y0	25178	D-ABAD
			N601TR
EC-GOC	Bell UH-1H (205)	unkn	EC-360
EC-GOD	Bell UH-1H (205)	4787	N92820
			65-09743
EC-GOE	Bell UH-1H (205)	5272	N19UH
			66-00789
EC-GOF	Bell UH-1H (205)	5580	N15UH
			66-01097
EC-GOG	Bell UH-1H (205)	9960	N17UH
			67-17762
EC-GOH	Bell UH-1H (205)	10484	N16UH
			68-15554
EC-GOI	DHC-4 Caribou	unkn	Sp.AF T.9-..
EC-GOJ	Boeing 767-204	23072	ZK-NBI
			G-BLKV
			N6067E
EC-GOK	Mitsubishi MU-2B-35	635	OY-ARV
			LN-MTU
			OY-ARV
			N485AH
			XA-DID
			N485MA
EC-GOL	Cameron C-80 Concept HAFB	3563	
EC-GOM	McDonnell-Douglas DC-9-83	49579	EC-EIG
			EC-148
EC-GON	Beech B24R Sierra 200	MC-228	N9PT

Regn.	Type	C/n	Prev.Id.
EC-GOO	Air Tractor AT-802	802-0047	N5007P
EC-GOP	Bell 412HP	36031	N4603T
EC-GOR	Bell 212	30931	C-GAEO
			XA-SSM
EC-GOS	Air Tractor AT-802	802-0042	N5005M
EC-GOT	Airbus A.310-324	455	N572SW
			C-GCIT
			N818PA
			F-WWCU
EC-GOU	McDonnell-Douglas DC-9-83	53198	SE-DLS
EC-GOV	Cessna 560 Citation V	0419	
EC-GOY	Beech C90 King Air	LJ-527	N55SG
			N55SQ
			N55SC
EC-GOZ	Cessna 182	unkn	
EC-GPA	Bell 412HP	36071	N7238Y
			OE-XPR
			N194SP
			OE-XPP
			D-HHQQ
			N2084D
EC-GPB	Airbus A.340-313	193	F-WWJR
EC-GPE	Fairchild-Swearingen SA.266TC Metro II	TC-273	OY-JER
			N5472M
EC-GPH	Beech E55 Baron	TE-1188	N38287
EC-GPI	Boeing 737-36Q	28661	
EC-GPJ	Cessna 172N	unkn	
EC-GPK	Bell 412	33048	N16HW
			VH-LHV
			9M-SSO
			JA9571
			B-12137
			JA9571
			N2239X
EC-GPL	PZL PW-5 Smyk	17.05.004	
EC-GPM	Cessna 172	unkn	
EC-GPN	Dassault Falcon 50	204	VP-CGP
	(Re-registered EC-HHS?)		VR-CGP
			F-GKAR
			F-WWHD
EC-GPP	Bell 205A-1	30290	EC-GCG
			EC-857
			LN-OPA
			OE-EXZ
			N2670N
			C-GUMJ
			OE-EXZ
EC-GPQ	Cessna 337 Super Skymaster	unkn	
EC-GPR	Cessna 182	unkn	
EC-GPS	Fairchild-Swearingen SA.227AC Metro III	AC-722	N439MA
EC-GPV	Cameron C-80 Concept HAFB	4176	
EC-GPY	Piper PA-32-301 Saratoga	unkn	
EC-GPZ-AJ	PZL PW-5 Smyk	17.07.023	
EC-GQA	Embraer EMB.120 Brasilia	120-027	EC-GMT
			N14033
			LN-KOD
			PT-SIW
EC-GQB	Cessna 210-5	unkn	
EC-GQE	Piper J-3C-65 Cub	10780	G-AKAA
			43-29489
EC-GQF	Aeritalia/SNIAS ATR-72-202	493	F-WWLN
EC-GQG	McDonnell-Douglas DC-9-83	49577	EC-FSY
			EC-463
			EC-EHT
			EC-147
EC-GQH	Bell 206B Jet Ranger II	578	HB-XDH
			EC-ENU
			HB-XDH
			OY-HSD
			HB-XDH
			(OY-HSW)
			HB-XDH
EC-GQI	Fokker F.27-050	20251	PH-WXH
			TF-FIU
			PH-EXU

Regn.	Type	C/n	Prev.Id.
EC-GQK	Airbus A.340-313	197	F-WWJL
EC-GQL	DHC-4 Caribou	unkn	Sp.AF T.9-..
EC-GQM	DHC-4 Caribou	unkn	Sp.AF T.9-..
EC-GQN	DHC-4 Caribou	unkn	Sp.AF T.9-..
EC-GQO	BAe.146-200QC	E-2086	D-ADEI
			SE-DEI
			G-5-086
			G-BNUA
			G-5-086
EC-GQP	BAe.146-200QC	E-2100	D-ANTJ
			G-TNTJ
			G-BOHK
			G-5-100
EC-GQT	Fokker F.27-050	20136	5Y-BFM
	(Reserved as PH-DML 4.99)		PH-EXJ
EC-GQU	Aeritalia/SNIAS ATR-72-201	198	F-WQGC
			B-22702
			F-WWEL
EC-GQV	Aeritalia/SNIAS ATR-72-201	210	F-WQGE
			B-22703
			F-WWEH
EC-GQX	Agusta A.109E	11013	
EC-GQZ	McDonnell-Douglas DC-9-81 *(unconfirmed)*	49571	HB-INY
EC-GRA	Agusta A.109C	7656	EC-GJD
			EC-380
			N45FB
			N1VN
EC-GRE	Airbus A.320-211	0134	EC-FAS
			EC-575
			F-WWIZ
EC-GRF	Airbus A.320-211	136	EC-FBQ
			EC-576
			F-WWDC
EC-GRG	Airbus A.320-211	143	EC-FBS
			EC-577
			F-WWDJ
EC-GRH	Airbus A.320-211	146	EC-FBR
			EC-578
			F-WWDM
EC-GRI	Airbus A.320-211	177	EC-FEO
			EC-582
			F-WWIP
EC-GRJ	Airbus A.320-211	246	EC-FKH
			EC-589
			F-WWII
EC-GRK	McDonnell-Douglas DC-9-87	49827	EC-EUE
			EC-290
EC-GRL	McDonnell-Douglas DC-9-87	49828	EC-EUD
			EC-291
EC-GRM	McDonnell-Douglas DC-9-87	49829	EC-EUC
			EC-292
EC-GRN	McDonnell-Douglas DC-9-87	49830	EC-EUL
			EC-293
EC-GRO	McDonnell-Douglas DC-9-87	49831	EC-EVB
			EC-294
EC-GRP	Aeritalia/SNIAS ATR-72-202	488	F-WWLI
EC-GRR	Cessna R172K Hawk XP	2270	N4077V
EC-GRU	Aeritalia/SNIAS ATR-72-202	493	F-WWLN
EC-GRX	Boeing 737-46B	24123	G-OBMN
			G-BOPJ
			N1790B
EC-GRY	Fokker F.27-050	20280	PH-LXU
			G-BWZL
			V8-RB1
			PH-LXU
EC-GRZ	Fokker F.27-050	20282	PH-MXE
			G-BWZM
			V8-RB2
			PH-MXE
EC-GSE	BAe .ATP	2038	EC-GKJ
			G-OEDI
			G-BTNI
			TC-THU
			G-BTNI
			(G-SLAM)
EC-GSF	BAe. ATP	2039	EC-GKI
			G-OEDH
			G-BTUE
			TC-THT
			G-BTUE
			G-11-039
EC-GSG	BAe. ATP	2041	EC-GLC
			G-BTPK
			G-11-041
EC-GSH	BAe. ATP	2043	EC-GNI
			G-BTPM
EC-GSI	BAe. ATP	2044	EC-GNJ
			G-BTPN
EC-GSJ	Convair 580	130	OO-HUB
			C-GGWG
			N5813
			N8419H
EC-GSK	Bell 412	33092	SE-HVL
			N3205S
			5N-AQS
EC-GSL	IAI-1124A Westwind	353	C-GRGE(2)
			N89UC
			N89UH
			N86UR
			N90CH
			N379JR
			4X-CTU
EC-GSM	Cessna 172N	70175	D-EEKS(2)
			N738RJ
EC-GSN	Cameron C-60 Concept HAFB	3640	
EC-GSQ	Beech B300 Super King Air	FL-128	N128FL
			D-CDDD
			N3157D
EC-GSU	Boeing 767-3Y0ER	26206	HL7269
EC-GSX	Boeing 727-256 *(Stored)*	20594	YV-126C
			EC-CAK
EC-GSY	Boeing 727-256 *(Stored)*	20597	YV-127C
			EC-CBC
			N1788B
EC-GSZ	Boeing 727-256 *(Stored)*	20599	YV-129C
			EC-CBE
			N1788B
EC-GTA	Boeing 727-256 *(Stored)*	20605	YV-128C
			EC-CBK
EC-GTB	McDonnell-Douglas DC-10-30	46556	YV-134C
			PH-DTG
EC-GTC	McDonnell-Douglas DC-10-30	46972	YV-136C
			PH-AAJ
			YV-136C
EC-GTD	McDonnell-Douglas DC-10-30	46982	YV-137C
			PH-AAK
			YV-137C
EC-GTI	Boeing 767-3Y0	26207	HL7286
EC-GTJ	Embraer EMB.120RT Brasilia	120.024	N72157
			LN-KOC
			PT-SIT
EC-GTM	Beech 1900C	UB-30	N7210R
EC-GTO	McDonnell-Douglas DC-9-81	49570	HB-INX
EC-GTR	Dassault Falcon 50EX	268	F-WWHS
EC-GTS	Cessna 500 Citation I	0037	N407SC
			N109AL
			SE-DPL
			N109AL
			N7CC
EC-GTV	Cessna 152	unkn	
EC-GTX	SOCATA TB-10 Tobago	unkn	
EC-GTY	PZL PW-5 Smyk	17.09.010	
EC-GTZ	PZL PW-5 Smyk	17.10.005	
EC-GUA	PZL PW-5 Smyk	17.10.006	
EC-GUB	PZL PW-5 Smyk	17.10.007	
EC-GUC	Robinson R-22 Beta	2222	EC-GPO
EC-GUD	Beech 1900C-1	UC-156	N156YV
EC-GUF	Air Tractor AT-802	802-0059	N51198

Regn.	Type	C/n	Prev.Id.
EC-GUG	Boeing 737-4S3	25116	EI-CNE, EC-GOA, EI-CNE, EC-GFE, EC-997, OO-LTR, 9M-MLF, N4249R, (G-BSRA), N1789B
EC-GUH	Aérospatiale AS.355F2 Ecureuil 2	5474	N6040U
EC-GUI	Boeing 737-4Y0	24690	EI-COU, SE-DRR, PT-TDC, EC-GHK, EC-308, PT-TDA, EC-FBP, EC-603, TC-AFL
EC-GUJ	Air Tractor AT-802A	802A-0064	N50756
EC-GUO	Boeing 737-4Q8	26285	N402KW
EC-GUP	Airbus A.340-313X	217	F-WWJG
EC-GUQ	Airbus A.340-313	221	F-WWJA
EC-GUR	Airbus A.320-231	308	G-BXRW, EC-GNB, N308RX, LZ-ABC, F-WWDL
EC-GUS	Fairchild-Swearingen SA.227AC Metro III	AC-648	N2685L
EC-GUT(2)	Bell UH-1H (205)	13367	N21UH, 73-21679
EC-GUX	BAe.ATP	2024	G-OEDJ, G-BURR, CS-TGC, G-BURR, CS-TGC, G-11-024
EC-GUZ	Aérospatiale AS.355F2 Ecureuil 2	5454	N26ET, PT-HXV, N84CC
EC-GVA	Cameron N-77 HAFB	4343	
EC-GVB	Boeing 737-4Y0	24689	PT-TDD, EC-EXY, EC-403
EC-GVD	Cessna 172	unkn	
EC-GVE	Fairchild-Swearingen SA.227AC Metro III	AC-669	N2702Z
EC-GVF	Robinson R-22 Beta	unkn	
EC-GVH	Aérospatiale AS.355N Ecureuil 2	5656	
EC-GVI	McDonnell-Douglas DC-9-83	49936	EI-CPA, TC-INB, G-HCRP, N3001D
EC-GVN	Air Tractor AT-802	802-0065	N5059X
EC-GVO	McDonnell-Douglas DC-9-83	49642	N462GE, SE-DHF, EC-GHJ, EC-323, EC-GBY, EC-807, EI-CGR, F-GMCD, EC-EMT, EC-257, XA-TUR, EC-EKT, EC-190, SE-DHF, (EC-EFL)
EC-GVP	Bell 212	30572	LN-OQG, SE-JCF, LN-OQG, N58024
EC-GVQ	SOCATA TB-10 Tobago	unkn	
EC-GVR	Robinson R-22 Beta	1489	HB-XYZ, N40233
EC-GVV	Bell 212	30584	N58121, HK-3729X, N58121, YS-1003P, N58121, C-FADC, N58121
EC-GVX	Reims/Cessna F.337F Super Skymaster	unkn	
EC-GVY	Cameron A-180 HAFB	4365	
EC-GXA	Bell 212	30812	LN-OQJ
EC-GXE	Fairchild-Swearingen SA.227AC Metro III	AC-694	N457AM
EC-GXF	Bell UH-1H (205)	12604	N22UH, 70-16299
EC-GXG	Bell 212	30759	N21601, C-GJDC, N21601, HC-BJQ, N49688
EC-GXJ	Fairchild-Swearingen SA.227AC Metro III	unkn	
EC-GXP	Fairchild 24R Argus	unkn	E.19-4, N14240
EC-GXQ	Beech T.34 Mentor	X-104	EC-750, E.17-24/'79- 24"
EC-GXR	Boeing 737-4Y0	24685	PT-TDB, EC-EVE, EC-402
EC-GXU	McDonnell-Douglas DC-9-83	49622	EC-FTT, EC-485, EC-FNU, EC-206, EC-EJZ, EC-382, EC-EJZ, EC-179
EC-GXV	Piper PA-28-	unkn	
EC-GXY	Aérospatiale AS.365N1 Dauphin 2	6242	N12AE, N365AS, F-WYME
EC-GYB	Fairchild-Swearingen SA.227AC Metro III	AC-699	N458AM
EC-GYC	SOCATA TB-10 Tobago	unkn	
EC-GYI	Canadair CL.600-2B19 Regional Jet	7249	C-GDDM, C-FMMQ
EC-GYL	Fokker F.27 Friendship 500	10381	G-BVOM, PH-FND, PT-LZN, F-BPNH, PH-FND
EC-GYU	Reims/Cessna F.337F Super Skymaster	unkn	
EC-GYX	Air Tractor AT-401	401-1068	
EC-GZA	Canadair CL.600-2B19 Regional Jet	7252	C-GDDO
EC-GZD	Airbus A.320-214	879	F-WWDD
EC-GZE	Airbus A.320-214	888	F-WWDG
EC-GZG	Beech 1900C	UC-161	N55635
EC-GZI	Embraer EMB.145U	145-098	PT-SBU
EC-GZL	Beech 1900D	UE-335	N23269
EC-GZO	Air Tractor AT-802	802-0071	N5166B
EC-GZP	Air Tractor AT-802	802-0072	N5176D
EC-GZT	UltraMagic HAFB	unkn	
EC-GZU	Embraer EMB.145EU	145-106	
EC-GZV	Boeing 757-256 (Reservation)	26247	N1795B
EC-GZZ	Boeing 757-256 (Reservation)	26248	
EC-HAA	Boeing 757-256 (Reservation)	26249	
EC-HAB	Airbus A.320-214	994	F-WWBM
EC-HAC	Airbus A.321-211	1021	D-AVZQ
EC-HAD	Airbus A.320-214	992	F-WWBJ
EC-HAE	Airbus A.321-211	1027	D-AVZL
EC-HAF	Airbus A.320-214	1047	F-WWIE
EC-HAG	Airbus A.320-214	1059	F-WWIP
EC-HAH	Boeing 727-223F	21084	OO-DHV, N857AA, N7AU
EC-HAI	Gates Learjet 55	55-112	LN-VIP, N325CP, (YV-325CP), N3802G

Regn.	Type	C/n	Prev.Id.
EC-HAL	Airbus A.310-324	594	LX-TXA
			(F-GJEY)
			F-WQHS
			VP-BCU
			VR-BCU
			HI-659CA
			HI-659
			VR-BMU
			F-WWCQ
EC-HAM	Comper CLA.7 Swift	S.32/5	G-ABUU
EC-HAP	CASA C.212-400	465	
EC-HAQ	Robin HR.200/120B	unkn	
EC-HAS	Cessna 172	unkn	
EC-HAT	Cessna 172RG	unkn	
EC-HAU	CASA/Nurtanio CN.235-200	C030	LV-VHM
			EC-FAE
EC-HAV	CASA/Nurtanio CN.235-200	C032	LV-VGV
			EC-FBD
EC-HBC	Cessna 525 CitationJet	0264	VP-CHV
EC-HBF	Embraer EMB.120ER Brasilia	120-008	N212AS
			PT-SIC
EC-HBG	Beech 1900D	UE-341	N23309
EC-HBH	Boeing 727-224	20661	N695CA
			N66732
EC-HBL	Boeing 737-85H	28381	N1787B
EC-HBM	Boeing 737-85H	28382	N1787B
EC-HBN	Boeing 737-8SH	28383	N1786B
EC-HBO	Reims/Cessna F.337FSuper Skymaster	unkn	
EC-HBR	Boeing 727-224	20662	N707CA
			N66733
EC-HBT	Boeing 737-4Y0	24545	PT-TDE
			G-OABE
			EC-ETB
			EC-401
			C-FVND
EC-HBU	Aeritalia/SNIAS ATR-72-212A	459	N12903
			F-WWLE
EC-HBX	Cessna 525 CitationJet	0304	N1128G
EC-HBY	Aeritalia/SNIAS ATR-72-212A	unkn	
EC-HBZ	Boeing 737-4Y0	25180	EC-GOB
			EI-CNF
			EC-GHT
			EC-348
			D-ABAJ
			EC-FLD
			EC-936
EC-HCA	Piper PA-34-200 Seneca	unkn	
EC-HCE	Aérospatiale AS.350	unkn	
EC-HCF	Embraer EMB.120RT Brasilia	120-007	N211AS
			PT-SIB
EC-HCG	Aeritalia/SNIAS ATR-72-212A	unkn	
EC-HCH	Fairchild-Swearingen SA.226TCMetro II	unkn	
EC-HCJ	SOCATA TB-10 Tobago	unkn	
EC-HCM	Beech 1900	unkn	
EC-HCN	Boeing 737-4Y0	24682	VT-JAH
			EC-FZX
			VT-JAH
			EC-FZX
			EC-737
			9M-MJK
			(C-FVNF)
EC-HCO	BAe. ATP	2052	G-BUKJ
			EC-GLD
			G-OEDF
			G-BUKJ
			TC-THZ
			G-BUKJ
EC-HCP	Boeing 737-4Y0	24124	EI-CRC
			EC-GNC
			SU-SAB
			EC-GHF
			EC-309
			SU-SAA
			EC-FYG,
			EC-655, N689MA, G-BOPK

Regn.	Type	C/n	Prev.Id.
EC-HCQ	Piper PA-31T Cheyenne	unkn	
EC-HCR	Airbus A.320-231	225	N225RX
			A40-MB
			N225RX
			SX-BSH
			N225RX
			F-WWIO
EC-HCT	Bell 206BJet Ranger	unkn	
EC-HCV	Piper PA-34-200 Seneca	unkn	
EC-HCX	Dassault Falcon 20 (identity unconfirmed)	184	OE-GCJ
			F-GAPC
			D-COMF
			F-BTMF
			F-WRQQ
EC-HCY	BAe. ATP	2013	G-BTPF
			G-11-103
			G-BPTF
			(N383AE)
EC-HCZ	Bell 212 (Code:"50")	30548	"EC-HCP"
			G-BGLJ
			(EC-GHP)
			EC-295
			G-BGLJ
			9Y-TIJ
			G-BGLJ
			5N-AJX
			G-BGLJ
			EP-HBZ
			VR-BEJ
			N2956W
EC-HDA	Cameron N-77 HAFB	4536	
EC-HDB	Cameron C-60 Concept HAFB	4550	
EC-HDC	Cameron N-77 HAFB	4560	
EC-HDE	Rockwell Commander 680V	1684-65	N10TG
			N1UT
			N1BA
			N81D
EC-HDF	Cessna 402B	unkn	
EC-HDG	Boeing 757-236	24794	EC-FEF
			EC-669
			G-BRJH
EC-HDH	BAe.146-200QT	E-2056	G-TNTA
			G-5-056
			(G-OTNT)
			N146QT
			N146FT
			G-5-056
EC-HDK	Airbus A.320-214	1067	F-WWBF
EC-HDL	Airbus A.320-214	1063	F-WWBL
EC-HDM	Boeing 757-256	26250	
EC-HDN	Airbus A.320-214	1087	F-WWIY
EC-HDO	Airbus A.320-214	1099	F-WWDR
EC-HDP	Airbus A.320-214	1101	F-WWDB
EC-HDQ	Airbus A.340-313X	302	F-WWJU
EC-HDR	Boeing 757-256	26251	
EC-HDS	Boeing 757-256	26252	
EC-HDT	Airbus A.320-214	1119	F-WWBO
EC-HDU	Boeing 757-256	26253	
EC-HDV	Boeing 757-256	26254	N1786B
EC-HEA	Aérospatiale SE.3160 Alouette III	unkn	
EC-HEG	Dassault Falcon 200	494	N204DD
			N49US
			LV-BAI
			LV-PFM
			N85LB
			N209FJ
			F-WZZD
EC-HEH	BAe. ATP	2014	G-BTPG
			(N384AE)
EC-HEI	Aeritalia/SNIAS ATR-72-212A	570	F-WWEG
EC-HEJ	Aeritalia/SNIAS ATR-72-212A	565	F-WWEE
EC-HEK	Canadair CL.600-2B19 Regional Jet	7320	C-GFCN
			C-FMLQ
EC-HEM	Cameron C-80 Concept HAFB	4535	
EC-HEP	Cameron C-80 Concept HAFB	4537	

Regn.	Type	C/n	Prev.Id.
EC-HEQ	Reims/Cessna F.337F Super Skymaster	unkn	
EC-HES	BAe. ATP	2042	G-BTPL
			EC-GLH
			G-BTPL
			G-11-042
EC-HFB	Airbus A.310-324	542	N824PA
			PK-MAX
			V2-LED
			N824PA
			F-WWCS
EC-HFD	Bell 412 *(identity unconfirmed)*	36183	N52247
EC-HFI	Airbus A.310-325	624	OE-LAD
			F-WWCE
EC-HFJ	Air Tractor AT-402A	402A-1056	N5020A
EC-HFM	BAe. ATP	2015	G-BTPH
			(N385AE)
EC-HFP	McDonnell-Douglas DC-9-82	53148	HL-7548
			HL-7204
EC-HFQ	Airbus A.310-324	492	OE-LAB
			F-WWCP
EC-HFR	BAe. ATP	2016	G-ATPJ
			(N386AE)
EC-HFS	McDonnell-Douglas DC-9-82	49517	EI-CTE
			B-540L
			B-2133
EC-HFT	McDonnell-Douglas DC-9-82	49521	EI-CTF
			B-2137
EC-HFY	Cessna 500 Citation*(Reservation)*	0157	CS-DCA
			N190AB
			PH-CTD
EC-HFZ	Embraer EMB.120RTBrasilia	120-...	
EC-HGA	McDonnell-Douglas DC-9-83	53052	N942AS
EC-HGB	BAe. ATP	2010	G-BTPC
			EC-GYF
			G-BTPC
			G-11-10
			(N380AE)
EC-HGC	BAe. ATP	2007	G-BTPA
			EC-GYE
			G-BTPA
			(N377AE)
EC-HGD	BAe. ATP	2011	G-BTPD
			EC-GYR
			G-BTPD
			(N381AE)
EC-HGE	BAe. ATP	2012	G-BTPE
			EC-GZH
			G-BTPE
			(N382AE)
EC-HGH	Grumman G-1159CGulfstream IV	1021	N3NU
			N3M
			N412GA
EC-HGI	Cessna 550 Citation II	0596	D-CAWA
			N96TD
			(N13026)
EC-HGJ	McDonnell-Douglas DC-9-82	49519	EI-CTQ
			B-2135
EC-HGK	Piper PA-34-200 Seneca	unkn	
EC-HGO	Boeing 737-85P	28384	
EC-HGP	Boeing 737-85P	28385	
EC-HGQ	Boeing 737-85P	28386	N1786B
EC-HGR	Airbus A.319-111	1154	D-AVYY
EC-HGS	Airbus A.319-111	1180	D-AVWR
EC-HGU	Airbus A.340-313X	318	F-WWJL
EC-HHF	McDonnell-Douglas DC-9-82	49509	EI-CTP
			B2125
EC-HHG	Boeing 737-86N	28608	N1786B
EC-HHH	Boeing 737-86N	26810	N1786B
EC-HHI	Canadair CL.600-2B19 Regional Jet	7343	C-GFKQ
EC-HHJ	Cessna 172	unkn	
EC-HHK	Dassault Falcon 900	151	G-OPWH
			F-WWFK
EC-HHN	Embraer EMB.120RTBrasilia	120-063	N7215U
			C-FZWF,
			LN-KOE, PT-SKG

Regn.	Type	C/n	Prev.Id.
EC-HHO	Beech 200 Super King Air	BB-262	N92V
			N18762
EC-HHP	McDonnell-Douglas DC-9-82	49501	EI-CTV
			B2107
EC-HHS	Dassault Falcon 50	204	EC-GPN
			VP-CGP
			VR-CGP
			F-GKAR
			F-WWHD
EC-HHU	Boeing 727-277F	22644	(OO-DLJ)
			N626DH
			N72381
			VH-ANF
EC-HHV	Canadair CL.600-2B19 Regional Jet	7350	C-GFKR
EC-HHX	Cessna 172RG	unkn	
EC-HHY	Cessna 172RG	unkn	
EC-HHZ	Aérospatiale SN.601 Corvette	15	F-GNAF
			D6-ECB
			F-GEQF
			N17AJ
			SE-DEN
			F-GDUB
			OO-MRE
			OO-MRA
			SE-DEN
			F-WIFA
EC-HIA	Aérospatiale SN.601 Corvette	19	F-GEPQ
			F-SEBH
			F-GDRC(1)
			TZ-PBF
			F-BVPL
			F-OCJL
			F-BVPL
EC-HIC	Cessna 172	unkn	
EC-HIG	Boeing 727-277	22641	N627DH
			N6393X
			VH-ANA
			N8278V
EC-HII	Piper PA-28R-200 Arrow	unkn	
EC-HIN	Cessna 525 CitationJet	0197	N525KH
			N5151S
EC-HJC	Fairchild-Swearingen SA.226TC Metro II	unkn	
EC-HJH	BAe.146 Series 200QC	E-2112	G-BOMK
			RP-C482
			F-GTNU
			G-5-112
			EC-231
			G-BOMK
EC-HJJ	Boeing 737-86N	28617	N1787B
EC-HJL	Hawker 800XP	258444	N40489
EC-HJP	Boeing 737-85P	28535	N1800B
			N1786B
EC-HJU	Convair CV-580	147	OO-DHF
			C-GQHA
			N5838
			N73158
			N2006
			N200A
			N100A
			N7600
EC-HJV	Boeing 727-200F *(Noted 3.00)*	unkn	

UNKNOWN AIRCRAFT

The following aircraft are known to have been exported to Spain but no Spanish marks are yet known due to the lack of published information. Any positive identifications would therefore be most welcome.

Regn.	Type	C/n	Prev.Id.
EC-...	Aérospatiale SA.318C Alouette Astazou	2170	F-GNCU
			TJ-AHW
			TR-LPE
EC-...	Aérospatiale AS.365C2 Dauphin 2	5055	PH-SSY
			EC-FOY
			EC-137
			CC-CJA
EC-...	Aérospatiale AS.365N2 Dauphin 2	6416	SE-JAE
			F-WYMM
EC-...	Aérospatiale AS.365N2 Dauphin 2	6478	SE-JCE
EC-...	Agusta A.109C	7642	D-HAAC(2)
			N1FD
EC-...	Agusta A.109C	7646	D-HBRK
			N1YE
EC-...	Agusta-Bell 206B Jet Ranger II	8620	G-BPIC
			D-HEAS
			I-CELT
EC-...	Air Command 532	PFA G/04-1147	G-BRKZ
EC-...	Air Tractor AT-301	301-0199	N8824S
EC-...	Air Tractor AT-802	802-0068	N5066S
EC-...	Antonov AN-2R	1G212-34	LY-AHH
			CCCP32729
EC-...	Avialsa-Scheibe A.60	87K	F-CDBO
EC-...	Beech 23 Musketeer	M-116	N2393Z
EC-...	Beech 65A80 Queen Air	LD-228	G-WJPN
			N197MC
EC-...	Beech 1900C-1	UC-124	N122GP
			(N529LX)
EC-...	Beech 1900D	UE-343	N22373
EC-...	Bell 206B Jet Ranger II	796	C-FOAS
			CF-OAS
EC-...	Bell 206L-4 Long Ranger IV	52062	G-BXMP
			N58968
			G-OCOP
			N58968
EC-...	Bell 212	30587	N605LH
			JA8517
			N58086
EC-...	Bell 212	30639	G-BCMC
			9Y-THL
			HK-4103X
			G-BCMC
			(EC-GHO)
			EC-294
			G-BCMC
			EC-GCS
			EC-932
			G-BCMC
			9Y-THL
			G-BCMC
			9M-ATU
			VR-BFI
			G-BCMC
			N18090
EC-...	Bell 212	30818	N25UH
			HK-....
			N69AL
EC-...	Bell UH-1H (205)	4787	N92820
			65-09743
EC-...	Bell UH-1H (205)	5057	N2218N
			65-10013
EC-...	Bell UH-1H (205)	5466	N1217A
			66-00983
EC-...	Bell UH-1H (205)	8853	N1206P
			66-16659
EC ...	Bell 412	36071	N7238Y
EC-...	Bell 412EP	36183	N52247
EC-...	Bölkow BO.105C	S-188	EC-234
			N3531T

Regn.	Type	C/n	Prev.Id.
EC-...	Cameron SS Packet HAFB	560	
EC-...	Cameron V-31 HAFB	867	
EC-...	Cameron R-60 HAFB	2057	
EC-...	Cameron C-60 HAFB	3477	
EC-...	Cameron C-60 HAFB	4355	
EC-...	Cameron N-77 HAFB	4738	
EC-...	Cameron C-80 Concept HAFB	4729	
EC-...	Cameron C-80 Concept HAFB	4739	
EC-...	Cameron RX-100 HAFB	2666	EC-937
			G-BTXP
EC-...	Cessna 150F	61943	N8643S
EC-...	Cessna 150L	74858	N10432
EC-...	Cessna 150M	77841	N7784U
EC-...	Cessna 152	84041	N4948H
EC-...	Reims/Cessna F.152	1606	D-EGUN(2)
EC-...	Reims/Cessna F.172H	0690	D-EBJK(2)
			HB-CUB
EC-...	Reims/Cessna F.172H	0721	D-ECHC
EC-...	Cessna 172M	62738	N13417
EC-...	Cessna 172M	63446	N5232R
EC-...	Cessna 172M	65188	N64356
EC-...	Reims/Cessna F.172M	0908	OH-CFZ
			SE-FZC
EC-...	Reims/Cessna F.172M	1404	D-ELJB
EC-...	Cessna 172N	68670	N104ES
EC-...	Cessna 172N	69055	N81709
			C-GYWU
			(N734RM)
EC-...	Cessna 172N	69275	N737AT
EC-...	Cessna 172N	70202	N738SN
EC-...	Cessna 172N	70379	D-EOEL(2)
			N739AA
EC-...	Cessna 172N	73303	D-EBER(3)
			N4677G
EC-...	Reims/Cessna F.172N	1560	D-EMDU(2)
EC-...	Reims/Cessna F.172N	1561	D-EKSM
EC-...	Reims/Cessna F.172N	1827	D-EIYG
EC-...	Reims/Cessna F.172N	1932	D-EHGP
EC-...	Cessna 172P	74314	N172U
			N51455
EC-...	Cessna 172P	75947	N66010
EC-...	Reims/Cessna F.172P	2098	D-EIKK
			(D-ELNU)
EC-...	Cessna 172R	80355	
EC-...	Cessna 172RG	0006	N4631R
EC-...	Cessna 172RG	0393	N4827V
EC-...	Cessna R172K Hawk XP	2544	N736HR
EC-...	Reims/Cessna FR.172H Rocket	0320	D-EEXP
EC-...	Cessna 177 Cardinal	00244	
EC-...	Reims/Cessna F.177RG	0131	D-EFMW
EC-...	Reims/Cessna F.177RG	0151	G-BFAC
			N177AB
			G-BFAC
			D-EDIS
EC-...	Cessna 182J Skylane	56994	N2894F
EC-...	Cessna 182P Skylane	63823	N6754M
EC-...	Cessna A188B	02700T	PH-YTA
			N4966Q
EC-...	Cessna 210D Centurion	58395	N3895Y
EC-...	Cessna 337B Super Skymaster	00619	N522TT
			N5222T
			N2319S
EC-...	Cessna 337E Super Skymaster	01203	N86480
EC-...	Cessna 337G Super Skymaster	01725	N53587
EC-...	Cessna 337G Super Skymaster	01815	N617L
			N1323L
EC-...	Reims/Cessna F.337F Super Skymaster	0033/01357	F-BSHU
EC-...	Reims/Cessna F.337G Super Skymaster	0059/01477	D-IOMS
			(N1877M)
EC-...	Cessna 402B	0581	N1436G
EC-	Cessna 411	0124	F-BSUT
			D-IFLA
			N4924T
EC-...	Challenger II	CH2-1189-0481	C-ICPZ

Regn.	Type	C/n	Prev.Id.
EC-...	Colt AS-56 Hot Air Airship	751	G-BMJP
			(PH-OET)
			G-BMJP,
EC-...	Colt 77A HAFB	2025	
EC-...	Colt 77A HAFB	4295	
EC-...	Colt 90A HAFB	2295	G-BUOU
EC-...	Consolidated PBY-5A Catalina	1960	EC-693
			EC-314
			C-FFFW
			N45998
			CF-FFW
			N6070C
			BuA46596
EC-...	Embraer EMB.120RT	120-103	N127AM
			PT-SMV
EC-...	Fairchild-Swearingen SA.226TC Metro II	TC-318	OY-JEO
			N5476M
EC-...	Fairchild-Swearingen SA.226TC Metro II	TC-374	OY-AUO
			D-IAEF
			OY-AUO
			SE-IKP
			LN-SAP
			OY-AUO
			N10104
EC-...	Fairchild-Swearingen SA.226TC Metro II	TC-390	N19WP
			C-FBWY
			N244AM
			N1012B
EC-...	Fairchild-Swearingen SA.227AC Metro III	AC-658B	N2692P
EC-...	Fairchild-Swearingen SA.227AC Metro III	AC-668	N358AE
EC-...	Fairchild-Swearingen SA.227AC Metro III	AC-694	N457AM
EC-...	Fairchild-Swearingen SA.227AC Metro III	AC-730	N2727B
EC-...	FLS OA-7 Optica	22	EC-438
			G-BOPP
EC-...	Fokker F.27 Friendship 500	10427	G-BVRN
			PH-FPB
			HL5211
			(HL5207)
			PH-FPB
EC-...	Glasflügel H201B Standard Libelle	523	PH-469
EC-...	Grob G.104 Speed Astir IIB	4012	OO-ZKT
			D-3837
EC-...	Grob G.109	6038	PH-789
			HB-2058
EC-...	Hughes 369D	108-0363D	N501RR
			N501RB
			N501RP
EC-...	LET L-23 Super Blanik	907807	
EC-...	LET L-23 Super Blanik	917818	
EC-...	McDonnell-Douglas DC-9-83	49624	EI-CGI
			EC-EKM
			EC-279
			EC-EKM
			EC-178
EC-...	Mooney M.20J Model 201	24-0518	N201YK
EC-...	Neico Lancair 320	001	N360LA
EC-...	Piper PA-23-250 Aztec C	27-3426	EC-831
			N6198Y
EC-...	Piper PA-23-250 Aztec D	27-4126	N6789Y
EC-...	Piper PA-28-140 Cherokee	28-20032	N6032W
			(N141DC)
			(N140HY)
			N6032W
EC-...	Piper PA-28-140 Cherokee	28-7525228	N33696
EC-...	Piper PA-28-151 Cherokee Warrior	28-7415142	N41227
EC-...	Piper PA-28-151 Cherokee Warrior	28-7515332	N33366
EC-150	Piper PA-28R-200 Arrow III	unkn	
EC-...	Piper PA-28R-200 Cherokee Arrow II	28R-7435019	N794AM
			C-GTOY
			N111RW
			N56620
EC-...	Piper PA-30-160 Twin Comanche C	30-1854	N8705Y

Regn.	Type	C/n	Prev.Id.
EC-...	Piper PA-31P Pressurized Navajo	31P-7300123	N888PD
			(N831SF)
			N888PD
			N7650L
EC-...	Piper PA-31T Cheyenne	31T-7520029	N43SC
			ZS-JLR
			N66854
EC-...	Piper PA-31T Cheyenne IA	31T-1104017	D-IEPA
			N91204
EC-...	Piper PA-32R-301 Saratoga SP	32R-8013132	G-TRIP
			G-HOSK
			PH-WET
			OO-HKN
			N8261X
EC-...	Piper PA-34-200 Seneca	34-7250191	9A-BPW
			RC-BPW
			YU-BPW
			D-GEAR
			N4978T
EC-...	Piper PA-34-200 Seneca	34-7350268	D-GMWU
			N55991
EC-...	Piper PA-34-220T Seneca V	3449126	N4141N
EC-...	Piper PA-36-300 Pawnee Brave	36-7360047	N6402P
EC-...	Piper PA-36-285 Pawnee Brave	36-7560099	N9984P
EC-...	Piper PA-36-375 Pawnee Brave	36-7802047	N3903E
EC-...	Piper PA-46-350P Malibu Mirage	4636235	N41653
EC-...	PZL-106BT-601 Turbo Kruk	10890228	SP-WAB
EC-...	PZL-106BT-601 Turbo Kruk	10890229	SP-WAC
EC-...	Raven S-60A HAFB	S60A-384	N2790Y
EC-...	Robin DR.400/180 Régent	1094	F-BXVG
EC-...	Robin DR.400/180 Régent	1301	F-GBAN
EC-...	Robinson R-22 Beta	1486	G-LOGS
EC-...	Robinson R-44 Astro	0454	
EC-...	Rolladen-Schneider LS-3A	3200	D-7804
EC-...	Scheibe SF-25D Falke	4834D	D-KHEQ
EC-...	Scheibe SF-28A Tandem-Falke	5768	D-KACU(2)
EC-...	Schempp-Hirth Discus 2b	49	
EC-...	Schempp-Hirth Janus C	110	
EC-...	Schempp-Hirth Standard Cirrus	15	D-0454
EC-...	Schleicher ASW-17	17013	OO-ZXF
			D-2112
EC-...	Schleicher ASW-19	19266	OY-XTP
			D-3588
			OE-5206
EC-...	Siren PIK-30	728	F-CFPK
EC-...	SOCATA MS.880B Rallye Club	1187	F-BPHM
EC-...	SOCATA MS.893A Rallye Commodore 180	10795	F-BPGJ
EC-...	SOCATA Rallye 180T Galérien	2774	F-GARS
EC-...	SOCATA TB-10 Tobago	245	F-GEFL
			6V-AFG
			F-OBLK
EC-...	SOCATA TB-10 Tobago	886	SE-KBI
EC-...	SOCATA TB-20 Trinidad	412	SE-IZV
			N141SW
			F-GDGK
EC-...	Stemme S-10V (Former c/n 14-007)	14-060M	D-KGCL(2)
EC-...	Sukhoi SU-31	unkn	RA-0402
EC-...	Sukhoi SU-31	unkn	RA-01278
EC-...	Sukhoi SU-31	unkn	RA-01296
EC-...	Sukhoi SU-26M2	unkn	
EC-...	Thunder AX7-77 SI	4451	
EC-...	Yakovlev YAK-52	unkn	LY-IZP

HOMEBUILT AIRCRAFT AND MICROLIGHTS

Regn.	Type	C/n	Prev.Id.
EC-YAA	Monnet Sonerai II	1	
EC-YAB	AX-9-140 Tramontana HAFB	001	
EC-YAC	Hosta JG-50A	001	
EC-YAD	Vidal JG-77A	001	
EC-YAE	Mendez JG-77C	001	
EC-YAF	Monnet Moni	203	ECT-440
EC-YAG	Roger D.31 Turbulent	01	ECT-706
EC-YAH	Rotorway Executive	3589	
EC-YAI	Rotorway Executive	31416	EC-199
EC-YAJ	Sallen 2-seat	001	
EC-YAK	Pendulaire	101	
EC-YAL	Copa	6/88	
EC-YAM	Copa	7/88	
EC-YAN	Eipper Quicksilver MXL-II	1361	
EC-YAO	Eipper Quicksilver MXL-II	1403	
EC-YAQ	Pitts S-1D Special	JFG 82/01	PP-ZZZ
EC-YAR	Eipper Quicksilver MXL-II	1521	
EC-YAS	Sallen Mach 10	16/87	
EC-YAT	Sallen Mach 15	1/89	
EC-YAU	Dynali Chickinox Kot Kot	31310417	
EC-YAV	Scheibe SF-25C Falke ? now "Singilia"	10/86	
EC-YAX	Light Aero Avid Flyer	20/88	
EC-YAY	Light Aero Avid Flyer	6/89	
EC-YAZ	Light Aero Avid Flyer	23/88	
EC-YBA	Light Aero Avid Flyer	44/89	
EC-YBB	Dynali Chickinox Kot Kot	6/90	
EC-YBC	Weedhopper	11/84	
EC-YBD	Rans S-6 Coyote II	79/90	
EC-YBE	Rans S-4 Coyote I	77/90	
EC-YBF	Brügger MB-2 Colibri	11/86	EC-386
EC-YBG	Flying Master	34/90	
EC-YBH	Comco Ikarus Fox-C22	10/90	
EC-YBI	Eipper Quicksilver MXL-II	70/90	
EC-YBJ	Cosmos Bidulum 50	28/90	
EC-YBK	Sallen Mach 15 Gyrocopter	29/90	ECT-444 ?
EC-YBL	LET L-13E Blanik M	28/89	EC-CQV
EC-YBM	Air Création GT BI Safari Quartz	8/90	
EC-YBN	Air Création Racer 12SX	43/90	
EC-YBO	Air Création GT BI Safari	25/90	
EC-YBP	Nicollier HN.700 Ménestrel II	18/90/001E	EC-605
EC-YBQ	Air Command 532 Elite	102/90	
EC-YBR	Rans S-4 Coyote I	16/91	
EC-YBS	Air Création Safari GT Quartz 16SX	38/90	EC-611
EC-YBT	Air Création Safari GT BI Fun 18	62/90	
EC-YBU	Air Création Racer Quartz 12SX	72/90	WAC-72
EC-YBV	Rans S-4 Coyote I	50/90	
EC-YBX	Eipper Quicksilver MXL-II	84/90	
EC-YBY	Light Aero Avid Flyer STOL	22/88	
EC-YBZ	VA-12C	21/89	
EC-YCA	Rotorway Executive	95/90	EC-656
EC-YCB	Cosmos Chronos 14	116/90	
EC-YCC	Light Aero Avid Flyer	17/88	
EC-YCD	Chickinox Tandem	21/91	
EC-YCE	Chickinox Tandem	20/91	
EC-YCF	Chickinox Monoplaza	53/90	
EC-YCG	Denney Kitfox	17/89	EC-661
EC-YCH	Sadler Vampire SV-2	11/91	
EC-YCI	AISA I-11B Peque (Replica)	7/89	
EC-YCJ	Rans S-7 Courier	17/91	EC-837
EC-YCK	Sirocco E	1/91	
EC-YCL	Pterodactyl Ascender	29/91	EC-724
EC-YCM	Air Command 582 Gyrocopter	114/90	
EC-YCN	Circa-Nieuport II	20/87	EC-201
EC-YCO	Eipper Quicksilver MXL-II	95/90	
EC-YCP	Light Aero Avid Flyer STOL	25/88	
EC-YCQ	Kolb Mk.II Twinstar	1/90	
EC-YCR	Air Création Safari GT BI	1	
EC-YCS	Air Création Safari Quartz 16SX	74/90	
EC-YCT	Chickinox Tandem	88/90	
EC-YCU	Air Création GT BIPlus 20	76/90	
EC-YCV	Kolb Twinstar Mk.II	55/90	EC-405
EC-YCX	Rans S-7 Courier	78/90	
EC-YCY	Rans S-10 Sakota	80/90	

Regn.	Type	C/n	Prev.Id.
EC-YCZ	Rans S-12 Airaile	38/91	
EC-YDA	TSA10 Flying Master	66/91	
EC-YDB	Rans S-4 Coyote I	139/91	
EC-YDC	Rans S-6 Coyote II	71/91	
EC-YDD	Sallen Mach 07 Gyrocopter	27/90	
EC-YDE	Rans S-6 Coyote II	80/91	
EC-YDF	Pendular Trike	13/91	
EC-YDG	Rans S-12 Airaile	83/91	
EC-YDH	Eipper Quicksilver MX-II	97/90	
EC-YDI	Volero Trike	27/91	
EC-YDJ	Air Création GT BI Quartz 16SX	63/91	
EC-YDK	Light Aero Avid Flyer	7/90	
EC-YDL	Zenair CH-701 STOL	154/91	EC-915 ?
EC-YDM	Safari GT BI Fun 18	3/91	
EC-YDN	Air Création Racer Fun 14	40/91	
EC-YDO	Eipper Quicksilver GT-500	68/91	
EC-YDP	Condor	119/90	
EC-YDQ	Rans S-6 Coyote II	58/91	
EC-YDR	JL Colibri 12SX	73/90	
EC-YDS	Dynali Chickinox Tandem	98/91	
EC-YDT	Light Aero Avid Flyer STOL	20/91	
EC-YDU	Rans S-6 Coyote II	117/91	
EC-YDV	Renegade Spirit	67/90	
EC-YDX	Aérienne Sirocco	45/91	
EC-YDY	Eipper Quicksilver MX-II	22/91	
EC-YDZ	Dynali Chickinox Kot-Kot	63/90	
EC-YEA	Safari GT BI Quartz 18 BI	64/90	
EC-YEB	Safari GT BI Plus 20	88/91	
EC-YEC	Colomban MC-15 Cri-Cri	15/87	EC-598
EC-YED	Safari GT BI Plus 20	113/90	
EC-YEE	Ultravia Pelican Club	33/89	EC-723
EC-YEF	Racer Fun 14	148/91	
EC-YEG	Rans S-4 Coyote I	97/91	
EC-YEH	Quad City Challenger II	116/91	EC-921 ?
EC-YEI	Flying Master	59/90	
EC-YEJ	Aériane Sirocco	66/90	EC-645
EC-YEK	Vector 610	113/90	
EC-YEL	Light Aero Avid Flyer STOL	40/89	
EC-YEM	Light Aero Avid Flyer STOL	31/89	
EC-YEN	Quad City Challenger II	62/91	EC-871 ?
EC-YEO	Light Aero Avid Flyer STOL	14/90	
EC-YEP	Light Aero Avid Flyer STOL	106/90	
EC-YEQ	Air Création Racer 12SX	42/92	
EC-YER	Quad City Challenger II Special	118/90	
EC-YES	Safari GT BI Fun	8/91	
EC-YET	Tierra II	110/91	
EC-YEU	Safari GT BI	61/91	
EC-YEV	Dynali Chickinox Kot-Kot	163/91	
EC-YEX	Rans S-4 Coyote I	144/91	
EC-YEY	Ménestrel II	002-E/58/90	
EC-YEZ	Rans S-6 Coyote II	139/91	
EC-YFA	Rans S-6 Coyote II	84/91	
EC-YFB	Kolb Twinstar Mk.II	115/90	
EC-YFC	Renegade Spirit (W/o 7.8.96)	2/89	
EC-YFD	Mini Maxi	56/90	EC-910
EC-YFE	Bragg	101/90	EC-143
EC-YFF	Van's RV-6A	44/90	EC-118
EC-YFG	Fischer FP-404 Classic	22/90	EC-398
EC-YFH	Capella XS	87/91	EC-200
EC-YFI	Ultravia Pelican Club	108/90	EC-846
EC-YFJ	Light Aero Avid Flyer	33/91	
EC-YFK	Rans S-12 Airaile	23/92	
EC-YFL	Rans S-12 Airaile	158/91	
EC-YFM	Air Création GT BI Fun 18	43/91	
EC-YFN	Air Command 582	165/91	
EC-YFO	Rans S-12 Airaile	123/91	
EC-YFP	Light Aero Avid Flyer STOL	115/91	
EC-YFQ	Rans S-6 Coyote II	33/92	
EC-YFR	Air Création GT BI Fun 18	145/91	
EC-YFS	Rans S-12 Airaile	74/92	
EC-YFT	Air Création GT BI Quartz SX-16	8/92	
EC-YFU	Air Création Racer Quartz SX12	121/91	
EC-YFV	Air Création Safari GT BI Quartz	105/91	
EC-YFX	Air Création GT BIFun 18	104/91	
EC-YFY	Air Création Safari GT BI Fun 18	166/91	

Regn.	Type	C/n	Prev.Id.
EC-YFZ	J.L.Colibri 2/Quartz SX-16	133/91	
EC-YGA	Air Création Racer Fun 14	53/91	
EC-YGB	Air Création Safari GT BI Quartz	131/91	
EC-YGC	Kolb Twinstar Mk.II	4/90	
EC-YGD	Kolb Twinstar Mk.II	3/90	
EC-YGE	Tango II	24/92	
EC-YGF	Air Création GT BI Quartz SX-16	168/91	
EC-YGG	Air Création Racer Quartz SX-12	124/91	
EC-YGH	Air Création GT BI Fun 18	54/91	
EC-YGI	Rans S-12 Airaile	70/91	
EC-YGJ	Rans S-10 Sakota	49/91	
EC-YGK	Cosmos Atlas 21	136/92	
EC-YGL	Rans S-6 Coyote II	132/92	
EC-YGM	Rans S-14	110/92	
EC-YGN	Rans S-6 Coyote II	52/92	
EC-YGO	Racer SX-12	2/92	
EC-YGP	Synairgie Jaguar 16	21/92	
EC-YGQ	Light Aero Avid Flyer STOL	30/89	
EC-YGR	Eipper Quicksilver Sprint II	21/93	
EC-YGS	Air Création GT BI Fun 18	175/92	
EC-YGT	Air Création Safari GT BI Plus 20	2/91	
EC-YGU	Rans S-6 Coyote II	5/93	
EC-YGV	Capella XSX	11/92	
EC-YGX	Minimax Fun-18	93/90	
EC-YGY	Zenair STOL	108/91	
EC-YGZ	TEAM Hi-Max	36/90	
EC-YHA	Rans S-6 Coyote II	153/91	
EC-YHB	Rans S-12 Airaile	169/91	
EC-YHC	Cosmos Echo-12	131/92	
EC-YHD	JN-1	57/90	
EC-YHE	Rans S-12 Airaile	106/92	
EC-YHF	Doleal DJP-03	35/89	
EC-YHG	Light Aero Avid Flyer STOL	51/90	
EC-YHH	Van's RV-4	18/87	EC-447
EC-YHI	Rans S-12 Airaile	167/91	
EC-YHJ	Mainair Gemini/Flash IIA	93088	
EC-YHK	Dynali Chickinox Kot-Kot	82/90	
EC-YHL	Eipper Quicksilver MX-II	93062	EC-671 ?
EC-YHM	Eipper Quicksilver MX-II	125/92	EC-675 ?
EC-YHN	Denney Kitfox	55/92	
EC-YHO	Mainair Gemini/Flash IIA	50/93	
EC-YHP	Air Création Safari GT BI Quartz	3/92	
EC-YHQ	Air Création Safari GT 1+1 Plus	56/93	
EC-YHR	Rans S-6 Coyote II	140/93	
EC-YHS	Lohele Sport Parasol	93119	
EC-YHT	TEAM Mini-Max	39/90	
EC-YHU	Light Aero Avid Flyer	40/90	
EC-YHV	Light Miniature LM-1	75/90	EC-710 ?
EC-YHX	Moni	35/88	
EC-YHY	Air Création Safari GT BI Quartz 18	22/93	
EC-YHZ	Bidulum-50 Turbo 17	60/92	
EC-YIA	Rans S-6 Coyote II	76/92	
EC-YIB	Cosmos Bidulum	123/92	
EC-YIC	Drifter ARV-582	142/92	
EC-YID	Pelican Club	23/89	
EC-YIE	Dynali Chickinox Kot-Kot	71/90	
EC-YIF	Vector 610	140/92	
EC-YIG	Rans S-12 Airaile	143/92	
EC-YIH	Sky Walker II-300	11/93	
EC-YII	Sky Walker II-300	99/91	
EC-YIJ	Capotilo	93112	
EC-YIK	Rans S-6 Coyote II	52/93	
EC-YIL	Air Création Racer Quartz SX12	94/92	
EC-YIM	Volero	93131	
EC-YIN	Drifter ARV-503	22/92	
EC-YIO	T-Bird II	101/91	
EC-YIP	TEAM Mini-Max	80/92	
EC-YIQ	Rans S-6 Coyote II	47/93	
EC-YIR	Denney Kitfox	128/91	
EC-YIS	Tierra II	119/92	
EC-YIT	Cosmos	93087	
EC-YIU	Neico Lancair 360	9/92	EC-537
EC-YIV	Sky Walker II-300	49/92	
EC-YIX	Teulai	26/90	EC-274
EC-YIY	Light Aero AvidMaster	17/92	
EC-YIZ	Light Aero AvidMaster	59/93	
EC-YJA	Eipper Quicksilver Sprint II-BI	93093	
EC-YJB	Rans S-6 Coyote II	115/92	
EC-YJC	Air Création Safari GT 1+1 Plus 17	137/92	
EC-YJD	Rans S-12 Airaile	44/92	
EC-YJE	Denney Kitfox	92/91	
EC-YJF	Rans S-6 Coyote II	93073	
EC-YJG	Rans S-4 Coyote I	107/91	
EC-YJH	Air Création Safari GT-BI	26/93	
EC-YJI	Fisher FP-404 Classic	37/92	
EC-YJJ	CFM Streak Shadow	93076	
EC-YJK	Rans S-14	93081	
EC-YJL	Rans S-6 Coyote II	41/93	
EC-YJM	Cosmos Chronos	69/92	
EC-YJN	Pelican Club	22/89	
EC-YJO	Pirriqui	93085	
EC-YJP	Preceptor Ultra-Pup	95/92	EC-108 ?
EC-YJQ	Rans S-12 Airaile	93130	
EC-YJR	Dynali Chickinox Tandem	122/92	
EC-YJS	Fisher FP.202 Super Koala	12/87	
EC-YJT	Cobra	161/91	
EC-YJU	Eipper Quicksilver Sprint II-BI	93100	
EC-YJV	Mosler N-32 Pup	23/90	
EC-YJX	Air Création Safari GT-BI Fun 18	162/91	
EC-YJY	Denney Kitfox	72/92	
EC-YJZ	Challenger II	93108	
EC-YKA	Rans S-6ES Coyote II	93099	
EC-YKB	TEAM Hi-Max	93127	
EC-YKC	Air Création Racer Fun 14	93114	
EC-YKD	Dynali Chickinox Kot-Kot	40/92	
EC-YKE	Titan Tornado	144/92	
EC-YKF	Rans S-6ES Coyote II	48/93	
EC-YKG	Icaro Quartz SX16	94077	
EC-YKH	Palomo	94030	
EC-YKI	TEAM Minimax Max	37/91	
EC-YKJ	Rans S-6ES Coyote II	27/93	
EC-YKK	Pendular Trike	94050	
EC-YKL	Hazard 15M	133/92	
EC-YKM	Rans S-4 Coyote I	93086	
EC-YKN	Aero Designs Pulsar XP	7/92	
EC-YKO	Light Aero Avid Flyer	117/92	
EC-YKP	MXP-640	93140	
EC-YKQ	Pendular Biplaza Cosmos	93134	
EC-YKR	Drifter ARV-582	93095	
EC-YKS	Neico Lancair 360	19/93	EC-537 ?
EC-YKT	Volero Cosmos Chronos	94087	
EC-YKU	Mosler Ultra Pup	94061	
EC-YKV	Stolp Starduster Too	36/92	EC-373 ?
	(Possibly c/n ACA-38, ex N9771A)		
EC-YKX	Burumballeta	9/88	EC-836
EC-YKY	Rans S-6ES Coyote II	57/93	
EC-YKZ	Tope 90	28/91	
EC-YLA	Terra-Bird 1	109/92	
EC-YLB	Rans S-6 Coyote II	93071	
EC-YLC	Rans S-4 Coyote I	122/91	
EC-YLD	Rans S-6 Coyote II	93068	
EC-YLE	Rans S-10 Sakota	94024	
EC-YLF	Phase IIChronos 16	95011-871	
EC-YLG	Eipper Quicksilver MX-II	94065	
EC-YLH	Bidulum Atlas-21	94067	
EC-YLI	TEAM Mini Max	72/91	
EC-YLJ	Rio Profil-27	44/93	
EC-YLK	Light Aero Avid Flyer	94019	
EC-YLL	Sky Walker	94096	
EC-YLM	Rans S-6 Coyote II	45/92	
EC-YLN	Villapar	60/93	
EC-YLO	Monnett Moni	93089	EC-788
EC-YLP	Anajopi GT-BI Hermes Turbo 16	35/92	
EC-YLQ	Dynali Chickinox Kot-Kot	82/92	
EC-YLR	Rans S-14	94118	EC-280 ?
EC-YLS	Flying Ghost	107/92	
EC-YLT	Pendular Fun 18	93125	
EC-YLU	Murphy Renegade Spirit	93133	
EC-YLV	Weedhopper	81/92	
EC-YLX	Polaris Cross Country Arie	94063	

Regn.	Type	C/n	Prev.Id.
EC-YLY	Rans S-12 Airaile	93082	
EC-YLZ	Gaviota	119/91	
EC-YMA	Weedhopper AX-3	94091	
EC-YMB	Pendular Tricido Hermes 17	95040-900	
EC-YMC	TEAM Z-Hi-Max	41/92	
EC-YMD	Capela XSX	53/93	
EC-YME	Rans S-12 Airaile	94010	
EC-YMF	Denney Kitfox	149/91	EC-466 ?
EC-YMG	Rans S-6 Coyote II	118/91	
EC-YMH	Solar Wings Pegasus XL	95047-907	
EC-YMI	Rans S-6 Coyote II	73/92	
EC-YMJ	Air Création Safari GT BI Fun 18	94044	
EC-YMK	Air Création Safari GT BI Fun 18	94043	
EC-YML	Cabanas Fun 18	94108	
EC-YMM	Autogyro TM-1	93067	
EC-YMN	Rans S-10 Sakota	94023	EC-901 ?
EC-YMO	Air Création Safari GT BI Fun 18	35/93	
EC-YMP	Denney Kitfox	6/93	
EC-YMQ	Maxair Drifter	95031-891	
EC-YMR	TEAM Mini-Max	94057	
EC-YMS	Eipper Quicksilver MX-II	93092	
EC-YMT	Rans S-6ES Coyote II	94102	
EC-YMU	Neico Lancair 320 Mk II	94008	
EC-YMV	Barom AGC-1 Pacific Wings	93083	
EC-YMX	Preceptor N-3 Pup	95036-896	EC-108 ?
EC-YMY	Formula Uno	94042	
EC-YMZ	Formula Uno	94117	
EC-YNA	Maxair 582 Drifter	95064-924	
EC-YNB	Rans S-12 Airaile	65/92	
EC-YNC	Pegasus Quasar	94066	
EC-YND	Rans S-4 Coyote I	94069	
EC-YNE	Neico Lancair 360	124/92	
EC-YNF	Echo-12 Trike	95037-897	
EC-YNG	Cosmos Chronos-14	95017-877	
EC-YNH	Cosmos Bidulum-50	95018-878	
EC-YNI	Cosmos Bidulum-50	95043-903	
EC-YNJ	Rans S-12 Airaile	94047	
EC-YNK	Neico Lancair 360	129/92	
EC-YNL	Volairo Cosmos	94112	
EC-YNM	Evans VP-1 Volksplane	4/81	
EC-YNN	Sky Jet II	94016	
EC-YNO	Sky Jet II	94015	
EC-YNP	Rutan LongEz	2/85	EC-676 ?
EC-YNQ	Eipper Quicksilver MX-II	93136	
EC-YNR	Preceptor Vagabond	96017-967	
EC-YNS	Rans S-6ES Coyote II	95068-928	
EC-YNU	AX-2 Le Guepard Autogyro	95050-910	
EC-YNV	Poisck 06A	95004-864	
EC-YNX	Commander 582 Elite gyrocopter	94026	
EC-YNY	Tango II-GT	94005-865	
EC-YNZ	Rans S-6ES Coyote II	93117	
EC-YOA	Precepter Maverick	96058-1008	
EC-YOB	TEAM Mini-Max	96021-971	EC-748 ?
EC-YOC	Air Création Safari GT BI Fun 18	94060	
EC-YOD	Synairgie Sky Ranger 912	95046-906	
EC-YOE	TEAM Mini-Max	95002-862	
EC-YOF	Strojnic S-2A	21/88	
EC-YOG	Van's RV-6	1/92	EC-432 ?
EC-YOH	Bragg A-3	94055	
EC-YOI	Maupin Woodstock One	unkn	
EC-YOY	Denney Kitfox	unkn	
EC-YQA	Jodel D.18	unkn	
EC-YRA	TEAM Mini-Max Sport	unkn	
EC-YSH	Van's RV-4	unkn	
EC-YTB	Denney Kitfox IV - 1200	unkn	
EC-YTC	CASAI-131E Jungmann	(built from spares)	

The following temporary registrations are also known - most have probably been re-regd in the above sequence :-

EC-043	Rans S-12XL Airaile		
EC-044	Rans S-6 Coyote IIXL		
EC-108	N-3 Pup (See EC-YMX)		
EC-152	Brügger MB-2 Colibri		

Regn.	Type	C/n	Prev.Id.
EC-160	Pterodactyl Ascender		
EC-164	Juvenavia Vulcano		
EC-173	Rand-Robinson KR-2		
EC-175	Neico Lancair 360		
EC-241	Brügger MB-2 Colibri	20	
EC-249	TEAM Mini-Max		
EC-250	Air Command Gyrocopter		
EC-300	Rans S-6 Coyote II		
EC-303	Pober Pixie		
EC-365	Light Aero Avid Flyer)		
EC-369	Light Aero Avid Flyer) (Probably re-registered in EC-YE. range)		
EC-370	Light Aero Avid Flyer)		
EC-414	Christen Eagle (Type unconfirmed)		
EC-432	Van's RV-6 (See EC-YOG)		
EC-444	Aviatika 890U Mai		
EC-459	Type unknown		
EC-466	Denney Kitfox III (See EC-YMF)		
EC-506	Rans S-6 Coyote II (W/o 19.6.94)		
EC-565	Light Aero Avid Flyer		
EC-573	Type unknown		
EC-579	Rotorway Executive 90 (Damaged 6.10.94)		
EC-581	Saltapraos		
EC-676	Rutan LongEz (See EC-YNP)		
EC-718	Eipper Quicksilver MXL-II Sport	029	
EC-741	Aero Designs Pulsar (See EC-CE8)		
EC-748	TEAM Mini-Max (See EC-YOB)		
EC-826	Rans S-6 Coyote II TD/912		
EC-847	Air Création		
EC-901	Rans S-10 Sakota (See EC-YMN)		
EC-926	Eipper Quicksilver MX		
EC-927	Rans S-12 Airaile		
EC-929	Jodel D.18		

MICROLIGHTS

EC-AA1	Ultralight Soaring Wizard J3		
EC-AA2	Pterodactyl Ascender 1		
EC-AA3	Pterodactyl Ascender 1		
EC-AA4	Ultralight Soaring Wizard		
EC-AA5	King Cobra		
EC-AA6	Cobra		
EC-AA7	Cobra		
EC-AA8	Condor III-2		
EC-AA9	Weedhopper JC-24C		
EC-AB1	Ultralight Soaring Wizard T-38B	66023	
EC-AB2	Ultralight Soaring Wizard T-38B	66024	
EC-AB3	King Cobra		
EC-AB4	Eipper Quicksilver MX-II	1222	
EC-AB5	Condor III 40		
EC-AB7	King Cobra		
EC-AB8	Mistral		
EC-AB9	Dragon 150	016	
EC-AC1	Dragon 150		
EC-AC2	Southdown Puma Sprint		
EC-AC3	Condor III 440		
EC-AC4	Eipper Quicksilver MX-IIAA	1909	
EC-AC5	Wizard T-38		
EC-AC6	Eipper Quicksilver MX-II	1910	
EC-AC7	Eipper Quicksilver MX-II	1940	
EC-AC8	Aquillon Etoile	B-19	
EC-AC9	Eipper Quicksilver MX-II	1943	
EC-AD1	Terratom Tierra II		
EC-AD2	Wizard T-38	66018	
EC-AD3	Rotec Rally III		
EC-AD4	Lazair II	B0-37	
EC-AD5	Jordan Aviation Duet	5	
EC-AD6	Wizard T-38	66069	
EC-AD7	Eipper Quicksilver MX-II	2000	
EC-AD8	Wizard J-3		

Regn.	Type	C/n	Prev.Id.
EC-AD9	Pterodactyl Ascender 2+2	83042092	
EC-AE1	Eipper Quicksilver MX		
EC-AE2	Eipper Quicksilver MX	3839	
EC-AE3	Eipper Quicksilver MX-I	3829	
EC-AE4	PumAll	109	
EC-AE5	Eipper Quicksilver MX-II	2082	
EC-AE6	Eipper Quicksilver MX	3693	
EC-AE7	Eipper Quicksilver MX-L	1386	
EC-AE8	Eipper Quicksilver MX	1809	
EC-AE9	Wizard T-38	44013	
EC-AF1	Wizard T-38B		
EC-AF2	Tango II-GT	108502	
EC-AF4	Pterodactyl Ascender II		
EC-AF5	Eipper Quicksilver MX-II	1955	
EC-AF6	Tango B-84	12841	
EC-AF7	Pterodactyl Ascender 2+2	1376	
EC-AF8	Pterodactyl Ascender 2+2	1407	
EC-AF9	Eipper Quicksilver MX-II	1781	
EC-AG1	Pterodactyl Ascender II		
EC-AG2	Aériane Sirocco		
EC-AG3	Eipper Quicksilver MX-II	1447	
EC-AG4	Sorrell SNA-8 Hiperlight	125	
EC-AG5	Sorrell SNA-8 Hiperlight	134	
EC-AG6	Challenger II		
EC-AG7	Challenger II		
EC-AG8	Interair F2	15/85	
EC-AG9	Wizard T-38	66036	
EC-AH1	Spitfire F2/55	85/16	
EC-AH2	Cosmos Hermes		
EC-AH3	Tango II	10842	
EC-AH4	Sky Jet IV	OLB/00501	
EC-AH5	Luroplane		
EC-AH6	La Moto del Cielo	8806	
EC-AH7	Interair F-2/55	SF-007	
EC-AH8	Interair F-2/55	SF-001	
EC-AH9	Interair F-2/55	SF-006	
EC-AI1	Interair F-2/55	85/00	
EC-AI2	Interair F-2/55	SF-003	
EC-AI3	Challenger	100B118103	
EC-AI4	Sky Jet II	MLB/0512A	
EC-AI5	Cosmos Bidulum 53		
EC-AI6	Tango II	5861	
EC-AI7	Sky Jet II A3	0101/85	
EC-AI9	Tango II-GT	10863	
EC-AJ1	Interair F-2/55	87/1	
EC-AJ2	Cosmos Bidulum 46	3585302	
EC-AJ3	Tango II	12855	
EC-AJ4	Sky Jet	00505A	
EC-AJ5	Hummer B		
EC-AJ8	Eipper Quicksilver MX-II	28AD	
EC-AJ9	Tango II-GT	2871	
EC-AK1	Tango II-GT	4871	
EC-AK3	Zodiac Twinstar	116	
EC-AK4	Aviasud Mistral	06.87/042	
EC-AK5	Aviasud Mistral	017	
EC-AK6	Eipper Quicksilver MX-II	2240	
EC-AK7	Cosmos Pendular	3585110	
EC-AK8	Tango II	2872	
EC-AK9	Tango II	9874	
EC-AL1	Tango II-GT	6875	
EC-AL2	Tango II	1882	
EC-AL3	Eipper Quicksilver MX-II	2216	
EC-AL4	Aviasud Mistral	034	
EC-AL5	Comco Ikarus Fox-C22	8803-3120	
EC-AL6	Comco Ikarus Fox-C22	8803-3121	
EC-AL7	Air Création GT BIPlus 20	042	
EC-AL8	Humbert La Moto del Cielo	8823	
EC-AL9	Tango II	5856	
EC-AM1	Tango II	4873	
EC-AM2	Tango II	6876	
EC-AM3	Rotec Panther 2	25733	
EC-AM4	Tango II-GT	3887	
EC-AM5	Eipper Quicksilver MX-II	1225	
EC-AM6	Tango II-GT	4882	
EC-AM7	Sallen Mach-15 Gyrocopter	129	
EC-AM8	Sallen Mach-15 Gyrocopter	119	
EC-AM9	Eipper Quicksilver MX-II	1994	
EC-AN1	Eipper Quicksilver MXL-II	3721	
EC-AN3	Sallen Mach-15 Gyrocopter	123	
EC-AN4	Sallen Mach-15 Gyrocopter	134	
EC-AN5	Sallen Mach-15 Gyrocopter	121	
EC-AN6	Colometa 52A	1511-8852002	
EC-AN7	Tango II-GT	9872	
EC-AN8	Sallen Mach 15 Gyrocopter	132	
EC-AN9	Eipper Quicksilver MX-II	2217	
EC-AO1	Sallen Mach-10	110	
EC-AO2	Dynali Chickinox Tandem	3693776	
EC-AO3	Tango II-GT	7871	
EC-AO4	Sallen Mach-15 Gyrocopter	120	
EC-AO5	Sallen Mach-15 Gyrocopter	114	
EC-AO6	Sallen Mach-15 Gyrocopter	130	
EC-AO7	Sallen Mach-15 Gyrocopter	133	
EC-AO8	Sallen Mach-15 Gyrocopter	136	
EC-AO9	Sallen Mach-15 Gyrocopter	137	
EC-AP1	Tango II-GT	6891	
EC-AP2	Tango II-GT	2885	
EC-AP4	Tango II-GT	3884	
EC-AP5	Tango II-GT	3881	
EC-AP6	Tango II-GT	3871	
EC-AP7	Colometa 52A	04049052003	
EC-AP8	Colometa 52A	04049052004	
EC-AP9	Tango II	3895	
EC-AQ1	Tango II	3894	
EC-AQ2	Tango II	1895	
EC-AQ3	Tango II	4893	
EC-AQ4	Tango II	6892	
EC-AQ5	Tango II	5856	
EC-AQ6	Sallen Mach-15 Gyrocopter	127	
EC-AQ7	Tango II-GT	1903	
EC-AQ8	Tango II	9877	
EC-AQ9	Tango II	1902	
EC-AR1	Tango II	4891	
EC-AR2	Tango II	5891	
EC-AR3	Tango II	6893	
EC-AR4	Tango II	2901	
EC-AR5	Tango II-GT	12854	
EC-AR6	Tango II	3905	
EC-AR8	Colometa 52V	09049052005	
EC-AR9	Tango II-GT	5892	
EC-AS1	Tango II	1905	
EC-AS2	Eipper Quicksilver MX-II	2327	
EC-AS3	Tango II-GT	5895	
EC-AS4	Tango II	3902	
EC-AS5	Sallen Mach 15 Gyrocopter	131	
EC-AS6	Tango II	5902	
EC-AS7	Tango II	1901	
EC-AS8	Tango II	2902	
EC-AS9	Tango II	2905	
EC-AT2	Tango II	5903	
EC-AT3	Tango II	1893	
EC-AT4	Tango II	3904	
EC-AT5	Colometa 52A	05119052006	
EC-AT6	Tango II	12852	
EC-AT7	Aerial Arts Chaser S	CH-779	EC-280
EC-AT8	Dynali Chickinox Kot-Kot	31191855	
EC-AU1	Dynali Chickinox Tandem II	292796	
EC-AU2	Tango II	4903	
EC-AU3	Tango II	9842	
EC-AU4	Dynali Chickinox Kot-Kot	31139741	
EC-AU5	Tango II	1913	
EC-AU6	Tango II	6904	
EC-AU7	Sallen Mach-15 Cyrocopter	138	
EC-AU8	Sallen Mach-15 Gyrocopter	118	
EC-AU9	Sallen Mach-10	115	
EC-AV1	Tango II	2882	
EC-AV2	Tango II	4905	
EC-AV3	Tango II	2904	
EC-AV4	Tango II	1912	
EC-AV5	Tango II	3876	
EC-AV6	Dynali Chickinox Kot-Kot	31256693	EC-606 ?

Regn.	Type	C/n	Prev.Id.
EC-AV7	Sallen Mach 15 Gyrocopter	15-142	
EC-AV8	Tango II	4904	
EC-AV9	Tango II	9876	
EC-AX1	Tango II	6902	
EC-AX2	Tango II	5901	
EC-AX3	Dynali Chickinox Tandem	219154	
EC-AX4	Tango II	2913	
EC-AX5	Tango II	2911	
EC-AX6	Tango II	2912	
EC-AX7	Tango II	4902	
EC-AX8	Tango II-GT	5904	
EC-AX9	Eipper Quicksilver MX-II	3876	
EC-AY1	Dynali Chickinox Kot-Kot	329846	
EC-AY2	Dynali Chickinox Tandem	2106128	
EC-AY3	Tango II	5851	
EC-AY4	Sallen Mach-15 Gyrocopter	15143	
EC-AY6	Tango II-GT	3912	
EC-AY7	Sallen Mach 10 Gyrocopter	10-111	
EC-AY8	Tango II-GT	2915	
EC-AY9	Tango II-GT	1914	
EC-AZ1	Sallen Mach 15 Gyrocopter	128	
EC-AZ2	Tango II-GT	3911	
EC-AZ3	Tango II-GT	4911	
EC-AZ4	Tango II-GT	1885	
EC-AZ5	Tango II	3853	
EC-AZ6	Eipper Quicksilver MXL-II	140	
EC-AZ7	Dynali Chickinox Kot-Kot	31086928	
EC-AZ8	Dynali Chickinox Monoplaza	11087812	
EC-AZ9	Dynali Chickinox Tandem	285787	
EC-BA1	Air Création Safari GT-BI Fun 18	191003	
EC-BA2	Air Création Safari GT-BI Fun 18	191007	
EC-BA3	Tango II	6903	
EC-BA4	Tango II	5893	
EC-BA5	Eipper Quicksilver MXL	3722	
EC-BA6	Eipper Quicksilver MX-Sprint II	212	
EC-BA7	Eipper Quicksilver MX-Sprint II	397018	
EC-BA8	Tango II	4901	
EC-BA9	Air Création Safari GT-BI Fun 18	191006	
EC-BB1	Tango II	4894	
EC-BB2	Air Création Safari GT-BI Fun 18	192013	
EC-BB3	Eipper Quicksilver MXL-II	78	
EC-BB4	Sallen Mach-15 Gyrocopter	15-144	
EC-BB5	Eipper Quicksilver MX-II	137	
EC-BB6	Dynali Chickinox	31220684	
EC-BB7	Eipper Quicksilver MXL-II	1353	
EC-BB8	Air Création Safari GT-BI Fun 18	192014	
EC-BB9	Sallen Mach-15 Gyrocopter	112	
EC-BC1	Eipper Quicksilver MXL	1212	
EC-BC2	Sallen Mach-10	140	
EC-BC3	Sallen Mach-15 Gyrocopter	15-145	
EC-BC4	Eipper Quicksilver MXL	1689	
EC-BC5	Tango II	4884	
EC-BC6	Tango II	6851	
EC-BC7	Eipper Quicksilver MX-II	237	
EC-BC8	Tango II	5912	
EC-BC9	Tango II	5913	
EC-BD1	Eipper Quicksilver MX-II	210	
EC-BD2	Sallen Mach-15 Gyrocopter	15-146	
EC-BD3	Tango II-GT	2914	
EC-BD4	Tango II-GT	4912	
EC-BD5	Tango II-GT	3913	
EC-BD6	Air Création Safari GT-BI Fun 18	191004	
EC-BD7	Dynali Chickinox Kot-Kot	354134	
EC-BD8	Eipper Quicksilver MXL	222	
EC-BD9	Eipper Quicksilver MX-II	1315	
EC-BE1	Air Création Safari GT-BI Fun 18	192017	
EC-BE2	Eipper Quicksilver MXL	1685	
EC-BE3	Tango II-GT	5914	
EC-BE4	Eipper Quicksilver MXL-II	143	
EC-BE5	Sallen Mach-15 Gyrocopter	15-147	
EC-BE6	Air Création Safari GT-BI Fun 18	191010	
EC-BE8	Air Création GT BIFun 18	19002	
EC-BE9	Air Création Safari GT-BI Fun 18	192015	
EC-BF1	Air Création Safari GT-BI Quartz	292008	
EC-BF2	Eipper Quicksilver MX	144	

Regn.	Type	C/n	Prev.Id.
EC-BF3	Eipper Quicksilver MXL	3260	
EC-BF4	Dynali Chickinox Tandem	258186	
EC-BF5	Air Création Safari GT-BI Quartz	292007	
EC-BF6	Sallen Mach-15 Gyrocopter	15-126	
EC-BF7	Sallen Mach-15 Gyrocopter	4016311	
EC-BF8	Eipper Quicksilver MX	3951428	
EC-BF9	Tango II-GT	1891	
EC-BG1	Tango II-GT	1926	
EC-BG2	Air Création GT BI Fun 18	19001	
EC-BG3	Air Création GT BI Quartz 16SX	291002	
EC-BG4	Tango II-GT	4914	
EC-BG5	Volero Jaguar-16	1921	
EC-BG6	Dynali Chickinox Kot-Kot	31060000	
EC-BG7	Tango II-GT	T2922	
EC-BG8	Tango II-GT	1921	
EC-BG9	Tango II-GT	1911	
EC-BH1	Dynali Chickinox Kot-Kot	2592E106	
EC-BH2	Dynali Chickinox Kot-Kot	32144536	
EC-BH3	Volero Jaguar-16	3922	
EC-BH4	Volero Jaguar-16	3921	
EC-BH5	Volero Jaguar-16	3924	
EC-BH6	Volero Jaguar-16	3923	
EC-BH7	Fly-Master TSA-10	003	
EC-BH8	Eipper Quicksilver MX-II	3269	
EC-BH9	Sallen Mach 15 Gyrocopter	15-148	
EC-BI1	Tango GT-II	T2921	
EC-BI2	Air Création GT BI Fun 18	192025	
EC-BI3	Volero Jaguar-16	V1923	
EC-BI4	Volero Jaguar-16	V4921	
EC-BI5	Volero Jaguar-16	V3925	
EC-BI6	Tango GT-II	2923	
EC-BI7	Air Création Safari GT-BI Quartz	291005	
EC-BI8	Eipper Quicksilver MX-II	0138	
EC-BJ1	Air Création Safari GT-BI Fun 18	192029	
EC-BJ2	Air Création Safari GT-BI Fun 18	192024	
EC-BJ3	Air Création Safari GT-BI Fun 18	192021	
EC-BJ4	Air Création Safari GT-BI Fun 18	191012	
EC-BJ5	Tango II-GT	T-1925	
EC-BJ7	Air Création Safari GT-BIFun 18	192031	
EC-BJ8	Eipper Quicksilver MX-II	5007	
EC-BJ9	Eipper Quicksilver MX-II	5008	
EC-BK1	Eipper Quicksilver MX-II	5009	
EC-BK2	Sallen Mach-15 Gyrocopter	15-150	
EC-BK3	Dynali Chickinox Kot-Kot	31216262	
EC-BK4	Dynali Chickinox Kot-Kot	31126409	
EC-BK5	Air Création Safari GT-BI Fun 18	192032	
EC-BK6	Volero Jaguar-16	V-1915	
EC-BK7	Air Création Safari GT-BI Fun 18	192018	
EC-BK8	Rans S-12 Airaile	S-12-100	
EC-BK9	Air Création Safari GT-BI Fun 18	192020	
EC-BL1	Volero Jaguar-16	V-1914	
EC-BL2	Volero Jaguar-16	V-1924	
EC-BL3	Air Création Safari GT-BI Fun 18	192022	
EC-BL4	Air Création Safari GT-BI Fun 18	193033	
EC-BL5	Fly-Master TSA-10	000	
EC-BL6	Eipper Quicksilver MX-Sprint II	0349	
EC-BL7	Eipper Quicksilver MX-Sprint II	289	
EC-BL8	Fly-Master TSA-10	016	
EC-BL9	Fly-Master TSA-10	012	
EC-BM1	Fly-Master TSA-10	015	
EC-BM2	Air Création Safari GT-BI Fun 18	192028	
EC-BM3	Tango II-GT	T-2925	
EC-BM4	Tango II-GT	T-2924	
EC-BM5	Eipper Quicksilver MX	0082	
EC-BM6	Fly-Master TSA-10	009	
EC-BM7	Eipper Quicksilver MX-Sprint II	364	
EC-BM8	Fly-Master TSA-10	007	
EC-BM9	Volero Jaguar-16	V-4923	
EC-BN1	Sallen Mach-15 Gyrocopter	15-151	
EC-BN2	Eipper Quicksilver MX-Sprint II	390	
EC-DN3	Volero Jaguar-16	V-1925	
EC-BN4	Eipper Quicksilver GT-500	0068	
EC-BN5	Eipper Quicksilver GT-500	0088	
EC-BN6	Volero Jaguar-16	V-1922	
EC-BN7	Volero Jaguar-16	V-2922	

Regn.	Type	C/n	Prev.Id.
EC-BN8	Volero Jaguar-16	V-2924	
EC-BN9	Dynali Chickinox Kot-Kot	1393-E-11	
EC-BO1	Air Création Safari GT-BI Fun 18	193034	
EC-BO2	Eipper Quicksilver GT-500	0089	
EC-BO3	Rans S-12 Airaile	S-12-115	
EC-BO4	Rans S-12 Airaile	S-12-108	
EC-BO5	Rans S-12 Airaile	S-12-103	
EC-BO6	Eipper Quicksilver MXL-Sport IIR	0328	
EC-BO8	Rans S-12 Airaile	S-12-117	
EC-BO9	Eipper Quicksilver MX-Sprint II	312	
EC-BP1	Eipper Quicksilver MX-Sprint II	0365	
EC-BP2	Eipper Quicksilver MX-Sprint II	309	
EC-BP3	Volero Jaguar-16	V-1916	
EC-BP4	Rans S-12 Airaile	S-12-114	
EC-BP5	Eipper Quicksilver MXL-Sport IIR	0353	
EC-BP6	Air Création Safari GT-BI Quartz	293010	
EC-BP7	Volero Jaguar-16	V-4925	
EC-BP8	Rans S-12 Airaile	S-12-112	
EC-BP9	Air Création Safari GT-BI Fun 18	193036	
EC-BQ1	Air Création Safari GT-BI Quartz	91004	
EC-BQ2	Eipper Quicksilver MX-Sprint II	350	
EC-BQ3	Eipper Quicksilver GT-500	0074	
EC-BQ4	Eipper Quicksilver MX-Sprint II	0388	
EC-BQ5	Rans S-12 Airaile	S-12-118	
EC-BQ6	Fly-Master TSA-10	14	
EC-BQ7	Eipper Quicksilver MX-Sprint II	0363	
EC-BQ9	Mainair Gemini/Flash IIA	934-01937-W732	
EC-BR1	Mainair Gemini/Flash IIA	914-07927-W713	
EC-BR2	Mainair Gemini/Flash IIA	871-12917-W666	
EC-BR3	Mainair Gemini/Flash IIA	847-07917-W641	
EC-BR4	Aviasud Mistral 582	157	
EC-BR5	Eipper Quicksilver MX-Sprint II	0392	
EC-BR6	Air Création Safari GT-BI Fun 18	191011	
EC-BR7	Air Création Safari GT-BI Quartz	291006	
EC-BR8	Eipper Quicksilver MX-Sprint II	0391	
EC-BR9	Rans S-12 Airaile	S-12-102	
EC-BS1	Sallen Mach-15 Gyrocopter	15-154	
EC-BS2	Air Création Safari GT-BI Quartz	293012	
EC-BS3	Tango II-GT	3915	
EC-BS4	Eipper Quicksilver MXL-II	1693	
EC-BS5	Dynali Chickinox Kot-Kot	3119196	
EC-BS6	Air Création Safari GT-BI Fun 18	193038	
EC-BS7	Eipper Quicksilver MX-Sprint II	0362	
EC-BS8	Rans S-12 Airaile	S-12-113	
EC-BS9	Air Création Safari GT-BI Fun 18	193037	
EC-BT1	Air Création Safari GT-BI Quartz	294015	
EC-BT2	Air Création Safari GT-BI Quartz	293013	
EC-BT3	Mainair Gemini/Flash IIA	952-06937-W747	
EC-BT5	Mainair Gemini/Flash IIA	782-02907-W575	
EC-BT6	Air Création Safari GT-BIFun 18	194040	
EC-BT7	Eipper Quicksilver MXL-Sport IIR	0409	
EC-BT8	Rans S-12 Airaile	S-12-111	
EC-BT9	Dynali Chickinox Kot-Kot	31149060	
EC-BU1	Tango II	3862	
EC-BU2	Eipper Quicksilver MXL-Sport IIR	0354	
EC-BU3	Rans S-12 Airaile	S-12-131	
EC-BU4	Mainair Gemini/Flash IIA	987-04947-W783	
EC-BU5	Rans S-12 Airaile	S-12-132	
EC-BU6	Mainair Gemini/Flash IIA	1005-08947-W80.	
EC-BU7	Air Création Safari GT-BI Fun 18	194041	
EC-BU8	Volero Jaguar-16	V-2923	
EC-BU9	Volero Jaguar-16	V-1931	
EC-BV1	Eipper Quicksilver MX-Sprint II	446	
EC-BV2	Eipper Quicksilver MXL-Sport IIR	0142	
EC-BV3	Aviasud Mistral Twin	146	
EC-BV4	Weedhopper AX-2	B-3043109	
EC-BV5	Rans S-12 Airaile	S-12-133	
EC-BV6	Rans S-12 Airaile	S-12-105	
EC-BV7	Rans S-12 Airaile	S-12-129	
EC-BV8	Tango II-GT	4915	
EC-BV9	Dynali Chickinox Kot-Kot	5192-E-108	
EC-BX1	Air Création Safari GT-BI Fun 18	194044	
EC-BX2	Air Création Safari GT-BI Quartz	293011	
EC-BX3	Rans S-12 Airaile	S-12-121	
EC-BX4	Eipper Quicksilver MXL-Sport IIR	0393	
EC-BX5	Rans S-12 Airaile	S-12-104	
EC-BX6	Eipper Quicksilver MX-Sprint IIR	211	
EC-BX7	Rans S-6 Coyote II	S-6A-100	
EC-BX8	Rans S-12 Airaile	S-12-130	
EC-BX9	Eipper Quicksilver GT-500	0082	
EC-BY1	Rans S-12 Airaile	S-12-136	
EC-BY2	Rans S-12 Airaile	S-12-135	
EC-BY4	Fly-Master TSA-10	011	
EC-BY5	Rans S-12 Airaile	S-12-106	
EC-BY6	Rans S-6 Coyote II	S-6A-101	
EC-BY7	Rans S-6 Coyote II	S-6A-102	
EC-BY8	Rans S-12 Airaile	S-12-124	
EC-BY9	Rans S-12 Airaile	S-12-138	
EC-BZ2	Eipper Quicksilver MXL-II	1214	
EC-BZ3	Eipper Quicksilver MX-II	3763640	
EC-BZ4	Rans S-6 Coyote II	S-6A-104	
EC-BZ5	Eipper Quicksilver MXL-Sport IIR	0350	
EC-BZ6	Rans S-12 Airaile	S-12-122	
EC-BZ7	Rans S-12 Airaile	S-12-127	
EC-BZ8	Rans S-6 Coyote II	S-6A-103	
EC-BZ9	Dynali Chickinox Kot-Kot	1392-E-103	
EC-CA1	Rans S-12 Airaile	S-12-141	
EC-CA2	Eipper Quicksilver GT-500	0079	
EC-CA3	Eipper Quicksilver MXL-II	1603	
EC-CA4	Air Création Safari GT-BI Fun 18	194045	
EC-CA5	Volero	V1932	
EC-CA6	Rans S-6 Coyote II	S-6A-105	
EC-CA7	Rans S-12 Airaile	S-12-140	
EC-CA8	Air Création Safari GT-BI Fun 18	195046	
EC-CA9	Sallen Mach-10	10-155	
EC-CB1	Sallen Mach-15 Gyrocopter	15-152	
EC-CB2	Aviasud Mistral	139	
EC-CB3	Eipper Quicksilver MXL-Sport IIR	0541	
EC-CB4	Tango II-GT	6894	
EC-CB5	Rans S-6ES Coyote II	S-6A-108	
EC-CB6	Eipper Quicksilver MXL-Sport IIR	0073	
EC-CB7	Weedhopper AX-3	C-3123195	
EC-CB8	Eipper Quicksilver MXL Sport IIR	0583	
EC-CB9	Eipper Quicksilver MX Sprint IIR	315	
EC-CC1	Air Création Safari GT-BI Fun 18	192019	
EC-CC2	Air Création Safari GT-BI Fun 18	194043	
EC-CC3	Air Création Safari GT-BI Fun 18	191008	
EC-CC4	Tango II-GT	T-1951	
EC-CC5	Air Création Safari GT-BI XP15	494004	
EC-CC6	Fly Master TSA-10	010	
EC-CC7	Fly Master TSA	002	
EC-CC8	Rans S-12 Airaile	S-12-142	
EC-CC9	Rans S-12 Airaile	S-12-146	
EC-CD1	Rans S-6 Coyote II	S-6A-111	
EC-CD2	Eipper Quicksilver MXL Sport II	0072	
EC-CD3	Eipper Quicksilver MXL-II	1357	
EC-CD4	Rans S-12 Airaile	S-12-116	
EC-CD5	Air Création Safari GT-BI M16	394001	
EC-CD6	Rans S-12 Airaile	S-12-144	
EC-CD7	Rans S-6 Coyote II	S-6A-110	
EC-CD8	Canelas Ranger	S-93-02	
EC-CD9	Rans S-12 Airaile	S-12-134	
EC-CE1	Rans S-12 Airaile	S-12-137	
EC-CE-2	Rans S-6 Coyote II	S-6A-109	
EC-CE3	Rans S-6ES Coyote II	S-6A-107	
EC-CE4	Eipper Quicksilver MXL Sport II	141	
EC-CE5	Air Création Safari GT-BI Fun 18	194042	
EC-CE6	Eipper Quicksilver GT-500	0301	
EC-CE7	Eipper Quicksilver MX Sprint IIR	0463	
EC-CE8	Aero Designs Pulsar II	0130	
EC-CE9	Mainair Blade 582	994-0694-7-W791	G-MYSH
EC-CF1	Volero	V1934	
EC-CF2	Dynali Chickinox Kot-Kot	5192-E-109	
EC-CF3	Rans S-12 Airaile	S-12-147	
EC-CF4	Mainair Blade 503	1073-0296-7-W875	
EC-CF6	Eipper Quicksilver MXL Sport IIR	0327	
EC-CF7	Eipper Quicksilver MXL Sport IIR	0326	
EC-CF8	Eipper Quicksilver MXL-II	1690	
EC-CF9	Eipper Quicksilver GT-500	043	
EC-CG1	Eipper Quicksilver GT-500	0070	

Regn.	Type	C/n	Prev.Id.
EC-CG2	Eipper Quicksilver MXL Sport IIR	0259	
EC-CG3	Eipper Quicksilver MXL Sport IIR	0593	
EC-CG4	Eipper Quicksilver MXL Sport IIR	0325	
EC-CG5	Eipper Quicksilver MXL Sport IIR	0410	
EC-CG6	Eipper Quicksilver MXL Sport IIR	0352	
EC-CG7	Dynali Chickinox Kot-Kot	2395-E-2	
EC-CG8	Dynali Chickinox Tandem	1195-E-1	
EC-CG9	Rans S-12 XL Airaile	S-12-150	
EC-CH1	Rans S-12 Airaile	S-12-145	
EC-CH2	Mainair Blade 503	1057-1195-7-W855	
EC-CH3	Rans S-12XL Airaile	S-12-153	
EC-CH4	Rans S-12XL Airaile	S-12-166	
EC-CH5	Rans S-12XL Airaile	S-12-165	
EC-CH6	Rans S-12XL Airaile	S-12-157	
EC-CH7	Rans S-12XL Airaile	S-12-162	
EC-CH8	Rans S-6ES Coyote II	S-6A-117	
EC-CH9	Rans S-12XL Airaile	S-12-172	
EC-CI1	Eipper Quicksilver Sprint II	0045	
EC-CI2	Sallen Mach-10	10-116	
EC-CI3	Rans S-12XL Airaile	S-12-154	
EC-CI4	Rans S-6ES Coyote II	S-6A-116	
EC-CI5	Rans S-6ES Coyote II	S-6A-112	
EC-CI6	Eipper Quicksilver MX Sprint IIR	0492	
EC-CI7	Rans S-12XL Airaile	S-12-159	
EC-CI8	Tango II-GT	6872	
EC-CI9	Rans S-12XL Airaile	S-12-151	
EC-CJ1	Rans S-12XL Airaile	S-12-173	
EC-CJ2	Rans S-6ES Coyote II	S-6A-120	
EC-CJ3	Flamingo	004	
EC-CJ4	Flamingo	003	
EC-CJ5	Flamingo	005	
EC-CJ6	Tango II-GT	2892	
EC-CJ7	Eipper Quicksilver GT-500	0305	
EC-CJ8	Rans S-12XL Airaile	S-12-156	
EC-CJ9	Dynali Chickinox Kot-Kot	31980	
EC-CK1	Rans S-6ES Coyote II	S-6A-115	
EC-CK2	Rans S-12XL Airaile	S-12-170	
EC-CK7	Dynali Chickinox Kot-Kot	1392-E-104	
EC-......	Powerchute Kestrel	00366	G-MWGS
EC-......	Mainair Gemini/Flash IIA	291-285-3-W27	G-MMUY
EC-......	Solar Wings Pegasus XL-R	SW-WA-1379	G-MVGP
EC-......	Solar Wings Pegasus Quasar IITC	6564	G-MYJV
EC-......	Solar Wings Pegasus Quatum 15	6651	G-MYLM

ES - ESTONIA

Regn.	Type	C/n	Prev.Id.
ES-ABC	Boeing 737-5Q8	26324	
ES-ABD	Boeing 737-5Q8	26323	
ES-ABE	Boeing 737-5L9	28083	OY-APA
ES-AFK	Fokker F.27-050	20126	OY-MMI
			PH-EXK
ES-AKE	Douglas C-47B	16697/33445	9Q-CUK
			N99665
			CAF:12906
			KP227
			44-77113
ES-ANS	Cessna 172R	unkn	
ES-BAB	Antonov AN-2	1G160-38	DOSAAF-O9
ES-BAC	Antonov AN-2	1G196-05	DOSAAF-67
ES-CAB	Antonov AN-2	1G219-07	CCCP32608
ES-CAC	Antonov AN-2	1G206-45	CCCP17940
ES-CAD	Antonov AN-2	1G194-36	CCCP68096
ES-CAJ	Antonov AN-2	1G137-49	CCCP70175
ES-CAK	Antonov AN-2	1G137-35	CCCP70161
ES-DAA	Antonov AN-28	unkn	
ES-ECA	Cessna 310K	0161	SE-GTY
			LN-TSA
			N7061L
ES-ECE	Reims/Cessna F.172P	2196	OH-BFO
			SE-IPN
			G-BKWH
ES-FCB	Cessna 150M	76454	OH-CMZ
			N8AZ
			(N3302V)
ES-FCC	Cessna 172M	62412	OH-CVX
			C-FIGO
			N12967
ES-FPC	Piper PA-28-140 Cherokee B	28-26267	OH-PCC
			N5544U
ES-FPM	Piper PA-34-200T Seneca II	34-8070191	D-GLHW
			N14EG
			N8191J
ES-FNO	Antonov AN-2	unkn	
ES-FNP	Antonov AN-2	unkn	
ES-FYA	Yakovlev YAK-54B	822002	FLARF-01087
ES-FYE	Yakovlev YAK-18T	22202034023	
ES-HRJ	Robinson R-22 Beta	1477	OH-HTA
ES-JRS	SAN Jodel D.117 Grand Tourisme	B729	F-BIDV
ES-LLB	LET L-410UVP-E20C	912608	CCCP67678
ES-LLC	LET L-410UVP-E20C	912609	OK-WDH
			CCCP67679
ES-LLD	LET L-410UVP	unkn	RA-.....
ES-LTA	Tupolev TU-134A	8360195	RA-65091
			LY-ABG
			CCCP65091
ES-LTP	Tupolev TU-154M	92A909	CCCP85727
ES-NIT	Ilyushin IL-76TD	1013409274	RA-76819
			76819
			CCCP76819
			UR-28759
ES-NOA	Antonov AN-28	1AJ004-08	CCCP28759
ES-NOB	Antonov AN-72	36572070695	CCCP72931
ES-NOC	Antonov AN-72	36572010952	"02-04"
ES-NOD	Antonov AN-28	1AJ002-06	UR-28759
			CCCP28759
ES-NOE	Antonov AN-74	36547097932	UR-74042
			CCCP74042
ES-NOF	Antonov AN-28	1AJ005-02	UR-28756
			CCCP28756
ES-NOG	Antonov AN-72	36572080786	RA-72942
			CCCP72942
ES-NOK	Antonov AN-72	36572080780	RA-72939
			CCCP72939
ES-NOL	Antonov AN-72	unkn	CCCP .....
ES-PAB	Yakovlev YAK-52	833113	CCCP05051
ES-PAE	Yakovlev YAK-52	9111412	CCCP05050
ES-PAH	Piper PA-31-350 Navajo Chieftain	31-7405156	SE-GDI

253

Regn.	Type	C/n	Prev.Id.
ES-PLI	LET L-410UVP	851438	LY-AIL / RA-67531 / CCCP67531
ES-PLW	LET L-410UVP (T)	810726	ES-EPA / 53+01 / LSK 313
ES-PLY	LET L-410UVP	810727	ES-EPI / 53+02 / LSK-316
ES-PMA	Mil Mi-8S	10532	93+42 / LSK-976
ES-PMB	Mil Mi-8TB	10588	93+88 / LSK-934
ES-PMC	Mil Mi-8TB	10579	93+71 / LSK-755
ES-PMD	Mil Mi-8T	10595	D-HOXE / DDR-SPE / DM-SPE
ES-PM.	Mil Mi-8T	10596	D-HOXF / DDR-SPF / DM-SPF
ES-PVV	Gates Learjet 55	55-011	N200BA / D-CREW / N574W / N411GL / (N57TA) / N37951
ES-RAB	PZL-04 Wilga 35A	107370	DOSAAF
ES-RAC	PZL-104 Wilga 35A	128435	DOSAAF
ES-RAD	PZL-104 Wilga 35A	16820660	DOSAAF
ES-RAF	PZL-104 Wilga 35A	17820668	DOSAAF
ES-RWA	PZL-104 Wilga 35A	96284	ES-RAE / DOSAAF
ES-SAE	PZL-104 Wilga 35A	140523	DOSAAF
ES-TAB	PZL-104 Wilga 35A	15800578	DOSAAF
ES-TAD	PZL-104 Wilga 35A	128433	DOSAAF-15
ES-TAE	PZL-104 Wilga 35A (Wfu?)	18840779	DOSAAF
ES-TAF	PZL-104 Wilga 35A	96285	DOSAAF
ES-TWG	PZL-104 Wilga 35A	18840781	DOSAAF
ES-UHA	X-32 Bekas	346	
ES-UHU	X-32 Bekas	348	
ES-VCW	Cessna 172M	60805	OH-CTZ / C-GEXJ / N19852
ES-XCL	Ryan NYP Replica	unkn	
ES-XLP	Aero L-29 Delfin	591683	Estonia AF / Soviet AF 46
ES-XYA	Yakovlev YAK-52	855707	DOSAAF
ES-XYK	Yakovlev YAK-18T	5201207	CCCP.....
ES-XYM	Yakovlev YAK-52	833206	DOSAAF
ES-XYN	Yakovlev YAK-52	844105	UR-B.. / DOSAAF
ES-XYP	Yakovlev YAK-52	844707	DOSAAF
ES-YLE	Aero L-29 Delfin	294872	Estonia AF / Soviet AF
ES-YLK	Aero L-29 Delfin	194521	Estonia AF / Soviet AF
ES-YLL	Aero L-39LO Albatros	731002	G-BWTS / 28+02 / EGAF 140
ES-YLO	Aero L-29 Delfin	294912	Estonia AF / Soviet AF
ES-YLT	Aero L-29 Delfin	094112	Estonia AF / Soviet AF
ES-YLU	Aero L-29 Delfin	194445	Estonia AF / Soviet AF
ES-YLX	Aero L-39C Albatros	432905	Khyrg.AF 105
ES-YLY	Aero L-39C Albatros	432936	Khyrg.AF 136?
ES-ZLB	Aero L-39 Albatros	31822	
ES-...	Antonov AN-2	1G160-28	DOSAAF
ES-...	Piper PA-34-200 Seneca	34-7250121	F-BTMG / F-BTDX / N4516T
ES-...	PZL-104 Wilga 35	96286	DOSAAF
ES-...	PZL-104 Wilga 35	139464	DOSAAF
ES-...	Schweizer 269C	S-1774	SE-JCZ / N69A
ES-...	Super Aero 45	03-007	OH-EFC / OY-EFC / (G-BFAZ) / D-GGAM / D-EGAM

GLIDERS

Regn.	Type	C/n	Prev.Id.
ES-1000	LAK-12 Lietuva	653	
ES-1001	LAK-12 Lietuva	6165	
ES-1002	LAK-12 Lietuva	6156	
ES-1003	LAK-12 Lietuva	6117	
ES-1004	SZD-48-3 Jantar Standard 3	B-1454	
ES-1005	SZD-48-1 Jantar Standard 2	B-1225	
ES-1006	SZD-48-1 Jantar Standard 2	B-1164	
ES-1007	SZD-41A Jantar Standard	B-912	
ES-1008	SZD-41A Jantar Standard	B-894	
ES-1009	SZD-48-3 Jantar Standard 3	B-1702	
ES-1010	Schleicher ASW-15	15092	
ES-1015	LET L-13 Blanik	171307	
ES-1016	LET L-13 Blanik	171313	
ES-1017	LET L-13 Blanik	171807	
ES-1018	LET L-13 Blanik	172221	
ES-1019	LET L-13 Blanik	172307	
ES-1020	LET L-13 Blanik	172956	
ES-1021	LET L-13 Blanik	173614	
ES-1022	LET L-13 Blanik	173621	
ES-1023	LET L-13 Blanik	173816	
ES-1024	LET L-13 Blanik	026214	
ES-1025	LET L-13 Blanik	026439	
ES-1501	SZD-36A Cobra 15	W-602	DOSAAF
ES-1602	SZD-30 Pirat	S-05.22	DOSAAF
ES-2001	LET L-13 Blanik	026437	
ES-2002	LET L-13 Blanik	026704	
ES-2003	LET L-13 Blanik	026706	
ES-2004	LET L-13 Blanik	026707	
ES-2006	LET L-13 Blanik	174518	
ES-2009-T99	SZD-42-2 Jantar 2B	B-1378	
ES-2010	LET L-13 Blanik	026951	
ES-2012	LET L-13 Blanik	026919	
ES-2021	SZD-48-3 Jantar Standard 3	B-1651	
ES-2023-KJ	SZD-48-3 Jantar Standard 3	B-1703	
ES-2024	SZD-48-3 Jantar Standard 3	B-1884	
ES-2026	SZD-41A Jantar Standard	B-928	
ES-2028	SZD-48-1 Jantar Standard 2	B-1058	
ES-2029	SZD-41A Jantar Standard	B-847	
ES-20..	SZD-48-1 Jantar Standard 2	B-1229	
ES-3117	LET L-13 Blanik	027317	
ES-3119	LET L-13 Blanik	027319	
ES-3120	LET L-13 Blanik	027320	
ES-3276	SZD-48-3 Jantar Standard 3	B-1576	ES-2022 / DOSAAF
ES-5301	LAK-12 Lietuva	6169	CCCP6169
ES-5302	LAK-12 Lietuva	6175	CCCP6175

BALLOONS

Regn.	Type	C/n	Prev.Id.
ES-HAA	Free Balloon TA-80	0270292	
ES-HAH	Free Balloon TA-80	0260292	
ES-HAR	Free Balloon TA-80	0221191	
ES-HAV	Free Balloon TA-61	0340692	

Regn.	Type	C/n	Prev.Id.

MICROLIGHTS

Regn.	Type	C/n	Prev.Id.
ES-KAS	Poisk-06 Hang Glider	R-1502	
ES-KAT	Powered Hang Glider	unkn	
ES-KDX	Poisk-06 Hang Glider	3062	
ES-KEN	Powered Hang Glider MD-20	3147	
ES-KES	Powered Hang Glider R-10D	20-1006	
ES-KEV	Powered Hang Glider MD-20	3139	
ES-KHK	Poisk-06 Powered Hang Glider	R-0210	
ES-KII	Powered Hang Glider	3034	
ES-KLM	Powered Hang Glider	unkn	
ES-KLY	Powered Hang Glider MD-20	3033	
ES-KPA	Powered Hang Glider	004	
ES-KRG	Poisk-06 Hang Glider	R-2518	
ES-KZ0	Pegasus Quasar	SW-WQQ-0452/	
		SW-TQC-0068	ES-YZO ?

F - FRANCE

Regn.	Type	C/n	Prev.Id.

CNRAC REGISTER
(HISTORIC AND VINTAGE AIRCRAFT)

Regn.	Type	C/n	Prev.Id.
F-AZAA	Morane-Saulnier MS.130 Et-2	02	F-APEK
	(Painted as French Navy "F28" - currently stored)		
F-AZAB	Salmson/CFAD 7 Cri-Cri Major *(Reservation)*	9	F-BFNG
F-AZAC(2)	SO.1221 Djinn	010/FC-18	F-BNDL
			F-BHHK
			F-WHHK
F-AZAD(2)	Procaer F-400 Cobra *(Reservation)*	02	(I-COBR)
F-AZAE	Morane-Saulnier MS.733 Alcyon *(Reservation)*	165	Fr.Navy
F-AZAF	Morane-Saulnier MS.733 Alcyon *(Reservation)*	190	Fr.Navy
F-AZAH	Morane-Saulnier MS.315	254	F-BBZO
F-AZAI (3)	Dassault MD.312 Flamant	228	Fr.AF
F-AZAJ	Morane-Saulnier MS.138 Ep-2	3220/138	F-AQDN
F-AZAK	Morane-Saulnier MS.230	403	F-BEJO
F-AZAL	Caudron C.275 Luciole	16	F-PJKE
			F-AOBS
F-AZAM	Caudron C.635 Simoun	7863	N85E
			F-ARCH
F-AZAN	Morane A-1 Replica	01	
F-AZAO	Morane A-1 Replica	3	
F-AZAP	Morane A-1 Replica	02	
F-AZAQ	Fokker DR-1 Replica	01	
F-AZAS	North American T-6G Texan	182-736	F-WZBN
	(Rebuilt using parts from F-BMJO - flew as		F-AZAS
	a Zero ReplicAIn 1987 as F-WZBN with c/n		F-BMJP
	SAM2-049)		Fr.AF
			51-15049
F-AZAT	North American Harvard IV	CCF4-550	F-BRGB
			(N73687)
			D-FABA
			AA+635
			53-4631
F-AZAU	North American AT-6G Texan	182-800	F-BNAU
			Fr.AF
			51-15113
F-AZAV	Albatros C-1 Replica	005	F-WZBH
	(Constructed from de Havilland DH.82A Tiger Moth components)		
F-AZAZ	Morane-Saulnier MS.185	3672/01	F-AJRQ
F-AZBA	Bleriot XI Replica	1	F-PERV
	(Ditched 26.7.98, for rebuild)		F-WERV
F-AZBD	Latécoère Laée 17P Replica	01	
	(Formerly Norseman c/n 778 ex.F-BSTC/F-OBTC/RNoAF/44-70513.		
	W/o in 1987 - wreck at La Ferté-Alais)		
F-AZBE	North American AT-6C Harvard IIA	88-12127	F-WJBI
	(Painted to represent NA-64 Yale)		F-BJBI
			H-29
			EX633
			41-33606
F-AZBG	SFCA/Peyrot Taupin G	10	F-PMEM
			F-APGB
F-AZBI	Spalinger S.18-III Glider	201	OO-ZPG
			HB-416
F-AZBJ	SG-38 Primary Glider (DFS 108-14)	19	F-WRRK
	(Displayed in RSA Museum)		
F-AZBK	North American AT-6G Texan	182-54	F-WZBK
	(Flew as a Zero Replica as F-WZBK in 1987		F-AZBK
	with c/n SAM2-367)		F-BVQD
			(PH-...)
			F-BVQD
			Fr.AF
			51-14367
F-AZBL	North American SNJ-5 Texan	88-17667	F-WZBM
	(Flew as a Zero Replica as F-WZBM in 1987		F-AZBL
	with c/n SAM2-669)		N9801C
			BuA90669
			42-85886
F-AZBM	Piper J-2 Cub	unkn	F-WZBM
	(Formerly Piper L-4H Cub c/n 12332 ex.F-BDTH/44-80036)		

Regn.	Type	C/n	Prev.Id.
F-AZBN	Noorduyn UC-64A Norseman *(Stored outside at La Ferté-Alais)*	774	CN-TEE / EC-ANO / I-AIAK / YE-AAD / I-AIAK / 44-70509
F-AZBO	Caudron C.635 Simoun *(Reservation)*	342	F-DADY
F-AZBP	Breguet XIVP Replica	02	
F-AZBQ	North American T-6G Texan	182-535	F-BOEO / Fr.AF / 51-14848
F-AZBS	Bücker Bü.133C Jungmeister	16	F-BOHK / HB-MIQ / U-69
F-AZBU	Bücker Bü.131 Jungmann	83	F-BOHF / HB-UTS / A-70
F-AZBV	Nord 1002 Pingouin	125	F-BDXV / Fr.Mil
F-AZBX	Nord 1002 Pingouin *(Reservation)*	282	F-BDJU / Fr.Mil
F-AZBZ	CASA I-131E Jungmann	2150?	E3B-549
F-AZCA	de Havilland DH.89A Dragon Rapide	6541	F-BGON / G-ALZF / X7381
F-AZCB	Dassault MD-311 Flamant	291	Fr.AF
F-AZCC	Pilatus P2-05	37	U-117
F-AZCD	Pilatus P2-05 *(Painted as Luftwaffe "116")*	36	U-116
F-AZCE	Pilatus P2-06 *(Painted in Japanese marks)*	72	U-152
F-AZCF	Fairchild F.24W-41A Argus II *(Identity as quoted is suspect - another possibility is that "314" as quoted is part of a serial number 314499)*	314	VH-AVN / G-AKJM / EV806 / 42-13578
F-AZCG	Pilatus P2-05	26	U-106
F-AZCH	DHC-1 Chipmunk 22 *(Painted as "WB557")*	C1/0702	OY-ALW / P-132
F-AZCI	Fairchild F.24R-46A Argus III *(c/n quoted as "33038AC1679" - while the above is thought correct another possible identity is c/n 999 ex.F-BFPD)*	998	F-BEXC / KK380 / 44-83037
F-AZCK	Boeing Stearman A75-N1	75-1653	N64926 / 41-8094
F-AZCM	North American/CCF Harvard 4 *(Painted as Swiss AF "U-301")*	CCF4-..?	G-BJMS / MM53802
F-AZCN	SE-5 Replica *(Stampe conversion)*	2	F-WZCN
F-AZCP	Morane-Saulnier MS.502 Criquet	320	F-BBUS
F-AZCQ	North American T-6G Texan	168-140	E.16-191 / 49-3037
F-AZCR	Holste MH-52 *(Reservation)*	4	F-BEAC / F-WEAC
F-AZCS	de Havilland DH.82A Tiger Moth *(Reservation)*	unkn	
F-AZCT	Caudron C-275 Luciole	7474	F-BBCF / F-APLM
F-AZCV	North American T-6G Texan	182-142	E.16-193 / 51-14456
F-AZCX	Morane-Saulnier MS.341/3 *(Reservation)*	4234	F-ANVS
F-AZCY	SE-5 Replica *(Stampe conversion)*	3	
F-WZCZ	Nord N.1101 Noralpha	77	CEV
F-AZDA	Morane-Saulnier MS.500 Criquet	226	F-BBUG
F-AZDB	Polikarpov Po-2W	0045	YU-CNS
F-AZDC	Chaize 'Pilatre de Rozier' 2200m3 Replica Balloon	01	F-WZDC
F-AZDD	Dassault MD.312 Flamant *(Painted as "138-DK")*	216	Fr.AF
F-AZDE	Dassault MD.312 Flamant	251	Fr.AF
F-AZDF	Dassault MD.454A Mystere IVA *(Painted as "1-DF")*	315	Fr.AF
F-AZDG	Erco 415C Ercoupe	3782	F-WZDG / F-BDPQ / NC3157H
F-AZDH(2)	de Havilland DH.82A Tiger Moth *(Reservation)*	unkn	
F-AZDI	Boeing Stearman E75/N2S-5	75-5238	N5817N / BuA61116 / 42-17075
F-AZDO	Auster J/1 Autocrat	2202	F-BFXO / G-AIPU
F-AZDP	Douglas AD-4 Skyraider *(Painted as "124143/205-RM")*	7449	F-WZDP / TR-KFP / (N91909) / Fr.AF'14' / BuA124143
F-AZDQ	Douglas AD-4 Skyraider	unkn	F-WZDQ / TR-K.. / Fr.AF '45' / BuA126956
F-AZDR	Dassault MD.312 Flamant	160	Fr.AF
F-AZDT	Bücker Bü.133E Jungmeister replica	3F	
F-AZDU	North American AT-6D Harvard III	88-14948	F-WZDU / G-AZJD / F-BJBF / H-9 / SAAF7509 / EX959 / 41-33932
F-AZDV	Morane-Saulnier MS.500 Criquet *(Reservation)* *(Painted as "AZ+DV")*	591	(F-BMHX) / F-BDHX
F-AZDX	Boeing B-17G-VE *(Painted as 48846 'Pink Lady')*	8246	ZS-DXM / F-BGSP / 44-8846A
F-AZDY	Dassault MD.312 Flamant *(Reservation)*	156	CEV
F-AZDZ	Auster J/2 Arrow	2354	F-BFVJ / OO-ABP
F-AZEA	Stampe SV.4B	unkn	
F-AZEB	UTVA Aero 3F	unkn	YU-DAJ / YU-CWA / JRV40156
F-AZEC	UTVA Aero 3F	65	YU-CYF / JRV40165
F-AZEE	Boeing Stearman A75N1 (PT-17) *(Painted as RAF "FK107")*	75-3286	F-WZEE / C-GBLQ / N65335 / BuA28011 / 41-25848
F-AZEF	North American T-6G Texan	182-74	Fr.AF / 51-14387
F-AZEG	Chance Vought F4U-5NL Corsair	unkn	FAH-605 / NX4901E / BuA124724
F-AZEH	Dassault MD.311 Flamant *(Reservation)*	274	Fr.AF
F-AZEI	de Havilland DH.82A Tiger Moth	84882	G-APIG / T6553
F-AZEJ	Beech E-18S	BA-359	F-BTCS / N23J
F-AZEK	SIPA S.903	99	F-BEJZ / F-BGHY
F-AZEL	Dassault MD.312 Flamant	177	F-WZEL / Fr.AF
F-AZEM	Bücker Bü.131D Jungmann	5	
F-AZEO	Dassault MD.312 Flamant	210	Fr.AF
F-AZER	Dassault MD.311 Flamant	276	(N276DF) / Fr.AF
F-AZES	Dassault MD.312 Flamant	226	Fr.AF
F-AZEU(2)	DHC-1 Chipmunk T.20	C1/0299	FAP1307
F-AZEX	Stampe & Renard/ SV.4B	"1194"	
F-AZEY	Nord 3202	20	F-WZBY / ALAT
F-AZEZ	North American T-6G Texan	182-361	Fr.AF / 51-14674
F-AZFA	Auster J/2 Arrow	2377	OO-ABV
F-AZFB	Yakovlev YAK-11 *(Reservation)*	25III/06	EAF-?
F-AZFE	Dassault MD.312 Flamant	237	Fr.AF
F-AZFF	LET L-13 Blanik	026750	OO-ZHG / LX-CAH
F-AZFG	Yakovlev YAK-18A	1609	EAF-640
F-AZFH	Brooks Pitts S-1S Special	K.027	F-WZAF / N835
F-AZFJ	Yakovlev YAK-11	25III/02	EAF-?
F-AZFL	Nord 3202	92	ALAT
F-AZFM	Nord 3400	122	ALAT

Regn.	Type	C/n	Prev.Id.
F-AZFN	Douglas AD-4 Skyraider	7609	ChadAF
			Fr.AF
			BuA125716
F-AZFO(2)	Nord 1201 Norécrin (Reservation)	6	F-BDSA
F-AZFP(2)	SPAD S-XIIIC1	4371	
F-AZFR	Soko J20 Kraguj	37	(F-AZGR)
			JRV30153
F-AZFS	Dassault MD-312 Flamant	217	Fr.AF
F-AZFT	Nord 3202	34	F-WYAY
			ALAT
F-AZFU	Nord 3202	37	F-WYAZ
			ALAT
F-AZFX	Dassault MD-311 Flamant	282	Fr.AF
F-AZFY	Moynet 360-6 Jupiter (Reservation)	03	F-BLKY
	(c/n quoted officially as "360.6")		F-WLKY
F-AZFZ	Payen PA-349 (Reservation)	01	
F-AZGB	North American T-6D Harvard IV	CCF4-175	N175JR
			CF-UNL
			RCAF20384
F-AZGC	EKW C-3605	273	F-WZII
			C-493
F-AZGD	EKW C-3605	330	F-WZIG
			C-550
F-AZGE	Dassault MD-312 Flamant	158	Fr.AF
F-AZGF	Nord 3202	80	G-BEFH
			N2255N
			ALAT
F-AZGG	CASA I-131E Jungmann	unkn	E3B-540
F-AZGH	CASA I-131E Jungmann	unkn	E3B-538
F-AZGI	CASA I-131E Jungmann	unkn	E3B-532
	(Painted in Sp.AF c/s as "781/13")		
F-AZGJ	Boeing Stearman E75	"75-SA28"	
F-AZGK(2)	Stinson V-77 Reliant	77-177	N77DB
			NC77DB
F-AZGL	CASA I-131E Jungmann (Reservation)	"1022"	
F-AZGM	Boeing Stearman A75-N1	75-589	G-BPEX
			N65D
			N61304
			40-2032
F-AZGN	Fokker DR.1 Replica	NS	
F-AZGO	DHC-1 Chipmunk T.20	C1/0346	F-WZGO
			FAP1308
F-AZGP	OGMA/DHC-1 Chipmunk T.20	OGMA-23	FAP1333
F-AZGQ	OGMA/DHC-1 Chipmunk T.20	OGMA-15	FAP1325
F-AZGR(2)	Boeing Stearman B75N1	75-2650	N62418
			BuA04320
F-AZGS	North American T-6G Texan	168-556	Fr.AF
			49-3432
F-AZGT	Nord 3202	94	F-WZBB
	(w/o 14.7.91)		ALAT
F-AZGU(3)	de Havilland DH.115 Vampire T.55	989	U-1229
F-AZGV	Payen PA-49 (Reservation)	B-02	
F-AZGX	Dassault MD.311 Flamant (Reservation)	290	Fr.AF
F-AZGY	Starck AS-70	unkn	
F-AZGZ	Pitts S-1S Special	288H	
F-AZHA	Nord NC.856A-1 Norvigie	25	F-BYCM
			F-BJLH
			ALAT
F-AZHB	Antonov AN-2	17309	LSK-452
F-AZHC	Bücker Bü.133E Jungmeister	F5-2009	
F-AZHD	North American NA-68 (Replica)	SA-30	
F-AZHE	North American NA-68 (Replica)	SA-31	
F-AZHF	Fouga CM8.13 Cyclone	01	F-CCHM
F-AZHG	Pilatus P3-03	322-4	A-805
F-AZHH	de Havilland DH.100 Vampire FB.6	708	J-1199
F-AZHI	de Havilland DH.100 Vampire FB.6 (Reservation)	652	J-1143
F-AZHJ	de Havilland DH.100 Vampire FB.6	668	J-1159
F-AZHK	Douglas AD-4N Skyraider	61/7802	N91989
			Fr.AF
			BuA127002
F-AZHL	Morane-Saulnier MS.315	350	F-BCNT
F-AZHM	Antonov AN-2	17311	D-FONH
			DDR-SKH(2)
			LSK453
F-AZHN	North American T-28C	226-124	N2800Q
	(Painted as 140547)		BuA140547
F-AZHO	Nord 3202	95	F-WZBC
			F-AZAC
			ALAT
			(F-BNRN)
			ALAT
F-AZHP	S.0.4050 Vautour IIN	348	CEV-"DP"
			Fr.AF
F-AZHR	North American T-28	135/174-602	Fr.AF
			51-7749
F-AZHS	Hawker Hunter F.Mk.58	41H-697462	F-WZHS
			J-4095
F-AZHT	Pilatus P.3-03	324-6	(F-AZGU)
			A-807
F-AZHU	de Havilland DH.115 Vampire T.55	870	U-1210
F-AZHV	de Havilland DH.115 Vampire T.55 (Reservation)	983	U-1223
F-AZHX	de Havilland DH.100 Vampire FB.6	624	J-1115
	(Painted as VZ192-"4-LH")		
F-AZHY	de Havilland DH.100 Vampire FB.6	610	J-1101
F-AZIA	Boisavia B.605 Mercurey (Reservation)	5	F-BHGA
F-AZIB	North American T-6G Texan	182-585	F-BMJQ
			Fr.AF
			51-14898
F-AZIC	Boeing Stearman PT-13D	75-5540	G-BTZM
			N4738V
			42-17377
F-AZID	North American B-25J Mitchell	108-47562	N9621C
			45-8811
F-AZIG	CCF Harvard Mk.4	CCF4-128	CF-UVQ
			RCAF20337
F-AZIH	Standard Austria (Reservation)	8	HB-680
F-AZII	Piper J-2 Cub (Identity uncertain)	5418	
F-AZIJ	Nord 3202	85	G-BRVA
			G-BIZL
			N2255Y
			ALAT
F-AZIK	de Havilland DH.100 Vampire FB.6	700	J-1191
F-AZIL	Nord 3202	18	ALAT
F-AZIM	Yakovlev YAK-3	9/04623	RomaniaAF
	(Same c/n quoted as F-AZIS)		
F-AZIN	Blériot XI	225	G-AVXV
F-AZIO	Yakovlev YAK-11	Y-5434	
F-AZIP	Boeing Stearman PT-17	75-341	N58712
			AN-BLL
			N58712
			40-1784
F-AZIR	Yakovlev YAK-11	unkn	
F-AZIS	Yakovlev YAK-3	9/04623	RomaniaAF
	(Same c/n quoted as F-AZIM)		
F-AZIT	Nord 3202	74	ALAT
F-AZIU	North American T-6G Texan	182-38	Fr.AF
			51-14351
F-AZIV	Nord 3400	123	ALAT
F-AZIY	Nord 3202	15	F-WZBA
			ALAT
F-AZIZ	Luscombe 8ASilvaire (Reservation 7.99)	3071	G-OWIZ
			N71644
			NC71644
F-AZJA	Grumman TBM-3E Avenger	85869	N9927Z
			BuA85869
F-AZJB	Yakovlev YAK-11	25III/03	EAF-533 ?
F-AZJC	WACO UPF-7	5495	N29998
			NC29998
F-AZJD	Dewoitine D.27-SA	SA-290/322	F-AZBF
			(F-AZBC)
			HB-RAC
			U-290
F-AZJE	Aero 3	unkn	YU-CXO
			JRV40174
F-AZJF	Hirth Hi.27 Akrostar II	4003	F-WZJF
			HB-MSA
			D-EBAZ
F-AZJG	Fokker DR.1 Replica	01JS	G-BTYV
			N152JS

Regn.	Type	C/n	Prev.Id.
F-AZJH	Morane-Saulnier MS.181 *(Reservation)*	unkn	
F-AZJI	North American T-6G Texan	182-407	Fr.AF 51-14720
F-AZJJ	North American P-51D-NA Mustang	122-41046	N335J, N6317T, CF-MWM, RCAF9231, 44-74506
F-AZJK	Nord 3202	64	ALAT
F-AZJL	DHC-1 Chipmunk 22 *(Painted as WP900-"V-15")*	C1/0771	G-BWRX, WP900
F-AZJN	Auster J/N Alpha	unkn	
F-AZJO	Nord 3202	101	F-WZBE, F-AZAI, F-BNRP, ALAT
F-AZJP	Beech D-17S	6738	(F-AZGU), N1126V, N4926V, XB-LEQ, NC67718, BuA23721, 44-76056, (BuA23721)
F-AZJQ	DHC-1 Chipmunk 22	C1/0829	WP967
F-AZJR	Boeing Stearman E75	75-5656	(F-AZJS), N5358N, 42-17493
F-AZJS	North American T-6 Harvard *(Reservation)*	unkn	
F-AZJT	Nord 3202BIB	71	F-WZBD, F-AZAD, ALAT
F-AZJU	CASA C.352L *(Painted as Luftwaffe "N9+AA")*	24	G-BECL, T2B-212
F-AZJV	DHC-1 Chipmunk	OGMA-65	CS-AZP, FAP1375
F-AZJX	Aero 45	4904	F-GFYA, I-CRES
F-AZJZ	Fokker DR.1.17 Replica	unkn	
F-AZKA	SZD-24C Foka	W-177	OO-ZJL, SP-1093
F-AZKD	Piaggio FWP.149D	141	D-EEWR, (G-BLOW), D-EEWR, 91+20, YA+457, YA+010, KB+118, 99+24
F-AZKM	North American OV-10B Bronco	338-9	
F-AZKQ	North American T-6 Harvard IV *(Also reserved as F-AZQK)*	"53796"	
F-AZKV	Nord 1200 *(Reservation)*	unkn	
F-AZKY(2)	Douglas AD-4N Skyraider *(Reservation)*	7798	Fr.AF, BuA126998
F-AZKZ	S.A.I. KZ-VIII *(Reservation)*	unkn	
F-AZLA	Beech D-17S	4829	N1255N, NC221, BuA33030, (F-AZJC), N32079, NC32079
F-AZLC	WACO UPF-7	5711	
F-AZLD	Stampe SV.4B	01-97	
F-AZLF	CASA I-131E Jungmann	2036	E3B-...
F-AZLG	Nord 3400 *(Reservation)*	89	ALAT
F-AZLI	DHC-1 Chipmunk T.10	C1/0915	WZ877
F-AZLL	Lockheed 12A	1287	F-BJJY, G-AGTL, N33615, BuA0294
F-AZLO	DHC-1 Chipmunk 22 *(Stored)*	C1/0529	WG479
F-AZMA	Nord 3202	65	G-BMBF, N2254X, EPNER, ALAT
F-AZMB	Caudron G-III	SA-33	
F-AZMC	OGMA/DHC-1 Chipmunk T.20	OGMA-11	FAP1321
F-AZMD	Morane-Saulnier MS.504 Criquet	600/01	F-BCME
F-AZMF	Pilatus P3-05	466-15	A-828
F-AZMG	Soko 522 Ikarus	068	JRV60168
F-AZMH	Mooney M.20B Mark 21	1778	HB-DUM
F-AZMI	Hunting Jet Provost T.3A	PAC/W/9269	G-BVBE, XM461
F-AZMJ	Soko 522 Ikarus *(Reservation)*	unkn	JRV .....
F-AZML	North American T-6D Harvard	unkn	
F-AZMO	Fouga CM.175 Zephyr	14	F-WQCG, Fr.Navy
F-AZMP	North American T-6D Harvard *(Reservation)*	168-160	SpAF AE.6-188, 49-3056
F-AZMR	Nord 1002	216	F-BFKR, Fr.Mil
F-AZMS	Morane-Saulnier H	Sams 22.01	
F-AZMT	de Havilland DH.82A Tiger Moth *(Identity unconfirmed)*	85983	F-BGEK, EM752
F-AZMU	North American P-51D-NA Mustang	122-31894	N5306M, HK-2812P, HK-2812X, N5411V, 44-72035
F-AZMZ	Boeing Stearman E75 (Salis rebuild) *(May have used parts of F-AZJR?)*	75-SA98	unkn
F-AZNA	Nord 2504 Noratlas *(Reservation)*	001	(F-GFTS), Fr.Navy, F-WIFU
F-AZNB	CASA I-1131E Jungmann	2149	E3B-...
F-AZNE	DHC-1 Chipmunk T.20	C1/0255	FAP1302
F-AZNN	Yakovlev YAK-11	25III/05	EAF-?
F-AZNP	Bleriot XI-2 *(Reservation)*	unkn	
F-AZNR	Nord 1110	150	F-WJDQ, Fr.Mil
F-AZNV	Breguet 905SA	24	F-CCIV
F-AZNX	Beech C-45B	5990	Fr.AF: 140, RCAF: HB140, 43-35553
F-AZOK	Yakovlev YAK-11	25III/19	EAF-?
F-AZOL	Aichi Type 99 Val Replica *(Converted from Vultee BT-13)*	308	N63163, 40-917
F-AZOO	de Havilland DH.100 Vampire FB.6	636	J-1127
F-AZOP	de Havilland DH.100 Vampire FB.6	701	J-1192
F-AZOU	North American T-6 Harvard	"AF33-038-21174"	
F-AZPB	CASA I-131E Jungmann	1036	F-WZPB, E3B-...
F-AZPD	DHC-1 Chipmunk T.10	C1/0027	WB575
F-AZPE	Yakovlev YAK-18	EM-019	SP-APR ?
F-AZPF	Fouga CM.175 Zephyr	28	Fr.Navy
F-AZPG	Blériot XII-2	SA-29	
F-AZPI	Fouga CM.175 Zephyr	5	
F-AZPK	Pilatus P.2-05	31	OO-PTO, U-111, A-111
F-AZPL	Nord NC.854	10	F-BDZT, F-BZBL, F-BDZT
F-AZPN	CSS-13 (Polikarpov Po.2)	8-0518	SP-APB(3), SP-AEP(2)
F-AZPO	CSS.13 (Polikarpov Po.2)	49-026	"PLW-5", SP-ANB
F-AZPP	de Havilland DH.82A Tiger Moth *(Painted as "T5857")*	PH-001	
F-AZPS	Bellanca 7KCAB Citabria	202	C-FDSF, CF-DSF
F-AZPT	Boeing Stearman A75N1 *(Reservation)*	unkn	
F-AZPY	Yakovlev YAK-18A	710	HB-RBD, EAF-710
F-AZQK	North American T-6 Harvard IV *(Also reserved as F-AZKQ)*	"53796"	
F-AZQL	Morane-Saulnier MS.131	4	
F-AZQZ	DHC-1 Chipmunk 22	C1/0916	WZ878
F-AZRB	North American AT-6D Harvard	88-17955	N3651F, BuA90747, 42-86174

Regn.	Type	C/n	Prev.Id.
F-AZRC	Nord N.3400	78	ALAT
F-AZRD	North American AT-6D Harvard	88-14510	F-BJBM
	(Painted as '14906/RD')		42-44467
F-AZRF	Pilatus P.3-05	507-56	A-869
F-AZRH	Nord 260	3	F-BKRH
F-AZRJ	Grumman F8F-2 Bearcat *(Reservation)*	D.1122	N200N
			N618F
			N1029B
			BuA121748
F-AZRS	Cessna 195B	7980	N3095B
F-AZSB	North American P-51 Mustang *(Reservation 2.99)*	unkn	N2251D
			44-74427
F-AZSC	North American T-6D Harvard	88-15943	
F-AZSI	SIPA S.903 *(Reservation)*	unkn	
F-AZSJ	Vickers-Supermarine 379 Spitfire F.XIVe	6S-663452	G-WWII
			IndianAF
			SM832
F-AZSK	Potez 60	4190	F-AOSK
F-AZSM	DHC-1 Chipmunk 22	C1/0789	WP914
F-AZSP	Morane-Saulnier MS.733 Alcyon	123	F-BLYI
			Fr.Mil
F-AZST	Boeing Stearman PT-18	75-2184	N61860
			41-8625
F-AZTC	Taylorcraft BC-12D1	10176	G-BTJZ
			N44376
			NC44376
F-AZTG	North American T-6 Harvard *(Reservation)*	unkn	
F-AZUR	DHC-1 Chipmunk 22	C1/0580	WK562
F-AZUV	CASA I-131E Jungmann	2190	OE-AUV
			D-EHFT(2)
			E3B-580
F-AZVA	DHC-1 Chipmunk 22	C1/0188	WB739
F-AZVJ	F-4U4 Corsair	9418	N5218V
			BuA97264
F-AZVM	Nord 2501 Noratlas	105	Fr.AF'63-VM'
F-AZVO	Caudron 270	6607/32	G-BDFM
			F-BBPT
			Fr.AF
			F-ALVO
			E3B-...
F-AZVS	CASA I-131E Jungmann	1035	WZ845
F-AZXM	DHC-1 Chipmunk 22	C1/0863	F-BLXU
F-AZXU	Morane-Saulnier MS.733 Alcyon *(Reservation 7.99)*	141	Fr.Mil
F-AZYK	Yakovlev YAK-18A *(Reservation)*	2624	
F-AZYT	North American T-6G Texan	unkn	41-32360
F-AZYU	UTVA-66F1	0807	YU-DLI
			JRV51104
F-AZ..	Spitfire XIV	6S-663452	G-WWII
			IAF ....
			SM832

METROPOLITAN FRANCE

Regn.	Type	C/n	Prev.Id.
F-AJAC	Albert 110 *(Under restoration .99)*	16	
F-AJFZ	Albert A.61 *(Under restoration .99)*	1	
F-AMJP	Potez 43.1 *(Under restoration .99)*	3322	
F-ASFA	Beech 65-E90 King Air	LW-47	(F-BUFY)
F-BAGK	AIAA/Stampe SV.4C	1110	Fr.Mil
F-BAGN	AIAA/Stampe SV.4C	1113	Fr.Mil
F-BAGY	AIAA/Stampe SV.4A	1116	Fr.Mil
F-BAHF	AIAA/Stampe SV.4C	1121	Fr.Mil
F-BAHG	AIAA/Stampe SV.4C	1122	Fr.Mil
F-BAHL	AIAA/Stampe SV.4C	1124	Fr.Mil
F-BAHV	AIAA/Stampe SV.4C	1130	Fr.Mil
F-BANI	AIAA/Stampe SV.4C	1140	Fr.Mil
F-BANX	AIAA/Stampe SV.4C	1143	Fr.Mil
F-BAOL(3)	SNCAN/Stampe SV.4C	207	F-BHEY
			ALAT
			F-BBLB
F-BAOM	AIAA/Stampe SV.4C	1146	Fr.Mil

Regn.	Type	C/n	Prev.Id.
F-BAQC	Poullin PJ.5B (Cub Conversion)	6	F-PAQC
F-BARP	Morane-Saulnier MS.505 Criquet	496/10	
F-BASF	Beech P35 Bonanza	D-7077	F-OBSF
			N9548Y
F-BASJ(3)	Morane-Saulnier MS.733 Alcyon	13	(F-BDZC(2))
			F-BDZY
F-BAUA	Beech D50 Twin Bonanza	DH-39	F-OAUA
F-BAVB	Morane-Saulnier MS.505 Criquet	633	Fr.Mil
F-BAVN	Agusta-Bell 47G-2	066	F-OAVF
F-BAVZ	Ryan Navion F	911	N8911H
F-BAYP	PA-18A-150 Super Cub	18-5486	(N6192D)
F-BBBL	SNCAN/Stampe SV.4A	156	CEV
			F-BFCE
			CEV
F-BBEG	Nord N.1203 Norécrin VI	295	
F-BBER	Nord N.1203 Norécrin VI	332	
F-BBES	Nord N.1203 Norécrin VI	333	
F-BBIK	Piper J-3C-65 Cub	11173	Fr.Mil
			43-29882
F-BBJZ	Nord NC.858S Norvigie	140	
F-BBOC	SAN Jodel D.117 Grand Tourisme	608	F-OBAC
F-BBOL	Cessna 182D	53391	F-OBTL
			N8991X
F-BBON	SNCAN/Stampe SV.4C	322	
F-BBPY	Bell 47G	490	F-OAPY
			OO-SHZ
			OO-UBC
F-BBQP	SNCAN/Stampe SV.4C	191	
F-BBQZ	Piper J-3C-65 Cub	12625	44-80329
F-BBTD	Piper J-3C-65 Cub	13148	HB-OVU
			45-4408
F-BBUJ	Morane-Saulnier MS.505 Criquet	263/23	
F-BBUU	SNCAN/Stampe SV.4A	85	Fr.Mil
F-BBVI	SNCAN/Stampe SV.4A	16	Fr.Mil
F-BBVM	SNCAN/Stampe SV.4A	199	
F-BBXU(3)	Morane-Saulnier MS.317	6522/268	F-BBZU
F-BBZR	Morane-Saulnier MS.317	6512/258	
F-BCBC	Morane-Saulnier MS.317	323	
F-BCBN	Piper PA-25-235 Pawnee B	25-3744	F-OCHN
			N7624Z
F-BCCB	Beech S35 Bonanza	D-7345	F-OCCB
F-BCDC	Piper PA-30-160 Twin Comanche	30-389	F-OCDC
			N7380Y
			N10F
F-BCDX	Piper J-3C-65 Cub	10528	43-29237
	(Officially quoted with f/n 10353)		
F-BCGS	SNCAN/Stampe SV.4C	281	
F-BCJJ	Piper PA-32-260 Cherokee Six	32-226	F-OCJJ
			N3800W
			(ZK-CNS)
F-BCKT	SNCAN/Stampe SV.4A	286	
F-BCLH	SNCAN/Stampe SV.4C	308	
F-BCLI	SNCAN/Stampe SV.4C	309	
F-BCNL	Morane-Saulnier MS.317	6527/273	
F-BCNN	Morane-Saulnier MS.317	6592/338	
F-BCOP	SNCAN/Stampe SV.4C	328	
F-BCOT	SNCAN/Stampe SV.4C	334	
F-BCPF	Piper J-3C-65 Cub	13251	45-4511
F-BCPK	Piper J-3C-65 Cub	13147	45-4407
F-BCPN	Piper J-3C-65 Cub	11801	OO-REA
			43-30510
F-BCPY	Piper J-3C-65 Cub	11531	43-30240
F-BCPZ	Piper PA-12 Super Cruiser	12-3485	NC4057H
F-BCQB	SNCAN/Stampe SV.4A	364	
F-BCQM	SNCAN/Stampe SV.4C	398	
F-BCQT	SNCAN/Stampe SV.4C	411	
F-BCUV	SNCAN/Stampe SV.4A	419	F-BCTC
F-BCVN	SNCAN/Stampe SV.4C	434	
F-BCXD	SNCAN/Stampe SV.4A	438	
F-BCZE	SNCAN/Stampe SV.4C	262	F-BCKH
F-BCZQ	Gardan GY-80 Horizon 160	7	F-OCBQ
F-BCZR	Piper PA-24-260 Comanche	24-4196	F-OCER
			N8751P
			N10F
F-BDCM	SNCAN/Stampe SV.4C	542	

Regn.	Type	C/n	Prev.Id.
F-BDCQ	SNCAN/Stampe SV.4A	546	
F-BDCV	SNCAN/Stampe SV.4C	551	
F-BDDD	SNCAN/Stampe SV.4C	558	
F-BDGL	SNCAN/Stampe SV.4C	493	
F-BDHC(4)	AIAA/Stampe SV.4A	1125	F-BAHN
			Fr.Mil
F-BDII	SNCAN/Stampe SV.4C	487	
F-BDJG	SNCAN/Stampe SV.4A	624	F-BDFT
F-BDJJ	SNCAN/Stampe SV.4A	516	F-BDGV
F-BDJP	Stampe SV.4C	591	F-GLHI (2)
			N591SV
			F-BGIX
			ALAT
			F-BDEL
F-BDME	SNCAN/Stampe SV.4A	635	
F-BDMI	SNCAN/Stampe SV.4A	639	
F-BDNF	SNCAN/Stampe SV.4A	661	
F-BDNM	SNCAN/Stampe SV.4A1	668	
F-BDNU	SNCAN/Stampe SV.4C	676	
F-BDOX	SNCAN/Stampe SV.4C	370	
F-BDOY	Zodiac-Vernanchet HG 380 Free Balloon	205/8888	
F-BDQI	Morane-Saulnier MS.505 Criquet	211/9	
F-BDTA	Piper J-3C-65 Cub	10174	43-1313
F-BDTI	Piper J-3C-65 Cub	13181	45-4441
F-BDTS	Piper J-3C-65 Cub	12526	44-80230
F-BDTT	Piper J-3C-65 Cub	12488	44-80192
F-BDUV	Piper J-3C-65 Cub	11653	OO-AVL
			43-30362
F-BDXM	Morane-Saulnier MS.506L Criquet	635	F-WDXM
	(Lycoming conversion)		F-BDHM
F-BDZP	Nord NC.854	6	
F-BEAU	Piper PA-20-135 Pacer	20-1057	
F-BECO	Stinson 108-3 Voyager	5105	N4105C
F-BEEV	Nord 1101 Noralpha	87	F-WZBI
			Fr.Mil
F-BEGD	Piper J-3C-65 Cub	9676	43-815
F-BEGG	Piper J-3C-65 Cub	12886	44-80590
F-BEGN	Piper PA-12 Super Cruiser	12-3472	NC4041H
F-BEGU	Piper J-3C-65 Cub	10384	F-OTAN-2
			F-BEGU
			43-29093
F-BEHG	Morane-Saulnier MS.733 Alcyon	6	Fr.AF
F-BEHM	Macchi MB.308	53/5826	F-OAHM
			I-LAGI
F-BEJF	Morane-Saulnier MS.505 Criquet	654/4	
F-BEJN	Morane-Saulnier MS.505 Criquet	602/23	F-ZJPZ
			F-BEJN
			Fr.Mil
F-BEJZ(3)	Piper J-3C-65 Cub	11457	F-BFCX
			43-30166
			Fr.Navy
			F-BCKE
F-BEKI	SNCAN/Stampe SV.4C	248	Fr.AF
F-BEKZ	Piper J-3C-65 Cub	11889	44-79593
F-BEOF	Nord N.1203 Norécrin VI	108	
F-BEOM	Nord N.1203 Norécrin VI	127	
F-BEPO	GY-30 Supercab (Stored)	01	F-WEPO
F-BEPY	AIAA/Stampe SV.4A	1056	Fr.Navy
F-BEPZ	Cessna 170B	26103	F-OAPZ
			N1958C
F-BERB	SAN Jodel D.140 Mousquetaire	33	F-OBRB
F-BETD	Piper PA-12 Super Cruiser	12-3557	
F-BETR	Piper J-3C-65 Cub	12164	44-79868
F-BETY	Piper J-3C-65 Cub	13177	45-4437
F-BEUS	Nord N.1203 Norécrin VI	180	
F-BEXZ	Bell 47G-2	148	
F-BEYR	SIPA S.903	15	
F-BEZG	Nord NC.858S	100	
F-BEZX	Nord NC.858S	116	
F-BFAM	Piper PA-24-250 Comanche	24-2802	F-OCCC
			N4636S
			LV-PQE
			N7591P
F-BFAR	Wassmer WA.41 Baladou	105	

Regn.	Type	C/n	Prev.Id.
F-BFBO	Piper J-3C-65 Cub	13153	NC74119
			45-4413
F-BFBP	Piper J-3C-65 Cub	13195	NC74118
			45-4455
F-BFBQ	Piper J-3C-90 Cub	12443	44-80147
	(Officially quoted as c/n 12959 which is HB-OGL)		
F-BFCC	Piper J-3C-65 Cub	11157	Fr.Mil
			43-29866
F-BFCF	SNCAN/Stampe SV.4C	58	Fr.Navy
			F-BDYN
F-BFDS	Jodel D.112 Club	485	
F-BFES	Piper PA-18A-150 Super Cub	18-3293	F-DAES
			N3295B
F-BFFJ	Piper J-3C-65 Cub	12679	44-80383
F-BFFN	Piper J-3C-65 Cub	13348	NC74115
			45-4608
F-BFFP	Piper PA-11 Cub Special	11-867	
F-BFFU	Piper PA-11 Cub Special	11-939	
F-BFFV	Piper PA-11 Cub Special	11-940	
F-BFHH	Piper PA-18 Super Cub 95	18-1537	ALAT
			51-15537
F-BFKL(3)	Holste MH.1521M Broussard	38	ALAT
F-BFLC	C.A.B .GY-20 Minicab	3	
F-BFMA	Piper PA-11 Cub Special	11-946	
F-BFMG	Piper PA-11 Cub Special	11-945	
F-BFML	Piper J-3C-65 Cub	12229	44-79933
F-BFMQ	Piper J-3C-65 Cub	12527	44-80231
F-BFOL	Beech D35 Bonanza	D-3606	F-OBOL
			OO-YAC
			(OO-SCF)
F-BFON	Boisavia B.601 Mercurey	01	F-WFON
F-BFOP	SNCAN/Stampe SV.4C	494	CEV
F-BFOZ	Piper J-3C-65 Cub	12696	N74123
			44-80400
F-BFPM	Stinson 108-3 Voyager	5080	N4080C
F-BFPX	Aeronca 7AC Champion	2192	OO-TWG
F-BFQD	Piper J-3C-65 Cub	13028	OO-SUD
			44-80732
F-BFQG	Piper J-3C-65 Cub	13289	45-4549
F-BFQL	Piper J-3C-65 Cub	12788	NC74124
			44-80492
F-BFQN	Piper J-3C-65 Cub	11725	N79815
			43-30434
F-BFQO	Piper PA-12 Super Cruiser	12-3492	N79814
			NC79814
			NC4059H
F-BFSY	Nord NC.858S	77	
F-BFTT	Wassmer Jodel D.112 Club	254	
F-BFXN	Morane-Saulnier MS.885 Super Rallye	90	F-OBXN
F-BFYD	Piper J-3C-65 Cub	"8979"	Fr.Mil
	(Quoted c/n is believed in error)		42-38410
F-BFYI	Piper J-3C-65 Cub	13054	OO-AVJ
			44-80758
F-BFYM	Piper J-3C-65 Cub	12166	OO-PCR
			44-79870
F-BFYU	Piper J-3C-65 Cub	12161	Fr.Mil
	(Officially quoted as 42-15216 but has f/n		44-79865
	11989,and is thus c/n 12161)		
F-BFZA	Piper PA-18 Super Cub 95	18-1338	ALAT
			51-15338
F-BFZK	Morane-Saulnier MS.317	6525/271	Fr.Mil
F-BFZN	SNCAN/Stampe SV.4C	71	Fr.Mil
F-BGCS	de Havilland DH.82A Tiger Moth	85946	Fr.AF
			DE210
F-BGGE	SNCAN/Stampe SV.4C	531	Fr.Mil
F-BGGP	SNCAN/Stampe SV.4C	41	Fr.Mil
F-BGJR	Nord N.1203 Norécrin VI	375	
F-BGKL	Jodel D.112 Club	618	
F-BGKX	Morane-Saulnier MS.317	6518/264	Fr.Mil
F-BGLM	Jodel D.112 Club	73	
F-BGOF	Bell 47G-2	1319	
F-BGOZ	Cessna 170A	19959	
F-BGPA	Piper J-3C-65 Cub	8531	OO-AVC
			42-36407
F-BGPO	Beech A35 Bonanza	D-1503	HB-ECB

Regn.	Type	C/n	Prev.Id.
F-BGPP	Beech 35 Bonanza	D-677	HB-ECS
			N90572
F-BGPT	Piper PA-18 Super Cub 125	18-1137	N1327A
F-BGQC	Piper J-3C-65 Cub	9001	Fr.Mil
			42-38432
F-BGQM	Piper J-3C-65 Cub	9920	43-1059
F-BGQY	Piper PA-12 Super Cruiser	12-1118	G-AJGY
F-BGSD	Aero Commander 560A	366	
F-BGTB	Cessna 310	35474	CN-TTB
			N5274A
F-BGTP	Piper J-3C-65 Cub	11967	F-BDRT
			OO-GAG
			44-79671
F-BGTR	Morane-Saulnier MS.733 Alcyon	9	Fr.AF
F-BGUV	Morane-Saulnier MS.317	6551/297	Fr.Mil
F-BGUZ	Morane-Saulnier MS.317	6560/306	Fr.Mil
F-BGXC	Piper J-3C-65 Cub	11446	43-30155
F-BGXS	Piper J-3C-65 Cub	10535	43-29244
F-BGZM(2)	Boisavia B.606 Mercurey	3	F-BHCH
F-BHCK	Jodel D.112 Club	483	
F-BHCR	Jodel D.112 Club	206	
F-BHDB	Bell 47G	19	OO-CSC
			N165B
F-BHDG	Wassmer Jodel D.112 Club	265	
F-BHDM(2)	Boisavia B.601L Mercurey	110	F-BIRF(2)
F-BHEG	Beech F35 Bonanza	D-4333	
F-BHFK(2)	Nord 1203 Norécrin	230	F-BEUU
F-BHGN	Jodel D.112 Club	379	
F-BHGX	Leopoldoff L.55 Colibri	5	
F-BHHD(3)	AIAA/Stampe SV.4C	119	F-BAHC
F-BHHF(2)	Morane-Saulnier MS.317	312	F-BCBR
F-BHHO	Piper PA-18-150 Super Cub	18-5319	
F-BHHP(2)	Piper PA-22-135 Tri-Pacer	22-2013	(F-BMXY)
			F-DAFE
			OO-HAA
			N3771A
F-BHHQ(2)	Pip-er J-3C-65 Cub	10272	(F-GJMQ)
			C-GVGM
			N46784
			NC46784
			43-1411
			(42-60221)
F-BHHV(2)	SNCAN/Stampe SV.4C	361	F-BGRN
			F-BCOJ
F-BHHX	Beech C35 Bonanza	D-2691	HB-EBC
F-BHJC	Piper PA-24-400 Comanche	26-51	N8524P
			N10F
F-BHKF	Wassmer Jodel D.112 Club	333	
F-BHKR	Wassmer Jodel D.112 Club	347	
F-BHLK	Piper PA-18A-135 Super Cub	18-3057	F-OALK
			F-DADN
			N3790A
F-BHLT	SAN Jodel D.140A Mousquetaire	25	F-OBLT
F-BHMM	Beech C-45G	AF-465	F-WHMM
			(OO-GET)?
			51-11908
F-BHOO	Hurel-Dubois HD.34	01	F-WHOO
F-BHOR	Rockwell Commander 112	0284	N1284J
F-BHOT	SO.1221-S Djinn	1006/FR-25	F-WHOT
F-BHOX	Rousseau Piel CP.301B Emeraude	111	
F-BHOY	Rousseau Piel CP.301B Emeraude	107	
F-BHPE	Piper PA-22-150 Tri-Pacer	22-2695	N1944P
F-BHPQ	Jodel D.112 Club	357	
F-BHPY	Jodel D.112 Club	550	
F-BHQO	Bell 47G-2	684	F-OAQO
F-BHQP	CEA Jodel DR.1051 Sicile	538	
F-BHTF	Nord N.1203 Norécrin III	358	
F-BHTO	Wassmer Jodel D.112 Club	518	
F-BHTP	Wassmer Jodel D.112 Club	519	
F-BHVD	Passot Jodel D.112 Club	521	
F-BHVG	Nord 1203 Norécrin III	361	
F-BHVM	Agusta-Bell 47G-2	097	
F-BHXK	SAN Jodel D.112 Club (ex D.117)	512	
F-BHXL	SAN Jodel D.117 Grand Tourisme	588	
F-BHXM	SAN Jodel D.117 Grand Tourisme	591	

Regn.	Type	C/n	Prev.Id.
F-BHYI	Wassmer Jodel D.119T (ex D.112 Club)	549	
F-BHYV	Nord N.1101 Noralpha	42	Fr.Mil
F-BHYZ	Wassmer Jodel D.120 Paris-Nice	69	
F-BHZK	SO.1221PS Djinn	1102/FR12	ALAT
F-BIAL	Beech D50 Twin Bonanza	DH-104	
F-BIAV	Passot Jodel D.112 Club	708	
F-BIAX	Passot Jodel D.112 Club	773	
F-BIBC	Jodel D.117 *(Being rebuilt)*	606	
F-BIBH	Jodel D.119D	626	
F-BIBI	SAN Jodel D.117 Grand Tourisme	612	
F-BICB	Agusta-Bell 47G-2	062	F-BHEO
F-BICC	Piper PA-23-160 Apache	23-777	N2017P
			N10F
F-BICE	Cessna 170B	26436	N2893C
F-BICK	Jodel D.112 Club	484	
F-BIDB	SAN Jodel D.117A Grand Tourisme	691	
F-BIDQ	SAN Jodel D.117 Grand Tourisme	721	
F-BIEJ	Bell 47G	1285	Fr.Mil
F-BIEQ	Bell 47G-2	1465	F-ZBAI
			F-BHKZ
F-BIEV	SO.1221-S Djinn	1019/FR-58	PB+158
			PB+120
F-BIEX	Jodel D.112 Club	568	F-BIKX
F-BIFB	Cessna 305C Bird Dog (L-19)	24582	ALAT
F-BIFH	Hiller UH-12B	273	Fr.AF
			51-16119
F-BIFN	Agusta-Bell 47G-2	209	Fr.Mil
F-BIFS	Hiller UH-12B	249	Fr.AF
			51-16095
F-BIFT	Aérospatiale SA.315B Lama	05	
F-BIGC	Jodel D.112D Club	849	
F-BIGF	Jodel D.112D Club	850	
F-BIGH	Jodel D.119 (ex D.112 Club)	857	
F-BIHC	Dornier Do.28A-1	3024	F-OBHC
			D-IDTF
F-BIHJ	Piper PA-24-260 Comanche B	24-4455	N8994P
F-BIHL	Piper PA-32-260 Cherokee Six	32-523	F-OCHL
			N3622W
			F-OCHT
F-BIHT	CEA DR.250/160 Capitaine	71	
F-BIKB	Wassmer Jodel D.112 Club	557	
F-BIKS	Wassmer Jodel D.112 Club	571	
F-BIMQ	Piel CP.301A Emeraude	244	
F-BINC	SAN Jodel D.140C Mousquetaire III	104	(D-EFVK)
			F-BINC
F-BINY	CEA DR.253 Régent	101	F-WINY
F-BIOE	SAN Jodel D.117 Grand Tourisme	755	
F-WIPA	Bell 47GRP	"01"	
F-BIPH	SE.313B Alouette II	1773	F-ZBBA
F-BIPI	SE.313B Alouette II	2147	IDFAF
F-BIPJ(3)	Morane-Saulnier MS.505 Criquet	149	F-BAOU
F-BIPL	Wassmer Jodel D.112 Club	897	
F-BIPP	North American Navion 4	277	OO-DEN
			OO-TWX
			N91470
F-BIPS	Morane-Saulnier MS.733 Alcyon	5	Fr.Mil
F-BIPU	Jodel D.112 Club	5	F-BIRU
F-BIQA	Wassmer Jodel D.112 Club	572	
F-BIQC	Wassmer Jodel D.119 (ex D.112)	576	
F-BIQL	Wassmer Jodel D.112 Club	581	
F-BIRL	Jodel D.112 Club	654	
F-BIRV	SNCAN/Stampe SV.4C	697	CEV
F-BISI	Piel CP.301A Emeraude	268	(D-EHBI)
F-BISN	Piel CP.301A Emeraude	284	
F-BITA	SAN Jodel DR.1050 Ambassadeur	52	
F-BITS	SAN Jodel DR.100A Ambassadeur	56	
F-BIUI	Jodel D.119	955	
F-BIUJ	Fournier RF-3	6	
F-BIUM	Jodel D.119DA	1198	F-BLEM
			F-WUM
			F-BIUM
F-BIUR	Rousseau Piel CP.301B Emeraude	116	
F-BIVI	SAN Jodel DR.100A Ambassadeur	65	
F-BIXA	Wassmer Jodel D.120 Paris-Nice	116	
F-BIXG	Wassmer Jodel D.112 Club	883	
F-BIXM	Wassmer Jodel D.112 Club	892	
F-BIXN	Wassmer Jodel D.112 Club	1001	

Regn.	Type	C/n	Prev.Id.
F-BIYZ	CEA DR.253 Régent	135	
F-BIZE	SAN Jodel D.140C Mousquetaire III	01	
F-BIZF	SAN Jodel D.140 Mousquetaire	20	
F-BIZH	SAN Jodel D.140A Mousquetaire	43	
F-BIZP	SAN Jodel D.140C Mousquetaire III	29	
F-BIZZ	SAN Jodel D.140 Mousquetaire	10	
F-BJAC	Piper PA-22-150 Tri-Pacer	22-5147	ALAT
F-BJAD	SE.313B Alouette II	1376	Austrian AF: 3D-XX
F-BJAG	Piper PA-24-250 Comanche	24-359	N10F
F-BJAX	Scintex Piel CP.301C-1 Emeraude	567	
F-BJBM	North American AT-6D Harvard (Under restoration)	88-14510	41-3 . . . .
F-BJCC	Piper PA-30-160 Twin Comanche B	30-1111	N8005Y
F-BJCL	Jodel DR100A Ambassadeur	8	
F-BJDA	Agusta-Bell 47G	038	ALAT
F-BJDB	Piper PA-18A-150 Super Cub	18-5877	F-OBDB
F-BJDC	Agusta-Bell 47G	052	ALAT
F-BJDD	Agusta-Bell 47G	054	ALAT
F-BJDE	Agusta-Bell 47G	067	ALAT F-BHPC
F-BJDR	SAN Jodel D.140 Mousquetaire	26	
F-BJDU	Gardan GY-80 Horizon 150	01	F-WJDU
F-BJEC	Cessna 182B Skylane	52214	N7214E
F-BJEE	Cessna 182B Skylane	52201	(N7201E)
F-BJEN	SE.210 Caravelle 10B3	185	OH-LSC
F-BJFN	Scintex Piel CP.301C Emeraude	538	
F-BJFR	Scintex Piel CP.301C-1 Emeraude	547	
F-BJFU	Scintex Piel CP.301C-1 Emeraude	554	
F-BJGM	Wassmer WA.41 Baladou	168	
F-BJGS	Piper PA-23-235 Apache	27-516	N4924P
F-BJHF	Cessna 210	57315	N9515T
F-BJHT	Cessna 310D	39143	N6843T
F-BJIC	Wassmer Jodel D.112A Club	1005	
F-BJIK	Wassmer Jodel D.112A Club	1010	
F-BJIY	Wassmer Jodel D.112A Club	1014	
F-BJJA	SAN Jodel DR.1050 Ambassadeur	92	
F-BJJG	SAN Jodel DR.1050 Ambassadeur	115	
F-BJJR	SAN Jodel DR.1050 Ambassadeur	107	
F-BJJV	Cessna 172B	48393	N7893X
F-BJJX	Jodel D.127	1048	
F-BJLK	Cessna 172B	48217	N7717X
F-BJLL	CEA Jodel DR.1050 Ambassadeur	13	
F-BJLP	CEA Jodel DR.1051-M1 Sicile Record	25	
F-BJMD	Scintex ML.250 Rubis	03	
F-BJME	Scintex ML.250 Rubis (Reserved as F-GRAZ)	101	
F-BJMG	Scintex ML.250 Rubis	103	
F-BJMH	Scintex ML.250 Rubis	104	
F-BJMO	Scintex CP.1310-C3 Super Emeraude (Wfu?)	907	
F-BJMQ	Scintex CP.1310-C3 Super Emeraude	911	
F-BJMR	Scintex CP.1310-C3 Super Emeraude	921	
F-BJMT	Scintex CP.1315-C3 Super Emeraude	922	
F-BJNT	SAN Jodel DR.1050 Ambassadeur	196	
F-BJNY	SAN Jodel DR.1051 Sicile	197	
F-BJOA	Jodel D.128	974	
F-BJOH	Cessna 182C Skylane	52986	N9086T
F-BJOO	Procaer F-15A Picchio	12	
F-BJOQ	Piel CP.301A Emeraude	349	
F-BJOS	Rousseau Piel CP.301B Emeraude	121	
F-BJOV	CEA Jodel DR.1050 Ambassadeur	24	
F-BJOZ	CEA Jodel DR.1050 Ambassadeur	30	
F-BJPE	Wassmer Jodel D.112 Club	1018	
F-BJPT	Wassmer Jodel D.112 Club	1064	
F-BJPV	Wassmer Jodel D.112 Club	1065	
F-BJPY	Wassmer Jodel D.112A Club	1066	
F-BJPZ	Wassmer WA.40 Super IV	6	
F-BJQK	SE.313B Alouette II	1979	Cambodian AF
F-BJQT	SAN Jodel D.140B Mousquetaire II	64	
F-BJQZ	SAN Jodel D.140B Mousquetaire II	70	
F-BJRG	Cessna 172B	48424	N7924X
F-BJRI	Cessna 182D Skylane	53041	N9941T
F-BJRN	Cessna 210A	57828	N9528X
F-BJRQ	Cessna 170B	26377	F-OAQV N2834C
F-BJRV	Cessna 172B	48592	N8092X

Regn.	Type	C/n	Prev.Id.
F-BJRX	Cessna 210A	57731	N9431X
F-BJSR	Fournier RF-2	01	F-WJSR
F-BJUB	CEA Jodel DR.1050 Ambassadeur	43	
F-BJUK	Piper PA-18-150 Super Cub	18-7549	N3812Z
F-BJUM	Procaer F.15A Picchio	11	
F-BJUN	Nord NC.858 (Reservation)	27	F-BFIV
F-BJUR	Cessna 172B	48725	N8225X
F-BJVB	Scintex Piel CP.315-C2 Emeraude	571	
F-BJVD	Scintex Piel CP.301-C2 Emeraude	576	
F-BJVE	Scintex Piel CP.301-C2 Emeraude	577	
F-BJVJ	Scintex CP.1310-C3 Super Emeraude	900	
F-BJVM	Scintex CP.301-C3 Emeraude	591	
F-BJVX	Scintex CP.1315-C3 Super Emeraude	912	
F-BJVY	Scintex CP.1315-C3 Super Emeraude	913	
F-BJVZ	Scintex CP.1315-C3 Super Emeraude	914	
F-BJYP	SAN Jodel DR.1050 Ambassadeur	254	
F-BJYV	SAN Jodel DR.1050 Ambassadeur	258	
F-BJZB	CEA Jodel DR.1051 Sicile	212	
F-BJZF	CEA Jodel DR.1050 Ambassadeur	213	
F-BJZG	CEA Jodel DR.1050 Ambassadeur	214	
F-BKAF	Wassmer WA.40 Super IV	18	
F-BKAI	Wassmer Jodel D.112 Club	1069	
F-BKAT	Wassmer Jodel D.112 Club	1075	
F-BKAU	Wassmer Jodel D.112 Club	1076	
F-BKBA	Cessna 172C	48784	N8284X
F-BKBB	Cessna 182D Skylane	53628	N9228X
F-BKBE	Piper PA-18-150 Super Cub	18-7658	
F-BKBH	Cessna 182B Skylane	52231	N7231E
F-BKBN	Beech D50E Twin Bonanza	DH-312	HB-GAR
F-BKBZ	SAN Jodel DR.1050 Ambassadeur	268	
F-BKCF	Wassmer Jodel D.112 Club	1080	
F-BKCT	Wassmer WA.40 Super IV	34	
F-BKDA	Morane-Saulnier MS.881 Rallye	1	
F-BKDD	Morane-Saulnier MS.880B Rallye Club	15	
F-BKDF	Morane-Saulnier MS.880B Rallye Club	17	
F-BKDV	Morane-Saulnier MS.880B Rallye Club	69	
F-BKEH	Morane-Saulnier MS.885 Super Rallye	54	
F-BKEO	Morane-Saulnier MS.885 Super Rallye	55	
F-BKEQ	Morane-Saulnier MS.885 Super Rallye	58	
F-BKES	Morane-Saulnier MS.885 Super Rallye	60	
F-BKFA	Beech S35 Bonanza	D-7432	HB-EFA
F-BKFC	Piper PA-23-250 Aztec C	27-3922	N6616Y
F-BKGL	CEA Jodel DR.1050-M1 Sicile Record	233	
F-BKGU	Cessna 172C	49387	N1687Y
F-BKHC	SANJodel DR.1051 Sicile	385	
F-BKHD	SAN Jodel DR.1050 Ambassadeur	366	
F-BKHF	SAN Jodel DR.1050 Ambassadeur	370	
F-BKHM	SAN Jodel DR.1051 Sicile	382	
F-BKHP	SAN Jodel DR.1050 Ambassadeur	368	
F-BKHS	SANJodel DR.1051 Sicile	387	
F-BKII	CEA Jodel DR.1051 Sicile	316	
F-BKIJ	CEA Jodel DR.1050 Ambassadeur	305	
F-BKIT	CEA Jodel DR.1051-M1 Sicile Record	329	
F-BKIU	CEA Jodel DR.1050 Ambassadeur	313	
F-BKIV	CEA Jodel DR.1050 Ambassadeur	309	
F-BKJE	Wassmer WA.40 Super IV	38	
F-BKJG	Wassmer WA.40A Super IV	39	
F-BKJT	Wassmer Jodel D.112 Club	1124	
F-BKJZ	Wassmer Jodel D.112 Club	1128	
F-BKKI	Morane-Saulnier MS.880B Rallye Club	75	
F-BKKP	Morane-Saulnier MS.880B Rallye Club	172	
F-BKKS	Morane-Saulnier MS.880B Rallye Club	175	
F-BKKU	Morane-Saulnier MS.886 Super Rallye	319	
F-BKKY	Morane-Saulnier MS.880B Rallye Club	190	
F-BKLA	Morane-Saulnier MS.885 Super Rallye	95	
F-BKLE	Morane-Saulnier MS.885 Super Rallye	124	
F-BKLG	Morane-Saulnier MS.885 Super Rallye	121	
F-BKLJ	Morane-Saulnier MS.885 Super Rallye	130	
F-BKLK	Morane-Saulnier MS.885 Super Rallye	131	
F-BKLN	Morane-Saulnier MS.885 Super Rallye	138	
F-BKLS	Morane-Saulnier MS.885 Super Rallye	167	
F-BKLT	Morane-Saulnier MS.885 Super Rallye	156	
F-BKLV	Morane-Saulnier MS.885 Super Rallye	162	
F-BKLZ	Morane-Saulnier MS.885 Super Rallye	157	
F-BKMO	Cessna 310Q	0999	

Regn.	Type	C/n	Prev.Id.
F-BKMP	AIAA/Stampe SV.4C	1091	Fr.Mil
F-BKMR	Agusta-Bell 206B Jet Ranger	8313	
F-BKNC	Wassmer Jodel D.120 Paris-Nice	215	
F-BKND	Wassmer WA.40A Super IV	50	
F-BKNI	Wassmer WA.40 Super IV	52	
F-BKNO	Piper J-3C-65 Cub	12784	F-BBOO
			OO-AVT
			44-80488
F-BKNY	Wassmer Jodel D.120 Paris-Nice	226	
F-BKOD	Morane-Saulnier MS.733 Alcyon	46	Fr.AF
F-BKOI	Morane-Saulnier MS.733 Alcyon	74	Fr.AF
F-BKOJ	Morane-Saulnier MS.733 Alcyon	138	Fr.AF
F-BKOK	Morane-Saulnier MS.733 Alcyon	139	Fr.AF
F-BKOM	Morane-Saulnier MS.733 Alcyon	36	Fr.AF
F-BKON	Morane-Saulnier MS.880B Rallye Club	64	F-BKDR
F-BKOZ	Morane-Saulnier MS.733 Alcyon	45	Fr.AF
			F-BHCV
			Fr.AF
F-BKPK	CEA Jodel DR.1050 Ambassadeur	332	
F-BKPN	CEA Jodel DR.1050-MI Sicile Record	336	
F-BKPS	CEA Jodel DR.1051 Sicile	324	
F-BKQN	Cessna 182F Skylane	54493	N3593Y
F-BKQQ	Cessna 182E Skylane	53793	N9393X
F-BKQU	Pilatus PC-6A/H2 Porter	534	
F-BKQY	Pilatus PC-6A/H2 Porter	549	
F-BKRA	Cessna 182E Skylane	54163	N3163Y
F-BKRC	Cessna 182F Skylane	54681	N3281U
F-BKRF	Cessna 172C	49241	N1541Y
F-BKRG	Cessna 182E Skylane	53914	N2914Y
F-BKRK	Piper PA-24-250 Comanche	24-3034	N7814P
F-BKRL	Piper PA-23-250 Aztec B	27-2082	N5068Y
F-BKRM	Cessna 310F	0074	HB-LBK
			N6774X
F-BKRZ	Cessna 182A Skylane	51468	F-DAFU
			N2168G
F-BKSB	SAN Jodel D.140B Mousquetaire II	85	
F-BKSD	SAN Jodel D.140C Mousquetaire III	91	
F-BKSH	SAN Jodel D.140B Mousquetaire II	94	
F-BKSJ	SAN Jodel D.140C Mousquetaire III	97	
F-BKSO	SAN Jodel D.140C Mousquetaire III	87	
F-BKSR	SAN Jodel D.140C Mousquetaire III	106	
F-BKSS	SAN Jodel D.140C Mousquetaire III	107	
F-BKTC	Morane-Saulnier MS.880B Rallye Club	191	(SE-EEG)
F-BKTD	SEEMS MS.880B Rallye Club	328	
F-BKTK	Morane-Saulnier MS.880B Rallye Club	215	
F-BKTN	Morane-Saulnier MS.880B Rallye Club	212	
F-BKTX	Morane-Saulnier MS.880B Rallye Club	288	
F-BKTZ	SEEMS MS.880B Rallye Club	315	
F-BKUC	Morane-Saulnier MS.885 Super Rallye	234	(D-ELVO)
F-BKUU	Morane-Saulnier MS.885 Super Rallye	268	
F-BKUV	SEEMS MS.885 Super Rallye	269	
F-BKVN	Beech P35 Bonanza	D-7114	
F-BKVY	SAN DR.1050-M Excellence	394	(G-.....)
			F-BKHX
F-BKXK	Morane-Saulnier MS.885 Super Rallye	232	F-OBXK
F-BKYB	SEEMS MS.880B Rallye Club	308	
F-BKYK	Morane-Saulnier MS.880B Rallye Club	303	
F-BKYQ	SEEMS MS.880B Rallye Club	299	
F-BKYU	SEEMS MS.880B Rallye Club	330	
F-BKZB	SEEMS MS.880B Rallye Club	337	
F-BKZG	SEEMS MS.880B Rallye Club	341	
F-BKZL	SEEMS MS.880B Rallye Club	380	
F-BKZM	SEEMS MS.880B Rallye Club (Wfu)	372	
F-BKZP	SEEMS MS.882 Rallye Club	313	
F-BLAD	CEA Jodel DR.1051 Sicile	404	
F-BLAN	CEA Jodel DR.1050 Ambassadeur	415	
F-BLAO	CEA Jodel DR.1051 Sicile	416	
F-BLAS	CEA Jodel DR.1051 Sicile	420	
F-BLAT	CEA Jodel DR.1051 Sicile	425	
F-BLAU	CEA Jodel DR.1051 Sicile	423	
F-BLAY	CEA Jodel DR.1051 Sicile	427	
F-BLBN	SEEMS MS.885 Super Rallye	5352	
F-BLBR	SEEMS MS.885 Super Rallye	364	
F-BLBU	SEEMS MS.885 Super Rallye	384	
F-BLBV	SEEMS MS.885 Super Rallye	383	

Regn.	Type	C/n	Prev.Id.
F-BLCM	Piper PA-18-150 Super Cub	18-5347	ALAT
F-BLCQ	Piper PA-18 Super Cub 95	18-1363	ALAT
			51-15363
F-BLDC	SAN Jodel D.150A Mascaret	05	
F-BLDN	SAN Jodel D.150A Mascaret	21	
F-BLDS	SAN Jodel D.150A Mascaret	23	
F-BLEB	Piper PA-23-250 Aztec B	27-2434	N5394Y
			N10F
F-BLEC	Cessna 182F Skylane	54872	N3472U
F-BLEH	Piper PA-23-250 Aztec B	27-2342	N5348Y
			N10F
F-BLEP	Fournier RF-3	8	
F-BLER	Fournier RF-3	10	
F-BLEV	Morane-Saulnier MS.733 Alcyon	68	Fr.AF
F-BLEY(3)	Piper PA-18-150 Super Cub (Written off)	18-5344	ALAT
F-BLFK	Wassmer Jodel D.112 Club	1177	
F-BLFP	Wassmer WA.40A Super IV	59	
F-BLFT	Wassmer WA.40A Super IV	55	
F-BLFX	Wassmer Jodel D.112 Club	1179	
F-BLGA	SOCATA Rallye 180T Galerien	3303	
F-BLGB	SOCATA Rallye 180T Galerien	3304	
F-BLGC	SOCATA Rallye 180T Galerien	3305	
F-BLGD	Beech 35-C33 Debonair	CD-867	
F-BLGE	Aermacchi AL.60B-2	31/6211	I-MACN
F-BLGN	Agusta-Bell 47G-2	283	
F-BLGO	Procaer F.15A Picchio	10	D-EBBE
F-BLGV	Cessna 182F Skylane	54703	N3303U
F-BLGY	Piper PA-24-250 Comanche	24-3076	N7853P
F-BLHA	Mooney M.20C Mark 21	2485	
F-BLHD	Cessna 172D	50009	N2409U
F-BLHJ	Piper PA-24-250 Comanche	24-3507	N8253P
F-BLHK	Mooney M.20E Super 21	279	
F-BLHP	Piper PA-18-150 Super Cub	18-5355	ALAT
F-BLIK	SOCATA Rallye 180T Galerien	3306	
F-BLIL	SOCATA Rallye 180T Galerien	3307	
F-BLIM	SOCATA Rallye 180T Galerien	3308	
F-BLIN	SOCATA Rallye 180T Galerien	3309	
F-BLIO	SOCATA Rallye 180T Galerien	3310	
F-BLIP	SOCATA Rallye 180T Galerien	3311	
F-BLIQ	SOCATA Rallye 180T Galerien	3312	
F-BLIS	SOCATA Rallye 180T Galerien	3314	
F-BLIT	SOCATA Rallye 180T Galerien	3315	
F-BLIV	SOCATA Rallye 180T Galerien	3316	
F-BLIX	Piper PA-28-160 Cherokee	28-8	F-OCIX
			N5007W
F-BLJL	SAN Jodel DR.1050 Ambassadeur	469	
F-BLJM	SAN Jodel DR.1050 Ambassadeur	470	
F-BLJN	SAN Jodel DR.1050M Excellence	474	
F-BLJO	SAN Jodel DR.1050M Excellence	475	
F-BLJT	SAN Jodel DR.1050M Excellence	484	
F-BLJV	SAN Jodel DR.105-M Excellence	482	
F-BLKC	Reims/Cessna FP.172D (Written off)	0001/57164	F-WLKC
F-BLKD	Reims/Cessna FP.172D	0003/57179	F-WLKD
F-BLKK	SAN Jodel D.140R Abeille	501	F-WLKK
F-BLKL	Morane-Saulnier MS.760C Paris III	01	F-WLKL
F-BLKM(2)	Bücker Bü 133E Jungmeister	39	F-BLGM
			HB-MIB
			U-92
F-BLKQ	CEA DR.200	02	F-WLKQ
F-BLKU	Gardan GY-80 Horizon 180	07	
F-BLLJ	Piper PA-23-250 Aztec C	27-3756	N6462Y
F-BLLP	Beech-SFERMA Marquis 60A	10	
F-BLLR	Beech-SFERMA Marquis 60A (Stored)	12	
F-BLMF	CEA Jodel DR.1050 Ambassadeur	434	
F-BLMI	CEA Jodel DR.1051 Sicile	438	
F-BLMK	CEA Jodel DR.1051 Sicile	440	
F-BLMO	CEA Jodel DR.1051 Sicile	445	
F-BLMR	CEA Jodel DR.1051 Sicile	441	
F-BLMS	CEA Jodel DR.1051 Sicile	448	
F-BLNA	Wassmer Jodel D.112 Club	1204	
F-BLND	Wassmer WA.40A Super IV	61	
F-BLNH	Wassmer WA.40A Super IV	63	
F-BLNM	Wassmer Jodel D.112 Club	1207	
F-BLNS	Wassmer Jodel D.112 Club	1210	
F-BLNY	Wassmer WA.40A Super IV	72	

Regn.	Type	C/n	Prev.Id.
F-BLOB	Mooney M.20C Mark 21	2613	
F-BLOD	Piper PA-22-150 Caribbean	22-7482	G-ARFA
			N3566Z
F-BLOK	Mooney M.20E Super 21	229	
F-BLON	Cessna 206	0081	N5081U
F-BLOQ	Piper PA-25-235 Pawnee	25-2400	N6824Z
F-BLOR	Piper PA-28-160 Cherokee	28-302	N10108
			LV-PRZ
F-BLOU	Gardan GY-80 Horizon 160	5	
F-BLPA	Gardan GY-80 Horizon 160	11	
F-BLPE	Gardan GY-80 Horizon 150	20	
F-BLPJ	Gardan GY-80 Horizon 160	44	
F-BLPK	Gardan GY-80 Horizon 160	41	
F-BLPM	Gardan GY-80 Horizon 180	06	
F-BLPQ	Gardan GY-80 Horizon 160	48	
F-BLPV	Gardan GY-80 Horizon 160	59	
F-BLPY	Gardan GY-80 Horizon 160	63	
F-BLRB	CEA Jodel DR.1051 Sicile	507	
F-BLRK	CEA Jodel DR.1051 Sicile	518	
F-BLRL	CEA Jodel DR.1050 Ambassadeur	516	
F-BLRN	CEA Jodel DR.1051 Sicile	514	
F-BLRQ	CEA Jodel DR.1051-M1 Sicile Record	524	
F-BLRR	CEA Jodel DR.1050 Ambassadeur	522	
F-BLRU	CEA Jodel DR.1050 Ambassadeur	525	
F-BLRY	CEA Jodel DR.1051 Sicile	523	
F-BLSI	SEEMS MS.892A Rallye Commodore 150	10453	
F-BLSK	SEEMS MS.892A Rallye Commodore 150	10450	
F-BLSO	SEEMS MS.892A Rallye Commodore 150	10485	
F-BLTS(2)	Aérospatiale AS.350B Ecureuil	1175	
F-BLUT	Wassmer WA.40A Super IV	104	F-OBUT
F-BLVC	Gardan GY-80 Horizon 160	32	
F-BLVE	Gardan GY-80 Horizon 160	66	
F-BLVG	Gardan GY-80 Horizon 160	72	
F-BLVI	Gardan GY-80 Horizon 160	31	
F-BLVQ	Gardan GY-80 Horizon 160	81	
F-BLVR	Gardan GY-80 Horizon 160	82	
F-BLVS	Gardan GY-80 Horizon 160	83	
F-BLVU	Gardan GY-80 Horizon 160	85	
F-BLVV	Gardan GY-80 Horizon 160	76	
F-BLXB	Fournier RF-3	19	
F-BLXC	Fournier RF-3	14	
F-BLXE	Fournier RF-3	13	
F-BLXF	Fournier RF-3	20	
F-BLXG	Fournier RF-3	15	
F-BLXL	Morane-Saulnier MS.733 Alcyon	76	Fr.Mil
F-BLXP	Morane-Saulnier MS.733 Alcyon	95	Fr.Mil
F-BLXU	Morane-Saulnier MS.733 Alcyon (Res as F-AZXU)	141	Fr.Mil
F-BLYP	Piper PA-28-180 Cherokee	28-1023	N7209W
F-BLYR	Cessna 182G Skylane	55263	N2063R
F-BLYZ	Piper PA-24-250 Comanche	24-2807	N4635S
			LV-PQD
			N7596P
F-BLZC	CEA Jodel DR.1051 Sicile	531	
F-BLZM	CEA Jodel DR.1050 Ambassadeur	544	
F-BLZS	CEA Jodel DR.1050 Ambassadeur	550	
F-BMAB	Wassmer Jodel D.112 Club	1214	
F-BMAC	Wassmer Jodel D.112 Club	1215	
F-BMAN	Wassmer Jodel D.112 Club	1221	
F-BMBE	SAN Jodel D.140C Mousquetaire III	120	
F-BMBM	SAN Jodel D.140C Mousquetaire III	129	
F-BMBS	SAN Jodel D.140C Mousquetaire III	126	
F-BMBV	SAN Jodel D.140C Mousquetaire III	134	
F-BMBX	SAN Jodel D.140C Mousquetaire III	142	
F-BMBY	SAN Jodel D.140C Mousquetaire III	137	
F-BMBZ	SAN Jodel D.140C Mousquetaire III	115	
F-BMCA	Piper PA-24-250 Comanche	24-3288	N8099P
			N10F
			(N8043P)
F-BMCB	Cessna 182F Skylane	54698	N3298U
F-BMCD	Beech 95-A55 Baron	TC-459	HB-GOM
F-BMCP	Reims/Cessna F.172E	0061	
F-BMCQ	Cessna 206	0003	N5003U
F-BMCR	Reims/Cessna F.172E	0062	
F-BMCT	Beech 95-B55 Baron	TC-524	HB-GBO

Regn.	Type	C/n	Prev.Id.
F-BMCU	Piper PA-18 Super Cub 95	18-1429	OO-MJD
			(OO-HNB)
			ALAT
			51-15429
F-BMDL	Fournier RF-3	33	
F-BMDM	Fournier RF-3	34	
F-BMDP	Fournier RF-3	37	
F-BMDY	Fournier RF-3	49	
F-BMEA	Cessna 182G Skylane	55832	F-OCEA
			N3432S
F-BMEE	SOCATA MS.893E Rallye 180GT Gaillard	12435	
F-BMFF	SAN Jodel D.140C Mousquetaire III	140	
F-BMFK	SAN Jodel D.140C Mousquetaire III	147	
F-BMFS	SAN Jodel D.140C Mousquetaire III	157	
F-BMFT	SAN Jodel D.140C Mousquetaire III	158	
F-BMFV	SAN Jodel D.140C Mousquetaire III	159	
F-BMFX	SAN Jodel D.140C Mousquetaire III	161	
F-BMGB	CEA Jodel DR.1051-M1 Sicile Record	570	
F-BMGE	CEA Jodel DR.1051 Sicile	562	
F-BMGG	CEA Jodel DR.1051 Sicile	574	
F-BMGH	CEA Jodel DR.1051 Sicile	567	
F-BMGK	CEA Jodel DR.1050 Ambassadeur	572	
F-BMGL	CEA Jodel DR.1050-M1 Sicile Record	576	
F-BMGM	CEA Jodel DR.1051-M1 Sicile Record	577	
F-BMGQ	CEA Jodel DR.1051-M1 Sicile Record	583	
F-BMHM	Piper J-3C-65 Cub	11907	Fr.Mil
			44-79611
	(Quoted officially with c/n 11157 - f/n 11735 confirms the true c/n as 11907)		
F-BMHO	SNCAN/Stampe SV.4A	154	Fr.Mil
F-BMIF	Wassmer Jodel D.112 Club	1258	
F-BMII	Wassmer WA.40A Super IV	80	
F-BMIL	Wassmer Jodel D.112 Club	1261	
F-BMIN	Wassmer WA.40A Super IV	81	
F-BMIT	Wassmer Jodel D.112 Club	1267	
F-BMIV	Wassmer Jodel D.112 Club	1269	
F-BMJB	Scintex CP.1310-C3 Super Emeraude	926	
F-BMJC	Scintex CP.1315-C3 Super Emeraude	930	
F-BMJD	Scintex CP.1310-C3 Super Emeraude	932	
F-BMJF	CAARP CP.1315-C3 Super Emeraude	933	
F-BMJM	CAARP CP.1330 Super Emeraude	942	
F-BMJN	Piper PA-18 Super Cub 95	18-1419	ALAT
			51-15419
F-BMJO	Holste MH.1521M Broussard	19	F-BNEN
			Fr.AF
F-BMJR	Piper PA-28-140 Cherokee	28-20191	5T-TJI
			HB-OLF
			N6174W
F-BMJU	Morane-Saulnier MS.733 Alcyon	189	Fr.Navy
F-BMJV	Piper PA-18 Super Cub 95	18-1356	ALAT
			51-15356
F-BMKB	Fournier RF-4D	4005	
F-BMKD	Fournier RF-4D	4007	
F-BMKL	AIAA/Stampe SV.4C	1078	F-BCDN
			Fr.Mil
F-BMKP	Piper PA-28R-180 Cherokee Arrow	28R-30086	(F-GBOP)
			F-OCKP
			N3774T
F-BMKS	SE.210 Caravelle 10B3	181	OH-LSA
F-BMLA	Reims/Cessna F.172E	0066	
F-BMLC	Cessna 336 Skymaster	0193	N3893U
F-BMLI	Mooney M.20C Mark 21	2775	
F-BMLJ	Mooney M.20E Super 21	425	
F-BMLS	Reims/Cessna F.172E	0073	
F-BMLT	Piper PA-24-250 Comanche	24-3573	N8322P
F-BMMD	SNCAN/Stampe SV.4C	56	ALAT
			F-BAYR
			CEV
F-BMMG	SNCAN/Stampe SV.4A	153	Fr.Mil
			F-BBAK
F-BMMH	SNCAN/Stampe SV.4A	247	Fr.Mil
			F-BCKE
F-BMMJ	SNCAN/Stampe SV.4C	691	Fr.Mil
F-BMMU	Morane-Saulnier MS.733 Alcyon	108	Fr.Mil
F-BMMY	Morane-Saulnier MS.733 Alcyon	128	Fr.Mil
F-BMNC	SEEMS MS.881 Rallye 105	408	

Regn.	Type	C/n	Prev.Id.
F-BMNE	GEMS MS.881 Rallye 105	410	
F-BMNL	SEEMS MS.893A Rallye Commodore 180	10489	
F-BMNM	SEEMS MS.892A Rallye Commodore 150 *(Stored)*	10490	
F-BMNN	SEEMS MS.892A Rallye Commodore 150	10491	
F-BMNO	SEEMS MS.892A Rallye Commodore 150	10492	
F-BMNP	SEEMS MS.892A Rallye Commodore 150	10493	
F-BMNQ	SEEMS MS.892A Rallye Commodore 150	10494	
F-BMNR	SEEMS MS.892A Rallye Commodore 150	10495	
F-BMNS	SEEMS MS.893A Rallye Commodore 180	10496	
F-BMNT	SEEMS MS.893A Rallye Commodore 180	10497	
F-BMNU	SEEMS MS.892A Rallye Commodore 150	10498	
F-BMNZ	SEEMS MS.892A Rallye Commodore 150	10502	
F-BMOC	Wassmer Jodel D.112 Club	1270	
F-BMOE	Wassmer Jodel D.120A Paris-Nice	268	
F-BMOM	Wassmer WA.40A Super IV	86	
F-BMOU	Wassmer Jodel D.112 Club	1300	
F-BMOY	Wassmer Jodel D.112 Club	1301	
F-BMPE	CEA Jodel DR.1051-M1 Sicile Record	596	
F-BMPH	CEA Jodel DR.1051-M1 Sicile Record	599	
F-BMPK	CEA Jodel DR.1050-M1 Sicile Record	602	
F-BMPM	CEA Jodel DR.1051-M1 Sicile Record	606	
F-BMPR	CEA Jodel DR.1051-M1 Sicile Record	613	
F-BMQC	Morane-Saulnier MS.733 Alcyon	200	Fr.Mil
F-BMQH	Morane-Saulnier MS.733 Alcyon	112	Fr.Mil
F-BMQQ	Zlin Z.326 Trenér Master	890	
F-BMQU	Zlin Z.326 Trenér Master	900	
F-BMQV	Zlin Z.326 Trenér Master	901	
F-BMRA	Cessna 210D Centurion	58295	N3795Y
F-BMRC	Piper PA-28-235 Cherokee	28-10272	N8800W
F-BMRH	Cessna 210E Centurion	58625	N4925U
F-BMRI	Cessna 310 I	0198	N8198M
F-BMRP	Cessna 182H Skylane	5947	N1847X
F-BMRT	SNCAN/Stampe SV.4A	686	Fr.Mil
F-BMRU	SNCAN/Stampe SV.4C	643	Fr.Mil
F-BMRV	Mooney M.20E Super 21	512	
F-BMSE	Cessna 210E Centurion	58622	N4922U
F-BMSK	Dornier Do.28A-1	3055	D-IBOR
F-BMSN	Cessna 182G Skylane	55120	N3720U
F-BMSO	Cessna 182H Skylane	56106	N2006X
F-BMSS	Dassault Falcon 20F	2/402	F-WMSS
F-BMSY	Piper PA-24-260 Comanche	24-4050	N8633P
			N10F
F-BMSZ	Piper PA-18-150 Super Cub	18-8156	N5409Y
F-BMTB	Fournier RF-3	53	
F-BMTD	Fournier RF-3	55	
F-BMTE	Fournier RF-3	60	
F-BMTK	Fournier RF-3	70	
F-BMTS	Fournier RF-3	85	
F-BMTU	Fournier RF-3	87	
F-BMUB	Gardan GY-80 Horizon 160	86	
F-BMUC	Gardan GY-80 Horizon 160	87	
F-BMUE	Gardan GY-80 Horizon 160	89	
F-BMUF	Gardan GY-80 Horizon 160	90	
F-BMUI	Gardan GY-80 Horizon 160	103	
F-BMUK	Gardan GY-80 Horizon 160	100	
F-BMUT	Gardan GY-80 Horizon 180	140	
F-BMUX	Gardan GY-80 Horizon 160D	154	
F-BMUZ	Gardan GY-80 Horizon 180	146	
F-BMVC	SEEMS MS.892A Rallye Commodore 150	10461	
F-BMVE	SEEMS MS.893A Rallye Commodore 180	10478	
F-BMVI	SEEMS MS.892A Rallye Commodore 150	10510	
F-BMVK	SEEMS MS.892A Rallye Commodore 150	10509	
F-BMVS	SEEMS MS.892A Rallye Commodore 150	10511	
F-BMVV	GEMS MS.892A Rallye Commodore 150	10538	
F-BMYG	Wassmer Jodel D.112 Club	1304	
F-BMYJ	Wassmer WA.40A Super IV	90	
F-BMYM	Wassmer WA.41 Baladou	94	
F-BMZD	CEA Jodel DR.1050-M1 Sicile Record	629	
F-BMZE	CEA DR.250 Capitaine	19	
F-BMZF	CEA DR.250 Capitaine	5	
F-BMZG	CEA DR.250/160 Capitaine	6	
F-BMZH	CEA DR.250/160 Capitaine	7	
F-BMZK	CEA DR.250/160 Capitaine	14	
F-BMZN	CEA DR.250/160 Capitaine	21	
F-BMZO	CEA DR.250/160 Capitaine	2	

Regn.	Type	C/n	Prev.Id.
F-BMZP	CEA DR.250/160 Capitaine	4	
F-BMZS	CEA DR.250 Capitaine	23	
F-BMZT	CEA DR.250A/160 Capitaine	3	
F-BMZU	CEA DR.250/160 Capitaine	34	
F-BMZX	CEA DR.250/160 Capitaine	26	
F-BMZY	CEA DR.250/160 Capitaine	24	
F-BMZZ	CEA DR.250 Capitaine	1	
F-BNAA	Cessna 210E Centurion	58697	N4997U
F-BNAB	Piper PA-24-260 Comanche	24-4156	N8709P
F-BNAE	Cessna U.206	0403	N8003Z
F-BNAF	Piper PA-30-160 Twin Comanche	30-17	N7016Y
F-BNAJ	Zlin Z.326 Trenér Master	906	
F-BNAL(2)	Reims/Cessna FR.172G Rocket	0162	D-EMZK
F-BNAQ	Cessna 210E Centurion	58678	N4978U
F-BNBA	SEEMS MS.892A Rallye Commodore 150	10514	
F-BNBJ	GEMS MS.892A Rallye Commodore 150	10542	
F-BNBN	GEMS MS.892A Rallye Commodore 150	10549	
F-BNBT	GEMS MS.892A Rallye Commodore 150	10557	
F-BNBZ	GEMS MS.880B Rallye Club	436	
F-BNCC	Wassmer Jodel D.120A Paris-Nice	291	
F-BNCJ	Wassmer Jodel D.112 Club	1311	
F-BNCK	Wassmer Jodel D.112A Club	1312	
F-BNCM	Wassmer Jodel D.112 Club	1313	
F-BNCO	Wassmer Jodel D.112 Club	1315	
F-BNCQ	Wassmer WA.40A Super IV	101	
F-BNCU	SNCAN/Stampe SV.4C	447	(F-GDXM)
			F-BCXM
F-BNDC	Mudry CAP.10B	39	CN-TBW
			F-BUDG
F-BNDD(4)	Holste MH.1521M Broussard	240	Fr.AF
F-BNDK	Piper PA-23-250 Aztec C	27-2598	N5527Y
			N10F
F-BNDM	Piper PA-22-150 Tri-Pacer	22-3990	TS-NPR
			ET-AAL
			N4837A
F-BNDT	Reims/Cessna F.172G	0198	
F-BNDU	Reims/Cessna F.172G	0202	
F-BNEB	Morane-Saulnier MS.733 Alcyon	124	Fr.Mil
F-BNEC	Morane-Saulnier MS.733 Alcyon	129	Fr.Mil
F-BNEK	Morane-Saulnier MS.733 Alcyon	158	Fr.Mil
F-BNEL	Morane-Saulnier MS.733 Alcyon	159	Fr.Mil
F-BNEX	Holste MH.1521C Broussard	108	Fr.AF
F-BNFC	Cessna 175A Skylark	56689	HB-CRI
			N7989T
F-BNFF	Reims/Cessna F.150F	0001/62312	F-WLIK
			(N3512L)
F-BNFH	Piper PA-30-160 Twin Comanche	30-571	F-OCDS
			N7508Y
F-BNFJ	Cessna 182J Skylane	56710	N2610F
F-BNFN	Reims/Cessna F.172G	0256	
F-BNFQ	Piper PA-28-140 Cherokee	28-20635	N6550W
			N11C
F-BNFR	Piper PA-23-235 Apache	27-567	N4972P
F-BNFS	Piper PA-32-260 Cherokee Six	32-191	N3376W
F-BNFX	Piper PA-28-180 Cherokee C	28-2489	N8316W
F-BNGL	Hiller UH-12B	667	ALAT
F-BNGM	Hiller UH-12B	699	ALAT
F-BNGP	CEA DR.220 2+2	01	F-WNGP
F-BNHE	Wassmer WA.41 Baladou	109	
F-BNHO	Wassmer Jodel D.112 Club	1345	
F-BNHS	Wassmer WA.41 Baladou	113	
F-BNIA	Mooney M.20E Super 21	624	
F-BNIC	SAN Jodel D.140C Mousquetaire III	165	
F-BNIF	SAN Jodel D.140C Mousquetaire III	168	
F-BNII	SAN Jodel D.140C Mousquetaire III	171	
F-BNIL	SAN Jodel D.140E Mousquetaire IV	174	
F-BNIM	SAN Jodel D.140E Mousquetaire IV	175	
F-BNIR	SAN Jodel D.140E Mousquetaire IV	177	
F-BNIV	SAN Jodel D.140E Mousquetaire IV	182	
F-BNIZ	SAN Jodel D.140E Mousquetaire IV	184	
F-BNJE	CEA DR.250/160 Capitaine	38	
F-BNJF	CEA DR.250/160 Capitaine	39	
F-BNJI	CEA DR.250/160 Capitaine	44	
F-BNJK	CEA DR.250/160 Capitaine	45	
F-BNJO	CEA DR.250/160 Capitaine	56	

Regn.	Type	C/n	Prev.Id.
F-BNJQ	CEA DR.250/160 Capitaine	55	
F-BNJX	CEA DR.250/160 Capitaine	63	
F-BNKM	Reims/Cessna F.172G	0205	
F-BNKO	Piper PA-24-260 Comanche B	24-4334	N8887P / N10F
F-BNKS	Piper PA-28-140 Cherokee	28-21180	N11C
F-BNLC	Cessna 185B	0533	TR-LLR / F-OBZU / N2533Z
F-BNLH	Cessna T.210F Turbo-System Centurion	0074	N6174R
F-BNLR	Piper PA-18 Super Cub 95	18-2076	(F-BNOH) / R-65 / 52-2476
F-BNMC	Beech 65-A90 King Air (w/o 27.8.97)	LJ-149	
F-BNMG	Cessna 172C	49164	HB-CRU / N1464Y
F-BNMJ	Beech A23-19 Musketeer Sport III	MB-116	
F-BNML	Cessna 182H Skylane	56678	N8578S
F-BNMP	Piper PA-18-150 Super Cub	18-1022	ALAT / 51-15325
F-BNMR	Piper PA-18 Super Cub 95	18-1388	ALAT / 51-15388
F-BNMT	Beech D95A Travel Air	TD-577	HB-GBU
F-BNMU	Zlin Z.326 Trenér Master	910	
F-BNMY	Zlin Z.526A Akrobat	1005	
F-BNNK	SOCATA MS.892A Rallye Commodore 150	10590	
F-BNNU	SOCATA MS.893A Rallye Commodore 180	10577	
F-BNNV	SOCATA MS.892A Rallye Commodore 180	10594	
F-BNNX	SOCATA MS.893A Rallye Commodore 180	10578	
F-BNOA	Mooney M.20E Super 21	919	
F-BNOB	Mooney M.20E Super 21	960	
F-BNOF	Jodel D.112D Club	1380	
F-BNOI	Beech 35-C33A Debonair	CE-39	
F-BNOK	Beech 95-C55 Baron	TE-54	
F-BNOL	Beech S35 Bonanza	D-7498	(F-ODOL) / HB-EFC
F-BNOM	Beech 35-C33 Debonair	CD-1029	
F-BNOP	Piper PA-23-250 Aztec B	27-2323	N5260Y
F-BNOR	Beech 35-C33 Debonair	CD-942	HB-ENI
F-BNOS	Beech S35 Bonanza	D-7944	HB-EFG
F-BNOV	Beech A23-19 Musketeer Sport	MB-30	
F-BNOZ	CEA DR.250/160 Capitaine	28	
F-BNPG	Beech A23 Musketeer	M-735	CN-TDP
F-BNPI	Piper PA-18-150 Super Cub	18-5396	ALAT
F-BNPM	CEA DR.220 2+2	2	F-WNPM
F-BNPQ	Bell 47J	1425	F-OBPQ / I-AGUS
F-BNPR	Piper PA-23-250 Aztec C	27-3297	N6091Y
F-BNPS	Agusta-Bell 206A Jet Ranger	8021	(G-AVSV)
F-BNQA	Gardan GY-80 Horizon 180	150	
F-BNQB	Gardan GY-80 Horizon 180	169	
F-BNQC	Gardan GY-80 Horizon 180	133	
F-BNQI	Gardan GY-80 Horizon 180	158	
F-BNQJ	Gardan GY-80 Horizon 180	170	
F-BNQL	Gardan GY-80 Horizon 180	155	
F-BNQO	Gardan GY-80 Horizon 150D	168	
F-BNQQ	Piper PA-18 Super Cub 95	18-1601	ALAT / 51-15601
F-BNQT	Gardan GY-80 Horizon 180	174	
F-BNQV	Gardan GY-80 Horizon 180	177	
F-BNQX	Gardan GY-80 Horizon 180	178	
F-BNQY	Gardan GY-80 Horizon 180	164	
F-BNQZ	Gardan GY-80 Horizon 180	161	
F-BNRI	Beech A23-24 Musketeer Super	MA-105	
F-BNRK	Beech V35 Bonanza	D-8238	
F-BNRM	Cessna 210E Centurion	58693	F-OCGG / N4993U
F-WNRQ(2)	Cessna 305C Bird Dog (L-19)	24519	ALAT
F-BNRR	Zlin Z.326 Trenér Master	913	F-WNRR / F-BNRR
F-BNRX	Fournier RF-6B-100 (Reservation)	14	HB-EZP / F-GANP / D-EGRF / (F-GADM)
F-BNRY	Nord NC.856A Norvigie	85	ALAT

Regn.	Type	C/n	Prev.Id.
F-BNRZ(2)	SNCAN/Stampe SV.4C	357	F-BCOF
F-BNSC	SOCATA MS.893A Rallye Commodore 180	10641	
F-BNSD	SOCATA MS.893A Rallye Commodore 180	10644	
F-BNSG	SOCATA MS.893A Rallye Commodore 180	10647	
F-BNSH	SOCATA MS.893A Rallye Commodore 180	10646	
F-BNSI	SOCATA MS.893A Rallye Commodore 180	10642	
F-BNSJ	SOCATA MS.893A Rallye Commodore 180	10648	
F-BNSK	SOCATA MS.892A Rallye Commodore 150	10626	
F-BNSN	SOCATA MS.893A Rallye Commodore 180	10600	
F-BNSQ	SOCATA MS.893A Rallye Commodore 180	10580	
F-BNST	SOCATA MS.893A Rallye Commodore 180	10583	
F-BNSV	SOCATA MS.893A Rallye Commodore 180	10596	
F-BNSX	SOCATA MS.893A Rallye Commodore 180	10597	
F-BNSZ	SOCATA MS.893A Rallye Commodore 180	10599	
F-BNTA	Piper PA-23-250 Aztec C	27-3256	N6061Y
F-BNTC	Piper PA-32-260 Cherokee Six	32-607	N3695W
F-BNTG	Beech A23-24 Musketeer Super	MA-33	
F-BNTL	Beech 35-C33 Debonair	CD-1049	
F-BNTM	Piper PA-32-300 Cherokee Six	32-40086	N4046W
F-BNTO	Agusta-Bell 47G-2	061	F-OATO
F-BNTP	Reims/Cessna F.172G	0239	
F-BNVA	CEA DR.250/160 Capitaine	64	
F-BNVB	CEA DR.220 2+2	3	
F-BNVC	CEA DR.250/160 Capitaine	67	
F-BNVD	CEA DR.250/160 Capitaine	66	
F-BNVE	CEA DR.250/160 Capitaine	61	
F-BNVL	CEA DR.250/160 Capitaine	72	
F-BNVO	CEA DR.220 2+2	8	
F-BNVS	CEA DR.250/160 Capitaine	78	
F-BNVT	CEA DR.220 2+2	9	
F-BNVU	CEA DR.250/160 Capitaine	80	
F-BNVY	CEA DR.220 2+2	11	
F-BNXB	SOCATA MS.893A Rallye Commodore 180	10652	
F-BNXD	AIAA/Stampe SV.4C	1090	Fr.Navy
F-BNXK	SOCATA MS.892A Rallye Commodore 150	10610	
F-BNXL	SOCATA MS.893A Rallye Commodore 180	10608	
F-BNXM	SOCATA MS.892A Rallye Commodore 150	10633	
F-BNXN	SOCATA MS.880B Rallye Club	844	
F-BNXO	SOCATA MS.880B Rallye Club	841	
F-BNXP	SOCATA MS.880B Rallye Club	839	
F-BNXY	SOCATA MS.880B Rallye Club	832	
F-BNYB	Gardan GY-80 Horizon 180	162	
F-BNYC	Gardan GY-80 Horizon 160D	152	
F-BNYE	Gardan GY-80 Horizon 180	185	
F-BNYG	Gardan GY-80 Horizon 180	184	
F-BNYI	Gardan GY-80 Horizon 180	189	
F-BNYJ	Gardan GY-80 Horizon 180	201	
F-BNYN	Gardan GY-80 Horizon 180	202	
F-BNYO	Gardan GY-80 Horizon 160D	219	
F-BNYQ	Gardan GY-80 Horizon 180	191	
F-BNYR	Gardan GY-80 Horizon 180	193	
F-BNYS	Gardan GY-80 Horizon 180	206	
F-BNYU	Gardan GY-80 Horizon 180	165	
F-BNYX	Gardan GY-80 Horizon 160D	181	
F-BNZB	Wassmer Jodel D.112 Club	1348	
F-BNZH	Wassmer WA.41 Baladou	120	
F-BNZU	Wassmer Jodel D.120A Paris-Nice	323	
F-BNZV	Wassmer WA.41 Baladou	125	
F-BOAF	Piper PA-28-180 Cherokee B	28-1130	F-OCAF / N7183W
F-BOBE	Wassmer WA.41 Baladou	131	
F-BOBF	Wassmer WA.40A Super IV	132	
F-BOBK	Wassmer WA.41 Baladou	135	
F-BOBN	Wassmer WA.41 Baladou	137	
F-BOBP	Wassmer WA.41 Baladou	129	
F-BOBQ	Wassmer WA.41 Baladou	140	
F-BOBV	Wassmer WA.41 Baladou	145	
F-BOBX	Wassmer Jodel D.120 Paris-Nice	334	
F-BOCA	CEA DR.250B/160 Capitaine	82	
F-BOCF	CEA DR.220 2+2	14	
F-BOCG	CEA DR.250/160 Capitaine	85	
F-BOCI	CEA DR.220A 2+2	50	
F-BOCJ	CEA DR.220 2+2	16	
F-BOCL	CEA DR.220 2+2	18	
F-BOCM	CEA DR.250/160 Capitaine	88	

Regn.	Type	C/n	Prev.Id.
F-BOCR	CEA DR.220 2+2	24	
F-BOCT	CEA DR.220 2+2	26	
F-BOCY	CEA DR.220 2+2	31	
F-BODD	SOCATA MS.893A Rallye Commodore 180	10661	
F-BODE	SOCATA MS.892A Rallye Commodore 150	10658	
F-BOEI	Piper PA-32-260 Cherokee Six	32-690	N3769W
F-BOEL	Reims/Cessna F.177RG Cardinal RG	0140	F-ODEA (F-BXQL)
F-BOER	Piper PA-18 Super Cub 95	18-1442	ALAT 51-15442
F-BOFA	SOCATA MS.893A Rallye Commodore 180	10825	F-OCMA
F-BOFC	Wassmer WA.421-250	401	F-BOBZ
F-BOFD	Wassmer WA.54 Atlantic	133	F-ODBD
F-BOFE	Cerva CE.43 Guepard	465	F-ODAI
F-BOFF	CEA DR.221 Dauphin	49	F-WOFF
F-BOFG	CEA DR.253 Régent	01	F-WOFG
F-BOFS	CEA DR.360 Chevalier	01	F-WOFS
F-BOFU	Agusta-Bell 47G-2	102	ALAT
F-BOFV	Agusta-Bell 47G-2	169	ALAT
F-BOFY	Piper PA-18 Super Cub 95	18-1378	F-BOMY ALAT 51-15378
F-BOGA	Reims/Cessna F.150G	0092	
F-BOGE	Reims/Cessna F.150G	0094	
F-BOGF	Reims/Cessna F.172G	0314	
F-BOGH	Reims/Cessna F.150G	0103	
F-BOGO	Reims/Cessna F.172H	0362	
F-BOGP	Reims/Cessna F.172H	0371	
F-BOGQ	Reims/Cessna F.172H	0384	
F-BOGT	Reims/Cessna F.172H	0340	
F-BOGV	Reims/Cessna F.150G	0178	
F-BOGX	Reims/Cessna F.150G	0179	
F-BOGZ	Reims/Cessna F.172H	0333	
F-BOHH	Nord 262-A35	49	F-WOFX
F-BOHI	Piper PA-23-250 Aztec	27-319	CN-TTX N4773P
F-BOHJ	Piper PA-18-150 Super Cub	18-5324	ALAT
F-BOHK(2)	Wassmer WA.40A Super IV	127	F-BOBA
F-BOHP	Holste MH.1521C.1 Broussard	10	Fr.AF
F-BOHS	Piper PA-23-250 Aztec C	27-3409	N6183Y
F-BOHT	Mooney M.20F Executive	670170	N9593M
F-BOHV	Piper PA-23-250 Aztec C	27-3442	N6215Y
F-BOHX	Cessna T.210G Turbo-System Centurion	0241	N6841R
F-BOID	Beech M35 Bonanza	D-6434	HB-EID
F-BOIS	Reims/Cessna F.172E	0082	F-OCIS
F-BOJK	SIAI-Marchetti S.205-18/F	240	(OO-HAP)
F-BOJN	Mooney M.20F Executive	670026	
F-BOJP	Mooney M.20F Executive	670216	N9639M
F-BOJQ	Piper PA-18-180M Super Cub	18-5325	F-WOJQ F-BOJQ ALAT
F-BOJU	Cessna 182K Skylane	57740	N2540Q
F-BOJX	Piper PA-30-160 Twin Comanche B	30-1318	N8199Y
F-BOJZ	Cessna 401	0072	N3272Q
F-BOKA	CEA DR.250/160 Capitaine	89	
F-BOKB	CEA DR.220 2+2	33	
F-BOKD	CEA DR.220 2+2	32	
F-BOKF	CEA DR.220 2+2	35	
F-BOKG	CEA DR.220 2+2	36	
F-BOKH	CEA DR.220 2+2	37	
F-BOKI	CEA DR.220 2+2	38	
F-BOKJ	CEA DR.220 2+2	39	
F-BOKK	CEA DR.220 2+2	40	
F-BOKN	CEA DR.220 2+2	43	
F-BOKO	CEA DR.220A 2+2	52	
F-BOKS	CEA DR.220 2+2	48	
F-BOKX	CEA DR.220A 2+2	54	
F-BOKY	CEA DR.220A 2+2	55	
F-BOKZ	CEA DR.221 Dauphin	56	
F-BOLC	Piper PA-23-250 Aztec C	27-3382	N6172Y N10F
F-BOLE	Piper PA-28-140 Cherokee	28-22847	N4442J
F-BOLN	SIAI-Marchetti S.205-20/R	363	
F-BOLO	Mooney M.20E Super 21	1177	OO-WA
F-BOLP	Beech 35-C33A Debonair	CE-147	
F-BOLR	Cessna 310L	0104	N3254X
F-BOLS	Aero Commander 200D	351	N2978T
F-BOLU	Piper PA-30-160 Twin Comanche B	30-1438	N8370Y N10F
F-BOLV	Mooney M.20F Executive	670296	
F-BOLY	Beech 35-C33 Debonair	CD-1081	
F-BOLZ	Piper PA-30-160 Twin Comanche B	30-1233	N8135Y (CF-.. E)
F-BOMB	Piper PA-18 Super Cub 95	18-1640	ALAT 51-15640
F-BOMC	Piper PA-18 Super Cub 95	18-1636	ALAT 51-15636
F-BOMF	Piper PA-18 Super Cub 95	18-1435	ALAT 51-15435
F-BOMH	Piper PA-18 Super Cub 95	18-2097	ALAT 52-2497
F-BOMI	Piper PA-18 Super Cub 95	18-1359	ALAT 51-15359
F-BOMK	Piper PA-18 Super Cub 95	18-1455	ALAT 51-15455
F-BOML	Piper PA-18 Super Cub 95	18-1367	ALAT 51-15367
F-BOMM	Piper P-A-18-95 Super Cub	18-1397	ALAT 51-15397
F-BOMP	Piper PA-18 Super Cub 95	18-1409	ALAT 51-15409
F-BOMT	Piper PA-18 Super Cub 95	18-1506	ALAT 51-15506
F-BOMV	Piper PA-18 Super Cub 95	18-1465	ALAT 51-15465
F-BOMX	Piper PA-18 Super Cub 95	18-1368	ALAT 51-15368
F-BONA	SOCATA MS.892A Rallye Commodore 150	10706	
F-BONE	SOCATA MS.893A Rallye Commodore 180	10686	
F-BONG	SOCATA MS.893A Rallye Commodore 180	10687	
F-BONH	SOCATA MS.893A Rallye Commodore 180	10688	
F-BONI	SOCATA MS.893A Rallye Commodore 180	10691	
F-BOOF	Beech V35A Bonanza	D-8635	
F-BOOG	Piper PA-23-250 Aztec C	27-3684	N6444Y N10F
F-BOOQ	Piper PA-18 Super Cub 95	18-1648	ALAT 51-15648
F-BOOR	Piper PA-18 Super Cub 95	18-2108	ALAT 52-2508
F-BOOV	Piper PA-18 Super Cub 95	18-1594	ALAT 51-15594
F-BOOX	Piper PA-18 Super Cub 95	18-1616	ALAT 51-15616
F-BOOZ	Beech 95-C55 Baron	TE-286	
F-BOPA	SAN Jodel D.140R Abeille	522	
F-BOPB	SAN Jodel D.140E Mousquetaire IV	186	
F-BOPF	SAN Jodel D.150 Mascaret	61	
F-BOPG	SAN Jodel D.140E Mousquetaire IV	188	
F-BOPH	SAN Jodel D.140E Mousquetaire IV	191	
F-BOPK	SAN Jodel D.140R Abeille	523	
F-BOPN	SAN Jodel D.140E Mousquetaire IV	213	
F-BOPO	SAN Jodel D.140R Abeille	526	
F-BOPS	SAN Jodel D.140E Mousquetaire IV	190	
F-BOPT	SAN Jodel D.140R Abeille	528	
F-BOPY	Beech V35 Bonanza	D-8383	
F-BOPZ	SAN Jodel D.140E Mousquetaire IV	189	F-WOPZ
F-BOQA	Reims/Cessna F.172H	0383	
F-BOQB	Reims/Cessna F.150G	0117	
F-BOQD	Reims/Cessna F.172H	0369	
F-BOQF	Reims/Cessna F.150G	0208	
F-BOQH	Reims/Cessna F.150G	0210	
F-BOQJ	Reims/Cessna F.150G	0212	
F-BOQK	Reims/Cessna F.150G	0213	
F-BOQN	Cessna R.172E (FR.172 Prototype)	0256	
F-BOQO	Reims/Cessna F.150G	0133	
F-BOQP	Reims/Cessna F.150G	0402	
F-BOQS	Reims/Cessna F.150H	0227	
F-BOQV	Reims/Cessna F.172H	0452	
F-BOQY	Reims/Cessna F.172H	0483	
F-BORA	Fournier RF-4D	4012	

Regn.	Type	C/n	Prev.Id.
F-BORB	Fournier RF-4D	4014	
F-BORC	Fournier RF-4D	4015	
F-BORG	Fournier RF-4D	4020	
F-BORI	Fournier RF-4D	4017	
F-BORO	Nord N.1101 Noralpha	180	Fr.Mil
F-BORY	Zlin Z.326 Trenér Master	927	
F-BOSI	Beech V35 Bonanza	D-8462	
F-BOSJ	Mooney M.20F Executive	670260	G-AVHD
F-BOSK	Club Aerostatique de France Free Balloon HG 600m3	8810	
F-BOSO	Piper PA-28-180 Cherokee C	28-3931	(G-AVBR) N9679J
F-BOSS	Club Aerostatique de France Free Balloon HG 600m3	1	
F-BOSX	SIAI-Marchetti S.205-20/R	376	
F-BOSY	Beech 65-A90 King Air	LJ-128	D-IMTW
F-BOSZ	Pilatus PC-6/B1-H2 Turbo Porter	636	
F-BOTB	SOCATA MS.893A Rallye Commodore 180	10671	
F-BOTC	SOCATA MS.893A Rallye Commodore 180	10672	
F-BOTD	SOCATA MS.893A Rallye Commodore 180	10673	
F-BOTF	SOCATA MS.893A Rallye Commodore 180	10675	
F-BOTG	SOCATA MS.893A Rallye Commodore 180	10676	
F-BOTH	SOCATA MS.893A Rallye Commodore 180	10677	
F-BOTI	SOCATA MS.893A Rallye Commodore 180	10678	
F-BOTJ	SOCATA MS.893A Rallye Commodore 180	10679	
F-BOTL	SOCATA MS.893A Rallye Commodore 180	10681	
F-BOTM	SOCATA MS.893A Rallye Commodore 180	10682	
F-BOTN	SOCATA MS.893A Rallye Commodore 180	10683	
F-BOTP	SOCATA MS.893A Rallye Commodore 180	10669	
F-BOTQ	SOCATA MS.892A Rallye Commodore 150	10712	
F-BOTU	SOCATA MS.893A Rallye Commodore 180	10696	
F-BOTX	SOCATA MS.880B Rallye Club	881	
F-BOUA	Piper PA-18 Super Cub 95	18-1417	ALAT 51-15417
F-BOUB	Piper PA-18 Super Cub 95	18-1422	ALAT 51-15422
F-BOUE	Piper PA-18 Super Cub 95	18-1470	ALAT 5I-15470
F-BOUF	Piper PA-18 Super Cub 95	18-1476	ALAT 51-15476
F-BOUH	Piper PA-18 Super Cub 95	18-1519	ALAT 51-15519
F-BOUK	Piper PA-18 Super Cub 95	18-1605	ALAT 51-15605
F-BOUL	Ballonfabrik Augsburg HG 1300 Free Balloon	10121	
F-BOUX	Piper PA-18 Super Cub 95	18-1587	ALAT 51-15587
F-BOUY	Piper PA-18 Super Cub 95	18-1611	ALAT 51-15611
F-BOUZ	Piper PA-18 Super Cub 95	18-1634	ALAT 51-15634
F-BOVA	SOCATA MS.892A Rallye Commodore 150	10711	
F-BOVD	SOCATA MS.893A Rallye Commodore 180	10698	
F-BOVH	SOCATA MS.893A Rallye Commodore 180	10718	
F-BOVI	SOCATA MS.880B Rallye Club	1142	
F-BOVJ	SOCATA MS.880B Rallye Club	892	
F-BOVM	SOCATA MS.880B Rallye Club	1114	
F-BOVP	SOCATA MS.880B Rallye Club	1107	
F-BOVR	SOCATA MS.880B Rallye Club	896	
F-BOVV	SOCATA MS.880B Rallye Club	1118	
F-BOVY	SOCATA MS.880B Rallye Club	895	
F-BOXB	Fournier RF-4D	4042	
F-BOXD	Fournier RF-4D	4044	
F-BOXI	Fournier RF-4D	4061	
F-BOXJ	Fournier RF-4D	4062	
F-BOXP	Morane-Saulnier MS.885 Super Rallye	93	F-OBXP
F-BOXR	Cessna T.210G Turbo-System Centurion	0248	N6848R
F-BOXT	Piper PA-28-140 Cherokee	28-23133	N9669W
F-BOXU	Piper PA-28R-180 Cherokee Arrow	28R-30290	N3947T
F-BOYC	Wassmer WA.40A Super IV	147	
F-BOYE	Wassmer WA.40A Super IV	150	
F-BOYG	Wassmer WA.41 Baladou	149	
F-BOYJ	Wassmer WA.41 Baladou	151	
F-BOYK	Wassmer WA.41 Baladou	152	
F-BOYR	Wassmer WA.41 Baladou	156	
F-BOYY	Wassmer WA.421-250	407	

Regn.	Type	C/n	Prev.Id.
F-BOZB	CEA DR.221 Dauphin	59	
F-BOZF	CEA DR.253 Régent	102	
F-BOZG	CEA DR.220A 2+2	63	
F-BOZH	CEA DR.221 Dauphin	64	
F-BOZJ	CEA DR.250/160 Capitaine	95	
F-BOZK	CEA DR.221 Dauphin	66	
F-BOZM	CEA DR.253 Régent	105	
F-BOZN	CEA DR.250/160 Capitaine	96	
F-BOZO	CEA DR.221 Dauphin	69	
F-BOZP	CEA DR.221 Dauphin	71	
F-BOZQ	CEA DR.221 Dauphin	72	
F-BOZS	CEA DR.221 Dauphin	74	
F-BOZT	CEA DR.220A 2+2	75	
F-BOZU	CEA DR.221 Dauphin	76	
F-BOZV	CEA DR.221 Dauphin	77	
F-BOZX	CEA DR.221 Dauphin	78	
F-BPAB	Gardan GY-80 Horizon 180	218	
F-BPAD	Gardan GY-80 Horizon 160D	137	
F-BPAI	SOCATA MS.880B Rallye Club	1253	
F-BPAJ	Gardan GY-80 Horizon 180	243	
F-BPAM	SOCATA MS.880B Rallye Club	1260	
F-BPAN	SOCATA MS.880B Rallye Club	1257	
F-BPAR	SOCATA MS.893A Rallye Commodore 180	10916	
F-BPAS	SOCATA MS.893A Rallye Commodore 180	11021	
F-BPAT	SOCATA MS.880B Rallye Club	1262	
F-BPAU	SOCATA MS.893A Rallye Commodore 180	11025	
F-BPAV	SOCATA MS.880B Rallye Club	1271	
F-BPAY	SOCATA MS.893A Rallye Commodore 180	10940	
F-BPBA	SOCATA MS.893A Rallye Commodore 180	10716	
F-BPBC	SOCATA MS.880B Rallye Club	1110	
F-BPBF	SOCATA MS.880B Rallye Club	1128	
F-BPBG	SOCATA MS.880B Rallye Club	1120	
F-BPBO	SOCATA MS.892A Rallye Commodore 150	10783	
F-BPBQ	SOCATA MS.893A Rallye Commodore 180	10733	
F-BPBT	SOCATA MS.893A Rallye Commodore 180	10730	
F-BPBX	SOCATA MS.893A Rallye Commodore 180	10738	
F-BPCA	CEA DR.253 Régent	108	
F-BPCC	CEA DR.253 Régent	109	
F-BPCE	CEA DR.253 Régent	110	
F-BPCG	CEA DR.221 Dauphin	84	
F-BPCH	CEA DR.220A 2+2	91	
F-BPCJ	CEA DR.221 Dauphin	86	
F-BPCK	CEA DR.221 Dauphin	87	
F-BPCL	CEA DR.221 Dauphin	88	
F-BPCN	CEA DR.221 Dauphin	117	
F-BPCO	CEA DR.221 Dauphin	92	
F-BPCT	CEA DR.221 Dauphin	97	
F-BPCY	CEA DR.221 Dauphin	101	
F-BPDA	SOCATA MS.893A Rallye Commodore 180	10734	
F-BPDK	SOCATA MS.893A Rallye Commodore 180	10773	
F-BPDP	SOCATA MS.893A Rallye Commodore 180	10790	
F-BPDR	SOCATA MS.880B Rallye Club	1140	
F-BPDT	SOCATA MS.880B Rallye Club	1146	
F-BPDY	SOCATA MS.880B Rallye Club	1155	
F-BPED	Reims/Cessna F.150H	0261	
F-BPEF	Reims/Cessna F.172H	0467	
F-BPEI	Reims/Cessna F.172H	0501	
F-BPEJ	Reims/Cessna F.150H	0282	
F-BPEK	Reims/Cessna F.150H	0287	
F-BPEO	Reims/Cessna F.172H	0496	
F-BPEP	Reims/Cessna F.172H	0493	
F-BPEQ	Reims/Cessna F.150H	0305	
F-BPES	Reims/Cessna FR.172E Rocket	0051	
F-BPET	Reims/Cessna F.172H	0551	
F-BPEU	Reims/Cessna F.150H	0311	
F-BPEV	Reims/Cessna F.150H	0385	
F-BPEX	Reims/Cessna F.150H	0388	
F-BPFD	Cessna 310N	0087	N4187Q
F-BPFF	SA.316B Alouette III	1100	F-BLOO
F-BPFH	Piper PA-23-250 Aztec C	27-3834	N6541Y
F-BPFI	Piper PA-23-250 Aztec C	27-3815	N6524Y
F-BPFJ	SIAI-Marchetti S.205-18/R	4-119	
F-BPFL	SIAI-Marchetti S.205-20/F	4-206	
F-BPFO	Beech 95-C55 Baron	TE-167	HB-GCO
F-BPFP	SA.318C Alouette Astazou	2006/15	

Regn.	Type	C/n	Prev.Id.
F-BPFR	Beech 35-C33A Debonair	CE-85	HB-EKZ
F-BPFS	Cessna 337C Skymaster	0839	N2539S
F-BPFX	Piper PA-28R-180 Cherokee Arrow	28R-30434	N4571J
F-BPGA	SOCATA MS.880B Rallye Club	1147	
F-BPGC	SOCATA MS.893A Rallye Commodore 180	10799	
F-BPGH	SOCATA MS.892A Rallye Commodore 150	10785	
F-BPGP	SOCATA MS.880B Rallye Club	1173	
F-BPGU	SOCATA MS.880B Rallye Club	1176	
F-BPGV	SOCATA MS.893A Rallye Commodore 180	10796	
F-BPHF	MS.B92A Rallye Commodore 150	10777	
F-BPHG	SOCATA MS.880B Rallye Club	1169	
F-BPHK	SOCATA MS.880B Rallye Club	1186	
F-BPHL	SOCATA MS.892A Rallye Commodore 150	10784	
F-BPHN	SOCATA MS.880B Rallye Club	1134	F-BPBN
F-BPHU	SOCATA MS.880B Rallye Club	1221	
F-BPHY	SOCATA MS.893A Rallye Commodore 180	10816	
F-BPIC	Piper PA-30-160 Twin Comanche B	30-1251	F-OCIP
			N8140Y
F-BPID	Bölkow BO.208C Junior	671	D-EGZB
F-BPIF	Piper PA-18 Super Cub 95	18-1462	ALAT
	(Quoted officially as c/n 18-1384,but the		51-15462
	f/n is 18-1359)		
F-BPIK	Piper PA-30-160 Twin Comanche B	30-1582	N8548Y
			N10F
F-BPIR	Piper PA-30-160 Twin Comanche B	30-1412	N8549Y
			N10F
F-BPIS	Beech 95-C55 Baron	TE-301	HB-GCX
F-BPIT	Beech 35-C33 Debonair	CD-852	HB-EKP
F-BPIU	Cessna 182L Skylane	58690	N3390R
F-BPIX	Cessna 310N	0140	N5040Q
F-BPJC	SIAI-Marchetti S.205-20/R	4-209	
F-BPJE	Piper PA-32-300 Cherokee Six	32-40388	N4148R
F-BPJF	Beech 95-B55 Baron	TC-1143	
F-BPKB	CEA DR.221 Dauphin	104	
F-BPKC	CEA DR.221 Dauphin	105	
F-BPKD	CEA DR.253 Régent	114	
F-BPKE	CEA DR.221 Dauphin	106	
F-BPKF	CEA DR.221 Dauphin	107	
F-BPKG	CEA DR.221 Dauphin	90	
F-BPKH	CEA DR.221 Dauphin	108	
F-BPKI	CEA DR.221 Dauphin	109	
F-BPKP	CEA DR.221 Dauphin	115	
F-BPKQ	CEA DR.253 Régent	119	
F-BPKS	CEA DR.221 Dauphin	116	
F-BPKU	CEA DR.221 Dauphin	119	
F-BPKX	CEA DR.221 Dauphin	120	
F-BPKY	CEA DR.315 Petit Prince	302	
F-BPKZ	CEA DR.253 Régent	122	
F-BPLG	Fournier RF-4D	4123	
F-BPLI	Fournier RF-4D	4121	
F-BPLJ	Fournier RF-4D	4125	
F-BPLL	CEA DR.253 Régent	124	
F-BPLO	Fournier RF-4D	4134	
F-BPLQ	Fournier RF-4D	4136	
F-BPLR	Fournier RF-5	5067	
F-BPLU	Fournier RF-5	5040	
F-BPLZ	Fournier RF-5	5079	
F-BPMB	SOCATA MS.893A Rallye Commodore 180	10755	
F-BPMD	SOCATA MS.893A Rallye Commodore 180	10757	
F-BPME	SOCATA MS.893A Rallye Commodore 180	10760	
F-BPMG	SOCATA MS.893A Rallye Commodore 180	10762	
F-BPMH	SOCATA MS.893A Rallye Commodore 180	10763	
F-BPMI	SOCATA MS.893A Rallye Commodore 180	10764	
F-BPMJ	SOCATA MS.893A Rallye Commodore 180	10765	
F-BPMK	SOCATA MS.893A Rallye Commodore 180	10766	
F-BPML	SOCATA MS.893A Rallye Commodore 180	10767	
F-BPMM	SOCATA MS.893A Rallye Commodore 180	10770	
F-BPMN	SOCATA MS.893A Rallye Commodore 180	10771	
F-BPMO	SOCATA MS.893A Rallye Commodore 180	10772	
F-BPMP	SOCATA MS.893A Rallye Commodore 180	10756	
F-BPMQ	SOCATA MS.880B Rallye Club	1200	
F-BPMT	SOCATA MS.880B Rallye Club	1201	
F-BPMU	SOCATA MS.893A Rallye Commodore 180	10819	
F-BPMV	SOCATA MS.892A Rallye Commodore 150	10778	
F-BPMZ	SOCATA MS.892A Rallye Commodore 150	10807	

Regn.	Type	C/n	Prev.Id.
F-BPNL	Ass.Aerostat.Nord France Free Balloon H.400	6	
F-BPNM	Zlin Z.326 Trenér Master	928	
F-BPNP	Zlin Z.326 Trenér Master	931	
F-BPNR	Zlin Z.326 Trenér Master	933	
F-BPOA	CEA DR.220A 2+2	121	
F-BPOB	CEA DR.315 Petit Prince	303	
F-BPOE	CEA DR.315 Petit Prince	305	
F-BPOH	CEA DR.315 Petit Prince	306	
F-BPOJ	CEA DR.253 Régent	127	
F-BPOL	CEA DR.253 Régent	128	
F-BPON	CEA DR.221 Dauphin	124	
F-BPOO	CEA DR.340 Major	301	
F-BPOQ	CEA DR.360 Chevalier	310	
F-BPOR	CEA DR.315 Petit Prince	309	
F-BPOV	CEA DR.253 Régent	131	
F-BPOZ	CEA DR.253 Régent	116	
F-BPPA	Aerospacelines Super Guppy 337SGT-201	002	N212AS
F-BPPH	SA.316B Alouette III	2245	
F-BPPK	Piper PA-24-180 Comanche	24-1749	F-OBPK
			N10F
F-BPPO	Piper PA-24-250 Comanche	24-1988	F-OBPO
			N10F
F-BPPY	Cessna 421A	0066	OO-LFD
			HB-LFD
			N2966Q
F-BPQE	SOCATA MS.892A Rallye Commodore 150	10781	
F-BPQF	SOCATA MS.892A Rallye Commodore 150	10782	
F-BPQL	SOCATA MS.892A Rallye Commodore 150	10911	
F-BPQM	SOCATA MS.892A Rallye Commodore 150	10912	
F-BPQO	SOCATA MS.880B Rallye Club	1202	
F-BPQX	SOCATA MS.880B Rallye Club	1243	
F-BPQY	SOCATA MS.880B Rallye Club	1185	
F-BPRC	CEA DR.315 Petit Prince	316	
F-BPRF	CEA DR.315 Petit Prince	319	
F-BPRG	CEA DR.253 Régent	134	
F-BPRI	CEA DR.315 Petit Prince	321	
F-BPRJ	CEA DR.315 Petit Prince	318	
F-BPRK	CEA DR.360 Chevalier	323	
F-BPRM	CEA DR.315 Petit Prince	325	
F-BPRN	CEA DR.220A 2+2	126	
F-BPRO	CEA DR.315 Petit Prince	326	
F-BPRP	CEA DR.315 Petit Prince	327	
F-BPRR	CEA DR.221 Dauphin	127	
F-BPRT	CEA DR.221 Dauphin	128	
F-BPRU	CEA DR.315 Petit Prince	330	
F-BPSB	SOCATA MS.880B Rallye Club	1215	
F-BPSC	SOCATA MS.893A Rallye Commodore 180	10824	
F-BPSE	SOCATA MS.892A Rallye Commodore 150	10810	
F-BPSF	SOCATA MS.880B Rallye Club	1191	
F-BPSI	SOCATA MS.880B Rallye Club	1193	
F-BPSL	SOCATA MS.894A Minerva 220	11010	
F-BPSP	SOCATA MS.893A Rallye Commodore 180	10826	
F-BPST	SOCATA MS.880B Rallye Club	1236	
F-BPTA	Wassmer WA.41 Baladou	160	
F-BPTC	Wassmer WA.421-250	411	
F-BPTF	Wassmer WA.41 Baladou	162	
F-BPTG	Wassmer WA.421-250	417	
F-BPTJ	Wassmer WA.421-250 (Written off)	412	
F-BPTK	Wassmer WA.41 Baladou	165	
F-BPTN	Wassmer WA.421-250	424	
F-BPTO	Wassmer WA.421-250	425	
F-BPTX	Wassmer WA.51 Pacific	04	
F-BPTY	Wassmer WA.51 Pacific	10	
F-BPUA	Fokker F.27 Friendship 500	10369	PH-FMR
F-BPUC	Fokker F.27 Friendship 500	10373	PH-FMV
F-BPUD	Fokker F.27 Friendship 500	10374	PH-FMW
F-BPUE	Fokker F.27 Friendship 500	10377	PH-FMZ
F-BPUF	Fokker F.27 Friendship 500	10378	PH-FNA
F-BPUG	Fokker F.27 Friendship 500	10379	PH-FNB
F-BPUH	Fokker F.27 Friendship 500 (Stored)	10382	PH-FNE
F-BPUJ	Fokker F.27 Friendship 500 (Stored)	10390	PH-FNN
F-BPVI	Wassmer WA.421-250	415	F-OCOK
F-BPVJ	Boeing 747-128B (Preserved, Le Bourget)	20541	N28903
			(F-BPVI)
F-BPVM	Boeing 747-128	20799	N63305

Regn.	Type	C/n	Prev.Id.
F-BPVP	Boeing 747-128	20954	
F-BPVR	Boeing 747-228F	21255	N1783B
F-BPVS	Boeing 747-228B Combi	21326	
F-BPVT	Boeing 747-228B Combi	21429	
F-BPVU	Boeing 747-228B Combi	21537	N1252E
F-BPVX	Boeing 747-228B Combi	21731	
F-BPVY	Boeing 747-228B Combi	21745	
F-BPVZ	Boeing 747-228F	21787	
F-BPXC	CEA DR.380 Prince	01	F-ZWRO
			F-WPXC
F-BPXN	SOCATA ST-60 Rallye 7-300	01	
F-BPXT	SOCATA MS.894A Minerva 220	11036	F-WPXT
F-BPXU	CAARP CAP.20	01	F-WPXU
F-BPXV	Fournier RF-6B-100	01	F-WPXV
F-BPXZ	Robin HR.100/200B Royale	01	F-WPXZ
F-BPYC	SOCATA MS.894A Minerva 220 (Cvtd.ex 893A)	11007	
F-BPYH	SOCATA MS.893A Rallye Commodore 180	10917	
F-BPYJ	SOCATA MS.880B Rallye Club	1247	
F-BPYM	SOCATA MS.880B Rallye Club	1245	
F-BPYN	SOCATA MS.880B Rallye Club	1250	
F-BPYO	SOCATA MS.880B Rallye Club	1249	
F-BPYP	SOCATA MS.880B Rallye Club	1246	
F-BPYQ	SOCATA MS.894A Minerva 220	11016	
F-BPYS	SOCATA MS.880B Rallye Club	1251	
F-BPYT	SOCATA MS.880B Rallye Club	1255	
F-BPYU	SOCATA MS.893A Rallye Commodore 180	10932	
F-BPYX	SOCATA MS.893A Rallye Commodore 180	10923	
F-BPYZ	SOCATA MS.880B Rallye Club	1252	
F-BPZP	Wassmer WA.421-250	430	
F-BRAC	Mooney M.20C Ranger	680141	N6860N
F-BRAE	Piper PA-28R-180 Cherokee Arrow	28R-30703	N4956J
F-BRAG	Bölkow BO.208C Junior	680	D-EGZN
F-BRAH	Cessna 182M Skylane	59320	N70598
F-BRAI	Cessna P.206C Super Skylane	0516	N8716Z
F-BRAJ	Agusta-Bell 206A Jet Ranger	8110	
F-BRAK	Beech 95-B55 Baron	TC-1170	
F-BRAU	Beech V35 Bonanza	D-8381	HB-EFL
F-BRAY	Piper PA-32-260 Cherokee Six	32-265	6V-AAY
			F-OCHD
			N3404W
F-BRAZ	Beech 36 Bonanza	E-110	
F-BRBA	Reims/Cessna FR.172F Rocket	0061	
F-BRBB	Reims/Cessna F.172H	0567	
F-BRBD	Reims/Cessna F.172H	0542	
F-BRBE	Reims/Cessna F.172H	0612	
F-BRBI	Reims/Cessna FR.172F Rocket	0099	
F-BRBL	Reims/Cessna F.150J	0518	
F-BRBN	Reims/Cessna F.150J	0520	
F-BRBO	Reims/Cessna FR.172F Rocket	0145	
F-BRBR	Reims/Cessna F.172H	0617	
F-BRBV	Reims/Cessna F.172H	0682	
F-BRBY	Reims/Cessna F.150K	0536	
F-BRBZ	Reims/Cessna F.172H	0673	
F-BRCD	CEA DR.315 Petit Prince	336	
F-BRCE	CEA DR.340 Major	337	
F-BRCF	CEA DR.340 Major	340	
F-BRCI	CEA DR.315 Petit Prince	341	
F-BRCL	CEA DR.315 Petit Prince	344	
F-BRCN	CEA DR.315 Petit Prince	346	
F-BRCO	CEA DR.340 Major	348	
F-BRCP	CEA DR.380 Prince	356	
F-BRCQ	CEA DR.340 Major	347	
F-BRCR	CEA DR.315 Petit Prince	349	
F-BRCT	CEA DR.340 Major	351	
F-BRCY	CEA DR.340 Major	353	
F-BRCZ	CEA DR.340 Major	354	
F-BRDB	SOCATA MS.892A Rallye Commodore 150	10910	
F-BRDE	SOCATA MS.880B Rallye Club	1279	
F-BRDG	SOCATA MS.893A Rallye Commodore 180	10975	
F-BRDH	SOCATA MS.880B Rallye Club	1276	
F-BRDI	Gardan GY-80 Horizon 180	250	
F-BRDJ	SOCATA MS.880B Rallye Club	1295	
F-BRDL	SOCATA MS.893A Rallye Commodore 180	10754	
F-BRDM	SOCATA MS.893A Rallye Commodore 180	10759	
F-BRDP	Gardan GY-80 Horizon 180	254	

Regn.	Type	C/n	Prev.Id.
F-BRDQ	SOCATA MS.880B Rallye Club	1285	
F-BRDS	SOCATA MS.893A Rallye Commodore 180	10941	
F-WRDT	SOCATA MS.892A Rallye Commodore (SACMA engine)	10951	F-BRDT
F-BRDX	SOCATA MS.880B Rallye Club	1275	
F-BREB	SOCATA MS.893A Rallye Commodore 180	10964	
F-BRED	SOCATA MS.880B Rallye Club	1290	
F-BREE	SOCATA MS.880B Rallye Club	1291	
F-BREG	SOCATA MS.893A Rallye Commodore 180	10948	
F-WREI	Gardan GY-80 Horizon 180	242	F-BREI
F-BREL	SOCATA MS.893A Rallye Commodore 180	10956	
F-BREN	SOCATA MS.893A Rallye Commodore 180	10651	F-OCHZ
F-BREP	SOCATA MS.880B Rallye Club	1287	
F-BRER	SOCATA MS.893A Rallye Commodore 180	10946	
F-BRET	SOCATA MS.893A Rallye Commodore 180	10967	
F-BRFA	CEA DR.340 Major	355	
F-BRFF	CEA DR.315 Petit Prince	359	
F-BRFH	CEA DR.315 Petit Prince	361	
F-BRFL	CEA DR.315 Petit Prince	366	
F-BRFN	CEA DR.340 Major	368	
F-BRFO	CEA DR.315 Petit Prince	369	
F-BRFP	CEA DR.315 Petit Prince	370	
F-BRFQ	CEA DR.340 Major	371	
F-BRFS	CEA DR.253B Régent	145	
F-BRFT	CEA DR.340 Major	373	
F-BRFU	CEA DR.315 Petit Prince	374	
F-BRFX	CEA DR.315 Petit Prince	375	
F-BRFY	CEA DR.253B Régent	140	
F-BRGB	SOCATA MS.880B Rallye Club	1296	F-BREJ
F-BRGD	Aero Resources Super J-2	043	F-WRGD
			N4333G
F-BRGN(4)	Gardan GY-100/135 Baghera	1	F-WRGA
			F-BRGA
F-BRGQ	SIAI-Marchetti S.208	2-48	OO-BMW
F-BRGS	SOCATA MS.893A Rallye Commodore 180	11064	D-EBVQ
F-BRGT	Piper PA-28R-200 Arrow	28R-35820	TJ-AEC
			N11C
			N5042S
			5T-TJP
F-BRGV	SAN Jodel D.140C Mousquetaire III	96	F-OCAN
			F-OCHA
F-BRHA	Mooney M.20E Super 21	810	N5891Q
F-BRHF	Piper PA-32-300 Cherokee Six	32-40467	N4152R
F-BRHH	Cessna 185C Skywagon	0660	TR-LKS
			F-OCBT
			N2660Z
F-BRHJ	SIAI-Marchetti S.205-18/F	4-268	
F-BRHK	Beech 95-B55 Baron	TC-1190	
F-BRHM	Bölkow BO.208C Junior	687	D-EEAJ
F-BRHT	Piper PA-28R-180 Cherokee Arrow	28R-30693	N4946J
F-BRIA	SOCATA Rallye 150SV Garnement	3366	F-OGLX
F-BRIB	Piper PA-28-235 Cherokee	28-10583	N9002W
F-BRIC	SEEMS MS.885 Super Rallye	5277	PH-MSC
F-BRIE	Aermacchi AL.60B-2	88/6268	
F-BRIF	Dornier Do.27Q-1	2022	
F-BRII	Cessna U.206D Stationair	1318	N72204
F-BRIL	Mooney M.20F Executive	690050	
F-BRIO	Beech 95-B55 Baron	TC-1201	N164V
F-BRIR	Piper PA-32-300B Cherokee	32-40635	N4261R
F-BRIZ	Beech E33A Bonanza	CE-271	(ZS-FLZ)
F-BRJL	SOCATA MS.892A Rallye Commodore 150	10972	
F-BRJO	Gardan GY-80 Horizon 180	240	
F-BRJP	Gardan GY-80 Horizon 180	255	
F-BRJX	SOCATA MS.892A Rallye Commodore 150	10970	
F-BRKA	SOCATA MS.893A Rallye Commodore 180	10937	
F-BRKB	SOCATA MS.893A Rallye Commodore 180	10949	
F-BRKC	SOCATA MS.893A Rallye Commodore 180	10958	
F-BRKE	SOCATA MS.893A Rallye Commodore 180	10959	
F-BRKF	SOCATA MS.893A Rallye Commodore 180	10960	
F-BRKG	SOCATA MS.893A Rallye Commodore 180	10961	
F-BRKH	SOCATA MS.893A Rallye Commodore 180	10965	
F-BRKI	SOCATA MS.893A Rallye Commodore 180	10998	
F-BRKK	SOCATA MS.893A Rallye Commodore 180	10977	
F-BRKL	SOCATA MS.893A Rallye Commodore 180	10978	
F-BRKP	SOCATA MS.893A Rallye Commodore 180	10985	

Regn.	Type	C/n	Prev.Id.
F-BRKR	SOCATA MS.893A Rallye Commodore 180	10987	
F-BRKS	SOCATA MS.893A Rallye Commodore 180	10995	
F-BRKT	SOCATA MS.893A Rallye Commodore 180	10996	
F-BRKU	SOCATA MS.893A Rallye Commodore 180	10997	
F-BRKV	SOCATA MS.893A Rallye Commodore 180	11046	
F-BRKZ	SOCATA MS.894A Minerva 220	11052	
F-BRLB	SOCATA MS.893A Rallye Commodore 180	11054	
F-BRLF	SOCATA MS.880B Rallye Club	1319	
F-BRLI	Gardan GY-80 Horizon 180	259	
F-BRLM	SOCATA MS.880B Rallye Club	1336	
F-BRLO	SOCATA MS.892A Rallye Commodore 150	10993	
F-BRLQ	SOCATA MS.893A Rallye Commodore 180	11415	
F-BRLV	SOCATA MS.893A Rallye Commodore 180	11058	
F-BRLZ	SOCATA MS.880B Rallye Club (W/o)	1347	
F-BRMD	SOCATA MS.880B Rallye Club	1351	
F-BRMG	SOCATA MS.893A Rallye Commodore 180	11413	
F-BRMH	SOCATA MS.893A Rallye Commodore 180	11414	
F-BRMJ	SOCATA MS.894A Minerva 220	11077	
F-BRMK	SOCATA MS.892A Rallye Commodore 150	11406	
F-BRML	SOCATA MS.894A Minerva 220	11055	
F-BRMO	SOCATA MS.883 Rallye 115	1362	
F-BRMU	SOCATA MS.883 Rallye 115	1380	
F-BRMV	SOCATA MS.883 Rallye 115	1513	
F-BRMZ	SOCATA MS.883 Rallye 115	1389	
F-BRNA	Zlin Z.526 Trenér Master	1063	
F-BRND	Zlin Z.526 Trenér Master	1080	
F-BRNQ	Piper PA-28R-200 Cherokee Arrow	28R-35714	N4988S
F-BRNU	Piper PA-23-250 Aztec C	27-3284	6V-ABJ 7T-VBG N6082Y
F-BROA	CEA DR.360 Chevalier	376	
F-BROC	CEA DR.360 Chevalier	379	
F-BROE	CEA DR.315 Petit Prince	381	
F-BROF	CEA DR.315 Petit Prince	394	
F-BROH	CEA DR.315 Petit Prince	387	
F-BROJ	CEA DR.315 Petit Prince	388	
F-BROK	CEA DR.340 Major	389	
F-BROR	CEA DR.340 Major	392	
F-BROS	CEA DR.340 Major	393	
F-BROT	CEA DR.380 Prince	395	
F-BROV	CEA DR.380 Prince	399	
F-BROX	CEA DR.360 Chevalier	400	
F-BROY	CEA DR.315 Petit Prince	365	F-OCMY
F-BRPD	Piper PA-28-140 Cherokee C	28-25740	N8877N
F-BRPQ	Cessna T.337D Super Skymaster	0995	N2695S
F-BRPS	Reims/Cessna FR.172F Rocket	0083	
F-BRPX	Piper PA-23-250 Aztec D	27-4285	N6928Y
F-BRPY	Piper PA-28-140 Cherokee C	28-26008	N98049
F-BRQA	Piper PA-25-260 Pawnee C	25-5205	N8752L
F-BRQB	SE.313B Alouette II	1502	CF-VKN F-BNGJ F-WNGJ H-8
F-BRQD	SAN Jodel D.140C Mousquetaire III	131	F-OCOD TT-AAB F-OCAX
F-BRQI	SE.3160 Alouette III	1915	FAP9399
F-BRQM	Piper PA-18-150 Super Cub	18-5322	(F-BRQH) ALAT
F-BRQN	Piper PA-18-150 Super Cub	18-5328	(F-BRQG) ALAT
F-BRRC	SOCATA MS.883 Rallye 115	1377	
F-BRRK	SOCATA MS.893A Rallye Commodore 180	11439	
F-BRRL	SOCATA MS.892A Rallye Commodore 150 (Stored)	11428	
F-BRRM	SOCATA MS.880B Rallye Club	1395	
F-BRRN	SOCATA MS.880B Rallye Club	1396	
F-BRRP	SOCATA MS.893A Rallye Commodore 180	11418	
F-BRRR	SOCATA MS.880B Rallye Club	1403	(D-ECCG)
F-BRRT	SOCATA MS.880B Rallye Club	1399	
F-BRRY	SOCATA MS.880B Rallye Club	1558	
F-BRSC	Beech 60 Duke	P-66	
F-BRSG	Cessna 182N Skylane	60154	N92328
F-BRSH	Cessna 414	0064	N8164Q
F-BRSV	Bellanca 17-30 Viking 300	30051	N6684V
F-BRSZ	Cessna 401B	0044	N7944Q
F-BRTB	CEA DR.315 Petit Prince	401	
F-BRTD	CEA DR.380 Prince	403	
F-BRTE	CEA DR.340 Major	402	
F-BRTF	CEA DR.340 Major	382	
F-BRTG	CEA DR.315 Petit Prince	404	
F-BRTJ	CEA DR.220A-B 2+2	133	
F-BRTK	CEA DR.315 Petit Prince	408	
F-BRTL	CEA DR.340 Major	413	
F-BRTM	CEA DR.253B Régent	152	
F-BRTN	CEA DR.380 Prince	410	
F-BRTO	CEA DR.315 Petit Prince	411	
F-BRTP	CEA DR.315 Petit Prince	412	
F-BRTQ	CEA DR.315 Petit Prince	414	
F-BRTR	CEA DR.315 Petit Prince	415	
F-BRTV	CEA DR.380 Prince	398	
F-BRTZ	CEA DR.253B Régent	150	
F-BRUA	Beech P35 Bonanza	D-7241	HB-EKI
F-BRUB	Piper PA-28R-200 Cherokee Arrow	28R-35239	N2645R
F-BRUC	Beech 95-B55 Baron	TC-1298	
F-BRUE	Piper PA-28R-200 Cherokee Arrow	28R-35364	N2949R
F-BRUH	Beech E33 Bonanza	CD-1230	N7770R
F-BRUK	Piper PA-30-160 Twin Comanche C	30-1990	N8832Y
F-BRUM	Cessna T.210J Turbo-System Centurion	0395	N2245R
F-BRUS	Piper PA-30-160 Twin Comanche C	30-1816	HB-LFG N8673Y
F-BRUU	Wassmer WA.421-250	418	
F-BRUV	Bellanca 17-30A Viking 300	30269	
F-BRVB	CEA DR.315 Petit Prince	438	
F-BRVC	CEA DR.315 Petit Prince	429	
F-BRVD	CEA DR.380 Prince	418	
F-BRVH	CEA DR.220A-B 2+2	134	
F-BRVI	CEA DR.360 Chevalier	427	
F-BRVJ	CEA DR.340 Major	430	
F-BRVK	CEA DR.315 Petit Prince	431	
F-BRVL	CEA DR.340 Major	432	
F-BRVP	CEA DR.340 Major	435	
F-BRVT	Robin DR.300/108 2+2 Tricycle	493	
F-BRVV	Robin DR.300/108 2+2 Tricycle	489	
F-BRVY	CEA DR.220A-B 2+2	136	
F-BRXA	Reims/Cessna F.150K	0533	
F-BRXC	Reims/Cessna FR.172G Rocket	0197	
F-BRXF	Reims/Cessna F.172H	0705	
F-BRXG	Reims/Cessna FR.172G Rocket	0204	
F-BRXK	Reims/Cessna F.150K	0615	
F-BRXN	Cessna U.206E Stationair	01674	N9474G
F-BRXO	Reims/Cessna F.150K	0624	
F-BRXQ	Reims/Cessna F.150K	0626	
F-BRXU	Reims/Cessna F.150K	0630	
F-BRXX	Reims/Cessna F.150K	0632	
F-BRYA	SOCATA MS.893A Rallye Commodore 180	11468	
F-BRYL	SOCATA MS.880B Rallye Club	1523	
F-BRYO	SOCATA MS.894C Minerva 220	11070	(G-AXOH)
F-BRYU	SOCATA MS.880B Rallye Club	1515	(G-AXHH)
F-BRZA	CEA DR.315 Petit Prince	445	
F-BRZB	CEA DR.315 Petit Prince	441	
F-BRZE	CEA DR.315 Petit Prince	450	
F-BRZI	CEA DR.340 Major	454	
F-BRZK	CEA DR.360 Chevalier	456	
F-BRZM	CEA DR.360 Chevalier	458	
F-BRZN	CEA DR.340 Major	459	
F-BRZO	CEA DR.315 Petit Prince	461	
F-BRZQ	CEA DR.315 Petit Prince	463	
F-BRZT	CEA DR.253B Régent	165	
F-BRZU	CEA DR.340 Major	466	
F-BRZY	CEA DR.220A-B 2+2	139	
F-BSAE	SOCATA MS.880B Rallye Club	1537	
F-BSAF	SOCATA MS.880B Rallye Club	1539	
F-BSAG	SOCATA MS.880B Rallye Club	1543	
F-BSAH	SOCATA MS.880B Rallye Club	1575	
F-BSAI	SOCATA MS.883 Rallye 115 (Dismantled)	1548	
F-BSAN	SOCATA MS.893A Rallye Commodore 180	11487	
F-BSAO	SOCATA MS.883 Rallye 115	1551	(D-EDDH)
F-BSAV	SOCATA MS.893A Rallye Commodore 180	11457	
F-BSAX	SOCATA MS.880B Rallye Club	1576	
F-BSAY	SOCATA MS.880B Rallye Club	1556	(G-AXHI)

Regn.	Type	C/n	Prev.Id.
F-BSBA	CEA DR.220A-B 2+2	141	
F-BSBG	CEA DR.315 Petit Prince	472	
F-BSBI	CEA DR.340 Major	473	
F-BSBL	CEA DR.315 Petit Prince	475	
F-BSBM	CEA DR.253B Régent	170	
F-BSBN	CEA DR.315 Petit Prince	480	
F-BSBR	CEA DR.315 Petit Prince	488	
F-BSBS	CEA DR.315 Petit Prince	491	
F-BSBT	Robin DR.300/108 2+2 Tricycle	492	
F-BSBV	Robin DR.300/108 2+2 Tricycle	494	
F-BSBX	Robin DR.300/108 2+2 Tricycle	499	
F-BSBY	CEA DR.315 Petit Prince	495	
F-BSBZ	CEA DR.340 Major	482	
F-BSCD	SOCATA MS.893A Rallye Commodore 180	11486	
F-BSCK	SOCATA MS.893A Rallye Commodore 180	11073	
F-BSCM	SOCATA MS.880B Rallye Club	1598	
F-BSCO	SOCATA MS.880B Rallye Club	1602	
F-BSDA	SOCATA MS.893A Rallye Commodore 180	11465	
F-BSDB	SOCATA MS.893A Rallye Commodore 180	11467	
F-BSDC	SOCATA MS.893A Rallye Commodore 180	11475	
F-BSDD	SOCATA MS.893A Rallye Commodore 180	11476	
F-BSDE	SOCATA MS.893A Rallye Commodore 180	11477	
F-BSDF	SOCATA MS.893A Rallye Commodore 180	11478	
F-BSDG	SOCATA MS.893A Rallye Commodore 180	11479	
F-BSDH	SOCATA MS.893A Rallye Commodore 180	11480	
F-BSDI	SOCATA MS.893A Rallye Commodore 180	11481	
F-BSDJ	SOCATA MS.893A Rallye Commodore 180	11482	
F-BSDK	SOCATA MS.893A Rallye Commodore 180	11483	
F-BSDL	SOCATA MS.893A Rallye Commodore 180	11484	
F-BSDM	SOCATA MS.893A Rallye Commodore 180	11499	
F-BSDN	SOCATA MS.893A Rallye Commodore 180	11500	
F-BSDR	SOCATA MS.880B Rallye Club	1604	
F-BSEA	Beech E33A Bonanza	CE-249	HB-EHI
F-BSEB	Piper PA-18-150 Super Cub	18-5353	ALAT
F-BSEC	Piper PA-18-150 Super Cub	18-5371	ALAT
F-BSEE	Piper PA-23-250 Aztec D	27-4557	N13923
F-BSEH	Piper PA-28R-200 Cherokee Arrow	28R-35233	HB-OZS
			N2628R
F-BSEK	SOCATA ST-10 Diplomate	118	OO-PLL
F-BSEN	Beech 95-B55 Baron	TC-1328	HB-GEL
F-BSEO	Piper PA-23-250 Aztec D	27-4428	N13778
F-BSEP	Cessna 150F	62954	G-ATLS
			(N8854G)
F-BSES	SO.1221-S Djinn	1001/FR7	G-AXFO
			F-BHOI
			F-WHOI
F-BSFE	SOCATA MS.880B Rallye Club	1613	
F-BSFF	SOCATA MS.880B Rallye Club	1614	
F-BSFQ	SOCATA MS.880B Rallye Club	1688	
F-BSFX	SOCATA ST-10 Diplomate	114	
F-BSFY	SOCATA ST-10 Diplomate	115	
F-BSGB	Agusta-Bell 206B Jet Ranger	8325	
F-BSGC	CAARP CAP.10B	04	
F-BSGD	Dornier Do.27A-4	383	56+77
			PZ+221
			QW+ . . .
			OE-VAI
			D-ELAW
			PG+104 ?
F-BSGF	Dornier Do.27A-4	416	56+99
			PJ+335
			GC+383
			GB+383 ?
F-BSGI	Dornier Do.27A-4	436	57+10
			PA+325
			QL+603 ?
F-BSGK	Dornier Do.27A-4	451	57+23
			PB+223
F-BSGM	Dornier Do.27A-4	524	57+63
			GB+375
F-BSGN	Deveque Free Balloon HG RD 700	8	
F-BSGO	Cessna 180A	32939	OO-SPO
			D-EGBE
			N9642B

Regn.	Type	C/n	Prev.Id.
F-BSGR	Cessna 310	35027	7T-VCD
			F-OCDZ
			HB-LBC
			(N2627C)
F-BSGS	Wassmer WA.421-250	428	
F-BSGX	SE.313B Alouette II	1341	Zaire 1341
			OL-A51
F-BSHB	Reims/Cessna F.177RG Cardinal RG	0001/00004	F-WLIR
			N8004G
F-BSHD	Reims/Cessna FR.172H Rocket	0255	
F-BSHF	Reims/Cessna F.172L	0808	F-BSHY
F-BSHM	Reims/Cessna FA.150K Aerobat	0077	
F-BSHQ	Reims/Cessna F.177RG Cardinal RG	0016/00133	
F-BSHV	Reims/Cessna F.177RG Cardinal RG	0032/00195	
F-BSIA	Bell 47G-2	1629	ALAT
			Fr.AF
			N2848B
F-BSIB	Reims/Cessna F.150K	0637	
F-BSID	Cessna A.188 Agwagon	0358	CN-TEK
			N8108V
F-BSIG	Reims/Cessna F.150K	0643	
F-BSIH	CEA Jodel DR.1050-M1 Sicile Record	634	HB-EEU
F-BSII	Reims/Cessna F.150K	0645	
F-BSIK	Reims/Cessna F.150K	0647	
F-BSIN	Reims/Cessna F.150K	0649	
F-BSIO	Reims/Cessna F.150K	0650	
F-BSIQ	Reims/Cessna F.150K	0652	
F-BSIR	Reims/Cessna F.150K	0653	
F-BSIS	Reims/Cessna FR.172H Rocket	0242	
F-BSIT	Reims/Cessna F.150K	0654	
F-BSIU	Reims/Cessna F.150K	0655	
F-BSIX	Reims/Cessna F.150K	0657	
F-BSIY	Reims/Cessna F.150K	0658	
F-BSJA	CEA DR.380 Prince	486	
F-BSJB	Robin DR.300/108 2+2 Tricycle	500	
F-BSJF	Robin DR.300/108 2+2 Tricycle	503	
F-BSJG	Robin DR.300/108 2+2 Tricycle	504	
F-BSJH	Robin DR.300/108 2+2 Tricycle	505	
F-BSJJ	Robin DR.300/108 2+2 Tricycle	506	
F-BSJN	Robin DR.300/108 2+2 Tricycle	512	
F-BSJQ	Robin DR.300/108 2+2 Tricycle	509	
F-BSJR	Robin DR.300/108 2+2 Tricycle	514	
F-BSJT	CEA DR.360 Chevalier	532	
F-BSJU	Robin DR.300/108 2+2 Tricycle	518	
F-BSJV	CEA DR.360 Chevalier	533	
F-BSJX	Robin DR.300/108 2+2 Tricycle	516	
F-BSJZ	CEA DR.315 Petit Prince	522	
F-BSKC	SOCATA MS.893A Rallye Commodore 180	11642	
F-BSKF	SOCATA MS.892A Rallye Commodore 150	11704	
F-BSKH	SOCATA MS.892A Rallye Commodore 150	11706	
F-BSKI	SOCATA MS.892A Rallye Commodore 150	11707	
F-BSKK	SOCATA MS.880B Rallye Club	1701	
F-BSKL	SOCATA MS.880B Rallye Club	1693	
F-BSKM	SOCATA MS.880B Rallye Club	1694	
F-BSKN	SOCATA MS.892A Rallye Commodore 150	11764	
F-BSKP	SOCATA MS.894A Minerva 220	11627	
F-BSKQ	SOCATA MS.880B Rallye Club	1697	
F-BSKV	SOCATA MS.880B Rallye Club	1692	
F-BSKY	SOCATA MS.880B Rallye Club	1696	
F-BSLC	Robin DR.300/108 2+2 Tricycle	527	
F-BSLF	Robin DR.300/108 2+2 Tricycle	537	
F-BSLG	Robin DR.300/108 2+2 Tricycle	538	
F-BSLJ	Robin DR.300/108 2+2 Tricycle	540	
F-BSLQ	Robin DR.300/108 2+2 Tricycle	552	
F-BSLR	Robin DR.300/108 2+2 Tricycle	551	
F-BSLT	CEA DR.253B Régent	184	
F-BSLU	Robin DR.300/108 2+2 Tricycle	557	
F-BSLX	Robin DR.300/108 2+2 Tricycle	559	
F-BSLY	Robin DR.300/140 Major	560	
F-BSLZ	Robin DR.300/108 2+2 Tricycle	561	
F-BSMA	SOCATA MS.893A Rallye Commodore 180	11768	
F-BSMB	SOCATA MS.893A Rallye Commodore 180	11769	
F-BSMC	SOCATA MS.893A Rallye Commodore 180	11770	
F-BSME	SOCATA MS.892A Rallye Commodore 150	11716	
F-BSMG	SOCATA MS.880B Rallye Club	1805	

Regn.	Type	C/n	Prev.Id.
F-BSMH	SOCATA MS.880B Rallye Club	1806	
F-BSMK	SOCATA MS.894A Minerva 220	11829	
F-BSMO	SOCATA ST-10 Diplomate	131	
F-BSMZ	SOCATA MS.892A Rallye Commodore 150	11817	
F-BSNA	Wassmer WA.51A Pacific	13	
F-BSND	Wassmer WA.421-250	427	
F-BSNE	Wassmer WA.51A Pacific	16	
F-BSNF	Wassmer WA.51A Pacific	17	
F-BSNJ	Enstrom F-28A	264	F-GATB
			3A-MJC
			(OO-BAO)
F-BSNL	Wassmer WA.52 Europa	24	
F-BSNM	Wassmer WA.51A Pacific	25	
F-BSNO	Wassmer WA.421-250	422	
F-BSNR	Wassmer WA.52 Europa	29	
F-BSNT	Wassmer WA.52 Europa	31	
F-BSNV	Wassmer WA.51A Pacific	34	
F-BSOA	Robin DR.300/108 2+2 Tricycle	562	
F-BSOB	Robin DR.300/108 2+2 Tricycle	563	
F-BSOC	Robin DR.300/108 2+2 Tricycle	564	
F-BSOD	Robin DR.300/108 2+2 Tricycle	565	
F-BSOE	Robin DR.300/108 2+2 Tricycle	566	
F-BSOF	Robin DR.300/108 2+2 Tricycle	567	
F-BSOI	Robin HR.100/200B Royal	04	
F-BSOJ	CEA DR.380 Prince	572	
F-BSOK	Robin DR.300/120 Petit Prince	574	
F-BSON	CEA DR.315 Petit Prince	579	
F-BSOP	Robin DR.300/120 Petit Prince	580	
F-BSOR	Robin DR.300/108 2+2 Tricycle	582	
F-BSOT	Robin DR.300/120 Petit Prince	585	
F-BSOU	CEA DR.315 Petit Prince	587	
F-BSOX	CEA DR.340 Major	588	
F-BSOY	Robin HR.100/200B Royal	07	
F-BSPA	Robin DR.300/108 2+2 Tricycle	575	
F-BSPE	Robin DR.300/120 Petit Prince	607	
F-BSPJ	Robin DR.300/108 2+2 Tricycle	612	
F-BSPK	Robin DR.300/140 Major	614	
F-BSPL	Robin DR.300/180R Remorqueur	591	
F-BSPM	Robin DR.300/120 Petit Prince	617	
F-BSPN	Robin DR.300/120 Petit Prince	618	
F-BSPO	Robin DR.300/120 Petit Prince	620	
F-BSPQ	Robin DR.300/120 Petit Prince	621	
F-BSPS	Robin DR.300/108 2+2 Tricycle	622	
F-BSPT	Robin DR.300/108 2+2 Tricycle	627	
F-BSPU	Robin HR.100/200B Royal	111	(D-EBAX)
F-BSPY	Robin DR.300/125 Petit Prince	30	
F-BSQJ	Cerva CE-43 Guepard	03/433	F-WSQF
F-BSQR	Robin HR.200/100 Club	01	F-WSQR
F-BSRE	Cessna 414	0156	N8226Q
F-BSRM	SE.313B Alouette II	1183	CF-YBV
			F-BIPV
F-BSRN	Agusta-Bell 206A Jet Ranger II	8278	
F-BSRQ	Cessna 185 Skywagon	0106	TR-LLQ
			F-OBVN
			N9906X
F-BSRS	Piper PA-18-150 Super Cub	18-4894	TR-LNS
			F-OAYV
F-BSST	Cessna 210L Centurion	61044	D-EARK
			N2077S
F-BSTD	Cessna 421B Golden Eagle	0106	N8076Q
F-BSTF	Pilatus PC-6/A2-H2 Turbo-Porter	654	HB-FDT
F-BSTL(2)	SNCAN/Stampe SV.4C	458	F-BCVZ
F-BSUB	Piper PA-28R-200 Cherokee Arrow	28R-7135071	N2128T
F-BSUI	Aérospatiale SA.315B Lama	2220	
F-BSUQ	SA.316B Alouette III	1779	HC-BOX
			F-BSUQ
F-BSUS	SIAI-Marchetti S.208	2-20	OO-HIJ
F-BSVI	SOCATA MS.880B Rallye Club	1735	
F-BSVN	SOCATA MS.892A Rallye Commodore 150 (Wfu)	11767	
F-BSVO	Beech A23-19 Musketeer Sport	MB-34	HB-ENR
F-BSVP	SOCATA MS.894A Minerva 220	11677	
F-BSVQ	SOCATA MS.893A Rallye Commodore 180	11632	
F-BSVR	SOCATA MS.893A Rallye Commodore 180	11666	
F-BSVS	SOCATA MS.893A Rallye Commodore 180	11715	
F-BSVT	SOCATA MS.893A Rallye Commodore 180	11743	
F-BSVU	SOCATA MS.893A Rallye Commodore 180	11744	
F-BSVV	SOCATA MS.893A Rallye Commodore 180	11745	
F-BSVX	SOCATA MS.893A Rallye Commodore 180	11746	
F-BSVY	SOCATA MS.893A Rallye Commodore 180	11747	
F-BSVZ	SOCATA MS.893A Rallye Commodore 180	11749	
F-BSXD	SOCATA MS.880B Rallye Club	1762	
F-BSXE	SOCATA MS.894A Minerva 220	11872	
F-BSXG	SOCATA MS.880B Rallye Club (Wfu)	1795	
F-BSXK	SOCATA ST-10 Diplomate	133	
F-BSXL	SOCATA MS.880B Rallye Club	1799	
F-BSXP	SOCATA MS.892A Rallye Commodore 150	11818	
F-BSXT	SOCATA MS.880B Rallye Club	1803	
F-BSXU	SOCATA MS.880B Rallye Club	1804	
F-BSXV	SOCATA MS.880B Rallye Club	1802	
F-BSYO	SOCATA MS.880B Rallye Club	1791	F-BSKO
F-BSYU	Gardan GY-80 Horizon 180	229	OO-UIL
F-BSZA	SOCATA MS.880B Rallye Club	1813	
F-BSZG	SOCATA MS.880B Rallye Club	1858	
F-BSZM	SOCATA ST-10 Diplomate	134	
F-BTAJ	Beech 58 Baron	TH-199	
F-BTAN	SIAI-Marchetti S.205-18/R	4-169	OO-HED
F-BTAS	Aérospatiale SA.315B Lama	2201/07	F-WIEO
	(Converted from SA.318C c/n 2201, 1.74)		
F-BTAU	DHC-6 Twin Otter 200	153	N246GW
			(N33TW)
			N246GW
F-BTBB	Robin DR.300/120 Petit Prince	636	
F-BTBC	Robin DR.300/120 Petit Prince	637	
F-BTBD	Robin DR.300/108 2+2 Tricycle	638	
F-BTBE	Robin DR.300/108 2+2 Tricycle	640	
F-BTBG	Robin DR.300/108 2+2 Tricycle	648	
F-BTBJ	Robin DR.300/120 Petit Prince	654	
F-BTBK	Robin DR.300/120 Petit Prince	655	
F-BTBM	CEA DR.253B Régent	197	
F-BTBO	Robin DR.300/180R Remorqueur	660	
F-BTBP	Robin HR.100/200B Royal	112	
F-BTBS	Robin DR.300/120 Petit Prince	664	
F-BTBV	CEA DR.360 Chevalier	666	
F-BTBX	Robin DR.300/108 2+2 Tricycle	668	
F-BTBZ	Robin DR.300/180R Remorqueur	671	
F-BTCF	SAN Jodel D.140B Mousquetaire II	98	PH-NVD
F-BTCG	Pilatus PC-6/A-H2 Porter	551	I-SORE
F-BTCN	Piper PA-28R-200 Cherokee Arrow	28R-7135182	N2289T
F-BTCP	Piper PA-31-310 Navajo	31-749	N7227L
F-BTCQ	Piper PA-34-200 Seneca	34-7250019	N2396T
F-BTCR	Beech 95-B55 Baron	TC-1351	HB-GES
F-BTCZ	Cessna 182P Skylane	60951	N7311Q
F-BTDD	McDonnell-Douglas DC-10-30	46963	
F-BTDE	McDonnell-Douglas DC-10-30	46853	N54639
			(F-BTDE)
F-BTDG	Boeing 747-3B3	22514	
F-BTDH	Boeing 747-3B3	22515	
F-BTDJ	Cessna 182H Skylane	56367	D-EHTY
			N2467X
F-BTDM	Mudry CAP.10B	29	
F-BTDN	Mudry CAP.10B	30	
F-BTDR	Cessna 182P Skylane	60869	N9329G
F-BTDY	Cessna 421B Golden Eagle	0233	G-AZPT
			N5990M
F-BTEE	Piper PA-31T Cheyenne	31T-7620045	F-ODEE
			N82053
F-BTEL	Cessna 550 Citation	0190	N98715
F-BTEM	Reims/Cessna FT.337GP Skymaster	0012/0159	D-IAPV
F-BTEN	Agusta-Bell 47G-2	251	74+11
			AS+373
			LA+102
			AS+052
F-BTEV	Cameron O-65 HAFB	49	F-WTEV
F-BTEX	SOCATA MS.893E Rallye 180GT Gaillard	12438	D-EGHH
			F-BVHX
F-BTEY	Piper PA-23-150 Apache	23-52	F-OCST
			OO-EHG
			HB-LBT
			F-OBOS,
			OO-CHF, N1075P

Regn.	Type	C/n	Prev.Id.
F-BTFA	Reims/Cessna FA.150L Aerobat	0121	F-WLIO
			(G-AZBJ)
			F-BSHP
F-BTFD	Reims/Cessna FR.172H Rocket	0309	
F-BTFE	Reims/Cessna F.150L	0786	
F-BTFH	Reims/Cessna F.150L	0789	
F-BTFI	Reims/Cessna F.150L	0802	
F-BTFJ	Reims/Cessna F.150L	0781	
F-BTFL	Reims/Cessna F.172L	0864	
F-BTFM	Reims/Cessna FR.172H Rocket	0317	
F-BTFN	Reims/Cessna F.150L	0782	
F-BTFQ	Reims/Cessna F.177RG Cardinal RG	0059	
F-BTFV	Reims/Cessna F.172L	0886	
F-BTFY	Reims/Cessna F.150L	0834	
F-BTGI	CEA DR.253B Régent	176	OO-ALM
F-BTGJ	Cessna 182C Skylane	53418	F-OBVC
			N9018X
F-BTGL	Beech 65-A80 Queen Air	LD-227	D-ILKE
F-BTGR	Agusta-Bell 47G-2	198	F-MJAF
F-BTGS	Cessna TU.206C	0929	N3929G
F-BTGT	Piper PA-23-250 Aztec C	27-3270	5R-MCE
			N6072Y
F-BTGU	Piper PA-28-140 Cherokee E	28-7225124	N11C
F-BTHC	SOCATA MS.880B Rallye Club	1902	
F-BTHG	SOCATA MS.883 Rallye 115	1392	
F-BTHM	SOCATA MS.883 Rallye 115	1644	
F-BTHO	SOCATA MS.883 Rallye 115	1646	
F-BTHV	SOCATA ST-10 Diplomate	142	
F-BTIA	SOCATA ST-10 Diplomate	143	
F-BTIC	SOCATA MS.880B Rallye Club	1905	
F-BTIE	SOCATA MS.880B Rallye Club	1903	
F-BTIG	SOCATA MS.893A Rallye Commodore 180	11892	
F-BTIH	SOCATA MS.880B Rallye Club	1923	
F-BTII	SOCATA MS.880B Rallye Club	1915	
F-BTIK	SOCATA MS.880B Rallye Club	1922	
F-BTIM	SOCATA MS.880B Rallye Club	1952	
F-BTIS	SOCATA MS.880B Rallye Club	1917	
F-BTIT	SOCATA MS.894A Minerva 220	11943	
F-BTIU	SOCATA MS.880B Rallye Club	1953	
F-BTIV	SOCATA MS.880B Rallye Club	1958	
F-BTJG	SOCATA MS.894A Minerva 220	11941	
F-BTJP	SOCATA MS.880B Rallye Club	1967	
F-BTJQ	SOCATA MS.880B Rallye Club	1959	
F-BTJV	SOCATA MS.893A Rallye Commodore 180	11979	
F-BTJZ	SOCATA MS.880B Rallye Club	2046	
F-BTKA	Robin DR.300/125 Petit Prince	670	
F-BTKC	Robin DR.400/120 Petit Prince	696	
F-BTKE	Robin DR.300/120 Petit Prince	695	
F-BTKF	CEA DR.360 Chevalier	698	
F-BTKG	Robin DR.300/120 Petit Prince	700	
F-BTKH	Robin DR.400/120 Petit Prince	701	
F-BTKK	Robin DR.300/108 2+2 Tricycle	711	
F-BTKL	Robin DR.300/108 2+2 Tricycle	713	
F-BTKN	Robin DR.400/160 Chevalier	715	
F-BTKP	Robin HR.100/210 Safari	143	
F-BTKQ	Robin DR.300/108 2+2 Tricycle	717	
F-BTKR	Robin DR.400/180 Régent	699	(D-ENTJ)
F-BTKT	Robin DR.400/120 Petit Prince	723	
F-BTKU	Robin DR.400/120 Petit Prince	719	
F-BTKX	Robin DR.400/120 Petit Prince	732	
F-BTLD	Wassmer WA.54 Atlantic	52	
F-BTLE	Wassmer WA.52 Europa	55	
F-BTLI	Wassmer WA.52 Europa	58	
F-BTLJ	Wassmer WA.52 Europa *(Wrecked)*	77	
F-BTLK	Wassmer WA.52 Europa	60	
F-BTLO	Wassmer WA.52 Europa	66	
F-BTLP	Wassmer WA.52 Europa	67	
F-BTLR	Wassmer WA.52 Europa	75	
F-BTLS	Wassmer WA.52 Europa	83	
F-BTLU	Cerva CE.43 Guepard	436	
F-BTLV	Wassmer WA.52 Europa	84	
F-BTLY	Cerva CE.43 Guepard	437	
F-BTME	Beech 99	U-79	N551GP
F-BTMH	Piper PA-34-200 Seneca	34-7250135	F-BTDY
			N4566T
F-BTMM	Piper PA-31-310 Navajo	31-480	N449TA
F-BTMN	Beech 36 Bonanza	E-43	HB-EHG
F-BTMS	Piper PA-23-250 Aztec E	27-7305053	N9738N
F-BTPA	SOCATA MS.893A Rallye Commodore 180	11981	
F-BTPB	SOCATA MS.893A Rallye Commodore 180	11982	
F-BTPC	SOCATA MS.893A Rallye Commodore 180	11983	
F-BTPD	SOCATA MS.893A Rallye Commodore 180	11984	
F-BTPE	SOCATA MS.893A Rallye Commodore 180	11985	
F-BTPH	SOCATA MS.893A Rallye Commodore 180	11988	
F-BTPI	SOCATA MS.893A Rallye Commodore 180	11989	
F-BTPJ	SOCATA MS.893A Rallye Commodore 180	11990	
F-BTPK	SOCATA MS.893A Rallye Commodore 180	11991	
F-BTPM	SOCATA MS.880B Rallye Club	2047	
F-BTPS	SOCATA MS.893A Rallye Commodore 180	11993	
F-BTPY	SOCATA MS.880B Rallye Club	2111	
F-BTQF	Piper PA-28R-200 Cherokee Arrow	28R-7235162	F-BTMU
F-BTQH	Piper PA-28R-200 Cherokee Arrow	28R-7235174	N11C
F-BTQJ	Piper PA-28R-200 Cherokee Arrow	28R-7235169	N11C
F-BTQM	Beech C23 Sundowner	M-1388	
F-BTQO	SE.313B Alouette II	1649	SVietnam AF
F-BTQP	Beech 65-90 King Air	LJ-40	I-GNIS
			HB-GCH
F-BTQV	Cessna 310K	0047	N6947L
F-BTQY	Cessna 182P Skylane	61517	N21249
F-BTRA	SOCATA MS.880B Rallye Club	2045	
F-BTRB	SOCATA MS.887 Rallye 125	2040	
F-BTRD	SOCATA MS.880B Rallye Club	2055	
F-BTRH	SOCATA MS.880B Rallye Club	2083	
F-BTRI	SOCATA MS.892A Rallye Commodore 150	12036	
F-BTRJ	SOCATA MS.894A Minerva 220	11995	
F-BTRN	SOCATA ST-10 Diplomate	151	
F-BTRO	SOCATA MS.880B Rallye Club	2085	(D-EMJD)
F-BTRZ	SOCATA ST-10 Diplomate	155	
F-BTSC	Aérospatiale/BAC Concorde 101	3	F-WTSC
F-BTSD	Aérospatiale/BAC Concorde 101	13	N94SD
			F-BTSD
			F-WJAM
F-BTSE	Bell 47G	483	ALAT
			Fr.AF
			Fr.Navy
F-BTSF	Agusta-Bell 47G-2	080	ALAT
F-BTSH	Bell 47G	709	ALAT
			Fr.AF
			Fr.Navy
F-BTSI	Bell 47G-2	1632	ALAT
			N2851B
F-BTSJ	Agusta-Bell 47G-2	131	ALAT
F-BTSM	Agusta-Bell 47G-2	117	ALAT
F-BTSN	Agusta-Bell 47G-2	126	ALAT
F-BTSP	Agusta-Bell 47G-2	201	ALAT
			Fr.AF
			ALAT
F-BTSQ	Agusta-Bell 47G-2	168	ALAT
F-BTSV	Agusta-Bell 47G-2	199	ALAT
F-BTSX	Agusta-Bell 47G-2	147	ALAT
F-BTSY	Agusta-Bell 47G-2	184	ALAT
			Fr.AF
F-BTTA	Dassault Mercure 100 *(Wfu, stored)*	1	F-WTTA
F-BTUB	Reims/Cessna F.150L	0858	
F-BTUD	Reims/Cessna FR.172H Rocket	0336	
F-BTUH	Reims/Cessna F.172L	0885	
F-BTUI	Reims/Cessna F.150L	0838	
F-BTUK	Reims/Cessna F.172L	0888	
F-BTUL	Reims/Cessna F.172L	0889	
F-BTUM	Reims/Cessna F.172L	0890	
F-BTUN	Reims/Cessna F.172L	0891	
F-BTUP	Reims/Cessna F.172L	0894	
F-BTUQ	Reims/Cessna F.150L	0837	
F-BTUY	Reims/Cessna F.172L	0901	
F-BTUZ	Reims/Cessna F.172L	0903	
F-BTVC	SOCATA MS.880B Rallye Club	2107	
F-BTVI	SOCATA MS.893E Rallye 180GT Gaillard	12126	
F-BTVJ	SOCATA MS.893E Rallye 180GT Gaillard	12127	
F-BTVN	SOCATA MS.880B Rallye Club	2120	
F-BTVR	SOCATA MS.880B Rallye Club	2109	

Regn.	Type	C/n	Prev.Id.
F-BTVS	SOCATA MS.880B Rallye Club	2110	
F-BTVU	SOCATA MS.880B Rallye Club	2086	
F-BTVX	SOCATA MS.880B Rallye Club	2113	
F-BTXD	SNCAN/Stampe SV.4A	595	CN-TTG
			F-BDEP
F-BTXS	Robin DR.300/120 Petit Prince	720	F-BTKS
F-BTYE	Piper PA-28-140 Cherokee E	28-7225484	N11C
F-BTYI	Piper PA-34-200 Seneca	34-7350077	F-BTMY
F-BTYK	Piper PA-34-200 Seneca	34-7250091	N4416T
F-BTYL	Beech V35B Bonanza	D-9468	
F-BTYP	Piper PA-28-180 Challenger	28-7305166	N11C
F-BTYQ	Piper PA-23-250 Aztec E	27-7304972	F-BTMV
			N9728N
F-BTYS	Beech F33A Bonanza	CE-433	(D-EHWB)
F-BTYY	Piper PA-23-250 Aztec E	27-4773	HB-LGX
			F-BTYY
			LV-PRT
			N14215
			N9674N
F-BTZF	Robin DR.400/160 Chevalier	754	
F-BTZI	Robin DR.400/120 Petit Prince	756	
F-BTZM	Robin DR.400/180 Régent	768	
F-BTZN	Robin DR.400/120 Petit Prince	769	
F-BTZO	Robin DR.400/140 Major	770	
F-BTZP	Robin DR.400/2+2 Tricycle	773	
F-BTZS	Robin HR.100/210 Safari	151	
F-BTZT	Robin HR.100/210 Safari	152	
F-BTZY	Robin DR.400/140 Major	799	
F-BTZZ	Robin DR.400/160 Chevalier	802	
F-BUAD	Airbus A.300B2-1C	3	F-WJAD
	(Airbus Industrie Testbed)		(F-ODCX)
			F-WJAD
F-BUAV	SA.316B Alouette III	1683	HC-BMP
			F-BUAV
			FAP9345
F-BUAZ	SNCAN/Stampe SV.4A	19	F-BBAB
F-BUBC	Reims/Cessna FR.172J Rocket	0363	
F-BUBF	Reims/Cessna F.150L	0841	
F-BUBI	Reims/Cessna F.172L	0892	
F-BUBJ	Reims/Cessna F.150L	0845	
F-BUBK	Reims/Cessna F.150L	0846	
F-BUBM	Reims/Cessna F.150L	0849	
F-BUBN	Reims/Cessna F.150L	0854	
F-BUBQ	Reims/Cessna F.172L	0898	
F-BUBR	Reims/Cessna F.150L	0851	
F-BUBS	Reims/Cessna F.150L	0855	
F-BUBT	Reims/Cessna FRA.150L Aerobat	0199	
F-BUBX	Reims/Cessna F.150L	0860	
F-BUBZ	Reims/Cessna F.150L	0856	
F-BUCE	SOCATA MS.880B Rallye Club	2116	
F-BUCG	SOCATA MS.880B Rallye Club	2222	
F-BUCI	SOCATA MS.880B Rallye Club	2227	
F-BUCJ	SOCATA MS.880B Rallye Club (Wfu)	2226	
F-BUCL	SOCATA MS.880B Rallye Club	2221	
F-BUCM	SOCATA MS.880B Rallye Club	2228	
F-BUCQ	SOCATA MS.880B Rallye Club	2242	
F-BUCT	SOCATA MS.893E Rallye 180GT Gaillard	12179	
F-BUCY	SOCATA MS.880B Rallye Club	2223	
F-BUCZ	SOCATA MS.892A Rallye Commodore 150	12037	
F-BUDJ	Mudry CAP.10B	41	
F-BUDL	Mudry CAP.10B	44	
F-BUDM	Mudry CAP.10B	45	
F-BUDQ	Mudry CAP.10B	49	
F-BUDU(2)	Wassmer WA.40 Super IV	36	F-BIUB
			F-OBUB
F-BUDY(2)	SNCAN/Stampe SV.4C1	634	F-BDMD
F-BUDZ(2)	Christen Pitts S-2B	5131	F-WVDZ
F-BUEB	Reims/Cessna F.172L	0902	
F-BUED	Reims/Cessna FR.172J Rocket	0371	
F-BUEG	Reims/Cessna F.177RG Cardinal RG	0085	
F-BUEH	Reims/Cessna FR.172J Rocket	0393	
F-BUEJ	Reims/Cessna F.150L	0995	
F-BUEK	Reims/Cessna F.150L	0996	
F-BUEL	Reims/Cessna F.150L	0997	
F-BUEM	Reims/Cessna F.150L	0998	
F-BUEO	Reims/Cessna F.172M	1136	
F-BUEQ	Reims/Cessna F.172M	1025	
F-BUER	Reims/Cessna F.172M	1026	
F-BUES	Reims/Cessna F.172M	1027	
F-BUET	Reims/Cessna F.172M	1028	
F-BUEY	Reims/Cessna F.172M	1032	
F-BUFK	Cessna 310Q	0711	N8234Q
F-BUFZ	Piper PA-28R-200 Cherokee Arrow	28R-35385	F-OCOP
			N3093R
F-BUGG	SOCATA MS.880B Rallye Club	2219	
F-BUGH	SOCATA MS.893E Rallye 180GT Gaillard	12184	
F-BUGI	SOCATA MS.893E Rallye 180GT Gaillard	12229	
F-BUGJ	SOCATA MS.893E Rallye 180GT Gaillard	12230	
F-BUGK	SOCATA MS.893E Rallye 180GT Gaillard	12231	
F-BUGL	SOCATA MS.893E Rallye 180GT Gaillard	12232	
F-BUGM	SOCATA MS.893E Rallye 180GT Gaillard	12233	
F-BUGO	SOCATA MS.893E Rallye 180GT Gaillard	12265	
F-BUGP	SOCATA MS.893E Rallye 180GT Gaillard	12266	
F-BUGQ	SOCATA MS.880B Rallye Club (Written off)	2240	
F-BUGS	SOCATA MS.880B Rallye Club	2241	
F-BUGU	SOCATA MS.880B Rallye Club	2258	
F-BUGV	SOCATA MS.880B Rallye Club	2244	
F-BUHA	Robin DR.400/120 Petit Prince	782	
F-BUHB	Robin DR.400/140 Major	783	
F-BUHC	Robin DR.400/180 Régent	785	
F-BUHD	Robin DR.400/2+2 Tricycle	787	
F-BUHE	Robin DR.400/140B Major	788	
F-BUHI	Robin DR.400/120 Petit Prince	792	
F-BUHJ	Robin DR.400/140 Major	793	
F-BUHL	Robin DR.400/160 Chevalier	795	
F-BUHN	Robin DR.400/2+2 Tricycle	801	
F-BUHO	Robin HR.100/210 Safari	158	
F-BUHP	Robin DR.400/140 Major	804	
F-BUHQ	Robin DR.400/120 Petit Prince	805	
F-BUHR	Robin DR.400/125 Petit Prince	806	
F-BUHT	Robin DR.400/140 Major	808	
F-BUHU	Robin DR.400/180 Régent	809	
F-BUHX	Robin DR.400/120 Petit Prince	810	
F-BUIB	Cessna 207 Skywagon	00217	N1617U
F-BUIH	Piper PA-28-140 Cherokee F	28-7325275	N11C
F-BUIJ	Piper PA-34-200 Seneca	34-7350204	F-ETAA
F-BUIN	Cessna A.185F Skywagon	02098	N70292
F-BUIQ	Piper PA-39 Twin Comanche C/R	39-80	N14473
			G-AYKO
			N892IY
F-BUIR	Beech 60 Duke	P-87	TU-TEV
			(HB-GDX)
			N2850B
F-BUJA	SOCATA MS.887 Rallye 125	2163	
F-BUJC	SOCATA MS.880B Rallye 100ST	2289	
F-BUJF	SOCATA MS.893E Rallye 180GT Gaillard	12268	
F-BUJH	SOCATA MS.880B Rallye Club	2259	
F-BUJP	SOCATA MS.880B Rallye Club	2282	
F-BUJQ	SOCATA MS.880B Rallye Club	2283	
F-BUJR	SOCATA MS.880B Rallye Club	2284	
F-BUKF	Wassmer WA.52 Europa	95	
F-BUKI	Wassmer WA.54 Atlantic	92	
F-BUKJ	Wassmer WA.52 Europa	98	
F-BUKK	Wassmer WA.54 Atlantic	99	
F-BUKL	Wassmer WA.52 Europa	101	
F-BUKP	Wassmer WA.54 Atlantic	97	
F-BUKS	Wassmer WA.52 Europa	108	
F-BUKT	Wassmer WA.54 Atlantic	94	
F-BUKV	Wassmer WA.52 Europa	118	
F-BULA	SOCATA MS.894A Minerva 220	12079	(D-ENMJ)
F-BULD	SOCATA MS.893E Rallye 180GT Gaillard	12305	
F-BULK	SOCATA Rallye 100S Sport	2293	
F-BULL	SOCATA Rallye 100S Sport	2294	
F-BULM	SOCATA Rallye 100ST	2295	
F-BULO	SOCATA Rallye 100S Sport	2297	
F-BULT	Procaer F.15A Picchio	15	H-INV
F-BULU	SOCATA MS.880B Rallye Club	2303	
F-BULX	SOCATA MS.893E Rallye 180GT Gaillard	12274	
F-BUMA	Reims/Cessna F.150L	1090	

Regn.	Type	C/n	Prev.Id.
F-BUMB	Reims/Cessna FR.172J Rocket	0423	
F-BUMC	Reims/Cessna F.150L	0863	
F-BUMD	Reims/Cessna F.172L	0904	
F-BUME	Reims/Cessna F.150L	0999	
F-BUMF	Reims/Cessna FR.172J Rocket	0403	
F-BUMH	Reims/Cessna FR.172J Rocket	0409	
F-BUMI	Reims/Cessna FR.172J Rocket	0408	
F-BUMJ	Reims/Cessna F.177RG Cardinal RG	0091	
F-BUMK	Reims/Cessna F.177RG Cardinal RG	0071	(G-BAIV)
F-BUML	Reims/Cessna FRA.150L Aerobat	0198	
F-BUMM	Reims/Cessna F.177RG Cardinal RG	0073	
F-BUMP	Reims/Cessna F.177RG Cardinal RG	0082	
F-BUMT	Reims/Cessna F.172M	1002	
F-BUMU	Reims/Cessna F.172M	1004	
F-BUMV	Reims/Cessna F.172M	1005	
F-BUMX	Piper PA-25-235 Pawnee C	25-5412	N8947L
F-BUMY	Reims/Cessna F.172M	1014	
F-BUNA	SOCATA MS.893E Rallye 180GT Gaillard	12275	(D-EKHL)
F-BUNB	SOCATA MS.893E Rallye 180GT Gaillard	12276	(D-EKHM)
F-BUND	SOCATA MS.893E Rallye 180GT Gaillard	12278	
F-BUNG	SOCATA MS.893E Rallye 180GT Gaillard	12306	
F-BUNH	SOCATA MS.880B Rallye Club	2347	
F-BUNK	SOCATA MS.880B Rallye Club	2351	
F-BUNL	SOCATA Rallye 100S Sport	2340	
F-BUNM	SOCATA MS.880B Rallye Club	2352	
F-BUNP	SOCATA Rallye 100S Sport	2337	
F-BUNQ	SOCATA Rallye 100ST	2338	
F-BUNR	SOCATA Rallye 100S Sport	2341	
F-BUNS	SOCATA Rallye 100S Sport	2342	
F-BUOA	Piper PA-34-200 Seneca	34-7350208	F-ETAB
F-BUOF	Piper PA-25-235 Pawnee C	25-4382	4X-APR
			N4660Y
F-BUOG	Piper PA-18-150 Super Cub	18-8057	F-OCSG
			TT-BAA
			F-OCCE
			N4062Z
F-BUOJ	Piper PA-28-180 Cherokee Challenger	28-7305463	F-ETAE
F-BUOL	Piper PA-28-140 Cherokee E	28-7225130	HB-OML
			N15778
F-BUON	Beech C23 Sundowner	M-1448	
F-BUOS	Beech 58 Baron	TH-401	(D-IDUA)
F-BUOT	Piper PA-28-180 Cherokee Challenger	28-7305508	F-ETAK
F-BUOV	Grumman AA-5 Traveler	0410	N7110L
F-BUOX	Grumman AA-IB Trainer	0240	N9940L
F-BUPA	Robin DR.400/120 Petit Prince	817	
F-BUPE	Robin DR.400/140 Major	823	
F-BUPK	Robin DR.400/180 Régent	831	
F-BUPL	Robin DR.400/120 Petit Prince	832	
F-BUPM	Robin DR.400/120 Petit Prince	833	
F-BUPO	Robin DR.400/120 Petit Prince	838	
F-BUPQ	Robin DR.400/120 Petit Prince	842	
F-BUPS	Robin DR.400/140 Major	852	
F-BUPT	Robin DR.400/140 Major	854	
F-BUPU	Robin DR.300/120 Petit Prince	635	PH-SRE
F-BUQB	Robin HR.200/120B	03	F-WUQB
F-BUQE	Piper PA-25-235 Pawnee C	25-4445	4X-APS
F-BUQF	Robin HR.200/120B Club	04	(D-ENQF)
			F-BUQF
			F-WUQF
F-BUQG	Robin HR.200/120	05	F-WUQG
F-BUQH	Robin HR.200/100 Club	06	F-WUQH
F-BUQL	Robin HR.200/100 Club	08	
F-BUQN	Aérospatiale SN.601 Corvette	3	F-WUQN
F-BUQP	Aérospatiale SN.601 Corvette	4	F-WUQP
F-BUQY	Montgolfière Moderne MM18 O-56 HAFB	01	F-WUQY
F-BURE	Reims/Cessna F.337G Skymaster	0062/01512	
F-BURL	Reims/Cessna F.150L	1019	
F-BURM	Reims/Cessna F.177RG Cardinal RG	0084	
F-BURN	Reims/Cessna F.150L	1028	
F-BURO	Reims/Cessna F.172M	1048	
F-BURP	Reims/Cessna FR.172J Rocket	0443	
F-BURQ	Reims/Cessna FR.172J Rocket	0451	
F-BURU	Reims/Cessna F.177RG Cardinal RG	0087	
F-BURV	Reims/Cessna F.172M	1068	
F-BUSC	Robin HR.100/210 Safari	170	

Regn.	Type	C/n	Prev.Id.
F-BUSE	Robin DR.400/160 Chevalier	865	
F-BUSF	Robin DR.400/2+2 Tricycle	869	
F-BUSG	Robin DR.400/160 Chevalier	871	
F-BUSH	Robin DR.400/140 Major	872	
F-BUSI	Robin HR.200/100 Club	10	
F-BUSM	Robin DR.400/180 Régent	878	
F-BUSN	Robin DR.400/140 Major	894	
F-BUSO	Robin DR.400/140 Major	904	
F-BUSP	Robin HR.100/210 Safari	179	
F-BUSU	Robin DR.400/180 Régent	881	
F-BUSV	Robin HR.200/100 Club	19	
F-BUSY	Robin DR.400/2+2 Tricycle	877	
F-BUTC	Cessna 182J Skylane	57250	N3150F
F-BUTG	Cessna U.206F Stationair	02123	N71140
F-BUTJ	Piper PA-28R-200 Cherokee Arrow	28R-7335406	F-ETAI
F-BUTL	Piper PA-28R-200 Cherokee Arrow	28R-7335010	N15063
F-BUTS	Beech 65-E90 King Air	LW-68	
F-BUTT	Piper PA-34-200 Seneca	34-7350320	F-ETAP
F-BUTZ	Beech 95-C55 Baron	TE-105	D-ILVA
F-BUUC	Piper PA-28-140 Cherokee F	28-7325567	N9506N
F-BUUD	Piper PA-28-140 Cherokee F	28-7325569	N9507N
F-BUUE	Piper PA-34-200 Seneca	34-7350336	F-ETAR
F-BUUH	Piper PA-28-180 Cherokee Archer	28-7405006	F-ETAT
F-BUUI	Piper PA-28R-200 Cherokee Arrow	28R-7435012	F-ETAU
F-BUUK	Cessna 310Q	0275	5H-MOW
			5Y-AOF
			N7775Q
F-BUUM	Cessna 310Q	0916	N69682
F-BUUN	Piper PA-28-180 Cherokee Challenger	28-7305597	N56467
F-BUUO	Rockwell S.2R-600 Thrush Commander	1902R	
F-BUVK	SOCATA MS.894A Minerva 220	12090	
F-BUVL	SOCATA MS.893E Rallye 180GT Gaillard	12327	
F-BUVR	SOCATA MS.880B Rallye Club	2334	
F-BUVT	SOCATA MS.880B Rallye Club	2331	
F-BUVU	SOCATA MS.880B Rallye Club	2357	
F-BUVV	SOCATA MS.880B Rallye Club	2358	
F-BUVZ	Piper PA-30-160 Twin Comanche B	30-1379	TR-LKK
			N8253Y
F-BUXA	SOCATA Rallye 100S Sport	2364	
F-BUXB	Bell 47G-2	2445	G-BBKW
			N6770D
			ZK-HAQ
			N6770D
F-BUXC	SOCATA Rallye 100S Sport	2366	
F-BUXG	SOCATA MS.880B Rallye Club	2373	
F-BUXI	SOCATA MS.880B Rallye Club (Written off)	2389	
F-BUXK	SOCATA MS.893E Rallye 180GT Gaillard	12208	
F-BUXM	SOCATA MS.893E Rallye 180GT Gaillard	12210	
F-BUXP	SOCATA MS.893E Rallye 180GT Gaillard	12329	
F-BUXV	SOCATA MS.880B Rallye Club	2397	
F-BUXY	SOCATA MS.880B Rallye Club	2399	
F-BUXZ	SOCATA MS.880B Rallye Club	2404	
F-BUYJ	Cessna 182P Skylane	62479	N52244
F-BUYK	Piper PA-23-250 Aztec E	27-7405263	F-ETAW
			N40528
F-BUYU	Agusta-Bell 47G-2	254	74+13
			AS+375
			LA+104
			AS+054
F-BUYX	Bell 47G-2	2007	74+38
			AS+399
			YA+033 ?
F-BUYY	Beech 95-B55 Baron	TC-1700	
F-BUZA	SOCATA MS.893E Rallye 180GT Gaillard	12213	
F-BUZB	SOCATA MS.893E Rallye 180GT Gaillard	12314	
F-BUZD	Bellanca 17-31ATC Turbo Viking	75-31109	OE-DYN
F-BUZE	Piper PA-28R-200 Cherokee Arrow	28R-35188	OO-LGH
			N9472N
F-BUZF	Bellanca 17-31ATC Turbo Viking	75-31119	N9744E
F-BUZG	SOCATA MS.880B Rallye Club	2401	
F-BUZH	SOCATA MS.880B Rallye Club	2402	
F-BUZK	SOCATA MS.880B Rallye Club	2405	
F-BUZL	SOCATA MS.893E Rallye 180GT Gaillard	12212	
F-BUZN	SOCATA MS.893E Rallye 180GT Gaillard	12320	
F-BUZP	SOCATA MS.880B Rallye Club	2428	

Regn.	Type	C/n	Prev.Id.
F-BUZQ	SOCATA MS.893E Rallye 180GT Gaillard	12380	
F-BUZR	SOCATA MS.892E Rallye 150GT	12237	
F-BUZS	SOCATA MS.880B Rallye Club	2453	
F-BUZV	SOCATA Rallye 100S	2395	
F-BUZY	SOCATA MS.880B Rallye Club	2407	
F-BUZZ	SOCATA MS.880B Rallye Club	2408	
F-BVAB	SOCATA MS.880B Rallye Club	2411	
F-BVAD	SOCATA MS.893E Rallye 180GT Gaillard	12381	
F-BVAI	SOCATA MS.880B Rallye Club	2416	
F-BVAJ	SOCATA MS.894A Minerva 220	12104	
F-BVAK	SOCATA MS.880B Rallye Club	2430	
F-BVAO	SOCATA MS.880B Rallye Club	2457	
F-BVAR	SOCATA MS.880B Rallye Club	2461	
F-BVAS	SOCATA MS.880B Rallye Club	2455	
F-BVAU	SOCATA MS.880B Rallye Club	2431	F-BVAL
F-BVAV	SOCATA MS.893E Rallye 180GT Gaillard	12375	
F-BVAX	SOCATA MS.893E Rallye 180GT Gaillard	12385	
F-BVBA	Reims/Cessna FR.172J Rocket	0460	
F-BVBC	Reims/Cessna F.177RG Cardinal RG	0094	
F-BVBF	Reims/Cessna F.150L	1085	
F-BVBI	Reims/Cessna F.172M	1109	
F-BVBK	Reims/Cessna F.150L	1065	
F-BVBL	Reims/Cessna F.150L	1077	
F-BVBM	Reims/Cessna FR.172J Rocket	0469	
F-BVBN	Reims/Cessna FR.172J Rocket	0480	
F-BVBO	Reims/Cessna F.177RG Cardinal RG	0100	
F-BVBP	Reims/Cessna F.172M	1057	
F-BVBQ	Reims/Cessna FR.172J Rocket	0488	
F-BVBR	Reims/Cessna FR.172J Rocket	0476	
F-BVBT	Reims/Cessna FR.172J Rocket	0458	
F-BVBU	Reims/Cessna F.150L	1082	
F-BVBV	Reims/Cessna F.150L	1104	
F-BVBX	Reims/Cessna F.150L	1114	
F-BVBY	Reims/Cessna F.150L	1120	
F-BVCA	Robin DR.400/2+2 Tricycle	897	
F-BVCB	Robin DR.400/2+2 Tricycle	907	
F-BVCE	Robin DR.400/140 Major	899	
F-BVCF	Robin DR.400/180 Régent	903	
F-BVCH	Robin HR.100/210 Safari (Stored)	185	
F-BVCJ	Robin DR.400/180 Régent	898	
F-BVCK	Robin DR.400/180 Régent	912	
F-BVCL	Robin DR.400/140 Major	909	
F-BVCN	Robin HR.200/100 Club	22	
F-BVCR	Robin DR.400/2+2 Tricycle	915	
F-BVCS	Robin DR.400/2+2 Tricycle	917	
F-BVCU	Robin DR.400/2+2 Tricycle	921	
F-BVCV	Robin DR.400/140 Major	919	
F-BVCY	Robin DR.400/125 Petit Prince	923	
F-BVDA	Robin DR.400/180 Régent	922	
F-BVDC	Robin DR.400/140 Major	927	
F-BVDD	Robin DR.400/2+2 Tricycle	930	
F-BVDI	Robin DR.400/140 Major	911	
F-BVDJ	Robin DR.400/180 Régent	910	
F-BVDL	Robin DR.400/2+2 Tricycle	934	
F-BVDO	Robin HR.200/100 Club	27	
F-BVDP	Robin DR.400/180 Régent	941	
F-BVDR	Robin DR.400/140 Major	939	
F-BVDX	Robin DR.400/2+2 Tricycle	947	
F-BVEA	Beech B24R Sierra 200	MC-235	
F-BVED	Beech 58 Baron	TH-443	
F-BVEE	Piper PA-34-200 Seneca	34-7450060	F-ETAY
F-BVEG	Cessna 182P Skylane	62700	N52601
F-BVEI	Aérospatiale SA.341G Gazelle	1087	
F-BVEJ	Aerotek Pitts S-2A	2067	F-WVEJ
			G-BCGF
			N80038
F-BVEK	Reims/Cessna F.172G	0217	CN-TZG
F-BVEL	Agusta-Bell 206B Jet Ranger	8402	
F-BVEP	Piper PA-28-140 Cherokee Cruiser	28-7425122	N9602N
			N54403
F-BVER	Mooney M.20C Aerostar 200	700045	F-OCRO
			N9432V
F-BVET	Beech 200 Super King Air	BB-21	
F-BVEU	Aérospatiale SA.315B Lama	2379	
F-BVEX	Aérospatiale SA.315B Lama	2342	

Regn.	Type	C/n	Prev.Id.
F-BVEY	Beech F33A Bonanza	CE-489	
F-BVFA	Aérospatiale/BAC Concorde 101	5	N94FA
			F-BVFA
F-BVFB	Aérospatiale/BAC Concorde 101	7	N94FB
			F-BVFB
F-BVFC	Aérospatiale/BAC Concorde 101	9	N94FC
			F-BVFC
F-BVFF	Aérospatiale/BAC Concorde 101	15	F-WJAN
F-BVFO	Agusta-Bell 47G	096	ALAT
			Fr.AF
F-BVFQ	Agusta-Bell 47G	072	ALAT
F-BVFR	Agusta-Bell 47G-2	143	F-BTSR
			(F-BTSL)
			ALAT
F-BVFU	Bell 47G	1313	ALAT
F-BVFY	Agusta-Bell 47G-2	211	G-AWSK
			AAF:3B-XB
F-BVFZ	Mooney M.20E Super 21	341	N6981U
F-BVGB	Airbus A.300B2-1C (Stored, Hurn)	06	F-WVGB
F-BVGC	Airbus A.300B2-1C (Stored, Hurn)	07	F-WVGC
F-BVHB	SOCATA MS.887 Rallye 125	2173	
F-BVHD	SOCATA MS.880B Rallye 100T	2503	
F-BVHG	SOCATA MS.893E Rallye 180GT	12439	
F-BVHH	SOCATA MS.893E Rallye 180GT	12440	
F-BVHI	SOCATA MS.893E Rallye 180GT	12441	
F-BVHJ	SOCATA MS.893E Rallye 180GT	12442	
F-BVHK	SOCATA MS.893E Rallye 180GT	12443	
F-BVHM	SOCATA MS.893E Rallye 180GT	12317	F-BUZE
F-BVHR	SOCATA MS.893E Rallye 180GT	12446	
F-BVHS	SOCATA MS.893E Rallye 180GT	12447	
F-BVHT	SOCATA MS.893E Rallye 180GT	12448	
F-BVHV	SOCATA MS.880B Rallye 100T	2514	
F-BVHY	SOCATA MS.880B Rallye 100T	2473	
F-BVHZ	SOCATA MS.880B Rallye 100S	2422	
F-BVIA	Reims/Cessna F.172M	1128	
F-BVIB	Reims/Cessna FRA.150L Aerobat	0235	
F-BVID	Reims/Cessna F.172M	1168	
F-BVIE	Reims/Cessna F.172M	1185	
F-BVIF	Reims/Cessna F.172M	1200	
F-BVIG	Reims/Cessna F.177RG Cardinal RG	0101	(G-BBUZ)
F-BVIH	Reims/Cessna F.150L	1087	
F-BVII	Reims/Cessna F.172M	1134	
F-BVIJ	Reims/Cessna F.177RG Cardinal RG	0081	(G-BAOR)
F-BVIK	Reims/Cessna F.177RG Cardinal RG	0103	
F-BVIM	Reims/Cessna F.177RG Cardinal RG	0111	
F-BVIP	Reims/Cessna F.177RG Cardinal RG	0104	
F-BVIR	Reims/Cessna F.177RG Cardinal RG	0089	(D-EJXO)
F-BVIS	Reims/Cessna FR.172J Rocket	0491	
F-BVIT	Reims/Cessna F.337G Skymaster	0066/01560	
F-BVIX	Reims/Cessna F.172M	1239	
F-BVIY	Reims/Cessna F.177RG Cardinal RG	0107	
F-BVIZ	Reims/Cessna F.177RG Cardinal RG	0110	
F-BVJA	Piper PA-28-140 Cherokee Cruiser	28-7425145	N9615N
F-BVJB	Piper PA-28-140 Cherokee Cruiser	28-7425179	N9639N
F-BVJC	Rockwell Commander 112A	0225	N1225J
F-BVJE	Piper PA-25-235 Pawnee C	25-7305545	N6813L
F-BVJG	Cessna 337D Skymaster	1048	OO-DMN
F-BVJJ	Piper PA-34-200 Seneca	34-7450090	F-ETAZ
F-BVJN	Grumman AA-IB Trainer	0369	N8869L
F-BVJS	Grumman AA-5 Traveler	0551	
F-BVJU	Cessna 185A	0500	TR-LKR
			F-OBYQ
			N2500Z
F-BVJY	Cessna A.188B Agtruck	01389T	N9133G
F-WVKE	Aérospatiale SA.365 Dauphin	004	
F-WVKI	Aérospatiale AS.350 Ecureuil	002	
F-BVKL	Robin HR.100/4+2	01	F-WVKL
F-BVKQ	Bell 47G	722	Fr.Mil
F-BVLA	SOCATA MS.880B Rallye Club	2515	
F-BVLD	SOCATA MS.880B Rallye Club	2476	
F-BVLE	SOCATA MS.880B Rallye Club	2502	
F-BVLF	SOCATA MS.894E Minerva 220GT	12199	
F-BVLH	SOCATA MS.893E Rallye 180GT Gaillard	12450	
F-BVLI	SOCATA MS.887 Rallye 125	2168	
F-BVLL	SOCATA MS.893A Rallye Commodore 180	12005	(D-ENMM)

Regn.	Type	C/n	Prev.Id.
F-BVLN	CEA DR.253B Régent	189	OO-RJB
F-BVLZ	SOCATA MS.894A Minerva 220	12081	
F-BVMB	Robin DR.400/2+2 Tricycle	949	
F-BVMC	Robin DR.400/180 Régent	955	
F-BVMD	Robin DR.400/140 Major	957	
F-BVMF	Robin DR.400/120 Petit Prince	945	
F-BVMG	Robin DR.400/140 Major	887	(G-BBOG)
F-BVMH	Robin DR.400/160 Chevalier	958	
F-BVMK	Robin DR.400/120 Petit Prince	961	
F-BVML	Robin DR.400/2+2 Tricycle	972	
F-BVMP	Robin DR.400/180 Régent	908	
F-BVMQ	Robin DR.400/140 Major	967	
F-BVMR	Robin DR.400/140 Major	882	(G-BBOF) (D-EFDC)
F-BVNE	MS.880B Rallye Club	2520	
F-BVNG	MS.880B Rallye Club	2537	
F-BVNH	MS.880B Rallye Club (Written off)	2538	
F-BVNJ	MS.880B Rallye Club	2540	
F-BVNK	MS.893E Rallye 180GT Gaillard	12495	
F-BVNX	MS.893E Rallye 180GT Gaillard	12528	
F-BVNZ	MS.880B Rallye Club	2543	
F-BVOB	Piper PA-28-180 Cherokee Archer	28-7405113	F-ETBJ
F-BVOC	Piper PA-28-180 Cherokee Archer	28-7405096	F-ETBN N9501N
F-BVOE	SNCAN/Stampe SV.4C	605	F-BDFA
F-BVOF	Piper PA-28-140 Cherokee	28-22046	6V-ACN 5T-TAJ F-OCJC N7492R
F-BVOI	Piper PA-28-180 Cherokee Archer	28-7405131	F-ETBV N9565N
F-BVOJ	Piper PA-28-180 Cherokee Archer	28-7405133	F-ETBW
F-BVOL	Piper PA-28-180 Cherokee Archer	28-7405149	F-ETBZ
F-BVON	Piper PA-34-200 Seneca	34-7450159	F-ETBT
F-BVOP	Piper PA-28-180 Cherokee Archer	28-7405117	F-ETBL
F-BVOR	SOCATA ST-10 Diplomate	109	TU-TFR F-OCPF
F-BVOS	Beech V35B Bonanza	D-9286	TN-AEP F-BVOS TR-LSC F-OCRY
F-BVOV	Piper PA-25-235 Pawnee C	25-4340	N4626Y
F-BVOZ	Piper PA-18 Super Cub 95	18-3162	OO-FBA OL-L84 L-84 53-4762
F-BVPB	Aérospatiale SN.601 Corvette (Wfu ?)	6	F-OGJL F-BVPB F-WJQR
F-BVPG	Aérospatiale SN.601 Corvette	25	F-WNGU
F-BVPK	Aérospatiale SN.601 Corvette	7	N611AC F-OBZR
F-BVPN	Dassault Falcon 20E	311/515	F-WRQS
F-BVPR	Dassault Falcon 10	5	F-WVPR F-BVPR (F-V10F) F-WLCT
F-BVQK	Cessna TU.206F Turbo Stationair	02251	N1544U
F-BVRC	Piper PA-28R-200 Cherokee Arrow	28R-7435174	F-ETBI
F-BVRF	Enstrom F-28A	213	
F-BVRN	Grumman AA-1B Trainer	0399	N8899L
F-BVRO	Grumman AA-1B Trainer	0400	N8950L
F-BVRT	Beech 58 Baron	TH-488	
F-BVRX	Cessna 182P Skylane	63110	N7326N
F-BVSA	Reims/Cessna FR.172J Rocket	0502	
F-BVSB	Reims/Cessna FR.172J Rocket	0504	
F-BVSC	Reims/Cessna FR.172J Rocket	0506	
F-BVSD	Reims/Cessna F.150L	1110	
F-BVSE	Reims/Cessna FTB.337G Skymaster	0001	F-WLIP
F-BVSG	Reims/Cessna FR.172J Rocket	0508	
F-BVSJ	Reims/Cessna F.172M	1187	
F-BVSK	Reims/Cessna FR.172J Rocket	0511	
F-BVSL	Reims/Cessna F.177RG Cardinal RG	0112	
F-BVSM	Reims/Cessna F.177RG Cardinal RG	0113	
F-BVSN	Reims/Cessna F.177RG Cardinal RG	0102	(G-BBNW)
F-BVSO	Reims/Cessna F.172M	1190	
F-BVSP	Reims/Cessna FRA.150L Aerobat	0248	
F-BVSR	Reims/Cessna F.172M	1195	
F-BVSS	Holste MH.1521M Broussard	021	ALAT
F-BVST	Reims/Cessna FR.172J Rocket	0513	
F-BVSU	Holste MH.1521 Broussard	022	ALAT
F-BVSV	Reims/Cessna F.150L	1117	
F-BVTB	Beech 65-C90 King Air	LJ-579	D-INAF
F-BVTF	Piper PA-28-180 Archer	28-7405142	F-ETBP
F-BVTH	Piper PA-28-151 Warrior	28-7415145	N9508N
F-BVTJ	Piper PA-28-140 Cruiser	28-7425248	N9541N
F-BVTK	Piper PA-28-140 Cruiser	28-7425255	N9549N
F-BVTL	Piper PA-28-180 Archer	28-7405125	F-ETBM
F-BVTM	Piper PA-28-180 Archer	28-7405147	F-ETBX
F-BVTN	Piper PA-28R-200 Arrow	28R-7435225	F-ETBY
F-BVTP	Piper PA-23-250 Aztec C	27-3901	N6598Y
F-BVTQ	Piper PA-28-180 Archer	28-7405153	F-ETBU
F-BVTT	Piper PA-28R-200 Arrow	28R-7435202	F-ETBO
F-BVTX	Piper PA-23-250 Aztec D	27-4560	N94476 HP-575 (PT-DPD) N13927
F-BVUC	Piper PA-23-250 Aztec E	27-7305225	G-BCDX N40495 N40504
F-BVUH	Beech C23 Sundowner	M-1408	F-BUIZ N58156
F-BVUJ	Piper PA-28-180 Archer	28-7405144	F-ETBQ
F-BVUK	Piper PA-28-140 Cruiser	28-7425262	N9532N
F-BVUL	Beech 58 Baron	TH-474	
F-BVUM	Mooney M.20E Chaparral	700032	F-OCRM
F-BVUN	Bell 206A Jet Ranger	247	D-HAMO
F-BVUO	Piper PA-32-300 Cherokee Six B	32-40646	F-OCRI 6V-ABX N4271R
F-BVUP	Piper PA-34-200 Seneca	34-7450199	F-VAAC
F-BVUS	Piper PA-28-151 Warrior	28-7415462	N9620N
F-BVUV	Cessna 310Q	1095	N1244G
F-BVVA	Piper PA-28-180 Archer	28-7505061	N9631N
F-BVVB	Piper PA-28-151 Warrior	28-7515165	N9636N
F-BVVC	Cessna 210L Centurion	61114	N2153S
F-BVVI	Grumman AA-5 Traveler	0686	
F-BVVJ	Grumman AA-5B Tiger	0008	N1508R
F-BVVT	Bellanca 7GCBC Citabria	845-75	OE-VPY
F-BVVX	Piper PA-28-235 Cherokee E	28-7110019	6V-ACO N11C
F-BVVY	Piper PA-28-180 Cherokee D	28-5336	6V-ADS TU-TEW N7925N
F-BVXB	Reims/Cessna F.172M	1204	
F-BVXC	Reims/Cessna F.150L	1123	
F-BVXE	Robin HR.100/250TR	502	D-EFIT F-BVDS
F-BVXF	Reims/Cessna F.150L	1129	
F-BVXG	Reims/Cessna F.150L	1131	
F-BVXN	Reims/Cessna F.172M	1277	
F-BVXO	Reims/Cessna FR.172J Rocket	0509	(D-EIQT)
F-BVXQ	Reims/Cessna FR.172J Rocket	0528	(F-BSGY)
F-BVXR	Reims/Cessna F.172M	1347	D-EBJA
F-BVXT	Reims/Cessna F.150L	1187	
F-BVXX	Reims/Cessna FR.172J Rocket	0523	
F-BVYC	Robin HR.200/100 Club	51	
F-BVYD	Robin DR.400/2+2 Tricycle	987	
F-BVYF	Robin DR.400/160 Chevalier	980	
F-BVYI	Robin HR.100/250TR	504	
F-BVYK	Robin DR.400/140 Major	995	
F-BVYP	Robin DR.400/2+2 Tricycle	1002	
F-BVYR	Robin DR.400/120 Petit Prince	984	
F-BVYS	Robin HR.200/100 Club	60	
F-BVYT	Robin DR.400/180 Régent	993	
F-BVYU	Robin HR.200/100 Club	57	
F-BVYV	Robin HR.200/100 Club	58	
F-BVYZ	Robin DR.400/140 Major	1003	
F-BVZC	SOCATA MS.893E Rallye 180GT Gaillard	12490	
F-BVZI	SOCATA MS.893E Rallye 180GT Gaillard	12488	

Regn.	Type	C/n	Prev.Id.
F-BVZP	SOCATA MS.892E Rallye 150GT	12497	
F-BVZU	SOCATA MS.893E Rallye 180GT Gaillard	12562	
F-BXAL	Reims/Cessna 182P Skylane	0006/63805	N6702M
F-BXAM	Cessna U.206F Stationair	02751	N35844
F-BXAN	Cessna T.210L Turbo Centurion	60812	N1792X
F-BXAP	Beech 65-C90 King Air	LJ-522	D-IHVB
F-BXAT	Cessna 172K	58289	N79964
F-BXAU	Cessna 182P Skylane	63417	N9651G
F-BXAV	SE.313B Alouette II	1932	AAF:3D-XO
F-BXAY	Cessna 340	0525	N1263G
F-BXBC	Montgolfière-Moderne MM20 O-65 HAFB	9	
F-BXBF	Montgolfière-Moderne MM18 O-65 HAFB	14	
F-BXBL	Montgolfière-Moderne MM20 O-70 HAFB	18	
	(Also has Cameron c/n 184)		
F-BXBS	Montgolfière-Moderne MM20 O-70 HAFB	25	
	(Also has Cameron c/n 222)		
F-BXBT	Montgolfière-Moderne MM20 O-70 HAFB	26	
F-BXCE	Cerva CE-43 Guepard (CE-44 prototype)	459	F-WXCE
F-BXCF	Wassmer WA.54 Atlantic	132	
F-BXCG	Wassmer WA.54 Atlantic	134	
F-BXCH	Wassmer WA.54 Atlantic	146	
F-BXCI	Cerva CE-43 Guepard	460	
F-BXCL	Wassmer WA.54 Atlantic	139	
F-BXCM	Wassmer WA.54 Atlantic	140	
F-BXCN	Cerva CE-43 Guepard	472	
F-BXCO	Cerva CE-43 Guepard	461	
F-BXCP	Holste MH.1521M Broussard	149	ALAT
F-BXCS	Holste MH.1521M Broussard	293	ALAT
F-BXCV	Cerva CE-43 Guepard	474	
F-BXDJ	SOCATA Rallye 100ST	2617	
F-BXDM	SOCATA MS.893E Rallye 180GT Gaillard	12636	
F-BXDN	SOCATA MS.893E Rallye 180GT Gaillard	12578	
F-BXDO	SOCATA MS.893E Rallye 180GT Gaillard	12579	
F-BXDP	SOCATA MS.893E Rallye 180GT Gaillard	12580	
F-BXDQ	SOCATA MS.893E Rallye 180GT Gaillard	12581	
F-BXDR	SOCATA MS.893E Rallye 180GT Gaillard	12602	
F-BXDS	SOCATA MS.893E Rallye 180GT Gaillard	12603	
F-BXEC	Robin DR.400/140 Major	954	
F-BXED	Robin DR.400/2+2 Tricycle	983	
F-BXEE	Robin DR.400/140 Major	999	
F-BXEK	Robin DR.400/120 Petit Prince	1011	
F-BXEN	Robin HR.200/120B	62	
F-BXEO	Robin DR.400/2+2 Tricycle	1017	
F-BXEQ	Robin DR.400/140 Major	1019	
F-BXET	Robin DR.400/2+2 Tricycle	1024	
F-BXEU	Robin DR.400/140 Major	1023	
F-BXEV	Robin HR.200/120B	65	
F-BXEX	Robin HR.200/120	52	(G-BCMX)
F-BXEZ	Robin DR.400/2+2 Tricycle	1026	
F-WXFK	Aérospatiale AS.332C Super Puma	2006	
F-BXGG	Robin HR.100/250TR Président	516	
F-BXGJ	Robin HR.100/250TR Président	518	
F-BXGM	Robin HR.100/250TR Président	521	
F-BXGN	Robin HR.100/250TR Président	522	
F-BXGP	Robin HR.100/250TR Président	541	
F-BXGQ	Robin HR.100/250TR Président	542	
F-BXGS	Robin HR.100/250TR Président	544	
F-BXGT	Robin HR.100/250TR Président	545	
F-BXGU	Robin HR.100/250TR Président	546	
F-BXGX	Robin HR.100/250TR Président	548	
F-BXGY	Robin HR.100/250TR Président	549	
F-BXHD	Mudry CAP.10B	60	
F-BXHE	Mudry CAP.10B	61	
F-BXHF	Mudry CAP.10B	63	
F-BXHG	Mudry CAP.10B	64	
F-BXHL	Mudry CAP.10B	69	
F-BXHN	Mudry CAP.10B	71	
F-BXHO	Mudry CAP.10B	75	
F-BXHR	Mudry CAP.10B	79	
F-BXHS	Mudry CAP.10B	81	
F-BXHT	Mudry CAP.10B	82	
F-BXHU	Mudry CAP.10B	83	
F-BXHV	Mudry CAP.10B	85	
F-BXHX	Mudry CAP.10B	90	
F-BXIB	Reims/Cessna F.172M	1307	
F-BXIE	Reims/Cessna F.177RG Cardinal RG	0130	
F-BXIF	Reims/Cessna F.150M	1179	
F-BXIG	Reims/Cessna F.150M	1162	
F-BXII	Reims/Cessna F.150M	1202	(OE-ATZ)
F-BXIJ	Reims/Cessna F.150M	1203	
F-BXIL	Reims/Cessna FTB.337G Skymaster	0034	
F-BXIN	Reims/Cessna F.172M	1331	
F-BXIP	Reims/Cessna FR.172J Rocket	0553	(F-BPQQ)
F-BXIS	Reims/Cessna F.150M	1213	
F-BXIT	Reims/Cessna F.172M	1345	
F-BXIU	Reims/Cessna F.172M	1351	
F-BXIV	Reims/Cessna F.172M	1349	
F-BXIX	Reims/Cessna F.172M	1357	
F-BXIY	Reims/Cessna F.172M	1359	
F-BXJB	Robin DR.400/180 Régent	1032	
F-BXJF	Robin DR.400/2+2 Tricycle	1035	
F-BXJG	Robin HR.200/100 Club	67	
F-BXJI	Robin DR.400/180 Régent	1040	
F-BXJK	Robin HR.200/120B	69	
F-BXJN	Robin DR.400/140 Major	1048	
F-BXJO	Robin DR.400/2+2 Tricycle	1046	
F-BXJP	Robin DR.400/180 Régent	1045	
F-BXJQ	Robin HR.200/100 Club	71	
F-BXJS	Robin HR.200/IOOS Club	73	
F-BXJU	Robin DR.400/120 Petit Prince	1054	
F-BXJV	Robin DR.400/180 Régent	1056	
F-BXJX	Robin DR.400/140 Major	1058	
F-BXJZ	Robin DR.400/2+2 Tricycle	1059	
F-BXKZ	Cameron D-96 Hot Air Airship	199	F-WXKZ
F-BXLB	Hughes 269C	94-0358	
F-BXLF	Beech 58 Baron	TH-647	
F-BXLL	Cessna A.185F Skywagon	02738	N1083F
F-BXLM	Mooney M.20E Chaparral	21-1177	
F-BXLP	Cessna 207 Skywagon	00287	N1687U
F-BXLQ	Reims/Cessna FT.337GP Skymaster	0009/0150	N14491
F-BXLR	Cessna 310R-II	0325	N87262
F-BXLV	Agusta-Bell 206B Jet Ranger	8508	
F-BXLZ	Piper PA-34-200 Seneca	34-7450216	F-VAAF
F-BXMA	SOCATA MS.893E Rallye 180GT Gaillard	12607	
F-BXMB	SOCATA MS.892E Rallye 150GT	2628	
F-BXME	SOCATA Rallye 100ST *(Dismantled)*	2619	
F-BXML	Reims/Cessna F.172G	0225	OO-WIG
			PH-AFF
F-BXMP	SOCATA MS.880B Rallye Club	2560	
F-BXMQ	SOCATA MS.880B Rallye Club	2588	
F-BXMS	SOCATA Rallye 235E Gabier	12691	
F-BXMT	SOCATA Rallye 235E Gabier	12692	
F-BXMU	SOCATA MS.880B Rallye Club	2589	
F-BXMV	SOCATA MS.892E Rallye 150GT	12500	
F-BXMX	SOCATA MS.880B Rallye Club	2590	
F-BXNB	Reims/Cessna F.177RG Cardinal RG	0134	
F-BXNC	Reims/Cessna F.337G Skymaster	0074/01614	F-WLIN
F-BXND	Cessna A.185F Skywagon	0001/02836	F-WLIQ
	(Reims-Assembled prototype)		N1368F
F-BXNE	Reims/Cessna F.177RG Cardinal RG	0132	
F-BXNH	Reims/Cessna F.150M	1244	
F-BXNM	Reims/Cessna FR.172J Rocket	0531	
F-BXNN	Reims/Cessna F.150M	1207	(G-BDEO)
F-BXNO	Reims/Cessna F.150M	1232	
F-BXNQ	Reims/Cessna F.150M	1211	
F-BXNR	Reims/Cessna F.150M	1282	
F-BXNS	Reims/Cessna F.150M	1150	(D-EDNW)
F-BXNT	Reims/Cessna F.150M	1167	
F-BXNU	Reims/Cessna F.150M	1246	
F-BXNV	Reims/Cessna F.150M	1209	(I-FFAH)
F-BXNX	Reims/Cessna F.150M	1218	(I-BONJ)
F-BXNZ	Reims/Cessna F.150M	1239	
F-BXOA	Piper PA-28-180 Archer	28-7505190	N9634N
F-BXOB	Piper PA-28R-200 Arrow	28R-7435198	OO-FEY
			N41551
F-BXON	Beech 65-E90 King Air	LW-161	
F-BXOR	Beech 58 Baron	TH-679	
F-BXOZ	Beech A36 Bonanza	E-782	
F-BXPF	Bell 206A Jet Ranger	306	G-AWRI
F-BXPI	Hughes 269C	16-0459	

Regn.	Type	C/n	Prev.Id.
F-BXPM	Piper PA-28R-200 Arrow	28R-7335127	LX-SIM
			N16323
F-BXPO	Cessna 340A	0053	N98599
F-BXPP	Piper PA-23-250 Aztec E	27-7654053	F-VAAI
			(N62572)
F-BXPQ	Piper PA-28-151 Warrior	28-7615122	N9521N
F-BXPR	Rockwell Commander 114	14054	F-WXPR
			N4724W
F-BXPS	Rockwell Commander 112TC	13026	F-WXPS
F-BXPT	Gates Learjet 23	23-014	JY-AEG
			(JY-AEF)
			N426EJ
			N814L
F-BXPX	Piper PA-39 Twin Comanche C/R	39-51	TR-LPH
			(F-OCOO)
			N8894Y
F-BXPY	Beech 65-C90 King Air	LJ-684	
F-BXQC	Zlin Z.526 Trenér Master	1289	D-EKOM
F-BXQD	Reims/Cessna F.172M	1412	
F-BXQE	Reims/Cessna F.172M	1424	
F-BXQG	Reims/Cessna F.177RG Cardinal RG	0141	F-WLIO
F-BXQH	Reims/Cessna F.150M	1253	
F-BXQI	Reims/Cessna F.172M	1386	
F-BXQJ	SE.313B Alouette II	1823	TR-LOM
			F-BMMB
			F-OBZF
F-BXQK	Reims/Cessna F.172M	1388	
F-BXQM	Reims/Cessna F.150M	1296	(F-BXZD)
F-BXQN	Reims/Cessna F.150M	1300	
F-BXQO	Reims/Cessna F.150M	1297	
F-BXQP	Reims/Cessna F.150M	1284	
F-BXQQ	Reims/Cessna F.172M	1434	
F-BXQT	Reims/Cessna F.150M	1307	
F-BXQV	Reims/Cessna F.172M	1464	
F-BXQX	Reims/Cessna F.177RG Cardinal RG	0145	
F-BXQZ	Reims/Cessna F.150M	1291	
F-BXRA	Robin DR.400/160 Chevalier	1062	
F-BXRB	Robin DR.400/140 Major	1063	
F-BXRD	Robin DR.400/140B Major	1064	
F-BXRG	Robin DR.400/160 Chevalier	1066	
F-BXRJ	Robin HR.200/100 Club	74	
F-BXRL	Robin HR.100/210 Safari	206	
F-BXRM	Robin DR.400/140 Major	1071	
F-BXRN	Robin DR.400/120 Petit Prince	1073	
F-BXRO	Robin DR.400/2+2 Tricycle	1074	
F-BXRP	Robin DR.400/160 Chevalier	1076	
F-BXRR	Robin DR.400/140B Major	1081	
F-BXRS	Robin DR.400/160 Chevalier	1082	
F-BXRU	Robin DR.400/2+2 Tricycle	1084	
F-BXRV	Robin DR.400/160 Chevalier	1086	
F-BXRX	Robin DR.400/2+2 Tricycle	1085	
F-BXRY	Robin DR.400/2+2 Tricycle	1089	
F-BXRZ	Robin DR.400/140B Major	1087	
F-BXSB	Piper PA-23-250 Aztec C	27-3655	6V-ADL
			TR-LPW
			6V-ABC
			N6447Y
			N10F
F-BXSC	Piper PA-28-181 Archer II	28-7690068	
F-BXSE	Piper PA-32R-300 Lance	32R-7680073	
F-BXSG	Reims/Cessna A.185F Skywagon	0002/02844	N1466F
F-BXSI	Beech 200 Super King Air	BB-128	
F-BXSK	Piper PA-31T Cheyenne	31T-7620020	
F-BXSL	Beech 65-C90 King Air	LJ-648	
F-BXSM	Piper PA-32R-300 Lance	32R-7680156	
F-BXSN	Beech 65-E90 King Air	LW-175	
F-BXSO	Beech A36 Bonanza	E-806	
F-BXSP	Beech V35B Bonanza	D-9615	N4372W
F-BXSQ	Piper PA-34-200T Seneca II	34-7670160	
	(Stored 6.99, but reserved as F-OHCR)		
F-BXSS	Robin DR.400/2+2 Tricycle	1109	
F-BXTD	SOCATA Rallye 100ST	2621	
F-BXTE	SOCATA Rallye 150ST	2662	
F-BXTF	SOCATA Rallye 100S Sport	2593	
F-BXTL	SOCATA MS.880B Rallye Club	2622	
F-BXTM	SOCATA MS.880B Rallye Club	2623	
F-BXTP	SOCATA Rallye 150ST	2668	
F-BXTS	SOCATA Rallye 150ST	2667	
F-BXTT	SOCATA MS.880B Rallye Club	2627	
F-BXTU	SOCATA MS.880B Rallye Club	2717	
F-BXTV	SOCATA MS.880B Rallye Club	2670	
F-BXTX	SOCATA Rallye 100ST	2716	
F-BXTZ	SOCATA MS.893E Rallye 180GT Gaillard	12676	
F-BXUB	Cameron A-105 HAFB	197	
F-BXUD	Cameron V-56 HAFB	229	
F-BXUG	Club Aerostatique de France Free Balloon HG 600m3	9885	F-OCUS
F-BXUH	Cameron V-56 HAFB	223	
F-BXUI	Raven S-60A HAFB	109	F-WXUI
			N51488
F-BXUJ	Cameron V-56 HAFB	206	
F-BXUM	Balloon Works Firefly 7 HAFB	725	N2008F
F-BXUQ	Cameron O-84 HAFB	282	
F-BXUR	Cameron V-56 HAFB	234	
F-BXUS	Chaize CS.2000F12 HAFB	006	
F-BXUT	Chaize CS.2000F12 HAFB	007	
F-BXUU	Cameron O-65 HAFB	281	
F-BXUX	Cameron O-77 HAFB	354	
F-BXUZ	Thunder AX7/65 HAFB	128	
F-BXVA	Robin DR.400/2+2 Tricycle	1088	
F-BXVE	Robin DR.400/140B Major	1096	
F-BXVF	Robin DR.400/140B Major	1097	
F-BXVI	Robin HR.200/100 Club	78	
F-BXVJ	Robin HR.100/285 Tiara	536	
F-BXVK	Robin HR.200/100 Club	80	
F-BXVM	Robin DR.400/2+2 Tricycle	1101	
F-BXVO	Robin HR.200/100S Club	79	
F-BXVP	Robin DR.400/120 Petit Prince	1104	
F-BXVQ	Robin HR.200/100 Club	85	
F-BXVT	Robin DR.400/120 Petit Prince	1105	
F-BXVV	Robin HR.200/100S Club	88	
F-BXVY	Robin DR.400/180 Régent	1111	
F-BXXG	Bell 47G-2	1638	ALAT
			N2857B
F-BXXH	Agusta-Bell 47G-2	055	ALAT
F-BXXJ	Agusta-Bell 47G-2	106	ALAT
F-BXXK	Agusta-Bell 47G	069	ALAT
			F-BHPG
F-BXXL	Agusta-Bell 47G-2	114	ALAT
F-BXXM	Agusta-Bell 47G-2	139	ALAT
F-BXXO	Agusta-Bell 47G-2	189	ALAT
F-BXXP	Bell 47G-2	1627	ALAT
			Fr.AF
			N2846B
F-BXXQ	Bell 47G-2	1639	ALAT
			Fr.AF
			N2858B
F-BXXR	Mudry CAP.10B	32	D-EGTR
			F-BUDB
F-BXXS	Agusta-Bell 47G	078	ALAT
F-BXXT	Agusta-Bell 47G-4	2517	G-AXHW
			9L-LAK
F-BXXU	Agusta-Bell 47G-2	154	ALAT
F-BXXV	Agusta-Bell 47G-2	161	ALAT
F-BXXY	Agusta-Bell 47G-2	203	F-MJAO
			ALAT
F-BXXZ	Bell 47G-2	1636	D-HAFU
			F-BILG
			Fr.Mil
			N2855B
F-BXYD	SOCATA Rallye 150ST	2693	
F-BXYE	SOCATA Rallye 235E Gabier	12699	
F-BXYH	SOCATA MS.880B Rallye Club	2720	
F-BXYI	SOCATA MS.880B Rallye Club	2721	
F-BXYJ	SOCATA MS.893E Rallye 180GT Gaillard	12570	Fr.AF
F-BXYP	SOCATA MS.892E Rallye 150GT	12189	
F-BXYS	SOCATA Rallye 235E Gabier	12709	
F-BXYU	SOCATA Rallye 235E Gabier	12711	
F-BXYV	SOCATA Rallye 235E Gabier	12712	
F-BXYY	SOCATA Rallye 235E Gabier	12769	

Regn.	Type	C/n	Prev.Id.
F-BXZB	Reims/Cessna F.150M	1242	
F-BXZD	Reims/Cessna F.150M	1245	
F-BXZF	Reims/Cessna F.172M	1268	
F-BXZG	Reims/Cessna F.150M	1278	
F-BXZH	Beech N35 Bonanza	D-6636	I-SCAI
			HB-EIH
F-BXZI	Reims/Cessna 182P Skylane	0046/64310	N1393M
F-BXZJ	Reims/Cessna F.172M	1403	
F-BXZL	Reims/Cessna F.172M	1245	
F-BXZM	Reims/Cessna F.172M	1247	
F-BXZO	Reims/Cessna F.172M	1274	
F-BXZP	Reims/Cessna F.172M	1283	
F-BXZQ	Reims/Cessna F.172M	1285	
F-BXZR	Reims/Cessna F.172M	1292	
F-BXZS	Reims/Cessna F.172M	1301	
F-BXZT	Reims/Cessna F.172M	1330	(G-BDEP)
			(OY-BIB)
F-BXZU	Bell 47G-2	1623	ALAT
			Fr.AF
			N2842B
F-BXZX	Reims/Cessna F.172M	1367	
F-BXZZ	Reims/Cessna F.172M	1383	
F-BYAJ	Aerotek Pitts S-2A	2195	G-BGSD
			N31458
F-BYAM	SE.313B Alouette II	1062	FinnishAF/HA-2
			SE-HDN
F-BYAO	Fokker F.27 Friendship 100	10127	F-WYAO
			F-BYAO
			VH-EWA
			VH-TFH
			PH-FAX
F-BYAS	Mooney M.20J Model 201	24-0380	
F-BYAV	Nord N.1101 Noralpha	13	CEV
F-BYAX	Nord N.1101 Noralpha	15	CEV
			F-BBJJ
F-BYCK	Wassmer WA.54 Atlantic	124	HB-DCN
			F-BUKY
F-BYCX	SE.313B Alouette II (W/o 28.4.97)	1647	F-ZBAF
			F-BIET
F-BYCZ	Aérospatiale SA.315B Lama	2395	OE-EXW
F-WZAV	Bede BD-5J	50005	N150BD
F-WZAZ	Stampe SV.4L (Lycoming conversion)	01	
F-WZCG	Mudry CAP.X	02	
F-WZCH	Mudry CAP.232	001	F-WWZH
			F-WZCH
F-WZCI	Mudry CAP.231EX	01	
F-WZCJ	Sukhoi SU.26MX	unkn	
F-WZCY	Aérospatiale SA.330 Puma	02	F-ZWWO
F-WZJF	Microjet 200	01	
F-BZJH	Grumman G.164C Agcat	11C	F-WZJH
			N6587K
F-WZJI	Aérospatiale AS.355 Ecureuil 2	002	
F-WZJY	Robin R.3000/140PRV	001	
F-WZLK	Aérospatiale AS.332L2 Super Puma	2298	
F-WZLQ(2)	Fouga CM-170 Magister	126	Fr.AF
F-BZZZ	Bellanca 8KCAB Decathlon	173-75	F-BZAA
			F-WZAA
F-EURO	Nord 2501 Noratlas	148	Fr.AF
F-GAAC	Reims/Cessna F.177RG Cardinal RG	0142	
F-GAAD	Reims/Cessna F.177RG Cardinal RG	0147	
F-GAAF	Reims/Cessna F.177RG Cardinal RG	0148	
F-GAAG	Reims/Cessna F.177RG Cardinal RG	0152	
F-GAAH	Reims/Cessna F.177RG Cardinal RG	0153	
F-GAAJ	Reims/Cessna F.172M	1462	
F-GAAK	Reims/Cessna F.172M	1465	
F-GAAN	Reims/Cessna FT.337GP Skymaster	0016/0229	
F-GAAO	Reims/Cessna F.177RG Cardinal RG	0150	
F-GAAV	Reims/Cessna F.150M	1324	
F-GAAY	Reims/Cessna F.150M	1327	
F-GABA	DR.400/120A Petit Prince	1123	
F-GABB	Robin DR.400/2+2 Tricycle	1114	

Regn.	Type	C/n	Prev.Id.
F-GABD	Robin DR.400/2+2 Tricycle	1118	
F-GABE	Robin DR.400/180 Régent	1119	
F-GABG	Robin DR.400/2+2 Tricycle	1121	
F-GABH	Robin DR.400/120 Petit Prince	1122	
F-GABJ	Robin DR.400/2+2 Tricycle	1125	
F-GABK	Robin DR.400/2+2 Tricycle	1126	
F-GABM	Robin HR.200/100S Club	94	
F-GABN	Robin DR.400/140B Major 80	1132	
F-GABQ	Robin DR.400/180 Régent	1135	
F-GABS	Robin DR.400/140B Major 80	1137	
F-GABT	Robin DR.400/180 Régent	1138	
F-GABV(2)	Beech E90 King Air	LW-102	CS-TFA
	(W/o 1.5.98)		N4423W
F-GABY	Robin DR.400/180 Régent	1112	
F-GABZ	Robin DR.400/160 Chevalier	1142	
F-GACB	SOCATA MS.880B Rallye Club	2745	
F-GACC	SOCATA MS.880B Rallye Club	2746	
F-GACF	SOCATA MS.880B Rallye Club	2780	
F-GACJ	SOCATA Rallye 100ST	2761	
F-GACK	SOCATA Rallye 100ST	2762	
F-GACL	SOCATA MS.880B Rallye Club	2781	
F-GACM	SOCATA MS.880B Rallye Club	2782	
F-GACO	SOCATA MS.880B Rallye Club	2778	
F-GACP	SOCATA Rallye 235E Gabier	12763	
F-GACQ	SOCATA Rallye 100ST	2752	
F-GACR	SOCATA Rallye 235E Gabier	12764	
F-GACS	SOCATA MS.893E Rallye 180GT Gaillard	12724	
F-GACY	SOCATA MS.880B Rallye Club	2808	
F-GADB	Fournier RF-6B-100	4	
F-GADC	Fournier RF-6B-100	15	
F-GADE	Fournier RF-6B-100	6	
F-GADH	Fournier RF-6B-100	10	
F-GADI	Fournier RF-6B-100	9	
F-GADJ	Fournier RF-6B-100	11	
F-GADK	Fournier RF-6B-100	12	
F-GADL	Fournier RF-6B-100	13	
F-GADM	Fournier RF-6B-100	29	
F-GADN	Fournier RF-6B-100	16	
F-GADQ	Fournier RF-6B-100	19	
F-GADS	Fournier RF-6B-100	20	
F-GADT	Fournier RF-6B-100	21	
F-GADV	Fournier RF-6B-100	23	
F-GADY	Fournier RF-6B-100	25	
F-GAED	Robin DR.400/140B Major 80	1146	
F-GAEE	Robin DR.400/160 Chevalier	1147	
F-GAEF	Robin DR.400/160 Chevalier	1148	
F-GAEG	Robin DR.400/120 Petit Prince	1149	
F-GAEJ	Robin DR.400/180 Régent	1156	
F-GAEK	Robin DR.400/120 Petit Prince	1151	
F-GAEP	Robin DR.400/140B Major 80	1159	
F-GAEQ	Robin HR.200/100S Club	99	
F-GAET	Robin DR.400/140B Major 80	1164	
F-GAEU	Robin DR.400/180 Régent	1165	
F-GAEV	Robin DR.400/120 Petit Prince	1167	
F-GAEX	Robin DR.400/140B Major 80	1168	
F-GAEZ	Robin DR.400/2+2 Tricycle	1170	
F-GAFB	SOCATA MS.880B Rallye Club	2811	
F-GAFG	SOCATA MS.880B Rallye Club	2815	
F-GAFN	SOCATA MS.893E Rallye 180GT Gaillard	12738	
F-GAFP	SOCATA MS.880B Rallye Club	2852	
F-GAFQ	SOCATA MS.892E Rallye 150GT	12823	
F-GAFU	SOCATA MS.880B Rallye Club	2850	
F-GAFV	SOCATA MS.880B Rallye Club	2851	
F-GAFZ	SOCATA MS.880B Rallye Club	2884	
F-GAGA	Reims/Cessna F.177RG Cardinal RG	0154	
F-GAGB	Reims/Cessna F.177RG Cardinal RG	0155	
F-GAGD	Reims/Cessna F.177RG Cardinal RG	0157	
F-GAGE	Reims/Cessna F.177RG Cardinal RG	0158	
F-GAGG	Reims/Cessna F.177RG Cardinal RG	0160	
F-GAGI	Reims/Cessna F.150M	1276	(G-BDPE)
F-GAGL	Reims/Cessna F.150M	1337	
F-GAGN	Reims/Cessna F.172M	1387	
F-GAGO	Reims/Cessna F.150M	1317	
F-GAGR	Reims/Cessna FR.172J Rocket	0583	
F-GAGS	Reims/Cessna FR.172J Rocket	0563	

Regn.	Type	C/n	Prev.Id.
F-GAGT	Reims/Cessna F.172M	1494	
F-GAGV	Reims/Cessna F.172N	1583	
F-GAGX	Reims/Cessna F.172M	1498	
F-GAGY	Reims/Cessna FR.172K-XP Hawk	0601	
F-GAHA	Robin DR.400/140B Major 80	1169	
F-GAHB	Robin DR.400/140B Major 80	1171	
F-GAHC	Robin DR.400/2+2 Tricycle	1172	
F-GAHE	Robin DR.400/2+2 Tricycle	1174	
F-GAHG	Robin DR.400/140B Major 80	1176	
F-GAHH	Robin DR.400/2+2 Tricycle	1177	
F-GAHK	Robin DR.400/140B Major 80	1180	
F-GAHN	Robin DR.400/140B Major 80	1184	
F-GAHP	Robin DR.400/2+2 Tricycle	1186	
F-GAHQ	Robin DR.400/2+2 Tricycle	1187	
F-GAHR	Robin DR.400/180 Régent	1188	
F-GAHS	Robin DR.400/2+2 Tricycle	1189	
F-GAHU	Robin HR.200/100 Club	102	
F-GAHV	Robin DP.400/2+2 Tricycle	1191	
F-GAHX	Robin DR.400/2+2 Tricycle	1192	
F-GAHY	Robin DR.400/160 Chevalier	1193	
F-GAHZ	Robin HR.200/100 Club	103	
F-GAIB	Wassmer WA.54 Atlantic	149	
F-GAIC	Wassmer WA.81 Piranha	803	F-WAIC
F-GAID	Cerva CE-43 Guepard	473	D-EACO
F-GAIE	Wassmer WA.54 Atlantic	150	
F-GAIF	Wassmer WA.81 Piranha	804	
F-GAIG	Wassmer WA.80 Piranha	806	
F-GAIK	Wassmer WA.81 Piranha	808	
F-GAIL	Wassmer WA.81 Piranha	809	
F-GAIO	Wassmer WA.80 Piranha	812	
F-GAIQ	Wassmer WA.81 Piranha	815	
F-GAIT	Wassmer WA.81 Piranha	820	
F-GAIU	Wassmer WA.81 Piranha	822	
F-GAJB	Piper PA-28-151 Cherokee Warrior	28-7615188	F-GALE N9550N
F-GAJF	Piper PA-28R-200 Cherokee Arrow	28R-7635357	
F-GAJM	Hughes 269C	114-0373	
F-GAJQ	Grumman G.164A Agcat	1277	N8903H
F-GAJU	Grumman AA-1B Trainer	0664	
F-GAJV	Hughes 269C	104-0363	
F-GAKA	SOCATA MS.880B Rallye Club	2886	
F-GAKB	SOCATA MS.880B Rallye Club	2887	
F-GAKD	SOCATA Rallye 235E Gabier	12830	
F-GAKF	SOCATA MS.880B Rallye Club	2890	
F-GAKG	SOCATA MS.893E Rallye 180GT Gaillard	12790	
F-GAKK	SOCATA MS.880B Rallye Club	2946	
F-GAKM	SOCATA MS.880B Rallye Club	2892	
F-GAKN	SOCATA MS.880B Rallye Club	2893	
F-GAKO	SOCATA MS.880B Rallye Club	2894	
F-GAKV	SOCATA MS.893E Rallye 180GT Gaillard	12792	
F-GAKX	SOCATA MS.880B Rallye Club	2912	
F-GAKY	SOCATA Rallye 100ST	2913	
F-GALA	Piper PA-28-181 Cherokee Archer II	28-7690210	N9541N
F-GALC	Piper PA-28-181 Cherokee Archer II	28-7690147	N9517N
F-GALD	Piper PA-31T Cheyenne	31T-7620032	
F-GALF	Piper PA-30-160 Twin Comanche B	30-1415	G-AVJT N8281Y
F-GALH	Piper PA-28R-200 Cherokee Arrow	28R-7635283	N75194
F-GALN	Beech 200T Super King Air	BB-186/BT-1	
F-GALP	Beech 200T Super King Air	BB-203/BT-2	
F-GALQ	Agusta-Bell 47G-2	108	I-MICO ALAT
F-GALV	IRMA/SA.316B Alouette III	5284	
F-GALY	Piper PA-23-250 Aztec E	27-7654101	F-VAAL (N62633)
F-GALZ	Beech 65-E90 King Air	LW-199	
F-GAMB	Aérospatiale SA.315B Lama	2457	
F-GAMC	IRMA/SA.316B Alouette III	5310	HC-BNU F-GAMC
F-GAMD	Bell 47G-2	2005	G-BAZO 9J-RAD VP-RAD ZS-HBE N5187B
F-GAME	Piper PA-38-112 Tomahawk	38-78A0655	PH-SRT N9704N
F-GAMG	Hughes 369D	106-0009D	
F-GAMJ	Cessna U.206G Stationair II	03638	F-WAMJ F-GAMJ N7369N
F-GAMO	Beech 58 Baron	TH-818	
F-GAMP	Piper PA-31T Cheyenne	31T-7720029	N82122
F-GAMQ	Piper PA-32R-300 Lance	32R-7780278	N9635N
F-GAMT	Enstrom F.280C Shark	1062	
F-GAMX	Cessna 182J Skylane	56812	CS-AGM F-OCKG 5N-AFU N2712F
F-GANB	Fournier RF-6B-100	30	
F-GANC	Fournier RF-6B-100	31	
F-GAND	Fournier RF-6B-100	32	
F-GANE	Fournier RF-6B-100	33	
F-GANF	Fournier RF-6B-120	44	F-WANF
F-GANG	Fournier RF-6B-100	35	
F-GANH	Fournier RF-6B-100	36	
F-GANK	Fournier RF-6B-100	41	
F-GANL	Fournier RF-6B-100	40	
F-GANQ	Chaize CS.2200F12 HAFB	061	
F-GANS	Agusta-Bell 47G-2	244	G-AXCF EP-HBA G-AXCF AAF:3B-XK
F-GANT	Agusta-Bell 47G-2	220	G-AXCD EP-HBC G-AXCD AAF:3B-XF
F-GANU	Bell 47G-2	1633	G-BEUG EP-HAV N6764 Fr.AF N2852B
F-GANV	Bell 47G-2	1628	G-BEUF EP-HAT N6762 Fr.AF N2847B
F-GANX	Bell 47G-2	2434	G-BBUK N6751D
F-GANY	Bell 47G-2	1635	G-BEUH EP-HAW N6765 Fr.AF N2854B
F-GANZ	Cessna 172RG Cutlass	0638	N6348V
F-GAOA	Robin DR.400/2+2 Tricycle	1237	
F-GAOB	Robin DR.400/180 Régent	1195	
F-GAOD	Robin DR.400/2+2 Tricycle	1201	
F-GAOE	Robin HR.200/100S Club	104	
F-GAOG	Robin DR.400/120A Petit Prince	1213	
F-GAOH	Robin DR.400/2+2 Tricycle	1217	
F-GAOJ	Robin HR.200/100 Club	105	
F-GAOK	Robin DR.400/2+2 Tricycle	1218	
F-GAOM	Robin DR.400/2+2 Tricycle	1220	
F-GAON	Robin DR.400/140B Major 80	1238	
F-GAOP	Robin DR.400/120 Petit Prince	1540	
F-GAOQ	Robin DR.400/2+2 Tricycle	1239	
F-GAOU	Robin DR.400/160 Chevalier	1226	
F-GAOV	Robin DR.400/140B Major 80	1232	
F-GAOX	Robin DR.400/2+2 Tricycle	1240	
F-GAOY	Robin DR.400/2+2 Tricycle	1253	
F-GAPB	Hughes 269C	47-0590	
F-GAPF	Piper PA-28R-201 Cherokee Arrow	28R-7737064	N9504N
F-GAPI	Aerotek Pitts S-2A	2089	N28MC
F-GAPL	Piper PA-25-235 Pawnee C	25-4714	N4907Y
F-GAPM	Cessna A.188B AgTruck	02851T	N731EY
F-GAPR	Cessna 421B Golden Eagle	0951	PH-VMX
F-GAPZ	Beech A36 Bonanza	E-1086	
F-GAQB	Reims/Cessna F.150M	1414	
F-GAQC	Reims/Cessna F.150M	1420	

Regn.	Type	C/n	Prev.Id.
F-GAQE	Reims/Cessna F.182Q Skyline	0040	
F-GAQG	Reims/Cessna FR.172K Hawk XP	0605	
F-GAQL	Reims/Cessna F.182Q Skyline	0036	
F-GAQO	Reims/Cessna F.172M	1501	
F-GAQP	Reims/Cessna F.172M	1391	
F-GAQQ	Reims/Cessna FR.172J Rocket	0580	
F-GAQR	Reims/Cessna F.182Q Skyline	0053	
F-GAQS	Reims/Cessna FRA.150M Aerobat	0324	
F-GAQT	Reims/Cessna FR.172J Rocket	0566	
F-GAQV	Reims/Cessna F.150M	1311	
F-GAQY	Reims/Cessna F.177RG Cardinal RG	0144	
F-GAQZ	Reims/Cessna F.172M	1496	
F-GARD	SOCATA MS.893E Rallye 180GT Gaillard	12960	
F-GARG	SOCATA Rallye 100ST	2918	
F-GARH	SOCATA MS.880B Rallye Club	2919	
F-GARI	SOCATA MS.880B Rallye Club	2920	
F-GARO	SOCATA MS.880B Rallye Club	2939	
F-GARP	SOCATA MS.880B Rallye Club	2940	
F-GARQ	SOCATA MS.880B Rallye Club	2941	
F-GASB	Reims/Cessna F.172M	1508	
F-GASE	Reims/Cessna F.172M	1390	
F-GASF	Reims/Cessna F.172M	1507	
F-GASH	Reims/Cessna F.172M	1511	
F-GASK	Reims/Cessna F.150M	1323	
F-GASM	Reims/Cessna F.150M	1401	
F-GASO	Reims/Cessna F.172N	1522	
F-GASS	Reims/Cessna F.150M	1378	
F-GASV	Reims/Cessna F.152	1435	(F-GAQH)
F-GASX	Reims/Cessna F.172N	1574	
F-GASY	Reims/Cessna F.150M	1386	F-WZDR
F-GASZ	Reims/Cessna F.152	1429	F-WZDA (N70791)
F-GATD	Piper PA-28-181 Cherokee Archer II	28-7890138	N9631N
F-GATE	Piper PA-28R-201T Turbo Arrow	28R-7803039	N9636N
F-GATJ	Cessna 210K Centurion	59380	OO-HGO OO-PAG N9480M
F-GATQ	SE.313B Alouette II	1550	F-ZBAE F-BIFK
F-GATT	Grumman AA-5B Tiger	0651	
F-GATU	Grumman AA-5A Cheetah	0532	
F-GATX	Partenavia P.68B	121	G-BFET
F-GAUA	Mudry CAP.20LS-200	02	
F-GAUE	Mudry CAP.10B	173	
F-GAUH	Mudry CAP.10B	106	
F-GAUL	Mudry CAP.20LS-200	6	
F-GAUN	Mudry CAP.20LS-200	9	
F-GAUO	Mudry CAP.10B	140	(PT-LCJ)
F-GAUP	Mudry CAP.21 (Assembled from kit)	1	
F-GAUR	Mudry CAP.10B	105	
F-GAUT	Mudry CAP.10B	174	
F-GAUY	Mudry CAP.10B	177	
F-GAVA	Robin DR.400/2+2 Tricycle	1254	
F-GAVC	Robin DR.400/180 Régent	1223	(F-BNPC)
F-GAVG	Robin DR.400/160 Chevalier	1259	
F-GAVH	Robin DR.400/160 Chevalier	1262	
F-GAVI	Robin DR.400/2+2 Tricycle	1263	
F-GAVJ	Robin DR.400/160 Chevalier	1265	F-WAVJ F-GAVJ
F-GAVK	Robin DR.400/2+2 Tricycle	1270	
F-GAVL	Robin DR.400/2+2 Tricycle	1271	
F-GAVM	Robin DR.400/180 Régent	1272	
F-GAVN	Robin DR.400/2+2 Tricycle	1273	
F-GAVO	Robin R.2100	125	
F-GAVP	Robin DR.400/2+2 Tricycle	1275	
F-GAVQ	Robin DR.400/2+2 Tricycle	1278	
F-GAVR	Robin DR.400/2+2 Tricycle	1277	
F-GAVS	Robin R.2100A	126	
F-GAVU	Robin DR.400/160 Chevalier	1229	
F-GAVV	Robin DR.400/120 Petit Prince	1280	
F-GAVX	Robin DR.400/2+2 Tricycle	1281	
F-GAVY	Robin DR.400/2+2 Tricycle	1282	
F-GAXA	Robin R.2160 Alpha Sport	112	
F-GAXB	Robin R.2160 Alpha Sport	113	
F-GAXC	Robin R.2160 Alpha Sport	144	
F-GAXD	Robin R.2160 Alpha Sport	142	
F-GAXE	Robin R.2160 Alpha Sport	143	
F-GAXF	Robin R.2160 Alpha Sport	141	
F-GAXG	Robin R.2160 Alpha Sport	145	
F-GAXH	Robin R.2160 Alpha Sport	146	
F-GAXI	Robin R.2160 Alpha Sport	147	
F-GAXJ	Robin R.2160 Alpha Sport	148	
F-GAXL	Robin R.2160 Alpha Sport	150	
F-GAXM	Robin R.2160 Alpha Sport	151	
F-GAXN	Robin R.2160 Alpha Sport	152	
F-GAXO	Robin R.2160 Alpha Sport	153	
F-GAXP	Robin R.2160 Alpha Sport	154	
F-GAXQ	Robin R.2160 Alpha Sport	155	
F-GAYF	SOCATA MS.880B Rallye Club	2953	
F-GAYH	SOCATA MS.880B Rallye Club	2955	
F-GAYJ	SOCATA Rallye 235E Gabier	12877	
F-GAYL	SOCATA MS.880B Rallye Club	2965	
F-GAYM	SOCATA MS.880B Rallye Club	2966	
F-GAYN	SOCATA Rallye 100ST	2967	
F-GAYO	SOCATA Rallye 100ST	2998	
F-GAYX	SOCATA Rallye 100ST	3003	
F-GAYY	SOCATA MS.880B Rallye Club	3004	
F-GAYZ	SOCATA MS.880B Rallye Club	3005	
F-GAZA	Thunder AX7/65 HAFB	132	
F-GAZB	Chaize CS.2000F12 HAFB	008	
F-GAZC	Cameron V-56 HAFB	352	
F-GAZD	Western 0-65 HAFB	012	G-AZLB
F-GAZE	Chaize CS.2200F32 HAFB	009	
F-GAZH	Cameron O-77 HAFB	425	
F-GAZK	Thunder AX7/65 HAFB	156	
F-GAZL	Cameron V-77 HAFB	443	
F-GAZN	Chaize CS.2000F12 HAFB	012	
F-GAZP	Cameron O-77 HAFB	462	
F-GAZQ	Cameron O-77 HAFB	463	
F-GAZR	Thunder AX7/65 HAFB	172	
F-GAZS	Thunder AX7/65Z HAFB	183	
F-GAZU	Cameron V-77 HAFB	467	
F-GAZV	Cameron V-65 HAFB	488	
F-GAZX	Cameron V-77 HAFB	489	
F-GAZY	Cameron O-77 HAFB	416	
F-GBAB	Robin DR.400/2+2 Tricycle	1284	
F-GBAE	Robin DR.400/180 Régent	1285	
F-GBAI	Robin DR.400/2+2 Tricycle	1289	
F-GBAJ	Robin R.2100A	132	
F-GBAK	Robin DR.400/2+2 Tricycle	1292	
F-GBAL	Robin R.2112	130	
F-GBAM	Robin R.1180T Aiglon	215	F-WZAO
F-GBAP	Robin DR.400/2+2 Tricycle	1302	
F-GBAQ	Robin DR.400/2+2 Tricycle	1305	
F-GBAR	Robin DR.400/2+2 Tricycle	1307	
F-GBAX	Robin DR.400/180R Remorqueur	1312	
F-GBAY	Robin DR.400/2+2 Tricycle	1316	
F-GBBM	Beech A36 Bonanza	E-1253	
F-GBBP	Bredanardi/Hughes NH.300C	BH-04	
F-GBBV(2)	Thunder AX7-65Z HAFB	406	G-BJWU
F-GBBY	Reims/Cessna U.206G Stationair	0007/04375	(N756UV)
F-GBCB	SOCATA Rallye 100ST	3029	
F-GBCH	SOCATA Rallye 180T Galérien	3134	
F-GBCI	SOCATA Rallye 100ST	3032	
F-GBCJ	SOCATA MS.880B Rallye Club	3033	
F-GBCP	SOCATA MS.893E Rallye 180GT Gaillard	13109	
F-GBCQ	SOCATA Rallye 100ST	3036	
F-GBCR	SOCATA MS.880B Rallye Club	3037	
F-GBCT	SOCATA Rallye 180T Galérien	3047	
F-GBCU	SOCATA Rallye 180T Galérien	3168	
F-GBCV	SOCATA Rallye 180T Galérien	3169	
F-GBCX	SOCATA Rallye 180T Galérien	3170	
F-GBCY	SOCATA Rallye 180T Galérien	3171	
F-GBCZ	SOCATA Rallye 180T Galérien	3172	
F-GBDC	SE.313B Alouette II	1820	F-ZBAN
F-GBDG	Beech 58 Baron	TH-944	
F-GBDL	Cessna 182N Skyline	60391	TR-LPF N92845
F-GBDQ	Piper PA-25-235 Pawnee B	25-3984	N7782Z
F-GBDR	Beech F33A Bonanza	CE-740	N98170

Regn.	Type	C/n	Prev.Id.
F-GBDT	SE.313B Alouette II	1744	F-ZBAK
F-GBDX	Grumman AA-5B Tiger	0936	
F-GBEB	Airbus A.300B2-1C	102	
F-GBED	Ayres S.2R Thrush Commander	1819R	G-BCKB / N5619X
F-GBEE(2)	Cameron O-77 HAFB	1349	
F-GBEG	Bell 47G-2	2588	G-LIFT / N6783D / CF-UAI / N6783D
F-GBEH	Grumman-American AA-5B Tiger	1092	OO-RTA / OO-HRT
F-GBEL	Cessna 182K Skylane	57747	F-BOEP / N2547Q
F-GBEM	Reims/Cessna FR.172K Hawk XP	0626	LX-JED
F-GBEN	Holste MH.1521M Broussard	224	Fr.AF
F-GBEQ	Piper PA-28-161 Warrior II	28-8416103	
F-GBEU	Bell 47G-2	1995	N5159B
F-GBEV	Cameron N-65 HAFB	1351	
F-GBEY(2)	Cameron V-77 HAFB	630	
F-GBEZ	SOCATA MS.880B Rallye-Club	1205	F-BPQZ
F-GBFA	Reims/Cessna F.152	1478	
F-GBFB	Reims/Cessna F.152	1491	
F-GBFD	Reims/Cessna F.150M	1356	
F-GBFG	Reims/Cessna F.172N	1688	
F-GBFI	Reims/Cessna F.177RG Cardinal RG	0171	
F-GBFL	Reims/Cessna F.152	1482	
F-GBFN	Reims/Cessna F.172N	1694	
F-GBFP	Reims/Cessna F.172N	1720	
F-GBFQ	Reims/Cessna F.152	1488	
F-GBFR	Reims/Cessna F.177RG Cardinal RG	0172	
F-GBFT	Reims/Cessna F.172N	1659	
F-GBFU	Reims/Cessna F.172N	1725	
F-GBFV	Reims/Cessna F.172N	1727	
F-GBFX	Reims/Cessna F.152	1486	
F-GBGC	Cessna 310R-II	0920	N3825G
F-GBGE	SOCATA Rallye 235E Gabier	12729	F-WBGE / F-GBGE / F-OAGE / ZS-JSP / F-ODCM
F-GBGF	Cessna 210L Centurion	59607	D-ECTP / (N5107Q)
F-GBGG	Cessna U.206G Stationair II	03712	N7660N
F-GBGM	Cessna A.185F Skywagon	03636	N8236Q
F-GBGQ	Grumman AA-5 Traveler	0202	N9991Q / CS-AHM / PH-ATO / N5300V
F-GBGZ	Cessna T.210L Turbo Centurion	60901	
F-GBHA	SOCATA TB-10 Tobago	5	
F-GBHB	SOCATA TB-10 Tobago	6	F-WBHB
F-GBHD	SOCATA TB-10 Tobago (Dismantled)	8	
F-GBHE	SOCATA TB-9 Tampico	9	
F-GBHG	SOCATA TB-10 Tobago	13	
F-GBHJ	SOCATA TB-10 Tobago	20	
F-GBHK	SOCATA TB-10 Tobago	21	
F-GBHL	SOCATA TB-10 Tobago	22	
F-GBHM	SOCATA TB-10 Tobago	28	
F-GBHO	SOCATA TB-10 Tobago	31	
F-GBHR	SOCATA TB-10 Tobago	32	
F-GBHS	SOCATA TB-10 Tobago	33	
F-GBHU	SOCATA TB-10 Tobago	36	
F-GBHX	SOCATA TB-10 Tobago	38	
F-GBHZ	SOCATA TB-10 Tobago	77	
F-GBIA	Robin DR.400/140B Major 80	1321	
F-GBIC	Robin DR.400/2+2 Tricycle	1309	
F-GBIE	Robin DR.400/2+2 Tricycle	1313	
F-GBIF	Robin R.2100A	158	
F-GBIH	Robin DR.400/160 Chevalier	1327	
F-GBIK	Robin R.2100A	156	
F-GBIM	Robin DR.400/180 Régent	1337	
F-GBIO	Robin DR.400/2+2 Tricycle	1333	
F-GBIP	Robin R.1180T Aiglon	221	
F-GBIQ	Robin R.2100A	162	
F-GBIR	Robin DR.400/180 Régent	1330	
F-GBIT	Robin DR.400/180 Régent	1335	
F-GBIU	Robin DR.400/140B Major 80	1338	
F-GBIV	Robin DR.400/120A Petit Prince	1339	
F-GBIX	Robin DR.400/180 Régent	1340	
F-GBIY	Robin DR.400/180 Régent	1344	
F-GBJA	Reims/Cessna F.152	1492	
F-GBJB	Reims/Cessna F.152	1509	
F-GBJF	Reims/Cessna F.152	1485	
F-GBJG	Reims/Cessna F.150M	1377	
F-GBJH	Reims/Cessna F.182Q Skylane	0093	
F-GBJI	Reims/Cessna F.182Q Skylane	0094	
F-GBJJ	Reims/Cessna F.152	1544	
F-GBJK	Reims/Cessna F.152	1548	
F-GBJM	Reims/Cessna F.152	1552	
F-GBJQ	Reims/Cessna F.172N	1771	
F-GBJR	Reims/Cessna F.152	1538	
F-GBJS	Reims/Cessna F.152	1610	
F-GBJV	Reims/Cessna F.152	1581	
F-GBJX	Reims/Cessna F.152	1568	
F-GBJY	Reims/Cessna F.172N	1778	
F-GBJZ	Reims/Cessna F.172N	1779	
F-GBKB	SOCATA Rallye 100ST	3059	
F-GBKC	SOCATA Rallye 100ST	3062	
F-GBKE	SOCATA Rallye 100ST	3063	
F-GBKF	SOCATA Rallye 100ST	3064	
F-GBKG	SOCATA Rallye 100T	3065	
F-GBKL	SOCATA Rallye 235E Gabier	13020	
F-GBKQ	SOCATA Rallye 235E Gabier	12899	(YV-1442P)
F-GBKS	SOCATA Rallye 150ST	3142	
F-GBKT	SOCATA Rallye 110ST Galopin	3214	
F-GBLF	Beech A36 Bonanza	E-1443	
F-GBLH(2)	Robin DR.400/180 Régent	790	D-EDGP
F-GBLJ	Piper PA-28-161 Warrior II	28-7916190	
F-GBLL(4)	Piper PA-28RT-201T Turbo Arrow IV	28R-7931269	N2944N
F-GBLO	Hughes 269C	56-0501	F-ODDO
F-GBLT	Hughes 269C	19-0757	N58205
F-GBLU	Beech 65-C90 King Air	LJ-822	
	(Reserved as F-GNCY, 4.99))		
F-GBLX	Cessna A.185F Skywagon (Dismantled)	03224	N93342
F-GBLZ	Cessna TU.206G Turbo Stationair II	05151	(N4894U)
F-GBML	Mooney M.20J Model 201	24-0530	
F-GBMM	Piper PA-38-112 Tomahawk	38-79A0531	N2456G
F-GBMO	Piper PA-28-181 Archer II	28-7990361	N9638N
F-GBMP	CEA DR.250/160 Capitaine	37	F-OCMP / SE-CIP / F-BNJP
F-GBMQ	Aérospatiale AS.350B Ecureuil	1042	F-WZFV
F-GBMT	Piper PA-30-160 Twin Comanche B	30-1488	N8342Y
F-GBMZ	Cessna 310R-II	1592	
F-GBOB	SE.3130 Alouette II	1845	D-HOFI
F-GBOE	SE.3130 Alouette II	1844	D-HOFE
F-GBOH	Bell 47G-2	2195	HB-XFB / OE-AXL / HB-XFB / N90799 / HB-XAX
F-GBOI	Agusta-Bell 47G-2	264	D-HORD / 74+22 / AS+378 / LA+107 / AS+064
F-GBOJ	Bell 47G-2	1621	D-HAIN / 74+30 / AS+384
F-GBOK	Piper PA-44-180 Seminole	44-8095001	TR-LZE / N8087B
F-GBOM	Reims/Cessna F.172M	1401	OO-WAW
F-GBOO	Bell 47G-2	2435	D-HEBA
F-GBOQ	Grumman AA-5B Tiger	1083	
F-GBOR	Cameron O-65 HAFB	426	
F-GBOV	Piper PA-38-112 Tomahawk 112	38-78A0801	N9718N
F-GBOX	Boeing 747-2B3F	21835	
F-GBOY	Piper PA-28-161 Warrior II	28-7916494	

Regn.	Type	C/n	Prev.Id.
F-GBPA	Piper PA-28R-201T Turbo Cherokee Arrow III		
		28R-7703190	OO-AWD
			OO-HCI
			N38230
F-GBPB	Beech 65-90 King Air	LJ-98	OY-ANP
			N158G
			N158GD
F-GBPF	Cessna 310R-II	1665	(N2638U)
F-GBPI	Piper PA-28RT-201T Turbo Arrow IV	28R-7931145	N29214
			N9640N
F-GBPK	Piper PA-44-180 Seminole	44-7995308	
F-GBPL	Mooney M.20K Model 231	25-0339	N231PJ
F-GBPN	Cessna A.185F Skywagon	03819	N4623E
F-GBPO	Bell 47G-2	2424	N6761D
F-GBPQ	Piper PA-38-112 Tomahawk	38-79A1046	
F-GBPR	Bell 47G-2	2179	N5188B
F-GBPS	Piper PA-38-112 Tomahawk	38-79A1047	
F-GBPT	Piper PA-38-112 Tomahawk	38-79A0488	N9663N
F-GBPU	Piper PA-38-112 Tomahawk	38-79A1105	
F-GBPX	Piper PA-38-112 Tomahawk	38-79A1037	
F-GBPY	Piper PA-34-200T Seneca II	34-7970284	N9562N
F-GBPZ	Beech 65-C90 King Air	LJ-860	
F-GBQA	Reims/Cessna F.182Q Skylane	0103	
F-GBQB	Reims/Cessna F.182Q Skylane	0104	
F-GBQD	Reims/Cessna F.152	1587	
F-GBQE	Reims/Cessna F.152	1593	
F-GBQF	Reims/Cessna F.152	1599	
F-GBQG	Reims/Cessna F.152	1620	
F-GBQH	Reims/Cessna F.172N	1807	
F-GBQI	Reims/Cessna F.172N	1822	
F-GBQJ	Reims/Cessna FR.182 Skylane RG	0027	(PH-AYA)
F-GBQL	Reims/Cessna F.150M	1344	
F-GBQO	Reims/Cessna F.152	1665	
F-GBQQ	Reims/Cessna F.172N	1848	
F-GBQR	Reims/Cessna F.182Q Skylane	0121	
F-GBQS	Reims/Cessna F.172N	1878	
F-GBQU	Reims/Cessna F.172N	1905	
F-GBQX	Reims/Cessna F.172N	1899	
F-GBQY	Reims/Cessna F.152	1641	
F-GBQZ	Reims/Cessna F.172N	1902	
F-GBRB	Aérospatiale SA.315B Lama	2547	
F-GBRF	Dassault Falcon 10	38	N20EE
			N20ET
			N2OES
			N127FJ
			F-WJMM
F-GBRG	Piper PA-38-112 Tomahawk	38-79A0535	N9726N
F-GBRI	Piper PA-38-112 Tomahawk	38-79A0799	N9707N
F-GBRK	Piper PA-28-161 Warrior II	28-7916448	
F-GBRL	Beech F33A Bonanza	CE-867	
F-GBRN	Robin HR.200/100 Club	46	D-EEWJ
F-GBRO	Bell 47G-2	2559	N8421E
F-GBRU	Fairchild F.27J	43	N2771R
			EL-AHI
			N2771R
F-GBSB	SOCATA MS.892E Rallye 150GT	13228	
F-GBSF	SOCATA Rallye 110ST Galopin	3234	
F-GBSG	SOCATA Rallye 110ST Galopin	3235	
F-GBSL	SOCATA Rallye 110ST Galopin	3254	
F-GBSN	SOCATA Rallye 110ST Galopin	3256	
F-GBSO	SOCATA Rallye 110ST Galopin	3257	
F-GBSP	SOCATA Rallye 110ST Galopin	3264	
F-GBSQ	SOCATA Rallye 110ST Galopin	3265	
F-GBSR	SOCATA Rallye 110ST Galopin	3266	
F-GBSS	SOCATA Rallye 110ST Galopin	3267	
F-GBST	SOCATA Rallye 110ST Galopin	3268	
F-GBSU	SOCATA Rallye 110ST Galopin	3269	
F-GBSV	SOCATA Rallye 110ST Galopin	3270	
F-GBSX	SOCATA Rallye 110ST Galopin	3271	
F-GBSZ	SOCATA Rallye 110ST Galopin	3273	
F-GBTD	Cessna T.210N Turbo Centurion II	63179	N6970N

Regn.	Type	C/n	Prev.Id.
F-GBTF	Aérospatiale SA.330J Puma	1307	HC-BNP
			F-GBTF
			PT-HSM
			F-GBTF
			PT-HPT
			F-GBTF
			F-ODEF
			LN-ORC
F-GBTG	Aérospatiale AS.350B Ecureuil	1092	
F-GBTJ	Piper PA-28RT-201T Turbo Arrow IV	28R-7931282	N9608N
F-GBTK	Piper PA-28-161 Warrior II	28-8016333	
F-GBTM	Dassault Falcon 20GF	397	F-WBTM
			F-GBTM
			F-WRQP
F-GBTN	Reims/Cessna F.172N	1834	LX-III
F-GBTP	Piper PA-34-200 Seneca	34-7250286	TR-LRA
			N1299T
F-GBTS	Reims/Cessna F.182P Skylane	0004	OO-WAS
			F-GAAA
F-GBTU	Piper PA-28-161 Warrior II	28-7916581	N8073S
			N9603N
F-GBTX	Reims/Cessna F.172M	1492	F-ODEK
F-GBTZ	Robin DR.400/2+2 Tricycle	1347	
F-GBUF	Robin DR.400/120A Petit Prince	1355	
F-GBUH	Robin DR.400/2+2 Tricycle	1359	
F-GBUJ	Robin DR.400/120 Petit Prince	1361	
F-GBUL	Robin DR.400/2+2 Tricycle	1356	
F-GBUM	Robin DR.400/120A Petit Prince	1365	
F-GBUP	Robin DR.400/140B Major 80	1364	
F-GBUQ	Robin DR.400/120A Petit Prince	1371	
F-GBUR	Robin DR.400/120 Petit Prince	1374	
F-GBUT	Robin DR.400/180 Régent	1377	
F-GBUU	Robin DR.400/140B Major 80	1379	
F-GBUV	Robin DR.400/2+2 Tricycle	1376	
F-GBUY	Robin DR.400/2+2 Tricycle	1382	
F-GBVB	Robin R.1180T Aiglon II	226	
F-GBVC	Robin DR.400/120A Petit Prince	1387	
F-GBVE	Robin DR.400/140B Major 80	1388	
F-GBVF	Robin DR.400/2+2 Tricycle	1390	
F-GBVG	Robin R.1180T Aiglon II	230	
F-GBVH	Robin DR.400/120A Petit Prince	1394	
F-GBVJ	Robin DR.400/2+2 Tricycle	1399	
F-GBVK	Robin DR.400/2+2 Tricycle	1393	
F-GBVL	Robin DR.400/120A Petit Prince	1406	
F-GBVM	Robin R.1180T Aiglon II	229	
F-GBVN	Robin DR.400/180 Régent	1408	
F-GBVP	Robin DR.400/120A Petit Prince	1407	
F-GBVR	Robin DR.400/120 Petit Prince	1415	
F-GBVS	Piper PA-30-160 Twin Comanche B	30-1293	I-KLKL
			N8178Y
F-GBVT	Robin DR.400/140B Major 80	1416	
F-GBVV	Robin DR.400/180R Remorqueur	1412	
F-GBVX	Robin DR.400/120A Petit Prince	1419	
F-GBVY	Robin DR.400/2+2 Tricycle *(Stored)*	1425	
F-GBXF	SOCATA Rallye 235CA Gaucho	13078	
F-GBXG	SOCATA Rallye 110ST Galopin	3283	
F-GBXN	SOCATA Rallye 110ST Galopin	3291	
F-GBXO	SOCATA Rallye 110ST Galopin	3292	
F-GBXQ	SOCATA Rallye 110ST Galopin	3294	
F-GBXR	SOCATA Rallye 110ST Galopin	3295	
F-GBXS	SOCATA Rallye 110ST Galopin	3296	
F-GBXV	SOCATA Rallye 235E Gabier	13338	
F-GBYA	Boeing 737-228	23000	N1787B
F-GBYB	Boeing 737-228	23001	
F-GBYC	Boeing 737-228	23002	
F-GBYD	Boeing 737-228	23003	
F-GBYF	Boeing 737-228	23005	
F-GBYJ	Boeing 737-228	23009	
F-GBYK	Boeing 737-228	23010	
F-GBYL	Boeing 737-228	23011	
F-GBYN	Boeing 737-228	23503	
F-GBYO	Boeing 737-228	23504	
F-GBYP	Boeing 737-228	23792	
F-GBYQ	Boeing 737-228	23793	
F-GBZC	Cameron V-56 HAFB	503	

Regn.	Type	C/n	Prev.Id.
F-GBZD	Cameron V-77 HAFB	504	
F-GBZE	Thunder AX7/65 Bolt HAFB	189	
F-GBZG	Cameron V-56 HAFB	523	
F-GBZH	Cameron V-77 HAFB	524	
F-GBZI	Cameron N-31 HAFB	525	
F-GBZM	Thunder AX7/65Z HAFB	208	
F-GBZN	Thunder AX7/65 Bolt HAFB	209	
F-GBZO	Chaize CS.4000F16 HAFB	017	
F-GBZS	Cameron V-65 HAFB	555	
F-GBZV	Cameron V-65 HAFB	564	
F-GBZY	Cameron V-77 HAFB	566	
F-GCAA	Robin DR.400/160 Chevalier	1410	
F-GCAB	Robin R.1180T Aiglon II	233	
F-GCAD	Robin R.1180T Aiglon II	234	
F-GCAE	Robin R.1180T Aiglon II	237	
F-GCAG	Robin R.1180T Aiglon II	235	
F-GCAH	Robin DR.400/160 Chevalier	1423	
F-GCAL	Robin DR.400/120 Petit Prince	1424	
F-GCAM	Robin DR.400/160 Chevalier	1422	
F-GCAN	Robin DR.400/180 Régent	1426	
F-GCAO	Robin DR.400/2+2 Tricycle	1428	
F-GCAQ	Robin DR.400/120 Petit Prince	1433	
F-GCAR	Robin R.1180T Aiglon II	240	
F-GCAT	Robin DR.400/120 Petit Prince	1436	
F-GCAU	Robin R.1180T Aiglon II	241	
F-GCAV	Robin DR.400/120 Petit Prince	1432	
F-GCAY	Robin DR.400/180 Régent	1442	
F-GCBA	Boeing 747-228B	21982	
F-GCBB	Boeing 747-228B	22272	N1289E
			(F-GCBB)
F-GCBD	Boeing 747-228B Combi	22428	N1305E
F-GCBE	Boeing 747-228F	22678	N4508E
			(F-GCBE)
F-GCBG	Boeing 747-228F	22939	N4544F
F-GCBH	Boeing 747-228B	23611	N6046P
F-GCBI	Boeing 747-228B Combi	23676	N6009F
F-GCBJ	Boeing 747-228B	24067	N6018N
F-GCBK	Boeing 747-228F	24158	N6055X
F-GCBL	Boeing 747-228F	24735	
F-GCBM	Boeing 747-228F	24879	
F-GCCB	Cessna 310Q	0925	PH-PLE
			D-IOLW
			G-BBKK
			N6969B
F-GCCD	Partenavia P.6BB	75	PH-RVR
F-GCCE	Reims/Cessna U.206G Stationair	0015/04818	N734BD
F-GCCF	Piper PA-38-112 Tomahawk	38-79A0738	N9674N
F-GCCG	Agusta-Bell 47G	095	ALAT
F-GCCJ	Bell 47G	723	ALAT
F-GCCK	Bell 47G	1316	ALAT
F-GCCL	Agusta-Bell 47G	047	ALAT
F-GCCM	Agusta-Bell 47G	085	ALAT
F-GCCN	Agusta-Bell 47G	087	ALAT
F-GCCT	Cessna 210N Centurion II	62969	N6198N
F-GCCU	Piper PA-25-235 Pawnee D	25-7405726	N9591P
F-GCCV	Piper PA-28-181 Archer II	28-8090005	N8073Z
			N9612N
F-GCCZ	Aérospatiale SA.342J Gazelle	1393	(KAF-401)
F-GCEA	SOCATA TB-10 Tobago	49	
F-GCEB	SOCATA TB-10 Tobago	50	
F-GCEE	SOCATA TB-10 Tobago	75	
F-GCEI	SOCATA TB-10 Tobago	96	
F-GCEJ	SOCATA TB-10 Tobago	91	
F-GCEL	SOCATA TB-10 Tobago	97	
F-GCEM	SOCATA TB-10 Tobago	112	
F-GCEN	SOCATA TB-10 Tobago	54	
F-GCEO	SOCATA TB-9 Tampico	120	
F-GCER	SOCATA TB-9 Tampico	70	
F-GCES	SOCATA TB-9 Tampico	121	
F-GCEU	SOCATA TB-10 Tobago	93	
F-GCEX	SOCATA TB-10 Tobago	98	
F-GCEZ	SOCATA TB-9 Tampico	123	
F-GCFA	Beech A36 Bonanza	E-1602	
F-GCFF	Bredanardi-Hughes NH.300C	BH-005	
F-GCFJ	Piper PA-38-112 Tomahawk	38-79A1021	N9712N

Regn.	Type	C/n	Prev.Id.
F-GCFL	Piper PA-38-112 Tomahawk	38-79A1147	N9680N
F-GCFN	Piper PA-38-112 Tomahawk	38-79A1148	N9681N
F-GCFP	Piper PA-38-112 Tomahawk	38-79A1157	N9699N
F-GCFQ	Aérospatiale AS.350B Ecureuil	1200	
F-GCFU	Piper PA-28-161 Warrior II	28-8016089	OO-HLD
			N8097D
F-GCFV	Cessna 421	0189	N4589L
F-GCFX	Piper PA-28-181 Archer II	28-8090266	N8177S
F-GCFZ	Agusta-Bell 206B Jet Ranger III	8578	
F-GCGA	Beech 65-C90 King Air	LJ-894	
F-GCGD	Piper PA-38-112 Tomahawk	38-80A0074	
F-GCGF	Piper PA-38-112 Tomahawk	38-80A0075	
F-GCGJ	Cessna 210N Centurion	63941	(N7350C)
F-GCGL	SE.313B Alouette II	1157	TR-LVA
			AAF: 3D-XW
F-GCGM	SE.313B Alouette II	1906	TR-LVB
			AAF: 3D-XJ
F-GCGN	SE.313B Alouette II	1911	TR-LVC
			AAF: 3D-XK
F-GCGQ	Boeing 727-227	20609	N411BN
F-GCGZ	Aérospatiale AS.350B Ecureuil	1068	TJ-AFU
			F-WZFR
F-GCHA	Reims/Cessna F.152	1648	
F-GCHB	Reims/Cessna F.152	1649	
F-GCHC	Reims/Cessna F.152	1650	
F-GCHD	Reims/Cessna F.152	1651	
F-GCHE	Reims/Cessna F.172N	1888	
F-GCHF	Reims/Cessna FR.182 Skylane RG	0044	
F-GCHG	Reims/Cessna F.152	1687	
F-GCHH	Reims/Cessna F.152	1693	
F-GCHJ	Reims/Cessna F.152	1702	
F-GCHL	Reims/Cessna F.152	1708	
F-GCHM	Reims/Cessna F.172N	1913	
F-GCHO	Reims/Cessna F.172N	1917	
F-GCHP	Reims/Cessna F.152	1748	
F-GCHR	Reims/Cessna F.172N	2009	
F-GCHS	Reims/Cessna F.152	1717	
F-GCHT	Reims/Cessna F.152	1722	
F-GCHU	Reims/Cessna F.152	1703	
F-GCHV	Reims/Cessna F.172N	1989	
F-GCHZ	Reims/Cessna F.152	1730	
F-GCIA	Robin DR.400/120 Petit Prince	1444	
F-GCIG	Robin DR.400/160 Chevalier	1453	
F-GCIH	Robin DR.400/120 Petit Prince	1454	
F-GCII	Robin DR.400/120 Petit Prince	1455	
F-GCIJ	Robin DR.400/120 Petit Prince	1456	
F-GCIK	Robin DR.400/120 Petit Prince	1459	
F-GCIL	Robin DR.400/160 Chevalier	1457	
F-GCIM	Robin DR.400/120 Petit Prince	1469	
F-GCIN	Robin DR.400/160 Chevalier	1467	
F-GCIP	Robin DR.400/120 Petit Prince	1458	
F-GCIQ	Robin DR.400/120 Petit Prince	1475	
F-GCIR	Robin DR.400/160 Chevalier	1473	
F-GCIS	Robin DR.400/120 Petit Prince	1468	
F-GCIT	Robin DR.400/120 Petit Prince	1474	
F-GCIU	Robin DR.400/120 Petit Prince	1479	
F-GCIX	Robin DR.400/120 Petit Prince	1480	
F-GCIY	Robin DR.400/120 Petit Prince	1488	
F-GCJB	Mooney M.20K Model 231	25-0248	N231GU
F-GCJC	Aérospatiale AS.350B Ecureuil	1257	
F-GCJD	Piper PA-28-161 Warrior II	28-8016251	N8148U
F-GCJE	Piper PA-44-180 Seminole	44-8095025	
F-GCJG	Piper PA-28-181 Archer II	28-8090219	N8146N
F-GCJH	Piper PA-28-161 Warrior II	28-8016326	N9555N
F-GCJK	Piper PA-28-181 Archer II	28-8090103	OO-HLF
			N8093Z
F-GCJL	Boeing 737-222	19067	N9029U
F-GCJM	Piper PA-28RT-201T Turbo Arrow IV	28R-7931245	OO-HCZ
			N2948B
			N9581N
F-GCJO	Fairchild-Hiller FH.227B	530	N703U
F-GCJP	Partenavia P.68B	190	
F-GCJR	Cessna P210N Pressurized Centurion II	00639	G-OSPL
			N5101W
F-GCJS	Mitsubishi MU-2B-40	406SA	N967MA

Regn.	Type	C/n	Prev.Id.
F-GCJU	Wassmer WA.54 Atlantic	144	G-MPWA
			F-GBIS
			F-OBUS
F-GCKA	Cameron V-65 HAFB	583	
F-GCKB	Cameron V-65 HAFB	594	
F-GCKC	Chaize CS.3000F16 HAFB	020	
F-GCKE	Thunder AX7/65Z HAFB	249	
F-GCKI	Thunder AX3/21C Sky Chariot HAFB	276	
F-GCKO	Thunder AX7/65 HAFB	286	
F-GCKQ	Cameron V-56 HAFB	650	
F-GCKR	Cameron A-140 HAFB	663	
F-GCKS	Chaize CS.2000F12 HAFB	025	F-WCKS
F-GCKU	Cameron V-77 HAFB	665	
F-GCKV	Cameron N-77 HAFB	666	
F-GCKZ	Balloon Works Firefly 7 HAFB	"10177"	
F-GCLD	Beech C90 King Air	LJ-637	N95DD
			N95BD
			N7311R
F-GCLH	Piper PA-31T Cheyenne	31T-8020044	N2330V
F-GCLI	Piper PA-28-161 Warrior II	28-8016236	OO-HLO
			N8141Y
F-GCLJ	Beech 76 Duchess	ME-347	
F-GCLR	Piper PA-28-161 Warrior II	28-8016228	OO-HLL
			N3578X
F-GCLT	Reims/Cessna F.172N	1894	XT-ABM
			F-ODKN
F-GCLU	Piper PA-28-181 Archer II	28-8090213	OO-HLP
			N81419
F-GCLV	Piper PA-28-181 Archer II	28-8090312	N8216V
F-GCLX	Cessna 172RG Cutlass	0553	(N5526V)
F-GCMB	Piper PA-28R-201T Turbo Cherokee Arrow III		
		28R-7703087	N3055Q
F-GCMC	Piper PA-28-181 Archer II	28-8090218	OO-HLS
			N8146B
F-GCMH	Piper PA-38-112 Tomahawk	38-80A0070	N9717N
F-GCMI	Piper PA-28-161 Warrior II	28-8016287	OO-HLU
			N81762
F-GCMK	Cessna 207 Skywagon	00248	TR-LTK
			N1648U
F-GCMM	Piper PA-23-250 Aztec E	27-7305134	N9118M
			F-GCMM
			TR-LRR
			N40371
F-GCMO	Agusta-Bell 206B Jet Ranger III	8602	
F-GCMP	Agusta-Bell 206B Jet Ranger III	8592	(G-LOCK)
F-GCMT(2)	Beech B24R Sierra	MC-158	G-BAXM
F-GCMZ	Piper PA-34-200 Seneca	34-7450055	PH-LPG
			N57377
F-GCNB	Reims/Cessna F.172N	1995	
F-GCNC	Reims/Cessna F.152	1729	D-EEFY
F-GCND	Reims/Cessna F.152	1779	
F-GCNG	Reims/Cessna F.152	1781	
F-GCNJ	Reims/Cessna F.152	1751	
F-GCNK	Reims/Cessna F.172N	2019	
F-GCNN	Reims/Cessna FR.182 Skylane RG	0050	
F-GCNP	Reims/Cessna F.152	1765	
F-GCNQ	Reims/Cessna F.172N	2017	PH-AYF
F-GCNS	Reims/Cessna F.152	1800	
F-GCNT	Reims/Cessna F.172N	2039	
F-GCNU	Reims/Cessna F.172N	2037	(OY-BNS)
F-GCNV	Reims/Cessna F.172P	2076	
F-GCNX	Reims/Cessna F.172P	2056	(D-EILC)
F-GCNZ	Reims/Cessna F.182Q Skylane	0150	
F-GCOA	SOCATA TB-10 Tobago	124	
F-GCOF	SOCATA TB-10 Tobago	135	
F-GCOI	SOCATA TB-10 Tobago	154	
F-GCOJ	SOCATA TB-9 Tampico	155	
F-GCOM	SOCATA TB-10 Tobago	161	
F-GCOQ	SOCATA TB-10 Tobago	172	
F-GCOS	SOCATA TB-10 Tobago (Derelict)	174	
F-GCOU	SOCATA TB-9 Tampico	202	
F-GCOX	SOCATA TB-9 Tampico	224	
F-GCOY	SOCATA TB-9 Tampico	233	
F-GCPB	Piper PA-28RT-201T Turbo Arrow IV	28R-8031124	N82318

Regn.	Type	C/n	Prev.Id.
F-GCPF	Piper PA-28-161 Warrior II	28-7916587	OO-HCG
			N8073T
			N9604N
F-GCPJ	Piper PA-32R-301 Saratoga	32R-8013120	N8252G
			N9578N
F-GCPK	Piper PA-34-200T Seneca II	34-8070332	N8252D
			N8250H
F-GCPN	SE.313B Alouette II	1697	D-HHAF
			76+54
			PL+209
			PK+141
F-GCPO	Piper PA-34-200T Seneca II	34-8070358	N8266V
F-GCQA	Reims/Cessna 172RG Cutlass	0001/0007	N4648R
F-GCQB	SOCATA MS.880B Rallye Club	853	F-BODP
F-GCQE	Piper PA-28-181 Archer II	28-8090370	N9582N
			N82525
F-GCQF	Reims/Cessna F.172M	0947	LX-AIJ
F-GCQH	Cessna 335	0059	F-WCQH
			F-GCQH
			N6801C
F-GCQI	Agusta-Bell 47G-2	027	(F-GDQI)
			I-COLO
			IDFAF
			Fr.AF
F-GCQJ	Piper PA-28RT-201 Arrow IV	28R-8118023	N82910
F-GCQM	Agusta-Bell 47G-2	148	F-BXXE
			ALAT
F-GCQO	Reims/Cessna FR.172J Rocket	0376	TU-TGC
F-GCQQ	Aérospatiale AS.350B Ecureuil	1363	
F-GCQR	Aérospatiale SA.365C2 Dauphin 2	5054	
F-GCQX	SE.313B Alouette II	1720	D-HHAG
			76+63
			PF+209
			PF+141
F-GCQZ	Aérospatiale AS.350B Ecureuil	1562	
F-GCRA	Robin R.1180TD Aiglon	245	
F-GCRD	Robin R.1180TD Aiglon	248	
F-GCRE	Robin R.1180TD Aiglon	249	
F-GCRF	Robin R.1180TD Aiglon	250	
F-GCRG	Robin R.1180TD Aiglon	251	
F-GCRH	Robin R.1180TD Aiglon	252	
F-GCRI	Robin R.1180TD Aiglon	253	
F-GCRJ	Robin R.1180TD Aiglon	254	
F-GCRL	Robin R.1180TD Aiglon	256	
F-GCRM	Robin R.1180TD Aiglon	257	
F-GCRN	Robin R.1180TD Aiglon	258	
F-GCRO	Robin R.1180TD Aiglon	259	
F-GCRP	Robin R.1180TD Aiglon	260	
F-GCRQ	Robin R.1180TD Aiglon	261	
F-GCRR	Robin R.1180TD Aiglon	263	
F-GCRS	Robin DR.400/120 Petit Prince	1485	
F-GCRT	Robin DR.400/120 Petit Prince	1495	
F-GCRU	Robin DR.400/120 Petit Prince	1481	
F-GCRV	Robin DR.400/120 Petit Prince	1487	
F-GCRX	Robin DR.400/120 Petit Prince	1491	
F-GCRY	Robin DR.400/120 Petit Prince	1492	
F-GCRZ	Robin DR.400/120 Petit Prince	1496	
F-GCSD	Cessna 172RG Cutlass (Reims assembled)	0008/0248	N5125U
F-GCSE	Cessna TU.206G Turbo Stationair II	05777	(N5463X)
F-GCSF	Cessna 207A Skywagon	00585	N73397
F-GCSG	Cessna T.210N Turbo Centurion II	63870	N6338C
F-GCSH	Cessna TR.182 Turbo Skylane RG	01051	N756EL
F-GCSI	Piper PA-38-112 Tomahawk	38-80A0073	N9652N
F-GCSL	Boeing 737-222	19066	N9028U
F-GCSM	Cessna 172RG Cutlass	0548	(N5511V)
F-GCSN	Piper PA-32-301 Saratoga	32-8006042	(OO-HKB)
			N8199H
F-GCSO	Beech 95-B55 Baron	TC-2311	
F-GCSP	Cessna 172RG Cutlass	0563	N5539V
F-GCSV	Cessna P210N Pressurized Centurion II	00528	N731QL
F-GCTD	Piper PA-28-161 Warrior II	28-7916212	OO-WPC
			OO-HCT
			N9554N

Regn.	Type	C/n	Prev.Id.
F-GCTF	Piper PA-39 Twin Comanche C/R	39-54	G-AZMW
			(D-GMWB)
			N8897Y
F-GCTI	Piper PA-28RT-201 Arrow IV	28R-7918242	N2969V
F-GCTK	Cessna 172RG Cutlass	0566	N5543V
F-GCTM	Aérospatiale AS.350B Ecureuil	1453	
F-GCTO	Aérospatiale AS.350B Ecureuil	1361	
F-GCTQ	Piper PA-28-181 Archer II	28-8090297	OO-HLZ
			(OO-HCZ)
			N82002
F-GCTR	Beech 65-F90 King Air	LA-115	
F-GCTU	Piper PA-38-112 Tomahawk	38-80A0085	N9694N
F-GCTV	Piper PA-38-112 Tomahawk	38-80A0087	N9695N
F-GCTX	Piper PA-38-112 Tomahawk	38-80A0088	N9696N
F-GCUA	Robin DR.400/120 Petit Prince	1498	
F-GCUB	Robin DR.400/180 Régent	1500	
F-GCUD	Robin DR.400/120 Petit Prince	1502	
F-GCUE	Robin DR.400/160 Chevalier	1503	
F-GCUF	Robin DR.400/160 Chevalier	1504	
F-GCUG	Robin DR.400/120 Petit Prince	1511	
F-GCUI	Robin DR.400/160 Chevalier	1518	
F-GCUK	Robin DR.400/120 Petit Prince	1515	
F-GCUM	Robin DR.400/180 Régent	1521	
F-GCUS	Robin DR.400/120 Petit Prince	1509	
F-GCUT	Robin DR.400/120 Petit Prince	1507	
F-GCUU	Robin DR.400/120 Petit Prince	1533	
F-GCVA	Mooney M.20K Model 231	25-0508	
F-GCVC	Cessna A.185F Skywagon	04045	N6463E
F-GCVF	Agusta-Bell 206B Jet Ranger III	8607	
F-GCVL	SE.210 Caravelle 12	273	OY-SAE
F-GCVM	SE.210 Caravelle 12	270	OY-SAA
F-GCVO	SE.313B Alouette II	1824	F-ODMO(1)
			TR-LYF
			F-OCNA
			TR-LLX
			F-BCZL
			F-OBZL
F-GCVS	Cessna A.185F Skywagon	04190	N61440
F-GCVU	Bell 206L-1 Long Ranger II	45456	HB-XLO
			(D-HIFA)
			HB-XLO
F-GCVV(2)	SE.3130 Alouette II	1010/10	Fr.AF
F-GCVX(2)	Cessna A.185F Skywagon	03383	N7379H
F-GCVY	Agusta-Bell 206B Jet Ranger III	8623	
F-GCXA	Thunder AX7/65Z HAFB	293	
F-GCXB	Deveque HG RD 700 Free Balloon	9	
F-GCXC	Thunder AX7/65Z HAFB	305	
F-GCXF	Chaize CS.2200F12 HAFB	027	
F-GCXG	Cameron N-77 HAFB	668	
F-GCXH	Thunder AX7/77 Bolt HAFB	326	
F-GCXJ	Raven S.60A HAFB	177	F-WCXJ
F-GCXK	Chaize CS.2200F32 HAFB	032	
F-GCXL(2)	Thunder AX7/77 HAFB	434	
F-GCXM	Cameron O-77 HAFB	721	
F-GCXN	Cameron N-77 HAFB	744	
F-GCXO	Chaize CS.2200F12 HAFB	033	
F-GCXP	Thunder AX7/65 HAFB	335	
F-GCXQ	Chaize CS.2200F12 HAFB	034	
F-GCXR	Thunder AX7/65 HAFB	285	
F-GCXT	Cameron V-65 HAFB	799	
F-GCXU	Deveque HG RD 700 Free Balloon	11	
F-GCXX	Chaize CS.2200F12 HAFB	037	
F-GCXZ	Cameron A-530 HAFB	701	G-BIWM
F-GCYB	Reims/Cessna FR.182 Skylane RG	0056	(PH-AXQ)
F-GCYD	Reims/Cessna F.152	1836	
F-GCYH	Reims/Cessna FR.182 Skylane RG	0066	
F-GCYL	Reims/Cessna F.172P	2086	
F-GCYP	Reims/Cessna F.182Q Skylane	0167	
F-GCYQ	Reims/Cessna FR.182 Skylane RG	0064	
F-GCYR	Reims/Cessna F.172P	2104	
F-GCYT	Reims/Cessna F.152	1851	
F-GCYX	Reims/Cessna FR.182 Skylane RG	0068	
F-GCYY	Reims/Cessna F.172P	2066	
F-GCZA	Thunder AX7/77 HAFB	371	
F-GCZB	Thunder AX6/56 HAFB	370	

Regn.	Type	C/n	Prev.Id.
F-GCZC	Thunder AX7/77A HAFB	110	G-BERR
F-GCZE	Deveque HG RD 700 Free Balloon	10	
F-GCZF	Thunder AX7/77 HAFB	432	
F-GCZG	Thunder AX7/77 S1 HAFB	415	
F-GCZN	Cameron N-77 HAFB	833	
F-GCZP	Cameron O-77 HAFB	795	
F-GCZQ	Cameron N-105 HAFB	827	
F-GCZR	Cameron O-56 HAFB	840	
F-GCZS	Cameron D-50 Hot Air Airship	818	G-BJXY
F-GCZU	Cameron O-84 HAFB	167	G-BDKT
F-GCZV	Cameron O-65 HAFB	857	
F-GCZX	Leys HG VL-248 Free Balloon	01	F-WCZX
F-GCZY	Cameron V-77 HAFB	461	G-BGEC
F-GCZZ	Cameron V-56 HAFB	704	
F-GDAA	Cessna U.206G Stationair II	06082	N5228Z
F-GDAB	Cessna 172RG Cutlass	0808	N9381B
F-GDAF	Enstrom F.280C Shark	1206	N5697T
F-GDAI	Piper PA-28-161 Warrior II	28-8116185	N8360V
F-GDAJ	Piper PA-28-181 Archer II	28-8090315	OO-HKC
			N8218A
F-GDAK	Beech 65-F90 King Air	LA-141	
F-GDAM	Aérospatiale AS.350B Ecureuil	1449	(F-GHYN)
			LV-ATW
			F-GDAM
F-GDAO	IRMA/SA.316B Alouette III	5400	HC-BMN
			F-GDAO
F-GDAP	Cessna U.206G Stationair II	05967	N6605X
F-GDAT	Piper PA-28-161 Warrior II	28-8116106	N8311V
F-GDBA	SOCATA TB-21 Trinidad TC	01	F-WDBA
F-GDBE	SOCATA TB-9 Tampico	223	
F-GDBG	SOCATA TB-10 Tobago	279	
F-GDBH	SOCATA TB-10 Tobago	280	
F-GDBK	SOCATA TB-10 Tobago	274	
F-GDBM	SOCATA TB-10 Tobago	304	
F-GDBP	SOCATA TB-9 Tampico	347	
F-GDBS	SOCATA TB-9 Tampico	365	
F-GDBU	SOCATA TB-9 Tampico	361	F-WGPL
F-GDBX	SOCATA TB-9 Tampico	364	
F-GDBZ	SOCATA TB-9 Tampico	373	
F-GDCE	Piper PA-28-181 Cherokee Archer II	28-7890538	OO-MLT
			N39524
F-GDCH	Piper PA-28-161 Warrior II	28-7916418	D-EIRI
			N29077
F-GDCI	Embraer EMB.110P2 Bandeirante	110-333	PT-SDJ
F-GDCJ	Aérospatiale SA.330J Puma	1665	
F-GDCM	SA.318C Alouette Astazou	1950	D-HI FO
F-GDCO	Robinson R-22	0122	
F-GDCT	Pilatus PC-6/B1-H2 Turbo-Porter	617	HB-FCL
F-GDCV	SOCATA TB-10 Tobago	204	F-ODOD
			F-GDBD
F-GDDB	Reims/Cessna F.152	1859	
F-GDDD	Reims/Cessna F.152	1849	
F-GDDH	Reims/Cessna F.172P	2130	
F-GDDI	Reims/Cessna F.152	1865	
F-GDDJ	Reims/Cessna F.152	1864	
F-GDDL	Reims/Cessna FR.182 Skylane RG	0062	
F-GDDM	Reims/Cessna F.152	1834	
F-GDDN	Reims/Cessna F.172P	2106	(G-BIYL)
			D-EEBT
F-GDDO	Reims/Cessna F.152	1891	
F-GDDP	Reims/Cessna F.152	1887	
F-GDDQ	Reims/Cessna F.152	1888	
F-GDDR	Reims/Cessna F.172P	2134	
F-GDDS	Reims/Cessna F.152	1862	(D-EANL)
F-GDDT	Reims/Cessna F.172P	2123	(D-EEJR)
F-GDDV	Reims/Cessna F.152	1871	D-EAND
F-GDDX	Reims/Cessna F.152	1905	
F-GDDY	Reims/Cessna F.152	1917	
F-GDDZ	Reims/Cessna F.172P	2132	
F-GDEA	Robin DR.400/120 Petit Prince	1531	
F-GDEB	Robin DR.400/180 Régent	1532	
F-GDEC	Robin DR.400/120 Petit Prince	1534	
F-GDED	Robin DR.400/180 Régent	1536	
F-GDEE	Robin DR.400/120 Petit Prince	1538	
F-GDEG	Robin DR.400/160 Chevalier	1554	

Regn.	Type	C/n	Prev.Id.
F-GDEH	Robin DR.400/120 Petit Prince	1556	
F-GDEJ	Robin DR.400/160 Chevalier	1561	
F-GDEM	Robin DR.400/120 Petit Prince	1563	
F-GDEN	Robin DR.400/120 Petit Prince	1573	
F-GDEO	Robin DR.400/120 Petit Prince	1580	
F-GDEP	Robin DR.400/180 Régent	1577	
F-GDEQ	Robin DR.400/120 Petit Prince	1566	D-EGDV
F-GDES	Robin DR.400/120 Petit Prince	1581	
F-GDET	Robin DR.400/120 Petit Prince	1539	
F-GDEU	Robin DR.400/120 Petit Prince	1567	
F-GDEV	Robin R.1180TD Aiglon	278	
F-GDEY	Robin DR.400/120 Petit Prince	1592	
F-GDEZ	Robin DR.400/120 Petit Prince	1579	
F-GDFA	Aérospatiale AS.355E Ecureuil 2	5018	
F-GDFC	Fokker F.28 Fellowship 4000	11133	G-WWJC
			PH-ZBU
			PH-EXO
F-GDFG	Aérospatiale AS.350B Ecureuil	1514	
F-WDFJ	Dassault Falcon 20G	362	F-GDFJ
			F-WDFJ
			F-WATF(1)
			F-WZAS
F-GDFM	Aérospatiale AS.350B Ecureuil	1007	G-BGHG
			F-GBBK
F-GDFN	Piper PA-34-200T Seneca II	34-7970169	N159CB
			N3066V
F-GDFP	Cessna T.303 Crusader	00127	(N4933C)
F-GDFQ	Piper PA-38-112 Tomahawk	38-81A0028	N25634
F-GDFU	Cessna 210N Centurion II	64215	(N5467Y)
F-GDGC	SOCATA Rallye 110ST Galopin	3347	
F-GDGF	SOCATA Rallye 110ST Galopin	3364	
F-GDGG	SOCATA TB-20 Trinidad	422	
F-GDGI	SOCATA Rallye 110ST Galopin	3377	
F-GDGJ	SOCATA Rallye 110ST Galopin	3378	
F-GDGL	SOCATA TB-9 Tampico	359	
F-GDGM	SOCATA TB-20 Trinidad	383	
F-GDGP	SOCATA TB-10 Tobago	392	
F-GDGQ	SOCATA TB-20 Trinidad	449	
F-GDGU	SOCATA TB-20 Trinidad	406	
F-GDGZ	SOCATA TB-20 Trinidad	419	
F-GDHB	Reims/Cessna F.172M	1467	TU-TJG
			(F-GAAQ)
F-GDHD	Britten-Norman BN-2A-9 Islander	591	F-WDHD
			9Q-CMJ
			G-BENU
F-GDHI	Cessna 172RG Cutlass	0819	(D-EANK)
			N9421B
F-GDHL	SE.3130 Alouette II	1325	D-HHAA
			75+33
			PK+201
			PL+131
			PH+135
F-GDHM	SE.3130 Alouette II	1545	D-HHAB
			76+00
			PZ+201
			PN+131
F-GDHO	SE.3130 Alouette II	1891	D-HOBY
F-GDHP	SE.3130 Alouette II	1864	D-HHAJ
			77+12
			AS+359
F-GDHX	Aérospatiale AS.350B Ecureuil	1662	
F-GDHY	Piper PA-28R-201T Turbo Arrow III	28R-7803333	HB-PCD
			N36688
F-GDIA	Reims/Cessna F.152	1895	
F-GDIB	Reims/Cessna F.172P	2141	
F-GDID	Reims/Cessna F.152	1911	
F-GDIE	Reims/Cessna F.152	1898	
F-GDIG	Reims/Cessna F.152	1909	
F-GDIH	Reims/Cessna F.172P	2138	
F-GDII	Reims/Cessna F.172P	2155	
F-GDIJ	Reims/Cessna F.152	1902	
F-GDIK	Reims/Cessna F.152	1817	
F-GDIL	Reims/Cessna F.152	1828	F-WZIX
F-GDIO	Reims/Cessna F.152	1892	
F-GDIP	Reims/Cessna F.152	1927	
F-GDIQ	Reims/Cessna F.152	1903	
F-GDIT	Reims/Cessna F.172P	2180	
F-GDIU	Reims/Cessna F.172P	2142	
F-GDIV	Reims/Cessna F.172P	2177	
F-GDIX	Reims/Cessna F.172P	2162	
F-GDIY	Reims/Cessna F.172P	2191	
F-GDIZ	Reims/Cessna F.152	1923	F-WZND
F-GDJB	SOCATA Rallye 150SV Garnement	3330	F-ODNH
F-GDJD	SOCATA Rallye 235E Gabier	13346	TU-VBK
			F-ODNZ
F-GDJE	Robin DR.400/120 Petit Prince	1527	D-EGWU
F-GDJF	Piper PA-28-161 Warrior II	28-8316042	N9631N
F-GDJL	Cessna A.185F Skywagon	04383	N714AA
F-GDJN	Agusta-Bell 47G-2	269	I-ESTA
F-GDJO	Agusta-Bell 47G-2	121	I-CIDI
			IDFAF
			Fr.AF
F-GDJP	Agusta-Bell 47G-2	141	I-TIEZ
			IDFAF
			Fr.AF
F-GDJQ	Agusta-Bell 47G-2	213	I-AGIR
F-GDJR	Bell 47G	1974	I-ONGO
			SE-HBH
			N2869B
F-GDJS	Beech 200B Super King Air	BB-1116	(D-ILOC)
F-GDJT	Cessna 172RG Cutlass	1022	N9768B
F-GDJV	SE.313B Alouette II	1680	D-HICU
F-GDJZ	Piper PA-28-161 Cherokee Warrior II	28-7816484	OO-AFL
			OO-HCM
			N9499C
F-GDKA	Robin DR.400/120 Petit Prince	1587	
F-GDKD	Robin DR.400/120 Petit Prince	1608	
F-GDKE	Robin DR.400/120 Petit Prince	1598	
F-GDKF	Robin DR.400/120 Petit Prince	1602	
F-GDKG	Robin DR.400/120 Petit Prince	1609	
F-GDKH	Robin DR.400/120 Petit Prince	1610	
F-GDKI	Robin DR.400/120 Petit Prince	1611	
F-GDKJ	Robin DR.400/120 Petit Prince	1612	
F-GDKL	Robin DR.400/160 Chevalier	1613	
F-GDKM	Robin DR.400/120 Petit Prince	1615	
F-GDKN	Robin DR.400/160 Chevalier	1616	
F-GDKP	Robin DR.400/120 Petit Prince	1620	
F-GDKQ	Robin DR.400/120 Petit Prince	1621	
F-GDKR	Robin DR.400/120 Petit Prince	1623	
F-GDKS	Robin DR.400/120 Petit Prince	1627	
F-GDKT	Robin DR.400/180 Régent	1624	
F-GDKV	Robin DR.400/160 Chevalier	1635	
F-GDKX	Robin DR.400/120 Petit Prince	1636	
F-GDKY	Robin DR.400/180 Régent	1626	
F-GDKZ	Robin DR.400/160 Chevalier	1637	
F-GDLC	SOCATA TB-10 Tobago	199	F-BNGQ
			PH-AFM
			F-BNGZ
F-GDLE	Beech 200 Super King Air	BB-230	G-BEHR
F-GDLG	Piper PA-28R-200 Cherokee Arrow	28R-7235308	OO-LDH
			PH-LDH
			N1508T
F-GDLH	Cessna 421B Golden Eagle	0320	3A-MDB
			F-BTQR
			N595OM
F-GDLI	CEA DR.220	29	(G-....)
			F-BOCV
F-GDLJ	Piper PA-38-112 Tomahawk	38-80A0078	OO-TIC
			PH-TMP
			OO-HKF
			N9660N
F-GDLK	Piper PA-44-180 Seminole	44-7995209	OO-ALK
			OO-HCR
			N2210K
F-GDLL	Agusta-Bell 47G	024	ALAT
			F-BDVC
			ALAT
F-GDLM	Cessna TR.182 Turbo Skylane RG	01115	G-OAST
			(N756MM)

Regn.	Type	C/n	Prev.Id.
F-GDLN	Piper PA-28RT-201 Arrow IV	28R-7918186	OO-PAR N2871N
F-GDLR	Dassault Falcon 10	121	HB-VFT (HB-VFS) F-WPUU
F-GDLS	Piper PA-38-112 Tomahawk	38-80A0093	OO-HKI N9685N
F-GDLV	Aérospatiale AS.355F Ecureuil 2	5265	F-WZKM
F-GDLX	Piper PA-44-180T Seminole	44-8107035	OO-GMH OO-HKR N8322X
F-GDLY	SOCATA Rallye 150SV Garnement	3345	TU-VBI F-ODNY
F-GDLZ	Piper PA-28RT-201 Arrow IV	28R-8218003	G-BJXE N8460L
F-GDMA	Cessna T.210N Turbo Centurion II	64251	N6101Y
F-GDMB	Piper PA-25-235 Pawnee	25-2612	N6884Z
F-GDMG	Bell 47G-2	1626	D-HABA F-BBOK F-OBOK Fr.Mil N2845B
F-GDMH	Agusta-Bell 47G-2	122	D-HAMG D-HNFC OE-AXT (OE-AXI) G-AYOF F-OCGB Fr.AF
F-GDMJ	Agusta-Bell 47G-2	242	D-HANY AAF: 3B-XI
F-GDMN	Piper PA-28-140 Cherokee	28-7725108	G-BEMV N9561N
F-GDMP	Fournier RF-5	5002	D-KIGA
F-GDMQ	SOCATA TB-20 Trinidad	282	F-OGLN
F-GDMS	Aérospatiale AS.355F Ecureuil 2	5063	
F-WDMT(2)	Microjet MJ.200B	3	
F-WDMU	Nord 1101 Noralpha	132	CAN: CAN-9
F-GDMV	Piper PA-38-112 Tomahawk	38-81A0029	N25635
F-WDMX	Microjet MJ-200B	2	
F-GDNA	SOCATA TB-20 Trinidad	320	
F-GDNC	SOCATA TB-20 Trinidad	327	
F-GDND	SOCATA TB-20 Trinidad	331	
F-GDNE	SOCATA TB-20 Trinidad	332	
F-GDNF	SOCATA TB-20 Trinidad	344	
F-GDNG	SOCATA TB-20 Trinidad	345	
F-GDNH	SOCATA TB-20 Trinidad	346	
F-GDNJ	SOCATA TB-20 Trinidad	402	
F-GDNK	SOCATA TB-20 Trinidad	403	
F-GDNL	SOCATA TB-20 Trinidad	434	
F-GDNM	SOCATA TB-20 Trinidad	435	
F-GDNN	SOCATA TB-20 Trinidad	436	
F-GDNO	SOCATA TB-20 Trinidad	437	
F-GDNP	SOCATA TB-20 Trinidad	438	
F-GDNQ	SOCATA TB-20 Trinidad	439	
F-GDNR	SOCATA TB-20 Trinidad	440	
F-GDNS	SOCATA TB-20 Trinidad	441	
F-GDNT	SOCATA TB-20 Trinidad	471	
F-GDNU	SOCATA TB-20 Trinidad	472	
F-GDNV	SOCATA TB-20 Trinidad	548	
F-GDNX	SOCATA TB-20 Trinidad	549	
F-GDNZ	SOCATA TB-20 Trinidad	551	
F-GDOA	Reims/Cessna F.152	1924	
F-GDOC	Reims/Cessna F.152	1926	
F-GDOE	Reims/Cessna F.152	1931	
F-GDOF	Reims/Cessna F.152	1913	
F-GDOG	Reims/Cessna F.152	1897	
F-GDOH	Reims/Cessna F.172P	2207	
F-GDOK	Reims/Cessna F.152	1938	
F-GDOL	Reims/Cessna F.172P	2210	
F-GDOM	Reims/Cessna F.172P	2216	
F-GDON	Reims/Cessna F.172P	2203	
F-GDOR	Reims/Cessna F.152	1948	
F-GDOX	Reims/Cessna F.152	1946	
F-GDOY	Reims/Cessna F.172P	2218	(F-WDOY)
F-GDPB	Piper PA-25-235 Pawnee B (Two-seat)	25-3109	F-WDPB N7202Z
F-GDPC	Cessna 305C/L-19E Bird Dog	24728	F-WDPC ALAT
F-GDPD	Bell 47G-2	689	G-AVKS 9J-RDE F-BHMH HB-XAE
F-GDPF	Cessna 305C/L-19E Bird Dog	24705	ALAT
F-GDPG	SE.313B Alouette II	1726	D-HIDO
F-GDPI	Beech 95-B55 Baron	TC-554	N8949M
F-GDPN	Piper PA-25-235 Pawnee B (Officially quoted as 25-3262)	25-3292	(F-BJQH) F-OGIG F-BOAT F-OCGT N7342Z
F-GDPO	Agusta-Bell 47G-2	265	HB-XHX D-HEKG 74+23 AS+065
F-GDPP	Douglas DC-3C	9172	(F-ODQE) TL-AAX TL-JBB F-BRGN Fr.AF G-AGZF WZ984 G-AGZF 42-23310
F-GDPU	Piper PA-31-310 Navajo	31-367	HP-...? I-CGAI N9244Y
F-WDPX	Holste MH.1521M Broussard	170	F-GDPX Fr.AF
F-GDQB	Agusta-Bell 47G-2	158	HB-XOP OE-AXY (F-BXZU) Fr.AF ALAT
F-GDQC	Bell 47G-4	3329	N1152W HC-AXA N1152W
F-GDQF	Piper PA-34-200T Seneca II	34-7770337	HB-LIY N38751
F-GDQL(2)	SE.313B Alouette II	1250	Gendarmerie Fr.AF
F-GDQN	SA.318C Alouette Astazou	2059	C-FZHM CF-ZHM F-BRPG
F-GDQR	SA.318C Alouette Astazou	2262	C-FMQP CF-MQP
F-GDQX	Agusta-Bell 206B Jet Ranger II	8517	3A-MFC F-BXSV
F-GDRA	Reims/Cessna F.152	1880	N9073F
F-GDRC(2)	Mudry CAP.10B	78	3A-MAV F-BXHP
F-GDRD	Agusta-Bell 206B Jet Ranger III	8641	
F-GDRE	Hughes 269C	43-0201	N8964F
F-GDRF	Agusta-Bell 47G-2	039	ALAT
F-GDRG	Piper PA-23-250 Aztec E	27-7305213	(D-IHBR) LX-HBR D-IHBR N40489
F-GDRH	Piper PA-28-161 Warrior II	28-7916003	PH-SBV N39735
F-GDRI	Morane-Saulnier MS.733 Alcyon	71	F-BLYA Fr.AF
F-GDRJ	Piper PA-31-310 Navajo	31-392	CN-TAI N9296Y
F-GDRO	Morane-Saulnier MS.733 Alcyon	97	F-BLXQ Fr.Mil
F-GDRQ	Aérospatiale AS.350B Ecureuil	1832	
F-GDRR	SE.3130 Alouette II	1671	F-MJAV F-MJBB
F-GDRS	Reims/Cessna F.152	1460	D-EAAQ

Regn.	Type	C/n	Prev.Id.
F-GDRU	Robin DR.400/2+2	1000	F-BXEA
F-GDRV	Bell 47G-2	1968	D-HORN
			74+31
			AS+386
F-GDRX	Reims/Cessna F.172M	0969	D-ECZL
F-GDSE	Piper PA-28-181 Cherokee Archer II	28-7790451	N3336Q
F-GDSF	CEA DR.250/160 Capitaine	97	OY-DNW
F-GDSH	Reims/Cessna F.172P	2224	
F-GDSI	Cameron O-77 HAFB	1157	
F-GDSJ	Cameron O-84 HAFB	607	N389CB
F-GDSN	Holste MH.1521M Broussard	247	Fr.AF
F-GDSP	Cameron O-77 HAFB	1255	
F-GDSR	Piper PA-28RT-201T Turbo Arrow IV	28R-7931155	D-EELW
			N2124Z
F-GDSS	Cameron O-77 HAFB	1390	
F-GDST	Cessna 172RG Cutlass	0831	N9469B
F-GDSU	Robin HR.100/210D Safari	144	D-EGOG
			F-BUPZ
			(G-AZZY)
F-GDSV	Beech 58 Baron	TH-667	TJ-AFD
			F-ODAZ
F-GDTA	Mudry CAP.10B	179	
F-GDTB	Mudry CAP.10B	180	
F-GDTF	Mudry CAP.10B	181	
F-GDTG	Mudry CAP.10B	191	
F-GDTI	Mudry CAP.10B *(Crashed)*	203	
F-GDTJ	Mudry CAP.10B	204	
F-GDTM	Mudry CAP.21	14	
F-GDTN	Mudry CAP.10B	73	OO-LAT
F-GDTO	Mudry CAP.10B	218	
F-GDTQ	Mudry CAP.10B	227	
F-GDTR	Mudry CAP.21	16	
F-GDTS	Mudry CAP.21	17	
F-GDTT	Mudry CAP.230	05	
F-GDTV	Mudry CAP.10B	231	
F-GDTX	Mudry CAP.10B	225	
F-GDTY	Mudry CAP.10B	226	
F-GDTZ	Mudry CAP.10B	230	
F-GDUE(2)	SE.313B Alouette II	1457/243	Fr.AF
F-GDUF(2)	SE.313B Alouette II *(W/o 12.6.97 ?)*	1727/336	Fr.AF
F-GDUG	SA.318C Alouette Astazou	1907	PT-HKN
			F-OGIH
			F-ZBAT
F-GDUM	SA.318C Alouette Astazou	2273	PT-HOK
			C-GAJK
			N10127
F-GDUN	SA.318C Alouette Astazou	2411	F-OGHV
			F-BXLJ
F-GDUO	SE.3130 Alouette II	1333/183	Fr.AF
F-GDUP	Aermacchi AL.60C5	68/6248	TL-KAO
			I-MANH
			CF-XKU
F-GDUQ	Aermacchi AL.60C5	95/6275	TL-KAM
			I-MANJ
F-GDUR	Chaize CS.2200F12 HAFB	062	
F-GDUS	Fokker F.28 Fellowship 2000	11053	5N-ANB
			PH-ZAX
			PH-EXF
F-GDUT	Fokker F.28 Fellowship 2000	11091	5N-ANH
			PH-EXT
F-GDUU	Fokker F.28 Fellowship 2000	11108	5N-ANI
			PH-EXF
F-GDUV	Fokker F.28 Fellowship 2000	11109	5N-ANJ
			PH-EXG
F-GDVY	Robin DR.400/140B Major 80	714	F-BTKM
F-GDXA	Aérospatiale AS.350B Ecureuil	1610	
F-GDXC	Cameron A-140 HAFB	1121	
F-GDXD	Cameron N-105 HAFB	1122	
F-GDXE	Cameron N-105 HAFB	1125	
F-GDXF	Cameron O-77 HAFB	1126	
F-WDXH	Fouga CM-170 Magister	2	Fr.AF
F-GDXJ	Bell 47G-2	1317	HB-XIE
			(F-BVFX)
			Fr.Mil
F-GDXK	Thunder AX7-77Z HAFB	830	

Regn.	Type	C/n	Prev.Id.
F-GDXN	Chaize CS.3000F16 HAFB	063	
F-GDXO	Chaize CS.2200F12 HAFB	064	
F-GDXQ	Thunder AX7-77 HAFB	805	
F-GDXR	Aérospatiale AS.350B Ecureuil	1912	F-OGNB
F-GDXS	SAN Jodel D.140B Mousquetaire II	74	D-EDHK
			OE-DHK
F-GDXT	Fairchild F-27J	126	N517T
F-GDYA	Robin DR.400/180 Régent	1639	
F-GDYC	Robin DR.400/120 Petit Prince	1641	
F-GDYD	Robin DR.400/180 Régent	1642	
F-GDYE	Robin DR.400/120 Petit Prince	1643	
F-GDYF	Robin R.3000/140	002	F-WZJZ
F-GDYG	Robin DR.400/120 Petit Prince	1648	
F-GDYH	Robin DR.400/120 Petit Prince	1649	
F-GDYI	Robin R.3000/140	101	
F-GDYK	Robin DR.400/120 Petit Prince	1661	
F-GDYM	Robin DR.400/180 Régent	1662	
F-GDYN	Robin DR.400/120 Petit Prince	1663	
F-GDYP	Robin DR.400/120 Petit Prince	1667	
F-GDYQ	Robin R.3000/120	105	F-WDYQ
			F-WEIA(1)
F-GDYR	Robin DR.400/120 Petit Prince	1669	
F-GDYS	Robin DR.400/160 Chevalier	1685	
F-GDYT	Robin DR.400/180 Régent	1675	
F-GDYU	Robin DR.400/120 Petit Prince	1654	
F-GDYV	Robin R.3000/140	104	
F-GDYX	Robin DR.400/120 Petit Prince	1673	
F-GDYY	Robin DR.400/160 Chevalier	1674	
F-GDZA	Thunder AX7-65 HAFB	470	
F-GDZB	Chaize CS.2200F12 HAFB	040	
F-GDZD	Chaize CS.3000F16 HAFB	041	
F-GDZE	Thunder AX7-77 HAFB	479	
F-GDZF	Cameron N-77 HAFB	886	
F-GDZG	Thunder AX7-77SI HAFB	471	
F-WDZI	Chaize CS.2300F24 HAFB	039	
F-GDZK	Cameron O-77 HAFB	858	
F-GDZM	Cameron V-56 HAFB	930	
F-GDZN	Chaize CS.2000F12 HAFB	043	
F-GDZO	Cameron V-65 HAFB	946	
F-GDZP	Cameron V-65 HAFB	903	
F-GDZQ	Chaize CS.2200F32 HAFB	051	
F-GDZR	Cameron V-77 HAFB	890	(F-GEAB)
F-GDZS	Thunder AX7-65Z HAFB	518	
F-GDZT	Thunder AX7-65 HAFB	516	
F-GDZU	Cameron V-65 HAFB	950	
F-GDZV	Cameron N-105 HAFB	944	
F-GDZX	Chaize CS.2200F12 HAFB	046	
F-GDZY	Aerostat Solaire Malleray	01	F-WDZY
F-GDZZ	Chaize CS.2000F12 HAFB	052	
F-GEAC	Ballonfabrik Augsburg HG K.630N Free Balloon	13336	
F-GEAE	Charles et Robert AX-3 HAFB	01	F-WEAE
F-GEAF	Zodiac MGZ 2-2-S Gas Balloon	010	
F-GEAG	Cameron V-77 HAFB	349	
F-GEAH	Cameron O-105 HAFB	1042	
F-GEAJ	Cameron V-77 HAFB	1014	
F-GEAL(2)	Christen Pitts S-2B	5197	
F-GEAO	Balloon Works Firefly 8-24 HAFB	F8-023	N37228
F-GEAP	Chaize CS.2200F32 HAFB	047	
F-GEAR	Chaize CS.2200F32 HAFB	048	
F-GEAS	Chaize CS.2200F12 CMM HAFB	049	
F-GEAT	Chaize CS.3000F16 HAFB	050	
F-GEAU	Cameron O-77 HAFB	1071	
F-GEAV	Bell 206B Jet Ranger II	1207	G-BBOS
			VR-BID
			G-BBOS
F-GEAY	Chaize CS.3000F16 HAFB	055	
F-GEAZ	Chaize CS.3000F16 HAFB	057	
F-GEBA	Piper PA-28-181 Cherokee Archer II	28-7890196	PH-LIA
			OO-HCK
			N9889K
F-GEBB	Cessna 310R	0584	HB-LMD
			N87473
F-GEBD	Beech A36 Bonanza	E-1592	D-EKBH
F-GEBE	Cessna 310Q	0731	N4568L
F-GEBG	Thunder AX8-84 HAFB	650	

Regn.	Type	C/n	Prev.Id.
F-GEBI	Thunder AX7-65 HAFB	630	
F-GEBK(2)	Cameron V-77 HAFB	1377	
F-GEBL	Thunder AX10-160 HAFB	643	
F-GEBM	Piper PA-18-150 Super Cub	18-1294	CS-ALJ
			FAP3205
F-GEBO	Reims/Cessna F.172M	1364	D-EEGN
F-GEBQ	Piper PA-38-112 Tomahawk	38-78A0293	D-EGXB
			N9678N
F-GEBR	Thunder AX7-77 HAFB	679	
F-GEBS	Pilatus PC-6/B1-H2 Turbo-Porter	702	HB-FFK
F-GEBT	Cessna 172RG Cutlass	0648	N6385Y
F-GEBV	SAN Jodel D.140C Mousquetaire III	128	CN-TZH
F-GEBX	Thunder AX8-105 HAFB	640	
F-GEBY	Thunder AX10-160A HAFB	677	
F-GECB	Cessna 305C/L-19E Bird Dog	24568	ALAT
F-GECF	Marks reserved for Ecole de Conduite France		
F-GECG	Thunder AX7-77 HAFB	675	
F-GECH	Thunder AX7-65Z HAFB	674	
F-GECJ	Thunder AX7-77 HAFB	688	
F-GECL	Mooney M.20J Model 201	24-1531	N57942
F-GECM	Aérospatiale AS.350B Ecureuil	1792	
F-GECO	Chaize CS.3000F16 HAFB	059	
F-GECP	Cessna U.206G Stationair II	04224	D-EKAX
			(OY-ASG)
			N756NM
F-GECQ	Chaize CS.3000F16 HAFB	060	
F-GECT	Aérospatiale SA.315B Lama	2666	
F-GECX	Thunder AX7-77 HAFB	741	
F-GECY	Robin DR.400/160 Chevalier	888	F-BUSQ
F-GECZ	Thunder AX7-77 HAFB	723	
F-GEDC	Holste MH.1521C Broussard	5	F-BICX
	(Identity also possibly MH.1521M c/n 5 ex.Fr.AF)		
F-GEDE	Aérospatiale SA.365C2 Dauphin 2	5078	(D-HMKA)
F-GEDF	Aérospatiale AS.350B Ecureuil	1820	
F-GEDG	Piper PA-18A-150 Super Cub	18-2849	CN-TDE
			F-DADF
F-GEDH	Piper PA-18A-150 Super Cub	18-558	PH-AAT
	(Officially quoted with f/n 18-490 - marks		R-207
	originally allotted to c/n 18-4606)		51-15672
			N7187K
F-GEDJ	Piper PA-18A-150 Super Cub	18-6373	CN-TDB
			F-DAFQ
F-GEDK	Thunder AX7-77 HAFB	748	
F-GEDL	Mooney M.20E Chaparral	21-0059	HB-DFG
			C-GNFJ
			N7179V
F-GEDM	Cessna 207A Skywagon	00209	D-EEDW
			N1609U
F-GEDN	SE.3130 Alouette II	1262/156	Fr.AF
F-GEDO	Piper PA-28-161 Warrior II	28-7916004	PH-SBW
			N39736
F-GEDT	Deveque HG RD 700 Free Balloon	12	
F-GEDU	Piper PA-32-300 Cherokee Six	32-7440007	TZ-ACK
			5U-AAQ
			6V-ADM
			N56601
F-GEDV	Beech 65-A90 King Air	LJ-150	D-ICPD
			SE-FNU
			N900W
			N4646S
			N1151S
F-GEDX	Cessna 210R Centurion II	64970	(N7596U)
F-GEEB	Thunder AX7-65 HAFB	543	
F-GEEC	Cameron O-65 HAFB	967	
F-GEED	Cameron V-65 HAFB	992	F-GDZQ(1)
F-GEEE	Thunder AX7-65 HAFB	548	
F-GEEG	Thunder AX8-140 HAFB	473	G-BKLK
F-GEEH	Thunder AX7-65 HAFB	550	
F-GEEI	Thunder AX7-65 HAFB	573	
F-GEEK(2)	Piper PA-28-161 Warrior II	28-8516012	N4380F
F-GEEL	Thunder AX7-65S1 HAFB	530	
F-GEEM	Cameron O-105 HAFB	1145	
F-GEEN	Cameron O-65 HAFB	1146	
F-GEEO	Pilatus PC-6/B1-H2 Turbo-Porter	676	HB-FEO
F-GEEP	Cameron O-77 HAFB	1147	
F-GEEQ	Chaize CS.2200F12 HAFB	058	
F-GEER	Chaize CS.2000F12 HAFB	065	
F-GEES	Durondeau L-180 HAFB	15	
F-GEET	Chaize CS.3000F16 HAFB	066	
F-GEEU	Chaize CS.3000F16 HAFB	067	
F-GEEV	Chaize CS.2200F12 HAFB	068	
F-GEEX	Chaize CS.2200F32 HAFB	069	
F-GEEY	Chaize CS.3000F16 HAFB	071	
F-GEFA	Piper PA-28RT-201T Turbo Arrow IV	28R- 8231036	N8176V
			N9643N
F-GEFC	Fournier RF-5	5087	F-OCPQ
F-GEFD	Morane-Saulnier MS.880B Rallye Club	77	HB-EDF
F-GEFG	Reims/Cessna F.152	1743	D-EFDW
F-GEFH	Reims/Cessna F.172M	1258	D-EESB
F-GEFI	Aérospatiale AS.350B Ecureuil	1787	D-HHCC
F-GEFJ	Rockwell S.2R-600 Thrush Commander	2183R	N8423V
F-GEFP	Reims/Cessna F.152	1704	OO-EDP
			(F-GCHK)
F-GEFQ	Thunder AX7-77 HAFB	859	
F-GEFT	Piper PA-31-310 Navajo	31-678	N4683
			D-IBRO
			F-BRQJ
			N6799L
F-GEFU(2)	Cessna 172N	72605	N6112D
F-WEFX(2)	Reserved by Europe Falcon Service		
F-WEFY(2)	Reserved by Europe Falcon Service		
F-GEFZ	Cessna 425 Corsair	0059	LN-AFB
			SE-IFM
			(N6777L)
F-WEGB	Aeritalia/SNIAS ATR-42	002	
F-GEGF	Aeritalia/SNIAS ATR-42-300	036	
F-GEGG	Thunder AX8-105 HAFB	1052	
F-GEGI	Cameron A-105 HAFB	1339	
F-GEGJ	Thunder AX7-77Z HAFB	941	
F-GEGK	Thunder AX7-77 HAFB	942	
F-GEGL	Thunder AX7-77 HAFB	923	
F-GEGM	Thunder AX10-160A HAFB	943	
F-GEGN	Thunder AX7-77 HAFB	985	
F-GEGO	Piper PA-28-181 Cherokee Archer II	28-7790320	TU-TMH
			F-ODFO
			N1639H
F-GEGP	Thunder AX8-90A HAFB	995	
F-GEGR	Thunder AX7-77Z HAFB	1001	
F-GEGS	Thunder AX7-77 HAFB	896	
F-GEGU	Cameron V-77 HAFB	730	N383CB
F-GEGV	Thunder AX7-77Z HAFB	1047	
F-GEGX	Thunder AX7-65Z HAFB	1046	
F-GEGY	Thunder AX7-65Z HAFB	1074	
F-GEGZ	Thunder AX7-77Z HAFB	1041	
F-GEHA	Aérospatiale SA.341G Gazelle	1064	N7721Y
			N6952
			F-WMHG
F-GEHB	Aérospatiale SA.341G Gazelle	1099	N266E
F-GEHC	Aérospatiale SA.341G Gazelle	1417	N341AT
			N49536
F-GEHD	Aérospatiale SA.341G Gazelle	1390	N6KT
			N49527
F-GEHE	Aérospatiale SA.341G Gazelle (Written off)	1170	N62416
F-GEHF	Aérospatiale SA.341G Gazelle	1320	N905XX
			N905X
			N49508
F-GEHH	SA.318C Alouette Astazou	1901	G-BDWN
			6W-S..
			(G-ATDT)
F-GEHM	Aérospatiale AS.350B Ecureuil	1722	
F-GEHN	Aérospatiale AS.350B Ecureuil	1027	F-ODIO
F-GEHO	SE.313B Alouette II	1628	F-MJAO
			ALAT
F-GEHQ	Aérospatiale SA.318C Alouette Astazou	2187	N8263
F-GEHU	Aérospatiale SA.330J Super Puma	1309	PT-HTX
			F-GEHU
			I- EHPG
			F-GAPQ
			(F-ODIA)
			F-GAPQ

Regn.	Type	C/n	Prev.Id.
F-GEHV	Aérospatiale AS.350B Ecureuil	1454	N5786B
F-GEHX	Cessna 177B Cardinal	02665	F-OGHX / N20379
F-GEHZ	Aérospatiale AS.350B Ecureuil	1291	N803DB / N3611T
F-WEIA	Robin R.3000Z	001	
F-GEIB	Robin DR.400/180 Régent	1676	
F-GEIC	Robin DR.400/120 Petit Prince	1678	
F-GEID	Robin DR.400/120 Petit Prince	1677	
F-GEIF	Robin DR.400/180 Régent	1690	
F-GEIH	Robin DR.400/180 Régent	1689	
F-GEII	Robin R.3000/120	108	
F-WEIJ	Robin DR.400/180R Remorqueur	1709	
F-WEIK	Robin R.3000/180R	107	
F-GEIL	Robin DR.400/180R Remorqueur	1693	
F-GEIM	Robin DR.400/180R Remorqueur	1694	
F-GEIN	Robin DR.400/120 Petit Prince	1696	
F-GEIO	Robin DR.400/120 Petit Prince	1699	
F-GEIP	Robin DR.400/160 Chevalier	1701	
F-WEIQ	Robin DR.400/180R (Porsche Test Bed)	1703	(D-EAFA) / F-WEIQ
F-GEIR	Robin DR.400/120 Petit Prince	1704	
F-GEIS	Robin DR.400/120 Petit Prince	1705	
F-GEIT	Robin DR.400/180R Remorqueur	1710	
F-GEIU	Robin DR.400/120 Petit Prince	1712	
F-GEIV	Robin R.3000/120	111	
F-GEIX	Robin DR.400/160 Chevalier	1716	
F-GEIY	Robin R.3000/120	113	
F-GEIZ	Robin R.3000/140	114	
F-GEJB	Aérospatiale AS.350B Ecureuil	1669	(JA9342)
F-GEJC	SE.313B Alouette II	1004	Fr.AF
F-GEJD	Cessna 172RG Cutlass	1158	D-EBDO / N9428D
F-GEJG	Cameron A-105 HAFB	1334	
F-GEJH	Cameron V-77 HAFB	734	
F-GEJJ	Beech A36TC Bonanza	EA-9	N6652Z
F-GEJK	Cessna 305C/L-19E Bird Dog	24588	ALAT
F-GEJO	Piper PA-28-181 Archer II	28-8690018	(F-GFEG) / N9097C
F-GEJQ	Piper PA-28-181 Archer II	2890030	N9123P
F-GEJV	Beech A100 King Air	B-129	N235B
F-GEJY(2)	Beech 200 Super King Air	BB-507	N600RM / N9OBR / (N80BR) / N66585
F-GEJZ	Reims/Cessna F.172M	1099	TU-TGT / F-OCVT
F-GEKA	Robin R.3000/120	115	
F-GEKB	Robin DR.400/120 Petit Prince	1720	
F-GEKC	Robin DR.400/120 Petit Prince	1722	
F-GEKD	Robin DR.400/120 Petit Prince	1728	
F-GEKE	Robin DR.400/160 Chevalier	1729	
F-GEKF	Robin DR.400/120 Petit Prince	1730	
F-GEKG	Robin DR.400/180 Régent	1732	
F-GEKH	Robin DR.400/120 Petit Prince	1733	
F-GEKI	Robin DR.400/120D	1734	
F-GEKJ	Robin R.3000/120	119	
F-GEKL	Robin DR.400/120 Petit Prince	1736	
F-GEKN	Robin DR.400/120 Petit Prince	1739	
F-GEKO	Robin DR.400/120 Petit Prince	1740	
F-GEKP	Robin DR.400/160 Chevalier	1741	
F-GEKT	Robin DR.400/120 Petit Prince	1745	
F-GEKV	Robin DR.400/120 Petit Prince	1746	
F-GEKY	Robin DR.400/180R Remorqueur	1748	
F-GEKZ	Robin R.3000/120	124	
F-GELA	Dassault Falcon 10	16	N48TT / N110FJ / F-WLCT
F-GELB	Agusta-Bell 47G-2	103	D-HFLA / ALAT
F-GELC	Agusta-Bell 47G	019	ALAT
F-GELD(2)	Bell 47G-4	1587	
	(c/n suspect - possibly AB.47G-3B1 ex.MM80410)		
F-GELF	Robinson R-22A Alpha	0444	N8555A
F-GELH	Fouga CM.170 Magister (Stored)	102	Fr.AF

Regn.	Type	C/n	Prev.Id.
F-GELJ	SE.313B Alouette II	85/1100	Fr.AF
F-GELK	Reims/Cessna F.172N	1811	D-EGLC
F-GELL	Beech 65-E90 King Air	LW-88	9Q-CTQ / N1TQ / N1LQ / N1LC / N9OCJ
F-GELM	Piper PA-34-200T Seneca II	34-7870040	N9833K
F-GELN	Bell 47G-4A	7668	N1438W
F-GELP	SE.210 Caravelle 10B3	187	I-GISO / OH-LSD
F-GELT	Dassault Falcon 10	211	F-WZGT
F-GELU	Piper PA-34-200 Seneca	34-7350147	N16463
F-GELX(2)	Piper PA-32R-301T Turbo Saratoga SP	32R-8529005	N4385D
F-GELY	Beech A-36 Bonanza	E-458	TN-ACZ / CR-LMX / N2893W
F-GEMA	Airbus A.310-203	316	
F-GEMB	Airbus A.310-203	326	
F-GEMC	Airbus A.310-203	335	
F-GEMD	Airbus A.310-203	355	
F-GEME	Airbus A.310-203	369	
F-GEMG	Airbus A.310-203	454	
F-GEMN	Airbus A.310-304	502	F-WWCD
F-GEMO	Airbus A .310-304	504	F-WWCF
F-GEMP	Airbus A.310-304	550	
F-GEMQ	Airbus A.310-304	551	
F-GENA	SOCATA TB-20 Trinidad	450	
F-GENB	SOCATA TB-20 Trinidad	460	
F-GENC	SOCATA Rallye 110ST Galopin	3384	
F-GENF	SOCATA TB-10 Tobago	474	
F-GENH	SOCATA TB-20 Trinidad	498	
F-GENI	SOCATA TB-21	500	
F-GENJ	SOCATA TB-20 Trinidad	499	
F-GENK	SOCATA TB-10 Tobago	506	
F-GENL	SOCATA TB-9 Tampico	519	
F-GENR	SOCATA TB-20 Trinidad	513	F-OGMS
F-GENS	SOCATA TB-20 Trinidad	588	
F-GENT	SOCATA TB-9 Tampico	587	
F-GENY	SOCATA TB-10 Tobago	640	
F-GEOE	Aérospatiale AS.350B1 Ecureuil	2024	
F-GEOF	Hughes 269C	S-1183	D-HIVE
F-GEON	Piper PA-28R-201T Turbo Cherokee Arrow II	28R-7703293	G-OTUX / SE-GPZ
F-GEOO	Piper PA-34-200T Seneca II	34-7870299	G-BMHP / 4X-CAW / N36160
F-GEOP	Thunder AX7-65Z HAFB	1088	
F-GEOQ	Piper PA-28R-201 Arrow III	28R-7837214	G-HIFI / G-BFTB / N9652C
F-GEOR	Mudry CAP.10B	77	G-WXY / F-BXHQ
F-GEOS	Cameron O-65 HAFB	1517	
F-GEOT	Reims/Cessna FR.172K Hawk XP	0649	OO-VNX / OO-HNX
F-GEOU	Beech 65-C90 King Air	LJ-941	N3804C
F-GEOV(2)	Piper PA-28R-201 Arrow III	28R-7837062	N4YN / N6207H
F-GEOY(2)	SA.316B Alouette III	5397	F-ODRU / D2-ESI / F-WTNF
F-GEPA	Chaize CS.3000F16 HAFB	074	
F-GEPB	Aérospatiale AS.350B Ecureuil	1893	
F-GEPE	Piper PA-31T Cheyenne	31T-7720031	HB-LIW / N82144
F-GEPG	Piper PA-28-161 Warrior II	28-8416108	N4367W
F-GEPI	Cessna T.210R Turbo Centurion II	65001	N9125U
F-GEPK	Piper PA-28RT-201T Turbo Arrow IV	28R-8031155	N8249Q
F-GEPN	Aérospatiale SA.365C2 Dauphin 2	5073	EC-DUT / D-HELY
F-GEPO	Beech 58 Baron	TH-112	G-AYGZ
F-GEPP	Hughes 269C	90-0044	D-HJUP / PH-NPL

Regn.	Type	C/n	Prev.Id.
F-GEPR	Wassmer WA.40A Super IV	82	OO-ROY
F-GEPT	SOCATA TB-10 Tobago	342	F-OGKD
F-GEPX	Thunder AX7-77 HAFB	76	
F-GEPY	Beech 200 Super King Air	BB-779	N811CB
			N197RB
F-GEPZ	SOCATA MS.892A Rallye Commodore 150	11948	TU-TKY
			F-BTJU
F-GEQE	Bell 206B Jet Ranger II	3163	N555BA
F-GEQG	Hughes 269C	42-0136	D-HADI (2)
			PH-EPL
			G-BAAN
F-GEQH(2)	Bell 47G-2	2420	N1044L
			CF-DTR
F-GEQI (2)	Aérospatiale SA.330J Puma	1590	F-ODJE
F-GEQJ	Aeritalia/SNIAS ATR-42-300	008	PH-ATR
			F-WWED
F-GEQL(3)	Cessna TR.182 Skylane RG	01327	N9193Y
F-GEQM(3)	Mitsubishi MU-2B-60	790SA	N279MA
			N279RB
			(N816RB)
			N279MA
F-GEQN(2)	Bell 47	26	N106L
			N106B
			NC106B
F-GEQO(2)	SOCATA TB-9 Tampico	294	6V-AFE
F-GEQS(2)	SE.3130 Alouette II	1142	ALAT
			Fr.AF
F-GEQT	Cessna 172RG Cutlass	0419	N4933V
F-GEQU	Cessna 172N	71982	N5996E
F-GEQV	Cessna 172N	71921	N5691E
F-GEQX	Piper PA-28-161 Cherokee Warrior II	28-7716080	N1038Q
F-GEQZ	SOCATA MS.880B Rallye-Club	1273	F-BRDN
F-GERB	Cessna U.206D Stationair	01385	LN-LJQ
			N72376
F-GERE	Cessna 305C/L-19E Bird Dog	24514	ALAT
F-GERF	Fournier RF-5	5021	D-KAHF
F-GERJ	Aérospatiale SA.365N Dauphin 2	6066	F-ODRA
			F-WXFH
F-GERK	Aérospatiale SA.365N Dauphin 2	6086	F-ODRB
F-GERM	Piper PA-28RT-201T Turbo Arrow IV	28R-8131122	N8382V
F-GERP	Fairchild-Swearingen SA.226AT Merlin IV	AT-012	N111MV
			N111MT
			N5320M
F-GERR	Thunder AX7-77 HAFB	977	
F-GERS	Beech 200 Super King Air	BB-753	N3705B
F-GERX	Thunder AX7-77 HAFB	1107	
F-GERZ	Thunder AX7-77Z HAFB	1102	
F-GESF	Cameron A-105 HAFB	1549	
F-GESG	Aérospatiale SA.341G Gazelle	1032	N57TT
			N57GT
			N341AH
			N223DB
			N223DP
			(N33623)
F-GESJ	Beech 65-E90 King Air	LW-97	F-WZIG(2)
			D-IDTB
			F-ODID
			TR-LRX
F-GESK	Thunder AX7-77 HAFB	775	
F-GESN	Piper PA-28R-200 Cherokee Arrow III	28R-7535364	N3948X
F-GESQ	Thunder AX11-240A HAFB	776	
F-GESR	SE.3130 Alouette II	1551	LQ-HIS
F-GESS	Thunder AX7-65 HAFB	767	
F-GEST	Aérospatiale SA.341G Gazelle	1113	EC-CUA
			F-BVRU
F-GESX	Piper PA-28RT-201T Turbo Arrow IV	28R-8431006	N4330Y
F-GETA	Boeing 747-3B3	23413	N6009F
			(F-GDUE)
F-GETB	Boeing 747-3B3	23480	(F-GDUF)
			N6018N
F-GETC	Reims/Cessna F.177RG Cardinal RG	0050	F-GETZ
			LX-RST
			G-AZKU
F-GETD	Thunder AX7-77 HAFB	804	
F-GETE	Thunder AX8-105Z HAFB	812	

Regn.	Type	C/n	Prev.Id.
F-GETF	Piper PA-23-250 Aztec F	27-7854011	G-BFKN
			N63890
F-GETG	Piper PA-28RT-201 Arrow IV	28R-8218009	N8040A
F-GETH	Piper PA-28RT-201T Turbo Arrow IV	28R-8031064	N8156Y
F-GETI	Beech F90 King Air	LA-19	N90NS
			N90MT
			N6686A
F-GETJ	Beech 65-E90 King Air	LW-296	N207CP
			N4424V
			YV-207CP
F-GETK	Piper PA-28-181 Archer II	28-8490059	N4350J
F-GETL	Reims/Cessna F.177RG Cardinal RG	0065	F-OCTL
F-GETQ	Piper PA-34-200T Seneca II	34-7870437	N30JA
F-GETR	Aérospatiale AS.355F Ecureuil 2	5060	F-OBUU
F-GETT	Piper PA-18 Super Cub 95	18-3230	OO-ACC
			OL-L56
			L-156
			53-4830
F-GETU	Agusta-Bell 47G-2	256	D-HEDU(2)
			D-HALM
			74+15
			AS+056
F-GETV	Thunder AX6-56 HAFB	845	
F-GETX	Thunder AX7-77 HAFB	816	
F-GETY	Thunder AX7-77 HAFB	799	
F-GETZ	Piper PA-28-181 Cherokee Archer II	28-7890085	N47511
F-GEUA	Reims/Cessna F.172P	2225	
F-GEUB	Reims/Cessna F.172P	2228	
F-GEUC	Reims/Cessna F.172P	2231	
F-GEVA	SOCATA TB-20 Trinidad	552	
F-GEVB	SOCATA TB-10 Tobago	561	
F-GEVC	SOCATA TB-10 Tobago	562	
F-GEVE	SOCATA TB-10 Tobago	564	
F-GEVF	SOCATA TB-10 Tobago	565	
F-GEVG	SOCATA TB-10 Tobago	566	
F-GEVH	SOCATA TB-10 Tobago	567	
F-GEVI	SOCATA TB-10 Tobago	568	
F-GEVJ	SOCATA TB-20 Trinidad	691	
F-GEVK	SOCATA TB-20 Trinidad	734	
F-GEVL	SOCATA TB-20 Trinidad	735	
F-GEVM	SOCATA TB-20 Trinidad	736	
F-GEVO	SOCATA TB-20 Trinidad	752	
F-GEVP	SOCATA TB-20 Trinidad	753	
F-GEVQ	SOCATA TB-20 Trinidad	796	
F-GEVR	SOCATA TB-20 Trinidad	797	
F-GEVS	SOCATA TB-20 Trinidad	798	
F-GEVT	SOCATA TB-20 Trinidad	799	
F-GEVU	SOCATA TB-20 Trinidad	800	
F-GEVV	SOCATA TB-20 Trinidad	801	
F-GEVX	SOCATA TB-20 Trinidad	802	
F-GEVY	SOCATA TB-20 Trinidad	803	
F-GEVZ	SOCATA TB-20 Trinidad	804	
F-GEXA	Boeing 747-4B3	24154	
F-GEXB	Boeing 747-4B3	24155	
F-GEXC	Hughes 269C	94-0352	N9584F
F-GEXG	Piper PA-34-200T Seneca II	34-7970078	N3007H
F-GEXH	Bell 206B Jet Ranger II	1236	N165HS
			N220CT
			N59449
F-GEXI	Boeing 737-2L9	22406	G-BNGK
	(Stored)		OY-APP
			N8295V
F-GEXL	Beech 200 Super King Air	BB-202	N2425X
			D-IBVW
F-GEXM	Piper PA-28RT-201T Turbo Arrow IV	28R-7931107	N3033U
F-GEXN	Hughes 269C	27-0578	D-HDAN(2)
			D-HMAP
F-GEXO	Thunder AX7-77 HAFB	963	
F-GEXQ	Agusta-Bell 47G-2	241	D-HIFA
			LN-ORT
			I-LOBY
F-GEXV	Beech A100 King Air	B-199	N110TD
			N600AC
			G-BBVL
			N85TC, G-BBVL

Regn.	Type	C/n	Prev.Id.
F-GEYA	Raven Europe S-55A HAFB	E-2	
F-GEYB	Raven Europe S-55A HAFB	E-4	
F-GEYC	Raven Europe S-55A HAFB	E-5	
F-GEYD	Raven Europe FS-57A HAFB	E-6	
F-GEYE	Raven Europe S-55A HAFB	E-7	
F-GEYF	Raven Europe S-55A HAFB	E-8	
F-GEYG	Raven Europe S-55A HAFB	E-9	
F-GEYH	Raven Europe S-55A HAFB	E-010	
F-GEYI	Raven Europe RX-65 HAFB	E-012	F-WEYI
			F-GEYI
			F-WEYI
F-GEYJ	Raven Europe S-55A HAFB	E-013	
F-GEYK	Raven Europe S-55A HAFB	E-015	
F-GEYL	Raven Europe FS-57A HAFB	E-016	
F-GEYM	Raven Europe FRX-65 HAFB	E-018	
F-GEYN	Raven Europe S-55A HAFB	E-019	
F-GEYQ	Raven Europe S-55A HAFB	E-025	
F-GEYR	Raven Europe S-55A HAFB	E-1	
F-GEYS	Raven Europe RX-7 HAFB	E-011	
F-GEYT	Raven Europe S-55A HAFB	E-021	
F-GEYU	Raven Europe S-60A HAFB	E-023	
F-GEYV	Raven Europe S-60A HAFB	E-027	
F-GEYX	Raven Europe FS-57A HAFB	E-028	
F-GEYY	Raven Europe S-55A HAFB	E-029	
F-GEYZ	Raven Europe S-55A HAFB	E-032	
F-GEZA	Raven Europe S-55A HAFB	E-026	
F-GEZB	Raven Europe S-55A HAFB	E-036	
F-GEZC	Raven Europe FRX-65 HAFB	E-038	
F-GEZD	Raven Europe FS-57A HAFB	E-050	
F-GEZE	Raven Europe S-55A HAFB	E-051	
F-GEZF	Raven Europe FS-57A HAFB	E-053	
F-GEZG	Raven Europe S-60A HAFB	E-055	
F-GEZI	Raven Europe S-55A HAFB	E-060	
F-GEZJ	Raven Europe S-55A HAFB	E-061	
F-GEZK	Raven Europe S-60A HAFB	E-068	
F-GEZM	Raven Europe RX-7 HAFB	E-064	
F-GEZN	Raven Europe RX-7 HAFB	E-097	
F-GEZO	Raven Europe FS-57A HAFB	E-103	
F-GEZP	Raven Europe RX-7 HAFB	E-079	
F-GEZQ	Raven Europe S-55A HAFB	E-104	
F-GEZR	Raven Europe FS-57A HAFB	E-098	
F-GEZS	Thunder AX7-77Z HAFB	678	
F-GEZT	Raven Europe S-66A HAFB	E-091	
F-GEZU	Raven Europe RX-7 HAFB	E-075	
F-GEZV	Raven Europe FS-57A HAFB	E-100	
F-GEZX	Raven Europe FS-57A HAFB	E-101	
F-GEZY	Raven Europe S-52A HAFB	E-102	
F-GEZZ	Raven Europe RX-7 HAFB	E-108	
F-GFAB	Aérospatiale AS.355F Ecureuil 2	5165	F-ODOM
F-WFAD	Ballon Commemoratif Dolfuss	unkn	
F-GFAN	Thunder AX7-77Z HAFB	498	OO-BCC
F-GFAQ	Aérospatiale AS.350B1 Ecureuil	2048	
F-GFAT	Reims/Cessna U.206G Stationair II	0014/04776	D-EOCY
			PH-AYH
			N733LU
F-GFAU	Beech 58 Baron	TH-1281	N1829D
F-GFAV	Robinson R-22 Beta	0560	
F-GFAX	Piper PA-28-161 Warrior II	28-8016090	OO-FLF
			OO-HLE
			N8097E
F-GFBB	Aérospatiale AS.350B Ecureuil	1831	
F-GFBC	Aérospatiale AS.350B Ecureuil	1850	
	(Reserved as D-HAUQ 10.93)		
F-GFBE	Fournier RF-5	5044	TR-LAO
			F-OCOM
F-GFBH(3)	Thunder AX7-77 HAFB	1874	
F-GFBI (2)	Piper PA-44-180 Seminole	4495010	D-GFPA
			N92076
F-GFBJ	Grumman G.164A Agcat	1124	N5168
F-GFBM	Aérospatiale SA.365C2 Dauphin 2	5070	F-OAYC
F-GFBN	Thunder AX7-77Z HAFB	1168	
F-GFBR	Cessna 172RG Cutlass	0668	N6406V
F-GFBS	Chaize CS.3000F16 HAFB	072	
F-GFBT	Beech V35B Bonanza	D-9727	N4079S
F-GFBU	Cessna 177RG Cardinal RG	0671	N2724V

Regn.	Type	C/n	Prev.Id.
F-GFBV	Hughes 269C	15-0383	D-HMAU
F-GFBY	Cameron N-65 HAFB	1636	
F-GFCC	Pilatus PC-6/B1-H2 Turbo-Porter	572	C-GWZO
			N2852T
F-GFCF	Hughes 269C	119-0853	N58390
F-GFCG	Cessna 210N Centurion	64148	OO-BIA
			N5275Y
F-GFCH	Aérospatiale SA.365C2 Dauphin 2	5072	F-OCCD
			F-WTNY
F-GFCI	Aérospatiale SA.341G Gazelle	1206	N3WU
			N3WL
			N55931
F-GFCJ	Cessna 310R	1519	D-ILCF
			N5229C
F-GFCK	Hughes 269C	104-0366	N9289F
F-GFCL	Hughes 269C	26-0471	N7418F
F-GFCM	Aérospatiale SA.315B Lama	2226	G-BLLX
			ZK-HDX
F-GFCP	Aérospatiale AS.355F1 Ecureuil 2	5292	F-WYMI
			PH-SLC
			F-WZFU
F-GFCQ	Grumman G-159 Gulfstream 1	140	N92SA
			N92K
			N300A
			N760G
F-GFCS	Aérospatiale AS.350B1 Ecureuil	1970	
F-GFCT	Cessna 172N	67974	N75817
F-GFCU	Cessna 172N	69612	N737RH
F-GFCV	Aérospatiale SA.315B Lama (Dbr 20.11.98?)	2497	N49531
F-GFCX	Cessna 305C/L-19E Bird Dog	24557	(F-GECD)
			ALAT
F-GFCY	Aérospatiale SA.315B Lama	2554	N3835W
			FAC-164
F-GFCZ	Cessna 172M	67413	N73380
F-GFDC	Pilatus PC-6/B1-H2 Turbo-Porter	656	ZK-PTP
			F-OCQV
			VH-SMA
			HB-FDC
F-GFDE	Cessna T.207A Turbo Stationair 8	00654	N75921
F-GFDG	Aérospatiale SA.342 Gazelle	1204	TG-KOV
F-GFDH	Aérospatiale SN.601 Corvette	13	N601AN
			F-BVPD
F-GFDI	Thunder AX7-77 HAFB	1187	
F-GFDJ	Beech 65-E90 King Air	LW-86	N410PB
			(N505N)
			N410PB
			(N429K)
			N410PD
			N410FD
			N3126W
F-GFDL	Aérospatiale AS.350B Ecureuil	1824	D-HHKK
F-GFDO	Agusta-Bell 206B Jet Ranger II	8531	G-BEKH
F-GFDP	Bell 47G	D-6	G-ARIA
			N4929V
			YI-ABY
			NC152B
F-GFDQ	CEA DR.360 Chevalier	524	OO-MAS
F-GFDR	Thunder AX7-65 HAFB	1097	
F-GFDS	Robin DR.400/120 Petit Prince	1528	EC-EAU
			F-OCJD
F-GFDT	Cameron O-77 HAFB	1651	
F-GFDY	Bell 206B Jet Ranger II	3600	G-OUPP
			N206SH
			N2261L
F-GFEA	Piper PA-31T Cheyenne	31T-7620011	N76PT
			N54990
F-GFEB	Aérospatiale SA.341G Gazelle	1491	N9002L
F-GFEC	Aérospatiale SA.365C2 Dauphin 2	5071	F-ODBV
			F-GDCT
F-GFED	Aérospatiale AS.350B Ecureuil	1473	D-HHPS(3)
F-GFEE	Piper PA-28R-180 Cherokee Arrow	28R-30350	5R-MEE
			N3995T

Regn.	Type	C/n	Prev.Id.
F-GFEF	Grumman G-159 Gulfstream 1	122	N707MP
			N152SR
			N153SR
			N738G
F-GFEG	Piper PA-28-181 Archer II	28-8090363	N8223H
F-GFEH	Robinson R-22 Beta	0769	
F-GFEM	Piper PA-34-200T Seneca II	34-8170017	N82772
F-GFEO	Embraer EMB.120 Brasilia	120-062	PT-SKF
F-GFET	SOCATA TB-10 Tobago	659	N20HY
F-GFEU	Robin ATL	77	
F-GFEX	Aérospatiale AS.355F Ecureuil 2	5217	ZS-HKZ
F-GFEY	Aérospatiale AS.355F Ecureuil 2	5046	N57826
F-GFFA	Robinson R-22B Beta	0665	
F-GFFC	Grumman AA-5A Cheetah	0573	TU-TMW
			F-OCBJ
			F-GBDJ
F-GFFD	Pilatus PC-6/B2-H2 Turbo-Porter	708	HB-FFD
F-GFFH	Beech 76 Duchess	ME-144	5T-AOH
			F-ODJQ
			F-GBLO
F-GFFI	Cameron A-140 HAFB	1561	
F-GFFJ	UltraMagic V-77 HAFB	77/18	
F-GFFK	UltraMagic M-77 HAFB	77/17	
F-GFFL	SOCATA TB-20 Trinidad	343	G-BNCD
			F-GDBY
F-GFFM	Cameron N-160 HAFB	1622	G-BOGH
F-GFFO	Cessna 150M	78660	N704JZ
F-GFFQ	SOCATA TB-20 Trinidad	647	N20GM
F-GFFR	SOCATA TB-20 Trinidad (Stored)	671	N20LJ
F-GFFT	SOCATA TB-20 Trinidad	672	N20LK
F-GFFU	Aérospatiale AS.350B Ecureuil	2083	
F-GFFV	Bell 47G-2	1987	N2874B
F-GFFX	Thunder AX8-90A SIII HAFB	1890	
F-GFFY	Chaize CS.2200F12 HAFB	080	
F-GFFZ	Cessna 172RG Cutlass	0375	N4754V
F-GFGA	Cessna P210N Pressurized Centurion II	00279	N210WC
			N4748K
F-GFGC	Robinson R-22B Beta	0687	
F-GFGH	SOCATA Rallye 235E Gabier	13337	F-ODNQ
F-GFGI (2)	Hughes 269C	117-0646	F-GDCF
			OE-CXN
F-GFGJ	Cessna U.206G Stationair II	04302	N756RT
F-GFGK(2)	Bell 47G-2	1990	CF-KAJ
F-GFGL	Beech 58 Baron	TH-360	TR-LSG
	(Reservation only - status uncertain)		F-OCTZ
F-GFGN	Piper PA-28-181 Archer II	2890056	
F-GFGO	Piper PA-28-181 Archer II	2890060	
F-GFGQ(2)	Cessna 172N	71595	N3576E
F-GFGR	Cessna T.303 Crusader	00054	N9908T
F-GFGS	Cessna 182N Skylane	60799	D-EFWG
			N9255G
F-GFGT	Grumman G-159 Gulfstream 1	5	N159AJ
			N925WL
			N159AJ
			N9EB
			N43AS
			N700PR
			N601HP
			N601HK
			N705G
F-GFGX	Piper PA-28-181 Cherokee Archer II	28-7690275	N9697K
F-GFGZ	Thunder AX8-90A HAFB	1235	
F-GFHA	Robinson R-22 Beta	0591	N24702
F-GFHC	Beech 65-C90 King Air	LJ-717	N200BX
F-GFHI	Cessna 172RG Cutlass	0332	N4595V
F-GFHJ	Beech 95-A55 Baron	TC-343	HB-GOZ
			N9770Y
F-GFHL	Bell 47G-2	2433	N5828K
			C-FLMZ
			CF-LMZ
F-GFHM(2)	Aérospatiale AS.350B Ecureuil	1560	F-WYMB
			MAAW H-05
			D-HEZE
F-GFHN(2)	Bell 47G-2	1489	N2805B
F-GFHO	Thunder AX10-160A HAFB	1246	

Regn.	Type	C/n	Prev.Id.
F-GFHQ	Beech 65-B90 King Air	LJ-347	N777SB
			N1TV
			N3290A
			N38RH
			N76AS
			N76RJ
			N333JJ
			D-IEVV
F-GFHS	Aérospatiale SA.318C Alouette Astazou	2233	N4683
F-GFHT	Cessna 172N	71679	N4938E
F-GFHU	Thunder AX7-77 HAFB	1253	
F-GFHX	Piper PA-12 Super Cruiser	12-3534	CN-TBS
			F-BFBK
			NC4102H
F-GFHY	Bell 206B Jet Ranger II	1673	N90224
F-GFIC	Grumman G-159 Gulfstream 1	49	N456
			N749G
F-GFID	Britten-Norman BN-2A-21 Islander	760	LN-MAG
			G-BCZE
F-GFIE	Piper PA-28-181 Archer II	2890071	
F-GFIF	Cessna 310R-II	0586	G-BEMA
			N87476
F-GFII	Hughes 369D	129-0628D	N58357
F-GFIL	Lake LA-4-200 Buccaneer	712	N1207L
			AN-BPP
			N1207L
F-GFIM	Piper PA-28RT-201T Turbo Arrow IV	28R-8331026	N923CC
			N9641N
			N4295T
F-GFIO	SNCAN Stampe SV.4C	695	F-BDOO
F-GFIP	Thunder AX8-105 HAFB	1262	
F-GFIQ	Thunder AX7-77 HAFB	1259	
F-GFIR	Beech 65-C90 King Air	LJ-434	OE-FDU
			HB-GDU
F-GFIS	Thunder AX7-77 HAFB	1268	
F-GFIT	Piper PA-28RT-201 Arrow IV	28R-8018023	N35747
F-GFIU	Piper PA-32R-301 Saratoga	32R-8113044	N8340D
F-GFIX	Thunder AX8-90A HAFB	1239	
F-GFIY	Chaize CS.3000F16 HAFB	084	
F-GFIZ	Piper PA-28RT-201T Turbo Arrow IV	28R-7931213	N2825N
F-GFJA	Piper PA-32R-300 Lance	32R-7680224	OO-BEL
			OY-BLR
F-GFJE	Piper PA-34-200 Seneca	34-7250169	TU-TFU
			N4838T
F-GFJG	Cessna TR.182 Turbo Skylane RG	01854	N5306T
F-GFJH	Aeritalia/SNIAS ATR-42-300	049	
F-GFJI	Reims/Cessna FRA.150L Aerobat	0139	TU-TFT
			F-OCPM
F-GFJJ(2)	Piper PA-28-181 Archer II	28-7990157	N321DG
F-GFJO	Bell 47G-2	2251	C-FKMX
			CF-KMX
F-GFJR	Cessna 425 Corsair	0032	N6773B
F-GFJY(2)	Piper PA-28-181 Archer II	28-8490111	N132AV
			N9637N
F-GFJZ	Thunder AX8-105 HAFB	1240	
F-GFKA	Airbus A.320-111	005	F-WWDI
F-GFKB	Airbus A.320-111	007	F-WWDJ
F-GFKD	Airbus A.320-111	014	F-WWDO
F-GFKE	Airbus A.320-111	019	
F-GFKF	Airbus A.320-111	020	
F-GFKG	Airbus A.320-111	021	
F-GFKH	Airbus A.320-211	061	
F-GFKI	Airbus A.320-211	062	
F-GFKJ	Airbus A.320-211	063	
F-GFKK	Airbus A.320-211	100	
F-GFKL	Airbus A.320-211	101	
F-GFKM	Airbus A.320-211	102	
F-GFKN	Airbus A.320-211	128	
F-GFKO	Airbus A.320-211	129	
F-GFKP	Airbus A.320-211	133	
F-GFKQ	Airbus A.320-111	002	F-WWDA
F-GFKR	Airbus A.320-211	186	
F-GFKS	Airbus A.320-211	187	
F-GFKT	Airbus A.320-211	188	
F-GFKU	Airbus A.320-211	226	

Regn.	Type	C/n	Prev.Id.
F-GFKV	Airbus A.320-211	227	
F-GFKX	Airbus A.320-211	228	
F-GFKY	Airbus A.320-211	285	
F-GFKZ	Airbus A.320-211	286	
F-GFLA	SOCATA TB-10 Tobago	85	F-ZVLA
F-GFLC	Piper PA-28-181 Archer II	28-8490047	TJ-AHB
			N4338E
F-GFLG	Piper PA-28RT-201 Arrow IV	28R-7918263	G-EDDY
			N8079E
F-GFLI	Bell 47G-2	670	N939B
F-GFLJ(2)	Nord 1101 Noralpha	141	N72SL
			F-BLTS
			Fr.Mil
F-GFLL	Aeritalia/SNIAS ATR-42	007	OY-CIB
	(Reservation only)		F-WWEC
F-GFLM	Bell 47G-2	1631	F-GBLM
			G-BEUE
			EP-HAU
			N6763
			Fr.AF
			N2850B
F-GFLR	Cessna 172RG Cutlass	0735	D-EOLR
			(D-EAYY)
			N6502V
F-GFLS	Cameron D-70 Hot Air Airship	1716	F-WFLS
			(LX-FLS)
F-GFLU	CEA DR.253 Régent	113	G-AWCD
F-GFLV	Boeing 737-2K5	22597	EC-DTR
			D-AHLE
F-GFLX	Boeing 737-2K5	22598	EC-DUB
			D-AHLF
			N5573B
F-GFLZ(2)	Piper PA-28-181 Archer II	28-8690049	N9082Z
F-GFMB	Beech C23 Sundowner 180	M-1501	TU-TGL
F-GFMC	Chaize CS.3000F16 HAFB	076	
F-GFMD	Dassault Falcon 10	136	F-WZGS
			I-MUDE
			F-WZGH
F-GFMF	Chaize CS.2200F12 HAFB	082	
F-GFMG	Robin DR.300/120 Petit Prince	615	F-ZVMG
F-GFMH	Grumman G-159 Gulfstream 1	20	N732US
			VR-CTN
			N5PC
			N250AL
			N227LA
			N227LS
			N226P
F-GFMK	Bell 206B Jet Ranger II	2386	N777TE
F-GFML	SOCATA MS.893E Rallye 180GT Gaillard	12386	F-ZVML
F-GFMM	Robin DR.400/2+2	1451	F-ZVMM
			F-GCIE
F-GFMO	Piper PA-28-181 Archer II	28-8390011	N8300Z
F-GFMQ	SOCATA ST-10 Diplomate	147	F-BTJM
F-GFMR	Cessna 310R	0696	PH-BLK
			D-IDGT
			N1286G
F-GFMT	Cessna 172N	68481	N733RC
F-GFMU	Reims/Cessna F.172H	0404	LX-AVB
			D-EMFC
F-GFMV	Beech 58 Baron	TH-745	OO-DUK
			F-ODCZ
F-GFMX	Agusta-Bell 206B Jet Ranger II	8305	OE-BXP
F-GFMY	Reims/Cessna F.182Q Skylane	0080	G-BLTE
			OO-TWR
			PH-AXC(2)
F-GFNA(2)	Mudry CAP.232	08	
F-GFNB	Robin ATL	01	F-WFNB
F-GFNC	Robin ATL	03	F-WFNC
F-GFNE	Robin ATL	05	F-WFNE
F-GFNG	Robin ATL	07	F-WFNG
F-GFNH	Robin ATL	08	F-WFNH
F-GFNI	Robin ATL	09	F-WFNI
F-GFNK	Robin ATL	11	F-WFNK
F-GFNL	Robin ATL	12	F-WFNL
F-GFNM	Robin ATL	13	F-WFNM

Regn.	Type	C/n	Prev.Id.
F-GFNO	Robin ATL	16	F-WFNO
F-GFNP	Robin ATL	20	F-WFNP
F-GFNQ	Robin ATL	17	F-WFNQ
F-WFNR	Robin ATL	02	
F-GFNS	Robin ATL	18	F-WFNS
F-GFNT	Robin ATL	19	F-WFNT
F-GFNX	Robin ATL	24	F-WFNX
F-GFNY	Robin ATL	21	F-WFNY
F-GFNZ	Robin ATL	25	F-WFNZ
F-GFOC	Robin ATL	27	F-WFOC
F-GFOD	Robin ATL	28	F-WFOD
F-GFOE	Robin ATL	29	F-WFOE
F-GFOF	Robin ATL	30	F-WFOF
F-GFOG	Robin ATL	31	F-WFOG
F-GFOH	Robin ATL	32	F-WFOH
F-GFOI	Robin ATL	33	F-WFOI
F-GFOJ	Robin ATL	34	F-WFOJ
F-GFOL	Robin ATL	36	F-WFOL
F-GFOM	Robin ATL	37	
F-GFON	Robin ATL	38	
F-GFOO	Robin ATL	39	
F-GFOQ	Robin ATL	41	
F-GFOR	Robin ATL	42	
F-GFOS	Robin ATL	43	
F-GFOT	Robin ATL	44	
F-GFOU	Robin ATL	45	
F-GFOV	Robin ATL	46	
F-GFOY	Robin ATL	48	
F-GFPA	Aérospatiale SA.365C2 Dauphin 2	5063	F-ODNK
			F-GCTL
F-GFPB	Aérospatiale SA.365C2 Dauphin 2	5064	F-ODNJ
			F-GCTM
F-GFPC	Chaize CS.2200F12 HAFB	085	
F-GFPD(2)	Piper PA-25-235 Pawnee	25-2685	N6940Z
F-GFPE	Beech 99	U-21	OO-WAY
			F-BSUK
			N1058C
F-GFPF	Dassault Falcon 10	68	N80MP
			N91DH
			N11DH
			(N7NL)
			N7NP
			N152FJ
			F-WLCV
F-GFPG	Aérospatiale AS.355F1 Ecureuil 2	5293	
F-GFPH	Piper PA-23-235 Apache	27-602	F-OBYY
			F-BMLL
			N4319Y
F-GFPI (2)	Cessna T.210M Turbo Centurion	62867	N6992B
F-GFPJ	Piper PA-18-135 Super Cub	18-3188	OO-WIK
	(Quoted officially with f/n 18-3191)		OO-HBB
			OL-L01
			L-114
			53-4788
F-GFPM	Aérospatiale AS.350B Ecureuil	1833	
F-GFPN	Robinson R-22 Beta	0848	
F-GFPP	Beech A36 Bonanza	E-1454	N6027M
F-GFPQ	Aérospatiale SA.318C Alouette Astazou	2247	C-FQMQ
			CF-QMQ
F-GFPS	Beech 76 Duchess	ME-209	N6626W
F-GFPX	Thunder AX10-160 HAFB	1295	
F-GFPY	CEA DR.315 Petit Prince	332	F-BPRY
F-GFPZ	Mudry CAP.20	5	Fr.AF: F-TFVY
			F-BTAG
			F-TFVY
F-GFQA	SOCATA TB-20 Trinidad	571	F-OGMT
F-GFQC	SOCATA TB-9 Tampico	699	
F-GFQD	SOCATA TB-20 Trinidad	707	
F-GFQE	SOCATA Rallye 180T Galérien	3386	
F-GFQF	SOCATA TB-20 Trinidad	709	
F-GFQG	SOCATA TB-10 Tobago	727	
F-GFQH	SOCATA TB-10 Tobago	733	
F-GFQJ	SOCATA TB-20 Trinidad	741	
F-GFQM	SOCATA TB-9 Tampico	742	
F-GFQO	SOCATA TB-10 Tobago	657	(N20HQ)

Regn.	Type	C/n	Prev.Id.
F-GFQQ	SOCATA TB-10 Tobago	658	(N20HX)
F-GFQU	SOCATA TB-10 Tobago	769	
F-GFQV	SOCATA TB-10 Tobago	661	(N20JQ)
F-GFQX	SOCATA TB-10 Tobago	663	(N20JY)
F-GFQY	SOCATA TB-20 Trinidad	779	
F-GFRA	Robin ATL	50	
F-GFRC	Robin ATL	52	
F-GFRD	Robin ATL	53	
F-GFRE	Robin ATL	54	
F-GFRF	Robin ATL	55	
F-GFRG	Robin ATL *(Wrecked, wings used by F-GFSH)*	56	
F-GFRH	Robin ATL	57	
F-GFRI	Robin ATL *(Wrecked)*	58	
F-GFRJ	Robin ATL	59	
F-GFRK	Robin ATL	60	
F-GFRL	Robin ATL	61	
F-GFRM	Robin ATL	62	
F-GFRN	Robin ATL	63	
F-GFRO	Robin ATL	64	
F-GFRP	Robin ATL	65	
F-GFRR	Robin ATL	67	
F-GFRS	Robin ATL	69	
F-GFRT	Robin ATL	70	
F-GFRU	Robin ATL	71	
F-GFRX	Robin ATL	72	
F-GFRY	Robin ATL	75	
F-GFRZ	Robin ATL	82	
F-GFSC	Robin ATL	79	
F-GFSD	Robin ATL	84	
F-GFSE	Robin ATL	85	
F-GFSF	Robin ATL	86	
F-GFSH	Robin ATL	88	
F-GFSJ	Robin ATL	90	
F-GFSK	Robin ATL	91	
F-GFSL	Robin ATL	92	
F-GFSN	Robin ATL	94	
F-GFSP	Robin ATL L	96	
F-GFSR	Robin ATL	98	
F-GFSS	Robin ATL	99	
F-GFST	Robin ATL	100	(I-....)
			F-GFST
F-GFSU	Robin ATL	101	
F-GFSV	Robin ATL	102	
F-GFSX	Robin ATL	104	
F-GFSY	Robin ATL	105	
F-GFSZ	Robin ATL	111	F-WFSZ
F-GFTD	SOCATA Rallye 100ST	2883	D-EDVW
F-GFTE	Cessna 177B Cardinal	02568	N19393
F-GFTF	Piper PA-34-200 Seneca	34-7350303	LX- IER
			OO- ITF
			N56197
F-GFTG	Mooney M.20J Model 205	24-3041	
F-GFTH	Cessna 177RG Cardinal RG	1005	N34560
F-GFTI	Piper PA-38-112 Tomahawk	38-78A0567	N4345E
F-GFTK	Ayres S.2R Thrush Commander	2518R	N4008D
F-GFTM	Thunder AX7-77Z HAFB	1302	
F-GFTN	Piper PA-28R-201T Turbo Arrow IV	28R-7931103	N3024U
F-GFTQ	Cameron O-105 HAFB	1712	
F-GFTR	Robin DR.400/180 Régent	1858	
F-GFTU	Agusta-Bell 47G-2	250	EC-DXB
			D-HIRT
			74+10
			AS+051
F-GFTV	Beech A36 Bonanza	E-1640	N6730L
F-WFTX	Fouga CM.170 Magister	522	Fr.AF
F-GFTY	Piper PA-25-235 Pawnee	25-2741	N6991Z
			(N585Z)
			N6991Z
F-GFTZ	Piper PA-28-161 Warrior II	28-8216093	N8053R
F-GFUA	Boeing 737-33A	23635	G-OUTA
			N6069D
			N3282Y
F-GFUD	Boeing 737-33A	24027	
F-GFUE	Boeing 737-33A	24387	
F-GFUF	Boeing 737-33A	24388	

Regn.	Type	C/n	Prev.Id.
F-GFUG	Boeing 737-4B3	24750	
F-GFUH	Boeing 737-4B3	24751	
F-GFUI	Boeing 737-3M8	24023	PH-TSR
			HB-IIA
			(OO-LTD)
			(OO-BTD)
F-GFUJ	Boeing 737-33A	25118	(F-GBYR)
F-GFUM	Pilatus PC-6/B2-H2 Turbo Porter	740	HA-YDB
F-GFUO	Piper PA-25-235 Pawnee	25-2141	N6585Z
F-GFUP	Piper PA-25-235 Pawnee	25-2841	N7061Z
F-WFUQ	Fouga CM-170 Magister	523	Fr.AF
F-GFUR	Robin ATL	80	
F-GFUS	Cameron N-90 HAFB	2376	
F-GFUV	Piper PA-31T Cheyenne	31T-7720063	N3948A
			YV-279CP
			N82185
F-GFUX	UltraMagic Label Rouge HAFB	6/01	
F-GFUY	Beech A36 Bonanza	E-2640	
F-GFUZ	Beech A36 Bonanza	E-2641	
F-GFVA	Cessna 305C/L-19E Bird Dog	24522	ALAT
F-GFVB	Cessna 305C/L-19E Bird Dog	24534	ALAT
F-GFVC	Cessna 305C/L-19E Bird Dog	24535	ALAT
F-GFVD	Cessna 305C/L-19E Bird Dog	24539	ALAT
F-GFVE	Cessna 305C/L-19E Bird Dog	24541	F-WFVE
			ALAT
F-GFVF	Cessna 305C/L-19E Bird Dog	24545	ALAT
F-GFVG	Agusta-Bell 206B Jet Ranger II	8414	YU-HBE
F-GFVI	Boeing 737-230C	20256	N304XV
			D-ABFE
F-GFVL	Thunder AX7-77Z HAFB	1242	
F-GFVN	Beech F90 King Air	LA-166	HB-GHM
			N6133H
F-GFVO	Piper PA-31T Cheyenne	31T-7920049	N500FE
			(N500FC)
			N500FE
			N23310
F-GFVP	Wassmer Jodel D.120A Paris-Nice	217	OO-PCJ
			LX-OUF(1)
			F-BKNF
F-GFVQ	Hughes 269C	12-0073	N9646F
F-GFVT	Dornier Do.27Q-5	2062	F-BKVT
			F-OBVT
			D-ENYQ
F-GFVV	Holste MH.1521M Broussard	298	Fr.AF
F-GFVZ	Robin DR.400/180 Régent	1113	F-BXVZ
F-GFXA	Robin DR.400/120 Petit Prince	1749	
F-GFXB	Robin DR.400/160 Chevalier	1750	
F-GFXC	Robin DR.400/120 Petit Prince	1752	
F-GFXD	Robin DR.400/120 Petit Prince	1751	
F-GFXE	Robin DR.400/180 Régent	1755	
F-GFXF	Robin DR.400/120 Petit Prince	1753	
F-GFXG	Robin DR.400/180 Régent	1756	
F-GFXH	Robin DR.400/120 Petit Prince	1757	
F-GFXI	Robin R.3000/120 Petit Prince	125	
F-GFXJ	Robin DR.400/120 Petit Prince	1772	
F-GFXK	Robin DR.400/180 Régent	1763	
F-GFXL	Robin DR.400/160 Chevalier	1761	
F-GFXN	Robin DR.400/120 Petit Prince	1768	
F-GFXO	Robin DR.400/120 Petit Prince	1770	
F-GFXP	Robin DR.400/120 Petit Prince	1771	
F-GFXQ	Robin R.3000/120	127	
F-GFXS	Robin DR.400/180 Régent	1774	
F-GFXT	Robin DR.400/100 Cadet	1775	F-WFXT
F-GFXV	Robin DR.400/180 Régent	1777	
F-GFXX	Robin DR.400/160 Chevalier	1779	
F-GFXY	Robin DR.400/180 Régent	1780	
F-GFXZ	Robin DR.400/120 Petit Prince	1782	
F-GFYD	Zlin Z.526F Trenér Master	1176	F-BTGD
			F-WTGD
F-GFYG	Chaize CS.2200F12 HAFB	094	
F-GFYJ(2)	Cessna T.210N Turbo Centurion II	63648	N4860C
F-GFYK	Piper PA-28-180 Cherokee C	28-3282	F-OCJV
			N9219J
F-GFYL	Boeing 737-2A9C	20205	N383PA
			CF-TAO

Regn.	Type	C/n	Prev.Id.
F-GFYO	Thunder AX7-77 HAFB	857	
F-GFYQ	Thunder AX7-77 HAFB	1366	
F-GFYR	Hughes 369D	39-0483D	N58262
F-GFYT	Piper PA-28-161 Cadet	2841060	
F-GFYU	Aérospatiale SA.365N Dauphin 2	6082	F-ODTC
F-GFYV	Piper PA-28-161 Cadet	2841059	
F-GFYY	Cessna 172M	67862	N75630
F-GFZA	Piper PA-28-181 Archer II	28-8390074	TJ-AGW
			N82608
			N9516N
F-GFZB	McDonnell-Douglas DC-9-83 (MD-83)	49707	(F-GIAL)
F-GFZC	Aérospatiale AS.350B Ecureuil	2163	
F-GFZD	Aérospatiale AS.350B Ecureuil	2195	
F-GFZF	Aérospatiale SA.318C Alouette Astazou	2352	D-HHFS
			SX-HAN
F-GFZG	Piper PA-28-140 Cherokee E	28-7225350	PH-LAM
			N11C
F-GFZH	Reims/Cessna FTB.337 Super Skymaster	0035	F-BXNL
F-GFZI	Zodiac MGZ 2-2-S Free Balloon	002	
F-GFZJ	SOCATA TB-20 Trinidad	626	(F-GFPO)
			N800X
F-GFZK	Piper PA-28-180 Cherokee Archer	28-7505247	6V-AFS
			OO-KIS
			OO-HAP
			N3919X
F-GFZL	Cessna 172F	53259	TN-AAS
			(F-GELD)
			TN-AAS
			F-OCGC
			(N5637R)
F-GFZN	Robinson R-22 Beta	1004	
F-GFZO	Morane-Saulnier MS.733 Alcyon	140	F-BNEE
			Fr.Mil
F-GFZP	Balloon Works Firefly 7 HAFB	F7-479	
F-GFZQ	SE.313B Alouette II	1813	F-MJBO
F-WFZR(2)	Chaize CS-500F12 HAFB	EX-001	
F-GFZS	Thunder AX7-77 HAFB	718	
F-GFZT	Bell 47G-4A	7726	N78HB
F-GFZU	Bell 47G-4A	7596	N6233N
F-GFZV	Piper PA-28-181 Archer II	2890117	
F-GFZX	Piper PA-28R-201T Turbo Cherokee Arrow III		
		28R-7703319	N43938
			(N748SB)
			N43938
F-GFZY	Cessna 172N	72390	N4902D
F-GGAA	Schweizer 269C	S-1308	
F-GGAC	Piper PA-28-181 Archer II	2890067	
F-GGAD	Zlin Z.526F Trenér Master	1177	(F-GGAA)
			F-BTGE
			F-WTGE
F-GGAE	Piper PA-28-161 Cadet	2841062	
F-GGAG	Bell 47G-2	665-10	CF-HFX
F-GGAH	Hughes 269C	61-0122	N9654F
F-GGAJ	Cessna T.210N Turbo Centurion II	63891	N6445C
F-GGAL	Cessna 650 Citation III	0117	N1321N
F-GGAM	Beech 65-90 King Air	LJ-32	F-BTOK
			PH-FSS
			HB-GCF
F-GGAN	Bell 47G-2	1965	N200J
F-GGAO	Aérospatiale AS.350B Ecureuil	2208	
F-GGAP	Chaize 3000 Ovrni Gas Balloon	001	F-WGAP
F-GGAR(2)	Aérospatiale AS.350B Ecureuil	1841	F-WYMC
			HB-XPG
F-GGAU	Reims/Cessna F.172N	1867	D-EKAU
F-GGAX	Agusta-Bell 206B Jet Ranger II	8020	D-HOOL
			SE-HPD
F-GGAY	Piper PA-28-181 Cherokee Archer II	28-7790461	N3493Q
F-GGAZ	Thunder AX7-77 HAFB	359	G-BJAZ
F-GGBA	Piper PA-28RT-201T Turbo Arrow IV	28R-8431002	N4324P
			N9547N
F-GGBB	Mudry CAP.10B	130	Fr.AF
F-GGBD	Piper PA-32R-301T Saratoga SP	32R-8129110	N8442U
F-GGBG	SE.313B Alouette II	1399	ALAT
F-GGBI	Thunder AX7-77 HAFB	1481	
F-GGBK	Rockwell S.2R Thrush Commander	1426R	
F-GGBM	Cameron N-77 HAFB	2067	
F-GGBN	Hughes 269C	20-0894	D-HKAG
F-GGBO	Holste MH.1521C-1 Broussard	262	F-WGBO
			Fr.AF
F-GGBQ	Piper PA-28-140 Cherokee	28-7625059	N921C
			N4580X
F-GGBR	SOCATA Rallye 150SV Garnement	3365	F-OGLV
F-GGBU	Cessna 172P	74044	N5284K
F-GGBX	SE.3130 Alouette II	1373	ALAT
F-GGBY	SE.313B Alouette II	1332	ALAT
F-GGBZ(2)	Cessna 172N	68486	N733RH
F-GGCB	Piper PA-28R-201 Arrow III	28R-7803290	N31650
F-GGCD	Chaize CS-2200F12 HAFB	81	
F-GGCE	Piper PA-28RT-201T Turbo Arrow IV	28R-8031111	N45KC
			N9566N
F-GGCF	Piper PA-28RT-201T Turbo Arrow IV	28R-7931310	N8094Q
F-GGCG	SE.313B Alouette II	1172	ALAT
F-GGCH	Piper PA-31T Cheyenne	31T-8120056	N51TW
F-GGCI	SE.313B Alouette II	1050	ALAT
F-GGCM	Cameron A-250 HAFB	1542	(F-GFGI)
			G-BNUD
F-GGCN	Holste MH.1521C1 Broussard	6	Fr.Mil
F-GGCO	SE.313B Alouette II	1132	ALAT
			Fr.AF
F-GGCP	Dassault Falcon 50	9	N100WJ
			VR-CBR
			(HB- IED)
			XA-LOH
			I- SAFP
			F-WZHD
F-GGCQ	SE.313B Alouette II	1348	ALAT
F-GGCR	Raven Europe FS-57A HAFB	E-092	
F-GGCS	Cessna 152	83555	N4622B
F-GGCT	Cessna 152	80130	N757ZH
F-GGCV	Cessna 172RG Cutlass	1111	N9997B
F-GGCX	Cessna 172RG Cutlass	1134	N9360D
F-GGCZ	Cessna 172RG Cutlass	0708	N6447V
F-GGDA	Piper PA-38-112 Tomahawk	38-82A0008	HB-PGK
F-GGDB	Piper PA-28RT-201 Arrow IV	28R-7918160	N2824R
F-GGDC	Piper PA-28-161 Cadet	2841063	
F-GGDE	Cessna A.185F Skywagon	04075	N60925
F-GGDF	Thunder AX7-65 HAFB	818	
F-GGDG	SE.313B Alouette II	1104	ALAT
			Fr.AF
F-GGDH	SE.313B Alouette II	1103	ALAT
F-GGDI	Hughes 369D	67-0149D	N444HM
			ZK-HJQ
F-GGDK	Thunder AX7-77 HAFB	1342	
F-GGDL	Piper PA-28-181 Archer II	28-8190242	N83912
F-GGDN	Thunder AX7-77 HAFB	1504	
F-GGDO	Thunder AX7-77Z HAFB	1515	
F-GGDQ	Robinson R-22 Beta	1042	
F-GGDR	Piper PA-28-181 Archer II	2890125	
F-GGDS	Chaize CS2000F12 HAFB	095	
F-GGDT	Hughes 369D	67-0154D	N81418
			TG-REY
			YS-1014P
F-GGDU	Bell 47G-2	1540	N5185B
F-GGDX	Cessna A.185F Skywagon	03538	N767RC
			N2901Q
F-GGDY	Hughes 269C	41-1043	D-HIMIG
F-GGEA	Airbus A.320-111	010	F-WWDL
F-GGEB	Airbus A.320-111	012	F-WWDM
F-GGEC	Airbus A.320-111	013	F-WWDN
F-GGEE	Airbus A.320-111	016	F-WWDQ
F-GGEF(2)	Airbus A.320-111	004	F-WWDC
F-GGEG(2)	Airbus A.320-111	003	F-WWDB
F-GGFC	Robinson R-22 Beta	0822	
F-GGFF	SNCAN Stampe SV.4C	610	F-BDFF
F-GGFG	Robinson R-22 Beta	1055	N8045U
F-GGFH	Bellanca 8KCAB Decathlon	27-72	C-GAYI
F-GGFK(2)	Colt Montgolfier SS HAFB	1281	G-BPHV
F-GGFL	Robinson R-22 Beta	1045	
F-GGFM	Chaize CS.2200F12 HAFB	093	

Regn.	Type	C/n	Prev.Id.
F-GGFN	Bell 47G	1708	OO-MMT
			PH-AAH
			D-HABO
F-GGFR	Cessna 310R	2103	(F-GFGD)
			N6830Q
F-GGFS	Piper PA-28-161 Cadet	2841068	
F-GGFT	Piper PA-28-161 Cadet	2841075	
F-GGFU	Piper PA-28-161 Cadet	2841076	
F-GGFV	Piper PA-28-161 Cadet	2841077	
F-GGFX	Piper PA-28-161 Cadet	2841078	
F-GGFY	Piper PA-28-161 Cadet	2841079	
F-GGFZ	Robinson R-22 Beta	0838	3A-MTU
F-GGGA	Cessna F.550 Citation	0586	N1301N
F-WGGC	Fouga CM-170 Magister	459	Fr.AF
F-WGGD	Holste MH.1521M Broussard	290	Fr.AF
F-WGGE	Mudry CAP.20	4	Fr.AF: F-TFVX
			F-BTAF
F-GGGG	Cessna T.310R	1805	N310AF
			N2642B
F-GGGI	Colt 21A HAFB	1554	
F-GGGJ	Colt 90A HAFB	1553	
F-WGGK	Holste MH.1521M Broussard	127	ALAT
F-GGGL	Mooney M.20J Model 205	24-3027	
F-GGGN	Cessna T.210N Turbo Centurion II	64426	N6537Y
F-GGGO	Colt 90A HAFB	1565	
F-GGGP	Beech A36 Bonanza	E-2200	N216JP
			N7212L
F-WGGQ	Holste MH.1521M Broussard	143	ALAT
F-GGGR	Boeing 727-2H3	20822	PH-AHD
			N191CB
			TS-JHP
			(F-ODSX)
F-GGGS	Robin HR.100/250TR	553	6V-AEK
			F-ODFX
F-GGGT	Cessna F550 Citation II	0611	
F-GGGZ	Piper PA-38-112 Tomahawk	38-81A0022	HB-PFT
F-GGHA	Robin ATL	106	
F-GGHB	Robin ATL	108	
F-GGHD	Robin ATL	110	
F-GGHE	Robin ATL	81	F-WZZX
			(PH-ATL)
F-GGHF	Robin ATL	116	
F-GGHG	Robin ATL	117	
F-GGHH	Robin ATL	118	
F-GGHI	Robin DR.400/180R Remorqueur	1833	
F-GGHJ	Robin DR.400/140B Major 80	1832	
F-GGHK	Robin DR.400/140B Major 80	1834	
F-GGHL	Robin DR.400/180 Régent	1835	
F-GGHM	Robin ATL	119	
F-GGHO	Robin R.3000/140	133	
F-GGHP	Robin ATL	120	
F-GGHQ	Robin ATL L	121	F-WGHQ
F-GGHR	Robin DR.400/180 Régent	1844	
F-GGHS	Robin ATL	122	
F-GGHT	Robin DR.400/180 Régent	1846	
F-GGHU	Robin DR.400/180 Régent	1848	
F-GGHV	Robin DR.400/120 Petit Prince	1849	
F-GGHX	Robin DR.400/120 Petit Prince	1850	
F-GGHY	Robin DR.400/160 Chevalier	1853	
F-GGHZ	Robin ATL	123	
F-GGIA	SOCATA TB-20 Trinidad	776	
F-GGIB	SOCATA TB-20 Trinidad	777	
F-GGIC	SOCATA TB-20 Trinidad	778	
F-GGID	SOCATA TB-20 Trinidad	790	
F-GGIE	SOCATA TB-20 Trinidad	854	
F-GGIF	SOCATA TB-20 Trinidad	855	
F-GGIG	SOCATA TB-20 Trinidad	859	
F-GGIH	SOCATA TB-20 Trinidad	990	
F-GGII	SOCATA TB-20 Trinidad	991	
F-GGIJ	SOCATA TB-20 Trinidad	996	
F-GGIK	SOCATA TB-10 Tobago	785	
F-GGIO	SOCATA TB-20 Trinidad	791	
F-GGIP	SOCATA TB-20 Trinidad	794	
F-GGIR	SOCATA TB-9 Tampico	809	
F-GGIS	SOCATA TB-9 Tampico	881	
F-GGIT	SOCATA TB-21 Trinidad TC	865	
F-GGIU	SOCATA TB-9 Tampico	885	
F-GGIV	SOCATA TB-9 Tampico	890	
F-GGIX	SOCATA TB-20 Trinidad	898	
F-GGIY	SOCATA TB-10 Tobago	906	
F-GGIZ	SOCATA TB-9 Tampico	908	
F-GGJB	Robin DR.400/120 Petit Prince	1788	
F-GGJC	Robin DR.400/120 Petit Prince	1791	
F-GGJD	Robin DR.400/180 Régent	1789	
F-GGJE	Robin DR.400/180R Remorqueur	1792	
F-GGJF	Robin DR.400/180 Régent	1796	
F-GGJG	Robin DR.400/120 Petit Prince	1799	
F-GGJH	Robin DR.400/160 Chevalier	1795	
F-GGJI	Robin DR.400/120 Petit Prince	1801	
F-GGJJ	Robin DR.400/180 Régent	1804	
F-GGJK	Robin DR.400/140B Major 80	1805	
F-GGJL	Robin DR.400/180 Régent	1807	
F-GGJM	Robin R.3000/140	131	
F-GGJO	Robin DR.400/120 Petit Prince	1814	
F-GGJP	Robin DR.400/180 Régent	1811	
F-GGJQ	Robin DR.400/120 Petit Prince	1813	
F-GGJR	Robin DR.400/120 Petit Prince	1815	
F-GGJS	Robin DR.400/120 Petit Prince	1816	
F-GGJT	Robin DR.400/180 Régent	1820	
F-GGJU	Robin DR.400/120 Petit Prince	1822	
F-GGJV	Robin DR.400/180 Régent	1840	
F-GGJX	Robin DR.400/120 Petit Prince	1823	
F-GGJY	Robin DR.400/160 Chevalier	1824	
F-GGKB	Piper J-3C-65 Cub	14986	N42690
			NC42690
F-GGKC(2)	Piper J-3C-65 Cub	5037	N30655
			NC30655
F-GGKH	Holste MH.1521C Broussard	32	F-WGKH
			Fr.AF
F-GGKI	Holste MH.1521M Broussard	53	F-WGKI
			Fr.AF
F-GGKK	Holste MH.1521C-1 Broussard	211M	F-WGKK
			Fr.AF
F-GGKL	Holste MH.1521C-1 Broussard	255	F-WGKL
			Fr.AF
F-WGKN	Holste MH.1521M Broussard	261	Fr.AF
F-GGKO	Holste MH.1521M Broussard	284	F-WGKO
			Fr.AF
F-GGKR	Holste MH.1521M Broussard	316	F-WGKR
			Fr.AF
F-GGKS	Holste MH.1521M Broussard	23	F-WGKS
			Fr.AF
F-GGKU	Aérospatiale SA.342 Gazelle	1186	TT-OAG
			F-WTNC
F-GGKV	Aérospatiale SA.342 Gazelle	1378	TT-OAF
F-GGKX	Aérospatiale SA.330B Puma	1021	TT-...
			ALAT
F-GGKY	Aérospatiale SA.330 Puma	1200	TT-...
			ALAT
F-GGKZ	Robinson R-22 Beta	1146	
F-GGLA	Beech 200 Super King Air	BB-744	N152WC
			N3702M
F-GGLB	Bell 47G-2	1056	N10194
F-GGLH	Robinson R-22 Beta	1065	N8046U
F-GGLI	Cessna 152	81685	N66950
F-GGLK	Aeritalia/SNIAS ATR-42-300	022	OH-LTB
			F-WWEI
F-GGLL	Piper PA-28-161 Warrior II	28-8116012	N8255A
F-GGLM	Thunder AX7-77Z HAFB	1450	
F-GGLN	Beech 200 Super King Air	BB-439	N500JA
			C-FMCF
			CF-MCF
			N110MJ
			N110JJ
F-GGLO	Piper PA-18-150 Super Cub	18-5329	TR-LBY
			F-BLOV
			ALAT
F-GGLP	Beech A36 Bonanza	E-1595	N19WH
			N66775
F-GGLR	Aeritalia/SNIAS ATR-42-300	043	

Regn.	Type	C/n	Prev.Id.
F-GGLS	Morane-Saulnier MS.885 Super Rallye	125	D-EMTE
F-GGLU	Morane-Saulnier MS.880B Rallye Club	68	D-EDRC
			F-BKDU
F-GGLV	Beech A100 King Air	B-150	N51BL
			N54MG
			N54KA
F-GGLX	Piper PA-38-112 Tomahawk	38-82A0109	TJ-AGO
			F-OCNB
F-GGLY	Cameron N-90 HAFB	2124	
F-GGLZ(2)	Holste MH.1521M Broussard	102	ALAT
F-GGMA	McDonnell-Douglas DC-9-83 (MD-83)	49399	EI-BTL
			N6200N
F-GGMB	McDonnell-Douglas DC-9-83 (MD-83)	49617	
F-GGMD	McDonnell-Douglas DC-9-83 (MD-83)	49618	
F-GGME	McDonnell-Douglas DC-9-83 (MD-83)	49855	
F-GGMF	McDonnell-Douglas DC-9-83 (MD-83)	53463	
F-WGMG	RJ-03A Roitelet Helicopter	unkn	
F-GGMH	Piper PA-28-181 Archer II	2890166	
F-GGMJ	Mooney M.20J Model 205	24-3045	N205DD
F-GGMK	Piper PA-18-150 Cub	1809051	N9522N
F-WGMO(2)	AS.300	008	
F-GGMP	Zodiac MGZ 3-0-S Free Balloon	012	
F-WGMQ	Aérospatiale AS.350Z Ecureuil	1013	F-WYMZ
			N134BH
			N90001
F-GGMS	Beech 200 Super King Air	BB-80	N444TW
			N200AL
			N78LC
			(N104AG)
			N78LC
			N73LC
			N925B
F-GGMT	Aerotek Pitts S.2A	2272	
F-GGMU	Piper PA-28RT-201T Turbo Arrow IV	28R-8031014	N8114P
F-GGMV	Beech 200 Super King Air	BB-616	SE-IUN
			N123AF
			N6693F
F-GGMY	Piper PA-28-181 Archer II	28-7990375	6V-AEP
			N2235X
F-GGNA	SOCATA TB-20 Trinidad	807	
F-GGNB	SOCATA TB-20 Trinidad	808	
F-GGNC	SOCATA TB-20 Trinidad	816	
F-GGND	SOCATA TB-20 Trinidad	817	
F-GGNE	SOCATA TB-20 Trinidad	818	
F-GGNF	SOCATA TB-20 Trinidad	819	
F-GGNG	SOCATA TB-10 Tobago	945	
F-GGNH	SOCATA TB-10 Tobago	946	
F-GGNI	SOCATA TB-10 Tobago	947	
F-GGNJ	SOCATA TB-10 Tobago	1172	
F-GGNK	SOCATA TB-10 Tobago	1173	
F-GGNL	SOCATA TB-10 Tobago	1174	
F-GGNM	SOCATA TB-10 Tobago	1175	
F-GGNN	SOCATA TB-10 Tobago	1176	
F-GGNO	SOCATA TB-20 Trinidad	1213	
F-GGNP	SOCATA TB-20 Trinidad	1264	
F-GGNQ	SOCATA TB-20 Trinidad	1265	
F-GGNR	SOCATA TB-20 Trinidad	1266	
F-GGNS	SOCATA TB-20 Trinidad	1267	
F-GGNT	SOCATA TB-20 Trinidad	1284	
F-GGNU	SOCATA TB-20 Trinidad	1285	
F-GGNV	SOCATA TB-20 Trinidad	1286	
F-GGNX	SOCATA TB-20 Trinidad	1287	
F-GGNY	SOCATA TB-20 Trinidad	1301	
F-GGNZ	SOCATA TB-20 Trinidad	1302	
F-GGOB	Grob G.115A	8027	F-WGOB
			D-EGVV
F-GGOC	Grob G.115A	8045	F-WGOC
			D-EGVV
F-GGOD	Grob G.115A	8036	F-WGOD
			D-EGVV
F-GGOH	Grob G.115A	8076	D-EGVV
F-GGOJ	Grob G.115A	8064	D-EIAW
F-GGOK	Grob G.115A	8096	
F-GGOL	Grob G.115A	8103	
F-GGON	Grob G.115A	8063	D-EIAU

Regn.	Type	C/n	Prev.Id.
F-GGOO	Grob G.115A	8018	D-EANP
F-GGOP	Grob G.115A	8106	
F-GGOQ	Grob G.115A	8107	
F-GGPH	Aérospatiale SA.341G Gazelle	1014	D-HMTC
F-GGPI	Agusta-Bell 206B Jet Ranger II	8169	G-BPHF
			SE-HGS
			D-HARU
F-GGPL(2)	Mooney M.20J Model 201	24-1632	
F-GGPO	Piper PA-28-161 Cadet	2841103	
F-GGPQ	SOCATA TB-20 Trinidad	972	
F-GGPR	Beech 200 Super King Air	BB-681	LN-AXA
			(LN-AAX)
			N200NF
			D-ILBO
			N6751T
F-GGPS	Aerotek Pitts S-2B	5015	N66LF
			N53206
F-WGPU(2)	Fouga CM.170R Magister	014	Fr.AF
F-GGPX	Cameron Paint-Tin 105SS HAFB	2239	
F-GGPY	Aérospatiale AS.350B Ecureuil	2361	
F-GGPZ	Robin DR.400/180 Régent	1134	6V-AFM
			F-GABP
F-GGQA	Robin DR.400/120 Petit Prince	1851	
F-GGQB	Robin DR.400/140B Major 80	1852	
F-GGQD	Robin DR.400/120 Petit Prince	1878	
F-GGQE	Robin DR.400/120 Petit Prince	1877	
F-GGQF	Robin DR.400/160 Chevalier	1856	
F-GGQG	Robin ATL	124	
F-GGQH	Robin R.3000/140	134	
F-GGQI	Robin ATL	125	
F-GGQJ	Robin ATL	126	
F-GGQK	Robin DR.400/180 Régent	1860	
F-GGQL	Robin DR.400/120 Petit Prince	1859	
F-GGQM	Robin DR.400/120 Petit Prince	1863	
F-GGQN	Robin DR.400/180 Régent	1867	
F-GGQO	Robin DR.400/100 Cadet	1864	
F-GGQP	Robin DR.400/100	1865	
F-GGQQ	Robin DR.400/180R Remorqueur	1868	
F-GGQR	Robin DR.400/120 Petit Prince	1866	
F-GGQS	Robin ATL	127	
F-GGQU	Robin DR.400/100 Cadet	1871	
F-GGQX	Robin DR.400/120 Petit Prince	1879	
F-GGQY	Robin DR.400/180 Régent	1873	
F-GGQZ	Robin DR.400/140B Major 80	1880	
F-GGRA	Thunder AX9-140 HAFB	427	G-CEZY
F-GGRB	Robinson R-22 Beta	0819	
F-GGRC	Chaize CS.2200F12 HAFB	092	
F-GGRD	Cessna 340A	0944	N2744Z
F-GGRE	Thunder AX-10-160Z HAFB	460	G-BKHH
F-GGRF	Cameron A-120 HAFB	2242	
F-GGRI	Chaize CS.3000F16 HAFB	097	
F-GGRK	Cessna 310R	0141	(F-GGRF)
			F-ODRK
			F-BXAK
			N5021J
F-GGRL	Mooney M.20J Model 201	24-1622	
F-GGRM	Beech F33A Bonanza	CE-993	N683IG
F-GGRN	Piper PA-28R-201 Arrow III	28R-7837283	N36544
F-GGRQ	UltraMagic H-77 HAFB	77/47	
F-GGRR	Schweizer 269C	S-1306	(F-GGSR)
F-GGRS	Aérospatiale AS.355F2 Ecureuil 2	5439	
F-GGRT	Chaize CS.3000F16 HAFB	086	
F-GGRU	Cameron N-65 HAFB	2287	
F-GGRV	Piper PA-31T Cheyenne II	31T-7720036	N41RC
			N1RA
			YV-123CP
			N9187Z
F-GGRX	Piper PA-28R-201 Arrow	2837035	
F-GGRY	Piper PA-28-161 Cadet	2841104	
F-GGSD	Cameron O-77 HAFB	1410	
F-GGSE	Cameron V-77 HAFB	1421	
F-GGSF	Cameron O-84 HAFB	1428	
F-GGSG	Cameron O-77 HAFB	1429	
F-GGSH	Schweizer 269C	S-1271	D-HDAM
F-GGSJ	Chaize CS.3000F16 HAFB	077	

Regn.	Type	C/n	Prev.Id.
F-GGSK	Piper PA-23-250 Aztec F	27-7854125	TJ-AFR
			N63996
F-GGSL	Robin DR.400/140B Major 80	1861	
F-GGSM	Aerotek Pitts S-2A	2151	N31502
F-GGSN	Robin DR.400/100 Cadet	1862	
F-GGSO	Cameron A-140 HAFB	2270	
F-GGSP	SOCATA TB-10 Tobago	271	D-EEVU
F-GGSQ	Robinson R-22 Beta	1346	
F-GGSR(2)	Hughes 269C	28-0667	D-HMAR
			D-HOYH
F-GGST	Cessna P210N Pressurized Centurion II	00319	G-BGVX
			(N4788K)
F-GGSU	Bell 47G	673	F-BMHY
			Fr.Mil
F-GGSY	Cessna 150M	78308	N9359U
F-GGTB	Aerotek Pitts S-2A	2160	N31429
F-GGTD	Embraer EMB.120 Brasilia	120-129	PT-SNV
F-WGTF/G/H	Re-useable test registrations for Falcon 20/TPE 731		
	modifications by Europe Falcon Service		
F-GGTJ	Aérospatiale SA.341G Gazelle	1473	C-GVWC
			F-WXFX
F-GGTK	Piper PA-28R-201 Cherokee Arrow III	28R-7737162	N47453
F-GGTL	Piper PA-46-310P Malibu	46-8508077	N6915C
F-WGTM(2)	Aérospatiale AS.355F Ecureuil 2	5264	G-BOSK
			D-HERP
F-GGTN	Reims/Cessna FTB.337G Skymaster	0003	FAP3702
			CS-AAW
F-GGTO	Reims/Cessna FTB.337G Skymaster	0004	FAP3703
			CS-AKK
F-GGTQ(2)	Aérospatiale AS.350D Ecureuil	1147	N35978
F-GGTR	Aerotek Pitts S-2A	2171	N31439
F-GGTS	Cameron O-77 HAFB	1460	
F-GGTU	Agusta-Bell 47G-4A	2533	I- SKAI
F-WGTX	Heli Atlas	01	
F-WGTY	Heli Atlas	02	
F-WGTZ	Heli Atlas	unkn	
F-GGUY	Cameron Concept 80 HAFB	3424	
F-GGVA	Cameron O-77 HAFB	1659	
F-GGVB	Dassault Falcon 50	11	N5739
			N203BT
			N501NC
			N50FH
			F-WZHE
F-GGVC	Cessna U.206F Stationair	02674	N33214
F-GGVD	Colt 21A HAFB	1609	
F-GGVG	Fairchild-Swearingen SA.226TB Merlin IIIB	T-293	D-IBBB(2)
			N5469M
F-GGVI	SNCAN/Stampe SV.4C	429	F-BCVI
F-GGVJ	Schweizer 269C	S-1448	D-HGUS
F-GGVK	Schweizer 269C	S-1449	D-HITA
F-GGVL	Piper PA-28-161 Cadet	2841105	
F-GGVM	UltraMagic HAFB	unkn	
F-GGVN	UltraMagic HAFB	unkn	
F-GGVO	UltraMagic HAFB	unkn	
F-GGVP	Boeing 737-2K2C	20943	VT-EKC
			PH-TVD
			G-BKBT
			PH-TVD
			G-BKBT
			PH-TVD
F-GGVQ	Boeing 737-2K2C	20944	VT-EKD
			PH-TVE
F-GGVS	Cameron N-90 HAFB	2312	
F-GGVT	Cameron N-105 HAFB	2303	
F-GGVU	Cameron N-90 HAFB	2318	
F-GGVZ	Piper PA-28-181 Archer II	28-8190289	N9195Y
			HR-AIR
			N8421H
F-GGXA	Robin DR.400/120 Petit Prince	1897	
F-GGXB	Robin ATL	128	
F-GGXC	Robin DR.400/120 Petit Prince	1888	
F-GGXD	Robin DR.400/120 Petit Prince	1882	
F-GGXE	Robin DR.400/180R Remorqueur	1883	
F-GGXF	Robin ATL	129	
F-GGXG	Robin DR.400/180 Régent	1891	
F-GGXI	Robin DR.400/120 Petit Prince	1895	
F-GGXJ	Robin DR.400/140B Major 80	1896	
F-GGXK	Robin DR.400/120 Petit Prince	1881	
F-GGXM	Robin DR.400/120 Petit Prince	1899	
F-GGXO	Robin DR.400/120 Petit Prince	1905	
F-GGXP	Robin DR.400/180 Régent	1907	
F-GGXQ	Robin DR.400/140B Major 80	1928	
F-GGXS	Robin DR.400/140B Major 80	1913	
F-WGXT	Robin DR.400/185V6	2287	
F-GGXU	Robin DR.400/100 Cadet	1909	
F-GGXX	Robin ATL L	131	
F-GGXY	Robin DR.400/140B Major 80	1923	
F-GGYA	Mudry CAP.10B	232	
F-GGYB	Mudry CAP.10B	233	
F-GGYC	Mudry CAP.10B	235	
F-GGYD	Mudry CAP.10B	234	
F-GGYE	Mudry CAP.10B	237	
F-GGYF	Mudry CAP.10B	238	
F-GGYG	Mudry CAP.10B	239	
F-GGYH	Mudry CAP.230	10	F-WZCJ
F-GGYI	Mudry CAP.10B	240	
F-GGYJ	Mudry CAP.10B	243	
F-GGYK	Mudry CAP.10B	247	
F-GGYL	Mudry CAP.10B	245	
F-GGYQ	Mudry CAP.231	14	F-WGZD
F-GGYS	Mudry CAP.231	16	
F-GGYT	Mudry CAP.10B	252	
F-GGYU	Mudry CAP.10B	253	
F-GGYV	Mudry CAP.10B	254	
F-GGYY	Mudry CAP.231	18	
F-GGYZ	Mudry CAP.231	20	
F-GGZB	Piper PA-28-181 Cherokee Archer II	28-7890105	N47624
F-GGZI	Gardan GY-80-160 Horizon	47	OO-GOD
			F-OCCV
F-GGZJ	Cessna 172N	69362	N737EN
F-GGZL	Thunder AX7-77 HAFB	1829	
F-GGZN	Piper PA-32R-301 Saratoga	32R-8313030	TR-LBD
			N8246A
F-GGZO	Reims/Cessna F.172N	1997	D-EIZO
F-GGZQ	Piper PA-38-112 Tomahawk	38-79A0485	N2571F
F-GGZR	Piper PA-38-112 Tomahawk	38-79A0213	N2518C
F-GGZS	Thunder AX8-105 HAFB	1505	
F-GGZT	Piper PA-38-112 Tomahawk	38-79A0401	N2354F
F-GGZU	UltraMagic S-105 HAFB	105/14	
F-GGZX	Christen A-1 Husky	1159	
F-GGZY	Schweizer 269C	S-1487	
F-GGZZ	Piper PA-32-300 Cherokee Six	32-7440110	N42160
F-GHAC	Mooney M.20J Model 201	24-1637	
F-GHAF(2)	Hughes 269C	61-1060	D-HIRN
			N5016R
F-WHAG	Raven Europe Aeroglobe Balloon	001	
F-GHAH	Bell 47G-2	1335	OO-RDG
			D-HAKI
			CF-GXL
F-GHAI	Bell 47G-2	1502	N2828B
F-GHAJ	Aérospatiale SA.318C Alouette Astazou	1806	Fr.Navy/806
F-GHAK	Aérospatiale AS.350B Ecureuil	1631	LN-OPQ
			SE-HSK
			LN-OPQ
			(D-HKXP)
			OE-KXP
			D-HLTJ
F-GHAM	Robin ATL	103	
F-GHAN	Aérospatiale SA.318C Alouette Astazou	2185	LV-ARI
			ZS-HKX
			CF-CWN
			N8659
F-GHAP	Bell 206B Jet Ranger II	1195	D-HIPY
F-GHAV	Reims/Cessna FR.172J Rocket	0489	N26674
			F-BVBH
F-GHAX	Chaize CS.2200F12 HAFB	089	
F-GHAY	Chaize CS.2200F12 HAFB	087	
F-GHAZ	Chaize CS.2200F12 HAFB	088	
F-GHBA	Piper PA-28-161 Cadet	2841162	
F-GHBB	Beech 65-C90 King Air	LJ-510	D-ILHB

Regn.	Type	C/n	Prev.Id.	Regn.	Type	C/n	Prev.Id.
F-GHBC	Chaize CS.3000F16 HAFB	073	F-WHBC	F-GHEI	McDonnell-Douglas DC-9-83 (MD-83)	49968	
F-GHBD	Beech 65-C90 King Air	LJ-545	D-ILHD	F-GHEK	McDonnell-Douglas DC-9-83 (MD-83)	49823	N83MV
F-GHBF	Robinson R-22M Mariner	1034M					G-BPSC
F-GHBG	Aérospatiale AS.350B Ecureuil	1109	N3602S				N6206F
F-GHBJ	Mooney M.20K Model 252	25-1127		F-GHEL	Mooney M.20J Model 205	24-3028	N205MJ
F-GHBK	Hughes 269C	90-0970	D-HGIN	F-GHEM	Beech 65-C90 King Air	LJ-760	N700JP
			SE-HLF				N707CB
			N1104N				(N9OAJ)
F-GHBL	Beech 76 Duchess	ME-89	N2074G				N707CB
F-GHBN	Cessna 172N	71123	N2026E				N319D
F-GHBO	Cameron N-77 HAFB	1643		F-GHEN	Cessna U.206F Stationair	03587	G-BOSC
F-GHBP	Cameron D-96 Hot Air Airship	536	SE-ZAD				5N-ASU
			G-BHBJ				N7256N
F-GHBQ	Piper PA-28-181 Archer II	28-8290018	N8406B	F-GHEO	Cessna R.182 Skylane RG	00453	N9833C
F-GHBR	Aérospatiale AS.350B Ecureuil	1600	(F-GHCO)	F-GHEQ	Embraer EMB.120RT Brasilia	120-...	PT-S..
			F-GGBR	F-GHES	Cessna T.210K Turbo Centurion	59444	CN-TES
			N58030				N8144G
F-GHBS	Mooney M.20F Executive	670142	D-EBBM(2)	F-GHEV	Cessna 172N	69730	N737WK
			N9565M	F-GHEX	Embraer EMB.120RT Brasilia	120-209	PT-SSD
F-GHBV	Aérospatiale AS.350B Ecureuil	1544	N323LB	F-GHEY	Embraer EMB.120RT Brasilia	120-214	PT-SSI
F-GHBX	Thunder AX7-77 HAFB	1808		F-GHFC	Cessna 172P	74447	N52229
F-GHBY	Piper J-3C-65 Cub	unkn	F-BFBY	F-GHFE	Beech 65-C90 King Air	LJ-544	(F-GHFC)
			"43-17737"				D-ILHC
F-GHCA	Cameron N-77 HAFB	1706		F-GHFG	Holste MH.1521M Broussard	104	Fr.AF
F-GHCC	Aérospatiale SA.315B Lama	2474	N49504	F-GHFI (2)	Aérospatiale SA.315B Lama	2476	D-HLEO
F-GHCE	Bell 206B Jet Ranger II	2092	N16701				F-GHCN
F-GHCG	Mooney M.20J Model 205	24-3075	N205RS				G-BLXJ
F-GHCI	Aérospatiale SA.315B Lama	1819/11	(F-ODSK)				N403AH
			TR-LXB				N47309
			F-GAMF	F-GHFJ	Aérospatiale AS.350B Ecureuil	2127	LN-OTP
			F-ZBAM	F-GHFR	Aérospatiale AS.350B Ecureuil	1374	N5779W
F-GHCK	Aérospatiale SA.360C Dauphin	1025	N213EH	F-GHFZ	SOCATA Rallye 235E Gabier	13013	N235G
	(Ditched 10.10.97)		N3597C				N477JH
			F-WXFA	F-GHGB	Holste MH.1521C1 Broussard	256	Fr.AF
F-GHCL	Reims/Cessna FT.337GP Skymaster	0008/0078	G-BBKJ	F-GHGF	Boeing 767-3Q8ER	24745	
F-GHCM	Cessna T.303 Crusader	00003	N9335T	F-GHGG	Boeing 767-3Q8ER	24746	
F-GHCO	Aérospatiale AS.350B Ecureuil	1467	(F-GHBR)	F-GHGH	Boeing 767-37E	25077	
			LN-OTC	F-GHGI	Boeing 767-328ER	27135	
F-GHCQ	SE.313B Alouette II	1607	XR382	F-GHGJ	Boeing 767-328ER	27136	
F-GHCS(2)	Beech 200 Super King Air	BB-303	N18345	F-GHGM(2)	Rockwell S.2R-600 Thrush Commander	1821R	CS-APO
F-GHCV	Beech 200 Super King Air (Reservation)	unkn					N5621X
F-GHCX	Wassmer Jodel D.120 Paris-Nice	305	F-BNCX	F-GHGN	Cameron N-105 HAFB	2091	
F-GHCY	SE.313B Alouette II (Reservation)	unkn		F-WHGQ	SOCATA TB-20 Trinidad (T-tail)	1227	
F-GHDD	Piper PA-28-161 Cadet	2841262		F-GHGU	Aérospatiale SA.341G Gazelle	1308	C-FWYN
F-GHDE	UltraMagic V-77 HAFB	77/24					N341JT
F-GHDF	UltraMagic S-105 HAFB	105/6					N49503
F-GHDH	Cessna 172P	76254	N93ER	F-GHGV	Chaize CS.3000F16 HAFB	083	
			(N98073)	F-GHGY	Hughes 269C	41-0109	D-HEXI
F-GHDI	UltraMagic M77 Air Balloon	77/38					OO-DLS
F-GHDJ	UltraMagic HAFB (Reservation)	unkn					D-HOYF
F-GHDL	Robinson R-22 Beta	1171					HB-XDU
F-GHDM	Piper PA-28-161 Cadet	2841263		F-GHGZ	Cessna 208 Caravan I	00188	
F-GHDN(2)	Cameron A-180 HAFB	2455	G-BTAO	F-GHHA	Colt 240A HAFB	1924	
F-GHDO	Beech 65-B90 King Air	LJ-206	3X-...	F-GHHB	Robinson R-22B Beta	0783	
			F-BTAK	F-GHHF	Aérospatiale AS.350B Ecureuil	2145	N373RE
			HB-GDG				N6024V
F-GHDQ	Cessna TR.182 Turbo Skylane RG	01331	N2330S	F-GHHJ	Cameron N-90 HAFB	2511	
F-GHDR	Agusta-Bell 206B Jet Ranger III	8693		F-GHHO	McDonnell-Douglas DC-9-83 (MD-83)	49985	
F-GHDT	Dassault Falcon 20C-5	176/458	F-WGTM	F-GHHP	McDonnell-Douglas DC-9-83 (MD-83)	49986	
			I- SNAM	F-GHHQ	Bell 205A-1	30092	C-GVHX
			F-WMKG				N8189J
F-GHDU	Piper PA-28R-201 Cherokee Arrow III	28R-7703233	N38520	F-GHHR	Bell 205A-1	30223	C-GFHN
F-GHDV	Cameron N-77 HAFB	1773					LN-OQP
F-GHDX	Dassault Falcon 10	140	N88WL				C-GIGC
			N70WC	F-GHHT	Robinson R-22 Beta	1815	
			N205FJ	F-GHHU	Zlin Z.526 Trenér Master	1081	F-BRNE
			F-WZGL	F-GHHV	Beech A100 King Air	B-91	N9050V
F-GHDY	Balloon Works Firefly F7-15 HAFB	F7-725		F-GHHX	Thunder AX7-77A HAFB	1954	
F-GHEB	McDonnell-Douglas DC-9-83 (MD-83)	49822	(F-GJAL)	F-GHHZ	Thunder AX7-77Z HAFB	1935	
F-GHEC	McDonnell-Douglas DC-9-83 (MD-83)	49662	G-PATC	F-GHIA	Embraer EMB.120RT Brasilia	120-154	PT-SPT
			N1005W	F-GHIB	Embraer EMB.120RT Brasilia	120-162	PT-SQA
			(N940MC)	F-GHIE	Robinson R-22 Mariner	1307M	
F-GHED	McDonnell-Douglas DC-9-83 (MD-83)	49576	EI-BWE	F-GHIG	SO.1221 Djinn	97/FR147	ALAT
			EC-EFK	F-GHIH	Piper J-3C-65 Cub	20546	N7242H
F-GHEE	Schweizer 269C	S-1307					NC7242H

Regn.	Type	C/n	Prev.Id.		Regn.	Type	C/n	Prev.Id.
F-GHIK	Robinson R-22 Beta	1750			F-GHKV	Beech 58 Baron	TH-1537	N31425
F-GHIL	Aérospatiale SA.318C Alouette Astazou	2323	LV-ARC		F-GHKY	Cessna R182 Skylane RG	00728	N736GF
			ZS-HIH		F-GHKZ	Robin DR.400/140B Major 80	924	F-BVCZ
			N9059H		F-GHLB	Beech 200 Super King Air	BB-349	D-IEXD
			C-GGNU			(Reserved as N349JW, 4.99)		N80GA
			N41171					G-BFEA
F-GHIM	Colt 160A HAFB	1834						G-BR0 N
F-GHIO	Bell 206B Jet Ranger II	2895	YU-HDG					G-BFEA
			N1067F		F-GHLE	Piper PA-28RT-201T Turbo Arrow IV	28R-8431012	N4334K
F-GHIP	Piper L-4B Cub	9357	N1138V					N9561N
			43-496		F-GHLF	Hughes 369E	0361E	
			(42-59306)		F-GHLJ	Chaize CS.2200F12 HAFB	099	
F-WHIQ	Holste MH.1521M Broussard	291	Fr.AF		F-GHLK	Piper PA-28-181 Archer II	28-7990391	N3065Y
F-GHIS	Hughes 269C	74-0325	N58161		F-GHLL	Balloon Works Firefly 7 HAFB	F7-603	N9041B
F-GHIU	Beech 58 Baron	TH-986	N2046E		F-GHLP	Beech A36 Bonanza	E-2283	N7230Z
F-GHIV	Beech 65-F90 King Air	LA-22	N4269Y		F-GHLQ	Piper J-3C-65 Cub	15243	N42908
			N444EM					NC42908
			N4269Y		F-GHLR	Bell 206B Jet Ranger II	2718	N2761B
			D-ICET		F-GHLU	Cessna 152	80860	N25923
F-GHIX	Piper PA-28-181 Archer II	28-8390042	N42940		F-GHLX(2)	Bell 47G-2	1388	C-FVTS
F-GHIY	Piper PA-28-181 Archer II	28-8490067	N131AV					CF-VTS
			N9592N					RCAF1388
			N43570					RCN . . . .
F-GHIZ	Hughes 269C	49-0765	D-HOOM		F-GHLY	Piper PA-28-161 Warrior II	2816055	
			N58340		F-GHLZ	Piper PA-38-112 Tomahawk	38-78A0642	N2327A
F-GHJB	Agusta-Bell 47G-2	210	EC-DGK		F-GHMA	Cessna 210L Centurion	60907	N5319V
			F-BTSR		F-GHMB	Mooney M.20K Model 231	25-0740	N5634Q
			ALAT		F-GHMC	Aérospatiale AS.355F Ecureuil 2	5108	(F-GHCH)
			Fr.AF					N57902
F-GHJC	Chaize CS.2200F12 HAFB	78			F-GHMG	Mooney M.20K Model 231	25-0515	N9758S
F-GHJG	Piper PA-28-181 Archer II	28-7990073	N22244		F-GHMH	Robinson R-22 Beta	1144	
F-GHJI	Piper PA-28-181 Archer II	28-7990023	N39958		F-GHMM	Beech 200 Super King Air (Reservation)	unkn	
F-GHJJ	Chaize CS.2200F12 HAFB	091			F-GHMQ	Aérospatiale AS.350B2 Ecureuil	2525	
F-GHJK	Reims/Cessna F.150L	0819	HB-CWH		F-GHMR	Thunder AX8-90A3 HAFB	1428	
F-GHJL	Dassault Falcon 10	58	N500FF		F-GHMS	Cessna T.210L Turbo Centurion	60012	N210ES
			N458A					N59003
			N58AS		F-GHMT	Cameron Bouchon 116 HAFB	2007	
			N76FJ		F-GHMU	SE.210 Caravelle 10B3	249	HB-IKD
			N143FJ					F-GCJT
			F-WJMM					TL-ABB
F-GHJM	Cessna 207A Skywagon	00635	F-OGJM					OY-STE
			(N75576)					F-WJAK
F-GHJN	Hughes 369D	1035D	SE-HVV		F-GHMV	Cameron O-65 HAFB	2112	
			ZK-HYT		F-GHMX(3)	Cameron A-230 HAFB (Reservation)	unkn	
			C-GPRU		F-GHNA	Piper PA-30-160 Twin Comanche C	30-1873	N8720Y
			N5079R		F-GHNB	Cameron V-90 HAFB	2502	
F-GHJO	Cessna 152	84330	C-GGEB		F-GHND	Colt 240A HAFB	665	G-BLXB
			(N5517L)		F-GHNE	Colt 240A HAFB	1230	G-BOOT
F-GHJQ	Colt 105A HAFB	1937			F-GHNF	Colt 240A HAFB	1229	G-BOOS
F-GHJT	Piper PA-28-181 Archer II	28-8090087	N8086L		F-GHNG	Thunder AX10-180 HAFB	626	G-BLUG
F-GHJU	Cessna 402C	0274	N6652C		F-GHNH	Thunder AX10-180 HAFB	625	G-BLUF
			YV-472C		F-GHNI	Thunder AX10-180 HAFB	627	G-BLUH
			YV-278CP		F-GHNJ	Thunder AX10-180 HAFB	940	G-BNHX
			N2741A		F-GHNK	Thunder AX10-180 HAFB	939	G-BNHW
F-GHJV	Piper PA-31T Cheyenne II	31T-7720067	N900SF		F-GHNL	Thunder AX10-180 HAFB	937	G-BNHU
			N999WS		F-GHNM	Thunder AX10-180 HAFB	938	G-BNHV
			N82186		F-GHNN	Thunder AX10-160 HAFB	565	G-BLKH
F-GHJY	Robinson R-22 Beta	1835	N23086		F-GHNO	Thunder AX10-160 HAFB	563	G-BLKF
F-GHJZ	Piper PA-28RT-201 Arrow III	28R-8118067	N8380Y		F-GHNP	Thunder AX10-160 HAFB	564	G-BLKG
F-GHKB	Piper PA-28-161 Cadet	2841253			F-GHNQ	Thunder AX10-160 HAFB	554	G-BLHA
F-GHKD	Cessna 152	80899	N25989		F-GHNR	Cameron O-105 HAFB	576	G-BMDG
F-GHKE	Cessna 152	80176	N24254					F-GCKH
F-GHKF	Schweizer 269C	S-1403	D-HDAN(3)		F-GHNS	Cameron O-84 HAFB	404	G-BNUK
F-GHKG	Beech V35B Bonanza	D-9488	D-EAPM					F-GCKY
			CS-AOK					N149CB
			N2881W		F-GHNX	Chaize CS.2200F12 HAFB	109	
F-GHKH	Chaize CS.2200F12 HAFB	107			F-GHNY	Cessna 152	84287	N5292L
F-GHKI	Piper PA-28-161 Warrior II	28-8516009	N4379S		F-GHNZ	Cessna 152	79559	N714ZJ
F-GHKJ	Piper PA-28-161 Warrior II	28-8216061	N8461Z		F-GHOC	Beech 200 Super King Air	BB-406	G-OEMS
F-WHKS	Bell 222A	47040	F-WQAA					N222PA
			F-WKHS		F-GHOD	Robinson R-22 Beta	1157	
			F-WYMA		F-GHOE	Aérospatiale AS.350B Ecureuil	1019	CS-HBJ
			SE-HSF					D-HMFG
			N1085G					G-BNAS
F-GHKU	Mudry CAP.10B	211	F-ZVMU					C-GMLT

Regn.	Type	C/n	Prev.Id.
F-GHOF	Raven Europe FS-57A HAFB	E-131	
F-GHOG	Cessna 172N	70189	N738RY
F-GHOH	Schweizer 269C	S-1272	D-HDAS
F-GHOI	McDonnell-Douglas DC-10-30	46870	OY-KDA
F-GHOK	Robinson R-22 Beta	1591	
F-GHOL	Boeing 737-53C	24825	
F-GHOM	SE.3130 Alouette II	1510	ALAT
F-GHON	AIAA Stampe SV.4C	1147	F-BAON
F-GHOO	Schweizer 269C	S-1302	
F-GHOP	Cessna 172RG Cutlass	0338	3A-MOP
			F-GCGO
			N4606V
F-GHOR	Cameron O-65 HAFB	1732	
F-GHOT	Robinson R-22 Beta	0707	N26203
F-GHOU	Cessna 150G	64617	N3217X
F-GHOV	SNCAN Stampe SV.4C	341	F-BCOV
F-GHOY	Nord 1101 Noralpha	53	F-BLQQ
			Fr.AF
F-GHOZ	Cameron O-160 HAFB	1308	G-BMOZ
F-GHPA	Dassault Falcon 20	170/455	I-EKET
			F-WPUV
F-GHPB	Dassault Falcon 10	215	
F-GHPD	SE.3130 Alouette II	1319	ALAT
F-GHPE	Cessna 150L	72136	N6636G
F-GHPG	Cessna R.172K Hawk XP	2300	TL-BPG
			TR-LXC
			N1598C
			N5492V
F-GHPH	Aérospatiale AS.350B2 Ecureuil	2365	
F-GHPI	Aeritalia/SNIAS ATR-42-300	214	F-WWEB
F-GHPJ	Robin DR.400/120 Petit Prince	1874	
F-GHPK	Aeritalia/SNIAS ATR-42-300	218	F-WWEC
F-GHPM	Mooney M.20J Model 201	24-1640	
F-GHPN	Piper PA-28-161 Cadet	2841252	
F-GHPP	Piper PA-32R-301 Saratoga	3213022	
F-GHPQ	Piper PA-28-161 Warrior II	28-7916492	N2867M
F-GHPS	Aeritalia/SNIAS ATR-42-300	006	B-2206
			F-GGFA
			OH-LTA
			F-WWEB
F-GHPT	Piper PA-28-181 Archer II	2890081	
F-GHPU	Aeritalia/SNIAS ATR-72-201	227	
F-GHPV	Aeritalia/SNIAS ATR-72-201	234	
F-GHPY	Aeritalia/SNIAS ATR-42-300	321	F-WWES
F-GHPZ	Aeritalia/SNIAS ATR-42-300	005	F-WGZH
	(Leased to Air Bosna)		YU-ALM
			F-GEDZ
			OY-CIA
			F-WWEA
F-GHQA	Airbus A.320-211	033	F-GGEF(1)
F-GHQB	Airbus A.320-211	036	F-GGEG(1)
F-GHQC	Airbus A.320-211	044	F-GGEH(1)
F-GHQD	Airbus A.320-211	108	
F-GHQE	Airbus A.320-211	115	
F-GHQF	Airbus A.320-211	130	
F-GHQG	Airbus A.320-211	155	
F-GHQH	Airbus A.320-211	156	
F-GHQI	Airbus A.320-211	184	
F-GHQJ	Airbus A.320-211	214	
F-GHQK	Airbus A.320-211	236	
F-GHQL	Airbus A.320-211	239	
F-GHQM	Airbus A.320-211	237	
F-GHQO	Airbus A.320-211	278	
F-GHQP	Airbus A.320-211	337	
F-GHQQ	Airbus A.320-211	352	
F-GHQR	Airbus A.320-211	377	
F-GHRA	SE.3130 Alouette II	1887	HB-XLG
			IDFAF
			D-HICI
F-GHRB	Thunder AX10-180 HAFB	1485	
F-GHRG	Piper PA-46-310P Malibu	46-8608067	N9099N
F-GHRH	Aérospatiale AS.350B Ecureuil	2504	F-WZKI
F-GHRI	Thunder AS-261 Hot Air Airship	1380	F-WGGM
			G-BPLD
F-GHRJ	Piper PA-28-181 Cherokee Archer II	28-7790360	N1950H

Regn.	Type	C/n	Prev.Id.
F-GHRK	DHC-6 Twin Otter 200	144	N202E
			(N871SA)
			N202E
F-GHRL	Piper PA-32R-301T Saratoga SP	32R-8429011	HB-PIA
			N43537
F-GHRM	Chaize CS.2200F12 HAFB	103	
F-GHRN	Chaize CS.2200F12 HAFB	102	
F-GHRO	Piper PA-38-112 Tomahawk	38-78A0660	6V-AEM
			N9706N
F-GHRP	SAN Jodel D.140E Mousquetaire IV	155	OO-JOS
F-GHRQ	Cameron O-105 HAFB	2459	
F-GHRR	Piper PA-46-310P Malibu	46-8608058	F-ODRR
			N9535N
F-GHRT	Cessna 310Q	0936	F-ODRT
			TT-BAE
			F-BUYQ
			N69714
F-GHRY	Aérospatiale AS.365N2 Dauphin 2	6412	LX-HUF
			F-GHRY
F-GHSB	Piper PA-38-112 Tomahawk	38-79A0760	HB-PEE
			N9681N
F-GHSE	Beech 1900C	UC-172	
F-GHSF	SE.3130 Alouette II	1297	ALAT
F-GHSH	Piper PA-25-260 Pawnee D	25-7656044	N54895
F-GHSI	Beech 1900C	UC-173	
F-GHSJ	Cessna P210N Pressurized Centurion II	00493	(F-GFMJ)
			CN-TCZ
			F-GCSY
			N731MH
F-GHSL	Robinson R-22M Mariner	0955M	
F-GHSM	SOCATA MS.880B Rallye Club	1559	F-GBSM
			F-BRYV
F-GHSN	Aérospatiale AS.350B Ecureuil	1905	N37AW
F-GHSP	Cessna 172N	72830	N6486D
F-GHSQ	Piper PA-25-235 Pawnee	25-2754	C-FRHP
			CF-RHP
			N7002Z
F-GHSR	Robinson R-22 Beta	1347	
F-GHSS	Schweizer 269C	S-1301	
F-GHST	Bell 206B Jet Ranger II	1104	D-HOCH
			SE-HLL
			LN-OSV
			G-BBES
			N18092
F-GHSU	Beech 76 Duchess	ME-343	N6722L
F-GHSV	Beech 200 Super King Air	BB-622	N212BF
			N7009J
			N7009
F-GHSX	Piper PA-25-235 Pawnee	25-2387	N6765Z
F-GHSZ	Piper PA-28-151 Cherokee Warrior	28-7415698	N44663
F-GHTA	Piper PA-31T Cheyenne	31T-7820015	N107BK
			N82217
F-GHTB	Robin HR.200/120B Club	23	HB-EXD
F-GHTC	Piper PA-28-161 Cadet	2841011	
F-GHTF	Aérospatiale AS.350B Ecureuil (Reservation)	unkn	
F-GHTH	Hughes 269C	47-0586	N7484F
F-GHTI	Cessna 421A Golden Eagle	0158	(F-GGFI)
			N777GP
			N3358Q
F-GHTJ(2)	CEA DR.250/160 Capitaine	41	F-OCIA
F-GHTL	Beech A36 Bonanza	E-799	N2545B
F-GHTM	Cessna TR.182 Turbo Skylane RG	01528	N5263S
F-GHTN	SE.3130 Alouette II	1401	ALAT
F-GHTO	SE.3130 Alouette II	1021	ALAT
F-GHTP	Bell 206B Jet Ranger II	1151	N1080Y
			N59405
			N414TV
			N59405
F-GHTQ(2)	Piper PA-25-235 Pawnee C	25-5074	N8637L
F-GHTR	Beech F33A Bonanza	CE-1054	N72167
F-GHTS	Cameron O-105 HAFB	1932	
F-GHTU	SE.3160 Alouette III	1429	ALAT
F-GHTY	Piper PA-28RT-201 Arrow IV	28R-8118013	N8282Z
F-GHTZ	Mooney M.20K Model 231	25-0322	N231NG
F-GHUE	Robinson R-22 Beta	1831	

Regn.	Type	C/n	Prev.Id.
F-GHUF	Aérospatiale SA.315B Lama	2540	N9006S
F-GHUH	Holste MH.1521C Broussard	275	ALAT
F-GHUJ	Holste MH.1521M Broussard	295	ALAT
F-GHUL	Boeing 737-53A	24826	
F-GHUM	Aérospatiale AS.350B Ecureuil (Written-off 9.3.98)	1448	F-ODQT / F-WIPB / F-WZLF
F-GHUN	Aérospatiale SA.315B Lama	2359	N7CH / N18857
F-GHUO	Holste MH.1521M Broussard	299	ALAT
F-GHUT	Aérospatiale AS.350B2 Ecureuil	2545	
F-GHUU	Aérospatiale AS.350B Ecureuil	1176	HB-XTS / G-BMWZ / F-GGDD / G-BMWZ / C-GBED
F-GHUV	Beech 65-E90 King Air	LW-278	YV-195CP / N4757C / N700MA
F-GHUY	Cessna 421B Golden Eagle	0417	I-MAME / N41049
F-GHUZ	Piper PA-28R-201 Arrow III	28R-7837020	N47972
F-GHVB	Cameron O-84 HAFB	1979	
F-GHVF	Fairchild-Swearingen SA.227AT Merlin IVC	AT-423	N10NB / N807M
F-GHVH	Fairchild PC-6/B2-H2 Turbo-Porter	2072	N530RQ / FAB-... / N5306F
F-GHVI	Piper PA-28-161 Cadet	2841165	
F-GHVJ	Mooney M.20J Model 201	24-1560	N5812Z
F-GHVL	Boeing 737-53A (Reservation)	unkn	
F-GHVM	Boeing 737-33A	24026	G-MONT / F-GFUC
F-GHVN	Boeing 737-33A	25138	F-OGRT
F-GHVO	Boeing 737-33A	24025	G-MONU / F-GFUB
F-GHVP	Chaize CS2200F12 HAFB	104	HB-BSJ
F-GHVQ	SE.313B Alouette II	1398	(F-GHSY) / ALAT
F-GHVT	SAAB-Scania SF.340B (Resvd as SE-KTK)	276	SE-G76
F-GHVV	Beech 200 Super King Air	BB-676	N970AA / N676DP / G-ONCA / N1362B / 9Y-TGR
F-GHVX	Cessna 152	85449	N93255
F-GHVY	Cessna 152	84585	N5426M
F-GHVZ	Cessna 152	85056	N4735Q
F-GHXC	Aérospatiale AS.350B Ecureuil	1093	N3594N
F-GHXD	Rockwell Commander 114	14134	N5463X / (N58230) / N5463X / YS-217P
F-GHXE	Christen A-1 Husky	1161	
F-GHXF	Aérospatiale SA.365C2 Dauphin 2	5017	LV-AID / F-ODJL / (F-GFIA) / F-ODJL / F-GBGV / F-WTNW
F-GHXI	Piper PA-22-150 Tri-Pacer	22-4476	PH-RCH / D-EANA / N5801D
F-GHXJ	Thunder AX8-90 HAFB	2126	
F-GHXK	Boeing 737-2A1C	21599	N171AW / YS-08C / N1247E
F-GHXL	Boeing 737-2S3	21775	G-BMOR / EI-BPR / (EI-BRR) / G-BMOR
F-GHXM	Boeing 737-53A	24788	
F-GHXQ(2)	Piper PA-28-181 Archer II	28-8090007	N2966W
F-GHXR	Aérospatiale SA.360C Dauphin	1010	(F-GHXQ) / G-BRMP / N49513
F-GHXT	Cameron A-105 HAFB	1755	
F-GHXX	Colt 90A HAFB	1703	
F-GHYA	Reims/Cessna F.150M	1206	F-BXIM
F-GHYC	Schweizer 269C	S-1532	N86G
F-GHYF	Piper PA-28-161 Warrior II	28-8516052	N69086
F-GHYG	Aérospatiale SA.315B Lama	2383	N85356 / F-BV VQ
F-WHYH	Zeppy II Airship	01	
F-GHYI	Dornier Do.28D-2 Skyservant	4199	59+24
F-GHYJ	Cameron O-77 HAFB	2632	
F-GHYK	Aérospatiale AS.350B Ecureuil	2624	
F-GHYL	Aérospatiale AS.350BA Ecureuil	2632	
F-GHYM(2)	Aérospatiale SA.315B Lama	13/2020	HB-XLT / F-OGIB / RP-C1202 / PI-C1202
F-GHYP	Hughes 269C	120-1012	N6593G / YV-206CP / YV-2092P / N1094T
F-GHYQ(2)	Robin DR.400/120 Petit Prince	2203	F-GMKK
F-GHYS	Agusta-Bell 47G-2	261	D-HCXB / OE-CXB / D-HCXB / OE-CXB / D-HAKM / 74+19 / AS+376 / LA+105 / AS+061
F-GHYT	Robinson R-22 Beta	1752	
F-GHYX	Piper PA-28-181 Archer II	28-8190101	N8302S
F-GHYY	Piper PA-28R-201T Arrow III	28R-7803232	N2121S / N9547N
F-GHYZ	Piper PA-28-181 Archer II	28-7990370	N2229X
F-GHZA	SOCATA TB-20 Trinidad	917	
F-GHZC	SOCATA TB-20 Trinidad	953	
F-GHZD	SOCATA TB-9 Tampico	925	
F-GHZG	SOCATA TB-9 Tampico	931	
F-GHZH	SOCATA TB-20 Trinidad	966	
F-GHZI	SOCATA TB-9 Tampico	940	
F-GHZK	SOCATA TB-9 Tampico	944	
F-GHZM	SOCATA TB-9 Tampico	993	
F-GHZO	SOCATA TB-20 Trinidad	1017	
F-GHZP	SOCATA TB-20 Trinidad	1031	
F-GHZS	SOCATA TB-9 Tampico	1015	
F-GHZU	SOCATA TB-20 Trinidad	1023	
F-GHZX	SOCATA TB-9 Tampico	1050	
F-GIAB	Piper PA-28-161 Cadet	2841066	
F-GIAD	Aérospatiale AS.350B Ecureuil	2112	
F-GIAE	Schweizer 269C	S-1414	
F-GIAI	Fokker F.28 Fellowship 1000	11013	C-GQBS / VH-MMJ / PH-EXA / LN-SUO / PH-ZAH
F-GIAL(2)	Beech 200 Super King Air (Damaged)	BB-844	SE-IGV
F-GIAM	Cessna 340A	0746	N2671X
F-GIAO(2)	Hughes 269C	16-0465	D-HABS / SE-HHB / G-BDOX
F-GIAQ(2)	Cessna 152	79649	N757DD
F-GIAS	Cessna 421C Golden Eagle	0300	N421YA / N8179G
F-GIAV	Cameron O-77 HAFB	1922	
F-GIAY	Piper PA-32R-301 Saratoga	32R-8313024	N4313T / N9518N
F-GIBA	Cessna 172N	73006	N1470F
F-GIBB	Aérospatiale SA.316B Alouette III	1241	JY-AEN / RJAF-308
F-GIBD	Robin HR.100/210 Safari	154	5T-TJB / F-BUHG

Regn.	Type	C/n	Prev.Id.
F-GIBE	Piper PA-28-161 Cadet	2841132	
F-GIBF(2)	UltraMagic S-130 HAFB	130/24	
F-GIBI	Aérospatiale AS.355F Ecureuil 2	5027	D-HAST(2)
			F-ODNS
F-GIBJ	Robin DR.400/120 Petit Prince	830	6V-AFP
			F-BUPJ
F-GIBK	Aérospatiale SA.315B Lama	2287/41	F-GEHY
			N65181
F-GIBM	Aérospatiale AS.350B Ecureuil	1424	N5784Y
F-GIBO	Cameron N-90 HAFB	2560	
F-GIBP	Zlin Z.526F Trenér Master	1082	F-BRNF
F-GIBQ	Piper PA-28-161 Cadet	2841324	N92156
F-GIBU	Aérospatiale SA.342J Gazelle	1470	HB-XMU
			N9000A
F-GIBV	Pilatus PC-6/B1-H2 Turbo-Porter	651	D-FLEV(2)
			OH-POB
			HB-FCZ
			ST-ADH
			HB-FCZ
F-GIBX	Piper PA-28-161 Cadet	2841323	N92155
F-GIBZ	Cameron N-65 HAFB	1439	OO-BON
F-GICA	Beech B300 Super King Air	FA-146	
F-GICC	Cessna 210N Centurion II	64046	N4918Y
F-GICE	Beech 65-B90 King Air	LJ-363	N303WJ
			N43TC
			N81648
			N95GR
			N959B
F-GICH	Bell 206B Jet Ranger II	2657	D-HOGA
F-GICJ	Cessna P210N Pressurized Centurion II	00678	(F-GFTY)
			N5358W
F-GICK	American AG-5B Tiger	10111	
F-GICL	Boeing 737-53A *(Reservation)*	unkn	
F-GICN	Dassault Falcon 50	210	F-WWHL
F-GICO	Bell 47G	1302	ALAT
F-GICP	Piper PA-28RT-201T Turbo Arrow IV	28R-8431004	N4327B
F-GICQ	Beech A36 Bonanza	E-2569	N8043E
F-GICR	Beech A36 Bonanza	E-2354	N3094T
F-GICU	Robin DR.400/180R Remorqueur	1483	EC-DKY
			D-EGPE
F-GICX	Hughes 269C	95-0432	F-BXOU
F-GICY	PZL-104 Wilga 35A	CF14800562	SP-TWS
F-GICZ	Maule MX-7-180 Star Rocket	11069C	G-MORL
F-GIDA	Robin DR.400/180 Régent	1838	
F-GIDD	Piper PA-28R-201 Arrow IV	2837060	(N181ND)
F-GIDE	Dassault Falcon 900	1	F-WIDE
F-GIDF	Piper PA-44-180 Seminole	44-8195005	N89PG
			(N256EP)
			N256ER
			N252ER
			N9628N
F-GIDG	Cessna 182P Skylane	61311	TJ-AET
			TL-AAL
			N20942
F-GIDI	Piper PA-28-181 Archer II	28-8290099	HB-PIE
			D-EIIT
			N9638N
F-GIDJ	Holste MH.1521M Broussard	283	ALAT
F-GIDK	Douglas C-47B	16604/33352	F-GIAZ
			C-GSCC
			C-GGJH
			CAF12965
			RCAF1000
			KN655
			44-77020
F-GIDR	Aérospatiale AS.350B Ecureuil	1993	N350TC
			N6008J
F-GIDS	Pilatus PC-6/B1-H2 Turbo-Porter	584	HB-FBZ
			P2-SEA
			P2-PNO
			P2-PNG(1)
			VH-PNG
			HB-FBZ

Regn.	Type	C/n	Prev.Id.
F-GIDV	Beech B200 Super King Air	BB-590	I-ALGH
			LN-AXC
			N514BV
			9M-UMW
			N6669T
F-GIDY	SA.316B Alouette III	2229	N84850
			IGM-229
			F-WXFD
F-GIEA	Piper PA-28-161 Cadet	2841106	
F-GIEB	Piper PA-28-161 Cadet	2841107	
F-GIEC	Piper PA-28-181 Archer II	2890105	N91634
F-GIED	Piper PA-28-161 Cadet	2841108	
F-GIEE	Piper PA-28-161 Cadet	2841109	
F-GIEF	Piper PA-28-161 Cadet	2841147	
F-GIEG	Piper PA-28-161 Cadet	2841149	(F-GIEH)
F-GIEH	Piper PA-28-161 Cadet	2841161	
F-GIEI	Piper PA-28-161 Cadet	2841164	
F-GIEJ	Piper PA-28-161 Cadet	2841169	
F-GIEK	Piper PA-28-161 Cadet	2841170	
F-GIEM	Piper PA-28-161 Cadet	2841267	
F-GIEO	Piper PA-28-161 Cadet	2841269	
F-GIEP	Piper PA-28-161 Cadet	2841270	
F-GIEQ	Piper PA-28-161 Cadet	2841271	
F-GIES	Piper PA-34-220T Seneca III	34-8333020	D-GABU(2)
			N83010
F-GIFA	Beech A36 Bonanza	E-1485	N6038M
F-GIFB	Beech 65-B90 King Air	LJ-453	(F-GFPI)
			D-ILTO
F-GIFC	Beech 65-B90 King Air	LJ-456	D-ILTY
F-GIFE	Piper PA-28R-201 Arrow III	28R-7837128	N3623M
F-GIFG	Beech A36 Bonanza	E-1814	N3825Z
F-GIFK	Beech F90 King Air	LA-62	D-ICBD
	(Reserved as F-HAAG .99)		N714D
F-GIFM	Beech F33A Bonanza	CE-1612	
F-GIFN	Piper PA-28-161 Cadet	2841133	
F-GIFO	Thunder AX7-65Z HAFB	2112	
F-GIFS	Cameron N-105 HAFB	2903	
F-WIFS	Aérospatiale AS.332L2 Super Puma	2167	
F-GIFX	Cameron N-105 HAFB	2597	
F-GIFZ	Holste MH.1521M Broussard	315	Fr.AF
F-GIGA	Aérospatiale AS.350B Ecureuil	1804	D-HOUA
F-GIGC	Cessna 310R	1824	N2640X
F-GIGD	Cessna 310R	1825	N2737T
F-GIGE	Cessna 172N	71560	N3473E
F-GIGF	Cessna 150L	74507	N19585
F-GIGH	Piper PA-18-150 Super Cub	1809027	
F-GIGJ	Fouga CM.170 Magister	561	F-WIGJ(2)
			Fr.AF
F-GIGK	Cessna P210N Pressurized Centurion II	00198	N521BB
			N6685P
F-GIGL	Robinson R-22 Beta	0873	
F-GIGQ	Colt 105A HAFB	2280	
F-GIGR	UltraMagic S90 HAFB	90/05	
F-GIGS	Thunder AX7-77 HAFB	1944	
F-GIGT	Aérospatiale AS.355F1 Ecureuil 2	5023	N355F
F-GIGX	Piper PA-25-260 Pawnee	25-4477	N4730Y
F-WIGY	Fouga CM.170 Magister *(Reserved as F-GLHO)*	331	Fr.AF
F-WIGZ	Fouga CM.170 Magister *(Reserved as F-GPHU)*	374	Fr.AF
F-GIHB	Cessna 172N *(Dismantled)*	68619	N733WZ
F-GIHC	Hughes 369E	0376E	
F-GIHD	Aérospatiale AS.350B Ecureuil	1100	N3598X
F-GIHE	Robinson R-22 Beta	0905	
F-GIHF	Robinson R-22 Beta	0900	
F-GIHG	Robinson R-22 Beta	0904	
F-GIHH	Robinson R.22 Beta	0814	N26417
F-GIHI	Aérospatiale AS.350B1 Ecureuil *(Dbr 4.1.98?)*	2086	
F-GIHJ	Aérospatiale AS.350B Ecureuil	1531	XA-MVA
F-GIHL(2)	Aérospatiale SA.360 Dauphin	1006	N49505
F-GIHM	Pilatus PC-6/B1-H2 Turbo-Porter	581	HS-TFD
			HS-SKE
			HS-CHE
			XW-PFB
			N13200
F-GIHN	Hughes 269C	65-0417	F-BXOS

Regn.	Type	C/n	Prev.Id.
F-GIHO	Morane-Saulnier MS.733 Alcyon	155	F-BMQB
			Fr.AF
F-GIHP	Schweizer 269C	S-1429	N429MS
F-GIHQ	Robin ATL	68	HB-SCA
F-GIHT(2)	Mudry CAP.10B	25	Fr.AF
F-GIHU(2)	Aérospatiale AS.355F2 Ecureuil 2	5313	XC-EDM
			F-WYMA
F-GIHV	Robinson R-22 Beta	2221	
F-GIIA	Aeritalia/SNIAS ATR-42-300	018	F-ODGM
			F-WDGM
F-GIIB	Aérospatiale SA.315B Lama	2461	CS-HBR
			F-GKSA
			TG-WAT
F-GIIC(2)	Thunder AX8-90SII HAFB	2343	
F-GIID	Cameron N-90 HAFB	2953	
F-GIIE	Aérospatiale SA.316B Alouette III	1885	(F-GIDD)
			Zimbabwe/RhAF
			N4965
F-GIIF	Robinson R-22 Beta	2245	
F-GIIG	Morane-Saulnier MS.885 Super Rallye	42	HB-EDP
F-GIII	Piper PA-31T2 Cheyenne	31T-8020037	N805SW
F-GIIK	Hughes 269C	16-0460	F-BXPJ
F-GIIL	Cessna 172N	72705	N6300D
F-GIIM	Colt 90A HAFB	2370	
F-GIIN	Cameron N-105 HAFB	3021	
F-GIIO	Piper PA-28-181 Archer II	2890190	
F-GIIP	Aérospatiale SA.365C3 Dauphin 2	5022	G-BJKA
			N3601S
F-GIIQ	Cessna 172M	66422	N80177
F-WIIR	Ballon Assimilable 1840m BCB	001	
F-GIIS	Reims/Cessna F.172P	2115	TU-TMG
			F-OCGJ(2)
F-GIIT	Cameron Concept 80 HAFB	3088	
F-GIIU	Chaize JZ25F16 HAFB	120	
F-GIIV	Cameron V-77 HAFB	1514	OO-BOR
F-GIIZ	Aerotek Pitts S-2A	2112	G-ODAH
			G-BDKS
F-GIJA	SE.313B Alouette II	1570	ALAT
F-GIJB	Beech 200 Super King Air	BB-13	N83MA
			N595A
			N200PB
F-GIJC	Mooney M.20K Model 231	25-0555	N1022G
F-GIJE	SE.313B Alouette II	1003	ALAT
F-GIJH	Robin DR.300/125	651	F-ODJH
			F-BTBH
F-GIJI	Mooney M.20J Model 205	24-3092	
F-GIJJ(2)	SE.313 Alouette II	1019	ALAT
F-GIJK(2)	SE.313 Alouette II	1087	F-MJAH
			F-MJSA
F-GIJL	SE.313B Alouette II	1556	ALAT
F-GIJM	Agusta-Bell 206B Jet Ranger III	8612	F-GCTJ
F-GIJN	SE.3130 Alouette II	1345	ALAT
F-GIJO	Piper PA-28-180 Cherokee E	28-5776	TR-LWU
			HB-OZY
			N3673R
F-GIJP	Aérospatiale AS.350B Ecureuil	1672	HK-3152X
			F-WZKH
F-GIJQ	Aérospatiale AS.350B Ecureuil	1647	EI-BYT
			(F-GIIC)
			EI-BYT
			G-JRBI
			EI-BNO
			G-BKJY
F-GIJZ	Maquette Frederic St.Denis	unkn	
F-GIKA	Robin DR.400/140B Major 80	1911	
F-GIKB	Robin DR.400/140B Major 80	1912	
F-GIKC	Robin DR.400/120 Petit Prince	1919	
F-GIKD	Robin DR.400/180 Régent	1914	
F-GIKE	Robin DR.400/120 Petit Prince	1929	
F-GIKG	Robin DR.400/140B Major 80	1930	
F-WIKI	Robin DR.400/120 Petit Prince	1931	F-GIKI
F-GIKJ	Robin DR.400/160 Chevalier	1941	
F-GIKK	Robin DR.400/120 Petit Prince	1942	
F-GIKL	Robin ATL L	132	
F-GIKM	Robin DR.400/120 Petit Prince	1945	
F-GIKN	Robin DR.400/140B Major 80	1946	
F-GIKO	Robin DR.400/120 Petit Prince	1947	
F-GIKP	Robin DR.400/120 Petit Prince	1948	
F-GIKQ	Robin DR.400/120 Petit Prince	1965	
F-GIKR	Robin ATL L	134	
F-GIKS	Robin DR.400/180 Régent	1950	
F-GIKT	Robin ATL L	130	
F-GIKU	Robin ATL L	135	
F-GIKV	Robin DR.400/180 Régent	1951	
F-GIKX	Robin DR.400/180 Régent	1952	
F-GIKY	Robin DR.400/120 Petit Prince	1954	
F-GIKZ	Robin DR.400/120 Petit Prince	1961	
F-GILA	Hughes 269C	110-0981	D-HAWK
			N1112N
F-GILF	Beech 200C Super King Air	BL-12	TR-LZH
			F-GCMT
F-GILG	Cameron O-105 HAFB	2188	
F-GILL	Aérospatiale AS.355F1 Ecureuil 2	5044	3A-MCC
			F-GBON
			F-WZKS
F-GILM	Aérospatiale SN.601A Corvette	32	EC-DUF
			OY-ARA
			SE-DED
			OY-ARA
			F-BTTQ
			F-WNGR
F-GILQ	Schweizer 269C-1	0036	
F-GILR	Robin R.216OD Acrobin	C209	HB-KBN
			N216MH
F-GILS	Robinson R-22 Beta	0601	G-BNBT
			N2530W
F-GILT	Piper PA-28-161 Cadet	2841067	
F-GILX	Aérospatiale SA.315B Lama	2366	N62190
F-GILZ	Beech A60 Duke	P-167	I-ENMA
			HB-GEX
F-GIMA	Cessna 414A Chancellor II	0446	N2732F
F-GIMB	Cameron V-65 HAFB	2055	
F-GIME	Thunder AX7-65 HAFB	1215	(F-GFFX)
F-GIMI	SA.330J Super Puma	1099	PH-SAZ
			9L-LBB
			PH-SAZ
			5N-AKG
			F-WKQA
F-GIML	Beech 65-E90 King Air	LW-180	N2180L
F-GIMM	Piper PA-28RT-201T Turbo Arrow IV	28R-8231067	N8261X
			N9583N
F-WIMN	Fouga CM-170 Magister	440	Fr.AF
F-WIMQ	Fouga CM-170 Magister	438	Fr.AF
F-GIMS	Mooney M.20J Model 201	24-1691	
F-GIMT	Thunder AX8-90S1 HAFB	2418	
F-GIMZ	Aérospatiale SA.315B Lama	2642	YV-350CP
			YV-428A
F-GINF	Thunder AX8-105Z HAFB	1785	
F-GINH	SOCATA MS.893A Rallye Commodore 180	10605	HB-EDZ
F-GINJ	Beech 58 Baron	TH-539	F-OANJ(2)
			5T-CJS
			F-BVUZ
F-GINL(2)	Boeing 737-53C	24827	
F-GINM	Robin DR.400/180 Régent	861	D-EDHN
F-GINP	Thunder AX7-65SI HAFB	446	G-LING
F-GINQ	Aérospatiale SA.330JPuma	1583	LX-HUL
	(Reservation .99)		PT-HAA
			LX-HUL
			F-GHYR
			I-EHPJ
			PH-SSB
			PK-TRF
			PH-SSB
			F-WXFM
F-GINR	Bell 47G	32	N112B
			NC112B
F-GINS	Schroeder Fire Balloons G30/24 HAFB	193	
F-GINT	Chaize JZ.25F16 HAFB	131	
F-GINU	Piper PA-32R-301 Saratoga SP	3213035	
F-GINV	Aérospatiale AS.350B Ecureuil	1153	

Regn.	Type	C/n	Prev.Id.
F-GINX	Chaize JZ.25F16 HAFB	132	
F-GINY	Cessna R.172K Hawk XP Floatplane	2676	C-GVIN
			(N736PG)
F-GIOA	Fokker F.28-0100	11261	PH-EZK
F-GIOG	Fokker F.28-0100	11364	(F-GIOH)
			PH-EZA
F-GIOH	Fokker F.28-0100	11424	PH-LXV
F-GIOI	Fokker F.28-0100	11433	PH-MXA
			PH-NXA
F-GIOJ	Fokker F.28-0100	11454	PH-EZF
F-GIOK	Fokker F.28-0100	11455	PH-EZG
F-GIOQ	Fokker F.28-0100 *(Reservation)*	unkn	
F-GIOR	Fokker F.28-0100 *(Reservation)*	unkn	
F-GIOS	Fokker F.28-0100 *(Reservation)*	unkn	
F-GIOT	Thunder AX7-77 HAFB	1474	
F-GIOU	Fokker F.28-0100 *(Reservation)*	unkn	
F-GIOY	Fokker F.28-0100	11259	C-FICP
			PH-EZJ
F-GIOZ	Fokker F.28-0100	11260	C-FICQ
			PH-EZK
F-GIPA	Mudry CAP.20	6	F-TFVZ
			F-BTAH
			F-TFVZ
F-GIPB	Fairchild F.27J	100	N384BA
			N471SP
			N2727R
F-GIPC	Piper PA-32R-301 Saratoga	32R-8313005	N82778
F-GIPD	Fairchild F.27J	92	F-OCVY
			N755L
			N155L
F-GIPE	Mooney M.20J Model 205	24-3066	
F-GIPF	Cameron O-65 HAFB	1925	
F-GIPG	Beech 65-90 King Air	LJ-83	N827T
			(YV-980P)
			N827F
F-GIPH	Dassault Falcon 10	194	N61FC
			N100FJ
			N260FJ
			F-WZGZ
F-GIPI	Aérospatiale SA.365C3 Dauphin 2	5020	(F-GIIP)
			G-BGKM
			F-WMHI
F-GIPJ	Aérospatiale SA.365N Dauphin 2 *(Reservation)*	unkn	
F-GIPL	Piper PA-31T Cheyenne	31T-8020091	N76SC
			N20AM
			N40TW
			N2334X
F-GIPM	Beech A36 Bonanza	E-2405	N3108F
F-GIPO	Gardan GY-80-180 Horizon	211	OO-KAG
			F-BPAG
F-GIPR	Piper PA-28-181 Archer II	28-8190312	N8433F
F-GIPS	Thunder AX7-77 HAFB	1807	
F-GIPT	Mooney M.20K Model 231	25-0172	N231RK
F-GIPU	Mudry CAP.10B	16	Fr.AF
F-GIPX	Thunder AX10-180SIII HAFB	3449	
F-GIPY	Aérospatiale AS.350B1 Ecureuil	2033	F-GHFY
			LN-OCA
F-GIPZ	SE.313B Alouette II	"076"	Fr.AF
F-GIQA	Cessna 172N	73536	N5087G
F-GIQK	Morane-Saulnier MS.733 Alcyon	149	F-BMQK
			Fr.AF
F-GIQL	SA.316B Alouette III	1836	EC-FEM
			F-GEPF
			HC-BOB
			F-GEPF
			F-ODTE
			FAP9380
F-GIQM	Cessna 152	80306	N24518
F-GIQN	Cessna 152	82366	N68766
F-GIQO	Cessna 172N	68742	N734CD
F-GIQR	Piper PA-28R-180 Cherokee Arrow	28R-30757	HB-OZL
			N7415J
F-GIQS	UltraMagic V-77 HAFB *(Reservation)*	77/112	
F-GIQT	HOAC DV-20 Katana	20078	D-EHLK
F-GIQU	Aérospatiale SA.315B Lama *(Reservation .99)*	2449	I-CTEC

Regn.	Type	C/n	Prev.Id.
F-GIQV	Beech 200 Super King Air	BB-529	N30AH
			F-GIIY
			EC-FPH
			EC-191
			F-GHPR
			N602MC
			N80LM
			N333SR
F-GIRB	Piper PA-22-160 Tri-Pacer	22-7499	OO-IRB
			I-AIRB
			N3669Z
F-GIRC	Aeritalia/SNIAS ATR-42-300	033	F-WIAF
			OH-LTC
			F-WWEO
F-GIRD	Beech 76 Duchess	ME-387	N3809N
F-GIRE	Wörner K-1000/3-Stu Gas Balloon	0323	
F-GIRF	Aérospatiale AS.350B2 Ecureuil	2411	
F-GIRG	Thunder AX8-105S2 HAFB	2402	
F-GIRH	Aérospatiale SN.601 Corvette	14	SP-FOA
	(Reservation, stored as SP-FOA)		F-BVPS
F-GIRI	Mooney M.20E Super 21	1978	HB-DUV
F-GIRJ	Piper PA-18 Super Cub	18-1010	SX-ADP
	(Quoted with f/n 18-1079)		RHAF115313
			51-15313
F-GIRP	Piper PA-28-161 Cherokee Warrior II	28-7816124	N2291F
			C-GIYC
			N9627N
F-GIRQ	Cessna 172R	80293	N9520P
F-GIRR	Cameron V-65 HAFB	1723	
F-GIRT	Bell 206B Jet Ranger II	1924	F-OGNI
			N49716
F-GIRU(2)	Mudry CAP.10B	14	Fr.AF
F-GIRV	Piper PA-28-181 Archer II	28-8590018	G-BPRW
			N43823
F-GISA	Boeing 747-428	25238	
F-GISB	Boeing 747-428	25302	
F-GISC	Boeing 747-428	25599	
F-GISD	Boeing 747-428	25628	
F-GISE	Boeing 747-428	25630	
F-GISF to GISZ	*Boeing 747-428 reservations for Air France (Combi)*		
F-GITA	Boeing 747-428	24969	
F-GITB	Boeing 747-428	24990	N6009F
F-GITC	Boeing 747-428	25344	
F-GITD	Boeing 747-428	25600	
F-GITE	Boeing 747-428	25601	
F-GITF	Boeing 747-428	25602	
F-GITH to GITZ	*Boeing 747-428 reservations for Air France (Passenger)*		
F-GIUB to GIUZ	*Boeing 747-428 reservations for Air France (Cargo)*		
F-GIVA	Piper PA-28-181 Archer II	2890108	
F-GIVB	Maule MX.7-235 Star Rocket	10083C	N9208V
F-GIVD(2)	Dassault Falcon 50EX *(Reservation)*	251	N870
			VP-CLN
			VR-CLN
			(F-GOND)
			F-WOND
F-GIVH	Bell 206B Jet Ranger II	4176	
F-GIVK	Embraer EMB.120RT Brasilia	120-112	C-FKOE
			LN-KOB
			PT-SNE
F-GIVL	Aérospatiale AS.355N Ecureuil	5603	
F-GIVM(2)	Aérospatiale AS.350B2 Ecureuil	2395	N350HH
F-GIVN	Bell 47G-2	2323	
F-GIVO	UltraMagic V-56 HAFB	56/13	
F-GIVQ	Westland/Aérospatiale SA.341GGazelle	WA/1073	I-ATOM
	(Reservation .99)		F-BXPG
			G-BAZL
F-GIVS	Cessna U.206G Soloy Turbine Pac	04881	HB-CKO
			N56HT
			(N734VR)
F-GIVU	SE.313 Alouette II	1473	Fr.AF
F-GIVV	Cessna 340A	1520	N34DA
			(N6871L)
F-GIVY	Robinson R-44 Astro	0035	
F-GIVZ	Robinson R-22B2 Beta	2689	

Regn.	Type	C/n	Prev.Id.
F-GIXA	Boeing 737-2K2C	20836	PH-TVC
			F-GGZA
			PH-TVC
			LV-MDB
			PH-TVC
F-GIXB	Boeing 737-33A	24789	F-OGSD
			F-GFUI
F-GIXC	Boeing 737-38B	25124	F-OGSS
			N4320B
			N1792B
F-GIXD	Boeing 737-33A	25744	N3213T
F-GIXE	Boeing 737-3B3	26850	N854WT
			F-GIXE
F-GIXF	Boeing 737-3B3	26851	N4361V
F-GIXG	Boeing 737-382	24364	F-OGSX
			CS-TIA
F-GIXH	Boeing 737-3S3	23788	5W-FAX
			N851LF
			G-NAFH
			G-BOYN
			EC-ECQ
			EC-277
			G-BOYN
			EC-ECQ
			N271LF
F-GIXI	Boeing 737-348	23809	F-OGSY
			EC-FQP
			EC-279
			EI- BUD
			N1786B
F-GIXJ	Boeing 737-3Y0	23685	G-MONH
F-GIXK	Boeing 737-33A	24028	G-MONP
F-GIXL	Boeing 737-348	23810	F-OHCS
			EC-FSC
			EC-375
			EI- BUE
			N1787B
F-GIXO	Boeing 737-3Q8	24132	N241LF
			EC-FET
			EC-593
			EC-EIR
			EC-160
F-GIXP	Boeing 737-3M8	24021	F-OHCQ
			9V-SQZ
			N40495
			OO-LTB
			(F-GKTE)
			OO-LTB
			(F-ODSU)
			(OO-BTB)
F-GIXQ to GIXT	Reserved for S.E.A./Aeropostale		
F-GIXU	Fairchild F.24R-46A Argus III	1063	F-BEXU
			F-OAAS
			F-BEXU
			KK445
			44-83102
F-GIXX	Pilatus PC-6/B2-H2 Turbo-Porter	564	N17XX
			N777XX
			N187H
F-GIXY	Mudry CAP.232	19	
F-GIXZ	Robin DR.315 Petit Prince	364	OO-NEW
			F-BRFK
F-GIYA	Reims/Cessna F.152	1854	HB-CKD
			F-GCYO
F-GIYB	Aérospatiale AS.355F1 Ecureuil 2	5142	N5793Z
F-GIYC	Schweizer 269CB	0036	F-GILQ
F-GIYD	Cessna 152	82164	C-GYRP
			N68175
F-GIYE	Aérospatiale SA.316B Alouette III	1452	A-452
F-GIYF	Aérospatiale SA.365C3 Dauphin 2	5068	VH-HCF
			9M-WYN
F-GIYG	Aérospatiale AS.350B Ecureuil	1410	HB-XLZ
F-GIYH	Embraer EMB.120RT Brasilia	120-239	LX-LGL
			PT-STL
F-GIYI	Embraer EMB.120RT Brasilia	120-244	LX-LGM
			(F-GHEZ)
			PT-STQ
F-GIYJ	Douglas DC-8-55F	45819	Fr.AF:F-RAFC
	(Reservation .99)		F-BNLD
			TU-TXK
			Fr.AF:F-RAFC
			F-BNLD
			TU-TXG
			F-BNLD
F-GIYL	Piper PA-28-180 Cherokee D	28-4540	HB-OZM
			N5245L
F-GIYM	Hughes 269C	25-0392	N269W
			N9290F
			N7484F
F-GIYN	Robinson R-22B2 Beta	2925	
F-GIYO	Cessna 172RG Cutlass	0558	D-EDYO
			N5532V
F-GIYP	Robinson R-22 Beta	1399	
F-GIYX	Reims/Cessna F.177RG (Reservation)	0114	F-BVIN
F-GIYY	Bell 47G-3B (Reservation 5.99)	"68043"	
	(Possibly Bell TH-13T Soloy N873M c/n 3476 ex 65-8043)		
F-GIYZ	Cameron A-105 HAFB	2931	
F-GIZA	Bell 47G-2 (Shelby Aero Rebuild)	SA-53	N1775
F-GIZB	Beech 65-C90 King Air	LJ-955	N768SB
			N678SB
F-GIZD	Reims/Cessna F.172M	1355	I- CCAV
			(D-EDZJ)
F-GIZE	CAARP CAP.10B	5	Fr.AF
F-GIZF	Aérospatiale AS.350B3 Ecureuil	3083	F-OIBU
F-GIZG	Aérospatiale AS.350B3 Ecureuil	3084	
F-GIZI	Cessna 172R	80435	N9328F
F-GIZJ	Thunder AX9-140ASII HAFB	4566	
	(This c/n also quoted for Cameron A-140 G-BYLU)		
F-GIZL	Mudry CAP.10B	18	Fr.AF
F-GIZM	UltraMagic H-65 HAFB (Also reserved as F-GJKX)	65/84	
F-GIZN	Schweizer 269C (Reservation .99)	S-1334	OH-HSP
			N7506U
F-GIZO	Robinson R-22 Beta	1814	F-ODZO
F-GIZR	Enstrom F.28A	223	OO-NMT
			G-RONT
F-GIZS(2)	Hughes 269C	72-0148	OH-HIY
			G-BAFC
F-GIZT	UltraMagic M-90 HAFB (Reservation 7.99)	90/35	
F-GIZU	Aérospatiale AS.365N2 Dauphin 2	6540	
F-GIZV	Bell 47G-2	2219	(F-GMPZ)
			G-ASYW
			VR-BBA
			CP-704
			VP-TCF
			CP-671
			VR-BBA
F-GIZY	UltraMagic H-77 HAFB	77/162	
F-GJAB	Aérospatiale AS.350B Ecureuil	1174	N3599U
F-GJAC	Holste MH.1521C Broussard	180	Fr.AF
F-GJAD	Beech 65-E90 King Air	LW-3	N888BH
			N9493Q
F-GJAE	Schroeder Fire Balloons G45/24 HAFB	125	
F-GJAH	Cessna 172N	72635	N6208D
F-GJAI	Rockwell S.2R-600 Thrush Commander	2434R	N5697X
F-GJAK	Embraer EMB.120RT Brasilia	120-215	PT-SSJ
F-GJAM	Aérospatiale AS.350B1 Ecureuil	1866	D-HILF
F-GJAN	SOCATA TB-20 Trinidad	965	
F-GJAP	Aérospatiale SN.601 Corvette	31	EC-DYE
			F-WZSB
			N602AN
			F-BTTK
			F-WNGZ
F-GJAR	Cessna 172N	69835	N738AX
F-GJAS	Aérospatiale SN.601 Corvette	8	6V-AEA
			F-WPTT
F-GJAT	Piper PA-34-200T Seneca II	34-7670342	D-GIRK
			D-IFFP
			PH-WON
			N4564F

Regn.	Type	C/n	Prev.Id.
F-GJAV	Cameron A-160 HAFB	1931	G-BPYF
F-GJAX	Aérospatiale AS.355N Ecureuil II	5543	I-IIII
			F-WYMH
			(F-GJAG)
F-GJAY	Robinson R-22 Beta	1001	
F-GJAZ	Leys HG VL-248 Free Balloon	2	
F-GJBA	Mooney M.20J Model 205	24-3132	N10675
F-GJBB	Colt 77A HAFB	1757	
F-GJBC	Pilatus PC-6/B2-H2 Turbo-Porter	868	
F-GJBD	Robinson R-22 Beta	1400	
F-GJBE	Robinson R-22 Beta	1348	
F-GJBF	Holste MH.1521C-1 Broussard	13	Fr.AF
	(Could possibly be c/n 013 ex. F-ZWTL)		
F-GJBH	SA.319B Alouette III	2102	(F-GGPU)
			Fr.AF
F-GJBI	Robinson R-22 Beta	1782	N40790
F-GJBK	Bell 47G-2	2428	N2883B
F-GJBL	Cessna A.185F Skywagon	04023	N6322E
F-GJBN	SE.313B Alouette II	1619	ALAT
F-GJBP	Pilatus PC-6/B2-H4 Turbo-Porter	716	HB-FFL
			9N-AAW
			HB-FFL
F-GJBQ	Nord 1101 Noralpha	177	F-ZJBQ
F-GJBR(2)	SE.3130 Alouette II	1357	ALAT
F-GJBS	Beech B200 Super King Air	BB-1181	N6725Y
F-GJBY	Airbus A.320-231	unkn	
F-GJBZ	Dassault Falcon 50EX	269	(F-GPBG)
			F-WWHT
F-GJCB	Piper PA-28R-201 Arrow III	28R-7837053	HB-PBR
			N6135H
F-GJCC	Dassault Falcon 20	72/413	N725P
			VH-DWA
			N99KT
			N1270F
			HB-VAW
			F-WNGO
F-GJCD	Beech 300 Super King Air	FA-7	N925AD
			ZS-LRG
			N6923Y
F-GJCG	Cessna R.182 Skylane RG	00340	N4234C
F-GJCI	Cessna 152	80674	N25467
F-GJCL	Piper PA-28R-201T Turbo Arrow IV	28R-8131004	N8275A
F-GJCM	Aérospatiale AS.350B1 Ecureuil	1988	LN-OMQ
F-GJCN	Cessna 152	83979	N4806H
F-GJCO	Cessna 152	81503	N64969
F-GJCP	Aérospatiale AS.350B1 Ecureuil	2172	JA9788
F-GJCQ	Aérospatiale SA.315B Lama	2526	
F-GJCR	Beech 65-E90 King Air	LW-251	N7ZU
			N483
			TG-BET
F-GJCS	Piper PA-28R-201 Cherokee Arrow III	28R-7737016	N1915H
F-GJCT	Cessna 172N	68897	N734JU
F-GJCU	Cameron N-105 HAFB	3964	
F-GJCV	SE.3130 Alouette II	1344	ALAT
F-GJCX(2)	Chaize JZ.25F12 HAFB	139	
F-GJCZ	Robinson R-44 Astro	0496	
F-GJDA	Pilatus PC-6A/B2-H2 Turbo Porter	721	HA-YDA
F-GJDB	Dassault Falcon 20	76	(F-GGFO)
			N776DS
			N937GC
			N970F
			F-WMKF
F-GJDC	Piper PA-28-161 Warrior II	2816100	N9222F
F-GJDD	Mooney M.20K Model 231	25-0776	(F-GJLU)
			LX-MLL
			N5696U
F-GJDF	Aérospatiale AS.350B2 Ecureuil	2642	F-WYMO
F-GJDG	Cessna F500 Citation	0312	N82AT
			N33MQ
			(N233ME)
			N33ME
			N5312J
F-GJDH	Piper PA-28-151 Cherokee Warrior	28-7415335	N41854
F-WJDI	Sikorsky S-76C	760269	N3123U
F-GJDJ	Cameron A-105 HAFB	2450	

Regn.	Type	C/n	Prev.Id.
F-GJDK(3)	Cessna 421A	0080	CN-TBH
			CN-MBD
			N2980Q
F-GJDN	Robin DR.400/120	1018	F-BXER
F-GJDO	Robin HR.100/210 Safari	203	TU-TMY
			F-BXJY
F-GJDP	Cessna T.303 Crusader	00032	N19HK
			N45526
			C-GNTK
			(N9636T)
F-GJDS	DHC-6 Twin Otter 300	375	TR-LDH
			C-FKDN
			F-GFAE
			SE-GEC
F-GJDT	Hughes 269C	99-0822	PH-HFH
F-GJDU	Cameron N-90 HAFB	3326	
F-GJDV	Aérospatiale SA.365N Dauphin 2	6065	I-SINV
F-GJDX	Robin DR.400/140B Major 80	781	F-BTZU
F-GJDZ	Cameron O-77 HAFB	2590	
F-GJEE	Aérospatiale AS.350B Ecureuil	1111	N400Q
			N400W
			N3596X
F-GJEF	Piper PA-28-181 Archer II	2890189	N9232N
F-GJEG	SE.3130 Alouette II	1229	V-45
			HB-XBK
			V-45
F-GJEH	Aviat Pitts S.2B	5255	N98AV
F-GJEI	Bell 47G-2	2426	N2889B
F-GJEJ	Beech K35 Bonanza	D-5912	HB-EGW
	(c/n correct but quoted as "D-59A2")		D-EGWA
			HB-EGW
F-WJEL	SOCATA TB-200 (Prototype)	1214	F-GKEC
F-GJEM	Piper J-3C-65 Cub	12963	HB-ONK
			44-80667
F-GJEN	Piper PA-28-181 Archer II	28-7990201	N3024H
F-GJEP	Christen Pitts S-2B	5156	
F-GJER	Maule MX-7-235 Star Rocket	10071C	N6127Q
F-GJET	Aeritalia/SNIAS ATR-42-300 *(Reservation)*	unkn	
F-GJEU	Aeritalia/SNIAS ATR-42-300 *(Reservation)*	unkn	
F-GJEV	Aeritalia/SNIAS ATR-42-300 *(Reservation)*	unkn	
F-GJEX	Aeritalia/SNIAS ATR-42-300 *(Reservation)*	unkn	
F-GJFA	Beech B200 Super King Air	BB-1270	N30391
F-GJFC	Beech B200 Super King Air	BB-1347	
F-GJFD	Beech B200 Super King Air	BB-1387	
F-GJFE	Beech B200 Super King Air	BB-1399	
F-GJFF to H	*Reserved for DGAC/SFACT*		
F-GJFI	Cessna 208B Grand Caravan	0230	N208GC
			(N4909B)
F-GJFJ	Aérospatiale AS.365N4 Dauphin 2 / EC.155	6557	
	(Reservation .99)		
F-GJFM	Chaize CS.2002F12 HAFB	100	
F-GJFN	Beech F33A Bonanza	CE-896	HB-EWA
F-GJFO	Thunder AX7-65Z HAFB	1743	
F-GJFP	Cessna T.210R Turbo Centurion II	64913	N6148U
F-GJFR	Cessna 172P	74712	N53258
F-GJFS	Chaize CS.4000F16 HAFB	101	
F-GJFT	Mooney M.20J Model 201	24-1134	N1085D
F-GJFU	Aérospatiale AS.355F1 Ecureuil 2	5079	G-BUZI
			N57894
F-GJFV	Bell 206B Jet Ranger II	2567	N501WN
			N5010N
F-GJFX	Beech 1900D	UE-106	N6011C
			TR-LET
			F-GMSM
			N15574
F-GJGF	Aérospatiale SA.315B Lama	2617	VT-BKM
			F-GHIJ
			N5785V
F-GJGG	Balloon Works Firefly F7R-15 HAFB	F/B-346	
F-GJGH	Piper PA-28R-201T Turbo Cherokee Arrow III		
		28R-7703396	N47548
F-GJGI	Chaize CS.2200F12 HAFB	112	
F-GJGJ	Piper PA-34-220T Seneca III	34-8133001	N8181C
F-GJGK	Mooney M.20J Model 205	24-3178	N9119N
F-GJGM	Mudry CAP.232	07	

Regn.	Type	C/n	Prev.Id.
F-GJGN	Mooney M.20J Model 205	24-3200	
F-GJGO	Beech 76 Duchess	ME-223	D-GBTC
F-GJGP	Bell 206L-1 Long Ranger II	45619	OH-HNE
F-GJGR	Beech A36 Bonanza	E-2221	N7223R
F-GJGT	Aérospatiale SA.342J Gazelle	1094	C-GSDZ
			N14416
F-GJGU	Aérospatiale AS.355F1 Ecureuil 2	5095	N7090T
			C-FMHP
			C-FVHQ
			N321HC
F-GJGV	Bell 206B Jet Ranger II	913	G-BALC
F-GJGX	Chaize JZX.22F12 HAFB	152	
F-GJGY	UltraMagic M-145 HAFB	145/10	
F-GJGZ	Cameron N-77 HAFB	2705	
F-GJHA	Reims/Cessna F.150G	0089	OO-SIQ
F-GJHB	Robinson R-22	0154	G-BJBR
			N9081N
F-GJHD	Piper PA-28R-201T Turbo Cherokee Arrow III		
		28R-7703135	G-RYAN
			G-BFMN
			OO-DGP
			N5622V
F-GJHE	Christen Pitts S-2B	5152	
F-GJHF	Piper PA-38-112 Tomahawk	38-78A0357	TJ-AHE
			F-OBNV
			N9667N
F-GJHH	Beech 300 Super King Air	FA-112	N324NE
			N2997Q
F-GJHJ	Dassault Falcon 2000	2	ZS-NNF
			F-WNEW
F-GJHK	Dassault Falcon 10	108	(F-GFJK)
			N88LD
			N91DH
			N11DH
			N246FJ
			F-BIPC
			F-WZGF
			HZ-AKI
			(HZ-KA1)
			F-WPUZ
F-GJHP	Schweizer 269C	S-1402	N424MS
F-GJHQ	McDonnell-Douglas DC-9-83	49668	N63050
			EC-GBV
			EC-898
			EI-CGA
			F-GMPP
			EI-CGA
			EC-EIK
			EC-289
			EC-EIK
			EC-163
			EI-BWC
			(N14845)
F-GJHR	Piper PA-28-181 Archer II	28-8090071	N876HR
			N8077T
F-GJHT	Piper PA-38-112 Tomahawk	38-79A0278	N2340D
F-GJHU	SANJodel D.140C Mousquetaire III	153	D-EIFI
F-GJHY	Agusta-Bell 206B Jet Ranger II	8426	EC-CPF
			F-BXAJ
F-GJHZ	Piper PA-46-310P Malibu	46-8508090	I-LRNZ
			I-DANB
			N2484X
F-GJIB	SE.313B Alouette II	1627	FAP9209
			76+30
F-GJID	Aerostar S-57A HAFB	3187	
F-GJIE	SE.3130 Alouette II	1902	V-56
F-GJIF	UltraMagic H-77 HAFB	77/126	
F-GJIG	SAAB 2000 (Reservation .99)	017	V7-9508
			SE-017
F-GJIH	Piper PA-28-236 Dakota	28-8111060	D-ENIH
			N8365D
F-GJII	Cameron V-77 HAFB	1915	OO-BRP
			(OO-BRR)
F-GJIJ	Fouga CM.170 Magister	482	Fr.AF

Regn.	Type	C/n	Prev.Id.
F-GJIM	Aérospatiale AS.350B Ecureuil	1489	N5434T
			XA-...
F-GJIN	UltraMagic M-77 HAFB	77/104	
F-GJIO	UltraMagic N-180 HAFB	180/19	
F-GJIR	Fouga CM.170 Magister (Reservation)	219	Fr.AF
F-GJIS	Beech B36TC Bonanza	EA-543	D-ECPK
			N333PK
F-GJIT	Piper PA-23-250 Aztec F	27-7954087	F-OGIT
			N6771A
F-GJIV	UltraMagic H-77 HAFB	77/170	
F-GJIX	Chaize JZ.25F16 HAFB (Reservation .99)	149	
F-GJIZ	Chaize JZ.22F24 HAFB	151	
F-GJJA	Cameron N-77 HAFB	2473	
F-GJJB	Thunder AX7-65 HAFB	1473	
F-GJJC	Piper PA-28RT-201T Turbo Arrow IV	28R-8531004	N4391D
			N9528N
F-GJJD	Cameron A-105 HAFB	2537	
F-GJJE	Chaize JZ.22F12 HAFB	141	
F-GJJG	Airbus A.300B4-103	069	G-BYYS
	(Reservation .99; also reserved as		5T-CLI
	F-WQKU and as F-OHLF)		N471AS
			RP-C3002
			F-WZEB
F-GJJH	Aérospatiale AS.350B2 Ecureuil	2584	
F-GJJJ	Beech A100 King Air	B-196	N773SK
			N5ST
F-GJJM	Holste MH.1521M Broussard	292	Fr.AF
F-GJJP	Piper PA-44-180T Turbo Seminole	44-8207008	N81487
F-GJJQ	Lindstrand LBL-180 HAFB	051	
F-GJJR	Piper PA-28RT-201T Turbo Arrow IV	28R-8431016	N4340K
F-GJJT	Chaize CS.2200F12 HAFB	106	
F-GJJX	Cessna 150M (Reservation .99)	78807	ZS-JWW
			(N704RE)
F-GJKA	Cameron N-77 HAFB	527	LX-PIN
F-GJKB	Chaize JZ.30F16 HAFB	136	
F-GJKC	Chaize JZ.30F16 HAFB	142	
F-GJKD	Robinson R-44 Astro (Reservation 12.99)	0114	D-HKAZ
			(ES-...)
			D-HKAZ
F-GJKE	Cameron N-65 HAFB	1861	LX-OKE
F-GJKL	SA.316B Allouette III	5277	F-ODLH
			N1037S
			TG-TEK
F-GJKM	Robin DR.400/160 Chevalier	2039	
F-GJKN	Robinson R-22 Beta	1349	
F-GJKP	SOCATA TB-20 Trinidad	503	N62TB
F-GJKQ	Airbus A.310-304 (Reservation)	571	TU-TAC
			F-WWYM
			F-GHYM
F-GJKR	Airbus A.310-304 (Reservation)	651	TU-TAD
			F-WWCC
F-GJKS	Airbus A.310-304 (Reservation)	652	TU-TAE
			F-WWCH
F-GJKT(2)	Airbus A.310-304 (Reservation)	671	TU-TAF
			F-WWCM
F-GJKX	UltraMagic H-65 HAFB (Also reserved as F-GIZM)	65/84	
F-GJLB	Aérospatiale SN.601 Corvette	39	TL-RCA
			TL-SMI
			F-OBYG
			F-WNGY
F-GJLC(2)	Reims/Cessna F.172H	0441	CN-TTU(2)
F-GJLE	Colt 105A HAFB	1596	
F-GJLF	Mooney M.20M TLS	27-0066	
F-GJLG	Cessna 172P	75063	N54836
F-GJLJ	Bell 206B Jet Ranger II	2748	YU-HCI
			N27668
F-GJLK	SE.3130 Alouette II (W/o 23.7.98)	1914	V-62
F-GJLL	Dassault Falcon 10	22	N48JC
			N44JC
			N114FJ
			F-WLCX
F-GJLM	Robin DR.400/180 Régent	1286	F-GBAG
F-GJLO	SOCATA MS.893A Rallye Commodore 180	11411	D-EAGQ
F-GJLP	Holste MH.1521C1 Broussard	279	Fr.AF
F-GJLR	Piper PA-28-161 Warrior II	28-7916231	N2236K

Regn.	Type	C/n	Prev.Id.
F-GJLS	Cessna 172R	80173	N9893F
F-GJLT	Holste MH.1521C Broussard	44C	F-BJLT
F-GJLX	Hughes 369D	91-1058D	(F-GHLX)
			N16DK
			N5107J
F-GJLZ	Cessna P210N Pressurized Centurion II	00423	N7757K
F-GJMB	SOCATA TB-20 Trinidad	909	
F-GJMC	SOCATA TB-20 Trinidad	910	
F-GJMD	SOCATA TB-20 Trinidad	911	
F-GJME	SOCATA TB-20 Trinidad	unkn	
F-GJMF	SOCATA TB-20 Trinidad	unkn	
F-GJMG	Mooney M.20M TLS	27-0032	
F-GJMI	Cameron N-105 HAFB	2519	
F-GJMJ	Beech B200 Super King Air	BB-1032	I-CUVI
			N6494S
F-GJMK	Cessna T.303 Crusader	00025	N9550T
F-GJML	Chaize CS.2200F12 HAFB	108	
F-GJMM	Beech 76 Duchess	ME-279	HB-GGV
F-GJMN	Fouga CM.170 Magister	424	F-WQCE
			Fr.AF
F-GJMO	Robinson R-22M Mariner	1296M	
F-GJMP	Bell 47G-2	7525	CF-CIU
F-GJMS	Piper PA-28-181 Archer II	28-8490103	N133AV
F-GJMU	Rockwell S.2R Thrush Commander	1689R	N5589X
F-GJMY	Cameron A-105 HAFB	2277	
F-GJMZ	Mooney M.20M TLS	27-0152	N9162D
F-GJNA	Boeing 737-528	25206	
F-GJNB	Boeing 737-528	25227	
F-GJNC	Boeing 737-528	25228	
F-GJND	Boeing 737-528	25229	
F-GJNE	Boeing 737-528	25230	
F-GJNF	Boeing 737-528	25231	
F-GJNG	Boeing 737-528	25232	
F-GJNH	Boeing 737-528	25233	
F-GJNI	Boeing 737-528	25234	
F-GJNJ	Boeing 737-528	25235	
F-GJNK	Boeing 737-528	25236	
F-GJNM	Boeing 737-528	25237	(F-GJNL)
F-GJNN	Boeing 737-528	27304	
F-GJNO	Boeing 737-528	27305	
F-GJNQ	Boeing 737-5H6	26445	9M-MFA
F-GJNR	Boeing 737-5H6	26446	9M-MFB
F-GJNS	Boeing 737-53S	29073	(F-GJNP)
			N1786B
F-GJNT	Boeing 737-53S	29074	N1786B
F-GJNU	Boeing 737-53S	29075	N1786B
F-GJNV	Boeing 737-548	26287	EI-CDS
F-GJNX	Boeing 737-5H6	26454	9M-MFE
F-GJNY	Boeing 737-5H6	26456	9M-MFF
F-GJOL	Wassmer WA.41 Baladou	163	TU-TLY
			F-OCOL
F-GJOM	Piper PA-28-181 Archer II	2890143	
F-GJOV	Piper PA-18-150 Super Cub	1809056	
F-GJOZ	SOCATA TB-10 Tobago	319	HB-EQU
F-GJPB	SOCATA TB-9 Tampico	896	
F-GJPC	Bell 47G-4	3141	N73281
F-GJPF	Mooney M.20L PFM	26-0019	(F-GPFM)
F-GJPG	SE.3130 Alouette II	1716	F-MJAN
F-GJPH	Piper J-3C-65 Cub	12416	OO-XYZ
			OO-REX
			44-80120
F-GJPJ	Piper PA-28-161 Warrior II	28-8516001	N4376U
F-GJPK	Cameron N-105 HAFB	2518	
F-GJPN	Fairchild-Swearingen SA.227AC Metro III	AC-757B	N57NE
F-GJPO	Piper PA-28RT-201T Turbo Arrow IV	28R-7931039	N2227L
F-GJPP	Cameron N-90 HAFB	1952	
F-GJPQ	Piper PA-28-236 Dakota	2811035	(HB-PNF)
F-GJPT	Cessna 310R	1817	N310LC
F-GJPV	Robinson R-22 Beta	1836	(F-GIVM)
			N23104
F-GJPY	SOCATA TBM-700	13	(F-GKDJ)
F-GJQA	Robin DR.400/140B Major 80	1955	
F-GJQB	Robin DR.400/140B Major 80	1956	
F-GJQC	Robin DR.400/140B Major 80	1970	
F-GJQE	Robin DR.400/120 Petit Prince	1966	

Regn.	Type	C/n	Prev.Id.
F-GJQF	Robin R.3000/140	143	
F-GJQG	Robin DR.400/180R Remorqueur	1963	
F-GJQH	Robin DR.400/180R Remorqueur	1964	
F-GJQI	Robin ATL L	133	
F-GJQJ	Robin DR.400/180 Régent	1967	
F-GJQK	Robin DR.400/120 Petit Prince	1962	
F-GJQL	Robin DR.400/120 Petit Prince	1968	
F-GJQN	Robin DR.400/180 Régent	1976	
F-GJQO	Robin DR.400/140B Major 80	1978	
F-GJQP	Robin DR.400/140B Major 80	1979	
F-GJQQ	Robin DR.400/140B Major 80	1986	
F-GJQR	Robin DR.400/140B Major 80	1971	
F-GJQS	Robin DR.400/140B Major 80	1977	
F-GJQT	Robin DR.400/120 Petit Prince	1987	
F-GJQU	Robin DR.400/120 Petit Prince	1983	
F-GJQV	Robin DR.400/120 Petit Prince	1975	
F-GJQX	Robin DR.400/120 Petit Prince	1993	
F-GJQY	Robin DR.400/160 Chevalier	1988	
F-GJQZ	Robin DR.400/120 Petit Prince	1989	
F-GJRA	Holste MH.1521C Broussard	282	Fr.AF
F-GJRB	SOCATA TB-10 Tobago	228	SE-GFV
			F-ODOE
F-GJRC	Piper J-3C-90 Cub	12028	(F-GJPR)
			HB-OIR
			44-79732
F-GJRD	Beech 65-A90 King Air	LJ-217	(F-GHRD)
			N601R
F-GJRE	Piper PA-28RT-201 Arrow IV	28R-8118059	N8354D
F-GJRF	CASA C.212-200CB	150	TR-LZJ
			F-WIPE
F-GJRG	Thunder AX7-77SI HAFB	1627	OO-BTA
F-GJRJ	Piper PA-28-181 Archer II	2890144	
F-GJRL	Thunder AX7-65 HAFB	1695	
F-GJRM	Piper 28-236 Dakota	28-8211033	N8200K
F-GJRP	Aérospatiale AS.350B Ecureuil	1926	D-HOST
F-GJRR	Piper PA-28RT-201T Turbo Arrow IV	28R-7931294	N8072D
F-GJRS	Piper PA-34-200T Seneca II	34-7670322	N3892F
F-GJRZ	Cessna 152	79724	D-EFRZ
			N757GG
F-GJSD	Beech 65-C90A King Air	LJ-1261	N56787
F-GJSI	Schweizer 269C	S-1390	
F-GJSJ	SE.3160 Alouette III (Reservation)	unkn	
F-GJSL	Aérospatiale SA.342J Gazelle	1052	C-GPGO
			N8350
F-GJSQ	Cessna 172N	72306	N1837C
F-GJSS	Schweizer 269C	S-1578	N110LU
F-GJSU	Piper PA-23-250 Aztec E	27-4776	F-ODSU
			TU-TJY
			TU-TIC
			N14219
F-GJTA	Robinson R-22 Beta	1187	
F-GJTC	Christen Pitts S-2B	5162	
F-GJTD	Cessna 150M	75860	TR-LTD
			N66132
F-GJTF to J	Embraer EMB.120RT Brasilia reservations		
F-GJTK to O	BAe.146 reservations		
F-GJTV	Dassault Falcon 50 (Reservation)	unkn	
F-WJTX/Y	Reserved for Transair France		
F-GJTZ	Cessna 172L	60417	N7117Q
F-GJUM	UltraMagic S-105 HAFB	105/01	EC-EGR
F-GJUP	Cameron N-133 HAFB	2563	
F-GJUS	Cameron O-84 HAFB	175	N83CB
F-GJUV	Piper PA-28-181 Archer II	28-8490060	N4350K
F-GJUX	Thunder AX7-77 HAFB	1745	
F-GJVA	Airbus A.320-211	144	F-WWDK
F-GJVB	Airbus A.320-211	145	F-WWDL
F-GJVC	Airbus A.320-211	204	
F-GJVD	Airbus A.320-211	211	
F-GJVE	Airbus A.320-211	215	
F-GJVF	Airbus A.320-211	244	
F-GJVG	Airbus A.320-211	270	
F-GJVU	Airbus A.320-212	436	G-BXAT
			F-GJVY
			(PH-GCL)
			F-WWDE

Regn.	Type	C/n	Prev.Id.
F-GJVW	Airbus A.320-211	491	N131LF
			F-WWBS
F-GJVX	Airbus A.320-211	420	PH-GCX
			N486GX
			F-WWIE
F-GJXA	SOCATA TB-20 Trinidad	1303	
F-GJXB	SOCATA TB-20 Trinidad	1304	
F-GJXC	SOCATA TB-10 Tobago	1496	
F-GJXD	SOCATA TB-10 Tobago	1497	
F-GJXE	SOCATA TB-10 Tobago	1498	
F-GJXF	SOCATA TB-10 Tobago	1500	
F-GJXG	SOCATA TB-10 Tobago	1504	
F-GJXH	SOCATA TB-10 Tobago	1505	
F-GJXI	SOCATA TB-10 Tobago	1591	
F-GJXJ	SOCATA TB-10 Tobago	1592	
F-GJXK	SOCATA TB-10 Tobago	1593	
F-GJXM	SOCATA TB-10 Tobago	1426	
F-GJXN	SOCATA TB-10 Tobago	1427	
F-GJXO	SOCATA TB-10 Tobago	1428	
F-GJXP	SOCATA TB-10 Tobago	1429	
F-GJXQ	SOCATA TB-10 Tobago	1430	
F-GJXR	SOCATA TB-10 Tobago	1431	
F-GJXS	SOCATA TB-10 Tobago	1432	
F-GJXT	SOCATA TB-10 Tobago	1433	
F-GJXU	SOCATA TB-10 Tobago	1491	
F-GJXV	SOCATA TB-10 Tobago	1493	
F-GJXX	Cessna 560 Citation III	0070	(N2725A)
F-GJXY	SOCATA TB-10 Tobago	1494	
F-GJXZ	SOCATA TB-10 Tobago	1495	
F-GJYD	Cessna 550 Citation II	0415	N1949M
			N1949B
			OH-CUT
			D-CNCI
			N12165
F-GJYG	Aérospatiale AS.350B Ecureuil	1244	F-WYMA
			N3607C
F-GJYL	Aerotek Pitts S-2A	2092	HB-MSD
			N8ED
F-GJYN	Robinson R-44 Astro	0418	
F-GJYY	Reims/Cessna F.152	1660	HB-CCM
F-GJYZ	Hughes 269C	65-0419	F-BXOT
F-GJZB	Robin DR.400/180 Régent	1982	
F-GJZD	Robin DR.400/140 Major	1994	
F-GJZE	Robin DR.400/120 Petit Prince	2005	
F-GJZF	Robin DR.400/140B Major 80	1999	
F-GJZG	Robin DR.400/120 Petit Prince	2003	
F-GJZH	Robin DR.400/120 Petit Prince	2002	
F-GJZI	Robin DR.400/140B Major 80	2016	
F-GJZJ	Robin DR.400/120 Petit Prince	2018	
F-GJZK	Robin DR.400/160 Chevalier	2000	
F-GJZL	Robin DR.400/120 Petit Prince	2009	
F-GJZM	Robin DR.400/120 Petit Prince	2010	
F-GJZN	Robin DR.400/140B Major 80	2019	
F-GJZO	Robin DR.400/120 Petit Prince	2023	
F-GJZP	Robin DR.400/120 Petit Prince	2028	
F-GJZQ	Robin DR.400/160 Chevalier	2030	
F-GJZR	Robin DR.400/120 Petit Prince	2034	
F-GJZS	Robin DR.400/120 Petit Prince	2033	
F-GJZT	Robin DR.400/140B Major 80	2025	
F-GJZU	Robin DR.400/120 Petit Prince	2031	
F-GJZV	Robin DR.400/160 Chevalier	2032	
F-GJZX	Robin DR.400/140B Major 80	2041	
F-GJZY	Robin R.3000/160	149	
F-GJZZ	Robin DR.400/120 Petit Prince	2036	
F-GKAB	Bell 206B Jet Ranger III	3763	G-SMCI
			N3183H
F-GKAC	Cameron N-77 HAFB	1958	
F-GKAD	SOCATA TB-20 Trinidad	954	
F-GKAF(2)	Balloon Works Firefly F8B-15 HAFB	410	OO-BWK
			N2523K
F-GKAH	Cessna 172N	73807	N5477J
F-GKAJ	Mudry CAP.10B	27	Fr.AF
F-GKAM	Mudry CAP.10B	114	HB-SAM
F-GKAP	Piper PA-28-161 Warrior II	28-8216072	N847AH
			N84727

Regn.	Type	C/n	Prev.Id.
F-GKAS	Aérospatiale AS.350B1 Ecureuil	2224	
F-GKAV	Colt 21A HAFB	1742	
F-GKBB	Cessna 172RG Cutlass	0222	N5085U
F-GKBC	Dassault Falcon 10	99	N67JW
			N500GM
			N656PC
			(N65HS)
			N10TJ
			N176FJ
			F-WPXH
F-GKBE	Aérospatiale AS.350B Ecureuil	2503	
F-GKBG	Rockwell 112 Commander	198	N1198J
F-GKBI	Cameron O-65 HAFB	2729	
F-GKBJ	Piper PA-12 Super Cruiser	12-3521	F-BFBJ
			NC4084H
F-GKBL	Cessna 172RG Cutlass	0609	N6289V
F-GKBM	Aérospatiale SA.318C Alouette Astazou	1786	F-MJAT
			F-MCSI
			F-MJAX
F-GKBN	Cameron A-105 HAFB	3289	
F-GKBP	SE.3130 Alouette II	1522	(F-GJMT)
			ALAT
F-GKBR	Piper PA-28-161 Cadet	2841320	N9213Z
F-GKBS	SE.313B Alouette II	1442	ALAT
F-GKBZ	Dassault Falcon 50	185	N238Y
			N23SY
			C-GDCO
			N184FJ
			F-WWHE
F-GKCA	Piper PA-18-150 Super Cub	18-8604	F-OCFI
F-GKCB	Piper PA-28RT-201T Turbo Arrow IV	28R-8131136	N83843
F-GKCF	Aérospatiale AS.350D Ecureuil	1452	N5797D
F-GKCG	Aérospatiale AS.350D Ecureuil	1352	N300HS
			XC-HEU
			N1350N
F-GKCH	Cameron O-84 HAFB	2552	
F-GKCK	SE.316V Alouette III	1256	ALAT
F-GKCM	Cameron Bouchon 116 HAFB	2021	
F-GKCN	Aérospatiale AS.350D Ecureuil	1098	N3596D
F-GKCO	Cessna 172R	80055	F-WKCO
			N374ES
F-GKCP	Robinson R-22 Beta	1401	
F-GKCQ	Thunder AX10-180A HAFB	1791	
F-GKCR	Piper PA-28RT-201T Turbo Arrow IV	28R-8131078	N8339H
F-GKCU	Aérospatiale SA.365N Dauphin 2	6011	PH-SEC
			F-GJEO
			F-ZWVT
			F-WZLG
			N6003L
			F-WZLG
F-GKCV	Beech 200 Super King Air	BB-251	I-BMPE
			HB-GGO
			N256TW
			N18251
F-GKDA	Piper PA-24-260 Comanche C	24-4847	5U-BAX
			5N-AHS
			N9348P
F-GKDB	Dassault Falcon 20E	271/493	(F-GHPO)
			7T-VRP
			F-WNGN
F-GKDE	Reims/Cessna F.152	1653	HB-CCK
F-GKDF	Mooney M.20M TLS	27-0109	
F-WKDL	SOCATA TBM-700	03	
F-GKDM	Pilatus PC-6/B1-H2 Turbo-Porter	670	S2-ACD
			AP-AVU
			HB-FES
F-GKDP	Helibras HB.350B Esquilo (Possible w/o 29.7.98)	1522	YV-569CP
			PT-HLX
F-GKDT	Aérospatiale SA.315B Lama	2562	HB-XUC
			XC-CAM
F-GKDU	Cessna R.182 Skylane RG	00316	N182KP
			(N3701C)
F-GKDX	Mudry CAP.232	10	
F-GKEA	Beech F33A Bonanza	CE-1628	
F-GKEB	SNCAN Stampe SV.4C	618	F-BDFN

Regn.	Type	C/n	Prev.Id.
F-GKEC(2)	Piper PA-28-181 Cherokee Archer II	28-7890218	N6221H
F-GKEF	Piper PA-28-181 Archer II	28-8290031	N8445U
F-GKEH	Dornier Do.27Q-1	2002	D-EKEH
F-GKEI	Fouga CM.170 Magister	479	Fr.AF
	(Previously reserved as F-GLEZ and F-GLSA, ntu)		
F-GKEJ	Piper PA-38-112 Tomahawk	38-82A0077	G-BPOW
			N2592V
F-GKEL	Beech A100 King Air	B-228	N23868
			ZS-XGB
			N23868
F-GKEM	Fokker F.27 Friendship 500	10596	TR-LCQ
			PH-FTX
			CN-CDC(2)
			PH-FTX
			N272SA
			N334MV
			PH-FTX
			PH-EXM
F-GKEN	Piper PA-23-250 Aztec E	27-4784	F-ODLN
			F-BTMQ
			F-BTDZ
			N14226
F-GKER	Cameron A-140 HAFB	2181	
F-GKET	Robin DR.300/108	599	F-BMRQ
			OO-JMM
F-GKEV	Cameron N-90 HAFB	2342	
F-GKFA	Raven Europe RX-7 HAFB	E-164	
F-GKFB	Raven Europe FS57A HAFB	E-172	
F-GKFD	Raven Europe S-60A HAFB	E-185	
F-GKFE	Raven Europe S-60A HAFB	E-177	
F-GKFF	Raven Europe FS-57A HAFB	E-195	
F-GKFG	Raven Europe S-55A HAFB	E-197	
F-GKFH	Raven Europe FS-57A HAFB	E-203	
F-GKFI	Raven Europe RX-7 HAFB	E-215	
F-GKFJ	Raven Europe RX-8 HAFB	E-223	
F-GKFK	Raven Europe FS-57A HAFB	E-210	
F-GKFL	Raven Europe S-49A HAFB	E-216	
F-GKFM	Raven Europe S-66A HAFB	E-225	
F-GKFN	Raven Europe FS-57A HAFB	E-226	
F-GKFO	Raven Europe FS-57A HAFB	E-228	
F-GKFP	Raven Europe FS-57A HAFB	E-229	
F-GKFQ	Raven Europe FS-57A HAFB	E-230	
F-GKFR	Raven Europe S-66A HAFB	E-231	
F-GKFS	Raven Europe S-60A HAFB	E-232	
F-GKFT	Raven Europe FS-57A HAFB	E-237	
F-GKFU	Raven Europe S-52A HAFB	E-204	
F-GKFV	Raven Europe S-55A HAFB	E-238	
F-GKFX	Raven Europe S-49A HAFB	E-239	
F-GKFY	Raven Europe RX-8 HAFB	E-241	
F-GKFZ	Raven Europe W-49A HAFB	E-242	
F-GKGA	Aérospatiale SN.601 Corvette	11	F-WFPD
			EI-BNY
			F-BTTV
			F-ODKS
			TR-LWY
			F-BTTS
			N613AC
			(F-WIFU)
F-GKGE	SE.3130 Alouette II	1541	ALAT
F-GKGF	Colt 90A HAFB	3888	
F-GKGG	Cessna A.185F Skywagon	03341	C-GYVZ
F-GKGI	Cameron N-77 HAFB	2123	
F-GKGJ	SNCAN Stampe SV.4C1	517	F-BDIA
F-GKGK	Cessna 182L Skylane	58851	TR-LCV
			TN-ABD
			TR-LNO
			N42095
F-GKGL	Cessna 560 Citation V	0058	N2686Y
F-GKGM	Bell 206B Jet Ranger II	335	N550JA
F-GKGN	Grumman-American AA-5B Tiger	0089	G-BDGN
			N6147A
F-GKGQ	SNCAN/Stampe SV.4C	54	F-BGGQ
			Fr.Mil
F-GKGR	Agusta-Bell 206B Jet Ranger II	8294	YU-HAP
F-GKGU	Cessna 172R	80338	

Regn.	Type	C/n	Prev.Id.
F-GKGX	Cessna 172R	80343	N9512W
F-GKGY	Colt 180A HAFB	1349	G-BRGY
F-GKGZ	Aerotek Pitts S-2A	2149	TU-TNY
			N31501
F-GKHA	Aérospatiale AS.350B2 Ecureuil	2359	
F-GKHB	Schweizer 269C	S-1438	(N431MS)
F-GKHD	Fokker F.28-0100	11381	HB-IVI
			PH-JXY
F-GKHE	Fokker F.28-0100	11386	HB-IVK
			PH-JXK
F-GKHF	SNCAN/Stampe SV.4C (Reservation .99)	300	F-BBAM
F-GKHG	Enstrom 280C Shark	1034	G-KLAY
			G-BGZD
F-GKHI	Cessna 172N	72688	N6281D
F-GKHL	Cessna 560 Citation V	0059	N2687L
F-GKHM	SE.3160 Alouette III	1088	ALAT
F-GKHP	Aérospatiale AS.350B Ecureuil	2357	
F-GKHR	SIAI S.205-20/R	4-211	OO-DLX
F-GKHT	Robin DR.400/120D	1726	HB-KBB
F-GKHU	Robin DR.400/120D	1723	HB-KBA
F-GKHV	Cameron Camembert SS HAFB	2516	
F-GKIC	Piper PA-46-350P Malibu Mirage	4622051	N927DC
			N91631
F-GKID	Cessna 500 Citation	0319	N94MA
			D-ICUW
			N22LH
			N5319J
			HZ-NC1
			N5319J
F-GKII	Beech 200 Super King Air	BB-515	N200HC
F-GKIJ	Piper PA-44-180 Seminole	44-7995193	N3010H
F-GKIM	Robin DR.400/160 Chevalier	2039	
F-GKIN	Dassault Falcon 50EX (Reservation)	286	
F-GKIP	Dassault Falcon 2000 (Reservation)	90	
F-GKIR	Cessna 500 Citation	0361	N90EB
			N5361J
			C-GOIL
			N5361J
			D-IKPW
			N5361J
F-GKIS	Dassault Falcon 20	307/513	OE-GLL
			I-GCAL
			HB-VDV
			F-WRQT
F-GKIT	Cameron V-77 HAFB	2230	
F-GKIV	Zlin Z.526F Trenér Master	1079	F-BRNC
F-GKIZ	Beech 350 Super King Air	FL-23	N1543Q
F-GKJB	Aérospatiale SN.601 Corvette	20	TR-LZT
			F-BTTN
			N616AC
			F-WNGS
F-GKJE	Aérospatiale AS.350B Ecureuil	1144	N350AJ
			N350S
			N3604D
F-GKJF	Cameron A-105 HAFB	2678	
F-GKJG(2)	Cessna 180A	50325	5R-MLO
			F-BJKE
			F-OBKE
			N5025E
F-GKJH	Piper PA-28RT-201T Turbo Arrow IV	28R-8231005	N8448H
F-WKJI	Raven Europe RXS-8 HAFB	E-333	
F-GKJJ	Cameron A-180 HAFB	2564	(F-GHMX)
F-GKJL	Cessna 560 Citation V	0093	
F-GKJN	Chaize CS.3000F16 HAFB	098	
F-GKJT	Holste MH.1521M Broussard	106	Fr.AF
F-GKJZ	Chaize JZ40F16 HAFB	111	
F-GKKA	Mudry CAP.10B	257	
F-GKKC	Mudry CAP.10B	59	D-EDKG
			F-BXHC
F-GKKE	Mudry CAP.10B	261	
F-CKKI	Mudry CAP.231EX	02	G-BVXL
			F-GKKF
			F-WGZC
F-GKKK	Beech F90 King Air	LA-129	OY-BEL
F-GKKM	Mudry CAP.10B	270	

Regn.	Type	C/n	Prev.Id.
F-GKKZ	Mudry CAP.10B	113	HB-SAL
F-GKLB to F	SAAB-Scania SF.340B reservations		
F-GKLJ	Boeing 747-121	19660	LX-GCV
			N770PA
F-GKLK	Schweizer 269C (Reservation?)	unkn	
F-GKLL	Aérospatiale AS.350B Ecureuil	1202	SE-HKH
F-GKLM	Beech F33A Bonanza	CE-1687	
F-GKLP	Aérospatiale AS.355F1 Ecureuil 2	5014	F-OGPY
			F-GJST
			N181DB
F-GKLS(2)	Agusta-Bell 206B Jet Ranger II	8441	G-JERY
			G-BDBR
F-GKLT	Piper PA-28-181 Archer II	2890124	F-ODLT
F-GKMA	Aérospatiale AS.350B Ecureuil	2285	
F-GKMB	Aérospatiale AS.350B Ecureuil	2304	F-WYMD
F-GKMC	Cameron Bouchon 82 HAFB	2020	
F-GKMF	Balloon Works Firefly F8 HAFB	F8-362	
F-GKMH	Robinson R-22 Beta	1589	
F-GKMI	SE.3130 Alouette II	1212	F-MJAM
			ALAT
F-GKMJ	Cameron N-77 HAFB	2530	
F-GKMK	Cameron Evian Bottle SS HAFB	2367	
F-GKMM	UltraMagic M-65 HAFB	65/76	
F-GKMN	SE.3130 Alouette II	1396	ALAT
F-GKMO	McDonnell-Douglas MD-11 (Reservation)	unkn	
F-GKMP	McDonnell-Douglas MD-11 (Reservation)	48526	
F-GKMQ	McDonnell-Douglas MD-11 (Reservation)	48482	
F-GKMS(2)	Christen A-1 Husky	1168	N9601C
F-GKMT	Chaize JZ25F16 HAFB	119	F-WKMT
F-GKMU	Westland SA.341G Gazelle 1	WA/1141	Q P-1
	(Also quoted as c/n 1181 ex C-FEDG)		G-BBSJ
	(No longer current?)		G-17-11
F-GKMV	Mooney M.20J Model 205	24-3210	
F-GKMX	Piper PA-28-161 Warrior II	28-8616048	N9084Z
			N9509N
F-GKMY	McDonnell-Douglas DC-10-30	47815	SE-DFF
			N5464M
			G-BGXI
F-GKMZ	Mudry CAP.232	09	
F-GKNB	Aeritalia/SNIAS ATR-42-300	226	
F-GKNC	Aeritalia/SNIAS ATR-42-300	230	
F-GKND	Aeritalia/SNIAS ATR-42-300	231	
F-GKNF	Aeritalia/SNIAS ATR-42-300	331	F-WWLP
F-GKNI to Z	Batch reserved for ATR-42-300's for T.A.T.		
F-GKOA	Aeritalia/SNIAS ATR-72-202	201	
F-GKOB	Aeritalia/SNIAS ATR-72-202	232	
F-GKOC	Aeritalia/SNIAS ATR-72-202	307	F-WWEG
F-GKOI	Aeritalia/SNIAS ATR-72-202	342	F-WWLX
F-GKOM to Q	Batch reserved for ATR-72-202's for T.A.T.		
F-GKOR	Cameron O-105 HAFB	2171	
F-GKOT	SE.3130 Alouette II	1243	ALAT
			Fr.AF
F-GKOY	Piper PA-28-161 Cadet	2841334	(N9217N)
F-GKOZ	Aérospatiale SA.360C Dauphin	1027	N49533
F-GKPA	Mooney M.20J Model 205	24-3166	N1079Y
F-GKPC	Aeritalia/SNIAS ATR-72-201	171	F-WWEA
F-GKPD	Aeritalia/SNIAS ATR-72-201	177	F-WWEH
F-GKPE	Aeritalia/SNIAS ATR-72-201	192	F-WWEE
F-GKPF	Aeritalia/SNIAS ATR-72-201	222	
F-WKPG	SOCATA TBM-700	002	
F-GKPH	Aeritalia/SNIAS ATR-72-201	352	F-WWEJ
F-GKPI	Aeritalia/SNIAS ATR-72-201	unkn	
F-GKPJ	Aeritalia/SNIAS ATR-72-201	unkn	
F-GKPO	Piper PA-28R-201 Turbo Arrow III	28R-7803274	N9693C
F-GKPR	Christen Pitts S-2B	5120	N6033Z
F-GKPS	Piper PA-28RT-201 Arrow IV	28R-7918128	N28456
F-GKPT	Reserved for Mr.De Queiroz		
F-WKPX	Fokker F.27 Friendship 100	10121	OO-SVM
			F-GAOT
			N1036U
			VH-TFF
			PH-FAR
F-GKPY	Fokker F.27 Friendship 100	10224	LX-LGA
			PH-FEO
F-GKQA	Robin DR.400/120 Petit Prince	2040	
F-GKQB	Robin DR.400/140B Major 80	2042	
F-GKQC	Robin DR.400/120 Petit Prince	2043	
F-GKQD	Robin DR.400/120 Petit Prince	2044	
F-GKQE	Robin DR.400/100 Cadet	2049	
F-GKQG	Robin DR.400/160 Chevalier	2064	
F-GKQH	Robin DR.400/120 Petit Prince	2053	
F-GKQI	Robin DR.400/180 Régent	2048	
F-GKQJ	Robin DR.400/180 Régent	2046	
F-GKQK	Robin DR.400/140B Major 80	2056	
F-GKQL	Robin DR.400/140B Major 80	2055	
F-GKQM	Robin DR.400/180 Régent	2057	
F-GKQN	Robin DR.400/160 Chevalier	2058	
F-GKQO	Robin DR.400/180 Régent	2087	
F-GKQP	Robin DR.400/120 Petit Prince	2060	
F-GKQQ	Robin DR.400/140B Major 80	2077	
F-GKQR	Robin DR.400/120 Petit Prince	2062	
F-GKQS	Robin DR.400/120 Petit Prince	2068	
F-GKQU	Robin DR.400/180 Régent	2065	
F-GKQV	Robin DR.400/120 Petit Prince	2037	
F-WKQX	Robin X-4	001	
F-GKQY	Robin DR.400/120 Petit Prince	2069	
F-GKQZ	Robin DR.400/120 Petit Prince	2070	
F-GKRB	Robin R.3000/160	141	
F-GKRD	Robin DR.400/120 Petit Prince	1992	
F-GKRF	Aérospatiale SA.342J Gazelle	1058	C-FEMF
F-GKRG	Cessna 172RG Cutlass	0500	N5297V
F-GKRH	Cessna 421C Golden Eagle	0008	D-IBUS(3)
			N87542
F-GKRM	Balloon Works Firefly F7B HAFB	F7B-316	
F-GKRN	SOCATA TB-21 Trinidad TC	520	I- SERN
			F-ODQO
F-GKRO	Holste MH.1521C1 Broussard	154	Fr.AF
F-GKRP	Mooney M.20J Model 205	24-3211	
F-GKRQ	Reserved for Kit Aircraft		
F-GKRR	Piper PA-31T Cheyenne	31T-8120015	N107TT
			HK-2617P
			N2411X
F-GKRS	Schweizer 269C	S-1499	
F-GKSB	Raven-Europe RX-8 HAFB	E-220	
F-GKSC	Thunder AX8-105Z HAFB	1763	
F-GKSF	Aérospatiale SA.315B Lama	2471	N471E
			TG-WAV
F-GKSH	Hughes 269C	120-1016	OO-KMD
			D-HNIG
F-GKSJ	Balloon Works Firefly F7B-15 HAFB	F7B-326	
F-GKSL	Raven-Europe S-60A HAFB	E-067	F-ODSL
F-GKSM	Cessna 182P Skylane	64935	N1373S
F-GKSP	Beech C90B King Air	LJ-1409	(F-GKDG)
F-GKSS	Beech 58 Baron	TH-154	3A-MON
			F-BSRF
F-GKTA	Boeing 737-3M8	24413	OO-LTH
F-GKTB	Boeing 737-3M8	24414	OO-LTI
F-GKTC	Robinson R-22 Beta	1369	
F-GKTH	Aérospatiale AS.355F2 Ecureuil 2	5493	
F-GKTJ	Thunder AX8-9OA S-III HAFB	1986	
F-GKTL	Mooney M.20K Model 231	25-0844	N5776Y
F-GKTM	Cameron A-210 HAFB	4660	
F-GKTN	Cameron A-120 HAFB	4659	
F-GKTO	DHC-6 Twin Otter 300	523	TR-LAL
			F-GAMR
F-GKTP	Cameron A-105 HAFB	4351	
F-GKTR	Bell 47G-2	2457	C-FCAD
			CF-CAD
F-GKTS	Aérospatiale AS.355F1 Ecureuil 2	5081	HB-XPF
			F-GDFH
F-GKUB	SOCATA TB-20 Trinidad	1124	
F-GKUD	SOCATA TB-9 Tampico Club	1128	
F-GKUE	SOCATA TB-9 Tampico Club	1129	
F-GKUF	SOCATA TB-9 Tampico Club	1147	
F-GKUG	SOCATA TB-9 Tampico Club	1148	
F-GKUH	SOCATA TB-9 Tampico Club	1149	
F-GKUI	SOCATA TB-10 Tobago	1150	
F-GKUM	SOCATA TB-20 Trinidad	1177	
F-GKUN	SOCATA TB-9 Tampico Club	1168	
F-GKUO	SOCATA TB-9 Tampico Club	1171	

Regn.	Type	C/n	Prev.Id.
F-GKUQ	SOCATA TB-9 Tampico	1180	
F-GKUR	SOCATA TB-20 Trinidad	1195	
F-GKUS	SOCATA TB-10 Tobago	1208	
F-GKUT	SOCATA TB-10 Tobago	1169	
F-GKUU	SOCATA TB-9 Tampico	1182	
F-GKUV	SOCATA TB-9 Tampico	1194	
F-GKUY	SOCATA TB-20 Trinidad	1179	
F-GKUZ	SOCATA TB-20 Trinidad	1196	
F-GKVA	SOCATA TB-10 Tobago	1230	
F-GKVE	SOCATA TB-20 Trinidad	1245	
F-GKVH	SOCATA TB-9 Tampico Club	1270	
F-GKVI	SOCATA TB-9 Tampico Club	1311	
F-GKVK	SOCATA TB-9 Tampico Club	1290	
F-GKVM	SOCATA TB-9 Tampico Club	1288	
F-GKVO	SOCATA TB-20 Trinidad	1330	
F-GKVS	SOCATA TB-9 Tampico Club	1310	
F-GKVT	SOCATA TB-9 Tampico Club	1312	
F-GKVU	SOCATA TB-9 Tampico Club	1313	
F-GKVV	SOCATA TB-9 Tampico Club	1314	
F-GKVY	SOCATA TB-9 Tampico Club	1347	
F-GKVZ	SOCATA TB-10 Tobago	1329	N5559U
F-GKXA	Airbus A.320-211	287	
F-GKXB to V	*Reserved for A.320's for Air France*		
F-GKXX	Aérospatiale AS.350D Ecureuil	1354	N5771H
F-GKXY/Z	*Reserved for A.320's for Air France*		
F-GKYC	Aérospatiale SA.341G Gazelle	1414	EC-EET
			F-GDFR
			I-ETBA
			F-WIPJ
F-GKYF	Fouga CM.170 Magister	315	F-WKYF
			Fr.AF
F-GKYG	Aérospatiale AS.350B Ecureuil	1536	JA9315
F-GKYH	Fouga CM.170 Magister	435	F-WKYH
			Fr.AF
F-GKYL	Piper PA-28RT-201T Turbo Arrow IV	28R-7931288	N4511U
F-GKYN	Aeritalia/SNIAS ATR-42-300	095	F-ODUL
F-GKZA	Beech 58 Baron	TH-1401	(F-GHHA)
			N104MK
			N6753K
F-GKZB	Beech 58 Baron	TH-1608	(F-GHYB)
F-GKZE	Beech 58 Baron	TH-1494	5V-MCB
F-GKZF	Beech 58 Baron	TH-1486	5V-MCA
F-GKZG	Beech 58 Baron *(Reservation)*	TH-....	
F-GKZH	Beech 58 Baron *(Reservation)*	TH-....	
F-GKZI	Beech 58 Baron *(Reservation)*	TH-....	
F-GKZJ	Beech 58 Baron *(Reservation)*	TH-....	
F-GKZL	McDonnell-Douglas DC-9-83	49402	D-ALLD(2)
F-GKZS	McDonnell-Douglas DC-10-30 *(Reservation 9.99)*	48252	D-ADSO
F-GKZT	Beech 58 Baron	TH-1557	G-BSDY
			N1557M
F-GLAB	SOCATA TB-9 Tampico Club	1074	
F-GLAE	SOCATA TB-9 Tampico Club	1051	
F-GLAF	SOCATA TB-9 Tampico Club	1093	
F-GLAG	SOCATA TB-9 Tampico Club	1094	
F-GLAH	SOCATA TB-20 Trinidad	1076	
F-GLAI	SOCATA TB-9 Tampico Club	1087	
F-GLAK	SOCATA TB-9 Tampico Club	1108	
F-GLAL	SOCATA TB-9 Tampico Club	1091	
F-GLAO	SOCATA TB-9 Tampico Club	1106	
F-GLAP	SOCATA TB-9 Tampico Club	1034	
F-GLAQ	SOCATA TB-9 Tampico Club	1035	
F-GLAR	SOCATA TB-9 Tampico Club	1165	
F-GLAS	SOCATA TB-10 Tobago	1166	
F-GLBL	SOCATA TBM-700	126	
F-GLBM	SOCATA TBM-700	22	F-OHBF
F-GLBN	SOCATA TBM-700	138	
F-GLBP	SOCATA TBM-700 *(Reservation 7.99)*	129	
F-GLBR	SOCATA TBM-700A	23	D-FSOC
			F-GLBF
			F-WNGO
			N700XL
F-GLCA	Raven Europe FS-57A HAFB	E-244	
F-GLCB	Raven Europe S-49A HAFB	E-252	
F-GLCC	Aérospatiale AS.350B Ecureuil	1020	C-GFVB
			N9001P
F-GLCD	Raven Europe FS-57A HAFB	E-256	
F-GLCF	Raven S-57S Fraise HAFB	3001	
F-GLCG	Raven Europe S-60A HAFB	E-262	
F-GLCH	Raven Europe FS-57A HAFB	E-264	
F-GLCI	Raven Europe S-60A HAFB	E-266	
F-GLCJ	Raven Europe S-66A HAFB	E-269	
F-GLCK	Raven Europe FS-57A HAFB	E-276	
F-GLCL	Raven Europe RX-7 HAFB	E-261	
F-GLCM	Raven Europe FS-57A HAFB	E-273	
F-GLCN	Raven Europe S-52A HAFB	E-259	
F-GLCO	Raven Europe S-55A HAFB	E-277	
F-GLCP	Raven Europe S-52A HAFB	E-278	
F-GLCQ	Raven Europe S-55A HAFB	E-285	
F-GLCR	Raven Europe FS-57A HAFB	E-286	
F-GLCS	Raven Europe S-60A HAFB	E-296	
F-GLCT	Raven Europe S-60A HAFB	E-295	
F-GLCU	Raven Europe S-55A HAFB	E-299	
F-GLCV	Raven Europe S-60A HAFB	E-300	
F-GLCY	Raven Europe S-55A HAFB	E-298	
F-GLCZ	Raven Europe S-71A HAFB	E-290	
F-GLDA	Robin DR.400/160 Chevalier	2074	
F-GLDB	Robin DR.400/120 Petit Prince	2072	
F-GLDC	Robin DR.400/120 Petit Prince	2082	
F-GLDD	Robin DR.400/120 Petit Prince	2083	
F-GLDE	Robin DR.400/140B Major 80	2075	
F-GLDF	Robin DR.400/140B Major 80	2091	
F-GLDG	Robin DR.400/140B Major 80	2092	
F-GLDH	Robin DR.400/180 Régent	2084	
F-GLDI	Robin DR.400/140B Major 80	2086	
F-GLDJ	Robin DR.400/120 Petit Prince	2094	
F-GLDK	Robin DR.400/120 Petit Prince	2090	
F-GLDL	Robin R.3000/160	155	
F-GLDM	Robin DR.400/180 Régent	2093	
F-GLDN	Robin DR.400/140B Major 80	2096	
F-GLDO	Robin DR.400/120 Petit Prince	2099	
F-GLDP	Robin DR.400/120 Petit Prince	2097	
F-GLDQ	Robin DR.400/140B Major 80	2098	
F-GLDR	Robin DR.400/180 Régent	2100	
F-GLDS	Robin DR.400/100 Cadet	2101	
F-GLDT	Robin DR.400/120 Petit Prince	2102	
F-GLDU	Robin DR.400/120 Petit Prince	2103	
F-GLDV	Robin DR.400/180 Régent	2120	
F-GLDX	Robin DR.400/120 Petit Prince	2110	
F-GLDY	Robin DR.400/160 Chevalier	2117	
F-GLDZ	Robin DR.400/180 Régent	2105	
F-GLEA	Cessna 172N	72260	N9425E
F-GLEB	American AG-5B Tiger	10100	N100AG
F-GLEC	Aérospatiale SN.601 Corvette	30	(F-GKGB)
			EC-DUE
			OO-MRC
			TR-LAH
			OO-MRC
			F-BTTP
			F-WNGQ
F-GLED(2)	SE.3130 Alouette II	1425	ALAT
F-GLEE	Bell 212	31149	C-GMUJ
F-GLEF(3)	Agusta A.109E	11027	
F-GLEG	Agusta A.109E	11030	
F-GLEH	Agusta A.109E	11037	
F-GLEJ	Mooney M.20K Model 252	25-1100	N252GD
			N252ZD
F-GLEK	UltraMagic N-180 HAFB *(Reservation .99)*	180/21	
F-GLEL	Cameron V-77 HAFB	2467	
F-GLEM	Piper PA-28-181 Archer	28-7990494	N2852K
F-GLEN	Piper PA-28RT-201T Turbo Arrow IV	28R-8231030	N81010
F-GLEP	Cameron A-180 HAFB	4510	
F-GLER	Cameron A-180 HAFB	4511	(F-GLEF)
F-GLET	Robinson R-22 Beta	1957	
F-GLEU	Pilatus PC-6/B1-H2 Turbo-Porter	627	I-SAEZ
			D-FLEV
			N4229S
			9M-APQ
			5Y-AHY
			HB-FDE,
			ST-ADJ(1), HB-FDE

Regn.	Type	C/n	Prev.Id.
F-GLEY	Agusta-Bell 206B Jet Ranger III	8558	3A-MRG
			(F-GBLB)
F-GLFA	SOCATA TB-9 Tampico Club	1363	
F-GLFB	SOCATA TB-200 Tobago XL *(Sold, USA?)*	1375	
F-GLFC	SOCATA TB-200 Tobago XL	1376	
F-GLFD	SOCATA TB-9 Tampico Club	1387	
F-GLFI	SOCATA TB-9 Tampico Club	1436	
F-GLFL	SOCATA TB-9 Tampico Club	1440	
F-GLFM	Aérospatiale AS.350BA Ecureuil	1395	F-WZJD(2)
			SE-HRR
			G-PDCC
			G-PORR
			F-WZFF
F-GLFS	SOCATA TB-20 Trinidad	1364	
F-GLFV	SOCATA TB-9 Tampico Club	1471	
F-GLFX	SOCATA TB-9 Tampico Club	1575	
F-GLFY	SOCATA TB-9 Tampico Club	1582	
F-GLFZ	SOCATA Rallye 235C	13075	
F-GLGA	SOCATA TB-10 Tobago	184	HB-EZU
F-GLGC	Piper PA-31-350 Chieftain	31-8052149	N3279H
			V2-LCC
			VP-LCC
F-GLGD	Bell 206L-1 Long Ranger II	45189	G-RASS
			G-JLBI
			D-HBBZ
			N5012L
			(D-HNRA)
F-GLGF	Robin DR.315 Petit Prince	484	OO-BIB
F-GLGG	Airbus A.320-211	203	ZS-NZP
			F-WWDN
F-GLGH	Airbus A.320-211	220	ZS-NZR
			F-WWIJ
F-GLGK	SOCATA MS.880B Rallye-Club	1584	LX-FBA
			F-BSCL
F-GLGL	Piper PA-28RT-201 Arrow IV	28R-7918250	N108CC
			N9624N
F-GLGM	Airbus A.320-212	131	N481GX
			F-WWIX
F-GLGN	Airbus A.320-211	132	N482GX
			F-WWIY
F-GLGO	Airbus A.320-211 *(Reservation)*	unkn	
F-GLGP	Airbus A.320-211 *(Reservation)*	unkn	
F-GLGQ	Airbus A.320-211 *(Reservation)*	unkn	
F-GLGR	Reims/Cessna FA.152 Aerobat	0384	(F-GLYB)
			3A-MPC
			F-GDOP
F-GLGT	Piper PA-32-301 Saratoga	3213081	N9249G
F-GLGU	Airbus A.320-211 *(Reservation)*	unkn	
F-GLGY	Dassault Falcon 900	11	UN-09002
			F-WEFX
			LX-AER
			F-WWFK
F-GLHA	Robin DR.400/120 Petit Prince	794	F-BUHK
F-GLHD	Aérospatiale SA.315B Lama	2647	VT-VKT
			F-GDJH
F-GLHF	Fouga CM.170 Magister	406	F-WLHF
			Fr.AF
F-GLHG	Piper PA-28R-200 Cherokee Arrow II	28R-7635051	N4461X
F-GLHH	Aérospatiale SA.360 Dauphin	1026	OH-HPM
			D-HACW
F-GLHJ	Dassault Falcon 2000	12	I-SNAW
			F-WWMM
F-GLHK	Mooney M.20M TLS	27-0176	
F-GLHL	Agusta-Bell 47J	1135	
F-GLHM	SOCATA Rallye 100ST	2587	Fr.Navy-87
F-GLHO	Fouga CM.170 Magister *(Reservation .99)*	331	F-WIGY
			Fr.AF
F-GLHP	Aérospatiale AS.350B2 Ecureuil	2609	
F-GLHT	Bell 407 *(Reservation 9.99)*	53294	N4442F
F-GLHV	Robinson R-22 Beta	2381	
F-GLHZ	Rockwell Commander 112	173	N1184J
F-GLIA	Aeritalia/SNIAS ATR-42-300	010	F-GDXL
			F-WDXL

Regn.	Type	C/n	Prev.Id.
F-GLIB	Aeritalia/SNIAS ATR-42-300	025	F-GHME
			DQ-FEK
			F-WWED
F-GLIC	Cameron A-180 HAFB	3344	G-BWBR
F-GLID	Bell 47G-2	2416	C-FLMD
			CF-LMD
F-GLIE	SOCATA TB-20 Trinidad	994	G-PLYD
F-GLIF	Beech 200 Super King Air	BB-192	F-OGPQ
			OY-CBV
			LN-KCI
			OY-CBV
			(EI-BGR)
			OY-CBV
			SE-GRP
F-GLIJ	Canadair CL.600-2B19 Regional Jet	7081	C-FM..
F-GLIK	Canadair CL.600-2B19 Regional Jet	7084	C-FMMT
F-GLIM(2)	Cessna 560 Citation V	0119	N6804N
F-GLIO	Cessna R.182 Skylane RG	01815	N510DC
			N5101T
F-GLIP	Aérospatiale AS.350B3 Ecureuil *(Reservation)*	unkn	
F-GLIQ	Cameron C-80 HAFB	3584	
F-GLIR	Fokker F.28-0100	11509	PH-EZF
F-GLIS	Fokker F.28-0070	11540	PH-RRS
			(F-GLIS)
			PH-EZS
F-GLIT	Fokker F.28-0070	11541	PH-RRT
			(F-GLIT)
			PH-EZN
F-GLIU	Fokker F.28-0070	11543	PH-RRU
			(F-GLIU)
			PH-EZM
F-GLIV	Fokker F.28-0070	11556	PH-RRV
			(F-GLIV)
			PH-RRV
F-GLIX	Fokker F.28-0070	11558	PH-RRW
			(F-GLIX)
			PH-RRW
F-GLIY	Canadair CL.600-2B19	7053	C-FMMQ
F-GLIZ	Canadair CL.600-2B19	7057	C-FM..
F-GLJB	SE.3130 Alouette II	1073	ALAT
F-GLJC	Piper PA-22-150 Caribbean	22-6854	N2857Z
F-GLJE	Aérospatiale AS.350B3 Ecureuil *(Reservation .99)*	3288	
F-GLJF	Schweizer 269C	S-1550	N41S
F-GLJH	Cameron N-120 HAFB *(Reservation 9.99)*	3416	G-BWJL
F-GLJJ	Cameron N-120 HAFB	3713	
F-GLJL	Beech 95-B55 Baron	TC-1718	HB-GDX
F-GLJM	Cameron N-77 HAFB	2659	
F-GLJO	Boeing 737-3B7	23380	N505AU
	(Reservation .99, identity suspect)		N374AU
F-GLJP	Agusta-Bell 206B Jet Ranger II	8315	(F-GGPD)
			YU-HAV
F-GLJR	Cameron A-105 HAFB	3367	
F-GLJS	SOCATA TBM-700	63	
F-GLKA	Robin DR.400/180R Remorqueur	2108	
F-GLKB	Robin DR.400/180R Remorqueur	2109	
F-GLKD	Robin DR.400/140B Major 80	2121	
F-GLKE	Robin DR.400/180 Régent	2119	
F-GLKF	Robin DR.400/120 Petit Prince	2122	
F-GLKG	Robin DR.400/180 Régent	2116	
F-GLKH	Robin R.3000/160	158	
F-GLKI	Robin DR.400/140B Major 80	2111	
F-GLKJ(2)	Robin DR.400/180 Régent	2216	
F-GLKK	Robin DR.400/180 Régent	2130	
F-GLKL	Robin DR.400/160 Chevalier	2129	
F-GLKO	Robin DR.400/120D Petit Prince	1604	HB-EQY
F-GLKP	Robin DR.400/180R Remorqueur	2131	
F-GLKQ	Robin DR.400/120D Petit Prince	1605	HB-EQZ
F-GLKR	Robin DR.400/120 Petit Prince	2134	
F-GLKS	Robin DR.400/120 Petit Prince	2126	
F-GLKT	Robin DR.400/180 Régent	2136	
F-GLKU	Robin DR.400/120 Petit Prince	2140	
F-GLKV	Robin DR.400/120 Petit Prince	2139	
F-GLKX	Robin DR.400/120 Petit Prince	2141	
F-GLKY	Robin DR.400/180 Régent	2127	
F-GLKZ	Robin DR.400/120 Petit Prince	2128	

Regn.	Type	C/n	Prev.Id.
F-GLLB	Piper PA-28-161 Warrior III	2842005	
F-GLLC	Schweizer 269C	S-1553	N41S
F-GLLF	Cessna 172S	172S8092	N681SP
F-GLLL	SOCATA TBM-700	107	F-GLBG
F-GLLR	Piper PA-32-300 Cherokee Six	32-7640093	N75183
F-GLLU	Mooney M.20J Model 201	unkn	
F-GLLY	UltraMagic S-130 HAFB (Reservation .99)	130/..	
F-GLMA	CEA DR.250/160 Capitaine	99	OO-LIP / D-EDLC
F-GLMB	Piper PA-34-220T Seneca III	34-8333087	N42996
F-GLMC	Wassmer Jodel D.120 Paris-Nice	82	F-BIKL
F-GLMD	Dassault Falcon 20C5	117	EC-FJP / EC-855 / HB-VKC / TS-IRS / N421ZC / N171PF / N995F / F-WMKH
F-GLME	Thunder AX7-65 HAFB	2064	
F-GLMF	Holste MH.1521M Broussard	289	ALAT
F-GLMG	Piper PA-32-300 Cherokee Six	32-40056	OO-DCR / TS-ASR / F-BOHQ / N4040W
F-GLMI	Bell 407 (Reservation)	53117	N14054
F-GLMJ	Balloon Works Firefly F8B HAFB	F8B-430	
F-GLMK	Thunder AX10-180A S3 HAFB	2183	
F-GLMO	Fouga CM.170 Magister	230	Fr.AF
F-GLMP	Aérospatiale AS.350B Ecureuil	1194	C-GBNH / N3603B
F-GLMR	Balloon Works Firefly 7B-15 HAFB	7B-336	
F-GLMS	Piper J-3C-65 Cub (L-4H)	12192	OO-GMS / (OO-LSD) / PH-CMS / D-EGUL / G-ANXP / N79819 / NC78919 / 44-79896
F-GLMT	Dassault Falcon 20F	246/482	F-BSTR / F-WJMK
F-GLMU	Dassault Falcon 900	35	HB-IAD / F-WWFC
F-GLMX	McDonnell-Douglas DC-10-30	47814	LN-RKC / N5463Y / G-BGXH
F-GLNA(2)	Boeing 747-206	20399	PH-BUE / HS-VGG / PH-BUE
F-GLNB	Reserved for Corse Air International		
F-GLNC	Reserved for Corse Air International		
F-GLND	Beech 1900D	UE-196	N3234G
F-GLNE	Beech 1900D	UE-197	N3234U
F-GLNF	Beech 1900D	UE-69	YR-RLA / YR-AAK / N82896
F-GLNG	Aérospatiale AS.350B Ecureuil	1415	F-OGNY / N114CT / N5784R
F-GLNH	Beech 1900D	UE-73	YR-RLB / YR-AAL / N82923
F-GLNI	BAe.146 Series 200QC	E-2188	G-BTDO / G-6-188
F-GLNJ	Beech 1900D	UE-258	N10936
F-GLNK	Beech 1900D	UE-269	N11017
F-GLNM	Cessna 340A	0351	G-BPNM / N989HC / N999HC / (N37331)
F-GLNY	Agusta-Bell 47G-2	260	9H-AAF / 74+18 / AS+060
F-GLNZ	SOCATA TB-10 Tobago	179	I-ODNZ / F-GAKU / OO-DAL
F-GLOA	Cessna 172RG Cutlass	0168	N6336R
F-GLOB	Cameron O-65 HAFB	2798	
F-GLOF	Schweizer 269C	S-1588	N69A
F-GLOH	Wassmer WA.54 Europa	93	F-BXOH(3) / F-BUKX / F-OCUY
F-GLOK	Cessna 172P	75517	N64080
F-GLOM	Cameron A-105 HAFB	2956	
F-GLOO	Reims/Cessna F.172N	1690	OO-VTG
F-GLOR(2)	Eurocopter EC.135T1	0041	
F-GLOT	Mudry CAP.21	6	F-ODOT
F-GLOU	Robinson R-44 Astro	0032	I-OOOI
F-GLPB	Robinson R-22 Beta	1967	
F-GLPC	Cameron Masque SS HAFB	2794	
F-GLPF	Cameron O-105 HAFB	2856	
F-GLPH	Aérospatiale AS.365N2 Dauphin 2	6439	F-WTNC
F-GLPI	SE.3130 Alouette II	1847	(FAP) / 77+00
F-GLPJ	Beech 1900C	UC-40	OY-BVG / OH-BPA / OY-BVG / N31101
F-GLPK	Beech 1900C	UC-74	N15528
F-GLPL	Beech 1900C	UC-92	
F-GLPM	Cessna 340A	0451	N6263X
F-GLPN	Cessna T.207A Turbo Stationair 8 /Soloy Pac	00595	N73469
F-GLPO	Cessna 152	80278	N24481
F-GLPR	Cessna 172N	67672	N73778
F-GLPS	SE.313B Alouette II	1527	FAP9210 / 75+92 / PL+139
F-GLPT	Fairchild-Swearingen SA.226T(B) Merlin IIIB (Reservation .99)	T-298	VH-AWU / N5495M
F-GLPV	SE.3130 Alouette II	1443	F-MJAZ
F-GLQJ	Piper PA-28R-201T Turbo Arrow III	28R-7803366	F-OGQJ / N22081
F-GLQQ	Piper J-3C-65 Cub	7396	C-GUQQ / N126RB / N40637 / NC40637
F-GLRC	SE.313B Alouette II	1117	F-MJAW
F-GLRD	Chaize CS.2200F12 HAFB	113	
F-GLRE	Fouga CM.170 Magister	217	Fr.AF
F-GLRF	SIGA MA-26 Pilatre de Rozier HAFB	114	
F-GLRG	Embraer EMB.120ER Brasilia	120-149	PH-MGX / OO-DTK / PT-SPO
F-GLRI	Piper PA-28RT-201T Turbo Arrow IV	28R-7931059	
F-GLRJ	Chaize CS.2200F12 HAFB	114	
F-GLRM	Cameron O-65 HAFB	2689	
F-GLRP	Piper PA-31T Cheyenne II (Reservation 10.99)	31T-8120064	F-ZBFZ / F-WFLQ / HK-2906P / HK-2906X / N9141Y
F-GLRR(2)	SE.313B Alouette II	1309	ALAT
F-GLRS	SE.313B Alouette II	1346	ALAT
F-GLRV	Piper J-3C-65 Cub	9440	N48526 / NC48526 / 43-579 / (42-59389)
F-GLRZ	Beech C90A King Air	LJ-1296	(F-GJDK) / F-OGRZ
F-GLSB	Cameron V-77 HAFB	3257	
F-GLSF	Robinson R-22 Beta	1813	(F-GHJY)
F-GLSI	Sikorsky S-76A	760170	F-GKSI / I-SKSA / F-GING / N76UT / C-GHVQ
F-GLSM	Mooney M.20C Ranger	20-0024	N7790M

Regn.	Type	C/n	Prev.Id.
F-GLSR	Beech A36 Bonanza	E-2120	OO-PBC
			F-GIBC
			N67578
F-GLST	Piper PA-28-161 Warrior II	28-7916306	N3036T
F-GLSV	Galaxy 7 HAFB	GLX-1737	
F-GLTC	Cessna T.210F Turbo-System Centurion	0188	CN-TZS
			N6788R
F-GLTH	Aérospatiale AS.350B Ecureuil	2701	
F-GLTK	Cessna 550 Citation II	0609	N344A
			D-CHOP
			N609TC
			(N1242A)
F-GLTL	Chaize JZ.30F16 HAFB	130	
F-GLTO	Fouga CM.170 Magister	471	F-WFPK
			Fr.AF
F-GLTP	Pilatus PC-6/B2-H2 Turbo-Porter	691	HB-FEV
			SX-AFC
			HB-FEV
F-GLTR	Cessna 172R	80833	
F-GLTZ	Piper PA-18A-150 Super Cub	18-5136	N7062B
F-GLUB	Piper J-3C-65 Cub	16395	N92002
			NC92002
F-GLUC	Raven-Europe S-55A HAFB	E-400	
F-GLUD	Robin DR.400/120 Petit Prince	2165	
F-GLUF	Jum J'Aie	001	
F-GLUI (2)	Sky 105-24 HAFB	143	
	(Originally allocated c/n 085 which became G-BXLC)		
F-GLVA	Robin DR.400/180 Régent	2146	
F-GLVB	Robin DR.400/120 Petit Prince	2148	
F-GLVC	Robin DR.400/120 Petit Prince	2149	
F-GLVD	Robin DR.400/120 Petit Prince	2147	
F-GLVE	Robin DR.400/120 Petit Prince	2151	
F-GLVF	Robin DR.400/120 Petit Prince	2150	
F-GLVG	Robin DR.400/120 Petit Prince	2153	
F-GLVI	Robin DR.400/120 Petit Prince	2138	
F-GLVJ	Robin DR.400/120 Petit Prince	2142	
F-GLVK	Robin DR.400/140B Major 80	2158	
F-GLVL	Robin DR.400/140B Major 80	2154	
F-GLVN	Robin DR.400/140B Major 80	2163	
F-GLVO	Robin DR.400/180 Régent	2155	
F-GLVP	Robin DR.400/140B Major 80	2164	
F-GLVQ	Robin DR.400/120 Petit Prince	2166	
F-GLVR	Robin DR.400/120 Petit Prince	2168	
F-GLVS	Robin DR.400/120 Petit Prince	2169	
F-GLVT	Robin DR.400/140B Major 80	2170	
F-GLVU	Robin DR.400/140B Major 80	2171	
F-GLVV	Robin DR.400/160 Chevalier	2172	
F-GLVX	Robin DR.400/140B Major 80	2175	
F-GLVY	Robin DR.400/120 Petit Prince	2173	
F-GLVZ	Robin DR.400/160 Chevalier	2174	
F-GLXD	SA.315BLama	2610	
F-GLXF	Boeing 737-219	22657	G-BJXJ
	(Stored)		N851L
			N6066Z
			(ZK-NAT)
			G-BMMZ
F-GLXH	Boeing 737-2D6	20544	TZ-ADL
			7T-VEC
F-GLXL	SE.3130 Alouette II	1612	76+25
			QW+218
			QW+743
F-GLXZ	SOCATA TB-200 Tobago XL	1448	F-ODXZ
F-GLYC	Cessna 560 Citation V	0205	
F-GLYG	Robinson R-22 Beta	0947	
F-GLYN	Robin DR.400/180R Remorqueur	1306	HB-EYN
F-GLYR	Aérospatiale AS.350B Ecureuil	1009	G-BWNA
			G-BFNC
			F-WXFH
F-GLYS	McDonnell-Douglas DC-10-30	46872	F-ODLX
			(F-GKMR)
			SE-DFE
			(SE-DEB)
F-GLZA	Airbus A.340-311	005	F-WWCA
F-GLZB	Airbus A.340-311	007	
F-GLZC	Airbus A.340-311	029	

Regn.	Type	C/n	Prev.Id.
F-GLZE	Airbus A.340-211	038	
F-GLZF	Airbus A.340-211	043	
F-GLZG	Airbus A.340-311	049	
F-GLZH	Airbus A.340-311	078	
F-GLZI	Airbus A.340-311	084	
F-GLZJ	Airbus A.340-313	186	(F-GLZN)
F-GLZK	Airbus A.340-313X	207	
F-GLZL	Airbus A.340-313X	210	
F-GLZM	Airbus A.340-313X	237	
F-GLZN	Airbus A.340-313X	245	
F-GLZO	Airbus A.340-313X	246	
F-GLZP	Airbus A.340-313X	260	
F-GLZQ	Airbus A.340-313X	289	
F-GLZR	Airbus A.340-313X	307	
F-GLZS	Airbus A.340-313X	310	
F-GLZT to Z	Reserved for A.340's for Air France		
F-GMAA	Cameron N-77 HAFB	2855	
F-GMAB	Piper PA-28-140 Cherokee	28-7625052	C-GGVB
F-GMAC	Cameron Concept 60 HAFB	3058	
F-GMAD	Beech 1900D	UE-290	N18153
F-GMAE	Zodiac MGZ 2.2.S Balloon	011	
F-GMAF	Robin DR.400/140B Major 80	2104	
F-GMAH	Balloon Works Firefly F7B HAFB	F7B-345	
F-GMAK	Cameron N-105 HAFB	3920	
F-GMAN	Cameron A-105 HAFB	4361	
F-GMAP	Cameron C-80 Concept HAFB	3380	
F-GMAS	Commander Aircraft 114B	14552	N60096
F-GMAT	Aérospatiale AS.350B3 Ecureuil	3202	
F-GMAU	Robinson R-22 Beta	2182	N23411
F-GMAX	UltraMagic V-105 HAFB (Reservation .99)	105/12	
F-GMAY	Aérospatiale SA.365N Dauphin 2	6137	
F-GMBA	Aérospatiale AS.355N Ecureuil 2	5320	N35EC
			YV-O-KWH-5
			F-WZKO
F-GMBB	Cessna P210NPressurized Centurion	00380	D-EAOH
			N4953K
F-GMBC	Piper PA-46-310P Malibu	46-8408039	G-BORP
			N4346M
F-GMBD	Piper PA-28-181 Archer II	2890062	HB-PLK
F-GMBE	Reims/Cessna FTB.337G Super Skymaster	0017	(F-GGTP)
			FAP3716
			CS-AAO
F-GMBF	Robinson R-22M Mariner	2193M	F-OGUV
			(F-GMAL)
F-GMBG	SE.3130 Alouette II	1643	76+38
F-GMBH	Aérospatiale AS.350B3 Ecureuil	3125	
F-GMBI	SIGA MA-30 Pilatre de Rozier HAFB	107	
F-GMBJ	Chaize CS.2200F12 HAFB	143	
F-GMBL	Aérospatiale AS.355N Ecureuil 2	5358	(N75EC)
			YV-O-KWH-6
F-GMBM	Robin DR.400/140B Major 80	2219	
F-GMBN	Aérospatiale AS.350B Ecureuil	1794	3A-MFC(2)
			3A-MSC
			F-GGSC
			3A-MSC
			F-GGSC
			3A-MSC
F-GMBO	Aérospatiale AS.350B2 Ecureuil	2253	SE-HUS
F-GMBP(2)	UltraMagic S-130 HAFB	130/18	
F-GMBS	Chaize CS.3000F16 HAFB	115	
F-GMBT	Robinson R-44 Astro	0123	
F-GMBV	Aérospatiale AS.350BA Ecureuil	1709	3A-MMC
			F-WZFU
F-GMBX	Lindstrand LBL-77A HAFB	515	
F-GMBZ	Aérospatiale AS.350B1 Ecureuil	2204	D-HBAS
			F-GHFL
			N607S
F-GMCA	Cameron N-77 HAFB	2714	
F-GMCB	Hughes 269C	21-1027	N1105U
F-GMCC	Rockwell Commander 112	294	N1294J
F-GMCE	Robinson R-22 Beta	2071	N23263
F-GMCF	Piper PA-28-181 Archer II	28-8290155	N8244D
F-GMCG	Christen Pitts S-2B	5243	
F-GMCH	Type unknown	1370	

Regn.	Type	C/n	Prev.Id.
F-GMCI	Cessna 550 Citation II	0050	F-ODUT
			N250CF
			(N259CF)
			D-CJJJ
			N362DJ
			N102FC
			(N3298M)
F-GMCJ	Eurocopter EC.135T1	(0020)	
F-GMCL	Piper PA-32R-301T Turbo Saratoga SP	32R-8129087	N8410B
F-GMCM	Piper PA-28RT-201T Turbo Arrow IV	28R-8531010	N6914K
F-GMCN	Piper PA-32R-301 Saratoga	3213049	N9221G
F-GMCO	Thunder AX6-56A HAFB	163	G-BRNY
F-GMCP	Piaggio P.180 Avanti	1022	I-RAIH
F-GMCT	Mudry CAP.10B	12	Fr.AF
F-GMCY	Nord 1101 Noralpha (Reservation)	67	CEV
F-GMCZ	Aérospatiale AS.350B2 Ecureuil	2641	D-HWCW
F-GMEA	Pilatus PC-7 Turbo Trainer	519	HB-HMA
F-GMEB	Pilatus PC-7 Turbo Trainer	520	HB-HMB
F-GMED	Pilatus PC-7 Turbo Trainer	480	HB-HMP
F-GMEE	Pilatus PC-7 Turbo Trainer	558	HB-HLE(5)
F-GMEF	Piper PA-38-112 Tomahawk	38-81A0057	N25701
F-GMEG	Piper PA-38-112 Tomahawk	38-80A0168	N25417
F-GMEL	Pilatus PC-6/B2-H2 Turbo-Porter	536	N4915
F-GMEN	Aérospatiale AS.350B3 Ecureuil	3115	
F-GMEP	Colt 69A HAFB	1960	
F-GMER	Cameron C-80 Concept HAFB	4655	
F-GMES	Robin ATL (Reservation)	73	F-GFRV
F-GMEU	SIGA MA-26 Pilatre de Rozier HAFB	102	F-WMEU
F-GMEZ	Cameron N-105 HAFB	4607	
	(Later reserved with c/n 4693 - as replacement?)		
F-GMFA	Raven Europe S-60A HAFB	E-110	
F-GMFB	Raven Europe RX-7 HAFB	E-111	
F-GMFD	Raven Europe FS-57A HAFB	E-122	
F-GMFE	Raven Europe FS-57A HAFB	E-125	
F-GMFF	Raven Europe FS-57A HAFB	E-129	
F-GMFG	Raven Europe RX-7 HAFB	E-156	
F-GMFH	Raven Europe RX-7 HAFB	E-162	
F-GMFI	Raven Europe RX-7 HAFB	E-132	
F-GMFJ	Raven Europe FS-55A HAFB	E-135	
F-GMFL	Raven Europe RX-7 HAFB	E-138	
F-GMFN	Raven Europe S-60A HAFB	E-139	
F-GMFO	Raven Europe FS-57A HAFB	E-144	
F-GMFP	Raven Europe RX-7 HAFB	E-133	
F-GMFQ	Raven Europe S-55A HAFB	E-141	
F-GMFR	Raven Europe S-55A HAFB	E-145	
F-GMFS	Raven Europe S-60A HAFB	E-163	
F-GMFT	Raven-Europe S-55A HAFB	E-157	
F-GMFU	Raven Europe FS-57A HAFB	E-158	
F-GMFV	Raven Europe FS-57A HAFB	E-140	
F-GMFX	Raven Europe S-52A HAFB	E-200	
F-GMFY	Raven Europe S-55A HAFB	E-161	
F-GMFZ	Raven Europe FS-57A HAFB	E-150	
F-GMGA	Dassault Falcon 50	51	N52DQ
			N52DC
			N70FJ
			F-WZHR
			(F-GLOP)
			F-ODZK
F-GMGB	Beech B200 Super King Air	BB-1390	N8043B
F-GMGC	Schweizer 269C	S-1631	N86G
F-GMGD	Dragonfly 333	3330093003	
F-GMGE	Dragonfly 333	3330093004	
F-GMGF	Cessna P210N Pressurized Centurion II	00253	I-NCVH
			N4665K
F-GMGG	Christen A-1 Husky	1091	HB-KCR
F-GMGH	Schweizer 269C	S-1535	
F-GMGK	Aeritalia/SNIAS ATR-72-202	365	F-OHAT
			F-WWEM
F-GMGM	SOCATA Rallye 100ST	2582	Fr.Navy-82
F-GMGN	SOCATA Rallye 100ST	2585	Fr.Navy-85
F-GMGO	Aerostar RX-8 HAFB	3298	
F-GMGP	Robin DR.400/140B Major 80	2231	
F-GMGS	Aerostar RX-8 HAFB	3258	
F-GMGT	Aerostar S-60A HAFB	3221	
F-GMGU	Raven S-57A HAFB	3195	

Regn.	Type	C/n	Prev.Id.
F-GMHA	Robinson R-22 Beta	2059	
F-GMHB	SIAI-Marchetti SF.260	358	Phil.AF
F-GMHC	Eurocopter EC.135T1	0036	
F-GMHD	Eurocopter EC.135T1 (Reserved as F-WQLA .99)	0037	
F-GMHE	Eurocopter EC.135T1	0048	
F-GMHF	Eurocopter EC.135T1	0056	
F-GHHG	Eurocopter EC.135T1	0066	
F-GMHH	Robin HR.100/210 Safari	155	3A-MUZ
			F-BUHH
F-GMHI	Aérospatiale SA.365N1 Dauphin 2	6037	PH-SED
			F-GNXB
			5N-...
			F-GDXB
			(F-ODSA)
			F-WTNV
F-GMHJ	Eurocopter EC.135T1	0032	
F-GMHK	Eurocopter EC.135T1	0081	D-HBYH
F-GMHM	SIGA MA-26 Pilatre de Rozier HAFB	101	
F-GMHP	SA.316B Alouette III	1780	EC-FST
			EC-456
			CC-CJD
			EC-EEB
			CC-CJD
			N39314
			PH-NNY
			5N-AEW
			PH-NNY
			F-WMHK
F-GMHR	Aérospatiale AS.350B Ecureuil	1921	OY-HEJ
F-GMHS	UltraMagic N-180 HAFB	180/10	
F-GMHY	Bell 47G	673	F-GGSU
			F-BMHY
			Fr.Mil
F-GMIA	Mooney M.20J Model 205	24-3358	
F-GMIB	Robin DR.500/200i Président	0002	
F-GMID	Hughes 369D	106-0007D	D-HDEK
			OE-DXN
F-GMIF	Cessna T.207A Turbo Stationair 7 /Soloy Pac	00416	HB-CJF
			N7138J
			N21190
			C-GBUZ
			N7352U
F-GMII	Piper PA-28-181 Archer III	2843029	LX-III
F-GMIK	Hughes 269C	96-0542	D-HGIS
			SE-HNX
			LN-OTX
			SE-HNX
			PH-HGH
			N5083U
			C-GGAN
			N7426F
F-GMIL	Robinson R-44 Astro	0283	
F-GMIM	Schweizer 269C	S-1239	D-HJON
F-GMIN	Cameron A-210 HAFB	4258	
F-GMIS	Cessna U.206F Stationair	02194	F-MJAD
			F-MJAJ
			F-BRGM
			N7411Q
F-GMIT	Cameron N-77 HAFB	1689	LX-FIT
F-GMIX	SOCATA TB-20 Trinidad	693	I-SDMB
			F-ODRQ
F-GMIZ	Aérospatiale SA.365C1 Dauphin 2	5018	
F-GMJA	Cessna 177B Cardinal	02254	N35188
F-GMJB	Thunder AX7-77 HAFB	2281	
F-GMJC	Eurocopter EC.135T1	0026	
F-GMJD	Boeing 737-2K5	22599	D-AHLG(2)
			CS-TMD
			D-AHLG(2)
F-GMJF	Rockwell Commander 112	289	N1289J
F-GMJG	Pilatus PC-6/B2-H2 Turbo Porter	659	HB-FFF
			F-GIMU
			HB-FEF
			EC-EHK
			HB-FEF

Regn.	Type	C/n	Prev.Id.
F-GMJL	Aérospatiale SA.341G Gazelle	1245	G-BKLT
	(W/o 18.6.98)		(F-GMJL)
			(F-GGGB)
			G-BKLT
			N15WC
			N47261
F-GMJM	SE.313B Alouette II	1714	Fr.AF
F-GMJR	Rockwell Commander 112TC	13072	N24WE
F-GMKA	Robin HR.200/120B	263	
F-GMKB	Robin HR.200/120B	253	
F-GMKC	Robin HR.200/120B	252	
F-GMKD	Robin HR.200/120B	256	
F-GMKE	Robin HR.200/120B	257	
F-GMKF	Robin HR.200/120B	258	
F-GMKG	Robin HR.200/120B	259	
F-GMKH	Robin HR.200/120B	261	
F-GMKI	Robin DR.400/120 Petit Prince	2206	
F-GMKJ	Robin DR.400/180 Régent	2204	
F-GMKL	Robin R.2160 Alpha Sport	265	
F-GMKM	Robin DR.400/140B Major 80	2202	
F-GMKN	Robin DR.400/120 Petit Prince	2199	
F-GMKO	Robin DR.400/140B Dauphin 4	2179	
F-GMKP	Robin DR.400/120 Petit Prince	2182	
F-GMKR	Robin DR.400/180 Régent	2186	
F-GMKS	Robin DR.400/120 Petit Prince	2177	
F-GMKT	Robin DR.400/180 Régent	2183	
F-GMKV	Robin DR.400/160 Chevalier	2195	
F-GMKX	Robin DR.400/140B Major 80	2194	
F-GMKY	Robin DR.400/180 Régent	2210	
F-GMKZ	Robin DR.400/180R Remorqueur	2189	
F-GMLC(2)	Robinson R-22 Beta	unkn	
F-GMLE	SA.318C Alouette Astazou	2151	F-GMLF
			9V-...
			F-GDQO
			C-FBMG
			CF-BMG
			F-WIEN
F-GMLJ	Cessna 414	0635	I-CCEE
			N69826
F-GMLM	Cessna 182F Skylane	54683	F-BKQM
			N3283U
F-GMLN	Cameron N-90 HAFB	4146	
F-GMLQ	Cameron N-77 HAFB	3859	
F-GMLT	Beech 200T Super King Air	BT-34/BB-1426	
F-GMLZ	Robinson R-22 Beta	0565	G-IEPF
			N2419X
F-GMMA	Pilatus PC-6/B1-H2 Turbo-Porter	714	HA-YDC
F-GMMB	Hughes 269C	129-0874	D-HHUT
			SE-HKN
F-GMMD	Cameron O-105 HAFB	3852	
F-GMMF	Chaize JZ.35F16 HAFB	133	
F-GMMG	Cameron N-105 HAFB	4318	
F-GMMJ	Chaize JZ.25F16 HAFB	121	
F-GMMN	Robin DR.400/180 Régent	2426	
F-GMMO	Lindstrand LBL-69A HAFB	313	
F-GMMP	BAe.146 Series 200QC	E-2176	G-BWLG
			VH-NJQ
			G-PRCS
F-GMMR	CEA Jodel DR.1051 Sicile	308	OO-GUY
			F-BKIN
F-GMMS	Mooney M.20R Ovation	29-0144	
F-GMMT	UltraMagic M-90 HAFB	90/15	
F-GMNA	Raven Europe FS-57A HAFB	E-307	
F-GMNB	Raven Europe S-71A HAFB	E-310	
F-GMND	Raven Europe S-52A HAFB	E-316	
F-GMNE	Raven Europe S-60A HAFB	E-334	
F-GMNF	Raven Europe FS-57A HAFB	E-317	
F-GMNG	Raven Europe RX-8 HAFB	E-328	
F-GMNH	Raven Europe S-49A HAFB	E-335	
F-GMNI	Raven Europe S-55A HAFB	E-326	
F-GMNJ	Raven Europe S-60A HAFB	E-336	
F-GMNK	Raven Europe S-60A HAFB	E-324	
F-GMNL	Raven Europe S-60A HAFB	E-325	
F-GMNM	Raven Europe FS-57A HAFB	E-340	
F-GMNN	Raven Europe FS-57A HAFB	E-346	
F-GMNP	Raven Europe S-55A HAFB	E-348	
F-GMNQ	Raven Europe FS-57A HAFB	E-308	
F-GMNR	Raven Europe FS-57A HAFB	E-354	
F-GMNS	Raven Europe S-52A HAFB	E-301	
F-GMNT	Raven Europe FS-57A HAFB	E-329	
F-GMNU	Raven Europe S-60A HAFB	E-355	
F-GMNV	Raven Europe FS-57A HAFB	E-352	
F-GMNX	Raven Europe S-52A HAFB	E-359	
F-GMNY	Raven Europe RX-7 HAFB	E-366	
F-GMNZ	Raven Europe RX-9 HAFB	E-362	F-WIMX
F-GMOA	Robin DR.400/120 Petit Prince	978	LX-RCA
			F-BVMT
F-GMOB	Morane-Saulnier MS.880B Rallye Club	3	HB-EDC
F-GMOD	Embraer EMB.120RT Brasilia	120-109	F-WQJV
			N128AM
			PT-SNB
F-GMOI	Cameron A-210 HAFB	4257	
F-GMOM	Eurocopter EC.135T1	0023	
F-GMON	Eurocopter EC.135T1	0024	
F-GMOP	Piper PA-23 Apache (Reservation)	unkn	
F-GMOR	Cameron Concept 60 HAFB	2976	
F-GMOT	Dassault Falcon 50	111	N50AH
			VR-CDF
			F-GKTV
			N297W
			F-WZHZ
F-GMOU	Reims/Cessna F.152	1925	HB-CKR
			F-GDOB
F-GMOV	Christen Pitts S-2B	5151	OO-MOV
			N10ZX
			(N71ZX)
			N10ZX
F-GMPA(2)	Aérospatiale AS.350B Ecureuil	1749	D-HSAN
			SE-HUV
			D-HCHL
			N2627A
F-GMPB	Cessna 182S	80217	
F-GMPD	SIGA MA-26 Pilatre de Rozier HAFB (Reservn .99)	unkn	
F-GMPE	Robinson R-22 Beta	2077	
F-GMPF	Maule MX-7-235 Star Rocket	10060C	D-ENLR
			N61113
F-GMPG	Fokker F.28-0100	11362	F-GIOF
			PH-EZT
F-GMPH	Piper PA-28-181 Archer II	2843085	
F-GMPJ	American AG-5B Tiger	10170	
F-GMPL	Bell 206B Jet Ranger II	4393	
F-GMPM	Beech C90B King Air	LJ-1303	(F-GIAO)
F-GMPN	SOCATA MS.893E Rallye 180GT Gaillard	12264	3A-MPO
			F-BUGN
F-GMPP	Beech M35 Bonanza	D-6451	(F-GNTP)
			I-TINE
			HB-EBH
			D-EBBA
F-GMPT	Partenavia P.68B	62	G-PART
			OY-CEY
			D-GATE
			PH-EEO
			(N718R)
F-GMPV	Mudry CAP.10B	260	
F-GMPY	Piper PA-28-151 Cherokee Warrior	28-7615037	HB-PAK
			N9637N
F-GMQA	SOCATA TB-10 Tobago	1594	
F-GMQB	SOCATA TB-10 Tobago	1595	
F-GMQC	SOCATA TB-20 Trinidad	1620	
F-GMQD	SOCATA TB-20 Trinidad	1621	
F-GMQE	SOCATA TB-20 Trinidad	1622	
F-GMQF	SOCATA TB-20 Trinidad	1623	
F-GMQG	SOCATA TB-20 Trinidad	1624	
F-GMQH	SOCATA TB-10 Tobago	1734	
F-GMQI	SOCATA TB-10 Tobago	1735	
F-GMQJ	SOCATA TB-10 Tobago	1736	
F-GMQK	SOCATA TB-20 Trinidad	1737	
F-GMQL	SOCATA TB-20 Trinidad	1738	
F-GMQM	SOCATA TB-20 Trinidad	1739	
F-GMQN	SOCATA TB-20 Trinidad	1740	
F-GMQO	SOCATA TB-20 Trinidad	1741	

Regn.	Type	C/n	Prev.Id.
F-GMRA	Robin DR.400/140B Major 80	2253	
F-GMRB	Maule MX-7-235 Star Rocket	10119C	
F-GMRC	Robinson R-22 Beta	2072	N23269
F-GMRD	Beech 58 Baron	TH-1459	3A-MON
			N851BE
F-GMRE	Reims/Cessna FR.182 Skylane RG	0016	HB-CCG
			D-EGTN
F-GMRF	SIAI-Marchetti SF.260	unkn	
F-GMRG	Mudry CAP.232	12	
F-GMRJ	Cameron A-120 HAFB	4477	
F-GMRM	Piaggio P.180 Avanti	1027	
F-GMRN	Beech E90 King Air	LW-304	G-SANB
			G-BGNU
F-GMRP	Aérospatiale AS.350B2 Ecureuil	3224	
F-GMRR	Robin DR.400/140B Dauphin 4	2430	
F-GMRS	McDonnell-Douglas DC-10-30 (Reservation)	unkn	
F-GMRT	SIGA MA-26 Pilatre de Rozier HAFB	115	
F-GMRV	Robin DR.400/160 Chevalier	1933	6V-AGB
F-GMSB	Mooney M.20MTLS (Reservation 10.99)	27-0126	OO-LSD
F-GMSC	Aérospatiale AS.355NEcureuil 2	5582	
F-GMSE	Piper PA-28RT-201T Turbo Arrow IV	28R-8131042	OO-GCI
			N83090
F-GMSF	SIAI-Marchetti SF.260	unkn	
F-GMSI	Schweizer 269C-1	0050	
F-GMSJ(2)	Piper PA-22-160 Tri-Pacer	22-6232	CN-TTF
F-GMSL	Robinson R-22 Beta	2216	(F-GMBL)
F-GMSR	Cessna 180E (Reservation .99)	51093	F-BFVX
			F-OBVX
			N8693X
F-GMSV	Sky 105-24 HAFB	081	
F-GMTA	SE.3160 Alouette III	1535	F-WQFJ
			A-535
F-GMTC	Robinson R-22 Beta	2078	
F-GMTF	Eurocopter EC-135	0012	
F-GMTH	Aérospatiale AS.350B Ecureuil	2700	
F-GMTL	UltraMagic H-77 HAFB	77/128	
F-GMTO	Fairchild-Swearingen SA.226AT Merlin IVA	AT-031	N22KW
			N95KY
			N5FW
			N44AG
			N5346M
F-GMTT	Schroeder Fire Balloons G HAFB	364	
F-WMTZ	Chaize JZ.F2212 HAFB	125	
F-GMUL	CEA Jodel DR.1050 Ambassadeur	15	HB-EUF
			F-BJHI
F-GMUP	Reims/Cessna F.150J (Reservation .99)	0431	LX-AVA
			D-EBML
F-GMUZ	Piper PA-28RT-201T Turbo Arrow IV	28R-8131143	N8396H
F-GMVB(2)	SAAB 2000	019	SE-019
F-GMVC(2)	SAAB 2000	021	SE-021
F-GMVD(2)	SAAB 2000	034	SE-034
F-GMVE	SAAB 2000	040	SE-040
F-GMVF	SAAB 2000	045	SE-045
F-GMVG	SAAB 2000	049	SE-049
F-GMVH	BAe. Jetstream Series 3206	974	G-BURU
			(F-OHFT)
			G-31-974
F-GMVI	BAe. Jetstream Series 3206	975	G-BUTW
			(F-OHFU)
			G-31-975
F-GMVJ	BAe. Jetstream Series 3206	976	G-BUUZ
			(F-OHFV)
			G-31-976
F-GMVK	BAe. Jetstream Series 3206	977	G-BUVD
			(F-OHFR)
			(F-OHFW)
			G-31-977
F-GMVL	BAe. Jetstream Series 3206	978	F-OHFX
			G-31-978
F-GMVM	BAe. Jetstream Series 3206	979	(F-OHFZ)
			G-31-979
F-GMVN	BAe. Jetstream Series 3206	980	G-31-980
F-GMVO	BAe. Jetstream Series 3206	982	G-31-982

Regn.	Type	C/n	Prev.Id.
F-GMVP(2)	BAe. Jetstream Series 3206	970	G-BUVC
			F-GLPY
			(F-OHFS)
			G-BUVC
			G-31-970
F-GMVS	Pilatus PC-6/B1-H2	518	N6251U
			PH-OTB
F-GMVT	Robinson R-44 Astro	0453	
F-GMVY	SAAB-Scania SF.340B	363	SE-C63
			(B-12264)
F-GMXA	Robin DR.400/140B Major 80	2211	
F-GMXB	Robin DR.400/120 Petit Prince	2212	
F-GMXD	Robin DR.400/140B Major 80	2214	
F-GMXE	Robin DR.400/180 Régent	2208	
F-GMXF	Robin DR.400/180 Régent	2218	
F-GMXG	Robin DR.400/120 Petit Prince	2223	
F-GMXH	Robin DR.400/120 Petit Prince	2132	F-WLKJ
F-GMXI	Robin DR.400/160 Chevalier	2220	
F-GMXJ	Robin DR.400/120 Petit Prince	2221	
F-GMXK	Robin HR.200/120B	266	
F-GMXL	Robin HR.200/120B	267	
F-GMXM	Robin DR.400/120 Petit Prince	2226	
F-GMXN	Robin DR.400/180 Régent	2222	
F-GMXO	Robin DR.400/180 Régent	2224	
F-GMXP	Robin DR.400/120 Petit Prince	2227	
F-GMXQ	Robin HR.200/120B	272	
F-GMXR	Robin DR.400/120 Petit Prince	2230	
F-GMXS	Robin DR.400/140B Major 80	2233	
F-GMXU	Robin HR.200/120B	277	
F-GMXV	Robin DR.400/180 Régent	2237	
F-GMXX	Robin DR.400/180 Régent	2238	
F-GMXY	Robin DR.400/140B Major 80	2239	
F-GMXZ	Robin DR.400/120 Petit Prince	2250	
F-GMYA to Z Reserved for Airbus A.321-100's for Air France			
F-GMZA	Airbus A.321-111	498	D-AVZK
F-GMZB	Airbus A.321-111	509	D-AVZN
F-GMZC	Airbus A.321-111	521	D-AVZW
F-GMZD	Airbus A.321-111	529	D-AVZA
F-GMZE	Airbus A.321-111	544	D-AVZF
F-GMZF	Airbus A.321-111 (Reservation)	unkn	
F-GNAD	Beech 1900C-1	UC-58	N1568G
			N15305
F-GNAE	Piaggio P.180 Avanti	1020	(D-ISAP)
F-GNAG	Beech A36 Bonanza	E-1653	CP-1566
F-GNAH	Beech 1900C-1	UC-131	N15486
F-GNAI	Aérospatiale SA.365C3 Dauphin 2	5026	G-BJKB
			N3601T
F-GNAJ	Beech 1900C-1	UC-163	N163AM
			N163YV
F-GNAL	Piper PA-32R-300 Lance	32R-7680422	N414AL
			N9626N
F-GNAM	Piper PA-28-181 Archer II	2890014	N9108Z
F-GNAP	Reims/Cessna F.150L	0843	F-BUBG
F-GNAR	Beech F33A Bonanza	CE-1735	
F-GNAS	CEA DR.253B Régent	157	CN-TAS
			F-BIFA
			D-EFCW
F-GNAT	Bell 47J	1134	
F-WNAV	Dassault Falcon 2000	1	(F-WNEW)
F-GNBA	Beech 65-A90 King Air	LJ-311	HB-GIN
			F-GIGP
			N114SV
			N10XL
			N909K
F-GNBC	Mooney M.20R Ovation	29-0034	
F-GNBD	Piper PA-28-181 Archer II	28-8090311	HB-PFD
			N8216T
F-GNBE	Piper PA-32RT-300 Lance	32R-7885042	N9299C
F-GNBF	Aérospatiale SA.316B Alouette III (Reservation .99)	1383	A-383
F-GNBG	Fouga CM-170 Magister	413	Fr.AF
F-GNBI	Grob G.115B (Reservation)	8010	D-ENZM
F-GNBJ	Robin DR.400/180 Régent (Reservation)	1744	(D-E...)
			F-GEKS
F-GNBK	Mooney M.20J Model 201	24-0417	F-GKDC
			N201AN

Regn.	Type	C/n	Prev.Id.
F-GNBM	Robinson R-22 Mariner	unkn	
F-GNBR	Beech 1900D	UE-327	N23154
F-GNBS	Dornier 328-100	3053	D-CDXU
F-GNBT	Aérospatiale AS.350B3 Ecureuil	3095	
F-GNCA	Cameron N-77 HAFB	3035	
F-GNCB	Thunder AX7-77A HAFB	2202	
F-GNCC	Cessna U.206F Stationair	02126	F-MJAA
			F-BRGI
			N71171
F-GNCD	Schweizer 269C	S-1362	G-FPEL
F-GNCE	Chaize JZX.18F12 HAFB	118	F-WNCE
F-GNCG	UltraMagic M77 HAFB	77/107	
F-GNCH	Piper PA-28-181 Archer III	2843074	
F-GNCK	Wassmer WA.51A Pacific	72	HB-DCK
F-GNCL	SOCATA TB-20 Trinidad	960	G-BRIN
F-GNCM	Piper PA-28-161 Cadet	2841292	N9202H
F-GNCN	UltraMagic S-90 HAFB	90-12	
F-GNCP	Cessna F550T Citation II	0004	N312GA
			C-GPAW
			N98786
F-GNCS	Thunder AX8-9OSI HAFB	2503	G-DAFL
F-GNCT	SA.318C Alouette Astazou	2265	TJ-AHP
			F-GBGX
			VR-HGX
F-GNCY	Beech 65-C90 Kinng Air (Reservation 4.99)	LJ-822	F-GBLU
F-GNDA	Dassault Falcon 900	88	VR-BLT
			F-WWFH
F-GNDB(2)	Fournier RF-3	21	I- BMDB
			F-BMDB
F-GNDC	McDonnell-Douglas DC-10-30	47849	F-GDJK
			(F-ODOV)
			ZK-NZR
F-WNDF	Fournier RF-47	01	
F-GNDH	Piper PA-34-220T Seneca II	34-8070359	D-GMFG
			N8248V
F-GNDI	Reserved for Dassault Aviation		
F-GNDJ	Piper PA-25-235 Pawnee C	25-5323	N8819L
F-GNDL	Mudry CAP.10B	269	
F-GNDP	Robin DR.400/120 Petit Prince	2073	
F-GNDR	UltraMagic S-90 HAFB	90/06	
F-GNDT	Cessna 340A	1008	TR-LCL
			G-SILV
			D-IHOS
			(N4272C)
F-GNDV	SA.318C Alouette Astazou	1988	F-GBDV
			F-ZBDB
F-GNDX	Cameron C-80 HAFB	4124	
F-GNDZ	Dassault Falcon 10	17	EC-949
			F-GHDZ
			N33HL
			N27DA
			N29966
			VH-FFB
			OH-FFB
			F-WLCS
F-GNEA	SE.3130 Alouette II	1841	FAP9208
			76+96
			PY+211
			PO+139
F-GNEB	Cessna U.206F Stationair II	03364	OO-SPA
			(N8507Q)
F-GNEC	Cameron V-90 HAFB	3022	
F-GNEE	Beech C90A King Air	LJ-1328	N90HB
			N8250K
F-GNEG	Beech B200 Super King Air	BB-1377	HB-GIR
			N56881
			(N65N)
F-GNEM	McDonnell-Douglas DC-10-30	46892	TU-TAM
			HS-TGB
			TU-TAM
			(TU-TBD)
F-GNET	Balloon Works Firefly 7 HAFB (Reservation .99)	unkn	
F-GNEV	Mudry CAP.10B	115	Fr.AF
F-GNFA	Cameron O-77 HAFB	4449	
F-GNFB	Piper PA-14 Family Cruiser	14-133	F-BFFB
F-GNFC	Boeing 737-36E	26315	EC-GAP
			EC-796
F-GNFD	Boeing 737-36E	26317	EC-GBU
			EC-797
F-GNFD	Douglas C-47B	15813/32561	G-BVRB
			F-GDXP
			Fr.Navy 729
			Fr.AF
			KN307
			44-76229
F-GNFE	Mudry CAP.10B	22	Fr.AF
F-GNFG	Chaize JZ.25F12 HAFB	134	
F-GNFJ	SE.3130 Alouette II	1908	V-59
F-GNFL	Piper PA-31-310 Navajo	31-7400986	I- ELET
			N7598L
F-GNFP	Bell 206B Jet Ranger II	1148	(F-GKLS)
			G-HUMT
			ZS-HDY
F-GNFR	Piper L-4H Cub	11114	EC-AKP
	(Identity highly suspect)		HB-OUC
			EC-AKP
			HB-OFC
			43-29823
F-GNFS	Boeing 737-4Y0	23981	SU-BLL
			EI-CEW
			EC-EMY
			EC-251
F-GNFU	Boeing 737-3Y0	24256	EC-GFU
			EC-204
			EC-FVJ
			EC-542
			G-MONM
F-GNGA	Piper PA-23- (Reservation .99)	unkn	
F-GNGC	Schweizer 269C	S-1632	
F-GNGG	Mooney M.20J Model 205	24-3216	F-GMOC
			N8VH
			F-GKBT
F-GNGH	Schweizer 269C	S-1535	D-HLIL
			N86G
F-GNGS	Boeing 727-260A	21978	SX-CAO
			ZS-OAO
			SX-BFM
			N978AL
			ET-AHL
F-GNGU	Grumman G.159 Gulfstream 1	101	4X-ARV
			F-GFGU
			N300SB
			N222H
			N716G
F-GNHB	SOCATA Rallye 235F	3388	
F-GNHD	SOCATA TB-200 Tobago XL	1459	
F-GNHE	SOCATA Rallye 235F	3389	
F-GNHF	SOCATA TB-10 Tobago	1315	(SX-...)
			F-GNHF
			F-OGSE
F-GNHG	SOCATA TB-200 Tobago XL	1633	
F-GNHI	Partenavia P.68B	169	G-WICK
			G-BGFZ
F-GNHK	SOCATA TB-20 Trinidad	1666	
F-GNHL	SOCATA Rallye 235F	3392	
F-GNHM	SOCATA Rallye 235F	3393	
F-GNHN	SOCATA Rallye 235F	3391	
F-GNHP	SOCATA TBM-700	102	
F-GNHQ	SOCATA TB-9 Tampico	1450	SE-KNT
F-GNHR	SOCATA TB-20 Trinidad	1358	SE-KNO
F-GNHS	SOCATA TB-200 Tobago XL	1761	
F-GNHV	SOCATA Rallye 235F	13396	
F-GNHY	SOCATA TB-20 Trinidad	1817	F-WWRD
F-GNIF	Airbus A.340-313X	168	(F-GLZL)
F-GNIG	Airbus A.340-313X	174	
F-GNJA	HOAC DV-20 Katana	20011	
F-GNJB	HOAC DV-20 Katana	20076	OE-ADV
F-GNLA	Aérospatiale SA.315B Lama	2165/32	F-GJRT
			Fr.AF
			ALAT

Regn.	Type	C/n	Prev.Id.
F-GNLB	SA.318C Alouette Astazou	2163	EC-FZH
			F-GDQP
			C-FBMU
			CF-BMU
F-GNLG	Fokker F.28-0100 (Reservation)	11363	D-ADFE
			F-GIOF
			PH-EZV
F-GNLH	Fokker F.28-0100	11311	D-ADFB
			F-GIOC
			PH-EZE
F-GNLI	Fokker F.28-0100	11315	D-ADFC
			F-GIOD
			PH-EZF
F-GNLJ	Fokker F.28-0100	11344	D-ADFD
			F-GIOE
			PH-EZD
F-GNLK	Fokker F.28-0100	11307	D-ADFA
			F-GIOB
			PH-EZX
F-GNLP	Aérospatiale AS.350B Ecureuil	1848	HB-XRO
			D-HONY
F-GNLT	Aérospatiale SA.365N Dauphin 2	6069	JA9585)
F-GNLV	SIGA MA-26 Pilatre de Rozier HAFB	103	(F-GNBR)
F-GNMA	Beech C90A King Air	LJ-1299	N8253D
F-GNMB	Aérospatiale AS.350B3 (Reservation .99)	3259	
F-GNMD	Piper PA-18-150 Super Cub	18-8209009	TR-LAX
			N91243
F-GNMG	Cessna U.206F Stationair	02173	F-MJAE
			F-BRGK
			N7325Q
F-GNMH	Nord 260 (Reservation)	8	CEV 'MC'
			F-BLHO
			LN-LME
			F-BLHO
F-GNMJ	Beech B36TC Bonanza	EA-517	D-ENMS
			(D-EOPL)
			D-ENMS
			N8217W
F-GNMP	Beech C90 King Air	LJ-828	(F-GPJC)
			I-BOMY
			F-GFME
			N6037C
F-GNNA	Robin DR.400/120 Petit Prince	2236	
F-GNNB	Robin HR.200/120B	278	
F-GNNC	Robin HR.200/120B	279	
F-GNND	Robin DR.400/160 Chevalier	2241	
F-GNNE	Robin DR.400/140B Major 80	2247	
F-GNNF	Robin HR.200/120B	280	
F-GNNH	Robin HR.200/120B	281	
F-GNNI	Robin DR.400/120 Petit Prince	2252	
F-GNNJ	Robin DR.400/180R Remorqueur	2254	
F-GNNK	Robin DR.400/125	2258	F-WNNK
F-GNNL	Robin DR.400/140B Major 80	2256	
F-GNNM	Robin DR.400/160 Chevalier	2259	
F-GNNN	Robin DR.400/180 Régent	2264	
F-GNNO	Robin HR.200/120B	283	
F-GNNP	Robin DR.400/140B Major 80	2257	
F-GNNQ	Robin HR.200/120B	284	
F-GNNR	Robin DR.400/180 Régent	2260	
F-GNNS	Robin DR.400/120 Petit Prince	2262	
F-GNNT	Robin HR.200/120B	285	
F-GNNU	Robin DR.400/120 Dauphin 2+2	2263	
F-GNNV	Robin HR.200/120B	286	
F-GNNX	Robin DR.400/120 Petit Prince	2265	
F-GNNY	Robin DR.400/120 Petit Prince	2267	
F-GNNZ	Robin DR.400/120 Petit Prince	2270	
F-GNOA	Beech 1900D (Reservation .99)	UE-51	N51YV
F-GNOM	Cameron O-84 HAFB	4624	
F-GNOO	Cameron Concept C-60 HAFB	3176	
F-GNOR	Cameron O-105 HAFB	3984	
F-GNOU	SIGA MA-26 Pilatre de Rozier HAFB	113	
F-GNOV	Aerotek Pitts S-2A	2202	OO-NOV
			N31469
F-GNPA	Dornier 328-100	3063	D-CDXK(2)
F-GNPC	UltraMagic N-160 HAFB	160/15	
F-GNPD	Beech 200 Super King Air	BB-199	LN-PAD
			OY-AUK
			N83DS
			N33DS
			N32KA
			N525BC
F-GNPE	Aérospatiale AS.350B2 Ecureuil (Reservation .99)	unkn	
F-GNPJ	Robin DR.400/140B Major 80	2261	
F-GNPL	Aeritalia/SNIAS ATR-42-320	063	F-ODUC(2)
F-GNPM	Beech1900C-1	UC-153	N153YV
F-GNPP	Chaize JZ.30F16 HAFB	129	
F-GNPR	Dornier 328-110	3088	
F-GNPS	Robinson R-22 Beta	2582	
F-GNPU(2)	Piper PA-23-250Aztec E (Reservation .99)	"27-4709"	
	(C/n suspect, this was PT-DMM w/o 3.4.73)		
F-GNPV	Piper PA-32R-301T Turbo Saratoga SP	32R-8329012	N4291Z
F-GNPZ	SE.3130 Alouette II (Reservation)	1382	ALAT
F-GNRA	Raven Europe RX-7 HAFB	E-368	
F-GNRB	Raven Europe RX-8 HAFB	E-369	
F-GNRC	Raven Europe S-52A HAFB	E-372	
F-GNRD	Raven Europe RX-7 HAFB	E-349	
F-GNRE	Raven Europe RX-8 HAFB	E-376	
F-GNRF	Raven Europe RX-8 HAFB	E-378	
F-GNRG	Raven Europe RXS-8 HAFB	E-382	
F-GNRH	Raven Europe S-66A HAFB	E-381	
F-GNRI	Raven Europe FS-57A HAFB	E-394	
F-GNRJ	Raven Europe S-55A HAFB	E-391	
F-GNRK	Raven Europe FS-57A HAFB	E-404	
F-GNRL	Raven Europe FS-57A HAFB	E-398	
F-GNRM	Raven Europe RXS-8 HAFB	E-392	
F-GNRO	Raven Europe S-52A HAFB	E-407	
F-GNRQ	Raven Europe S-55A HAFB	E-402	
F-GNRS	Raven Europe S-55A HAFB	E-353	
F-GNRV	Raven Europe S-55A HAFB	E-380	
F-GNRY	Raven Europe FS-57A HAFB	E-396	
F-GNRZ	Raven Europe S-60A HAFB	E-397	
F-GNSA	Beech 58 Baron	TH-1701	
F-GNSB	Beech 58 Baron	TH-1702	
F-GNSC	Beech 58 Baron	TH-1703	
F-GNSD	Beech 58 Baron	TH-1704	
F-GNSE	Beech 58 Baron	TH-1705	
F-GNSF	Beech 58 Baron	TH-1706	
F-GNSG	Beech 58 Baron	TH-1734	
F-GNSH	Beech 58 Baron	TH-1736	
F-GNSI	Beech 58 Baron	TH-1510	N3178P
F-GNSJ	Beech 58 Baron	TH-1515	N3076B
F-GNTA	Embraer EMB-145 (Reservation)	145-...	
F-GNTB	Embraer EMB-145 (Reservation)	145-...	
F-GNTC to GNTO Reserved for Embraer EMB.145's			
F-GNTV	Cameron N-77 HAFB	3900	
F-GNUJ	Robin ATL L	22	EC-FKB
			F-GFNU
			F-WFNU
F-GNVA	CAARP CAP.10	02	F-TFVA
	(Reserved as D-EQVA 6.99)		F-TFVQ
			F-ZWRM
F-GNVB	SE.3130 Alouette II	1920	V-66
F-GNVE	UltraMagic H-77 HAFB	77/98	
F-GNVN	Mudry CAP.10B	278	Fr.AF
F-GNVV	Chaize JZ.25F16 HAFB	126	
F-GNXB	Aérospatiale SA.365N Dauphin 2	6037	5N-...
			F-GDXB
			(F-ODSA)
			F-WTNV
F-GNXX	UltraMagic M-105 HAFB	105/37	
F-GNYC	Robinson R-44 Astro	0390	
F-GNYD	Fouga CM.170 Magister (Reservation)	232	Fr.AF
F-GNYG	Raven-Europe FS-57A HAFB	E-408	
F-GNYK	Robinson R-44 Clipper	0319	N7132M
F-GNYL	Beech 1900C-1	UC-134	N134YV
F-GNYN	Fouga CM.170 Magister	532	Fr.AF
F-GNYQ	Robinson R-44 Astro	0388	
F-GNZA	Morane-Saulnier MS.885 Super Rallye	274	F-BHZA
			F-OBZA

Regn.	Type	C/n	Prev.Id.
F-GNZB	Fokker F.28 Fellowship 1000C	11073	F-ODZB
			F-GJLC
			(F-GGKC)
			PK-PJV
			PH-EXT
F-GNZC	Cessna R.182 Skylane RG	01199	TR-LZC
			(N756ZA)
F-GNZK	Cessna 414	0277	G-AZZK
			N1562T
F-GOAC	Dornier 328-100	3084	
F-GOAD	Piper J-3C-65 Cub (Reservation)	10293	HB-OCW
			HB-OUF
			43-1432
F-GOAE	Beech 350CSuper King Air (Reservation 12.99)	FM-1	V5-RTZ
			N1564D
F-GOAF	Boeing 737-242C	19847	N847TA
			F-GGPA
			(F-GFVK)
			C-FNAB
			CF-NAB
			N6241
F-GOAG	Pilatus PC-6/B1-H2 Turbo Porter	658	D-FDHP
			HB-FDH
F-GOAH	Dornier 228-201	8056	F-GPIV
			F-OGOQ
			7P-LAL
			D-CAMI
F-GOAK	Bombardier BD.700 Global Express (Reservation)		
F-GOAL	Dassault Falcon 50	131	F-WGTF
			(F-GPLH)
			I-ADAG
			HZ-BB2
			F-WPXD
F-GOAM	Beech A36 Bonanza	E-2427	
F-GOAP	Cessna 172R	80423	N9540Q
F-GOAS	Mudry CAP.10B (Reservation)	133	F-WQHT
			Fr.AF
F-GOAT	Cessna 402C Utiliner (Reservation .99)	0015	TT-DAQ
			TT-BAC(3)
			G-OFAR
			(N4656A)
F-GOAV	Reims/Cessna F.152	1757	HB-CNT
F-GOAZ	SIGA MA-22 Pilatre de Rozier HAFB	105	
F-GOBB	Robin DR.400/140B Major 80	729	F-BUHS
			D-EBAZ
F-GOBF	SIAI-Marchetti SF.260	116	BF8431
			Philippines AF
F-GOBI	UltraMagic S-130 HAFB (Reservation .99)	130/25	
F-GOBJ	Mooney M.20M TLS	27-0199	LX-PAL
F-GOBM	Reims/Cessna F.150G	0215	F-BOQM
F-GOBO	SIGA MA-26 Pilatre de Rozier HAFB (Reservn 11.99)	125	
F-GOBP	CASA C.212-CB	10	TC-AOS
			EC-CRX
			EC-102
F-GOBR	Boeing 727-256	20601	EC-CBG
			N1790B
F-GOBS	Chaize JZ.30F16 HAFB	146	
F-GOBY	Cameron O-90 HAFB	2813	G-OREY
F-GOCA	Piper PA-28-151 Cherokee Warrior	28-7615380	HB-PBD
			N9609N
F-GOCB	Mudry CAP.10	28	Fr.AF
F-GOCC	Pilatus PC-6/B1-H2 Turbo Porter	667	SE-IRR
			C-GXIJ
			N62156
			XW-PFQ
			HB-FDR
F-GOCD	Chaize JZ25F16 HAFB	127	
F-GOCE	Cameron N-77 HAFB	3630	
F-GOCH	Aérospatiale AS.350B Ecureuil	1010	G-BMIF
	(Damaged 15.4.97)		LN-OTW
			SE-HHS
			F-WZFB
F-WOCM	Chaize JZ.13F16 HAFB	122	
F-GOCN	Piper PA-34-220T Seneca III	3433138	F-GPCN
			N274CP
			YV-274CP
			N9170Z
			N9637N
F-GOCP	Cameron V-90 HAFB	3415	
F-GOCS	SOCATA MS.880B Rallye Club	1579	OO-CCS
			F-BSCB
F-GOCV	Aérospatiale SA.341G Gazelle	1010	F-GFFN
			D-HMTB
			F-GBOP
			D-HMTB
F-GODA	Reserved for Heli-Inter		
F-GODC	Cameron V-90 HAFB	3325	
F-GODD	HS.748 Series 2A	1658	G-BFLL
			HK-1409
F-GODF	Cameron A-105 HAFB	3315	
F-GODR	Mudry CAP.232 (Dbf 15.12.95)	03	
F-GODZ	Pilatus PC-6/340 Porter (Reservation)	340	(N340N)
			ST-AFR
			HB-FAR
F-GOES	Reims/Cessna FRA.150L Aerobat (Reservn)	0179	TT-CAJ
			F-OCTP
F-GOFA	Scintex Piel CP.301C Emeraude	511	F-BJFA
F-GOFB	Dornier 328-11	3087	
F-GOFD	Chaize JZ.25F16 HAFB	135	
F-GOFF	SOCATA TB-20 Trinidad	306	HB-EQS
F-GOFL	Cameron A-160 HAFB	4159	
F-GOFM	Piper PA-34-200 Seneca	34-7570285	F-BXAA
			HB-LEY
F-GOFP	Reims/Cessna F.152	1752	6V-AGK
			F-GCNL
F-GOFY	Cameron N-77 HAFB	3052	
F-GOGC	Cameron O-84 HAFB	4379	
F-GOGG	Balloon Works Firefly 7-15 HAFB	F7-1037	
F-GOGI	Cameron SS HAFB	"447"	
F-GOGN	CASA C.212-200CB	92	(F-GOBP)
			TC-AOC
F-GOGO	Cameron A-105 HAFB	3207	
F-GOGT	Fouga CM.170 Magister	545	Fr.AF
F-GOHA	Embraer EMB.135ER (Reservation)	145-189	
F-GOHB	Embraer EMB.135ER (Reservation)	145-198	
F-GOJB	Mudry CAP.231EX	04	OO-CAP
			F-GNCF
			F-WZCF
F-GOJC	Robin R.2160 Alpha Sport (Reservation)	unkn	
F-GOJD	Cameron V-56 HAFB	554	OO-SOM
F-GOJE	Cameron N-56 HAFB	645	OO-CLA
F-GOJL	Schweizer 269C	S-1525	D-HHAK
F-GOJM	Cameron O-90 HAFB	3336	
F-GOJP	Chaize JZ.22F12 HAFB	157	
F-GOJR	Chaize CS.2200F12 HAFB	123	
F-GOKQ	Robin DR.400/120 (Reservation .99)	unkn	
F-GOLA	Thunder AX7—77A HAFB	4230	
F-GOLB	Colt Bibendum 110 SS HAFB	4221	G-BXNR
F-GOLC	Thunder AX10-160 HAFB	4260	
F-GOLD	Aérospatiale AS.350B2 Ecureuil (W/o 26.6.98)	2590	(F-GMTS)
F-GOLE	SA.316B Alouette III	1353	ALAT
F-GOLF	Cessna 310R	1638	N179MP
			N2634N
F-GOLL	Zlin Z.726K Universal	1069	OK-DXA
			OK-YRB
			OK-95
F-GOLP	Aérospatiale AS.355N Ecureuil 2	5588	
F-GOMA	BAe.146 Series 200QC	E-2211	G-BVCD
			G-6-211
F-GOMC	Zlin Z.526F Trenér Master	1078	F-BRNB
F-GOMD	Aviat Pitts S-2B	5213	N319JM
F-GOME	Pilatus PC-6/B2-H2 Turbo Porter (Reservation .99)	543	N4911
F-GOMF	Cessna 210 (Reservation)	"0012"	
F-WOMG	SOCATA TP-319 Omega	01	
F-GOMJ	Christen Pitts S-2B	5176	EC-EXV
			N6081F
F-GOMM	Cessna 414	0831	I-CCMM
			N98745

Regn.	Type	C/n	Prev.Id.
F-GOMP	Piper PA-28R-201 Arrow IV	2844001	
F-GOMS	Robin DR.400/120 Petit Prince	2316	
F-GONA	Cameron N-105 HAFB *(Reservation .99)*	1446	PH-ISO
F-GONC	Cessna T.210N Turbo Centurion II	64544	F-GHNC
			N9543Y
F-GONG	SAN Jodel D.140R Abeille	506	OO-VVN
F-GONT	Cameron O-65 HAFB	60	G-BANT
			F-GDZH
			G-BANT
F-GONZ	Robinson R-22B2 Beta	2693	
F-GOOG	Cameron A-105 HAFB	4645	
F-GOOI	Cameron C-60 Concept HAFB	3160	LX-OOI
F-GOOO	Beech 300 Super King Air	FA-175	N175NJ
			JA8868
			N1558Y
F-GOPA	Chaize JZ.30F16 HAFB	128	
F-GOPB(2)	Cameron A-210 HAFB	3672	
F-GOPC	Robinson R-22 Mariner	1648M	3A-MBC
F-GOPE	Beech 1900D	UE-103	N82930
			(F-GMSA)
F-GOPG	Eurocopter EC.135T1 *(Reservation)*	0062	
F-GOPI	SIGA MA-26 Pilatre de Rozier HAFB	108	
F-GOPK	Beech 1900C1	UC-74	TR-LEO
			F-GLPK
			N15528
F-GOPM	Dassault Falcon 20E	302/510	F-WQBM
			N84V
			OE-GDP
			D-COMM
			F-WRQP
F-GOPP	Chaize JZ.30F16 HAFB	150	
F-GOPR	Piper PA-23-250 Aztec E	27-4727	G-AZWW
			N14161
F-GOPX	CAARP CAP.10	01	F-ZAGO
			F-BOPX
F-GOPY	Bell 206B Jet Ranger II	2584	G-RSMA
			G-SHZZ
			G-BNUW
			N5018B
F-GORA	Robin DR.400/160 Chevalier	2271	
F-GORB	Robin DR.400/140B Major 80	2272	
F-GORC	Robin DR.400/120 Petit Prince	2276	
F-GORD	Robin DR.400/180 Régent	2277	
F-GORG	Robin DR.400/140B Major 80	1034	F-BXJE
F-GORH	Robin DR.400/160 Chevalier	2279	
F-GORI	Robin DR.400/120 Petit Prince	2283	
F-GORJ	Robin DR.400 NGL Régent 3	2278	
F-GORK	Robin DR.400/140B Major 80	2286	
F-GORL	Robin DR.400/140B Major 80	2288	
F-GORM	Robin DR.400/120 Petit Prince	2289	
F-GORN	Robin DR.400/120 Petit Prince	2300	
F-GORO	Robin DR.400/180 Régent	2292	
F-GORP	Robin DR.400/120 Petit Princ	2295	
F-GORQ	Robin DR.400/120 Petit Prince	2297	
F-GORR	Robin DR.400/140B Major 80	2298	
F-GORS	Robin HR.200/120B	292	
F-GORT	Robin DR.400/180 Régent	2299	
F-GORU	Robin HR.200/120B	294	
F-GORX	Robin DR.400/160 Chevalier	2302	
F-GORY	Robin DR.400/180 Régent	2301	
F-GORZ	Robin DR.400/120 Petit Prince	2284	
F-GOSA(2)	General Avia F.22 Pinguino *(Reservation .99)*	016	
F-GOSE	Piper PA-46-310P Malibu	4608010	N770MR
			N146DS
			G-DODS
			N9100N
F-GOSF	Beech A36 Bonanza	E-3259	N41020
F-GOST	Cessna A.152 Aerobat	0774	N7587B
F-GOTA(2)	Aérospatiale SA.365N Dauphin 2 *(Reservation .99)*	6147	TN-AES
F-GOTC	Mudry CAP.232	15	
F-GOTE	Cameron A-180 HAFB	3144	G-TATE
F-GOTM	Hughes 369E	0259E	C-FYTZ
			N535JP
			N1603K
F-GOTO	Reims/Cessna FR.172J Rocket	0532	TR-LTO
F-GOTT	Cessna T.207 Turbo Skywagon/ Soloy Pac	00323	
F-GOTU	Hughes 369E	0248E	C-FXQH
			N132KC
			N16028
F-GOUD	Cameron Nivea SSHAFB	4576	
F-GOUE	SIGA MA-26 Pilatre de Rozier HAFB	112	
F-GOUM	Mudry CAP.10B	122	Fr.AF
F-GOUN	Mudry CAP.10B *(Reservation .99)*	129	Fr.AF
F-GOUP	Mudry CAP.10B	138	Fr.AF
F-GOUT	Aérospatiale AS.355F1 Ecureuil 2	5141	N5793Y
F-GOVA	Robin DR.400/120 Petit Prince	2303	
F-GOVB	Robin DR.400/120 Petit Prince	2304	
F-GOVC	Robin HR.200/120B	297	
F-GOVD	Robin DR.400/180 Régent	2106	G-MRSL
			G-BUAP
F-GOVE	Robin DR.400/120 Petit Prince	2307	
F-GOVF	Robin DR.400/120 Petit Prince	2315	
F-GOVG	Robin DR.400/140B Major 80	2314	
F-GOVI	Robin DR.400/120 Petit Prince	2310	
F-GOVJ	Robin HR.200/120B	301	
F-GOVK	Robin HR.200/120B	303	
F-GOVL	Robin DR.400/120 Petit Prince	2312	
F-GOVM	Robin DR.400/160 Chevalier	2317	
F-GOVN	Robin DR.400/120 Petit Prince	2318	
F-GOVO	Robin DR.400/120 Petit Prince	2322	
F-GOVP	Robin DR.400/180 Régent	2328	
F-GOVQ	Robin DR.400/160 Chevalier	2321	
F-GOVR	Robin DR.400/140B Major 80	1345	I-GUCC
			F-GBUC
F-GOVS	Robin DR.400/180 Régent	2323	
F-GOVT	Robin DR.400/140B Major 80	2325	
F-GOVU	Robin DR.400/120 Petit Prince	2326	
F-GOVX	Robin DR.400/120 Petit Prince	2330	
F-GOYA	Dassault Falcon 900EX	11	F-WWFI
F-GOYC	Robinson R-44 Astro	0511	
F-GOYD	Fouga CM.170 Magister *(Reservation)*	203	Fr.AF
F-GOYE	Pilatus PC-6/B2-H2 Turbo Porter *(Reservation 9.99)*	517	N617SA
			XW-PDG
			HB-FCI
			D-ENLJ
F-GOZA	Airbus A.300B4-103	148	SX-BEG
			F-WZMB
F-GOZB	Airbus A.300B4-103	184	SX-BEH
			F-WZMA
F-GOZC	Airbus A.300B4-103	189	SX-BEI
			F-WZMG
F-GOZZ	Robin DR.400/160 Chevalier	2306	
F-GPAA	Dassault Falcon 20/CC117ECM	103/423	G-FRAV
			CAF117505
			CAF20505
			F-WMKH
F-GPAB	Dassault Falcon 20F	254	G-FRAC
			(N910FR)
			C-FYPB
			CF-YPB
			N4423F
			F-WNGO
F-GPAC to E	*Reserved for Dassault Falcon 20's for P.A.S.*		
F-GPAF	Piper PA-34-200T Seneca II	34-7670005	N3953X
F-GPAI	UltraMagic S-90 HAFB	90/17	
F-GPAJ	Christen Pitts S-2B	5286	(N98AV)
F-GPAK	Grumman G-1159C Gulfstream IV	1061	N457GA
F-GPAL	SOCATA Rallye 100ST	2583	F-WQFQ
			Fr.Navy 83
F-GPAR	Robinson R-22 Beta	2439	(F-GLHI)
F-GPAS	Beech 200 Super King Air	BB-209	D-IACS
			N545GM
			N5450M
			EB-001
			ZP-PTC
			ZP-TTC
F-GPBA	Cessna 172N	72517	C-FEIQ
			N5322D
F-GPBB	Piper PA-28-181 Archer III	2843196	N41332
			N9503N

Regn.	Type	C/n	Prev.Id.
F-GPBF	Piper PA-31T Cheyenne	31T-7920094	OH-PYE
	(Reservation 11.99; officially c/n 31T-79294)		SE-ICS
F-GPBJ	Lindstrand LBL-77A HAFB	272	
F-GPBM	Beech 1900D	UE-305	N22546
F-GPBO	Aérospatiale SA.316BLama (Reservation .99)	1414	A-414
F-GPBZ	Piper PA-24-260 Comanche	24-4766	HB-PBZ
			5U-AAG
			F-OCLU
			N9298P
F-GPCA	Cameron N-105 HAFB	3421	
F-GPCB	Beech 58 Baron	TH-1467	HB-GHX
			N72281
F-GPCC	Mooney M.20K Model 231	25-0359	N231QJ
F-GPCD	Aérospatiale AS.350BA Ecureuil	2658	F-ODYY
F-GPCE	Cameron N-105 HAFB	3720	
F-GPCH	Beech 58 Baron (Reservation)	TH-404	F-BUYT
F-GPCJ	Fouga CM.170 Magister	369	Fr.AF
F-GPCP	SE.313B Alouette II	1046	ALAT
F-GPCS	Lindstrand LBL-105A HAFB	327	
F-GPCT	Cameron A-120 HAFB	4151	
F-GPDA	Durondeau L-300 HAFB	22	
F-GPDB	Cameron A-120 HAFB	4473	
F-GPDC	HS.748 Series 2A	1612	G-AZSU
			A2-ABB
			G-AZSU
			VP-BCM
F-GPDL	Reims/Cessna F.150M	1229	TN-ADL
			F-BXNK
F-GPDM	UltraMagic S-90 HAFB	90/16	
F-GPDP	Lindstrand LBL-105A HAFB	251	
F-GPDR	SIGA MA-26 Pilatre de Rozier HAFB	100	
F-GPDT	Robin DR.500 Super Régent	0014	
F-GPEE	Cameron N-90 HAFB	4573	
F-GPET	Piper PA-28R-200 Cherokee Arrow	28R-7135174	HB-OHG
			N2149T
F-GPFA	Cessna 172S	172S8159	N7280N
F-GPFC	Cessna 525 CitationJet	0101	
F-GPFD	Dassault Falcon 100	221	OE-GHA
			F-WZGH
F-GPFF	Cessna 421A (Reservation .99)	0080	CN-TBH
	(Officially regd as model 421)		CN-MBD
			N2980Q
F-GPFM(2)	Mooney M.20L PFM	26-0031	
F-GPFN	Schweizer 269C	S-1627	
F-GPGA	Pilatus PC-6/B2-H4 Turbo-Porter	862	D-FAXI
			G-ITPS
F-GPGC	Bell 206LT Twin Ranger	52069	N41061
F-GPGM	SE.3160 Alouette III	1536	A-536
F-GPGO	Cameron 105 Ronald SS HAFB	4047	
F-GPGP	SE.3130 Alouette II	1475	ALAT
F-GPHB	Balloon Works Firefly 7-15 HAFB	F7-911	
F-GPHC(2)	Cessna T206H	T20608078	N4206V
F-GPHD	Fouga CM.170 Magister (Reservation)	445	Fr.AF
F-GPHG	SIGA MA-18 Pilatre de Rozier HAFB	104	
F-GPHI	Aérophile 5500 Tethered Gas Balloon	1	
F-GPHL	Robin DR.400/120 Dauphin 2+2	2428	
F-GPHM	Beech C24R Sierra	MC-507	N18818
F-GPHP	Piper PA-38-112 Tomahawk	38-80A0102	D-EKEF(2)
			N9691N
F-GPHS	Robinson R-44 Astro	0124	
F-GPHU	Fouga CM.170 Magister (Reservation .99)	374	F-WIGZ
			Fr.AF
F-GPHV	Cameron N-77 HAFB	3821	
F-GPIA	Aeritalia/SNIAS ATR-42-300	018	TR-LEW
			F-GIIA
			F-ODGM
F-GPIC	SIGA MA-26 Pilatre de Roxier HAFB	119	
F-GPJA	Beech 58 Baron	TH-1532	G-BPJA
			N3102A
F-GPJB	Robin DR.400/120 Petit Prince	2235	
F-GPJC(2)	Chaize JZX.20F12 HAFB (Reservation .99)	155	
F-GPJD	Beech E90 King Air	LW-328	N551M
			N797PA
			N1AM
F-GPJG	Robinson R-44 Astro	0567	

Regn.	Type	C/n	Prev.Id.
F-GPJL	Robin DR.400/180 Régent	2349	
F-GPJM	Boeing 747-206B	20427	PH-BUG
F-GPJN	Colt 105A HAFB (Reservation .00)	4783	
F-GPJR	Robinson R-44 Astro	0036	HB-XZX
F-GPJS	Stinson SR-10C Reliant	3-5846	F-BBCS
F-GPKB	Aérophile 5500 Tethered Gas Balloon	3	
F-GPKD	SAAB-Scania 340B	173	HB-AKD
			SE-F73
F-GPKF	Robin DR.400/140B Major 80	2385	(F-GVAB)
F-GPKG	SAAB-Scania 340B	185	HB-AKG
			SE-F85
F-GPKL	Piper PA-46-350P Malibu Mirage	4622194	
F-GPLA	Aérospatiale SN.601 Corvette	28	F-BTTL
			(OO-TTL)
			F-BTTL
			F-WNGX
F-GPLB	SIGAMA-26 Pilatre de Rozier HAFB	122	
F-GPLC	Piper PA-28-235 Cherokee	28-7710021	5Y-GWB
			N2929Q
F-GPLF	Cessna 525 CitationJet	0291	N51744
F-GPLM	Durondeau HAFB (Reservation .99)	unkn	
F-GPLS	Cameron V-90 HAFB	4439	
F-GPMA	Airbus A.319-113	598	D-AVYD
F-GPMB	Airbus A2.319-113	600	D-AVYC
F-GPMC	Airbus A.319-113	608	D-AVYE
F-GPMD	Airbus A.319-113	618	D-AVYJ
F-GPME	Airbus A.319-113	625	D-AVYQ
F-GPMF	Airbus A.319-113	637	D-AVYT
F-GPMG	Airbus A.319-113	644	D-AVYA
F-GPMH	Airbus A.319-113	647	D-AVYD
F-GPMI	Airbus A.319-113	660	D-AVYC
F-GPNA	Aérospatiale AS.355F1 Ecureuil 2	5207	N5802B
F-GPNJ	Dassault Falcon 900EX	50	F-WWFS
F-GPOA to GPOH Reserved for ATR-72s for Aéropostale			
F-GPOA	Aeritalia/SNIAS ATR-72-202	204	F-ORAC
			(XU-RAC)
			F-GKJK
			F-WQAG
			ZS-NDI
			F-WWER
			(N7270)
			F-WWER
F-GPOC	Aeritalia/SNIAS ATR-72-202	311	B-22707
			F-WWED
F-GPOD	Aeritalia/SNIASATR-72-202	361	B-22711
			F-WWEX
F-GPOP	Mudry CAP.10B	10	Fr.AF
F-GPOR	Thunder AX8-84 HAFB	853	
F-GPPA(2)	Holste MH.1521MBroussard (Reservation .99)	38	F-BFKL
			ALAT
F-GPPE	Agusta A.109A	7173	F-WQBP
			(F-GRMA)
			F-WQBP(2)
			F-GRMK
			G-HWBK
F-GPPF	Dassault Falcon 50	65	N1EV
			N50LV
			D-BFFB
			N65HS
			N90FJ
			N50FJ
			F-WZHT
F-GPPM	CAARP CAP.10	1	Fr.AF
F-GPPP	Robinson R-22 Beta	0526	HB-XZZ
			N99PS
			TG-..-
			N2363C
F-GPPR	Cessna 177A Cardinal	01370	OO-MAC
			(N30631)
F-GPPZ	Schroeder Fire Balloons G HAFB	560	
F-GPRA	Reims/Cessna F.406 Caravan II	0013	5Y-JJA
			OO-TIY
			F-WZDV
F-GPRC	Mudry CAP.232 (w/o 24.10.95)	02	
F-GPRD	Chaize JZ.22F12 HAFB	140	

Regn.	Type	C/n	Prev.Id.
F-GPRJ	Raven Europe S-40A HAFB	E-312	
F-GPRM	Cessna U.206F Stationair	02125	CN-TFL
			F-GPCM
			F-MJAF
			F-BRGH
			N71163
F-GPRO	Pilatus PC-6/B1-H2 Turbo Porter	524	HB-FHL
			OO-POF
			F-BKRR
F-GPRP	Aérospatiale AS.350B2 Ecureuil	3129	
F-GPRS	Aérophile 5500 Tethered Gas Balloon	6	
F-GPRT	Cessna 152	79995	OO-GPJ
			N757TQ
F-GPSA	Dassault Falcon 50	123	N211EF
			VH-SFJ
			(F-GDSC)
			F-WZHH
F-GPSD	Beech 1900D	UE-303	N11249
F-GPSK	Cameron N-90 HAFB	4242	
F-GPSL	Cameron V-77 HAFB	4243	
F-GPSN	Fairchild-Swearingen SA.227AC Metro III	AC-758B	N58NE
F-GPSO	SOCATA Rallye 100ST	2584	Fr.Navy 84
F-GPTB	Canadair CL.600-2B19 Regional Jet	7177	
F-GPTC	Canadair CL.600-2B19 Regional Jet	7182	
F-GPTD	Canadair CL.600-2B19 Regional Jet	7184	
F-GPTE	Canadair CL.600-2B19 Regional Jet	7183	
F-GPTF	Canadair CL.600-2B19 Regional Jet	7197	C-FMLB
F-GPTG	Canadair CL.600-2B19 Regional Jet	7223	
F-GPTH	Canadair CL.600-2B19 Regional Jet	7309	C-FMMQ
F-GPTI	Canadair CL.600-2B19 Regional Jet	7316	C-FMKZ
F-GPTJ	Canadair CL.600-2B19 Regional Jet	7323	
F-GPTK	Canadair CL.600-2B19 Regional Jet	7332	
F-GPTL	Beech A100 King Air (Reservation)	B-109	N78MK
			N78CA
			N51VK
			N51V
			N1GX
			N1GT
F-GPTM	Canadair CL.600-2B19 Regional Jet	7020	EC-GTG
			F-GNME
			C-FMMB
F-GPUH	SE.3130 Alouette II (Reservation 12.99)	1523	ALAT
F-GPUM	Aérospatiale SA.330J Puma	1652	HB-XUV
			I-EHPD
F-GPUY	Cameron N-105 HAFB	4693	
F-GPVA	McDonnell-Douglas DC-10-30	47956	OH-LHA
F-GPVC	McDonnell-Douglas DC-10-30	48265	N345HC
			(OH-LHC)
F-GPVD	McDonnell-Douglas DC-10-30	47865	OH-LHD
			I-DYNU
F-GPVF	McDonnell-Douglas DC-10-30 (Reservation)	unkn	
F-GPVI	Mudry CAP.10B	21	Fr.AF
F-GPVM	Robinson R-44 Astro	0056	
F-GPVV	Boeing 747-228F	21576	N536MC
			F-BPVV
F-GPXA	Fokker F.28-0100	11487	PH-EZW
F-GPXB	Fokker F.28-0100	11492	PH-EZK
F-GPXC	Fokker F.28-0100	11493	PH-EZY
F-GPXD	Fokker F.28-0100	11494	PH-EZO
F-GPXE	Fokker F.28-0100	11495	PH-EZP
F-GPXF	Fokker F.28-0100	11330	F-WQJX
			N133ML
			SE-DUG
			PH-CFH
			(PH-LNY)
			(G-FIOA)
			PH-EZB
F-GPYA	Aeritalia/SNIAS ATR-42-512	457	(G-ZAPJ)
			F-WWET
F-GPYB	Aeritalia/SNIAS ATR-42-512	480	F-WWLZ
F-GPYC	Aeritalia/SNIAS ATR-42-512	404	F-WWEB
F-GPYD	Aeritalia/SNIAS ATR-42-512	490	F-WWLJ
F-GPYF	Aeritalia/SNIAS ATR-42-512	495	F-WWLM
F-GPYG	Aeritalia/SNIAS ATR-42-512	516	F-WWLU
F-GPYH	Aeritalia/SNIAS ATR-42-512	522	F-WWLC
F-GPYI	Aeritalia/SNIAS ATR-42-512	526	F-WWLM
F-GPYJ	Aeritalia/SNIAS ATR-42-512	530	F-WWLH
F-GPYK	Aeritalia/SNIAS ATR-42-512	537	F-WWLC
F-GPYL	Aeritalia/SNIAS ATR-42-512	542	F-WWLH
F-GPYM	Aeritalia/SNIAS ATR-42-512	520	F-WWLR
F-GPYN	Aeritalia/SNIAS ATR-42-512	539	F-WWL.
F-GPYO	Aeritalia/SNIAS ATR-42-512	544	F-WWL.
F-GPYP	Canadair CL.600-2B19 Regional Jet	7126	C-FM..
F-GPYQ	Canadair CL.600-2B19 Regional Jet	7144	C-FMMT
F-GPYR	Canadair CL.600-2B19 Regional Jet	7164	C-FMND
F-GPYS	Beech 1900C-1	UC-69	N69ZR
			N520LX
			N15466
F-GPYT	Beech 1900C-1	UC-80	N80ZR
			N522LX
			N15337
F-GPYU	Beech 1900C-1	UC-109	N109YV
F-GPYV	Beech 1900C-1	UC-121	N121ZR
			N528LX
F-GPYX	Beech 1900C-1	UC-I11	N111YV
F-GPYY	Beech 1900C-1	UC-115	N115YV
F-GPZA	McDonnell-Douglas DC-9-83	49943	EI-CBX
			TC-INA
			EI-CBX
F-GPZB	Aeritalia/SNIAS ATR-42-300	027	F-OGOE
			F-GEQK
			F-WWEF
			PH-IFH
			F-WWEF

TEMPORARY REGISTRATIONS:
The F-WQ . . series is used mainly for delivery or ferry flights.

Regn.	Type	C/n	Prev.Id.
F-WQAN	Eurocopter AS.355N Ecureuil 2	5308	F-WEQC(3)
			Fr.AF
F-WQAP	Aérospatiale SA.365N Dauphin 2	6001	F-WZJJ
F-WQAQ	Aérospatiale SA.365N Dauphin 2	6015	F-WDFK
			F-GDFK
F-WQCF	Fouga CM.175 Zephyr	unkn	Fr.Navy
F-WQEY	Eurocopter EC.155B/SA.365 Dauphin 2	6542	
F-WQFI	Eurocopter EC-120 Colibri	1001	
F-WQFX(2)	Airbus A.310-304	435	C-GRYD
			TU-TAU
			B-2304
			F-WWCD
F-WQFY(2)	Airbus A.310-304	440	C-GRYV
			TU-TAR
			B-2305
			F-WWCF
F-WQHA	Aeritalia/SNIAS ATR-42-300	298	PP-ATV
			F-GIVG
			C-GICY
			F-WWLA
F-WQHV	Aeritalia/SNIAS ATR-42-320	343	PK-HJF
			F-WQAC
			ZS-NKZ
			F-WQAC
			F-GKNG
			F-WWED
F-WQHZ	Aeritalia/SNIAS ATR-42-300	406	EC-GFY
			EC-123
			F-WWLY
F-WQIA	Aeritalia/SNIAS ATR-42-300	128	N428MQ
			F-WWEA
F-WQIB	Aeritalia/SNIAS ATR-42-300	091	N427MQ
			F-GFIN
			F-WWEQ
F-WQIH	Aeritalia/SNIAS ATR-42-300	144	N432MQ
			F-WWEP
F-WQII	Aeritalia/SNIAS ATR-42-300	151	N133MQ
	(Sold to Honduras?)		(N148DD)
			F-WWEW
F-WQIJ	Aeritalia/SNIAS ATR-42-300	136	N430MQ
			F-WWEH

Regn.	Type	C/n	Prev.Id.
F-WQIN	Fokker F.27 Friendship 600	10401	9Q-CBP
			PH-FNZ
			PT-LDT
			N379BS
			C9-AMD
			CR-AMD
			PH-FNZ
F-WQIO	Aeritalia/SNIAS ATR-42-300	028	N422MQ
			F-WW..
F-WQIQ	Aeritalia/SNIAS ATR-42-300	015	N19AE
	(Sold to Cuba?)		N141DD
			F-WWEA
F-WQIX	Aeritalia/SNIAS ATR-72-202	365	F-OHAT
			F-WWEM
F-WQJC	Aeritalia/SNIAS ATR-42-400	466	F-WWEX
F-GQJD	Beech C90A King Air	LJ-667	N888GN
			G-BMZD
			N9067S
F-WQJM	Aeritalia/SNIAS ATR-42-300 (Reservation .99)	077	YR-ATX
			F-WQBU
			N4205G
			F-WWEC
F-WQJN	Aeritalia/SNIAS ATR-42-300 (Reservation .99)	083	YR-ATY
			F-WQBV
			N4207G
			F-WWEI
F-WQJO	Aeritalia/SNIAS ATR-42-300 (Reservation .99)	384	PT-MFF
			F-WWEG
F-WQJP	Aeritalia/SNIAS ATR-42-300 (Reservation .99)	388	PT-MFG
			F-WWLA
F-WQJS	Fokker F.28-0100 (Reservation .99)	11329	G-BYDN
			N130ML
			SE-DUF
			PH-CFG
			PH-EZV
			(G-FIOZ)
			PH-EZV
F-WQJT	Aeritalia/SNIAS ATR-72-201 (Reservation .99)	210	EC-GQV
			F-WQGE
			B-22703
			F-WWEH
F-WQJU	Aeritalia/SNIAS ATR-72-201 (Reservation .99)	198	EC-GQU
			F-WQGC
			B-22702
			F-WWEL
F-WQJZ	Aeritalia/SNIAS ATR-42-300 (Reservation 7.99)	304	G-BUEB
			F-WWLE
F-WQKN	Bell 407 (Reservation 9.99)	53306	
F-WQKO	Aérospatiale SA.316B Alouette III (Reservation .99)	1226	A-226
F-WQKR	Airbus A.310-304 (Reservation 10.99)	651	F-GJKR
			TU-TAD
			F-WWCC
F-WQKU	Airbus A.300B4-103 (Reservation .99)	069	G-BYYS
	(Also reserved as F-GJJG and F-OHLF)		5T-CLI
			N471AS
			RP-C3002
			F-WZEB
F-WQKX	Aeritalia/SNIAS ATR-42-300 (Reservation .99)	148	D-BGGG
			F-WWEU
F-WQLA	Eurocopter EC.135T1 (Reservation .99)	0037	F-GMHD
F-WQLD	Airbus A.310-322 (Reservation 12.99)	409	A40-OA
			HB-IPH
			F-WWCE
F-WQLE	Airbus A.310-322 (Reservation 12.99)	410	A40-OB
			HB-IPI
			F-WWCF
F-WQLF	Aeritalia/SNIAS ATR-42-300 (Reservation 12.99)	087	TR-LEZ
			F-OICA
			(F-OIET)
			F-WQCS
			OK-TFF
			F-WQAF
			TC-AGC
			F-WIYB
			B-2202

Regn.	Type	C/n	Prev.Id.
F-WQLI	Aeritalia/SNIAS ATR-42-512 (Reservation .99)	503	N14445
			F-WWEN
F-WQLJ	Aeritalia/SNIAS ATR-42-512 (Reservation .99)	504	N19446
			F-WWEO
F-GRAB	Cameron A-120 HAFB	3447	
F-GRAC	Aérospatiale AS.350BA Ecureuil	1652	(F-GPUM)
			SX-HBP
F-GRAD	Piper PA-28-180 Cherokee Challenger	28-7305060	F-OGFW
F-GRAE(2)	Eurocopter EC.120B Colibri	1049	
F-GRAF	Cessna 172R	80232	(N415ES)
F-GRAK	Bell 412EP	36191	N70722
F-GRAL	Cameron O-105 HAFB	3908	
F-GRAM	Chaize CS.2200F12 HAFB	144	
F-GRAP	Lindstrand LBL-105A HAFB	208	
F-GRAR	CEA Jodel DR.1051 Sicile	346	OO-YVE
			F-BKPX
F-GRAS	Cameron V-77 HAFB	3930	
F-GRAT	Cameron V-90 HAFB (Reservation .99)	4771	
F-GRAU	Aérospatiale SA.365C3 Dauphin 2	5023	G-BGNM
			EC-DOQ
			G-BGNM
			EC-DOQ
			G-BGNM
			EC-DOQ
			G-BGNM
			EC-DOQ
			G-BGNM
			(G-BGPU)
F-WRAV	Raven Europe EU-250 Balloon	E-309	
F-GRAY	Cessna T.207A Turbo Stationair 8/ Soloy Pac	00777	HB-CLV
			N9992M
F-GRAZ	Scintex ML.250 Rubis (Reservation .99)	101	F-BJME
F-GRBD	SOCATA TB-9 Tampico	1092	EC-EYM
			F-GKUK
F-GRBG	SOCATA TB-9 Tampico	1348	EC-FLE
			F-GKVX
F-GRBH	SOCATA TB-10 Tobago	1807	
F-GRBI	SOCATA TB-20 Trinidad	1821	
F-GRBJ	SOCATA TB-20 Trinidad	1822	
F-GRBK	SOCATA TB-20 Trinidad	1825	F-WWRB
F-GRBL	SOCATA TB-20 Trinidad	1827	
F-GRBN	SOCATA TB-20 Trinidad	1830	F-WWRF
F-GRBO	SOCATA TB-200 Tobago XL	1812	
F-GRBQ	SOCATA TB-200 Tobago XL	1811	
F-GRBT	SOCATA TB-20 Trinidad	1109	I-FMLV
			F-ODTY
F-GRBW	SOCATA TB-20 Trinidad	1874	
F-GRBY	SOCATA TB-200 Tobago XL	1813	
F-GRCA	Schweizer 269C	S-1551	G-BTTV
			N86G
F-GRCC	SIGA MA-26 Pilatre de Rozier HAFB	123	(F-GNUI)
F-GRCD	Beech 1900D	UE-311	N10984
F-GRCE	Bell 206B Jet Ranger II	1679	F-BXLG
			N90070
F-GRCG	Cameron A-210 HAFB (Reservation .99)	4728	
F-GRCJ	Antonov AN-2 (See F-OHRJ)	unkn	
F-GRCM	Schweizer 269C (Reservation)	unkn	
F-GRCP	Pilatus PC-6/B2-H2 Turbo Porter	2071	N392AC
			N392CA
			OB-....
			N5305F
F-GRCR	Hughes 269C	39-0781	D-HESP
			PH-WPL
F-GRCY	Agusta-Bell 206B Jet Ranger III	8690	I-ELEP
F-GRDC	Chaize JZ.25F16 HAFB	147	
F-GRDF	Chaize CS.2200F12 HAFB (Reservation 12.99)	158	
F-GRDJ	Piper PA-36-285 Pawnee Brave	36-7660123	N57803
	(Reservation 11.99)		
F-GRDR	Cessna 150L	74024	G-BSBY
			N18662
F-GRDT	Piper PA-31-310 Navajo	31-7300931	F-WQCB
			Fr.Navy 931
			F-BTMU
F-GRDX	Aérophile 5500 Tethered Gas Balloon	4	(F-GSMA)

Regn.	Type	C/n	Prev.Id.
F-GREA	Beech 1900D	UE-307	N22761
F-GREB	Mooney M.20M TLS	27-0025	OO-GJS
			(OO-MEY)
			(OO-GJS)
			F-GJSM
			N10901
F-GREC	Hughes 269C	S-1711	N41S
F-GREF	Cameron N-65 HAFB	3024	
F-GREL	Mooney M.20J Model 205 (Reservation 6.99)	24-3403	N2138W
F-GREP	Robin DR.400/160 Major	2439	
F-GRES	Holste MH.1521M Broussard	124	Fr.AF
F-GREV	Cameron N-77 HAFB	1704	LX-REV
F-GREY	Robinson R-44 Astro	0090	
F-GRFA	Boeing 737-36N	28672	
F-GRFB	Boeing 737-36N	28673	
F-GRFC	Boeing 737-36N	28569	
F-GRFD to F-GRFZ Reserved for Boeing 737-300 for Air France			
F-GRGA	Embraer EMB.145	145-008	
F-GRGB	Embraer EMB.145	145-010	PT-SYG
F-GRGC	Embraer EMB.145	145-012	PT-SYI
F-GRGD	Embraer EMB.145	145-043	PT-S..
F-GRGE	Embraer EMB.145EU	145-047	PT-S..
F-GRGF	Embraer EMB.145EU	145-050	PT-SZP
F-GRGG	Embraer EMB.145EU	145-118	PT-S..
F-GRGH	Embraer EMB.145EU	145-120	PT-S..
F-GRGI	Embraer EMB.145EU	145-152	PT-SED
F-GRGP	Embraer EMB.135ER	145-188	
F-GRHA	Airbus A.319-111	0938	D-AVYS
F-GRHB	Airbus A.319-111	0985	D-AVYO
F-GRHC	Airbus A.319-111	0998	D-AVYW
F-GRHD	Airbus A.319-111	1000	D-AVYP
F-GRHE	Airbus A.319-111	1020	D-AVYX
F-GRHF	Airbus A.319-111	1025	D-AVYE
F-GRHG	Airbus A.319-111	1036	D-AVYS
F-GRHH	Airbus A.319-111	1151	D-AVWK
F-GRHI	Airbus A.319-111	1169	D-AVYX
F-GRHJ	Airbus A.319-111	1176	D-AV..
F-GRHK to F-GRHZ Reserved for Airbus A.319s for Air France			
F-GRIC	Cameron N-90 HAFB	4143	CS-BAR
F-GRIF	Robinson R-22 Beta	0526	(F-GPPP)
			HB-XZZ
			N999PS
			TG-...
			N23667
F-GRIS	Cameron N-90 HAFB	3811	
F-GRIT	Mudry CAP.10B	277	
F-GRIX	SIGA MA-26 Pilatre de Rozier HAFB	118	
F-GRJA	Canadair CL.600-2B19 Regional Jet	7070	C-FMKW(3)
F-GRJB	Canadair CL.600-2B19 Regional Jet	7076	C-FMLS(3)
F-GRJC	Canadair CL.600-2B19 Regional Jet	7085	C-FM..
F-GRJD	Canadair CL.600-2B19 Regional Jet	7088	C-FMLU(4)
F-GRJE	Canadair CL.600-2B19 Regional Jet	7106	C-FMNQ(4)
F-GRJF	Canadair CL.600-2B19 Regional Jet	7108	C-FMLU(5)
F-GRJG	Canadair CL.600-2B19 Regional Jet	7143	C-FM..
F-GRJH	Canadair CL.600-2B19 Regional Jet	7162	C-FM..
F-GRJI	Canadair CL.600-2B19 Regional Jet	7147	C-FZAL
			C-FMMY(4)
F-GRJJ	Canadair CL.600-2B19 Regional Jet	7190	C-GBFF
F-GRJK	Canadair CL.600-2B19 Regional Jet	7219	C-FMMQ
F-GRJL	Canadair CL.600-2B19 Regional Jet	7221	C-....
F-GRJM	Canadair CL.600-2B19 Regional Jet	7222	C-....
F-GRJN	Canadair CL.600-2B19 Regional Jet	7262	C-FMLT
F-GRJO	Canadair CL.600-2B19 Regional Jet	7296	C-....
F-GRJP	Canadair CL.600-2B19 Regional Jet	7301	C-....
F-GRJQ	Canadair CL.600-2B19 Regional Jet	7321	C-FMLS
F-GRLC	Piper PA-28RT-201T Turbo Arrow IV	28R-7931100	I-ARLC
			N2158U
F-GRLN	Beech F90 King Air	LA-191	TR-LAJ
F-GRLO	SIGA MA-30 Pilatre de Rozier HAFB	111	
F-GRLT	Mooney M.20K Model 231	25-0141	N40WE
			N4758Y
			YV-1805P
F-GRMB	Beech A36 Bonanza	E-2292	F-GRST
			F-ODST
			D-EBVS(2)
F-GRMC	McDonnell-Douglas DC-9-83	53466	
F-GRMD	Beech 1900D	UE-296	N21572
F-GRMF	Schweizer 269C	S-1395	D-HEYN
			HB-XUP
F-GRMG	McDonnell-Douglas DC-9-83	53464	
F-GRMH	McDonnell-Douglas DC-9-83	53465	
F-GRMI	McDonnell-Douglas DC-9-83	53488	
F-GRMJ(2)	McDonnell-Douglas DC-9-83	53520	
F-GRML	McDonnell-Douglas DC-9-83	49628	F-WQFN
			EC-FVB
			EC-524
			VR-BMH
			EC-EOM
			EC-260
F-GRMM to GRMO Reserved for AOM Minerve			
F-GRMP	Cessna 310R	1250	(F-GFZR)
			TJ-AHA
			PH-VWM
			N98997
F-GRMR	Robin DR.400/160 Major	2429	
F-GRNA	Boeing 737-85F	28823	N1795B
F-GRNB	Boeing 737-85F	28824	N500GX
F-GRNC	Boeing 737-85F	28821	N1786B
F-GRND	Boeing 737-85F	28827	
F-GRNO	Embraer EMB.120RT Brasilia	120-144	PT-OZM
	(Reservation .99)		F-GGTE
			PT-SPK
F-GRNY	Aérophile 5500 Tethered Gas Balloon	2	
F-GROA	Robin DR.400/180 Régent	2423	
F-GROB	Grumman AA-5A Cheetah	0301	LX-AVC
			D-EJMT
F-GROK	Cameron N-65 HAFB	4654	
F-GRON	HS.125 Series 700B	257166	F-BYFB
			G-5-18
F-GROS	Cameron N-77 HAFB	4677	
F-GROT	Mudry CAP.10B	11	Fr.AF
F-GROU	Mudry CAP.10B	24	F-WQCM
			Fr.AF
F-GROV	Piper PA-28RT-201T Turbo Arrow IV	28R-8131009	N8277H
F-GROY	UltraMagic S-90 HAFB (Reservation .99)	90/..	
F-GRPA	Mudry CAP.232	06	
F-GRPC	Nord 1101 Noralpha (Reservation .99)	113	F-BFNJ
			F-ZJPS
F-GRPM	Beech 1900D	UE-300	N22120
F-GRRA	Mudry CAP.10B	119	Fr.AF
F-GRRB	Aérospatiale SA.315B Lama	2475	CNET/F-SEBO
F-GRRG	Mudry CAP.232	11	F-GKCK
	(Reserved as F-GXRB .99)		ALAT
F-GRRM	Cessna 525 CitationJet	0166	N343PJ
			N5148N
F-GRRT	Mudry CAP.10B	116	(F-GIPQ)
			Fr.AF
F-GRSD	Airbus A.320-214	653	F-WWIF
			F-GJDY
			F-WWIF
F-GRSE	Airbus A.320-214	657	F-WWIR
F-GRSF	SIGA MA-22 Pilatre de Rozier HAFB	106	
F-GRSG	Airbus A.320-214	737	F-WWBS
F-GRSH	Airbus A.320-214	749	F-WWIK
F-GRSI	Airbus A.320-214	973	F-WWBR
F-GRSJ	Reserved for Airbus A.320 for Star Europe		
F-GRSK	Grumman G.164 AgCat (Reservation .99)	unkn	
F-GRSL	Mudry CAP.231	17	HB-MSR
			F-GGYX
F-GRSO	Cessna 150M	78171	G-BTSO
			N9221U
F-GRSP	CEA DR.250/160 Capitaine	13	OO-BOY
F-GRSV	Robin DR.500 Super Régent	0009	
F-GRTA	Euravial RF-47	3	F-WWNG
F-GRTB to GRTZ Reserved for Euravial RF-47s			
F-GRUE	Aérospatiale AS.350B2 Ecureuil	2462	F-GHUP
F-GRVA	UltraMagic V-105 HAFB	105/36	
F-GRVB	Robinson R-44 Astro	0042	D-HTUT
F-GRVC	Aérospatiale SA.341G Gazelle	1164	JRV126..
			JRV12013

Regn.	Type	C/n	Prev.Id.
F-GRVN	Piper J-3C-65 Cub *(Reservation)*	11343	F-BHEB
			F-OAEB
			43-30052
F-GRVZ	Pilatus PC-6/B2-H4 Turbo-Porter	901	
F-GRXA to F-GRXZ *Reserved for Airbus A.319s for Air France*			
F-GRYD	Fouga CM.170 Magister *(Reservation)*	393	Fr.AF
F-GRYL	Beech 1900D	UE-301	N22161
F-GRYR	Raven Europe S-55A HAFB	E-357	
F-GSAA	Dassault Falcon 2000	36	
F-GSAC	Pilatus PC-6/B2-H4 Turbo-Porter	902	HB-FIJ
F-GSAG	Nord 1203 Norécrin	104	F-BEOQ
F-GSAK	SAAB S.91B Safir	91229	F-BHAK
F-GSAL	American Champion 8KCAB Decathlon	unkn	
F-GSAM	Lindstrand LBL-120A	448	
F-GSAN	Beech 1900D	UE-54	(F-GNOC)
			N54YV
F-GSAO	SOCATA TB-20 Trinidad	1801	
F-GSAP	Bell 214 *(Reservation 9.99)*	28039	JA6189
F-GSAS	Aérospatiale AS.355F1 Ecureuil 2	5159	N5796B
F-GSAT	Pilatus PC-6/B2-H4 Turbo Porter	904	HB-FLC
F-GSBA	Robin DR.400/140B Major 80	2342	
F-GSBB	Robin DR.400/120 Petit Prince	2334	
F-GSBC	Robin DR.400/180 Régent	2340	
F-GSBD	Robin DR.400/180 Régent	2329	
F-GSBE	Robin DR.400/120 Petit Prince	2337	
F-GSBF	Robin DR.400/120 Petit Prince	2335	
F-GSBG	Robin DR.400/180 Régent	2336	
F-GSBH	Robin DR.400/180 Régent	2341	
F-GSBI	Robin DR.400/120 Petit Prince	2352	
F-GSBJ	Robin DR.400/140B Major 80	2350	
F-GSBK	Robin DR.400/120 Dauphin 2+2	2351	
F-GSBL	Robin HR.200/120B	314	
F-GSBM	Robin DR.400/180 Régent	2353	
F-GSBN	Robin DR.400/120 Petit Prince	2355	
F-GSBO	Robin DR.400/180 Régent	2358	
F-GSBP	Robin DR.400/120 Petit Prince	2356	
F-GSBQ	Robin DR.400/120 Petit Prince	2374	
F-GSBR	Robin DR.400/140B Major	2344	
F-GSBS	Robin DR.400/140B Major	2357	
F-GSBT	Robin DR.400/120 Petit Prince	2359	
F-GSBU	Robin DR.400/140B Major 80	2369	
F-GSBV	Robin DR.400/180 Régent	2364	
F-GSBX	Robin DR.400/180 Régent	2366	
F-GSBY	Robin HR.200/120B	319	
F-GSBZ	Robin DR.400/180 Régent	2362	
F-GSCA	Cessna 404 Titan	0052	TR-LCY
			OH-CHN
			N5434G
F-GSCB	Piper PA-18-135 Super Cub	18-4006	TC-CUB
	(Officially quoted with f/n 18-4577 as c/n)		Turkish AF
			54-2606
F-GSCC	Mudry CAP.10B	127	F-WQCN
			Fr.AF
F-GSCD	SAN Jodel D.140E Mousquetaire IV	180	D-EDHL
F-GSCE	Aérospatiale AS.350BA Ecureuil	9009	
F-GSCH	Schroeder Fire Balloons G HAFB	480	
F-GSCI	SIGA MA-30 Pilatre de Rozier HAFB	121	
F-GSCJ	Cessna 182S	80194	N2638A
F-GSCN	Dassault Falcon 900	62	F-WQBL
			N62FJ
			F-GIVR
			F-WWFJ
F-GSCP	Cessna 172R	80170	N9890F
F-GSDB	Piper PA-28R-200 Cherokee Arrow	28R-35039	TU-TMT
			F-BVFT
			TU-TFA
			N9339N
F-GSDL	Mooney M.20R Ovation	29-0027	
F-GSDM	Beech C90B King Air	LJ-1441	N995TA
			ZS-NUE
			N3271S
F-GSDP	Dassault Falcon 900EX	43	F-WWFE
F-GSDR	UltraMagic M-77 HAFB	77/130	
F-GSDV	Commander Aircraft 114B	14601	N6018F
F-GSEA	Boeing 747-312	23032	N121KG
			(9V-SKG)
			(9V-SQZ)
F-GSEB	Beech B200 Super King Air	BB-1110	TR-LDU
			N110GA
			N7045C
			(F-GGAR)
			HZ-MW2
			N200MW
F-GSEE	Robin DR.400/140B Major 80	2360	
F-GSER	Dassault Falcon 50	2	F-BINR
			F-RAFJ
			F-BINR
			F-WINR
F-GSET	SOCATA Rallye 100ST	2586	Fr.Navy 86
F-GSEX	Boeing 747-312	23028	F-WSEX
			N117KC
			VH-INK
			N117KC
			(9V-SKC)
			(9V-SQV)
F-GSFD	Beech 1900D	UE-252	N10907
F-GSFO	Reims/Cessna F.152	1774	D-EGNW
F-GSFR	Cameron N-77 HAFB	3783	
F-GSFT	SIGAMA-26 Pilatre de Rozier HAFB	120	
F-GSGG	Aérospatiale SA.332C Super Puma	2033	HB-XVY
			N5795P
			N300US
			N5795P
F-GSGS	Piper PA-46-350P Malibu	4622154	D-EBPA
			N92421
F-GSGZ	Mudry CAP.232	08	
F-GSHB	Robinson R-22M Mariner	2101M	3A-MJM
F-GSHD	Fouga CM.170 Magister *(Reservation)*	529	Fr.AF
F-GSHG	Fouga CM.170 Magister *(Reservation .99)*	045	G-FUGA
			G-BSCT
			Fr.AF
F-GSHK	Airbus A.320-231	326	SU-RAB
			F-WWDK
F-GSID	Cameron O-120 HAFB	3420	HB-QAI
F-GSIN	Beech 200 Super King Air	BB-239	N517JM
			G-WWHL
			G-BLAE
			I-ELCO
			N17649
F-GSIR	Thunder AX8-105SII HAFB	3591	
F-GSIT	SIGA MA-30 Pilatre de Rozier HAFB	124	
F-GSIU	Robin R.2000/120	312	
F-GSIX	Piper PA-32-260 Cherokee Six	32-59	HB-OLZ
			N3313W
F-GSJA	SAN Jodel D.140 Mousquetaire	39	D-EBAQ
F-GSJB	UltraMagic S-105 HAFB *(Reservation .99)*	105/59	
F-GSJD	Beech 58PBaron	TJ-74	G-PAPU
F-GSJF	Sky 77/24 HAFB	128	
F-GSJL	Beech B90 King Air *(Reservation)*	LJ-393	N221NC
			N800CT
			N300CT
			N757K
F-GSJR	Piper PA-46-350P Malibu	4636112	
F-GSJS	Bell 206L-4 Long Ranger IV	52059	N96V
			N90C
			N62LH
F-GSKA to GSKF *Reserved for DC-10-30s for Sky Jet*			
F-GSKX	Robin DR.400/120 Dauphin 2+2	2415	
F-GSLC	Thunder AX8-90 SI HAFB	1624	G-SLCI
F-GSLT	Robinson R-44 Astro	0470	
F-GSLZ	Dassault Falcon 100	208	F-WQBJ
			N71M
			I-OANN
			F-GELS
			F-WZGO
F-GSMA	Aérophile 5500 Tethered Gas Balloon	5	
	(Originally allocated to c/n 4 which is F-GRDX)		

Regn.	Type	C/n	Prev.Id.
F-GSMC	Cessna F500 Citation	0308	F-GMLH
			(F-GIRS)
			N6525J
			N70TG
			N38CJ
			N308CC
			(N5308J)
F-GSMD	Piper PA-28-181 Archer III	2843066	N9282N
F-GSMP	Agusta A.109E	11028	
F-GSMR	Piper PA-34-200T Seneca II	34-8070208	D-GORS
			N8195L
F-GSMU	Eurocopter EC.135T1	0043	
F-GSMV	Robin DR.400/180 Régent	2361	
F-GSOL	Cameron N-90 HAFB	3769	
F-GSON	Cameron N-90 HAFB	4373	
F-GSOP	Schroeder Fire Balloons G HAFB	376	PH-BIM
F-GSPA	Boeing 777-228	29002	
F-GSPB	Boeing 777-228	29003	
F-GSPC	Boeing 777-228	29004	
F-GSPD	Boeing 777-228ER	29005	
F-GSPE	Boeing 777-228ER	29006	
F-GSPF	Boeing 777-228ER	29007	
F-GSPG	Boeing 777-228ER	27609	
F-GSPH	Boeing 777-228ER	28675	
F-GSPI	Boeing 777-228	29008	
F-GSPJ	Boeing 777-228	29009	
F-GSPK	Boeing 777-228	29010	
F-GSRA	Robin DR.400/140B Major 80	2372	
F-GSRB	Robin R.2160 Alpha Sport	320	
F-GSRC	Robin DR.400/120 Petit Prince	2370	
F-GSRD	Robin R.2160 Alpha Sport	322	
F-GSRE	Robin DR.400/160 Chevalier	2386	
F-GSRF	Robin DR.400/120 Petit Prince	2390	
F-GSRG	Robin DR.400/120 Petit Prince	2373	
F-GSRH	Robin R.2160 Alpha Sport	325	
F-GSRI	Robin DR.400/160 Chevalier	2394	
F-GSRJ	Robin DR.400/120 Petit Prince	2380	
F-GSRK	Robin DR.400/120 Dauphin 2+2	2395	
F-GSRL	Robin DR.400/180 Régent	2368	
F-GSRM	Robin DR.400/200R Remorqueur 200	2287	
F-GSRN	Robin DR.400/120 Petit Prince	2396	
F-GSRO	Robin DR.400/120 Petit Prince	2377	
F-GSRP	Robin DR.400/120 Petit Prince	2397	
F-GSRQ	Robin DR.400/120 Petit Prince	2400	
F-GSRR	Robin DR.400/140B Dauphin 4	2393	
F-GSRS	Robin DR.400/120 Petit Prince	2378	
F-GSRT	Robin DR.400/180 Régent	2399	
F-GSRU	Robin DR.400/120 Petit Prince	2404	
F-GSRX	Robin HR.200/120B	330	
F-GSRY	Robin HR.200/120B	327	
F-GSRZ	Robin HR.200/120B	328	
F-GSSA	Boeing 737-2K5	22596	N231TA
			YU-AOF
			D-AHLD
			N2941W
			D-AHLD
			N8279V
F-GSSB	Thunder AX7-77A HAFB	4065	
F-GSSC	Robin DR.400/120 Petit Prince	2338	
F-GSSF	Chaize JZ.40F16 HAFB	154	(F-GPSF)
F-GSTA	Airbus A.300-608ST Beluga	001/655	F-WAST
F-GSTB	Airbus A.300-608ST Beluga	002/751	F-WSTB
F-GSTC	Airbus A.300-608ST Beluga	003/765	F-WSTC
F-GSTD	Airbus A.300-608ST Beluga	004/776	F-WSTD
F-GSTE	Schroeder Fire Balloons G HAFB	679	
F-GSTF	Airbus A.300-600ST Beluga (Reservation)	005/796	F-W . . .
F-GSTH	Aérospatiale AS.355N Ecureuil 2	5649	
F-GSTJ	Fournier/Euravial RF.47	02	F-WWTJ
F-GSTM	Mudry CAP.10B	128	Fr.AF
F-GSTZ	Mauls MX-7-180 Star Rocket	11045C	OO-LVL
F-GSUN	Boeing 747-312	23030	N119KE
			(9V-SKE)
			(9V-SQX)
F-GSUP	Mudry CAP.10B	7	Fr.AF

Regn.	Type	C/n	Prev.Id.
F-GSVA	Piper PA-28-181 Archer II	28-8190111	HB-PFX
			N8309K
F-GSVC	Beech 1900D (Reservation)	UE-340	N23317
F-GSVI	SIGA MA-26 Pilatre de Rozier HAFB	110	
F-GSVM	Balloon reservation		
F-GSXF	Dassault Falcon 20E-5	315/517	F-SEBI
			F-GDLO
			OO-VPQ
			F-BVPQ
			F-WRQP
F-GSYD	Fouga CM.170 Magister (Reservation)	455	Fr.AF
F-GSZA	SOCATA TB-200 Tobago XL	1597	F-OHDL
F-GSZB	SOCATA TB-20 Trinidad	1886	
F-GSZC	SOCATA TB-10 Tobago	1823	
F-GSZD	SOCATA TB-20 Trinidad	1904	
F-GSZF	SOCATA TB-20 Trinidad	1910	
F-GSZG	SOCATA TB-20 Trinidad	1437	CS-D . .
			F-GLFJ
			(N678TB)
F-GSZI	SOCATA TB-20 Trinidad	1916	
F-GSZY	SOCATA TB-10 Trinidad	1892	
F-GTAA	Airbus A.321-131	674	D-AVZP
F-GTAB	Airbus A.321-131	675	D-AVZS
F-GTAC	Airbus A.321-131	684	D-AVZQ
F-GTAD	Airbus A.321-111	777	D-AVZI
F-GTAE	Airbus A.321-211	796	D-AVZN
F-GTAF	Airbus A.321-211	761	D-AVZJ
F-GTAG	Airbus A.321-211	956	D-AVZO
F-GTAH	Airbus A.321-211	1133	D-AVZD
F-GTAI to GTAZ Reserved for A.321's for Air France			
F-GTBA	Aérospatiale AS.350B2 Ecureuil	2577	F-OGRY
F-GTBC	Airbus A.300B4-203 (Reservation .99)	203	N473AS
			F-GOAA
			RP-C3004
			F-WZMO
F-GTBE	Aérospatiale AS.350B2 Ecureuil	3215	
F-WTBM	SOCATA TBM-700	01	
F-GTBR	Robin DR.500 Super Régent	0008	
F-GTBS	Thunder AX7-77A HAFB	4292	
F-GTCB	Boeing 727-200 (Reservation)		
F-GTCC	Airbus A.300B4-203 (Reservation .99)	219	N474AS
			RP-C3005
			F-WZMV
F-GTCE	SA.316B Alouette III	1271	F-GJCX
			ALAT
F-GTCF	Piper PA-34-220T Seneca V	3449145	N9521N
			N41635
F-GTCG	Chaize JZ22F12 HAFB	145	
F-GTCM	Schweizer 300CB	0072	N69A
F-GTCS	Piper PA-32R-301T SaratogAII TC	3257038	N9503N
F-GTDC	Airbus A.300B4-203 (Reservation .99)	unkn	
F-GTDD	Robin DR.400/180 Régent	2398	
F-GTDF	McDonnell-Douglas DC-10-30	46854	(F-GRMR)
			N54649
			(F-GHOJ)
			(F-BTDF)
			(N54649)
F-GTDG	McDonnell-Douglas DC-10-30	46997	TU-TAN
F-GTDH	McDonnell-Douglas DC-10-30	46851	F-BTDC
			HS-TGA
			F-BTDC
			N1350U
F-GTDN	SIGA MA-40 Pilatre de Rozier HAFB	109	D-OTAB(2)
F-GTDR	Robinson R-22M2 Mariner	2604M	(F-GRLB)
F-GTDS	Cessna 421B Golden Eagle (Reservation)	0233	F-BTDY
			G-AZPT
			N5990M
F-GTEF	Beech 200 Super King Air	BB-560	LN-MAA
			N200NA
			N72GA
			C-FDLO
			N38DD
F-GTEM	Beech 300 Super King Air	FL-80	PH-BRN
			N8275D
F-GTEZ	Piper PA-28-181 Archer II	2890165	D-ETAP
			N9195B

Regn.	Type	C/n	Prev.Id.
F-GTFA	Robin DR.400/160 Chevalier	2376	
F-GTGE	Cameron Z-105 HAFB (Reservation 12.99)	4749	
F-GTHD	Fouga CM.170 Magister (Reservation 1.99)	530	Fr.AF
F-GTIM	Lindstrand LBL-69A HAFB	491	
F-GTIV	Cameron N-77 HAFB	4606	
F-GTJB	Cameron A-250 HAFB	3928	
F-GTJC	Cessna 172S	172S08277	N7273H
F-GTJM	SOCATA TBM-700	145	
F-GTJP	Robinson R-44 Astro	0590	
F-GTKJ	Beech 1900D	UE-348	N23406
F-GTLC	UltraMagic N-210 HAFB	210/08	
F-GTLY	McDonnell-Douglas DC-10-30 (Reservation .99)	46954	F-ODLY F-GKMS SE-DFH ZK-NZS CC-CJS ZK-NZS (N85NA) ZK-NZS
F-GTLZ	McDonnell-Douglas DC-10-30 (Reservation .99)	46869	F-ODLZ SE-DFD (SE-DEA)
F-GTMA	Chaize JZ.25F12 HAFB	148	
F-GTMD	Cessna 525 CitationJet	0312	
F-GTMP	Robin DR.400/120 Dauphin 2+2	2444	
F-GTMR	Robin DR.500 Super Régent (Reservation .99)	20	
F-GTNY	Schroeder Fire Balloons Gas Bottle SS HAFB	680	
F-GTOB	Cessna 421C Golden Eagle (Reservation 12.99)	0896	RA-01559 HB-LOB D-ILAA (N6170C)
F-GTOD	Dassault Falcon 10	155	N725PA D-CIEL (N220FJ) F-WZGC
F-GTOM	Boeing 747SP-44 (Damaged 6.6.99)	21253	LX-ACO CN-RMS ZS-SPD
F-GTOP	Beech 95-B55 Baron	TC-649	F-BOST D-ILPU
F-GTOU	Cameron C-80 HAFB	4177	
F-GTOY	Aérospatiale AS.350B Ecureuil	1030	C-FBKW N7091U C-FBKW N90033
F-GTPA	Robin DR.400/180 Régent	2405	
F-GTPB	Robin DR.400/180 Régent	2406	
F-GTPC	Robin DR.400/120 Dauphin 2+2	2404	
F-GTPD	Robin DR.400/120 Dauphin 2+2	2417	
F-GTPE	Robin DR.400/160 Major	2413	
F-GTPF	Robin DR.400/120 Dauphin 2+2	2416	
F-GTPG	Robin DR.400/160 Major	2409	
F-GTPH	Robin DR.400/180 Régent	2410	
F-GTPI	Robin DR.400/140B Dauphin 4	2422	
F-GTPJ	Robin DR.400/140B Dauphin 4	2432	
F-GTPK	Robin DR.400/140B Major 80	2421	
F-GTPL	Robin DR.400/160 Major	2408	
F-GTPM	Robin DR.400/120 Dauphin 2+2	2425	
F-GTPN	Robin DR.400/180 Régent	2435	
F-GTPO	Robin HR.200/120B	340	
F-GTPP	Robin DR.400/160 Major	2411	
F-GTPQ	Robin DR.400/180 Régent	2414	
F-GTPR	Robin HR.200/120B	333	
F-GTPS	Robin DR.400/120 Dauphin 2+2	2427	
F-GTPT	Robin DR.400/180 Régent	2440	
F-GTPU	Robin DR.400/160 Major	2424	
F-GTPV	Robin DR.400/180 Régent	2438	
F-GTPX	Robin DR.400/180 Régent	2436	
F-GTPY	Robin DR.400/120 Dauphin 2+2	2437	
F-GTPZ	Robin DR.400/160 Major	2403	
F-GTRA	UltraMagic S-105 HAFB	105/51	
F-GTRB	Fairchild-Swearingen SA-227AC Metro III	AC-519	EC-GJV F-GHVE HB-LNE N31083
F-GTRY	Cessna 525 CitationJet	0359	
F-GTSB	SAAB 2000	014	D-ADSB SE-014
F-GTSG	Embraer EMB.120ER Brasilia	120-087	PH-BRS OO-DTG PT-SME
F-GTSH	Embraer EMB.120RT Brasilia	120-104	OO-DTH PT-SMW
F-GTSI	Embraer EMB.120RT Brasilia	120-123	OO-DTJ PT-SNP
F-GTSJ	Embraer EMB.120RT Brasilia	120-176	OO-DTL PT-SQO
F-GTSK	Embraer EMB.120RT Brasilia	120-213	OO-MTD (OO-DTM) PT-SSH
F-GTSL	SAAB 2000	013	EI-CPQ F-GTSA D-ADSA SE-013
F-GTSM	Aeritalia/SNIAS ATR-42-300	026	F-OGNE
F-GTTT	Pilatus PC-12/45 (Reservation, originally for c/n 249)	247	HB-FRR
F-GTVC	Beech 1900D	UE-349	N23430
F-GTVE	Aerospatiale AS.355F2 Ecureuil 2	5378	DQ-FGH F-WYMT
F-GTXU	Robin DR.400/120 Dauphin 2+2	2419	
F-GTXV	Robin DR.400/120 Dauphin 2+2	2420	
F-GTYT	Cameron N-90 HAFB	4461	
F-GTZA to F-GTZZ Reserved for Avions Pierre Robin:			
F-GTZA	Robin R.2160	341	
F-GTZB	Robin DR.500 Super Régent	45	
F-GTZC	Robin DR.500 Super Régent	22	
F-GTZD	Robin DR.400/160 Major	2442	
F-GTZE	Robin HR.200/120B	342	
F-GTZF	Robin R.2160	343	
F-GTZG	Robin HR.200/120B	345	
F-GTZI	Robin DR.400/120 Dauphin 2+2	2443	
F-GTZK	Robin DR.400/120 Dauphin 2+2	2451	
F-GTZQ	Robin DR.400/180 Régent	2446	
F-GTZY	Robin DR.400/160 Major	2445	
F-GUAB	SOCATA TB-10 Tobago	1721	
F-GUAC	SOCATA TB-10 Tobago	1720	
F-GUAL	Robin HR.100-210	169	F-OCQU
F-GUAM	Embraer EMB.135ER (Reservation .99)	145-...	
F-GUAS	Pilatus PC-6/B2-H2 Turbo Porter	557	N184L ST-AGR N184L
F-GUAT	Mudry CAP.10B	8	Fr.AF
F-GUAY	Cameron N-105 HAFB	4694	
F-GUCB	Beech 1900D	UE-308	N22841
F-GUCE	Robinson R-44 Astro	0551	
F-GUEQ	Dassault Falcon 900B	167	F-WWFO
F-GUFA	Cessna 182S	80437	N4219M
F-GUFD	Embraer EMB.145MP	145-197	
F-GUFR	SIGA MA-30 Pilatre de Rozier HAFB	116	
F-GUGA to F-GUGZ Reserved for Airbus A.318s for Air France			
F-GUHD	Fouga CM.170 Magister (Reservation)	533	Fr.AF
F-GUIL	Mooney M.20J Model 205	24-3131	
F-GUIX	Cessna 172R	80207	N9402F
F-GUJL	SIGA MA-22 Pilatre de Rozier HAFB (Res 12.99)	126	
F-GUJM	Mudry CAP.232 (Reservation .99)	unkn	
F-GUMD	Piper PA-28-181 Archer III	2843243	N9524N
F-GUNA to F-GUNZ Reserved for Airbus A.318s for Air France			
F-GUPE	Beech 1900D	UE-248	N10882
F-GUPF	Aérospatiale AS.350B1 Ecureuil	1191	F-GIPN N3599X
F-GUPT	Embraer EMB.145MP (Reservation .99)	unkn	
F-GURU	Sky 105-24 HAFB	152	
F-WUSH	Ballon Helium Globe Trott'Air 2	001	
F-GUST	Cessna 421B Golden Eagle	0968	OE-FMZ D-IGPZ G-BLAZ ZS-JOL N87534
F-GUUU	Pilatus PC-12/45 (Reservation, originally for c/n 250)	299	
F-GUYD	Fouga CM.170 Magister (Reservation)	465	Fr.AF

Regn.	Type	C/n	Prev.Id.
F-GVAB(2)	SIAI-Marchetti SF.260C	361	Phil. AF
F-GVAC	Boeing 737-229	20907	OO-SDA
			LX-LGN
			OO-SDA
F-GVAD	Robin DR.400/140B Major	1717	HB-KAZ
F-GVAL	UltraMagic S-90 HAFB	90/29	
F-GVAP	Bell 206L3 Long Ranger III	51248	N2217V
			D-HHOO
			C-FBZM
F-GVAR	Aérospatiale SA.365N1 Dauphin 2	6256	JA6694
			N29TH
			N6024P
F-GVCE	Aérospatiale AS.350B3 Ecureuil	3227	
	(Also reserved as F-GKCE)		
F-GVCT	Piper PA-38-112 Tomahawk	38-82A0105	HB-PGV
F-GVDP	Dassault Falcon 900EX	51	F-WWFU
F-GVHD	Embraer EMB.145MP	145-178	
F-GVIP	Aérospatiale SA.365C1 Dauphin 2	5045	RP-C365
F-GVIT	SIGA MA-30 Pilatre de Rozier HAFB	117	
F-GVLL	Aérospatiale SA.316B Alouette III	1081	F-GSOS
			ALAT
F-GVMD	Robinson R-44 Astro	0699	
F-GVNT	Lindstrand LBL-180A HAFB *(Reservation .99)*	071	G-EVNT
F-GVOL	UltraMagic M-130 HAFB	130/17	
F-GVPE	Beech 300 Super King Air	FA-94	I-AZME
			N25219
F-GVRA	Cessna 172SP	172S08278	N2386L
F-GVUE	Robinson R-44 Astro	0621	
TEST REGISTRATIONS:			
F-WWMB	Dassault Falcon 2000	58	
F-WWMP	Moniot APM-20 Lionceau	01	
F-WWMQ	Raven Europe FS-64A Hot Air Balloon	E-405	
F-WWMY	Aerotech Europe G.222 (ex CAP.222)	01	
F-WWRG	SOCATA TB-20NG Trinidad NG	1900	
F-WWXX	Moniot APM-20 Lionceau	03	
F-GXAB	Beech A100 King Air	B-193	EC-CHD
			E.23-1
			EC-CHD
F-GXCM	Mudry CAP.232	14	
F-GXRB	Mudry CAP.232 *(Reservation .99)*	11	F-GRRG
F-GYAB	Beech 1900D	UE-58	F-OHRV
			N83022
F-GYCC	Hughes 369E *(Reservation 11.99)*	0325E	D-HASP
			I-BNAR
F-GYOL	Dassault Falcon 50	88	LZ-010
			F-GYOL
			F-WQBK
			N588FJ
			VP-CRT
			VR-CRT
			F-WQCP
			N188FJ
			XA-OVR
			N92FJ
			F-WZHU
F-GYRA	Schweizer 269C	S-1604	N86G
F-GYSL	Dassault Falcon 20F	341	F-OHCJ
			VR-CDT
			N31IJS
			N78BC
			N51IWR
			N511WP
			N66GA
			N20FJ
			N4462F
			F-WMKF
F-GZOB	Colt 69A HAFB	2601	
F-GZOO	Aérospatiale AS.350B2 Ecureuil	9012	
F-HAAG	Beech F90 King Air *(Reservation .99)*	LA-62	F-GIFK
			D-ICBD
			N714D

Regn.	Type	C/n	Prev.Id.
F-HAAP	Dassault Falcon 900	142	TC-CAG
			F-GSMF
			F-WSMF
			N10AT
			N142FJ
			F-WWFN
F-HAOC	Embraer EMB.120RTBrasilia	120-014	LX-PTU
	(Reservation 7.99)		OY-JRT
			F-GFIN
			PT-SIJ
F-HAPE	Beech 1900D	UE-367	N30515
F-HASI	Mitsubishi MU-2B-60 Marquise	1515SA	N802SM
	(Reservation .99)		N910DA
			N426MA
F-HAXA	Dassault Falcon 900EX	12	F-WQBL
			N912EX
			(N900SB)
			N900EX
			N913FJ
			F-WWFJ
F-HBCA	Beech 1900D	UE-188	SE-KXV
			N1564J
F-HBIL	Airbus A.330-200 *(Reservation .99 for Corsair)*	unkn	
F-HCAT	Airbus A.330-243	285	F-WWKB
F-HCHA	Beech 1900D	UE-37	N37YV

FRANCE d'OUTREMER

Regn.	Type	C/n	Prev.Id.
F-OAIZ	Raven-Europe S.60A HAFB	E-040	
F-OBAS	Reims/Cessna F.182Q Skylane	0045	
F-OBFT	SAN Jodel D.117A Grand Tourisme	911	
F-OBJR	SOCATA MS.893E Rallye 180GT Gaillard	12647	F-BXMR
F-OBYN	Piper PA-31-350 Chieftain	31-8152005	N4046M
F-OCEO	Piper PA-34-200 Seneca	34-7350229	F-BUOO
			F-ETAF
F-OCEY	Piper PA-38-112 Tomahawk	38-78A0692	N2442A
F-OCFA	Piper PA-23-250 Aztec C	27-2788	N10F
			(N5674Y)
F-OCFE	Cessna 150E	61471	N4071U
F-OCFK	Cessna 310P	0053	N5753M
F-OCFL	Piper PA-23-250 Aztec C	27-3856	VH-SVZ
			N6560Y
F-OCFN	Piper PA-28-140 Cherokee	28-24166	N11C
F-OCFP	Piper PA-31-310 Navajo	31-370	VH-SVY
			N9279Y
F-OCGU	Cessna U.206	0492	N8092Z
F-OCIT	Piper PA-23-250 Aztec C	27-3425	N6197Y
F-OCKA	CEA DR.220A 2+2	57	
F-OCLJ	Piper PA-32-260 Cherokee Six	32-1015	
F-OCMJ	Cessna 182J Skylane	57111	N3011F
F-OCNA	Piper PA-34-200 Seneca	34-7250342	F-GCCA
			F-OCNA
			F-BTQS
			F-BTMS
F-OCNX	Cessna 172K	58463	N84411
F-OCOY	Britten-Norman BN-2Aislander	131	G-51-53
F-OCPR	Piper PA-28-140 Cherokee C	28-26922	N11C
F-OCPS	SOCATA MS.893A Rallye Commodore 180	11635	
F-OCPT	SOCATA MS.893A Rallye Commodore 180	11665	
F-OCQC	SA.318C Alouette Astazou	2171	
F-OCQE	CEA DR.253B Régent	179	
F-OCQG	SA.318C Alouette Astazou	2219	
F-OCQO	Reims/Cessna F.337F Super Skymaster	0045/01385	
F-OCQQ	Robin DR.400/180 Régent	740	
F-OCQS	Piper PA-32-260 Cherokee Six	32-375	5R-MCD
			N3495W
F-OCQX	Robin DR.400/180 Régent	916	
F-OCQZ	DHC-6 Twin Otter 300	412	
F-OCSO	Piper PA-23-160 Apache H	23-1988	CF-NMP
			N4463P

Regn.	Type	C/n	Prev.Id.
F-OCSP	SOCATA MS.894A Minerva 220	11997	(D-EMJJ)
F-OCTU	Reims/Cessna FR.172J Rocket	0570	(F-BXQC)
F-OCUX	Reims/Cessna F.172M	1009	
F-OCXA	Cessna 177B Cardinal	02092	ZK-DSF
F-OCXB	Cessna 310Q	1075	ZK-DRK
			N1222G
F-OCXE	Piper PA-32-300 Cherokee Six	32-7340049	VH-MIO
			N11C
F-OCXL	Piper PA-31-310 Navajo	31-7512068	N59701
F-OCXP	Britten-Norman BN-2A-21 Islander	483	G-BDLF
F-OCXQ	Aérospatiale SA.342J Gazelle	1602	
F-OCXS	Hughes 369HS	106-0865S	
F-OCXU	Piper PA-28-161 Cherokee Warrior II	28-7816534	N9572N
F-ODAN	Robin DR.400/180 Régent	1043	
F-ODBN	DHC-6 Twin Otter 300	470	
F-ODDZ	Cessna U.206E Stationair	01633	5R-MEV
			(N9433G)
F-ODFC	Reims/Cessna F.150M	1338	
F-ODGD	Cessna 152	83539	ZK-EOZ
			(N53379)
F-ODGF	Cessna 152	83590	ZK-ETB
			(N4710B)
F-ODGH	Cessna 207A Skywagon	00650	ZK-EOE
			N85020
			(N75894)
F-ODGJ	Hughes 269C	70-0937	ZK-HPM
F-ODGK	Hughes 369HS	85-0763S	ZK-HPE
			(N222PF)
			N900Q
F-ODGN	Aeritalia/SNIAS ATR-42-300	097	
F-ODGQ	Aérospatiale AS.350B Ecureuil	2263	
F-ODGS	Piper PA-31T Cheyenne II	31T-7720041	TS-LAZ
			LN-PAE
			(N82144)
F-ODGT	Piper PA-28-161 Warrior II	28-8616050	N9294A
			N9511N
F-ODGU	Beech 65-F90 King Air	LA-88	F-GCTB
F-ODGV	Robin ATL L	97	F-GFSQ
F-ODGX	Boeing 737-33A	24094	
F-ODHE	Cessna 172RG Cutlass	0503	(N5300V)
F-ODHL	Robin R.2112 Alpha	123	
F-ODHS	Cessna U.206G Stationair II	03900	N7362C
F-ODIN	Cessna TU.206G Turbo Stationair II	04722	(N732TZ)
F-ODIV	Piper PA-38-112 Tomahawk	38-80A0058	N9656N
F-ODIX	Beech 58 Baron	TH-1016	
F-ODJD	SOCATA MS.893E Rallye 180GT Gaillard floatplane	13202	
F-ODJG	Boeing 747-2Q2B	21468	(TR-LXK)
			N1248E
F-ODJJ	Cessna 172G	54376	5R-MDR
			N11B
			(N4307L)
F-ODKR	Cessna TU.206G Turbo Stationair II	04562	N9757M
F-ODLB	Cessna 150K	71137	ZS-FXM
			N5637G
F-ODLC	Aérospatiale SA.315B Lama	2635	
F-ODLE	Aérospatiale SA.315B Lama	2250/25	5V-MAJ
F-ODLF	Beech 58 Baron	TH-310	ZS-PTE
			N1041W
F-ODLI	Aérospatiale AS.350B1 Ecureuil	2063	F-WYMC
F-ODLJ	Aérospatiale SA.365C3 Dauphin 2	5079	D-HMKB
F-ODLL	Aérospatiale AS.350B Ecureuil	1192	(N215EH)
			N3602V
F-ODLP	Piper PA-31-310 Navajo	31-756	F-BTCX
			N7234L
F-ODLR	Piper PA-28-161 Cadet	2841153	(F-GHBI)
F-ODLS	Piper PA-28-181 Archer II	2890084	F-GFYB
F-ODLU	Aérospatiale AS.350B1 Ecureuil	2242	
F-ODLV	Robinson R-22 Beta	1035	N8043E
F-ODLY	McDonnell-Douglas DC-10-30	46954	F-GKMS
	(Reserved as F-GTLY .99)		SE-DFH
			ZK-NZS
			CC-CJS
			ZK-NZS
			(N85NA)
			ZK-NZS

Regn.	Type	C/n	Prev.Id.
F-ODLZ	McDonnell-Douglas DC-10-30	46869	SE-DFD
	(Reserved as F-GTLZ .99)		(SE-DEA)
F-ODMM	Piper PA-31T Cheyenne	31T-8020084	N2592V
F-ODMN	Aérospatiale SA.365C1 Dauphin 2	5047	F-GCJR
F-ODNI	Reims/Cessna F.152	1749	(F-GCNI)
F-ODNL	Mudry CAP.10B	70	HB-SAI
F-ODNR	Mudry CAP.10B	139	
F-ODOX	SOCATA TB-20 Trinidad (Wfu)	312	
F-ODPA	Centrair ASW-20F	20151	
F-ODQI	Piper PA-31-350 Navajo Chieftain	31-7305065	F-BUOI
			F-ETAH
F-ODQN	Chaize CS.3000F16 HAFB	056	
F-ODSE	Chaize CS.3000F16 HAFB	079	
F-ODSM	Piper PA-28R-201 Cherokee Arrow III	28R-7737084	N38223
F-ODSN	Beech 58 Baron	TH-413	N401RC
F-ODSP	Piper PA-28-161 Warrior II	28-8016137	C-GBHY
F-ODSR	Aérospatiale SN.601 Corvette	35	YV-01CP
			YV-589CP
			F-GDAZ
			PH-JSC
F-ODSZ	SOCATA TB-10 Tobago	660	SE-IMZ
			N20HZ
F-ODTD	Raven-Europe S.60A HAFB	E-049	
F-ODTI	SE.3130 Alouette II	1852	F-GBOC
			D-HOFO
F-ODTK	Airbus A.300-B4-622	252	F-WZLR
F-ODTS	Raven Europe S-66A HAFB	E-048	
F-ODTU	Raven Europe FS-83A HAFB	E-076	
F-ODTV	Raven-Europe S-60A HAFB	E-077	
F-ODUI	Beech 58 Baron	TH-1205	N1821T
F-ODUM	Aérospatiale AS.350B Ecureuil	1834	VH-LEW
F-ODUN	Dornier 228-212	8197	D-CATS(1)
			D-CBDH(3)
F-ODUO	Piper PA-28-181 Archer II	28-8490065	N4355B
F-ODUP	Pilatus Britten-Norman BN-2B-26 Islander	2219	G-BRGB
F-ODUQ	Pilatus Britten-Norman BN-2B-26 Islander	2220	G-BRGC
F-ODUR	Pilatus Britten-Norman BN-2B-26 Islander	2217	G-BRFZ
F-ODUS	Aérospatiale AS.350B Ecureuil	2098	
F-ODUY	Piper PA-28-181 Archer II	2890092	N9152X
F-ODUZ	Aérospatiale SA.365N1 Dauphin 2	6264	
F-ODVA	Raven-Europe S-66A HAFB	E-045	
F-ODVF	Airbus A.310-304	445	
F-ODVG	Airbus A.310-304	490	
F-ODVH	Airbus A.310-304	491	
F-ODVI	Airbus A.310-304	531	
F-ODYB	Dornier 228-212	8191	D-CORK
			D-CBDA(4)
F-ODYD	Aeritalia/SNIAS ATR-42-300	221	
F-ODYE	Aeritalia/SNIAS ATR-42-300	335	F-WWLW
F-ODYF	Britten-Norman BN-2A-26 Islander	309	G-BADK
			G-51-309
F-ODYG	Cessna 402B	0931	ZK-KAN
			N87138
F-ODYH	Cessna 402B	0585	ZK-DSB
			N1457G
F-ODYI	Aérospatiale AS.355F1 Ecureuil 2	5068	N800HH
			N5787N
F-ODYJ	SOCATA TB-10 Tobago	1193	
F-ODYK	Cessna 340	0041	F-BTDS
			N5753M
F-ODYL	SOCATA TB-10 Tobago	1192	
F-ODYM	Robinson R-22 Mariner	1908M	
F-ODYN	Cessna 152	82982	C-GRXZ
			N46008
F-ODYO	Piper PA-28-151 Cherokee Warrior	28-7515153	ZK-DUV
			N9628N
F-ODYP	Aérospatiale AS.350B1 Ecureuil	2303	
F-ODYQ	SOCATA TB-20 Trinidad	1118	VH-LQJ
F-ODYS	Piper PA-28-161 Cherokee Warrior II	28-7816621	C-GDJQ
			N36208
F-ODYT	Reims/Cessna 182P Skylane	0056/64397	F-GALB
			(F-GAAL)
			N1630M
F-ODYU	Aérospatiale AS.350BA Ecureuil	1998	ZK-HZH
F-ODYZ	Reims/Cessna F.406 Caravan	0057	N31226

Regn.	Type	C/n	Prev.Id.
F-ODZC	Piper PA-31-350 Navajo Chieftain	31-7652095	F-OAFH
			F-GCQV
			F-OAFH
			F-GAJH
			F-VAAK
F-ODZF	Dornier 228-201	8107	LN-NVH
			D-COHH
F-ODZG	Dornier 228-202K	8123	N2255E
			VH-NSH
			D-CEZH
			(D-CBDC)
F-ODZH	Dornier 228-202K (wfu?)	8077	N2255Y
			VH-NSZ
			G-BMND
			D-CESI
			D-IESI
F-ODZI	Cessna 152	82520	N69162
F-ODZJ	Boeing 737-53A	24877	F-GHXN
F-ODZM	Aérospatiale AS.350B Ecureuil	1045	N9006X
F-ODZP	SE.3130 Alouette II	1573	ALAT
F-ODZQ	Robinson R-22 Beta	2094	N23340
F-ODZR	SE.3130 Alouette II	1359	ALAT
F-ODZT	Schweizer 269C	S-1650	N86G
F-ODZU	Bell 47G-4A	7592	F-GFLP
			N225FD
			N6211N
F-ODZV	Aérospatiale AS.355F2 Ecureuil 2	5310	JA9611
F-ODZX	Aerotek Pitts S-2	2122	N5SV
F-ODZY	Boeing 737-33A	27452	
F-ODZZ	Boeing 737-39M	28898	N35153
			N1786B
F-OGBL	Piper PA-23-160 Apache G	23-2006	N4484P
F-OGDS	Cessna 150H	67214	N6414S
F-OGES	DHC-6 Twin Otter 300	254	N302MA
F-OGEV	Cessna 150K	71815	N6315G
F-OGFC	Cessna P.206E Super Skylane	0627	N5727J
F-OGFF	Piper PA-28-180 Cherokee F	28-7105138	
F-OGFL	Cessna 402B	1369	N418JB
F-OGFR	Piper PA-28-140 Cherokee E	28-7225294	
F-OGFS	Piper PA-28-140 Cherokee E	28-7225296	
F-OGGT	Beech 58 Baron	TH-514	
F-OGGX	Beech C23 Sundowner	M-1649	
F-OGHF	Partenavia P.68B	58	
F-OGHN	Piper PA-28R-200 Cherokee Arrow	28R-7635342	
F-OGHQ	Cessna 177B Cardinal	02522	N17238
F-OGHT	Hughes 269C	117-0643	F-GATL
F-OGHZ	Piper PA-28-181 Cherokee Archer II	28-7690351	N6142J
F-OGIA	Piper PA-28-181 Archer II	28-7990351	
F-OGIC	Cessna A.185F Skywagon	03348	N6990H
F-OGIO	Piper PA-32-301 Saratoga	32-8006078	N82425
F-OGIP	SOCATA Rallye 110ST Galopin	3060	
F-OGIU	Cessna A.188B Agtru k	02399T	N4880R
F-OGIZ	DHC-6 Twin Otter 300	675	
F-OGJC	Fairchild F.27J	107	F-GBRT
			N1782
			N4306F
			N2734R
F-OGJF	Piper PA-28-181 Archer II	28-8090333	
F-OGJG	Piper PA-28-236 Dakota	28-8011119	
F-OGJJ	Robin R.2160 Alpha Sport	184	
F-OGJP	Rockwell S.2R Thrush Commander	2255R	N8495V
F-OGJR	Piper PA-28-181 Archer II	28-8090293	N8198A
F-OGJT	Piper PA-23-250 Aztec E	27-7305050	N40245
F-OGJU	Piper PA-32-301 Saratoga	32-8106006	N8290U
F-OGJV	DHC-6 Twin Otter 300	422	EC-CJI
F-OGKB	Piper PA-32-300 Cherokee Six	32-40749	F-BUOC
			OO-KAA
			N8945N
F-OGKO	Piper PA-28-151 Cherokee Warrior	28-7715109	N5358F
F-OGKQ	Cessna 172P	76311	N98571
F-OGKR	Rockwell S.2R Thrush Commander	1979R	N4220X
F-OGKU	Cessna 152	82981	N46006
F-OGNG	Cessna 152	83030	N46319
F-OGNJ	Piper PA-28-161 Cherokee Warrior II	28-7816079	N47475
F-OGNK	Piper PA-23-250 Aztec F	27-7854054	N63917

Regn.	Type	C/n	Prev.Id.
F-OGNP	Cessna T.188C AgHusky	03636T	N3372J
F-OGNQ	Cessna U.206G Stationair II	07015	N9302W
F-OGNZ	Piper PA-32-300 Cherokee Six	32-7440037	N56939
F-OGOB	Cessna 152	81780	N67363
F-OGOC	Cessna 172M	63038	N13913
F-OGOD	Cessna 208 Caravan I	00166	N9743F
F-OGOF	Dornier 228-202	8143	D-CBCB
			D-CBDW
F-OGOG	Reims/Cessna F.406 Caravan II	0026	
F-OGOI	Britten-Norman BN-2A-III-2 Trislander	1037	V2-LCI
			VP-VAG
			G-BEDN
F-OGOJ	Dornier 228-202	8136	D-CIRA(2)
			D-CBCA
			D-CBDP(1)
F-OGOK	Hughes 269C	11-0080	N9650F
F-OGOL	Dornier 228-202K	8139	D-CACC
			(D-CBDS)
F-OGOM	Piper PA-28-151 Cherokee Warrior	28-7515020	N44739
F-OGON	Grumman G.164B Agcat	54B	- ? -
			N48503
F-OGOP	Robin R.2160D	163	HB-EXM
F-OGOQ	Dornier 228-201	8056	7P-LAL
			D-CAMI
F-OGOU	Aérospatiale AS.355F2 Ecureuil 2	5051	N281DB
			C-GLCA
			N281DB
			N5778C
F-OGOV	Britten-Norman BN-2A-26 Islander	399	G-BJWP
			4X-AYP
			SX-BFF
			4X-AYP
			SX-BFD
			4X-AYP
			SX-BFA
			4X-AYP
			N57JA(2)
			G-BCEJ
F-OGOZ	Dornier 228-202K	8161	D-CBDR(2)
F-OGPB	Hughes 269C	76-0521	N42JW
F-OGPI	Dornier 228-202	8169	D-COCA(2)
			D-CBDL(3)
F-OGPJ	Piper PA-28-161 Warrior II	28-7916379	V2-LCA
			VP-LCA
			N9507N
F-OGPM	Beech 58 Baron	TH-345	N1896W
F-OGPP	Piper PA-23-250 Aztec F	27-7654152	C-GPXX
F-OGPS	Aérospatiale AS.350B2 Ecureuil	2412	
F-OGPV	Piper PA-28-181 Archer II	28-8190091	N82978
F-OGPZ	Mooney M.20J Model 205	24-3194	N91284
F-OGQQ	Airbus A.310-304	592	F-WWCN
F-OGQR	Airbus A.310-304	593	F-WWCP
F-OGQT	Airbus A.310-304	622	F-WWCD
F-OGQU	Airbus A.310-304	646	F-WWCT
F-OGRA	Piper PA-28-181 Archer II	28-8090354	N8233S
F-OGRB	Piper PA-23-250 Aztec F	27-7754102	N6570X
			- ? -
			N63771
F-OGRH	Piper PA-28-161 Cherokee Warrior II	28-7716282	N38864
F-OGRI	Aérospatiale AS.350B Ecureuil	1282	F-GHHK
			N3610U
F-OGRN	Ayres S.2R-T34 Turbo Thrush	T34-163	N3096S
F-OGRP	Aérospatiale AS.355F1 Ecureuil 2	5085	N900HH
			N57876
F-OGRT	Boeing 737-341	26854	(PP-VPC)
F-OGRV	Cessna 150L	75755	N65980
F-OGRX	SOCATA TB-9 Tampico Club	1349	
F-OGSB	Raven Europe S-60A HAFB	E-191	
F-OGSC	Raven Europe S-60A HAFB	E-196	
F-OGSK	Raven Europe S-66A HAFB	E-246	
F-OGSL	Raven Europe S-60A HAFB	E-235	
F-OGSU	Raven Europe S-60A HAFB	E-263	
F-OGUA	Robinson R-22 Mariner	2025M	
F-OGUH	Piper PA-32-301 Saratoga	32-8106031	N8320S
F-OGUJ	Cessna 172M	62019	N12494

Regn.	Type	C/n	Prev.Id.
F-OGUK	Piper PA-28-180 Cherokee G	28-7305323	CF-CCP
F-OGUO(2)	Aeritalia/SNIAS ATR-72-212	475	F-WWEH
F-OGUP	Cessna 172N	71961	N5820E
F-OGUQ	Bell 47G-4	3369	N65168
			CF-RXR
F-OGUR	Piper PA-28R-201 Arrow III	28R-7837041	C-FGWJ
			N9852K
F-OGUS	Aérospatiale AS.350B Ecureuil	1379	F-GIHA
			N5449C
F-OGUT	Cessna 152	85711	N566V
			(N94541)
F-OGUZ	Aérospatiale AS.350B2 Ecureuil	2684	(D-HWPA)
F-OGVA(2)	Dornier 228-212	8236	D-CBDB(7)
F-OGVB	GAF N-24A Nomad	0076FA	N4816C
	(Dismantled)		VH- IIK
F-OGVC	GAF N-24A Nomad	0098FA	N419NE
			VH- IIQ
F-OGVD	GAF N-24A Nomad	0064FA	N4807W
			VH-COV
F-OGVE(2)	Dornier 228-212	8237	D-CBDD(7)
F-OGVF	Cessna 150M	78963	N704XU
F-OGVG	Piper PA-23-160 Apache	23-1412	N3443P
F-OGVI (2)	Cessna U.206G Stationair II	04849	N734LN
F-OGVK	Cessna 150M	78184	N9234U
F-OGVL	Cessna U.206G Stationair II	05207	N5326U
F-OGVM	Cessna A.188B Agtruck	02804T	N731DA
F-OGVN	Partenavia P.68B	155	F-GBLY
F-OGVO	Hughes 269C	86-0539	N911PD
			TF-ELI
			N911PD
F-OGVQ	Cessna TU.206G Turbo Stationair II	04854	N734NZ
			XB-ANA
			N734NZ
F-OGVS	Reims/Cessna F.406 Caravan II	0061	N3121X
F-OGVT	Cessna 172N	68788	N143ER
			N734EB
F-OGVV	Piper PA-28-181 Archer III	2843016	
	(Originally c/n 2890249)		
F-OGVX	Partenavia P.68B	39	G-BFVO
			SE-FUK
F-OGVZ	Bell 205A-1	30109	F-GHHN(2)
			C-FJSI
			N2969W
F-OGXB	Britten-Norman BN-2A-2 Islander	303	D-IHVH
			G-AZUS
			G-51-303
			(N58JA)
F-OGXC	Aérospatiale AS.350BA Ecureuil	1300	F-GJHI
F-OGXD	Cessna U.206G Stationair II	05007	N4622U
F-OGXE	Robin R.2160 Alpha Sport	290	F-GORE
F-OGXF	Aeritalia/SNIAS ATR-72-212	461	F-WWLP
F-OGXG	Dornier 228-212	8176	F-WGXG
			D-CDDB
			D-CBDG(3)
F-OGXH	Cessna 172	unkn	
F-OGXI	Cessna 208B Grand Caravan	0485	N2647Y
F-OGXJ	Cessna 208B Grand Caravan	0497	N12289
F-OGXK	Cessna 208B Grand Caravan	0459	N2646X
F-OGXL	Cessna U.206G Stationair II	04129	F-GOSA
			OO-MTC
			N756JN
F-OGXM	Pilatus PC-6/B2-H4 Turbo Porter	915	
F-OGXN	CAARP CAP.10B	4	Fr.AF
F-OGXQ	Cessna 172N	68492	N733RP
F-OGXS	Hughes 269C	56-0502	N7445F
F-OGXT	Piper PA-28-236 Dakota	28-7911116	N3009T
F-OGXU	Hughes 269C	118-0734	N58281
F-OGXV	Piper PA-28-181 Archer III	2843065	
F-OGXX	Cessna 208B Grand Caravan	0557	(F-OHXI)
			N1268N
F-OGXY	Cessna 208B Grand Caravan	0574	(F-OHXJ)
			N1207A
F-OGXZ	Cessna 208B Grand Caravan	0586	(F-OHXK)
			N12160
F-OGYA	Airbus A.320-211	087	F-WWDM

Regn.	Type	C/n	Prev.Id.
F-OGYB	Airbus A.320-211	088	F-WWDN
F-OGYC	Airbus A.320-212	569	(JY-CAS)
			F-WWDG
F-OGYM	Airbus A.310-324	457	F-WGYM
			N820PA
			F-WWCD
F-OGYN	Airbus A.310-324	458	N821PA
			F-WWCF
F-OGYP(2)	Airbus A.310-324	442	N812PA
			F-WWCZ
F-OGYQ	Airbus A.310-324	453	N817PA
			F-WWCK
F-OGYR	Airbus A.310-324	456	N819PA
			F-WWCV
F-OGYS	Airbus A.310-324	467	N822PA
			F-WWCG
F-OGYT	Airbus A.310-324	660	N836AB
			F-WWCF
F-OGYU	Airbus A.310-324	687	N842AB
			F-WWCE
F-OGYV	Airbus A.310-324	689	N843AB
			F-WWCG
F-OGYW	Airbus A.310-222	276	F-WGYN
			A7-ABB
			F-WAYB
			F-WGYO
			9K-AHB
			YI-AOB
			9K-AHB
			F-WZEP
F-OHAA	Dornier 228-212	8198	D-CDWK
			D-CBDK(4)
F-OHAE	Aérospatiale AS.355F1 Ecureuil 2	5070	N200HH
			N5787P
F-OHAF	Dornier 228-212	8199	D-CLOG
			D-CBDZ(2)
F-OHAJ	Piper PA-28R-201 Arrow III	28R-7837014	N47911
F-OHAK	Cessna 152	85907	N95499
F-OHAL	Robin DR.400/160 Chevalier	812	F-BUHY
F-OHAM	Aérospatiale AS.350BA Ecureuil	2633	F-WYMP
F-OHAO	Aérospatiale AS.355F2 Ecureuil 2 *(Resvn)*	unkn	
F-OHAP	Piper PA-28-161 Warrior II	28-8516022	N43820
F-OHAR	Schweizer 269C	S-1626	
F-OHAV	Cessna 404 Titan	0216	HB-LOY
			OY-GAZ
			LN-MAI
			(SE-GYF)
			N88676
F-OHAY	Cessna U.206G Stationair II	04683	N732JK
F-OHAZ	Cessna 172N	71145	N2077E
F-OHCB	Piper PA-28R-200 Cherokee Arrow II	28R-7635100	F-BXSD
			N9642N
F-OHCE(2)	Raven-Europe S-60A HAFB	E-288	
F-OHCH	Raven Europe S-60A HAFB	E-320	
F-OHCI	Raven-Europe S-60A HAFB	E-314	
F-OHCP	Beech 200 Super King Air	BB-831	F-ODUA
			N43WB
			N78011
			N7801L
F-OHCR	Piper PA-34-200T Seneca II	34-7670160	F-BXSQ
	(Reservation, not yet taken up)		
F-OHCT	Partenavia P.68B	13	F-WQHL
			G-MOET
			G-HPVC
			OH-PVB
F-OHCV	Maule MXT-7-180 Star Rocket	14016C	F-GHJX
			N9210T
F-OHCX	Airbus A.320-232	709	B-2348
			F-WWIP
F-OHDZ	SOCATA Rallye 235F *(CofA Expired)*	3390	
F-OHED	Aérospatiale AS.350B2 Ecureuil	2597	
F-OHEN	Aérospatiale AS.355F2 Ecureuil 2	5515	
F-OHEO	Aérospatiale AS.350B2 Ecureuil	2679	
F-OHFA(2)	Aeritalia/SNIAS ATR-42-320	363	F-WWLC
F-OHFB	Aeritalia/SNIAS ATR-42-320	366	F-WWLE

Regn.	Type	C/n	Prev.Id.
F-OHFC	Aeritalia/SNIAS ATR-42-320	351	F-WWER
F-OHFD	Aeritalia/SNIAS ATR-42-320	374	F-WWLQ
F-OHFE	Aeritalia/SNIAS ATR-42-320	378	F-WWLA
F-OHFH	Aeritalia/SNIAS ATR-42-300	067	I-ATRK
			F-WWER
F-OHFK	SA.316B Alouette III	1510	JRV23157
F-OHFO	Dassault Falcon 50EX	267	F-WWHR
F-OHFR(2)	Airbus A.320-212	189	G-UKLL
			C-GRYY
			G-BWCP
			N483GX
			F-WWDC
F-OHFS	Aeritalia/SNIAS ATR-72-210	393	F-WWLI
F-OHFT	Airbus A.320-212	343	G-UKLK
			G-BWKO
			N485GX
			F-WWDH
F-OHFU	Airbus A.320-212	190	PH-DVR
			(SE-DVH)
			G-UKLJ
			G-BWKN
			N484GX
			F-WWDD
F-OHFV	Aeritalia/SNIAS ATR-42-300	012	F-WQJB
	(W/o in Kosovo 13.11.99)		N12MQ
			N420MQ
			F-WWED
F-OHFY	Britten-Norman BN-2A-9 Islander	829	F-GFDK
	(W/o 5.9.97)		TR-LXX
			G-BELM
			YR-BNX(1)
F-OHGB	Airbus A.320-212	289	A40-MC
			TC-ONC
			9H-ABX
			F-WWBX
F-OHGC	Airbus A.320-211	407	CS-TNF
			F-WWDH
F-OHGD	Beech 1900D *(Reservation 12.99)*	UE-370	
F-OHGE	Beech 1900D *(Reservation 12.99)*	UE-380	
F-OHGF	Beech 1900D *(Reservation 12.99)*	UE-383	
F-OHGH	Beech 1900D *(Reservation 12.99)*	UE-384	
F-OHGH	Robinson R-44 Clipper	0446	
F-OHGL	Aeritalia/SNIAS ATR-42-320	323	F-WWET
F-OHJA	Aeritalia/SNIAS ATR-72-202	456	F-WWLN
F-OHJB	Aeritalia/SNIAS ATR-42-512	513	F-WWLL
F-OHJC	Aeritalia/SNIAS ATR-42-512	528	F-WWLF
F-OHJD	Aeritalia/SNIAS ATR-42-500	556	F-WW..
F-OHJF	DHC-6 Twin Otter 300	500	N929MA
F-OHJJ	Aeritalia/SNIAS ATR-72-212A *(Reservation .99)*	unkn	
F-OHJK	Beech B200 Super King Air	BB-1544	N1094S
F-OHJL	Beech B200 Super King Air /Raisbeck	BB-1592	N6148X
F-OHJM	Dornier 328-300	3129	D-BDXL(1)
F-OHJN	Aeritalia/SNIAS ATR-72-210	535	F-WWEC
F-OHJO	Aeritalia/SNIAS ATR-72-212A	553	F-WWLC
F-OHJP	Cessna R.182 Skylane RG	00128	N7363Y
F-OHJR	Piper PA-23-250 Aztec E	27-7554087	VH-WJJ
			N54785
F-OHJT	Aeritalia/SNIAS ATR-72-212A	590	
F-OHJU	Aeritalia/SNIAS ATR-72-212A	563	F-WWEA
F-OHKG to OHKZ *Reservations for Eurocopter*			
F-OHLE	Airbus A.300B4-2C	031	EL-LIC
			G-BXRU
			N63661
			HL7238
			F-WZEQ
			F-WJAY
			F-WLGC
F-OHLF	Airbus A.300B4-103	069	G-BYYS
	(Reservation .99, also reserved as		5T-CLI
	F-GJJG and F-WQKU)		N471AS
			RP-C3002
			F-WZEB
F-OHLG	Cessna 208 Caravan	00061	N9463F
F-OHLH	Airbus A.310-304	447	D-APOL
			A6-KUA
			C-GCWD
			F-WWCN
F-OHLI	Airbus A.310-304	481	D-APOP
			A6-KUD
			C-GKWD
			F-WWCQ
F-OHMA	Airbus A.320-231	368	F-WWIF
F-OHMB	Airbus A.320-231	376	F-WWIK
F-OHMC	Airbus A.320-231	386	F-WWBI
F-OHMD	Airbus A.320-231	433	F-WWDC
F-OHME	Airbus A.320-231	252	XA-RZU
			F-WWBD
F-OHMF	Airbus A.320-231	259	XA-RYQ
			F-WWBK
F-OHMG	Airbus A.320-231	260	XA-RYS
			F-WWBL
F-OHMH	Airbus A.320-231	261	XA-RYT
			F-WWBM
F-OHMI	Airbus A.320-231	275	XA-RJW
			F-WWIG
F-OHMJ	Airbus A.320-231	276	XA-RJX
			F-WWIM
F-OHMK	Airbus A.320-231	296	XA-RJY
			F-WWIH
F-OHML	Airbus A.320-231	320	XA-RJZ
			F-WWBI
F-OHMM	Airbus A.320-231	321	XA-RKA
			F-WWBK
F-OHMN	Airbus A.320-231	353	XA-RKB
			F-WWDV
F-OHMO	Airbus A.320-231	640	F-WWDF
F-OHMP	Airbus A.321-211	663	D-AVZK
F-OHMQ	Airbus A.321-211	668	D-AVZN
F-OHMR	Airbus A.320-231	676	F-WW..
F-OHNE	Aérospatiale AS.355N Ecureuil 2	5584	
F-OHNR	Aérospatiale AS.350BA Ecureuil	2922	
F-OHNS	Aérospatiale AS.350BA Ecureuil	2925	
F-OHNV(2)	Aérospatiale AS.350BA Ecureuil	2981	
F-OHNX	Aérospatiale AS.350B Ecureuil	1612	
F-OHOB	Aeritalia/SNIAS ATR-72-202	316	(F-OHFA)
			(F-GKOE)
			F-WWEJ
F-OHPB	Airbus A.300B4-203	235	N211PA
			F-WZMG
F-OHPC	Airbus A.300B4-203	304	N208PA
			F-WZMD
F-OHPD	Airbus A.300B4-203	305	N209PA
			F-WZMV
F-OHPJ(2)	Airbus A.340-313X	173	F-WWJG
F-OHPK	Airbus A.340-212	176	F-WWJE
F-OHPL	Airbus A.340-313X	187	F-WWJO
F-OHPM	Airbus A.340-313X	196	F-WWJI
F-OHPP(2)	Airbus A.310-222	331	F-WGYR
			OO-SCI
			F-WGYT
			9K-AHE
			YI-AOD
			9K-AHE
			F-WZEO
F-OHPQ	Airbus A.310-222	318	F-WGYQ
			9K-AHD
			YI-AOA
			9K-AHD
			F-WZEL
F-OHPR	Airbus A.310-325	702	F-WWCG
F-OHPS	Airbus A.310-325	704	F-WWCL
F-OHPT	Airbus A.310-304	526	F-WHPT
			D-AIDK
			F-WWCC
F-OHPU	Airbus A.310-324	439	F-WHPU
			C-GCIL
			N811PA
			F-WWCI

Regn.	Type	C/n	Prev.Id.
F-OHPV	Airbus A.310-324	449	F-WHPV
			C-GCIO
			N813PA
			F-WWCG
F-OHQA	Cessna 208 Caravan	00260	N12324
F-OHQB	Ayres S.2R-T34	226	
F-OHQC	Ayres S.2R-T34	227	N2269V
F-OHQD	Ayres S.2R-T34	243DC	N2045D
F-OHQE	Cessna A188B AgTruck	02623T	N4887Q
F-OHQF	Short SD.3-60	SH.3743	N824BE
			N743CC
			(G-BOWG)
			G-14-3743
F-OHQG	Short SD.3-60	SH.3721	N121PC
			G-BNFE
			G-14-3721
F-OHQH	Short SD.3-60	SH.3722	N722PC
			G-BNMS
			G-14-3722
F-OHQI	Cessna 172R	80214	N9403F
F-OHQJ	Dornier 228-212	8239	
F-OHQK	Dornier 228-212	8238	
F-OHQL(2)	Aeritalia/SNIAS ATR-42-512	524	F-WWEF
F-OHQM(2)	Cessna 208B Grand Caravan	0726	
F-OHQN(2)	Cessna 208B Grand Caravan	0715	N1258H
			N52627
F-OHQO	Pilatus PC-6/B2-H4 Turbo Porter	924	
F-OHQQ	Cessna A188B AgTruck	03900T	N9971J
F-OHQR	Cessna 150M	79102	N714DT
F-OHQS	Cessna 182S (Reservation)	80177	N9525P
F-OHQT	Hughes 269C (Reservation)	34-0288	YV-245E
			N9574F
F-OHQU	Cessna 208B Grand Caravan	0725	N12326
F-OHQV	Aeritalia/SNIAS ATR-42-512	571	F-WWEM
F-OHQX	Pilatus Britten-Norman BN-2A-26 Islander	3009	"F-OHQW"
			D-IORC
			OY-CEG
			G-BLNR
			RP-C184
F-OHRA	Piper PA-32-300 Cherokee Six B	32-40635	F-BRIR
			N4261R
F-OHRB	Nord 262C Frégate	74	F-BSUF
F-OHRE	Piper PA-28-181 Archer II	28-8590087	N2537Y
F-OHRJ	Antonov AN-2 (See F-GRCJ)	unkn	
F-OHRM	Cessna 208 Caravan	00142	N208RM
			HK-3467P
			HK-3467X
F-OHRR	Grumman G.164 AgCat (Reservation 11.99)	216	N406Y
F-OHRT	Beech 300 Super King Air	FA-226	N80907
F-OHRU	Cessna 560 Citation III	0407	N1218Y
			N5204D
F-OHRX	Beech 1900D	UE-282	N11296
F-OHSA	Piper PA-23-250 Aztec C	27-3862	5R-MCP
			N6565Y
F-OHSB	Aérospatiale SA.365C3 Dauphin 2	5014	G-BFVW
			F-WXFO
F-OHSC	Aérospatiale AS.350BA Ecureuil (Cr. 8.9.98)	2333	HB-XXV
			N60BW
F-OHSE	Aérospatiale AS.350B2 Ecureuil	2291	VH-EEA
			ZK-IWI
F-OHSM	Aérospatiale AS.355F2 Ecureuil 2	5510	OE-BXV
			F-WYMA
F-OHTJ	SOCATA TB-200 Tobago XL	1770	
F-OHUY	SOCATA TB-20 Trinidad	1815	F-WWRG
F-OHVC	Aérospatiale AS.355N Ecureuil 2	5643	
F-OHVE	Aérospatiale AS.355N Ecureuil 2	5647	
F-OHVJ(2)	Aérospatiale AS.350B2 Ecureuil	3275	
F-OHVM	Aérospatiale AS.350B2 Ecureuil	3237	
F-OHVN	Aérospatiale AS.350B3 Ecureuil	3255	
F-OHVP	Aérospatiale AS.365N3 Dauphin 2	6567	
F-OHVQ	Eurocopter EC.120B Colibri	1057	
F-OHYA	Cessna U.206F Stationair	03130	N52EC
			(N8269Q)
F-OHZM	Airbus A.330-301	183	F-WWKP
F-OHZN	Airbus A.330-301	184	F-WWKG
F-OHZO	Airbus A.330-301	188	F-WWKQ
F-OHZP	Airbus A.330-301	191	F-WWKR
F-OHZQ	Airbus A.330-301	189	F-WWKS
F-OHZR	Airbus A.330-301	198	F-WWKT
F-OHZS	Airbus A.330-301	200	F-WWKH
F-OHZT	Airbus A.330-301	203	F-WWKI
F-OIAB	Cessna 172N	68209	VH-KJJ
			N1748C
			(N733DF)
F-OIAC	Piper PA-34-200 Seneca	34-7350277	VH-RRS
			OY-DZP
			HB-LEK
			N56054
F-OIAG	Aérospatiale AS.350B2 Ecureuil	2170	
F-OIAH	Aérospatiale AS.350B2 Ecureuil	9004	
F-OIAJ	Aérospatiale AS.350BA Ecureuil	1296	- ? -
			F-OIAE
			ZK-HLX
			F-ODGE
F-OIAL	Cessna 421C Golden Eagle II	0455	ZK-JBF
			N6771C
F-OIAM	Aeritalia/SNIAS ATR-42-320	403	F-WWLD
F-OIAP	Cessna 182P Skylane	62717	VH-IRN
			N52619
F-OIAR	Pilatus Britten-Norman BN-2T Turbo Islander	2287	G-BVSK
F-OIAT	Mooney M.20J Model 205	24-3370	
F-OIAU	Aérospatiale AS.350B2 Ecureuil	2978	
F-OIAV	DHC-6 Twin Otter Srs 300 (Reservation)	559	N74GC
			J8-SVD
			N74GC
			9M-BCP
			N74GC
			N63RA
F-OIBD	Robinson R-22B2 Beta	2921	
F-OICG	Aeritalia/SNIAS ATR-42-300	003	F-GEGE
			PH-HWJ
			F-GEGC
			F-WEGC
F-OIFB	Cessna 182Q Skylane	67570	TU-TLZ
			TU-TXZ
			(F-OBYY)
			N5204N
F-OIGC to F-OIGZ Reservations for SOCATA			
F-OIHA	Airbus A.300B4-622R	530	HL7582
			F-ODSX
			F-WWAL
F-OIHB	Airbus A.300B4-605R	505	F-WIHB
			A6-EKC
			F-WWAO
F-OIHC	Airbus A.320-231	344	OO-COL
			F-WIHX
			B-22308
			F-WGYU
			SU-RAG
			F-WWDS
F-OIHD to OIHZ Reserved for Airbus Industrie			
F-OIHS	Airbus A.310-325	674	N837AB
			F-WWCH
F-WIHT	Airbus A.310-322	404	HB-IPG
			F-WWCD
F-OIJA	Cessna 172SP	172S08154	N954SP
			F-WWLF
			F-WWEZ
F-OIJB	Aeritalia/SNIAS ATR-42-500	579	
F-OIJC	Cessna 172SP	172S08303	N2461N
F-OIKA to F-OILZ Reserved for SOCATA			
F-OILC	SOCATA TB-10 Tobago	1826	
F-OILH	SOCATA TB-20 Trinidad	1923	
F-OINC	Beech B200 Super King Air	BB-1244	F-GSFA
			G-RIOO
			N251DL
			N72357
F-OIOL	Bell 412	33160	N4380K
			F-GKAK
			N3207D

Regn.	Type	C/n	Prev.Id.
F-OIOM	Aérospatiale SA.315B Lama	2423	EC-DNZ
			N47065
F-OIPA	Robin DR.400/200R Remo 200	2375	
F-OIPB	Pilatus PC-6/B1-H2 Turbo Porter	661	HB-FKQ
			A14-661
			HB-FDM
F-OIRA	Aeritalia/SNIAS ATR-72-212A	562	F-WWLZ
F-OIRB	Aeritalia/SNIAS ATR-72-212A	573	F-WWEK
F-OITN	Airbus A.340-211	031	(F-OJTN)
			F-GLZD
F-OIYA	Aeritalia/SNIAS ATR-72-212	479	F-WWEL
F-OIYB	Aeritalia/SNIAS ATR-72-212	481	F-WWEQ
F-OIYL	Aérospatiale AS.350B2 Ecureuil	9008	
F-OJAF	Airbus A.310-324	638	F-GJEZ
			F-WQHN
			EC-FXB
			EC-640
			VR-BOU
			EC-FNI
			EC-117
			F-WWCK
F-OJAS	Beech 1900C	UB-66	N823BE
			N3044C
F-OJIJ	Piper PA-32-300 Cherokee Six	32-40451	F-BPIJ
			N4134R
F-OKSY	Dassault Falcon 50EX	257	F-WWHE
F-OKVL	Aeritalia/SNIAS ATR-72-201	215	(F-OHCE)
			F-WWEK
F-OKVM	Aeritalia/SNIAS ATR-72-201	341	F-WW..
F-OMAR	Aeritalia/SNIAS ATR-72-201	108	F-GIGO
			F-WWEZ
F-ONAT	Schroeder Fire Balloons GHAFB	743	
F-ONCI	Chaize JZ.30F16 HAFB (Reservation .99)	156	
F-ONLY	Cessna 404 Titan (Reservation 11.99)	0692	F-ZBDX
			F-GCQM
			N6764C
F-OPCL	Partenavia P.68B	142	
F-ORAN	Aeritalia/SNIAS ATR-72-202	207	(XU-RAN)
			F-WQAH
			ZS-NDJ
			F-WWEF
			(N7271)
			F-WWEF
F-OTDH	Cessna U.206F Stationair	02794	N35912

CNRA REGISTER (Homebuilt Aircraft)

Regn.	Type	C/n	Prev.Id.
F-PAAC(2)	Stern ST-87 Europlane	27	
F-PAAF(2)	Cassutt III	284	
F-PAAS	Piel CP.320 Super Emeraude (Reservation)	426	
F-PABC	Jodel DR.250	02	
F-PABD	Pena Bilouis	03	
F-PABF	Pottier P.230S Panda	443	
F-PABJ	Pottier P.220S Koala	245	
F-PABL	Nicollier HN.434 Super Ménestrel	17	
F-PABN	Jodel D.113 (Reservation)	1744	
F-PACA	Jodel D.18	206	
F-PACB	Pottier P.230S Panda	1	
F-PACE	Jodel D.18	147	
F-PACI	Guy Paci GP.01 Caracara	01	
F-PACK	Jodel D.113 (Reservation .99)	1802	
F-PACM	Jodel D.18	169	
F-PACO	Druine D.5 Turbi	67	
F-PACS	Pottier P.230S Panda (Reservation)	unkn	
F-PACV	Vandamme TPL-1	01	
F-PADB	Nicollier HN.700 Ménestrel II	79	
F-PADE	Jodel D.18	327	
F-PADJ	Pottier P.80S	56	

Regn.	Type	C/n	Prev.Id.
F-PADY	Jodel D.112 Club	1626	
F-PAED	Rutan Cozy (Reservation)	CC-1037	
F-WAEO	Revolution Mini-500	0230	
F-PAFE	Rutan LongEz (Reservation)	1673	
F-PAFK	Kessler FK-001	01	
F-PAGA	Pottier P.180S	167	
F-PAGB	Jurca MJ.77 Gnatsum	15	
F-PAGD	Auster J/1 Autocrat	2218	G-AJID
F-PAGE	Nicollier HN-434 Super Ménestrel	61	F-WAGE
F-PAGI	Piel CP.320-100 Super Emeraude	446	
F-PAGM	Jodel D.19	120T	
F-PAHM	Acrolaram (Reservation)	01	
F-PAIA	Nicollier HN-700 Ménestrel II (Reservation .99)	124	
F-PAJC	Pottier P.250S (Reservation .99)	01	
F-PAJD	Didier AH-01	02	
	(Also reported as Wag Aero Wag-a-Bond)		
F-PAJN	Ollivier CO-04 Collivier	01	
F-PAJP	Cariou CL-3	19	
F-PALB	Jodel DR.1054M Ambassadeur (Reservation 6.99)	848	
F-PALC	Heintz Tri-Z	3-1356	
F-PALS	Jeannet JH-01 Le Courlis	01	F-WALS ?
F-PALU	Colomban MC-100 Banbi	04	
F-PAMB	G.802B Gerfaut (Reservation)	02	
F-PAMC	Nicollier HN-700 Ménestrel II	103	
F-PAMD	Brügger MB-2 Colibri	261	
F-PAMI	Assi Aeri Asso V (Reservation .99)	238	
F-PAML	Pottier P.180S	202	
F-PAMT	Rand-Robinson KR-1	5469	
F-PANG	Jurca MJ.77 Gnatsum	04	
F-PAOI	Mauboussin M.202S	001	F-WAOI
			F-BAOI
F-PAON	Jodel D.18	329	
F-PAPA	Colomban MC-15 Cri-Cri	224	
F-PAPE	Blavier 8C2	01	
F-PAPI	Caudron C.272/5 Luciole	6799	F-PMMI
			F-AMMI
F-PAPY	Pottier P.80SM	59	
F-PARA	Ameur Balbuzard	01	F-WARA
F-PARB	Jodel DR.1054M	862	
F-PARD	Pottier P.180S (Reservation)	21	
F-PARI	Richet Cobra 200DR	01	
F-PARJ	Kieger AK-2R (Reservation)	01	
F-PARK	Pottier P.180S	112	F-PYZQ
F-PARM	Nicollier HN.700 Ménestrel	27	
F-PARS	Pottier P.230S Panda	421	
F-PASB	Steen Aero Skybolt	341	
F-PASC	Jodel D.92 Bébé	818	F-WASC
			F-PASC
F-PASD	WagAero Sport Trainer (Reservation)	3122	
F-PASE	Saint-Ex AT-02	01	
F-WASK	Stoddard-Hamilton Glastar (Reservation .99)	5719	
F-PASM	Rutan Vari-eze	1794	F-WASM
F-PASO	Jodel D.150 (Reservation .99)	142	
F-PASR	Rolland RS-3000	01	
F-PASS	Colomban MC-15 Cri-Cri	308	
F-PAST	Croses EC-6 Criquet	06	
F-PATM	Autogyre Libellule	01	
F-PATR	Feugray TR-200	04	
F-PAUL	Feugray TR-200	2	
F-PAUR	Van's RV-4	309	
F-PAVC	Notteghem Occitan Club	04	
F-PAVM	Jodel D.19	22T	
F-PAVU	Jodel D.112 Club (Reservation)	1709	
F-PAVX	Nicollier HN.700 Ménestrel II	15	
F-PAXF	Aero Designs Pulsar	101	F-WRXF
F-PAYC	Pottier P.80S	68	
F-PAYM	Piel CP.1320 Super Emeraude (Reservation .99)	36	
F-PAYS	Pottier P.60A Minacro	14	
F-PBAG	Pottier P.60 Minacro	15	
F-PBAL	Ameur Balbuzard	MP100/01	
F-PBAM	Nicollier HN.700 Ménestrel II (Reservation)	02	
F-PBAR(2)	Jodel D.19	09-T	
F-PBAT	Stampe LBP (Reservation)	01	
F-PBAY	Farman 404 (Under rebuild .99)	7358.1	F-AMGY
F-PBBC	WAR Sea Fury	25	

Regn.	Type	C/n	Prev.Id.
F-PBBF	Jodel D.112 Club	01	F-BBBF
			F-WBBF
F-PBBK	Aero 101C	01	F-BBBK
F-PBBM	Rutan Cozy	436	
F-PBBR	Piel CP.320 Super Emeraude	443	
F-WBBY	Tesson La Persévérance (Reservation)	01	
F-PBCA	Rutan Cozy (Reservation)	CC-1021	
F-PBCB	Nicollier HN.700 Ménestrel II	116	
F-PBCH	Piel CP.320 Super Emeraude (Reservation)	452	
F-PBCJ	Pottier P.130L	1000	
F-PBCM	Fairchild 24 Argus (UC-61)	01-1996	
	(Possibly a rebuild of 43-14531 c/n 495)		
F-PBCO	Ollivier DR.100 Collivier	01	
F-PBCQ	Coq (Reservation)	unkn	
F-PBCT	Piel CP.751B Beryl II	37	
F-WBDO	Bulle d'Orage Montgolfiere	01	
F-PBDR	Jodel D.18 (Reservation)	98	
F-PBDS	Aeronca 7ACChampion (Reservation .99)	2501	F-BLLI
			N83821
			NC83821
F-PBEC	F-8L-BX Falco	233-1	F-BNAS
	(Rebuild of Aeromere Falco F-8L c/n 233)		LX-AIY
			I- LEPG
			(D-EBQE)
F-PBER	WAR FW-190A Replica	339	
F-PBFD	Evans VP-2 Volksplane	0781-FD	
F-PBFJ	Pena Bilouis	1	
F-PBGD	Starck AS.70 Jac	07	
F-PBGS	Starck AS.70L Jac	12	
F-PBGT(2)	Air Camper J-3 Torpedo (Reservation)	2533	
F-WBGX(2)	Stolp SA.300Starduster Too	36	G-BPCE
	(Reservation, from storage at Barcelona)		N8HM
F-PBHC	Mauboussin 125 Corsaire	208	F-BBHC
F-PBHQ	Grenet PG-2 Bison (cvtd from Mauboussin	01	F-BBHQ
	126 c/n 182, then back to M.123, 11.90)		
F-PBIS	Junqua RJ-03 1 bis (Reservation)	02	
F-PBIX	Druine Fradon D.60 Condor	01	F-BBIX
F-PBJC	Fournier RF-5	RF-3A	
F-PBJE	Jodel D.18	259	
F-PBJL	Rutan Vari-eze	1449	
F-PBJP	Jodel D.112 Club	1630	
F-PBJR	Pottier P.180S	132	
F-PBLB	Geronimo LB-1	01	
F-PBMC	WAR F-4U Corsair	559/512	
F-PBMD	Nicollier HN.700 Ménestrel II	29	
F-PBME	Pottier P.230S Panda (Reservation .99)	473	
F-PBMG	Mugnier L'Embellie Balloon	01	
F-PBMJ	Rutan LongEz	184	
F-PBMS	Heintz Zenith CH250-160	2-1605	
F-PBNO	Jodel DR.1053M	832	
F-PBNP	Jodel DR.1050M	701	
F-PBNS	Piel CP.80 (Reservation .99)	64	
F-PBOB(2)	Pottier P.80S	66	
F-PBOI	Jodel D.92 Bébé	40	
F-PBOL	Jodel D.92 Bébé	UAC.33	
F-PBOS	Jodel D.92 Bébé	23	
F-PBOV	Jodel D.112 Club	27	
F-PBOX	Jodel D.92 Bébé	115	
F-WBPA	Rans S-6 Coyote II (Reservation .99)	03981209	
F-WBPC	Dyn'Aero MCR-01 Banbi (Reservation .99)	46	
F-PBPF	Jodel D.150 Mascaret (Reservation)	147	
F-PBPY	Jodel D.92 Bébé	38	
F-PBRD	Club des Ballons Libre du Nord XW-340	01	
F-PBRG	Apodo (Reservation)	01	
F-PBRI	Bücker Bü.133C Jungmeister	2008	F-AZLB
			F-AZEU
F-PBRL	Pottier P.230S Panda	426	
F-PBRU	Brügger MB.8 (Reservation .99)	01	
F-PBSC	Amphibie Esperanza 4	05	
F-PBSG	Viking Dragonfly Mk.2	824	
F-PBSH	Nicollier HN.700 Ménestrel II	113	
F-PBSM	Junqua RJ-03 Ibis	21	F-WBSM
F-PBSQ	Druine D.3 Turbulent (Reservation)	127	
F-PBSY	Adam RA.14 Loisirs	121	F-WBSY
F-PBTO	Jodel D.18	192	
F-PBUG	Jodel DR.251	1	
F-PBUL	Balatchev Centaure (Reservation .99)	01	
F-PBUS	Jodel D.150/120 Mascaret	149	
F-PBXM	Jodel D.921 Bébé	198	
F-PBXS	Druine D.31 Turbulent	03	
F-PBXU	Jodel D.92 Bébé	126	
F-PBYM	Starck AS.80 Holiday	NJ-1	
F-PBZE	Piel CP.320 Super Emeraude	429	
F-PBZH	Brändli BX-2 Cherry (Reservation)	94	
F-PBZT	Jodel D.112 Club	unkn	
F-PCAA	Pottier P.180S	169	
F-PCAB	WAR P-47D Thunderbolt	60	F-WCAB
F-PCAC	Nicollier HN.434 Super Ménestrel	14	F-WCAC
F-PCAD	Jodel D.18	89	
F-PCAL	Jodel D.18	122	F-WCAL
F-PCAN	Midgy LD.261	2	F-BCAN
F-PCAO	Jodel D.18	79	
F-PCAR	Carriou CL-8 RSA Club	01	F-PSAG ?
F-PCAS	Jurca MJ.5G2 Sirocco	62	
F-WCAT	Pottier P.180S	90	
F-PCBC	Colomban MC-15 Cri-Cri	360	
F-PCBD	Jodel D.18 (Reservation)	367	
F-PCBM	Autoplan CBM-01	01	
F-PCBN	Jodel D.119D (formerly D.113, D.112)	4	F-WCBN
F-PCBY	Rutan LongEz	1803	
F-PCBZ	Jodel D.19	145T	
F-PCCA	Jodel DR.100T	803	
F-PCCL	Nicollier HN-700 Ménestrel II	33	
F-PCCM	Croibier-Muscat CCM 01	01	
F-PCCU	Jodel D.112 Club	40	
F-PCDB	Speedy RG (Destroyed 9.9.95)	01	
F-PCDO	Jodel D.140R Abeille (Reservation .99)	454	
F-PCDQ	Chapeau JC.1 Levrier	01	F-WCDQ
F-PCDY	Jodel D.128	973	
F-PCEA	Jodel D.18	177	
F-PCEK	Mauboussin 123C Corsaire	179	F-BCEK
F-PCES	Mauboussin 125 Corsaire	177	F-BCES
F-PCET	Vintras ET-01	01	
F-PCEU	Piel CP.80	68	
F-PCFD	Viking Dragonfly Mk.2	572	F-WCFD
F-PCFK	Paumier MP.02 Baladin	09	
F-PCFM	Jodel D.19	146T	
F-PCGB	Viking Dragonfly Mk.2	802	
F-PCGG	Rutan LongEz	1655	
F-PCGJ	Jodel D.19	123T	
F-PCGK	Jodel D.112 Club	1679	
F-PCGO	Jodel de Havilland DH.251	07	
F-PCGS	Pottier P.180S	89	
F-PCGT	Zenair CH-601 Zodiac	6-2060	
F-PCHB	Brändli BX-2 Cherry	141	
F-PCHJ	Jodel D.18	368	
F-PCHN	Pechon JP-01 (Reservation)	01	
F-PCHR	SIPA S.903 (Reservation)	01	
F-PCIM	Starck AS.57	11	F-BCIM
F-PCIO	Mauboussin 127 Corsaire	181	F-BCIO
F-PCIP	Mauboussin 123C Corsaire	183	F-BCIP
F-PCIR	Jodel D.92 Bébé	826	
F-PCJB	Gardan GY-21 Minicab	27	
F-PCJC	Viking Dragonfly Mk.1	1115	
F-PCJD	Colomban MC-100 Banbi	07	
F-PCJG	Grinvalds G-801 Orion	54	
F-PCJH	Brügger MB-2 Colibri	269	
F-PCJL	Jodel D.19	156T	
F-PCJM	Nicollier HN.700 Ménestrel II (Reservation)	147	
F-PCJP	Pocino PJ-1A Toucan	01	
F-PCLB	Dyn'Aero MCR-01 Banbi	60	
F-PCLD	Quaissard Monogast	5	
F-PCLF	Colomban MC-15 Cri-Cri	533	
F-PCLG	Jodel D.113 (Reservation .99)	1673	
F-PCLM	Jodel D.19T	260-T	
F-PCLR	Croses LC-6 Criquet (Reservation)	60	
F-PCMB	Jodel D.19	170-T	
F-PCME	Nottegherm Occitan 01 Club	05	
F-PCMG	Ollivier CO-02 Collivier	01	
F-PCMH	Jodel D.18	105	

Regn.	Type	C/n	Prev.Id.
F-PCMJ	Jodel D.18	16	
F-PCML	Canu 3J	01	
F-PCMM	Piper J-3C-65 Cub *(Rebuilt)*	S.1	
F-PCMN	Jodel D.113	1629	
F-PCMS	Jodel DR.1050M	791	
F-PCMT	Jodel D.19	95	
F-PCMV	Cassutt IIIM	646	
F-PCOL	Fournier RF-5	2A	
F-PCOM	Viking Dragonfly Mk.2F	825	
F-WCOO	Grandjean DG.01 Alcyon	21	
F-PCOS	Jodel D.92 Bébé	141	
F-PCOU	Pecou SP-230 *(Also reserved as F-PCSC?)*	001	
F-PCOZ	Rutan Cozy *(Reservation .99)*	CC-1042	
F-PCPA	Jodel D.18	143	
F-PCPC	Jodel D.18	240	
F-PCPD	Jodel D.18	49	
F-PCPG	Jodel D.18	333	
F-PCPJ	Jodel D.113	1639	
F-PCPL	Pottier P.60A Minacro *(Reservation .99)*	17	
F-PCPR	Jurca MJ.5 Sirocco	25	
F-PCPS	Pottier P.70S	29	(F-PROO)
F-PCQR(2)	Val Lot JG-01 *(Reservation .99)*	01	
F-PCRA	Van's RV-4	714	
F-PCRH	Henetier Gold HCR-2900 (HAFB?)	01	
F-PCRI	Colomban MC-15 Cri-Cri	405	
F-PCRQ	Quercy CQR.01 Cadi	01	
F-PCRT	Jodel DR.1053MV	772	
F-PCRY	Brändli BX-2 Cherry	113	
F-PCSA	Marie JPM-01 Médoc	22	
F-PCSC	Pecou SP-250 *(also reserved as F-PCOU?)*	001	
F-PCSJ	Jodel D.19	261-T	F-WCSJ
F-PCSM	Stern ST-87C Europlane	18	
F-PCSR	Pottier P.230S Panda	430	F-WCSR
F-PCSY	Bücker Bü.131D Jungmann	01	F-BCSY
F-PCTF	Van's RV-4 *(Reservation)*	3903	
F-PCTY	Nicollier HN-433 Ménestrel	67	
F-PCUB	Wag-A-Bond *(Reservation)*	412	
F-WCUV	Mignet HM.290 *(Reservation)*	419	
F-PCUX	Jodel D.112 Club	181	
F-PCYG	Monnett Sonerai II LS *(Reservation)*	836	
F-PCYM	Jodel D.18	133	F-WCYM
F-WCZD	CJ-200	01	
F-PCZF	Brochet MB-72 *(Reservation)*	01	F-BCZF
			F-WCZF
F-PDAB	Rutan Cozy	E-717	
F-PDAC	Arlais-Chasle AC-210	001	
F-PDAF	Jodel D.18	71	
F-PDAN	Jodel de Havilland DH.251 *(Reservation)*	05	
F-PDAT	Humbert Tetras	07	
F-PDAX	Jodel D.113	1588	
F-PDBB	WagAero Sportsman 2+2	568	
F-WDBG	Deborde-Rolland Cobra 201AC	01	F-PDBG
F-PDBL	Piel CP.320 Super Emeraude	398	
F-PDCB	Jodel DR.1051M	770	
F-PDDR	Didier AH-01	01	
F-PDEB	Rutan LongEz	2113	
F-PDEL	Jodel D.18	05	
F-PDEM	Viking Dragonfly *(Reservation)*	1009	
F-PDES	Pottier P.180S	130	F-WDES
F-PDGM	Jodel D.140C Mousquetaire III	445	
F-PDHE	SIPA 200 Minijet	7	F-BDHE
F-PDHF	Jodel D.92 Bébé	W6	
F-PDHI	Jodel D.92 Bébé	603	
F-PDHK	Jodel D.92 Bébé	M.11	F-WDHK
F-PDID	Aeronca 0-58B-L3 Grasshopper	8092	F-BELT
	(Res., c/n quoted as '30123')		42-36123
F-PDJC	Jodel DR.1051T *(Reservation)*	875	
F-PDJV	Delvion DV-01 Zephyr	01	
F-PDKL	Aurensan KG-1 *(Reservation .99)*	01	
F-PDKY	Jodel D.112 Club	42	
F-PDLC	Jodel D.18	14	
F-PDLF	Junqua RJ-03 Ibis *(Reservation .99)*	31	
F-PDLJ	Liberty APL-01 *(Reservation .99)*	01	
F-PDLQ	Marie JPM-01 Médoc	38	
F-PDMC	Nicollier HN.700 Ménestrel II	67	

Regn.	Type	C/n	Prev.Id.
F-PDNE	Le Goeland	02	F-WDNE
F-PDOF	Leopoldoff L-3 Colibri *(Reservation)*	127	F-BGFS
F-PDOG	Dyn'Aero MCR-01 Banbi	18	F-WQUF
F-PDOL	CAP Dole	01	
F-PDPZ	Holleville RH.1 Banbi	01	F-WDPZ
F-PDRA	Jodel-Miettaux DM02 Bébé Special	01	
F-PDSD	Jodel D.18	116	
F-PDTC	Jodel DR.1050M Sicile Record	781	
F-PDTG	Dyn'Aero CR-100C	04	
F-PDTL	Brügger MB-2 Colibri	249	
F-PDUD	Zenair CH-701 STOL	7-1543	
F-PDVD	Poulin PJ.5A (Cub conversion)	1	F-WDVD
	(f/n 11614 - thus formerly L-4H c/n 11788 ex.43-30497)		
F-PDVN	Marie JPM-01 Médoc *(Reservation .99)*	44	
F-PDVO	Poulin PJ.5A	03	
F-PDVP	Poulin PJ.5A	4	
F-PDVV	Jodel D.112 Club	A.103	
F-PDYN	Christophe Robin CR.100	01	
F-PDZN	Junqua RJ-03 Ibis Canard	23	
F-PEAH	Colomban MC-15 Cri-Cri	69	
F-PEAK	BRT Eider	02	
F-PEAM	Jodel D.18	252	
F-PEBP	Jodel D.113 *(Reservation .99)*	1707	
F-PEBZ	Brochet MB-50 Pipistrelle	52	F-PHBZ
F-PECA	Pena Le Joker *(Reservation .99)*	02	
F-PECB	Sable-Bouchon SB-2	01	
F-PECH	Colomban MC-100 Banbi	01	F-WECH
F-PECQ	Nicollier HN-434 Super Ménestrel	02	
F-PECS	Jodel D.18	18	
F-PEDF	Nicollier HN-700 Ménestrel II	54	
F-PEGH	Jodel D.113 *(Reservation)*	1650	
F-PEGR	Jodel D.18 *(Reservation)*	428	
F-PEGY	Jodel D.19	101	
F-PEHO	Jodel D.92 Bébé	43	
F-PEHV	Gardan GY-201 Minicab	A-216	
F-PEJC	Rutan Cozy Mk.4	83	
F-PEJH	Dyn'Aero CR.100C	28	
F-PEJR	Rand-Robinson KR-2	7854	
F-PELB	Dyn'Aero MCR-01 VLA Banbi	94	F-WELB
F-PELD	Jurca MJ.2H Tempête	48	
F-PELR	Jodel D.19	364-T	
F-PEMY	Jodel D.18	162	
F-PENA	Pena Bilouis	01	
F-PENO	Jodel D.19	13T	F-WENO
F-PEOO	SFAN-4 *(Reservation .99)*	01	F-PFOO
			F-WFOO
F-PEPE	Jodel D.116T	01	F-WEPE
	(Formerly reserved as Anquetil JA-1 Kiout)		
F-PEPM(2)	Nicollier HN.700 Ménestrel II *(Reservation)*	26	
F-PEPS	Pottier P-220D Koala *(Reservation)*	415	
F-PERB	Rhone et Sud-Est J-3 Cub	01	
F-PERD	Jodel D.119T Club (conv from D.112)	202	
F-PERG	C.A.B. GY-20 Minicab	A-162	
F-PERK	Jodel D.113V (ex D.112, D.127, D.119V)	196	
F-PERL	Jodel D.92 Bébé	213	
F-PERT	Jodel D.116 Club (ex D.112)	54	
F-PERU	Jodel D.112 Club	47	F-WERU
F-PERY	Jodel D.92 Bébé	306	
F-PERZ	Jodel D.112 Club	231	
F-PESK	Pottier P.180SP	33	
F-PESL	Nicollier HN-434 Super Ménestrel	21	
F-PESM	Jodel D.121 (ex D.11, D.115)	64	
F-PESV	Van's RV-4 *(Reservation .99)*	3594	
F-PESY	Jodel D.92 Bébé	175	F-WESY
F-PETI	Colomban MC-100 Banbi	03	
F-PEUG	Pottier P.180S	176	F-PMCR
F-PEVF	Jodel D.112 Club	275	
F-PEVH	Jodel D.92 Bébé	332	
F-PEVL	Jodel D.112 Club	221	
F-PEVN	Jodel D.126 (ex D.112)	12	
F-PEVX	Jodel D.112 Club	A.193	
F-PEVY(2)	Boudeau MB.16 Mickevy	01	
F-PEYA	Jodel DR.1053M *(Reservation)*	849	
F-PEZE	Rutan Vari-eze	2194	
F-PFAB	Jodel D.19	390T	F-WFAB

Regn.	Type	C/n	Prev.Id.
F-PFAD	Nicollier HN-700 Ménestrel II	96	
F-PFAG	Notteghem Occitan Club (Reservation)	12	
F-PFAI	Dyn'Aero MCR-01UL Banbi	23	F-WFAI
	(Also recorded as Colomban MC-100 and as MCR-01 c/n 01, regd. 3.6.97)		
F-PFAM	Pottier P.130L (Reservation .99)	1047	
F-PFAR	Bagimer II Alouette	01	F-WFAR
F-PFAX	Rand-Robinson KR-2 (Reservation)	01	
F-PFBA	Sequoia F.8LFalco (Reservation .99)	1266	F-WFBA
F-PFBB	Adam RA.14 Loisirs	01	F-WFBB
F-PFBE	Jodel D.112 Club	1719	
F-PFBM	Rutan Cozy	E-736	
F-PFBR	Grinvalds G-801 Orion	38	
F-PFCA	Jodel D.112 Club	1648	
F-PFCR	Jodel D.119T	09A	
F-PFCZ	Jodel D.112 Club	32	
F-PFDA	Gatard Statoplan AG 01 Alouette	01	F-WFDA
F-PFDD	Druine D.31 Turbulent	106	
F-PFEN	Jodel D.112 Club	111	
F-PFET	Jodel D.112 Club	112	
F-PFGJ	Coupe JC-3	04	
F-PFHC	Dyn'Aero CR.100C	27	
F-PFHM	Nicollier HN-700 Ménestrel II	32	
F-PFHN	Nicollier HN-500 Bengali	01	
F-PFHV	Colomban MC-15 Cri-Cri	304	
F-PFIF	Rutan Cozy (Reservation)	597	
F-PFIN	Jodel D.112 Club (Reservation)	1770	
F-PFJB	Fresion Omega (Reservation .99)	01	
F-PFJC	Quercy CQR-01 (Reservation)	02	
F-PFJD	Darcissac-Grinvalds DG-87 Goeland	01	F-WFJD
F-PFJJ	Rutan LongEz	1358	
F-PFJL	Colomban MC-15 Cri-Cri	175	
F-PFJP	Stolp SA.300 Starduster Too	265	
F-WFKA	Allard D-40 Puck	unkn	
F-PFKC	Mignet HM.360	1	F-WFKC
F-PFKU	WAR F-4UCorsair (Reservation .99)	242	
F-PFLB	Caudron C.601 Aiglon	7102/18	F-BFLB, F-ANXX
F-PFLC	Jodel D.11 (Reservation .99)	1789	
F-PFLL	Croses LC-6 (Reservation)	87	
F-PFLM	Rutan Vari-eze	1928	
F-PFLO	Jodel D.18 (Reservation .99)	04	
F-PFLX	Trotobas Le Felix TF-01 (Reservation)	01	
F-PFLY	Jodel D.112 Club (Reservation .99)	1785	
F-PFMJ	Lucas L-7	01	
F-PFMP	Rutan Cozy	20	
F-PFMR	Pietenpol Aircamper	0041	
F-PFMT	Croses LC-6M Criquet	28	
F-PFMX	Jurca MJ.5F1 Sirocco (Reservation .99)	14	
F-PFOX(2)	Rand-Robinson KR-2	01	
F-PFPB	Flamant-Peignant-Pijean (autogiro?) (Res.)	01	
F-PFPS	Viking Dragonfly Mk.3	101	
F-PFPV	Jodel D.18	237	
F-PFPZ	Stern ST-87 (Reservation)	06	
F-PFQA	Piper J-3C-65 Cub	9929	(F-BFQA) 43-1068
	(Quoted officially with f/n 9761)		
F-PFRA	SAN.01 Piper Cub	01	F-BFRA
F-PFRB	Jodel D.92 Bébé	354	
F-PFRC	Nicollier HN.434 Super Ménestrel (Reservn)	82	
F-PFRE	Stark AS.80 Holiday (ex c/n 01)	5201	F-WFRE
F-PFSU	EAAAcrosport II (Reservation .99)	1654	
F-PFSV	Jodel D.140E Mousquetaire IV (Reservn)	415	
F-PFTY	Jurca MJ-12 (Reservation .99)	03	
F-PFVA	Potez 36/13	3203	F-PEVA, F-AMEI
F-PFVG	Alpha HB-207 (Reservation)	207-030	
F-PFVS	Soccol VS.01 Gascon	01	
F-PFVV	Adam RA-14 Loisirs (Reservation .99)	35bis	F-PEVV
F-PFXG	Pottier P.220S Koala	409	
F-PFYC	Chasle YC-15 Tourbillon II	01	
F-PFYS	Nord NC.854S	146	
	(Built from spares using wings from F-BFIL c/n 21)		
F-PFYY	Piel CP.30 Emeraude	01	F-PFVY
F-PGAD	SIPA S.903	40	F-PGAO, F-BGAO
F-PGAF	Jodel D.113 (Reserved originally as D.119A)	1733	
F-PGAG	Colomban MC-15 Cri-Cri (Reservation .99)	571	
F-PGAH	SIPA S.903	33	F-BGAH
F-WGAJ	Stoddard-Hamilton Glastar (Reservation .99)	5047	
F-PGAM	Brochet MB.80	3	F-WGAM, F-BGLC
F-PGAS	Pottier P.180S	115	
F-PGAT	Jodel D.19 (Reservation)	267-T	
F-PGAY	Jurca MJ.77 Gnatsum	10	
F-PGAZ	Parker Teenie Two	15-1627	
F-PGBC	Stoddard-Hamilton Glastar GS-1	5074	
F-PGBJ	Jodel D.112 Club	1610	
F-PGBS	Pottier P.60A Minacro	09	
F-PGBT	Jurca MJ.54 (Reservation)	01	
F-PGCC	Brändli BX-2 Cherry	22	
F-PGCD	Nord NC.856A (Reservation)	33	ALAT
F-PGCI	Guilie CAP TR	01	
F-PGCR	Stolp SA.300 Starduster Too	254	
F-PGDF	Pottier P.230S Panda	423	
F-PGDG	Nicollier HN-700 Ménestrel II	25	
F-PGDL	DG-01 Leader	01	
F-PGEL	Colomban MC-15 Cri-Cri	201	
F-PGEV	Rutan LongEz	2106L	
F-PGFO	Jodel D.92 Bébé	121	
F-PGGG	Grinvalds G-801 Orion (Res., or F-PGGR?)	13	
F-PGGO	Coupe JC.200	4	
F-PGGP	Jodel D.18 (Reservation)	413	
F-PGGT	Jodel DR.1053M	742	
F-PGGZ	Jodel D.92 Bébé	34	
F-PGHG	Pottier P.230S Panda (Reservation)	455	
F-PGHS	Mignet HM.293A (Reservation)	01	
F-PGIC	Aero 101	3	F-BGIC
F-PGIE	Jodel D.18	08	F-WGIE
F-PGIL	Jurca MJ.2D Tempête	82	
F-PGJB	Rand-Robinson KR-2	8006	
F-PGJJ	Rutan Cozy Mk.4 (Reservation)	162	F-PCOQ
F-PGJP	Rand-Robinson KR-2	8612	
F-PGJY	Rutan Cozy	337	
F-PGKH	Piper J-3 Marabout	EN2	F-BGKH, ALAT
	(f/n 8456 - L-4A c/n 8321 ex.42-15202)		
F-PGLF	Brochet MB.83D	6	F-BGLF
F-PGLH	Brochet MB.83D	8	F-BGLH
F-PGLM	Jodel D.18	310	
F-PGLX	Jodel D.113	55	
F-PGMB	Marie JPM.01 Médoc	06	
F-PGMF	Jodel D.18	163	
F-PGMG	Jodel D.119	1197	
F-PGMH	Jodel D.18	75	
F-PGMI	Jurca MJ.77 Gnatsum (Reservation)	21	
F-WGML	Jurca MJ.100D Spitfire	2	
F-PGMN	C.A.B. GY-201 Minicab (ex c/n 16)	A.124	F-BGMN
F-PGMS	Rutan LongEz	358	
F-PGNA	Jodel D.11 T28	07A	
F-PGOA	Pottier P.180S	76	
F-PGOM	Pottier P.180S (Reservation .99)	200	
F-PGPA	Boisavia B.601L Mercurey (Reservation .99)	110	F-GPPA, F-BHDM, F-BIRF
F-PGRA	Velocity STD (Reservation)	179	F-WGRA
F-PGRB	Nicollier HN.434 Super Ménestrel	22	
F-PGRE	Jodel D.112 Club	115	
F-PGRG	Dyn'Aero CR-100	05	
F-PGRK	Starck AS-80 Holiday	56	
F-PGRP	Jodel DB-1101	001	
F-PGRS	Stern ST-87 (Reservation)	43	
F-PGSG	Pottier P.230S Panda	444	
F-PGSH	Pereira Osprey GP-4 (Reservation)	71	
F-PGSJ	Horizon 2	AH-0082	
F-PGSY	Dyn'Aero MCR-01 Banbi (Reservation .99)	97	
F-PGTC	Piel CP.1320 Super Emeraude	05	
F-PGTE	Jodel D.112 Club	137	
F-PGTL	Guillotel DG-1	01	
F-PGTM	Junqua RJ-03 Ibis	01	
F-PGTU	Ambrosini F.4 Rondone 1	019	F-BGTU
F-PGTY	Jurca MJ.2 Tempête	54	
F-PGUI	Evans VP-1 Volksplane	V-1382-GD	

Regn.	Type	C/n	Prev.Id.
F-PGUY	Nicollier HN.434 Super Ménestrel	03	
F-PGVR	Piel CP.30A Emeraude	2	F-WGVR
F-PGYA	Mignet HM.293	JH-3/37	F-WGYA
F-PGYB	Jodel D.112 Club	122	
F-PGYH	Jodel D.92 Bébé *(Stored)*	133	
F-PGYN	Jodel D.92 Bébé	124	
F-PGYR	Druine D.5 Turbi	02	F-WGYR
F-PHAM	Stolp SA.300 Starduster Too	785	N6099
F-PHBT	Feugray TR-200	06	
F-PHCB	Jodel D.19	268	
F-PHCD	Deschamps / Charles Dolfus HG-760 Balloon	01	
F-PHCH	Nicollier HN-700 Ménestrel II	61	
F-PHDJ	Pottier P.220S Koala	410	
F-PHDP	Jurca MJ.77 Gnatsum	11	
F-PHEL	Zenair CH-601HDS Zodiac	"601"	
F-PHFB	Jodel D.112 Club	268	
F-PHFG	Couyaud GC-01	01	
F-PHFK	Caudron C.232 *(Res., probably ntu)*	6486/1	F-AJSS
F-PHFL	Jodel D.112 Club	184	
F-PHGT	Leopoldoff L.55 Colibri	2	F-BHGT
F-PHIL	Piel CP.615A Super Diamant	55	
F-PHIM	Stoddard-Hamilton Glastar *(Reservation .99)*	5525	
F-PHJB	Jodel D.112 Club	374	
F-PHJJ	Jodel D.113 Club (ex D.112)	A.204	
F-PHJK	Jodel D.112 Club	212	
F-PHJL	Jodel D.112 Club	159	
F-PHJN	Jodel D.112 Club (ex D.118, D.121)	104	
F-PHJO	Jodel D.112 Club	281	
F-PHJP	Jodel D.112 Club	211	
F-PHJS	Jodel D.92 Bébé	349	
F-PHJX	Jodel D.112 Club	A.386	
F-PHJY	Jodel D.112 Club	328	
F-PHLA	Jodel D.112 Club	304	
F-PHLB	Jodel D.112 Club	A.14	F-WHLB
F-PHLC	Jodel D.119C (ex D.112, D.113C)	329	
F-PHLF	Jodel D.112 Club	284	
F-PHLJ	Jodel D.92 Bébé	350	
	(Also carries ULM marks W62-AAB)		
F-PHLL	Druine Martin (D.61 Condor variant)	02	F-WBIY ?
F-PHLM	Piel CP.30 Emeraude	4	
F-PHLN	Piel CP.301 Emeraude	5	
F-PHLO	Piel CP.30 Emeraude	10	
F-PHLP	Jodel D.112 Club	383	
F-PHLQ	Jodel D.112 Club	282	
F-WHLR	Jodel D.112 Club	290	F-PHLR
F-PHLS	Jodel D.112 Club	136	F-WHLS
F-PHMC	Croses LC-6W Criquet *(Reservation .99)*	122	
F-PHME	Nicollier HN.700 Ménestrel II *(Reservation .99)*	181	
F-PHMH	Rutan Cozy	E-706	
F-PHMN	Colomban MC-15 Cri-Cri *(Reservation .99)*	120	
F-PHMP	Pottier P.270S	432	
F-PHOK	Jodel D.113 *(Reservation)*	1751	
F-PHOQ	Rippert A.1-65 Cub	1	F-BEKV
	(converted from Piper L-4 c/n 12154)		44-79858
F-PHPC	Piel CP.615 Super Diamant	50	
F-PHPG	Helicoptère Autour 01	01	
F-PHQA	Jodel D.92 Bébé	263	
F-PHQC	Jodel D.112 Club	317	
F-PHQE	Jodel D.119 (ex D.121)	44	
F-PHQG	Leopoldoff L.4 Colibri (ex L.3 rebuilt)	24	F-APZN
F-PHQH	Larrieu JL.2	01	F-WHQH
	(converted from D.112 c/n 77)		F-BGMA
F-PHQI	Piel CP.301 Emeraude	38	
F-PHQK	Jodel D.119A	472	(F-BHAE)
F-PHQN	Planchais LD-45/4	4	
F-PHQO	Chatelain AC.5 Bijou	01	
F-PHQP	Jodel D.92 Bébé	390	
F-PHQS	Jodel D.112 Club	468	
F-PHQZ	Druine D.5 Turbi	48	
F-PHRS	Piel CP.320 Super Emeraude	420	
F-PHUD	Jodel D.112 Club	398	
F-PHUF	Camandre 1 (Cub conversion)	01	
F-PHUI	Jodel D.119	460	
F-PHUL	Jodel D.112 Club	360	
F-PHUM	Jodel D.112 Club	404	

Regn.	Type	C/n	Prev.Id.
F-PHUO	Gatard Statoplan AG 02 Poussin	01	
F-PHUP	Jodel D.112 Club	375	
F-PHUQ	Jodel D.119 (ex D.112)	291	
F-PHUS	Jodel D.112 Club	220	
F-PHUV	Jodel D.119	A.392	
F-PHYN	Brügger MB-2 Colibri	21	
F-PHZC	Adam RA.15/1 Major	1	
	(Possibly rebuild of F-PEPD, F-WEPD ?)		
F-PHZD	Piel CP.30 Emeraude	75	
F-PHZG	Jodel D.112 Club	213	
F-PHZM	Jodel D.113 (ex D.119)	318	
F-PHZN	Potez 36/14	3207	F-AMEM
F-PHZO	Piel CP.301 Emeraude	11	
F-PHZX	Jodel D.113 (ex D.119)	A.97	
F-PHZY	Marabout M (Cub conversion)	01	
F-PIAB	Rutan Cozy	45	
F-PIAF	Viking Dragonfly Mk.2	1024	
F-PIAN	Boisavia B.601L Mercurey *(Reservation)*	25	(F-GLNA)
			F-BIAN
F-PICG	Rand-Robinson KR-2	7499	
F-PICO	Jodel D.18	60	
F-PIDZ	Jodel D.119V *(Reservation)*	1772	
F-PIED	Pottier P.180S	111	
F-PIEL	Piel CP.320 Super Emeraude *(Reservation)*	416	
F-PIET	Zenair CH-701 STOL	1298	
F-PIFE	Pottier P.180S	27	
F-PIHF	Jodel D.113 (ex D.119)	663	
F-PIHH	Jodel D.112 Club (ex D.123)	279	
F-PIHI	Piel CP.301 Emeraude	34	
F-PIHL	Croses EC-1	02	F-WIHL
F-PIHV	Jodel D.112 Club (ex D.119)	619	
F-PIHX	Jodel D.113 (ex D.119)	621	
F-PIHY	Jodel D.119	653	
F-PIID	Jodel D.112 Club	660	
F-PIIE	Jodel D.92 Bébé	292	
F-PIIM	Jodel D.112 Club	749	
F-PIIO	Jodel D.112 Club (ex D.119)	319	
F-PIIS	Druine D.5 Turbi	26	
F-PIIX	Piel CP.30 Emeraude	19	
F-PIIY	Jodel D.112 Club	536	
F-PIJH	Jurca MJ.5G2 Sirocco	60	
F-PILA	Guimbal G2 Cabri	01	
F-PILD	Neico Lancair 320 *(Reservation .99)*	640	
F-WILO	Jodel D.112 Club *(Reservation)*	1769	
F-PILP	Jodel D.119 *(Reservation)*	1746	
F-PIMA	Jodel D.113	1760	
F-PINB	Jodel D.112 Club	769	
F-PINE	Jodel D.112 Club (ex D.124)	782	
F-PINI	Jodel D.119 (ex D.112)	57	
F-PINJ	Piel CP.310 Emeraude (ex CP.301)	49	
F-PINK	Piel CP.301 Emeraude	08	
F-PINM	Gardan GY-201-90 Minicab	A144	
F-PINP	Jodel D.119 (ex D.112)	387	
F-PINR	Piel CP.310 Emeraude (ex CP.308)	27	
F-PINV	Jodel D.92 Bébé	391	
F-PINY	Jodel D.119 (ex D.112)	449	
F-PIOI	Wadsworth PW-01 *(Reservation)*	01	
F-PIOL	Jurca MJ.2P Tempête *(Reservation)*	47	
F-PIPO	Jodel D.19	359T	
F-PIPR	Altair 2PL *(Reservation)*	01	
F-PIRA	Pereira Osprey 2	752	F-WIRA
F-PIRI	Jodel D.150 *(Reservation .99)*	146	
F-PITR	Techaero Feugray TR-200 *(Reservation)*	09	
F-PITS	Cousin DFC-01 Optima *(Reservation)*	01	
F-PIVA	Colomban MC-15 Cri-Cri *(Reservation)*	428	
F-PIXX	Jodel D.140C Mousquetaire III	433	
F-PIYA	Druine D.5 Turbi	46	
F-PIYB	C.A.B. GY-201 Minicab	A.159	
F-PIYC	Jodel D.113 (ex D.112)	713	
F-PIYJ	Jodel D.119	864	
F-PIYM	Jodel D.112 Club	748	
F-PIYN	Piel CP.301 Emeraude	178	
F-PIYO	Jodel D.119	739	
F-PIYP	Jodel D.92 Bébé	398	
F-PIYR	Jodel D.119G (ex D.112)	676	

Regn.	Type	C/n	Prev.Id.
F-PIYS	Jodel D.112 Club	513	
F-PIYT	Jodel D.119	102	
F-PIYV	Brochet MB.76	23	
F-PIYY	Piel CP.315 Emeraude	16	
F-PIYZ	Jodel D.113 (ex D.119)	620	
F-PJAC	Jodel D.92 Bébé (Reservation 3.99)	657	
F-PJAG	Jodel DR.1050MT (Reservation)	792	
F-PJAK	Rutan Cozy	190	
F-PJAR	Du Dognon 01	01	
F-PJBC	Jodel DR.1051 Ambassadeur	788	
F-PJBD	Morin M-82 (Reservation)	02	
F-PJBG	Jurca MJ.5 Sirocco	19	
F-PJBH	Belin Zephyr	01	F-WJBH
F-PJBL	Jodel D.18 (Reservation)	11	
F-PJBR	Jodel DR.1051M	827	
F-PJBS	WagAero Sport Trainer (Reservation)	3303	
F-PJBV	Jodel D.18	349	
F-PJBY	Blenet RB-1 Joze	01	F-WJBY
F-PJCA	Jodel D.112 Club	943	
F-PJCB	Piel CP.750A Beryl II (Reservation)	06	
F-PJCD	Jurca MJ.2 Tempête	66	
F-PJCG	CEA Jodel DR.105S Ambassadeur (ex DR.100A)	4	
F-PJCK	Aero Club Lons/Leglise L-400	01	
F-PJCL	Dyn'Aero MCR-01 Banbi (Reservation .99)	65	
F-PJCN	Adam RA.14 Loisirs	110	
F-PJCX	Jodel D.119 (ex D.112)	671	
F-PJDH	Mauboussin 123C Corsaire	159	F-ARDR
F-PJDL	Grinvalds G-801 Orion	16	F-WJDL
F-WJDR	Dyn'Aero MCR-01 Banbi (Reservation .99)	7	
F-PJDV	Van's RV-4 (Reservation)	44062	
F-PJDY(2)	Mignet HM.390 Auto-Ciel (Reservation)	1 bis	
F-PJDZ	Nord NC.858	64	F-BFSK
F-PJEB	Rutan Vari-eze (Reservation .99)	1962	
F-PJFK	Notteghem Occitan	02	
F-PJFT	Van's RV-6 (Reservation .99)	22419	
F-PJGC	Jodel D.119	529	F-WJGC
F-PJGI	Adam RA.14 Loisirs	45	
F-PJGJ	Jodel D.119 (ex D.112)	952	
F-PJGM	Jodel D.112 Club	682	
F-PJGO	Jodel D.119	975	
F-PJGP	Gatard Statoplan AG 02 Poussin	02	
F-PJGQ	Damoure-Fabre-Lacroix DFL-6 Saphir	01	F-WJGQ
F-PJGR	Jodel D.112 Club	147	
F-PJGS	Jodel D.119	994	
F-PJGZ	Jodel D.112 Club	403	
F-PJHG	Pottier P.80S	69	
F-PJHJ	Pottier P.80S	156	
F-PJIC	Jodel DR.1056MAmbassadeur (Reservation .99)	886	
F-PJIM	Stolp SA.300 Starduster Too	2105	
F-PJJB	Robin CR.100	06	
F-PJJC	Rutan Cozy (Reservation)	CC-1056	
F-PJJG	Jurca MJ.5H1 Sirocco	52	
F-PJJR	Jurca MJ.55	01	
F-PJKB	Jodel D.119 (ex D.111)	790	
F-PJKD	Druine D.31 Turbulent	93	
F-PJKG	CEA Jodel DR.101 Ambassadeur	31	
F-PJKL	Piel CP.301 Emeraude	192	
F-PJKM	Jodel D.119L (ex D.112)	617	
F-PJKN	Jodel D.112 Club	963	
F-PJKP	Jodel D.121 (ex D.112)	191	
F-PJKR	Piel CP.301 Emeraude	343	
F-PJKS	Jodel D.92 Bébé	88	
F-PJKV	Paumier MP-21 Baladin	01	
F-PJKY	Jodel D.112 Club	1037	
F-PJLB	Rutan LongEz	1344	
F-PJLC	JLC-01 Abeille (Reservation)	01	
F-PJLG	Nicollier HN-700 Ménestrel II (Reservation)	76	
F-PJLH	Taylor Coot Amphibian (Reservation .99)	106	
F-WJLM	Piel CP.1320 Saphir	1	
F-PJLO	Nicollier HN.434 Super Ménestrel (Reservn)	53	
F-PJLT	Pottier P.270S (Reservation .99)	436	
F-PJMA	Dyn'Aero MCR-01 VLA Banbi	54	F-WSLK
F-PJMC	Jodel D.119	390	F-PIHO
F-PJMD	Jodel DR.1050M (Reservation)	726	
F-PJML	Colomban MC-15 Cri-Cri (Reservation)	unkn	
F-PJMM	Neico Lancair 320	547	
F-PJMP	Nicollier HN-434 Super Ménestrel	48	
F-PJMS	Sauval SE-5A (Reservation .99)	01	
F-PJMT	Jodel D.18	45	F-WJMT
F-PJNL	DS-150 (Reservation)	unkn	
F-PJOB	Lucas L.5-200	2	F-WJOB
F-PJOC	Gravereau Box'Air Racer	01	F-WJOC ?
F-PJOD	Jodel DR.1054 Ambassadeur	857	
F-PJOE	Jurca MJ.2E Tempête	96	
F-PJOH	Rutan Cozy (Reservation .99)	CC-1021	
F-PJOJ	C.A.B. GY-201 Minicab (ex.c/n 722)	A.204	
F-PJOR	Nicollier HN-434 Super Ménestrel (Reservn)	74	
F-PJOS	Piel CP.301A Emeraude	445	
F-PJPB	Nicollier HN-434 Super Ménestrel	73	
F-PJPC	CAPENA	05	
F-PJPD	Marie JPM-01 Médoc	21	F-WJPD
F-PJPF	WAR FW-190 Replica	184	
F-PJPG	Croses EC-6 Criquet (Reservation)	47	
F-PJPL	Pottier P.70S	30	
F-PJPR	Jodel D.92 Bébé	801	
F-PJPS	EAA Acrosport II	602	
F-PJQA	Junqua RJ.02 Volucelle	01	F-WJQA
F-PJRA	Jodel DR.1050M	760	
F-PJRC	Chalard JRC-01	01	
F-PJRD	Jodel D-20 (Reservation .99)	04	
F-PJRH	Marcel 01	01	
F-PJRM	Colomban MC-15 Cri-Cri (Reservation)	294	
F-PJRP	Croses LC-6 Criquet	100	
F-PJSA	Legrand-Simon LS.60	01	F-BJSA F-WJSA
F-PJSB	Schepers Job M-16 Trainer (Was earlier reserved as Magni M-16 Gyrocopter)	01	
F-PJSF	Jodel D.18	371	
F-PJSM	Godbille GJJ	01	F-WJSM
F-PJST	Rand-Robinson KR-2S (Reservation .99)	447	
F-PJSX	Jurca MJ.5K2 Sirocco	01	F-WJSX
F-PJTA	Jodel D.18	189	
F-PJUL	Jodel D.18 (Reservation)	418	
F-PJUP	Schwind Autogyre JS-01 (Reservation)	01	
F-PJXA	Jodel D.112 Club	941	
F-PJXB	Jodel D.92 Bébé	422	
F-PJXC	Jodel D.112 Club	971	
F-PJXD	Jodel D.112 Club	1054	
F-PJXE	Jodel D.112 Club	1041	
F-PJXF	Jodel D.119	1032	
F-PJXG	Jodel D.119	984	
F-PJXH	Jodel DR100A Ambassadeur	202	
F-PJXJ	Jodel D.112 Club	1034	
F-PJXN	Jodel D.112 Club	1101	
F-PJXO	Jodel D.112 Club	1087	
F-PJXP	Piel CP.60 Diamant	01	F-WJXP
F-PJXR	Jodel D.112 Club	1107	
F-PJXS	Jodel D.112 Club	214	
F-PJXV	Jodel D.112 Club	1104	
F-PJXX	Jodel D.119	451	
F-PJXZ	Piel CP.301 Emeraude	200	
F-PJYA	Natin JNB-01 (Reservation)	01	
F-PJYB	Colomban MC-15 Cri-Cri	57	
F-PJZG	Nicollier HN-700 Ménestrel II	89	
F-PKAD	Rutan LongEz	1059	
F-PKCF	Piel CP.1320 Saphir	57	
F-PKEN	Jodel D.119 (Reservation .99)	1551	
F-PKER	Gasnier "2 Kerdonis" GG-01 (Reservation .99)	01	
F-PKFC	Jodel D.112 Club	972	
F-PKFG	Jodel D.112 Club	950	
F-PKFH	Jodel D.112 Club	1095	
F-PKFI	Druine D.31 Turbulent	115	
F-PKFJ	Piel CP.301 Emeraude	32	
F-PKFL	Jodel D.112 Club	391	
F-PKFN	Mignet HM.380B	12	F-WKFN
F-PKFO	Jodel D.92 Bébé	446	
F-PKFT	Jodel D.112 Club	985	
F-PKFU	Lucas L.4 Baby	01	F-WKFU
F-PKFY	Jodel D.112 Club	1050	
F-PKFZ	C.A.B. GY-201-90 Minicab	A.233	

Regn.	Type	C/n	Prev.Id.
F-PKGQ	Jodel DRM (converted DR.1050/239)	01	F-BKGQ
F-PKIT	Colomban-Robin MCR-01 (Dyn'Aero constr)	01	
F-PKLE	Pottier P.220S Koala (Reservation .99)	461	
F-PKMB	Jodel D.112 Club	1085	
F-PKMC	Jodel D.112 Club	271	
F-PKMD	Jodel D.119	1044	
F-PKMF	Jodel D.112 Club	986	
F-PKMG	Piel CP.301A Emeraude	353	
F-PKMH	Jodel D.119 (ex D.112)	777	
F-PKMJ	Jodel D.119 (ex D.112)	1135	
F-PKMK	Jodel D.119	1154	
F-PKMN	Jodel D.119	678	
F-PKMP	Jodel D.113 (ex D.112)	793	
F-PKMR	Jodel D.119	741	
F-PKMT	Druine D.31 Turbulent	248	
F-PKMV	Damoure-Fabre DF-5C	01	
F-PKMX	Piel CP.316 Emeraude	352	F-WKMX
F-PKPL	Jodel DR.1050 Ambassadeur	778	
F-PKRJ	Light Aero Avid Flyer (Reservation .99)	798	F-PRKJ
			F-WRKJ
F-PKSE	Jodel D.112 Club	1765	
F-PKUJ	Europa Aviation Europa	297	F-WKUJ
F-PKVB	Piel CP.301 Emeraude	93	
F-PKVC	Tipsy T.66 Nipper III	7	OO-NIG
F-PKVD	Jodel D.112 Club	1182	
F-PKVF	Duruble RD.02 Edelweiss	01	
F-PKVI	Jodel D.92 Bébé	460	
F-PKVH	Junca-Steiner JS (Reservation)	01	
F-PKVU	Druine D.31 Turbulent	96	
F-PKVX	Jodel D.112 Club	1195	
F-PKVZ	Piel CP.325 Super Emeraude	359	F-WKVZ
F-PKXA	Piel CP.301A Emeraude	322	
F-PKXC	Jodel D.119	1139	
F-PKXL	Jodel D.112 Club	1224	
F-PKXQ	Druine D.5C Turbi	60	
F-PKXR	Jodel D.113	1142	
F-PKXV	Jodel D.112 Club	1201	
F-PKXX	Piel CP.601 Diamant	5	
F-PKXY	Aero 20	1	F-WKXY
F-PLAB	Jodel D.19	253-T	
F-PLAJ	Jaillet AJ-160 (Reservation)	1	
F-PLAL	Leblanc L-06	01	
F-PLAM	Lamaziere AL-01 (Reservation .99)	01	
F-PLAU	Pena Bilouis	27	
F-PLAY	Piel CP.320 Super Emeraude	439	
F-PLBC	Pottier P.220S Koala	469	
F-PLBM	Jodel D.119 (Reservation)	1763	(F-PBPM)
F-PLBT	Wittman W8 Tailwind	522	
F-PLCA	Druine-Lucas D.31 LP1 Turbulent	01	F-WLCA
	(Originally regd as Druine-Colombier D.31 Turbulent c/n 392)		
F-PLCB	Jodel D.18 (Reservation)	444	
F-PLCD	Ollivier C0-03 Collivier	01	
F-PLCL	Piel CP.90 Pinocchio II	7	
F-PLCM	Colomban MC-15 Cri-Cri	11	
F-PLCT	Jodel D.18	412	
F-PLDS	Rutan Cozy (Reservation)	CC-1038	
F-PLDV	Pottier P.210S	01	
F-PLEA	Robin (Dyn'Aero) CR-100	26	
F-PLEF	Brügger MB-2 Colibri	242	
F-PLEJ	Godbille JG.IB	01	
F-PLEO	Viking Dragonfly Mk.I	1116	
F-PLFC	Lucas L-5 (Reservation, actually wears F-WLMC)	61	
F-PLGC	Tormancy LR-01	01	
F-PLGL	Jurca MJ.2 Tempête	44	F-WLGL
F-PLGO	Nicollier HN.700 Ménestrel II (Reservation)	128	
F-PLGZ	Jodel D.18	402	
F-PLHB	Alpha HB-207 (Reservation)	207-019	
F-PLJB	Nicollier HN.434 Super Ménestrel	31	
F-PLJC	Jodel D.113	1635	
F-PLJM	Jodel D.19	424-T	
F-PLKP	Jodel DR.200P	01	F-BLKP
			F-WLKP
F-PLKQ	CPG 150 (Reservation .99)	01	
F-PLMB	Leopoldoff LMB	04.98	
F-WLMC	Lucas L-5 (Officially regd F-PLFC)	61	(F-PLFC)

Regn.	Type	C/n	Prev.Id.
F-PLMJ	Pottier P.270S	438	
F-PLMK	Laigniel-Mathely-Klinka LMK-1 Oryx	01	F-WLMK
F-PLMP	Heinz Zenith 100	2-128	
F-PLMS	Lucas L-5	46	
F-PLNA	Monobi MC-210 (Reservation .99)	01	
F-PLPG	Denize RD-20 Raid-Driver	27	F-WLPG
F-PLPH	EAA Acrosport 2	1222	
F-PLPP	Jodel D.18	106	
F-PLPR	Pottier P.180S	135	
F-PLRJ	Gombert Pena "Le Dahu"	01	
F-PLSA	Nicollier HN-700 Ménestrel II	142	
F-PLSD	Nicollier HN-700 Ménestrel II	104	
F-PLUA	Druine D.31B Turbulent	249	
F-PLUB	Jurca MJ.2D Tempête	3	
F-PLUF	Jodel D.119	1132	
F-WLUG(2)	Akrotech G-202 (Reservation .99)	029	
F-PLUI	Jodel D.119	1226	
F-PLUJ	Mignet HM.381	51	F-WLUJ
F-PLUK	Jodel D.113 (ex D.112)	1186	
F-PLUL	Jodel D.113 (ex D.119)	1027	
F-PLUM	Jodel D.119 (ex D.112)	187	
F-PLUN	Piel CP.301D Emeraude	361	
F-PLUP	Jodel D.112 Club	1193	
F-PLUQ	Jodel D.119	995	
F-PLUR	Jodel D.113E (ex D.119A)	1230	
F-PLUS	Jodel D.119	530	
F-PLUU	Jodel D.112 Club	1244	
F-WLUV	Bensen B.8ML Gyrocopter (ex B.7M)	01	
F-PLUX	Piel CP.301A Emeraude	348	
F-PLYM	Duruble RD-02 Edelweiss	02	
F-PLYT	Heintz Zenith (Reservation)	122	
F-PMAA	Piel CP.323 Super Emeraude	428	
F-PMAC	Jodel D.114 3L	1670	
F-PMAK	Jodel DR.1050M1 Sicile Record (Reservation .99)	887	
F-PMAR	Nicollier HN-700 Ménestrel II	14	
F-PMAS	Jodel D.18 (Reservation)	388	
F-PMAX	Stolp SA.750 Acroduster Two	529	
F-PMAY	Colomban MC-15 Cri-Cri	499	
F-PMAZ	Jodel D.18	53	
F-PMBL	Marie JPM-01 Médoc (Reservation .99)	51	
F-PMCA	Pitts S-1DSpecial (Reservation .99)	07342	
F-PMCB	Nord NC.854CM (Reservation .99)	01	
F-PMCC	Piel CP.320 Super Emeraude	431	
F-PMCD	Luscombe 8A Silvaire	895	C-FRNJ
			CF-RNJ
			NC22069
F-PMCE	Jodel D.18 (Reservation)	352	
F-PMCF	Laigniel-Mathely-Klinka LMK-1	01-LPCA	
F-PMCG	WagAero Wagabond (Reservation .99)	1007	
F-PMCL	Nicollier HN-700 Ménestrel II	133	
F-PMCM	Jodel D.140E Mousquetaire IV (Reservation 3.99)	460	
F-PMCR	Pottier P.180S (Reserved as F-PEUG)	176	
F-PMCS	Jurca MJ.5 Sirocco (Reservation)	127	
F-PMDA	Jodel DA-01 (Reservation)	01	
F-PMDK	WAR F-4U Corsair (Reservation)	477	
F-PMDL	Jodel DR.1050 (Reservation)	852	
F-PMDS	deHavilland DH.82ATiger Moth	83741	F-BGZY
	(Reservation .99; officially registered		(G-ATWI)
	with c/n "7400")		F-BGZY
			(F-OAPT)
			T7400
F-PMEB	Jodel D.112 Club	1245	
F-PMED	Jodel D.119	1092	
F-PMEH	Croses EC-6 Criquet	37	
F-PMEN	Jodel D.119	219	
F-PMEO	Jodel D.119C	1249	
F-PMER	Jodel D.112 Club	1136	
F-PMES	Leger RL-3	01	
F-PMEU	Jodel D.112 Club	1328	
F-PMEZ	Jodel D.119	718	
F-PMFH	Viking Dragonfly Mk 2	MH-5015-V	
F-PMGA	Nicollier HN-700 Ménestrel II	71	
F-PMGE	Mayence MP-01 (Reservation .99)	01	
F-PMGT	Rutan Cozy (Reservation)	627	

Regn.	Type	C/n	Prev.Id.
F-PMIC	BRT Eider (Reservation)	01	
	(Previously reserved as Murphy Rebel)		
F-PMIE	Pena Bilouis (Reservation .99)	30	
F-PMIL	Junqua RJ-03	25	
F-PMJA	Jodel D.20	02	
F-PMJC	Jodel D.140R Abeille	416	
F-PMJF	Jurca MJ.5 Sirocco (Reservation)	94	
F-PMJG	Kelly Hatz CB-1 (Reservation .99)	326	
F-PMJP	Rutan Cozy Mk IV	32	
F-PMJR	Jodel D.19	279-T	
F-PMKI	E Racer Mk.1 (Reservation)	ER-263	
F-PMLC	Pottier P.230S Panda (Reservation)	448	
F-PMLD	Jodel de Havilland DH.251 (Reservation)	06	
F-PMLG	Fournier RF-5	A-04	F-WMLG
	(Originally c/n 5084)		F-BSGA
F-PMLO	Colomban MC-15 Cri-Cri	482	
F-PMLR	Van's RV-8	80592	
F-PMLS	Melos DFB-1A (Reservation .99)	01	
F-PMLT	Nicollier HN.701TM Ménestrel II	166-01	
F-PMMB	Stern ST-87 Europlane (Reservation .99)	35	
F-PMMC	Jodel D.112 Club (Reservation .99)	1784	
F-PMOA	Jodel D.18 (Reservation)	450	
F-PMOH	Jodel D.112 Club (Reservation)	1327	
F-PMOR	Dyn'Aero MCR-01 Banbi	22	F-WQUH
F-PMOS	Nicollier HN.700 Ménestrel II (Reservation .99)	43	
F-PMPG	Pottier P.180S	133	
F-PMPJ	Jodel D.113-3L	1723	
F-PMPL	Jodel D.92 Bébé	509	
F-PMPZ	Rutan Vari-eze (Reservation)	1736	
F-PMQJ	Jodel D.128 (Reservation .99)	1764	
F-PMRD	Duruble RD-03 Edelweiss (Reservation)	26	
F-PMRJ	Jodel D.140E Mousquetaire IV (Reservation)	430	
F-PMRR	Rutan Cozy (Reservation)	CC-1051	
F-PMRV	Van's RV-4 (Reservation)	3466	
F-PMRY	Nicollier HN.700 Ménestrel II (Reservation)	63	
F-PMSC	Omega CS-900 (Reservation)	01	
F-PMSE	Jodel D.112 Club	1700	
F-PMSJ	Moliere Blue Djinn (Reservation)	01	
F-PMSZ	Nicollier HN.700 Ménestrel II (Reservation)	163	
F-PMTB	Marie JPM-01 Médoc (Reservation .99)	34	
F-PMTS	Stern ST-87 Europlane	30	
F-PMTY	EAA Acrosport II (Reservation .99)	2063	
F-PMVT	Maunoury DM-01 (Reservation .99)	01	
F-PMXA	Jodel D.112 Club	1291	
F-PMXB	Jodel D.119D	1337	
F-PMXF	Jodel D.119	1335	
F-PMXH	Jodel D.112 Club	1191	
F-PMXJ	Jodel D.112 Club	1192	
F-PMXK	Chatelain AC.9	01	
F-PMXL	Vintras-Bouiller VB.20 Isard	01	F-WMXL
F-PMXO	Jurca MJ.2D Tempête	20	
F-PMXQ	Chasle YC-12 Tourbillon	01	F-WMXQ
F-PMXR	C.A.B. GY-201 Minicab	A.170	
F-PMXT	Piel CP.301 Emeraude	366	
F-PMXU	Jodel D.92 Bébé	494	
F-PMXX	Jodel D.92 Bébé	495	
F-WMXZ	Fourneron CF-2 Gyrocopter	02	
F-WMYB	Dyn'Aero MCR-01 Banbi (Reservation .99)	68	
F-PMYD	Rutan LongEz	1797L	F-WMYD
F-PMYG	Notteghem Occitan Club (Reservation)	03	
F-PMYV	Piel CP.605 Diamant (Reservation)	34	
F-PNAC	Jodel D.113 (Reservation)	1619	
F-PNBC	Nicollier HN-700 Ménestrel II	70	
F-PNBG	Piel CP.1321B Super Emeraude (Reservn)	40	
F-PNDF	Fournier RF-47	01	F-WNDF
F-PNDL	Colomban MC-100 Banbi (Reservation)	06	
F-PNEU	Jodel D.113	1773	
F-PNGT	Leduc RL-19 (Reservation .99)	1	F-PAGT
F-PNHJ	Nicollier HN.700 Ménestrel II (Reservation .99)	137	
F-PNIC	Nicollier HN-434 Super Ménestrel	50	
F-PNJD	Lucas L-5	19	
F-PNJL	Neico Lancair LC.30 (Reservation)	225	
F-PNJP	Kurun JPR-01 (Reservation .99)	01	
F-PNJY	Caudron JN-760 (Reservation)	01	
F-PNKU	Fouga CM-8R Sylphe IIIB	1	F-CRRE

Regn.	Type	C/n	Prev.Id.
F-PNLG	Jodel D.92 (Reservation)	41 ?	
F-PNLY	Coupe C-423G	02	F-WNLY
F-PNMI	Jodel D.112 Club	522	F-BHVE
F-PNOG	ACBA-8 Midour 2 (ACBA-7 modified)	01	F-PRNG
F-PNRJ	Jodel D.19	110T	
F-PNSG	Jodel D.19	416T	
F-PNUB	Jodel D.119	1289	
F-PNUF	Jodel D.119A	983	
F-PNUG	Jodel D.112 Club	1155	
F-PNUH	Jodel D.113 (ex D.119)	1325	
F-PNUI	Jodel D.112 Club	1194	
F-PNUL	Jodel D.119D	1383	
F-PNUN	Piel CP.605B Diamant (ex CP.603)	10	F-WNUN
F-PNUT	Piel CP.319 Emeraude	367	
F-PNUY	Neau RN-01 Farfadet (modified Turbulent)	01	
F-POAI	Jodel D.18	87	F-WOAI
F-POBG	Jodel D.18	166	F-WOBG
F-POBY	Jurca MJ.5 Sirocco	50	
F-POCC	Notteghem Occitan Club	01	
F-POCU	SNCAN/Stampe SV.4C	229	F-BOCU
F-POEL	Pottier P.230S Panda (Reservation)	456	
F-POEM	Jodel D.113 3L	1609	
F-POET	Heintz CH-180 Zenith (Reservation)	18-841	
F-POFG	Farigoux FG-01 Origan	01	
F-POIA	Jodel D.92 Bébé	466	
F-POIB	Jodel D.112 Club	1377	
F-POIC	Jodel D.119 (ex D.112)	1275	
F-POID	Jodel D.119	1133	
F-POIF	Jodel D.112 Club	965	
F-POIH	Jodel D.119	714	
F-POII	Jodel D.119DA	1287	
F-POIL	Jurca MJ.5G2 Sirocco	17	F-WOIL
F-POIP	Jurca MJ.5 Sirocco	11	
F-POIX	Piel CP.301A Emeraude	356	
F-POIZ	Piel CP.301A Emeraude	196	
F-POLE	Bushby Midget Mustang II	1708	
F-POLI	Van's RV-6 (Reservation)	24044	
F-POLO (2)	Jodel DR.1053	865	
	(Previously reserved for Brügger MB-2 Colibri c/n 196)		
F-POLU	Deramecourt D16/1600	01	
F-POLV	Pottier P.230S Panda (Reservation)	431	
F-POMF	Jodel D.18 (Reservation)	125	
F-POOO	Nord NC.854S	78	F-BFSZ
F-POPB	Jodel D.140E Mousquetaire IV (Reservation .99)	461	
F-POPG	CATA L Mk.1 Oryx	02-LPCA	
F-POPI	Colomban MC-15 Cri-Cri (Reservation)	286	
F-PORM	Lucas L-5	03	
F-POSE	Potez 60 Sauterelle	4184	F-WOSE
			F-AOSE
F-POSO	Rutan Cozy Mk.4 (Reservation)	443	
F-POST	Breguet 14P (Reservation .99)	150-AB	
F-POTE	Pottier P.180S	180	F-WOTE
F-POUA	Barry Souricette (Reservation)	168	
F-POUF	Jodel de Havilland DH.251PR	03	
F-POUM	Barry Souricette	67	
F-POUN	Pottier P.220S Koala (Reservation)	414	
F-POUS	Gatard AG-02 Poussin (Reservation .99)	53	
F-PPAP	Fisher Celebrity (Dismantled)	56	F-WPAP
F-WPAT	Jabiru SK-80 (Reservation .99)	101	
F-PPBH	Pottier P.230S Panda	449	
F-PPCM	Zenair CH-300 Tri-Z	3.97	
F-PPCR	Robin (Dyn'Aero) CR 120	01	
F-PPCY	Boland 48.12 Hot Air Bag Balloon	01	
F-PPDI	Nicollier HN-700 Ménestrel II	123	
F-PPDY	Dyn'Aero MCR-01 Banbi	101	F-WPDY
F-PPEJ	Jodel D.113VTC (Reservation)	27-A	
F-PPHC	Nicollier HN-700 Ménestrel II	115	
F-PPHJ	Jodel D.113A (Reservation .99)	1790	
F-PPIA	Charles LMC-1 (Reservation .99)	04	
F-PPJJ	Jodel D.18	274	
F-PPJM	Jodel D.119 (Reservation)	1599	
F-PPJR	Renaud 01	01	
F-PPMU	Pottier P.180S	110	
F-PPOT	Rutan LongEz (Reservation)	1950-L	
F-PPPD	Jodel D.119 (ex D.121)	1405	

Regn.	Type	C/n	Prev.Id.
F-PPPG	Damoure-Fabre-Lacroix DFL-6 Saphir	2	
F-PPPK	Druine D.31 Turbulent	207	
F-PPPL	Leglaive Miniplane	1	
F-PPPO	Druine D.31 Turbulent	316	
F-PPPP	Jurca MJ.2E Tempête	26	
F-PPPS	Jodel D.113 (ex D.119)	1427	
F-PPPV	Jodel D.92 Bébé (ex D.95)	532	
F-PPPX	Jodel D.119	1039	
F-PPRB	Jodel D.112 Club (Reservation)	1767	
F-PPRC	Pena Bilouis	26	
F-PPRP	Piel CP.320 Super Emeraude	434	
F-PPSA	Sens AS-05	01	
F-PPSE	Leys VL1050 Le Petit Prince Balloon	01	
F-PPTL	Colomban CR-100C (Reservation .99)	30	
F-PPYL	Luciani PL-160	01	
F-PPYS	Jodel D.112 Club	1778	
F-WPZA	Rebas-Courcel Gyrocopter (Reservation)	01	
F-PPZB	Jurca MJ.2D Tempête	13	F-WPZB
F-PPZD	Jurca MJ.5F1 Sirocco	26	
F-PPZF	Jodel D.119 (ex D.112)	1426	
F-PPZG	Barbaro RB-60	01	
	(Rebuilt 1976-86 with fuselage of Auster J/5 F-BEAV c/n 2028)		
F-PPZH	Jodel D.119	1433	
F-PPZI	Gazuit-Valladeau GV-1031	01	F-WPZI
F-PPZK	Jodel D.112 Club	1414	
F-PPZL	Jodel D.119	1290	
F-PPZM	Croses EAC-3 (Reservation)	5	
F-PPZP	Jodel D.113 (ex D.119)	1419	
F-PPZX	Druine D.31B2 Turbulent	60	
F-PQNO	Dyn'Aéro MCR-01 Banbi	14	F-WSLI
F-PQUA	Dyn'Aéro MCR-01 Banbi	21	F-WQUA
F-WQUB	KIS TR-1 (Reservation)	034	
F-WQUC	Dyn'Aéro MCR-01 Banbi (Reservation)	26	
F-WQUD	Dyn'Aéro MCR-01 Banbi (Reservation)	10	
F-PQUE	Dyn'Aéro MCR-01 Banbi	25	F-WQUE
F-WQUF	Dyn'Aéro MCR-01 Banbi (Reserved as F-PDOG)	18	
F-WQUG	Dyn'Aéro MCR-01 Banbi (Reservation)	16	
F-WQUH	Dyn'Aéro MCR-01 Banbi (Reserved as F-PMOR)	22	
F-PQUI	Dyn'Aéro MCR-01 Banbi	29	F-WQUI
F-WQUJ	Europa Aviation Europa (Reservation)	297	
F-WQUK	Murphy Rebel (Reservation)	490	
F-WQUL	Europa Aviation Europa (Reservation)	184	
F-WQUM	Dyn'Aéro MCR-01 Banbi (Reservation)	70	
F-PQUN	Dyn'Aéro MCR-01 Banbi	04	F-WQUN
F-WQUO	Light Aero AvidSpeed Wing (Reservation)	1507	
F-PQUP	Dyn'Aéro MCR-01 Banbi	09	F-WQUP
F-PQUQ	Dyn'Aéro MCR-01 Banbi	55	F-WQUQ
F-WQUR	Dyn'Aéro MCR-01 Banbi (Reservation)	72	
F-PQUS	Jodel D.20 (Reservation .99)	11	
F-PQUT	Jodel D.20	09	F-WQUT
F-PQUU	Neico Lancair 320 (Reservation .99)	691	
F-PQUV	Dyn'Aéro MCR-01 Banbi	42	F-WQUV
F-PQUX	Akrotech G-202 (Reservation .99)	K-05	
F-PRAA	Jodel D.19	288	
F-PRAB	Jodel D.18	90	
F-PRAC	Pottier P.180S	206	
F-PRAD	Colomban MC-15 Cri-Cri	389	
F-PRAE	Jodel D.19T	220-T	
F-PRAF	Jodel D.18	47	
F-PRAG	Rutan Cozy	279	
F-PRAH	Jurca MJ.53 Autan	1	
F-PRAI	Jodel D.18V	227	
F-PRAJ	Jodel D.18	131	
F-PRAK	Piel CP.402 Donald	9	
F-PRAL	Pottier P.180S	195	F-WRAL
F-PRAM	Jodel D.19	196-T	
F-PRAN	Wittman Tailwind	124	
F-PRAO	Jodel D.18	315	
F-PRAP	GR.90 Condor (Reservation)	01	
F-PRAQ	Jodel D.19T	24	
F-PRAR	Rutan LongEz	2039L	F-WRAR
F-PRAS	Viking Dragonfly Mk.3	966	
F-PRAT	Jodel D.113	1671	
F-PRAU	Jodel D.113	1550	
F-PRAV	Jodel DR.1053M	795	
F-PRAX	Jodel D.19	271	
F-PRAY	Jodel D.18	245	
F-PRAZ	Gardan GY-201 Minicab	A-243	
F-PRBA	Druine D.31 Turbulent	414	F-WRBA
F-PRBB	Bücker Bü .131 Jungmann	R-1	F-WRBB
	(Believed to be a rebuild of CASA I-131E Jungmann ex E3B-459, G-BECY)		
F-PRBC	Jodel D.119	1675	
F-WRBD	Quickie Quickie Q-1	31154-84	
F-PRBE	Stolp SA.750 Acroduster Too	224	
F-PRBF	Jodel D.18	311	
F-PRBI	Olagnier Pélican	01	
F-PRBJ	Avaram	01	
F-PRBK	Evans VP-1 Volksplane	2344	
F-PRBL	Deborde-Rolland Cobra 200A	01	
F-PRBM	Piel CP-750 Beryl	14	
F-PRBN	Croses EC-3 Pouplume	58	
F-PRBO	Jodel D.19	309	
F-PRBP	Rutan LongEz	2080L	
F-PRBQ	Cassutt IIIM	169	
F-PRBR	Jodel D.18	176	
F-PRBS	Sens 01 (formerly LC-3 Sagittaire c/n 23)	01	
F-PRBT	Colomban MC-15 Cri-Cri	301	D-GLMH F-PZIX
F-PRBU	Zenair CH-600 Zodiac	6-1	
F-PRBV	Gatard AG.02 Poussin	33	
F-PRBX	Jodel D.113	1654	
F-PRBY	Pena Capena	10	
F-PRBZ	Colomban MC-15 Cri-Cri	471	
F-PRCA	Jodel D.92 Bébé	692	
F-PRCB	K&S Jungster 1J1	8001	
F-PRCC	Viking Dragonfly Mk.3	0538	
F-PRCD	Jurca MJ.53 Autan	02	
F-WRCE	Pottier P.180S	007	
F-PRCF	Pottier P.180S	96	
F-PRCG	Pottier P.180S	92	
F-PRCH	Piel CP.1320 Saphir	34	
F-PRCI	Lucas L-6	01	F-WRCI
F-PRCJ	Jodel D.18	96	
F-PRCK	Lucas L-5-03	47	F-WRCK
F-PRCL	Brügger MB.2 Colibri	71	
F-PRCM	Piel CP.80	73	
F-PRCN	Jodel D.119D	1642	
F-PRCO	Jodel D.18	56	
F-PRCP	Stern ST-87 Europlane	01	
F-PRCQ	Colomban MC-15 Cri-Cri	171	F-WRCQ
F-PRCR	Jodel D.19	297	
F-PRCS	Taylor JT.2 Titch	F4	
F-PRCT	CAP-XB	01	F-WRCT
F-PRCU	Jeoffroy JJ-01	01	F-WRCU
	(Modified Jodel DR.1052 c/n 773)		
F-PRCV	Nicollier HN-700 Ménestrel II	17	
F-PRCY	Lucas L-5	44	
F-PRCZ	Viking Dragonfly Mk.II	640	
F-PRDA	Jodel D.19T	318-T	
F-PRDB	Brügger MB.2 Colibri	171	F-WRDB
F-PRDC	Jodel D.18	126	
F-PRDD	Ferrière LF-04	01	
F-PRDE	Jodel D.18	134	
F-PRDF	Jodel D.18	281	
F-PRDG	Colomban MC-15 Cri-Cri	314	
F-PRDH	Jodel D.150/120	129	
F-PRDI	Stern ST-85 Evasion	01	F-WRDI
F-PRDJ	WagAero Sport Trainer	842	
F-PRDK	Rutan LongEz	1197	
F-PRDL	Rutan Cozy	E-731	F-WRDL
F-WRDM	Deborde-Rolland Cobra 260	01	
F-PRDN	Daurelle AD-02	01	
F-PRDP	Nicollier HN-700 Ménestrel II	6	
F-PRDQ	Colomban MC-15 Cri-Cri	114	
F-PRDR	Pottier P.180S	185	
F-PRDS	Rutan LongEz	1859L	
F-WRDT	Jurca MJ.10 Spitfire	1	
F-PRDU	Denize RD-105 Raid Driver	24	
F-PRDV	Croses EC-6 Criquet	84	
F-PRDX	Nicollier HN-434 Super Ménestrel	29	

Regn.	Type	C/n	Prev.Id.
F-PRDY	Nicollier HN-700 Ménestrel II	38	
F-PRDZ	Jodel D.18	269	
F-WREA	DGH-02 Gyrocopter	2	
F-WREB	Tadrent TA-01 Gyrocopter	01	
F-WREC	Quetzal Gyrocopter	01	
F-WRED	Averso AX-02 Gyrocopter	22	
F-WREE	CFB-01 Gyrocopter	01	
F-PREF	Nicollier HN.434 Super Ménestrel (Reservn)	75	
F-WREF	Bensen-B-8 Gyrocopter	8-104-100	
	(Same c/n as quoted for F-WYUV)		
F-WREG	La Colombe Gyrocopter (former c/n 01)	02	
F-PREH	Druine D.5 Turbi	25	
F-WREI	Rouet JR Guêpe Gyrocopter	01	
F-WREJ	Averso AX-02 Gyrocopter	20	
F-PREK	Humbert Moto du Ciel DA	8807	
F-WREL	Fauvette Gyrocopter	01	
F-WREM	Averso AX-02 Gyrocopter	23	
F-WREN	Averso AX-02 Gyrocopter	24	
F-WREO	Averso AX-02 Gyrocopter	21	
F-WREP	Bensen B-8 Gyrocopter	104-OF	
F-WREQ	Averso AX-02 Gyrocopter	26	
F-WRER	Averso AX-02 Gyrocopter	25	
F-PRES	Jodel D.19	I99-T	
F-WRET	Auque AM-01 Gyrocopter	01	
F-PRET(2)	Murphy Rebel (Reservation .99)	526R	
F-WREU	Elixir Gyrocopter	1	
F-PREU(2)	Pottier P.220S Koala	463	
F-WREV	Vigneron POMV Gyrocopter	01	
F-PREV(2)	Rutan Vari-eze	1961	
F-WREX	Averso AX-02 Gyrocopter	28	
F-WREY	TUR-1 Gyrocopter	001	
F-WREZ	Averso AX-02 Gyrocopter	29	
F-WRFA	Light Aero Avid Flyer	539	
F-WRFB	Light Aero Avid Amphibian	78-A	
F-PRFC	Light Aero Avid Flyer	695	F-WRFC
F-WRFD	Light Aero Avid Flyer	646	
F-WRFE	Light Aero Avid Amphibian	061	
F-WRFF	Light Aero Avid Flyer	543	
F-WRFG	Light Aero Avid Flyer	479	
F-WRFH	Aviasud Mistral Mk.10	130	
F-WRFI	Light Aero Avid Amphibian	63	
F-PRFK	Neico Lancair 235	197	F-WRFK
F-WRFL	Christen Eagle 2	TA-3	
F-WRFM	Light Aero Avid Flyer	729	
F-WRFN	Light Aero Avid Flyer	797	
F-WRFO	Light Aero Avid Flyer	537	
F-WRFP	Light Aero Avid Flyer	727	
F-WRFQ	Light Aero Avid Flyer	728	
F-PRFR	Neico Lancair 235	195	F-WRFR
F-WRFS	Rans S-10 Sakota	05-911-33	
F-WRFT	Rans S-10 Sakota	04-911-29	
F-WRFU	Light Aero Avid Flyer	645	
F-PRFV	Light Aero Avid Flyer	723	F-WRFV
F-PRFX	Light Aero Avid Flyer	536	F-WRFX
F-PRFY	Light Aero Avid Flyer	690	F-WRFY
F-WRFZ	Christen Eagle 2	MG-2	
F-WRGA	Franck Gyrocopter	002	
F-WRGB	Doucet DP-1 Gyrocopter	01	
F-WRGC	Averso AX-02 Gyrocopter	27	
F-WRGD	Herzig HF-1 Gyrocopter	01	
F-WRGE	Averso AX-02 Gyrocopter	31	
F-WRGF	Averso AX-02 Gyrocopter	30	
F-WRGG	GA-LAPA-1 Gyrocopter	01	
F-WRGH	Radas RR-2 Gyrocopter	01	
F-WRGI	Rabillard CR-02 Gyrocopter	01	
F-WRGJ	Sagittaire Gyrocopter	02	
F-WRGK	Cartier-Traverse CT1 Gyrocopter	01	
F-WRGL	Chauvin & Changeur CHA-2 Gyrocopter	01	
F-WRGM	Playe PL-B-1 Gyrocopter	01	
F-WRGN	Flying Dream Gyrocopter	01	
F-WRGO	Averso AX-06 Guepard Gyrocopter	01	
F-WRGP	Weinbrenner J.W.Gyrocopter	004	
F-WRGQ	Nieddu NA-01 Gyrocopter	01	
F-WRGR	Averso AX-02 Gyrocopter / Snoopy	1	
F-WRGS	Ceyrat JC Gyrocopter	01	

Regn.	Type	C/n	Prev.Id.
F-WRGT	Colibri Gyrocopter	02	
F-WRGU	Averso AX-02 Gyrocopter	32	
F-WRGV	Maisonhaute MB-1 Gyrocopter	01	
F-WRGX	Max-1 Gyrocopter	1	
F-WRGY	Averso AX-06 Guepard Gyrocopter	2	
F-WRGZ	DGH-02 Gyrocopter	1	
F-WRHA	Gisquet JG-1 Gyrocopter	01	
F-WRHB	Roum TOW Gyrocopter	01	
F-WRHC	Ledent LL-1 Gyrocopter	01	
F-WRHD	Eclair Gyrocopter	01	
F-WRHE	Soubsol S-1S Gyrocopter	01	
F-PRHF	Gyrocopter Mk.1	01	F-WRHF
F-WRHG	B.TPR Gyrocopter	01	
F-WRHH	Doleac DJP-03 Gyrocopter	02	
F-WRHI	Mehault MN-1 Gyrocopter	01	
F-WRHJ	GRB Gyrocopter	01	
F-WRHK	Averso AX-02 Gyrocopter	33	
F-WRHL	Jeanneau JC-0001 Gyrocopter	01	
F-WRHM	JG-01 Gyrocopter	01	
F-WRHN	Mammouth Gyrocopter	01	
F-WRHO	Tadrent AT-1 Gyrocopter	01	
F-WRHP	Pellefigue PJF Gyrocopter	01	
F-WRHQ	DGH-03 Gyrocopter	01	
F-WRHR	Duflos DR-01 Gyrocopter	01	
F-WRHS	Averso AX-02 Gyrocopter	34	
F-WRHT	La Gazelle 01 Gyrocopter	01	
F-WRHU	Boillon RB-03 Gyrocopter	1	
F-WRHV	Lacoste HL-01 Gyrocopter	1	
F-WRHX	DGH-03 Gyrocopter	03	
F-WRHY	RM-02 Gyrocopter	1	
F-WRHZ	Averso AX-02 Gyrocopter	01	
F-PRIA	Pitts S-1D Special	7-0503	
F-PRIB	Brügger MB-2 Colibri	240	F-WRIB
F-PRIC	Pottier P.80S	024	
F-PRID	Heintz Zenith	2-124	
F-PRIE	Jodel D.19	1681	
F-PRIF	Jodel DR.1050	739	
F-PRIG	Nicollier HN-700 Ménestrel II	81	
F-PRIH	Rutan LongEz	2203	
F-PRII	Pena Capena	9	
F-PRIJ	Pottier P.60 Minacro	03	
F-PRIK	Colomban MC-15 Cri-Cri	67	F-WRIK
F-PRIL	Colomban MC-15 Cri-Cri	492	
F-PRIM	Zenair CH-600 Zodiac	6-1003	
F-PRIN	Piel CP.90 Pinocchio II	10	F-WRIN
F-PRIO	Jodel D.18	342	
F-PRIP	Darcissac-Grinvalds DG-87 Goëland	02	
F-PRIQ	Rutan Vari-eze	1563	
F-PRIR	Vare JCV-24 Tangara	01	F-WRIR
F-PRIS	Rutan LongEz	1272	
F-PRIT	Croses Criquet L	75	
F-PRIU	Nicollier HN-700 Ménestrel II	05	
F-PRIV	Damoure-Fabre-Lacroix DFL-6 Saphir	3	
F-PRIX	Pottier P.180S	20	F-WRIX
F-PRIZ	Jodel D.92 Bébé	811	
F-PRJA	Jodel D.18	46	
F-PRJB	Colomban MC-15 Cri-Cri	341	
F-PRJC	Deborde-Rolande Cobra 201A	1	
F-PRJD	Alexandre Dewoitine D-501	01	F-WRJD
	(Constructed from Mauboussin-Beaujard 130 F-PCIZ c/n 01,		
	formerly Mauboussin 129/48 F-BCIZ c/n 226)		
F-PRJE	Jurca MJ.5H1 Sirocco	21F	
F-PRJF	Colomban MC-12 Cri-Cri	21	
F-PRJG	Piel CP-320 Super Emeraude	437	
F-PRJH	Helf-Aubertin HA Flieger	01	
F-PRJI	Jodel D.18	48	
F-PRJJ	Leopoldoff L-55 Colibri	LF-01-93	F-WVZR
	(Rebuild of Leopoldoff L-56 F-BHGU c/n 03)		
F-PRJK	Jodel D.18	17	
F-PRJL	Deborde-Rolande Cobra L-160 (Reservn)	01	
F-PRJM	Jess Canard (Reservation)	1	
F-PRJN	Jodel DR100MJJ	01	
F-PRJO	Jodel D.150 Mascaret	119	
F-PRJP	Jodel D.18	214	
F-PRJQ	Colomban MC-15 Cri-Cri (Reservation)	56	

Regn.	Type	C/n	Prev.Id.
F-PRJR	Max Plan MP.205 Busard	25	F-WRJR
F-PRJS	Rutan LongEz	2073-L	
F-PRJT	Jodel D.18	301	
F-PRJU	Viking Dragonfly Mk.3	1133	
F-PRJV	Jodel D.9 Bébé	83	
F-PRJX	Pottier P.230S Panda	409	
F-PRJY	Zenair CH-701 STOL *(Reservation)*	1302	
F-PRJZ	Marie JPM-01 Médoc	36	
F-WRKA	Light Aero Avid Flyer	696	
F-WRKB	Light Aero Avid Flyer	687	
F-WRKC	Denney Kitfox	410	
F-WRKD	Light Aero Avid Flyer	725	
F-PRKF	Light Aero Avid Flyer	979	F-WRKF
F-WRKG	Neico Lancair 320	547	
F-WRKI	Neico Lancair 320	552	
F-PRKJ	Light Aero Avid Flyer *(Reserved as F-PKRJ)*	798	F-WRKJ
F-WRKK	Light Aero Avid Flyer IV	1097	
F-WRKL	Light Aero Avid Flyer	981	
F-WRKM	Light Aero Avid Flyer	472	
F-WRKN	Light Aero Avid Flyer	726	
F-WRKO	Light Aero Avid Flyer	799	
F-WRKP	Light Aero Avid Flyer	692	
F-WRKQ	Light Aero Avid Flyer IV	1099	
F-PRKR	Light Aero Avid Flyer	696	F-WRKR
F-WRKS	Murphy Rebel	136	
	(Appears to have become F-WSDO, then C-FJCS)		
F-WRKT	Light Aero Avid Flyer	1095	
F-WRKU	Murphy Rebel	141	
F-WRKV	Light Aero Avid Flyer	1212	
F-WRKX	Light Aero Avid Flyer	724	
F-WRKY	Pelican Club PL	438	
F-PRKZ	Neico Lancair 360	248	F-WRKZ
F-PRLA	Laplace RL-221	01	
F-PRLB	Jodel D.113	1702	
F-PRLC	Brändli BX-2 Cherry	110	
F-PRLD	Peters PGK-1 Hirondelle	183	F-WRLD
F-PRLE	Nicollier HN.434 Super Ménestrel	27	F-WRLE
F-PRLF	Nicollier HN.700 Ménestrel II	50	
F-PRLG	Colomban MC-15 Cri-Cri	23	F-WRLG
F-PRLH	Deborde-Rolland Cobra 202 *(Reservation)*	01	
FWRLI	Steen Skybolt CJ-250	325	
F-PRLJ	CJL-100	01	
F-PRLK	Brändli BX-2 Cherry	145	
F-PRLL	Jodel D.113	1666	
F-PRLM	Pottier P.70S	38	
F-PRLN	Stolp SA-750 Acroduster Too	528	
F-PRLO	Stolp Starduster Too ? *(Reservation)*	unkn	
F-PRLP	Marie JPM-01 Médoc	26	
F-PRLQ	Brändli BX-2 Cherry	13	
F-PRLR	Brändli BX-2 Cherry	111	
F-PRLS	Zenair CH-701 STOL	7-1349	
F-PRLT	Darcissac-Grinvalds DG-87 Goeland	03	
F-PRLU	Jodel D.113	1637	
F-PRLV	Couderc Vagabond *(Reservation)*	001	
F-PRLX	Jodel D.18	386	
F-PRLY	Decoiro DRC-01	01	
F-PRLZ	Kieger AK-01	2	
F-PRMA	Nicollier HN.434 Super Ménestrel	23	
F-PRMB	Jodel D.150	123	
F-PRMC	Microgy MK-20	01	
F-PRMD	Pottier P.230S Panda	442	
F-PRME	Rutan Cozy	455	
F-PRMG	Stern ST-87C Europlane	11	
F-PRMH	Pottier P.220S Koala	446	
F-PRMI	Helicoptere Cicare CH-7 Angel *(Reservation)*	unkn	
F-PRMJ	Jodel D.18	320	
F-PRMK	Nicollier HN.700 Ménestrel II	53	
F-PRML	Viking Dragonfly Mk.2	950	
F-PRMM	Colomban MC-15 Cri-Cri	200	
F-PRMN	Brügger MB.2 Colibri	123	
F-PRMO	Lucas L-6B	01	
F-PRMR	Stern-Mallick SM Vega	01	
F-PRMS	Grinvalds G-801 Orion	21	F-WRMS
F-PRMT	Filcoa J-6 Karatoo	2907885	
F-WRMU	Piel CP.1320 Saphir	32	
F-PRMV	Piel CP.320 Super Emeraude	409	
F-PRMX	Rutan LongEz	2179	
F-PRMY	Piel CP.1321 Saphir	37	
F-PRMZ	WagAero Sportsman 2+2	885	
F-PRNA	Jodel D.140E Mousquetaire IV	431	
F-PRNB	Nicollier HN-434 Super Ménestrel	45	
F-PRNC	Zenair CH-600 Zodiac	6-3	
F-PRND	Protech PT-2	1070	
F-PRNE	Jodel DR.1053P	735	F-WRNE
F-PROB	Rutan Vari-eze	1432	OO-101 (OO-76)
F-PROC	Pottier P.80S	65	
F-PROD	Jodel D.113	1721	
F-PROF	Salvato SVO	1	
F-PROI	Heintz Zenith 100	2.127	
F-PROO(2)	Brügger MB-2 Colibri *(Reservation)*	275	
F-PROQ	Pottier P.180S *(Reservation)*	171	
F-PROS	Lucas L.5	033	
F-PROU	Piel CP.322-120 Super Emeraude	424	
F-PROV	Colomban MC-15 Cri-Cri	311	
F-PROY	Jodel D.113 *(regd as D.119)*	1605	
F-WRPA	Berset BR-01 Gyrocopter	01	
F-PRPB	Jodel D.18	343	
F-PRPC	Pottier P.70S	15	
F-WRPH	Lucas LP-01 Gyrocopter	01	
F-PRPL	Jodel DR.1055M	811	
F-PRPM	Jodel D.140R Abeille	400	
F-PRPT	Nicollier HN-700 Ménestrel II	16	
F-PRPY	Colomban MC-12 Cri-Cri	24	
F-WRQA	Duquenne DM-01 Gyrocopter	1	
F-WRQB	Carbonnel CR-01 Gyrocopter	1	
F-WRQC	Averso AX-02 Gyrocopter	02	
F-WRQD	Averso AX-02G Gyrocopter	03	
F-WRQE	Vassot PV-01 Gyrocopter	001	
F-WRQF	Gyrolet 1 Gyrocopter	01	
F-WRQG	Labussiere LC-01 Gyrocopter	01	
F-WRQH	Doleac DJP-03C Gyrocopter	01	
F-WRQI	Bonnot BP-01 Gyrocopter	01	
F-WRQJ	Libellule Gyrocopter	1	
F-WRQK	Raspberry Gyrocopter	1	
F-WRQL	Doleac DJP-Max Gyrocopter	1	
F-WRQM	Hanneton Gyrocopter	1	
F-WRQN	Dupin Bizuth Gyrocopter	DD-01	
F-WRQO	Guepard Gyrocopter	01	
F-WRQP	Caylus Gyrocopter	2	
F-WRQQ	Aquila Gyrocopter	1	
F-WRQR	Pennec-Peden PP-01 Gyrcopter	01	
F-WRQS	Icarus Gyrocopter	01	
F-WRQT	Boinon GB Gyrocopter	01	
F-WRQU	Bonnafous BC Gyrocopter	02	
F-WRQV	Cherokee Gyrocopter	FK-500	
F-WRQX	Averso AX-02G Gyrocopter	GM-01	
F-WRQY	Averso AX-02 Gyrocopter	MM-01	
F-WRQZ	Bonnafous BC-2 Gyrocopter	02	
F-PRRD	Rutan Cozy	E-751	
F-PRRG	Jodel D.18	180	
F-PRRK	Rand-Robinson KR-1 *(Reservation)*	4928	
F-PRRM	Gravereau GD-2001 Milan Royale	01	
F-PRRV	Gerfan RV02	01	F-WRRV
F-PRSA	Jodel D.18	23	
F-PRSB	Jodel D.18	370	
F-PRSC	Rutan Cozy	593	
F-PRSG	Jodel D.119	1385	
F-PRSH	Jodel D.18	277	
F-PRSJ	Rolland RC-65	01	
F-PRSK	Van's RV-6 *(Reservation)*	23914	
F-PRST	Colomban MC-15 Cri-Cri	410	
F-PRSZ	Piel CP.320 Super Emeraude	427	
F-WRTD	Coupe JC-3-80 *(Reservation)* (or c/n 5?)	8	
F-PRTJ	Godbille JG-03	01	
F-PRUD	Nickel-Foucard NF-02 Asterix	01	
F-PRUQ	Aeromarine Skyote *(Reservation)*	63	
F-PRVI	Pottier P.180S	94	
F-PRVJ	Rutan Cozy *(Reservation)*	384	

Regn.	Type	C/n	Prev.Id.
F-PRVL	Van Lith IX bis	01	F-PYSZ F-WYSZ
F-PRVS	Van's RV-6 (Reservation)	22239	
F-WRXA	Rans S-6ES SQFT Coyote II	0192262	
F-WRXB	Aero Designs Pulsar	7F	
F-PRXC	Light Aero Avid Flyer	1219	F-WRXC
F-WRXD	Stoddard Hamilton Glasair RG-II	1060	
F-WRXE	Light Aero Avid Flyer	1214	
F-WRXF	Aero Designs Pulsar (Reserved as F-PAXF)	101	
F-WRXG	Murphy Rebel	14 . ?	
F-WRXH	Light Aero Avid Flyer	977	
F-PRXI	Light Aero Avid Flyer	795	F-WRXI
F-PRXJ	Aero Designs Pulsar 582	255-2F	F-WRXJ
F-WRXK	Light Aero Avid Flyer	1096	
F-WRXL	Light Aero Avid Flyer	976	
F-WRXM	Light Aero Avid Flyer Mk.IV	1094	
F-WRXN	Light Aero Avid Flyer	1098	
F-WRX0	Rans S-9 Chaos	0790092	
F-WRXP	Light Aero Avid Flyer	1302	
F-WRXQ	Light Aero Avid Flyer	1220-D	
F-WRXR	Denney Kitfox	785	
F-WRXS	Light Aero Avid Flyer	1372	
F-WRXT	CFM Streak Shadow SA	K192-SA	
F-WRXU	Light Aero Avid Flyer	800	
F-WRXV	Light Aero Avid Flyer	1370	
F-PRXX	Aero Designs Pulsar	12-F	
F-WRXY	Murphy Rebel	263	F-WRXY
F-WRXZ	Dyn'Aero CR.100C	05	
F-WRYA	Roitelet Gyrocopter	CA-01	
F-WRYB	Averso AX-02 Gyrocopter	GC-01	
F-WRYC	Rodriguez RH Gyrocopter	01	
F-WRYD	Ricard Jokari Gyrocopter	1	
F-WRYE	Averso AX-02 Gyrocopter	JB	
F-WRYF	Kimpe KM Gyrocopter	1	
F-PRYG	Jodel DR.1050	814	
F-WRYH	Portespane Gyrocopter	03	
F-WRYI	Delsol MD Gyrocopter	2703	
F-WRYJ	Pasquier PJ Gyrocopter	01	
F-WRYK	Vimon-Hoffmann VHB-1 Gyrocopter	01	
F-WRYL	AB-01 Gyrocopter	01	
F-WRYM	REL Gyrocopter	01	
F-WRYN	Dieudonne RD Gyrocopter	01	
F-WRYO	Bimbo Gyrocopter	01	
F-PRYP	Potez 60 Sauterelle	P-1991-1	
F-WRYQ	Elite 80 Gyrocopter	01	
F-WRYR	Gyrolet 3 Gyrocopter	01	
F-WRYS	Mistral 01 Gyrocopter	01	
F-WRYT	AST-1 Gyrocopter	01	
F-WRYU	Esposito GSE-01 Gyrocopter	01	
F-WRYV	Callauzene JC Gyrocopter	01	
F-WRYX	Le Gaulois 01 Gyrocopter	01	
F-WRYY	Dal-Bor 01 Gyrocopter	01	
F-WRYZ	MS-01 Abeille Gyrocopter	01	
F-PRZB	Brochet MB-50 Pipistrelle	8	F-PHZB
F-PRZZ	Rutan Cozy	414	
F-PSAB	Jodel D.20 Jubilé	01	F-WSAB
F-PSAC	Jodel D.18 (Reservation)	257	
F-PSAD	Delustre DD-100 (Reservation)	001	
F-PSAF	Mignet HM.360	166	
F-PSAG	RSA Carriou CL-3 (Reservn, to F-PCAR?)	01	
F-PSAM	Piel CP.322 Super Emeraude (Reservation)	451	
F-WSAM	Rutan Vari-eze	1794	
F-PSAR	Jodel D.119	1756	
F-PSBC	Pottier P.230S Panda	422	
F-PSBI	Soyer-Barritault SB-1/160	01	F-WSBI
F-PSBR	Marie JPM 01 Tanagra	19	
F-PSCC	Cassutt 3M (Reservation)	589	
F-PSCF	Rutan Cozy	128	
F-PSCG	Jodel D.18	193	
F-PSCJ	Pottier P.180S	52	
F-WSDA	Light Aero Avid Amphibian	75	
F-WSDB	Light Aero Avid Flyer	1371	
F-WSDC	Light Aero Avid Flyer	423	
F-WSDD	Light Aero Avid Flyer	1369	
F-WSDE	Rans S-6ES Coyote II	0193428	
F-WSDF	Light Aero Avid Flyer	980	
F-WSDG	Light Aero Avid Flyer	1210 or 1290?	
F-WSDH	Light Aero Avid Flyer	1315	
F-WSDI	Light Aero Avid Flyer	481	
F-WSDJ	Light Aero Avid Flyer	540	
F-WSDK	Light Aero Avid Flyer	1405	
F-WSDL	Light Aero Avid Flyer	1406	
F-WSDM	Aero Visions Celebrity	54	
F-WSDN	Light Aero AvidMagnum	26	
F-WSDO	Murphy Rebel	0136-R	
F-WSDP	Light Aero AvidMagnum	07	
F-PSDQ	Aero Designs Pulsar	111-F	F-WSDQ
F-PSDR	Aero Designs Pulsar 582	106-F	F-WSDR
F-WSDS	Light Aero Avid Flyer Bandit	1403	
F-WSDT	Aero Designs Pulsar	103-F	
F-PSDU	Murphy Rebel	269	F-WSDU
F-WSDV	Neico Lancair 320	651	
F-WSDX	Denney Kitfox Speedster	AC-5093/4152518	
F-WSDY	Murphy Rebel	352	
F-WSDZ	Aero Designs Pulsar	114-F	
F-PSEA	Tissot-Charbonnier TC-160 Oceanair	01	
F-PSEB	Jodel DR.1054	732	
F-PSFE	Jodel D.112 Club	1729	
F-PSFG	Tech'Aero Feugray TR-200	05	
F-PSFS	Bonnet BLJ-01	01	
F-PSGG	Grinvalds G-801 Orion (Reservation)	48	
F-PSIC	Jodel DR.1050M	821	
F-PSIM	Tech'Aero TR-200	07	
F-PSIR	Fournier RF-7	03	
F-PSJB	Croses LC-6 Criquet	63	
F-PSJH	JR-01 Mancha	01	
F-PSJM	CATA LMK-1 Oryx (Reservation)	LPCA-03	
F-PSJP	DRLS 250 (Reservation .99)	01	
F-WSKA	Light Aero Avid Flyer	1404	
F-WSKB	Aero Designs Pulsar	109-F	
F-WSKC	Murphy Rebel	415	
F-WSKD	Wheeler Express	1133	
F-WSKE	Denney Kitfox	4156	
F-WSKF	Light Aero Avid Flyer	1218	
F-PSKG	Dyn'Aero CR.100	24	F-WSKG
F-WSKH	Light Aero Avid Flyer	1502	
F-WSKI	Murphy Rebel	434	
F-PSKJ	Denney Kitfox Vixen 912	KCV-024	F-WSKJ
F-WSKK	Stoddard-Hamilton Glasair IIFT	2249-FT	
F-PSKL	Stoddard-Hamilton Glasair IIRG	2250-RG	F-WSKL
F-WSKM	Stoddard-Hamilton Glasair IIRG	unkn-RG	
F-PSKN	Stoddard-Hamilton Glasair IIFT	2305-FT	F-WSKN
F-WSKO	Stoddard-Hamilton Glasair IITD (Res as F-PSUZ)	1109-TD	
F-WSKP	Rans S-10 Sakota	988030	
F-WSKQ	Murphy Rebel	262	
F-WSKR	Aero Designs Pulsar	320-2J	
F-WSKS	Light Aero Avid Flyer Speedwing	1415	
F-PSKT	Ultravia Pélican PL-914	624	F-WSKT
F-WSKU	Light Aero Avid Flyer	978	
F-WSKV	Dyn'Aero CR.100C (Reservation)	25	
F-WSKX	Murphy Rebel (Rebuild of c/n 256)	538	C-FPNT
F-WSKY	Akrotech G-202 (Reservation)	030	
F-WSKZ	Light Aero Avid Flyer (Reservation)	1501	
F-PSLA	Dyn'Aéro MCR-01 VLA Banbi	52	F-WSLA
F-WSLB	Akrotech G-202 (Reservation)	27	
F-WSLC	Stoddart-Hamilton Glastar (Reservation)	5074	
F-WSLD	Dyn'Aéro MCR-01 Banbi (Reservation)	8	
F-WSLE	Rans S-6 Coyote II S-116 (Reservation)	07961016	
F-WSLF	Dyn'Aéro MCR-01 Banbi (Reservation)	17	
F-WSLG	Dyn'Aéro MCR-01 Banbi (Reservation)	5	
F-PSLH	Europa Aviation Europa	273	F-WSLH
F-WSLI	Dyn'Aéro MCR-01 Banbi (Reserved as F-PQNO)	14	
F-PSLJ	Stoddart-Hamilton Glastar GS-1	5079	F-WSLJ
F-WSLL	Dyn'Aéro MCR-01 Banbi (Reservation)	41	
F-PSLM	Rand-Robinson KR-2	66	
F-PSLN	Europa Aviation Europa	98	F-WSLN
F-WSLO	Europa Aviation Europa (Reservation)	108	
F-WSLP	Pottier P.230S Panda	427	
F-PSLQ	Dyn'Aéro MCR-01 Banbi	30	F-WSLQ
F-PSLR	Dyn'Aéro MCR-01 Banbi	33	F-WSLR

Regn.	Type	C/n	Prev.Id.
F-PSLS	Dyn'Aéro MCR-01 Banbi	44	F-WSLS
F-WSLT	Rans S-7 Courier (Reservation)	1295167	
F-PSLU	Light Aero AvidMagnum	97	F-WSLU
F-WSLV	Akrotech G-202 (Reservation)	K-04	
F-WSLX	Dyn'Aéro MCR-01 Banbi (Reservation)	37	
F-PSLY	Europa Aviation Europa	275	F-WSLY
F-PSLZ	Dyn'Aéro MCR-01 Banbi	35	F-WSLZ
F-PSMB	Nicollier HN-700 Ménestrel II	88	
F-PSMJ	Piel CP.1320 Saphir (Reservation)	25	
F-PSMU	Europa Aviation Europa XS (Reservation .99)	439	
F-PSPF	Rouet MR-01	01	
F-PSPL	Druine D.5 Turbi (Reservation)	77	
F-PSRD	Nicollier HN-700 Ménestrel II	127	
F-PSRG	EAA Acrosport II	964	
F-PSSA	Jodel D.119	1278-1	
F-WSSB	Bensen B-8MV Gyrocopter	unkn	
F-WSSC	Bensen B-8 Gyrocopter	unkn	
F-WSSE	Laboye-Bensen Gyrocopter	1	
F-PSSF	Druine D.31 Turbulent	182	
F-WSSG	Bensen-Testa 70 Gyrocopter	001	
F-PSSH	Jodel D.119V	1428	
F-WSSL	Raybout D-2 Autogyre	01	
F-PSSN	Jodel D.119	1399	
F-PSSO	Leblanc L.52	1	
F-WSSP	Bensen/Nuville JN-2 Gyrocopter	01	
F-PSSQ	Duranton DE Junior	01	
F-PSSR	Druine D.5 Turbi	50	F-WSSR
			F-PSSR
F-PSSS	Seckler SS-02 (Reservation)	01	
F-WSSS	Bensen B-8M Gyrocopter (Cld?)	3213	
F-WSSU	Bensen B.8MC Gyrocopter	01	
F-PSSV	Jodel D.119	1413	
F-PSSX	Gazuit-Valladeau GV-1031	02	F-BSSX
			F-WSSX
F-WSTA	Arneur Aviation Baljims (Reservation .99)	001	
F-PSTC	Ultimate 20.300T (Reservation)	130 393 004	
F-PSTO	Jodel D.11T (Reservation)	01	
F-PSUN	Jurca MJ.77 Gnatsum (Reservation)	09	
F-PSUZ	Stoddard-Hamilton Glasair II-TD (Reservn .99)	1109TD	F-WSKO
F-PSVR	Jodel DR.100	843	
F-WSYB	Gyrol L-2 Autogyre	002	
F-PSYD	Jodel D.112 Club	1472	
F-PSYE	Starck AS.80 Holiday	58	
F-PSYH	Druine D.5 Turbi	27	
F-WSYJ	Bensen B.8M Gyrocopter	01	
F-PSYN	Mignet HM.360	128	F-WSYN
F-PSYP	Jodel D.112 Club	1447	
F-WSYR	Campbell Cricket Gyrocopter	CA/342	G-AYHJ
F-WSYS	Bensen B-8M Gyrocopter	01	
F-PSYT	Roy Mignet GR	01	F-WSYT
F-WSYZ	Bensen B-8M	01	
F-WSZA	Bouget-Capdeville BC-1 Gyrocopter	01	
F-WSZB	Scheila Gyrocopter	001	
F-WSZC	Fardeau Gyrocopter	001	
F-WSZD	Colin CX Gyrocopter	01	
F-WSZE	Garnin H-16 Gyrocopter	01	
F-WSZF	Lion Gyrocopter	001	
F-WSZG	Cobra Gyrocopter	01	
F-WSZH	Marquion-Dreyer MD-05B Gyrocopter	001	
F-WSZI	Bouilin BJM-III Gyrocopter	001	
F-WSZJ	Averso AX-02 Gyrocopter	LJS-01	
F-WSZK	Averso AX-02 Gyrocopter	unkn	
F-WSZL	Rapetout Gyrocopter	01	
F-WSZM	Albatros Gyrocopter	02	
F-WSZN	Arc en Ciel Gyrocopter	01	
F-WSZO	Dieudonne RD-02 Gyrocopter	01	
F-WSZP	GS-01 Gyrocopter	01	
F-WSZQ	Maury M-1 Gyrocopter	001	
F-WSZR	Martins OM Gyrocopter	01	
F-WSZS	Rivollier-Bernardi RB Gyrocopter	01	
F-WSZT	Le Sommer ALS Gyrocopter	001	
F-WSZU	Averso AX-02 Gyrocopter	001	
F-WSZV	Faure JPF-002 Gyrocopter	002	
F-WSZX	Libellule Gyrocopter	01	
F-WSZY	Colibri Gyrocopter	01	
F-WSZZ	Palombe Gyrocopter	01	
F-PTAH	Startrap FG-01	01	
F-PTAJ	Piel CP.615 Super Diamant (Reservation .99)	57	
F-PTAM	Rutan LongEz (Reservation)	1515	
F-PTAT	W.A.R. FW.190A Replica	117	F-WTAT
F-PTAV	Pottier P.230S Panda (Reservation)	452	
F-WTBS	Steen Skybolt	478	
F-PTCA	Stern ST-87 Europlane (Reservation .99)	47	
F-PTCD	Arneur Avn Baljims 1A	01	
F-PTCM	Jurca MJ.77 Gnatsum (Reservation)	02	
F-PTCR	Robin (Dyn'Aero) CR-120 (Reservation)	02	
F-PTDD	G-802 Gerfaut (Reservation .99)	04	
F-PTDI	Pennec-Lucas Dieselis PL-2	01	
F-PTDM	Jurca MJ.2HTempête	10	
F-WTEA	Queniet QG-01 Gyrocopter	04	
F-WTEB	Descatha DB Gyroglider	01	
F-WTEC	Bensen B-8M Gyrocopter	01	
F-WTED	Danis DB Giroplaneur	01	
F-WTEE	Danis DB Giroplaneur Nautic	03	
F-WTEF	Danis DB Giroplaneur Nautic	02	
F-WTEG	Danis DB Autogire	01	
F-PTEJ	Jurca MJ.5-K2 Sirocco	16	
F-PTEK	Jodel D.112 Club	1459	
F-WTEM	Bensen B.8MG Gyrocopter	1	
F-PTER	Jurca MJ.2D Tempête	34	
F-WTEY	Bensen B.8MB Gyrocopter	01	
F-WTEZ	Bensen B.8MT Gyrocopter	01	
F-PTEZ(2)	Potez 60EF (Reservation .99)	01	
F-PTJB	G-802B Gerfaut (Reservation .99)	03	
F-PTJC	Rutan Cozy (Reservation)	E-716	
F-PTJM	Rutan Vari-eze	1756	
F-PTLC	WagAero Sport Trainer	1240	
F-PTLF	G-802L Gypaete (Reservation .99)	01	
F-PTMV	Rutan Cozy (Reservation .99)	CC-1058	
F-PTNF	Tipsy Nipper Marquis	01	
F-PTOP	Jodel DR.1050M (Reservation)	783	
F-PTOY	Clenet DC-01 Baboo (Reservation)	01	
F-PTRA	Jodel de Havilland DH.251 (Reservation)	08	
F-PTRB	Bodenan CRD-01 (Reservation)	01	
F-PTRC	Parker Teenie Two (Reservation)	15-1838	
F-PTSH	Jodel D.140R Abeille (Reservation)	464	
F-PTVH	Dyn'Aéro CR-100 (Reservation)	29	
F-PTXC	Croses EC.8 Tourisme	18	F-WTXC
F-PTXE	Vintras JPV.30 Joker	01	F-WTXE
F-PTXG	Heintz Zenith	16	
F-WTXI	Bensen B.8M Gyroplaneur	01	
F-PTXM	Jurca MJ.2D Tempête	21	
F-WTXN	Bensen-Sica SP-01 Gyrocopter	01	
F-PTXO	Druine D.31 Turbulent	359	
F-PTXP	Jodel D.119A	1341	
F-WTXQ	Bensen B.8MB Gyrocopter	01	
F-PTXR	Jodel D.119	1502	
F-PTXU	Piel CP.320A Super Emeraude	83	F-WTXU
F-WTXV	Bensen JC-01 Gyrocopter	01	
F-WTXZ	Rouaux RB-01 Gyrocopter	01	
F-WTYA	Onauros Gyrocopter	01	
F-WTYB	Bonnafous B-5 Gyrocopter	01	
F-WTYC	Le Roitelet Gyrocopter	01	
F-WTYD	Krukowsky VK Gyrocopter	01	
F-WTYE	FGA Gyrocopter	01	
F-WTYF	Flying Dream Gyrocopter	02	
F-WTYG	Vignan JPV Corfou Gyrocopter	01	
F-WTYH	Despaux DR Gyrocopter	01	
F-WTYI	BMW Gyrocopter	01	
F-WTYJ	Lacombe Gyrocopter	01	
F-WTYK	Colibri Gyrocopter	01	
F-WTYL	Mondary JM Gyrocopter	01	
F-WTYM	Zéphir Gyrocopter	01	
F-WTYN	Tête Brûlée Gyrocopter	01	
F-WTYO	Averso AX-02 Gyrocopter	01	
F-WTYP	Tigre Opter Gyrocopter	07	
F-WTYQ	Phénix Gyrocopter	01	
F-WTYR	OK Gyrocopter	01	
F-WTYS	AG-15 Gyrocopter	15	
F-WTYT	Puente PR Gyrocopter	01	

Regn.	Type	C/n	Prev.Id.
F-WTYU	Aubin DA Gyrocopter	01	
F-WTYV	Ousset OA Gyrocopter	01	
F-WTYX	Galaxy Gyrocopter	01	
F-WTYY	Averso AX-02 Gyrocopter	01	
F-WTYZ	Weinbrenner Gyrocopter	05	
F-WTZA	Mila 01 Gyrocopter	01	
F-WTZB	Beltrando BD-01 Gyrocopter	01	
F-WTZC	Python Gyrocopter	01	
F-WTZD	Dilal Gyrocopter	01	
F-WTZE	Picsou Gyrocopter	01	
F-WTZF	GJ Gyrocopter	02	
F-WTZG	Glemet GJL Gyrocopter	01	
F-WTZH	Dessart-Larioze DL Gyrocopter	01	
F-WTZI	Enfossi EJM Gyrocopter	01	
F-WTZJ	VHM Gyrocopter	01	
F-WTZK	Averso AX-02 Gyrocopter	01	
F-WTZL	Evenot EL-02 Gyrocopter	01	
F-WTZM	Derlan Gyrocopter	01	
F-WTZN	Michelot DM Gyrocopter	01	
F-WTZO	Kloeti RK Gyrocopter	01	
F-WTZP	Magni Gyrocopter	01	
F-WTZQ	Colombie OC Gyrocopter	01	
F-WTZR	Raoul Gyrocopter	01	
F-WTZS	Berger BX Guepard Gyrocopter	01	
F-WTZT	Romagnoli RJ Gyrocopter	01	
F-WTZU	Le Loup Gyrocopter	01	
F-WTZV	Maffre Gyrocopter	01	
F-WTZX	Tiercelin GT Gyrocopter	01	
	(Noted marked as Averso AX07, 8.99)		
F-WTZY	Navarro Gyrocopter (Reservation)	01	
F-WTZZ	Ducos G-3 Gyrocopter (Reservation)	01	
F-WUCE	Dyn'Aero MCR-01 Banbi (Reservation .99)	36	
F-PUCH	Brändli BX-2 Cherry (Reservation)	151	
F-PUCK	Motopompe (Reservation)	01	
F-PUCY	Bonnavaud LB-01	01	
F-PUIG	Brügger MB-2 Colibri (Reservation .99)	102	
F-PUJG	Colomban MC-15 Cri-Cri (Res)	110	
F-PULC	Nicollier HN.700 Ménestrel II	37	
F-PULP	Ferrier AAL-01	01	
F-PUMA	Piel CP.320 Super Emeraude	440	
F-PUNK	Jurca MJ.52 Zephyr (Reservation .99)	01	
F-PUPY	Preceptor Ultra Pup (Reservn., or F-PUPI ?)	129	
F-WUQQ	Scorpion Gyrocopter	01	
F-PURG	Jodel D.119A (Reservation)	1699	F-PHUG
F-WURR	Murphy Rebel (Reservation .99)	268R	
F-WUSA	Bervat Gyrocopter (Reservation)	01	
F-WUSB	Ferrie FB Gyrocopter (Reservation)	01	
F-WUSC	Durand DC Gyrocopter (Reservation)	01	
F-WUSD	Gurau GG Gyrocopter (Reservation)	01	
F-WUSE	Gayaud GR Gyrocopter (Reservation)	01	
F-WUSF	Kerchaun KD Gyrocopter (Reservation)	01	
F-WUSG	Palavadeau Bensen 002 Gyrocopter (Res.)	02	
F-WUSH	Delfour DC Gyrocopter (Reservation)	01	
F-WUSI	Averso AX Gyrocopter (Reservation)	06	
F-WUSJ	Max Gyrocopter (Reservation)	001	
F-WUSK	Averso Guepard Gyrocopter (Reservation)	01	
F-WUSL	Fior Gyrocopter (Reservation)	01	
F-WUSM	Averso AX-02 Gyrocopter (Reservation)	01	
F-WUSN	Averso AX-02 Gyrocopter (Reservation)	01	
F-WUSO	VHB-1 Supercopter (Reservation)	01	
F-WUSP	Bonnafous BC03 Gyrocopter (Reservation)	01	
F-WUSQ	Daubert DF Gyrocopter (Reservation)	01	
F-WUSR	Magni Gyrocopter (Reservation)	01	
F-WUSS	Aerogi Gyrocopter (Reservation)	01	
F-WUST	Snoopy Gyrocopter (Reservation)	01	
F-WUSU	Equilibre 2 Gyrocopter (Reservation)	01	
F-WUSV	Odorico R-003 Gyrocopter (Reservation)	03	
F-WUSX	Delawind Gyrocopter (Reservation)	01	
F-WUSY	Rangers Gyrocopter (Reservation)	001	
F-WUSZ	Pisoni P-01 Gyrocopter (Reservation)	01	
F-WUTA	Sorrano GSXR Gyrocopter (Reservation)	01	
F-WUTB	Moustique Gyrocopter (Reservation)	001	
F-WUTC	Averso Guepard Gyrocopter (Reservation)	01	
F-WUTD	Lopez Gyrocopter (Reservation)	001	
F-WUTE	Faulcon Gyrocopter (Reservation)	01	
F-WUTF	Averso AX-2 Guepard Gyrocopter (Res.)	01	
F-WUTG	Averso AX-2 Guepard Gyrocopter (Res.)	01	
F-WUTH	Progressor Pou Gyrocopter (Reservation)	01	
F-WUTI	Maya Gyrocopter (Reservation)	001	
F-WUTJ	Jacquelin JMJ Gyrocopter (Reservation)	001	
F-WUTK	Lignac J'Ais'Quirm'Faut Gyrocopter (Res.)	001	
F-WUTL	Betaille BG Gyrocopter (Reservation)	01	
F-WUTM	Creusot HC Gyrocopter (Reservation)	01	
F-WUTN	Martins OM-02 Gyrocopter (Reservation)	unkn	
F-WUTO	Benus Gyrocopter (Reservation)	002	
F-WUTP	Techer JYT Gyrocopter (Reservation)	01	
F-WUTQ	Petitgirard VP-01 Gyrocopter (Reservation)	01	
F-WUTR	Kloeti RK-02 Gyrocopter (Reservation)	02	
F-WUTS	Averso AX-02 Guepard Gyrocopter (Res.)	01	
F-WUTT	Schaeffer MS-01 Gyrocopter (Reservation)	01	
F-WUTU	Magni M-16 Trainer Gyrocopter (Reservn)	01	
F-WUTV	Averso AX-02 Guepard Gyrocopter (Res.)	01	
F-WUTX	Air Command 582 Gyrocopter (Reservn)	KC-164	
F-WUTY	Cena CP-003 Gyrocopter (Reservation)	03	
F-WUTZ	Averso AX-02 Guepard Gyrocopter (Res.)	01	
F-WUUA	Bensen B-8 Gyrocopter (Reservation)	01	
F-WUUB	Berva Gyrocopter (Reservation)	03	
F-WUUC	Colibri 2 Gyrocopter (Reservation)	01	
F-WUUD	Sundarp MS-1 Gyrocopter (Reservation)	01	
F-WUUE	(Agnelet) Autogyre (Reservation)	01	
F-WUUF	Mosquito Killer Gyrocopter (Reservation)	001	
F-WUUG	Fourlade JF Dominator Gyrocopter (Res.)	01	
F-WUUH	Gabi Gyrocopter (Reservation)	02	
F-WUUI	X2 Gyrocopter (Reservation)	001	
F-WUUJ	Vil Coyote Gyrocopter (Reservation)	unkn	
F-WUUK	Magni M-14 Gyrocopter (Reservation)	01	
F-WUUL	Magni M-18 Gyrocopter (Reservation)	01	
F-WUUM	Magni M-16 Gyrocopter (Reservation)	01	
F-WUUN	Monoplace CBGyrocopter (Reservation .99)	01	
F-WUUO	Gisquet JG Gyrocopter (Reservation .99)	01	
F-WUUP	Magni M-16 Gyrocopter (Reservation .99)	01	
F-WUUQ	Mourier Gyrocopter (Reservation .99)	01	
F-WUUR	Polge Gyrocopter (Reservation .99)	01	
F-PVAJ	Jodel D.113	1669	
F-PVAL	Disdier JD-01 (Reservation)	01	
F-PVAP	Jodel DR.1052MAmbassadeur (Reservation .99)	851	
F-PVBC	Druine D.5 Turbi	97	
F-PVBN	Pamany PL-4A (Reservation)	420	
F-PVDB	Vandenbrock VDB-01 Gyrocopter	01	
F-PVDG	Piel CP.320 Super Emeraude (Reservation)	442	
F-PVDM	Piel CP.618A Super Diamant	59	
F-PVDV	Delvion DVDiesel (Reservation .99)	01	
F-PVGB	Autogyre PVGB-01	01	
F-PVIL	Velocity STD (Reservation)	046	
F-PVIN	Stolp SA.750 Acroduster Too	150	
F-PVIP	Van's RV-4	730	
F-PVJF	Viking Dragonfly Mk 1 (Reservation)	1017	
F-PVLS	Piel CP.320 Super Emeraude	435	
F-PVLT	Notteghem Occitan Club	06	F-WVLT
F-PVMA	Jurca MJ.5L2 Sirocco (Reservation)	113	
F-PVMC	Rutan Cozy	E-747	
F-PVMM	Lucas L-8	01	
F-PVQB	Delattre/Potez 60 Sauterelle	1	
F-PVQC	Druine D.31 Turbulent	49	
F-PVQE	Piel CP.310 Emeraude	364	
F-PVQG	Pottier P.70	01	
F-WVQH	Laboye HL-01 Gyrocopter	01, or 2 ?	
F-PVQM	Mignet HM.293M	600	F-WVQM
F-PVQN	Druine D.5 Turbi	9	
F-PVQO	Gatard Statoplan AG-02 Poussin	12	
F-PVQP	Jurca MJ.2D Tempète	17	
F-PVQQ	Chatelain AC.11	01	
F-PVQR	Roloff RLU-1 Breezy	FE1/01	
F-PVQS	Heintz Zenith 100LR	03	F-WVQS
F-PVQT	Heintz Zenith	7	
F-PVQU	Heintz Zenith 130	22MF	
F-PVQV	Heintz Zenith 125 FLR	04	
F-PVQX	Leger JCL 01	1	F-WVQX
F-WVQZ	Geiser G-10 Motodelta	01	
F-PVRD	Druine D.31 Turbulent (Reservation)	395	F-PZRD

Regn.	Type	C/n	Prev.Id.
F-PVRO	Colomban MC-15 Cri-Cri (Reservation .99)	379	
F-PVVA	ACBA-7 Midour (Reservation .99)	03	
F-PVVP	ACBA-7 Midour	02	
F-WWNA	Murphy Rebel 912	485	
F-WWNB	Murphy Rebel 912	486	
F-WWUU	Dyn'Aero MCR-01 Ban-bi	69	
F-PXAD	ACALLA-Jodel D.140E Mousquetaire	428	
F-PXAK	Jodel D.112 Club	1660	
F-PXAV	BKSud Eleisson (Reservation .99)	01	
F-PXDV	Landray GL.1	01	F-WXDV
F-PXGX	Guillaumaud GX-01 (Reservation)	01	
	(Probably Guillaumaud Glasair II N111XG c/n 3071)		
F-PXKA	Jurca MJ.2D Tempête	8	
F-PXKB	Gatard Statoplan AG-02 Poussin	19	F-WXKB
F-PXKC(2)	Jurca MJ.2A Tempête	42	F-WXKC (F-PYBR(1))
F-PXKE	Mudry CAP.10B	A-1	
F-PXKI	Jurca MJ.5 Sirocco	27	
F-PXKJ	Jodel D.112 Club	1488	
F-PXKK	Croses LC.10 Criquet	01	F-WXKK
F-WXKM	Eysseric F Gyrocopter	01	
F-WXKN	Bos AB-01 Gyrocopter	01	
F-PXKO	Brügger MB-2 Colibri	46	
F-WXKP	Rigaud RD Gyrocopter	06	
F-PXKQ	Heintz Zenith 90LR	20	F-WXKQ
F-PXKR	Mignet HM.382	115	
F-PXKS	Jodel D.92 Bébé	486	
F-WXKT	Averso Epervier XA Gyrocopter	01	
F-PXKU	Jurca MJ.2 Tempête	4	F-WXKU
F-PXKV	Coupe JC-01	001	
F-PXKY	Jodel D.92 Bébé	648	(F-PXKC)
F-PXXL	Gatard AG-02 Poussin (Reservation)	35	
F-PXYZ	Jurca MJ.2 Tempête (Reservation)	101	
F-PYAE	Jodel D.113 (ex D.119)	1026	F-POAE
F-PYAF	Jodel D.18 (Reservation)	248	
F-PYAM	Colomban MC-15 Cri-Cri (Reservation .99)	513	
F-PYAN	Jodel D.18 (Reservation)	329	
F-PYAS	Max Plan MP-207 Busard (Reservation .99)	19	
F-PYAV	Quercy CQR-01 (Reservation .99)	06	
F-PYBA	Jodel D.92 Bébé	658	
F-PYBB	Gatard AG 04 Pigeon	1	F-WYBB
F-PYBC	Heintz Zenith 100	28	
F-PYBD	Heintz Zenith 100BF	47	
F-PYBE	Lucas L-5	02	F-WYBE
F-PYBG	Croses-Bujon BEC-9 Paras-Cargo (on rebuild)	01	
F-PYBH	Piel CP.80 (Dismantled)	08	
F-PYBJ	Jodel D.119	1517	
F-PYBK	Piel CP.80	12	
F-PYBL	Jodel D.92 Bébé	638	
F-PYBN	Heintz Zenith 105	21	
F-PYBP	Piel CP.80	06	F-WYBP
F-PYBQ	Starck Nickel SN.01	1	F-WYBQ
	(Conversion of Starck AS.37 c/n 14)		
F-PYBR(2)	Heintz Zenith 100MF	5	
F-PYBS	Gatard Statoplan AG 02 Poussin	7	
	(Formerly Gatard GF-02T)		
F-PYBV	Terrade AT Diamant	01	
	(Jodel derivative built from D.120s F-BHYD and F-BNHK)		
F-PYBX	Jurca MJ.5G1 Sirocco	15	
F-PYBZ	Dyke JD-2 Manta	1239	F-WYBZ
F-PYCC	Quercy CQR-01 (Reservation .99)	8	
F-PYCG	Pottier P.180S	209	F-WYCG
F-WYDA	Megret-Amy ML-02 Gyrocopter	02	
F-WYDB	Ferrer La Darnaga Gyrocopter	01	
F-WYDC	Faure Bensen B.8 JPF Gyrocopter	01	
F-WYDE	Py MP-01 Alouette Gyrocopter	01	
F-WYDF	Chamanier AC-01 Gyrocopter	01	
F-WYDG	Sudres GS PPMB Gyrocopter	01	
F-WYDH	Faure AF-01 Gyrocopter	01	
F-WYDJ	Massemin JM-01 Gyrocopter	01	
F-WYDK	Debout AD-01 Gyrocopter	01	
F-WYDL	Callaugene JC-01 Gyrocopter	01	
F-WYDM	Lapierre Bensen RL-01 Gyroglider	01	
F-WYDN	Clerc JMC-01 Gyrocopter	01	
F-WYDO	Audrouhin AAG Gyrocopter	01, later 3	
F-WYDP	Bastet RB-01 Gyrocopter	01	
F-WYDQ	Bensen B.8MS Gyrocopter	01	
F-WYDR	Lix-01 Gyrocopter	01	
F-WYDS	Bensen B.8MH Gyrocopter	01	
F-WYDT	Henric CH-01 Gyrocopter	01	
F-WYDU	Bensen AR-01 Gyrocopter	01	
F-WYDV	Schleiss PS-01 Gyrocopter	01	
F-WYDX	Dabian GD-01 Gyrocopter	01	
F-WYDZ	Canville JMC-01 Gyrocopter	01	
F-PYEA	Colomban MC-15 Cri-Cri	4	F-WYEA
	(Formerly MC-11, MC-12B)		
F-PYEC	Rand-Robinson KR-2	4391	F-WYEC
F-PYEE	Jurca MJ.5H2 Sirocco	35	
F-PYEF	Pottier P.70S	25	F-WYEF
F-PYEG	Heintz Zenith 125	31	
F-PYEH	Brügger MB-2 Colibri	55	
F-PYEI	Evans VP-1 Volksplane	2069	
F-PYEJ	Jurca MJ.5K1 Sirocco	41	
F-PYEK	Druine D.31 Turbulent	384	
F-WYEN	Mignet HM.293	31	
F-PYEP	Jodel D.112 Club	1401	
F-PYEQ	Evans VP-1 Volksplane	V-2251	
F-PYER	Jodel D.112 Club	1434	
F-PYET	Jodel DR.1051M1 Sicile	700	
F-PYEU	Druine D.31 Turbulent	379	
F-PYEX	Parker Teenie Two	5891	
F-WYEY(2)	Dyn'Aero MCR-01 Banbi (Reservation .99)	92	
F-PYEZ	Brügger MB-2 Colibri (accident 30.8.87)	100	
F-PYFA	Jurca MJ.2 Tempête	29	
F-PYFB	Piel CP.70 Béryl	03	
F-PYFD	Jurca MJ.2D Tempête	52	
F-PYFE	Brügger MB-2 Colibri	88	F-WYFE
F-PYFH	Delaunay JDA-01	01	
F-PYFM	Ferriere LF 02 (Jodel variant)	01	
F-PYFO	Milon PMB-78 Faucon	01	
F-PYFP	Rutan Vari-Viggen SP	072	F-WYFP
F-PYFQ	Max Plan MP.205 Busard	17	
F-PYFR	Jodel D.119	1514	
F-PYFS	Jodel D.92 Bébé	686	
F-PYFT	Croses LC-6 Criquet	72	
F-PYFU	Delemontez-Cauchy DC-01	01	
F-PYFV	Croses LC-6 Criquet	22	
F-PYFX	Jurca MJ.2 Tempête	59	
F-PYFY	Piel CP.80TR	3	
F-PYFZ	Croses LC-6 Criquet	42	
F-WYGA	Carayon LC-01 Gyrocopter	01	
F-WYGB	Dedieu DF-01 Gyrocopter	01	
F-WYGD	St.Lary ISL-01 Gyrocopter	01	
F-WYGF	Laugier AL-01 Gyroglider	01	
F-WYGH	Audrouhin AAG-01 Gyrocopter	01	
F-WYGI	Daubian GD-02 Roitelet Gyrocopter	01	
F-WYGJ	Bordes RB-01 Gyrocopter	01	
F-WYGK	Odorico RO-01 Eole Gyrocopter	01	
F-WYGL	Bex DB-01 Gyrocopter	01	
F-WYGM	Rodriguez JCR-01 Gyrocopter	01	
F-WYGO	Durieux MD-01 Gyrocopter	01	
F-WYGP	Bensen B.8MP Gyrocopter	577	
F-WYGQ	Bor BJ-01 Gyrocopter	01	
F-WYGR	Bournery DB-47 Gyrocopter	01	
F-WYGS	Pequignot MP-01 Gyrocopter	01	
F-WYGT	Forich JCF-01 Gyrocopter	01	
F-WYGU	Bensen B.8MP Gyrocopter	01	
F-WYGV	Averso-Loupiac AL-01 Gyrocopter	01	
F-WYGX(2)	Montbazon BLVM-01 Gyrocopter	01	
F-WYGY	Bouchiba JB-01 Gyrocopter	01	
F-WYGZ	Meyrou JBM-01 Gyrocopter	01	(F-WYGX)
F-PYHB	Jurca MJ.5K1 Sirocco	7	
F-PYHC	Mignet HM.360	97	
F-PYHD	Mignet HM.293W	01	F-WYHD
F-PYHG(2)	Nickel-Foucard Asterix NF	001	F-WYHG
F-PYHI	Croses LC-6 Criquet	23	
F-PYHK	Jurca MJ.2D Tempête	49	
F-PYHM	Piel CP.751 Béryl	4	F-WYHM
F-PYHO	Jodel DR.1051-M1 Sicile Record	713	
F-PYHQ	Croses-Noel CN-1	01	

Regn.	Type	C/n	Prev.Id.
F-PYHR	Rutan Vari-eze	1991	
F-PYHS	Rutan Vari-eze	1697	F-WYHS
F-PYHT	Rutan Vari-eze	1384	
F-PYHV	Jodel D.119	1573	
F-PYHX	St Germain Raz-Mut	55	
F-PYHY	Jodel D.119-3L	1504	F-WYHY
F-PYHZ	Rutan Vari-eze	1694	(F-PYHG(1))
F-PYIB	Rutan Vari-eze	1609	F-WYIB
F-PYIC	Heintz-Zenith 100LR	84	
F-PYIE	Piel CP.1320 Saphir	3	F-WYIE
F-PYIF	Mudry CAP.10A	A.2	
F-PYIG	Pottier P.80S	8	
F-PYIH	Heintz Zenith 125	15	
F-PYII	Pottier P.70S	02	F-WYII
F-PYIJ	Colomban MC-15 Cri-Cri (ex MC-12)	14	F-WYIJ
F-PYIK	Pottier P.170S	004	
F-PYIM	Lucas LL-5	1	F-WYIM
			F-PYIM
			F-WYIM
F-PYIN	Tsilefski TG-01 Malech	01	
F-PYIP	Rutan Vari-eze	1457	
F-PYIS	Pottier P.70S	32	
F-PYIT	Duruble RD-03 Edelweiss 150	1	F-WYIT
F-PYIV	Brügger MB-2 Colibri	107	
F-PYIX	Piel CP.607 Diamant	11	
F-PYIY	Cassutt IIIM	548	
F-PYIZ	Cassutt IIIM	585	
F-PYJA	Croses LC-6 Criquet	75	
F-PYJC	Pottier P.100TS	01	F-WYJC
F-PYJD	Jodel DR.1052-M2	715	
F-PYJF	Fere F.3	1	
F-PYJG	Jurca MJ.2 Tempête	7W6	
F-PYJI	Dessevres-Coupe JCD	1	F-WYJI
F-PYJJ	Brügger MB-2 Colibri	149	
F-PYJK	Heintz Zenith 120	77	
F-PYJM	Minina MG.2	1	
F-PYJN	Jodel D.119	1555	
F-PYJO	Rutan Vari-eze	1775	
F-PYJP	Piel CP.80	51	
F-PYJR	Pottier P.80S	23	
F-PYJS	Piel CP.1320 Saphir	14	
F-PYJU	Pottier P.80S	19	
F-PYJV	Brügger MB-2 Colibri	114	
F-PYJX	Boyer BF	02	F-WYJX
F-PYJY	Gardan-Laverlochere GL.10	01	
F-PYJZ	Nicollier HN433 Ménestrel	37	F-WYJZ
F-PYKA	Nicollier HN433 Ménestrel	43	F-WYKA
F-PYKB	Brügger MB-2 Colibri	145	
F-PYKC	Jodel D.112 Club	1570	
F-PYKD	Croses LC.6 Criquet	83	
F-PYKE	Chasle YC.10 Migrateur	01	F-WYKE
F-PYKG	St Germain Raz Mut 440A	31	F-WYKG
F-PYKI	Mignet HM.360	158	F-WYKI
F-PYKK	Piel CP.801 Racer	17	
F-PYKO	Colomban MC-15 Cri-Cri	08	
F-PYKP	Pottier P.70S	011	
F-PYKQ	Rutan Vari-eze	1989	
F-PYKR	Piel CP.80	15	
F-PYKS	Brügger MB-2 Colibri	66	
F-PYKT	Pottier P.180S	012	F-WYKT
F-PYKU	Jodel DR.1052	704	
F-PYKV	Jodel D.92 Bébé	711	
F-PYKX	Jodel D.92 Bébé	615	
F-PYLD	Jodel D.113	1574	
F-PYLF	Croses LC.6 Criquet	79	
F-PYLG	Pottier P.170B (ex P.170S)	012	
F-PYLH	Colomban MC-15 Cri-Cri (ex MC-12)	6	
F-PYLJ	Piel CP.80	66	
F-PYLK	Piel CP.70 Beryl	06	F-WYLK
F-PYLL	Jodel D.92 Bébé	713	
F-PYLM	Stark AS-37B (originally c/n '77')	36	
F-PYLO	Brügger MB-2 Colibri	134	
F-PYLP	Jodel DR.1050M Excellence	718	
F-PYLQ	Jurca MJ5-G2 Sirocco	47	F-WYLQ
F-PYLR(2)	Evans VP-2 Volksplane	V2-0179HJ	F-WYLR

Regn.	Type	C/n	Prev.Id.
F-PYLT	Evans VP-1 Volksplane	V-1712	
F-PYLX	Pottier P.180S	06	
F-PYLY	Rutan Vari-eze	2043	
F-PYLZ	Pottier P.80S	44	F-WYLZ
F-PYMV	Stern ST-87 Europlane	33	
F-PYNA	Grinvalds G-801ST Orion	28	F-WYNA
F-PYNC	Jodel D.92 Bébé	729	
F-PYND	Cavarroc RC-01	01	
F-PYNE	Jodel D.92 Bébé	766	
F-PYNF	Brügger MB-2 Colibri (accident 23.2.97)	58	
F-PYNG	Jodel D.18	91	
F-PYNH	Brügger MB-2 Colibri	116	
F-PYNJ	Jodel D.18	20	
F-PYNK	Colomban MC-15 Cri-Cri	135	
F-PYNL	Jodel D.112 Club	1645	
F-PYNM	Cassutt IIIM	282	
F-PYNN	Colomban MC-15 Cri-Cri	269	
F-PYNP	Jodel D.18	137	
F-PYNQ	Jodel DR.1050M	753	
F-PYNR	Colomban MC-15 Cri-Cri	262	
F-PYNS	Feugray TR-200 (accident 5.6.93)	1	
F-PYNT	Colomban MC-15 Cri-Cri	47	
F-PYNU	Jodel D.112 Club	1616	
F-PYNX	Jodel D.18	119	
F-PYNY	Piel CP.320A Super Emeraude	412	
F-PYNZ	Pottier P.180S	139	F-WYNZ
F-PYOB	Pottier P.80S	38	
F-PYOC	Collard CSR-1 Tsétsé	01	F-WYOC
F-PYOD	Rutan Vari-eze	1385	
F-PYOE	Croses LC-6 Criquet	88	
F-PYOF	Rutan LongEz	1047	
F-PYOG	Evans VP-1 Volksplane	V-2589	
F-PYOI	Brügger MB-2 Colibri	180	
	(also wears marks 27-MB)		
F-PYOK	Brügger MB-2 Colibri	106	
F-PYOL	Gros-Bredelet GB-01	01	
F-PYOM	Pottier P.70S	40	
F-PYON	Jodel DR.1050 Ambassadeur	723	
F-PYOO	Rutan Vari-eze	2164	
F-PYOP	Rutan Vari-eze	2042	
F-PYOQ	Rutan LongEz	355	F-WYOQ
F-PYOT	Piel CP.320 Super Emeraude	386	
F-PYOU	Jodel D.112 Club	1386	
F-PYOX	Jodel D.113	1444	
F-PYOY	Heintz Zenith 100	52	
F-PYPB	Pottier P.80S	40	
F-PYPC	Pottier P.180S	36	F-WYPC
F-PYPD	Marquion RM-01 Helicopter	01	
F-PYPE	Courtes JCC-01	1	
F-PYPF	Stolp SA-750 Acroduster Too	359	
F-PYPH	Jurca MJ.5G Sirocco (accident 8.6.89)	30	F-WYPH
F-PYPI	Pottier P.180S	41	
F-PYPJ	Pottier P.180S	51	
F-PYPK	Mudry-Canu CAP.10B	A-4	F-WYPK
	(Built using parts of CAP.10B F-BUDN c/n 46, 1983)		
F-PYPL	Fournier RF-7	02	
F-PYPM	Colomban MC-15 Cri-Cri	20	
F-PYPN	Colomban MC-15 Cri-Cri	74	
F-PYPO	Brügger MB-2 Colibri	87	
F-PYPP	Evans VP-1 Volksplane	2258	F-WYPP
F-PYPQ	Piel CP.80SC (accident 24.5.93)	02	
F-PYPR	Jurca MJ.5L2 Sirocco	37	
F-PYPT	Jodel D.119	1563	
F-PYPY	Rutan LongEz	1163	F-WYPY
F-PYPZ	Piel CP.605C Diamant	45	
F-PYQA	Stern/Staudt ST-80 Balade	01	
F-PYQC	Proust Lespace Helicopter	001	F-WYQC
F-PYQD	Colomban MC-15 Cri-Cri	177	
F-PYQE	Rutan LongEz	809	
F-PYQF	Jodel D.92 Bébé	725	
F-PYQG	Croses LC-6 Criquet	69	
F-PYQI	Pottier P.180S (accident 30.4.90)	34	
F-PYQJ	Jodel D.112 Club	1521	
F-PYQK	Colomban MC-12 Cri-Cri	46	
F-PYQL	Rutan Vari-eze	2010	

Regn.	Type	C/n	Prev.Id.
F-PYQM	Jodel D.18	01	(F-WZDH)
F-PYQN(2)	Rutan Vari-eze	2134	
F-PYQO	Piel CP.605B Super Diamant	21	
F-PYQP	Colomban MC-15 Cri-Cri	10	
F-PYQQ	WAR P-47 Thunderbolt	71	
F-PYQS	Lendepergt LP-01 Sibylle	01	
F-PYQT	Quaissard GQ Monogast	01	F-WYQT
F-WYQU	Quickie Q2 (Reservation)	01	
F-PYQV	Brochet MB-72	9	F-BGTG
F-PYQX	Mignet HM-384	1235	
F-PYQY	Jodel D.119TK	04	

The following registration batches, suffixed (2), were originally used by ULMs but were re-allocated as shown from 1985 onwards:

Regn.	Type	C/n	Prev.Id.
F-WYRA(2)	Bensen-Francois B-PF Gyrocopter	1	
F-WYRB(2)	Averso AAD La Guepe Gyrocopter	01	
F-WYRC(2)	Gros GG-01 Gyrocopter	01	
F-WYRD(2)	Phoenix Gyrocopter	01	
F-WYRE(2)	Lejeune RL Gyrocopter	02	
F-WYRF(2)	Raymond RR-01 Gyrocopter	01	
F-WYRG(2)	Varga VJM-01 Gyrocopter	01	
F-WYRH(2)	Bensen-Germain BG Gyrocopter	1	
F-WYRI(2)	Rameil RF-01 Gyrocopter	01	
F-WYRJ(2)	Rodrigue-Souza SDDS Gyrocopter	001	
F-WYRK(2)	Bensen-SENA CP Gyrocopter	01	
F-WYRL(2)	Roy RJ-01 Gyrocopter	01	
F-WYRM(2)	Santos Marques SM Gyrocopter	1	
F-WYRN(2)	Castagnet SLC-11 Gyrocopter	1	
F-WYRO(2)	Beillard Avril Gyrocopter	001	
F-WYRP(2)	Bouchiba JB Gyrocopter	03	
F-WYRQ(2)	Bensen-Ruchonnet B.8M-BR Gyrocopter	1	
F-WYRR(2)	Doleac DJP-01 Space Gyrocopter	01	
F-WYRS(2)	Averso AX Le Guepard Gyrcopter	02	
F-WYRT(2)	Bot BF-2 Gyrocopter	1	
F-WYRU(2)	Fournier FAA Gyrocopter	01	
F-WYRV(2)	Cros CM-01 Gyrocopter	01	
F-WYRX(2)	Dougnac CD-01 Libellule Gyrocopter	01	
F-WYRY(2)	Labit LR Gyrocopter	2	
F-WYRZ(2)	Baudry-Bourgon-Bouchet-Lachaise BBBL	1	
F-PYSA(2)	Piel CP.80	59	
F-PYSB(2)	Parker Teenie Two	5-1203	
F-PYSC(2)	Jodel D.119 (ex D.112)	1579	
F-PYSE(2)	Pottier P.180S	48	
F-PYSF(2)	Rutan LongEz	1433	
F-PYSG(2)	Brügger MB-2 Colibri	175	
F-PYSH(2)	Colomban MC-15 Cri-Cri	127	
F-PYSJ(2)	Pottier P.80S	50	
F-PYSK(2)	Colomban MC-15 Cri-Cri	336	
F-PYSL(2)	Jurca MJ.5K1 Sirocco	57	
F-PYSM(2)	Rutan Vari-eze	2048	
F-PYSN(2)	Colomban MC-15 Cri-Cri	65	
F-PYSO(2)	Piel CP.1320D Saphir	18	
F-PYSR(2)	Jodel D.92 Bébé	84	
F-PYSS(2)	Piel CP.70 Béryl	7	
F-PYST(2)	Pottier P.70S	47	
F-PYSU(2)	Jodel D.92 Bébé	746	
F-PYSV(2)	Stolp SA.300 Starduster Too	1677	
F-PYSY(2)	Rutan LongEz	1094	
F-PYTA(2)	Mignet HM-8	L-1	F-WYTA
F-PYTB(2)	Sauzeau Eres-II Coquin	01	F-WYTB
F-PYTC(2)	Colomban MC-15 Cri-Cri	104	
F-PYTD(2)	Lucas L-5	4	
F-PYTG(2)	Leglaive-Gautier LG-150	01	F-WYTG
F-PYTH(2)	Colomban MC-15 Cri-Cri	156	
F-PYTI (2)	Jodel DR.1051M	762	
F-PYTJ (2)	Descatoire CD-01 Astuss	01	
F-PYTL(2)	Pottier P.80S	48	
F-PYTM(2)	Jodel D.18 (accident 18.3.90)	9	
F-PYTN(2)	Jurca MJ.5K1 Sirocco	92	
F-PYTO(2)	Jodel DR.1050M	745	
F-PYTP(2)	Piel CP.751B Béryl	02	
F-PYTQ (2)	Pena Capena	02	
F-PYTR (2)	Brügger MB-2 Colibri	115	
F-PYTT (2)	Gatard AG-02SP Poussin	22	
F-PYTU (2)	Mudry CAP.10B	A-3	
F-PYTV (2)	Rutan Vari-eze	2008	F-WYTV
F-PYTX (2)	Colomban MC-15 Cri-Cri	248	
F-PYTY (2)	Colomban MC-15 Cri-Cri	278	
F-PYTZ (2)	Rutan LongEz	2117	
F-WYUA	Bensen B.8MJ Gyrocopter	01	
F-WYUB	Franclet PF-01 Gyrocopter	01	
F-WYUC	Soulignac BS-01 Gyrocopter	01	
F-WYUD	Loupiac AL Gyrocopter	02	
F-WYUE	Sers AS-01 Gyrocopter	01	
F-WYUF	Antome Gyrocopter	01	
F-WYUG	Durand Gyrocopter	01	
F-WYUH	Baldy LB-01 Gyrocopter	01	
F-WYUI	Ocon AO-01 Gyrocopter	01	
F-WYUJ	Idrac A-1 Gyrocopter	02	
F-WYUK	Galea BG-01 Gyrocopter	01	
F-WYUL	Jurquet JJ-01 Gyrocopter	01	
F-WYUM	Puente Gyrocopter	01	
F-WYUN	Chrysalide Gyrocopter	01	
F-WYUO	Bonnafous-Chapuis BC-1 Gyrocopter	1	
F-WYUP	Paques PB-8 Gyrocopter	1	
F-WYUQ	Doucet DR-01 Gyrocopter	01	
F-WYUR	Bensen DB Gyrocopter	001	
F-WYUS	Bensen-Clisson BC-1 Gyrocopter	01	
F-WYUT	Bensen LG Gyrocopter	1	
F-WYUU	Bensen-Miquel B-CM Gyrocopter	1	
F-WYUV	Bensen B-8 Gyrocopter (same c/n as F-WREF)	8-104100	
F-WYUX	Zago AZ-01 Gyrocopter	01	
F-WYUY	Rives RR-01 Gyrocopter	01	
F-WYUZ	Andre JPA-01 Gyrocopter	001	
F-PYVA (2)	Colomban MC-15 Cri-Cri	371	
F-PYVB (2)	Jodel DR.1050M	765	
F-PYVC (2)	Piel CP.321 Super Emeraude	400	
F-PYVD (2)	Colomban MC-15 Cri-Cri	16	
F-PYVE (2)	WAR P-47D Thunderbolt	95	F-WYVE
F-PYVG (2)	Jodel D.113 (ex D.112)	1231	
F-PYVH (2)	Rutan LongEz	1218	
F-PYVI (2)	K & S Jungster 1	J1-76003R	F-WYVI
F-PYVJ (2)	Verges VJ-01 Gringo	01	
F-PYVK (2)	Colomban MC-15 Cri-Cri	160	
F-PYVL (2)	Pottier P.180S	97	
F-PYVM (2)	Jodel D.19	01	
F-PYVN (2)	Colomban MC-15 Cri-Cri	194	F-WYVN
F-PYVO (2)	Pottier P.180S	46	F-WYVO
F-PYVP (2)	Viking Dragonfly Mk.2	511	
F-PYVQ (2)	Colomban MC-15 Cri-Cri	77	
F-PYVS (2)	Adam RA.14 Loisirs	17	F-PGKC
F-PYVT (2)	Jurca MJ.2E Tempête	18	LX-PUT F-PNUD
F-PYVV (2)	Brügger MB-2 Colibri	104	
F-PYVY (2)	Jodel D.18	06	
F-PYVZ (2)	Colomban MC-15 Cri-Cri	400	
F-PYXA (2)	Pitts S-1D Special	7-0492	F-WYXA
F-PYXB (2)	Starck AS.71	32R	F-WYXB
F-PYXC (2)	Kreimendahl Shoestring	054	F-WYXC "F-WXYC"
F-PYXD (2)	Pottier P.180S	119	
F-PYXE (2)	Nicollier HN434 Super Ménestrel	1	
F-PYXF (2)	Pottier P.180S	24	
F-PYXG (2)	Colomban MC-15 Cri-Cri	180	
F-PYXH (2)	Jodel DR.1050M	733	
F-PYXJ (2)	Rutan Vari-eze	2092	
F-PYXK (2)	Jodel D.150-B3 Mascaret	106	
F-PYXL (2)	Jodel D.18	33	
F-PYXM (2)	Rutan LongEz	1688	
F-PYXN (2)	Piel CP.320 Super Emeraude	415	
F-PYXO (2)	Piel CP.80	20	
F-PYXP (2)	Jodel D.18	80	
F-PYXQ (2)	Chudzik CC-01 (ULM)	01	F-WYXQ "F-WYRB(1)"
F-PYXS (2)	Heintz Zenith 150 Tri-Z	3-111	F-WYXS
F-PYXT (2)	Viking Dragonfly Mk-3TH	551	
F-PYXU (2)	Jodel DR.1050M	769	
F-PYXV (2)	Jodel DR.1051M	729	
F-PYXX (2)	Jodel D.19	2	
F-PYXY (2)	Colomban MC-15 Cri-Cri	264	F-WYXY
F-PYXZ (2)	Jodel D.92 Bébé	17	

Regn.	Type	C/n	Prev.Id.
F-PYYA (2)	Coupe-Brault JCFB 01	1	
F-PYYB (2)	Piel CP.80	62	
F-PYYC (2)	Pottier P.180S	91	F-WYYC
F-PYYE (2)	Croses LC-6 Criquet	116	
F-PYYF (2)	Piel CP.320 Super Emeraude	383	
F-PYYG (2)	Van's RV-4	474	F-WYYG
F-PYYH (2)	Pottier P.80S	18	
F-PYYI (2)	Rutan LongEz	1575	
F-PYYJ (2)	Colomban MC-15 Cri-Cri	344	
F-PYYK (2)	Colomban MC-15 Cri-Cri	86	
F-PYYL (2)	Jodel D.92 Bébé (accident 14.1.90)	645	
F-PYYM (2)	Piel CP.801	72	
F-PYYN (2)	Brügger MB-2 Colibri	228	
F-WYYO (2)	Feugray TR260 Faucon	001-J	
F-PYYP (2)	Jodel D.18	82	
F-PYYQ (2)	Jodel D.18V	84	
F-PYYR (2)	Croses LC-6 Criquet	62	
F-WYYS (2)	HLM-01 Helicopter	01 or 02 ?	
F-PYYT (2)	Viking Dragonfly Mk2	103	F-WYYT
F-PYYU (2)	Motoplaneur Clave Le Goeland	01	
F-PYYV (2)	Rutan LongEz	1046	
F-PYYX (2)	Pottier P.180S	98	
F-PYYY (2)	Druine D.31 Turbulent	356	
F-PYYZ (2)	Rutan Vari-eze	1959	
F-PYZB (2)	Rutan Vari-eze	2013	
F-PYZC (2)	Legallois RL	1	
F-PYZD (2)	Rutan LongEz	624	
F-PYZE (2)	Pottier P.180S	80	
F-PYZF (2)	Rutan LongEz	734	
F-PYZG (2)	Rutan LongEz (accident 16.6.90)	1703	
F-PYZH (2)	Jodel DR.1050M	766	F-WYZH
F-PYZI (2)	SA.300 Starduster Too	1690	
F-PYZJ (2)	Jodel DR.1050M	764	
F-PYZK (2)	Minina MG.3 Harmattan	001	
F-PYZL (2)	Pottier P.180S	66	F-WYZL
F-PYZO (2)	Viking Dragonfly Mk.2	1007	
F-PYZP (2)	Jodel D.119V	1569	
F-PYZR (2)	Brugger MB.2 Colibri	168	
F-PYZS (2)	Piel CP.80	18	
F-PYZT (2)	Chaboud CJC-01	01	
F-PYZU (2)	Rutan Vari-eze	1850	
F-PYZV (2)	Monnet Moni	327	F-WYZV
F-PYZX (2)	Pottier P.80S	57	
F-PYZY (2)	Pottier P.180S	67	
F-PZAG	Jurca MJ.2H Tempête	30	
F-PZAR	Darcissac-Grinvalds DG-87 Goëland (Res.)	04	
F-PZAZ	Piel CP.320 Super Emeraude	454	
F-PZBA	Jodel D.18	247	
F-PZBB	Jodel D.19	108T	
F-WZBC (3)	SOFCA Paramoteur Agrion	0001	
F-WZBD (3)	SOFCA Paramoteur Agrion	1	
F-WZBG (2)	SOFCA Paramoteur Agrion	002	
F-WZBH (2)	SOGCA Paramoteur Agrion	003	
F-PZBM	Colomban MC-15 Cri-Cri	429	F-WZBM
F-PZBO	Piel CP.1321 Saphir	24	
F-PZBP	Jodel D.119	1161	
F-PZBQ	Jodel D.119T	05-A	F-WZBQ (F-PART)
F-PZBR	De La Calle CRT-01 Amphibian	01	F-WZBR
F-PZBS	Colomban MC-15 Cri-Cri	417	
F-PZBT	Pottier P.180S	44	
F-WZBU	Feugray (Tech'Aero) TR.300 (Reservation)	3	
F-PZBV	Rutan Vari-eze	1939	F-WZBV
F-PZBX	Rutan LongEz	1565	
F-PZBY	Jodel DR.1053M	746	
F-PZBZ	Jodel D.18	183	
F-WZEA	Borel JPB-30 Gyrocopter	01	
F-WZEB	Mompo AM-01 Gyrocopter	01	
F-WZEC	Le Bauzec Moustique Gyrocopter	01	
F-WZED	Combon-Bonnafous BCGyrocopter	02	
F-WZEE	Averso Train'Air XA-03 Gyrocopter	03	
F-WZEF	Doleac DJP-2 Gyrocopter	01	
F-WZEG	Revol RG Gyrocopter	01	
F-WZEH	Savez SGB Gyrocopter	01	
F-WZEI	Cobra Gyrocopter	01	

Regn.	Type	C/n	Prev.Id.
F-WZEJ	Verdan VG-1 Gyrocopter	01	
F-WZEK	Domme JD Gyrocopter	01	
F-WZEL	Naja Gyrocopter	01	
F-WZEM	Poma Gyrocopter	001	
F-WZEN	Moustic Gyrocopter	01	
F-WZEO	Strupp Gyrocopter	01	
F-WZEP	Lix Condor Gyrocopter	002	
F-WZEQ	Durant DJL Gyrocopter	03	
F-WZER	Chanet JCC.2000 Gyrocopter	1	
F-WZES	Gregnanin GE Gyrocopter	01	
F-WZET	Franck Gyrocopter	001	
F-WZEU	Mono 87 Gyrocopter	001	
F-WZEV	HRP Gyrocopter	01	
F-WZEX	Stuani SR-1 Gyrocopter	01	
F-WZEY	Weinbrenner JW Gyrocopter	03	
F-WZEZ	Bouche BB Gyrocopter	01	
F-PZGL	Valladeau RV-12 (Polikarpov 1-15 replica)	01	
F-WZGM	Carro Quickie 1 (Reservation)	C-1	
F-PZGN	Wittmann W.8 Tailwind	622	
F-PZGO	Colomban MC-15 Cri-Cri	207	
F-PZGP	Pottier P.180S	159	
F-PZGQ	Adam RA-14 Loisirs	132	F-PAHD
F-PZGR	Jodel D.112 Club	1678	
F-PZGS	Pottier P.180S	161	F-WZGS
F-PZGT	Loriot DG-01	01	
F-PZGU	Brändli BX-2 Cherry (Reservation)	58	
F-PZGV	Chasle YC-320 (Reservation)	001	
F-PZGX	Rand-Robinson KR-2	7975	
F-PZGZ	Denize RD.205 Raid Driver	2	
F-WZHA	AB-53 Gyrocopter	0	
F-WZHB	Averso AX-02 Gyrocopter	17	
F-WZHC	Averso AX-02 Gyrocopter	19	
F-WZHD	Pouilles GP Gyrocopter	01	
F-WZHE	Hoffmann VHB-1 Gyrocopter	01	
F-WZHF	Huvier HR-1 Gyrocopter	02-M	
F-WZHG	AU SR Gyrocopter	01	
F-WZHH	Vandenbulke VG-1 Gyrocopter	01	
F-WZHI	Faucher PF-1 Gyrocopter	001	
F-WZHJ	Darrozes MD Gyrocopter	01	
F-WZHK	Le Bigourdin Gyrocopter	1	
F-WZHL	Colibri Gyrocopter	01	
F-WZHM	Bensen-Vandamme B-VG Gyrocopter	01	
F-WZHN	Tessier YT-1 Gyrocopter	2	
F-WZHO	Revol GR Gyrocopter	02	
F-WZHP	AX-1 Gyrocopter	01	
F-WZHQ	Bonnafous BC-2 Gyrocopter	02	
F-WZHR	Krauss BK-1 Gyrocopter	1	
F-WZHS	Krauss GK-1	1	
F-WZHT	Averso AX-02 Gyrocopter	18	
F-WZHU	JF-1 Gyrocopter	01	
F-WZHV	Aubert AJL-2 Gyrocopter	001	
F-WZHX	Courgey HC-1 Gyrocopter	001	
F-WZHY	Ingrassia IS-1 Gyrocopter	1	
F-PZHZ	Mercier IX Gyrocopter	01	F-WZHZ
F-WZID	2CV Eau Volante	unkn	
F-PZIG	Jurca MJ.2P Tempête (Reservation)	28	
F-PZIK	Desjardins D-01 Ibis	01	F-WZIK
F-PZIL	Piel CP.605B Super Diamant	48	
F-PZIM	Croses LC-6 Criquet	97	
F-PZIN	Jurca MJ.2E Tempête	74	
F-PZIO	Croses LC-10 Criquet	32	
F-PZIP	Piel CP.803	70	
F-PZIQ	Colomban MC-15 Cri-Cri	282	F-WZIQ
F-PZIT	Evans VP-1 Volksplane	V-1583	
F-PZIU	Pottier PRM.180	045	
F-PZIV	Colomban MC-15 Cri-Cri	41	F-WZIV
F-PZIZ	Brügger MB-2 Colibri	209	
F-WZJG	Auricoste AA-01 Gyrocopter	unkn	
F-PZLD	Salis AJBS 10 (Modified CAP 10)	01	F-WZLD
F-WZLH(3)	Rotorway Executive	938	
F-WZLI (3)	Geiser Zeppy Airship	01	
F-PZLJ	Jodel D.112 Club	125	F-PKMM
F-PZLL	Constantini STC-1 Magic	1	
F-PZLM	Serleg 225EX Amphibian	001	F-WZLM
F-WZLN(2)	Lanot Aquitain	003	

Regn.	Type	C/n	Prev.Id.
F-WZLP(2)	Lanot Aquitain	002	
F-WZLS(4)	Grillon 120	01	(F-GESP)
F-WZLU	Gardan GY-120 Microlight	001	
F-WZLY	Homet S-10	unkn	
F-WZLZ	Loravia ULI-2	01	
F-PZMA	Heintz Zenith 100CP	2123	
F-PZMB	Jodel D.92 Bébé	730	
F-PZMC	Gatard AG-02 Poussin	34	
F-PZMD	Pottier P.180S	47	
F-PZMF	Colomban MC-15 Cri-Cri	51	
F-WZMG	Rutan Defiant	119	
F-PZMH	Pottier P.180S	144	F-WZMH
F-PZMI	Lacroix L-16 Autoplan	01	
F-PZMJ	Dupau MD-12 Papillon	01	
F-PZMK	Dedon Quickie 2	02-F	
F-PZML	Colomban MC-15 Cri-Cri	440	
F-PZMM	Rutan Vari-eze (Reservation)	1847	
F-PZMN	Colomban MC-15 Cri-Cri	68	
F-PZMO	Kieger AK-01	01	
F-PZMP	Grinvalds G-801 Orion (accident)	9	
F-PZMQ	Taylor JT.2 Titch	108	
F-PZMT	Rutan LongEz	7801L	
F-PZMU	Jodel D.18	34	
F-PZMV	Nicollier HN-700 Ménestrel II	001	
F-PZMZ	Viking Dragonfly Mk.1	678	
F-WZNL	Capdevielle CPCL Gyrocopter	1	
F-WZNM	Sudre SRE Gyrocopter	01	
F-WZNN	Guillaume DG Gyrocopter	01	
F-WZNO	Darmanne Gyrocopter	01	
F-WZNP	Fournier FAA Gyrocopter	02	
F-WZNQ	GG-200 Gyrocopter	01	
F-WZNR	Averso AX-02 Gyrocopter	8	
F-WZNS	Lambour-Deudon LLD Gyrocopter	1	
F-WZNT	Duhamel-Greaux-Huber DGH-01 Gyrocopter	01	
F-WZNU	Duhamel-Greaux-Huber DGH-02 Gyrocopter	01	
F-WZNX	Coqu Bensen B-8 Gyrocopter	C-1	
F-WZNY	Averso AX-02 Gyrocopter	10	
F-WZNZ	Averso AX-02 Gyrocopter	11	
F-WZOA(2)	Hard HP Gyrocopter	01	
F-PZOB(1)	Le Ventilateur ULM	01	
F-PZOB(2)	Van's RV-4 (Reservation)	3091	
F-WZOC(2)	Mono LG Gyrocopter	01	
F-WZOD(2)	Blandy AB-1 Gyrocopter	01	
F-WZOE(2)	Lejeune RL-2 Gyrocopter	03	
F-WZOF(2)	HIR-1 Gyrocopter	01	
F-WZOG(2)	Bluebird Gyrocopter	01	
F-WZOH(2)	Redbird Gyrocopter	01	
F-WZOI(2)	Averso AX-02 Gyrocopter	1	
F-WZOJ(2)	Bensen B-8JLG Gyrocopter (w/o 27.1.91?)	1	
F-WZOK(2)	HTV Gyrocopter	2	
F-WZOL(2)	Liberty Gyrocopter	01	
F-WZOM(2)	Cena CP-02 Gyrocopter	1	
F-WZON(2)	Averso AX-02 Gyrocopter	2	
F-WZOO(2)	Beart JMB-1 Gyrocopter	01	
F-WZOP(2)	Averso AX-02 Gyrocopter	4	
F-WZOQ(2)	Gil Gyrocopter	01	
F-WZOT(2)	Cros CM-2 Gyrocopter	02	
F-WZOU(2)	Chevallot Bensen B-8	CD-01	
F-WZOV(2)	Bourgue BP-01 Gyrocopter	01	
F-WZOY(2)	Barbier CB Gyrocopter	01	
F-WZOZ(2)	Averso AX-02 Gyrocopter	5	
F-PZPA(2)	Chambon-Koenig CK-01 Profil	001	F-WZPA
F-PZPB(2)	Jodel D.18	43	F-WZPB
F-PZPD	Gatard AG-02CR Poussin	40	
F-PZPE	Kreimendahl K-10 Shoestring	48	
F-PZPF(2)	Colomban MC-15 Cri-Cri	84	
F-PZPG(2)	Jodel D.112 Club	767	F-PCDV
F-PZPH(2)	Pottier P.180S (accident 31.12.89)	99	
F-PZPI(2)	Pottier P.180S	25	
F-PZPJ(2)	Brügger MB-2 Colibri	172	
F-PZPK(2)	Colomban MC-15 Cri-Cri	81	
F-PZPM(2)	Dopouridis DV.219 (Jodel variant)	01	F-WZPM
F-PZPN(2)	Rutan LongEz	2115	
F-PZPO(2)	Jurca MJ.7 Gnatsum	2	F-WZPO
F-PZPP(2)	Jodel D.19	15T	F-WZPP
F-PZPQ(2)	Daurelle AD-01	01	
F-PZPR(2)	Colomban MC-15 Cri-Cri	306	
F-PZPS(2)	Jodel D.18	124	
F-PZPT(2)	Jodel DR.100 Ambassadeur	763	
F-PZPU(2)	Jodel D.92 Bébé	758	
F-PZPV(2)	Pottier P.180S	32	F-WZPV
F-PZPX(2)	Jodel D.18	112	
F-PZPY(2)	Croses LC-6 Criquet	59	
F-PZPZ(2)	Landray GL-07	01	
F-WZQA(2)	Bernardeau Bensen B-8B Gyrocopter	B-1	
F-WZQB(2)	Portal-Revertegat HRP Gyrocopter	02	
F-WZQC(2)	Averso AX-02 Gyrocopter	6	
F-WZQD(2)	Bourdon B-2 Gyrocopter	01	
F-WZQE(2)	Sanchez SB-01 Gyrocopter	1	
F-WZQF(2)	Baldy LB-02 Gyrocopter	1	
F-WZQG(2)	Bastien BH-2 Gyrocopter	01	
F-WZQH(2)	Doleac Aircopter DJP Max	03	
F-WZQI(2)	Tenneguin TT-01 Gyrocopter	01	
F-WZQK(2)	Lettinger LC Gyrocopter	01	
F-WZQL(2)	Passot MP-02 Morgon Gyrocopter	2	
F-WZQM(2)	Averso AX-04 Le Guépard Gyrocopter	01	
F-WZQN(2)	Averso AX-05 Léopard Gyrocopter	01	
F-WZQO(2)	Phénix Gyrocopter	SC-01	
F-WZQP(2)	Romero JR-1 Gyrocopter	001	
F-WZQQ(2)	Kraetter AK Gyrocopter	1	
F-WZQR(2)	Tenneguin TT-02 Gyrocopter	01	
F-WZQS(2)	Bourgues BP-02 Gyrocopter	1	
F-WZQT(2)	Fortunato ERF Gyrocopter	01	
F-WZQU(2)	Averso AX-02 Gyrocopter	7	
F-WZQV(2)	Pate NP-001 Gyrocopter	001	
F-WZQX(2)	Bond Gyrocopter	007	
F-WZQY(2)	Mousticq Gyrocopter	01	
F-WZQZ(2)	Bensen B-8 Gyrocopter	104-V1	
F-PZRA	Jodel D.92 Bébé	719	
F-PZRC	Brügger MB-2 Colibri	51	
F-PZRF	Jodel D.112 Club	1602	
F-PZRH	Croise AC-1 (1/2 scale Spitfire)	01	
F-PZRI	Evans VP-2B Volksplane	2130	
F-PZRJ	Christen Eagle II	01	
F-PZRL	Monnereau MG-01	01	
F-PZRM	Brügger MB-2 Colibri	108	
F-PZRN	Pottier P.80S	015	
F-PZRO	Pottier P.180S	77	
F-PZRP	Rutan LongEz	621	
F-PZRQ	Lucas L-5	24	F-WZRQ
F-PZRR	Croses LC-6 Criquet	104	
F-PZRT	Jodel DR.1050M (Reservation)	721	
F-PZRU	Rutan Vari-eze (Reservation)	1843	
F-PZRX	Rutan LongEz	2114	
F-PZRY	Albarde Ruty	01	F-WZRY
F-PZRZ	Evans VP-2 Volksplane	2201	
F-PZSF (2)	Pottier P.80S	28	
F-PZSG (2)	Jurca MJ.5K1 Sirocco	20	
F-PZSH (2)	Jodel D.112 Club	453	
F-PZSI (2)	Max Plan MP-207 Busard	20	F-WZSI
F-WZSK(2)	Quenaud 50	01	
F-PZSL (2)	Colomban MC-15 Cri-Cri	270	
F-PZSM (2)	Jodel DR.1053M Sicile Record	737	
F-PZSN (2)	Colomban MC-15 Cri-Cri	25	
F-PZSO (2)	Colomban MC-15 Cri-Cri	36	
F-PZSP (2)	Colomban MC-15 Cri-Cri	39	
F-PZSS (2)	Brügger MB-2 Colibri	85	
F-PZST (2)	Colomban MC-15 Cri-Cri	147	
F-PZSU (2)	Druine D.31B2 Turbulent	409	
F-PZSV (2)	Jodel DR.100A	754	
F-PZSY (2)	Rand-Robinson KR-2	5256	
F-PZSZ (2)	Pottier P.80S	58	
F-PZTA (2)	Fournier RF-5	01	F-WZTA
F-PZTB (2)	Jodel DR 1050M1 Sicile Record	744	
F-PZTC (2)	Pena Capena (Modified CAP-20)	01	F-WZTC
F-PZTD (2)	Colomban MC-15 Cri-Cri	64	F-WZTD
F-PZTE (2)	Jurca MJ.2E Tempête	43	
F-PZTF (2)	Pottier P.70S	49	
F-PZTG (2)	Colomban MC-15 Cri-Cri	113	
F-PZTI (2)	Colomban MC-15 Cri-Cri	63	

Regn.	Type	C/n	Prev.Id.
F-PZTJ (2)	Mignet HM.381 Pou-du-Ciel	85	F-WZTJ
F-PZTL (2)	Piel CP.320A Super Emeraude	382	
F-PZTM (2)	Rutan Vari-eze	277	
F-PZTN (2)	Pottier P.80SR	14	F-WZTN
F-PZTO (2)	Colomban MC-15 Cri-Cri	85	
F-PZTP (2)	Colomban MC-15 Cri-Cri	66	
F-PZTQ (2)	Taylor JT-2 Titch Mk.3	CB-5	
F-PZTR (2)	Colomban MC-15 Cri-Cri	121	
F-PZTS (2)	Evans VP-2 Volksplane	V2-1521	F-WZTS
F-WZTT (2)	Watson Windwagon	JW-573	F-PZTT
F-PZTU (2)	Colomban MC-15 Cri-Cri	27	F-WZTU / F-PZTU
F-PZTV (2)	Pottier P.180S	42	
F-PZTY (2)	Pottier P.70S	28	
F-PZTZ (2)	Druine D.31 Turbulent	358	
F-WZUA(2)	Light Aero Avid Flyer	CP84-1	
F-WZUB(2)	Light Aero Avid Flyer	263	
F-WZUD(2)	Light Aero Avid Flyer	264	
F-WZUE(2)	Janowski J-5 Marco	F-2	
F-WZUF(2)	Light Aero Avid Amphibian	24	
F-WZUG(2)	Light Aero Avid Flyer	327	
F-WZUH(2)	Light Aero Avid Flyer	422	
F-WZUI (2)	Light Aero Avid Amphibian	25	
F-WZUJ(2)	Janowski J-5 Marco	6	
F-WZUK(2)	Light Aero Avid Flyer	323	
F-WZUL(2)	Janowski J-5 Marco	8	
F-WZUM(2)	Light Aero Avid Flyer	476	
F-WZUN(2)	Light Aero Avid Flyer	541	
F-WZUO(2)	Light Aero Avid Flyer	538	
F-WZUP(2)	Light Aero Avid Flyer	421	
F-WZUQ(2)	Light Aero Avid Flyer	473	
F-WZUR(2)	Light Aero Avid Flyer	471	
F-WZUS(2)	Light Aero Avid Flyer	542	
F-WZUT(2)	Light Aero Avid Flyer	424	
F-WZUU(2)	Light Aero Avid Flyer	319	
F-PZUV	Light Aero Avid Flyer	475	F-WZUV(2)
F-WZUX(2)	Light Aero Avid Amphibian	41	
F-WZUY(2)	Light Aero Avid Flyer	647	
F-WZUZ(2)	Light Aero Avid Flyer	694	
F-WZVA(2)	Bensen GGMS Gyrocopter	01	
F-WZVB(2)	Sicard JMS-01 Gyrocopter	01	
F-WZVC(2)	Onyx Gyrocopter	01	
F-WZVD(2)	Hernando FH-1 Gyrocopter	1	
F-WZVE(2)	Condomine YC-2 Gyrocopter	1	
F-WZVF(2)	Mouchel BM-01 Gyrocopter	01	
F-WZVG(2)	Cauchy CM-01 Gyrocopter	01	
F-WZVH(2)	Flip Gyrocopter	1	
F-WZVI (2)	Hostein AH-01 Gyrocopter	01	
F-WZVJ(2)	Laboye-Meygret LMN-1 Gyrocopter	01	
F-WZVK(2)	Viala HTV Gyrocopter	1	
F-WZVL(2)	Bouchiba JB Gyrocopter	2	
F-WZVM(2)	Mace MA-01 Gyrocopter	01	
F-WZVN(2)	Proust DP-3 Gyrocopter	1	
F-WZVO(2)	Odorico OR-02 Gyrocopter	02	
F-WZVP(2)	Beaudoin GB-01 Beaugiro	01	
F-WZVQ(2)	Zamponi CZ-01 Gyrocopter	01	
F-WZVR(2)	Pascal JP-01 Gyrocopter	01	
F-WZVS(2)	Seidner AS-100 Gyrocopter	01	
F-WZVT(2)	Passot MP-01 Gyrocopter	1	
F-WZVU(2)	Lejeune RL-01 Gyrocopter	01	
F-WZVV(2)	Lambelin Bensen BML Gyrocopter	001	
F-WZVX(2)	Desauge Bensen JD Gyrocopter	01	
F-WZVY(2)	Oudoul GO Gyrocopter	1	
F-WZVZ(2)	Dumon B-RD Gyrocopter	1	
F-PZXD (2)	ACBA-4 Pipit Véloce	01	
F-PZXE (2)	Croses EC-7 Tous Terrains	01	F-PPPM ?
F-PZXF (2)	Jodel D.119T	1562	
F-PZXH (2)	Nicollier HN-434 Super Ménestrel	36	
F-PZXI (2)	Lucas L-5	28	F-WZXI
F-PZXJ (2)	Colomban MC-15 Cri-Cri	268	F-WZXJ
F-PZXK (2)	Rutan Cozy	310	
F-PZXL (2)	Zenair CH-600 Zodiac	6-1001	F-WZXL
F-PZXM (2)	Colomban MC-15 Cri-Cri	443	
F-PZXN (2)	Pottier P.180S	88	F-WZXN
F-PZXO (2)	Jodel D.18	07	
F-PZXQ (2)	Rutan Vari-eze	2200	
F-PZXR (2)	Jodel D.18	92	
F-PZXT (2)	Descubes III	01	
F-PZXU (2)	Colomban MC-15 Cri-Cri (Reservation)	352	
F-PZXV (2)	Colomban MC-15 Cri-Cri (Reservation)	247	
F-WZXX (2)	Dirigeable DIPA Aeromodelisme Balloon	unkn	
F-WZXY (2)	Dirigeable DIPA Aeromodelisme Balloon	unkn	
F-PZXZ (2)	Viking Dragonfly Mk.2 (SB-2)	771	
F-WZYA	Portespane DP Requin Blanc Gyrocopter	01	
F-PZYB	Averso AX-02 Guepard Gyrocopter	09	F-WZYB
F-WZYC	Deluc MD-2 Black Panther Gyrocopter	01	
F-WZYD	Gyro Club Gascon GCG-2 Gyrocopter	01	
F-WZYE	Carletti Bensen B-8AC Gyrocopter	01	
F-WZYF	Casset RC-01 Gyrocopter	01	
F-WZYG	Lagarde AL-01 Gyrocopter	01	
F-WZYH	Laboye Bensen B-8LH Gyrocopter	006	
F-WZYI	CD Gyrocopter	01	
F-WZYJ	Averso AX-02 Gyrocopter	12	
F-PZYK	Jodel DR.1054M (ex DR.1051)	757-13A	
F-WZYL	Telegoni ATM-01 Gyrocopter	1	
F-WZYM	Meygret CHM-2 Gyrocopter	01	
F-WZYN	Fuertes JF-1 Gyrocopter	1	
F-WZYO	Gerard Bensen G-800MV Gyrocopter	GR-01	
F-WZYP	Averso AX-02 Gyrocopter	13	
F-WZYQ	Averso AX-02 Gyrocopter	14	
F-WZYR	Averso AX-02 Gyrocopter	15	
F-WZYS	Benoit L-1 Gyrocopter	1	
F-WZYT	Arnould JPA-001 Gyrocopter	001	
F-WZYU	Averso AX-02 Gyrocopter	16	
F-WZYV	Rabillard CR-1 Gyrocopter	01	
F-WZYX	Duhamel-Greaux-Hubert DGH-03 Gyrocopter	01	
F-WZYY	Paraire PG Gyrocopter	01	
F-WZYZ	Arnaud AR-1 Gyrocopter	01	
F-PZZL	Piel CP.615 Diamant	46	
F-PZZM	Jodel D.18	216	
F-PZZN	Jodel DR.1051	786	
F-PZZO	Brändli BX-2 Cherry	28	F-WZZO
F-PZZP	Jodel D.18	141	
F-PZZQ	Jurca MJ.5 Sirocco	46	
F-PZZR	Lannier LA Bengali	01	
F-PZZS	Colomban MC-15 Cri-Cri	94	F-WZZS
F-WZZY	Robin DR.400/200i	2354	

CURRENT TEST REGISTRATIONS

F-WWAI	Airbus A.340-311 (Stored)	001	
F-WWEY	Aeritalia/SNIAS ATR-72-201	098	
F-WWFA-Z	Dassault for Falcon 900s		
F-WWFT	Airbus A.320-231	001	F-WWAI
F-WWHA-Z	Dassault for Falcon 50s		
F-WWMA-W	Dassault for Falcon 2000s		
F-WWMX-Z	Aerotech Europe for CAP.222s		
F-WWNG-I	Euravial for RF-47s		
F-WWOA-Z	Eurocopter/Aérospatiale		
F-WWPA	Eurocopter EC-120 Colibri	01	
F-WWPB-Z	Eurocopter/Aérospatiale		
F-WWRA-Z	SOCATA for TB- and TBM- series		
F-WWUX-Y	Dyn'Aero for MCR-01s		
F-WWVA-Z	Dassault for Falcon 2000s		

GLIDERS AND MOTOR GLIDERS

Most recently reported tail codes are shown next to the registration where space permits.

Regn.	Type	C/n	Prev.Id.
F-CAAB	Scheibe SF-28A Tandem-Falke	5772	PH-635
			PH-TER
			D-KCLB
F-CAAH	Arsenal 4111	02	
F-CAAZ	Eiri PIK-20E	20274	
F-CABI	Glaser Dirks DG-200	2-117	
F-CABK	Schleicher ASW-19B	19309	
F-CABO	Air 100	4	
F-CABY	Breguet 900	1	
F-CACC	Grob G.103 Twin Astir II	3515	
F-CACI-K06	Glaser Dirks DG-200/17	2-121/1724	
F-CACJ	Wassmer WA.22A Super Javelot	143	Fr.AF
F-CACK	Wassmer WA.30 Bijave	232	Fr.AF
F-CACL	Wassmer WA.22A Super Javelot	115	Fr.AF
F-CACM	Wassmer WA.22A Super Javelot	124	Fr.AF
F-CACN	ICA/Brasov IS.28B2	224	
F-CADC	Air 100	12	
F-CADE	Avialsa-Scheibe A.60 Fauconnet	135K	
F-CADN	Grob G.102/77J Astir Jeans	2099	
F-CADO	Grob G.102/77J Astir Jeans	2 03	
F-CADP	Grob G.103 Twin Astir	3197	
F-CADQ(2)	Grob G.102/77J Astir Jeans	2248	D-2396
F-CADS(2)	Grob G.102/77J Astir Jeans	unkn	
F-CADT(2)	Rolladen-Schneider LS-4	4212	BGA2933/ETF
F-CAEA	Wassmer WA.22 Super Javelot	126	Fr.AF
F-CAEC	Grob G.102/77J Astir CS Jeans	2135	
F-CAEM	Grob G.102/77J Astir CS Jeans	2061	D-7579
F-CAEN	Rolladen-Schneider LS-6	6067	F-WAEN(2)
			D-1504
F-CAEO	Rolladen-Schneider LS-IC	113	D-1044
F-CAEQ-37	Rolladen-Schneider LS-4	4264	D-5530
F-CAES	Wassmer WA.30 Bijave	162	Fr.AF
F-CAFA	Scheibe SF-28A Tandem-Falke	5747	HB-2029
			D-KOEY
F-CAFI	Carmam M.100S Mésange	57	OO-ZFE
			F-CDDN
F-CAFJ	Rolladen-Schneider LS-1D	137	OO-ZMH
F-CAFK	SZD-50-3 Puchacz	B-2060	
F-CAFL	Scheibe SF-28A Tandem-Falke	5712	OE-9069
			D-KDAL
F-CAFZ	Wassmer WA.22A	151	Fr.AF
F-CAGI	Wassmer WA.22A	153	Fr.AF
F-CAGK	Wassmer WA.30 Bijave	231	Fr.AF
F-CAGL	Fauvel AV.22S	2	
F-CAGQ	Air 102	26	
F-CAGU	Breguet 904S	11	F-CCFU
F-CAHD	Caudron C.800	230	
F-CAHJ	Fournier RF-9	1	
F-CAHL(2)	Fournier RF-9	9	
F-CAHM(2)	Fournier RF-9	3	
F-CAHP(2)	Fournier RF-9	5	
F-CAHY	Fournier RF-9	2	
F-CAIA	Issoire D.77 Iris	01	F-WAQA
F-CAIC	Schempp-Hirth Ventus A	298	F-WAIC
			N125SG
F-CAID	Scheibe SF-28A Tandem-Falke	5761	HB-2007
			(D-KACN)
F-CAIR	Wassmer WA.22	145	Fr.AF
F-CAJB-T74	Grob G.103 Twin Astir II	3206	OO-ZMA
F-CAJC(2)	SZD-51-1 Junior	B-2020	
F-CAJE	Nord 2000	35	F-CAJD
F-CAJJ	Caudron C.800	9780/120	
F-CAJM(2)	Rolladen-Schneider LS-6A	6084	F-WAJM(2)
			OH-738
F-CAKO-8X	Rolladen-Schneider LS-4A	4674	D-0124
F-CALA	Schleicher ASK-14	14032	D-KOHC
F-CALB	Scheibe SF-25B Falke	46128	D-KADD
F-CALG	Schleicher ASK-14	14050	G-AYRN
			D-KISA
F-CALH	Schempp-Hirth Janus	181	D-2814
F-CAMD	Avialsa-Scheibe A.60 (Damaged, wfu)	2	

Regn.	Type	C/n	Prev.Id.
F-CAMF	Avialsa-Scheibe A.60	4	
F-CAOB(2)	Schempp-Hirth Janus CM	37/290	D-KAOK(2)
F-CAOP	Nord 2000	60/10390	
F-CAOT	Stemme S-10	10-53	
F-CAPB	Schempp-Hirth Janus A	34	OO-ZDC
F-CAPF	Caudron C.800 (Being restored)	181/9841	
F-CAPX	Wassmer WA.21 Javelot II	51	Fr.AF
F-CAQA(4)	Scheibe SF-25C Falke 2000	44324	F-WAQA(4)
			D-KOOQ
F-CAQB-2A	SZD-42-1 Jantar 2A	B-784	F-WAQB
			LX-CMD
			F-WAQB
F-CAQC	Schleicher ASW-17	17051	F-WAQC
F-CAQE	ICA/Brasov IS.28B2	118	F-WAQE
F-CAQF(3)	Scheibe SF-25B Falke	46148	F-WAQY
			D-KCAN
F-WAQG	Carmam C-38	25	
F-WAQH(5)	A.S.D.Glider	1	
F-WAQI	KV-3A	01	
F-CAQJ	Carmam C-38	03	F-WAQJ
F-CAQN(2)	Grob G.109B	6239	F-WAQN
F-CAQO	Grob G.109B	6333	F-WAQO
F-CAQP	Grob G.109B	6374	F-WAQP
F-CAQQ	Scheibe SF-25C Falke	4483	F-WAQQ
			OY-VXV
			(D-KEIC(1))
F-CAQS(2)	Scheibe SF-28A Tandem-Falke	5799	OY-XJB
			(D-KDCZ)
F-CAQT	Scheibe SF-28A Tandem-Falke	5741	HB-2023
			(D-KOEB(2))
F-CAQU	Loravia SFL-25R Remorqueur	4813	F-WAQU(2)
	(Converted SF-25C Falke for glider towing)		D-KBAV
F-CAQV(2)	Scheibe SF-25A Falke	4545	F-WAQV(2)
			D-KANY
F-CAQX	Scheibe SF-25C Falke	4404	F-WAQX(2)
			D-KAAM
F-WAQY(2)	Centrair 201C Marianne	201C-095	
F-CAQZ	Scheibe SF-25E Super Falke	4364	D-KNIY(2)
F-CARA	Schempp-Hirth Nimbus IIB	162	PH-599
F-CARB	Schempp-Hirth Nimbus III	21	Fr.AF
F-CARC	Castel C.311P	16	F-CALS
F-CARD	Scheibe SF-25B Falke	4863	F-WARD
			D-KAEB
F-CARF	Fournier RF-9	02	F-WARF
F-CARH	Fournier RF-10	02	F-WARH
F-WARI	Fournier RF-10	03	
F-WARJ	Fournier RF-10	4	F-WARJ
F-CARK	Schleicher ASW-22A	22022	D-9394
F-CARL(2)	Scheibe SF-28A Tandem-Falke	5717	D-KOAI
F-CARM	Schempp-Hirth Janus C	91	D-3198
F-CARN	Grob G.102 Astir CS	1494	HB-1375
F-CARP	Scheibe SF-25B Falke	46205	D-KASW
			(D-KAST)
F-CARS	Scheibe SF-25E Super Falke	4348	D-KDGA
F-CARZ	Nord 2000	70/10400	
F-CASB	Air 102	36	
F-CASD	Schleicher ASK-14	14026	D-KOIA
F-WASE	KV-5	001	
F-CASF	Grob G.103 Twin II	3674	D-8697
F-WASG	Scheibe SF-34A	5110	D-3340
F-CASH	Schleicher ASH-25	25127	
F-CATA	Grob G.103 Twin Astir	3168	D-7805
F-CATC	Rolladen-Schneider LS-4	4051	D-4189
F-CATD(2)	Schleicher ASH-25E	25030	D-4705
F-CATE(2)	Valentin Taifun 17E	1041	HB-2099
			D-KDSF
F-CATI-4W	Rolladen-Schneider LS-4	4558	D-8922
F-CATT -2	Rolladen-Schneider LS-6C	6227	
F-CATU-T72	Grob G.103 Twin Astir II	3236	
F-CATY(2)	Rolladen-Schneider LS-4	4248	I-GATS
			D-9108
F-CAUB(2)	Caudron C.800	310/9970	F-CAUA
F-CAVY	Schleicher K.8B	8170	
F-CAXA	Schempp-Hirth Janus CE	183	OO-ZXA
F-CAYD-JB	Glaser Dirks DG-200/17	2-112/1719	

Regn.	Type	C/n	Prev.Id.
F-CAYM	Castel C.311P	23/294	
F-CAYU	Air 102	39	
F-CBAN	Caudron C.800	9985/325	F-CBXA
F-CBBA	IAR-Brasov IS.28M2	53	
F-CBBB	Schleicher K.8B	815	
F-CBBC	IAR-Brasov IS.28M2	61	
F-CBBD	IAR-Brasov IS.28B2	345	
F-CBBF	IAR-Brasov IS.28M2	51	
F-CBBG	IAR-Brasov IS.28M2	55	
F-CBBN(2)	Schleicher K.8B	8755	D-1039
F-CBCA	Glaser Dirks DG-200/17	2-127/1729	
F-WBCB	Stralpes ST-II Minimus	01	
F-CBCC(2)	Glaser Dirks DG-200/17	2-172/1755	
F-WBCD	Stralpes ST-15 Crystal	01	
F-CBCE	Stralpes ST-15 Crystal	1	F-WBCE
F-CBCF	Stralpes ST-15 Crystal	2	F-WBCF
F-WBCG	Stralpes ST-15 Crystal	3	
F-CBCI	Stralpes ST-15 Crystal	8	
F-CBCJ	Stralpes ST-15 Crystal	9	
F-CBCK	Stralpes ST-15 Crystal	10	
F-CBCN	Stralpes ST-15 Crystal	6	
F-CBCO(2)	Stralpes ST-15 Crystal	7	
F-CBDA-YV	Schleicher ASW-20L	20460	
F-CBDB	Schleicher ASW-22	22024	F-WBDB
F-CBDC(2)	Schleicher ASW-20L (Code 'JA')	20319	
F-CBDD	Schleicher ASW-20BL	20648	F-WBDD
F-CBDE	Schleicher ASW-22	22016	F-WBDE
F-CBDF	Schleicher ASW-20	20576	
F-CBDH	Schleicher ASW-20CL	20710	F-WBDH
F-CBDI	Schleicher ASW-20CL	20744	F-WBDI
F-CBDK	Schleicher ASW-19B	19365	
F-CBDM	Schleicher ASW-20CL	20743	F-WBDM
F-CBDN	Schleicher ASW-20C	20761	F-WBDN
F-CBDO	Schleicher ASW-20	20130	
F-CBDP	Schleicher ASK-21	21105	F-WBDP
F-CBDQ	Schleicher ASK-21	21209	
F-CBDR	Schleicher ASK-21	21146	F-WBDR
F-CBDS	Schleicher ASK-21	21183	
F-CBDT	Schleicher ASK-21	21184	
F-CBDU	Schleicher ASK-21	21186	
F-CBDV	Schleicher ASK-21	21187	
F-CBDX	Schleicher ASK-21	21188	
F-CBDY	Schleicher ASK-21	21202	
F-CBDZ	Schleicher ASK-21	21203	
F-CBEA	Carmam M.100S Mésange	62	F-CDHB
F-CBET(2)	Rolladen-Schneider LS-6B	6202	
F-CBFF(2)	Schleicher ASW-22	22021	D-2282
F-CBFP	Nord 2000	34/10364	
F-CBFR	Nord 2000 (Being restored)	13/10343	
F-CBGE	Nord 2000	48/10378	
F-CBGV	Wassmer WA.20 Javelot 1	3	
F-CBGZ -7	Wassmer WA.20 Javelot 1	7	
F-CBHD	Air 100	13	
F-CBHN	Stralpes ST-15 Crystal	5	
F-CBHR	Schempp-Hirth Standard Cirrus	250	D-1122
F-CBII	Caudron C.800	9788/128	
F-CBJR(2)	Scheibe SF-25B Falke	46161	LX-CAB D-KOXY (D-KBIF)
F-CBKA	Caudron C.800	140	
F-CBLA	Centrair C-201A Marianne	201A-027	
F-CBLB(2)	Centrair C-201A Marianne	201A-028	
F-CBLC	Centrair C-201A Marianne	201A-029	
F-CBLD(2)	Centrair C-201A Marianne	201A-032	
F-CBLF	Centrair C-201A Marianne	201A-031	
F-CBLG	Centrair C-201A Marianne	201A-033	
F-CBLH	Centrair C-201A Marianne	201A-034	
F-CBLI	Centrair C-201A Marianne	201A-035	
F-CBLJ	Centrair C-201A Marianne	201A-036	
F-CBLK(2)	Centrair C-201A Marianne	201A-038	
F-CBLL(2)	Centrair C-201A Marianne	201A-039	
F-CBLM(2)	Centrair C-201A Marianne	201A-040	
F-CBLN(2)	Centrair C-201A Marianne	201A-041	
F-CBLO	Centrair C-201A Marianne	201A-042	
F-CBLP	Centrair C-201B Marianne	201B-043	

Regn.	Type	C/n	Prev.Id.
F-CBLQ(2)	Centrair C-201A Marianne	201A-044	
F-CBLR(2)	Centrair C-201A Marianne	201A-045	
F-CBLS(2)	Centrair C-201B Marianne	201B-046	
F-CBLT(2)	Centrair C-201B Marianne	201B-047	
F-CBLU(2)	Centrair C-201B Marianne	201B-048	F-WBLU
F-CBLV(2)	Centrair C-201B Marianne	201B-051	
F-CBLX	Centrair C-201B Marianne	201B-049	
F-CBLY(2)	Centrair C-201B Marianne	201B-050	
F-CBLZ	Centrair C-201B Marianne	201B-059	
F-CBMA	Castel C.310P	117	
F-CBNV(2)	Schempp-Hirth Nimbus 2	52	F-CEDB
F-CBOT	Sportavia-Pützer RF-5B Sperber	51055	D-KENT
F-CBPF(2)	Fournier RF-9	4	EC-DML F-ODPB F-WDPB
F-CBPJ-PJ	Glaser Dirks DG-200	2-52	
F-CBPM	Schleicher ASH-25	25038	F-WBPM D-4756
F-CBPR	Wassmer WA.28E	117	D-4231
F-CBQO	Wassmer WA.20 Javelot 1	1	
F-CBQR	Wassmer WA.20 Javelot 1	8	
F-CBQS	Wassmer WA.20 Javelot 1	9	
F-CBQZ	Air 102	25	
F-CBRK	Fauvel AV.36	111	
F-CBRS	Fauvel AV.36	119	
F-CBRX	Fauvel AV.36 (Being restored)	123	
F-CBSM	Fauvel AV.36	138	
F-CBUU	Wassmer WA.22A	152	Fr.AF
F-CBVP	Nord 2000	93/10423	
F-CBVR	Nord 2000	50/10380	
F-CBVV	Wassmer WA.30	175	Fr.AF
F-CBYK	Merville SM.31	01	
F-CBYR	Wassmer WA.21 Javelot II (Being restored)	02	
F-CBYV	Caudron C.800	9891/231	
F-CBZU	Schleicher Ka.6E	4211	
F-CBZX	Schleicher Ka.6CR Rhönsegler	6609	
F-CCAA(2)	Schempp-Hirth Janus B	08	HB-1325 D-3115
F-CCAB	Rolladen Schneider LS-1D	26	
F-WCAF	Carmam JP.15/34	01	
F-WCAR	Carmam JP.15/36 Aiglon	02	
F-CCAS	Centre Aer. Beynes KBK 10	02	
F-CCAV	Schleicher Ka.6CR Rhönsegler	6545	
F-CCBC	Wassmer WA.28 Espadon	01	F-WCBC
F-CCBD	Eiri PIK-20E-II	20294	F-WCBD
F-CCBT	Schempp-Hirth Nimbus IIC	56	OO-HZG
F-CCCB	Wassmer WA.22 Super Javelot	01	F-WCCB
F-CCCC	Wassmer WA.22A (Dismantled)	154	Fr.AF
F-CCCF	Breguet 901S Mouette	1	
F-CCCG	Breguet 901S Mouette	3	
F-CCCL	Breguet 901S Mouette	9	
F-CCCM	Breguet 901S Mouette	10	
F-CCCO	Breguet 901S Mouette	12	
F-CCCP	Breguet 901S Mouette	13	
F-CCCQ	Breguet 901S Mouette	14	
F-CCCR	Breguet 901S Mouette	15	
F-CCCU	Breguet 901S Mouette	18	
F-CCCX	Breguet 901S Mouette	20	
F-CCCY	Breguet 901S Mouette (Dismantled)	21	
F-CCDB	Breguet 901S Mouette	6	
F-CCDI	Caproni A.21S Calif	208	I-SERI
F-CCDK	Scheibe Bergfalke 11/55	207	
F-CCEA	Wassmer WA.20 Javelot	01	F-WCEA
F-CCEE	Wassmer WA.21 Javelot II	2	
F-CCEH	Wassmer WA.21 Javelot II (Dismantled)	14	
F-CCEO	Wassmer WA.21 Javelot II	18	
F-CCER	Wassmer WA.21 Javelot II	24	
F-CCEU	Wassmer WA.21 Javelot II	30	
F-CCEX	Wassmer WA.21 Javelot II	32	
F-CCFA	FFA Diamant 18	70	
F-WCFC	Carmam JP.15/36 Aiglon	04	
F-CCFF	Issoire E.78 Silene	01	
F-CCFK	Breguet 904S Nymphale (Dismantled)	1	
F-CCFN	Breguet 904S Nymphale	4	
F-CCFO	Breguet 904S Nymphale	5	

Regn.	Type	C/n	Prev.Id.
F-CCFP	Breguet 904S Nymphale (Dismantled)	6	
F-CCFQ	Breguet 904S Nymphale	7	
F-CCFR	Breguet 904S Nymphale	8	
F-CCFY	Breguet 904S Nymphale	14	
F-CCFZ	Breguet 904S Nymphale	15	
F-CCGE	Breguet 901S1	34	
F-CCGK	Fauvel AV.22S	1	
F-CCHC	Wassmer WA.21 Javelot II	7	
F-CCHD	Wassmer WA.21 Javelot II	8	
F-CCHF	Wassmer WA.21 Javelot II	17	
F-CCHG	Wassmer WA.21 Javelot II	19	
F-CCHJ	Wassmer WA.21 Javelot II	27	
F-CCHK	Wassmer WA.21 Javelot II	28	
F-CCHL	Wassmer WA.21 Javelot II	29	
F-CCHN	Merville SM.30	01	Fr.Mil
F-CCHO	Breguet Br.901.07	01	
F-CCHR-WH	Schempp-Hirth Janus B	03	D-3110
F-CCHY	Carmam M.100S Mésange	01	F-WCHY
F-CCJX	Schleicher ASK-21	21040	(F-CBDQ) F-WCJX
F-CCJY	Scheibe SF-28A Tandem-Falke	5763	D-KACP
F-CCKE	Wassmer WA.21 Javelot II	39	
F-CCKI	Wassmer WA.21 Javelot II	43	
F-CCKL	Wassmer WA.21 Javelot II	47	
F-CCKO	Wassmer WA.21 Javelot II	50	
F-CCKQ	Wassmer WA.21A Javelot II	53	
F-CCKU	Wassmer WA.21 Javelot II	59	Fr.AF
F-CCLC	Avialsa-Scheibe A.60 Fauconnet	7	
F-CCLI	Avialsa-Scheibe A.60 Fauconnet (Being restored)	13	
F-CCLJ	Avialsa-Scheibe A.60 Fauconnet	14	
F-CCLL	Avialsa-Scheibe A.60 Fauconnet	16	
F-CCLM	Wassmer WA.22 Super Javelot	63	
F-CCLO	Wassmer WA.22 Super Javelot	62	
F-CCLS	Wassmer WA.22 Super Javelot	66	
F-CCLZ	Wassmer WA.22 Super Javelot	70	
F-CCME	Wassmer WA.30 Bijave	8	
F-CCMG	Wassmer WA.30 Bijave	10	
F-CCMH	Wassmer WA.30 Bijave	11	
F-CCMI	Wassmer WA.30 Bijave	13	
F-CCML	Wassmer WA.30 Bijave	15	
F-CCMR	Wassmer WA.30 Bijave	20	
F-CCMU	Wassmer WA.30 Bijave	24	
F-CCMY	Wassmer WA.30 Bijave	31	
F-CCMZ	Wassmer WA.30 Bijave	27	
F-CCNB	Wassmer WA.30 Bijave	52	
F-CCNC	Wassmer WA.30 Bijave	53	
F-CCND	Wassmer WA.30 Bijave	54	
F-CCNF	Wassmer WA.30 Bijave	56	
F-CCNH	Wassmer WA.30 Bijave	58	
F-CCNI	Wassmer WA.30 Bijave	59	
F-CCNJ	Wassmer WA.30 Bijave	60	
F-CCNK	Wassmer WA.30 Bijave	61	
F-CCNL	Wassmer WA.30 Bijave (Dismantled)	62	
F-CCNM	Wassmer WA.30 Bijave	63	
F-CCNN	Wassmer WA.30 Bijave	64	
F-CCNP	Wassmer WA.30 Bijave	66	
F-CCNQ	Wassmer WA.30 Bijave	67	
F-CCNR	Wassmer WA.30 Bijave	68	
F-CCNS	Wassmer WA.30 Bijave	69	
F-CCNT	Wassmer WA.30 Bijave	70	
F-CCNU	Wassmer WA.30 Bijave	71	
F-CCNZ	Wassmer WA.30 Bijave	75	
F-CCOC	Wassmer WA.22 Super Javelot	75	
F-CCOD	Wassmer WA.22 Super Javelot (Dismantled)	76	
F-CCOF	Wassmer WA.22 Super Javelot (Dismantled)	78	
F-CCOH	Wassmer WA.22 Super Javelot	80	
F-CCOI	Wassmer WA.22 Super Javelot	81	
F-CCOL	Wassmer WA.22 Super Javelot	84	
F-CCOQ	Wassmer WA.30 Bijave	30	
F-CCOR	Wassmer WA.22 Super Javelot	86	
F-CCOS	Wassmer WA.22 Super Javelot	87	
F-CCOT	Wassmer WA.22 Super Javelot	88	
F-CCOU	Wassmer WA.22 Super Javelot	89	
F-CCPI	Carmam M.100S Mésange	10	
F-CCPP	Avialsa-Scheibe A.60 Fauconnet	22	
F-CCPS	Vasama PIK-16C	22	F-WCPS
F-CCPT	Scheibe Zugvogel IIIB	1084	
F-CCPV	Standard Austria S	42	
F-CCQC	Avialsa-Scheibe A.60 Fauconnet	25	
F-CCQD	Avialsa-Scheibe A.60 Fauconnet	26	
F-CCQF	Avialsa-Scheibe A.60 Fauconnet	28K	
F-CCQK	Avialsa-Scheibe A.60 Fauconnet	33K	
F-CCQT	Avialsa-Scheibe A.60 Fauconnet	42K	
F-CCQX	Avialsa-Scheibe A.60 Fauconnet	45	
F-CCRA	Wassmer WA.30 Bijave	32	
F-CCRB	Wassmer WA.22A Super Javelot	94	
F-CCRC	Wassmer WA.30 Bijave	34	
F-CCRD	Wassmer WA.30 Bijave	35	
F-CCRI	Wassmer WA.30 Bijave	38	
F-CCRJ	Wassmer WA.30 Bijave	33	
F-CCRL	Wassmer WA.30 Bijave	40	
F-CCRM	Wassmer WA.30 Bijave	41	
F-CCRN	Wassmer WA.30 Bijave	42	
F-CCRO(2)	Mouisset AP	01	
F-CCRP	Wassmer WA.30 Bijave	43	
F-CCRQ	Wassmer WA.30 Bijave	44	
F-CCRS	Wassmer WA.30 Bijave	46	
F-CCRU	Wassmer WA.30 Bijave	47	
F-CCRV	Wassmer WA.30 Bijave	48	
F-CCRZ	Wassmer WA.22A Super Javelot	97	
F-CCSE	Carmam M.100S Mésange	16	
F-CCSP	Carmam M.100S Mésange	27	
F-CCSY	Carmam M.100S Mésange	35	
F-CCTA	Wassmer WA.30 Bijave	77	
F-CCTE	Wassmer WA.30 Bijave	80	
F-CCTF	Wassmer WA.30 Bijave	81	
F-CCTH	Wassmer WA.30 Bijave	83	
F-CCTI	Wassmer WA.22A Super Javelot	100	
F-CCTK	Wassmer WA.30 Bijave	85	
F-CCTN	Wassmer WA.30 Bijave	88	
F-CCTO	Wassmer WA.22A Super Javelot	101	
F-CCTP	Wassmer WA.30 Bijave	89	
F-CCTR	Wassmer WA.30 Bijave	91	
F-CCTZ	Wassmer WA.30 Bijave	98	
F-CCUC	Siren C.30S Edelweiss	3	
F-CCUD	Siren C.30S Edelweiss	4	
F-CCUI	Siren C.30S Edelweiss	10	
F-CCUM	Siren C.30S Edelweiss	15	
F-CCUV	Siren C.30S Edelweiss	24	
F-CCVF	Avialsa-Scheibe A.60 Fauconnet	53K	
F-CCVO	Avialsa-Scheibe A.60 Fauconnet	62	
F-CCVP	Avialsa-Scheibe A.60 Fauconnet	63K	
F-CCVQ	Avialsa-Scheibe A.60 Fauconnet	64	
F-CCVS	Avialsa-Scheibe A.60 Fauconnet	66K	
F-CCVT	Avialsa-Scheibe A.60 Fauconnet	67	
F-CCVX	Avialsa-Scheibe A.60 Fauconnet	70	
F-CCVY	Avialsa-Scheibe A.60 Fauconnet	71	
F-CCXH	Carmam M.100S Mésange (Dismantled)	43	
F-CCXJ	Carmam M.100S Mésange	45	
F-CCXR	Carmam M.100S Mésange	51	
F-CCXT	Carmam M.200 Foehn	5	
F-CCXX	Carmam M.200 Foehn	7	
F-CCXY	Carmam M.200 Foehn (Dismantled)	9	
F-CCXZ	Carmam M.200 Foehn	10	
F-CCYA	Wassmer WA.30 Bijave	97	
F-CCYB	Wassmer WA.30 Bijave	99	
F-CCYD	Wassmer WA.30 Bijave	101	
F-CCYF	Wassmer WA.30 Bijave	103	
F-CCYI	Wassmer WA.30 Bijave	106	
F-CCYJ	Wassmer WA.30 Bijave	107	
F-CCYK	Wassmer WA.30 Bijave	108	
F-CCYL	Wassmer WA.30 Bijave	109	
F-CCYM	Wassmer WA.30 Bijave	110	
F-CCYO	Wassmer WA.30 Bijave	112	
F-CCYP	Wassmer WA.30 Bijave	115	
F-CCYQ	Wassmer WA.30 Bijave	114	
F-CCYS	Wassmer WA.30 Bijave	116	
F-CCYT	Wassmer WA.30 Bijave	117	
F-CCYU	Wassmer WA.30 Bijave	118	

Regn.	Type	C/n	Prev.Id.
F-CCYV	Wassmer WA.30 Bijave	119	
F-CCYX	Wassmer WA.30 Bijave	120	
F-CCYZ	Wassmer WA.30 Bijave	122	
F-CCZC	Wassmer WA.30 Bijave	125	
F-CCZE	Wassmer WA.30 Bijave	127	
F-CCZI	Wassmer WA.30 Bijave	130	
F-CCZJ	Wassmer WA.30 Bijave	131	
F-CCZK	Wassmer WA.30 Bijave	132	
F-CCZM	Wassmer WA.30 Bijave	133	
F-CCZO	Wassmer WA.30 Bijave	135	
F-CCZU	Wassmer WA.30 Bijave	138	
F-CCZX	Wassmer WA.22A Super Javelot	108	
F-CCZY	Wassmer WA.30 Bijave	141	
F-CCZZ	Wassmer WA.22A Super Javelot	105	
F-CDAF	Glasflügel H201B Standard Libelle	557	
F-CDAH	Schempp-Hirth SHK-1	15	
F-CDAI	Siren C.30S Edelweiss	28	
F-CDAK	Siren C.30S Edelweiss	30	
F-CDAL	Siren C.30S Edelweiss	31	
F-CDAM	Siren C.30S Edelweiss	32	
F-CDAU	Siren C.30S Edelweiss	40	
F-CDAV	Siren C.30S Edelweiss	41	
F-CDAY	LCA-Scheibe 10 Topaze	001	F-WDAY
F-CDBC	Avialsa-Scheibe A.60 Fauconnet (Dismantled)	75K	
F-CDBG	Avialsa-Scheibe A.60 Fauconnet	79K	
F-CDBV	Avialsa-Scheibe A.60 Fauconnet	94	
F-CDBY	Avialsa-Scheibe A.60 Fauconnet	96	
F-CDCB	Wassmer WA.30 Bijave	143	
F-CDCC	Wassmer WA.30 Bijave	144	
F-CDCD	Wassmer WA.30 Bijave	145	
F-CDCE	Wassmer WA.30 Bijave	146	
F-CDCF	Wassmer WA.22A Super Javelot	109	
F-CDCI	Wassmer WA.22A Super Javelot	111	
F-CDCL	Wassmer WA.30 Bijave	150	
F-CDCP	Wassmer WA.30 Bijave	156	
F-CDCQ	Wassmer WA.30 Bijave	157	
F-CDCS	Wassmer WA.22A Super Javelot	117	
F-CDCU	Wassmer WA.30 Bijave	160	
F-CDCV	Wassmer WA.30 Bijave	161	
F-CDCZ	Wassmer WA.30 Bijave	166	
F-CDDD	Carmam M.200 Foehn	13	
F-CDDO	Carmam M.200 Foehn	22	
F-CDDQ	Carmam M.200 Foehn	23	
F-CDDU	Carmam M.200 Foehn	26	
F-CDED	Wassmer WA.22A Super Javelot	122	
F-CDEE	Wassmer WA.22A Super Javelot	123	
F-CDEF	Wassmer WA.30 Bijave	169	
F-CDEG	Wassmer WA.30 Bijave	170	
F-CDEH	Wassmer WA.30 Bijave	172	
F-CDEI	Wassmer WA.30 Bijave	173	
F-CDEJ	Wassmer WA.22A Super Javelot	125	
F-CDEK	Wassmer WA.22A Super Javelot	127	
F-CDEO	Wassmer WA.22A Super Javelot	131	
F-CDEQ	Wassmer WA.30 Bijave	177	
F-CDES	Wassmer WA.22A Super Javelot	130	
F-CDET	Wassmer WA.30 Bijave	180	
F-CDEU	Wassmer WA.30 Bijave	183	
F-CDEY	Wassmer WA.30 Bijave	186	
F-CDFD	Avialsa-Scheibe A.60 Fauconnet	101	
F-CDFH	Avialsa-Scheibe A.60 Fauconnet	105K	
F-CDFK	Avialsa-Scheibe A.60 Fauconnet	108K	
F-CDFL	Avialsa-Scheibe A.60 Fauconnet	109K	
F-CDFM	Avialsa-Scheibe A.60 Fauconnet	110K	
F-CDFQ	Avialsa-Scheibe A.60 Fauconnet	114	
F-CDFR	Avialsa-Scheibe A.60 Fauconnet	115K	
F-CDFT-M7	Avialsa-Scheibe A.60 Fauconnet	117	
F-CDFV	Avialsa-Scheibe A.60 Fauconnet	119	
F-CDFZ	Avialsa-Scheibe A.60 Fauconnet	122	
F-CDGA	Siren C.30S Edelweiss	42	
F-CDGB	Siren C.30S Edelweiss	43	
F-CDGG	Siren C.30S Edelweiss	48	
F-CDGN	Rocheteau-Scheibe CRA.60	12K	
F-CDHC	Carmam M.200 Foehn	30	
F-CDHE	Carmam M.200 Foehn	31	
F-CDHI	Carmam M.200 Foehn	35	
F-CDHO	Carmam M.200 Foehn	40	
F-CDHQ	Carmam M.100S Mésange	67	
F-CDHR	Carmam M.100S Mésange (Dismantled)	68	
F-CDHS	Carmam M.200 Foehn	43	
F-CDHT	Carmam M.100S Mésange	69	
F-CDHU	Carmam M.200 Foehn	44	
F-CDHX	Carmam M.100S Mésange	70	
F-CDIB	Wassmer WA.30 Bijave	188	
F-CDIC	Wassmer WA.30 Bijave	189	
F-CDID	Wassmer WA.22A Super Javelot	136	
F-CDIE	Wassmer WA.30 Bijave	191	
F-CDIF	Wassmer WA.30 Bijave	192	
F-CDIG	Wassmer WA.30 Bijave	193	
F-CDIH	Wassmer WA.30 Bijave	194	
F-CDIJ	Wassmer WA.30 Bijave	195	
F-CDIL	Wassmer WA.30 Bijave	197	
F-CDIN	Wassmer WA.22A Super Javelot	141	
F-CDIP	Wassmer WA.30 Bijave	200	
F-CDIQ	Wassmer WA.30 Bijave	201	
F-CDIS	Wassmer WA.30 Bijave	203	
F-CDIT	Wassmer WA.22A Super Javelot	142	
F-CDIZ	Wassmer WA.22A Super Javelot	146	
F-CDJA	Wassmer WA.30 Bijave	208	
F-CDJB	Wassmer WA.22A Super Javelot	147	
F-CDJC	Wassmer WA.30 Bijave	209	
F-CDJE	Wassmer WA.30 Bijave	211	
F-CDJF	Wassmer WA.30 Bijave	212	
F-CDJG	Wassmer WA.30 Bijave	213	
F-CDJK	Wassmer WA.30 Bijave	215	
F-CDJL	Wassmer WA.30 Bijave	216	
F-CDJM	Wassmer WA.30 Bijave	217	
F-CDJN	Wassmer WA.22A Super Javelot	150	
F-CDJO	Wassmer WA.30 Bijave	218	
F-CDJQ	Wassmer WA.30 Bijave	220	
F-CDJR	Wassmer WA.30 Bijave	221	
F-CDJT	Wassmer WA.30 Bijave	223	
F-CDJX	Wassmer WA.30 Bijave	225	
F-CDKB	Carmam M.200 Foehn	48	
F-CDKF	Carmam M.100S Mésange	74	
F-CDKH	Carmam M100S Mésange	75	
F-CDKI	Carmam M.200 Foehn (Dismantled)	51	
F-CDKN	Carmam M.200 Foehn	53	
F-CDKS	Carmam M.100S Mésange	82	
F-CDKU	Carmam M.100S Mésange	83K	
F-CDKV	Carmam M.200 Foehn	56	
F-CDLC	Avialsa-Scheibe A.60 Fauconnet	125K	
	(Being restored)		
F-CDLF	Avialsa-Scheibe A.60 Fauconnet	128	
F-CDLG	Avialsa-Scheibe A.60 Fauconnet	129K	
F-CDLN	Avialsa-Scheibe A.60 Fauconnet	136K	
F-CDLR	Avialsa-Scheibe A.60 Fauconnet	140	
F-CDLT	Avialsa-Scheibe A.60 Fauconnet	142	
F-CDLU	Avialsa-Scheibe A.60 Fauconnet	143K	
F-CDMA	Wassmer WA.30 Bijave	229	
F-CDMB	Wassmer WA.30 Bijave	234	
F-CDMC	Wassmer WA.30 Bijave	235	
F-CDMJ	Wassmer WA.30 Bijave	240	
F-CDMN	Wassmer WA.30 Bijave	242	
F-CDMP	Wassmer WA.30 Bijave	244	
F-CDMQ	Wassmer WA.26P Squale	06	
F-CDMT	Wassmer WA.30 Bijave	247	
F-CDMU	Wassmer WA.26P Squale	07	
F-CDMV	Wassmer WA.30 Bijave	248	
F-CDMY	Wassmer WA.26P Squale	08	
F-CDND	Avialsa-Scheibe A.60 Fauconnet	151K	
F-CDNF	Avialsa-Scheibe A.60 Fauconnet	153	
F-CDNH	Avialsa-Scheibe A.60 Fauconnet	155K	
F-CDNT	Rocheteau-Scheibe CRA.60	05	
F-CDNX	Rocheteau-Scheibe CRA.60	08	
F-CDNY	Rocheteau-Scheibe CRA.60	09	
F-CDOC	Bölkow Phoebus C	889	
F-CDOF	Bölkow Phoebus C	902	
F-CDOG	Bölkow Phoebus C	906	
F-CDOJ	Bölkow Phoebus C	915	
F-CDOL	Bölkow Phoebus CWB	925	

Regn.	Type	C/n	Prev.Id.
F-CDOO	Bölkow Phoebus C	932	
F-CDOP	Bölkow Phoebus C	926	
F-CDOQ	Bölkow Phoebus CWB	937	
F-CDOR	Bölkow Phoebus CWB	941	
F-CDOS	Bölkow Phoebus B1	943	
F-CDOT	Bölkow Phoebus C	944	
F-CDOU	VTC-75 Standard Cirrus	227	
F-CDOV	VTC-75 Standard Cirrus	229	
F-CDOX	VTC-75 Standard Cirrus	239	
F-CDOY	VTC-75 Standard Cirrus	240	
F-CDOZ	VTC-75 Standard Cirrus	241	
F-CDPB	Schempp-Hirth L265 Cirrus	75	
F-CDPC	Glasflügel H201 Standard Libelle	70	
F-CDPD	Schempp-Hirth L265 Cirrus	29	
F-CDPF-701	Glasflügel H201 Standard Libelle	150	
F-CDPG-702	Glasflügel H201B Standard Libelle	151	
F-CDPH-703	Glasflügel H201B Standard Libelle	152	
F-CDPJ	Glasflügel H201B Standard Libelle	160	
F-CDPK	Carmam M.200 Foehn	59	
F-CDPP-20	Schempp-Hirth Standard Cirrus	74	
F-CDPR	Glasflügel H201B Standard Libelle	226	
F-CDPS-707	Glasflügel H201 Standard Libelle	227	
F-CDPT	Glasflügel H201B Standard Libelle	230	
F-CDPU	Glasflügel H201 Standard Libelle	231	
F-CDPX	Glasflügel H201 Standard Libelle	247	
F-CDPY-712	Glasflügel H201B Standard Libelle	255	
F-CDQA	Wassmer WA.30 Bijave	251	
F-CDQF	Wassmer WA.30 Bijave	254	
F-CDQG	Wassmer WA.26P Squale	11	
F-CDQH	Wassmer WA.26P Squale	12	
F-CDQK	Wassmer WA.30 Bijave	255	
F-CDQN	Wassmer WA.26P Squale	16	
F-CDQO	Wassmer WA.26P Squale	17	
F-CDQQ-819	Wassmer WA.26P Squale	19	
F-CDQT	Wassmer WA.26P Squale	22	
F-CDQU	Wassmer WA.30 Bijave	257	
F-CDQX	Wassmer WA.30 Bijave	259	
F-CDQZ	Wassmer WA.30 Bijave	261	
F-CDRA	Schleicher Ka.6E	4278	
F-CDRD	Schleicher Ka.6E	4293	
F-CDRG	Schleicher Ka.6E	4296	
F-CDRH	Schleicher Ka.6E	4298	
F-CDRI	Schleicher Ka.6E	4299	
F-CDRK	Schleicher Ka.6E	4302	
F-CDRL	Schleicher Ka.6E	4289	
F-CDRM	Schleicher Ka.6E	4290	
F-CDRN	Schleicher Ka.6E	4303	
F-CDRT	Schleicher Ka.6E	4319	
F-CDRU	Schleicher Ka.6E	4320	
F-CDRX	Schleicher Ka.6E	4323	
F-CDRY	Schleicher ASW-15	15029	
F-CDRZ	Schleicher ASK-14	14035	D-KECH
F-CDSA	Wassmer WA.30 Bijave	262	
F-CDSD	Wassmer WA.26P Squale	25	
F-CDSH	Wassmer WA.30 Bijave	263	
F-CDSI	Wassmer WA.26P Squale	29	
F-CDSJ	Wassmer WA.26P Squale	30	
F-CDSK	Wassmer WA.30 Bijave	264	
F-CDSN	Wassmer WA.26P Squale	32	
F-CDSP	Wassmer WA.26P Squale	34	
F-CDSQ	Wassmer WA.30 Bijave	266	
F-CDSU	Wassmer WA.30 Bijave	270	
F-CDSV	Wassmer WA.26P Squale	35	
F-CDTA	Schleicher Ka.6E	4322	
F-CDTB	Schleicher Ka.6E	4324	
F-CDTC	Schleicher Ka.6E	4328	
F-CDTG	Schleicher Ka.6E	4332	
F-CDTH	Schleicher Ka.6E	4333	
F-CDTI	Schleicher Ka.6E	4337	
F-CDTM	Schleicher Ka.6E	4350	
F-CDTN	Schleicher Ka.6E	4351	
F-CDTP	Schleicher Ka.6E	4354	
F-CDTQ	Schleicher ASK-13	13275	
F-CDTR	Schleicher Ka.6E	4355	
F-CDTS	Schleicher Ka.6E	4356	
F-CDTT	Schleicher Ka.6E	4358	
F-CDTU	Schleicher Ka.6E	4359	
F-CDTV	Schleicher ASW-15	15117	
F-CDTY	Schleicher Ka.6E	4361	
F-CDUA	Wassmer WA.30 Bijave	271	
F-CDUB	Wassmer WA.30 Bijave	272	
F-CDUC	Wassmer WA.30 Bijave	273	
F-CDUD	Wassmer WA.26P Squale	39	
F-CDUE	Wassmer WA.26P Squale	40	
F-CDUI	Wassmer WA.26CM	01	
F-CDUJ	Wassmer WA.26P Squale	44	
F-CDUN	Wassmer WA.26P Squale	47	
F-CDUO	Wassmer WA.30 Bijave	274	
F-CDUP	Wassmer WA.30 Bijave	275	
F-CDUR	Wassmer WA.26P Squale	48	
F-CDUS	Wassmer WA.26P Squale	49	
F-CDUU	Wassmer WA.26CM	03	
F-CDUX	Wassmer WA.30 Bijave	278	
F-CDVB	Rolladen-Schneider LS-1C	53	
F-CDVC	Rolladen-Schneider LS-1C	47	
F-CDVE-L04	Rolladen-Schneider LS-1C	201	
F-CDVG	Rolladen-Schneider LS-1D	203	
F-CDVJ	Rolladen-Schneider LS-1C	206	
F-CDVM	Rolladen-Schneider LS-1D	209	
F-CDVN	Rolladen-Schneider LS-1D	210	
F-CDVQ	Rolladen-Schneider LS-1C	213	
F-CDVS-L18	Rolladen-Schneider LS-1D	128	
F-CDVT	Rolladen-Schneider LS-1D	141	
F-CDVU-L20	Rolladen-Schneider LS-1C	148	
F-CDVV	Rolladen-Schneider LS-1C	156	
F-CDVW-L22	Rolladen-Schneider LS-1C	157	
F-CDVX	Rolladen-Schneider LS-1D	158	
F-CDVY-L34	Rolladen-Schneider LS-1D	190	
F-CDVZ	Rolladen-Schneider LS-1D	191	
F-CDXC	Wassmer WA.26P Squale (Dismantled)	54	
F-CDXD	Wassmer WA.26CM	05	
F-CDXH	Wassmer WA.26CM	09	
F-CDXK	Wassmer WA.26P Squale	55	
F-CDXL	Wassmer WA.26P Squale	56	
F-CDXM	Wassmer WA.30 Bijave	279	
F-CDXN	Wassmer WA.30 Bijave	280	
F-CDXO	Wassmer WA.26P Squale	57	
F-CDXS	Wassmer WA.26P Squale	60	
F-CDXU	Wassmer WA.30 Bijave	282	
F-CDXV	Wassmer WA.26P Squale	62	
F-CDYA	Schleicher ASK-13	13296	
F-CDYB	Schleicher ASK-13	13297	
F-CDYC	Schleicher ASK-13	13298	
F-CDYD	Schleicher ASK-13	13299	
F-CDYG	Schleicher Ka.6E	4367	
F-CDYI	Schleicher Ka.6E	4369	
F-CDYJ	Schleicher Ka.6E	4370	
F-CDYL	Schleicher Ka.6E	4372	
F-CDYM	Schleicher ASK-13	13316	
F-CDYO	Schleicher ASK-13	13322	
F-CDYP	Schleicher ASK-13	13323	
F-CDYS	Schleicher ASK-13	13326	
F-CDYT	Schleicher ASK-13	13327	
F-CDYU	Schleicher ASW-15	15123	
F-CDYX	Schleicher ASK-13	13332	
F-CDYY	Schleicher ASK-13	13336	
F-CDYZ	Schleicher ASK-13	13334	
F-CDZA	Wassmer WA.26P Squale	66	
F-CDZC	Wassmer WA.26P Squale	68	
F-CDZD	Wassmer WA.26P Squale	69	
F-CDZG	Wassmer WA.26P Squale	72	
F-CDZJ	Wassmer WA.26P Squale	75	
F-CDZK	Wassmer WA.28 Espadon	93	
F-CDZM	Wassmer WA.28 Espadon	91	
F-CDZO	Wassmer WA.28 Espadon	95	
F-CDZR	Wassmer WA.28F	98	
F-CDZT	Wassmer WA.28 Espadon	100	
F-CDZU	Wassmer WA.28F	101	
F-CDZV	Wassmer WA.28F	102	
F-CDZZ-W15	Wassmer WA.28 Espadon	105	

Regn.	Type	C/n	Prev.Id.
F-CEAA	Schleicher ASK-13	13337	
F-CEAB	Schleicher ASK-13	13338	
F-CEAC	Schleicher ASK-13	13339	
F-CEAD	Schleicher ASK-13	13340	
F-CEAE	Schleicher ASK-13	13343	
F-CEAF	Schleicher ASK-13	13344	
F-CEAG	Schleicher ASK-13	13347	
F-CEAI	Schleicher ASK-13	13349	
F-CEAJ	Schleicher ASK-13	13350	
F-CEAK	Schleicher ASK-13	13353	
F-CEAL	Schleicher ASK-13	13355	
F-CEAM	Schleicher ASK-13	13356	
F-CEAO	Schleicher Ka.6E	4379	
F-CEAP	Schleicher ASK-13	13365	
F-CEAQ	Schleicher ASW-15	15167	
F-CEAS	Schleicher ASW-15	15169	
F-CEAT	Schleicher ASK-13	13371	
F-CEAU	Schleicher Ka.6E	4380	
F-CEAV	Schleicher ASK-13	13372	
F-CEAX	Schleicher ASK-13	13373	
F-CEAY	Schleicher ASK-14	14062	D-KICI
F-CEAZ	Schleicher ASW-15	15171	
F-CEBB	Glasflügel H201 Standard Libelle	302	
F-CEBC-716	Glasflügel H201 Standard Libelle	303	
F-CEBE	Glasflügel H201B Standard Libelle	318	
F-CEBG-720	Glasflügel H201B Standard Libelle	320	
F-CEBH	Glasflügel H201 Standard Libelle	321	
F-CEBJ-723	Glasflügel H201B Standard Libelle	360	
F-CEBK	Glasflügel H201B Standard Libelle	361	
F-CEBM	Glasflügel H201 Standard Libelle	421	
F-CEBN	Glasflügel H201B Standard Libelle	427	
F-CEBQ	Glasflügel H201 Standard Libelle	431	
F-CEBS-M21	Glasflügel H304	246	
F-CEBU	Glasflügel H304	252	
F-CEBV	VTC-75 Standard Cirrus	242	
F-CEBX	VTC-75 Standard Cirrus	243	
F-CECC	Schleicher ASK-13	13381	
F-CECD	Schleicher ASK-13	13382	
F-CECE	Schleicher Ka.6E	4381	
F-CECF	Schleicher Ka.6E	4382	
F-CECG	Schleicher ASW-17	17005	
F-CECH	Schleicher Ka.6E	4383	
F-CECI	Schleicher ASK-13	13383	
F-CECJ	Schleicher ASK-13	13384	
F-CECK	Schleicher ASK-13	13385	
F-CECL	Schleicher ASK-13	13387	
F-CECM	Schleicher ASK-13	13388	
F-CECN	Schleicher Ka.6E	4386	
F-CECO	Schleicher ASK-13	13389	
F-CECQ	Schleicher ASK-13	13390	
F-CECS-K89	Schleicher Ka.6E	4389	
F-CECT	Schleicher ASK-13	13402	
F-CECU	Schleicher ASK-13	13405	
F-CECV	Schleicher ASW-15B	15229	
F-CECY	Schleicher ASK-13	13407	
F-CEDA-N1	Schempp-Hirth Nimbus II	8	
F-CEDC	Schempp-Hirth Nimbus II	53	
F-CEDD	Schempp-Hirth Nimbus II	54	
F-CEDF-N8	Schempp-Hirth Nimbus IIC	71	
F-CEDG-N9	Schempp-Hirth Nimbus IIC	73	
F-CEDH-N10	Schempp-Hirth Nimbus IIC	74	
F-CEDI-19	Schempp-Hirth Nimbus IIC	81	
F-CEDJ-SA	Schempp-Hirth Nimbus IIC	92	
F-CEDK-N14	Schempp-Hirth Nimbus IID	112	
F-CEDL-N15	Schempp-Hirth Nimbus IID	120	
F-CEDM-N17	Schempp-Hirth Nimbus IIB	137	F-WEDM
F-CEDO-W	Schempp-Hirth Ventus A	25	F-WEDO
F-CEDQ-14	Schempp-Hirth Ventus b	52	F-WEDQ
F-CEDS-28	Schempp-Hirth Ventus b	44	F-WEDS
F-CEDT	Schempp-Hirth Ventus bT	31/202	F-WEDT
F-CEDU	Schempp-Hirth Ventus b	95	F-WEDU D-4305
F-CEDV	Schempp-Hirth Ventus b	235	F-WEDV
F-CEDX	Glasflügel H303B Mosquito	128	
F-CEDZ-M05	Glasflügel H303B Mosquito	154	

Regn.	Type	C/n	Prev.Id.
F-CEEA	LCA-Scheibe 10 Topaze	1	
F-CEEC	LCA-Scheibe 10 Topaze	3	
F-CEED	LCA-Scheibe 10 Topaze	4	
F-CEEE	LCA-Scheibe 11 Topaze	5	
F-CEEG	LCA-Scheibe 10 Topaze	7	
F-CEEL	LCA-Scheibe 11 Topaze	12	
F-CEEM	LCA-Scheibe 11 Topaze	13	
F-CEEN	LCA-Scheibe 11 Topaze	14	
F-CEEO	LCA-Scheibe 11 Topaze	15	
F-CEEQ	LCA-Scheibe 11 Topaze	17	
F-CEET	LCA-Scheibe 11 Topaze	20	
F-CEEY	LCA-Scheibe 11 Topaze	24	
F-CEFB-C04	Schempp-Hirth CS-11 St.Cirrus	326G	
F-CEFD-C05	Schempp-Hirth CS-11 St.Cirrus	342G	
F-CEFE	Schempp-Hirth CS-11 St.Cirrus	344G	
F-CEFF-CI	Schempp-Hirth CS-11 St.Cirrus	371G	
F-CEFG-C10	Schempp-Hirth CS-11 St.Cirrus	387G	
F-CEFH	Schempp-Hirth CS-11 St.Cirrus	401G	
F-CEFI-C12	Schempp-Hirth CS-11 St.Cirrus	404G	
F-CEFK	Schempp-Hirth CS-11 St.Cirrus	406G	
F-CEFN-N	Schempp-Hirth CS-11 St.Cirrus	436G	
F-CEFQ-C13	Schempp-Hirth CS-11 St.Cirrus	453G	
F-CEFS-C22	Schempp-Hirth CS-11 St.Cirrus	462G	
F-CEFU	Schempp-Hirth CS-11 St.Cirrus	468G	
F-CEFV	Schempp-Hirth CS-11 St.Cirrus	469G	
F-CEFZ	Schempp-Hirth CS-11 St.Cirrus	512G	
F-CEGA	Schleicher ASK-13	13404	
F-CEGC	Schleicher ASK-13	13410	
F-CEGD	Schleicher ASK-13	13412	
F-CEGE	Schleicher ASW-15B	15269	
F-CEGG	Schleicher ASW-15B	15271	
F-CEGH	Schleicher ASW-15B	15272	
F-CEGI	Schleicher ASW-15B	15273	
F-CEGK	Schleicher ASW-13	13411	
F-CEGM	Schleicher ASW-15B	15281	
F-CEGN	Schleicher ASW-15B	15297	
F-CEGO	Schleicher ASW-15B	15291	
F-CEGP	Schleicher ASW-15B	15292	
F-CEGQ	Schleicher ASW-15B	15293	
F-CEGS	Schleicher ASW-15B	15295	
F-CEGT	Schleicher ASW-15B	15296	
F-CEGU	Schleicher K.8B	8933	
F-CEGV	Schleicher K.8B	8934	
F-CEGX	Schleicher K.8B	8935	
F-CEGZ	Schleicher Ka.6E	4186	
F-CEHA	Rolladen-Schneider LS-1D	192	
F-CEHC	Rolladen-Schneider LS-1D	216	
F-CEHD	Rolladen-Schneider LS-1D	217	
F-CEHF	Rolladen-Schneider LS-1D	219	
F-CEHG	Rolladen-Schneider LS-1D	220	
F-CEHI	Rolladen-Schneider LS-1D	222	
F-CEHJ	Rolladen-Schneider LS-1D	223	
F-CEHK	Rolladen-Schneider LS-1D	224	
F-CEHL	Rolladen-Schneider LS-1D	225	
F-CEHM-L35	Rolladen-Schneider LS-1D *(Dismantled)*	226	
F-CEHO-L39	Rolladen-Schneider LS-1D	228	
F-CEHQ	Rolladen-Schneider LS-1D	230	
F-CEHR	Rolladen-Schneider LS-1D	231	
F-CEHS-L43	Rolladen-Schneider LS-1D	232	
F-CEHT	Rolladen-Schneider LS-1D	233	
F-CEHU	Rolladen-Schneider LS-1D	234	
F-CEHV	Rolladen-Schneider LS-1D	235	
F-CEHY	Rolladen-Schneider LS-1D	237	
F-CEHZ-L49	Rolladen-Schneider LS-1F	375	
F-CEIB-SG	Rolladen-Schneider LS-4	4012	
F-CEIC	Rolladen-Schneider LS-4	4013	
F-CEID-FL	Rolladen-Schneider LS-4	4020	
F-CEIE	Rolladen-Schneider LS-4	4053	
F-CEIF	Rolladen-Schneider LS-4	4056	
F-CEIG-V08	Rolladen-Schneider LS-4	4057	
F-CEIH	Rolladen-Schneider LS-4	4058	
F-CEII-V10	Rolladen-Schneider LS-4	4059	
F-CEIJ-V11	Rolladen-Schneider LS-4	4138	
F-CEIK-V12	Rolladen-Schneider LS-4	4139	
F-CEIL	Rolladen-Schneider LS-4	4245	

Regn.	Type	C/n	Prev.Id.
F-CEIM-V14	Rolladen-Schneider LS-4	4140	
F-CEIN	Rolladen-Schneider LS-4	4141	
F-CEIP-V20	Rolladen-Schneider LS-4	4231	
F-CEIQ-CA	Rolladen-Schneider LS-4	4292	
F-CEIR-TC	Rolladen-Schneider LS-4	4232	
F-CEIS-V22	Rolladen-Schneider LS-4	4233	
F-CEIT-V23	Rolladen-Schneider LS-4	4234	
F-CEIU-V24	Rolladen-Schneider LS-4	4235	
F-CEIV-V25	Rolladen-Schneider LS-4	4236	
F-CEIX	Rolladen-Schneider LS-4	4237	
F-CEIY-V27	Rolladen-Schneider LS-4	4238	
F-CEIZ-V49	Rolladen-Schneider LS-4	4239	
F-CEJA	Schleicher K.8B	8936	
F-CEJB	Schleicher K.8B	8937	
F-CEJC	Schleicher K.8B	8939	
F-CEJD	Schleicher K.8B	8940	
F-CEJE	Schleicher K.8B	8938	
F-CEJF	Schleicher K.8B	8955	
F-CEJG	Schleicher ASW-17	17022	
F-CEJH	Schleicher K.8B	8956	
F-CEJI	Schleicher K.8B	8957	
F-CEJJ	Schleicher ASK-13	13461	
F-CEJK	Schleicher ASK-13	13462	
F-CEJM	Schleicher ASW-15B	15349	
F-CEJN	Schleicher ASW-15B	15350	
F-CEJP	Schleicher K.88	8976	
F-CEJQ	Schleicher K.8B	8977	
F-CEJR	Schleicher ASK-13	13497	
F-CEJS	Schleicher K.8B	8979	
F-CEJT	Schleicher ASK-13	13509	
F-CEJU	Schleicher ASK-13	13520	
F-CEJV	Schleicher K.8B	8982	
F-CEJW	Schleicher ASK-13	13521	
F-CEJX	Schleicher ASK-13	13522	
F-CEJY	Schleicher K.8B	8984	
F-CEJZ	Schleicher K.8B	8983	
F-CEKA	Rolladen-Schneider LS-1F	376	
F-CEKB-L51	Rolladen-Schneider LS-1F	377	
F-CEKC	Rolladen-Schneider LS-1F	380	
F-CEKD	Rolladen-Schneider LS-1F	387	
F-CEKE-L54	Rolladen-Schneider LS-1F	388	
F-CEKF-L55	Rolladen-Schneider LS-1F	389	
F-CEKH-L57	Rolladen-Schneider LS-1F	391	
F-CEKJ-L59	Rolladen-Schneider LS-1F	393	
F-CEKL-L61	Rolladen-Schneider LS-1F	396	
F-CEKM-L62	Rolladen-Schneider LS-1F	397	
F-CEKN	Rolladen-Schneider LS-1F	398	
F-CEKO	Rolladen-Schneider LS-1F	399	
F-CEKP	Rolladen-Schneider LS-1F	400	
F-CEKQ-L66	Rolladen-Schneider LS-1F	401	
F-CEKR	Rolladen-Schneider LS-1F	402	
F-CEKS-F1	Rolladen-Schneider LS-1F	403	
F-CEKT	Rolladen-Schneider LS-1F	404	
F-CEKU-L70	Rolladen-Schneider LS-1F	405	
F-CEKV-L72	Rolladen-Schneider LS-1F	439	
F-CEKX-L73	Rolladen-Schneider LS-1F	440	
F-CEKY	Rolladen-Schneider LS-1F	451	
F-CEKZ	Rolladen-Schneider LS-1F	452	
F-CELA	Glasflügel H201B Standard Libelle	498	
F-CELB	Glasflügel H201B Standard Libelle	531	
F-CELC-758	Glasflügel H201B Standard Libelle	558	
F-CELD	Wassmer WA.26P Squale	64	F-CDXY
F-CELE	Glasflügel H201B Standard Libelle	590	
F-CELF	Glasflügel H201 Standard Libelle	428	
F-CELG	Glasflügel H201B Standard Libelle	600	
F-CELH-709	Glasflügel H201B Standard Libelle	599	
F-CELJ	Glasflügel H201B Standard Libelle	589	
F-CELK	Glasflügel H303B Mosquito	156	
F-CELL-M07	Glasflügel H303B Mosquito	168	
F-CELM-M08	Glasflügel H303B Mosquito	169	
F-CELN	Glasflügel H303B Mosquito	175	
F-CELP	Glasflügel H303B Mosquito	182	
F-CELQ-M12	Glasflügel H303B Mosquito	183	
F-CELR	Glasflügel H201B Standard Libelle	598	
F-CELS	Glasflügel H303B Mosquito	188	

Regn.	Type	C/n	Prev.Id.
F-CELT	Glasflügel H303B Mosquito	189	
F-CELU	Glasflügel H303B Mosquito	197	
F-CELV	Glasflügel H303B Mosquito	198	
F-CELX-M17	Glasflügel H303B Mosquito	199	
F-CELY	Glasflügel H303B Mosquito	202	
F-CELZ	Glasflügel H304	235	
F-CEMA	Schempp-Hirth CS-11 St.Cirrus	513G	
F-CEMB-C30	Schempp-Hirth CS-11 St.Cirrus	551G	
F-CEMC	Schempp-Hirth CS-11 St.Cirrus	552G	
F-CEMD-C32	Schempp-Hirth CS-11 St.Cirrus	562G	
F-CEME	Schempp-Hirth CS-11 St.Cirrus	563G	
F-CEMG-C35	Schempp-Hirth CS-11 St.Cirrus	577G	
F-CEMJ	Schempp-Hirth CS-11 St.Cirrus	584G	
F-CEMM	Schempp-Hirth CS-11/75 St.Cirrus	589	
F-CEMN	Schempp-Hirth CS-11/75 St.Cirrus	616	
F-CEMO	Schmepp-Hirth CS-11/75 St.Cirrus	617	
F-CEMP	Schempp-Hirth CS-11/75 St.Cirrus	643	
F-CEMS	Schempp-Hirth CS-11/75 St.Cirrus	649	
F-CEMU	Schempp-Hirth CS-11/75 St.Cirrus	657	
F-CEMX-C51	Schempp-Hirth CS-11/75 St.Cirrus	669	
F-CEMZ	Schempp-Hirth CS-11/75 St.Cirrus	679	
F-CENA	LCA-Scheibe 12	26	
F-CENB	LCA-Scheibe 12	27	
F-CENF	LCA-Scheibe 12	31	
F-CEOD	Wassmer WA.28 Espadon	109	
F-CEOE	Wassmer WA.28F	110	
F-CEOF	Wassmer WA.28 Espadon	111	
F-CEOG	Wassmer WA.28 Espadon	112	
F-CEOH	Wassmer WA.28 Espadon	113	
F-CEPA	Schempp-Hirth Janus A	05	F-WEPA
F-CEPB	Schempp-Hirth Janus A	14	
F-CEPC-3C	Schempp-Hirth Janus A	17	
F-CEPD	Schempp-Hirth Janus A	21	
F-CEPE	Schempp-Hirth Janus A	22	
F-CEPF	Schempp-Hirth Janus A	33	
F-CEPG	Schempp-Hirth Janus A	32	
F-CEPH	Schempp-Hirth Janus A	38	
F-CEPI	Schempp-Hirth Janus B	46	
F-CEPJ	Schempp-Hirth Janus B	67	
F-CEPK	Schempp-Hirth Janus B	81	
F-CEPL	Schempp-Hirth Janus B	82	
F-CEPM	Schempp-Hirth Janus B	84	
F-CEPN	Schempp-Hirth Janus B	85	
F-CEPO	Schempp-Hirth Janus B	94	
F-CEPP	Schempp-Hirth Janus B	95	
F-CEPQ	Schempp-Hirth Janus B	100	
F-CEPR	Schempp-Hirth Janus B	102	
F-CEPS-J22	Schempp-Hirth Janus B	101	
F-CEPT	Schempp-Hirth Janus B	105	
F-CEPU-U	Schempp-Hirth Janus B	107	
F-CEPV	Schempp-Hirth Janus B	108	
F-CEPX	Schempp-Hirth Janus B	109	
F-CEPY	Schempp-Hirth Janus B	114	
F-CEPZ	Schempp-Hirth Janus B	115	
F-CEQC	Glasflügel H205 Libelle	146	
F-CEQD	Glasflügel H205 Libelle	147	
F-CEQE-H05	Glasflügel H205 Libelle	148	
F-CEQF-H06	Glasflügel H205 Libelle	149	
F-CEQG	Glasflügel H205 Libelle	150	
F-CEQH	Glasflügel H205 Libelle	151	
F-CEQI	Glasflügel H205 Libelle	152	
F-CEQJ	Glasflügel H205 Libelle	156	
F-CEQK	Glasflügel H205 Libelle	157	
F-CEQL	Glasflügel H205 Libelle	159	
F-CEQN	Glasflügel H205 Libelle	161	
F-CEQO	Glasflügel H205 Libelle	162	
F-CEQQ	Glasflügel H205 Libelle	166	
F-CEQR	Glasflügel H205 Libelle	167	
F-CEQT	Glasflügel H205 Libelle	169	
F-CEQU	Glasflügel H205 Libelle	170	
F-CEQV	Glasflügel H303 Mosquito	16	
F-CEQX-M2	Glasflügel H303 Mosquito	41	F-WEQX
F-CEQY	Lanaverre CS-11/75L Standard Cirrus	37	
F-CEQZ	Lanaverre CS-11/75L Standard Cirrus	38	
F-CERA	Schleicher ASK-13	13523	

Regn.	Type	C/n	Prev.Id.	Regn.	Type	C/n	Prev.Id.
F-CERB	Schleicher ASK-13	13531		F-CEXE	Grob G.102 Astir CS	1525	
F-CERD	Schleicher ASK-13	13532		F-CEXF	Grob G.102 Astir CS	1526	
F-CERE	Schleicher ASK-13	13541		F-CEXG	Grob G.102 Astir CS	1527	
F-CERF	Schleicher ASK-13	13542		F-CEXH-R07	Grob G.102/77 Astir CS	1654	
F-CERG	Schleicher K.8B	8985		F-CEXK	Grob G.102 Astir CS	1535	
F-CERH	Schleicher K.8B	8986		F-CEXL	Grob G.102 Astir CS	1536	
F-CERI	Schleicher ASK-18	18032		F-CEXM	Grob G.102/77 Astir CS	1688	
F-CERJ	Schleicher ASK-18	18033		F-CEXN	Grob G.102/77 Astir CS	1697	
F-CERK	Schleicher ASK-13	13545		F-CEXO-R20	Grob G.102/77 Astir CS	1706	
F-CERL	Schleicher ASK-18	18035		F-CEXP	Grob G.102/77 Astir CS	1699	
F-CERM	Schleicher ASW-19	19041		F-CEXQ-R26	Grob G.102/77 Astir CS	1730	
F-CERN	Schleicher ASK-13	13544		F-CEXR-R29	Grob G.102/77 Astir CS	1743	
F-CERO	Schleicher ASK-13	13573		F-CEXS	Grob G.102/77 Astir CS	1759	
F-CERP-X01	Schleicher ASW-20	20024		F-CEXT	Grob G.102/77 Astir CS	1775	
F-CERQ-X00	Schleicher ASW-20	20048		F-CEXU-R31	Grob G.102/77 Astir CS	1773	
F-CERS-F04	Schleicher ASW-19	19241		F-CEXV-R32	Grob G.102/77 Astir CS	1779	
F-CERT	Schleicher ASW-19	19242		F-CEXX	Grob G.102/77 Astir CS	1774	
F-CERU	Schleicher ASW-19B	19326		F-CEXY	Grob G.102/77 Astir CS	1794	
F-CERV-X99	Centrair ASW-20F	20500		F-CEXZ	Grob G.102/77 Astir CS	1795	
F-CERX	Centrair ASW-20F	20513		F-CEYA	Scheibe SF-28A Tandem-Falke	5756	D-KMOS
F-CERY-X117	Centrair ASW-20F	20517					(D-KMGF)
F-CESA	Rolladen-Schneider LS-1F	469		F-CEYB	Scheibe SF-28A Tandem-Falke	5781	D-KCIR(2)
F-CESB	Rolladen-Schneider LS-1F	455		F-CEYC	Scheibe SF-28A Tandem-Falke	5783	(D-KDFM(1))
F-CESD	Rolladen-Schneider LS-3	3203		F-CEYD	Scheibe SF-28A Tandem-Falke	5784	(D-KDFN(1))
F-CESE-S02	Rolladen-Schneider LS-3A	3303		F-CEYE	Scheibe SF-28A Tandem-Falke	5785	(D-KDFQ(1))
F-CESF-S03	Rolladen-Schneider LS-3A	3204		F-CEYF	Scheibe SF-28A Tandem-Falke	5786	(D-KDFW(1))
F-CESG-S04	Rolladen-Schneider LS-3A	3205		F-CEYG	Scheibe SF-28A Tandem-Falke	5787	(D-KDFY(1))
F-CESH	Rolladen-Schneider LS-3A	3157		F-CEYH	Scheibe SF-28A Tandem-Falke	5788	(D-KDFZ(1))
F-CESI	Rolladen-Schneider LS-3A	3187		F-CEYI	Scheibe SF-28A Tandem-Falke	5789	(D-KDFX(3))
F-CESJ-S07	Rolladen-Schneider LS-3A	3383		F-CEYJ	Scheibe SF-28A Tandem-Falke	5790	(D-KDFY(3))
F-CESK-S08	Rolladen-Schneider LS-3A	3384		F-CEYK	Scheibe SF-28A Tandem-Falke	5792	(D-KDCJ(1))
F-CESL-S09	Rolladen-Schneider LS-3A	3385		F-CEYL	Scheibe SF-28A Tandem-Falke	5793	(D-KDCK(1))
F-CESM-S10	Rolladen-Schneider LS-3A	3419		F-CEYM	Scheibe SF-28A Tandem-Falke	5794	(D-KDCQ(1))
F-CESO-S14	Rolladen-Schneider LS-3A	3438		F-CEYN	Scheibe SF-28A Tandem-Falke	5795	(D-KDCU(2))
F-CESQ	Rolladen-Schneider LS-3A	3452		F-CEYO	Scheibe SF-28A Tandem-Falke	5796	(D-KDCW)
F-CESR	Rolladen-Schneider LS-3A-17	3453		F-CEYP	Scheibe SF-28A Tandem-Falke	5797	(D-KDCX)
F-CESS	Rolladen-Schneider LS-3A	3454		F-CEYQ	Scheibe SF-28A Tandem-Falke	5798	(D-KDCY)
F-CEST-S17	Rolladen-Schneider LS-3A	3455		F-CEYR	Scheibe SF-28A Tandem-Falke	57100	(D-KDBS(1))
F-CESU-S19	Rolladen-Schneider LS-3A	3460		F-CEYS	Scheibe SF-28A Tandem-Falke	57101	(D-KDBR(1))
F-CETG	Carmam JP.15/36A Aiglon	9		F-CEYT	Scheibe SF-28A Tandem-Falke	57104	(D-KDBY(1))
F-CETI	Carmam JP.15/36A Aiglon	11		F-CEYU	Scheibe SF-28A Tandem-Falke	57105	(D-KDBU(2))
F-CETJ	Carmam JP.15/36A Aiglon	12		F-CEYV	Scheibe SF-28A Tandem-Falke	5734	HB-2022
F-CETL	Carmam JP.15/36A Aiglon	14					(D-KOED(1))
F-CETN	Carmam JP.15/36AR Aiglon	16	F-WETN	F-CEYY	Scheibe SF-28A Tandem-Falke	57109	(D-KDGS(1))
F-CETP	Carmam JP.15/36A Aiglon	18		F-CEZA	Scheibe Bergfalke IV	5861	
F-CETR	Carmam JP.15/36A Aiglon	20		F-CEZB	Scheibe Bergfalke IV	5865	
F-CETT	Carmam JP.15/36AR Aiglon	22		F-CFAA	Schempp-Hirth HS-7 Mini-Nimbus	17	F-WFAA
F-CETV	Carmam JP.15/36A Aiglon	24		F-CFAB-101	Schempp-Hirth HS-7 Mini-Nimbus	130	
F-CETY	Carmam JP.15/36AR Aiglon	29		F-CFAC	Schempp-Hirth Janus B	121	
F-CETZ	Carmam JP.15/36A Aiglon	30		F-CFAD	Schempp-Hirth Janus B	124	
F-CEUB	Caproni A.21S Calif	236		F-CFAE-E	Schempp-Hirth Janus B	128	
F-CEUC	Caproni A.21S Calif	237		F-CFAF	Schempp-Hirth Janus B	131	
F-CEUE	Caproni A.21S Calif	240		F-CFAG	Schempp-Hirth Janus B	135	
F-CEUF	Caproni A.21S Calif	241		F-CFAH	Schempp-Hirth Janus B	137	
F-CEUH	Caproni A.21S Calif	244		F-CFAI	Schempp-Hirth Janus B	139	
F-CEUJ	Centrair ASW-20FL	20174		F-CFAJ-J39	Schempp-Hirth Janus B	153	
F-CEUK	Centrair ASW-20F	20168		F-CFAK	Schempp-Hirth Janus B	57	D-7950
F-CEVA	Schempp-Hirth CS-11/75 Standard Cirrus	698		F-CFAL	Schempp-Hirth Janus C	154	
F-CEVF	Lanaverre CS-11/75L Standard Cirrus	5		F-CFAM-M	Schempp-Hirth Janus C	155	
F-CEVI	Lanaverre CS-11/75L Standard Cirrus	8		F-CFAN-J43	Schempp-Hirth Janus C	159	
F-CEVJ	Lanaverre CS-11/75L Standard Cirrus	9		F-CFAO-PTT	Schempp-Hirth Janus C	160	
F-CEVL	Lanaverre CS-11/75L Standard Cirrus	11		F-CFAP	Schempp-Hirth Janus C	164	
F-CEVM	Lanaverre CS-11/75L Standard Cirrus	12		F-CFAQ	Schempp-Hirth Janus C	173	
F-CEVN-C68	Lanaverre CS-11/75L Standard Cirrus	13		F-CFAR-IN	Schempp-Hirth Janus C	166	
F-CEVP	Lanaverre CS-11/75L Standard Cirrus	23		F-CFAS	Schempp-Hirth Janus B	175	
F-CEVQ-C71	Lanaverre CS-11/75L Standard Cirrus	24		F-CFAT	Schempp-Hirth Janus B	180	
F-CEVT	Lanaverre CS-11/75L Standard Cirrus	28		F-CFAU-J50	Schempp-Hirth Janus B	192	
F-CEVU	Lanaverre CS-11/75L Standard Cirrus	29		F-CFAV	Schempp-Hirth Janus CT	3/195	F-WFAV
F-CEVV-C76	Lanaverre CS-11/75L Standard Cirrus	30					D-KFAV
F-CEVY-RR	Lanaverre CS-11/78L Standard Cirrus	32	F-WEVY				F-WFAV
F-CEVZ-C7	Lanaverre CS-11/75L Standard Cirrus	34		F-CFAX-73	Schempp-Hirth Janus B	204	
F-CEXA-R01	Grob G.102 Astir CS	1459		F-CFAY	Schempp-Hirth Janus B	207	
F-CEXB	Grob G.102 Astir CS	1522		F-CFAZ	Schempp-Hirth Janus B	221	
F-CEXC	Grob G.102 Astir CS	1523		F-CFBA-T01	Grob G.103 Twin Astir	3055	
F-CEXD-R04	Grob G.102 Astir CS	1524		F-CFBB-T02	Grob G.103 Twin Astir	3082	

Regn.	Type	C/n	Prev.Id.
F-CFBC-T03	Grob G.103T Twin Astir Trainer	3124	
F-CFBD	Grob G.103 Twin Astir	3119	
F-CFBE	Grob G.103 Twin Astir	3120	
F-CFBG	Grob G.103 Twin Astir	3107	
F-CFBH-T08	Grob G.103 Twin Astir	3123	
F-CFBI	Grob G.103 Twin Astir	3131	
F-CFBJ-T10	Grob G.103 Twin Astir	3132	
F-CFBK-T11	Grob G.103 Twin Astir	3133	
F-CFBL	Grob G.103 Twin Astir	3114	
F-CFBM-T13	Grob G.103 Twin Astir	3135	
F-CFBN	Grob G.103 Twin Astir	3158	
F-CFBO-T15	Grob G.103T Twin Astir Trainer	3128	
F-CFBP-T16	Grob G.103T Twin Astir Trainer	3144	
F-CFBQ	Grob G.103 Twin Astir	3134	
F-CFBR-T18	Grob G.103 Twin Astir	3161	
F-CFBS-T19	Grob G.103 Twin Astir	3162	
F-CFBT-T20	Grob G.103 Twin Astir	3125	
F-CFBU-T21	Grob G.103 Twin Astir	3183	
F-CFBV	Grob G.103 Twin Astir	3153	
F-CFBX	Grob G.103 Twin Astir	3281	
F-CFBZ	Grob G.103T Twin Astir Trainer	3201	
F-CFCB-R15	Grob G.102/77J Astir Jeans	2079	
F-CFCC	Grob G.102/77J Astir Jeans	2084	
F-CFCD-R21	Grob G.102/77J Astir Jeans	2111	
F-CFCE	Grob G.102/77J Astir Jeans	2094	
F-CFCF	Grob G.102/77J Astir Jeans	2098	
F-CFCH-R34	Grob G.102/77J Astir Jeans	2115	
F-CFCI-R25	Grob G.102/77J Astir Jeans	2123	
F-CFCJ	Grob G.102/77J Astir Jeans	2144	
F-CFCK	Grob G.102/77J Astir Jeans	2145	
F-CFCL-R36	Grob G.102/77J Astir Jeans	2163	
F-CFCM-R37	Grob G.102/77J Astir Jeans	2177	
F-CFCO-R40	Grob G.102/77J Astir Jeans	2179	
F-CFCQ	Grob G.102/77J Astir Jeans	2200	
F-CFCR-R43	Grob G.102/77J Astir Jeans	2201	
F-CFCS	Grob G.102/77J Astir Jeans	2204	
F-CFCU-R46	Grob G.102/77J Astir Jeans	2231	
F-CFCX	Grob G.102C Club Astir II	5021C	
F-CFCY-R49	Grob G.102C Club Astir II	5022C	
F-CFCZ-60	Grob G.102C Club Astir II	5023C	
F-CFDA	Schempp-Hirth Standard Cirrus G/81	256	F-WFDA
F-CFDB-C89	Schempp-Hirth Standard Cirrus G/81	257	F-WFDB
F-CFDC	Schempp-Hirth Standard Cirrus G/81	260	F-WFDC
F-CFDD	Scheibe SF-34B	5136	
F-CFDE	Scheibe SF-34B	5140	
F-CFDF	Schempp-Hirth Discus CS	017CS	
F-CFDG	Rolladen-Schneider LS-6C	6301	
F-CFDH	Schempp-Hirth Discus b	509	
F-CFDI	Schempp-Hirth Discus b	513	
F-CFDJ	Schempp-Hirth Discus CS	175CS	
F-CFDK	Schempp-Hirth Discus CS	180CS	
F-CFDL-D31	Schempp-Hirth Discus CS	221CS	
F-CFDM	Schempp-Hirth Discus b	139	D-4693
F-CFDN	Schempp-Hirth Discus CS	235	
F-CFEB	Issoire E-78B Silène	5	
F-CFED	Issoire E-78 Silène	9	
F-CFER	Issoire E-78B Silène	10	
F-CFFA-X02	Centrair ASW-20FL	20101	
F-CFFB	Centrair ASW-20F	20102	
F-CFFD	Centrair ASW-20F	20104	
F-CFFE	Centrair ASW-20F	20105	
F-CFFF	Centrair ASW-20F	20106	
F-CFFH	Centrair ASW-20F	20111	
F-CFFI-JM	Centrair ASW-20F	20112	
F-CFFN-X18	Centrair ASW-20FL	20117	
F-CFFP	Centrair ASW-20F	20120	
F-CFFS-X24	Centrair ASW-20FL	20124	
F-CFFT	Centrair ASW-20FL	20125	
F-CFFU	Centrair ASW-20F	20126	
F-CFFV-X29	Centrair ASW-20F	20129	
F-CFFY	Centrair ASW-20F	20134	
F-CFFZ	Centrair ASW-20F	20135	
F-CFGC	Carmam JP.15/36AR Aiglon	35	
F-CFGE	Pottier 15/34 Kit Club	50-38	
F-CFGI	Pottier 15/34 Kit Club	50-44	

Regn.	Type	C/n	Prev.Id.
F-CFGJ	Pottier 15/34 Kit Club	50-46	
F-CFGK	Pottier 15/34 Kit Club	50-48	
F-CFGM	Pottier 15/34 Kit Club	50-49	
F-CFHB	Grob G.103 Twin Astir	3229	
F-CFHD	Grob G.103 Twin Astir	3234	
F-CFHE-T30	Grob G.103 Twin Astir	3241	
F-CFHF-T31	Grob G.103 Twin Astir	3244	
F-CFHG	Grob G.103T Twin Astir Trainer	3243	
F-CFHH	Grob G.103 Twin Astir	3250	
F-CFHI -T34	Grob G.103 Twin Astir	3255	
F-CFHJ	Grob G.103T Twin Astir Trainer	3283	
F-CFHK	Grob G.103T Twin Astir Trainer	3282	
F-CFHM	Grob G.103 Twin Astir II	3530	
F-CFHO	Grob G.103 Twin Astir II	3566	
F-CFHP	Grob G.103 Twin Astir II	3567	
F-CFHQ	Grob G.103 Twin Astir II	3568	
F-CFHR	Grob G.103 Twin Astir II	3569	
F-CFHS	Grob G.103 Twin Astir II	3578	
F-CFHT	Grob G.103 Twin Astir II	3579	
F-CFHU	Grob G.103 Twin Astir II	3580	
F-CFHX-T48	Grob G.103 Twin Astir II	3582	
F-CFHY-T49	Grob G.103 Twin Astir II	3583	
F-CFHZ	Grob G.103 Twin Astir II	3584	
F-CFIA	Grob G.102/77 Astir CS	1801	
F-CFIB	Grob G.102/77 Astir CS	1802	
F-CFIC	Grob G.102/77 Astir CS	1807	
F-CFID	Grob G.102/77 Astir CS	1810	
F-CFIE-R54	Grob G.102/77 Astir CS	1811	
F-CFIF-R55	Grob G.102/77 Astir CS	1815	
F-CFIG-R56	Grob G.102/77 Astir CS	1821	
F-CFII	Grob G.102S Speed Astir	5034S	
F-CFIJ	Grob G.102S Speed Astir	5035S	
F-CFIK	Grob G.102S Speed Astir	5036S	
F-CFIL	Grob G.102S Speed Astir	5037S	
F-CFIM	Grob G.102S Speed Astir	5038S	
F-CFIN-R73	Grob G.102S Speed Astir	5039S	
F-CFIO	Grob G.102S Speed Astir	5042S	
F-CFIP	Grob G.102S Speed Astir II	5043S	
F-CFIQ-R76	Grob G.102 Astir CS 77	1817	
F-CFIR	Grob G.102 Astir CS 77	1637	PH-572
F-CFJA	Scheibe SF-28A Tandem-Falke	57115	(D-KDGX(2))
F-CFJB	Scheibe SF-28A Tandem-Falke	57117	(D-KOOH(1))
F-CFJC	Scheibe SF-28A Tandem-Falke	57119	(D-KNAU(1))
F-CFJD	Scheibe SF-28A Tandem-Falke	57121	D-KNIH
F-CFJE	Scheibe SF-28A Tandem-Falke	5769	D-KACV
F-CFJF	Scheibe SF-28A Tandem-Falke	5726	D-KOAO
F-CFJG	Scheibe SF-28A Tandem-Falke	5725	D-KOAM
F-CFJH	Scheibe SF-28A Tandem-Falke	5709	D-KHOS
F-CFJJ	Scheibe SF-28A Tandem-Falke	5720	D-KOAL
F-WFJK	Scheibe SF-28A Tandem-Falke	5705	D-KHOO
F-CFJL	Scheibe SF-28A Tandem-Falke	5737	D-KOEG
F-CFKA	Grob G.103 Twin Astir II	3585	
F-CFKB	Grob G.103 Twin Astir II	3586	
F-CFKC-T53	Grob G.103 Twin Astir II	3587	
F-CFKD	Grob G.103 Twin Astir II	3588	
F-CFKE	Grob G.103 Twin Astir II	3589	
F-CFKF-T56	Grob G.103 Twin Astir II	3590	
F-CFKG	Grob G.103 Twin Astir II	3591	
F-CFKH	Grob G.103 Twin Astir II	3592	
F-CFKI	Grob G.103 Twin Astir II	3627	
F-CFKJ-T60	Grob G.103 Twin Astir II	3628	
F-CFKK-T61	Grob G.103 Twin Astir II	3629	
F-CFKL-T62	Grob G.103 Twin Astir II	3630	
F-CFKM	Grob G.103 Twin Astir II	3631	
F-CFKN	Grob G.103 Twin Astir II	3693	
F-CFKO-T65	Grob G.103 Twin Astir II	3694	
F-CFKP	Grob G.103 Twin Astir II	3695	
F-CFKQ-T67	Grob G.103 Twin Astir II	3704	
F-CFKR-T68	Grob G.103 Twin Astir II	3705	
F-CFKS	Grob G.103 Twin Astir II	3706	
F-CFKT	Grob G.103 Twin Astir II	3707	
F-CFKU	Grob G.103 Twin Astir II	3715	
F-CFKV-T75	Grob G.103 Twin Astir II	3759	
F-CFKY-T77	Grob G.103 Twin Astir II	3834	
F-CFKZ-T78	Grob G.103 Twin Astir II	3835	

Regn.	Type	C/n	Prev.Id.
F-CFLC	Centrair ASW-20FL	20138	
F-CFLD-X41	Centrair ASW-20FL	20141	
F-CFLE	Centrair ASW-20F	20142	
F-CFLF-X43	Centrair ASW-20F	20143	
F-CFLG	Centrair ASW-20F	20144	
F-CFLH	Centrair ASW-20FL	20146	
F-CFLI- LI	Centrair ASW-20FL	20148	
F-CFLJ	Centrair ASW-20F	20147	
F-CFLK-X49	Centrair ASW-20F	20149	
F-CFLM	Centrair ASW-20F	20152	
F-CFLN	Centrair ASW-20FL	20153	
F-CFLP-AV	Centrair ASW-20F	20157	
F-CFLO	Centrair ASW-20F	20158	
F-CFLR	Centrair ASW-20F	20159	
F-CFLT-X61	Centrair ASW-20FL	20161	
F-CFLX-X86	Centrair ASW-20FL	20186	
F-CFLY	Centrair ASW-20F	20170	
F-CFMA	Grob G.102C Club Astir II	5024C	
F-CFMC-R63	Grob G.102C Club Astir II	5053C	
F-CFMD	Grob G.102C Club Astir II	5054C	
F-CFMF	Grob G.102C Club Astir IIIB	5509CB	
F-CFMG	Grob G.102C Club Astir IIIB	5544CB	
F-CFMI	Grob G.102C Club Astir IIIB	5565CB	
F-CFMJ	Grob G.102C Club Astir IIIB	5582CB	
F-CFMK	Grob G.102/77J Astir Jeans	2240	D-5946
F-CFML-R86	Grob G.102/77J Astir Jeans	2245	
F-CFMM	Grob G.102/77J Astir Jeans	2093	D-7535
F-CFMN	Grob G.102/77J Astir Jeans	2055	D-7576
F-CFMO	Grob G.102/77J Astir Jeans	2023	D-4828
F-CFMP	Grob G.102/77J Astir Jeans	2036	D-3882
F-CFMQ	Grob G.102/77J Astir Jeans	2092	D-7534
F-CFMR	Grob G.102/77J Astir Jeans	2159	D-4555
F-CFMS	Grob G.102/77J Astir Jeans	2202	D-3821
F-CFMT	Grob G.102/77J Astir Jeans	2071	HB-1399
F-CFMU	Grob G.102/77J Astir Jeans	2102	D-7630
F-CFNA	Pottier 15/34 Kit Club	50-57	
F-CFNB	Pottier 15/34 Kit Club	50-59	
F-CFPD	Siren PIK-20E2-F	710	
F-CFPE	Siren PIK-30	713	
F-CFPG	Siren PIK-30	723	
F-CFPH	Siren PIK-30	724	
F-CFPI	Siren PIK-30	725	
F-CFPJ	Siren PIK-30	727	
F-CFPO	Siren PIK-30	712	F-WFPO
F-CFQB-B35	Centrair 101A Pégase	101A-035	
F-CFQD	Centrair 101A Pégase	101A-036	
F-CFQE	Centrair 101A Pégase	101A-038	
F-CFQG-B43	Centrair 101A Pégase	101A-043	
F-CFQH	Centrair 101A Pégase	101A-037	
F-CFQK-B47	Centrair 101A Pégase	101A-047	
F-CFQM-B50	Centrair 101A Pégase	101A-050	
F-CFQN-B51	Centrair 101A Pégase	101A-051	
F-CFQO-B52	Centrair 101A Pégase	101A-052	
F-CFQP	Centrair 101A Pégase	101A-053	
F-CFQR	Centrair 101A Pégase	101A-055	
F-CFQS	Centrair 101A Pégase	101A-059	
F-CFQT	Centrair 101A Pégase	101A-044	
F-CFQV	Centrair 101A Pégase	101A-056	
F-CFQZ	Centrair 101A Pégase	101A-067	
F-CFRA	Centrair 101A Pégase	101A-001	F-WFRA
F-CFRB	Centrair 101A Pégase	101A-005	
F-CFRC-B06	Centrair 101A Pégase	101A-006	
F-CFRD	Centrair 101A Pégase	101A-007	
F-CFRE	Centrair 101A Pégase	101A-008	
F-CFRF	Centrair 101A Pégase	101A-009	
F-CFRG	Centrair 101A Pégase	101A-010	
F-CFRH-B14	Centrair 101A Pégase	101A-014	
F-CFRI	Centrair 101A Pégase	101A-011	
F-CFRJ	Centrair 101A Pégase	101A-013	
F-CFRK	Centrair 101A Pégase	101A-015	
F-CFRL	Centrair 101A Pégase	101A-018	
F-CFRM	Centrair 101A Pégase	101A-019	
F-CFR0	Centrair 101A Pégase	101A-017	
F-CFRQ	Centrair 101A Pégase	101A-021	
F-CFRT-B22	Centrair 101A Pégase	101A-022	

Regn.	Type	C/n	Prev.Id.
F-CFRU-B25	Centrair 101A Pégase	101A-025	
F-CFRV-B30	Centrair 101A Pégase	101A-030	
F-CFRX-B31	Centrair 101A Pégase	101A-031	
F-CFSA	Centrair ASW-20FL	20516	
F-CFSB	Centrair ASW-20F	20519	
F-CFSC	Centrair ASW-20F	20521	
F-CFSE	Centrair ASW-20F	20523	
F-CFSF	Centrair ASW-20F	20524	
F-CFSG	Centrair ASW-20F	20525	
F-CFSH	Centrair ASW-20F	20511	
F-CFTA	Centrair ASW-20FL	20107	EI-126 F-CFFG
F-CFTB	Grob G.103 Twin Astir II	3212	
F-CFTC	Schleicher K.8B	8422	
F-CFTD	Scheibe SF-28A Tandem-Falke	5719	D-KOAK
F-CFTE	Scheibe Bergfalke IV	5844	
F-CFTF	Scheibe Bergfalke IV	5827	D-KOLT
F-CFTH	Schleicher K.8B	8450SH	HB-823
F-CFTI	Scheibe SF-28A Tandem-Falke	5780	OY-XDD D-KCLJ
F-CFTJ	Scheibe SF-28A Tandem-Falke	5738	D-KOEH
F-CFTK	Scheibe SF-28A Tandem-Falke	5758	HB-2032 D-KMGH
F-CFTL-R23	Grob G.102/77J Astir Jeans	2113	3A-MCG F-CFCG
F-CFTM	Scheibe SF-28A Tandem-Falke	5702/V-2	D-KAOQ
F-CFTN	Scheibe SF-28A Tandem-Falke	5762	OY-XHG D-KAWU (D-KACO(2))
F-CFTO	Schempp-Hirth Nimbus 3/24.5	33	BGA3102/FAH N17UF
F-CFTU	Scheibe SF-28A Tandem-Falke	5722	D-KAUM
F-CFUA	Schempp-Hirth Nimbus 3	35	
F-CFUB	Schempp-Hirth Nimbus 3/24.5	38	F-WFUB
F-CFUC	Schempp-Hirth Nimbus 2	176	D-6851
F-CFUD	Schempp-Hirth Nimbus 3DT	4	F-WFUD D-KFJM
F-CFUE	Schempp-Hirth Nimbus 3DT	10	F-WFUE D-KFUE
F-CFUF	Schempp-Hirth Nimbus 3DM	10/28	D-KCUF
F-CFUG	Schempp-Hirth Nimbus 3D	6/33	D-1753
F-CFUH	Schempp-Hirth Nimbus 3DM	8/24	D-KFUH
F-CFUI -EN	Schempp-Hirth Nimbus 3D	8/41	
F-CFUJ-SFA	Schempp-Hirth Nimbus 3D	7/35	
F-CFUN	Schempp-Hirth Nimbus 3/24.5	50	F-WFUN
F-CFUO	Schempp-Hirth Nimbus 3DT	55	
F-CFUP	Schempp-Hirth Nimbus 3DT	60	
F-CFUQ	Schempp-Hirth Nimbus 3DT	62	
F-CFUR	Schempp-Hirth Nimbus 3/24.5	34	D-1151
F-CFUS	Schempp-Hirth Nimbus 4DT	1/1	D-KFUS D-2111
F-CFUT	Schempp-Hirth Nimbus 3D	10/50	D-2872
F-CFUU	Schempp-Hirth Nimbus 4 DM	2/6	D-KFUU
F-CFUV	Schempp-Hirth Nimbus 4D	3/11	D-8563
F-CFUX	Schempp-Hirth Nimbus 4 DM	6/14	D-KLUX
F-CFUY	Schempp-Hirth Nimbus 4D	5/29	
	(Intended for modification to Nimbus 4DT c/n 8/29)		
F-CFUZ-EN	Schempp-Hirth Nimbus 4D	6/36	
F-CFVA-PP	Glaser-Dirks DG-400	4-52	F-WFVA
F-CFVC	Glaser-Dirks DG-400	4-109	F-WFVC
F-CFVD	Glaser-Dirks DG-400	4-110	F-WFVD
F-CFVE	Glaser-Dirks DG-400	4-121	F-WFVE
F-CFVF	Glaser-Dirks DG-400	4-122	F-WFVF
F-CFVG	Glaser-Dirks DG-400	4-140	F-WFVG
F-CFVH	Glaser-Dirks DG-400	4-157	
F-CFVI	Glaser-Dirks DG-400	4-172	
F-CFVJ	Glaser-Dirks DG-400	4-173	
F-CFVK-K17	Glaser-Dirks DG-300 Elan	3E-36	F-WFVK
F-CFVL	Glaser-Dirks DG-300 Elan	3E-88	F-WFVL
F-CFVM	Glaser-Dirks DG-300 Elan	3E-137	F-WFVM
F-CFVN	Glaser-Dirks DG-300 Elan	3E-153	F-WFVN
F-WFVO	Glaser-Dirks DG-300 Elan	3E-171	
F-CFVP	Glaser-Dirks DG-300 Elan	3E-170	F-WFVP
F-CFVQ	Glaser-Dirks DG-300 Elan	3E-202	F-WFVQ
F-CFVR	Glaser-Dirks DG-300 Elan	3E-212	F-WFVR

Regn.	Type	C/n	Prev.Id.
F-CFVS	Glaser-Dirks DG-300 Elan	3E-229	F-WFVS
F-CFVT	Glaser-Dirks DG-300 Elan	3E-245	F-WFVT
F-CFVU	Glaser-Dirks DG-300 Elan	3E-276	F-WFVU
F-WFXA	Centrair 101C Pégase	101C-901	
F-WFXB	Centrair 101C Pégase	101C-902	
F-CFXC-B72	Centrair 101A Pégase	101A-072	
F-CFXF	Centrair 101A Pégase	101A-075	
F-CFXG	Centrair 101A Pégase	101A-076	
F-CFXI	Centrair 101A Pégase	101A-092	
F-CFXJ-B93	Centrair 101A Pégase	101A-093	
F-CFXK	Centrair 101A Pégase	101A-085	
F-CFXM	Centrair 101A Pégase	101A-0106	
F-CFXN	Centrair 101A Pégase	101A-0104	
F-CFX0	Centrair 101A Pégase	101A-0103	
F-CFXP	Centrair 101A Pégase	101A-0101	
F-CFXQ	Centrair 101A Pégase	101A-0113	
F-CFXR-B114	Centrair 101A Pégase	101A-0114	
F-CFXS	Centrair 101A Pégase	101A-0115	
F-CFXT	Centrair 101A Pégase	101A-0116	
F-CFXV-XV	Centrair 101A Pégase	101A-0134	
F-CFXX	Centrair 101A Pégase	101A-0133	
F-CFXY	Centrair ASW-20F	20531	
F-CFXZ-B135	Centrair 101A Pégase	101A-0135	
F-CFYA-T79	Grob G.103 Twin Astir II	3838	
F-CFYB	Grob G.103 Twin Astir II	3766	
F-CFYC	Grob G.103 Twin II Acro	33951-K-184	
F-CFYD-T83	Grob G.103 Twin II Acro	33952-K-185	
F-CFYE	Grob G.103 Twin II Acro	33963-K-196	
F-CFYF-T85	Grob G.103 Twin II Acro	33968-K-201	
F-CFYG	Grob G.103 Twin II Acro	34052-K-282	
F-CFYH	Grob G.103 Twin II Acro	34058-K-288	
F-CFYI	Grob G.103 Twin Astir II	3570	D-6640
F-CFYJ	Grob G.103 Twin Astir II	3596	D-3963
F-CFYK	Grob G.103 Twin Astir II	3556	D-8764
F-CFYL	Grob G.103 Twin Astir II	3845-K-91	PH-744
F-CFYM	Grob G.103 Twin Astir II	33965-K-198	D-8067
F-CFYN	Grob G.103 Twin Astir II	3594	D-4867
F-CFYO	Grob G.103 Twin Astir II	3523	D-4772
F-CFYP	Grob G.103 Twin Astir II	3675	D-8703
F-CFYQ	Grob G.103 Twin Astir II	3188	HB-1442
F-CFYR	Grob G.103 Twin Astir II	3663	D-2600
F-CFYS-T99	Grob G.103 Twin Astir	3078	D-3949
F-CFYT	Grob G.103A Twin II Acro	3732-K-47	D-1604
			PL-90
			D-6189
F-CFZA-J	Rolladen-Schneider LS-4	4336	
F-CFZB	Rolladen-Schneider LS-4	4358	
F-CFZC-V30	Rolladen-Schneider LS-4	4359	
F-CFZD	Rolladen-Schneider LS-4	4397	
F-CFZE-V33	Rolladen-Schneider LS-4	4409	
F-CFZF	Rolladen-Schneider LS-4	4425	
F-CFZG	Rolladen-Schneider LS-4	4441	
F-CFZH-V36	Rolladen-Schneider LS-4	4476	
F-CFZI	Rolladen-Schneider LS-4	4487	
F-CFZJ-V38	Rolladen-Schneider LS-4	4488	
F-CFZK	Rolladen-Schneider LS-4	4499	
F-CFZL	Rolladen-Schneider LS-4	4500	
F-CFZM	Rolladen-Schneider LS-4	4509	
F-CFZN	Rolladen-Schneider LS-4	4517	
F-CFZO	Rolladen-Schneider LS-4	4535	
F-CFZP-LI	Rolladen-Schneider LS-4	4645	
F-CFZQ	Rolladen-Schneider LS-4	4644	
F-CFZR	Rolladen-Schneider LS-4	4643	
F-CFZS	Rolladen-Schneider LS-4	4680	
F-CFZT	Rolladen-Schneider LS-4	4639	
F-CFZU	Rolladen-Schneider LS-4	4678	
F-CFZV	Rolladen-Schneider LS-4	4707	
F-CFZX	Rolladen-Schneider LS-4	4779	
F-CFZY	Rolladen-Schneider LS-4	4142	3A-MCD
F-CFZZ	Rolladen-Schneider LS-4B	4938	
F-CGAB	Valentin Taifun 17E	1027	F-WGAB
			D-KCCF
F-CGAC	Valentin Taifun 17E	1037	F-WGAC
			D-KDSE

Regn.	Type	C/n	Prev.Id.
F-CGAD	Valentin Taifun 17E	1049	F-WGAD
			D-KDSO
F-CGAF	Valentin Taifun 17E	1073	F-WGAF
			D-KHVA
F-CGAG	Valentin Taifun 17E	1100	F-WGAG
			D-KHVA
F-CGAJ	Valentin Taifun 17E-II	1124	F-WGAJ
			D-KHVA
F-CGAK	Hoffmann H-36 Dimona	3524	F-WGAK
F-CGAM	Hoffmann H-36 Dimona	36206	F-WGAM
F-CGAN	Hoffmann H-36 Dimona	36237	F-WGAN
F-CGAP	Hoffmann H-36 Dimona	36225	F-WGAP
F-CGAQ	Hoffmann H-36 Dimona	36226	F-WGAQ
F-CGAR	Hoffmann H-36 Dimona	36228	F-WGAR
F-CGAS	Hoffmann H-36 Dimona	36229	F-WGAS
F-CGAT	Hoffmann H-36 Dimona	36258	F-WGAT
F-CGAU	Hoffmann H-36 Dimona	36260	F-WGAU
F-CGAV	Hoffmann H-36 Dimona	36265	F-WGAV
F-CGAX	Hoffmann H-36 Dimona	36270	F-WGAX
F-CGBA-B13	Centrair 101A Pégase	101A-0136	
F-CGBB-TB	Centrair 101A Pégase	101A-0137	
F-CGBC-TC	Centrair 101A Pégase	101A-0138	
F-CGBD-TD	Centrair 101A Pégase	101A-0139	
F-CGBE	Centrair 101A Pégase	101A-0140	
F-CGBF	Centrair 101B Pégase	101B-0143	F-WGBF
F-CGBG	Centrair 101BC Pégase	101B-0148	F-WGBG
F-CGBH	Centrair 101A Pégase	101A-0144	
F-CGBI	Centrair 101A Pégase	101A-0145	
F-CGBJ-B146	Centrair 101A Pégase	101A-0146	
F-CGBK	Centrair 101A Pégase	101A-0147	
F-CGBL-I	Centrair 101A Pégase	101A-0150	
F-CGBM	Centrair 101A Pégase	101A-0151	
F-CGBN-B152	Centrair 101A Pégase	101A-0152	
F-CGBO	Centrair 101A Pégase	101A-0153	
F-CGBP-BP	Centrair 101A Pégase	101A-0171	
F-CGBQ	Centrair 101A Pégase	101A-0158	
F-CGBR	Centrair 101A Pégase	101A-0159	
F-CGBS	Centrair 101A Pégase	101A-0160	
F-CGBT	Centrair 101A Pégase	101A-0162	
F-CGBU	Centrair 101A Pégase	101A-0163	
F-CGBV	Centrair 101A Pégase	101A-0164	
F-CGBX	Centrair 101A Pégase	101A-0165	
F-CGBY-J8	Centrair 101A Pégase	101A-0168	
F-CGBZ	Centrair 101A Pégase	101A-0169	
F-CGCA-BYO	Schleicher ASW-20C	20762	F-WGCA
F-CGCB	Schleicher ASW-20L	20381	
F-CGCC	Schleicher ASK-21	21244	
F-CGCD	Schleicher ASW-22	22046	F-WGCD
F-CGCE	Schleicher ASH-25	25006	F-WGCE
F-CGCF	Schleicher ASW-22	22026	F-WGCF
F-CGCG	Schleicher ASK-21	21245	
F-CGCH	Schleicher ASK-21	21269	
F-CGCI	Schleicher ASK-21	21264	
F-CGCJ	Schleicher ASK-21	21270	
F-CGCK	Schleicher ASK-21	21277	
F-CGCL	Schleicher ASK-21	21298	
F-CGCM	Schleicher ASK-21	21344	
F-CGCN	Schleicher ASW-20C	20817	
F-CGCO	Schleicher ASW-20C	20818	
F-CGCP	Schleicher ASW-20C	20819	
F-CGCQ	Schleicher ASW-20CL	20860	
F-CGCR	Schleicher ASW-20CL	20829	F-WGCR
F-CGCT	Schleicher ASK-23	23034	F-WGCT
F-CGCU	Schleicher ASK-23	23053	F-WGCU
F-CGCV	Schleicher ASK-23B	23063	F-WGCV
F-CGCX	Schleicher ASK-23B	23064	F-WGCX
F-CGCY	Schleicher ASW-15	15170	FrAF
F-CGCZ	Schleicher ASK-23B	23072	F-WGCZ
F-CGDB	Aerostructure-Fournier RF-10	8	F-WGDB
F-CGDC	Aerostructure-Fournier RF-10	9	F-WGDC
F-CGDD	Aerostructure-Fournier RF-10	10	F-WGDD
F-CGDE	Aerostructure-Fournier RF-10	14	
F-CGEB	Centrair 101A Pégase (Code 'B170')	101A-0170	
F-CGEC	Centrair 101A Pégase	101A-0172	
F-CGED	Centrair 101A Pégase	101A-0173	

Regn.	Type	C/n	Prev.Id.
F-CGEE-FF	Centrair 101A Pégase	101A-0179	
F-CGEF	Centrair 101A Pégase (Code 'B174')	101A-0174	
F-CGEG	Centrair 101A Pégase	101A-0180	
F-CGEH-EZ	Centrair 101A Pégase	101A-0167	
F-CGEI	Centrair 101A Pégase	101A-0181	
F-CGEJ	Centrair 101A Pégase	101A-0183	
F-CGEL	Centrair 101A Pégase	101A-0192	
F-CGEM-EM	Centrair 101A Pégase	101A-0191	
F-CGEN-B196	Centrair 101A Pégase	101A-0196	
F-CGEO	Centrair 101A Pégase	101A-0194	
F-CGEP	Centrair 101A Pégase	101A-0193	
F-CGEQ	Centrair 101A Pégase	101A-0197	
F-CGER	Centrair 101A Pégase	101A-0195	
F-CGES	Centrair 101A Pégase	101A-0205	
F-CGET	Centrair 101A Pégase	101A-0206	
F-CGEU	Centrair 101A Pégase	101A-0210	
F-CGEV	Centrair 101A Pégase	101A-0212	
F-CGEX	Centrair 101A Pégase	101A-0215	
F-CGEY	Centrair 101A Pégase	101A-0216	
F-CGFB-B213	Centrair 101B Pégase	101B-0213	F-WGFB
F-CGFC	Centrair 101A Pégase	101A-0217	
F-CGFD	Centrair 101A Pégase	101A-0211	
F-CGFE-E	Centrair 101A Pégase	101A-0219	
F-CGFF-Z	Centrair 101A Pégase	101A-0220	
F-CGFG	Centrair 101A Pégase	101A-0221	
F-CGFH	Centrair 101A Pégase	101A-0222	
F-CGFI	Centrair 101A Pégase	101A-0223	
F-CGFJ	Centrair 101A Pégase	101A-0226	
F-CGFK	Centrair 101A Pégase	101A-0232	
F-CGFL	Centrair 101A Pégase	101A-0227	
F-CGFM	Centrair 101A Pégase	101A-0228	
F-CGFN	Centrair 101A Pégase	101A-0231	
F-CGFO	Centrair 101A Pégase	101A-0229	
F-CGFP	Centrair 101A Pégase (Code 'B230')	101A-0230	
F-CGFQ	Centrair 101A Pégase	101A-0233	
F-CGFR	Centrair 101A Pégase	101A-0234	
F-CGFS	Centrair 101A Pégase	101A-0235	
F-CGFT	Centrair 101A Pégase	101A-0236	
F-CGFU	Centrair 101A Pégase	101A-0237	
F-CGFV	Centrair 101A Pégase	101A-0238	
F-CGFX	Centrair 101A Pégase	101A-0239	
F-CGFY	Centrair 101A Pégase	101A-0241	
F-CGFZ-T	Centrair 101A Pégase	101A-0242	
F-CGGA-DO	Schempp-Hirth Discus b	35	F-WGGA
F-CGGB	Schempp-Hirth Discus b	36	F-WGGB
F-CGGC	Schempp-Hirth Discus b	89	F-WGGC
F-CGGD	Schempp-Hirth Discus b	90	F-WGGD
F-CGGE	Schempp-Hirth Discus b	102	F-WGGE
F-CGGF-SJ	Schempp-Hirth Discus b	117	F-WGGF
F-CGGG	Schempp-Hirth Discus b	129	F-WGGG
F-CGGH	Schempp-Hirth Discus b	163	F-WGGH
F-CGGI	Schempp-Hirth Discus b	177	F-WGGI
F-CGGK	Schempp-Hirth Discus b	191	F-WGGK
F-CGGL	Schempp-Hirth Discus b	192	F-WGGL
F-CGGM	Schempp-Hirth Discus b	213	F-WGGM
F-CGGN	Schempp-Hirth Discus b	225	F-WGGN
F-CGGO	Schempp-Hirth Discus b	148	F-WGGO
F-CGGP	Schempp-Hirth Discus bT	33/335	
F-CGGQ	Schempp-Hirth Discus b	340	
F-CGGR	Schempp-Hirth Discus b	91	D-5239
F-CGGS	Schempp-Hirth Discus CS	037CS	
F-CGGT	Schempp-Hirth Discus CS	039CS	
F-CGGU	Schempp-Hirth Discus CS	105CS	
F-CGGV	Schempp-Hirth Discus CS	106CS	
F-CGGX	Schempp-Hirth Discus bT	108/455	
F-CGGY	Schempp-Hirth Discus CS	117CS	
F-CGGZ	Schempp-Hirth Discus CS	118CS	
F-CGHA-E1	Centrair 101BC Pégase	101BC-0501	F-WGHA
F-CGHB-E5	Centrair 101BC Pégase	101BC-0504	F-WGHB
F-CGHC	Centrair 101BC Pégase	101BC-0507	
F-CGHD	Centrair 101BC Pégase	101BC-0509	
F-CGHF	Centrair 101BC Pégase	101BC-0508	
F-CGHG-E12	Centrair 101D Pégase	101D-0512	
F-CGHH	Centrair 101D Pégase	101D-0511	
F-CGHJ-E14	Centrair 101D Pégase	101D-0514	
F-CGHK	Centrair 101D Pégase	101D-0517	
F-CGHL	Centrair 101D Pégase	101D-0515	
F-CGHM	Centrair 101D Pégase	101D-0516	
F-CGHN	Centrair 101D Pégase	101D-0518	
F-CGHO	Centrair 101D Pégase	101D-0521	
F-CGHQ	Centrair 101D Pégase	101D-0522	
F-CGHR-F	Centrair 101D Pégase	101D-0520	
F-CGHS	Centrair 101D Pégase	101D-0524	
F-CGIA	Schempp-Hirth Janus A	41	D-3786
F-CGIB	Wassmer WA.30 Bijave	222	F-CDJS
F-CGIC	Wassmer WA.22A	119	Fr.AF
F-CGKA	Schleicher ASW-20CL	20856	
F-CGKB	Schleicher ASW-20CL	20847	
F-CGKC	Schleicher ASK-21	21414	
F-CGKD	Schleicher ASK-21	21427	
F-CGKF	Schleicher ASK-21	21445	
F-CGKG	Schleicher ASW-24	24007	F-WGKG
F-CGKH	Schleicher ASW-24	24008	F-WGKH
F-CGKI	Schleicher ASW-24	24053	
F-CGKJ	Schleicher ASW-24	24054	F-WGKJ
F-CGKK	Schleicher ASW-24	24056	F-WGKK
F-CGKL	Schleicher ASW-24E	24814	D-KAXG
F-CGKM	Schleicher ASW-24	24102	
F-CGKN	Schleicher ASW-24	24084	F-WGKN
F-CGKO	Schleicher ASW-24	24088	
F-CGKP	Schleicher ASW-24	24095	
F-CGKQ	Schleicher ASW-24	24103	
F-CGKR	Schleicher ASW-24E	24813	D-KAXF(2)
F-CGKS	Schleicher ASW-20	20583	D-4690
F-CGKT	Schleicher ASH-25	25022	F-WGKT
F-CGKU	Schleicher ASH-25	25028	F-WGKU
F-CGKV-CHN	Schleicher ASH-25E	25046	F-WGKV D-KFAX(2)
F-CGKX	Schleicher ASH-25	25075	F-WGKX
F-CGKY	Schleicher ASH-25	25009	F-WGKY
	(Reserved as F-CIVH .99)		D-5242
F-CGKZ	Schleicher ASH-25	25094	
F-CGLA	Schempp-Hirth Ventus b	236	F-WGLA
F-CGLB	Schempp-Hirth Ventus b	238	F-WGLB
F-CGLC	Schempp-Hirth Ventus b	245	F-WGLC
F-CGLD	Schempp-Hirth Ventus b	260	F-WGLD
F-CGLE	Schempp-Hirth Ventus b	268	F-WGLE
F-CGLF	Schempp-Hirth Ventus b	269	F-WGLF
F-CGLH	Schempp-Hirth Ventus b	291	F-WGLH
F-CGLI	Schempp-Hirth Ventus b/16.6	313	F-WGLI
F-CGLJ-EQ	Schempp-Hirth Ventus 2a	72	
	(F-WGLJ, Schempp-Hirth Ventus b/16.6 c/n 315 also believed current)		
F-CGLK	Schempp-Hirth Ventus b/16.6	316	F-WGLK
F-WGLL	Schempp-Hirth Ventus bT	336/89	
F-CGLM	Schempp-Hirth Ventus b/16.6	339	F-WGLM
F-CGLN	Schempp-Hirth Ventus b/16.6	361	F-WGLN
F-CGLO	Schempp-Hirth Ventus c/17.6	433	F-WGLO
F-WGLQ	Schempp-Hirth Ventus cM	6/417	D-KGLQ
F-CGLS-EN	Schmepp-Hirth Ventus 2a	07	
F-CGLT	Schmepp-Hirth Ventus 2a	08	D-8560
F-CGLV	Schmepp-Hirth Ventus 2b	29	
F-CGLX	Schmepp-Hirth Ventus 2b	69	
F-CGLY	Schempp-Hirth Ventus c/17.6	425	F-WGLY
F-CGLZ	Schempp-Hirth Ventus 2c	21/52	
F-WGMA	Centrair 201 Marianne	201-001	
F-CGMB	Centrair 201 Marianne	201-002	F-WGMB
F-CGMC	Centrair 201B1 Marianne	201-003	F-WGMC
F-CGMD	Centrair 201B1 Marianne	201-004	
F-CGME	Centrair 201B1 Marianne	201-005	
F-CGMF	Centrair 201B1 Marianne	201-006	
F-CGMG	Centrair 201B1 Marianne	201-007	
F-CGMH-E8	Centrair 201B1 Marianne	201-008	
F-CGMI	Centrair 201B1 Marianne	201-009	
F-CGMJ	Centrair 201B1 Marianne	201-010	
F-CGMK	Centrair 201B1 Marianne	201-011	F-WGMK
F-CGMN	Centrair 201B1 Marianne	201-015	
F-CGMO	Centrair 201B1 Marianne	201-016	
F-CGMP	Centrair 201B1 Marianne	201-017	F-WGMP
F-CGMQ	Centrair 201B1 Marianne	201-018	F-WGMQ
F-CGMR	Centrair 201B1 Marianne	201-019	F-WGMR

Regn.	Type	C/n	Prev.Id.
F-CGMS	Centrair 201B1 Marianne	201-020	F-WGMS
F-CGMT	Centrair 201B1 Marianne	201-021	F-WGMT
F-CGMU	Centrair 201B1 Marianne	201-022	F-WGMU
F-CGMV	Centrair 201B1 Marianne	201-023	
F-CGMX	Centrair 201B1 Marianne	201-024	
F-CGMY	Centrair 201B1 Marianne	201-025	
F-CGMZ	Centrair 201B Marianne	201-026	F-WGMZ
F-CGNA	Centrair 101A Pégase	101A-0248	
F-CGNB-B240	Centrair 101A Pégase	101A-0240	
F-CGNC	Centrair 101A Pégase	101A-0256	
F-CGND	Centrair 101A Pégase	101A-0246	
F-CGNE	Centrair 101A Pégase	101A-0249	
F-CGNF	Centrair 101A Pégase	101A-0247	
F-CGNG	Centrair 101A Pégase	101A-0251	
F-CGNH	Centrair 101A Pégase	101A-0257	
F-CGNI	Centrair 101A Pégase	101A-0258	
F-CGNJ	Centrair 101A Pégase	101A-0259	
F-CGNK-LV	Centrair 101A Pégase	101A-0270	
F-CGNL	Centrair 101A Pégase	101A-0271	
F-CGNN	Centrair 101A Pégase	101A-0263	
F-CGNO	Centrair 101A Pégase	101A-0272	
F-CGNP-Y31	Centrair 101A Pégase	101A-0266	
F-CGNR	Centrair 101C Pégase	101C-0903	
F-CGNS	Centrair 101C Pégase	101C-0904	
F-CGNT	Centrair 101A Pégase	101A-0267	
F-CGNU	Centrair 101A Pégase	101A-0250	
F-CGNV	Centrair 101A Pégase	101A-0277	
F-CGNX	Centrair 101B Pégase	101B-0279	
F-CGNY	Centrair 101B Pégase	101B-0280	
F-CGNZ	Centrair 101A Pégase	101A-0281	
F-CGOB	Centrair 101A Pégase	101A-0316	
F-CGOC	Centrair 101A Pégase	101A-0317	
F-CGOD-OD	Centrair 101A Pégase	101A-0318	
F-CGOE	Centrair 101A Pégase	101A-0320	
F-CGOF	Centrair 101A Pégase	101A-0326	
F-CGOG	Centrair 101A Pégase	101A-0327	
F-CGOH	Centrair 101A Pégase	101A-0328	
F-CGOI	Centrair 101A Pégase	101A-0329	
F-CGOJ	Centrair 101A Pégase	101A-0330	
F-CGOK	Centrair 101A Pégase	101A-0324	
F-CGOL	Centrair 101A Pégase	101A-0331	
F-CGOM-3M	Centrair 101A Pégase	101A-0332	
F-CGON	Centrair 101A Pégase	101A-0333	
F-CGOP	Centrair 101A Pégase	101A-0335	
F-CGOQ	Centrair 101A Pégase	101A-0336	
F-CGOR	Centrair 101A Pégase	101A-0337	
F-CGOS	Centrair 101A Pégase	101A-0338	
F-CGOT	Centrair 101A Pégase	101A-0339	
F-CGOU	Centrair 101A Pégase	101A-0340	
F-CGOV-ED	Centrair 101A Pégase	101A-0341	
F-CGOX	Centrair 101A Pégase	101A-0342	
F-CGOZ	Centrair 101A Pégase	101A-0354	
F-CGPA	Rolladen-Schneider LS-3A	3162	
F-CGPN	Wassmer WA.22A	155	Fr.AF
F-CGQA-J57	Schempp-Hirth Janus C	224	
F-CGQC	Schempp-Hirth Janus CM	229/28	
F-CGQD	Schempp-Hirth Janus B	231	
F-CGQE	Schempp-Hirth Janus CM	234/29	F-WGQE
			D-KHIA(5)
F-CGQF	Schempp-Hirth Janus CM	246/31	F-WGQF
F-CGQG	Schempp-Hirth Janus CM	33/250	F-WGQG
			D-KGQG
F-CGQH	Schempp-Hirth Janus C	258	
F-CGQI	Schempp-Hirth Janus CM	34/259	F-WGQI
			D-KGQI
F-CGQJ	Schempp-Hirth Janus C	267	
F-CGQK	Schempp-Hirth Janus CT	12/271	F-WGQK
			D-KGQK
F-CGQL	Schempp-Hirth Janus CE	287	
F-CGQM	Schempp-Hirth Janus CE	295	
F-CGQN	Schempp-Hirth Janus B	37	D-7849
F-CGQO	Schempp-Hirth Janus CE	293	D-7460
F-CGQP	Schempp-Hirth Janus C	219	D-3949
F-CGQQ-Q2	Schempp-Hirth Janus CE	306	
F-CGQR	Schempp-Hirth Janus CE	307	

Regn.	Type	C/n	Prev.Id.
F-CGQS	Schempp-Hirth Discus CS	262CS	
F-CGRA	Glaser-Dirks DG-400	4-181	
F-CGRC	Glaser-Dirks DG-400	4-202	
F-CGRD	Glaser-Dirks DG-400	4-203	
F-CGRE	Glaser-Dirks DG-400	4-215	
F-CGRG	Glaser-Dirks DG-400	4-243	
F-CGRH	Glaser-Dirks DG-400	4-257	
F-CGRI	Glaser-Dirks DG-400	4-283	D-KSPL
F-CGRJ	Glaser-Dirks DG-400	4-262	
F-CGRO	Glaser-Dirks DG-600	6-51	
F-CGRP	Glaser-Dirks DG-600	6-59	
F-CGRR	Glaser-Dirks DG-600	6-60	
F-CGRS	Glaser-Dirks DG-600M	6-86M32	
F-CGRT	Glaser-Dirks DG-600M	6-83M29	
F-CGRU	Hoffmann HK-36R Super Dimona	36388	
F-CGRV	Glaser-Dirks DG-400	4-112	N2JW
F-CGRX	Glaser-Dirks DG-800	8-23A20	D-KAPS
F-CGRY	Glaser-Dirks DG-800S	8-73S19	
F-CGRZ	HOAC H-36TTC Super Dimona	36524	
F-CGSA	Centrair 101A Pégase	101A-0282	
F-CGSB	Centrair 101A Pégase	101A-0288	
F-CGSC	Centrair 101A Pégase	101A-0287	
F-CGSD	Centrair 101A Pégase	101A-0292	
F-CGSF	Centrair 101A Pégase	101A-0291	
F-CGSG	Centrair 101A Pégase	101A-0294	
F-CGSH	Centrair 101A Pégase	101A-0295	
F-CGSJ	Centrair 101A Pégase	101A-0297	
F-CGSK	Centrair 101A Pégase	101A-0298	
F-CGSL	Centrair 101A Pégase	101A-0300	
F-CGSM(2)	Centrair 101A Pégase	101A-0301	
F-CGSN	Centrair 101A Pégase	101A-0302	
F-CGSO	Centrair 101A Pégase	101A-0303	
F-CGSP	Centrair 101A Pégase	101A-0304	
F-CGSQ	Centrair 101A Pégase	101A-0305	
F-CGSR	Centrair 101A Pégase	101A-0306	
F-CGSS	Centrair 101A Pégase	101A-0308	
F-CGST	Centrair 101A Pégase	101A-0309	
F-CGSU	Centrair 101A Pégase (Code 'PₕV')	101A-0310	
F-CGSV	Centrair 101A Pégase	101A-0269	
F-CGSX	Centrair 101A Pégase	101A-0312	
F-CGSY	Centrair 101A Pégase	101A-0313	
F-CGSZ	Centrair 101A Pégase	101A-0314	
F-CGTA	Centrair 201B Marianne	201B-060	
F-CGTB	Centrair 201B Marianne	201B-062	
F-CGTC	Centrair 201B Marianne	201B-063	
F-CGTD	Centrair 201B Marianne	201B-065	
F-CGTE	Centrair 201B Marianne	201B-067	
F-CGTF	Centrair 201B Marianne	201B-071	
F-CGTG-CA	Centrair 201B Marianne	201B-073	
F-CGTH	Centrair 201B Marianne	201B-075	
F-CGTI	Centrair 201B Marianne	201B-076	
F-CGTJ	Centrair 201B Marianne	201B-077	
F-CGTK	Centrair 201B Marianne	201B-079	
F-CGTL	Centrair 201B Marianne	201B-080	
F-CGTM	Centrair 201B Marianne	201B-030	
F-CGTN	Centrair 201B Marianne	201B-083	
F-CGTO	Centrair 201B Marianne	201B-084	
F-CGTP	Centrair 201B Marianne	201B-087	
F-CGTQ	Centrair 201B Marianne	201B-089	
F-CGTR	Centrair 201B Marianne	201B-091	
F-CGTS	Centrair 201B Marianne	201B-092	
F-CGUA	Rolladen-Schneider LS-6A	6093	F-WGUA
F-CGUB	Rolladen-Schneider LS-6	6097	F-WGUB
F-CGUC	Rolladen-Schneider LS-6	6099	F-WGUC
F-CGUD	Rolladen-Schneider LS-6	6130	F-WGUD
F-CGUE-CA	Rolladen-Schneider LS-6B	6137	F-WGUE
F-CGUF	Rolladen-Schneider LS-6B	6141	F-WGUF
F-CGUG-D	Rolladen-Schneider LS-6B	6142	F-WGUG
F-CGUH-72	Rolladen-Schneider LS-6B	6179	F-WGUH
F-CGUI	Rolladen-Schneider LS-6B	6188	F-WGUI
			D-5017
F-CGUJ	Rolladen-Schneider LS-6C	6206	
F-CGUK	Rolladen-Schneider LS-6C	6208	
F-CGUL	Rolladen-Schneider LS-6C	6222	
F-CGUM	Rolladen-Schneider LS-6C	6221	

Regn.	Type	C/n	Prev.Id.
F-CGUN	Rolladen-Schneider LS-6B	6087	F-WGUN
F-CGUO	Rolladen-Schneider LS-6C	6243	
F-CGUP	Rolladen-Schneider LS-6C	6244	
F-CGUQ	Rolladen-Schneider LS-6C	6255	
F-CGUR	Rolladen-Schneider LS-6C	6268	
F-CGUS	Rolladen-Schneider LS-6C	6312	
F-CGUT-RC	Rolladen-Schneider LS-6C	6300	
F-CGUU	Rolladen-Schneider LS-6C	6304	
F-CGUV	Rolladen-Schneider LS-6C	6305	
F-CGUX	Rolladen-Schneider LS-6C	6320	
F-CGUY-Z27	Rolladen-Schneider LS-6C	6321	
F-CGUZ-Z28	Rolladen-Schneider LS-6C	6322	
F-CGVA	Grob G.102 Astir CS	1063	D-3287
F-CGVL	Schempp-Hirth Ventus 2b	45	
F-CGVN	Wassmer WA.30 Bijave	206	Fr.AF
F-CGVO	Centrair C-201B Marianne	201B-064	
F-CGVV	Rolladen-Schneider LS-7	7106	D-9777
F-CGXA	Grob G.103C Twin III	36002	
F-CGXB	Grob G.103C Twin III Acro	34119	D-5214
F-CGXC	Grob G.103C Twin III Acro	34122	D-3698
F-CGXD-TD	Grob G.103C Twin III Acro	34136	D-4034
F-CGXE	Grob G.103C Twin III Acro	34138	D-4343
F-CGXF	Grob G.103C Twin III Acro	34140	D-4344
F-CGXG	Grob G.103C Twin III	36008	
F-CGXH	Grob G.103C Twin III	34178	
F-CGXI	Grob G.103C Twin III Acro	34184	
F-CGXJ	Grob G.103C Twin III Acro	34114	D-1833
F-CGYB	Rolladen-Schneider LS-7	7014	F-WGYB / D-4644
F-CGYC	Rolladen-Schneider LS-7	7015	F-WGYC / D-4663
F-CGYD	Rolladen-Schneider LS-7	7103	
F-CGYE	Rolladen-Schneider LS-7	7120	
F-CGYF-EB	Rolladen-Schneider LS-7	7155	
F-CGYG-Y55	Rolladen-Schneider LS-4B	4988	
F-CGYH	Rolladen-Schneider LS-4B	4985	
F-CGYI	Rolladen-Schneider LS-4B	4999	
F-CGYJ	Rolladen-Schneider LS-4B	41003	
F-CGYL	Stemme S-10	10-33	D-KGCI (2)
F-CGYM	Stemme S-10V	10-55	D-KGCU(2)
F-CGZA	Rolladen-Schneider LS-6C-18	6327	
F-CGZB	Rolladen-Schneider LS-6C-18	6325	
F-CGZC	Rolladen-Schneider LS-6C-18	6326	D-7141
F-CGZD	Rolladen-Schneider LS-6C-18	6335	D-1681
F-CGZE	Rolladen-Schneider LS-6-18W	6368	
F-CGZF	Rolladen-Schneider LS-6C-18	6376	
F-CGZI	Rolladen-Schneider LS-8A (see F-CGZY below)	8231	
F-CGZK-2M	Rolladen-Schneider LS-8A	8041	D-3571
F-CGZL	Rolladen-Schneider LS-8A	8043	
F-CGZM-EU	Rolladen-Schneider LS-8A	8045	
F-CGZN	Rolladen-Schneider LS-8A	8061	
F-CGZO	Rolladen-Schneider LS-8A	8063	
F-CGZP	Rolladen-Schneider LS-8A	8077	
F-CGZQ	Rolladen-Schneider LS-8A	8082	
F-CGZR	Rolladen-Schneider LS-8A	8137	
F-CGZS	Rolladen-Schneider LS-8A	8138	
F-CGZT	Rolladen-Schneider LS-8A	8143	
F-CGZU	Rolladen-Schneider LS-8A	8170	
F-CGZX	Rolladen-Schneider LS-8A	8192	
F-CGZY	Rolladen-Schneider LS-8A (Officially registered as F-CGZI)	8231	
F-CHAA	Schleicher ASW-24	24106	
F-CHAB	Schleicher ASW-24	24107	
F-CHAC	Schleicher ASW-24	24117	
F-CHAD	Schleicher ASW-24	24126	
F-CHAE	Schleicher ASW-24	24127	
F-CHAF	Schleicher ASW-24	24145	
F-CHAG	Schleicher ASW-24E	24843	
F-CHAH	Schleicher ASW-24E	24852	
F-CHAI	Schleicher ASW-24	24147	
F-CHAJ	Schleicher ASW-24	24148	
F-CHAL	Schleicher ASH-25	25121	
F-CHAM	Schleicher ASK-21	21504	
F-CHAN	Schleicher ASK-21	21505	
F-CHAO	Schleicher ASH-25	25092	
F-CHAP	Schleicher ASH-25	25099	
F-CHAQ	Schleicher ASW-25	25123	
F-CHAR	Schleicher ASH-25	25137	
F-CHAS	Schleicher ASK-23B	23009	BGA2999/EVZ
F-CHAT	Schleicher ASH-25	25080	F-WHAT
F-CHAU	Schleicher ASH-25E	25090	F-WHAU
F-CHAV	Schleicher ASH-25	25136	
F-CHAX	Schleicher ASH-25E	25065	D-KFAX
F-CHAY	Schleicher ASH-25E	25139	
F-CHAZ	Schleicher ASH-25	25156	
F-CHBA	Swift S-1A	0108	
F-CHBC	Schleicher ASH-25E	25055	F-WHBC / D-KBBC
F-CHBJ	Glaser-Dirks DG-200/17	2-122/1726	3A-MBJ
F-CHBL	Rolladen-Schneider LS-4	4435	D-3441
F-CHBY	Schleicher ASK-21	21619	
F-CHCA	Scheibe SF-25B Falke	4827	D-KHEG
F-CHCB	Scheibe SF-25E Super Falke	4351	D-KDGK
F-CHCC	Scheibe SF-25E Super Falke	4365	D-KIOK(2)
F-CHCD	Scheibe SF-25D Falke	4825D	D-KHEE
F-CHCE	Scheibe SF-25B Falke	4630	D-KOKE / (D-KIMJ)
F-CHCF	Scheibe SF-25C Falke	4242	D-KAJD
F-CHCH	Scheibe SF-25B Falke	AB46302	D-KAFI (2)
F-CHCI	Scheibe SF-25E Super Falke	4329	D-KDFO
F-CHCJ	Scheibe SF-25E Super Falke	4361	D-KLUE
F-CHCK	Scheibe SF-25B Falke	46177	D-KAGK
F-CHCL	Scheibe SF-25D Falke	AB46305	D-KOAN
F-CHCM	Scheibe SF-25B Falke	46173	D-KURT / OE-9038 / D-KIBS
F-CHCN	Scheibe SF-25C Falke 1700	44107	D-KMJG
F-CHCO	Scheibe SF-25E Super Falke	4321	G-BDZS / (D-KECX)
F-CHCP	Scheibe SF-25E Super Falke	4356	D-KOOZ(2)
F-CHCQ	Scheibe SF-25E Super Falke	4344	D-KDBG
F-CHCR	Scheibe SFL-25R Falke	4619	D-KEGA
F-CHDA	Centrair 101A Pégase	101A-0355	
F-CHDB	Centrair 101A Pégase	101A-0356	
F-CHDC	Centrair 101A Pégase	101A-0357	
F-CHDD	Centrair 101A Pégase	101A-0358	
F-CHDE	Centrair 101A Pégase	101A-0359	
F-CHDF	Centrair 101A Pégase	101A-0360	
F-CHDG	Centrair 101A Pégase	101A-0361	
F-CHDH	Centrair 101A Pégase	101A-0362	
F-CHDI -Si	Centrair 101A Pégase	101A-0363	
F-CHDJ	Centrair 101A Pégase	101A-0366	
F-CHDK	Centrair 101A Pégase	101A-0367	
F-CHDL	Centrair 101A Pégase	101A-0369	
F-CHDM	Centrair 101A Pégase	101A-0370	
F-CHDN	Centrair 101A Pégase	101A-0372	
F-CHDO	Centrair 101A Pégase	101A-0373	
F-CHDP	Centrair 101A Pégase	101A-0374	
F-CHDQ	Centrair 101A Pégase	101A-0375	
F-CHDR	Centrair 101A Pégase	101A-0376	
F-CHDS	Centrair 101A Pégase	101A-0349	
F-CHDT	Centrair 101A Pégase	101A-0377	
F-CHDU	Centrair 101A Pégase	101A-0364	
F-CHDV	Centrair 101A Pégase	101A-0365	
F-CHDX	Centrair 101A Pégase	101A-0368	
F-CHDY	Centrair 101A Pégase	101A-0371	
F-CHDZ	Centrair 101A Pégase	101A-0379	
F-CHEA	Centrair 101A Pégase	101A-0380	
F-CHEB	Centrair 101A Pégase	101A-0378	
F-CHEC	Centrair 101A Pégase	101A-0381	
F-CHED	Centrair 101A Pégase	101A-0382	
F-CHEE	Centrair 101A Pégase	101A-0383	
F-CHEF	Centrair 101A Pégase	101A-0384	
F-CHEG	Centrair 101A Pégase	101A-0385	
F-CHEH	Centrair 101A Pégase	101A-0386	
F-CHEI	Centrair 101A Pégase	101A-0387	
F-CHEJ	Centrair 101A Pégase	101A-0388	
F-CHEK	Centrair 101A Pégase	101A-0389	
F-CHEL -L	Centrair 101A Pégase	101A-0390	
F-CHEM	Centrair 101A Pégase	101A-0391	

Regn.	Type	C/n	Prev.Id.
F-CHEN	Centrair 101A Pégase	101A-0393	
F-CHEO	Centrair 101A Pégase	101A-0395	
F-CHEP	Centrair 101A Pégase	101A-0396	
F-CHEQ	Centrair 101A Pégase	101A-0397	
F-CHER	Centrair 101A Pégase	101A-0398	
F-CHES	Centrair 101A Pégase	101A-0399	
F-CHEU	Centrair 101A Pégase	101A-0401	
F-CHEV	Centrair 101A Pégase	101A-0402	
F-CHEX	Centrair 101A Pégase	101A-0405	
F-CHEY	Centrair 101A Pégase	101A-0406	
F-CHEZ -5	Centrair 101A Pégase	101A-0407	
F-CHFA	Centrair 101A Pégase	101A-0466	
F-CHFC	Centrair 101A Pégase	101A-0468	
F-CHFD	Centrair 101A Pégase	101A-0469	
F-CHFE	Centrair 101A Pégase	101A-0470	
F-CHFF	Centrair 101A Pégase	101A-0471	
F-CHFG	Centrair 101A Pégase	101A-0472	
F-CHFH	Centrair 101A Pégase	101A-0474	
F-CHFI	Centrair 101A Pégase	101A-0473	
F-CHFK	Centrair 101A Pégase	101A-0480	
F-CHFL	Centrair 101A Pégase	101A-0481	
F-CHFM	Centrair 101A Pégase	101A-0480	
F-CHFN	Centrair 101A Pégase	101A-0483	
F-CHFO	Centrair 101A Pégase	101A-0485	
F-CHFP	Centrair 101A Pégase	101A-0486	
F-CHFQ	Centrair 101A Pégase	101A-0487	
F-CHFR	Centrair 101A Pégase	101A-0488	
F-CHFS	Centrair 101A Pégase	101A-0489	
F-CHFT	Centrair 101A Pégase	101A-0494	
F-CHFU	Centrair 101A Pégase	101A-0496	
F-CHFV	Centrair 101A Pégase	101A-0497	
F-CHFX	Centrair 101A Pégase	101A-0498	
F-CHFY	Centrair 101A Pégase	101A-0499	
F-CHFZ	Centrair 101A Pégase	101A-0600	
F-CHGA	Centrair 101A Pégase	101A-0601	
F-CHGB	Centrair 101A Pégase	101A-0602	
F-CHGC	Centrair 101A Pégase	101A-0603	
F-CHGD	Centrair 101A Pégase	101A-0604	
F-CHGE	Centrair 101A Pégase	101A-0605	
F-CHGF	Centrair 101A Pégase	101A-0606	
F-CHGG	Centrair 101A Pégase	101A-0490	
F-CHGH	Centrair 101A Pégase	101A-0607	
F-CHGI	Centrair 101A Pégase	101A-0612	
F-CHGJ -V	Centrair 101A Pégase	101A-0614	
F-CHGK	Centrair 101A Pégase	101A-0615	
F-CHGL	Centrair 101A Pégase	101A-0616	
F-CHGM	Centrair 101A Pégase	101A-0617	
F-CHGN	Centrair 101A Pégase	101A-0618	
F-CHGO	Centrair 101A Pégase	101A-0622	
F-CHGP	Centrair 101A Pégase	101A-0621	
F-CHGQ-IS	Centrair 101A Pégase	101A-0623	
F-CHGR	Centrair 101A Pégase	101A-0624	
F-CHGS	Centrair 101A Pégase	101A-0625	
F-CHGT	Centrair 101A Pégase	101A-0626	
F-CHGU	Centrair 101A Pégase	101A-0627	
F-CHGV	Centrair 101A Pégase	101A-0630	
F-CHGX	Centrair 101A Pégase	101A-0629	
F-CHGY	Centrair 101A Pégase	101A-0631	
F-CHGZ	Centrair 101A Pégase	101A-0632	
F-CHHA	Scheibe SF-25B Falke	46144	D-KJHM
			OE-9138
			D-KCAK
F-CHHB	Schempp-Hirth Janus C	187	D-7718
F-CHHC	Glaser-Dirks DG-800	8-31A23	
F-CHHD	SZD-51-1 Junior	B-2138	
F-CHHE	Schleicher Ka.6E	4240	HB-961
F-CHHF	Caproni A-21S Calif	218	HB-1180
F-CHHG	Schleicher K.8B	883	HB-682
F-CHHH	Grob G.102/77 Astir CS	1808	HB-1470
F-CHHI	Schleicher ASK-13	13232	D-0512
F-CHHJ	Grob G.102/77J Astir CS Jeans	2239	D-5943
F-CHIIIK	Scheibe SF-28A Tandem-Falke	5749	D-KOFF
F-CHHM	Marganski MDM-1 Fox	221	
F-CHHN	Schleicher Ka.6E	4041	D-1932
F-CHHO	Schleicher ASH-25	25002	D-2522

Regn.	Type	C/n	Prev.Id.
F-CHHP	Grob G.102 Astir Jeans 77J	2234	D-5949
F-CHHR	Grob G.102 Astir Jeans 77J	2237	D-5917
F-CHHY	Glaser-Dirks DG-400 (Reservation 9.99)	4-6	D-KINS
F-CHIA	Schleicher ASK-21	21526	
F-CHIB	Schleicher ASK-21	21540	
F-CHIC	Schleicher ASK-21	21549	
F-CHID	Schleicher ASK-21	21547	
F-CHIE	Schleicher ASK-21	21080	PH-711
F-CHIF	Schleicher ASW-24	24176	
F-CHIG	Schleicher ASW-24	24178	
F-CHIL	Schleicher ASK-21	21553	
F-CHIM	Schleicher ASK-21	21614	
F-CHIN	Schleicher ASK-21	21625	
F-CHIS	Schleicher ASW-19B	19128	D-7560
F-CHIT	Schleicher ASH-25	25100	
F-CHIU	Schleicher ASH-25	25157	
F-CHJA	Glaser-Dirks DG-500M Elan	5E-6M4	D-KGBE
F-CHJB	Glaser-Dirks DG-500T Elan Trainer	5E-22T4	
F-CHJC	Glaser-Dirks DG-500T Elan Trainer	5E-27T7	
F-CHJD	Glaser-Dirks DG-500T Elan Trainer	5E-49T19	
F-CHJE	Glaser-Dirks DG-500T Elan Trainer	5E-73T30	
F-CHJF	Glaser-Dirks DG-500M Elan	5E-83M35	
F-CHJG-DD	Glaser-Dirks DG-500T Elan Trainer	5E-88T38	
F-CHJH	Glaser-Dirks DG-500/22 Elan	5E-102S15	
F-CHJI	Glaser-Dirks DG-500 Elan Trainer	5E-129T55	
F-CHJJ	Glaser-Dirks DG-500 Elan Orion	5E-168X23	(D-0168)
F-CHJK	Glaser-Dirks DG-500 Elan Orion	5E-172X25	
F-CHJL	Glaser-Dirks DG-500M Elan	5E-82M34	
F-CHJM	Schempp-Hirth Nimbus 3DM	6/20	D-KAJM
F-CHJN	Glaser-Dirks DG-500M Elan	5E-96M42	OH-857
F-CHKA	Centrair 101A Pégase	101A-0408	
F-CHKB	Centrair 101A Pégase	101A-0410	
F-CHKC	Centrair 101A Pégase	101A-0412	
F-CHKD	Centrair 101A Pégase	101A-0411	
F-CHKE	Centrair 101A Pégase	101A-0413	
F-CHKF	Centrair 101A Pégase	101A-0414	
F-CHKG	Centrair 101A Pégase	101A-0415	
F-CHKH	Centrair 101A Pégase	101A-0416	
F-CHKI	Centrair 101A Pégase	101A-0417	
F-CHKJ-AM	Centrair 101A Pégase	101A-0418	
F-CHKK	Centrair 101A Pégase	101A-0419	
F-CHKL	Centrair 101A Pégase	101A-0409	
F-CHKM	Centrair 101A Pégase	101A-0420	
F-CHKN	Centrair 101A Pégase	101A-0421	
F-CHKO	Centrair 101A Pégase	101A-0422	
F-CHKP	Centrair 101A Pégase	101A-0423	
F-CHKQ	Centrair 101A Pégase	101A-0424	
F-CHKR	Centrair 101A Pégase	101A-0428	
F-CHKS-KS	Centrair 101A Pégase	101A-0429	
F-CHKT	Centrair 101A Pégase	101A-0430	
F-CHKU	Centrair 101A Pégase	101A-0431	
F-CHKV	Centrair 101A Pégase	101A-0432	
F-WHKV	Windex 1200C (Reservation .99)	unkn	
F-CHKX	Centrair 101A Pégase	101A-0433	
F-CHKY	Centrair 101A Pégase	101A-0434	
F-CHLA-3A	Centrair 101A Pégase	101A-0436	
F-CHLB	Centrair 101A Pégase	101A-0438	
F-CHLC	Centrair 101A Pégase	101A-0439	
F-CHLD	Centrair 101A Pégase	101A-0440	
F-CHLE-B02	Centrair 101A Pégase	101A-0441	
F-CHLF	Centrair 101A Pégase	101A-0443	
F-CHLG	Centrair 101A Pégase	101A-0442	
F-CHLH	Centrair 101A Pégase	101A-0444	
F-CHLI	Centrair 101A Pégase	101A-0446	
F-CHLJ	Centrair 101A Pégase	101A-0445	
F-CHLK	Centrair 101A Pégase	101A-0447	
F-CHLL	Centrair 101A Pégase	101A-0452	
F-CHLM-EO	Centrair 101A Pégase	101A-0453	
F-CHLN	Centrair 101A Pégase	101A-0454	
F-CHLO	Centrair 101A Pégase	101A-0455	
F-CHLP	Centrair 101A Pégase	101A-0456	
F-CHLQ	Centrair 101A Pégase	101A-0457	
F-CHLR	Centrair 101A Pégase	101A-0458	
F-CHLS	Centrair 101A Pégase	101A-0459	
F-CHLT	Centrair 101A Pégase	101A-0460	

Regn.	Type	C/n	Prev.Id.
F-CHLU	Centrair 101A Pégase	101A-0461	
F-CHLV	Centrair 101A Pégase	101A-0462	
F-CHLX	Centrair 101A Pégase	101A-0463	
F-CHLY	Centrair 101A Pégase	101A-0464	
F-CHLZ	Centrair 101A Pégase	101A-0465	
F-CHMA	Schleicher ASW-24	24174	
F-CHMB	Schleicher ASW-24	24175	
F-CHMD	Schleicher ASH-25	25193	
F-CHMP	Schleicher ASH-25	25181	
F-CHNA	Grob G.102 Astir CS	1456	D-7447
F-CHNB	Scheibe SF-25B Falke	46116	D-KABN
F-CHNC	Rolladen-Schneider LS-4	4510	3A-MSS
F-CHND	Schempp-Hirth Janus C	165	HB-1672
F-CHNE-87	Bölkow Phoebus C	910	
F-CHNN	Wassmer WA.30 Bijave	168	Fr.AF
F-CHOA	Grob G.103C Twin IIISL	35051	D-KPIC
F-CHOB	Grob G.103C Twin IIISL	35003	D-KLSA
F-CHPA	Grob G.102 Astir CS	1017	D-6996
F-CHPB	Rolladen-Schneider LS-4B	41010	BGA4281
F-CHPC	Bréguet Br.904S Nymphale *(Reservation .99)*	9	F-CCFS
F-CHPG	Schempp-Hirth Duo Discus	198	
F-CHPH	Wassmer WA.22A Super Javelot	137	Fr.AF
F-CHPV	Caproni-Vizzola A-21S Calif	46	
F-CHQA	HOAC HK-36TTCSuper Dimona	36544	OE-9444
F-CHQB	HOAC HK-36TTCSuper Dimona	36558	
F-CHQC	HOAC HK-36TTCSuper Dimona	36607	
F-CHQD	HOAC HK-36TTC Super Dimona *(Res .99)*	36610	
F-CHQE	HOAC HK-36TTC Super Dimona *(Res .99)*	36612	OE-9409
F-CHQF to F-CHQZ *Reserved for HK-36 Super Dimonas*			
F-CHRA	Schleicher ASK-14	14023	D-KEBB
F-CHRC	Schempp-Hirth Ventus c	376	F-WHRC
F-CHRD	Glaser-Dirks DG.505MB *(Reservation 11.99)*	unkn	
F-CHRE	Wassmer WA.22A Super Javelot	134	Fr.AF?
F-CHRF	Bréguet Br.901F Mouette *(Reservation .99)*	2	F-ZABX
F-CHRG	Rolladen-Schneider LS-8A	8149	
F-CHRH	Schleicher ASK-18	18014	D-6883
F-CHRS	Wassmer WA.30	165	Fr.AF
F-CHSA	Grob G.102 Astir CS	1256	D-7350
F-CHSB	Schleicher ASK-13 *(Reservation .99)*	13670AB	D-5800
F-CHSC	Scheibe SF-25E Super Falke	4323	N250BA (D-KECZ)
F-CHSE	Schleicher ASK-13 *(Reservation .99)*	13175	D-0265
F-CHSF	Schleicher K.8B *(Reservation .99)*	8206	D-8465
F-CHSG	Stralpes ST-15 Crystal	4	
F-CHSM	Rolladen-Schneider LS-6-18W	6380	
F-CHSN	SZD-55-1	551191031	F-WHSN
F-CHSO-5.5	SZD-55-1	551192042	F-WHSO
F-CHSP	SZD-55-1	551193056	F-WHSP
F-CHTA-CHN	Schempp-Hirth Duo Discus	09	
F-CHTB	Schempp-Hirth Duo Discus	40	
F-CHTC	Schempp-Hirth Duo Discus	67	
F-CHTD	Schempp-Hirth Duo Discus	88	
F-CHTE	Schempp-Hirth Duo Discus	106	
F-CHTF	Schempp-Hirth Duo Discus	120	
F-CHTG	Schempp-Hirth Duo Discus	134	
F-CHTH	Schempp-Hirth Duo Discus	221	
F-CHTI	Schempp-Hirth Duo Discus	145	
F-CHTJ	Schempp-Hirth Duo Discus	151	
F-CHTK	Schempp-Hirth Duo Discus	155	
F-CHTL	Schempp-Hirth Duo Discus	167	
F-CHTM	Schempp-Hirth Duo Discus	190	
F-CHUA	Centrair 101A Pégase	101A-0633	
F-CHUB	Centrair 101A Pégase	101A-0628	
F-CHUC	Centrair 101A Pégase	101A-0634	
F-CHUD	Centrair 101A Pégase	101A-0635	
F-CHUE	Centrair 101A Pégase	101A-0636	
F-CHUF to F-CHUZ *Reserved for Centrair 101A Pégase production*			
F-CHVE-197	Schempp-Hirth Janus C	144	
F-CHVU	Schempp-Hirth Janus B	66	D-7770
F-CHXA	Aeromot AMT.100 Ximango	100023	PT-PMV
F-CHXB	Aeromot AMT.100 Ximango	100024	PT-PMU
F-CHXC	Aeromot AMT.100 Ximango	100025	PT-PMX
F-CHXD	Aeromot AMT.100 Ximango	100027	PT-PMZ
F-CHXE	Aeromot AMT.100 Ximango	100031	PT-POO
F-CHXF	Aeromot AMT.100 Ximango	100032	PT-POP

Regn.	Type	C/n	Prev.Id.
F-CHXG	Aeromot AMT.200 Super Ximango	200040	
F-CHYA to F-CHYZ *Reserved for Aerosport*			
F-CHZA to F-CHZZ *Reserved for Centrair SNC-34C Alliance production*			
F-CIAB	Swift S-1A	119	
F-CIAF	Bölkow Phoebus C	898	HB-960
F-CIAI	Grob G.102 Astir CS 77	1750	D-4565
F-CIAJ	Schleicher ASK-14	14051	D-KISE
F-CIBA	Rolladen-Schneider LS-8A	8250	
F-CIBB	Rolladen-Schneider LS-8A	8262	
F-CIBN	Scheibe SF-25E Falke	4803	D-KABQ
F-CIBO	Grob G.102/77J Astir Jeans	2128	D-2536
F-CIBZ	Grob G.102 Astir CS	1381	D-7408
F-CICA	PZL PW-5 Smyk	17.02.004	
F-CICB-EZ	PZL PW-5 Smyk	17.07.012	
F-CICC	PZL PW-5 Smyk	17.07.013	
F-CICD-FH	PZL PW-5 Smyk	17.09.011	
F-CICE	PZL PW-5 Smyk	17.10.022	
F-CIED	Glaser-Dirks DG.500 Elan Trainer	5E-20T2	D-0262
F-CIEL	Swift S-1A	106	SP-3574
F-CIGC	Schleicher K.8B	506	HB-620
F-CIHB	Centrair SNC-34C Alliance	34003	
F-CIHC	Centrair SNC-34C Alliance	34001	
F-CIHD	Centrair SNC-34C Alliance	34004	
F-CIHE	Centrair SNC-34C Alliance	34005	
F-CIHF	Centrair SNC-34C Alliance	34006	
F-CIHG	Centrair SNC-34C Alliance	34007	
F-CIHH	Centrair SNC-34C Alliance	34008	
F-CIHI	Centrair SNC-34C Alliance	34009	
F-CIHJ	Centrair SNC-34C Alliance	34010	
F-CIHK	Centrair SNC-34C Alliance	34011	
F-CIHL	Centrair SNC-34C Alliance	34012	
F-CIHM	Centrair SNC-34C Alliance	34014	
F-CIHN	Centrair SNC-34C Alliance	34015	
F-CIHO	Centrair SNC-34C Alliance	34016	
F-CIHP	Centrair SNC-34C Alliance	34017	
F-CIHQ	Centrair SNC-34C Alliance	34018	
F-CIHR	Centrair SNC-34C Alliance	34019	
F-CIHS	Centrair SNC-34C Alliance	34020	
F-CIHT	Centrair SNC-34C Alliance	34021	
F-CIHU	Centrair SNC-34C Alliance	34022	
F-CIHV	Centrair SNC-34C Alliance	34023	
F-CIHX	Centrair SNC-34C Alliance	34024	
F-CIHY	Centrair SNC-34C Alliance	34025	
F-CIHZ	Centrair SNC-34C Alliance	34027	
F-CIIT	Schempp-Hirth Nimbus 4 D	4/15	D-9153 (D-KFVA)
F-CIJA	Schempp-Hirth Ventus 2c	23/59	
F-CIJB	Schempp-Hirth Ventus 2c	26/71	
F-CIJC	Schempp-Hirth Ventus 2c	39/113	
	(To become Ventus 2cM c/n 57/113 on conversion)		
F-CIJD	Schempp-Hirth Ventus 2cT	27/96	
F-CIJE	Schempp-Hirth Ventus 2c	40/119	
	(To become Ventus 2cT c/n 35/119 on conversion)		
F-CIJF	Schempp-Hirth Ventus 2cT	42/137	
F-CIJG	Schempp-Hirth Ventus 2cT	55/164	
F-CIJH	Schempp-Hirth Ventus 2c	47/145	
	(To become Ventus 2cT c/n 46/145 on conversion)		
F-CILC	Schleicher ASH-25	25130	
F-CILH	Schempp-Hirth Janus CM	36	
F-CIMC	Schleicher ASK-21	21700	
F-CIME	Schempp-Hirth Duo Discus	218	
F-CIML	Schempp-Hirth Janus C	217	D-7180
F-CIMM	Rolladen-Schneider LS-8A *(Reservation 7.99)*	8270	
F-CIPH	Schleicher ASK-14 *(Reservation .99)*	14015	D-KILY
F-CIPV	Schleicher ASK-21 *(Reservation 12.99)*	21001	OE-5245
F-CIRH	Stemme S-10V	14-028M	
F-CIRS	Schempp-Hirth Duo Discus	130	
F-CIVH	Schleicher ASH-25 *(Reservation .99)*	25009	F-CGKY F-WGKY D-5242
F-CJAA to F-CJAY *Reserved for Schempp-Hirth Nimbus production*			
F-CJAB	Schempp-Hirth Nimbus 4D	10	
F-CJAZ	Schempp-Hirth Nimbus 4D	8/39	D-8157
F-CJBA	Centrair SNC-34C Alliance	34028	
F-CJBB	Centrair SNC-34C Alliance	34029	

Regn.	Type	C/n	Prev.Id.
F-CJBC	Centrair SNC-34C Alliance	34030	
F-CJBD	Centrair SNC-34C Alliance	34031	
F-CJBE	Centrair SNC-34C Alliance	34032	
F-CJBF	Centrair SNC-34C Alliance	34033	
F-CJBG	Centrair SNC-34C Alliance	34034	
F-CJBH	Centrair SNC-34CAlliance	34035	
F-CJCD	Rolladen-Schneider LS-8A	8139	
F-CJCN	Schleicher ASK-21	21621	HB-3178
F-CJCM	Castel C.25S	60	F-CRNK
	(Also reserved as F-CRMC(2))		
F-CJEF	SZD-51-1 Junior	W-950	HB-1895
F-CJEM	Schleicher ASK-21	21439	HB-3023
F-CJFB	Avialsa-Scheibe A.60 Fauconnet	59K	OO-ZCX
			F-CCVL
F-CJGC	Schempp-Hirth Duo Discus	225	
F-CJHA	Grob G.102 Astir CS	1100	D-6994
F-CJHD	Castel C.311P	16	(F-CARC)
			F-CALS
F-CJIM	SZD-51-1 Junior	B-1500	HB-1797
F-CJLS	Grob G.109B	6394	HB-2111
F-CJOE	Scheibe SF-25B Falke	4668	D-KAPD
F-CJPB	LF-3 (Reservation 7.99)	317	
F-CJPG	Schleicher ASH-25E	25119	F-CHHL
			HB-2197
F-CJPJ	Rolladen-Schneider LS-6C	6195	PH-913

GLIDERS/MOTOR-GLIDERS WITH RESTRICTED CofA

Regn.	Type	C/n	Prev.Id.
F-CRAG(2)	Pottier JP15/34R Kit Club	60-43	
F-CRAH(2)	Boulay Condor	01	
F-CRAI (2)	Pottier JP15-34R Kit Club	60-58	
F-CRBA(2)	Rutan 77-6	F1	
F-CRBG(2)	Fournier RF-9	13	
F-CRBJ	Castel C.301S	1127	F-CAKD
F-CRBL	Fauvel AV.36 (Modified)	131	F-CBSF
F-CRBM(2)	Sirius C (Homebuilt)	19	
F-CRDQ	Castel 25S	139	F-CAMX
F-CRDU(2)	ACBA 3A	01	
F-CREB	Peyronnenc PP.1	01	F-WREB
F-CREV(2)	Nord 1300	228	F-CREU
			F-CBXE
F-CREZ(2)	Rolladen/Mudry LS1-SP-1	01	F-CREK(2)
			F-WRKE
F-CRFK	Emouchet SA.104	282	
F-CRFM(2)	Akaschtroumpf Cuervo FS-25	1	
F-CRFU	Nord 1300	197	F-CAXI
F-CRGC	Fauvel AV-222 (Reservation .99)	07	
F-CRGF	Fournier RF-9	12	
F-CRGL	Nord 1300	94	F-CBXR
F-CRGN	Nord 1300	177	F-CBET
F-CRHK	Castel 25S	175	
F-CRHL	Nord 1300	60	F-CBXV
F-CRHT	Castel C.301S	1133	
F-CRHX	Castel 25S	150	
F-CRII	Nord 1300	203	F-CBUZ
F-CRIN	Castel 25S (Dismantled)	124	F-CBOS
F-CRJM(2)	Castel C.301S (Being restored)	1050	F-CRHQ
			F-CBLA
F-CRLO	Nord 1300	123	F-CAGX
F-CRMB	Sablier 18 (Reservation .99)	01	
F-CRML	Castel 25S	115	F-CBOU
F-CRMU(2)	Castel 25S	172	F-CRMA
			F-CBAP
F-CRMX(2)	DFS Weihe	3	F-CBGT
			F-CRMD
			F-CBGT
F-CRND(2)	Pottier 15/34R	60-60	
F-CRNR	Nord 1300	65	F-CAAN
F-CROI (2)	Fouga CM.8W	01	
F-CROL(2)	Neukom AN-20B (Stored)	7	
F-CRON	Fauvel AV.221 (Dismantled)	01	F-CCON
			F-WCON
F-CRQX	Fauvel AV.361	323	

Regn.	Type	C/n	Prev.Id.
F-CRRA	Scheibe Mu.13D	03	
F-CRRG	Fauvel AV.45	3	F-WRRG
			F-CCHS
F-CRRH	Trucavaysse GEP TCV 03	1	
F-CRRI	Bouley Menin BM 1	01	F-WRRI
F-CRRJ	Vaysse TCV 03	PS-1	
F-CRRL	Compact	1	
F-CRRM	Fauvel AV.451	13	F-WRRM
F-CRRN	Emouchet SA.104	233	F-CRNJ
			F-CBJH
F-CRRO	Mouisset	01	
F-CRRP	Rambaud Fournier RF-9	03-A	F-CAHK
F-CRRY	Fauvel AV.45	01	(F-PYEY)
			F-WCAG
			F-CCAG

GOVERNMENT-OPERATED AIRCRAFT: SECURITÉ CIVILE, FIRE SERVICE AND CUSTOMS

Regn.	Type	C/n	Prev.Id.
F-ZBAA(4)	Conair Turbo-Firecat (Code " T-22")	456/027	F-WEOL
	(Grumman US-2B Tracker conversion)		C-FQCW
			F-WEOL
			F-ZBAA(4)
			F-WEOL
			C-GYQN
			BuA136547
F-ZBAB(3)	Reims/Cessna F.406 Vigilant	0025	F-GEUL
			F-WZDV
F-ZBAC(3)	Aérospatiale AS.355F2 Ecureuil 2	5026	C-GFSI
F-ZBAD(3)	Aérospatiale AS.355F2 Ecureuil 2	5156	N5796A
F-ZBAF(2)	SE.3160 Alouette III	1075	F-RAFO
F-ZBAH(2)	SE.3160 Alouette III	1790	EI-AVI
F-ZBAJ(2)	SA.316B Alouette III	2224	
F-ZBAK(2)	SE.3160 Alouette III	1076	F-RAFP
F-ZBAN(2)	SE.316B Alouette III	1115	F-RAFQ
F-ZBAP(3)	Conair Turbo Firecat (Code "T- 12")	567/026	F-ZBDA
	(Grumman US-2BTracker conversion)		F-WEOK
			C-FOKN
			F-WEOK
			F-ZBDA
			F-WEOK
			C-GYQS
			BuA136658
F-ZBAR(3)	Canadair CL.215 1A-10 (Code " 21") (For sale)	1021	
F-ZBAU(2)	Conair Firecat (Code " T-2")	DH-32/009	F-WZLQ
	(Grumman CS-2F1 Tracker conversion)		C-FOPW
			CF-OPW
			RCN1533
F-ZBAV(2)	SA.316B Alouette III	2252	
F-ZBAW	SA.316B Alouette III	2306	
F-ZBAY(2)	Canadair CL.215 1A-10 (Code " 23") (For sale)	1023	
F-ZBAZ(2)	Conair Turbo Firecat (Code " T-1")	DH-57/008	F-WEOL
	(Grumman CS-2F1 Tracker conversion)		C-FVPK
	(Damaged 19.9.98, repair under consideration)		F-WEOL
			F-ZBAZ
			F-WZLS
			(F-WZLR)
			C-FOPZ
			CF-OPZ
			RCN1558
F-ZBBB(2)	Reims/Cessna F.406 Vigilant	0039	F-WZDS
F-ZBBC(2)	SE.3160 Alouette III	1791	
F-ZBBD(2)	Canadair CL.215 1A-10 (Code " 29") (For sale)	1029	
F-ZBBE(2)	Canadair CL.215 1A-10 (Code " 5") (For sale)	1005	CF-YWN
			CF-PQJ-X
F-ZBBH	Canadair CL.215 1A-10 (Code " 26") (For sale)	1026	

Regn.	Type	C/n	Prev.Id.
F-ZBBJ	Canadair CL.215 1A-10 (Code "28") (For sale)	1028	
F-ZBBL(2)	Conair Turbo Firecat (Code "T-19") (Grumman US-2A Tracker conversion)	626/024	F-WEOK C-FTFC F-WEOJ F-ZBBL F-WDQD C-GHPV BuA136717
F-ZBBN(2)	Aérospatiale AS.350B1 Ecureuil	1951	F-ZKBT D-HHZZ(2)
F-ZBBP	SE.316B Alouette III	1795	
F-ZBBQ	SE.316B Alouette III	1798	
F-ZBBS	SE.316B Alouette III	1978	
F-ZBBT	Canadair CL.215 1A-10 (Code "40") (Wfu 10.96, to Ontario Museum)	1040	
F-ZBBV	Canadair CL.215 1A-10 (Code "46") (For sale)	1046	C-GAOS
F-ZBBW	Canadair CL.215 1A-10 (Code "47") (For sale)	1047	
F-ZBBX	SOCATA MS.893E Rallye 180GT Gaillard	12532	F-BVZL
F-ZBCE	Reims/Cessna F.406 Vigilant	0042	F-GKRA F-WKRA F-GKRA
F-ZBCF	Reims/Cessna F.406 SurMar	0077	F-WZDZ
F-ZBCG	Reims/Cessna F.406 PolMar II	0066	F-WZDT
F-ZBCH	Reims/Cessna F.406 SurMar	0075	
F-ZBCI	Reims/Cessna F.406 Vigilant	0070	
F-ZBCJ	Reims/Cessna F.406 Vigilant	0074	F-WZDJ
F-ZBCZ	Conair Turbo Firecat (Code "T-23") (Grumman CS2F-3 Tracker conversion)	DH-94/036	F-ZBCA (F-ZBBF) C-FKUF CAF12195 RCN1595
F-ZBDC	SE.316B Alouette III	1435	
F-ZBDD	Canadair CL.215 1A-10 (Code "24") (For sale)	1024	
F-ZBDE	SE.316B Alouette III	1630	FAP9331
F-ZBDF	SE.316B Alouette III	1646	FAP9346
F-ZBDG	SE.316B Alouette III	1749	FAP9357
F-ZBDH	SE.316B Alouette III	1784	FAP9366
F-ZBDI	SA.316B Alouette III	1878	FAP9388
F-ZBDJ	SE.316B Alouette III	1879	FAP9389
F-ZBDL	SE.3160 Alouette III	1611	XC-FAR
F-ZBDM	SA.319B Alouette III	1610	XC-FAS
F-ZBDN	SE.316B Alouette III	1854	XC-FIB
F-ZBDQ	SE.316B Alouette III	2357	
F-ZBDR	SOCATA MS.893E Rallye 180GT Gaillard	12725	F-GAFJ
F-ZBDT	SOCATA Rallye 235E Gabier	12869	F-GAYQ
F-ZBDV	Aérospatiale AS.350BA Ecureuil	1157	F-GCFR
F-ZBDW	Cessna 404 Titan	0640	F-BIPJ N5293J
F-ZBDX	Cessna 404 Titan (Reserved as F-ONLY 11.99)	0692	F-GCQM N6764C
F-ZBDY	Cessna 404 Titan	0815	F-GCVR N67664
F-ZBDZ	Cessna 310R-II	0569	F-GAJI N87455
F-ZBEA	Aérospatiale AS.350B Ecureuil	1003	F-GBBQ F-WZAL
F-ZBEC	Aérospatiale SA.365C2 Dauphin 2	5027	N122ME (N3594D)
F-ZBED	Aérospatiale SA.365C2 Dauphin 2	5040	N123ME
F-ZBEF	Aérospatiale AS.355F2 Ecureuil 2	5236	
F-ZBEG	Canadair CL.415 6B-11 (Code "39")	2015	C-FXBH
F-ZBEH(2)	Conair Turbo Firecat (Code "T-20") (Grumman US-2A Tracker conversion)	410/035	F-WEOJ C-FCAD N435DF BuA136501
F-ZBEJ	Aérospatiale AS.355F1 Ecureuil 2	5003	F-WZKI
F-ZBEK	Aérospatiale AS.355F2 Ecureuil 2	5298	
F-ZBEL	Aérospatiale AS.355F2 Ecureuil 2	5299	
F-ZBEM	SOCATA TB-20 Trinidad	384	
F-ZBEN	Piper PA-28-161 Warrior II	28-8016245	D-EINK N9614N
F-ZBEO	Canadair CL.415 6B-11 (Code "36")	2011	C-FWPD
F-ZBEP	Reims/Cessna F.406 Vigilant	0006	

Regn.	Type	C/n	Prev.Id.
F-ZBEQ	Cessna 210L Centurion	60712	OO-DIL N1677X
F-ZBER	Cessna 404 Titan	0608	F-GAMZ LN-KAG SE-IBL (N2683Y)
F-ZBES	Reims/Cessna F.406 Vigilant	0017	
F-ZBET	Conair Turbo Firecat (Code "T-15") (Grumman US-2A Tracker conversion)	703/028	F-WEOJ(3) C-GHYH F-ZBET F-WEOJ C-GHYH BuA147559
F-ZBEU	Canadair CL..4156B-11 (Code "41")	2024	C-FZDE
F-ZBEV	Aérospatiale SA.365C1 Dauphin 2	5043	F-GBEP F-WPJ F-GBLL
F-ZBEW	Conair Turbo Firecat (Code "T-11") (Grumman US-2B Tracker conversion)	621/025	F-WEOL C-FSPK F-WEOL F-ZBEW F-WEOJ C-GYQY BuA136712
F-ZBEX	Conair Turbo Firecat (Code "T-09") (Grumman US-2B Tracker conversion) (Scheduled for delivery 6.00)	461/021	F-WEOL F-ZBEX F-WDSX(2) C-GQCW N4477Z BuA136552
F-ZBEY	Conair Turbo Firecat (Code "T-07") (Grumman US-2A Tracker conversion)	400/017	C-FYHB F-WEOK F-ZBEY F-WDQD C-GRXU BuA136491
F-ZBEZ	Canadair CL..415 6B-11 (Code "40")	2018	C-FXBX
F-ZBFA	Reims/Cessna F.406 PolMar I	001	F-GGRA(2) F-GGAN F-GFLT F-WZLT
F-ZBFC	Aérospatiale AS.350B1 Ecureuil	2109	
F-ZBFD	Aérospatiale AS.350B1 Ecureuil	2114	F-GIRO
F-ZBFE	Conair Turbo Firecat (Code "T-17") (Grumman US-2A Tracker conversion)	656/032	F-WEOK(3) C-FFQM N437DF BuA136747
F-ZBFF	Conair F.27-600 Firefighter (Code "71")	10432/003	C-FGDS OY-CCM CN-CDA PH-FPG
F-ZBFG	Conair F.27-600 Firefighter (Code "72")	10440/002	C-FBDY VH-TQR PH-EXB JA9771
F-ZBFH	Aérospatiale AS.350BA Ecureuil	2110	
F-ZBFJ	Beech B200 Super King Air (Code "98")	BB-1102	(F-GKDO) D-IWAN HB-GHI N147D
F-ZBFK	Beech B200 Super King Air (Code "96")	BB-876	F-GHSC N52BC
F-ZBFL	SA.316B Alouette III	1121	ALAT
F-ZBFM	SA.316B Alouette III	1280	ALAT
F-ZBFN	Canadair CL.415 6B-11 (Code "33")	2006	C-FVUK
F-ZBFP	Canadair CL.415 6B-11 (Code "31")	2002	C-FBET
F-ZBFS	Canadair CL.415 6B-11 (Code "32")	2001	C-GSCT
F-ZBFT	Aérospatiale AS.350B2 Ecureuil	2380	
F-ZBFU	IRMA/SA.316B Alouette III	5386	F-GBLC HC-BMY F-GBLC
F-ZBFV	Canadair CL.415 6B-11 (Code "37")	2013	C-FWPE
F-ZBFW	Canadair CL.415 6B-11 (Code "38")	2014	C-FWZH
F-ZBFX	Canadair CL.415 6B-11 (Code "34")	2007	C-FVUJ
F-ZBFY	Canadair CL.415 6B-11 (Code "35")	2010	C-FVDY

Regn.	Type	C/n	Prev.Id.
F-ZBFZ	Piper PA-31T Cheyenne II (Reserved as F-GLRP 10.99)	31T-8120064	F-WFLQ HK-2906P HK-2906X N9141Y
F-ZBGA	Reims/Cessna F.406 SurMar	0086	F-WWSR
F-ZB . . .	Aérospatiale SA.365N Dauphin 2	6091	F-GFBX OY-HMZ F-GEDQ F-WYME TF-SIF F-WXFJ

GENDARMERIE AIRCRAFT

In most cases only the last 3 letters of the " Registration" are actually carried on the aircraft.

Regn.	Type	C/n	Prev.Id.
F-MJBL	SA.319B Alouette III	2009	
F-MJBN	SA.319B Alouette III	2033	
F-MJBP	SA.319B Alouette III	2057	
F-MJBQ	SA.319B Alouette III	1956	ZaireAF:9T-HT6
F-MJBS	SA.319B Alouette III	2202	F-BVVH
F-MJBT	SA.316B Alouette III	1122	F-MJBG F-BVVH
F-MJBU	SA.316B Alouette III	2330	F-MCSG F-BYAQ
F-MJBV	SA.319B Alouette III	2125	Fr.AF
F-MJBW	SE.3160 Alouette III	1120	ALAT
F-MJBX	SE.3160 Alouette III	1693	ALAT
F-MJBY	SA.319B Alouette III	2338	Fr.AF
F-MJBZ	SA.319B Alouette III	2101	Fr.AF
F-MJCA	Aérospatiale AS.350B Ecureuil	1028	F-GBLQ
F-MJCB	Aérospatiale AS.350B Ecureuil	1574	
F-MJCC	Aérospatiale AS.350B Ecureuil	1916	
F-MJCD	Aérospatiale AS.350B Ecureuil	1576	
F-MJCE	Aérospatiale AS.350B Ecureuil	1812	F-MCSC F-MJCM
F-MJCF	Aérospatiale AS.350B Ecureuil	1810	F-MCSA F-MJCK
F-MJCG	Aérospatiale AS.350B Ecureuil	1753	
F-MJCH	Aérospatiale AS.350B Ecureuil	1756	
F-MJCJ	Aérospatiale AS.350B Ecureuil	1809	
F-MJCK	Aérospatiale AS.350B Ecureuil	1953	
F-MJCL	Aérospatiale AS.350B Ecureuil	1811	
F-MJCM	Aérospatiale AS.350B Ecureuil	1952	
F-MJCN	Aérospatiale AS.350B Ecureuil	2044	
F-MJCO	Aérospatiale AS.350B Ecureuil	1917	
F-MJCP	Aérospatiale AS.350B Ecureuil	2045	
F-MJCQ	Aérospatiale AS.350B Ecureuil	2057	
F-MJCR	Aérospatiale AS.350B Ecureuil	2088	
F-MJCS	Aérospatiale AS.350B Ecureuil	1575	F-MCSE F-MJCC
F-MJCT	Aérospatiale AS.350B Ecureuil	2104	
F-MJCU	Aérospatiale AS.350B Ecureuil	2117	
F-MJCV	Aérospatiale AS.350B Ecureuil	2118	
F-MJCW	Aérospatiale AS.350B Ecureuil	2218	
F-MJCX	Aérospatiale AS.350B Ecureuil	2219	
F-MJCY	Aérospatiale AS.350B Ecureuil	2221	
F-MJCZ	Aérospatiale AS.350B1 Ecureuil	2423	
F-MCSA	Aérospatiale AS.350B Ecureuil	1692	F-MJCF
F-MCSC	Aérospatiale AS.350B Ecureuil	1691	F-MJCE
F-MCSF	Aérospatiale AS.350B1 Ecureuil	2225	F-MJBZ
F-MCSG	SE.3160 Alouette III	1160	F-MJBU F-MCSK F-MCSH F-MJBE
F-MCSL	Aérospatiale AS.350B1 Ecureuil	2096	F-MJCS F-ZKCP
F-MCSM	Aérospatiale AS.350B1 Ecureuil	2222	F-MJCZ

Regn.	Type	C/n	Prev.Id.

MICROLIGHTS / ULM

Registration is by the prefix number of the Département in which the owner lives, administered on a regional basis. The F-J... marks are portable radio call-signs rather than aircraft registrations, they may therefore remain with an owner and be transferred to other aircraft. No complete ULM listing is as yet available and what follows is made up largely of reported sightings. As in the main register the letter W is used for test flying, although it may be applied before, after, or in the middle of the registration! Only confirmed types are now included and the editor would welcome any additional reports and sightings.

01-T	Baroudeur		
01-AD	Perouges X-15		
WAV-01	Murphy Rebel		
W01-BM	Fox Tristar		
01-BP	Air Création GT BI Quartz		
01-CG	Airplumb		
01-CQ	Weedhopper		
01-DA	Dynali Chickinox (F-JAFY)		
01-DE	Aviasud Mistral		
01-DJ	Air Création		
01-DZ	Aviasud Mistral		
01-EB	Dynali Chickinox		
01-FA	Denney Kitfox		
01-GB	Denney Kitfox		
01-W-GE	Tecnam P.96 Golf		
01-GI	Dynali Chickinox		
01-HF	Micro Aviation Pulsar 2		
01-HU	Air Création GTE Clipper		
01-HV	Dynali Chickinox		
01-II	Synairgie Sky Ranger		
01-IJ	Arrow Caprice 21		
01-JS	Soubeyrat Albatros paramotor		
01-KF	Rans S-6ESD Coyote II (F-JCKL)		
01-KG	Rans S-7 Courier (F-JCKM)		
01-KH	Rans S-6ESD Coyote IIXL (F-JCKO)		
01-LB	Tecnam P.92 Echo (F-JCUM)		
01-LG	Air Création		
01-LJ	Rans S-6 Coyote II		
01-MB	Tecnam P.92S Echo		
01-MC	Rans S-7 Courier (F-JEIU)		
01-MQ	Flight Design CT		
01-MR	Tecnam P.92 Echo (J-EIK)		
01-NH	Flight Design CT		
W-PA-01	Icarus Jet Fox 97		
02-CN	Cosmos		
02-CO	JCC Aviation J-300 Joker Kit (F-JAOP)		
02-HB	III Sky Arrow 500TF		
03-AD	Baroudeur		
03-AF	Baroudeur		
03-AJ	Air Création GT BI Quartz		
03-AQ	Aermas 386 (F-JABA)		
03-BC	Air Création		
03-BG	Air Création SX		
03-CG	Dynali Chickinox		
03-CO	Air Création		
03-DE	Quicksilver		
03-DL	Tandem Air Sunny		
03-ET	Tandem Air Sunny		
03-IH	Aviasud AE-209 Albatross	10	
03-II	Airwave Rave Jet Pocket paraglider		
03-RA	Rans S-5 Coyote		
04-AQ	Weedhopper Europa		
04-BP	Mignet HM.1100 Cordouan (F-JCTJ)		
04-BQ	Cosmos		
W04-DT	Dynamic 912		
04-HM	Mignet HM.14 Pou-du-Ciel		
04-SH	Quicksilver		
05-I	CLN-1		
05-BD	Sirius		
05 CO	Claude Noin Choucas	01	
05-DE	Air Création Clipper		
05-DI	Synairgie Sky Ranger		
05-DP	Rajhamsa X'Air		
05-EH	Synairgie Sky Ranger		

Regn.	Type	C/n	Prev.Id.
05-EL	Funk FK-9		
05-EN	Cosmos		
5-KZ	Skyranger		
05-UG	Synairgie Sky Ranger		
06-C	ULAC X-99 (2-seater)	163	
06-M	Eipper Quicksilver MX		
06-N	Pioneer Flightstar		
06-AE	Arrow F2 Foxcat (2-seater)		
06-AF	Skycraft AJS.2000		
06-AR	Weedhopper		
06-CA	PGO Cobra		
06-CD	Murphy Renegade Floatplane		
06-CZ	Air's Maestro		
06-DG	Aviasud Albatross		
06-FM	Pendulaire		
07-F	Air Création Quartz		
07-M	Titan Tornado		
07-AA	Air Création		
07-AQ	Quartz SX		
07-AX	Air Création		
07-BB	Air Création SX		
07-BC	Air Création Racer SX 12		
07-BL	Air Création Quartz		
07-BM	Aviasud Mistral	50	
07-BO	Air Création		
07-CS	Air Création SX-12		
07-DG	Butterfly		
07-DH	Air Création Fun		
07-EC	Weedhopper Europa		
07-EI	Air Création Fun		
07-EQ	Air Création Safari		
07-ES	Weedhopper		
07-FQ	Rans S-6 Coyote II		
07-FU	Air Création Quartz		
07-GA	Air Création Clipper XP		
07-GT	Air Création Fun GT		
07-HC	Air Création XP12 Buggy		
07-HM	Fly Synthesis Storch (F-JCUE)		
08-CM	Air Création		
08-CV	Air Création XP		
09-AC	Tempest (Modified)		
WAE-09	Aviasud Albatross AE-209 (sold as PH-2R2 ?)	0009	
10-C	Huntair Pathfinder		
10-E	Huntair Pathfinder		
10-R	Eipper Quicksilver MX		
10-T	Zenith	021	
10-Z	Dynali Chickinox		
10-AC	RP.82 Oméga		
10-AL	Aviasud Mistral		
10-BG	Previot Helios IV		
10-DH	Safari		
10-FJ	Aviakit Hermés		
10-FN	Quicksilver GT500		
10-FY	Air Création Hermes		
10-GH	Quicksilver GT500		
10-GJ	Light Aero Avid Flyer		
10-GL	Light Aero AvidLite		
10-GM	Humbert Moto-du-Ciel		
10-GS-W	SG Aviation Storm 300		
10-HB	Air Création		
10-HC	Aviakit Hermés Vega 2000		
10-HN	Fantasy air cora CT (F-JEJC)		
10-LA	Zenair MXD 740		
11-AJ	Weedhopper		
11-BY	Ikarus C-22 Extreme		
11-DB	Sunwheel		
12-AU	Weedhopper		
12-BE	Aviasud Mistral		
12-BU	Cosmos		
12-BV	Cosmos Echo 12		
12-CF	Weedhopper		
12-CI	Aviasud Albatros AE.209		
12-CZ	Croses Air Plume		26-CL
13-CH	Croses Airplume	15	
13-CZ	Filcon J-6 Karatoo		
13-DD	J-3 Kitten		
13-DN	Air's Maestro		
13-DT	Aviasud Mistral		
13-DZ	Cosmos Chronos		
13-EC	Baroudeur		
13-GD	Oméga paraglider		
13-IO	Baroudeur Zenith		
13-JF	Air Création Clipper GTE		
13-JM	Synairgie Sky Ranger		
14-F	Condor		
14-I	Air Création		
14-K	Lega Avia		
14-AB	Air Création Quartz		
14-AG	Super O		
14-BC	Air Création Trike		
14-BE	Air Création XS		
14-BS	Air Création Trike		33-AP
14-BV	Air Création GT BI Fun		
14-CA	Cosmos		
14-CB	Mignet HM.1000 Balèrit	51	
14-CD	Cosmos		
14-DH	ACGE		
14-DM	Weedhopper		
14-FI	AX-3		
15-KM	Corsair JPX Souricette		
16-AC	Ultrastar		
16-AK	Ultrastar		
16-BF	Weedhopper AX-3		
16-DA	Squale		
16-DH	Micro Aviation Pulsar		
16-DX	Piel CP.150 Onyx		
W16-JE	Magni M20 Talon	409	
17-G	Mignet HM.1000 Balèrit 3X		
17-L	Huntair Pathfinder		
17-S	Trike 44PM	8300351	
17-X	Eipper Quicksilver MX-II		
17-AA	Léger Frères		
17-AS	Mignet HM.1000 Balèrit 3X		
17-AU	Baroudeur LS-120		
17-BB	Quartz		
17-BD	Air Création		
17-CB	Baroudeur		
17-CC	Weedhopper AX-3		
17-CV	Mignet HM.1000 Balèrit 3X (sold as 95-GU?)	24	
17-CY	Weedhopper AX-3		
17-DA	Mustang	044	
17-DC	Top Concept Hurricane		
17-DG	Mignet HM.1000 Balèrit 3X (sold as 52-BF ?)	28	
17-DJ	Weedhopper Europa 1		
17-DM	Weedhopper Europa 2		
17-DY	Air Création Quartz		
17-EA	Weedhopper AX-3		
17-EE	Weedhopper AX-3		
17-EF	Weedhopper Europa 2		
17-EJ	Micro Aviation Pulsar III		
17-FN	Mignet HM.1000 Balèrit 3X	64	
17-FR	Weedhopper AX-3		
17-FU	Weedhopper AX-3		
17-GD	Le Petaplume		
17-GE	Buccaneer II Floatplane		
17-GF	Mignet HM.1000 Balèrit (F-JAMJ)	80	
17-HS	Mignet HM.1000 Balèrit		
17-HU	Zenair ZH.701		
17-HZ	Europa		
17-JJ	Skyranger		
17-JL	Mignet HM.1000 Balèrit		
17-JY	Mignet HM.1000 Balèrit	122	
17-LG	Mignet HM.1100 Cordouan (F-JCIZ)		
17-MC	Chereau J.300 Joker		
17-ME	Mignet HM.1100 Cordouan (F-JCZS)	8	
17-MJ	Weedhopper AX-3		
17-NF	Mignet HM.1100 Cordouan (F-JBQD)	17	
18-AM	Club 18SL		
18-AS	Aériane Sirocco		
18-BB	Dynali Chickinox		

Regn.	Type	C/n	Prev.Id.
18-BJ	JCC Aviation J-300 Joker		
18-CO	Air Création		
18-CU	Air Création		
18-DP	Dynali Chickinox		
18-EO	JCC Aviation J-300 Joker (F-JART)		
18-ER	Quicksilver GT500		
18-EX	Rans S-6 Coyote II		
19-W	Trike		
19-DE	Quartz Trike		
19-EB	MD.03 (Biplane Amphibian)	01	
20-H	Aériane Sirocco		
20-GS	SG Aviation Storm 300 Special (F-JBXV)		
21-AH	Cosmos Profile		
21-AJ	Mono Dragster		
21-AK	Aériane Sirocco		
21-AP	JC.24 Weedhopper		
21-AR	Pendulaire		
21-BC	La Mouette Cosmos		
21-BN	Croses Air Plume		
21-CB	Cosmos		
21-DR	Rans S-6ESDCoyote II		
21-EQ	Cosmos		
21-FH	Cosmos		
21-GB	Trike		
21-GG	Cosmos		
21-HC	Chariot		
21-HS	Air Création		
21-HT	Air Création		
21-HV	Cosmos		
21-IM	Cosmos		
21-KJ	Air Création Ibis Quartz		
21-KL	Cosmos		
21-KM	Cosmos / La Mouette		
21-LC	Cosmos		
21-LD	Cosmos Chronos 16		
21-LH	Cosmos		
21-LU	Cosmos		
21-NJ	III Sky Arrow 500TF	017	
21-NO	Rans S-7 Courier		
21-NP	Zenair CH.601 Zodiac		
21-OJ	Cosmos		
21-OR	Rans S-6ESDCoyote II		
21-OT	Ecolight X'Air		
21-QP	Dyn'Aero MCR-01 Banbi		
W22-C	SCA Lone Ranger		
22-M	Veliplane		
22-AP	Weedhopper		
22-DE	Humbert Moto-du-Ciel		
22-EA	Rans S-6ESD Coyote II (F-JCDE)		
22-EL	Rans S-6 Coyote II		
22-GV	Rans S-12 Airaile		
24	Aériane Sirocco 377		
24-R	Baroudeur		
24-AP	Air's Maestro		
24-AS	Eipper Quicksilver MX-II		
24-AX	Eipper Quicksilver MX-II		
24-BD	Soprano		
24-BE	J-3 Kitten		
24-BH	de Havilland DH.82A Tiger Moth (Scale Replica)		
24-BT	Top Concept Hurricane		
24-CG	Toper Tielman ?		
24-CO	Pegaso		
24-EE	Top Concept Hurricane		
24-GH	Weedhopper		
25-J	ASW Microstar		
25-R	Mini Spitfire		
25-BD	SEP		
25-BM	Air Composite		
25-CD	Baroudeur		
25-CE	Air Création		
25-CI	Cosmos Chronos		
25-CR	Cosmos Chronos		
25-DF	Cosmos Chronos		
25-DG	Air Création		
25-DJ	Cosmos		
25-DQ	Air Création XP		
25-DR	Rans S-6 Coyote II		
25-DV	Moto du Ciel		
25-EG	Airborne Australia Cosmos Chronos		
25-FP	Air Création SX-II		
25-GE	Cosmos Chronos		
25-GV	Comco Ikarus Fox-C22		
25-HL	Air Création GTE Clipper XP		
25-HN	Air Création		
25-HO	Comco Ikarus Fox-C22		
25-HV	Cosmos Merlin		D-MMWW ?
	(Now reported as Sun & Moon Titan)		
25-IC	Rans S-6ESD Coyote II		
25-IE	Rans S-6ESD Coyote II		
25-IJ	Zenair CH-701 STOL		
25-IV	Funk FK-9	81	
25-JQ	Comco Ikarus Fox-C22		
25-JS	Hermes Adventure		
25-KB	Rans S-6ESDCoyote II (F-JDFK)		
26-G	Air Création		
26-AJ	Quartz 18		
26-AP	Air Création Alpair Chariot		
26-AS	Air Création		
26-BL	Air Création		
26-BO	Air Création XP		
26-BP	Air Création		
26-BU	Air Création SX		
26-CR	Air Création Alpair Chariot		
26-DD	Air Création Fun		
26-DE	Air Création XS		
26-EC	Air Création		
26-EE	Cosmos		
26-EJ	Air Création Fun		
26-ES	Quicksilver		
26-EV	Quicksilver GT-500		
26-FF	Air Création S		
26-FG	Air Création SX		
26-FK	Weedhopper		
26-FR	Air Création Fun		
26-FS	Air Création Fun		
26-FY	Weedhopper		
26-GB	Bifly	1	
26-GD	Air Création XP		
26-GE	Weedhopper		
26-GS	Air Création Quartz		
26-GT	Aviasud		
26-GU	Air Création SX		
26-GX	Mignet HM.1000 Balèrit		
26-HG	Air Création		
26-IB	Airwave		
26-IL	Zenair CH-701 STOL (F-JCTY)		
26-JO	Sirius		
26-JS	Pegasus		07-OT
26-JV	Air Création XP		
27-H	Synairgie Puma BI		
27-AC	Aerospecial Airpuce		
27-BG	Eipper Quicksilver MXL-II		
27-CG	JPK		
27-DG	Cosmos		
27-DH	Synairgie		
27-DV	Air Création		
27-DY	Synairgie		
27-EM	Puma		
27-EX	La Mouette		
27-FB	Synairgie		
27-FI	Puma		
27-FK	Mignet HM.14		
27-FS	Air's Maestro 2		
27-FZ	Cosmos		
27-GA	Weedhopper		
27-GP	Allogro 1		
27-GT	Air's		
27-GU	Air Création XS		
27-GW	Puma		
27-GZ	Aviasud Mistral		

Regn.	Type	C/n	Prev.Id.
27-HD	Cosmos		
27-HS	Europa		
27-IC	Mignet HM.1000 Balèrit		
27-IH	Aviasud Albatross		
27-IN	Cosmos		
27-JN	Zenair CH-701 STOL		
27-KS	Zenair CH.700 STOL (F-JCLG)	A6-04-91-1060	
27-LE	Zenair MXP-740 Savannah (F-JCQA)	12-97-50-072	
27-MA	ICP MXP.740 Savannah	12-96-50-049	
27-MB	Brügger MB.2 Colibri	180	F-PYOI
	(wears both marks)		
27-MC	ICP MXP.740 Savannah	01-98-50-077	
28-D	Pendulaire Azur		
28-U	Skycraft AJS.2000		
28-V	Eipper Quicksilver MX		
28-AC	Aiglon 01		
28-AO	Charcoal Raven X	HN003	
28-BG	Allegro		
28-BJ	Air's Maestro 2		
28-BL	Air's Maestro		
28-DE	Weedhopper JC-24	9072521	
28-DQ	Weedhopper JC-24		
28-EP	Renegade 503		
28-EY	Pegasus		
28-FC	Comco Ikarus Fox-C22		
28-FJ	Allegro II		
28-FM	Springbok		91-IF
28-FN	Top Commander Tempest		
28-FT	Comco Ikarus Fox-C22		
28-GJ	JCC J-300 Joker (F-JALL)		
28-GN	Weedhopper		
28-GS	Renegade 503		
28-GT	Air Création GT Fun		
28-HO	Air's Maestro 2		
28-HP	Aviasud Mistral		
28-HS	Epervier		
28-HY	Aviasud Albatros		
28-IM	Weedhopper		
28-JL	Renegade 503		
28-JS	Aviasud Mistral		
28-KD	Rans S-6 Coyote II		
28-KN	Falcon Daxiwing		
28-KW	Murphy Renegade Spirit		
28-LB	Comco Ikarus Fox-C22		
28-LI	Comco Ikarus Fox-C22	9411-3637	
28-LV	Synairgie		
28-LW	Humbert Tetras (F-JBJE)		
28-ME	Rans S-6 Coyote II		
28-MO	Comco Ikarus Fox-C22		
28-MZ	Rans S-6 Coyote II		
28-NA	Aviasud Mistral		
28-NM	Comco Ikarus C-42 Cyclone		
28-NN	Air Création Clipper GTE		
28-NX	Funk FK-9	76	
28-NZ	Funk FK-9TG	67	
28-PE	Funk FK-9	74	
28-PM	Comco Ikarus Fox C-22	9511-3696	
28-PP	III Sky Arrow 500TF	040	
28-QP	Rans S-6ESD Coyote IIXL		
28-RR	Comco Ikarus C-42 Cyclone		
28-RV	Zenair CH.701 STOL		
28-SA	Comco Ikarus Fox C-22	9501-3638	
28-SK	Comco Ikarus C-42 Cyclone (F-JBGS)		
28-ST	Comco Ikarus Fox C-22		
29-H	Eipper Quicksilver MX		
29-AA	Bidulum		
29-AF	Air Création		
29-AX	Air Création		
29-AZ	Flipper		
29-BI	Air Création		
29-CD	Cosmos Echo 12		
29-CG	Rans S-6 Coyote II		
29-CH	Rans S-12 Airaile		
29-CR	Air Création		
29-CS	Mignet HM.14		

Regn.	Type	C/n	Prev.Id.
29-CZ	Weedhopper AX-3		
29-DJ	Rans S-6 Coyote II		
29-FM	Chereau J-300 Joker		
29-FO	Rans S-6 Coyote II		
29-HD	Aviasud Mistral		
29-PO	Cosmos		
30-U	Funfly		
30-AD	Eipper Quicksilver MX-II		
30-AO	Sirocco		
30-BM	JC-24 Weedhopper Europa II		
30-BN	Air Création XS		
30-BX	Dynali Chickinox		
W30-CE	AX-3 Weedhopper Ultracam (F-JAAS)		
30-CH	Pegasus		
30-CN	Dynali Chickinox		
30-CP	Tefou Trike		17-AR
30-CT	Air Création Quartz SX		
30-CX	Air Création		
30-DC	Dynali Chickinox		
30-DD	Quicksilver MX		
30-DE	Air Création		
30-DF	Mignet HM.1000 Balèrit	55	
30-DH	JC-24 Weedhopper Europa II		
30-DK	Air Création		
30-DP	Rans (exact type unknown)		
30-DQ	SE-5A Replica		
30-DS	Air Création		
30-EB	Dynali Chickinox		
30-ED	Air Création		
30-EF	Air Création Plus		
30-EG	Air Création Quartz		
30-EY	(Cessna 150 Replica)		
30-FD	Rossi 503S Pegasus		
30-FJ	Criquet		
30-FN	Air Création GTI		
30-FT	Air Création		
30-FU	Quicksilver GT		
30-FV	Aquilair		
30-FY	La Mouette		
30-GB	Air Création SX		
W30-GE	Solar Wings Pegasus Quasar IITC	6662	G-MYOD
30-GX	Fly Synthesis Storch		
30-KA	Albatros		
31-T	Eipper Quicksilver MX		
31-AI	Funk FK-9		
31-CD	Weedhopper		
31-DL	Eipper Quicksilver MX		
31-DT	Le Raitelet	CQR/1	
31-DV	Eipper Quicksilver MX-II	1053	
31-EJ	Eipper Quicksilver		
31-EN	JC-31D Weedhopper		
31-GX	Denney Kitfox		
31-HA	Denney Kitfox		
31-HI	Denney Minifox		
31-JV	Air Création XPII		
31-JZ	Tecnam P.92 Echo		
31-KP	Synairgie Sky Ranger 503		
31-OO	Baroudeur Aeronautique 2000		
31-TU	Air Création Clipper GTE		
31-UM	Weedhopper AX-3		
31-UZ	Funk FK 9 Mk3		
32-AH	Cosmos		
32-BT	Moto du Ciel		
32-CV	Ultralair JC.24 Weedhopper Sport (F-JBCC)	9122574	
33-BL	Bombardier		
33-CO	Mustang		
33-CQ	Eipper Quicksilver MX		
33-CS	Eipper Quicksilver MX		
33-CU	Mustang		
33-CY	Mustang		
33-DD	Eipper Quicksilver MX-II		
33-DU	Aériane Sirocco	54	
33-DX	Top Concept Hurricane		
33-EB	Air's Allegro/La Mouette Hermes 16		
33-EG	Bidulum 43		

382

Regn.	Type	C/n	Prev.Id.
33-ES	JC.31 Weedhopper		
33-FC	Cobra		
33-FL	PGO Cobra		
33-FR	Eipper Quicksilver MX-II	1848	
33-FT	Pou du Ciel MF-02		
33-FZ	Mignet HM.14		
33-GJ	Aviasud Mistral		
33-GK	PGO Cobra		
33-GM	Mignet HM.1000 Balèrit	14	
33-GX	Mignet HM.1000 Balèrit	23	
33-MT	Mignet HM.1100 Cordouan (F-JKAG)		
34-E	J-3		
34-V	Eipper Quicksilver		
34-AC	Aériane Sirocco		
34-AL	Aeropiel CP.150G Onyx		
34-AM	Mignet HM.14		
34-BB	Aériane Sirocco		
34-BD	Mignet HM.1000 Balèrit 3X		
34-BO	Weedhopper		
34-BR	Air's Maestro		
34-CC	Eipper Quicksilver MX		
34-CD	Quicksilver		
34-CE	Eipper Quicksilver MX-II		
34-DJ	Renegade		
34-DU	Air's Allegro		
34-DV	Air's Allegro		
34-DX	Air's Maestro		
34-DY	Air's Allegro		
34-EA	Air's Maestro		
34-EB	Air's Allegro		
34-EF	Eipper Quicksilver MX		
34-EG	J-3 Kitten		
34-EH	Eipper Quicksilver MX		
34-EL	JC-31 Weedhopper		
34-EP	Dynali Chickinox		
34-EQ	Dynali Chickinox		
34-ER	Eipper Quicksilver MX-II		
34-EY	Weedhopper JC-24 Sport		
34-FB	Top Concept Hurricane		
34-FI	Eipper Quicksilver MX-II		
34-FJ	Thruster TST		
34-FL	Eipper Quicksilver GT-400		
34-WFM	Air Création GT BI Quartz		
34-FP	Air Création		
34-FQ	Eipper Quicksilver MX		
34-GC	La Mouette Cosmos		
34-GD	Cobra		W34-GD
34-GG	Weedhopper		
34-GJ	Weedhopper 1		
34-GQ	AX-3 Weedhopper Twin		
34-GU	AX-3 Weedhopper		
34-GV	Eipper Quicksilver MX-II		
34-G.	GT-BI X5		
34-HB	Aériane Sirocco		
34-HC	AX-3 Weedhopper Amphibian		
34-HF	Weedhopper		
34-HL	Eipper Quicksilver MX-II	1262	
34-HU	Tempête		
34-HX	AX-3 Weedhopper		
34-IC	AX-3 Weedhopper		
34-ID	Weedhopper		
34-IE	Weedhopper		
34-IH	AX-3 Weedhopper		
34-II	AX-3 Weedhopper		
34-IK	Weedhopper		
34-IM	AX-3 Weedhopper		
34-IT	AX-3 Weedhopper		
34-OO	Air Création XPClipper		
34-A	Mignet		
35-E	ULM 35/Djinn 300		
35-AK	Mignet HM.14		
35-AY	Air Création		
35-AZ	Air Création GT BI		
35-BD	Mignet HM.1000 Balèrit 3X	60	
35-BF	Weedhopper		
35-BH	Air Création		
35-BM	Weedhopper		
35-BO	Croses Criquet	60	
35-BV	Air Création GT BI Quartz		
35-CP	Rans S-12 Airaile		
35-DA	Air Création		
36-AA	Trike		
36-AD	Trike		
36-AG	Air Création GT BI Quartz		
36-AJ	Trike		
36-AL	Air Création GT BI Quartz		
36-BA	Air Création GT BI Quartz		
36-BF	Air Création GT BI Quartz		
36-BO	Air Création GT BI Quartz		
36-BX	Breezy RLU.1		
36-CC	Trike		
36-DS	Air Création Quartz		
36-DT	Air Création		
36-EJ	Air Création		
36-EK	Ikel		
36-ER	Pegasus Quantum		
36-EY	Cosmos Trike		
36-FF	Synairgie Puma		
36-FH	Synairgie		
36-FQ	Air Création		
36-LB	Corrado		
37-B	Trike		
37-H	Baroudeur Veliplane		
37-N	Trike		
37-X	Aeropiel CP.150 Onyx	48	
37-AA	RH.02		93-AD
37-AD	Azur		
37-AK	Synairgie		
37-BI	Weedhopper	8032376	
37-BP	Plus		
37-BR	Air Création Quartz		
37-BS	Air Création		
37-BT	Air Création		
37-BU	Air Création		
37-CA	Air Création		
37-CC	JCC Aviation J-300 Joker		
37-CD	Air Création Quartz X5		
37-CE	Air Création		
37-CO	PGO Cobra		
37-CP	Mudry Baroudeur	319	
37-CS	Air Création		
37-CU	Patrifor		
37-DI	Safari		
37-DJ	Air Création Quartz		
37-DP	Air Création Quartz		
37-DT	Air Création Quartz		
37-DU	Air's Maestro 2		
37-DX	JCC Aviation J-300 Joker (F-JARN)		
37-EA	Kolb Twinstar		
37-EB	Safari		
37-EC	Pagojet		
37-EP	Air Création GT-BI Quartz X5		
37-EU	Safari		
37-FA	Weedhopper		
37-FB	L.X.P.		
37-FK	Air Création Quartz X5		
37-GB	Cosmos Trike		
37-GP	Pagojet		
37-GR	(F-JAOU) Type unknown		
37-GS	Air's Maestro 2		61-CA
37-HC	Air's Maestro 2		
37-HD	Air Création Quartz		
37-HL	JCC Aviation J-300 Joker (F-JATT)		
37-HU	Ultrastar		
37-JD	Aviasud Albatros AE-209	57	
37-JE	Cosmos		
37-JF	Weedhopper		
37-JU	Air Création GT-BI		
37-JW	Colibri		
37-KD	Weedhopper		

Regn.	Type	C/n	Prev.Id.
37-KN	Air Création GTE Clipper XP		
37-KP	Synairgie Sky Ranger		
37-KS	Caprice 21		
37-KU	Aviasud Mistral		
37-KY	Air Création GTE Clipper XP		
37-LA	Synairgie Sky Ranger		
37-LB	Synthesis Storch		
37-LH	Pelican		
37-LK	Air Création GT-BI		
37-LS	Synthesis Storch		
37-MH	"Hydravion"		
37-MX	JCC J-300 Joker (F-JCUF)		
38-V	JC-31 Weedhopper		
38-AQ	Aerosport Puma	S.195/365	G-MBBU
38-AV	Croses Air Plume	18	
38-BG	Solar Wings Puma		55-Y
38-BH	Cosmos Elf		
38-CE	Cosmos Chronos		
38-CM	SMAN Pétrel (F-JAVL), noted 4.00	045 ?	54-PL
			56-CM
38-CQ	Air Création Racer A6		
38-CR	Cosmos		
38-DQ	Weedhopper		
38-ER	Pegasus Quantum		
38-FC	Weedhopper	B1101148	72-ED
38-FT	Pendulaire		
38-FU	Pendulaire		
38-GY	CP.152B Onyx	140	
38-HV	Rans S-6 Coyote II		
38-IA	Air's Maestro 2		
38-ID	Quicksilver MXE Sport		
38-JG	Synairgie Skyranger		
38-KK	Air Création		
38-KQ	TEAM MiniMax		
38-LC	Rans S-6ESDCoyote II		
38-LM	Light Aero Avid Flyer	692	
39-J	Safari		
39-AF	Eipper Quicksilver MX-II	1776	
39-BL	JC.31 Weedhopper		
39-BP	Cosmos/Atlas		
39-BV	Renegade 503		
39-BY	Renegade 503		
39-CC	Renegade 503	328	
39-FC	Light Aero Avid Flyer		
39-FO	Humbert Tetras (F-JCYT)		
39-FR	ICP MXP.740 Savannah		
39-IT	Dynali Chickinox		
40-J	Aériane Sirocco		
40-L	JC.24 Weedhopper		
40-M	Eipper Quicksilver MX		
40-S	Dynali Chickinox		
40-AP	Trike		
40-AX	Trike		
40-UL	Twin Weedhopper		
41-G	Pelican		
41-K	Antar		
41-AH	Labasse Griffon 41		
41-BI	Air Création Quartz		
41-CD	Air Création GT BI Quartz		
41-DB	Air Création GT BI Quartz		
41-ED	Air Création Quartz		
41-HG	Fly Synthesis Storch HS		
42-N	JC.31C Weedhopper		
42-0	Baroudeur		
42-AJ	Baroudeur		
42-BA	HFL Stratos 300		
42-BY	Weedhopper		
42-CK	Weedhopper		
42-DM	Aviasud Mistral		
42-DX	Synairgie Skyranger		
43-J	J-3 Kitten		
43-N	Aquila S-440		
43-BMW	Air Création GT BI Quartz		
43-BS	Denney Kitfox		
43-BT	Helios		

Regn.	Type	C/n	Prev.Id.
43-DK	Aquilair		
44-L	Cosmos Chronos		
44-0	Concept		
44-S	Vector		
44-AF	Weedhopper		
44-AM	Dragon 150		
44-CD	Polaris		
44-DL	Sirocco		
44-DU	Huiles Loto		
44-FT	Cosmos Chronos		
44-FV	La Mouette Cosmos		
44-GB	AX-3		
44-GO	Cosmos		
44-HF	Cosmos Chronos		
44-HJ	Cosmos		
44-HK	Cosmos		
44-HR	"La Poste"		
44-HS	Cosmos		
44-HY	AX-3		
44-IC	Cosmos		
44-IL	Cosmos		
44-IU	Cosmos		
44-JM	Weedhopper AX-3		
44-KB	Rand-Kar X-Air		
44-KC	AX-3		
44-KU	Weedhopper		
44-LA	AX-3		
44-LF	Chronos		
44-LK	Cosmos		
44-LO	Rans S-6 Coyote II		
44-LS	Chronos		
44-LO	Rans S-6 Coyote II		
44-MB	Rans S-6 Coyote II		
44-MK	Cosmos		
44-MS	Aviasud Albatros		
44-MT	Air Création Mild		
44-ND	Rand-Kar X-Air		
44-OB	Cosmos		
44-OK	Quicksilver GT500		
44-OL	Rand-Kar X-Air		
44-OO	AX-3		
44-OU	Rand-Kar X-Air		
44-OV	Rand-Kar X-Air		
44-PH	Rand-Kar X-Air		
44-PN	Rans S-6 Coyote II		
44-PO	Buse'Air 150		
44-PR	AX-3		
44-PX	HMD.380		
44-PY	Aviasud Albatros		
44-RH	Solar Wings Pegasus Quantum 15	6952	G-MYVF
44-RM	Cosmos		
44-RN	Aviasud Albatros		
44-RV	Rand-Kar X-Air		
44-SF	Rand-Kar X-Air		
44-SU	Rand-Kar X-Air		
44-UQ	Trophy TT2000		
45-AP	Mustang		
45-BP	Air Création Racer SX 12		
45-BV	Synairgie		
45-CU	Piel CP.15 B	50	
45-EH	Cosmos		
45-EX	SCEP Mustang		
45-FM	Air Création Quartz		
45-FO	Air Création		
45-GG	AX-3		
45-GR	Air Création GT BI Quartz		
W-45-HY	Air Création XP		
45-JA	Air Création		
45-KG	Mignet HM.293 Pou du Ciel		
45-KL	III Sky Arrow 501TF		
47-P	La Mouette Cosmos		57-AK
47-BJ	Atlas Wing		
47-BL	Air Création		
47-BY	ADR-20		
47-CR	Cosmos		

Regn.	Type	C/n	Prev.Id.
47-DG	Mignet HM.14		
47-EB	Air Création GT BI Quartz		
47-EC	Air Création GT BI Quartz		
47-EI	Air Création Racer		
47-FK	La Moto du Ciel		
47-FN	Rans S-6 Coyote II (F-JBBZ)		
47-FW	Air Création GT BI Quartz		
47-FY	Cosmos Chronos 16		
47-GE	Dauphin/Synairgie		
47-GG	Buccaneer II Amphibian		
47-GH	Air Création Racer		
47-GN	Air Création Racer		
47-GU	Weedhopper	B1081143	
47-GW	Air Création GT		
47-GY	Air Création GT		
47-HB	Weedhopper	0011129	
47-HD	Air Création GT BI X5		
47-HF	Air Création		
47-HY	Rans S-6 Coyote II		
48	Dragon 150		
49-A	Air Création GT BI Quartz		
49-AL	Air Création GT BI Quartz		
49-BF	Ropulcia Colt		
49-BG	Microbel Must		
49-BP	Microbel Must		
49-BV	Synairgie		
49-EU	Aerial Arts Chaser 377		
49-FO	CP.152B Onyx	50	
49-GB	Fulmar		
49-HO	Synairgie		
49-VU	Air Création GT BI Quartz		
50-U	Aerodyne Vector 627SR		
50-AF	Aerodyne 627SR Vector TM		40-D
50-AG	Air Création Quartz 180SX		
50-AI	Aerodyne Vector 627SR		
50-AJ	Air Création Trike		
50-AN	Quartz X5		
50-AO	Synairgie Trike		
50-AQ	Quartz X5		
50-AV	Lemmonier Maestro		
50-BH	Fischer FP-202 Super Koala		
50-BL	Air Création		
50-CG	Aviasud Mistral		
50-CJ	SE-5A Replica		
50-CN	Air Création GT BI SX		
50-CU	Air Création		
50-CX	Air Création SX		
50-CY	Dynali Chickinox		
50-DF	Air Création		
50-DI	Air Création SX		
50-DP	Air Création GT BI		
50-DY	Air Création		
50-DZ	Air Création		
50-ED	Parapente		
50-EI	Air Création		
50-EN	Humbert Tetras		
50-EQ	Moto du Cie		
50-EX	Air Création SXI		
50-FD	Mignet HM.1000 Balèrit	114	
50-FM	Air Création SX		
50-FN	Air Création GTE		
50-FO	Avions Guepard 912		
50-FR	Air Création Quartz		
50-FZ	Air Création		76-FE
50-GC	Air Création GT BI		
50-GJ	Raj Hamsa X-Air		
50-GK	Air Création SX		
50-GO	Rans S-6 Coyote II		
50-GQ	Humbert Tetras		
50-GT	Air Création		
50-GU	Air Création GYBI		50-DS
51-AA	Egrett Sophie		
51-DJ	Breezy RLU.1		
51-DN	Air Création Fun GT		
51-EQ	Mignet HM.1000 Balèrit	41	

Regn.	Type	C/n	Prev.Id.
51-ET	Rans S-12 Airaile		
51-FY	Humbert Tetras (F-JBGL)		
51-GP	Mignet HM.293 Pou du Ciel		
51-GT	Interplane Skyboy		
52-AD	Cosmos		
52-AL	Cosmos		
52-AP	Cosmos		
52-AT	Cosmos		
52-AW	Cosmos		
52-BC	Air Création GT BI		
52-BE	Air Création GT BI		
52-BF	Mignet HM.1000 Balèrit	28	17-DG
52-BH	Weedhopper		
52-BQ	Synairgie		
52-BR	Cosmos		
52-CA	Air Création		54-FV
52-CI	Air Création		
52-CK	Air Création Fun		
52-CL	Cosmos		
52-CO	Air Création		
52-CQ	Air Création SX		
52-EC	Cosmos		
52-GG	Cosmos		
53-AJ	Mignet HM.1000 Balèrit		
54-V	Cosmos 250/Azure		
54-AC	Eipper Quicksilver MX		
54-AK	AEIM Epsilon		
54-AT	"Fujicolor"		
54-DT	Moto-du-Ciel (F-JAYT)		
54-FX	Air Création		
54-GR	Murphy Renegade Spirit	241	
54-HL	Weedhopper JC.31		
54-IB	Cosmos		
54-JE	Aviasud Albatros AE.209 (F-JAPR)		
54-JL	Murphy Renegade Spirit		
54-KA	Ultralair AX-3 Weedhopper	0062663	LX-XGK
54-KG	Air's Maestro		
54-KN	(F-JBWK) Type unknown		
54-KP	Guerpont Autoplum 04	01	
54-KS	Murphy Renegade Spirit		
54-KV	Air Création		
54-KX	Rans S-6 Coyote II		
54-LA	Air Création		
54-LB	Air Création Clipper GTE		
54-LI	Air Création Clipper GTE		
54-LT	Denney Kitfox		
54-ME	Air Création Clipper XP		
54-NN	Cosmos		
54-NY	Trophy TT2000 STOL		
54-OA	Micro Aviation Pulsar 2		
54-OP	Air Création GT		
54-OR	Air Création		
54-PL	SMAN Pétrel (F-JAVL) probably now 38-CM	045	56-CM
54-QA	Air Création Clipper XP		
55-AD	Ultralair JC.31C Weedhopper		
55-CE	Mignet HM.1000 Balèrit	18	
55-CL	Aviasud Mistral		
55-CT	Ultralair JC.24 Weedhopper Sport		
55-CU	Dynali Chickinox		
55-CX	Denney Kitfox		
55-DB	Sky System		
55-DN	Air Création		
55-DP	Weedhopper	9042580	
55-EB	Huntair Pathfinder		
55-EI	Ultralair JC24 Weedhopper Sport		
55-EV	Mignet HM.293A Pou-du-Ciel		
55-FA	Rans S-6ESD Coyote II		
55-FE	Eipper Quicksilver GT-500		
55-FO	Humbert Tetras (F-JAPB)		
55-FR	Ultravia PL-914 Pelican Super Sport (F-JBME)		
55-FS	Moto-du-Ciel		
55-FT	Cosmos Chronos 12		
55-FX	Eipper Quicksilver GT-500		
55-GF	Rans S-6ESD Coyote II (F-JAMV)		
55-GM	Micro Aviation Pulsar II		

Regn.	Type	C/n	Prev.Id.
55-GS	Rans S-7 Courier (F-JCKR)		
55-GT	HM.293A Pou-du-Ciel		55-FC
55-HA	Light Aero Avid Flyer		
55-HG	Ecolight X'Air		
55-HH	Rans S-6ESDCoyote II *(Also wears regn F-WRKH -*		
	which was reserved 1991 for Light Aero Avid Flyer c/n 801)		
55-HN	Moto-du-Ciel (F-JBAL)		
55-HY	Mignet HM.1100 Cordouan	11	
56	Baroudeur		
56-G	Baroudeur		
56-J	Veliplane		
56-K	Baroudeur		
56-L	Baroudeur		
56-N	SMAN	01	
56-U	Wida		
56-X	Danis Jumbo		
56-AJ	Weedhopper		
56-AR	SMAN Pétrel	01	
56-AV	SMAN Pétrel	001	
56-BA	SMAN Pétrel		
56-BK	Air Création Biplace		
56-BS	Denney Kitfox		
56-CH	SMAN Pétrel	044	
56-DR	SMAN Pétrel (F-JBSW)	061	
57-F	Aériane Sirocco 377		
57-AM	Dynali Chickinox		
57-BC	Moto-du-Ciel (F-JBJQ)		
57-BD	Huntair Pathfinder		
57-BK	Aviasud Mistral		
57-BM	Air Création Quartz		
57-BP	Huntair Pathfinder		
57-EL	Weedhopper		
57-FL	Cosmos Chronos		
57-GG	Synairgie		
57-GP	Air Création		
57-GQ	Aviasud Mistral		
57-GV	Tandem Air Sunny Sport RV		
57-HT	Rans S-14		
57-JB	Weedhopper AX-3		
57-JC	Weedhopper AX-3		
57-JD	Cosmos Chronos 16		
57-JF	AX-3 Weedhopper		
57-JK	Dynali Chickinox		
57-KA	Zodiac Ultrastar		
57-KC	Dynali Chickinox		
57-KF	Rans S-6 Coyote II		
57-LI	Pegasus Quasar		
57-LK	Cosmos		
57-LP	Cosmos		
57-LR	Air Création GTE Clipper XP (F-JBLU)		
57-LT	Euronef ATTL-1		
57-LX	Technoflug Piccolo	103	D-MTOH
57-LY	Air's Maestro		
57-MD	Comco Ikarus Fox-C22		
57-MJ	Rans S-6 Coyote II		
57-MK	Solar Wings Pegasus XL-Quantum 15		
57-ML	Hermes		
57-MN	Murphy Renegade Spirit		
57-MS	Rans S-6 Coyote II		
57-NM	Air Création GTE Clipper		
57-NS	Air Création XP		
57-NX	Tulak		
57-OG	HM.293 Pou du Ciel		
57-OK	Comco Ikarus Fox-D	8510-FD34	LX-XOE
			D-MBOE
57-OY	Comco Ikarus Jet Fox		
57-PE	Light Aero Avid Flyer		
57-PI	Dynali Chickinox		
57-PJ	"E.C.L." Pou-type	116	
57-PK	Albatross		
57-PO	Ecolight X'Air		
57-PP	Cosmos		
57-PQ	Air Création XP		
57-PR	Cosmos		
57-PU	Humbert Tetras		

Regn.	Type	C/n	Prev.Id.
57-PX	Denney Kitfox		
57-PY	Dynali Chickinox		
57-QA	Jet Fox		
57-QC	Humbert Tetras		
57-QD	Aviakit Hermés Vega		
57-RF	Rans S-6 Coyote II		
58-AG	Eipper Quicksilver MX	5805	
58-AH	Eipper Quicksilver MX-II	1178	
58-AI	Eipper Quicksilver MX		
58-AS	Eipper Quicksilver MX		
58-AV	Baroudeur		
58-EK	Dynamic 582 DT/15		
58-ID	Air Création		
58-QY	HM. Pou du Ciel		
59-C	Air Création		
59-H	Dynali Chickinox Kot-Kot *(not airworthy)*		
W59-AA	Rans S.6 Coyote II		
59-AM	JC-24 Weedhopper		
59-AN	JC-31C Weedhopper Europa II		
59-BF	Ultralair SE.5A Replica *(Painted as "F760")*		
59-BZ	Lemonnier Maestro	86.102	
59-CA	Dynali Chickinox		
59-CK	Weedhopper		
59-DD	Kolb Twinstar		
59-DP	Quicksilver GT-500		
59-DJ	Weedhopper	904112	55-DY?
59-DV	Rans S-12 Airaile		
59-DY	AX-3 Weedhopper		
59-EA	Weedhopper 1		
59-EB	Weedhopper		
59-EE	Premier Cyclone AX-3 / 503		
59-EF	Cosmos trike		
59-EP	Aerolac MD04 Airland		
59-ES	Dynali Chickinox		
59-EX	Dynali Chickinox		
59-EZ	Marquart Charger		
59-FD	Air Création Quartz		
59-FJ	Dynali Chickinox Kot-Kot		
59-FU	Weedhopper		
59-FZ	Dynali Chickinox Kot-Kot		
59-GB	Dynali Chickinox		
59-GC	Weedhopper		
59-GP	Quartz		
59-GQ	Weedhopper		
59-GT	HM.293A Pou du Ciel		55-FC
59-HB	Macair 1142 Merlin		
59-HC	Aviasud Mistral		
59-HI	Dynali Chickinox Kot-Kot		
59-HV	Air Création		
59-HX	Weedhopper JC-24D Sport *(Stored)*	B1071142	
59-IG	Dynali Chickinox Kot-Kot		
59-IL	Eipper Quicksilver GT500		
59-IN	Eipper Quicksilver Mk.IIHP		
59-IO	Eipper Quicksilver MX		
59-IP	Mignet HM.293 Poudu-Ciel		
59-IT	Dynali Chickinox		
59-JE	Dynali Chickinox Kot-Kot		
59-JG	Weedhopper		
59-JH	Weedhopper		
59-JO	Citizen Flyer Twin JL9		
59-KC	Cosmos GT		
59-KG	Weedhopper		
59-KK	Epervier		
59-KN	Mignet HM.1000 Balèrit	46	
59-KP	Eipper Quicksilver GT500		
59-KU	Aviasud AE209 Albatros	46	PH-2M5
59-LJ	TEAMMinimax		
59-LY	Rans S-12 Airaile		
59-LZ	Aviasud AE209 Albatros	50	
59-MB	Aviasud AE209 Albatros	51	
59-MH	Zenair CH.701		
59-MI	Zenair CH.701 STOL		
59-MJ	Zenair CH.701 STOL	003	(OO-B67)
59-MN	F.2 Foxcat *(Damaged, stored)*		
59-MO	Rans S-6 Coyote II	0192261	OO-A52

Regn.	Type	C/n	Prev.Id.
59-MP	Rans S-6 Coyote II		
59-MQ	Cyclone AX-3 / 503		
59-MT	Zenair CH.701 STOL		
59-MU	Zenair CH.701 *(painted as 59/72014)*	7-2014?	
59-MW	Zenair CH.701		
59-MX	Fly Synthesis/Rodaro Storch	22?	
59-MZ	Rans S-6 Coyote II		
59-NA	Dynali Chickinox Kot Kot		
59-NE	Rans S-6 Coyote II		
59-NG	Dynali Chickinox Tandem		
59-NI	Zenair CH.701 STOL		
59-NJ	Rans S-6 Coyote II		
59-NK	Rans S-6ESD Coyote II	0891214	OO-A60
59-NL	AMFChevvron 2-32		
59-NQ	Aviatika Locafly		
59-NS	Synairgie		
59-NU	Mignet HM.1000 Balèrit	92	
59-OK	Zenair CH.601 Zodiac		
59-OL	Rans S-6 Coyote II		
59-OO	Air Création		
59-OP	Rans S-6 Coyote II		
59-OR	Fly Synthesis Storch		
59-OS	Zenair CH-601 Zodiac		
59-OV	Rans S-12 Airaile	0792245	OO-B08
59-PB	Dynali Chickinox		
59-PD	Mignet HM.1000 Balèrit	111	
59-PG	Rans S-6 Coyote II		
59-PI	Fly Synthesis Storch		
59-PK	Zenair CH.701 STOL		
59-PP	Macair 1142 Merlin		
59-PQ	Dynali Chickinox Kot-Kot		
59-PS	Eipper Quicksilver GT500	202	OO-B01
59-PV	Rans S-6 Coyote II (OQ-AYV)		
59-QC	Zenair CH-601 Zodiac		
59-QD	Rans S-6 Coyote II		
59-QE	Rans S-6 Coyote II		
59-QF	Zenair CH-701 STOL		
59-QI	Chasser		
59-QJ	Zenair CH-701 STOL		
59-QM	Rans S-6 Coyote II	1091222	OO-A53
59-QR	AES Sky Ranger		
59-QS	Rans S-6 Coyote II	295732ES	OO-C06
59-QT	Zenair CH-701 STOL		
59-QX	Dynali Chickinox		
59-QY	Mignet HM.293 Pou du Ciel		
59-RA	Rans S-6 Coyote II		
59-RC	Aviasud AE.209 Albatros		
59-RJ	Air Création		
59-RL	Weedhopper AX-3		59-RH?
59-RN	Evans VP-2 Volksplane		
59-RR	Rans S-6 Coyote II		
59-RT	Zenair CH-701 STOL		
59-RU	Zenair CH-701 STOL		
59-RY	Mignet HM.1000 Balèrit	115	
59-RZ	Croses Airplume	23	OO-833
59-SA	Rans S-6 Coyote II		
59-SE	Dynali Chickinox Kot-Kot		
59-SF	Mignet HM.1000 Balèrit	119	
59-SH	Zenair CH-601HD Zodiac (F-JCPP)	6-1780	59-OJ
			C-FMXN
59-SN	Zenair CH-701 STOL		
59-SR	Zenair CH-601 Zodiac		
59-SW	Zenair CH-701 STOL		
59-TD	Fly Synthesis Storch		
59-TF	Murphy Renegade Spirit	PFA/188-11562	G-MWHK
59-TH	Rans S-7 Courier (F-JCBU)		
59-TL	Zenair CH.601 Zodiac		
59-TM	Zenair CH.601 Zodiac (F-JDEI)		
59-TN	Rans S-6 Coyote II (OQ-AXH)		
59-TZ	Air Création Fun GT BI (F-JCCR)		
59-UA	Mignet Proto		
59-UC	Zenair CH.601 Zodiac (F-JCLU)		
59-UD	Aérianne Swift	45	
59-UG	Mignet HM.1000 Balèrit	127	
59-UI	Air Création Racer XS		

Regn.	Type	C/n	Prev.Id.
59-UJ	Rans S-6 Coyote II		
59-UK	Rans S-6 Coyote II		
59-UO	Air Création Fun GT		
59-US	Air Création Fun GT		
59-UU	Air Création		
59-VB	DPM Cosmos	21225	
59-VJ	Air Création GTE Clipper		
59-VN	Zenair CH-601 Zodiac		
W59-VO	Fly Synthesis Storch		
59-VQ	TL-132 Condor	94016	
59-VV	Zenair CH-601 Zodiac		
59-VX	Zenair CH-601 Zodiac		
59-VZ	Dynali Chickinox		74-AQ
59-WA	Rans S-6 Coyote II		
59-WD	Air Création XS		
59-WE	Rans S-6 Coyote II		
59-WF	Zenair CH.601HD Zodiac1 (F-JDCH)	6-3592	
59-WI	Mignet HM.1100 Corduan (F-JDBB)	05	
59-WP	Dynali Chickinox Tandem		
59-WW	Zenair CH.601 Zodiac		
59-XA	ICP Torino MXP-740 Savannah	09-97-50-060	
59-XD	Fly Synnthesis Storch		
59-XI	Air Création		
59-XS	Zodiac CH.701 STOL		
59-XU	Zenair CH-601 Zodiac		
59-XX	Skyranger		
59-YF	Air Création		
59-YJ	Mignet HM.1100 Cordouan		
59-YK	Fly Synthesis Storch 88		
59-YN	Rans S-6 Coyote II		
59-YP	Rans S-6 Coyote II		
59-ZK	Air Création XP		
59-ZN	Quicksilver GT500		
59-ZR	Mignet HM.293 Pou du Ciel		
59-ZS	SE.5A replica		
59-ZV	Fly Synthesis Storch		
59-ZW	Fantasy Air Cora		
59-AAC	Air Création Quartz		
59-AAG	Rans S-6 Coyote II		
59-AAI	Rans S-6 Coyote II		
59-AAJ	Fly Synthesis Storch SS		
59-AAM	Fly Synthesis Storch		
59-AAY	Air Création Fun		35-CC
59-CAM	Eurofox		
60-AQ	Quartz Air Création SX		
60-AU	Baroudeur Veliplane		
60-BC	Air Création Fun		
60-BH	Air Création		
60-DK	Air Création Fun GT BI		
60-GV	Aviasud AE.209 Albatros		
61-L	Zodiac Ultrastar 500	145	
61-AE	Air Création		
61-AH	Air Création		
61-AN	Dynali Chickinox		
61-AP	Aviasud Mistral		
61-AS	Eipper Quicksilver MX-II		
61-AX	Quartz		
61-BG	X5 Racer		
61-BK	JCC J-300 Joker		
61-BN	Dynali Chickinox (previously reported as Thruster)		
61-BT	Air Création GT BI		
61-CB	Dynali Chickinox		
61-CF	Aviasud Mistral		
61-CH	Air Création		
61-DB	Dynali Chickinox		
61-DD	Air Création Mild		
61-DH	Air Création GT		
61-DS	Air Création GT BI Quartz		
61-EC	Biplume		
61-EF	Buse Air 150 (F-JBSA)		
61-EH	Buse Air 150		
61-EL	Dynali Chickinox		
61-EP	Air's Allegro 2		
61-ER	Dynali Chickinox		
61-ET	Air Création GT Mild		

Regn.	Type	C/n	Prev.Id.
61-FG	Humbert Tetras (F-JCAJ)		
61-FM	Air Création GT BI		
61-FO	Air Création GT XS		
61-FR	J-6 Karatoo		
61-FU	Raj Hamsa X-Air		
61-GJ	Zenair MXP-740 Savannah		
62-P	Djinn 300		
62-BN	Eipper Quicksilver		
62-CD	JC-24 Weedhopper AX-3		
62-CU	Cosmos Chronos		
62-DC	Air Création Fun		
62-DG	Weedhopper		
62-DW	Air Création Fun		
62-ED	Rans S-6 Coyote II		
62-EE	Rans S-6 Coyote II		
62-EG	J-3 Kitten		
62-EK	Synairgie		
62-FH	Synairgie		
62-FJ	Eipper Quicksilver		
62-FS	Weedhopper		
62-FT	AES Sky Ranger		
62-FX	Zenair CH-701 STOL (F-JBUL)		
62-GI	Rans S-6 Coyote II		
62-GJ	Synairgie Sky Ranger	SR05-17057	
62-GK	Zenair CH.601 Zodiac		
62-GN	Rans S-6 Coyote II		
62-GW	Air Création		
62-GY	Synairgie		
62-HA	Light Aero Avid Light		
62-AAA	Funk FK.9 Mk.3		
W62-AAB	Jodel D.92	350	F-PHLJ
63-AK	Pendulaire		
63-AQ	Pendulaire		
63-CB	Air Création Cosmos		
63-CC	JCC Aviation J-300 Joker		
63-CS	Air Création Quartz		
63-EA	Air Création SX		
63-EG	Air Création		
63-FJ	Denney Kitfox (F-JAZN)		
63-GE	Denney Kitfox		
64-AX	Pendulaire		
64-DR	Air's Maestro 2		
64-GN	Aeriane		
64-HD	Aurore Souris Bulle		
65-N	Eipper Quicksilver MX		
65-AG	Chasle YC.100 Hirondelle		
65-CV	Aviasud Albatros AE-209	28	
W65-DY	Dufau M.80		
65-ED	Campana Observer (F-JBCP)		
65-EM	Titan Tornado 912		
66-AD	Baroudeur		
66-AJ	Weedhopper		
66-BN	Eipper Quicksilver GT		
66-BX	Weedhopper		
66-CH	Weedhopper		
66-CQ	Weedhopper		
66-CR	Air Création Quartz		
66-CT	Weedhopper		
66-CU	Weedhopper		
66-DB	Weedhopper (F-JAOB)		
66-DD	Air Création GT18 Quartz		
66-DK	Pelican (F-JBDW)		
66-DO	Weedhopper		
W66-DT	Hélios		
66-EX	Weedhopper		
66-FK	Air Création Quartz		
66-FU	unknown (F-JCXR)		
66-GB	Zenair CH- ?		
66-GG	Storch		
66-GH	Denney Kitfox	693	
66-GI	Weedhopper		
66-GM	Air Création Quartz		
66-QC	Weedhopper		
67-V	Pioneer Flightstar		
67-AG	Falcon		

Regn.	Type	C/n	Prev.Id.
67-AK	Baroudeur		
67-BJ	La Mouette		
67-BK	Pioneer Flightstar		
67-CL	Pioneer Flightstar		
67-DS	Rans S-6 Coyote II (F-JCOO)		
67-EF	Sky Pup		
67-EI	Denney Kitfox		
67-EM	Rans S-6 Coyote II (F-JAKQ)		
67-ES	Weedhopper		
67-FG	Epervier		
67-FK	Mignet HM.293 Pou-du-Ciel	86	
67-FM	Rans S-12 Airaile		
67-GO	Airwave/CEM Rave paraglider		
67-GU	J.300 Joker ?		
67-GZ	Rans S-6 Coyote II (F-JBTG)		
67-HB	Rans S-12 Airaile		
67-HG	Mignet HM.1000 Balèrit	114	
67-HT	Mignet HM.293 Pou-du-Ciel		
67-IA	Tipsy T.66 Nipper 2	59	D-ECPU(1) LX-AIG
67-IB	Mignet HM.293 Pou-du-Ciel		
67-IR	Skyboy		
67-IS	Rans S-6 Coyote II		
67-JC	Voilerie du Vent Phebus		
67-JD	Rans S-6ESD Coyote II		
67-JE	Sky Ranger		
67-JM	Avion JC Nacelle		
67-KU	Fantasy Air Allegro ST	98-101	
67-KW	Voilerie du Vent Phebus		
67-KZ	Rans S-6 Coyote II		
67-LE	Weedhopper		
67-LG	Murphy Maverick 503 (F-JCFN)		
67-LQ	Weedhopper AX-3		
67-NN	Voilerie du Vent Phebus		
68-AO	Skycraft AJS2000		
68-BO	Comco Ikarus Fox II	8604-3015	D-MJGH
68-CN	Weedhopper		
68-CQ	Weedhopper		
68-DJ	Ultralair JC.24 Weedhopper Sport		
68-DQ	Ultralair JC.24 Weedhopper Sport		
68-EJ	Cosmos Trike		
68-EL	Weedhopper		
68-FE	Weedhopper AX.3		
68-FF	Cosmos Trike		
68-FH	Rans S-6 Coyote II		
68-FI	Aviasud AE.209 Albatros		
68-FS	Croses Ultra Loisiere		
68-GB	Aviasud Albatros		
68-GH	Rans S-12 Airaile (Also registered D-MNBI)	1292-356	
68-GK	Synairgie Sky Ranger		
68-HC	Mignet HM.1000 Balèrit	114	
68-HK	Comco Ikarus Fox-C22		
68-HV	Weedhopper AX-3		
68-HY	Cosmos		
68-IL	Air Création		
68-IN	Light Aero Avid Lite		
68-IO	Skyboy		
68-IP	Air Création XP		
68-IQ	Synairgie Sky Ranger		
68-JA	Mignet HM.293 Pou-du-Ciel		
68-JM	Synairgie Sky Ranger		
68-KK	Synairgie Sky Ranger		
68-KR	Humbert Tetras (F-JDAB)		
68-KS	Quicksilver ?		
68-LC	Synairgie Sky Ranger		
68-LD	Aquilair XP		
68-LF	Weedhopper AX-3		
68-TN	Light Aero Avid Flyer		
69-M	Southdown Puma		
69-AE	Weedhopper JC-31		
69-AK	J-3 Kitten		
69-AR	Cosmos		
69-AU	Croses Air Plume	19	
69-BI	Aerial Arts Chaser		
69-BO	Croses Air Plume		

Regn.	Type	C/n	Prev.Id.
69-BX	Microbel Must		
69-CA	Pendulaire		
69-CX	Solar Wings Pegasus XL-Q		
69-DG	Weedhopper AX-3		62-DG
69-EG	Synairgie Trike		
69-EI	Weedhopper		
69-EQ	Biplum		
69-ER	Tandem Air Sunny		
69-ET	Weedhopper		
69-EX	Weedhopper		
69-GB	Aviasud AE.209 Albatros		
69-GV	Micro Aviation Pulsar 2		
69-HV	Air Création		
69-IJ	Air Création		
70-AB	Eipper Quicksilver MX		
70-AX	Raven		
70-BS	Cosmos Chronos		
70-CN	Air Composite		
70-DK	Humbert Moto-du-Ciel		
70-DR	Dynamic 15		
71-F	Southdown Puma		
71-N	Mavic		
71-AE	Mustang		
71-AF	Air's Maestro		
71-AH	Mustang		
71-BA	Europa Malik		
71-BJ	Cosmos		
71-BK	Aviasud Mistral		
71-BL	Aviasud Mistral		
71-CJ	Aviasud Mistral	100	
71-CO	Weedhopper		
71-CP	Aviasud Mistral	110	
71-CV	Mignet HM.1000 Balèrit 3X		
71-EA	Croses (Pou du Ciel)		
71-EG	Air Création GT		
71-FC	Tecnam P.92 Echo (F-JBWE)	100	
71-FG	Air Création Clipper GTE		
71-KD	Voyageur 172		
72-K	Aerokart		
72-L	JC-24 Weedhopper		
72-AA	JC-24 Weedhopper		
72-AM	Air Création Safari		
72-BC	Mignet HM.1000 Balèrit 3X	20	
72-BJ	JC-24 Weedhopper Europa 2		
72-BK	JC-24 Weedhopper Europa 1		
72-CA	Solar Wings Pegasus XL-R	SW-WA-1253 / SW-TB-1248	
72-FV	Humbert Tetras (F-JBIS)		
72-GB	Maxair Drifter XP503		
72-GV	JCC J-300 Joker		
73-AB	Air's Maestro (Single-seat)		
73-BU	Renegade 503		
73-CI	Weedhopper		
73-DG	Rans S-6 Coyote II	0293-44 .	
73-EF	Rans S-6 Coyote II (F-JBEC)		
73-EN	Zenair CH-701		
73-ER	Rans S-6 Coyote II (F-JBOK)		
74-Y	Aériane Sirocco		
74-AM	Zodiac Ultrastar	122	
74-CQ	Paraplane		
W74-DG	Paraplane		
74-DO	Sirius		
74-DX	Denney Minifox	519	
74-EG	Denney Minifox		
74-EO	Rans S-6 Coyote II		
74-EV	Mignet HM.14		
74-FH	Albatros		
74-GB	Cosmos Profil/La Mouette		
74-HG	Synairgie		
74-HK	Technic'air F40GT parachute		
74-KF	Rans S-6ESD Coyote II		
74-PF	Rans S-6ESD Coyote II		
75-H	Eipper Quicksilver MX		
75-Y	Aériane Sirocco		
75-AJ	Guerpont Biplum		
75-DN	Doutart Le Chevron Volant		

Regn.	Type	C/n	Prev.Id.
75-EI	Baroudeur Zenith	016	
75-FL	Mignet HM.100 Balèrit		
75-GF	Air Création		
75-GG	Air Création Racer SX 12		
75-GIW	Inovatic		
75-GJ	Baroudeur		
75-GV	J.2		
75-HP	Pegasus Le Volant		
75-HV	Synairgie		
75-II	Air's Maestro		
75-KC	Air Création Cosmos		
75-KM	Johnathan Souricette		
75-KU	Adventure paraglider		
75-LG	Barodeur		
75-LQ	Synairgie Sky Ranger		
75-MH	Aero Kuhlmann SCUB	2	
75-MI	Scub MTR-75 (F-JBVS)		
75-MT	Rans S-6 Coyote II		
75-NK	Weedhopper		
76-AX	Vector		
76-CG	Weedhopper (F-JAEN)		
76-DL	Synairgie		
76-EG	Foxi Puma 14		
76-FA	Synairgie		
76-GD	Synairgie		
76-HR	Air Création		
77-N	Baroudeur Veliplane		
77-BA	Baroudeur Veliplane		
77-BH	Comco Ikarus Fox-C22		
77-BJ	Falcon		
77-BN	Baroudeur Veliplane		
77-BS	Croses Airplume	10	
77-BT	Profile Trike		
77-CH	Baroudeur Zenith		
77-CK	Baroudeur Veliplane		
77-CL	Baroudeur Veliplane		
77-CP	Type unknown		
77-CU	Baroudeur Aeronautique 2000		
77-DC	Baroudeur Veliplane		
77-DI	Baroudeur Veliplane		
77-DN	Mignet HM.1000 Balèrit	02	
77-DQ	Aviasud Mistral		
77-DY	Baroudeur		
77-EA	Baroudeur		
77-EE	Baroudeur		
77-EG	Air Création		
77-ES	Etendard 493 (also reported as Air Création)		
77-FD	Trike		
77-GD	Mainair Gemini/Flash IIA		
77-GP	Paraman Powerchute		
77-GS	Mainair Gemini/Flash IIA		
77-HH	Mainair Gemini/Flash IIA		
77-ID	Air Création		
77-IK	Air's Maestro		
77-IS	Powerchute		
77-JA	Barodeur		
77-JF	Air Création GT BI Quartz		
77-JH	La Mouette Cosmos		
77-JV	Baroudeur		
77-KA	Air's Maestro		
77-KC	Challenger		
77-LB	Air Création Cosmos		
77-LC	Baroudeur		
W77-LD	Baroudeur		
77-LF	C.Jupitor		
77-LL	Rans S-6 Coyote II		
77-LQ	Air Création Cosmos Chronos		
77-LY	Safari		
77-MD	TEAM Mini-Max		
77-MH	Air Création Cosmos		
77-MJ	Weedhopper		
77-MQ	(powered parachute)		
77-MS	Air Création Fun GT		
77-MU	Air Création Fun GT BI		
77-MX	Air Création Cosmos		

Regn.	Type	C/n	Prev.Id.
77-NB	Chronos		
77-NS	Cosmos Chronos 16		
77-NX	Adventure 210 paraglider		
77-PJ	Dynali Chickinox (or Barodeur ?)		
77-PK	Dynali Chickinox		
77-RS	Rans S-6 Coyote II		
77-RT	Rans S-6 Coyote II		
77-SK	Rans S-6 Coyote II		
77-SL	Rans S-6ESD Coyote II		
77-ST	Aviasud AE209 Albatros	107	
77-TK	Rans S-7 Courier		
77-TX	Rans S-6ESD Coyote II		
77-TY	Rans S-6ESD Coyote II		
77-UD	Rans S-12 Airaile		
77-US	Cosmos Aeros		
78-CM	Mignet Touraco		
78-DM	Baroudeur		
78-DS	Air's Maestro		
78-FG	Safari		
78-FY	Eipper Quicksilver MXL-II		
78-GK	Aviasud Mistral		
F-78HV	Murphy Renegade Spirit		
78-JE	Icarus Comco Fox-C22		
78-JR	Powerchute		
78-KJ	Weedhopper		
78-KR	Zodiac Ultra Star		
78-MI	Rans S-6 Coyote II		
78-MT	Zenair CH-601		
79-R	Mustang		
79-S	Quartz		
79-X	Trike		
79-AB	Aviasud Mistral		
79-BE	Air Création XS		
79-BF	Air Création XS		
79-BG	Air Création XS		
79-BJ	Air Création Quartz		
79-BM	Air Création Quartz		
79-BN	JC-24 Weedhopper		
79-BS	Air Création XS		
79-CB	Air Création XS		
79-FA	TL-232 Condor		
79-FC	Light Aero Avid Flyer		
79-FE	Air Création Quartz		
80-D	Air Création		
80-AB	Aviasud Mistral		
80-BI	Synairgie		
80-BO	Synairgie		
80-CC	Synairgie Sky Ranger		
80-CE	Synairgie Dauphin		
80-CG	Synairgie/Air Action		
80-CH	Synairgie/Air Action		
80-CK	Synairgie Dauphin		
80-CP	Synairgie Dauphin		
80-CR	Quartz ZSX		
80-CS	Synairgie Sky Ranger		
80-DF	Cyclone AX-3		C3073132
80-DK	Lorafly		
80-DW	Air Création Fun GTE		
80-DX	Synairgie Sky Ranger		
80-EB	Air Création Fun GTE Mild		
80-EH	"Little Mouse" (Homebuilt)		
80-EO	Cyclone AX-3		
80-EQ	Air Création Fun		
80-ES	Air Création Fun GTE Mild		
80-ET	Air Création Fun GTE Mild		
80-EU	Air Création		
80-FO	Air Création		
80-FQ	Air Création Quartz		
80-FS	Sky Ranger		
80-GA	Synairgie Sky Ranger		
80-GB	Cyclone AX-3		C3123184
80-GE	Synairgie Sky Ranger		
81-S	Air Création		
81-U	Air Création		
81-V	Baroudeur		
81-AC	Aviasud Mistral		
81-CT	Chereau J.300 Joker (F-JAUK)		
81-FC	Chereau J.300 Joker (F-JBHY)		
81-QE	Dynamic (F-JIQE)		
81-QF	Rajhamsa X'Air		
81-UC	Air Création		
82-AF	Dynali Chickinox		
82-AG	Weedhopper JC-31D		
W82-BQ	Croses Criquet L		
82-CE	Sky Ranger		
82-DM	Top Concept Hurricane		
82-FO	Sky Ranger		
83-H	Aériane Sirocco		
83-T	Eipper Quicksilver MX		
83-AE	Aériane Sirocco		
83-AK	Aviasud Mistral		
83-AP	Air's Maestro (Two-seat)		
83-BB	Aviasud Mistral		
83-BC	KFM		
83-BE	Nike Aeronautica		
83-BG	Aériane Sirocco		
83-BP	Aviasud Mistral		
83-BQ	Aviasud Mistral		
83-BV	Patrilor		
83-CB	Aviasud Mistral		
83-CC	Air's Maestro		
83-CF	Avcan		
83-CI	Aviasud AE.209 Albatros		
83-CJ	Aviasud Mistral		
83-CK	Air Création		
83-CL	Aviasud Mistral		
83-CP	Aviasud Mistral		
83-CT	Air's Maestro (Seaplane)		
83-DB	ULM Rapid		
83-DG	Weedhopper		
83-DN	Aviasud Mistral		
83-DO	Aviasud Mistral		
83-DP	Mignet HM.1000 Balèrit 3X	45	
83-DV	PGO Cobra		
83-DY	Aviasud Mistral		
83-EG	Denney Kitfox III	993	
83-EP	Paraplume		
83-EU	Aviasud Albatross	95	
83-EV	Aviasud Albatross 62-CV	32	
W83-FI	Croses Airplume		
83-GD	Rans S-6 Coyote II		
83-GJ	Zenair CH-601 Zodiac		
83-GO	Aviasud Albatros		
83-GP	Synairgie Sky Ranger		
83-HF	Air Création		
83-HR	Mignet HM.1100 (F-JDBG)	07	
83-JP	Guepard 912		
83-RM	Synairgie Sky Ranger		
83-SE	III Sky Arrow 500TF	070/98.017	
84-J	Huntair		
84-0	Airplast Prima		
84-Y	Albatross Delta Pilot		
84-AE	Pipistrelle		
84-AJ	Croses Airplume		
84-AL	Aviasud Mistral		
84-AP	Weedhopper Europa II		
84-AS	Eipper Quicksilver MX		
84-AT	Weedhopper JC.31		
84-BA	Moto du Ciel		
84-BB	Croses Airplume		
84-BY	AMF Chevvron Amphibian		
84-CB	Weedhopper AX-3		
84-CC	Weedhopper JC.31		
84-CW	Air Micro		
84-DF	Albatros		
84-DG	Air Création		
84-DI	Rans S-6 Coyote II		
84-DO	Air Création GT BI		
84-EA	Dynali Chickinox		
84-GY	Mignet HM.14		

Regn.	Type	C/n	Prev.Id.
85-A	Allegro		
85-AA	Quartz		
85-AD	Agriplane Condor		
85-AE	Weedhopper		
85-AL	Quartz		
85-AT	Weedhopper Europa II		
85-AX	Allegro		
85-BF	SMAN Pétrel Amphibian (F-JATC)	026	
85-BH	Synairgie Puma		
85-BJ	Synairgie Puma		
85-BK	Weedhopper		
85-BL	Weedhopper		
85-BT	Weedhopper		
85-BX	Weedhopper		
85-BY	Weedhopper		
85-CD	Trike		
85-CL	Air Création		
85-CV	Air Création		
85-CX	Air Création		
85-DC	Air Création Quartz		
85-DD	Weedhopper		
85-DG	Weedhopper		
85-DJ	Moto du Ciel		
85-DS	Hermes		
85-EL	Quicksilver GT-500		
85-EN	Quicksilver MXL-III Sport		
85-EP	Air Création Quartz		
85-ES	Synairgie Puma		
85-EU	AX-3		
85-EX	Synairgie Sky Ranger		
85-FB	Synairgie Trike		
85-FJ	Synairgie Sky Ranger		
85-FN	Kitfox		
85-FT	Technic' ULM		
85-GA	Humbert Tetras (F-JCJS)		
86-AA	Aile Stryker 19		
86-BX	Quasar		
86-CN	Air Création Quartz		
86-DU	Zodiac Twinstar		
86-EC	Dynali Chickinox		
86-EN	X5		
86-GK	Weedhopper		
86-GR	Air Création SX		
86-JJ	Synairgie		
86-..	Aviasud Albatros AE-209	24	
87-M	Eipper Quicksilver		
87-JM	Funk FK.9		
88-I	Humbert 02 Moto du Ciel		
88-AJ	Moto du Ciel	WHB-1	
88-AK	Humbert Moto du Ciel		
88-DD	Weedhopper		
88-DF	Moto du Ciel		
88-DM	Humbert Tetras (F-JBRJ)		
88-EC	Humbert Moto du Ciel		
88-EE	Humbert Tetras		
88-EF	Humbert Moto du Ciel (F-JBZE)		
88-EQ	Humbert Tetras		
88-ES	Gemini		
88-ET	Humbert Tetras (F-JASO)		
88-EX	Weedhopper		
88-FB	Humbert Tetras		
88-GA	Humbert Tetras (F-JCXX)		
88-GB	Humbert Moto du Ciel (F-JBDP)		
89-AA	Etendard		
89-BC	Air Création Quartz		
89-BH	Air Création Quartz		
89-BS	Air Création Quartz		
89-FY	Rans S-6 Coyote II		
89-GK	Buse'Air 150		
89-GO	Cosmos		
89-HM	Zenair CH-601 Zodiac		
89-HN	Zenair CH-601 Zodiac		
89-HR	Buse'Air 150		
90-CC	Humbert Tetras (F-JGCV)		
90-CI	Icarus Eurofox Savane		
90-CK	Cosmos Merlin		
91-M	Ulac Aviation X99	169	
91-N	Landray GL.4 Visa		
91-S	Antar		
91-V	Antar		
91-X	Antar		
91-Y	Antar		
91-AK	Trike		
91-BL	Baroudeur Veliplane		
91-BN	FT-91 Renegade		
91-CB	FT-91 Renegade		
91-CF	Eipper Quicksilver		
91-CV	Mervay		
91-DU	FT-91 Renegade		
91-ED	Quartz 2 XS		
91-FN	Eipper Quicksilver MX		
91-FT	Renegade Spirit 503		
91-GF	Eipper Quicksilver MX		
91-GH	La Mouette		
91-GK	Air Création		
91-GQ	Maestro		
91-HA	Chariot		
91-HY	Allegro 2-seater		
91-IJ	Air Création SX		
91-IO	Cyclone AX-3		
91-JE	Barry Souricette		
91-JM	Sky Ranger		
91-KJ	Aero Kuhlmann SCUB / AK		
91-KP	Sky Ranger		
91-LE	Sky Ranger		
91-LP	Comco Ikarus Fox C-22		
91-NG	Air Domi Trophy TT2000		
91-TB	Landray GL-06 Papillon		
92-AE	Baroudeur Veliplane		
92-AK	Baroudeur Veliplane		
92-AN	Eipper Quicksilver MX		
92-BM	Baroudeur		
92-BS	Baroudeur		
92-BU	Baroudeur		
92-CT	Aviasud Mistral		
92-CU	CFM Shadow Series B	010	G-MNES
92-CX	Air's Maestro		
92-DF	Baroudeur	123	
92-DN	Baroudeur		56-G
92-EB	Air Création		
92-EP	Air Création		
92-EQ	Baroudeur		
92-EV	Baroudeur Veliplane		
92-FF	JC.31 Weedhopper		
92-FG	GT-BI Quartz		
92-FN	Baroudeur		
92-FP	Baroudeur		
92-GD	Air's Maestro		
92-GM	Quartz		
92-GN	Air's Maestro II		
92-GS	Air Création Cosmos 14		
92-GU	Aviasud Mistral		83-DA
92-HD	Weedhopper		
92-HE	Air Création Cosmos		
92-HJ	Solar Wings Pegasus Quantum		
92-HU	Air Création Fun GT		
92-HV	Aviasud Albatros	383	
92-II	Air Création Ghost 12		
92-IR	Rans S-6ESD Coyote II		
92-IY	TEAM Minimax		
92-JA	Air Création Cosmos Chronos		
93-AJ	Mignet HM.293		
93-AK	ULAC X99		
93-BB	Baroudeur ? ('Thompson')		
93-BG	Aériane Sirocco		
03-BY	Air Création		
93-CU	Cosmos Trike		
93-ET	Rans S-6ESD Coyote II		
93-FM	Curtiss Jenny replica		
93-LO	Air Création Quartz		

Regn.	Type	C/n	Prev.Id.
94-AQ	Air Création		
94-BD	Aériane Sirocco		
94-BE	Coutrot Pou du Ciel		
94-CH	Pacific		
94-DT	JCC Aviation J-300 Joker		
94-EC	Quartz X5		
94-EF	Mainair Gemini/Flash IIA		
94-EH	Veliplane		
94-EV	Air Création Cosmos		
94-EX	Weedhopper AX-3		
94-FA	Baroudeur		
94-FB	Air Création Cosmos Fun GT BI		
94-FG	Mignet HM.1000 Balèrit	71	
94-GK	Air Création Fun GTE		
94-IJ	Tecnam P.92 Echo		
95-0	Bee		
95-AM	Air Création		
95-CH	ASEA 3-axis		
95-CY	Aviasud Mistral		
95-DD	Quartz SX		
95-DN	Doutart Chevron Volant		
95-EA	Quartz		
95-EH	Quartz X5		
95-EV	Baroudeur		
95-FM	Aviasud Mistral	121	
95-GJ	Air Création		
95-GS	Cyclone AX-3 / 503		
95-GU	Mignet HM.1000 Balèrit	24	17-CV
95-HA	Air Création Cosmos		
95-HI	Weedhopper Europa II		
95-HN	Air Création Fun GT BI		
95-HP	Air Création Cosmos		
95-HX	Air Création Cosmos		
95-IA	Air Création Clipper		
95-II	Micro Aviation Pulsar 2 (F-JBSN)		
95-IK	Aquilair Swing 14		
95-IN	Air Création Fun GT		
95-IX	Siriu		
95-JF	Rans S-6ESD Coyote II		
95-KV	Buse Air 150		
AD-97-1	Weedhopper Amphibian		
97-BA	Air's Maestro		
971-AL	Buccaneer		
974-D	Mustang		
974-J	Quartz 18		
974-AA	Quartz		
974-DH	Zenair CH-701 STOL		
2A-G	Cosmos		
2A-AU	Synairgie 2-seater		
2B-AA	Hydroplum Amphibian		

Cross-reference for observed F-J . . . tie-ups (see note at start of this section):

F-JAAS	30-CE		F-JABA	03-AQ
F-JAEN	76-CG		F-JAFY	01-DA
F-JAKQ	67-EM		F-JALL	28-GJ
F-JAMJ	17-GF		F-JAMV	55-GF
F-JAOB	66-DB		F-JAOP	02-CO
F-JAPB	55-FO		F-JAPR	54-JE
F-JARN	37-DX		F-JART	18-EO
F-JASO	88-ET		F-JATC	85-BF
F-JATT	37-HL		F-JAUK	81-CT
F-JAVL	38CM and ex 54-PL		F-JAYT	54-DT
F-JAZN	63-FJ		F-JBAL	55-HN
F-JBBZ	47-FN		F-JBCC	32-CV
F-JBCP	65-ED		F-JBDP	88-GB
F-JBDW	66-DK		F-JBEC	73-EF
F-JBGL	51-FY		F-JBGS	28-SK
F-JBGT	67-GZ		F-JBHY	81-FC
F-JBIS	72-FV		F-JBJE	28-LW
F-JBJQ	57-BC		F-JBLU	57-LR
F-JBME	55-FR		F-JBOK	73-ER
F-JBRJ	88-DM		F-JBSA	61-EF
F-JBSN	95-II		F-JBSW	56-DR
F-JBUL	62-FX		F-JBVS	75-MI

Regn.	Type	C/n	Prev.Id.
F-JBWE	71-FC	F-JBXV	20-GS
F-JBZE	88-EF	F-JCAJ	61-FG
F-JCBU	59-TH	F-JCCR	59-TZ
F-JCDE	22-EA	F-JCFN	67-LG
F-JCJS	85-GA	F-JCKL	01-KF
F-JCKM	01-KG	F-JCKO	01-KH
F-JCKR	55-GS	F-JCLG	27-KS
F-JCLU	59-UC	F-JCOO	67-DS
F-JCPP	59-SH	F-JCQA	27-LE
F-JCTJ	04-BP	F-JCTY	26-IL
F-JCUE	07-HM	F-JCUF	37-MX
F-JCUM	01-LB	F-JCXR	66-FU
F-JCXX	88-GA	F-JCYT	39-FO
F-JDAB	68-KR	F-JDBB	59-WI
F-JDBG	83-HR	F-JDCH	59-WF
F-JDEI	59-TM	F-JDFK	25-KB
F-JEIK	01-MR	F-JEIU	01-MC
F-JEJC	10-HN	F-JGCV	90-CC
F-JIQE	81-QE		

Registration/call-sign tie-ups unknown:

F-JBCM	Rans S-6 Coyote II		
F-JBQI	HM.100 Balèrit	117	
F-JCQJ	Rans S-6 Coyote II		

Type unidentified:

F-JAOU / 37-GR		F-JBWK	54-KN

See also end of Belgian ULM section for OQ- call signs used by French aircraft.

Regn.	Type	C/n	Prev.Id.
HA-AAI	Gerle II	F-04	
HA-ABA	Antonov AN-2P	1G234-23	
HA-ABC	Antonov AN-2P	1G235-20	
HA-ABD	Antonov AN-2P	1G235-21	
HA-ABG	Antonov AN-2R	1G151-13	CCCP07438
HA-ABJ	Antonov AN-2	1G201-40	RA-84722
			CCCP84722
HA-ABK	Antonov AN-2	1G235-37	DOSAAF'12'
HA-ABN	Antonov AN-2	1G152-47	RA-07519
			CCCP07519
HA-ABP	Antonov AN-2R	1G185-52	RA-54885
			CCCP54885
HA-ABR	Antonov AN-2	1G174-08	RA-40830
			CCCP40830
HA-ABS	Antonov AN-2T	1G76-15	RA-09681
			CCCP09681
HA-ABT	Antonov AN-2	1G170-42	CCCP07883
HA-ACF	Cessna 421	0048	N4048L
			N209PP
			N4048L
HA-ACG	Cessna 402B	1222	N4421Z
			C-GYJQ
			(N4176G)
HA-ACL	Dornier Do.28D-2 Skyservant	4125	D-IDRC
			58+50
HA-ACM	Dornier Do.28D-2 Skyservant	4134	D-IDRD
			58+59
HA-ACN	Cessna 402B	1037	OO-SVD
			(OO-SVO)
			G-BENE
			N98668
HA-ACT	Beech B60 Duke	P-434	N9046Z
			TG-VBA
HA-ACU	Dornier Do.28D-2 Skyservant (Walter M601 turbo conversion)	4121	D-IDRS 58+46
HA-ANC	Antonov AN-2T	1G27-21	
HA-ANG	Antonov AN-2P	1G132-53	
HA-ANI	Antonov AN-2P	1G132-55	
HA-ANK	Antonov AN-2P	1G174-42	
HA-ANM	Antonov AN-2P	1G187-35	
HA-ANO	Antonov AN-2P (Accident 10.99)	1G188-33	
HA-ANP	Antonov AN-2P	1G224-09	
HA-ANR	Antonov AN-2P	1G224-10	
HA-ANS	Antonov AN-2P	1G230-21	
HA-ANT	Antonov AN-2P	1G230-22	
HA-ANV	Antonov AN-2P	1G231-48	
HA-ANX	Antonov AN-2P	1G232-57	
HA-ANZ	Antonov AN-2P	1G232-56	
HA-APA	Piper PA-28R-200 Cherokee Arrow	28R-7535328	OY-BLM (SE-GLK)
HA-APC	Piper PA-28R-200 Cherokee Arrow	28R-7135009	SE-FPN
HA-APF	Piper PA-28-140 Cherokee	28-23765	SE-FAE
HA-APG	Piper PA-32-300 Cherokee Six	32-40333	C-FYDY
HA-APH	Piper PA-28-180 Cherokee C	28-2381	N5863W
HA-API	Piper PA-32-300 Cherokee Six	32-40220	N4149W
HA-APJ	Piper PA-28-140 Cherokee F	28-7325128	SE-GAS
HA-APK	Piper PA-28-140 Cherokee B	28-26700	D-EEFI N5868U
HA-ARA	Aero Commander 500A	1113-55	SE-GUR N1527T G-ASIO N4441 N6236X
HA-BCA	Mil Mi-2 (Preserved)	516301099	
HA-BCB	Mil Mi-2 (Wrecked)	516302099	
HA-BCE	Mil Mi-2	5111201011	
HA-BCF	Mil Mi-2	5111202011	
HA-BCG	Mil Mi-2	511543080	DOSAAF-42
HA-BCH	Mil Mi-2	543723084	DOSAAF-41
HA-BCI	Mil Mi-2	562247032	D-HVAD 94+81 LSK-377
HA-BCJ	Mil Mi-2	562818043	D-HVAA 94+64 NVA-423
HA-BCL	Mil Mi-2	563820114	D-HVAC 94+53 LSK-306
HA-BCM	Mil Mi-2 (Reservation)	unkn	
HA-BCQ	Mil Mi-2	524707036	UR-20583 CCCP20583
HA-BCR	Mil Mi-2	546743080	DOSAAF-O9
HA-BCS	Mil Mi-2	5210005106	UR-15620 CCCP15620
HA-BCT	Mil Mi-2	547716062	RA-20761 CCCP20761
HA-BDA	Aérospatiale AS.350B2 Ecureuil	2472	F-WYME
HA-BDB	Aérospatiale AS.350B2 Ecureuil	2607	
HA-BDC	Aérospatiale AS.350B Ecureuil	1715	OO-VCZ D-HLOS
HA-BFA	Mil Mi-2	545049017	UR-14351 CCCP14351
HA-BFB	Mil Mi-2	547805082	UR-20768 CCCP20768
HA-BFC	Mil Mi-2	549245065	UR-23337 CCCP23337
HA-BFG	Mil Mi-2	52100033106	UR-15618 CCCP15618
HA-BFK	Mil Mi-2	525916128	UR-23513 CCCP23513
HA-BFM	Mil Mi-2 (Reservation)	unkn	
HA-BFN	Mil Mi-2 (Reservation)	unkn	
HA-BFO	Mil Mi-2 (Reservation)	unkn	
HA-BFP	Mil Mi-2 (Reservation)	unkn	
HA-BFR	Mil Mi-2	528021013	UR-20817 EW-20817 CCCP20817
HA-BFS	Mil Mi-2 (Reservation)	unkn	
HA-BFT	Mil Mi-2	526534020	UR-20657 CCCP20657
HA-BFU	Mil Mi-2	525108017	UR-14360 CCCP14360
HA-BFV	Mil Mi-2 (Wfu)	529812056	UR-20365 CCCP20365
HA-BFY	Mil Mi-2	5411038109	DOSAAF
HA-BFZ	Mil Mi-2	526442010	CCCP20653
HA-BGA	Mil Mi-2	5411039109	DOSAAF
HA-BGC	Mil Mi-2	543722084	Sov.mil:31 red
HA-BGD	Mil Mi-2	548633044	RA-01149 Sov.mil.
HA-BGE	Mil Mi-2	568942124	Slovak:8942 Czech:8942
HA-BGF	Mil Mi-2	518215053	Slovak:8215 Czech:8215
HA-BGH	Mil Mi-2	unkn	
HA-BGI	Mil Mi-2	unkn	SlovakAF
HA-BGJ	Mil Mi-2	5110717098	Czech:0717
HA-BGK	Mil Mi-2	518915104	HAF: 8915
HA-DAC	Antonov AN-2	1G229-02	CCCP33510
HA-DAD	Antonov AN-2R	1G122-14	RA-02603 CCCP02603
HA-DAE	Antonov AN-2R	1G164-06	RA-16053 CCCP16053
HA-DAF	Antonov AN-2R	1G169-26	RA-07811 CCCP07811
HA-ELA	WagAero CUBy II (To HA-Y . . . . ?)	AAH-O10	
HA-FAA	Reims/Cessna FA.337G Super Skymaster	0073/01609	OE-FAH (F-BJDI)
HA-FAB	Fokker F.27 Friendship 500	10370	HB-ISY F-BPUB PH-FMS
HA-FBA	Zlin Z.43	0060	
HA-HUY	Yakovlev YAK-52	unkn	
HA-HUZ	Yakovlev YAK-52	unkn	
HA-JAA	Yakovlev YAK-52	899802	DOSAAF-74
HA-JAB	Yakovlev YAK-18T	22202023842	FLA-02160 CCCP44420

Regn.	Type	C/n	Prev.Id.
HA-JAD	Yakovlev YAK-18T	5200509	FLA-02161
HA-JAE	Yakovlev YAK-52	9011011	DOSAAF-113
HA-JAJ(2)	Cessna 177RG Cardinal RG	1193	C-GLMD
			N52394
HA-JAL	Yakovlev YAK-18T	22202047216	DOSAAF
HA-JDU	Reims/Cessna F.177RG	0063	N43AG
			D-EANY
			N10632
HA-LAD	LET L-410UVP-E8A	902516	
HA-LAE	LET L-410UVP-E8A	902517	
HA-LAF	LET L-410UVP-E8A	902518	
HA-LAG(2)	LET L-410UVP	800425	CCCP67159
HA-LAL	LET L-410UVP	841317	RA-67492
			CCCP67492
HA-LAN	LET L-410UVP	851408	UR-67504
			CCCP67504
HA-LAO	LET L-410UVP-E	902501	RA-67648
			CCCP67648
HA-LAP	LET L-410UVP	unkn	
HA-LAQ	LET L-410UVP-E4	841332	HAF-332
			HA-YFB
HA-LAR	LET L-410UVP-E4	871923	HAF-923
HA-LAS	LET L-410UVP-E4	871924	HAF-924
HA-LAV	LET L-410UVP-E	882215	RA-67604
			CCCP67604
HA-LAY	LET L-410UVP	841326	UR-67100
			CCCP67100
HA-LBN	Tupolev TU-134A-3	12096	HA-YSA
			HA-926
HA-LBO	Tupolev TU-134A-3	17103	HA-YSB
			HA-927
HA-LBR	Tupolev TU-134A-3	63580	
HA-LCM	Tupolev TU-154B-2	325	
HA-LCN	Tupolev TU-154B-2	326	
HA-LCO	Tupolev TU-154B-2	473	
HA-LCP	Tupolev TU-154B-2	474	
HA-LCR	Tupolev TU-154B-2	543	
HA-LCU	Tupolev TU-154B-2	531	CCCP85531
HA-LCV	Tupolev TU-154B-2	544	CCCP85544
HA-LDB	LET L.200D Morava	171127	
HA-LDF	LET L.200D Morava	171408	
HA-LDG	LET L.200D Morava	171411	S5-CAH
			SL-CAH
			YU-BBF
HA-LEB	Boeing 737-2M8	22090	OO-TE0
			TC-AJK
			OO-TE0
			4X-ABM
			OO-TE0
HA-LED	Boeing 737-3Y0	24909	
HA-LEF	Boeing 737-3Y0	24914	
HA-LEG	Boeing 737-3Y0	24916	
HA-LEI	Boeing 737-2T4	22803	B-614L
			B-2502
			N6018N
HA-LEJ	Boeing 737-3Q8	26303	
HA-LEK	Boeing 737-2K9	23404	TC-JUU
			VR-BMX
			TC-JUU
			N700ML
HA-LEM	Boeing 737-2T4	22804	B-615L
			B-2503
			N6038E
HA-LEN	Boeing 737-4Y0	26069	UR-GAA
			N3509J
HA-LEO	Boeing 737-4Y0	26071	UR-GAB
			N35108
HA-LEP	Boeing 737-5K5	24776	D-AHLE
HA-LER	Boeing 737-5K5	24926	D-AHLD
HA-LES	Boeing 737-3Y0	24676	TC-SUN
			(PT-TEO)
HA-LFN	Soko SA.341G Gazelle	045	JRV....
HA-LFO	Soko SA.341G Gazelle	022	JRV....
HA-LFP	Soko SA.341G Gazelle	008	JRV12616
HA-LHA	Boeing 767-27GER	27048	

Regn.	Type	C/n	Prev.Id.
HA-LHB	Boeing 767-27GER	27049	
HA-LJB	Yakovlev YAK-40	9640851	CCCP87214
HA-LJC	Yakovlev YAK-40	9440937	4K-87218
			HA-LJC
			CCCP87218
			OK-EEF
HA-LJF	Yakovlev YAK-40	unkn	
HA-LMA	Fokker F.28-0070	11564	PH-EZR
HA-LMB	Fokker F.28-0070	11565	PH-EZX
HA-LMC	Fokker F.28-0070	11569	PH-EZA
HA-LMD	Fokker F.28-0070	11563	PH-WXD
			I-REJA
			PH-EZT
HA-LME	Fokker F.28-0070	11575	PH-WXB
			I-REJU
			PH-EZB
HA-LRA	Yakovlev YAK-40	9440837	OK-EED
HA-MAB	Antonov AN-2 (Reservation)	unkn	
HA-MAC	Antonov AN-2 (Reservation)	unkn	
HA-MAD	Antonov AN-2 (Reservation)	unkn	
HA-MAE	Antonov AN-2 (Reservation)	unkn	
HA-MAF	Antonov AN-2R	1G190-45	LY-ACN
			CCCP84613
HA-MAG	Antonov AN-2P	1G114-36	RA-35524
			CCCP35524
HA-MAH	Antonov AN-2R	1G178-39	RA-62647
			CCCP62647
HA-MAL	Antonov AN-2R	1G225-15	RA-40498
			CCCP40498
HA-MAM	Antonov AN-2R	1G208-44	CCCP81540
HA-MAR	Antonov AN-2R	1G205-39	RA-17898
			CCCP17898
HA-MAS	Antonov AN-2 (Reservation)	unkn	
HA-MAT	Antonov AN-2 (Reservation)	unkn	
HA-MAV	Antonov AN-2R	1G211-15	RA-43996
			CCCP43996
HA-MAW	Antonov AN-2R	1G166-57	RA-.....
			CCCP.....
HA-MAX	Antonov AN-2R	1G167-59	RA-82845
			CCCP82845
HA-MAY	Antonov AN-2R	1G185-40	CCCP54880
HA-MBA	Antonov AN-2R	1G161-06	
HA-MBB	Antonov AN-2R	1G161-07	
HA-MBC	Antonov AN-2R	1G161-08	
HA-MBD	Antonov AN-2R	1G161-09	
HA-MBE	Antonov AN-2R	1G161-10	
HA-MBF	Antonov AN-2R	1G161-11	
HA-MBG	Antonov AN-2R	1G163-29	
HA-MBJ	Antonov AN-2R	1G166-28	
HA-MBK	Antonov AN-2R	1G166-29	
HA-MBL	Antonov AN-2R	1G166-30	
HA-MBN	Antonov AN-2R (Wfu)	1G166-32	
HA-MBO	Antonov AN-2R	1G166-33	
HA-MBP	Antonov AN-2R	1G167-46	
HA-MBR	Antonov AN-2R (Wfu)	1G168-14	
HA-MBT	Antonov AN-2R	1G172-53	
HA-MBV	Antonov AN-2R	1G172-54	
HA-MBZ	Antonov AN-2R	1G191-14	RA-84636
			CCCP84636
HA-MCB(2)	Kamov Ka.26	7303410	RA-.....
HA-MCD(2)	Kamov Ka.26	7404717	RA-19558
			CCCP19558
HA-MCE(2)	Kamov Ka.26	7605519	RA-.....
HA-MCF(2)	Kamov Ka.26	7505306	RA-.....
HA-MCH	Kamov Ka.26	7404620	CCCP19...
HA-MCI	Kamon Ka.26	7303406	D-HOAV
			DDR-SPV
			DM-SPV
HA-MCJ	Kamov Ka.26	7303502	CCCP19...
HA-MCK	Kamov Ka.26	7404408	CCCP19414
HA-MCL	Kamov Ka.26	7404420	CCCP19...
HA-MCM	Kamov Ka.26	7202904	CCCP19...
HA-MCN	Kamov Ka.26	7102104	CCCP19...
HA-MCO	Kamov Ka.26	7101804	CCCP-19291
HA-MDA	Antonov AN-2R	1G176-23	

Regn.	Type	C/n	Prev.Id.
HA-MDB	Antonov AN-2R	1G176-24	
HA-MDE	Antonov AN-2R	1G177-20	
HA-MDF	Antonov AN-2R	1G181-37	
HA-MDG	Antonov AN-2R	1G181-38	
HA-MDH	Antonov AN-2R	1G181-39	
HA-MDI	Antonov AN-2R	1G181-40	
HA-MDK	Antonov AN-2R *(Wfu)*	1G181-42	
HA-MDM	Antonov AN-2R *(Wfu)*	1G183-20	
HA-MDN	Antonov AN-2R *(Wfu)*	1G183-21	
HA-MDO	Antonov AN-2R	1G185-43	
HA-MDP	Antonov AN-2R *(Wfu)*	1G185-44	
HA-MDQ	Antonov AN-2R *(Wfu)*	1G185-45	
HA-MDR	Antonov AN-2R	1G185-46	
HA-MDS	Antonov AN-2R	1G185-47	
HA-MDT	Antonov AN-2R	1G185-53	
HA-MDU	Antonov AN-2R	1G186-02	
HA-MDX	Antonov AN-2R	1G186-05	
HA-MDY	Antonov AN-2R	1G186-06	
HA-MDZ	Antonov AN-2R	1G186-04	
HA-MEA	Antonov AN-2R	1G186-07	
HA-MEB	Antonov AN-2R	1G186-08	
HA-MEC	Antonov AN-2R	1G187-28	
HA-MED	Antonov AN-2R	1G187-29	
HA-MEF	Antonov AN-2R	1G187-30	
HA-MEG	Antonov AN-2R	1G187-31	
HA-MEI	Antonov AN-2R	1G190-18	
HA-MEJ	Antonov AN-2R	1GI90-19	
HA-MEK	Antonov AN-2R	1G190-20	
HA-MEL	Antonov AN-2R	1G190-21	
HA-MEM	Antonov AN-2R	1G190-22	
HA-MEN	Antonov AN-2R	1G190-23	
HA-MEO	Antonov AN-2R	1G190-24	
HA-MEP	Antonov AN-2R	1G190-25	
HA-MES	Antonov AN-2R	1G194-28	
HA-MEX	Antonov AN-2R	1G217-53	
HA-MEY	Antonov AN-2R	1G217-54	
HA-MEZ	Antonov AN-2R	1G127-27	RA-..... / CCCP..... / OK-UJJ
HA-MFA	Z-137T Agro Turbo	026	OM-UJJ
HA-MFB	LET Z-37AC-2 Cmelák	unkn	
HA-MFC	Z-137T Agro Turbo	030	OM-UJN / OK-UJN
HA-MFD	Z-137T Agro Turbo	034	OM-VIK / OK-VIC
HA-MGA	LET Z-37A Cmelák	10-03	OK-ZJS
HA-MGD(2)	LET Z-37A Cmelák	17-19	OK-DJR
HA-MGE(2)	Z-137T Agro Turbo	045	OK-XJB
HA-MGH(2)	LET Z-37T Agro Turbo	021	OK-SJN
HA-MGJ(2)	Z-137T Agro Turbo	025	OK-UJI
HA-MGN(2)	Z-137T Agro Turbo	035	OK-VID
HA-MGO	LET Z-37AC-2 Cmelák	10-12	OK-ZXW / OK-ZJW
HA-MGP(2)	LET Z-37 Cmelák	09-13	OK-ZJR
HA-MGR	LET Z-37AC-2 Cmelák	16-28	OK-CJJ
HA-MGS(2)	LET Z-37T Agro Turbo	005	OK-PJC
HA-MGV(2)	LET Z-37T Agro Turbo	009	OK-RJC
HA-MGX(2)	Z-137T Agro Turbo	049	OK-YJI
HA-MGY	LET Z-37T Agro Turbo	008	OK-RJB
HA-MGZ	LET Z-37T Agro Turbo	015	OK-RJI
HA-MHN	Antonov AN-2R *(Wfu)*	1G126-02	
HA-MHQ	Antonov AN-2R	1G145-42	
HA-MHS	Antonov AN-2R	1G145-44	
HA-MHT	Antonov AN-2R	1G155-11	
HA-MHU	Antonov AN-2R	1G155-12	
HA-MHV	Antonov AN-2R	1G154-05	
HA-MHW	Antonov AN-2R	1G158-60	
HA-MIA	Hiller UH-12E	1329	N14CU / N13CU / 61-3143
HA-MIB(2)	Rogerson-Hiller UH-12E *(W/o 15.5.93)*	5224	
HA-MIC	Rogerson Hiller UH-12E	5225	
HA-MID	Hiller UH-12E *(Wreck)*	HA3018	G-BLDM / N118HA, / G-BCXK, N118HA
HA-MIF	Robinson R-22 Beta	1872	N700VG / N23159
HA-MIH	Rogerson-Hiller UH-12E	5226	
HA-MIJ	Hiller UH-12E	2262	G-BDOI / XS166
HA-MIK	Enstrom F-28A	124	G-BASB
HA-MIL	Enstrom 280	1021	G-BTLF / N43RG
HA-MIM	Hiller UH-12E4	2315	OH-HKT / G-BPKP / S3-BAS / S2-ABE / AP-ATV
HA-MIO	Robinson R-22 Beta	2256	N2354F
HA-MIT	Enstrom 280C	1138	N51732
HA-MJA	Piper PA-25-235 Pawnee	25-2908	YU-BOK / N7110Z
HA-MJB	Piper PA-25-235 Pawnee	25-2403	YU-BKH / YU-BBA / N6828Z
HA-MJC	Piper PA-25-235 Pawnee	25-3178	YU-BDB / N7272Z
HA-MJE	Cessna A.188B Agtruck	02833T	YU-B.. / N73IEF
HA-MJF	Cessna A.188B Agtruck	02343T	YU-B.. / N4824R
HA-MKA	Antonov AN-2R	1G186-29	OM-JIR / OK-JIR
HA-MKB	Antonov AN-2R	1G190-15	OM-KIU / OK-KIU
HA-MKC	Antonov AN-2R	1G186-30	OM-JIS / OK-JIS
HA-HMD	Antonov AN-2R	1G186-31	OM-JIT / OK-JIT
HA-MKE	Antonov AN-2R	1G158-34	UR-07714 / CCCP07714
HA-MKF	Antonov AN-2	1G233-43	OM-248 / OM-UIN / OK-UIN
HA-MKG	Antonov AN-2	1G158-16	(HA-DAG) ? / CCCP07696
HA-MKI	Antonov AN-2R	1G153-36	LY-ANV / CCCP05723
HA-MMC	Kamov Ka.26 *(Wfu)*	7001002	
HA-MMD	Kamov Ka.26 *(Wfu)*	7001003	
HA-MME	Kamov Ka.26	7001102	
HA-MMF	Kamov Ka.26	7001103	
HA-MMG	Kamov Ka.26	7001105	
HA-MMK	Kamov Ka.26	7303301	
HA-MMO	Kamov Ka.26	7303304	
HA-MMQ	Kamov Ka.26	7404305	
HA-MMS	Kamov Ka.26	7303307	
HA-MMT	Kamov Ka.26 *(Wfu)*	7303906	
HA-MMW	Kamov Ka.26 *(Wfu)*	7303909	
HA-MMX	Kamov Ka.26	7404302	
HA-MMY	Kamov Ka.26	7404303	
HA-MMZ	Kamov Ka.26 *(Wfu)*	7404304	
HA-MNA	Kamov Ka.26 *(Wfu)*	7404306	
HA-MNB	Kamov Ka.26	7404307	
HA-MNE	Kamov Ka.26 *(Wfu)*	7404418	
HA-MNF	Kamov Ka.26 *(Wfu)*	7505001	
HA-MNH	Kamov Ka.26 *(Wfu)*	7505010	
HA-MNI	Kamov Ka.26 *(Wfu)*	7505011	
HA-MNL	Kamov Ka.26	7505203	
HA-MNM	Kamov Ka.26	7505204	
HA-MNO	Kamov Ka.26	7505205	
HA-MNQ	Kamov Ka.26 *(Wfu)*	7605402	
HA-MNT	Kamov Ka.26	7605603	
HA-MNU	Kamov Ka.26	7605607	
HA-MNV	Kamov Ka.26	7605608	
HA-MNW	Kamov Ka.26	7605609	
HA-MNX	Kamov Ka.26 *(Wfu)*	7605610	
HA-MNY	Kamov Ka.26	7605611	
HA-MPA	Kamov Ka.26 *(Wfu)*	7706108	
HA-MPB	Kamov Ka.26	7706109	

Regn.	Type	C/n	Prev.Id.
HA-MPC	Kamov Ka.26 (Wfu)	7706110	
HA-MPD	Kamov Ka.26	7706111	
HA-MPE	Kamov Ka.26 (Wfu)	7706112	
HA-MPI	Kamov Ka.26 (Wfu)	7706307	
HA-MPJ	Kamov Ka.26 (Wfu)	7806308	
HA-MPL	Kamov Ka.26	7806310	
HA-MPM	Kamov Ka.26 (Wfu)	7806311	
HA-MPN	Kamov Ka.26	7806312	
HA-MPO	Kamov Ka.26 (Wfu)	7806314	
HA-MPR	Kamov Ka.26	7806315	
HA-MPS	Kamov Ka.26	7806316	
HA-MPT	Kamov Ka.26	7806317	
HA-MPU	Kamov Ka.26	7806318	
HA-MPV	Kamov Ka.26	7806319	
HA-MPW	Kamov Ka.26 (Wfu)	7806320	
HA-MPY	Kamov Ka.26 (Wfu)	7806402	
HA-MPZ	Kamov Ka.26	7806403	
HA-MRA	Kamov Ka.26	7806404	
HA-MRB	Kamov Ka.26	7806408	
HA-MRC	Kamov Ka.26	7806409	
HA-MRD	Kamov Ka.26 (Wfu)	7806410	
HA-MRE	Kamov Ka.26	7806502	
HA-MRF	Kamov Ka.26	7806503	
HA-MRG	Kamov Ka.26 (Wfu)	7806506	
HA-MRH	Kamov Ka.26	7806507	
HA-MRI	Kamov Ka.26	7806508	
HA-MRJ	Kamov Ka.26 (Wfu)	7001401	HAF-401
HA-MRK	Kamov Ka.26	7001402	HAF-402
HA-MRL	Kamov Ka.26 (Wfu)	7001405	HAF-405
HA-MRM	Kamov Ka.26 (Wfu)	7001406	HAF-406
HA-MRN	Kamov Ka.26	7001506	HAF-506
HA-MRO	Kamov Ka.26 (Wfu)	7001604	HAF-604
HA-MRP	Kamov Ka.26	7101701	HAF-701
HA-MRQ	Kamov Ka.26	7001510	HAF-510
HA-MRS	Kamov Ka.26	7001501	HAF-501
HA-MRT	Kamov Ka.26	7101702	HAF-702
HA-MRV	Kamov Ka.26	7001601	HAF-601
HA-MRW	Kamov Ka.26	7001509	HAF-509
HA-MRX	Kamov Ka.26 (Wfu)	7001602	HAF-602
HA-MRY	Kamov Ka.26	7001403	HAF-403
HA-MRZ	Kamov Ka.26	7001508	HAF-508
HA-MSA	Hughes 369E	0015E	SE-HNA
HA-MSH	Hughes 369E	0309E	
HA-MSI	Hughes 369E	0310E	
HA-MSL	Hughes 269C	30-0890	D-HRIO
			D-HMAX
			PH-HCH
			TF-ATH
HA-MSR	Hughes 269C	117-0650	SE-HNH
			OY-HSG
			SE-HNH
			OY-HCG
			HB-XHF
HA-MST	Hughes 269C	110-0067	PH-HIH
			(PH-HHH)
			N9640F
			C-....
			N9640F
HA-MSU	Hughes 269B	116-0277	SE-HCU
HA-MTG	PZL M-18 Dromader	1Z006-01	
HA-MTK	PZL M-18 Dromader	1Z006-05	
HA-MTP	PZL M-18 Dromader	1Z007-20	
HA-MTY(2)	PZL M-18A Dromader	1Z017-21	OM-SGC
			OK-SGC
HA-MUI	PZL M-18 Dromader	1Z009-10	
HA-MUR	PZL M-18 Dromader	1Z011-10	
HA-MVA	PZL M-18 Dromader	1Z007-06	SP-FCE
			SP-DBY
			SP-PBC
			OK-LZP
HA-MVB	PZL M-18A Dromader	1Z017-15	OM-SGN
			OK-SGN
HA-MVC	PZL M-18A Dromader	1Z018-17	OM-TGH
			OK-TGH
HA-MVD	PZL M-18A Dromader	1Z018-30	OM-TGP
			OK-TGP
HA-MZB	Kamov Ka.26	7404710	LY-HAC
			CCCP19551
HA-MZC	Kamov Ka.26	7605514	LY-HAF
			CCCP24336
HA-MZD	Kamov Ka.26	7303501	LY-HAA
			CCCP19335
HA-MZE	Kamov Ka.26	7304004	LY-HAB
			CCCP19481
HA-MZF	Kamov Ka.26	7504904	LY-HAE
			CCCP19577
HA-MZG	Kamov Ka.26	7101705	HAF-705
HA-MZH	Kamov Ka.26	7202510	LY-HAL
			CCCP19371
HA-MZI	Kamov Ka.26	7303408	
HA-MZJ	Kamov Ka.26	7404716	RA-19557
			CCCP19557
HA-MZK	Kamov Ka.26	7404010	
HA-MZL	Kamov Ka.26	7202805	
HA-MZN	Kamov Ka.26	7404712	LY-HAD
			CCCP19553
HA-MZO	Kamov Ka.26	7505111	
HA-MZP	Kamov Ka.26	7605416	
HA-MZR	Kamov Ka.26	7505114	
HA-MZS	Kamov Ka.26	7505105	
HA-MZT	Kamov Ka.26	7605420	
HA-MZU	Kamov Ka.26	7705911	
HA-MZV	Kamov Ka.26	7404516	
HA-MZW	Kamov Ka.26	7304006	
HA-OME	Super Aero 045	unkn	
HA-PAO	CSS-13 (Polikarpov Po-2)	0448	HAF-'48'
HA-PPY	Soko 341G Gazelle	021	HA-LFR
	(Also has Aérospatiale c/n 1118)		HA-VLA
			YU-HDN
			JRV
HA-PYC	PZL-101 Gawron	119292	
HA-PZK	PZL-101 Gawron (Derelict 6.97)	21012	
HA-SABA	Neico Lancair IV	HSH-LIV-0001	
HA-SABC	Van's RV-4	779	N13HW
HA-SAC	Zlin Z.526A Akrobat	1019	
HA-SAF	Zlin Z.526A Akrobat	1055	N1189X
			HA-SAF
HA-SAU	Zlin Z.526F Trenér Master	1292	
HA-SAV	Zlin Z.526F Trenér Master	1293	
HA-SBA	PZL-101A Gawron	107199	
HA-SBB	PZL-101A Gawron	107200	
HA-SBC	PZL-101A Gawron	107201	
HA-SBD	PZL-101A Gawron	107230	
HA-SBE	PZL-101A Gawron	107231	
HA-SBF	PZL-101A Gawron	107232	
HA-SBG	PZL-101A Gawron	107233	
HA-SBH	PZL-101A Gawron	107234	
HA-SBI	PZL-101A Gawron	107235	
HA-SBK	PZL-101A Gawron	107237	
HA-SBL	PZL-101A Gawron	119294	
HA-SBM	PZL-101A Gawron	119295	
HA-SBN	PZL-101A Gawron	119296	
HA-SBP	PZL-101A Gawron	107236	HA-YGA
HA-SDA	Zlin Z.726 Universal	1333	
HA-SDE	Zlin Z.726 Universal	1357	
HA-SDF	Zlin Z.726 Universal	1358	
HA-SDG	Zlin Z.726 Universal	1359	
HA-SEA	PZL-104 Wilga 35A	96315	
HA-SEB	PZL-104 Wilga 35A	118374	
HA-SEC	PZL-104 Wilga 35A	129451	
HA-SED	PZL-104 Wilga 35A	149544	
HA-SEF	PZL-104 Wilga 35	59064	Police R-07
HA-SEH	PZL-104 Wilga 35A	17820684	
HA-SEJ	PZL-104 Wilga 35A	18840772	
HA-SEK	PZL-104 Wilga 35A (Accident 7.99)	19870852	
HA-SEL	PZL-104 Wilga 35A	19880864	
HA-SEM	PZL-104 Wilga 35A	19880865	
HA-SEN	PZL-104 Wilga 35A	19880866	
HA-SEO	PZL-104 Wilga 35A (W/o 15.7.96)	19880867	

Regn.	Type	C/n	Prev.Id.
HA-SEP	PZL-104 Wilga 35A	19880868	
HA-SER	PZL-104 Wilga 35A	20890876	
HA-SES	PZL-104 Wilga 35A	20890875	
HA-SET	PZL-104 Wilga 35A	20900899	
HA-SEU	PZL-104 Wilga 35A	CF15810606	YU-DHU
HA-SEW	PZL-104 Wilga 35A	15800576	DOSAAF'45'
HA-SFA	Zlin Z.42M	0175	
HA-SFB	Zlin Z.42M	0176	
HA-SFE	Zlin Z.42M	0179	
HA-SFG	Zlin Z.42M	0180	
HA-SFH	Zlin Z.142	0217	
HA-SFJ	Zlin Z.142	0219	
HA-SFK	Zlin Z.142	0220	
HA-SFL	Zlin Z.142	0223	
HA-SFM	Zlin Z.142	0224	
HA-SFN	Zlin Z.142	0225	
HA-SFO	Zlin Z.142	0226	
HA-SFR	Zlin Z.142	0236	
HA-SFS	Zlin Z.142	0237	
HA-SFU	Zlin Z.142	0239	
HA-SFV	Zlin Z.142	0240	
HA-SFX	Zlin Z.142	0243	
HA-SFY	Zlin Z.142	0255	
HA-SFZ	Zlin Z.142	0241	
HA-SGA	Zlin Z.142	0256	
HA-SGC	Zlin Z.142	0273	
HA-SGD	Zlin Z.142	0274	
HA-SGE	Zlin Z.142	0275	
HA-SGF	Zlin Z.142	0282	
HA-SGH	Zlin Z.142	0313	
HA-SGI	Zlin Z.142	0314	
HA-SGJ	Zlin Z.142	0315	
HA-SGK	Zlin Z.142	0346	
HA-SGL	Zlin Z.142	0374	
HA-SGM	Zlin Z.142	0419	
HA-SGN	Zlin Z.142	0420	
HA-SGP	Zlin Z.142	0441	
HA-SGR	Zlin Z.142	0459	
HA-SGU	Zlin Z.142	0483	
HA-SGV	Zlin Z.142	0484	
HA-SGX	Zlin Z.142	0486	
HA-SGY	Zlin Z.142	0487	
HA-SGZ	Zlin Z.142	0516	
HA-SIF	Zlin Z.50LS	0033	
HA-SIH	Zlin Z.50LS	0050	
HA-SIJ	Zlin Z.50LS	0056	
HA-SJA	Reims/Cessna FR.172J Rocket	0412	D-ECXQ
HA-SJB	Cessna 150D	60596	OE-AYN
			N4596U
HA-SJC	Cessna 172N	69115	N734UB
HA-SJD	Cessna 172N	69825	N738AM
HA-SJE	Cessna 172N	68295	N733GY
HA-SJF	Cessna 172N	73311	N4685G
HA-SJG	Cessna 152	84015	N4909H
HA-SJH	Cessna 152	85024	N6477P
HA-SJI	Cessna 152	84544	N5338M
HA-SJK	Cessna 152	84860	N4960P
HA-SJL	Cessna 172M	65068	N64179
HA-SJM	Cessna 172M	61908	N12251
HA-SJN	Cessna R.172K Hawk XP	2349	N9729V
HA-SJO	Cessna 172N	71843	N5398E
			(N944SA)
			N5398E
HA-SJP	Cessna 177RG Cardinal RG	1226	N52644
HA-SJQ	SOCATA MS.883 Rallye 115	1531	SE-KNN
			OY-DJO
HA-SJR	SOCATA MS.893E Rallye 180GT Gaillard	12531	F-BVZK
HA-SJS	Cessna 150	17389	N5889E
HA-SJT	Cessna 150G	66914	N3014S
HA-SJU	Cessna 150M	76687	N4056V
HA-SJV	Cessna 150M	76400	N3142V
HA-SJW	Cessna 150H	68122	N22184
HA-SJX	Cessna 172N	70653	N31EF
			N739MQ
HA-SJY	Cessna 172N	68609	N733WP

Regn.	Type	C/n	Prev.Id.
HA-SJZ	Reims/Cessna F.150K	0486	F-BRBJ
HA-SKA	Cessna 210H Centurion	59024	C-GKPG
			N6124F
HA-SKC	Cessna P.206E	0618	N5718J
HA-SKD	Cessna 172N	69712	N737VQ
HA-SKE	Cessna 150G	66532	N8632J
HA-SKF	Cessna 150M	77223	N63275
HA-SKG	Cessna 182A Skylane	34371	N72DC
			N9971B
HA-SKI	Cessna 150G	65401	N2201J
HA-SKJ	Cessna 185C Skywagon	0712	F-BMCV
			N5812T
HA-SKL	Cessna 172M	64904	N61944
HA-SKM	Cessna 172K	58947	N800TS
			(N7247G)
HA-SKN	Cessna R.172K Hawk XP	2402	SE-IYV
			N736BS
HA-SKO	Cessna 172N	69692	SE-KLM
			N737UU
HA-SKP	Reims/Cessna F.172H	0739	OO-NZV
HA-SKR	Cessna 175C Skylark	57110	N8510X
HA-SKS	Cessna 152	85904	N95491
HA-SKT	Cessna 182Q Skylane	66280	N759UX
HA-SKU	Piper PA-28-140 Cherokee E	28-7225304	C-FTVX
			CF-TVX
HA-SKV	Cessna 152	85545	C-FAFS
			N93742
HA-SKW	Cessna 210	57526	F-BFRQ(2)
			F-OBRQ
			N6526X
HA-SKX	Cessna U.206 Skywagon	0433	OO-SPR
			LN-HHL
			N8033Z
HA-SKY	Cessna T.210K Turbo Centurion	59306	LN-RTG
			SE-FTC
			G-AYCL
			(N9406M)
HA-SKZ	Cessna (Model unknown)	unkn	
HA-SLA	Reims/Cessna F.150L	0788	OO-CLO
			F-BTFF
HA-SLC	Morane-Saulnier MS.885 Super Rallye	142	D-EJPW
			HB-EDM
HA-SLD	Cessna 150M	77875	N7986U
HA-SLE	Cessna 172L	59309	N1201H
			CF-AZC
			(N7609G)
HA-SLF	Reims/Cessna F.172F	0140	OO-CMT
			(HB-CMT)
HA-SLG	Cessna 172C	48772	N8272X
HA-SLH	Cessna 182P Skylane	63126	SE-GGE
			(N7342N)
HA-SLJ	Cessna 150F	62039	OO-SPC
			PH-ICA
			N8739S
HA-SLK	Reims/Cessna FR.172K Hawk XP	0643	D-EIYP
HA-SLM	Cessna 182P	62838	D-ELOM(3)
			N52778
HA-SLN	Cessna 150	unkn	
HA-SLP	Cessna 150	unkn	
HA-SLU	Cessna 150	unkn	
HA-SLZ	Reims/Cessna F.172G	0262	N600MK
			OO-VEV
			F-BNLB
HA-TCB	Ilyushin IL-76TD	1013408257	UR-78736
			CCCP78736(2)
HA-TCG	Ilyushin IL-76TD	23436048	RA-76382
HA-TCI	Ilyushin IL-76	unkn	
HA-TRA	Zlin Z.226MS Trenér	322	
HA-TRD	Zlin Z.226T Trenér 6	350	
HA-TRL	Zlin Z.226T Trenér 6	370	G-BEZA
			D-EMUD
			OK-MUA
HA-TRM	Zlin Z.226MS Trenér	369	
HA-TRT	Zlin Z.326 Trenér Master	833	

Regn.	Type	C/n	Prev.Id.
HA-VEI	Fuji FA.200-160 Aero Subaru	150	OO-YAP
			N19AP
			OO-YAP
HA-XAD	A-01 Farnadár	01/1986	
HA-XAE	Vector 610	1394	
HA-XAJ	Rubik R-32	01	
HA-XAK	Light Aero Avid Flyer	unkn	
HA-XAU	Rotorway Executive 90	5085	
HA-XAV	Taylorcraft LM-2X-2P	AR 92/2	
HA-XAW	Taylorcraft LM-2X-2P	AR 92/1	
HA-XAX	Rotorway Executive 90	unkn	
HA-XBC	RAF-2000GTX	H2-94-5-113	
HA-XBE	RAF-2000GTX	H2-92-3-56	
HA-XBF	RAF-2000GTX	H2-92-3-57	
HA-XBG	Rotorway Executive 90	5130	
HA-XBM	V-001 Vereb	001	
HA-YAK	Yakovlev YAK-18T	unkn	
HA-YBA	Piper PA-60 Aerostar 601P	61P-0780-8063393	N3831Y
			D-IFWF
			N3636D
HA-YCD	Piper PA-23-250 Aztec E	27-4700	OH-PKS
			SE-FYI
HA-YCE	Piper PA-23-250 Aztec E	27-7405341	N5132G
			C-GRFF
			N40594
HA-YCF	Piper PA-23-250 Aztec E	27-4684	D-IDMV
			N14081
HA-YDE	Pilatus PC-6/B2-H2 Turbo-Porter	814	
HA-YFC	LET L-410-FG	851528	
HA-YFD	LET L-410UVP-E17	892324	
HA-YHA	Antonoc AN-2R	1G151-53	
HA-YHB	Antonov AN-2PF	1G181-44	
HA-YHC	Antonov AN-2PF	1G181-45	
HA-YHD	Antonov AN-2PF	1G187-36	
HA-YHE	Antonov AN-2PF	1G187-37	
HA-YHF	Antonov AN-2PF	1G224-13	
HA-YHG	Antonov AN-2PF	1G234-08	
HA-YLR	Yakovlev YAK-40	9541044	
HA-YMA	Maule M-7-235C Super Rocket	4079C	
HA-YMB	Maule M-7-235C Super Rocket	4081C	
HA-YMC	Maule M-5-235C Lunar Rocket	7336C	SE-IGD
HA-YTV	Kamov Ka.26	7001504	HAF-504
HA-...	Agusta-Bell 206A Jet Ranger II	8108	PH-HHG
			OH-HRJ
			HB-1
HA-...	Beech 200 Super King Air	BB-306	N500HY
			N274K
HA-...	Cessna 150F	64094	OO-VLA
			N7994F
HA-...	Reims/Cessna F.150L	0922	OO-KAI
			PH-KAG
			OO-WIJ
HA-...	Reims/Cessna FRA.150L Aerobat	0186	SE-FZF
HA-...	Cessna 172	28311	N5711A
HA-...	Reims/Cessna F.172H	0353	OO-LKC
			F-BOQE
HA-...	Cessna 172M	64977	C-GKHH
			N64032
HA-...	Cessna 172N	69338	OY-JRA
			N737DM
HA-...	Cessna 172N	72218	OO-GAL
			N9306E
HA-...	Cessna 172P	75867	N65763
HA-...	Reims/Cessna F.177RG	0063	N43AG
			D-EANY
			N10632
HA-...	Dornier Do.28D-2 Skyservant	4335	G-BWCN
			5N-AYE
			D-ILID
			9V-BKL
			D-ILID
HA-...	Enstrom F-28C	138	G-OSWA
			G-BZZZ
			G-BBBZ

Regn.	Type	C/n	Prev.Id.
HA-...	Hughes 269C	61-1055	PH-HHD
			OY-HSF
			D-HDEA
			N5017V
HA-...	Luscombe 8A Silvaire	2891	N71464
			NC71464
HA-...	Mitsubishi MU-2B-20	191	SE-GHG
			N99EE
			N112MA
HA-...	Piper PA-28-140 Cherokee B	28-25362	D-EBTB
			N8166N
HA-...	Piper PA-28-181 Archer II	28-8090277	D-EAHP(2)
			N8179X
HA-...	Robinson R-44 Astro	0666	D-HKAA(2)
HA-...	Schempp-Hirth Nimbus 4T	1/1	D-KBXX
HA-...	SOCATA MS.893A Rallye Commodore 180	10650	OO-RED
HA-...	SOCATA MS.893E Rallye 180GT Gaillard	12865	OO-LVG
			F-GAKJ

BALLOONS AND AIRSHIPS

Regn.	Type	C/n	Prev.Id.
HA-X01	SCB AX-6 Bottle SS Balloon	SCBO90/1991	
HA-002	Tomi AX-10 HAFB	BAV064/1989	
HA-003	Sup-Air E-AX-10 HAFB	1994/SA2	
HA-301	SCB AX-3 Sky Walker Balloon	SCBO96/1991	
HA-401	SCB SX-4 Sky Rider Balloon	SCBO91/1991	
HA-501	Mecsek AX-5 HAFB	BAV006/1984	
HA-502	Supa Air D (AX-5) Balloon	005/1991	
HA-602	MHSZ AX-6 HAFB	8/1981	
HA-603	SCB AX-6 HAFB	SCB093/1991	
HA-604	SCB AX-6 HAFB	SCB106/1993	
HA-605	Tomi AX-6 HAFB	unkn	
HA-701	AX-7 HAFB	4/1981	
HA-702	RSZ-05 HAFB	9/1982	
HA-703	MHSZ AX-7 HAFB	10/1982	
HA-704	Colt 77A HAFB	759	
HA-705	RSZ-05 HAFB	BAV021/1986	
HA-707	Tomi AX-7 HAFB	BAV023/1986	
HA-708	Tomi AX-7 HAFB	BAV024/1986	
HA-710	Tomi AX-7 HAFB	BAV031/1987	
HA-711	Tomi AX-7 HAFB	BAV032/1987	
HA-712	Tomi AX-7 HAFB	BAV052/1988	
HA-713	Mecsek AX-7 HAFB	BAV056/1988	
HA-715	Tomi AX-7 HAFB	BAV062/1989	
HA-716	RSZ-05/1 HAFB	1989/001	(G-BRSZ)
			HA-716
HA-717	Tomi AX-7 HAFB	BAV073/1989	
HA-718	Tomi AX-7 HAFB	BAV077/1989	
HA-719	Tomi AX-7 HAFB	SCB086/1990	
HA-720	Tomi AX-7 HAFB	SCB087/1990	
HA-721	SCB AX-7 HAFB	SCB094/1991	
HA-722	SCB AX-7 HAFB	SCB092/1991	
HA-723	Tomi AX-7 HAFB	unkn	
HA-724	SCB AX-7 HAFB	SCB098/1991	
HA-725	Tomi AX-7 HAFB	004/92	
HA-726	Tomi AX-7 HAFB	005/92	
HA-727	Tomi AX-7 HAFB	006/92	
HA-728	SCB AX-7 HAFB	SCB100/1992	
HA-729	SCB AX-7 HAFB	SCB104/1993	
HA-731	Tomi AX-7 HAFB	8/1993	
HA-732	Tomi AX-7 HAFB	9/1993	
HA-733	Tomi AX-7 HAFB	11/1993	
HA-735	SCB AX-7 HAFB	SCB107/1994	
HA-736	Tomi AX-7 HAFB	17/1994	
HA-737	Tomi AX-7 HAFB	15/1994	
HA-738	Tomi AX-7 HAFB	16/1994	
HA-739	Cameron C-60 HAFB	3342	
HA-740	Tomi AX-7 HAFB	20/1995	
HA-741	Kubicek BB-22 HAFB	40	

Regn.	Type	C/n	Prev.Id.
HA-742	Tomi AX-7 HAFB	002/95	
HA-743	Tomi AX-7 HAFB	22/1995	
HA-746	SCB AX-7 HAFB	SCB111/1995	
HA-747	Tomi AX-7 HAFB	unkn	
HA-749	HAFB, type unknown	unkn	
HA-807	Tomi AX-8 HAFB	3/1981	
HA-808	Tomi AX-8 HAFB	4/1980	
HA-813	Tomi AX-8 HAFB	3/1982	
HA-815	Tomi AX-8 HAFB	5/1982	
HA-819	Tomi AX-8 HAFB	1/1983	
HA-820	Tomi AX-8 HAFB	1/1984	
HA-821	RSZ-03/1 HAFB	KÖ ÉV 1/1986	
HA-822	Tomi AX-8 HAFB	BAV004/1983	
HA-823	Tomi AX-8 HAFB	BAV008/1984	
HA-824	Tomi AX-8 HAFB	BAV010/1985	
HA-825	RSZ-03/1 HAFB	1985/MMRK/01	
HA-826	Tomi AX-8 HAFB	BAV012/1985	
HA-827	Tomi AX-8 HAFB	BAV019/1986	
HA-828	Tomi AX-8 HAFB	BAV020/1986	
HA-829	RSZ-03/1 HAFB	1986/001	
HA-830	RSZ-03/1 HAFB	1988/001	
HA-831	RSZ-03/1 HAFB	1990/001	
HA-832	Tomi AX-8 HAFB	BAV030/1986	
HA-833	Tomi AX-8 HAFB	BAV022/1986	
HA-834	Tomi AX-8 HAFB	BAV039/1987	
HA-835	Tomi AX-8 HAFB	BAV049/1988	
HA-836	Tomi AX-8 HAFB	BAV050/1988	
HA-837	Tomi AX-8 HAFB	BAV051/1988	
HA-838	Tomi AX-8 HAFB	BAV058/1988	
HA-839	Tomi AX-8 HAFB	BAV083/1990	
HA-840	Tomi AX-8 HAFB	BAV071/1989	
HA-841	Tomi AX-8 HAFB	BAV072/1989	
HA-842	RSZ-03/1 HAFB	1990/003	
HA-843	RSZ-03/1 HAFB	1990/002	
HA-844	Tomi AX-8 HAFB	BAV085/1990	
HA-845	RSZ-03/1 HAFB	1991/001	
HA-846	RSZ-03/1 HAFB	1990/004	
HA-847	RSZ-03/1 HAFB	1991/002	
HA-848	RSZ-03/1 HAFB	1991/004	
HA-849	SCB AX-8 HAFB	SCB095/1991	
HA-850	SCB AX-8 HAFB	SCB097/1991	
HA-851	Tomi AX-8 HAFB	003/1991	
HA-852	SCB AX-8 HAFB	SCBO99/1992	
HA-853	SCB AX-8 HAFB	SCB101/1992	
HA-854	SCB AX-8 HAFB	SCB102/1993	
HA-855	Tomi AX-8 HAFB	007/1993	
HA-856	SCB AX-8 HAFB	SCB103/1993	
HA-857	Tomi AX-8 HAFB	10/1993	
HA-858	Tomi AX-8 HAFB	13/1994	
HA-859	HAFB, type unknown	unkn	
HA-860	SCB AX-8 HAFB	SCB109/1995	
HA-861	SCB AX-8 HAFB	SCB110/1995	
HA-903	RSZ-04/1 HAFB	BAV011/1985	
HA-904	Tomi AX-9 HAFB	BAV063/1989	
HA-905	Tomi AX-9 HAFB	BAV070/1989	
HA-906	Tomi AX-9 HAFB	SCB089/1990	
HA-907	SCB AX-9 HAFB	SCB088/1991	
HA-908	SCB AX-9 HAFB	SCB089/1991	
HA-909	RSZ 04/1 HAFB	1991/01	
HA-910	Sup-Air C HAFB	1994/SA1	
HA-911	Kubicek BB-37 HAFB	41	
HA-912	HAFB, type unknown	unkn	
HA-913	Nothiesz AX-8 HAFB	unkn	
HA-B-401	Cameron DP-90 Hot Air Airship	3233	
HA-B-501	MEM RSZ BX-5 Hot Air Airship	2/1981	
HA-B-601	Jakab Airship	L01/95	

GLIDERS

Regn.	Type	C/n	Prev.Id.
HA-X001	KM400	unkn	
HA-1039	R-16 Lepke	E-1000	
HA-2336	R-07 Vocsok 81	F-01	
HA-3175	Schempp-Hirth Nimbus 3/24.5	36	D-3175
HA-3176	Schempp-Hirth Nimbus 4T	1	D-KBXX
HA-3409	E-31 Esztergom	E-1289	
HA-3426	E-31 Esztergom	E-1306	
HA-3429	E-31 Esztergom	E-1309	
HA-3430	E-31 Esztergom	E-1310	
HA-3500	LET L-33 Solo	960404	
HA-3600	PZL PW-5 Smyk	17.08.018	
HA-4059	R-22 Futár	E-741	
HA-4133	R-22g Junius 18	E-1026	
HA-4155	Cinke *(Wfu)*	E-1088	
HA-4211	R-22SV Super Futár	E-1152	HB-670
			OE-0404
HA-4235	SZD-22C Mucha Standard	787	
HA-4239	SZD-24-4C Foka	W-201	
HA-4244	SZD-24-4A Foka 4	W-231	
HA-4247	SZD-24-4A Foka 4	W-330	
HA-4248	SZD-24-4A Foka 4	W-371	
HA-4249	SZD-24-4A Foka 4	W-372	
HA-4250	SZD-32A Foka 5	W-419	
HA-4251	SZD-32A Foka 5	W-473	
HA-4252	SZD-32A Foka 5	W-516	
HA-4253	SZD-32A Foka 5	W-512	
HA-4254	SZD-32A Foka 5	W-517	
HA-4255	SZD-32A Foka 5 *(Wfu)*	W-528	
HA-4256	SZD-36A Foka 5	W-548	
HA-4257	SZD-32A Foka 5	W-549	
HA-4258	SZD-32A Foka 5	W-550	
HA-4260	SZD-32A Foka 5	W-552	
HA-4261	SZD-32A Foka 5	W-553	
HA-4262	SZD-32A Foka 5	W-465	YR-183
HA-4263	SZD-32A Foka 5	W-464	YR-182
HA-4264	Schleicher K.8B	814	HB-673
HA-4265	Schleicher K.8B	8787	D-0264
HA-4268	Schleicher K.8B	8027	D-4002
HA-4276	VTC-75 Standard Cirrus	246	
HA-4277	VTC-75 Standard Cirrus	247	
HA-4279	VTC-75 Standard Cirrus	249	
HA-4280	VTC-75 Standard Cirrus	250	
HA-4281	VTC-75 Standard Cirrus	282	
HA-4282	VTC-75 Standard Cirrus	283	
HA-4283	VTC-75 Standard Cirrus	294	
HA-4284	VTC-75 Standard Cirrus	295	
HA-4285	VTC-75 Standard Cirrus	362	
HA-4287	VTC-75 Standard Cirrus	364	
HA-4288	VTC-75 Standard Cirrus	365	
HA-4289	VTC-75 Standard Cirrus	366	
HA-4290	VTC-75 Standard Cirrus	367	
HA-4291	VTC-75 Standard Cirrus	368	
HA-4292	VTC-75 Standard Cirrus	369	
HA-4293	VTC-75 Standard Cirrus	370	
HA-4294	VTC-75 Standard Cirrus	371	
HA-4295	VTC-75 Standard Cirrus	248	HA-4278
HA-4307	SZD-36 Cobra 15	W-771	
HA-4308	SZD-36 Cobra 15	W-768	
HA-4311	SZD-36 Cobra 15	W-566	
HA-4312	SZD-36 Cobra 15	W-661	
HA-4313	SZD-36 Cobra 15	W-726	
HA-4314	SZD-36 Cobra 15	W-688	
HA-4315	SZD-36 Cobra 15 *(Wfu)*	W-773	
HA-4316	SZD-36 Cobra 15	W-774	
HA-4317	SZD-36 Cobra 15	W-784	
HA-4318	SZD-36 Cobra 15	W-785	
HA-4319	SZD-36 Cobra 15	W-799	
HA-4321	VTC-75 Cirrus 17	142	
HA-4322	VTC-75 Cirrus 17	143	
HA-4323	VTC-75 Cirrus 17	144	
HA-4324	VTC-75 Cirrus 17	146	
HA-4325	VTC-75 Cirrus 17	147	

Regn.	Type	C/n	Prev.Id.
HA-4326-VZ	VTC-75 Cirrus 17	161	
HA-4328	Schempp-Hirth Standard Cirrus	615	
HA-4329	SZD-30 Pirat	S-07.04	
HA-4330	SZD-30 Pirat	S-03.27	
HA-4331	SZD-30 Pirat	S-04.03	
HA-4333	SZD-30 Pirat	S-04.24	
HA-4334	SZD-30 Pirat	S-04.50	
HA-4335	SZD-30 Pirat	S-04.49	
HA-4336	SZD-30 Pirat	S-05.19	
HA-4337	SZD-30 Pirat	S-05.37	
HA-4338	SZD-30 Pirat	S-05.38	
HA-4339	SZD-30 Pirat	S-05.39	
HA-4340	SZD-30 Pirat	S-05.40	
HA-4341	SZD-30 Pirat	S-05.41	
HA-4342	SZD-30 Pirat	S-05.42	
HA-4343	SZD-30 Pirat	S-05.43	
HA-4344	SZD-30 Pirat	S-05.44	
HA-4345	SZD-30 Pirat	S-07.05	
HA-4347	SZD-30 Pirat	S-07.07	
HA-4348	SZD-30 Pirat	S-07.08	
HA-4353	SZD-38A Jantar 1	B-673	
HA-4354	SZD-38A Jantar 1	B-674	
HA-4356	SZD-38A Jantar 1	B-687	
HA-4357	SZD-38A Jantar 1	B-688	
HA-4358	SZD-30 Pirat	S-07.01	
HA-4359	SZD-30 Pirat	S-07.02	
HA-4360	SZD-41A Jantar Standard	B-690	
HA-4361	SZD-41A Jantar Standard	B-692	
HA-4362	SZD-30 Pirat	S-07.26	
HA-4363	SZD-36A Cobra 15	W-800	
HA-4364	SZD-30 Pirat	S-08.17	
HA-4365	SZD-30 Pirat	S-08.18	
HA-4368	SZD-30 Pirat	S-08.21	
HA-4369	SZD-30 Pirat	S-08.22	
HA-4370	SZD-30 Pirat	S-08.23	
HA-4371	SZD-30 Pirat	S-08.24	
HA-4372	SZD-30 Pirat	S-08.25	
HA-4373	SZD-30 Pirat	S-08.26	
HA-4374	SZD-30 Pirat	S-08.27	
HA-4375	SZD-30 Pirat	S-08.28	
HA-4376	SZD-30 Pirat (Wfu)	S-08.16	
HA-4377	SZD-30 Pirat	S-08.29	
HA-4378	SZD-30 Pirat	S-08.30	
HA-4379	SZD-30 Pirat	S-08.31	
HA-4380	SZD-30 Pirat	S-08.32	
HA-4381	SZD-30 Pirat	S-08.33	
HA-4382	SZD-30 Pirat	S-08.34	
HA-4383	SZD-30 Pirat	S-08.35	
HA-4384	SZD-30 Pirat	S-08.36	
HA-4385	SZD-30 Pirat	S-08.37	
HA-4386	SZD-30 Pirat	S-08.38	
HA-4388	SZD-30 Pirat (Dismantled)	S-08.40	
HA-4389	SZD-30 Pirat	S-08.41	
HA-4390	SZD-30 Pirat	S-08.42	
HA-4391	SZD-30 Pirat	S-08.43	
HA-4392	SZD-30 Pirat	S-08.44	
HA-4393	SZD-30 Pirat	S-08.45	
HA-4394	SZD-30 Pirat C	P-801	
HA-4395	SZD-30 Pirat C	P-832	
HA-4396	SZD-30 Pirat C	P-835	
HA-4397	VTC-75 Cirrus 17	178	YU-4302
HA-4398	SZD-36A Cobra 15	W-573	OE-0938
HA-4399	SZD-30 Pirat	B-568	OE-0973
HA-4400	SZD-48-1 Jantar Standard 2	B-1184	
HA-4401	SZD-48-1 Jantar Standard 2	B-1224	
HA-4402	SZD-48-1 Jantar Standard 2	B-1223	
HA-4403	SZD-41A Jantar Standard	B-737	
HA-4404	SZD-41A Jantar Standard	B-740	
HA-4406	Eiravion PIK-20D	20614	
HA-4407	Eiravion PIK-20D	20610	
HA-4408	Eiravion PIK-20D	20612	
HA-4409	Eiravion PIK-20D	20611	
HA-4410	Eiravion PIK-20D	20627	
HA-4411	Eiravion PIK-20D	20633	
HA-4412	Eiravion PIK-20D	20634	
HA-4413	Eiravion PIK-20D	20647	
HA-4414	Eiravion PIK-20D	20551	
HA-4415	Eiravion PIK-20D	20667	
HA-4416	SZD-48-1 Jantar Standard	B-1096	
HA-4417	SZD-48-1 Jantar Standard	B-1051	
HA-4418	SZD-42-2 Jantar 2B	B-943	
HA-4419	SZD-42-2 Jantar 2B	B-945	
HA-4420	SZD-42-2 Jantar 2B	B-950	
HA-4421	SZD-42-2 Jantar 2B	B-1127	
HA-4422	SZD-42-2 Jantar 2B	B-1129	
HA-4423	SZD-42-2 Jantar 2B	B-1307	
HA-4424	SZD-42-2 Jantar 2B	B-1130	
HA-4425	SZD-48-1 Jantar Standard 2	B-1136	
HA-4426	SZD-48-1 Jantar Standard 2	B-1185	
HA-4427	SZD-48-1 Jantar Standard 2	B-1188	
HA-4428	SZD-42-2 Jantar 2B	B-1309	
HA-4429	SZD-48-1 Jantar Standard	B-1189	
HA-4432	IAR-Brasov IS.29D2	133	
HA-4433	IAR-Brasov IS.29D2	161	
HA-4435	IAR-Brasov IS.29D2 (Wrecked)	164	
HA-4436	IAR-Brasov IS.29D2	165	
HA-4437	IAR-Brasov IS.29D2	166	
HA-4438	IAR-Brasov IS.29D2	167	
HA-4439	IAR-Brasov IS.29D2	168	
HA-4440	IAR-Brasov IS.29D2	169	
HA-4441	IAR-Brasov IS.29D	170	
HA-4442	IAR-Brasov IS.29D2	171	
HA-4443	IAR-Brasov IS.29D2	172	
HA-4444	IAR-Brasov IS.29D2	173	
HA-4445	IAR-Brasov IS.29D2	174	
HA-4446	IAR-Brasov IS.29D2	175	
HA-4447	IAR-Brasov IS.29D2	176	
HA-4449	IAR-Brasov IS.29D2	178	
HA-4450	SZD-42-2 Jantar 2B	B-1308	
HA-4451	SZD-42-2 Jantar 2B	B-1132	
HA-4452	SZD-42-2 Jantar 2B	B-1133	
HA-4453	SZD-42-2 Jantar 2B	B-1310	
HA-4454	SZD-42-2 Jantar 2B	B-1322	
HA-4455	SZD-42-2 Jantar 2B	B-1324	
HA-4456	SZD-42-2 Jantar 2B	B-1487	
HA-4457	SZD-42-2 Jantar 2B	B-1488	
HA-4459	SZD-48-3 Jantar Standard 3	B-1453	
HA-4460	SZD-48-3 Jantar Standard 3	B-1571	
HA-4461	SZD-48-3 Jantar Standard 3	B-1652	
HA-4462	SZD-42-2 Jantar 2B	B-1674	
HA-4464	LAK-12 Lietuva	6122	
HA-4465-KT	LAK-12 Lietuva	6132	
HA-4466	LAK-12 Lietuva	6134	
HA-4467	SZD-48-3 Jantar Standard 3	B-1906	
HA-4468	SZD-48-3 Jantar Standard 3	B-1907	
HA-4469	SZD-42-2 Jantar 2B	B-1680	
HA-4470	SZD-48-3 Jantar Standard 3	B-1452	HA-4458
HA-4471-BM	Schempp-Hirth Discus CS	093CS	
HA-4472-KB	Schempp-Hirth Discus CS	094CS	
HA-4473	Schempp-Hirth Discus CS	098CS	
HA-4474	SZD-48-1 Jantar Standard 2	B-1234	DOSAAF
HA-4478	IAR-Brasov IS.29D2	182	
HA-4479	IAR-Brasov IS.29D2	183	
HA-4481	IAR-Brasov IS.29D2	199A	
HA-4482	Schempp-Hirth Discus CS	215CS	
HA-4483	Schempp-Hirth Ventus 2b	40	
HA-4484	SZD-48-1 Jantar Standard 2	B-985	
HA-4485	Schempp-Hirth Nimbus 2	20	D-2091
HA-4487	SZD-48-1 Jantar Standard 2	B-1198	HB-1644
HA-4488	SZD-48-1 Jantar Standard 2	B-1026	OE-5296
			OE-5155
HA-4489	SZD-48-3 Jantar Standard 3	B-1959	PH-917
HA-5000	IAR-Brasov IS.28B2	240	
HA-5001	IAR-Brasov IS.28B2	243	
HA-5002	IAR-Brasov IS.28B2 (Dismantled)	244	
HA-5003	IAR-Brasov IS.28B2	252	
HA-5004	IAR-Brasov IS.28B2	272	
HA-5005	IAR-Brasov IS.28B2	273	
HA-5006	IAR-Brasov IS.28B2	274	
HA-5007	IAR-Brasov IS.28B2	275	

Regn.	Type	C/n	Prev.Id.
HA-5008	IAR-Brasov IS.28B2	278	
HA-5009	IAR-Brasov IS.28B2	279	
HA-5010	IAR-Brasov IS.28B2	280	
HA-5011	IAR-Brasov IS.28B2	289	
HA-5012	IAR-Brasov IS.28B2	229	
HA-5013	IAR-Brasov IS.28B2	241	
HA-5014	IAR-Brasov IS.28B2	301	
HA-5015	IAR-Brasov IS.28B2	303	
HA-5016	IAR-Brasov IS.28B2	304	
HA-5017	IAR-Brasov IS.28B2	323	
HA-5018	IAR-Brasov IS.28B2	331	
HA-5019	IAR-Brasov IS.28B2	333	
HA-5020	IAR-Brasov IS.28B2	334	
HA-5021	IAR-Brasov IS.28B2	335	
HA-5022	IAR-Brasov IS.28B2	328	
HA-5023	IAR-Brasov IS.28B2	329	
HA-5024	IAR-Brasov IS.28B2	330	
HA-5026	IAR-Brasov IS.28B2	337	
HA-5027	IAR-Brasov IS.28B2	338	
HA-5028	IAR-Brasov IS.28B2	340	
HA-5030	IAR-Brasov IS.28B2	332	
HA-5031	IAR-Brasov IS.28B2	343	
HA-5032	IAR-Brasov IS.28B2	344	
HA-5033	IAR-Brasov IS.28B2	346	
HA-5034	IAR-Brasov IS.28B2	347	
HA-5035	R-IIb Cimbora 84	F-03	
HA-5036	IAR-Brasov IS.28B2	348	
HA-5037	IAR-Brasov IS.28B2	349	
HA-5038	IAR-Brasov IS.28B2	352	
HA-5040	IAR-Brasov IS.28B2	350	
HA-5050	Schleicher K7 Rhönadler	693	HB-660
HA-5051	Schleicher K7 Rhönadler	1084	HB-694
HA-5052	Schleicher K7 Rhönadler	464	D-9110
HA-5055	Schleicher K7 Rhönadler	7086	D-8880
HA-5175	LET L-13 Blanik	027359	
HA-5176	LET L-13 Blanik	027360	
HA-5177	LET L-13 Blanik	170511	DOSAAF
HA-5190	LET L-13 Blanik	170210	OK-9834
HA-5192	LET L-13 Blanik	026244	
HA-5193	LET L-13 Blanik	026804	
HA-5195	SZD-9bis Bocian IE	P-442	
HA-5196	SZD-9bis Bocian IE	P-687	
HA-5200	LET L-23 Super Blanik	897517	
HA-5201	LET L-23 Super Blanik	897519	
HA-5202	LET L-23 Super Blanik	897520	
HA-5304	R-26S Góbé	E-1172	
HA-5311	R-26S Góbé	E-1179	
HA-5313	R-26S Góbé	E-1182	
HA-5314	R-26S Góbé	E-1183	
HA-5315	R-26S Góbé	E-1184	
HA-5316	R-26S Góbé	E-1185	
HA-5317	R-26S Góbé	E-1186	
HA-5319	R-26S Góbé	E-1188	
HA-5321	R-26S Góbé	E-1190	
HA-5323	R-26S Góbé	E-1192	
HA-5326	R-26S Góbé	E-1195	
HA-5328	R-26S Góbé	E-1197	
HA-5329	R-26S Góbé	E-1198	
HA-5330	R-26S Góbé	E-1199	
HA-5331	R-26S Góbé	E-1200	
HA-5334	R-26S Góbé	E-1203	
HA-5335	R-26S Góbé	E-1204	
HA-5336	R-26S Góbé	E-1205	
HA-5337	R-26S Góbé	E-1206	
HA-5340	R-26S Góbé	E-1209	
HA-5341	R-26S Góbé	E-1210	
HA-5343	R-26S Góbé	E-1212	
HA-5344	R-26S Góbé	E-1213	
HA-5346	R-26S Góbé	E-1215	
HA-5347	R-26S Góbé	E-1216	
HA-5349	R-26S Góbé	E-1218	
HA-5350	R-26S Góbé	E-1219	
HA-5353	R-26S Góbé	E-1222	
HA-5355	R-26S Góbé	E-1224	
HA-5357	R-26S Góbé	E-1226	
HA-5358	R-26S Góbé	E-1227	
HA-5360	R-26S Góbé	E-1229	
HA-5362	R-26S Góbé	E-1231	
HA-5363	R-26S Góbé	E-1232	
HA-5365	R-26S Góbé	E-1234	
HA-5366	R-26S Góbé	E-1235	
HA-5367	R-26S Góbé	E-1236	
HA-5370	R-26S Góbé	E-1239	
HA-5372	R-26S Góbé	E-1241	
HA-5374	R-26S Góbé	E-1243	
HA-5376	R-26S Góbé	E-1245	
HA-5377	R-26S Góbé	E-1246	
HA-5378	R-26S Góbé	E-1247	
HA-5379	R-26S Góbé	E-1248	
HA-5380	R-26S Góbé	E-1249	
HA-5382	R-26S Góbé	E-1251	
HA-5384	R-26S Góbé	E-1253	
HA-5385	R-26S Góbé	E-1254	
HA-5386	R-26S Góbé	E-1255	
HA-5387	R-26S Góbé	E-1256	
HA-5388	R-26S Góbé	E-1257	
HA-5390	R-26S Góbé	E-1259	
HA-5392	R-26S Góbé	E-1261	
HA-5393	R-26S Góbé	E-1262	
HA-5395	R-26S Góbé	E-1264	
HA-5396	R-26S Góbé	E-1265	
HA-5398	R-26S Góbé	E-1267	
HA-5399	R-26S Góbé	E-1268	
HA-5400	R-26S Góbé	E-1269	
HA-5401	R-26S Góbé	E-1270	
HA-5402	R-26S Góbé	E-1271	
HA-5403	R-26S Góbé	E-1272	
HA-5404	R-26S Góbé	E-1273	
HA-5405	R-26S Góbé	E-1274	
HA-5407	R-26S Góbé	E-1276	
HA-5408	R-26S Góbé	E-1277	
HA-5500	R-26SU Góbé	A800001	
HA-5501	R-26SU Góbé	A800002	
HA-5502	R-26SU Góbé	A800003	
HA-5503	R-26SU Góbé	A800004	
HA-5504	R-26SU Góbé	A800005	
HA-5505	R-26SU Góbé	A800006	
HA-5506	R-26SU Góbé	A800007	
HA-5507	R-26SU Góbé	A800023	
HA-5508	R-26SU Góbé	A800024	
HA-5509	R-26SU Góbé	A800025	
HA-5510	R-26SU Góbé	A800026	
HA-5511	R-26SU Góbé	A800027	
HA-5512	R-26SU Góbé	A800028	
HA-5513	R-26SU Góbé	A800029	
HA-5514	R-26SU Góbé	A800030	
HA-5515	R-26SU Góbé	A800031	
HA-5516	R-26SU Góbé	A800032	
HA-5517	R-26SU Góbé 82	A800033	
HA-5518	R-26SU Góbé 82	A800034	
HA-5519	R-26SU Góbé 82	A800035	
HA-5520	R-26SU Góbé 82	A800036	
HA-5521	R-26SU Góbé 82	A800037	
HA-5522	R-26SU Góbé 82	A800038	
HA-5523	R-26SU Góbé 82	A800039	
HA-5524	R-26SU Góbé 82	A800040	
HA-5525	R-26SU Góbé 82	A800041	
HA-5526	R-26SU Góbé 82	A800042	
HA-5527	R-26SU Góbé 82	A800043	
HA-5528	R-26SU Góbé 82	A800044	
HA-5529	R-26SU Góbé 82	A800045	
HA-5531	R-26SU Góbé 82	A800047	
HA-5532	R-26SU Góbé 82	A800048	
HA-5533	R-26SU Góbé	A800049	
HA-5534	R-26SU Góbé	A800050	
HA-5535	R-26SU Góbé	A800051	
HA-5536	R-26SU Góbé	A800052	
HA-5537	R-26SU Góbé	A800053	
HA-5538	R-26SU Góbé	A800054	
HA-5539	R-26SU Góbé	A800055	

Regn.	Type	C/n	Prev.Id.
HA-5540	R-26SU Góbé	A800056	
HA-5541	R-26SU Góbé	A800057	
HA-5542	R-26SU Góbé	A800058	
HA-5543	R-26SU Góbé	A800059	
HA-5544	R-26SU Góbé	A800060	
HA-5545	R-26SU Góbé (Wfu)	A800061	
HA-5546	R-26SU Góbé	A800062	
HA-5547	R-26SU Góbé	A800064	
HA-5548	R-26SU Góbé	A800066	
HA-5549	R-26SU Góbé	A800067	
HA-5550	R-26SU Góbé	A800068	
HA-5551	R-26SU Góbé	A800069	
HA-5558	R-26SU Góbé	A800070	
HA-5559	R-26SU Góbé	A800073	
HA-5560	R-26SU Góbé	A800063	BGA3473/FRU
HA-5561	R-26SU Góbé	A800071	
HA-5562	R-26SU Góbé	A800072	
HA-7019	A-15	0305	
HA-7020	A-15	0306	
HA-7022	Swift S-1A	113	
HA-....	Avialsa/Scheibe A.60 Fauconnet	32	F-CCQJ
HA-....	SZD-48-3 Jantar Standard 3	B-1959	PH-917

MOTOR GLIDERS

Regn.	Type	C/n	Prev.Id.
HA-1001	Brditschka HB-21	21029	OE-9226

MICROLIGHTS (Alphabetical series)

Regn.	Type	C/n	Prev.Id.
HA-YABB	MAN-89	07	
HA-YABC	KSML-IM Nyirseg -2	001/P	
HA-YABD	CFM Shadow Series BD	093	G-MVLN
HA-YABF	Apollo CX/IIOO Tandem/T	MZ87/03	
HA-YABG	Apollo CX/15p.0 Racer/GT/R	MZ29/89	
HA-YABH	Apollo CX/R Okoplan	MZ16/90	
HA-YABI	Apollo CX Racer GT/R	MZ34/90	
HA-YABJ	Denney Kitfox III	972	
HA-YABK	Denney Kitfox III	973	
HA-YABL	Apollo CX Racer GT/R	MZ48/91	
HA-YABM	Apollo CX Racer GT/R	MZ49/91	
HA-YABN	Apollo CX Racer GT/R	MZ50/91	
HA-YABP	Apollo CX Racer GT/R	MZ42/91	
HA-YABQ	Apollo CX Tandem/R	MZ19/86	
HA-YABR	Apollo CX Racer GT/R	MZ58/90	
HA-YABT	Apollo CX Tandem/R	MZ02/87	
HA-YABV	Aviatek MAI-890 Junior	07	
HA-YABY	Light Aero Avid Flyer	824	
HA-YABZ	Pelikan Agricole/R	01/90	
HA-YACA	Light Aero Avid Flyer Mk.IV	1166	
HA-YACB	Light Aero Avid Flyer D	1167	
HA-YACD	Apollo CX Racer GT/R	MZ86/91	
HA-YACE	Apollo CX Racer GT/R	MZ14/92	
HA-YACF	Apollo CX Tandem/R	MZ89040	
HA-YACG	Apollo CX Racer GT/R	MZ118/91	
HA-YACH	Apollo CX Racer GT/R	MZ107/91	
HA-YACI	Apollo CXM Racer GT	180495	
HA-YACJ /57-05	Apollo CX Racer GT/R	MZ47/92	
HA-YACK	Apollo CX Racer GT/R	MZ92/91	
HA-YACL	Apollo CX Racer GT	MZ16/92	
HA-YACM	Apollo CX Racer GT/R	MZ03/87	
HA-YACO	Apollo CX Racer GT/R	MZ111/91	
HA-YACP	Apollo CXM Racer GT/R	MZ51/91	
HA-YACR	Apollo CXM Racer GT/R	100693	
HA-YACS	Apollo CX Racer GT/R	MZ124/91	
HA-YACT	GAK-22 Dino	001-93	HA-XBP
HA-YAWF	Type unknown		
HA-YCAB	BB-01 Bence	BB 01-09	
HA-YCAC	Apollo CXM Racer GT/R	100394	
HA-YEAC	Apollo CX Aircross	AS/01-014-89	
HA-YEAD	Apollo CX Tandem/R	46-002	
HA-YEAE	Apollo Star-Bike/R	SB 001/92	
HA-YEAF	Apollo Star-Bi ke/R	SB 002/92	
HA-YEAG	Apollo Star-Bike/R	SB 003/92	
HA-YEAI	Apollo Star-Bi ke/R	SB 004/92	
HA-YEAJ	Apollo CX Racer GT	"MZ36/9"	
HA-YEAK	Apollo Aercross HodgeP	KSE 1/1991	
HA-YEAM	Apollo Star-Bike/R	SB 005/92	
HA-YEA0	BB-01 Bence	BB 01-08	
HA-YEAR	Apollo CXM Tandem/R	MZ74/92	
HA-YEAS	Kolibri AK-3	unkn	
HA-YGAB	Apollo CX Racer GT/R	MZ45/91	
HA-YGAC	Apollo CX Racer GT/R	MZ119/91	
HA-YHAB	Apollo CXM Racer GT/R	MZ73/92	
HA-YHAC	Apollo CX Aircross	AV0100987	
HA-YHAD	Apollo CXM Racer GT/R	010793	
HA-YHAE	Apollo CXM Racer GT/R	050293	
HA-YJAB	Kolibri AK-3	002	
HA-YNAA	Apollo CX Tandem/R	MZ001/87	
HA-YNAB	Apollo CX Tandem/R	MZ002/87	
HA-YNAE	Apollo CX Tandem R	MZ17/88	
HA-YNAF	Apollo CX Tandem R	MZ18/88	
HA-YNAG	Apollo CX Tandem R	MZ01/89	
HA-YNAH	Apollo CX Racer GT/R	MZ33/89	
HA-YNAI	Apollo CX Racer GT/R	MZ74/91	
HA-YNAJ	Apollo CX Aircross P1	MZ890620	
HA-YNAK	Apollo CX Aircross/R	AT 001005/87	
HA-YNAL	Apollo CX Racer GT/R	MZ112/91	
HA-YNAM	Apollo CX Racer GT/R	MZ116/91	
HA-YNAN	Apollo CX Racer GT/R	MZ27/91	
HA-YNAO	Apollo CXM Racer GT/A	MZ49/91	
HA-YNAP	RAF-2000GTX	H2-94-5-111	
HA-YNAQ	RAF-2000GTX	H2-92-3-56	
HA-YNAR	RAF-2000GTX	H2-94-5-110	
HA-YNAS	RAF-2000GTX	H2-94-5-112	
HA-YOAB	Apollo CX Racer GT/R	MZ06/90	
HA-YOAC	Apollo CX Racer GT/R	MZ07/90	
HA-YOAD	Apollo CXM Aircross	MZ28/92	
HA-YRAA	Apollo CX Aircross	AT 01016	
HA-YRAB	Apollo CXM Racer GT/R	100194	
HA-YRAC	Apollo CXM Racer GT/R	110194	
HA-YRAD	Apollo CX Racer GT/R	MZ113/91	
HA-YRAE	Apollo CX Racer GT/R	MZ900212	
HA-YRAF	Apollo CX Racer GT/R	MZ87/91	
HA-YRAG	Apollo CX Tandem/R	MZ89/0710	
HA-YRAH	Apollo CXM Racer GT	MZ68/1992	
HA-YRAI	Apollo	unkn	
HA-YRAJ	Diamond DA.20 Katana	unkn	
HA-YSAA	Apollo CX Racer GT/R	MZ46/91	
HA-YSAB	Apollo CX Racer GT/R	MZ21/91	
HA-YSAC	Apollo CX Racer GT/R	MZ28/91	
HA-YSAD	Apollo CX Racer GT/R	MZ29/91	
HA-YSAE	Apollo CX Racer GT/R	MZ30/91	
HA-YSAF	Apollo CX Racer GT/R	MZ23/90	
HA-YSAG	Apollo CX Racer GT/R	MZ31/9O	
HA-YSAH	Apollo CX Racer GT/R	MZ51/90	
HA-YSAI	Apollo CX Aircross R	AS01-002	
HA-YSAL	Apollo CX Racer GT/R	MZ88/91	
HA-YSAM	Apollo CX Aircross	MZ27/89	
HA-YSAN	Apollo CX Aircross	AT01-030	
HA-YSAO	Apollo CX Racer GT/R	MZ122/91	
HA-YSAP	Apollo CX Racer GT/R	MZ115/91	
HA-YSAQ	Apollo CX Racer GT/R	MZ39/92	
HA-YSAR	Apollo CX Racer GT/R	MZ62/91	
HA-YSAS	Apollo CXM Racer GT/R	MZ235/92	
HA-YSAT	Apollo CX Racer GT/R	MZ89/91	
HA-YSAU	Apollo CX Racer GT/R	MZ104/91	
HA-YSAV	Apollo CX Racer GT/R	MZ05/91	
HA-YSAW	Apollo CX Racer GT/R	MZ106/91	
HA-YSAX	Apollo CX Tandem/R	MZ45/90	
HA-YSAZ	Tandem Air Sunny Sport 582UL	43/93	
HA-YSBA	Apollo CX Racer GT/R	MZ29/92	
HA-YSBC	Apollo CXM Racer GT/R	070393	

402

Regn.	Type	C/n	Prev.Id.
HA-YSBD	Apollo CXM Racer GT/R	MZ69/92	
HA-YTAA	KSML-IM Nyirség-2	001	
HA-YTAB	KSML-IM Nyirség-2	002	
HA-YTAC	KSML-IM Nyirség-2	003	
HA-YTAD	KSML-IM Nyirség-2	004	
HA-YTAE	KSML-IM Nyirség-2	005	
HA-YUAB	Apollo CX Aircross 1400	3 68 2823	
HA-YUAC	Apollo CXM Racer GT/R	150693	
HA-YUAD	Apollo CX Racer GT/R	MZ37/91	
HA-YVAB	OCSI SZ-01	AA-90-01M	
HA-YVAC	Apollo CX Tandem R	MZ21/88	
HA-YVAD	Apollo CX Tandem R	MZ66/90	
HA-YVAE	Apollo CX Racer GT/R	MZ33/90	
HA-YWAB	Apollo CX Racer GT/R	MZ108/91	
HA-YWAC	Apollo CXM Racer GT/R	030193	
HA-YWAD	Apollo CXM Racer/T	170194	
HA-YWAE	Apollo CXM Racer	MZ70/92	
HA-YWAF	Apollo CX Racer GT/R	MZ33/92	
HA-YWAG	Apollo CXM Racer GT/R	MZ1205/93	
HA-YWAI	Apollo CX Racer GT/R	190994	
HA-YXAA	Apollo CX Racer GT/R	MZO9/89	
HA-YXAB	Apollo CX Racer GT/R	MZ08/89	
HA-YXAC	Apollo CX Racer GT/R	MZ04/88	
HA-YXAD	Apollo CX Racer GT/R	MZ105/91	
HA-YXAE	Apollo CX Racer GT/R	MZ123/91	
HA-YXAF	Apollo CXM Racer GT/R	MZ54/92	
HA-YXAG	Apollo CXM Racer GT/R	MZ53/92	
HA-YXAH	Apollo CX Racer GT/R	1305/93	
HA-YZAA	Apollo CX Tandem/R	MZ26/89	
HA-YZAB	Apollo CX Racer GT/R	MZ129/90	
HA-YZAD	Apollo CX Racer GT/R	MZ53/91	
HA-YZAE	Apollo CX Racer GT/R	MZ54/91	
HA-YZAF	Apollo CX Racer GT/R	MZ55/91	
HA-YZAG	Apollo CX Racer GT/R	MZ60/91	
HA-YZAH	Apollo CX Racer GT/R	MZ900130	
HA-YZAI	Apollo CX Racer GT/R	MZ44/91	
HA-YZAJ	Apollo CX Racer GT/R	MZ61/91	
HA-YZAK	Apollo CX Racer GT/R	MZ33/91	
HA-YZAL	Apollo CX Racer GT/R	MZ109/91	
HA-YZAM	Pipistrel-15	TRMM 0900580392	
HA-YZAN	Apollo CX Racer GT/R	MZ121/91	
HA-YZAO	Apollo CX Racer GT/R	MZ25/92	
HA-YZAP	Apollo CX Racer GT/R	MZ125/91	
HA-YZAQ	Apollo CX Aircross/R	AV 01025	
HA-YZAR	Apollo C4M Racer GT/R	MZ31/92	
HA-YZAS	Apollo C4M Racer GT/R	MZ41/92	
HA-YZAT	Apollo CX Racer GT/R	MZ43/91	
HA-YZAV	Apollo C4M Racer GT/R	MZ44/92	
HA-YZBA	Apollo CXM Racer GT/R	0201/93	
HA-YZBC	Pipistrel-15	15H0041192	
HA-YZBD	Pipistrel-15	0870961291	
HA-YZBE	Apollo CXM Racer GT/R	110493	
HA-YZBF	BB-01 Bence	01/14	
HA-YZBG	Apollo CXM Racer GT/R	120495	
HA-YZBH	Type unknown		

Regn.	Type	C/n	Prev.Id.
25-08	Apollo CX		
25-11	Apollo		
25-13	Air Création Quartz SX-II		
25-14	Apollo		
25-15	TL-22 Duo	95C04	
25-25	Apollo CX		
25-30	Apollo CX		
36-24	Type unknown		
40- 17	Homebuilt CX		
44-001	Apollo CX		
44-003	Apollo CX		
44-004	Apollo CX	44-004	
44-005	Apollo CX		
44-006	Apollo CX		
44-007	Apollo CX		
44-008	Apollo CX		
44-009	Apollo CX		
44-011	Apollo CX		
44-012	Apollo CX		
44-22	Apollo CX	MZ 890821	
44-023	Apollo CX		
45-101	Apollo CX		
45-108	Apollo CX		
45-111	Apollo CX		
45-112	Apollo CX		
59-69	unkn		
61-10	Apollo C15		
67-09	Apollo CX		
75-07	Apollo CX		
75-10	Apollo CX		
139-12	Apollo Tandem C4		

MICROLIGHTS (Numerical series)

Regn.	Type	C/n	Prev.Id.
00-11	Air Création		25-16
00-13	Apollo CX		
3-49	Apollo CX		
3-75	Apollo		
12-1	MZ Produkt ZX		
15-10	Apollo CX		
15-12	Apollo CX		
18-001	Apollo CX		
22-45	Apollo CX Racer GT/R	MZ117/91	
25-1	Apollo CX	25-001	
25-2	Apollo CX		
25-3	Apollo CX		
25-6	Apollo CX		

HB - SWITZERLAND

(*) Aircraft Registered in Liechtenstein

Regn.	Type	C/n	Prev.Id.
HB-AAM	Short SD.3-60 *(W/o 13.1.00)*	SH.3763	G-BRMY
HB-AAS	Fokker F.28 Fellowship 2000	11110	F-GDUX
			5N-ANK
			PH-ZB0
			PH-EXL
HB-AEE	Dornier 328-100	3005	D-CITA(2)
HB-AEF	Dornier 328-100	3017	D-CDHB
			(D-CERL)
HB-AEG	Dornier 328-100	3011	D-CDOG
HB-AEI	Dornier 328-100	3041	D-CDXH
HB-AFE	Bücker Bü.131 Jungmann	36	G-ATJX
			D-EDMI
			HB-AFE
			A-88
			HB-AFE
HB-AHF	SAAB-Scania SF.340A	026	D-CDIE
			HB-AHF
HB-AKA	SAAB-Scania SF.340B	160	SE-F60
HB-AKB	SAAB-Scania SF.340B	161	SE-F61
HB-AKC	SAAB-Scania SF.340B	164	SE-F64
HB-AKE	SAAB-Scania SF.340B	176	SE-F76
HB-AKF	SAAB-Scania SF.340B	182	SE-F82
HB-AKH	SAAB-Scania SF.340B	200	SE-E02
HB-AKI	SAAB-Scania SF.340B	208	SE-G08
HB-AKK	SAAB-Scania SF.340B *(W/o 10.1.00)*	213	SE-G13
HB-AKL	SAAB-Scania SF.340B	215	SE-G15
HB-AKM	SAAB-Scania SF.340B	221	SE-G21
HB-AKN	SAAB-Scania SF.340B	225	SE-G25
HB-AKO	SAAB-Scania SF.340B	228	SE-G28
HB-ALP	Piper J-3C-100 Cub	12026	44-79730
HB-CAB	Cessna 140	10119	
HB-CAD	Cessna 140	13033	
HB-CAF	Cessna 140	12839	
HB-CAG	Cessna 140	14236	
HB-CAO	Cessna 170	18720	
HB-CAX	Cessna 170A	19644	
HB-CBA	Cessna 150D	60123	OE-AYR
			N4123U
HB-CBF	Reims/Cessna F.150F	0005	
HB-CBG	Cessna 182J Skylane	56707	N2607F
HB-CBK	Reims/Cessna F.150F	0026	
HB-CBS	Cessna 172	46428	N6328E
HB-CBX	Reims/Cessna F.150G	0069	
HB-CBZ	Cessna 182J Skylane	57233	N3133F
HB-CCA	Reims/Cessna FR.172K Hawk XP	0621	(D-EIIH)
HB-CCD	Reims/Cessna F.152	1565	
HB-CCF	Reims/Cessna F.152	1629	
HB-CCH	Cessna P210N Pressurized Centurion II	00294	N4763K
HB-CCN	Reims/Cessna F.152	1621	
HB-CCO	Reims/Cessna F.172N	1763	
HB-CCR	Cessna T.210N Turbo Centurion II	63489	(N5545A)
HB-CCT	Reims/Cessna F.172N	1885	
HB-CCV(*)	Reims/Cessna F.172M	1476	D-EKOC(2)
HB-CCZ	Reims/Cessna F.152	1609	
HB-CDA	Reims/Cessna F.150L	0775	
HB-CDB	Reims/Cessna F.150L	0870	
HB-CDC	Reims/Cessna F.172M	0945	
HB-CDE	Reims/Cessna F.177RG Cardinal RG	0077	
HB-CDF	Reims/Cessna F.172M	0926	
HB-CDH	Reims/Cessna F.150L	0924	
HB-CDL	Reims/Cessna F.172M	0955	
HB-CDN	Reims/Cessna F.172H	0570	G-AXSO
HB-CDP	Reims/Cessna F.150L	0923	
HB-CDR	Reims/Cessna F.150L	1105	
HB-CDS	Reims/Cessna F.172M	1153	
HB-CDU	Cessna 182P Skylane	62790	
HB-CEC	Cessna 182P Skylane	62474	N52235
HB-CED	Reims/Cessna F.177RG Cardinal RG	0075	(D-ECYM)
HB-CEE	Reims/Cessna F.150L	1115	
HB-CEO	Cessna 172M	65929	N9079H
HB-CEU	Reims/Cessna F.172L	0879	D-EEZI
HB-CFA	Reims/Cessna F.152	1801	D-ECEO
HB-CFB	Cessna 172RG Cutlass	0520	N5402V
HB-CFE	Reims/Cessna FR.172J Rocket	0429	D-EGJT
HB-CFF	Reims/Cessna F.152	1869	
HB-CFG	Reims/Cessna F.152	1970	
HB-CFH	Reims/Cessna F.152	1809	D-EBHJ
			N8495L
HB-CFN	Reims/Cessna F.172P	2113	
HB-CFO	Cessna 172RG Cutlass	0804	N9358B
HB-CFP	Cessna TR.182 Turbo Skylane RG	01348	N2539S
HB-CFR	Reims/Cessna F.172P	2053	
HB-CFS	Cessna 182R Skylane	67859	N5075H
HB-CFT	Reims/Cessna F.172P	2133	
HB-CFW	Reims/Cessna F.152	1907	
HB-CFX	Reims/Cessna F.152	1885	
HB-CFY	Reims/Cessna F.172M	1123	D-EENO
HB-CFZ	Cessna TR.182 Turbo Skylane RG	01660	N6317S
HB-CGB	Reims/Cessna F.172P	2137	(D-EIKH)
HB-CGD	Reims/Cessna FR.182 Skylane RG	0067	F-GCYM
HB-CGE	Reims/Cessna FR.172J Rocket	0536	D-EHCW
HB-CGF	Reims/Cessna F.172P	2040	N37797
			PH-AYN
HB-CGH	Reims/Cessna F.152	1860	
HB-CGI	Reims/Cessna F.172P	2129	D-EGOY
HB-CGK	Cessna 152	84522	N5305M
HB-CGM	Reims/Cessna F.177RG Cardinal RG	0136	D-EHRB
HB-CGN	Reims/Cessna F.172P	2139	
HB-CGR	Cessna 172RG Cutlass	0688	N6427V
HB-CGS	Cessna 172RG Cutlass	1076	N9908B
HB-CGT	Reims/Cessna F.152	1952	
HB-CGU	Reims/Cessna F.172P	2194	LX-III
HB-CGW	Reims/Cessna U.206G Stationair	0016/04822	D-ELML
			N1659C
			(OY-BNK)
			N734CN
HB-CGX	Cessna TR.182 Turbo Skylane RG	01949	(N6257T)
HB-CHA	Reims/Cessna F.152	1901	
HB-CHB	Reims/Cessna FR.182 Skylane RG	0043	G-ILLI
			(HB-CCU)
			N1660C
HB-CHJ	Cessna P210N Pressurized Centurion II	00522	D-EATD
			(F-GCQG)
			N731PG
HB-CHM	Reims/Cessna FR.182 Skylane RG	0035	D-EIEG
HB-CHP	Cessna 172RG Cutlass	0429	D-EHNL
			(N4961V)
HB-CHS	Cessna 182R Skylane	68189	D-EEFG
			N2231E
			D-EJAV
			N2231E
HB-CHV	Reims/Cessna F.152	1553	F-GBJN
HB-CHW	Reims/Cessna F.172P	2208	
HB-CHZ	Cessna 210L Centurion	61320	D-EARB
			N2534S
HB-CIA	Reims/Cessna F.172P	2219	
HB-CIC	Cessna TR.182 Turbo Skylane RG	01847	(D-EITW)
			N5275T
			(D-EITW)
HB-CIE	Reims/Cessna F.172P	2221	
HB-CIF	Reims/Cessna F.177RG Cardinal RG	0123	D-EFMV
			F-WLIQ
HB-CIH	Reims/Cessna F.172P	2178	OE-KAB
HB-CII	Cessna 210D Centurion	58321	D-EDEG
			OE-DEG
			N3821Y
HB-CIM	Reims/Cessna F.152	1679	D-EEQR
HB-CIN	Cessna TR.182 Turbo Skylane RG	01402	D-EGPY
			N4722S
HB-CIO	Reims/Cessna F.172P	2235	
HB-CIP	Reims/Cessna F.172P	2153	OO-TRG
			OO-XRG
HB-CIR	Cessna 182Q Skylane	66647	N95832
HB-CIS	Cessna 172N	73679	N4800J
HB-CIT	Reims/Cessna F.172P	2248	
HB-CIU	Reims/Cessna FR.172J Rocket	0437	D-EJXX

Regn.	Type	C/n	Prev.Id.
HB-CIV	Cessna 182R Skylane	68557	D-EDEC(3) N9564X
HB-CIW	Reims/Cessna F.152	1980	
HB-CIX	Reims/Cessna F.152	1966	
HB-CIY	Reims/Cessna F.152	1955	D-EFIT
HB-CJA	Cessna 172N	70935	N739ZK
HB-CJB	Cessna 182R Skylane	68406	N9394E
HB-CJC	Cessna TR.182 Turbo Skylane RG	01992	N6352T
HB-CJI	Cessna TU.206G Soloy	05938	N6527X
HB-CJJ	Reims/Cessna F.182Q Skylane	0076	D-ECUG(3) PH-AYO
HB-CJK	Reims/Cessna F.182Q Skylane	0156	D-EFQN
HB-CJM	Cessna 172P	76310	N98564
HB-CJO	Cessna U.206G Soloy	04101	C-GJKD N206DG C-GBBV N756HJ
HB-CJP	Cessna TU.206G Soloy	06048	N4914Z
HB-CJQ	Cessna 172N	71531	D-EAOT N3397Q
HB-CJR	Cessna 172P	74303	N51370
HB-CJU	Cessna R.182 Skylane RG	01685	N6488S
HB-CJV	Reims/Cessna F.152	1564	D-EFGR
HB-CJW	Cessna 152	83388	N48904
HB-CJX	Cessna 182Q Skylane	66703	D-ERAP N96379
HB-CKA	Cessna 170A	19135	OO-GAY N11B N9574A
HB-CKB	Cessna 182P (Reims-assembled)	0021/63933	D-EIGS (D-EEOB) N9872E
HB-CKF	Cessna TR.182 Turbo Skylane RG	01365	D-EFNF N4642S
HB-CKG	Reims/Cessna F.172P	2251	G-BMPB
HB-CKH	Cessna P210N Pressurized Centurion II	00613	N734VR
HB-CKI	Reims/Cessna F.152	1969	
HB-CKL	Reims/Cessna F.182Q Skylane	0109	D-EIYK
HB-CKP	Reims/Cessna F.152	1944	F-GEUE
HB-CKT	Cessna 172RG Cutlass	1163	F-GEBP N9441D
HB-CKU	Reims/Cessna F.172P	2195	F-GDOQ F-WZDR
HB-CKV	Cessna TR.182 Turbo Skylane RG	00898	C-FHPC N757ZH
HB-CKY	Reims/Cessna F.172P	2211	D-EAEL(2)
HB-CLA	Cessna R.182 Skylane RG	01701	N7181S
HB-CLB	Cessna 182Q Skylane	67423	N4857N
HB-CLE	Reims/Cessna F.182Q Skylane	0166	D-EOOK N182PL D-EOOK
HB-CLL	Cessna 172P	76572	N9538L
HB-CLN	Cessna 172RG Cutlass	0970	N9690B
HB-CLO	Cessna 172P	76627	N9830L
HB-CLP	Cessna 172P	76461	N99528
HB-CLS	Cessna 172P	76640	N9855L
HB-CLU	Cessna R.182 Skylane RG	01776	N4848T
HB-CLW	Cessna 172P	74391	N51993
HB-CLY	Reims/Cessna F.172M	0976	D-ECXL
HB-CMC	Cessna 175 Skylark	56111	OY-AED N6611E
HB-CMK	Cessna 175B Skylark	56791	N8091T
HB-CML	Cessna 182F Skylane	54812	N3412U
HB-CMO	Reims/Cessna F.172E	0041	
HB-CMS	Cessna 150D	60517	OE-AYT N4517U
HB-CMZ	Cessna 182H Skylane	56287	N2387X
HB-CNC	Cessna 150J	70521	N60715
HB-CNE	Reims/Cessna F.150M	1309	
HB-CNF	Reims/Cessna F.172H	0653	D-EABZ
HB-CNG	Cessna 210L Centurion	00208	OE-DFE (N59309)
HB-CNI	Reims/Cessna F.152	1494	(D-EAAX)
HB-CNK	Reims/Cessna F.152	1445	
HB-CNM	Cessna 177RG Cardinal RG	1335	N53062
HB-CNN	Cessna TR.182 Turbo Skylane RG	1045	(N756DC)
HB-CNO	Cessna 182P Skylane	64838	N1270S
HB-CNS	Reims/Cessna F.152	1741	
HB-CNY	Reims/Cessna F.172N	1681	D-EIIF
HB-COE	Cessna 180	30465	N1765C
HB-COK	Cessna 170B	26445	N3402C
HB-COR	Cessna 140A	15351	N9630A
HB-CPJ	Cessna TR.182 Turbo Skylane RG	01654	N6252S
HB-CPL	Cessna 172	29046	N6946A
HB-CPP	Cessna 172	29928	N8128B
HB-CPU	Cessna 150	17036	N5536E
HB-CPX	Cessna 182B Skylane	51964	N2664G
HB-CQA	Cessna 172N	70725	N739QR
HB-CQB	Cessna A.185F Skywagon	04093	N60998
HB-CQC	Cessna R.182 Skylane RG	02034	N6474T
HB-CQE	Cessna U.206G Soloy Stationair II	05976	N7371X
HB-CQF	Cessna 172M	61782	N5375Q
HB-CQI	Cessna 152	80211	N24314
HB-CQJ	Cessna 152	80131	N757ZJ
HB-CQL	Cessna 172P	74190	N6393K
HB-CQM	Cessna 172N	73010	N1916F
HB-CQN	Cessna 150L	74264	N19239
HB-CQO	Cessna 150L	74592	N21988
HB-CQQ	Cessna 172R	80102	
HB-CQR	Cessna 172R	80506	
HB-CQS	Cessna P210N Pressurized Centurion II	00167	N6307P
HB-CQT	Cessna A.185F Skywagon	04263	PH-BAK N61826 N70PF N61826
HB-CQU	Cessna 182Q Skylane	66611	D-EFST(3) N95727
HB-CQW	Cessna 172S	172S8288	
HB-CQ .	Cessna U.206G Stationair II	04373	F-GGVY N756UT
HB-CRD	Cessna 172	36339	N8639B
HB-CRE	Cessna 172RG Cutlass	0634	(N6341V)
HB-CRG	Cessna 182A Skylane	51429	N2129G
HB-CRL	Cessna 175A Skylark	56752	N8052T
HB-CRM	Cessna 175B Skylark	56959	N8259T
HB-CRR	Cessna 150B	59485	N7385X
HB-CRS	Cessna 172C	49162	N1462Y
HB-CRZ	Cessna 182E Skylane	54203	N3203Y
HB-CSD	Reims/Cessna F.150G	0101	
HB-CSE	Reims/Cessna F.172H	0329	
HB-CSF	Reims/Cessna F.150G	0123	
HB-CSM	Reims/Cessna F.150G	0189	
HB-CSR	Cessna 182H Skylane	55849	D-EFHY N3449S
HB-CSS	Cessna 210F	58757	N1857F
HB-CST	Cessna 182G Skylane	55388	OE-DDM N2188R
HB-CSW	Reims/Cessna F.150H	0223	
HB-CSZ	Reims/Cessna F.150H	0265	
HB-CTD	Reims/Cessna F.150H	0296	
HB-CTF	Reims/Cessna F.150H	0336	
HB-CTL	Cessna 182L Skylane	58953	(D-EFMJ) (D-EDCD) N42301
HB-CTR	Reims/Cessna F.172H	0582	
HB-CTS	Cessna 150F	62938	D-ECYQ N8838G
HB-CTU	Reims/Cessna F.150J	0476	
HB-CTW	Reims/Cessna F.150J	0491	
HB-CUA	Reims/Cessna F.150K	0590	
HB-CUD	Reims/Cessna F.172H	0560	
HB-CUE	Cessna 182M Skylane	59376	N70814
HB-CUI	Reims/Cessna F.150K	0618	
HB-CUQ	Reims/Cessna FA.150K Aerobat	0009	
HB-CUR	Reims/Cessna F.150K	0534	
HB-CVD	Reims/Cessna F.150L	0684	
HB-CVF	Reims/Cessna FR.172H Rocket	0241	
HB-CVI	Reims/Cessna F.177RG Cardinal RG	0011	
HB-CVK	Cessna 182N Skylane	60526	N8986G
HB-CVL	Reims/Cessna FA.150K Aerobat	0054	D-ECAD

Regn.	Type	C/n	Prev.Id.
HB-CVM	Reims/Cessna F.172K	0796	
HB-CVR	Cessna 182A Skylane	34126	OE-DBK
			N6126B
HB-CVT	Reims/Cessna F.150L	0721	
HB-CVU	Reims/Cessna F.172K	0783	
HB-CVV	Cessna 182L Skylane	58763	D-EDHY
			N3463R
HB-CVZ	Reims/Cessna F.150J	0497	F-WLIT
			G-AXUG
			F-BRBF
HB-CWA	Reims/Cessna FRA.150L Aerobat	0134	
HB-CWC	Cessna 177B Cardinal	01690	
HB-CWD	Reims/Cessna F.177RG Cardinal RG	0047	
HB-CWE	Reims/Cessna F.172L	0829	
HB-CWI	Reims/Cessna FRA.150L Aerobat	0147	
HB-CWN	Cessna 182P Skylane	61794	
HB-CWR	Reims/Cessna F.15 L	0669	I-NOLE
HB-CWT	Reims/Cessna F.150M	1208	
HB-CWX	Cessna 182P Skylane	63399	N9511G
HB-CWY	Cessna 182P (Reims-assembled)	0010/63877	N6882M
HB-CWZ	Cessna A.185F	02641	N4879C
HB-CXA	Cessna 177B Cardinal	02234	N35150
HB-CXD	Reims/Cessna F.172M	1426	
HB-CXE	Cessna 182P (Reims-assembled)	0051/64380	N1590M
HB-CXF	Cessna T.210L Turbo Centurion	61259	N2378S
HB-CXK	Cessna T.210L Turbo Centurion	59922	N41CF
			N30428
HB-CXN	Reims/Cessna F.150M	1343	
HB-CXV	Reims/Cessna F.152	1504	
HB-CXW	Reims/Cessna F.152	1499	
HB-CXZ	Reims/Cessna F.172N	1630	
HB-CYC	Cessna 172RG Cutlass	0556	N5529V
HB-CYE	Cessna 152	84056	N4981H
HB-CYF	Reims/Cessna F.152	1792	
HB-CYK	Cessna TU.206G Turbo Stationair II	06155	SE-III
			N6134Z
HB-DAI	Nord 1203 Norécrin II	307	
HB-DAR	Nord 1203 Norécrin II	318	OE-DAR
			HB-DAR
HB-DBC	Ruschmeyer R.90-230RG	012	D-EEBX
HB-DBF	Ruschmeyer R.90-230RG	006	D-EEHY
HB-DBL	Saab S.91D Safir	91439	
HB-DCA	Wassmer WA.40 Super IV	45	
HB-DCB	Wassmer WA.40A Super IV	68	
HB-DCE	Wassmer WA.421/250	420	
HB-DCF	Gardan GY-80 Horizon 160	24	F-BLPG
HB-DCI	Gardan GY-80 Horizon 160	62	F-BLVM
HB-DCM	Gardan GY-80 Horizon 160	88	PH-AAZ
			OO-FRA
			F-BMUD
HB-DCQ	Gardan GY-80 Horizon 150	112	F-BMUN
HB-DCR	Varga 2150A Kachina	154-80	OO-HTB
			N80716
HB-DCU	Varga 2180 Kachina	180-82	
HB-DED	Mooney M.20E Super 21	213	
HB-DEG	Mooney M.20E Super 21	345	
HB-DEK	Mooney M.20C Mark 21	2594	N6890U
HB-DEN	Mooney M.20E Super 21	714	
HB-DET	Mooney M.20E Super 21	947	
HB-DEU	Mooney M.20E Super 21	1053	
HB-DEV	Mooney M.20F Executive	670058	N3520X
HB-DEW	Mooney M.22	670002	N7706M
HB-DEZ	Mooney M.20F Executive	670187	N9610M
HB-DFA	Mooney M.20J Model 201	24-0262	
HB-DFB	Mooney M.20J Model 201	24-0263	
HB-DFF	Mooney M.20J Model 201	24-0545	
HB-DFI	Mooney M.20K Model 231	25-0104	
HB-DFK	Mooney M.20J Model 201	24-0796	
HB-DFL	Mooney M.20J Model 201	24-0764	N4548H
HB-DFM	Mooney M.20J Model 201	24-0775	
HB-DFN	Mooney M.20J Model 201	24-0801	
HB-DFO	Mooney M.20K Model 231	25-0129	
HB-DFP	Mooney M.20J Model 201	24-0817	
HB-DFR	Mooney M.20K Model 231	25-0027	N4564H
HB-DFS	Mooney M.20J Model 201	24-0824	
HB-DFT	Mooney M.20J Model 201	24-0837	
HB-DFU	Mooney M.20J Model 201	24-0859	
HB-DFV	Mooney M.20F Executive	700051	D-EHOF
			N9497V
HB-DFW	Mooney M.20C Ranger	690088	N9305V
HB-DFX	Mooney M.20J Model 201	24-0967	(N3866H)
HB-DFY	Mooney M.20K Model 231	25-0366	N231QS
HB-DFZ	Mooney M.20K Model 231	25-0368	N231QU
HB-DGB	Mooney M.20K Model 231	25-0523	
HB-DGC	Mooney M.20K Model 231	25-0539	
HB-DGD	Mooney M.20K Model 231	25-0816	
HB-DGE	Mooney M.20K Model 231	25-0389	EI-BJD
			C-GMWH
			(N4024H)
HB-DGF	Mooney M.20J Model 201	24-0947	SE-GXS
			(N3813H)
HB-DGG	Mooney M.20J Model 201	24-0804	SE-GXF
HB-DGI	Mooney M.20K Model 231	25-0693	G-BKMC
			N1167W
HB-DGL	Mooney M.20K Model 231	25-0887	
HB-DGM	Mooney M.20K Model 252	25-1036	
HB-DGN	Mooney M.20K Model 252	25-1037	
HB-DGP	Varga 2150A Kachina	158-80	G-BLHT
			OO-RTW
HB-DGR	Mooney M.20K Model 231	25-0709	N9042G
			YV-2310P
HB-DGS	Mooney M.20J Model 201	24-1615	
HB-DGV	Mooney M.20J Model 201	24-1624	
HB-DGW	Mooney M.20J Model 201	24-1621	
HB-DGZ	Mooney M.20J Model 205	24-3035	
HB-DHA	Mooney M.20K Model 252	25-1155	
HB-DHF	Mooney M.20L PFM	26-0022	
HB-DHG	Mooney M.20K Model 252	25-1170	
HB-DHH	Mooney M.20K Model 231	25-0554	N2XK
HB-DHI	Mooney M.20J Model 201	24-1039	D-EESU
			N3683H
HB-DHK	Mooney M.20K Model 252	25-1185	
HB-DHL	Mooney M.20J Model 201	24-1685	
HB-DHM	Mooney M.20K Model 252	25-1152	(D-EAMT)
			N252MT
HB-DHO	Mooney M.20L PFM	26-0036	N155MP
HB-DHP	Mooney M.20M TLS	27-0015	
HB-DHT	Mooney M.20J Model 205	24-3177	N9125N
HB-DHV	Mooney M.20M TLS	27-0056	
HB-DHW	Mooney M.20J Model 201	24-1579	N58152
HB-DHY	Mooney M.20S	30-0015	
HB-DHZ	Mooney M.20M TLS	27-0046	
HB-DIA	Mooney M.20J Model 205	24-3288	
HB-DIB	Mooney M.20M TLS	27-0078	I-SEVE
			N9124N
HB-DIC	Mooney M.20J Model 205	24-3240	D-ECZL
			N9139V
HB-DIE	Mooney M.20R Ovation	29-0015	
HB-DIF	Mooney M.20M TLS	27-0206	
HB-DIG	Mooney M.20J Model 205	24-3379	
HB-DIH	Mooney M.20J Model 205	24-3385	
HB-DIK	Mooney M.20J Model 205	24-3392	
HB-DIL	Mooney M.20R Ovation	29-0102	
HB-DIM	Mooney M.20MTLS	27-0202	N202VL
			OE-KGG
HB-DUH	Mooney M.20	1133	(N5270B)
HB-DUK	Mooney M.20A	1531	(N8353E)
HB-DUN	Bellanca 14-13-3 Cruisair Senior	1637	N6516N
HB-DUP	Mooney M.20A	1658	
HB-DUX	Luscombe 8A Silvaire	2835	NC71408
HB-DUZ	Gardan GY-80 Horizon 160	02	
HB-DVD	Gardan GY-80 Horizon 180	192	
HB-DVE	Gardan GY-80 Horizon 180	148	
HB-DVF	Mooney M.20F Executive	670298	N2904L
HB-DVG	Mooney M.20F Executive	670313	N2919L
HB-DVK	Mooney M.20F Executive	670348	N2989L
HB-DVM	Mooney M.20E Super 21	670003	
HB-DVN	Mooney M.20E Super 21	807	N5885Q
HB-DVR	Mooney M.20C Mark 21	2882	N78867
HB-DVV	Mooney M.20B Mark 21	1831	D-ECTO

Regn.	Type	C/n	Prev.Id.
HB-DVW	Luscombe 8A Silvaire	946	TU-TLS
			5Y-KDD
			VP-KDD
			K-?
			VP-KCW
			NC23023
HB-DVY	Mooney M.22	690004	N7729M
HB-DVZ	Mooney M.22	700001	N7734M
HB-DWC	Mooney M.20C Mark 21	3269	
HB-DWD	Mooney M.20E Super 21	1003	N2684W
HB-DWF	Luscombe 8A Silvaire	1230	N25354
			NC25354
HB-DWH	Mooney M.20C Mark 21	1205	(N7047V)
HB-DWI	Mooney M.20F Executive	22-1411	
HB-EAC	Meteor FL.55B	1119	I-FELH
HB-EAE	Meteor FL.55CM	1134	
HB-EAG	SAN Jodel DR.1050 Ambassadeur	100	
HB-EAI	CEA Jodel DR.1050 Ambassadeur	16	
HB-EBG	Beech G35 Bonanza	D-4523	
HB-EBK	CEA Jodel DR.1050 Ambassadeur	533	F-BLZE
HB-EBM	CEA Jodel DR.1051 Sicile	446	
HB-EBQ	Piaggio P.149E	348	
HB-EBS	CEA Jodel DR.1050 Ambassadeur	231	
HB-EBV	Piaggio P.149E	346	
HB-EBZ	CEA Jodel DR.1051 Sicile	426	
HB-ECD	Beech B35 Bonanza	D-2271	
HB-ECF	Beech A35 Bonanza	D-1827	
HB-ECG	Beech A35 Bonanza	D-1828	
HB-ECX	Beech B35 Bonanza	D-2656	
HB-EDB	Robin DR.300/180R Remorqueur	613	(D-EHDV)
			F-BSPP
HB-EDD	Morane-Saulnier MS.885 Super Rallye	56	
HB-EDE	Morane-Saulnier MS.880B Rallye Club	76	
HB-EDH	Morane-Saulnier MS.885 Super Rallye	43	
HB-EDK	Morane-Saulnier MS.880B Rallye Club	107	
HB-EDY	Morane-Saulnier MS.880B Rallye Club	207	
HB-EEI	CEA Jodel DR.1050 Ambassadeur	549	
HB-EEM	CEA Jodel DR.1050M Sicile	575	
HB-EEN	CEA Jodel DR.1050M1 Sicile Record	610	
HB-EEP	CEA Jodel DR.1051 Sicile	617	
HB-EEQ	SOCATA MS.880B Rallye-Club	1268	
HB-EER	Piaggio P.149E	350	
HB-EEV	CEA DR.250/160 Capitaine	27	
HB-EEW	CEA Jodel DR.1050 Ambassadeur	568	F-OCCZ
HB-EEX	CEA DR.250/160 Capitaine	31	
HB-EEZ	CEA DR.250/160 Capitaine	48	
HB-EFB	Beech F35 Bonanza	D-4132	
HB-EFH	Beech V35 Bonanza	D-8072	
HB-EFM	Beech V35 Bonanza	D-8414	
HB-EFP	CEA Jodel DR.1050 Ambassadeur	338	
HB-EFR	CEA Jodel DR.1051 Sicile	318	F-BKPA
HB-EFS	CEA DR.220 2+2	17	F-BOCK
HB-EFT	CEA Jodel DR.1050M1 Sicile Record	619	F-BMPX
HB-EFW	Piaggio FWP.149D	102	90+83
			AC+436
			JB+394
			(D-EKAG)
			AS+406
HB-EFX	Piaggio P.149D	266	91+82
			AC+417
			AS+417
HB-EFZ	Piaggio P.149D	321	92+24
			AC+425
			AS+472
HB-EGB	Beech C35 Bonanza	D-2761	
HB-EGC	Beech C35 Bonanza	D-2766	
HB-EGE	Beech A35 Bonanza	D-2045	
HB-EGF	Beech D35 Bonanza	D-3540	
HB-EGP	Beech H35 Bonanza	D-4930	
HB-EGS	Beech D35 Bonanza	D-3637	PH-NFF
HB-EGW	Beech K35 Bonanza	D-5912	D-EGWA
			HB-EGW
HB-EHB	Beech 35-C33 Debonair	CD-1085	
HB-EHF	Beech 35-C33A Debonair	CE-103	
HB-EHK	Beech V35B Bonanza	D-9330	D-EHKK

Regn.	Type	C/n	Prev.Id.
HB-EHL	Beech 35-F33 Bonanza	CD-1254	
HB-EHN(*)	Beech V35B Bonanza	D-9180	
HB-EHO	Beech 35-33 Debonair	CD-132	OE-DNE
HB-EHP	Beech 35-A33 Debonair	CD-344	I-ZEZE
			HB-EIO
HB-EHR	Beech V35B Bonanza	D-9439	
HB-EHS	Beech C23 Sundowner	M-1451	
HB-EHW	Beech C23 Sundowner	M-1571	
HB-EIF	Beech 35-33 Debonair	CD-211	
HB-EII	Beech F35 Bonanza	D-4019	N3353C
HB-EIQ	Piaggio P.149D	262	91+80
			AC+413
			AS+413
HB-EIT	Beech 35-A33 Debonair	CD-377	
HB-EIU	Beech 35-B33 Debonair	CD-438	
HB-EIX	Beech E35 Bonanza	D-3788	N7325B
HB-EIZ	Beech P35 Bonanza	D-7105	D-EEIZ
			HB-EIZ
HB-EJA(*)	Beech A36 Bonanza	E-1669	
HB-EJB	Beech V35 Bonanza	D-7978	D-EFTH
HB-EJD	Beech 77 Skipper	WA-136	
HB-EJE	Beech A36TC Bonanza	EA-118	
HB-EJH	Beech C23 Sundowner	M-2216	
HB-EJJ	Morane-Saulnier MS.505 Criquet	590	F-BCMQ
HB-EJM	Beech F33A Bonanza	CE-962	
HB-EJN	Beech V35B Bonanza	D-9907	D-EOLM
HB-EJP	Beech A36 Bonanza	E-951	D-EICH
			N4296S
HB-EJR	SOCATA TB-10 Tobago	370	
HB-EJV	Beech 35-C33A Debonair	CD-1028	OE-DYT
			D-EKVO
HB-EJW	Beech B36TC Bonanza	EA-292	N150CB
			N6398U
			YV-2305P
HB-EJX	Piaggio P.149D	070	D-EEIH
			90+53
			JA+390
HB-EKC	Aero 45S	51195	
HB-EKN	Beech S35 Bonanza	D-7675	I-FARE
			HB-EKN
HB-EKW	Beech 35-C33A Debonair	CE-57	
HB-EKX(*)	Beech 35-C33A Debonair	CE-78	
HB-ELD	Oberlerchner JOB 15-180/2	069	OE-DOA
HB-ELH	SIAI-Marchetti SF.260	106	
HB-ELI	Piper J-3C-90 Cub	13129	44-80833
HB-ELK	SIAI-Marchetti S.205-18/R	104	
HB-ELL	SIAI-Marchetti S.205-18/R	211	
HB-ELO	Piper J-3C-65 Cub	13237	45-4497
HB-ELP	SIAI-Marchetti S.205-20/R	231	
HB-ELT	SIAI-Marchetti S.205-20/R	237	
HB-ELX	SIAI-Marchetti S.205-22/R	383	
HB-EMI	Fairchild F.24W-41A Argus II	767	FZ827
			43-14803
HB-EML	SIAI-Marchetti SF.260	502	F-BSRV
			OO-LLA
			I-ALLA
HB-EMM	Partenavia P.66B Oscar 150	18	I-BIRT
HB-EMN	Robin DR.300/180R Remorqueur	544	
HB-EMP	Robin DR.300/180R Remorqueur	550	
HB-EMQ	Robin DR.300/180R Remorqueur	571	
HB-EMR	CEA DR.250/160 Capitaine	57	F-BNJS
HB-EMS	SAN Jodel DR.105A Ambassadeur	63	F-BIVN
HB-EMW	Robin HR.100/200B Royale	114	
HB-EMX	CEA DR.250/160 Capitaine	25	F-BMZV
HB-EMZ	CEA DR.221 Dauphin	79	F-BPCB
HB-ENA	Beech 23 Musketeer	M-12	
HB-ENK	Beech S35 Bonanza	D-7848	
HB-ENM	Beech A23-19 Musketeer Sport III	MB-118	
HB-ENP	Beech A23-19 Musketeer Sport III	MB-33	
HB-ENS	Beech A23-19 Musketeer Sport III	MB-35	
HB ENV	Beech A23-24 Musketeer Super III	MA-108	
HB-ENW	Beech A23-24 Musketeer Super III	MA-107	
HB-ENX	Beech A23-19 Musketeer Sport III	MB-141	
HB-EOF	Auster J/1 Autocrat	1981	
HB-EOP	Auster J/1 Autocrat (Lycoming)	1974	

Regn.	Type	C/n	Prev.Id.
HB-EOW	Auster Mk.5	1004	NJ611
HB-E..	Auster Mk.5	1753	G-ANHZ
			TW384
HB-EPG	Robin DR.300/180R Remorqueur	649	
HB-EPK	Partenavia P.64B Oscar 200	62	
HB-EPL	Partenavia P.66B Oscar 150	39	
HB-EPN	Ryan Navion A	881	F-BESJ
			N8881H
HB-EPS	S.A.I. KZ-VII Laerke	188	
HB-EQA	SOCATA MS.880B Rallye Club	1179	F-BPGZ
HB-EQB	Robin DR.400/180 Régent	1389	D-EJRZ
HB-EQC	Robin DR.400/180R Remorqueur	1028	D-EGPR
HB-EQD	Robin DR.400/180R Remorqueur	1564	
HB-EQE	Robin DR.400/180R Remorqueur	1464	
HB-EQG	Robin DR.400/180R Remorqueur	1476	
HB-EQI	Robin R.1180TD Aiglon	242	
HB-EQK	Robin HR.100/250TR	537	G-BFPG
			ZS-JSU
			F-ODCS
HB-EQL	Robin DR.400/180R Remorqueur	1529	F-GCUX
HB-EQM	Robin DR.300/180R Remorqueur	710	D-ELAR
HB-EQN	Robin DR.400/180R Remorqueur	1569	
HB-EQR	SOCATA TB-20 Trinidad	293	F-BNGQ
HB-EQV	Robin HR.100/250TR	550	OY-POD
HB-ERB	Erco 415C Ercoupe	4367	OO-EXA
HB-ERH	Erco 415C Ercoupe	1751	D-ELEN
			N99128
HB-ERK	SOCATA MS.893A Rallye Commodore 180	10933	
HB-ERM	SOCATA MS.893A Rallye Commodore 180	10939	
HB-ERO	Fairchild F.24R-46A Argus III	891	HB653
			43-14927
HB-ERP	SOCATA MS.883 Rallye 115	1364	
HB-ERQ	Robin DR.380 Prince	546	F-BSLM
HB-ERT	SOCATA MS.894A Minerva 220	11075	
HB-ERV	SOCATA MS.893A Rallye Commodore 180	10616	F-BNNO
HB-ESB	North American Navion 4	4-331	LR-AAU
HB-ESO	North American Navion 4	4-1361	OE-DYD
			HB-ESO
			N4361K
HB-ESR	Fuji FA-200-160 Aero Subaru	86	
HB-ESU	Fuji FA-200-180 Aero Subaru	192	
HB-ETD	Aeronca 7BCM Champion	3490	N84777
			NC84777
HB-ETF	Aeronca 7AC Champion	1792	OO-TWB
HB-ETI	Comte AC-4	15	CH-180
HB-ETM	SOCATA MS.894A Minerva 220	12096	
HB-ETN	Maule M-4-210 Rocket	1035	
HB-ETR	Maule M-4-210C Rocket	1033C	
HB-ETS	Maule M-4-220C Strata Rocket	2020C	
HB-ETX	Fuji FA-200-180AO Aero Subaru	246	
HB-ETY	SOCATA MS.894A Minerva 220	12089	F-BUNV
HB-EUD	Beagle A.61 Terrier 2	B.616	G-ASCE
			WE571
HB-EUG	CEA DR.221 Dauphin	99	F-BPCV
HB-EUI	Robin HR.100-200B Royal	129	D-EEDD
HB-EUK	CEA Jodel DR.1051M1 Sicile Record	609	F-BMPO
HB-EUL	Taylorcraft Plus D	176	LB317
HB-EUM	Robin HR.100-200D Royal	174	
HB-EUN	Robin DR.300/108 2+2	523	F-BSJM
HB-EUO	CEA Jodel DR.1050M1 Sicile Record	625	5A-CAA
			G-ATBR
HB-EUP	Robin DR.400/180R Remorqueur	780	
HB-EUQ	Robin DR.400/180R Remorqueur	786	
HB-EUV	Robin DR.400/180R Remorqueur	820	
HB-EUW	Robin DR.400/180R Remorqueur	855	
HB-EUX	CEA DR.340 Major	462	D-EERT
HB-EUZ	CEA DR.250/160 Capitaine	70	F-BNVI
HB-EVB	SIAT 223K-1 Flamingo	018	D-ENBP
HB-EVP	SIAI-Marchetti S.208	1-04	
HB-EVQ	Maule M-5-235C Lunar Rocket	7282C	
HB-EVT	SIAI-Marchetti SF.260	2-57	I-RAIB
HB-EVW	Procaer F.15 Picchio	05	I-LONI
HB-EVY	Maule M-5-235C Lunar Rocket	7302C	N56364
HB-EWE	Beech 23 Musketeer	M-504	OE-DMK
			D-ENXU
HB-EWF	Beech A23-24 Musketeer Super III	MA-313	
HB-EWG	Beech F33A Bonanza	CE-513	OE-DMN
			D-EBNP
HB-EWH	Beech F33A Bonanza	CE-844	
HB-EWM	Beech B24R Sierra	MC-237	
HB-EWP	SIAI-Marchetti SF.260	2-29	D-EBAA
HB-EWQ	SIAI-Marchetti SF.260C	636/46-002	I-APAB
HB-EWR	Beech F33A Bonanza	CE-609	
HB-EWS	SOCATA MS.893E Rallye 180GT Gaillard	12844	
HB-EWU	Beech A36 Bonanza	E-854	
HB-EWY	Sportavia-Pützer RS.180 Sportsman	6017	D-EFBJ
HB-EXC	Fuji FA-200-180 Aero Subaru	98	D-EMYV
HB-EXF	Robin HR.200/120 Acrobin	25	
HB-EXG	Robin DR.400/180 Régent	943	
HB-EXH	Robin HR.200/120 Acrobin	28	
HB-EXL	Robin DR.400/180R Remorqueur	959	
HB-EXQ	Robin DR.400/180R Remorqueur	1037	
HB-EXT	Robin DR.400/180R Remorqueur	1027	D-EGPQ
HB-EXU	Robin DR.400/180R Remorqueur	1199	
HB-EXV	CEA DR.250/160 Capitaine	68	F-BNJV
HB-EXW	Robin DR.400/180R Remorqueur	1257	
HB-EXX	Robin R.2160	124	
HB-EXY	Robin DR.400/180R Remorqueur	1227	
HB-EYD	SOCATA MS.893E Rallye 180GT Gaillard	12680	F-BXYZ
HB-EYK	SOCATA Rallye 235E Gabier	13114	
HB-EYN	Robin DR.400/180R Remorqueur	1306	
HB-EYO	Robin DR.400/180R Remorqueur	1372	
HB-EYP	Robin R.1180T	222	
HB-EYS	Robin DR.400/180R Remorqueur	1297	
HB-EYV	Maule M-5-235C Lunar Rocket	7300C	N56362
HB-EYX	SOCATA TB-10 Tobago	110	
HB-EYY	SOCATA TB-10 Tobago	111	
HB-EYZ	SOCATA TB-10 Tobago	183	
HB-EZG	PZL-104 Wilga 35A	86275	SP-WRF
HB-EZM	SOCATA TB-10 Tobago	103	
HB-EZN	SOCATA Rallye 180TS Galérien	3320	
HB-EZR	SOCATA TB-10 Tobago	129	
HB-EZS	Maule M-5-235C Lunar Rocket	7355C	
HB-EZW	SOCATA TB-10 Tobago	351	
HB-EZX	Robin DR.400/180R Remorqueur	1349	D-EEGE
HB-FCF	Pilatus PC-6/B1-H2 Turbo Porter	614	
HB-FCT	Pilatus PC-6/B2-H2 Turbo Porter	637	
HB-FDU	Pilatus PC-6/B1-H2 Turbo Porter	663	
HB-FEZ	Pilatus PC-6/B1-H2 Turbo Porter	699	
HB-FFA	Pilatus PC-6/B1-H2 Turbo Porter	700	
HB-FFI	Pilatus PC-6/B1-H2 Turbo Porter	671	
HB-FFV	Pilatus PC-6/B2-H2 Turbo Porter	817	9Q-CTH(2)
			HB-FFV
HB-FFW	Pilatus PC-6/B2-H2 Turbo Porter	735	
HB-FGI	Pilatus PC-6/B2-H2 Turbo Porter	810	
HB-FHZ	Pilatus PC-6/B2-H2 Turbo Porter	840	ZS-MTP
			HB-FHZ
HB-FIE	Pilatus PC-6/B2-H2 Turbo Porter	748	A40-AL
HB-FKC	Pilatus PC-6/B2-H4 Turbo Porter	844	
HB-FKF	Pilatus PC-6/B2-H4 Turbo Porter	815	G-OAPA
HB-FKH	Pilatus PC-6/B2-H4 Turbo Porter	865	
HB-FKJ	Pilatus PC-6/B2-H4 Turbo Porter (W/o 12.99)	895	
HB-FKL	Pilatus PC-6/B2-H4 Turbo Porter	867	
HB-FKM	Pilatus PC-6/B2-H4 Turbo Porter	873	
HB-FKO	Pilatus PC-6/B2-H4 Turbo Porter	874	V5-ODH
			HB-FKO
HB-FKP	Pilatus PC-6/B2-H4 Turbo Porter	877	
HB-FKR	Pilatus PC-6/B2-H4 Turbo Porter	872	
HB-FKT(*)	Pilatus PC-6/B2-H4 Turbo Porter	876	
HB-FKZ	Pilatus PC-6/B2-H4 Turbo Porter	892	
HB-FLA	Pilatus PC-6/B2-H4 Turbo Porter	905	
HB-FLB	Pilatus PC-6/B2-H4 Turbo Porter	906	
HB-FLD	Pilatus PC-6/B2-H4 Turbo Porter	913	
HB-FLE	Pilatus PC-6/B2-H4 Turbo Porter	912	
HB-FLG	Pilatus PC-6/B2-H4 Turbo Porter	910	
HB-FLH	Pilatus PC-6/B2-H4 Turbo Porter	918	
HB-FLI	Pilatus PC-6/B2-H4 Turbo Porter	893	F-GONE
HB-FLK	Pilatus PC-6/B2-H4 Turbo Porter	779	D-FACT
			N119SA
			LV-MAF

Regn.	Type	C/n	Prev.Id.
HB-FMB	Pilatus PC-6/B2-H4 Turbo Porter	932	
HB-FMC	Pilatus PC-6/B2-H4 Turbo Porter	938	
HB-FOB	Pilatus PC-XII	P-02	
HB-FOM	Pilatus PC-12/45	201	
HB-FON	Pilatus PC-12/45	213	
HB-FOO	Pilatus PC-12/45	290	
HB-FOP	Pilatus PC-12/45	291	
HB-FQI	Pilatus PC-12/45	294	
HB-FQO(2)	Pilatus PC-12/45	302	
HB-FQP	Pilatus PC-12/45	124	
HB-FQQ(2)	Pilatus PC-12/45	303	
HB-FQR(2)	Pilatus PC-12/45	304	
HB-FQS(2)	Pilatus PC-12/45	305	
HB-FQT(2)	Pilatus PC-12/45	306	
HB-FQU(2)	Pilatus PC-12/45	307	
HB-FQV(2)	Pilatus PC-12/45	308	
HB-FQW(2)	Pilatus PC-12/45	310	
HB-FRC	Pilatus PC-12/45	232	
HB-FRR	Pilatus PC-12/45 *(Reserved as F-GTTT)*	247	
HB-FSA	Pilatus PC-12/45	256	
HB-FSB	Pilatus PC-12/45	257	
HB-GAF	Beech C50 Twin Bonanza	CH-144	
HB-GBL	Beech 95 Travel Air	TD-222	N2043C
HB-GBS	Beech 95-B55 Baron	TC-564	I-ALGE
			HB-GBS
			N6845Q
HB-GCE	Beech 95 Travel Air	TD-216	N657Q
HB-GCG	Beech 95-55 Baron	TC-76	D-ICAX
			I-VICO
			HB-GOI
HB-GDA	Beech C90 King Air	LJ-996	N600SB
			N34TM
			N150TH
HB-GDL	Beech B200 Super King Air	BB-1079	
HB-GDS	Beech 95-B55 Baron	TC-850	5Y-AGT
			VQ-ZEG
			ZS-DVO
HB-GEA	Beech 95-55 Baron	TC-64	N1221Z
HB-GEC	Beech 95-B55 Baron	TC-1272	
HB-GEV	Beech 65-A90 King Air	LJ-215	D-IEVW
HB-GFA	Beech A60 Duke	P-172	
HB-GFF	Beech D95A Travel Air	TD-584	SE-EWT
			OH-BTA
HB-GGM	Beech 58P Baron	TJ-103	
HB-GGP	Beech 58P Baron	TJ-157	
HB-GGU	Beech 65-E90 King Air	LW-315	
HB-GHD	Beech 65-F90 King Air	LA-50	F-GCLS
HB-GHF(*)	Beech 200 Super King Air	BB-417	G-BFVZ
HB-GHG	Beech 95-B55 Baron	TC-1616	G-BBEM
HB-GHK	Rockwell Commander 695	96023	ZS-KZV
			(N9943S)
HB-GHN	Beech C90A King Air	LJ-1093	N70PJ
			HB-GHN
			D-IDSR
			N720DK
			N7204V
HB-GHO	Beech F90 King Air	LA-111	G-BIEZ
HB-GHS	Beech 200 Super King Air	BB-1039	N6572K
			(N69F)
			(N62828)
HB-GHV	Beech 300 Super King Air	FA-170	
HB-GIA	Beech 95-B55 Baron	TC-1825	N7220R
HB-GII	Beech 350C Super King Air	FN-1	
HB-GIL	Beech 200 Super King Air	BB-194	N502EB
			N300PH
			N200PH
HB-GIP	Beech 300 Super King Air	FA-202	
HB-GIT	Beech 300 Super King Air	FA-142	N987BT
			N3081Z
HB-GIX	Beech E95 Travel Air	TD-717	G-AWCW
HB-GJD	Beech 200C Super King Air	BL-7	F-GJBJ
			N6690E
HB-GJF(*)	Beech C90B King Air	LJ-1407	

Regn.	Type	C/n	Prev.Id.
HB-GJG	Beech E-18S	BA-328	N328N
			N621AA
			N729KB
			N561FD
			N5619D
HB-GJH	Beech C90 King Air	LJ-972	N18080
HB-GJI	Beech 200 Super King Air	BB-451	D-IBOW(3)
HB-GJJ	Beech B60 Duke	P-272	D-INMC
			N30MC
			N4470W
HB-GJK	Beech B60 Duke	P-274	D-INAR(2)
HB-GJL	Beech B300 Super King Air	FL-183	
HB-GJM	Beech 200 Super King Air	BB-255	N32KD
			N32KC
			N820DY
			N920DY
HB-GOD	Beech 95 Travel Air	TD-247	
HB-GPC	Beech 58P Baron	TJ-463	
HB-GPD	Beech 58P Baron	TJ-281	N369RS
			N4097M
			ZS-MMM
			N123CR
HB-GPF	Beech B300 Super King Air	FL-224	N2217C
HB-GPG	Beech 200 Super King Air	BB-307	N703HT
			N921S
			N23687
HB-G..	Beech B200 Super King Air	BB-531	SE-LDM
			VH-XFB
			N2657
			C-GBWO
			N2657
HB-HAB	Dornier Do.27H-2	2012	V-605
			HB-HAB
			V-605
HB-HAO	Pilatus PC-7 Turbo Trainer	101	
HB-HEC	FFA AS.202/15 Bravo	V-3	
HB-HEF	FFA AS.202/15 Bravo	002	
HB-HEG	FFA AS.202/15 Bravo	003	
HB-HEH	FFA AS.202/15 Bravo	004	
HB-HEI	FFA AS.202/15 Bravo	006	
HB-HEM	FFA AS.202/15 Bravo	007	
HB-HEO	FFA AS.202/15 Bravo	009	
HB-HEP	FFA AS.202/15 Bravo	010	
HB-HER	FFA AS.202/15 Bravo	011	
HB-HES	FFA AS.202/15 Bravo	012	
HB-HET	FFA AS.202/15 Bravo	014	
HB-HEW	FFA AS.202/15 Bravo	018	
HB-HEY	FFA AS.202/18 Bravo	015	
HB-HEZ	FFA AS.202/15 Bravo	019	
HB-HFD	FFA AS.202/18A Bravo	023	
HB-HFF	FFA AS.202/15-1 Bravo	107	
HB-HFH	FFA AS.202/15-1 Bravo	108	
HB-HFI	FFA AS.202/15-1 Bravo	109	
HB-HFJ	FFA AS.202/18A4 Bravo	243	
HB-HFK	FFA AS.202/15-1 Bravo	112	
HB-HFV	FFA AS.202/15-1 Bravo	127	
HB-HFW	FFA AS.202/15-1 Bravo	129	
HB-HFX	FFA AS.202/15-1 Bravo	124	
HB-HFY	FFA AS.202/18A-1 Bravo	135	
HB-HFZ	FFA AS.202/18A-2 Bravo	237	
HB-HGA	FFA AS.202/18A-1 Bravo	134	
HB-HGB	FFA AS.202/15-1 Bravo	130	
HB-HLA(5)	Pilatus PC-7 Mk II	601	
HB-HLB(5)	Pilatus PC-7 Mk II	602	
HB-HLC(5)	Pilatus PC-7 Mk II	603	
HB-HLD(5)	Pilatus PC-7 Mk II	604	
HB-HMR	Pilatus PC-7 Mk II	010	
HB-HMS	Pilatus PC-7 Mk II Plus	011	
HB-HOH	Dätwyler MD-3-160	001	
HB-HOJ	Dätwyler MD-3-160	002	
HB-HOO	Pilatus PC-7 Turbo Trainer	394	
HB-HOP	Junkers Ju 52/3mg4e	6610	A-703
	(c/n officially quoted as 3385, which was probably a Luftwaffe aircraft)		HB-HOP

Regn.	Type	C/n	Prev.Id.
HB-HOS	Junkers Ju 52/3mg4e	6580	A-701
			HB-HOS
			A-701
HB-HOT	Junkers Ju 52/3mg4e	6595	A-702
			HB-HOT
			A-702
HB-HOY	CASA 352A-3 (Junkers Ju 52/3m)	96	D-CIAK
			T.2B-165
HB-HPA	Pilatus PC-9 Turbo Trainer	001	
HB-HPE	Pilatus PC-9 Turbo Trainer	176	
HB-HRE(3)	Pilatus PC-9 Turbo Trainer	617	
HB-HRF(3)	Pilatus PC-9 Turbo Trainer	618	
HB-IAH	Dassault Falcon 900EX	28	F-WWFZ
HB-IAQ	Dassault Falcon 900EX	35	N2BD
			F-WWFJ
HB-IAW	Dassault Falcon 2000	16	F-WWMB
HB-IAX	Dassault Falcon 2000	33	F-WWME
HB-IAY	Dassault Falcon 2000	34	F-WWMF
HB-IAZ	Dassault Falcon 2000	30	F-WWMB
HB-IBH	Dassault Falcon 2000	42	F-WWMG
HB-IBX	Grumman G.1159C Gulfstream IVSP	1183	VR-BDC
			N476GA
HB-IDJ	Canadair CL.600-2B19 Regional Jet	7136	VP-CRJ
			VR-CRJ
HB-IEE	Boeing 757-23A	24527	HB-IHU
HB-IEJ	Grumman G.1159C Gulfstream IV	1148	N427GA
			JA8380
			N427GA
HB-IES(*)	Dassault Falcon 50	61	F-WZHI
HB-IGE	Boeing 747-357	22995	N221GE
			(HB-IGE)
HB-IGF	Boeing 747-357	22996	N221GF
			(HB-IGF)
HB-IHR	Boeing 757-2G5	29379	
HB-IHT	Boeing 767-35H	26387	EI-CJA
			S7-AAQ
			(I-AEJD)
HB-IHU	Boeing 767-35H	26388	EI-CJB
			S7-AAV
			(I-AEJE)
HB-IHX	Airbus A.320-214	942	F-WWIU
HB-IHY	Airbus A.320-214	947	F-WWIY
HB-IHZ	Airbus A.320-214	1026	F-WWDD
HB-IIB	Boeing 737-3M8	24024	(OO-LTE)
HB-IIE	Boeing 737-3Q8	26307	N721LF
			(HB-IIE)
HB-III	Boeing 737-33V	29338	G-EZYN
HB-IIJ	Boeing 737-33V	29342	G-EZYS
HB-IIN	Boeing 737-3L9	27924	OY-MAT
HB-IIO	Boeing 737-7AK	29865	N1786B
HB-IIP	Boeing 737-7AK	29866	
HB-IIQ	Boeing 737-7AK	29752	
HB-IJA	Airbus A.320-214	533	F-WWIF
HB-IJB	Airbus A.320-214	545	F-WWII
HB-IJC	Airbus A.320-214	548	F-WWIJ
HB-IJD	Airbus A.320-214	553	F-WWBI
HB-IJE	Airbus A.320-214	559	F-WWIP
HB-IJF	Airbus A.320-214	562	F-WWDQ
HB-IJG	Airbus A.320-214	566	F-WWIN
HB-IJH	Airbus A.320-214	574	F-WWDN
HB-IJI	Airbus A.320-214	577	F-WWDT
HB-IJJ	Airbus A.320-214	585	F-WWIV
HB-IJK	Airbus A.320-214	596	F-WWBH
HB-IJL	Airbus A.320-214	603	F-WWBK
HB-IJM	Airbus A.320-214	635	F-WWDD
HB-IJN	Airbus A.320-214	643	F-WWDI
HB-IJO	Airbus A.320-214	673	F-WWBF
HB-IJP	Airbus A.320-214	681	F-WWBH
HB-IJQ	Airbus A.320-214	701	F-WWDL
HB-IJR	Airbus A.320-214	703	F-WWDS
HB-IJS	Airbus A.320-214	782	F-WWDS
HB-IJT	Airbus A.320-214	870	F-WWBX
HB-IKN	McDonnell-Douglas DC-9-83	49951	G-GMJM
			N13627

Regn.	Type	C/n	Prev.Id.
HB-IKO	Comte AC-4	034	D-ELIS
			HB-IKO
			CH-262
HB-IKS	Canadair CL.600-2B16 Challenger	5042	C-FEUV
HB-IKT	Canadair CL.600-2B16 Challenger	5003	N778XX
			C-GDHP
HB-ILJ	Fokker F.27 Friendship 500	10596	F-SEBJ
			CN-CDC
			PH-FTX
			N334MV
			PH-FTX
			PH-EXM
HB-ILK(*)	Canadair CL.600-1A11 Challenger	3033	N601TJ
			C-GLXQ
HB-ILL	Canadair CL.600-2B16 Challenger	5373	C-GCVZ
HB-ILQ	Fokker F.27 Friendship 500	10389/10528	F-BPUI
			PH-FNM
HB-IMJ	Grumman Gulfstream V	517	N517GA
HB-IMY	Grumman G-1159C Gulfstream IV	1084	N448GA
HB-INR	McDonnell-Douglas DC-9-82	49277	
HB-INV	McDonnell-Douglas DC-9-81	49359	
HB-INW	McDonnell-Douglas DC-9-81	49569	
HB-INZ	McDonnell-Douglas DC-9-81	49572	
HB-IOA	Airbus A.321-111	517	D-AVZS
HB-IOB	Airbus A.321-111	519	D-AVZU
HB-IOC	Airbus A.321-111	520	D-AVZV
HB-IOD	Airbus A.321-111	522	D-AVZX
HB-IOE	Airbus A.321-111	535	D-AVZC
HB-IOF	Airbus A.321-111	541	D-AVZE
HB-IOG	Airbus A.321-111	642	D-AVZH
HB-IOH	Airbus A.321-111	664	D-AVZL
HB-IOI	Airbus A.321-111	827	D-AVZY
HB-IOJ	Airbus A.321-111	891	D-AVZJ
HB-IOK	Airbus A.321-111	987	D-AVZC
HB-IOL	Airbus A.321-111	1144	D-AVZE
HB-IPN	Airbus A.310-325	672	F-WWCD
HB-IPR	Airbus A.319-112	1018	D-AVYQ
HB-IPS	Airbus A.319-112	734	D-AVYZ
HB-IPT	Airbus A.319-112	727	D-AVYC
HB-IPU	Airbus A.319-112	713	D-AVYB
HB-IPV	Airbus A.319-112	578	F-WWTA
			D-AVYA
HB-IPW	Airbus A.319-112	588	D-AVYB
HB-IPX	Airbus A.319-112	612	D-AVYH
HB-IPY	Airbus A.319-112	621	D-AVYK
HB-IPZ	Airbus A.319-113	629	D-AVYR
HB-IQA	Airbus A.330-223	229	F-WWKS
HB-IQB	Airbus A.330-223	240	F-WWKZ
HB-IQC	Airbus A.330-223	249	F-WWKI
HB-IQD	Airbus A.330-223	253	F-WWKM
HB-IQE	Airbus A.330-223	255	F-WWKB
HB-IQF	Airbus A.330-223	262	F-WWKS
HB-IQG	Airbus A.330-223	275	F-WWKF
HB-IQH	Airbus A.330-223	288	F-WWKK
HB-IQI	Airbus A.330-223	291	F-WWKS
HB-IQJ	Airbus A.330-223	294	F-WWYJ
HB-IQK	Airbus A.330-223	299	F-WWYD
HB-IQL	Airbus A.330-223	305	F-WWYI
HB-IQM	Airbus A.330-223	308	F-WWYK
HB-IQN	Airbus A.330-223	312	F-WWYO
HB-ISB	Douglas DC-3C	4666	C-FTAS
			CF-TAS
			CF-CPW
			41 -18541
HB-ISC	Douglas DC-3C	9995	G-BMCR
			N88YA
			N88Y
			NC6K
			NC65266
			42-24133
HB-ISQ	Fokker F.27 Friendship 500	10447	F-BSUM
	(Rebuilt 1974 with new c/n 10506)		(PH-FPX)
HB-ISX	McDonnell-Douglas DC-9-81	49844	
HB-ISZ	McDonnell-Douglas DC-9-83	49930	
HB-ITX	Grumman G-1159C Gulfstream IV	1093	VR-BLC

Regn.	Type	C/n	Prev.Id.
HB-IUG	McDonnell-Douglas DC-9-81	53149	
HB-IUH	McDonnell-Douglas DC-9-81	53150	
HB-IUM	McDonnell-Douglas DC-9-83	49847	D-AGWC
			N62020
HB-IUN	McDonnell-Douglas DC-9-83	49769	D-ALLK
HB-IUO	McDonnell-Douglas DC-9-83	49857	D-ALLN
HB-IUP	McDonnell-Douglas DC-9-83	49856	D-ALLM
HB-IUR	Bombardier BD.700-1A10 Global Express	9013	C-GDXU
HB-IUW	Dassault Falcon 900	150	N335MC
			N150FJ
			F-WWFC
HB-IUX	Dassault Falcon 900EX	54	F-WWFY
HB-IUZ	Dassault Falcon 2000	74	F-WWMH
HB-IVL	Grumman Gulfstream V	513	N513GA
HB-IVM	Dassault Falcon 2000	55	F-WWMM
HB-IVN	Dassault Falcon 2000	61	F-WWME
HB-IVO	Dassault Falcon 2000	62	F-WWMF
HB-IVP	Canadair CL.600-2B16 Challenger	5369	C-GCQB
			(D-AZPP)
			C-GCQB
HB-IVQ	Fokker F.27 Friendship 500	10425	PH-FOZ
			G-BVZW
			9Q-CBU
			PH-FOZ
			VH-EWS
			F-BYAF
			OY-APA
			(OY-DKR)
			PH-FOZ
HB-IVR	Canadair CL.600-2B16 Challenger	5318	HB-IKQ
			C-FYYH
			C-GLXO
HB-IVS	Canadair CL.600-2B16 Challenger	5166	N601A
			9M-NSK
			N618CC
			C-GLWT
HB-IVT	Canadair CL.600-2B16 Challenger	5394	N604CH
			C-GLXS
HB-IVU	Canadair CL.600-2B19 Regional Jet	7176	N176SE
HB-IVV	Canadair CL.600-2B16 Challenger	5384	C-GDLH
HB-IVX	DHC-7-102	91	VP-CDZ
			SU-MAC
			LN-WFG
			C-GFUM
HB-IVY	DHC-7-102	74	C-GFFL
			A6-ADA
			N6541C
			C-GHRV
			N903HA
			C-GEWQ
HB-IVZ	Grumman Gulfstream V	577	N577GA
HB-IWA	McDonnell-Douglas MD-11	48443	N517MD
HB-IWB	McDonnell-Douglas MD-11	48444	
HB-IWC	McDonnell-Douglas MD-11	48445	
HB-IWD	McDonnell-Douglas MD-11	48446	
HB-IWE	McDonnell-Douglas MD-11	48447	
HB-IWG	McDonnell-Douglas MD-11	48452	
HB-IWH	McDonnell-Douglas MD-11	48453	
HB-IWI	McDonnell-Douglas MD-11	48454	
HB-IWK	McDonnell-Douglas MD-11	48455	
HB-IWL	McDonnell-Douglas MD-11	48456	
HB-IWM	McDonnell-Douglas MD-11	48457	
HB-IWN	McDonnell-Douglas MD-11	48539	
HB-IWO	McDonnell-Douglas MD-11	48540	
HB-IWP	McDonnell-Douglas MD-11	48634	
HB-IWQ	McDonnell-Douglas MD-11	48541	(HB-IWP)
HB-IWR	McDonnell-Douglas MD-11	48484	D-AERB
HB-IWS	McDonnell-Douglas MD-11P	48485	D-AERW
HB-IWT	McDonnell-Douglas MD-11P	48486	D-AERX
HB-IWU	McDonnell-Douglas MD-11	48538	D-AERZ
HB-IXF	BAe.146 Series RJ85	E-2226	G-CROS
HB-IXG	BAe.146 Series RJ85	E-2231	G-6-231
HB-IXH	BAe.146 Series RJ85	E-2233	G-6-233
			G-XARJ
			G-6-233

Regn.	Type	C/n	Prev.Id.
HB-IXK	BAe.146 Series RJ85	E-2235	G-XAIR
			G-6-235
HB-IXM	Avro 146-RJ100	E-3291	G-6-291
HB-IXN	Avro 146-RJ100	E-3286	G-6-286
HB-IXO	Avro 146-RJ100	E-3284	G-6-284
HB-IXP	Avro 146-RJ100	E-3283	G-6-283
HB-IXQ	Avro 146-RJ100	E-3282	G-6-282
HB-IXR	Avro 146-RJ100	E-3281	G-6-281
HB-IXS	Avro 146-RJ100	E-3280	G-6-280
HB-IXT	Avro 146-RJ100	E-3259	G-BVYS
HB-IXU	Avro 146-RJ100	E-3276	G-6-276
HB-IXV	Avro 146-RJ100	E-3274	G-6-274
HB-IXW	Avro 146-RJ100	E-3272	G-6-272
HB-IXX	Avro 146-RJ100	E-3262	G-6-262
HB-IYA	SAAB 2000	056	SE-056
HB-IYB	SAAB 2000	057	SE-057
HB-IYC	SAAB 2000	058	SE-058
HB-IYD	SAAB 2000	059	SE-059
HB-IYE	SAAB 2000	060	SE-060
HB-IYF	SAAB 2000	061	SE-061
HB-IYG	SAAB 2000	062	SE-062
HB-IYH	SAAB 2000	063	SE-063
HB-IYV	Avro 146-RJ100	E-3359	G-6-359
HB-IYX	Avro 146-RJ100	E-3357	G-6-357
HB-IYY	Avro 146-RJ100	E-3339	G-6-339
HB-IYZ	Avro 146-RJ100	E-3338	G-6-338
HB-IZA	SAAB 2000	004	SE-004
HB-IZB	SAAB 2000	005	SE-005
HB-IZC	SAAB 2000	006	SE-006
HB-IZD	SAAB 2000	007	(D-ADIA)
			SE-007
HB-IZE	SAAB 2000	008	(D-ADIB)
			SE-008
HB-IZF	SAAB 2000	009	SE-009
HB-IZG	SAAB 2000	010	SE-010
HB-IZH	SAAB 2000	011	SE-011
HB-IZI	SAAB 2000	012	SE-012
HB-IZJ	SAAB 2000	015	SE-015
HB-IZK	SAAB 2000	018	SE-018
HB-IZL	SAAB 2000	022	SE-022
HB-IZM	SAAB 2000	024	SE-024
HB-IZN	SAAB 2000	026	SE-026
HB-IZO	SAAB 2000	029	SE-029
HB-IZP	SAAB 2000	031	SE-031
HB-IZQ	SAAB 2000	032	SE-032
HB-IZR	SAAB 2000	033	SE-033
HB-IZS	SAAB 2000	035	SE-035
HB-IZT	SAAB 2000	036	SE-036
HB-IZU	SAAB 2000	037	SE-037
HB-IZV	SAAB 2000	038	SE-038
HB-IZW	SAAB 2000	039	SE-039
HB-IZX	SAAB 2000	041	SE-041
HB-IZY	SAAB 2000	047	SE-047
HB-IZZ	SAAB 2000	048	SE-048
HB-JAA	Embraer EMB.145 (Reservation)		
HB-JAB	Embraer EMB.145 (Reservation)		
HB-JAC	Embraer EMB.145 (Reservation)		
HB-JAD	Embraer EMB.145 (Reservation)		
HB-JAE	Embraer EMB.145 (Reservation)		
HB-JAF	Embraer EMB.145 (Reservation)		
HB-JAG	Embraer EMB.145 (Reservation)		
HB-JAH to -JAO Embraer EMB.145 reservations for Crossair in 2001.			
HB-KAB	SOCATA TB-20 Trinidad	377	
HB-KAC	Robin R.2160D	134	F-GBAU
HB-KAD	Robin DR.400/120D	1632	
HB-KAF	Robin R.1180TD Aiglon	283	
HB-KAH	SOCATA TB-20 Trinidad	425	
HB-KAJ	SOCATA TB-10 Tobago	431	
HB-KAL	CEA DR.250/160 Capitaine	47	F-BNJM
HB-KAM(2)	Beech F33A Bonanza	CE-1292	OY-BVO
HB-KAP	Robin DR.400/180R Remorqueur	1686	
HB-KAR	Robin DR.400/120D	1688	
HB-KAU	SOCATA TB-10 Tobago	515	
HB-KAW	Robin DR.400/180R Remorqueur	1707	
HB-KAY	SOCATA TB-20 Trinidad	578	

Regn.	Type	C/n	Prev.Id.
HB-KBC	Robin R.3000/120D	118	
HB-KBH	SOCATA TB-20 Trinidad	700	
HB-KBJ	CEA DR.250/160 Capitaine	42	F-BNJJ
HB-KBK	Robin DR.400/180R Remorqueur	779	F-BTZQ
HB-KBM	Robin DR.400/RP Remorqueur	1785	D-EAJB(2)
HB-KBP	Robin DR.400/180R Remorqueur	1769	
HB-KBS	SOCATA TB-20 Trinidad	774	
HB-KBV	Robin DR.400/120D Petit Prince	1819	
HB-KBX	Robin DR.400/120D Petit Prince	1843	
HB-KBY(*)	Maule M-7-235 Super Rocket	4059C	N54361
HB-KBZ	Beech F33A Bonanza	CE-1213	N3102V
HB-KCB	Maule MX.7-235 Star Rocket	10069C	N6124C
HB-KCC	CEA Jodel DR.1050 Ambassadeur	535	D-EBEI
			F-BLZF
HB-KCE	Maule MX.7-235 Star Rocket	10072C	N6117T
HB-KCF	Robin DR.400/160D Chevalier	1890	
HB-KCG	Robin DR.400/140B Major	1885	
HB-KCH	Robin DR.400/180S	1900	
HB-KCI	Christen A-1 Husky	1079	
HB-KCJ	Robin DR.400/140B Major	1916	
HB-KCK	Beech C33A Debonair	CE-67	D-ECMI
HB-KCL	Maule M-7-235 Super Rocket	4054C	N6108X
HB-KCO	Robin R.3000/160S	135	F-GGXN
HB-KCQ	Maule M-7-235 Super Rocket	4066C	N6130Q
HB-KCS	Robin DR.400/180R Remorqueur	1934	
HB-KCV	SOCATA TB-20 Trinidad	997	(D-EAOQ)
HB-KDA	Robin DR.400/140B Major	2124	
HB-KDB	Robin DR.400/140B Major	2125	
HB-KDC	SOCATA TB-200	1444	
HB-KDD	Robin DR.400/140B Major	2152	
HB-KDF	Maule MX.7-235 Star Rocket	10117C	
HB-KDG	Robin DR.400/140B Major	2156	
HB-KDH	Robin DR.400/140B Major	2161	
HB-KDK	Beech F33A Bonanza	CE-815	N2036M
HB-KDL	Maule MXT.7-180 Star Rocket	14054C	
HB-KDM	Maule M-7-235 Super Rocket	4110C	
HB-KDN	SOCATA TB-200 Tobago XL	1558	
HB-KDO	Robin DR.400/200R Remorqueur	2133	F-WZZX
			F-GLKN
HB-KDP	Robin DR.400/200R Remorqueur	2190	
HB-KDT	PZL-104 Wilga 80	CF14800563	I-MATE
			SP-TWT
HB-KDV	Robin DR.400/140B Major	2240	
HB-KDW	Robin DR.400/140B Major	2266	
HB-KDY	Robin DR.400/200R	2242	
HB-KEA	Robin DR.400/140B Major	2274	
HB-KEB	Robin DR.400/140B Major	2275	
HB-KEC	Robin R.3000/160	160	F-GLVM
HB-KED	Robin DR.400/180 Régent	2294	
HB-KEE(*)	Robin DR.400/180 Régent	2290	
HB-KEF	Aviat A-1 Husky	1292	
HB-KEG	Aviat A-1 Husky	1293X	
HB-KEH	Robin R.3000/160	169	
HB-KEI	SOCATA TBM-700	3	F-GJTS
HB-KEJ	Beech A36 Bonanza	E-2720	D-EJVD
			N56465
HB-KEK	Aviat A-1 Husky	1279	
HB-KEL	Robin R.3000/160	123	
HB-KEM	Tecnam P-92J Echo	003	
HB-KEN	Maule M-7-235C Super Rocket	25003C	N1025C
HB-KEO	Aviat A-1 Husky	1324	
HB-KEP	Robin R.2160	318	
HB-KEQ	Robin R.3000/160	146	F-GJZC
HB-KER	Maule MX.7-235 Star Rocket	10066C	HB-KDS
			(D-EVAM)
			N6112Y
HB-KET	CEA Jodel DR.250/160 Capitaine	76	D-ENVQ
			F-BNVQ
HB-KEV	Oberlerchner JOB 15-180/2	064	D-EKWK
			D-EHGE
			OE-CAW
HB-KEW	American 8KCAB Decathlon	763-96	N69BP
HB-KEX	Robin DR.400/140BDauphin 4	2407	
HB-KEY	Robin DR.500 Super Régent	0011	
HB-KEZ	Robin DR.500 Super Régent	0012	

Regn.	Type	C/n	Prev.Id.
HB-KFA	Robin HR.200/160	331	
HB-KFB	Robin HR.200/160	332	
HB-KFC	Maule MX.7-235 Star Rocket	10053C	N5668Y
HB-KFD	Robin DR.400/140B Dauphin 4	2431	
HB-KFE	Robin DR.500 Super Régent	15	
HB-KFF	Maule M-7-235CSuper Rocket	4048C	D-EHVW
			N6109V
HB-KFM	SOCATATB-20 Trinidad	1921	
HB-KIA	Beech A36 Bonanza	E-2522	N5664F
HB-KIE	Robin R.3000/160	144	
HB-KIF(*)	Maule MX.7-420	13002C	N9204Y
HB-KIJ	Robin R.3000/160	150	
HB-KIO	Maule MX.7-235 Star Rocket	10094C	
HB-KIP	Christen A-1 Husky	1153	
HB-KIQ	Maule MX.7-235 Star Rocket	10095C	
HB-KIS	Piaggio FWP.149D	089	D-EFON(2)
			90+71
			DA+390
			DA+498
			AS+498
HB-KIU	Piaggio FWP.149D	175	D-EFCT
			91+53
			DF+394
			AS+0..
			KB+141
HB-KIV	Christen A-1 Husky	1156	N9609G
HB-KIW	Beech F33A Bonanza	CE-1286	N1527P
HB-KIY	Robin DR.400/140B Major	2135	
HB-K..	Maule MX.7-235 Star Rocket	10053C	N5668Y
HB-LAD	Piper PA-30-160 Twin Comanche	30-434	N7423Y
HB-LBH	Piper PA-23-160 Apache	23-1625	N4144P
HB-LBI	LET L-200A Morava	170702	
HB-LBM	Cessna 310F	0147	N6847X
HB-LCY	Cessna 320C Skyknight	0054	N3054T
HB-LDE	Piper PA-30-160 Twin Comanche B	30-1121	N8014Y
HB-LDH	Piper PA-23-250 Aztec C	27-3305	N6098Y
HB-LDU	Piper PA-30-160 Twin Comanche B	30-1413	N8279Y
HB-LEH	Cessna 340	0075	D-ILEH
			HB-LEH
			N5940M
HB-LEL	Piper PA-34-200 Seneca	34-7350313	N56296
HB-LEM	Piper PA-34-200 Seneca	34-7350327	(4X-CAK)
			HB-LEM
			N56394
HB-LER	Piper PA-34-200 Seneca	34-7450014	N56645
HB-LEU	Piper PA-34-200 Seneca	34-7450076	N40751
HB-LFP	Cessna T.310P	0207	N5907M
HB-LFU	Cessna 401B	0048	N7948Q
HB-LGH	Cessna 310Q	0051	OY-AKD
HB-LGR	Cessna 340	0068	(I-MELE)
			N5916M
			(I-ALBB)
HB-LHA	Cessna 335 Crusader	0030	N2708D
HB-LHW	Cessna 402B	0926	N87130
HB-LID	DHC-6 Twin Otter 300	466	C-GPXO-X
HB-LIG	Piper PA-34-200T Seneca II	34-7670262	N6146J
HB-LIN	Piper PA-60 Aerostar 601P	61P-571-7963248	D-IEWF
			N8085J
HB-LIP	Piper PA-34-200T Seneca II	34-7770198	N2798Q
HB-LKA	Piper PA-34-200T Seneca II	34-7770049	N6945F
HB-LKB	Piper PA-34-200T Seneca II	34-7870183	N9364C
HB-LKF	Cessna 340A	0096	OE-FBS
			N1529G
HB-LKG	Gulfstream GA-7 Cougar	0089	N798GA
HB-LKL	Piper PA-23-250 Aztec F	27-7754153	N63836
HB-LKM	Piper PA-34-200T Seneca II	34-7970106	N3056K
HB-LKT	Piper PA-34-200T Seneca II	34-7970193	N2135Y
HB-LKU	Cessna 340A	0493	N6322X
HB-LLK	Piper PA-31T1 Cheyenne	31T-7904014	N401PT
HB-LLM	Piper PA-34-200T Seneca II	34-7970108	N2077N
HB-LLR	Piper PA-34-200T Seneca II	34-7970242	D-IMOC
			N29254
HB-LLW	Piper PA-34-200T Seneca II	34-8070170	N8176T
HB-LLX(*)	Piper PA-34-200T Seneca II	34-8070232	

Regn.	Type	C/n	Prev.Id.
HB-LMC	Piper PA-34-200 Seneca	34-7450008	OO-GPA / N56622
HB-LMF	Cessna 414A Chancellor	0296	OO-HFN / N26197
HB-LML	Piper PA-34-200 Seneca	34-7250341	N3094T
HB-LMM	Piper PA-34-200T Seneca II	34-8170029	N8292T
HB-LMN	Cessna 340A	0945	N2745D
HB-LMR	Cessna 421C Golden Eagle	0111	N421PB
HB-LMS	Piper PA-34-220T Seneca III	34-8133105	
HB-LNN	Cessna T.303 Crusader	00089	D-IJAA / N2289C
HB-LNX	Piper PA-31T2 Cheyenne	31T-8166050	N700XL
HB-LOA	Partenavia P.68B	35	D-GITE
HB-LOE	Cessna 425 Corsair	0016	ZS-KST / N6771L
HB-LOG	Piper PA-34-200T Seneca II	34-7870415	OE-FSS / N39677
HB-LOK	DHC-6 Twin Otter 300	658	D-IASL
HB-LOO	Piper PA-23-250 Aztec B	27-2250	F-GDAG / F-BMSF / F-OBZY / N5221Y
HB-LOR	Piper PA-23-250 Aztec E	27-7305192	D-IFGE / N40474
HB-LOT	Piper PA-31-310 Navajo B	31-7400981	D-IDRA / N7589L
HB-LPD	Cessna 421C Golden Eagle	0206	D-IOSR / N98486
HB-LPE	Piper PA-34-200 Seneca	34-7250293	D-GOBI / N1344T
HB-LPI	Cessna 340	0070	D-ICEF / (N5929M)
HB-LPK	Cessna 340A	0235	D-IEVO / N3925G
HB-LPT	Cessna 414A Chancellor	0054	N62PC / N6673C
HB-LPZ	Partenavia P.68B	44	OY-CEP / OH-PVC
HB-LQA	Gulfstream Commander 695	95069	VR-CBP / N14CX / N14CN / N982IS
HB-LQJ	Piper PA-34-200 Seneca	34-7350164	D-GNUT / EI-AWT / N55034
HB-LQK	Piper PA-44-180T Turbo Seminole	44-8207010	N81610
HB-LQM	Piper PA-34-220T Seneca III	3433129	
HB-LQP	Piper PA-31T1 Cheyenne 1	31T-8004044	OO-JMR / N180SW
HB-LQQ	Piper PA-34-200T Seneca II	34-7570281	N1544X
HB-LQR	Piper PA-34-220T Seneca III	3433130	
HB-LQT	Cessna 421C Golden Eagle	0337	F-GATY / (N37396)
HB-LQV	DHC-6 Twin Otter 300	643	5Y-LQV / HB-LQV / F-GFAJ / TT-EAI / Chad Army / 5A-DCY
HB-LQY	Piper PA-34-220T Seneca III	3448006	
HB-LQZ	Cessna 421C Golden Eagle	1237	N811SW / (N2724L)
HB-LRC	Piper PA-34-220T Seneca IV	3448026	N93KH
HB-LRD	Piper PA-34-220T Seneca III	3448015	N9208X
HB-LRF	DHC-6 Twin Otter 300	794	N794CC / N27278 / C-GESR
HB-LRL	Cessna 421B	0398	N205PV / N203PV / (N41010)
HB-LRN	DHC-6 Twin Otter 310	630	PK-YPE / HB-LRN / N636WJ / 3B-NAD
HB-LRO	DHC-6 Twin Otter 300	523	F-GKTO / TR-LAL / F-GAMR
HB-LRR	DHC-6 Twin Otter 300	505	5Y-KZT / N888WJ / F-ODGP / N505GH / J6-SLH / C-GPJA
HB-LRS	DHC-6 Twin Otter 300	502	5Y-UAU / N555WJ / F-ODGI / D-IASD / OY-ATB
HB-LRU	Piper PA-34-220T Seneca III	3433171	I-CGAQ / N91970
HB-LRV	Piper PA-31T Cheyenne	31T-7820017	N82222
HB-LRW	Cessna 421C Golden Eagle II	0633	N421KK / (N421JW) / N421KK / N47WK / N511HB / N88651
HB-LRY	Piper PA-34-220T Seneca III	3433132	N919IP
HB-LSC	Piper PA-34-220T Seneca III	34-8333004	N8240G
HB-LSD	Piper PA-34-200T Seneca II	34-7970098	D-ICTM / N2192K
HB-LSE	Cessna T.310R	0276	D-ICYF / (N5478J)
HB-LSG	Piper PA-60 Aerostar 602P	60-8265033	D-IGGG / N6901Z
HB-LSH	Cessna 340A	0477	F-GESV / D-IAWL / N6306X
HB-LSI	Cessna 421C Golden Eagle II	0140	N3913C
HB-LSK	STOL UC-1 Twin Bee	018	N9512U
HB-LSM	Cessna 340A	0701	N8515G
HB-LSO	Piper PA-34-200T Seneca IV	3448032	I-SELA / N9181G
HB-LSP	DHC-6 Twin Otter 300	288	VH-TGC / C-FCUS / N288Z / C-GFXJ / N288Z / N26TC / HC-ASJ
HB-LSQ	Cessna 340A	0661	N1891E / D-ICMF / N1661C / N1891E
HB-LSR	Cessna 340	0180	D-IGOL(2) / D-ICOP / N7641Q
HB-LSS	Piper PA-34-220T Seneca IV	3447015	N947G
HB-LST	Cessna 340A	0545	N4553N
HB-LSU	DHC-6 Twin Otter 300	277	VH-TGG / N8861
HB-LSV	DHC-6 Twin Otter 300	281	N616BA / VH-TGH / N8336
HB-LSW	Piper PA-34-220T Seneca V	3449111	
HB-LSY	DHC-6 Twin Otter 300	283	VH-TGI / (N616BA) / VH-TGI / N8339
HB-LTA	Piper PA-34-200T Seneca II	34-8070122	D-GASC / N8156C
HB-MIU	Bücker Bü.133 Jungmeister	29	U-82
HB-MIV	Bücker Bü.133 Jungmeister	32	OE-AKC / HB-MIV / U-85
HB-MIZ	Bücker Bü.133 Jungmeister	1003	U-53
HB-MKH	Bücker Bü.133 Jungmeister	40	U-93
HB-MKN	Bücker Bü.133 Jungmeister	23	U-76
HB-MKP	Bücker Bü.133 Jungmeister	28	U-81

Regn.	Type	C/n	Prev.Id.
HB-MKR	Bücker Bü.133 Jungmeister	WD29A	U-..
HB-MKZ	Bücker Bü.133 Jungmeister	09	U-62
HB-MSE	Aerotek Pitts S-2S	3001	
HB-MSF	Mudry CAP.20LS-200	8	OO-BNG
HB-MSH	Aviat Pitts S-2B	5238	I-PJTS
HB-MSK	Hirth Hi.27 Akrostar Mk.II	4009	D-EOIG
HB-MSL	Extra EA.300	05	D-ELET(2)
HB-MSN	Sukhoi SU-26MX	5205	CCCP5205
HB-MSO	Sukhoi SU-26M	0604	RA-0604
HB-MSS	Sukhoi SU-26M	0704	RA-0704
HB-MST	Sukhoi SU-26M	0602	RA-0602
HB-MSX	Extra EA.300/L	026	
HB-MSY	Extra EA.300/200	028	
HB-M..	Christen Eagle	L0026	N246RL
HB-NAB	Beagle B.121 Pup 150	043	G-35-043
HB-NBB	Slingsby T.67M Firefly	2003	G-SFTW
HB-NBC	Slingsby T.67M Firefly	2018	G-BMIT
HB-NCB	Rockwell Commander 112	165	(N1165J)
HB-NCE	Rockwell Commander 112TC	13018	
HB-NCF	Rockwell Commander 114	14034	
HB-NCG	Rockwell Commander 112TC	13074	
HB-NCH	Rockwell Commander 114	14050	
HB-NCI	Rockwell Commander 114	14208	N4878W
HB-NCK	Rockwell Commander 112	384	N1384J
HB-NCN	Rockwell Commander 112TCA	13151	N4620W
HB-NCO	Rockwell Commander 114	14183	D-EIXD / HB-NCO
HB-NCP	Rockwell Commander 114	14374	N5806N
HB-NCR	Rockwell Commander 112TCA	13251	N4675W
HB-NCS	Rockwell Commander 114	14356	N114TC / N5772N
HB-NCT	Rockwell Commander 112	442	N1442J
HB-NCU	Rockwell Commander 114A	14532	
HB-NCV	Rockwell Commander 114	14407	D-EJAB
HB-NCX	Rockwell Commander 112TC	13014	N1824J
HB-NCY(*)	Rockwell Commander 112A	188	OE-DYB
HB-NCZ	Rockwell Commander 114	14527	G-BGTE / N5910N
HB-NDA	Rockwell Commander 112TC	13070	D-EIXM / N4580W
HB-NDC	Commander Aircraft 114B	14550	N184A
HB-NDD	Commander Aircraft 114B	14587	N589CA / - ? - / N583CA
HB-NDE	Rockwell Commander 114	14150	OO-EJL / N4820W / VH-MCN / N4820W
HB-OAG	Piper J-3C-100 Cub	12897	44-80601
HB-OAP	Piper PA-12 Super Cruiser	12-2245	OO-XAZ / NC2239M
HB-OBF	Piper J-3C-85 Cub	13257	45-4517
HB-OBG	Piper J-3C-65 Cub	13231	45-4491
HB-OBL	Piper J-3C-65 Cub	12575	44-80279
HB-OBP	Piper J-3C-90 Cub	11709	43-30418
HB-OCI	Piper J-3C-65 Cub	12704	44-80408
HB-OCP	Piper J-3C-90 Cub	10937	43-29646
HB-OCR	Piper J-3C-90 Cub	11059	43-29768
HB-OCU	Piper J-3C-100 Cub	12842	44-80546
HB-ODC	Piper J-3C-90 Cub	12892	44-80596
HB-ODE	Piper J-3C-85 Cub	12866	44-80570
HB-ODH	Piper J-3C-90 Cub	13342	45-4602
HB-ODL	Piper PA-22-108 Colt	22-9336	D-EHRO
HB-ODN	Piper J-3C-65 Cub	10457	43-29166
HB-ODW	Piper J-3C-90 Cub	12542	HB-OEL / 44-80246
HB-ODX	Piper J-3C-65 Cub	13130	44-80834
HB-ODZ	Piper J-3C-90 Cub (original c/n 11651)	MDC-1049	43-30360
HB-OEI	Piper J-3C-90 Cub	11382	43-30091
HB-OEN	Piper J-3C-65 Cub	11842	44-79546
HB-OER	Piper J-3C-90 Cub	12595	44-80299
HB-OEY	Piper J-3C-90 Cub	12440	44-80144
HB-OFK	Piper J-3C-65 Cub	13131	44-80835
HB-OFP	Piper J-3C-90 Cub	12092	44-79796
HB-OFR	Piper J-3C-65 Cub	13285	45-4545
HB-OFV	Piper J-3C-65 Cub	13188	45-4448
HB-OFW	Piper J-3C-90 Cub	12273	44-79977
HB-OGA	Piper J-3C-90 Cub	13123	44-80827
HB-OGC	Piper J-3C-65 Cub	11486	43-30195
HB-OGG	Piper J-3C-65 Cub	10993	D-EHAL / G-AIYX / 43-29702
HB-OGX	Piper PA-18 Super Cub 95 (true c/n either 18-1623 or 18-1625)	f/n 18-1622	F-BRUL / ALAT
HB-OGZ	Piper J-3C-90 Cub	12648	44-80352
HB-OHC	Piper PA-28-180 Cherokee C	28-3623	F-OAYB / TJ-ADI / N9503J
HB-OHN	Piper PA-28-140 Cherokee C	28-26401	N5615U
HB-OHT	Piper PA-28-140 Cherokee C	28-26484	N5687U
HB-OHW	Piper PA-28R-200 Cherokee Arrow	28R-35609	N4968S
HB-OHX	Piper PA-28-180 Cherokee F	28-7105220	N11C
HB-OIA	Piper J-3C-90 Cub	12619	44-80323
HB-OIC	Piper J-3C-90 Cub	12372	SE-ATX / 44-80076
HB-OID	Piper PA-28R-200 Cherokee Arrow B	28R-7135226	N2389T
HB-OIH	Piper PA-28R-200 Cherokee Arrow II	28R-7235096	N4569T
HB-OIN	Piper J-3C-65 Cub	12119	44-79823
HB-OIO	Piper J-3C-90 Cub	11231	43-29940
HB-OIX	Rösgen EPR.301	1	
HB-OKB	Piper PA-18-150 Super Cub	18-8884	N8573Y
HB-OKD	Piper PA-28-180 Cherokee G	28-7205182	
HB-OKG	Piper PA-28-180 Cherokee G	28-7205176	N4848T
HB-OKH	Piper PA-28R-200 Cherokee Arrow II	28R-7235020	N4370T
HB-OKK	Piper PA-28R-200 Cherokee Arrow B	28R-7335009	N11C
HB-OKL	Piper PA-28R-200 Cherokee Arrow B	28R-7335008	N11C
HB-OKN	Piper J-3C-90 Cub	12333	OO-SAM / OO-AVO / 44-80037
HB-OKP	Piper J-3C-65 Cub	12810	F-BFQH / 44-80514
HB-OKR	Piper PA-28R-200 Cherokee Arrow B	28R-7435170	N41354 / N9501N
HB-OKT	Piper PA-28R-200 Cherokee Arrow B	28R-7435181	N9526N
HB-OKX	Piper PA-28-180 Cherokee Challenger	28-7305007	N11C
HB-OLH	Piper PA-28R-200 Cherokee Arrow II	28R-7535156	N33492
HB-OLP	Piper PA-28-140 Cherokee	28-20495	N6425W
HB-OLR	Piper PA-18-150 Super Cub	18-8278	N5514Y
HB-OLW	Piper PA-18-180 Super Cub	18-8337	N4171Z
HB-OLX	Piper PA-18-180 Super Cub	18-8446	N4222Z
HB-OMF	Piper PA-32-300 Cherokee Six	32-40148	N4097W
HB-OMN	Piper PA-28-140 Cherokee E	28-7225118	N15777
HB-OMP	Piper PA-28-140 Cherokee E	28-7225232	N15458 / (XB-ZIP)
HB-OMS	Piper PA-28-180 Cherokee Challenger	28-7305437	N11C
HB-OMV	Piper PA-18 Super Cub 95	18-6327	D-EDOK
HB-OMW	Piper PA-28-180 Cherokee Challenger	28-7305572	N9551N
HB-OMX	Piper PA-28-180 Cherokee Challenger	28-7305575	N9548N
HB-OMZ	Piper PA-28-151 Cherokee Warrior	28-7415283	N9553N
HB-ONA	Piper J-3C-100 Cub	12867	44-80571
HB-ONB	Piper J-3C-90 Cub	12063	44-79767
HB-ONC	Piper J-3C-90 Cub	12027	44-79731
HB-ONE	Piper J-3C-90 Cub	12661	44-80365
HB-ONG	Piper J-3C-90 Cub	13032	44-80736
HB-ONH	Piper J-3C-100 Cub	12519	44-80223
HB-ONM	Piper J-3C-90 Cub	12298	44-80002
HB-ONW	Piper J-3C-65 Cub	12144	D-ELRO / F-BFNM / F-OBAX / Fr.AF / 44-79848
HB-ONY	Piper J-3C-100 Cub	18601	N98414 / NC98414
HB-OOC	Piper PA-12 Super Cruiser	12-2306	NC2653M
HB-OOF	Piper PA-16 Clipper	16-502	
HB-OOP	Piper PA-22-135 Tri-Pacer	22-985	
HB-OPH	Piper PA-18-150 Super Cub	18-5517	N6982D
HB-OPL	Piper PA-22-150 Tri-Pacer	22-2865	N2504P
HB-OPP	Piper PA-18-150 Super Cub	18-5784	
HB-OPU	Piper PA-18-150 Super Cub	18-5938	

Regn.	Type	C/n	Prev.Id.
HB-OQA	Piper PA-18-150 Super Cub	18-5375	D-ECBX
HB-OQB	Piper PA-18-150 Super Cub	18-8991	(PT-IGG)
HB-OQE	Piper PA-28-180 Cherokee Archer	28-7405011	N9568N
HB-OQG	Piper PA-28-151 Cherokee Warrior	28-7415089	N9629N
HB-OQH	Piper PA-28R-200 Cherokee Arrow B	28R-7435230	N41941
HB-OQK	Piper PA-28-151 Cherokee Warrior	28-7415439	N9612N
HB-OQL	Piper PA-18 Super Cub 95	18-1613	(D-EOCG)
			ALAT
			51-15613
HB-OQN	Piper PA-28R-200 Cherokee Arrow B	28R-7435093	N54381
HB-OQO	Piper PA-28-235 Cherokee Pathfinder	28-7410096	N44559
HB-OQP	Piper PA-28-180 Cherokee Archer	28-7405119	N9557N
HB-OQR	Piper PA-28R-200 Cherokee Arrow II	28R-7535011	N9591N
HB-OQS	Piper PA-28-151 Cherokee Warrior	28-7515009	N9572N
HB-OQT	Piper PA-28-180 Cherokee Archer	28-7505016	N9593N
HB-OQU(*)	Piper PA-28-140 Cherokee Cruiser	28-7525061	N9625N
HB-OQV	Piper PA-28-151 Cherokee Warrior	28-7515204	N9507N
HB-OQW	Piper PA-28-181 Cherokee Archer II	28-7690049	N9640N
HB-OQY	Piper PA-28-140 Cherokee Cruiser	28-7525190	N9605N
HB-ORA	Piper PA-18-150 Super Cub	18-7049	
HB-ORH	Piper PA-18-150 Super Cub	18-7408	
HB-ORK	Piper PA-18-150 Super Cub	18-7035	D-ENAG
HB-ORL	Piper PA-18-150 Super Cub	18-5301	F-BBOM
			F-OBDM
HB-ORM	Piper PA-18-150 Super Cub	18-7478	
HB-ORN	Piper PA-18-150 Super Cub	18-7514	
HB-ORT	Piper PA-18-150 Super Cub	18-6433	D-ENAT
			N9068D
HB-ORV	Dätwyler/PA-18-150 Super Cub	MDC-1040	
HB-ORW	Dätwyler/PA-18-150 Super Cub	MDC-1041	
HB-ORY	Piper PA-18-180M Super Cub	18-4639	D-ENOL
HB-ORZ	Piper PA-18-180M Super Cub	18-7938	N4013Z
HB-OSK	Piper J-3C-90 Cub	13139	44-80843
HB-OSM	Piper J-3C-90 Cub	12252	44-79956
HB-OSW	Piper J-3C-65 Cub	13262	45-4522
HB-OSY	Piper J-3C-90 Cub	11805	D-ECYF
			(SL-ABD)
			HB-OUG
			43-30514
HB-OTB	Piper PA-24-180 Comanche	24-189	
HB-OTF	Piper PA-24-260 Comanche C	24-4915	D-EHGM
			N9410P
HB-OTG	Piper J-3C-100 Cub	11626	OO-FAB
			F-BDRQ
			F-OADH
			43-30335
HB-OTN	Piper PA-22-108 Colt	22-8221	
HB-OTR	Piper PA-22-150 Caribbean	22-7525	LN-BWE
HB-OTS	Piper PA-24-250 Comanche	24-2320	N7155P
HB-OTW	Piper PA-24-250 Comanche	24-2643	
HB-OUA	Piper J-3C-100 Cub	12809	44-80513
HB-OUD	Piper J-3C-90 Cub	11854	44-79558
HB-OUE	Piper J-3C-100 Cub	12315	44-80019
HB-OUN	Piper J-3C-100 Cub	12316	44-80020
HB-OUP	Piper J-3C-65 Cub	12530	44-80234
HB-OUR	Piper J-3C-100 Cub	10853	44-29562
HB-OUS	Piper J-3C-100 Cub	11502	43-30211
HB-OUV	Piper J-3C-90 Cub	11756	F-BFMP
			43-30465
HB-OVC	Piper PA-12 Super Cruiser	12-540	F-BFQZ
			OO-PDO
			OO-PDC
HB-OVE	Piper J-3C-90 Cub	12264	44-79968
HB-OVF	Piper J-3C-90 Cub	12492	F-BEGR
			NC74116
			44-80196
HB-OVH	Piper PA-28-160 Cherokee	28-554	N5472W
HB-OVR	Piper PA-24-250 Comanche	24-1595	N6478P
HB-OVS	Piper PA-24-250 Comanche	24-3251	N8039P
			(ZS-CWH)
HB-OVT	Piper PA-28-180 Cherokee B	28-1174	N7312W
HB-OVW	Piper PA-24-250 Comanche	24-3498	N8296P
HB-OVX	Piper PA-28-180 Cherokee B	28-1258	N7419W
HB-OWB	Piper PA-22-108 Colt	2-9565	N5726Z
HB-OWE	Piper PA-28-160 Cherokee B	28-1127	N5702W

Regn.	Type	C/n	Prev.Id.
HB-OWI	Piper PA-28-180 Cherokee B	28-795	N7042W
HB-OWL	Piper PA-28-180 Cherokee B	28-1514	N7571W
HB-OWM	Piper PA-28-180 Cherokee B	28-1689	N7750W
HB-OWO	Piper J-3C-90 Cub	12132	44-79836
HB-OWS	Piper J-3C-90 Cub	11379	D-ENIX
			PH-NAB
			43-30088
HB-OXD	Piper J-3C-90 Cub	G-215	N49625
	(Rebuilt Piper TG-8)		NC49625
			43-3223
HB-OXI	Piper J-3C-100 Cub	12896	F-BFQM
			HB-OGE
			44-80600
HB-OXL	Dätwyler/Piper J-3C-90 Cub	MDC-1039	
HB-OXR	Piper J-3C-100 Cub	12611	D-EMYT
			LX-ACL
			OO-VIR
			44-80315
HB-OXT	Piper J-3C-90 Cub (Rebuilt)	1 bis	F-PFQR
	(c/n also quoted as 9014 - this is the		42-36803
	original f/n thus true c/n is 8927)		
HB-OXY	Piper J-3C-100 Cub	13223	F-BDTO
	(c/n not confirmed - officially 12223)		45-4483
HB-OXZ	Piper J-3C-90 Cub	12986	F-BFMM
			HB-OGY
			44-80690
HB-OYB	Piper PA-18-150 Super Cub	18-1192	V-652
			KAB-102
			HB-OOM
HB-OYH	Piper PA-28-140 Cherokee	28-20959	N6821W
HB-OYI	Piper PA-28-140 Cherokee	28-21466	N11C
HB-OYK	Piper PA-18-150 Super Cub	18-4509	D-EBYL
			N2995P
HB-OYM	Piper PA-18-150 Super Cub	18-8324	N5750Y
HB-OYN	Piper PA-28-180 Cherokee C	28-3100	N9065J
HB-OYT	Piper PA-28-140 Cherokee	28-22577	N4228J
HB-OYW	Piper PA-28R-180 Cherokee Arrow	28R-30100	N3787T
HB-OYX	Piper PA-28R-180 Cherokee Arrow	28R-30065	N3756T
HB-OYZ	Piper PA-28R-180 Cherokee Arrow	28R-30014	N3710T
HB-OZB	Piper PA-28-140 Cherokee	28-24135	N1723J
HB-OZC	Piper PA-18 Super Cub 95	18-5598	D-EKAG
			OE-AEM
			2A-AR
HB-OZD	Piper PA-28-180 Cherokee D	28-4564	N5266L
HB-OZF	Piper PA-28-140 Cherokee	28-23088	N9631W
HB-OZG	Piper PA-28-140 Cherokee	28-21528	OO-DPD
			G-AVDD
			OE-DPD
			(OE-APD)
			N11C
HB-OZI	Piper PA-28R-180 Cherokee Arrow	28R-30769	N7425J
HB-OZK	Piper PA-28-180 Cherokee D	28-4702	N5393L
HB-OZP	Piper PA-28R-200 Cherokee Arrow	28R-35155	N9441N
HB-OZT	Piper PA-28-140 Cherokee B	28-26092	N98188
HB-OZU	Piper PA-28R-200 Cherokee Arrow	28R-35221	N9454N
HB-OZV	Piper PA-28-180 Cherokee D	28-4613	N5310L
HB-OZX	Piper PA-28R-200 Cherokee Arrow	28R-35319	N2982R
HB-PAB	Piper PA-28-161 Cherokee Warrior II	28-7816495	D-ELET
			N9564N
HB-PAD	Piper PA-28R-200 Cherokee Arrow B	28R-7435157	N41219
HB-PAE	Piper PA-28-180 Cherokee Archer	28-7505098	N9527N
HB-PAF	Piper PA-28-180 Cherokee Archer	28-7505200	N1047X
HB-PAI	Piper PA-18-150 Super Cub	18-7509081	N66804
HB-PAL	Piper PA-28R-200 Cherokee Arrow B	28R-7635125	N7975C
HB-PAO	Piper PA-32R-300 Lance	32R-7680253	N75062
HB-PAP	Piper PA-28-140 Cherokee Cruiser	28-7625115	N9514N
HB-PAR	Piper PA-18-180M Super Cub	18-7609050	N83278
HB-PAT	Piper PA-28-181 Cherokee Archer II	28-7690245	N9343K
HB-PAV	Piper PA-18-150 Super Cub	18-8055	V-654
HB-PAW	Piper PA-18-150 Super Cub	18-8192	V-655
HB-PAX	Piper PA-18-150 Super Cub	18-8193	V-656
HB-PAY	Piper PA-18-135 Super Cub	18-2548	D-ELNL
			ALAT
			52-6230

Regn.	Type	C/n	Prev.Id.
HB-PAZ	Piper PA-32-301T Turbo Saratoga	32-8024019	G-BSMC N8190Y
HB-PBA	Piper PA-18-150 Super Cub *(Quoted c/n is a spare fuselage number)*	18-4922	D-ENDE (D-EIOT) RBAF
HB-PBB	Piper PA-28-151 Cherokee Warrior	28-7415062	N54437
HB-PBE	Piper PA-28-181 Cherokee Archer II	28-7690349	N6134J
HB-PBF	Piper PA-28R-201 Cherokee Arrow	28R-7737012	N1764H
HB-PBH	Piper PA-28-181 Cherokee Archer II	28-7790151	N5995F
HB-PBK	Piper PA-32R-300 Lance	32R-7780141	N1174H
HB-PBO	Piper PA-28-235 Pathfinder	28-7710022	N3063Q
HB-PBP	Piper PA-28R-201T Turbo Cherokee Arrow III	28R-7703205	N38350
HB-PBS	Piper PA-28R-201T Turbo Cherokee Arrow III	28R-7703294	N40027
HB-PBV	Piper PA-28-181 Cherokee Archer II	28-7790562	N38552
HB-PBW	Piper PA-28-181 Cherokee Archer II	28-7790603	N38899
HB-PBX	Piper PA-28R-200 Cherokee Arrow	28R-7135207	D-ENOL N2266T
HB-PBY	Piper PA-28R-201 Arrow III	28R-7837144	N3963M
HB-PBZ	Piper PA-24-260 Comanche B	24-4766	5U-AAG F-OCLU N9298P
HB-PCA	Piper PA-28-181 Cherokee Archer II	28-7890230	N2138M
HB-PCB	Piper PA-28-181 Cherokee Archer II	28-7890389	N6989C
HB-PCC	Piper PA-28R-201 Turbo Arrow III	28R-7803321	N36329
HB-PCE	Piper PA-32-300 Cherokee Six	32-40332	F-BIEP F-OCLG N4035R
HB-PCH	Piper PA-28-161 Cherokee Warrior II	28-7816611	N36093
HB-PCI	Piper PA-28-180 Cherokee E	28-5745	D-EEFU N3648R
HB-PCM	Piper PA-18-150 Super Cub	18-7809037	N82964
HB-PCN	Piper PA-18-150 Super Cub	18-7809038	N82968
HB-PCS	Piper PA-38-112 Tomahawk	38-78A0520	N4411E
HB-PCU	Piper PA-32-300 Cherokee Six	32-7840097	N9382C
HB-PCV	Piper PA-28-140 Cherokee Cruiser	28-7725096	N9544N
HB-PCZ	Piper PA-28-181 Cherokee Archer II	28-7890529	N36763
HB-PDC	Piper PA-28R-201 Arrow IV	28R-7837269	N36212
HB-PDD	Piper PA-28-181 Cherokee Archer II	28-7890528	N36744
HB-PDH	Piper PA-28-181 Archer II	28-7990159	N2141D
HB-PDI	Piper PA-28-181 Archer II	28-7990338	N2088V
HB-PDL	Piper PA-18-150 Super Cub	18-7909016	N9750N
HB-PDS	Piper PA-28-236 Dakota	28-7911217	N2871Z
HB-PDU	Piper PA-28RT-201 Arrow IV	28R-7918201	N2887Y
HB-PDV	Piper PA-28-236 Dakota	28-7911246	N2920G
HB-PDW	Piper PA-28RT-201T Turbo Arrow IV	28R-7931169	N2221Z
HB-PDX	Piper PA-28RT-201T Turbo Arrow IV	28R-7931183	N28511
HB-PDZ	Piper PA-28-181 Archer II	28-7990402	N2156Z
HB-PEA	Piper PA-28-181 Archer II	28-7990350	
HB-PEC	Piper PA-28-236 Dakota	28-7911188	N29680
HB-PEH	Piper PA-28-181 Archer II	28-7990531	N2886Z
HB-PEJ	Piper PA-32R-301 Saratoga	3213007	G-YUCS G-BSOL N9130Z N9590N
HB-PEL	Piper PA-28RT-201 Arrow IV	28R-7918262	N8079B
HB-PEM	Piper PA-28-140 Cherokee	28-20920	D-EMHA N6790W
HB-PEN	Piper PA-28-236 Dakota	28-8011011	N9501N
HB-PEO	Piper PA-28RT-201 Arrow IV	28R-8018039	N8153H
HB-PER	Piper PA-28-181 Archer II	28-8090221	N8146R
HB-PES	Piper PA-32R-301 Saratoga	32R-8013042	N81437
HB-PEU	Piper PA-28RT-201T Turbo Arrow IV	28R-8131019	N8287X
HB-PEW	Piper PA-28-181 Archer II	28-8190005	
HB-PEX	Piper PA-28-161 Warrior II	28-8016295	N8181W
HB-PEY	Piper PA-28-161 Warrior II	28-8016323	N82112
HB-PEZ	Piper PA-28-236 Dakota	28-8011091	N81682
HB-PFA	Piper PA-28-181 Archer II	28-8090159	N8129M
HB-PFE	Piper PA-28-181 Archer II	28-8090314	N82173
HB-PFK	Piper PA-18-150 Super Cub	18-8009059	N9767N
HB-PFP	Piper PA-32RT-300 Lance	32R-7885243	N78LD N39750
HB-PFS	Piper PA-28-181 Archer II	28-8190083	N82895
HB-PFW	Piper PA-25-235 Pawnee D	25-8056047	N90819
HB-PFY	Piper PA-32-301T Turbo Saratoga	32-8124004	N83166
HB-PFZ	Piper PA-28-236 Dakota	28-8111033	N8308L
HB-PGA	Piper PA-32R-301 Saratoga	32R-8113045	
HB-PGB	Piper PA-28-181 Archer II	28-8190142	
HB-PGC	Piper PA-28-181 Archer II	28-8190172	
HB-PGE	Piper PA-28-181 Archer II	28-8190204	
HB-PGF	Piper PA-28RT-201T Turbo Arrow IV	28R-8131121	
HB-PGG	Piper PA-28-161 Warrior II	28-8116236	
HB-PGL	Piper PA-38-112 Tomahawk	38-82A0011	
HB-PGM	Piper PA-28-181 Archer II	28-8190245	N8392A
HB-PGN	Piper PA-28-161 Warrior II	28-8216134	
HB-PGP	Piper PA-28-236 Dakota	28-8211030	
HB-PGR	Piper PA-28RT-201T Turbo Arrow IV	28R-8231045	
HB-PGS	Piper PA-28-181 Archer II	28-8290113	
HB-PGU	Piper PA-38-112 Tomahawk	38-82A0104	
HB-PGX	Piper PA-28-181 Archer II	28-8290121	
HB-PGY	Piper PA-28-236 Dakota	28-8311009	
HB-PGZ	Piper PA-28-236 Dakota	28-8211036	
HB-PHB	Piper PA-28-181 Archer II	28-8190208	D-EEJT N83666
HB-PHC	Piper PA-28-181 Archer II	28-8290168	
HB-PHD	Piper PA-28-161 Warrior II	28-8016246	D-EGWL N9615N
HB-PHE	Piper PA-38-112 Tomahawk *(Wfu)*	38-80A0067	D-ECIZ N9721N
HB-PHG	Piper PA-28-181 Archer II	28-8190221	D-EFXP N8380H
HB-PHH	Piper PA-28-161 Warrior II	28-8316034	
HB-PHL	Piper PA-28-161 Warrior II	28-8116222	D-EBKC N9537N N8383S
HB-PHM	Piper PA-28-181 Archer II	28-8390038	
HB-PHO	Piper PA-28-181 Archer II	28-8390030	
HB-PHP	Piper PA-18-125 Super Cub	18-7901	(D-ELIY) EL-AEB
HB-PHR	Piper PA-28-181 Archer II	28-8190141	D-EIFP N83235
HB-PHT	Piper PA-28-181 Archer II	28-7990564	OY-BRZ
HB-PHU	Piper PA-28-181 Archer II	28-8490010	N4359N
HB-PHV	Piper PA-28-161 Warrior II	28-8416082	N4329J
HB-PHW	Piper PA-28-236 Dakota	28-7911212	OY-BRW
HB-PHX	Piper PA-18-180M Super Cub	18-8431	(F-GBEE) 5R-MEC N4212Z
HB-PHZ	Piper PA-18-150 Super Cub	18-8009039	D-EMII N2320P
HB-PIB	Piper PA-28-161 Warrior II	28-8416104	N4341Y
HB-PIC	Piper PA-18-150 Super Cub	18-8309025	N91293
HB-PID	Piper PA-28-181 Archer II	28-8490084	N4365U
HB-PIG	Piper PA-28R-201 Arrow IV	28R-7837261	OE-DUG N31991
HB-PIJ	Piper PA-18-135 Super Cub	18-4036	G-BLFB (G-AOSG) OO-ALH (OO-LVV) EI-291 I-EIVT MM542436 54-2436
HB-PIK	Piper PA-28R-201T Turbo Arrow III	28R-7803343	D-EKTP N36803
HB-PIL	Piper PA-28-181 Cherokee Archer II	28-7790190	9V-BHJ N9538N
HB-PIM	Piper PA-28-161 Warrior II	28-8216114	D-EFFJ N9629N
HB-PIN	Piper PA-28RT-201 Arrow IV	28R-8018057	D-EIHU N9086Z
HB-PIR	Piper PA-28-181 Archer II	28-8690048	N9514N
HB-PIT	Piper PA-28RT-201T Turbo Arrow IV	28R-8031047	OY-GKF
HB-PIU	Piper PA-46-310P Malibu	46-8608047	
HB-PIV	Piper PA-28-181 Archer II	28-8190002	D-EFSP N8247C
HB-PIX	Piper PA-28RT-201 Arrow IV	28R-7918100	D-EFKI N2187Y
HB-PIZ	Piper PA-32R-301 Saratoga	32R-8513007	N9539N

Regn.	Type	C/n	Prev.Id.
HB-PKC	Piper PA-46-310P Malibu	46-8608033	N9296M
HB-PKD	Piper PA-46-310P Malibu	46-8608028	N9282Y
HB-PKE	Piper PA-28-181 Archer II	2890087	D-ELLT
			N9149Z
HB-PKF	Piper PA-28-236 Dakota	2811004	N9110R
HB-PKG	Piper PA-28-181 Archer II	2890008	N9106Z
HB-PKH	Piper PA-28RT-201T Turbo Arrow IV	28R-8231048	N8205H
HB-PKI	Piper PA-18-150 Super Cub	18-7692	D-EDFE
HB-PKK	Piper PA-28-181 Archer II	28-8690012	N90831
HB-PKL	Piper PA-28-181 Archer II	2890031	N9124N
HB-PKM	Piper PA-28-181 Archer II	2890026	N9217T
HB-PKN	Piper PA-28-181 Archer II	2890028	N9104F
HB-PKP	Piper PA-46-310P Malibu	46-8408022	G-SOFY
			N910LE
			N4336P
HB-PKR	Piper PA-28-181 Cherokee Archer II	28-7890544	D-EDES(3)
			N39624
HB-PKS	Piper PA-46-350P Malibu	4636180	
HB-PKT	Piper PA-28RT-201T Turbo Arrow IV	28R-8031129	N8235W
HB-PKU	Piper PA-32RT-300T Lance	32R-7887046	G-WROY
			G-WRAY
			OY-BRD
HB-PKV	Piper PA-28R-201T Turbo Arrow IV	28R-8331039	G-BSRS
			ZS-LGJ
			N4307U
HB-PKW	Piper PA-24-260 Comanche C	24-4959	N9452P
HB-PKX	Piper PA-28RT-201T Turbo Arrow IV	28R-8331032	G-BNIG
			N4299S
HB-PLA	Piper PA-28-236 Dakota	28-7911109	N3017R
HB-PLC	Piper PA-28RT-201T Turbo Arrow IV	28R-8231056	N8216Q
HB-PLD	Piper PA-46-310P Malibu	4608123	
HB-PLE	Piper PA-46-310P Malibu	4608121	
HB-PLF	Piper PA-28-236 Dakota	2811017	N9136N
HB-PLG	Piper PA-18-150 Super Cub	18-7949	I-MAMJ
HB-PLI	Piper PA-28-181 Archer II	2890063	
HB-PLJ	Piper PA-28-181 Archer II	2890061	N9136B
HB-PLL	Piper PA-28-161 Warrior II	2816057	
HB-PLO	Piper PA-24-250 Comanche	24-269	F-BBFV
			F-DAFV
			N10F
HB-PLP	Piper PA-28-181 Archer II	2890074	
HB-PLQ	Piper PA-18-150 Super Cub	1809112	N4159Z
HB-PLR	Piper PA-28-181 Archer II	2890094	
HB-PLU	Piper PA-28-161 Warrior II	2816065	
HB-PLV	Piper PA-28RT-201T Turbo Arrow IV	28R-8131080	N83423
HB-PLW	Piper PA-28-181 Archer II	2890085	
HB-PLY	Piper PA-28-181 Archer II	2890095	
HB-PLZ	Piper PA-28-181 Archer II	2890099	
HB-PMB	Piper PA-28R-201T Cherokee Arrow III	28R-7703114	N3565Q
HB-PMC	Piper PA-28-161 Warrior II	2816077	
HB-PMD	Piper PA-28-181 Archer II	2890097	(HB-PLH)
HB-PME	Piper PA-28-161 Cadet	2841110	
HB-PMF	Piper PA-28-161 Warrior II	2816078	
HB-PMG	Piper PA-28-181 Archer II	2890109	
HB-PMH	Piper PA-28-181 Archer II	2890112	
HB-PMI	Piper PA-28-161 Cadet	2841111	
HB-PMJ	Piper PA-28-236 Dakota	2811027	
HB-PMK	Piper PA-28-181 Archer II	2890130	
HB-PML	Piper PA-28-161 Warrior II	2816094	
HB-PMM	Piper PA-18-150 Super Cub	1809052	
HB-PMN	Piper PA-18-150 Super Cub	1809053	
HB-PMP	Piper PA-28-236 Dakota	2811030	
HB-PMR	Piper PA-28-181 Archer II	2890131	
HB-PMS	Piper PA-28R-201T Turbo Arrow III	28R-7803212	N6238C
HB-PMT	Piper PA-28-181 Archer II	2890151	
HB-PMU	Piper PA-32RT-300T Turbo Lance	32R-7887073	N36735
HB-PMV	Piper PA-28R-201T Turbo Cherokee Arrow III		
		28R-7703231	D-EKJW
			N38503
HB-PMX	Piper PA-28-151 Cherokee Warrior	28-7415228	D-EHRH
			N9537N
HB-PMY	Piper PA-28-181 Warrior II	2890191	
HB-PMZ	Piper PA-28-181 Archer II	28-7990548	N2910G
HB-PNA	Piper PA-28-181 Archer II	2890185	
HB-PNB	Piper PA-28-181 Archer III	2890218	

Regn.	Type	C/n	Prev.Id.
HB-PNC	Piper PA-28-181 Archer III	2843004	
HB-PND	Piper PA-28-181 Archer III	2843006	
HB-PNG	Piper PA-28-161 Warrior II	2816109	
HB-PNH	Piper PA-46-350P Malibu Mirage	4636003	
HB-PNI	Piper PA-28RT-201T Turbo Arrow IV	28R-8431018	N4349D
			N9574N
HB-PNJ	Piper PA-28-181 Archer III	2843025	
HB-PNL	Piper PA-28-161 Warrior II	2816108	
HB-PNM	Piper PA-28-161 Warrior II	28-8616046	N7TY
			C-FUNY
			N9507N
HB-PNN	Piper PA-28-161 Warrior II	2816103	(HB-PNG)
HB-PNP	Piper PA-28RT-201T Turbo Arrow IV	28R-8131037	D-EANB
			N8304T
HB-PNR	Piper PA-28-161 Cadet	2841080	D-EFCF
			N9166Z
HB-PNT	Piper PA-28RT-201T Turbo Arrow IV	28R-8431031	G-BOGJ
			N4376E
HB-PNU	Piper PA-18-150 Super Cub	18-7883	D-ENSU
			N8019P
HB-PNV	Piper PA-25-235 Pawnee D	25-8056042	I-SLAM
			N9770N
HB-PNW	Piper PA-32R-301 Saratoga SP	3213053	
HB-PNX	Piper PA-32R-301T Turbo Saratoga SP	32R-8029040	N3579S
			SE-KKL
			N3579S
HB-PNZ	Piper PA-24-260 Comanche C	24-4934	F-BRUO
			N9426P
HB-POB	Piper PA-28R-201T Turbo Cherokee Arrow III		
		28R-7703245	N38571
HB-POC	Piper PA-28-161 Cadet	2841291	N9200J
HB-POD	Piper PA-18-180M Super Cub	18-7409045	I-FOSS
HB-POE	Piper PA-28-161 Cadet	2841296	N9207Z
HB-POF	Piper PA-28-161 Cadet	2841294	N9204N
HB-POG	Piper PA-18-150 Super Cub	18-2538	D-ELNK
			ALAT
			52-6220
HB-POI	Piper PA-28-236 Dakota	28-8311025	N4314A
HB-POJ	Piper PA-28-236 Dakota	28-8411030	N4370G
HB-POK	Piper PA-28R-201T Arrow IV	2803005	F-GIGM
			N9178N
HB-POL	Piper PA-28-181 Archer II	28-8490016	N4326M
HB-PON	Piper PA-24-260 Comanche C	24-4868	N9368P
HB-POP	Piper PA-46-350P Malibu Mirage	4622077	N9185B
HB-POQ	Piper J-3C-65 Cub	17650	OE-AAS
			N70638
			NC70638
HB-POR	Piper PA-28-236 Dakota	28-8011056	N8089Y
HB-POU	Piper PA-18-180 Super Cub	18-5655	D-EIRG
			(SE-...)
			PH-LUB
			N7189D
HB-POV	Piper PA-28-161 Warrior II	28-8316106	N4314K
HB-POW	Piper PA-28-181 Archer II	2890158	N91892
			(OH-PBM)
			(SE-KMI)
HB-POX	Piper PA-28-181 Archer II	2890159	SE-KMK
HB-POY	Piper PA-46-350P Malibu Mirage	4622090	N836AJ
HB-POZ	Piper PA-18-150 Super Cub	18-8877	F-BTCO
			N8480Y
HB-PPB	Piper PA-28RT-201T Turbo Arrow IV	28R-7931278	N700CT
			N2963Q
HB-PPD	Piper PA-24-260 Comanche C	24-5016	D-EDAS
			N9498P
HB-PPF	Piper PA-28-161 Warrior III	2842011	
HB-PPG	Piper PA-28-161 Warrior III	2842012	
HB-PPH	Piper PA-46-350P Malibu Mirage	4636045	
HB-PPI	Piper PA-28-181 Archer III	2843045	
HB-PPJ	Piper PA-18-150 Super Cub	18-5342	I-EAEW
			D-EAEW
			ALAT
HB-PPK	Piper PA-28-181 Archer III	2843084	
HB-PPL	Piper PA-18-150 Super Cub	18-7299	F-GERI
			F-OBOJ
HB-PPM	Piper PA-28-181 Archer III	2843095	

Regn.	Type	C/n	Prev.Id.
HB-PPN	Piper PA-28-181 Archer III	2843140	N9509N
HB-PPO	Piper PA-28-161 Warrior III	2842032	N9518N
HB-PPR	Piper PA-28R-201 Arrow	2844018	N9518N
HB-PPS	Piper PA-28-181 Archer III	2843259	N9519N
HB-PPT	Piper PA-28-181 Archer II	2890163	D-ETAM
			N9224D
			(SE-KMF)
HB-PPU	Piper PA-46-350P Malibu Mirage	4636227	N4140S
HB-RAI	Dewoitine D.26	276	U-284
HB-RAJ	CCF-4/North American Harvard IV	CCF4-384	I-RYGA
			51-17202
HB-RAL	MDC-Trailer	MDC-1038	
	(Built from PA-18 parts by Dätwyler)		
HB-RAM	Pilatus P.2-06	64	U-144
HB-RAN	Morane-Saulnier MS.733 Alcyon	134	F-BNED
			Fr.Mil
HB-RAO	Morane-Saulnier MS.317	329	F-BCBI
HB-RAP	Pilatus P.2-06	75	U-155
HB-RAR	Pilatus P.2-06	56	U-136
HB-RAV	Pilatus P.2-06	48	U-128
HB-RAW	Pilatus P.2-06	49	U-129
HB-RAX	Pilatus P.2-05	23	U-103
HB-RAY	Pilatus P.2-05	35	U-115
HB-RAZ	Pilatus P.2-05	46	U-126
HB-RBC	Pilatus P.2-05	42	U-122
HB-RBG	Boeing Stearman E75	75-5345	N68489
			42-17182
HB-RBI	EKW C-3605	327	C-547
HB-RBK	Pilatus P.3-03	327-9	A-810
HB-RBN	Pilatus P.3-03	330-12	A-813
HB-RBP	Pilatus P.3-05	473-22	A-835
HB-RBR	Pilatus P.3-05	508-57	A-870
HB-RBT	Pilatus P.3-05	504-53	A-866
HB-RBU	Pilatus P.3-05	484-33	A-846
HB-RBV	Pilatus P.3-05	468-17	A-830
HB-RBX	Pilatus P.3-05	493-42	A-855
HB-RBY	Pilatus P.3-05	510-59	A-872
HB-RCC	Pilatus P.3-05	465-14	A-827
HB-RCD	Pilatus P.3-05	505-54	G-BUKM
			A-867
HB-RCE	Pilatus P.3-05	457-6	A-819
HB-RCF	D-3801 (Morane-Saulnier MS.406C)	unkn	J-143
	(Composite rebuild also using parts from J-276)		
HB-RCG	Pilatus P.3-05	483-32	A-845
HB-RCH	Pilatus P.3-05	456-5	A-818
HB-RCI	Pilatus P.3-05	502-51	A-864
HB-RCJ	Pilatus P.3-05	467-16	A-829
HB-RCK	Pilatus P.3-05	452-1	A-814
HB-RCL	Pilatus P.3-05	511-60	A-873
HB-RCO	Pilatus P.3-05	486-35	A-848
HB-RCP	Noorduyn AT-16 Harvard IIB	14A-868	G-BAFM
			PH-SKL
			B-104
			FS728
			43-15269
HB-RCQ	Pilatus P.3-05	453-2	A-815
HB-RCS	Pilatus P.3-05	490-39	A-852
HB-RCT	North American T-28B Trojan	200-337	N391W
			BuA138266
HB-RCV	Bleriot XI Replica	1	
HB-RCX	Yakovlev YAK-18A	607	F-AZFK
			EAF: ....
HB-RVA	de Havilland DH.112 Venom FB.50	840	J-1630
HB-RVC	de Havilland DH.112 Venom FB.50	841	J-1631
HB-RVE	de Havilland DH.100 Vampire FB.6	993	J-1082
HB-RVF	de Havilland DH.115 Vampire T.55	868	U-1208
HB-RVH	de Havilland DH.100 Vampire FB.6	612	J-1103
HB-RVI	de Havilland DH.115 Vampire T.55	DHP.44352	U-1235
HB-RVJ	de Havilland DH.115 Vampire T.55	988	U-1228
HB-RVK	de Havilland DH.115 Vampire T.55	DH.37	U-1233
HB-RVN	de Havilland DH.100 Vampire FB.6	706	J-1197
HB-RVP	Hawker Hunter T.Mk.68	HABL-003221	J-4205
	(Identity unconfirmed - c/n quoted		G-6-412
	officially as " 41HR/003206")		Fv.34086
			G-9-62

Regn.	Type	C/n	Prev.Id.
HB-RVQ	Hawker Hunter F.Mk.58	41H-697451	J-4084
HB-RVR	Hawker Hunter T.Mk.68	41HR/670803X	J-420 .
HB-RVT	Hawker Hunter F.Mk.58	41H-697447	J-4080
HB-RVU	Hawker Hunter F.Mk.58	41H-697453	J-4086
HB-RXA	Bristol 171B Sycamore Mk.52	13483	D-HELM
			78+25
			GD+102
			LB+102
			CD+090
			BD+178
			G-18-156
HB-RXB	Bristol 171B Sycamore Mk.52	13475	D-HALD
	(Painted as "XG544")		78+17
			GD+112
			WE+545
			SC+206
			AS+
			CA+328
			G-18-148
HB-SAC	Gardan GY-20/1 Minicab	RHR-1	
HB-SAE	Jodel D.9 Bébé	AB-11	D-EHAX
HB-SAF	Jodel D.9 Bébé	501	
HB-SAG	Gardan GY-20 Minicab	V-11	F-BEYG
HB-SAN	Mudry CAP.10B	147	
HB-SAO	Mudry CAP.10B	123	
HB-SAP	Mudry CAP.10B	186	F-WZCG
HB-SAS	Mudry CAP.10B	182	
HB-SAV	Mudry CAP.10B	185	F-GDTE
HB-SAW	Mudry CAP.10B	209	
HB-SAX	Mudry CAP.10B	246	
HB-SAY	Mudry CAP.10B	96	F-BXHZ
HB-SBC	Mudry CAP.231EX	05	F-GKKG
			F-WGZE
HB-SBD	Mudry CAP.10B	268	
HB-SCB	Robin ATL	74	
HB-SCD	Robin ATL	107	
HB-SCF	Calair CA-25 Skyfox	CA25007	
HB-SCG	Skyfox CA25N Gazelle	CA25N027	
HB-SCL	HOAC DV-20 Katana	20046	
HB-SCM	HOAC DV-20 Katana	20074	
HB-SCN	HOAC DV-20 Katana	20124	
HB-SCO	HOAC DV-20 Katana	20115	
HB-SCP	HOAC DV-20 Katana	20077	
HB-SCR	HOAC DV-20 Katana	20136	
HB-SCS	HOAC DV-20 Katana	20131	
HB-SCT	HOAC DV-20 Katana	20112	
HB-SCU	HOAC DV-20 Katana	20143	
HB-SCV	Diamond DA.20-A1 Katana	10101	
HB-SCW	Diamond DA.20-A1 Katana	10138	
HB-SCX	Diamond DA.20-A1 Katana	10142	
HB-SCY	Diamond DA.20-A1 Katana	10264	
HB-SCZ	Diamond DA.20-A1 Katana	10298	N298DA
HB-SEE	Binder CP.301S Smaragd	115	
HB-SEF	Binder CP.301S Smaragd	116	D-EDRI
HB-SEH	SAN Jodel D.140C Mousquetaire III	50	F-BHQV
			F-OBQV
HB-SEL	Binder CP.301S Smaragd	004	
HB-SEW	CEA Jodel DR.1050 Ambassadeur	223	F-BKGE
HB-SEX	Erla 5A	14	D-ENAL
			D-YBIT
HB-SEY	Wassmer Jodel D.120 Paris-Nice	154	D-EJIZ
HB-SEZ	SAN Jodel D.117 Grand Tourisme	801	F-BIOM
HB-SFA	SAN Jodel D.140E Mousquetaire IV	187	F-BOPD
HB-SFB	SAN Jodel D.140E Mousquetaire IV	176	F-BNIQ
HB-SFC	SAN Jodel D.140C Mousquetaire III	127	F-BMBL
HB-SFD	SAN Jodel D.140C Mousquetaire III	167	F-BNIE
HB-SFE	SAN Jodel D.140C Mousquetaire III	160	F-BMFU
HB-SFF	SAN Jodel D.140C Mousquetaire III	19	D-EIZD
			F-BIZD
HB-SFG	SAN Jodel D.140R Abeille	505	OO-VVM
HB-SFH	SAN Jodel D.140C Mousquetaire III	130	D-EHBG
			F-BMBN
HB-SFI	SAN Jodel D.140R Abeille	525	F-BOPM
HB-SOA	Gardan GY-201 Minicab (Wfu?)	A-213	
HB-SOG	Jodel D.112 Club	490	

Regn.	Type	C/n	Prev.Id.
HB-SOH	Jodel D.11	489	
HB-SOI	Druine D.31 Turbulent	00	
HB-SOK	Piel CP.301A Emeraude	74	
HB-SOU	Jodel D.112 Club	unkn	
HB-SPH	Gardan GY-201 Minicab	05	F-BFLK
HB-SPI	Brügger Kolibri MB-2	2	
HB-SPM	Potez 600 Sauterelle	3998	F-PIIN
			F-AOET
HB-SPN	Slingsby T.66 Nipper Mk.III	S.132/1708	G-AXLJ
HB-SPO	SAN Jodel D.117 Grand Tourisme	605	F-BIBB
HB-SPP	SIPA S.903	48	F-BGAX
HB-SPQ	Slingsby T.66 Nipper Mk.III	S.118/1625	G-AWDB
HB-SPS	Jodel D.112 Club	350	F-BHKT
HB-SPT	SIPA S.903	88	F-BGHM
HB-SPU	SIPA S.903	76	F-BGHA
HB-SPX	Wassmer Jodel D.120 Paris-Nice	211	F-BKJM
HB-SUD	Jodel D.11	399	
HB-SUF	Jodel D.112 Club	163	
HB-SUG	Gardan GY-201 Minicab	unkn	
HB-SUH	Jodel D.11	286	
HB-SUI	Gardan GY-20 Minicab	A126	
HB-SUK	Gardan GY-201 Minicab	210	
HB-SUL	Jodel D.11	172	
HB-SUM	Gardan GY-201 Minicab	A211	
HB-SUN	Jodel D.9 Bébé	73	
HB-SUT	Gardan GY-201 Minicab	212/1	
HB-SUU	Jodel D.112 Club	316	
HB-SUV	Jodel D.11	487-5	
HB-SUX	Gardan GY-201 Minicab	1	
HB-SUY	Jodel D.11	315-24	
HB-SVB	Druine D.31 Turbulent	287	
HB-SVL	Jodel D.112 Club	459	TS-ABC
			F-PHFF
HB-SVM	Uetz Jodel U.2V	22	
HB-SVT	Uetz Jodel U.2V	23	
HB-SVV	Wassmer Jodel D.112 Club	1121	F-BKJO
HB-SVX	SAN Jodel D.117A Grand Tourisme	889	
	(c/n is probably wrong as 889 was D.112 F-BIXK)		
HB-TAP	Mraz Sokol M.1C	218	F-BCSU
HB-TBD	Uetz Marabu	01	
HB-TBU	Uetz U4M Pelikan	7303	
HB-TBV	Uetz U3M Pelikan	25	
HB-TBX	Uetz U4M Pelikan	05	
HB-TBY	Uetz U4M Pelikan	27	
HB-TBZ	Uetz U4M Pelikan	29	
HB-TCA	Orlican L-40 Meta-Sokol	150410	D-EHOL
HB-TCB	Zlin Z.326 Trenér Master	902	F-BMQX
HB-TCC	Zlin Z.326 Trenér Master	925	F-BORV
HB-TCD	Zlin Z.143L	0022	
HB-TCE	Zlin Z.143L	0006	
HB-TCG	Zlin Z526F Trenér Master	1238/26	I-GIRE
HB-TCH	Zlin Z.143L	0029	
HB-TRG	Zlin Z.526F Trenér Master	1232	YR-ZLR
HB-TRJ	Zlin Z.526F Trenér Master	1287	YR-ZLW
HB-TRQ	Zlin Z.526ASM Akrobat Special	1027	OK-WXB
HB-TRS	Stinson 108-3 Voyager	108-4419	F-BBSV
			HB-TRH
			N6419M
HB-TUG	DHC-1 Chipmunk 22	C1/0731	WP847
HB-TUM	OGMA/DHC-1 Chipmunk 20	OGMA-62	OO-NPO
			FAP1372
HB-UAD	Praga E-114 Air Baby	122	F-BCSQ
HB-UAF	Praga E-114M Air Baby	119	F-BCSN
HB-UAL	Champion 7GCB Challenger	40	
HB-UAO	Champion 7FC Tri-Traveller	446	
HB-UAW	Champion 7ECA Citabria	238	
HB-UBC	de Havilland DH.82A Tiger Moth	3956	G-AOUX
			N6652
HB-UBK	Klemm Kl.35D	1918	D-EJUL
			SE-BGB
			Fv5029
HB-UBN	American AA-1A Trainer	0166	N9266L
HB-UBP	American AA-1A Trainer	0167	N9267L
HB-UBS	American AA-1A Trainer	0353	
HB-UBT	American AA-1A Trainer	0354	
HB-UBV	Grumman-American AA-5 Traveler	0036	N5836L
HB-UBW	Grumman-American AA-5 Traveler	0035	N5835L
HB-UCA	Grumman-American AA-5 Traveler	0581	N9581L
HB-UCC	Grumman-American AA-5 Traveler	0540	N9540L
HB-UCD	Grumman-American AA-5 Traveler	0541	(N9541L)
HB-UCE	Grumman-American AA-5A Cheetah	0054	
HB-UCF(*)	Grumman-American AA-5B Tiger	0170	
HB-UCH	Grumman-American AA-5B Tiger	0465	
HB-UCL	Grumman-American AA-5B Tiger	0904	
HB-UCM	Grumman-American AA-5B Tiger	0924	
HB-UCO	Grumman-American AA-5B Tiger	1078	
HB-UCR	Grumman-American AA-5B Tiger	1101	OO-RTL
			(OO-HRU)
			(N4524L)
HB-UCT	Gyroflug SC-01 Speed Canard	S-16	
HB-UCU	Gyroflug SC-01B Speed Canard	S-27	D-EAND(2)
HB-UCV	Gyroflug SC-01B Speed Canard	S-33	(D-EAMR)
HB-UCW	Grumman-American AA-5B Tiger	1027	D-EEJW
			(D-EAZG)
			N4517E
HB-UCX	de Havilland DH.82A Tiger Moth	83683	D-EHAL(2)
			(D-EAKP)
			D-EKAL(1)
			G-ANGD
			T7213
HB-UCY	Gyroflug SC-01B-160 Speed Canard	S-34	
HB-UCZ	Gyroflug SC-01B-160 Speed Canard	S-35	
HB-UDA	American AG-5B Tiger	10135	SP-FYC
HB-UDB	CASA I-131E Jungmann	2147	E3B-...
HB-UDE	CASA I-131E Jungmann	2194	E3B-...
HB-UEA	Bölkow BO.209 Monsun	103	(D-EBOF)
HB-UEB	Bölkow BO.209 Monsun	124	(D-EFJB)
HB-UEC	Bölkow BO.209 Monsun	51	(D-EBJK)
HB-UEG	Bölkow BO.209 Monsun	195	(D-EAIK)
HB-UGA	Grob G.115	8011	(D-EGVV)
HB-UGB	Grob G.115	8020	(D-EGVV)
HB-UGC	Grob G.115	8021	(D-EGVV)
HB-UGD	Grob G.115	8023	(D-EGVV)
HB-UGE	Grob G.115A	8026	(D-EGVV)
HB-UGF	Grob G.115A	8037	(D-EGVV)
HB-UOD	Laverda F.8L Falco IV	402	D-ELXE
HB-UOE	Laverda F.8L Falco IV	410	OY-DKH
HB-UOG	Aeromere F.8L Falco	230	G-AZAY
			D-EFAK
HB-UOK	Aviamilano F.8L Falco I	115	I-DARE
HB-UPD	Bölkow BO.208C Junior	584	D-EJMO
HB-UPF	Bölkow BO.208C Junior	637	(D-EGFE)
HB-UPH	Bölkow BO.208C Junior	676	(D-EGZJ)
HB-UPM	de Havilland DH.82A Tiger Moth	DHNZ-135R	G-BJLI
			ZK-ATM
			NZ1455
HB-UPP	de Havilland DH.82A Tiger Moth	1000	G-BCRD
			N17565
			VH-FBR
			A17-565
HB-UPR	SNCAN/ Stampe SV.4A	662	F-BDNG
HB-UPS	SNCAN/ Stampe SV.4A	243	OO-EFD
			F-BCKC
HB-UPZ	Waco YMF (F5C)	F5C-055	
HB-URD	Bücker Bü.131 Jungmann	33	A-24
HB-URF	Bücker Bü.131 Jungmann	47	A-36
HB-URH	Bücker Bü.131 Jungmann	61	A-49
HB-URM	Bücker Bü.131 Jungmann	60	A 48
HB-USD	Bücker Bü. APM 131-150 Jungmann	65	A-52
HB-UTH	Bücker Bü. APM 131-150 Jungmann	51	OE-AKH
			HB-UTH
			A-40
HB-UTN	Bücker Bü.131 Jungmann	87	A-74
HB-UUA	Bücker Bü. APM 131-150 Jungmann	8	A-1
			HB-UTE
			A-1
HB-UUC	Bücker Bü.131 Jungmann	13	A-6
HB-UUD	Bücker Bü. APM 131-150 Jungmann	16	A-9
HB-UUE	Bücker Bü. APM 131-150 Jungmann	24	A-15
HB-UUF	Bücker Bü.131 Jungmann	71	A-58

Regn.	Type	C/n	Prev.Id.
HB-UUI	Bücker Bü.APM 131-150 Jungmann *(c/n officially quoted as 94)*	95	A-82 HB-USM A-82
HB-UUL	Bücker Bü. APM 131-150 Jungmann	29	A-20
HB-UUM	Bücker Bü. APM 131-150 Jungmann	31	A-22 HB-UFI A-22
HB-UUN	Bücker Bü. APM 131-150 Jungmann	41	A-30
HB-UUO	Bücker Bü. APM 131-150 Jungmann	42	A-31
HB-UUP	Bücker Bü. APM 131-150 Jungmann *(c/n officially quoted as 59)*	50	G-BHGZ HB-UUP A-39 HB-UTF A-39
HB-UUR	Bücker Bü.131 Jungmann	73	A-60
HB-UUS	Bücker Bü. APM 131-150 Jungmann	79	A-66
HB-UUT	Bücker Bü.131 Jungmann	81	A-68
HB-UUU	Bücker Bü. APM 131-150 Jungmann	84	A-71
HB-UUV	Bücker Bü. APM 131-150 Jungmann	18	A-11
HB-UUW	Bücker Bü. APM 131-150 Jungmann	11	A-4
HB-UUY	Bücker Bü. APM 131-150 Jungmann	10	A-3
HB-UVB	Bücker Bü. APM 131-150 Jungmann	39	A-28
HB-UVC	Bücker Bü.131 Jungmann *(c/n officially quoted as 53)*	66	A-53 HB-HEL
HB-UVE	Bücker Bü. APM 131-150 Jungmann	69	A-56
HB-UVF	Bücker Bü. APM 131-150 Jungmann	93	A-80
HB-UVG	Bücker Bü.131 Jungmann	30	A-21
HB-UVH	CASA I-131E Jungmann	2152	
HB-UVI	CASA I-131E Jungmann	2178	D-EEEQ E3B-562
HB-UVK	CASA I-131E Jungmann	2115	I-FERT E3B-...
HB-UVM	CASA I-131E Jungmann	unkn	E3B-484
HB-UVP	CASA I-131E Jungmann	"466"	E3B-466
HB-UVZ	Bücker Bü.131 Jungmann	43	A-32
HB-UXL	Bölkow BO.207	208	(D-EHUM)
HB-UXN	Bölkow BO.208C Junior	513	D-ENCU
HB-UXW	Bölkow BO.208C Junior	594	(D-EKDO)
HB-VCN(2)	North American NA265-65 Sabreliner 65	645-32	N303A N97RE (XC-DUF) N98630
HB-VGS	Cessna 550 Citation II	0183	
HB-VHV	BAe.125 Series 800B	258153	G-5-627
HB-VIA	Mitsubishi MU-300 Diamond	A.087SA	N487DM
HB-VIF	Gates Learjet 36A	36A-057	
HB-VIK	BAe.125 Series 800B	258091	G-5-560
HB-VIL	BAe.125 Series 800B	258097	G-5-567
HB-VIO	Cessna 551 Citation II	0205	N342DA N3951Z XA-KIQ N999AU N88732
HB-VIS	Cessna 550 Citation II	0447	(N447CJ) N12482
HB-VIT	Cessna 550 Citation II	0197	N44FC (N30F) N6798Z
HB-VJB	Cessna 501 Citation 1/SP	0067	VR-BLW HB-VJB D-IGMB SE-DEO N2959A
HB-VJI	Gates Learjet 31	31-011	N3803G
HB-VJJ	Gates Learjet 35A	35A-649	N10870
HB-VJK	Gates Learjet 35A	35A-651	
HB-VJL	Gates Learjet 35A	35A-653	
HB-VJV	Dassault Falcon 20D	237/476	VR-BKH VR-CBT N4227Y D-CITY (D-CALM) (D-CHCH) F-WPXF
HB-VKB	Cessna 525 CitationJet	0037	N1820E
HB-VKE	Dassault Falcon 10	7	D-CASH HB-VKE I-LUBE HB-VDE F-BXAG VR-BFF F-WJMN
HB-VKI	Bombardier Learjet 60	60-019	N40366
HB-VKK	Cessna 500 Citation	0178	I-FBCK D-IKFJ N178CC
HB-VKO	Dassault Falcon 20F-5	257	F-GKDD F-GJPI C-GNTL N300CC N781W N4425F F-WMKH
HB-VKP	Cessna 550 Citation II	0622	N826EW N326EW (N1255J)
HB-VKW	BAe.125 Series 800B	258246	N387H G-5-782
HB-VLA	HS.125 Series 700B	257031	N89TJ G-5-701 G-BFSP D-CBAE G-5-701 G-BFSP G-PRMC G-BFSP
HB-VLE	Cessna 500 Citation	0313	N313BA XA-SDS XB-DYF XA-KUJ N76GT (N5313J)
HB-VLF	BAe.125 Series 800	258264	N805H G-5-806
HB-VLG	BAe.125 Series 800	258265	N806H G-5-809
HB-VLP	Cessna 650 Citation III	7064	N52626
HB-VLQ	Cessna 550 Citation II	0324	N23W I-JESJ N171LE N5873C
HB-VLR	Gates Learjet 31	31-127	N80727
HB-VLS	Cessna 550 Citation II	0196	N400DK N88ML N800EC N1212H N68DS N6798Y
HB-VLV	Cessna 560 Citation V	0077	N42NA C-GNND G-BSVL N2745R
HB-VLW	Beech 400A Beechjet	RK-103	D-CIGM
HB-VLZ	Cessna 560 Citation V	0446	
HB-VMA	Bombardier Learjet 45	45-020	N5000E
HB-VMB	Bombardier Learjet 45	45-021	N5009T
HB-VMF	BAe.125 Series 800A	258175	N204JC VR-BLQ (VR-BPB) N598BA G-5-650
HB-VMG	IAI-1125 Astra SPX	105	N217PT
HB-VMH	Cessna 550 Citation II	0649	N44LQ
HB-VMI	BAe.125 Series 800B	258210	G-RAAR G-5-705
HB-VMJ	Cessna S550 Citation II	0029	N608LB N185SF (N1260N)

Regn.	Type	C/n	Prev.Id.
HB-VMN	Dassault Falcon 20	240	N240AT / I-SNAG / F-WLCX
HB-VMO	Cessna 560XLCitation Excel	5061	N5200R
HB-VMP	Cessna 550 Citation II	0697	N697EA / ZS-NFL / N6851C
HB-VMT	Cessna 525 CitationJet	0250	N250CJ
HB-XAJ	Enstrom 280FX	2078	
HB-XAQ	SE.3130 Alouette II	1932	F-BXAV / 3D-XO
HB-XBA	Agusta-Bell 206B Jet Ranger III	8593	G-HYDE
HB-XBF	SE.3130 Alouette II	1236	N92785 / HB-XBF / V-48
HB-XBJ	SE.313B Alouette II	1929	V-51
HB-XBQ	Schweizer/Hughes 269D	0024	N69A
HB-XBZ	Agusta-Bell 47G-3B1	1594	(D-HZKA) / HB-XBZ
HB-XCB	SA.316B Alouette III (Stored, 9.99)	1259	
HB-XCJ	Aérospatiale AS.350B2 Ecureuil	2557	F-GJOK
HB-XCM	SE.3160 Alouette III (Wreck noted 9.99)	1443	
HB-XDA	SE.3160 Alouette III	1609	
HB-XDG	Aérospatiale SA.315B Lama	2221	F-WIEL
HB-XDI	Aérospatiale SA.315B Lama	2207	
HB-XDJ	Aérospatiale SA.365N Dauphin 2	6151	F-OHCF / F-WYMB / JA9625
HB-XDN	Aérospatiale SA.315B Lama	2232	
HB-XDQ	Schweizer 269C	S-1732	
HB-XDY	Agusta-Bell 206A Jet Ranger II	8335	
HB-XEJ	Schweizer 269C	S-1733	N41S
HB-XEO	Aérospatiale SA.315B Lama (Stored, 9.99)	2321	F-BUYA
HB-XES	Enstrom F-28C	353	
HB-XFE	Aérospatiale SA.315B Lama	2436	OE-EXB / HB-XFE
HB-XFQ	Schweizer 269C	S-1687	N69A
HB-XFX	Aérospatiale SA.315B Lama	2445	
HB-XGD	Bell 206B Jet Ranger II	106	D-HABL
HB-XGJ	Schweizer 269C	S-1688	N41S
HB-XGP	Aérospatiale SA.315B Lama	2349	F-BVUG / HB-XDZ
HB-XHB	Westland-Bell 47G-3B1	WA/424	G-BEPA / XT512
HB-XHD	Aérospatiale SA.315B Lama	2460	OE-EXL
HB-XHN	Aérospatiale SA.315B Lama	1083/04	F-BIEC
HB-XHO	Agusta-Bell 206A Jet Ranger II	8155	OE-DXS / D-HBBZ
HB-XHQ	Robinson R-22 Beta	2169	G-BULX
HB-XIA	Aérospatiale SA.315B Lama	2552	
HB-XIB	Aérospatiale SA.315B Lama	2531	
HB-XIJ	Hughes 369E	0454E	SE-JAM
HB-XII	Aérospatiale SA.315B Lama	2551	
HB-XIQ	Aérospatiale AS.355N Ecureuil 2	5557	VR-BQM / G-BVNW / (D-HWPC)
HB-XJA	Agusta A.109A-II	7317	N295CA / JA9695 / N1CL / N109GG
HB-XJC	Aérospatiale AS.350B2 Ecureuil	2382	G-BWLI / G-IINA / N908BA
HB-XJE	Westland-Bell 47G-3B1 Soloy	WA/352	D-HAHE(2) / (D-HAFM) / XT193
HB-XJF	McDonnell-Douglas MD-900 Explorer	00017	N9213Z
HB-XJH	Robinson R-22 Beta	2551	
HB-XJJ	SE.313B Alouette II	1903	V-57
HB-XJK	SA.319B Alouette III	2273	I-OYEN / N1044N / ZK-HNY
HB-XJN	Aérospatiale SA.315B Lama	2609	I-BREY
HB-XJP	Schweizer 269C	S-1731	
HB-XJQ	Enstrom 480	5018	
HB-XJR	SA.316B Alouette III	1781	I-LESY / HB-XOT / D-HADX / F-GBGJ / XC-FEZ
HB-XJS	Robinson R-44 Astro	0083	D-HRHP
HB-XJT	Schweizer 269D	0018	
HB-XJW	Aérospatiale AS.350B Ecureuil	1802	OE-KXB / D-HHFF
HB-XJX	Bell 407	53169	
HB-XJY	Schweizer 269C	S-1781	N69A
HB-XJZ	Robinson R-22 Beta	2674	
HB-XKE	Kamov Ka.32A12	8709/02	
HB-XKJ	SE.3130 Alouette II	1910	V-61
HB-XKN	Bell 206B Jet Ranger II	1205	G-BBTV / N18092
HB-XLA	Agusta-Bell 206B Jet Ranger III	8616	
HB-XLL	Agusta-Bell 206B Jet Ranger III	8609	P2-XLL / HB-XLL
HB-XLM	Robinson R-22	0072	
HB-XLN	Robinson R-22	0073	
HB-XLS	Enstrom 280C Shark	1211	N5695K
HB-XMC	Aérospatiale SA.315B Lama	2527	ZK-HNW
HB-XMJ	Bell 206B Jet Ranger II	4302	N112AJ
HB-XMO	Enstrom 280C Shark	1213	N5697N
HB-XMR	Aérospatiale SA.315B Lama (W/o 22.1.98)	2512	OE-EXY
HB-XMT	Bell 206B Jet Ranger II	866	D-HKLI
HB-XND	Aérospatiale SA.315B Lama	2624	
HB-XNE	Aérospatiale AS.332C Super Puma	2002	F-WZJM
HB-XNI	Enstrom F.280F Shark	1509	D-HGIL / HB-XNI
HB-XNM	Bell 206L-3 Long Ranger III	51332	N105PS / N21921 / C-FHHZ
HB-XNR	Enstrom 280F	1512	
HB-XNS	SA.319B Alouette III	2389	
HB-XNU	Agusta-Bell 206B Jet Ranger II	8289	D-HASA / LN-OSI / D-HAWA
HB-XNW	SA.316B Alouette III	2265	N49543
HB-XNZ	SE.3160 Alouette III	1071	LX-EEE / RDAF:M-071
HB-XOE	SE.3160 Alouette III	1019	LX-AAA / RDAF:M-019
HB-XOF	SE.3160 Alouette III	1439	LX-OOO / RDAF:M-439
HB-XOO	SA.319B Alouette III	1959	D-HAAK
HB-XOV	Bell 214ST	28129	N13158
HB-XOY	Aérospatiale SA.315B Lama	2508	ZK-HNV
HB-XPD	Aérospatiale SA.315B Lama	2167/22	F-WIPE / D-HNRW
HB-XPE	Aérospatiale SA.365N Dauphin 2	6146	
HB-XPJ	Aérospatiale SA.315B Lama	2368	(N315TM) / 9M-SAB / F-GAML / LN-OSO
HB-XPK	Aérospatiale AS.350B1 Ecureuil	1903	
HB-XPL	Aérospatiale SA.315B Lama	2560	OE-EXD / HB-XPL / I-STEC
HB-XPN	Aérospatiale AS.350B Ecureuil	1328	F-GCQU
HB-XPP	Aérospatiale SA.315B Lama	2679	
HB-XPQ	Agusta-Bell 206B Jet Ranger III	8606	OE-DXV
HB-XPS	Hughes 269C	S-1228	
HB-XPT	Hughes 269C	S-1229	
HB-XPU	Schweizer 269C	S-1233	
HB-XPW	Agusta-Bell 206B Jet Ranger III	8557	G-TKHM / G-MKAN / G-DOUG
HB-XPY	Aérospatiale SA.315B Lama	2542	N9007N
HB-XQA	Kaman K-1200 K-Max	A94-0008	N136KA
HB-XQB	McDonnell-Douglas MD.600N	RN-007	N92007
HB-XQC	Bell 407	53132	
HB-XQD	SA.316B Alouette III	1324	A-324
HB-XQE	Agusta A.109E Power	11016	

Regn.	Type	C/n	Prev.Id.
HB-XQF	Schweizer 269C	S-1635	D-HMPI (2)
		N41S	
HB-XQI	Agusta-Bell 206B Jet Ranger II	8326	I-MIPE
			D-HMOS
HB-XQJ	Aérospatiale AS.350B3 Ecureuil	3093	
HB-XQK	RobinsonR-22B2 Beta	2757	
HB-XQL	Robinson R-44 Astro	0408	
HB-XQM	Agusta A.109E Power	11017	
HB-XQO	Bell 206B Jet Ranger II	3934	OE-XRH
			N42TM
			D-HMTM
HB-XQP	Bell 206L-4 Long Ranger IV	52016	D-HOBC(2)
HB-XQQ	Bell 206L-4 Long Ranger IV	52167	D-HMIS
			N72167
HB-XQR	Aérospatiale AS.350B2 Ecureuil	9000	
HB-XQS	Aérospatiale AS.365N3 Dauphin 2	6539	
HB-XQT	SE.313B Alouette II	1650	F-GNPX
			ALAT
HB-XQU	Aérospatiale AS.350B2 Ecureuil	2629	OE-XHK
HB-XQV	Bell 407	53259	
HB-XQW	Aérospatiale AS.365N1 Dauphin 2	6350	N610LH
			JA6609
HB-XQY	Bell 407	53299	N8226X
HB-XQZ	McDonnell-Douglas MD-900	00037	N9199X
HB-XRA	Aérospatiale SA.315B Lama	1542/17	F-GHCG
			F-ODSJ
			(F-GHCG)
			TR-LZR
			TR-LUY
			3D-XZ
HB-XRD	Aérospatiale SA.315B Lama	2400	OE-EXV
HB-XRE	Aérospatiale SA.315B Lama	2462	G-BMSN
			N47319
HB-XRF	Aérospatiale SA.315B Lama	2490	OE-KXD
			HB-XRF
			G-BMUA
			N49524
HB-XRK	Agusta A.109A-II	7352	I-AGSC
HB-XRL	Aérospatiale SA.315B Lama	2291	C-GDWD
			HB-XFO
			OE-EXA
HB-XRN	Aérospatiale SA.315B Lama	2309	N6390
HB-XRW	Hughes 369E	0231E	
HB-XSE	Aérospatiale AS.350B1 Ecureuil	2133	
HB-XSH	Bell 206B Jet Ranger II	2337	N215GP
HB-XSI	Bell 206B Jet Ranger II	3091	
HB-XSK	Schweizer 269C	S-1329	
HB-XSL	Bell 206B Jet Ranger II	1516	D-HCBB
			N111RL
			N111WH
HB-XSM	Agusta-Bell 206B Jet Ranger II	8550	OE-BXW
HB-XSO	Aérospatiale AS.350B1 Ecureuil	1950	D-HACC
			D-HAHI (2)
			F-WZKX
HB-XSP	Bell 206L-3 Long Ranger III	51158	N3199J
HB-XSR	Robinson R-22 Beta	0774	
HB-XSU	Aérospatiale AS.350B1 Ecureuil	2115	
HB-XSV	Aérospatiale SA.315B Lama	2421	LN-ORU
			N67103
HB-XSW	Aérospatiale SA.315B Lama	2563	
HB-XTA	Bell 412	33168	EI-BVL
			N3207Q
HB-XTB	Bell 412	33177	
HB-XTC	Aérospatiale SA.315B Lama	2521	N90016
HB-XTD	Aérospatiale SA.315B Lama	2596	N70283
			XC-...
HB-XTM	Aérospatiale SA.315B Lama	2654	LN-OMW
HB-XTN	Aérospatiale SA.315B Lama	2407	N62345
HB-XTO	Aérospatiale SA.315B Lama	2633	LN-OTE
HB-XTQ	Robinson R-22 Beta	1014	N8040A
HB-XTU	Aérospatiale SA.315B Lama	2614	F-GEHJ
			I-FAVA
HB-XTW	Aérospatiale SA.315B Lama	2537	F-GCLB
			G-DASL
HB-XTY	Aérospatiale SA.315B Lama	2645	LN-OMO
			(LN-OLM)
			F-WXFG
HB-XTZ	Robinson R-22 Beta	1064	
HB-XUA	Aérospatiale SA.315B Lama	2595	F-GHCP
			ZK-HBR(2)
			XC-DOS
HB-XUE	Bell 206B Jet Ranger	3080	OE-KXR
			N5744M
HB-XUG	Robinson R-22 Beta	1081	
HB-XUI	Agusta-Bell 206B Jet Ranger II	8337	G-BKDA
			LN-OQX
HB-XUK	Aérospatiale AS.350B2 Ecureuil	2230	
HB-XUN	Hughes 369E	0358E	VR-BLS
			HB-XUN
			(D-HILV)
HB-XUO	Hughes 369E	0357E	
HB-XUQ	Schweizer 269C	S-1394	
HB-XUU	Aérospatiale AS.350B2 Ecureuil	2598	F-WYME
HB-XUW	Agusta-Bell 206B Jet Ranger III	8722	
HB-XUZ	Aérospatiale AS.350B2 Ecureuil	2381	
HB-XVA	Aérospatiale AS.350B2 Ecureuil	2387	F-WYME
HB-XVB	Aérospatiale AS.350B2 Ecureuil	2340	
HB-XVK	Schweizer 269C	S-1401	
HB-XVL	Aérospatiale SA.315B Lama	2334	F-GEOI
			N62250
			(N502HA)
			N62250
HB-XVM	Aérospatiale AS.350B2 Ecureuil	2399	F-WYMO
HB-XVS	Bell 206L-3 Long Ranger III	51358	N7133D
			C-FIFV
HB-XVV	Aérospatiale SA.315B Lama	2382	OE-OXB
			HB-XVV
			JA9134
			N382HS
HB-XVZ	Bell 214B-1	28048	LN-OPV
			N3127U
			C-GTWH
HB-XWA	Agusta A.109K2	10001	I-RAIE
HB-XWB	Agusta A.109K2	10002	
HB-XWC	Agusta A.109K2	10003	
HB-XWD	Agusta A.109K2	10004	
HB-XWG	Agusta A.109K2	10007	
HB-XWH	Agusta A.109K2	10008	
HB-XWI	Agusta A.109K2	10009	
HB-XWJ	Agusta A.109K2	10010	
HB-XWK	Agusta A.109K2	10011	
HB-XWL	Agusta A.109K2	10012	
HB-XWM	Agusta A.109K2	10013	
HB-XWN	Agusta A.109K2	10014	
HB-XWO	Agusta A.109K2	10015	
HB-XWP	Agusta A.109K2	10027	
HB-XXC	Aérospatiale SA.316B Alouette III	1592	OE-EXT
			G-BMMS
			N4261E
			C-GXGW
			N65376
			9M-ASI
			FM1097
HB-XXE	Aérospatiale SA.315B Lama	2331	PT-HFK
HB-XXJ	Aérospatiale SA.315B Lama	1155/16	F-GFFG
			TR-LZQ
			TR-LUZ
			3D-XU
			F-WMES
HB-XXL	Aérospatiale AS.350B2 Ecureuil	2432	
HB-XXN	Bell 206B Jet Ranger II	4123	
HB-XXO	Bell 206B Jet Ranger II	3595	N22988
			(N101DG)
			N22988
HB-XXQ	Robinson R-22 Beta	1538	
HB-XXS	Aérospatiale SA.315B Lama	2470	OE-OXI
			HB-XXS
			YV-318A
			F-WTND

Regn.	Type	C/n	Prev.Id.
HB-XXW	Aérospatiale AS.350B2 Ecureuil	2405	N450HH
HB-XXY	Bell 206B Jet Ranger II	4131	D-HHBI
HB-XYA	Bell 206B Jet Ranger II	3067	SE-HUH
			G-BPZH
			ZK-HWL
HB-XYB	SE.3130 Alouette II	1915	V-63
HB-XYG	Bell 214B-1	28044	LN-OPR
			C-GLCA
			N214PH
			N5015G
HB-XYI	Schweizer 269C	S-1538	N41S
HB-XYL	Schweizer 269C	S-1648	
HB-XYM	Hughes H.369E	0461E	
HB-XYP	McDonnell-Douglas MD.520N	LN-052	N5204P
HB-XYR	Aérospatiale AS.350B2 Ecureuil	2420	N6037N
HB-XYT	Aérospatiale SA.315B Lama	2439	D-HBRA
			G-BMUB
			N47276
HB-XYW	Bell 206B Jet Ranger II	4180	
HB-XZB	Agusta-Bell 206B Jet Ranger III	8735	
HB-XZC	Hughes 269C	67-0601	(D-HURE)
			OE-AXM
			N7499F
HB-XZE	Robinson R-22HP	0316	N8415L
			N8327B
HB-XZF	Hughes 269C	39-0772	OY-HCW
HB-XZH	Robinson R-22 Beta	2195	N23412
HB-XZK	Robinson R-22 Beta	2213	N23488
HB-XZN	Robinson R-22 Beta	2332	N81907
HB-XZR	Robinson R-22 Beta	2369	N8033J
HB-XZS	Robinson R-22 Beta	2368	
HB-XZT	Robinson R-22 Beta	2365	
HB-XZU	Aérospatiale SA.315B Lama	2522	JA9190
HB-XZV	Robinson R-22 Beta	2380	N83094
HB-ZBA	Bell 407	53324	C-GEGC
HB-ZBB	Eurocopter EC.120B Colibri	1067	
HB-ZBC	Agusta A.109E	11032	
HB-ZBD	Eurocopter EC.120B Colibri	1009	D-HACO(2)
HB-ZBE	SE.313B Alouette II	1666	F-WQIV
			F-GPEP
			OL-A23
			OT-AAQ/A23
HB-ZBF	Westland-Bell 47G-3B1	WA/403	D-HISE
			OE-AXZ
			D-HLBS
			OE-AXZ
			HB-XIF
			D-HATW
			XT244
HB-ZBG	Aérospatiale SA.365N1 Dauphin 2	6251	N600GN
HB-ZBH	Aérospatiale AS.350B3 Ecureuil	3190	
HB-ZBJ	Aérospatiale AS.350B3 Ecureuil	3204	
HB-ZBL	SA.316B Alouette III	1101	F-ZLAR
HB-ZBN	Aérospatiale AS.350B3 Ecureuil	3209	
HB-ZBO	Schweizer 269C	S-1782	N69A
HB-ZBP	Hughes 269C	23-0184	G-BAUK
HB-ZBQ	Hughes 369D	70-0748D	OE-KXW
			G-BNMY
			N1091A
HB-ZBR	Aérospatiale AA.350B1 Ecureuil	3195	
HB-ZBU	Agusta-Bell 206B Jet Ranger 3	8649	I-SIMB
			I-MIST
HB-ZBV	Bell 430	49017	N1207V
HB-ZBW	Aérospatiale AS.350B3 Ecureuil	3266	
HB-ZBX	Bell 206B Jet Ranger II	480	N203WB
			C-CRGP
			N2502M
HB-ZBZ	Bell 430	49057	N6389Z
			C-FOEP
HB-ZCC	Aérospatiale AS.350B2 Ecureuil	2107	OE-OXC
HB-ZCD(*)	Agusta A.109C	7663	N109JN
			OO-AAI

Regn.	Type	C/n	Prev.Id.

EXPERIMENTAL AND HOMEBUILT AIRCRAFT

Regn.	Type	C/n	Prev.Id.
HB-XVC	Brügger MB.1 Kolibri	1	
HB-YAH	Luton LA.5 Major	1	
HB-YAL	Brügger MB.2 Kolibri	43	
HB-YAN	Aero 101 (Rebuilt)	011	F-PGYO
HB-YAS	Jodel D.9 Bébé	570	
HB-YAU	Bede BD-5B	281	
HB-YAV	Brügger MB.2 Kolibri	41	
HB-YAW	Tipsy T.66 Nipper Mk.2	69	OO-WOT
			PH-MEV
HB-YBA	Evans VP-1 Volksplane	V-1622	
HB-YBC	Brügger MB.2 Kolibri	27	
HB-YBD	Monnet Sonerai 1	290	
HB-YBG	Rutan Vari-eze	1236	
HB-YBI	Prometheus PV	001	
HB-YBK	Mignet HM.380	31	
HB-YBL	Rutan Vari-eze	511	
HB-YBO	Rutan Vari-eze	1513	
HB-YBP	Rotorway Exec 90	5222	
HB-YBS	Rutan Vari-eze	1924	
HB-YBV	Rutan Vari-eze	2145	
HB-YBW	Rutan LongEz	353	
HB-YBX	Brändli BX-2 Cherry	001	
HB-YBY	Rutan LongEz	1137	
HB-YCA	Neukom AN-20B	03	
HB-YCB	Neukom AN-20B	20-08	
HB-YCC	Quickie Quickie	475	
HB-YCD	Polliwagen	1103	
HB-YCE	Rutan Vari-eze	2174	
HB-YCF	Rutan Vari-eze	2178	
HB-YCG	Rutan LongEz	1293	
HB-YCH	Neukom AN-20B	20-09	
HB-YCI	Rutan LongEz	1701	
HB-YCK	Vetro GB-3 Twin Baby	01	
HB-YCM	Rutan Vari-eze	2202V	
HB-YCO	Vetro	03	
HB-YCP	Neukom AN-22	001	
HB-YCT	Rutan LongEz	1759L	
HB-YCU	Zenair Tri-Z	3-440	
HB-YCW	Colomban MC-15 Cri-Cri	12-0016	
HB-YCY	Brändli BX-2 Cherry	01-A	
HB-YDA	Rutan Vari-eze	2049	
HB-YDB	Rutan LongEz	1665	
HB-YDC	Rutan LongEz	1828	
HB-YDD	Rutan Vari-eze	2210-V	
HB-YDE	Rutan Vari-eze	1991	
HB-YDF	Rutan Vari-eze	2187	
HB-YDH	Brändli BX-2 Cherry	142	
HB-YDJ	Stoddard-Hamilton Glasair RG	790	
HB-YDL	Rutan Vari-eze	2115	
HB-YDN	Brügger MB-2 Colibri D	225-001	
HB-YDO	Van's RV-3	597	
HB-YDR	AFM	01	
HB-YDS	Brändli BX-2 Cherry	3	
HB-YDT	Marco J-5	03	
HB-YDU	Brändli BX-2 Cherry	031	
HB-YDW	Brändli BX-2 Cherry	038	
HB-YDX	Brändli BX-2 Cherry	057	
HB-YDY	Brändli BX-2 Cherry	049	
HB-YEA	Stoddard-Hamilton Glasair RG	750	
HB-YEB	Neico Lancair 235	150	
HB-YEC	Colomban MC-15 Cri-Cri	134	
HB-YEE	Light Aero Avid Flyer	269	
HB-YEF	Rutan Vari-eze	6801D	
HB-YEG	Viking Dragonfly II	748	
HB-YEI	Mignet HM-8 Avionette	FS-01	
HB-YEK	Pottier P.180	73	
HB-YEL	WAR FW-190	289	
HB-YEM	Light Aero Avid Hauler	482	
HB-YEN	Rotorway Executive	2951	
HB-YEO	Light Aero Avid Hauler	535	
HB-YEQ	Light Aero Avid Hauler	483	
HB-YER	Denney Kitfox II	408	
HB-YEU	Rutan LongEz	1938-L	

Regn.	Type	C/n	Prev.Id.
HB-YEV	Brügger MB-2 Kolibri	160	
HB-YEW	Mad Whisky	SR01	
HB-YEY	Brändli BX-2 Cherry	27	
HB-YEZ	Light Aero Avid Hauler	962	
HB-YFB	Denney Kitfox III	890	
HB-YFC	Light Aero Avid Hauler	833	
HB-YFD	TEAM Mini Max	352	
HB-YFE	Denney Kitfox III	971	
HB-YFF	Evans VP-1 Volksplane	V-2304	
HB-YFH	Denney Kitfox III	1194	
HB-YFI	Denney Kitfox IV	1193	
HB-YFJ	Rotorway Executive 90	5122	
HB-YFK	Stoddard-Hamilton Glasair IIRG	1116	
HB-YFL	Rotorway Executive 90	28609	
HB-YFM	Air Command 532 Elite	001	
HB-YFO	Light Aero Avid Hauler	963	
HB-YFP	Light Aero Avid Hauler	1104	
HB-YFQ	Light Aero Avid Hauler	566	
HB-YFR	Neico Lancair 320	503	
HB-YFS	Denney Kitfox IV	1856	
HB-YFT	Light Aero Avid Flyer Mk.IV	925	
HB-YFU	Denney Kitfox III	1167	
HB-YFV	Neico Lancair 320	366	
HB-YFW	Rotorway Executive 90	5156	
HB-YFX	Denney Kitfox IV	1881	
HB-YFY	Rutan LongEz	1279	
HB-YFZ	Denney Kitfox IV-1200	1903	
HB-YGA	Denney Kitfox IV	1581	
HB-YGB	Light Aero Avid Hauler	961	
HB-YGC	Ultravia Pelican GS	377	
HB-YGF	Light Aero Avid Flyer Mk IV	778	
HB-YGG	Brändli BX-2 Cherry	112	
HB-YGH	Rotorway Executive 90	8-01	
HB-YGJ	Neico Lancair 235	227	
HB-YGK	Rotorway Executive 90	5121	
HB-YGL	Stoddard-Hamilton Glasair II-FT	1096	
HB-YGN	Titan Tornado	0068	
HB-YGQ	Dallach Sunrise II	00	
HB-YGR	Rotorway Executive 90	5240	
HB-YGS	Brändli BX-3	001	
HB-YGT	Denney Kitfox IV-1200	1893	
HB-YGU	Rotorway Executive 90	5201	
HB-YGV	Light Aero Avid Flyer Mk.IV	1319D	
HB-YGW	Denney Kitfox IV	S9411-0061	
HB-YGX	Denney Kitfox IV-1200 Speed	KCS140	
HB-YGZ	Mustang	unkn	
HB-YHA	Mühlemann M-1	1	
HB-YHB	Velocity 173RGElite	DMO 078	
HB-YHD	Light Aero Avid Flyer Mk IV	1240	
HB-YHG	Neukom AN-20C	unkn	
HB-YHH	WARFocke Wulf FW-190	288	
HB-YHK	Light Aero Avid Hauler	534	
HB-YHL	Aero Designs Pulsar XP	363	
HB-YHP	Elisport CH-7 Angel	82	
HB-YHR	Brändli BX-2 Cherry	150	
HB-YHS	Rotorway Executive 90	5237	
HB-YHT	Brändli BX-2 Cherry	84	
HB-YHU	Skystar Aero Designs Pulsar XP	331	
HB-YHV	Velocity 173FG	92	
HB-YHW	Aero Designs Pulsar XP	287	
HB-YHZ	Light Aero Avid Flyer	1499D	
HB-YIC	Zenair CH-701 STOL	7-1712	
HB-YIH	Light Aero AvidMagnum	M008	
HB-YIJ	Rotorway Exec 162F	6068	
HB-YIL	Esprit VF-II	001	
HB-YIN	Aero Designs Pulsar XP	369	
HB-YIQ	Brditschka HB-207 Alfa	207009	
HB-YIR	Denney Kitfox Vixen	V94090017	
HB-YIX	Aero Designs/Skystar Pulsar XP	192-15	
HB-YJA	Stoddard-Hamilton Glasair IIRG	3282	
HB-YJK	Brinkert Mini-500	480	
HB-YJM	One Design MSW	95-0278	

Regn.	Type	C/n	Prev.Id.
BALLOONS AND AIRSHIPS			
HB-BAJ	Cameron N-90 HAFB	3348	
HB-BAL	Stuttgart K-780/2-STU Gas Balloon	0282	
HB-BAO	Stuttgart K-1260/3-STU Gas Balloon	0281	
HB-BAQ	Cameron N-133 HAFB	3359	
HB-BAS	Raven S-55A HAFB	626	
HB-BAW(2)	Cameron N-105 HAFB	1526	
	(Formerly c/n 505)		
HB-BAX	Colt 77A HAFB	045	
HB-BAY	Raven S-60A HAFB	138	
HB-BBA	Stuttgart K-945/2-STU Gas Balloon	0283	
HB-BBE(4)	Colt 105A HAFB	1193	
	(Formerly c/ns 054,322,and 714)		
HB-BBF	Stuttgart K-1000/3-STU Gas Balloon	0284	
HB-BBG	Augsburg K-1260/3-RI Gas Balloon	10512	
HB-BBH(3)	Colt 77A HAFB	1608	
	(Formerly c/ns 055,and 709)		
HB-BBL	Stuttgart K-1000/3-STU Gas Balloon	0288	
HB-BBQ	UltraMagic M-130 HAFB	130/05	
HB-BBU	Cameron O-84 HAFB	648	
HB-BBV	Cameron V-77 HAFB	649	
HB-BBW	Raven RX-7 HAFB	238	
HB-BBY	Raven RX-7 HAFB	240	
HB-BCE	Cameron V-77 HAFB	764	
HB-BCG	Raven S-55A HAFB	732	
HB-BCH	Thunder AX8-90 HAFB	330	
HB-BCJ	Cameron N-160 HAFB	3341	
HB-BCM	Thunder AX8-105 HAFB	356	
HB-BCN	Cameron N-105 HAFB	1966	
HB-BCQ	Galaxy-8B HAFB	GLX-1018B	
HB-BCV(2)	Thunder AX7-77Z HAFB	1301	
	(Formerly c/n 409)		
HB-BCY	Cameron O-84 HAFB	838	
HB-BDA	Cameron O-84 HAFB	883	
HB-BDD	Cameron O-84 HAFB	1068	
HB-BDF	Cameron O-84 HAFB	913	
HB-BDG	Cameron O-84 HAFB	928	
HB-BDH	Cameron N-105 HAFB	927	
HB-BDJ	Cameron A-140 HAFB	3329	
HB-BDK	Colt 21A HAFB	1031	
HB-BDP	Cameron O-84 HAFB	952	
HB-BDR(2)	Cameron O-84 HAFB	3030	
	(Formerly c/n 955)		
HB-BDV	Thunder Colt AX8-105Z HAFB	425	
HB-BEA	Stuttgart K-780/2-STU Gas Balloon	0235	
HB-BEJ	Cameron N-133 HAFB	3338	
HB-BEM	Stuttgart K-945/2-STU Gas Balloon	0262	
HB-BEQ(2)	Colt 210A HAFB	4208	
	(Formerly used envelope c/n 2635)		
HB-BER	Stuttgart K-1000/3-STU Gas Balloon	0266	
HB-BFA	Cameron N-90 HAFB	1019	
HB-BFB(3)	Cameron N-90 HAFB	3407	
	(Formerly c/ns 1016 and 2170)		
HB-BFD	Cameron N-90 HAFB	1046	
HB-BFE	Cameron N-105 HAFB	902	
HB-BFF	Raven RX-7 HAFB	359	
HB-BFJ	Cameron O-120 HAFB	3364	
HB-BFQ	Raven-Europe S-66A HAFB	E-383	
HB-BFR	Cameron O-84 HAFB	1087	
HB-BFU(2)	Cameron N-90 HAFB	3060	
	(Formerly c/n 1083)		
HB-BFX	Colt 90A HAFB	622	
HB-BFY	Cameron N-90 HAFB	1102	
HB-BGD(2)	Thunder Colt AX8-90 HAFB	1664	
	(Formerly c/n 637 ex G-BLYN)		
HB-BGH	Balloon Works Firefly F7B HAFB	F7B-052	G-BKOO N3609T
HB-BGJ	UltraMagic M-160 HAFB	160/04	
HB-BGN	Augsburg K-1050/3-RI Gas Balloon	43041	
HB-BGP	Colt 105A HAFB	729	
HB-BGQ	Raven Europe RX-9 HAFB	E-371	
HB-BGS	Raven S-60A HAFB	S60A-410	
HB-BGT	Colt 90A HAFB	730	
HB-BGU	Bronschhofen 1050 Gas Balloon	8403	

Regn.	Type	C/n	Prev.Id.
HB-BGV	Augsburg K-1680/4-RI Gas Balloon	10415	
HB-BGW	Cameron N-120 HAFB	3390	
HB-BGX	Cameron O-105 HAFB	1220	
HB-BGY	Aerostar S-55A HAFB	3001	
HB-BHF	Cameron O-105 HAFB	1286	
HB-BHH	Colt 90A HAFB	824	
HB-BHJ	Cameron O-56 HAFB	1318	
HB-BHL	Colt 90A HAFB	848	
HB-BHN	Cameron V-56 HAFB	1293	
HB-BHO	Cameron N-105 HAFB	1292	
HB-BHP(2)	Cameron N-105 HAFB	2326	
	(Formerly c/n 1285)		
HB-BHQ	Raven-Europe S-66A HAFB	E-395	
HB-BHR	Cameron O-84 HAFB	1989	
HB-BHS	Raven-Europe MFM FRX-65 HAFB	E-034	
HB-BHT	Cameron O-105 HAFB	1372	
HB-BHY	Cameron A-105 HAFB	1392	
HB-BIJ	Cameron N-105 HAFB	1371	
HB-BJB	Bronschhofen 1050 Gas Balloon	8404	
HB-BJC	Cameron N-105 HAFB	1382	
HB-BJE	Cameron N-105 HAFB	1391	
HB-BJG	Colt 105A HAFB	935	
HB-BJH	Colt 105A HAFB	921	
HB-BJI	Cameron O-84 HAFB	1417	
HB-BJM	Cameron N-133 Bird SS HAFB	1458	
HB-BJO	Bronschhofen 1050 Gas Balloon	8406	
HB-BJP	Cameron O-84 HAFB	1393	
HB-BJQ	Colt 21A HAFB	1030	
HB-BJS	Bronschhofen 1050 Gas Balloon	8405	
HB-BJU	Raven-Europe MFM FS-57A HAFB	E-058	
HB-BJX	Raven-Europe MFM FS-57A HAFB	E-107	
HB-BJY	Cameron N-105 HAFB	1496	
HB-BJZ(2)	Raven-Europe S-66A HAFB	E-294	
	(Formerly c/n E-069)		
HB-BKA(2)	Cameron N-180 HAFB	2371	
	(Formerly c/n 1438)		
HB-BKD	Cameron N-105 HAFB	1521	
HB-BKE	Colt 105A HAFB	1560	
HB-BKH	Cameron N-105 HAFB	1532	
HB-BKJ	Schroeder Fire Balloons 26/24 HAFB	282	
HB-BKK	Cameron N-105 HAFB	1587	
HB-BKL	Cameron O-105 HAFB	1581	
HB-BKM	Colt 160A HAFB	1108	
HB-BKR	Cameron DP-70 Hot Air Airship	1558	G-BNXG
HB-BKS	Bronschhofen 1350 Gas Balloon	88-401	
HB-BKU	Bronschhofen 780 Gas Balloon	88-201	
HB-BKV	Cameron A-105 HAFB	1637	
HB-BKW	Schroeder Fire Balloons G HAFB	372	D-OGUY
HB-BLA	Cameron Watch SS-90 HAFB	1592	G-BOCJ
HB-BLB	Bronschhofen 1050 Gas Balloon	8408	
HB-BLE	Colt 21A Cloudhopper HAFB	1110	
HB-BLF	Cameron N-145 HAFB	1684	
HB-BLG	Cameron N-105 HAFB	1661	
HB-BLJ	Cameron N-145 HAFB	1695	
HB-BLM	Raven-Europe S-60A HAFB	E-095	
HB-BLN	Cameron N-105 HAFB	1707	
HB-BLP	Cameron A-105 HAFB	1696	
HB-BLT(2)	Raven-Europe S-66A HAFB	E-265	
HB-BLU	Cameron N-105 HAFB	1743	
HB-BLY	Colt 120A HAFB	1276	
HB-BLZ	Thunder AX8-105 HAFB	1270	
HB-BMB	Aerostar S-66A HAFB	3028	
HB-BMC	Chaize CS.3000F16 HAFB	90	
HB-BMD	Schroeder Fire Balloons 26/24 HAFB	38	
HB-BME	Cameron A-250 HAFB	1697	
HB-BMG	Lindstrand LBL-240A HAFB	192	
HB-BML	Cameron N-105 HAFB	1850	
HB-BMN	Cameron SS HAFB	1797	
HB-BMO	Raven-Europe FS-57A HAFB	E-113	
HB-BMQ	Cameron A-210SV HAFB	3428	
HB-BMR	Raven-Europe S-60A HAFB	E-116	
HB-BMX	Aerostar S-60A HAFB	3115	
HB-BMY	Aerostar S-60A HAFB	3116	
HB-BMZ	Raven-Europe S-55A HAFB	E-147	
HB-BNA	Cameron N-77 HAFB	2033	
HB-BNB	Schroeder Fire Balloons 45/24 HAFB	76	
HB-BNE	Schroeder Fire Balloons 30/24 HAFB	81	
HB-BNG	Cameron O-105 HAFB	2074	
HB-BNI	Cameron N-105 HAFB	2052	
HB-BNJ	Cameron N-105 HAFB	2051	
HB-BNK	Cameron N-105 HAFB	2053	
HB-BNL	Cameron A-375 HAFB	4620	
	(New envelope replacing c/n 2132)		
HB-BNO	Cameron N-105 HAFB	2143	
HB-BNQ	Cameron A-300 HAFB	2156	
HB-BNR	Colt 105A HAFB	1613	
HB-BNT	Raven-Eurpe S-66A HAFB	E-149	
HB-BNU	Thunder AX8-105 HAFB	1640	
HB-BNY	Raven-Europe S-60A HAFB	E-155	
HB-BNZ	Colt 90A HAFB	1621	
HB-BOD	Stuttgart K-630/1-STU Gas Balloon	0129	
HB-BOF	Stuttgart K-945/2-STU Gas Balloon	0201	
HB-BOH	Augsburg K-1260/3-RI Gas Balloon	8747	
HB-BOJ	Thunder AX8-90 SI HAFB	2678/3512	
HB-BOQ	Thunder AX10-210 SII HAFB	2679/3513	
HB-BOS	Stuttgart K-945/2-STU Gas Balloon	0220	
HB-BPA	Colt 90A HAFB	1442	
HB-BPB	Raven-Europe S-66A HAFB	E-127	
HB-BPD	Cameron V-77 HAFB	1926	
HB-BPG	Thunder AX8-105 HAFB	1432	
HB-BPH	Cameron N-105 HAFB	1923	
HB-BPJ	Cameron N-105 HAFB	1939	
HB-BPK	Colt 120A HAFB	3446	
HB-BPO	Cameron N-105 HAFB	2244	
HB-BPS(2)	Raven-Europe S-66A HAFB	E-171	
	(Formerly c/n E-134)		
HB-BPT	Schroeder Fire Balloons 40/24 HAFB	461	
HB-BPU	UltraMagic S-130 HAFB	130/01	
HB-BPW	Cameron O-90 HAFB	1997	
HB-BPY	Raven-Europe FS-57A HAFB	E-154	
HB-BQA	Cameron A-105 HAFB	2306	
HB-BQC	Cameron N-56 HAFB	2205	
HB-BQF	Thunder AX8-105 HAFB	1653	
HB-BQH	Colt 105A HAFB	1661	
HB-BQJ	Colt 120A HAFB	1821	
HB-BQK	Colt 120A HAFB	1681	
HB-BQL	Raven-Europe RX-7 HAFB	E-112	F-GMFC
HB-BQM	Thunder AX10-180 HAFB	1660	
HB-BQO	Balloon Works Firefly 8 HAFB	F8-360	
HB-BQP	Schroeder Fire Balloons 36/24 HAFB	123	
HB-BQU	UltraMagic V-105 HAFB	105/10	
HB-BQV	Schroeder Fire Balloons 30/24 HAFB	127	
HB-BQW	Colt 105A HAFB	1756	
HB-BQX	Cameron N-105 HAFB	2305	
HB-BQY	Stuttgart K-1000/3-STU Gas Balloon	0327	
HB-BRC	Cameron N-120 HAFB	2272	
HB-BRE	Aerostar S-66A HAFB	3057	
HB-BRF	Stuttgart K-1260/3-STU Gas Balloon	1025	
HB-BRH	Raven-Europe S-60A HAFB	E-188	
HB-BRI	Raven-Europe S-60A HAFB	E-205	
HB-BRJ	Thunder AX9-140 SII HAFB	3616	
HB-BRK	Raven-Europe RX-8 HAFB	E-190	
HB-BRL	Cameron N-120 HAFB	2323	
HB-BRN	Cameron V-77 HAFB	5222	N29919
HB-BRO	Aerostar S-77A HAFB	3014	
HB-BRP	UltraMagic M-105 HAFB	105/13	
HB-BRU	Cameron A-105 HAFB	2329	
HB-BRV	Schroeder Fire Balloons 36/24 HAFB	136	
HB-BRY	Balloon Works Firefly 7 HAFB	F7-720	
HB-BRZ	Cameron N-120 HAFB	2385	
HB-BSF	Cameron V-56 HAFB	2396	
HB-BSH	Thunder AX8-90 HAFB	1988	
HB-BSI	Colt 105A HAFB	1852	
HB-BSK	Schroeder Fire Balloons 40/24 HAFB	208	
HB-BSL	Stuttgart K-1000/3-STU Gas Balloon	1026	
HB-BSM	Colt 105A I HAFB	1844	
HB-BSN	Thunder AX8-90 HAFB	1875	
HB-BSP	Schroeder Fire Balloons 50/24 HAFB	154	
HB-BST	Cameron O-90 HAFB	3069	
HB-BSU	Thunder AX8-105 HAFB	1842	

Regn.	Type	C/n	Prev.Id.
HB-BSW	Schroeder Fire Balloons 40/24 HAFB	175	
HB-BSY	Raven-Europe FS-57A HAFB	E-221	
HB-BSZ	Aerostar S-49A HAFB	3035	
HB-BTA	Raven-Europe S-55A HAFB	E-224	
HB-BTB	Raven-Europe S-60A HAFB	E-223	
HB-BTD	Cameron A-140 HAFB	2485	
HB-BTE	Stuttgart K-1000/3-STU Gas Balloon	1027	
HB-BTF	Cameron N-90 HAFB	2517	
HB-BTG	Schroeder Fire Balloons 36/24 HAFB	158	
HB-BTH	Balloon Works Firefly F7-15 HAFB	F7-736	
HB-BTJ	Thunder AX10-180 HAFB	1917	
HB-BTL	Thunder AX8-90 SI HAFB	4663	
	(New envelope replacing c/n 1926)		
HB-BTM	Cameron N-77 HAFB	2523	
HB-BTN(2)	Colt 120A HAFB	4497	
	(Replaces envelope c/n 1918)		
HB-BTO(2)	UltraMagic M-105 HAFB	105/22	
	(Formerly c/n 105/11)		
HB-BTP	Raven-Europe S-60A HAFB	E-234	
HB-BTQ	Cameron N-145 HAFB	2540	
HB-BTR	Schroeder Fire Balloons 30/24 HAFB	488	
HB-BTS	Schroeder Fire Balloons 36/24 HAFB	182	
HB-BTV	Cameron O-105 HAFB	2553	
HB-BTW	UltraMagic M-160 HAFB	160/08	
HB-BTX	UltraMagic V-105 HAFB	105/16	
HB-BTZ	Aerostar S-49A HAFB	3065	
HB-BUA	Aerostar S-49A HAFB	3066	
HB-BUB	Schroeder Fire Balloons 30/24 HAFB	199	
HB-BUC	Aerostar S-49A HAFB	3080	
HB-BUD	Colt 160A HAFB	1973	
HB-BUF	Colt 120A HAFB	2013	
HB-BUG	Colt 31A HAFB	2020	
HB-BUH	Cameron O-90 HAFB	2604	
HB-BUI	Cameron N-105 HAFB	2605	
HB-BUK	Raven-Europe S-49A HAFB	E-251	
HB-BUL	Raven-Europe S-60A HAFB	E-250	
HB-BUM	Aerostar S-49A HAFB	3085	
HB-BUN	Thunder AX7-65 HAFB	2035	
HB-BUO	Colt 105A HAFB	2061	
HB-BUP	Cameron N-145 HAFB	2684	
HB-BUQ	Cameron N-145 HAFB	2706	
HB-BUR	Cameron N-105 HAFB	2708	
HB-BUT	Cameron N-160 HAFB	2648	
HB-BUU	Lindstrand LBL-150A HAFB	273	
HB-BUV(2)	Cameron N-160 HAFB	3321	
	(Formerly c/n 2710)		
HB-BUW	UltraMagic N-180 HAFB	180/13	
HB-BUX	Cameron A-180 HAFB	2682	
HB-BUZ	Raven-Europe FS-57A HAFB	E-255	
HB-BVA	Raven-Europe S-60A HAFB	E-254	
HB-BVB	Aerostar S-49A HAFB	3142	
HB-BVC	Balloon Works Firefly 8 HAFB	F8-380	
HB-BVD	Cameron N-120 HAFB	2731	
HB-BVE	Cameron O-120 HAFB	2732	
HB-BVG	Colt 105A HAFB	2117	
HB-BVI	Colt AS.105 Mk II Hot Air Airship	2069	G-BUAD
HB-BVJ	Balloon Works Firefly 8 HAFB	F8-383	
HB-BVK	Cameron A-105 HAFB	2740	
HB-BVL	Balloon Works Firefly 8 HAFB	F8-384	
HB-BVM	Bronschhofen 780 Gas Balloon	88-202	
HB-BVN	Cameron A-105 HAFB	2743	
HB-BVO	Schroeder Fire Balloons 24/24 HAFB	254	
HB-BVP	Cameron N-105 HAFB	2752	
HB-BVS	Aerostar S-71A HAFB	3009	
HB-BVT	Raven-Europe RX-8 HAFB	E-267	
HB-BVU	Raven-Europe S-66A HAFB	E-271	
HB-BVV	Thunder AX9-140 SII HAFB	2124	
HB-BVW	Raven-Europe RX-8 HAFB	E-291	
HB-BVX	Raven-Europe S-66A HAFB	E-360	
HB-BVY	Cameron Battery SS HAFB	2762	
HB-BVZ	Bronschhofen 1050 Gas Balloon	8409	
HB-BWA	Cameron DP-90 Hot Air Airship	2771	
HB-BWC	Cameron O-105 HAFB	2788	
HB-BWD	UltraMagic S-130 HAFB	130/06	
HB-BWE	UltraMagic M-105 HAFB	105/21	
HB-BWF	Schroeder Fire Balloons 36/24 HAFB	245	
HB-BWG	Schroeder Fire Balloons 22/24 HAFB	276	
HB-BWH	Cameron V-90 HAFB	2811	
HB-BWK	Cameron N-105 HAFB	2792	
HB-BWM	Balloon Works Firefly 10 HAFB	F10-002	
HB-BWN	Cameron N-105 HAFB	2842	
HB-BWP	Schroeder Fire Balloons "Kater" SS HAFB	311	
HB-BWQ	Cameron A-105 HAFB	2757	
HB-BWS	Schroeder Fire Balloons 30/24 HAFB	261	
HB-BWT	Colt 90A HAFB	2217	
HB-BWU	Balloon Works Firefly 8 HAFB	F8-390	
HB-BWW	Balloon Works Firefly 10 HAFB	F10-006	
HB-BXA	Raven-Europe S-60A HAFB	E-303	
HB-BXC	Raven-Europe FS-57A HAFB	E-257	F-GLCE
HB-BXE	Balloon Works Firefly 8 HAFB	F8-392	
HB-BXG	Colt 105A HAFB	2286	
HB-BXH	Cameron A-300 HAFB	2914	
HB-BXI	Cameron N-133 HAFB	2921	
HB-BXK	Cameron N-120 HAFB	2941	
HB-BXL	Cameron SS HAFB	2947	
HB-BXM	Cameron O-77 HAFB	2923	
HB-BXN	Cameron O-77 HAFB	2950	
HB-BXO	Chaize JZ30 F16 HAFB	117	
HB-BXP	Thunder AX9-140 SII HAFB	2304	
HB-BXQ	Cameron N-145 HAFB	2948	
HB-BXR	Colt 77A HAFB	2040	
HB-BXS	Colt 120A HAFB	2354	
HB-BXU	Cameron N-90 HAFB	2979	
HB-BXV	Colt 120A HAFB	2303	
HB-BXW	Balloon Works Firefly Bottle SS HAFB	Bottle 01	
HB-BXX	Schroeder Fire Balloons "Vase" SS HAFB	462	
HB-BYA	Schroeder Fire Balloons G HAFB	326	
HB-BYB	Cameron N-160 HAFB	2990	
HB-BYD	Cameron N-120 HAFB	2998	
HB-BYE	Cameron N-105 HAFB	3011	
HB-BYF	Schroeder Fire Balloons G HAFB	428	
HB-BYG	Chaize CS.3000F16 HAFB	116	F-GMAJ
HB-BYH	Cameron N-77 HAFB	3007	
HB-BYI	Cameron A-160 HAFB	3041	
HB-BYJ	Cameron N-90 HAFB	3042	
HB-BYK	Thunder AX8-105 SII HAFB	2373	
HB-BYL	Raven Europe RXS-8 HAFB	E-333	F-WKJI
HB-BYM	Raven Europe RXS-8 HAFB	E-331	
HB-BYN	Raven Europe S-66A HAFB	E-332	
HB-BYO	Colt 77A HAFB	1912	
HB-BYQ	Cameron O-120 HAFB	3074	
HB-BYR	Thunder AX8-105 HAFB	2435	
HB-BYS	Schroeder Fire Balloons 36/24 HAFB	343	
HB-BYT	Cameron N-160 HAFB	3101	
HB-BYU	Thunder AX8-9O SII HAFB	2438	
HB-BYW	Cameron N-120 HAFB	4678	
	(New envelope replacing c/n 3119)		
HB-BYX	Balloon Works Firefly F-11 HAFB	F11-001	N2594U
HB-BYY	Raven Europe S-66A HAFB	E-330	
HB-BYZ	Cameron N-120 HAFB	3165	
HB-BZA	Cameron O-120 HAFB	3127	
HB-BZB	Cameron A-210 HAFB	3188	
HB-BZC	Cameron A-180 HAFB	3201	
HB-BZD	Cameron N-105 HAFB	3147	
HB-BZE	Cameron N-105 HAFB	3183	
HB-BZF	Chaize JZ.22F12 HAFB	125	F-WMTZ
HB-BZG	Cameron A-300 HAFB	4669	
	(New envelope replacing c/n 3259)		
HB-BZH	Bronschhofen 1050 Gas Balloon	8411	
HB-BZI	Bronschhofen 780 Gas Balloon	88-203	
HB-BZJ	Schroeder Fire Balloons G HAFB	423	
HB-BZK	Cameron N-120 HAFB	3327	
HB-BZL	Thunder AX9-120SII HAFB	2593	
HB-BZM	Colt 105A HAFB	2602	
HB-BZN	Cameron A-140 HAFB	3335	
HB-BZO	Schroeder Fire Balloons G HAFB	431	
HB-BZP	Cameron O-120 HAFB	3309	
HB-BZQ	Raven Europe RX-8 HAFB	E-364	
HB-BZR	Raven Europe S-49A HAFB	E-365	
HB-BZT	Raven Europe S-77A HAFB	E-375	F-WQAO

Regn.	Type	C/n	Prev.Id.
HB-BZU	Raven Europe RX-9 HAFB	E-373	
HB-BZV	Cameron A-300 HAFB	3297	
HB-BZW	Thunder AX8-105 SI HAFB	2410	D-OMAA
HB-BZX	Cameron N-145 HAFB	3310	
HB-BZY	Balloon Works Firefly 11 HAFB	F11-003	
HB-BZZ	Raven Europe S-60A HAFB	E-356	
HB-QAA	Lindstrand LBL-105A HAFB	163	
HB-QAB	Lindstrand LBL-105A HAFB	159	
HB-QAC	Lindstrand LBL-105A HAFB	160	
HB-QAD	Lindstrand LBL-105A HAFB	161	
HB-QAE	Lindstrand LBL-105A HAFB	162	
HB-QAF	Lindstrand LBL-105A HAFB	139	
HB-QAG	Lindstrand LBL-310A HAFB	355	
HB-QAH	Lindstrand LBL-120A HAFB	373	
HB-QAJ	UltraMagic M-145 HAFB	145/01	
HB-QAK	UltraMagic N-250 HAFB	250/02	
HB-QAL	Cameron A-375 HAFB	3440	
HB-QAM	Cameron A-250 HAFB	4690	
	(New envelope replacing c/n 3476)		
HB-QAN	Cameron N-120 HAFB	3474	
HB-QAO	Cameron SS HAFB	3642	
HB-QAQ	Cameron N-120 HAFB	3562	
HB-QAS	Thunder AX9-120 SII HAFB	3597	
HB-QAT	Wörner NL-640/STU Gas Balloon	1047	
HB-QAU	UltraMagic M-130 HAFB	130/10	
HB-QAV	UltraMagic M-130 HAFB	130/07	
HB-QAW	UltraMagic M-145 HAFB	145/03	
HB-QAX	Thunder AX8-105 SI HAFB	3578	
HB-QAY	Cameron N-120 HAFB	3593	
HB-QAZ	Schroeder Fire Balloons 40/24 HAFB	481	
HB-QBA	Raven-Europe S-66A HAFB	E-315	
HB-QBB	Balloon Works Firefly 10 HAFB	F10-017	
HB-QBD	Colt 160A HAFB	3577	
HB-QBF	Colt AS-105 Mk.2 Hot Air Airship	3570	
HB-QBG	Schroeder Fire Balloons G HAFB	504	
HB-QBH	Lindstrand LBL-150A HAFB	348	
HB-QBI	Lindstrand LBL-120A HAFB	303	
HB-QBJ	Aerostar S-60A HAFB	3209	
HB-QBK	Lindstrand LBL-210A HAFB	455	
HB-QBL	Lindstrand LBL-310A HAFB	330	
HB-QBN	Cameron 105SS HAFB	3680	G-LOKO
HB-QBO	Colt 120A HAFB	3670	
HB-QBP	Cameron A-160 HAFB	3675	
HB-QBQ	Cameron N-56 HAFB	3674	
HB-QBR	Chaize JZ.30F16 HAFB	137	
HB-QBS	Thunder AX9-120 SII HAFB	3718	
HB-QBT	Colt 42A HAFB	3719	
HB-QBU	Colt 31A HAFB	3681	
HB-QBW	Colt AS105 Mk 2 Hot Air Airship	3665	
HB-QBX	Cameron N-145 HAFB	3711	
HB-QBY	Cameron N-145 HAFB	3340	
HB-QBZ	Cameron N-160 HAFB	3776	
HB-QCA	Cameron A-180SV HAFB	3865	
HB-QCB	Cameron N-120 HAFB	3764	
HB-QCC	Cameron N-120 HAFB	3831	
HB-QCD	Thunder AX8-90 SII HAFB	3752	
HB-QCE	Cameron A-160SV HAFB	3872	
HB-QCF	Cameron N-120 HAFB	3959	
HB-QCG	Cameron N-120 HAFB	3968	
HB-QCH	Cameron N-120 HAFB	3937	
HB-QCI	Colt 120A HAFB	3840	
HB-QCJ	Thunder AX9-120 SIITV HAFB	3845	
HB-QCK	Colt 69A HAFB	2581	G-BVKY
HB-QCM	Cameron N-120 HAFB	3854	
HB-QCN	Colt 105A HAFB	3851	
HB-QCO	Thunder AX8-105A HAFB	1407	OO-BVP
HB-QCP	Cameron O-105 HAFB	3145	F-GOOR
HB-QCQ	Lindstrand LBL-120A HAFB	485	
HB-QCR	Lindstrand LBL-120A HAFB	481	
HB-QCS	Augsburg K-945/2-RI Gas Balloon	8908	
HB-QCT	Lindstrand LBL-150A HAFB	472	
HB-QCU	Cameron A-210 HAFB	4014	
HB-QCV	Colt 180A HAFB	3949	
HB-QCW	Cameron O-90 HAFB	3988	
HB-QCX	Balloon Works Firefly 9B-15 HAFB	F9B-015	
HB-QCY	Cameron A-180 HAFB	3993	
HB-QCZ	Cameron A-160 HAFB	3998	
HB-QDB	Sky 65-24 HAFB	058	
HB-QDC	Schroeder Fire Balloons G HAFB	580	
HB-QDD	UltraMagic V-90 HAFB	90/22	
HB-QDE	Balloon Works Firefly 9B-15 HAFB	F9B-018	
HB-QDF	Cameron N-105 HAFB	4074	
HB-QDG	Schroeder Fire Balloons G HAFB	584	
HB-QDH	Cameron A-160 HAFB	4091	
HB-QDI	Aerostar S-66A HAFB	3009	
HB-QDJ	Cameron A-120 HAFB	4110	
HB-QDK	Cameron A-300 HAFB	4009	
HB-QDL	Colt 120A HAFB	4109	D-OTOE
HB-QDM	Schroeder Fire Balloons G HAFB	586	
HB-QDN(2)	Cameron N-90 HAFB	4428	
	(Replacing envelope c/n 4097)		
HB-QDO(2)	Cameron N-160 HAFB	4430	
	(Replacing envelope c/n 4098)		
HB-QDP	Cameron A-120 HAFB	4114	
HB-QDQ	UltraMagic S-130 HAFB	130/12	
HB-QDR	UltraMagic M-90 HAFB	90/23	
HB-QDS	Aerostar RX-9 HAFB	3009	
HB-QDT	Lindstrand LNBL-105A HAFB	147	G-BVTU
HB-QDU	Cameron N-180 HAFB	4174	
HB-QDV	Cameron N-120 HAFB	4209	
HB-QDX	Cameron N-120 HAFB	4219	
HB-QDY	UltraMagic M-65C HAFB	65/70	
	(Reserved as D-OOHP 2.98)		
HB-QDZ	Sky 105-24 HAFB	091	
HB-QEB	Colt 120A HAFB	4152	
HB-QEC	Lindstrand LBL-150A HAFB	502	
HB-QEE	Lindstrand LBL-180A HAFB	517	
HB-QEH	Schroeder Fire Balloons G HAFB	643	
HB-QEJ	Sky 105-24 HAFB	097	
HB-QEK	Schroeder Fire Balloons G HAFB	362	D-OVON
HB-QEL	Sky 105-24 HAFB	093	
HB-QEM	Sky 105-24 HAFB	094	
HB-QEN	Balloon Works Firefly 8 HAFB	F8-425	
HB-QEO	Colt 105A HAFB	4306	
HB-QEP	Cameron N-133 HAFB	4281	
HB-QEQ	Colt 120A HAFB	4283	
HB-QER	Colt 210A HAFB	4307	
HB-QES	Schroeder Fire Balloons G HAFB	669	
HB-QET	Cameron Concept C-60 HAFB	3453	G-BWAM
HB-QEU	Cameron O-105 HAFB	4381	
HB-QEV	Schroeder Fire Balloons G HAFB	700	
HB-QEW	Cameron A-120 HAFB	4413	
HB-QEX	Schroeder Fire Balloons G HAFB	702	
HB-QEY	Colt 120A HAFB	4429	
HB-QEZ	Aerostar RX-9 HAFB	3008	
HB-QFA	Cameron Concept C-60 HAFB	4364	
HB-QFB	Sky 105-24 HAFB	127	
HB-QFC	Aerostar S-66A HAFB	3063	
HB-QFD	Aerostar RX-9 HAFB	3014	
HB-QFE	Schroeder Fire Balloons G HAFB	717	
HB-QFF	Cameron A-120 HAFB	4481	
HB-QFG	Thunder AX7-77ZHAFB	795	F-GFAM
HB-QFH	Sky 105-24 HAFB	141	
HB-QFI	Colt 120A HAFB	4515	
HB-QFJ	Cameron V-65 HAFB	4542	
HB-QFK	Cameron N-120 HAFB	4527	
HB-QFL	Cameron Cows' Heads SS HAFB	4517	
HB-QFM	Aerostar RX-9 HAFB	3016	
HB-QFN	Schroeder Fire Balloons GHAFB	749	
HB-QFO	Aerostar RX-9 HAFB	3017	
HB-QFP	Thunder AX9-120 SII HAFB	4617	
HB-QFQ	Cameron A-400 HAFB	4621	
HB-QFR	Schroeder Fire Balloons G HAFB	778	
HB-QFS	Schroeder Fire Balloons GHAFB	785	
HB-QFT	Cameron O-160 HAFB	4685	
HB-QFU	Lindstrand LBL-105A HAFB	556	
HB-QFV	Sky 90-24 HAFB	169	
HB-QFW	Colt 120A HAFB	4709	
HB-QFX	Cameron N-120 HAFB	4697	
HB-QFY	Cameron A-300 HAFB	4446	

Regn.	Type	C/n	Prev.Id.
HB-QFZ	Cameron A-160 HAFB	4727	
HB-QGC	Sky 105-24 HAFB	180	
HB-QGF	Cameron RX-120 Roziere Replica HAFB	4748	
HB-Q ..	Cameron A-120 HAFB	4011	
HB-...	Cameron V-77 HAFB	2166	
HB-...	Colt 31A Cloudhopper HAFB	1109	
HB-...	Colt 31A Cloudhopper HAFB	1397	
HB-...	Colt 21A HAFB	1032	G-BNFX

MOTOR-GLIDERS

Regn.	Type	C/n	Prev.Id.
HB-2001	Schleicher ASK-14	14054	(D-KISU)
HB-2002	Schleicher ASK-16	16008	(D-KAVQ)
HB-2004	Fournier RF-4D	4097	
HB-2005	Fournier RF-3	28	F-BMDI
HB-2006	Fournier RF-4D	4141	
HB-2010	Scheibe SF-25B Falke	4692	(D-KOSF)
HB-2013	Fournier RF-3	29	F-BMDG
HB-2014	Schleicher ASK-14	14056	(D-KISY)
HB-2018	Sportavia-Pützer RF-5B Sperber	51010	
HB-2025	Glaser-Dirks DG-800A	8-64A38	D-KIIS
HB-2030	Schleicher ASK-16	16016	(D-KIVU)
HB-2031	Schleicher ASK-16	16017	(D-KAAQ)
HB-2033	Schleicher ASK-16	16026	(D-KITU)
HB-2036	Farner Colibri SL-1	001	
HB-2038	Schleicher ASK-16	16037	(D-KIWO)
HB-2040	SZD-45A Ogar	B-660	
HB-2042	Scheibe SF-28A Tandem-Falke	5782	(D-KDFD)
HB-2045	Scheibe SF-25E Super Falke	4340	D-KIOJ HB-2045 (D-KDCN)
HB-2048	Scheibe SF-28A Tandem-Falke	5704	D-KAVM
HB-2053	Eiri PIK-20E	20260	
HB-2055	Eiri PIK-20E	20283	
HB-2057	Eiri PIK-20E	20285	
HB-2059	Hoffmann H-36 Dimona	3523	
HB-2061	Siren/Eiri PIK-20E-IIF	701	F-WANC
HB-2063	Grob G.109	6115	
HB-2068	Glaser-Dirks DG-400	4-8	
HB-2069	Glaser-Dirks DG-400	4-43	
HB-2070	Glaser-Dirks DG-400	4-40	
HB-2073	Glaser-Dirks DG-400	4-57	
HB-2074	Glaser-Dirks DG-400	4-49	
HB-2077	Glaser-Dirks DG-400	4-61	
HB-2082	Glaser-Dirks DG-400	4-90	(PH-742)
HB-2083	Grob G.109B	6231	
HB-2084	Grob G.109B	6220	
HB-2087	Grob G.109B	6258	
HB-2088	Grob G.109B	6270	
HB-2089	Glaser-Dirks DG-400	4-115	
HB-2092	Glaser-Dirks DG-400	4-89	
HB-2094	Valentin Taifun 17E	1029	D-KDSA
HB-2096	Hoffmann H-36 Dimona	36101	
HB-2097	Grob G.109B	6280	
HB-2098	Schempp-Hirth Ventus bT	9/136	HB-1658
HB-2100	Schempp-Hirth Ventus bT	47/242	
HB-2101	Glaser-Dirks DG-400	4-118	
HB-2103	Grob G.109B	6355	
HB-2107	Scheibe SF-25C Falke	44376	(D-KNBB)
HB-2109	Glaser-Dirks DG-400	4-135	
HB-2112	Glaser-Dirks DG-400	4-154	
HB-2114	Schempp-Hirth Ventus bT	282/67	
HB-2116	Schempp-Hirth Ventus bT	303/73	D-KBHC D-KASE(3)
HB-2117	Valentin Taifun 17E	1080	D-KHVA(16)
HB-2119	Hoffmann H-36 Dimona	36215	
HB-2120	Schempp-Hirth Ventus bT	311/75	
HB-2121	Raab Krähe IV	Liz.015	D-KADY(2)
HB-2122	Schempp-Hirth Ventus bT	338/91	
HB-2123	Glaser-Dirks DG-400	4-31	D-KIDG(2)
HB-2125	Glaser-Dirks DG-400	4-206	
HB-2126	Scheibe SF-25C Falke	44436	(D-KIAC)
HB-2127	Glaser-Dirks DG-400	4-210	
HB-2128	Schempp-Hirth Ventus cT	125/399	
HB-2129	Technoflug Piccolo	008	D-KACT(2)
HB-2130	Technoflug Piccolo	010	D-KACL
HB-2131	Technoflug Piccolo	005	D-KAFT
HB-2132	Schleicher ASH-25E	25039	D-KBEB
HB-2134	Glaser-Dirks DG-400	4-227	(D-KIDG)
HB-2135	Schempp-Hirth Ventus cM	15/442	D-KCPB
HB-2136	Schleicher ASW-20L TOP	20403	HB-1569
HB-2138	Schleicher ASW-20 TOP	20053	HB-1417
HB-2139	Glaser-Dirks DG-400	4-47	ZS-VKN D-KBOL
HB-2140	Schleicher ASW-20BL TOP	20955	
HB-2141	Schempp-Hirth Ventus cT	119/393	
HB-2142	Technoflug Piccolo	021	D-KCTB
HB-2144	Schempp-Hirth Nimbus 3T	11/68	D-KHIH
HB-2145	Schempp-Hirth Ventus cT	124/398	
HB-2146	Neukom Elfe S4A/TOP	63	HB-1236
HB-2149	Technoflug Piccolo	024	D-KCFA
HB-2150	Technoflug Piccolo	037	D-KOIB (2)
HB-2151	Technoflug Piccolo	030	D-KCFG
HB-2152	Canard SC	V-01	
HB-2153	Glaser-Dirks DG-400	4-244	
HB-2154	Glaser-Dirks DG-400	4-246	
HB-2155	Hoffmann H-36 Dimona	36277	
HB-2156	Technoflug Piccolo	031	D-KCFH
HB-2157	Schempp-Hirth Discus bT	11/282	D-KCCE(2)
HB-2159	Schempp-Hirth Discus bT	12/287	D-KIDE(2)
HB-2160	Schempp-Hirth Nimbus 3DT	30	
HB-2161	Glaser-Dirks DG-400	4-253	
HB-2163	Valentin Kiwi	K3013	D-KEGX(1)
HB-2164	Schempp-Hirth Ventus cM	18/447	(D-KCPF)
HB-2167	Glaser-Dirks DG-400	4-274	
HB-2168	Schleicher ASW-20L/TOP	20498	HB-1613
HB-2169	Schempp-Hirth Ventus bT	41/231	HB-1788
HB-2170	Schempp-Hirth Ventus cT	149/475	
HB-2171	Schleicher ASH-25E	25050	D-KCCH
HB-2172	Schleicher ASH-25E	25071	D-KBFA
HB-2173	Schempp-Hirth Ventus cT	150/476	
HB-2174	Schempp-Hirth Ventus cM	32/465	
HB-2175	Schempp-Hirth Ventus cM	16/443	D-KCPE
HB-2176	Glaser-Dirks DG-400	4-271	
HB-2177	Stemme S-10	10-20	D-KGCI
HB-2178	Schleicher ASW-20/TOP	20757	HB-1740
HB-2180	Glaser-Dirks DG-500M	5E-25M13	
HB-2181	Schleicher ASW-24E	24830	
HB-2182	Schleicher ASW-24E	24831	
HB-2184	Schempp-Hirth Ventus cM	47/488	
HB-2185	Stemme S-10	10-16	D-KGCD(1)
HB-2187	Stemme S-10	10-08	D-KKBH
HB-2188	Schempp-Hirth Discus bT	40/352	
HB-2189	Scheibe SF-25C Falke	44497	D-KIOG(2)
HB-2191	Hoffmann HK-36R Super Dimona	36316	
HB-2192	Schleicher ASW-24E	24820	D-KAXH
HB-2193	Schempp-Hirth Discus bT	97/436	
HB-2194	Schempp-Hirth Discus bT	70/397	
HB-2198	Schempp-Hirth Discus bT	54/372	
HB-2199	Stemme S-10	10-21	D-KGCH
HB-2201	Glaser-Dirks DG-500M	5E-43M21	
HB-2202	Glaser-Dirks DG-400	4-282	(D-KIDG)
HB-2203	Glaser-Dirks DG-600M	6-63M14	
HB-2204	Glaser-Dirks DG-600M	6-82M28	
HB-2205	Hoffmann HK-36R Super Dimona	36338	
HB-2206	Schempp-Hirth Ventus cT	163/530	
HB-2207	Schempp-Hirth Ventus cT	78/409	
HB-2208	Hoffmann HK-36R Super Dimona	36349	
HB-2210	Schempp-Hirth Ventus cM	67/529	
HB-2211	Glaser-Dirks DG-400	4-289	
HB-2213	Valentin Kiwi	K3015	D-KEGX(3)
HB-2214	Technoflug Piccolo B	061	D-KIMW(2)
HB-2217	Stemme S-10	10-14	D-KDNE
HB-2218	Schempp-Hirth Nimbus 3DM	3/16	D-KEML

Regn.	Type	C/n	Prev.Id.
HB-2219	Grob G.103C Twin IIISL	35013	
HB-2220	Valentin Kiwi	K3017	D-KEGX(5)
HB-2222	Glaser-Dirks DG-600M	6-64M15	
HB-2223	Schempp-Hirth Ventus cM	86/567	
HB-2224	Grob G.103C Twin IIISL	35032	
HB-2225	Technoflug Piccolo B	064	
HB-2226	Schempp-Hirth Discus bT	85/420	
HB-2229	Schempp-Hirth Ventus cT	173/564	
HB-2230	Stemme S-10	10-44	D-KGCD(4)
HB-2231	Technoflug Piccolo B	067	D-KAAL(3)
HB-2232	Schempp-Hirth Nimbus 3DT	59	
HB-2233	Schempp-Hirth Ventus cT	175/572	
HB-2234	Glaser-Dirks DG-400	4-96	OO-DGI
HB-2235	Stemme S-10	10-48	
HB-2236	Glaser-Dirks DG-500M	5E-79M32	
HB-2239	Glaser-Dirks DG-500M	5E-95M41	
HB-2240	Schleicher ASW-22BE	22067	
HB-2241	Stemme S-10	10-7	D-KARD
HB-2243	Schempp-Hirth Discus bT	115/468	
HB-2245	Schempp-Hirth Ventus cM	101/593	
HB-2248	Stemme S-10	10-9	D-KOHM(2)
HB-2249	Glaser-Dirks DG-500M	5E-93M40	
HB-2251	Schempp-Hirth Ventus cT	183/601	
HB-2252	Technoflug Piccolo B	084	D-KIMZ
HB-2253	Schleicher ASH-25E	25171	
HB-2254	Schempp-Hirth Nimbus 4M	27/10	
HB-2255	Technoflug Piccolo B	100	D-KENZ
HB-2256	Glaser-Dirks DG-500M	5E-122M52	
HB-2258	Schempp-Hirth Ventus cM	63/524	D-KALE(2)
HB-2260	Technoflug Piccolo B	093	D-KIIB
HB-2261	Scheibe SF-25C Falke	44570	D-KTIH
HB-2262	Schleicher ASH-26E	26037	D-KHHE
HB-2263	Schempp-Hirth Ventus 2cT	9/33	D-KCUP
HB-2264	Glaser-Dirks DG-500M	5E-113M50	(D-KNDG)
HB-2266	Schleicher ASH-26E	26057	D-KLEH(1)
HB-2268	Technoflug Piccolo B	101	D-KIKC
HB-2269	Schleicher ASH-26E	26055	D-KKTG
HB-2270	Schleicher ASH-26E	26053	D-KMML(1)
			D-2270
HB-2271-38	Glaser-Dirks DG-500M	5E-148M60	
HB-2272	Technoflug Piccolo B	102	D-KAIW
HB-2273	Valentin Kiwi	3008	D-KBEI
HB-2274	Technoflug Piccolo B	041	D-KAIY
			D-MAIY
			D-KAIY
HB-2275	Glaser-Dirks DG-800A	8-61A36	
HB-2276	Schleicher ASH-26E	26074	
HB-2277	Schempp-Hirth Discus bT	157/558	
HB-2278	Glaser-Dirks DG-800B	8-51B5	D-KKDG
			D-KEBC
HB-2279	Scheibe SF-25C Falke	44351	D-KNAI
HB-2280	Scheibe SF-25C Rotax-Falke	44595	D-KTIT(1)
HB-2281	Schleicher ASH-25E	25052	D-KKHB
HB-2282	Technoflug Piccolo B	108	D-KIHI (2)
HB-2283	Schleicher ASH-26E	26088	(D-5222)
HB-2284	Schempp-Hirth Nimbus 4 DM	10/18	D-KCUC
HB-2285	Glaser-Dirks DG-500M	5E-2M01	JRV . . . .
			D-5007
HB-2286	Schempp-Hirth Ventus 2cT	14/54	
HB-2287	Schempp-Hirth Nimbus 4 DM	2/6	F-CFUU
			D-KFUU
HB-2288-VZ	Schleicher ASH-26E	26122	
HB-2289	Schempp-Hirth Ventus 2cT	11/42	D-KAFT(2)
HB-2290	Schempp-Hirth Ventus 2cM	32/56	D-KSEE
HB-2291	Glaser-Dirks DG-800B	8-83B20	D-KDFF(3)
HB-2292	Glaser-Dirks DG-800B	8-93B28	D-KMEG
HB-2293	Schempp-Hirth Ventus 2cM	24/46	D-KFFH
HB-2294	Schempp-Hirth Ventus 2cM	26/48	D-KPUE
HB-2295	Technoflug Piccolo B	113	
HB-2296	HOAC HK-36TTC Super Dimona	36564	
HB-2297	HOAC HK-36TTC Super Dimona	36535	
HB-2298	Schempp-Hirth Ventus 2cM	40/70	
HB-2299	Technoflug Piccolo B	114	
HB-2300	Glaser-Dirks DG-800B	8-76B17	D-KTHG
HB-2301	Technoflug Piccolo B	112	

Regn.	Type	C/n	Prev.Id.
HB-2302	Technoflug Piccolo B	057	D-KIMF(2)
HB-2303	Glaser-Dirks DG-400	4-214	D-KEDI (2)
HB-2304	Schleicher ASH-26E	26139	
HB-2305	Stemme S-10VT	11-003	
HB-2306	Schleicher ASH-26E	26127	
HB-2307	Glaser-Dirks DG-800B	8-82B19	D-KIBU(2)
HB-2308	Glaser-Dirks DG-800B	8-122B51	
HB-2310	HOAC HK-36TTC Super Dimona	36570	
HB-2311	Glaser-Dirks DG-800B	8-118B47	
HB-2312	Glaser-Dirks DG-800B	8-116B45	D-KRDS
HB-2313	Glaser-Dirks DG-800B	8-98B33	D-KTAR
HB-2314	HOAC HK-36TTC Super Dimona	36580	
HB-2315	Schleicher ASW-24/TOP	24811	D-KKDK
HB-2316	Schleicher ASH-26E	26142	
HB-2317	Schempp-Hirth Ventus 2cM	51/105	D-7317
	(Formerly Ventus 2c c/n 37/105)		
HB-2318	Schleicher ASH-25E	25019	D-KEMU
HB-2319	Glaser-Dirks DG-800B	8-101B35	D-KNTT
HB-2320	Glaser-Dirks DG-800B	8-50B4	D-KBDW
HB-2321	IAR IS.28M2/GR	76	
HB-2322	Glaser-Dirks DG-800B	8-135B64	
HB-2323	Glaser-Dirks DG-800B	8-123B52	
HB-2324	HOAC HK-36TTC Super Dimona	36594	
HB-2325	Schempp-Hirth Ventus 2cT	32/111	
HB-2327	Glaser-Dirks DG-800B	8-153B77	
HB-2328	HOAC HK-36TTC Super Dimona	36619	
HB-2329	Schleicher ASH-26E	26096	HB-3203
HB-2330	Schleicher ASH-26E	26033	D-KJAS
HB-2331	Glaser-Dirks DG-800B	8-173B97	
HB-2332	Glaser-Dirks DG-800B	8-129B56	
HB-2333	Glaser-Dirks DG-500MB	5E-190MB5	D-KLOC
HB-2335	HOAC HK-36TC-Eco Super Dimona	36581	
HB-2336	Glaser-Dirks DG-800B	8-87B23	D-KFMA
HB-2237	Schempp-Hirth Ventuc 2cT	45/144	
HB-2338	HOACHK-36TTC Super Dimona	36652	
HB-2339	Schempp-Hirth Nimbus 4 DM	38/54	
HB-2340	Glaser-Dirks DG-800B	8-117B46	D-KBPM
HB-2341	Glaser-Dirks DG-800B	8-183B107	
HB-2343	Technoflug Piccolo B	105	D-KAIX(2)
HB-2344	Glaser-Dirks DG-800B	8-170B94	
HB-2346	Glaser-Dirks DG-800B	8-177B101	
HB-2347	Glaser-Dirks DG-800B	8-182B106	

GLIDERS

Regn.	Type	C/n	Prev.Id.
HB-87	Grünau Baby II	90	
HB-120	Grünau Baby II	281	
HB-183	Grünau Baby II	unkn	
HB-190	RRG Zögling	HS1	
HB-223	Hütter H.28	unkn	
HB-225	Spalinger S-19	unkn	
HB-234	Grünau Baby II	unkn	
HB-257	Moswey IIa	unkn	
HB-280	Spalinger S-21H	280	
HB-289	Grünau Baby IIb	AB201	
HB-309	Moswey IIa	unkn	
HB-336	Spyr IV	unkn	
HB-348	Nord 1300	210	F-CRJP
			F-CAQV
HB-366	Spalinger S-22 II	unkn	
HB-369	Spyr V Replica	unkn	
HB-373	Moswey III	44	
HB-374	Moswey III	unkn	
HB-376	Moswey III	unkn	
HB-380	Moswey III	unkn	
HB-381	DFS-Meise	unkn	
I ID-304	DFS-Meise	unkn	
HB-411	Spalinger S-18 IIB	unkn	
HB-418	Spalinger S-16 II	unkn	
HB-437	Spalinger S-25M	unkn	
HB-442	Karpf Baby	unkn	

Regn.	Type	C/n	Prev.Id.
HB-444	Karpf Baby	unkn	
HB-458	Spalinger S-18 III	unkn	
HB-461	Karpf Zögling	unkn	
HB-462	Karpf Baby	unkn	
HB-465	Schleicher Ka.2 Rhönschwalbe	122	
HB-475	Kranich III	1167	
HB-485	Moswey III	unkn	
HB-486	Spalinger S-18 III	unkn	
HB-491	Olympia-DFS Meise	unkn	
HB-494	Karpf Baby	1	
HB-505	Karpf Baby	unkn	
HB-509	Spyr 5A	unkn	
HB-510	Spalinger S-18 III	unkn	
HB-522	Müller Moswey IVA	4/2	BGA2277/DPS HB-522
HB-532	Fauvel AV-36	unkn	
HB-534	Neukom Elfe M	unkn	
HB-535	Schleicher Ka.2B	unkn	
HB-545	Moswey III	unkn	
HB-552	Weber-Landolf-Münch WLM-1	03	
HB-556	Weihe 50	unkn	
HB-560	Fauvel AV.36	31	
HB-562	WLM-2	01	
HB-574	Schleicher Ka.6 Rhönsegler	175	
HB-575	Scheibe L-Spatz 55	unkn	
HB-576	Schleicher Rhönlerche II *(Dismantled)*	182	
HB-580	Grünau Baby IIB	unkn	
HB-586	Schleicher Rhönlerche II	238	
HB-587	Schleicher Ka.2B Rhönschwalbe	254	
HB-588	Schleicher Ka.6 Rhönsegler	249	
HB-592	Schleicher Rhönlerche II	230	
HB-593	Scheibe L-Spatz 55	unkn	
HB-595	Schleicher Rhönlerche II	261	
HB-597	Schleicher Rhönlerche II	266	
HB-602	Schleicher Ka.6BR Rhönsegler	335	
HB-608	Schleicher Rhönlerche II	379	
HB-609	Schleicher Ka.6BR Rhönsegler	356	
HB-610	Schleicher Rhönlerche II	401	
HB-612	Scheibe L-Spatz 55	646	
HB-617	Schleicher Ka.6BR Rhönsegler	457	
HB-637	Schleicher K.8B	636	
HB-643	Schleicher Ka.6CR Rhönsegler	620	
HB-645	Schleicher Ka.2B Rhönschwalbe	633	
HB-649	Schleicher Rhönlerche II	797	
HB-651	Schleicher Ka.6CR Rhönsegler	722	
HB-652	Schleicher K7 Rhönadler	765	
HB-653	Schleicher K7 Rhönadler	777	
HB-654	Schleicher Ka.6CR Rhönsegler	675	
HB-655	Schleicher Rhönlerche II	710	
HB-656	SZD-12A Mucha 100A	492	
HB-663	Schleicher K.8B	669	
HB-664	Schleicher Rhönlerche II	672	
HB-671	Schleicher K.8B	838	
HB-672	Schleicher Rhönlerche II	798	
HB-677	Schleicher K7 Rhönadler	891	
HB-686	SZD-22C Mucha Standard	614	
HB-687	Schleicher K7 Rhönadler	933	
HB-689	Schleicher K.8B	994	
HB-690	Scheibe Bergfalke II/55	340	
HB-692	Schleicher Rhönlerche II	956	
HB-693	SZD-22C Mucha Standard	F-676	
HB-695	Schleicher K.8B	1053	
HB-697	Schleicher Rhönlerche II	1120	
HB-701	Schleicher K.8B	1059	
HB-703	Schleicher Ka.6CR Rhönsegler	6006	
HB-704	Schleicher K.8B	1123	
HB-706	SZD-22C Mucha Standard	F-675	
HB-708	Schleicher Rhönlerche II	3003	
HB-710	Schleicher K.8B	8004	
HB-711	Schleicher Ka.6CR Rhönsegler	6065	
HB-712	Schleicher K.8B	8351	
HB-713	Schleicher K.8B	1106	
HB-714	SZD-24C Foka	W-142	
HB-724	Schleicher Ka.2B Rhönschwalbe	1064	
HB-730	Schleicher Ka.6CR Rhönsegler	6049	
HB-733	Schleicher Ka.2B Rhönschwalbe	2005	
HB-734	Götz/Schleicher K.8B	04	
HB-736	Neukom Elfe MN	unkn	
HB-737	Scheibe L-Spatz 55	551	D-1770
HB-742	Glasflügel H.301 Libelle	01	
HB-744	Slingsby T-31B Cadet TX.3	908	BGA3251/FGN XE795
HB-745	Scheibe SF-26A Standard	5033	
HB-747	SZD-22C Mucha Standard	790	
HB-748	Slingsby T.50 Skylark 4	1371	
HB-750	SZD-25A Lis	727	SP-2343
HB-752	Schleicher K.8B	8184	
HB-753	Schleicher K.8B	8263	
HB-757	Schleicher Rhönlerche II	3033	
HB-759	SZD-22C Mucha Standard	778	
HB-760	Schleicher K.8B	8280	
HB-762	HBV Diamant	V-3	
HB-764	Schleicher K.8B	8281	
HB-765	Schleicher K.8B	8254	
HB-767	Slingsby T.50 Skylark 4	1401	
HB-768	Schleicher K7 Rhönadler	7112	
HB-771	Schleicher Ka.6CR Rhönsegler	6236	
HB-778	Schleicher K.8B	8328	
HB-781	Neukom Elfe MN-R	3	
HB-786	Schleicher Rhönlerche II	3054	
HB-787	Schleicher K.8B	8420	
HB-789	Schleicher Ka.6CR-PE Rhönsegler	6143	
HB-790	Schleicher K.8B	8409	
HB-795	Scheibe SF-26A	5051	D-1801
HB-796	Schleicher Ka.6CR Rhönsegler	6008	
HB-798	Glasflügel H.301 Libelle	47	
HB-803	Neukom Elfe Standard S2/3P	7	
HB-804	Neukom Elfe Standard S2/3V	8	
HB-805	Schleicher Ka.6CR Rhönsegler	6431/Si	
HB-806	Schleicher K.8B	8384/SH	
HB-807	Schleicher Rhönlerche II	3064Br	
HB-811	Götz/Schleicher K.8B	8363Go	
HB-816	Schleicher Ka.6CR Rhönsegler	682	
HB-825	Schleicher K.8B	8494	
HB-827	Schleicher Rhönlerche II	3073Br	
HB-828	Götz/Schleicher K.8B	8504Go	
HB-829	Götz/Schleicher K.8B	8528Go	
HB-830	Schleicher K.8B	8518	
HB-833	Musger Mg 23SL Arrow	25	
HB-834	Schleicher K.8B	8548	
HB-839	Schleicher Ka.6E	4025	
HB-840	Schleicher K.8B	8555	
HB-841	Neukom Elfe S3P	9	
HB-842	Neukom Elfe S2/3P	11	
HB-845	Neukom Elfe S3P	13	
HB-846	Götz/Schleicher K.8B	8527Go	
HB-847	Götz/Schleicher K.8B	8526Go	
HB-848	Schleicher Rhönlerche II	3057Br	
HB-850	Schleicher Ka.6E	4018	
HB-851	Schleicher Ka.6CR Rhönsegler	824	
HB-857	Akaflieg Braunschweig SB-7A	4	
HB-859	Neukom Elfe S2/3	unkn	
HB-860	Schleicher Rhönlerche II	955	
HB-871	Schleicher Ka.6CR Rhönsegler	6620	
HB-872	Neukom AN-66	14	
HB-873	Neukom Elfe S3	16	
HB-878	Schleicher Ka.6CR Rhönsegler	6584	
HB-880	Götz/Schleicher K.8B	8640Go	
HB-884	Schleicher K.8B	8694	
HB-887	Castel C.25S	189	BGA2113/DGW F-CRKI
HB-888	Schleicher K.8B	8692	
HB-893	HBV Diamant 16.5	017	
HB-896	Schleicher Ka.6E	4105	
HB-899	Schleicher K.8B	8728	
HB-901-NN	Neukom AN-66	20	
HB-902	Neukom Elfe S3P	18	
HB-903	Neukom Elfe S3P	17	
HB-904	Neukom AN-66B	22	
HB-908	Götz/Schleicher K.8B	8727	

Regn.	Type	C/n	Prev.Id.
HB-909	Glasflügel H.301 Libelle	58	
HB-911	Schempp-Hirth Cirrus	11	
HB-916	HBV Diamant 18	030	
HB-917	HBV Diamant 18	036	
HB-919	Bölkow Phoebus A-1	793	
HB-924	Schleicher Ka.6CR Rhönsegler	6646	
HB-933	Bölkow Phoebus B-1	794	
HB-940	HBV Diamant 16-5	060	
HB-943	Schleicher K.8B	8601/A	
HB-945	Slingsby T-53B	1702	
HB-946	Rolladen-Schneider LS-1A	17	
HB-949	Glasflügel H201B Standard Libelle	48	
HB-953	Schleicher ASW-12	12010	
HB-956	Rolladen-Schneider LS-1C	16/69	
HB-957	Schiller FS-1	1	
HB-968	Glasflügel H201B Standard Libelle	104	
HB-969	Schleicher Rhönlerche II	3031	
HB-970	Schleicher ASW-15	15012	
HB-972	Glasflügel H201B Standard Libelle	67	
HB-976	Glasflügel H201B Standard Libelle	164	
HB-977	Neukom Elfe S4	23	
HB-978	Schleicher Ka.6E	4312	
HB-979	Schleicher Ka.6E	4048	
HB-982	Neukom Elfe 17	46	
HB-983	Rolladen-Schneider LS-1B	33	
HB-992	Schleicher ASW-15	15042	
HB-996	Schleicher Ka.6CR Rhönsegler	6534	
HB-1004	Rolladen-Schneider LS-1C	37	
HB-1008	Schleicher ASW-15	15105	
HB-1010	Glasflügel H201B Standard Libelle	202	
HB-1011	Schleicher ASW-15	15121	
HB-1013	Schleicher ASW-15	15065	
HB-1014	SZD-12 Mucha 100	87	F-CCDU
			SP-1461
HB-1015	Schempp-Hirth Standard Cirrus	113	
HB-1016	Glasflügel H201B Standard Libelle	195	
HB-1018	Schleicher ASW-15	15111	
HB-1019	Schleicher ASW-15	15104	
HB-1020	Schleicher ASW-15	15119	
HB-1029	Schleicher ASW-15	15143	
HB-1030	Schleicher ASW-15	15094	
HB-1033	Schempp-Hirth Standard Cirrus	170	
HB-1036	Glasflügel H201B Standard Libelle	201	
HB-1042	Rolladen-Schneider LS-1C	84	
HB-1043	Neukom AN-17	27	
HB-1044	Neukom AN-66C	26	
HB-1052	Schleicher Ka.6CR Rhönsegler	6014	
HB-1055	Glasflügel H201B Standard Libelle	287	
HB-1056	Glasflügel H201B Standard Libelle	288	
HB-1057	Glasflügel H401 Kestrel	63	
HB-1058	Glasflügel H201B Standard Libelle	312	
HB-1061	Rolladen-Schneider LS-1D	89	
HB-1062	Glasflügel H202 Standard Libelle	169	D-0649
HB-1064	Schleicher Ka.6E	4384	
HB-1066	Glasflügel H201B Standard Libelle	296	
HB-1068	Rolladen-Schneider LS-1D	111	
HB-1070	Glasflügel H201B Standard Libelle	311	
HB-1072	LET L-13 Blanik	175106	
HB-1074	Neukom Elfe 17	8/36	
HB-1075	LET L-13 Blanik	175113	
HB-1078	Schleicher ASK-13	13675AB	
HB-1079	Neukom Elfe 17	31	
HB-1080	Neukom Elfe MK	1	
HB-1081	Neukom Elfe 17	6/39	
HB-1082	Glasflügel H201B Standard Libelle	332	
HB-1085	Glasflügel H201B Standard Libelle	407	
HB-1086	Glasflügel H201B Standard Libelle	351	
HB-1087	Neukom Elfe 17	11	
HB-1089	Glasflügel H201B Standard Libelle	357	
HB-1091	Glasflügel H201B Standard Libelle	397	
HB-1100	Pilatus B4-PC11AF	001	
HB-1101	Pilatus B4-PC11	002	
HB-1103	Pilatus B4-PC11	004	
HB-1105	Pilatus B4-PC11	006	
HB-1106	Pilatus B4-PC11	007	
HB-1108	Pilatus B4-PC11	009	
HB-1112	Pilatus B4-PC11	013	
HB-1116	Pilatus B4-PC11	024	
HB-1120	Pilatus B4-PC11	044	
HB-1122	Pilatus B4-PC11	056	
HB-1123	Pilatus B4-PC11	057	
HB-1125	Pilatus B4-PC11	064	
HB-1126	Pilatus B4-PC11A	068	
HB-1128	Pilatus B4-PC11	079	
HB-1130	Pilatus B4-PC11	118	
HB-1131	Pilatus B4-PC11AF	119	
HB-1132	Pilatus B4-PC11	120	
HB-1133	Pilatus B4-PC11	014	
HB-1139	Pilatus B4-PC11AF	095	
HB-1143	Pilatus B4-PC11	117	
HB-1148	Pilatus B4-PC11	143	
HB-1156	Glasflügel H201B Standard Libelle	403	
HB-1163	Neukom Elfe S4	55	
HB-1165	Neukom Elfe 17	34	
HB-1166	Neukom Elfe 17	32	
HB-1167	Neukom Elfe 17	15/35	
HB-1168	Glasflügel H201B Standard Libelle	443	
HB-1169	Neukom Elfe S4	unkn	
HB-1171	G.Steiner SB-7	701	
HB-1173(*)	Bölkow Phoebus C	934	
HB-1174	Glasflügel H401 Kestrel	95	
HB-1176	Neukom Elfe 17	16/33	
HB-1177	Glasflügel H201B Standard Libelle	505	
HB-1178	Neukom Elfe 17	40	
HB-1179	Schleicher ASW-15B	15306	
HB-1182	Neukom Elfe 17A	42	
HB-1185	SZD-30 Pirat	S.01-33	
HB-1186	Schempp-Hirth Nimbus 2	67	
HB-1189	Glasflügel H201B Standard Libelle	506	
HB-1190	Neukom Elfe S4	82	
HB-1192	Glasflügel H201B Standard Libelle	520	
HB-1193	Schempp-Hirth Standard Cirrus	418	
HB-1199	Neukom Elfe S4A	47	
HB-1212	Schempp-Hirth Standard Cirrus	383	
HB-1213	SZD-36 Cobra 15	W-667	
HB-1218	Neukom Elfe 17A	61	
HB-1219	Neukom Elfe S4A	53	
HB-1220	Neukom Elfe S4A	48	
HB-1225	Glasflügel H401 Kestrel	124	
HB-1227	Sperber	1	
HB-1230	SZD-38A Jantar 1	B-615	
HB-1231	Glasflügel H401 Kestrel	119	
HB-1232	Glasflügel H101 Salto	43	
HB-1233	Schempp-Hirth Standard Cirrus	530	
HB-1235	Eiri PIK-20B	20037	
HB-1238	Rolladen-Schneider LS-1F	258	
HB-1239	Glasflügel H401 Kestrel	70	
HB-1242	Grob Standard Cirrus	564G	
HB-1245	Schleicher Rhönlerche II	116	
HB-1247	Neukom Elfe S4A	72	
HB-1248	Schempp-Hirth Standard Cirrus	87	D-0688
HB-1249	Glasflügel H205 Club Libelle	85	
HB-1252	Pilatus B4-PC11	172	
HB-1253	Pilatus B4-PC11AF	175	
HB-1255	Pilatus B4-PC11A	196	
HB-1257	Pilatus B4-PC11AF	188	
HB-1260	Glasflügel H205 Club Libelle (Mod)	46	
HB-1266	Glasflügel H205 Club Libelle	59	
HB-1267	Neukom Elfe S4A	68	
HB-1268	Glasflügel H205 Club Libelle	60	
HB-1273	Neukom Elfe 17A	49	
HB-1275	Neukom Elfe 17A	75	
HB-1276	Glaser-Dirks DG-100	17	
HB-1279	Neukom Elfe S4A	70	
HB-1283	Neukom Elfe S4A	80	
HB-1292	HBV Diamant 16.5	68	
HB-1293	Schempp-Hirth Standard Cirrus	625	
HB-1294	Glasflügel H206 Hornet	30	
HB-1295	Glasflügel H206 Hornet	6	
HB-1296	Glasflügel H206 Hornet	2	

Regn.	Type	C/n	Prev.Id.
HB-1299	Standard Austria S	44	F-CCPU
HB-1301	Grob G.102 Astir CS	1126	
HB-1302	Neukom Elfe 17A	85	
HB-1303	LET L-13 Blanik	026351	
HB-1305	Neukom Elfe S4A	62	
HB-1314	Pilatus B4-PC11AF	129	
HB-1317	Pilatus B4-PC11AF	242	
HB-1318	Pilatus B4-PC11	244	
HB-1319	Pilatus B4-PC11AF	247	
HB-1320	Pilatus B4-PC11AF	258	
HB-1321	Pilatus B4-PC11AF	276	
HB-1329	Glaser-Dirks DG-100	69	
HB-1331	Glaser-Dirks DG-100	77	
HB-1333	Grob G.102 Astir CS	1380	
HB-1334	Glaser-Dirks DG-200	2-2	
HB-1337	Grob G.102 Astir CS	1334	
HB-1340	Delphin	001	
HB-1341	Grob G.102 Astir CS	1432	
HB-1343	Schempp-Hirth Standard Cirrus B	693	
HB-1346	Glaser-Dirks DG-100	93	
HB-1347	Glaser-Dirks DG-100	96	
HB-1351	Grob G.102 Astir CS	1473	
HB-1353	Rolladen-Schneider LS-3	3005	
HB-1354	Rolladen-Schneider LS-3	3008	
HB-1357	Rolladen-Schneider LS-3	3025	
HB-1358	Rolladen-Schneider LS-3	3026	
HB-1359	Rolladen-Schneider LS-3	3033	
HB-1361	Rolladen-Schneider LS-3	3036	
HB-1364	Rolladen-Schneider LS-3	3046	
HB-1366	Rolladen-Schneider LS-3	3066	
HB-1371	Rolladen-Schneider LS-3A	3201	
HB-1372	Rolladen-Schneider LS-3A	3095	
HB-1373	Glasflügel H201B Standard Libelle	414	
HB-1374	Glasflügel H303 Mosquito	14	
HB-1376	Grob G.102 Astir CS	1490	
HB-1379	Schleicher ASW-19B	19110	
HB-1381	Grob G.102 Astir CS	1629	
HB-1388	SZD-41A Jantar Standard	B-796	
HB-1394	Grob G.102 Astir CS 77	1687	
HB-1395	Schempp-Hirth Mini-Nimbus HS-7	35	
HB-1396	SZD-41A Jantar Standard	B-809	
HB-1398	Grob G.103 Twin Astir II	3044	
HB-1405	Schempp-Hirth Mini-Nimbus HS-7	44	
HB-1406	Grob G.103 Twin Astir II	3088	
HB-1407	Glaser-Dirks DG-200	2-14	
HB-1408	Glaser-Dirks DG-200	2-16	
HB-1409	Glaser-Dirks DG-200	2-18	
HB-1410	Glaser-Dirks DG-200	2-20	
HB-1414	Schempp-Hirth Mini-Nimbus HS-7	46	
HB-1418	Rolladen-Schneider LS-3	3312	
HB-1419	Glasflügel H303 Mosquito	91	
HB-1421	Grob G.103 Twin Astir II	3090	
HB-1422	Schleicher ASW-19	19179	
HB-1423	Glasflügel H303B Mosquito	115	
HB-1425	Schempp-Hirth Mini-Nimbus C	107	
HB-1428	Glaser-Dirks DG-200	2-37	
HB-1429	Valentin Mistral C	MC 012/78	
HB-1430	Grob G.102 Astir CS 77	1726	
HB-1432	Glasflügel H303B Mosquito	118	
HB-1433	Rolladen-Schneider LS-3A	3137	
HB-1434	Grob G.102 Astir CS 77	1731	
HB-1437	Schempp-Hirth Mini-Nimbus C	106	
HB-1438	Grob G.102 Astir CS 77	1771	
HB-1439	Glaser-Dirks DG-100	104	
HB-1440	Schempp-Hirth Mini-Nimbus C	87	
HB-1444	Glaser-Dirks DG-200	2-55	
HB-1446	Grob G.102 Astir CS 77	1772	
HB-1449	Schleicher ASW-20	20129	
HB-1450	Schleicher ASW-20	20118	
HB-1452	Schempp-Hirth Mini-Nimbus C	111	
HB-1453	Schempp-Hirth Mini-Nimbus B	92	
HB-1458	Grob G.102 Astir CS 77	1812	
HB-1459	Grob G.102 Astir CS 77	1804	
HB-1460	Molino PIK-20D	20646	
HB-1463	Rolladen-Schneider LS-3A	3148	
HB-1464	Glaser-Dirks DG-100G	E11-G5	
HB-1467	Grob G.102 Astir CS 77	1786	
HB-1468	Glaser-Dirks DG-100 Elan	E-13	
HB-1469	Rolladen-Schneider LS-3-17	3270	
HB-1473	Grob G.103 Twin Astir II	3226	
HB-1475	Rolladen-Schneider LS-3A	3240	
HB-1478	Schleicher ASW-19B	19259	
HB-1479	Schleicher ASK-18B	18039	
HB-1480	Schempp-Hirth Nimbus 2C	189	
HB-1486	Club Libelle 205	28	
HB-1490	Schempp-Hirth Mini-Nimbus C	131	
HB-1491	Grob G.102 Astir CS 77	1605	
HB-1492	SZD-42-2 Jantar 2B	B-873	
HB-1493	SZD-42-2 Jantar 2B	B-874	
HB-1496	Schempp-Hirth Nimbus 2	44	D-1229
HB-1498	Grob G.102 Speed Astir IIB	4066	
HB-1501	Rolladen-Schneider LS-3-17	3238	
HB-1503	Schempp-Hirth Mini-Nimbus C	137	
HB-1504	Grob G.102 Astir CS 77	1836	
HB-1505	Pilatus B4-PC11AF	309	D-1161
			HB-1505
HB-1507	SZD-48-1 Jantar Standard 2	W-918	
HB-1508	Schempp-Hirth Mini-Nimbus C	147	
HB-1513	Schempp-Hirth Mini-Nimbus C	146	
HB-1515	Glaser-Dirks DG-100 Elan	E-28	
HB-1519	Schleicher ASW-20	20292	
HB-1525	Rolladen-Schneider LS-3A	3451	
HB-1527	Rhönlerche II	10060	
HB-1530	Grob G.103 Standard Astir II	5045S	
HB-1533	Schempp-Hirth Nimbus 2C	227	
HB-1537	Schleicher ASW-19B	19320	
HB-1538	Glaser-Dirks DG-100G Elan	E31-G16	
HB-1540	Grob G.103 Twin Astir II	3537	
HB-1544	Glaser-Dirks DG-200/17	2-120/1725	
HB-1545	Schleicher ASK-21	21027	
HB-1546	Schempp-Hirth Nimbus 2C	231	
HB-1547	Glaser-Dirks DG-100G Elan	E40-G22	
HB-1548	Standard Libelle	309	
HB-1549	Kranich III	080	
HB-1550	Valentin Mistral C	MC 033/81	
HB-1551	Rolladen-Schneider LS-4	4010	
HB-1552	Delphin	02	
HB-1553	SZD-48-1 Jantar Standard 2	B-1145	
HB-1554	Schleicher ASK-21	21053	
HB-1556	Glasflügel H201B Standard Libelle	582	
HB-1557	Schempp-Hirth Janus C	110	
HB-1560	SZD-48-1 Jantar Standard 2	B-1162	
HB-1561	Rolladen-Schneider LS-4	4050	
HB-1563	Grob G.103 Twin Astir II	3600	
HB-1564	Rolladen-Schneider LS-4	4025	
HB-1567	Rolladen-Schneider LS-4	4060	
HB-1568	Schempp-Hirth Janus C	149	
HB-1570	Schempp-Hirth Ventus A	18	
HB-1574	Rolladen-Schneider LS-4	4107	
HB-1575	Glaser-Dirks DG-100G Elan	E69-G44	
HB-1576	Glaser-Dirks DG-100G Elan	E58-G34	
HB-1577	Glasflügel H304	241	
HB-1579	Glaser-Dirks DG-100 Elan	E64-G39	
HB-1581	Grob G.103 Twin II Acro	3654-K-23	
HB-1582	Valentin Mistral C	MC 040/81	
HB-1583	Rolladen-Schneider LS-4	4120	
HB-1585	SZD-48-1 Jantar Standard 2	B-1170	
HB-1586	Glaser-Dirks DG-100G Elan	E66-G41	
HB-1588	Glasflügel H304	237	
HB-1589	Schleicher ASK-21	21078	
HB-1590	Schleicher ASK-21	21101	
HB-1591	Schleicher ASK-21	21102	
HB-1592	Glaser-Dirks DG-100G Elan	E78-G53	
HB-1593	Glaser-Dirks DG-200/17	2-160/1751	
HB-1594	Rolladen-Schneider LS-4	4158	
HB-1595	Rolladen-Schneider LS-4	4112	
HB-1596	Valentin Mistral C	MC 042/81	
HB-1598	Schempp-Hirth Mini-Nimbus C	159	
HB-1599	Schempp-Hirth Ventus b	75	
HB-1601	Schleicher ASW-20	20428	

Regn.	Type	C/n	Prev.Id.
HB-1602	Rolladen-Schneider LS-4	4174	
HB-1605	Grob G.103A Twin II Acro	3678-K-29	
HB-1606	Glasflügel H304B	349	D-9375
HB-1607	Glasflügel H304	250	
HB-1608	SZD-48-1 Jantar Standard 2	B-1194	
HB-1609	Glaser-Dirks DG-100 Elan	E-87	
HB-1610	Glasflügel H304	253	
HB-1611	Glaser-Dirks DG-200	2-159	
HB-1612	Glaser-Dirks DG-100 Elan	E-94	
HB-1615	Rolladen-Schneider LS-1F	371	
HB-1618	Grob G.102 Club Astir IIIB	5568CB	
HB-1619	Rolladen-Schneider LS-4	4080	
HB-1620	Schleicher ASK-21	21111	
HB-1622	Schleicher ASK-21	21088	
HB-1623	Schleicher ASW-20L	20578	
HB-1624	Schleicher ASK-21	21103	
HB-1629	Schleicher ASK-21	21097	
HB-1630	Schleicher ASK-21	21095	
HB-1632	Schleicher ASK-21	21092	
HB-1633	Rolladen-Schneider LS-4	4133	
HB-1635	Schleicher ASK-21	21100	
HB-1636	Glaser-Dirks DG-200	2-167	
HB-1638	Schempp-Hirth Nimbus 3	15	
HB-1639	Glaser-Dirks DG-200/17	2-174/1757	
HB-1641	Rolladen-Schneider LS-4	4152	
HB-1642	Glaser-Dirks DG-100G Elan	E95-G65	
HB-1643	Rolladen-Schneider LS-4	4168	
HB-1646	Schempp-Hirth Ventus b/16.6	118	
HB-1647	Rolladen-Schneider LS-4	4128	
HB-1649-AJ	Schleicher ASK-21	21114	
HB-1650	Schempp-Hirth Ventus b	90	
HB-1651	Grob G.103 Twin Astir II	3703	
HB-1653	Schleicher K.8B	8012SH/A	
HB-1654	Schleicher ASK-21	21138	
HB-1655	Rolladen-Schneider LS-4	4169	
HB-1660	Schleicher ASW-20L	20595	
HB-1661	Schempp-Hirth Nimbus 3/24.5	29	
HB-1662	Rolladen-Schneider LS-4	4155	
HB-1664	Centrair 101AP Pégase	101A-029	
HB-1665	Centrair 101AP Pégase	101A-026	
HB-1666-1K	Centrair 101A Pégase	101A-027	
HB-1667	Centrair 101A Pégase	101A-028	
HB-1668	Rolladen-Schneider LS-4	4324	
HB-1669	Schleicher ASK-21	21139	
HB-1670	Schempp-Hirth Ventus b/16.6	123	
HB-1671	Rolladen-Schneider LS-4	4154	
HB-1673	Rolladen-Schneider LS-4	4176	
HB-1676	Schempp-Hirth Nimbus 3/24.5	14	
HB-1678	Rolladen-Schneider LS-4	4193	
HB-1680	Rolladen-Schneider LS-4	4270	
HB-1681	Schempp-Hirth Nimbus 2C	200	
HB-1682	Schleicher ASK-21	21140	
HB-1683	Rolladen-Schneider LS-4	4210	
HB-1684	Schempp-Hirth Ventus b	138	
HB-1685	Schleicher ASK-21	21161	
HB-1686	Rolladen-Schneider LS-4	4170	
HB-1687	Rolladen-Schneider LS-4	4320	
HB-1688	Centrair 101A Pégase	101A-042	
HB-1689	Centrair 101A Pégase	101A-063	
HB-1690	Schleicher ASK-21	21163	
HB-1695	Rolladen-Schneider LS-4	4333	
HB-1697	Grob G.103A Twin II Acro	3785-K-63	
HB-1698	Centrair 101AP Pégase	101A-060	
HB-1699	Schleicher ASK-21	21171	
HB-1700	Schleicher ASK-21	21164	
HB-1701	Schleicher ASW-22	22031	
HB-1702	Schleicher ASK-21	21168	
HB-1703	Glaser-Dirks DG-100G Elan	E136-G104	
HB-1704	Schempp-Hirth Janus B	174	
HB-1705	Rolladen-Schneider LS-4	4332	
HB-1708	Schleicher ASK-21	21175	
HB-1710	Centrair 101A Pégase	101A-077	
HB-1714	Schleicher ASW-19B	19396	
HB-1715	Rolladen-Schneider LS-4	4357	
HB-1716	Schempp-Hirth Nimbus 3/24.5	63	
HB-1720	Centrair 101A Pégase	101A-107	
HB-1722	Schleicher ASK-21	21192	
HB-1723	Rolladen-Schneider LS-4	4374	
HB-1724	Schleicher ASW-19B	19398	
HB-1725	Centrair 101A Pégase	101A-105	
HB-1726	Grob G.103A Twin II Acro	3818-K-79	
HB-1727	Schleicher ASW-20C	20718	
HB-1729	Glaser-Dirks DG-300 Elan	3E-21	
HB-1730	Schleicher ASW-19B	19399	
HB-1732	Glaser-Dirks DG-300 Elan	3E-98	
HB-1733	Glaser-Dirks DG-100G Elan	E159-G126	
HB-1735	Schleicher ASW-20C	20731	
HB-1736	Glaser-Dirks DG-300	3E-37	
HB-1737	SZD-48-3 Jantar Standard 3	B-1372	
HB-1738	Schempp-Hirth Discus b	22	
HB-1739	Glaser-Dirks DG-300	3E-33	
HB-1741	Schempp-Hirth Ventus b/16.6	193	
HB-1745	Glaser-Dirks DG-300 Elan	3E-42	
HB-1746	Grob G.103 Standard Astir	5044S	
HB-1747	Rolladen-Schneider LS-4	4471	
HB-1748	Valentin Mistral C	MC 052/84	
HB-1749	Rolladen-Schneider LS-4	4417	
HB-1750	Schempp-Hirth Nimbus 2B	150	D-7507
HB-1751	Glaser-Dirks DG-300 Elan	3E-48	
HB-1752-IB	Glaser-Dirks DG-300 Elan	3E-43	
HB-1753	Rolladen-Schneider LS-4	4423	
HB-1754	Glaser-Dirks DG-300 Elan	3E-49	
HB-1755	Glaser-Dirks DG-300 Elan	3E-51	
HB-1756	Glaser-Dirks DG-300 Elan	3E-52	
HB-1757	Glaser-Dirks DG-300 Elan	3E-46	
HB-1758	Schleicher ASW-20CL	20708	D-KAAL D-7474
HB-1759	Rolladen-Schneider LS-4	4458	
HB-1762	Schempp-Hirth Janus C	203	
HB-1763	Rolladen-Schneider LS-4	4459	
HB-1764	Rolladen-Schneider LS-4	4446	
HB-1765	Glaser-Dirks DG-300 Elan	3E-58	
HB-1766	Schleicher ASK-21	21232	
HB-1767	Rolladen-Schneider LS-4	4484	
HB-1768	Neukom Elfe S4A	90	
HB-1769	Schempp-Hirth Nimbus 2C	236	D-1809
HB-1770	Schempp-Hirth Ventus b/16.6	224	
HB-1773	Schleicher ASW-19B	19413	
HB-1774	Schempp-Hirth Nimbus 3/24.5	78	
HB-1775	Schleicher ASW-19B	19409	
HB-1776-BE	Glaser-Dirks DG-300 Elan	3E-74	
HB-1777	Centrair 101A Pégase	101-0166	
HB-1778	Grob G.103 Twin II Acro	33950-K-183	
HB-1779	Schleicher ASK-23	23014	
HB-1781	SZD-48-3 Jantar Standard 3	B-1449	
HB-1782	Schempp-Hirth Mini-Nimbus C	99	D-6741
HB-1783-XD	Schempp-Hirth Discus A	1	D-6111
HB-1784	Schleicher ASW-20CL	20795	
HB-1786	Schleicher ASK-23	23012	
HB-1787	Schempp-Hirth Discus b	14	BGA3253/FGQ HB-1787
HB-1789	Glaser-Dirks DG-300 Elan	3E-90	
HB-1790	Schleicher ASK-23	23015	
HB-1792-BY	Rolladen-Schneider LS-6	6026	
HB-1793	Schleicher ASK-21	21246	
HB-1794	Glaser-Dirks DG-300 Elan	3E-121	
HB-1796	Schleicher ASK-23	23016	
HB-1798	Schleicher ASW-20B	20672	
HB-1799	Rolladen-Schneider LS-4	4504	
HB-1800	Glaser-Dirks DG-300 Elan	3E-100	
HB-1801	Schempp-Hirth Discus b	39	
HB-1802	Schempp-Hirth Discus b	25	
HB-1803	Rolladen-Schneider LS-6	6025	
HB-1804	Rolladen-Schneider LS-4	4514	
HB-1805	Schempp-Hirth Discus b	43	
HB-1806	Schempp-Hirth Discus b	19	
HB-1807	SZD-48-3 Jantar Standard 3	B-1463	
HB-1808	Schleicher ASW-20CL	20816	
HB-1809	SZD-51-1 Junior	B-1503	
HB-1810	Schempp-Hirth Ventus b/16.6	287	

Regn.	Type	C/n	Prev.Id.
HB-1811	Schleicher ASK-21	21258	
HB-1812	Schempp-Hirth Discus b	46	
HB-1813	Rolladen-Schneider LS-6	6083	
HB-1815	Schleicher ASW-19B	19417	
HB-1818	Rolladen-Schneider LS-4	4523	
HB-1819	Glaser-Dirks DG-300 Elan	3E-135	
HB-1820-3E	Schempp-Hirth Discus b	60	
HB-1822	Schempp-Hirth Discus b	56	
HB-1824	Rolladen-Schneider LS-4	4515	
HB-1825	Schleicher ASW-20CL	20821	
HB-1826	Schempp-Hirth Discus b	59	
HB-1827	Schempp-Hirth Discus b	61	
HB-1828	Rolladen-Schneider LS-4	4527	
HB-1830	Schempp-Hirth Discus b	73	
HB-1832	Rolladen-Schneider LS-4	4551	
HB-1833	Glaser-Dirks DG-300 Elan	3E-158	
HB-1834	Schleicher ASK-21	21300	
HB-1835	Rolladen-Schneider LS-4	4525	
HB-1836	SZD-48-3 Jantar Standard 3	B-1566	
HB-1837	Schempp-Hirth Ventus b/16.6	294	D-3086
HB-1838	Schempp-Hirth Discus b	165	
HB-1839	Schleicher ASK-21	21283	
HB-1840	Rolladen-Schneider LS-4	4537	
HB-1841	Glaser-Dirks DG-300 Elan	3E-159	
HB-1842	Glaser-Dirks DG-300 Elan	3E-168	
HB-1843	Glaser-Dirks DG-300 Elan	3E-146	
HB-1845	Glaser-Dirks DG-300 Elan	3E-150	
HB-1847	SZD-51-1 Junior	W-940	
HB-1848	SZD-51-1 Junior	W-939	
HB-1850	Schempp-Hirth Ventus b/16.6	272	
HB-1851	SZD-48-3 Jantar Standard 3	B-1572	
HB-1852	ICA-Brasov IS.28B2	320	D-2843
HB-1854	Schleicher ASK-21	21290	
HB-1856	Schleicher ASW-19B	19423	
HB-1857	Rolladen-Schneider LS-4	4577	
HB-1858	Rolladen-Schneider LS-6	6063	
HB-1859	Rolladen-Schneider LS-6	6079	
HB-1860	Schempp-Hirth Discus b	106	
HB-1861	Glaser-Dirks DG-300 Elan	3E-166	
HB-1862	Schleicher ASK-23	23060	
HB-1864	Schempp-Hirth Discus b	115	
HB-1865	Rolladen-Schneider LS-4	4588	
HB-1866	Rolladen-Schneider LS-3A	3192	
HB-1867	Schleicher ASK-23B	23071	
HB-1868	Schempp-Hirth Janus C	226	
HB-1870	Rolladen-Schneider LS-4	4586	
HB-1871	Schleicher ASW-20CL	20842	
HB-1872	Glaser-Dirks DG-300 Elan	3E-205	
HB-1873	Glaser-Dirks DG-300 Elan	3E-191	
HB-1875	Rolladen-Schneider LS-4	4592	
HB-1876	Rolladen-Schneider LS-6A	6124	
HB-1877	Schempp-Hirth Discus b	116	
HB-1878	Glaser-Dirks DG-300 Elan	3E-193	
HB-1879	Schleicher ASK-23B	23078	
HB-1880	Schleicher ASK-23B	23083	
HB-1881	Glaser-Dirks DG-300 Elan	3E-197	
HB-1882	Rolladen-Schneider LS-4	4587	
HB-1883	Schleicher ASK-23B	23079	
HB-1884	Schleicher ASK-21	21311	
HB-1885	Schempp-Hirth Discus b	127	
HB-1886	Rolladen-Schneider LS-6	6096	
HB-1890	Schleicher ASK-23B	23081	
HB-1892	Rolladen-Schneider LS-4	4621	
HB-1893	Rolladen-Schneider LS-4	4618	
HB-1894	Glaser-Dirks DG-300 Elan	3E-228	
HB-1896	Schempp-Hirth Discus b	137	
HB-1898	Glaser-Dirks DG-300 Elan	3E-211	
HB-1899	Schempp-Hirth Janus C	243	
HB-1900	Rolladen-Schneider LS-6	6094	
HB-1901	Schleicher ASK-23B	23090	
HB-1902	Glaser-Dirks DG-300 Elan	3E-223	
HB-1904	Schempp-Hirth Discus b	218	
HB-1905	Schempp-Hirth Janus C	226	
HB-1906	SZD-51-1 Junior	W-957	
HB-1907	Schempp-Hirth Discus b	150	
HB-1908	Schempp-Hirth Discus b	154	
HB-1909	Rolladen-Schneider LS-4	4648	
HB-1910	Rolladen-Schneider LS-4	4650	
HB-1912	Schempp-Hirth Discus b	159	
HB-1913	Centrair 101D Pégase	101D-0527	
HB-1915	Schempp-Hirth Discus b	183	
HB-1916	Rolladen-Schneider LS-1F	331	D-2738
HB-1917	Glaser-Dirks DG-300 Elan	3E-252	
HB-1918	SZD-51-1 Junior	W-968	
HB-1919	Glaser-Dirks DG-300 Elan	3E-238	
HB-1923	Glaser-Dirks DG-300 Elan	3E-254	
HB-1924	Rolladen-Schneider LS-6	6009	D-6590
HB-1925	Schempp-Hirth Ventus b	184	D-7721
HB-1926	Glaser-Dirks DG-300 Elan	3E-253	
HB-1928	SZD-51-1 Junior	B-1775	
HB-1929	Schleicher ASH-25	25026	
HB-1931	SZD-51-1 Junior	B-1785	
HB-1932	Centrair 101A Pégase	101A-045	F-CFQU
HB-1933	Glaser-Dirks DG-300 Elan	3E-256	
HB-1934	Glaser-Dirks DG-300 Elan	3E-262	
HB-1936	Schempp-Hirth Ventus c	358	
HB-1937	Rolladen-Schneider LS-4	4664	
HB-1939-3L	Rolladen-Schneider LS-6B	6154	
HB-1940	Schleicher ASH-25E	25024	
HB-1941	Glaser-Dirks DG-300 Elan	3E-264	
HB-1942	Rolladen-Schneider LS-6B	6155	
HB-1943	Glaser-Dirks DG-300 Elan	3E-318	
HB-1944	Glaser-Dirks DG-600	6-2	D-0626
HB-1945	Schempp-Hirth Ventus c	363	
HB-1946	Schempp-Hirth Ventus c	356	
HB-1948	Schempp-Hirth Discus b	208	
HB-1949	Schempp-Hirth Discus b	210	
HB-1950	Glaser-Dirks DG-300 Elan	3E-272	
HB-1951	Schempp-Hirth Discus b	281	
HB-1952	Schempp-Hirth Discus b	199	
HB-1953	Schempp-Hirth Nimbus S-3D	2/8	D-1973
HB-1954	Glaser-Dirks DG-600	6-31	
HB-1955	Centrair 201B Marianne	201B-068	
HB-1956	Centrair 101B Pégase	101B-0283	
HB-1958	Schempp-Hirth Discus b	228	
HB-1959	Schleicher ASK-21	21368	
HB-1961	Schempp-Hirth Discus b	24	D-4124
HB-1962	Schleicher ASK-21	21366	
HB-1963	Schempp-Hirth Ventus c	368	
HB-1965	Schempp-Hirth Discus b	229	
HB-1966	Schempp-Hirth Discus b	231	
HB-1967	Schleicher ASK-23B	23104	
HB-1969	Glaser-Dirks DG-300 Club Elan	3E-299/C17	
HB-1970	Schleicher ASK-21	21384	
HB-1972	Glaser-Dirks DG-300 Elan	3E-289	
HB-1973	Schempp-Hirth Discus b	236	
HB-1975	Schempp-Hirth Ventus c	328	D-1975
HB-1976	Schleicher ASK-23B	23105	
HB-1977	Rolladen-Schneider LS-7	7020	D-4587
HB-1978	Schleicher ASW-20	20121	D-2660
HB-1979	Rolladen-Schneider LS-7	7012	
HB-1980	Glaser-Dirks DG-300 Elan	3E-321	
HB-1981	Rolladen-Schneider LS-7	7002	
HB-1982	Schleicher ASK-21	21377	
HB-1983	Glaser-Dirks DG-300 Elan	3E-308	
HB-1984	Glaser-Dirks DG-300 Elan	3E-316	
	(C/n 3E-316/C25 is also quoted for D-5564, both are current)		
HB-1987	SZD-51-1 Junior	B-1827	
HB-1988	Rolladen-Schneider LS-7	7010	D-1275
HB-1989	Schempp-Hirth Ventus c	405	
HB-1990	Schempp-Hirth Discus b	267	
HB-1991	Glaser-Dirks DG-300 Elan	3E-322	
HB-1992	Schempp-Hirth Ventus c	416	
HB-1993	Rolladen-Schneider LS-7	7034	D-1671
HB-1994	Glaser-Dirks DG-500/22	5E-13S4	
HB-1995	Rolladen-Schneider LS-6A	6189	D-5020
HB-1996	Rolladen-Schneider LS-7	7042	D-5156
HB-1997	SZD-51-1 Junior	B-1843	
HB-1998	Rolladen-Schneider LS-7	7047	
HB-1999	Schempp-Hirth Janus C	253	

Regn.	Type	C/n	Prev.Id.
HB-3004	Avafiber Canard SC (Solar powered)	01	
HB-3005	Glaser-Dirks DG-300 Elan	3E-345	
HB-3006	Rolladen-Schneider LS-7	7063	
HB-3007	Glaser-Dirks DG-300 Elan	3E-244	HB-007 ?
HB-3008	Schleicher ASW-24	24047	
HB-3009	Schleicher ASW-24	24045	
HB-3011	Rolladen-Schneider LS-4	4760	
HB-3012	SZD-51-1 Junior	B-1851	
HB-3013	SZD-51-1 Junior	B-1846	
HB-3014	SZD-51-1 Junior	B-1850	
HB-3015	Schleicher ASK-23B	23047	N923KS
HB-3016	Grob G.103 Twin III Acro	34129	
HB-3017	SZD-51-1 Junior	B-1859	
HB-3018	Grob G.103 Twin III Acro	34132	
HB-3019	Rolladen-Schneider LS-6B	6191	D-5026
HB-3021	Rolladen-Schneider LS-7	7072	
HB-3022	Schempp-Hirth Discus b	325	
HB-3024	Schleicher ASW-24	24016	D-3463
HB-3025	Rolladen-Schneider LS-4A	4770	
HB-3026	Schleicher ASK-21	21438	
HB-3027	Schempp-Hirth Discus b	309	
HB-3028	Celstar GA-1	S001	ZS-GTC
HB-3029	Schleicher ASK-21	21466	
HB-3031	Rolladen-Schneider LS-6A	6010	HB-1795
HB-3032	Rolladen-Schneider LS-7	7096	
HB-3033	Glaser-Dirks DG-600	6-61	
HB-3034	Rolladen-Schneider LS-4A	4782	
HB-3035	Rolladen-Schneider LS-7	7098	
HB-3036	SZD-51-1 Junior	B-1927	
HB-3037	Glaser-Dirks DG-300 Elan	3E-96	
HB-3038	Schleicher ASK-21	21452	
HB-3039	Glaser-Dirks DG-600	6-49	
HB-3040	SZD-55-1	551190003	
HB-3041	Schempp-Hirth Discus b	341	
HB-3042	Schempp-Hirth Discus b	385	
HB-3044	Schempp-Hirth Discus b	410	
HB-3045	SZD-55-1	551190006	
HB-3046	SZD-55-1	551190009	
HB-3047	Schleicher ASH-25	25051	D-3460
HB-3048-NY	Rolladen-Schneider LS-7	7141	
HB-3049	Schleicher ASH-25	25103	
HB-3050	Glaser-Dirks DG-500/22	5E-44T14	
HB-3051	Pilatus B4-PC11AF	282	D-2230
HB-3052	Schempp-Hirth Ventus c	499	
HB-3053	Grob G.103A Twin II Acro	3622-K-9	D-3071
HB-3054	Schleicher ASK-23B	23122	
HB-3055	Schleicher ASK-23B	23130	
HB-3056	SZD-55-1	551191012	
HB-3057	Neukom Elfe 17	89	HB-2047
HB-3058	Schempp-Hirth Discus b	374	
HB-3059	Glaser-Dirks DG-600	6-65	
HB-3060	Rolladen-Schneider LS-7	7133	
HB-3062	Schempp-Hirth Discus b	354	
HB-3064	Schleicher ASH-25	25128	
HB-3065	Rolladen-Schneider LS-7	7132	
HB-3066	Rolladen-Schneider LS-7	7136	
HB-3068	Rolladen-Schneider LS-7	7151	
HB-3069	Schleicher ASK-23B	23123	
HB-3070	Schleicher ASK-23B	23128	
HB-3071	Schempp-Hirth Ventus c	518	
HB-3073	SZD-55-1	551192034	
HB-3074	Rolladen-Schneider LS-4B	4842	
HB-3075	Schleicher ASK-21	21507	
HB-3076	Rolladen-Schneider LS-4B	4834	
HB-3077	Schleicher ASW-24	24139	
HB-3080	SZD-55-1	551191021	
HB-3081	Schempp-Hirth Janus CE	278	
HB-3082	Rolladen-Schneider LS-4B	4847	
HB-3083	Glaser-Dirks DG-500/22	5E-52S9	
HB-3084	SZD-55-1	551191027	
HB-3085	Rolladen-Schneider LS-6C	6272	
HB-3086	Schempp-Hirth Ventus c	549	
HB-3087	Schempp-Hirth Janus CE	288	
HB-3088	Schempp-Hirth Duo Discus	56	
HB-3089	Centrair 101A Pégase	101A-0426	
HB-3090	Centrair 101A Pégase	101A-0427	
HB-3091	Schleicher ASK-23B	23133	
HB-3092	Glaser-Dirks DG-600/18	6-107	
HB-3093	Schleicher ASH-25	25134	
HB-3094	Schempp-Hirth Discus CS	076CS	
HB-3095	Scheibe SF-34	5139	
HB-3096	Centrair 101A Pégase	101A-0435	
HB-3098	Schempp-Hirth Discus CS	080CS	
HB-3099	Schleicher ASK-21	21546	
HB-3100	Schempp-Hirth Janus CE	289	
HB-3101	Schempp-Hirth Discus CS	083CS	
HB-3102	Grob G.103C Twin III	34171	
HB-3104	Schleicher ASW-24	24182	
HB-3105	Schempp-Hirth Discus CS	085CS	
HB-3106	SZD-55-1	551192043	
HB-3107	SZD-55-1	551192045	
HB-3108	Schempp-Hirth Discus b	450	
HB-3109	Schempp-Hirth Discus b	238	D-1029
HB-3110	Glaser-Dirks DG-600/18	6-113	
HB-3111	Glaser-Dirks DG-300 Elan Acro	3E-437A5	
HB-3112	SZD-51-1 Junior	B-2016	
HB-3113	Rolladen-Schneider LS-6C	6297	
HB-3114	Swift S-1	109	
HB-3115	Rolladen-Schneider LS-6C	6298	
HB-3116	LET L-23 Super Blanik	928005	D-8065
HB-3117	Rolladen-Schneider LS-4B	4966	
HB-3118	SZD-55-1	551192048	
HB-3119	Rolladen-Schneider LS-6C	6307	
HB-3120	Rolladen-Schneider LS-4B	4908	
HB-3121	Schempp-Hirth Discus CS	164CS	
HB-3122	Glaser-Dirks DG-300 Elan	3E-439	
HB-3123	Swift S-1	107	(D-9107)
HB-3125	Swift S-1	103	
HB-3126	Swift S-1	101	SP-3536
HB-3127	Rolladen-Schneider LS-6C	6309	
HB-3128	Schleicher ASW-20FL	20116	F-CFFM
HB-3129	Glaser-Dirks DG-200/17C	2-130/CL-07	D-0695
			PH-695
HB-3130	Schleicher ASW-22	22006	D-2270
HB-3131	Schempp-Hirth Duo Discus	24	
HB-3132	Schempp-Hirth Janus CE	296	
HB-3134	Glaser-Dirks DG-500 Elan Trainer	5E-104T41	
HB-3135	Swift S-1	115	
HB-3136	SZD-51-1 Junior	B-2130	
HB-3137	Glaser-Dirks DG-500 Elan	5E-109S16	
HB-3138	Swift S-1	116	
HB-3139	Swift S-1	105	SP-3573
HB-3141	Rolladen-Schneider LS-6C	6330	
HB-3142	Schempp-Hirth Discus CS	153CS	
HB-3143	Schleicher ASK-21	21601	
HB-3144	Rolladen-Schneider LS-4B	4936	
HB-3145	Rolladen-Schneider LS-4B	4924	
HB-3146	Rolladen-Schneider LS-6C-18	6334	D-1832
HB-3147	Centrair 101B Pégase	101B-0484	
HB-3148	Schempp-Hirth Discus CS	167CS	
HB-3149	Rolladen-Schneider LS-6C	6339	D-1868
HB-3150	Glaser-Dirks DG-500 Elan Trainer	5E-123T53	
HB-3151	Glaser-Dirks DG-800S	8-29S6	D-5093
HB-3152	Glaser-Dirks DG-800S	8-30S7	D-5559
HB-3153	Schempp-Hirth Duo Discus	14	
HB-3154	Schempp-Hirth Discus b	519	
HB-3155	Glaser-Dirks DG-300 Elan	3E-450	S5-3155
HB-3156	Schleicher ASW-24B	24228	D-3156
HB-3157	Scheibe SF-27A	6037	D-1205
HB-3158	Rolladen-Schneider LS-6-18W	6317	D-1789
HB-3160	Schempp-Hirth Duo Discus	20	
HB-3161	Rolladen-Schneider LS-6-18W	6336	D-8035
HB-3162	Schempp-Hirth Discus CS	185CS	
HB-3163	Swift S-1	120	
HB-3165	Glaser-Dirks DG-800S	8-37S8	D-8180
HB-3166	Schempp-Hirth Duo-Discus	27	
HB-3167	Rolladen-Schneider LS-6C-18	6347	D-1772
HB-3168	Glaser-Dirks DG-800S	8-43S12	D-5647
HB-3169	Swift S-1	122	
HB-3170	Rolladen-Schneider LS-8A	8020	D-2035

435

Regn.	Type	C/n	Prev.Id.
HB-3171	Rolladen-Schenider LS-4B	4977	
HB-3173	Glaser-Dirks DG-800S	8-55S14	
HB-3174	Rolladen-Schneider LS-4B	4986	
HB-3175	Rolladen-Schneider LS-6C-18	6357	
HB-3176	Rolladen-Schneider LS-4B	4985	
HB-3177	Rolladen-Schneider LS-6-18W	6356	
HB-3179	Glasflügel H304	257	D-5827
HB-3180	Glaser-Dirks DG-800S	8-57S16	
HB-3181	Schempp-Hirth Discus CS	197CS	
HB-3182	Rolladen-Schneider LS-8A	8021	D-2171
HB-3183	SZD-51-1 Junior	B-2140	
HB-3185	Glaser-Dirks DG-500	5E-151X8	
HB-3186	Rolladen-Schneider LS-8A	8078	
HB-3187	Rolladen-Schneider LS-4B	4990	
HB-3188	Schleicher ASH-25	25185	
HB-3189	Schleicher ASH-26	26073	D-5775
HB-3190	Glaser-Dirks DG-300 Elan	3E-464A18	
HB-3191 -IQ	Schleicher ASH-25	25020	D-2519
HB-3192	Schempp-Hirth Ventus 2c	6/9	D-2389
HB-3193	Schempp-Hirth Duo Discus	152	
HB-3194	Schempp-Hirth Ventus 2a	26	
HB-3196	Schempp-Hirth Duo Discus	77	
HB-3197	Glaser-Dirks DG-500 Elan	5E-157X14	
HB-3198	Rolladen-Schneider LS-7WL	7059	D-5775
HB-3199	Schleicher ASW-27	27027	D-7453
HB-3200	Glaser-Dirks DG-300 Elan	3E-465	
HB-3201	Glaser-Dirks DG-500/20	5E-124W1	D-7320 (D-0219)
HB-3202	Glaser-Dirks DG-300 Elan	3E-466	
HB-3204	Glaser-Dirks DG-500 Elan	5E-163X18	
HB-3205	Glaser-Dirks DG-500 Elan	5E-146X6	D-2988
HB-3206	Rolladen-Schneider LS-8A	8052	D-3719
HB-3207	Schempp-Hirth Ventus 2c	10/22	D-5206
HB-3208	Schleicher ASW-24B	24243	
HB-3209	Schleicher ASW-27	27028	D-7456
HB-3210	Rolladen-Schneider LS-6C-18	6373	
HB-3211	Rolladen-Schneider LS-8A	8067	
HB-3212	Centrair 101A Pégase	101A-0613	
HB-3214	Schmepp-Hirth Duo Discus	87	
HB-3215	Schleicher ASH-26	26094	
HB-3216	Rolladen-Schneider LS-8A	8070	
HB-3217	Schempp-Hirth Ventus 2a	39	
HB-3218	Schempp-Hirth Ventus 2a	30	
HB-3219	Rolladen-Schneider LS-6C	6375	
HB-3220	Rolladen-Schneider LS-4B	41008	
HB-3221	Pilatus B4-PC11AF	111	
HB-3222	Schmepp-Hirth Nimbus 3D	9/44	D-4346
HB-3223	Schempp-Hirth Duo Discus	102	
HB-3224	Schempp-Hirth Duo Discus	9	F-CHTA
HB-3225	Schleicher ASK-21	21642	
HB-3226-C6	Rolladen-Schneider LS-8A	8121	
HB-3227	Glaser-Dirks DG-500 Elan	5E-166X21	
HB-3229	Glaser-Dirks DG-500 Elan	5E-155X12	D-3680
HB-3230	Rolladen-Schneider LS-8A	8098	
HB-3231	Schempp-Hirth Duo Discus	111	
HB-3232	Schempp-Hirth Duo Discus	113	
HB-3233	Schempp-Hirth Duo Discus	115	
HB-3234	Schempp-Hirth Ventus 2c	20/51	
HB-3235	Schmepp-Hirth Ventus 2c	19/49	
HB-3236-ZP	Schleicher ASW-27	27048	
HB-3237	Rolladen-Schneider LS-8A	8127	
HB-3238	Rolladen-Schneider LS-8A	8126	
HB-3239	Schleicher ASW-27	27049	
HB-3240	Schleicher ASW-27	27038	
HB-3241	Marganski MDM-1 Fox	216	
HB-3243	Caproni A.21S Calif	211	D-6613 I-VIZR
HB-3245	Centrair 101A Pégase	101A-0467	F-CHFB
HB-3246	Schempp-Hirth Ventus 2c	25	
HB-3248	Swift S-1	123	
HB-3249	Rolladen-Schneider LS-8A	8140	
HB-3250	Glaser-Dirks DG-800S	8-110S26	
HB-3251	PZL PW-5 Smyk	17.08.019	
HB-3252	Glaser-Dirks DG-800S	8-111S27	
HB-3253	Glaser-Dirks DG-800S	8-112S28	

Regn.	Type	C/n	Prev.Id.
HB-3254	Rolladen-Schneider LS-8A	8194	
HB-3255	Rolladen-Schneider LS-8A	8168	
HB-3256	Glaser-Dirks DG-500 Elan	5E-179X30	
HB-3257	Schempp-Hirth Ventus 2b	67	
HB-3258	Schleicher ASW-27	27090	
HB-3259	Schleicher ASW-24B	24249	
HB-3260	Schempp-Hirth Duo Discus	114	D-3887
HB-3261	Schleicher ASW-27	27087	
HB-3263	Schempp-Hirth Duo Discus	182	
HB-3264	Schleicher ASW-27	27095	
HB-3265	Schleicher ASW-27	27079	
HB-3266	Glaser-Dirks DG-500 Elan Orion	5E-184X35	
HB-3269	Schleicher ASW-27	27107	
HB-3270	Schleicher ASH-25	25048	D-4959
HB-3271	Rolladen-Schneider LS-4B	41027	
HB-3272	Schempp-Hirth Duo Discus	207	
HB-3273	Glaser-Dirks DG-500 Elan Orion	5E196X40	
HB-3276	Glaser-Dirks DG-500 Elan Orion	5E176X28	D-4629
HB-3277-IY	Schempp-Hirth Duo Discus	206	
HB-3278-EQ	Schleicher ASH-25	25210	
HB-3279	Schempp-Hirth Duo Discus	213	
HB-3280	Glaser-Dirks DG-800S	8-138S31	
HB-3281	Schempp-Hirth Discus 2b	26	
HB-3282	Glaser-Dirks DG-800S	8-139S32	
HB-3283	Schempp-Hirth Discus 2b	37	
HB-3285	Glaser-Dirks DG-800S	8-140S33	
HB-3286	Glaser-Dirks DG-800S	8-141S34	
HB-3290	Schempp-Hirth Discus 2b	43	
HB-3291	Schempp-Hirth Discus 2b	44	
HB-3292	Glaser-Dirks DG-500 Elan Orion	5E-197X41	
HB-3295	Glaser-Dirks DG-500 Elan Orion	5E-203X47	
HB-3299	Glaser-Dirks DG-800S	8-9S2	D-8027
HB-3300	Schempp-Hirth Discus 2b	29	
HB-3303	Schempp-Hirth Ventus 2c	50/151	
HB-3311	Schempp-Hirth Ventus 2c	57/168	

MICROLIGHTS

Microlights may not be registered in Switzerland as a result of a national referendum. The reported allocation of U-1081 is thought to represent an example on trials with the Swiss Air Force. A number of three-axis machines classified as ULMs in other countries nevertheless appear in the Swiss homebuilt category.

Regn.	Type	C/n	Prev.Id.
I-AASV	S.A.I. F.7 Rondone I	9	
I-ABCA	Beech E33A Bonanza	CE-235	HB-EHH
I-ABOU	Caproni CA.100 Idro	3992	MM65156
I-ABRH	WagAero CUBy Sport Trainer	1	
I-ACCU	Cessna 150M	77136	N63298
I-ACCV	Dragon Fly DF333AC	EB060	
I-ACIR	Piper PA-28-140 Cherokee C	28-26747	N5953U
I-ACLU	Piper PA-28RT-201 Arrow IV	28R-8018021	N35720
I-ACMG	Cessna 172M	66875	N1174U
I-ACMH	Piper PA-28-161 Warrior II	28-8216024	G-BMNM
			N8447N
I-ACMI	Partenavia P.64 Oscar	06	
I-ACMM	Piper PA-28-180 Cherokee F	28-7105230	N11C
I-ACMN	Piper PA-28-180 Cherokee G	28-7205106	N11C
I-ACMP	Piper PA-28-140 Cherokee C	28-26724	N5913U
I-ACMQ	Reims/Cessna F.172L	0868	(I-CCAD)
I-ACMR	Cessna 172M	63056	N4302R
I-ACMS	Piper PA-28-161 Warrior II (Wrecked)	28-8416060	N4345D
I-ACMT	SIAI-Marchetti S.205-20/R	4-113	
I-ACMV	SIAI-Marchetti S.205-20/R	4-108	
I-ACMX	Cessna 172M	67500	N73485
I-ACNU	Partenavia P.64B Oscar B-1155	68	
I-ACPD	Piper PA-28R-200 Cherokee Arrow	28R-7535080	N32705
I-ACRS	Reims/Cessna F.172P	2067	
I-ACRV	Partenavia P.66B Oscar 150	16	
I-ACRY	Partenavia P.66B Oscar 150	21	
I-ACSI	Macchi MB.308	101/5874	MM53055
I-ACST	Maule MXT-7-180 Star Rocket	14002C	N9213A
I-ACTC	Piaggio P.180 Avanti	1014	
I-ACTD	Piper PA-34-220T Seneca III	34-8233174	N8242A
I-ACTV	Partenavia P.66B Oscar 150	01	
I-ACUB	SOCATA MS.880B Rallye Club	902	
I-ACUD	SOCATA MS.893A Rallye Commodore 180	10692	
I-ACVB	Partenavia P.66B Oscar 100	77	
I-ACVI	Partenavia P.66B Oscar 100	76	
I-ACVZ	Cessna 172P	74861	N54054
I-ADAA	Reims/Cessna F.152-II	1914	
I-ADAB	Aerotek Pitts S-2A	2252	
I-ADAC	Cessna 182R Skylane	67826	N6327N
I-ADAP	Robinson R-22B2 Beta	2986	
I-ADCR	Piper PA-18-150 Super Cub	18-8109027	N6501A
I-ADLF	Aeritalia/SNIAS ATR-42-500	462	F-OHFF
			F-WWLL
I-ADLG	Aeritalia/SNIAS ATR-42-500	476	F-OHFG
			F-WWLX
I-ADLH	Aeritalia/SNIAS ATR-42-512	445	F-OHFM
			F-WWLZ
			F-GJMV
			F-WWER
I-ADLI	Aeritalia/SNIAS ATR-42-512	515	F-OHFN
			F-WWLP
I-ADLL	Aeritalia/SNIAS ATR-42-512	518	F-OHFP
			(I-ADLL)
			F-WWLX
I-ADLM	Aeritalia/SNIAS ATR-72-212	543	F-WW..
I-ADLN	Aeritalia/SNIAS ATR-72-212	557	F-WWLX
I-ADLO	Aeritalia/SNIAS ATR-72-212A	585	F-WWEQ
I-ADLP	Aeritalia/SNIAS ATR-42-512	604	F-WQKY
			F-WWLH
I-ADOA	Avia FL.3	87	
I-ADRE	S.A.I. F.7 Rondone II	020	
I-ADRY	Partenavia P.64B Oscar 200	09	
I-AEAL	Cessna 500 Citation	0053	HB-VGO
			I-KUNA
			N9OWJ
			I-CITY
			N553CC
I-AEEA	Stinson L-5 Sentinel	unkn	MM52963
I-AEEE	Stinson L-5 Sentinel	unkn	MM52956
I-AEEG	Stinson L-5 Sentinel	unkn	MM56686
I-AEEI	Stinson L-5 Sentinel	unkn	MM52958
I-AEEM	Stinson L-5 Sentinel	unkn	MM52881
I-AEEP	Stinson L-5 Sentinel (Stored)	unkn	MM52839
I-AEEX	Stinson L-5 Sentinel (Stored)	unkn	MM52884
I-AEFE	Stinson L-5 Sentinel (SSVV conversion)	unkn	MM53454
I-AEFF	Stinson L-5 Sentinel	unkn	MM52967
I-AEFH	Stinson L-5B Sentinel	unkn	MM52892
I-AEFJ	Stinson L-5 Sentinel	unkn	MM52877
I-AEFO	Stinson L-5 Sentinel	unkn	MM56694
I-AEFU	Stinson L-5 Sentinel	unkn	MM52873
	(Flies marked as 298592-"5M")		42-98596
I-AEFX	Stinson L-5 Sentinel	unkn	MM52840
I-AEFZ	Stinson L-5 Sentinel	unkn	MM52970
I-AEGB	Stinson L-5 Sentinel	unkn	MM52863
I-AEGC	Stinson L-5 Sentinel	unkn	MM52891
I-AEGD	Stinson L-5 Sentinel (SSVV conversion)	unkn	MM52847
I-AEGI	Stinson L-5 Sentinel (SSVV conversion)	unkn	MM52876
I-AEGN	Stinson L-5 Sentinel (SSVV conversion)	unkn	MM52846
I-AEGR	Stinson L-5 Sentinel	unkn	MM52854
I-AEGS	Stinson L-5 Sentinel	unkn	MM52979
I-AEGZ	Stinson L-5 Sentinel (SSVV conversion)	unkn	MM52952
I-AEIY	Boeing 767-3Q8	25208	EI-CIY
			D-ABUY
I-AEKA	Fiat G.46-4B-V	180	I-LSBA
			I-AEKA
			MM53304
I-AEKT	Fiat G.46-4A Series 6	216	MM53491
I-AERG	SOCATA MS.892A Rallye Commodore 150	11638	
I-AERQ	SOCATA MS.892A Rallye Commodore 150	11641	
I-AERZ	SOCATA MS.880B Rallye Club	1794	
I-AESC	Piper PA-28RT-201T Turbo Arrow IV	28R-7931095	N500DS
			N500DU
			N2137U
I-AETA	Piper PA-18-150 Super Cub	18-7909050	N9751N
I-AETB	Piper PA-18-150 Super Cub	18-7909080	N9753N
I-AFAB	Reims/Cessna FR.172H Rocket	0281	N5448
I-AFAC	Reims/Cessna F.152	1875	
I-AFAE	Cessna U.206G Stationair II	06479	N9419Z
I-AFAF	Reims/Cessna F.172M	1281	D-EECR
I-AFCN	Aérospatiale AS.350B2 Ecureuil	1997	JA9461
I-AFET	Aérospatiale SA.315B Lama	2663	
I-AGAA	Piper J-3C-65 Cub	12079	44-79783
I-AGAE	Partenavia P.68B	183	I-GYAN
I-AGFA	Aérospatiale SA.365N1 Dauphin 2	6229	
I-AGKK	Agusta A.109K2	10021	
I-AGKL	Agusta A.109K2	10020	
I-AGMP	Agusta-MD.500N	301	
I-AGSD	Partenavia P.68TC	248-10-TC	(EC-DOI)
I-AGSE	Agusta A.109A-II	7354	
I-AGSF	Agusta-Bell AB.412	25542	
I-AGSH	Agusta A.109A-II	7384	
I-AGSL	Agusta A.109A-II	7391	
I-AGSN	Agusta A.109A-II	7396	
I-AGSO	Agusta-Bell AB.412	25560	
I-AGUI	Agusta-Bell AB.412	25507	Fv11337
			I-DACB
I-AGUN	Agusta-Bell 206B-1 Jet Ranger	9010	
I-AGUO	Bell 206B Jet Ranger II	1102	G-BBET
			N18091
I-AGVE	Cessna 152 (Crashed)	84580	N5402M
I-AGWH	Agusta EH.101/510	510-001	
I-AIAA	Avia LM.5	5	
I-AIIA	Lake LA-4-200 Buccaneer (Sank, Lake Como 9.99)	1010	N80029
I-AIKE	Mudry CAP.10B	222	
I-AIMA	Maule MX-7-180 Star Rocket	11068C	N9206R
I-AIMQ	Boeing 767-3Q8ER	27993	EI-CMQ
I-AINA	Cessna 172N	69301	N737BX
I-AINB	Cessna 172RG Cutlass	0131	N6269R
I-AINC	Cessna 172M	64625	N61540
I-AIND	Cessna 172M	61243	N20383
I-AIOI	Aérospatiale AS.350B2 Ecureuil	2535	
I-AIRC	Piper PA-24-250 Comanche (Damaged)	24-1605	N6894P
			(G-APZI)
I-AIRG	Robinson R-22 Beta	1277	I-MIAC
			N8066V
I-AIRI	Piper PA-23-250 Aztec B	27-2010	N5098Y
			LV-PST
I-AIRP	Piper PA-22-108 Colt	22-9595	N5753Z

Regn.	Type	C/n	Prev.Id.
I-AIRQ	Eurocopter EC.135P1	0101	
I-AIRR	Agusta-Bell 412	25577	HB-XVU
I-AIRW	Gates Learjet 31	31-025	N39399
I-AIRY	Aérospatiale AS.350B2 Ecureuil	2193	HB-XTF
			F-WZTB
I-AITE	Aeritalia-Partenavia AP.68TP-600 Viator	9006	
I-AITT	Aeritalia-Partenavia AP.68TP-300 Spartacus	8011	
I-AIVO	Bell 412	33014	HB-XRP
			N2070E
			(ZK-HNF)
			N2070E
			ZS-HKG
			A2-HKG
			ZS-HKG
			N2070E
I-AKAI	Piper PA-34-200 Seneca	34-7350045	N15269
I-AKRM	T-30 Katana	003	
I-AKRO	Mudry CAP.10B	42	F-BUDK(1)
I-ALAA	Reims/Cessna F.172H	0566	
I-ALAB	Reims/Cessna F.150J	0442	
I-ALAD	Reims/Cessna F.150J	0400	
I-ALAG	Reims/Cessna F.150H	0382	(I-FAUL)
I-ALAJ	Reims/Cessna F.150L	0667	
I-ALAK	Beech 95-B55 Baron	TC-1218	HB-GDR
I-ALAO	Reims/Cessna FR.172H Rocket	0235	
I-ALAV	Reims/Cessna F.150K	0544	
I-ALBA	Beech 35-C33 Debonair	CD-876	HB-EKO
I-ALBJ	S.A.I. F.4 Rondone 1	013	
I-ALBN	Reims/Cessna F.172M	0954	(I-FFST)
I-ALCA	Cessna 182P Skylane	60947	N7307Q
I-ALCH	SOCATA Rallye 235E Gabier	12907	F-GBXC
I-ALCI	Robinson R-44 Astro	0163	
I-ALCO	Aviamilano F.8L Falco	120	
I-ALDO	Piper J-3C-65 Cub	13071	HB-OES
			44-80775
I-ALEU	Cessna 172RG Cutlass	0757	N6532V
I-ALGB	Reims/Cessna FR.172J Rocket	0434	
I-ALGC	Cessna A.185F Skywagon	02912	N8766Z
I-ALIF	Partenavia P.57 Fachiro IIf	26	
I-ALJC	Cessna 182E Skylane	53969	N2969Y
I-ALJG	Cessna 172D	49643	N2143Y
I-ALJK	Cessna 337A Super Skymaster	0471	N5371S
I-ALJM	Reims/Cessna F.172G	0249	
I-ALJO	Reims/Cessna F.172F	0131	
I-ALJP	Reims/Cessna F.172G	0192	
I-ALJS	Cessna 210F	58748	N1848F
I-ALJT	Reims/Cessna F.150F	63079/0030	
I-ALJZ	Reims/Cessna F.172H	0361	(I-AIJZ)
I-ALKE	Aérospatiale AS.355F2 Ecureuil 2	5478	
I-ALKI	Cessna 210H	58985	N5985F
I-ALOO	Piper PA-28-180 Cherokee Archer	28-7505064	N32491
I-ALPC	SIAI-Marchetti SF.260C	713/47-002	
I-ALPD	SIAI-Marchetti SF.260C	714/47-003	
I-ALPF	SIAI-Marchetti SF.260C	715/47-004	
I-ALPG	Cessna 551 Citation	0355	N551AS
			N5451G
I-ALPK	Fokker F.28-0100	11244	F-WQHE
			HB-IVA
			PH-EZB
I-ALPL	Fokker F.28-0100	11250	F-WQHG
			HB-IVB
			PH-EZC
I-ALPP	Reims/Cessna F.150J	0434	
I-ALPQ	Fokker F.28-0100	11256	F-WQFP
			HB-IVH
			PH-EZI
I-ALPR	Gates Learjet 55	55-078	N56TG
			(N120GR)
			N56TG
			N55GV
			(N55GJ)
I-ALPS	Fokker F.28-0100	11254	F-WQHK
			HB-IVF
			PH-EZG
I-ALPX	Fokker F.28-0100	11251	F-WQFL
			HB-IVC
			PH-EZD
I-ALPY	Piper PA-28-180 Cherokee E	28-5843	G-AYIE
			N11C
I-ALPZ	Fokker F.28-0100	11252	F-WQBP
			HB-IVD
			PH-EZE
I-ALRO	Beech F33A Bonanza	CE-1444	N5644J
I-ALWA	Reims/Cessna F.172D	50285/0017	
I-ALWE	Aérospatiale AS.350B2 Ecureuil	2468	F-WQ..
			C-FJXY
I-ALWI	Mudry CAP.10B	228	
I-AMAA	Reims/Cessna F.172M	1275	D-EEVK
I-AMAB	Reims/Cessna F.150M	1175	D-EEVF
I-AMAD	Cessna 182P (Reims assembled)	0036/64100	D-EGWZ
			PH-MYL
			D-EJPD
			N6085F
I-AMAG	Beech F33A Bonanza	CE-650	D-ELKA
I-AMAI	Reims/Cessna FR.172H Rocket	0298	D-ECRP
I-AMAJ	Cessna 182P (Reims assembled)	0039/64125	D-EDRV
			N6215F
I-AMAP	Reims/Cessna F.150L	0895	D-ECTW
I-AMAQ	Cessna 182K Skylane	57798	D-EHSV
			N2598Q
I-AMAS	Reims/Cessna FR.172H Rocket	0326	D-EEYL
I-AMAT	Cessna 152	80995	D-EOHN
			N48839
I-AMAU	Piper PA-28R-200 Cherokee Arrow II	28R-7635234	N234SW
			N9377K
			G-BMJF
			ZS-JUF
			N9377K
I-AMAV	Reims/Cessna F.152	1973	
I-AMAX	Cessna 182P Skylane	64283	N71671
I-AMAY	Aérospatiale SA.315B Lama	2607	
I-AMAZ	Maule MXT-7-180 Star Rocket	11046C	N6116U
I-AMCB	Cessna R.172K Hawk XP	2399	N736BP
I-AMCG	Cessna R.172K Hawk XP	3321	N758SJ
I-AMCH	Cessna 152	85885	N95400
I-AMCJ	Cessna U.206F Stationair	03127	N8266Q
I-AMCK	Cessna U.206F Stationair	03430	N8574Q
I-AMCO	Cessna 172N	69064	N734RW
I-AMCP	Cessna 152	80197	N24289
I-AMCQ	Cessna 152	80639	N25411
I-AMCR	Cessna 152	85267	N6528Q
I-AMCV	Cessna R.172K Hawk XP	2972	N58ER
			(N758BU)
I-AMCW	Cessna 182P Skylane	63396	N9471G
I-AMCZ	Cessna 152	81481	N64931
I-AMDA	Macchi MB.339C	147/6775	
I-AMDB	Cessna 152	81044	N48911
I-AMDC	Cessna A152	0865	N4683A
I-AMDD	Cessna 152 (Wreck noted 11.94)	80494	N24985
I-AMDE	Cessna 152	84137	N6157H
I-AMDF	Cessna 152	80055	N757WE
I-AMDG	Cessna 150M	76585	N3675V
I-AMDH	Cessna 172RG Cutlass	0512	N5350V
I-AMDI	Cessna 172RG Cutlass	0887	N9568B
I-AMDJ	Cessna 152	81764	N67336
I-AMDK	Cessna 152	85603	N94128
I-AMDM	Mooney M.20K Model 231	25-0424	N3570H
I-AMDY	Cessna 172RG Cutlass	0502	N5297V
I-AMII	Bell 206B Jet Ranger II	3821	I-MIDD
			N3199B
I-AMOK	Eurocopter EC.120B Colibri	1031	
I-AMOM	Piper PA-28RT-201T Turbo Arrow IV	28R-7931227	N2858A
I-AMON	Piper PA-28RT-201T Turbo Arrow IV	28R-8231032	N81293
I-AMRS	Neico Lancair 320	1313	
I-AMVD	Schweizer 269C	S-1540	HB-XYJ
			N69A
I-AMVE	Aérospatiale AS.350B2 Ecureuil	2640	F-WYMQ
I-AMVG	Aérospatiale AS.350B3 Ecureuil	3071	
I-AMVI	Schweizer 269C	S-1649	HB-XFJ

Regn.	Type	C/n	Prev.Id.
I-ANBE	Hughes 369D	1127D	N5183Y
I-ANCP	Partenavia P.68B	17	
I-ANDR	Reims/Cessna F.172P	2209	
I-ANDY	Piper PA-28-181 Archer II	28-8590066	N6920S
I-ANFE	SIAI-Marchetti S.205-20/R	103	
I-ANGI	Piper PA-23-235 Apache	27-564	N4963P
I-ANIA	Agusta A.109A-II	7286	
I-ANLA	Piper PA-28RT-201T Turbo Arrow IV	28R-8331049	N43155
I-ANNE	Cessna 182M Skylane	59398	N70864
I-ANNJ	Beech 35-33 Debonair	CD-62	
I-ANNY	Gardan GY-80 Horizon 160	23	
I-ANPD	Reims/Cessna FR.172G Rocket	0170	
I-AOLA	Aérospatiale AS.350B3 Ecureuil	3105	
I-AOPA	Robin ATL	6	F-GFNF
			F-WFNF
I-APCE	Piper PA-28-161 Cadet	2841045	N9161Z
I-APEX	Aérospatiale SA.315B Lama	2491	F-GFCA
			N40IAH
			N218RM
			N47314
I-APGN	Raz-Mut	unkn	
I-APLI	de Havilland DH.82A Tiger Moth	86562	I-RIBU
			G-APLV
			PG653
I-APUS	Aérospatiale SA.315B Lama	2539	N9005Q
			VR-HIL
			N9005Q
I-AQLA	Partenavia P.66B Oscar 150	32	
I-AQLE	Partenavia P.66B Oscar 150	49	
I-AQUI	Cessna 172N	71207	N2254E
I-AQVA	Lake LA-4-250 Renegade	10	N1401G
I-ARAM	Bölkow BO.207	243	D-EJBO
I-ARAS	Cessna 172C	49312	N1612Y
I-ARDA	Piper PA-24-250 Comanche	24-1305	N6324P
I-ARDO	Cessna U.206F Stationair	02809	N35934
I-ARME	Piper PA-22-160 Tri-Pacer	22-7357	
I-ARMY	Piper PA-18-135 Super Cub	18-2002	EI-75
			I-EIDI
			MM522402
			52-2402
I-AROO	Cessna 550 Citation II	0081	N254AM
			I-FBCT
			N26626
I-AROS	Piper PA-18-150 Super Cub	18-4912	N4729
I-ARPI	Piper PA-28RT-201T Turbo Arrow IV	28R-7931273	N2955A
I-ARRO	III Sky Arrow 650T	001	
I-ARWI	Procaer F.15A Picchio	07	
I-ASCA	Avia FL.3	A.51-29-48	MM51810
I-ASER	Beech 400ABeechjet	RK-204	N2357K
I-ASIO	Aérospatiale SA.315B Lama	1923/21	D-HODU
I-ASKI	Piper PA-34-200 Seneca	34-7250115	N4572T
I-ASKY	Christen A-1 Husky	1155	
I-ASSW	Asso V Whisky	unkn	
I-ATAK	Reims/Cessna F.172K	0790	
I-ATAL	Stinson L-5 Sentinel (Euravia covn)	001	
I-ATAQ	Reims/Cessna F.177RG Cardinal RG	00197/0034	
I-ATAR	Cessna 337C Super Skymaster	0846	N2546S
I-ATAT	Partenavia P.68TC	254-14-TC	
I-ATMC	Aeritalia/SNIASATR-72-212A	588	F-WWED
I-ATOM	Westland-SNIAS SA.341G Gazelle	WA/1073	F-BXPG
			G-BAZL
I-ATPA	Aeritalia/SNIAS ATR-72-212A	626	F-WQKZ
			F-WWLC
I-ATPI	Beech F33A Bonanza	CE-464	HB-EHT
I-ATRD	Aeritalia/SNIAS ATR-42-300	032	F-WWEN
I-ATRF	Aeritalia/SNIAS ATR-42-300	034	F-WWEP
I-ATRG	Aeritalia/SNIAS ATR-42-300	042	F-WWEW
I-ATRJ	Aeritalia/SNIAS ATR-42-300	057	F-WWEL
I-ATRL	Aeritalia/SNIAS ATR-42-300	068	F-WWES
I-ATRM	Aeritalia/SNIAS ATR-42-300	114	F-WWEK
I-ATRN	Aeritalia/SNIAS ATR-42-300	020	SX-BIX
			I-ATRB
			F-WWEG

Regn.	Type	C/n	Prev.Id.
I-ATRP	Aeritalia/SNIAS ATR-42-300	021	SX-BIY
			I-ATRC
			F-WWEH
I-ATSL	Aeritalia/SNIAS ATR-72-212A	592	F-WWEM
I-AUNI	Robinson R-22 Beta	1769	
I-AUNY	Cessna 501 Citation	0213	N6785D
I-AVAA	Mudry CAP.10B	38	F-BUDH
I-AVAB	Piper PA-18-150 Super Cub	18-7909097	N9750N
I-AVAM	Piper PA-18 Super Cub 95	18-7363	
I-AVGM	Cessna 550 Citation II	0492	
I-AVIF	Aérospatiale SA.315B Lama	2566	
I-AVIU	Cessna TR.182 Turbo Skylane RG	01372	N4665S
I-AVIV	Reims/Cessna F.152	1831	
I-AVJC	Bell 206B Jet Ranger II	1491	N100FW
			N777FW
			N777FL
I-AVJF	MBB-Kawasaki BK.117C-1	7525	D-HBKX(2)
I-AVJG	Gates Learjet 35A	35A-189	N727JP
	(W/o, Geneva 24.10.99)		N18NM
			N35KC
			N32FN
			N32TC
			(N189TC)
			N39292
			VH-AJV
			N381IG
I-AVON	Partenavia P.64B Oscar B	52	
I-AVRM	Cessna 550 Citation	0491	
I-AVVM	Cessna S550 Citation	0062	N12715
I-AXLE	Agusta A.109A-II	7436	
I-AXOO	Agusta A.109C	7648	OO-AAY
			D-HMET
I-AZRO	Piper PA-28RT-201T Turbo Arrow IV	28R-8031025	N2852S
I-AZUL	SOCATA Rallye 180T Galérien	3090	F-GAYS
I-BADB	Piper PA-18-150 Super Cub	18-8764	N4426Z
I-BADC	Piper PA-18-150 Super Cub	18-8770	N4437Z
I-BADF	Robin DR.300/180R Remorqueur	573	
I-BAEB	Piper PA-18-150 Super Cub	18-7609021	N9773P
I-BAEL	Dassault Falcon 20F	426	N416RM
			N555PT
			N123WH
			N427F
			F-WJMK
I-BAKE	Aero Designs Pulsar	01	
I-BALF	Piper PA-18-150 Super Cub	18-7609149	N9691P
I-BALG	Piper PA-18-150 Super Cub	18-7609129	I-ALGD
			N83443
I-BALK	Piper PA-18-150 Super Cub	18-7709032	N66842
I-BALM	Piper PA-18-150 Super Cub	18-7809035	N82961
I-BALN	Piper PA-18-150 Super Cub	18-7809033	N82951
I-BALP	Piper PA-18-150 Super Cub	18-8009044	N9757N
I-BALS	Piper PA-18-150 Super Cub	18-8109080	N91192
I-BALT	Piper PA-18-150 Super Cub	18-8109082	N91201
I-BALW	Christen A-1 Husky	1133	
I-BALZ	Christen A-1 Husky	1157	
I-BAND	Cessna R.172K Hawk XP	3081	N758GH
I-BANG	de Havilland DH.82A Tiger Moth	85482	G-APRY
			DE486
I-BATR	Piper PA-18-150 Super Cub	18-8699	N4377Z
I-BAZZ	S.A.I. F.4 Rondone I	021	
I-BBAK	Cessna 182R Skylane	68475	N9936E
I-BBMM	Christen Pitts S-2B	5196	N317JK
I-BDUE	Piper PA-18-135 Super Cub	18-2013	EI-83
			I-EIPU
			MM522413
			52-2413
I-BEAR	Piper PA-28RT-201 Arrow IV	28R-7918129	N28471
I-BEAS	Piper PA-34-220T Seneca III	34-8133248	N711KB
			(D-GKBL)
			N711KB
			N9589N
I-BEAU	Dassault Falcon 900	23	F-WWFK
I-BEBO	Piper PA-24-260 Comanche B	24-4759	N9260P
I-BECS	Schweizer 269C	S-1261	N75045

Regn.	Type	C/n	Prev.id.
I-BEKT	Beech 76 Duchess	ME-85	HB-GGR
			F-GBRO
I-BEMF	Cessna 182Q Skylane	65216	N7567S
I-BENN	Cessna 550 Citation Bravo	0859	(N550KH)
			N551KH
I-BERL	SOCATA Rallye 100S Sport	2359	HB-ERL
			I-RALR
I-BEST	Cessna 320B Skyknight	0006	N9806L
I-BETT	Piper PA-28RT-201T Turbo Arrow IV	28R-8331023	N4293K
I-BETV	Cessna 650 Citation III	0104	N13195
I-BEWW	Canadair CL-600-2B16	5020	C-FBKR
			C-GLYA
I-BFIZ	Reims/Cessna FT.337GP Super Skymaster	0021	G-BFIZ
I-BGBG	Cessna 152	83080	N46605
I-BGFE	Piper PA-31-350 Navajo Chieftain	31-7652043	N59772
I-BGMT	Piper PA-18-150 Super Cub	18-7545	
I-BGTT	SE.313B Alouette II	1115	F-GMJT
			(F-GMLC)
			CNET/F-SEBN
I-BIAP	Piper PA-28-140 Cherokee	28-24326	N1882J
I-BIAR	Piper PA-28-140 Cherokee	28-24336	N1891J
I-BIAT	Piper PA-28-140 Cherokee	28-24572	N7235J
I-BIFA	Enstrom 280FX Shark	2065	(JA7857)
I-BIKA	Airbus A.320-214	951	F-WWBT
I-BIKE	Airbus A.320-214	999	F-WWBZ
I-BIKI	Airbus A.320-214	1138	F-WWDJ
I-BIOH	Macchi MB.308 (Current but CoA exp 6.77)	121/5894	MM53074
I-BIOI	Macchi MB.308	122/5895	MM53075
I-BIRS	Partenavia P.64B Oscar B-1155	56	
I-BISB	Cessna 172P Floatplane	75014	N54630
I-BITT	Partenavia P.64B Oscar 200	01	
I-BIXA	Airbus A.321-112	477	D-AVZE
I-BIXB	Airbus A.321-112	524	D-AVZY
I-BIXC	Airbus A.321-112	526	D-AVZZ
I-BIXD	Airbus A.321-112	532	D-AVZB
I-BIXE	Airbus A.321-112	488	D-AVZG
I-BIXF	Airbus A.321-112	515	D-AVZQ
I-BIXG	Airbus A.321-112	516	D-AVZR
I-BIXH	Airbus A.321-112	940	D-AVZS
I-BIXI	Airbus A.321-112	494	D-AVZI
I-BIXJ	Airbus A.321-112	959	D-AVZP
I-BIXL	Airbus A.321-112	513	D-AVZO
I-BIXM	Airbus A.321-112	514	D-AVZP
I-BIXN	Airbus A.321-112	576	D-AVZR
I-BIXO	Airbus A.321-112	495	D-AVZJ
I-BIXP	Airbus A.321-112	583	D-AVZT
I-BIXQ	Airbus A.321-112	586	D-AVZU
I-BIXR	Airbus A.321-112	593	D-AVZW
I-BIXS	Airbus A.321-112	599	D-AVZZ
I-BIXT	Airbus A.321-112	765	D-AVZW
I-BIXU	Airbus A.321-111	434	D-AVZB
			F-WWID
I-BIXV	Airbus A.321-112	819	D-AVZU
I-BIXZ	Airbus A.321-112	848	D-AVZC
I-BJBB	Cessna 152	84252	G-BJBB
			N5086L
I-BKAK	Rutan LongEz	001	
I-BKBO	MBB-Kawasaki BK.117B-1	7199	D-HIMP
			N54114
			D-HIMP
I-BKBS	MBB-Kawasaki BK.117C-1	7504	D-HOTZ
			XA-...
			D-HOTZ
			D-HECA(3)
			D-HMBF
I-BLAC	Cessna 182P Skylane	64498	N1948M
I-BLAE	Piper PA-28-161 Cadet	2841054	N9163V
I-BLAS	Mudry CAP.10B	151	N151AS
			F-WZCG
I-BLIM	SE.313B Alouette II	1242	F-GHUQ
			ALAT
I-BLIP	Aérospatiale SA.315B Lama	2495	
I-BLIV	Piper PA-31P-425 Pressurized Navajo	31P-7300122	HB-LIV
			N7350L
I-BLUB	Cessna 650 Citation VI	0216	N68269
I-BLUX	Aérospatiale AS.350B2 Ecureuil	2506	SE-JAF
			F-WYMN
I-BMBN	Beech V35 Bonanza	D-8133	N9046S
I-BMFE	Gates Learjet 25C	25C-146	N6KJ
			N9HN
			C-GRQX
			N9HN
			N9HM
			N146LJ
I-BNAA	Hughes 369HS	71-0331S	
I-BNAP	Bredanardi NH-500D	BH-12	
I-BNBH	Hughes 269C	24-0274	
I-BNBI	Hughes 269C	24-0275	
I-BNBV	Bredanardi NH-300C	BH-01	
I-BNCC	Bredanardi NH-300C	003	
I-BNCD	Bredanardi NH-300C	004	
I-BNCH	Bredanardi NH-300C	008	
I-BNCI	Bredanardi NH-300C	009	
I-BNCN	Bredanardi NH-300C	015	
I-BNCR	Bredanardi NH-300C	018	
I-BNCS	Bredanardi NH-300C	019	
I-BNCV	Bredanardi NH-300C	025	
I-BNDA	Schweizer 269C	S-1473	N69A
I-BNDB	Schweizer 269C	S-1560	N104LU
I-BNDC	Schweizer 269C	S-1576	N69A
I-BNDD	Schweizer 269C	S-1599	N69A
I-BOBO	Piper J-3C-65 Cub	12128	I-PIST
			44-79832
I-BOCA	Piper J-3C-65 Cub	20141	N6910H
I-BODE	Stolp SA.750 Starduster Too	400	
I-BOGO	Reims/Cessna FR.172J Rocket	0568	(I-AIIA)
			(I-CCAJ)
			(D-EALR)
			(I-CCAJ)
			(D-EOGV)
I-BOLK	Robin DR.400/180R Remorqueur	1706	
I-BONG	Reims/Cessna F.150K Floatplane	0621	(I-ALAT)
I-BONU	Piper PA-28-161 Cadet	2841274	N91966
I-BOYA	Cessna A.152 Aerobat	0966	G-BOYA
			N761ML
I-BPAA	Bredanardi NH-300C	023	I-BNCT
I-BPBP	Robinson R-22 Beta	1276	I-MIBP
			N8076R
I-BRAL	Aérospatiale AS.350B Ecureuil	1904	
I-BRBR	Beech 35-C33A Debonair	CE-35	HB-EKV
I-BRIG	Partenavia P.64B Oscar 200	03	
I-BRIP	Partenavia P.66B Oscar 150	43	
I-BRIS	Partenavia P.66B Oscar 100	39	
I-BRJN	Reims/Cessna F.150L	1025	
I-BRJO	Partenavia P.64B Oscar B	49	
I-BRMA	Agusta-Bell AB.412	25626	
I-BRUZ	SE.5A Replica	unkn	
I-BSAB	Piper PA-46-350P Malibu Mirage	4622049	G-BSAB
			N9161N
I-BSAM	Robinson R-22B Beta	1076	N8048U
I-BSCR	Beech B24R Sierra	MC-351	
I-BSHV	Bell 206B Jet Ranger II	909	HB-XHV
			D-HORY
I-BSTI	Fairchild-Swearingen SA.227AC Metro III	AC-470	N581BT
			C-FAFM
			C-FJLX
			N470A
			(N470CA)
			N470A
			HB-LNB
			N30486
I-BSTS	Fairchild-Swearingen SA.227AC Metro III	AC-603	N3117S
I-BTRE	Piper PA-18-135 Super Cub	18-3339	EI-120
			I-EIKR
			MM537739
			53-7739
I-BUCK	Bücker Bü.131 Jungmann	46	HB-UTM
			A-35
I-BUFF	Piper PA-18S-150 Super Cub Floatplane	1809008	N9616N
I-BULG	SIAI-Marchetti S.205-20/R	215	

Regn.	Type	C/n	Prev.Id.
I-BUNN	Reims/Cessna FR.172H Rocket	0289	D-ECQN
I-BUNO	Piper PA-18-135 Super Cub	18-3982	EI-260
			I-EIUJ
			MM542582
			54-2582
I-BURI	Avia FL.54 Meteor	1126	OE-ABR
			I-FELO
I-BURL	Stinson L-5 Sentinel	unkn	MM52883
I-BURY	Piper PA-23-250 Aztec D	27-4400	N6628Y
I-BUSM	Airbus A.300B2-203 (Stored)	049	N291EA
			F-GBNI
			F-ODHY
			F-WZES
			F-WUAV
I-BUSN	Airbus A.300B4-203 (Stored)	051	N292EA
			F-GBNJ
			F-ODHZ
			(F-WZEA)
I-BUSP	Airbus A.300B4-203 (Stored)	067	N207EA
			F-GBNC
			F-WZEP
I-BUSQ	Airbus A.300B4-103 (Stored)	118	N401UA
			N216EA
			F-GBNL
I-BUSR	Airbus A.300B4-103	120	N402UA
			N219EA
			F-GBNN
I-BUST	Airbus A.300B4-103	068	N403UA
			N208EA
			F-GBND
			F-WZEA
I-BVUL	Piper PA-34-200T Seneca II	34-7570128	G-BVUL
			OY-PEA
			N33531
I-BXPD	Beech P35 Bonanza	D-7025	CN-TYI
I-BXWA	SA.316B Alouette III	1307	F-GIBY
			A-307
I-BXWB	SA.315B Lama	2453	HB-XGG
I-BZEB	Reims/Cessna FR.172J Rocket	0490	D-EDCC
			D-EECC
I-BZEC	Reims/Cessna FR.172J Rocket	0379	D-ECVG
I-CAAL	Robin DR.400/140 Major	863	
I-CACR	Maule MX-7-180 Star Rocket	11060C	N9204U
I-CADF	Dragon Fly 333AC	EB063	
I-CAFD	Dassault Falcon 50	183	F-WWHC
I-CAMI	Aviamilano F.14 Nibbio	207	
I-CAMY	Mooney M.20J Model 205	24-3205	N9132N
I-CANO	Cessna U.206G Stationair II	06003	N4692Z
I-CAPC	CAP.1	unkn	
I-CAPH	Evans VP-1 Volksplane	V-8-78-AC	
I-CAPJ	Ianotta I-66 San Francesco	001	
I-CAPK	Sparviero	unkn	
I-CAPM	Jodel D.92 Bébé	unkn	
I-CAPS	Brügger MB-2 Colibri	002	
I-CARQ	General Avia F.22B Pinguino	010	
I-CARR	Agusta A.109A-II	7319	
I-CASP	Piper PA-28R-200 Cherokee Arrow	28R-7335155	N333RG
I-CATF	Evans VP-1 Volksplane	unkn	
I-CATS	Robinson R-44 Astro	0546	
I-CATW	Reims/Cessna F.150M	1188	
I-CAVE	Partenavia P.64B Oscar B-1155	69	
I-CAVI	Piper PA-28-180 Cherokee Archer	28-7505171	N4436X
			N9622N
I-CAVL	Aviamilano P.19 Scricciolo	341	
I-CAVM	Piper PA-28-161 Cadet	2841090	N9170N
I-CBLT	Agusta A.109A	7175	
I-CBSQ	Mooney M.20R Ovation	29-0116	N323SQ
			N716MA
I-CCAA	Mooney M.20E Chaparral	700028	N943IV
I-CCAB	Reims/Cessna FR.172H Rocket	0312	
I-CCAD	Reims/Cessna FR.172J Rocket	0357	
I-CCAE	Reims/Cessna FR.172J Rocket	0413	
I-CCAF	Reims/Cessna FR.172J Rocket	0404	
I-CCAH	Reims/Cessna F.172M	1056	
I-CCAL	Reims/Cessna FR.172J Rocket	0483	
I-CCAN	Reims/Cessna FR.172J Rocket	0556	
I-CCAP	Reims/Cessna FR.172J Rocket	0438	(D-EJXY)
I-CCAQ	Reims/Cessna F.172M	1336	
I-CCAR	Reims/Cessna F.172M	1135	(F-BSGU)
I-CCAS	Reims/Cessna FR.172J Rocket	0527	
I-CCAT	Reims/Cessna F.172M	1358	
I-CCAW	Reims/Cessna F.172M	1427	
I-CCBA	Reims/Cessna FR.172J Rocket	0541	
I-CCBC	Cessna U.206F Stationair	03232	N8371Q
I-CCBF	Reims/Cessna F.172N	1550	
I-CCBG	Reims/Cessna FR.172K Hawk XP	0599	
I-CCBI	Maule MX.7-235 Star Rocket	10075C	N92047
I-CCDC	Reims/Cessna FR.172J Rocket	0571	
I-CCFF	Cessna 340A	0223	N3888G
I-CCIM	Piper PA-28-161 Cadet	2841091	N9170R
I-CCSV	Piper PA-28-161 Cadet	2841096	N9173R
I-CCWW	Piper PA-24-260 Comanche	24-4048	N8589P
			HB-OYA
			N8589P
I-CDXV	SOCATA TB-20 Trinidad	536	F-GENO
I-CECC	SOCATA MS.883 Rallye 115	1510	F-BRYK
I-CECI	Aeromere F.8L Falco	202	
I-CEDA	SOCATA TB-10 Tobago	759	
I-CEDI	de Havilland DH.82A Tiger Moth	85374	G-AOUI
			DE352
I-CELF	Bell 206B Jet Ranger II	1605	N77884
			N333PA
			N90108
I-CELI	Macchi AL.60B-2	50/6230	I-CELE
			I-CELI
I-CELJ	Piper PA-28-180 Cherokee Archer	28-7405263	N44594
I-CELU	Cessna 172RG Cutlass	0326	N5293U
I-CELY	Piper PA-34-200T Seneca II	34-8070255	
I-CEMX	SIAI-Marchetti SF.260	2-48	
I-CENB	Reims/Cessna F.150L	0943	
I-CEND	Reims/Cessna FR.172J Rocket	0401	(I-CENC)
I-CENE	Reims/Cessna F.150L	0986	
I-CEPI	Robin DR.380 Prince	609	
I-CERL	Piper J-3C-65 Cub	17372	HB-OWY
			N70386
I-CERR	Piper PA-20 Pacer 125	20-796	HB-OON
I-CERX	Aeritalia-Fiat G.222	4043	
I-CESY	Piper PA-28-161 Cadet	2841097	N9173X
I-CFAA	Agusta-Bell AB.412	25610	
I-CFAB	Agusta-Bell AB.412	25614	
I-CFAC	Agusta-Bell AB.412	25615	
I-CFAD	Agusta-Bell AB.412	25618	
I-CFBU	Agusta A.109C	7656	
I-CFSB	Hughes 369HS	84-0634S	I-BNAD
I-CFSC	Hughes 369HS	94-0648S	
I-CFSD	Bredanardi NH-500D	BH-01	
I-CFSE	Bredanardi NH-500D	BH-02	
I-CFSF	Bredanardi NH-500D	BH-03	
I-CFSG	Bredanardi NH-500D	BH-04	
I-CFSH	Bredanardi NH-500D	BH-05	
I-CFSI	Bredanardi NH-500D	BH-06	
I-CFSJ	Agusta-Bell 412	25561	
I-CFSK	Bredanardi NH-500D	BH-07	
I-CFSL	Bredanardi NH-500D	BH-15	
I-CFSM	Bredanardi NH-500D	BH-16	
I-CFSN	Bredanardi NH-500D	BH-17	
I-CFSO	Agusta-Bell 412	25562	
I-CFSP	Agusta-Bell 412	25563	
I-CFST	Canadair CL-215-1A10	1072	MM62019
			I-CFSR
			C-GKDP
I-CFSW	Agusta-Bell 412	25564	
I-CFSX	Agusta-Bell 412	25572	
I-CFSZ	Canadair CL-215-1A10	1108	C-FFYO
			C-FBNJ
			C-GKEE
I-CGAB	Piper PA-28-140 Cherokee E	28-7225166	N11C
I-CGAD	Piper PA-28-140 Cherokee F	28-7325020	N11C
I-CGAG	Piper PA-18-150 Super Cub	18-9000	
I-CGAM	Piper PA-28-151 Cherokee Warrior	28-7715151	N9523N

Regn.	Type	C/n	Prev.Id.
I-CGAN	Piper PA-18S-150 Super Cub Floatplane	18-8109003	N24310
I-CGAO	Piper PA-18-150 Super Cub	18-8109085	(LN-FAL)
			N91205
I-CGAR	Piper PA-34-220T Seneca III	34-8233081	N8096B
I-CGAS	Piper PA-28-181 Archer II	28-8690020	N9102T
I-CGAT	Piper PA-31T-620 Cheyenne	31T-7520033	N54964
I-CGAV	Piper PA-34-220T Seneca III	34-8433021	N4312E
I-CGAZ	Piper PA-28RT-201 Arrow IV	28R-7918247	N4507U
I-CGBB	Mooney M.20J Model 205	24-3129	N1067S
I-CGCC	Christen A-1 Husky	1158	
I-CGCL	Agusta-Bell 412	25600	
I-CGDD	Christen A-1 Husky	1181	
I-CGFE	Aérospatiale AS.365N2 Dauphin 2	6494	F-WQDI
I-CGTT	Piper PA-31T-620 Cheyenne	31T-7820045	N82288
I-CHEK	Piper PA-28R-201 Arrow	2844017	N4136W
I-CHIM	Aviamilano F.8L Falco	112	
I-CHNR	Beech 95 Travel Air	TD-299	N9623R
I-CHOP	Bell 206B Jet Ranger II	2523	G-BSUG
			N888GC
			N222PF
			N315GC
I-CHTH	Grumman AA-5A Cheetah	0659	
I-CICC	Partenavia P.66B Oscar 100	13	
I-CICO	Procaer F.15B Picchio	20	
I-CIGB	Cessna 501 Citation	0163	(I-AGIK)
			N1354G
I-CIGH	HS.125 Series 700A	257201	N2KW
			N710BV
			G-5-19
I-CILL	Mudry CAP.21	8	F-GDTC
I-CIND	Beech A36TC Bonanza	EA-31	N817BK
			N6695Z
I-CIOH	Aérospatiale SA.365N Dauphin 2	6004	F-WYMI
			F-WZJS
I-CIRE	Aviamilano F.8L Falco	111	
I-CIST	Cessna 650 Citation III	0085	N650DA
			JA8249
			N1317G
I-CITS	Robinson R-22 Beta	1374	
I-CITT	Partenavia P.68C	217	G-TELE
			G-DORE
			OY-CAD
I-CITU	Aerotek Pitts S-2A	2199	G-BGSF
I-CJAO	Cessna U.206B	0782	N3482L
I-CLAD	Cessna 500 Citation I	0223	N223P
			OH-COC
			N400SA
			N444KV
			N444LP
			N223CC
I-CLAM	Robinson R-22 Mariner	2490M	N83206
I-CLEO	Schweizer 269C	S-1490	N86G
I-CLLO	Cessna 172M	66468	N80240
I-CLON	American AA-5B Tiger	0432	N81110
I-CLRM	Agusta A.109E	11042	
I-CMAO	Reims/Cessna F.150L	0748	D-ECQB
I-CMDA	Cessna 172A	46883	HB-CMD
			OE-DGW
			N7283T
I-CMDV	Agusta A.109A	7128	
I-CMMA	Piper PA-46-350P Malibu Mirage	4622062	N9178D
I-CMMB	Piper PA-28RT-201T Turbo Arrow IV	28R-8231029	N8101C
I-CMUT	Dassault Falcon 20F	389	F-WRQV
I-CNPG	Piper PA-28-161 Warrior II	28-7916394	N424RP
			N16PA
			N9514N
I-COAE	Agusta A.109A	7180	LX-HRG
			3A-MGI
			I-GAME
			N284CN
			D-HACP
			HB-XKZ
I-COBY	Piper PA-34-200T Seneca II	34-7670026	N9244K
			N9611N

Regn.	Type	C/n	Prev.Id.
I-COCE	Aérospatiale SA.365N Dauphin 2	6099	F-WYMD
			G-BLWC
I-COKK	Beech F33A Bonanza	CE-1307	N524PD
I-COLL	Piper PA-28-181 Archer II	28-8190074	N82854
I-COMB	Piper PA-18 Super Cub 95	18-3656	F-DADQ
I-COND	Hughes 269C	117-0644	
I-COOP	Aérospatiale SA.315B Lama	2668	
I-CORB	Piper PA-28R-200 Cherokee Arrow	28R-7635072	N4535X
I-CORR	Partenavia P.57 Fachiro IIf	33	
I-COTT	Beech 77 Skipper	WA-292	HB-EJK
I-CRAB	Reims/Cessna F.150L	1032	
I-CRAC	Reims/Cessna F.150L	1098	
I-CRBM	Agusta A.109C	7623	I-CRBN
I-CRBO	Partenavia P.66C Charlie	104	
I-CRCA	Piper PA-28-181 Archer II	2890153	N9211G
I-CREM	Dassault Falcon 10	161	N50SL
			N30CN
			N230FJ
			F-WZGM
I-CRIC	Mudry CAP.231EX	001	F-GRLR
			F-WZCI
I-CRMC	Aérospatiale AS.350B Ecureuil	1272	F-GCJZ
I-CRMA	Hughes 269C	99-0831	HB-XKV
I-CRMD	Agusta A.109A-II	7301	
I-CRPI	Piper PA-28-180 Cherokee Archer	28-7505254	N3992X
I-CRSE	Piper PA-28RT-201T Turbo Arrow IV	28R-7931225	N2853W
I-CRSR	SA.316B Alouette III	1949	F-OCUR
I-CSAB	Schweizer 269C	S-1598	N41S
I-CSAM	Aérospatiale AS.350B1 Ecureuil	2233	
I-CSMA	Reims/Cessna F.152	1889	
I-CSNA	Cessna 310N	0141	HB-LHB
			I-ALCC
			N5041Q
I-CTGM	Robinson R-44 Astro	0481	
I-CUCC	Cessna 172M	62671	N13326
I-CUDP	SE.313 Alouette II	1165	F-ZBAA
			F-BIFM
			F-WIFM
I-CVMD	Agusta A.109A	7107	N109JD
			(N1091F)
			N109JD
			I-DCMV
I-CWSA	Piper PA-18-150 Super Cub	18-8109002	N24291
I-CYRN	Partenavia P.64B Oscar B	37	
I-CZAJ	Monnet Sonerai IILS	51LS	
I-DACD	Agusta A.109A-II	7258	(N9047U)
I-DACE	Agusta A.109A-II (A.109K)	7340	
I-DACG	Agusta-Bell 206B Jet Ranger III	8652	
I-DACM	McDonnell-Douglas DC-9-82	49971	
I-DACN	McDonnell-Douglas DC-9-82	49972	
I-DACP	McDonnell-Douglas DC-9-82	49973	
I-DACQ	McDonnell-Douglas DC-9-82	49974	
I-DACR	McDonnell-Douglas DC-9-82	49975	
I-DACS	McDonnell-Douglas DC-9-82	53053	
I-DACT	McDonnell-Douglas DC-9-82	53054	
I-DACU	McDonnell-Douglas DC-9-82	53055	
I-DACV	McDonnell-Douglas DC-9-82	53056	
I-DACW	McDonnell-Douglas DC-9-82	53057	
I-DACX	McDonnell-Douglas DC-9-82	53060	
I-DACY	McDonnell-Douglas DC-9-82	53059	
I-DACZ	McDonnell-Douglas DC-9-82	53058	
I-DAFE	Cessna 172N	72647	N6229D
I-DAGF	Cessna 525 CitationJet	0347	N1133G
I-DAGI	Neico Lancair 235	1	
I-DALS	Piper PA-28-161 Warrior II	28-8016171	D-EWII
			N8144Z
			N9525N
I-DANC	Piper PA-32-301T Saratoga	32-8324007	N4292C
I-DAND	McDonnell-Douglas DC-9-82	53061	
I-DANF	McDonnell-Douglas DC-9-82	53062	
I-DANG	McDonnell-Douglas DC-9-82	53176	
I-DANH	McDonnell-Douglas DC-9-82	53177	
I-DANL	McDonnell-Douglas DC-9-82	53178	
I-DANM	McDonnell-Douglas DC-9-82	53179	
I-DANP	McDonnell-Douglas DC-9-82	53180	

Regn.	Type	C/n	Prev.Id.
I-DANQ	McDonnell-Douglas DC-9-82	53181	
I-DANR	McDonnell-Douglas DC-9-82	53203	
I-DANS	Piper PA-28-161 Warrior II	28-8316054	N42952
I-DANU	McDonnell-Douglas DC-9-82	53204	
I-DANV	McDonnell-Douglas DC-9-82	53205	
I-DANW	McDonnell-Douglas DC-9-82	53206	
I-DARD	Piper PA-28-161 Warrior II	28-8216172	N8224V
I-DASO	Aérospatiale SA.316B Alouette III	1318	F-GJCY
			ALAT
I-DATA	McDonnell-Douglas DC-9-82	53216	
I-DATB	McDonnell-Douglas DC-9-82	53221	
I-DATC	McDonnell-Douglas DC-9-82	53222	
I-DATD	McDonnell-Douglas DC-9-82	53223	
I-DATE	McDonnell-Douglas DC-9-82	53217	
I-DATF	McDonnell-Douglas DC-9-82	53224	
I-DATG	McDonnell-Douglas DC-9-82	53225	
I-DATH	McDonnell-Douglas DC-9-82	53226	
I-DATI	McDonnell-Douglas DC-9-82	53218	
I-DATJ	McDonnell-Douglas DC-9-82	53227	
I-DATK	McDonnell-Douglas DC-9-82	53228	
I-DATL	McDonnell-Douglas DC-9-82	53229	
I-DATM	McDonnell-Douglas DC-9-82	53230	
I-DATN	McDonnell-Douglas DC-9-82	53231	
I-DATO	McDonnell-Douglas DC-9-82	53219	
I-DATP	McDonnell-Douglas DC-9-82	53232	
I-DATQ	McDonnell-Douglas DC-9-82	53233	
I-DATR	McDonnell-Douglas DC-9-82	53234	
I-DATS	McDonnell-Douglas DC-9-82	53235	
I-DATU	McDonnell-Douglas DC-9-82	53220	
I-DAVA	McDonnell-Douglas DC-9-82	49215	
I-DAVB	McDonnell-Douglas DC-9-82	49216	
I-DAVC	McDonnell-Douglas DC-9-82	49217	
I-DAVD	McDonnell-Douglas DC-9-82	49218	N6203D
I-DAVF	McDonnell-Douglas DC-9-82	49219	
I-DAVG	McDonnell-Douglas DC-9-82	49220	
I-DAVH	McDonnell-Douglas DC-9-82	49221	
I-DAVI	McDonnell-Douglas DC-9-82	49430	
I-DAVJ	McDonnell-Douglas DC-9-82	49431	
I-DAVK	McDonnell-Douglas DC-9-82	49432	
I-DAVL	McDonnell-Douglas DC-9-82	49433	
I-DAVM	McDonnell-Douglas DC-9-82	49434	
I-DAVN	McDonnell-Douglas DC-9-82	49435	
I-DAVP	McDonnell-Douglas DC-9-82	49549	
I-DAVR	McDonnell-Douglas DC-9-82	49550	
I-DAVS	McDonnell-Douglas DC-9-82	49551	
I-DAVT	McDonnell-Douglas DC-9-82	49552	
I-DAVU	McDonnell-Douglas DC-9-82	49794	
I-DAVV	McDonnell-Douglas DC-9-82	49795	
I-DAVW	McDonnell-Douglas DC-9-82	49796	
I-DAVX	McDonnell-Douglas DC-9-82	49969	
I-DAVZ	McDonnell-Douglas DC-9-82	49970	
I-DAWA	McDonnell-Douglas DC-9-82	49192	N19B
I-DAWB	McDonnell-Douglas DC-9-82	49197	
I-DAWC	McDonnell-Douglas DC-9-82	49198	
I-DAWD	McDonnell-Douglas DC-9-82	49199	
I-DAWE	McDonnell-Douglas DC-9-82	49193	
I-DAWF	McDonnell-Douglas DC-9-82	49200	
I-DAWG	McDonnell-Douglas DC-9-82	49201	
I-DAWH	McDonnell-Douglas DC-9-82	49202	
I-DAWI	McDonnell-Douglas DC-9-82	49194	
I-DAWJ	McDonnell-Douglas DC-9-82	49203	
I-DAWL	McDonnell-Douglas DC-9-82	49204	
I-DAWM	McDonnell-Douglas DC-9-82	49205	
I-DAWO	McDonnell-Douglas DC-9-82	49195	
I-DAWP	McDonnell-Douglas DC-9-82	49206	
I-DAWQ	McDonnell-Douglas DC-9-82	49207	
I-DAWR	McDonnell-Douglas DC-9-82	49208	
I-DAWS	McDonnell-Douglas DC-9-82	49209	
I-DAWT	McDonnell-Douglas DC-9-82	49210	
I-DAWU	McDonnell-Douglas DC-9-82	49196	
I-DAWV	McDonnell-Douglas DC-9-82	49211	
I-DAWW	McDonnell-Douglas DC-9-82	49212	
I-DAWY	McDonnell-Douglas DC-9-82	49213	
I-DAWZ	McDonnell-Douglas DC-9-82	49214	
I-DCVM	Agusta A.109A	7109	
I-DDVA	Hawker 800XP	258389	N23493
I-DDVE	Aérospatiale AS.365N2 Dauphin 2	6414	G-CBRA
			I-GRDN
			F-WYMJ
I-DEBO	Hughes 369D	39-0480D	HB-XIR
I-DECA	Piper PA-28R-200 Cherokee Arrow	28R-7635300	N6125J
I-DECR	Piper PA-28-181 Cherokee Archer II	28-7690448	N6981J
I-DEEN	Cessna TR.182 Turbo Skylane RG	00665	N9150R
I-DEIB	Boeing 767-33AER	27376	G-OITA
			VH-ITA
			N276AW
			N1794B
I-DEIC	Boeing 767-33AER	27377	G-OITB
			VH-ITB
			N361AW
			N6009F
I-DEID	Boeing 767-33A	27468	G-OITC
			(VH-ITH)
I-DEIF	Boeing 767-33A	27908	G-OITF
			N6055X
I-DEIG	Boeing 767-33AER	27918	G-OITG
I-DEIL	Boeing 767-33AER	28147	G-OITL
I-DELA	Mooney M.20J Model 205	24-3349	N612SB
I-DELF	Robinson R-22 Beta	1091	
I-DEMC	Boeing 747-243B Combi	22506	
I-DEMF	Boeing 747-243B Combi	22508	
I-DEMG	Boeing 747-243B	22510	
I-DEML	Boeing 747-243B	22511	
I-DEMN	Boeing 747-243B	22512	
I-DEMP	Boeing 747-243B	22513	
I-DEMR	Boeing 747-243B	22545	
I-DEMS	Boeing 747-243B	22969	N8289V
I-DEMV	Boeing 747-243B Combi	23301	N6018N
I-DEMY	Boeing 747-230B	21589	D-ABYN(2)
I-DENR	Dassault Falcon 50	125	N711KT
			N118FJ
			F-WZHB
I-DENY	Aérospatiale SA.315B Lama	2525	G-BMKT
			N9002K
I-DEPE	Pilatus Britten-Norman BN-2B-26 Islander	2253	G-BTLY
I-DEPL	Polliwagen	unkn	
I-DERT	SIAI-Marchetti S.205-18/R	357	
I-DESO	Agusta A.109A-II	7401	
I-DEST	Piper PA-28-140 Cherokee	28-7525085	N9503N
I-DEVE	Dragon Fly DF333AC	EB054	
I-DFCA	Dragon Fly DF333	EB030	
I-DIAV	Partenavia P.57 Fachiro IIf	18	
I-DIDE	Piper PA-24-250 Comanche	24-158	I-DIDJ
			HB-OTC
			N5199P
I-DIDU	Brugger MB-2 Colibri	40	
I-DIEL	Robinson R-22	0104	HB-XMK
			N9041Q
I-DIES	Dassault Falcon 900	30	F-WGTH
			HB-IAF
			F-WWFL
I-DIGI	Partenavia P.57 Fachiro IIf	12	
I-DINA	Stinson L-5 Sentinel (Euravia conversion)	004	
I-DINU	Robin DR.400/160	711	
I-DIPA	SEEMS MS.885 Super Rallye	353	
I-DISI	Reims/Cessna F.150L	1027	
I-DIZE	McDonnell-Douglas DC-9-32	47502	
I-DJNO	SA.316B Alouette III	5411	F-WTNB
I-DLAB	Piper J-3C-65 Cub	9495	43-634
I-DLON	Gates Learjet 35A	35A-346	N35AJ
			C-GMGA
			N3803G
I-DMPL	Partenavia P.68C	350	
I-DODE	Piper J-3C-65 Cub	9664	43-803
			(42-59613)
I-DOIT	Zorzoli PRG-1	02	
I-DONY	Cessna 207 Skywagon	00261	F-BXAI
			N1661U
I-DPCA	Agusta A.109A-II	7322	MM81223
I-DPCB	Agusta A.109A-II	7323	MM81224

Regn.	Type	C/n	Prev.Id.
I-DPCC	Agusta A.109A	7226	MM80752
			I-DACK
			N9046Z
I-DPCD	Canadair CL.215-6B11	2003	C-FTUA
I-DPCE	Canadair CL.215-6B11	2004	C-FTUS
I-DPCJ	Agusta A.109K	10034	
I-DPCL	Agusta CH-47C Chinook	172	
I-DPCM	Agusta CH-47C Chinook	173	
I-DPCN	Canadair CL.215-6B11	2008	C-FUAK
I-DPCO	Canadair CL.215-6B11	2009	C-FVRA
I-DPCP	Canadair CL.215-6B11	2020	C-FYCY
I-DPCQ	Canadair CL.215-6B11	2021	C-FYDA
I-DPCR(2)	Piaggio P.180 Avanti	1032	D-IMLP
I-DPCS(2)	Piaggio P.180 Avanti	1033	
I-DPCT	Canadair CL.215-6B11	2029	C-FZYS
I-DPCU	Canadair CL.215-6B11	2030	C-GALV
I-DPCV	Canadair CL.215-6B11	2035	C-GCXG
I-DPCW	Canadair CL215-6B11	2036	C-GDHW
I-DRAC	Cessna T.310Q	0078	(N7578Q)
I-DRAW	Zlin Z.50L	0011	OK-HZD
I-DRIS	Partenavia P.66B Oscar 100	51	
I-DROP	Piper PA-28-140 Cherokee D	28-7125238	N5076S
I-DSAM	Aérospatiale AS.350B Ecureuil	2296	F-WYMA
I-DSPV	Neico Lancair 320	670/A	
I-DUCL	Rand-Robinson KR-2	6657/001	
I-DUPA	McDonnell-Douglas MD-11F	48426	
I-DUPB	McDonnell-Douglas MD-11F	48431	
I-DUPC	McDonnell-Douglas MD-11F	48581	
I-DUPD	McDonnell-Douglas MD-11F	48630	
I-DUPE	McDonnell-Douglas MD-11F	48427	
I-DUPI	McDonnell-Douglas MD-11F	48428	
I-DUPO	McDonnell-Douglas MD-11F	48429	
I-DUPU	McDonnell-Douglas MD-11F	48430	
I-DUST	Stolp SA-700 Acroduster One	020	
I-DVCM	Agusta A.109A	7156	
I-DYAL	Aérospatiale SA.315B Lama	2670	
I-EADU	Robin DR.400/180R Remorqueur	800	D-EADU
I-EAGR	Enstrom 280FX Shark	2027	N8624T
I-EAGS	Agusta A.109A-II	7426	N1YU
I-EASY	Rutan LongEz	unkn	
I-EBSS	Piper PA-28RT-201T Turbo Arrow IV	28R-8031013	D-EBSS
			N8106J
I-EBXK	Reims/Cessna F.150M	1373	D-EBXK
I-ECAX	SIAI-Marchetti S.205-20/R	038/06-38	I-ICAX
I-ECID	Piper PA-18-150 Super Cub	18-4549	D-ECID(2)
			OE-CID
			OE-BID
			N10F
I-ECOA	PZL M-18B Dromader	1Z024-28	SP-DED(2)
I-ECOC	PZL M-18B Dromader	1Z024-30	SP-DEF(2)
I-ECOH	PZL M-18B Dromader	1Z024-29	SP-DEE(2)
I-ECOL	Agusta A.109C	7608	
I-ECOS	Robinson R-22 Beta	1006	N8039M
I-ECOW	PZL-104 Wilga 80	CF21990939	SP-WDG
I-ECSI	Reims/Cessna F.152	1937	G-BKTT
I-ECSO	Cessna 152	83856	G-BOTC
			N5385B
I-ECUR	Aérospatiale AS.355F Ecureuil 2	5285	I-BSBS
			F-WZKK
I-EDAI	de Havilland DH.82A Tiger Moth	86560	G-AYUX
	(Accident 6.7.96)		F-BDOQ
			Fr.AF
			PG651
I-EDEM	Cessna 525 CitationJet	0155	N155CJ
I-EDIK	Dassault Falcon 50	132	F-WPXF
I-EDLB	Cessna 182E Skylane	54262	D-EDLB
			D-ECZE
			HB-CMA
			N3262Y
I-EDUE	Agusta-Bell 47J	1066	MM80193
			I-EDUE
			MM80193
I-EEYA	Cessna 182P Skylane	60833	D-EEYA
			N9293G
I-EFCN	Aérospatiale AS.350B Ecureuil	1445	

Regn.	Type	C/n	Prev.Id.
I-EFCT	Piper PA-28-180 Cherokee F	28-7105122	N5097S
I-EGDO	SOCATA Rallye 235E Gabier	12905	F-GBKZ
I-EGEB	Beech 95-B55 Baron	TC-1261	HB-GEB
I-EHAC	Agusta-Bell 412	25504	(G-BKNS)
I-EHRB	Cessna 182P Skylane	64372	D-EHRB(2)
			D-EDRB(2)
			I-EKRB
			D-EKRB(1)
			N1565M
I-EIAD	Cessna 305C (L-19E) Bird Dog	0030	EI-5
	(Regal Air conversion)		MM612984
			61-2984
I-EIAE	Cessna 305C (L-19E) Bird Dog	0044	EI-9
	(Regal Air conversion)		MM6212282
			62-12282
I-EIAF	Cessna 305C (L-19E) Bird Dog	0011	EI-13
	(Regal Air conversion)		MM612965
			61-2965
I-EIAG	Cessna 305C (L-19E) Bird Dog	0012	EI-15
	(Regal Air conversion)		MM612966
			61-2966
I-EIAH	Cessna 305C (L-19E) Bird Dog	0008	EI-18
	(Regal Air conversion)		MM612962
			61-2962
I-EIAI	Cessna 305C (L-19E) Bird Dog	0033	EI-20
	(Regal Air conversion)		MM612987
			61-2987
I-EIAJ	Cessna 305C (L-19E) Bird Dog	0005	EI-24
	(Regal Air conversion)		MM612959
			61-2959
I-EIAK	Cessna 305C (L-19E) Bird Dog	0031	EI-29
	(Regal Air conversion)		MM612985
			61-2985
I-EIAN	Cessna 305C (L-19E) Bird Dog	0006	EI-30
	(Regal Air conversion)		MM612960
			61-2960
I-EIAP	Cessna 305C (L-19E) Bird Dog	0027	EI-32
	(Regal Air conversion)		MM612981
			61-2981
I-EIAQ	Cessna 305C (L-19E) Bird Dog Floatplane	0013	EI-33
	(Regal Air conversion)		MM612967
			61-2967
I-EIAS	Cessna 305C (L-19E) Bird Dog	0028	EI-37
	(Regal Air conversion)		MM612982
			61-2982
I-EIAU	Cessna 305C (L-19E) Bird Dog	0001	EI-39
	(Regal Air conversion)		MM612955
			61-2955
I-EIAV	Cessna 305C (L-19E) Bird Dog	0004	EI-19
	(Regal Air conversion)		MM612958
			61-2958
I-EIAW	Cessna 305C (L-19E) Bird Dog	0009	EI-36
	(Regal Air conversion)		MM612963
			61-2963
I-EIAX	Cessna 305C (L-19E) Bird Dog	0019	EI-35
	(Regal Air conversion)		MM612973
			61-2973
I-EIAY	Cessna 305C (L-19E) Bird Dog	0020	EI-41
	(Regal Air conversion)		MM612974
			61-2974
I-EIAZ	Cessna 305C (L-19E) Bird Dog	0022	EI-17
	(Regal Air conversion)		MM612976
			61-2976
I-EIBG	Cessna 305C (L-19E) Bird Dog	0024	EI-42
	(Regal Air conversion)		MM612978
			61-2978
I-EIBK	Cessna 305C (L-19E) Bird Dog	0043	EI-44
	(Regal Air conversion)		MM612995
			61-2995
I-EIPP	Eipper Quicksilver MX-II	001	
I-EJRA	Cessna 402B	0918	N82931
I-EKOR	Partenavia P.64B Oscar B	45	
I-ELAP	Hughes 269C	67-0608	HB-XGR
I-ELBA	Beech 95-B55 Baron	TC-1291	HB-GEF
I-ELBR	Aérospatiale AS.350B2 Ecureuil	2502	

Regn.	Type	C/n	Prev.Id.
I-ELBY	Robinson R-22B2 Beta	2876	
I-ELCA	Beech 95-B55 Baron	TC-540	HB-GBR
I-ELDE	Westland-Bell 47G-3B1	WA/519	(D-HOAA)
			XT812
I-ELEM	Aérospatiale AS.350B1 Ecureuil	2095	
I-ELES	Robinson R-22 Beta	2546	
I-ELIG	Hughes 269C	117-0653	HB-XHL
I-ELIM	Partenavia P.68C	293	N39278
I-ELLY	Cessna 182Q Skylane	65876	N759CA
I-ELMR	Aérospatiale AS.350B Ecureuil	1751	F-GFCB
	(w/o 17.11.94)		
I-ELPA	Aérospatiale SA.315B Lama	2568	F-GCFO
I-ELPO	SIAI-Marchetti S.205-18/F	229	
I-ELSE	Piper PA-28-180 Cherokee Archer	28-7405008	N9563N
I-ELTA	Aérospatiale SA.315B Lama	2507	HB-XPC
			N49558
I-ELTE	Aérospatiale AS.350B Ecureuil	1477	HB-XMI
I-ELTO	SA.316B Alouette III	2310	N9002G
I-ELTW	Bredanardi NH.300C	022	I-BNCP
I-ELZA	Laverda F.8L Falco	407	
I-EMAH	Cessna U.206F Stationair	02309	N1958U
I-EMAS	Bell 206B Jet Ranger II	286	N4761R
I-EMEB	Aérospatiale AS.332CSuper Puma	2001	F-WQDA
			C-GOOH
			F-WZJK
I-EMME	Aeromere F.8L Falco	225	
I-ENAL	Tecnam P.92J Echo	007	
I-ENDE	Piper PA-28-140 Cherokee B	28-25320	N8070N
I-ENDO	Agusta-Bell 47J3B1	2063	OE-DXD
			OE-BXF
I-ENDR	Robinson R-22 Beta	0875	N26627
I-ENRJ	Cessna 172N	70663	N739NA
I-EOLN	Reims/Cessna F.182Q Skylane	0158	D-EOLN
I-EPEP	Aérospatiale SA.315B Lama	2661	
I-EPIA	Agusta-Bell 206B Jet Ranger III	8701	F-GEJM
I-EPIB	Bell 407	53260	C-GDSZ
I-EPTL	Piper PA-28RT-201T Turbo Arrow IV	28R-7931116	N2215V
I-EPUS	Bredanardi NH-300C	020	
I-EPWR	Agusta A.109E	11005	
I-EQUR	Aérospatiale AS.350B2 Ecureuil	2579	
I-ERID	Partenavia P.64B Oscar B-1155	60	
I-ERJA	Cessna 501 Citation I/SP	0006	N93TJ
			N5016P
			(N1236P)
			N121UW
			N121JW
			N358CC
			(N5358J)
I-ERJB	Gates Learjet 31A	31A-167	N167LJ
I-ERJD	Bombardier Learjet 45	068	
I-ERMS	Aérospatiale AS.350B3 Ecureuil	3214	
I-ERNE	Piper PA-28-161 Cadet	2841272	N91955
I-ESAI	Cessna 525 CitationJet	0235	VP-BZZ
			N5246Z
I-ESAU	Piper PA-30-160 Twin Comanche	30-203	N7221Y
I-ESEV	Robinson R-22B2 Beta	2669	
I-ESSO	Cessna 182L Skylane	58957	N42309
I-ETAL	Reims/Cessna F.150L	1099	HB-CEA
I-ETAR	Cessna 172M	66658	N80580
I-ETBR	Bell 206B Jet Ranger II	484	HB-XXH
			C-GFAJ
			N112FL
I-ETIA	Aérospatiale SA.315B Lama	2548	
I-ETIB	Aérospatiale SA.315B Lama	2090/14	IDFAF
I-ETID	Aérospatiale SA.315B Lama	2615	F-GDFB
I-ETIK	SOCATA Rallye 235EGabier	12831	F-GAKS
I-ETOB	Robinson R-22B2 Beta	2938	
I-ETOP	Robinson R-22 Mariner	2086M	
I-ETOS	Partenavia P.68	11	
I-ETTO	Rutan Vari-eze	02	
I-EVIT	Hughes 369D	39-0478D	HB-XIO
I-EWAA	Cessna 182Q Skylane	65935	N182FM
			(N759EM)
I-EWAB	Cessna 172N	73714	N5147J
I-EWAD	Cessna 152	83059	N46482

Regn.	Type	C/n	Prev.Id.
I-EWAE	Cessna 172N	72711	N6310D
I-EXPA	Piper PA-46-350P Malibu	4622128	D-EXPA
			N9217Z
			(N339W)
I-FABR	Macchi MB.308	001	
I-FACN	Cessna 172R	80147	
I-FADI	Piper PA-18-135 Super Cub	18-4017	OO-LWA
	(f/n 18-5261 quoted officially as c/n)		EI-274
			I-EIVA
			MM542617
			54-2617
I-FADL	SIAI-Marchetti S.205-20/R	4-248	
I-FAGE	Piper PA-28R-200 Cherokee Arrow	28R-7435149	N40994
I-FAIV	Agusta-Bell 204B	3048	OE-EXO
			HB-XBO
I-FANA	Partenavia P.57 Fachiro IIf	03	
I-FARA	Piper PA-28-140 Cherokee	28-24296	N1858J
I-FARB	DHC-7 Series 102	22	OE-LLS
			OE-HLS
I-FARI	Piper PA-34-220T Seneca III (Damaged)	34-8133213	N8422Y
I-FARM	SOCATA TB-10 Tobago	775	
I-FARN	Cessna 500 Citation	0401	N2651
			N2617K
I-FELN	Meteor FL.54	1125	
I-FERR	Procaer F.15B Picchio	26	
I-FEST	Piper PA-31P-425 Pressurized Navajo	31P-19	N12434
			CF-AYA
I-FEVM	Partenavia P.66B Oscar 150	19	
I-FFAC	Reims/Cessna FR.172J Rocket	0365	
I-FFAE	Reims/Cessna F.172M	1087	
I-FFAF	Reims/Cessna F.150L	1033	
I-FFAG	Reims/Cessna F.150L	1052	
I-FFAZ	Cessna 310Q	0749	N7500Q
I-FFSC	Reims/Cessna FR.172F Rocket	0135	
I-FFSD	Reims/Cessna F.172H	0621	
I-FFSG	Reims/Cessna FA.150K Aerobat	0016	
I-FFSH	Reims/Cessna FA.150K	0568	
I-FFSJ	Reims/Cessna FA.150K Aerobat	0005	
I-FFSM	Reims/Cessna FR.172G Rocket	0181	
I-FFSO	Reims/Cessna F.150L	0832	F-WLIO
I-FFSP	Reims/Cessna FR.172H Rocket	0304	
I-FFSQ	Reims/Cessna FA.150L Aerobat	0082	
I-FFSR	Reims/Cessna F.150L	0696	
I-FFSV	Reims/Cessna F.172L	0865	
I-FFSW	Reims/Cessna FR.172H Rocket	0257	D-ECGF
I-FFVC	Piper PA-28RT-201T Turbo Arrow IV	28R-8031070	N81640
I-FGEX	Van's RV-4	01	
I-FGPB	General Avia F.22C Pinguino	024	
I-FIAM	Piper PA-30-160 Twin Comanche B	30-1718	N8570Y
I-FICV	Dassault Falcon 900	54	F-WWFC
I-FJTO	Cessna 550 Citation II	0679	N6776P
I-FLAG	Aérospatiale AS.350B2 Ecureuil	2621	F-GPFE
			G-BWAZ
			OO-AKK
			OO-XKK
			F-WYML
I-FLAI	Aérospatiale SA.315B Lama	2605	F-GDCX
I-FLAN	Agusta A.109E	11038	
I-FLAO	Aérospatiale AS.350B1 Ecureuil	2097	
I-FLAP	Aérospatiale AS.350B2 Ecureuil	2487	G-BTLS
I-FLAR	Aérospatiale SA.315B Lama	2662	
I-FLAX	Aérospatiale SA.315B Lama	2029/A	F-GIXV
			F-OGVY
			3A-MLB
			VH-PDU
			P2-PDU
			VH-PDU
			VH=FJS
			F-WKQF
I-FLDA	Dragon Fly DF333AC	EB056	
I-FLIP	Robinson R-22 Beta	0812	
I-FLOP	Bell 206B Jet Ranger II	2959	I-MIBI
			(F-GOOD)
			I-MIBI,
			N333WM, N5763P

Regn.	Type	C/n	Prev.Id.
I-FLRE	BAe.146 Series 200	E-2210	G-BVMP
			G-6-210
I-FLRI	BAe.146 Series 200	E-2220	G-BVMT
			G-6-220
I-FLRO	BAe.146 Series 200	E-2227	G-BVMS
I-FLRU	BAe.146 Series 200	E-2204	I-FLRA
			G-OSAS
			G-6-204
I-FLYA	Cessna 501 Citation	0099	N3170A
I-FLYJ	Gates Learjet 55	55-084	N740AC
			N85643
I-FLYM	Mooney M.20M TLS	27-0128	N9155G
I-FLYP	Dassault Falcon 2000	103	F-WW..
I-FLYR	Robinson R-22B2 Beta	2734	
I-FLYV	Dassault Falcon 2000	108	F-WW..
I-FLYW	Cessna 551 Citation II/SP	unkn	
I-FLYY	McDonnell-Douglas DC-9-51	47754	N56UA
			YU-AJU
I-FLYZ	McDonnell-Douglas DC-9-51	47697	N54UA
			YU-AJT
			N8709Q
I-FNMD	Aérospatiale AS.350BA Ecureuil	2729	F-WYMO
I-FOGS	Piper PA-28-140 Cherokee D	28-7125079	N1761T
I-FORA	Rand-Robinson KR-2S	9122-6746	
I-FOSG	Turnercraft D7	unkn	
I-FREA	Bell 206B Jet Ranger II	463	N2671Q
			(N999SD)
			N267IQ
			C-FTPP
			CF-TPP
			N2264W
I-FREB	Bell 206B Jet Ranger II	3105	I-MIAB
			N5760U
I-FREC	Bell 407	53241	C-GBLC
			(N42978)
I-FREF	Bell 430	49023	N7204R
I-FREG	Bell 430	49025	N7244N
I-FREL	Bell 412	33047	N2152V
I-FREM	Bell 212	30685	C-GCVF
			ZK-HFG
			I-DVMC
I-FRRE	Christen A-1 Husky	1132	
I-FSAD	Fairchild-Swearingen SA.227AT Metro IV	AT-440B	N36JP
			N56TA
I-FSTK	Fokker F.27 Friendship 600	10409	OY-FCM
			F-SEBG
			PH-EXX
			TY-BBI
			TY-ATM
			TY-AAG
			PH-FOH
			PK-GFE
			PH-FOH
I-FULZ	Meteor FL.55	1109	
I-FURB	Cessna 152	80885	OY-JRC
			N25967
I-FVBD	Aérospatiale SA.315B Lama	2620	
I-FVDB	Aérospatiale SA.315B Lama	2636	
I-FVPD	Hughes 269C	120-1011	N1107U
I-FXRA	Piaggio P.180 Avanti	1013	I-PJAP
			N180AZ
I-FZIT	Agusta A.109E	11062	
I-GAGI	Aviamilano P.19 Scricciolo	320	
I-GALB	Bellanca 7ECA Citabria	1182-77	
I-GALD	SIAI-Marchetti S.208	4-227	OE-DLU
			ET-ACT
	(Converted from S.205-22/R ET-ACT)		
I-GAMP	Piper PA-28-180 Cherokee Archer	28-7505231	N1465X
I-GANP	Hughes 269C	59-0785	D-HERW
I-GARL	Hughes 269C	17-0575	N7481F
I-GASD	Cessna 650 Citation III	0037	N37VP
			VH-OZI
			N37CD
			N411BB
I-GATE	Agusta A.109A-II	7285	N3235A
I-GATO	de Havilland DH.82A Tiger Moth	85253	DE193

Regn.	Type	C/n	Prev.Id.
I-GAUS	Partenavia P.68	02	
I-GAYD	MS.893E Rallye 180GT Gaillard	12987	F-GAYD
I-GBGI	Cessna 152	80822	N25857
I-GBSD	SOCATA MS.893E Rallye 180GT Gaillard	13230	F-GBSD
I-GBXK	SOCATA MS.892E Rallye 150GT Gaillard	13288	F-GBXK
I-GEAA	General Avia F.20 Pegaso	003	
I-GEAD	General Avia F.22 Pinguino	001	
I-GEAE	General Avia F.22R Pinguino Sprint	002	
I-GEAG	General Avia F.22B Pinguino	004	
I-GEAH	General Avia F.22C Pinguino	005	
I-GEAM	Piper PA-28R-200 Cherokee Arrow	28R-7435006	N9569N
I-GEAN	General Avia F.22A Pinguino	011	
I-GEAZ	General Avia F.22C Pinguino	007	
I-GELP	Aérospatiale SA.315B Lama	2237	TG-H-FEM-CP
			(TG-H-JOO-CP)
I-GEMA	Piper PA-23-150 Apache	23-618	YV-T-ATP
I-GEOK	Tecnam P.92J Echo	010	
I-GEOR	Aeromere F.8L Falco	215	
I-GETA	Hughes 269C	87-0624	G-BFDH
I-GEVI	Partenavia P.66B Oscar 150	40	
I-GGAA	Piper PA-28-151 Cherokee Warrior	28-7415341	N41868
I-GGGG	Christen A-1 Husky	1052	
I-GGMS	Piper PA-34-220T Seneca V	3449016	N9284N
I-GHEE	SIAI-Marchetti S.205-20/R	4-270	
I-GHEP	Piper PA-31P-425 Pressurized Navajo	31P-7630016	N540L
			N57552
I-GHIA	Piper PA-32R-300T Lance	32R-7887154	HB-PCW
			N39710
I-GHIB	Cessna T.210M Turbo Centurion	61971	I-GHII
			N815HG
			N1997M
I-GICA	Robinson R-22 Mariner	2260M	
I-GICO	Aérospatiale AS.350B Ecureuil	2229	
I-GIFE	Partenavia P.68C	335	
I-GIGJ	SOCATA MS.894A Minerva 220	12196	
I-GIGY	SIAI-Marchetti S.208	2-27	
I-GILO	Reims/Cessna F.172H	0454	
I-GIOM	Cessna 172RG Cutlass	0733	N6500V
I-GIPA	Beech 58P Baron	TJ-148	N48TX
			N10021
I-GIPS	CASA I-131E Jungmann	2116	E3B-...
I-GITA	Piper PA-28R-201 Arrow	2844011	N9280N
I-GIUN	Maule MX-7-235 Star Rocket	10080C	N6133H
			(D-EVEP)
			N6133H
I-GIVW	Cessna 550 Citation II	0871	N871CB
I-GJUL	Partenavia P.68B	206	
I-GLAM	Robinson R-22B2 Beta	2716	
I-GLAS	Piper PA-18-150 Super Cub	18-7809117	N82058
I-GLGM	Aérospatiale AS.350B2 Ecureuil	2332	F-WYMK
I-GLTS	Aérospatiale AS.350B2 Ecureuil	2627	
I-GLUE	Jodel D.18B	381	
I-GMBT	Piper PA-18-150 Super Cub	18-7421	
I-GNAP	Hughes 269C	S-1312	
I-GOBJ	Dassault Falcon 20C-5	460/180	OY-BDS
			F-WMKF
I-GOBZ	Dassault Falcon 20E-5	293	F-GOBZ
			F-WQBN
			OY-CKY
			HB-VJX
			HZ-PL1
			N2613
			N2615
			N4442F
			F-WMKJ
I-GODF	Piper PA-32-300 Cherokee Six	32-7540169	N1524X
I-GOES	Piper PA-32-260 Cherokee Six	32-223	G-AVTK
	(Rebuilt using spare fuselage 32-856S)		I-....,
			G-AVTK
			N3266W
I-GOFA	Rotorway Executive 90	01	
I-GOLF	Piper PA-18-150 Super Cub	18-8871	N8465Y
I-GOLP	Mooney M.20M TLS	27-0113	N9149Z
I-GONG	Robinson R-22 Mariner	2649M	
I-GONI	Agusta-Bell AB.412	25506	(G-BKNU)

Regn.	Type	C/n	Prev.Id.
I-GORB	Sukhoi SU-29	76-04	RA7604
I-GPAP	Robinson R-22 Mariner	1410M	I-MIAD
			N4009A
I-GPAR	Agusta-Bell 206B Jet Ranger III	8714	
I-GPBP	Aérospatiale AS.350B2 Ecureuil	2345	I-BPGP
I-GRAB	Hughes 269C	48-0683	N58172
I-GRAD	Partenavia P.68TC	222	
I-GRAE	Aérospatiale SA.315B Lama	1807/37	HB-XYQ
			(SE-HUN)
			F-MJAX
I-GRAL	Hughes 269C	S-1299	N7506H
I-GRAR	Hughes 269C	36-0485	N7420F
I-GREG	Partenavia P.66B Oscar 150	23	
I-GREN	Aérospatiale SA.315B Lama	2482	F-GELX
			N223RM
I-GRIG	Robinson R-22 Beta	1869	N23105
I-GRIM	Maule MXT-7-180 Star Rocket	14006C	
I-GRIP	Piper PA-32-301 Saratoga	32-8006099	N8264G
I-GRIS	Reims/Cessna F.172P	2233	PH-AVD
			PH-AXT(4)
I-GROB	Grob G.115A	8019	
I-GROC	Grob G.115A	8035	(D-EGVV)
I-GROE	Grob G.115A	8054	(D-EGVV)
I-GROF	Grob G.115A	8060	(D-EGVV)
I-GROW	Macchi MB.339A	106/6711	MM54502
I-GSGS	Piper PA-32R-301 Saratoga IITC	3257052	N41276
I-GUGU	Cessna 172M	65576	N6770H
I-GUMA	SIAI-Marchetti S.205-20/R	4-112	
I-GUYD	Piper PA-28R-201 Arrow	2844009	N9278Q
I-HANS	Zlin Z.50LA	0002	D-EFHJ
			OK-IRK
			OK-FSA
			OK-072
I-HAVE	Aérospatiale AS.350B3 Ecureuil	3205	
I-HBAS	Sikorsky S-76A	760298	VR-HZC
			HKG-16
I-HBFI	Agusta A.109E	11048	
I-HBHA	Agusta A.109K2	10023	I-ECAM
I-HBHB	Agusta A.109K2	10025	
I-HBHC	MBB-Kawasaki BK.117B-2	7251	D-HITZ
I-HBMC	MBB-Kawasaki BK.117C-1	7528	D-HBMC
I-HEDA	Robinson R-22 Beta	1074	N80354
I-HEDB	Robinson R-22 Beta	1302	N8069U
I-HEDC	Robinson R-22 Beta	1352	N8080N
I-HEDD	Aérospatiale AS.350B2 Ecureuil	2479	F-WYMU
I-HEDO	Robinson R-22 Beta	0764	
I-HEDY	Cessna 172RG Cutlass	1045	N9799B
I-HELI	Robinson R-22 Beta	2519	
I-HELY	Robinson R-22 Beta	2501	
I-HEMS	Eurocopter EC.135T1	0035	
	(Reserved as D-HEOY 7.99 but ntu by 2.00)		
I-HENO	Hughes 369E	0281E	
I-HESP	Robinson R.22B Beta	0572	N2440Q
I-HHHH	Christen A-1 Husky	1051	N11N
I-HIFI	Eurocopter EC.135T1	0085	
I-HIGH	Reims/Cessna FT.337GP Skymaster	0007/0060	G-HIGH
			OO-KAL
I-HIOI	Agusta EH-101	50007	
I-HMED	Eurocopter EC.135T1	0082	
I-HOOK	Aérospatiale AS.350B3 Ecureuil	3090	
I-HPWG	Bell 206B Jet Ranger II	3297	I-MIGE
			D-HHCW
			N39105
I-HUFF	Robinson R-22B2 Beta	2942	
I-HUPF	Mooney M.20	1169	D-ECYR
			N6502B
I-HVEN	MBB-Kawasaki BK.117C-1	7526	D-HVEN
			(D-HBKY)
I-HYDR	Piper PA-31T-620 Cheyenne	31T-7520034	N54966
I-HAAA	Partenavia P.66C Charlie	01	
I-HAAB	Partenavia P.66C Charlie	02	
I-HAAD	Partenavia P.66C Charlie	04	
I-HAAF	Partenavia P.66C Charlie	06	
I-HAAG	Partenavia P.66C Charlie	07	
I-HAAH	Partenavia P.66C Charlie	08	

Regn.	Type	C/n	Prev.Id.
I-HAAK	Partenavia P.66C Charlie	11	
I-HAAL	Partenavia P.66C Charlie	12	
I-HAAM	Partenavia P.66C Charlie	13	
I-HAAN	Partenavia P.66C Charlie	14	
I-HAAO	Partenavia P.66C Charlie	15	
I-HAAR	Partenavia P.66C Charlie	18	
I-HAAS	Partenavia P.66C Charlie	19	
I-HAAT	Partenavia P.66C Charlie	20	
I-HAAU	Partenavia P.66C Charlie	21	
I-HAAV	Partenavia P.66C Charlie	22	
I-HAAX	Partenavia P.66C Charlie	24	
I-HAAZ	Partenavia P.66C Charlie	26	
I-HABA	Partenavia P.66C Charlie	27	
I-HABB	Partenavia P.66C Charlie	28	
I-HABF	Partenavia P.66C Charlie	32	
I-HABG	Partenavia P.66C Charlie	33	
I-HABI	Partenavia P.66C Charlie	35	
I-HABK	Partenavia P.66C Charlie	37	
I-HABL	Partenavia P.66C Charlie	38	
I-HABN	Partenavia P.66C Charlie	40	
I-HABO	Partenavia P.66C Charlie	41	
I-HABP	Partenavia P.66C Charlie	42	
I-HABQ	Partenavia P.66C Charlie	43	
I-HABS	Partenavia P.66C Charlie	45	
I-HABT	Partenavia P.66C Charlie	46	
I-HABW	Partenavia P.66C Charlie	49	
I-HABX	Partenavia P.66C Charlie	50	
I-HACB	Partenavia P.66C Charlie	55	
I-HACC	Partenavia P.66C Charlie	56	
I-HACE	Partenavia P.66C Charlie	58	
I-HACF	Partenavia P.66C Charlie	59	
I-HACG	Partenavia P.66C Charlie	60	
I-HACI	Partenavia P.66C Charlie	62	
I-HACJ	Partenavia P.66C Charlie	63	
I-HACK	Partenavia P.66C Charlie	64	
I-HACL	Partenavia P.66C Charlie	65	
I-HACN	Partenavia P.66C Charlie	67	
I-HACO	Partenavia P.66C Charlie	68	
I-HACQ	Partenavia P.66C Charlie	70	
I-HACS	Partenavia P.66C Charlie	72	
I-HACT	Partenavia P.66C Charlie	73	
I-HACU	Partenavia P.66C Charlie	74	
I-HACV	Partenavia P.66C Charlie	75	
I-HACW	Partenavia P.66C Charlie	76	
I-HACX	Partenavia P.66C Charlie	77	
I-HACZ	Partenavia P.66C Charlie	79	
I-HADA	Partenavia P.66C Charlie	80	
I-HADE	Partenavia P.66C Charlie	84	
I-HADF	Partenavia P.66C Charlie	85	
I-HADH	Partenavia P.66C Charlie	87	
I-HADI	Partenavia P.66C Charlie	88	
I-HADL	Partenavia P.66C Charlie	89	
I-HADM	Partenavia P.66C Charlie	90	
I-HADN	Partenavia P.66C Charlie	91	
I-HADO	Partenavia P.66C Charlie	92	
I-HADR	Partenavia P.66C Charlie	95	I-RAIP
I-HADS	Partenavia P.66C Charlie	97	
I-HADT	Partenavia P.66C Charlie	98	
I-HADU	Partenavia P.66C Charlie	99	
I-HADW	Partenavia P.66C Charlie	101	
I-HADX	Partenavia P.66C Charlie	102	
I-HAEA	SOCATA TB-9 Tampico Club	1143	
I-HAEC	SOCATA TB-9 Tampico Club	1202	
I-HAED	SOCATA TB-9 Tampico Club	1203	
I-HAEE	SOCATA TB-9 Tampico Club (Wrecked)	1204	
I-HAEF	SOCATA TB-9 Tampico Club	1207	
I-HAEG	SOCATA TB-9 Tampico Club	1215	
I-HAEH	SOCATA TB-9 Tampico Club	1216	
I-HAEI	SOCATA TB-9 Tampico Club	1217	
I-HAEJ	SOCATA TB-9 Tampico Club	1218	
I-HAEK	SOCATA TB-9 Tampico Club	1219	
I-HAEL	SOCATA TB-9 Tampico Club	1220	
I-HAEM	SOCATA TB-9 Tampico Club	1221	
I-HAEO	SOCATA TB-9 Tampico Club	1238	
I-HAEP	SOCATA TB-9 Tampico Club	1254	

Regn.	Type	C/n	Prev.Id.
I-IAEQ	SOCATA TB-9 Tampico Club	1255	
I-IAER	SOCATA TB-9 Tampico Club	1256	
I-IAES	SOCATA TB-9 Tampico Club	1257	
I-IAET	SOCATA TB-9 Tampico Club	1260	
I-IAEU	SOCATA TB-9 Tampico Club	1261	
I-IAEV	SOCATA TB-9 Tampico Club	1262	
I-IAEW	SOCATA TB-9 Tampico Club	1263	
I-IAEX	SOCATA TB-9 Tampico Club	1274	
I-IAEY	SOCATA TB-9 Tampico Club	1281	
I-IAEZ	SOCATA TB-9 Tampico Club	1282	
I-IAFA	SOCATA TB-9 Tampico Club	1283	
I-IAFB	SOCATA TB-9 Tampico Club	1291	
I-IAFC	SOCATA TB-9 Tampico Club	1292	
I-IAFD	SOCATA TB-9 Tampico Club	1293	
I-IAFE	SOCATA TB-9 Tampico Club	1294	
I-IAFF	SOCATA TB-9 Tampico Club	1321	
I-IAFG	SOCATA TB-9 Tampico Club	1322	
I-IAFH	SOCATA TB-9 Tampico Club	1323	
I-IAFI	SOCATA TB-9 Tampico Club	1324	
I-IAFJ	SOCATA TB-9 Tampico Club	1343	
I-IAFK	SOCATA TB-9 Tampico Club	1344	
I-IAFL	SOCATA TB-9 Tampico Club	1345	
I-IAFM	SOCATA TB-9 Tampico Club	1346	
I-IAFN	SOCATA TB-9 Tampico Club	1365	
I-IAFO	SOCATA TB-9 Tampico Club	1366	
I-IAFP	SOCATA TB-9 Tampico Club	1367	
I-IAFQ	SOCATA TB-9 Tampico Club	1368	
I-IAFS	SOCATA TB-9 Tampico Club	1384	
I-IAFT	SOCATA TB-9 Tampico Club	1385	
I-IAFU	SOCATA TB-9 Tampico Club	1386	
I-IAFV	SOCATA TB-9 Tampico Club	1370	
I-IAFW	SOCATA TB-9 Tampico Club	1371	
I-IAFX	SOCATA TB-9 Tampico Club	1372	
I-IAFY	SOCATA TB-9 Tampico Club	1373	
I-IAFZ	SOCATA TB-9 Tampico Club	1374	
I-IAGA	SOCATA TB-9 Tampico Club	1388	
I-IAGB	SOCATA TB-9 Tampico Club	1389	
I-IAGC	SOCATA TB-9 Tampico Club	1390	
I-IAGD	SOCATA TB-9 Tampico Club	1391	
I-IAGE	SOCATA TB-9 Tampico Club	1392	
I-IAGF	SOCATA TB-9 Tampico Club	1393	
I-IAGG	SOCATA TB-9 Tampico Club	1394	
I-IAGH	SOCATA TB-9 Tampico Club	1395	
I-IAGI	SOCATA TB-9 Tampico Club	1396	
I-IAGJ	SOCATA TB-9 Tampico Club	1397	
I-IAGK	SOCATA TB-9 Tampico Club	1410	
I-IAGL	SOCATA TB-9 Tampico Club	1411	
I-IAGM	SOCATA TB-9 Tampico Club	1412	
I-IAGN	SOCATA TB-9 Tampico Club	1413	
I-IAGO	SOCATA TB-9 Tampico Club	1414	
I-IAGP	SOCATA TB-9 Tampico Club	1415	
I-IAGQ	SOCATA TB-9 Tampico Club	1416	
I-IAGR	SOCATA TB-9 Tampico Club	1417	
I-IAGS	SOCATA TB-9 Tampico Club	1418	
I-IAGT	SOCATA TB-9 Tampico Club	1419	
I-IAGU	SOCATA TB-9 Tampico Club	1420	
I-IAGV	SOCATA TB-9 Tampico Club	1535	
I-IAGW	SOCATA TB-9 Tampico Club	1536	
I-IAGX	SOCATA TB-9 Tampico Club	1537	
I-IAGY	SOCATA TB-9 Tampico Club	1538	
I-IAGZ	SOCATA TB-9 Tampico Club	1548	
I-IAHA	SOCATA TB-9 Tampico Club	1549	
I-IAHB	SOCATA TB-9 Tampico Club	1550	
I-IAHC	SOCATA TB-9 Tampico Club	1551	
I-IAID	General Avia F.22C Pinguino	025	
I-IBAA	SIAI-Marchetti S.205-20/R	001/06-001	
I-IBAB	SIAI-Marchetti S.205-20/R	002/06-002	
I-IBAD	SIAI-Marchetti S.205-20/R	004/06-004	
I-IBAF	SIAI-Marchetti S.205-20/R	007/06-007	
I-IBAG	SIAI-Marchetti S.205-20/R	008/06-008	
I-IBAI	SIAI-Marchetti S.205-20/R	015/06-015	
I-IBAJ	SIAI-Marchetti S.205-20/R	016/06-016	
I-IBAK	SIAI-Marchetti S.205-20/R	017/06-017	
I-IBAN	SIAI-Marchetti S.205-20/R	025/06-025	
I-IBLE	Aérospatiale SA.315B Lama	2483	

Regn.	Type	C/n	Prev.Id.
I-ICAB	SIAI-Marchetti S.205-20/R	011/06-011	
I-ICAF	SIAI-Marchetti S.205-20/R	014/06-014	
I-ICAK	SIAI-Marchetti S.205-20/R	021/06-021	
I-ICAO	SIAI-Marchetti S.205-20/R	029/06-029	
I-ICAP	SIAI-Marchetti S.205-20/R	030/06-030	
I-ICAQ	SIAI-Marchetti S.205-20/R	031/06-031	
I-ICAS	SIAI-Marchetti S.205-20/R	033/06-033	
I-ICBA	SIAI-Marchetti S.205-20/R	040/06-040	
I-ICES	Piper PA-28-140 Cherokee D	28-7125233	N5073S
I-ICGR	Aérospatiale SA.315B Lama	2671	
I-IEAA	Partenavia P.68B	87	
I-IEAD	Partenavia P.68B	150	
I-IEAF	Partenavia P.68B	161	
I-IEAG	Partenavia P.68B	234	
I-IEAH	Partenavia P.68C	387	
I-IFRE	Robinson R-22 Beta	2437	
I-IHAA	Bredanardi NH-300C	010	
I-IHAB	Bredanardi NH-300C	011	
I-IHAC	Schweizer 269C	S-1491	N41S
I-IHAD	Schweizer 269C	S-1498	N69A
I-IHAE	Schweizer 269C	S-1602	N86G
I-IKIM	Piper PA-28-181 Archer II	28-7990524	N2877W
I-ILLL	Hughes 269C	110-0985	N7011X
			YV-594CP
			YV-175E
			YV-2091P
			N1094N
I-IMEC	Reims/Cessna FR.172H Rocket	0311	
I-IMPE	Piper PA-38-112 Tomahawk	38-82A0055	N2395V
I-INAA	Piper PA-18-150 Super Cub	18-7809148	N63922
I-INAB	Piper PA-18-150 Super Cub	18-7809175	N82213
I-INAC	Piper PA-18-150 Super Cub	18-7809176	N82301
I-INAD	Piper PA-18-150 Super Cub	18-8009043	N82696
I-INKA	Piper PA-28-180 Cherokee Challenger	28-7305011	N15098
I-INTR	Agusta A.129DE	29800	
I-IOIO	Zlin Z.526AFS Akrobat	1330	
I-IOLE	Cessna 172RG Cutlass	0166	N6333R
I-IPAA	Cessna TU.206G Turbo Stationair II	03601	N7283N
I-IPAB	Cessna TU.206G Turbo Stationair II	04026	(N756EF)
I-IPAD	Cessna TU.206G Turbo Stationair II	03881	(N7341C)
I-IPAF	Cessna TU.206G Turbo Stationair II	03913	(N7383C)
I-IPAJ	Cessna TU.206G Turbo Stationair II	04152	N756KM
I-IPAK	Cessna TU.206G Turbo Stationair II	05613	N5294X
I-IPAL	Cessna TU.206G Turbo Stationair II	05654	(N5336X)
I-IPAQ	Cessna TU.206G Turbo Stationair II	04390	N756VL
I-IPAR	Cessna TU.206G Turbo Stationair II	04291	N756RG
I-IPIZ	Beech 400A Beechjet	RK-29	N15693
I-IRCA	Cessna 182J Skylane	57172	N3072F
I-IRNO	Partenavia P.66B Oscar 150	41	
I-IRPI	Aérospatiale SA.315B Lama	2672	
I-ISAA	SIAI-Marchetti SF.260D	830	
I-ISAB	SIAI-Marchetti SF.260D	831	
I-ISAC	SIAI-Marchetti SF.260D	832	
I-ISAD	SIAI-Marchetti SF.260D	833	
I-ISAE	SIAI-Marchetti SF.260D	834	
I-ISAF	Aérospatiale SA.315B Lama	2148	IDFAF
I-ISAG	SIAI-Marchetti SF.260D	835	
I-ISAH	SIAI-Marchetti SF.260D	836	
I-ISAI	SIAI-Marchetti SF.260D	837	
I-ISAJ	SIAI-Marchetti SF.260D	838	
I-ISAK	SIAI-Marchetti SF.260D	839	
I-ISAL	SIAI-Marchetti SF.260D	849	
I-ISAM	SIAI-Marchetti SF.260D	850	
I-ISAR	Aérospatiale AS.350B2 Ecureuil	2576	OE-XHG
I-ISEO	Reims/Cessna F.150J	0471	
I-ISKY	Monnet Sonerai IIL	unkn	
I-ISOR	Cessna 402B	0438	
I-ITAA	Robin DR.400/180R Remorqueur	1241	
I-ITAB	Robin DR.400/180R Remorqueur	1242	
I-ITAD	Robin DR.400/180R Remorqueur	1244	
I-ITAE	Robin DR.400/180R Remorqueur	1245	
I-ITAF	Robin DR.400/180R Remorqueur	1246	
I-ITAG	Robin DR.400/180R Remorqueur	1247	
I-ITAJ	Robin DR.400/180R Remorqueur	1249	
I-ITAK	Robin DR.400/180R Remorqueur	1250	

Regn.	Type	C/n	Prev.Id.
I-TAO	Robin DR.400/180R Remorqueur	1350	
I-TAP	Robin DR.400/180R Remorqueur	1351	
I-TAQ	Robin DR.400/180R Remorqueur	1352	
I-TAR	Robin DR.400/180R Remorqueur	1353	
I-TAS	Robin DR.400/180R Remorqueur	1489	
I-TAT	Robin DR.400/180R Remorqueur	1490	
I-TAU	Robin DR.400/180R Remorqueur	1505	
I-TAV	Robin DR.400/180R Remorqueur	1506	
I-TAW	Robin DR.400/180R Remorqueur	1548	
I-TAX	Robin DR.400/180R Remorqueur	1568	
I-TAY	Robin DR.400/180R Remorqueur	1519	
I-TAZ	Robin DR.400/180R Remorqueur	1601	
I-TBA	Robin DR.400/180R Remorqueur	1721	F-WZZV
I-TBB	Robin DR.400/180R Remorqueur	2001	
I-TBC	Robin DR.400/180R Remorqueur	2007	
I-TBD	Robin DR.400/180R Remorqueur	2008	
I-TBE	Robin DR.400/180R Remorqueur	2013	
I-TBF	Robin DR.400/180R Remorqueur	2014	
I-TBG	Robin DR.400/180R Remorqueur	2020	
I-TSA	Piper PA-30-160 Twin Comanche B	30-1282	N8169Y
I-VIV	Robinson R-44 Astro	0216	
I-ZAA	Mudry CAP.20LS-200	11	
I-ZAB	Mudry CAP.20LS-200	12	
I-ZAF	Mudry CAP.10B	95	F-WZCH
I-ZAG	Mudry CAP.10B	145	F-WZCG
I-ZAI	Mudry CAP.10B	242	
I-ZAJ	Mudry CAP.10B	251	
I-ZAK	Mudry CAP.21	4	F-GAUQ
I-ZAL	Mudry CAP.10B	255	
I-ZAM	Mudry CAP.10B	258	
I-ZAN	Mudry CAP.10B	271	
I-JACO	Schweizer 269C	S-1332	HB-XSY
I-JAHO	Robinson R-22B2 Beta	2951	
I-JALU	Piper PA-28RT-201T Turbo Arrow IV	28R-8531003	N4385N
I-JANN	Iannotta I.66 San Francesco	unkn	
I-JANS	Aérospatiale SA.316B Alouette III	1226	A-226
I-JANV	Iannotta I.66L San Francesco	01	
I-JARR	Sivel SD.27	001	
I-JCRT	Robinson R-22 Mariner	3004M	
I-JECT	Sukhoi SU-31M	N-05	RA-01688
I-JEMP	Rand-Robinson KR-2	8123	
I-JENA	de Havilland DH.82A Tiger Moth (Accident 14.5.96)	84682	G-APLR / T6256
I-JESA	Cessna 551 Citation II	0133	N222TG / G-JRCT / N2663N
I-JESB	Piper PA-18-150 Cub	1809009	N9617N
I-JESC	Piper PA-28R-201 Arrow IV	2837020	N9178R
I-JESD	Piper PA-28-181 Archer II	2890154	N9211D
I-JESO	Cessna 550 Citation II	0255	N28GA / I-DEAF / N6861L
I-JETA	Boeing 737-229	21839	OO-SBS / LX-OOO / OO-SBS / LX-OOO / OO-SBS
I-JETC	Boeing 737-230	23153	D-ABMA
I-JETD	Boeing 737-230	23158	D-ABMF
I-JETS	Cessna 560XL Citation Excel	5012	N561DA
I-JJOY	de Havilland DH.82A Tiger Moth	86550	G-APGM / EI-AHM / EI-AHH / PG641
I-JOBE	Mooney M.20R Ovation	29-0085	N9147F
I-JOGG	Reims/Cessna F.152	1688	N8064X
I-JOKE	Zlin Z.526F Trenér Master	1298	
I-JOLE	Macchi MB.308	unkn	
I-JOPS	Aérospatiale AS.350B3 Ecureuil	3191	
I-JPAT	SIAI-Marchetti S.211A	202	
I-JUKY	SAN Jodel DR.1050 Ambassadeur	293	
I-JULI	Beech 95-B55 Baron	TC-629	HB-GBH
I-JULY	Piper PA-32-300 Lance (Dismantled)	32R-7680045	N7298C
I-JURA	Rand-Robinson KR-2	unkn	
I-KALU	Rutan Vari-eze	001	

Regn.	Type	C/n	Prev.Id.
I-KARL	Rutan LongEz	001	
I-KATA	HOAC DV-20 Katana	20119	
I-KAVA	Piper PA-28-161 Cadet	2841275	N91968
I-KEIT	Piper PA-23-250 Aztec E	27-7305040	N40237
I-KELE	Agusta A.109A-II	7315	
I-KELM	Gates Learjet 35A	35A-406	N35Q / N764G
I-KGKM	Aérospatiale SA.315B Lama	1241/48	Fr.AF
I-KIDA	Piper PA-28-161 Warrior II	28-7916264	N2220N
I-KIDE	Piper PA-34-220T Seneca III	3433140	N91648
I-KIIS	Cessna T.210N Turbo Centurion II	63986	LX-III (2) / TR-LBN / F-GCSC / (N4683Y)
I-KILE	Piper PA-28R-201 Arrow IV	2837050	N92067
I-KIMM	Piper PA-23-250 Aztec E	27-7405434	N54127
I-KISE	Piper PA-34-220T Seneca IV	2848065	N9251V / (N295PS) / N9251R
I-KITO	Piper PA-24-260 Comanche B	24-4386	I-GIOV / N8930P
I-KITT	Piper PA-28R-201T Turbo Cherokee Arrow III	28R-7703029	N1651H
I-KJNG	Boeing Stearman E-75	005	
I-KKLT	Aviat Pitts S-2B	5248	
I-KKVB	Piper PA-34-220T Seneca IV	3447012	N9262B
I-KNOW	Agusta A.119	14005	
I-KOME	Piper PA-24-250 Comanche	24-837	N6099P
I-KORR	Piper PA-32RT-300T Turbo Lance	32R-7987102	D-EIRR / N2209P
I-KQUO	Cessna 152	82875	N89806
I-KRAY	Rand-Robinson KR-2	5412	
I-KRLI	Rand-Robinson KR-2	8191	
I-KRLS	Piper PA-28-161 Cadet	2841033	N9157J
I-KRNL	Piper PA-34-200T Seneca II	34-7870449	N21703
I-KTAN	Terzi T-30 Katana	001	
I-KYKO	Christen Pitts S-2B	5167	
I-LAAC	Piper PA-28RT-201T Turbo Arrow IV	28R-8031126	N8233X
I-LAAS	Robinson R-44 Astro	0191	
I-LABO	Piper PA-18 Super Cub 95	18-2018	I-EIRI / MM522418 / 52-2418
I-LACA	Piper PA-34-220T Seneca III	34-8133011	N83311
I-LACI	Piper PA-38-112 Tomahawk	38-78A0027	N9317T
I-LACO	Britten-Norman BN-2A-6 Islander	17	G-AWBY
I-LAER	Piper PA-18-150 Super Cub	18-7871	
I-LAGE	Schweizer 269C	S-1357	N75069
I-LAGY	Piper PA-34-200T Seneca II	34-7970353	N2912U
I-LAKI	Rutan LongEz	unkn	
I-LALE	Cessna 172K	58379	N84208
I-LALI	Robinson R.22 Beta	0632	
I-LALM	Robinson R-22B2 Beta	2987	
I-LAMC	Robinson R-44 Astro	0274	
I-LAMO	Aérospatiale AS.350B Ecureuil	2171	
I-LANC	Piper PA-32RT-300 Lance	32R-7985100	N2078X
I-LARJ	SIAI-Marchetti S.205-18/R	4-204	
I-LASA	Robinson R-22B2 Beta	2922	
I-LASC	Piper PA-28-236 Dakota	28-7911209	N2854G
I-LASD	Aérospatiale AS.350B2 Ecureuil	2410	F-GHHL
I-LASG	Aérospatiale AS.350B2 Ecureuil	3217	
I-LASP	Aérospatiale AS.350B1 Ecureuil	1822	JA9779 / N6004C / F-WJUL / F-GJUL / F-WJUL / F-WYMK
I-LAZZ	Aérospatiale SA.315B Lama	2653	
I-LDAP	Piper PA-28-181 Archer II	28-8390072	N4309N
I-LDAV	Aérospatiale SA.341G Gazelle	1034	F-BUFB / F-WMHC
I-LEAN	Schweizer 269C	S-1472	
I-LEAS	Cessna 182K Skylane	58416	N2816R
I-LECI	Piper PA-28RT-201T Turbo Arrow IV	28R-8031138	N82396
I-LECN	Piper PA-28RT-201T Turbo Arrow IV	28R-7931192	N29040
I-LEDI	Xausa X-001	unkn	

Regn.	Type	C/n	Prev.Id.
I-ELB	SIAI-Marchetti SF.260C	563/41-001	
I-ELC	SIAI-Marchetti SF.260C	566/41-002	
I-ELD	SIAI-Marchetti SF.260C	567/41-003	
I-ELF	SIAI-Marchetti SF.260C	568/41-004	
I-ELG	SIAI-Marchetti SF.260D	735/41-005	
I-ELH	SIAI-Marchetti SF.260D	764	
I-ELM	SIAI-Marchetti SF.260D	765	
I-ELO	Piper PA-18-150 Super Cub	18-7809034	N82956
I-EMO	Piper PA-24-250 Comanche	24-1278	N6298P
I-EOG	Agusta A.109C	7602	
I-EOZ	Partenavia P.66B Oscar 100	58	
I-ETI	Schweizer 269C	S-1276	HB-XRT
			N7504Z
I-ETY	Piper PA-18-150 Super Cub	18-7909095	N82384
I-FSA	Cessna 177B Cardinal	02080	N34906
I-GAW	Christen Eagle	unkn	
I-GET	Robin DR.400/180 Régent	1525	
I-GUE	Piper PA-18-150 Super Cub	18-5263	N5761D
I-IAB	Dassault Falcon 20	172/456	F-BRHB
			F-WNGM
I-IAC	Dassault Falcon 20D	234/475	D-COLL
			(D-CIBM)
			F-WLCU
I-IAD	Gates Learjet 35A	35A-111	OE-GMA
			(I-SIDU)
			(HB-VFE)
			N3815G
I-IAO	Schweizer 269C	S-1445	
I-IAT	Piper PA-31T1 Cheyenne	31T-8004052	N2316X
I-IDB	Schweizer 269C	S-1325	
I-IDY	Quickie Quickie Q.2	unkn	
I-IMG	Piper PA-32RT-300T Turbo Lance	32R-7887288	N3001A
I-INK	Bredanardi NH-300C	006	I-BNCF
I-INO	Evans VP-1 Volksplane	unkn	
I-IOI	Agusta E-101	50009	
I-IPO	Beech 65-C90 King Air	LJ-616	SE-GXD
			N1MX
			N1MB
			N1970T
I-IPS	Piper PA-22-150 Tri-Pacer	22-5488	HB-OPS
I-ITT	Robinson R-22 Beta	2345	N83081
I-IVO	Piper PA-28-181 Archer III	2843052	N92768
I-IZZ	Piper PA-34-220T Seneca III	34-8133156	N8410D
I-JFE	Macchi AL.60B-2	89/6269	
I-LBB	Agusta A.109C	7625	
I-LEA	Schweizer 269C	S-1743	
I-LEO	Bell 206B Jet Ranger	4077	N63AJ
			N21463
			C-FHBC
I-LES	Hiller UH-12E	5141	
I-MAX	Steen Skybolt	unkn	
I-OBO	Piper PA-18-135 Super Cub	18-3318	I-EIKA
			MM537718
			53-7718
I-OBY	Agusta-Bell 47G-2	241	LN-ORT
			D-HIFA
I-OGI	Aérospatiale SA.315B Lama	2489	(F-GEEK)
			N49521
I-ONE	Jodel D.18	01	
I-OOK	Gates Learjet 55	55-021	EI-BSA
			N700TG
			N3794B
I-ORI	Piper PA-28-151 Cherokee Warrior	28-7415666	N9555N
I-ORY	Monnett Sonerai II	1008	
I-RMS	Piper PA-28-181 Cherokee Archer II	28-7890152	N47921
I-SBB	Cessna 208B Caravan	0712	N1268C
			N5264U
I-SBD	Christen A-1 Husky	1024	N2910F
I-SBV	Beech A36TC Bonanza	EA-144	HB-EJF
I-SEE	Cessna 172N Floatplane	73797	N5442J
I-SEI	Piper PA-28RT-201T Turbo Arrow IV	28R-8231040	
I-SMA	Mooney M.20K Model 231	25-0862	N888DK
I-TOP	Aérospatiale AS.355F1 Ecureuil	5106	N5792X
I-TRY	Piper PA-28-181 Archer II	28-8590013	N4381M
I-UAN	Piper PA-31-325 Navajo	31-7512027	N59950

Regn.	Type	C/n	Prev.Id.
I-LUBA	Reims/Cessna F.150L	1103	
I-LUBB	Cessna 172P	74485	N52294
I-LUBI	Grumman G.1159C Gulfstream IV	1123	N457GA
I-LUDA	General Avia F.22B Pinguino	012	
I-LUEL	Piper PA-30-160 Twin Comanche C	30-1760	N8649Y
I-LUGA	Agusta-Bell 47G-2	165	MM80093
I-LUMM	Cessna 172P	74307	N51388
I-LUNE	Reims/Cessna F.150J	0477	
I-LUNJ	Reims/Cessna F.150J	0485	
I-LUPP	Cessna 182Q Skylane	67596	N5247N
I-LURR	Cessna 172P	74450	N52235
I-LURY	SA.316B Alouette III	1365	HB-XPB
			D-HFRD
			ZAF: 9T-HT4
I-LUSA	Robinson R.22B Beta	0571	N2436W
I-LUST	Enstrom 280FX Shark	2026	N88CV
I-LXCA	Sikorsky S-76B	760403	N5008L
I-LXGR	Grumman G.1159C Gulfstream IV	1234	N924ML
			N475GA
I-LYDU	Piper PA-28RT-201 Arrow IV	28R-8118047	N83198
I-LYFE	Partenavia P.68	12	
I-LYLY	Champion 7ECA Citabria	512	
I-LYNC	Fokker DR.I M Replica	01/84M	
I-MABR	MBB-Kawasaki BK.117A-4	7047	D-HBMV
I-MACE	Macchi AL.60B-2	36/6216	
I-MACM	Macchi AL.60B-2	40/6220	
I-MADD	Partenavia P.66B Oscar 150	46	
I-MADS	Piper PA-28R-201T Turbo Cherokee Arrow III		
		28R-7703166	N5919V
I-MAED	Cessna 172RG Cutlass	1157	N9426D
I-MAEL	Aérospatiale SA.315B Lama	2510	F-GEEZ
			N49564
I-MAFE	CASA C.212-CC	273	EC-DVD
			(N431CA)
I-MAFI	Robinson R-22 Beta	2428	N83106
I-MAFR	Bredanardi NH-500D	BH-13	
I-MAGB	Schweizer 269C	S-1603	N41S
I-MAGH	Piper PA-28-181 Archer II	28-7990213	N2129J
I-MAGM	Agusta-Bell AB.412	25602	Fv11338
			I-LEMA
I-MAGN	Magni MT-5 Autogyro (Rebuild of Termavaki JT-5)	01	OH-XYS
I-MAIC	Helibras HB.350B Esquilo	HB1086/1942	LV-AZX
			PT-HMJ
I-MAIP	Partenavia P.66B Oscar 150	10	
I-MAKT	Partenavia P.68C	209	
I-MALC	Robinson R-22 Mariner	2432M	N8254Z
I-MALG	Robinson R-44 Astro	0628	
	(Also quoted as c/n 0624)		
I-MALL	Agusta A.109E	11023	
I-MALO	Piper J-3C-65 Cub (Rebuilt)	001M	
I-MALU	Piper J-3C-65 Cub	11950	44-79654
I-MAMI	Cessna 210C	58134	N3634Y
I-MAMM	Partenavia P.64 Oscar	07	
I-MAMO	Brügger MB-2 Colibri	231	
I-MAMY	Laverda F.8L Falco	419	
I-MAPE	Piper PA-28R-201 Arrow IV	2844007	N9275P
	(Registration worn simultaneously by two aircraft, 9.99)		
I-MARA	Macchi MB.308 (Rebuilt)	01	
I-MARJ	CEA DR.340 Major	320	F-OCMG
I-MARK	SIAI-Marchetti SF.260	2-35	
I-MARL	SIAI-Marchetti S.205-18/F	343	
I-MARM	Aviamilano P.19R Scricciolo	331	
I-MASE	Piper PA-23-160 Apache	23-1720	
I-MASF	SOCATA MS.880B Rallye Club	1222	
I-MASK	SOCATA MS.880B Rallye Club	1294	
I-MASQ	SOCATA MS.880B Rallye Club	1324	
I-MASV	SOCATA MS.892A Rallye Commodore 150	10992	
I-MASX	SOCATA MS.880B Rallye Club	1536	
I-MASY	SOCATA MS.880B Rallye Club	1519	
I-MATJ	Aérospatiale AS.350B3 Ecureuil	3189	
I-MATU	Reims/Cessna FRA.150L Aerobat	0204	
I-MAUL	Maule MX-7-180 Star Rocket	11036C	N61086
I-MAWW	Beech 58P Baron	TJ-55	
I-MBER	Partenavia P.66B Oscar 150	24	
I-MDNA	Piper PA-38-112 Tomahawk	38-82A0048	N2326V

Regn.	Type	C/n	Prev.Id.
I-MDVC	Agusta A.109A	7225	N9046Y
I-MDVI	Partenavia P.66B Oscar 150	50	
I-MEAS	Cessna 421B Golden Eagle	0251	(N3367Q)
I-MEDT	Aérospatiale AS.350B2 Ecureuil	2766	F-WYMI
I-MEMA	Stinson L-5 Sentinel (Euravia)	003	
I-MENC	Cessna 172R	80148	
I-MEPI	Piper PA-34-200T Seneca II	34-7970355	N2184K
I-MERG	Partenavia P.66B Oscar 150	48	
I-MERL	Piper PA-32-300 Cherokee Six	32-7940258	
I-MEZE	Rutan LongEz	001	
I-MIAA	Bell 206B Jet Ranger II	2916	D-HEPI
			N206TG
			N1085V
I-MIAE	Aérospatiale AS.350B Ecureuil	1774	N8837K
			N516FB
			RP-C668
I-MIAS	Robinson R-22 Beta	1134	N8044X
I-MICI	Piper J-3C-65 Cub	10900	43-29609
I-MICK	Mooney M.20M TLS	27-0166	
I-MICU	Aérospatiale SA.315B Lama	2295	F-GEJU
			N62886
I-MIFA	Beech 23 Musketeer	M-337	N2373J
I-MIGL	CEA DR.300/125 Petit Prince	658	
I-MIGO	Piper PA-18-150 Super Cub	18-7409041	
I-MIIS	Hughes 369E	0110E	N5223X
I-MIKE	Schweizer 269C	S-1413	I-MIAR
			N75076
I-MIKI	Aviamilano F.8L Falco	119	
I-MILI	Aeromere F.8L Falco	219	
I-MILK	Canadair CL.600-2B16	5304	C-FXHE
I-MIMU	Piper PA-34-200 Seneca	34-7350330	N56424
I-MIPS	Monnet Sonerai IILS	001	
	(Believed to be N17DB, c/n 1545L exported to Italy)		
I-MIRK	Piper PA-34-200T Seneca II	34-8170053	N8306P
I-MISA	Cessna 172C	49520	N2020Y
I-MISE	Partenavia P.66B Oscar 150	47	
I-MISS	Reims/Cessna FR.172J Rocket	0415	
I-MITI	Piper PA-23-250 Aztec E	27-7304943	N14358
I-MIZA	Aviamilano P.19TR Scricciolo	349	
I-MLAT	Aerotek Pitts S-2A	2226	
I-MLQT	Fokker F.27 Friendship 400	10295	HB-ITQ
			HA-ACK
			HB-ITQ
			PH-SFB
			N714A
			PH-FIO
I-MMAA	Robinson R-22 Beta	1164	N8062L
I-MMAB	Robinson R-22 Beta	1186	
I-MMAC	Robinson R-22 Beta	2127	
I-MMAF	Robinson R-22 Beta	2514	
I-MMAG	Robinson R-22 Beta	2502	N83240
I-MMAH	Robinson R-22B2 Beta	2658	
I-MMBA	Robinson R-44 Astro	0112	
I-MMEM	SIAI-Marchetti SF.260	2-43	
I-MMES	Robinson R.22B Beta	0551	
I-MMRR	Piper PA-28RT-201 Arrow IV	28R-8218023	N539FT
			N9519N
I-MOCO	Gates Learjet 35A	35A-445	HB-VHG
			N3802G
I-MODC	Piper PA-32-301 Saratoga	32-8506017	N2541Y
			N9597N
I-MODD	SA.318C Alouette Astazou	2186	F-GDQS
			C-GNQX
			N8262
I-MODJ	Bücker Bü.131 Jungmann	001	
I-MODN	Piper PA-38-112 Tomahawk	38-82A0042	N91514
I-MODU	Piper PA-28-181 Archer II	28-8190188	N83527
I-MOEN	Beech 77 Skipper	WA-135	HB-EJC
I-MOKA	SIAI-Marchetti S.205-20/R	4-159	
I-MOKE	Agusta A.109C	7660	
I-MOLG	Procaer F.15B Picchio	21	
I-MONY	Mooney M.20K Model 252	25-1217	
I-MOSS	AIAA Stampe SV.4C	1049	F-BBGQ
I-MROS	Aérospatiale SA.315B Lama	2498	G-BMUC
			N49529

Regn.	Type	C/n	Prev.Id.
I-MRSV	Fiat G.59B	181	MM53774
I-MSPG	Reims/Cessna F.150G	0119	
I-MSTR	Agusta A.109A	7227	N4256P
			I-KTRE
I-MUGH	Mooney M.20J Model 205	24-3175	N1067L
I-MUNI	Mooney M.20K Model 231	25-0597	N1147P
I-MUNY	Mooney M.20K Model 231	25-0483	N94471
I-MURE	Aérospatiale SA.315B Lama	2509	N72590
I-MUSE	Partenavia P.64 Oscar	10	
I-MUTO	Eurocopter EC.120B Colibri	1046	
I-MYCL	Mooney M.20M TLS	27-0134	N9159Q
I-MYKY	Robinson R-22 Beta	1447	
I-MYRO	Robinson R-22 Beta	1723	N4075S
I-NACA	Piper PA-18 Super Cub 95	18-2023	EI-92
			I-EITA
			MM522423
			52-2423
I-NAIG	Robinson R-22 Beta	2440	
I-NAIS	Piper PA-24-260 Comanche B	24-4777	N9299P
I-NARC	Fairchild-Swearingen SA.226AT Merlin IV	AT-035	N90090
			ZS-LJR
			SAAF-10
			N5350M
I-NARE	Aérospatiale AS.350B Ecureuil	1266	
I-NASA	Piper PA-30-160 Twin Comanche C	30-1864	N8715Y
I-NCAA	Cessna A.150M Aerobat	0633	N9824J
I-NCCA	Cessna 414A Chancellor	0282	N2618C
I-NDIO	Aérospatiale AS.350B1 Ecureuil	2308	
I-NEGL	Cessna 421A	0138	OO-EDB
			OO-LFC
			HB-LFL
			(N4048L)
I-NEKI	Piper PA-32-301 Saratoga	32-8106009	N8294B
I-NENA	Piper PA-18-150 Super Cub	18-7709074	N83550
I-NERO	Reims/Cessna F.150L	0950	
I-NERY	Aérospatiale SA.315B Lama	2437	
I-NEWA	Piper PA-28R-201T Turbo Arrow	2803004	N9176Q
I-NGPR	Piper PA-28-181 Archer II	28-8090368	N8241A
I-NIAR	Cessna 551 Citation II/SP	0056	N214AM
			I-GAMB
			(N312CC)
			N6864X
I-NIKI	Piper PA-18-150 Super Cub	18-7509064	N7480L
I-NILE	Piper PA-25-235 Pawnee D	25-7756061	N82549
I-NITA	Piper J-3C-65 Cub	10905	43-29614
	(Identity quoted officially as 44-79610 = c/n 11906)		
I-NIVE	Cessna 172C	49541	N2041Y
I-NJNO	SA.318C Alouette Astazou	1804	F-BMRG
			Cambodia AF
I-NOLB	Reims/Cessna F.150K	0640	
I-NOLD	Reims/Cessna F.150L	0668	
I-NOLJ	Reims/Cessna F.150L	0948	
I-NOLL	Reims/Cessna F.150L	0989	
I-NOLP	Reims/Cessna F.150L	0755	
I-NOLQ	Reims/Cessna F.150M	1217	
I-NOLS	Reims/Cessna F.150L	1070	
I-NOLT	Reims/Cessna F.150L	1084	
I-NOLV	Reims/Cessna F.150L	1116	(OE-ATO)
I-NOPA	Piper PA-34-200T Seneca II	34-8170048	N8303U
I-NORA	Piper PA-32-300 Cherokee Six	32-7640088	N75009
I-NOWA	SNIAS/Aeritalia ATR-42-300	051	F-WWEF
I-NOWT	SNIAS/Aeritalia ATR-42-300	054	F-WWEI
I-NSEM	Robinson R-22 Beta	2517	N83298
I-NUDO	Partenavia P.64B Oscar B	30	
I-NUMI	Dassault Falcon 900	89	F-WWFB
I-NUVE	Partenavia P.66B Oscar 150	05	
I-OBBY	Piper PA-32-300 Cherokee Six E	32-7340119	N55463
I-OBER	Piper PA-46-350P Malibu	4622013	N9154N
I-OBPC	Partenavia P.68 Observer	261-08-OB	
I-OBSR	Partenavia P.68 Observer	236-01-OB	
I-OBSW	Partenavia P.68 Observer	331-21-OB	
I-ODHK	SOCATA Rallye 235E Gabier	12881	F-ODHK
I-ODKF	SOCATA TB-10 Tobago	17	F-ODKF
I-ODNV	SOCATA TB-9 Tampico	216	F-ODNV
I-ODQD	SOCATA TB-20 Trinidad	385	F-ODQD

Regn.	Type	C/n	Prev.Id.
I-ODSO	SOCATA TB-20 Trinidad	761	F-ODSO
I-ODTZ	SOCATA TB-9 Tampico	1095	F-ODTZ
I-OETE	Aérospatiale AS.350B Ecureuil	1103	F-WZFH
I-OGAM	Beech F50 Twin Bonanza	FH-90	HB-GAM
I-OGLT	SOCATA TB-9 Tampico	321	F-OGLT
I-OGQH	SOCATA TB-10 Tobago	1007	F-OGQH
I-OHDB	SOCATA TB-20 Trinidad	1469	F-OHDB
I-OLEY	Aérospatiale AS.315B Lama	2369	
I-OLLY	Westland/SNIAS SA.341G Gazelle	WA/1065	F-GBMC
			G-BAGK
I-OMAT	Piper PA-18 Super Cub 95	18-3356	EI-134
	(Officially quoted with f/n 18-3299 as c/n)		I-EIHI
			MM537756
			53-7756
I-OMET	Aérospatiale AS.350B Ecureuil	2490	F-WYMQ
I-OMGA	Piper PA-32-301 Saratoga	32-8306032	N8156U
			N9512N
I-ONYX	Hughes 369E	0483E	OY-HEM
I-OPCV	Cessna 182N Skylane	60467	N8927G
I-OPES	Avia FL.3	A.7	
I-ORAO	Aérospatiale AS.355N Ecureuil 2	5583	
I-ORAS	Agusta A.109A	7183	
I-ORBE	Piper PA-28-161 Warrior II	28-8016368	N8240X
			(N8240V)
I-ORLY	Aérospatiale SA.315B Lama	2627	
I-OSIR	Partenavia P.66B Oscar 100	45	
I-OTEL	Cessna 501 Citation	0048	(I-DAEP)
			N414CC
			N87510
I-OTIS	SIAI-Marchetti S.208	4-52	MM61939
I-OTMA	Cessna P210N Pressurized Centurion II	00339	N4832K
I-OTTY	Beech 400A Beechjet	RJ-25	N125RJ
			I-MPIZ
			N3025T
I-OXAL	SOCATA MS.893A Rallye Commodore 180	10945	
I-PACC	Partenavia P.57 Fachiro IIf	28	
I-PADI	Rockwell 114 Commander	14388	G-PADY
			(G-BFXT)
			N5840N
I-PAEA	Piper PA-28-181 Archer III	2843069	N92834
I-PAFI	Piper PA-28RT-201T Turbo Arrow IV	28R-8231059	N8238X
I-PAGG	Partenavia P.57 Fachiro IIf	32	
I-PAHH	Partenavia P.64 Oscar	12	
I-PAIA	SIAI-Marchetti S.205-18/R	4-292	
I-PALS	Piper PA-31T Cheyenne	31T-7620005	N54979
I-PAMY	Piper PA-28-180 Cherokee F	28-7105039	N5185S
I-PAPA	Macchi AL.60B-2	17/6162	
I-PARJ	Partenavia P.68	06	
I-PASC	Piper PA-28-181 Archer III	2843162	N41226
I-PATE	Aérospatiale SA.365N2 Dauphin 2	6356	
I-PATI	Aérospatiale SA.315B Lama	2651	
I-PATS	Agusta S.211A	201	
I-PAVR	Cessna U.206G Stationair II	06011	(D-EOMG)
			N4746Z
I-PAVV	Piper PA-18-150 Super Cub	18-8006	HB-OWK
			N6785Z
I-PCLE	Agusta A.109A	7164	
I-PDAC	Piper PA-34-200 Seneca	34-7450145	I-SIMO
			N41653
I-PDRG	SOCATA TB-21 Trinidad TC	1040	
I-PEGA	Cessna 500 Citation	0081	HB-VDA
			N5B
			N581CC
I-PEKA	Airbus A.320-214	1132	(HB-IJU)
			F-WWIS
I-PEKC	Airbus A.320-214	1179	F-WWDQ
I-PELE	Piper PA-28R-200 Cherokee Arrow	28R-7635360	N6915J
I-PELL	Aérospatiale SA.315B Lama	2621	
I-PELO	SNCAN/ Stampe SV.4C	375	F-BBFI
			Fr.Mil
I-PENN	Partenavia P.57 Fachiro IIf	36	
I-PEPE	Piper PA-22-108 Colt	22-8242	
I-PEPI	SOCATA MS.880B Rallye Club	885	
I-PFDC	Aérospatiale AS.355N Ecureuil 2	5514	F-WYMF
			F-WYMB
			F-WYMC
I-PGAB	Cessna 172R	80421	N26624
			N41227
I-PGAR	Piper PA-28RT-201T Turbo Arrow IV	28R-8231063	G-BNBX
			N8257H
I-PGCC	Pitts S-1S Special	101	
I-PIAH	Beech 200 Super King Air	BB-777	
I-PIAT	Piper PA-18-150 Super Cub	18-7509138	N9714P
I-PICA	Partenavia P.66B Oscar 150	37	
I-PICC	Procaer F.15 Picchio	02	
I-PIDR	Piper PA-28-181 Archer II	28-8490083	N4365K
I-PIER	Avia LM.5	3	
I-PIGA	Schweizer 269C	S-1281	HB-XRR
I-PIKY	Piper PA-28RT-201 Arrow IV	28R-7918106	N2102Z
I-PILA	Piper PA-18-150 Super Cub	18-6696	N9453D
I-PILL	Robinson R-22 Beta	1167	N8055J
I-PIOT	Piper PA-28-161 Warrior II	28-7916388	HB-PDP
			N2210Z
I-PITS	Christen Pitts S-2B	5140	
I-PITT	Pitts S-1T Special	001	
I-PJAR	Piaggio P.180 Avanti	1002	
I-PJCG	Series 341GC (Modified SA.341GGazelle)	001	
I-PJNO	Piper PA-28-181 Archer II	28-8190157	N8331A
I-PLAM	Reims/Cessna FR.182 Skylane RG	0037	F-BVOE
			(PH-AYA)
I-PLAS	Reims/Cessna FT.337GP Super Skymaster	P.0004	(G-BAVV)
I-PMPM	Piper PA-28-181 Archer II	28-8190251	N8397A
	(w/o 25.6.95)		
I-PNCA	Cessna 550 Citation II	0235	N67SG
			(N6803T)
I-PNIN	Piper PA-34-200T Seneca II	34-7570160	N33785
I-PNTG	SOCATA TB-10 Tobago	805	
I-POBA	CEA DR.1051 Sicile	543	
I-POGI	Partenavia P.66C Charlie	94	
I-POHE	Piper PA-18-150 Super Cub	18-8458	HB-POH
			D-EBYK(2)
			N4232Z
I-POMI	Cessna 320D Skyknight	0002	N4102T
I-POMO	Piper PA-31T1 Cheyenne	31T-7904030	N601PT
I-PONC	Reims/Cessna F.172H	0668	
I-PONJ	Champion 7ECA Citabria	119	
I-POPA	Bell 412SP	33199	N14UV
I-POPY	Cessna T.210N Turbo Centurion II	63966	N4638Y
I-PORL	Piper PA-28-161 Cadet	2841289	N9199X
I-PORR	Cessna 152	81301	N49482
I-POSI	Partenavia P.66B Oscar 150	22	
I-POXY	Rutan LongEz	001	
I-PRAL	SIAI-Marchetti S.208	369	
I-PRBE	Bredanardi NH-300C	016	I-BNCO
I-PRCO	Hughes 269C	14-0268	I-BNBE
I-PRIM	Partenavia P.66B Oscar 100	43	
I-PRMA	SGAviation Storm 280SI	62	
I-PROD	General Avia F.15E Picchio	38-GA	
I-PRSC	Piper PA-34-200 Seneca	34-7450154	N41853
I-PRVV	Aérospatiale SA.315B Lama	2418	
I-PSCM	Cessna P210R Pressurized Centurion II	00862	D-EDDS(3)
			N5530A
I-PSMR	SOCATA MS.880B Rallye Club	1133	OY-DFG
I-PUBB	Champion 7GCAA Citabria	125	
I-PUCK	Aviamilano F.8L Falco	116	
I-PULI	Cessna 340A	0019	HB-LMW
			D-IMJP
			(N98528)
I-PVAE	Piper PA-34-220TSeneca V	3449041	N92865
I-PVLA	Cessna 172N	72322	HB-CLZ
			N4639D
I-PWER	Agusta A.109E Power	11001	
I-PYCG	47TT	001	
	(1999 rebuild of Agusta-Bell 47G-3B1 MM80490)		
I-PYRO	SE.3130 Alouette II	1558	F-GLNO
			XR376
			(XJ376)
I-RACC	Partenavia P.64B Oscar 200	10	

Regn.	Type	C/n	Prev.Id.
I-RAGC	Piper PA-31-350 Navajo Chieftain	31-7552024	9Q-CSI
			N61520
I-RAIA to RAIZ	*Test Registrations used for type certification by R.A.I.*		
I-RALC	SOCATA MS.894E Minerva 220GT	12137	
I-RALE	SOCATA MS.880B Rallye Club	2052	(D-EMJB)
I-RALF	SOCATA MS.880B Rallye Club	2087	
I-RALI	SOCATA MS.880B Rallye Club	2324	
I-RALJ	SOCATA MS.880B Rallye Club	2391	F-BUXU
I-RALK	SOCATA MS.880B Rallye Club	2410	
I-RALL	Morane-Saulnier MS.885 Super Rallye	45	(D-EMPA)
I-RALQ	SOCATA Rallye 100S Sport	2345	
I-RALS	SOCATA Rallye 100S Sport	2360	
I-RAMT	Piper PA-32RT-300T Turbo Lance	32R-7887054	N36576
I-RAPI	Piper PA-23-250 Aztec B	27-2415	N5341Y
I-RATO	Pitts S-2A Special	012	
I-RAUL	Beech F33C Bonanza	CJ-27	HB-EKH
I-RAVN	Piper PA-28-161 Warrior II	28-8216090	N80510
I-RAVU	Reims/Cessna F.150J	0443	(G-AXBR)
I-RBII	Robinson R-22B2 Beta	2733	
I-RCNF	Aero Designs Pulsar 912	01	
I-RDGO	Valmet L-90TP Redigo	S016	OH-VTS
I-RDUE	Robinson R-22 Beta	1871	N23152
I-REAL	Dassault Falcon 20E	267/491	F-WRQZ
I-RECE	Agusta-Bell AB.412	25571	
I-RECL	Aérospatiale AS.350B2 Ecureuil	2107	OE-OXC
I-REDO	Piper J-3C-65 Cub	"11438"	
	(c/n as quoted is in error - true c/n unknown)		
I-REDV	Agusta A.109A Hirundo	7223	N9547S
I-REGO	Aviamilano P.19 Scriccolo	215/339	
I-REIL	Aérospatiale AS.350B2 Ecureuil	2379	
I-RELT	North American NA.265-40 Sabreliner	282-133	N41NR
			N65740
I-RESG	Colomban MC-15 Cri-Cri	unkn	
I-RFSZ	Piper PA-28-181 Cherokee Archer II	28-7690069	N7593C
I-RGDT	Piel CP.80	80	
I-RGGG	Cessna T.337G Turbo Skymaster	0285	N46JA
			N2QN
I-RGRB	Rockwell Commander 114	14188	N4858W
I-RIBO	Cessna 170B	25557	HB-COD
			(N4613C)
I-RICI	Cessna 182R Skylane	68105	N9909H
I-RICK	Rand-Robinson KR-2S	9270-768	
I-RIEZ	Cessna 175C Skylark	57098	N8398T
I-RIFA	Aviamilano P.19 Scriccolo	351	
I-RIFI	Reims/Cessna F.150L	0962	
I-RIKJ	Piper PA-28-181 Archer II	28-8490068	N4359K
I-RIKK	Robinson R-22 Beta	1446	
I-RIML	Aeritalia/SNIAS ATR-42-300	206	G-BYHB
			HS-TRL
			F-WWEU
I-RIMS	Aeritalia/SNIAS ATR-42-300	190	G-BYHA
			HS-TRK
			F-WWEF
I-RISI	Hughes 369E	0235E	I-MIIR
			HB-XRS
I-RJGA	Pitts S-1E Special	78001	
I-RMDV	Sikorsky S-76A	760235	N760P
I-ROBH	Robinson R-22 Beta	1870	N23143
I-ROBJ	Piper PA-18-150 Super Cub	18-7893	N3977Z
I-ROBO	Robin R.2160D	186	D-EFQM
I-ROCH	Cessna 172RG Cutlass	0984	N9713B
I-ROCK	Parker Teenie Two	unkn	
I-RODY	Robinson R-22 Beta	1054	
I-ROLI	Piper PA-30-160 Twin Comanche	30-639	N7613Y
I-ROLL	SIAI-Marchetti SF.260	112	HB-EV V
			OO-HAZ
			I-SJAD
I-ROSA	Piper PA-22-150 Tri-Pacer	22-2804	N2433P
I-ROTA	Vag-A-Bond	unkn	
I-ROYA	Mudry CAP.10B	53	F-BUDS
I-ROYJ	Piper PA-18-150 Super Cub	18-7709066	N83549
I-ROYS	Piper PA-18-150 Super Cub	18-7509124	N40575
I-ROYY	Piper PA-18-150 Super Cub	18-7509122	N40573
I-ROZO	SOCATA TB-20 Trinidad	1258	G-POZO
			I-POZO
I-RPLL	Cessna R.172K Hawk XP	3290	N758RB
I-RRAA	Cessna 172N	72073	N6839E
I-RRPG	Partenavia P.68B	193	
I-RRRR	Robinson R-22M Mariner	1305M	
I-RTAA	Partenavia P.68B	181	
I-RWLT	Piper PA-28-161 Archer II	28-8390085	N4313Z
I-SAAB	Cessna 172N Floatplane	69026	N734QG
I-SAAV	SIAI-Marchetti SF.260B	2-58	
I-SABR	Piper PA-28RT-201T Turbo Arrow IV	28R-8031076	N81774
I-SABY	Piper PA-28-180 Cherokee E	28-5852	N3892R
I-SADG	Aérospatiale AS.350B3 Ecureuil	3120	
I-SADP	Bredanardi NH-300C	014	
I-SALE	Laverda F.8L Falco	408	
I-SAMA	Laverda F.8L Falco	409	I-LACH
I-SAME	Dassault Falcon 50	37	(I-CAIK)
			F-WZHM
I-SANA	Partenavia P.57 Fachiro II	10	
I-SARB	Bell 412	33078	
I-SARI	Piper J-3C-65 Cub	12612	D-ELIC
			SE-BFE
			44-80316
I-SARU	Beech 65-80 Queen Air	LD-37	HB-GBC
			D-ILLU
I-SARY	SNCAN/ Stampe SV.4C	379	I-SARC
			F-BDIS
I-SASA	Piper PA-31T1 Cheyenne	31T-8004024	
I-SATL	Partenavia P.66C Charlie	103	
I-SAXS	Piper PA-34-220T Seneca III	34-8233175	D-GENT
			N8249Y
I-SBIR	Cessna 152	82029	OY-JRB
			N67804
I-SBMG	Jungster 1	C005	
I-SBRG	Piper PA-34-220T Seneca III	34-8133094	N83872
I-SCAN	Heintz Zenith CH-200	unkn	
I-SCAP	Cessna 182P Skylane	61064	N7424Q
I-SCDT	Piper PA-18-150 Super Cub	18-7909174	N9754N
I-SCDX	Reims/Cessna F.152	1455	
I-SCUD	Piper PA-28-140 Cherokee D	28-7125245	N5079S
I-SDCR	Piper PA-34-200T Seneca II	34-8070254	N8230S
I-SDFG	BAe.125 Series 800A	NA0424/258136	N452SM
			N569BA
			G-5-609
I-SEAL	Reims/Cessna FR.172H Rocket	0314	D-EARY
I-SEEL	Robinson R-22 Beta	2390	N2364D
I-SEIA	Agusta A.109A-II	7388	
I-SEIB	Agusta A.109A-II	7366	
I-SEIC	Agusta A.109A-II	7293	D-HJFF(2)
I-SEID	Agusta A.109A-II	7429	N1VQ
I-SEIQ	Agusta-Bell AB.412	25603	
I-SEPA	Partenavia P.68	08	
I-SERY	Aérospatiale SA.315B Lama	2603	F-GDCY
I-SESE	Mooney M.20K Model 252	25-1219	N1068G
I-SESI	Aérospatiale SA.315B Lama	2053/20	N29907
			D-HASO
I-SEXI	Aero L-29 Delfin	591235	-?-
I-SFTP	SIAI-Marchetti SF.260TP	661/60-004	
I-SHOW	Zlin Z.50LS	0054	
I-SIAF	SIAI-Marchetti S.205-22/R	378	
I-SIAR	SIAI-Marchetti S.205-20/R	003	
I-SIAW	SIAI-Marchetti SF.260	102	
I-SIBD	American AG-5B Tiger	10089	N11947
I-SIBM	Mudry CAP.10B	146	
I-SIBY	Robinson R-22M Mariner	2830M	
I-SIEL	Robinson R-22B2 Beta	2719	
I-SIEM	Piper PA-28-180 Cherokee Challenger	28-7305541	N56151
I-SILK	Partenavia P.57 Fachiro IIf	23	
I-SILL	Aérospatiale AS.350B2 Ecureuil	2456	F-WYMT
I-SIMI	Piper PA-28R-180 Cherokee Arrow	28R-30600	N4697J
I-SIMP	Robin ATL L	40	F-GFOP
I-SINE	SE.3160 Alouette II	1203	
I-SINK	SIAI-Marchetti SF.260B	3-84	
I-SINS	Aérospatiale SA.365N1 Dauphin 2	6306	
I-SINT	Aérospatiale SA.360C Dauphin	5030	
I-SISB	Canadair CL.215-1A10	1034	UD.13-6
I-SISC	Canadair CL.215-1A10	1038	UD.13-10

Regn.	Type	C/n	Prev.Id.
I-SISI	Piper J-3C-65 Cub	12474	44-80178
I-SISO	SOCATA MS.880B Rallye Club	894	
I-SIVI	Piper PA-28-161 Cadet	2841026	N9155G
I-SIVM	Mudry CAP.21DS	OK3	
I-SJAB	SIAI-Marchetti S.205-20/R	4-199	
I-SJAE	SIAI-Marchetti S.208	1-10	
I-SJAG	SIAI-Marchetti S.205-18/R	4-105	
I-SJAU	SIAI-Marchetti S.208A	1-13	
I-SJAY	SIAI-Marchetti SF.260B	3-78	
I-SJAZ	SIAI-Marchetti S.208	2-22	
I-SKIM	Cessna 182H Skylane	56597	N8497S
I-SKYD	Cessna 207 Skywagon	00337	N1737U
I-SLIM	Piper PA-22-108 Colt	22-9496	N5690Z
I-SLOT	SOCATA MS.893A Rallye Commodore 180	11003	OO-DAX F-BRLU
I-SLVN	940A-Zefiro	unkn	
I-SMAA	SIAI-Marchetti SF.260C	369/42-001	
I-SMAB	SIAI-Marchetti SF.260C	370/42-006	
I-SMAU	Reims/Cessna F.172P	2077	
I-SMBR	Piper PA-28-161 Warrior II	28-8016103	N8102Q
I-SMCE	SIAI-Marchetti SF.260E	784	I-RAIE I-RAIC
I-SMEB	McDonnell-Douglas DC-9-82	53064	B-28001 N6203D (N812ML)
I-SMEC	McDonnell-Douglas DC-9-83	49808	N183NA N3010G
I-SMED	McDonnell-Douglas DC-9-83	53182	N875RA N456AW
I-SMEF	Robinson R-22 Beta	1770	
I-SMEL	McDonnell-Douglas DC-9-82	49247	HB-IKK
I-SMEM	McDonnell-Douglas DC-9-82	49248	HB-IKL
I-SMEP	McDonnell-Douglas DC-9-82	49740	
I-SMER	McDonnell-Douglas DC-9-82	49901	N6202S
I-SMES	McDonnell-Douglas DC-9-82	49902	
I-SMET	McDonnell-Douglas DC-9-82	49531	
I-SMEV	McDonnell-Douglas DC-9-82	49669	
I-SMEZ	McDonnell-Douglas DC-9-82	49903	PH-SEZ I-SMEZ N3010C (I-SMEZ)
I-SNAB	Dassault Falcon 50	169	F-WPXD
I-SNAW	Dassault Falcon 2000	12	F-WWMM
I-SNAX	Dassault Falcon 900	69	F-WWFD
I-SOCC	Agusta A.109A-II	7399	N1VG (D-HEEP) (D-HARK) N1VG
I-SOCO	Aérospatiale SA.315B Lama	2183/39	F-GMET F-OCFX
I-SOFI	Aérospatiale AS.315BLama	2604	LN-OTB SE-HSP LN-OTB
I-SOGA	Piper PA-30-160 Twin Comanche	30-377	HB-LCP N7360Y N10F
I-SOLG	Piper PA-28-181 Archer II	28-8190086	N8293L
I-SOND	Aérospatiale SA.315B Lama	2481	N221RM
I-SORA	Piper PA-23-250 Aztec C	27-3595	N6396Y
I-SOUL	Bell 206B Jet Ranger II	1599	I-MIBE N90104
I-SPAA	Cessna 172P	74919	N54211
I-SPAB	Cessna 172P	75083	N54942
I-SPAE	Cessna 172P	75873	N65769
I-SPAF	Cessna 172P	75817	N65680
I-SPAH	Cessna 150L	74326	N19309
I-SPAR	Pagani Condor 150	001	
I-SPAX	Piper PA-28RT-201T Turbo Arrow IV	28-7931017	N2101G
I-SPBI	Robinson R-22 Beta	0746	
I-SPFO	SOCATA Rallye 235E Gabier	12872	
I-SPID	Procaer F.15B Picchio	17	
I-SPIN	Piper PA-28-161 Warrior II	28-7916498	N2875A
I-SPOT	Agusta-Bell 412	25601	
I-SRAL	Partenavia P.66B Oscar 100	40	
I-SRHA	Robinson R-22 Beta	1403	N40225 (N4021A)
I-SSKK	Piper PA-28RT-201T Turbo Arrow IV	28R-7931304	N8090Q
I-STAF	Cessna 182N Skylane	60209	N92453
I-STAS	Beech S35 Bonanza	D-7617	
I-STEN	Piper PA-28RT-201T Turbo Arrow IV	28R-8131120	N8380Z
I-STET	Piper PA-28R-200 Cherokee Arrow	28R-7335016	N15099
I-STIL	Sivel T-9 Stiletto	01	
I-SUCK	Bell 47G-2	2149	MM80809 57-6220
I-SUDE	SOCATA MS.880B Rallye Club	1855	
I-SUDH	SOCATA MS.892A Rallye Commodore 180	11868	
I-SUDI	SOCATA MS.880B Rallye Club	1956	
I-SUDL	SOCATA MS.880B Rallye Club	1957	
I-SUDM	SOCATA MS.893A Rallye Commodore 180	11973	
I-SUDN	SOCATA MS.892A Rallye Commodore 150	12038	
I-SUDP	SOCATA MS.894A Minerva 220	12001	
I-SUDQ	SOCATA MS.880B Rallye Club	2084	(D-EMJC)
I-SUDS	SOCATA MS.887 Rallye 125	2118	F-OCTC
I-SUDU	SOCATA MS.887 Rallye 125	2159	F-OCTH
I-SUDV	SOCATA MS.880B Rallye Club	2152	
I-SUDX	SOCATA MS.880B Rallye Club	2153	
I-SUDY	SOCATA MS.880B Rallye Club	2156	
I-SUED	Cessna 340A	1247	OE-FPN (N87453)
I-SUKO	Sukhoi SU-31	04-01	
I-SUSY	S.A.I. F.7 Rondone II	02	
I-SUVE	Piper PA-28-180 Cherokee F	28-7105163	N1949T
I-SVFA	Cessna 172RG Cutlass	1062	N9867B
I-SVFB	Cessna 172RG Cutlass	0968	N9687B
I-SVFC	Cessna 172M	65378	N5220H
I-SVFD	Cessna 172L	59615	N7915G
I-SVFE	Cessna 172RG Cutlass	0903	N9590B
I-SVFF	Cessna 172M	66963	N1268U
I-SVFG	Cessna 152	83749	N5108B
I-SVFH	Cessna 152	83939	N6484B
I-SVFI	Cessna 152	82437	N69018
I-SVFL	Cessna 152	82636	N89112
I-SWIM	Lake LA-4-250 Renegade	47	N14042
I-SWSA	Aérospatiale SA.318C Alouette Astazou	2143	F-GEFF N6184
I-SWSB	Aérospatiale SA.318C Alouette Astazou	2281	I-SWOK F-GBDD VR-HGY (RP-C . . .)
I-SYAI	SIAI-Marchetti SF.260	2-36	
I-SYAK	SIAI-Marchetti S.205-20/R	4-272	
I-SYAW	SIAI-Marchetti S.205-20/R	4-253	
I-SYLV	Tecnam P.92J Echo	008	
I-SYNT	Piper PA-34-200T Seneca II	34-7970258	N29472
I-SYST	Bredanardi NH-300C	021	
I-TALE	Aérospatiale SA.318C Alouette Astazou	2025	
I-TALL	Beech 58P Baron	TJ-93	HB-GGK I-TINT HB-GGK
I-TAMM	Partenavia P.66B Oscar 150	44	
I-TASE	Rockwell Commander 690A	11260	(N891WA) I-TASE N324BT N6B N57097
I-TATU	Piper PA-22-108 Colt	22-9295	N5567Z
I-TEAK	Cessna 182R Skylane	68246	N4585E
I-TEBO	Piper PA-22-150 Caribbean	22-7336	N3423Z
I-TECK	Tecnam P.92J Echo	002	
I-TECM	Piper PA-34-220T Seneca III	34-8133189	N8424K
I-TECN	Tecnam P.92J Echo	001	
I-TECO	Piper PA-32R-301 Saratoga	32R-8113038	N31HB N8331R
I-TEMI	Partenavia P.66B Oscar 100	75	
I-TEST	Aérospatiale AS.355F1 Ecureuil 2	5119	N5791Z
I-TGZA	AS-10 Microlight	C006	
I-THRS	Piper PA-28-180 Cherokee D	28-5399	N2374R
I-TIBI	Cessna T.210N Turbo Centurion II	63432	D-EIME(2) N5429A

Regn.	Type	C/n	Prev.Id.
I-TILE	Piper PA-28R-200 Cherokee Arrow	28R-7635395	N4067F
I-TINI	Aviamilano F.8L Falco	118	
I-TINX	Agusta-Bell 206B Jet Ranger II	8520	HB-XFS
I-TITT	Piper PA-34-200 Seneca	34-7250351	N15048
I-TITY	Robinson R-22B2 Beta	2857	
I-TIZY	Partenavia P.68B	67	
I-TLRN	Partenavia AP.68TP-600 Viator	9005	I-RAIL
I-TLRS	Cessna TU.206G Turbo Stationair II	04000	TF-UPP(2)
			N7560D
I-TLST	Mooney M.20M TLS	27-0135	N9159D
I-TNAC	SOCATA TB-9 Tampico Club	1110	F-OGSA
I-TNTC	BAe.146 Series 200QT	E.2078	G-5-078
			G-BNPJ
I-TOAD	Cessna T.207A Turbo Stationair 8	00642	G-NJAP
			(N75768)
I-TOBI	Jodel D.18B	347	
I-TOGI	Schweizer 269C	S-1552	N69A
I-TOIO	Cessna 501 Citation	0252	N825HL
			N2628Z
I-TOLI	Schweizer 269C	S-1391	
I-TOLL	Mooney M.20J Model 201	24-1518	N5784R
I-TOLU	Agusta A.109A-II	7424	
I-TOMJ	Piper PA-38-112 Tomahawk	38-78A0677	N9712N
I-TOMK	Schweizer 269C	S-1562	N69A
I-TOND	Piper PA-28-161 Cadet	2841273	N91956
I-TONT	Mudry CAP.10B	190	
I-TOPA	Piper PA-28-181 Archer II	28-8390027	N8328H
I-TOPJ	Beech 400 Beechjet	RJ-44	N22WJ
			I-GCFA
			N3144A
			HB-VJE
			N3144A
I-TORD	Cessna 152	79668	N757DY
I-TOSY	Cessna 172M	62349	PH-JJG
			N12894
I-TOTE	Piper PA-24-250 Comanche	24-1853	HB-OTE
			N6726P
I-TREE	Cessna 172N	72944	N1069F
I-TREG	SOCATA MS.894A Minerva 220	12092	
I-TREH	SOCATA MS.894A Minerva 220	12093	
I-TREI	III Sky Arrow 650TC	C001	
I-TREM	III Sky Arrow 650TC	C002	
I-TREO	III Sky Arrow 650TC	C009	
I-TREP	Piper PA-42-720 Cheyenne IIIA	42-5501045	
I-TREQ	Piper PA-42-720 Cheyenne IIIA	42-5501046	
I-TRER	Piper PA-42-720 Cheyenne IIIA	42-5501047	
I-TRET	III Sky Arrow 650TC	C010	
I-TREX	III Sky Arrow 650TC	C005	
I-TRIB	Bell 47G3B1	2926	N1130W
I-TRIG	Partenavia P.66B Oscar 100	42	
I-TRIP	Aviamilano F.8L Falco	102	
I-TRUE	Partenavia P.64B Oscar 200	04	
I-TSNP	Robinson R-22 Beta	1411	N4009F
I-TTAM	Robinson R-44 Astro	0547	
I-TTCC	Robinson R-22 Mariner	0803M	
I-TTEB	Piper PA-28R-201T Turbo Arrow III	28R-7803071	N9854K
I-TTLL	Aérospatiale SA.365N1 Dauphin 2	6325	F-WTNV
I-TVMA	Piper PA-28-161 Warrior II	28-8416042	N4337M
I-TWIN	Partenavia P.68	01	
I-TYKE	Gates Learjet 31A	31A-120	N5020Y
I-UDDY	Reims/Cessna F.172M	1514	F-GAQN
I-UDLB	SOCATA Rallye 110ST Galopin	3318	
I-UBFC	Agusta A.109E	11031	
I-UMPL	SOCATA Rallye 110ST Galopin	3272	
I-UUNY	Cessna 500 Citation	0358	SE-DEP
			N82MJ
			N36870
			EP-PAQ
			N36870
I-UVAM	Robin DR.400/180R Remorqueur	880	
I-VAGO	Pereira Osprey Amphibian	unkn	
I-VALO	Piper PA-18A-150 Super Cub	18-4263	N2487P
I-VALP	Piper PA-18A-150 Super Cub	18-4264	N2488P
I-VAMA	SOCATA Rallye 150ST	3102	
I-VANO	Mitchell-Wing B-10	unkn	

Regn.	Type	C/n	Prev.Id.
I-VANZ	Cessna 182P Skylane	64562	OY-PEC
			N8204M
I-VAST	Volmer VJ-22 Sportsman	RV-0001	
I-VBIG	Van's RV-4	1985	
I-VBIT	Aérospatiale AS.350B Ecureuil	1553	
I-VBMP	Pitts S.2E Special	274	
I-VEBA	Piper PA-30-160 Twin Comanche	30-773	N7797Y
I-VEIC	Piper PA-34-200T Seneca II	34-7770011	N5364F
I-VENT	Piper PA-28-140 Cherokee	28-24576	N7239J
I-VEPP	Reims/Cessna F.172H	0696	
I-VERL	SIAI-Marchetti S.205-18/F	4-246	
I-VIBA	Piper PA-22-160 Tri-Pacer	22-6544	
I-VICC	Partenavia P.68B	16	
I-VICH	Cessna 172M	66222	N9550H
I-VICK	Cessna 172M	64307	N8951V
I-VICP	Piper PA-34-200 Seneca	34-7450015	N56646
I-VICR	Partenavia P.68R	40	
I-VICT	Partenavia P.68	03	
I-VICY	Fairchild-Swearingen SA.227DC Metro 23	DC-849B	N451LA
			N3024V
I-VIGI	Mitsubishi MU.300 Diamond	A.013SA	N81HH
I-VIGN	Piper PA-28RT-201 Arrow IV	28R-7918107	OY-CEI
			TF-TMG
			N2114Z
I-VIMU	Aérospatiale AS.355F2 Ecureuil 2	5443	
I-VINC	Aviamilano F.8L Falco	106	ET-ABZ
			OE-ACW
			I-MOGA
I-VINI	SOCATA MS.892A Rallye Commodore 150	11876	
I-VINO	Aérospatiale AS.350B2 Ecureuil	3213	
I-VIOL	Aérospatiale SA.315B Lama	2501	
I-VIOU	SA.316B Alouette III	2179	
I-VISI	Beech 35-B33 Debonair	CD-552	HB-EIW
I-VITB	Piper PA-18 Super Cub 95	18-2011	I-EIPI
			MM522411
			52-2411
I-VIZZ	Zlin Z.526F Trenér Master	1162	
I-VLEO	Airbus A.320-214	1125	HB-IGZ
			F-WWIH
I-VLLE	SA.319B Alouette III	1999	HB-XUM
			FAP-636
I-VMAB	Rutan Vari-eze	unkn	
I-VOGH	Cessna 182R Skylane	67749	N5480N
I-VOLE	Piper J-3C-65 Cub	11587	D-ELEM
	(Officially quoted with its f/n 11412)		HB-OUL
			43-30296
I-VOLG	Piper PA-32R-300 Lance	32R-7680295	N75347
I-VOLP	Piper PA-32-300 Cherokee Six	32-7940142	N2821X
I-VORA	Piper PA-18-150 Super Cub	18-7909137	N9753N
I-VRCW	Cessna P210N Pressurized Centurion II	00790	N6504W
I-VREM	Aérospatiale AS.355F Ecureuil 2	5297	F-GEHL
I-VRST	SIAI-Marchetti S.205-20/R	4-138	
I-VRVR	Aérospatiale AS.355F Ecureuil 2	5180	
I-VSEM	Robinson R-22 Beta	2563	
I-VULA	SIAI-Marchetti SF.600A Canguro	10	
I-VULC	Gates Learjet 35A	35A-421	N413JP
			N3AH
			(N88AH)
			N85QA
			N85CA
			N44MJ
I-VVEE	Beech 58P Baron	TJ-320	N3707N
I-ZACM	Piper PA-28RT-201T Turbo Arrow IV	28R-8631005	N9085Z
I-ZANC	Robinson R-22 Beta	2561	
I-ZARO	Christen A-1 Husky	1042	
I-ZARY	Maule MXT-7-180 Star Rocket	14011C	N9225S
I-ZEND	Zlin Z.526F Trenér Master	1311	
I-ZEUS	Partenavia P.66B Oscar 100	44	
I-ZKRC	Agusta-Bell 206B Jet Ranger III	8731	
I-ZLIN	Zlin Z.526 Trenér Master	1070	
I-ZNTH	Zenair CH-250 Zenith	A114	
I-ZOLI	Rutan LongEz	unkn	

Regn.	Type	C/n	Prev.Id.
I-ZOOM	Gates Learjet 35A	35A-135	N11AK
			N719US
			D-CDAX
			N22MJ
			(OO-LFX)
I-ZUBO	Partenavia P.64B Oscar B-1155	03	
I-ZVPC	PZ.150	001	
I-ZZIO	Robin DR.400/180R Remorqueur	990	OE-DUO
			D-EOKB

GLIDERS AND MOTOR-GLIDERS

Regn.	Type	C/n	Prev.Id.
I-ACOS	Bölkow Phoebus B-1	769	
I-ACRN	Scheibe Bergfalke IV	5835	
I-ACRO	Schleicher ASK-13	13195	
I-ACRQ	LET L-13 Blanik	175116	
I-ADRT	Schempp-Hirth Nimbus 2B	153	
I-AECX	Velino (Homebuilt)	101	
I-AESV	AS 10 Microlight motorglider	001	
I-AFFE	Grob G.102 Astir Club IIIB	5553CB	
I-AIRZ	Bölkow Phoebus A-1	755	D-1349
I-AJTB	Grob G.109B	6384	
I-ALIA	Schleicher ASW-19B	19014	
I-ALOE	Glasflügel H205 Club Libelle	29	
I-ALOR	Grob G.103 Twin Astir II	3533	
I-ALTI	Glasflügel 604	10	
I-ANEA	Glaser-Dirks DG-300 Elan	3E-372	
I-ANKA	Schempp-Hirth Nimbus 2	9	D-0884
I-ANNC	Glaser-Dirks DG-200	2-56	
I-ANTO	Schempp-Hirth Standard Cirrus	510	
I-ANUS	Schempp-Hirth Janus	59	
I-APBK	Scheibe SF-25C Falke 2000	44435	(D-KIAB(1))
I-ASAV	Glaser-Dirks DG-400	4-235	(D-KIDG)
I-ASEN	Glasflügel H.301 Libelle	87	
I-ASET	Schempp-Hirth Cirrus	7	
I-ASPE	Hoffmann H-36 Dimona	36241	
I-ASVV	Scheibe Zugvogel IIIA	1035	OE-0416
I-AUAA	Aeronautica Umbra AU-SF-25B Falke	001	
I-AUAD	Aeronautica Umbra AU-SF-25B Falke	006	
I-AUAG	Aeronautica Umbra AU-SF-25B Falke	005	
I-AVAD	Grob G.109B	6331	
I-AVAG	Scheibe Bergfalke III	5598	D-1289
I-AVAH	Glaser-Dirks DG-300 Elan	3E-365	
I-AVAK	Glaser-Dirks DG-300 Elan	3E-306	
I-AVAO	Glasflügel H.301B Libelle	106	
I-AVAR	Glaser-Dirks DG-300 Elan	3E-251	
I-AVAS	Glaser-Dirks DG-300 Elan	3E-408	
I-AVAT	Glaser-Dirks DG-300 Elan	3E-366	
I-AVCZ	Glasflügel H201B Standard Libelle	141	
I-AVVA	Hoffmann H-36 Dimona	36268	
I-AVVB	Grob G.103 Twin Astir	3166	D-7796
I-AYAX	Glaser-Dirks DG-100G Elan	E61-G37	
I-BAUU	Schleicher K.8B	8777	
I-BEPO	Schempp-Hirth Standard Cirrus	529	
I-BINE	Glasflügel H201B Standard Libelle	434	
I-BITO	Glasflügel H401 Kestrel	8	
I-BLEK	Fournier RF-3	02	F-BLEK
I-BLOB	Glaser-Dirks DG-300 Elan	3E-430	
I-BOOK	Glaser-Dirks DG-300 Elan	3E-411	
I-BOOM	Glaser-Dirks DG-300 Elan	3E-432	
I-BOYS	Schempp-Hirth Standard Cirrus	585	
I-BOZZ	Schempp-Hirth Discus b	216	
I-BRAE	Schempp-Hirth Janus B	147	
I-BRAN	Schleicher Ka.6E	4378	
I-BREM	Grob G.109B	6442	
I-BROC	Glasflügel H.301B Libelle	96	
I-BRRR	AS 10 Microlight motorglider	0009	
I-BRUT	Glaser-Dirks DG-300 Elan	3E-409	
I-BSTR	Grob G.102 Astir III	5599S	
I-BZAC	LET L-13 Blanik	026528	D-3349

Regn.	Type	C/n	Prev.Id.
I-BZAF	Scheibe SF-25C Falke	4470	D-KOBL
I-BZAI	Schleicher K.8B	8919	
I-BZAP	Grob G.102 Astir CS 77	1676	D-3879
I-BZAR	Glaser-Dirks DG-300 Elan	3E-422	
I-BZAS	Schleicher ASK-21	21610	
I-BZEL	LET L-13 Blanik	026529	
I-BZUM	Grob G.102 Astir CS 77	1714	
I-CAIO	Schleicher ASK-14	14006	D-KOIB
I-CAJO	Glaser-Dirks DG-400	4-241	
I-CALM	Glasflügel H206 Hornet	31	
I-CAOS	Glasflügel H401 Kestrel	40	
I-CCCP	Caproni Vizzola A.21S Calif	229	
I-CCLO	Scheibe SF-25C Falke	4212	D-KAWA
I-CECJ	Glaser-Dirks DG-300 Elan	3E-384	
I-CEMM	Glaser-Dirks DG-200	2-61	D-7776
I-CENN	Schleicher ASK-13	13117	
I-CENO	Schleicher Ka.6E	4260	
I-CEUO	Centrair ASW-20F	20179	F-CEUO
I-CIAU	Schempp-Hirth SHK-1	18	
I-CILY	Schleicher ASW-15B	15218	
I-CINK	Glaser-Dirks DG-300 Elan	3E-235	
I-CIOK	Schleicher ASW-20	20092	
I-CIOT	Schleicher Ka.6E	4267	
I-CIUK	SZD-30 Pirat	B-566	
I-CJSA	LET L-13 Blanik	026110	
I-CLAB	Glasflügel H205 Club Libelle	41	
I-CLUB	Scheibe SF-27A	6053	
I-CNVV	Aeromere M.100S	000	
I-CRBB	Glasflügel H201B Standard Libelle	475	
I-CRBV	Glasflügel H206 Hornet	46	
I-CROZ	Scheibe Mü.13E Bergfalke	01	
I-CRVV	LET L-13 Blanik	025420	
I-CSWP	Glasflügel H401 Kestrel	1	
I-CYAO	Schempp-Hirth Cirrus	V-2	D-8437
			D-9406
I-DAMJ	Schleicher ASW-15B	15430	
I-DAVY	Grob G.109B	6417	
I-DAYS	Schempp-Hirth Standard Cirrus	618	
I-DEKA	Grob G.109	6127	D-KCOT
			(I-.....)
I-DENT	Glasflügel H401 Kestrel	22	
I-DEUX	Glasflügel H206 Hornet	57	D-7260
I-DGAM	Glaser-Dirks DG-200	2-85	
I-DHEM	AS 10 Microlight motorglider	C011	
I-DIAW	Rolladen-Schneider LS-3A	3410	D-4297
I-DIGY	Glaser-Dirks DG-300 Elan	3E-39	
I-DISK-LB	Schempp-Hirth Discus A	03	D-6095
I-DLEA	Glasflügel H201B Standard Libelle	50	
I-DOSE	LET L-13 Blanik	175102	
I-DUEP	Glaser-Dirks DG-300 Elan	3E-410	
I-DUKI	Schleicher ASK-13	13148	
I-DUNO	Rolladen-Schneider LS-3-17	3457	D-6684
I-DURI	Avionautica Rio CVV.8	012	
I-DURT	Schleicher ASW-24E	24848	(D-KAXS)
I-EDEC	Schleicher Ka.6CR Rhönsegler	568	
I-EDEL	Schleicher K-7	405	
I-ELAN	Glaser-Dirks DG-300 Elan	3E-75	
I-ELJO	Schleicher ASW-24	24149	
I-ENCA	Schleicher ASK-13	13280	
I-EREL	Schleicher ASW-20	20421	
I-ERSI	Schempp-Hirth Standard Cirrus B	595	
I-EUGI	Schempp-Hirth Ventus c	110/377	
I-EVAI	Scheibe Zugvogel IIIB	1070	
I-EVAM	Scheibe Bergfalke IIt55	391	
I-EVIO	LET L-13 Blanik	173212	HB-832
I-FACG	Rolladen-Schneider LS-4	4363	
I-FALL	Glaser-Dirks DG-300 Elan	3E-274	
I-FEVV	Schleicher ASK-13	13158	
I-FEWW	Fournier RF-4D	4019	F-BORF
I-FGTM	Rolladen-Schneider LS-4	4362	
I-FIUR	Glasflügel H201B Standard Libelle	72	
I-FLAV	Glasflügel H206 Hornet	4	
I-FLUG	Schleicher ASW-19B	19052	
I-FOFI-64	Schempp-Hirth Standard Cirrus	417	
I-FOLE	Meteor MS.30L Passero	50005	

Regn.	Type	C/n	Prev.Id.
I-FOLL	L-Spatz (Motor conversion)	unkn	
I-FOXY	Glaser-Dirks DG-300 Elan	3E-382	
I-FRAU	Eiri PIK-20E-II	20304	OH-624
I-FRYY	Rolladen-Schneider LS-4	4306	HB-1712
I-GATS	Rolladen-Schneider LS-4	4248	D-9108
I-GCCP	Caproni Vizzola A.21S Calif	253	
I-GEDE	Sportavia-Pützer RF-5B Sperber	51035	(D-KEAQ)
I-GELO	Grob G.109B	6273	
I-GGBP	Glaser-Dirks DG-300 Elan	3E-379	
I-GHES	Schleicher ASW-20L	20455	D-3248
I-GIMY	Aeromere M.100S	024	
I-GIDI	LET L-13 Blanik	171612	D-9811
			OK-1811
I-GIOO	Glaser-Dirks DG-400	4-130	D-KERO
I-GIRI	Schleicher ASK-13	13394	
I-GITO	Schleicher ASK-21	21486	
I-GLAD	Schleicher ASW-20C	20716	D-7875
I-GLOO	Schleicher ASW-15B	15242	
I-GNEO	Schempp-Hirth Standard Cirrus	473	
I-GOAL	Schleicher Ka.6E	4376	
I-GOST	Schleicher ASW-24	24146	
I-GOUP	Glasflügel H201B Standard Libelle	365	
I-GROG	Schempp-Hirth Discus A	111	
I-GRRR	Glaser-Dirks DG-300 Elan	3E-428	
I-GULP	LET L-13 Blanik	175007	
I-GVAM	Scheibe SF-26A	5052	
I-HEXE	Bölkow Phoebus C	942	
I-HOBO	Glaser-Dirks DG-200	2-54	
I-HOPS	Glaser-Dirks DG-300 Elan	3E-339	
I-HOWA	Grob G.102 Astir CS	1098	
I-HVAR	EC.39D Uribel D	030	
I-HBTS	Glaser-Dirks DG-200	2-53	
I-HDEA	Schempp-Hirth Standard Cirrus	91	
I-HDOT	Schleicher Ka.6E	4353	
I-HILY	Schempp-Hirth Ventus b/16.6	122	D-3153
I-HLMA	Hoffmann H-36 Dimona	36274	
I-HLPO	Schleicher ASK-21	21239	
I-HMAA	Scheibe SF-25C Falke	44253	D-KDBI
I-HMAB	Scheibe SF-25C Falke	44254	D-KDBL
I-HMAC	Scheibe SF-25C Falke	44256	D-KDBM
I-HMAD	Scheibe SF-25C Falke	44257	D-KDBN
I-HMAF	Scheibe SF-25C Falke	44260	D-KDBP
I-HMAH	Scheibe SF-25C Falke	44306	(D-KOOE)
I-HMBG	Schempp-Hirth Ventus cM	95/585	
I-HMRH	Rolladen-Schneider LS-6A	6106	
I-HNES	Glasflügel H205 Club Libelle	4	
I-HOOO-VS	Rolladen-Schneider LS-6A	6023	D-6334
I-HPER	Glaser-Dirks DG-300 Elan	3E-305	
I-HUUH	Schleicher ASW-19B	19115	
I-HVAA	Schleicher ASK-13	13562	
I-HVAB	Grob G.103 Twin Astir	3145	
I-HVAC	Grob G.103 Twin Astir	3146	
I-HVAD	Grob G.103 Twin Astir	3164	
I-HVAE	Grob G.103 Twin Astir	3165	
I-HVAF	Grob G.103 Twin Astir	3180	
I-HVAG	Grob G.103 Twin Astir	3175	
I-HVAH	Grob G.103 Twin Astir	3184	
I-HVAI	Grob G.103 Twin Astir	3185	
I-HVAJ	Grob G.103 Twin Astir	3259	
I-HVAK	Grob G.103 Twin Astir	3258	
I-HVAM	Glasflügel H201 Standard Libelle	19	
I-HVAQ	Grob G.103 Twin Astir	3214	
I-HVAR	Grob G.103 Twin Astir	3215	
I-HVAS	Grob G.103 Twin Astir	3216	
I-HVAT	Grob G.103 Twin Astir	3204	
I-HVAU	Grob G.103 Twin Astir	3276	
I-HVAV	Grob G.103 Twin Astir	3277	
I-HVAW	Grob G.103 Twin Astir	3278	
I-HVAY	Grob G.103 Twin Astir	3280	
I-HVBA	Grob G.102 Astir CS 77	1734	
I-HVBB	Grob G.102 Astir CS 77	1735	
I-HVBC	Grob G.102 Astir CS 77	1755	
I-HVBD	Grob G.102 Astir CS 77	1754	
I-HVBE	Grob G.102 Astir CS 77	1765	
I-HVBF	Grob G.102 Astir CS 77	1766	

Regn.	Type	C/n	Prev.Id.
I-HVBH	Grob G.102 Astir CS 77	1778	
I-HVBI	Grob G.102 Standard Astir II	5026S	
I-HVBJ	Grob G.102 Standard Astir II	5027S	
I-HVBK	Grob G.102 Standard Astir II	5028S	
I-HVBL	Grob G.102 Standard Astir II	5029S	
I-HVBN	Grob G.102 Standard Astir II	5048S	
I-HVBP	Grob G.102 Standard Astir II	5524S	
I-HVBQ	Grob G.102 Standard Astir II	5525S	
I-HVCB	Caproni Vizzola A.21S Calif	251	
I-HVDB	Schempp-Hirth Janus	77	
I-HVDC	Schempp-Hirth Janus B	130	
I-HVDE	Schempp-Hirth Janus B	134	
I-HVDF	Schempp-Hirth Janus B	140	
I-HVDG	Schempp-Hirth Janus B	141	
I-HVEA	Centrair ASW-20F	20193	F-CEUV
I-HVEC-S2	Centrair ASW-20F	20195	F-CEUY
I-HVED	Centrair ASW-20F	20196	F-CEUZ
I-HVFA-C5	Rolladen-Schneider LS-4	4276	
I-HVFB-C6	Rolladen-Schneider LS-4	4277	
I-HVFC	Rolladen-Schneider LS-4	4278	
I-HVPA-P1	Glaser-Dirks DG-300 Club Elan	3E-346/C35	
I-HVPB-P2	Glaser-Dirks DG-300 Club Elan	3E-347/C36	
I-HVPC	Glaser-Dirks DG-300 Club Elan	3E-348/C37	
I-HVPE-P5	Glaser-Dirks DG-300 Club Elan	3E-363/C48	
I-HVPF-PI	Glaser-Dirks DG-300 Club Elan	3E-375/C51	
I-HVPG-P7	Glaser-Dirks DG-300 Elan	3E-386	
I-HVPH-Z	Glaser-Dirks DG-300 Elan	3E-387	
I-HVPI	Glaser-Dirks DG-300 Elan	3E-390	
I-HVPK	Glaser-Dirks DG-300 Club Elan	3E-440/C75	
I-HVVA	Grob G.103 Twin Astir II	3698	
I-HVVB	Grob G.103 Twin Astir II	3699	
I-HVVC	Grob G.103 Twin Astir II	3700	
I-HVVE	Grob G.103 Twin Astir II	3758	
I-HVVF	Grob G.103 Twin Astir II	3836	
I-HVVG	Grob G.103 Twin Astir II	3837	
I-HVVH	Grob G.103 Twin III Acro	34159	
I-HVVI	Grob G.103 Twin III Acro	34160	
I-HVVJ	Grob G.103 Twin III Acro	34161	
I-HVVK	Grob G.103 Twin III Acro	34162	
I-HVVL	Grob G.103 Twin III Acro	34163	
I-HVVM	Grob G.103 Twin III Acro	34164	
I-HVVN	Grob G.103 Twin III Acro	34165	
I-HVVO	Grob G.103 Twin III Acro	34166	
I-HVVP	Grob G.103 Twin III Acro	34167	
I-HVVQ	Grob G.103 Twin III Acro	34168	
I-HVVR	Grob G.103 Twin III Acro	34169	
I-HVVS	Grob G.103 Twin III Acro	34181	
I-HVVT	Grob G.103 Twin III Acro	34182	
I-HVVU	Grob G.103 Twin III Acro	34183	
I-HVVV	Grob G.103 Twin III Acro	34188	
I-HVVW	Grob G.103 Twin III Acro	34189	
I-HVVX	Grob G.103 Twin III Acro	34190	
I-HVVY	Grob G.103 Twin III Acro	34191	
I-HVVZ	Grob G.103 Twin III Acro	34192	
I-HVWA	Schleicher ASK-21	21474	
I-HVWB	Schleicher ASK-21	21475	
I-HVWC	Schleicher ASK-21	21476	
I-HVWD	Schleicher ASK-21	21477	
I-HVWE	Schleicher ASK-21	21478	
I-HVWF	Schleicher ASK-21	21479	
I-HVWG	Schleicher ASK-21	21480	
I-HVWH	Schleicher ASK-21	21481	
I-HVWI	Schleicher ASK-21	21482	
I-HVWJ	Schleicher ASK-21	21483	
I-HVWK	Schleicher ASK-21	21484	
I-HVWL	Schleicher ASK-21	21685	
I-HVWM	Schleicher ASK-21	21687	
I-HVWN	Schleicher ASK-21	21690	
I-HVWO	Schleicher ASK-21	21691	
I-HVWP	Schleicher ASK-21	21692	
I-HVWQ	Schleicher ASK-21	21693	
I-HVWR	Schleicher ASK-21	21695	
I-HVWS	Schleicher ASK-21	21697	
I-JANE	Grob G.109	6034	OO-PRY
			D-KGRO

Regn.	Type	C/n	Prev.Id.
I-JANO	Schempp-Hirth Janus	11	D-2476
I-JOLI	Schleicher ASW-15B	15316	
I-JOSE	Schleicher ASW-20	20448	
I-JOUX	Glasflügel H201B Standard Libelle	476	
I-JUCK	Glaser-Dirks DG-300 Elan	3E-162	
I-JULO	AM-11 Motorglider	unkn	
I-JURI	Glasflügel H201 Standard Libelle	73	
I-KAIB	Scheibe SF-25B Falke	46234	D-KAIB
I-KAND	Scheibe SF-25C Falke	44425	
I-KAOS	Rolladen Schneider LS-1F	322	
I-KARO	Glasflügel H201B Standard Libelle	473	
I-KASA	SZD-48-3 Jantar Standard 3	B-1953	
I-KASB	SZD-51-1 Junior	B-1930	
I-KAZZ	Rolladen-Schneider LS-3A	3437	D-3540
I-KBDG	Glaser-Dirks DG-400	4-165	D-KBDG
I-KCEO	Glaser-Dirks DG-400	4-193	D-KCEO
I-KCIP	Grob G.109	6016	D-KCIP(2)
I-KDFD	Scheibe SF-25C Falke 1700	44209	D-KDFD(2)
I-KDHA	Valentin Taifun 17E	1059	D-KDHA
I-KEEN-52	Glaser-Dirks DG-300 Elan	3E-340	
I-KEOG	Grob G.109B	6307	D-KEOG
I-KFAP	Glaser-Dirks DG-400 (Reserved as D-KUKI 11.99)	4-156	D-KFAP
I-KHHB	Valentin Taifun 17E	1067	D-KHHB
I-KICO	Glasflügel H401 Kestrel	12	
I-KIDC	Glaser-Dirks DG-400	4-125	D-KIDC
I-KIKA	Glasflügel H201B Standard Libelle	35	
I-KILC	Grob G.109	6108	D-KILC
I-KILF	Glaser-Dirks DG-400	4-177	D-KILF
I-KIPR	Valentin Taifun 17E	1083	D-KIPR
I-KIRA	Glasflügel H201B Standard Libelle	280	
I-KKFA	Schleicher ASW-24E	24815	D-KKFA
I-KLEO	Hoffmann HK-36R Super Dimona	36352	
I-KMAP	Schempp-Hirth Ventus cM	38/474	D-KMAP
I-KOKI	Glasflügel H401 Kestrel	9	
I-KOLL	Schleicher ASW-20L	20551	
I-KRYS	Glaser-Dirks DG-300 Elan	3E-255	
I-LADJ	Aeronautica Umbria AU-SF-25B Falke	001	
	(Amateur-built version, not related to I-AUAA c/n 001)		
I-LAMP	Schleicher ASW-20	20249	
I-LARY	Schempp-Hirth SHK-1	59	
I-LAVU	Schleicher ASW-15	15056	D-0542
I-LBIS	Scheibe Bergfalke IV	5826	
I-LBOB	Schleicher ASW-20	20375	
I-LBOS	Bölkow Phoebus B-1	805	D-1458
I-LEFA	EC.39C Uribel C	024	
I-LERE	Schleicher ASW-15B	15267	
I-LETJ	Schempp-Hirth Standard Cirrus	315	D-2949
I-LFOX	Glaser-Dirks DG-200	2-60	
I-LGEP	Schempp-Hirth Discus b	408	
I-LGIO-Y	Rolladen-Schneider LS-6A	6127	D-0665
I-LGVA	Glasflügel H205 Club Libelle	70	
I-LIPA	Schempp-Hirth Nimbus 2B	169	D-2206
I-LIVE	Schleicher ASW-19B	19026	
I-LJET	Schempp-Hirth SHK-1	56	
I-LMAT	Glasflügel H206 Hornet	48	
I-LMIG	Schempp-Hirth Discus b	249	
I-LOIS	Schempp-Hirth Ventus A	73	D-0150
I-LOOP	Schempp-Hirth Standard Cirrus	478	
I-LORA	Glaser-Dirks DG-200	2-25	D-6782
I-LORJ	Rolladen-Schneider LS-3A	3443	D-6923
I-LPIU	Schleicher ASW-15B	15238	
I-LRIP	Schempp-Hirth Discus b	323	
I-LUCB	Sportavia-Fournier RF-4D	4092	D-KALD
I-LUKA	Glaser-Dirks DG-200	2-92	
I-LUKO-B	Glaser-Dirks DG-100G Elan (Dismantled)	E217-G183	
I-LULU	Glasflügel H201B Standard Libelle	554	
I-LUSO	Bölkow Phoebus C	928	
I-LVBG	Grob G.102 Astir CS 77	1777	I-IVBG
I-LVIG	Schleicher ASK-21	21430	
I-LVIP	Glaser-Dirks DG-300 Elan	3E-230	
I-LVIT	Rolladen-Schneider LS-6A	6076	D-3398
I-LYMA	Rolladen-Schneider LS-4	4039	D-3356
I-LYNO	Glaser-Dirks DG-100G Elan	E222-G188	
I-MACH	Schempp-Hirth Standard Cirrus	331	D-3024
I-MAEN	LET L-13 Blanik	173455	
I-MAGO	Bölkow Phoebus A-1	758	
I-MAIA	Rolladen-Schneider LS-6A	6181	
I-MBIG	Schempp-Hirth Discus b	200	D-8111
I-MEIO	LET L-13 Blanik	026250	
I-MEKI	Schleicher ASW-20L	20279	
I-MERY	Glaser-Dirks DG-300 Elan	3E-420	
I-MEZZ	Scheibe Bergfalke IV	5836	
I-MIGG	Glaser-Dirks DG-300 Elan	3E-412	
I-MIMO	Rolladen-Schneider LS-3A	3435	D-2866
I-MISU	Aviamilano A-2	601	
I-MMST	Rolladen-Schneider LS-3A	3166	HB-1362
I-MONJ	AS 10 Microlight motorglider	unkn	
I-MOSK	Schleicher ASW-20	20422	
I-MUGE	Grob G.103 Twin Astir	3187	D-5953
I-MVAM	Scheibe SF-25A Motorfalke	4524	D-KAJY
I-NANQ	Glasflügel H201B Standard Libelle	474	
I-NAOS	Hoffmann HK-36R Super Dimona	36319	OE-9351
I-NERI	AS 10 Microlight motorglider	unkn	
I-NEVI-47	Schempp-Hirth Nimbus 2	109	D-7246
I-NEWD	Glasflügel H205 Club Libelle	56	
I-NIBO	Schleicher ASK-21	21327	
I-NIKO	SZD-36 Cobra 15	W-695	
I-NIMB	Rolladen-Schneider LS-3A	3431	D-4584
I-NMCV	Grob Standard Cirrus	461G	
I-NOIR	Schleicher ASW-15	15106	
I-NONI	Schempp-Hirth Janus C	106	D-4519
I-NOVL	LET L-13 Blanik	025421	
I-NYKE	Glaser-Dirks DG-300 Elan	3E-424	
I-NYKK	Schleicher Ka.6E	4338	D-0544
I-NYNO	Glaser-Dirks DG-100G Elan	E218-G184	
I-OASI	Glasflügel H401 Kestrel	10	
I-OCIO	Glasflügel H205 Club Libelle	55	
I-OGHY	Schempp-Hirth Standard Cirrus	553G	
I-OKAY	Schleicher ASW-20	20373	
I-OKEY	Schempp-Hirth Standard Cirrus	509	
I-OKYO	Schleicher ASW-15B	15198	
I-OOSO	Schleicher ASW-24	24136	
I-OPEL	Bölkow Phoebus C	818	
I-ORNI	Rolladen-Schneider LS-3A	3459	D-3393
I-ORPO	Scheibe SF-25B Falke	4612	D-KODB
I-OSSO	Schleicher ASW-15B	15266	
I-PAIS	Schleicher ASK-21	21349	
I-PAIU	Scheibe SF-25B Falke	4682	D-KBAH
I-PAMI	Schempp-Hirth Ventus b	49	D-2925
I-PATR	Grob G.103 Twin Astir	3242	
I-PBEI	Glaser-Dirks DG-300 Elan	3E-377	
I-PEAW	Glasflügel H201B Standard Libelle	553	
I-PECK	Schempp-Hirth Ventus c	538	
I-PHIL	Schempp-Hirth Standard Cirrus	541G	
I-PICK	Schleicher ASK-21	21405	
I-PICW	Eiri PIK-20E	20256	OH-563
I-PIKA	Hoffmann HK-36R Super Dimona	36320	
I-PIKE	Eiri PIK-20E-II	20295	OH-615
I-PIKK	Eiri PIK-20E	20259	OH-559
I-PINE	Glaser-Dirks DG-200	2-46	D-6661
I-PING	Scheibe Bergfalke IV	5837	
I-PINK	Schleicher ASW-19B	19178	
I-PLAN	Grob G.109	6156	D-KCEC
I-PLOC	Schleicher ASK-13	13120	
I-PLOK	Schleicher ASK-13	13213	
I-PLOQ	Schleicher ASK-13 (Dismantled)	13271	
I-PORK	Hoffman H-36 Dimona	3519	OE-9219 (D-KBIN)
I-PUCI	Glasflügel H201B Standard Libelle	316	
I-PUSC	Glasflügel H206 Hornet	32	
I-RANI	EC.39C Uribel C	028	
I-RATA	Glaser-Dirks DG-200	2-5	D-4509
I-RDPR	AS 10 Microlight motorglider	unkn	
I-RECM	Schleicher ASW-24	24137	
I-RGOT	Rolladen-Schneider LS-4	4136	D-0531
I-RHEM	Aeromere M-100S	030	
I-RHEN	Schempp-Hirth Discus b	223	
I-RIAS	Hoffman HK-36R Super Dimona	36375	HB-2238
I-RIET	Hoffmann H-36 Dimona	36224	
I-RIFF	Caproni-Vizzola A-3	607	

Regn.	Type	C/n	Prev.Id.
I-RISE	Glaser-Dirks DG-200	2-177	
I-RIZO	Eiri PIK-20D	20653	
I-ROAR	LET L-13 Blanik	175030	
I-ROCQ	Schleicher ASK-13	13263	
I-ROKI	Glasflügel H206 Hornet	47	
I-ROPA	Schempp-Hirth Janus	13	
I-RORI	EC-39C Uribel C	021	
I-ROSL	Schleicher ASW-15B	15370	
I-RUMA	Schleicher ASW-20	20574	
I-RYZZ	Glaser-Dirks DG-300 Elan	3E-426	
I-SAIL	Schempp-Hirth Standard Cirrus B	686	
I-SANO	Schleicher ASK-13	13118	
I-SCFL	Schleicher ASW-20	20316	
I-SCPV	Caproni Vizzola A-2	610	
I-SEGI	Hoffman HK-36R Super Dimona	36301	OE-9350
I-SEGL	Bölkow Phoebus C	808	
I-SELL	Schleicher ASK-13	13264	
I-SELZ	Schleicher ASW-20L	20423	D-2604
I-SETA	Avionautica Rio M-HOOS	072	
I-SEXY	HBV Diamant	006	
I-SIRV	Schleicher ASK-21	21308	
I-SKYY	Schleicher ASW-24	24129	
I-SNIF	LET L-13 Blanik	175103	
I-SNOB	Schempp-Hirth Nimbus 2B	155	
I-SOLO	Glasflügel H201B Standard Libelle	396	
I-SONG	Schleicher ASW-19B	19369	
I-SOUF	Schleicher ASW-24	24138	
I-STMA	Hoffmann H-36 Dimona	36117	HB-2072
I-SURC	LET L-13 Blanik	175003	
I-SYBI	Glaser-Dirks DG-300 Elan	3E-369	
I-TAFA	Grob G.103 Twin Astir	3023	
I-TASS	Rolladen-Schneider LS-6	6038	D-3652
I-TEAM	Glaser-Dirks DG-200	2-33	
I-TILU	Sportavia-Pützer RF-5B Sperber	51047	D-KITZ
I-TORR	Sportavia-Fournier RF-5	5026	
I-TOTI	Slingsby T.51 Dart 17R	1511	
I-TREK	Schleicher ASW-24	24153	
I-TRIK	Glasflügel H201B Standard Libelle	59	
I-TWJN	Grob G.103 Twin Astir II	3572	
I-TWYN	Grob G.103 Twin Astir	3058	D-4848
I-UKSI	Rolladen-Schneider LS-4	4706	D-0527
I-URKA	Glasflügel H201B Standard Libelle	363	
I-USAF	Glaser-Dirks DG-300 Elan	3E-243	
I-VELU	Aeromere M-100S	015	
I-VIEL	Glaser-Dirks DG-300 Elan	3E-355	
I-VITA	Schempp-Hirth Cirrus	9	
I-VIUS	Glasflügel H303 Mosquito	83	
I-VIZQ	Caproni Vizzola A-21S Calif	219	
I-VLEN	Rolladen Schneider LS-1F	313	
I-VOLK	Sportavia-Fournier RF-4D	4045	
I-VORY	Glasflügel H201B Standard Libelle	588	
I-VVSS-55	Schleicher ASW-20L	20558	D-0882
I-ZAKK	AS 10 Microlight motorglider	C021	
I-ZAKO	Schleicher ASK-16	16018	D-KAAR
I-ZANI	Schempp-Hirth Standard Cirrus	474	
I-ZAVA	Glasflügel H205 Club Libelle	53	
I-ZBOW	Schleicher ASW-24	24128	D-6132
I-ZEDA	Schleicher ASK-21	21304	
I-ZITA	Glasflügel H206 Hornet	33	
I-ZOOW	Schleicher ASW-20	20397	
I-ZWEI	Schempp-Hirth Janus	43	D-4816
I-ZWYK	Schempp-Hirth Discus b	332	
I-ZUCK	Hoffman H-36 Dimona	36205	D-KFGT
I-ZZIP	Eiri PIK-20D	20586	

BALLOONS AND AIRSHIPS

Regn.	Type	C/n	Prev.Id.
I-AIMO(4)	Cameron O-77 HAFB	4206	
	(Formerly c/ns 912, 1472 and 2083)		
I-AJMO	Cameron N-105 HAFB	1868	
I-ALBB	Thunder AX7-77 SI HAFB	1289	
I-ANTC	Cameron V-77 HAFB	1556	(I-ANTO)
I-APAI	Cameron V-77 HAFB	2423	
I-APIS	Cameron O-84 HAFB	2677	
I-AZIT	Cameron N-105 HAFB	4326	
I-BGEJ	Cameron N-105 HAFB	2002	
I-BINN	Colt 105A HAFB	4689	
	(Replaces c/n 1739)		
I-BOPA	Bonanno X-7 Homebuilt HAFB	009	
I-BRIT	Colt 120A HAFB	1706	G-BSCJ
I-BZLA	Thunder AX7-77 HAFB	1634	
I-CAIT	Augsburg K-1050/3-RI Gas Balloon	9866	
I-CCNE	UltraMagic M-130	130/16	
I-CHAR	Thunder AX7-77 HAFB	1343	
I-CHBC	Cameron O-120 HAFB	2340	
I-CING(2)	Cameron N-90 HAFB	1675	
	(Formerly c/n 1129)		
I-COCK	Cameron V-77 HAFB	1281	
I-COTE	Cameron O-77 HAFB	1210	
I-DLOG	Cameron N-105 HAFB	2284	
I-DUCK(2)	Cameron O-77 HAFB	905	
I-FEED(2)	Cameron O-77 HAFB	3156	
	(Formerly c/n 1117)		
I-FLEG	Cameron N-90 HAFB	2778	
I-FMCL	Thunder AX7-77 HAFB	1685	
I-FRIK(2)	Cameron O-84 HAFB	2935	
	(Formerly c/n 1509)		
I-FRIM	Cameron O-105 HAFB	1266	
I-FROG(3)	Cameron V-77 HAFB	2926	
	(Formerly V-77 c/ns 848 and 1455)		
I-FROK(2)	Cameron O-84 HAFB	4440	
	(Formerly c/n 2425)		
I-FRQM	Cameron O-84 HAFB	1546	
I-GASI	Thunder AX7-77 HAFB	2116	
I-GIVJ	Cameron N-105 HAFB	3171	
I-GSCN	Cameron O-77 HAFB	1137	
I-GUFY	Cameron V-77 HAFB	2514	
I-IFIM	Cameron O-84 HAFB	2044	
I-KAMI (2)	Cameron O-84 HAFB	4205	
	(Formerly c/n 1507)		
I-KBPC	Cameron V-77 HAFB	3312	
I-KIKE(2)	Cameron N-105 HAFB	2363	
	(Formerly c/n 1167)		
I-KONG	Cameron O-105 HAFB	2578	
I-LAMB	Cameron O-105 HAFB	2685	
I-LBAA	Cameron O-105 HAFB	2080	
I-LBIG	Cameron N-90 HAFB	2443	
I-LBLU	Cameron O-105 HAFB	4529	
I-LBUS	Cameron A-210 HAFB	1789	
I-LDOC	Cameron O-120 HAFB	3586	
I-LMAL	Cameron V-77 HAFB	2491	
I-LMEL(2)	Cameron V-77 HAFB	3121	
	(Formerly c/n 1454)		
I-LOSI	Cameron N-105 HAFB	2657	
I-MMAP	Colt 77A HAFB	1040	G-BNEY
I-MOVI	Cameron O-77 HAFB	2039	
I-NELL(2)	Cameron O-77 HAFB	1287	
	(Formerly c/n 906)		
I-NIER	Colt 105A HAFB	1675	
I-NISE	Cameron N-105 HAFB	3594	
I-NOVG	Colt 90A HAFB	1540	
I-NPUT	Cameron V-77 HAFB	2424	
I-OMFS(3)	Cameron V-77 HAFB	4207	
	(Formerly c/ns 1177 and 1906)		
I-PAAM	Bonanno X-8 Homebuilt HAFB	007	
I-PACA	UltraMagic M-105 HAFB	105/41	
I-PARK	Augsburg K-1260/3-RI Gas Balloon	10007	D-OUTE
			D-Auguste X
I-PERC	UltraMagic V-105 HAFB	105/33	
I-RERE	Cameron V-77 HAFB	1113	(OO-BCL)

Regn.	Type	C/n	Prev.Id.
I-RIKY	Thunder AX7-77 HAFB	895	G-BNDU
I-ROLO	UltraMagic M-105 HAFB	105/55	
I-RORY	Cameron O-84 HAFB	1847	
I-SGMA	Cameron O-84 HAFB	4027	
	(Formerly c/n 2753)		
I-SIFO	UltraMagic S-90 HAFB	90/30	
I-SOLL(3)	Colt 77A HAFB	810	
	(Formerly c/ns 265 and 499)		
I-TETO	Cameron V-77 HAFB	4195	
I-TIRE	American Blimp Co A-60+ Airship	003	N2017A
I-VANI	Cameron N-105 HAFB	3460	
I-VESP(2)	Cameron V-31 HAFB	3081	
	(Formerly c/n 831)		
I-VSGE	Cameron O-105 HAFB	2382	G-BSSD
I-....	Cameron N-105 HAFB	3736	
I-....	Colt AS.80 Mk II Hot Air Airship	1248	G-BPGT
I-....	Colt Apple SS HAFB	756	G-BMKU
I-....	Colt 56A HAFB	2198	
I-....	Thunder AX7-77 SI HAFB	1222	
I-....	Thunder AX7-77 SI HAFB	1289	
I-....	Thunder AX7-77 SI HAFB	1341	
I-....	Thunder AX7-77 SI HAFB	1533	

MICROLIGHTS

Most Ultralights and Microlights are now registered in a numerical series, if indeed they carry any registrations at all. The following are known so far and details of other sightings would be welcome.

Regn.	Type	C/n	Prev.Id.
I-1006	Polaris		
I-0026	Golf 19		
I-0214	Murphy Maverick *(Wrecked)*		
I-0391	Pepistrone		
I-1242	Sky Walker		
I-1465	Europe Aviation Tucano		
I-1521	Sky Sports Europe Buccaneer		
I-1772	La Mouette Trike		
I-1962	Denney Kitfox		
I-2099	Aviatika MAI-89		
I-2153	Type unknown (Pusher microlight)		
I-2285	Dragon Fly		
I-2433	Tipsy T.66 Nipper	40	I-FAIB
			OO-ITB
			OY-AEV
I-2579	Euro ALA Jetfox JF.91S		
I-2580	Denney Kitfox		
I-2600	III Sky Arrow 450T		
I-2608	Cormorano		
I-2638	Macchi MB.308 (rebuild)		
I-2692	Dragon Fly		
I-2808	Cormorano		
I-3000	III Sky Arrow 500A		
I-3001	Curtiss Jenny (scale replica)		
I-3037	VPM M-16 Gyrocopter		
I-3121	Top Fun		
I-3130	Denney Kitfox		
I-3136	Cormorano		
I-3176	Elisport CH-7 Angel		
I-3189	Rodaro Storch		
I-3290	III Sky Arrow 650TC	12	
I-3348	Ferrari Tucano		
I-3416	Type unknown		
I-3443	Vidor Guiseppe Asso IV Wisky		
I-3453	CG-10 Ultralight		
I-3456	Ferrari Tucano		
I-3490	Pottier P.180		
I-3542	III Sky Arrow 450T		
I-3544	FGX Ultralight		
I-3556	Type unknown		
I-3566	Rans S-6 Coyote II		
I-3584	Nando Groppo Groppino		

Regn.	Type	C/n	Prev.Id.
I-3615	Type unknown		
I-3655	Dragon Fly		
I-3676	Mig		
I-3709	Condo		
I-3754	Europe Aviation Storm P280		
I-3764	SG Aviation Storm 280 SI		
I-3842	Tecnam P.92 Echo		
I-3854	Blue Sky Storch		
I-3858	Dragon Fly		
I-3901	Sparrow Effe		
I-3915	Dragon Fly		
I-3941	Cram		
I-3985	Dragon Light		
I-3994	GTAir		
I-4000	Air Command Gyrocopter		
I-4215	JEOF Candania GV 1		
I-4270	Dragon Fly		
I-4276	Dragon Fly		
I-4293	Tecnam P.92 Echo		
I-4312	Denney Kitfox		
I-4316	Tecnam Sky Arrow 450T		
I-4320	Tecnam P.92 Echo	086	
I-4322	SG Aviation Storm 280		
I-4394	SG Aviation Storm 280		
I-4401	Dragon Fly		
I-4430	Vidor Guiseppe Asso III	35	
I-4432	Dragon Fly		
I-4456	Zenair CH-701 STOL		
I-4462	Tecnam P.92 Echo		
I-4465	Dragon Fly		
I-4486	III Sky Arrow		
I-4493	Zenair CH-601UL Zodiac		
I-4505	Lombardi FL-5		
I-4554	Vidor Guiseppe Asso III	37	
I-4555	Salsedo Elpo 6		
I-4576	SG Aviation Storm 400 Special	179	
I-4583	SG Aviation Storm 280-51		
I-4598	Type unknown		
I-4660	Drafon Fly 333		
I-4665	Dragon Fly		
I-4683	Magni M-16 Gyrocopter		
I-4702	Dragon Fly 333		
I-4814	III Sky Arrow 450T		
I-4842	Dragon Fly		
I-4932	Selenia Moto Rider		
I-4940	Raj Hamsa X-Air		
I-4955	Tecnam P-96 Golf (Prototype)		
I-5067	SG Aviation Storm 280		
I-5104	Type unknown		
I-5105	Numberone		
I-5148	Raj Hamsa X-Air		
I-5169	Type unknown		
I-5227	Helicopter, type unknown		
I-5228	SG Aviation Storm 280TF-1		
I-5249	SG Aviation Storm 280SI		
I-5250	Tecnam P-96 Golf		
I-5272	Tecnam P.92 Echo		
I-5318	SG Aviation Storm 500 Special		
I-5335	Numberone		
I-5374	SG Aviation Storm		
I-5382	Ferrari Tucano		
I-5403	Polaris		
I-5436	Aerotechnica-CZ (Pottier P.220-4L)		
I-5576	Polaris		
I-5615	Euroala Jet Fox 97		
I-5752	Polaris MO		
I-5770	Asso Aeri Asso V		

Regn.	Type	C/n	Prev.Id.
LN-AAA(4)	Cessna 650 Citation III	0187	N39VP
			D-CAYK
			(N78PT)
			N70PT
			(N55PC)
			N500RP
			N187CM
			N2617K
LN-AAE(2)	Cessna 175C Skylark	57093	SE-FTG
			LN-HHA
			(SE-FTG)
			D-EHVO
			N8393T
LN-AAF(2)	Cessna 500 Citation	0311	SE-DRT
			(OY-VIP)
			SE-DRT
			N39RE
			N501RL
			OH-COL
			N818CD
			N5311J
LN-AAJ	Lake LA-4-200 Buccaneer	976	OY-JRH
			N3085P
LN-AAK	Aviat A-1AHusky	1458	N58AW
LN-AAL	Van's RV-6	21149	
LN-ABS(2)	Van's RV-4	1416	
LN-ACB	Aero Composites/Grefstad Sea Hawker	210	
LN-ACF	Piper PA-18 Super Cub 95	18-3232	RNoAF34832/
			'FA-F'
			53-4832
LN-ACG	Piper PA-18 Super Cub 95	18-3237	RNoAF34837/
			'FA-O'
			53-4837
LN-ACH	Piper PA-18 Super Cub 95	18-3238	RNoAF34838/
			'FA-P'
			53-4838
LN-ACI	Piper PA-18 Super Cub 95	18-3239	RNoAF34839/
			'FA-H'
			53-4839
LN-ACJ	Piper PA-18 Super Cub 95	18-3241	RNoAF34841/
			'FA-C'
			53-4841
LN-ACK	Piper PA-18 Super Cub 95	18-3244	RNoAF34844/
			'FA-S'
			53-4844
LN-ACL	Piper PA-18 Super Cub 95	18-3248	RNoAF34848/
			'FA-N'
			53-4848
LN-ACN(2)	Extra EA.230	004	OO-PAB
			D-ELBS
LN-AEA(3)	SOCATA MS.892E Rallye 150T	2803	SE-GTF
LN-AEC(2)	Piper PA-28-180 Cherokee G	28-7205275	
LN-AED(8)	Cessna 172N	68157	N733BA
LN-AEF(7)	Denney Kitfox II	462	
LN-AEG(2)	Cessna 172E	50985	(N3785S)
LN-AEH(2)	Piper PA-18-150 Super Cub	18-8472	N4244Z
LN-AEI (2)	Piper PA-23-250 Aztec C	27-3390	N6169Y
LN-AEJ	Reims/Cessna F.172E (Stored)	50691/0036	OY-DCD
LN-AEK(3)	Piper PA-18-150 Super Cub	18-8531	
LN-AEP	Cessna 170B (Stored)	26196	N2552C
LN-AER(2)	Piper PA-18-150 Super Cub	18-8150	
LN-AEV(3)	Grumman GA-7 Cougar	0041	N417GA
			C-GVOZ
			N751GA
LN-AEW(3)	Maule MX.7-180 Star Rocket	11025C	N5668N
LN-AEX	Piper PA-23-250 Aztec C (Stored)	27-2538	SE-EMG
LN-AEY	Piper PA-31-310 Navajo	31-457	
LN-AEZ(2)	Cessna U.206G Stationair II	06796	N9986Z
LN-AFH	Torbjorn Aaker Bowers IA Fly Baby	74-09	
LN AKE	Beech 58 Baron	TH-967	OY-ARZ
LN-AKH	Van's RV-4	2751	
LN-AKT	Rutan LongEz	1043	

Regn.	Type	C/n	Prev.Id.
LN-AKU	Morane-Saulnier MS.885 Super Rallye	266	D-EKUE
			F-BKUP
			(D-EMVE)
LN-ALA	Cessna A.185F Floatplane	03201	N93249
LN-ALB	Reims/Cessna F.172N	1566	
LN-ALD	Cessna U.206G Floatplane	03628	N7355N
LN-ALE	Reims/Cessna F.172M	1385	N31058
LN-ALF	Reims/Cessna FA.152 Aerobat	0341	
LN-ALG	Reims/Cessna F.172N	1668	
LN-ALH(2)	Cessna 172N	70475	N739EB
LN-ALI (3)	Piper PA-34-200T Seneca II	34-7970259	N2822A
LN-ALK	Reims/Cessna F.177RG Cardinal RG	0149	(F-BJDJ)
			N91049
LN-ALL	Cessna 210M Centurion (Cr 27.3.90)	61645	N732NP
LN-ALM(3)	Bellanca 8KCAB Decathlon	553-79	SE-GXR
LN-ALO(2)	Cessna 140	9032	OY-AVO
			D-EKUH
			N89980
LN-ALP(2)	Cessna U.206G Floatplane (Dbr 7.8.84)	05175	N4951U
LN-ALR	Reims/Cessna F.177RG Cardinal RG	0170	(G-....)
LN-ALS	Cessna U.206G Floatplane (Cr., stored)	05230	N5349U
LN-ALT	Piper PA-28-181 Archer II	28-7990435	N28924
LN-ALU	Reims/Cessna F.172P	2103	
LN-ALV	Reims/Cessna F.172P	2118	
LN-ALX	Cessna U.206G Stationair II	05407	N6300U
LN-ALY(2)	Grumman GA-7 Cougar	0057	OY-GAV
			N770GA
LN-ALZ	Reims/Cessna F.172P	2125	
LN-AMY	North American AT-6D Harvard	88-16849	(LN-LCS)
			(LN-LCN)
			N10595
LN-ASA	Reims/Cessna F.172M	1107	
LN-ASB	Reims/Cessna F.172M	1151	
LN-ASC	Cessna U.206F Stationair (W/o 12.9.90)	02308	N1957U
LN-ASD	Cessna 182P Skylane	63104	(N7320N)
LN-ASF	Reims/Cessna F.172M	1083	
LN-ASH	Reims/Cessna F.172M	1240	
LN-ASJ	Reims/Cessna F.172M	1303	
LN-ASM	Cessna 182P (Reims assembled)	63880/0012	(N6887M)
LN-ASN	Reims/Cessna F.172M	1414	
LN-ASO	Cessna 180B	50534	LN-HHO
			SE-CTR
			N5234E
LN-ASP	Reims/Cessna F.172M	1466	
LN-ASQ	Reims/Cessna F.172M	1448	
LN-ASR	Cessna U.206F Floatplane	03141	N8280Q
LN-ASS	Cessna 182P (Reims assembled)	64412/0056	N1677M
LN-AST	Reims/Cessna F.172N	1524	
LN-ASW	Cessna A.185F	03906	I-AGEL
			N4918E
LN-ASY	Reims/Cessna F.172N	1591	
LN-ATF	Rutan LongEz	1567	
LN-ATR	Piper PA-28-181 Archer II (W/o 15.6.93)	28-7990093	N30466
LN-AUD	Neico Lancair 320 (Reservation)	unkn	
LN-AZN	Piper PA-31-310 Navajo	31-491	OY-AZN
			G-BGYI
			F-BYCQ
			F-OCPC
			N6600L
LN-BAK(2)	SOCATA TB-10 Tobago	619	OY-GCL
			D-EOQC(3)
			SE-IMU
LN-BAT(2)	Cessna 421B Golden Eagle	0915	N421L
			OO-DFE
			D-IMMI
			N5457J
LN-BBA	Fokker F.27-050	20130	(LN-AKE)
			PH-EXC
LN-BBB	Fokker F.27-050	20131	(LN-AKF)
			PH-EXE
LN-BBC	Fokker F.27-050	20134	(LN-AKG)
			PH-EXH
LN-BBU	Piper PA-28-140 Cherokee	28-21094	OY-BBU
			N11C
LN-BDA(4)	Piper PA-28-161 Cherokee Warrior II	28-7816512	N9664C

Regn.	Type	C/n	Prev.Id.
LN-BDB(6)	Piper PA-28-140 Cherokee E	28-7225392	
LN-BDC	Reims/Cessna F.172H (Scrapped .90)	0588	
LN-BDD(3)	Dornier Do.27Q-5 (Stored)	2042	(TF-FHK)
			LN-BDD(3)
			OY-AFZ
			D-EKOC
LN-BDE(5)	Fuji FA-200-160 Aero Subaru (Stored)	220	D-EBPV
			PH-LEA
LN-BDF(3)	Cessna A.185E	1047	N11B
			(N4450F)
LN-BDG	Cessna 180	32150	N3352D
LN-BDH(2)	Piper PA-28-140 Cherokee	28-23019	N9577W
LN-BDI (3)	SAAB S.91B-2 Safir	91328	RNoAF57328
			328/UA-I'
LN-BDJ (2)	SOCATA MS.880B Rallye-Club	1909	SE-FSL
LN-BDL (3)	Cessna 172P	74491	N52302
LN-BDM	de Havilland DH.82A Tiger Moth	85294	G-ANSC
			DE248
LN-BDO(3)	Cessna 170B	27048	N3505D
LN-BDV(3)	Piper PA-28-180 Cherokee D	28-5394	
LN-BDX(2)	Reims/Cessna F.172M	0916	
LN-BDY	Piper PA-28-140 Cherokee B (Stored)	28-25602	
LN-BDZ	Piper PA-28-140 Cherokee B	28-25644	
LN-BEA(2)	Piper J-3C-90 Cub	16353	SE-BCT
LN-BED(2)	Maule M-5-180C	8061C	OY-CPM
	(Rebuilt with parts from LN-AEU c/n 8021C)		N749RC
LN-BEE(4)	SOCATA MS.893A Rallye Commodore 180	10929	SE-CIW
LN-BEF	Lake LA-4 Buccaneer (W/o 12.6.88)	411	N7638L
LN-BEG(2)	SIAI FN-333 Riviera (Stored)	009	SE-CWN
			I-SIAU
LN-BEH	Reims/Cessna F.150L	0707	
LN-BEL	Cessna I50F	61903	SE-ESN
			N8603S
LN-BEM	Cessna U.206E Stationair	01530	N9130M
LN-BEN(2)	Cessna T.210M Turbo Centurion	61584	OH-CHP
			N732KY
LN-BEQ(2)	Dornier DO 228-201	8016	SE-IKY
			(D-IBLH)
LN-BER(2)	Dornier DO 228-212	8192	F-ODYC
			D-CJKM
			D-CBDB(4)
LN-BET	Piper PA-32-260 Cherokee Six	32-7100016	
LN-BEV(2)	Cessna 180H (Stored)	51550	N2750X
LN-BEW(2)	Cessna U.206G Stationair II (W/o 13.8.86)	04664	N732EG
LN-BEX	Cessna 177A Cardinal (W/o .84)	01264	SE-FEF
			N30453
LN-BFC	Aero Commander 100 Darter (Cr.85)	254	
LN-BFD(4)	Piper PA-18-I50 Super Cub	18-7663	SE-CRY
			OH-CPM
LN-BFG (4)	Piper PA-38-112 Tomahawk (W/o 29.9.90)	38-79A0881	SE-ICH
LN-BFH(4)	Rockwell Commander 112A (W/o 14.1.88)	422	OY-AZY
			N1422J
LN-BFK (3)	Piper PA-28-140 Cherokee F	28-7325139	N15689
LN-BFL (3)	Piper PA-38-112 Tomahawk	38-79A1025	
LN-BFN(3)	Piper PA-28-140 Cherokee F	28-7325140	N15690
LN-BFO (3)	Piper PA-38-112 Tomahawk	38-79A1026	
LN-BFP (3)	Cessna U.206F Stationair	01928	(N50479)
LN-BFQ	Cessna U.206D Stationair	1352	(N72286)
LN-BFS(3)	Auster 5	1788	SE-BZL
			TW440
LN-BFT (2)	Piper J-3C-65 Cub	12811	LN-OAE
	(t/n 12641 officially quoted as c/n)		44-80515
LN-BFU(3)	Cessna U.206G Floatplane	04763	N733EX
LN-BFV	Auster J/1 Autocrat	2005	(LN-BFT)
			G-AGYN
LN-BFY	de Havilland DH.114 Heron 1B	14015	"LN-PSG"
			G-AOXL
			(LN-BFY)
			G-AOXL
			PK-GHB
LN-BGA(2)	Piper PA-23-180 Cherokee Challenger	28-7305525	(SE-GDL)
LN-BGB	Cessna U.206F Stationair	01757	
LN-BGE	Cessna 172L	59927	N3827Q
LN-BGG	Cessna 172K	58781	N7081G
LN-BGH	Cessna 172K	57409	N46648

Regn.	Type	C/n	Prev.Id.
LN-BGI	Piper PA-28-151 Cherokee Warrior (Wfu)	28-7415068	
LN-BGJ	Cessna 180H	52565	(N9910N)
LN-BGK	EAA Acro Sport	01	
LN-BGL	Cessna U.206F Stationair (W/o 11.6.83)	02853	N1168Q
LN-BGM	Reims/Cessna F.172M	1070	
LN-BGO	Cessna A.185F	02437	(N1716R)
LN-BGP	Cessna U.206F Stationair (W/o 13.4.95)	02254	(N1548U)
LN-BGQ(2)	Piper PA-28-161 Warrior II	28-8116219	(SE-IKA)
LN-BGR	Cessna 150D	60457	SE-EHL
			OY-TRI
			N4557U
LN-BGS	Reims/Cessna F.172M (W/o 2.10.93)	1306	
LN-BGT	Piper PA-28-151 Cherokee Warrior	28-7515208	
LN-BGY	Bowers Fly-Baby 1A (W/o 7.5.88)	71-8	
LN-BGZ	Piper PA-28RT-201 Arrow IV	28R-7918251	SE-ICR
LN-BIA(2)	Piper PA-39 Twin Comanche C/R	39-129	G-AZIA
	(W/o 7.6.90)		N8966Y
LN-BIB(2)	SOCATA MS.893A Rallye Commodore 180	12063	
	(W/o 8.9.90)		
LN-BIC	Reims/Cessna F.172L (Stored)	0812	(D-ECHL)
LN-BID(3)	SOCATA Rallye 100ST (Stored)	3045	
LN-BIG(4)	Aerotek Pitts S-2A (Stored)	2042	N42PS
LN-BIH(2)	Cessna 172B	48149	SE-CXH
			N7649X
LN-BII (3)	SAAB S.91B Safir	91284	RNoAF0074
			Fv50074
LN-BIK(2)	Cessna 180H	52105	(LN-UXZ)
			N9005M
LN-BIL(3)	SOCATA MS.880B Rallye Club	2963	
LN-BIM(2)	Cessna 180H (Stored)	51566	N2766X
LN-BIQ(2)	SOCATA Rallye 235E Gabier	13326	
LN-BIS(3)	SOCATA MS.880B Rallye Club	2950	
LN-BIT(2)	Piper PA-28-140 Cherokee	28-23520	N11C
			N9973W
LN-BIV(5)	SAAB MFI-15-200A	15801	SE-S31
LN-BIX(2)	Cessna 172N	68317	TF-BHX
			N733HX
LN-BIZ	SOCATA Rallye 150T	2656	
LN-BJV	Van's RV-4	1446	
LN-BND	Piper PA-22-108 Colt (W/o 10.12.92)	22-8947	(N10F)
LN-BNE	Stinson 108-1 Voyager	1793	N8793K
LN-BNG(3)	SAAB MFI-9B Trainer	061	SE-EUG
LN-BNL	Piper PA-22-108 Colt (Stored)	22-9170	
LN-BNR(4)	Cessna 177RG Cardinal RG	0809	TF-IOO(3)
			TF-SPE
			N7511V
LN-BNS(3)	Orlican L-40 Meta-Sokol	150713	LN-BNS(1)
			OK-NMR
LN-BNW	Piper PA-22-108 Colt (Wfu .90)	22-8987	(N10F)
LN-BOL	Cessna U.206G Stationair II	05504	SE-INO
			LN-ALY
			N6616U
LN-BOS	Neico Lancair 320	318	
LN-BRC	Boeing 737-505	24650	N5573K
LN-BRD	Boeing 737-505	24651	
LN-BRE	Boeing 737-405	24643	
LN-BRF	Boeing 737-505	24652	D-ACBA
			LN-BRF
LN-BRG	Boeing 737-505	24272	
LN-BRH	Boeing 737-505	24828	D-ACBB
			LN-BRH
LN-BRI	Boeing 737-405	24644	9M-MLL
			LN-BRI
LN-BRJ	Boeing 737-505	24273	D-ACBC
			(LN-BRJ)
LN-BRK	Boeing 737-505	24274	
LN-BRM	Boeing 737-505	24645	
LN-BRN	Boeing 737-505	24646	
LN-BRO	Boeing 737-505	24647	
LN-BRP	Boeing 737-405	25303	9M-MLK
			LN-BRP
LN-BRQ	Boeing 737-505	25348	
LN-BRR	Boeing 737-505	24648	
LN-BRS	Boeing 737-505	24649	
LN-BRU	Boeing 737-505	25790	

Regn.	Type	C/n	Prev.Id.
LN-BRV	Boeing 737-505	25791	
LN-BRX	Boeing 737-505	25797	
LN-BSB	Quickie Q-1	262	
LN-BSN	Svein Nordahl Quickie Q-2 (Stored)	261	
LN-BUC	Boeing 737-505	26304	
LN-BUD	Boeing 737-505	25794	(LN-BUA)
LN-BUE	Boeing 737-505	27627	
LN-BUF	Boeing 737-405	25795	
LN-BUG	Boeing 737-505	27631	
LN-BWE(2)	Piper PA-23-160 Apache	23-1509	N4033P
LN-BWF(2)	Cessna 180	50813	SE-CTY
			N9313T
LN-BWH(2)	Cessna 180H	51995	N3495Y
			N29205
LN-BWL	Luscombe 8F Silvaire Floatplane	S-76	N3544G
LN-BWM	Cessna 180	50986	N6486X
LN-BWO	Reims/Cessna FRA.150L Aerobat	0154	
LN-BWU(2)	Piper J-3C-65 Cub	13202	SE-CGU
			LN-RAI
			45-4462
LN-BWW(2)	Cessna U.206F Floatplane	01994	(N51300)
LN-BWY	Reims/Cessna FRA.150L Aerobat (Stored)	0172	
LN-BWZ	Reims/Cessna FR.172J Rocket	0374	
LN-DAA(2)	Cessna 172N	69065	SE-GOX
	(Rebuilt with new fuselage 1978-9)		N734RX
LN-DAC(2)	Cessna 182M Skylane	59391	SE-FEO
			N70847
LN-DAE(2)	Reims/Cessna F.172M	1201	(LN-BGS)
			D-EOQN
LN-DAG(2)	Reims/Cessna F.172M	1219	(OY-BIN)
LN-DAH(2)	Reims/Cessna F.172M	1471	SE-GMB
LN-DAL(2)	Reims/Cessna F.172H	0681	SE-FMS
LN-DAO(2)	Reims/Cessna F.172M (W/o 31.7.88)	1431	
LN-DAP(2)	MFI-9B Trainer	036	(LN-BFL)
			SE-ENA
LN-DAV(2)	Reims/Cessna F.172M	1479	
LN-DAW	Reims/Cessna F.172N	1573	
LN-DAX	Piper PA-28-151 Cherokee Warrior	28-7515176	N32529
LN-DAY	Reims/Cessna F.172N	1608	
LN-DAZ	Reims/Cessna F.172N	1620	
LN-DBA(2)	Cessna 180C	50810	SE-CXA
			N9310T
LN-DBC(2)	Cessna 172P	75187	OY-CJC
			N55471
LN-DBF(2)	Cessna U.206B	0779	N3479L
LN-DBG	Cessna 185	0136	N9936X
LN-DBI (2)	Piper PA-28-140 Cherokee F	28-7325219	
	(Wfu .86, to instructional airframe)		
LN-DBJ(2)	Cessna A.185F	03369	(N7347H)
LN-DBK(2)	Beech A23-24 Musketeer (Dam. 6.9.96)	MA-228	
LN-DBM(2)	Cessna 206	0117	N5117U
LN-DBQ	Cessna U.206F Stationair (W/o 30.9.87)	03563	N7206N
LN-DBR	Cessna 172D	50165	(N2565U)
LN-DBU	Cessna 172C	49398	N1698Y
LN-DBY	Cessna 182N Skylane	60103	N92231
LN-DDD	Rutan Defiant	0024B	
LN-DHC	DHC-1 Chipmunk 22	C1/0038	WB586
LN-DRF	Viking Dragonfly Mk.2 (Cr. 1.6.97)	594	
LN-FAA	Piper PA-22-108 Colt	22-9353	
LN-FAB	Taylor J-2 Cub	980	
LN-FAD(3)	Piel CP.301C Emeraude (To museum)	L-355/67	
LN-FAE(3)	Piper PA-28-151 Cherokee Warrior	28-7615379	N5905F
	(W/o 5.8.86)		N9608N
LN-FAF	Cessna 150 (Stored)	17257	SE-CNN
			OY-AEF
			N5757E
LN-FAG(3)	Reims/Cessna F.172M	1485	
LN-FAH(3)	Rockwell Commander 690B	11367	OY-BEJ
			N888TB
			D-IAWW
			N81547
LN-FAJ	BAe. Jetstream Series 3102	621	G-BTXL
			(D-C . . .)
			G-BTXL
			G-BLDO
			(G-BLCY)
			G-31-621
LN-FAK(2)	SOCATA MS.893E Rallye 180GT Gaillard	13008	
LN-FAL(3)	BAe. Jetstream Series 3101	604	OY-CLC
			SE-IPC
			G-BKHI
			SE-IPC
			G-BKHI
LN-FAM(3)	BAe. Jetstream Series 3112	740	C-GJPO
			(N2247R)
			C-GJPO
			(N331QC)
			G-31-740
LN-FAT(2)	SOCATA Rallye 180T Galérien	2972	
LN-FAU(2)	Reims/Cessna F.172N (W/o 25.8.85)	1644	
LN-FAV(4)	BAe. Jetstream Series 3102	606	OY-CLB
			SE-KHA
			G-BKKY
			(SE-IZA)
			G-BKKY
			G-31-46
LN-FAW(2)	Reims/Cessna F.172N	1703	
LN-FAX	Cessna U.206G Stationair II (W/o 21.3.82)	04100	(N756HH)
LN-FAY	Cessna U.206G Stationair II	04326	
LN-FAZ(2)	BAe. Jetstream Series 3112	749	C-GJPU
			(N839JS)
			G-31-749
LN-FIX	Cessna T337GP Pressurised Skymaster / Riley Rocket	P337-0265	N772H
			N1ZG
LN-FKE	Piper PA-31-310 Navajo	31-293	SE-FFE
			LN-NPL
			SE-FFE
LN-FKL	SOCATA MS.893A Rallye Commodore 180	11471	SE-FNL
			OY-DJT
LN-FLY	Denney Kitfox III	1066	
LN-FMU	SAAB S.91B Safir	91267	RNoAF058
	(Painted as RNoAF "FM-U")		Fv.50058
LN-FOB	Piper PA-28-151 Cherokee Warrior	28-7415344	SE-GBN
LN-FOC	Cessna 210H	59007	SE-FBY
			N6107F
LN-FOF(3)	Piper PA-28-180 Cherokee Challenger	28-7305404	SE-GDY
LN-FOI (3)	Lockheed L-188CF Electra	2005	(LN-MOF)
			N31231
			ZK-TEA
			(ZK-BMP)
			N9724C
LN-FOK(2)	Piper PA-28-180 Cherokee B	28-1061	
LN-FOL(2)	Lockheed L-188C Electra	1116	N669F
			N404GN
			N6126A
LN-FON(2)	Lockheed L-188C Electra	1128	N342HA
			N417MA
			OB-R-1138
			HP-684
			N417MA
			CF-ZST
			N7142C
LN-FOP(2)	Piper PA-28-140 Cherokee	28-22922	SE-EYP
LN-FSA	Piper PA 28-181 Cherokee Archer II	28-7890549	OY-BRH
LN-FSB	Piper PA-28-140 Cherokee	28-23870	OY-DNM
			(LN-VYR)
LN-FTN	Cessna U.206C Stationair	1116	LN-LMW
	(painted but not yet re-regd)		N29146
LN-FWA	Gulfstream Commander 690C	11681	(LN-FAN)
			SE-IUV
			N110WE
			ZS-KZO
			N5933K
LN-HAB(2)	Cessna 150F	63502	N11B
			N6902F

Regn.	Type	C/n	Prev.Id.
LN-HAE(4)	Cessna 310R	0525	TF-EUT
			TF-ELT
			OY-BJN
			N87353
LN-HAF(2)	Piper PA-22-150 Caribbean	22-7359	SE-CSY
LN-HAG(4)	Pottier P.180S	148	
LN-HAH(2)	Cessna 210L Centurion	60751	
LN-HAI (3)	Cessna U.206F Stationair	03058	N4696Q
LN HAJ(2)	Light Aero Avid Magnum	43	
LN-HAK(2)	Piper PA-28-140 Cherokee *(Museum, Bodo)*	28-20733	(SE-EOF)
LN-HAM(3)	Cessna U.206F Stationair	02689	N33244
LN-HAN(2)	Piper PA-28-140 Cherokee	28-20353	(SE-EML)
LN-HAR(4)	Piper PA-18-150 Super Cub	18-1566	(LN-HHN)
			D-ELTB
			ALAT
			51-15566
LN-HAS(2)	Cessna 150D	60568	LN-BIE
			N4568U
LN-HAU(2)	Piper PA-18A-150 Super Cub	18-6642	SE-CLE
LN-HAV(2)	Piper PA-18-150 Super Cub *(W/o 20.11.88)*	18-7247	SE-CSS
LN-HAW(2)	Cessna 150F	62678	N11B
			N8578G
LN-HAX	Piper J-3C-65 Cub *(Stored)*	12874	D-EBIW
	(Officially quoted as Dätwyler c/n 12500)		HB-ONO
			44-80578
LN-HFK	SOCATA TB-10 Tobago *(Stored)*	78	SE-GFK
LN-HHA(4)	Piper PA-18-150 Super Cub	18-1570	(LN-HHA(2))
			D-EMTJ
			ALAT
			51-15570
LN-HHH	Piper PA-28-140 Cherokee	28-20950	
LN-HHI (2)	Piper PA-18S-135 Super Cub	18-2094	(LN-HHE)
			D-ELTG
			ALAT
			52-2494
LN-HHK(2)	Piper PA-28-180 Cherokee C *(Cr 25.8.91)*	28-3170	(SE-EYK)
LN-HHO(2)	Piper PA-18-150 Super Cub	18-1450	D-ELTN
	(Destroyed 25.12.86)		ALAT
			51-15450
LN-HHR	Piper PA-28-140 Cherokee	28-21085	
LN-HHS(2)	SAAB S.91B-2 Safir	91210	Fv50010
LN-HHW(2)	SAAB S.91B-2 Safir	91252	(SE-LBG)
	(Stored)		LN-HHW(2)
			RNoAF:040
			Fv50040
LN-HIH	Cessna 182M Skylane	59653	SE-LDF
			(SE-LEM)
			OY-AGR
			N71528
LN-HOA(2)	Reims/Cessna F.182Q Skylane	0154	
LN-HOE	Cessna U.206G Stationair II	05143	(N4885U)
LN-HOF	Reims/Cessna F.172N	1896	
LN-HOG	Cessna 172N	72740	N6354D
LN-HOK	Rockwell Commander 114	14111	N4781W
LN-HON	Cessna U.206G Stationair II	05475	(N6397U)
LN-HOO	Cessna TU.206G Floatplane	05490	(N6493U)
LN-HOQ	Reims/Cessna F.172P *(Dbr? 13.2.88)*	2035	
LN-HOR	Piper PA-28-140 Cherokee E	28-7225264	SE-FYX
LN-HOV(2)	Rand-Robinson KR-2	10057	
LN-HOX	Reims/Cessna F.172P	2029	
LN-HOY	Reims/Cessna F.172N	1928	
LN-HOZ	Cessna U.206G Floatplane	04279	SE-GYK
			N756QU
LN-HPB	Rutan LongEz	190	
LN-HPC	Grumman-American AA-5A Cheetah	0841	G-BGCN
LN-HPD	SAAB S.91B-2 Safir *(W/o 5.3.89)*	91345	RNoAF57345
			345/UA-Z
LN-HPJ	Cessna TP.206C Turbo Super Skylane	0502	SE-FED
	(Under restoration)		N8702Z
LN-HPT	Cessna 310R	0083	OY-BIW
			(SE-GKA)
LN-HTA	Dornier DO 228-202	8127	(VT-...?)
			D-CBDE(5)
			N262MC
			D-CBDG(1)

Regn.	Type	C/n	Prev.Id.
LN-HUS	Vans' RV-4 *(Reservation)*	1486	
LN- IGA	Jungster 1	J1-73012R	(LN-HOT(2))
LN- IGB	Condor YAK-52	888814	UR-BEO
			UR-BTN
			DOSAAF-86
LN- IKA	Cessna TU.206G Turbo Stationair II	06251	(N6356Z)
LN- IKB(3)	Auster Mk.5	1550	SE-BZC
	(Wfu .77, for rebuild)		G-AJLE
			TJ541
LN- IKD(2)	Cessna 150F	62147	(SE-ESP)
			N8847S
LN- IKG(2)	Cessna 172C	49042	OY-AFI
			N1342Y
LN- IKJ	Piper J-3C-65 Cub (L-4J)	12081	(SE-ASO)
			LN-IKJ
			SE-ASO
			44-79785
LN- IKK	Republic RC-3 Seabee	270	SE-AXR
LN- IKO	Cessna 180B	50435	SE-CLS
			N5135E
LN- IKP	Piper PA-22-108 Colt *(Stored)*	22-9128	(LN-IKI)
			LN-IKP
			(SE-CZH)
LN- IKQ	Reims/Cessna FR.172F Rocket	0101	(G-AWYC)
LN- IKS	Cessna 172C *(W/o 22.1.94)*	49255	N1555Y
LN- IKX	Reims/Cessna F.150J	0420	
LN- IKY	Cessna 172P	74139	N5473K
LN- ILS	DHC-8 Series 103	396	(LN-WIL)
LN-JAN	Sequoia F.8L Falco	626	
LN-JBL	Cessna 172G	54437	N4362L
LN-JET	de Havilland DH.100 Vampire Mk.6	655	LN-17
	(Flies as RNoAF "ZK-P")		(LN-JET)
			J-1146
LN-JYS	Van's RV-4 *(Reservation)*	unkn	
LN-KAC	Piper PA-22-150 Tri-Pacer	22-5368	SE-CDC
			N7658D
LN-KAD(4)	Piper PA-18-150 Super Cub	18-7809141	(OY-CGS(3))
			SE-IAO
LN-KAE(3)	SOCATA TB-10 Tobago	27	F-ODKL
LN-KAF(4)	Piper PA-28-181 Cherokee Archer II	28-7690341	(LN-AED)
			OY-CTW
			N6101J
LN-KAH	Auster J/1 Autocrat	2044	SE-ARM
LN-KAI (3)	Piper PA-23-250 Aztec E	27-7304954	SE-KHV
			OY-RPW
			G-BARU
			N14367
LN-KAJ	Grumman-American AA-5 Traveler	0372	(OY-GAA)
			(N5472L)
LN-KAK	Piper J-3C-65 Cub *(Rebuilt)*	LFS-1/56	SE-CBR
LN-KAL(2)	Aero Designs Pulsar	179	
LN-KAM	Reims/Cessna F.150G	0111	
LN-KAN	Cessna P.206A Super Skylane *(W/o 4.7.94)*	0270	N4670F
LN-KAO	Cessna A.185E	1187	N4733Q
LN-KAQ	Champion 7ECA Citabria	540	N5107T
LN-KAY	de Havilland DH.82A Tiger Moth	84616	SE-COL
	(Cr 14.7.90, rebuilding)		T6168
LN-KCA	Cessna A.185F	01302	N335OL
LN-KCC	Cessna 177 Cardinal	00995	N29618
LN-KCD	Reims/Cessna F.150H	0312	
LN-KCE	Reims/Cessna F.150H	0333	
LN-KCF	Cessna 180H	51952	N3452Y
LN-KCG(3)	Beech 65-C90 King Air	LJ-768	OY-SBU
LN-KCH	Piper PA-18-150 Super Cub	18-8579	(SE-...)
			N4995P
LN-KCJ	Cessna 140	8529	LN-TSV
	(Quoted officially as c/n 11721)		SE-AZZ
			LN-NAK
LN-KCL	Piper PA-28-140 Cherokee	28-23576	N11C
			N3527K
LN-KCM(2)	Piper PA-18A-150 Super Cub	18-5878	D-EGCI
			N7582D
LN-KCN	Auster 6A Tugmaster	3743	SE-ELM
			VF514

Regn.	Type	C/n	Prev.Id.
LN-KCO	Piper PA-18 Super Cub 95	18-2051	(LN-BFR)
			R-42
			52-2451
LN-KCR(2)	Beech 65-C90 King Air (W/o 2.4.87)	LJ-793	
LN-KCU	Piper PA-18 Super Cub 95	18-2053	R-68
			52-2453
LN-KCX	Piper PA-18 Super Cub 95	18-2062	R-76
			52-2462
LN-KCY(2)	Maule M-7-235 Super Rocket	4014C	OY-CRZ
			HR-AKY
			N5657H
LN-KIT	Denney Kitfox 1 (W/o 25.6.94)	157	
LN-KJK	Cessna 208B Grand Caravan	0554	N1267A
LN-KKA	Fokker F.27-050	20117	PH-DLT
			D-AFKY
			PH-DLT
			OE-LFZ
			(VH-FNL)
			PH-EXA
LN-KKD	Fokker F.27-050	20230	PT-SLR
			PH-JXF
LN-KKE	Fokker F.27-050	20226	PT-SLQ
			PH-JXC
			PH-EXC
LN-KKK	Piper PA-34-220T Seneca V	3449010	SE-KEP
			N92865
LN-KLB(2)	Grumman-American AA-5B Tiger	0729	
LN-KLC	Grumman-American AA-5A Cheetah	0549	F-GBDK
LN-KLD(2)	SOCATA TB-9 Tampico	225	
LN-KLE(3)	SOCATA TB-9 Tampico	127	F-GCOE
LN-KLF(2)	Grumman-American AA-5A Cheetah	0610	
LN-KLG(2)	Grumman-American AA-5A Cheetah	0014	SE-GRF
			OY-GAH
LN-KLH(2)	Grumman-American AA-5A Cheetah	0844	
LN-KLI(2)	Grumman-American AA-5B Tiger	1131	
LN-KLM	SOCATA TB-9 Tampico	303	
LN-KLO	SOCATA TB-9 Tampico	692	
LN-KLP(2)	SOCATA TB-10 Tobago	390	
LN-KLQ	Mooney M.20J Model 201	24-1597	OY-CGK
LN-KLR(2)	SOCATA TB-9 Tampico	738	
LN-KLW	Piel CP.301 Emeraude	1-79A	
LN-LAG(2)	Neico Lancair 320	1	
LN-LFB	Mooney M.20C Ranger	690028	N9157V
LN-LFG	SOCATA MS.893E Rallye 180GT Gaillard	3242	SE-GFD
LN-LFI	Piper PA-24-250 Comanche	24-2898	SE-EPA
	(W/o 18.10.92)		N7688P
LN-LFJ	Pottier P.180S	162	
LN-LFK	SAAB S.91B-2 Safir	91341	RNoAF:57341
			341/UA-V
LN-LFM	SOCATA MS.880B Rallye-Club	1522	OY-DJM
LN-LGB	Cessna 150G	66260	N8360J
LN-LGC	Cessna 172B	47960	SE-CXU
			N7460X
LN-LGF	Reims/Cessna F.172P (W/o 29.6.88)	2050	(EI-BIN)
			(EI-BIC)
LN-LGG	Reims/Cessna F.172N	1929	SE-IFG
LN-LJB	Cessna 210G	58936	SE-FBC
			N5936F
LN-LJD	Piper PA-18-150 Super Cub	18-8541	SE-GCA
			Fv51234
LN-LJF	Reims/Cessna F.172H	0572	(G-AXBI)
LN-LJJ	Piper PA-18 Super Cub 95	18-3088	OL-L14
			53-4688
LN-LJK	Piper PA-18 Super Cub 95 (Stored)	18-3103	OL-L29
			53-4703
LN-LJM	Piper PA-18 Super Cub 95	18-3122	OL-L48
			53-4722
LN-LJT	Cessna 180H (W/o 8.9.86)	52088	N91450
LN-LJZ	Cessna A.185E (W/o 9.8.90)	01841	(N1629M)
LN-LMA(2)	Denney Kitfox IV	1635	
LN-LMB(2)	Piper PA-28-140 Cherokee	28-24421	
LN-LMD(2)	Aero Commander 680FL	1401-56	N8484A
	(To museum, Sola)	CF-SHC	
LN-LME(2)	Piper PA-28-140 Cherokee	28-24441	
LN-LMG(3)	Cessna A.185F	03278	SE-GZN

Regn.	Type	C/n	Prev.Id.
LN-LMH(2)	Cessna TU.206B Turbo Stationair	0850	N3850G
	(W/o 30.7.90)		
LN-LMI (2)	C.L.Larsen Special II (Cr. 6.8.82, wfu)	02	LN-11
LN-LMJ	Cessna U.206C Super Skywagon Floatplane	1163	N29205
LN-LMK(5)	Piper PA-34-200T Seneca	34-7870278	OY-AUC
			5Y-BCW
			N31940
			N8885D
LN-LMM(2)	Aero Commander 680FL (Stored)	1355-34	N6335U
LN-LMN(2)	Aero Commander 680FL (Dism. 87)	1202-106	N78342
LN-LMO(3)	Grumman-American AA-5 Traveler	0262	OY-AYU
LN-LMP(4)	Reims/Cessna FRA.150L Aerobat	0131	SE-GFY
			LN-BWJ
LN-LMR(3)	Piper PA-28R-180 Cherokee Arrow	28R-30976	
LN-LMV	Cessna U.206C Stationair (W/o 18.8.89)	1118	N29148
LN-LMX(2)	Aeritalia/Partenavia AP.68TP Spartacus	8006	I-RA1Z
LN-LMY(2)	SAAB S.91B-2 Safir (Wfu .84)	91281	RNoAF:071
			Fv50071
LN-LMZ(2)	Dornier Do.28A-1 (Stored)	3003	D-IHOL
LN-LOK	Cessna P210N Pressurized Centurion II	00394	N6181K
LN-LTH	Cessna 182E	54027	(OY-EHL)
			(LN-EHL)
			N3027Y
LN-LTP	Van's RV-4	1403	
LN-LYR	Dornier 228-202K	8166	D-CTCA
			TC-FBP
			D-CBCE
			D-CBDW
LN-MAB(3)	Rutan LongEz	2072	
LN-MAE(3)	Beagle A.61 Terrier	3740	(LN-MAU)
			(LN-BNH)
			SE-ELL
			VF543
LN-MAH(2)	Cessna 441 Conquest	0002	(SE-IBI)
	(W/o 17.7.86, remains sold to USA)		N9175G
LN-MAI (3)	MFI-9B Trainer (Dbf c.89)	017	SE-EFD
LN-MAJ	Cessna 310R	0627	(N98871)
LN-MAK(2)	Cessna U.206F Stationair (W/o 19.11.76)	03143	(N8282Q)
LN-MAL (2)	Cessna U.206F Stationair (Dbr .86)	03153	(N8292Q)
LN-MAQ	Cessna U.206G Stationair II	03733	SE-GZY
			(N9933N)
LN-MAR(3)	SkyStar Denney Kitfox IV	1636	
LN-MAS(2)	Cessna A.185E (W/o 11.10.86 Tanzania)	01938	SE-FXN
			N70068
LN-MAT(3)	Piper PA-34-200T Seneca II	34-7670341	OY-BLW
LN-MAV	Piper J-3C-65 Cub (L-4J)	13157	45-4417
LN-MAX(2)	de Havilland DH.82A Tiger Moth	84167	(G-ASPV)
	(Constructed from the original frame of c/n		T7794
	84167 but uses paperwork of c/n 85738		
	LN-BDO, G-ANSE, DE840))		
LN-MAZ	SAAB S.91D Safir	91433	G-BCFS
			PH-RLV
LN-MOA(3)	Beech 200 Super King Air	BB-582	N47PA
			N78LB
			N82LB
LN-MOB(3)	Beech 200 Super King Air	BB-584	(N490WP)
			N400WP
			N6679H
LN-MOC(2)	Beech B200 Super King Air	BB-1449	N200KA
LN-MOD(4)	Beech B200 Super King Air	BB-1459	N8163R
LN-MOE(2)	Beech B200 Super King Air	BB-1460	N8164G
LN-MOF(3)	Beech B200 Super King Air	BB-1461	N8261E
LN-MOG(3)	Beech B200 Super King Air	BB-1465	N8214T
LN-MOH(3)	Beech B200 Super King Air	BB-1466	N8216Z
LN-MOI (2)	Beech B200 Super King Air	BB-1470	N8225Z
LN-MOK	Cessna 182 Skylane	33768	(LN-ATS)
			(LN-IKJ)
			OY-BZG
			D-EBRX
			OE-DKS
			N5768B
LN-MOM	Piper PA-28-180 Cherokee C	28-3981	SE-EZR
LN-MOZ	Grumman-American AA-5B Tiger	0053	OY-GAF
LN-MTA(4)	Cessna U.206G Stationair II	05641	N5322X
LN-MTC(2)	Reims/Cessna F.172M	1261	

Regn.	Type	C/n	Prev.Id.
LN-MTD(3)	Cessna 177RG Cardinal RG	0895	N7627V
	(Rebuilt using front section of c/n 0846 ex N7549V)		
LN-MTE(2)	Cessna 182N Skylane	60245	SE-FXU
			OH-CDR
			N92525
LN-MTF(2)	Cessna R.182 Skylane RG	00551	N1763R
LN-MTG(2)	Cessna 172P (W/o 27.8.93)	74775	N53533
LN-MTH(2)	Cessna 172N	72201	N8443E
			(OY-CYK)
			N8443E
LN-MTI	Cessna U.206F Stationair	03170	N8309Q
LN-MTJ	Piper PA-28-161 Warrior II	28-8216021	N8330G
LN-MTM(2)	Cessna 172P	74333	N51639
LN-MTN	Piper PA-28-140 Cherokee D	28-7125348	
LN-MTO	Cessna 140	8864	LN-BNT
			N89815
LN-MTP(2)	Cessna 172P	75197	N55522
LN-MTQ	Cessna A.185E	01839	N1625M
LN-MTR	Cessna R.172K Hawk XP	2423	N736CP
LN-MTS(2)	Cessna 182Q Skylane	65900	N759DA
LN-MTT(2)	Cessna 172M	63835	N20781
LN-MTU(3)	Cessna 172P	75510	N64050
LN-MTV(2)	Piper PA-23-250 Aztec E	27-4741	SE-IMC
			PH-DEN
			D-IHFF
			N14177
LN-MTW	Cessna 182N Skylane	60459	N8919G
LN-MTX	Cessna 172P	74671	N53043
LN-NAA(2)	Cessna U.206F Stationair	03199	N11KB
			(N8338Q)
LN-NAB(3)	Piper PA-31-310 Navajo C	31-8012029	OY-BYJ
			PH-URI
			N1002W
			PH-URI
			N3552V
LN-NAD(3)	Cessna TU.206G Turbo Stationair II	05639	(N5320X)
	(W/o 8.6.84)		
LN-NAE(2)	Cessna 177RG Cardinal RG	1009	N34611
LN-NAG(2)	Piper PA-28-161 Cherokee Warrior II	28-7816376	
LN-NAH(2)	Piper PA-28-181 Cherokee Archer II	28-7690194	
LN-NAK(2)	Reims/Cessna F.172H (W/o 29.10.85)	0604	(LN-RTJ)
LN-NAL(2)	Piper PA-28-151 Cherokee Warrior	28-7615377	
LN-NAM(2)	Piper PA-28-181 Cherokee Archer II	28-7690386	
LN-NAN(2)	Piper PA-28-151 Cherokee Warrior	28-7715212	
	(W/o 20.10.77)		
LN-NAO(2)	Piper PA-28-161 Cherokee Warrior II	28-7716166	
LN-NAQ	Piper PA-28-181 Cherokee Archer II	28-7790302	
LN-NAR	Piper PA-28-161 Cherokee Warrior II	28-7716054	
LN-NAS(2)	Piper PA-28-161 Cherokee Warrior II	28-7716055	
LN-NAU	Piper J-3C-65 Cub (L-4H) (Stored)	11673	43-30482
LN-NAV(2)	Piper PA-18-90 Super Cub	18-1342	D-EAEQ
			ALAT
			51-15342
LN-NAW(2)	Piper PA-32R-300 Lance (W/o 25.7.97)	32R-7780281	
LN-NAY	Piper PA-28-181 Cherokee Archer II	28-7790488	
LN-NAZ	Piper PA-28-161 Cherokee Warrior II	28-7816220	
LN-NFA(2)	Cessna 182Q Skylane	66169	D-EAGW
	(Rebuilt 1992 using fuselage from		N759QF
	Cessna 182P D-EDVF c/n 64428)		
LN-NFB	Reims/Cessna F.172P	2111	D-EGWJ
LN-NFC(2)	Cessna U.206G Stationair	06489	D-EGOP(3)
			N27173
			(N9437Z)
LN-NFD	Cessna A.185F	04152	N61342
LN-NFF	Cessna 177RG Cardinal RG (Stored)	1309	N8707Z
LN-NFG	Cessna 172P	74277	N51194
LN-NFH	Piper PA-28-140 Cherokee E (Stored)	28-7225299	SE-GAG
LN-NFI	Reims/Cessna F.152	1766	D-EITF
LN-NFJ (2)	Reims/Cessna F.172M	1483	D-EOXY
			(G-BDZE)
LN-NFK(3)	SOCATA MS.Rallye 235E	12798	SE-GTC
LN-NFL	Reims/Cessna F.172L	0807	D-EHMS
			PH-JBA
LN-NFN(2)	Piper PA-23-235 Apache (Stored)	27-533	TF-ELL
			N4948P

Regn.	Type	C/n	Prev.Id.
LN-NFP(2)	Cessna 177RG Cardinal RG	1336	N53070
LN-NFQ	Cessna 172B (W/o 25.7.86)	48351	SE-CPX
			OY-EAE
			N7851X
LN-NFS	Grumman-American AA-5B Tiger	1208	(N5481V)
			D-EGFC
LN-NFU	Piper PA-38-112 Tomahawk	38-79A0938	D-ELMC
			N9681N
LN-NFW	Reims/Cessna F.172N	1683	SE-FOT
			LN-FAV
LN-NFX	Cessna 172P	74239	N50950
LN-NFY	Piper PA-38-112 Tomahawk	38-79A0775	N2598L
LN-NLC	Cessna 650 Citation III	0028	N328QS
			N148C
LN-NLD	Cessna 650 Citation III	0070	N370TG
			N370QS
			N149C
			(N1315A)
LN-NOA	Beech 200 Super King Air	BB-829	N829AJ
			SE-KVL
			C9-SWE
			N225JL
			N225HP
LN-NOK	Piper PA-18-150 Super Cub	1809054	
LN-NPJ	Auster Mk.5 (Wfu .87)	1410	SE-CDL
			TJ340
LN-NPK	Cessna 172B	48518	SE-CTK
			N8018X
LN-NPN(2)	Piper PA-28-180 Cherokee C (W/o 13.11.78)	28-3247	(SE-EYT)
LN-NPO(2)	Piper PA-28-181 Archer 11	28-8090012	(SE-ICX)
LN-NPQ(2)	Piper PA-28-181 Cherokee Archer 11	28-7890340	
LN-NPR(2)	Piper PA-28R-201 Arrow 111	28R-7837247	
LN-NPS(2)	Piper PA-28-161 Cherokee Warrior 11	28-7816449	
LN-NPT	Piper PA-28-140 Cherokee	28-22832	
LN-NPV	Piper PA-28-140 Cherokee	28-22902	
LN-NPW	Piper PA-28-140 Cherokee	28-22917	
LN-NPX(2)	Cessna 310P	0229	(OY-AKB)
			(LN-TUV)
			N5729M
LN-NPZ	Piper PA-31-310 Navajo	31-7512047	(SE-GIY)
LN-NTH	Piper PA-25-235 Pawnee C	25-4505	SE-FCX
			OH-PIS
			SE-FCX
LN-NVK	Cessna 152	81089	OY-CTY
			(N48988)
LN-OAC	Aérospatiale AS.350B2 Ecureuil	2511	N350R
			D-HMIR
			N6042S
LN-OAD(2)	Robinson R-22B2 Beta	2755	
LN-OAE(2)	Robinson R-44 Astro	0397	
LN-OAF	Rotorway Exec 162F	6208	
LN-OAG	Robinson R-22 Beta	2912	
LN-OAH	Robinson R-22 Beta	2919	
LN-OAI(2)	Robinson R-44 Astro	0608	
LN-OAJ	Robinson R-22 Beta	2051	N62900
LN-OAK(3)	Aérospatiale AS.350B3 Ecureuil	3212	
LN-OAL	Robinson R-44 Astro	0580	
LN-OAM	Robinson R-44 Astro	0452	
LN-OAN	Aérospatiale AS.350B3 Ecureuil	3199	
LN-OAP(2)	Schweizer 269C-1	0057	N297TH
LN-OAQ	Bölkow BO.105S	S-147	D-HCCA
			N90740
			D-HDEO
LN-OAR(2)	Bell 206BJet Ranger II	3616	RP-C1156
			N2271Z
LN-OAS(2)	Bell 206BJet Ranger III	2369	JA9200
LN-OAT(2)	Agusta-Bell 204B	3231	SE-HRL
			LN-OQT
LN-OAV(2)	Aérospatiale AS.350B2 Ecureuil	9015	
LN-OAW(2)	Aérospatiale AS.332L Super Puma	2053	OY-HMH
			LN-OME
LN-OAY	Robinson R-22B2 Beta	3025	
LN-OBA(2)	Aérospatiale AS.332L1 Super Puma	2384	
LN-OBC	Robinson R-22 Beta	1340	
LN-OBE(2)	Robinson R-44 Astro	0078	

Regn.	Type	C/n	Prev.Id.
LN-OBF	Aérospatiale AS.332L1 Super Puma	2381	
LN-OBL	Hughes 269C *(Stored, to Sweden)*	70-0024	(SE-HTY)
			N9615F
LN-OBM	Robinson R-44 Astro	0197	
LN-OBQ	Aérospatiale AS.332L Super Puma	2312	
LN-OBR(2)	Eurocopter EC.120B Colibri	1064	
LN-OBS	Bell 206L-3 Long Ranger III	51235	(LN-OPP)
			C-FBBW
LN-OCB	Aérospatiale AS.350B Ecureuil	1786	D-HAFP
	(W/o 28.7.88)		
LN-OCC	Hughes 369E	0252E	
LN-OCD	Aérospatiale AS.350B1 Ecureuil	2207	
LN-OCE	Aérospatiale SA.315B Lama	2179	5V-MAF
			F-WKQI
LN-OCF	Aérospatiale AS.350B2 Ecureuil	2478	
LN-ODB	Aérospatiale AS.365N2 Dauphin 2	6358	G-NTWO
LN-ODD	Aérospatiale SA.315B Lama	2578	SE-HRX
			(LN-O . .)
			SE-HRX
			F-GEHI
			LN-OSQ
LN-OED	Schweizer 269C	S-1352	OH-HHY
			SE-HTO
			N41S
LN-OEF	Robinson R-44 Astro	0239	
LN-OGT	Robinson R-44 Astro	0484	N7052V
LN-OHA	Aérospatiale AS.332L2 Super Puma	2396	F-WYMS
LN-OHB	Aérospatiale AS.332L2 Super Puma	2398	F-WYMD
LN-OHC	Aérospatiale AS.332L2 Super Puma	2393	F-W . . .
LN-OHD	Aérospatiale AS.332L2 Super Puma	2395	F-WQDN
LN-OHE	Aérospatiale AS.332L2 Super Puma	2474	
LN-OHG	Aérospatiale AS.332L2 Super Puma	2493	
LN-OLB	Aérospatiale AS.332L Super Puma	2082	OY-HMJ
			LN-OLB
			F-WKQA
LN-OLC	Aérospatiale AS.332L Super Puma	2083	(LN-ONE)
			JA6782
			LN-OLC
			F-WKQB
LN-OLD	Aérospatiale AS.332L Super Puma	2103	OY-HMI
			LN-OLD
LN-OLG	Aérospatiale AS.350B1 Ecureuil	2198	
LN-OLK	Bell 212	30722	C-GOKT
			YV-324C
			C-GOKT
LN-OLN	Aérospatiale SA.365N1 Dauphin 2	6115	G-BLUO
LN-OLT	Aérospatiale SA.365N Dauphin 2	6140	G-BLUP
LN-OMB(2)	Aérospatiale AS.350B2 Ecureuil	2514	F-WYMO
LN-OMC	Aérospatiale AS.332L Super Puma	2114	G-BMBV
	(W/o 18.3.96)		LN-OMC
LN-OME(3)	Hughes 369E	0335E	SE-JBV
			N10NT
			C-FFOY
LN-OMG(2)	Aérospatiale SA.315B Lama	2443	SE-HGY
LN-OMH	Aérospatiale AS.332L Super Puma	2113	HZ-RH4
			LN-OMH
LN-OMI	Aérospatiale AS.332L Super Puma	2123	G-PUMJ
			LN-OMI
			G-PUMJ
			LN-OMI
			G-BLZJ
			LN-OMI
			G-BLZJ
			LN-OMI
			F-W . . .
LN-OMJ	Aérospatiale AS.365N2 Dauphin 2	6301	F-WQEZ
			F-WIPI
			G-BVME
			F-WKAY
			F-WYML
LN-OML(2)	McDonnell-Douglas MD.520N	LN-054	
LN-OMM	Bell 214ST	28199	N3216U

Regn.	Type	C/n	Prev.Id.
LN-OMN	Aérospatiale AS.365N2 Dauphin 2	6423	F-GHXG
			(LN-OMN)
			F-GHXG
			F-WYMS
LN-OMP(2)	Hughes 369E	0177E	SE-HRB
LN-OMS	Hughes 369D	91-1067D	SE-HMB
			N5294X
LN-OMT(2)	Aérospatiale AS.332L-1 Super Puma	2468	
LN-OMU	Aérospatiale SA.315B Lama	2643	(LN-OLL)
			F-WXFC
LN-OMW(2)	Hughes 369E	0498E	SE-JBA
			OY-HEI
			N1610Z
LN-OMX(2)	Aérospatiale AS.332L-1 Super Puma	2351	G-BTNZ
			F-WYMA
			G-BTNZ
LN-OMY(2)	Aérospatiale AS.350B Ecureuil	1017	SE-HIA
LN-OMZ(2)	Hughes 369E	0344E	SE-JAR
			OH-HET
LN-ONA	Aérospatiale AS.332L Super Puma	2111	G-BLRY
			LN-ONA
			G-BLRY
			P2-PHP
			VR-BIJ
			G-BLRY
			C-GQGL
			G-BLRY
LN-ONB	Aérospatiale AS.332L Super Puma	2122	G-BLPM
			LN-ONB
			G-BLPM
			C-GQCB
			G-BLPM
LN-OND	Aérospatiale AS.332L Super Puma	2157	G-BLXS
LN-ONH	Aérospatiale AS.332L2 Super Puma	2488	
LN-ONI	Aérospatiale AS.332L2 Super Puma	2500	
LN-ONZ	Sikorsky S-76C	760456	
LN-OOO	Hughes 369HS *(W/o 12.8.91)*	46-0810S	ZK-HJH
LN-OPB	Aérospatiale AS.350B1 Ecureuil	1940	
LN-OPD	Aérospatiale SA.365N Dauphin 2	6067	
LN-OPE	Aérospatiale AS.350B1 Ecureuil	2183	
LN-OPH	Aérospatiale AS.332L1 Super Puma	2347	
LN-OPI	Aérospatiale AS.350B2 Ecureuil	2616	OY-HEL
LN-OPJ	Aérospatiale SA.365N1 Dauphin 2	6228	9M-TAF
LN-OPK	Aérospatiale AS.350B3 Ecureuil	3091	
LN-OPL	Aérospatiale SA.365N1 Dauphin 2	6346	F-OGSV(2)
			LX-HUP
			F-OGSV(2)
			JA9970
LN-OPM(2)	Aérospatiale SA.365N1 Dauphin 2	6264	CS-HCG
			F-WYMI
			F-ODUZ
LN-OPP	Aérospatiale AS.350B1 Ecureuil	2020	SE-HRT
LN-OPQ(2)	Aérospatiale SA.365N1 Dauphin 2	6319	G-THGS
			G-BPOJ
LN-OPR(2)	Aérospatiale SA.365N Dauphin 2	6028	I-AGFN
	(W/o 14.10.96)		G-DFIN
			F-WTNO
			(G-DFIN)
LN-OPS(2)	Aérospatiale AS.350B Ecureuil	1849	SE-HTS
			D-HHTT
LN-OPT	Aérospatiale AS.350B1 Ecureuil	1881	D-HHPS
LN-OPU(2)	Aérospatiale SA.315B Lama	2316/33	HB-XVW
			F-GDUJ
			PT-HKI
			C-GGNT
			N48017
LN-OPV(2)	Aérospatiale AS.350B2 Ecureuil	2378	HB-XUS
LN-OPX(2)	Aérospatiale AS.350B2 Ecureuil	2346	
LN-OQB(2)	Sikorsky S-61N	61807	
LN-OQM	Sikorsky S-61N	61764	(D-HOSA)
LN-OQQ(2)	Sikorsky S-61N	61814	
LN-OQR	Bell 214B-1	28040	N2673Q
			JA9227
			N5009F
LN-OQU(2)	Sikorsky S-61N	61816	(LN-ORC)

Regn.	Type	C/n	Prev.Id.
LN-ORA(5)	Aérospatiale SA.315B Lama	2665	F-GECS
LN-ORC(3)	Sikorsky S-61N	61817	(LN-OQU)
LN-ORD(2)	Aérospatiale SA.315B Lama	2172/18	F-GHCJ
			N1356A
			HB-XBP
			G-BBJE
			N8268
LN-ORH(4)	Aérospatiale AS.350B2 Ecureuil	2843	OY-HJC
LN-ORJ(3)	Aérospatiale AS.350B1 Ecureuil	2212	N501RP
			C-GFIN
LN-ORK(3)	Aérospatiale AS.350BA Ecureuil	1056	SE-JDE
			LN-ORK
			F-WZFT
LN-ORS(2)	Agusta-Bell 206A Jet Ranger	8212	D-HEZF
	(W/o 13.12.86)		(D-HAVA)
LN-ORW(3)	Bell 204 /UH-1B	1087	(LN-10)
	(Under rebuild using parts of c/n 297,		(LN-ORN)
	RNoAF699/SI-L, 61-0699)		RNoAF963/JT-F
			64-13963
LN-OSA(3)	Hughes 269C	40-0918	PH-HJH
			C-GBSA
			N10970
LN-OSB(3)	Bölkow BO.105S	S-606	N2913Z
			N132EH
			D-HDSB
LN-OSD(2)	Bölkow BO.105S (W/o 4.1.91)	S-607	N2914W
			D-HDSC
LN-OSE(3)	Bölkow BO.105S	S-634	N2784V
			D-HDTD
LN-OSF(2)	Aérospatiale SA.315B Lama (Floats)	2580	
LN-OSI (2)	Bölkow BO.105CBS	S-609	N29144
			D-HDSE
LN-OSJ	Sikorsky S-61N	61715	N53094
LN-OSK(2)	Hughes 369E	0261E	SE-HSR
			LN-OBA
			SE-HSR
LN-OSM(3)	Aérospatiale AS.350B1 Ecureuil	1966	SE-HUT
			HB-XP I
LN-OSN(2)	Robinson R-22 Beta (Reservation)	unkn	
LN-OSP(2)	Bell 214B-1 (w/o 5.8.98)	28045	I-CODA
			LN-OSP
			N2757G
LN-OSR(4)	Rotorway Exec 162F	6095	
LN-OST	Sikorsky S-61N	61738	
LN-OSZ(2)	Bölkow BO.105S	S-666	N4573A
			HK-3225
			N4573A
			D-HDUH
LN-OTA(2)	Aérospatiale AS.350B1 Ecureuil	1902	SE-JAC
			LN-OBD
			(F-GHYU)
			LN-OBD
			SE-JAC
			HB-XPH
LN-OTC(2)	Hughes 369HS	89-0112S	N2171Z
			VH-PMY
			G-AXPL
LN-OTD	Bölkow BO.105CBS	S-433	D-HDMG
LN-OTE(2)	Aérospatiale SA.315B	2338/36	SE-JDN
			F-GLEV
			XB-LAE
LN-OTG(2)	Robinson R-44 Astro	0113	D-HLAX
LN-OTK(2)	Schweizer 269C (W/o 3.11.88)	S-1278	SE-HSK
LN-OTL(3)	Bell 206B Jet Ranger II	234	OH-HHW
			PH-HNH
			N4071G
LN-OTQ	Bölkow BO.105CBS (W/o 12.4.89)	S-582	D-HDQE
LN-OTV(2)	Robinson R-22 Beta	2184	G-BVLY
			SP-GSA
LN-PAL (2)	Piper PA-28-161 Cherokee Warrior II	28-7816500	
LN-PAM(2)	Piper J-3C-65 Cub (Stored)	12807	SE-CGY
			LN-RTM
			44-80511
LN-PAQ	Piper PA-38-112 Tomahawk (W/o 6.5.87)	38-78A0533	

Regn.	Type	C/n	Prev.Id.
LN-PBB	Cessna 208B Grand Caravan	0302	OY-TCB
	(Accident 6.9.99)		N1002D
LN-PBD	Cessna 208 Caravan	00105	OY-TCA
			(LN-PBA)
			OY-TCA
			(OY-CJL)
			N9604F
			N105YV
			N9604F
LN-PBE	Cessna 208B Grand Caravan	0587	N9782X
			N7229Z
LN-PWA	Cessna 172R	80168	
LN-RAA(2)	Cessna 182P Skylane	62731	SE-GGC
			N52365
LN-RAB(2)	Cessna 172P	74101	N5412K
LN-RAF(3)	Van's RV-4	1553	
LN-RAG(2)	Cessna 180 (W/o 17.7.84)	32556	(LN-HAT)
			D-EHTA
			N7659A
LN-RAI (2)	Cessna 172N	72812	N6461D
LN-RAJ	Cessna U.206G Stationair II (W/o 16.4.83)	04701	N732NH
LN-RAK	Piper J-3C-65 Cub (L-4J) (Under restoration)	12889	44-80593
LN-RAL(2)	Reims/Cessna F.172H	0676	SE-FUI
			D-EBLQ
LN-RAM	Reims/Cessna F.172M	1454	SE-GMY
LN-RAN(2)	Piper PA-28-161 Cherokee Warrior II	28-7816501	LN-PAN(2)
LN-RAP	Piper J-3C-65 Cub (L-4J)	12583	SE-CDH
	(Flies as "43-E")		LN-RAP
			44-80287
LN-RAR(2)	Bellanca 7GCBC Citabria	1209-80	
LN-RBI	Piper J-3C-65 Cub	12640	(SE-IML)
			OY-ALN
			D-EDUH
			SL-ABC
			SL-AAC
			F-BDTL
			44-80344
LN-RCD	Boeing 767-383ER	24847	
LN-RCE	Boeing 767-383ER	24846	SE-DKR
			N60697
LN-RCG	Boeing 767-383ER	24475	SE-DOA
			(N7638T)
			SE-DOA
			OY-KDI
LN-RCH	Boeing 767-383ER	24318	SE-DKO
LN-RCI	Boeing 767-383ER	24476	SE-DOB
			OY-KDK
LN-RCK	Boeing 767-383ER	24729	SE-DKU
			(LN-RCD)
LN-RCL	Boeing 767-383ER	25365	SE-DKX
LN-RCM	Boeing 767-383ER	26544	SE-DOC
			N6055X
LN-REB	Pazmany PL-4A	682	
LN-RET	Cessna 140	8784	LN-TSI
			N89735
LN-RIC	Grefstad Sea Hawker (W/o 18.6.97)	91	
LN-RLE	McDonnell-Douglas DC-9-82	49382	
LN-RLF	McDonnell-Douglas DC-9-82	49383	VH-LNJ
			LN-RLF
LN-RLG	McDonnell-Douglas DC-9-82	49423	N844RA
			LN-RLG
			VH-LNK
			LN-RLG
LN-RLR(2)	McDonnell-Douglas DC-9-82	49437	VH-LNL
			LN-RLR(2)
LN-RMA	McDonnell-Douglas DC-9-81	49554	(LN-RLI)
LN-RMD	McDonnell-Douglas DC-9-82	49555	(OY-KHD)
LN-RMF	McDonnell-Douglas DC-9-83	49556	(SE-DFP)
LN-RMG	McDonnell-Douglas DC-9-87	49611	
LN-RMH	McDonnell-Douglas DC-9-87	49612	N6203U
LN-RMJ	McDonnell-Douglas DC-9-81	49912	
LN-RMK	McDonnell-Douglas DC-9-87	49610	
LN-RML	McDonnell-Douglas DC-9-81	53002	
LN-RMM	McDonnell-Douglas DC-9-81	53005	
LN-RMN	McDonnell-Douglas DC-9-82	53295	

Regn.	Type	C/n	Prev.Id.
LN-RMO	McDonnell-Douglas DC-9-81	53315	
LN-RMP	McDonnell-Douglas DC-9-87	53337	
LN-RMR	McDonnell-Douglas DC-9-81	53365	
LN-RMS	McDonnell-Douglas DC-9-81	53368	
LN-RMT	McDonnell-Douglas DC-9-81	53001	OY-KHS
			(SE-DIP)
LN-RMU	McDonnell-Douglas DC-9-87	53340	SE-DMC
LN-RMX	McDonnell-Douglas DC-9-87	49585	HB-IUA
LN-RMY	McDonnell-Douglas DC-9-87	49586	HB-IUB
LN-RNB	Fokker F.27-050	20173	PH-EXX
LN-RNC	Fokker F.27-050	20176	PH-EXY
LN-RND	Fokker F.27-050	20178	PH-EXZ
LN-RNE	Fokker F.27-050	20179	PH-EXE
LN-RNF	Fokker F.27-050	20183	PH-EXI
LN-RNG	Fokker F.27-050	20184	PH-EXJ
LN-RNH	Fokker F.27-050	20172	PH-EXW
LN-ROA	McDonnell-Douglas MD-90-30	53459	
LN-ROB	McDonnell-Douglas MD-90-30	53462	
LN-ROM	McDonnell-Douglas DC-9-81	53008	SE-DIY
LN-RON	McDonnell-Douglas DC-9-81	53347	SE-DMD
			N90125
LN-ROO	McDonnell-Douglas DC-9-81	53366	SE-DME
LN-ROP	McDonnell-Douglas DC-9-81	49384	SE-DFS
LN-ROR	McDonnell-Douglas DC-9-81	49385	SE-DFT
LN-ROS	McDonnell-Douglas DC-9-81	49421	SE-DFU
			N841RA
			SE-DFU
LN-ROT	McDonnell-Douglas DC-9-81	49422	SE-DFR
			SE-DFV
			(SE-DFW)
LN-ROU	McDonnell-Douglas DC-9-81	49424	SE-DFX
			N840RA
			SE-DFX
LN-ROW	McDonnell-Douglas DC-9-81	49438	SE-DFY
LN-ROX	McDonnell-Douglas DC-9-81	49603	SE-DIA
			N19B
LN-ROY	McDonnell-Douglas DC-9-81	49615	SE-DID
			N843RA
			SE-DID
LN-ROZ	McDonnell-Douglas DC-9-81	49608	SE-DIH
LN-RPA	Boeing 737-683	28290	
LN-RPB	Boeing 737-683	28294	N1787B
LN-RPE	Boeing 737-683	28306	N1795B
LN-RPF	Boeing 737-683	28307	N1786B
LN-RPG	Boeing 737-683	28310	
LN-RPH	Boeing 737-683	28605	
LN-RPW	Boeing 737-683	28289	OY-KKA
			N5002K
LN-RPX	Boeing 737-683	28291	SE-DNN
			N1787B
LN-RPY	Boeing 737-683	28292	SE-DNO
			N1780B
LN-RPZ	Boeing 737-683	28293	OY-KKB
			N1787B
LN-RTA(3)	Cessna A.185F Skywagon (W/o 10.10.86)	02257	N2649S
LN-RTB	Piper PA-18 Super Cub 95	18-1593	ALAT
			51-15593
LN-RTC	Piper PA-18 Super Cub 95	18-1480	ALAT
	(W/o 15.11.81, used to repair LN-VYP)	51-15480	
LN-RTH(2)	Piper PA-18 Super Cub 95	18-1408	D-ENLI
			ALAT
			51-15408
LN-RTI (2)	Rutan Defiant	0023B	
LN-RTJ (3)	Denney Kitfox II	463	
LN-RTQ	Cessna U.206E Stationair Floatplane	01449	
	(W/o 2.10.89, stored)		
LN-RTV	Rockwell Lark Commander 100-180	5162	
LN-RTY	Cessna U.206E Stationair (W/o 4.11.81)	01491	
LN-SAC	Cessna TP.337G Super Skymaster (Stored)	0169	N68S
LN-SAD	SAAB-MFI-15-200A Safari	15814	SE-FIR
LN-SAF	SAAB S.91B-2 Safir	91330	RNoAF:5/330
	(Under restoration)		330/'UA-K'
LN-SAG(2)	Cessna 172M (W/o 1.10.83)	63760	N1815V
LN-SAI	Piper J-3C-65 Cub (L-4J)	12579	44-80283

Regn.	Type	C/n	Prev.Id.
LN-SAK	SAAB S.91B-2 Safir (W/o 12.11.83)	91340	RNoAF:57340
			340/'UA-U'
LN-SAL(2)	SAAB S.91B Safir (Stored)	91286	Fv50076
LN-SAM(2)	SAAB S.91B-2 Safir	91342	RNoAF:57342
	(Under restoration)		342/'UA-W'
LN-SAO(2)	SAAB S.91B-2 Safir	91344	RNoAF:57344
			344/'UA-Y'
LN-SAP(3)	SAAB S.91B-2 Safir	91333	RNoAF:57333
			333/'UA-N'
LN-SAQ	SAAB S.91B-2 Safir	91322	RNoAF:57322
	(W/o 15.8.87, to Sweden)		322/'UA-C'
LN-SAS(3)	PZL-150 Koliber	19005	SE-KHG
			SP-PHA
			SP-ZKC
LN-SAU	Schweizer TSC-1A1 Teal	23	G-BAVK
			N41S
			N2023T
LN-SFK	Cessna 182M Skylane	59952	N91918
LN-SFT	Fairchild-Swearingen SA.226T Merlin IIIB	T-342	N342NX
			9Q-CQP
			G- IIIA
			N1008S
LN-SHA	Neico Lancair 320	582-320-329FB	
LN-SNI	Rans S-9 Chaos	1098112	
LN-SVF	Denney Kitfox II (Reservation)	unkn	
LN-SVO	Piper PA-28-181 Cherokee Archer II	28-7790101	OY-CTG
			C-GUST
			N5368F
LN-SXY	Neico Lancair 360	630	
LN-TAU	Piper PA-25-235 Pawnee D	25-7756038	G-BFBX
			N82504
LN-TDY	Embraer EMB.110P1 Bandeirante	110-456	N220EB
			PT-SHK
LN-TEK	Cessna U.206F Stationair	02858	C-GTHK
			N1179Q
LN-TEP	Cessna U.206G Stationair II	05186	N5305U
LN-TET	Piper J-3C-65 Cub	18020	LN-BWU
			N71006
LN-TEX	North American T-6G Harvard	14A-2268	FAP1794
			D-FIBU
			OO-AAR
			H-58
			KF568
LN-TEZ	Fuji FA-200-160 Aero Subaru (Stored)	295	G-BMLN
			(G-BIMR)
LN-TFA	Slingsby T-67M/200 Firefly	2045	SE-LBA
			LN-TFA
			G-7-121
LN-TFC(2)	Piper PA-34-220T Seneca V	3449094	
LN-TFF	Slingsby T-67M/200 Firefly	2051	SE-LBF
			LN-TFF
			G-7-126
LN-TFI	Cessna T.210N Turbo Centurion II	63836	N6224C
LN-TFJ	Cessna T.210N Turbo Centurion II	63655	N4879C
LN-TFM	Cessna P210N Pressurized Centurion II	00268	N4737K
LN-TFN	MFI-15-200A	15-803	RNoAF0803
LN-TFO	MFI-15-200A	15-810	RNoAF0810
LN-TFP	MFI-15-200A	15-815	RNoAF0815
LN-TFQ	Piper PA-28-181 Archer III	2843265	N9524N
LN-TFR	Piper PA-28-181 Archer III	2843269	N9526N
LN-TFS	Piper PA-28-181 Archer III	2843273	
LN-TFT	Piper PA-28-181 Archer III	2843274	
LN-TFU	Piper PA-28-181 Archer III	2843285	
LN-TFV	Piper PA-28-181 Archer III	2843293	N9522N
LN-TFW	Grob G.115D	82078	D-EZAN
LN-TFX	Grob G.115D	82067	N115MH
LN-TFY	Grob G.115D	82052	N115AD
LN-TFZ	Grob G.115D	82014	D-EXEC
LN-TIM	Denney Kitfox IV	1520	
LN-TSA(2)	Beech 200 Super King Air (W/o 19.3.93)	BB-308	N98WP
			N9OWP
LN-TSB	Cessna 182A Skylane	33977	N5977B
LN-TSE(2)	Cessna 150F	62137	(SE-ESS)
			N8837S
LN-TSF	Cessna 180 (Damaged 12.5.96)	32473	N6576A

Regn.	Type	C/n	Prev.Id.
LN-TSG(2)	Cessna U.206	0388	N11B
			(N2188F)
LN-TSK(4)	SOCATA Rallye 180T Galérien	2973	SE-GTH
LN-TSL	Cessna 172	36540	N8840B
LN-TSM(2)	Cessna 185	0046	N9846X
LN-TSP	Cessna 180	50262	N5364D
LN-TSR(2)	Piper PA-12 Super Cruiser *(W/o 25.8.85)*	12-205	SE-AZX
LN-TST(3)	Cessna 177A Cardinal	01343	SE-ELX
			N30583
LN-TSU	Cessna 175A Skylark *(Scrapped 4.88)*	56701	N8001T
LN-TSV(2)	Piper PA-28-140 Cherokee	28-22312	(SE-...)
LN-TSW	Cessna 150E	61451	N11B
			(N4051U)
LN-TSX	Piper PA-18 Super Cub 95 *(Under restoration)*	18-1545	OO-HMV
			ALAT
			51-15545
LN-TSZ	Piper PA-18 Super Cub 95	18-1579	OO-HMN
			ALAT
			51-15579
LN-TUA	Boeing 737-705	28211	(LN-SUA)
LN-TUB	Boeing 737-705	29089	(LN-SUB)
LN-TUC	Boeing 737-705	29090	(LN-SUC)
LN-TUD	Boeing 737-705	28217	N1786B
LN-TUE	Boeing 737-705	29091	
LN-TUF	Boeing 737-705	28222	
LN-TUG	Boeing 737-705	29092	
LN-TUH	Boeing 737-705	29093	
LN-TUX	Boeing 737-548	25165	EI-CDT
			PT-MNC
			EI-CDT
LN-TVB(3)	Beech A23 Musketeer *(Under restoration)*	M-788	OH-BMC
			N1447L
LN-TVD	Cessna 172D	50004	(OY-TRE)
			N2404U
LN-TVE(2)	Beagle A.61 Terrier 2	B.626	SE-ELR
			(SE-ELJ)
			G-ASIE
			G-35-11
			VX924
LN-TVI	Malmö MFI-9 Junior	013	(SE-EBZ)
LN-TVK	Piper PA-22-160 Tri-Pacer	22-5680	N8425D
LN-TVO(2)	Cessna 150D *(W/o 14.7.94)*	60532	N4532U
LN-TVQ	Reims/Cessna F.150J	0413	
LN-TVR(4)	Orlican L-40 Meta-Sokol	150615	OY-ADC
			LN-TVR(2)
			OY-ADC
LN-TVS	Cessna 180 *(Dbf 6.9.92)*	30454	N1754C
LN-TVZ	Reims/Cessna F.150J *(Stored)*	0487	
LN-TWA	Piper PA-28RT-201T Turbo Arrow IV	28R-8231012	N4327X
			LN-TWA
			N8467J
LN-TWB	Piper PA-31-325 Navajo	31-8212025	N4083T
LN-TWH	Reims/Cessna F.406 Caravan II	0032	PH-CLE
			AP-BFA
			N422AB
			G-BPSW
			F-WZDU
LN-TWL	Beech B200 Super King Air	BB-144	N120AJ
			ZS-NWT
			D-IBHF
			N62BE
			N221P
LN-ULF	Cessna 182P	64448	OY-CKL
			OH-CVF
			N1795M
LN-USA	Rutan Cozy	112	
LN-UXA	Piper PA-28-140 Cherokee	28-23020	
LN-UXB	Piper PA-28-140 Cherokee *(W/o 24.7.96)*	28-23108	
LN-UXC	Piper PA-18-150 Super Cub	18-3213	OL-L10
			L-139
			53-4813
LN-UXD	Piper PA-28-140 Cherokee *(Dbr 12.2.82)*	28-23113	
LN-UXE	Piper PA-28-140 Cherokee	28-23118	
LN-UXF	Piper PA-28-140 Cherokee	28-23168	
LN-UXG	Piper PA-28-140 Cherokee *(W/o 8.7.79)*	28-23188	

Regn.	Type	C/n	Prev.Id.
LN-UXK	Piper PA-28-140 Cherokee	28-23263	
LN-UXQ(2)	Grumman-American AA-5 Traveler	0198	(OY-AYS)
LN-UXR	Piper PA-28-180 Cherokee C	28-4292	
LN-UXT	Piper PA-28-140 Cherokee *(W/o 1.1.92)*	28-23785	
LN-UXY	Cessna 180H Floatplane	52106	N9006M
LN-UXZ	Cessna U.206G Stationair II *(W/o 2.9.82)*	05694	SE-IFI
			(N5378X)
LN-VIE	Reims/Cessna F.172G *(W/o 22.5.77)*	0231	OY-DOW
LN-VIF	Cessna 180H	52004	(N91217)
LN-VIG	Rutan Vari-eze	1879	
LN-VIK	Quickie 2	058	
LN-VIU	Beech 200 Super King Air	BB-216	OY-AUZ
			N600LR
			N700CP
LN-VIZ(2)	Beech B200 Super King Air	BB-1136	D-IDOK
			N62KL
			N62KM
			N83KA
LN-VYA	Cessna 172H (Atlas Skyrocket) *(W/o 18.6.84)*	55170	N1775F
LN-VYC	Piper PA-38-112 Tomahawk	38-79A0880	(SE-ICO)
LN-VYE	Cessna 150F *(W/o 22.5.81)*	62643	N8543G
LN-VYG	de Havilland DH.82A Tiger Moth *(Stored)*	85328	LN-BDN
			G-ANSB
			DE282
LN-VYI	Piper PA-23-250 Aztec C	27-3873	
LN-VYJ	Cessna 180 Floatplane	32096	OY-DGF
			OE-DBE
			HB-CPB
			N3298D
LN-VYM(2)	Grumman GA-7 Cougar	0047	N760GA
LN-VYN(2)	Cessna U.206E Stationair	01490	N1490M
LN-VYP	Piper PA-18-150 Super Cub	18-8328	(SE-EPP)
LN-VYU	Piper PA-28-140 Cherokee *(W/o 13.12.82)*	28-23845	
LN-VYX	Piper PA-18-150 Super Cub	18-1772	N1937A
LN-VYZ	Reims/Cessna F.172H	0414	OY-EGT
LN-WFA	DHC-8 Series 311	342	C-FTUY
			EI-CIS
			D-BOBS
			C-GFHZ
LN-WFB	DHC-8 Series 311	293	PH-SDS
			EI-CIU
			PT-OKD
			C-GDIU
LN-WFC(3)	DHC-8 Series 311	236	D-BEYT
			C-GFCF
LN-WFD	DHC-6 Twin Otter 300	700	
LN-WFE(2)	DHC-8 Series 311	491	C-GFCA
LN-WFH	DHC-8 Series 311	238	C-FZOH
			PH-SDJ
			C-GFYI
LN-WFO(2)	DHC-8 Series 311	493	C-GERC
LN-WFP(2)	DHC-8 Series 311	495	C-GFUM
LN-WFR	DHC-8 Series 311	385	N383DC
			ZS-NME
			C-GFUM
LN-WFS	DHC-8 Series 311	535	
LN-WIA	DHC-8 Series 103	359	C-GHRI
LN-WIB	DHC-8 Series 103	360	C-GFBW
LN-WIC	DHC-8 Series 103	367	C-GDNG
LN-WID	DHC-8 Series 103	369	C-FDHD
LN-WIE	DHC-8 Series 103	371	C-GFYI
LN-WIF	DHC-8 Series 103	372	C-GFOD
LN-WIG	DHC-8 Series 103	382	C-GLOT
LN-WIH	DHC-8 Series 103	383	C-GFYI
LN-WII	DHC-8 Series 103	384	C-GFOD
LN-WIJ	DHC-8 Series 103	386	C-G...
LN-WIK	DHC-8 Series 103	394	C-GDNG
LN-WIL	DHC-8 Series 103	398	C-GFCF
LN-WIM	DHC-8 Series 103	403	C-GDIU
LN-WIN	DHC-8 Series 103	409	C-G...
LN-WIO	DHC-8 Series 103	417	C-G...
LN-WIP	DHC-8 Series 106	239	C-FXNE
			OE-LLK
			C-GETI

Regn.	Type	C/n	Prev.Id.
LN-WIR	DHC-8 Series 103	273	C-FZNU
			OE-LRT
			OE-HRT
			C-GFYI
LN-WIS	DHC-8 Series 103	247	N813AW
			C-GFRP
			N813AW
			C-GFRP
LN-WNA	Holste MH.1521M Broussard	78	(G-....)
			(LN-WNA)
			F-GHUG
			ALAT
LN-WNB	Holste MH.1521M Broussard	16	F-GHJH
			ALAT
LN-WND	Douglas C-53D	11750	N59NA
			G-BLYA
			DO-9
			OH-LCG
			42-68823
LN-WNH	North American AT-6D Harvard	88-14552	(LN-LFW)
	(Flown as FS907/AJ)		G-SUES
			FAP1506
			74+24
			EX881
			41-33854
LN-WWP	Steen Skybolt (Reservation)	unkn	

GLIDERS AND MOTOR-GLIDERS

Regn.	Type	C/n	Prev.Id.
LN-GAA(2)	Eiri PIK-3B	1	
LN-GAB(3)	Grob G.103 Twin II Acro	34063-K-293	
LN-GAC	Scheibe Zugvogel IIIB	1074	D-8460
LN-GAD(2)	Scheibe Specht	410/1957	
LN-GAE(4)	LET L-13 Blanik	026315	D-3300
LN-GAF(5)	Rolladen-Schneider LS-1F	180	
LN-GAG(2)	Schleicher K.7 Rhönadler	7266	
LN-GAH(3)	Grob G.102 Astir CS	1162	D-4183
LN-GAI (2)	Scheibe Bergfalke IIa (Stored)	343	
LN-GAM(4)	Schleicher ASK-21	21132	
LN-GAN(5)	Grob G.103C Twin III SL	35049	
LN-GAO(4)	Slingsby T.21B Sedbergh (Stored)	MHL 2496	BGA3423/FPS
			WB974
LN-GAP(2)	Schleicher K.7 Rhö nadler	7246	
LN-GAQ(2)	Schleicher K.8B	8217	D-1900
LN-GAR(3)	Bölkow Phoebus C	810	SE-TFP
LN-GAS(2)	LET L-13 Blanik	026127	
LN-GAT(3)	Scheibe SF-28A Tandem-Falke	5765	OY-XMV
			D-KACR
LN-GAU(2)	Scheibe L-Spatz 55 (Stored)	676	
LN-GAV(2)	LET L-13 Blanik	025810	
LN-GAW(4)	LET L-13SL Vivat	930508	D-KACH(3)
LN-GAX	Schleicher ASK-13	13171	
LN-GAY	Glasflügel H201B Standard Libelle (Stored)	480	OH-429
LN-GBA(3)	Grob G.102 Astir CS77	1625	D-4799
LN-GBB(2)	Rolladen-Schneider LS-6 "BB"	6014	D-4975
LN-GBC	Schleicher Rhönlerche II (Wfu)	3010	D-3595
LN-GBD(3)	Scheibe SF-25C Falke	4499	SE-TLV
			D-KEIQ
LN-GBE(4)	Brditschka HB-21/2400	21027	SE-TUM
LN-GBF(3)	Pilatus B4-PC11	107	
LN-GBG(3)	Schleicher ASK-13	13103	
LN-GBH(2)	Rolladen-Schneider LS-6 "BH"	6022	
LN-GBJ	LET L-13 Blanik (Dbr 25.7.92)	026555	
LN-GBK(3)	Schleicher K.8B (Dbr 16.10.93)	1	D-6077
LN-GBM(4)	LET L-13 Blanik	026124	OY-XRK
			HB-1243
LN-GBN(2)	Schleicher K.7 Rhönadler (Wfu)	7236	
LN-GBO(2)	Eiri PIK-20D	20548	
LN-GBQ	Schleicher ASK-13	13190	
LN-GBR(3)	Schleicher K.8B	8754	
LN-GBS(2)	SZD-30 Pirat (W/o 21.9.97)	S-02.20	
LN-GBT(2)	Schleicher K.7 Rhönadler	7237	
LN-GBU(3)	Scheibe Bergfalke II/55	247	(LN-GBM)
			D-8268
LN-GBV(3)	Schleicher K.8B	1088	D-1731
LN-GBW(4)	Scheibe Bergfalke III	5578	SE-TEM
LN-GBX	Grob G.102 Astir CS	1519	
LN-GBY	Rolladen-Schneider LS-3	3065	
LN-GDB	Schleicher ASW-15B	15382	OY-XNJ
			D-9271
LN-GDD	Schempp-Hirth Duo Discus	211	
LN-GDF	Schempp-Hirth Janus C	152	BGA2823/ENR
LN-GDM	Schempp-Hirth Nimbus 4 DM	36/51	
LN-GDW	Schempp-Hirth Discus bT	163/571	
LN-GEE	SZD-45A Ogar	X-133	SP-0027
LN-GEL	LET L-23 Super Blanik	978308	
LN-GEM	Schleicher K.8B (Under restoration)	151	OY-XEM
			D-5198
LN-GER	Rolladen-Schneider LS-8A	8129	
LN-GET	SZD-48-1 Jantar Standard	B-1034	SE-UMR
			OH-585
LN-GFE	Schempp-Hirth Discus b	166	SE-UFE
LN-GFI	LET L-13 Blanik	171520	LY-10013
			DOSAAF
LN-GFJ	LET L-13 Blanik	027260	LY-GAC
			DOSAAF
LN-GFK	LET L-13 Blanik	026243	OY-XGB
LN-GFN	Monnett Moni	369	
LN-GFT	LET L-13 Blanik	026415	LY-GLC
			DOSAAF
LN-GGA(3)	Pilatus B-4/PC-11	209	
LN-GGB(3)	SZD-36A Cobra	W-796	LY-...
			DOSAAF
LN-GGC(2)	Bölkow Phoebus C (Wfu)	888	OH-379
			OH-PHC
LN-GGD(2)	Schleicher K.8B	8610	
LN-GGF(2)	Bölkow Phoebus B-1	738	HB-855
LN-GGG(3)	Schleicher K.8B	8682/A	D-5834
LN-GGH(3)	Scheibe SF-34	5109	D-1114
LN-GGI (2)	Schleicher K.8B	12	OY-BXG
LN-GGJ	Bölkow Phoebus A-1	809	D-5488
LN-GGK(2)	SZD-30 Pirat	S-07.03	
LN-GGM(3)	Schempp-Hirth Nimbus II	121	OY-XGR
LN-GGN(2)	Pilatus B-4/PC-11AF	256	
LN-GGO(2)	Grob G.102 Astir CS	1198	OY-XOP
			LN-GGO(2)
LN-GGP(2)	PIK-16C Vasama	19	OY-BXB
LN-GGR(2)	Rolladen-Schneider LS-3	3052	
LN-GGS(2)	Schleicher K.8B	04	
LN-GGT	Schleicher K.8	521/59	
LN-GGU(2)	Grob G.102 Astir CS 77	1711	
LN-GGV(2)	Grob G.102 Astir CS 77 (Stored)	1640	D-7471
LN-GGW(2)	Grob G.102 Astir CS	1488	
LN-GGX(2)	Grob G.102 Astir CS Jeans	2185	(OY-XMZ)
			D-7760
LN-GGY	Rolladen-Schneider LS-3	3058	HB-1355
LN-GGZ	Schleicher K.8B	8913	D-0991
LN-GHA	Rolladen-Schneider LS-1F	329	(LN-GHO)
			SE-TON
LN-GHB	Scheibe Bergfalke III	5583	D-5771
LN-GHC	Rolladen-Schneider LS-3A	3339	(D-3183)
LN-GHD	Rolladen-Schneider LS-3A	3363	
LN-GHE	Schleicher K.8B	8380	D-6345
LN-GHF	Glasflügel H303 Mosquito B	180	
LN-GHG	Grob G.102 Astir CS	1182	OY-XJM
			D-4192
LN-GHH	Schleicher Rhönlerche II	104/61	D-6253
LN-GHI	Scheibe Bergfalke II/55	84	D-1492
LN-GHK	Rolladen-Schneider LS-6	6034	
LN-GHL	Schleicher ASW-19B	19402	
LN-GHM(2)	Monerai Max	378	
LN-GHO	Grob G.103 Club Astir II	5055C	D-3060
LN-GHR(2)	Slingsby T.21B Sedbergh	"FF1161"	BGA3338/FLD
			WB987
LN-GHS	Rolladen-Schneider LS-6	6095	

Regn.	Type	C/n	Prev.Id.
LN-GHT	Grünau 9 *(Stored)*	01 EB	D-1161
			(LN-GHT)
LN-GHV	Scheibe SF-25C Falke	4208	OY-XHM
			D-KAIJ
LN-GHX	Grob G.102 Astir CS *(Dbr 31.5.92)*	1115	OY-XKJ
			D-4175
LN-GHY	Rolladen-Schneider LS-6	6107	
LN-GIA(2)	LET L-23 Super Blanik	988409	
LN-GIB	Schleicher ASK-21	21293	
LN-GIC	Schempp-Hirth Discus b	153	
LN-GID	Valentin Mistral C	MC050/82	D-4950
LN-GIE(2)	Scheibe Bergfalke III	5520	SE-TBY
LN-GIF	Schleicher ASK-21	21554	
LN-GII	Schleicher ASW-19B	19272	OY-XJS
LN-GIK	Rolladen-Schneider LS-4A	4720	
LN-GIL	Scheibe Bergfalke II/55	3	D-1683
LN-GIM	Rolladen-Schneider LS-7	7028	D-1317
LN-GIN	Rolladen-Schneider LS-7	7127	
LN-GIO	Lunds Tekniske Kern-Silhouette SA-60	LTSA-1	
LN-GIR	Rolladen-Schneider LS-7	7049	D-5175
LN-GIW	Schempp-Hirth Discus 8	290	
LN-GLA	Scheibe Bergfalke IV *(W/o 21.7.94)*	5840	D-3698
LN-GLB	Scheibe L-Spatz	01	SE-TIP
LN-GLD	LET L-13 Blanik *(Stored, Denmark)*	026007	D-3708
LN-GLE	Rolladen-Schneider LS-4	4062	(D-5989)
LN-GLF	Rolladen-Schneider LS-4	4061	(D-5988)
LN-GLG	Rolladen-Schneider LS-4	4064	
LN-GLH	Rolladen-Schneider LS-3A	3365	
LN-GLI	Schleicher K7 Rhönadler	771	D-5763
LN-GLJ	SZD-41A Jantar Standard	B-813	OY-XII
LN-GLK	Scheibe SF-25B Falke	4641	SE-UAM
			D-KEDF
LN-GLL	Schleicher K7 Rhönadler	7186	D-3031
LN-GLM	Glasflügel H303 Mosquito	24	SE-TTG
LN-GLN	Scheibe Bergfalke IV	5812	D-0309
LN-GLO	Jastreb Standard Cirrus G/81	278	
LN-GLS	Scheibe Bergfalke III	5542	D-6370
LN-GLT(2)	Schleicher K.8B	8462	SE-TCM
LN-GLU(2)	LET L-23 Super Blanik	978309	
LN-GLV	Slingsby T.30B Prefect Mk.2	1132	BGA853
LN-GLW	Eiri PIK-20B	20129C	OY-XIH
			OH-488
LN-GLX	Grob G.103A Twin II Acro	3878-K-116	
LN-GLZ	Grob G.103 Twin Astir	3539	OY-XOU
			D-8732
LN-GMA	Scheibe SF-28A Tandem-Falke	57112	(OY-...)
			(D-KDGY)
LN-GMB	Eiri PIK-20E	20289	
LN-GMC(2)	Scheibe SF-25B Falke	46202	(LN-GDX)
			SE-UBM
			D-KASQ
LN-GMD	Grob G.109	6001	D-KECG(2)
			D-KBGF
LN-GMF	Scheibe SF-25B Falke	46125	D-KABZ
LN-GMK	Monnett Moni	00328	
LN-GMR	Valentin Taifun 17E	1053	D-KDST
LN-GMT	IAR IS.28M2	043	
LN-GMV	Eiri PIK-20E	20286	D-KARM
LN-GMY	Hoffmann H-36 Dimona	3653	SE-TUS
LN-GMZ	Hoffmann H-36 Dimona	3690	SE-TUZ
			D-KLBD
LN-GOD	LET L-13 Blanik	026246	HB-1287
LN-GOL	Schleicher ASW-20	20322	SE-UGH
			OH-580
LN-GOR	LET L-13 Blanik	026610	LY-GJQ
			DOSAAF
LN-GOS	Schleicher K7 Rhönadler	162/59	BGA2665/EGB
			D-5743
LN-GOY	Scheibe SF-36A	4104	D-KOOY
			(OY-XMI)
LN-GPA	Glaser-Dirks DG-300 Elan	3E-303	
LN-GPE	Rolladen-Schneider LS-7	7077	
LN-GPF	Grob G.109	6110	OH-782
			D-KBGF
LN-GPO	Schempp-Hirth Discus b	334	SE-UIK

Regn.	Type	C/n	Prev.Id.
LN-GPP	Grob G.103C Twin III Acro	34105	
LN-GPR	LET L-23 Super Blanik	978310	
LN-GPS	Schempp-Hirth Discus bT	155/555	
	(Possibly conversion of Discus B c/n 555 D-8261?)		
LN-GRJ	SZD-48-3 Jantar Standard 3	B-1275	HB-1706
			SP-3243
LN-GRR	Schempp-Hirth Ventus 2cT	43/139	
LN-GRY	Fournier RF-5	5113	G-AZZW
LN-GSS	Schempp-Hirth Ventus 2cT	34/118	
LN-GSW	Schleicher ASW-15B	15244	OY-XBN
LN-GTE	Schleicher ASW-20	20325	OH-526
LN-GTI	Grü nau Bay II b	504	
LN-GTT	Rolladen-Schneider LS-8A	8177	
LN-GWA	PZL PW-5 Smyk	17.08.001	
LN-GWC	PZL PW-5 Smyk	17.03.018	
LN-GWS	PZL PW-5 Smyk	17.05.011	
LN-GWW	PZL PW-5 Smyk	17.05.008	
LN-HAA	SZD-22C Mucha Standard *(Wfu)*	F-616	

BALLOONS

Regn.	Type	C/n	Prev.Id.
LN-ASU	Cameron D-77 HAFB *(Wfu)*	212	
LN-ASX	Cameron O-56 HAFB *(Wfu)*	98	SE-ZZE
LN-CBA	Cameron V-77 HAFB	614	
LN-CBD	Cameron O-42 HAFB	183	SE-ZZK
LN-CBE	Cameron V-77 HAFB	1101	
LN-CBF	Cameron N-105 HAFB	943	
LN-CBG	Cameron V-77 HAFB	1694	
LN-CBH	Cameron A-120 HAFB	2830	
LN-CBI	Cameron V-77 HAFB	3635	
LN-CBJ	Colt 77A HAFB	4073	
LN-CBK	Aerostar RX-7 HAFB *(Dbf .89)*	3086	
LN-CBM	Cameron V-77 HAFB	3715	
LN-CBS	Colt 77A HAFB	1904	
LN-CBV	Cameron Concept 60 SS HAFB	2758	
LN-CBX	Cameron O-77 HAFB	1277	SE-ZBX

MICROLIGHTS

Regn.	Type	C/n	Prev.Id.
LN-YAA	La Mouette Cosmos	N1-86	
LN-YAB(2)	Mainair Gemini/Flash II	KR-425-386-4/W-183-386-2	
LN-YAC	Aerodyne Vector 610 *(To Sola museum)*	1389	
LN-YAD	Teratorn Tierra 2	844020	
LN-YAG	La Mouette Cosmos Dragster Comet 2	83-1	
LN-YAI (2)	Solar Wings Pegasus XL-R	SW-TB-1065/SW-WA-1072	
LN-YAJ	Solar Wings Typhoon XL	N-2-85/SW-WA-1023	
	(Wing has same c/n as LN-YCB, mated with local trike)		
LN-YAK	CFM Shadow	003/2	
LN-YAL	Solar Wings Pegasus XL-R	SW-TB-1089/SW-WA-1137	
LN-YAM(2)	Zodiac Ultrastar	151	
LN-YAN	Mainair Triflyer 330/Flash IIA	355-785-1/W-28-285-1	
	(Registered as Mainair Gemini trike unit, trike c/n same as LN-YBN)		
LN-YAO	Solar Wings Pegasus XL-R	SW-TB-1067/SW-WA-1316	
	(Used parts and trike c/n SW-TB-1067 from LN-YBC)		
LN-YAP	Solar Wings Pegasus XL-R/Se	SW-TB-1156/SW-WA-1154	
LN-YAQ	Pioneer Flightstar	673	D-M...
LN-YAR(3)	Solar Wings Typhoon 180 *(Reservation)*	unkn	
LN-YAS(2)	Solar Wings Pegasus Flash 1	SW-TB-1017/SW-WF-0002	
LN-YAT(2)	Solar Wings Pegasus XL *(Reservation)*	unkn	
LN-YAU	Birdman Chinook WT-II	03507	
LN-YAV	Birdman Chinook WT-2S *(Cr 1990)*	00952	
LN-YAX	Steinbach Firebird/Austro Sierra 170	2204	
LN-YBB	Solar Wings Pegasus XL-R	SW-TB-1019/SW-WA-1037	
LN-YBD	Solar Wings Pegasus Photon	SW-TP-0017/SW-WP-0017	
LN-YBF	Solar Wings Pegasus XL-R	SW-TB-1051/SW-WA-1068	

Regn.	Type	C/n	Prev.Id.
LN-YBG	Solar Wings Pegasus XL-R	SW-TB-1052/SW-WA-1069	
	(Wing c/n also quoted for LN-YCR)		
LN-YBH	La Mouette Cosmos Profil 19M	unkn	
LN-YBI	Solar Wings Pegasus XL-R	SW-TB-1064/SW-WA-1071	
LN-YBJ	Rotec Panther 2 Plus	69055	
LN-YBK	Pioneer Flightstar	669	
LN-YBL	Thruster Gemini	086-119	
LN-YBM	Mainair Gemini/Flash II	4335-864/W-191-586-2	
LN-YBN	Mainair Triflyer 330	KR-355-785-3/W-190-586-1	
	(Registered as Merlin Scorcher)		
LN-YBO	Mainair Merlin Solo / Flash	KR 354-785-1/W-215-686-1	
LN-YBQ	Mainair Gemini Flash II	530-387-5/W232	
LN-YBS	Manta Tripacer Fledge III	BF02/BF27	
LN-YBU	La Mouette Profil 17	V001 P003	
LN-YBV	Pioneer Flightstar	674	
LN-YBW(2)	Pioneer Flightstar	unkn	
LN-YBX	Mainair Gemini/Flash II	438-686-4/W-157-386-2	
LN-YBY(2)	Rotec Rally Sport	72295	
LN-YBZ	La Mouette Maxi Hermes 15M	GA-1551-H15-85141	
LN-YCA	Ultrasports Tripacer/ Hiway Demon	TA12/1	
LN-YCB	Solar Wings Pegasus XL-R	SW-TB-1001/SW-WA-1023	
	(Wing c/n same as that given for LN-YAJ)		
LN-YCC	Solar Wings Pegasus XL-S /Ultrasports trike	TA 12/4	
LN-YCD	Solar Wings Pegasus XL-R /Ultrasports trike	TA 12/5	
LN-YCE	Solar Wings Typhoon XL /Ultrasports trike	T1084-1228XL	
LN-YCF	Solar Wings Demon /Ultrasports trike ?	TA 12/3	
LN-YCG	Solar Wings Panther/Southdown Puma Sprint	- /83-00293	
LN-YCH	Solar Wings Typhoon S4+	82-00084	
	(C/n quoted is Fuji-Robin engine serial)		
LN-YCI	Skyhook Pixie	1785	
	(C/n is date of sale, trike c/n probably TR1-57)		
LN-YCJ	Solar Wings Hiway Skytrike Photon	SW-WP-0016/TA 12/9	
	(Appears to have been mated with Ultrasports trike after sale)		
LN-YCK	Aerodyne Vector 610 *(Sola museum)*	1203-270	
LN-YCM	Mainair Gemini/Flash II	439-786-3/W-221	
LN-YCN	Rotec Panther 2 Plus	19863	
LN-YCO	Solar Wings Pegasus Flash 2	SW-TB-1010/SW-WF-0115	
	(Trike c/n is G-MNAW, wing originally supplied with trike of LN-YAL)		
LN-YCP	Solar Wings Pegasus XL-R	SW-TB-1088/SW-WA-1084	
LN-YCQ	Ultrasports Tripacer /La Mouette	T EVE 1/W EVE 1	
LN-YCR	Solar Wings Eagle 3XL	SW-WA-1069	
	(C/n also quoted for LN-YBG)		
LN-YCS	La Mouette Protax Mini /Profil 17	BR 001 BR 1306	
LN-YCT	Mainair Gemini/Flash II W	448-786-4/W-222	
	(Trike c/n same as LN-YCX, wing c/n same as LN-YES)		
LN-YCU	Solar Wings Pegasus XL-R	SW-TB-1086/SW-WA-1082	
LN-YCV	Quad City Ultralight Challenger 1	0987-0-0230	
LN-YCX	Mainair Gemini/Flash II	448-786-4/W-300-1186-2	
	(Trike c/n same as LN-YCT)		
LN-YCY	Mainair Merlin Scorcher	505-1286-1/W308	
LN-YCZ	Mainair Merlin/La Mouette Cronos	352-785-2/116	
LN-YDB	Solar Wings Pegasus XL-R	SW-TB-1087/SW-WA-1083	
LN-YDC	Birdman Chinook (Reservation)	unkn	
LN-YDD	Rotec Panther 2 Plus	69066	
LN-YDE	Manta Fledge III /Cosmos Dragster	FC 10/125	
LN-YDF	Solar Wings Panther XL-2	T 7841150 XL	
LN-YDG	La Mouette Minimum /Profil 15	N 201/87	
LN-YDH	La Mouette Cosmos	N 387 T184 W	
LN-YDI	Mainair Merlin/Flash II	KR-353-785-1 /W211-686-1	
	(Wing formerly SW-WF-0123 / G-MNYY rebuilt and re-sold)		
LN-YDJ	Mikrofly Stratus 1	GF 01/87	
LN-YDK	Zodiac Ultrastar	137	
LN-YDL	Eipper Quicksilver MXL-II	1196	
LN-YDM	Aerial Arts Chaser S	TR 678/ W 678 388	
	(Not a Chaser c/n, possibly local trike and Aerial Arts 130SX wing)		
LN-YDN	Pioneer Dualstar	DS 104	
LN-YDO(2)	Kolb Twinstar *(Reservation)*	unkn	
LN-YDP	Birdman Chinook WT-IS	3757	
LN-YDQ	Birdman Chinook WT-IIS	3747	
LN-YDR	Solar Wings Pegasus XL-RSE	SW-TB-1155/SW-WA-1153	
LN-YDS	Mainair Merlin Scorcher	KR-356-7853/W-205-686-1	
LN-YDT	Quad City Ultralight Challenger 2	0587 R0 257	
LN-YDU	Hiway Skytrike 160 Mk.2/Excalibur	unkn	
LN-YDV	Birdman Chinook WT-II	03687	
LN-YDW	Thruster Gemini TST Mk.1	867-TST-023	
LN-YDY	Solar Wings Pegasus TSR	T285 1328 TSR	
LN-YEA	La Mouette Schwartze Minimum	204-87	
LN-YED	La Mouette Cosmos Hermes 15 Dragster	N 188 TN 188W	
LN-YEE	Solar Wings Pegasus XL-SE	TB-1154 /WA 1152	
LN-YEF	La Mouette Minimum Hermes 16	N 20388	
LN-YEG	La Mouette Cosmos Dragster Turbo 16	N-228	
LN-YEH	Teratorn Tierra II	880313 07	
LN-YEI	La Mouette Minimum Hermes 15	2-88	
LN-YEK	La Mouette Cosmos Magnum 21	308/001	
LN-YEM	La Mouette Cosmos Turbo 15 Dragster	110	
LN-YEO	La Mouette Cosmos Turbo 15 Dragster	N113 88	
LN-YEP	La Mouette Cosmos Turbo 15	N112 88	
LN-YEQ	La Mouette Cosmos Bidulm Turbo 15	N3 88	
LN-YER	La Mouette Cosmos Dragster Hermes 15	11088	
LN-YES	Mainair Gemini/Flash II	KR-441-780-4/W-222-1186-2	
	(Wing has same c/n as LN-YCT)		
LN-YET	Teratorn Tierra I	860805009	
LN-YEU	La Mouette Minimum Profil 17	5 88	
LN-YEV	La Mouette Minimum Hermes 16	6 88	
LN-YEW	La Mouette Hermes 16	6 89	
LN-YEX	Mikrofly Stratus 2	MFP 02 88	
LN-YEY	La Mouette Minimum Hermes 15	3 87	
LN-YEZ	Teratorn Tierra II	880712021	
LN-YFA	La Mouette Minimum Profil 17	3 87	
LN-YFB	La Mouette Minimum Hermes 16	9 88	
LN-YFC	La Mouette Minimum Hermes 15	10 88	
LN-YFD	Aerial Arts Chaser S	TR 674 W 674	
	(Not a Chaser c/n, possibly local trike and Aerial Arts 130SX wing)		
LN-YFE	La Mouette Cosmos Bidulm Turbo 15	029	
LN-YFF	Fisher Super Koala	1	
LN-YFG	Aviasud Mistral *(Cr 9.7.95)*	12-88-71	
LN-YFH	Air Création GT-BI Quartz 16SX	501	
LN-YFI	La Mouette Minimum Bidulm Turbo 16	0052	
LN-YFJ	Aerial Arts Chaser S	CH 795	
LN-YFK	Aerial Arts Chaser S	CH 793	
LN-YFL	Aerial Arts Chaser S	CH 794	
LN-YFM	Zodiac Ultrastar	148	
LN-YFN	La Mouette Cosmos Bidulm Chronos	208	
LN-YFO	Teratorn Tierra IA	890319039	
LN-YFP	La Mouette Cosmos Bidulm Chronos	198	
LN-YFQ	Solar Wings Pegasus XL-Q	SW-TE-219/SW-Q-0233	
LN-YFR	Quad City Ultralight Challenger II	CH2-0289-CW-0398	
LN-YFS	Fisher Super Koala *(Reservation)*	unkn	
LN-YFT	Air Création SX GT 503	104	
LN-YFU	Air Création SX GT 462	102	
LN-YFV	Air Création GT BI /Quartz SX 16	103	
LN-YFX	Hovey Delta Bird	unkn	
LN-YFY	TEAM Mini Max	223-4-90	
LN-YFZ	Mikrofly Stratus 1	MFP 04 89	
LN-YGA	Mosler N-3-2 Pup	0021 LAS-2	
LN-YGB	S.M.A.N. Petrel	52083	
LN-YGE	Mainair Gemini/Flash IIA	KR-297-385-3/W31-3851	
LN-YGF	Mikrofly Stratus 1	MFP 03 89	
LN-YGG	Kolb Twinstar Mk.2	M2-154	
LN-YGH	Furuheim Mikromoth 1-503	BF 00390	
LN-YGI	Rans S-6ES Coyote II	1089089	
LN-YGJ	Pioneer Flightstar	675	
LN-YGK	Quad City Ultralight Challenger II	CH2-0388-CW-....	
LN-YGL	Quad City Ultralight Challenger II Special	H2-1289 CW-0493	
LN-YGM	Air Création Racer SX 12	106	
LN-YGN	Quad City Ultralight Challenger II Special	CH2-1289 CW-0494	
LN-YGO	Zodiac Twin Star	011	
LN-YGP	Mikrofly Stratus 1	MFP 05 90	
LN-YGQ	Quad City Ultralight Challenger II Special	CH-21189 CW-0429	
LN-YGR	Rans S-5 Coyote I	90124	
LN-YGS	Aerial Arts Chaser S	W 459 TR 459	
LN-YGT(2)	Eipper Quicksilver GT-400	unkn	
LN-YGU	Quad City Ultralight Challenger II Special	CH2-1189 CW-0478	
	(Possibly sold as N101SV?)		
LN-YGV	Mikrofly Stratus 2B	MFP 06 91	
LN-YGW	Quad City Ultralight Challenger II Special	CH2-0890 CW-0553	
LN-YGX	Aerial Arts Chaser S	CH 592	
	(Not a Chaser c/n, possibly local trike and Aerial Arts 130SX wing)		
LN-YGY	Rans S-6 Coyote II	0989079	
LN-YGZ	Rans S-6ES Coyote II	191155	

Regn.	Type	C/n	Prev.Id.
LN-YHA	Rans S-5 Coyote I	090148	
LN-YHB	Rans S-6 Coyote II	0191158	
LN-YHC	Eipper Quicksilver GT-500	0065	
LN-YHD	Kolb Firestar	3607811	
LN-YHE	Rans S-12 Airaile	0491073	
LN-YHF	Quad City Ultralight Challenger II Special	CH2-0890 CW-0552	
LN-YHG	Mikrofly Stratus 2B	MFP 07 91	
LN-YHH	Rans S-5 Coyote I	90136	
	(C/n probably incorrect, 90136 is Rans S-4 N2131A)		
LN-YHI	Rans S-6 Coyote II *(Damaged 2.8.95)*	591190	
LN-YHJ	Rans S-12 Airaile	591074	
LN-YHK	Solar Wings Pegasus Quasar	SW-WQQ-0465/SW-TQC-0071	
LN-YHL	Eipper Quicksilver MX	3016	
LN-YHM	Teratorn Tierra I	88030718	
LN-YHN	Mikrofly Stratus 1	MFP 08 91	
LN-YHO	European CUBy 2	C 06	
LN-YHQ	Light Aero Avid High Gross STOL	1471 HGS	
	(Damaged 28.7.96)		
LN-YHR	Rans S-12 Airaile	491070	
LN-YHS	Fisher Classic	C-053	
LN-YHT	Quad City Ultralight Challenger II Special	CH-20688 CW-0330	
LN-YHU	Rans S-7 Courier	0991087	
LN-YHW(2)	Rans S-6S Super Six	0495795	
LN-YHX	Rans S-6 Coyote II	1091232	
LN-YHY	Murphy Renegade II	386	
LN-YHZ	Rans S-12 Airaile	9-120	
LN-YIA	Rans S-7 Courier	1291090	
LN-YIB	Mikrofly Stratus 2B	MFP 09 92	
LN-YIC	Mikrofly Stratus 2B	MFP 10 92	
LN-YID	TEAM Mini Max *(Reservation)*	unkn	
LN-YIE	Rans S-6 Coyote II *(Reservation)*	unkn	
LN-YIF	Trike?Turbo 15 *(Reservation)*	unkn	
LN-YIG	Rans S-12 Airaile	1292352	
LN-YIH	Rans S-6ES Coyote II	0990140	
LN-YII	Quad City Ultralight Challenger II Special	CH-20589 CW-0421	
LN-YIJ	Fisher FP101 Koala	N-3	
LN-YIK	Fisher Super Koala	N-2	
LN-YIL	Edra Sao Paulo Seabird	049	
LN-YIM	Mikrofly Stratus 2B	MFP 11 92	
LN-YIN	Atlas *(Reservation)*	unkn	
LN-YIO	Kolb Firestar	193	
LN-YIP	Mikrofly Stratus 1B	MFP 12 93	
LN-YIQ	Noim Sirius C	C15	
LN-YIR	TEAM Hi-Max	811P	
LN-YIS	TEAM Hi-Max *(Reservation)*	unkn	
LN-YIT	Teratorn Tierra 2	920627157	
LN-YIU	Rans S-12 Airaile	0293378	
LN-YIV	Rans S-12 Airaile	unkn	
LN-YIW	Rans S-12 Airaile	0193370	
LN-YIX	Mikrofly Twin Stratus	MFP 13 93	
LN-YIY	TEAM Hi-Max	232	
LN-YJA	Mainair Sports Scorcher	639-588-4/W427	
	(C/n quoted as W428 which is G-MTXS)		
LN-YJB(2)	Murphy Renegade Spirit	336	
LN-YJC	Rans S-12 Airaile	C493409	
LN-YJD	TEAM Z-Max	764P	
LN-YJE	TEAM Z-Max	763P	
LN-YJF	Rans S-6 Coyote II	0392281	
LN-YJG	TEAM Hi-Max *(Reservation)*	unkn	
LN-YJH(2)	Rans S-6ES Coyote II	0195721ES	
LN-YJI	Skystar Denney Kitfox III	902	
LN-YJK	La Mouette Cosmos Dragster Turbo 15	N115	
LN-YJL	TEAM Z-Max	525P	
LN-YJN	TEAM Z-Max *(Reservation)*	unkn	
LN-YJO	Teratorn Tierra II	880317106	
LN-YJR	Jodel D.18 *(Reservation)*	unkn	
LN-YJS	Fisher FP404	N4-404	
LN-YKA	Type unknown *(Reservation)*	unkn	
LN-YKB	Preceptor N3-2 Pup	0122	
LN-YKC	Preceptor N3-2 Pup *(Reservation)*	unkn	
LN-YKD	Mikrofly Twin Stratus	unkn	
LN-YKE	Rans S-6 Coyote II	0460117	
LN-YKF	Denney Kitfox III	1065	
LN-YKG	Falken *(Reservation)*	unkn	
LN-YKH	Rans S-6ES Coyote II	0795857	
LN-YKI	Edra Sao Paulo Seabird *(Reservation)*	unkn	
LN-YKJ	Rans S-6ES Coyote II	1295907ES	
LN-YKL	Rans S-6 Coyote II *(Reservation)*	unkn	
LN-YKM	Rans S-6 Coyote II	1095887	
LN-YKN	Denney Kitfox IV	1517	(LN-AEO)
LN-YKO	Kolb Ultrastar	unkn	
LN-YKP	Rans S-6ES Coyote II	0395775	
LN-YKR(2)	Light Aero Avid Flyer Bandit	1417E	
LN-YKS	Denney Kitfox III	unkn	
LN-YKT	Edra Sao Paulo Seabird *(Reservation)*	unkn	
LN-YKU	Rans S-6ES Coyote II	9961036ES	
LN-YKV	Jora *(Reservation)*	unkn	
LN-YKW	Murphy Maverick	unkn	
LN-YKX	Light Aero Avid Flyer	394	LN-PET
LN-YKY	Rans S-12 Airaile *(Reservation)*	unkn	
LN-YKZ	Rans S-6S Super Six	unkn	
LN-YLA	TEAM Hi-Max *(Reservation)*	unkn	
LN-YLB	Rans S-6S Super Six	unkn	
LN-YLC	Rans S-6 Coyote II	0592301	
LN-YLD	TEAM Hi-Max *(Reservation)*	unkn	
LN-YLE	La Mouette Cosmos Bidulm Chronos	0228/960 425 8	
LN-YLF	Rans S-6 Coyote II	unkn	
LN-YLG	Bailey-Moyes Dragonfly	26	
LN-YLH	Rans S-6ES Coyote II	0195720ES	
LN-YLI	Fisher FP-303 *(Reservation)*	unkn	
LN-YLL	Quad City Ultralight Challenger I Special	CHCW 0488-105	
	(C/n as quoted. Possibly CH2-0484-0105, ex N105PL, or possibly		
	could be CH2-0488-CW-0305))		
LN-YLM	Rans S-6 Coyote II	1292402	
LN-YLN	Merlin (Whittaker MW-6 ?)	M1138	
LN-YLR	Rans S-6ES Coyote II	unkn	
LN-YLS	Teratorn Tierra 1A	900121060	
LN-YLT	Austro Turbo 16 *(Reservation)*	unkn	
LN-YLV	Rans S-6S Super Six *(Reservation)*	unkn	
LN-YMA	Teratorn Tierra 1	870806017	
LN-YMB	Teratorn Tierra 1	860404005	
LN-YMC	Teratorn Tierra 1	860302004	
LN-YME	Teratorn Tierra 1	900222065	
LN-YMF	Teratorn Tierra 1	901026091	
LN-YMG	Teratorn Tierra 1A	880715019	
LN-YMH	Rans S-6 Coyote II	0990140	
LN-YML	Teratorn Tierra 1	860301002	
LN-YMN	Denney Kitfox III	1031	LN-AKF
LN-YMO	Preceptor/Mosler N3-2 Ultra Pup	LA065UP	
LN-YMP	Jabiru UL	0287/UL0075	
LN-YMR	Denney Kitfox IV *(Reservation)*	unkn	
LN-YMU	Murphy Maverick	002M-UL	C-FPSJ
LN-YMX	Eipper Quicksilver MXL-2	365	
LN-YNB	Kolb Twinstar III	M3-032	
LN-YNH	Light Aero Avid Flyer *(Reservation)*	unkn	
LN-YNK	Skystar Denney Kitfox IV	DCU-016	
LN-YNN	Jabiru UL	0286/UL-74	
LN-YOA	Quad City Ultralight Challenger II Special	CH2-1188- CW 0371	
	(Correct c/n may be CH2-0888-0371)		
LN-YOB	Quad City Ultralight Challenger II *(Reservn)*	unkn	
LN-YOC	Rans S-12 Airaile	unkn	
LN-YOJ	Solar Wings Pegasus XL-Q	SW-TE-218/SW-Q-0024	
	(Wing SW-Q-0024 originally sold with trike SW-TE-0029 as LN-YKR,		
	sold as SE-YRC)		
LN-YOL	Rans S-12 Airaile	0493396	
LN-YOM	Quad City Ultralight Challenger II	01871 R 0231	
	(C/n 0231 also quoted for LN-YOR and for N231SP)		
LN-YOO	Light Aero Avid Flyer IV *(Damaged 13.9.97)*	1491 HGS	
LN-YOR	Quad City Ultralight Challenger I	0987 R 0231	
	(C/n 0231 also quoted for LN-YOM and for N231SP)		
LN-YOS	First Strike Supercat	474	
LN-YOU	Mainair Gemini Southdown Sprint	241384	
LN-YOY	Jora	008-1995	
LN-YPC	Lamco Euro Cub Mk.1	CAH-011	
LN-YPG	Teratorn Tierra 1A	880714017	
LN-YPH	Rans S-6 Coyote II	1093549	
LN-YPK	Eipper Quicksilver GT-400S	GT 2801206	
LN-YPO	Mikrofly Twin Stratus	unkn	
LN-YPP	Teratorn Tierra 1A	880316106	
LN-YPS	Mainair Gemini/Flash 1	294-0385-W29	

Regn.	Type	C/n	Prev.Id.
LN-YPX	Solar Wings Pegasus Q	SW-WQ-0024	
LN-YPZ	Rans S-6S Super Six	1294715S	
LN-YQS	Eipper Quicksilver MX-II	3981	
LN-YQT	Rans S-12 Airaile	0292189	
LN-YQW(2)	La Mouette Cosmos Chronos 14	unkn	
LN-YRE	Teratorn Tierra 1A	900723078	
LN-YRH	Teratorn Tierra 1 (to museum, Sola)	860303003	
LN-YRJ	Skystar Denney Kitfox IV	DCV 018	
LN-YRR	Lamco Eurocub Mk.1 (Accident 23.5.98)	CAH 008	
LN-YRS	Murphy Renegade Spirit	AC-385	
LN-YRW	Ragwing Special (Reservation)	unkn	
LN-YRY	Rans S-6S Super Six	1294711	
LN-YSA	III Sky Arrow 450T	030	
LN-YSB(2)	III Sky Arrow 450T	unkn	
LN-YSC	III Sky Arrow 450T	unkn	
LN-YSD	Fisher FP-404 Classic (Reservation)	unkn	
LN-YSE	Zenair CH-701 STOL	7-1263	LN-PSB
LN-YSF	La Mouette Cosmos Dragster Hermes 16	N2 87	
LN-YSI	Light Aero Avid Flyer	354	LN-HAL
LN-YSJ	Murphy Renegade Spirit 2	379	
LN-YSK	La Mouette Cosmos Dragster Turbo 16	189	
LN-YSL	Denney Kitfox IV (Reservation)	unkn	
LN-YSN	Fisher FP-202 Super Koala	unkn	
LN-YSP(2)	Ikarus C42 Cyclone (Reservation)	unkn	
LN-YSR	La Mouette Cosmos Dragster Turbo 16	83-2	
LN-YSS	Rans S-7 Courier	0390074	
	(Correct c/n believed to be 0989.057)		
LN-YST	Fisher Super Koala	unkn	
LN-YSW	Aériane Sirocco	11/84	
LN-YTA	Birdman Chinook WT-IIS	01212	
LN-YTB	Birdman Chinook WT-II	03667	
LN-YTC	Birdman Chinook WT-II	03657	
LN-YTE	Rans S-6 ES Coyote II	0191156	
LN-YTF	Birdman Chinook WT-IIS	00512	
LN-YTG	Mainair Gemini/Flash 2	293-0385-3W-28	
LN-YTH	Fisher FP-202 Super Koala	2-90	
LN-YTI	Light Aero Avid Flyer	863	(LN-TTI)
LN-YTJ	Fisher FP-202 UL Koala	2196	
LN-YTL	Teratorn Tierra 1A Special	901025090	
LN-YTM	Rans S-6ES Coyote II	0596992ES	
LN-YTO	Rans S-7 Courier	0989057	LN-ATC
LN-YTP	Light Aero Avid Flyer Mk.4 STOL	1201	
LN-YTR	Denney Kitfox IV (Reservation)	unkn	
LN-YTS(2)	Rans S-14	0895088	
LN-YTT	Teratorn Tierra 1	unkn	
LN-YTW	Rans S-6 ES Coyote II	0191159	
	(Same c/n as N42739, possibly ex and returned to?)		
LN-YTY	Titan Tornado 912 (Reservation)	unkn	
LN-YVE	Eipper Quicksilver MXL Sport	162	
LN-YVI	Rans S-12 Airaile	0892254	
LN-YVL	Rans S-6ES Coyote II (Damaged 3.6.95)	0195718ES	
LN-YVT	Light Aero Avid Flyer	158	
LN-YVW	Denney Kitfox (Reservation)	unkn	
LN-YWA	Rans S-6 Coyote II	0192266	
LN-YWW	Lamco Eurocub Mk.1	CAH-004	
LN-YWY	Murphy Renegade Spirit	unkn	
LN-YXX	Teratorn Tierra 1A	890820058	
LN-YYW	Rans S-12 Airaile	1294542	
LN-YYY(2)	Denney Kitfox III	858	LX-FOX
LN-YZL	Eipper Quicksilver MX2	QS.83.3264.1	
LN-YZP	Rans S-6S Super Six	0195716	
LN-YZX	Type unknown	unkn	

LX - LUXEMBOURG

Regn.	Type	C/n	Prev.Id.
LX-ABC	Short SC.7 Skyvan 3M	SH.1888	PA-51
			G-14-60
LX-ACD	Cerva CE-43 Guepard	466	F-BXCD
LX-ACE	Rutan Cozy Classic	CC.1002	N52CZ
LX-ACR	Piper PA-31T1 Cheyenne I	31T-8104067	D-IACR
			N52TW
			N2608Y
LX-AGM	Mooney M.20K Model 231	25-0636	N1154P
LX-AHI	Cessna A.188B Agtruck	01818T	N70042
LX-AHN	Cessna A.188B Agtruck	03491T	CN-THN
			LX-AHN
			N2640J
LX-AHP	Cessna A.188B Agtruck	03118T	SX-AMP
			N731SL
LX-AHT	Cessna A.188B Agtruck	0008/03120T	CN-THT
	(Reims assembled)		LX-AHT
			SX-AHT
			N73ISN
LX-AHZ	Cessna T.210N Turbo Centurion II	63672	I-KKIS
			N4918C
LX-AIA	Piper PA-18 Super Cub 95	18-1011	ALAT
			51-15314
LX-AIB(2)	Piper PA-28-161 Cadet	2841086	N91692
LX-AIC	Reims/Cessna F.172L	0852	
LX-AID	Reims/Cessna F.172N	1972	D-EOOT
LX-AIE	Piper PA-28-161 Cadet	2841346	D-ESTG
			N92294
			N151ND
			N92294
LX-AIF	Piper PA-28-161 Cadet	2841173	N9185V
LX-AIG(2)	Piper PA-28-161 Cadet	2841315	N9211Q
LX-AIL	Bellanca 7ECA Scout	1055-74	N88301
LX-AIP	Reims/Cessna F.152	1432	
LX-AIQ	Reims/Cessna F.152	1868	
LX-AIR	Piper PA-28-235 Cherokee	28-10586	N9005W
LX-AIS	Reims/Cessna F.152	1617	
LX-AIT	Cessna TR.182 Turbo Skylane RG	01415	F-GCVZ
			N4753S
LX-AIX	Reims/Cessna F.182Q Skylane	0102	
LX-AIZ	Reims/Cessna F.172N	1968	D-EAKU
LX-ALF	Grob G.115A	8030	(OO-PHD)
			(D-EGVV)
LX-ARA	Beech F33A Bonanza	CE-861	N222FT
			N31228
			D-EHVE
LX-ARS	Grumman-American AA-1B Trainer	0556	D-EHLD
			(N1456R)
LX-ATT	Piper PA-28-181 Archer II	28-8090096	OO-PAQ
			OO-HLC
			N80922
LX-AVA(2)	Piper PA-28-181 Archer II	2890157	D-ETAH
			N9214X
LX-AVE	Grob G.115A	8055	(D-EGV V)
LX-AVF	Grob G.115A	8067	(D-EGV V)
LX-AVG	Piper PA-28-236 Dakota	28-8611006	OY-CEC
LX-AWD	American AG-5B Tiger	10054	N11927
LX-AWY	Grumman AA-5 Traveler	0723	
LX-BOY	Robin HR.100/200B Royale	119	D-EOCY
LX-BSM(2)	Colomban MC-15 Cri-Cri	421	
LX-BUG	Commander Aircraft 114B	14549	D-ERPA
			N172A
LX-DIS	Cessna 140	12409	C-FELQ
			CF-ELQ
LX-DPA	Dassault Falcon 10	113	F-GFHH(2)
			(F-GFHG)
			HB-VIW
			I-CHOC
			(I-SHOP)
			F-WPXE
LX-DUC	Beech B200 Super King Air	BB-1369	D-IVHM
			N778HP
			N5649V

474

Regn.	Type	C/n	Prev.Id.
LX-EAC	Embraer EMB.120RT Brasilia	120-184	N288UE
			PT-SQW
LX-EJW	Cessna T.310R	1628	N72JW
			N2632Z
LX-FAC	Piper PA-18 Super Cub 95	18-2132	Army 841
			52-2532
LX-FAR	SOCATA TB-200 Tobago XL	1445	
LX-FCA	Piper PA-32R-301T Turbo Saratoga	32R-8129099	N8430H
LX-FCV(4)	Boeing 747-4R7F	25866	N17856
LX-FLO	Piper PA-28-181 Archer II	28-8190084	OO-ESC
			OO-HKO
			N8291Y
LX-FLY(2)	Piper PA-28RT-201 Arrow IV	28R-7918165	N2839K
LX-FMR	Dassault Falcon 50	165	HZ-SM3
			F-WZHF
LX-FRZ	Beech C90 King Air	LJ-898	N113AP
			YV-741CP
			N41AJ
			OH-BKI
			N67599
LX-FTJ	Dassault Falcon 50	144	N544RA
			VP-BZE
			VR-BZE
			N70FL
			N133FJ
			F-WZHL
LX-GBY	Hawker 800XP	258392	N23569
LX-GCV(3)	Boeing 747-4R7F	25867	
LX-GDB	Beech 200 Super King Air	BB-397	D-IAMW
			F-GFIV
			PH-SLG
			5N-ALF
			PH-SLG
LX-GDL	Cessna 550 Citation II	0033	(N526CA)
			F-WPLT
			F-GPLT
			N46DA
			N755CM
			N59MJ
			TR-LYE
			(N3252M)
LX-GER	Aero Designs Pulsar	379	
LX-GHI	Short SC.7 Skyvan 3M	SH.1890	PA-53
			G-14-62
LX-GHL	Cessna TR.182 (Reims assembled)	0002/00860	N737NK
LX-HEP	Bell 212	30972	N606LH
			JA9545
			N1071G
LX-HEX	Revolution Mini-500	349	
LX-HGR	Aérospatiale SA.365NDauphin 2	6307	JA9902
LX-HMD	McDonnell-Douglas MD.900	00033	D-HRTA
LX-HOR	Bell 205A-1	30159	C-GMOR
			VH-JOR
			C-GMOR
			N367EH
LX-HRI	Bell 205A-1	30019	HB-XRI
			N4774R
			C-GXXH
			N4774R
			HC-BDT
			N4774R
			YV-O-MOP-9
			N4774R
LX-HUA	Sikorsky S-76+	760170	F-GLSI
			I-SKSA
			F-GING
			N76UT
			C-GHVQ
LX-HUD	Sikorsky S-76A +	760042	F-GILD
			N9007N
			PH-NZN
			N5009V

Regn.	Type	C/n	Prev.Id.
LX-HUE	Sikorsky S-76A	760186	ZS-RKH
			LX-HUE
			F-GDHU
			F-WZSB
			F-GDHU
LX-HUF	Aérospatiale AS.365N2 Dauphin 2	6412	F-GHRY
LX-HUL	Aérospatiale SA.330J Puma	1583	F-GHYR
	(Reserved as F-GINQ .99)		I-EHPJ
			PH-SSB
			PK-TRF
			PH-SSB
			F-WXFM
LX-HUN	Aérospatiale AS.365N2 Dauphin 2	6468	F-GMBU
			LX-H ..
			F-GJBU
LX-HUP	Aérospatiale SA.365N1 Dauphin 2	6346	F-....
			JA9970
LX-HXU	Bell 205A-1	30288	HB-XXU
			OE-EXR
			C-GLMC
			N2750L
LX-IAL	Dassault Falcon 20C	136/439	SP-FCP
			HB-VBM
			F-GCGU
			9K-ACQ
			HB-VBM
			F-WJMJ
LX-ICV	Boeing 747-428F	25632	(F-GIUA)
			N6005C
LX-JCG	Dassault Falcon 10	160	F-GFFP
			N31TM
			N223HS
			N225FJ
			F-WZGK
LX-JCO	Mooney M.20R Ovation	29-0071	D-EICO(3)
LX-JOE	Brändli BX-2 Cherry	13	
LX-JOS	Reims/Cessna FR.172J Rocket	0453	OO-WAI
LX-JWT	Cessna 421C Golden Eagle II	0473	D-IUNP
			N888JS
			(N808JS)
			N888JS
			N666HS
			D-IOLI
			HB-LKI
			N6815C
LX-KCV	Boeing 747-4R7F	25868	
LX-KEN	Reims/Cessna F.172E	0055	D-EMAX
LX-KEV	Pilatus Britten-Norman BN-2T Islander	2102	LX- III
			V2-LDF
			(OB-T-1282)
			V2-LDF
			VP-LMF
			N660J
			G-BIIO
LX-KVF	SOCATA TB-21 Trinidad TC	721	D-EFMV
LX-LCL	Piper PA-28R-201T Turbo Arrow III	28R-7803083	N6050H
LX-LCO	Cessna P210N Pressurized Centurion II	00104	N4781P
			C-GVVY
			N478IP
LX-LCT	Mooney M.20K Model 231	25-0811	N5741A
			D-EMEM
			N574IA
LX-LCV	Boeing 747-4R7F	29053	
LX-LGB(2)	Fokker F.27-050	20221	PH-EXU
			(PH-RRC)
LX-LGC	Fokker F.27-050	20168	PH-EXH
LX-LGD	Fokker F.27-050	20171	PH-EXJ
LX-LGE	Fokker F.27-050	20180	PH-EXF
LX-LGF	Boeing 737-4C9	25429	
LX-LGG	Boeing 737-4C9	26437	
LX-LGK	Embraer EMB.120RT Brasilia	120-261	PT-SUH
LX-LGO	Boeing 737-5C9	26438	
LX-LGP(2)	Boeing 737-5C9	26439	
LX-LGR	Boeing 737-528	27424	(F-GJNP)
LX-LGS	Boeing 737-528	27425	(F-GJNQ)

Regn.	Type	C/n	Prev.Id.
LX-LGT	Embraer EMB.145	145-076	PT-SAU
LX-LGU	Embraer EMB.145	145-084	PT-S ..
LX-LGV	Embraer EMB.145ER	145-129	PT-S ..
LX-LGW	Embraer EMB.145ER	145-135	PT-S ..
LX-LGX	Embraer EMB.145ER	145-147	
LX-LTX	Beech E90 King Air	LW-297	SE-IKD
			OY-AZG
LX-MAX	Holste MH.152IM Broussard	312	F-GGKQ
			(LX- III)
			F-WGKQ
			Fr.AF
LX-MCV	Boeing 747-4R7F	29729	
LX-MEN	Reims/Cessna F.177RG Cardinal RG	0051	
LX-MMB	Canadair CL.600-2B16 Challenger	5146	C-FRQA
LX-NAN	Dassault Falcon 900	159	F-WQPL
			LX-NAN
			N263PW
			P4-NAN
			F-WWFD
LX-NCV	Boeing 747-4R7F	29730	
LX-NVL	Embraer EMB.120RT Brasilia	120-097	F-GFEQ
			PT-SMP
LX-OCV	Boeing 747-4R7F	29731	
LX-OKC	Piper PA-28-160 Cherokee	28-7225328	HB-OKC
			N11C
LX-ONE	Gates Learjet 35A	35A-417	N281CD
			(N37HR)
			HC-BTN
			N90RK
			N97D
			D-CONO
			(N117RJ)
			N117FJ
			N934GL
LX-OUF(3)	Grumman AA-5B Tiger	0275	G-BDYB
LX-PAA	Piper PA-18-135 Super Cub	18-3815	(PH-KNC)
			R-125
			54-2415
LX-PAB	Cessna 305C (L-19E) Bird Dog	23312	ALAT
			51-12855
LX-PAC	Cessna 305C (L-19E) Bird Dog	24566	F-GHDK
			ALAT
LX-PAD	Pilatus P.3-05	497-46	HB-RCB
			A-859
LX-PAE	North American T-6G Texan	168-587	E16-106
			49-3453
LX-PAV	Piper PA-32R-301T Saratoga IITC	3257097	N9513N
LX-PCT	Gates Learjet 31A	31A-112	N5082S
LX-PCV	Boeing 747-4R7F	29732	
LX-PCW	Cessna 182Q Skylane	66467	N94630
LX-PEZ	Gyrocopter	unkn	
LX-POL	Pitts S-1S Special	789H	
LX-PRA	Bombardier Learjet 60	60-145	N145LJ
LX-PRS	Cessna 551 Citation II	0496	N999GH
			N8008F
			N232CC
			(N12543)
LX-PTC	Piper PA-28RT-201T Turbo Arrow IV	28R-7931157	N100US
			N9645N
LX-PTU	Embraer EMB.120RT Brasilia	120-014	OY-JRT
	(Reserved as F-HAOC 7.99)		F-GFIN
			PT-SIJ
LX-RCC	Robin DR.400/120 Dauphin 2+2	2319	
LX-RCD	Robin DR.400/180 Régent	2320	
LX-RCE	Robin DR.400/180 Régent	2313	D-ECJH
LX-RCV	Boeing 747-4R7F	30400	
LX-RGI	Embraer EMB.120ER Brasilia	120-099	F-GFER
			PT-S ..
LX-ROH	Robin R.3000/160	153	(D-EKKS(2))
LX-RST	Piper PA-31T Cheyenne II	31T-7820027	F-GGPJ
			N61RA
			N22CA
			N82231
LX-SAS	Pilatus P.3-05	489-38	A-851

Regn.	Type	C/n	Prev.Id.
LX-SKS	Embraer EMB.110P1 Bandeirante	110-381	F-GFYZ
			F-WFYZ
			TR-LAG
			PT-SEY
LX-SKY	Cessna 421C Golden Eagle II	0621	D-ISAL
			N88636
LX-SUD	Piper PA-22-135 Tri-Pacer	22-295	D-EFUV
			N983A
LX-TAT	Bushby Mustang II	961	
LX-TFA	Cessna TU206C Super Skywagon	0946	CN-TFA
			C-FPSI
			CF-PSI
			N3946G
LX-THF	Mooney M.20R Ovation	29-0047	
LX-THS	Cessna 550 Citation II	0074	D-CIFA
			(N10GN)
			(N551GN)
			N386MA
			LN-AAI
			(N86JM)
			N48ND
			N4754G
LX-TLA	McDonnell-Douglas DC-8-62FC	45960	F-GDJM
			I-DIWC
LX-TLB	McDonnell-Douglas DC-8-62	45925	N922BV
			CX-BQN
			CX-BQN-F
			C-GMXR
			N922CL
			HB-IDG
LX-TLC	McDonnell-Douglas DC-8-62F	45920	N924BV
			C-GMXY
			N923CL
			HB-IDF
LX-TLD	McDonnell-Douglas DC-10-30CF *(Reservn)*	47831	G-BHDI
LX-TLE	McDonnell-Douglas DC-10-30CF *(Reservation)*	46949	G-BEBL
			N54643
LX-TPL	SOCATA MS.880B Rallye-Club	2041	F-BTPL
LX-TRG	Dassault Falcon 10	19	3A-MGT
			F-GJFZ
			N937J
			N36JM
			(N36KA)
			(N30JH)
			N30JM
			N112FJ
			F-WLCU
LX-TWN	Beech 76 Duchess	ME-404	F-GKDH
			N771AW
			EI-BKW
			ST-AKB
			EI-BKW
			N3834Z
LX-TWO	Mitsubishi MU-2B-60 Marquise	1515SA	N802SM
			N910DA
			N426MA
LX-UAE	Dassault Falcon 50	104	N351JS
			SE-DVG
			N50VG
			F-WWHK
			F-GFGQ
			N90AE
			N105FJ
			F-WZHR
LX-UGO	Short SC.7 Skyvan Series 3-100	SH.1945	5T-MAN
			G-14-113
LX-ULI	Piper PA-28RT-201T Turbo Arrow IV	28R-8031112	N8223V
LX-UXM	Bölkow BO.207	290	HB-UXM
			(D-ENWO)
LX-VAN	Reims/Cessna FR.172H Rocket	0300	LX-PCL
			D-ECRR
LX-VDV	Embraer EMB.120RT Brasilia	120-119	N129AM
			PT-SNL
LX-VIV	Pottier P.230S Panda	430	
LX-WOW	Beech C24R Sierra	MC-754	N3846Q

Regn.	Type	C/n	Prev.Id.
LX-YKH	Cessna 500 Citation	0086	C-FMAN
			N503GP
			N586CC
LX-ZAZ	CASA I-131E Jungmann	2032	D-EKPH
			G-BECX
			E3B-430
LX-...	Reims/Cessna F406 Caravan II	0007	PH-FWC
			EC-ESF
			PH-FWC
			OO-TIR
			(OO-TIA)
			F-WZDT
LX-...	Piper PA-28-161 Warrior III	2842040	

MICROLIGHTS

Regn.	Type	C/n	Prev.Id.
LX-XAA	Cosmos BI 17	21300	
LX-XAE	Comco Ikarus Fox C-22	unkn	
LX-XAM	Fly Synthesis Storch 503	113/60	
LX-XAP	Sky Walker 1+1	26104	
LX-XBB	Light Aero Avid Mk.IV STOL	1583D	
LX-XCB	Zenair CH-701 STOL	7-3183	
LX-XCD	Kolb Firestar	KXP-254	
LX-XER	Continental Aerolights Eagle XL	85071015	PH-1R2
LX-XGH	Dynali Chickinox Kot-Kot	3192B91	
LX-XHO	Cosmos DPM	B0174	
LX-XII	Air Création Quartz GT-BI 503	046	
LX-XOK	Letov ST-4 Aztek	unkn	
LX-XPP	Weedhopper AX-3	unkn	
LX-XRE	Rans S-6 Coyote II	unkn	
LX-XSH	Air's Maestro	8809187	
LX-XTT	Air's Maestro	128-87	
LX-X..	AMFChevron 2-32	031	OO-A29

BALLOONS AND AIRSHIPS

Regn.	Type	C/n	Prev.Id.
LX-ASS	Raven S-49A HAFB	3042	
LX-AXA	Cameron A-120 HAFB	3944	
LX-BAG	Cameron N-90 HAFB	2348	LX-MTC
			(OO-BLX)
LX-BCC	Cameron N-65 HAFB	3037	
LX-BCE	Cameron N-77 HAFB	4501	
LX-BCP	Cameron V-77 HAFB	3124	
LX-BEG	Cameron N-90 HAFB	4432	
LX-BES	Cameron N-90 HAFB	3618	LX-SES
LX-BIG(2)	Schroeder Fire Balloons G HAFB	704	
LX-BIL(3)	Cameron N-77 HAFB	4075	
LX-BIS	Cameron N-90 HAFB	4367	
LX-BMG	Cameron N-77 HAFB	3059	
LX-BML	Cameron N-77 HAFB	4551	
LX-BMM	Cameron Z-77 HAFB	4719	
LX-BOS	Cameron V-65 HAFB	4271	
LX-BST	Schroeder Fire Balloons G HAFB	767	
LX-BTL	Cameron N-77 HAFB	2507	LX-BIL(2)
LX-BUL	Cameron N-77 HAFB	1726	
LX-BUS	Cameron A-140 HAFB	1550	
LX-DBI	Cameron A-140 HAFB	2660	
LX-EUR	Cameron N-77 HAFB	3320	
LX-EXP	Cameron A-105 HAFB	2728	
LX-FES	Cameron V-65 HAFB	3051	
LX-GSM	Cameron N-90 HAFB	3072	
LX-GUY	Cameron DP-80 Hot Air Airship	3083	
LX-HAI	Cameron N-90 HAFB	1869	

Regn.	Type	C/n	Prev.Id.
LX-HBT(2)	Cameron DP-90 Hot Air Airship	3333	
LX-HIT	Cameron V-65 HAFB	4720	
LX-HOT(2)	Cameron O-77 HAFB	925	
LX-JLW	Cameron H-24 HAFB	2665	
LX-JOY	Cameron V-77 HAFB	5549	N61267
LX-LUX	Cameron O-105 HAFB	2500	
LX-MAT(2)	Cameron N-90 HAFB	3702	
	(Formerly c/n 2347)		
LX-MOB	Schroeder Fire Balloons G HAFB	498	
LX-MWL	Cameron N-77 HAFB	2506	
LX-OIO	Cameron C-60 Concept HAFB	3880	
LX-OKE(2)	Cameron N-77 HAFB	2676	
LX-OLE	Cameron N-65 HAFB	2066	
LX-PFX	Cameron A-120 HAFB	4148	
LX-PST	Cameron DP-80 Hot Air Airship	2611	
LX-ROM	Cameron H-34 HAFB	2366	
LX-RTL	Cameron N-90 HAFB	3253	
LX-TNT	Cameron N-90 HAFB	3969	
LX-TOP	Cameron A-180 HAFB	2234	
LX-ZEP	Cameron N-90 HAFB	1870	

GLIDERS AND MOTOR-GLIDERS

Regn.	Type	C/n	Prev.Id.
LX-CAC	Valentin Mistral C	MC 053/84	
LX-CAG	Schleicher ASW-19B	19253	
LX-CAM	Grob G.109B	6266	
LX-CAT(2)	Scheibe SF-25B Falke	46175	D-KAGJ
LX-CAX	Glasflügel H303 Mosquito	165	D-7521
LX-CHJ	Schempp-Hirth Nimbus 3DM	59/26	
LX-CLV	Schleicher ASK-21	21379	
LX-CMB	Schmepp-Hirth Nimbus 2B	165	D-2791
LX-CMN	Rolladen-Schneider LS-4	4330	D-0400
LX-CMW	Rolladen-Schneider LS-4	4319	PH-732
			D-2512
LX-COE	Schleicher ASK-21	21585	
LX-COY	Glaser-Dirks DG-400	4-162	OY-XOY
LX-CPB	Schleicher ASW-20	20257	D-7645
LX-CPF	Glaser-Dirks DG-500M	5E-40M18	
LX-CPG	Scheibe Bergfalke III	AB-5649	
LX-CRP	Glaser-Dirks DG-300 Elan	3E-444A7	
LX-CVN	Hoffman H-36 Dimona	36244	D-KLSW
LX-UCL(2)	Grob G.103C Twin IIISL	35048	
LX-...	Rolladen-Schneider LS-4	4319	PH-732
			D-2512

LY - LITHUANIA

Regn.	Type	C/n	Prev.Id.
LY-AAA	Yakovlev YAK-40	9720154	CCCP86729
LY-AAB	Yakovlev YAK-40	9520940	CCCP87507
LY-AAC	Yakovlev YAK-40	9530344	CCCP87980
LY-AAD	Yakovlev YAK-40	9412032	CCCP87388
LY-AAE	Yakovlev YAK-52	899311	N2183F
			LY-AAE
			DOSAAF-08
LY-AAO	Yakovlev YAK-42	4520423606237	CCCP42339
LY-AAQ	Yakovlev YAK-42	4520422708295	CCCP42344
LY-AAR	Yakovlev YAK-42	4520422708304	CCCP42345
LY-AAT	Yakovlev YAK-42	4520424711396	CCCP42353
LY-AAU	Yakovlev YAK-42	4520424711397	CCCP42354
LY-AAV	Yakovlev YAK-42	4520424711399	CCCP42355
LY-AAW	Yakovlev YAK-42	4520423811417	CCCP42359
LY-AAX	Yakovlev YAK-42	4520424811431	CCCP42362
LY-AAY	Yakovlev YAK-40	9720753	CCCP88269
LY-ABA	Tupolev TU-134A	3352003	CCCP65973
LY-ABJ	Antonov AN-2	1G223-23	(SE-KYZ)
			SP-FAI
LY-ABK(2)	Antonov AN-2	1G238-11	(SE-LCG)
			SP-FBG
LY-ABP	Yakovlev YAK-52	800810	DOSAAF
LY-ABQ	Yakovlev Yak-52	866915	DOSAAF-111
LY-ABS	Antonov AN-2	1G234-01	(SE-KZY)
			SP-FAN
LY-ABT	Antonov AN-2	1G233-20	(SE-KZV)
			SP-FAG
LY-ABU	Antonov AN-2	1G233-24	(SE-KZX)
			SP-FAK
LY-ABV	Yakovlev YAK-52	8910004	DOSAAF
LY-ABW	Antonov AN-2	1G195-26	DOSAAF
			CCCP68121
LY-ABX	Antonov AN-2TP	1G238-12	SE-LCH
			SP-FBH(1)
LY-ABY	Antonov AN-2TP	1G238-13	SE-LCI
			SP-FBI
LY-ABZ	Yakovlev YAK-52	9611914	
LY-ACV	Antonov AN-2	1G185-24	CCCP54864
LY-ACW	Antonov AN-2	1G185-26	CCCP54866
LY-ACY	Antonov AN-2R	1G190-46	CCCP84614
LY-ACZ	Antonov AN-2	1G191-11	CCCP84633
LY-ADG	Antonov AN-2	1G201-02	CCCP71219
LY-ADI	Antonov AN-2 (Stored)	1G206-46	CCCP17941
LY-ADJ	Antonov AN-2	1G206-47	CCCP17942
LY-ADM	Antonov AN-2	1G211-18	CCCP43989
LY-ADN	Antonov AN-2	1G211-07	CCCP43988
LY-ADQ	Antonov AN-2	1G220-38	CCCP40248
LY-ADR	Antonov AN-2	1G220-39	CCCP40249
LY-ADS	Antonov AN-2	1G225-37	CCCP33318
LY-AEH	Antonov AN-2	115547304	CCCP01902
LY-AEI	Antonov AN-2 (Stored)	1G168-39	CCCP82863
LY-AEJ	Antonov AN-2	1G168-44	CCCP82868
LY-AEK	Antonov AN-2	1G168-45	CCCP82869
LY-AEL	Antonov AN-2	1G171-35	CCCP92978
LY-AEN	Antonov AN-2	1G182-31	HA-ABI
			LY-AEN
			CCCP56474
LY-AEO	Antonov AN-2	1G185-14	CCCP54854
LY-AEP	Antonov AN-2	1G185-18	CCCP54858
LY-AER	Antonov AN-2	1G191-15	CCCP84637
LY-AES	Antonov AN-2	1G191-16	CCCP84638
LY-AET	Antonov AN-2	1G192-07	CCCP84689
LY-AEV	Antonov AN-2	1G201-40	HA-ABJ
			LY-AEV
			CCCP84722
LY-AEW	Antonov AN-2	1G206-60	CCCP17955
LY-AEX	Antonov AN-2	1G227-03	CCCP33404
LY-AEY	PZL-104 Wilga 35A	17820673	DOSAAF
LY-AFA	Yakovlev YAK-52	822608	DOSAAF-110
LY-AFB	Yakovlev YAK-52	822610	DOSAAF-112
LY-AFF	Yakovlev YAK-12M	512764	DOSAAF
LY-AFI	LET L-410UVP-E	872021	RusAF 2021
LY-AFJ	Yakovlev YAK-52	9712003	

Regn.	Type	C/n	Prev.Id.
LY-AFK	Yakovlev YAK-52	877415	DOSAAF-27
LY-AFO	Antonov AN-2	1G211-42	LY-ADL
			CCCP32683
LY-AFQ	Yakovlev YAK-52	8910206	DOSAAF-138
LY-AFR	Yakovlev YAK-52	899912	DOSAAF-99
LY-AFS	Yakovlev YAK-18T	22202044785	DOSAAF
LY-AFT	Antonov AN-2	1G178-16	LY-ACT
	(Reserved as SP-FNS, 2.99)		CCCP62624
LY-AFU	Antonov AN-2R	1G178-15	LY-ACU
			CCCP62623
LY-AFV	Yakovlev YAK-52	899915	DOSAAF-102
LY-AFW	Yakovlev YAK-18T	721515	
LY-AFX	Yakovlev YAK-52	899413	DOSAAF-25
LY-AFZ	Yakovlev YAK-50	842706	DOSAAF-24
LY-AGB	PZL-104 Wilga 35A	15810581	DOSAAF
LY-AGC	PZL-104 Wilga 35A	15810595	DOSAAF
LY-AGD	PZL-104 Wilga 35A	18830743	DOSAAF
LY-AGE	PZL-104 Wilga 35A	18840793	DOSAAF
LY-AGF	Antonov AN-2	1G138-42	CCCP70224
LY-AHB	Yakovlev YAK-52	9812106	DOSAAF
LY-AHC	Yakovlev YAK-50	853007	G-BVVO
			LY-AMO
			DOSAAF
LY-AHD	Yakovlev YAK-12A	30119	SP-CXW
			PLW-...
LY-AHE	Yakovlev YAK-52	822710	DOSAAF-100
LY-AHF	Yakovlev YAK-52	unkn	DOSAAF
LY-AHJ	PZL-104 Wilga 35A	18830737	DOSAAF
	(C/n previously reported as 107373)		
LY-AHK	PZL-104 Wilga 35A	96305	DOSAAF-26
LY-AHL	PZL-104 Wilga 35A	128461	DOSAAF
LY-AHM	PZL-104 Wilga 35A	128462	DOSAAF
LY-AHN	PZL-104 Wilga 35A	18840789	DOSAAF
LY-AHO	Antonov AN-2	1G160-39	DOSAAF
LY-AHP	Antonov AN-2	1G194-45	DOSAAF
LY-AHQ	Antonov AN-2	1G194-46	DOSAAF
LY-AHR	Yakovlev YAK-50	801809	DOSAAF
LY-AHS	Yakovlev YAK-52	888815	DOSAAF
LY-AHT	Yakovlev YAK-52	833804	DOSAAF
LY-AHW	Yakovlev YAK-52	844405	DOSAAF
LY-AHY	Yakovlev YAK-52	877406	DOSAAF
LY-AHZ	Yakovlev YAK-52	877608	DOSAAF
LY-AIA	Yakovlev YAK-52	899606	DOSAAF
LY-AIC	Yakovlev YAK-18T	5201508	DOSAAF
LY-AID	Yakovlev YAK-52	822603	DOSAAF-105
LY-AIE	Yakovlev YAK-52	899907	
LY-AIF	Yakovlev YAK-52	822010	DOSAAF
LY-AIH	Yakovlev YAK-52	unkn	
LY-AII	Yakovlev YAK-50	842608	DOSAAF-16
LY-AIN	Antonov AN-2DT	1G174-29	DOSAAF
LY-AIO	Antonov AN-2DT	1G160-43	DOSAAF
LY-AIP	Yakovlev YAK-18T	5200709	DOSAAF
LY-AIQ	Yakovlev YAK-52	833610	DOSAAF
LY-AIR	Yakovlev YAK-52	844012	DOSAAF
LY-AIW	Yakovlev YAK-52	877704	DOSAAF
LY-AIX	Yakovlev YAK-52	866802	DOSAAF
LY-AJC	PZL-104 Wilga 35A	85240	DOSAAF
LY-AJD	PZL-104 Wilga 35A	128439	DOSAAF
LY-AJE	PZL-104 Wilga 35A	139481	DOSAAF
LY-AJF	PZL-104 Wilga 35A	16810616	DOSAAF
LY-AJG	Antonov AN-2	1G178-48	CCCP62656
LY-AJH	PZL-104 Wilga 35A	128434	DOSAAF
LY-AJI	Antonov AN-2	1G194-44	DOSAAF-42
LY-AJJ	Antonov AN-2	1G28-06	DOSAAF-08
LY-AJK	PZL-104 Wilga 35A	15810584	DOSAAF
LY-AJL	PZL-104 Wilga 35A	96290	DOSAAF
LY-AJM	PZL-104 Wilga 35A	85249	DOSAAF
LY-AJN	PZL-104 Wilga 35A	128458	DOSAAF
LY-AJO	PZL-104 Wilga 35A	16810622	DOSAAF
LY-AJP	PZL-104 Wilga 35A	139492	DOSAAF
LY-AJT	PZL-104 Wilga 35A	139494	DOSAAF
LY-AJU	PZL-104 Wilga 35A	18840784	DOSAAF
LY-AJV	PZL-104 Wilga 35A	107365	DOSAAF
LY-AJW	PZL-104 Wilga 35A	96298	DOSAAF
LY-AJX	PZL-104 Wilga 35A	96309	DOSAAF

Regn.	Type	C/n	Prev.Id.
LY-AJZ	PZL-104 Wilga 35A	17820669	DOSAAF
LY-AKC	Yakovlev YAK-52	867212	DOSAAF
LY-AKG	Sukhoi SU-26	06-03	RA-0603
	(C/n previously reported as 35130)		
LY-AKI	PZL-104 Wilga 35A	85243	DOSAAF
LY-AKJ	PZL-104 Wilga 35A	128417	DOSAAF
LY-AKM	Antonov AN-2	1G85-44	DOSAAF-08
LY-AKP	Yakovlev YAK-52	844403	DOSAAF
LY-AKS	PZL-104 Wilga 35A	16820650	DOSAAF
LY-AKT	PZL-104 Wilga 35A	17830700	DOSAAF
LY-AKW	Yakovlev YAK-52	855601	DOSAAF-56
LY-ALA	Antonov AN-2 (Wfu)	1G170-07	CCCP07848
LY-ALB	Yakovlev YAK-18T	7201814	DOSAAF
LY-ALH	Cessna 172B	47836	N6936X
LY-ALI	Erco Ercoupe 415C	2516	N99893
			NC99893
LY-ALN	Yakovlev YAK-52	800910	DOSAAF
LY-ALO	Yakovlev YAK-52	844815	DOSAAF-135
LY-ALP	Yakovlev YAK-52	844414	DOSAAF
LY-ALQ	Yakovlev YAK-52	844010	DOSAAF
LY-ALR	Yakovlev YAK-52	833609	DOSAAF
LY-ALS	Yakovlev YAK-52	855509	DOSAAF
LY-ALT	Yakovlev YAK-52	822704	DOSAAF
LY-ALU	Yakovlev YAK-52	9011107	DOSAAF
LY-ALW	Yakovlev YAK-18T	22202044595	LY-XLW
			LY-30
LY-ALX	Piper PA-28-140 Cherokee	28-23313	SE-FAP
LY-AMA	Yakovlev YAK-52	877111	DOSAAF-137
LY-AMC	Yakovlev YAK-52	9011001	DOSAAF-103
LY-AMG	Yakovlev YAK-18T	22202034016	DOSAAF
LY-AMH	Yakovlev YAK-18T	034089	DOSAAF
LY-AMJ	Yakovlev YAK-18T	22202047812	DOSAAF
LY-AMM	Cessna 172I	56618	N8418L
LY-AMN	Cessna 172K	59102	N7402G
LY-AMP	Yakovlev YAK-52	800708	DOSAAF-52
LY-AMS	Yakovlev YAK-52	844306	DOSAAF-51
LY-AMT	Yakovlev YAK-55	920410	DOSAAF-35
LY-AMU	Yakovlev Yak-52	833901	DOSAAF-42
LY-AMV	Yakovlev YAK-52	889109	DOSAAF
LY-AMW	Antonov AN-2	1G186-40	CCCP54892
LY-AMX	Yakovlev YAK-52	878014	DOSAAF-116
LY-AMY	Antonov AN-2T	1G43-30	DOSAAF
LY-AMZ	PZL-104 Wilga 35A	85251	DOSAAF
LY-ANA	PZL-104 Wilga 35A	15810591	DOSAAF
LY-ANB	PZL-104 Wilga 35A	96292	DOSAAF
LY-ANC	PZL-104 Wilga 35A	85250	DOSAAF
LY-AND	PZL-104 Wilga 35A	85252	DOSAAF
LY-ANE	Yakovlev YAK-52	9411711	G-BVJR
			Rom. AF-48
LY-ANF	Yakovlev YAK-52	9411810	DOSAAF
LY-ANG	Yakovlev YAK-52	832409	DOSAAF-81
LY-ANI	Yakovlev YAK-52	9411812	DOSAAF
LY-ANK	Antonov AN-2	1G170-31	CCCP07872
LY-ANP	Yakovlev YAK-52	811907	DOSAAF
LY-ANT	Yakovlev YAK-52	888901	DOSAAF-86
LY-ANW	Yakovlev YAK-52	9111510	YL-CAD
			DOSAAF-60
LY-ANY	Yakovlev YAK-52	811704	DOSAAF
LY-AOA	Cessna 150G	64647	N3247X
LY-AOB	Yakovlev YAK-52	9211517	DOSAAF
LY-AOC	Yakovlev YAK-52	811308	DOSAAF
LY-AOH	Piper PA-28RT-201T Turbo Arrow IV	28R-8031145	N82392
LY-AOK	Yakovlev YAK-52	877404	DOSAAF-16
LY-AOO	Yakovlev YAK-18T	22202040425	LY-AOG
LY-AOP	Antonov AN-2P	1G141-49	RA-70395
			CCCP70395
LY-AOQ	Antonov AN-2	1G170-33	CCCP07874
LY-AOR	Antonov AN-2	1G201-34	RA-71306
			CCCP71306
LY-AOS	Antonov AN-2	1G187-56	CCCP54947
LY-AOT	Yakovlev YAK-50	853101	
LY-AOX	Yakovlev YAK-52	833708	DOSAAF-122
LY-APA	SOCATA MS.880B Rallye Club	1725	I-AERP
LY-APS	Yakovlev YAK-18T	4200703	
LY-APW	Yakovlev YAK-52	unkn	DOSAAF
LY-AQA	Antonov AN-2	1G201-09	LithAF 03
			(LY-ADX)
			CCCP71226
LY-ARA	Beech 95-B55A Baron	TC-1389	G-AYPD
LY-ARI	Aeritalia/SNIAS ATR-42-300	012A	F-WQBT
			OY-CIF
			YU-ALK
			VH-AQC
			F-WWEI
LY-ARU	SOCATA Rallye 235E Gabier	12836	OH-SEV
			OY-CAU
			F-GARU
LY-ASA	Antonov AN-2 (Damaged 22.6.99)	1G139-49	UR-70290
			CCCP70290
LY-ASB	LET L-410UVP	851426	CCCP67522
LY-ASG	Yakovlev YAK-50	812101	DOSAAF
LY-ASK	Tupolev TU-134A	60054	LY-ABD
			CCCP65079
LY-ASS	Antonov AN-2	1G205-55	UR-17914
			CCCP17914
LY-ATF	Yakovlev YAK-18T	"07-31"	
LY-AVA	LET L-410UVP-E	882036	RusAF 2036
LY-AVS	Yakovlev YAK-52	9111509	DOSAAF-59
LY-AVT	LET L-410UVP-E	882033	RusAF 2033
LY-AVX	LET L-410UVP-E	872015	RusAF 2015
LY-AVY	LET L-410UVP-E	851413	CCCP67509
LY-AYT	Cessna 421B Golden Eagle	0248	(N2137E)
			OY-RYT
			N1560T
LY-AZK	LET L-410UVP-E	unkn	RA-.....
LY-AZM	LET L-410UVP-E	unkn	RA-.....
LY-AZN	LET L-410UVP	unkn	
LY-BAG	Boeing 737-382	24449	CS-TID
LY-BFV	Boeing 737-59D	26419	OY-SEG
			G-OBMY
			SE-DNI
LY-BJK	Yakovlev YAK-52	867002	LY-ALK
			DOSAAF-113
LY-BRE	Yakovlev YAK-50	801808	DOSAAF
LY-BSD	Boeing 737-2T4	22701	N4569N
			(N85AF)
LY-BSG	Boeing 737-2T2	22793	N457IM
			(C-GDPG)
			N1779B
			(C-GDPG)
LY-CAT	Yakovlev YAK-52	822011	DOSAAF
LY-COX	Antonov AN-2R	1G206-48	(LY-ADK)
			CCCP17943
LY-CRI	Yakovlev YAK-52	833006	DOSAAF-16
LY-EGO	PZL-101A Gawron	85162	SP-FGB
			SP-KXI (2)
LY-FKD	Yakovlev YAK-12M	210999	SP-FKD
			SP-AAD(3)
			PLW-...
LY-FLY	Yakovlev YAK-52	9111503	YL-CAA
			DOSAAF-53
LY-FUN	Yakovlev YAK-52	867211	DOSAAF
LY-GPA	Boeing 737-2Q8	22453	(LY-ABL)
			HA-LEH
			TC-JUS
			(F-GHXH)
			VR-HYZ
			G-BKMS
			N143AW
			G-BKMS
			OO-RVM
			TF-VLK
			OO-RVM
LY-HAI	Kamov Ka.26	7706010	CCCP24308
LY-HAK	Kamov Ka.26	7605813	CCCP24381
LY-HAM	Kamov Ka.26	7505210	CCCP19630
LY-HAN	Kamov Ka.26	7505211	CCCP19631
LY-HAO	Mil Mi-8T	3029	
LY-HAP	Mil Mi-8T	22613	
LY-HAQ	Mil Mi-8T	5876	

Regn.	Type	C/n	Prev.Id.
LY-HAW	Mill Mi-2 *(possibly LY-HBW re-regd)*	unkn	
LY-HAX	Mill Mi-8PS	105107	
LY-HAY	Mill Mi-8PS	105108	
LY-HBA	Mill Mi-8T	4886	
LY-HBB	Mill Mi-8PS	unkn	
LY-HBK	Mill Mi-8T	4887	
LY-HBW	Mill Mi-2	543719094	YL-LHK
			CCCP23951
LY-HBX	Mill Mi-2	542910043	Sov AF
LY-HBY	Mill Mi-2	543630064	Sov AF
LY-IZP	Yakovlev YAK-52	877912	DOSAAF-99
LY-JDR	Yakovlev YAK-50	792006	DOSAAF
LY-JJK	Yakovlev YAK-50	842801	DOSAAF-29
LY-KAG	Antonov AN-2	1G195-22	LithAF:04
			LY-ADV
			CCCP08117
LY-LJK	Sukhoi SU-31	01-03	
	(C/n previously reported as 35125)		
LY-LMA	Cessna A.150L Aerobat	00433	N6156F
LY-LMB	Cessna 152	79681	N757EM
LY-LMC	Cessna 152	79498	N714WV
LY-LMD	Cessna 152	80525	N25065
LY-LME	Cessna 152	79626	N757CE
LY-LMF	Cessna 152	79554	N714ZD
LY-LMG	Cessna 172M	61239	C-FCZS
LY-LMH	Cessna 172M	65307	C-GIWP
LY-LMI	Cessna 310Q	0951	N1974B
			(N69734)
LY-LMJ	Cessna 310Q	0996	N310JE
			N888L
			N888PD
			N69815
LY-LVR	Antonov AN-26	unkn	
LY-MAA	LET L-410UVP	810634	CCCP67058
LY-MJR	LET L-410UVP	841318	CCCP67493
LY-MMR	LET L-410UVP	841314	CCCP67489
LY-MRA	LET L-410UVP	810622	CCCP67021
LY-SBA	SAAB-Scania 340B	248	SE-G48
			EC-349
			N248PX
			EI-CFA
			SE-G48
LY-SBB	SAAB-Scania 340B	255	OH-FAH
			(N255PX)
			EI-CFC
			SE-G55
LY-SBC	SAAB 2000	025	F-GTSE
			D-ADSE
			SE-025
LY-SKY	Yakovlev YAK-52	9011108	
LY-SNW	Piper PA-28-140 Cherokee	28-20691	N6600W
LY-TED	Antonov AN-2	1G235-51	Sov.AF-17
LY-YAK	Yakovlev YAK-18T	22202034006	
LY-...	Beech B23 Musketeer Custom	M-1266	N7652R
LY-...	Beech 65-90 King Air	LJ-107	N78Q
			N7BF
			N157CA
			N1183S
			N1153S
LY-...	Cessna 150L	72219	N6719G
LY-...	Cessna 150L	73341	N5441Q
LY-...	Decourt DMS.884-1	1	F-BRMA
	(Modified MS.883 c/n 1337)		
LY-...	HS.125-700B	257212	OH-BAP
			G-5-659
			G-IJET
			N81CN
			N81CH
			G-RACL
			G-5-12
LY-...	Piper PA-28-140 Cherokee E	28-7225081	C-GPZM
			N2663C

BALLOONS

Regn.	Type	C/n	Prev.Id.
LY-OAA	Cameron O-120 HAFB	1670	D-OAOB
			G-BOHE
LY-OAB	Cameron A-160 HAFB	1968	D-OPTW
			G-BPTW
LY-OBA	AX-7 "Moletai" HAFB	004	
LY-OBB	Aerotechnik AB-2a HAFB	880312	
LY-OBC	Raven S-55A HAFB	853	
LY-OBD	Aerotechnik AB-8 HAFB	890419	
LY-OBE	Tomi AX-7 HAFB	BAV048/1988	LOD-0002
LY-OBF	Cameron O-84 HAFB	2031	LOD-0009
LY-OBH	Free Balloon TA-61	0470992	
LY-OBI	Free Balloon TA-80	0410692	
LY-OBJ	Tomi AX-7 HAFB	BAV080/1990	LY-PRI
LY-OBK	Cameron O-120 HAFB	3489	
LY-OBL	Free Balloon TA-61	0471032	
LY-OBM	LS-7 HAFB	LS-002	
LY-OBO	Tomi AX-7 HAFB	BAV047/1988	LOD-0001
LY-OBP	Experimental B HAFB	unkn	
LY-OBQ	Interavia 80TA Free Balloon	310492	
LY-OBR	Free Balloon TA-80	0541292	
LY-OBS	Aerotechnik AB-8 HAFB	200489	
LY-OBT	Cameron N-70 HAFB	3244	
LY-OBU	Cameron N-77 HAFB	3258	
LY-OBV	Cameron C-80 Concept HAFB	3433	
LY-OBW	Raven RX-7 HAFB	377	
LY-OBX	Colt 77A HAFB	1350	LOD-0003
LY-OBY	Colt SS Pepsi Can HAFB	1448	G-BRFK
LY-OBZ	Tomi AX-7 HAFB	BAV060/1988	
LY-OCA	Cameron C-80 Concept HAFB	3605	
LY-OCB	Cameron C-80 Concept HAFB	3960	
LY-OCC	Cameron C-80 Concept HAFB	4008	
LY-OCE	Cameron C-80 Concept HAFB	4346	
LY-OCH	UltraMagic HAFB	unkn	
LY-OCR	Cameron C-80 Concept HAFB	4594	
LY-ODE	Cameron N-105 HAFB	2886	PH-FWW
LY-ODO	Cameron N-90 HAFB	4490	
LY-O..	Raven S-49AHAFB	S-49A-3122	N9006W

EXPERIMENTAL SERIES

Regn.	Type	C/n	Prev.Id.
LY-XAA	Lituanica		
LY-XAB	Experimental Type	004	
LY-XAJ	Experimental Type		
LY-XAM	Yakovlev YAK-12	212615	
LY-XAT	TL-132/232 Condor	95C17	SP-FPB
LY-XBK	Experimental Type		
LY-XBR	Experimental Type unknown		
LY-XKU	LET L-13 Blanik	174203	LY-GKU
			DOSAAF
LY-XLM	Zuvedra		
LY-XLN	Vladas Kensgaila VK-8 Ausra	unkn	LY-21
LY-XLP	Experimental Type		
LY-XMC	Zilvinas		
LY-XMD	Gandras		
LY-XME	SAS / LET L-13 Blanik	027118	DOSAAF
LY-XMF	Kregzdute		
LY-XMH	Aeroplastika LAK-X	001	
LY-XMI	SML		
LY-XMJ	L-14		
LY-XMK	RB-19		
LY-XMM	R-1		
LY-XMR	Experimental Type		
LY-XMT	LET L-13 Blanik	171309	LY-GGG
			DOSAAF
LY-XMV	Zlin Z.326T Trenér	823-14	DOSAAF
LY-XNB	LET L-13 Blanik	172619	DOSAAF

Regn.	Type	C/n	Prev.Id.
LY-XNR	Experimental Type		
LY-XNT	Experimental Type		
LY-XNU	Experimental Type		
LY-XPA	Yakovlev YAK-18A	2624	
LY-XPV	A-15		0505
LY-XVD	Moravan Z.326A Akrobat	585-05	DOSAAF

MICROLIGHTS

Regn.	Type	C/n	Prev.Id.
LY-SAA	T-2	0431	
LY-SAB	T-2	0432	
LY-SAC	Skraidykle	XA3-29	
LY-SAD	Skraidykle		
LY-SAE	Skraidykle		
LY-SAF	Skraidykle		
LY-SAG	Skraidykle		
LY-SAH	Skraidykle		
LY-SAI	Skraidykle		
LY-SAJ	Skraidykle		
LY-SAK	Skraidykle		
LY-SAL	Skraidykle		
LY-SAM	Skraidykle		
LY-SAN	Skraidykle		
LY-SAO	Skraidykle		
LY-SAP	Skraidykle		
LY-SAQ	Skraidykle		
LY-SAR	Skraidykle		
LY-SAS	Skraidykle		
LY-SAW	Skraidykle		
LY-SAX	Skraidykle		

GLIDERS

Regn.	Type	C/n	Prev.Id.
LY-GAA	LAK-12 Lietuva	650	DOSAAF
LY-GAB	LAK-12 Lietuva	635	DOSAAF
LY-GAC(2)	LET L-13 Blanik	174230	DOSAAF
LY-GAD	LET L-13 Blanik	174304	DOSAAF
LY-GAE	LET L-13 Blanik	027148	DOSAAF
LY-GAF	LET L-13 Blanik	027311	DOSAAF
LY-GAG	LET L-13 Blanik	174508	DOSAAF
LY-GAH	LET L-13 Blanik	174511	DOSAAF
LY-GAI	LET L-13 Blanik	174510	DOSAAF
LY-GAJ	LET L-13 Blanik	174514	DOSAAF
LY-GAK	LET L-13 Blanik	174513	DOSAAF
LY-GAL	LET L-13 Blanik	026444	DOSAAF
LY-GAM	LET L-13 Blanik	026445	DOSAAF
LY-GAN	LET L-13 Blanik	026446	DOSAAF
LY-GAO	LET L-13 Blanik	173708	DOSAAF
LY-GAP	LET L-13 Blanik	026948	DOSAAF
LY-GAQ	LET L-13 Blanik	173525	DOSAAF
LY-GAR	LET L-13 Blanik	026949	DOSAAF
LY-GAS	LET L-13 Blanik	027149	DOSAAF
LY-GAT	LET L-13 Blanik	027150	DOSAAF
LY-GAU	LET L-13 Blanik	027151	DOSAAF
LY-GAV	LET L-13 Blanik	027313	DOSAAF
LY-GAW	LAK-12 Lietuva	669	DOSAAF
LY-GAX	LAK-12 Lietuva	675	DOSAAF
LY-GAY	LAK-12 Lietuva	6102	DOSAAF
LY-GAZ	LAK-12 Lietuva	6118	DOSAAF
LY-GBA	LAK-12 Lietuva	6140	DOSAAF
LY-GBB	LAK-12 Lietuva	6147	DOSAAF
LY-GBC	LAK-12 Lietuva	6151	DOSAAF
LY-GBD	SZD-41A Jantar Standard	B-923	DOSAAF
LY-GBE	SZD-48-1 Jantar Standard 2	B-1029	DOSAAF
LY-GBF	SZD-48-1 Jantar Standard 2	B-1235	DOSAAF
LY-GBG	SZD-48-3 Jantar Standard 3	B-1283	DOSAAF
LY-GBH	SZD-48-3 Jantar Standard 3	B-1422	DOSAAF
LY-GBI	SZD-48-3 Jantar Standard 3	B-1423	DOSAAF
LY-GBJ	SZD-48-3 Jantar Standard 3	B-1520	DOSAAF
LY-GBK	SZD-48-3 Jantar Standard 3	B-1763	DOSAAF
LY-GBL	SZD-42-2 Jantar 2B	B-868	DOSAAF
LY-GBM	SZD-50-3 Puchacz	B-1078	DOSAAF
LY-GBO	LET L-13 Blanik	174524	DOSAAF
LY-GBP	LET L-13 Blanik	174523	DOSAAF
LY-GBQ	LET L-13 Blanik	026213	DOSAAF
LY-GBR	LET L-13 Blanik	026625	DOSAAF
LY-GBS	LET L-13 Blanik	026624	DOSAAF
LY-GBT	LET L-13 Blanik	026441	DOSAAF
LY-GBU	LET L-13 Blanik	174637	DOSAAF
LY-GBV	LET L-13 Blanik	174634	DOSAAF
LY-GBW	LET L-13 Blanik	026212	DOSAAF
LY-GBX	LET L-13 Blanik	027309	DOSAAF
LY-GBY	LET L-13 Blanik	027310	DOSAAF
LY-GBZ	LET L-13 Blanik	027307	DOSAAF
LY-GCA	LET L-13 Blanik	027146	DOSAAF
LY-GCB	LET L-13 Blanik	027308	DOSAAF
LY-GCC	LET L-13 Blanik	027147	DOSAAF
LY-GCD	LET L-13 Blanik	027306	DOSAAF
LY-GCE/2-07	LET L-13 Blanik	027305	DOSAAF
LY-GCF	LET L-13 Blanik	173806	DOSAAF
LY-GCG	SZD-48-1 Jantar Standard 2	B-1212	DOSAAF
LY-GCH	SZD-48-1 Jantar Standard 2	B-1196	DOSAAF
LY-GCI	SZD-48-3 Jantar Standard 3	B-1405	DOSAAF
LY-GCJ-W	SZD-48-3 Jantar Standard 3	B-1506	DOSAAF
LY-GCK-J	SZD-48-3 Jantar Standard 3	B-1460	DOSAAF
LY-GCL-DR	SZD-48-3 Jantar Standard 3	B-1407	DOSAAF
LY-GCM	SZD-48-3 Jantar Standard 3	B-1643	DOSAAF
LY-GCN-CN	SZD-48-3 Jantar Standard 3	B-1284	DOSAAF
	(Previously quoted as c/n B-1530)		
LY-GCO	SZD-48-3 Jantar Standard 3	B-1765	DOSAAF
LY-GCP	SZD-48-3 Jantar Standard 3	B-1697	DOSAAF
LY-GCQ	SZD-42-2 Jantar 2B	B-946	DOSAAF
LY-GCR	SZD-42-2 Jantar 2B	B-1315	DOSAAF
LY-GCU	LAK-12 Lietuva	616	DOSAAF
LY-GCV	LAK-12 Lietuva	663	DOSAAF
LY-GCW	LAK-12 Lietuva	664	DOSAAF
LY-GCX	LAK-12 Lietuva	685	DOSAAF
LY-GCY-S	LAK-12 Lietuva	6100	DOSAAF CCCP6100
LY-GCZ-O	LAK-12 Lietuva	6116	DOSAAF
LY-GDA-DA	LAK-12 Lietuva	6137	DOSAAF CCCP6137
LY-GDB-P	LAK-12 Lietuva	6131	DOSAAF CCCP6131
LY-GDC-SV	LAK-12 Lietuva	6142	DOSAAF
LY-GDD-KR	LAK-12 Lietuva	6125	DOSAAF
LY-GDE	LAK-12 Lietuva	6148	DOSAAF
LY-GDF-DF	LAK-12 Lietuva	6153	DOSAAF
LY-GDG	LAK-12 Lietuva	6154	DOSAAF
LY-GDH-DH	LAK-12 Lietuva	6155	DOSAAF
LY-GDI-DI	LAK-12 Lietuva	6163	DOSAAF
LY-GDJ-MZ	LAK-12 Lietuva	679	DOSAAF CCCP679
LY-GDK	SZD-50-3 Puchacz	B-1077	DOSAAF
LY-GDL	SZD-30 Pirat	S.06-30	DOSAAF
LY-GDM	LAK-16	220	
LY-GDQ	LAK-16	003	DOSAAF
LY-GDS	LAK-16	010	DOSAAF
LY-GDV	LAK-12 Lietuva	6227	DOSAAF
LY-GEN	LAK Gemini		
LY-GFA-SV	LAK-17A	unkn	
LY-GFF	PZL PW-5 Smyk	17.08.020	
LY-GFG	LET L-13 Blanik	174638	DOSAAF
LY-GFH	LET L-13 Blanik	170614	DOSAAF
LY-GFI	LET L-13 Blanik	173462	DOSAAF
LY-GFJ	LET L-13 Blanik	173711	DOSAAF
LY-GFK	LET L-13 Blanik	173210	DOSAAF
LY-GFL	SZD-48-1 Jantar Standard 2	B-1030	DOSAAF
LY-GFM-DG	SZD-48-1 Jantar Standard 2	B-1054	DOSAAF
LY-GFN	LAK-12 Lietuva	632	DOSAAF

Regn.	Type	C/n	Prev.Id.
LY-GFO	LAK-12 Lietuva	6126	DOSAAF
LY-GFP	LET L-13 Blanik	170406	DOSAAF
LY-GFQ	LET L-13 Blanik	172230	DOSAAF
LY-GFR	LET L-13 Blanik	172323	DOSAAF
LY-GFS	LET L-13 Blanik	173610	DOSAAF
LY-GFT	LET L-13 Blanik	174118	DOSAAF
LY-GFU	LET L-13 Blanik	174206	DOSAAF
LY-GFV	LET L-13 Blanik	174321	DOSAAF
LY-GFW	LET L-13 Blanik	174520	DOSAAF
LY-GFX	LET L-13 Blanik	026915	DOSAAF
LY-GFY	LET L-13 Blanik	026916	DOSAAF
LY-GFZ	LET L-13 Blanik	174128	DOSAAF
LY-GGA	LET L-13 Blanik	173713	DOSAAF
LY-GGB	LET L-13 Blanik	171011	DOSAAF
LY-GGC	LET L-13 Blanik	171506	DOSAAF
LY-GGD	LET L-13 Blanik	026443	DOSAAF
LY-GGE	LET L-13 Blanik	172949	DOSAAF
LY-GGH	LET L-13 Blanik	172228	DOSAAF
LY-GGI	LET L-13 Blanik	173020	DOSAAF
LY-GGJ	LET L-13 Blanik	172526	DOSAAF
LY-GGK	LET L-13 Blanik	026449	DOSAAF
LY-GGL	LET L-13 Blanik	174116	DOSAAF
LY-GGM	LET L-13 Blanik	173137	DOSAAF
LY-GGN	LET L-13 Blanik	026716	DOSAAF
LY-GGO	LET L-13 Blanik	026717	DOSAAF
LY-GGP	LET L-13 Blanik	174229	DOSAAF
LY-GGQ	LET L-13 Blanik	173618	DOSAAF
LY-GGR	LET L-13 Blanik	172915	DOSAAF
LY-GGS	LET L-13 Blanik	027135	DOSAAF
LY-GGT	SZD-48-1 Jantar Standard 2	W-920	DOSAAF
LY-GGU	LET L-13 Blanik	026947	DOSAAF
LY-GGV	LET L-13 Blanik	173709	DOSAAF
LY-GGW	LET L-13 Blanik	172427	DOSAAF
LY-GGX	LET L-13 Blanik	027316	DOSAAF
LY-GGY	LET L-13 Blanik	027315	DOSAAF
LY-GGZ	LET L-13 Blanik	171116	DOSAAF
LY-GHA	LET L-13 Blanik	026946	DOSAAF
LY-GHB	LET L-13 Blanik	026447	DOSAAF
LY-GHC	LET L-13 Blanik	173609	DOSAAF
LY-GHD	LET L-13 Blanik	173714	DOSAAF
LY-GHE	SZD-48-1 Jantar Standard 2	B-1182	DOSAAF
LY-GHF	SZD-48-1 Jantar Standard 2	B-1020	DOSAAF
LY-GHG	SZD-48-1 Jantar Standard 2	B-1186	DOSAAF
LY-GHH	SZD-48-3 Jantar Standard 3	B-1696	DOSAAF
LY-GHI	LAK-12 Lietuva	6110	DOSAAF
LY-GHJ	LET L-13 Blanik	173523	DOSAAF
LY-GHK	LET L-13 Blanik	171715	DOSAAF
LY-GHL	LET L-13 Blanik	173018	DOSAAF
LY-GHM	LET L-13 Blanik	171808	DOSAAF
LY-GHN	LET L-13 Blanik	172311	DOSAAF
LY-GHO	LET L-13 Blanik	172950	DOSAAF
LY-GHP	LET L-13 Blanik	027145	DOSAAF
LY-GHQ	LET L-13 Blanik	027144	DOSAAF
LY-GHR	LET L-13 Blanik	027314	DOSAAF
LY-GHS	LET L-13 Blanik	026713	DOSAAF
LY-GHT	LET L-13 Blanik	027312	DOSAAF
LY-GHU	LET L-13 Blanik	026712	DOSAAF
LY-GHW	LAK-12 Lietuva	691	DOSAAF
LY-GHX	SZD-41A Jantar Standard	B-919	DOSAAF
LY-GHY	SZD-48-3 Jantar Standard 3	B-1518	DOSAAF
LY-GHZ	LET L-13 Blanik	171003	DOSAAF
LY-GIA	LET L-13 Blanik	172209	DOSAAF
LY-GIB	LET L-13 Blanik	172306	DOSAAF
LY-GIC	LET L-13 Blanik	172519	DOSAAF
LY-GID	LET L-13 Blanik	172617	DOSAAF
LY-GIE	LET L-13 Blanik	173134	DOSAAF
LY-GIF	LET L-13 Blanik	172923	DOSAAF
LY-GIG	LET L-13 Blanik	173468	DOSAAF
LY-GIH	LET L-13 Blanik	026709	DOSAAF
LY-GII	LET L-13 Blanik	026911	DOSAAF
LY-GIJ	LET L-13 Blanik	026913	DOSAAF
LY-GIK	LET L-13 Blanik	026914	DOSAAF
LY-GIL	LET L-13 Blanik	171816	DOSAAF
LY-GIN	SZD-41A Jantar Standard	B-845	DOSAAF
LY-GIO	SZD-41A Jantar Standard	B-893	DOSAAF

Regn.	Type	C/n	Prev.Id.
LY-GIP	SZD-48-1 Jantar Standard 2	B-1022	DOSAAF
LY-GIR	LAK-12 Lietuva	642	DOSAAF
LY-GJI	SZD-48-3 Jantar Standard 3	B-1406	DOSAAF
LY-GJJ	LET L-13 Blanik	172716	DOSAAF
LY-GJK	LET L-13 Blanik	173712	DOSAAF
LY-GJM	LET L-13 Blanik	171620	DOSAAF
LY-GJN	LET L-13 Blanik	027303	DOSAAF
LY-GJR	SZD-36A Cobra 15	W-633	DOSAAF
LY-GJU	SZD-41A Jantar Standard	B-745	DOSAAF
	(c/n unconfirmed - B-748 quoted officially)		
LY-GJV	LET L-13 Blanik	173113	DOSAAF
LY-GJY	SZD-36A Cobra 15	W-640	DOSAAF
LY-GJZ	SZD-41A Jantar Standard	B-924	LY-GJL
			DOSAAF
LY-GKB	LAK-12 Lietuva	6215	
LY-GKD	SZD-30 Pirat	S-06.35	DOSAAF 8-18
LY-GKE	LAK-16	011	
LY-GKF	LAK-12 Lietuva	6214	LY-GKA
LY-GKH	LET L-13 Blanik	172424	DOSAAF
LY-GKI	LET L-13 Blanik	026448	DOSAAF
LY-GKJ	LET L-13 Blanik	174317	DOSAAF
LY-GKK	LET L-13 Blanik	174318	DOSAAF
LY-GKL	LET L-13 Blanik	026711	DOSAAF
LY-GKM	LET L-13 Blanik	026714	DOSAAF
LY-GKN	LET L-13 Blanik	026715	DOSAAF
LY-GKO	LET L-13 Blanik	027156	DOSAAF
LY-GKP	LET L-13 Blanik	027157	DOSAAF
LY-GKQ	LET L-13 Blanik	172511	DOSAAF
LY-GKR	LET L-13 Blanik	173501	DOSAAF
LY-GKT	SZD-48-3 Jantar Standard 3	B-1644	DOSAAF
LY-GKV	LET L-13 Blanik	173705	DOSAAF
LY-GKW	LET L-13 Blanik	027136	DOSAAF
LY-GKX	SZD-48-1 Jantar Standard 2	B-1227	DOSAAF
LY-GKY	LAK-12 Lietuva	681	DOSAAF
LY-GKZ	LAK-12 Lietuva	8105	DOSAAF
LY-GLA	LAK-12 Lietuva	6184	DOSAAF
LY-GLB	LAK-16A	105	
LY-GLE	BRO-11M	90006	
LY-GLG	SZD-36A Cobra 15	W-600	DOSAAF
LY-GLH	LAK-16	310	
LY-GLI	LAK-16	217	
LY-GLK	LAK-16	238	
LY-GLL	BRO-11M	900011	
LY-GLM	BRO-11M	900009	
LY-GLN	LAK-16	297	
LY-GLQ	LAK-12 Lietuva	6225	
LY-GLS	BRO-11M	910087	
LY-GLT	LAK-16	90374	
LY-GLU	LAK-16A	001	
LY-GLV	LAK-16A	104	
LY-GLW	LAK-16A	101/A	
LY-GLX	LAK-16A	102	
LY-GLY	LAK-16A	103/A	
LY-GPV	LET L-13 Blanik (Experimental)	unkn	
LY-GUA	PZL PW-5 Smyk	17.08.021	
LY-GUB	SZD-36A Cobra 15	W-728	DOSAAF
LY-G..	SZD-36A Cobra 15	W-778	DOSAAF
LY-G..	SZD-36A Cobra 15	W-780	DOSAAF
LY-G..	SZD-36A Cobra 15	W-781	DOSAAF
LY-G..	SZD-30 Pirat	B-547	DOSAAF
LY-G..	SZD-30 Pirat	S-03.11	DOSAAF

LZ - BULGARIA

Regn.	Type	C/n	Prev.Id.
LZ-ANB	Antonov AN-24V	67302710	
LZ-ANC	Antonov AN-24V	67302808	
LZ-AND	Antonov AN-24V	77303301	
LZ-ANG	Antonov AN-24V	77303408	
LZ-ANK	Antonov AN-24RV	17307005	
LZ-ANL	Antonov AN-24V	57302206	DM-SBA
LZ-ANM	Antonov AN-24V	77302905	SP-LTL
LZ-ANO	Antonov AN-24V	87304406	SP-LTM
LZ-ANP	Antonov AN-24	97305402	
LZ-ANR	Antonov AN-24	07306001	
LZ-ANS	Antonov AN-24	97306006	SP-LTR
LZ-ANT	Antonov AN-24	97307903	SP-LTS
LZ-AZC	Ilyushin IL-18D	184006903	CCCP75530
LZ-AZO	Ilyushin IL-18D	184007405	RA-75553
			D-AOAO
			DM-STF
			CCCP75553
LZ-BAC	Antonov AN-12	5343708	CCCP1100 .
LZ-BAE	Antonov AN-12	402001	CCCP113 ..
LZ-BAF	Antonov AN-12	402408	CCCP113 ..
LZ-BEA	Ilyushin IL-18D	188010802	
LZ-BEH	Ilyushin IL-18D	185008905	SP-LSI
LZ-BEI	Ilyushin IL-18V	181002805	SP-LSC
LZ-BEU	Ilyushin IL-18V	183005905	4W-ABO
			YE-AYE
			CCCP75870
LZ-BEZ	Ilyushin IL-18D	185008603	SP-LSG
LZ-BFC	Antonov AN-12	2400502	RA-48970
			CCCP48970
LZ-BFD	Antonov AN-12	5343005	RA-98102
			CCCP98102
			SovietAF-17
LZ-BFG	Antonov AN-12BT	6344305	LZ-BAG
			RA-11650
			CCCP11650
			YI-AES
			IAF-685
LZ-BOA	Boeing 737-53A	24881	
LZ-BOB	Boeing 737-53A	24921	
LZ-BOC	Boeing 737-53A	25425	
LZ-BOD	Boeing 737-3Y0	23749	EC-FKJ
			EC-781
			EC-ECR
LZ-BOE	Boeing 737-3Y0	23923	EC-FJZ
			EC-898
			EI-CEE
			G-TEAB
			EI-BZP
			(N117AW)
			EI-BZP
			(LN-AEQ)
			EC-EIA
			EC-152
LZ-BTA	Tupolev TU-154B	72A-026	
LZ-BTC	Tupolev TU-154B	73A-036	
LZ-BTE	Tupolev TU-154B	74A-073	
LZ-BTF	Tupolev TU-154B	74A-077	
LZ-BTG	Tupolev TU-154A	75A-095	
LZ-BTH	Tupolev TU-154M	87A-754	
LZ-BTJ	Tupolev TU-154B-1	78A-270	
LZ-BTK	Tupolev TU-154B	76A-144	
LZ-BTL(2)	Tupolev TU-154B	77A-208	
LZ-BTM(2)	Tupolev TU-154B	77A-209	
LZ-BTN(2)	Tupolev TU-154M	90A-832	
LZ-BTO	Tupolev TU-154B-1	78A-258	
LZ-BTP	Tupolev TU-154B-1	78A-278	
LZ-BTS	Tupolev TU-154B-2	80A-422	
LZ-BTT	Tupolev TU-154B-2	81A-483	
LZ-BTU	Tupolev TU-154B-2 *(Museum)*	81A-484	
LZ-BTV	Tupolev TU-154B-2	82A-569	CCCP85569
LZ-BTW	Tupolev TU-154M	85A-707	
LZ-BTY	Tupolev TU-154M	89A-800	
LZ-BTZ	Tupolev TU-154M	88A-781	

Regn.	Type	C/n	Prev.Id.
LZ-BZB	Antonov AN-2	unkn	
LZ-CAA	Mil Mi-8	10311	
LZ-CAC	Mil Mi-8	10309	
LZ-CAE	Mil Mi-8	10312	
LZ-CAF	Mil Mi-8	10314	
LZ-CAG	Mil Mi-8	103 . .	
LZ-CAH	Mil Mi-8	unkn	
LZ-CAK	Mil Mi-8	10316	
LZ-CAL	Mil Mi-8	10317	
LZ-CAM	Mil Mi-8	10318	
LZ-CAO	Mil Mi-8	10307	
LZ-CAP	Mil Mi-8	10320	
LZ-CAT	Mil Mi-8	103 . .	
LZ-CAZ	Mil Mi-8	unkn	
LZ-CBA	Antonov AN-26	unkn	
LZ-CCE	LET L-410UVP-E3	871816	SovietAF
LZ-CCL	LET L-410UVP-E3	871827	SovietAF
LZ-DOA	Yakovlev YAK-40	9341431	
LZ-DOB	Yakovlev YAK-40	9340432	
LZ-DOC	Yakovlev YAK-40	9340532	
LZ-DOD	Yakovlev YAK-40	9340631	
LZ-DOE	Yakovlev YAK-40	9521441	
LZ-DOF	Yakovlev YAK-40	9521541	
LZ-DOL	Yakovlev YAK-40	9620347	
LZ-DOM	Yakovlev YAK-40	9620447	
LZ-DON	Yakovlev YAK-40	9620547	
LZ-DOR	Yakovlev YAK-40	9231623	
LZ-DOS	Yakovlev YAK-40	9231423	
LZ-FAA	Mil Mi-17	unkn	
LZ-FEO	Beech 200 Super King Air	BB-82	LZ-RGP
			N788AA
			8R-GFB
LZ-ITA	Antonov AN-12	unkn	
LZ-KLA	LET L-410UVP-E	902506	CCCP67653
LZ-KLB	LET L-410UVP-E	902507	CCCP67654
LZ-KLC	LET L-410UVP-E	902514	CCCP67660
LZ-LSB	LET L-410UVP-E1	861802	
LZ-LSC	LET L-410UVP-E12	882207	
LZ-LTB	Tupolev TU-154B-2	79A-365	RA-85365
			CCCP85365
LZ-LTC	Tupolev TU-154M	93A-974	RA-85790
			85790
LZ-LTD	Tupolev TU-154M	89A-802	RA-85657
			CCCP85657
LZ-LTE	Tupolev TU-154M	90A-848	EP-LAU
			RA-85681
			CCCP85681
LZ-LTF	Tupolev TU-154M	88A-794	RA-85652
			CCCP85652
LZ-LTG	Tupolev TU-154M	92A-927	LZ-LTA
			RA-85744
			UN-85744
			CCCP85744
LZ-MAN	LET L-410UVP	unkn	
LZ-MIA	Mil Mi-2	543541054	
LZ-MIB	Mil Mi-2	544516115	
LZ-MIC	Mil Mi-2	526015029	LZ-5029
LZ-MID	Mil Mi-2	526020029	LZ-5034
LZ-MIG	Tupolev TU-154M	90A-840	
LZ-MIK	Tupolev TU-154M	90A-844	
LZ-MIL	Tupolev TU-154M	90A-845	
LZ-MIR	Tupolev TU-154M	90A-852	
LZ-MIS	Tupolev TU-154M	90A-863	
LZ-MIV	Tupolev TU-154M	92A-920	CCCP85737
			LZ-MIV
			CCCP-85737
LZ-MNB	LET L-410UVP	unkn	
LZ-MNC	LET L-410UVP	unkn	
LZ-MND	Antonov AN-24	97305307	UR-46311
			CCCP46311
LZ-MNE	Antonov AN-24RV	37308605	UR-46608
			CCCP46608
LZ-MNG	LET L-410UVP	841326	UR-67100
			CCCP67100

Regn.	Type	C/n	Prev.Id.
LZ-MNI	Antonov AN-24B	07305810	040
			LZ-040
LZ-MNL	Antonov AN-26	1309	PWL-1309
LZ-MOA	Mil Mi-26	226206	
LZ-MOB	Mil Mi-26	226207	
LZ-MOE	Mil Mi-8MTV-1	415M01	
LZ-MOF	Mil Mi-8MTV-1	103M15	
LZ-MOG	Mil Mi-8MTV-1	415M02	
LZ-MOH	Mil Mi-8MTV-1	103M14	
LZ-MOL	Mil Mi-8	unkn	
LZ-MON	Mil Mi-8	unkn	
LZ-MOO	Mil Mi-8	unkn	
LZ-MOR	Kamov Ka.32	unkn	
LZ-MOS	Mil Mi-8	unkn	
LZ-MSF	Mil Mi-8	99150935	
LZ-MSG	Mil Mi-8	99150928	
LZ-MSK	Kamov Ka.32T	unkn	
LZ-MSM	Kamov Ka.32T	8702	
LZ-MSN	Mil Mi-8MTV-1	95919	UR-27083
			CCCP27083
LZ-MSQ	Mil Mi-17	unkn	
LZ-MSR	Mil Mi-17	unkn	
LZ-MSS	Kamov Ka.32T	unkn	
LZ-MSW	Kamov Ka.32T	8610	
LZ-MSZ	Mil Mi-17	unkn	
LZ-NHA	Antonov AN-26	unkn	
LZ-OKC	Kamov Ka.26	7303501	
LZ-PHA	Antonov AN-2	unkn	
LZ-PIA	Piaggio P.180 Avanti	1008	LZ-VPC
			EC-FKL
			EC-619
			I-RAIP
LZ-PVM	Antonov AN-32B	3005	RA-48068
			CCCP48068
LZ-PVN	Antonov AN-32B	3006	RA-48069
			CCCP48069
LZ-SFA	Antonov AN-12	02348007	LZ-SGA
			YU-AIC
			(JRV73311)
LZ-SFB	Antonov AN-22	unkn	LZ-SGB
LZ-SFC	Antonov AN-12	402913	LZ-SGC
			Soviet AF
LZ-SFK	Antonov AN-12	2341901	CCCP11511
LZ-SFL	Antonov AN-12	4342101	
LZ-SFM	Antonov AN-12	401705	Soviet AF
LZ-SFN	Antonov AN-12	2340806	
LZ-SFP	Antonov AN-24RV	67302308	
LZ-SFS	Antonov AN-12	5344308	SP-LZB
			PLW-51
			SP-LZB
			PLW-51
			SP-LZB
			PLW-51
LZ-SNA	Antonov AN-2	1G149-01	
LZ-SNB	Antonov AN-2	1G149-02	
LZ-SNC	Antonov AN-2	1G56-48	LZ-1074
LZ-SND	Antonov AN-2	1G55-20	LZ-1039
			LZ-916
LZ-SNG	Antonov AN-2	1G82-47	
LZ-TCA	Yakovlev YAK-18T	22202050376	
LZ-TCB	Yakovlev YAK-18T	22202034068	
LZ-TCC	Yakovlev YAK-18T	13-35	
LZ-TEA	Antonov AN-14	601613	LZ-7001
LZ-TEB	Antonov AN-14	601610	LZ-7002
LZ-TEC	Antonov AN-14	601606	LZ-7003
LZ-TED	Antonov AN-14	601607	LZ-7004
LZ-TEE	Antonov AN-14	601609	LZ-7005
LZ-TEF	Antonov AN-14	603101	LZ-7006
LZ-TEG	Antonov AN-14	003309	LZ-7007
LZ-TEK	Antonov AN-14	unkn	
LZ-TUC	Tupolev TU-134	9350807	
LZ-TUD	Tupolev TU-134	9350808	
LZ-TUE	Tupolev TU-134	9350914	
LZ-TUG	Tupolev TU-134A-3	49858	OK-BYT
LZ-TUH	Tupolev TU-134A	7360142	OK-HFM
LZ-TUJ	Tupolev TU-134A	7349913	OK-HFL
LZ-TUK	Tupolev TU-134A (Wfu)	1351209	
LZ-TUL	Tupolev TU-134A-3	4352303	
LZ-TUM	Tupolev TU-134A-3	3351906	
LZ-TUN	Tupolev TU-134A-3	4352307	
LZ-TUO	Tupolev TU-134	0350922	BAF-050(1)
LZ-TUP	Tupolev TU-134A	1351303	LZ-TUP
			LZ D050
			LZ-TUP
			BAF: 050
			LZ-TUP
LZ-TUT	Tupolev TU-134B-3	unkn	
LZ-VEA	Antonov AN-12	unkn	
LZ-VEB	Antonov AN-12	unkn	
LZ-010	Dassault Falcon 50	88	F-GYOL
			F-WQBK
			N588FJ
LZ-103	PZL-101 Gawron	74123	LZ-GA..
LZ-104	PZL-101 Gawron	74124	LZ-GA..
LZ-105	PZL-101 Gawron	74125	LZ-GA..
LZ-106	PZL-101 Gawron	74126	LZ-GA..
LZ-107	PZL-101 Gawron	63108	LZ-GA..
LZ-108	PZL-101 Gawron	85139	LZ-GA..
LZ-109	PZL-101 Gawron	85140	LZ-GA..
LZ-110	PZL-101 Gawron	52075	LZ-GA..
			SP-CFK
LZ-111	PZL-101 Gawron	107228	LZ-GA..
LZ-113	PZL-101 Gawron	107229	LZ-GA..
LZ-114	PZL-101 Gawron	107226	LZ-GA..
LZ-115	PZL-101 Gawron	119269	LZ-GA..
LZ-116	PZL-101 Gawron	119270	LZ-GA..
LZ-117	PZL-101 Gawron	119275	LZ-GA..
LZ-118	PZL-101 Gawron	119257	LZ-GA..
LZ-119	PZL-101 Gawron	119258	LZ-GA..
LZ-120	PZL-101 Gawron	119259	LZ-GA..
LZ-121	PZL-101 Gawron	119261	LZ-GA..
LZ-122	PZL-101 Gawron	119264	LZ-GA..
LZ-123	PZL-101 Gawron	119265	LZ-GA..
LZ-124	PZL-101 Gawron	119266	LZ-GA..
LZ-125	PZL-101 Gawron	119272	LZ-GA..
LZ-126	PZL-101 Gawron	119256	LZ-GA..
LZ-127	PZL-101 Gawron	119260	LZ-GA..
LZ-129	PZL-101 Gawron	119263	LZ-GA..
LZ-130	PZL-101 Gawron	119271	LZ-GA..
LZ-131	PZL-101 Gawron	119267	LZ-GA..
LZ-132	PZL-101 Gawron	107227	LZ-112
			LZ-GA..
LZ-133	PZL-101 Gawron	119298	LZ-GA..
LZ-134	PZL-101 Gawron	119273	LZ-GA..
LZ-135	PZL-101 Gawron	119274	LZ-GA..
LZ-136	PZL-101 Gawron	119278	LZ-GA..
LZ-137	PZL-101 Gawron	119276	LZ-GA..
LZ-138	PZL-101 Gawron	118243	LZ-GA..
LZ-210	Yakovlev YAK-52	822713	
LZ-211	Yakovlev YAK-52	822715	
LZ-400	PZL-104 Wilga 35	48041	
LZ-401	PZL-104 Wilga 35	48042	
LZ-402	PZL-104 Wilga 35	48043	
LZ-404	PZL-104 Wilga 35	59047	
LZ-405	PZL-104 Wilga 35A	18830761	
LZ-406	PZL-104 Wilga 35A	19840815	
LZ-407	PZL-104 Wilga 35A	19840816	
LZ-408	PZL-104 Wilga 35A	19840817	
LZ-409	PZL-104 Wilga 35A	19840818	
LZ-410	PZL-104 Wilga 35A	19840819	
LZ-411	PZL-104 Wilga 35A	19840820	
LZ-412	PZL-104 Wilga 35A	19860842	
LZ-413	PZL-104 Wilga 35A	19860843	
LZ-414	PZL-104 Wilga 35A	19860844	(Z3 DCJ)
			LZ-414
LZ-415	PZL-104 Wilga 35A	19860845	
LZ-416	PZL-104 Wilga 35A	19870859	
LZ-417	PZL-104 Wilga 35A	19880869	
LZ-418	PZL-104 Wilga 35A	85245	DOSAAF

Regn.	Type	C/n	Prev.Id.
LZ-419	PZL-104 Wilga 35A	85238	DOSAAF
LZ-521	Yakovlev YAK-18T	unkn	
LZ-522	Yakovlev YAK-18T	unkn	
LZ-524	Yakovlev YAK-18T	unkn	
LZ-525	Yakovlev YAK-18T	unkn	
LZ-526	Yakovlev YAK-18T	unkn	
LZ-527	Yakovlev YAK-18T	22202034090	
LZ-528	Yakovlev YAK-18T	unkn	(Z3-DCK) LZ-528
LZ-530	Yakovlev YAK-18T	unkn	
LZ-551	Zlin Z.50LS	unkn	
LZ-554	Zlin Z.50LS	0049	
LZ-801	Zlin Z.42	0055	
LZ-802	Zlin Z.42MU	0058	
LZ-803	Zlin Z.42M	0057	OK-ELB
LZ-804	Zlin Z.42	0059	
LZ-805	Zlin Z.42	0056	
LZ-806	Zlin Z.42	0136	
LZ-807	Zlin Z.42	0137	
LZ-810	Zlin Z.42	0442	
LZ-811	Zlin Z.42	0466	
LZ-901	Antonov AN-2	110406	
LZ-902	Antonov AN-2	113616	
LZ-903	Antonov AN-2M	500308	
LZ-904	Antonov AN-2M	500304	
LZ-905	Antonov AN-2	1G147-18	
LZ-906	Antonov AN-2	115708	
LZ-907	Antonov AN-2	117005	
LZ-908	Antonov AN-2	1G55-17	
LZ-909	Antonov AN-2	1G56-44	
LZ-911	Antonov AN-2	1G181-60	
LZ-912	Antonov AN-2	1G33-13	
LZ-914	Antonov AN-2R	1G55-26	
LZ-915	Antonov AN-2R	1G55-29	
LZ-923	Antonov AN-2	1G55-09	
LZ-1008	Antonov AN-2	1G55-01	
LZ-1018	Antonov AN-2	1G55-11	(Z3-DCI) LZ-918
LZ-1021	Antonov AN-2	1G79-23	
LZ-1022	Antonov AN-2	1G79-29	
LZ-1023	Antonov AN-2	1G79-30	
LZ-1024	Antonov AN-2	1G79-31	
LZ-1033	Antonov AN-2	unkn	
LZ-1040	Antonov AN-2	unkn	
LZ-1044	Antonov AN-2R	unkn	
LZ-1057	Antonov AN-2	1G92-05	
LZ-1081	Antonov AN-2R	1G93-46	LZ-030
LZ-1084	Antonov AN-2	1G93-49	
LZ-1088	Antonov AN-2	1G79-28	
LZ-1089	Antonov AN-2R (Museum)	1G82-46	
LZ-1090	Antonov AN-2R	1G86-02	
LZ-1091	Antonov AN-2R	1G86-04	
LZ-1092	Antonov AN-2R	1G86-05	
LZ-1093	Antonov AN-2R	1G86-06	
LZ-1095	Antonov AN-2R	1G92-03	
LZ-1098	Antonov AN-2T	117412	
LZ-1099	Antonov AN-2R	1G135-51	
LZ-1100	Antonov AN-2R	1G135-52	
LZ-1101	Antonov AN-2R	1G135-53	
LZ-1103	Antonov AN-2R	1G135-55	
LZ-1106	Antonov AN-2R	1G135-58	
LZ-1107	Antonov AN-2R	1G135-59	
LZ-1108	Antonov AN-2R	1G135-60	
LZ-1109	Antonov AN-2R	1G145-48	
LZ-1110	Antonov AN-2R	1G145-49	
LZ-1111	Antonov AN-2R	1G145-50	
LZ-1112	Antonov AN-2R	1G145-51	
LZ-1113	Antonov AN-2R	1G145-52	
LZ-1114	Antonov AN-2R	1G145-53	
LZ-1115	Antonov AN-2R	1G145-54	
LZ-1116	Antonov AN-2R	1G145-45	
LZ-1117	Antonov AN-2R	1G145-46	
LZ-1118	Antonov AN-2R	1G145-47	LZ-1097 ?
LZ-1119	Antonov AN-2 (Awaiting rebuild 11.99)	17904	DM-SKF
LZ-1122	Antonov AN-2R	1G155-01	
LZ-1123	Antonov AN-2R	1G155-02	
LZ-1124	Antonov AN-2R	1G155-03	
LZ-1125	Antonov AN-2R	1G155-04	
LZ-1126	Antonov AN-2R	1G155-05	
LZ-1127	Antonov AN-2R	1G155-06	
LZ-1128	Antonov AN-2R	1G155-07	
LZ-1129	Antonov AN-2R	1G155-08	
LZ-1130	Antonov AN-2R	1G155-09	
LZ-1131	Antonov AN-2R	1G155-10	
LZ-1133	Antonov AN-2	unkn	
LZ-1134	Antonov AN-2	114616	DM-SKO
LZ-1135	Antonov AN-2R	1G158-39	
LZ-1136	Antonov AN-2R	1G158-40	
LZ-1138	Antonov AN-2R	1G158-42	
LZ-1140	Antonov AN-2R	1G158-44	
LZ-1141	Antonov AN-2R	1G158-45	
LZ-1142	Antonov AN-2R	1G158-46	
LZ-1144	Antonov AN-2R	1G158-48	
LZ-1145	Antonov AN-2R	1G160-04	
LZ-1146	Antonov AN-2R	1G160-05	
LZ-1147	Antonov AN-2R	1G160-06	
LZ-1149	Antonov AN-2R	1G161-01	
LZ-1150	Antonov AN-2R	1G160-09	
LZ-1151	Antonov AN-2R	1G160-10	
LZ-1152	Antonov AN-2R	1G160-11	
LZ-1153	Antonov AN-2R	1G160-12	
LZ-1154	Antonov AN-2R	1G160-13	
LZ-1156	Antonov AN-2R	1G163-57	
LZ-1157	Antonov AN-2R	1G163-58	
LZ-1158	Antonov AN-2R	1G163-59	
LZ-1159	Antonov AN-2R	1G163-60	
LZ-1160	Antonov AN-2R	1G166-11	
LZ-1161	Antonov AN-2R	1G166-12	
LZ-1162	Antonov AN-2R	1G166-13	
LZ-1163	Antonov AN-2R	1G166-14	
LZ-1164	Antonov AN-2R	1G166-15	
LZ-1166	Antonov AN-2R	1G168-16	
LZ-1167	Antonov AN-2R	1G168-17	
LZ-1168	Antonov AN-2R	1G168-18	
LZ-1169	Antonov AN-2R	1G169-10	
LZ-1171	Antonov AN-2	116803	DM-SKR
LZ-1173	Antonov AN-2	19506	DM-SKL
LZ-1175	Antonov AN-2	19503	DM-SKQ(2) DM-SKJ(1)
LZ-1177	Antonov AN-2	117316	DM-SKV
LZ-1178	Antonov AN-2	117417	DM-SKX
LZ-1180	Antonov AN-2R	1G181-47	
LZ-1185	Antonov AN-2R	1G181-55	
LZ-1186	Antonov AN-2R	1G181-56	
LZ-1187	Antonov AN-2R	1G181-57	
LZ-1188	Antonov AN-2R	1G181-58	
LZ-1189	Antonov AN-2R	1G181-59	
LZ-1190	Antonov AN-2R	1G182-01	
LZ-1191	Antonov AN-2R	1G182-02	
LZ-1194	Antonov AN-2R	1G182-05	
LZ-1195	Antonov AN-2R	1G206-12	
LZ-1196	Antonov AN-2R	1G206-13	
LZ-1197	Antonov AN-2R	1G206-14	
LZ-1198	Antonov AN-2R	1G206-15	
LZ-1199	Antonov AN-2R	1G206-16	
LZ-1200	Antonov AN-2R	1G206-17	
LZ-1201	Antonov AN-2R	1G206-18	
LZ-1203	Antonov AN-2R	1G206-20	
LZ-1204	Antonov AN-2R	1G206-21	
LZ-1205	Antonov AN-2R	1G206-22	
LZ-1206	Antonov AN-2R	1G206-23	
LZ-1210	Antonov AN-2TP	1G129-04	CCCP.....
LZ-1211	Antonov AN-2TP	1G119-40	CCCP02497
LZ-1212	Antonov AN-2TP	1G125-08	CCCP02730
LZ-1213	Antonov AN-2TP	1G125-26	CCCP.....
LZ-1214	Antonov AN-2TP	1G125-33	CCCP.....
LZ-1215	Antonov AN-2	unkn	
LZ-1216	Antonov AN-2TP	1G146-13	CCCP07184
LZ-1217	Antonov AN-2R	1G213-08	
LZ-1218	Antonov AN-2R	1G213-09	

Regn.	Type	C/n	Prev.Id.
LZ-1220	Antonov AN-2R	1G213-11	
LZ-1221	Antonov AN-2R	1G213-12	
LZ-1222	Antonov AN-2R	1G213-13	
LZ-1223	Antonov AN-2R	1G213-14	
LZ-1224	Antonov AN-2R	1G213-15	
LZ-1225	Antonov AN-2R	1G213-16	
LZ-1226	Antonov AN-2R	1G213-17	
LZ-1227	Antonov AN-2R	1G213-18	
LZ-1228	Antonov AN-2R	1G213-19	
LZ-1231	Antonov AN-2R	1G216-18	
LZ-1236	Antonov AN-2R	1G216-23	
LZ-1237	Antonov AN-2R	1G216-24	
LZ-1238	Antonov AN-2R	1G216-25	
LZ-1239	Antonov AN-2R	1G216-26	
LZ-1240	Antonov AN-2R	1G216-27	
LZ-1241	Antonov AN-2R	1G216-28	
LZ-1242	Antonov AN-2R	1G216-29	
LZ-1243	Antonov AN-2R	1G216-30	
LZ-1244	Antonov AN-2R	1G216-31	
LZ-1245	Antonov AN-2R	1G216-32	
LZ-1246	Antonov AN-2R	1G216-33	
LZ-1248	Antonov AN-2R	1G216-35	
LZ-1502	Antonov AN-2	1G166-04	RA-19750
			CCCP19750
LZ-1503	Antonov AN-2	1G148-33	RA-07272
			CCCP07272
LZ-1504	Antonov AN-2	1G199-12	Z3-BGO
			LZ-1504
			CCCP31503
LZ-1505	Antonov AN-2	1G189-22	Z3-BGP
			LZ-1505
			RA-84555
			CCCP84555
LZ-2002	Antonov AN-2	unkn	
LZ-2006	Antonov AN-2M	unkn	
LZ-2010	Antonov AN-2M	801825	
LZ-3013	LET Z-37 Cmelák	14-26	
LZ-3040	LET Z-37 Cmelák	14-28	
LZ-....	LET Z-37A Cmelák	17-29	D-ENSK
			DDR-SSK
			DM-SSK
LZ-5021	Mil Mi-2	544721036	
LZ-5022	Mil Mi-2	544722036	
LZ-5023	Mil Mi-2	544723046	
LZ-5024	Mil Mi-2	525928128	
LZ-5025	Mil Mi-2	525929128	
LZ-5027	Mil Mi-2	526008039	
LZ-5028	Mil Mi-2	526014029	
LZ-5030	Mil Mi-2	526016029	
LZ-5031	Mil Mi-2	526017029	
LZ-5032	Mil Mi-2	526018029	
LZ-5033	Mil Mi-2	526019029	
LZ-5035	Mil Mi-2	526021029	
LZ-5036	Mil Mi-2	526022029	
LZ-5037	Mil Mi-2	526445010	
LZ-5038	Mil Mi-2	526446010	
LZ-5039	Mil Mi-2	526447010	
LZ-5040	Mil Mi-2	526448010	
LZ-5041	Mil Mi-2	526449010	
LZ-5042	Mil Mi-2	526450010	
LZ-5043	Mil Mi-2	526501010	
LZ-5044	Mil Mi-2	526502010	
LZ-5045	Mil Mi-2	526503010	
LZ-6003	Kamov Ka.26	7101703	
LZ-6012	Kamov Ka.26	unkn	
LZ-6013	Kamov Ka.26	7202407	
LZ-6015	Kamov Ka.26	unkn	
LZ-6017	Kamov Ka.26	unkn	
LZ-6019	Kamov Ka.26	unkn	
LZ-6025	Kamov Ka.26	unkn	
LZ-6027	Kamov Ka.26	7404310	
LZ-6030	Kamov Ka.26	7504808	
LZ-6031	Kamov Ka.26	7504809	
LZ-6032	Kamov Ka.26	7504810	
LZ-6033	Kamov Ka.26	7504811	

Regn.	Type	C/n	Prev.Id.
LZ-6036	Kamov Ka.26	7504819	
LZ-6042	Kamov Ka.26	7505314	
LZ-6044	Kamov Ka.26	unkn	
LZ-6045	Kamov Ka.26	7605502	
LZ-6047	Kamov Ka.26	unkn	
LZ-6048	Kamov Ka.26	unkn	
LZ-6049	Kamov Ka.26	unkn	
LZ-6050	Kamov Ka.26	unkn	
LZ-6052	Kamov Ka.26	unkn	
LZ-6053	Kamov Ka.26	unkn	
LZ-6056	Kamov Ka.26	7615807	
LZ-6059	Kamov Ka.26	unkn	
LZ-6061	Kamov Ka.26	unkn	
LZ-6063	Kamov Ka.26	7706002	
LZ-6066	Kamov Ka.26	7706005	
LZ-6067	Kamov Ka.26	unkn	
LZ-6069	Kamov Ka.26	7806407	Z3-HHC
			LZ-6069
LZ-6071	Kamov Ka.26	unkn	
LZ-6072	Kamov Ka.26	unkn	
LZ-6073	Kamov Ka.26	7102207	
LZ-8001	PZL M-18 Dromader *(Museum)*	1Z008-11	
LZ-8002	PZL M-18 Dromader	1Z008-12	
LZ-8003	PZL M-18 Dromader	1Z008-13	
LZ-8004	PZL M-18 Dromader	1Z008-14	
LZ-8005	PZL M-18 Dromader	1Z009-07	
LZ-8006	PZL M-18 Dromader	1Z009-08	
LZ-8007	PZL M-18 Dromader	1Z009-11	Z3-BGK
			LZ-8007
LZ-8008	PZL M-18 Dromader	1Z009-12	Z3-BGL
			LZ-8008
LZ-8009	PZL M-18 Dromader	1Z009-21	
LZ-8010	PZL M-18 Dromader	1Z009-22	
LZ-8011	PZL M-18 Dromader	1Z009-23	Z3-BGM
			LZ-8011
LZ-8012	PZL M-18 Dromader	1Z009-24	
LZ-8013	PZL M-18 Dromader	1Z009-25	
LZ-8014	PZL M-18 Dromader	1Z009-26	
LZ-8015	PZL M-18 Dromader	1Z009-27	
LZ-8016	PZL M-18 Dromader	1Z009-28	
LZ-8017	PZL M-18 Dromader	1Z009-29	Z3-BGN
			LZ-8017
LZ-8018	PZL M-18 Dromader	1Z009-30	
LZ-9001	Ayres S.2R-T34 Turbo Thrush	unkn	
LZ-9002	Ayres S.2R-T34 Turbo Thrush	unkn	
LZ-9003	Ayres S.2R-T34 Turbo Thrush	T34-60	
LZ-9006	Ayres S.2R-T34 Turbo Thrush	unkn	
Police 501	Mil Mi-2	543303123	
Police 502	Mil Mi-2	543304123	
Police 503	Mil Mi-2	526007039	LZ-5026
Police 504	Mil Mi-2	539009124	
Police 505	Mil Mi-2	539010124	
LZ-...	Bell 206B Jet Ranger II	4504	N82407
			C-GFNU
LZ-...	Bell 206B Jet Ranger II	4506	N82401
			C-FOEP
LZ-...	Bell 206B Jet Ranger II	4508	N8264U
			C-GFNQ
LZ-...	Bell 206B Jet Ranger II	4510	N82744
			C-FOFB
LZ-...	Bell 206B Jet Ranger II	4512	N8268J
			C-GBUP
LZ-...	Bell 206B Jet Ranger II	4514	N8267W
			C-GAJN
LZ-...	Cessna 421C Golden Eagle II	0272	N6390G

Regn.	Type	Cn	Prev.Id.

BALLOONS

LZ-001	Cameron A-210 HAFB	1437	
LZ-002	Cameron V-56 HAFB	1721	
LZ-004	Tomi AX-7 HAFB	BAV067/1989	
LZ-005	Tomi AX-7 HAFB	BAV068/1989	
LZ-006	Tomi AX-7 HAFB	BAV069/1989	
LZ-007	Tomi AX-7 HAFB	BAV076/1989	
LZ-008	Cameron V-77 HAFB	3034	

GLIDERS

LZ-02	LET L-13 Blanik	172530	
LZ-06	LET L-13 Blanik	173926	
LZ-07	LET L-13 Blanik	173826	
LZ-09	LET L-13 Blanik	174029	
LZ-10	LET L-13 Blanik	174030	
LZ-11	LET L-13 Blanik	174112	
LZ-12	LET L-13 Blanik	174113	
LZ-16	LET L-13 Blanik	174716	
LZ-18	LET L-13 Blanik	174725	
LZ-19	LET L-13 Blanik (Wfu)	174728	
LZ-22	LET L-13 Blanik	174727	
LZ-23	LET L-13 Blanik	026843	
LZ-25	LET L-13 Blanik	174726	
LZ-26	LET L-13 Blanik	026429	DOSAAF
LZ-200	SZD-36 Cobra 15	W-570	
LZ-201	SZD-36 Cobra 15	W-571	
LZ-304	SZD-32A Foka 5 (Museum)	W-421	
LZ-305	SZD-32A Foka 5 (Wfu)	W-422	
LZ-306	SZD-32A Foka 5 (Wfu)	W-423	
LZ-307	SZD-32A Foka 5	W-467	
LZ-308	SZD-32A Foka 5	W-468	
LZ-309	SZD-32A Foka 5	W-545	
LZ-601	SZD-38A Jantar 1	B-669	
LZ-602	SZD-38A Jantar 1	B-670	
LZ-603	SZD-41A Jantar Standard	B-794	
LZ-604	SZD-41A Jantar Standard	B-885	
LZ-606	SZD-42-2 Jantar 2B	B-964	
LZ-607	SZD-48-1 Jantar Standard 2	W-910	
LZ-608	SZD-48-1 Jantar Standard 2	W-923	
LZ-609	SZD-42-2 Jantar 2B	B-940	
LZ-610	SZD-42-2 Jantar 2B	B-949	
LZ-611	SZD-48-1 Jantar Standard 2	B-1032	
LZ-612	SZD-42-2 Jantar 2B	B-1381	
LZ-613	Rolladen-Schneider LS-4A	4659	
LZ-614	Rolladen-Schneider LS-4A	4660	

Other marks known include Kometa 1 Standard LZ-901, Kometa 2 Standards LZ-902-911, and Kometa 3 Standards LZ-912-931 of which some of the latter may still be extant

MICROLIGHTS

LZ-X01	Optimum-88 Microlight	unkn	
LZ-....	Funk FK-9	71	
LZ-....	Funk FK-9	79	
LZ-....	Mainair Sea Alpha 582	903-0492-W698	
LZ-....	Mainair Gemini 462 Flash IIA	586-1087-W375	

OE - AUSTRIA

Regn.	Type	Cn	Prev.Id.
OE-AAA	Diamond DA.20-A1 Katana	10064	N844DF
OE-AAB	Piper J-3C-65 Cub	11717	HB-OBK
			43-30426
OE-AAG	Piper J-3C-65 Cub	13120	HB-OUW
			44-80824
OE-AAK(2)	Pottier P.50P	014	
OE-AAR	HOAC DV-20 Katana	20114	
OE-AAT	Auster Mk.5	845	G-ANGW
			MS980
OE-AAX	Jodel D.95	189	
OE-ABA	Meteor FL.54	1114	I-FELC
OE-ABB	Jodel D.112 Club	661/7	
OE-ABE	Piper J-3C-90 Cub	11210	D-EKWU
			OE-ABE
			HB-ONN
			43-29919
OE-ABH(2)	Europa Aviation Europa	194	
OE-ABJ	Bücker T.131P Jungmann	T-101	OE-VPI
OE-ABL	Jodel D.112 Club	672/8	
OE-ABV(2)	Christen A-1 Husky	1152	N9608B
OE-ABX	Piper PA-18-150 Super Cub	18-7694	N10F
OE-ABZ	Piper J-5A Cub Cruiser	5-814	N35926
			NC35926
OE-ACC	Piper PA-18-150 Super Cub	MDC-1042	HB-ORX
OE-ACE	Zlin 381 Bestmann	16	OK-ZFQ
OE-ACF	Piper PA-18 Super Cub 95	18-6112	AAF:2A-AU ?
OE-ACK	Meteor FL.53BM	1135	I-FELX
OE-ACR	Piper J-3C-65 Cub	12863	HB-OSS
			44-80567
OE-ADA(2)	HOAC DV-20 Katana	20150	
OE-ADB	Tipsy T.66H Nipper	17	
OE-ADD(2)	Europa Aviation Europa	133	
OE-ADE	Champion 7GCB Challenger 180	53	
OE-ADF	Piper PA-18-150 Super Cub	18-7510	
OE-ADI (2)	HOAC DV-20 Katana	20060	D-ENMH
OE-ADK	Piper PA-18-150 Super Cub	18-4291	(D-ELTE)
			N2416P
OE-ADV(3)	HOAC DV-20 Katana	20006	C-FSBY
			OE-CDY
OE-AEA(2)	HOAC DV-20 Katana	20120	D-ESIM
OE-AEO	Piper PA-18 Super Cub 95	18-6111	AAF:2A-AV
OE-AEP	HOAC DV-20 Katana	20113	
OE-AER	Piper PA-18 Super Cub 95	18-5587	AAF:2A-AP
OE-AEW	Pitts S-1H Special	69IH	
OE-AEZ	Champion 7GCBC Citabria	097	D-ENBR
OE-AFB	PZL-101A Gawron	119325	
OE-AFC	Piper PA-18 Super Cub 95	18-5500	AAF:2A-AO
OE-AFD	Cessna 150	17802	N6402T
OE-AFE	Piper PA-18-150 Super Cub	18-6336	AAF:2A-BJ
OE-AFF	PZL-101A Gawron	52076	
OE-AFG(2)	HOAC DV-20 Katana	20071	
OE-AFK	Piper PA-18-105 Super Cub	18-2415	N301T
OE-AFP	PZL-101A Gawron	63090	
OE-AFT	PZL-101A Gawron	63102	
OE-AFU	Piper PA-18-150 Super Cub	18-5513	AAF:2A-AT
OE-AFV	Taylorcraft BC-12D	10218	D-EMAF
			N44418
OE-AGA(2)	HOAC DV-20 Katana	20009	
OE-AGB	Piper PA-18-150 Super Cub	18-7445	
OE-AGC	Binder CP.301S Smaragd	106	D-EFIR
OE-AGE	Aviamilano P.19 Scricciolo	326	
OE-AGG(2)	HOAC DV-20 Katana	20054	N54DV
OE-AGH(2)	HOAC DV-20 Katana	20147	G-BWIO
OE-AGI	Piper PA-18-150 Super Cub	18-7609058	
OE-AGL	Aero C-104 Jungmann	166	(D-EEST)
			OE-AGL
			OK-...
			Czech AF
OE-AGN	First Strike Super Cat	1	
OE-AGO	Piper PA-18 Super Cub 95	18-156	F-BIRP
			F-DAAA
			HB-OOK

Regn.	Type	C/n	Prev.Id.
OE-AGP	Piper PA-38-112 Tomahawk	38-78A0176	N9700N
OE-AGS	HOAC DV-20 Katana	20032	
OE-AGT	HOAC DV-20 Katana	20109	
OE-AGU	Robin HR.200/120 Club	13	
OE-AGW	Piper PA-18-90 Super Cub	18-6882	OE-AGV
OE-AGX	HOAC DV-20 Katana	20047	
OE-AGY	HOAC DV-20 Katana	20145	D-EDSV
OE-AHB(2)	Brditschka HB-202 VI	202-001	
OE-AHC	Cessna 150M	78589	N704GA
OE-AHE	Champion 7GCBC Citabria	227-70	N7566F
OE-AHG	Cessna 150A	59176	N7076X
OE-AHK	Cessna A.152 Aerobat	0989	N761VG
OE-AHL	SAN Jodel DR.1050 Ambassadeur	177	OE-AWG
OE-AHO	HOAC DV-20 Katana	20138	
OE-AHR	Rand-Robinson KR-2	3317	
OE-AHT	HOAC DV-22 Speed Katana	22002	
OE-AIF	Piper PA-18-150 Super Cub	18-4401	OE-BIF
			N2772P
OE-AIL	Piper PA-18-180 Super Cub	18-7505	OE-BIL
			N3747Z
OE-AIN	Piper PA-18-150 Super Cub	18-7803	OE-BIN
OE-AIO	Piper PA-18-180 Super Cub	18-8115	OE-BIO
			N7273Y
OE-AIR(2)	HOAC DV-20 Katana	20007	
OE-AIS	Cessna 150B	59433	N7333X
OE-AIW	HOAC DV-20 Katana	20126	
OE-AIZ	Piper PA-22-108 Colt	22-8475	OE-BIZ
OE-AJK	Aero Designs Pulsar XP	469	
OE-AKA	Fieseler Fi.156C Storch S-14b	110202	Fv3814
OE-AKF	Bücker Bü.133 Jungmeister	18	HB-MIR
			U-71
OE-AKK	Bücker-Lerche R-180	96	HB-URT
	(Lycoming Bü 131 conversion)		A-83
OE-AKL	HOAC DV-20 Katana	20003	
OE-AKM(2)	HAOC DV-20 Katana	20087	N87DV
OE-AKN	Diamond DA-20-A1 Katana	10172	N152SE
OE-AKT	Bücker Bü.133C Jungmeister	43	HB-MKD
			U-96
OE-AKY	Diamond DA-20-A1 Katana	10059	N199DA
OE-ALA	Piper J-3C-65 Cub	8637	N62752
			42-36513
OE-ALB	Reims/Cessna F.150H	0343	(D-EGAA)
OE-ALD	Reims/Cessna F.150J	0470	
OE-ALE	Reims/Cessna F.150J	0403	
OE-ALF	Reims/Cessna FA.150K Aerobat	0006	
OE-ALG(2)	Brditschka HB-207 Alfa	005	
OE-ALH	Reims/Cessna FA.150K Aerobat	0050	
OE-ALI	Aero Jodel D.IIA Club	614	
OE-ALJ	HOAC DV-20 Katana	20089	
OE-ALN	Reims/Cessna F.150K	0607	D-ECEY
OE-ALO	Reims/Cessna F.150K	0642	F-BSIF
OE-ALP	Reims/Cessna F.150K	0639	F-BRXI
OE-ALR	Reims/Cessna F.150L	0694	
OE-ALS	HOAC DV-20 Katana	20118	
OE-ALU	Reims/Cessna F.150L	0732	
OE-ALY	HOAC DV-20 Katana	20119	
OE-ALZ	Reims/Cessna FRA.150L Aerobat	0137	
OE-AMA	Beech 77 Skipper	WA-251	D-EFCQ
OE-AMB	Bölkow BO.208C Junior	597	(D-ECGE)
OE-AMD	HOAC DV-20 Katana	20066	D-EKKH(2)
OE-AMH	HOAC DV-20 Katana	20063	
OE-AMI	Starlite SL-1	113	
OE-AML	Piel CP.301A Emeraude	02	
OE-AMN	Jodel D.95	673	
OE-AMS	Europa Aviation Europa	183	
OE-AMW(2)	Christen Pitts S-2B Special	5158	
OE-ANB	Piper PA-18 Super Cub 95	18-1459	D-ENCB
			ALAT
			51-15459
OE-AND	Piper PA-18 Super Cub 95	18-1582	D-EETL
			ALAT
			51-15582
OE-ANF	Piper PA-18 Super Cub 95	18-2056	D-ENAW
			R-71
			52-2456

Regn.	Type	C/n	Prev.Id.
OE-ANX	Diamond DA-20-A1 Katana	10313	N313DA
OE-AOB	Bellanca 7GCBC Citabria	678-74	
OE-AOC	Bellanca 7GCBC Citabria	696-74	
OE-AOD	Bellanca 7GCBC Citab ia	697-74	
OE-AON	Bellanca 7GCBC Citabria	760-74	
OE-AOT	SAN Jodel DR.1050 Ambassadeur	147	
OE-APA	Piper PA-18-150 Super Cub	18-8872	N8474Y
OE-APG	Piper PA-18-150 Super Cub	18-8691	N4369Z
OE-APK	Piper PA-18-150 Super Cub	18-8629	N4317Z
OE-APL	Christen A-1 Husky	1104	D-EBAD(5)
OE-APN	Piper PA-18-150 Super Cub	18-8119	N4112Z
OE-APW	Piper PA-18-150 Super Cub	18-8672	N4354Z
OE-ARD	Christen A-1 Husky	1112	D-EARD
OE-ARE	Aero Designs Pulsar XP	429	
OE-ARF	Piel CP.301A Emeraude	048	
OE-ARG	Piper PA-38-112 Tomahawk II	38-81A0102	(D-ECZW)
OE-ARK	Denney Kitfox II	471	
OE-ASA	Bölkow BO.208C Junior	698	(D-EABL)
OE-ASK(2)	Cessna 150M	75982	N66311
OE-ASN	Piper PA-38-112 Tomahawk	38-78A0463	N9723N
OE-ASP(2)	HOAC DV-22 Speed Katana	22001	
OE-ASR	Bölkow BO.208C Junior	695	D-EABI
OE-ASS	Aero-Jodel D.11A Club	604	
OE-AST	Pitts S-1S Special	1-0039	VH-KGZ
			N8068
OE-ASW	Aero-Jodel D.11A Club	632	
OE-ATB	Reims/Cessna F.150L	0867	
OE-ATD	Reims/Cessna F.150L	0937	
OE-ATF	Reims/Cessna FRA.150L Aerobat	0197	
OE-ATG	Reims/Cessna F.150L	0955	
OE-ATL	Reims/Cessna F.150L	0936	
OE-ATM	Reims/Cessna F.150L	1039	
OE-ATN	Reims/Cessna F.150L	1079	
OE-ATO	Reims/Cessna F.150L	1081	
OE-ATT	Reims/Cessna F.150L	1010	
OE-ATV	Reims/Cessna F.150L	1057	
OE-ATW	Reims/Cessna FRA.150L Aerobat	0225	(G-BBTC)
OE-ATX	Reims/Cessna F.150L	1047	(G-BBTD)
OE-AUA	Reims/Cessna F.150L	0790	OE-BUA
			OE-ATA
OE-AUE(2)	Piper PA-18-150 Super Cub	18-8009053	OE-BUE
			(D-EFSC)
			N2351P
OE-AUL(2)	Piper PA-18-150 Super Cub	18-8826	OE-BUL
			N4491Z
OE-AUR	Reims/Cessna F.152	1951	OE-BUR
OE-AUS	Pitts S-1S Special	K-101	
OE-AUW	CASA I-131E Jungmann	2059	D-EDFD
			(D-EOOL)
			E3B-510
OE-AVD	Reims/Cessna F.150F	0027/63012	
OE-AVE	Reims/Cessna F.150F	0034/63107	
OE-AVG	Reims/Cessna F.150F	0028/63028	
OE-AVI	Reims/Cessna F.150F	0033/63104	
OE-AVR	Reims/Cessna F.150G	0138	
OE-AVV	Reims/Cessna F.150H	0229	
OE-AXB(2)	Westermayer WE.4 Gyrocopter	03	
OE-AXF	Frank TSF.02 Gyrocopter	02	
OE-AXR	Westermayer WE.4 Gyrocopter	04	
OE-AXW	Bensen B.8M Austria Gyrocopter	01	
OE-AYE	Cessna 150C	59841	N2041Z
OE-AYI	Cessna 150C	59991	N7891Z
OE-AYK	Cessna 150C	60006	N7906Z
OE-AYX	Cessna 150E	61494	N4094U
OE-BAX	Cessna 182P Skylane	62985	OE-DGF
			N52982
OE-BBB	Beech 200 Super King Air	BB-526	
OE-BBL	Pilatus PC-6/B2-H2 Turbo-Porter	664	
OE-BIP	Cessna 182P Skylane	0058/64384	OE-DGX
	(Reims-assembled)		N1594M
OE-BIR	Reims/Cessna F.182Q Skylane	0042	
OE-BIT	Reims/Cessna F.182Q Skylane	0111	
OE-BIU	Reims/Cessna F.182Q Skylane	0120	
OE-BXA	Agusta-Bell 206B Jet Ranger III	8613	
OE-BXB(2)	Agusta-Bell 206B Jet Ranger III	8644	

Regn.	Type	C/n	Prev.Id.
OE-BXC(2)	Agusta-Bell 206B Jet Ranger III	8618	
OE-BXD(4)	Aérospatiale AS.355N Ecureuil 2	5581	F-WYMK
OE-BXE(2)	Agusta-Bell 206B Jet Ranger III	8666	
OE-BXF(2)	Bell 206L-3 Long Ranger III	51112	
OE-BXH	Aérospatiale AS.350B1 Ecureuil	1898	
OE-BXI	Aérospatiale AS.350B1 Ecureuil	1899	
OE-BXK	Aérospatiale AS.350B1 Ecuerui	1900	
OE-BXL	Aérospatiale AS.350B1 Ecureuil	2049	
OE-BXM(2)	Aérospatiale AS.350B1 Ecureuil	2113	
OE-BXN(2)	Aérospatiale AS.350B1 Ecureuil	2214	
OE-BXO(2)	Bell 206B3 Jet Ranger III	4440	
OE-BXP(2)	Bell 206B3 Jet Ranger III	4410	C-FYDD
OE-BXR(3)	Bell 206B3 Jet Ranger III	4413	C-FYDH
OE-BXS	Agusta-Bell 206B Jet Ranger II	8403	
OE-BXT(2)	Bell 206B3 Jet Ranger III	4441	
OE-BXU(3)	Aérospatiale AS.355F2 Ecureuil 2	5485	F-WYMA
OE-BXW(2)	Aérospatiale AS.355F2 Ecureuil 2	5528	F-WYMA
OE-BXX(2)	Aérospatiale AS.355N Ecureuil 2	5558	F-WYMF
OE-BXY	Agusta-Bell 206B Jet Ranger III	8604	
OE-BXZ	Agusta-Bell 206B Jet Ranger III	8605	
OE-CAA(2)	Brditschka HB 207VRG	207-002	
OE-CAL	Oberlerchner-Job 15-150	051	OE-VAL
OE-CBE	Reims/Cessna F.150J	0396	(D-EWOR)
			HB-CBE
			OE-AVZ
OE-CBH	Brändli BX-2 Cherry	78	
OE-CBK	Brditschka HB-207 Alpha *(Exhibited 4.99)*	unkn	
OE-CBL	Reims/Cessna F.150J	0509	D-EBBL
OE-CBR	HOAC DV-20 Katana	20010	
OE-CBS	Piper PA-18-150 Super Cub	18-8083	N4092Z
OE-CBW	HOAC DV-20 Katana	20160	
OE-CCB	Cessna L-19A Bird Dog (305A)	21510	AAF:3A-CB
			51-4625
OE-CCC	HOAC DV-20 Katana	20095	N95DV
OE-CCF	Cessna L-19E Bird Dog (305C)	23933	AAF:3A-BF
			57-6019
OE-CCG	Cessna L-19A Bird Dog (305A)	22589	AAF:3A-CG
			51-12275
OE-CCH	Pitts S-1S Special	001	
OE-CCM	Cessna L-19A Bird Dog (305A)	22085	AAF:3A-CM
			51-7351
OE-CCO	Cessna L-19A Bird Dog (305A)	22216	AAF:3A-CO
			51-7477
OE-CCP	Cessna L-19A Bird Dog (305A)	22395	AAF:3A-CQ
			51-12081
OE-CCS	HOAC DV-20 Katana	20097	N197DV
OE-CCW	Beech B45 Mentor	G-2	OE-BAP
			OE-VAA
			HB-EGM
			N8592A
			51-74598
OE-CDA	HOAC DV-20 Katana	20154	
OE-CDF	Viking Dragonfly	EDO-1	
OE-CDM(2)	Piper PA-18-150 Super Cub	1809019	N189PC
OE-CDP	Piper PA-18-150 Super Cub	18-5664	D-EADP
			OE-ADH
			(D-ECEQ)
			N7196D
OE-CDV(2)	HOAC DV-20 Katana	20081	OY-JAC
			OE-AII
OE-CEA	Cessna 152	80019	D-EBKF
			N757US
OE-CEB	Cessna 152	80994	D-EDLO
			N48838
OE-CEF	HOAC DV-20 Katana	20014	
OE-CEL	Denney Kitfox	PA470.001	
OE-CEM	HOAC DV-20 Katana	20099	N199DV
OE-CEO	Bellanca 7GCAA Citabria	362-78	VH-WEO
OE-CEP(2)	Brändli BX-2 Cherry	91	
OE-CES	HOAC DV-20 Katana	20035	C-FSBS
OE-CET	Etrich-Taube F Replica	01	
OE-CEW(2)	Diamond DA-20-A1 Katana	10156	
OE-CEX	Piper J-3C-65 Cub	11030	D-EGIS
			HB-OHD
			43-29739

Regn.	Type	C/n	Prev.Id.
OE-CFB	Europa Aviation Europa	174	
OE-CFC	Reims/Cessna F.152	1596	
OE-CFE	Reims/Cessna F.152	1639	
OE-CFF	Reims/Cessna F.152	1719	
OE-CFH	Binder CP.301S Smaragd	008	
OE-CFK	Reims/Cessna F.152	1760	
OE-CFN	Cessna 152	84468	N6623L
OE-CFT	Cessna 150E	61097	D-EDTD
			N2597J
OE-CFW	Jodel D.1190-S Compostela	E-95	D-EBDX
			EC-BDX
OE-CGA	Cessna 152 *(W/o 18.7.98)*	81867	N67497
OE-CGC	Cessna A.152 Aerobat	0984	N761TA
OE-CGD	Cessna 152	85793	N94817
OE-CGH	Stoddard-Hamilton Glasair II-S RG	2025	
OE-CGO	Reims/Cessna F.150L	0905	N9693N
			D-ECVV
OE-CGW(2)	Brditschka HB-202-V1	202-003	
OE-CHA	Brditschka HB.207V-RG Alpha	207003	
OE-CHC	Brditschka HB-207V-RG Alpha	20701	
OE-CHE	Polliwagen Supernova PW235	0613	
OE-CHG	Brändli BX-2 Cherry	64	
OE-CHI	Brändli BX-2 Cherry	98	
OE-CHK	Piper PA-38-112 Tomahawk	38-82A0047	HB-PHK
			N91535
OE-CHL	Europa Aviation Europa	227	
OE-CHM	Bede BD-5B	2537	
OE-CHR	Christen A-1 Husky	1240	D-EXAD
OE-CHW	Denney Kitfox IV	HCU-078	
OE-CIC	HOAC DV-20 Katana	20073	
OE-CIF	Denney Kitfox III	642	
OE-CIG	Denney Kitfox II/IV	641	
OE-CIH	Piper PA-18-150 Super Cub	18-6765	OE-BIH
OE-CIK	Piper PA-18-180 Super Cub	18-7414	OE-BIK
OE-CIW	HOAC DV-20 Katana	20070	
OE-CKD	Europa Aviation Europa	134	
OE-CKF	Denney Kitfox Classic	C9412-0086	
	(Accident 10.8.98, probable write-off)		
OE-CKH	Brändli BX-2 Cherry	106	
OE-CKL	HOAC DV-20 Katana	20125	TF-FTZ
			OY-JAK
OE-CKR	Rutan LongEz	1201	
OE-CLA	Cessna 152	84007	N4898H
OE-CLW	Lischak LW-02	01	
OE-CMB	Reims/Cessna F.150M	1226	
OE-CMD	Reims/Cessna F.150M	1283	
OE-CME	Reims/Cessna F.150M	1227	
OE-CMG	Reims/Cessna F.150M	1305	
OE-CMH	Reims/Cessna F.150M	1271	(F-BXQJ)
OE-CMI	Reims/Cessna F.150M	1397	
OE-CMK	Reims/Cessna F.150M	1384	
OE-CML	Reims/Cessna F.150M	1410	
OE-CMM	Reims/Cessna F.150M	1409	
OE-CMN	Reims/Cessna F.150M	1387	
OE-CMP	Reims/Cessna FA.152	0342	
OE-CMR	Reims/Cessna F.152	1446	
OE-CMS	Reims/Cessna F.152	1456	
OE-CMW	Europa Aviation Europa	173	
OE-CMX	Reims/Cessna F.150M	1413	
OE-CMY	Reims/Cessna F.152	1449	
OE-CNC	Reims/Cessna F.152	1853	D-EANC(2)
OE-CNH	Europa Aviation Europa	132	
OE-COC	HOAC DV-20 Katana	20111	
OE-COG	HOAC DV-20 Katana	20100	
OE-CON	HOAC DV-20 Katana	20108	
OE-COO	Cessna 150M	77772	N7618U
OE-COS	Piper PA-18-180 Super Cub	18-7552	OE-BIM
			N3814Z
OE-CPC	Piper PA-38-112 Tomahawk	38-80A0091	N9682N
OE-CPE	Reims/Cessna F.150M	1374	F-GAQS
OE-CPL	Wassmer WA.81 Piranha	819	D-EERB
OE-CPU	HOAC LF-2 (DV-20 Katana)	20002	
OE-CPW	Piper PA-18A-150 Super Cub	18-5859	N7572D
OE-CRF	Light Aero Avid Flyer-Speedwing	1038	
OE-CRK	Zlin Z.326 Trenér Master	646-08	HA-TRK

Regn.	Type	C/n	Prev.Id.
OE-CRN	Denney Kitfox-Mk IV Speedster	FCS118	
OE-CRP	SOCATA MS.883 Rallye 115	1687	F-BTHU
OE-CRS	Reims/Cessna F.152	1954	
OE-CRW	Brändli BX-2 Cherry	93	
OE-CSA	Zlin Z.526F Trenér Master	1242	HA-SAR
OE-CSK	Quickie Quickie Q.2	2284	
OE-CSM	Cessna 152	84433	D-EKCU(2)
			PH-SCU
			N6555L
OE-CST	Brändli BX-2 Cherry	125	
OE-CSW	Light Aero Avid Flyer-Speedwing	459	
OE-CSZ	Bellanca 8KCAB Decathlon	349-77	
OE-CTO	Brändli BX-2 Cherry	115	
OE-CUB	Piper J-3C-65 Cub	18282	N98128
			NC98128
OE-CUC	Reims/Cessna F.150H	0304	OE-BUC
			OE-ALC
OE-CUG	Reims/Cessna FA.152	0381	OE-BUG
			OE-AIM
OE-CUM	Cessna 150M	77165	D-EFJF
			N63191
OE-CUS	Cessna 152	84488	N4889M
OE-CVB	Light Aero Avid Flyer Mk.IV	1050D	
OE-CVC	Reims/Cessna F.150L	0719	HB-CVQ
OE-CVY	Reims/Cessna F.150L	0740	HB-CVY
OE-CXG	Hughes 269C	71-1063	N1110K
OE-CXR	Hughes 269C	129-0859	D-HAKO(3)
OE-CXT	Robinson R-22	0126	D-HEMI
			SE-HOD
OE-CXX	Robinson R-22 Beta	1570	
OE-CXY	Robinson R-22 Beta	0692	
OE-CYZ	Rutan Cozy	E-730	
OE-...	Diamond DA.20-A1 Katana	10298	N298DA
OE-...	Diamond DA.20-A1 Katana	10314	N644DA
OE-...	Diamond DA.20-A1 Katana	10315	N315DA
OE-...	Diamond DA.20-A1 Katana	10316	N646DA
OE-...	HOAC DV-20 Katana	20096	N96DV
OE-DAA(2)	Piper PA-32RT-300T Turbo Lance	32R-7887053	D-ETAS
			OE-KRR
			D-EJHW
			PH-BRO
			N36552
OE-DAD	Cessna 170B	26920	HB-COV
			N2977D
OE-DAI	Cessna 172B	47801	N6901X
OE-DAS	Neico Lancair Super ES	A-ES-01	
OE-DAW	Reims/Cessna F.182Q Skylane	0065	OE-BAW
			OE-DOL
OE-DBR	Cessna 182B Skylane	51700	N2400G
OE-DBU(2)	Reims/Cessna FR.172K Hawk XP	0661	N988PK
			(D-EBKP)
			HB-CNU
OE-DBW	Cessna 170B	26490	D-EFYL
			N3447C
OE-DCC	Robin DR.400/180R Remorqueur	1030	D-EGPS
OE-DCD	SOCATA MS.893E Rallye 180GT Gaillard	12492	F-BVLK
OE-DCG	Cessna 175B Skylark	56856	N8156T
OE-DCN	Cessna P.172D	57170	N8570X
OE-DCS	Reims/Cessna F.172E	0060	OE-DOS
OE-DCV	Reims/Cessna F.172E	0065	
OE-DCW	Reims/Cessna F.172D	0003/50001	F-WLIS
			(N2401U)
OE-DDC	Cessna 182E Skylane	54279	N3279Y
OE-DDK	Cessna 182G Skylane	55195	N3795U
OE-DDN	Cessna 182H Skylane	55998	N1898X
OE-DDT	Cessna 182K Skylane	57779	N2579Q
OE-DDU	Cessna 182L Skylane	58898	
OE-DDV	Cessna 182M Skylane	59404	N70881
OE-DDW	Cessna 182K Skylane	58365	N2665R
OE-DDY	Cessna 182N Skylane	60200	
OE-DEC	Cessna 210	57259	D-EJAV
			N9459T
OE-DEF(2)	Diamond DA.40-V1 Star	40001	OE-VPC
OE-DEH	SOCATA MS.893A Rallye Commodore 180	12031	F-BTPQ
OE-DEI	Cessna 210E	58615	N4915U
OE-DEP	Piper PA-28R-201 Arrow III	28R-7837282	N36512
OE-DER	Cessna P.206B Super Skylane	0342	N4742F
OE-DES	Cessna 210G	58835	N5835F
OE-DEU	Piper PA-24-250 Comanche	24-1931	N6798P
OE-DEX	Cessna 207A Skywagon	00165	N1565U
OE-DFC	SOCATA MS.893A Rallye Commodore 180	10568	
OE-DFD	Diamond DA-40-V2 Star	40002	OE-DED(3)
			OE-VPE
OE-DFL	Piper PA-28-180 Cherokee G	28-7205008	N2158T
OE-DFO	Morane-Saulnier MS.885 Super Rallye	253	D-EDFO
			F-BKUG
OE-DFR	GEMS MS.893A Rallye Commodore 180	10601	(D-EHYN)
OE-DFS	Robin DR.400/180R Remorqueur	970	
OE-DFV	Cessna T.207A Turbo Skywagon	0370	N1770U
OE-DFX	Piper PA-28-181 Cherokee Archer II	28-7790239	N8439F
OE-DFZ	Beech 35-C33A Debonair	CE-152	D-EKVY
OE-DGA	Cessna 182P Skylane	60911	
OE-DGB	Cessna 182P Skylane	61104	
OE-DGC	Cessna 182P Skylane	61534	
OE-DGH	Reims/Cessna F.172D	0001/49991	F-WLIK
OE-DGI	Cessna 182P Skylane	62878	
OE-DGM	SOCATA MS.893A Rallye Commodore 180	10639	
OE-DGN	Cessna 182P Skylane	63534	N5785J
OE-DGP	Cessna T.210L Turbo Centurion	60102	N59118
OE-DGR	Cessna 182P (Reims-assembled)	0007/63835	N6786M
OE-DGU	Cessna 182P Skylane	63497	N5717J
OE-DGW	Cessna TR.182 Turbo Skylane RG	01391	N4705S
OE-DGZ	Piper PA-28-151 Cherokee Warrior	28-7415396	N9585N
OE-DHA	Piper PA-28-151 Cherokee Warrior	28-7615220	N9560N
OE-DHB	Reims/Cessna F.172N	1800	
OE-DHF	Reims/Cessna F.172N	1861	
OE-DHH	Piper PA-28-161 Cherokee Warrior II	28-7816076	N9615N
OE-DHO(2)	Cessna P210N Pressurized Centurion	00322	D-EDEN(3)
			N4794K
OE-DHT	SOCATA ST.10 Diplomate	145	F-BTIP
OE-DHU	Piper PA-28-151 Cherokee Warrior	28-7415449	N9616N
OE-DHV	Reims/Cessna F.172N	1950	
OE-DHX	Reims/Cessna FR.172K Hawk XP	0619	
OE-DHY	Piper PA-32-300 Cherokee Six	32-7940119	N28581
OE-DID	Cessna 182P (Reims-assembled)	0062/64446	N1789M
OE-DIG	Reims/Cessna F.182Q Skylane	0035	
OE-DIH	SOCATA MS.893A Rallye Commodore 180	12030	F-BTJD
OE-DII	SOCATA MS.892E Rallye 150ST	2818	
OE-DIK	GEMS MS.892A Rallye Commodore 150	10526	D-EDNY
OE-DIM	SOCATA MS.893E Rallye 180GT Gaillard	12843	
OE-DIN	Robin DR.400/180R Remorqueur	1235	
OE-DIR	Reims/Cessna F.182Q Skylane	0046	(G-BENA)
OE-DIU	Piper PA-28R-200 Cherokee Arrow II	28R-7535036	N32236
OE-DIV	Reims/Cessna F.182Q Skylane	0058	(F-GAQH)
			(D-EBXP)
OE-DIX	Reims/Cessna FR.172K Hawk XP	0594	
OE-DIZ	SOCATA MS.893E Rallye 180GT Gaillard	13050	
OE-DKB	Robin DR.400/140 Major	885	
OE-DKD	Cessna 210M Centurion	62358	(N761MF)
OE-DKF	Robin DR.400/180R Remorqueur	750	
OE-DKG	Cessna 175 Skylark	55612	N7312M
OE-DKN	Cessna U.206G Stationair II	03690	N7585N
OE-DKS(2)	SOCATA Rallye 235F	3390	F-OHDZ
			F-WNGX
OE-DKT	Piper PA-28-181 Cherokee Archer II	28-7890244	N9517N
OE-DKV	SOCATA Rallye 180T Galérien	3240	
OE-DKY	SOCATA Rallye 180T Galérien	3223	
OE-DKZ	Piper PA-32-300 Cherokee Six	32-7440057	N40729
OE-DLA	Reims/Cessna F.172F	0132	
OE-DLH	Reims/Cessna F.172F	0323	
OE-DLI	Reims/Cessna F.172H	0435	
OE-DLL	Cessna 177A Cardinal	01285	
OE-DLP	Reims/Cessna FR.172G Rocket	0179	
OE-DLR	Reims/Cessna F.172K	0764	
OE-DLS	Reims/Cessna FR.172H Rocket	0236	
OE-DLW	Reims/Cessna F.172K	0771	
OE-DLY	Reims/Cessna F.172L	0821	
OE-DLZ	Reims/Cessna FR.172H Rocket	0279	

Regn.	Type	C/n	Prev.Id.
OE-DMF	Beech B19 Musketeer Sport	MB-674	
OE-DMH	Beech C23 Sundowner	M-1549	
OE-DMP	Beech C23 Sundowner	M-1818	
OE-DMR	Reims/Cessna FR.172H Rocket	0258	D-ELAL
OE-DMS	Cessna 175A Skylark	56288	N6788E
OE-DMV	Piper PA-28-151 Cherokee Warrior	28-7415293	N9560N
OE-DMW	Piper PA-28-151 Cherokee Warrior	28-7415364	N9581N
OE-DMZ	Robin DR.400/180R Remorqueur	979	
OE-DNA	SOCATA MS.893E Rallye 180GT Gaillard	12194	F-BVHC
OE-DNB	Reims/Cessna F.182Q Skylane	0066	
OE-DND	Reims/Cessna F.182Q Skylane	0083	
OE-DNF	Reims/Cessna F.182Q Skylane	0125	(D-EKEB)
OE-DNI (2)	Cessna TR.182 Turbo Skylane RG	00866	(N737PN)
OE-DNK	Piper PA-28-180 Cherokee Challenger	28-7305309	N11C
OE-DNL	Reims/Cessna F.182Q Skylane	0117	
OE-DNM	Robin DR.400/180R Remorqueur	1219	
OE-DNN	Piper PA-28RT-201 Arrow IV	28R-7918261	N9631N
OE-DNP	Robin DR.400/180R Remorqueur	1200	
OE-DNR	Piper PA-28-200 Cherokee Arrow II	28R-7435111	N54484
OE-DNS	Reims/Cessna FR.172H Rocket	0273	D-ECNS
OE-DNW	Robin DR.400/180R Remorqueur	1158	
OE-DNY	Reims/Cessna FR.182 Skylane RG	0030	PH-AYG
OE-DOC	Oberlerchner Job 15-150/2	071	(D-EKEP) OE-DOC
OE-DOD	Oberlerchner Job 15-150/2	072	(D-EKET) OE-DOD
OE-DOE	Oberlerchner Job 15-150/2	073	
OE-DOI	Piper PA-28-236 Dakota	28-7911249	N2921F
OE-DOK	SIAI-Marchetti S.205-20/R	4-218	
OE-DON(2)	Cessna 182R Skylane	67887	D-EDGN N2287U
OE-DOS(2)	SOCATA TB-10 Tobago	102	HB-EZL
OE-DOT	Reims/Cessna F.182Q Skylane	0143	
OE-DOU	Piper PA-28RT-201 Arrow IV	28R-8018038	N8153E
OE-DOX	Cessna T.210N Turbo Centurion	62757	N6394B
OE-DPA	Piper PA-28-140 Cherokee	28-21500	N11C
OE-DPB	Piper PA-28-180 Cherokee B	28-1664	N7759W
OE-DPC	Piper PA-32-300 Cherokee Six	32-40070	N4042W
OE-DPD	Piper PA-28-140 Cherokee	28-22232	HB-OYR N11C
OE-DPF	Piper PA-28-140 Cherokee D Fliteliner	28-7125242	N5078S
OE-DPL	Piper PA-28-180 Cherokee D	28-4500	N5312L N11C
OE-DPM	Piaggio P.149D	344	AAF:3E-AB
OE-DPW	Piper PA-28R-200 Cherokee Arrow B	28R-35680	N4908S
OE-DPX	Piper PA-28-140 Cherokee E	28-7225427	N11C
OE-DRA	Piper PA-28RT-201 Arrow IV	28R-7918235	N2954S
OE-DRB	SOCATA MS.880B Rallye Club	2951	
OE-DRE	Robin HR.100/210 Safari	146	
OE-DRN	Piper PA-28RT-201 Arrow IV	28R-7918050	N2192P
OE-DRU	Piper PA-28-161 Warrior II	28-8116281	N2397U
OE-DRV	Robin DR.400/180R Remorqueur	1446	
OE-DRY	SOCATA MS.894A Minerva 220	12016	F-BTRY
OE-DSB	Robin DR.400/180R Remorqueur	734	
OE-DSC	Cessna 182C Skylane	52757	D-EBCE N8857T
OE-DSD	Cessna 210B	57947	N9647X
OE-DSE	Robin DR.400/180R Remorqueur	1155	
OE-DSL	Piper PA-28-180 Cherokee Archer	28-7405009	N9564N
OE-DSN	Piper PA-28R-201 Arrow III	28R-7737118	N38774
OE-DSY	SOCATA MS.893A Rallye Commodore 180	12068	F-BTRV
OE-DSZ	SOCATA MS.893E Rallye 180GT Gaillard	12962	
OE-DTA	Reims/Cessna F.172L	0857	
OE-DTB	Reims/Cessna F.172M	0939	
OE-DTE	Reims/Cessna F.172M	0998	
OE-DTI	Robin DR.400/180R Remorqueur	757	
OE-DTL	GEMS MS.892A Rallye Commodore 150	10506	
OE-DTN	Reims/Cessna F.172M	1090	
OE-DTP	Reims/Cessna F.172M	1102	
OE-DTT	Reims/Cessna F.172M	1114	
OE-DTV	Reims/Cessna F.172M	1429	
OE-DTX	Robin DR.400/180R Remorqueur	1095	
OE-DTY	Reims/Cessna F.172N	1577	
OE-DTZ	Piper PA-28R-200 Cherokee Arrow II	28R-7335376	D-EAYE N56185
OE-DUE	Piper PA-32-300 Cherokee Six	32-7940213	N2928F
OE-DUF	Cessna T.210N Turbo Centurion II	63973	(N4665Y)
OE-DUI	Piper PA-28RT-201 Arrow IV	28R-8018076	N8217Z
OE-DUM	Cessna U.206F Stationair	01806	
OE-DUR	Cessna T.210N Turbo Centurion II	63862	(N6317C)
OE-DUT	SOCATA TB-10 Tobago	23	F-ODKA
OE-DUU	SOCATA Rallye 110ST Galopin	3319	
OE-DUW	SOCATA MS.893E Rallye 180GT Gaillard	12845	
OE-DUY	SOCATA TB-10 Tobago	198	
OE-DVD	Reims/Cessna F.172N	1568	
OE-DVE	Reims/Cessna F.172N	1578	
OE-DVF	Piper PA-28-180 Cherokee Challenger	28-7305399	N55616
OE-DVG	Reims/Cessna F.172N	1623	(OE-DWC)
OE-DVH	Reims/Cessna F.172N	1615	(SX-...)
OE-DVI	Reims/Cessna F.172N	1672	(HB-CCC) (LN-ALH)
OE-DVK	Reims/Cessna F.172N	1761	
OE-DVL	Cessna U.206E Stationair	01638	D-EDWJ OY-AKN
OE-DVM	Piper PA-28-160 Cherokee B	28-784	HB-OVM N5679W
OE-DVO	Reims/Cessna F.182Q Skylane	0136	
OE-DVR	Cessna 172RG Cutlass	0133	N627IR
OE-DVV	Reims/Cessna FR.172K Hawk XP	0670	
OE-DVW	Robin DR.400/180R Remorqueur	1069	
OE-DVX	Reims/Cessna FR.172K Hawk XP	0620	
OE-DXM	Bell 206A Jet Ranger	42	D-HEAS N9B
OE-DYF	Rockwell Commander 112A	0216	
OE-DYI	Robin DR.400/180R Remorqueur	1233	D-EEPG
OE-DYK	Mooney M.20J Model 201	24-0889	D-ENMF(2) N4770H (N4822H)
OE-DYM	Piper PA-28R-201 Arrow III	28R-7837072	N2233M
OE-DYP	Piper PA-28-181 Archer II	28-8190219	N83795
OE-DYR	SOCATA MS.892E Rallye 150T	2777	
OE-DYS	SOCATA TB-9 Tampico	237	
OE-DYU	Reims/Cessna F.172N	1883	D-EOWW
OE-DYV	Robin DR.400/180R Remorqueur	1562	
OE-DYX	Robin DR.400/120D Petit Prince	1559	
OE-EAS	Chance-Vought F4U-4 Corsair	"96995"	N4908M BuA96995
OE-EKD	Pilatus PC-12 /45	142	HB-FRD
OE-ESA	North American T-28B	200-250	N3905H BuA138179
OE-EXE	Aérospatiale SA.315B Lama	2406	F-WXFS
OE-EXF	Aérospatiale SA.315B Lama	2278	F-BVUF LN-OQD
OE-EXS	Bell 205A-1	30265	N5002N
OE-EXU	Aérospatiale SA.315B Lama	2478	
OE-FAM(2)	Cessna 425 Conquest 1	0131	OE-FIB N385MA N977MP (N489BC) N54BC N6883L
OE-FAN	Cessna 500 Citation	0289	N939KS XA-KAH N5591A YV-50CP N5289J N289CC
OE-FAR(2)	Piper PA-34-200T Seneca II	34-8070053	D-GMOX N8134A
OE-FBF	Cessna 414A Chancellor	0415	(N26918)
OE-FBI (2)	Piper PA-34-220T Seneca III	34-8433062	N4361N
OE-FBO	Piper PA-31T Cheyenne	31T-7820051	D-IGAK LN-AET OY-BRL
OE-FBR(2)	Piper PA-34-220T Seneca III	3448009	D-GCWO N9197Z
OE-FBS(2)	Cessna 551 Citation II	0574	N60GF N60GL (N1299B)

Regn.	Type	C/n	Prev.Id.
OE-FBY	Cessna 421B Golden Eagle	0931	OE-BAY, OE-FLK, N5381J
OE-FCA(2)	Cessna 421C Golden Eagle II	0099	D-IACS(2), N978AC, D-IFLS, OE-FLS, N98800
OE-FCI	Cessna 340A	0690	N6347X
OE-FCK	Cessna 310R	1837	N2739D
OE-FCV	Cessna 340A	1263	(N88557)
OE-FDE	Short SC-7 Skyvan Series 3	SH.1886	C9-ASN, G-BKMF, A40-SO, G-AYJO, G-14-58
OE-FDF	Short SC-7 Skyvan Series 3	SH.1958	ZS-MJP, N981GA, PMU-1, 7P-AAB, G-BFIA, G-14-126
OE-FDM	Cessna 501 Citation 1/SP	0140	N96CF, N96TD, (N99TD), (N2651R)
OE-FDO	Piper PA-34-220T Seneca III	3433158	N9176B
OE-FDR	Cessna 421C Golden Eagle II	1413	N1205P
OE-FDS	Piper PA-31T Cheyenne	31T-7720056	(N82169)
OE-FEE	Piper PA-34-220T Seneca III	34-8133066	D-GILS, D-IILS, N8372B
OE-FEG	Cessna 421C Golden Eagle II	1078	D-IBMF(2), N6866X
OE-FEI	Cessna 421C Golden Eagle II	0881	N5705C
OE-FEP	Piper PA-60-601P Aerostar	61P-0623-7963283	HB-LKZ, N8222J
OE-FFE	Cessna 421C Golden Eagle II	0120	N811VQ, N3853C
OE-FFP	Cessna 340A	1503	D-IAEH, OE-FFP, D-IAMO, N68696
OE-FFS	Piper PA-23-250 Aztec F	27-7754073	D-IDAC, N62838
OE-FFY	Piper PA-23-250 Aztec E	27-7405365	HB-LHY, N54016
OE-FGA	Piper PA-34-200T Seneca II	34-7870207	N9661C
OE-FGI	Cessna 525 CitationJet	0254	N5183V
OE-FGL	Cessna 414A Chancellor	0450	D-IFEP, OE-FBH, (N2732X)
OE-FGN	Cessna 500 Citation	0291	N291DS, ZS-JOO, N5291J
OE-FGO	Cessna 414	0608	N1980G
OE-FGT	Cessna T.303 Crusader	00086	(N2277C)
OE-FGW	Partenavia P.68B Victor	122	D-GERO
OE-FHA	Beech B60 Duke	P-502	D-IHCI
OE-FHD	Piper PA-44-180 Seminole	44-7995111	N61624, C-GUPJ, N3017B
OE-FHE	Cessna 421B Golden Eagle	0111	(D-IREG), HB-LFZ, (N808IQ)
OE-FHH	Cessna 501 Citation	0246	N26LC, N85RS, N2627N
OE-FHL	Beech C90A King Air	LJ-1115	D-IBPE
OE-FHM(2)	Beech C90A King Air	LJ-1284	N25GA, OY-GEM
OE-FHW	Cessna 501 Citation 1/SP	0121	D-IANO, HB-VID, D-IANO, N26506
OE-FHZ	Piper PA-34-200 Seneca	34-7350098	D-GHSI, N15829
OE-FIL	Partenavia P.68C	226	HB-LPW, I-KDUE
OE-FJU	Cessna 525 CitationJet	0295	N295CM, N5209E
OE-FKG	Piper PA-31T-620 Cheyenne	31T-8020036	N30DJ, N2570W
OE-FKH(2)	Piper PA-31T1 Cheyenne I	31T-8104029	N803CA, (N90WA), N2484X
OE-FKL	Piper PA-34-220T Seneca III	3433021	D-GOAT, N9091N
OE-FKV	Piper PA-23-250 Aztec C	27-2743	D-IBIW, N5660Y
OE-FLD	Piper PA-34-200T Seneca II	34-7870076	N2271M
OE-FLG(2)	Cessna 525 CitationJet	0103	D-IVHA, (N203CJ), N5204D
OE-FLN	Cessna T.303 Crusader	00080	OO-VJI, N2266C
OE-FLT(2)	Rockwell Commander 685	12027	HB-GGN, OO-JPP, G-BBHA, N9161N
OE-FLX	Cessna 421C Golden Eagle	0248	(D-IDEM), N5536G
OE-FME(2)	Beech 300LW Super King Air	FA-228	HB-GJC, N80806
OE-FMH	Cessna 340A	0289	D-IAAB, N4117G
OE-FMM	Piper PA-42-720 Cheyenne III	42-5501030	N5022M, G-BLTB
OE-FMO	Piper PA-31T Cheyenne II	31T-8120058	N3GF, N9114Y
OE-FMS	Cessna 501 Citation I/SP	0239	N164CB, LV-MYN, LV-PDZ, N26497
OE-FNA	Piper PA-34-220T Seneca III	34-8433024	N4301U
OE-FOW	Fairchild-Swearingen SA-226T Merlin IIIB	T-318	D-IBBD, N1006F
OE-FPA	Cessna 551 Citation II	0552	
OE-FPC	Piper PA-34-200T Seneca II	34-8070286	N8241Z
OE-FPK	Piper PA-30-160 Twin Comanche	30-351	HB-LAA, N7363Y
OE-FPT	Cessna 337D Skymaster	1177	N86405
OE-FPU	Cessna 414A Chancellor	0505	D-IHAB(2), N36993
OE-FPY	Piper PA-44-180 Seminole	44-7995247	
OE-FRD(2)	Piper PA-34-220T Seneca III	34-8133069	D-GESN, N8372R
OE-FRE	Piper PA-30-160 Twin Comanche B	30-998	N7909Y
OE-FRF	Beech B200 Super King Air	BB-933	D-IAWS(2), N200LP
OE-FRH	Cessna 414A Chancellor	0027	
OE-FRW	Cessna 414	0825	N98726
OE-FSK(2)	Cessna 340A	0607	D-IFAW, N8661K
OE-FSL	Piper PA-31-310 Navajo	31-7912058	N3519C
OE-FSM	Piper PA-34-200T Seneca II	34-7970359	D-GIAS, D-IGAS, N2918U
OE-FSO	Beech 300LW Super King Air	FA-215	N8017G
OE-FTE	Piper PA-31-310 Navajo	31-7400978	D-IHOY, N7586L
OE-FTI	Piper PA-34-220T Seneca III	34-8533002	N4376N
OE-FTM	Piper PA-34-200T Seneca II	34-7870093	N2786M
OE-FTW	Piper PA-34-200T Seneca II	34-7570288	D-INIX, N1566X
OE-FWS	Grumman G.44A Widgeon (SCAN-30)	30	N151SA, N2814D
OE-FXA	Aérospatiale AS.355F1 Ecureuil 2	5056	
OE-FXB	Aérospatiale AS.355F1 Ecureuil 2	5252	D-HLTK
OE-FXH	Aérospatiale AS.355F2 Ecureuil 2	5429	

Regn.	Type	C/n	Prev.Id.
OE-GAA	Cessna 560 Citation V	0111	(N91AN)
			(N6802T)
OE-GAP(2)	Cessna 560XL Citation Excel	5004	N5148N
OE-GBA	Cessna 550 Citation II	0085	N57AJ
			OY-GKC
			(N2663Y)
OE-GBB	Dornier 328-100	3078	D-CDXG
OE-GCC	Cessna 560 Citation V	0125	N6809V
OE-GCF	Gates Learjet 55C	55C-136	N155PS
			N767NY
			N767AZ
			N3811G
OE-GCI	Cessna 550 Citation II	0041	N177HH
			N985BA
			N341AG
			N8418B
			N3279M
OE-GCO	Cessna 650 Citation III	0012	N15VF
			N1305V
OE-GCP(2)	Cessna 560 Citation V	0214	(N1285D)
OE-GDA	Cessna 560 Citation V	0200	
OE-GDI	Bombardier Learjet 45	45-037	
OE-GDM	Cessna 550 Citation II	0707	(SE-DYY)
			N707EA
			RP-C4654
			N1202T
OE-GHA	Dassault Falcon 100	221	F-WZGH
OE-GHS	BAe.125 Series 800B	258078	ZS-FSI
			G-BNEH
			G-5-713
			G-BNEH
			G-5-544
OE-GII	Bombardier Learjet 60	60-169	N5014F
OE-GIL	Cessna 550 Citation II	0060	N315CK
			N98BE
			N75KR
			(N550KR)
			N26610
OE-GKK	Cessna 550 Citation II	0872	N5093L
OE-GLZ	Cessna 550 Citation II	0690	N6780C
OE-GMD	Gates Learjet 36A	36A-047	N36SK
	(Damaged, 9.99)		N14CN
			N2972Q
			G-ZEIZ
OE-GMI	Cessna 560 Citation V	0362	N5183U
OE-GNL(2)	Gates Learjet 60	60-032	N5013D
OE-GPS(2)	Cessna 550 Citation II	0837	N5185J
OE-GRO	Gates Learjet 55	55-122	N622LJ
			C-FHJB
			N99KV
			N99KW
			N18ZD
			N8568P
			N10870
OE-GRR	Gates Learjet 55C	55C-059	D-CAEP
			(N211BY)
OE-GSC	Dassault Falcon 10	122	N312AT
			N312A
			N22ES
			N193FJ
			F-WPUV
OE-GSW	Cessna 560 Citation V	0088	(N6783X)
OE-GTZ	Cessna 550 Citation II	0864	N864CB
OE-HET	Canadair CL.600-1A11 Challenger	1085	N600ST
			N20GX
			N20G
			C-GLXQ
OE-HIT	Dassault Falcon 50	222	D-BELL
			F-WWHM
OE-HLE	Canadair CL.600-2A12 Challenger	3047	N602TJ
			N602HJ
			B-4006
			C-GBZQ
			C-GLXM
OE-HTJ	Dornier 328-300	3114	D-BDXA(1)

Regn.	Type	C/n	Prev.Id.
OE-ILA	Lockheed L.188C Electra	1145	LN-FOH
			LN-MOI
			N9746C
			N5767
			CF-IJJ
			N9746C
OE-ILB(2)	Lockheed L.188AF Electra	1039	N356Q
			N355WS
			N356Q
			VH-RMA
OE-ILF	Boeing 737-3Z9	23601	
OE-ILG	Boeing 737-3Z9	24081	
OE-ILS	Dassault Falcon 900	58	F-WWFE
OE-ILW	Fokker F.27 Friendship 500	10681	N505AW
			PH-EXN
OE-IMI	Dassault Falcon 900B	147	(N901FJ)
			N900FJ
			N147FJ
			F-WWFG
OE-KAA	Reims/Cessna F.172P	2145	
OE-KAC	Piper PA-28RT-201 Arrow IV	28R-8218013	N8156L
OE-KAE	SIAI-Marchetti S.208	1-14	D-EATS(2)
			LX-FLY(1)
			OO-IAT
			I-SJAT
OE-KAH	SAAB S.91D Safir	91470	3F-SL
OE-KAM	Robin DR.400/180R Remorqueur	1482	D-EKFM(2)
OE-KAR	Cessna 210M Centurion	61741	N732SQ
OE-KAW	Cessna 182Q Skylane	66383	N759ZF
OE-KAZ	Piper PA-32-301 Saratoga	3206044	N9150G
OE-KBC	Piper PA-28RT-201T Turbo Arrow IV	28R-8331017	D-ELUR(2)
			N4292P
OE-KBD	Rockwell Commander 114B	14522	D-EIKU
			(N5905N)
OE-KBE	Beech F33A Bonanza	CE-1226	N23EL
OE-KBF	Robin DR.400/180R Remorqueur	1708	D-EEWF(2)
OE-KBS	Piper PA-28-181 Archer II	28-8390087	N43149
OE-KBW	Piper PA-28R-201T Turbo Cherokee Arrow III		
		28R-7703407	D-EMOC(2)
			N47606
OE-KCA	Cessna 182N Skylane	60411	HB-CGG
			G-AYIU
			N92885
OE-KCC	Reims/Cessna F.172N	1942	D-EKCC
OE-KCD	SAAB S.91D Safir	91459	3F-SU
OE-KCM	Piper PA-28R-201 Arrow IV	2837041	D-EBLH(2)
			N9191X
OE-KDA	Cessna U.206G Stationair II	05848	C-GIIW
			(N6265X)
OE-KEC	Mooney M.20J Model 205	24-3011	N205ME
OE-KEH	Cessna 182R Skylane	68387	N8187E
OE-KEM	Piper PA-28-181 Cherokee Archer II	28-7890072	N47434
OE-KEP	Cessna P210N Pressurized Centurion II	00777	D-EAMP(2)
			N4563P
			C-GOPM
			(N6435W)
OE-KES	Piper PA-28R-201T Turbo Arrow IV	2803007	D-EALV
			N9182N
OE-KEX	Cessna 172P	74957	D-EVIP
			N54323
OE-KEZ	Robin DR.400/180R Remorqueur	1665	D-EEWZ
OE-KFA(2)	SOCATA TB-20 Trinidad	442	D-EIPW
OE-KFE	SOCATA TB-20 Trinidad	481	
OE-KFG	Cessna 182J Skylane	57234	D-EMCA
			N3134F
OE-KFK	Reims/Cessna F.172M	1447	D-EECZ
OE-KFO	Robin DR.400/RP Remorqueur	1828	D-EIOA
OE-KFR	SOCATA TB-20 Trinidad	1340	
OE-KFS	Cessna TU.206G Turbo Stationair II	05232	N5351U
OE-KFT	Piper PA-28RT-201T Turbo Arrow IV	28R-8431030	D-ETUL
			N4372Z
			N9605N
OE-KFU	Robin DR.400/180R Remorqueur	725	
OE-KFW	Cessna 172P	75823	N65701
OE-KGE	Mooney M.22 Mustang	680009	N7718M

Regn.	Type	C/n	Prev.ld.
OE-KGF	Beech K35 Bonanza	D-5793	N5328E
OE-KGH	Cessna 177RG Cardinal RG	1120	N45469
OE-KGK	SAAB S.91D Safir	91449	3F-SN
OE-KGM	Cessna 182M Skylane	59721	D-EAGM
			N71696
OE-KGN	Cessna 182J Skylane	57199	D-ECGY(2)
			N3099F
OE-KGO	Cessna 182H Skylane	56179	D-EEJM
			N2079X
OE-KGP	Zlin Z.143L	0009	OK-AGP
OE-KGS	Rockwell Commander 112TCA	13177	(D-E . . .)
			ZS-MBF
			N4647W
OE-KHF	Cessna 172RG Cutlass	0177	F-GHXU
			N6394R
OE-KHK	Reims/Cessna F.172H	0615	D-EDMR
			PH-TGU
OE-KHL	Robin DR.400/180R Remorqueur	1303	D-EHWN
OE-KHO	SAAB S.91D Safir	91452	3F-SQ
OE-KHR	Cessna R.182 Skylane RG	01844	N5257T
OE-KHS	Mooney M.20K Model 231	25-0465	N4088H
OE-KHW	Robin DR.400/180R Remorqueur	2269	
OE-KIK	Cessna P210N Pressurized Centurion	00445	N731DP
OE-KIM	Cessna P210N Pressurized Centurion II	00211	N4583K
OE-KIR	Robin DR.400/180R Remorqueur	918	D-EAWR
OE-KIS	Piper PA-28RT-201T Turbo Arrow IV	28R-8531012	N2506V
OE-KIT	Cessna 182P Skylane (Reims-assembled)	0005/63819	D-EGAS
			(SE-GKK)
			N6737M
OE-KJE	Reims/Cessna FR.172J Rocket	0569	D-EKJE
OE-KKK	SOCATA TB-9 Tampico	927	
OE-KLB	Robin DR.400/180R Remorqueur	2180	
OE-KLM	Piper PA-24-250 Comanche	24-1184	D-EBEW
			N6299P
OE-KLR	Piper PA-28RT-201T Turbo Arrow IV	28R-8231018	D-EKCM
			N80225
OE-KLS	Piper PA-28R-201T Arrow IV	2803009	D-ENXH
			N9184D
OE-KLW	Robin DR.400/180R Remorqueur	2198	
OE-KLZ	Reims/Cessna F.182Q Skylane	0107	D-EFGS
OE-KMA	Piper PA-28-181 Archer II	28-8590001	N4377Z
OE-KMC	Piper PA-28-181 Cherokee Archer II	28-7790368	D-EBBI
			OE-DOW
			N1994H
OE-KMD	SOCATA TB-9 Tampico	212	D-EBZD
OE-KME	SOCATA TB-9 Tampico	1273	
OE-KMF	SOCATA TB-10 Tobago	451	
OE-KMG	Commander Aircraft 114B	14578	D-EJDM
OE-KMH	Piper PA-32R-301T Turbo Saratoga SP	32R-8529007	N6912B
			N9529N
OE-KMI	Cessna P210N Pressurized Centurion II	00685	N5411W
OE-KML	Mooney M.20J Model 205	24-3025	N205MG
OE-KMM	Piper PA-28RT-201T Turbo Arrow IV	28R-8531005	N4388F
			N9533N
OE-KMO(2)	Mooney M.20 Ovation	29-0094	
OE-KMP	Robin DR.400/RP Remorqueur	1841	D-EGMP
OE-KMS	Piper PA-32R-301T Turbo Saratoga SP	32R-8029090	D-EDET(3)
			N82009
OE-KMT	Cessna R.172K Hawk XP	2434	D-EBGF
			N736DA
OE-KMU	Piper PA-32R-301T Saratoga	32R-8229046	HB-PHA
OE-KMV	Piper PA-28-181 Archer III	2843012	N9258L
OE-KMW	Piper PA-32R-301T Saratoga	32R-8329035	N4314B
OE-KMX	Beech F33A Bonanza	CE-1711	
OE-KMZ	Beech A36 Bonanza	E-1505	D-EMVA(2)
			N6056U
OE-KND	Robin DR.400/180R Remorqueur	834	D-EIVU
OE-KNI	Mooney M.20M TLS	27-0194	
OE-KOG	Mooney M.20K Model 252	25-1066	N252SS
OE-KOL	Piper PA-28-181 Archer II	2890182	D-ETCF
			N9169Z
OE-KOM	Robin R.3000/160	167	
OE-KOS	Piper PA-28-181 Cherokee Archer II	28-7790591	OY-BTL
OE-KPA	SOCATA MS.893E Rallye 180GT Gaillard	12989	D-EGYO
OE-KPC	Cessna TU.206F Turbo Stationair	02898	N1451Q

Regn.	Type	C/n	Prev.ld.
OE-KPG	Reims/Cessna F.182Q Skylane	0153	D-EBMW(3)
			(HB-CNY)
OE-KPM	Diamond DA-40-P4 Star	40004	OE-VPM
OE-KRH	Beech F33A Bonanza	CE-1703	N55572
OE-KRP	Cessna 172R	80394	D-EKRP
			N9552B
OE-KRS	Piper PA-32-301 Saratoga	32-8106096	N8435H
OE-KRT	Piper PA-28R-201T Cherokee Arrow III	28R-7703150	D-EHRW
			N5691V
OE-KSD	SAAB S.91D Safir	91466	3F-SH
OE-KSE	Robin DR.400/180R Remorqueur	1396	D-EISE
OE-KSF	Piper PA-28RT-201T Turbo Arrow IV	28R-8331016	N8346Y
OE-KSI	Cessna T.182 Turbo Skylane	68368	HB-CHE
			(N6416E)
OE-KSL	Reims/Cessna FR.172K Hawk XP	0618	D-EGTC
OE-KSM	Piper PA-28-161 Cadet	2841012	D-EFXB
			N9140X
OE-KSR	Robin DR.400/180R Remorqueur	1786	G-BNRB
OE-KSS	SAAB S.91D Safir	91456	3F-SS
OE-KSV	SAAB S.91D Safir	91461	3F-SV
OE-KSW	Reims/Cessna FR.172G Rocket	0172	D-EBLM
OE-KTC	Robin DR.400/180R Remorqueur	1655	
OE-KTH	SOCATA MS.893A Rallye Commodore 180	12078	HB-ETH
	(Built as MS.894A Minerva 220, mod 7.99)		SE-FSX
OE-KTP	SAAB S.91D Safir	91464	3F-SX
OE-KTS	Mooney M.20M TLS	27-0190	(OE-KID)
OE-KTW	Mooney M.20M TLS	27-0130	D-ETFC
			N92VR
OE-KUB	Robin DR.400/180R Remorqueur	1256	OE-BUB
OE-KUD	Robin DR.400/180R Remorqueur	1447	OE-BUD
OE-KUI	Robin DR.400/180R Remorqueur	2059	OE-BUI
OE-KUM	Robin DR.400/180R Remorqueur	1671	D-EDQG(2)
OE-KUN	Reims/Cessna FR.182 Skylane RG	0026	OE-BUN
			(OE-DNI)
OE-KUS	Robin DR.400/180R Remorqueur	1892	F-GGXH
OE-KVT	Mooney M.20J Model 205	24-3395	
OE-KXE	Bell 206L Long Ranger	45028	D-HAVS
			C-GSHX
			N9945K
			(N87TA)
OE-KXH	Aérospatiale AS.350B Ecureuil	1761	D-HAFP
OE-KXM	Bell 206B Jet Ranger II	2997	D-HMHS(2)
			N904SD
			N1086D
OE-KYH	SOCATA TB-21 Trinidad TC	555	D-EDED(2)
OE-KYK	Piper PA-28-181 Archer II	28-7990304	D-ECYK
			N2179R
OE-KYV	Cessna 172N	73693	YV-178E
			YV-623P
OE-LAA	Airbus A.310-324	489	F-WWCK
OE-LAC	Airbus A.310-324	568	F-WWCE
OE-LAG	Airbus A.340-212	075	F-WWJR
OE-LAH	Airbus A.340-212	081	F-WWJO
OE-LAK(2)	Airbus A.340-313X	169	F-WWJC
OE-LAL(2)	Airbus A.340-313X	263	F-WWJU
OE-LAM(2)	Airbus A.330-223	223	F-WWKQ
OE-LAN(2)	Airbus A.330-223	195	F-WWKJ
OE-LAO(2)	Airbus A.330-223	181	F-WWKA
OE-LAP	Airbus A.330-223	0317	F-WWYQ
OE-LAS	Boeing 767-33AER	27909	
OE-LAT	Boeing 767-31AER	25273	PH-MCK
			I-LAUD
			OE-LAT
			PH-MCK
			N6046P
OE-LAU	Boeing 767-3Z9ER	23765	N6009F
			N767PW
OE-LAW	Boeing 767-3Z9ER	26417	
OE-LAX	Boeing 767-3Z9ER	27095	
OE-LAY	Boeing 767-3Z9	29867	
OE-LAZ	Boeing 767-3Z9ER	30331	
OE-LBA(2)	Airbus A.321-111	552	D-AVZH
OE-LBB	Airbus A.321-111	570	D-AVZQ
OE-LBC	Airbus A.321-111	581	D-AVZS
OE-LBD(2)	Airbus A.321-211	920	D-AVZN

Regn.	Type	C/n	Prev.Id.
OE-LBE	Airbus A.321-211	935	D-AVZR
OE-LBN(2)	Airbus A.320-214	768	F-WWDH
OE-LBO	Airbus A.320-214	776	F-WWDM
OE-LBP	Airbus A.320-214	797	F-WWDV
OE-LBQ	Airbus A.320-214	1137	F-WWDF
OE-LBR	Airbus A.320-214	1150	F-WWBP
OE-LCF	Canadair CL.600-2B19 Regional Jet	7094	
OE-LCG	Canadair CL.600-2B19 Regional Jet	7103	
OE-LCH	Canadair CL.600-2B19 Regional Jet	7110	
OE-LCI	Canadair CL.600-2B19 Regional Jet	7133	(OE-LCK) / C-FMNB
OE-LCJ	Canadair CL.600-2B19 Regional Jet	7142	(OE-LCL)
OE-LCK	Canadair CL.600-2B19 Regional Jet	7133	C-FMNB
OE-LCL	Canadair CL.600-2B19 Regional Jet	7167	
OE-LCM	Canadair CL.600-2B19 Regional Jet	7205	
OE-LCN	Canadair CL.600-2B19 Regional Jet	7365	
OE-LCO(2)	Canadair CL.600-2B19 Regional Jet	7371	
OE-LDY	McDonnell-Douglas DC-9-82	49115	
OE-LDZ	McDonnell-Douglas DC-9-82	49164	
OE-LEA(2)	Beech 200 Super King Air	BB-468	TF-ELI / TF-ELT(4) / N204KA / N2KH / N6056T
OE-LFG	Fokker F.28-0070	11549	PH-EZW
OE-LFH	Fokker F.28-0070	11554	PH-EZN
OE-LFI	Fokker F.28-0070	11529	PH-WXF / PK-JGI / PH-EZL
OE-LFJ	Fokker F.28-0070	11532	PH-WXG / PK-JGJ / PH-EZR
OE-LFK	Fokker F.28-0070	11555	PH-EZP
OE-LFL	Fokker F.28-0070	11573	PH-WXE / I-REJE / PH-EZW
OE-LFO	Fokker F.28-0070	11559	PH-EZV
OE-LFP	Fokker F.28-0070	11560	PH-EZW
OE-LFQ	Fokker F.28-0070	11568	PH-EZC
OE-LFR	Fokker F.28-0070	11572	PH-EZD
OE-LFS	Fokker F.28-0070	11528	PH-JCH / N528YV / PH-JCH / PH-EZS
OE-LFT	Fokker F.28-0070	11537	PH-JCT / N537YV / PH-JCT / PH-EZV
OE-LKA	Dornier 328-100	3110	D-CDXI
OE-LKB	Dornier 328-100	3036	HB-AEH / D-CDXB(1) / (D-CDHV)
OE-LKC	Dornier 328-100	3119	D-CDXK(4)
OE-LKD	Dornier 328-110	3072	HS-PBB / D-CDXY(2)
OE-LLE	DHC-8 Series 106B	355	C-GFEN
OE-LLF	DHC-8 Series 106	351	C-FWBB
OE-LLG	DHC-8 Series 106	345	C-GFQL
OE-LLH	DHC-8 Series 106	268	C-GFBW
OE-LLJ	DHC-8 Series 106	317	OE-LRU / OE-HRU / C-GDKL
OE-LLY	DHC-8 Series 314	370	C-GFUM
OE-LLZ	DHC-8 Series 314	340	(N437AW) / C-GLOT
OE-LMA	McDonnell-Douglas DC-9-82	49278	
OE-LMB	McDonnell-Douglas DC-9-82	49279	(OE-LDQ)
OE-LMC	McDonnell-Douglas DC-9-82	49372	
OE-LMD	McDonnell-Douglas DC-9-83	49933	
OE-LME	McDonnell-Douglas DC-9-83	53377	
OE-LMK	McDonnell-Douglas DC-9-87	49411	
OE-LML	McDonnell-Douglas DC-9-87	49412	
OE-LMM	McDonnell-Douglas DC-9-87	49413	
OE-LMN	McDonnell-Douglas DC-9-87	49414	
OE-LMO	McDonnell-Douglas DC-9-87	49888	

Regn.	Type	C/n	Prev.Id.
OE-LNH	Boeing 737-4Z9	25147	
OE-LNI	Boeing 737-4Z9	27094	
OE-LNJ	Boeing 737-8Z9	28177	(OE-LAY)
OE-LNK	Boeing 737-8Z9	28178	N1768B
OE-LPA	Boeing 777-2Z9	28698	
OE-LPB	Boeing 777-2Z9IGW	28699	
OE-LRA	Canadair CL.600-2B19 Regional Jet	7032	C-FRKQ / C-FMNW
OE-LRB	Canadair CL.600-2B19 Regional Jet	7033	C-FRSA / C-FMNX
OE-LRC	Canadair CL.600-2B19 Regional Jet	7036	D-ACLX / OE-LRC / C-FMOL
OE-LRD	Canadair CL.600-2B19 Regional Jet	7052	C-FMMN
OE-LRE	Canadair CL.600-2B19 Regional Jet	7059	
OE-LRF	Canadair CL.600-2B19 Regional Jet	7061	C-FMNQ
OE-LRG	Canadair CL.600-2B19 Regional Jet	7063	C-FMNY
OE-LRH	Canadair CL.600-2B19 Regional Jet	7125	C-FMMB
OE-LRS	DHC-8 Series 103	175	OE-HRS / C-GFOD
OE-LRW	DHC-8 Series 311	307	C-FTUX / EI-CIT / D-BOBE / C-GEOA
OE-LSA(2)	DHC-8 Series 314	487	C-GEWM
OE-LSB	DHC-8 Series 314	525	C-FDHY
OE-LSR	Embraer EMB.145MP	145-203	
OE-LTD	DHC-8 Series 314	400	C-GFQL
OE-LTF	DHC-8 Series 314	423	C-GDIU
OE-LTG	DHC-8 Series 314	438	C-GDFT
OE-LTH	DHC-8 Series 314Q	442	C-GFUM
OE-LTI	DHC-8 Series 314Q	466	C-GFQL
OE-LTJ	DHC-8 Series 314Q	481	C-GDOE
OE-LTK	DHC-8 Series 314Q	483	(YR-GPO) / C-GDFT
OE-LTL	DHC-8 Series 314Q	485	C-GFYI
OE-LTM	DHC-8 Series 314Q	527	C-FGNP
OE-LTN	DHC-8 Series 314Q	531	C-GDNK
OE-OXA	Aérospatiale AS.350B2 Ecureuil	2158	F-WIPI / OE-OXA / F-WYMD
OE-OXR	Aérospatiale SA.315B Lama	1025	Fr.AF
OE-OXT	Aérospatiale AS.350B2 Ecureuil	2393	F-WYMN
OE-VPB	Aero Designs Pulsar	unkn	
OE-VPC	Diamond DA-40-V1 Star	40001	
OE-VPH	Neico Lancair IV	unkn	
OE-VPI	T-131PA Jungmann	101	
OE-VPM	Diamond DA-40-180 Star (Reservation)	unkn	
OE-VPP	Diamond DA-20-100 Katana (Reservation)	20125	
OE-VPX	HOAC DV-20 Katana	20001	
	(Formerly designated HOAC LF-2000 Turbo prototype)		
OE-VPY	HOAC F-15F Excalibur	unkn	
OE-XAC	Bell 206B Jet Ranger II	4480	D-HIFI (2)
OE-XAK	Schweizer 269C	S-1595	D-HMIX / N69A
OE-XAW	WE-04 Gyrocopter	05	
OE-XBG	Aérospatiale SA.316B Alouette III	2361	F-GIFQ / CS-HBI / F-GBGS
OE-XBP	Robinson R-22B2 Beta	2834	
OE-XCC	Bell 206B Jet Ranger II	4256	
OE-XCD	Bell 206B Jet Ranger II	3750	N76AJ / N45EA / JA9356
OE-XCH	Aérospatiale AS.350B2 Ecureuil	2799	F-WYMU
OE-XDD	Agusta-Bell 206BJet Ranger II	8434	HA-LFA(2) / OE-XDD / G-OABY / G-BCWM
OE-XEA	Eurocopter EC-135T1	0025	
OE-XEB	Eurocopter EC-135T1	0050	
OE-XEC	Eurocopter EC-135T1	0053	
OE-XED	Eurocopter EC-135T1	0072	
OE-XEE	Eurocopter EC-135T1	0097	
OE-XEF	Eurocopter EC-135T1	0127	

Regn.	Type	C/n	Prev.Id.
OE-XEG	Eurocopter EC-135T1	0128	
OE-XFH	Agusta A.109A-II	7318	VH-AUG
			ZK-HXI
			N109BL
			N109BA
OE-XFK	Klampfl K-236	01	
OE-XFW	Robinson R-22 Beta	1966	N2318S
OE-XGG	McDonnell-Douglas MD.520N	LN-053	HB-XUL
OE-XHA	Hughes 369E	0336E	D-HABC
			F-GGCJ
OE-XHB	Aérospatiale AS.350B2 Ecureuil	2536	
OE-XHD	Agusta A.109E	11033	
OE-XHE	Hughes 369D	77-0166D	D-HHOP
			OO-VCH
OE-XHH	Robinson R-44 Astro	0518	
OE-XHL	Robinson R-44 Astro	0070	
OE-XIW	Robinson R-22 Beta	1483	G-DAMI
OE-XKH	Bell 206B Jet Ranger II	3814	N3189T
	(Reserved as D-HHTC 6.99)		
OE-XKI	McDonnell-Douglas MD.520N	LN-033	OO-MRI
			N52024
OE-XLA	Robinson R-22B2 Beta	2966	
OE-XLB	Aérospatiale AS.350BA Ecureuil	2881	
OE-XLM	Agusta-Bell 206B Jet Ranger	8046	G-COUR
			G-FSDG
			G-ROOT
			G-JETR
			G-BKBR
			OO-CDP
OE-XMF	Hughes 269C	114-0372	N9585F
OE-XMH	Aérospatiale SA.315B Lama	2587	HB-XTR
			XC-DOQ
OE-XMI	Schweizer 269C	S-1640	D-HMIE
OE-XNY	Robinson R-22B2 Beta	2985	
OE-XQQ	Robinson R-44 Astro	0245	
OE-XRA	Bell 206B Jet Ranger II	3968	N206RP
			C-FTOU
			N67CT
			N67AJ
			N3DU
OE-XRB	Bell 206B Jet Ranger II	2311	D-HAUO
			EC-FBX
			EC-496
			D-HEDO(2)
			HB-XLB
			D-HHPS
OE-XRC	Agusta A.109C	7639	N5QS
			N1EQ
OE-XRF	Agusta-Bell 206A Jet Ranger II	8246	G-BNRE
			Oman-603
OE-XRS	Aérospatiale AS.350B1 Ecureuil	2021	F-GEOD
OE-XSP	Robinson R-44 Astro	0364	
OE-XXL(2)	Aérospatiale AS.350B2	9014	
OE-XXY	Aérospatiale AS.350B2 Ecureuil	2652	D-HWPH
OE-XXZ	Aérospatiale AS.355F1 Ecureuil 2	5214	N378E
OE-XYZ	Robinson R-22 Beta	2536	
OE-XZZ	Robinson R-22 Beta	2694	

BALLOONS AND AIRSHIPS

Austrian balloons belonging to the same owner may carry the same registration marks at the same time. This has led to duplications which will be evident below from the suffix letters.

Regn.	Type	C/n	Prev.Id.
OE-AZA	Cameron V-56 HAFB	579	G-BHAE
OE-AZC	Cameron V-31 HAFB	2147	
OE-AZK(a)	Colt 77A HAFB	073	
OE-AZK(b)	Schön-Neptun 3000 HAFB	S033/5/98	
OE-AZM	Cameron Cow-105 SS HAFB	1886	
OE-AZS	Thunder AX6-56A HAFB	104	
OE-AZU	Thunder-Colt AS-56 Hot Air Airship	663	

Regn.	Type	C/n	Prev.Id.
OE-AZW	Thunder AX6-56A HAFB	684	
OE-AZZ	Raven RX-6 HAFB	298	HB-BAB
OE-CZA	Cameron O-84 HAFB	1299	
OE-CZE	Cameron Cometto-66 SS HAFB	1489	
OE-CZH	Colt 21A HAFB	689	G-BMBG
OE-CZS	Colt AX7-77A HAFB	538	
OE-CZX	Cameron O-56 HAFB	1355	
OE-DZC	Stuttgart K-945/2-Stu Gas Balloon	0222	
OE-DZD	Cameron O-77 HAFB	151	
OE-DZG	Augsburg K-945/2-Ri Gas Balloon	8525	
OE-DZI	Cameron O-105 HAFB	824	
OE-DZK	Cameron N-77 HAFB	293	G-BTOY
OE-DZL	Cameron V-77 HAFB	783	
OE-DZO	Cameron N-77 HAFB	559	
OE-DZP	Thunder AX7-77 HAFB	199	
OE-DZS	Cameron O-77 HAFB	65	G-BAMA
OE-DZT	Cameron O-84 HAFB	373	
OE-DZU	Colt 77A HAFB	614	
OE-DZW	Thunder AX8-105 HAFB	372	
OE-DZY	Cameron O-105 HAFB	845	
OE-DZZ	Cameron N-77 HAFB	550	
OE-KZA	Cameron O-105 HAFB	1237	
OE-KZB	Thunder AX7-77Si HAFB	803	
OE-KZC	Cameron N-90 HAFB	1295	
OE-KZD	Cameron N-90 SS HAFB	1394	G-BNGI
OE-KZE(a)	Cameron N-105 HAFB	1345	
OE-KZE(c)	Kubicek BB-30 HAFB	89	
OE-KZF	Thunder AX7-77Z HAFB	486	
OE-KZI	Cameron O-105 HAFB	1056	
OE-KZL	Cameron O-84 HAFB	1435	
OE-KZN	Cameron N-105 HAFB	976	
OE-KZO	Cameron O-84 HAFB	1165	
OE-KZP(a)	Cameron O-77 HAFB	1081	
OE-KZP(b)	Cameron O-120 HAFB	4681	
OE-KZR	Cameron N-105 HAFB	1075	
OE-KZS	Thunder AX8-105S2 HAFB	452	
OE-KZT	Thunder AX7-77Si HAFB	872	
OE-KZU	Colt 105A HAFB	591	
OE-MZA	Venus 2600 HAFB	100.187	
OE-MZC	Cameron V-77 HAFB	1576	
OE-MZD	Cameron A-105 HAFB	1584	
OE-MZE(b)	Cameron A-120 HAFB	4391	OE-MZR(c)
OE-MZF	Cameron O-84 HAFB	1501	
OE-MZH(a)	Cameron A-105 HAFB	1591	
OE-MZH(b)	Cameron Mug-90 SS HAFB	2154	OE-CZG
OE-MZI	Cameron O-105 HAFB	1170	
OE-MZL(a)	Colt 105A HAFB	1127	
OE-MZL(b)	Balloon Works Firefly 8 HAFB	F8-416	
OE-MZM(a)	Cameron A-140 HAFB	2017	
OE-MZM(b)	Colt 77A HAFB	1551	OE-ZCC(a)
			OE-SZY
			G-BRRV
OE-MZO	Cameron N-90 HAFB	1383	
OE-MZR(a)	Cameron N-105 HAFB	1516	
OE-MZR(b)	Cameron Bee-105 SS HAFB	1884	OE-CZR
OE-MZS	Cameron O-105 HAFB	1325	
OE-MZX	Thunder AX8-105SI HAFB	1148	
OE-MZY	Cameron N-90 HAFB	1544	
OE-MZZ	Cameron A-105 HAFB	1589	
OE-PZA	Cameron A-105 HAFB	1728	
OE-PZB	Schroeder Fire Balloons G HAFB	50	
OE-PZC	Thunder AX7-77 HAFB	1181	
OE-PZD	Cameron N-105 HAFB	1676	
OE-PZE	Cameron O-105 HAFB	1787	
OE-PZF	Thunder SS-77 HAFB	1218	
OE-PZG	Cameron A-140 HAFB	1782	
OE-PZH	Cameron A-105 HAFB	1680	
OE-PZI	Cameron A-120 HAFB	1756	
OE-PZK	Cameron A-105 HAFB	1774	
OE-PZL	Cameron A-105 HAFB	1621	
OE-PZO(a)	Cameron O-120 HAFB	1735	
OE-PZO(b)	Kubicek BB-37 HAFB	122	
OE-PZP	Cameron N-90 HAFB	1580	
OE-PZR	Cameron A-105 HAFB	1909	
OE-PZS	AA-1050/1 Gas Balloon	1269	

Regn.	Type	C/n	Prev.Id.
OE-PZT(a)	Cameron O-105 HAFB	1624	
OE-PZT(b)	Sky 105-24 HAFB	066	
OE-PZT(c)	Kubicek BB-37 HAFB	111	
OE-PZU	Cameron A-105 HAFB	1882	
OE-PZV	Cameron A-105 HAFB	1883	
OE-PZY	Cameron O-120 HAFB	1722	
OE-PZZ	Cameron N-77 HAFB	1763	
OE-RHZ	Thunder AX10-180 SII HAFB	4634	
OE-RZA(a)	Thunder AX8-105/II HAFB	1391	
OE-RZA(b)	Cameron N-105 HAFB	2879	OE-ZZU(b)
OE-RZB	Cameron O-105 HAFB	1981	
OE-RZD	Cameron N-105 HAFB	2062	
OE-RZE	Raven-Europe S-60A HAFB	E-143	
OE-RZF(a)	Cameron A-105 HAFB	1916	
OE-RZF(b)	Schön-Saturn 3500 HAFB	S021/3/98	
OE-RZG	Cameron Bulb-120 SS HAFB	2219	
OE-RZH	Colt 160A HAFB	1562	
OE-RZI	Saturn 3400 HAFB	S-001	
OE-RZK	Cameron O-120 HAFB	1957	
OE-RZM	Schroeder Fire Balloons G HAFB	90	
OE-RZN	Saturn 3000 HAFB	S-002	
OE-RZR	Cameron N-105 HAFB	2359	
OE-RZS	Cameron N-90 HAFB	2090	
OE-RZU	Schroeder Fire Balloons G HAFB	109	
OE-RZV(b)	Cameron N-133 HAFB	3740	
OE-RZX(b)	Cameron A-140 HAFB	4093	
OE-RZY	Cameron O-105 HAFB	2111	
OE-RZZ(a)	Cameron A-120 HAFB	2015	
OE-RZZ(b)	Cameron N-133 HAFB	3739	
OE-SZA	Cameron O-105 HAFB	2228	
OE-SZB	Cameron A-105 HAFB	2339	
OE-SZC	Cameron A-105 HAFB	2137	G-BRSB
OE-SZE	Schroeder Fire Balloons G HAFB	163	
OE-SZF	Saturn 2400 HAFB	S002/5/90	
OE-SZH	Colt 77A HAFB	1688	
OE-SZK(a)	Neptune 3000 HAFB	S002/5/90	
OE-SZK(b)	Cameron A-105 HAFB	4538	
OE-SZM	Cameron A-105 HAFB	2285	
OE-SZN	Schroeder Fire Balloons G HAFB	106	
OE-SZP(a)	Saturn 3400 HAFB	S001/3/90	
OE-SZP(b)	Schön Saturn 3000 HAFB	S016/3/95	
OE-SZU	Cameron N-105 HAFB	2179	
OE-SZV	Cameron N-105 HAFB	2503	
OE-SZW	Neptun 3400 HAFB	S001/5/90	
OE-SZZ	Neptun 3000 HAFB	S004/5/90	
OE-ZAA(a)	Schroeder Fire Balloons G HAFB	449	
OE-ZAA(b)	Cameron A-160 HAFB	4331	
	(Reported by Camerons to be OE-ZZA)		
OE-ZAB	Cameron O-105 HAFB	3355	
OE-ZAC	Schön-Neptun 4000 HAFB	S035/5/98	
OE-ZAD(a)	Cameron A-120 HAFB	2567	
OE-ZAD(b)	Schön-Neptun 2500 HAFB	S010/5/93	
OE-ZAF	Thunder AX7-77 SI HAFB	2386	OE-KZE(b) OE-ZAK
OE-ZAG	Cameron A-105 HAFB	3230	
OE-ZAH	Colt 105A HAFB	1564	D-Telgate/1
OE-ZAI	Schön-Saturn 3000 HAFB	S020/3/97	
OE-ZAP	Cameron A-105 HAFB	3661	
OE-ZAQ	Schön-Saturn 3400 HAFB	S014/3/94	
OE-ZAR	Schön-Saturn 3000 HAFB	S015/3/94	
OE-ZAS	Colt 105A HAFB	2340	
OE-ZAT	Schön Saturn 4000 HAFB	S017/3/95	
OE-ZAW	Cameron A-120 HAFB	2966	
OE-ZBA(a)	Kubicek BB-30 HAFB	33	
OE-ZBA(b)	Schön-Neptun 3000 HAFB	S026/5/97	
OE-ZBB(a)	Colt Baren Bear SS HAFB	1336	OE-AZB G-BPVS
OE-ZBB(b)	Cameron N-90 HAFB	1547	OE-ZMK(a) OE-MZK
OE-ZBM	Schroeder Fire Balloons G HAFB	348	
OE-ZBR	Cameron N-105 HAFB	3046	
OE-ZBS(a)	Cameron O-90 HAFB	1824	OE-PZX
OE-ZBS(b)	Cameron N-120 HAFB	2663	OE-ZOP(a)
OE-ZBS(c)	Cameron O-65 HAFB	1503	OE-AZE
OE-ZBT	Cameron N-105 HAFB	2587	G-BTMM
OE-ZBW	Schön-Neptun 3000 HAFB	S024/5/97	
OE-ZCB(a)	Cameron N-90 HAFB	2760	G-BUHN
OE-ZCB(b)	Cameron Gosser Glass SS-90 HAFB	3268	OE-ZGO
OE-ZCC(b)	Thunder AX8-90SII HAFB	2401	
OE-ZCD	Schön-Neptun 3000 HAFB	S008/5/92	
OE-ZCE(a)	Cameron Cornetto-66 SS HAFB	1250	G-BMVZ
OE-ZCE(b)	Cameron O-77 HAFB	949	OE-ZCU(b) OE-KZX
OE-ZCF	Schön-Neptun 3000 HAFB	S037/5/98	
OE-ZCH	Cameron N-56 HAFB	3172	
OE-ZCK(a)	Cameron N-77 HAFB	1335	
OE-ZCK(b)	Cameron O-105 HAFB	4186	
OE-ZCM	Cameron A-105 HAFB	3043	
OE-ZCP(a)	Cameron A-105 HAFB	2018	OE-RZC
OE-ZCP(b)	Thunder AX7-77 HAFB	207	OE-AZP
OE-ZCS	Schroeder Fire Balloons G HAFB	355	D-OTEO
OE-ZCU(a)	Cameron Can-100 SS HAFB	2178	OE-CZU
OE-ZCU(c)	Cameron N-105 HAFB	3738	
OE-ZCW(a)	Cameron A-105 HAFB	2099	OE-RZL
OE-ZCW(b)	JM-22 BNT HAFB	01	
OE-ZDF(a)	Schön-Saturn 3000 HAFB	S012/3/94	
OE-ZDF(b)	Schön-Neptun 3000 HAFB	S016/5/95	
OE-ZDV	Schön-Neptun 3000 HAFB	S044/5/99	
OE-ZDW	Raven-Europe S-55A HAFB	E-070	OE-ZPW(a) OE-MZW
OE-ZEB	Balloon Works Firefly 7 HAFB	F7-130	
OE-ZEG	Cameron N-145 HAFB	4107	
OE-ZES	Schroeder Fire Balloons GHAFB	708	
OE-ZEW(a)	Kubicek BB-30 HAFB	12	
OE-ZEW(b)	Kubicek BB-30 HAFB	59	
OE-ZFA	Schön-Saturn 3000 HAFB	S001/3/91	
OE-ZFF	Schön-Neptun 3000 HAFB	S030/5/97	
OE-ZFG	Cameron A-105 HAFB	3015	
OE-ZFH	Schön-Saturn 3000 HAFB	S011/3/93	
OE-ZFM	Cameron V-90 HAFB	3135	
OE-ZFW	Schön-Neptun 3000 HAFB	S045/5/99	
OE-ZGB	Schön-Neptun 3000 HAFB	S031/5/97	
OE-ZGE	Schön-Neptun 3000 HAFB	S023/5/97	
OE-ZGG(a)	Cameron O-105 HAFB	1506	OE-MZG
OE-ZGG(b)	Cameron O-90 HAFB	2982	
OE-ZGH	Schön-Saturn 3400 HAFB	S010/3/92	
OE-ZGI	Kubicek BB-30 HAFB	64	
OE-ZGP	Schön-Neptun 3500 HAFB	S025/5/97	
OE-ZGS(a)	Colt 56A HAFB	761	OE-CZC
OE-ZGS(b)	Schön-Neptun 1800 HAFB	S006/5/92	
OE-ZGW	Cameron N-105 HAFB	4422	
OE-ZHB	Schön-Neptun 3500 HAFB	S012/5/94	
OE-ZHF	Cameron N-105 HAFB	4248	
OE-ZHH	Kubicek BB-37 HAFB	124	OK-0124
OE-ZHP	Schroeder Fire Balloons GHAFB	695	
OE-ZHS	Schön-Saturn 3000 HAFB	S009/3/92	
OE-ZHT(a)	Schön-Neptun 3400 HAFB	S020/5/96	
OE-ZHT(b)	Cameron O-84 HAFB	929	OE-ZMM(a) OE-KZW
OE-ZHZ	Cameron DP-70 Hot Air Airship	1504	HB-BKQ G-BNVA
OE-ZII	Cameron N-120 HAFB	4539	
OE-ZIN	Schön-Neptun 3500 HAFB	S036/5/98	
OE-ZIW	Cameron N-90 HAFB	3189	OE-ZKW(b) G-BVGU
OE-ZJM	Cameron N-105SV HAFB	3371	
OE-ZJS	Kubicek BB-30 HAFB	72	
OE-ZKA	Cameron N-145SV HAFB	3938	
OE-ZKE	Schön-Neptun 3000 HAFB	S027/5/97	
OE-ZKK	Colt 90A HAFB	851	D-Proghea
OE-ZKM(a)	Schön-Neptun 3000 HAFB	S015/5/95	
OE-ZKM(b)	Schön-Neptun 3500 HAFB	S041/5/98	
OE-ZKW(a)	Cameron N-105 HAFB	3657	
OE-ZLC	Cameron A-105 HAFB	2520	
OE-ZLM(b)	Sky 120-24 HAFB	107	
OE-ZLW	Schön-Neptun 3400 HAFB	SOO9/5/93	
OE-ZLZ	Cameron Newspaper SS HAFB	4679	
OE-ZMB(a)	Thunder AX7-77 HAFB	841	OE-MZB
OE-ZMB(b)	Schön-Neptun 3000 HAFB	S014/5/95	
OE-ZMF	Neptun 3000 HAFB	S001/5/91	

Regn.	Type	C/n	Prev.Id.
OE-ZMH	Schön-Neptun 3000 HAFB	S019/5/96	
OE-ZMI (a)	Schön-Saturn 3400 HAFB	S018/3/95	
OE-ZMI (b)	Cameron Mickey-90 HAFB	2671	OE-ZMM(b)
OE-ZMK(a)	Cameron O-65 HAFB	1057	
OE-ZMK(c)	Cameron N-120 HAFB	3452	
OE-ZML(a)	Cameron N-145 HAFB	3946	
OE-ZML(b)	Cameron N-120 HAFB	4333	
OE-ZMP(b)	Cameron V-90 HAFB	2681	
OE-ZMR(a)	Thunder AX7-77Z HAFB	228	OE-AZR
OE-ZMR(b)	Schön-Neptun 3000 HAFB	S007/5/92	
OE-ZMR(c)	Sky 105-24 HAFB	132	
OE-ZNA	Cameron V-77 HAFB	2639	
OE-ZNO	Tomi AX-7 HAFB	12/1993	
OE-ZNS	Schön-Neptun 3500 HAFB	S040/5/98	
OE-ZNW	Cameron A-105 HAFB	3419	
OE-ZOO(a)	Cameron O-140 HAFB	2197	OE-ZSG(b)
			OE-SZG
OE-ZOO(b)	Lindstrand LBL-48LHAFB	552	
OE-ZOP(c)	Lindstrand LBL-48L HAFB	553	
OE-ZOS	Schroeder Fire Balloons G HAFB	377	
OE-ZPA	Schön-Neptun 3500 HAFB	S018/5/95	
OE-ZPE	Kubicek BB-60 HAFB	127	OK-0127
OE-ZPF	Aerotechnik AB-8 HAFB	910.542	
OE-ZPG	Cameron A-105 HAFB	3173	
OE-ZPM	Cameron N-77 HAFB	3223	
OE-ZPN(a)	Schön-Saturn 2550 HAFB	S013/3/94	
OE-ZPN(b)	Colt 77A HAFB	984	OE-PZN
OE-ZPO(a)	Cameron A-140 HAFB	2576	
OE-ZPO(b)	Cameron A-140SV HAFB	3813	
OE-ZPP	Cameron A-140 HAFB	2832	
OE-ZPQ	Cameron A-140 HAFB	3620	
OE-ZPW(b)	Raven Europe RX-8 HAFB	E-243	
OE-ZRA	Augsburg K-1260/3-Ri Gas Balloon	8127	
OE-ZRB	Colt 21A Cloudhopper HAFB	2534	G-BVGV
OE-ZRD	Schön-Neptun 3000 HAFB	S034/5/98	
OE-ZRE	Kubicek BB-37 HAFB	27	
OE-ZRG	Schön-Neptun 3000 HAFB	S021/5/96	
OE-ZRI	Schön-Neptun 3000 HAFB	S022/5/97	
OE-ZRS	Cameron O-105 HAFB	1978	D-OGOL
			D-Mengede
OE-ZRW	Schön-Neptun 3000 HAFB	S029/5/97	
OE-ZRX	Cameron O-105 HAFB	3000	
OE-ZSA(a)	Cameron V-77 HAFB	1080	OE-ZMP(a)
			OE-MZP
OE-ZSB	Schön-Saturn 2400 HAFB	S008/3/92	
OE-ZSE(b)	Cameron A-210 HAFB	4378	
OE-ZSF	Cameron A-140 HAFB	3814	
OE-ZSG(b)	Lindstrand LBL-210A HAFB	097	
OE-ZSG(d)	Thunder AX-11-250SII HAFB	4015	
OE-ZSG(e)	Sky 200-24 HAFB	146	
OE-ZSH	Cameron A-105 HAFB	2859	D-OREX
OE-ZSI (a)	Aerotechnik AB-2c N-30 HAFB	400.591	
OE-ZSI (b)	Aerotechnik AB-8 N-30 HAFB	410.591	
OE-ZSL(a)	Cameron A-180 HAFB	2292	OE-SZL
OE-ZSL(c)	Cameron A-180 HAFB	3758	
OE-ZSO	Schön-Neptun 3000 HAFB	S038/5/98	
OE-ZSP	Kubicek BB-30 HAFB	6	
OE-ZSS	Schön-Saturn 3000 HAFB	S019/3/96	OE-ZSA(b)
OE-ZSV	Cameron N-133 HAFB	2907	
OE-ZSW(a)	Schön-Neptun 3400 HAFB	S011/5/93	
OE-ZSW(b)	Cameron A-140 HAFB	2061	OE-RZX(a)
OE-ZSZ	Cameron N-105 HAFB	4459	
OE-ZTB	Aerotechnik AB.2c HAFB	230.589	
OE-ZTH(a)	Cameron N-133 HAFB	3454	OE-ZKG(b)
OE-ZTH(b)	Tomi AX-8 HAFB	001/1991	OE-ZKG(a)
OE-ZTL(a)	Colt 105A HAFB	1552	OE-RZP
OE-ZTL(b)	Schön-Neptun 3000 HAFB	S003/5/90	OE-SZS
OE-ZTL(c)	Schön-Neptun 3000 HAFB	S013/5/95	
OE-ZTT	Cameron N-105 HAFB	4293	
OE-ZUA	Cameron N-105 HAFB	4387	
OE-ZUP	Cameron V-90 HAFB	2531	
OE-ZUS	Schön-Neptun 4000 HAFB	S028/5/97	
OE-ZUW	Cameron O-120 HAFB	2600	
OE-ZVA	Schön-Neptun 3000 HAFB	S017/5/95	
OE-ZVM	Schön-Neptun 3000 HAFB	S039/5/98	

Regn.	Type	C/n	Prev.Id.
OE-ZVP	Schön-Neptun 3500 HAFB	S043/5/99	
OE-ZVS	Cameron N-145 HAFB	3965	
OE-ZYY	Cameron O-65 HAFB	2577	
OE-ZZA	Cameron A-160 HAFB *(Res., see OE-ZAA)*	4331	
OE-ZZB(a)	Cameron V-77 HAFB	1652	OE-ZZU(a)
			OE-MZU
OE-ZZB(b)	Colt 105A HAFB	1098	OE-MZT
OE-ZZB(c)	Cameron A-140 HAFB	2698	OE-ZMZ
OE-ZZG(a)	Schön-Neptun 3500 HAFB	S032/5/97	
OE-ZZG(b)	Cameron O-120 HAFB	4745	
OE-ZZI (a)	Stuttgart K-945/2-Stu Gas Balloon	0211	OE-SZI
OE-ZZI (b)	Colt AA-1050 Gas Balloon	2151	
OE-ZZK	Kubicek BB-45 HAFB	117	
OE-ZZT	Cameron N-133 HAFB	3384	
OE-ZZU(c)	Cameron N-105 HAFB	3654	
OE-ZZU(d)	Cameron O-140 HAFB	4390	
OE-ZZV(a)	Cameron N-105 HAFB	1477	OE-MZV
OE-ZZW	Cameron A-140 HAFB	3354	
OE-ZZX(a)	Saturn 3400 HAFB	S003/3/90	OE-SZX
OE-ZZX(b)	Cameron V-77 HAFB	652	OE-DZX

MOTOR-GLIDERS

Regn.	Type	C/n	Prev.Id.
OE-9002	Raab Krähe II	V-3	D-KGAZ
			D-EGAZ
OE-9003	Raab Krähe IV	021	D-KADY
OE-9006	Scheibe SF-24B Motorspatz	4027	(D-KACY)
OE-9009	Raab Krähe V	2	
OE-9014	Scheibe SF-24B Motorspatz	4046	(D-KOBA)
OE-9017	Raab Austro Krähe	027	
OE-9021	Scheibe SF-25A Motorfalke	4554	(D-KOGO)
OE-9022	Raab Krähe V	024	
OE-9023	Brditschka HB-3AR	51	
OE-9024	Schleicher Kaiser Ka.2 Rhönschwalbe	V-1	D-KAIS
OE-9026	Scheibe SF-25B Falke	4659	(D-KABK)
OE-9027	Scheibe SF-25B Falke	4665	(D-KACJ)
OE-9032	Raab Krähe IV	12	D-KAGO
OE-9037	Scheibe SF-25B Falke	46153	(D-KCAS)
OE-9042	Scheibe SF-25B Falke	46218	(D-KAAT)
OE-9043	Scheibe SF-25B Falke	46216	(D-KASX)
OE-9046	Sportavia-Pützer RF-5B Sperber	51018	
OE-9047	Scheibe SF-25B Falke	46239	(D-KAIE)
OE-9052	Scheibe SF-25C Falke	46249	(D-KAVI)
OE-9053	Brditschka HB-3BR	057	
OE-9054	Scheibe SF-25B Falke	46246	(D-KAVF)
OE-9058	Scheibe SF-25C Falke	4445	(D-KDAE)
OE-9059	Scheibe SF-25C Falke	4444	(D-KDAD)
OE-9061	Brditschka HB-3 BR	058	
OE-9062	Scheibe SF-25C Falke	4423	(D-KHOG)
OE-9065	Scheibe SF-28A Tandem-Falke	5729	(D-KOAR)
OE-9067	Scheibe SF-25C Falke	4465	(D-KOAX)
OE-9068	Scheibe SF-25C Falke	4466	(D-KOAY)
OE-9072	Scheibe SF-28A Tandem-Falke	5743	(D-KOEE(2))
OE-9073	Scheibe SF-28A Tandem-Falke	5701	D-KAFJ
OE-9074	Scheibe SF-28A Tandem-Falke	5723	(D-KAUN)
OE-9075	Scheibe SF-25C Falke	4481	(D-KEIA)
OE-9077	Scheibe SF-28A Tandem-Falke	5748	(D-KOEZ)
OE-9079	Brditschka HB-3AR	061	
OE-9082	Scheibe SF-25C Falke	4489	(D-KEII)
OE-9085	Fournier RF-4D	4056	D-KAQU
OE-9086	Scheibe SF-25C Falke	4495	(D-KEIM)
OE-9087	Scheibe SF-25C Falke	4497	(D-KEIO)
OE-9090	Brditschka HB-3 BR	060	
OE-9091	Scheibe SF-25B Falke	4675	D-KATD
OE-9096	Scheibe SF-25B Falke	46169D	D-KBIO
OE-9097	Scheibe SF-25C Falke	44117	(D-KNOX)
OE-9098	Scheibe SF-28A Tandem-Falke	5778	D-KCLH
OE-9099	Scheibe SF-25C Falke	44126	D-KLDC
OE-9103	Scheibe SF-25D Falke	4670D	D-KFFD
	(SE-TUL quoted with same c/n or 4670-1D)		D-KFFB

Regn.	Type	C/n	Prev.Id.
OE-9104	Alpla AVO 68 Samburo	003	
OE-9106	Alpla AVO 68v Samburo	002	
OE-9107	Scheibe SF-25C Falke	44135	(D-KDDJ)
OE-9109	Alpla AVO 68 Samburo	005	
OE-9111	Alpla AVO 68 Samburo	006	
OE-9112	Brditschka HB-21-V2	21005	
OE-9113	Brditschka HB-3BR	055	
OE-9116	Scheibe SF-25C Falke	44148	D-KLUG
			(D-KDEF)
OE-9125	Scheibe SF-25B Falke	4831	D-KANF
			HB-2011
			(D-KAHP)
OE-9126	Scheibe SF-25C Falke	44192	(D-KADO)
OE-9127	Scheibe SF-25E Super-Falke	4328	(D-KDFF)
OE-9129	Brditschka HB-21/2400	21009	
OE-9130	Scheibe SF-25B Falke	46258	D-KEAR
OE-9131	Brditschka HB-21	21008	
OE-9133	Scheibe SF-25C Falke	44204	(D-KDFJ)
OE-9136	Scheibe SF-25C Falke	44145	D-KDEC
OE-9137	Scheibe SF-25C Falke	44213	(D-KDFU)
OE-9141	Scheibe SF-25C Falke	44226	(D-KDFX)
OE-9143	Brditschka HB-21/2400	21011	
OE-9145	Scheibe SF-25C Falke	44125	D-KLDB
OE-9147	Scheibe SF-25C Falke	44133	D-KDDH
OE-9148	Scheibe SF-25C Falke	44230	(D-KDCC)
OE-9149	Fournier RF-4D	4130	D-KALH
OE-9153	Brditschka HB-21/2400	21012	
OE-9154	Scheibe SF-28A Tandem-Falke	5791	(D-KDFZ)
OE-9155	Fournier RF-3	22	D-KEHL
			F-BMDC
OE-9157	Brditschka HB-21	21014	
OE-9158	Scheibe SF-25D Falke	4838D	D-KHEU
OE-9160	Brditschka HB-21/2400	21023	
OE-9161	Scheibe SF-25D Falke	46137D	D-KCAD
OE-9162	Scheibe SF-25B Falke	46192	D-KASG
OE-9164	Scheibe SF-25C Falke	44275	(D-KDBX)
OE-9170	Scheibe SF-25B Falke	4844	D-KHFB
OE-9171	Scheibe SF-25C Falke	44233	D-KDCC
OE-9173	Scheibe SF-25B Falke	4626	D-KIMA
			(D-KIMG)
OE-9175	Scheibe SF-25B Falke	4861	D-KAEH
OE-9176	Scheibe SF-25C Falke	44300	(D-KDGU)
OE-9177	Scheibe SF-25C Falke	44297	(D-KDGQ)
OE-9179	Scheibe SF-25D Falke	46157D	D-KBIB
OE-9180	Scheibe SF-25C Falke	44301	(D-KDGW)
OE-9181	Scheibe SF-25D Falke	AB46308D	(D-KDGG(3))
OE-9185	Scheibe SF-25D Falke	46164D	HB-2015
			(D-KBII)
OE-9186	Scheibe SF-25C Falke	44309	D-KOOB
OE-9189	Scheibe SF-25D Falke	4679D	D-KBAE
OE-9191	Grob G.109	6014	(D-KISI)
OE-9193	Grob G.109	6061	
OE-9194	Brditschka HB-21	21025	
OE-9197	Scheibe SF-25C Falke	44147	D-KDAT
			(D-KDEE)
OE-9201	Scheibe SF-25B Falke	46209	OE-9156
			D-KFVN
			(D-KASE)
OE-9204	Hoffmann H-36 Dimona	3502	
OE-9205	Eiri PIK-20E	20277	D-KIDM
OE-9206	Hoffmann H-36 Dimona	3615	
OE-9207	Hoffmann H-36 Dimona	3504	
OE-9208	Hoffmann H-36 Dimona	3621	
OE-9209	Hoffmann H-36 Dimona	3631	
OE-9210	Hoffmann H-36 Dimona	3624	
OE-9211	Hoffmann H-36 Dimona	3648	
OE-9214	Hoffmann H-36 Dimona	3652	
OE-9217	Brditschka HB-21/2400	21028	
OE-9218	Hoffmann H-36 Dimona	3530	
OE-9220	Scheibe SF-25C Falke	44231	D-KDCF
OE-9221	Hoffmann H-36 Dimona	3675	
OE-9222	Scheibe SF-25D Falke	4858D	D-KAAH
OE-9223	Hoffmann H-36 Dimona	3637	
OE-9224	Fournier RF-5	5048	OE-9101
			D-KLUB
OE-9226	Brditschka HB-21/2400	21029	
OE-9227	Hoffmann H-36 Dimona	3645	
OE-9228	Brditschka HB-23-V2	23002	
OE-9229	Schempp-Hirth Janus CM	06	D-KBOS
			OO-BPC
			(D-KIBC)
OE-9230	Grob G.109B	6242	
OE-9231	Grob G.109B	6244	
OE-9233	Hoffmann H-36 Dimona	36138	
OE-9235	Grob G.109B	6272	
OE-9238	Hoffmann H-36 Dimona	3672	
OE-9242	Brditschka HB-23 Scanliner	23003	
OE-9246	Brditschka HB-21	21004	
OE-9247	Grob G.109B	6230	D-KGFN
OE-9249	Scheibe SF-25C Falke	44137	D-KDDL
OE-9250	Grob G.109B	6341	
OE-9251	Fournier RF-5	5062	D-KBAL
OE-9252	Brditschka HB-23/2400	23007	
OE-9256	Grob G.109B	6386	
OE-9258	Grob G.109B	6373	
OE-9260	Scheibe SF-25C Falke	44191	HB-2037
			D-KADI
OE-9261	Scheibe SF-25C Falke	44382	(D-KNIE)
OE-9262	Brditschka HB-23/2400	23009	
OE-9263	Brditschka HB-23/2400	23014	
OE-9265	Brditschka HB-23/2400	23015	
OE-9266	Brditschka HB-23/2400	23010	
OE-9271	Brditschka HB-23/2400	23016	
OE-9272	Brditschka HB-23/2400	23017	
OE-9273	Glaser-Dirks DG-400	4-188	
OE-9274	Grob G.109	6078	D-KCBF
OE-9275	AVO-68V Samburo	022	D-KAGM(2)
OE-9277	Brditschka HB-23/2400	23018	
OE-9278	Hoffmann H-36 Dimona	36221	
OE-9279	Brditschka HB-23/2400	23019	
OE-9280	Scheibe SF-25C Falke	44401	(D-KNIJ)
OE-9282	Hoffmann H-36 Dimona	36239	
OE-9283	Brditschka HB-23/2400	23020	
OE-9287	Brditschka HB-23/2400	23022	
OE-9292	Valentin Taifun 17E-II	1094	D-KEWI (1)
OE-9293	Valentin Taifun 17E-II	1106	D-KHVA(31)
OE-9296	Brditschka HB-23/2400	23027	
OE-9298	Brditschka HB-23/2400	23024-S-6	
OE-9299	Scheibe SF-28A Tandem-Falke	5708	D-KHOR
OE-9302	Brditschka HB-23/2400	23031	
OE-9303	Scheibe SF-25C Falke	44262	D-KDOX
OE-9305	Hoffmann H-36 Dimona	36262	
OE-9306	Brditschka HB-21	21018	PH-677
OE-9309	Hoffmann H-36 Dimona	36266	
OE-9310	Brditschka HB-23/2400	23032	
OE-9311	Brditschka HB-23/2400	23033	
OE-9312	Brditschka HB-23/2400	23028-S-7	
OE-9313	Valentin Taifun 17E-II	1118	(D-KHVA)
OE-9314	Brditschka HB-23/2400	23036	
OE-9315	Brditschka HB-23/2400	23035	
OE-9317	Brditschka HB-23/2400	23038	
OE-9320	Scheibe SF-25C Falke	44150	D-KDEH
OE-9321	Brditschka HB-23/2400SP	23041	
OE-9322	Brditschka HB-23/2400SP	23040	
OE-9326	Skyhopper	001	
OE-9328	Brditschka HB-23/2400 Scanliner	23037-S-8	
OE-9331	Brditschka HB-23/2400SP	23045	
OE-9333	Aeronautica-Umbra AU-SF-25B Falke	AU-008D	D-KIAY
			I-AUAB
OE-9335	Hoffmann H-36 Dimona	3525	D-KESI
OE-9336	Brditschka HB-23/2400 Scanliner	23047-S9	
OE-9337	Schleicher ASW-24E	24812	
OE-9338	Schleicher ASH-25E	25091	
OE-9339	Scheibe SF-25C Falke	44278	D-KDBT(3)
OE-9342	Scheibe SF-25C Falke	44274	D-KABL(2)
OE-9344	Hoffmann HK-36R Super Dimona	36302	
OE-9345	Schempp-Hirth Nimbus 3DT	4/15	OE-5445
			D-0962
OE-9348	Brditschka HB-23/2400	23034	HB-2143
OE-9353	Schempp-Hirth Discus bT	53/371	

Regn.	Type	C/n	Prev.Id.
OE-9354	Hoffmann HK-36R Super Dimona	36307	
OE-9356	Schempp-Hirth Discus bT	52/369	
OE-9357	Schempp-Hirth Ventus cM	56/506	(D-KDHH)
OE-9358	Scheibe SF-25C Falke	4202	D-KAOG
OE-9359	Schleicher ASH-25E	25114	
OE-9360	Hoffmann HK-36R Super Dimona	36324	
OE-9362	Hoffmann HK-36R Super Dimona	36326	
OE-9364	Schempp-Hirth Nimbus 3T	5	D-KGZT
OE-9367	Schempp-Hirth Discus bT	75/403	
OE-9369	Grob G.103C Twin IIISL	35021	
OE-9370	Schempp-Hirth Ventus cM	83/559	
OE-9372	Scheibe SF-25C Falke	44459	D-KIAJ(2)
OE-9373	Technoflug Piccolo	059	D-KIMV
OE-9374	Grob G.103C Twin IIISL	35014	
OE-9376	Hoffmann HK-36R Super Dimona	36353	
OE-9377	Schempp-Hirth Ventus cM	87/569	
OE-9378	Schempp-Hirth Discus bT	89/426	
OE-9380	Valentin Kiwi	K3016	D-KEGX(4)
OE-9381	Scheibe SF-25C Falke	44283	D-KDGC(2)
OE-9382	Hoffmann HK-36R Super Dimona	36374	
OE-9384	Schempp-Hirth Discus bT	114/467	
OE-9385	Schempp-Hirth Discus bT	119/475	
OE-9386	Schempp-Hirth Discus bT	123/481	
OE-9387	Schempp-Hirth Ventus cT	80/321	D-KMMY
OE-9389	Scheibe SF-25C Falke	44433	D-KIAO
			(D-KNIY)
OE-9390	Eiri PIK-20E	20220	HB-2049
OE-9391	Schempp-Hirth Discus bT	140/518	
OE-9392	Hoffmann HK-36R Super Dimona	36392	
OE-9396	Technoflug Piccolo B	095	(D-KIIC)
OE-9398	Hoffmann H-36 Dimona	3696	HB-2091
OE-9399	Schempp-Hirth Discus bT	129/491	
OE-9400	HOAC HK-36R Super Dimona	36386	F-CGAZ
OE-9404	Scheibe SF-25C Rotax Falke	44601	D-KTIV(1)
OE-9405	Schempp-Hirth Discus bT	143/521	
OE-9408	HOAC HK-36TTC Super Dimona	36540	
OE-9410	HOAC HK-36TTC Super Dimona	36545	
OE-9411	Schempp-Hirth Ventus 2cM	78/161	
OE-9412	HOAC HK-36TTC Super Dimona	36542	
OE-9413	HOAC HK-36TTC Super Dimona	36620	
OE-9414(2)	HOAC HK-36TTC Super Dimona	36561	
OE-9417	HOAC HK-36TC Super Dimona	36517	
OE-9418	HOAC HK-36TTC Super Dimona	36606	
OE-9420	Scheibe SF-25C Falke	44339	D-KBCL
OE-9421	HOAC HK-36TTC Super Dimona	36590	
OE-9423	Schempp-Hirth Discus bT	28/324	D-KEBG
OE-9424	HOAC HK-36TTS Super Dimona	36624	
OE-9425	HOAC HK-36TTC Super Dimona	36525	
OE-9426	Schleicher ASH-26E	26062	
OE-9431	HOAC HK-36TTC Super Dimona	36531	
OE-9432	HOAC HK-36TTC Super Dimona	36532	
OE-9433	HOAC HK-36TTC Super Dimona	36533	
OE-9436	HOAC HK-36TTC Super Dimona	36636	
OE-9438	HOAC HK-36TTC Super Dimona	36538	
OE-9440	LET L-13SL Vivat	940519	
OE-9441	HOAC HK-36TTC Super Dimona	36541	
OE-9445	HOAC HK-36TC Super Dimona	36650	
OE-9446	HOAC HK-36TTC Super Dimona	36546	
OE-9449	Scheibe SF-25C Falke 1700	44344	D-KBCO
OE-9450	HOAC HK-36TTC Super Dimona	36565	
OE-9452	HOAC HK-36TTC Super Dimona	36552	
OE-9453	HOAC HK-36TTC Super Dimona 115	36653	
OE-9454	HOAC HK-36TTS Super Dimona	36514	
OE-9455	HOAC HK-36TC Super Dimona	36529	
OE-9456	HOAC HK-36TTC Super Dimona	36656	
OE-9457	HOAC HK-36TTC Super Dimona	36557	
OE-9459	HOAC HK-36TTC Super Dimona	36559	
OE-9460	HOAC HK-36TTC Super Dimona	36665	
OE-9461	Schleicher ASH-26E	26161	
OE-9462	HOAC HK-36TTC Super Dimona	36562	
OE-9466	HOAC HK-36TTC Super Dimona	36659	
OE-9467	Technoflug Piccolo B	086	D-KIIA
OE-9470	Schempp-Hirth Ventus 2cM	69/141	
OE-9476	Scheibe SF-25C Rotax Falke	44600	D-KTIU(2)
OE-9477	HOAC HK-36TS Super Dimona	36502	

Regn.	Type	C/n	Prev.Id.
OE-9484	Brditschka HB-23/2400 Scanliner	23012-S2	OE-9284
OE-9489	HOAC HK-36TTC Super Dimona	36589	
OE-9490	Schempp-Hirth Ventus cT	151/480	
OE-9493	HOAC HK-36R Super Dimona	36393	
OE-9497	Valentin Taifun 17E-II	1111	D-KRRK
			OE-9297
			D-KHVA
OE-9500	HOAC HK-36TTC Super Dimona	36549	
OE-9573	Schempp-Hirth Discus bT	51/368	OE-5573
			D-4504

GLIDERS

Regn.	Type	C/n	Prev.Id.
OE-0001	Grunau Baby IIb	unkn	
OE-0004	Grunau Baby IIb	30340	
OE-0038	Grunau Baby IIb	004290	
OE-0041	Grunau Baby IIb	003374	
OE-0061	Grunau Baby IIb	005	
OE-0070	DFS-Weihe	139	
OE-0097	SG-38 Schulgleiter	7	
OE-0124	DFS-Olympia-Meise	635	
OE-0126	Grunau Baby IIb	01	
OE-0129	Grunau Baby IIb Edelweiss	007	
OE-0135	Grunau Baby IIb	011	
OE-0169	SG-38 Schulgleiter	1	
OE-0187	Scheibe Bergfalke II/55	04/261	
OE-0190	Grunau Baby IIb	002	
OE-0204	Scheibe Bergfalke II/55	05	
OE-0217	Grunau Baby IIb	017	
OE-0227	Grunau Baby IIb	unkn	
OE-0238	Scheibe Bergfalke II/55	02/U	
OE-0241	DFS-Weihe	408	
OE-0243	Schneider ESG.31 Grunau Baby IIB	unkn	
OE-0248	Scheibe L-Spatz W	268	
OE-0249	Scheibe Bergfalke II/55	4	
OE-0252	Doppelraab IV	007	
OE-0254	Grunau Baby IIb	023	
OE-0256	Scheibe Spatz B	104/54	
OE-0261	Grunau Baby IIb	024	
OE-0266	Mü.13E Bergfalke	3	
OE-0271	Grunau Baby IIb	1	
OE-0277	DFS-Weihe 50	490	
OE-0284	Scheibe Bergfalke II	110/54	
OE-0288	Musger Mg.19 Steinadler	09	
OE-0298	Scheibe Bergfalke II	114/55	
OE-0299	Scheibe L-Spatz 55	542	
OE-0302	Scheibe Bergfalke II	3	
OE-0306	Musger Mg.19 Steinadler	11	
OE-0307	Scheibe Bergfalke II	03	
OE-0314	Musger Mg.23	01	
OE-0333	Doppelraab IV	37	
OE-0338	Musger Mg.23	02	
OE-0345	Musger Mg.19b	017	
OE-0346	Grunau Baby IIb Edelweiss	031	
OE-0362	Scheibe L-Spatz	03	
OE-0363	Scheibe Bergfalke II	2	
OE-0367	Scheibe L-Spatz	205	
OE-0372	Zsebo-Bohn Z-03b Ifjusag	103	
OE-0374	Grunau Baby IIb	032	
OE-0377	Scheibe L-Spatz 55	207	
OE-0380	Dora 5b	0001	
OE-0387	Scheibe Spatz B	1	
OE-0390	Musger Mg.19a	025	
OE-0394	Grunau Baby IIb	051	
OE-0396	Musger Mg.19b	030	
OE-0398	Musger Mg.19b	032	
OE-0400	Musger Mg.19b	034	
OE-0401	Musger Mg.19b	035	
OE-0402	Super Futar R 22S	E-1147	
OE-0405	Lo-100 Zwergreiher	015	

Regn.	Type	C/n	Prev.Id.
OE-0407	Musger Mg.23	06	
OE-0408	Musger Mg.23	008	
OE-0409	Musger Mg.19a	040	
OE-0412	Grunau Baby IIb	38	
OE-0415	Musger Mg.19a	036	
OE-0423	Grunau Baby IIb	01	
OE-0425	Musger Mg.23	05	
OE-0427	Scheibe Bergfalke II/55	047	
OE-0428	Scheibe Bergfalke II/55	048	
OE-0430	Scheibe L-Spatz 55	544	
OE-0431	Scheibe L-Spatz 55	03	
OE-0435	Schleicher Ka.6BR Rhönsegler	463	
OE-0437	Scheibe L-Spatz 55	214	
OE-0442	Grunau Baby IIb	42	
OE-0448	Grunau Baby IIb	41	
OE-0449	Grunau Baby IIb	44	
OE-0457	Scheibe L-Spatz 55	215/503	
OE-0460	Scheibe L-Spatz 55	R219/H234	
OE-0463	Scheibe L-Spatz 55	3	
OE-0465	Scheibe Zugvogel IV	1040	
OE-0466	Scheibe L-Spatz 55	679	
OE-0467	Scheibe L-Spatz 55	208	
OE-0470	Scheibe L-Spatz 55	R58/H230	
OE-0472	Grunau Baby IIb	unkn	
OE-0475	Schleicher Ka.6CR Rhönsegler	569	
OE-0477	Olympia-Meise 51	17	
OE-0478	Scheibe L-Spatz 55	R56/H229	
OE-0479	Scheibe L-Spatz 55	R55/H227	
OE-0480	SZD-9 bis Bocian 1D	P-349	
OE-0485	Musger Mg.19a	20	
OE-0486	Schleicher Ka.6CR Rhönsegler	643	
OE-0488	Schleicher K.8	666	
OE-0490	Schleicher K.7 Rhönadler	632	
OE-0498	Schleicher K.8B	830	
OE-0500	Scheibe L-Spatz	R844/H193	
OE-0501	Grunau Baby IIb	47	
OE-0502	Scheibe Bergfalke II/55	224	
OE-0505	Scheibe L-Spatz 55	20	
OE-0506	Fauvel AV-36C	201	
OE-0508	Scheibe L-Spatz 55	R218/H232	
OE-0510	Scheibe L-Spatz 55	21	
OE-0511	Scheibe L-Spatz 55	22	
OE-0518	Scheibe L-Spatz 55	719	
OE-0520	Scheibe Bergfalke II/55	305	
OE-0523	Akaflieg Wien AFW.8	2	
OE-0526	Scheibe L-Spatz 55	R229/H234	
OE-0529	Schleicher K.8B	910	
OE-0530	Scheibe L-Spatz 55	R228/H248	
OE-0532	SZD-22C Mucha Standard	598	
OE-0534	SZD-22C Mucha Standard	600	
OE-0536	SZD-22C Mucha Standard	599	
OE-0537	Scheibe L-Spatz	R230/H249	
OE-0538	SZD-22C Mucha Standard	610	
OE-0540	SZD-9bis Bocian 1D	P-387	
	(c/n quoted officially as F-873 ex SP-2506)		
OE-0544	Scheibe Spatz A	509	
OE-0547	Scheibe L-Spatz	R232/H244	
OE-0548	Scheibe L-Spatz	R234/H254	
OE-0551	Schleicher Ka.6CR Rhönsegler	1077	
OE-0552	Doppelraab	E-1	
OE-0556	Schleicher K.7 Rhönadler	1007	
OE-0561	Schleicher K.8B	1017	
OE-0562	SZD-9bis Bocian 1D	P-392	
OE-0567	Schleicher K.8B	1098	
OE-0573	Musger Mg.23SL	09	
OE-0575	Lehrmeister FES.530/1	232	
OE-0578	Schleicher K.8B	1152	
OE-0579	Schleicher K.8B	1154	
OE-0583	Rhönlerche II	3018	
OE-0584	Schleicher K.8B	8153	
OE-0585	Schleicher K.7 Rhönadler	7002	
OE-0587	Schleicher K.7 Rhönadler	7060	
OE-0588	Schleicher Ka.6CR Rhönsegler	1130	
OE-0594	Scheibe L-Spatz	539	
OE-0595	Schleicher K.7 Rhönadler	24	
OE-0596	Schleicher K.8B	25	
OE-0597	Schleicher K.8B	26	
OE-0600	Musger Mg.23SL	13	
OE-0602	Scheibe L-Spatz 55	R53/H240	
OE-0610	Grunau Baby IIb	45	
OE-0616	Grunau Baby IIb	597	
OE-0617	Meise	196	
OE-0620	Scheibe L-Spatz 55	762	
OE-0625	Scheibe SF-26 Standard	5006	
OE-0626	Musger Mg.23SL	12	
OE-0628	Schleicher K.8B	KR-1	
OE-0630	Schleicher Ka.6CR Rhönsegler	6147	
OE-0633	Schleicher K.8B	8160	
OE-0636	Schleicher Ka.6CR Rhönsegler	6205	
OE-0637	Schleicher K.8B	8158	
OE-0639	Schleicher Ka.6CR Rhönsegler	6134	
OE-0640	Schleicher Ka.6CR Rhönsegler	6204	
OE-0641	Schleicher K.8B	8179	
OE-0642	Schleicher K.8B	8180	
OE-0644	Schleicher Ka.6CR Rhönsegler	6164	
OE-0645	Schleicher K.8B	8251	
OE-0652	Schleicher K.7 Rhönadler	7085	
OE-0653	Schleicher K.8B	8804	
OE-0654	Schleicher K.8B	8314	
OE-0655	Schleicher K.8B	8303	
OE-0657	Schleicher K.7 Rhönadler	7097	
OE-0658	Schleicher K.8B	8322	
OE-0659	Schleicher Ka.6CR Rhönsegler	6275	
OE-0660	Schleicher Ka.6CR Rhönsegler	6232	
OE-0661	Musger Mg.23SL	16	
OE-0662	Standard Austria	13	
OE-0665	LG-125 Sohaj 2	519	
OE-0672	Schleicher K.8B	8315	
OE-0673	Schleicher K.8B	8325	
OE-0675	Schleicher Ka.6CR Rhönsegler	6276	
OE-0677	Schleicher K.7 Rhönadler	7140	
OE-0678	Schleicher K.8B	8363	
OE-0679	Schleicher Ka.6CR Rhönsegler	6405	
OE-0682	Scheibe L-Spatz-W	258	
OE-0683	Scheibe Zugvogel IIIB	1083	
OE-0684	Scheibe Zugvogel IIIA	1048	
OE-0687	Fauvel AV-36CR	216	
OE-0690	Musger Mg.23SL	17	
OE-0693	Schleicher K.8B	8230	
OE-0695	Bölkow Phoebus B-1	946	
OE-0699	Scheibe L-Spatz W	259	
OE-0700	Scheibe Bergfalke III	5565	
OE-0702	Lehrmeister IIFES.530/II	214	
OE-0703	Schleicher K.8B	8232	
OE-0704	Glasflügel H.301 Libelle	16	
OE-0710	Schleicher K.10	10011	
OE-0712	LET L-13 Blanik	174506	
OE-0713	SZD-30 Pirat	B-328	
OE-0714	FFA-Diamant 16.5	066	
OE-0715	Schleicher Ka.6CR Rhönsegler	6532/Si	
OE-0716	Rolladen-Schneider LS-1A	15	
OE-0717	SZD-30 Pirat	B-336	
OE-0718	Bölkow Phoebus C	770	
OE-0719	Scheibe Spatz A	103/54	OE-0276
OE-0721	Schleicher K.8B	8413	
OE-0722	Schleicher Ka.6CR Rhönsegler	6351	
OE-0724	Schleicher Ka.6CR Rhönsegler	6406	
OE-0725	Schleicher Ka.6CR Rhönsegler	6420	
	(same c/n as OY-XMJ)		
OE-0726	Schleicher Ka.6CR Rhönsegler	6440	
OE-0727	Schleicher Ka.6E	4016	
OE-0728	Schleicher K.8B (W/o 18.7.93)	8474	
OE-0730	Schleicher K.8B	8476	
OE-0731	Schleicher K.8B	8231	
OE-0733	Scheibe Bergfalke III	5523	
OE-0735	Grunau Baby IIb	03	
OE-0737(2)	LET L-13 Blanik	175019	D-1067
OE-0738	Schleicher Ka.6CR Rhönsegler	7	
OE-0739	LET L-13 Blanik	173219	
OE-0741	Schleicher Ka.6CR Rhönsegler	6364	

Regn.	Type	C/n	Prev.Id.
OE-0743	Schleicher K.8B	8463	
OE-0747	Schleicher Ka.6E	4017	
OE-0748	Schleicher K.8B	8546	
OE-0749	Schleicher K.8B	8545	
OE-0751	Standard Austria SH.1	66	
OE-0752	Musger Mg.23SL	24	
OE-0753	Schleicher K.8B	8434/ZW	
OE-0754	Schleicher K.8B	8233	
OE-0756	Grunau Baby IIb Edelweiss	51	
OE-0757	Scheibe SF-26 Standard	5053	
OE-0758	LET L-13 Blanik	173311	
OE-0759	Scheibe L-Spatz 55	527	
OE-0760	Schleicher K.8B	8234	
OE-0763	SZD-9 bis Bocian 1D	875	
OE-0765	Schleicher K.8B	8483	
OE-0769	Scheibe L-Spatz 55	551	
OE-0771	Schleicher Ka.6E	4023	
OE-0772	Schleicher K.8B	8554	
OE-0773	Schleicher Ka.6CR Rhönsegler	6498	
OE-0777	Schleicher K.8B	8597	
OE-0778	Schleicher K.8B	8598	
OE-0779	Schleicher K.8B	8599	
OE-0781	Scheibe SF-27	6026	
OE-0782	Scheibe Bergfalke II/55	2	
OE-0783	Schleicher K.8B	8506/ZW	
OE-0784	Schleicher K.8B	8507/ZW	
OE-0785	Schleicher K.8B	8484/A	
OE-0788	LET L-13 Blanik	173330	
OE-0789	Scheibe SF-27A	1702E	
OE-0791	Musger Mg.23SL	26	
OE-0793	Scheibe SF-27A	1701E	
OE-0794	Schleicher K.8	8430a	
OE-0797	Schleicher Ka.6E	4064	
OE-0798	Scheibe L-Spatz 55	740	
OE-0800	Schleicher K.8B	8731	
OE-0801	Schleicher Rhönlerche II	3070/BR	
OE-0802	Schleicher K.8B	8648	
OE-0803	Schleicher K.8B	8649	
OE-0804	Schleicher K7 Rhönadler	7219A	
OE-0805	Scheibe SF-27	6056	
OE-0806	Schleicher Ka.6E	4063	
OE-0810	Schleicher Rhönlerche	3075/BR	
OE-0811	Schleicher Ka.6E	4089	
OE-0814	Schleicher K.8B	8686	
OE-0815	Schleicher ASK-13	13043	
OE-0820	Bölkow Phoebus C	924	
OE-0822	Scheibe SF-27	1703E	
OE-0824	Schleicher Ka.6BR Rhönsegler	570	
OE-0826	Schleicher Ka.6E	4003	D-4401
OE-0828	Bölkow Phoebus B-1	780	
OE-0829	Scheibe Bergfalke III	5603	
OE-0830	Schleicher K.8B	8050A	
OE-0833	Scheibe L-Spatz 55	01	
OE-0834	Schleicher Rhönlerche II	3076/BR	
OE-0838	Bölkow Phoebus C	799	
OE-0840	Bölkow Phoebus A-1	803	
OE-0844	Bölkow Phoebus B-1	761	
OE-0846	Bölkow Phoebus C	821	
OE-0847	SZD-22C Mucha Standard	753	OE-0601
OE-0848	Schempp-Hirth SHK.1	48	D-8187
OE-0850	Scheibe Specht	812	
OE-0851	Bölkow Phoebus B-1	757	
OE-0853	Glasflügel H401 Kestrel	55	
OE-0854	Bölkow Phoebus C	842	
OE-0855	Bölkow Phoebus C	832	
OE-0856	Schleicher K.7 Rhönadler	7106	
OE-0858	Schleicher Rhönlerche II	102/60	D-5058
OE-0859	Schleicher K.8B	8440	
OE-0860	Bölkow Phoebus C	848	
OE-0861	Schleicher K.8B	8830	
OE-0862	Schleicher ASW-15	15008	
OE-0864	Schleicher ASW-15	15067	
OE-0865	VT-109 Pioneer	212	
OE-0866	VT-125 Sohaj	211	
OE-0868	Bölkow Phoebus C	950	

Regn.	Type	C/n	Prev.Id.
OE-0871	Schleicher K.8B	8540/A	
OE-0872	Bölkow Phoebus B-1	855	
OE-0873	Glasflügel H201B Standard Libelle	042	
OE-0875	Schempp-Hirth SH.2 Cirrus	35	
OE-0877	Schleicher Ka.6CR Rhönsegler	6325	
OE-0881	Scheibe Bergfalke III	5624	
OE-0882	Glasflügel H201B Standard Libelle	15	
OE-0884	Schleicher Rhönlerche II	659	
OE-0887	Glasflügel H201B Standard Libelle	53	
OE-0889	Schleicher K.8B	8664	
OE-0895	Scheibe Bergfalke III	5639	
OE-0897	Schempp-Hirth SH.2 Cirrus *(W/o 23.2.97)*	97	
OE-0898	SZD-22C Mucha Standard	609	OE-0541
OE-0899	Rolladen-Schneider LS-1D	79	
OE-0900	Bölkow Phoebus C-1	804	
OE-0901	Schleicher K.8B	8033A	
OE-0905	Schleicher K.8B	8852	
OE-0907	LET L-13 Blanik	174810	
OE-0908	FFA-Diamant 18	78	
OE-0911	Schleicher ASK-13	13306	
OE-0912	Schleicher K.8B	8371	
OE-0913	Glasflügel H201B Standard Libelle	220	
OE-0914	Glasflügel H201B Standard Libelle	221	
OE-0917	FFA-Diamant 18	079	
OE-0918	Schleicher ASK-13	13320	
OE-0920	Schempp-Hirth Cirrus	57	D-0220
OE-0921	Schleicher ASW-15	15162	
OE-0922	Glasflügel H201B Standard Libelle	262	
OE-0923	Glasflügel H201B Standard Libelle	257	
OE-0924	Glasflügel H201B Standard Libelle	256	
OE-0925	Glasflügel H201B Standard Libelle	198	
OE-0926	Schleicher ASK-13	13376	
OE-0928	Bölkow Phoebus B-1	730	
OE-0931	LET L-13 Blanik	175119	
OE-0932	LET L-13 Blanik	175120	
OE-0933	LET L-13 Blanik	175121	
OE-0934	LET L-13 Blanik	175122	
OE-0935	LET L-13 Blanik	175117	
OE-0936	Glasflügel H201B Standard Libelle	307	
OE-0943	SZD-30 Pirat	B-493	
OE-0945	Glasflügel H201B Standard Libelle	333	
OE-0946	Schleicher ASW-15B	15224	
OE-0947	Schleicher K.8B	8905	
OE-0949	Glasflügel H401 Kestrel 17	71	
OE-0953	Glasflügel H401 Kestrel 17	74	
OE-0955	Schleicher ASW-15B	15260	
OE-0957	Schleicher K.8B	844	OE-0525
OE-0958	Glasflügel H401 Kestrel	76	
OE-0960	Schleicher Ka.6CR Rhönsegler	6286	D-4673
OE-0961	Schleicher ASW-15B	15259	
OE-0963	Schleicher ASW-15B	15256	
OE-0965	Pilatus B4-PC11	052	
OE-0967	Glasflügel H401 Kestrel	53	
OE-0968	SZD-30 Pirat	W-315	OY-DXP
OE-0969	Glasflügel H401 Kestrel	84	
OE-0971	Pilatus B4-PC11	012	
OE-0974	Bölkow Phoebus C	874	OE-0876
OE-0975	Standard Austria	4	OE-0555
OE-0976	Schleicher ASW-15B	15283	
OE-0978	Schleicher ASW-15B	15289	
OE-0980	Pilatus B4-PC11	076	
OE-0981	Condor IV	3	
OE-0985	Pilatus B4-PC11	099	
OE-0987	LET L-13 Blanik	025718	
OE-0988	Glasflügel H401 Kestrel	102	
OE-0989	Glasflügel H201BStandard Libelle	514	
OE-0990	Scheibe L-Spatz 55 *(same c/n as D-7138)*	549	
OE-0992	LET L-13 Blanik	025915	
OE-0993	LET L-13 Blanik	025929	
OE-0994	SZD-9bis Bocian 1E	P-640	
OE-0996	Schempp-Hirth Nimbus II	63	
OE-0998	Glasflügel H201B Standard Libelle	545	
OE-5002	Schleicher ASW-15B	15366	
OE-5003	Schleicher K.7 Rhönadler	7248	
OE-5004	Glasflügel H401 Kestrel	111	

Regn.	Type	C/n	Prev.Id.
OE-5007	Rollanden-Schneider LS-1C	140	
OE-5008	Schleicher Ka.6BR Rhönsegler	491	
OE-5009	LET L-13 Blanik	026042	
OE-5013	Schleicher ASW-15B	15367	
OE-5014	Glasflügel H201B Standard Libelle	584	
OE-5015	Schleicher K.8B	W-18	
OE-5017	Glasflügel H401 Kestrel	117	
OE-5018	Glasflügel H201B Standard Libelle	583	
OE-5020	Glasflügel H401 Kestrel 17m	121	
OE-5022	LET L-13 Blanik	026136	
OE-5023	Schleicher ASW-15B	15385	
OE-5024	Glasflügel H401 Kestrel	120	
OE-5025	Schleicher ASW-15B	15413	
OE-5026	Glasflügel H401 Kestrel	58	
OE-5031	Schleicher ASK-13	13496	
OE-5034	LET L-13 Blanik	026150	
OE-5036	LET L-13 Blanik	026225	
OE-5039	Schleicher ASK-18	18003	
OE-5040	Schleicher K.8C	81005	
OE-5041	Schleicher K.8B	8893/AB	
OE-5042	LET L-13 Blanik	026248	
OE-5043	Scheibe Bergfalke III	5652	
OE-5045	Schleicher ASK-18	18011	
OE-5046	Grunau Baby IIb	3366	OE-0092
OE-5047	Schleicher ASK-18	18010	
OE-5048	Glaser-Dirks DG-100	33	
OE-5050	SZD-9 bis Bocian 1E	P-712	
OE-5051	Schleicher ASW-15	15046	
OE-5052	LET L-13 Blanik	026501	
OE-5053	Grob G.102 Astir CS	1049	
OE-5054	Grob G.102 Astir CS	1058	
OE-5055	Grob G.102 Astir CS	1060	
OE-5056	Schempp-Hirth Standard Cirrus	594	
OE-5057	Glaser-Dirks DG-100	43	
OE-5058	Schleicher K.8B	8823AB	
OE-5059	Schleicher K.8B	8824AB	
OE-5064	Grob G.102 Astir CS	1152	
OE-5069	Schleicher Rhonlerche II	unkn	
OE-5070	Schleicher ASW-19	19024	
OE-5071	Glaser-Dirks DG-100	59	
OE-5072	Schempp-Hirth Standard Cirrus	650	
OE-5073	Schleicher Ka.6E	4042	HB-853
OE-5076	Pilatus B4-PC11	191	
OE-5078	Grob G.102 Astir CS	1283	
OE-5079	Standard Cirrus 75	670	
OE-5080	Grob G.102 Astir CS	1255	
OE-5083	Schleicher ASK-13	13553	
OE-5084	Grob G.102 Astir CS	1324	
OE-5087	Grob G.102 Astir CS	1357	
OE-5089	Scheibe Spatz	F-1	
OE-5091	Grob G.102 Astir CS	1395	
OE-5092	Grob G.102 Astir CS	1384	
OE-5094	Glaser-Dirks DG-100G	85G6	
OE-5096	LET L-13 Blanik	026647	
OE-5098	Eiri PIK-20D	20515	
OE-5099	Eiri PIK-20D	20516	
OE-5101	Eiri PIK-20D	20518	
OE-5102	Eiri PIK-20D	20519	
OE-5104	Schleicher ASW-15	15102	
OE-5105	Grob G.102 Astir CS	1466	
OE-5108	Glaser-Dirks DG-200	2-4	
OE-5109	Pilatus B4-PC11AF	230	
OE-5112	Grob G.102 Astir CS	1496	
OE-5113	Grob G.102 Astir CS	1483	
OE-5117	Schleicher ASW-19	19104	
OE-5119	Grob G.102 Astir CS 77	1627	
OE-5120	Grob G.102 Astir CS	1531	
OE-5121	Grob G.102 Astir CS 77	1621	
OE-5122	Schempp-Hirth Mini-Nimbus HS-7	14	
OE-5123	Grob G.102 Astir CS 77	1630	
OE-5124	Glaser-Dirks DG-100	95G-12	
OE-5126	Grob G.102 Astir CS 77	1659	
OE-5129	Grob G.102 Astir CS Jeans	2009	
OE-5131	Schleicher ASW-19	19147	
OE-5133	Eiri PIK-20D	20559	
OE-5134	Schleicher K.8B	8718	
OE-5135	Schempp-Hirth Mini-Nimbus HS-7	8	D-3793
OE-5137	Grob G.102 Astir CS Jeans	2038	
OE-5138	Grob G.102 Astir CS Jeans	2045	
OE-5139	Grob G.102 Astir CS Jeans	2046	
OE-5141	Glaser-Dirks DG-200	2-15	
OE-5145-6	Schleicher ASW-20	20040	
OE-5146	Valentin Mistral C	MC 009/77	
OE-5147	Lanaverre CS-11/75L St.Cirrus	15	
OE-5149	SZD-41A Jantar Standard	B-811	
OE-5150	Grob G.103 Twin Astir	3022	
OE-5151	Grob G.102 Astir CS Jeans	2062	
OE-5158	Schleicher ASW-19B	19162	
OE-5159	Schleicher ASW-15B	15310	OE-0986
OE-5160	Schempp-Hirth Mini-Nimbus HS-7	42	
OE-5161	LET L-13 Blanik	026927	
OE-5164	Schleicher ASK-13	13586	
OE-5165	Grob G.102 Astir CS Jeans	2060	
OE-5166	Schleicher ASW-19	19164	
OE-5167	Grob G.102 Astir CS Jeans	2044	
OE-5169	Glaser-Dirks DG-100	46	
OE-5172	Glasflügel H206 Hornet	50	
OE-5174	Schleicher ASW-19	19168	
OE-5176	Lanaverre CS-11/75L St.Cirrus	33	
OE-5177	Grob G.103 Twin Astir	3176	
OE-5178	Scheibe L-Spatz III	822	
OE-5179	Schleicher Ka.6CR Rhönsegler	6279	
OE-5180	Schleicher ASW-19	19200	
OE-5181	Scheibe Specht	EB-001	
OE-5182	Grob G.102 Astir CS Jeans	2153	
OE-5183	LET L-13 Blanik	027064	
OE-5184	Glasflügel H303 Mosquito B	129	
OE-5185	Grob G.102 Astir CS Jeans	2161	
OE-5186	Grob G.102 Astir CS 77	1742	
OE-5187	SZD-48 Jantar Standard 2	W-879	
OE-5189	Grob G.102 Astir CS 77	1780	
OE-5190	Grob G 103 Twin Astir	3208	
OE-5191	Schleicher Rhönlerche II	3069/Br	
OE-5192	Schleicher K.8B	8266	
OE-5193	Grob G.102 Astir CS 77	1787	
OE-5194	SZD-48 Jantar Standard 2	W-883	
OE-5195	SZD-48 Jantar Standard 2	W-888	
OE-5198	SZD-48 Jantar Standard 2	W-890	
OE-5200	Glaser-Dirks DG-100 Elan	E-4	
OE-5201	Grob G.103 Twin Astir Trainer	3245-T27	
OE-5202	Schleicher K.8B	AB 81002	
OE-5203	Glaser-Dirks DG-100G	E9-G3	
OE-5205	Schempp-Hirth Standard Cirrus	393	D-9225
OE-5207	SZD-48 Jantar Standard 2	W-894	
OE-5209	Grob G.102 Astir CS 77	1820	
OE-5210	Bölkow Phoebus B-1	722	
OE-5211	Schleicher ASK-13	13569	
OE-5212	Grob G.102 Astir CS 77	1826	
OE-5213	Grob G.102 Astir CS Jeans	2241	
OE-5214	Schleicher ASW-17	17037	
OE-5215	Schleicher K.8B	8479/A	VH-GPA
	(Identity suspect)		VH-GMA
OE-5217	Schempp-Hirth Mini-Nimbus C	132	
OE-5218	Grob G.102 Speed Astir	4057	
OE-5219	Schleicher ASW-20	20223	
OE-5221	Scheibe Bergfalke III	5656	
OE-5225	Grob G.102 Astir CS 77	1838	
OE-5226	Grob G.102 Astir CS Jeans	2037	
OE-5228	Schleicher ASW-19B	19290	
OE-5229	SZD-41A Jantar Standard	B-931	
OE-5235	Schleicher ASW-19B	19293	
OE-5236-BF	PZL PW-5 Smyk	17.04.016	
OE-5239	Glasflügel Mosquito B	177	
OE-5240	Glaser-Dirks DG-200/17	2-105/1716	
OE-5244	Grob G.103 Twin Astir	3172	
OE-5246	Schleicher ASK-21	21022	
OE-5248	Glaser-Dirks DG-100G Elan	E30-G15	
OE-5249	SZD-48-1 Jantar Standard 2	B-1024	
OE-5253	SZD-42-2 Jantar 2B	B-947	
OE-5254	SZD-48-1 Jantar Standard 2	B-1037	

Regn.	Type	C/n	Prev.Id.
OE-5257	Pilatus B4-PC11AF	073	
OE-5258	Grob G.103 Twin II	3522	
OE-5259	Grob G.103 Twin Astir	3074	D-4859
OE-5261	Rolladen-Schneider LS-1F	310	
OE-5262	Schleicher K.8B	8642/19	
OE-5263	Schleicher ASK-21	21041	
OE-5264	Schleicher K.8B	8369	
OE-5265	SZD-48-1 Jantar Standard 2	B-1135	
OE-5267	Grob G.103 Twin II Acro	3620-K-7	
OE-5270	Glaser-Dirks DG-100G	E50-G28	
OE-5272	Rolladen-Schneider LS-4	4048	
OE-5273	Glaser-Dirks DG-100G	E51-G29	
OE-5274	Grob G.103A Twin II Acro	3634-K-21	
OE-5275	Grob G.102 Club IIIB	5516CB	
OE-5276	Grob G.102 Standard Astir III	5536S	
OE-5278	Rolladen-Schneider LS-3A	3076	
OE-5279	Grob G.103A Twin II Acro	3655-K-24	
OE-5280	Schleicher ASK-21	21070	
OE-5281	Schleicher ASK-21	21064	
OE-5286	SZD-48-1 Jantar Standard 2	B-1179	
OE-5287	Schleicher K.8B	222/61	
OE-5288	Rolladen-Schneider LS-4	4145	
OE-5290	Glaser-Dirks DG-200/17	2-96/1711	
OE-5291	SZD-50-3 Puchacz	B-976	
	(W/o 10.7.93 and old but re-appeared in 1.00 register)		
OE-5292	Schleicher ASW-20	20484	
OE-5293	Schempp-Hirth Ventus b/16.6	93	
OE-5295	Schleicher K.8B	8081	
OE-5298	Glaser-Dirks DG-100G Elan	E109-G79	
OE-5299	SZD-48-1 Jantar Standard 2	B-1219	
OE-5300-53	Rolladen-Schneider LS-4	4267	
OE-5301	SZD-48-1 Jantar Standard 2	B-1220	
OE-5305	Grob G.102 Club IIIB	5585CB	
OE-5306	Rolladen-Schneider LS-4	4255	
OE-5308	Rolladen-Schneider LS-4	4295	
OE-5309	Grob G.102 Speed Astir IIB	4034	
OE-5310-KB	Schempp-Hirth Nimbus III	39	
OE-5312	Grob G.103 Twin II	3746	
OE-5313	Grob G.102 Club IIIB	5592CB	
OE-5314	Rolladen-Schneider LS-4	4175	
OE-5315	Schempp-Hirth Ventus b	135	
OE-5316	Schleicher K.7 Rhönadler	7198	
OE-5317	Schleicher Rhönlerche II	05/Liz.103	
OE-5318	Rolladen-Schneider LS-4	4298	
OE-5319	Valentin Mistral C	MC 022/79	PH-674
OE-5320	Schleicher Ka.6CR Rhönsegler	827	
OE-5321	Rolladen-Schneider LS-4	4219	
OE-5322	Centrair 101A Pégase	101A-057	
OE-5323	Centrair 101A Pégase	101A-064	
OE-5324	Schempp-Hirth Ventus b	87	D-3200
OE-5325	Rolladen-Schneider LS-4	4308	
OE-5328	Scheibe Specht	64	
OE-5329	Scheibe L-Spatz	233	OE-0607
OE-5330	Valentin Mistral C	MC 054/83	
OE-5331	Schleicher ASW-15B	15347	OE-5001
OE-5332	Schempp-Hirth Ventus b/16.6	167	
OE-5333	LET L-13 Blanik	025508	D-....
OE-5334	Schempp-Hirth Nimbus 3/24.5	54	
OE-5335	Grob G.102 Speed Astir IIB	4033	
OE-5336	Schempp-Hirth Ventus b/16.6	168	
OE-5337	Scheibe Spatz A	2	OE-5067
OE-5338	Rolladen-Schneider LS-4	4377	
OE-5339	Schleicher ASW-20C	20709	
OE-5340	Rolladen-Schneider LS-4	4369	
OE-5343	Schempp-Hirth Ventus b/16.6	195	
OE-5344	Glasflügel H.401 Kestrel	81	
OE-5345	Schempp-Hirth Ventus b	188	
OE-5346	Grob G.103 Twin Astir	3110	PH-614
OE-5348-HO	Schempp-Hirth Nimbus 3	64	
OE-5349	Scheibe Bergfalke III	5521	
OE-5351	SZD-48-3 Jantar Standard 3	B-1409	
OE-5353	Rolladen-Schneider LS-4	4434	
OE-5354	Glaser-Dirks DG-300 Elan	3E-68	
OE-5357	Glaser-Dirks DG-300 Elan	3E-63	
OE-5358	Schleicher ASK-13	13639AB	
OE-5359	Rolladen-Schneider LS-4	4456	
OE-5361	Glaser-Dirks DG-100G Elan	E175-G141	
OE-5362	Glaser-Dirks DG-100G Elan	E176-G142	
OE-5364-C6	Rolladen-Schneider LS-6	6015	
OE-5365	Glaser-Dirks DG-300 Elan	3E-85	
OE-5366	Schleicher ASK-21	21262	
OE-5367	Grob G.102 Astir Standard III	5631S	
OE-5369	Glasflügel H-101 Salto	24	D-2994
OE-5370	Schleicher ASW-15B	15418	D-8663
OE-5372	Scheibe Bergfalke II	317	
OE-5374	Pilatus B4-PC11AF	122	HB-1134
OE-5375	Schleicher K.7 Rhönadler	7160	
OE-5376	Schempp-Hirth Ventus b	267	
OE-5377	Rolladen-Schneider LS-6	6058	
OE-5378	Schleicher ASK-21	21271	
OE-5382	Grob G.102 Club Astir II	5011C	
OE-5383	Rolladen-Schneider LS-6	6078	
OE-5384	Grob G.103A Twin II Acro	34068-K-298	
OE-5385	Schleicher K.8B	8535	PH-347
OE-5387	Glaser-Dirks DG-100G Elan	E193-G159	
OE-5388	Glasflügel H303 Mosquito	101	
OE-5389	Schleicher K.7 Rhönadler	345	
OE-5390	Schempp-Hirth Discus b	107	
OE-5391	Rolladen-Schneider LS-4	4545	
OE-5392	Schleicher Rhönlerche II	712	
OE-5393	Glaser-Dirks DG-300 Elan	3E-195	
OE-5394	Glaser-Dirks DG-300 Elan	3E-194	
OE-5395	Schleicher ASK-23	23075	
OE-5396	Schleicher K.8B	8872	D-3901 PH-420
OE-5397	Scheibe SF-34B	5125	
OE-5398	Rolladen-Schneider LS-4	4593	
OE-5399	Scheibe SF-34	5113	D-1477
OE-5401	Rolladen-Schneider LS-4	4606	
OE-5402	Glaser-Dirks DG-100G Elan	E203-G169	
OE-5403	Glaser-Dirks DG-100G Elan	E204-G170	
OE-5406	Rolladen-Schneider LS-4	4628	
OE-5407	Glaser-Dirks DG-100G Elan	E198-G164	
OE-5410	SG-38 Schulgleiter	01	
OE-5411	Schempp-Hirth Ventus b	63	D-7711
OE-5412	Glaser-Dirks DG-300 Elan	3E-231	
OE-5414	Rolladen-Schneider LS-6A	6133	
OE-5415	Glasflügel H201B Standard Libelle	352	D-1112
OE-5416	Schleicher K.8B	FWB.20	
OE-5418	Glasflügel H.304B	351	
OE-5419	Grob G.102 Astir CS Jeans	2157	D-4553
OE-5421	Schleicher K.8B	518	HB-681
OE-5422	Schleicher ASK-21	21354	
OE-5423	Schleicher ASK-23B	23098	
OE-5424	SZD-50-3 Puchacz	B-1629	
OE-5425	Pilatus B4-PC11	071	HB-1888 D-2200
OE-5426	Rolladen-Schneider LS-4A	4672	
OE-5428	Schleicher ASW-20CL	20861	
OE-5429	Schleicher Rhönlerche II	486	OE-0929
OE-5430	Schleicher ASW-24	24063	
OE-5431	Glaser-Dirks DG-300 Elan	3E-280C6	
OE-5432	Schleicher ASH-25	25036	
OE-5433	Grob G.102 Astir CS	1276	D-7370
OE-5434	Glaser-Dirks DG-100G Elan	E43-G24	
OE-5435	Schleicher K.8B	181/60	D-5797
OE-5436	SG-38A Schulgleiter	unkn	
OE-5437	Glaser-Dirks DG-300 Elan	3E-294	
OE-5438	LET L-13 Blanik	026026	D-9295
OE-5439	Scheibe SF-34B	5131	
OE-5440	Musger Mg.19a Steinadler	039	OE-0440
OE-5441	SZD-50-3 Puchacz	B-1721	
OE-5443	SZD-50-3 Puchacz	B-1724	
OE-5444	Glaser-Dirks DG-300 Club Elan (W/o 10.94)	3E-315/C24	
OE-5446	Schleicher ASK-21	21400	
OE-544/	Glaser-Dirks DG-300 Elan	3E-317	
OE-5448	Glaser-Dirks DG-100G Elan	E7-G1	D-6448
OE-5449-MI	Rolladen-Schneider LS-7	7035	D-1672
OE-5450	Glaser-Dirks DG-600	6-25	
OE-5451	R-26SU Gobé	AA800.065	

Regn.	Type	C/n	Prev.Id.
OE-5452	SZD-51-1 Junior	B-1830	
OE-5453	Glaser-Dirks DG-300 Club Elan	3E-333/C30	
OE-5454	Schempp-Hirth Discus b	263	
OE-5455-ZL	Rolladen-Schneider LS-7	7040	D-1689
OE-5456	Glaser-Dirks DG-100G Elan	E221-G187	
OE-5457	Glaser-Dirks DG-300 Club Elan	3E-328/C27	
OE-5458	Glaser-Dirks DG-300 Club Elan	3E-332/C29	
OE-5461	Glaser-Dirks DG-300 Club Elan	3E-331/C28	
OE-5462	Glaser-Dirks DG-300 Elan	3E-329	
OE-5463	Glaser-Dirks DG-300 Elan	3E-334	
OE-5464	Schleicher ASW-24	24038	
OE-5465	Schempp-Hirth Nimbus 2B	135	D-2202
OE-5466	SZD-36 Cobra 15A	W-670	OE-5005
OE-5468	Scheibe Bergfalke III	5597	D-6006
OE-5469	Grob G.103C Twin III A ro	34 34	
OE-5470	Rolladen-Schneider LS-4	4754	
OE-5471	Glaser-Dirks DG-300 Elan	3E-41	
OE-5472	Glaser-Dirks DG-300 Elan	3E-324	D-8300
OE-5473	Glaser-Dirks DG-300 Club Elan	3E-361/C46	
OE-5474-BL	Glaser-Dirks DG-600	6-47	
OE-5475	SZD-36A Cobra 15	W-658	D-2243
OE-5476	Grob G.102 Astir CS Jeans	2151	D-4892
OE-5479	Rolladen-Schneider LS-4	4477	D-3457
OE-5480	Schleicher ASW-24	24078	
OE-5481	Grob G.103A Twin II Acro	3688-K-39	D-8693
OE-5482	Rolladen-Schneider LS-7	7117	BGA3672/GAE
OE-5483	Rolladen-Schneider LS-7	7100	
OE-5484	Schleicher ASK-21	21446	
OE-5485	Glaser-Dirks DG-300 Elan	3E-358	
OE-5486	Schleicher K.8B	8693	D-9171
OE-5487	Schleicher K7 Rhönadler	7277	D-5222
OE-5488	Schleicher K.8B	843	D-5788
OE-5489	Rolladen-Schneider LS-7	7113	
OE-5490	Schleicher ASK-13	13290	D-0661
OE-5491	Glaser-Dirks DG-300 Elan	3E-400	
OE-5492	Schleicher K.8B	610	HB-630
OE-5493	Rolladen-Schneider LS-7	7105	
OE-5494	Glaser-Dirks DG-300 Elan	3E-399	
OE-5495	Grob G.102 Astir CS	1005	D-8942
OE-5496	Schleicher K.8B	8197	D-2064
			OE-0643
OE-5498	Glaser-Dirks DG-300 Elan	3E-393	
OE-5499	LET L-13 Blanik	027015	OE-5175
OE-5500	Schempp-Hirth Janus B	158	D-3146
OE-5501	LET L-23 Super Blanik	917812	
OE-5502	LET L-23 Super Blanik	917822	
OE-5503	Rolladen-Schneider LS-7	7158	
OE-5504	Grob Standard Cirrus	550G	D-4754
OE-5505	Glaser-Dirks DG-300 Club Elan	3E-418/C69	
OE-5506	Rolladen-Schneider LS-4B	4838	
OE-5507	Schleicher ASW-24	24165	
OE-5508	LET L-23 Super Blanik	917902	
OE-5509	Glaser-Dirks DG-300 Elan	3E-219	D-7187
OE-5510	Glaser-Dirks DG-300 Elan	3E-416	
OE-5511	Schempp-Hirth Discus CS	048CS	
OE-5512	Schleicher Rhönlerche II	3044/Br	D-4108
OE-5513	Glaser-Dirks DG-300 Elan	3E-72	
OE-5514	LET L-23 Super Blanik	917907	
OE-5515	Glaser-Dirks DG-300 Elan	3E-281	
OE-5516	Glaser-Dirks DG-300 Elan	3E-224	OY-XYZ
OE-5517	Valentin Mistral C	MC 036/81	D-4936
OE-5518	Schleicher ASW-24	24173	
OE-5519	Schleicher ASW-19	19056	D-6718
OE-5520	Glaser-Dirks DG-300 Club Elan	3E-421/C70	
OE-5521	Schleicher ASH-25	25154	
OE-5523	Glaser-Dirks DG-300 Elan	3E-368	
OE-5524	Schleicher ASW-24	24162	
OE-5526	Schempp-Hirth Ventus c	570	
OE-5527	Grob G.102 Astir CS Jeans	2030	D-3877
OE-5528	Rolladen-Schneider LS-7	7045	D-5162
OE-5529	Schempp-Hirth Discus CS	115CS	
OE-5531	Grob G.102 Astir CS Jeans	2206	D-3823
OE-5533	Schleicher ASW-15B	15404	D-8651
OE-5534	Schempp-Hirth Discus CS	109CS	
OE-5535	Schleicher ASK-21	21560	
OE-5536	Schleicher ASK-21	21564	
OE-5537	LET L-23 Super Blanik	928003	
OE-5538	Schleicher ASW-24	24033	D-2615
OE-5541	Glasflügel H205 Club Libelle	105	HB-1261
OE-5542	Swift S-1	112	
OE-5543	Schempp-Hirth Discus CS	131CS	
OE-5544	Glaser-Dirks DG-300 Club Elan	3E-438/C74	
OE-5545	Glaser-Dirks DG-300 Club Elan	3E-338/C33	BGA3766/GED
OE-5546	Rolladen-Schneider LS-6B	6152	D-8090
OE-5547	Schempp-Hirth Discus CS	138CS	
OE-5548	Bölkow Phoebus C	852	D-0089
OE-5549	Schempp-Hirth Discus CS	146CS	
OE-5550	LET L-23 Super Blanik	917908	
OE-5551	Pilatus B4-PC11	169	HB-1251
OE-5553	SZD-55-1	551192049	
OE-5554	Swift S-1	P-07/P-02	SP-3533
OE-5555	Standard Austria	14	OE-0669
OE-5556	Glasflügel H401 Kestrel	21	D-0518
OE-5557	Schempp-Hirth Discus CS	154CS	
OE-5558	Schleicher ASW-20CL	20855	D-4758
OE-5560	Rolladen-Schneider LS-4B	4922	
OE-5561	LET L-23 Super Blanik	938102	
OE-5562	Schleicher ASH-25	25085	D-2509
OE-5563	Rolladen-Schneider LS-4B	4945	
OE-5564	Schempp-Hirth Discus b	503	
OE-5565	SZD-55-1	551193053	SP-3584
OE-5566	Schleicher ASW-20L	20434	D-8953
OE-5567	Schleicher ASW-15B	15361	D-2369
OE-5568	Schempp-Hirth Discus CS	038CS	
OE-5569	Rolladen-Schneider LS-4B	4957	
OE-5570	Schempp-Hirth Discus CS	158CS	
OE-5571	Rolladen-Schneider LS-4B	4978	D-5544
OE-5572	Glaser-Dirks DG-300 Club Elan Acro	3E-447C77A10	
	(Believed w/o 1.8.98)		
OE-5574	Grob G.103C Twin III Acro	34200	
OE-5576	Grob G.103 Twin Astir	3057	OE-5347
			D-4847
OE-5577	Schleicher ASH-25	25007	D-4810
OE-5578	Grob G.103 Twin Astir	3199	D-5958
OE-5579	PZL PW-5 Smyk	17.03.015	
OE-5580	Schleicher ASK-13	13426	D-2134
OE-5581	Schempp-Hirth Discus CS	173CS	
OE-5582	SZD-51-1 Junior	B-2136	SP-3609
OE-5583	Schempp-Hirth Duo Discus	188	
OE-5584	Schempp-Hirth Discus CS	202CS	
OE-5585	SZD-55-1	551195064	
OE-5586	SZD-59 Acro	B-2165	
OE-5588	Rolladen-Schneider LS-8A	8...	
OE-5589	PZL PW-5 Smyk	17.04.004	
OE-5590	SZD-55-1	551194063	
OE-5591	Grob G.102 Astir CS	1253	HB-1310
OE-5592	Schempp-Hirth Discus CS	088CS	D-1374
OE-5593	Schleicher K.8B	8200	HB-717
OE-5594	Glaser-Dirks DG-300 Club Elan	3E-458/C81	
OE-5596	PZL PW-5 Smyk	17.03.019	
OE-5597	Schempp-Hirth Ventus 2c	5	
OE-5598	Marganski MDM-1 Fox	206	
OE-5599	SZD-51-1 Junior	B-2145	
OE-5600	Schempp-Hirth Discus CS	194CS	
OE-5601	Marganski MDM-1 Fox	P15	SP-3604
OE-5603	Schempp-Hirth Ventus 2b	24	
OE-5604	PZL PW-5 Smyk	17.03.007	
OE-5605	Glaser-Dirks DG-300 Club Elan Acro	3E-457C80A15	
OE-5606	Marganski MDM-1 Fox	202	
OE-5607	Swift S-1	102	SP-3537
OE-5608	Marganski MDM-1 Fox	P14	SP-3598
			SP-P598
OE-5610	Marganski MDM-1 Fox	205	
OE-5611	Schempp-Hirth Duo Discus	59	
OE-5612	Glaser-Dirks DG-303 Elan	3E-467	
OE-5613	Schempp-Hirth Discus CS	212CS	
OE-5614	SZD-51-1 Junior	B-2142	SP-3612
OE-5615	Glaser-Dirks DG-500 Elan Orion	5E-160X16	
OE-5616	Rolladen-Schneider LS-8A	8051	
OE-5617	Rolladen-Schneider LS-8A	8054	D-3751

Regn.	Type	C/n	Prev.Id.
OE-5618	LET L-23 Super Blanik	948205	
OE-5619	Rolladen-Schneider LS-4B	41002	
OE-5621	Rolladen-Schneider LS-4B	41001	
OE-5622	Grob G.102 Astir CS	1240	D-7321
OE-5623	Schleicher ASW-15B	15344	I-ORCO
OE-5627	Glaser-Dirks DG-300 Elan	3E-471	
OE-5629	Marganski MDM-1 Fox	212	
OE-5630	SZD-55-1	551196090	
OE-5631	Grob G.103C Twin III	34201	D-8687
OE-5632	PZL PW-5 Smyk	17.04.013	
OE-5633	Grob G.102 Astir CS Jeans	2078	D-5791
OE-5634	Glaser-Dirks DG-300 Club Elan	3E-474C84	
OE-5635	Schleicher ASW-24B	24247	
OE-5636	Schleicher ASW-27	27045	
OE-5637	Rolladen-Schneider LS-4	4406	D-9144
OE-5638	PZL PW-5 Smyk	17.05.010	
OE-5639	Schempp-Hirth Discus CS	084CS	D-2084
OE-5640	Grob G.102 Astir CS	1174	OE-5074
OE-5641	Glaser-Dirks DG-300 Elan Acro	3E-475A20	
OE-5642	LET L-13 Blanik	171413	I-MAX
			OM-1805
			OK-1805
OE-5643	Glaser-Dirks DG-100	4	HB-1264
OE-5644	SZD-59 Acro	B-2167	SP-3614
OE-5645	Rolladen-Schneider LS-8A	8103	
OE-5646	Rolladen-Schneider LS-4B	4871	D-8103
OE-5647	PZL PW-5 Smyk	17.05.14	
OE-5649-W1	PZL PW-5 Smyk	17.07.024	
OE-5650-W2	PZL PW-5 Smyk	17.07.025	
OE-5651	PZL PW-5 Smyk	17.08.010	
OE-5652	SZD-55-1	551197095	
OE-5653	Grob G.103A Twin II Acro	3635-K-16	D-3075
OE-5654	Schempp-Hirth Ventus 2b	65	
OE-5655	SZD-51-1 Junior	B-2155	
OE-5656	Glasflügel H201B Standard Libelle	283	D-0380
OE-5657	Schempp-Hirth Duo Discus	161	
OE-5658	Glaser-Dirks DG-100	15	D-3731
OE-5659	Schempp-Hirth Discus b	103	D-2952
OE-5660	Grob G.103 Twin Astir	3105	D-3962
OE-5661	Grob G.102 Club Astir II	5019C	D-6816
OE-5662	Schleicher ASK-21	21552	D-9331
OE-5663	Marganski MDM-1 Fox	222	
OE-5664	Rolladen-Schneider LS-8A	8202	
OE-5665	Grob G.102 Standard Astir III	5502	D-3080
OE-5666	Marganski MDM-1 Fox	225	
OE-5667	LET L-23 Super Blanik	988414	
OE-5668	Rolladen-Schneider LS-4B	41032	
OE-5669	Rolladen-Schneider LS-3	3037	D-2803
OE-5671	Schempp-Hirth Discus CS	060CS	D7114
OE-5672	Schempp-Hirth Discus CS	256CS	
OE-5673	SZD-51-1 Junior	B-2193	
OE-5674	LET L-23 Super Blanik	998411	
OE-5675	SZD-55-1	551191016	HB-3061
OE-5676	LET L-13 Blanik	026529	I-BZEL
OE-5677	SZD-51-1 Junior	511199244	
OE-5678	Schleicher ASW-15	15089	D-1019
OE-5...	PZL PW-5 Smyk	17.10.008	

MICROLIGHTS

OE-6000 class (Powered Hang-gliders, not self-launching)

OE-6003	Sport 167/HHM 210/1	16090/109	
OE-6016	Super Sport 163/HHM 210/1	18906	OE-8116

Regn.	Type	C/n	Prev.Id.

OE-7000 class (Three-axis Microlights)

OE-7003	Pioneer Flightstar	373	
OE-7006	Pioneer Flightstar	369	
OE-7007	Comco Ikarus Fox-C22	3063	
OE-7008	Albatros	111	
OE-7009	Sky-Walker II-300E	191	
OE-7010	Albatros	117	
OE-7011	Thruster T.500	88-295	
OE-7012	Rotec Rally 2B	7012	
OE-7015	Thruster T.300	88-330	
OE-7016	Platzer Kiebitz-B	89	
OE-7017	Rotec Rally 2B	65626/154	
OE-7018	Bronco	M02	
OE-7019	Comco Ikarus Fox-C22	9206-3433	
OE-7020	Tandem Air Sunny Sport	4092	
OE-7021	Comco Ikarus Fox-C22	9303-3493	
OE-7022	Sunwheel R	011	
OE-7025	Comco Ikarus Fox-C22	9201-3383	
OE-7026	Comco Ikarus Fox-C22	9402-3568	
OE-7027	Comco Ikarus Fox-C22	9209-3406	
OE-7028	Resurgam Mk 2	unkn	
OE-7029	Comco Ikarus Fox-C22B	9502-3652	
OE-7030	Sunwheel R	033	
OE-7031	Comco Ikarus Fox-C22B	9503-3674	
OE-7032	Comco Ikarus Fox-C22B	9505-3673	
OE-7033	Rodaro Storch	7IA16	
OE-7034	Sunwheel	034	
OE-7035	Comco Ikarus Fox-C22	9603-3705	
OE-7037	Comco Ikarus C-42 Cyclone	9610-6010	
OE-7038	Comco Ikarus C-42 Cyclone	9702-6007	
OE-7039	Comco Ikarus C-42 Cyclone	9708-6051	
OE-7040	Comco Ikarus C-42 Cyclone	9704-6020	
OE-7041	Comco Ikarus C-42 Cyclone	9801-6079	
OE-7042	Flight Design CT	98-02-03-23	
OE-7043	Zenair CH-601OE Zodiac	6-3654	
OE-7045	Comco Ikarus C-42 Cyclone	9902-6151	
OE-7046	Flight Design CT	98.12.02.43	

OE-8000 class (Flex-wing types)

OE-8011	Agro-Trike	OE-01	
OE-8012	Saturn 165/Hortner-Trike	1	
OE-8013	Nimbus 62/Minimum	120532	
OE-8015	Vega Duo Trike	88423/1	
OE-8017	Nimbus 62/Minimum	120711	
OE-8023	Austro Trike/Euro IIIM	1924	
OE-8025	Austro Trike/Euro IIIM	1123	
OE-8026	Vega 16/Minimum	87/372	
OE-8028	Vega 16PR/Minimum	86/351	
OE-8029	Vega 16M	21/84	
OE-8035	Vega 16M/Steinbach	88/428	
OE-8038	Apollo CX/1500 Racer GT	MZE 20/88	
OE-8040	Apollo CX/1500 Racer GT	MZEA 15/89	
OE-8041	Vega Duo Trike	89/510/DO02	
OE-8042	Vega Duo Trike	89/509/D01	
OE-8043	Apollo CX/1500 Racer GT	MZEA 45/89	
OE-8044	Apollo CX/1500 Racer GT	MZEA 21/88	
OE-8045	Apollo CX/1500 Racer GT	MZEA 13/90	
OE-8046	Apollo CX/1500 Racer GT	MZEA 22/89	
OE-8048	Apollo CX/1500 Racer GT	MZEA 23/90	
OE-8049	Apollo CX/1500 Racer GT	MZEA 14/90	
OE-8050	Vega Duo Trike (cancelled ?)	06/84	
OE-8051	Vega Duo Trike	90/566D03	
OE-8052	Apollo CX/1500 Racer GT	MZEA 24/90	
OE-8053	Apollo CX/1500 Racer GT	MZEA 22/90	
OE-8054	Vega 16M Trike	85/301	
OE-8055	Nimbus 62/Minimum	120618	
OE-8057	Apollo CX/1500 Racer GT	MZEA 43/90	
OE-8058	Apollo CX/1500 Racer GT	MZEA 42/901	
OE-8059	Apollo CX/1500 Racer GT	A220494	
OE-8060	Apollo CX/1500 RacerGT	MZEA 13/91	
OE-8061	Hazard 15M/Racer GT	03/922015	
OE-8062	CX II 23/Pago Jet	89804	

Regn.	Type	C/n	Prev.Id.
OE-8063	Apollo CX/1500 Racer GT	MZEA 85/91	
OE-8064	Apollo CX/1500 Racer GT	MZEA 84/91	
OE-8065	Sport 167AT/HHM210/1	17205/101	
OE-8066	HP-AT158/HHM210/1	23112	
OE-8067	Apollo CX/1500 Racer GT	MZEA 15/91	
OE-8068	Apollo CX/1500 Racer GT	MZEA 07/91	
OE-8070	Saphir 17/Minimum	15265	
OE-8071	Sport 167/HHM 210/1	17525	
OE-8072	Apollo CX/1500 Racer GT	A290693	
OE-8073	Apollo CX/1500 Racer GT	A280693	
OE-8074	Sport 167 AT/HHM 210/1	17276	
OE-8075	Super Sport 163/HHM 210/1	18410	
OE-8076	Apollo CX/1500 Racer GT	A021293	
OE-8077	Sport 167/HHM 210/1	16075	
OE-8078	Sport 167/HHM 210/1	14577	
OE-8079	Comet II 165	CMT2-1652018	
OE-8080	Apollo CX/1500 Racer GT	MZ 06/91	
OE-8081	Apollo CXM/Racer GT/R	MZ/37/92	
OE-8083	Pipistrel Spider 8F/Hazard 13M	1931610296/8083	
OE-8084	Apollo CX/1500 Racer GT	A191093	
OE-8085	Royal/Hazard 15M	6751	
OE-8086	Apollo CXM Racer GT	A280494	
OE-8087	Royal Trike R503/Karat 13	04-9409	
OE-8088	Neurajet Solo 210/Compact 35	49403329	
OE-8090	Apollo CXM Racer GT	A010894	
OE-8091	Apollo CXM Racer GT	A030295	
OE-8093	Apollo CXM Racer GT	A220395	
OE-8094	Spider/Hazard 13M	097/93/2707	
OE-8095	Apollo CXM/Racer GT	A020595	
OE-8096	Sport 167/HHM 210/1	15424/118	
OE-8097	Spider/Hazard 15M	05/93/0105	
OE-8100	Super Sport 163/HHM 210/1	18135/115	
OE-8101	Apollo C-15/Racer GT-X (c/n as OE-8108)	A020295	
OE-8102	Spider/Hazard 15M	048/95/1905	
OE-8103	Apollo CXM/Racer GT	A240795	
OE-8104	Apollo CX/1500 Racer GT	MZEA 82/91	
OE-8105	Sport 167/HHM 210/1	15112	
OE-8107	Royal/Hazard 13M	144/95	
OE-8108	Apollo CXM/Racer GT (c/n as OE-8101)	A020295	
OE-8109	Apollo CXM/Racer GT	A00196	
OE-8110	Apollo CXM/Racer GT	A00296	
OE-8111	Laser 14/HHM 210/1	050-2/7123	
OE-8112	Apollo CXM/Racer GT	A071195	
OE-8113	Spider 6D/Hazard 15M	196	
OE-8114	Apollo CXMD/Delta Jet/R	A0396	
OE-8115	Sport 180/HHM 210/1	16109	
OE-8117	Super Sport 167/HHM 210/1	15613	
OE-8118	Apollo CXM/Racer GT	A0496	
OE-8119	Apollo C15/Racer GT/R	141194	
OE-8121	Apollo CXMD/Delta Jet/R	A0397	
OE-8123	Merlin Karat 13	160995	
OE-8124	Sport 167/HHM 210/1	14538	
OE-8125	Apollo CXM/Racer GT/R	A0597	
OE-8126	Apollo CXM/Racer GT/R	A0697	
OE-8127	Apollo CXM/Racer GT/R	A0797	
OE-8128	Apollo CXM/Racer GT/R	A0198	
OE-8129	Apollo CX/1500 Racer GT	A11591	
OE-8130	Apollo CXMD Delta Jet/R	A0298/1998	

OH - FINLAND

Regn.	Type	C/n	Prev.Id.
OH-ACA	Aero Commander 500	803-80	N8464C
OH-ACN	Rockwell Commander 690A	11301	(N81405)
OH-ACO	Aero Commander 680FL	1373-46	OY-DLL
			N899NA
			N414N
OH-ADA	Fairchild-Swearingen SA.226T Merlin III	T-248	N120TT
			F-GGGH
			N10WL
			N5338M
OH-AIL	Cessna T.303 Crusader	00060	EC-ETD
			N1426C
OH-AKD	Lake LA-4-200 Buccaneer	592	N65660
OH-AKF	Lake LA-4-200 Buccaneer	710	N1205L
OH-AKI	Lake LA-4-200 Buccaneer	764	SE-GRM
			N6009V
OH-AMB	Dassault Falcon 10	193	N3BY
			N259FJ
			F-WZGY
OH-AUA	Auster Mk.5	1556	G-AJFI
			TJ531
OH-AUE	Auster 6A Tugmaster	3734	SE-ELE
			WJ373
OH-AUF	Auster Mk.4	856	G-AKRC
			MT100
OH-AVB	Auster J/5P Autocar	3275	OY-AVB
			D-EJUX
OH-AWA	Cessna 172P	74155	N5489K
OH-AWB	Cessna 152	83512	C-GMYM
			N49754
OH-AYA	American AA-1 Yankee	0402	(LN-KAZ)
			(N6202L)
OH-AYC	Grumman-American AA-1A Trainer	0088	
OH-AYE	Grumman-American AA-1A Trainer	0301	
OH-AYF	American AA-1 Yankee	0404	(LN-BFP)
			N6204L
OH-AYG	Grumman AA-1B Trainer 2	0039	
OH-AYH	Grumman AA-5 Traveler	0196	
OH-AYJ	Grumman AA-5 Traveler	0296	
OH-AYK	Grumman AA-5 Traveler	0334	N5434L
OH-AYM	Grumman AA-5 Traveler	0431	N7131L
OH-AYO	Grumman AA-5 Traveler	0478	N7178L
OH-AYP	Grumman AA-5 Traveler	0765	
OH-AYR	Grumman AA-5 Traveler	0762	
OH-AYS	Grumman AA-5B Tiger	0117	N6145A
OH-AYT	Grumman AA-5B Tiger	0219	
OH-AYU	Grumman AA-5A Cheetah	0099	
OH-BAB	Beech 23-B19 Musketeer Sport	MB-822	
OH-BAR	Beech B60 Duke	P-477	N100CD
OH-BAX	Beech 65-C90 King Air	LJ-984	LN-FOD
			N1823A
OH-BBK	Beech A36 Bonanza	E-2374	
OH-BBL	Beech A36 Bonanza	E-2375	
OH-BBM	Beech A36 Bonanza	E-2376	
OH-BBN	Beech A36 Bonanza	E-2497	
OH-BBX	Beech 95-B55 Baron	TC-1279	
OH-BCA	Bellanca 7ECA Citabria	1198-77	N4212Y
OH-BCK	Stinson 108-2 Voyager	863	SE-BCK
			NC97863
OH-BCX	Beech 65-C90 King Air	LJ-770	N88CG
			N4770M
OH-BDA	Beech 35-B33 Debonair	CD-789	
OH-BDX	Beech 60 Duke	P-194	N4AJ
			(N5AJ)
			N86TP
OH-BEX	Beech 65-C90 King Air	LJ-978	N725KR
			ZS-LBF
			N3835Z
OH-BGB	Beagle B.121 Pup 100	059	G-35-059
OH-BGE	Beagle B.121 Pup 100	098	G-35-098
OH-BJK	Bellanca 8GCBC Citabria	115-74	C-GBMZ
			N88346
OH-BJT	Bellanca 8KCAB Decathlon	26-72	N11716
OH-BKA	Beech 100 King Air	B-39	HB-GEN

Regn.	Type	C/n	Prev.Id.
OH-BLK	Beech 65-B80 Queen Air *(Wfu)*	LD-298	SE-EUU
OH-BMD	Beech A23-19 Musketeer Sport	MB-163	
OH-BMH	Beech A23-19 Musketeer Sport	MB-225	
OH-BMK	Beech A23-19A Musketeer Sport	MB-298	
OH-BML	Beech A23-19A Musketeer Sport	MB-299	
OH-BND	Pilatus Britten-Norman BN-2B-21 Islander	2171	G-BKOH
OH-BSA	Beech 300 Super King Air	FA-205	N5672A
OH-BSB	Beech 300 Super King Air	FA-206	N5672J
OH-CAC	Cessna U.206F Stationair	02364	SE-GGI
			N2387U
OH-CAD	Cessna 182F Skylane	54999	SE-EHS
			N3599U
OH-CAE	Reims/Cessna F.172H	0670	SE-FMB
			LN-LJP
OH-CAF	Reims/Cessna F.172M	1184	SE-FMF
			D-EEIA
OH-CAH	Reims/Cessna FR.172F Rocket	0065	SE-FEY
OH-CAJ	Cessna 172N	72593	N5529D
OH-CAK	Cessna 172N	73208	C-GBGT
			(N6373F)
OH-CAL	Cessna 172H	55695	9J-RFH
			ZS-ETE
			N2495L
OH-CAM	Cessna 172P	74753	N53455
OH-CAN	Cessna 172N	69701	N737VD
OH-CAO	Cessna 152	81506	C-GYBK
			(N64973)
OH-CAP	Cessna 152	79955	C-GVGD
			N757RY
OH-CAQ	Cessna 152-II	84712	N6404M
OH-CAS	Cessna 152-II	85573	N93919
OH-CAV	Cessna 172N	70621	N739LE
OH-CAW	Cessna 172N	70218	N738TE
OH-CAX	Cessna 172N	71573	N3524E
OH-CAY	Cessna 172P	74597	N555RT
			N52744
OH-CAZ	Cessna 172N	73806	N5476J
OH-CBA	Cessna A.185E	1458	N2297T
OH-CBC	Cessna 421A	0013	N2213Q
OH-CBI	Reims/Cessna F.150J	0448	
OH-CBJ	Reims/Cessna F.150J	0458	
OH-CBL	Reims/Cessna F.150J	0468	
OH-CBO	Reims/Cessna F.150J	0452	
OH-CBP	Reims/Cessna F.150J	0478	
OH-CBR	Cessna 180H	52071	N91404
OH-CBV	Reims/Cessna FA.150K Aerobat	0019	
OH-CBW	Reims/Cessna FA.150K Aerobat	0025	
OH-CBX	Reims/Cessna FA.150K Aerobat	0026	
OH-CBZ	Reims/Cessna FA.150K Aerobat	0033	
OH-CCA	Cessna 182F Skylane	54522	SE-EAD
			N3122U
OH-CCF	Reims/Cessna F.172H	0455	
OH-CCK	Reims/Cessna F.150H *(Wreck noted 1.00)*	0251	
OH-CCL	Reims/Cessna F.150H	0279	
OH-CCO	Reims/Cessna F.150H	0253	
OH-CCS	Reims/Cessna F.150H	0323	
OH-CCY	Cessna A.185E	1352	N2200T
OH-CCZ	Reims/Cessna FR.172E Rocket	0017	(G-AVYJ)
			F-WLIS
OH-CDA	Reims/Cessna FA.150K Aerobat	0034	
OH-CDD	Reims/Cessna FA.150K Aerobat	0037	
OH-CDE	Reims/Cessna FA.150K Aerobat	0038	
OH-CDF	Reims/Cessna FR.172G Rocket	0188	
OH-CDH	Cessna 310K	0090	G-ATPS
			N6990L
OH-CDI	Cessna A.185E	01529	N2779J
OH-CDK	Cessna A.185E (Robertson STOL)	01675	N1959U
OH-CDN	Cessna 180H *(Awaiting rebuild)*	52134	N9034M
OH-CDO	Cessna A.185E	01773	N5804J
OH-CDW	Reims/Cessna F.172H	0679	
OH-CEB	Reims/Cessna F.172F	0118	
OH-CEE	Reims/Cessna F.150G (Taildragger mod.)	0075	
OH-CEF	Cessna 150E	61433	N4033U
OH-CEG	Cessna 185D	0863	
OH-CEM	Reims/Cessna F.172G	0254	

Regn.	Type	C/n	Prev.Id.
OH-CEN	Reims/Cessna F.150F	63540/0061	(G-ATNF)
OH-CER	Cessna 180H	51823	N7920V
OH-CES	Reims/Cessna F.150G	0162	
OH-CET	Reims/Cessna F.150G	0142	
OH-CEU	Reims/Cessna F.150F	63470/0056	(EI-APF)
OH-CEV	Cessna A.185E	1180	N4726Q
OH-CEW	Reims/Cessna F.172H	0344	
OH-CEX	Cessna 180H	51856	N7956V
OH-CEZ	Reims/Cessna F.172H (Modified)	0386	
OH-CFA	Reims/Cessna FR.172G Rocket	0180	
OH-CFF	Reims/Cessna F.172H	0753	
OH-CFG	Cessna A.188 Agwagon	00275	SE-ETI
			N8025V
OH-CFJ	Reims/Cessna F.172L	0834	
OH-CFN	Cessna 170B	26636	D-EDBB
			OE-DBA
			HB-COO
			N3592C
OH-CFO	Cessna A.188 Agwagon	00789	N9989G
OH-CFP	Reims/Cessna F.172L	0873	
OH-CFQ	Reims/Cessna F.172M	0962	
OH-CFS	Reims/Cessna F.172M	0963	
OH-CFT	Reims/Cessna F.150L	0891	
OH-CFW	Reims/Cessna FR.172J Rocket	0416	
OH-CGA	Cessna 402B	0208	SE-FXO
			N7880Q
OH-CGB	Cessna U.206F Stationair	02237	N1526U
OH-CGC	Reims/Cessna F.150M	1147	
OH-CGD	Reims/Cessna F.150M	1177	
OH-CGH	Reims/Cessna F.172M	1045	(SE-FZL)
OH-CGI	Reims/Cessna F.172H (Modified)	0595	SE-FME
			LN-AEF
OH-CGJ	Reims/Cessna F.150L	0674	SE-FRH
OH-CGL	Reims/Cessna FA.150L Aerobat	0089	SE-FXA
OH-CGM	Cessna A.188B Agtruck	01506T	N9507G
OH-CGO	Cessna A.185E	02010	SE-FXM
			N70130
OH-CGT	Cessna A.188B Agtruck	01959T	(OH-CGQ)
			N78763
OH-CGU	Cessna A.188B Agtruck	01502T	N9497G
OH-CGW	Cessna 401B	0009	G-AXVA
			N7909Q
OH-CGX	Reims/Cessna F.172M	1449	
OH-CHD	Cessna 170B	26528	D-EFYT
			N3485C
OH-CHE	Cessna 175A Skylark	56727	SE-CTT
			N8927T
OH-CHM	Cessna 401A	0125	LN-TVN
			(LN-VYM)
			N3151K
OH-CHO	Cessna TU.206G Turbo Stationair II	03634	N7364N
OH-CHQ	Reims/Cessna F.182P Skylane	0024	
OH-CHS	Cessna 402B	1082	CB-52
			OH-CHS
			N1780G
OH-CHU	Cessna TU.206G Turbo Stationair II	04332	(N756SZ)
OH-CHV	Reims/Cessna F.182Q Skylane	0071	
OH-CHY	Reims/Cessna F.172N	1893	
OH-CHZ	Cessna TU.206G Turbo Stationair II	04970	(N735VJ)
OH-CIA	Champion 7ECA Citabria	279	
OH-CIC	Champion 7ECA Citabria	288	
OH-CID	Reims/Cessna F.172N	1897	
OH-CII	Cessna TU.206G Turbo Stationair II	05466	N6385U
OH-CIJ	Cessna A.185F	04004	(N6149E)
OH-CIL	Reims/Cessna F.172P	2080	
OH-CIN	Reims/Cessna F.152	1874	
OH-CIO	Cessna TU.206G Turbo Stationair II	06090	(N5269Z)
OH-CIP	Reims/Cessna F.152	1857	
OH-CIR	Reims/Cessna FR.172K Hawk XP	0673	D-EANJ
			(D-EDMY)
OH-CIS	Reims/Cessna F.152-II	1900	
OH-CIV	Cessna 402B	0219	SE-IHP
			PH-MAZ
OH-CIW	Cessna 172M	65340	SE-GCZ
			N5097H

Regn.	Type	C/n	Prev.Id.
OH-CIY	Cessna A.188B Agtruck	03917T	G-BKKA
			N9988J
OH-CJJ	Cessna A.185E	1418	LN-VIX
			N2260T
OH-CJM	Cessna 152	83317	N48277
OH-CKB	Reims/Cessna FA.152	0388	
OH-CKC	Reims/Cessna FA.152	0389	
OH-CKE	Reims/Cessna FA.152	0419	
OH-CKF	Reims/Cessna FA.152	0420	
OH-CKH	Cessna 172N	70074	SE-KKG
			N738LZ
OH-CKI	Cessna 182R Skylane	68278	N4855E
OH-CKK	Cessna 172N	67772	N75512
OH-CKL	Cessna 172K	59090	N7390G
OH-CKN	Cessna 177B Cardinal	02264	N35204
OH-CKO	Cessna 152	83579	C-GQQD
			N4687B
OH-CKQ	Cessna 172M	67244	C-GDRP
			N73033
OH-CKR	Cessna A.185F Skywagon	03548	N4686Q
OH-CKT	Cessna 172F	52009	SE-EAO
			N8109U
OH-CKU	Cessna 172N	73892	C-FJIK
			N6567J
OH-CKV	Cessna 150M	76935	C-GEDJ
			(N45461)
OH-CKW	Cessna 180K Skywagon	53053	N2739K
OH-CKY	Cessna 150M	76334	N2959V
OH-CLE	Cessna 152	80803	(SE-IXM)
			OH-CLE
			N25828
OH-CLO	Cessna 172P	74464	OY-CPO
			N15BH
			N52260
OH-CLT	Reims/Cessna F.172H	0738	D-ECIT
OH-CMD	Cessna 172N	68649	N733YF
OH-CME	Cessna 172N	66014	N9205H
OH-CMG	Cessna T.210N Turbo Centurion II	64546	N9550Y
OH-CMH	Cessna 172N	68309	N733HP
OH-CMI	Cessna 172N	71770	N5209E
OH-CMJ	Cessna 152-II	85425	N93162
OH-CMK	Cessna 152	80276	N24479
OH-CML	Cessna 152	81594	N65507
OH-CMM	Cessna 152	81774	N67356
OH-CMO	Cessna 172P	74899	N54169
OH-CMP	Cessna 172P	74422	N52141
OH-CMR	Cessna 182P Skylane	64924	N1361S
OH-CMT	Cessna U.206F Stationair	02702	LN-HAP
			(N33266)
OH-CMU	Cessna 152	83464	C-GQOG
			(N49503)
OH-CMV	Cessna 152-II	82281	N68355
OH-CMX	Cessna 150L	73228	N5328Q
OH-CMY	Cessna R.172K Hawk XP	3005	N758DD
OH-CNB	Reims/Cessna FR.172E Rocket	0042	
OH-CNJ	Reims/Cessna FR.172E Rocket	0001	F-WLJK
			N20001
OH-CNM	Cessna 177A Cardinal	01349	N30594
OH-CNN	Cessna 177A Cardinal	01301	N30522
OH-CNO	Cessna 150J	70066	N60099
OH-CNQ	Reims/Cessna FR.172F Rocket	0077	
OH-CNR	Cessna 150J	70065	N60092
OH-CNU	Reims/Cessna FR.172F Rocket	0100	
OH-CNV	Reims/Cessna F.150J	0459	
OH-CNW	Cessna 180H	52002	N91215
OH-CNX	Cessna 150J	70304	N60436
OH-COA	Cessna 152	81987	N67737
OH-COD	Cessna 152	82645	N89137
OH-COE	Cessna 152	81990	N67744
OH-COF	Cessna 152	81698	C-GLNJ
			N66973
OH-COG	Cessna 152	83780	C-GULK
			N5156B
OH-COK	Cessna 172N	67709	C-GYDH
			(N73835)

Regn.	Type	C/n	Prev.Id.
OH-CON	Cessna 172N	73561	C-GDGY
			(N5542G)
OH-COO	Cessna 172C	48855	SE-CYN
			N8355X
OH-COQ	Cessna 150L	72425	N6925G
OH-COR	Reims/Cessna F.172L	0833	SE-FXL
OH-COT	Cessna 172N	69416	N737GW
OH-COU	Reims/Cessna F.172H	0624	SE-FEX
OH-COV	Cessna 172N	70301	N738WU
OH-COX	Cessna A.152 Aerobat	0897	N4809A
OH-COY	Cessna 152	79480	C-GRDC
			N714WA
OH-COZ	Cessna 182P Skylane	64069	C-GWXC
			(N6052F)
OH-CPA	Piper J-3C-65 Cub	12471	SE-ATF
			44-80175
OH-CPE	Piper J-2 Cub (Modified)	1157	OH-LPA
			OH-SNB
OH-CPG	Piper J-3C-85 Cub	16879	D-EDIP
			N92415
OH-CPO	Piper PA-22-108 Colt	22-9122	SE-CZB
OH-CPP(2)	Cessna 150G	66344	C-FHCF
			CF-HCF
			N8444J
OH-CPT	Piper PA-18A-150 Super Cub	18-2632	SE-BXW
OH-CPW	Piper PA-28-180 Cherokee B	28-1518	N7572W
OH-CPX	Piper PA-18-150 Super Cub	18-8189	
OH-CQF	Cessna 172R	80230	
OH-CRA	Cessna 152	81374	N49873
OH-CRG	Cessna 177RG Cardinal RG	0654	N333WE
			N2681V
OH-CRH	Cessna 170B	20918	C-GJZM
			N8066A
OH-CSC	Cessna 195B	16067	LN-BDR
			N4483C
OH-CSG	Reims/Cessna F.172F	0100	
OH-CSN	Cessna 180	30797	N2497C
OH-CSO	Cessna 170B	26766	N4422B
OH-CSP	Cessna 170B (Modified)	25167	N1111
			N8315A
OH-CSU	Cessna U.206A	0620	N4920F
OH-CSW	Cessna 150D	60598	N4598U
OH-CSX	Cessna 140	8899	N89854
OH-CSY	Cessna 140	8292	N89268
OH-CTC	Cessna 152	82266	C-GZZS
			N68339
OH-CTD	Cessna 172N	68254	C-GWZQ
			N733FD
OH-CTE	Cessna TU.206G Turbo Stationair II	06883	OY-CGE
			N9534R
OH-CTH	Cessna 152	83570	C-GDZL
			(N46628)
OH-CTK	Cessna 150M	78426	C-GFVL
			(N9478U)
OH-CTL	Cessna 172M	66211	N9537H
OH-CTM	Cessna 152	79733	C-GPSS
			N757GR
OH-CTO	Cessna 152	85423	OY-CSS
			N93158
OH-CTP	Cessna 172N	73624	N9173G
OH-CTQ	Cessna 182P Skylane	64729	C-GVPF
			N9184M
OH-CTS	Cessna 182P Skylane	62018	N7029Q
OH-CTT	Cessna 150J	70776	C-GASR
			N61065
OH-CTU	Cessna 172M	67525	C-GQNP
			N73517
OH-CTW	Cessna 150H	67736	CF-WPW
			N7036S
OH-CTY	Cessna 182Q Skylane	67492	N4971N
OH-CUB	Piper J-3C-65D Cub	12320	D-EFIL
			HB-OBT
			44-80024
OH-CVA	Cessna 150F	63334	N699LC
			N6734F

Regn.	Type	C/n	Prev.Id.
OH-CVB	Cessna 172P	75246	N62286
OH-CVD	Cessna 172P	75310	N62610
OH-CVE	Cessna 182P Skylane	63510	N5741J
OH-CVK	Cessna 172N	73786	N5418J
OH-CVL	Cessna 172M	65792	C-GVOT
			N9848Q
OH-CVM	Cessna 172P	74014	N5214K
OH-CVO	Reims/Cessna F.150J	0417	LN-NFR
			SE-FKP
			N13724
OH-CVP	Cessna 152	83201	N47258
OH-CVQ	Cessna 172P	74072	N5342K
OH-CVS	Cessna 172RG Cutlass	0327	N5295U
OH-CVT	Cessna A.185F Skywagon	02977	N500BW
			C-GJBI
			N102WC
			(N5012R)
OH-CVY	Cessna 152	82185	C-GYRY
			(N68207)
OH-CVZ	Cessna 172P	75663	C-FHXS
			N64979
OH-CWB	Cessna 172M	62571	C-GCZC
			N13204
OH-CWE	Cessna 182H Skylane	56418	D-EKWE
			N8318S
OH-CWH	Cessna 175C Skylark	57108	SE-EAI
			N8508X
OH-CWM	Cessna 152	80391	N204JA
			(N24808)
OH-CWO	Cessna 152	82757	N89465
OH-CWQ	Cessna 170B	25798	C-GMJJ
			N3154A
OH-CWW	Cessna U.206C Stationair	1076	LN-IKC
			N29106
OH-CWY	Cessna A.150L Aerobat	0368	C-GGYM
			N70CA
			N40CF
			N6068J
OH-CXO	Cessna 750 Citation X	0022	N10JM
			(N722CX)
			N52639
			(N5116)
			N51313
OH-CYY	Cessna R.172K Hawk XP	3121	N232JA
			N758HZ
OH-CZG	Cessna 404 Titan	0033	SE-GZG
			Navy 87001
			SE-GZG
			(N5414G)
OH-DAA	Diamond DA.20-A1 Katana	10249	
OH-DAK	Cessna A.185F Skywagon	02880	LN-DAK
			(N3445Y)
OH-EBC	Embraer EMB.110P1 Bandeirante	110-258	PT-SAX
OH-EBD	Embraer EMB.110P1 Bandeirante	110-439	N110EB
OH-EKR	Cessna 421C Golden Eagle II	1235	N421MJ
			N421CF
			N396CC
			(N236MA)
			(N8BV)
			N2723C
OH-EMA	Scintex Piel CP.301C2 Emeraude	574	
OH-ESM	Piper PA-32R-301T Turbo Saratoga	32R-8429026	N4377D
			N9630N
OH-EWA	Extra EA.300	020	D-EFCS
OH-FAE	SAAB-Scania SF.340A	139	SE-F39
OH-FAF	SAAB-Scania SF.340B	167	SE-F67
OH-FMA	Fouga CM-17D Magister	37	FM-37
OH-FMM	Fouga CM-17D Magister	51	FM-51
OH-FPC	Dassault Falcon 20F	345	N133AP
			F-GHMD
			N678BM
			N4463F
			F-WMKI

Regn.	Type	C/n	Prev.Id.
OH-GLB	Gates Learjet 24D	24D-262	N110PS
			N38788
			OH-GLB
			N2GR
			N2GP
OH-HAC	Bell 206B Jet Ranger II	1007	SE-HPI
OH-HAF	Robinson R-22 Beta	0655	
OH-HAP	Hughes 369HM	44-0247M	HH-1
OH-HAQ	Aérospatiale AS.355F Ecureuil 2	5090	N500HH
OH-HAT(2)	Agusta-Bell 206B Jet Ranger III	8720	
OH-HAU	Agusta-Bell 206B Jet Ranger II	8257	LN-OTK
			SE-HGB
			D-HAVU
OH-HAV	Schweizer 269C	S-1277	SE-HUY
			OY-HED
OH-HAW	Agusta A.109A-II	7327	N1BN
			N109NA
OH-HAX	Hughes 269C	120-0078	SE-HDX
OH-HAY	Hughes 269C	127-0662	SE-HNK
			N58210
OH-HCB	Bölkow BO.105S	S-396	N10360
OH-HCC	Bölkow BO.105CBS	S-546	AB-6
			Dubai Pol:106
			D-HDNU
OH-HCD	Bölkow BO.105CBS	S-547	AB-7
			Dubai Pol:107
			D-HDNV
OH-HCE	Hughes 269C	S-1316	SE-HTA
OH-HCF	DHC-1 Chipmunk	C1/0016	OH-HCD
	(Lycoming 0-360-A3A)		G-AOSV
			WB564
OH-HCG	Aérospatiale AS.350B2 Ecureuil	2710	SE-JBX
OH-HCH	Eurocopter EC.135P1	0008	D-HPOZ
			D-HECH
OH-HED	Robinson R-44 Clipper	0298	
OH-HEK	Robinson R-22 Beta	0742	
OH-HES	Robinson R-44 Astro	0273	LN-OAB
			(SE-JDH)
OH-HEW	Robinson R-22 Mariner	2420M	
OH-HHC	Hiller UH-12B	732	RNethAF:O-4
			54-2938
OH-HHP	Hughes 269C	70-0022	SE-HNI
			PH-HDH
			(PH-GEA)
			G-BBIW
			N9613F
OH-HHS	Schweizer 269C	S-1230	N7504L
OH-HHT	Robinson R-44 Astro	0014	SE-JDG
			N144CH
OH-HIE	Agusta-Bell 206A Jet Ranger II	8177	
OH-HIF	Agusta-Bell 206B Jet Ranger II	8372	
OH-HIN	Hughes 269C	60-0931	SE-HLC
			N1098Y
OH-HJL	Bell 206L Long Ranger	45084	SE-HSO
			C-GISM
			N16628
OH-HKC	Heinonen HK-1B	003	
OH-HKI	Bölkow BO.105S	S-731	D-HECB
			Fv.09415
			D-HDRS
OH-HKP	Robinson R-22 Beta	0730	
OH-HKX	Heinonen HK-2 Valkuainen	1	
OH-HKY	Bell 206A Jet Ranger	125	G-BPKU
			N26BF
			N6251N
OH-HLB	Robinson R-22	0131	SE-HOH
OH-HLK	Agusta-Bell 206B Jet Ranger II	8532	G-BEPP
			F-GAML
OH-HLP	Bell 206B Jet Ranger II	1766	N49587
OH-HLT	Hughes 269C	128-0737	N58222
OH-HMA	Bölkow BO.105C	S-88	D-HDCM
			HB-XEI
			D-HDCM
OH-HME	Robinson R-22 Beta	1357	LN-OBO
			N8081J

Regn.	Type	C/n	Prev.Id.
OH-HMP	Hughes 369D	51-0981D	N7102G
			N5012G
OH-HMS	Bölkow BO.105S	S-703	D-HMBV(3)
			Fv09414
			D-HNRK
			(D-HDRK)
OH-HMT	Schweizer 269C	S-1447	
OH-HMZ	Robinson R-22 Beta	1881	G-RZZB
OH-HNS	Bölkow BO.105S	S-762	D-HNWI
			D-HDXX
OH-HOC	Robinson R-22 Beta	1339	
OH-HOD	Robinson R-22 Beta	1601	
OH-HOE	Robinson R-22 Beta	1979	
OH-HOH	Bell 206L Long Ranger	45030	C-GIIP
			N221AM
			N66BH
			N66LJ
			N49770
OH-HOT	Bell 206B Jet Ranger II	3552	JA9321
			N2230W
OH-HPJ	Robinson R-22 Beta	2411	LN-OBD
			N8152H
OH-HPK	Robinson R-22 Beta	1991	N2345P
OH-HPO	Robinson R-22 Beta	0828	G-WAGI
			N26584
OH-HPV	Robinson R-22 Beta	1735	
OH-HPY	Enstrom F-28A	136	N9579
OH-HRF	Agusta-Bell 206A Jet Ranger II	8286	
OH-HRG	Agusta-Bell 206A Jet Ranger II	8295	
OH-HRH	Agusta-Bell 206B Jet Ranger II	8380	
OH-HRI	Agusta-Bell 206B Jet Ranger III	8599	
OH-HSR	Bell 206B Jet Ranger II	1494	SE-HOX
			N200PC
			N59626
OH-HSS	Enstrom F-28A	075	
OH-HTE	Robinson R-22 Mariner	1771M	G-ISPL
			SE-JAL
OH-HTR	Aérospatiale SA.360C Dauphin	1024	
OH-HUG	Enstrom 280C Shark	1123	SE-HGN
OH-HVD	Agusta-Bell AB.412	25540	
OH-HVE	Agusta-Bell AB.412	25541	
OH-HVF	Aérospatiale AS.332L Super Puma	2218	F-WMHE
			F-WYMI
OH-HVG	Aérospatiale AS.332L Super Puma	2221	
OH-HVH	Agusta-Bell AB.412	25609	
OH-HVI	Aérospatiale AS.332L1 Super Puma	2341	
OH-HVJ	Agusta-Bell AB.412EP	25903	
OH-HWA	Hughes 369E	0487E	D-HWAG
OH-HWC	Robinson R-22 Mariner	2055M	OY-HFS
OH-HWD	Robinson R-22 Beta	1270	HB-XVG
OH-HWE	Hughes 369E	0427E	D-HFAZ
OH-HWF	Robinson R-22 Beta	1702	HB-XXX
OH-HWG	Robinson R-22 Beta	2176	G-BVCI
OH-HWH	Hughes 369D	50-0702D	D-HSUR
			CS-HCU
			D-HSUR
			G-HEWT
			N808F
			N1095D
OH-HYY	Enstrom 280C Shark	1083	N280EC
			TG-WEY
OH-ILI	Klemm Kl.25D.VIIR	1129	
OH-JAB	BAe. Jetstream Series 3202	835	G-BUIO
			C-GZRT
			G-31-835
OH-JET	BAe.125 Series 700B	257136	G-5-545
			G-BIRU
OH-JLK	Cessna TU.206G Turbo Stationair II	06134	LN-IKT
			(N6088Z)
OH-JOB	CEA Jodel DR.1050 Ambassadeur (Modified)	204	
OH-JUS	Maule M-4-210C Rocket	1047C	SE- IGF
			LN-VYD
OH-KLS	Cessna 152	82409	SE-KLS
			N68940

Regn.	Type	C/n	Prev.Id.
OH-KNE	Mitsubishi MU-300 Diamond	A.014SA	N339DM
			N15TW
OH-KOG	DHC-6 Twin Otter 310	642	
OH-KOT	Cessna 150M	76768	C-GMFZ
			N45171
OH-KRA	Aeritalia/SNIAS ATR-72-201	126	F-WWEM
OH-KRB	Aeritalia/SNIAS ATR-72-201	140	F-WWER
OH-KRC	Aeritalia/SNIAS ATR-72-201	145	F-WWES
OH-KRD	Aeritalia/SNIAS ATR-72-201	162	F-WWEM
OH-KRE	Aeritalia/SNIAS ATR-72-201	174	F-WWEE
OH-KRF	Aeritalia/SNIAS ATR-72-201	324	F-WWEU
OH-KRH	Aeritalia/SNIAS ATR-72-201	212	B-22705
			F-WWEB
OH-KRK	Aeritalia/SNIAS ATR-72-201	251	B-22706
			F-WWEV
OH-KRL	Aeritalia/SNIAS ATR-72-201	332	B-22710
			F-WWLN
OH-KYC	Piper PA-31-350 Chieftain	31-8052186	SE-KYC
			N4502V
OH-KZC	S.A.I. KZ-VII Laerke	195	
OH-KZE	S.A.I. KZ-VII Laerke	168	OY-ABC
OH-LBO	Boeing 757-2Q8	28172	N1789B
OH-LBR	Boeing 757-2Q8	28167	
OH-LBS	Boeing 757-2Q8	27623	N5573K
OH-LBT	Boeing 757-2Q8	28170	
OH-LBU	Boeing 757-2Q8	29377	
OH-LCH	Douglas DC-3C	6346	DO-11
			OH-LCH
			42-2033
			(NC34953)
OH-LGA	McDonnell-Douglas MD-11	48449	
OH-LGB	McDonnell-Douglas MD-11	48450	
OH-LGC	McDonnell-Douglas MD-11	48512	
OH-LGD	McDonnell-Douglas MD-11	48513	
OH-LMA	McDonnell-Douglas DC-9-87	49403	
OH-LMB	McDonnell-Douglas DC-9-87	49404	
OH-LMC	McDonnell-Douglas DC-9-87	49405	
OH-LMG	McDonnell-Douglas DC-9-87	49625	
OH-LMH	McDonnell-Douglas DC-9-83	53245	
OH-LMN	McDonnell-Douglas DC-9-82	49150	(XA-AMP)
OH-LMO	McDonnell-Douglas DC-9-82	49151	(XA-AMQ)
OH-LMP	McDonnell-Douglas DC-9-82	49152	
OH-LMR	McDonnell-Douglas DC-9-82	49284	
OH-LMS	McDonnell-Douglas DC-9-82	49252	
OH-LMT	McDonnell-Douglas DC-9-82	49877	
OH-LMU	McDonnell-Douglas DC-9-83	49741	
OH-LMV	McDonnell-Douglas DC-9-83	49904	
OH-LMW	McDonnell-Douglas DC-9-82	49905	
OH-LMX	McDonnell-Douglas DC-9-82	49906	
OH-LMY	McDonnell-Douglas DC-9-82	53244	
OH-LMZ	McDonnell-Douglas DC-9-82	53246	
OH-LPA	McDonnell-Douglas DC-9-82	49900	EC-FJQ
			EC-893
			N64480
			N6202D
OH-LPB	McDonnell-Douglas DC-9-82	49966	SE-DLX
			N6204N
OH-LPC	McDonnell-Douglas DC-9-82	49965	SE-DLV
			N6204C
OH-LPD	McDonnell-Douglas DC-9-83	49710	EC-GFJ
			EC-159
			SX-BAQ
			HB-IUI
			XA-TOR
OH-LPE	McDonnell-Douglas DC-9-83	49401	EC-FZQ
			EC-749
			N902PJ
			EI-CBN
			EC-FEQ
			EC-714
			EI-CBN
			EC-ECN
			N6200N

Regn.	Type	C/n	Prev.Id.
OH-LPF	McDonnell-Douglas DC-9-83	49574	EC-FVR EC-591 N574PJ EC-EFU EC-348 EC-EFU
OH-LPG	McDonnell-Douglas DC-9-83	49708	EC-GKS EC-440 EC-FVV EC-607 TC-RTU XA-TUR N6203U
OH-LPH	McDonnell-Douglas DC-9-83	49623	SE-DHN
OH-LVA	Airbus A.319-112	1073	F-WWID D-AVWG
OH-LVB	Airbus A.319-112	1107	D-AVWS
OH-LYP	McDonnell-Douglas DC-9-51	47696	N9MD OH-LYP
OH-LYR	McDonnell-Douglas DC-9-51	47736	
OH-LYS	McDonnell-Douglas DC-9-51	47737	9Y-TFF (OH-LYS)
OH-LYT	McDonnell-Douglas DC-9-51	47738	
OH-LYU	McDonnell-Douglas DC-9-51	47771	
OH-LYV	McDonnell-Douglas DC-9-51	47772	N8713Q
OH-LYW	McDonnell-Douglas DC-9-51	47773	N8714Q
OH-LYX	McDonnell-Douglas DC-9-51	48134	
OH-LYY	McDonnell-Douglas DC-9-51	48135	
OH-LYZ	McDonnell-Douglas DC-9-51	48136	
OH-LZA	Airbus A.321-211	0941	D-AVZT
OH-LZB	Airbus A.321-211	0961	D-AVZU
OH-MAB	Maule M-6-235CSuper Rocket	7384C	N49646
OH-MAC	Maule M-5-235C Lunar Rocket	7333C	N275RX
OH-MAF	Cessna U.206A	0639	N4939F 5Y-ANK N4939F
OH-MAI	Maule M-5-235C Lunar Rocket	7314C	N5638M
OH-MAJ	Maule MX.7-180 Star Rocket	11064C	
OH-MAT	Maule M-7-235 Super Rocket	4030C	N56636
OH-MAU	Maule MX.7-235 Star Rocket	10068C	
OH-MAX	Maule M-5-235C Lunar Rocket	7318C	N5639L
OH-MIA	Maule M-5-235C Lunar Rocket	7181C	SE-GTR
OH-MIB	Mitsubishi MU-2B-30	532	N30SA N8400E (N444UP) N8400E N156MA
OH-MIC	Mitsubishi MU-2B-30	557	OY-CUG N314MA N73MC N192MA C-GWID N192MA
OH-MIK	Maule M-6-235C Super Rocket	7392C	N5649D
OH-MIL	Maule M-6-235CSuper Rocket	7427C	N56485
OH-MIV	Piper PA-32R-301 Saratoga SP	32R-8213035	SE-KRU N8146R
OH-MOI	Maule M-6-235CSuper Rocket	7189C	N235LY
OH-MRS	Piper PA-31-310 Navajo	31-7400984	SE-GBS
OH-MVN	Dornier 228-212	8233	D-CBDB(4) D-CATE(2)
OH-MVO	Dornier 228-212	8232	D-CATD(2)
OH-MXN	Lake LA-4-200 Buccaneer	934	G-BMXN EC-DHI N2872P
OH-NAD	Cessna 170A	19600	N5547C
OH-NBB	Cessna 172M	63963	N21526
OH-NBE	Piper PA-34-200T Seneca II	34-8170050	OY-NBB (OY-CJN) N8306H C-GSVL N8306H
OH-NEU	Reims/Cessna FA.152 Aerobat	0422	
OH-PAB	Piper PA-28-151 Cherokee Warrior	28-7515201	
OH-PAC	Piper PA-28-180 Cherokee Archer	28-7505109	
OH-PAD	Piper J-3C-65 Cub	12522	D-EJIB LN-SAG 44-80226
OH-PAE	Piper J-3C-65 Cub	13137	D-EMYR OO-AVZ 44-80841
OH-PAM	Piper PA-28R-200 Cherokee Arrow	28R-7635265	SE-GNK
OH-PAN	Piper PA-28-151 Cherokee Warrior	28-7615164	
OH-PAR	Piper PA-30-160 Twin Comanche B	30-1597	(G-BBYN) OH-PAR G-BBYN PH-ATS N8437Y
OH-PAY	Piper PA-42-1000 Cheyenne 400	42-5527040	JA8870 N9219G N9524N
OH-PBA	Piper PA-28RT-201T Turbo Arrow IV	28R-8431007	N4332J
OH-PCB	Piper PA-28-140 Cherokee B	28-26116	
OH-PCE	Piper PA-28-140 Cherokee B	28-26276	N5552U
OH-PCH	Piper PA-28-160 Cherokee B	28-26296	
OH-PCI	Piper PA-28-160 Cherokee B	28-26297	
OH-PCJ	Piper PA-28-140 Cherokee B	28-26298	
OH-PCK	Piper PA-28-140 Cherokee B	28-26309	
OH-PCL	Piper PA-28-140 Cherokee C	28-26605	
OH-PCN	Piper PA-28-140 Cherokee C	28-26699	N5867U
OH-PCO	Piper PA-28-140 Cherokee C	28-26763	
OH-PCP	Piper PA-28-140 Cherokee C	28-26774	
OH-PCQ	Piper PA-28-140 Cherokee C	28-26604	N5779U
OH-PCU	Piper PA-32-260 Cherokee Six	32-1281	
OH-PCW	Piper PA-28-140 Cherokee C	28-26411	(SE-FHI)
OH-PDB	Piper PA-28-140 Cherokee C	28-26610	
OH-PDD	Piper PA-28R-200 Cherokee Arrow	28R-7135010	(SE-FPP)
OH-PDF	Piper PA-28-140 Cherokee E	28-7325150	
OH-PDG	Piper PA-28R-200 Cherokee Arrow	28R-7335165	PA-6 OH-PDG
OH-PDH	Piper PA-28-140 Cherokee E	28-7325217	
OH-PDI	Piper PA-28-140 Cherokee E	28-7325337	
OH-PDJ	Piper PA-28-160E Cherokee	28-7325330	
OH-PDL	Piper PA-28-160F Cherokee	28-7425006	
OH-PDO	Piper PA-18-150 Super Cub	18-1446	D-EKQB ALAT 51-15446
OH-PDP	Piper PA-28-160E Cherokee	28-7325323	(SE-GAV)
OH-PDQ	Piper PA-28-140 Cherokee (Modified)	28-20094	SE-EIT
OH-PDT	Piper PA-28-140 Cherokee Cruiser	28-7525077	
OH-PDU	Piper PA-28-160F Cherokee	28-7425414	
OH-PDV	Piper PA-28-161 Warrior II	28-7916336	(SE-ICI)
OH-PDW	Piper PA-25-235 Pawnee B	25-3673	SE-EPX
OH-PDX	Piper J-3C-85 Cub	15179	D-EFIB N42857
OH-PDZ	Piper PA-25-235 Pawnee C	25-4163	SE-EZA
OH-PEA	Piper PA-28R-201 Cherokee Arrow III	28R-7737036	C-GQHD
OH-PEM	Piper PA-28R-180 Cherokee Arrow	28R-30406	SE-FDM N4545J
OH-PEN	Piper PA-28-181 Archer II	2890113	SE-KIC
OH-PEO	Piper PA-23-250 Aztec B	27-2104	SE-ECO
OH-PEP	Piper PA-18-135 Super Cub	18-3105	LN-LJL OL-L31 53-4705
OH-PET	Piper PA-28-181 Cherokee Archer II	28-7690067	OY-BLC
OH-PEU	Piper PA-28-161 Warrior II	28-8116165	N8345T
OH-PEV	Piper PA-28-180 Cherokee C	28-2133	SE-EMT
OH-PEW	Piper PA-25-235 Pawnee	25-2579	SE-IUR G-ATYA 5B-CAA N6885Z
OH-PGA	Piper PA-28RT-201T Turbo Arrow IV	28R-8331014	N8341F
OH-PHA	Piper PA-31T Cheyenne	31T-7620001	OY-BSB C-GNPT N54976
OH-PHE	Piper PA-28-161 Cherokee Warrior II	28-7716103	SE-GPS N9622N
OH-PIA	Piper PA-28-140 Cherokee	28-21561	(SE-EYF)
OH-PIF	Piper PA-28-140 Cherokee	28-21864	(SE-EYW)
OH-PIG	Piper PA-25-235 Pawnee B	25-3959	N7766Z

Regn.	Type	C/n	Prev.Id.
OH-PIJ	Piper PA-28-140 Cherokee	28-23353	
OH-PIL	Piper PA-25-235 Pawnee C	25-4164	
OH-PIO	Piper PA-28-140 Cherokee	28-22707	N4332J
OH-PIR	Piper PA-28-140 Cherokee	28-23580	
OH-PIT	Piper PA-18-150 Super Cub	18-8598	
OH-PIY	Piper PA-28-235 Cherokee B	28-10919	(SE-EYK)
OH-PJC	Piper PA-28-140 Cherokee	28-24341	
OH-PJD	Piper PA-28-140 Cherokee	28-24426	SE-FDK
OH-PJE	Piper PA-28-140 Cherokee	28-24196	N1774J
OH-PJF	Piper PA-28-140 Cherokee B	28-25482	
OH-PJH	Piper PA-28-140 Cherokee B	28-25590	
OH-PJJ	Piper PA-28-140 Cherokee B	28-25686	
OH-PJK	Piper PA-18-150 Super Cub	18-8787	
OH-PJO	Piper PA-28-140 Cherokee B	28-26050	
OH-PJQ	Piper PA-28-140 Cherokee B	28-25290	(SE-FHH)
OH-PJR	Piper PA-28R-200 Cherokee Arrow	28R-35257	(SE-FFX)
OH-PJS	Piper PA-28-140 Cherokee B	28-25698	(SE-FHF)
OH-PJU	Piper PA-28R-200 Cherokee Arrow	28R-35286	
OH-PJV	Piper PA-28R-200 Cherokee Arrow	28R-35267	
OH-PJW	Piper PA-28R-200 Cherokee Arrow	28R-35289	
OH-PJX	Piper PA-28R-200 Cherokee Arrow	28R-35383	
OH-PJY	Piper PA-28-140 Cherokee B	28-26009	
OH-PKT	Piper PA-28-181 Archer II	28-8490093	N4368M
OH-PMI	Piper PA-28R-180 Cherokee Arrow	28R-30225	LN-UXN
OH-PMK	Piper PA-28R-200 Cherokee Arrow	28R-7335030	N15161
OH-PMU	Piper PA-32R-301T Turbo Saratoga	32R-8129083	N8409B
OH-PNB	Piper PA-31-310 Navajo	31-609	N6714L
OH-PNG	Piper PA-31-310 Navajo	31-825	
OH-PNJ	Piper PA-23-250 Aztec E	27-7304983	N14388
OH-PNL	Piper PA-31-310 Navajo	31-253	SE-FLE
			D-INKA
			(D-IDUL)
			N9190Y
OH-PNO	Piper PA-31-310 Navajo	31-273	SE-FDR
OH-PNU	Piper PA-31-350 Navajo Chieftain	31-7752027	N62993
OH-PNX	Piper PA-31-350 Chieftain	31-8052040	ES-PAG
			SE-IDC
OH-PNY	Piper PA-31-350 Navajo Chieftain	31-7652079	LN-SAB
			(SE-GNX)
OH-POK	Piper PA-18-150 Super Cub	18-8509	C-GUUL
			N4270Z
OH-POM	Piper PA-20 Pacer (Cvtd. from PA-22-150)	22-4250	SE-CDO
OH-PPG	Piper PA-36-300 Pawnee Brave	36-7560005	SE-GIV
"OH-PPS"	Piper PA-23-250 Aztec D	27-4017	N612RS
			N6744Y
	(Painted as such but not officially regd.)		
OH-PRB	Piper PA-31-310 Navajo	31-7812124	N27793
OH-PRK	Piper PA-28RT-201 Arrow IV	28R-8118064	N83730
OH-PRS	Piper PA-28-140 Cherokee	28-20305	LN-AEB
			N11C
OH-PRT	Piper PA-32T-300 Lance	32R-7885011	N3602M
OH-PSA	Piper PA-18A-150 Super Cub	18-6900	LN-BDL
			OY-AIM
			N9878D
OH-PST	Piper PA-23-250 Aztec E	27-7305013	OY-BJR
	(Wreck noted 1.00)		G-BASK
			N40214
OH-PTA	Piper PA-38-112 Tomahawk	38-78A0056	
OH-PTG	Piper PA-28-140 Cherokee Fliteliner	28-7125604	OY-DTG
			N675FL
OH-PTH	Piper PA-28-161 Warrior II	28-8016293	SE-IDL
OH-PTI	Piper PA-28-180 Cherokee	28-1650	SE-EIL
OH-PTJ	Piper PA-28R-200 Cherokee Arrow	28R-7235221	(SE-KLP)
			N5299T
OH-PTU	Piper PA-23-250 Aztec C	27-3677	SE-EYE
OH-PUL	Piper PA-24-180 Comanche	24-3021	N7802P
OH-PUM	Piper PA-20 Pacer	20-341	SE-CTC
			N7431K
OH-PVA	Partenavia P.68	10	
OH-PVD	Piper PA-34-200 Seneca	34-7250186	OY-MVD
			D-GHFC
			N4939T
OH-PVL	Piper PA-28-151 Cherokee Warrior	28-7415493	C-GCXZ
			N43442
OH-PVN	Piper PA-28R-180 Cherokee Arrow	28R-30484	SE-FCF
OH-PWB	Piper PA-28-161 Warrior II	28-8616030	N9258A
OH-PVW	Piper PA-28R-180 Cherokee Arrow	28R-31011	D-EMWE
			N7693J
OH-PYM	Piper PA-28RT-201T Turbo Arrow IV	28R-8131139	N8392M
OH-PYW	Piper PA-28-181 Cherokee Archer II	28-7790557	N81AB
OH-PZL	Piper PA-34-200T Seneca II	34-7970047	SE-IZL
			N2120H
OH-RAA	Robin HR.200/160	75	
OH-RAB	Robin HR.200/120B	81	
OH-SAC	SAAB-Scania SF.340A	081	N374DC
			F-GELG
			SE-E81
OH-SAD	SAAB-Scania SF.340A	083	N376DC
			F-GFBZ
			SE-E83
OH-SAE	SAAB-Scania SF.340A	117	N378DC
			F-GHDB
			SE-F17
OH-SAF	SAAB-Scania SF.340A	143	N375DC
			F-GHMK
			SE-F43
OH-SAG	SAAB-Scania SF.340A	007	YL-BAG
			SE-LBP
			HB-AHB
			SE-E07
OH-SBA	Short SC.7 Skyliner 3A-100	SH.1908	SE-GEY
			LN-NPC
			G-BAIT
			G-14-80
OH-SCB	SOCATA MS.893A Rallye Commodore 180	10654	
OH-SCC	SOCATA MS.893A Rallye Commodore 180	10697	
OH-SCF	SOCATA MS.893A Rallye Commodore 180	10720	
OH-SCH	SOCATA MS.880B Rallye-Club	1208	
OH-SCK	SOCATA MS.880B Rallye-Club	1286	
OH-SCM	SOCATA MS.880B Rallye-Club	1320	
OH-SCN	SOCATA MS.880B Rallye-Club	1330	
OH-SCT	SOCATA MS.880B Rallye-Club	1343	
OH-SCU	SOCATA MS.893A Rallye Commodore 180	10994	
OH-SCV	SOCATA MS.883 Rallye 115	1367	
OH-SCW	SOCATA MS.880B Rallye-Club	1373	
OH-SCX	SOCATA MS.880B Rallye-Club	1375	(G-AXHH)
OH-SCZ	SOCATA MS.894A Minerva 220	11069	
OH-SDA	SOCATA MS.893A Rallye Commodore 180	11447	
OH-SDC	SOCATA MS.892A Rallye Commodore 150	11444	
OH-SDG	SOCATA MS.880B Rallye-Club	1563	
OH-SDI	SOCATA MS.880B Rallye-Club	1650	
OH-SDJ	SOCATA MS.892A Rallye Commodore 150	11490	
OH-SDK	SOCATA MS.883 Rallye 115	1514	
OH-SDL	SOCATA MS.892A Rallye Commodore 150	11429	
OH-SDM	SOCATA MS.893A Rallye Commodore 180	11449	
OH-SDN	SOCATA MS.892A Rallye Commodore 150	11640	F-BSFH
OH-SDO	SOCATA MS.892A Rallye Commodore 150	11717	
OH-SDR	SOCATA MS.880B Rallye-Club	1737	
OH-SDT	SOCATA MS.894A Minerva 220	11674	F-OCPM
OH-SDU	SOCATA MS.880B Rallye-Club	1962	
OH-SDV	SOCATA MS.893A Rallye Commodore 180	11925	
OH-SDW	SOCATA MS.894A Minerva 220	11974	
OH-SDX	SOCATA MS.894A Minerva 220	11942	
OH-SDZ	SOCATA MS.880B Rallye-Club	1964	
OH-SEA	SOCATA MS.892A Rallye Commodore 150	11878	
OH-SEB	SOCATA MS.893A Rallye Commodore 180	11976	
OH-SED	SOCATA MS.893A Rallye Commodore 180	11867	F-BTHX
OH-SEE	SOCATA MS.893E Rallye 180GT Gaillard	12530	
OH-SEG	SOCATA MS.892E Rallye 150T	2652	
OH-SEH	SOCATA MS.880B Rallye Club	2557	
OH-SEI	SOCATA Rallye 235E Gabier	12800	
OH-SEK	SEEMS MS.885 Super Rallye	271	EL-AFX
			SE-EEG(2)
OH-SEW	SOCATA Rallye 235E-D Gabier	12799	D-EDRK
OH-SFF	SAAB S.91D Safir	91350	SF-4
OH-SFJ	SAAB S.91D Safir	91412	SF-24
OH-SFN	SAAB S.91D Safir	91362	SF-16
OH-SFP	SAAB S.91D Safir	91410	SF-22
OH-SLK	DHC-6 Twin Otter 300	260	SE-GEG
			CF-JCH

Regn.	Type	C/n	Prev.Id.
OH-SPA	Gyroflug SC.01B-160 Speed Canard	S-30	SE-IVB
			(OH-SPA)
OH-SUN	Cessna 182Q Skylane	65392	SE-KUL
			N735FQ
OH-SZJ	Focke-Wulf FW.44J Stieglitz	2927	SZ-24
OH-SZR	Focke-Wulf FW.44J Stieglitz	unkn	SZ-10
OH-TBC	SOCATA TB-9 Tampico	882	SE-KBC
OH-TBD	SOCATA TB-9 Tampico	197	SE-GFU
			F-ODNU
			(SE-GFU)
OH-TBG	SOCATA TB-10 Tobago	631	SE-KBE
			F-GFDX
			N20EY
OH-TJS	SOCATA TB-21 Trinidad TC	744	F-GFQL
OH-TOW	Valmet PIK-23 Towmaster	001	
OH-TUG	Valmet PIK-23 Suhinu	002	N255H
	(W/o 11.6.91)		OH-TUG
OH-TZA	Zlin 126 (Lycoming, modified)	847	
OH-UDZ	Cessna T.207A Turbo Skywagon/ Soloy Pac	00388	D-EXWG
			HB-CLR
			N1788U
OH-USI	Cessna 208 Caravan	00275	
OH-UTI	Rockwell Commander 690A	11204	SE-GSR
			D-IGAA
OH-VAA	Valmet L-70	31	
OH-VJL	PZL-104 Wilga 35A	20890874	
OH-VKW	Cessna T.188C Husky	03674T	N3842J
OH-VTP	Valmet L-90TP Redigo	001	
OH-WAA	Wassmer CE-43 Guepard	440	
OH-WAC	Wassmer WA.54 Atlantic	138	
OH-WBA	Mitsubishi MU-2N (MU-2B-36A)	718SA	N150BA
			C-GJSD
			N715US
			VH-ENH
			N889MA
OH-WIH	Canadair CL.600-1A11 Challenger	1029	N205A
			D-BMTM
			HB-VGA
			C-GLXO
OH-WIN	Dassault Falcon 20F	481	N250RA
			N502F
			F-WLCS
OH-WIP	Dassault Falcon 20F	359	N369CE
			N369CA
			(N508L)
			N50SL
			N35RZ
			N647JP
			N64769
			HZ-AO1
			HZ-TAG
			(N64769)
			F-WRQR
OH-XAB	Corby Starlet	492	
OH-XAL	Brügger MB-2 Colibri	04	
OH-XAM	Rotorway Scorpion II	A1	
OH-XAS	Rand-Robinson KR-2	01	
OH-XCH	Denney Kitfox III	961	9H-ACH
OH-XCO	Brügger MB-2 Colibri	1	
OH-XCY	Kaipainen PK-3 Rallyette	01	
	(built from MS.883 Rallye 115 c/n 1361 ex OH-SCY)		
OH-XEA	Christen Eagle II	01	
OH-XEC	Fox Christen Eagle II	002	N444LF
OH-XES	Druine D.31 Turbulent (Modified)	01	
OH-XFA	Bowers Fly-Baby A-1	02	
OH-XFK	Rotorway Exec	226	
OH-XGK	Stoddard-Hamilton Glasair ITD	355	
OH-XGT	Gloster Gauntlet II (Modified)	G5/35957	GT-400
	(Painted as GT-400)		K5271
OH-XHC	Revolution Mini 500	0110	
OH-XHI	Rotorway Exec	223	
OH-XHN	Christen Eagle II	2	
OH-XHO	Rotorway Exec	1059	
OH-XHU	Denney Kitfox	334	
OH-XHW	Rotorway Exec	6232	

Regn.	Type	C/n	Prev.Id.
OH-XII	Corby Starlet	247	
OH-XJH	Bowers Fly Baby 1A	85-1	
OH-XJK	Acey Deucy P-70	01	
OH-XJP	Neico Lancair 320	169	
OH-XKD	Van's RV-4	3006	
OH-XKJ	Neico Lancair 320	1	
OH-XKK	Pereira Osprey 2	01	
OH-XKR	Denney Kitfox IV	1617	
OH-XKS	Rans S-10 Sakota	0291126	
OH-XKV	Rotorway Exec	855	
OH-XLA	de Havilland DH.82A Tiger Moth (Lycoming Mod)	85167	OH-ELA
			G-AMJR
			T6958
OH-XLS	Cessna 150XL	0317	OH-CTT
OH-XLT	Taylor JT-1 Monoplane	01	
OH-XMA	Monnett Sonerai I	123	
OH-XMT	Van's RV-6	1	
OH-XOH	Rotorway Exec 162F	6119	
OH-XOO	Rans S-10 Sakota	0709106	
OH-XOT	Van's RV-6	20261	
OH-XPA	Pitts S-1 Special	01	
OH-XPB	Pitts S-1 Special	02	
OH-XPC	Pitts S-1S Special	04	
OH-XPF	Pitts S-1 Special	541-H	N51DM
OH-XPS	EAA Biplane B2	1-596	SE-XHF
			N3DB
OH-XQA	Rutan Quickie	01	
OH-XRK	Tervamaki JT-5	01	
OH-XSF	Ultimate 10-300S	300-003	
OH-XSH	Aero Designs Pulsar XP	137	
OH-XSS	Smyth Sidewinder RG	01	
OH-XST	Light Aero Avid Flyer Speed Wing	344	
OH-XSW	Sorrell SNS-7 Hiperbipe	294	
OH-XTA	Taylor JT.1 Monoplane	01	
OH-XTI	PIK-18	01	
OH-XTJ	Rans S-10 Sakota	0709108	
OH-XTK	Van's RV-4	1945	
OH-XTM	PIK-21 Super-Sytky	01	
OH-XTP	Evans VP-2 Mod.	8693	
OH-XVB	Evans VP-2	02	
OH-XVO	Rand-Robinson KR-2	01	
OH-XVX	Tervamaki JT-5	04	
OH-XVY	HAT-4 gyrocopter	03	
OH-XWY	Rotorway Exec 90	6021	
OH-XYM	Tervamaki JT-5	02	
OH-XYQ	Tervamaki-Eerola ATE-3	02	
OH-XYR	Tervamaki-Eerola ATE-3	03	
OH-YHB	PIK-15 Hinu	002	
OH-YHD	PIK-15 Hinu	006	
OH-YHE	PIK-15 Hinu	005	
OH-YHF	PIK-15 Hinu	004	
OH-YMC	PIK-11 Tumppu	3	
OH-YMD	PIK-11 Tumppu	4	

HOT-AIR BALLOONS AND AIRSHIPS

Regn.	Type	C/n	Prev.Id.
OH-APU	Cameron N-65 HAFB	4586	
OH-ARM	UltraMagic V-77 HAFB	77/31	
OH-BKK	Lindstrand LBL-120A HAFB	527	
OH-DBF	UltraMagic N-180 HAFB	180/12	
OH-DCF	UltraMagic M-65 HAFB	65/80	
OH-DFA	Thunder AX7-65 HAFB	1176	
OH-DIN	Colt 77A HAFB	1957	
OH-DUO	Lindstrand LBL-150A	590	
OH-ENV	UltraMagic V-90 HAFB	90/18	
OH-ERI	Lindstrand LBL-150A HAFB	449	
OH-ESO	Cameron N-90 HAFB	4030	
OH-FUN	Colt 105A HAFB	992	G-TALK
OH-GAS	Colt 69A HAFB	1800	
OH-GAZ	Lindstrand LBL-77A HAFB	567	

Regn.	Type	C/n	Prev.Id.
OH-GSM	Lindstrand LBL-120A HAFB	031	
OH-IDA	Cameron A-140 HAFB	4062	
OH-ISO	Lindstrand LBL-210A HAFB	522	
OH-JEP	Cameron Concept C-70 HAFB	4417	
OH-JOY	Colt 77A HAFB	1106	
OH-JTI	Cameron A-180 HAFB	2107	G-TIBC
OH-JUL	Cameron O-77 HAFB	1498	
OH-KID	Thunder AX7-77 HAFB	1288	
OH-KUU	UltraMagic H-65 HAFB	65/53	
OH-KVT	Colt 69A HAFB	1949	
OH-KWH	Cameron Concept C-70 HAFB	4418	
OH-MAA	UltraMagic V-56 HAFB	56/07	
OH-MHZ	Thunder AX3 HAFB	262	G-BHOP
OH-MMH	Cameron A-275 HAFB	4574	
OH-MPM	Lindstrand LBL-77A HAFB	610	
OH-MUS	Cameron N-90 HAFB	1791	
OH-NMT	Lindstrand LBL-56A HAFB	030	
OH-OHO	Cameron N-77 HAFB	3388	G-BVVJ
OH-OKK	Lindstrand LBL-77A HAFB	539	
OH-OPE	UltraMagic H-65 HAFB	65/32	
OH-POP	Cameron O-77 HAFB	510	
OH-ROP	Colt 77A HAFB	1396	
OH-RSC	UltraMagic V-65 HAFB	65/61	
OH-SEX	UltraMagic M-120 HAFB	120/01	
OH-SIL	Colt 69A HAFB	2229	
OH-SOL	Ultramagic S-130 HAFB	130/09	
OH-TAO	Cameron V-77 HAFB	885	
OH-TKK	Lindstrand LBL-56A HAFB	081	
OH-TKP	Lindstrand LBL-77B HAFB	206	
OH-TOK	Colt 105A HAFB	1367	
OH-TON	Colt 56A HAFB	1541	
OH-TOP	Cameron V-77 HAFB	580	
OH-TOY	Colt 69A HAFB	739	
OH-TPM	Colt 77A HAFB	1665	
OH-TRE	Colt 90A HAFB	1659	
OH-TSS	Thunder AX7-77 HAFB	692	
OH-TTR	Thunder AX7-77 HAFB	1221	
OH-TWS	Thunder AX7-77 HAFB	686	
OH-TWW	Thunder AX7-77 HAFB	1142	
OH-TYA	Colt 56A HAFB	1816	
OH-VAL	Colt 77A HAFB	1285	
OH-VIP	Colt 77A HAFB	904	
OH-XSK	Cameron O-56 HAFB	419	
OH-YIT	UltraMagic M-77 HAFB	77/157	
OH-ZDD	Viking 69A HAFB	SLB-007	SE-ZDD
OH-...	Colt 42A HAFB	821	G-BMUM

GLIDERS AND MOTOR-GLIDERS

Regn.	Type	C/n	Prev.Id.
OH-034	Harakka II	5	H-35
OH-170	Schleicher Ka.2B Rhönschwalbe	23	OH-KKA
OH-171	Schleicher Ka.2B Rhönschwalbe	24	OH-KKB
OH-207	Rhönlerche II	591	OH-KRB
OH-213X	Motorlerche	671	OH-KRE
OH-216	Schleicher Ka.6CR Rhönsegler	684	OH-RSD
OH-218	Schleicher Ka.6CR Rhönsegler	683	OH-RSC
OH-220	Schleicher Ka.6CR Rhönsegler	720	OH-RSF
OH-221	Schleicher Ka.6CR Rhönsegler	728	OH-RSE
OH-222	Schleicher Ka.6CR Rhönsegler	729	OH-RSH
OH-230X	Schleicher Rhönlerche II	761	OH-KRL
OH-231	Schleicher Ka.6CR Rhönsegler	719	OH-RSG
OH-237	PIK-5c	31	OH-PBI
OH-239	Schleicher Ka.6CR Rhönsegler	971	OH-RSK
OH-242	Schleicher Ka.6CR Rhönsegler	961	OH-RSI
OH-244	PIK-3c Kajava	6	OH-YKU
OH-245	PIK-3c Kajava	8	OH-YKS
OH-249X	Schleicher Rhönlerche II Mod.	1/61	OH-KRJ
OH-250	PIK-3c Kajava	13	OH-YKM
OH-255	Schleicher K.8B	990	OH-RTD

Regn.	Type	C/n	Prev.Id.
OH-257X	Rhönlerche II (Mod)	4/61	OH-KRO
OH-260-'6'	Schleicher Ka.6CR Rhönsegler	969	OH-RSJ
OH-262X	Motorlerche	5	OH-KRP
OH-265	Schleicher K.8B	8033	OH-RTF
OH-268X	Schleicher Ka.6CR Rhönsegler (Motorised)	6034	OH-RSL
OH-270	Schleicher K.8B	8058	OH-RTG
OH-276	Schleicher Ka.6CR Rhönsegler	6046	OH-RSO
OH-277	PIK-3c Kajava	16	OH-YKJ
OH-280	PIK-16c Vasama	8	OH-VAH
OH-281	PIK-16c Vasama	9	OH-VAI
OH-282	LET L-13 Blanik	172620	OH-VLK
OH-284	PIK-16c Vasama	7	OH-VAG
OH-285	PIK-12	4	OH-KYD
OH-287	Schleicher K.8B	8185	OH-RTH
OH-296	Schleicher K7 Rhönadler	7081	OH-KKI
OH-301	Schleicher Ka.6CR Rhönsegler	6269	OH-RSR
OH-303	PIK-16c Vasama	27	OH-VAM
OH-304	PIK-3c Kajava	17	OH-YKI
OH-305	Schleicher K7 Rhönadler	7146	OH-KKK
OH-310	Schleicher K.8B	8324	OH-RTJ
OH-312	Schleicher K.8B	02	OH-RTL
OH-313	Schleicher K.8B	01	OH-RTK
OH-314	Schleicher K.8B	03	OH-RTM
OH-324	Schleicher Ka.6CR Rhönsegler	6407	OH-RST
OH-325	Schleicher Ka.6CR Rhönsegler	6408	OH-RSU
OH-326	Schleicher K.8B	06	OH-RTO
OH-327X	LET L-13M Blanik	173318	OH-BLB
OH-332	Schleicher K7 Rhönadler	7250	OH-KKN
OH-339	SZD-9bis Bocian 1D	F-878	OH-KBO
OH-344	Schleicher K.8B	24	OH-RTV
OH-348	Schleicher K.8B	14	OH-RTU
OH-350	PIK-5C	24	OH-PBO
			OH-PBB
OH-352	Schleicher K.8B	23	OH-RTY
OH-353	PIK-16c Vasama	35	OH-VAO
OH-354	Schleicher Ka.6E	4102	OH-RSZ
OH-356	Schleicher Ka.6E	4146	OH-REA
OH-365	Schleicher K.8B	19	OH-RTZ
OH-367X	Fournier RF-4D Mod.	4096	OH-FIA
OH-369	Schleicher Ka.6E	4190	OH-REB
OH-371	Fournier RF-4D	4106	OH-FIC
OH-374	Fournier RF-4D	4110	OH-FIF
OH-378	Bölkow Phoebus C	886	OH-PHB
OH-380	Fournier RF-4D	4144	OH-FIH
OH-381X	Fournier RF-4D	4143	OH-FIG
OH-382	Fournier RF-4D	4145	OH-FII
OH-383	Fournier RF-5	5023	OH-FKA
OH-385	Fournier RF-5	5027	OH-FKB
OH-386	Fournier RF-5	5019	OH-FKC
OH-389	Fournier RF-5	5035	OH-FKD
OH-390	Fournier RF-4D	4142	OH-FIJ
			(SE-TGT)
OH-392	Fournier RF-5	5043	OH-FKE
OH-393	SZD-30 Pirat	B-335	OH-FPB
OH-397	Schleicher K.8B	17	OH-RTQ
OH-401	Scheibe SF-25B Falke	46130	OH-FLA
			(D-KADG)
OH-404	SZD-9bis Bocian 1E	P-498	OH-KBM
OH-405	Schleicher ASK-13	13301	OH-KKT
OH-406	Schleicher ASK-13	13328	OH-KKU
OH-407	Schleicher ASW-15	15174	
OH-411	Schempp-Hirth Standard Cirrus	352	
OH-413	LET L-13 Blanik	175108	
OH-414	LET L-13 Blanik	175109	
OH-415	Slingsby T-61C Falke	1754	
OH-417	Glasflügel H201 Standard Libelle	398	
OH-422	Glasflügel H20I Standard Libelle	331	
OH-426X	Pilatus B4-PC11 (Motorised)	49	
OH-427	LET L-13 Blanik	025416	
OH-428	LET L-13 Blanik	025417	
OH-434	LET L-13 Blanik	025717	
OH-436	LET L-13 Blanik	025515	
OH-438-WA	PIK-16c Vasama	53	
OH-440	Schleicher ASK-14	14011	D-KANK
OH-442	Eiri PIK-20	20022	

Regn.	Type	C/n	Prev.Id.
OH-454	Eiri PIK-20	20007	
OH-458	Scheibe SF-28A Tandem-Falke	5775	(D-KCLE)
OH-463	Schleicher ASW-15B	15406	
OH-466-TM	Eiri PIK-20	20028	
OH-469	Eiri PIK-20	20035	
OH-470	Eiri PIK-20	20032	
OH-476	Eiri PIK-20D	20527	BGA2233
OH-477	Eiri PIK-20B	20106	
OH-480	Glaser-Dirks DG-100	2	D-7099
OH-482	Eiri PIK-20	20041	
OH-484	Eiri PIK-20B	20113	
OH-486	Eiri PIK-20B	20137C	
OH-489-TS	Eiri PIK-20B	20133C	
OH-493	Eiri PIK-20	20066	
OH-496X	Motorlerche	417	D-0022
OH-501	LET L-13 Blanik	026239	
OH-502	Eiri PIK-20D	20624	
OH-503	Schleicher Ka.6E	4394/AB	
OH-504	Glasflügel H206 Hornet	53	
OH-506	SZD-30 Pirat	S-06.46	
OH-507	Eiri PIK-20B	20142C	
OH-510X	Eiri PIK-20D	20501	
OH-511-MA	Schleicher ASW-20	20056	
OH-512-PI	Eiri PIK-20D	20529	
OH-513	LET L-13 Blanik	026603	
OH-514	LET L-13 Blanik	026604	
OH-516	Eiri PIK-20D	20536	
OH-518	Schleicher K.8B	15	OY-DXF
OH-519	LET L-13 Blanik	026851	
OH-520X-T6	Tervamäki JT-6	01	
OH-521-FL	Eiri PIK-20D	20547	
OH-522	Eiri PIK-20D	20554	
OH-532	Schleicher ASW-19B	19246	
OH-536	Eiri PIK-20D	20648	
OH-537	Grob G.102 Astir CS Jeans	2207	
OH-540	Grob G.102 Astir CS Jeans	2142	
OH-542	SZD-41A Jantar Standard	B-843	
OH-543-TIY	Schleicher ASK-21	21026	
OH-546	Schleicher ASK-21	21259	
OH-547	Schleicher ASK-21	21133	
OH-549	Eiri PIK-20D	20639	
OH-552	Grob G.102 Astir CS Jeans	2233	
OH-556	Schleicher ASW-19B	19328	
OH-557	Schleicher ASK-21	21115	
OH-561	Eiri PIK-20E	20270	
OH-562	Eiri PIK-20D	20603	
OH-565	Eiri PIK-20D	20533	BGA2236
OH-571	PIK-16c Vasama	38	
OH-572	Schleicher ASW-20	20212	
OH-573	Schleicher ASK-21	21038	
OH-582	Eiri PIK-20E	20272	
OH-583	Eiri PIK-20E	20290	
OH-586	SZD-48-1 Jantar Standard 2	B-1044	
OH-587	SZD-48-1 Jantar Standard 2	B-1097	
OH-588	SZD-48-1 Jantar Standard 2	B-1035	
OH-591-EE	Grob G.102 Astir CS Jeans	2210	
OH-592	Schleicher ASW-19	19017	D-4529
OH-598	Scheibe SF-25C Falke	4487	D-KEIG
OH-602	Eiri PIK-20E	20279	
OH-604	Schleicher ASW-20	20379	
OH-605	Eiri PIK-20E	20213	G-OCPA
OH-607	Eiri PIK-20E	20292	
OH-608-PC	Glasflügel H304	217	
OH-609	Schleicher ASW-20	20420	
OH-610	Eiri PIK-20D	20665	
OH-614	SZD-48-1 Jantar Standard	B-1163	
OH-619	Rolladen-Schneider LS-4A	4124	
OH-622	Grob G.102 Club Astir IIIB	5514CB	
OH-623	Scheibe SF-25C Falke	4432	OY-XLA D-KMSO
OH-625	Valentin Mistral C	MC 035/81	
OH-627	Scheibe SF-25C Falke	4462	OE-9064 (D-KOAV)
OH-628	Grob G.103 Twin Astir II	3660	
OH-631	LET L-13 Blanik	026640	

Regn.	Type	C/n	Prev.Id.
OH-632X	Schleicher Ka.6EM	1	
OH-636	Glaser-Dirks DG-100G Elan	E68-G43	
OH-637	Scheibe SF-25C Falke	4458	D-KOAE
OH-639	Grob G.102 Club Astir II	5569C	
OH-642	Glasflügel H304	260	
OH-643	Grob G.109	6088	
OH-646	Grob G.109	6092	
OH-647	Grob G.109	6094	
OH-648	Grob G.102 Club Astir II	5052C	
OH-649	Grob G.109	6073	
OH-650-FK	Grob G.102 Club Astir II	5574C	
OH-651X	Motorlerche (Rhönlerche II)	3043/Br	
OH-653	Grob G.109	6114	
OH-655	Rolladen-Schneider LS-4A	4345	
OH-657-PV	Grob G.102 Club Astir IIIB	5590CB	
OH-658-ST	Grob G.102 Astir CS	1088	D-6988
OH-659	Grob G.109	6097	D-KENA
OH-661	Grob G.102 Club Astir II	5059C	
OH-664	Glaser-Dirks DG-300	3E-31	
OH-665	Grob G.109	6107	
OH-667	Grob G.102 Club Astir IIIB	5575CB	
OH-668-OW	Rolladen-Schneider LS-4A	4346	
OH-669	Rolladen-Schneider LS-4A	4344	
OH-670-T8	Grob G.102 Astir CS Jeans	2025	
OH-671	Grob G.109	6020	D-KETO
OH-672	Schleicher ASW-20	20568	
OH-674	Grob G.109	6031	OE-9192
OH-675	SZD-50-3 Puchacz	B-973	
OH-676	Centrair 101 Pégase	101-062	
OH-677	Schleicher ASK-21	21190	
OH-679	Rolladen-Schneider LS-4	4533	
OH-680-TO	Schleicher ASW-20	20208	
OH-681-TK	Centrair 101A Pégase	101A-0109	
OH-684-VW	Rolladen-Schneider LS-4A	4343	
OH-685	Schempp-Hirth Janus B	186	
OH-686	Grob G.109B	6217	
OH-687	Grob G.109	6111	
OH-688	Valentin Taifun 17E	1022	D-KIHL
OH-691	Rolladen-Schneider LS-4A	4347	
OH-692	Glaser-Dirks DG-300	3E-30	
OH-693	Rolladen-Schneider LS-4A	4396	
OH-694	Eiri PIK-20E	20288	PH-694
OH-695	Schleicher ASK-23	23031	
OH-696	Schleicher ASK-23	23029	
OH-697	Schleicher ASK-23	23026	
OH-699	Schleicher ASK-23B	23065	
OH-701	SZD-51-1 Junior	W-960	
OH-703	Schleicher ASK-23B	23069	
OH-704	Schleicher ASK-23B	23070	
OH-705	Scheibe SF-25C Falke	4427	D-KHOK
OH-707	Glaser-Dirks DG-300	3E-25	
OH-710	Rolladen-Schneider LS-4A	4393	
OH-711	Schleicher ASW-20B	20646	
OH-712	Glasflügel H304B	347	
OH-713	Rolladen-Schneider LS-4A	4462	
OH-715	Rolladen-Schneider LS-6	6024	
OH-716	Grob G.109B	6339	
OH-717	Rolladen-Schneider LS-4	4391	
OH-719	Schempp-Hirth Janus C	222	
OH-721	Grob G.109	6032	D-KELC
OH-723	Rolladen-Schneider LS-4A	4578	
OH-724	SZD-50-3 Puchacz	B-1601	
OH-726	Rolladen-Schneider LS-6B	6081	
OH-727	Grob G.109	6050	D-KLFM
OH-728	SZD-51-1 Junior	W-948	
OH-729	Schempp-Hirth Discus b	124	
OH-730	Schempp-Hirth Discus b	30	
OH-732-PD	Schempp-Hirth Ventus b	307	
OH-733-FQ	Grob G.103A Twin II Acro	34049-K-280	
OH-735	Rolladen-Schneider LS-6	6047	
OH-737	Grob G.109B	6338	
OH-739	Schempp-Hirth Discus b	169	
OH-740	Grob G.109B	6413	
OH-741-BX	Schempp-Hirth Discus b	168	
OH-742	SZD-51-1 Junior	W-958	

Regn.	Type	C/n	Prev.Id.
OH-743	SZD-51-1 Junior	B-1769	
OH-744	SZD-51-1 Junior	W-949	
OH-745	SZD-50-3 Puchacz	B-1608	
OH-746	Grob G.102 Astir CS Jeans	2156	OE-5373
			HB-1441
OH-747	Grob G.109B	6398	
OH-748	Schempp-Hirth Ventus c	374	
OH-749	SZD-50-3 Puchacz	B-1620	
OH-750	SZD-51-1 Junior	W-942	
OH-751	SZD-50-3 Puchacz	B-1618	
OH-752	SZD-51-1 Junior	B-1776	
OH-753	SZD-48-3 Jantar Standard 3	B-1661	
OH-754	Rolladen-Schneider LS-6B	6134	
OH-755	Rolladen-Schneider LS-4A	4600	
OH-756	SZD-50-3 Puchacz	B-1627	
OH-758	SZD-51-1 Junior	B-1768	
OH-760-PH	Schleicher ASW-20BL	20952	
OH-763-P1	Schempp-Hirth Discus b	214	
OH-765	Rolladen-Schneider LS-6B	6162	
OH-767	Rolladen-Schneider LS-6B	6132	
OH-768	Schleicher ASK-21	21362	
OH-769	Schempp-Hirth Discus b	226	
OH-770-PO	Schempp-Hirth Discus b	235	
OH-772	SZD-50-3 Puchacz	B-1720	
OH-773	SZD-51-1 Junior	B-1814	
OH-776	SZD-51-1 Junior	B-1815	
OH-778	Rolladen-Schneider LS-4A	4691	
OH-779	SZD-50-3 Puchacz	B-1617	
OH-780	Schempp-Hirth Discus b	2	D-8111
OH-783	Schleicher ASK-21	21380	
OH-784	SZD-50-3 Puchacz	B-1723	
OH-785	SZD-48-3 Jantar Standard 3	B-1713	
OH-786	SZD-50-3 Puchacz	B-1722	
OH-787-FM	Rolladen-Schneider LS-4A	4715	
OH-788	Rolladen-Schneider LS-7	7003	D-1254
OH-790	Schleicher ASW-24	24020	
OH-791-PP	Schleicher ASW-24	24025	
OH-792-HB	Schleicher ASW-24	24057	
OH-794-TI	Schleicher ASW-24	24058	
OH-795	Hoffmann HK-36R Super Dimona	36312	
OH-796	Glaser-Dirks DG-600	6...	
OH-797	Grob G.109B	6528	
OH-798	SZD-51-1 Junior	B-1935	
OH-799	SZD-55-1	551190007	
OH-801	SZD-50-3 Puchacz	B-1875	
OH-802	SZD-51-1 Junior	B-1852	
OH-804	SZD-51-1 Junior	B-1853	
OH-805	Rolladen-Schneider LS-7	7019	D-4635
OH-806	Rolladen-Schneider LS-6B	6149	D-8077
OH-807-A2	Schempp-Hirth Discus A	279	
OH-808	SZD-55-1	X-146	
OH-810	Grob G.103C Twin III Acro	34125	
OH-811	Schleicher ASW-24	24070	
OH-812	Rolladen-Schneider LS-7	7056	
OH-813	Hoffmann H-36 Dimona	3661	SE-TUT
OH-814	Brditschka HB-21/2400B	21019	LN-GAK
			OE-9178
OH-815	Grob G.103C Twin III Acro	34120	
OH-816	SZD-50-3 Puchacz	B-1877	
OH-817	Schleicher ASK-21	21455	
OH-818	Grob G.102 Astir CS	1243	D-4212
OH-820-FS	Rolladen-Schneider LS-7	7078	
OH-821	Schempp-Hirth Ventus c	470	
OH-822-IY	Rolladen-Schneider LS-4A	4785	
OH-823	Rolladen-Schneider LS-7	7092	
OH-824	SZD-55-1	551190005	
OH-827	Schempp-Hirth Discus A	331	
OH-828	SZD-50-3 Puchacz	B-2026	
OH-829	SZD-51-1 Junior	B-1929	
OH-831	LAK-12 Lietuva	unkn	
OH-832	SZD-50-3 Puchacz	B-2027	
OH-834	Rolladen-Schneider LS-6C	6220	
OH-835	SZD-55-1	551191013	
OH-836	Schempp-Hirth Discus A	376	
OH-837	Rolladen-Schneider LS-6C	6225	

Regn.	Type	C/n	Prev.Id.
OH-838	Grob G.109B	6227	D-KGFJ
OH-839	SZD-51-1 Junior	B-1992	
OH-840	Schempp-Hirth Nimbus 3DM	18/42	
OH-842	SZD-51-1 Junior	B-1816	SE-UGO
OH-844	Rolladen-Schneider LS-6C	6...	
OH-845	SZD-55-1	551191025	
OH-846	SZD-55-1	551191026	
OH-848	Schempp-Hirth Discus b	407	
OH-849	SZD-51-1 Junior	B-2004	
OH-850	LET L-23 Super Blanik	917918	
OH-851	LET L-13 Blanik	026611	DOSAAF
OH-852	Schempp-Hirth Janus CT	18/281	
OH-853	Schempp-Hirth Janus CT	19/282	
OH-855	SZD-55-1	551191022	
OH-856	SZD-55-1	551192040	
OH-858	Grob G.102 Club Astir IIIB	5627CB	D-7603
OH-859	SZD-50-3 Puchacz	B-2084	
OH-860	LET L-13 Blanik	174210	DOSAAF
OH-862	SZD-55-1	551192046	
OH-863	SZD-51-1 Junior	B-2018	
OH-864	SZD-51-1 Junior	B-2128	
OH-865	Rolladen-Schneider LS-6-18W	6315	
OH-866	Rolladen-Schneider LS-6-18W	6316	D-4518
OH-867	LET L-23 Super Blanik	938108	
OH-868	LET L-23 Super Blanik	938109	
OH-869	Schleicher ASW-24	24226	
OH-870	LET L-33 Solo	940219	
OH-871	SZD-42-1 Jantar 2	B-777	SE-TPX
OH-872	PZL PW-5 Smyk	17.04.008	
OH-875	PZL PW-5 Smyk	17.03.016	
OH-876	PZL PW-5 Smyk	17.04.009	
OH-877	Schempp-Hirth Ventus 2c	3	
OH-878	Rolladen-Schneider LS-7	7083	SE-UPP
OH-879	Rolladen-Schneider LS-6-18W	6372	
OH-880	PZL PW-5 Smyk	17.04.015	
OH-881	Grob G.102 Astir CS77	1739	SE-UEB
			D-4898
OH-882	Rolladen-Schneider LS-8A	8062	
OH-883	Rolladen-Schneider LS-8A	8101	
OH-884	Rolladen Schneider LS-8A	8119	
OH-885	PZL PW-5 Smyk	17.05.007	
OH-886	Schleicher ASH-25	25165	BGA4026/HLJ
			(BGA4023)
OH-887	SZD-36A Cobra 15	W-731	LY-GIT
			DOSAAF
OH-889	Grob G.109A	6046	SE-UAG
			OY-XLW
OH-890	Rolladen-Schneider LS-4B	41015	
OH-891	SZD-42-2 Jantar 2B	B-1376	LY-G..
			DOSAAF
OH-892	Schleicher Ka.6E	4026	OY-XGH
			D-6475
			D-9375
OH-893	Schleicher ASH-26E	26136	
OH-894	Rolladen-Schneider LS-8A	8175	
OH-895	Rolladen-Schneider LS-8A	8196	
OH-896	Rolladen-Schneider LS-7WL	7016	SE-UGX
			D-4639
OH-897	Rolladen Schneider LS-8A	8195	
OH-898	Rolladen-Schneider LS-8A	8134	D-3382
OH-899	Schempp-Hirth Nimbus 2	85	D-2784
OH-900	Schempp-Hirth Ventus 2b	68	
OH-901	Glaser-Dirks DG-800B	8-90B26	D-KWDG(1)
OH-902	Schempp-Hirth Ventus 2c	42/122	
OH-904	Schempp-Hirth Ventus 2a	88	
OH-905	Eiri PIK-20B	20101	LN-GAZ

MICROLIGHTS

Regn.	Type	C/n	Prev.Id.
OH-U009	American Aerolights Eagle XL430	300371	
OH-U013	Dragon 150	0071	
OH-U017	Comco Ikarus Fox C-22	8808-3151	
OH-U029	La Mouette Cosmos Hermes 14-BID	unkn	
OH-U030	La Mouette Cosmos Hermes 16	unkn	
OH-U035	Air Création Safari GT-BI	unkn	
OH-U036	Southdown Puma Raven	unkn	
OH-U039	Southdown Puma Raven	unkn	
OH-U040	Air Création Safari GT-BI	3530163	
OH-U043	Southdown Puma Raven X	unkn	
OH-U045	Hiway Trike	21T5	OH-U001
OH-U047	Mainair Gemini/Flash	491-1086-4/W255	
OH-U048	Southdown Puma Raven X	unkn	
OH-U050	La Mouette Azur 17/Trike	unkn	
OH-U051	Sky-Walker II	26150	
OH-U053	Southdown Puma Raven X	unkn	
OH-U055	Comco Ikarus Fox C-22	8701-3057	
OH-U056	Comco Ikarus Fox C-22	8701-3058	
OH-U057	Southdown Raven Trike	001	
OH-U058	Southdown Raven X462LQ	P19351	
OH-U060	Southdown Raven X462	3585264	
OH-U062	Southdown Raven	unkn.	
OH-U063	Southdown Puma Raven X462	unkn	
OH-U065	Renegade Spirit	370	
OH-U070	Fisher FP-404 Classic	4053	
OH-U073	Air Création Safari BI-GT	unkn	
OH-U075	Sky-Walker II	172	
OH-U076	Comco Ikarus Fox C-22	8711-3114	
OH-U080	Raven	EJ-001	
OH-U082	Raven 447	unkn	
OH-U084	Comco Ikarus Fox C-22	8804-3127	
OH-U087	La Mouette Cosmos Azur 19/Trike	unkn	
OH-U088	Mainair Gemini/Flash IIA	619-188-5/W408	
OH-U092	Mainair Gemini/Flash IIA	644-588-6/W434	
OH-U094	Comco Ikarus Fox C-22	8810-3157	
OH-U095	Comco Ikarus Fox C-22	035-115	
OH-U096	Comco Ikarus Fox C-22	8805-3131	
OH-U100	Murphy Renegade Spirit	107	
OH-U103	Murphy Renegade Spirit	195	
OH-U105	Murphy Renegade II Mod.	140	
OH-U106	Kolb Twinstar Mark II	TX 2501 1188	
OH-U110	Comco Ikarus Fox C-22	8808-3150	
OH-U111	Comco Ikarus Fox C-22	8809-3155	
OH-U113	Medway Hybred R447	MR.030/47	
OH-U119	Southdown Puma Sprint	T29	
OH-U120	Murphy Renegade II	175	
OH-U121	Firebird Sierra	unkn	
OH-U123	Firebird Sierra	364	
OH-U126	Medway Hybred R447/R503	MR . . ./54 ?	
OH-U127	Southdown Puma Sprint	unkn	
OH-U128	Kolb Twinstar	194	
OH-U129	Firebird Sierra	300/84	
OH-U130	Murphy Renegade II	377	
OH-U132	Comco Ikarus Fox C-22	8903-3194	
OH-U133	Southdown Puma Sprint	unkn	
OH-U134	Medway Hybred R503	MR . . ./67 ?	
OH-U138	Kolb Twinstar Mark II	193	
OH-U141	Beaver RX-550	0013	
OH-U142	Southdown Puma Sprint	unkn	
OH-U143	Beaver RX-550 Mod.	0014	
OH-U144	Murphy Renegade Spirit	225	
OH-U146	Southdown Puma Sprint	unkn	
OH-U148	Southdown Puma Sprint	1	
OH-U150	Southdown Puma Sprint	44	
OH-U151	Southdown Puma Sprint	T45	
OH-U153	Kolb Twinstar Mark II	TX 255	
OH-U154	Murphy Renegade II	0142	
OH-U155	La Mouette Cosmos Profil 19M	T47	
OH-U157	Southdown Puma Sprint	unkn	
OH-U158	Southdown Puma Sprint	1231-0052	
OH-U159	Murphy Renegade II	197	
OH-U161	Murphy Renegade II	223	
OH-U166	Southdown Puma Sprint	unkn	

Regn.	Type	C/n	Prev.Id.
OH-U168	Beaver RX-550	0056	
OH-U169	Beaver RX-550	0053	
OH-U173	Beaver RX-550	0051	
OH-U174	Beaver RX-550	0054	
OH-U177	Southdown Puma Raven	unkn	
OH-U178	Beaver RX-550	0055	
OH-U179	La Mouette Cosmos Hermes Profil 19/Chronos 16	3549726	
OH-U180	Cosmos Profil 19/Chronos 16	unkn	
OH-U182	Southdown Puma Raven	SN 2232-0093	
OH-U183	Rans S-6 Coyote II	0389027	
OH-U184	Rans S-6 Coyote II	0689041	
OH-U186	Mainair Gemini/Flash	396-186-4/W142	
OH-U187	Southdown Puma Raven X	unkn	
OH-U188	Murphy Renegade Spirit	263	
OH-U189	Murphy Renegade Spirit	246	
OH-U190	Southdown Puma Raven	unkn	
OH-U192	Southdown Raven Sprint	T67	
OH-U193	Kolb Twinstar Mark II	TS II 226	
OH-U196	Kolb Twinstar Mark II	196	
OH-U202	Murphy Renegade II	198	
OH-U204	Murphy Renegade Spirit	226	
OH-U205	Murphy Renegade Spirit	205	
OH-U206	Beaver RX-550	0010	
OH-U207	Comco Ikarus Fox C-22	8906-3205	
OH-U208	Comco Ikarus Fox C-22	8903-3206	
OH-U209	Comco Ikarus Fox C-22	8906-3208	
OH-U210	Comco Ikarus Fox C-22	8906-3207	
OH-U211	Beaver RX-650	0003	
OH-U212	Rans S-6 Coyote II	0689035	
OH-U214	Rans S-6 Coyote IIES	1190147	
OH-U215	Azur 17/Trike	003-90	
OH-U216	Rans S-6 Coyote IIES	1190146	
OH-U217	Rans S-6 Coyote II	1089092	
OH-U218	Rans S-6 Coyote II	1289103	
OH-U219	Rans S-6 Coyote II	1089096	
OH-U220	HFL Stratos IIE	006	D-MAKT
OH-U221	Murphy Renegade II	199	
OH-U222	Rans S-6 Coyote II	0489022	
OH-U223	Rans S-6 Coyote II	0790132	
OH-U224	Rans S-6 Coyote II	1089088	
OH-U225	Rans S-6 Coyote II	0989069	
OH-U227	Rans S-6 Coyote II	0989071	
OH-U229	Rans S-6 Coyote II	1089091	
OH-U232	Beaver RX-550	0108	
OH-U235	Mosler N3-2 Pup	0043LA-2	
OH-U236	Beaver RX-550	0103	
OH-U238	Sky Sports Yarrow Arrow 2	016	
OH-U240	Rans S-7 Courier	1189059	
OH-U243	Rans S-6 Coyote II	1289100	
OH-U244	Rans S-6 Coyote II Mod.	1289099	
OH-U246	Comco Ikarus Fox C-22	9007-3277	
OH-U247	Rans S-6 Coyote II	1289102	
OH-U248	Rans S-7L Courier	0190065	
OH-U249	Rans S-6 Coyote II	1289105	
OH-U248	Rans S-7L Courier	0190065	
OH-U251	Murphy Renegade Spirit	0247	
OH-U254	Rans S-6 Coyote II	0690126	
OH-U255	Rans S-6 Coyote II	0490118	
OH-U256	Rans S-6 Coyote II	0190110	
OH-U258	Rans S-6 Coyote II Mod.	0490121	
OH-U262	Beaver RX-650	0002	
OH-U263	Beaver RX-650	0014	
OH-U264	Beaver RX-650 Mod.	0004	
OH-U265	Beaver RX-650	0006	
OH-U266	Beaver RX-650	0007	
OH-U268	Beaver RX-650	0009	
OH-U269	Beaver RX-650	0010	
OH-U270	Beaver RX-650	0011	
OH-U271	Beaver RX-650	0012	
OH-U274	Beaver RX-650	0015	
OH-U275	Rans S-6 Coyote IIES	0890137	
OH-U276	Alanne Moottoriharakka	1	
OH-U277	Rans S-4 Coyote I	90138	
OH-U278	Rans S-6 Coyote II Mod	0690123	

Regn.	Type	C/n	Prev.Id.
OH-U280	LAK-16AM	001	LY-GLU?
OH-U281	Rans S-6 Coyote II Mod.	0790130	
OH-U285	Aviasud Mistral 582	134	
OH-U291	Rans S-6 Coyote II ES	0291164	
OH-U292	Kolb Twinstar Mark III Mod.	M3-018	
OH-U293	Rans S-6 Coyote II	1289101	
OH-U297	Rans S-6 Coyote II ES	0491179	
OH-U298	Rans S-6 Coyote II ES	0491180	
OH-U299	Rans S-6 Coyote II ES	0491181	
OH-U303	Light Aero Avid Flyer STOL	923	
OH-U304	Kolb Twinstar Mark III Mod.	M3R5001	
OH-U305	Kolb Twinstar Mark II	TS-166	
OH-U306	Murphy Renegade Spirit	273	
OH-U311	Rans S-6 Coyote II ES	1190145	
OH-U312	S.M.A.N. Pétrel	031	
OH-U313	Rans S-12 Airaile Ultramarin	1090.033	
OH-U320	Counts Wolfen Pup	85001	
OH-U321	Rans S-6 Coyote II ES	1190144	
OH-U323	Circa Nieuport 17	266	
OH-U333	Murphy Renegade Spirit	381	
OH-U345	Zenair CH-701 STOL	7-1593	
OH-U346	Chronos ULM Cosmos	426	
OH-U347	Lamco Eurocub Mk.1	CAH-002	SE-YSF ?
OH-U348	Kolb Twinstar Mark III Mod.	M3-069	
OH-U349	Zenair CH-701 STOL	7-3049	
OH-U350	Nieuport II	198	OH-U1064
OH-U351	Beaver RX-650	BRX-016	
OH-U352	Lamco Eurocub 912Mk.1	CAH-001	
OH-U353	Lamco Eurocub 912 Mk.1	CAH-007	SE-...?
OH-U354	Kolb Twinstar Mark II	unkn	
OH-U355	PIK-26 Mini-Sytky	387	
OH-U356	PIK-26 Mini-Sytky	392	
OH-U358	Denney Kitfox II	325	OH-XKF
OH-U360	SMAM Petrel	69	(France)
OH-U362	Martenko ATOL 500	446	
OH-U365	Cora 200 Arius	98-301	
OH-U366	Polaris Motor SRL	983709	
OH-U367	Cora 200 Arius	99-303	
OH-U368	Cora 200 Arius	99-304	
OH-U369	Comco Ikarus C-42 Cyclone	9907-6203	
OH-U370	Cora 200 Arius	99-303	
OH-U475	Martenko ATOL 475 LT	0905	

OK - CZECH REPUBLIC

Regn.	Type	C/n	Prev.Id.
OK-AAG	Cessna TU.206G Turbo Stationair II	04336	HPAP
			N756TD
OK-ABA	Fokker F.27 Friendship 500RF	10530	N737A
			PH-EXK
OK-ABB	Fokker F.27 Friendship 500RF	10531	N739A
			PH-EXM
OK-ADO	LET L-410A Turbolet (Preserved)	710005	
OK-ADP	LET L-410A Turbolet (Preserved)	710101	OK-IYV
			OK-ADP
OK-ADQ	LET L-410A Turbolet (Preserved)	700003	OK-AZA
			OK-AKG
			OK-176
OK-AFE	Aeritalia/SNIAS ATR-42-420	487	F-WWEF
OK-AFF	Aeritalia/SNIAS ATR-42-420	491	F-WWLC
OK-AIA	Aérospatiale AS.355F2 Ecureuil 2	5512	RP-C355
			F-OHEM
OK-AIH	Mil Mi-2	542209121	SP-FDH
			SP-FSH
			PWL-2209
OK-AIO	LET Z-37A Cmelák	14-10	
OK-AIP	LET Z-37A Cmelák	14-09	
OK-AIZ	LET Z-37A Cmelák	14-12	
OK-AJC	LET Z-37 Cmelák	13-12	HA-MCE
OK-AJE	LET Z-37 Cmelák	13-19	HA-MCJ
OK-AJF	LET Z-37 Cmelák	13-02	HA-MCA
OK-AJG	LET Z-37 Cmelák	13-04	OM-AJG
			OK-AJG
			HA-MCC
OK-AJI	LET Z-37 Cmelák	13-03	HA-MCB
OK-AJJ	LET Z-37 Cmelák	13-13	HA-MCF
OK-AJK	LET Z-37A Cmelák	13-15	HA-MCH
OK-AJM	LET Z-37 Cmelák	13-29	HA-MCO
OK-AJP	LET Z-37 Cmelák	11-16	
OK-AJQ	LET Z-37 Cmelák	11-17	
OK-AJR	LET Z-37 Cmelák	11-18	
OK-AJS	LET Z-37A-C3 Cmelák	11-24	
OK-AJX	LET Z-37 Cmelák	12-05	
OK-AKA	Piper PA-28-161 Warrior III	2842004	N9257B
			OK-AKA
OK-AKC	LET Z-37A Cmelák	11-22	
OK-AKE	LET Z-37A Cmelák	11-19	
OK-AKF	LET Z-37A Cmelák	13-26	
OK-AKH	LET Z-37A Cmelák	14-05	HA-MCQ
OK-AKI	LET Z-37 Cmelák	14-07	HA-MCS
OK-AKL	Cessna 172L	59772	CF-ZZO
			(N9872G)
OK-AKM	Reims/Cessna F.172H	0250	D-ECMZ
OK-AKN	LET Z-37 Cmelák	12-15	
OK-AKQ	LET Z-37 Cmelák	12-23	
OK-AKR	LET Z-37 Cmelák	12-24	
OK-AKS	LET Z-37A-C2 Cmelák	12-25	
OK-AKV	LET Z-37A Cmelák	12-28	
OK-AKZ	LET Z-37 Cmelák	13-08	
OK-ALN	LET Z-37 Cmelák	13-18	
OK-ANA	Zlin Z.242LA	0690	
OK-AYA	Letov L.11	960001	
OK-BFG	Aeritalia/SNIAS ATR-42-320	409	F-OKMR
			F-WWEA
OK-BFH	Aeritalia/SNIAS ATR-42-202	412	F-OKMS
			F-WWEC
OK-BIC	Aérospatiale AS.355F2 Ecureuil 2	5388	F-WQED
			GN-8884
OK-BIG	Robinson R-22B2 Beta	2611	
OK-BKS	Beech C90B King Air	LJ-1430	N3251U
OK-BLC	Diamond DA-20-A1 Katana	10178	C-GRUV
OK-BLD	Diamond DA-20-A1 Katana	10160	N181DA
OK-BYV	Ilyushin IL-62M	3850145	
OK-BZF	Reims/Cessna F.172M	1266	D-EBZF
OK-CDB	LET L-410UVP-E20	972730	
OK-CGH	Boeing 737-55S	28469	
OK-CGJ	Boeing 737-55S	28470	
OK-CGK	Boeing 737-55S	28471	
OK-CJA	LET Z-37A Cmelák	16-16	

Regn.	Type	C/n	Prev.Id.
OK-CJB	LET Z-37A Cmelák (Stored)	16-17	
OK-CJC	LET Z-37A Cmelák	16-18	OM-CJA
	(C/n now quoted as 14-24; rebuild?)		OK-CJC
OK-CJD	LET Z-37A Cmelák	16-14	
OK-CJE	LET Z-37A Cmelák	16-21	
OK-CJF	LET Z-37A Cmelák	16-22	
OK-CJG	LET Z-37A Cmelák (Stored)	16-23	
OK-CJH	LET Z-37 Cmelák	16-24	
OK-CJL	LET Z-37A Cmelák	17-01	
OK-CJM	LET Z-37A-2 Cmelák	16-02	HA-SCE
OK-CJS	LET Z-37 Cmelák	15-06	
OK-CJT	LET Z-37 Cmelák	15-07	
OK-CJV	LET Z-37A Cmelák	15-09	
OK-CJW	LET Z-37 Cmelák	15-10	
OK-CJY	LET Z-37A Cmelák (Stored)	15-27	
OK-CJZ	LET Z-37A Cmelák	15-28	
OK-CKN	LET Z-37A Cmelák	15-29	
OK-CKP	LET Z-37 Cmelák	16-15	
OK-CKR	LET Z-37A Cmelák	16-26	
OK-CKU	LET Z-37 Cmelák	17-06	
OK-CKW	LET Z-37A Cmelák	17-08	
OK-COA	Zlin Z.43	0001	
OK-COB	Zlin Z.43	0002	
OK-COC	Zlin Z.43 (Stored)	0004	
OK-COD	Zlin Z.43	0005	
OK-COE	Zlin Z.43	0007	
OK-COG	Zlin Z.43	0010	
OK-CRA	Zlin Z.526F Trenér Master	1251	
OK-CSR	Mraz M.1 Sokol	0142	
OK-CTA	Zlin Z.226MS Trenér	0104	
OK-CTB	Zlin Z.226MS Trenér	0105	
OK-CXA	Zlin Z.526AFS-V Akrobat	1218	
OK-CXB	Zlin Z.526AFS-V Akrobat	1219	
OK-CXC	Zlin Z.526AFS-V Akrobat	1220	
OK-CXF	Zlin Z.526AFS-V Akrobat	1224	
OK-CXQ	Z.37A-C2 Cmelák	16-25	OK-CKQ
OK-CZB	PZL-104 Wilga 35A	62152	
OK-CZD	LET L-610G	970301	
OK-DGL	Boeing 737-55S	28472	
OK-DGM	Boeing 737-45S	28473	
OK-DGN	Boeing 737-45S	28474	
OK-DJN	LET Z-37A Cmelák	17-15	
OK-DJO	LET Z-37A Cmelák	17-16	
OK-DJP	LET Z-37A Cmelák	17-17	
OK-DJS	LET Z-37A Cmelák	17-20	
OK-DJY	LET Z-37A Cmelák	19-12	
OK-DKJ	Cessna 172M	62698	N13360
OK-DKK	Cessna 172M	62539	N13161
OK-DKP	Piper PA-34-200 Seneca	34-7350288	D-GCZA
			N7130G
			D-GCZA
			N56133
OK-DKS	LET Z-37A Cmelák (Wfu)	19-25	
OK-DKT	LET Z-37 Cmelák	19-26	
OK-DKU	LET Z-37A Cmelák	19-27	
OK-DKV	LET Z-37A Cmelák	19-28	
OK-DKW	LET Z-37A Cmelák	19-29	
OK-DKZ	LET Z-37A Cmelák	19-30	
OK-DLO	LET Z-37A-2 Cmelák	19-06	
OK-DOA	Zlin Z.43	0011	
OK-DOB	Zlin Z.43	0013	
OK-DOC	Zlin Z.43	0014	
OK-DOD	Zlin Z.43	0016	
OK-DOE	Zlin Z.43	0028	
OK-DOF	Zlin Z.43	0029	
OK-DOG	Zlin Z.43	0032	
OK-DOH	Zlin Z.43	0033	
OK-DOI	Zlin Z.43	0035	
OK-DOJ	Zlin Z.43	0036	
OK-DOS(2)	Zlin Z.43MAF	0033	
OK-DRC	Zlin Z.726 Universal	1075	OK-078
OK-DVG	Zlin Z.126 Trenér 2	525	
OK-DVM	Reims/Cessna FR.172J Rocket	0425	D-EGJI
OK-DZA	LET L-410MA Turbolet	730207	OK-158
OK-EGO	Boeing 737-55S	28475	
OK-EGP	Boeing 737-45S	28476	N1786B
OK-EIN	Robinson R-44 Astro	0662	
OK-EJA	Z-137T Agro-Turbo	052	
OK-EKD	Reims/Cessna F.172M	1125	D-EENM
OK-EKI	Reims/Cessna F.150L	1053	D-EENV
OK-EKK	Cessna 172M	61924	N12320
OK-EKM	Reims/Cessna FR.172J Rocket	0471	D-EENS
OK-EKR	Cessna 172M	63033	N13896
OK-EKS	Beech 95-B55 Baron	TC-1686	N4482W
OK-EKT	Cessna U.206F Stationair	02276	D-EEVR
			(D-EAHP)
			N1906U
OK-EKU	Piper PA-23-250 Aztec E	27-7405402	G-JASP
			C-GREG
			N9669N
OK-ELM	Reims/Cessna F.172M	1193	D-EOQI
OK-EOA	Zlin Z.43	0045	
OK-EOC	Zlin Z.43	0048	
OK-EOD	Zlin Z.43	0049	
OK-EOE	Zlin Z.43	0051	
OK-EOF	Zlin Z.43	0053	
OK-EOG	Zlin Z.43	0054	
OK-EOH	Zlin Z.43	0056	
OK-EOI	Zlin Z.43	0057	
OK-ERE	Zlin Z.526AFS-V Akrobat	1307	HA-SAW
			OK-DHB
			OK-ERE
OK-ESO	Zlin Z.42MU	0054	LZ-800
OK-EUR	Europa Avn Europa XSTurbo	370	
OK-EXC	Mil Mi-8T	9743714	
OK-FAN	Boeing 737-33A	27469	
OK-FBI	Cessna 340	0114	OY-RPV
			OE-FKI
			N4576L
OK-FGR	Boeing 737-45S (Reservation .00)	28477	N1786B
OK-FGS	Boeing 737-45S (Reservation .00)	28478	
OK-FHP	Aero 45	51179	
OK-FIT	Boeing 737-36N	28590	N1787B
OK-FJB	LET Z-37A Cmelák	22-01	
OK-FJO	LET Z-37A Cmelák	21-09	
OK-FJP	LET Z-37A Cmelák (Stored)	21-10	
OK-FJT	LET Z-37A Cmelák	21-14	
OK-FJY	LET Z-37A Cmelák	21-19	
OK-FJZ	LET Z-37A Cmelák	21-20	
OK-FKD	Cessna 172N	66144	N9403H
OK-FKL	Cessna 150M	76965	N45540
OK-FKU	Cessna 172M	65255	D-EXEL
			N64474
OK-FLB	Aero 45	51188	
OK-FOF	Zlin Z.43	0061	
OK-FOG	Zlin Z.43	0063	
OK-FOH	Zlin Z.43	0064	
OK-FOI	Zlin Z.43	0067	
OK-FOJ	Zlin Z.43	0068	
OK-FOK	Zlin Z.43	0069	
OK-FOL	Zlin Z.43	0070	
OK-FOM	Zlin Z.43	0072	
OK-FUN	Boeing 737-33A	27910	
OK-GIB	Antonov AN-2	1G168-01	
OK-GIC	Antonov AN-2TD	1G168-03	
OK-GJC	LET Z-37A Cmelák	22-18	
OK-GJS	LET Z-37A Cmelák	22-11	
OK-GJU	LET Z-37A Cmelák	22-13	
OK-GJV	LET Z-37A Cmelák	22-14	
OK-GJW	LET Z-37A-C2 Cmelák	22-15	
OK-GKA	Cessna 172M	66459	N80228
OK-GKG	Cessna 172M	66111	N9354H
OK-GKH	Cessna 172M	65979	D-ETRW
			N9154H
OK-GKO	Piper PA-28R-200 Cherokee Arrow II	28R-7635119	D-EFEI
			N7828C
OK-GTJ	Beech 300LW Super King Air	FA-223	D-IHHB
			N80775
OK-HGC	Aero 45	51158	

Regn.	Type	C/n	Prev.Id.
OK-HIR	Antonov AN-2	1G176-39	UR-62570
			CCCP62570
OK-HJB	LET Z-37A Cmelák	23-02	
OK-HJC	LET Z-37 Cmelák	23-03	
OK-HJD	LET Z-37A Cmelák	23-04	
OK-HJE	LET Z-37A Cmelák	23-05	
OK-HJF	LET Z-37A Cmelák	23-07	
OK-HJG	LET Z-37A Cmelák	23-10	
OK-HJH	LET Z-37 Cmelák	23-11	
OK-HJI	LET Z-37A Cmelák *(Stored)*	23-14	
OK-HJJ	LET Z-37 Cmelák *(Stored)*	23-15	
OK-HJK	LET Z-37A Cmelák	23-17	
OK-HJM	LET Z-37A Cmelák	23-19	
OK-HJU	LET Z-37 Cmelák	23-23	
OK-HKC	Reims/Cessna F.150M	1422	D-EBXD
OK-HKD	Cessna 172N	68857	TF-IDA
			N734HB
OK-HKE	Cessna TU.206G Turbo Stationair II	03877	I-IPAC
			(N7336C)
OK-HKS	Piper PA-23-250 Aztec F	27-7754134	N95EB
			N63811
OK-HLF	Zlin Z.126 Trenér 2	715	CzAF213
OK-HLH	Zlin Z.126 Trenér 2	716	CzAF216
OK-HLJ	Zlin Z.126 Trenér 2	721	CzAF219
OK-HLK	Zlin Z.126 Trenér 2	722	CzAF220
OK-HRE	Zlin Z.50LA	0010	OK-HZE
OK-HYA	LET Z-37-2C Cmelák	23-08	
OK-IFG	Zlin Z.126 Trenér 2	746	
OK-IFH	Zlin Z.126 Trenér 2	748	
OK-IGL	Zlin Z.126 Trenér 2	796	
OK-IHK	Zlin Z.126 Trenér 2	731	CzAF229
OK-IHM	Zlin Z.126 Trenér 2	733	CzAF231
OK-IHQ	Zlin Z.126 Trenér 2	778	CzAF243
OK-IHR	Zlin Z.126 Trenér 2	773	CzAF238
OK-IKA	Cessna 152	82048	N67837
OK-IKC	Cessna 152	81978	N67713
OK-IKF	Cessna 152	81144	D-EYAP(1)
			OH-CKX
			C-GGTJ
			N49091
OK-IKH	Cessna 152	82176	N68193
OK-IKL	Cessna R.182 Skylane RG	00161	D-ETAT
			N222CM
			N2361C
OK-IKQ	Cessna 172N	71299	N2487E
OK-ILP	Zlin Z.42M	0158	
OK-ILQ	Zlin Z.42M	0159	
OK-IMG	Zlin Z.126 Trenér 2	776	CzAF241
OK-IMI	Zlin Z.126T Trenér 2	780	CzAF245
OK-IRF	Zlin Z.50LA	0016	
OK-IRG	Zlin Z.50LA	0017	
OK-IRJ	Zlin Z.50LA	0020	
OK-IYA	LET L-410UVP	770101	OK-026
			OK-IYA
			OK-160
OK-JAS	Reims/Cessna FR.172G Rocket	0222	D-ECKG
OK-JCA	Zlin Z.226MS Trenér	839	
OK-JGD	Zlin Z.126 Trenér 2	860	
OK-JGL	Zlin Z.126 Trenér 2	801	
OK-JGT	Zlin Z.226MS Trenér	804	
OK-JHA	Zlin Z.126 Trenér 2	811	
OK-JHC	Zlin Z.126 Trenér 2	816	DM-WAR
			OK-JHC
OK-JHE	Zlin Z.126 Trenér 2	818	
OK-JID	Antonov AN-2R	1G186-18	
OK-JIF	Antonov AN-2T	1G186-20	OM-JIF
			OK-JIF
			OM-JIF
			OK-JIF
OK-JIH	Antonov AN-2R	1G186-22	OM-JIH
			OK-JIH
OK-JIJ	Antonov AN-2R	1G186-24	
OK-JIL	Antonov AN-2R *(Stored)*	1G186-26	
OK-JIM	Antonov AN-2R *(Stored)*	1G186-27	
OK-JIQ	Antonov AN-2R	1G186-28	

Regn.	Type	C/n	Prev.Id.
OK-JIX	Mil Mi-2	536012029	OM-JIX
			OK-JIX
OK-JJA	LET Z-37A Cmelák	24-08	
OK-JJB	LET Z-37A Cmelák	24-02	
OK-JJC	LET Z-37A Cmelák	24-09	
OK-JJD	LET Z-37A Cmelák	24-05	
OK-JKA	LET Z-37A Cmelák	24-01	
	(C/n now quoted as 23-21, possibly a rebuild?)		
OK-JKF	Cessna 172N	71045	D-EVOA
			N1556E
OK-JKS	Piper PA-34-200T Seneca II	34-7970494	D-GELD
			N8080Y
OK-JLA	Zlin Z.126 Trenér 2	781	CzAF246
OK-JLB	Zlin Z.126 Trenér 2	785	CzAF250
OK-JLE	Zlin Z.126 Trenér 2	827	CzAF259
OK-JLF	Zlin Z.126 Trenér 2	820	CzAF252
OK-JLU	Zlin Z.42M	0189	
OK-JOA	Aero L-60S Brigadyr	03	
OK-JSB	Zlin Z.42M	0182	
OK-JSC	Zlin Z.42M	0183	
OK-JSD	Zlin Z.42M	0185	
OK-JSE	Zlin Z.42M	0186	
OK-JSF	Zlin Z.42M	0187	
OK-JXA	SK.1 Trempik (Homebuilt)	unkn	OK-006
OK-JZE	Yakovlev YAK-C11	171511	OK-242
			OK-JIL
OK-KAT	Diamond DA.20-A1 Katana	10021	N322FT
OK-KGB	Aero 45S	04016	
OK-KIC	Antonov AN-2R	1G186-34	
OK-KID	Antonov AN-2RD	1G186-35	
OK-KIE(2)	Antonov AN-2R	1G186-36	
OK-KIF	Antonov AN-2R *(Derelict)*	1G186-37	
OK-KII	Antonov AN-2R	1G190-04	
OK-KIJ	Antonov AN-2R	1G190-05	OM-KIJ
			OK-KIJ
OK-KIK	Antonov AN-2R	1G190-06	
OK-KIL	Antonov AN-2R	1G190-07	
OK-KIN	Antonov AN-2R	1G190-09	OM-KIN
			OK-KIN
OK-KIP	Antonov AN-2R	1G190-10	
OK-KIQ	Antonov AN-2R	1G190-11	
OK-KIR	Antonov AN-2R	1G190-12	OM-KIR
			OK-KIR
OK-KIT	Antonov AN-2R	1G190-14	OM-KIT
			OK-KIT
OK-KIV	Antonov AN-2R *(Stored)*	1G190-16	
OK-KIZ(2)	Mil Mi-2	526847100	RA-20208
			CCCP20208
OK-KJA	Aero L-60SF Brigadyr	150205	
OK-KJB	LET Z-37A Cmelák	23-28	
OK-KJT	LET Z-37A Cmelák	24-16	
OK-KKA	Cessna 127RG Cutlass	0128	N6266R
OK-KKB	LET Z-37A Cmelák	24-10	
OK-KKD	Cessna 172N	73712	N5138J
OK-KLN	LET Z.37A-2 Cmelák *(c/n 11-11 OK-AJO rebuild)*	24-19	OM-KLN
			OK-KLN
OK-KMB	Zlin Z.226AS Akrobat Special	02-08	
OK-KMJ	Zlin Z.226MS Trenér	11-08	
OK-KMK	Zlin Z.226T Trenér 6	08-12	
OK-KMM	Zlin Z.126T Trenér 2	814	DM-WAJ
			OK-JFP
OK-KMO	Zlin Z.226M Trenér	0016	
OK-KMP	Zlin Z.226MS Trenér	0017	
	(C/n formerly quoted as 08-07)		
OK-KMR	Zlin Z.226MS Trenér	0019	
OK-KMS	Zlin Z.226M Trenér	08-21	
	(C/n formerly quoted as 09-21; most likely 0021)		
OK-KMT	Zlin Z.226MS Trenér	0022	
OK-KNA	Zlin Z.226M Trenér	0028	
OK-KNB	Zlin Z.226M Trenér	09-29	
OK-KNC(2)	Zlin Z.142	0206	
OK-KND	Zlin Z.226M Trenér	0031	
OK-KNE	Zlin Z.142	0222	
OK-KNF	Zlin Z.226MS Trenér	0033	
OK-KNG	Zlin Z.226 MS Trenér	0034	

Regn.	Type	C/n	Prev.Id.
OK-KNH	Zlin Z.142	0221	
OK-KNK	Zlin Z.142	0228	
OK-KNL	Zlin Z.142	0229	
OK-KNM	Zlin Z.226M Trenér	0040	
OK-KNN	Zlin Z.226MS Trenér	0041	
OK-KNR	Zlin Z.126T Trenér 2	103	
OK-KNX	Zlin Z.226MS Trenér	0047	
OK-KOS	Zlin Z.43	0083	
OK-LAB	Piper PA-32R-301 Saratoga II TC	3257098	OY-JAG
			N9515N
OK-LHA	Zlin Z.326M Trenér Master	301	
OK-LJA	LET Z-37A Cmelák	24-14	
OK-LJR	Mil Mi-2	537327091	OM-LJR
			OK-LJR
OK-LKA	LET Z-37A Cmelák	24-12	
OK-LKF	Aero L-60S Brigadyr	150727	
OK-LKG	Aero L-60S Brigadyr	150728	
OK-LKH	Aero L-60S Brigadyr	150729	
OK-LKJ	Aero L-60S Brigadyr	150801	
OK-LKN	Aero L-60 Brigadyr	150507	
OK-LKP	Cessna 182R Skylane	67924	D-EXAP
			SE-IHB
			(N9063H)
OK-LKR	Aero L-60S Brigadyr	150413	
OK-LLF	Zlin Z.226MS Trenér	121	
OK-LLH	Zlin Z.226T Trenér 6	123	
OK-LLK	Zlin Z.226MS Trenér	126	
OK-LMB	Zlin Z.226MS Trenér	124	OK-LLI
OK-LMD	Zlin Z.226M Trenér	120	OK-LLE
OK-LME	Zlin Z.226MS Trenér	119	
OK-LMF	Zlin Z.226MS Trenér	139	
OK-LMG	Zlin Z.226M Trenér	135	OK-LLS
OK-LMH	Zlin Z.226M Trenér	118	
OK-LMI	Zlin Z.226MS Trenér	128	OK-LLM
OK-LMJ	Zlin Z.226MS Trenér	137	
OK-LNA	Zlin Z.142	0231	
OK-LNB	Zlin Z.142	0232	
OK-LNC	Zlin Z.142	0235	
OK-LND	Zlin Z.142	0242	
OK-LNE	Zlin Z.142	0247	
OK-LNG	Zlin Z.142	0251	
OK-LNH	Zlin Z.142	0252	
OK-LNI	Zlin Z.142	0253	
OK-LNJ	Zlin Z.142	0254	
OK-LNK	Zlin Z.142	0258	
OK-LNL	Zlin Z.142	0259	
OK-LNM	Zlin Z.142	0262	
OK-LNN	Zlin Z.226MS Trenér	105	
OK-LRA	LET L-410UVP-E	882216	CCCP67605
OK-LSV	Maule MX-7-235 Star Rocket	10062C	D-EKMM(2)
			OE-KUW
OK-MDC	Antonov AN-2R	1G176-25	HA-MDC
OK-MDV	Antonov AN-2R	1G186-03	HA-MDV
OK-MFE	Zlin Z.226MS Trenér	149	
OK-MFK	Zlin Z.226MS Trenér	155	
OK-MFO	Zlin Z.226M Trenér	159	
OK-MFP	Zlin Z.226T Trenér 6	160	
OK-MFQ	Zlin Z.226MS Trenér	161	
OK-MFV	Zlin Z.226MS Trenér	168	
OK-MFX	Zlin Z.226T Trenér 6	163	
OK-MFY	Zlin Z.226MS Trenér	170	
OK-MGD	Zlin Z.226MS Trenér	175	
OK-MGF	Zlin Z.226T Trenér 6	177	
OK-MGJ	Zlin Z.226MS Trenér	181	
OK-MGK	Zlin Z.226MS Trenér	182	
OK-MGM	Zlin Z.226MS Trenér	184	
OK-MGQ	Zlin Z.226M Trenér	188	
OK-MGR	Zlin Z.226MS Trenér	189	
OK-MGU	Zlin Z.226MS Trenér	193	
OK-MGV	Zlin Z.226MS Trenér	194	
OK-MGX	Zlin Z.226MS Trenér	190	
OK-MIA	Aérospatiale AS.355F2 Ecureuil 2	5187	N5799W
OK-MIK	PZL Kania	900103	SP-SSA
OK-MJL	Aero L-60S Brigadyr	151011	
OK-MJN	Aero L-60 Brigadyr	150826	

Regn.	Type	C/n	Prev.Id.
OK-MJO	Aero L-60SF Brigadyr (Stored)	150822	
OK-MJP	Aero L-60 Brigadyr	151128	
OK-MJQ	Aero L-60S Brigadyr	150827	
OK-MJS	Aero L-60 Brigadyr	151127	
OK-MKR	Piper PA-44-180 T Seminole	44-8207014	D-GJOY
			F-GJOY
			N82067
OK-MLA	Cessna 172P	75132	G-BTGF
			N55195
OK-MME	Orlican L-40 Meta-Sokol	150203	
OK-MML	Orlican L-40 Meta-Sokol	150607	
OK-MMM	Orlican L-40 Meta-Sokol	150608	
OK-MMN	Orlican L-40 Meta-Sokol	150609	
OK-MMQ	Orlican L-40 Meta-Sokol	150207	
OK-MMR	Orlican L-40 Meta-Sokol	150612	
OK-MMT	Orlican L-40 Meta-Sokol	150307	
OK-MNA	Zlin Z.142	0266	
OK-MNB	Zlin Z.142	0267	
OK-MNC	Zlin Z.142	0279	
OK-MND	Zlin Z.142	0280	
OK-MNE	Zlin Z.142	0306	
OK-MNF	Zlin Z.142	0283	
OK-MNG	Zlin Z.142	0285	
OK-MNH	Zlin Z.142	0286	
OK-MNI	Zlin Z.142	0288	
OK-MNJ	Zlin Z.142	0289	
OK-MNK	Zlin Z.142	0291	
OK-MNL	Zlin Z.142	0295	
OK-MNM	Zlin Z.142	0302	
OK-MNU	Zlin Z.142	0301	
OK-MPA	Zlin Z.226MS Trenér	246	
OK-MPB	Zlin Z.226MS Trenér	247	
OK-MPG	Zlin Z.226MS Trenér	252	
OK-MPJ	Zlin Z.226B Trenér	255	
OK-MPK	Zlin Z.226MS Trenér	256	
OK-MPP	Zlin Z.226MS Trenér	261	
OK-MPT	Zlin Z.226MS Trenér	266	
OK-MPV	Zlin Z.226MS Trenér	268	
OK-MQB	Zlin Z.226MS Trenér	273	
OK-MQE	Zlin Z.226MS Trenér	276	
OK-MQG	Zlin Z.226B Trenér	278	
OK-MQH	Zlin Z.226MS Trenér	279	
OK-MQI	Zlin Z.226B-SL Trenér	280	
OK-MQJ	Zlin Z.226MS Trenér	281	
OK-MQL	Zlin Z.226B Trenér	283	
OK-MQM	Zlin Z.226MS Trenér	284	
OK-MQN	Zlin Z.226MS Trenér	285	
OK-MRA	Zlin Z.226MS Trenér	198	OK-MHA
OK-MTA	Aero L-60S Brigadyr	150820	
OK-MTF	Aero L-60S Brigadyr	151202	
OK-MTG	Aero L-60S Brigadyr	151203	
OK-MTH	Aero L-60S Brigadyr	150813	
OK-MTI	Aero L-60S Brigadyr	150815	
OK-MTK	Aero L-60S Brigadyr	150810	
OK-MYA	Antonov AN-2 (Scrapped)	19507	
OK-NDG	LET L-410UVP	831138	OK-NZG
			OK-OZG
OK-NEW	Piper PA-28-181 Archer III	2843271	N4147V
			N9507N
OK-NHE	Aero 145 Super Aero	19013	
OK-NJA	LET Z-37A Cmelák	25-01	
OK-NJB	LET Z-37A Cmelák	25-02	
OK-NJD	LET Z-37A Cmelák	25-06	
OK-NJE	LET Z-37 Cmelák (Stored)	25-07	
OK-NJG	LET Z-37A Cmelák	25-09	
OK-NJH	LET Z-37A Cmelák	25-10	
OK-NJI	LET Z-37A Cmelák	25-11	
OK-NJJ	LET Z-37A Cmelák	25-13	
OK-NJK	LET Z-37A Cmelák	25-14	
OK-NJL	LET Z-37A Cmelák	25-15	
OK-NJM	LET Z-37A Cmelák	25-17	
OK-NJN	LET Z-37A Cmelák	25-18	
OK-NJO	LET Z-37A Cmelák	25-19	
OK-NJP	LET Z-37A Cmelák	25-20	

Regn.	Type	C/n	Prev.Id.
OK-NJR	LET Z-37A Cmelák	25-04	OM-NJR
			OK-NJR
OK-NMO	Orlican L-40 Meta-Sokol	150308	
OK-NNB	Aero L-60S Brigadyr	151207	
OK-NNG	Aero L-60S Brigadyr	151212	
OK-NNH	Aero L-60S Brigadyr	151213	
OK-NNI	Aero L-60S Brigadyr	151214	
OK-NNJ	Aero L-60S Brigadyr	151215	
OK-NNN	Zlin Z.142	0311	
OK-NOA	Zlin Z.142	0309	
OK-NOB	Zlin Z.142	0310	
OK-NOC	Zlin Z.142	0312	
OK-NOD	Zlin Z.142	0327	
OK-NOE	Zlin Z.142	0328	
OK-NOF	Zlin Z.142	0330	
OK-NOG	Zlin Z.142	0320	
OK-NOH	Zlin Z.142	0331	
OK-NOI	Zlin Z.142	0335	
OK-NOJ	Zlin Z.142	0337	
OK-NOK	Zlin Z.142	0338	
OK-NOL	Zlin Z.142	0340	
OK-NOM	Zlin Z.142	0341	
OK-NON	Zlin Z.142	0349	
OK-NOO	Zlin Z.142	0350	
OK-NOP	Zlin Z.142	0352	
OK-NPE	Orlican L-40 Meta-Sokol	150504	
OK-NPF	Orlican L-40 Meta-Sokol	150714	
OK-NPK	Orlican L-40 Meta-Sokol	150804	
OK-NPL	Orlican L-40 Meta-Sokol	150805	
OK-NPM	Orlican L-40 Meta-Sokol	150907	G-ARSP
OK-NPN	Orlican L-40 Meta-Sokol	150807	
OK-NPR	Orlican L-40 Meta-Sokol	150811	
OK-NPU	Orlican L-40 Meta-Sokol	150814	OM-NPU
			OK-NPU
OK-NPV	Orlican L-40 Meta-Sokol	150815	
OK-OFB	LET L.200A Morava	170606	OM-OFB
			OK-OFB
			OE-FSE
			OK-OFB
OK-OFI	LET L.200A Morava	170614	OE-FSC
			OK-OFI
OK-OFK	LET L.200A Morava	170620	
OK-OFL	LET L.200A Morava	170618	CzAF0618
OK-OGA	LET L.200D Morava	170317	OK-BYB
OK-OGB	LET L.200D Morava	170318	OK-BYC
OK-OHD	LET L.200D Morava	170212	
OK-OHE	LET L.200A Morava	170102	
OK-OHF	LET L.200A Morava	170215	
OK-OHG	LET L.200A Morava	170617	
OK-OHH	LET L.200A Morava	170619	
OK-OIT	Mil Mi-2	528919104	OM-OIT
			OK-OIT
OK-OJA	LET Z-37A Cmelák	25-25	
OK-OJB	LET Z-37A Cmelák	25-26	
OK-OJC	LET Z-37A Cmelák	25-27	
OK-OJD	LET Z-37A Cmelák	25-29	
OK-OJE	LET Z-37A Cmelák (Stored)	25-30	
OK-OJF	LET Z-37A Cmelák	25-31	
OK-OJG	LET Z-37A Cmelák (Stored)	25-33	
OK-OJH	LET Z-37A Cmelák	25-34	
OK-OJI	LET Z-37A Cmelák	25-35	
OK-OJJ	LET Z-37A Cmelák	25-37	
OK-OJK	LET Z-37A Cmelák (Stored)	25-38	
OK-OJL	LET Z-37A Cmelák	25-39	
OK-OKR	Piper PA-34-220T Seneca V	3449163	
OK-OKZ	LET L.200A Morava	170320	
OK-ONR	Zlin Z.142	0381	
OK-OPA	Zlin Z.142	0357	
OK-OPB	Zlin Z.142	0358	
OK-OPC	Zlin Z.142	0360	
OK-OPD	Zlin Z.142	0361	
OK-OPE	Zlin Z.142	0363	
OK-OPG	Zlin Z.142	0371	
OK-OPH	Zlin Z.142	0372	
OK-OPI	Zlin Z.142	0379	

Regn.	Type	C/n	Prev.Id.
OK-OPJ	Zlin Z.142	0380	
OK-OPK	Zlin Z.142	0382	
OK-OPL	Zlin Z.142	0383	
OK-OPM	Zlin Z.142	0385	
OK-OPN	Zlin Z.142	0386	
OK-OTA	Zlin Z.326M Trenér Master	604	CzAF0604
OK-OTB	Zlin Z.326 Trenér Master	605	CzAF0605
OK-OTD	Zlin Z.326 Trenér Master	609	CzAF0609
OK-OTE	Zlin Z.326 Trenér Master	610	CzAF0610
OK-PDB	LET L-410FG	851522	CzAF1522
OK-PDC	LET L-410FG	851524	CzAF1524
OK-PDO	LET L-410UVP	851411	UR-67507
			CCCP67507
OK-PEK	SOCATA TB-10 Tobago	420	HB-KAG
OK-PEP	SAAB-Scania SF.340A	018	HB-AHD
			SE-E18
OK-PFM	LET L.200A Morava	170710	
OK-PHG	LET L.200A Morava	170805	
OK-PHJ	LET L.200A Morava	170802	
OK-PHK	LET L.200A Morava	170704	
OK-PHR	Beech 58P Baron	TJ-237	D-IBEE
			OE-FKP
			N600PA
			4X-DZG
			N6680L
OK-PIM	Schweizer 269C	S-1185	SE-JAB
			N7503Q
OK-PJA	LET Z-37T Agro-Turbo	001	
OK-PJB	LET Z-37T Agro-Turbo	003	
OK-PJD	LET Z-37T Agro Turbo	006	
OK-PJN	LET Z-37T Agro-Turbo	002	OK-PXH
OK-PLA	LET L.200A Morava	170713	
OK-PLC	LET L.200A Morava	170715	
OK-PLE	LET L.200A Morava	170718	
OK-PLG	LET L.200A Morava	170720	
OK-PLH	LET L.200A Morava	170722	
OK-PLI	LET L.200D Morava	170723	
OK-PLJ	LET L.200D Morava	170724	
OK-PLL	LET L.200D Morava	170726	
OK-PLN	LET L.200A Morava	170728	
OK-PLO	LET L.200A Morava	170729	
OK-PLR	LET L.200A Morava	170801	
OK-PLS	LET L.200A Morava	170803	
OK-PLV	LET L.200D Morava	170815	SP-NXX
			SP-GBA
			CCCP-34454
OK-PNB	Zlin Z.142	0393	
OK-PNC	Zlin Z.142	0395	
OK-PND	Zlin Z.142	0399	
OK-PNE	Zlin Z.142	0401	
OK-PNF	Zlin Z.142	0402	
OK-PNG	Zlin Z.142	0404	
OK-PNH	Zlin Z.142	0407	
OK-PNI	Zlin Z.142	0409	
OK-PNJ	Zlin Z.142	0410	
OK-PNK	Zlin Z.142	0412	
OK-PNL	Zlin Z.142	0418	
OK-PNM	Zlin Z.142	0415	
OK-PPA	Zlin Z.142	0416	
OK-PPM	Zlin Z.142	0413	
OK-PRO	LET L.200A Morava	170705	CCCP-34387
	(C/n previously listed as 170105)		
OK-PYA	Antonov AN-2	115718	
OK-RDA	LET L-410UVP-E5	861813	OM-RAY
			OM-RDA
			OK-RDA
OK-RDE	LET L-410UVP-E1	861801	LZ-LSA
OK-REK	SAAB-Scania SF.340A	071	SE-E71
			D-CDIA
			SE-E71
OK-RFP	LET L.200D Morava	171114	
OK-RHH	LET L.200D Morava	171418	YU-BBI
OK-RID	Antonov AN-2	117008	CzAF7008
OK-RIE	Antonov AN-2	117413	CzAF7413
OK-RJA	LET Z-37T Agro-Turbo	007	

Regn.	Type	C/n	Prev.Id.
OK-RJD	LET Z-37T Agro-Turbo	010	
OK-RJF	LET Z-37T Agro-Turbo	012	
OK-RJG	LET Z-37T Agro-Turbo	013	
OK-RJH	LET Z-37T Agro-Turbo	014	
OK-RJJ	LET Z-37T Agro-Turbo	016	
OK-RJK	LET Z-37T Agro-Turbo	017	
OK-RJL	LET Z-37T Agro-Turbo	018	
OK-RJM	LET Z-37T Agro-Turbo	019	
OK-RJN	LET Z-37T Agro-Turbo	020	
OK-RMA	LET L.200D Morava	171124	
OK-RRD	Zlin Z.50LS	0047	
OK-RXE	Aero C-104S (Jungmann)	X001	OK-AXT
OK-RYA	Antonov AN-2 (Derelict)	117010	
OK-SDJ	LET L-410UVP-E	871925	SovAF 1925
OK-SEN	Zlin Z.326 Trenér Master	893	F-BMQR
OK-SJA	Z-137T Agro-Turbo	022	
OK-SJB	Z-137T Agro-Turbo	023	
OK-SJC	Z-137T Agro-Turbo	024	
OK-SLI	Beech 58 Baron	TH-1757	N3257N
OK-SNZ	Zlin Z.142	0441	
OK-TCD	Tupolev TU-154M	792	
OK-TEC	Reims/Cessna FR.172K Hawk XP	0627	D-EOMS
OK-TGA	PZL M-18A Dromader (Preserved)	1Z018-10	
OK-TGD	PZL M-18A Dromader	1Z018-13	
OK-TGG	PZL M-18A Dromader	1Z018-16	OM-TGG OK-TGG
OK-TGL	PZL M-18A Dromader	1Z018-26	
OK-TGR	PZL M-18A Dromader	1Z019-16	OM-TGR OK-TGR (G-MATE)
OK-TRO	Zlin Z.50LS	0055	
OK-TRP	Zlin Z.50L	0059	
OK-TRQ	Zlin Z.50L	0060	
OK-TVQ	Boeing 737-86N (Reservation .00)	28618	N1786B
OK-TVR	Boeing 737-4Y0	23870	G-OBMG
OK-TVS	Boeing 737-4Y0	24911	SE-DTB EI-CIX OY-MBK PT-WBJ PP-SOJ (TC-ADA)
OK-UCE	Tupolev TU-154M	89A804	
OK-UDS	LET L-410UVP-E13	892321	
OK-UFO	SAAB-Scania SF.340A	141	ZK-NSL SE-KRS D-CHBA SE-F41
OK-UIA	Antonov AN-2	1G237-36	
OK-UJD	LET Z-37 Cmelák	005	
OK-UJK	Z-137T Agro-Turbo	027	
OK-UJL	Z-137T Agro-Turbo	028	
OK-UJO	Z-137T Agro-Turbo	031	
OK-UKB	PZL-104 Wilga 80	20890882	SP-FWS
OK-UKC	Reims/Cessna F.172G	0233	HB-CBO
OK-UKD	Piper PA-28-180 Cherokee C	28-2318	HB-OLN N819IW
OK-UKJ	Cessna 172F	52606	N172DP N8702U
OK-UXA	Aerotechnik XL-113	X 01	
OK-UXE	Piper J-3C-65 Cub (L-4J) (C/n quoted as 001/89 after rebuild)	12254	OK-YIE 44-79958
OK-UZB	LET L-610M	900003/X-03	OK-024 OK-132
OK-UZI	Beech 400 Beechjet	RJ-56	G-BSZP N1556W
OK-VGB	PZL M-18A Dromader	1Z021-19	
OK-VHA	Antonov AN-2	1G238-53	
OK-VHB	Antonov AN-2	1G238-54	
OK-VHC	Antonov AN-2TP	1G238-24	
OK-VHD	Antonov AN-2TP	1G238-25	
OK-VHJ	Antonov AN-2TP	1G234-02	
OK-VIB	Z-137T Agro-Turbo	033	
OK-VIH	Z-137T Agro-Turbo	039	
OK-VII	Z-137T Agro-Turbo	040	
OK-VIL	PZL Kania	900305	
OK-VJP	LET Z-37 Cmelák	01-08	

Regn.	Type	C/n	Prev.Id.
OK-VJT	LET Z-37A Cmelák	01-12	
OK-VJV	LET Z-37C-3 Cmelák	01-14	
OK-VJX	LET Z-37 Cmelák	01-16	
OK-VKF	Reims/Cessna F.172G	0277	D-EKER(2)
OK-VNB	Zlin Z.142	0514	
OK-VNC	Zlin Z.142	0515	
OK-VNF	Zlin Z.142	0528	
OK-VNH	Zlin Z.142	0527	
OK-VNJ	Zlin Z.142	0517	HA-SHA
OK-VNP	Zlin Z.242L	P001/0490	OK-076
OK-VZB	Zlin Z.50LE	0052	OK-072
OK-WAA	Airbus A.310-304	564	F-WWCB
OK-WAB	Airbus A.310-304	567	F-WWCD
OK-WDC	LET L-410UVP-E8D	912531	
OK-WDR	LET L-410UVP-E20C	912607	CCCP67677
OK-WDT	LET L-410UVP-E20C	912615	CCCP67684
OK-WEL	Zlin Z.43	0089	
OK-WGF	Boeing 737-4Y0	24903	9M-MJN
OK-WGG	Boeing 737-4Y0	24693	9M-MJM
OK-WHB	Antonov AN-2	1G85-55	
OK-WHN	LET L.200D Morava	171415	
OK-WIQ	Aérospatiale AS.355F2 Ecureuil 2	5483	OM-WIQ OK-WIQ SE-JET F-WYMA
OK-WIR	Bell 206L-3 Long Ranger III	51511	C-FLSV
OK-WJD	LET Z-37 Cmelák	02-04	
OK-WJI	LET Z-37 Cmelák	02-10	
OK-WJQ	LET Z-37 Cmelák	03-11	
OK-WJT	LET Z-37 Cmelák	03-14	
OK-WJU	LET Z-37 Cmelák	03-17	HA-MGC
OK-WKF	Cessna 150G	66672	C-FWBL CF-WBL (N2772S)
OK-WKQ	LET Z-37 Cmelák (Wfu)	02-26	
OK-WNL	Zlin Z.142C	0525	C-FKII
OK-WNN	Zlin Z.142L	0534	
OK-WOA	Zlin Z.43	0090	
OK-WOB	Zlin Z.43	0085	
OK-WOC	Zlin Z.43	0086	
OK-WOD	Zlin Z.43	0087	
OK-WOE	Zlin Z.43	0088	
OK-WOF	Zlin Z.43	0091	
OK-WOH	Zlin Z.43	0101	
OK-WOI	Zlin Z.43	0102	
OK-WOJ	Zlin Z.43	0103	
OK-WOK	Zlin Z.43	0095	
OK-WOL	Zlin Z.43	0104	
OK-WRK	Zlin Z.50LS	0065	
OK-WRL	Zlin Z.50LS	0066	
OK-WXA	Zlin Z.526ASM Akrobat	1026	
OK-WXE(2)	Extra EA.300	026	D-EIUE
OK-WYI	LET L-410UVP	912616	CCCP67685
OK-XFA	Aeritalia/SNIAS ATR-72-201	285	(F-GIGU) F-WWLO
OK-XFB	Aeritalia/SNIAS ATR-72-201	297	F-WWLW
OK-XFC	Aeritalia/SNIAS ATR-72-201	299	F-WWLX
OK-XFD	Aeritalia/SNIAS ATR-72-201	303	F-WWLB
OK-XGA	Boeing 737-55S	26539	(OO-SYL) N1790B
OK-XGB	Boeing 737-55S	26540	(OO-SYM)
OK-XGC	Boeing 737-55S	26541	(OO-SYN)
OK-XGD	Boeing 737-55S	26542	(OO-SYO)
OK-XGE	Boeing 737-55S	26543	(OO-SYP)
OK-XIA	Robinson R-22 Beta	2115	
OK-XIB	Robinson R-22 Beta (W/o 19.12.99)	2120	
OK-XIF	Robinson R-22M Mariner	2233M	N2352Y
OK-XIG	Antonov AN-2T	1G98-70	
OK-XIS	Bell 206L-3 Long Ranger III	51602	N5129G
OK-XJA	Zlin Z.137T Agro-Turbo	046	
OK-XJI	LET Z-37 Cmelák	07-10	
OK-XKB(2)	Cessna 150H	69265	N91AV
OK-XKG	Reims/Cessna F.172G	0201	G-ATKS
OK-XKH	Cessna 150J	69891	N51280
OK-XKJ	Reims/Cessna F.150H	0325	HB-CTE

Regn.	Type	C/n	Prev.Id.
OK-XNB	Zlin Z.142C	0550	
OK-XOA	Zlin Z.43	0105	
OK-XOB	Zlin Z.43	0106	
OK-XOC	Zlin Z.43	0107	
OK-XOD	Zlin Z.43	0108	
OK-XOE	Zlin Z.43	0111	
OK-XOG	Zlin Z.43	0112	
OK-XOH	Zlin Z.43	0113	
OK-XRA	Zlin Z.50LX	0071	
OK-XRB	Zlin Z.50LX	0072	
OK-XRC	Zlin Z.50LX	0073	
OK-XRD	Zlin Z.50LX	0074	
OK-XRG	Zlin Z.50LS	0070	SE-KMY
OK-XRK	Zlin Z.50M	0078	
OK-XTA	Extra EA .300/S	004	D-EBEW(3)
OK-XYB	Mil Mi-8T	99254381	27014 / CCCP27014
OK-XYC	Mil Mi-8T	99250952	RA-27004 / CCCP27004
OK-XYD	Mil Mi-8TP	99254392	RA-27015 / CCCP27015
OK-XYJ	Zlin Z.143L	0093/04	
OK-XZA	LET L-610G	920102	OK-136
	(Originally reported as c/n 910101)		
OK-YES	Beech B300 Super King Air	FL-221	N3030S
OK-YIJ	Robinson R-22 Beta	2366	N8029Q
OK-YIK	Robinson R-44 Astro	0021	
OK-YIP	Bell 206L-4 Long Ranger IV	52068	N2137P
OK-YIR	Bell 206LT Twin Ranger	52061	N6252Q
OK-YJA	LET Z-37 Cmelák	08-03	
OK-YJC	LET Z-37 Cmelák	08-05	
OK-YJD	LET Z-37 Cmelák	05-02	HA-MGE / (YU-BFF)
OK-YJF	LET Z-37 Cmelák	08-01	HA-SCA
OK-YJH	Z-137T Agro Turbo	047	
OK-YKD	LET Z-37A-2 Cmelák	07-19	
OK-YNB	Zlin Z.242L	0655	
OK-YNE	Zlin Z.242L	0659	
OK-YNG	Zlin Z.242L	0654	
OK-YOA	Zlin Z.143L	0001	
OK-YXA	Brouchek W-01 (Homebuilt)	unkn	
OK-YXB	Mil Mi-8T	041032	CzAF1032
OK-YXC	Mil Mi-8T	051632	CzAF1632
OK-YXJ	Jodel/Falconar F-11	6268	
OK-ZIL	Robinson R-22 Beta	2400	N8101G
OK-ZIO	Robinson R-44 Astro	0150	
OK-ZIU	Bell 206LT Twin Ranger	52032	N93LT
OK-ZJC	LET Z-37A Cmelák	09-10	HA-MGP
OK-ZJD	LET Z-37A Cmelák	09-17	HA-MGJ
OK-ZJF	LET Z-37 Cmelák	10-01	HA-MGM
OK-ZJH	LET Z-37A-C3 Cmelák	10-27	HA-MGS
OK-ZJO	LET Z-37 Cmelák	09-11	
OK-ZJP	LET Z-37 Cmelák	09-12	
OK-ZJQ	LET Z-37 Cmelák	10-13	
OK-ZJV	LET Z-37 Cmelák	10-11	
OK-ZKB	LET Z-37A Cmelák	09-02	
OK-ZKC	LET Z-37 Cmelák (Wfu)	09-03	
OK-ZKN	LET Z-37 Cmelák	11-01	
OK-ZLA	Diamond DA.20-A1 Katana	10006	N106CM
OK-ZOE	Zlin Z.143L	0003	
OK-ZRA	Zlin Z.526AFS-V Akrobat	1118	
OK-ZRB	Zlin Z.526AFS-V Akrobat	1119	
OK-ZRC	Zlin Z.526AFS Akrobat	1125	
OK-ZRD	Zlin Z.526F Trenér Master	1147	
OK-ZSC	Zlin Z.42MU	0003	OK-XSB
OK-ZSD	Zlin Z.42MU	0004	
OK-ZSE	Zlin Z.42MU	0006	
OK-ZSF	Zlin Z.42MU	0007	
OK-ZSG	Zlin Z.42MU	0009	
OK-ZSH	Zlin Z.42MU	0010	
OK-ZYV	Inteco VM-23 Variant	23 X 01	

Regn.	Type	C/n	Prev.Id.
OK-...	Bell 206L-3 Long Ranger III	51239	N2271M / TC-HTH
OK-...	Cessna 172P	74664	D-EVAD / N53020
OK-...	Cessna 414	0505	OY-BSD / (N505ML) / D-IGOR / OY-BSD / G-BBYT / (G-BBRK) / N9092Q
OK-...	Diamond DA-20-A1 Katana	10212	N812CH
OK-...	Diamond DA-20-A1 Katana	10228	N228DA
OK-...	Hughes 369D	106-0007D	D-HDEK(3) / OE-DXN
OK-...	Orlican L-40 Meta-Sokol	150905	G-AROF
OK-...	Robinson R-22 Beta	2201	
OK-...	Robinson R-22 Beta	2322	N23627

PROTOTYPE SERIES

OK-016	Mikoyan Mig-21U	unkn	CzAF
OK-018	Ilyushin IL-18D	18002202	DDR-STC / DM-STC
OK-020	Yakovlev YAK-40	9431436	OK-EXB / OK-EEA / OK-020
OK-028	LET L-410UVP Turbolet	810625	
OK-042	VSO-10 Gradient	150001	
OK-044	VSO-10 Gradient	unkn	
OK-064	LET L-13SW Vivat	920425	
OK-066	LET L-13SE Vivat	unkn	
OK-070	Zlin Z.50LS (Prototype)	0001	
OK-072	Zlin Z.143	0031	
OK-074	Zlin Z.143L	0092	
OK-080	Zlin Z.50M	unkn	
OK-112	Zlin Z.142	unkn	
OK-120	LET L-33 Solo (Prototype)	unkn	
OK-126	LET L-23 Blanik T	unkn	
OK-130	LET L-610	880001/X-01	OK-TZB / OK-038 / OK-130
OK-162	LET L-410UVP	X02	
OK-164	LET L-410UVP	770103	OK-IYC / OK-164
OK-182	Aero L-39MS Albatros	X-24	
OK-184	Aero L-39MS Albatros	X-22	
OK-186	Aero L-39ZA Albatros	533216	
OK-188	Aero L-39ZA Albatros	X-10	
OK-190	Aero L-39 Albatros	X-11	CzAF 3911 / OK-HXA
OK-192	Aero L-39 Albatros	unkn	
OK-194	Aero L-39 Albatros	4853	
OK-198	Aero L-39 Albatros	unkn	
OK-208	Aero L-39 Albatros	unkn	
OK-230	Aero Designs Pulsar	001	
OK-230	Alpha Air J-1B Don Quixote	unkn	
OK-238	LET L-213A	unkn	

MICROLIGHTS

OK-004	SP-1 Spunt		
OK-006	ZA-01 Microlight		
OK-008	Letov LK-2 Sluka		
OK-066	Type unknown		
OK-122	ULM-1 Gryff		
OK-210	Type unknown		
OK-212	Type unknown		OK-21

Regn.	Type	C/n	Prev.Id.
OK-220	Letov LK-2 Sluka		
OK-AUA-01	Toresi Straton D8 Moby Dick		
OK-AUA-09	Fantasy Air Cora Legato		
OK-AUD-07	J-3 Kitten		
OK-AUD-19	Pegass		
OK-AUE-28	Letov LK-2 Sluka	01-03	
OK-AUI-05	Type unknown		
OK-AUL-01	WK-94		
OK-AUO-11	CRO SPOL Swing		
OK-AUO-14	Rhönlerche		
OK-AUO-15	Rhönlerche		
OK-AUR-01	Ungo		
OK-AUR-05	Aeropro Fox		
OK-AUR-06	Aeropro Fox		
OK-AUR-07	Type unknown		
OK-AUR-10	Aeropro Fox		
OK-AUR-11	Aeropro Fox (?)		
OK-AUR-12	Vektor		
OK-AUR-17	Aeropro Fox	EV9507	
OK-AUR-25	Letov LK-2 Sluka		
OK-AUU-03	TL Ultralight TL-132 Condor	95C03	
OK-AUU-05	TL Ultralight TL-132 Condor		
OK-AUU-06	Letov LK-2M Sluka	829409x16	OK-WXA-O
OK-AUU-07	Letov ST-4 Aztek		
OK-AUU-09	Fantasy Air Cora		
OK-AUU-12	TL Ultralight TL-132 Condor		
OK-AUU-15	Rans S-6ES Coyote II		
OK-AUU-20	Fantasy Air Cora		
OK-AUU-25	TL Ultralight TL-132 Condor II	95C07	
OK-AUU-37	Letov LK-2M Sluka		
OK-AUU-39	TL Ultralight TL-132 Condor		
OK-AUU-43	TEAM Hi-Max		
OK-AZU-08	Junkers Profly II	20	
OK-AZU-O9	Junkers Profly II		
OK-BGA-1	Powered Para-Glider (Type unknown)		
OK-BPM-02	Jet Pocket (Para-Glider)		
OK-BUA-04	Fantasy Air Cora		
OK-BUA-16	Fantasy Air Cora		
OK-BUE-29	Letov LK-2M Sluka		OK-XXAV
OK-BUI-05	Test-1 Alpin glider		
OK-BUL-06	Fantasy Air Cora Legato		
OK-BUO-10	Rhönlerche		
OK-BUO-11	TL Ultralight TL-532 Fresh		
OK-BUR-01	Aeropro Fox	EV9508	
OK-BUR-03	Aeropro Fox	EV9609	
OK-BUR-04	Evektor Eurofox	EV9610	
OK-BUR-08	Rans S-6 Coyote II (Mod - unconfirmed)		
OK-BUR-09	Evektor EV-97 Eurostar		
OK-BUR-20	Kompakt		
OK-BUS-02	CR-090P		
OK-BUU-02	TL Ultralight TL-132 Condor		
OK-BUU-10	TL Ultralight TL-232 Condor Plus		
OK-BUU-16	Type unknown		
OK-BUU-18	Fantasy Air Cora		
OK-BUU-19	Fantasy Air Cora		
OK-BUU-21	Urban Air UFM Lambada		
OK-BUU-23	Kappa KP2V Sova		
OK-BUU-29	TL Ultralight TL-232 Condor Plus	96C10	
OK-BUU-30	Letov LK-2M Sluka	82-960001	
OK-BUU-31	Fisher FP-404 Classic		
OK-BUU-34	Straton D.8 Moby Dick		
OK-BUU-35	TEAM Hi-Max		
OK-BUU-40	TL Ultralight TL-32 Typhoon	9601	
OK-BUU-51	Urban Air UFM Lambada	13	
OK-BUY-02	Aeropro Fox	1501	
OK-BUY-07	Aeropro Fox		
OK-BZC-02	TL Ultralight TL-1/E90	D17	
OK-BZC-04	TL Ultralight TL-2/E90		
OK-BZC-05	TL Ultralight TL-22 Duo		
OK-BZF-02	Junkers Pro-Fly II		
OK-BZF-08	Type unknown		
OK-BZG-11	Super Wing MW-155		
OK-COR-97	Aerotecknik EV97 Eurostar		
OK-CUA-01	Atec Zephyr	BA-96	
OK-CUA-02	Fantasy Air Cora Legato		
OK-CUA-22	Fantasy Air Cora Legato		
OK-CUD-02	LET-Mont Tulak		
OK-CUO-07	CRO SPOL Swing		
OK-CUO-17	Powered glider, type unknown		
OK-CUR-08	CRO Metallica LG 2		
OK-CUR-09	Type unknown		
OK-CUR-11	Aerotecknik CZ		
OK-CUR-17	Aerotecknik P.220SKoala	9701-09	
OK-CUR-25	Aerotecknik CZ		
OK-CUR-97	Aerotecknik Eurostar		
OK-CUU-O9	Kappa-2 Sova		
OK-CUU-12	Fantasy Air Cora Legato		
OK-CUU-15	TL Ultralight TL-232 Condor Plus		
OK-CUU-18	Type unknown		
OK-CUU-27	Lazava		
OK-CUU-40	Type unknown		
OK-CUU-45	Fantasy Air Cora Legato		
OK-CUY-02	Type unknown		
OK-DUA-06	Toresi Straton Tukan		
OK-DUD-06	Storm		
OK-DUL-02	TL Ultralight TL-132 Condor		
OK-DUL-11	Tulak		
OK-DUO-04	Piper J-3CCub (Mikron engine)		
OK-DUO-09	TL Ultralight TL-132 Condor		
OK-DUR-12	Aerotecknik EV-97 Eurostar	980307	
OK-DUR-19	Evektor PEV-19 Eurostar		
OK-DUR-99	Zenair CH-601UL Zodiac	6-9071	
OK-DUU-06	Letov		
OK-DUU-07	Type unknown		
OK-DUU-14	TL Ultralight TL-96 Star		
OK-DUU-15	Urban Air UFM Lambada		
OK-DUU-16	Kappa-2U Sova		
OK-DUU-25	ATEC Zephyr		
OK-DUU-26	Kappa 77AS		
OK-DUU-37	Tecnam P.96 Golf		
OK-DUU-55	Moira Lambada		
OK-DZF-04	TL Ultralight TL-32 Typhoon		
OK-EUD-08	SG Aviation Storm 280G		
OK-EUL-05	Type unknown		
OK-EUL-10	Qualt 235MX		
OK-EUR-07	Evektor EV-97 Eurostar	99-0508	
OK-EUU-05	Kapa 77 KP-2USova		
OK-EUU-38	Urban UFM-10 Samba		
OK-EUU-39	Urban UFM-10 Samba		
OK-SXAA	WT-2S Chinook		
OK-WUA-12	Denney Kitfox		
OK-WUC-01	LET ULM-01 Aspic		
OK-WUD-02	V-tail Homebuilt Glider (Trabant)		
OK-WUE-02	Bugic UL Sarancha	03	
OK-WUI-1	TST Klokon	02	
OK-WXAF	Letov LK-2 Sluka	01910900004	
OK-WXAJ	Letov LK-2 Sluka		
OK-WZA-01	Jan Bern Cosmos Wing		N901ME
OK-WZD-2	Type unknown		
OK-WZF-4	Type unknown		
OK-WZG-8	Type unknown		
OK-WZJ-15	Type unknown "Opel Decker"		
OK-WZL-9	Aerodelta		
OK-XUA-11	Toresi Straton Moby Dick		
OK-XUD-05	TEAM MiniMax (Cr 13.5.97)		
OK-XUE-05	Gryf T.I.B.	191	OK-WUC-02
OK-XUE-06	Type unknown		
OK-XUE-012	Letov LK-2 Sluka		
OK-XUJ-20	TL Ultralight TL-32 Typhoon		
OK-XUU-02	Letov LK-3 Nova		
OK-XUU-05	Letov LK-2M Sluka		
OK-XUU-10	TL Ultralight TL-32 Typhoon		
OK-XUU-20	TL Ultralight TL-32 Typhoon		
OK-XUU-70	Letov LK-2 Sluka	8192090114	
OK-XXAB	Denney Kitfox II	1501	
OK-XXAC	Denney Kitfox II	1502	
OK-XXAE	Denney Kitfox II	1504	
OK-XXAS	Letov LK-2 Sluka		
OK-XZD-13	Type unknown		
OK-XZF-13	TL Ultralight TL-32 Typhoon		

Regn.	Type	C/n	Prev.Id.
OK-XZF-19	Type unknown		
OK-XZF-20	Type unknown		
OK-XZG-07	Mara Wing 155		
OK-YUA-11	Motor Glider (Type unknown)		
OK-YUD-10	Aeropro Fox		
OK-YUD-15	Lasotronic CS		
OK-YUD-17	Type unknown		
OK-YUD-23	Motor Glider (Type unknown)		
OK-YUE-011	Type unknown		
OK-YUK	Pelican	02	
OK-YUP-03	TEAM Hi-Max		
OK-YUU-01	Type unknown		
OK-YUU-02	Letov LK-2M Sluka		
OK-YUU-03	Denney Kitfox		
OK-YUU-15	Aeropro Fox		
OK-YUU-19	Denney Kitfox		
OK-YUU-20	TL Ultralight TL-32 Typhoon		
OK-YUU-27	Interplane Skyboy		
OK-YUU-28	TL Ultralight TL-32 Typhoon		
OK-YUU-36	Type unknown		
OK-YUU-38	Type unknown		
OK-YUU-54	JORA Jora		
OK-YUU-57	Denney Kitfox		
OK-YUU-66	Rans S-12 Airaile		
OK-YUU-67	Rans S-6ES Coyote II		
OK-YUU-71	TL Ultralight TL-32 Typhoon Sprint	93A040	
OK-YZG-08	MW767		
OK-ZBF-08	Junkers		
OK-ZUA	Motor Glider (Type unknown)		
OK-ZUA-03	Type unknown		
OK-ZUD-09	Type unknown		
OK-ZUD-17	Aeropro Fox		
OK-ZUE-21	Letov LK-2 Sluka		
OK-ZUI-01	Toresi Straton D8 Moby Dick *(Cr 8.6.97)*		
OK-ZUK	Pelican VS		
OK-ZUK-03	Ultravia Pelican		
OK-ZUO-15	Scheibe Spatz A (Wankel engine)	02	OE-0292
OK-ZUP-03	Rans S-6XL Supra		
OK-ZUR-03	J-03 Yetti		
OK-ZUR-04	Type unknown		
OK-ZUU-01	Type unknown		
OK-ZUU-03	Type unknown		
OK-ZUU-07	JORA 199		
OK-ZUU-08	TL Ultralight TL-32 Typhoon		
OK-ZUU-09	TL Ultralight TL-32 Typhoon Sprint		
OK-ZUU-10	Letov LK-3 Nova		
OK-ZUU-29	Rans S-6 Coyote II		
OK-ZUU-35	Letov LK-2M Sluka		
OK-ZUU-36	Type unknown		
OK-ZUU-37	Type unknown		
OK-ZUU-41	Letov LK-2M Sluka	829409X04	
OK-ZUU-45	TL Ultralight TL-132 Condor		
OK-ZUU-55	Ikarus C-22		
OK-ZUU-61	TL Ultralight TL-132 Condor "Autoprim"	94C09	
OK-ZYV	VM-23 Variant	23X01	
OK-ZZC-02	TL Ultralight TL-1/K21		
OK-ZZF-09	VM Brothers Triumph 142 Viper		
OK-ZZF-10	VM Brothers Triumph 142 Viper		
OK-ZZF-11	Justra Stratos	037.92	
OK-ZZG-09	Type unknown		
OK-ZZG-29	Super Wing MW-155		
OK-ZZL-07	TL Ultralight TL-22 Duo	95C08	

BALLOONS AND AIRSHIPS

Regn.	Type	C/n	Prev.Id.
OK-0002	Gas Balloon (Type unknown - believed WFU)		
OK-0008	Hot Air Balloon (Type unknown)		
OK-0020	Hot Air Balloon (Type unknown)		
OK-0026	Kubicek BB-26 HAFB	126	
OK-1011	Hot Air Balloon (Type unknown)		
OK-1012	Hot Air Balloon (Type unknown)		

Regn.	Type	C/n	Prev.Id.
OK-1014	Aerotechnik N-22 HAFB	460591	
OK-1017	Hot Air Balloon (Type unknown)		
OK-1018	Hot Air Balloon (Type unknown)		
OK-1021	Hot Air Balloon (Type unknown)		
OK-1024	Hot Air Balloon (Type unknown)		
OK-1026	Hot Air Balloon (Type unknown)		
OK-2001	Gas Balloon (Type unknown - believed WFU).		
OK-2002	Kubicek BB-12 HAFB		
OK-2003	Kubicek Poppetje-SS HAFB	2	
OK-2004	Kubicek Beer Keg SS HAFB	3	
OK-2005	Kubicek BB-30 HAFB	4	
OK-2010	Hot Air Balloon (Type unknown)		
OK-2017	Kubicek BB-30 HAFB	7	
OK-2018	Kubicek BB-20 HAFB	10	
OK-2019	Kubicek BB-12 HAFB	9	
OK-2020	Kubicek BB-30 HAFB	11	
OK-2021	Kubicek BB-30 HAFB	16	
OK-2022	Kubicek BB-16 HAFB	14	
OK-3010(2)	Aerotechnik AB-2 HAFB	01/86	
OK-3023	Kubicek Hart-SS HAFB	15	
OK-3025	Kubicek BB-30 HAFB	18	
OK-3027	Kubicek BB-12 HAFB	20	
OK-3028	Kubicek BB-30 HAFB	21	
OK-3029	Kubicek BB-22 HAFB	22	
OK-3030	Kubicek BB-20 HAFB	23	
OK-3031	Kubicek BB-20 HAFB	24	
OK-3032	Kubicek BB-30 HAFB	25	
OK-3036	Kubicek BB-30 HAFB	26	
OK-3038	Kubicek BB-30 HAFB	28	
OK-3039	Kubicek BB-22 HAFB	29	
OK-3040	Kubicek AV-1 Hot Air Airship	30	
OK-3041	Kubicek BB-26 HAFB	31	
OK-3046	Cameron N-105 HAFB	3073	
OK-4000	Cameron DP-90 Hot Air Airship	3214	
OK-4012	Aviatik AB-2 HAFB	02	
OK-4014(2)	Aviatik AB-2 HAFB	06/87	
OK-4016	Aviatik AB-2 HAFB	04	
OK-4018	Aviatik AB-2 HAFB	05/86	
OK-4044	Kubicek BB-22 HAFB	34	
OK-4045	Kubicek BB-22 HAFB	35	
OK-4046	Kubicek BB-22 HAFB	36	
OK-4047	Kubicek BB-22 HAFB	37	
OK-4048	Kubicek BB-30 HAFB	38	
OK-4049	Kubicek BB-30 HAFB	39	
OK-5052	Kubicek BB Kriglok SS HAFB	42	
OK-5054	Kubicek BB-22 HAFB	44	
OK-5055	Kubicek BB-30 HAFB	45	
OK-5056	Kubicek BB-22 HAFB	46	
OK-5057	Kubicek BB-20 HAFB	47	
OK-5058	Kubicek BB-22 HAFB	48	
OK-5059	Kubicek BB-30 HAFB	49	
OK-5060	Kubicek BB-30 HAFB	50	
OK-6052	Kubicek BB-45 HAFB	52	
OK-6056	Kubicek BB-22 HAFB	56	
OK-6057	Kubicek BB Vorwerk SS HAFB	57	
OK-6060	Kubicek BB-22 HAFB	60	
OK-6061	Kubicek BB-22 HAFB	61	
OK-6062	Kubicek BB-22 HAFB	62	
OK-6063	Kubicek BB-30 HAFB	63	
OK-6068	Kubicek BB-37 HAFB	68	
OK-7002	Aerotechnik AB-2a HAFB	02/87	
OK-7004	Aerotechnik AB-2a HAFB	03/87	
OK-7005	Aerotechnik AB-2a HAFB	unkn	
OK-7006	Aerotechnik AB-2a HAFB	020587	
OK-7008	Hot Air Balloon (Type unknown)		
OK-7071	Kubicek BB-22 HAFB	71	
OK-7075	Kubicek BBLIAZ HAFB	75	
OK-7079	Kubicek BB-22 HAFB	79	
OK-7082	Kubicek BB-30 HAFB	82	
OK-7083	Kubicek BB-22 HAFB	83	
OK-8001	Kubicek BB-37 HAFB	87	
OK-8003	Gas Balloon 945m "Cedok"	unkn	
OK-8006	Cameron O-77 HAFB	387	
OK-8007	Aviatik AB-2A HAFB	unkn	
OK-8008	Aerotechnik AB-2a HAFB	04/87	

Regn.	Type	C/n	Prev.Id.
OK-8009	Hot Air Balloon (Type unknown)		
OK-8018	Kubicek BB-37 HAFB	88	
OK-8020	Kubicek BB-22 HAFB	90	
OK-8024	Kubicek BB-30 HAFB	94	
OK-8025	Kubicek BB-26 HAFB	95	
OK-8038	Kubicek BB-37 HAFB	108	
OK-9001	Hot Air Balloon (Type unknown)		
OK-9002	Hot Air Balloon (Type unknown)		
OK-9003	Hot Air Balloon (Type unknown)		
OK-9004	Hot Air Balloon (Type unknown)		
OK-9005	Hot Air Balloon (Type unknown)		
OK-9039	Kubicek BB-26 HAFB	109	
OK-9045	Kubicek BB-30 HAFB	115	
OK-9046	Kubicek BB BEMB SSHAFB	116	
OK-9050	Kubicek BB Krigl SSHAFB	120	
OK-9053	Kubicek Jäger Bottle SS HAFB	123	
OK-....	Cameron O-77 HAFB	3540	S5-OHB
OK-....	Cameron N-90 HAFB	3152	
OK-....	Colt 21A Cloudhopper HAFB	1446	G-LUGG

GLIDERS

Regn.	Type	C/n	Prev.Id.
OK-0105	LET L-13SE Vivat	900402	
OK-0107	LET L-13SE Vivat	900404	
OK-0108	LET L-13SE Vivat	900405	
OK-0115	LET L-13SE Vivat	900412	
OK-0116	LET L-13SW Vivat		
OK-0117	LET L-13SL Vivat		
OK-0120	LET L-13SL Vivat		
OK-0200	LET L-23 Super Blanik	897518	C-GLET
OK-0201-X	LET L-23 Super Blanik	907601	
OK-0205	LET L-13 Blanik		
OK-0208-Z	LET L-13 Blanik	170916	OK-0908
OK-0210	LET L-23 Super Blanik	907613	
OK-0211-N	LET L-23 Super Blanik	907614	
OK-0214	LET L-23 Super Blanik	907617	
OK-0216-K4	LET L-23 Super Blanik	907619	
OK-0219-V1	LET L-23 Super Blanik	907711	
OK-0222-T	LET L-23 Super Blanik	907714	
OK-0223	LET L-23 Super Blanik	907715	
OK-0225	LET L-23 Super Blanik	907722	
OK-0230	LET L-23 Super Blanik	907727	
OK-0234	LET L-23 Super Blanik	907717	
OK-0235-B2	LET L-23 Super Blanik	907706	
OK-0365	Schempp-Hirth Discus		
OK-0367	Type unknown		
OK-0372	Schempp-Hirth Discus		
OK-0402	VT-16 Standard		
OK-0507	VSO-10 Gradient	150023	
OK-0514	VSO-10 Gradient		
OK-0520	VSO-10 Gradient		
OK-0522	VSO-10 Gradient	150022	
OK-0524-C8	VSO-10C Gradient	150024	
OK-0526	VSO-10 Gradient	150025	
OK-0528	VSO-10 Gradient	150026	
OK-0530-D2	VSO-10 Gradient	150028	
OK-0730-CE	Schempp-Hirth Discus CS		
OK-0793	VT-125 (Stored)	594	
OK-0796	Letov Lunak		
OK-0802	Type unknown		
OK-0816	Lunak VT-7		
OK-0820	Type unknown		
OK-0833	Lunak VT-7		
OK-0902	LET L-13 Blanik	170910	
OK-0904	LET L-13 Blanik	170912	
OK-0911	LET L-13 Blanik	170919	
OK-0914	LET L-13 Blanik	171106	
OK-0915	LET L-13 Blanik	171107	
OK-0921	LET L-13 Blanik	171304	
OK-0937	LG.125 Sohaj	537	

Regn.	Type	C/n	Prev.Id.
OK-0975	Lunak LF107	12	
OK-1101	LET L-13SW Vivat		
OK-1242	LG.130	VC13	
OK-1400	VT-18		
OK-1411	VSO-10 Gradient	150107	
OK-1420	VSO-10B Gradient	150116	
OK-1500	VSO-10 Gradient	150029	
OK-1502-E2	VSO-10 Gradient	150030	
OK-1504-E3	VSO-10 Gradient		
OK-1505	VSO-10 Gradient		
OK-1506-E4	VSO-10 Gradient	150032	
OK-1508	VSO-10 Gradient	150035	
OK-1509	VSO-10 Gradient	150044	
OK-1516-E9	VSO-10 Gradient	150041	
OK-1518	VSO-10 Gradient		
OK-1522	VSO-10 Gradient	150045	
OK-1524	VSO-10 Gradient	150046	
OK-1526	VSO-10 Gradient	150047	
OK-1528	VSO-10 Gradient	150048	
OK-1600-A1	Schleicher ASW-19B		
OK-1707	LET L-13 Blanik	175023	
OK-1800	LET L-13 Blanik	171408	
OK-1801	LET L-13 Blanik	171409	
OK-1803-L1	LET L-13 Blanik	171411	
OK-1812	LET L-13 Blanik	171613	
OK-1816	LET L-13 Blanik	171617	
OK-1817	LET L-13 Blanik	171618	
OK-1820	LET L-13 Blanik	171912	
OK-1823	LET L-13M Blanik	171915	
OK-1824	LET L-13 Blanik	171930	
OK-1825	LET L-13 Blanik	172001	
OK-1827	LET L-13 Blanik	172003	
OK-1834	LET L-13 Blanik	172010	
OK-1839	LET L-13 Blanik	172015	
OK-1850	LET L-13 Blanik	175005	
OK-1852-H	LET L-13 Blanik	175025	
OK-1968	LG-125 Sohaj		
OK-1969	LG-125 Sohaj		
OK-2101	LET L-13SEH Vivat		
OK-2300	LET L-23 Super Blanik		
OK-2433	VT-16 Orlik	150505	
OK-2500	VSO-10 Gradient	150050	
OK-2502	VSO-10A Gradient	150051	
OK-2504	VSO-10 Gradient	150053	
OK-2505	VSO-10 Gradient		
OK-2510	VSO-10 Gradient		
OK-2530-LF	Schempp-Hirth Ventus c		
OK-2700	LET L-13 Blanik	175215	
OK-2702	LET L-13 Blanik	175216	
OK-2704	LET L-13 Blanik	175217	
OK-2706	LET L-13 Blanik	827404	
OK-2710-Z	LET L-13 Blanik	827407	
OK-2714-T1	LET L-13 Blanik	827410	
OK-2716	LET L-13 Blanik	827411	
OK-2720	LET L-13 Blanik	827414	
OK-2722	LET L-13 Blanik	827416	
OK-2728	LET L-13 Blanik	827420	
OK-2802	LET L-13 Blanik	172030	
OK-2803	LET L-13 Blanik	172101	
OK-2805	LET L-13 Blanik	172103	
OK-2806	LET L-13 Blanik	172104	
OK-2807	LET L-13 Blanik	172105	
OK-2809-I	LET L-13 Blanik	172107	
OK-2813	LET L-13 Blanik	172111	
OK-2814	LET L-13 Blanik	172112	
OK-2815	LET L-13 Blanik	172113	
OK-2817	LET L-13 Blanik	172115	
OK-2819	LET L-13 Blanik	172117	
OK-2823	LET L-13 Blanik	172421	
OK-2900	SZD-36A Cobra 15	W-574	OM-2900
			OK-2900
OK-2901	SZD-36A Cobra 15		
OK-2902	SZD-36A Cobra 15	W-575	
OK-2903	M-28		
OK-2916	M-25 Standard		

529

Regn.	Type	C/n	Prev.Id.
OK-2918	M-25 Standard		
OK-2921	LET L-33 Solo (prototype)		
OK-3102	LET L-13SW Vivat		
OK-3104	LET L-13SEW Vivat	930512	
OK-3137-LT	Rolladen-Schneider LS-1	379 ?	D-3137 ?
OK-3304-17	Schleicher ASW-15B		
OK-3306-X	Schleicher ASW-15B		
OK-3418	VT-16 Orlik		
OK-3508	VSO-10 Gradient		
OK-3518	VSO-10 Gradient		
OK-3520	VSO-10 Gradient		
OK-3522-G9	VSO-10B Gradient	150064	
OK-3535-LI	Schempp-Hirth Ventus c		
OK-3600	LET L-13SW Vivat	830001	
OK-3702	LET L-13 Blanik	025806	
OK-3719	LET L-13 Blanik		
OK-3800	LET L-13 Blanik	172613	
OK-3801	LET L-13 Blanik	172602	
OK-3802	LET L-13 Blanik	172614	
OK-3805	LET L-13 Blanik	172607	
OK-3806	LET L-13 Blanik	172616	
OK-3807	LET L-13 Blanik	172608	
OK-3808	LET L-13 Blanik	172609	
OK-3809-V	LET L-13 Blanik	172610	
OK-3819	LET L-13 Blanik	172827	
OK-3822	LET L-13 Blanik	172830	
OK-3825	LET L-13 Blanik	172903	
OK-3827	LET L-13 Blanik	172905	
OK-3900	LET L-13SW Vivat		
OK-3901	SZD-48-1 Jantar Standard	B-1269	DOSAAF
OK-3902	LET L-13SW Vivat		
OK-3903	LF-109 Pionyr		
OK-3905	LET L-13SDM Super Vivat		
OK-4106	LET L-13SEH Vivat		
OK-4214	LET L-23 Super Blanik	948124	
OK-4300-VL	Schempp-Hirth Discus		
OK-4402	LET L-33 Solo	940212	
OK-4407	LET L-33 Solo	940305	
OK-4408	LET L-33 Solo	940301	
OK-4409	LET L-33 Solo	940303	
OK-4503	VSO-10 Gradient		
OK-4504	VSO-10B Gradient	150089	
OK-4510	VSO-10 Gradient		
OK-4512-J2	VSO-10 Gradient		
OK-4516	VSO-10 Gradient	150098	
OK-4518-J5	VSO-10 Gradient	150099	
OK-4520-J6	VSO-10B Gradient	150101	
OK-4522	VSO-10 Gradient	150102	
OK-4530-L1	VSO-10B Gradient	150108	
OK-4600	LET L-13SW Vivat	840002	
OK-4602	LET L-13SW Vivat		
OK-4603	LET L-13SW Vivat	840006	
OK-4604	LET L-13SW Vivat	840005	
OK-4606	LET L-13SW Vivat		
OK-4608	LET L-13SW Vivat	840008	
OK-4610-7F	Schempp-Hirth Ventus b/16.6	220	
OK-4700	LET L-13 Blanik	025924	
OK-4704	LET L-13 Blanik	025928	
OK-4706-0	LET L-13 Blanik	026030	OE-5010
OK-4708	LET L-13 Blanik	026229	
OK-4710	LET L-13 Blanik	026230	
OK-4712	LET L-13 Blanik	026231	
OK-4714	LET L-13 Blanik	026232	
OK-4716	LET L-13 Blanik	026233	
OK-4718	LET L-13 Blanik		
OK-4720	LET L-13 Blanik	026107	
OK-4800	LET L-13 Blanik	173021	
OK-4801	LET L-13 Blanik	173023	
OK-4802	LET L-13 Blanik	173024	
OK-4805-FL	LET L-13 Blanik		
OK-4806	LET L-13 Blanik	173028	
OK-4808	LET L-13 Blanik	173030	
OK-4809-MT	LET L-13 Blanik		
OK-4810	LET L-13 Blanik	173036	
OK-4811	LET L-13 Blanik	173037	
OK-4812	LET L-13 Blanik	173038	
OK-4815-T5	LET L-13 Blanik	173048	
OK-4816	LET L-13 Blanik	173050	
OK-4817	LET L-13 Blanik	173051	
OK-4818	LET L-13 Blanik	173053	
OK-4820	LET L-13 Blanik	173055	
OK-4821	LET L-13 Blanik	173056	
OK-4830	LET L-13SW Vivat		
OK-4831-H	LET L-13 Blanik	173106	
OK-4833	LET L-13 Blanik	173108	
OK-4837	LET L-13 Blanik		
OK-5100	LET L-13SW Vivat	850101	
OK-5102	LET L-13SW Vivat	850102	
OK-5103	LET L-13SW Vivat		
OK-5112	LET L-13SW Vivat	850110	
OK-5114	LET L-13SW Vivat	850111	
OK-5115	LET L-13DM Vivat	950606	
OK-5309	Type unknown	0205	
OK-5310-Y	Schleicher ASW-15B		
OK-5326-JC	Schempp-Hirth Discus CS		
OK-5341	Type unknown (Wrecked)		
OK-5500	VT-116 Orlik II ZK	151207	
OK-5504	VT-116 Orlik II ZK	151211	
OK-5510	VT-116 Orlik II ZK	151217	
OK-5511	VT-116 Orlik II ZK (Dismantled)	151218	
OK-5512-ZV	Schempp-Hirth Ventus b	253	
OK-5513	VT-116 Orlik II ZK	151220	
OK-5521-12	VT-116 Orlik II ZK (Dismantled)	151408	
OK-5603	VSO-10 Gradient		
OK-5606	VSO-10B Gradient	150114	
OK-5608	VSO-10 Gradient		
OK-5616-LO	VSO-10B Gradient	150122	
OK-5622	VSO-10 Gradient	150126	
OK-5626	VSO-10B Gradient	150129	
OK-5630-4	VSO-10 Gradient		
OK-5702	LET L-13 Blanik	175806	
OK-5988	LG.425 Sohaj 3	0510	
OK-6100	LET L-13SW Vivat		
OK-6104	LET L-13SW Vivat	860117	
OK-6106	LET L-13SW Vivat		
OK-6108	LET L-13SW Vivat	860120	
OK-6110	LET L-13SW Vivat		
OK-6114	LET L-13SW Vivat	860124	
OK-6116	LET L-13SW Vivat	860126	
OK-6118	LET L-13SW Vivat	860127	
OK-6200	SZD-48-3 Jantar Standard 3	B-1581	
OK-6201	LET L-13 Blanik		
OK-6202	LET XL-13M Blanik		
OK-6300-L7	Schempp-Hirth Discus b	130	
OK-6410	VT-116 Orlik II ZK	151510	
OK-6412	VT-116 Orlik II ZK	151512	
OK-6415	VT-116 Orlik II ZK	151515	
OK-6426	LET L-33 Solo	950402	
OK-6429	VT-116 Orlik II ZK	151609	
OK-6434	VT-116 Orlik II ZK		
OK-6437	VT-116 Orlik II ZK		
OK-6440-4	VT-116 Orlik II ZK (Dismantled)	151626	
OK-6441	VT-116 Orlik II ZK (Dismantled)		
OK-6444	VT-116 Orlik II ZK (Dismantled)	151624	
OK-6502-8	VSO-10B Gradient	150138	
OK-6504	VSO-10B Gradient		
OK-6510	VSO-10B Gradient	150144	
OK-6512	VSO-10B Gradient	150145	
OK-6514-Z4	VSO-10B Gradient	150147	
OK-6516-25	VSO-10B Gradient		
OK-6518	VSO-10B Gradient	150150	
OK-6520-27	VSO-10B Gradient	150151	
OK-6526	VSO-10B Gradient	150156	
OK-6528-31	VSO-10B Gradient	150157	
OK-6530-32	VSO-10B Gradient	150159	
OK-6618	Schempp-Hirth Nimbus		
OK-6700	LET L-13 Blanik	026815	
OK-6701	LET L-21 Sportak		
OK-6802	LET L-13 Blanik	173422	
OK-6804	LET L-13 Blanik	173424	

Regn.	Type	C/n	Prev.Id.
OK-6806	LET L-13 Blanik	173426	
OK-6807	LET L-13 Blanik	173427	
OK-6808-L	LET L-13 Blanik	173428	
OK-6817	LET L-13 Blanik	173437	
OK-6818	LET L-13 Blanik	173438	
OK-6831	LET L-13 Blanik	173408	
OK-6901	LET L-13 Blanik		
OK-6902	SZD-45A Ogar	B-658	SP-0019
OK-6907-UO	VT-116 Orlik II ZK	151507	
OK-6911	LET L-13 Blanik		
OK-6922	VT-116 Orlik II		
OK-7104	LET L-13SW Vivat		
OK-7106	LET L-13SW Vivat	870204	
OK-7108	LET L-13SW Vivat		
OK-7110	LET L-13SW Vivat	870207	
OK-7112-ZV	LET L-13SW Vivat	870208	
OK-7114	LET L-13SW Vivat	870210	
OK-7116	LET L-13SW Vivat		
OK-7304-IH	Glasflügel H304CZ		
OK-7399	Schempp-Hirth Janus	49	
OK-7400	VT-116 Orlik II ZK (Dismantled)		
OK-7404-14	VT-116 Orlik II ZK (Dismantled)	151704	
OK-7416	VT-116 Orlik II ZK (Dismantled)		
OK-7418	VT-116 Orlik II ZK	151718	
OK-7419	VT-116 Orlik II ZK	151719	
OK-7425	VT-116 Orlik II ZK	151805	
OK-7433	VT-116 Orlik II ZK (Dismantled)		
OK-7445	VT-116 Orlik II ZK (Dismantled)	151825	
OK-7502	VSO-10 Gradient	150078	
OK-7505	VSO-10B Gradient	150171	
OK-7506-36	VSO-10B Gradient	150166	
OK-7508-37	VSO-10B Gradient	150167	
OK-7520-53	VSO-10B Gradient	150176	
OK-7522	VSO-10 Gradient		
OK-7526-56	VSO-10B Gradient	150181	
OK-7528	VSO-10 Gradient		
OK-7531-60	VSO-10B Gradient	150186	
OK-7542	VSO-10 Gradient	150003	OK-044
OK-7700	LET L-13 Blanik	027069	
OK-7702	LET L-13 Blanik	027070	
OK-7704	LET L-13 Blanik (Damaged)	027101	
OK-7706	LET L-13 Blanik	026852	
OK-7801	Marganski MDM-1 Fox	220	
OK-7901	LET L-23 Super Blanik		
OK-7906	Antonov A-15		
OK-8027	Grunau Baby IIB		
OK-8055	Grunau Baby IIB		
OK-8101	LET L-13SW Vivat	880217	
OK-8103	LET L-13SW Vivat		
OK-8104	LET L-13SW Vivat	880220	
OK-8106	LET L-13SW Vivat		
OK-8107	LET L-13SW Vivat		
OK-8108	LET L-13SW Vivat		
OK-8109	LET L-13SW Vivat	880225	
OK-8113	LET L-13SW Vivat	880229	
OK-8116	LET L-13SWvivat	880302	
OK-8117	LET L-13SW Vivat	880303	
OK-8200	LET L-23 Super Blanik		
OK-8233	Krajánek		
OK-8310-PD	Schempp-Hirth Duo Discus		
OK-8412	Grunau Baby IIB		
OK-8418-81	VT-116 Orlik II ZK	151918	
OK-8419	VT-116 Orlik II ZK	151919	
OK-8424	VT-116 Orlik II ZK (Dismantled)		
OK-8425	VT-116 Orlik II ZK		
OK-8432	VT-116 Orlik II ZK		
OK-8433	VT-116 Orlik II ZK	152003	
OK-8462	Grunau Baby IIB		
OK-8502	VSO-10B Gradient	150188	
OK-8508	VSO-10B Gradient	150194	
OK-8511	VSO-10B Gradient	150197	
OK-8516	VSO-10B Gradient	150202	
OK-8600-AX	Schempp-Hirth Nimbus 2B	182	
OK-8602-AZ	Schempp-Hirth Ventus 2a		
OK-8621	LET L-23 Super Blanik		
OK-8708-KV	LET L-13 Blanik		
OK-8805	LET L-13 Blanik	170105	
OK-8822	LET L-13 Blanik	173818	
OK-8825	LET L-13 Blanik	173822	
OK-8826	LET L-13 Blanik	173823	
OK-8828	LET L-13 Blanik	173825	
OK-8830	LET L-13 Blanik	173907	
OK-8847	LET L-13 Blanik		
OK-8853	Zlin Z.25 Sohaj		
OK-8900	LET L-13SW Vivat		
OK-8902	LET L-13 Blanik		
OK-8903	SZD-45A Ogar	B-773	SP-0022
OK-9103	LET L-13SW Vivat	890310	
OK-9104	LET L-13SW Vivat	890311	
OK-9106	LET L-13SW Vivat	890313	
OK-9113	LET L-13SE Vivat	890322	
OK-9114	LET L-13SW Vivat		
OK-9117	LET L-13SW Vivat	890316	
OK-9118	LET L-13SW Vivat	890317	
OK-9119	LET L-13SW Vivat	890326	
OK-9200	LET L-23 Super Blanik	897501	
OK-9204	LET L-23 Super Blanik	897505	
OK-9252	LET L-13 Blanik		
OK-9301-L3	Schempp-Hirth Discus b	305	
OK-9303-MD	Schempp-Hirth Discus		
OK-9401	VT-116 Orlik II ZK	152011	
OK-9402	VT-116 Orlik II ZK (Dismantled)	152012	
OK-9405	VT-116 Orlik II ZK	152015	
OK-9407	VT-116 Orlik II ZK	152017	
OK-9415	VT-116 Orlik II ZK	152025	
OK-9502	VSO-10C Gradient		
OK-9506	VSO-10C Gradient		
OK-9508	VSO-10C Gradient	150012	
OK-9509	VSO-10C Gradient	150011	
OK-9510	VSO-10C Gradient	150013	
OK-9608	VSO-10B Gradient	150...	
OK-9618-95	VSO-10B Gradient	150222	
OK-9703-V1	LET L-13 Blanik	173914	
OK-9705	LET L-13 Blanik	173916	
OK-9706-I	LET L-13 Blanik	173917	
OK-9707	LET L-13 Blanik	174003	
OK-9712	LET L-13 Blanik	174008	
OK-9717	LET L-13 Blanik	174013	
OK-9719-4	LET L-13 Blanik	174015	
OK-9811	IS-3d		
OK-9826	LET L-13 Blanik	170202	
OK-9829	LET L-13 Blanik	170205	
OK-9847	LET L-13 Blanik	170716	
OK-9851	LET L-13 Blanik	170801	
OK-9902	VSM-40 Demant	08	
OK-....	Grob G.103 Twin Astir	3104	D-3961
OK-....	LET L-13SEH Vivat	930513	G-BVGD
OK-....	LET L-13SEH Vivat	940517	D-KXYZ
OK-....	Rolladen-Schneider LS-1F	379	D-3137
OK-....	Schempp-Hirth Standard Cirrus	448	PH-655
OK-....	Schempp-Hirth Nimbus 2	62	D-3118
OK-....	Schempp-Hirth Ventus 2a	63	
OK-....	Schleicher ASW-15	15399	D-2029
OK-....	Schleicher ASW-19	19088	D-4489
OK-....	Schleicher ASW-19B	19393	D-5712
OK-....	Schleicher ASW-27	27100	
OK-....	VT-16 Standard	150309	

OM - SLOVAKIA

Regn.	Type	C/n	Prev.Id.
OM-ABC	WagAero CUBy *(Type unconfirmed)*	1909/07	
OM-AIX	LET Z-37 Cmelák	3-17	OK-AIX
OM-AJA	LET Z-37A Cmelák	11-21	OK-AJA
			HA-MGX
OM-AJB	LET Z-37A Cmelák	13-11	OK-AJB
			HA-MCD
OM-AJY	LET Z-37 Cmelák	12-06	OK-AJY
OM-AKP	LET Z-37 Cmelák	12-18	OK-AKP
OM-AKU	LET Z-37 Cmelák	12-27	OK-AKU
OM-AKW	LET Z-37 Cmelák	13-05	OK-AKW
OM-AMI	Zlin Z.226 Trenér 6	unkn	
OM-ARD	Zlin Z.50LS	0069	
OM-ARH	Zlin Z.50LS	0076	
OM-ARU	Zlin Z.526ALS-V Akrobat	unkn	
OM-ARV	Zlin Z.526AFS Akrobat	unkn	
OM-AYF	Aero Designs Pulsar	unkn	
OM-BYE	Yakovlev YAK-40	9440338	OK-BYE
OM-BYL	Yakovlev YAK-40	9940560	OK-BYL
OM-BYO	Tupolev TU-154M	89A-803	OK-BYO
OM-BYR	Tupolev TU-154M	98A-1012	
OM-CJH	LET Z-37 Cmelák	16-24	OK-CJH
OM-CJI	LET Z-37 Cmelák	16-27	OK-CJI
OM-CJQ	LET Z-37 Cmelák	15-04	OK-CJQ
OM-CKS	LET Z-37 Cmelák	16-29	OK-CKS
OM-CKT	LET Z-37 Cmelák	17-02	OK-CKT
OM-CKY	LET Z-37 Cmelák	17-10	OK-CKY
OM-COP	Zlin Z.43	0009	OK-COP
OM-CRO	Zlin Z.526F Trenér Master	unkn	
OM-CWJ	Boeing 737-230	22116	9A-CTB
			RC-CTB
			D-ABFD
OM-CYL	Neico Lancair 320ES	046-08-96	
OM-CZA	PZL-104 Wilga 35A	62151	OK-CZA
OM-DJA	LET Z-37 Cmelák	unkn	
OM-DJT	LET Z-37 Cmelák	18-04	OK-DJT
OM-DJU	LET Z-37 Cmelák	18-05	OK-DJU
OM-DJW	LET Z-37 Cmelák	18-19	OK-DJW
OM-DJX	LET Z-37 Cmelák	19-11	OK-DJX
OM-DKN	LET Z-37 Cmelák	19-22	OK-DKN
OM-DOU	Zlin Z.43	0037	OK-DOU
OM-DXO	Mil Mi-8	10825	OK-DXO
OM-DYA	Yakovlev YAK-40	9231230	OK-DHA
OM-EGA	SAAB 2000	unkn	
OM-EIA	Antonov AN-2T	1G157-03	OK-EIA
OM-EIB	Antonov AN-2P	1G151-53	HA-YHA
OM-EIP	Mil Mi-2	513830114	OK-EIP
OM-EIR	Mil Mi-2	513831114	OK-EIR
OM-EIT	Mil Mi-2	533501054	OK-EIT
			B-2401
OM-EOV	Zlin Z.43	unkn	
OM-EOW	Zlin Z.43	0050	OK-EOW
OM-ERS	Zlin Z.526AFS	1306	OK-ERS
OM-EXR	Mil Mi-8	10862	OK-EXR
			B-8426
OM-FCB	Cessna U206F Skywagon	02718	HA-SKB
			SE-KUR
			LN-ASL
			(SE-KLY)
			LN-ASL
			(N33297)
OM-FEH	Hughes 269C	unkn	
OM-FIN	Mil Mi-2	514307095	OK-FIN
OM-FIO	Mil Mi-2	514308085	OK-FIO
OM-FIQ	Mil Mi-2	514517115	OK-FIQ
OM-FIS	Mil Mi-2	514518115	OK-FIS
OM-FIT	SA.316B Alouette III	2257	OK-FIT
			F-WYMY
			F-GHBH
			N47317
OM-FIU	Mil Mi-2	534542125	OK-FIU
			B-2542
OM-FJC	LET Z-37A Cmelák	unkn	
OM-FJQ	LET Z-37 Cmelák	21-11	OK-FJQ

Regn.	Type	C/n	Prev.Id.
OM-FJR	LET Z-37 Cmelák	21-12	OK-FJR
OM-FJU	LET Z-37 Cmelák	21-15	OK-FJU
OM-FJX	LET Z-37 Cmelák	21-18	OK-FJX
OM-FKO	Piper PA-34-200T Seneca II	34-7570019	OK-FKO
			N32407
OM-FON	Zlin Z.43	0062	OK-FON
OM-FOO	Zlin Z.43	0065	OK-FOO
OM-FOP	Zlin Z.43	0066	OK-FOP
OM-FOR	Zlin Z.43	0073	OK-FOR
OM-GAT	Tupolev TU-134A	48565	ES-AAF
			CCCP65034
OM-GHN	Antonov AN-2T	1G168-02	OK-GHN
OM-GIT	Mil Mi-2	514807066	OK-GIT
OM-GIU	Mil Mi-2	514808076	OK-GIU
OM-GJA	LET Z-37 Cmelák	22-16	OK-GJA
OM-GJO	LET Z-37 Cmelák	22-07	OK-GJO
OM-GJR	LET Z-37 Cmelák	22-10	OK-GJR
OM-GJT	LET Z-37A Cmelák	22-12	OK-GJT
OM-HIV	Mil Mi-2	515442018	OK-HIV
OM-HIW	Mil Mi-2	515440018	OK-HIW
OM-HJQ	LET Z-37 Cmelák	23-13	OK-HJQ
OM-HJT	LET Z-37 Cmelák	23-22	OK-HJT
OM-HJX	LET Z-37 Cmelák	23-25	OK-HJX
OM-HLB	LET L-410UVP-E10A	871914	Russian AF
			1914/89 red
OM-HSI	Zlin Z.42M	0134	OK-HSI
OM-HYU	LET Z-37-2C Cmelák	23-09	OK-HYU
OM-IFE	Zlin Z.126 Trenér 2	741	OK-IFE
OM-JIE	Antonov AN-2R	1G186-19	OK-JIE
OM-JIG	Antonov AN-2R	1G186-21	OK-JIG
OM-JIY	Mil Mi-2	536013029	OK-JIY
OM-JLV	Zlin Z.42M	0190	OK-JLV
OM-JSP	Zlin Z.42		unkn
OM-KIH	Mil Mi-2		unkn
OM-KIX	Mil Mi-2	526643050	OK-KIX
			CCCP20678
OM-KJN	Mil Mi-2	516625040	OK-KJN
OM-KJO	Mil Mi-2	516626040	OK-KJO
OM-KJP	Mil Mi-2	516641040	OK-KJP
OM-KJV	LET Z-37 Cmelák	unkn	
OM-KNQ	Zlin Z.142	0204	OK-KNQ
OM-KNS	Zlin Z.142	0203	OK-KNS
OM-KNT	Zlin Z.226M Trenér	104	OK-KNT
OM-KNU	Zlin Z.142	0205	OK-KNU
OM-KNW	Zlin Z.226MS Trenér	107	OK-KNW
OM-KOR	Zlin Z.43	0082	OK-KOR
OM-LIA	Antonov AN-2R	1G194-30	HA-MEU
OM-LJN	Mil Mi-2	527224071	OK-LJN
OM-LJO	Mil Mi-2	527225071	OK-LJO
OM-LJP	Mil Mi-2	527226071	OK-LJP
OM-LJQ	Mil Mi-2	537326101	OK-LJQ
OM-LKE	Aero L-60S Brigadyr	150726	OK-LKE
OM-LKG	Aero L-60S Brigadyr	150728	OK-LKG
OM-LKL	Aero L-60S Brigadyr *(Wfu)*	150803	OK-LKL
OM-LLO	Zlin Z.226MS Trenér *(Wrecked)*	130	OK-LLO
OM-LMJ	Sukhoi SU-31M	unkn	
OM-LNQ	Zlin Z.142	0234	OK-LNQ
OM-LNR	Zlin Z.142	0248	OK-LNR
OM-LNS	Zlin Z.142	0249	OK-LNS
OM-LNT	Zlin Z.142	0260	OK-LNT
OM-LNV	Zlin Z.142	0263	OK-LNV
OM-LOW	Zlin Z.43L	0084	OK-LOW
OM-MDD	Hughes 369D	91-1077D	D-HMAU
			N9114Y
			C-GZXX
			N5284C
OM-MDF	LET L-410UVP	unkn	
OM-MFN	Zlin Z.226MS	158	OK-MFN
OM-MIN	Mil Mi-2	527734072	OK-MIN
OM-MIO	Mil Mi-2	527735072	OK-MIO
OM-MIQ	Aérospatiale AS.355F Ecureuil 2	5160	F-GEXD
			F-ODDH
OM-MMS	Orlican L-40 Meta-Sokol	150305	OK-MMS
OM-MNP	Zlin Z.142	0281	OK-MNP

Regn.	Type	C/n	Prev.Id.
OM-MNQ	Zlin Z.142	0284	OK-MNQ
OM-MNT	Zlin Z.142	0296	OK-MNT
OM-MPX	Zlin Z.226MS Trenér	264	OK-MPX
OM-MQC	Zlin Z.226M Trenér	274	OK-MQC
OM-MQD	Zlin Z.226 Trenér	275	OK-MQD
OM-MQK	Zlin Z 226 Trenér	unkn	
OM-MRK	Orlican L-40 Meta-Sokol	150302	OK-MRK
			HB-TAZ
			OK-MMG
OM-MYN	Mil Mi-8	98203673	OK-MYN
			CCCP25301
OM-NDP	LET L-410UVP	831028	OK-NDP
			CCCP67400
OM-NHS	Aero 145 Super Aero	171422	OK-NHS
OM-NIN	Mil Mi-2	528348103	OK-NIN
OM-NIS	Mil Mi-2	528233073	OK-NIS
			CCCP20872
OM-NJS	LET Z-37 Cmelák	25-12	OK-NJS
OM-NKD	BAe. Jetstream Series 3102	612	HB-AEA
			G-BKTN
			G-31-612
OM-NNP	Zlin Z.142	0329	OK-NNP
OM-NNQ	Zlin Z.142	0334	OK-NNQ
OM-NNR	Zlin Z.142	0336	OK-NNR
OM-NNT	Zlin Z.142	0348	OK-NNT
OM-NNU	Zlin Z.142	0351	OK-NNU
OM-NPJ	Orlican L-40 Meta-Sokol	150803	OK-NPJ
OM-ODQ	LET L-410UVP	841320	OK-ODQ
			CCCP67096
OM-OFH	LET L.200A Morava	170613	OK-OFH
			OE-FSF
			OK-OFH
OM-OFS	LET L.200D Morava	170213	OK-OFS
OM-OIM	Mil Mi-2	unkn	
OM-OIN	Mil Mi-2	528522014	OK-OIN
OM-OIO	Mil Mi-2	528523014	OK-OIO
OM-OIP	Mil Mi-2	528524014	OK-OIP
OM-OIQ	Mil Mi-2	528620034	OK-OIQ
OM-OIR	Mil Mi-2	528621034	OK-OIR
OM-OIS	Mil Mi-2	528622034	OK-OIS
OM-OIU	Mil Mi-2	529012124	OK-OIU
			CCCP23417
OM-OIV	Mil Mi-2	528603034	OK-OIV
			CCCP20921
OM-OIW	Mil Mi-2	529013124	OK-OIW
			CCCP23418
OM-OIZ	Mil Mi-2	unkn	
OM-OJN	LET Z-37 Cmelák	25-21	OK-OJN
OM-OJO	LET Z-37 Cmelák	25-22	OK-OJO
OM-OJP	LET Z-37A Cmelák	25-23	OK-OJP
OM-OJQ	LET Z-37 Cmelák	25-24	OK-OJQ
OM-OJS	LET Z-37 Cmelák	25-32	OK-OJS
OM-ONN	Zlin Z.142	0359	OK-ONN
OM-ONS	Zlin Z.142	0384	OK-ONS
OM-ONT	Zlin Z.142	0387	OK-ONT
OM-OYO	Mil Mi-8	98417135	OK-OYO
OM-PII	Schweizer 269C	S-1197	PH-HYH
			LN-ORA
			SE-HNV
			N41S
OM-PIN	Mil Mi-2	529307065	OK-PIN
OM-PIO	Mil Mi-2	529308065	OK-PIO
OM-PIP	Mil Mi-2	529309065	OK-PIP
OM-PIQ	Mil Mi-2	529310065	OK-PIQ
OM-PIR	Mil Mi-2	529311065	OK-PIR
OM-PIS	Mil Mi-2	529312065	OK-PIS
OM-PIT	Mil Mi-2	529313065	OK-PIT
OM-PLF	LET L.200A Morava	170719	OK-PLF
OM-PLK	LET L.200A Morava	170725	OK-PLK
OM-PLM	LET L.200A Morava	170727	OK-PLM
OM-PLP	LET L.200A Morava	170730	OK-PLP
OM-PLQ	LET L.200A Morava	170731	OK-PLQ
OM-PNN	Zlin Z.142	0394	OK-PNN
OM-PNO	Zlin Z.142	0400	OK-PNO
OM-PNQ	Zlin Z.142	0408	OK-PNQ

Regn.	Type	C/n	Prev.Id.
OM-PNS	Zlin Z.142	0414	OK-PNS
OM-PNV	Zlin Z.142	0417	OK-PNV
OM-PYB	Antonov AN-2	115720	OK-PYB
OM-RDE	LET L-410UVP-E1	861801	LZ-LSA
OM-RFK	LET L.200D Morava	171109	OK-RFK
			OE-FSG
			OK-RFK
OM-RIO	Antonov AN-2	117003	OK-RIO
			CzAF7003
OM-RIP	Antonov AN-2	117410	OK-RIP
			CzAF7410
OM-RIQ	Antonov AN-2	117414	OK-RIQ
			CzAF7414
OM-SDA	LET L-410UVP	unkn	
OM-SGA	PZL M-18A Dromader	1Z017-19	OK-SGA
OM-SGB	PZL M-18A Dromader	1Z017-20	OK-SGB
OM-SGE	PZL M-18A Dromader	1Z017-23	OK-SGE
OM-SIF	Aérospatiale AS.350B2 Ecureuil	3066	
OM-SYI	LET L-410UVP-E6	882019	OK-SYI
OM-TFA	PZL Kania	900202	SP-SSE
			B-3211
			SP-SSE
OM-TGF	PZL M-18A Dromader	1Z018-15	OK-TGF
OM-TRM	Zlin Z.50M	0053	OK-080
			OK-TRM
OM-TXB	Janowski J-1B Don Quixote	unkn	
OM-UIC	Mil Mi-2	548149053	OK-UIC
	(Unconfirmed)		LY-HBL
			YL-LHL
			Soviet Mil
OM-UJG	LET Z-37 Kurier	009P	OK-UJG
OM-UJL	Z-137T Agro-Turbo	028	OK-UJL
OM-UJO	Z-137T Agro-Turbo	031	OK-UJO
OM-UKA	Piper PA-34-220T Seneca III	3433160	OK-UKA
			N9182B
OM-UNO	Zlin Z.142	0502	OK-UNO
OM-VEA	Tupolev TU-154M	90A-866	EP-ITG
			RA-85693
			CCCP85693
OM-VGA	PZL M-18A Dromader	1Z021-18	OK-VGA
OM-VKE	Beech C90A King Air	LJ-1222	OK-VKE
			N15627
OM-VOR	Zlin Z.526M Trenér Master (cvtd from Z.326)	909	F-BNMX
OM-WDA	LET L-410UVP-E8B	912540	OK-WDA
OM-WMN	Zlin Z.226T Trenér 6	102	OK-WMN
			EAF-...
OM-XOM	Zlin Z.43	0114	OK-XOM
OM-XON	Zlin Z.43	0109	OK-XON
OM-XYP	Aero Designs Pulsar	235/001	OK-XYP
OM-YIT	Robinson R-22 Beta	unkn	OK-YIT
OM-YJE	LET Z-37 Cmelák	05-01	OK-YJE
			HA-MGD
OM-YJG	LET Z-37 Cmelák	08-07	OK-YJG
			HA-SCB
OM-YJP	LET Z-37 Cmelák	08-24	OK-YJP
OM-YXQ	LET Z-37A-3 Cmelák	30-38	OK-YXQ
OM-ZJA	LET Z-37 Cmelák	10-02	OK-ZJA
			HA-MGN
OM-ZJE	LET Z-37 Cmelák	09-18	OK-ZJE
			HA-MGK
OM-ZJN	LET Z-37A Cmelák	09-01	OK-ZJN
OM-ZJY	LET Z-37 Cmelák	10-14	OK-ZJY
OM-ZKP	LET Z-37A Cmelák	11-03	OK-ZKP
OM-ZNP	LET Z-37 Cmelák	09-30	OK-ZNP
			HA-SCD
OM-ZXP	Mil Mi-8	10821	OK-ZXP
			B-8022
			OK-BYL
OM-...	Reims/Cessna FR.172K Hawk XP	0602	D-EOHY(2)
OM-...	Cessna T.303	00148	D-IKER(2)
			N6179C

MICROLIGHTS

Regn.	Type	C/n	Prev.Id.
OM-AUB-01	Sky Pup TP		
OM-AUD-01	Type unknown		
OM-AUQ-0	Aviatik JORA		
OM-AUQ-03	Toresi Straton D8 Moby Dick		
OM-AUQ-04	Type unknown		
OM-AUQ-06	Type unknown		
OM-AXAB	Denney Kitfox (?)		
OM-AXM	MXP-741	A8-03-95-50-026	
OM-CXAR	Ikarus EV-97 Eurostar		
OM-DXBP	DSBS-01 Koma Twin		
OM-DXCH	Aeropro Fox		
OM-HCRM	Type unknown		
OM-VLAV	Evektor EV-97		
OM-WZG-7	Type unknown		OK-WZG-7
OM-XUL-02	Toresi Straton D8 Moby Dick		
OM-XZB-13	Type unknown		
OM-YUA-07	Toresi Straton D8 Moby Dick		
OM-YUB-06	AeroPro Fox		OK-YUB-06
OM-YUB-14	Letov LK-21 Sluka	829309X02	
OM-YUD	Zenith MXP-740	A6-07-93-50-007	OK-YUD
OM-YUF-01	Type unknown		
OM-YUL-01	Type unknown		
OM-YUU-50	TL Ultralight TL-32 Typhoon		OK-YUU-50
OM-YUU-53	TL Ultralight TL-32 Typhoon		
OM-YUU-59	TL Ultralight TL-32 Typhoon		OK-YUU-59
OM-YXR	Murphy Rebel	096	OK-YXR-002
OM-YZB-1	Type unknown		
OM-YZG-17	Type unknown		
OM-ZUB-01	Aeropro Fox		OK-ZUB-01
OM-ZUB-07	Rans S-6 Coyote II	1193559	
OM-ZUC-02	AgroLET Junior		OK-ZUC-02
OM-ZUC-04	AgroLET Junior		
OM-ZUQ-01	Type unknown		
OM-ZXAH	Aeropro Fox		
OM-ZXSV	Type unknown		
OM-ZZB-2	MZK Skypala		
OM-ZZB-3	MZ Apollo		

BALLOONS AND AIRSHIPS

Regn.	Type	C/n	Prev.Id.
OM-ADS	Kubicek AV 2 Hot Air Airship	106	OK-8036
OM-3033	Kubicek BB-26 HAFB	19	OK-3033
OM-6001	Kubicek BB-30 HAFB	55	
OM-6002	Kubicek BB Pneu-SS HAFB	53	
OM-6003	Kubicek BB Pneu-SS HAFB	54	
OM-6004	Kubicek BB-22 HAFB	65	
OM-6005	Kubicek BB-22 HAFB	66	
OM-6006	Kubicek BB-22 HAFB	67	
OM-7007	Kubicek VS SSHAFB	73	
OM-8001	Kubicek BB-37 HAFB	87	
OM-8002	Kubicek BB-37 HAFB	97	
OM-8003	Kubicek BB-37 HAFB	98	
OM-8004	Kubicek BB-22 HAFB	103	
OM-8005	Kubicek BB-22 HAFB	104	
OM-9007	Kubicek BB-26 HAFB	118	
OM-9009	Kubicek BB-26 HAFB	121	

GLIDERS

Regn.	Type	C/n	Prev.Id.
OM-0106	LET L-13SE Vivat	900403	OK-0106
OM-0112	LET L-13SE Vivat	900409	OK-0112
OM-0114	LET L-13SW Vivat	900411	OK-0114
OM-0203	LET L-13 Blanik	unkn	OK-0203
OM-0903	LET L-13 Blanik	170911	OK-0903
OM-0913	LET L-13 Blanik	171105	OK-0913
OM-0972	Lunak LF-107	unkn	OK-0972
OM-1503	VSO-10 Gradient	150034	OK-1503
OM-1602-A4	Type unknown		
OM-1709	LET L-13 Blanik	175024	OK-1709
OM-1713	LET L-13 Blanik	817403	OK-1713
OM-1836	LET L-13 Blanik	172012	OK-1836
OM-2512	VSO-10 Gradient	150058	OK-2512
OM-2705	LET L-13 Blanik	175330	OK-2705
OM-2707	LET L-13 Blanik	827406	OK-2707
OM-2709	LET L-13 Blanik	827409	OK-2709
OM-2715	LET L-13 Blanik	827418	OK-2715
OM-2812	LET L-13 Blanik	172110	OK-2812
OM-3701	LET L-13 Blanik	025427	OK-3701
OM-3818	LET L-13 Blanik	172826	OK-3818
OM-4400	Schempp-Hirth Nimbus	unkn	
OM-4507-M2	VSO-10 Gradient	150097	OK-4507
OM-4511	VSO-10 Gradient	unkn	OK-4511
OM-4603	LET L-13SW Vivat	unkn	OK-4603
OM-4607	LET L-13SW Vivat	840010	OK-4607
OM-5107	LET L-13SW Vivat	850112	OK-5107
OM-5401-M	Type unknown		OK-5401
OM-6509-16	Type unknown		
OM-6834	LET L-13 Blanik	173411	
OM-7102	LET L-13SE Vivat	unkn	
OM-7103	LET L-13SW Vivat	unkn	OK-7103
OM-7105	LET L-13SW Vivat	870209	OK-7105
OM-7301	Schempp-Hirth Janus	53	OK-7301
OM-9102	LET L-13SW Vivat	890309	OK-9102
OM-9115	LET L-13SE Vivat	890324	OK-9115
OM-9601	Schempp-Hirth Janus	unkn	OK-9601
OM-9610-87	VSO-10B Gradient	150214	OK-9610
OM-9700	LET L-13 Blanik	173911	OK-9700
OM-9702	LET L-13A Blanik	173913	OK-9702

Regn.	Type	C/h	Prev.Id.
OO-AAP	Piper PA-18 Super Cub 95	18-3214	(OO-ACF)
			OL-L40
			L-140
			53-4814
OO-ABO	CEA Jodel DR.1051M1 Sicile Record	591	PH-ABC
			OO-JOZ
OO-ABS	Mooney M.20F Executive	22-1219	N7442V
OO-ABU	Auster J/2 Arrow	2375	
OO-ABZ	Beech 35-C33 Debonair	CD-890	G-BABZ
			SE-EKI
OO-ACG	Piper PA-18 Super Cub 95	18-3216	OL-L42
			L-142
			53-4816
OO-ACK	Piper PA-18 Super Cub 95	18-3146	OL-L72
			53-4746
OO-ACN	Piper PA-18-150 Super Cub	18-5392	D-EIWW
			ALAT
OO-ACS	Reims/Cessna F.152	1758	D-EIYU
OO-ADC	Piper PA-28-180 Cherokee B	28-1638	5N-ADC
			N7758W
OO-ADO	Reims/Cessna FR.172H Rocket	0260	F-BSHF
OO-AED	Piper J-3C-90 Cub	12379	OO-LIL
			44-80083
OO-AEM	SEEMS MS.892B Rallye Commodore 150	10281	F-BLBA
			F-WLBA
OO-AEP	Mooney M.20K Model 231	25-0537	N9871P
OO-AET	Grumman-American AA-5 Traveler	0083	G-KASH
			G-AZUG
OO-AEY	Airbus A.320-212	348	G-TPTT
			F-GLGE
			F-WWBT
OO-AEZ	Airbus A.320-212	349	OY-CNR
			G-DACR
			G-OEXC
			F-WWBU
OO-AFB	Piper PA-28-180 Cherokee Archer	28-7505184	(OO-AFP)
			N51JD
OO-AFJ	SNCAN/ Stampe SV.4C	197	F-BCFJ
OO-AFK	Piper PA-28RT-201 Arrow IV	28R-7918249	OO-HLB
			N2969Y
OO-AGP	Cessna 172H	54976	EL-AGP
			5N-AHJ
			N1481F
OO-AGU	Junkers JU-52/3mG (Reservation)	unkn	FAP6310
OO-AHE	Agusta A.109A-II	7325	OO-XHE
			N109LA
OO-AHH	Wassmer WA.40A Super IV	124	F-BNZR
OO-AHO	Scintex CP.1330 Super Emeraude	924	F-BJMY
OO-AHY	Cessna 182P Skylane	61644	G-BAHY
			N21460
OO-AIF	Piper PA-28-140 Cherokee	28-24668	CS-AIF
OO-AJK	Nord 1203 Norécrin	261	F-BFJE
	(Instructional airframe in Antwerp school)		
OO-ALC	Reims/Cessna F.150L	0953	
OO-ALD	Reims/Cessna F.150L	0951	
OO-ALE	Reims/Cessna F.172M	1126	
OO-ALT	Cessna 177RG Cardinal RG	0571	N2171Q
OO-ALW	Reims/Cessna F.177RG Cardinal RG	0097	D-EIQT
OO-ALZ	Piper PA-18 Super Cub 95	18-2083	ALAT. F-MAKA
			52-2483
	(Also using parts of 18-2116)		
OO-AME	Boeing-Stearman E75N1	75-190	NC55389
			40-1633
OO-ANI	Piper PA-28-161 Warrior II	28-8016321	OO-HLW
			N8200Y
OO-ANM	Cessna 152 -II	81455	N648CA
			N64871
OO-ANO	Reims/Cessna F.152	1745	OO-HNQ
OO-ANR	Zlin Z.526F Trenér Master	1265	YR-ZAM
OO-API	SOCATA Rallye 110ST Galopin	3289	PH-AFI
OO-APV	Cessna 152	79842	D-EAPV
			OH-CQC
			C-GQSW
			(N757ME)

Regn.	Type	C/h	Prev.Id.
OO-ARA	Grumman-American AA-5B Tiger	1203	(OO-RTJ)
OO-ARD	SOCATA MS.880B Rallye Club	1659	F-BSKB
OO-ARM	SOCATA Rallye 110ST Galopin	3293	F-GBXP
OO-ASE	Beech 77 Skipper	WA-149	D-EBCS
OO-ATN	SOCATA MS.880B Rallye Club	2624	F-BXTN
OO-ATP	SOCATA MS.883 Rallye 115	1568	
OO-ATY	Piper PA-18 Super Cub 95	18-3221	OL-L47
			L-147
			53-4821
OO-AUW	Brändli BX-2 Cherry	117	OO-137
OO-AVA	Piper PA-34-200T Seneca II	34-7970301	N2872C
OO-AWC	Reims/Cessna F.152-II	1614	PH-AXJ
OO-AWT	Reims/Cessna F.172M	1236	N94723
OO-AWY	Reims/Cessna F.172H	0563	
OO-AYA	Reims/Cessna F.150M	1290	F-BUDY
			(F-GAAR)
OO-AYZ	Beech A36 Bonanza	E-454	(OO-PYZ)
			D-EHWC
OO-BAK	Enstrom F.28A	168	
OO-BBY	Piper PA-23-250 Aztec E	27-7305049	G-BAWY
			N40244
OO-BDV	Wassmer Jodel D.120 Paris-Nice	316	F-BNZE
OO-BEA	Reims/Cessna F.150J	0506	
OO-BET	Reims/Cessna F.152-II	1716	LX-XYZ
OO-BFC	Piper PA-38-112 Tomahawk	38-79A0003	N9690N
OO-BFZ	Piper PA-28R-200 Cherokee Arrow II	28R-7335337	G-BBFZ
			N9516N
OO-BIR	Piper PA-28-181 Archer II	28-7990189	N2136F
OO-BLD	Robin HR.100/210 Royale	197	
OO-BLY	SEEMS MS.885 Super Rallye (Wfu)	5389	F-BLBY
OO-BNO	Bellanca 8KCAB Decathlon	610-80	
OO-BOM	SOCATA Rallye 150T	2775	
OO-BPL	Stampe & Renard/ SV.4B	1194	(OO-GWC)
			OO-BPL
			V-52
OO-BPW	Piper PA-32-300 Cherokee Six B	32-40765	N8970N
OO-BTL	SOCATA Rallye 100ST	2424	F-BVZN
OO-BUC	Piper PA-32-260 Cherokee Six	32-833	(OO-MRA)
			LN-UXP
			N3887W
OO-BUK	CEA DR.315 Petit Prince	443	
OO-BVT	Grumman-American AA-5A Cheetah	0719	OO-HRB(1)
OO-BYL	de Havilland DH.82A Tiger Moth	3882	G-ANBU
			W7952
			G-AFNR
OO-CAR	CEA Jodel DR.1051M1 Sicile Record	605	
OO-CAT	Jodel D.112 Club	88	OO-HDD
			F-BHDD
OO-CCB	SOCATA MS.894A Minerva 220	11051	F-BRJY
OO-CCD	CEA DR.220A/2+2	83	F-BPCF
OO-CEA	CEA DR.315 Petit Prince	409	
OO-CEK	Piper J-3C-65 Cub	"12760"	9Q-CEK
			9O-CEK
			OO-CEK
			OO-GEK
			44-80464
OO-CGD	Cessna A.150M Aerobat	0647	N9839J
OO-CGH	Beech 95-B55 Baron	TC-766	9Q-CXH
OO-CHA	Robinson R-22	0124	
OO-CHD	Cessna 150M	76554	N3586V
OO-CIA	Grumman-American AA-5 Traveler	0705	
OO-CID	Cessna 172N	70050	N738KZ
OO-CIN	Piper J-3C-85 Cub	11644	D-ECIN
	(t/n 11818,thus c/n is suspect)		HB-ODS
			43-30527
OO-CIR	Cessna 172N	73282	N172N
			N4656G
OO-CJD	Robin HR.200/120B	255	
OO-CJF	Piper PA-28RT-201 Arrow IV	28R-8018044	F-GCJF
			N8164D
OO-CJP	Cessna 414A Chancellor	0229	G-WITE
			G-LOVO
			G-KENT
			N8828K
OO-CKD	Robin R.2112 Alpha	189	PH-SBV

Regn.	Type	C/n	Prev.Id.
OO-CLD	Robin DR.400/180RP Remorqueur	1922	F-GGXR
OO-CLM	Beech 35-C33 Debonair	CD-1021	D-ECLM
OO-CLP	Cessna 182P Skylane	62694	G-BCBW
			N52593
OO-CLS	SOCATA MS.880B Rallye Club	1194	
OO-CMD	Beech A36 Bonanza	E-1784	N3803Y
OO-CNA	Reims/Cessna F.150M	1198	HB-CNA
OO-CNC	Reims/Cessna F.172M	1440	
OO-CNH	Reims/Cessna FR.172K Hawk XP	0596	N96098
OO-CNO	Reims/Cessna F.152	1472	(OO-HNO)
OO-CNP	Reims/Cessna F.152	1497	OO-HNP
OO-CNW	Reims/Cessna F.172N	2032	PH-AYM(3)
OO-COA	Cessna 172N	73978	N5133K
OO-COB	Bell 206B Jet Ranger II	385	G-AYTF
			N1453W
OO-COC	Piper PA-28-181 Cherokee Archer II	28-7890496	N36143
OO-COD	Agusta-Bell 206B Jet Ranger II	8378	D-HCAC(2)
			G-BBXM
			HP-635
			G-BBXM
OO-COE	Cessna 172N	70095	N738MY
OO-COP	Agusta-Bell 206A Jet Ranger	8284	D-HAVA
OO-COV	Reims/Cessna FR.182 Skylane RG	0008	PH-LTN
OO-CPC	Reims/Cessna FRA.150M Aerobat	0292	(OO-WAX)
OO-CPD	Robin DR.400/120 Petit Prince	2215	
OO-CPS	Airbus A.321-131	591	TC-ABC
			N591KB
			TC-ONH
			D-AVZV
OO-CPW	Cessna 182B Skylane	51584	HB-CPW
			N2284G
OO-CQD	Robin DR.400/120 Petit Prince	2273	
OO-CRG	Reims/Cessna F.152	1524	
OO-CRO	Robinson R-22 Beta	1745	F-GHKK
OO-CRZ	Piper PA-38-112 Tomahawk	38-78A0729	N9746N
OO-CSD	Robin DR.400/160 Major	2392	
OO-CTB	McDonnell-Douglas MD-11	48766	N6203U
OO-CTC	McDonnell-Douglas MD-11	48780	
OO-CTD	Robin DR.400/140B Major	2201	
OO-CTQ	Boeing 767-33AER	28159	(OO-CPQ)
OO-CTR	Boeing 767-33AER	28495	VH-NOA
			(VH-BZI)
			N6009F
OO-CTS	McDonnell-Douglas MD-11	48756	
OO-CTT	Airbus A.300C4-605R	755	F-WWAX
OO-CTU	Airbus A.300C4-605R	758	F-WWAR
OO-CTV	Boeing 737-46Q	29000	N283CD
			(N463PR)
			TC-IAA
OO-CTW	Boeing 737-46Q	29001	N284CD
			(N464PR)
			TC-IAB
OO-CUD	Cessna 172N	70426	N739CA
OO-CVT	Cessna 150H	67974	N7274S
OO-CXD	Robin DR.400/180RP Remorqueur 212	1817	HB-KBU
			D-EAJD
OO-CYD	Cessna 150M	77540	N6131K
OO-CYF	SOCATA MS.894A Minerva 220	11078	F-BSCP
OO-CZD	Robin DR.400/140B Dauphin 4	2401	
OO-DAD	Cessna T.303 Crusader	00281	N4837V
OO-DAF	Noorduyn/ N.American AT-16 Harvard IIB	14A-1494	MLD/KM:098
			B-84
			FT454
			43-13195
OO-DAJ	Mooney M.20J Model 201	24-0422	F-GJSB
			N201AY
OO-DAN	Wassmer Jodel D.112 Club	1305	F-BMYQ
OO-DAP	Mooney M.20K Model 231	25-0572	G-BJGT
			N10485
OO-DAR	Cessna 150L	73982	N18607
OO-DAS	Piper PA-18 Super Cub 95	18-1558	OO-HMP
			ALAT
			51-15558
OO-DAT	Piper PA-28-161 Warrior II	28-8016066	N8085D

Regn.	Type	C/n	Prev.Id.
OO-DAV	Piper PA-38-112 Tomahawk	38-79A0956	OO-HLJ
			N9702N
OO-DAY	SOCATA MS.893A Rallye Commodore 180	11453	F-BSAZ
OO-DAZ	Cessna 182P Skylane	64103	N6088F
OO-DBM	Boeing-Stearman A75N1	75-5714	G-BPMD
			N5084N
			42-17551
OO-DBR	Grumman-American AA-5A Cheetah	0634	(OO-HRH)
OO-DBW	Robinson R-22 Beta	2539	
OO-DCJ	Grumman-American AA-5 Traveler	0591	N9591L
OO-DCL	Taylorcraft Plus D	156	G-AHHB
			LB285
OO-DCM	Cessna 500 Citation	0182	N13HJ
			N590EA
			C-FNOC
			N525GA
			D-IABC
OO-DDC	Piper PA-28-235 Pathfinder	28-7410083	TU-TDC
			6V-ADR
			N43450
OO-DDF	Bell 206B Jet Ranger II	3179	3A-MTR
			N6TR
			N3895C
OO-DEB	Beech 95-B55 Baron	TC-1224	OY-DSC
OO-DEC	Piper PA-28R-200 Cherokee Arrow	28R-35694	D-EEFQ
			N4974S
OO-DEM	Cessna 182P (Reims-assembled)	0042/64142	N6259F
OO-DFB	Piper PA-28R-201T Turbo Arrow III	28R-7803280	F-GEPH
			N9819C
OO-DFJ	Mooney M.20J Model 201	24-0717	D-EDFN(2)
			HB-DFH
			(N4352H)
OO-DFK	Piper PA-38-112 Tomahawk	38-79A0004	N9657N
OO-DFL	Piper PA-38-112 Tomahawk	38-79A0084	N2486B
OO-DFM	Piper PA-28-151 Cherokee Warrior	28-7615093	N8336C
OO-DFN	Piper PA-28R-200 Cherokee Arrow II	28R-7335265	N55651
OO-DFS	Piper PA-18 Super Cub 95	18-1637	ALAT
			51-15637
OO-DHA	Robinson R-22	0160	
OO-DHC	Convair CV-580	68	N535SA
			N5841
			N73131
OO-DHE	Convair CV-580	52	C-GDTE
			N5845
			N73125
OO-DHJ	Convair CV-580	361	N73162
			OO-DHJ
			N73162
			OO-SCN
OO-DHK	Boeing 727-277	22643	N70415
			VH-ANE
OO-DHL	Convair CV-580	459	C-GGWF
			N5811
			N8420H
			VH-BZI
OO-DHM	Boeing 727-31	20114	N7892
OO-DHN	Boeing 727-31	20113	N260NE
			N97891
OO-DHO	Boeing 727-31	20112	N250NE
			N7890
OO-DHR	Boeing 727-35F	19834	N932FT
			(N526FE)
			N932FT
			N1958
OO-DHS	Boeing 727-223F	20189	N6836
OO-DHT	Boeing 727-223F	19489	N6814
OO-DHU	Boeing 727-223F	20992	N851AA
OO-DHW	Boeing 727-223F	20993	N852AA
OO-DHX	Boeing 727-223F	20994	N853AA
OO-DHY	Boeing 727-230F	20905	N626DH
			TC-AFV
			N866SY
			YV-855C
			N860SY
			D-ABKG

Regn.	Type	C/n	Prev.Id.
OO-DHZ	Boeing 727-2Q4	22424	N7563Q
			XA-SIV
			XA-MEQ
			(PT-TCE)
OO-DIA	Beech 35-C33 Debonair	CD-886	D-EKVI
OO-DJE	BAe.146 Series 200	E-2164	G-6-164
OO-DJF	BAe.146 Series 200	E-2167	G-6-167
OO-DJG	BAe.146 Series 200	E-2180	(G-BSZZ)
			G-6-180
OO-DJH	BAe.146 Series 200	E-2172	G-BSSG
			G-6-172
OO-DJJ	BAe.146 Series 200	E-2196	G-6-196
OO-DJK	Avro 146-RJ85	E-2271	G-6-271
OO-DJL	Avro 146-RJ85	E-2273	G-6-273
OO-DJN	Avro 146-RJ85	E-2275	G-6-275
OO-DJO	Avro 146-RJ85	E-2279	G-6-279
OO-DJP	Avro 146-RJ85	E-2287	G-6-287
OO-DJQ	Avro 146-RJ85	E-2289	G-6-289
OO-DJR	Avro 146-RJ85	E-2290	G-6-290
OO-DJS	Avro 146-RJ85 (Damaged 5..99)	E-2292	G-6-292
OO-DJT	Avro 146-RJ85	E-2294	G-6-294
OO-DJV	Avro 146-RJ85	E-2295	G-6-295
OO-DJW	Avro 146-RJ85	E-2296	G-6-296
OO-DJX	Avro 146-RJ85	E-2297	G-6-297
OO-DJY	Avro 146-RJ85	E-2302	G-6-302
OO-DJZ	Avro 146-RJ85	E-2305	G-6-305
OO-DKM	Piper PA-28-181 Cherokee Archer II	28-7690296	C-GXEE
			N75113
OO-DKT	SOCATA TB-10 Tobago	87	PH-AKT
			EC-DKT
			F-ODMQ
OO-DLB	Boeing 727-277	22642	N86330
			VH-ANB
OO-DLC	Airbus A.300B4-203F	152	N221EA
			F-GBNP
OO-DLD	Airbus A.300B4-203F	259	N865PA
			TC-ALG
			OB-1634
			(AP-BFG)
			SE-DSG
			N72990
			(N990C)
			N232EA
			F-GBNZ
OO-DLE	Airbus A.300B4-203F	236	N222KW
			N207PA
			F-WZMI
OO-DLG	Airbus A.300B4-203F	208	N212PA
			F-OHPN
			F-WHPJ
			SX-BAY
			N212PA
			F-WZMQ
OO-DLH	Piper PA-22-160 Tri-Pacer	22-7419	G-ARAL
OO-DLI	Airbus A.300B4-203F	234	N206PA
			F-OHPA
			F-WZMF
OO-DLJ	Boeing 757-23APF	24971	N573CA
			G-OBOZ
			N5002K
OO-DLK	Boeing 757-23APF (Reservation .00)	24635	VH-AWE
			9J-AFO
			(N3502P)
			PT-TDA
OO-DLM	Hughes 269C	64-0323	G-OSHC
			N8989F
OO-DMB	SOCATA TB-20 Trinidad	560	D-EPMT
			F-GJGL
			N43AS
OO-DMC	Beech F33A Bonanza	CE-1273	G-JBET
			N15574
OO-DMF	Reims/Cessna F.172M	1015	D-EJXA
OO-DMS	Reims/Cessna FA.150L Aerobat	0087	(OO-WJ)
OO-DMT	Robinson R-44 Astro	0413	D-HIFF
OO-DNB	SOCATA TB-9 Tampico	1541	F-GLFR

Regn.	Type	C/n	Prev.Id.
OO-DOC	Robin DR.300/125 Petit Prince	623	
OO-DOD	Mooney M.20K Model 231	25-0414	N4076H
OO-DOU	Agusta-Bell 206B Jet Ranger III	8718	G-RNGR
OO-DPG	Grumman-American AA-5 Traveler	0647	OO-HAE
			(OO-WAE)
OO-DPH	Schweizer 269C (w/o 8.2.92)	S-1467	D-HHOF
OO-DPS	SOCATA MS.894A Minerva 220	11676	F-BSKX
OO-DRB	SOCATA TB-9 Tampico	1631	D-EMIC(2)
OO-DSA	Robin DR.400/180R Remorqueur	1703	(OO-FWC)
			F-WEIQ
			(D-EAFA)
			F-WEIQ
OO-DSD	Piper PA-28-181 Archer II	2843075	
OO-DTJ	Embraer EMB.120RT Brasilia	120-123	PT-SNP
OO-DTT	Robinson R-44 Astro	0230	
OO-DVJ	Cessna R.182 Skylane RG	00142	N129
			N7594Y
OO-DWA	Avro 146-RJ100	E-3308	G-6-308
OO-DWB	Avro 146-RJ100	E-3315	G-6-315
OO-DWC	Avro 146-RJ100	E-3322	G-6-322
OO-DWD	Avro 146-RJ100	E-3324	G-6-324
OO-DWE	Avro 146-RJ100	E-3327	G-6-327
OO-DWF	Avro 146-RJ100	E3332	G-6-332
OO-DWG	Avro 146-RJ100	E-3336	G-6-336
OO-DWH	Avro 146-RJ100	E-3340	G-6-340
OO-DWI	Avro 146-RJ100	E-3342	G-6-342
OO-DWJ	Avro 146-RJ100	E-3355	G-6-355
OO-DWK	Avro 146-RJ100	E-3360	G-6-360
OO-DWL	Avro 146-RJ100	E-3361	G-6-361
OO-DXZ	Beech F33A Bonanza	CE-500	D-EDXZ
OO-DYN	Gyroflug SC.01B-160 Speed Canard	S-24	D-ECES
OO-EAB	Piper J-3C-65 Cub	12220	44-79924
OO-EAM	Piper PA-34-200T Seneca II	34-8070308	OO-HKL
			N8244D
OO-EAN	Bell 206B Jet Ranger II	1595	G-BORX
			C-GHYQ
OO-EBH	Robinson R-22	0064	D-HEXE
			N9033Y
OO-EBL	Valtion Viiima II	VI-3	G-BAAY
			OH-VIG
			VI-3
OO-EBS	Beech A24R Sierra	MC-426	N1984L
OO-EBT	Beech A24R Sierra	MC-745	N3711G
OO-EBU	Piper PA-28-161 Cadet	2841246	(OO-PRO)
OO-ECF	SOCATA MS.883 Rallye 115	1549	F-BSAJ
OO-ECS	Cessna 172RG Cutlass	1126	N9338D
OO-EDM	Gyroflug SC-01B-160 Speed Canard	S-31	D-EJDB
			(PH-AVO)
OO-EDY	SEEMS MS.892A Rallye Commodore 150	10459	F-BLSJ
OO-EEJ	SIAI-Marchetti SF.260	2-41	(OO-EEG)
OO-EET	Reims/Cessna F.172H	0602	D-EETB
OO-EFA	Tipsy T.66 Nipper II	75	
OO-EGB	Robinson R-22 Beta	1840	
OO-EGC	Robinson R-22 Beta	1839	
OO-EGH	Robinson R-22 Beta	1360	
OO-EGJ	Robinson R-44 Astro	0284	G-BWWR
OO-EGM	Bell 206B Jet Ranger II	1097	G-BBBM
			N18090
OO-EHO	Reims/Cessna F.172H	0381	D-EHOH(2)
OO-EII	Bücker B.133C Jungmeister	51	D-EIII (2)
			SpAF:E.1-...
OO-EIR	Stampe & Renard/ SV.4B	1144	V-4
OO-EKT	Robin DR.400/2+2 Tricycle	892	F-BUSL
OO-ELV	Jodel D.112 Club	310	F-BHGD
OO-EMF	Beech V35B Bonanza	D-10076	D-EEMF(2)
OO-EMG	Tipsy T.66 Nipper II (Cr., reserved as PH-EMG)	60	
OO-EMS	MD.900 Explorer	00020	SE-JCG
OO-ENO	Beech A23 Musketeer	M-790	D-EMNI
OO-EOD	Beech F33A Bonanza	CE-291	N3797A
OO-EOT	Tipsy D	18	G-AISB
OO-EPV	Epervier	01	OO-964
OO-ERD	Beech 76 Duchess	ME-374	(OO-VHE)
			(OO-RDE)
			N3706L

Regn.	Type	C/n	Prev.Id.
OO-ERG	Hughes 269A	66-0602	G-FSDH
			N602CH
			66-18319
OO-ESA	Piper PA-38-112 Tomahawk	38-78A0733	N9747N
OO-ESB	Piper PA-28-161 Warrior II	28-7916111	N9537N
OO-ESV	Stampe & Renard/ SV.4B	1165	V-23
OO-ETF	Reims/Cessna F.150L	0704	
OO-ETW	Beech F33A Bonanza	CE-1108	D-EBUM(3)
OO-EUR	CEA Jodel DR.1051 Sicile	249	F-BKIE
OO-EVE	de Havilland DH.82A Tiger Moth	85953	T-25
			ETA-25
			EM722
OO-EVJ	de Havilland DH.82A Tiger Moth	82712	T-29
			R4771
OO-EVM	Piper PA-28-236 Dakota	28-7911181	OO-HCW
			N29599
OO-EVZ	Morane-Saulnier MS.885 Super Rallye	233	F-BKUA
OO-EWL	Robin HR.100/200B Royale	125	D-EJYJ
			(OO-NDW)
			D-EJYJ
OO-FAC	Nord NC.858D	12	F-BFIA
OO-FAS	Nord NC.858D	104	F-BEZK
OO-FBL	Agusta-Bell 47G-2 (Reservation)	111	F-BXXD
			ALAT
OO-FBV	Reims/Cessna F.150F	0023/62918	OO-SIJ
			(N8818G)
OO-FCA	Reims/Cessna F.177RG Cardinal RG	0040/00204	
OO-FCD	Piper PA-28-181 Cherokee Archer II	28-7790285	N1085H
OO-FCE	Reims/Cessna F.172M	1470	
OO-FDN	Wassmer Jodel D.120A Paris-Nice	265	
OO-FDQ	Wassmer Jodel D.120A Paris-Nice	270	
OO-FDS	Wassmer Jodel D.120A Paris-Nice	272	
OO-FDU	Wassmer Jodel D.120A Paris-Nice	276	
OO-FDV	Wassmer Jodel D.120A Paris-Nice	277	
OO-FEE	Schweizer 269C	S-1596	D-HHEX
			N41S
OO-FES	Beech 35-C33 Debonair	CD-1011	D-ECLC
OO-FFI	Robin DR.360 Chevalier	702	OO-BOB
			D-ENTG
OO-FFT	DHC-1 Chipmunk 22A	C1/0475	G-AOTZ
			WG401
OO-FGW	Beech F33A Bonanza	CE-982	N1849Z
			(F-GGBM)
			N1849Z
OO-FIC	Rockwell 114 Commander	14089	N4759W
OO-FIF	GEMS MS.892A Rallye Commodore 150	10534	F-BNBF
OO-FIR	Piper PA-18 Super Cub 95	18-1371	OO-HMZ
			ALAT
			51-15371
OO-FJL	Schweizer 269C	S-1636	D-HMAC
			N69A
OO-FJZ	Cessna 182P Skylane	62728	F-BVJZ
			N52631
OO-FKV	Cessna R.182 Skylane RG	01429	N4788S
OO-FLA	Piper PA-28-140 Cherokee	28-7625105	OO-HAX
			N9509N
OO-FLC	Reims/Cessna F.152	1624	OO-HNS
OO-FLE	Piper PA-34-200T Seneca II	34-7770135	OO-HCC
			N1693H
OO-FLM	Piper PA-28-181 Archer II	28-7990544	OO-HCE
			N2907T
OO-FLS	Piper PA-32-300 Cherokee Six	32-7940074	N2226W
OO-FLW	Piper PA-18 Super Cub 95	18-1562	OO-HMS
			ALAT
			51-15562
OO-FLZ	SOCATA Rallye 180T Galérien	3207	
OO-FMC	Reims/Cessna F.172H	0614	
OO-FMX	Reims/Cessna F.172N	2031	D-EFMX
OO-FNL	Cessna 525 CitationJet	0332	N5161J
OO-FOR	Douglas AD-4NA Skyraider	7765	(OO-SKY)
			F-ZVMM
			ChadAF126956
			Fr.AF
			BuA126956
OO-FOX	Enstrom 280 Shark (Reservation)	unkn	

Regn.	Type	C/n	Prev.Id.
OO-FSI	Reims/Cessna F.150M	1399	F-GASN
OO-FST	Reims/Cessna F.150H	0350	
OO-FTL	SEEMS MS.885 Super Rallye	5395	F-BLSZ
OO-FUL	Akrotech CAP-222	001	F-WWMY
OO-FUS	Cessna 208B Grand Caravan (Reservn .00)	0794	N13047
OO-FVR	Agusta-Bell 206B Jet Ranger III (Cr. 4.99)	8590	D-HORA(2)
			HB-XIV
OO-FWA	Robin R.3000/160	136	
OO-FWB	Robin DR.300/108	510	F-BSLB
OO-FWD	Robin DR.400RP Remorqueur	1872	F-GGQV
OO-FWJ	Pilatus PC-6/B1-H2 Turbo-Porter	710	HB-FFP
OO-FWP	Piaggio FWP.149D	059	D-EEHH
			90+45
			JD+390
			BF+702
			BC+702
			AS+486
OO-GAC	SOCATA MS.880B Rallye Club	2302	(F-BULT)
OO-GAI	Cessna 182P (Reims-assembled)	0015/63909	OO-CKC
			HB-CKC
			OO-GAI
			N6988M
OO-GAM	Grumman-American AA-5A Cheetah	0011	OO-HAZ
OO-GAQ	Cessna 172N	68074	N75968
OO-GAS	SOCATA MS.880B Rallye Club	1700	F-BSZS
			F-BSKS
OO-GAZ	Grumman-American AA-5B Tiger	0971	OO-HRD
OO-GBL	Gates Learjet 35A	35A-284	D-CCAX
			(D-CEFL)
OO-GCA	Piper PA-28-140 Cherokee C	28-26573	N5750U
OO-GCO	Grumman-American AA-5A Cheetah	0526	OO-HGB
OO-GCZ	Hughes 269B	25-0163	D-HCOC
			PH-HOP
			D-HESW
OO-GDE	Piper PA-18-100 Super Cub	18-3106	OL-L32
			53-4706
OO-GDH	Piper PA-18-135 Super Cub	18-3131	OL-L57
	(Painted as "L-57")		53-4731
OO-GEL	Piper J-3C-85 Cub	12682	OO-AVP
	(Believed rebuilt using parts from OO-GEK)		44-80386
OO-GEM	Beech 35-C33 Debonair	CD-1090	G-AVHG
OO-GEO	Dornier Do.28D-1 Skyservant	4023	OY-DLS
			D-IDWM
			PH-NVB
			D-IDWM
			(N6774)
OO-GET	Beech F33A Bonanza	CE-1285	(OO-EOS)
			D-EOGH
OO-GFC	SOCATA MS.880B Rallye Club	1796	
OO-GFD	Dassault Falcon 2000	101	N399FA
			N2093
OO-GHM	Piper PA-34-220T Seneca III	34-8133021	N8341U
OO-GIN	Wassmer WA.52 Europa (Crashed)	71	F-BTLT
OO-GIO	Aeronca 7AC Champion	4458	
OO-GJY	Reims/Cessna F.150L	0975	D-EGJY
OO-GLB	Grob G.115C2	82045	D-EXGR
OO-GLO	Robin HR.100/210 Royale	172	
OO-GLR	Wassmer Jodel D.112 Club	1002	F-BIXO
OO-GMC	Piper PA-34-200T Seneca II	34-7970007	N2213B
OO-GMD	Piper PA-38-112 Tomahawk	38-79A0487	(OO-TLT)
			N9661N
OO-GMX	Maule MX.7-180 Star Rocket	11034C	F-GGMX
			F-WGMX
			N61071
OO-GPS	Cessna 404 Titan	0609	
OO-GRH	Wassmer WA.40A Super IV	102	
OO-GRT	Morane-Saulnier MS.880B Rallye Club	223	OO-JGN
OO-GSM	Reims/Cessna FR.182 Skylane RG	0013	OO-HNN
OO-GTR	SAN Jodel D.117 Grand Tourisme	694	F-BIDE
OO-GUN	Schweizer 269CB-300	0022	
OO-GUY	CEA Jodel DR.1051 Sicile	308	F-BKIN
OO-GVA	SOCATA MS.883 Rallye 115	1391	F-BRRJ
OO-GVE	Beech 77 Skipper	WA-293	HB-EJL
OO-GWA	SNCAN/ Stampe SV.4C	478	N1024N
			F-BDBO

Regn.	Type	C/n	Prev.Id.
OO-GWB	Stampe & Renard/ SV.4B	1171	(OO-GWR)
			V-29
OO-GWC	SNCAN/ Stampe SV.4A	1	N9480A
			F-BFVA
			AeN
			Adl'A
OO-GWD	Stampe & Renard/ SV.4B	1160	G-BRMC
			SLN-03
			V-18
OO-GYM	Cessna 170B	25509	D-EMIT
			N4565C
OO-GYS	SOCATA MS.880B Rallye Club	2857	
OO-GYT	SOCATA MS.880B Rallye Club	2260	
OO-GZM	Reims/Cessna FR.182 Skylane	0045	D-EIYO
OO-HBD	Reims/Cessna F.150J	0464	(D-EBUA)
OO-HBG	Piper PA-18 Super Cub 95	18-3228	OL-L18
			L-154
			53-4828
OO-HBH	Piper PA-18 Super Cub 95	18-3142	OL-L68
	(Officially quoted with c/n 18-3194 but f/n is		L-68
	18-3110 matching c/n above)		53-4742
OO-HBI	Reims/Cessna F.150L	0747	
OO-HBQ	Piper PA-18 Super Cub 95	18-3130	OL-L56
			53-4730
OO-HBR	Reims/Cessna F.172M	1484	(D-EITA)
OO-HBS	Piper PA-18 Super Cub 95	18-1511	OO-SPK
	(c/n quoted officially as 18-3080)		ALAT
			51-15511
OO-HBT	Reims/Cessna F.150M	1254	D-EIHF
			(F-BXQA)
OO-HBU	Reims/Cessna F.172N	1916	(F-GCHN)
OO-HBW	Reims/Cessna F.150G	0144	D-EJRO
OO-HEO	SIAI-Marchetti S.208 (cvtd from 205-22/R)	4-231	
OO-HER	Cessna 172M	63034	N13899
OO-HFA	Reims/Cessna F.152-II	1866	
OO-HFD	Hughes 269C	47-0585	G-BMGP
			ZS-HMK
			N7496F
OO-HFE	Reims/Cessna F.152-II	1877	
OO-HFI	Cessna 172N	72136	C-GLIV
			N8084E
OO-HFS	Hughes 369D	120-0880D	LX-HLE
			OO-HFS
			G-BIOA
OO-HFZ	Hughes 269C	99-0823	(OO-DMG)
			G-BOVZ
			VH-TID
OO-HGZ	CEA Jodel DR.1051 Sicile	301	F-BKIG
OO-HOP	Agusta-Bell 206B Jet Ranger II	8418	PH-HAP
			SX-HAP
			(HB-XEX)
OO-HPK	Cessna U.206G Stationair Soloy	05788	(OO-HSD)
			D-EATU
			HB-CJG
			N5474X
OO-HSB	Aérospatiale AS.355F1 Ecureuil 2	5223	G-PLAX
			G-BPMT
			N380E
OO-HSG	Aérospatiale AS.355F1 Ecureuil 2	5116	N5791M
OO-HSS	Robinson R-22 Beta	0913	(N . . . . .)
			PH-THA
			(PH-VLO)
OO-HUS	Christen A-1 Husky	1128	N9603R
OO-HVC	Cessna 150M	78359	N9411U
OO-HYW	SNCAN/ Stampe SV.4C	552	F-BDCX
OO-IBL	HP.137 Jetstream 200	241	G-GLOS
			G-BCGU
			G-AXRI
			N8469A
			N8459A
OO-IBR	Piper PA-32R-301 Saratoga	32R-8213002	N69135
OO-IFR	Piper PA-28-181 Archer II	28-8590056	
OO-IKA	Grumman-American AA-5B Tiger	0543	OO-HGA
OO-ILJ	Boeing 737-46B	25262	
OO-ING	Airbus A.300B4-2C	066	HS-TAZ
			N405UA
			N206EA
			F-GBNB
			F-WZEO
OO-IPZ	CEA Jodel DR.1050-M1 Sicile Record	02	F-BIPZ
			F-WIPZ
OO-ISE	Cessna T303 Crusader	00160	LX-YNC
			N65NC
			G-BPZN
			G-RSUL
			(G-BPZN)
			N6610C
OO-IVB	Cessna T.210L Turbo Centurion	61063	D-ELSY(2)
			N2097S
OO-IXY	Wassmer Jodel D.120A Paris-Nice	145	F-BIXY
OO-JAC(5)	Beech V35A Bonanza	D-8745	
OO-JAE	Piper PA-28R-200 Cherokee Arrow	28R-35676	D-EJAE
			N4904S
OO-JAG	Piper PA-28-161 Cadet	2841247	N9192Z
OO-JAK(3)	Piper PA-22-150 Tri-Pacer	22-7640	F-BJAK
			ALAT
OO-JAL	Wassmer Jodel D.120A Paris-Nice	59	(OO-CMF)
			F-BHYP
OO-JBH	SAN Jodel D.150 Mascaret	51	
OO-JCJ	Piper PA-28-140 Cherokee	28-25242	(OO-NEW)
			N8001N
OO-JCM	Piper PA-28-181 Archer II	28-7990499	N2853D
OO-JCO	Wassmer WA.51 Pacific	03	F-BPTU
OO-JDA	Robinson R-22 Beta	0840	G-JWSD
OO-JDC	Piper J-3C-65 Cub	12476	OO-AJK
			44-80180
OO-JDG	Robinson R-22 Beta	0821	F-GICD
OO-JDV	Pilatus PC-6/B2-H4 Turbo-Porter	911	
OO-JEN	SAAB S.91A Safir	91140	PH-UEF
			SE-BNU
OO-JEP	Piel CP.301A Emeraude	231	F-BIMF
OO-JGA	Piper PA-28-181 Archer II	28-8090313	N87GA
			CX-BNB-F
			N9558N
OO-JIM	Robinson R-22 Beta	1512	G-BUZW
			OH-HJA
			(N151NH)
OO-JIR	Wassmer WA.40 Super IV	3	F-BJIR
OO-JKM	Beech F33 Bonanza	CE-487	N4386W
OO-JKT(2)	Focke-Wulf FW.44J Stieglitz	183	D-EHDH(2)
			LV-YYX
OO-JLJ	Beech 95-A55 Baron	TC-450	D-ILDU
OO-JLM	Cessna 177RG Cardinal RG	1295	PH-BRA
			N52874
OO-JMA	SOCATA MS.893E Rallye 180GT Gaillard	12273	F-BUJX
OO-JMB	Piper PA-32R-300 Lance	32R-7780226	N1226Q
OO-JMC	Piper PA-28-181 Archer II	28-7990550	N2910H
OO-JMF	Piper PA-28-140 Cherokee D	28-7125468	PH-SRB
			N11C
OO-JMI	Reims/Cessna F.172M	1437	F-BXQR
OO-JMK	Mooney M.20K Model 231	25-0734	N5615G
OO-JML	Piper PA-32R-301 Saratoga	3213073	N9235X
OO-JMS	Robin DR.300/108 2+2	586	
OO-JMW	Mooney M.20J Model 201	24-1633	
OO-JNH	SOCATA MS.883 Rallye 115	1550	F-BSAK
OO-JNS	Beech A36 Bonanza	E-1108	C-GJLS
			N18380
OO-JOA	CEA Jodel DR.1051 Sicile (W/o 11.8.92)	220	
OO-JOB	Wassmer Jodel D.112F Club	1119	
OO-JOG	Piper PA-32R-301T Turbo Saratoga	32R-8329022	N42989
OO-JPD	Piper PA-28-140 Cherokee	28-7425107	N9593N
OO-JPF	Piper PA-28-140 Cherokee	28-7625062	OO-HAV
			N9636N
OO-JPL	Boisavia B.601L Mercurey	115	(OO-UPL)
			F-BIGZ
OO-JPR	Piper PA-28-151 Cherokee Warrior	28-7415538	N9513N
OO-JPS	Piper PA-28-140 Cherokee E	28-7225575	N15460
OO-JPW	Piper PA-28R-200 Cherokee Arrow II	28R-7635397	N4209F
OO-JRB	Reims/Cessna F.150J	0510	(HB-CTX)

Regn.	Type	C/n	Prev.Id.
OO-JRD	Reims/Cessna F.177RG Cardinal RG	0046	
OO-JSG	Piper PA-38-112 Tomahawk	38-79A0250	N2594C
OO-JSY	Robinson R-44 Astro	0463	D-HIBB
OO-JUL	Morane-Saulnier MS.317	6530/276	(OO-MIL)
	(Wears French Navy c/s as "3S2")		F-BFZO
OO-JUN	Tipsy Junior (Reservation)	unkn	G-AMVP ?
OO-JUS	Naval Aircraft Factory N3N-3	2909	N45172
			BuA .....
OO-JVE	Piper PA-28-235 Cherokee	28-10894	OO-HSL
			N9226W
OO-JVO	Reims/Cessna F.172G	0281	
OO-JVS	Beech 95-E55 Baron	TE-1099	D-IKLM
OO-KAA	Beech A36 Bonanza	E-445	N808T
OO-KAC	Robin DR.400/180R Remorqueur	1404	OE-DKU
OO-KAJ	PZL-110 Koliber 150	03900039	(OO-CAJ)
			PH-BEE
OO-KAM	Tipsy T.66 Nipper II	29	OO-69
OO-KAT	SNCAN/ Stampe SV.4C (Lycoming 0-360)	416	F-BCQZ
OO-KAY	Mooney M.20K Model 231	25-0332	N231NV
OO-KBM	Bell 206B Jet Ranger II	1788	G-BVWS
			C-GGXX
			N49610
OO-KEA	SOCATA Rallye 110ST Galopin	3302	D-EGRJ
OO-KER	de Havilland DH.115 Vampire T.55	22277	N4368F
			U-1237
OO-KES	Piper PA-28-140 Cherokee F	28-7325013	N15196
OO-KEY	Beech A36 Bonanza	E-1150	(OO-AZM)
			D-EFIT(4)
			OE-KMK
			D-EEHZ
			HB-EHZ
OO-KFC	Piper PA-18-135 Super Cub	18-1633	OO-HNH
			ALAT
			51-15633
OO-KID	Grumman-American AA-5A Cheetah	0661	(OO-HRI)
OO-KIW	Piper PA-18 Super Cub 95	18-1573	OO-HSC
			OL-L04
			51-15573
OO-KIX	Aeronca Champion 8KCAB Decathlon	799-97	(OO-XIX)
			N799AC
OO-KKK	Piper PA-18 Super Cub 95	18-3155	D-EKKK
			OL-L77
			53-4755
OO-KLO	Boisavia B.601L Mercurey	22	F-BHVH
OO-KMA	Robinson R-22 Beta	1501	N4033S
OO-KMP	Cessna 152	83278	D-EMKF
			N48080
OO-KMS	Cessna 152	82406	N68927
OO-KMT	American Champion 8GCBC Scout	383-97	
OO-KMZ	SOCATA MS.893A Rallye Commodore 180	11842	(OO-HUB)
			D-EODJ
OO-KNK	SOCATA TB-20 Trinidad	1013	SE-KNK
OO-KPA	Cessna 172R	80521	D-EPRP
			N9573G
OO-KPM	Cessna 152 (Damaged 5.99)	81190	N49201
OO-KPW	Cessna 172R	80065	N697SC
OO-KTJ	Morane-Saulnier MS.880B Rallye Club	214	F-BKTJ
OO-KVU	Beech 35-C33 Debonair (Reservn .00)	CD-1036	D-EKVU
OO-KWP	Cessna 152	85995	(OO-KWT)
			N95992
OO-KWS	Cessna 152	85985	N95920
OO-KWT	Cessna 172N	68274	N733GA
OO-LAA	Piper J-5A Cub Coupé	5-868	N38057
			NC38057
OO-LAK	Grumman-American AA-5B Tiger	0099	
OO-LAP	Piper PA-18-150 Super Cub	18-8780	D-ECOL(2)
			N4444Z
			N10F
OO-LBC	SEEMS MS.890A Rallye Commodore 150	10283	F-BLBC
			(D-ECKY)
			F-BLBC
OO-LCA	SAN Jodel D.140A Mousquetaire	46	F-BIZK
OO-LCB	Jodel D.112 Club	669	F-BIGM

Regn.	Type	C/n	Prev.Id.
OO-LCM	Cessna 500 Citation	0036	N18HJ
			D-IEXC
			SE-DEU
			OY-DVL
			N536CC
OO-LDR	Robin R.3000/140	101	F-GDYI
OO-LEA	Robinson R-22HP	0207	F-GIVI
			HB-XMW
OO-LED	SNCAN/ Stampe SV.4C	388	F-BBTR
			Fr.AF
OO-LEE	SNCAN/ Stampe SV.4E (Lycoming 0-360)	99	F-BNDA
			F-BJCF
			F-BBAG
OO-LEL	Stampe & Renard/ SV.4B	1197	PH-BOZ
			OO-RLC
			V-55
OO-LEM	Aeronca 11AC Chief	1607	
OO-LEO	Tipsy T.66 Nipper II	62	
OO-LER	Bell 206B Jet Ranger II	2043	G-BVWT
			C-GUXC
			N9965K
OO-LES	Reims/Cessna F.150G	0072	PH-LES
OO-LET	Beech B200 Super King Air	BB-1473	N8210X
			PT-OXG
			N8064Q
OO-LEV	Schweizer 269C-300	S-1726	
OO-LEX	Robinson R-44 Astro	0367	D-HISS
OO-LFM	Piper PA-18-135 Super Cub	18-2543	(OO-VVQ)
			OO-HMC
			ALAT
			52-6225
OO-LFS	Bombardier Learjet 45	45-018	N418LJ
OO-LFT	Dassault Falcon 50	42	OE-HCS
			D-BDWO
			N82MP
			N61FJ
			F-WZHE
OO-LFV	Gates Learjet 35A	35A-481	N27NR
			N729HS
			HK-3122/X
			N729HS
			N728MP
			N666KK
			N6666K
OO-LGB	Piper PA-18 Super Cub 95	18-2060	OO-SPG
	(Exchanged fuselages with c/n 18-1650 -		R-53
	see OO-SPG)		52-2460
OO-LGD	Reims/Cessna F.150H	0351	
OO-LHM	Dornier Do.27A-3	417	57+00
			CA+047
			GB+384
OO-LIB	Wassmer WA.41 Baladou	96	F-BMYV
OO-LJR	Robinson R-22 Beta	1844	G-EDDI
OO-LMC	Fokker S.11- 1 Instructor	6216	(PH-HOB)
			E-25
OO-LME	CEA Jodel DR.1051M1 Sicile Record	432	F-BLME
OO-LMI	Bell 206B Jet Ranger II	1231	G-BRMH
			N39AH
			G-BRMH
			G-BBUX
			N18091
OO-LMO	Reims/Cessna F.406 Caravan II	0034	D-ILIM
			OY-PAB
			PH-PHO
			AP-BFB
			N443AB
			G-BPSX
			F-WZDX
OO-LMZ	Piper PA-18 Super Cub 95	18-1474	ALAT
			51-15474
OO-LNA	SOCATA MS.893E Rallye 180GT Gaillard	12270	F-BUJT
OO-LNC	Reims/Cessna F.172M	1510	F-BUDU
OO-LOP	Robin R.2112 Alpha	178	F-GCAC
OO-LOQ	Gyroflug SC-01 Speed Canard	S-12	

Regn.	Type	C/n	Prev.Id.
OO-LOT	Piper PA-18 Super Cub 95	18-3218	OL-L12 / L-144 / 53-4818
OO-LOU	Piper PA-18 Super Cub 95	18-1617	OO-HNF / ALAT / 51-15617
OO-LOV	Beech V35A Bonanza	D-8799	F-GCME / N8464N
OO-LPE	Grumman AA-5B Tiger (Reservation .00)	0468	D-ELPE(2)
OO-LRF	CEA Jodel DR.1051 Sicile	511	F-BLRF
OO-LRM	McDonnell-Douglas DC-10-30	46998	N526MD / PH-MCO / HB-IHK
OO-LSA	Partenavia P.68C	279	D-GIMI
OO-LSY	SEEMS MS.892A Rallye Commodore 150	10448	F-BLSY
OO-LTH	Hughes 369E	0469E	OO-XTH
OO-LTM	Boeing 737-3M8	25070	F-GMTM / OO-LTM / F-GLTM / OO-LTM
OO-LTP	Boeing 737-33A	25032	N228AW / PP-SOG
OO-LTV	Boeing 737-3Y0	23924	XA-SEM / G-BNGL
OO-LTW	Boeing 737-33A	25010	VH-OAM / N226AW
OO-LTY	Boeing 737-3Y0	23925	PP-SOE / XA-SEO / G-BNGM
OO-LUC	Percival P.40 Prentice 1	5840/18	G-AOLM / VS396 / V-41
OO-LUK	Stampe & Renard/ SV.4B	1183	
OO-LUX	Alpavia Jodel D.117A Grand Tourisme	1060	F-BJEL
OO-LUY	Schweizer 269C	S-1780	(OO-LEC) / N41S
OO-LVB	Cessna 152-II	84883	N5124P
OO-LVD	Reims/Cessna F.172P	2126	D-EILV / (D-EDDL)
OO-LVJ	Reims/Cessna FA.152 Aerobat	0378	HB-CHL / N96954 / (D-EJDG) / N96954
OO-LVK	Hughes 369D	120-0881D	OE-XBB / N190CA / N5293E / C-GHVK
OO-LVL	Maule MX7-180 Star Rocket	11045C	
OO-LVN	Piper PA-25-235 Pawnee D	25-7656121	N82407
OO-LVP	Piper PA-18-135 Super Cub	18-3593	EI-202 / I-EIYW / MM542393 / 54-2393
OO-LVW	Mooney M.20J Model 205	24-3250	D-ESEO
OO-LVZ	Piper PA-18 Super Cub 95 (Dismantled)	18-1405	ALAT / 51-15405
OO-LWI	Piaggio FWP.149D (Displayed in garden at Zenst)	154	91+32 / BF+701 / KB+131
OO-LXV	Cessna 172N	73261	N7575F
OO-LYR	SNCAN/ Stampe SV.4C	109	F-BMME / Fr.Mil
OO-LYT	Robinson R-44 Astro	0634	
OO-MAD	Beech A24R Musketeer Super R	MC-91	(OO-LCC) / G-USTO / (OO-...) / G-USTO / G-AYPA
OO-MAF	Hispano HA.1112MIL	201	C4K-121
OO-MAK	Piaggio FWP.149D	056	90+42 / AS+407 / AS+483 / OO-HNK(2)
OO-MAM	Reims/Cessna F.182Q Skylane	0144	
OO-MAN	SOCATA MS.880B Rallye Club	2251	G-BAOI
OO-MAR	Grumman-American AA-5 Traveler	0424	N7124L
OO-MAY	SAN Jodel DR.105A Ambassadeur	98	LX-MAY
OO-MBS	Piper PA-18-150 Super Cub	18-4046	(OO-LVT) / EI-297 / I-EIZC / MM542646 / 54-2646
OO-MBV	SOCATA Rallye 110ST Galopin	3210	
OO-MCA	Piper PA-32-301 Saratoga	32-8006013	N81648
OO-MCD	Reims/Cessna F.182Q Skylane	0151	F-BJCE
OO-MCH	Fokker S-11-1 Instructor	6208	(PH-HOE) / E-17
OO-MCL	Morane-Saulnier MS.733 Alcyon	186	Fr.Navy
OO-MCP	Cessna TU.206G Turbo Stationair II	03642	N545AC / N7377N
OO-MCT	Robinson R-22 Beta	2333	PH-THB / (OO-...) / N82246 / N2352Y
OO-MDA	Cessna R.182 Skylane RG	01057	N182MR / (N756EX)
OO-MDF	Reims/Cessna F.172N	1890	OO-HNV
OO-MDG	Cessna 172N	73913	F-GJAA / N7378J
OO-MDM	Aeronca 7AC Champion	3623	
OO-MDP	Schweizer 269C	S-1787	N69A
OO-MEA	SIAI-Marchetti S.205-18/R	4-164	OO-HEA
OO-MEC	SIAI-Marchetti S.205-18/R	4-167	OO-HEC
OO-MEV	Piaggio FWP.149D	053	90+39 / BF+405 / AS+480
OO-MFG	Zlin Z.526F Trenér Master	1266	YR-ZAN
OO-MGA	CEA Jodel DR.1051 Sicile	557	F-BMGA
OO-MGM	Cessna 182P Skylane	64973	OH-COP / N1415S
OO-MHB	Piper PA-28-236 Dakota	28-8011143	G-BMHB / D6-PAD / N81321 / N9593N
OO-MIA/B/D/E	Reserved for Air Mercuery International		
OO-MIL	SEEMS MS.885 Super Rallye	5390	F-BLSD
OO-MJE	BAe.146 Series 200	E-2192	(OO-DJI) / G-6-192
OO-MJN	Reserved for DAT Wallonie SA		
OO-MKD	Reims/Cessna F.150K	0546	
OO-MLB	Reims/Cessna F.150M	1335	
OO-MLD	Tipsy T.66S Nipper III	2071	
OO-MLF	Piper PA-34-200T Seneca II	34-7970216	N2245Z
OO-MLS	Piper PA-28R-200 Cherokee Arrow II	28R-7335221	D-EORW / N55358
OO-MMD	SNCAN/Stampe SV.4C (Reservation)	56	F-BMMD / ALAT / F-BAYR / CEV
OO-MMP	Cessna 551 Citation II/SP	0559	D-ICHE / VR-CHB / G-BNSC / N1298H
OO-MNM	Piper PA-18-150 Super Cub	18-8009035	N82675
OO-MOG	Wassmer Jodel D.112 Club	1293	F-BMOG
OO-MOI	Wassmer Jodel D.120A Paris-Nice	273	F-BMOI
OO-MOM	Commander Aircraft 114B	14615	N6031Y
OO-MON	Stampe & Renard/ SV.4B	1172	V-30
OO-MOR	Morane-Saulnier MS.315	6533/279	N315MS / F-BGIL / Fr.AF
OO-MOU	SAN Jodel DR.1050 Ambassadeur	399	F-BLJC
OO-MPG	Beech A36 Bonanza	E-2461	G-BPHM / N1558W
OO-MPJ	Holste MH.1521M Broussard	195	F-GDPY / Fr.AF
OO-MPK	Cessna 172RG Cutlass	0057	N5359R
OO-MQA	Cessna 150M	77810	N7684U
OO-MQB	Cessna 150M	78537	N704DV
OO-MQD	Cessna 172M	61945	N12355
OO-MSA	Morane-Saulnier MS.733 Alcyon	178	Fr.Navy
OO-MSG	Piper PA-38-112 Tomahawk	38-79A1113	N24355

Regn.	Type	C/n	Prev.Id.
OO-MSH	Fokker S-11-1 Instructor	6269	(PH-HOC)
	(Painted as "E-26")		E-26
			PH-NEK
OO-MSN	Cessna T.310R	0562	LX- III (6)
			5B-CGN
			D-IFOP
			N87743
OO-MTW	Piper PA-28-181 Archer II	2890091	N9151Z
OO-MUA	Reims/Cessna F.172N	1801	OO-HNT
OO-MVG	Reims/Cessna F.172M	1130	
OO-MVH	Cessna 182P Skylane	62473	G-BBSG
			N52234
OO-MWM	Piper PA-28-180 Cherokee E	28-5777	D-EMWM
			N3674R
OO-MYR	Piper PA-28-140 Cherokee F	28-7325568	N56084
OO-NAC	Tipsy T.66 Nipper II (Reservation)	58	
OO-NAP	Pilatus PC-6/B2-H4 Turbo-Porter	914	
OO-NAT	SOCATA MS.880B Rallye Club	2253	G-BAOK
OO-NEA	Hughes 369E	0419E	HB-XQG
			D-HJAA
			F-GMMC
			D-HJAA
OO-NEN	SIAI-Marchetti S.208 (Cvtd 205-20/R)	4-250	OO-HEN
OO-NHV	Aérospatiale AS.365N3 Dauphin 2	6510	F-WWOZ
OO-NIK	Reims/Cessna F.172M	1018	PH-GUS
OO-NIQ	North American Navion 4	NAV-4-1259	HB-ESE
			N4259K
OO-NKN	Schweizer 269C	S-1498	D-HHOB
OO-NLG	Piper PA-18 Super Cub 95	18-2044	PH-NLG
			R-67
			52-2444
OO-NLW	Piper PA-28-140 Cherokee	28-25368	PH-NLW
			N8172N
OO-NNA	SOCATA MS.893A Rallye Commodore 180	10604	F-BNNA
OO-NPT	Beech A23-19 Musketeer Sport	MB-31	(OO-NBS)
			F-BNOX
OO-NQD	Schweizer 269C	S-1745	
OO-NRJ	Cessna U.206G Stationair II	03579	G-BNRJ
			N7242N
OO-NSA	SOCATA MS.893A Rallye Commodore 180	10612	F-BNSA
OO-NSD	SOCATA MS.880B Rallye Club	2301	F-BULS
OO-NTB	Robin DR.400/180R Remorqueur	1441	PH-NTR
OO-NTF	Reims/Cessna FR.172H Rocket	0244	
OO-NUE	Aerotek Pitts S-2A	2078	(OO-RUT)
			N5VC
			N4C
OO-NVM	SOCATA MS.894A Minerva 220	11008	
OO-NVT	Reims/Cessna F.172H	0392	PH-MIB
OO-NYL	Piper PA-28-180 Cherokee D	28-4654	N5351L
OO-NZA	Reims/Cessna FRA.150M Aerobat	0336	
OO-NZB	Cessna 172P	75025	G-BNYW
			N54655
OO-NZD	Grob G.115A	8068	OO-XZD
			G-BPSY
			D-EAMH
OO-NZF	Piper PA-28-181 Archer II	28-8590043	G-BRLE
			OY-CGY
			N152AV
OO-NZG	Piper PA-28-161 Warrior II	28-8316050	G-LADN
			G-BOLK
			N4295C
OO-NZM	Mooney M.20K Model 231	25-0295	N231LD
OO-OAA	Piper PA-18-135 Super Cub	18-568	(OO-OOA)
			R-213
			51-15682
			N7197K
OO-OAC	Robin HR.200/120B Club	298	
OO-OAW	Piper PA-18-150 Super Cub	18-5346	D-EOAW
			ALAT
OO-OBC	Robin R.2160 Acrobin	07	
OO-OFD	Mudry CAP.10B	220	
OO-OLD	Piper J-3C-65 Cub	3307	N24619
			NC24619
OO-OLE	CASA I-131E Jungmann	1078	EC-DKV
			E3B-379
OO-OLI	Grumman-American AA-5A Cheetah	0010	OO-HAL
OO-OMA	Cessna 172N	70037	C-GQPQ
			N738KL
OO-ONG	Cessna 207A Stationair 8	00601	D-EEFB(2)
			N73512
OO-OPA	Reims/Cessna F.172N	1670	OO-HNK(1)
OO-OSA	Cessna S550 Citation II	0147	(OO-SAL)
			N1296N
OO-OSM	SAN Jodel DR.1050 Ambassadeur	113	D-EINN
			F-BJJD
OO-OTO	SOCATA MS.880B Rallye Club	1264	
OO-OUI	SOCATA MS.893A Rallye Commodore 180	11710	N4389
			F-BSTL
OO-OVB	Beech F33A Bonanza	CE-1282	TU-TNC
OO-PAL	Piper PA-25-235 Pawnee D	25-7556112	N267JW
			N9799P
OO-PAM	Stampe & Renard SV.4B	1190	V-48
OO-PAS	Grumman-American AA-5 Traveler	0507	
OO-PAW	Piper PA-25-235 Pawnee C	25-5396	N8932L
OO-PAX	Stampe & Renard/ SV.4B	1147	V-5
OO-PCA	Cessna A.185F Skywagon	03151	C-GYFY
			(N84725)
OO-PCH	Fokker S-11-1 Instructor	6199	(PH-HOA)
OO-PCL	Cessna U.206G Stationair II	0011/04724	(OO-LPK)
			N732UF
OO-PCT	Piper PA-32-260 Cherokee Six	32-7400002	N56630
OO-PCV	Pilatus PC-6/B2-H4 Turbo Porter	882	D-FSPA
OO-PCZ	Cessna T.207A Turbo Stationair 7 / Soloy	00520	HB-CJL
			VH-SUQ
			N6425H
OO-PDP	Schweizer 269D	0010	N6139U
OO-PEF	Gulfstream-American AA-5B Tiger	1128	OO-HRG
OO-PEP	SOCATA MS.880B Rallye Club	1814	F-BSZK
OO-PET	Piper PA-32-260 Cherokee Six	32-708	N3785W
OO-PEV	Hughes 269B	128-0402	
OO-PHI	Cessna 525 CitationJet	0115	(OO-TAU)
			N52141
OO-PHR	SAN Jodel DR.1050 Ambassadeur	97	F-BJJB
OO-PIF	Piper PA-32-300 Cherokee Six	32-7440073	N552TW
OO-PJC	Piel CP.301A Emeraude	211	F BIJK
OO-PJG	CEA DR.221 Dauphin	89	F-BPCM
OO-PKS	Cessna TU.206G Turbo Stationair II	05455	N4375G
			C-FJFK
			N6371U
OO-PLC	SIAI-Marchetti S.208	2-21	OO-HIK
OO-PLG	Tipsy T.66 Nipper II	37	
OO-PLM	SIAI-Marchetti S.205-18/F	002	OO-HAG
			I-SIAA
OO-PLR	Wassmer WA.40 Super IV	47	PH-PUT
OO-PMA	Enstrom F-28A	263	(OO-BAN)
OO-PMB	Robin DR.400/180R Remorqueur	1366	
OO-PMH	Robinson R-22B2 Beta	2832	
OO-PMK	Beech F33A Bonanza	CE-1578	F-GJGA
			N81701
OO-PMS	Grumman-American AA-1B Trainer	0354	
OO-PMT	Robinson R-22B2 Beta (Reservation)	unkn	
OO-POS	SAN Jodel D.117 Grand Tourisme	430	F-BHNO
OO-POU	Piper PA-18-150 Super Cub	18-7865	D-EHRY
OO-PPD	Schweizer 269C	S-1295	D-HLAB
OO-PPE	Reims/Cessna F.172H	0557	
OO-PPR	Piper PA-38-112 Tomahawk	38-79A1128	G-BTMZ
			N24529
OO-PRA	Piper PA-28-140 Cherokee D	28-7125218	PH-SRA
			N11C
OO-PRF	Reims/Cessna F.150L	0840	F-BTUA
OO-PRG	Reims/Cessna F.150M	1185	F-BVXS
OO-PRH	Reims/Cessna F.150M	1183	F-BVXP
OO-PRK	Cessna 150M (Wfu)	77811	N7685U
OO-PRL	Reims/Cessna FA.150K Aerobat	0008	
OO-PRN	Reims/Cessna FA.150K Aerobat	0031	
OO-PRO	Robin HR.100/210 Safari	210	F-ODDK
OO-PRS	Reims/Cessna F.172M	1044	N14498
OO-PRV	Enstrom F-28A	146	F-BUIL
OO-PRW	Enstrom F-28A	258	G-LERN
			G-BBRS

Regn.	Type	C/n	Prev.Id.
OO-PTC	Grumman-American AA-1B Trainer	0466	D-EFDM (N9866L)
OO-PTF	Piper PA-30-160 Twin Comanche B	30-1586	I-JUMBO N8429Y
OO-PUS	Erco 415CD Ercoupe	4577	NC3876H
OO-PVA	Tipsy T.66 Nipper III	A-116	OO-79
	(Used wings of c/n 78 (OO-69) in construction)		
OO-PWW	Cessna 182P	61095	G-LSKW OO-PWW N7455Q
OO-PZG	Cessna 207A Skywagon	00582	(OO-ONG) LX-ASF OO-PZG 9Q-CKD N73379
OO-RAA	Piper PA-38-112 Tomahawk	38-79A0625	N2426K
OO-RAB	Piper PA-38-112 Tomahawk	38-79A0569	D-EKTS N2313K
OO-RAC	CEA DR.220 2+2	4	F-BNVF
OO-RAF	SOCATA MS.880B Rallye Club	1195	
OO-RAG	Piper PA-32R-301 Saratoga	3213004	G-WILI N9128N N9582N
OO-RAK	Erco 415CD Ercoupe	4789	NC94678
OO-RAQ	Reims/Cessna F.172K	0788	(D-ECKJ)
OO-RAV	Piper PA-32R-300 Lance	32R-7680031	OO-HAQ N4578X
OO-RCY	Piper PA-28-161 Cadet	2841166	G-RCYI N9185F
OO-REL	Cessna 140	9067	OO-ACA
OO-RES	Rockwell Commander 112A	373	(OO-CWR) G-NELL OY-DLJ N1373J
OO-RGW	Wassmer WA.40 Super IV	42	F-BKJB
OO-RHB	Robinson R-44 Astro	0034	
OO-RIK	Aeronca 11AC Chief	1598	
OO-RJA	Robinson R-22 Beta	1838	
OO-RJC	Robin DR.300/125 Petit Prince	646	
OO-RJL	Robinson R-22 Beta	2319	
OO-RJM	Bellanca 7KCAB Citabria	486-74	OE-AOP
OO-RJP	Robinson R-22 Beta	1867	N4063C
OO-RJQ	Robinson R-22 Beta	1931	
OO-RJR	Robinson R-22 Beta	1624	
OO-RLD	Miles M.65 Gemini 1A	6285	G-AISD OO-RLD (OO-PRD) VP-KDH G-AISD
OO-RMA	SOCATA TB-9 Tampico	80	G-BKPL SE-GFL
OO-RMB	Reims/Cessna FA.150K Aerobat	0079	
OO-RMF	SNCAN/ Stampe SV.4C	480	F-BDBQ
OO-RMU	Reims/Cessna F.150M	1339	(N1646C) N96103
OO-ROB	Rockwell 690B Commander	11409	N81646
OO-ROC	Maule M-7-235C Super Rocket	4037C	(OO-NDA) N5671R
OO-ROD	Beech A36 Bonanza	E-316	N9488D
OO-ROM	Cessna 150M	77521	N6092K
OO-ROS	Mooney M.20J Model 201	24-0592	N6201S
OO-RSJ	Reims/Cessna FA.150L Aerobat	0110	(OO-BSJ) PH-BSJ D-ECPN
OO-RTC	Reims/Cessna FR.172H Rocket	0265	F-BSHK
OO-RTD	Gulfstream-American AA-5A Cheetah	0826	OO-HRP
OO-RTE	Gulfstream-American AA-5B Tiger	1135	(OO-HRV)
OO-RTF	Reims/Cessna F.177RG Cardinal RG	0033/00196	(N8296G)
OO-RTK	Gulfstream-American AA-5A Cheetah	0766	(OO-HRO)
OO-RTN	Varga 2150A Kachina	152-80	OO-HTA N3360J
OO-RTO	Gulfstream-American AA-5A Cheetah	0726	OO-HRE
OO-RTP	Bellanca 8GCBC Scout	342-80	OO-HTF
OO-RUD	Robin HR.100/200B Royale	123	

Regn.	Type	C/n	Prev.Id.
OO-RVP	Piper PA-46-310P Malibu	46-8408062	G-BLIZ N4364D
OO-RWB	Robinson R-22 Beta	1868	N4076A
OO-RWF	Robinson R-44 Astro	0458	
OO-RWG	Cessna 401	0204	D-IAMG G-AWDM (N7836F)
OO-RWH	Robinson R-22 Beta	1632	N4040R
OO-RYL	Mooney M.20J Model 201	24-1010	(N4004H)
OO-RYP	Rockwell 112 Commander	167	D-EGHT LX-GHB N1167J
OO-RZZ	Robinson R-22 Beta	1461	N4023K
OO-SAB	Piper PA-23-250 Aztec	27-152	OY-AFE N4633P
OO-SAN	Piper PA-32-260 Cherokee Six	32-646	G-AZYE 5Y-AEA N3732W
OO-SAP	Piper PA-24-260 Comanche C	24-4805	N9309P
OO-SAT	Bell 407	53061	C-GFNQ
OO-SBJ	Boeing 737-46B	24573	G-BROC
OO-SBM	Boeing 737-429	25729	
OO-SBX	Boeing 737-3M8	25040	TC-BIR VR-CRC PH-YAA OO-LTK
OO-SBY	Boeing 767-33A	27310	
OO-SBZ	Boeing 737-329	23775	
OO-SCI	Airbus A.310-222	331	F WGYT 9K-AHE YI-AOD 9K-AHE F-WZEO
OO-SCW	Airbus A.340-211	014	F-GNIB (OO-SLG) F-WWJF
OO-SCX	Airbus A.340-211	022	F-GNIC (OO-SLH) F-WWJM
OO-SCY	Airbus A.340-311	047	F-GNID (OO-SLI)
OO-SCZ	Airbus A.340-311	051	F-GNIE (OO-SLJ)
OO-SDG	Boeing 737-229	21135	
OO-SDJ	Boeing 737-229C	20915	
OO-SDL	Boeing 737-229	21136	
OO-SDN	Boeing 737-229	21176	9M-MBP OO-SDN
OO-SDO	Boeing 737-229	21177	
OO-SDV	Boeing 737-329	23771	
OO-SDW	Boeing 737-329	23772	
OO-SDX	Boeing 737-329	23773	
OO-SDY	Boeing 737-329	23774	
OO-SEP	Reims/Cessna F.172G	0183	
OO-SER	Cessna 152	79819	N757LF
OO-SEU	Cessna 172M	61130	(OO-SEX) N20249
OO-SEV	Cessna 152	81644	N65603
OO-SEW	Reims/Cessna F.150M	1172	(YU-CCW) F-BVXJ
OO-SEY	Reims/Cessna F.172G	0214	
OO-SEZ	Cessna 150E	61495	N4095U
OO-SFL	Rockwell Commander 114	14018	N10481 D-EFWH
OO-SFM	Airbus A.330-301	030	F-GMDA F-WWKD
OO-SFN	Airbus A.330-301	037	F-GMDB
OO-SFO	Airbus A.330-301	045	F-GMDC
OO-SFP	Airbus A.330-222	230	FWWKT
OO-SFQ	Airbus A.330-223	290	F-WWKQ
OO-SFR	Airbus A.330-223	296	F-WWKO
OO-SFS	Airbus A.330-223	300	F-WWYC
OO-SFT	Airbus A.330-223	322	F-WWYT
OO-SFU	Airbus A.330-223 *(Reservation .00)*	324	F-WWYU

Regn.	Type	C/n	Prev.Id.
OO-SFX	Airbus A.330-322	096	9M-MKZ
			F-WWKP
OO-SGI	Cessna P210N Pressurized Centurion II	00753	N6333W
OO-SHB	Reims/Cessna F.152	1570	
OO-SHC	Reims/Cessna F.172N	1770	
OO-SHD	Reims/Cessna F.172N	1773	
OO-SHE	Reims/Cessna F.182Q Skylane	0098	
OO-SIC	Cessna 150E	61490	N4090U
OO-SII	Cessna 150F	62208	N8908S
OO-SIL	Reims/Cessna F.150F	0022/62890	(N8790G)
OO-SKB	Reims/Cessna F.150J	0423	
OO-SKG	Reims/Cessna F.172M	1091	
OO-SKI	Robin HR.100/250TR	540	F-GFBD
			F-OCAM
			F-GAEM
OO-SKS	Cessna 551 Citation II	0117	N11AB
			C-GHYD
			(N26616)
OO-SKX	Piper PA-18-150 Super Cub	18-4920	D-EHCP
	(c/n quoted is f/n - built from spares)		
OO-SLK	Boeing 737-33S	29072	
OO-SLR	Boeing 767-3BGER	30563	
OO-SML	SIAI-Marchetti SF.260	2-33	
OO-SMM	SIAI-Marchetti SF.260	2-47	
OO-SMO	SIAI-Marchetti SF.260	2-53	
OO-SNA	Beech A100 King Air	B-217	
OO-SNE	Airbus A.320-214	1054	F-WWIN
OO-SNF	Airbus A.320-214	1081	F-WWIT
OO-SOO	Hughes 369E	0447E	D-HGWM(2)
OO-SOT	Westland Lysander Mk.IIIA	unkn	
	(Painted as RCAF2442-"D-MA")		
OO-SPC	Cessna 150F	62039	PH-ICA
			N8739S
OO-SPD	GEMS MS.892A Rallye Commodore 150	10531	F-BNBC
OO-SPE	Reims/Cessna F.150G	0191	SE-FBB
			LN-BDO
			SE-FBB
OO-SPG	Piper PA-18 Super Cub 95	18-1650	(OO-VIC)
	(Exchanged fuselage with c/n 18-2060 -		OO-LGB
	see OO-LGB)		OO-HMU
			ALAT
			51-15650
OO-SPJ	Piper PA-18 Super Cub 95	18-1547	ALAT
			51-15547
OO-SPM	SNCAN/ Stampe SV.4C	349	F-BCOC
OO-SPP	Cessna 152	85903	PH-PJM
			G-BRCB
			N95490
OO-SPQ	Piper PA-18 Super Cub 95	18-3118	LN-LJI
			OL-L.44
			L-44
			53-4718
OO-SPU	Cessna U.206G Stationair II	05375	F-GMSA
			N6189U
OO-SPY	Reims/Cessna F.172H	0569	
OO-SQA	General Avia F.1300 Jet Squalus	001	I-SQAL
			(OO-SQA)
OO-SSA	Airbus A.319-112	1048	D-AVYT
OO-SSB	Airbus A.319-112	1068	D-AVWD
OO-SSC	Airbus A.319-112	1086	D-AVWL
OO-SSD	Airbus A.319-112	1102	D-AVWN
OO-SSE	Airbus A.319-112	1124	D-AVYV
OO-SSF	Airbus A.319-112	1145	D-AVWH
OO-SSG	Airbus A.319-112	1160	D-AVWL
OO-SSH	Airbus A.319-112	1184	D-AVYR
OO-STF	Boeing 767-328ER	27212	F-GHGK
OO-STG	Cessna 421C Golden Eagle II	0879	D-IXXX
			N5638C
			(N80WD)
			N5638C
OO-STM	Boeing-Stearman N2S-2	75-1391	N59257
			(OO-JKT)
			N59257
			BuA03614
OO-STO	Morane-Saulnier MS.505 Criquet	269/6	F-BBUK

Regn.	Type	C/n	Prev.Id.
OO-STS	Cessna 172RG Cutlass RG	0962	N9677B
OO-STY	Cessna 172N	70980	N1381E
OO-SUA	Airbus A.321-211	970	D-AVZY
OO-SUB	Airbus A.321-211	995	D-AVZG
OO-SUC	Airbus A.321-211	1012	D-AVZH
OO-SUN	Beech C23 Sundowner 180	M-1484	G-BBAT
OO-SUP	Schweizer 269C	S-1495	G-BSUP
OO-SVA	Stampe & Renard/ SV.4B	1191	V-49
OO-SVB	Stampe & Renard/ SV.4B	1185	PH-ZLS
			OO-SVB
			V-43
OO-SVF	AIAA/ Stampe SV.4C	1086	Fr.Navy
OO-SVG	Stampe & Renard/ SV.4B (Preserved)	1163	V-21
OO-SVH	Stampe & Renard/ SV.4B	1168	N-26
OO-SVK	Robin HR.200/120B	250	PH-SVK
OO-SVS	SNCAN/ Stampe SV.4C	320	N2272K
			N320RL
			N10WN
			F-BCLT
OO-SVT	SNCAN/ Stampe SV.4E	9	N9SV
			N15JJ
			N17810
			F-BGGO
			Fr.Mil
OO-SVV	Stampe & Renard/ SV.4B	1200	G-DANN
			OO-SVV
			V-58
OO-SXA	Embraer EMB.121 Xingu	121038	PT-MBF
OO-SXB	Embraer EMB.121 Xingu	21040	PT-MBH
OO-SXC	Embraer EMB.121 Xingu	121042	PT-MBJ
OO-SXD	Embraer EMB.121 Xingu	121043	PT-MBK
OO-SXE	Embraer EMB.121 Xingu	121045	PT-MBM
OO-SYA	Boeing 737-329	24355	(OO-SQA)
OO-SYB	Boeing 737-329	24356	(OO-SQB)
OO-SYC	Boeing 737-429	25226	(OO-SQC)
OO-SYD	Boeing 737-429	25247	(OO-SQD)
OO-SYE	Boeing 737-529	25218	(OO-SQE)
OO-SYF	Boeing 737-429	25248	(OO-SQF)
OO-SYG	Boeing 737-529	25249	(OO-SQG)
OO-SYH	Boeing 737-529	25418	(OO-SQH)
OO-SYI	Boeing 737-529	25419	(OO-SQI)
OO-SYJ	Boeing 737-529	26537	
OO-SYK	Boeing 737-529	26538	
OO-SZO	McDonnell-Douglas MD.520N	LN-027	OY-HEN
			N5212N
OO-TAA	BAe. 146 Series 300QT	E-3151	G-TNTR
			SE-DIT
			G-BRGM
OO-TAB	SOCATA TB-9 Tampico	130	
OO-TAC	SEEMS MS.892A Rallye Commodore 150	10473	
OO-TAO	SEEMS MS.892A Rallye Commodore 150	10457	(OO-TAC)
OO-TBB	SOCATA TB-10 Tobago	1449	
OO-TDA	Robin R.2160 Acrobin	310	
OO-TDF	SOCATA MS.894A Minerva 220	12136	F-BUGF
OO-TDO	Mudry CAP.20	7	F-BTDO
OO-TGM	de Havilland DH.82A Tiger Moth	3318	G-ADCG
			A2126
			A728
			BB731
			G-ADCG
OO-TGW	Reims/Cessna F.172M	1294	PH-TGW
OO-THL	Schweizer 269C	S-1400	HB-XVJ
OO-THO	SOCATA MS.887 Rallye 125	2171	F-OCYR
OO-TIT	SOCATA Rallye 110ST Galopin	3212	
OO-TIX	Tipsy Junior III (Reservation)	J.112	G-TIPS
OO-TJK	Partenavia P.68B Observer	372-28-OB	
OO-TMM	Beech 35-C33 Debonair	CD-1050	F-BNTH
OO-TMT	Piper PA-28-161 Warrior II	28-7916112	N9538N
OO-TOB	SOCATA TB-10 Tobago	26	
OO-TOP	Britten-Norman BN-2A-27 Islander	424	G-BCSI
OO-TOT	SOCATA MS.880B Rallye Club	1226	
OO-TOX	SNCAN/ Stampe SV.4C	150	F-BMMF
			Fr.Mil
OO-TOY	Robin DR.400/120 Petit Prince	1042	F-BXJJ
OO-TPA	Cessna T.210N Turbo Centurion II	64604	N9808Y

Regn.	Type	C/n	Prev.Id.
OO-TRB	Reims/Cessna F.172P	2108	OO-HRB(2)
OO-TRD	Reims/Cessna F.152	1950	
OO-TRJ	Reims/Cessna F.172P	2140	(OO-XRJ)
OO-TRU	SOCATA Rallye 110ST Galopin	3209	F-GBKR
OO-TST	Rockwell 114 Commander	14409	N5864N
OO-TTD	Aérospatiale AS.350BA Ecureuil	9017	
OO-TUG	Piper PA-25-235 Pawnee C	25-4088	N4447Y
OO-TUJ	Reims/Cessna F.177RG Cardinal RG	0064	F-BTUJ
OO-TUT	SOCATA Rallye 100ST-D	2888	D-EDVO(2)
OO-TVB	Reims/Cessna F.150L	1118	
OO-TVH	Cessna T.210N Turbo Centurion II (Robertson-STOL conversion)	63796	N6083C
OO-TVI	Robinson R-22 Beta	0824	G-OLIE
			G-BOUW
OO-TVO	Piper PA-28-140 Cherokee F	28-7325008	N15158
OO-TWA	Piper PA-28-180 Cherokee E	28-5608	(D-EHGC)
			N2394R
OO-TWJ	Aeronca 7AC Champion	3625	
OO-TWP	Aeronca 7AC Champion	3624	
OO-TYP	CEA DR.250/160 Capitaine	81	F-BNVV
OO-TZZ	Schweizer 269C	S-1464	(OO-GBZ)
			G-BSLR
			N69A
OO-UAR	CEA Jodel DR.1051 Sicile	419	F-BLAR
OO-UBY	Reims/Cessna FR.172J Rocket	0498	D-EDJV
OO-UNY	Schweizer 269CB-300	0012	
OO-UOZ	Robin HR.100/210 Safari	165	F-BUOZ
OO-URS	Mooney M.20J Model 201	24-1138	N952AP
OO-USA	Piper PA-18-150 Super Cub	18-3824	R-134
			54-2424
OO-USK	Christen A-1 Husky	1056	F-GGAQ
			F-WGAQ
			N9590C
OO-USN	Boeing-Stearman E75N1	75-4695	N17PT
			N37744
			YS-272P
			N54280
			42-16532
OO-VAB	SOCATA MS.880B Rallye Club	879	(TU-TDW)
OO-VAD	Slingsby T-67M Firefly	2010	G-BLER
OO-VAF	Nord 1101 Noralpha	119	F-BHER
			F-ZJDG
OO-VAG	Tipsy T.66 Nipper I	15	OO-LYS
OO-VAK	Reims/Cessna FR.182 Skylane RG	0001	(F-GDPL)
			TR-LBF
			F-GBFH
			F-WZAU
OO-VAL	Tipsy T.66 Nipper II	50	9Q-CYJ
			9O-CYJ
			OO-CYJ
OO-VAS	Boeing 767-33AER (Reservation)	25535	F-GKAU
			VH-NOE
			N768TA
			N6018N
OO-VBR	Boeing 737-4YO	24314	F-GMBR
			HL7256
OO-VCB	Robinson R-22 Beta	0697	
OO-VCC	Bell 206B Jet Ranger II	4057	(OO-RJL)
			PH-VCK
			(PH-VCH)
			(PH-VCK)
			OO-VCC
			C-FFNM
OO-VCD	Robinson R-22 Beta	1063	N8046J
OO-VCE	Robinson R-22 Beta	0505	OO-XCE
			G-BMIZ
			N2270B
OO-VCF	Robinson R-22 Beta	1437	N40244
OO-VCG	Cessna 152	79528	C-GUSO
OO-VCI	Agusta-Bell 206B Jet Ranger III	8732	PH-VCP
			OO-VCI
			(OO-XCI)
OO-VCJ	Robinson R-22 Beta	1817	
OO-VCP	Robinson R-22 Alpha	0353	N8408T
OO-VCR	Cessna 152-II	83529	N53295

Regn.	Type	C/n	Prev.Id.
OO-VCT	Piper PA-28-140 Cherokee	28-22552	PH-VCT
OO-VCU	Piper PA-28-161 Warrior II	2841245	(OO-PRO)
OO-VCY	MBB-Kawasaki BK.117A-3	7056	OO-XCY
			(OO-VCY)
			(N156BK)
			D-HBND
OO-VDB	Cessna 210F Centurion	58726	N1826F
OO-VDG	Piper PA-28RT-201 Arrow IV	28R-7918228	N2936F
			(N999EA)
			N2936F
OO-VDK	Enstrom F.28F	765	G-BSAU
			N5FX
OO-VDS	Jodel D.112 Club (Type "D.11-09")	1461	
OO-VDV	CEA Jodel DR.1050 Ambassadeur	46	F-BJUE
OO-VEE	Boeing 737-3YO	23922	TF-ABK
			N922AB
			(PH-...)
			PP-VOM
			EI-BZO
			EC-EHZ
			EC-151
OO-VEF	Boeing 737-430	27000	D-ABKA
OO-VEH	Boeing 737-36N	28571	
OO-VEJ	Boeing 737-405	24271	LN-BRB
OO-VEK	Boeing 737-405	24270	LN-BRA
OO-VEX	Boeing 737-36N	28670	
OO-VFB	Beech A36 Bonanza	E-1910	N1835P
OO-VFI	Beech A36 Bonanza	E-926	F-GJFY
			OO-CJA
			F-GCJA
			F-ODDL
OO-VFK	Piper PA-28-181 Archer II	28-8390004	N82674
OO-VFR	Piper PA-28-181 Archer II	2890200	LX-EDZ
			N9247Q
OO-VGV	Rockwell Commander 112	196	OO-HRF
			N1196J
OO-VHB	Piper PA-28RT-201 Arrow IV	28R-7918079	N2212W
OO-VHL	SOCATA MS.880B Rallye Club	2558	F-BXDI
OO-VIK	Piper PA-18 Super Cub 95	18-5822	N7484D
OO-VIM	Piper PA-18 Super Cub 95 (Crashed)	18-1622	ALAT
			51-15622
OO-VIP	Piper PA-32RT-300 Lance	32R-7985066	OO-HCU
			N3050K
OO-VIW	Piper PA-18 Super Cub 95	18-1544	OO-HMW
			ALAT
			51-15544
OO-VIX	Piper PA-18 Super Cub 95 (Crashed)	18-1366	ALAT
			51-15366
OO-VJO	Boeing 737-4YO	23980	F-GMJO
			HL7255
OO-VKB	Beech A36 Bonanza	E-994	N17602
OO-VLE	Fokker F.27-050	20132	PH-ARG
			D-AFKD
			(LN-AKG)
			PH-EXF
OO-VLG	Fokker F.27-050	20104	PH-ARD
			Z-WPG
			PH-ARD
			SX-BSE
			PH-ARD
			D-AFKA
			(PH-DLT)
			PH-EXC
OO-VLH	Piper PA-31-310 Navajo	31-7812073	N27636
OO-VLJ	Fokker F.27-050	20105	PH-ARE
			Z-WPH
			PH-ARE
			SX-BSF
			PH-ARE
			D-AFKB
			PH-EXE
OO-VLK	Fokker F.27-050	20122	PH-FZF
			OE-LFA
			PH-EXG

Regn.	Type	C/n	Prev.Id.
OO-VLO	Fokker F.27-050	20127	ES-AFL
			OY-MMJ
			PH-EXL
OO-VLR	Fokker F.27-050	20121	PH-ARF
			(OO-VLJ)
			PT-SLL
			PH-ARF
			D-AFKC
			PH-EXF
OO-VLU	Robin R.2160	115	
OO-VLW	Enstrom 480	5008	G-BWHE
OO-VMC	Piper PA-28-161 Warrior III	2842016	N9262L
OO-VMH	Piaggio FWP.149D	026	90+16
			AC+402
			DE+392
OO-VMR	Hughes 269C	71-1086	D-HESY
OO-VMS	Robin DR.400/160 Chevalier	1124	
OO-VMX	Piper PA-28-261 Warrior III	2842040	N9506N
			N41225
OO-VOP	Piel CP.301A Emeraude	238	OO-VOR(1)
			OO-ANA
OO-VOR	Fiat G.46-4A	199	I-AEKI
			MM53293
OO-VOS	SAAB S.91D Safir	91434	PH-RLW
OO-VPA	Robin HR.200/100 Club	91	
OO-VPC	Cessna 182P (Reims-assembled)	0019/63928	D-EHTW
			N9859E
OO-VPH	Dornier Do.27A-3	411	56+95
			SA+116
			SB+734
			GA+387
OO-VPI	Robin DR.400/180 Régent	1216	
OO-VPJ	Dornier Do.27A-4	446	57+18
			PY+223
			PD+101
OO-VRE	Reims/Cessna F.172M	1287	(OO-WAO)
OO-VRM	Cessna 152	81478	D-EBTF
			N64922
OO-VRV	Jodel D-11 Club	CD.02	
OO-VSA	Robin HR.200/100 Club	63	
OO-VSC	Robin HR.200/100 Club	66	
OO-VSL	Robin DR.400/160 Chevalier	875	
OO-VTA	Piper PA-34-220T Seneca III	34-8133049	N8357Z
OO-VTS	Cessna 172L	59253	N7553G
OO-VVA	Piper PA-18-150 Super Cub	18-8281	
OO-VVB	Piper PA-18-150 Super Cub	18-8282	
OO-VVC	Piper PA-18-150 Super Cub	18-8286	
OO-VVD	Piper PA-18-150 Super Cub	18-8304	
OO-VVF	Piper PA-18-150 Super Cub	18-8319	
OO-VVG	Piper PA-18-150 Super Cub	18-8332	
OO-VVH	Piper PA-18-150 Super Cub	18-8381	
OO-VVJ	SAN Jodel D.140R Abeille (Written-off)	502	
OO-VVK	SAN Jodel D.140R Abeille	503	
OO-VVP	Piper PA-18-135 Super Cub	18-2539	OO-HMB
			ALAT
			52-6221
OO-VVE	Agusta-Bell 206B Jet Ranger III	8563	G-NATO
			G-FLCH
			G-BGGX
OO-VVK	Piper PA-34-220T Seneca III	34-8133182	HB-LQL
			N2913L
OO-VXB	Agusta A.109C	7635	HB-XXB
OO-VZZ	Robin DR.400/180R Remorqueur	962	D-EEJA
OO-WAC	Reims/Cessna F.150M	1250	
OO-WAD	Reims/Cessna F.172M	1342	
OO-WAE	Reims/Cessna FRA.150M Aerobat	0274	
OO-WAF	Reims/Cessna FRA.150L Aerobat	0148	PH-WAE
OO-WAJ	Reims/Cessna F.172M	1196	
OO-WAL	Cessna 182R Skylane	68083	N9870H
OO-WAN	Grumman-American AA-5 Traveler	0517	
OO-WAO	Reims/Cessna F.172M	1324	
OO-WAR	Piper PA-28-161 Warrior II	2816112	N9252Q
OO-WDB	Robinson R-22 Beta	2081	N23272

Regn.	Type	C/n	Prev.Id.
OO-WDM	Aerotek Pitts S-2A	2046	OO-XDM
			D-EILH
			YV-38P
			YV-TAEF
OO-WEA	Beagle B.121 Pup 100	012	G-AWEA
OO-WEJ	Robin R.1180TD Aiglon	275	F-GCUJ
OO-WEO	Reims/Cessna FA.150K Aerobat	0002	D-EKKF
OO-WGW	Agusta A.109C	7647	I-SEIG
OO-WIE	Reims/Cessna F.150L	0889	
OO-WIF	Grumman-American AA-1B Trainer	0264	
OO-WIH	Cessna 150F	62054	OO-SIH
			N8754S
OO-WIL	Stampe & Renard SV.4B	1184	V-42
OO-WIM	SEEMS MS.880B Rallye Club	342	F-BKZH
OO-WIN	Reims/Cessna F.172K	0760	F-WLIO
OO-WIO	Reims/Cessna FRA.150L Aerobat	0183	
OO-WIQ	Reims/Cessna FRA.150L Aerobat	0158	
OO-WIU	Reims/Cessna F.172M	0912	
OO-WIV	Reims/Cessna FRA.150L Aerobat	0123	(D-ECGJ)
OO-WIW	Reims/Cessna F.177RG Cardinal RG	0053	
OO-WIX	Reims/Cessna F.150L	0890	
OO-WIY	Reims/Cessna FR.172J Rocket	0353	
OO-WLF	Grob G.115A	8032	D-EOFT(2)
OO-WMB	Wassmer WA.41 Baladou	153	F-BOYN
OO-WOT	Tipsy T.66 Nipper II	49	PH-MEV
	(cr.7.7.84 - under rebuild using fuselage		(PH-MES)
	of kit c/n 71, OO-69 ntu)		(PH-SUS)
			EL-AEV
			OO-MON
			(OY-AEU)
OO-WOU	SEEMS MS.880B Rallye Club	329	F-BKYX
OO-WPS	Piper PA-32-301T Turbo Saratoga SP	32-8024011	N8169Y
OO-WVS	Cessna 172N	69394	C-GZJI
			(N737FY)
OO-XOU	Reims/Cessna F.150M	1293	F-BXQU
OO-XTH	Hughes 369E	0469E	HB-X..
OO-YAC	Piper PA-28-161 Warrior II	28-8316019	N83094
OO-YAK	Yakovlev YAK-11 (Reservation)	unkn	EAF-079
OO-YAO	Reims/Cessna F.172H (Robertson STOL)	0695	G-AYAO
OO-YET	Piper PA-24-260 Comanche B	24-4213	(G-AVCL)
			N8763P
OO-YIO	Robin DR.400/120 Petit Prince	2038	
OO-YOB	Robin DR.400/160 Chevalier	1943	
OO-YOL	Piper J-3C-65 Cub	12949	F-BCPD
			44-80653
OO-YUG	Zlin Z.526F Trenér Master	1031	YU-DJX
			JRV41106
OO-YVO	SOCATA MS.880B Rallye Club	2848	
OO-...	Christen A-1 Husky (Reservation)	1056	F-GGAQ
			F-WGAQ
			N9590C
OO-...	Extra EA.300/L (Reservation .00)	039	D-ETZX
OO-...	Piper PA-25-235 Pawnee B (Reservn .00)	25-3119	N7208Z
OO-...	SNCAN/Stampe SV.4C (Reservation)	279	N4BH
			F-BCKQ

BALLOONS AND AIRSHIPS

Regn.	Type	C/n	Prev.Id.
OO-ADL	Cameron V-56 HAFB	496	
OO-AFC	Cameron N-77 HAFB	1077	G-JAFC
OO-ARK	Cameron N-56 HAFB	276	
OO-BAA	Thunder/Colt 77A HAFB	653	(OO-BEM)
OO-BAD	Cameron O-77 HAFB	1103	
OO-BAF	Schroeder Fire Balloons G HAFB	414	
OO-BAG	Cameron V-56 HAFB	417	
OO-BAH	Cameron A-315 HAFB	4255	
OO-BAI	Duronadeau L-250 HAFB	21	
OO-BAJ	Cameron N-77 HAFB	1163	
OO-BAL	Van dem Bemden 460m3 Gas Balloon	VDB.86	
OO-BAU	Cameron N-77 HAFB	2354	

Regn.	Type	C/n	Prev.Id.
OO-BAV	UltraMagic M-77 HAFB	77/41	
OO-BAX	Cameron N-56 HAFB	385	G-BSUN
OO-BAY	Cameron N-65 HAFB	1032	
OO-BAZ	Stuttgart 360m3 Gas Balloon	unkn	
OO-BBB	Raven S-60A HAFB	179	D-Ruttgers-Club
OO-BBD	Cameron N-90 HAFB	2607	
OO-BBE	Chaize AX-8 HAFB	110	
OO-BBF	Cameron V-77 HAFB	1715	
OO-BBG	Cameron A-210 HAFB	2846	G-BUGF
OO-BBH	Cameron A-180 HAFB	3243	G-BVIU
OO-BBI	Cameron N-77 HAFB	1483	(OO-BDS)
OO-BBJ	Durondeau L-250 HAFB	19	
OO-BBK	Raven Europe FS-57A HAFB	E-390	
OO-BBL	Cameron V-56 HAFB	1243	(OO-BOS)
OO-BBM	Colt 90A HAFB	2129	
OO-BBN	Cameron V-77 HAFB	1671	
OO-BBO	Cameron N-160 HAFB	1908	(OO-BOY)
OO-BBP	Cameron N-77 HAFB	1513	
OO-BBQ	Cameron O-120 HAFB	3103	G-BUYZ
OO-BBR	Colt A-120 HAFB	2206	
OO-BBS	Cameron O-90 HAFB	2054	
OO-BBT	Kubicek BB-45 HAFB	52	OK-6052
OO-BBU	Kubicek Orangina SS HAFB	43	
OO-BBV	Kubicek BB-37 HAFB	17	OK-3024
OO-BBW	Kubicek BB-60 HAFB	92	
OO-BBX	Aviatik B&B Ax8 HAFB	5	
OO-BCA	Cameron V-77 HAFB	596	
OO-BCD	Libert L.3000 HAFB	006	
OO-BCE	UltraMagic M-105 HAFB	105/03	EC-021
OO-BCF	UltraMagic H-77 HAFB	77/51	
OO-BCG	Raven-Europe S-60A HAFB	E-293	
OO-BCH	Lindstrand LBL-105A HAFB	158	
OO-BCI	Durondeau L.250 HAFB	006	
OO-BCJ	Cameron N-77 HAFB	2243	
OO-BCK	Schroeder Fire Balloons GHAFB	769	
OO-BCL	Cameron V-90 HAFB	2853	
OO-BCM	Durondeau L-220 HAFB	003	
OO-BCN	Durondeau L.180 HAFB	001	
OO-BCO	Schroeder Fire Balloons G HAFB	748	
OO-BCP	Aerostar RX-7 HAFB	3233	
OO-BCR	UltraMagic V-105 HAFB	105/17	
OO-BCT	Schroeder Fire Balloons G HAFB	742	
OO-BCV	Cameron N-105 HAFB	1852	
OO-BCW	Kubicek BB-30 HAFB	101	
OO-BCY	Libert L.3000 HAFB	286-011	
OO-BDA	Cameron N-105 HAFB	3087	
OO-BDB	Cameron O-105 HAFB	3130	
OO-BDC	Lindstrand LBL-105A HAFB	530	
OO-BDD	Cameron O-77 HAFB	1734	(OO-BTJ)
OO-BDE	Cameron N-120 HAFB	3755	
OO-BDG	Cameron A-210 HAFB	3728	
OO-BDH	Kubicek BB-45 HAFB	93	
OO-BDI	Lindstrand LBL-150A HAFB	616	
OO-BDJ	Lindstrand LBL-105A HAFB	571	
OO-BDK	Thunder/Colt AX8-90 S-II HAFB	1135	
OO-BDL	Raven-Europe S-55A HAFB	E-114	
OO-BDM	UltraMagic M-77 HAFB	77/48	
OO-BDO(3)	HAFB, details unknown	unkn	
OO-BDP	Lindstrand HS-110 Hot Air Airship	362	G-BWOO
OO-BDS	Raven-Europe S-55A HAFB	E-082	
OO-BDT	Thunder AX10-160 HAFB	1388	G-BPLU
OO-BDU	Cameron N-105 HAFB	3463	
OO-BDW	UltraMagic M-77 HAFB	77/50	
OO-BDZ	Cameron N-90 HAFB	1961	(LX-DLH)
OO-BEB	Raven-Europe FS-57A HAFB	E-099	
OO-BED	Cameron O-77 HAFB	4487	
	(Replaces envelope c/n 1262)		
OO-BEF	Kubicek BB-26 HAFB	76	
OO-BEI	Kubicek BB-30 HAFB	74	OK-7074
OO-BEJ	Cameron N-120 HAFB	4605	
OO-BEM(2)	UltraMagic M-105 HAFB	105/18	
OO-BEO	Cameron O-77 HAFB	1384	
OO-BEP	Schroeder Fire Balloons G HAFB	437	
OO-BER	Cameron N-77 HAFB	2279	
OO-BES	Thunder AX7-77 HAFB	950	PH-JVH

Regn.	Type	C/n	Prev.Id.
OO-BEU	Libert L.3000 HAFB	286-009	
OO-BEW	Cameron A-105 HAFB	2940	
OO-BEX	Cameron N-90 HAFB	2722	PH-BIH
OO-BFB	Cameron N-90 HAFB	2521	
OO-BFD	Cameron N-90 HAFB	2725	
OO-BFE	Cameron V-90 HAFB	3132	
OO-BFF	Cameron N-145 HAFB	2466	
OO-BFG(2)	HAFB, type unknown	unkn	
OO-BFH	Cameron N-90 HAFB	3543	
OO-BFM	Thunder AX7-77 HAFB	1311	
OO-BFO	Aerostar S-60A HAFB	3219	
OO-BFP	Colt 105A HAFB	1781	
OO-BFR	Colt 105A HAFB	711	PH-IFR
			G-BMHO
OO-BFT	Cameron N-90 HAFB	2594	
OO-BFU	Durondeau L.250 HAFB	007	
OO-BFV	Cameron N-120 HAFB	4263	
OO-BGA	Cameron SS Montgolfiere HAFB	806	
OO-BGB	Schroeder Fire Balloons G HAFB	545	
OO-BGC	Cameron N-90 HAFB	2608	
OO-BGD	Cameron N-145 HAFB	3547	
OO-BGG	Cameron V-65 HAFB	2765	
OO-BGH	Cameron N-90 HAFB	3249	G-BVKI
OO-BGI	Cameron N-90 HAFB	2307	
OO-BHA	Kubicek BB-37 HAFB	112	
OO-BHB	Libert L.800 HAFB	140	
OO-BHC	Cameron Smurf SS HAFB	4266	
OO-BHD	Durondeau L-300 HAFB	20	
OO-BHF	Thunder AX6-56Z HAFB	355	G-DOLL
OO-BHG	Cameron Hex-Glass 84SS HAFB	3272	
OO-BHH	Cameron V-65 HAFB	2766	
OO-BHI	Raven S-60A HAFB	244	F-GIBH
			HB-BDI
OO-BHJ	Cameron N-77 HAFB	1314	G-OOFI
OO-BHK	Kubicek BB-22 HAFB	113	
OO-BHL	Cameron O-90 HAFB	2865	
OO-BHM	Raven Europe S-60A HAFB	E-389	
OO-BHP	Raven Europe RX-7 HAFB	E-337	
OO-BHR	Raven Europe FS-57A HAFB	E-363	
OO-BHS	Lindstrand LBL-77B HAFB	444	
OO-BHU	Cameron N-105 HAFB	3413	
OO-BIC	Durondeau L.220 HAFB	014	
OO-BID	UltraMagic N-180 HAFB	180/18	
OO-BIE	Cameron A-180 HAFB	2869	
OO-BIG	Cameron N-77 HAFB	798	
OO-BIH	Cameron Hex Glass 84SS HAFB	2618	
OO-BII	UltraMagic M-65C HAFB	65/74	
OO-BIL	Cameron O-65 HAFB	265	
OO-BIM	Cameron Salami SS HAFB	1048	
OO-BIN	Cameron N-77 HAFB	1608	
OO-BIO	Cameron O-77 HAFB	1405	
OO-BIP	Schroeder Fire Balloons HAFB	223	
OO-BIS	Thunder AX8-90 SII HAFB	1129	
OO-BIT	Cameron O-160 HAFB	4119	
OO-BIV	Cameron N-90 HAFB	2584	
OO-BIW	Cameron N-160 HAFB	1967	
OO-BJA	Raven Europe FS-57A HAFB	E-227	
OO-BJB	Cameron O-77 HAFB	2224	
OO-BJD	Schroeder Fire Balloons G HAFB	671	
OO-BJF	Cameron N-105 HAFB	4615	
OO-BJH	Durondeau L.220 HAFB	011	
OO-BJI	Thunder AX7-77Z HAFB	1549	PH-JIM
OO-BJJ	Cameron N-90 HAFB	2094	
OO-BJK	Cameron A-140 HAFB	4087	
OO-BJL	Cameron N-77 HAFB	1128	
OO-BJN	Libert L.3000 HAFB	249004	
OO-BJO	Cameron O-105 HAFB	1239	
OO-BJP	Thunder AX7-65 HAFB	500	
OO-BJR	Cameron N-77 HAFB	1887	
OO-BJT	Raven Europe S-57A HAFB	E-219	
OO-BJV	Durondeau E.220 HAFB	010	
OO-BJZ(2)	HAFB, type unknown	unkn	
OO-BKA	UltraMagic H-77 HAFB	77/60	
OO-BKB	Cameron O-90 HAFB	3231	G-BVIJ
OO-BKC	Cameron A-120 HAFB	4637	

Regn.	Type	C/n	Prev.id.
OO-BKD	Cameron N-90 HAFB	2430	
OO-BKE	Cameron A-105 HAFB	3745	
OO-BKG	USSR Airship Works Association		
	DC-AT8.0000-0 Balloon	0791-02-008	
OO-BKH	Cameron N-90 HAFB	2193	(OO-BWB)
OO-BKJ	Lindstrand LBL-90A HAFB	073	
OO-BKL	Colt 77A HAFB	4457	
	(New envelope replacing c/n 1477)		
OO-BKN	Cameron A-210 HAFB	4765	
OO-BKO	Cameron A-210 HAFB	4718	
OO-BKR	Cameron A-210 HAFB	3316	
OO-BKW	Cameron V-77 HAFB	1905	G-BPVV
OO-BKY	Cameron N-105 HAFB	4716	
OO-BLA	Cameron N-77 HAFB	1267	
OO-BLB	Cameron N-90 HAFB	2346	
OO-BLC	Raven-Europe S-50A HAFB	E-017	
OO-BLE	Colt 77A HAFB	016	G-NILE
OO-BLF	Kubicek BB-30 HAFB	96	
OO-BLJ	Cameron N-56 HAFB	518	
OO-BLK	Cameron N-105 HAFB	3048	
OO-BLL	Cameron O-90 HAFB	2297	
OO-BLN	Cameron N-65 HAFB	742	
OO-BLO	Kubichek BB-37 HAFB	119	
OO-BLP	Raven-Europe S-55A HAFB	E-081	
OO-BLQ	Lindstrand LBL-105A HAFB	035	G-BVAR
OO-BLS	Libert L-600 HAFB	200-002	
OO-BLT	Raven-Europe S-52A HAFB	E-146	
OO-BLU	Cameron A-210 HAFB	4760	
	(New envelope replacing c/n 4575, .99)		
OO-BLW	UltraMagic M-77 HAFB	77/25	
OO-BMA	Cameron N-77 HAFB	841	(OO-BVR)
OO-BMB	Lindstrand Salami SS HAFB	033	G-BUYP
OO-BMC	UltraMagic SS HAFB	F7/01	
OO-BMD	Cameron N-105 HAFB	2283	
OO-BME	Cameron N-90 HAFB	2422	
OO-BMF	Sky 140-24 HAFB	122	
OO-BMG	Durondeau L.220 HAFB	005	
OO-BMH	UltraMagic V-105 HAFB	105/30	
OO-BMI	Durondeau L.220 HAFB	016	
OO-BMK	Schroeder Fire Balloons SS HAFB	622	D-OKOP
			(OO-BMK)
OO-BML	Cameron O-56 HAFB	31	G-AZNR
OO-BMM	Cameron N-105 HAFB	3281	
OO-BMN	Cameron N-133 HAFB	3905	
OO-BMO	Cameron N-120 HAFB	4337	
OO-BMP	Cameron V-77 HAFB	478	
OO-BMQ	Kubicek BB-26 HAFB	105	OM-8006
OO-BMR	Cameron O-77 HAFB	1253	
OO-BMS	Chaize CS.2200 F32 HAFB	22	
OO-BMU	Raven Europe S-60A HAFB	E-057	F-GEZH
OO-BMV	Cameron DP-70 Hot Air Airship	1612	
OO-BNA	Cameron A-210 HAFB	4760	
OO-BNB	Raven-Europe S-60A HAFB	E-044	
OO-BNC	Thunder AX3-17 Sky Chariot HAFB	01	
OO-BNI	Cameron N-180 HAFB	4651	
OO-BNJ	Cameron N-90 HAFB	1533	
OO-BNK	Cameron A-160 HAFB	4717	
OO-BNL(2)	Thunder AX7-77 HAFB	1050	
OO-BNM	Cameron N-105 HAFB	3495	
OO-BNN	UltraMagic N-180 HAFB	180/15	
OO-BNP	Cameron N-77 HAFB	856	
OO-BNS	Schroeder Fire Balloons G HAFB	450	
OO-BNT	Cameron N-160 HAFB	4540	
OO-BNY	Cameron A-160 HAFB	3025	G-BUVU
OO-BOA	Durondeau L.220 HAFB	009	
OO-BOC	Schaut 450m3 Gas Balloon	unkn	
OO-BOD	Schroeder Fire Balloons 30/24 HAFB	323	
OO-BOJ	Cameron N-90 HAFB	2922	
OO-BOK	UltraMagic M-77 HAFB	77/21	
OO-BOL	Cameron O-65 HAFB	189	
OO-BOO	Colt 21A Cloudhopper HAFB	480	
OO-BOP	Raven Europe RX-7 HAFB	E-403	
OO-BOT	Raven-Europe RX-7 HAFB	E-083	
OO-BOU	Cameron V-77 HAFB	727	G-BMOU
OO-BOW	Kubicek BB-26 HAFB	100	

Regn.	Type	C/n	Prev.id.
OO-BOX	Ultramagic M-77 HAFB	77/30	
OO-BPA	Cameron N-90 HAFB	3040	G-BUVV
OO-BPB	Cameron N-77 HAFB	379	
OO-BPD	Cameron N-105 HAFB	3005	
OO-BPE	Cameron O-65 HAFB	125	G-BCOA
OO-BPF	Raven Europe FS-57A HAFB	E-119	
OO-BPG	Cameron O-77 HAFB	1411	
OO-BPH	Libert L.3000 HAFB	251-005	
OO-BPI	Libert L.3000 HAFB	287-010	
OO-BPJ	Cameron V-77 HAFB	1195	
OO-BPK	Kubicek BB-37 HAFB	85	
OO-BPM	Durondeau L.220 HAFB	013	
OO-BPN	Durondeau E-220 HAFB	008	(F-GMEM)
			OO-BPN
OO-BPP	Cameron V-77 HAFB	964	
OO-BPR	UltraMagic M-77 HAFB	77/28	
OO-BPS	Cameron A-105 HAFB	3656	
OO-BPT	Raven-Europe S-57A HAFB	E-189	
OO-BPV	Raven-Europe S-55A HAFB	E-218	
OO-BPX	Schroeder Fire Balloons G HAFB	653	
OO-BPY	Thunder AX7-77 HAFB	1005	
OO-BPZ	Raven Europe S-57A HAFB	E-247	
OO-BQU	Lindstrand LBL-150A HAFB	631	
OO-BQQ	Cameron O-120 HAFB	2579	G-BTKN
OO-BRA	Thunder AX8-90 HAFB	1376	
OO-BRB	Cameron V-77 HAFB	1804	G-BPBX
			(G-BPCU)
OO-BRC	UltraMagic M-65C HAFB	65/75	
OO-BRD	Lindstrand LBL-120A HAFB	255	
OO-BRE	Cameron N-145 HAFB	2812	
OO-BRI	Cameron V-77 HAFB	1202	
OO-BRJ	Cameron V-90 HAFB	2699	
OO-BRL	Lindstrand LBL-105A HAFB	414	
OO-BRM	Thunder-Colt AX-7 Fiesta HAFB	1111	
OO-BRN	Cameron N-120 HAFB	4761	
OO-BRO	Cameron N-90 HAFB	2750	
OO-BRR	Thunder AX8-90 HAFB	1223	
OO-BRS	Durondeau L.220 HAFB	018	
OO-BRT	Cameron O-77 HAFB	1367	
OO-BRU	Thunder AX3-17A Sky Chariot HAFB	292	
OO-BRV	Colt 17A Cloudhopper HAFB	1245	G-DIPZ
OO-BRW	Cameron N-90 HAFB	2118	
OO-BRX	Lindstrand LBL-120A HAFB	454	
OO-BSB	Schroeder Fire Balloons G HAFB	732	
OO-BSD	Raven-Europe FS-57A HAFB	E-120	
OO-BSE	Balloon Works Firefly F7 HAFB	F7-859	
OO-BSF	Raven-Europe FS-55A HAFB	E-151	
OO-BSG	Cameron N-90 HAFB	2866	G-BUPD
OO-BSH	Raven Europe RX-7 HAFB	E-306	
OO-BSI	Cameron V-77 HAFB	1783	
OO-BSJ	Thunder AX3-17A Sky Chariot HAFB	279	F-GCKP
			G-BHVW
OO-BSK	Cameron N-145 HAFB	4294	
OO-BSL	Cameron N-90 HAFB	1815	
OO-BSM	Adams LD.S HAFB	072	
OO-BSN	Cameron N-180 HAFB	2613	
OO-BSO	Aerostar S-60A HAFB	3244	
OO-BSP	Aviatik B&B Ax8 Replika SS HAFB	8	
OO-BSR	Cameron A-105 HAFB	2695	
OO-BSS	Cameron O-42 HAFB	1072	
OO-BST	Cameron N-105 HAFB	3246	
OO-BSU	Cameron Marshmallow 105SS HAFB	2362	G-BSOP
OO-BSV	Raven Europe FS-57A HAFB	E-379	
OO-BSW	Cameron N-90 HAFB	2226	
OO-BSY	Durondeau L-250 HAFB	017	
OO-BSZ	Raven Europe Aurora 54K HAFB	E-387	
OO-BTB	Cameron O-77 HAFB	1001	
OO-BTC	Raven RX-65 HAFB	E-014	
OO-BTD	Kubicek BB-37 HAFB	78	
OO-BTE	Cameron N-90 HAFB	3556	
OO-BTF	Cameron N-90 HAFB	2551	
OO-BTH	Thunder AX3-21A HAFB	1196	PH-WEK
OO-BTI	Cameron V-77 HAFB	1892	
OO-BTJ	Cameron V-77 HAFB	1823	
OO-BTK	Cameron N-180 HAFB	2403	

Regn.	Type	C/n	Prev.Id.
OO-BTM	Cameron A-250 HAFB	3378	
OO-BTN	Thunder AX7-77 HAFB	976	G-BTWH
OO-BTO	Lindstrand LBL-90A HAFB	177	
OO-BTP	Lindstrand LBL-150A HAFB	495	
OO-BTR	Cameron V-77 HAFB	2809	
OO-BTS	Cameron N-90 HAFB	2627	
OO-BTT	Cameron A-140 HAFB	4415	
OO-BTV	UltraMagic V-90 HAFB	90/02	
OO-BTW	Cameron O-77 HAFB	1481	
OO-BUB	Cameron A-105 HAFB	2787	
OO-BUE	Colt Orangina SS HAFB	1247	G-PULP
OO-BUF	Cameron O-90 HAFB	3385	
OO-BUG	Cameron V-77 HAFB	1812	
OO-BUL	Raven S-55A HAFB	855	N4047G
OO-BUM	UltraMagic M-77 HAFB	77/20	
OO-BUN	Cameron N-90 HAFB	2175	
OO-BUR	Cameron V-77 HAFB	787	
OO-BUS	Cameron O-140 HAFB	2282	
OO-BUU	Kubicek BB-37 HAFB	81	OK-7081
OO-BUZ	Cameron N-145 HAFB	4363	
OO-BVA(2)	Thunder AX8-90 HAFB	1576	(OO-BVT)
OO-BVB	Raven-Europe RX-7 HAFB	E-071	
OO-BVD	Cameron N-90 HAFB	3212	G-BVII
OO-BVE	Cameron N-90 HAFB	1873	
OO-BVG	Cameron N-145 HAFB	4117	(OO-BVN)
OO-BVH	UltraMagic M-105 HAFB	105/20	
OO-BVI	UltraMagic M-77 HAFB	77/22	
OO-BVK	Schroeder Fire Balloons GHAFB	770	
OO-BVL	Colt 90A HAFB	1698	
OO-BVM	Raven-Europe S-57A HAFB	E-258	
OO-BVN	Raven-Europe S-55A HAFB	E-182	
OO-BVR	Durondeau L.180 HAFB	012	
OO-BVS	Cameron V-90 HAFB	3151	
OO-BVV	Libert L.2200 HAFB	003	
OO-BVW	Cameron N-90 HAFB	1938	
OO-BWB	Aerostar S-60A HAFB	3231	
OO-BWJ	Cameron V-90 HAFB	2733	
OO-BWL	Cameron N-90 HAFB	2880	
OO-BWM	Cameron V-77 HAFB	872	
OO-BWP	Cameron N-105 HAFB	1951	
OO-BWS	Libert L.3000 HAFB	265-007	
OO-BWT	Kubicek BB-60 HAFB	91	OK-8021
OO-BWV	Cameron N-90 HAFB	1714	
OO-BWW	Cameron O-105 HAFB	1059	G-BLIV
OO-BXI	Lindstrand LBL-105A HAFB	113	
OO-BXL	Cameron N-77 HAFB	662	LX-BIL
OO-BXX	Lindstrand LBL-31A HAFB	140	
OO-BYA	Raven-Europe S-67 HAFB	E-186	
OO-BYE	Cameron V-65 HAFB	773	
OO-BYK	Cameron N-145 HAFB	4259	
OO-BYS	Cameron V-77 HAFB	3076	
OO-BYV	Cameron N-133 HAFB	4642	
OO-BYW	Cameron O-90 HAFB	3049	G-BUWB
OO-BYY	Cameron O-160 HAFB	1595	PH-YUP
			G-BOBE
OO-BYZ	Raven Europe S-55A HAFB	E-118	
OO-BZB	Cameron N-133 HAFB	4598	
OO-BZW	Lindstrand LBL-120A HAFB	585	
OO-BZZ	Thunder AX7-77 HAFB	010	G-BBKO
OO-CBE	Cameron N-90 HAFB	1316	
OO-CGM	Raven S-55A HAFB	655	
OO-EOL	Cameron O-84 HAFB	27	
OO-GDB	Cameron S-65 HAFB	14	
OO-GDC	Cameron S-65 HAFB	20	
OO-GDF	Cameron O-77 HAFB	155	
OO-GKB	Raven S.55A HAFB	686	
OO-JBC	Cameron N-56 HAFB	506	
OO-JOH	Thunder AX6-56 HAFB	264	
OO-LAM	Cameron N-77 HAFB	584	
OO-LAN	Cameron V-65 HAFB	646	
OO-LOM	Cameron V-77 HAFB	1273	
OO-LON	Cameron N-77 HAFB	381	
OO-MRA	Cameron O-77 HAFB	364	
OO-RUP	Cameron O-77 HAFB	437	
OO-SAX	Cameron O-77 HAFB	244	

Regn.	Type	C/n	Prev.Id.
OO-SWF	Schaut 1500m3 Gas Balloon	unkn	
OO-WFS	Cameron O-77 HAFB	1328	
OO-WTM	Cameron V-56 HAFB	651	
OO-YAN	Cameron N-77 HAFB	374	
OO-...	Cameron A-120 HAFB	4760	
OO-...	Thunder AX8-90 HAFB	2006	G-BTNL
OO-...	Thunder AX9-120 SII HAFB	4786	

GLIDERS AND MOTOR-GLIDERS

Regn.	Type	C/n	Prev.Id.
OO-CDG	Glaser-Dirks DG-400	4-14	LX-CDG
			D-KEBM
OO-CHM	Grob G.103 Twin Astir II	3750	(OO-ZKG)
OO-DAC	Schweizer SGU-2-22	19	
OO-DRS	Scheibe SF-24B Motorspatz	4043	D-KBWS
			D-KIDI
OO-ELG	Eiri PIK-20E	20231	D-KLMO
OO-ERA	Fournier RF-5	5085	
OO-FPJ	Schempp-Hirth Nimbus 4 DM	37-52-868	
OO-FRA	Grob G.103 Twin Astir II	3701	
OO-FRI	Eiri PIK-20E	20262	D-KOSO
OO-ICD	Schleicher ASK-14	14057	D-KICD
OO-JAZ	Fournier RF-3	78	D-KILA
OO-JLB	Fournier RF-4D	4088	
OO-JVM	Scheibe SF-24B Motorspatz	4020	D-KECI
OO-KCB-CK	Schempp-Hirth Ventus cM	85/565	(OO-CKB)
OO-KDB-KB	Schempp-Hirth Janus CT	233/6	(OO-ZDK)
OO-KEI	Schleicher Rhönlerche II	unkn	OO-ZUA(1)
OO-KUL	Grob G.102 Astir Jeans	2066	
OO-LEI	Scheibe SF.27M-A	6307	D-KIML
OO-LGA-GA	Schempp-Hirth HS.7 Mini-Nimbus	54	
OO-LIT-IT	Schempp-Hirth Ventus b	132	D-3518
OO-LNO	LET L-13SL Vivat	900415	OK-0118
OO-LUS	Fournier RF-4D	4036	F-BOXE
OO-MFS	Scheibe SF-25C Falke	4213	D-KAWB
OO-MIC	Schleicher Ka.6E Rhönsegler	4109	
OO-MIG-4	LET L-13 Blanik	026134	
OO-MJC	Schempp-Hirth Ventus cM	17/444	
OO-MLV	Scheibe SF-25B Falke	44281	D-KDGH
OO-MRM	Sportavia-Pützer RF-5B Sperber	51034	N55SH
			(D-KEAP)
OO-MTA	Fournier RF-3	30	F-BMDJ
OO-MVA	Scheibe SF-25B Falke (Wfu)	4650	D-KEBJ
OO-MVB	Scheibe SF-25B Falke	4654	D-KICG
OO-MVC	Scheibe SF-25C Falke	44287	D-KDGO
OO-MVF	Scheibe SF-25C Falke	46121	D-KABT
OO-NAM-AM	Schleicher ASW-20	20139	
OO-NKD	Schempp-Hirth Nimbus 4 DM	35/50	
OO-NKL	Sportavia-Pützer RF-5B Sperber	51022	D-KCAW
OO-NMC	Scheibe SF-28A Tandem-Falke	5755	D-KMGE
OO-NSC	Fournier RF-3	64	F-BMTI
OO-NZT-ZT	Schleicher ASW-20	20086	
OO-OSI	Stemme S-10	10-43	D-KGCU
OO-PCP	Eiri PIK-20E	20244	D-KEMA
OO-PDM	Glaser-Dirks DG-300 Elan	3E-330	
OO-PIK	Eiri PIK-20E	20235	
OO-PRJ	Stemme S-10VT	11-017	
OO-SZA	Scheibe Spatz A	515	
OO-SZB	Scheibe Spatz A	517	
OO-SZD	Schleicher Ka.2B Rhönschwalbe	196/56	
OO-SZE	SZD-9 bis Bocian 1C	P-311	
OO-SZP	Schleicher Ka.6CR Rhönsegler	196	
OO-SZW	Hoffmann H-36 Dimona	3609	(OO-LCL)
OO-ULB	Fournier RF-3	71	OO-WAA
OO-VCN	Stemme S-10V	14-003	(OO-VCI)
			D-KGCI (4)
OO-VHA	Stemme S-10	10-15	G-BSVU
			D-KGCS
			G-BSVU
			D-KDLF

Regn.	Type	C/n	Prev.Id.
OO-WCA	LET L-13SL Vivat *(Crashed 7.99)*	930515	(OO-ZFX)
OO-YAA	Rolladen-Schneider LS-1C	43	D-0558
OO-YAB	Scheibe Bergfalke II/55	04	D-6259
OO-YAD	SZD-48-3 Jantar Standard 3	B-1971	F-CBZD
OO-YAR	Schleicher Ka.6ERhönsegler	4317	F-CDRS
OO-YAS	Schleicher Ka.6E Rhönsegler	4011	D-9362
OO-YAZ	Eiri PIK-20D	20632	D-6584
OO-YBB	Scheibe L-Spatz 55	726	D-8592
OO-YBL	Glaser-Dirks DG-200/17	2-175/1758	D-5892
OO-YBM	Rolladen-Schneider LS-8A	8209	
OO-YBW	Rolladen-Schneider LS-1C	69	D-0672
OO-YCM	Carmam M.100S Mésange	48	F-CCXM
OO-YCP	Schleicher Ka.6CR Rhönsegler	1027	D-9092
OO-YCR	Valentin Mistral C	MC 011/78	D-4911
OO-YDD	Rolladen-Schneider LS-1C	161	OE-5297
OO-YDS	Schleicher ASH-26	26133	
OO-YDV	Schleicher ASW-19B	19237	PH-640
OO-YDW	Schleicher ASW-20L	20261	D-6540
OO-YEA	SZD-48-1 Jantar Standard II	B-1101	LX-CBO
			HB-1555
OO-YEC	Glaser-Dirks DG-300	3E-260	LX-CDE
OO-YEK	Centrair 101A Pégase	101A-Ol90	F-CGEK
OO-YEN	Schempp-Hirth Nimbus 3T	77/16	D-KOTT
OO-YGG	Schempp-Hirth Ventus b	40	D-4060
OO-YHN	Rolladen-Schneider LS-6	6040	D-6258
OO-YHP	Schempp-Hirth Standard Cirrus	460	D-3690
OO-YIL	Rolladen-Schneider LS-8A	8093	
OO-YIN	Rolladen-Schneider LS-6C-18w	6381	
OO-YJH	Rolladen-Schneider LS-8A	8084	D-1617
OO-YJJ	Schleicher ASK-13	13478	D-2366
OO-YJR	Eiri PIK-20D	20543	D-7652
OO-YKA	Schleicher ASK-13	13094	D-2018
OO-YKC	Schleivher K.8B	122	D-1670
OO-YKP	Schleicher ASK-13	13550	D-6717
OO-YLA	SZD-48-1 Jantar Standard	B-1000	LX-CHO
			HB-1523
OO-YLB	Schleicher ASW-15B	15358	D-2348
OO-YLE	Centrair 201A Marianne	201A-037	F-CBLE(2)
OO-YLL	Schempp-Hirth Janus C	241	
OO-YLS	Rolladen-Schneider LS-6	6064	D2567
OO-YMA	Schempp-Hirth Nimbus 3T	13/82	D-KCMA
			D-KHIA(4)
OO-YMM	Grob G.103 Twin Astir	3042	BGA3128/FBK
			RAFGSA-R59
			RAFGSA-529
OO-YOU	Grob G.102 Astir CS Jeans	2080	PH-600
OO-YPH	Glaser-Dirks DG-600	6-42	D-4882
OO-YPJ	Schleicher Ka.6CR Rhönsegler	853	D5540
OO-YPR	Rolladen-Schneider LS-3-17	3226	D-4573
OO-YRD	Rolladen-Schneider LS-1D	138	D-0957
OO-YRG	SZD-50-3 Puchacz	B-1876	HB-3010
OO-YRL	Centrair 101AP Pégase	101AP-0214	F-CGFA
OO-YRV	Schleicher K.8B	182/60	
OO-YSM	Schempp-Hirth Nimbus 2B	170	LX-CRC
			D-6442
OO-YVA	Grob G.103 Twin Astir	3051	D-4843
OO-YVD	Schempp-Hirth Ventus 2b	91	
OO-YVM	Schleicher ASK-18	18013	
OO-YXL	Schempp-Hirth Nimbus 4M *(Reservation)*	12/34	OO-XXL
	(Built as Nimbus 4 c/n 14/34)		D-4789
OO-YYP	Rolladen-Schneider LS-4	4119	D-5985
OO-YYV	Schleicher ASW-15	15108	OE-0909
OO-YZW	Scheibe SF-34	5105	D-1134
OO-ZAA-AA	Schempp-Hirth Standard Cirrus 75	695	
OO-ZAB	Schleicher Ka.6B Rhönsegler	204	D-8352
OO-ZAC	Schleicher K.7 Rhönadler	7025	D-5231
OO-ZAF	Schleicher K.7 Rhönadler	7169	
OO-ZAH	Schleicher K.7 Rhönadler	7221	
OO-ZAI	Grob G.102 Astir CS 77	1736	
OO-ZAJ	Schleicher K.7 Rhönadler	7267	
OO-ZAK	Schleicher K.7 Rhönadler	7268	
OO-ZAL	Schleicher K.7 Rhönadler	7269	
OO-ZAM	Schleicher K.7 Rhönadler	631	D-5758
OO-ZAN	Schleicher K.7 Rhönadler	7270	
OO-ZAO-AO	Schleicher K.8B	8628	

Regn.	Type	C/n	Prev.Id.
OO-ZAP	Schleicher K.8B	8629	
OO-ZAQ	Schleicher K.8B	8630	
OO-ZAR	Schleicher K.8B	8703	
OO-ZAS	Schleicher K.8B	8704	
OO-ZAT	Schleicher K.8B	8705	
OO-ZAU	Schleicher K.8B *(Dbr 5.99)*	8706	
OO-ZAV	Schleicher K.8B	8707	
OO-ZAW	Schleicher K.8B	8708	
OO-ZAX	Schleicher K.8B	143/59	D-5139
			D-KACH
OO-ZAY	Schleicher K.7 Rhönadler	700	D-4042
OO-ZAZ	Schleicher K.8B	unkn	D-6271
OO-ZBA-BA	Schleicher ASW-15	15025	
OO-ZBB	Schleicher K.7 Rhönadler	7273	
OO-ZBC	Schleicher Ka.6CR Rhönsegler	6103	D-5898
OO-ZBD	Schleicher Ka.6E Rhönsegler	4086	
OO-ZBE	Schleicher K.7 Rhönadler	447	D-6263
OO-ZBF-BF	Schleicher Ka.6E Rhönsegler	4066	
OO-ZBH	Schleicher K.8B	8764	
OO-ZBK	Rolladen-Schneider LS-1F	189	
OO-ZBL	Schleicher Ka.6CR Rhönsegler	854	D-5800
OO-ZBO-BO	Rolladen-Schneider LS-3	3014	
OO-ZBP-NP	Rolladen-Schneider LS-1D	94	
OO-ZBQ-2G	Rolladen-Schneider LS-3A	3128	D-6834
OO-ZBR	Glasflügel H.301 Libelle	56	
OO-ZBS-7	Rolladen-Schneider LS-1F	353	
OO-ZBU	Schleicher K.8B	8311	D-5390
OO-ZBW-WW	Schleicher Ka.6CR Rhönsegler	6331	D-4651
OO-ZBX-JB	Schempp-Hirth Standard Cirrus	223	D-0973
OO-ZBY-Y	Rolladen-Schneider LS-1D	93	
OO-ZCB	SZD-9 bis Bocian 1C	P-274	F-CCDM
	(Believed w/o 16.8.82)		SP-1569
OO-ZCC-A6	Grob Standard Cirrus	451G	
OO-ZCD	SZD-24C Foka C	W-193	
OO-ZCF	Schleicher Ka.6CR Rhönsegler	101/43	D-8382
OO-ZCG-Z2	Rolladen-Schneider LS-4	4413	
OO-ZCI	Schempp-Hirth Standard Cirrus 75	699	
OO-ZCJ-CJ	Schempp-Hirth Standard Cirrus B	694	
OO-ZCK-CK	Schleicher K.8B	8608	D-4042
OO-ZCL	Avialsa-Scheibe A.60 Fauconnet	12	F-CCLH
OO-ZCN	Scheibe Specht	822	D-5588
OO-ZCP	Scheibe L-Spatz 55	02/658	D-7131
OO-ZCQ	Bölkow Phoebus C	882	F-CDOB
OO-ZCR	Avialsa-Scheibe A.60	113K	F-CDFP
OO-ZCS	LET L-13 Blanik	026111	
OO-ZCU-719	Glasflügel H201 Standard Libelle	319	F-CEBF
OO-ZCV	Grob Standard Cirrus	389G	
OO-ZCW	Scheibe L-Spatz B-13	600	D-5511
OO-ZCX	Avialsa-Scheibe A.60 Fauconnet	59K	F-CCVL
OO-ZCY	Schleicher ASW-19B	19296	D-7940
OO-ZDB	Schleicher Ka.6E Rhönsegler	265	HB-582
OO-ZDF	Schleicher K.7 Rhönadler	7173	
OO-ZDG-268	Slingsby T-59F Kestrel	1786	BGA1682
OO-ZDH	Caudron C.800	354/10314	F-CAPI
			Fr.Navy
OO-ZDK-AH	Glaser-Dirks DG-300 Elan	3E-17	D-4450
OO-ZDM	Siren C.30S Edelweiss	39	F-CDAT
OO-ZDO-E7	Schleicher ASW-15	15043	D-0490
OO-ZDQ	Slingsby T.31B Cadet TX.3	904	XE791
OO-ZDR	Schleicher Ka.6E Rhönsegler	4316	F-CDRR
OO-ZDT	Schleicher K.8B	8909	PH-452
OO-ZDU-DU	Grob G.102 Astir Jeans	2118	D-7643
OO-ZDW	Avialsa-Scheibe A.60 Fauconnet	102K	F-CDFE
OO-ZDX	Bölkow Phoebus C	782	D-9210
OO-ZDZ	Scheibe L-Spatz 55	570	(OO-JDL)
			D-5089
OO-ZEA	Schleicher Rhönlerche II	611/59	PL-1
OO-ZEC	Schleicher Rhönlerche II	706/60	PL-3
OO-ZED	Schleicher Rhönlerche II	707/60	PL-4
OO-ZEE	Schleicher Ka.6CR Rhönsegler	6106	D-5253
OO-ZEF	LET L-13 Blanik	025413	
OO-ZEH	Schleicher Rhönlerche II	799/60	
OO-ZEI	Schleicher Rhönlerche II	872/60	
OO-ZEK	Schleicher Rhönlerche II	874/60	
OO-ZEL	Schleicher Rhönlerche II	915/60	PL-5

Regn.	Type	C/n	Prev.Id.
OO-ZEN	Schleicher K.8B	8929	
OO-ZEO	Siebert Sie 3 *(w/o)*	3020	
OO-ZEP-3D	Schleicher Ka.6CR Rhönsegler	901	D-7122
OO-ZEQ-EQ	Schleicher Ka.6CR Rhönsegler	6263	(OO-ZGI)
			(OO-ZXW)
			D-5093
OO-ZER-L1	PIK-16C Vasama	41	LX-CEH
OO-ZES	Schleicher K.7 Rhönadler	398	OY-GUX
OO-ZET-ET	Schleicher K.7 Rhönadler	7079	
OO-ZEU	SZD-24C Foka C	W-174	
OO-ZEV	Grob G.102 Astir Standard III	5614S	
OO-ZEW	Schleicher Rhönlerche II	3063/Br	D-5461
OO-ZEX-EX	Grob G.102 Astir Jeans	2175	
OO-ZEY-EY	Grob G.103 Twin Astir II	3618	
OO-ZEZ	Carmam M.100S Mésange	36	F-CCSZ
OO-ZFA	Schleicher Ka.2B Rhönschwalbe	01	D-6743
OO-ZFB-FB	Grob G.102 Astir Standard	1377	
OO-ZFC	SZD-22C Mucha Standard	F-526	OO-ZSM
	(Rebuilt using parts from OO-ZSU c/n 532 - q.v.)		
OO-ZFD	Scheibe Zugvogel IIIB	1105	D-6364
OO-ZFG	Schleicher K.8	102/58	D-5719
OO-ZFH	Grunau Baby III	unkn	
OO-ZFI	Schempp-Hirth Standard Cirrus	85	BGA1633/CLS
OO-ZFK	Grob G.103 Twin Astir	3096	D-3952
OO-ZFM	Schleicher Ka.6CR Rhönsegler	6241	D-4101
OO-ZFN-FN	Rolladen-Schneider LS-3A	3145	
OO-ZFO	Issoire E78 Silène	6	F-CFEC
OO-ZFP-70	Schleicher ASW-19	19065	D-4470
OO-ZFQ-WF	Schempp-Hirth Janus C	122	D-6848
OO-ZFR	Schleicher Ka.6CR Rhönsegler	6097/Si	D-5280
OO-ZFS-717	Glasflügel H201B Standard Libelle	304	F-CEBD
OO-ZFT	Lanaverre CS-11/75 Standard Cirrus	341G	(OO-ZFC)
			(OO-EFC)
			F-CEFC
OO-ZFU	Grob G.103 Twin Astir	3072	D-4857
OO-ZFV-J3	Eiri PIK-20D	20651	
OO-ZFW	Schleicher ASK-21	21417	
OO-ZFX	Schempp-Hirth Discus b	256	BGA3405/FNY
OO-ZFZ	Grob G.103 Twin Astir	3069	D-4855
OO-ZGA	ICA-Brasov IS.28B2	126	(OO-ZEA)
			PH-627
OO-ZGC	Carmam M.200 Foehn	46	F-CDHY
OO-ZGD	Schleicher Ka.6E Rhönsegler	4151	LX-CBP
OO-ZGE-GE	Schleicher ASW-20L	20238	LX-CGE
OO-ZGG	Siren C.30S Edelweiss	53	F-CDGL
OO-ZGH	Schleicher ASW-20	20207	
OO-ZGI-X118	Centrair ASW-20F	20518	F-CERZ
OO-ZGJ	Schleicher Ka.6CR Rhönsegler	6228/Si	D-9104
OO-ZGK-CB	Rolladen-Schneider LS-3-17	3250	D-3185
OO-ZGM-AM	Glasflügel H.201B Standard Libelle	596	OO-NAM(1)
OO-ZGO-L32	Rolladen-Schneider LS-1D	221	F-CEHH
OO-ZGP-777	Glasflügel H.201B Standard Libelle	49	
OO-ZGR	SZD-48-3 Jantar Standard 3	B-1638	
OO-ZGS-PG	Schempp-Hirth Cirrus	60	D-0189
OO-ZGT-GT	Lanaverre CS11/75L Standard Cirrus	2	F-CEVC
OO-ZGU	Schempp-Hirth Cirrus	48	D-0179
OO-ZGV-GV	Schleicher K.8B	8911	D-0990
OO-ZGW-HE	Rolladen-Schneider LS-7	7031	D-1301
OO-ZGX	Avialsa-Scheibe A.60	154	F-CDNG
OO-ZHA-HA	Schleicher Rhönlerche II	549	D-4362
OO-ZHB	Schleicher ASW-20	20132	
OO-ZHC	Centrair 101A Pégase	101A-046	F-CFQI
OO-ZHD-17	Schempp-Hirth Standard Cirrus	568G	
OO-ZHE	Schleicher Rhönlerche II	216/57	PL-7
OO-ZHH	Carmam M.200 Foehn	34	F-CDHH
OO-ZHI	Valentin Mistral C	MC 057/85	D-4957
OO-ZHJ	Schleicher Ka.6E	4375	D-0759
OO-ZHK	Schleicher ASW-15	15137	HB-1028
OO-ZHL	LET L-13 Blanik	175129	
OO-ZHM	Bölkow Phoebus C-1	787	D-9204
OO-ZHO	Schleicher Ka.6E	4284	D-0231
OO-ZHQ	Nord 2000	63/10393	F-CAYP
OO-ZHR	Fauvel AV.36	1	D-5513
OO-ZHS	Grob G.103 Twin Astir	3070	PH-591
OO-ZHU-MR	Start & Flug H-101 Salto	39	D-9239

Regn.	Type	C/n	Prev.Id.
OO-ZHV	Neukom S4D Elfe 16	409AB	D-7700
OO-ZHX	Rolladen-Schneider LS-6	6032	PH-761
OO-ZHY	Schempp-Hirth Nimbus 2	115	OE-5075
OO-ZHZ-F1	Schempp-Hirth Discus CS	057CS	
OO-ZIC	Hutter Hu-17B Nimbus	unkn	
OO-ZID	Karpf Baby II	unkn	
OO-ZIE	Scheibe L-Spatz 55	503B	
OO-ZIF	LET L-13 Blanik	026857	
OO-ZIG	Fauvel AV.36	1	D-5510
OO-ZII	FFA Diamant 16.5	038	BGA1471
OO-ZIJ-IJ	Schleicher K.8B	8733	D-4416
OO-ZIK-26	Schleicher ASW-17	17039	
OO-ZIO	DFS Grunau Baby III	unkn	
OO-ZIP	Breguet 905PS Fauvette	1	F-CCIA
OO-ZIS-IS	SZD-22C Mucha Standard	F-756	
OO-ZIT	EoN Olympia	EON/0/052	
OO-ZIV	Schleicher ASW-20	20304	
OO-ZIW	Spalinger S-15	unkn	
OO-ZIX	Akaflieg München Mü.13E Bergfalke	unkn	D-6050
OO-ZIZ	Doppelraab VI	unkn	D-1206
OO-ZJA-JA	Eiri PIK-20D	20635	
OO-ZJC-19	Scheibe Zugvogel IIIB	1089	
OO-ZJD	Wassmer WA.30 Bijave	210	F-CDJD
OO-ZJF-99	Schleicher Ka.6E Rhönsegler	4094	D-3243
OO-ZJG-45	Bölkow Phoebus C	894	F-CDOD
OO-ZJI	Centrair ASW-20F	20189	F-CEUT
OO-ZJK	Schempp-Hirth Janus C	218	HB-1829
OO-ZJN	Breguet 905S Fauvette	45	F-CCJO
OO-ZJP	Schleicher Ka.6CR Rhönsegler	676	D-5737
OO-ZJQ	LET L-13 Blanik	026928	D-0935
			OE-5236
OO-ZJT	Valentin Mistral C	MC005/77	D-4900
OO-ZJU	Rolladen-Schneider LS-3-17	3405	D-7893
OO-ZJV	Scheibe L-Spatz 55	2	D-5608
OO-ZJW	Scheibe Spatz 55	SF-01	D-1233
OO-ZJX-25	Glasflügel H201B Standard Libelle	362	F-CEBL
OO-ZJY	Schempp-Hirth Janus B	79	D-1153
			N177BC
OO-ZJZ	Rolladen-Schneider LS-3-17	3269	D-2868
OO-ZKB	Schleicher K.8B	8822	
OO-ZKC	Schleicher ASK-23	23058	
OO-ZKD	LET L-13 Blanik	025707	D-2298
OO-ZKE-66	Schempp-Hirth Standard Cirrus 75	696	
OO-ZKF-66	Schleicher K.8B	8449/SH	D-5807
OO-ZKG	Schempp-Hirth Nimbus 3T	59/7	D-KHRG
			D-3111
OO-ZKI	Schleicher Rhönlerche II	01	D-8835
OO-ZKJ-111	Schleicher Ka.6BR Rhönsegler	408	D-5628
OO-ZKK	LET L-13 Blanik	026146	
OO-ZKL-KL	Grob G.103 Twin Astir II	3619	
OO-ZKM	Avialsa-Scheibe A.60 Fauconnet	36K	F-CCQN
OO-ZKN	Schleicher ASK-13	13254	
OO-ZKO	Schleicher ASK-13	13244	
OO-ZKP	Schleicher ASK-13	13261	
OO-ZKQ-B2	Schleicher K.8B	8685/A	D-5158
OO-ZKR-11	Schleicher K.8B	8347	D-4635
OO-ZKS-KS	Schleicher ASK-13	13239	OH-396
			OH-KKS
OO-ZKU	Schleicher K.8B	8155	OY-XFF
			RDAF:Z-966
OO-ZKV-KV	Grob G.103 Twin Astir II	3644	
OO-ZKW-KW	Grob G.103 Twin Astir	3231	
OO-ZKX	Grob G.102 Astir CS	1426	PH-560
OO-ZKY	Schleicher ASK-23B	23091	
OO-ZKZ	Centrair 101A Pégase	101A-0273	
OO-ZLB-GB	Schempp-Hirth Nimbus III	27	
OO-ZLC-VP	Schempp-Hirth Ventus b	153	D-2521
OO-ZLD	Schleicher K.8B	8055/A	D-5466
OO-ZLE-A7	VTC-75 Cirrus	114Y	D-0503
OO-ZLF	Carmam M.200	45	F-CDHV
OO-ZLG-LG	Schempp-Hirth Standard Cirrus	189	D-0704
OO-ZLH-3D	SZD-36A Cobra 15	W-721	
OO-ZLI	Rolladen-Schneider LS-4	4001	D-2628
OO-ZLJ-LJ	Glasflügel H.201B Standard Libelle	378	
OO-ZLK	Schempp-Hirth Standard Cirrus	268	D-1981

Regn.	Type	C/n	Prev.Id.
OO-ZLL	Schempp-Hirth Standard Cirrus	62	
OO-ZLM	Akaflieg München Mü.13E Bergfalke	8	D-5236
OO-ZLN	Schleicher ASK-21	21007	
OO-ZLO	Schempp-Hirth Nimbus II	47	
OO-ZLP	Olympia Meise 52	unkn	D-6434
OO-ZLQ	Schempp-Hirth Ventus cT	152/487	
OO-ZLR	Schleicher Ka.6CR Rhönsegler	6186	D-5347
OO-ZLT-LT	Schempp-Hirth Standard Cirrus	102	D-0735
OO-ZLU	Schleicher Rhönlerche II	90/55	D-5418
OO-ZLV	Schleicher K.8B	8709	
OO-ZLW	Schleicher K.7 Rhönadler	7196	
OO-ZLX-LX	Schempp-Hirth Standard Cirrus	416	D-4750
OO-ZLY	Carmam M.200 Foehn	28	F-CDDY
OO-ZLZ	Scheibe L-Spatz 55	534	D-1215
OO-ZMB	Schleicher ASW-15A	15166	D-0827
OO-ZMC	Scheibe L-Spatz 55	515	D-4018
OO-ZMD	Schleicher K.7 Rhönadler	1093	D-5072
OO-ZME	Scheibe L-Spatz 55	669	D-1722
OO-ZMG	Scheibe L-Spatz 55	1	D-5166
OO-ZMJ	Schleicher K.7 Rhönadler	2/59	D-5650
OO-ZMK	Schleicher Ka.6CR Rhönsegler	6114	D-1897
OO-ZMM	Glasflügel H.301 Libelle	11	D-8897
OO-ZMN	Scheibe SF-27A	6019	D-9374
OO-ZMO-JY	Grob G.102 Astir Club Standard	1396	
OO-ZMP	Carmam M.200 Foehn	58	F-CDPO
OO-ZMQ	Slingsby T.31B Cadet TX.3	853	XA311
OO-ZMR-P	SZD-48-1 Jantar Standard 2	W-895	
OO-ZMS-52	Schempp-Hirth Mini-Nimbus B	74	
OO-ZMT-MT	Schleicher Ka.6CR Rhönsegler	6464	D-5104
OO-ZMV	Schleicher K.8B	175/60	D-6390
OO-ZMW	Grob G.102 Astir CS Jeans	2205	
OO-ZMX-MG	Schempp-Hirth Ventus A	92	D-1480
OO-ZMY-MY	Rolladen-Schneider LS-1D	97	D-0436
OO-ZNB-729	Glasflügel H.201B Standard Libelle	258	
OO-ZNC	Schleicher K.7 Rhönadler	835	D-5787
OO-ZND-YT	ICA-Brasov IS.28B-2	271	
OO-ZNE	Scheibe/LCA.11 Topaze	23	F-CEEX
OO-ZNF	Eiri PIK-20D	20544	OH-535
OO-ZNG-MG	Grob G.102 Speed Astir IIB	4103	D-6817
OO-ZNH-NH	Rolladen-Schneider LS-1F	412	D-2753
OO-ZNK	Grob G.102 Standard Astir II	5033S	D-6265
OO-ZNL-U2	Schempp-Hirth Janus	31	LX-CPC OO-ZPY (OO-ZMN) D-4091
OO-ZNM-JL	Schleicher Ka.6CR Rhönsegler	6001	
OO-ZNO-3M	Grob G.102 Astir CS Jeans	2158	D-4554
OO-ZNP	Schleicher K7 Rhönadler	284	D-5544
OO-ZNQ	LET L-23 Super Blanik	907624	OK-0238 (BGA3666/FZY)
OO-ZNR	SZD-48-1 Jantar Standard 2	B-1025	OE-5250
OO-ZNS	Schleicher ASW-19	19221	
OO-ZNT	Scheibe Bergfalke IV	5860	(OO-ZJT(2)) D-5941
OO-ZNU-NU	Pilatus B4-PC11AF	257	LX-CVA
OO-ZNV-13	Rolladen-Schneider LS-1D	87	D-4440
OO-ZNW-NW	SZD-51-1 Junior	B-1993	
OO-ZNX	SZD-50-3 Puchacz	B-1391	SP-3284
OO-ZNY	Grob Standard Cirrus	425G	F-CEFL
OO-ZNZ	Schleicher ASW-20	20437	PH-703
OO-ZOA	Schleicher K.8B	746/60	D-4034
OO-ZOB	Aeromere M.100S	054	
OO-ZOC	Scheibe L-Spatz 55	561	D-5441
OO-ZOD-21	Schleicher K.6E Rhönsegler	4032	
OO-ZOE	Schleicher K.8B	8734	D-5847
OO-ZOG-OG	Grob G.102 Speed Astir IIB	4049	D-8715
OO-ZOI	Schleicher K.8B	8953	PH-476
OO-ZOJ	Schleicher K.8B	586	D-5706
OO-ZOK	LET L-13 Blanik	175018	
OO-ZOL-AB	Schleicher K.8B	8891	
OO-ZOM	Schleicher K.8B	8654	PL-58
OO-ZON	Schleicher K.8B	8573	
OO-ZOP	Breguet 905S Fauvette	3	F-CCIG
OO-ZOQ-114	Schleicher Ka.6E Rhönsegler	4163	
OO-ZOT	Schempp-Hirth Janus CM	5	D-KONI (D-KJMD)

Regn.	Type	C/n	Prev.Id.
OO-ZOV-AV	Schempp-Hirth Janus C	103	D-7997
OO-ZOW	Schleicher K7 Rhönadler	2	D-5754
OO-ZOX	Schleicher K.8B	173/01AB	D-0131
OO-ZOY	Wassmer WA.30 Bijave	17	F-CCMN
OO-ZPC-PC	Schleicher ASW-20	20049	
OO-ZPE	Akaflieg München Mü.13E Bergfalke	186	D-6090
OO-ZPF-PF	Grob G.102 Speed Astir IIB	4104	D-6818
OO-ZPH	Akaflieg München Mü.13E Bergfalke	131	LX-CBA
OO-ZPJ	Akaflieg Braunschweig SB-5B Sperber	5025	D-8617
OO-ZPK	Scheibe Zugvogel IIIB	1077	D-1975
OO-ZPM-PM	Rolladen-Schneider LS-4	4049	
OO-ZPO	Zsebo-Bohn Z-03B Ifjusag	unkn	
OO-ZPP-PP	Schleicher ASW-15	15157	D-0807
OO-ZPQ-HB	SZD-48-3 Jantar Standard 3	B-1961	(OO-ZCY)
OO-ZPR	Grunau Baby III	unkn	
OO-ZPS-PS	SZD-48-3 Jantar Standard 3	B-1346	(OO-ZTD) SP-3232
OO-ZPT	Schleicher K.8B	8075	PH-289
OO-ZPU	Schleicher ASW-15	15140	D-0790
OO-ZPV	Schleicher Rhönlerche II	234/56	
OO-ZQA	Schleicher Ka.2B Rhönschwalbe	69/55	PL-10
OO-ZQB	Schleicher Ka.2B Rhönschwalbe	71/55	PL-11
OO-ZQE	VTC Cirrus	136Y	D-2968
OO-ZQF	SZD-55-1	551193057	
OO-ZQG-GG	Neukom S4D Elfe 15	401	D-4599
OO-ZQH	Eiri PIK-20D	20568	D-6703
OO-ZQI-QI	Schempp-Hirth Discus bT	81/414	
OO-ZQJ	Schleicher ASW-15B	15270	F-CEGF
OO-ZQK	Glasflügel H303 Mosquito	46	D-8986
OO-ZQL	SZD-59 Acro	B-2163	
OO-ZQM	Grob G.102 Astir CS Jeans	2070	D-7584
OO-ZQN	Grob G.102 Standard Astir II	5007S	D-4884
OO-ZQO	Schleicher K7 Rhönadler	7224	D-5819
OO-ZQP	Grob G.102 Astir CS 77	1818	D-6754
OO-ZQQ	Schleicher ASW-27	27016	
OO-ZQU	Schleicher K7 Rhönadler	698	D-5753
OO-ZQV	Glasflügel H201B Standard Libelle	601	F-CELI
OO-ZQW	Wassmer WA.30 Bijave	78	F-CCTB
OO-ZQY	Schleicher K7 Rhönadler	10	D-5667
OO-ZRA	Schleicher ASW-20L	20553	
OO-ZRB	Schleicher K.8B	12	D-1130
OO-ZRC	Rolladen-Schneider LS-6	6056	D-6522
OO-ZRD	Avialsa-Scheibe A.60	47K	F-CCQZ
OO-ZRE	Schleicher Ka.2B Rhönschwalbe	319	D-6216
OO-ZRG	Wassmer WA.22A Super Javelot	96	F-CCRG
OO-ZRI	Schleicher ASW-20	20235	
OO-ZRK-23	Glasflügel H.201B Standard Libelle	16	D-0108
OO-ZRL	LET L-13 Blanik	026639	
OO-ZRM	Schleicher K.7 Rhönadler	7135/A	D-5415
OO-ZRN	Schleicher ASH-25	25012	
OO-ZRO-57	Glasflügel H.201B Standard Libelle	8	
OO-ZRP	Carmam M.100S Mésange	13	F-CCSB
OO-ZRQ	Rolladen-Schneider LS-6B	6126	
OO-ZRR-LV	Schempp-Hirth Standard Cirrus 75	614	
OO-ZRU	Schleicher K.8B	8438GV	D-8815
OO-ZRV	Brieglieb BG.12-16	236	(OO-ZJK) (OO-51)
OO-ZRW	Schleicher K7 Rhönadler	7050	LX-CAE
OO-ZRX-01	Rolladen-Schneider LS-1C	88	D-0305
OO-ZRY-78	Rolladen-Schneider LS-6	6035	
OO-ZRZ-70	Schleicher ASW-20	20299	
OO-ZSA	SZD-8ter-Z0 Jaskolka	247	
	(Displayed in AELR Museum Brussels)		
OO-ZSB	Akaflieg Braunschweig SB-5B Sperber	5009	
OO-ZSC	SZD-8ter-Z0 Jaskolka	254	
OO-ZSD	SZD-8ter-Z0 Jaskolka	255	
OO-ZSE	SZD-8ter-Z0 Jaskolka	256	
OO-ZSG-V	Grob G.103 Twin Astir	3137	
OO-ZSH	Slingsby T.30B Prefect	880	OO-SZH
OO-Z SI	SZD-22B Mucha Standard	518 ?	
OO-ZSM-SM	Rolladen-Schneider LS-4	4172	(OO-ZDG)
OO-ZSO	SZD-22C Mucha Standard	525	
OO-ZSS	SZD-22C Mucha Standard	530	
OO-ZST	SZD-22C Mucha Standard (w/o in 1988)	531	

Regn.	Type	C/n	Prev.Id.
OO-ZSU	SZD-22C Mucha Standard	532	
	(Rebuilt using parts from OO-ZSM/OO-ZFC c/n 526 - which is still current as OO-ZFC)		
OO-ZSX	SZD-9 bis Bocian 1D	P-393	
OO-ZTA	Carmam M.200 Foehn	17	F-CDDI
OO-ZTB	Carmam M.100S Mésange	84	F-CDKY
OO-ZTC	Schleicher K.8B	8047/EI	D-5189
OO-ZTD	Grob G.103 Twin Astir	3016	HB-1389
OO-ZTE	Schempp-Hirth SHK-1	V-2	OY-BXP
			D-6438
			D-9338
OO-ZTF-21	Glasflügel H.201B Standard Libelle	490	PH-475
OO-ZTG	Schleicher Ka.6CR Rhönsegler	6179	OY-XFO
			RDAF:Z-967
OO-ZTH	LET L-13 Blanik	170711	D-0138
			SP-1795
OO-ZTI	Schleicher Ka.6CR Rhönsegler	6132	D-4350
OO-ZTJ	Schleicher K.7 Rhönadler	7096	D-8884
OO-ZTK-C87	Standard Cirrus VTC-75	244	F-CEBY
OO-ZTL	Schempp-Hirth SH.1 Standard Austria	55	
OO-ZTM	Schleicher Ka.6CR Rhönsegler	492	D-4004
OO-ZTN	Schempp-Hirth Nimbus 3T	26/92	(OO-ZJT)
OO-ZTO	Schempp-Hirth Ventus cT	102/362	D-KFAH
OO-ZTP	Glaser-Dirks DG-300 Elan	3E-207	D-8957
OO-ZTQ-TQ	Rolladen-Schneider LS-4	4113	PH-716
OO-ZTS	Schleicher Ka.6E Rhönsegler	4197	D-1100
OO-ZTT	Schleicher Ka.2B Rhönschwalbe	03	D-9107
OO-ZTU-DJ	Schempp-Hirth Discus CS	114CS	
OO-ZTV-T1	Valentin Mistral C	059/85	D-4959
OO-ZTY	Glasflügel H201 Standard Libelle	301	F-CEBA
OO-ZUA	Schleicher Rhönlerche II	unkn	
OO-ZUB	Schleicher Rhönlerche II	unkn	
OO-ZUC	Schleicher Rhönlerche II	426/58	
OO-ZUD	SZD-22C Mucha Standard	F-776	
OO-ZUE	Schleicher Rhönlerche II	428/58	
OO-ZUH	Schleicher Rhönlerche II	431/58	
OO-ZUJ	Schleicher Rhönlerche II	594/59	
OO-ZUK	Schleicher Rhönlerche II	595/59	
OO-ZUL	Schleicher Rhönlerche II	596/59	
OO-ZUM	Schleicher Rhönlerche II	425/58	
OO-ZUO	Schempp-Hirth SH-1 Standard Austria	78	D-4004
			LX-CWW
OO-ZUQ-JU	Rolladen-Schneider LS-3	3100	D-1151
			D-2859
			OO-ZOZ
OO-ZUR	Scheibe L-Spatz 55	680	
OO-ZUS	Grob G.103 Twin Astir II	3645	
OO-ZUV	Wassmer WA.26CM	04	F-CDUV
OO-ZUW-UW	Neukom S-4A Elfe	45	HB-1224
OO-ZUX	SZD-8ter-Z0 Jaskolka	240	
OO-ZUY	Schleicher Rhönlerche II	409	
OO-ZVC	Grob G.103 Twin Astir	3238	
OO-ZVF	Grob G.103 Twin Astir II	3517	
OO-ZVG	Schleicher K.8B	8335/A	D-5451
OO-ZVH-VH	Schleicher ASW-19	19239	
OO-ZVI	Grob Standard Cirrus	296G	D-2055
OO-ZVJ	Grob G.103 Twin Astir	3260	
OO-ZVK-VK	Schempp-Hirth Janus C	205	
OO-ZVM-76	Schleicher ASW-20	20047	
OO-ZVN-VN	Schleicher Ka.6CR Rhönsegler	6336	PH-336
OO-ZVO	Schleicher Rhönbussard	unkn	(OO-ZJH)
			OO-ZVA(1)
OO-ZVP	Glasflügel H.201B Standard Libelle	17	OE-0880
OO-ZVR	Grob G.102 Astir Club IIIB	5589	
OO-ZVS	Grob G.102 Astir Club II	5057C	
OO-ZVT	Scheibe L-Spatz 55	667	
OO-ZVU	Scheibe L-Spatz 55	4	D-5505
OO-ZVV	Bölkow Phoebus B-1	737	D-5733
OO-ZVX	Grob G.102 Astir Club Standard	1813	
OO-ZVY	Grob G.102 Astir Standard Jeans	2048	
OO-ZVZ	Grob G.102 Astir Standard Jeans	2047	
OO-ZWA	Schleicher Ka.6CR Rhönsegler	6591	D-3659
OO-ZWB	Grob G.102 Astir CS Jeans	2137	
OO-ZWD	Schleicher K.8B	8816	
OO-ZWF-7	Avialsa-Scheibe A.60	8	F-CCLD
OO-ZWG	Grob G.102 Astir Club Standard Jeans	2182	
OO-ZWH	Schleicher Ka.6CR Rhönsegler	6224	D-1853
OO-ZWJ	SZD-48 Jantar Standard 2 *(Dbr 5.99)*	W-884	
OO-ZWK	Wassmer WA.30 Bijave	25	F-CCMV
OO-ZWL	Wassmer WA.30 Bijave	12	F-CCMJ
OO-ZWM	SZD-48-3 Jantar Standard 3	B-1419	
OO-ZWP-LL	Schleicher ASW-15	15163	D-0808
OO-ZWR	Schleicher K7 Rhönadler	7042	D-5206
OO-ZWT-WT	Schleicher ASW-19	19054	
OO-ZWU-WU	Schleicher ASK-13	13485	OH-441
OO-ZWV	Schleicher K.7 Rhönadler	886	D-5003
OO-ZWW	Scheibe SF-30A	6806	
OO-ZWX-49	Rolladen-Schneider LS-3A	3403	
OO-ZWZ	Grob G.102 Astir Club Standard	1776	
OO-ZXC	Schempp-Hirth Duo Discus	44	
OO-ZXD	Schleicher K.8B	8255	D-5387
OO-ZXE	SZD-24C Foka	W-158	SP-2376
OO-ZXG	Wassmer WA.28F	106	F-CEOA
OO-ZXH	Carmam M.100S Mésange	47	F-CCXL
OO-ZXI	Schleicher K.8B	8293	D-6032
OO-ZXJ	Schleicher K7 Rhönadler	7103	D-3608
OO-ZXK-K	Schleicher ASK-21	21511	
OO-ZXM	Schleicher ASK-21	21535	
OO-ZXN	Slingsby T-31B Cadet	1179	XN240
OO-ZXO-XO	Glaser-Dirks DG-300 Elan	3E-128	D-2857
OO-ZXP-XP	Schempp-Hirth Discus bT	61/383	D-KHEI (2)
OO-ZXR-OB	Schempp-Hirth Discus b	217	
OO-ZXS-Z	Rolladen-Schneider LS-6C/17.5	6267	D-4350
OO-ZXT-XT	Schleicher ASW-20L	20243	D-3373
OO-ZXU	Glaser-Dirks DG-200	2-184	PH-722
OO-ZXV	Rolladen-Schneider LS-4A	4731	D-1377
OO-ZXW	Schleicher K.8B	8269	HB-763
OO-ZXX-JA	Rolladen-Schneider LS-3A	3229	
OO-ZYA	Schleicher Ka.6CR Rhönsegler	6615	
OO-ZYB-HO	Glasflügel H.205 Libelle	145	(OO-ZQB)
			(OO-EQB)
			F-CEQB
OO-ZYC	Grob G.102 Speed Astir IIB	4032	D-4504
OO-ZYD-P8	Rolladen-Schneider LS-1D	110	D-1072
OO-ZYE	Schleicher Ka.6BR Rhönsegler	527	D-8130
OO-ZYF	Schleicher K7 Rhönadler	7013	D-1785
OO-ZYG	Schleicher Ka.6CR-PE Rhönsegler	6112	D-8457
OO-ZYH-64	Schempp-Hirth Janus	29	OY-XDH
OO-ZYJ	SZD-48-3 Jantar Standard 3	B-1968	LX-CEE
OO-ZYK-YK	Schleicher ASH-25	25008	D-4741
OO-ZYL	Glasflügel H.303 Mosquito	88	
OO-ZYM	VTC-75 Cirrus *(W/o 7.99)*	113Y	D-0502
OO-ZYO	Rolladen-Schneider LS-1D	5	D-0125
OO-ZYP	ICA-Brasov IS.28B2	311	
OO-ZYQ-CG	Rolladen-Schneider LS-1F	352	D-2744
OO-ZYR	SZD-48-3 Jantar Standard 3 *(Damaged)*	B-1956	
OO-ZYS-PT	Rolladen-Schneider LS-1F	410	D-3144
OO-ZYU-YU	Schempp-Hirth Ventus cT	71/295	D-KMHN
OO-ZYV	Schleicher Ka.6CR Rhönsegler	6182	D-4679
OO-ZYX	Pilatus B4-PC11	155	HB-1147
OO-ZZA	Rolladen-Schneider LS-3A	3150	
OO-ZZC	Grob G.102 Astir CS 77	1665	
OO-ZZD	Glaser-Dirks DG.100 Club Elan	E34-G18	
OO-ZZG	Glaser-Dirks DG-300 Elan	3E-179	D-5702
OO-ZZI-ZI	Rolladen-Schneider LS-1F	159	D-2427
OO-ZZJ	Schleicher K7 Rhönadler	699	D-5745
OO-ZZK-K3	Glasflügel H303 Mosquito	3	D-4321
OO-ZZL	Schleicher K7 Rhönadler	892	(OO-ZZK)
			D-8359
OO-ZZN	Rolladen-Schneider LS-3A	3118	D-3899
OO-ZZO-51	Schleicher Ka.6CR Rhönsegler	60/2	D-5792
OO-ZZP-DM	Rolladen-Schneider LS-3A	3301	D-6953
OO-ZZQ	Rolladen-Schneider LS-1C	124	D-0886
OO-ZZR-ZR	Glaser-Dirks DG-300 Elan	3E-133	D-9353
OO-ZZS-7	Rolladen-Schneider LS-4	4126	
OO-ZZT-C52	Lanaverre CS-11/75 Standard Cirrus	678	F-CEMY
OO-ZZU-L11	Schempp-Hirth Discus b	180	F-CGGJ
			F-WGGJ
OO-ZZV	Schleicher K.8B	8820	PH-417
OO-ZZW-ZW	Schleicher ASH-25E	25126	

Regn.	Type	C/n	Prev.Id.
OO-ZZX	Glaser-Dirks DG-300 Elan	3E-125	N301LA
OO-ZZY	Schleicher K.8B	8952	PH-478
OO-ZZZ-13	Schleicher Ka.6E Rhönsegler	192/56	
OO-Z..	Slingsby T-38 Grasshopper TX.1	1263	BGA3439/FQJ
			XP464

HOMEBUILT AIRCRAFT

Regn.	Type	C/n	Prev.Id.
OO-11	Mignet HM.293 Pou-du-Ciel	unkn	
	(On display in AELR Museum)		
OO-15	Jodel D.9 Bébé	unkn	
	(On display in AELR Museum)		
OO-19	Jodel D.92 Bébé (CofA exp 4.85)	CD-03	
OO-20	Jodel D.9 Bébé (CofA exp 8.72)	CD-04	
OO-22	Jodel D.9 Bébé (W/o 3.5.89)	386	
OO-29	Pottier P.80S	47	
OO-30	Druine D.31 Turbulent	378	
OO-31	Jodel D.9 Bébé	487	
	(Built using parts from OO-14 and OO-26)		
OO-32	Mignet HM.293 Pou-du-Ciel (Stored)	821	F-PKFK
OO-33	Mignet HM.293 Pou-du-Ciel	unkn	
	(Stored at AELR Museum marked as OO-BAM)		
OO-35	Mignet HM.360 Pou-du-Ciel (Wfu)	40	
OO-43(2)	Breezy RLU-1	5537	
OO-45	Jodel D.9 Bébé	629	
OO-54	Pottier P.80S	54	PH-SOM
			(PH-NOK)
			(OO-89)
OO-59	Croses EAC-3 Pouplume (CofA exp 8.81)	41	
OO-63	Cvjetkovic CA-65 (Under construction)	unkn	
OO-66	Evans VP-1 Volksplane	V-2574	
OO-69	Tipsy T.66 Nipper 1L	29	
	(Also regd as G-BWHR with c/n PFA/25-12843)		
OO-70	Monerai S	190	
OO-71	Monnet Monerai S	241	
OO-72	Monerai S	265	
OO-78	Bede BD-5B (CofA exp 5.82)	unkn	(OO-LWL)
OO-80	EAA Super Acro Sport	864	(OO-RAG)
OO-83	Evans VP-2 (Stored at Overmere)	3730	
OO-88	Evans VP-2 (CofA exp 9.88)	V2-3274	
OO-90	WAR FW190	209	
OO-93	Pober P-9 Pixie	unkn	
OO-96	Mignet HM.293A Pou-du-Ciel (W/o 8.99)	B-001	
OO-99	Monnet Sonerai IIL	919	
OO-100	Mass 302	001	
OO-102	Rutan Vari-eze	1434	
OO-103	Rutan Vari-eze	1433	
OO-104	Rutan Vari-eze (CofA exp 11.88)	1847	
OO-106	Colomban MC-15 Cri-Cri	163	
OO-107	SCWALL 101 ATL	001	
OO-108	Pottier P.80S	052	
OO-111	Grinvalds G-802 Orion	80/014	(OO-ION)
			(N802JS)
OO-118	JP.II (Homebuilt)	01	OO-LJP
OO-119	Marco J-5	05	(OO-GUN)
OO-122	Murphy Renegade Spirit	0292	
OO-125	Rand-Robinson KR-2	001	
OO-126	Stoddard-Hamilton Glasair III	3143	
OO-128	Murphy Renegade Spirit	388	
OO-129	CFM Streak Shadow	K156-SA	(OO-A62)
OO-130	Neico Lancair 320	363	
OO-132	Brändli BX-2 Cherry	157	
OO-134	Rans S-10 Sakota	0892.143	
	(C/n quoted as 0892.145 which is ZK-SWJ, above believed correct)		
OO-135	Rans S-10 Sakota	0494.172	
OO-138	Rotorway Exec 162F	6045	
OO-...	Tipsy T.66 Nipper II (Reservation)	28	(OY-AEN)
			OO-SRY
			F-BMLV

Regn.	Type	C/n	Prev.Id.
MICROLIGHTS			
OO-501	Grasshopper Model Mono 01	GH/01/81/00	
OO-502	Weedhopper JC.24B	873	
OO-503	Grasshopper Model Mono 01	GH/01/81/001	
OO-504	Romibutter (Modified Butterfly)	0101	(OO-753)
OO-505	Microbel	unkn	
OO-506	Fulmar Trident I	unkn	
OO-507	Fulmar Trident I	unkn	
OO-508	Véliplane Mosquito	340	
OO-509	JC.24B Weedhopper B	972	
OO-510	Aero-Marcq Marcq 1	0001	
OO-511	Fulmar Tricycle	81-012	
OO-512	Franken FR-II	unkn	
OO-513(2)	Micronef BI Hi	0839	
OO-514	Microbel SC-330	unkn	
OO-515	Cosmos/La Mouette Dragster	90/2618	
OO-516	JC.31A Weedhopper Two	unkn	
OO-517	JC.24B Weedhopper B	1597	
OO-518	Fulmar Tyger II	82-8230051	
OO-519	Butterfly	03	
OO-520	JC.24C Weedhopper C	2210	
OO-523	Microbel/Hiway Trike	unkn	
OO-524	Fulmar Trident I	T1-81-005	
OO-525	Fulmar Trident I	82-006	
OO-526	JC.24C Weedhopper C	108	
OO-527	JC.24C Weedhopper C	unkn	
OO-528	Fulmar Trident I	82-013	
OO-529	Fulmar Trident I	82-012	
OO-530	Rotec Rally 3B	25037	
OO-531	Fulmar Trident I	82-015	
OO-532	B.Danis Aile Delta	001	
OO-533	Eipper Quicksilver MX-II	1101	
OO-534	Fulmar Standart	TS-8003	
OO-535	Danis-Sabre	1018	
OO-536	Mainair Triflyer 440/Lightning DS	105121182	
	(Registered as a Southdown Puma, above correct)		
OO-537	Fulmar Tyger I	82-017	
OO-538	Microbel SC-250	20-28	
OO-539	Microbel SC-250	8000085	
OO-540	Microbel Big Fun	83-00296	
OO-541	Weedhopper Moustique	001	
OO-542	Fulmar Tricycle KDA	1143	
OO-543	Microbel Super Costaud SC-250	82-00503	
OO-544	Eipper Quicksilver MX-II	1174	
OO-545	Microbel SC-250	923/651	
OO-546	Microbel SL-20CV	83-102	
OO-547	Butterfly	04	
OO-548	Microbel SC-250	MR-8290	
OO-549	Fulmar Tyger I	TT-83-023	
OO-550	Microbel SC-440	82-001	
OO-551	Microbel SC-250	unkn	
OO-552	Sofrec Mustang	unkn	
OO-553	Baroudeur	83-3004	
OO-554	Cosmos/La Mouette Dragster 25	83-4156	
OO-556	Fulmar Heron MP15	001	
OO-557	Fulmar Tyger I	unkn	
OO-558	Fulmar Trident I	unkn	
OO-559	Microbel SC-503	83-113	
OO-560	Southdown Puma MS	83-2696	
OO-561	Southdown Puma MS	KR 1377383	
	(Probably Mainair Triflyer 440 Dual trike unit)		
OO-562	Fulmar Trident	82-007	
OO-563	Fulmar Tyger I	TTB-83030	
OO-564	Hunter Pathfinder II	110	
OO-565	Fulmar Tyger I	TTB-82018	
OO-567	Eipper Quicksilver MX-L	unkn	
OO-568	Microbel SC-250	unkn	
OO-569	Butterfly	03-01	
OO-570	Hunter Pathfinder II	124	
OO-571	Eipper Quicksilver MX-II	unkn	
OO-572	Véliplane OQ	248/82	
OO-573	Dragon 150	043	
OO-574	Microbel Big Fun	unkn	
OO-576	Microbel SC-432	02783	

Regn.	Type	C/n	Prev.Id.
OO-577	Microbel SC-440	unkn	
OO-578	Rotec Rally 3B	25039	
OO-579	Rotec Rally 3B	25056	
OO-581	Dragon 150	049	
OO-582	Dragon 150	050	
OO-583	Fulmar Tricycle	unkn	
OO-584	Fulmar Trident II	82-1003	
OO-585	JC.24C Weedhopper C	2052	
OO-586	Southdown Puma MS	830076	
OO-587	Mainair Triflyer 440/Lightning DS	177-287-3	
OO-588	Southdown Puma MS	8300146	
OO-589	ULAC X99	187	
OO-590	Airion Lezart Volant	B-11	
OO-592	Fulmar Gold Tricycle	63M2135	
OO-593	Fulmar Tyger I	321	
OO-594	Fulmar Tyger I	TTB-83035	
OO-595	Eipper Quicksilver MX-II	1751	
OO-596	Southdown Puma MS	8300017	
OO-597	Butterfly	31-02	
OO-598	Microbel SC-250	unkn	
OO-599	Fulmar Tyger II	TTB-83039	
OO-600	Fulmar Tyger I	TTB-83032	
OO-601	Butterfly 04	001	
OO-602	Mitchell Wing P-38 Lightning	5602	
OO-603	Fulmar Tyger 1	TTB-83040	
OO-604	Microbel SC-250	82-00317	
OO-605	JC.31C Weedhopper	4010020	
OO-606	Phoenix SR44	0016	
OO-607	Eipper Quicksilver MX-II	1750	
OO-608	Eipper Quicksilver MX-II	1755	
OO-609	American Aircraft Falcon	500180	
OO-611	American Aircraft Falcon	500182	
OO-612	American Aircraft Falcon	500187	
OO-613	JC.31C Weedhopper	4010017	
OO-614	Microbel SC-250	83-121	
OO-615	Southdown Puma MS	8300022	
OO-616	Aériane Sirocco	048	
OO-617	Microbel SC-440	111	
OO-618	Microbel SC-440	83-00849	
OO-619	Fulmar Tyger II	84-3070	
OO-620	Southdown Puma MS	8200151	
OO-621	JC.31C Weedhopper	3486385	
OO-623	JC.31C Weedhopper	4040034	
OO-625	Huntair Pathfinder II	154	
OO-626	Huntair Pathfinder II	155	
OO-627	Southdown Puma MS	84-3249	
OO-628	Baroudeur	499C00-401-43	
OO-629	Chickinox 34	3478171	
OO-630	Weedhopper JC-24D	4040047	
OO-631	Microbel SC-330	83602	
OO-632	Southdown Puma Sprint MS	8300208	
OO-633	Eipper Quicksilver MX-II	1756	
OO-634	JC.31C Weedhopper	4040035	
OO-635	Weedhopper Gipsy	001	
OO-636	JC.24D Weedhopper	4040052	
OO-637	JC.31C Weedhopper	4050070	
OO-638	Phoenix SR44	unkn	
OO-639	Butterfly 03	04	
OO-640	Southdown Puma MS	unkn	
OO-641	Butterfly 03	20	
OO-642	Microbel SC	863753	
OO-643	American Aircraft Falcon	500192	(OO-ETA)
OO-644	JC.31C Weedhopper	4050057	
OO-645	Fulmar Trident	TT-84048	
OO-646	Fulmar Trident	TT-83	
OO-647	Fulmar Tyger I	TTB-084	
OO-648	Microbel Mono	unkn	
OO-649	Butterfly	02	
OO-650	Fulmar Standard	28183	
OO-651	Sofrec Baroudeur	56-2050955	
OO-653	Microbel SC-440	8402	
OO-654	Microbel SC-250	84315	
OO-656	JC.31C Weedhopper	4050068	
OO-657	Aériane Sirocco	unkn	
OO-659	Eipper Quicksilver MX-II	1816	
OO-660	Southdown Puma Sprint MS	8300142	
OO-662	Fulmar Tyger I	270-IA-03E	
OO-663	JC.31C Weedhopper	4072001	
OO-664	Microbel	RK-01-1984	
OO-665	Microbel	NP-70ZN2	
OO-666	Microbel	82-00457	
OO-667	Fulmar Tyger I	TTB83038	
OO-668	Microbel	82-00472	
OO-669	Microbel	863673	
OO-670	Cosmos/La Mouette Bidulum 44	83-00011	
OO-671	Zodiac Ultrastar	123	
OO-672	Microbel SC-250	unkn	
OO-673	Fulmar Tyger II	85-2608	
OO-674	Aériane Sirocco	123	
OO-675	Albatros 83/003	unkn	(OO-108)
OO-676	Dynali Chickinox	unkn	
OO-677	Dynali Chickinox	077	
OO-678	Dynali Chickinox	004	
OO-679	Microbel SC-337	8503	
OO-680	Solar Wings Pegasus XL-R	T1084-1224	
OO-681	JC.24D Weedhopper	4040048	
OO-682	Southdown Puma Sprint MS	T-519	
OO-683	Southdown Puma Sprint MS	P-554/T-516	
OO-684	Aériane Sirocco	99	
OO-686	Dynali Chickinox	AAB-40	
OO-687	Fulmar R	82-496	
OO-688	Microbel	unkn	
OO-689	Dynali Chickinox	AAA-00	
OO-690	Microbel SC-447	8561	
OO-691	Butterfly 03	018	
OO-692	Baroudeur	095	
OO-693	Microbel SC-493	864474	
OO-694	Dynali Chickinox Bi	31	
OO-695	Dynali Chickinox Tandem	035	
OO-696	Dynali Chickinox	032	
OO-697	JC.31D Weedhopper	5072150	
OO-698	Microbel Bi	26-12-84-861	
OO-699	Microbel	unkn	
OO-700	Fulmar Tyger I	83044	
OO-701	JC.24D Weedhopper	404-0051	
OO-703	Microbel Big Fun	86-5166	
OO-704	Fulmar Tyger II	865116	
OO-705	Fulmar Tyger III	T3-85101	
OO-707	Fulmar Tyger I	86-1244	
OO-708	Dynali Chickinox	061	
OO-709	Microbel SC-330	001	
OO-710	Microbel SC-330	002	
OO-711	Fulmar Trident I	TT-83-019	
OO-712	Lejong I	001	
OO-713	Microbel SC-447	8621	
OO-714	Dynali Chickinox Bi	0063	
OO-716	Aériane Sirocco	unkn	
OO-717	Microbel SC-440 Big Fun	8401	OO-652
OO-718	Microfun SC-330 Typhoon	MF-850501	
OO-719	JC.24D Weedhopper	4040053	
OO-720	Dragon 150	024	
OO-721	IPES 1	86-4019	
OO-722	Lux 1	001	
OO-723	Microbel SL-447	8651	
OO-724	Microbel SL-447	8509	
OO-725	Dynali Chickinox	070	
OO-726	Dynali Chickinox Kot Kot	084	
OO-727	Microbel SC-330	003	
OO-728	Solar Wings Pegasus Panther XL	86-6277	
OO-729	Dynali Chickinox	075	
OO-730	Eipper Quicksilver MX-II	1754	
OO-731	Cosmos Bidulum	005	
OO-732	Cosmos Bidulum	006	
OO-734	Dynali Chickinox Tandem	036	
OO-735	Fulmar Tyger III	T3-86106	
OO-736	Centrair Paraffan	03	
OO-737	Dynali Chickinox Kot Kot	86-3231	
OO-738	Fulmar Tyger III	T3-86105	
OO-739	Eipper Quicksilver MX-II	1896	
OO-740	Dynali Chickinox Kot Kot	86-2832	

Regn.	Type	C/n	Prev.id.
OO-742	Fulmar Tyger III	T3-85102	
OO-743	Fulmar Tyger	unkn	
OO-744	Microbel SC-330	83601	
OO-745	Cabis II	001	
OO-746	JC.24D Weedhopper	5031032	
OO-747	Centrair Parafan 1	41045	
OO-748	Dynali Chickinox Tandem	AAD-00	
OO-749	Microbel Chaser 377	86121	
OO-750	Microbel Trident II	86107	
OO-751	Durondeau 377 Parafan	1	
OO-752	Southdown Raven X	2000/0143	
OO-753	Baroudeur Biplace	142	
OO-754	Dynali Chickinox Kot Kot	210187012	
OO-755	Micronef Sc.Bi.Fu	008	
OO-756	Micronef Cosmos Bidulum	007	
OO-757	Microlight Trident II	87-108	
OO-758	Southdown Raven X	unkn	
OO-759	Microbel Cosmos Dragster	333-66	
OO-760	Fulmar Tyger III	T3-86103	
OO-761	Weedhopper Europa II	612-2255	
OO-762	Dynali Chickinox Kot Kot	31016691	
OO-763	Aériane Sirocco	148	
OO-764	JC.24D Weedhopper	6081069	
OO-765	Microbel CH-447	87503	
OO-766	Dynali Chickinox	040	
OO-767	Microbel CH-447	87501	
OO-768	Microbel CH-447	87502	
OO-769	Micronef Cosmos SC BI-FU	009	
OO-770	Micronef Cosmos	011	
OO-771	Microbel SC-330	86121	
OO-772	Dynali Chickinox Kot Kot	31014948	
OO-773	Dynali Chickinox Kot Kot	087	
OO-774	Dynali Chickinox Kot Kot	3950823	
OO-776	Centrair Parafan 1	41039	
OO-777	Weedhopper Europa II	7032300	
OO-778	Southdown Puma MS	87-5929	
OO-779	J-3 Kitten	242861	
OO-781	Microbel SL-503	86101	
OO-782	Microbel CH-377	87801	
OO-783	JC.31C Weedhopper	4040030	
OO-784	American Aircraft Falcon	0019	
OO-785	Fulmar Trident I	unkn	
OO-786	Dynali Chickinox Kot Kot	3102109	
OO-787	Rotec Rally 3B	65176	
OO-788	Dynali Chickinox	21045876	
OO-789	Dynali Chickinox Kot Kot	AAC-00	
OO-790	Solar Wings Pegasus XL-R	T-1287/87	
OO-791	Aerokart 4320	B83	
OO-792	Dynali Chickinox Kot Kot	3982423	
OO-793	Dynali Chickinox Kot Kot	3965960	
OO-794	Dynali Chickinox	21033455	
OO-795	Centrair Parafan 1	41035	
OO-796	Durondeau 447	M37711	
OO-797	American Aircraft Falcon	SM-016	
OO-798	American Aircraft Falcon XP	SMB01-PX	
OO-799	Micronef SC BI-FU	013	
OO-800	Micronef Cosmos	012	
OO-801	Fulmar Trident I	TT-82014	
OO-802	Dynali Chickinox Kot Kot	31035487	
OO-803	Dynali Chickinox Tandem	unkn	
OO-804	Cosmos Micronef	014	
OO-805	Cosmos Micronef Racer SX12	016	
OO-806	Dynali Chickinox Kot Kot	3109596	
OO-807	Microbel TD 1+1	88101	
OO-808	JC.24D Weedhopper	7071079	
OO-809	Aviasud Mistral 532	46	83-CR
OO-810	Microbel SC-330	83-101	
OO-811	Microbel Tandem 1+1	88-301	
OO-812	Dynali Chickinox Tandem	21008533	
OO-813	Aeronautic 2000 Baroudeur	28	
OO-814	Cosmos Bidulum	015	
OO-815	Cosmos Bidulum	017	
OO-816	Zodiac Ultrastar	unkn	
OO-817	Microbel SC-330	unkn	
OO-818	Aériane Sirocco	069	83-BN
OO-819	Air Création Safari GT-BI 462	unkn	
OO-820	Air Création Racer	019	
OO-821	Microbel SL-503	88402	
OO-823	Pterodactyl Ascender II	unkn	
OO-824	Microbel SC-447	88601	
OO-825	Dynali Chickinox Tandem	21176133	
OO-826	Dynali Chickinox Kot Kot	31075538	
OO-827	Dynali Chickinox Kot Kot	3115062	
OO-828	Solar Wings Pegasus XL-Q	SW-WQ-0072/SW-TB-1353	
OO-829	Aermas 386	03	
OO-830	Cosmos Bidulum	020	
OO-832	Aviasud Mistral 532	0388/57	WAE-57
OO-833	Croses Airplume	23	
OO-834	Dynali Chickinox Kot Kot	31138394	
OO-835	Dynali Chickinox Kot Kot	31099441	
OO-836	Dynali Chickinox Kot Kot	31111730	
OO-837	Centrair Parafan B1	43006	
OO-838	Centrair Parafan	43008	
OO-839	Fulmar Trident II	TR2-88109	
OO-840	Aviasud Mistral 532	58	WAE-58
OO-842	Centrair Parafan B1	43009	
OO-843	Air Création GT RO 503	021	
OO-844	Fulmar Tyger I	F-01	OO-513
OO-845	Dynali Chickinox Kot Kot	31177480	
OO-846	Dynali Chickinox Tandem	21060765	
OO-847	Microbel TD 1+1	88901	
OO-848	Dynali Chickinox Kot Kot	31100392	
OO-849	Solar Wings Pegasus Quasar XL-Q	SW-WQ-0085/SW-TE-0081	
OO-850	JC-24D Weedhopper D	4072016	
OO-851	Air Création	022	
OO-852	Manta Fledge	unkn	
OO-853	Air Création Racer SX12	023	
OO-854	Eipper Quicksilver MX-II	2426	
OO-855	Dynali Chickinox	31139873	
OO-856	Dynali Chickinox	31178826	
OO-857	Dynali Chickinox	31073464	
OO-858	Dynali Chickinox	31073596	
OO-859	H.M.14	001	
OO-860	Cosmos Micronef	025	
OO-861	Microbel	88903	
OO-862	Microbel TD 1+1	88121	
OO-863	Microbel TD 1+1	88122	
OO-864	Air Création GT BI RO 462	024	
OO-866	Air Création GT BI RO 462	026	
OO-867	Dynali Chickinox	31061478	
OO-868	Dynali Chickinox	31180952	
OO-870	Microbel TD 1+1	88111	
OO-871	Dynali Chickinox	31063736	
OO-872	Dynali Chickinox	21293226	
OO-873	Air Création GT BI RO 503-2	028	
OO-874	Air Création GT BI RO 503-2	027	
OO-875	Microbel TD 1+1	89031	
OO-876	Weedhopper Europa II	9022462	
OO-877	Dynali Chickinox	31227996	
OO-878	Weedhopper AX-2	9032466	
OO-879	Air Création GT BI 503-2	030	
OO-880	Micronef Cosmos BI RO 503-2	033	
OO-881	Air Création GT BI RO 503	029	
OO-882	Dynali Chickinox	31268256	
OO-883	Microbel	89041	
OO-884	Aviasud Mistral 532	02/89/73	
OO-885	Dynali Chickinox	31241592	
OO-886	Weedhopper Europa II	9022463	
OO-887	Microbel TD 1+1	89034	
OO-888	Dynali Chickinox	31089621	
OO-889	Dynali Chickinox	31063604	
OO-890	Zodiac Ultrastar (W/o 1.5.97)	118	
OO-891	JC.31C Weedhopper	5042102	
OO-892	Microbel Pendulaire	89090	
OO-893	Microbel	89091	
OO-894	Microbel TD 1+1	88801	
OO-895	Aviasud Mistral 532	079	
OO-896	Euronef ATTL-1	1	

Regn.	Type	C/n	Prev.Id.
OO-897	Fulmar	8200733	
OO-898	Dynali Chickinox	1601833	
OO-899	Microbel TD 1+1	89601	
OO-900	Dynali Chickinox	31203880	
OO-901	Air Création Racer SX12	031	
OO-902	Air Création Racer SX12	032	
OO-903	Air Création Racer SX12	034	
OO-904	Air Création GT BI RO 532	035	
OO-905	Microbel TD 1+1	89603	
OO-906	Microbel TD 1+1	89604	
OO-907	Weedhopper Europa II	99052501	
OO-908	Dynali Chickinox Kot Kot	31231072	
OO-909	Aériane Sirocco	B89/100	
OO-910	Microbel TD 1+1	89602	
OO-911	Weedhopper AX-2	9062508	
OO-912	Fulmar Tyger 1	90-2684	
OO-913	Zodiac Ultrastar	106	
OO-914	J-3 Kitten	242868	
OO-915	Air Création GT BI AR 500	043	
OO-916	Air Création GT BI SX 16	036	
OO-917	Air Création GT BI SX 16	038	
OO-918	Dynali Chickinox Kot Kot	31111598	
OO-919	Microbel TD 1+1	89-101	
OO-920	Dynali Chickinox Kot Kot	31312014	
OO-921	Microbel SL-447	89-901	
OO-922	Solar Wings Pegasus Quasar XL-Q	SW-WQ-0236/SW-TE-0221	
OO-923	Dynali Chickinox Kot Kot	31193069	
OO-924	Aviasud Mistral 532	098	
OO-925	Cosmos Bidulum	039	
OO-926	Microbel TD 1+1	89-111	
OO-927	Dynali Chickinox Tandem	21191987	
OO-928	Dynali Chickinox Kot Kot	31193624	
OO-929	Weedhopper AX-3	9092547	
OO-930	Solar Wings Pegasus Quasar XL-Q	SW-WQ-0254/SW-TE-0231	
OO-931	Dynali Chickinox Kot Kot	31244404	
OO-932	Dynali Chickinox Kot Kot	3120552	
OO-933	JC.31 Weedhopper	9112562	
OO-934	Kaiman 462 Cosmos	982807	
OO-935	Air Création Racer 447	041	
OO-936	Air Création Racer 447	042	
OO-937	Dynali Chickinox Kot Kot	31296821	
OO-938	Dynali Chickinox Kot Kot	31231890	
OO-939	Microbel TD 1+1	89121	
OO-940	JC.31 Weedhopper	9122578	
OO-941	Air Création Racer 447	045	
OO-942	Air Création Racer 447	050	
OO-943	Air Création GT BI	041	
OO-944	Air Création Racer 447	048	
OO-945	Air Création Racer 447	049	
OO-946	Air Création Racer 447	047	
OO-947	Cosmos Bidulum 50	B0294	
OO-948	Weedhopper AX-2	0022600	
OO-949	Dynali Chickinox Tandem	32112	
OO-950	Dynali Chickinox Tandem	37933	
OO-951	Dynali Chickinox	31245354	
OO-952	Weedhopper AX-3	0022604	
OO-953	Dynali Chickinox	3788844	
OO-954	Solar Wings Pegasus Quasar XL-Q	SW-WQ-0300	
	(C/n refers to wing only, trike unit type and c/n unidentified)		
OO-955	Dynali Chickinox	328776	
OO-956	Dynali Chickinox Tandem	31296821	
OO-957	Microbel TD 1+1	90501	
OO-958	Solar Wings Pegasus Quasar	SW-WQQ-0310/SW-TQ-0003	
OO-959	Aériane Sirocco	B-90041	
OO-960	Microbel TD 1+1	90502	
OO-961	Weedhopper AX-3	0062662	
OO-962	Microbel TD 1+1	90601	
OO-963	Microbel TD 1+1	90602	
OO-965	Air Création GT BI	052	
OO-966	Eipper Quicksilver MX-II	2436	
OO-967	Eipper Quicksilver MX-II	2437	
OO-968	Dynali Chickinox	241712	

Regn.	Type	C/n	Prev.Id.
OO-969	Dynali Chickinox	369327	
OO-970	Mignet HM.14	02	OO-123 OO-970
OO-971	Microbel TD 1+1	90801	
OO-972	Dynali Chickinox	21205319	
OO-973	Dynali Chickinox	356826	
OO-974	Dynali Chickinox	3119342	
OO-975	Air Création GT BI 582-ES	055	
OO-976	Air Création Cosmos BI 503-2E	051	
OO-977	Air Création GT BI 502-2E	054	
OO-978	Weedhopper AX-2	0042643	
OO-979	Dynali Chickinox	344537	
OO-981	Dynali Chickinox	384282	
OO-982	Dynali Chickinox	370554	
OO-983	Eipper Quicksilver MX-II	2438	
OO-984	Solar Wings Pegasus XL-Q	SW-WQ-0010/SW-TE-0036	G-MTTV
OO-985	Microbel TD 1+1	90-1001	
OO-986	Microbel TD 1+1	90-1002	
OO-987	Weedhopper AX-2	9032465	
OO-988	Dynali Chickinox	345237	
OO-989	Microbel XL TD 1+1	90-1003	
OO-990	Dynali Chickinox	344405	
OO-991	Dynali Chickinox	3110168	
OO-992	Microbel TD 1+1	90-1101	
OO-993	Eipper Quicksilver MXL-II	178	
OO-994	Air Création GT BI 582-ES	053	
OO-995	Air Création GT BI 503-2	056	
OO-996	Weedhopper AX-2	0102821	
OO-997	Weedhopper Europa II	0112839	
OO-998	Aériane Sirocco	90-101	
	(Possibly sold as PH-1Z2 which is c/n 89-101 ?)		
OO-999	Weedhopper AX-2	0092801	
OO-A01	Solar Wings Pegasus XL-R	SW-WA-1343/SW-TB-1356	G-MVBX
OO-A02	CFM Shadow Series CD	155CD	
OO-A03	Eipper Quicksilver MX-IIHP	5004	
OO-A04	Micronef Cosmos BI RO	059	
OO-A05	Aviasud Mistral	0142	
OO-A06	Dynali Chickinox	319454	
OO-A07	Aériane Sirocco	87	
OO-A08	Dynali Chickinox	32521332	
OO-A09	Air Création Safari GT BI	unkn	
OO-A10	Aviasud Mistral	141	
OO-A11	Air Création GT BI 582-ES	060	
OO-A12	Air Création Racer 503-1	058	
OO-A14	Microbel	91/0502	
OO-A15	Micronef Cosmos	8579	
OO-A16	Air Création GT BI 582-ES	062	
OO-A17	Dynali Chickinox	912053738	
OO-A18	Rans S-12 Airaile	10090027	
OO-A19	Aviasud Mistral	148	
OO-A20	Dynali Chickinox	2391872	
OO-A21	Fulmar	341406	
OO-A22	Kolb Firestar	unkn	
OO-A23	CFM Streak Shadow	K103	
OO-A24	Dynali Chickinox	3191874	
OO-A25	Cosmos Bidulum 447	8667	
OO-A26	Microbel TS 1+1	91/0901	
OO-A27	Micronef SC BI RO 503	603	
OO-A28	Dynali Chickinox	3391879	
OO-A30	Air Création GT BI 582-ES	064	
OO-A31	Air Création GT BI 582-ES	065	
OO-A32	Dynali Chickinox	21109064	
OO-A33	Dynali Chickinox	358001	
OO-A34	Air Création GT BI 503S	066	
OO-A35	Aviasud Mistral	0156	
OO-A36	Aviasud Mistral	0155	
OO-A37	Micronef Cosmos 503-1	068	
OO-A38	Air Création GT BI	070	
OO-A39	Microbel TD 1+1	910501	
OO-A40	Dynali Chickinox	0792889	
OO-A41	Dynali Chickinox	0792890	
OO-A43	Dynali Chickinox	3891B84	
OO-A44	Air Création GT BI 503S	069	
OO-A45	Micronef Cosmos BI 582-2S	071	

Regn.	Type	C/n	Prev.Id.
OO-A46	HM.1000 Balèrit	HM.1000/52	
OO-A47	Microbel TD 1+1	92/0401	
OO-A48	Dynali Chickinox	3591B78	
OO-A50	HM.1000 Balèrit	69	
OO-A51	Racer SX2-503S	072	
OO-A53	Rans S-6 Coyote II *(Also flies as 59-QM)*	1091222	
OO-A54	Rans S-12 Airaile	0991126	N61ME?
OO-A55	Merlin Stoll	A0006	
OO-A56	Weedhopper AX-3	B1032881	
OO-A57	Dynali Chickinox	1792892	
OO-A58	Dynali Chickinox	3980021	
OO-A59	Dynali Chickinox	393240	
OO-A60	Rans S-6 Coyote II *(Now/also 59-NK)*	0891214	
OO-A61	Dynali Chickinox Kot-Kot	0492885	
OO-A63	Eipper Quicksilver MX-II Sprint	323	
OO-A64	CFM Shadow Series CD	189CD	
OO-A65	Air Création GT BI 582ES	073	
OO-A66	Rans S-6 Coyote II ESD	0292271	
OO-A67	Cosmos Trike	0791241	
OO-A68	Air Création GT BI 582ES	074	
OO-A69	Dynali Chickinox	2692B99	
OO-A70	Air Création Safari GT BI 503	075	
OO-A71	Weedhopper AX-3	B2043009	
OO-A72	Dynali Chickinox	2592B98	
OO-A73	Air Création Racer 447	079	
OO-A74	Dynali Chickinox	2692B96	
OO-A75	Air Création Safari GT BI 503S	081	
OO-A76	Air Création Safari GT BI 582	078	
OO-A77	Air Création Safari GT BI 503S	076	
OO-A78	Air Création Racer 447	077	
OO-A79	Solar Wings Pegasus Quasar II.TC		
		SW-WQT-0548/SW-TQD-0109	
OO-A81	Mignet HM.1000 Balèrit	72	
OO-A82	Air Création Safari GT BI 503S	080	
OO-A83	Dynali Chickinox	0392F92	
OO-A84	Dynali Chickinox	4092B105	
OO-A85	Cosmos BI II	B971	
OO-A86	Cosmos BI II 582	B983	
OO-A87	Dynali Chickinox	5092B110	
OO-A88	Weedhopper AX2-503	B1032886	
OO-A89	Mignet HM.1000 Balèrit	75	
OO-A90	Air Création GT BI	082	
OO-A91	Dynali Chickinox	5092B109	
OO-A92	Minimax 1500	610	
OO-A93	Dynali Chickinox	2491B71	
OO-A94	Air Création Racer SX 12	3909789	PH-2F9
OO-A95	CFM Shadow Series CD	200CD	
OO-A96	Dynali Chickinox	4192B106	
OO-A97	Air Création GT BI 503	084	
OO-A98	Rans S-6 Coyote II ESD	Co 93/0201	
OO-A99	Dynali Chickinox	4792B111	
OO-B01	Eipper Quicksilver GT-500	202	
OO-B02	Mignet HM.1000 Balèrit	76	
OO-B03	Dynali Chickinox	D3079B00114	
OO-B04	Dynali Chickinox Kot-Kot	4092B103	
OO-B05	Pendulaire Quasar QII 582	"93/0401"	
	(Possibly c/n SW-WQQ-0528/SW-TQD-0128)		
OO-B06	Weedhopper AX-3	C3023096	
OO-B07	Murphy Renegade Spirit	unkn	68-EB
OO-B09	Dynali Chickinox	312131341	
OO-B12	Weedhopper JC-31	4010018	
OO-B13	Air Création GT BI 582S	086	
OO-B14	Rans S-5 Coyote I	92191	
OO-B15	Microbel SC-447	921101	
OO-B16	Eipper Quicksilver MX-IIHP	5006	
OO-B17	Weedhopper AX-3	C3033098	
OO-B18	Rans S-6ESD Coyote II	1292413	
OO-B19	Rans S-6ESD Coyote II	1192394	
OO-B20	Dynali Chickinox	1693B121	
OO-B21	Cosmos Phase II	978	
OO-B22	Rans S-12 Airaile	1192321	
OO-B23	Air Création GT BI 503-2	085	
OO-B24	Quasar Q II	930601	
OO-B25	Microbel Q II	930401	
OO-B26	Microbel TD 1+1	920801	

Regn.	Type	C/n	Prev.Id.
OO-B27	Rans S-6 Coyote II	1092370	
OO-B28	Zenair CH-701 STOL	7-2012	
OO-B29	American Aircraft Falcon	018	
OO-B30	Weedhopper AX-3	C3063118	
OO-B31	Solar Wings Pegasus Q-462	93/0701	
OO-B32	Rans S-6ES Coyote II	1192382	
OO-B33	Rans S-6ES Coyote II	0393456	
OO-B34	Zenair CH-701 STOL	7-2014	
OO-B35	Rans S-6ES Coyote II	0393461	
OO-B36	Weedhopper AX-3	C3073127	
OO-B37	Rans S-6ES Coyote II	1192391	
OO-B38	Dynali Chickinox	1693B117	
OO-B39	CFM Shadow Series CD	K216	
OO-B40	Air Création GT BI 582S	087	
OO-B41	Air Création GT BI 582S	088	
OO-B43	Rans S-6ESD Coyote II	1192390	
OO-B44	Air Création SX2 Racer 503S	083	
OO-B45	Aviasud Albatros 522	008	
OO-B46	Dynali Chickinox Kot-Kot	3393B123	
OO-B48	Rans S-6ESD Coyote II	0793518	
OO-B49	Dynali Chickinox	3692B102	
OO-B50	Weedhopper JC.31D-BI	4072020	
OO-B51	Air Création GT BI 503-S	089	
OO-B52	Aviasud Mistral	194	
OO-B53	Air Création GT BI 582-S	092	
OO-B54	Weedhopper AX3/503	C3093150	
OO-B55	Air Création GT BI 582S	094	
OO-B56	Dynali Chickinox	3792B100	
OO-B57	Weedhopper AX-3	C3113172	
OO-B58	Weedhopper AX-3	C3113171	
OO-B59	UltraCraft Calypso	001	
OO-B60	Weedhopper AX3-503	C3113170	
OO-B61	Dynali Chickinox Kot Kot	4793B127	
OO-B62	Aviasud Mistral 582	199	
OO-B63	Weedhopper AX-3	C3113182	
OO-B64	Rans S-4 Coyote I	93204	
OO-B65	Air Création GT BI 582S	093	
OO-B66	Rans S-6ES Coyote II	0993534	
OO-B67	Zenair CH-701 STOL	003	
OO-B68	Pegasus Quantum	6782	
OO-B69	Rans S-6ES Coyote II	0394601	
OO-B70	Aviasud Mistral 582	201	
OO-B71	Noble Hardman Snowbird Mk.IV	SB-008	G-MTXV
OO-B72	Air Création GT BI 503S	095	
OO-B73	Cosmos BI 503-2	096	
OO-B74	CFM Shadow Series CD	K219/1	
OO-B75	Air Création GT BI 582S XP	097	
OO-B76	Minimax 1600	779	
OO-B77	CFM Shadow Series CD	K229/CD	
OO-B78	CFM Shadow Series CD	247/1	
OO-B79	Air Création 582S	098	
OO-B80	Air Création GT BI 503S	099	
OO-B81	Dynali Chickinox	2992P6	
OO-B82	Rans S-6 Coyote II	0294586	
OO-B83	Weedhopper AX-3	C3103164	
OO-B84	Rans S-6ES Coyote II	0594619	
OO-B86	Aviasud Mistral	0686/012	D-MTIF
OO-B87	Rans S-6ES Coyote II	0393468	
OO-B88	Dynali Chickinox *(Crashed 8.99)*	2391F73	
OO-B89	Solar Wings Pegasus Quantum 15	6794	
OO-B90	Rans S-5 Coyote I	93194	
OO-B91	Air Création GT BI 503S	100	
OO-B92	Air Création Racer 337 Fun 14	101	
OO-B93	Dynali Chickinox	3891B82	
OO-B94	CFM Shadow Series CD	K226/1	
OO-B95	Rans S-6ES Coyote II	0594621	
OO-B96	Weedhopper 55ES Europa II	8022383	
OO-B97	Cosmos Phase II	B913	
OO-B98	Rans S-6 Coyote II	0994673	
OO-B99	Rans S-6ES Coyote II	1194685	
OO-C01	Rans S-6ES Coyote II	0994674	
OO-C02	Rans S-6ES Coyote II	0195725	
OO-C03	Microbel Q TD 1+1	950101	
OO-C04	Microbel Bandit TD 1+1	950301	
OO-C05	Air Création GT BI 503-S	102	

Regn.	Type	C/n	Prev.Id.
OO-C07	Weedhopper AX-3	B3023097	
OO-C08	Rans S-6ES Coyote II-582	0295737	
OO-C09	Cosmos Phase II Chronos 16M	21078	
OO-C10	Aviasud Mistral	55	55-DC
OO-C11	Rans S-6ES Coyote II	0395780	
OO-C12	Rans S-6ES Coyote II	0595816	
OO-C13	Rans S-6ES Coyote II	0595822	
OO-C15	Eipper Quicksilver GT-500	0123	
OO-C16	Racer Fun 14	105	
OO-C17	Rans S-6ES Coyote II-582TD	0595821	
OO-C18	Weedhopper AX-3	0082792	
OO-C20	Weedhopper Europa II	9022464	
OO-C21	Rans S-6ES Coyote II	1195892	
OO-C22	Aviasud Mistral	195	D-MNAT
	(Still shown as current in Germany)		
OO-C23	Air Création Clipper 582-SXP 15	104	
OO-C24	Air Création Clipper 582-SXP 15	106	
OO-C25	Mainair Kolb Twinstar 3	Kit 0021	
OO-C26	Air Création GTE 582S Mild	109	
OO-C27	Aviasud Mistral	184	D-MBTH
OO-C28	Cosmos BI 90	964	PH-2M7
OO-C29	Rans S-6ES Coyote II	46545051	
OO-C30	TEAM Minimax 1500R	854	
OO-C31	Rans S-6ES Coyote II	0496976	
OO-C32	TEAM Minimax 1100	1552P	
OO-C33	CFM Streak Shadow	K267CD	
OO-C34	Cosmos Phase II 582	B-21165	
OO-C35	Rans S-6ESD Coyote IITD	0496981	
OO-C36	Air Création GTE-503S XP	108	
OO-C37	Air Création GTE-503S Mild	110	
OO-C38	Air Création GTE-582S Clipper	114	
OO-C39	Rans S-6ES Coyote IIXL	0396955	
OO-C40	Air Création GTE-503S	111	
OO-C41	Air Création GTE-503S Mild	112	
OO-C42	Rans S-6ES Coyote II	07961017	
OO-C43	Rans S-6 Coyote II	0596994	
OO-C44	Mainair Blade 582	1099-1096-7-W902	
OO-C45	Microbel TD 1+1	960301	
OO-C46	Rans S-6ES Coyote II	09961037	
OO-C48	Air Création GTE 582-S XP15	119	
OO-C49	Dynali Chickinox Tandem	1993B115	
OO-C50	Pegasus Quantum 582	7294	
OO-C51	CFM Shadow Series CD	K285/1	
OO-C52	Rans S-6 Coyote II	02971090	
OO-C54	Rans S-6ES Coyote II	08961029	
OO-C55	Rans S-6ES Coyote II	0696996	
OO-C56	UltraCraft Calypso	002	
OO-C57	Air Création GTE 503-S	122	
OO-C58	Air Création GTE 582-S	115	
OO-C60	Rans S-6ES Coyote II	01971087	
OO-C61	Air Création GTE 503-SL Mild	123	
OO-C62	Air Création GTE 503S	126	
OO-C63	Air Création GTE 582S Clipper	125	
OO-C64	Air Création GTE 582S XP-15	128	
OO-C65	Murphy Renegade Spirit	R583	
OO-C66	Dynali Chickinox Tandem	2692B962	
OO-C67	Rans S-5 Coyote I	089111	OO-C53 LX-XJS
OO-C68	UltraCraft Calypso 1A	003	
OO-C69	Air Création GTE 503S	130	
OO-C70	Air Création Safari GT 1+1	unkn	
OO-C71	Rans S-6ES Coyote II	0295752ES	47-HY
OO-C72	Zenair CH-701 STOL	7-2886	59-SN
OO-C73	Air Création GTE 503S	132	
OO-C74	Paramotor Solo 210	unkn	
OO-C75	Pegasus Quantum 15	7089	
OO-C76	JC.24D Weedhopper D	10.1138	PH-1F9
OO-C77	UltraCraft Calypso	007	
OO-C78	Rans S-6ESCoyote II	08961030	
OO-C79	Adventure F3	L1906	
OO-C80	Adventure Z4	8261	
OO-C81	Adventure F3	L1926	
OO-C82	Adventure F3	N2046	
OO-C83	Adventure F3	N2004	
OO-C84	Adventure F3	N2042	

Regn.	Type	C/n	Prev.Id.
OO-C85	Adventure F3	N2041	
OO-C86	Adventure F3	N2003	
OO-C87	Adventure F3	1641	
OO-C88	Adventure F3	1611	
OO-C89	Murphy Maverick	97	
OO-C90	TEAM Minimax 1600	967	
OO-C91	Adventure F3	2018N	
OO-C92	Adventure F3	Q2193	
OO-C93	Adventure F3	02148	
OO-C94	Adventure F3	2168	
OO-C95	Adventure F3	1959	
OO-C96	Adventure F3	2017N	
OO-C97	Air Création Micronef GTE	135	
OO-C98	Air Création GTE	136	
OO-C99	Air Création GTE	133	
OO-D01	Air Création Micronef GT BI	137	

A number of French registered microlights based in Belgium have been noted using radio call-signs with a Belgian OQ- prefix. Known examples are as follows and, as usual, additions would be gratefully received.

OQ-AXH	Rans S-6 Coyote II		also 59-TN
OQ-AYW	Rans S-6 Coyote II		also 59-PV

OY - DENMARK

Regn.	Type	C/n	Prev.ld.
OY-AAC	S.A.I. KZ-III U-2	108	
OY-AAD	S.A.I. KZ-VII U-4 Laerke	157	
OY-AAM	Piper PA-22-125 Tri-Pacer	22-113	SE-CLU
			EI-AJU
			XB-NOU
			N811A
OY-AAU	S.A.I. KZ-VII U-4 Laerke	158	
OY-AAV	S.A.I. KZ-VII U-4 Laerke	160	D-EHED
			OY-AAV
OY-AAZ	S.A.I. KZ-VII U-4 Laerke	165	
OY-ABF	S.A.I. KZ-VII U-4 Laerke	164	
OY-ABG	S.A.I. KZ-VII U-4 Laerke	167	
OY-ABJ	Piper PA-22-150 Caribbean	22-6918	
OY-ABL	S.A.I. KZ-VII U-4 Laerke	171	D-EABE
			OY-ABL
OY-ABM	S.A.I. KZ-VII U-4 Laerke	172	D-EFIF(2)
			OY-ABM
			ZS-BXX
			OY-ABM
OY-ABT	Piper J-3F-50 Cub	2475	
OY-ABY	Auster J/2 Arrow	2355	D-EGIL
			OY-ABY
OY-ACG	S.A.I. KZ-III U	51	RDAF:612
			RDAF:51
OY-ACH	S.A.I. KZ-VII U-7 Laerke	200	
OY-ACO	S.A.I. KZ-VII U-4 Laerke	166	
OY-ACS	Piper PA-22-108 Colt	22-9116	(SE-CRY)
OY-ACW	Piper PA-22-150 Caribbean	22-7538	G-ARHO
			N3643Z
OY-ADR	Mooney M.20A	1532	N8354E
OY-ADW	Cessna 172B	48072	(N7572X)
OY-AEA	S.A.I. KZ-II Coupé	27	OH-KZT
			OH-SPJ
			SE-ANR
			(OY-DUY)
OY-AFD	Piper PA-22-108 Colt	22-9388	LN-IKM
OY-AFH	Morane-Saulnier MS.885 Super Rallye	11	
OY-AFP	Cessna 172D	47957	SE-CXG
			N7457X
OY-AFT	Piper PA-22-108 Colt	22-8284	
OY-AFV	Cessna 172C	49168	N1468Y
OY-AFW	Piper/Taylor J-2 Cub	S.559	SE-AEW
OY-AGB	Reims/Cessna F.172H	0527	
OY-AGF	Reims/Cessna F.172H	0552	
OY-AGG	Reims/Cessna F.172H	0539	(SE-FMP)
OY-AGH	Reims/Cessna F.172H	0485	
OY-AGI	Reims/Cessna F.150H	0327	
OY-AGL	Reims/Cessna F.172H	0589	
OY-AGW	Reims/Cessna F.172M	1131	
OY-AHD	Reims/Cessna F.172H	0473	
OY-AHF	Reims/Cessna F.172H	0434	
OY-AHM	Reims/Cessna F.150H	0316	
OY-AHW	Reims/Cessna F.172H	0513	
OY-AHY	Reims/Cessna F.172H	0494	
OY-AIE	Scintex Piel CP.301C-1 Emeraude	555	
OY-AIH	Messerschmitt Bf.108 Taifun	1561	F-BBRH
			Luftwaffe
OY-AIK	Piper PA-23-180 Apache	23-1759	OH-PNU
			OY-AIK
			N4260P
OY-AIN	Piper PA-20 Pacer 125	20-42	VP-KIR
			ZS-DDU
OY-AJI	Piper PA-34-200 Seneca	34-7250312	SE-FND
			N1413T
OY-AJJ	SOCATA MS.880B Rallye Club	3031	
OY-AJL	Cessna 172N	69173	N734WM
OY-AJM	Reims/Cessna F.172N	1682	(D-EIIC)
OY-AJN	SOCATA MS.893E Rallye 180GT Gaillard	13087	
	(Dam. 20.11.96)		
OY-AJS	Piper PA-18-150 Super Cub	18-8280	PH-NKG
	(Written-off 15.5.83)		N7157Z
OY-AJU	Reims/Cessna F.150L	0673	D-EKNC
			PH-GKG

Regn.	Type	C/n	Prev.ld.
OY-AKE	Reims/Cessna FA.150L Aerobat	0100	
OY-AKG	Cessna 182N Skylane	60163	N92342
OY-AKH	Reims/Cessna F.172K	0775	
OY-AKM	Piper PA-16 Clipper	16-101	D-EKUW
			N9979F
			HB-OOE
OY-AKP	Cessna 337D Skymaster	1076	(G-AWYD)
			N86095
OY-AKR	Reims/Cessna F.172L	0817	
OY-AKT	Reims/Cessna F.172H	0532	D-EMTG
OY-AKY	Reims/Cessna F.172L	0819	
OY-ALA	Aeronca 7AC Champion	1024	N9120U
			G-TINE
			(OY-ALA)
			D-EBGF(2)
			N82391
OY-ALB	Piper PA-18 Super Cub 95	18-1355	D-EFCZ
			ALAT
			51-15355
OY-ALC	Piper PA-12 Super Cruiser	12-2838	D-ELEB
			N3950M
			NC3950M
OY-ALD	DHC-1 Chipmunk 22	C1/0902	RDAF: P-147
OY-ALF	Piper J-3C-65 Cub	12591	D-EGAR
			HB-OBR
			44-80295
OY-ALJ	Piper PA-18-150 Super Cub	18-8220	PH-NKF
OY-ALL	DHC-1 Chipmunk 22	C1/0881	RDAF: P-142
OY-ALM	Piper J-3C-65 Cub	8766	D-EMOG
			OO-AAH
			42-36642
OY-ALO	Piper PA-14 Family Cruiser	14-192	D-EMOB
			SL-AAH
			F-BFFC
OY-ALR	Piper J-3C-65 Cub	12987	D-EDMA
			D-ECYC
			HB-OCL
			44-80691
OY-ALW	Miles M.28 Mercury 6	6268	D-EHAB
			G-AHAA
OY-ALZ	DHC-1 Chipmunk 22	C1/0067	RDAF: P-121
OY-AME	Jodel D.112 Club	1152	
OY-AMG	Druine D.31 Turbulent	274	
OY-AMJ	Druine D.31 Turbulent	1	
OY-AMO	Jodel D.112 Club	956	
OY-AMR	Druine D.31 Turbulent	282	
OY-AMS	Druine D.31 Turbulent	1	
OY-ANF	Piper J-3C-65 Cub	13052	D-EFPE
			(D-EGPI)
			OE-AAR
			(D-EDYR)
			44-80756
OY-ANG	Reims/Cessna F.172M	1232	
OY-ANH	Reims/Cessna F.172M	1224	(OY-RYZ)
OY-ANS	SOCATA MS.893A Rallye Commodore 180	11891	SE-FSH
OY-AOL	S.A.I. KZ-X Mk II	205	OY-ACL
OY-AOW	Beech 23 Musketeer	M-14	(SE-EDE)
OY-AOZ	Beech 23 Musketeer	M-446	
OY-APC	Boeing 737-5L9	28129	
OY-APD	Boeing 737-5L9	28130	
OY-APG	Boeing 737-5L9	28131	
OY-APH	Boeing 737-5L9	28721	
OY-API	Boeing 737-5L9	28722	
OY-APK	Boeing 737-5L9	28995	
OY-APL	Boeing 737-5L9	28996	
OY-APM	Canadair CL.600-2B16 Challenger	5153	N604BA
			VR-CHA
			N601EB
			C-GLXH
OY-APN	Boeing 737-5L9	28997	
OY-APP(2)	Boeing 737-5L9	29234	
OY-APR	Boeing 737-5L9	29235	N1786B
OY-ARJ	Cessna 414	0614	D-IAWM
			N69397

Regn.	Type	C/n	Prev.Id.
OY-ARL	Cessna 182P (Reims assembled)	0028/63958	D-EATU
			N9938E
OY-ARV	Mitsubishi MU-2B-35	635	LN-MTU
	(Sold to Spain 4.97)		OY-ARV
			N485AH
			XA-DID
			N485MA
OY-ARY	Grumman AA-IA Trainer	0420	SE-FTU
			(N6220L)
OY-ASJ	Beech D95A Travel Air	TD-541	SE-EEX
			OY-DCM
OY-ASM	Reims/Cessna F.172M	1316	
OY-ASW	Piper PA-34-200T Seneca II	34-7670105	D-ILBI
			N7843C
OY-ASY	Embraer EMB.110P1 Bandeirante	110-308	EI- BPI
			OY-ASY
			PT-SCO
OY-ATC	Reims/Cessna F.172L	0853	D-ECSB
OY-ATD	DHC-1 Chipmunk 22	C1/0891	RDAF: P-145
OY-ATE	DHC-1 Chipmunk 22	C1/0885	RDAF: P-144
OY-ATF(2)	DHC-1 Chipmunk 22 *(Reservation)*		
	(Presumably replacement for OY-ATF c/n C1/0787 damaged 29.7.97)		
OY-ATI	S.A.I. KZ-VII Laerke	178	RDAF: 0-616
			RDAF: 63-616
OY-ATJ	S.A.I. KZ-VII Laerke	186	RDAF: 0-623
			RDAF: 63-623
OY-ATL	DHC-1 Chipmunk 22	C1/0897	RDAF: P-146
OY-ATM	S.A.I. KZ-VII Laerke	181	RDAF: 0-619
			RDAF: 63-619
OY-ATO	DHC-1 Chipmunk 22	C1/0108	RDAF: P-129
OY-ATR	DHC-1 Chipmunk 22	C1/0802	RDAF: P-140
OY-ATT	Piper PA-28-180 Cherokee Challenger	28-7305118	G-BASF
			N11C
OY-ATY	DHC-6 Twin Otter 300	561	C-GRZH-X
OY-AUH	Piper PA-31-310 Navajo	31-7512072	LN-PAB
			(SE-GLI)
OY-AUN	Piper PA-28-181 Archer II	28-8090021	N2974L
OY-AUR	SOCATA Rallye 235C	13261	N354RA
OY-AUS	Piper PA-31-310 Navajo	31-647	LN-KCM
			N6741L
OY-AUU	Cessna 172L	59274	LN-BGF
			N7574G
OY-AUW	SOCATA MS.893E Rallye 180GT Gaillard	13085	F-GBCE
OY-AUY	Auster J/1 Autocrat	2241	D-EJSA
			OE-AAH
			G-AJAI
			44-80537
OY-AVC	Piper J-3C-65 Cub	12833	D-EBES
OY-AVF	DHC-1 Chipmunk 22	C1/0794	RDAF: P-139
OY-AVG	Piper J-4 Cub Coupé	4-441	D-EDED
			G-AFPP
OY-AVH(2)	S.A.I. KZ-VII U-8	183	RDAF: 0-621
			RDAF: 63-621
OY-AVK	S.A.I. KZ-VII Laerke U-8	197	D-ENIM
			LX-AIT
OY-AVL	DHC-1 Chipmunk 22	C1/0107	RDAF: P-128
OY-AVN	Aeronca 11AC Chief	1601	D-EKUD
			HB-UPK
			D-ECAB
			N9953F
			LX-AID
OY-AVR	S.A.I. KZ-VII	176	RDAF: 0-615
			RDAF: 63-615
OY-AVT	Piper PA-18 Super Cub 95	18-3202	D-ELFT
			OL-L05
			L-128
			53-4802
OY-AVU	Piper PA-12 Super Cruiser	12-1272	D-ELKE
			N2835M
OY-AVV	Beagle A.61 Terrier 2	B.612	D-EBMU
			(D-ECKO)
			G-ASBT
			WE603

Regn.	Type	C/n	Prev.Id.
OY-AVY	Auster Mk.5	1400	D-EJON
			PH-NEG
			PH-NAD
			G-AJYH
			TJ352
OY-AVZ	Bücker Bü.181B Bestmann	25073	D-ELET
			Fv25073
OY-AYA	American AA-1 Yankee	0411	
OY-AYF	American AA-1 Yankee	0446	SE-INF
			OY-AYF
			(N6246L)
OY-AYI	American AA-1 Yankee	0449	SE-FTL
			OY-AYI
			SE-FTL
			(N6249L)
OY-AYL	Grumman-American AA-5 Traveler	0021	
OY-AYM	Grumman-American AA-5 Traveler	0020	
OY-AYN	Grumman-American AA-1B Trainer 2	0311	
OY-AYP	Grumman-American AA-5 Traveler	0359	(N5459L)
OY-AYR	Grumman-American AA-5 Traveler	0360	(N5460L)
OY-AYS	Grumman-American AA-5 Traveler	0420	(N7120L)
OY-AYW	Grumman-American AA-5 Traveler	0264	
OY-AYY	Grumman-American AA-5 Traveler	0265	
OY-AYZ	Grumman-American AA-5 Traveler	0361	(N5461L)
OY-AZB	Reims/Cessna F.172N	1657	
OY-AZC	Reims/Cessna F.150L	0683	PH-EHD
OY-AZD	Reims/Cessna F.150L	1078	PH-GDR
OY-AZE	Reims/Cessna F.172N	1021	PH-SMH
OY-AZH	Reims/Cessna F.172E	0058	PH-LZE
	(Written-off 10.8.92)		D-ELZE
OY-AZK	Reims/Cessna F.172M	1072	PH-ADF
OY-AZM	Reims/Cessna F.172N	1718	PH-AXA(2)
OY-AZR	Piper PA-18 Super Cub 95	18-3151	Y-652
			66-652
			L-89
			53-4751
OY-AZU	Robin DR.400/160 Chevalier	1144	LN-BEZ
OY-AZZ	Piper PA-18-135 Super Cub	18-3165	RDAF:Y-654
			RDAF:66-654
			OL-L91
			53-4765
OY-BAB	Piper PA-28-235 Cherokee	28-10143	N8628W
OY-BAF	Piper PA-28-140 Cherokee	28-20680	
OY-BAG	Piper PA-28-235 Cherokee	28-10640	LN-BEC
			OY-BAG
OY-BAR	Piper PA-22-160 Tri-Pacer	22-6476	D-EJBA
			N9559D
OY-BAZ	Piper PA-28-180 Cherokee C	28-2497	
OY-BBA	Piper PA-28-140 Cherokee	28-21160	
OY-BBB	Piper PA-28-180 Cherokee C	28-2589	(SE-EPH)
OY-BBC	Piper PA-28-140 Cherokee	28-21145	
OY-BBD	Piper PA-28-140 Cherokee	28-20972	(SE-EOF)
OY-BBE	Piper PA-28-140 Cherokee	28-20987	(SE-EPL)
OY-BBI	Piper PA-28-140 Cherokee	28-21451	
OY-BBJ	Piper PA-28-180 Cherokee C	28-3205	(SE-EYP)
OY-BBK	Piper PA-28-140 Cherokee	28-21064	
OY-BBM	Piper PA-28-140 Cherokee	28-22412	(SE-EPP)
OY-BBN	Piper PA-28-140 Cherokee	28-22502	(SE-EPH)
OY-BBP	Piper PA-23-250 Aztec C	27-3038	
OY-BBR	Piper PA-28-140 Cherokee	28-22877	
	(Damaged 20.8.95)		
OY-BBS	Piper PA-28-180 Cherokee C	28-4209	
OY-BBT	Piper PA-28-180 Cherokee C	28-3487	
OY-BBV	Piper PA-28-140 Cherokee	28-22977	
OY-BBW	Piper PA-28-180 Cherokee C	28-2737	
OY-BBY	Piper PA-28-180 Cherokee C	28-3663	
OY-BCA	Piper PA-28-180 Cherokee C	28-3971	
OY-BCB	Piper PA-28-140 Cherokee	28-22942	
OY-BCF	Piper PA-28-140 Cherokee	28-22842	
OY-BCG	Piper PA-28-180 Cherokee C	28-3966	
OY-BCK	Piper PA-28-140 Cherokee	28-22997	N560W
			OY-BCK
			N9560W
OY-BCL	Piper PA-28R-180 Cherokee Arrow	28R-30156	
OY-BCP	Piper PA-28-140 Cherokee	28-23391	N9872W

Regn.	Type	C/n	Prev.Id.
OY-BCR	Piper PA-32-260 Cherokee Six	32-838	N3892W
OY-BCU	Piper PA-28-180 Cherokee D	28-4814	
OY-BCY	Piper PA-28-140 Cherokee	28-24406	
OY-BDC	Piper PA-28R-200 Cherokee Arrow	28R-35313	(OY-BDG)
OY-BDF	Piper PA-28-140 Cherokee B *(Dbr 1.8.98)*	28-26074	
OY-BDG	Piper PA-28-180 Cherokee D	28-5456	
OY-BDI	Piper PA-28R-180 Cherokee Arrow	28R-31079	
OY-BDP	Piper PA-23-250 Aztec D	27-4527	
OY-BDU	Piper PA-28-140 Cherokee E	28-7225140	
OY-BDV	Piper PA-28R-200 Cherokee Arrow II	28R-7235068	
OY-BDW	Piper PA-23-250 Aztec D	27-4112	N6778Y
OY-BDY	Piper PA-28-140 Cherokee E	28-7225343	
OY-BED	Beech 76 Duchess	ME-352	EI-BHS
OY-BEF	Piper PA-23-250 Aztec F	27-7654185	LN-NAX
			N62734
OY-BEI	Reims/Cessna F.177RG Cardinal RG	0125	LN-ASZ
			N94721
OY-BFE	Cessna 182P Skylane	62478	SE-GXZ
			OY-BFE
			N52243
OY-BFI	Reims/Cessna F.172M	1079	
OY-BFK	Reims/Cessna F.172M	1094	
OY-BFL	Cessna 182P Skylane	61610	N21399
OY-BFM	Reims/Cessna F.172M	1096	
OY-BFO	Reims/Cessna FR.172J Rocket	0479	
OY-BFP	Reims/Cessna F.172M	1104	
OY-BFS	Piper PA-28-140 Cherokee	28-24371	SE-EYK
OY-BFV	Reims/Cessna F.172M	0942	(OY-RYV)
OY-BFW	Reims/Cessna F.172M	0997	
OY-BFY	Reims/Cessna F.172M	1142	
OY-BGB	Piper PA-28-140 Cherokee E	28-7225285	(SE-FYZ)
OY-BGC	Piper PA-28-180 Cherokee Challenger	28-7305290	
OY-BGI	Piper PA-34-200 Seneca	34-7250260	(SE-GAI)
OY-BGN	Piper PA-28-140 Cherokee	28-7425151	
OY-BGP	Piper PA-28R-200 Cherokee Arrow II	28R-7335170	(SE-GDF)
OY-BGR	Piper PA-28-140 Cherokee Cruiser	28-7425257	
OY-BGS	Piper PA-28-151 Cherokee Warrior	28-7415258	
OY-BGT	Piper PA-28R-200 Cherokee Arrow II	28R-7435131	
OY-BGW	Piper PA-28-140 Cherokee Cruiser	28-7425100	
OY-BGZ	Piper PA-28-140 Cherokee Cruiser *(Damaged 6.7.96)*	28-7425104	
OY-BHF	Piper PA-31-310 Navajo	31-245	G-BXAZ
			G-AXAZ
			N9184Y
OY-BHI	Cessna 172N	73831	5H-OCG
			N5744J
OY-BHN	Piper PA-44-180T Turbo Seminole	44-8107012	N8244T
OY-BHS	Viking Dragonfly	480	
OY-BHT	Embraer EMB.110-P2 Bandeirante	110-161	N4942S
			G-CELT
OY-BHU	Piper PA-31T1 Cheyenne	31T-7904004	N131SW
OY-BHZ	de Havilland DH.104 Dove 8 *(Wfu)*	04270	G-BLPZ
			WB534
OY-BIE	Reims/Cessna F.172M	1220	
OY-BIJ	Cessna 182P Skylane	63703	N4704K
OY-BIK	Reims/Cessna F.172M	1333	(SE-GKH)
OY-BIL	Reims/Cessna F.177RG Cardinal RG	0122	SE-GKN
OY-BIM	Cessna 421B Golden Eagle	0878	(N5419J)
OY-BIU	Reims/Cessna F.172M	1179	(F-BVSF)
OY-BIV	Reims/Cessna F.337G Super Skymaster	0064	LN-NPE
			OY-BIV
			N14500
OY-BIY	Cessna 182P (Reims assembled)	0017/63917	SE-GKI
			N9810E
OY-BJC	Malmö MFI-9B Trainer	70	SE-EWG
OY-BJD	Reims/Cessna F.150H	0270	SE-IYA
			OY-BJD
			SE-FBX
OY-BJF	Reims/Cessna F.150M	1421	
OY-BJJ	Cessna 182E Skylane	54667	D-ELZA
			N3267U
OY-BJL	Reims/Cessna F.172N	1654	
OY-BJM	Reims/Cessna F.150M	1427	
OY-BJO	Piper PA-28RT-201T Turbo Arrow IV	28R-7931051	G-BGNX
			N2191N

Regn.	Type	C/n	Prev.Id.
OY-BJP	Fairchild-Swearingen SA.227AC Metro III	AC-499	F-GHVG
			SE-KHH
			LN-HPF
			OY-BJP
			N3106D
OY-BJW	Reims/Cessna F.172N	1649	(D-EGQE)
OY-BKA	Piper PA-28-140 Cherokee	28-24436	
OY-BKC	Laverda F.8L Falco IV	414	
OY-BKD	Piper PA-28-180 Cherokee D	28-4774	
OY-BKG	Piper PA-28R-180 Cherokee Arrow	28R-30680	
OY-BKI	Piper PA-23-250 Aztec C	27-3207	(D-IMUN)
			N6023Y
OY-BKJ	Piper PA-28-180 Cherokee D	28-5132	
OY-BKK	Piper PA-28-140 Cherokee	28-25009	
OY-BKL	Piper PA-28R-180 Cherokee Arrow	28R-30869	
OY-BKM	Piper PA-28-140 Cherokee	28-24821	
OY-BKN	Piper PA-28-140 Cherokee B	28-25398	
OY-BKP	Piper PA-28-180 Cherokee D	28-5255	
OY-BKS	Piper PA-28-140 Cherokee B	28-25680	
OY-BKU	Piper PA-28-140 Cherokee B *(Dam.12.5.95)*	28-25554	
OY-BKW	Piper PA-28-140 Cherokee B	28-25254	
OY-BKY	Piper PA-28-140 Cherokee B	28-25338	
OY-BLA	Piper PA-28-180 Cherokee Archer	28-7505234	
OY-BLB	Piper PA-28-151 Cherokee Warrior	28-7515420	
OY-BLH	Cessna 150L	74145	SE-FMI
			N19074
OY-BLI	Cessna 150L	73891	SE-FMH
			N18238
OY-BLL	Piper PA-28-181 Cherokee Archer II	28-7690145	
OY-BLN	Piper PA-28-151 Cherokee Warrior	28-7615120	
OY-BLO	Piper PA-28-151 Cherokee Warrior	28-7615217	
OY-BLP	Piper PA-28-151 Cherokee Warrior	28-7615218	
OY-BLS	Piper PA-28-181 Cherokee Archer II	28-7690269	
OY-BLU	Piper PA-28-181 Cherokee Archer II	28-7690457	
OY-BLY	Piper PA-28-181 Cherokee Archer II	28-7790121	
OY-BLZ	Piper PA-28-151 Cherokee Warrior	28-7715092	(N5321F)
OY-BMC	Druine D.31 Turbulent	334	
OY-BMH	Druine D.31 Turbulent	325	
OY-BMI	Druine D.31 Turbulent	328	
OY-BMR	Jodel D.112 Club (Modified)	1435	
OY-BMU	Jodel D.112 Club	1463	
OY-BMW	Jurca MJ.2 Tempète *(Reservation)*	25	
OY-BNE	Reims/Cessna F.172N	1860	
OY-BNF	Reims/Cessna F.172N	1854	
OY-BNG	Reims/Cessna F.182Q Skylane	0126	
OY-BNH	Reims/Cessna F.172N	1983	
OY-BNL	Piper PA-28-161 Warrior II	28-8016299	D-EICI
OY-BNM	Embraer EMB.110P2 Bandeirante	110-200	N5071N
			G-BFZK
			PT-GLS
OY-BNP	Rutan Cozy Mk IV *(Reservation)*	0688	
OY-BNR	Reims/Cessna FR.172K Hawk XP	0674	
OY-BNW	Tri-R Kis *(Reservation)*	0394	
OY-BPB	Douglas C-47A	20019	RDAF:K-682
			RDAF:682
			LN-IAT
			43-15553
OY-BPH	Fairchild-Swearingen SA.227AC Metro III	AC-580B	TC-FBU
			OY-BPH
			N3115A
OY-BPT	Grumman-American AA-5B Tiger	1165	HB-UCP
OY-BRA	Piper PA-28-181 Cherokee Archer II	28-7890426	
OY-BRC	Piper PA-28R-201T Turbo Arrow III	28R-7803322	
OY-BRE	Piper PA-28-181 Cherokee Archer II	28-7890532	
OY-BRI	Piper PA-28-181 Cherokee Archer II	28-7890502	
OY-BRO	Piper PA-38-112 Tomahawk	38-79A0266	
OY-BRT	Piper PA-28-181 Archer II	28-7990266	
OY-BRY	Piper PA-28-181 Archer II	28-8090220	
OY-BSA	Champion 7GCBC Citabria	155	D-EGPB
OY-BSE	Partenavia P.68B	174	SE-GEU
OY-BSF	Piper PA-34-200 Seneca	34-7350073	SE-GAK
			OH-PND
			SE-GAK
OY-BSI	Piper PA-34-200 Seneca	34-7350334	OO-TNT
			N56458

Regn.	Type	C/n	Prev.Id.
OY-BSL	Beech E95 Travel Air	TD-715	D-GECA
OY-BSM	Rutan LongEz	8202/715	OY-82X02
			(OY-8202)
OY-BSO	Cessna 340A	0666	D-IGMN
			(LN-LFA)
			D-IGMN
			PH-LTR
			N1913E
OY-BSR	Cessna 172D	49702	SE-EHR
			LN-DBM
			N2402Y
OY-BSS	Piper PA-11 Cub Special	11-914	D-EMIX
			N5034H
OY-BSV	Reims/Cessna F.172M	1435	SE-GOF
OY-BSZ	Piper PA-28R-180 Cherokee Arrow	28R-30332	SE-FCU
OY-BTD	Piper PA-28-161 Cherokee Warrior II	28-7716118	
OY-BTE	Piper PA-28-161 Cherokee Warrior II	28-7716161	
OY-BTF	Piper PA-28-181 Cherokee Archer II	28-7790288	
OY-BTH	Piper PA-28-161 Cherokee Warrior II	28-7716117	
OY-BTI	Piper PA-28-161 Cherokee Warrior II	28-7816146	
OY-BTJ	Piper PA-28-181 Cherokee Archer II	28-7790371	
OY-BTM	Piper PA-28R-201T Turbo Cherokee Arrow III	28R-7703215	
OY-BTN	Piper PA-28-161 Cherokee Warrior II	28-7816147	
OY-BTO	Piper PA-28-181 Cherokee Archer II	28-7790586	
OY-BTS	Piper PA-18-150 Super Cub	18-7709065	
OY-BTT	Piper PA-28-181 Cherokee Archer II	28-7890245	
OY-BTU	Piper PA-28-161 Cherokee Warrior II	28-7816374	
OY-BTV	Piper PA-28-161 Cherokee Warrior II	28-7816375	
OY-BTY	Piper PA-32RT-300 Lance	32R-7885038	
OY-BTZ	Piper PA-31-350 Navajo Chieftain	31-7752031	SE-GPM
OY-BUA	Reims/Cessna F.172M	1477	
OY-BUD	Cessna 210L Centurion	61351	N5421S
OY-BUE	Reims/Cessna F.172M	1446	
OY-BUF	Reims/Cessna F.172M	1453	
OY-BUG	Reims/Cessna F.182P Skylane	0010	
OY-BUI	Piper PA-28-140 Cherokee F	28-7325344	SE-GAX
OY-BUJ	Cessna 182P (Reims assembled)	0064/64453	N1802M
OY-BUK	Reims/Cessna F.172M	1398	
OY-BUM	Reims/Cessna F.172M	1468	
OY-BUR	Reims/Cessna F.172N	1588	
OY-BUV	Reims/Cessna F.172N	1536	
OY-BUY	Cessna U.206G Stationair II	03631	N7359N
OY-BVA	Beech 65-90 King Air (Wfu)	LJ-68	D-IKAO
			D-ILNE
OY-BVB	Beech 200 Super King Air	BB-419	N256EN
			N555FP
OY-BVH	Fokker F.27 Friendship 200	10200	A2-ADG
	(Used for fire training at CPH)		PH-KFC
			HB-AAU
			D-BAKE
			PH-FDO
			LV-PTO
			PH-FDO
OY-BVM	Beech A36 Bonanza	E-1982	N6227M
OY-BVN	Beech F33A Bonanza	CE-783	N4806M
OY-BVP	Bölkow BO.208C Junior	588	D-EJNE
OY-BVR	Beech F33A Bonanza	CE-1200	
OY-BVS	Beech B90 King Air	LJ-418	SE-LEN
			OK-XKN
			OY-BVS
			N49CM
			(N49CN)
			N715K
			N725K
OY-BVT	Beech F33A Bonanza (W/o 13.12.89)	CE-1151	
OY-BVU	Beech F33A Bonanza	CE-1139	
OY-BVV	Beech E33A Bonanza	CE-1123	
OY-BVW	Beech 200 Super King Air	BB-705	D-IBAB
			G-GKNB
OY-BYA	Reims/Cessna F.182Q Skylane	0114	SE-IBA
OY-BYB	Reims/Cessna F.172G	0306	D-EJKI
OY-BYC	Piper PA-28R-201T Turbo Arrow III	28R-7803246	SE-GVP
OY-BYD	Reims/Cessna F.150G	0168	D-EGEW

Regn.	Type	C/n	Prev.Id.
OY-BYE	Cessna 150L	72775	LN-KAD
			N1475Q
OY-BYI	Piper PA-34-200T Seneca II	34-7570249	SE-ITG
			OY-BYI
			PH-PEM
			OO-HAM
			N1452X
OY-BYK	Cessna 421B Golden Eagle	0593	SE-IND
			OO-LFG
			PH-PLT
			OO-LFG
OY-BYR	Reims/Cessna F.337G Super Skymaster	0069/01584	C5-CLD
	(Wfu 1990)		N1025A
			ST-AFM
			D-IKED
OY-BYT	Beech A23 Musketeer (Dbr 19.6.95)	M-677	D-EHWU
OY-BYV	Bölkow BO.208C Junior	706	D-ENYU
OY-BYW	Cessna 140A	15426	OO-BNV
			N5306C
OY-BYY	Reims/Cessna F.150L (Sold to Germany)	0776	D-ECRF
OY-BYZ	Reims/Cessna F.337F Super Skymaster	0025/01333	D-IHAW
			(N1733M)
OY-BZA	Reims/Cessna F.150G	0113	D-EGDA
OY-BZB	Reims/Cessna F.150G	0141	D-EFSE
OY-BZC	Reims/Cessna F.150L	0671	D-ECJW
OY-BZE	Reims/Cessna F.172N	1600	D-EOTA
OY-BZN	Cessna 421C Golden Eagle II	0045	SE-INC
			LN-VIH
			N112GA
			D-ICST
			N98448
OY-BZO	Cessna 337D Super Skymaster	0991	G-AWVS
	(W/o 3.10.86)		N2691S
OY-BZT	Cessna 550 Citation II	0259	N810JT
			VH-KDP
			N68617
OY-BZW	Fairchild-Swearingen SA.226TC Metro II	TC-328	N917MM
	(Dbr 16.2.91, stored CPH)		(D-IKOO)
			ZS-LJH
			D-IKOO
			OE-LSB
			N10110
OY-BZZ	Reims/Cessna F.172M	1475	D-EEPV
OY-CAA	Partenavia P.68B	48	
OY-CAB	Partenavia P.68B	72	
OY-CAC	Partenavia P.68B	179	
OY-CAE	Partenavia P.68B (Dbr 8.8.98)	199	(G-BHEF)
OY-CAF	Partenavia P.68B	196	(G-BHEE)
OY-CAG	Partenavia P.68 Observer	243-03-OB	
OY-CAH	SOCATA TB-10 Tobago	395	
OY-CAK	SOCATA TB-10 Tobago	185	
OY-CAL	SOCATA TB-9 Tampico (W/o 28.7.91)	175	
OY-CAM	SOCATA TB-9 Tampico	51	F-GCEC
OY-CAN	SOCATA TB-9 Tampico	132	
OY-CAO	SOCATA TB-10 Tobago	133	
OY-CAP	SOCATA TB-9 Tampico	52	
OY-CAR	SOCATA TB-10 Tobago	53	
OY-CAW	SOCATA MS.880B Rallye Club	3030	
OY-CAZ	SOCATA MS.880B Rallye Club (W/o 6.10.86)	2891	
OY-CBA	Mooney M.20J Model 201	24-0735	(N4449H)
OY-CBB	Cessna T.337D Turbo Skymaster	1000	OH-CBB
	(Wfu, stored)		N85850
OY-CBN	SOCATA MS.894A Minerva 220	12019	LN-BIQ
OY-CBP	Beech 200 Super King Air	BB-235	N9BK
OY-CBR	Reims/Cessna F.182Q Skylane	0112	PH-AYD(2)
OY-CBT	DHC-7 Series 103	10	C-GRQB-X
OY-CBU	DHC-7 Series 103	20	
OY-CCG	Cessna 650 Citation III	0003	N92LA
			N187CP
			HZ-AAA
			N653CC
OY-CCJ	Gates Learjet 35A	35A-468	N468LM
			VH-ANI
OY-CDB	SOCATA TB-20 Trinidad	553	
OY-CDC	Partenavia P.68C	211	D-GEMD

Regn.	Type	Cn	Prev.Id.
OY-CDD	SOCATA TB-9 Tampico	158	SE-GFM
OY-CDF	Reims/Cessna F.182Q Skylane	0124	LN-KAF
	(W/o 6.4.87)		(D-EOKE)
OY-CDH	SOCATA TB-10 Tobago	629	N20EV
OY-CDI	Partenavia P.68C-TC	392-46-TC	
OY-CDJ	SOCATA TB-9 Tampico Club	1271	
OY-CDL	SOCATA TB-9 Tampico Club	1272	
OY-CDN	SOCATA TB-21 Trinidad TC	969	F-GKVQ
			N25198
OY-CDO	SOCATA TB-9 Tampico	883	F-OIDM
			SE-KBD
OY-CDS	SOCATA TB-20 Trinidad	1912	F-OIGY
OY-CEA	Piper PA-34-200 Seneca	34-7250109	G-BBFX
	(Instructional airframe at Copenhagen)		5Y-APJ
			N4586T
OY-CEE	Piper PA-28-181 Archer II	2890053	
OY-CEN	Piper PA-31-310 Navajo	31-7612028	TF-ODE
			OY-CEN
			LN-PAC
			SE-GLY
			N9665N
OY-CET	Piper PA-34-200T Seneca II	34-7570240	D-IHGB
			N1415X
OY-CEV	Cessna 500 Citation	0329	N4999H
			XC-PPM
			XC-IPP
			N5329J
			ZS-JOK
			N5329J
OY-CFA	PZL-104 Wilga 35A (Wfu, stored)	118403	HB-EZI
OY-CFB	Bellanca 8KCAB Decathlon	487-79	SE-GEZ
OY-CFC	Cessna 414 Chancellor	0067	(LN-...)
			OY-CFC
			SE-GOT
			G-BAXO
			9J-ACI
			A2-ZFP
			ZS-IDP
			N8167Q
OY-CFH	PZL-104 Wilga 35A (Wfu, stored)	18840811	SP-ZOD
OY-CFJ	Cessna 172P	75198	N62023
OY-CFL	Grumman AA-5B Tiger	0565	LN-NFY
			(N5479Y)
			D-EFZW
			N28333
OY-CFM	Maule M-5-235C Lunar Rocket	7369C	N56423
OY-CFN	Piaggio FWP.149D	172	D-EHLG
			EB+390
			DA+386
			KB+148
OY-CFT	Partenavia P.68C	213	I-VCID
			I-VICD
OY-CFU	Mooney M.20J Model 201	24-0841	LN-MON
			(LN-RAN)
			SE-GXH
OY-CFV	Pilatus Britten-Norman BN-2B-27 Islander	2174	G-BKOK
OY-CFW	Cessna 182D Skylane	52048	D-EGLT
			N2748G
OY-CFY	Reims/Cessna F.172P	2239	
OY-CFZ	Piper PA-28-181 Archer II	2890004	N9090D
OY-CGB	Reims/Cessna F.172M	1296	D-EEON
OY-CGD	WAR FW190 Replica (Reservation)	unkn	
OY-CGF	Maule M-5-235C Lunar Rocket	7325C	SE-IEL
OY-CGG	Bellanca (Reservation)	unkn	
OY-CGL	Cessna 150B	59395	D-EBIX
			OE-AYB
			N7295X
OY-CGP	Piper PA-23-250 Aztec E	27-4614	N1JX
			N1JG
			N13996
OY-CGS(4)	Brändli BX-2 Cherry (Reservation)	188	
OY-CGV	Piper PA-28-180 Cherokee Archer	28-7505088	LN-BGV
OY-CGZ	Reims/Cessna F.150L	0909	D-ECVW
OY-CHD	Cessna 172L	59403	N1003M
OY-CHL	Beech 58 Baron	TH-747	N1847L
OY-CHM	Cessna 172N	69528	N737MT
OY-CHO	Piper PA-28R-200 Cherokee Arrow II	28R-7235076	SE-FYM
OY-CHP	Cessna 207 Skywagon	00049	SE-IOA
			LN-HAC
			N36207
			(N91062)
OY-CHR	Piper PA-28-151 Cherokee Warrior	28-7715089	SE-GNY
OY-CHV	Gardan GY-80 Horizon (Reservation)	unkn	
OY-CIB	Aeritalia/SNIAS ATR-42-300	007	F-WWEC
OY-CID	Aeritalia/SNIAS ATR-42-300	079	D-BATA(2)
			F-WWEE
OY-CIE	Aeritalia/SNIAS ATR-42-300	082	D-BATB
			F-WWEH
OY-CIG	Aeritalia/SNIAS ATR-42-300	019	YU-ALL
			VH-AQD
			F-WWEF
OY-CIH	Aeritalia/SNIAS ATR-42-300	238	F-WWEC
OY-CIJ	Aeritalia/SNIAS ATR-42-512	497	F-WWLR
OY-CIK	Aeritalia/SNIAS ATR-42-512	501	F-WWEE
OY-CIL	Aeritalia/SNIAS ATR-42-512	514	F-WWLO
OY-CIM	Aeritalia/SNIAS ATR-72-212A	468	F-WWLV
OY-CIN	Aeritalia/SNIAS ATR-72-212	568	F-WWEH
OY-CIO	Aeritalia/SNIAS ATR-72-212	595	F-WWEB
OY-CIR	Aeritalia/SNIAS ATR-42-310	107	F-GHPX
			EI-BXR
			F-WWEE
OY-CIS	Aeritalia/SNIAS ATR-42-310	161	EI-BYO
			F-WWEH
OY-CIT	Aeritalia/SNIAS ATR-42-300	196	C-FZVZ
			C-GITI
			F-WWEK
OY-CIU	Aeritalia/SNIAS ATR-42-300	112	C-FIQB
			F-WWEI
OY-CJB	Piper PA-28R-201 Arrow III	28R-7837285	N36586
OY-CJE	Grumman AA-5A Cheetah	0590	N26434
OY-CJG	Cessna U.206E Stationair	01567	LN-BEI
			(SE-KLL)
			LN-BEI
			(N9167M)
OY-CJH	Piper PA-17 Vagabond (Reservation)	unkn	
OY-CJI	Piper PA-28-181 Archer II	28-8290134	N8209A
OY-CJK	Piper PA-34-200T Seneca II	34-7570245	N854WM
OY-CJL	Aero Designs Pulsar	0292/174	
OY-CJO	Polliwagen (Reservation)	8501-1753N	
OY-CJP	Piper PA-28R-200 Cherokee Arrow	28R-35141	N9429N
OY-CJT	Piper PA-25-235 Pawnee B (Reservation)	unkn	
OY-CJW	Beech F33A Bonanza	CE-1409	N5543T
OY-CKA	Piper PA-31P-425 Pressurized Navajo	31P-7300136	N150TT
	(Reserved as PH-CRL, 5.99)		N666BC
			(N444PM)
			N666BC
			N36PC
			N7657L
OY-CKB	Piper PA-18-150 Super Cub	18-1463	D-ELTC
			ALAT
			51-15463
OY-CKC	Cessna U.206G Stationair II/Soloy	03724	N7993N
OY-CKG	Piper PA-32R-300 Lance	32R-7680134	SE-GNC
OY-CKK	Dassault Falcon 900B	110	F-WWFH
OY-CKN	Dassault Falcon 2000	76	F-WWMZ
OY-CKT	Cessna 560 Citation V	0078	SE-DLI
			N2846B
OY-CKU	Piper PA-32R-300 Lance	32R-7780491	N38966
OY-CKV	Cessna T.210N Turbo Centurion II	64184	D-EHSD
			(N5368Y)
OY-CLA	Cessna 172N	69903	N738DU
OY-CLD	Canadair CL.600-2B16 Challenger 3A	5070	(D-AAFX)
			N305FX
			N780HC
			N980HC
			C-GLXO
OY-CLH	Grumman-American AA-1B Trainer	0184	N9684L
OY-CLJ	Grumman-American AA-1B Trainer	0106	N9606L

Regn.	Type	C/n	Prev.Id.
OY-CLM	Short SC-7 Skyvan (Reservation)	SH.1913	VH-WGG / SAF-700 / G-14-85
OY-CLW	Piper PA-30-160 Twin Comanche C	30-1856	G-RNTV / G-AXDL / N8707Y
OY-CMB	Jodel D.112M Club	1470	
OY-CMH	Jodel D.112M Club	1491	
OY-CMO	Jodel D.112 Club	1445	
OY-CMP	Ultimate 10-20 (Reservation)	2	
OY-CMR	Denney Kitfox 1200 (Reservation)	1689	
OY-CMS	Rans S-10 Sakota (Reservation)	unkn	
OY-CMV	Van's RV-6 (Reservation)	unkn	
OY-CMY	Rand-Robinson KR-1 (Reservation)	0886	
OY-CMZ(2)	Rand-Robinson KR-2	8802-5275	
OY-CNA	Airbus A.300B4-120	079	LN-RCA / F-WZEN
OY-CNB	Airbus A.320-212	221	G-DRVE / F-GLGI / ZS-NZS / F-WWIK
OY-CNC	Airbus A.320-212	222	G-RRJE / F-GLGJ / ZS-NZT / F-WWIL
OY-CNK	Airbus A.300B4-120	094	SE-DFK / F-WZEJ
OY-CNL	Airbus A.300B4-120	128	SE-DFL / F-WZEE
OY-CNM	Airbus A.320-212	301	G-JANM / G-KMAM / F-WWIX
OY-CNP	Airbus A.320-212	294	G-HBAP / G-HAGT / F-WWID
OY-CNR	Airbus A.320-212	349	G-DACR / G-OEXC / F-WWBU
OY-CNS	McDonnell-Douglas DC-10-10	46646	SE-DHS / N913WA
OY-CNT	McDonnell-Douglas DC-10-10	47833	SE-DHT / N915WA
OY-CNU	McDonnell-Douglas DC-10-10	47832	SE-DHU / N914WA
OY-CNW	Airbus A.320-212	299	G-JDFW / G-SCSR / F-WWIQ
OY-CNY	McDonnell-Douglas DC-10-10	46983	SE-DHY / N909WA
OY-CPB	Cessna 172N	72960	N1115F
OY-CPC	Piper PA-28-181 Archer II	28-8090175	N8136T
OY-CPD	Beech A36 Bonanza	E-990	N17606
OY-CPH	Cessna 172E	51334	N5434T
OY-CPI	Cessna 172F	52887	N5357R
OY-CPP	Christen Eagle II	0001	N22JF
OY-CPR	Reims/Cessna F.150M	1310	SE-GMR
OY-CPZ	Reims/Cessna F.172F	0158	D-EMGI
OY-CRA	Maule M-7-235 Super Rocket	4056C	N6122Q
OY-CRB	Piper PA-34-220T Seneca III	34-8133006	N8329B
OY-CRC	Cessna 177RG Cardinal RG	0700	N1524H
OY-CRD	Piper PA-34-200T Seneca II (W/o 1.9.97)	34-7970167	N205DM / N3048V
OY-CRF	Grob G.115	8033	(LN-AES)
OY-CRG	BAe.146 Series 200	E.2075	N193US / N369PS / (G-5-075)
OY-CRP	HP.137 Jetstream 1 (Wfu)	209	N2209 / N5VH / N5VP / N74169 / N5V / G-AXEP / G-8-7
OY-CRR	HP.137 Jetstream 1 (Wfu)	217	N12217 / G-AXHJ
OY-CRS	HP.137 Jetstream 1 (Wfu)	225	N12225 / N10AB / G-AXON / G-8-10
OY-CRT	HP.137 Jetstream 1 (Wfu)	233	N33233 / N815M / (N2ES) / N815M / N8943 / G-AXLP
OY-CRV	Gates Learjet 35 (Reservation)	unkn	
OY-CRW	Piper PA-32-300 Cherokee Six	32-7240118	SE-KRZ / OY-CRW / SE-FLF / G-BAHV / N1400T
OY-CSA	Piper PA-28RT-201T Turbo Arrow IV	28R-7931198	N29333
OY-CSC	Piper PA-28RT-201 Arrow IV	28R-7918135	N29026
OY-CSE	Cessna 152	82883	N89824
OY-CSF	Piper PA-28-140 Cherokee	28-25033	SE-FFN
OY-CSG	Piper PA-28-140 Cherokee	28-7125294	SE-FYD
OY-CSK	Cessna 182A Skylane	34083	SE-CDY / N6083B
OY-CSL	Cessna 152	83210	N47295
OY-CSM	Cessna 172N	73854	N6089J
OY-CSP	Cessna 172N	70336	N738YF
OY-CSV	Piper PA-28R-201 Cherokee Arrow III	28R-7737107	N16DB / N728P
OY-CTC	DHC-7 Series 102	101	G-BNDC / ZK-NEW / C-GFQL
OY-CTH	Cessna R.172K Hawk XP	2236	SE-GOU / N2998V
OY-CTI	Piper PA-28-181 Archer II	28-8090045	N2433U
OY-CTL	Pützer Elster B	018	D-ECAY / 97+11 / D-EDUF
OY-CTR	Piper PA-31-310 Navajo	31-8012066	LN-SAY / (SE-IDI)
OY-CTT	Maule M-7-235 Super Rocket	4043C	N56700
OY-CTU	Cessna R.172K Hawk XP	3348	N758TM
OY-CTV	Cessna 172P	74255	N51037
OY-CTZ	Cessna 172M	67356	N73300
OY-CUA	Neico Lancair 320	01289-408	
OY-CUC	Christen Pitts S-2B	5220	
OY-CUD	Cessna 172N	68483	N733RE
OY-CUE	Druine D.31 Turbulent	329	
OY-CUL	Maule M-5-180C (Reservation)	unkn	
OY-CYA	Pützer Elster B (Reservation)	unkn	
OY-CYF	Piper PA-28-140 Cherokee	28-7625122	N8523C
OY-CYK	Cessna 172N	72201	N8443E
OY-CYL	Cessna 172N	73590	N6360G
OY-CYN	Grumman AA-5B Tiger	1251	N4559Z
OY-CYP	Piper PA-25-235 Pawnee C	25-4760	G-BDCT / CS-AIV
OY-CYR	Jodel D.18	73	
OY-CYS	Polliwagen	8607-1794N	
OY-CYU	Rand-Robinson KR-2 (Reservation)	6513	
OY-CYV	Cessna 550 Citation II	0440	N120TC / N31FT / N31F / (N1220D)
OY-CYY	Piper PA-25-235 Pawnee C	25-4018	G-AXFD / OH-PIK / N4502Y
OY-CYZ	Christensen Opus 3	0188-001/92	
OY-DAB	S.A.I. KZ-III U-2	82	
OY-DAE	S.A.I. KZ-III U-2	87	D-EHYC / OY-DAE
OY-DBC	Stampe & Renard/ SV.4B	1204	RBAF:V-62
OY-DBK	Cessna 150L	72077	XB-CXY / XC-FUQ / XB-NUA / (N6577G)
OY-DBM	Champion 7FC Tri-Traveler	454	N9922Y

Regn.	Type	C/n	Prev.Id.
OY-DBZ	Cessna 170A	19758	D-ENQI / D-EHON / N1204D
OY-DCB	Piper PA-22-150 Tri-Pacer	22-5233	N7506D
OY-DCC	Piper PA-23-250 Aztec B	27-2473	(N5398Y)
OY-DCH	Cessna 172	28858	SE-CMN / N6758A
OY-DCL	Piper PA-22-160 Tri-Pacer	22-6874	
OY-DCR	Piper PA-22-160 Tri-Pacer	22-7469	G-ARES / N3558Z
OY-DCV	Piper PA-22-108 Colt	22-9133	(SE-CZN)
OY-DCW	Reims/Cessna F.172E	50575/0020	
OY-DDF	Gardan GY-80 Horizon 180	186	
OY-DDH	Piper PA-30-160 Twin Comanche	30-113	OE-FPA / N7142Y
OY-DDJ	Champion 7GCAA Citabria	97	
OY-DDL	Mooney M.20C Mark 21	2920	N79805
OY-DDT	SOCATA MS.880B Rallye-Club	845	
OY-DEB	S.A.I. KZ-III U-2	94	D-EJUM / OY-DEB
OY-DEJ	S.A.I. KZ-III U-2	54	D-EDUD / OY-DHI
OY-DEU	Scintex Piel CP.301C Emeraude	516	F-BJFD
OY-DEW	Reims/Cessna F.172D	50181/0011	
OY-DEY	Scintex Piel CP.301C-2 Emeraude	587	OH-EMB
OY-DEZ	de Havilland DH.87B Hornet Moth	8040	G-AMZO / SE-ALD / OY-DEZ / VR-RAI
OY-DFD	Mooney M.20F Executive	670327	N2968L
OY-DFF	SOCATA MS.880B Rallye-Club	1124	
OY-DFP	Piper PA-28-140 Cherokee B	28-25422	LN-BNX
OY-DGD	CEA DR.250/160 Capitaine	83	
OY-DGH	de Havilland DH.82A Tiger Moth	85939/E-8	D-EDAS / DF203
OY-DGP	Reims/Cessna F.172G	0226	
OY-DGT	Cessna 172 I (Dbr 24.12.88)	57001	N46031
OY-DGV	S.A.I. KZ-III U	47	SE-APT
OY-DGY	Auster J/1 Autocrat	2025	
OY-DHC	Piper J-3C-65 Cub	13173	D-EBER / HB-OSC / 45-4433
OY-DHD	Piper PA-28-140 Cherokee	28-24829	LN-LMQ
OY-DHG	Cessna 150B	59575	LN-IKT / N1175Y
OY-DHK	S.A.I. KZ-II Coupé Series 3	23	SE-ANN / (OY-DEY)
OY-DHM	Piper PA-28-140 Cherokee	28-20694	LN-BFH / (SE-EOI)
OY-DHP	Polyt V	70-1	
OY-DHR	Reims/Cessna FR.172F Rocket (W/o 10.8.94)	0093	
OY-DHV	Wassmer WA.40 Super IV	40	D-EHJP
OY-DHY	S.A.I. KZ-III U-1	55	
OY-DIV	Piper PA-22-150 Tri-Pacer	22-6639	LN-HAH / N9727D
OY-DIZ	S.A.I. KZ-IV	43	
OY-DJD	SOCATA MS.880B Rallye-Club	1284	
OY-DJG	SOCATA MS.892A Rallye Commodore 150	10952	
OY-DJK	Beagle A.61 Terrier 1	3741	SE-ELN / WE554
OY-DJS	SOCATA MS.880B Rallye-Club	1907	SE-FSI
OY-DJU	SOCATA MS.883 Rallye 115	1505	
OY-DJV	Partenavia P.68B	22	
OY-DJW	SOCATA MS.892A Rallye Commodore 150	11460	D-ENAB(2) / F-BSZE / OY-DJW / F-BNGV
OY-DJZ	Beech V35B Bonanza	D-9528	N115TW
OY-DKF	Beech A23-24 Musketeer Super	MA-190	
OY-DKK	Piper PA-28-180 Cherokee C	28-3671	LN-AEF / N9542J
OY-DKM	Beech A23-19 Musketeer Sport	MB-193	
OY-DKO	S.A.I. KZ-III U-2	61	
OY-DKU	S.A.I. KZ-III U-2	107	
OY-DKV	Cessna 150F	61763	N8163S
OY-DKW	Cessna 150	17143	OE-AHP / N5643E
OY-DLB	Cessna 177 Cardinal	00504	N3204T
OY-DLF	Mraz M.1C Sokol	270	D-ENOV / OK-DHK
OY-DLY	Piper PA-31-310 Navajo	31-229	G-AWOW / N9172Y
OY-DMD	SOCATA MS.892A Rallye Commodore I50	10541	
OY-DME	S.A.I. KZ-III	67	
OY-DMG	Piper PA-22-150 Tri-Pacer	22-5337	SE-CEI
OY-DMJ	S.A.I. KZ-VII U-9 Laerke	174	D-ECOC / HB-EPZ
OY-DMK	Beech 35-B33 Debonair	CD-745	SE-EKD
OY-DML	S.A.I. KZ-VII U-10 Laerke	163	LN-RAE
OY-DMM	Piper PA-22-150 Tri-Pacer	22-5842	LN-AEF / SE-CEL
OY-DMO	S.A.I. KZ-III U-2	105	
OY-DMY	Piper PA-22-150 Tri-Pacer	22-4295	LN-AEH / TG-CIR
OY-DMZ	Piper PA-24-250 Comanche	24-759	SE-CKT / N5687P
OY-DNK	Beech 35-C33A Debonair	CE-163	
OY-DNN	Reims/Cessna F.172H	0523	LN-FKT / SE-FMV / (LN-TST) / OY-DNN / LN-LMT
OY-DNO	Auster J/1 Autocrat	2110	
OY-DNT	Reims/Cessna F.172F	0115	D-ENNY
OY-DOE	S.A.I. KZ-III U-2	99	
OY-DOJ	Piper PA-28-140 Cherokee	28-20373	
OY-DOZ	S.A.I. KZ-III	42	
OY-DPF	Cessna 210-5	0294	HB-CMW / N8294Z
OY-DPI	Auster J/1 Autocrat	2129	
OY-DPL	Beech A23 Musketeer	M-637	
OY-DPS	Gardan GY-80 Horizon 160	93	
OY-DRG	SAAB-MFI-9B Junior	067	SE-FIE / OY-DRG
OY-DRH	Cessna 310 (Riley 65) (Wfu)	35407	G-ASSZ / N5207A
OY-DRI	Piper PA-28-140 Cherokee	28-23815	LN-UXV
OY-DRR	S.A.I. KZ-VIII	203	D-EBIZ
OY-DRS	Reims/Cessna F.172K	0786	LN-LJY
OY-DRZ	Piper PA-28-140 Cherokee B	28-25608	LN-BDX
OY-DSA	Beech A23-19A Musketeer Sport	MB-300	
OY-DSB	S.A.I. KZ-VII Laerke	191	HB-EPT
OY-DSD	Reims/Cessna F.172K (W/o 10.1.97)	0756	LN-BES / N9443
OY-DSF	Piper PA-28-140 Cherokee D	28-7125326	LN-MTK
OY-DSH	Taylorcraft Plus D	228	D-ECOD / G-AHKO / LB381
OY-DSI	S.A.I. KZ-III U-2 (Damaged 12.7.94)	64	D-EDEP / OY-DSI
OY-DSN	Piper PA-28-140 Cherokee	28-23283	LN-UXL
OY-DSO	S.A.I. KZ-III U-2	65	
OY-DSS	Piper PA-28-180 Cherokee C	28-3655	LN-NPS
OY-DSV	Auster J/1 Autocrat	1824	D-ENUM / G-AGTR
OY-DSZ	Taylorcraft Plus D	173	D-ELUV / N .?. / D-ELUS / G-AHHX / LB314
OY-DTL	SOCATA MS.880B Rallye Club	1108	
OY-DTP	Auster J/1 Autocrat	2332	D-EJYN / G-AJIN
OY-DTS	SOCATA MS.880B Rallye Club	1180	
OY-DTY	S.A.I. KZ-VII U-4 Laerke	159	D-EGAH / OY-DTY
OY-DUS	Piper PA-22-150 Caribbean	22-7588	LN-BDB / SE-CUN / N3717Z

Regn.	Type	C/n	Prev.ld.
OY-DVA	S.A.I. KZ-III U-2	74	D-ENYL / OY-DVA
OY-DVB	Beagle B.121 Pup 150	107	SE-FOB / G-35-107
OY-DVG	Piper PA-32-260 Cherokee Six	32-455	LN-HHU / N11C
OY-DVI	S.A.I. KZ-III U-2	75	D-ECOT / OY-DVI
OY-DVZ	Transavia PL-12 Airtruk	1238	VH-ETZ
OY-DZA	S.A.I. KZ-III U-3 Ambulance	66	
OY-DZB	S.A.I. KZ-VII U-9 Laerke	198	OH-KZB
OY-DZD	Piper PA-28-140 Cherokee F	28-7325226	LN-DBJ
OY-DZF	Piper PA-28-140 Cherokee	28-21815	LN-NPL / (SE-EYX)
OY-DZJ	Cessna 182M Skylane	59434	N70954
OY-DZT	SOCATA MS.880B Rallye-Club	2406	
OY-DZW	Beech B95A Travel Air	TD-529	OE-FSA
OY-EAH	Piper PA-23-150 Apache	23-575	SE-CRR / OY-EAH / SE-CBM
OY-EAI	Cessna 150C	59809	N2009Z
OY-EAM	Piper PA-18A-150 Super Cub	18-6796	N9694D
OY-EAT	Piper PA-22-108 Colt	22-9253	
OY-EAV	Piper PA-22-108 Colt	22-9144	
OY-EAY	Mooney M.20C Mark 21	2144	SE-EDK
OY-EBB	Fokker F.27-050	20118	EI-FKA / PH-LMA / PH-EXB
OY-EBC	Fokker F.27 Friendship 200	10675	LN-AKD / (SE-KXZ) / LN-AKD / PH-EXL / (PH-EXB)
OY-EBD	Fokker F.27-050	20119	EI-FKB / PH-LMB / (VH-FNN) / PH-EXC
OY-ECC	Piper PA-28-235 Cherokee	28-10435	LN-AEE / SE-EMU / N8919W
OY-ECD	Cessna 172M	61536	N92007
OY-ECE	Cessna 172M	62101	N12596
OY-ECF	Piper PA-28-235 Cherokee	28-10964	LN-LMF / N9293W
OY-ECG	Auster J/4	2071	D-EFYW / D-ECYS / LX-REX / G-AIJO
OY-ECH	de Havilland DH.82A Tiger Moth	85234	OO-DLA / G-ANCY / DE164
OY-ECI	Piper PA-32-260 Cherokee Six E	32-7300024	LN-BNR
OY-ECJ	Cessna 421B Golden Eagle (Dbr 28.1.94)	0508	D-ICOA / N69855
OY-ECN	Reims/Cessna F.172M	1041	(D-EIQI)
OY-ECO	Piper PA-18 Super Cub 95	18-3209	D-ELFZ / OL-LO9 / L-135 / 53-4809
OY-ECR	S.A.I. KZ-III U-2	106	
OY-ECS	Piper J-3C-65 Cub	13367	D-EGPL / D-EGPI / (D-EDUX) / PH-UCO / 45-4627
OY-ECT	Piper J-3C-65 Cub	22617	D-EDAP / N4492M / NC4492M
OY-ECU	Piper PA-28-140 Cherokee E Fliteliner	28-7225541	N736FL
OY-ECV	Piper J-3C-65 Cub (Painted as "215272")	8391	D-ECIZ / NC49642 / 42-15272
OY-ECY	Robin HR.100/210 Royale	189	
OY-ECZ	Piper PA-28-140 Cherokee E Fliteliner	28-7225559	N738FL
OY-EDG	Cessna 182S Skylane	80139	N9522J
OY-EEF	Beech B200 Super King Air	BB-1548	
OY-EEZ	Rutan LongEz	245	N245R
OY-EFA	Piper PA-18 Super Cub 95	18-1477	D-EKMM / OO-SPE / ALAT / 51-15477
OY-EFB	Cessna 140	9203	D-EGAN / NC90142
OY-EFE	Piper J-3C-65 Cub	11578	D-EBIR / HB-OAM / 43-30287
OY-EFF	SNCAN/ Stampe SV.4C (Wfu and stored)	222	G-BUNA / N10SV / F-BCBG
OY-EFI	Auster 5	1815	D-ENIR / G-AOSL / TW477
OY-EFJ	Wassmer Jodel D.120A Paris-Nice	292	D-EMTL / F-BMYZ
OY-EFN	SNCAN/ Stampe SV.4C	625	D-EDEN / F-BDFU
OY-EFP	Stinson HW-75 Reliant	7249	D-EMUB / SL-AAN / F-BESY / Fr.Navy / 5143
OY-EFR	Cessna 170A	18832	D-EKIS / N9073A
OY-EFU	Beagle-Auster A.61 Terrier 2	2296/B.630	D-EDTU / (OH-BEA) / G-ARRN / VF527
OY-EFV	Stinson 108-2 Voyager	353	D-EFAD / HB-TRO / N97353
OY-EFY	Piper PA-18 Super Cub 95	18-6039	D-EJEQ / SE-CLH / N7879D
OY-EFZ	Beagle A.61 Terrier 2	B.644	D-EEBN / VF624
OY-EGG	Reims/Cessna F.172H	0330	
OY-EGJ	Reims/Cessna F.150G	0087	
OY-EGK	Reims/Cessna F.150G	0163	
OY-EGL	Reims/Cessna F.172H (W/o 12.8.95)	0349	
OY-EGM	Reims/Cessna F.172H	0391	
OY-EGP	Reims/Cessna F.172H	0356	
OY-EGU	Reims/Cessna F.172H	0396	
OY-EGV	Reims/Cessna F.172H	0410	
OY-EGZ	Reims/Cessna F.172H	0324	N17013
OY-EHL	Cessna 182E Skylane	54027	LN-EHL / N3027Y
OY-EHM	Cessna 172 (Reservation)	unkn	
OY-EIG	Mooney M.20J Model 201	24-1674	N5274V
OY-EJJ	Epervier	1	OO-EPB
OY-EKA	Piper PA-28RT-201 Arrow IV	28R-8018075	N8212S
OY-EKU	Reims/Cessna F.172H	0691	SE-FKU
OY-ELW	Mooney M.20R Ovation	29-0045	G-BVZY
OY-EMC	Yakovlev YAK-52	801002	SE-KDC / UR-BNQ / DOSAAF
OY-ENG	Piper PA-32R-300 Lance (W/o 8.9.96)	32R-7680115	SE-GDS
OY-ENV	Reims/Cessna F.172M	1055	G-BBPJ
OY-ERD	Van's RV-4 (Reservation)	9507	
OY-ERI	Piper PA-28R-201 Arrow III	28R-7837299	OO-TRI / N39501
OY-ESA	Cessna 182P Skylane	63601	TF-ACC(2) / N5989J
OY-ESB	Reims/Cessna F.172M	1133	SE-FZT
OY-ESI	Europa Aviation Europa (Reservation)	300	
OY-ESK	Rans S-10E Sakota (Reservation)	1189069	
OY-EUR	Europa Aviation Europa (Reservation)	158	
OY-EYA	Stoddard-Hamilton Glasair II-S RG	unkn	
OY-FAA	Piper J-2 Cub	964	LN-EAP
OY-FAK	S.A.I. KZ-II Trainer	115	RDAF:107 / RDAF:115

Regn.	Type	C/n	Prev.Id.
OY-FAT	S.A.I. KZ-II Trainer	109	RDAF:101
			RDAF:109
OY-FAW	Piper PA-28-160 Cherokee *(W/o 21.5.94)*	28-588	
OY-FCJ	Cessna T.182R Turbo Skylane	67996	N9751H
OY-FCK	Maule MX-7-235 Star Rocket *(Reservation)*	10012C	N15CK
			N56589
OY-FCT	Beech 200 Super King Air	BB-389	N859CC
	(Reservation)		N510WR
			N510WP
			N5082M
OY-FDS	Piper PA-28R-180 Cherokee Arrow	28R-30683	SE-FDS
OY-FFB	Cessna 500 Citation	0406	SE-DET
			(N67829)
OY-FHM	Cessna 172 *(Reservation)*	unkn	
OY-FKA	Aeritalia/SNIAS ATR-42-300 *(Reservation)*	095	F-GKYN
			F-ODUL
OY-FLI	Piper PA-38-112 Tomahawk	38-78A0138	G-BOEC
			N9587T
OY-FLK	Gates Learjet 55	55-050	N122JD
			D-CARP
			N4289X
OY-FLV	DHC-1 Chipmunk 22 *(Reservation)*	C1/0878	RDAF: P-143
OY-FRA	Piper PA-34-200 Seneca	34-7250017	G-AZJB
			N1036U
OY-FRB	Piper PA-28-140 Cherokee	28-7725152	N1607H
OY-FRC	Piper PA-28-140 Cherokee	28-7325016	SE-GAP
OY-FRD	Grumman AA-1C Trainer 2	0133	LN-KLA
			(D-EGDB)
OY-FRE	Piper PA-31-310 Navajo	31-632	G-AXYA
			N6731L
OY-FRG	Piper PA-28-140 Cherokee	28-7325407	D-ELLF
			N11C
OY-FRK	Bölkow BO.208C Junior	691	D-ENVD
OY-FRO	Piper PA-28-151 Cherokee Warrior	28-7415428	SE-GLD
OY-FRV	Van's RV-4 *(W/o 16.4.96)*	1720	
OY-FUN	Rans S-10 Sakota *(Reservation)*	unkn	
OY-FUR	Cessna 172P	75370	LN-MTL
			N62969
OY-GAB	Grumman-American AA-5 Traveler	0421	N7121L
OY-GAC	Grumman-American AA-1 Yankee	0405	LN-UXQ
			(N8955L)
OY-GAE	Piper PA-28-140 Cherokee C	28-26718	SE-FPH
			N5927U
OY-GAI	Grumman-American AA-5B Tiger	0131	
OY-GAJ	Grumman-American AA-5A Cheetah	0083	
OY-GAL	Grumman-American AA-5B Tiger	0197	
OY-GAN	Grumman-American AA-5 Traveler	0199	SE-FTR
			N6099L
OY-GAT	Grumman-American GA-7 Cougar	0048	
OY-GBH	SOCATA Rallye 110ST Galopin	3297	D-EGRH
OY-GBK	Reims/Cessna F.337F Skymaster	0030/01349	SE-GOK
	(Reservation)		D-ICEL
			N1749M
OY-GDA	Dassault Falcon 50 *(Reservation)*	54	LX-GED
			N130A
			N392U
			N202DD
			N204DD
			(N50EF)
			N450X
			N71FJ
			(F-WZHT)
OY-GDB	Cessna U.206F Stationair	01750	SE-LFL
			OH-CFL
			N9550G
OY-GDS	Europa Aviation Europa *(Reservation)*	unkn	
OY-GEB	Beech 200C Super King Air	BL-40	VH-NSR
			N44344
			VH-OTH
			N3837R
OY-GEG	Beech 1900C-1	UC-132	YemenAF:1180
			OY-GEG
			N55201
OY-GEO	Beech 58 Baron	TH-1647	
OY-GEP	Beech 1900D	UE-31	N31YV

Regn.	Type	C/n	Prev.Id.
OY-GET	Beech F33A Bonanza	CE-1358	
OY-GEU	Beech 1300 Super King Air	BB-1341	VT-SAD
			N41AV
			N341YV
OY-GEV	Beech F33A Bonanza	CE-1370	
OY-GEW	Beech 1300 Super King Air	BB-1342	VT-SAE
			N99DX
			N250AF
			N342YV
OY-GGG	Cessna 650 Citation VII	7039	D-CACM
			N12643
OY-GHC	Reims/Cessna FR.182 Skylane RG	0038	D-EIYI
OY-GIG	Beech B300 Super King Air	FL-167	
OY-GJA	Rans S-10 Sakota *(Reservation)*	0790109	
OY-GKE	Piper PA-18-150 Super Cub	18-8109024	
OY-GKL	Cessna 650 Citation III	0043	
OY-GKM	Piper PA-32R-301T Saratoga II TC	3257071	
OY-GMA	Beech B200 Super King Air	BB-1340	N256AF
			N340YV
OY-GPC	Pereira GP-4 Osprey	0692	
OY-GPD	CEA Jodel DR.1050 Ambassadeur	528	OO-GPD
			F-BLRX
OY-GRB	Beech 200 Super King Air	BB-845	N486DC
			N38535
OY-GRD	DHC-7 Series 101	9	A6-ALM
OY-GRE	DHC-7 Series 102	106	N54026
			(N53994)
			C-GFYI
OY-GRF	DHC-7 Series 102	113	OE-LLU
			C-GFCF
			(G-BOAZ)
OY-GRL	Boeing 757-236	25620	TF-GRL
			G-CSVS
			G-IEAC
OY-GSC	Rockwell 112 Commander	487	SE-GSC
OY-GTE	Grumman AA-5 Traveler	0299/0197	G-BAOV
OY-GTM	Reims/Cessna F.172P	2026	SE-IFE
OY-GUM	Cessna 550 Citation II *(Reservation)*	unkn	
OY-GVD	Piper PA-32RT-300 Lance	32R-7885130	D-EBRB
			G-XMAS
			N31793
OY-GZE	Reims/Cessna FRA.150M Aerobat	0287	SE-GZE
			(F-BOFD)
OY-HAF	Sikorsky S-61N	61267	N10045
OY-HAG	Sikorsky S-61N	61268	N10046
OY-HAH	Sikorsky S-61N	61365	
OY-HAJ	Bell 47G-5	25003	N8170J
OY-HBF	Bell 206B Jet Ranger II	1468	
OY-HCY	Bell 212	31166	
OY-HDC	Agusta-Bell 206B Jet Ranger II	8499	SE-HGU
OY-HDD	Bell 206B Jet Ranger II	3649	N130S
			C-GTXA
			N3982M
OY-HDM	Bell 212	31142	N57545
OY-HDN	Bell 212	31136	N5752K
OY-HDO	Sikorsky S-61N	61740	LN-OSU
OY-HDT	Aérospatiale AS.332L Super Puma	2017	G-BWHN
			C-GSLC
			HC-BQJ
			C-GSLC
			HC-BNC
			C-GSLC
OY-HDV	Schweizer 269C	S-1380	D-HBIG
			N7508E
OY-HEA	Bell 212	30914	N5009L
OY-HEC	Aérospatiale AS.350B1 Ecureuil	1999	
	(W/o 13.9.96)		
OY-HEG	Schweizer 269C *(Damaged 14.12.96)*	S-1706	N41S
OY-HEO	Aérospatiale AS.332LSuper Puma	2007	G-CHCA
			F-WQDZ
			C-GSEM
			HC-B..
			C-GSEM
			HC-BPE,
			C-GSEM, HK-3197X, C-GSEM, N332CH, OE-GXB

Regn.	Type	C/n	Prev.Id.
OY-HEP(2)	McDonnell-Douglas MD-500N	LN-022	G-NOTA
			VR-CPD
			N520QP
			N52113
OY-HES	Hughes 369D	40-0714D	G-BHST
OY-HET	Bell 407	53066	YR-ANA
			C-FZPQ
OY-HEY	Aérospatiale AS.350B2 Ecureuil	2904	N4027Q
OY-HEZ	Sikorsky S-76A -II +	760101	G-CHCD
			G-CBJB
			N288SP
			C-GIMN
			YV-326C
OY-HFC	Robinson R-22 Beta	1251	
OY-HFE	Robinson R-22 Beta	1480	
OY-HFF	Robinson R-22M Mariner	1629M	
OY-HFI	Robinson R-22M Mariner	1708M	
OY-HFJ	Robinson R-22M Mariner	1777M	
OY-HFK	Robinson R-22M Mariner	1948M	
OY-HFL	Robinson R-22M Mariner	1778M	
OY-HFM	Robinson R-22M Mariner	1170M	
OY-HFU	Robinson R-44 Astro	0028	
OY-HFW	Robinson R-44 Astro	0195	
OY-HGA	Aérospatiale AS.350B2 Ecureuil	2600	
OY-HGB	Hughes 369D	1146D	CS-HCI
			G-ONTA
OY-HGD	Hughes 369D	48-0294D	SE-JBU
			(PH-....)
			G-GOGO
			(G-BFSM)
OY-HGE	Hughes 369D	47-0112D	D-HOLG
			CS-HCD
			D-HOLG
			C-GYXP
OY-HGF	Hughes 369D	98-0347D	D-HILS
			LY-H..
			D-HILS
			CS-HCV
			D-HILS
			N8634F
			YV-146CP
			YV-285CP
			N8634F
OY-HGJ	Aérospatiale AS.350B2 Ecureuil	2401	C-GHMD
OY-HGK	Aérospatiale AS.350B2 Ecureuil	2570	C-FNJW
OY-HGL	Aérospatiale AS.350B2 Ecureuil	2950	N4074E
OY-HHA	Aérospatiale AS.332L Super Puma	2015	G-CHCB
			F-....
			C-GQYX
			HC-BRH
			C-GQYX
			HC-BRH
			C-GQYX
			P2-PHY
			C-GQYX
			N5789M
OY-HHT	Bell 206B Jet Ranger II	3128	G-BWBX
			D-HOLY
			N20WW
			N57521
OY-HIA	Bell 222U	47529	(N3188V)
			TC-HCS
			N3188V
OY-HIB	Bell 222U	47519	D-HCED
			C-FVUZ
			JA9961
			N8154Q
			VH-LAJ
OY-HII	Bell 206L-1 Long Ranger II	45339	SE-HVH
			N6592X
			G-BSSH
			RP-C675
OY-HIW	Sikorsky S-76A +	760183	G-BVCX
			N951L
			N5450M

Regn.	Type	C/n	Prev.Id.
OY-HJN	Eurocopter EC.120B Colibri	1072	
OY-HJS	Rotorway Exec 90	9305-5128	
OY-HJW	Schweizer 269C	S-1651	OO-HJW
			N69A
OY-HLK	Robinson R-22	0086	D-HHOI
OY-HMB	Bell 212	30686	LN-OSR
OY-HMW	Aérospatiale AS.365N2 Dauphin 2	6448	F-WYMR
OY-HMY	Aérospatiale AS.365N2 Dauphin 2	6446	F-WYMN
OY-HOY	Aérospatiale AS.355F2 Ecureuil 2	5598	HB-XJI
OY-HPA	Schweizer 269C	S-1620	F-GMMM
			D-HCMF
			N41S
OY-HPB	Agusta A.109A-II (Reservation)	7344	N109PB
			OH-HEI
			N109PD
OY-HRA	Sikorsky S-61N (Reservation)	unkn	
OY-HSH	Bell 206L Long Ranger	45014	SE-HOL
			N49695
OY-HSM	Hughes 269C	S-1773	N69A
OY-HSV	Robinson R-44 Astro	0616	
OY-HVD	Aérospatiale SA.315B Lama (Reservation)	2453	HB-XGG
OY-HVM	Rotorway Exec 162F (Reservation)	9409	
OY-IBM	Cessna 172RG Cutlass	0567	PH-TWD
			D-EIZZ
			N5545V
OY-IDB	Piper PA-28-236 Dakota	28-8011043	SE-IDB
OY-IHB	Rans S-10 Sakota (Reservation)	unkn	
OY-IIB	Noorduyn/ N.American AT-16 Harvard IIB (Reservation)	14-426	Fv16126
			FE692
			42-889
OY-III	Reims/Cessna F.172H	0377	SE-EXB
			OH-CSQ
OY-IMR	SOCATA TB-9 Tampico (Reservation)	413	SE-IMR
OY-INI	Cessna 501 Citation I/SP (Reserved as N166FA, 8.99)	0166/0559	I-CIPA
			(N30AF)
			(OY- INI)
			I- CIPA
			N476X
			N2614C
OY-IPI	Reims/Cessna FR.172KHawk XP	0616	D-EIPI
OY-IVA	Nord 262A-42	57	
OY-JAA	Piper PA-28-181 Archer III	2843176	N9501N
OY-JAB	Beech C90A King Air	LJ-1223	N5522X
OY-JAD	Piper PA-32R-301T Saratoga II TC	3257065	
OY-JAE	Piper PA-28-181 Archer III	2843101	
OY-JAH	Piper PA-32R-301T Saratoga IITC	3257103	N9527N
OY-JAI	Cessna 500 Citation	0193	N293S
			XA-SQZ
			XC-GOW
			N193CC
OY-JAL	Piper PA-28-181 Archer III	2843046	
OY-JAN	Cessna 177B Cardinal (Damaged 10.6.97)	01917	TF-RUN
			TF-ILO
			TF-IOO(2)
			N34640
OY-JAR	Beech 200C Super King Air	BL-13	PH-ILG
OY-JAU	Piper PA-34-200T Seneca V	3449136	
OY-JAV	Piper PA-28-181 Archer III	2843093	
OY-JAY	Piper PA-28-181 Archer III	2843241	N9520N
OY-JAZ	Piper PA-28-140 Cherokee	28-23885	LN-VYO
OY-JBB	Europa Aviation Europa (Reservation)	unkn	
OY-JBC	Rutan LongEz (Reservation)	97-03	
OY-JBI	Piper PA-34-220T Seneca III	3433090	D-GCPA
			N9135B
OY-JBO	Brändli BX-2 Cherry (Reservation)	unkn	
OY-JCP	Neico Lancair 320 (Reservation)	unkn	
OY-JEC	Piper PA-28-161 Cadet	2841099	
OY-JED	Piper PA-28-161 Cadet	2841177	
OY-JEE	Piper PA-28-161 Cadet	2841175	
OY-JES	Van's RV-6 (Reservation)	9401-2306	
OY-JEV	Cessna 550 Citation II	0284	I-ARIB
			N6801R
OY-JEZ	Piper PA-28R-200 Cherokee Arrow II (W/o 9.11.90)	28R-7535024	N32104
OY-JHS	Piper PA-34-220T Seneca V	3449056	

Regn.	Type	C/n	Prev.Id.	Regn.	Type	C/n	Prev.Id.
OY-JKA	Cessna 172N	73613	C-GDKJ	OY-KHK	McDonnell-Douglas DC-9-81	49910	
			(N7022G)	OY-KHL	McDonnell-Douglas DC-9-81	49911	
OY-JKH	Bombardier Learjet 60	60-141	N141LJ	OY-KHM	McDonnell-Douglas DC-9-81	49914	
			N234FX	OY-KHN	McDonnell-Douglas DC-9-81	53000	
OY-JMC	Cessna 525 CitationJet	0277	N277CJ	OY-KHP	McDonnell-Douglas DC-9-81	53007	
OY-JMP	Cessna TP.206D Turbo Skywagon	0537	D-ECAJ	OY-KHR	McDonnell-Douglas DC-9-81	53275	
			N8737Z	OY-KHT	McDonnell-Douglas DC-9-82	53296	
OY-JPC	Cessna 172M	67193	N70102	OY-KHU	McDonnell-Douglas DC-9-87	53336	
OY-JRF	Beech 1900C	UB-66	F-OJAS	OY-KHW	McDonnell-Douglas DC-9-87	53348	
			F-GTOT	OY-KID	McDonnell-Douglas DC-9-21	47360	SE-DBP
			N823BE	OY-KIE	McDonnell-Douglas DC-9-21	47306	SE-DBR
			N3044C	OY-KIG	McDonnell-Douglas DC-9-81	48006	HB-ING
OY-JRJ	Aeritalia/SNIAS ATR-42-320	036	F-WQIS	OY-KIH	McDonnell-Douglas DC-9-81	48007	HB-INH
			9J-HFJ	OY-KII	McDonnell-Douglas DC-9-81	48008	HB-INI
			F-OHFJ	OY-KIK	McDonnell-Douglas DC-9-81	48004	HB-INE
			F-GEGF	OY-KIL	McDonnell-Douglas MD-90-30	53458	
			F-WWER	OY-KIM	McDonnell-Douglas MD-90-30	53460	
OY-JRK	Short SC.7 Skyvan 3A-100	SH.1901	N8117V	OY-KIN	McDonnell-Douglas MD-90-30	53544	
			9M-AXT	OY-KKC	Boeing 737-683	28298	
			SE-GEX	OY-KKD	Boeing 737-683	28299	
			LN-NPA	OY-KKE	Boeing 737-683	28305	
			G-AZRY	OY-KKF	Boeing 737-683	30189	
			G-14-73	OY-KKG	Boeing 737-683	28300	(LN-RPC)
OY-JRN	Beech 200 Super King Air	BB-364	(OY-JRB)	OY-KKH	Boeing 737-683	28301	(LN-RPD)
			F-GHYV	OY-KKK	Boeing 737-683 (Reservation)	28316	
			N66171	OY-KKL	Boeing 737-683 (Reservation)	28321	
			XC-DIK	OY-KKM	Boeing 737-683 (Reservation)	30193	
			N18450	OY-KKP	Boeing 737-683	28312	
OY-JRO	Beech 65-B90 King Air	LJ-327	N827K	OY-KZI	S.A.I. KZ-I Replica	8605/2	(OY-CMZ)
			(N507M)	OY-KZS	S.A.I. KZ-VIII Replica	8703, formerly KZ8R-001	
			N827K	OY-LAJ	SOCATA TB-9 Tampico	1090	F-GLAJ
OY-JRR	DHC-2 Turbo-Beaver III	1632/TB-18	N911CC	OY-LAN	Neico Lancair 360 (Reservation)	473	
			C-FUKK	OY-LEK	Van's RV-8 (Reservation)	1197	
			CF-UKK	OY-LEL	Beech B300 Super King Air	FL-161	N11196
OY-JRU	Lockheed T-33 (Reservation)	unkn		OY-LEN	G-200 (Reservation)	unkn	
OY-JRV	Beech 1900D	UE-338	N23381	OY-LEO	Rans S-10E Sakota	unkn	9-111
OY-JRW	GAF N-24A Nomad	117	VH-KNA	OY-LIN	Dassault Falcon 50	230	3B-NSY
			ZK-ECM				HB-IAV
			VH-PGW				F-GNGL
			(N415NE)				F-WWHD
			VH-PGW	OY-LJA	Gates Lear Jet 35A	35A-594	N7007V
			(VH-AUR)				(ZS-EFD)
OY-JSN	Piper J-3C-65 Cub	5368	N311PB				(ZS-PTL)
			N31154				N7007V
			NC31154				N72596
OY-KAG	Fokker F.27-050	20185	PH-EXL				N1088C
OY-KAH	Fokker F.27-050	20186	PH-EXM	OY-LJB	Gates Learjet 31A	31A-086	N105FX
OY-KAI	Fokker F.27-050	20194	PH-EXS				N867JS
OY-KAK	Fokker F.27-050	20195	PH-EXA				N2603Q
OY-KCA	DHC-8 Series 402	4012	C-FWBB	OY-LJC	Gates Learjet 31A	31A-087	N106FX
OY-KDH	Boeing 767-383ER	24358	I-AEJB				N868JS
			OY-KDH				N9173T
OY-KDL	Boeing 767-383ER	24477		OY-LJD	Bombardier Learjet 60	60-005	N205FX
OY-KDM	Boeing 767-383ER	25088					N869JS
OY-KDN	Boeing 767-383ER	24848	SE-DKS				N610TM
OY-KDO	Boeing 767-383ER	24849	SE-DKT				N5011L
OY-KGF	McDonnell-Douglas DC-9-21	47308		OY-LJE	Bombardier Learjet 60	60-011	N60T
OY-KGL	McDonnell-Douglas DC-9-41	47597	N54631				N5013U
OY-KGM	McDonnell-Douglas DC-9-41	47624		OY-LJF	Bombardier Learjet 60	60-173	
OY-KGO	McDonnell-Douglas DC-9-41	47632		OY-LKA	Zenair CH-601HD Zodiac (Reservation)	unkn	
OY-KGP	McDonnell-Douglas DC-9-41	47646		OY-LKH	Beech B200 Super King Air	BB-1325	G-KMCD
OY-KGR	McDonnell-Douglas DC-9-41	47725					V5-BDL
OY-KGS	McDonnell-Douglas DC-9-41	47766					N15587
OY-KGT	McDonnell-Douglas DC-9-82	49380	N845RA	OY-LLE	Aero Designs Pulsar XP (Reservation)	0396	
			OY-KGT	OY-LPJ	Fairchild F.24W-41A Argus II	834	(OY-ANO)
			N19B		(Reservation)		D-EHIB
OY-KGY	McDonnell-Douglas DC-9-81	49420					HB-EAK
OY-KGZ	McDonnell-Douglas DC-9-82	49381					HB597
OY-KHC	McDonnell-Douglas DC-9-81	49436					43-14870
OY-KHE	McDonnell-Douglas DC-9-82	49604	N842RA	OY-LUI	Van's RV-6 (Reservation)	unkn	
			OY-KHE	OY-LYK	Cessna 150 (Reservation)	unkn	
			N6200N	OY-LYN	Rans S-10 Sakota	0189048	
OY-KHF	McDonnell-Douglas DC-9-87	49609		OY-MAF	Boeing 737-5L9	28128	
OY-KHG	McDonnell-Douglas DC-9-81	49613		OY-MDC	Bede BD-5B (Reservation)	2235D	
OY-KHI	McDonnell-Douglas DC-9-87	49614		OY-MED	Zenair CH-701 STOL (Reservation)	unkn	

Regn.	Type	C/n	Prev.Id.
OY-MEI	Piper PA-28-181 Archer III	2843036	
OY-MEN	Beech B300 Super King Air	FL-229	N9WV
OY-MKA	Piper PA-22-108 Colt (Reservation)	22-9069	LN-IKE
			N10F
OY-MMH	Fokker F.27-050	20125	PH-EXJ
OY-MMS	Fokker F.27-050	20148	PH-EXU
OY-MMV	Fokker F.27-050	20154	G-BXZW
			OY-MMV
			PH-EXO
OY-MNA	Piper PA-28-181 Archer III	2890215	G-PIPA
			N92516
OY-MRB	Boeing 737-7L9	28005	
OY-MRC	Boeing 737-7L9	28006	N5573K
OY-MRD	Boeing 737-7L9	28007	N1786B
OY-MRE	Boeing 737-7L9	28008	
OY-MRF	Boeing 737-7L9	28009	
OY-MST	Piper PA-31-310 Navajo	31-7300967	G-BNDD
			G-BBMK
			N7571L
OY-MUA	Embraer EMB.110P1 Bandeirante	110-263	N431A
			PT-SBC
OY-MUB	Short SD.3-30	SH.3069	G-BITX
			G-14-3069
OY-MUD	Short SD.3-60	SH.3692	N693PC
			G-BMNH
			G-14-3692
OY-MUE	BAe.Jetstream Series 3102	758	G-BTAI
			(OM-SKY)
			G-BTAI
			I-ALKD
			G-BTAI
			I- BLUI
			G-31-758
OY-MUF	Fairchild F.27	40	LN-BSE
			OY-MUF
			LN-BSD
			SE-INB
			N3225
			HK-1137
			N3225
			CF-QBE
			N5095A
			N2712
			N5095A
OY-MUG	Short SD.3-60 Variant 100	SH.3716	G-BNDM
			EI-CMG
			N360AR
			G-BNDM
			G-14-3716
OY-MUH	Aeritalia/SNIAS ATR-42-300	125	N425TE
			F-WWEV
OY-MUK	Aeritalia/SNIAS ATR-42-300	176	EI-CBF
			(N426TE)
			F-WWEG
OY-NFK	Cessna TU206G Stationair/ Soloy	04287	HB-CLG
			VH-SUL
			N756RC
OY-NHF	Piper PA-28-161 Warrior II (Dam. 27.9.97)	28-8316072	N4306W
OY-NIF	Aero Designs Pulsar (Reservation)	unkn	
OY-NIW	Canard 77 (Reservation)	unkn	
OY-NPA	Fairchild-Swearingen SA.226TC Metro II	TC-258	C-GBDF
			4X-CSA
			N5463M
OY-NPB(2)	Fairchild-Swearingen SA.227AC Metro III	AC-420	N67TC
			(N568G)
			N67TC
			N1014D
OY-NPC(2)	Fairchild-Swearingen SA.227AC Metro III	AC-748B	OE-LIZ
			OY-FCM
			OE-GMT
			I-SASR
			N274IA
OY-NPD(2)	Fairchild-Swearingen SA.227DC Metro 23	DC-865B	9M-BCH
			N30289

Regn.	Type	C/n	Prev.Id.
OY-NPE	Fairchild-Swearingen SA.227DC Metro 23	DC-867B	N23VJ
			9M-APA
			(VH-MYE)
			9M-APA
			N3029R
OY-NUK	Beech 200 Super King Air	BB-634	N101CP
			N6692D
OY-OCM	Partenavia P.68B	180	PH-SPB
			D-GEKA
OY-OIV	Jurca MJ.52 Sirocco (Reservation)	101	(OY-CGS)
OY-OKC	Cessna 177B Cardinal	02663	N20373
OY-OKI	Cessna 337 Skymaster (Reservation)	unkn	
OY-OLE	Piper PA-31-350 Navajo Chieftain	31-7752061	PH-DAE
			N353AC
			N63748
OY-ONE	Cessna 501 Citation 1/SP	0143	D-IGGK
			N26523
OY-PAC	LET L-410UVP-R20	871812	OK-SDP
			RA-67599
			CCCP-67599
OY-PAF	LET L-410UVP-E9	892325	S9-TBG
			SovAF:2325
OY-PBA	Pilatus PC-6/B4-H2 Turbo Porter	678	LN-VIT
			HB-FEY
			I-ALPJ
			HB-FEY
OY-PBF	Cessna 208B Grand Caravan	0584	G-MART
OY-PBG	Reims/Cessna F.406 Caravan	0015	G-TINI
			PH-FWE
			EC-FOH
			EC-177
			PH-FWE
			F-WZDX
OY-PBH(2)	LET L-410UVP-E20	972736	OK-DDC
OY-PBS	Cessna 172R	80087	
OY-PCA	Piper PA-32RT-300 Lance	32R-7885087	SE-GXA
			N1822C
OY-PCC	Reims/Cessna F.172M	1486	SE-GMV
OY-PCF	Piper PA-32-300 Cherokee Six	32-40755	OH-PCF
OY-PCL	Beech B200 Super King Air	BB-1675	N2355Z
OY-PDN	Cessna 551 Citation II	0412	N413VP
			G-OMCL
			N12160
OY-PEB	Beech 200 Super King Air	BB-309	5Y-NUR
			OY-PEB
			D-ILNY
			G-BEUZ
OY-PEL	Piper PA-28RT-201 Arrow IV	28R-8018024	SE-IDE
OY-PEM	Piper PA-44-180 Seminole	44-8195020	N333X
			N8383A
OY-PEN	Cessna 172M	64743	N61702
OY-PET	Piper PA-34-200T Seneca II	34-7570011	N32174
OY-PEU	Reims/Cessna F.406 Caravan II	0045	5Y-LAN
			G-FIND
			PH-ALV
			F-WZDT
OY-PEV	Cessna 172P	74367	LN-MTA
			N51872
OY-PEW	Reims/Cessna F.172N	1599	LN-MTZ
			SE-GOV
OY-PHN	Dassault Falcon 10	209	HB-VKR
			N312AT
			(N312AR)
			N312AT
			N272FJ
			F-WZGP
OY-PIL	Cessna 177RG Cardinal RG	0422	SE-KRP
			N2022Q
OY-PIN	Rutan LongEz	103	SE XFG
OY-PJA	Maule M-7-235 Super Rocket	4004C	N56562
OY-PJH	Maule M-7-235 Super Rocket	4023C	N56616
OY-PJJ	Piper J-3C-65 Cub	12417	G-BKGO
			CN-TVO
			F-DACK
			CN-TUK, F-BDTK, 44-80121

Regn.	Type	C/n	Prev.Id.
OY-PJP	SOCATA MS.894A Minerva 220	12077	SE-FSV
OY-PLL	SOCATA TB-10 Tobago	547	LN-KLL
OY-PMT	Cessna R.172K Hawk XP	2688	YN-CEK
			N736PU
OY-POE	Cessna 182P Skylane	61335	N20977
			(G-BAFJ)
OY-POF	DHC-6 Twin Otter 300	235	N6868
OY-POJ	Beech 95-B55 Baron (W/o 18.7.90)	TC-579	SE-EEZ
OY-POS	SOCATA MS.893E Rallye 180GT Gaillard	12674	
OY-POT	Piaggio FWP.149D	016	D-EOPG
	(Built from Piaggio airframe c/n 340)		90+08
			BD+392
OY-POW	Piper PA-28R-200 Cherokee Arrow II	28R-7435267	G-BCKR
			N9633N
OY-POZ	Piper PA-28-151 Cherokee Warrior	28-7415248	D-EOEP
			N9547N
OY-PRA	Piper PA-28R-180 Cherokee Arrow	28R-30464	SE-FCE
OY-PRB	Piper PA-28-140 Cherokee Cruiser	28-7425394	N44199
OY-PRE	Rockwell Commander 112A	480	
OY-PRF	SOCATA MS.893A Rallye Commodore 180	11924	SE-FSK
OY-PRG	SOCATA MS.880B Rallye Club	2779	
OY-PRI	SOCATA MS.892E Rallye 150ST	2687	
OY-PRJ	SOCATA MS.893E Rallye 180GT Gaillard	12727	
OY-PRK	SOCATA MS.880B Rallye-Club	2925	
OY-PRL	SOCATA Rallye 100ST-D	2744	D-EBWN
			F-ODDH
OY-PRM	SOCATA MS.893E Rallye 180GT Gaillard	12736	
OY-PRS	SOCATA MS.880B Rallye Club	2948	
OY-PRU	SOCATA MS.893E Rallye 180GT Gaillard	12959	
OY-PRZ	SOCATA MS.893E Rallye 180GT Gaillard	12754	
OY-PUP	Beagle B.121 Pup 150 (Reservation)	105	LN-HHC
			G-AXNO
OY-PYY	Piper PA-61-601P Aerostar	61P-0768-8063382	EC-DJS
	(Damaged 26.7.97)		N3634M
OY-RAC	Hawker 800XP	258335	(LN-AAA(3))
			N335XP
OY-RAF	Europa Aviation Europa (Reservation)	313	
OY-RAM	Boeing Stearman A75N1	75-2186	41-8627
OY-RAV	Cessna 340A/RAM	0716	N98976
			F-GCSQ
			N98976
OY-RCA	BAe.146 Series 200	E-2045	G-DEBH
			N185US
			N362PS
OY-RGB	VFW-Fokker VFW-614 (Reservation)	G-018	D-AXDB
			17+02
OY-RLN	Piper PA-28-181 Archer II	28-7990518	G-BTKY
			N2877D
OY-RPE	Aeronca 11AC Chief	1603	D-EJUN
			OO-GUS
			OO-USG
OY-RPH	Cessna 150L	73011	N1711Q
OY-RPJ	Reims/Cessna F.172M	1206	
OY-RPM	Piper PA-39 Twin Comanche C/R	39-4	OO-RPM
			OY-RPM
			D-GFHW
			OE-FCG
			N8845Y
OY-RPO	Piper PA-23-250 Aztec E	27-7554144	N54845
OY-RPR	SOCATA MS.880B Rallye-Club	1283	SE-CIU
OY-RPT	Beech 35-E33 Bonanza	CD-1213	D-EKXI
OY-RPU	Piper PA-28-180 Cherokee Archer	28-7405016	N56548
OY-RPV	Cessna 340	0114	OE-FKI
			N4576L
OY-RPY	Piper PA-18-150 Super Cub	18-8092	PH-NKE
OY-RRG	Cessna 177RG Cardinal RG	1214	LN-LGP
			N52609
OY-RRW	VFW-Fokker VFW-614 (Reservation)	G-019	D-ASDB
			17+03
OY-RSC	Cessna TR.182 Turbo Skylane RG	01575	N5455S
OY-RVA	Van's RV-8A (Reservation)	unkn	
OY-RYB	Reims/Cessna F.172L	0862	
OY-RYE	Reims/Cessna F.172M	0927	
OY-RYI	Cessna 182P Skylane	61811	N79309
OY-RYJ	Cessna 182P Skylane	62271	
OY-RYN	Cessna 182P Skylane	62267	N58738
OY-RYO	Reims/Cessna F.172M	1053	
OY-RYP	Reims/Cessna F.172M	0944	
OY-RYU	Reims/Cessna F.172M	1140	
OY-RYW	Cessna U.206F Stationair	01776	
OY-RYY	Reims/Cessna F.172M	1116	
OY-SAV	Cessna 402B	0201	
OY-SBR	Aérospatiale SN.601 Corvette	23	F-BVPF
OY-SBT	Aérospatiale SN.601 Corvette	33	F-BTTT
OY-SEA	Boeing 737-8Q8	28213	N3521N
OY-SEC	Boeing 737-8Q8	28221	N17878
OY-SEE	Boeing 737-3YO	24463	N955WP
			EI-BZR
			YV-99C
			EI-BZR
			EC-ENT
			EC-245
			N1779B
OY-SEF	Boeing 737-382	25162	CS-TIL
OY-SEG	Boeing 737-59D	26419	G-OBMY
			SE-DNI
OY-SEH	Boeing 737-85H	28444	N1787B
OY-SEI	Boeing 737-85H	28445	N1786B
OY-SER	Boeing 727-232A	20639	N16784
			N516PE
			(N506PE)
			N457DA
			(N466DA)
OY-SES	Boeing 727-251	19977	N258US
			(N258KP)
			N258US
OY-SET	Boeing 727-227F	21245	EI-PAK
			N16762
			N569PE
			(N443PS)
			N444BN
OY-SEV	Boeing 727-281F	20571	EI-SKY
			N905PG
			N530MD
			HL7367
			JA8341
OY-SEW	Boeing 727-287F	21688	N920PG
			LV-MIM
OY-SEY	Boeing 727-224F	20659	N29730
			(N24730)
OY-SFH	Pilatus PC-6/B2-H4 Turbo Porter	778	N117SA
			(D-FHPK)
			LV-MAE
OY-SFK	Cessna TR.182 Turbo Skylane RG	00667	N9194R
OY-SFU	Cessna TR.182 Turbo Skylane RG	01113	G-BOYE
			N756MK
OY-SMI	Yakovlev YAK-52 (Reservation)	unkn	
OY-SMP	Piper PA-34-220T Seneca III	3448007	G-BSMP
			N9196W
OY-SPL	Piper PA-28-181 Archer III	2843164	N9502N
OY-STJ	S.A.I. KZ-VII U-8 Laerke	199	D-EKID
			HB-EPA
			OH-KZG
OY-SUA	Mooney M.20K Model 231	25-0875	SE-KZU
			OY-SUA
			N5809Y
OY-SUC	Cessna 207A Skywagon	00781	N9999M
OY-SUK	Cessna 152	82543	TF-FTG
			N69194
OY-SUN	Cessna 402C	0461	ZS-KUU
			N6837C
OY-SUP	Reims/Cessna FRA.150M Aerobat	0323	PH-KDI
			PH-AXQ
OY-SUR	Partenavia P.68C Observer	246-04-OB	D-GEMG
OY-SUW	Piper PA-34-200 Seneca	34-7250257	G-BADF
			N5446T
OY-SVC	Piper PA-31-310 Navajo	31-722	LN-RAZ
	(Wfu in Sweden)		SE-FYV
OY-SVD	Piper PA-28-180 Cherokee G	28-7305490	SE-GDK

Regn.	Type	C/n	Prev.Id.
OY-SVF	BAe. Jetstream Series 3102	686	G-BSFG
			PH-KJF
			G-31-686
OY-SVI	BAe. ATP	2061	G-BUYW
			HL5227
			G-BUYW
			G-11-061
OY-SVJ	BAe. Jetstream Series 3102	711	G-BTYG
			N415MX
			G-31-711
OY-SVL	Cessna 501 Citation SP	0049	(N347DA)
			(N36WS)
			N2ZC
			N98586
OY-SVM	Cessna 172P	74818	N53796
OY-SVR	BAe. Jetstream Series 3100	701	D-CONA
			(PH-KJH)
			G-31-701
OY-SVS	BAe. Jetstream Series 4100	41014	G-4-014
OY-SVT	BAe, ATP	2062	G-11-062
OY-SVU	BAe. ATP	2063	G-BWYT
			HL5228
			G-11-063
OY-SVW	BAe. Jetstream Series 4102	41047	(OY-SVT)
			G-BVZC
			G-4-047
			(N29226)
OY-TAC	Cessna U.206C Stationair	01178	LN-VIY
OY-TAO	Rutan Cozy Mk IV (Reservation)	9410-0349	
OY-TAW	Aviat A-1 Husky	1279	D-EJHU(2)
OY-TBS	Rutan LongEz (Reservation)	9503	
OY-TCL	LET L-410UVP-E20C	912533	OK-WDL
			(PT-...)
			OK-WDL
OY-TCM	LET L-410UVP-E20C	912532	OK-WDJ
			PT-WLS
			OK-WDJ
OY-TCP	Cessna 500 Citation (Reservation)	0315	SE-DRZ
			N55SH
			N55SK
			N5315J
OY-TEA	Piper PA-28-181 Archer III	2843313	
OY-TEI	Piper PA-28-181 Archer III	2843040	
OY-TFB	Beech A36 Bonanza	E-3003	N821SA
OY-TFC	Beech A36 Bonanza	E-3009	N1109Q
OY-TFD	Beech A36 Bonanza	E-3013	N1113J
OY-TFE	Beech A36 Bonanza	E-3034	N1096Y
OY-TFT	Piper PA-32-301T Turbo Saratoga II TC	3257050	
OY-TIN	Erco 415 Ercoupe (Reservation)	unkn	
OY-TKI	Cessna 500 Citation	0299	N80364
			PT-OZX
			YV-940CP
			N5133K
			ZS-MGH
			N55AK
			N66TR
			N3JJ
			HB-VEO
			N5299J
OY-TLC	Partenavia P.68B	147	G-CNIS
			G-BJOF
			EI-BKH
			G-PAUL
OY-TMA	Cessna 550 Citation II (Reservation)	0457	N63TM
			N457CF
			N220CC
			N1250L
			EI-TNT
OY-TNT	Boeing 727-281F	20725	N902PG
			N526MD
			HL/366
			JA8346
OY-TOE	Piper PA-28-151 Cherokee Warrior	28-7415656	
OY-TOF	Piper PA-28-140 Cherokee Cruiser	28-7425324	N9597N
OY-TOG	Piper PA-28-180 Cherokee Archer	28-7505142	

Regn.	Type	C/n	Prev.Id.
OY-TOH	Piper PA-28-151 Cherokee Warrior	28-7515329	
OY-TOI	Piper PA-28-140 Cherokee Cruiser	28-7525045	
OY-TOJ	Piper PA-28-140 Cherokee Cruiser	28-7525049	
OY-TOM	Piper PA-18 Super Cub 105	18-1639	OO-SPN
			ALAT
			51-15639
OY-TON	Piper PA-31-310 Navajo	31-414	D-ILTD
			N6458L
OY-TOS	Piper PA-28-180 Cherokee Archer	28-7505177	
OY-TOT	Piper PA-28-151 Cherokee Warrior	28-7515096	(OY-TOL)
OY-TOU	Piper PA-28R-200 Cherokee Arrow II	28R-7535262	
OY-TOZ	Piper PA-28-151 Cherokee Warrior	28-7515419	
OY-TRD	Cessna 150C	59770	N1970Z
OY-TRE	Reims/Cessna F.172E	0044	
OY-TRP	Piper J-3C-65 Cub (L-4H)	11964	OO-MCG
			44-79668
OY-TRR	Reims/Cessna F.172M	0991	LN-BFD
OY-TRY	Piper PA-28R-200 Cherokee Arrow	28R-35167	OO-ISF
			N9452N
OY-TRZ	Cessna P.206E Super Skylane	00621	D-EDEV
			OE-DEY
			N5721J
OY-TSI	Piper PA-28 Cherokee (Reservation)	unkn	
OY-TUS	Pilatus PC-12/45	230	HB-FSY
OY-TVA	Reims/Cessna F.152	1525	D-EACY
OY-UPA	Boeing 727-31C	19233	N926UP
			N894TW
OY-UPB	Boeing 727-180V	19874	N921UP
			N9515T
OY-UPD	Boeing 727-22C	19103	N944UP
			N431EX
			N7415U
OY-UPJ	Boeing 727-22C	19102	N943UP
			N420EX
			HK-2476
			N7414U
OY-UPM	Boeing 727-31QC	19229	N923UP
			N890TW
OY-UPS	Boeing 727-31QC	19232	N927UP
			N893TW
OY-UPT	Boeing 727-22QC	19094	N945UP
			N422EX
			HK-2475
			N7406U
OY-VAF	Cessna TR.182 Turbo Skylane RG	01458	N4919S
OY-VAM	de Havilland DH.100 Vampire FB.6	693	SE-DXY
			J-1184
OY-VIB	Stoddart-Hamilton Glastar (Reservation)	unkn	
OY-VIP	Cessna 500 Citation (Reservation)	0311	SE-DRT
			N39RE
			N501RL
			OH-COL
			N818CD
			N5311J
OY-VSG	Hummelbird (Reservation)	SR3019-P	
OY-YAC	Yakovlev YAK-52	9511904	LY-AOD
OY-YAK	Yakovlev YAK-52	899408	RA-01364 / 20
OY-YYY	Cessna P210N Pressurized Centurion II	00438	SE-KGT
			N3RS
			N731CG
OY-...	Beech B200 Super King Air	BB-1144	N120AJ
			ZS-NWT
			D-IBHF
			N62BE
			N221P
OY-...	Beech 1900D	UE-29	N29YV
OY-...	Cessna 195	7358	N117DH
OY-...	Lockheed T-33A	580-697. ?	N49239
	(Probably the intended OY-JRU ?)		51-91..
OY-...	Piper PA-28-236 Dakota	28-8111017	D-EVAP(2)
			G-BOUI
			N84017

Regn.	Type	C/n	Prev.Id.
OY-...	S.A.I. KZ-III/U2	103	SE-AMF
			OY-DUI
			D-ECUF
			OY-DUI
OY-...	Schempp-Hirth Standard Cirrus	641	PH-533

BALLOONS

Regn.	Type	C/n	Prev.Id.
OY-BOA	Piccard AX-6 HAFB	106	
OY-BOD	Cameron V-77 HAFB	2288	
OY-BOE	Thunder AX7-65 HAFB	062	
OY-BOF	Cameron V-77 HAFB	881	
OY-BOH	Cameron V-77 HAFB	757	
OY-BOL	Cameron N-77 HAFB	1891	
OY-BOM	Cameron O-105 HAFB	4156	
OY-BOO	Cameron N-56 HAFB	393	
OY-BOR	Cameron Tuborg Bottle SS 52 HAFB	809	
OY-BOT	Cameron N-77 HAFB	569	
OY-BOU	Colt 77A HAFB	1357	
OY-BOW(2)	Colt 77A HAFB	014	SE-ZVB
OY-BOZ	Colt 77A HAFB	1359	
OY-COA	Balloon Works Firefly F7 HAFB	F7-601	
OY-COB	Galaxy 7 HAFB	GLX-1197	VH-HGX
OY-COC	Cameron N-90 HAFB	2006	
OY-COD	Cameron N-77 HAFB	2320	
OY-COE	Lindstrand LBL-60A HAFB	210	G-BWDK
OY-COG	Cameron V-77 HAFB	3232	
OY-COH	Colt 77A HAFB	1325	
OY-COI	Thunder AX7-77 HAFB	2081	
OY-COJ	Lindstrand LBL-21A HAFB	083	
OY-COK	Colt 77A HAFB	1914	
OY-COL	Cameron O-120 HAFB	2327	
OY-COM	Cameron N-77 HAFB	2801	
OY-CON	Cameron N-77 HAFB	3904	
OY-COO	Colt 56A HAFB	1379	
OY-COP	Thunder AX7-77SI HAFB	1889	
OY-COR	Lindstrand LBL-21A HAFB	080	
OY-COS	Sky 77-24 HAFB	037	
OY-COT(2)	Cameron O-77 HAFB	2620	
OY-COU	Cameron V-90 HAFB (Reservation)	3583	G-BWBN
OY-COW	Colt 77A HAFB	1980	
OY-COY	Colt 77A HAFB	757	
OY-COZ	Cameron V-77 HAFB	3009	
OY-GOB	Cameron V-77 HAFB	3699	
OY-GOF	Cameron V-77 HAFB	3248	
OY-GOG	Sky 77-24 HAFB	024	
OY-GOK	Cameron N-77 HAFB	3286	
OY-GOM	Cameron N-77 HAFB	3701	
OY-GON	Balloon Works Firefly C8 HAFB	FC8-001	HB-BRX
OY-GOP	Lindstrand LBL-77A HAFB	366	
OY-GOS	Cameron V-77 HAFB	2963	
OY-GOV	Lindstrand LBL-90A HAFB	045	
OY-SOB	SLB Viking 180A HAFB	SLB-020	SE-ZFK
OY-SON	Lindstrand LBL-77A HAFB	unkn	

GLIDERS AND MOTOR-GLIDERS

Regn.	Type	C/n	Prev.Id.
OY-AEX	Schleicher Ka.6 Rhönsegler	279	
OY-AIX	Hoglund/Traugott-Olsen 2G	1	OY-123
OY-AJX	Schleicher Ka.6BR Rhönsegler	339	D-5812
			D-3561
OY-AVX	Hoglund/Traugott-Olsen 2G	DA-7	OY-121
OY-AXE	Grunau Baby IIb	3	
OY-AXN	Grunau Baby IIb	12	
OY-AXO	Grunau Baby IIb	3	OY-93
OY-AXR	Scheibe Spatz	526	

Regn.	Type	C/n	Prev.Id.
OY-AXV	Scheibe L-Spatz 55	525	
OY-AXY	Scheibe L-Spatz 55	527	
OY-AXZ	Schleicher K.8B	8106	
OY-AYX	Schleicher K.8B	1104	
OY-AZX	Schleicher K.8B	8175	
OY-BAX	VEB FES.530/1 Lehrmeister	0178	
OY-BCX	Grunau Baby IIb	2	OY-120
OY-BJX	Scheibe SF-26A Standard	5022	
OY-BNX	Scheibe Bergfalke II	188	D-4617
OY-BOX	Scheibe Bergfalke II	249	
OY-BVX	Schleicher Rhönlerche II	522	
OY-BXA	PIK-16C Vasama	34	
OY-BXD	Schleicher K.8B	5	
OY-BXE	Schleicher K.8B	9	
OY-BXF	Aeromere M-100S	055	
OY-BXJ	Schleicher K.8B	8647	
OY-BXK	Schleicher K.8B	839	D-1675
OY-BXL	Schleicher K.7 Rhönadler	7261	
OY-BXN	Scheibe Bergfalke II	102	D-5394
			D-9338
OY-BXS	Schleicher K.8B	1	D-3606
OY-BXT	Schleicher K.8B	8714	
OY-BXU	PIK-16C Vasama	36	
OY-BXV	Schleicher K.8B	8	
OY-BYX	Schleicher Ka.6CR Rhönsegler	6059	
OY-CBX	Schempp-Hirth Ventus b/16.6	51	OH-606
OY-CCX	Schempp-Hirth Ventus c	510	
OY-CRX	Schempp-Hirth Mini-Nimbus HS-7	59	SE-TSP
OY-DBX	SZD-22C Mucha Standard	672	
OY-DCX	SZD-24C Foka	W-146	
OY-DDX	Schleicher Ka.6CR Rhönsegler	6120	
OY-DGX	Scheibe Bergfalke II/55	392	
OY-DHX	Schleicher K.8B	8699	
OY-DJX	Schleicher Ka.6CR Rhönsegler	6177	
OY-DKX	Schleicher K.8B	8368	
OY-DMX	Schleicher Ka.6CR Rhönsegler	6358	
OY-DNX	Schleicher Rhönlerche II	139	D-4340
OY-DSX	SZD-9 bis Bocian 1D	861	
OY-DTX	Burgfalke Lo 150B	27	D-8279
OY-DVX	SZD-25A Lis	762	
OY-DXB	Schleicher Ka.6E	4207	
OY-DXC	Glasflügel H.201B Standard Libelle	422	
OY-DXG	Schleicher Ka.6E	4168	
OY-DXK	FES.530/1 Lehrmeister	0223	
OY-DXM	Standard Austria SH-1	72	HB-799
OY-DXN	Scheibe Zugvogel IV	1506	LN-GAW
OY-DXS	Scheibe L-Spatz 55	668	D-4701
OY-DXX	SZD-25A Lis	757	
OY-EDX	Schleicher Ka.6CR Rhönsegler	6309	
OY-EEX	Schleicher K.8B	8471	D-4062
OY-EGX	Scheibe Bergfalke II/55	344	D-6154
OY-EHX	SZD-22C Mucha Standard	589	SP-2167
OY-EIX	Schleicher Ka.6CR Rhönsegler	6413	
OY-EKX	Schleicher K.8B	8549	
OY-EMX	SZD-9 bis Bocian 1D	870	
OY-EOX	SZD-22C Mucha Standard	539	SP-2121
OY-EPX	SZD-24 Foka	200	
OY-ETX	SZD-25A Lis	759	
OY-EUX	Schleicher K.8	742	
OY-EXC	Rolladen-Schneider LS-8A	8122	
OY-EZX	Schleicher Ka.6CR Rhönsegler	6513	
OY-FAX	Schleicher K.8B	658	
OY-FBX	Scheibe Bergfalke III	5517	D-3201
OY-FEX	Aeromere M-100S Series V	052	
OY-FFX-71	SZD-9bis Bocian 1E	P-440	
OY-FHX	Scheibe Bergfalke II	5630	
OY-FIX	EoN Olympia 2	EON/056	RDAF: Z-963
			RDAF: 96-963
OY-FJX	Schleicher Ka.6CR Rhönsegler	6146	D-6034
OY-FMX	Schempp-Hirth SHK-1	41	OO-ZLJ
OY-FOX	SZD-25A Lis	765	
OY-FPX	Schempp-Hirth SHK-1	23	D-8807
OY-FTX	Scheibe Zugvogel IIIB	1068	D-1888
OY-FXF	Rolladen-Schneider LS-8A	8242	
OY-FXS	Glasflügel H.201B Standard Libelle	103	SE-TIN

Regn.	Type	C/n	Prev.Id.
OY-FYX	Schleicher Ka.6E	4158	
OY-FZX	Schleicher Ka.6CR Rhönsegler	6575	D-1019
OY-HAX	Schleicher K.8B	8129/A	D-1939
OY-HBX	Schempp-Hirth Standard Cirrus	30	
OY-HEX	Schleicher ASW-24	24075	D-9022
OY-HFX	SZD-9 bis Bocian 1E	P-462	
OY-HSX	Schempp-Hirth Ventus b	206	D-8422
OY-IBX	Schempp-Hirth Ventus 2cT	22/86	
OY-JIX	Eiri PIK-20D	20622	SE-TVO
OY-JXF	Schempp-Hirth Janus C	256	D-5062
OY-KFX	Schleicher K.8B	8758	SE-TFW
OY-KHX-3T	Schempp-Hirth Nimbus 3T	6/57	
OY-LEX	Schempp-Hirth Janus CE	302	SE-UKZ
OY-LFX	Grob G.103 Twin II	3511	D-3064
OY-LMX	Schleicher K.8B	8574/A	D-5299
OY-LUX	Schleicher ASW-20	20324	SE-UIT
			OH-539
OY-LVX	Schleicher ASK-21	21326	D-5421
OY-LXT	Schleicher K.8B	8482	SE-TCL
OY-MBX	Aeromere M-100S Series V	060	D-1095
OY-MCX	Scheibe L-Spatz 55	758	D-3599
OY-MEX	Scheibe Spatz A	01	D-3206
OY-MHX	Scheibe Zugvogel IIIB	1067	SE-TCE
			OY-EFX
			D-1814
OY-MIX	Glasflügel H201 Standard Libelle	209	
OY-MKX	Rolladen-Schneider LS-1C	83	
OY-MLX	Scheibe Bergfalke II	185	D-3655
			D-3209
OY-MMX	Rolladen-Schneider LS-1-0	2	D-4734
OY-MNX	Schleicher K.7 Rhönadler	7104	D-3609
OY-MRX	Glasflügel H201 Standard Libelle	251	
OY-MSX	Schleicher Ka.6E	4277	D-0204
OY-MTX	Glasflügel H201 Standard Libelle	261	
OY-MXX	Schleicher Ka.6CR Rhönsegler	6510-Si	D-3642
OY-MYX	Schleicher Ka.6CR Rhönsegler	6386	SE-TCO
OY-NIX	LET L-13 Blanik	173004	OE-0697
OY-NXS	Schempp-Hirth Ventus 2cM	48/99	
	(Formerly Ventus 2c c/n 36/99)		
OY-OXO	Scheibe SF-25E4 Super Falke	4312	D-KDDB
OY-PAX	Rolladen-Schneider LS-3A	3191	D-5894
OY-PEX	Schempp-Hirth Ventus bT	15/152	
OY-PFX	Schempp-Hirth Discus CS	139CS	
OY-PHX	Schempp-Hirth Ventus cT	118/392	LX-CDT
			D-KHUM
OY-PJX	Schleicher ASK-13	13607	D-6969
OY-PKX	SZD-51-1 Junior	B-2187	
OY-RBX	Rolladen-Schneider LS-8A	8176	
OY-RFX	LET L-13SDM Vivat	950609	D-KLIH
OY-RKX	Schleicher ASK-23	23149	
OY-RLX	Schleicher ASW-24	24083	SE-UIC
OY-RMX	Schempp-Hirth Duo Discus	208	
OY-SBX	LET L-23 Super Blanik	917910	OE-5540
OY-SEX	Rolladen-Schneider LS-8A	8201	
OY-SXG	Schempp-Hirth Discus b	487	D7302
OY-VBX	Schleicher K.8B	8238	
OY-VCX	Schleicher Ka.6CR Rhönsegler	6465-Si	D-4404
OY-VFX	Scheibe Bergfalke III	5571	
OY-VHX	Schleicher Ka.6E	4169	
OY-VJX	Schleicher ASW-15	15017	D-0344
OY-VLX	Schleicher Ka.6BR Rhönsegler	617	D-6144
OY-VMX	Schleicher Ka.6E	4077	
OY-VRX	Schleicher ASK-13	13342	
OY-VSX	Grob G.103 Twin Astir *(Reservation)*	3770-K-56	D-1311
OY-VXB	Schleicher Ka.6CR Rhönsegler	986	D-5046
OY-VXC	Schleicher ASK-13	13448	
OY-VXD	Slingsby T-61A Falke	1741	G-AYZV
OY-VXG	Rolladen-Schneider LS-1F	183	
OY-VXI	Schempp-Hirth Cirrus	106	D-0788
OY-VXJ	Scheibe Bergfalke II	101	D-5349
OY-VXK	Glasflügel H201B Standard Libelle	439	
OY-VXN	Schempp-Hirth Standard Cirrus	639	
OY-VXP	Pilatus B4-PC11	139	
OY-VXS	Glasflügel H201 Standard Libelle	276	(BGA1520)
OY-VXT	Pilatus B4-PC11	105	

Regn.	Type	C/n	Prev.Id.
OY-VXW	Glasflügel H205 Club Libelle	43	
OY-VXX	Glasflügel H201 Standard Libelle	268	BGA1710
OY-VXY	Schleicher Ka.6CR Rhönsegler	6043	D-6821
OY-VXZ	Rolladen-Schneider LS-1F	171	
OY-VYX	Schleicher Ka.6CR Rhönsegler	6121	
OY-XAB	Schleicher Rhönlerche II	709	
OY-XAE	LOM 57 Libelle	039	
OY-XAI	SZD-22B Mucha Standard	512	
OY-XAO	Schleicher K.8B	749	
OY-XAR	FES.530/1 Lehrmeister	0222	
OY-XAS	SZD-22A Mucha Standard	264	
OY-XAU	FES.530/1 Lehrmeister	0219	
OY-XAY	FES.530/1 Lehrmeister	0220	
OY-XAZ	Schleicher K.8B	8063	
OY-XBB	Carman M-200 Foehn	01	F-CCXG
			F-WCXG
OY-XBD	Glasflügel H201B Standard Libelle	354	
OY-XBE	Scheibe Bergfalke II/55	351	OH-KBE
OY-XBF	Glasflügel H201B Standard Libelle	406	
OY-XBG	Glasflügel H201B Standard Libelle	411	
OY-XBH	Pilatus B4-PC11	058	
OY-XBI	Pilatus B4-PC11	059	
OY-XBM	Glasflügel H201B Standard Libelle	423	
OY-XBO	PIK-16C Vasama	21	OO-ZER
OY-XBP	Pilatus B4-PC11	054	
OY-XBR	Pilatus B4-PC11	055	
OY-XBS	Scheibe L-Spatz 55	66	D-1506
OY-XBT	Scheibe Bergfalke II/55	308	D-1615
OY-XBU	Pilatus B4-PC11	060	
OY-XBX	Pilatus B4-PC11	082	
OY-XBY	Rolladen-Schneider LS-1C	187	
OY-XBZ	Glasflügel H201B Standard Libelle	405	
OY-XCA	SZD-36A Cobra 15	W-691	
OY-XCC	Glasflügel H201B Standard Libelle	595	
OY-XCD	Glasflügel H205 Club Libelle	62	
OY-XCE	Glasflügel H201B Standard Libelle	567	
OY-XCF	LET L-13 Blanik	173319	SE-TDH
OY-XCG	Grob Standard Cirrus	565G	
OY-XCH	Schempp-Hirth Standard Cirrus	505	
OY-XCI	Rolladen-Schneider LS-1D	136	D-2048
OY-XCM	SZD-36A Cobra 15	W-690	
OY-XCP	Eiri PIK-20	20058	
OY-XCT	Grob Standard Cirrus	569G	
OY-XCV	Scheibe SF-28A Tandem-Falke	5742	D-KOED
OY-XCW	Glasflügel H205 Club Libelle	106	
OY-XCX	Pilatus B4-PC11	142	
OY-XCY	Schleicher K.7 Rhönadler	7194	D-4074
OY-XDA	Scheibe SF-27	6035	D-5551
OY-XDB	Grob G.102 Astir CS	1094	
OY-XDC	Schempp-Hirth Standard Cirrus	637	
OY-XDE	Grob G.102 Astir CS	1112	
OY-XDF	Eiri PIK-20B	20090	
OY-XDG	Glasflügel H205 Club Libelle	142	
OY-XDJ	Grob G.102 Astir CS	1079	
OY-XDK	Grob G.102 Astir CS	1129	
OY-XDL	Grob G.102 Astir CS	1095	
OY-XDM	Grob G.102 Astir CS	1406	
OY-XDN	Grob G.102 Astir CS	1096	
OY-XDO	Grob G.102 Astir CS	1080	
OY-XDP	Grob G.102 Astir CS	1097	
OY-XDR	Schleicher K.7 Rhönadler	7128/A	D-5421
OY-XDS	Grob G.102 Astir CS	1131	
OY-XDT	Schleicher K.7 Rhönadler	7071	D-5265
OY-XDU	Standard Cirrus B	634	
OY-XDV	Glaser-Dirks DG-100	44	
OY-XDW	Grob G.102 Astir CS	1132	
OY-XDX	Scheibe SF-25B Falke	46141	D-KCAH
OY-XDY	Grob G.102 Astir CS	1361	
OY-XEA	Schleicher Ka.6CR Rhönsegler	6237	
OY-XEC	SZD-22C Mucha Standard	528	OO-ZSQ
OY-XED	Scheibe L-Spatz 55	794	D-1530
OY-XEF	EoN Olympia Series 2	EON/059	RDAF: Z-962
			OY-BKX
			RDAF: Z-962
OY-XEG	Schleicher ASK-13	13313	

Regn.	Type	C/n	Prev.Id.
OY-XEH	Schleicher ASW-15	15016	
OY-XEI	Scheibe Zugvogel IIIB	1069	SE-TCI
OY-XEJ	SZD-24C Foka	W-196	
OY-XEL	Schleicher Ka.6CR Rhönsegler	645	D-3208
OY-XEN	Grunau Baby IIb	unkn	
OY-XEO	Ka-2 Rhönschwalbe	223	D-5495
OY-XES	Mü.13E Bergfalke	107	D-6312
OY-XET	Siebert SIE-3	3011	
OY-XEW	Scheibe Bergfalke IV	5819	
OY-XEZ	Schempp-Hirth Standard Cirrus	40	
OY-XFA	Polyt III	1	RDAF: Z-931
OY-XFC	Schleicher K.7 Rhönadler	476	RDAF: Z-982
OY-XFD	Schleicher K.7 Rhönadler	477	RDAF: Z-983
OY-XFE	Schleicher K.8B	973	RDAF: Z-965
OY-XFH	Schleicher K.8B	8370	RDAF: Z-969
OY-XFI	Schleicher K.8B	8495	RDAF: Z-970
OY-XFK	Schleicher K.8B	8496	RDAF: Z-971
OY-XFL	Schleicher K.8B	8497	RDAF: Z-973
OY-XFM	Schleicher K.8B	8498	RDAF: Z-972
OY-XFN	Schleicher Ka.6CR Rhönsegler	779	RDAF: Z-964
			OY-XAD
			RDAF: Z-964
			OY-XAD
			RDAF: Z-964
OY-XGA	Schleicher ASK-14	14021	D-KOMI
OY-XGF	Grob G.102 Astir CS	1427	
OY-XGG	Grob G.102 Astir CS	1476	
OY-XGI	Scheibe SF-25B Falke	4829	D-KHEI
OY-XGJ	Scheibe SF-25B Falke	46120	D-KABS
OY-XGK	Schempp-Hirth Cirrus	86	SE-TIR
OY-XGL	Grob G.102 Astir CS	1472	
OY-XGM	Schleicher Ka.6CR Rhönsegler	6640-Si	D-8581
OY-XGN	Schleicher Ka.6CR Rhönsegler	1111	D-5012
OY-XGO	Standard Cirrus B	666	
OY-XGP	Scheibe SF-25B Falke	4689	D-KOSC
OY-XGT	Grob G.102 Astir CS	1185	
OY-XGV	Grob G.102 Astir CS	1279	
OY-XGW	Grob Standard Cirrus	414G	D-9247
OY-XGY	Grob G.102 Astir CS	1471	
OY-XHA	Grob G.102 Astir CS	1474	
OY-XHB	Grob G.102 Astir CS	1052	D-7236
OY-XHC	Schempp-Hirth Standard Cirrus	198	D-0882
OY-XHE	Grob G.102 Astir CS	1344	
OY-XHH	Eiri PIK-20B	20025	
OY-XHI	Scheibe SF-25C Falke	4493	D-KAUV
OY-XHK	Schempp-Hirth Standard Cirrus	537	D-3097
OY-XHL	Glasflügel H201B Standard Libelle	135	SE-TKF
OY-XHN	Eiri PIK-20D	20545	
OY-XHP	Grob G.102 Astir CS	1418	
OY-XHR	Grob G.102 Astir CS	1484	
OY-XHS	Schempp-Hirth Standard Cirrus	43	SE-TIZ
OY-XHT	Eiri PIK-20D	20546	
OY-XHU	Schempp-Hirth Cirrus 18	6	D-9319
OY-XHV	Grob G.103 Twin Astir	3008	
OY-XHW	Schempp-Hirth Standard Cirrus	142	SE-TKV
OY-XHX	Eiri PIK-20D	20552	
OY-XHY	Eiri PIK-20B	20083	
OY-XIA	Grob G.102 Astir CS 77	1650	
OY-XIC	Grob G.103 Twin Astir	3049	
OY-XID	Scheibe SF-25A Motorfalke	4541	D-KALU
OY-XIF	Glasflügel H303 Mosquito	61	
OY-XIG	Glasflügel H303 Mosquito	59	
OY-XIJ	Schempp-Hirth Standard Cirrus	258	D-1137
OY-XIK	Grob G.102 Astir CS	2107	
OY-XIL	Schleicher ASW-19	19192	
OY-XIM	Schleicher ASW-20	20091	
OY-XIN	Schleicher ASK-13	13594	
OY-XIO	Grob G.103 Twin Astir	3080	
OY-XIP	Schleicher ASW-19	19198	
OY-XIU	Scheibe SF-25B Falke	46252	D-KEAS
OY-XIV	Eiri PIK-20B	20021	OH-461
OY-XIW	Grob G.102 Astir CS 77	1710	
OY-XIZ	Eiri PIK-20D	20616	
OY-XJA	Grob G.103 Twin Astir	3126	
OY-XJC	Eiri PIK-20D	20631	

Regn.	Type	C/n	Prev.Id.
OY-XJD	Grob G.103 Twin Astir	3192	
OY-XJE	Schleicher ASW-20	20215	
OY-XJI	Schleicher ASW-19B	19224	
OY-XJJ	Schleicher ASW-24	24143	D-7263
OY-XJK	Glasflügel H201B Standard Libelle	509	D-2409
OY-XJL	Schleicher ASW-19B	19234	
OY-XJP	Rolladen-Schneider LS-3A	3380	
OY-XJR	Rolladen-Schneider LS-1C	175	D-2950
OY-XJV	Hogslund/Traugott-Olsen 2G	unkn	RDAF: Z-923
			RDAF: 92-923
OY-XJX	Eiri PIK-20D	20521	D-4778
OY-XJY	Rolladen-Schneider LS-3A	3345	
OY-XJZ	Schleicher ASW-19B	19271	
OY-XKB	Glasflügel H201B Standard Libelle	566	SE-TNT
OY-XKC	Sportavia RF-5B Sperber	51013	D-KCIL
OY-XKD	Centrair ASW-20F	20130	
OY-XKF	Schleicher ASW-20F	20131	
OY-XKH	Rolladen-Schneider LS-3A	3412	
OY-XKI	Schleicher ASK-21	21023	
OY-XKK	Rolladen-Schneider LS-1C	117	D-0698
OY-XKL	Rolladen-Schneider LS-1F	309	D-2761
OY-XKM	Schleicher ASW-20	20441	
OY-XKO	Schleicher ASK-21	21056	
OY-XKP	Rolladen-Schneider LS-3A	3414	
OY-XKS	Schleicher ASW-20	20415	
OY-XKT	Schleicher ASW-20	20301	
OY-XKV	Rolladen-Schneider LS-4	4108	
OY-XKW	Schleicher ASW-20	20278	
OY-XKX	Rolladen-Schneider LS-4	4011	
OY-XKZ	Grob G.103 Twin II	3575	D-6436
OY-XLD	Rolladen-Schneider LS-4	4216	
OY-XLE	Schleicher Ka.6CR Rhönsegler	6384	D-0071
			OO-ZAA
OY-XLH	Centrair ASW-20F	20504	
OY-XLI	Rolladen-Schneider LS-4	4215	D-0510
OY-XLK	Rolladen-Schneider LS-4	4217	
OY-XLL	Centrair ASW-20F	20199	
OY-XLM	Rolladen-Schneider LS-4	4159	D-0296
OY-XLN	Centrair ASW-20F	20514	
OY-XLO	Schleicher Ka.6CR Rhönsegler	6015	D-5860
OY-XLP	Rolladen-Schneider LS-4	4296	D-2897
OY-XLS	Grob G.102 Astir CS	1220	D-7284
OY-XLT	Schleicher/ASK-13	13484	D-2381
OY-XLV	Grob G.102 Astir CS	1284	D-7376
OY-XLZ	Grob G.103 Twin Astir II	3697	
OY-XMA	IAR IS.28M2	54	YR-1982
OY-XMB	Schleicher Ka.6CR Rhönsegler	6365Si	D-5636
OY-XMC	Scheibe SF-34	5114	
OY-XMD	Rolladen-Schneider LS-4	4392	D-4582
OY-XME	Schleicher K.8C	81011	D-3765
OY-XMF	Schleicher ASK-21	21205	
OY-XMH	Schleicher ASW-19B	19400	
OY-XMJ	Schleicher Ka.6CR Rhönsegler	6420	OH-306
	(Same c/n as OE-0725)		OH-RSS
OY-XMK	Schleicher K.7 Rhönadler	AB 7282	D-8673
OY-XML	Rolladen-Schneider LS-4	4307	
OY-XMM	Centrair 101AP Pégase	101-041	
OY-XMO	Rolladen-Schneider LS-4	4375	D-9101
OY XMS	Schleicher ASW-19B	19401	
OY-XMT	Schempp-Hirth Nimbus 2	29	OO-ZGB
			D-2942
OY-XMU	Grob G.109B	6225	
OY-XMW	Grob G.109	6149	
OY-XMX	Schempp-Hirth Ventus b	137	
OY-XMY	Grob G.103A Twin II Acro	3743-K-49	D-0820
OY-XNB	Grob G.109B	6232	
OY-XNC	Grob G.109	6033	D-KAZE
OY-XND	Grob G.109B	6286	
OY-XNE-NE	Rolladen-Schneider LS-4	4404	
OY-XNF	Schleicher ASW-20L	20284	D-6553
OY-XNG	Scheibe SF-25B Falke	46135	D-KADM
OY-XNH	Glaser-Dirks DG-200/17C	2-163/CL-14	D-9428
OY-XNK	Glaser-Dirks DG-300 Elan	3E-64	
OY-XNL	Glaser-Dirks DG-300 Elan	3E-91	
OY-XNM	Rolladen-Schneider LS-1F	478	D-6520

Regn.	Type	C/n	Prev.Id.
OY-XNN	Grob G.109B	6202	D-KGFB
OY-XNO	Hoffmann H-36 Dimona	3691	
OY-XNP	Grob G.102 Astir CS	1400	D-7432
OY-XNR	Rolladen-Schneider LS-6	6016	
OY-XNS	Schleicher K.7 Rhönadler	7143	D-5471
OY-XNT	Jastreb Standard Cirrus G/81	307	
OY-XNU	Centrair 101A Pégase	101A-0208	
OY-XNV	Rolladen-Schneider LS-4	4470	D-5172
OY-XNX	Schleicher ASK-21	21240	
OY-XNY	Glaser-Dirks DG-400	4-136	
OY-XNZ	Grob G.103 Twin Astir	3643	D-6157
OY-XOA	Scheibe SF-25E Super Falke	4336	D-KDCG
OY-XOB	SZD-50-3 Puchacz	B-1483	
OY-XOC	Schleicher ASK-21	21276	
OY-XOD	Schleicher ASK-23	23050	
OY-XOF	Glaser-Dirks DG-100G	E60-G36	D-6846
OY-XOG	Glaser-Dirks DG-200	2-64	D-1171
OY-XOH	Schempp-Hirth Nimbus II	96	D-8930
OY-XOJ	Grob G.103A Twin II Acro	34057-K-287	
OY-XOK	Schempp-Hirth Discus b	32	
OY-XOL	Schempp-Hirth Discus b	95	
OY-XOM	Schempp-Hirth Nimbus 2B	147	D-3366
OY-XOS	Glaser-Dirks DG-300 Elan	3E-176	
OY-XOT	Scheibe SF-25E Super Falke	4327	D-KEBS
OY-XOV	Scheibe SF-25E Super Falke	4339	D-KIEL
OY-XOW	Glaser-Dirks DG-400	4-184	
OY-XOZ	Glaser-Dirks DG-200/17C	2-165/CL-15	HB-1627
OY-XPA	SZD-51-1 Junior	W-951	
OY-XPB	Glaser-Dirks DG-600	6-36	
OY-XPC	Schleicher ASK-21	21316	
OY-XPD	Glaser-Dirks DG-400	4-183	
OY-XPE	Schleicher ASW-20L	20853	
OY-XPF	Schleicher ASW-20CL	20858	
OY-XPG	Sportavia-Pützer RF-5B Sperber	1005	D-KLL I
			EAF-...
OY-XPH	Schempp-Hirth Ventus c (Reservation)	unkn	
OY-XPI	Glaser-Dirks DG-300 Elan	3E-285	
OY-XPJ	Schleicher ASK-13	13423	D-2125
OY-XPK	Schleicher ASW-20CL	20852	
OY-XPL	Schleicher ASK-21	21356	
OY-XPM	Schempp-Hirth Discus	112	
OY-XPN	Scheibe SF-25C Falke	44176	D-KDEI
OY-XPO	Glaser-Dirks DG-300 Elan	3E-278	
OY-XPP	Glaser-Dirks DG-300 Elan	3E-165	D-7213
OY-XPS	Glaser-Dirks DG-400	4-230	(D-KIDG)
OY-XPT	Glasflügel H201B Standard Libelle	65	LN-GIE
			SE-TIE
OY-XPU-PU	Rolladen-Schneider LS-6A	6160	
OY-XPV	Scheibe SF-25B Falke	4837	D-KHET
OY-XPW	Rolladen-Schneider LS-1F	180	LN-GAF
OY-XPX	Rolladen-Schneider LS-4A	4654	D-8028
OY-XPY	Schleicher ASW-19B	19372	D-1488
OY-XPZ	Glaser-Dirks DG-300 Elan	3E-301	
OY-XRA	SZD-50-3 Puchacz	B-1725	
OY-XRB	Rolladen-Schneider LS-6B (Reservation)	unkn	
OY-XRC	Rolladen-Schneider LS-7	7048	D-5168
OY-XRD	Schleicher Ka.2 Rhönschwalbe	48	D-8757
OY-XRE-55	Schempp-Hirth Ventus c	419	
OY-XRF	Rolladen-Schneider LS-4A	4788	
OY-XRG	Rolladen-Schneider LS-6C	6217	
OY-XRI	Scheibe SF-25C Falke	4238	D-KAJA(2)
OY-XRL	Schempp-Hirth Janus CE	199	N911RR
OY-XRM	Schempp-Hirth Ventus cM	41/479	
OY-XRN	Schempp-Hirth Discus CS	026CS	
OY-XRO	Schleicher ASW-24	24022	
OY-XRP	SZD-50-3 Puchacz	B-1991	
OY-XRR	Schempp-Hirth Janus C	257	
OY-XRS-27	Schempp-Hirth Discus b	270	
OY-XRU	Glaser-Dirks DG-300 Elan	3E-403	
OY-XRW	SZD-55-1	551191028	
OY-XRX	Schempp-Hirth Ventus c	380	
OY-XRY	Eiri PIK-20	20060	SE-TOO
OY-XRZ	Schempp-Hirth Ventus cT	166/543	D-KNMA
OY-XSA	Schempp-Hirth Janus CT	160CS	
OY-XSD	Grob G.102 Astir CS	1173	D-7294
OY-XSE	Stamer-Lippisch	01-92	
OY-XSF	Schempp-Hirth Janus C	260	
OY-XSG	Scheibe SF-25B Falke	4666	D-KAPB
OY-XSH	Rolladen-Schneider LS-7	7139	
OY-XSI	Slingsby T.21B Sedbergh	MHL.012	SE-SMA
			WB985
OY-XSK	Schempp-Hirth Ventus bT	32/211	PH-747
OY-XSL	Scheibe SF-25E Super Falke	4355	D-KDGO
OY-XSM	Schempp-Hirth Ventus c	550	
OY-XSN	SZD-51-1 Junior	B-2014	SP-3576
			SP-P576
OY-XSO	Schempp-Hirth Ventus 2cT	7/15	
OY-XSP	SZD-50-3 Puchacz	B-2094	
OY-XSR	Rolladen-Schneider LS-8A	8120	
OY-XST	Schempp-Hirth Discus b	478	
OY-XSU	Schempp-Hirth Discus CS	183CS	
OY-XSV	PZL PW-5 Smyk	17.03.017	
OY-XSW	Schempp-Hirth Ventus 2c	18	
OY-XSX	Schempp-Hirth Nimbus 4DT	02	D-KKFM
OY-XTA	Schempp-Hirth Nimbus 3T	2/44	N45U
			N806MD
			D-KHIA
OY-XTB	Schempp-Hirth Ventus c	542	
OY-XTD	Schleicher K7 Rhönadler	7059/A	D-5472
OY-XTE	Scheibe SF-25B Falke	4611	D-KOGY
OY-XTF	Rolladen-Schneider LS-4B	4857	
OY-XTG	Grob G.103C Twin III	34180	
OY-XTH	Schempp-Hirth Standard Cirrus	363	D-2153
OY-XTI	Schempp-Hirth Ventus cT	176/577	
OY-XTJ	Rolladen-Schneider LS-3A	3430	D-8990
OY-XTK	SZD-51-1 Junior	B-2011	
OY-XTL	Rolladen-Schneider LS-4A	4815	
OY-XTM	Rolladen-Schnieder LS-3A	3147	SE-TTK
OY-XTN	Rolladen-Schneider LS-7	7138	(D-3674)
OY-XTO	Scheibe SF-25E Super Falke	4354	G-BHAG
			(D-KDGO)
OY-XTS	Glaser-Dirks DG-500-22 Elan	5E-118S17	
OY-XTT	Scheibe SF-34	5103	SE-UEA
			D-3337
OY-XTU	Schempp-Hirth Nimbus 3DM	21/49	
OY-XTV	Hoffmann H-36 Dimona	36220	SE-UBO
OY-XTX	Schempp-Hirth Ventus c	469	
OY-XTY	Rolladen-Schneider LS-4A	4812	
OY-XTZ	Schleicher ASK-23B	23125	
OY-XUA	Schleicher ASK-21	21666	
OY-XUB	Schempp-Hirth Discus CS	046C	D-2172
OY-XUC	PZL PW-5 Smyk	17.04.011	
OY-XUE	Schempp-Hirth Discus b	452	D-7955
OY-XUG	Schempp-Hirth Discus CS	181CS	
OY-XUU	Schempp-Hirth Ventus cT	184/604	
OY-XUV	Schempp-Hirth Discus CS	210CS	
OY-XUW	Schempp-Hirth Nimbus 4T	10	D-KJAA
OY-XVA	Grob G.103 Twin III	35006	D-KLMA
OY-XVC	Schleicher ASK-21	21415	D-6254
OY-XVE	Schleicher ASW-24	24212	D-6962
OY-XVH	Scheibe SF-25C Falke	44342	D-KNAF
OY-XVI	Schleicher ASW-24	24061	D-7724
OY-XVJ	Schempp-Hirth Ventus 2cT	38/128	
OY-XVK	Schempp-Hirth Duo Discus	057	
OY-XVL	Schleicher ASH-25E	25033	D-KKSR
OY-XVM	SZD-55-1	551196082	D-9551
OY-XVN	Schempp-Hirth Duo Discus	228	
OY-XVS	Schleicher ASW-24B	24245	
OY-XVV	Schleicher ASW-20	20378	SE-TVN
OY-XVX	Schempp-Hirth Discus CS	162CS	
OY-XVZ	Schleicher ASK-21	21670	
OY-XXA	Schempp-Hirth Ventus 2a	70	
OY-XXD	PZL PW-5 Smyk	17.06.022	
OY-XXI	Schempp-Hirth Discus CS	071CS	D-3934
OY-XXL	Schempp-Hirth Ventus 2 (Reservation)	unkn	
OY-XYB	Hoffmann H-36 Dimona	36217	
OY-XYC	Valentin Taifun 17E	1091	
OY-XYD	Glaser-Dirks DG-300 Elan	3E-192	
OY-XYE	PZL PW-5 Smyk	17.04.010	
OY-XYF	Rolladen-Schneider LS-6	6258	

Regn.	Type	C/n	Prev.Id.
OY-XYH	Schempp-Hirth Ventus b/16.6	228	D-5237
OY-XYJ	Schleicher ASW-15	15153	D-0801
OY-XYK	Schempp-Hirth Discus b	172	
OY-XYL	Rolladen-Schneider LS-4	4568	
OY-XYM	Grob Standard Cirrus	493G	D-9443
OY-XYN	Rolladen-Schneider LS-6A	6129	
OY-XYO	Grob G.102 Astir CS	1191	D-7308
OY-XYP	Scheibe SF-25C Falke	44164	D-KEFP
OY-XYR	Centrair 101A Pégase	101-0276	
OY-XYT	Scheibe SF-25E Super Falke	4316	D-KEFL
OY-XYU	Schleicher ASK-21	21310	
OY-XYV	Schempp-Hirth Standard Cirrus	653	D-7248
OY-XYY	Schempp-Hirth Janus CM	227/27	
OY-XZB	SZD-48-3 Jantar Standard 3	B-1737	SE-UGM
OY-XZG	Scheibe SF-25C Falke	44509	D-KIOJ(3)
OY-XZM	HOAC HK-36TTC Super Dimona	36618	
OY-XZO	Hoffmann H-36 Dimona	3514	SE-UCK
			N408DH
OY-XZP	HOAC HK-36TTC Super Dimona	36536	
OY-XZT	Schempp-Hirth Discus CS	191CS	
OY-XZW	Glaser-Dirks DG-800	unkn	
OY-XZZ	Rolladen-Schneider LS-7WL	7165	

MICROLIGHTS

KLASSE A (Weightshift control)

8-1	Demon Hiway
8-2	Solar Wing/Ultra Sport Trike
8-3	Fledgewing
8-4	Airwave Gliders UP Comet
8-5	Solar Wing/Mainair Trike
8-6	Demon Hiway/Hiway Trike
8-7	Flexiform Striker/Mainair Trike
8-8	Southdown Puma Sprint
8-9	Azur/Trifun
8-10	Airwave Gliders UP Comet
8-11	Solar Wing/Hiway Trike
8-12	Typhoon/Trifun
8-13	Southdown Puma Sprint
8-14	Typhoon/Trifun
8-15	Typhoon/Trifun
8-16	Azur/Trifun
8-17	Demon Hiway/Monopole Trike
8-18	Demon Hiway/Hiway Trike
8-19	Firebird Sierra/Monopole Trike
8-20	Flexiform Striker/Air Play Trike
8-21	Lightning 2
8-22	Typhoon Solar Wing/Hiway Trike
8-23	Lightning/Air Play Trike
8-24	Firebird Sierra
8-25	Typhoon Trifun
8-26	Typhoon XL
8-27	Southdown Puma Sprint
8-28	Southdown Puma DS
8-29	Moyes Missiles GT
8-30	Firebird Sierra
8-31	Flexiform Striker/Mainair Trike
8-32	Gold Marque Sports/Hiway Skymaster
8-33	Solar Wings/Trifun 330
8-34	Southdown Puma Sprint
8-35	Firebird Sierra/Air Play Trike
8-36	Airplay Magic 3
8-37	Dual Strike
8-38	Southdown Puma Sprint
8-39	Flexiform Striker/Mainair Sport Trike
8-40	Flexiform Striker
8-41	Southdown Puma Sprint
8-42	Mainair Gemini/Flash
8-43	Southdown Puma Sprint/Air Play Trike
8-44	Typhoon S Medium

8-45	Firebird Sierra
8-46	Typhoon S Medium/Kopi Air Play Trike
8-47	Lite Air/Air Play Trike
8-48	Southdown Puma Sprint/Air Play Trike
8-49	Striker/Air Play Trike
8-50	Striker/Air Play Trike
8-51	Typhoon 180/Hiway Trike
8-52	Striker/Air Play Trike
8-53	Southdown Puma Sprint
8-54	Striker/Air Play Trike
8-55	Southdown Puma Sprint
8-56	Raven T15/Air Play Trike
8-57	Raven/Air Play Trike
8-58	Raven/Air Play Trike
8-59	Raven 25 Two-seater
8-60	Demon-JTM
8-61	Firebird Sierra
8-62	Fledgwing
8-63	La Mouette Tri Fun
8-64	Pegasus/Air Play Trike
8-65	Chaser JTM
8-66	Alpha JTM A130XL
8-68	Mistral GTR/Taifun
8-69	Typhoon Trifun
8-70	Solar Wings Pegasus XL
8-71	Striker/Air Play Trike
8-72	Solar Wings Pegasus XL
8-73	Firebird Sierra/Air Play Trike
8-74	Southdown Puma Sport
8-75	Solar Wings Pegasus XL
8-77	Steinbach Delta
8-79	Mainair Gemini/Flash II
8-80	Aerial Arts 130SX
8-81	Aerial Arts 130SX
8-82	Aerial Arts Winder JTM
8-83	Raven/Air Play Trike
8-84	Aerial Arts 110LX JTM
8-85	Bida OSS
8-86	Solar Wings Pegasus XL-Q
8-87	Aerial Arts 130SX
8-88	Aerial Arts 110SX JTM
8-89	Solar Wings Pegasus XL-Q
8-90	Aerial Arts Chaser 110
8-91	Solar Wings Pegasus XL
8-92	Solar Wings Pegasus XL-Q
8-93	Typhoon TH
8-94	Aerial Arts Power W
8-95	Solar Wings Pegasus XL
8-96	Tyhoon S4
8-97	Demon Trifun
8-98	Solar Wings Pegasus XL
8-99	Aerial Arts 130SX
8-100	Aerial Arts Chaser 110SX JTM
8-101	Aerial Arts Chaser 110SX JTM
8-102	Bida Spider
8-103	C-S Prototype 1
8-105	Solar Wings Pegasus XL
8-106	Solar Wings Pegasus XL (Crashed)
8-107	Solar Wings Pegasus XL
8-108	Airwave Magic III
8-109	Lotni Polen
8-110	Magic 165
8-111	Solar Wings Pegasus XL
8-112	Magic III 166
8-113	Solar Wings Pegasus XL
8-114	Hiway Demon
8-115	JTM IIOSX
8-116	JTM IIOSX
8-117	Solar Wings Pegasus XL
8-118	Solar Wings Typhoon 180B
8-119	Solar Wings Pegasus XL
8-120	Solar Wings Pegasus XL
8-121	Solar Wings Pegasus XL
8-122	Solar Wings Pegasus XL
8-123	Solar Wings Pegasus XL

Regn.	Type	C/n	Prev.Id.
8-124	Solar Wings Pegasus XL/JTM		
8-125	JTM 110		
8-126	Solar Wings Pegasus XL		
8-127	JTM Spar 2		
8-128	Southdown Puma Sprint		
8-129	Southdown Puma Sprint		
8-130	Aerial Arts JTM		
8-131	Aerial Arts		
8-132	JTM Spar 2		
8-133	Solar Wings Pegasus XL		
8-134	JTM Spar 2		
8-135	Southdown Raven/Airplay Trike		
8-136	Solar Wings Pegasus XL		
8-137	Solar Wings Pegasus XL/Airplay Trike		
8-138	JTM		
8-139	Southdown Raven		
8-140	JTM 130SX		
8-141	JTM 115SX		
8-142	Solar Wings Pegasus XL-Q		
8-143	Solar Wings Pegasus XL-Q		
8-144	Southdown Puma Sprint 2 seat		
8-145	Aerial Arts Chaser 2		
8-146	Solar Wings Pegasus XL-Q		
8-147	JTM 110SX		
8-148	Solar Wings Pegasus XL		
8-149	Magic 4 Christian		
8-150	Aerial Arts Chaser 110SX		
8-151	Solar Wings Pegasus Quasar		
8-152	Solar Wings Pegasus XL		
8-153	Raven		
8-154	Solar Wings Pegasus XL-Q		
8-156	Chaser S		
8-157	Pegasus Quasar		
8-158	Deltalet Record MD-20		
8-159	La Mouette Chronos 16		
8-160	La Mouette		
8-161	Pai Aero		
8-162	JTM Spar 2		
8-163	Solar Wings Pegasus XL-Q Mk2		
8-164	La Mouette		
8-165	Aerial Arts JTM		
8-166	Solar Wings Pegasus XL-Q Mk2		
8-167	Lotni Polen Airo		
8-168	Southdown Puma Sprint		

KLASSE B (Conventional 3-axis control)

Regn.	Type	C/n	Prev.Id.
9-1	Eipper Quicksilver MX-II		
9-2	Huntair Pathfinder 2 (Crashed)		
9-3	Huntair Pathfinder 2 (Crashed)		
9-4	Dragon 150		
9-5	Sirocco		
9-6	Dragon 150		
9-7	Dragon 150		
9-8	Eipper Quicksilver MX-II		
9-9	Scout		
9-10	Dragon 150		
9-11	Sirocco		
9-12	Eipper Quicksilver MX		
9-13	Dragon 150 (Crashed)	064	
9-14	Rotec Rally 3		
9-15	Rotec Rally Sport		
9-16	Eipper Quicksilver MX		
9-17	Dragon 150 (Believed c/n 068, now G-MNJF)		
9-18	Dragon 150		
9-19	Eipper Quicksilver MX-II		
9-20	Eipper Quicksilver MX-II		
9-21	Eipper Quicksilver MX-II		
9-22	Sirocco		
9-23	Eipper Quicksilver MX-II		
9-24	Dragon 150-M1		
9-25	Pioneer Flightstar		
9-26	Robertson B1-RD (Single seat) (Crashed)		
9-27	Robertson B1-RD (Two-seat)		

Regn.	Type	C/n	Prev.Id.
9-28	Rotec Rally 2B		
9-29	Rotec Rally 3		
9-30	Pioneer Flightstar		
9-31	Eipper Quicksilver MX-II		
9-32	Sherpa II		
9-33	Sherpa II		
9-34	Sherpa Fox I		
9-35	BUF-1 (Crashed)		
9-36	Eipper Quicksilver MX-II		
9-37	Comco Ikarus Fox-C22		
9-38	Midit FS		
9-39	Eipper Quicksilver MX-II		
9-40	Comco Ikarus Fox C-22		
9-41	Comco Ikarus Fox-C22		
9-42	Comco Ikarus Fox-C22		
9-43	Comco Ikarus Fox-C22		
9-44	Pioneer Flightstar		
9-45	Challenger Two-seater		
9-46	Pioneer Flightstar		
9-47	Skywalker II		
9-49	Comco Ikarus Fox-C22		
9-50	J-3 Kitten		
9-51	J-3 Kitten (Crashed)		
9-52	Comco Ikarus Fox-C22		
9-53	Comco Ikarus Fox-C22		
9-54	Albatros		
9-55	Albatros		
9-56	Eipper Quicksilver GT-400		
9-58	Comco Ikarus Fox-C22		
9-60	SE5A Replica (Wfu)		
9-61	Comco Ikarus Fox-C22		
9-62	Eipper Quicksilver MX-II		
9-64	Pioneer Flightstar		
9-65	Spectrum RX-550		
9-66	Comco Ikarus Fox-C22		
9-67	Eipper Quicksilver 1		
9-68	Comco Ikarus Fox-C22		
9-70	Quad City Challenger II		
9-71	Quad City Challenger II		
9-72	Quad City Challenger II		
9-73	Comco Ikarus Fox-C22		
9-74	Comco Ikarus Fox-C22		
9-75	Albatros		
9-76	Comco Ikarus Fox-C22		
9-77	Quad City Challenger II (Crashed)		
9-78	Sky Walker II		
9-79	Rans S-6E Coyote II (Crashed)		
9-80	Rans S-6E Coyote II		
9-81	Rans S-6E Coyote II		
9-82	Skywalker II		
9-83	Rans S-6E Coyote II		
9-84	Quad City Challenger II		
9-85	Kolb Twinstar II		
9-86	HFL Stratos 300		300-017K
9-88	Rans S-6E Coyote II (Crashed)		
9-89	Rans S-6E Coyote II		
9-90	Spectrum Beaver RX-550E		
9-91	Rans S-6E Coyote II		
9-92	Fischer FP-303		
9-93	Rans S-10E Sakota		
9-94	CZ-ULF 1		
9-95	Rans S-6E Coyote II		
9-96	Rans S-6E Coyote II		
9-97	Sky Walker II (Crashed)		
9-98	Rans S-10E Sakota		
9-99	Rans S-6E Coyote II		
9-100	HFL Stratos 300		300-023K
9-101	Rans S-6E Coyote II		
9-102	Rans S-6E Coyote II		
9-103	Aviasud Mistral		
9-104	Rans S-6E Coyote II		
9-105	Rotec Panther 2 Plus		
9-106	Sky Walker II		
9-107	Rans S-7E		
9-108	Rans S-9 Chaos (or S-10E Sakota ?)		

Regn.	Type	C/n	Prev.Id.
9-109	Sky Walker II		
9-110	Pioneer Flightstar		
9-111	Rans S-10E Sakota *(Re-regd OY-LEO ?)*		
9-112	TEAM Mini-Max		
9-113	Rans S-12E Airaile		
9-114	Rans S-12E Airaile		
9-115	Rans S-6ES Coyote II		
9-116	Rans S-7E Courier		
9-117	Rans S-10E Sakota		
9-118	Rans S-12E Airaile		
9-119	Bobcat Special		
9-120	Rans S-12E Airaile		
9-121	Rans S-12E Airaile		
9-122	Rans S-5 Coyote I		
9-123	Rans S-10E Sakota		
9-124	Rans S-12ES Airaile		
9-125	Comco Ikarus Fox-C-22		
9-126	Rans S-12E Airaile		
9-127	Rans S-6E Coyote II		
9-128	TEAM Mini-Max *(Crashed)*		
9-129	Rans S-12E Airaile		
9-130	Rans S-12E Airaile (mod.)		
9-131	Rans S-6ES Coyote II		
9-132	Mosler N3-2 Pup		
9-133	Rans S-12E Airaile		
9-134	Rans S-12ES Airaile		
9-135	Comco Ikarus Fox-C-22		
9-136	Rans S-12ES Airaile *(Crashed)*		
9-137	Rans S-6ES Coyote II *(Crashed)*		
9-139	Rans S-12ES Airaile		
9-140	Explorer Airaile		
9-142	Rans S-12ES Airaile		
9-143	Rans S-12E Airaile		
9-146	CUBy 2		
9-148	Tandem Air Sunny Sport		
9-149	Comco Ikarus Fox C-22		
9-150	Rans S-12E Airaile		
9-152	Rans S-12E Airaile		
9-153	Quad City Challenger II		
9-154	Comco Ikarus Fox C-22		
9-155	Quad City Challenger II		
9-157	Rans S-12E Airaile		
9-158	Rans S-12E Airaile		
9-159	CUBy 2		
9-160	Comco Ikarus Fox C-22		
9-161	Rans S-6ES Coyote II		
9-162	Z-Max		
9-163	Comco Ikarus Fox C-22		
9-164	Rans S-6ES Coyote II		
9-165	Z-Max 1300		
9-166	CFM Shadow		
9-167	Quad City Challenger II		
9-168	Rans S-12ES Airaile		
9-171	Comco Ikarus Fox C-22		
9-173	Rans S-6ES Coyote II		
9-175	Mosler N3 Pup		
9-176	Kolb Twinstar Mk.3		
9-177	CFM Streak Shadow	K.234-SA	
9-178	Quad City Challenger II		
9-179	Kolb Twinstar Mk 3		
9-180	Comco Ikarus Fox C-22		
9-181	Rans S-12ES Airaile		
9-183	Rans S-12ES Airaile		
9-184	TEAM Mini-Max		
9-185	TEAM Mini-Max		
9-187	JORA Jora		
9-188	Comco Ikarus Fox C-22		
9-189	Wendell WAP 200		
9-190	Renagade 2		
9-191	Rans S-6ES Coyote II		
9-192	Rans S-6ES Coyote II XL		
9-193	Rans S-6ES Coyote II		
9-197	Rans S-6ES Coyote II XL		
9-198	Rans S-6ES Coyote II		
9-201	Rans S-6ES Coyote II		

Regn.	Type	C/n	Prev.Id.
9-202	Denney Kitfox		
9-205	Pioneer Flightstar		

GYROCOPTERS

10-1	Air Command 532		
10-2	Air Command 532 *(Crashed)*		
10-3	Air Command 532		
10-4	Humlan		
10-5	Air Command 532		
10-6	Campbell Cricket *(Crashed)*		
10-7	Air Command 532 *(Crashed)*		
10-8	PL Air Command		
10-9	Campbell-Bensen B.8		
10-10	Parson Trainer		
10-11	Humlan		
10-12	Air Command 532		
10-14	Tornado 2		
10-15	Air Command 532		
10-16	PL Air Command 2		
10-17	PL Air Command 2		
10-18	PL Air Command 2		

NON-CURRENT AIRCRAFT

The following Aircraft are known to exist in Denmark - most are held by members of the KZ-Club for storage or rebuild.

OY-AAP	S.A.I. KZ-VII U-4 Laerke	152	
OY-AAS	S.A.I. KZ-VII U-4 Laerke	155	D-EMES
			OY-AAS
OY-ACC	S.A.I. KZ-VII U-4 Laerke	177	D-EDOP
			OY-ACC
OY-ACE	S.A.I. KZ-IX Ellehammer (Replica)	204	
OY-ACT	S.A.I. KZ-III U	50	RDAF:611
			RDAF:50
OY-AFG	Piper J-3C-65 Cub	10858	SE-CEW
			LN-MAP
			43-29567
OY-AIG	Scintex Piel CP.301C-1 Emeraude	557	
OY-ALA	Aeronca 7AC Champion	1024	D-EBGF
			N82391
OY-ALT	de Havilland DH.82A Tiger Moth	85621	D-ELYG
			(SL-AAF)
			G-ANBZ
			DE680
OY-ALV	Auster Mk.4	906	D-ELIT
			G-ANHP
			MT170
OY-ANO	Fairchild F.24W-41A Argus II	834	D-EHIB
			HB-EAK
			HB597
			43-14870
OY-ANV	Auster Mk.5	1159	D-EGAT
			I- METE
			HB-EON
			G-AKSI
			RT497
OY-ANY	S.A.I. KZ-III U	52	SE-ASH
OY-AVH(1)	Piper J-4 Cub Coupé	4-449	D-EBYP
			N22765
			NC22765
OY-AVJ	Rearwin 9000	567D	SE-AGB
OY-AVM	Auster J/1N Alpha	1980	G-AHCN
OY-AVW	Piper PA-17 Vagabond	17-70	D-EEMM
			N4665H
OY-BMY	Druine D.31 Turbulent	unkn	
OY-CMD	Druine D.31 Turbulent	326	
OY-CME	Jodel D.112 Club	1448	
OY-CMI	Jodel D.112 Club	1440	
OY-CMJ	Druine D.31 Turbulent	342	

Regn.	Type	C/n	Prev.Id.
OY-CMM	Jurca MJ.2D Tempête	unkn	
OY-CMN	Jodel D.112 Club	S55/FR.1501	
OY-DGU	Auster J/1 Autocrat	2031	D-ENIT
			OY-DGU
OY-DHN	Piper J-3C-65 Cub	11065	SE-AWE
			43-29774
OY-DIA	S.A.I. KZ-III U-2	79	
OY-DMB	S.A.I. KZ-III U-2	90	9M-AMF
			(VR-RCW)
			VR-OAD
			VR-RBK
			VR-SCH
OY-DNR	de Havilland DH.82A Tiger Moth	82104	G-AHRV
			N6849
OY-DRA	Auster J/1 Autocrat	2142	
OY-DTE	S.A.I. KZ-III U-2	71	
OY-DVR	de Havilland DH.82A Tiger Moth	83223	D-EBUN
			G-ANVE
			T5490
OY-DYZ	S.A.I. KZ-III U-1	56	D-EFID
			OY-DYZ
OY-EFG	Globe GC-1B Swift	1325	D-ECEZ
			N3323K
OY-EFL	Cessna 140	10220	D-EHEP
			N73015
OY-EFM	Piper TG-8 Cub	G1	D-EMUG
			N46490
			NC46490
			43-3009
OY-FAN	S.A.I. KZ-II Trainer	110	RDAF: 102
			RDAF: 110
OY-POL	Piper J-3C-65 Cub	12818	44-80522

PH - NETHERLANDS

Regn.	Type	C/n	Prev.Id.
PH-ABB	Piper PA-38-112 Tomahawk	38-82A0005	N91340
			(PH-ABB)
			N91340
PH-ABD	Piper PA-31-350 Navajo Chieftain	31-7305048	F-BTMU
PH-ABL	Piper PA-28-235 Cherokee	28-10648	F-BNFY
			N9054W
PH-ABV	Cessna 172P Skyhawk	74260	N51054
PH-ACG	Fokker S.11.1 Instructor	6279	MLD:179/K
			E-36
PH-ACH	Reims/Cessna F.152-II	1838	OO-HRD(2)
	(Rebuilt 1985-6 using fuselage of F.152		(OO-JDH)
	D-EOWT c/n 1883)		(OO-HDO)
			OO-HRD(2)
PH-ACI	Cessna T.303 Crusader	00236	N9914C
			JA5295
			N9914C
PH-ACM	Cessna 172P	75454	N63602
PH-ACW	Velocity (Reservation)	unkn	
PH-ACY	Beech 1900D	UE-44	D-CBSG
			OK-YES
			D-CBSG
			N80683
PH-ACZ	Beech B200 Super King Air	BB-1215	D-IEEE(2)
			F-GICV
			G-BPLC
			N7225V
PH-ADE	Reims/Cessna F.172M	1118	D-EENJ
PH-ADP	Piper PA-32RT-300 Lance II	32R-7885061	N9619C
PH-ADW	Reims/Cessna F.172L	0841	OK-CKB
			PH-ADW
PH-ADY	Murphy Elite (Reservation 10.99)	unkn	
PH-AEA	Commander Aircraft 114B	14574	
PH-AEC	Piper PA-28-181 Archer III	2843039	(PH-AEG)
PH-AED	Piper PA-28-181 Archer III	2843089	N92883
PH-AEE	Piper PA-28-181 Archer III	2843076	OY-JAZ
PH-AEF	Piper PA-28-181 Archer III	2843149	N9291S
PH-AEM	Piper PA-46-350P Malibu	4636169	N41222
			PH-AEG
PH-AFA	SOCATA Rallye 180T Galérien	2685	
PH-AFD	SOCATA Rallye 100ST (Reservation for restoration)	2787	
PH-AFG	SOCATA Rallye 150ST	3174	
PH-AFK	SOCATA TB-9 Tampico	182	F-BNGX
PH-AFP	Pottier P.170S	020	
PH-AFS	Fokker S.11.1 Instructor	6205	(PH-HOO)
			E-14
PH-AHE	Boeing 757-27B	24135	OY-SHE
			PH-AHE
			OY-SHE
			PH-AHE
PH-AHI	Boeing 757-27B	24137	G-OAHI
			(G-BSUB)
			PH-AHI
			OY-SHI
			PH-AHI
PH-AHP	Boeing 757-23A	24528	G-BXOL
			SE-DSM
			OO-ILI
PH-AIG	Robin R.1180TD Aiglon	270	
PH-AIJ	Piper PA-34-200T Seneca II	34-7870029	LN-AKP
			N9030K
PH-AIL	SIAI-Marchetti S.208 (Formerly S.205-22/R)	4-232	OO-HEP
PH-AIP	Robin DR.400/120 Dauphin 80	1797	
PH-AJA	Brändli BX-2 Cherry	71/NVAV-101	
PH-AJB	Piper PA-36-285 Pawnee Brave	36-7560040	N9929P
PH-AJC	Brändli BX-2 Cherry	67/NVAV-103	
PH-AJD	Piper PA-34-220T Seneca IV	3448044	N9246N
PH-AJK	Robinson R-22 Beta	1738	G-MISR
PH-AJS	SOCATA TBM-700	24	F-GLBD
PH-AJU	Douglas DC-2	1288	VH-CRH/
	(Reservation 2.87 for Dutch Dakota Assn BV,		A30-14
	under restoration)		NC13738

Regn.	Type	C/n	Prev.Id.
PH-AKJ	Cessna 177RG Cardinal RG	1019	N34907
			(PH-RAP)
			N34907
PH-ALI	Reims/Cessna F.150M Commuter	1161	
PH-ALL	Piper PA-28RT-201T Turbo Arrow IV	28R-8331048	OY-CEH
			N4315Z
			ZS-LGK
			N4315Z
PH-ALT	Piper PA-38-112 Tomahawk	38-79A0801	OO-TLT
			N9651N
PH-ALW	Reims/Cessna F.172M Skyhawk II	1226	
PH-AMA	Piper PA-18-150 Super Cub	18-8009042	N82678
PH-AMB	Reims/Cessna F.172N Skyhawk II	1921	PH-AXM(3)
PH-AMD	Europa Aviation Europa	322	
PH-AMR	Piper PA-28-161 Warrior II	28-8416077	N4353B
PH-AMT	Cessna 340A	0963	D-ICMA
			N4621G
			N981JC
			N4621G
PH-ANF	Piper PA-28RT-201 Arrow IV	28R-8018004	N8099H
PH-ANG	Cessna 172M Skyhawk	67384	N73336
PH-ANH	Reims/Cessna F.172P Skyhawk II	2244	PH-AXP(5)
PH-ANI	Piper PA-28-161 Cherokee Warrior II	28-7816576	N31685
PH-ANJ	Cessna 150M	77028	N45706
PH-ANM	American AG-5B Tiger	10122	N5021T
PH-ANW	Cessna 152	85766	N94689
PH-AOA to -AOZ	*Reserved for Airbus aircraft for KLM*		
PH-APA	Piper PA-18-135 Super Cub	18-3814	R-124
			54-2414
PH-APE	Reims/Cessna FRA.150L Aerobat	0247	D-EDJJ
PH-APR	Grumman G.164B Agcat	204B	G-BFTN
			N6687Q
PH-ARC	SOCATA TB-10 Tobago	12	F-ODKB
PH-ARJ	Cessna 150M	78911	N704VQ
PH-ARK	Fuji FA-200-160 Aero Subaru	174	
PH-ARM	Mooney M.20K Model 231	25-0431	N3691H
PH-ART(2)	Neico Lancair 360	246	
PH-ARV	ARV Super 2	015	G-BMWH
PH-ASE	SAN Jodel DR.1050 Ambassadeur	142	
PH-ASL	Piper PA-28-161 Warrior II	28-8016289	D-EALY
			N8177C
PH-AST	Piper PA-31-350 Navajo Chieftain	31-7752046	N63722
PH-ASY	Cessna 172P Skyhawk	75551	N64375
PH-ATM	Beech 200 Super King Air	BB-123	N120DA
			N123YV
			N911LR
			N711AR
			N9123S
PH-ATW	Reims/Cessna F.172N Skyhawk II	1802	(PH-AYB(2))
PH-AVA	Reims/Cessna F.172P Skyhawk II	2184	PH-AXN(4)
			F-WZDD
PH-AVB	Reims/Cessna F.172P Skyhawk II	2185	PH-AXM(4)
PH-AVF	Reims/Cessna F.172P Skyhawk II	2212	PH-AXR(4)
PH-AVG	Fokker F.27-050	20278	(PH-LXS)
PH-AVH	Fokker F.27-050	20281	
PH-AVJ	Fokker F.27-050	20285	
PH-AVN	Fokker F.27-050	20296	
PH-AVO	Fokker F.27-050	20297	
PH-AVT	Piper PA-28-181 Archer II	28-7990075	N22324
PH-AWH	Aviat A-1 Husky	1261	
PH-AWI	Reims/Cessna F.172M Skyhawk II	1343	D-EDHZ
			(F-BXZU)
			(D-EDQJ)
PH-AWR	SR-20 Cirrus *(Reservation)*	unkn	(PH-AWS)
PH-BAD	Reims/Cessna F.172M Skyhawk II	1284	
PH-BAI	Cessna 172P Skyhawk	74695	(PH-BIS)
			N53167
PH-BAW	SOCATA TB-9 Tampico Club	1470	OE-KMN
PH-BCF	Skystar Kitfox Classic IV	C95120133	(PH-BCZ)
PH-BDA	Boeing 737-306	23537	
PH-BDB	Boeing 737-306	23538	
PH-BDC	Boeing 737-306	23539	
PH-BDD	Boeing 737-306	23540	
PH-BDE	Boeing 737-306	23541	
PH-BDG	Boeing 737-306	23542	
PH-BDH	Boeing 737-306	23543	
PH-BDI	Boeing 737-306	23544	
PH-BDK	Boeing 737-306	23545	
PH-BDL	Boeing 737-306	23546	
PH-BDN	Boeing 737-306	24261	
PH-BDO	Boeing 737-306	24262	
PH-BDP	Boeing 737-306	24404	
PH-BDR	Boeing 737-406	24514	
PH-BDS	Boeing 737-406	24529	
PH-BDT	Boeing 737-406	24530	
PH-BDU	Boeing 737-406	24857	
PH-BDW	Boeing 737-406	24858	
PH-BDY	Boeing 737-406	24959	
PH-BDZ	Boeing 737-406	25355	
PH-BEA	SOCATA TB-9 Tampico	1130	
PH-BEC	Piper PA-28RT-201T Turbo Arrow IV	28R-8131041	D-EIJK
			N8308H
PH-BEG	Piper PA-28-181 Cherokee Archer II	28-7890419	G-BTGE
			N9514C
PH-BFA	Boeing 747-406	23999	N6018N
PH-BFB	Boeing 747-406	24000	
PH-BFC	Boeing 747-406 Combi	23982	N6038E
PH-BFD	Boeing 747-406 Combi	24001	
PH-BFE	Boeing 747-406 Combi	24201	N6046P
PH-BFF	Boeing 747-406 Combi	24202	N6046P
PH-BFG	Boeing 747-406	24517	
PH-BFH	Boeing 747-406 Combi	24518	N60668
PH-BFI	Boeing 747-406 Combi	25086	
PH-BFK	Boeing 747-406 Combi	25087	
PH-BFL	Boeing 747-406	25356	
PH-BFM	Boeing 747-406 Combi	26373	
PH-BFN	Boeing 747-406	26372	
PH-BFO	Boeing 747-406 Combi	25413	
PH-BFP	Boeing 747-406 Combi	26374	
PH-BFR	Boeing 747-406 Combi	27202	
PH-BFS	Boeing 747-406 Combi	28195	
PH-BFT	Boeing 747-406	28459	
PH-BFU	Boeing 747-406 Combi	28196	(PH-BFT)
PH-BFV	Boeing 747-406 *Combi*	28460	
PH-BGB to -BGR	*Reserved for Boeing 747-406s for KLM*		
PH-BGS	Aérospatiale AS.350B2 Ecureuil	3107	
PH-BGV	Europa Aviation Europa	264	
PH-BIK	Reims/Cessna F.150M Commuter	1256	D-EIHC
			(F-BJDK)
PH-BIT	Reims/Cessna F.172N Skyhawk II	1863	
PH-BLE	Blériot XI replica	NVAV-78	
PH-BLM	SOCATA TB-21 Trinidad TC	710	D-EFAK(4)
PH-BLO	Robin R.2160D	171	
PH-BMA	American AG-5B Tiger	10097	N1195Q
PH-BNK	Beech F33C Bonanza	CJ-140	
PH-BNZ	Beech B36TC Bonanza	EA-398	N641PA
PH-BOA	Mitsubishi MU-2B-60 Marquise	1507SA	N888FS
			(N415HH)
			N888FS
			N976MA
			N612CC
			N413MA
PH-BON	Aviat A-1 Husky	1212	D-EXON
PH-BOS	Piper PA-28-151 Cherokee Warrior	28-7615375	OO-HAZ
			N9605N
PH-BPA	Boeing 737-4Y0	23865	G-UKLA
			VT-MGE
			G-UKLA
			9M-MLC
			G-UKLA
PH-BPB	Boeing 737-4Y0	24344	G-UKLB
			VT-MGF
			G-UKLB
			9M-MLI
			G-UKLB
			9M-MJL
			G-UKLB
			C-GATJ
			C-FVNC
			G-UKLB

Regn.	Type	C/n	Prev.Id.
PH-BPC	Boeing 737-4Y0	24468	G-UKLE
			VT-MGG
			G-UKLE
PH-BPD	Boeing 737-42C	24231	G-UKLC
PH-BPE	Boeing 737-42C	24232	G-UKLD
PH-BPF	Boeing 737-42C	24813	G-UKLF
PH-BPG	Boeing 737-42C	24814	G-UKLG
PH-BPM	Neico Lancair 360	747	
PH-BPS	Dassault Falcon 20F	321	N104SB
			(PH-BPS)
			N20FM
			N244CA
			N702SC
			N2525
			N4454F
			F-WJMJ
PH-BQA to -BQZ *Reserved for Boeing 737-806s for KLM*			
PH-BRI	Embraer EMB.120ER Brasilia	120.235	OO-DTN
			PT-STH
PH-BRK	Embraer EMB.120ER Brasilia	120.253	(PH-BRJ)
			OO-DTO
			PT-STZ
PH-BRL	Embraer EMB.120RTBrasilia	120.083	N278UE
			PT-SMA
PH-BRM	Embraer EMB.120RTBrasilia *(Reservation 1.99)*	120.090	N280UE
			PT-SMH
PH-BRP	Embraer EMB.120RTBrasilia	120.175	N286UE
			PT-SQN
PH-BRT	SOCATA TB-9 Tampico	125	F-GCOC
PH-BRU	Bensen B.8MV gyrocopter	5210108061	
PH-BSM	Cessna 182Q Skylane	66773	N96596
PH-BSV	Cessna 152	81403	N521DG
			N49932
PH-BSX	Reims/Cessna F.177RG Cardinal RG	0095	
PH-BTA	Boeing 737-406	25412	
PH-BTB	Boeing 737-406	25423	
PH-BTC	Boeing 737-406	25424	
PH-BTD	Boeing 737-306	27420	
PH-BTE	Boeing 737-306	27421	
PH-BTF	Boeing 737-406	27232	
PH-BTG	Boeing 737-406	27233	
PH-BTH	Boeing 737-306	28719	
PH-BTI	Boeing 737-306	28720	N1786B
PH-BTK to -BTO *Reserved for Boeing 737s for KLM*			
PH-BUH	Boeing 747-206B Combi (EUD)	21110	
PH-BUI	Boeing 747-206B Combi (EUD)	21111	N8279V
PH-BUK	Boeing 747-206B Combi (EUD)	21549	
PH-BUL	Boeing 747-206B Combi (EUD)	21550	
PH-BUM	Boeing 747-206B Combi (EUD)	21659	N1729B
PH-BUN	Boeing 747-206B Combi (EUD)	21660	
PH-BUO	Boeing 747-206B Combi (EUD)	21848	
PH-BUP	Boeing 747-206B (EUD)	22376	N1295E
			(PH-BUP)
			N1295E
			N57004
PH-BUR	Boeing 747-206B (EUD)	22379	N1298E
			(PH-BUR)
PH-BUT	Boeing 747-206B Combi (EUD)	22380	N1309E
			(PH-BUT)
			N1309E
			(PH-BUT)
			N1309E
			(N1301E)
PH-BUU	Boeing 747-306 Combi	23056	N4548M
			(PH-BUU)
PH-BUV	Boeing 747-306 Combi	23137	N4551N
			(PH-BUV)
PH-BUW	Boeing 747-306 Combi	23508	N6055X
PH-BVE	Cessna 172R Skyhawk	80188	N9941F
PH-BVL	Reims/Cessna F.172N Skyhawk	1868	PH-AXE
			(PH-AXC)
			N9149R
PH-BVT	Piper PA-28-181 Archer II	2890086	
PH-BWA	Beech A36AT Bonanza	E-2581	
PH-BWC	Beech A36AT Bonanza	E-2609	
PH-BWD	Beech A36AT Bonanza	E-2611	
PH-BWF	Beech A36AT Bonanza	E-2617	
PH-BWG	Beech A36AT Bonanza	E-2619	
PH-BWR	Reims/Cessna F.150H Commuter	0365	D-ELND
PH-BXA	Boeing 737-8K2	29131	(PH-EBA)
			N1786B
PH-BXB	Boeing 737-8K2	29132	(PH-EBB)
			N1786B
PH-BXC	Boeing 737-8K2	29133	(PH-EBC)
PH-BXD	Boeing 737-8K2	29134	(PH-EBD)
PH-BXE	Boeing 737-8K2 *(Reservation 10.99)*	29595	
PH-BXF	Boeing 737-8K2 *(Reservation 10.99)*	29596	
PH-BXG	Boeing 737-8K2 *(Reservation 10.99)*	30357	
PH-BXH	Boeing 737-8K2 *(Reservation 10.99)*	29597	
PH-BXI	Boeing 737-8K2 *(Reservation 10.99)*	30358	
PH-BXK	Boeing 737-8K2 *(Reservation 10.99)*	29598	
PH-BXL	Boeing 737-8K2 *(Reservation 10.99)*	30359	
PH-BXM	Boeing 737-8K2 *(Reservation 10.99)*	30355	
PH-BXN	Boeing 737-8K2 *(Reservation 10.99)*	30356	
PH-BXO - BXP, BXR - BXW, Y, Z *Reserved for Boeing 737s for KLM*			
PH-BYA	Beech 58 Baron	TH-1609	F-GKZC
			(F-GIIC)
PH-BYB	Beech 58 Baron	TH-1613	F-GKZD
			(F-GJED)
PH-BZA	Boeing 767-306ER	27957	
PH-BZB	Boeing 767-306ER	27958	
PH-BZC	Boeing 767-306ER	26263	
PH-BZD	Boeing 767-306ER	27610	
PH-BZE	Boeing 767-306ER	28098	
PH-BZF	Boeing 767-306ER	27959	(PH-BZE)
PH-BZG	Boeing 767-306ER	27960	N6009F
			(PH-BZF)
PH-BZH	Boeing 767-306ER	27611	(PH-BZG)
PH-BZI	Boeing 767-306ER	27612	
PH-BZK	Boeing 767-306ER	27614	
PH-BZM	Boeing 767-306ER	28884	
PH-BZN	Fuji FA-200-180AO Aero Subaru	278	D-EFSH
PH-BZO	Boeing 767-306ER	30393	
PH-BZP to BZZ *Reserved for Boeing 767-306ERs for KLM*			
PH-CAG	SOCATA TB-9 Tampico	131	
PH-CAN	Cessna 150M	76686	C-GDQX
			N4053V
PH-CAR	Fuji FA-200-160 Aero Subaru	210	
PH-CBB	Reims/Cessna F.152-II	1782	
PH-CBD	Reims/Cessna F.152-II	1791	
PH-CBF	Reims/Cessna F.152-II	1799	
PH-CBG	Reims/Cessna F.152-II	1803	
PH-CBN	Reims/Cessna F.172N Skyhawk	1985	PH-AYA(3)
PH-CBU	Piper PA-32RT-300 Lance II	32R-7985102	N2113Z
PH-CBX	Brändli BX-2 Cherry *(Reservation)*	NVAV-142	
PH-CDL	Piper PA-34-220T Seneca III	32-8233053	D-GFKI
			N8011Q
PH-CDS	Cessna 152	79972	D-EADZ
			N757SR
PH-CIO	Reims/Cessna F.172N	1556	PH-AXU(1)
PH-CLA	Airbus A.300B4-103	44	N204EA
			F-WJAX
PH-CLE	Reims/Cessna F.406 Caravan II	0032	LN-TWH
			PH-CLE
			AP-BFA
			N442AB
			G-BPSW
			F-WZDU
PH-CMC	Beech F33A Bonanza	CE-1598	
PH-COA	Cessna 140	14737	HB-COA
			N2469V
PH-COL	Neico Lancair 320	399	
PH-COM	Piper PA-30-160 Twin Comanche	30-279	G-MAAG
			G-ASOB
PH-COP	SR-20 Cirrus *(Reservation 7.99)*	unkn	
PH-COR	Dijkhaster CWH	001	
PH-COU	Cessna 172M	67385	(PH-MUG)
			N73337
PH-COZ	Reims/Cessna F.172M	1256	
PH-CPL	Piper PA-28-151 Cherokee Warrior	28-7415050	G-BBXW
			N9599N

Regn.	Type	C/n	Prev.Id.
PH-CRI	Colomban MC-15 Cri-Cri	2 / NVAV-130	
PH-CRJ	Van's RV-6A	23773	
PH-CRL	Piper PA-31P-425 Pressurized Navajo *(Reservation 10.99)*	31P-7300136	OY-CKA N150TT N666BC (N444PM) N666BC N36PC N7657L
PH-CSE	Cessna U206G Stationair 6 II (Robertson STOL)	05952	OO-CAD N6570X
PH-CSL	de Havilland DH.82A Tiger Moth	86609	OO-DJU A-2 PG712
PH-CTW	Cessna 500 Citation *(Reservation 12.99)*	0296	D-ICCC N5269J
PH-CTX	Cessna 550 Citation II	0398	N398S (N550SC) I-KESO N101DD VH-BRX N6889T
PH-CTY	Cessna 500 Citation	0044	OO-ATS N501WW VR-CWW N892CA N712US N942B N544CC
PH-CTZ	Cessna 550 Citation II	0052	N67TM N534MV N90MJ OY-ASV (OO-LFX) N4620G
PH-CUR	Curtiss P-40 *(Reservation 6.99)*	unkn	
PH-CVH	Bowers Fly-Baby 1B	3	
PH-CVT	Cessna 172P Skyhawk	75333	N62766
PH-DAG	Mooney M.20J Model 201	24-1614	N56921
PH-DAY	Ultravia Pelican PL-914	637	
PH-DBO	Neico Lancair 360	245	
PH-DDB	Beech 200 Super King Air	BB-221	SE-KYL F-GJEB N711FD N711UE N20004 N200PB
PH-DDD	Piper PA-28R-201T Cherokee Arrow III	28R-7703348	N40F N9608N
PH-DDS	Douglas DC-4-1009	42934	ZS-NUR SAAF6901 ZS-AUA SAAF6901 ZS-AUA (EI-BSJ)
PH-DDZ	Douglas DC-3C	19754	SU-BFY N920 6O-SAA 6OS-AAA N161 43-15288
PH-DES	Cessna 182P Skylane (Reims-assembled)	0016/63920	N9816E
PH-DGY	Mooney M.20K Model 252	25-1145	HB-DGY
PH-DHC	DHC-2 Beaver 1	965	G-BUVF S-9 55-4585
PH-DIB	Schweizer 269C	S-1612	N86G
PH-DIX	Pilatus PC-12/45 *(Reservation 11.99)*	unkn	
PH-DJM	Skystar Denney Kitfox Mk IV	1412/ NVAV-124	
PH-DKE	Reims/Cessna F.152	1832	OO-TRH
PH-DKF	Reims/Cessna F.172P Skyhawk	2124	G-BJCE
PH-DKG	Cessna 172P Skyhawk	75386	N63052
PH-DKH	Cessna 172P Skyhawk	75655	N64933
PH-DKI	Partenavia P.68C	297	F-GEGT G-BKTD

Regn.	Type	C/n	Prev.Id.
PH-DKJ	Reims/Cessna F.150M	1347	HB-CXM
PH-DKS	Cessna 182P Skylane	62475	D-EDZP (G-BBUN) N52238
PH-DLA	Reims/Cessna FR.172K Hawk XP	0608	PH-AXR(1)
PH-DMB	Fokker F.27-050	20264	OE-LFF PH-EXA
PH-DMC	Fokker F.27-050	20227	OE-LFE PH-EXY (PH-EXJ)
PH-DMD	Fokker F.27-050	20144	SE-LEM (PH-DMI) OE-LFD PH-EXS
PH-DMG	Fokker F.27-050	20203	(PH-DMD) EC-GTE 5Y-BHK (5Y-BHI) PH-EXR
PH-DMK	Fokker F.27-050	20137	EC-GUT 5Y-BFN PH-EXM
PH-DML	Fokker F.27-050 *(Reservation 4.99)*	20136	(PH-DKL) EC-GQT 5Y-BFM PH-EXJ
PH-DMO	Fokker F.27-050	20103	OY-MBM PH-DMO OO-VLC PH-DMO
PH-DON	Cessna 172P Skyhawk	74985	N54484
PH-DPC	Cessna 172RG Cutlass	0369	PH-AYH(3) N4717V
PH-DPL	Reims/Cessna F.172N	1775	PH-AXY(2)
PH-DPX	Cessna T.207A Turbo Stationair 8 II	0727	D-EBMO(2) OE-KMG N9769M
PH-DRI	Fokker DR.1 (Replica)	152/17	
PH-DRN	SOCATA TB-10 Tobago	1135	D-ENFG
PH-DRT	Piper PA-28-181 Archer II	28-8490055	(D-EXUL) N4347Y
PH-DUB	Piper PA-28R-200 Cherokee Arrow II *(Reservation 9.99)*	28R-7435139	D-EBFF N40898
PH-DUC	Stoddard-Hamilton Glasair IIRG-S	2069	
PH-DUS	Beech B200 Super King Air	BB-1296	N296YV
PH-DVE	Piper PA-28-181 Cherokee Archer II	28-7790478	N4581Q
PH-DVW	Reims/Cessna FR.172H Rocket	0342	
PH-DWH	SOCATA TB-9 Tampico	1438	D-EVHN
PH-DZE	Piper PA-24-250 Comanche	24-1877	D-EIEI N6749P
PH-EAG	Euro-ENAER EE-10 Eaglet	04	
PH-EAH	Piper PA-28-181 Archer II	28-7990445	N29517
PH-EAL	Grumman AA-5B Tiger	0703	G-MURF G-JOAN G-BFML
PH-EAM	Reims/Cessna F.172N Skyhawk	1602	PH-AXP(1)
PH-EAN	Airbus A.300B4-103	041	N201EA F-WUAZ
PH-EBF	Fokker DR.1 (Replica) *(Carries c/n 1867 but believed by builder to be 102)*	155/17	N6178N N5505V
PH-ECF	Beech B200 Super King Air	BB-956	D-IAMK N72SE N956WT N193K N19CK
PH-ECI	Cessna 525 CitationJet	0321	D-IAAS
PH-ECN	Robin R.1180TD Aiglon	228	F-GBVD
PH-EDD	Piper PA-28-161 Warrior II	28-8116202	N83726
PH-EDH	Piper PA-24-250 Comanche	24-3361	N8111P
PH-EEE	Piper PA-28-161 Warrior II	28-8316088	N4310M
PH-EEF	Piper PA-31-350 Navajo Chieftain	31-7552017	SE-GIM
PH-EGC	Piper PA-34-220T Seneca III	34-8133115	N83658 (N996N) (N888PC), N83658, N9542N

Regn.	Type	C/n	Prev.Id.
PH-EHN	Reims/Cessna F.172M Skyhawk	1186	D-EEIB
PH-EHO	Cessna 172M Skyhawk	67148	N1481U
PH-EHV	Cessna 172M Skyhawk	64973	N64027
PH-EIJ	SOCATA Rallye 150ST	3141	
PH-ELI	Robinson R-44 Astro	0656	
PH-ELL(3)	Piper PA-28RT-201T Turbo Arrow IV	28R-8131167	N8412N
PH-ELT	Christen A-1 Husky	1131	G-BSVA
			N9604X
PH-EMC	Partenavia P.68B	253	G-OLES
			G-JAJV
			OO-TJG
			(OO-XJG)
PH-EMG	Tipsy T.66S Nipper IIB *(Reservation)*	60	OO-EMG
PH-END	Bölkow BO.208 Junior	515	D-ENDA
			VH-UES
			D-ENDA
PH-ENG	Bölkow BO.208 Junior	510	D-ENCE
PH-EPO	Piper PA-28-181 Archer II	28-7990557	N2919N
PH-ERO	Cessna 182R Skylane	67960	(PH-HBP)
			N9530H
PH-ESP	Robinson R-44 Astro	0506	
PH-EVF	Reims/Cessna F.152	1770	PH-AYI (3)
PH-EWK	Tecnam P.92J Echo	011	
PH-FAM(2)	Piper PA-28RT-201T Turbo Arrow IV	28R-8031123	(PH-VAM)
			N222SQ
			(PH-ELL)
			N222SQ
			N82283
PH-FEA	SOCATA TB-20 Trinidad	1920	F-OIGZ
PH-FHC	Robinson R-22B2 Beta	3010	
PH-FHG	Piper PA-46-350P Malibu Mirage	4636022	
PH-FHL	Fokker F.27 Friendship 500	10634	PT-LAK
			PH-FSL
			(N426SA)
			PH-EXD
PH-FHS	Cessna R.182 Skylane RG	01890	D-EFPW
			N5540T
PH-FLM	Fokker F.27 Friendship 500	10341	PT-LAL
			N272FA
			PH-EXM
			VH-EWO
			OY-STO
			PH-FLM
PH-FNV	Fokker F.27 Friendship 500	10397	F-BPUK
			PH-FNV
PH-FNW	Fokker F.27 Friendship 500	10398	F-BPUL
			PH-FNW
PH-FUN	Aeronca 7AC Champion	2002/NVAV-46	D-EGUP
			N83335
			NC83335
PH-FUT	Velocity 173RG	F02RG-001	(PH-FAE)
PH-FVA	Embraer EMB.110P1B Bandeirante	110-198	N522MW
			PT-GLQ
PH-FWM	Mitsubishi MU-2B Marquise	1548SA	N474MA
PH-FYC	Fokker F.27 Friendship 500	10632	F-WQKM
			PH-FYC
			PT-LAJ
			PH-FSJ
			PH-EXB
PH-FZE	Fokker F.27-050	20182	PT-MLA
	(Reservation 1.00)		PH-FZE
			HB-IAN
			PH-EXH
PH-FZG	Fokker F.27-050	20202	PT-MLC
	(Reservation 1.00)		PH-FZG
			HB-IAP
			PH-EXL
PH-FZH	Fokker F.27-050	20210	PT-MLD
	(Reservation 1.00)		PH-FZH
			HB-IAR
			PH-EXB
PH-GAU	Piper PA-18-135 Super Cub	18-3871	R-181
			54-2471
PH-GAW	Reims/Cessna F.172E	0083	OO-PAT

Regn.	Type	C/n	Prev.Id.
PH-GAZ	Piper PA-18-135 Super Cub	18-3537	R-109
			54-2337
PH-GBS	Cessna T.210N Turbo Centurion II	63846	F-GICM
			N6257C
PH-GDH	SOCATA TB-10 Tobago	750	(PH-GID)
			D-EHJF(2)
PH-GEN	Piper J-3C-90 Cub	12893	(PH-CUB)
			PH-GEN
			OO-SKY
			D-EGUH
			HB-OWN
			44-80597
PH-GEO	Reims/Cessna F.172N Skyhawk	1837	
PH-GFK	Neico Lancair Columbia 300 *(Reservation)*	unkn	
PH-GGG	Piper PA-28RT-201T Turbo Arrow IV	28R-8131186	N8442N
	(Reservation 6.97)		N9562N
			N84207
PH-GGT	Denney Kitfox III	1079	
PH-GIL	Neico Lancair 360	243	
PH-GIN	Fuji FA-200-180 Aero Subaru	255	
PH-GIR	Airbus A.300B4-103	042	N202EA
			F-WJAU
PH-GLG	SOCATA TB-20 Trinidad	1907	F-OIGX
PH-GOM	RAF 2000 GTX-SE	H2-97-8-300	
PH-GOZ	Aviat A-1 Husky	1211	D-EVII
PH-GPX	Reims/Cessna F.406 Caravan II	0058	F-OGPX
			F-GEUD
			F-WZDJ
PH-GRA	Reims/Cessna F.150L Commuter	1006	F-BUMZ
PH-GRB	Fokker S 11-I Instructor	6211	(PH-GRA)
			E-20
PH-GRC	Piper PA-18-135 Super Cub	18-3829	R-139
	(Still officially regd as c/n 18-3828)		54-2429
PH-GRG	American AG-5B Tiger	10174	D-ELYN
			N1198Z
PH-GRH	Cessna 172P Skyhawk	74269	N51114
PH-GRY	Fokker S.11.1 Instructor	6280	MLD 197/K
			E-37
PH-GUG	Reims/Cessna F.406 Caravan II	0060	F-OGUG
			N6660A
			F-WZDR
PH-GUT	Cessna 150M	78155	N9204U
PH-GVB	Cessna 172SP	172S8231	N282SP
PH-GVE	Cessna 172N Skyhawk	71494	N3296E
PH-GVN	Piper PA-32-260 Cherokee Six	32-582	(PH-GEM)
			(PH-GRD)
			(PH-SET)
			N3673W
PH-GWW	Ruschmeyer R.90-230RG	014	D-EECJ(2)
PH-GYN	Piper PA-31-350 Navajo Chieftain	31-7305119	G-BDMD
			N608HR
			(N74968)
PH-GYS	Reims/Cessna F.172N Skyhawk	1871	D-EFOU
PH-GZC	Bellanca 8GCBC Scout	344-80	OO-VVX
PH-HAN	Neico Lancair 360	248	
PH-HBB	SOCATA TB-20 Trinidad	1079	D-EAGT(2)
PH-HBH	Hughes 269C	110-0986	SE-HNC
			PH-HBH
			C-GDLW
			N1108T
PH-HBR	Viking Dragonfly II	124/NVAV-48	
PH-HCG	Reims/Cessna FR.172J Rocket	0400	(PH-HGC)
			D-ECXH
PH-HCW	Reims/Cessna F.172M	1011	D-EJXF
PH-HDE	Cessna P210N Pressurized Centurion II	0709	N210MN
			JA4019
			N5537W
PH-HDW	Brock KB-2	NVAV-76	(PH-JDW)
PH-HGO	Reims/Cessna F.152-II	1701	(PH-AXI (3))
PH-HHA	Schweizer 269D	S-0014	N86G
PH-HHB	Schweizer 269D	S-0016	N69A
PH-HHC	Aérospatiale AS.355F1 Ecureuil 2	5049	I-VIEY
			N357E
PH-HHE	Reims/Cessna F.172N Skyhawk	1617	PH-AXW(1)
PH-HHF	Schweizer 269D	S-0022	N41S

Regn.	Type	C/n	Prev.Id.
PH-HIL	Cessna 150L	75161	(PH-SKN)
			N19050
PH-HJM	Piper PA-28RT-201T Turbo Arrow IV	28R-8231051	N8206B
PH-HKH	Hughes 269C	31-1032	C-GBUS
			N11043
PH-HLF	Cessna 182P Skylane II	0034/64085	N6069F
	(Reims-assembled)		
PH-HLM	Piper PA-34-200T Seneca II	34-7770393	OO-HCJ
			N47405
PH-HLS	Rutan LongEz *(Reservation 9.96)*	unkn	
PH-HLW	Neico Lancair Columbia 300 *(Reservation)*	unkn	
PH-HMK	Reims/Cessna F.172N	1836	
PH-HNK	Cessna 340A	0546	OO-DKE
			D-IHAF
			N4554N
PH-HOG	Fokker S.11.1 Instructor	6275	(PH-HOH)
			MLD:199/K
			E-39
			PH-NFA
			(E-32)
PH-HOI	Fokker S.11.1 Instructor	6282	(PH-DHF)
			PH-HOI
			MLD:175/K
			E-32
PH-HOK	Fokker S.11.1 Instructor	6272	E-29
PH-HOL	Fokker S.11.1 Instructor	6270	E-27
PH-HOY	SkyStar Denney Kitfox IV Speedster	GBS029	
PH-HPH	Hughes 269B	128-0400	D-HARA
			(D-HCRB)
PH-HPL	Schweizer 269C	S-1600	N69A
PH-HTC	Fokker S.11.1 Instructor	6209	E-18
PH-HTH	Hughes 369HS	53-0478S	N9143F
PH-HTM	Reims/Cessna F.182P Skylane II	0008	D-EJCH
PH-HUB	SOCATA TBM-700	127	F-OHBV
			F-WWRL
PH-HVD	Bölkow BO.208C Junior	616	(D-EHET)
PH-HVH	Aérospatiale AS.355F Ecureuil 2	5215	ZS-HMF
PH-HVM	Boeing 737-3K2	24326	
PH-HVN	Boeing 737-3K2	24327	
PH-HVP	Reims/Cessna F.150M Commuter	1194	
PH-HVT	Boeing 737-3K2	24328	
PH-HVV	Boeing 737-3K2	24329	
PH-HVZ	Robinson R-22B2 Beta	2979	
PH-HWH	Agusta-Bell 206B Jet Ranger II	8076	(PH-HXH)
			G-AWLL
PH-HXH	Bell 206L Long Ranger	45103	SE-HSA
			N16773
PH-HZA	Boeing 737-8K2	28373	
PH-HZB	Boeing 737-8K2	28374	
PH-HZC	Boeing 737-8K2	28375	N1786B
PH-HZD	Boeing 737-8K2	28376	N1786B
PH-HZE	Boeing 737-8K2	28377	N1786B
PH-HZF	Boeing 737-8K2	28378	N1796B
PH-HZG	Boeing 737-8K2 *(Reservation .00)*	28379	
PH-HZI	Boeing 737-8K2 *(Reservation .00)*	28380	
PH-HZJ	Boeing 737-8K2 *(Reservation .00)*	30389	
PH-HZK	Boeing 737-8K2 *(Reservation .00)*	30390	
PH-HZL to HLZ	*Batch reserved for Transavia*		
PH-IBI	Noorduyn/ N.American AT-16ND Harvard IIB	14-543	B-181
	(Reservation)		FE809
			42-12296
PH-IBL	Pottier P.220S Koala	467	(PH-MAY)
PH-IBU	SOCATA Rallye 235E Gabier	13125	
PH-IBY	Noorduyn/ N.American AT-16ND Harvard IIB	14A-1100	B-194
	(Reservation)		FS960
			43-12901
PH-ICN	Piper PA-32R-301 Saratoga SP	32R-8013004	D-ERUM
			N8112A
			N9639N
PH-IDA	Piper PA-31-350 Navajo Chieftain	31-7852160	N27806
PH-IIB	Noorduyn/ N.American AT-16ND Harvard IIB	14A-1467	B-118
			FT427
			43-13168
PH-III	de Havilland DH.82A Tiger Moth	86403	D-EDEM
			NL971

Regn.	Type	C/n	Prev.Id.
PH-ILC	Dassault Falcon 900B	161	G-GSEB
			VP-CTT
			F-GSAA
			F-WWFF
PH-IMR	Mooney M.20K Model 231	25-0817	(PH-INR)
			N231VH
PH-INE	Cvjetkovic CA-65	NL-001/ NVAV-117	
PH-INS	Aerosport Scamp	001/ NVAV-25	
PH-IRO	Reims/Cessna F.172M Skyhawk	1088	D-EIQX
PH-ITC	Piper PA-31-350 Navajo Chieftain	31-7405491	N61479
PH-JAC	Piper PA-28-161 Warrior II	28-8416130	N122AV
			N9631N
PH-JAK	Reims/Cessna F.172M Skyhawk	1313	G-BCUI
PH-JAP	Piper PA-25-260 Pawnee C	25-3811	SE-EZI
	(Rebuilt from original PA-25-235B standard		N7666Z
	using parts of PH-APB)		
PH-JAS	Cessna 208 Caravan I	0226	(N9823F)
PH-JBB	Reims/Cessna F.172M	0971	
PH-JBC	Reims/Cessna F.172M	0960	
PH-JBF	Reims/Cessna F.172N Skyhawk	1757	
PH-JBG	Reims/Cessna F.172P Skyhawk II	2072	PH-AYE(4)
PH-JBH	Reims/Cessna F.172M Skyhawk II	1182	D-EDJS
PH-JBI	Cessna R.172K Hawk XP	2969	N758BR
PH-JBJ	Piper PA-34-220T Seneca III	3433157	
PH-JBW	SOCATA TB-20 Trinidad	389	(PH-JWB)
PH-JBY	Cessna U.206F Stationair	3230	OO-CNF
			N8369Q
PH-JDG	Reims/Cessna F.152	1558	D-EEJP
PH-JDL	Ruschmeyer R.90-230G	010	D-EEAU(2)
PH-JDM	Reims/Cessna F.150M Commuter	1391	PH-AXM(2)
PH-JED	SOCATA TB-20 Trinidad	1181	F-GKUP
PH-JEJ	Fuji FA.200-180AO Aero Subaru	253	(PH-BOG)
PH-JFB	Sequoia F.8L Falco	1228	(PH-JSF)
PH-JFD	Pilatus PC-6/B2-H4 Turbo Porter	909	(PH-JRK/-KST/
			-YRK)
			OO-PKZ
PH-JFH	Cessna P210N Pressurized Centurion II Soloy	00726	HB-CQK
			N6185W
PH-JGR	Robinson R-22B2 Beta	2920	
PH-JGS	Robinson R-22B2 Beta	2817	
PH-JGT	Robinson R-22 Beta *(Reservation 3.99)*	unkn	(PH-JRT)
PH-JGW	Europa Aviation Europa *(Reservation 2.99)*	206	
PH-JJM	Reims/Cessna F.152-II	1673	PH-AXC(3)
			(D-EIVR)
PH-JLH	Airbus A.300B4-203F	123	N59123
			(SU-BMZ)
			N59123
			I-BUSF
			F-WZET
PH-JLI	Airbus A.300B4-203F	129	N825SC
	(Reserved for Jet Link, now SU-BMZ ?)		F-BVGO
PH-JMB	Piper PA-28RT-201T Turbo Arrow IV	28R-7931061	N3061N
PH-JML	Pottier P.80S	NVAV-34	
PH-JMP	Cessna 208B Grand Caravan	0583	(PH-JLP)
			N52645
			N1115P
PH-JMS	Reims/Cessna F.182Q Skylane	0168	SX-AJR
			F-WZIZ
PH-JMV	Piper PA-31-350 Chieftain	31-8052088	N180CR
PH-JNA	Cessna 172P	75773	N65524
			LN-NFK
			N65524
PH-JNP	Cessna 172N Skyhawk	67803	N75554
PH-JOE	Cessna 425 Conquest I	0168	G-BJYC
			(N6872T)
PH-JOS	Reims/Cessna F.150L Commuter	1016	
PH-JPO	Reims/Cessna F.172N Skyhawk	2010	
PH-JPR	Neico Lancair *(Reservation)*	unkn	
PH-JSA	Cessna 182N Skylane	60367	N92809
PH-JSL	Mitsubishi MU-300 Diamond *(Reservation)*	A.087SA	HB-VIA
			N487DM
PH-JSP	Mooney M.20J Model 201	24-1269	N1159N
PH-JUR	Piper PA-32R-301T Turbo Saratoga SP	32R-8229033	N8107T
PH-JVB	Cessna 152	80786	D-EADX
			N25789

Regn.	Type	C/n	Prev.Id.
PH-JVG	Piper PA-28-161 Warrior II	28-7916008	N28VG / N39769
PH-JVL	Murphy Rebel	504REB	
PH-JVO	Reims/Cessna FA.150K Aerobat	0041	
PH-JXJ	Fokker F.27-050	20232	PT-SLJ / (PT-OQB) / PH-JXJ
PH-JXK	Fokker F.27-050	20233	PT-SLK / (PT-OQA) / PH-JXK
PH-JXW	Fokker F.28-0100	11390	XA-SGS / PH-JXW
PH-KAC	Cessna 172M Skyhawk	62999	N13758
PH-KAD	Reims/Cessna F.172N Skyhawk	1532	PH-AXD(1)
PH-KAI	Slingsby T.67M Firefly	2038	G-7-116
PH-KAJ	Slingsby T.67M Firefly	2039	G-7-117
PH-KAN	Cessna 172M Skyhawk	64143	C-GCRP
PH-KAO	Robin R.3140	112	
PH-KAU	Slingsby T.67M Firefly	2040	G-7-118
PH-KAX	Piper PA-28-181 Archer II	2890001	N9087U
PH-KBA	Cessna 172P	75109	N55106
PH-KBS	Schweizer 269C	S-1545	N41S
PH-KBX	Fokker F.28-0070	11547	(PH-PCL) / (PH-PBY) / (PH-PWA)
PH-KBY	Cessna 172R Skyhawk	80482	N9537F
PH-KCA	McDonnell-Douglas MD-11P	48555	N6202D
PH-KCB	McDonnell-Douglas MD-11P	48556	
PH-KCC	McDonnell-Douglas MD-11P	48557	
PH-KCD	McDonnell-Douglas MD-11P	48558	
PH-KCE	McDonnell-Douglas MD-11P	48559	N91566
PH-KCF	McDonnell-Douglas MD-11P	48560	
PH-KCG	McDonnell-Douglas MD-11P	48561	
PH-KCH	McDonnell-Douglas MD-11P	48562	
PH-KCI	McDonnell-Douglas MD-11P	48563	PP-SPM / PH-KCI
PH-KCK	McDonnell-Douglas MD-11P	48564	
PH-KCL to -KCP, -KCR to -KCZ *Reserved for MD-11s for KLM*			
PH-KDF	Reims/Cessna F.150L Commuter	1111	D-EDJF / (F-BSGP)
PH-KDL	Reims/Cessna F.152-II	1489	PH-AXH(1)
PH-KDM	Piper PA-28-161 Warrior II	28-8016286	OO-HLT / N81748
PH-KDN	Reims/Cessna F.172N Skyhawk II	1735	D-EFEA
PH-KED	Piper PA-23-250 Aztec E	27-7305116	(PH-KNP) / N40357
PH-KHA	Sikorsky S-76B	760310	N638ME / N638MF / N3124K
PH-KHD	MBB-Bölkow BO.105CBS-4	S-324	HB-XGM / D-HDJD / (D-HDJB)
PH-KHE	MBB-Bölkow BO.105CBS-4	S-329	HB-XGT / D-HDJG
PH-KHV	Beech 3NM / D-18S *(Reservation)*	CA-254	N5369X / (PH-DDB) / N5369X / C-FAID / N7820 / CF-AID / RCAF:2375
PH-KID	Piper PA-31-350 Navajo Chieftain *(Reservation .00)*	31-7305038	N78CF / PJ-PLA / PH-KID / PJ-PLA / PH-KID / G-BBEJ / N74905
PH-KIK	Piper PA-28-181 Archer II	2890155	D-ETAN / N92117
PH-KIS	Christen A-1 Husky	1109	
PH-KJB	BAe. Jetstream Series 3108	648	(PH-KJA) / (N408MX) / G-31-648

Regn.	Type	C/n	Prev.Id.
PH-KJG	BAe. Jetstream Series 3108	690	G-LOGT / G-BSFH / PH-KJG / G-31-690
PH-KLA	Piper PA-18-150 Super Cub *(Officially quoted with f/n 18-1582)*	18-1595	ALAT / 51-15595
PH-KLU	Noorduyn/ N.American AT-16ND Harvard IIB *(Officially regd.with incorrect c/n 14-664)*	14A-1184	B-59 / FT144 / 43-12885
PH-KMP	Beech F33A Bonanza	CE-1623	N8244H
PH-KMS	Cessna P210N Pressurized Centurion	0626	N322KD / N232W / N255TJ / XC-FUV / (N4785W)
PH-KNE(2)	Piper PA-18-135 Super Cub	18-3825	(PH-KNF) / (OO-TAN) / R-135 / 54-2425
PH-KNF(2)	Piper PA-18-135 Super Cub	18-3826	(PH-KNG) / R-136 / 54-2426
PH-KNG(3)	Piper PA-18-135 Super Cub	18-3816	(PH-KND) / R-126 / 54-2416
PH-KNL(2)	Piper PA-18-135 Super Cub	18-3849	(PH-KNN) / R-159 / 54-2449
PH-KNR(2)	Piper PA-18-135 Super Cub	18-3867	(PH-KNT) / R-177 / 54-2467
PH-KOR	Dijkhastar III	001/ NVAV-100	
PH-KPD	Piper PA-32RT-300T Turbo Lance II	32R-7887236	N21880
PH-KRI	Reims/Cessna F.172G	0218	
PH-KSL	SAAB-Scania SF.340B	270	SE-G70
PH-KVA	Fokker F.27-050	20189	PH-EXC
PH-KVB	Fokker F.27-050	20190	PH-EXD
PH-KVC	Fokker F.27-050	20191	PH-EXF
PH-KVD	Fokker F.27-050	20197	
PH-KVE	Fokker F.27-050	20206	
PH-KVF	Fokker F.27-050	20207	
PH-KVG	Fokker F.27-050	20211	
PH-KVH	Fokker F.27-050	20217	
PH-KVI	Fokker F.27-050	20218	
PH-KVK	Fokker F.27-050	20219	
PH-KXJ	Fokker F.28-0100	11400	XA-SGT / PH-KXJ
PH-KXM	Fokker F.27-050	20252	PT-SLO / (PT-OQC) / PH-KXM
PH-KXR	Fokker F.28-0100	11410	XA-SHG / PH-KXR
PH-KYK	Bellanca 8KCAB-180CS Super Decathlon	606-80	N5069K
PH-KZA	Fokker F.28-0070	11567	(PK-JGM)
PH-KZB	Fokker F.28-0070	11562	(PK-JGK)
PH-KZC	Fokker F.28-0070	11566	(PK-JGL)
PH-KZD	Fokker F.28-0070	11582	(PK-JGN)
PH-KZE	Fokker F.28-0070	11576	(PH-EZF)
PH-KZF	Fokker F.28-0070	11577	(G-BVTH) / (PH-EZG)
PH-KZG	Fokker F.28-0070	11578	(G-BWKI) / (PH-EZI)
PH-KZH	Fokker F.28-0070	11583	
PH-KZI	Fokker F.28-0070	11579	(I-REJC) / (PH-EZK)
PH-KZK	Fokker F.28-0070	11581	(I-REJD) / (PH-EZM)
PH-LAB	Cessna 550 Citation II	0712	(PH-LNR/-NLY/-SLV) / N12030
PH-LAG	Piper PA-28-181 Archer II	28-8090296	OO-HLY / N82001
PH-LAT	Piper PA-25-235 Pawnee	25-2596	D-EFPX / SE-FPX / OY-DCS

Regn.	Type	C/n	Prev.Id.
PH-LAW	Cessna T.310R	0096	D-IARW
			N5449X
PH-LBA	Dassault Falcon 900B	173	F-WWFI
PH-LEF	Cessna 182Q Skylane	67283	N4645N
PH-LEN	Reims/Cessna F.172N Skyhawk	1619	
PH-LFA	Cessna 172P Skyhawk	74058	N5309K
PH-LFB	Cessna 172P Skyhawk	75363	N62943
PH-LFC	Fuji FA-200-160 Aero Subaru	181	D-EIDD
PH-LFX	Cessna R.182 Skylane RG	1823	N5149T
PH-LIN	Cessna 172H	56239	N8039L
PH-LJM	Piper PA-28-181 Archer III	2843235	N4126V
			(PH-LJM)
			N4126V
PH-LLU	Piper PA-34-200 Seneca	34-7450185	HB-LLU
			D-GDEB
			EI-BAC
			N43320
PH-LMJ	Reims/Cessna FA.150L Aerobat	0112	D-ECGJ
PH-LMR	Piper PA-32-260 Cherokee Six	32-7700021	(PH-TES)
			N38982
PH-LMT	Fokker F.27-050	20192	PT-MLB
	(Reservation 1.00)		PH-LMT
			HB-IAO
			PH-LMT
			PH-EXO
PH-LPO	Reims/Cessna F.172M Skyhawk	1500	
PH-LSK	Noorduyn/ N.American AT-16-ND Harvard IIB	14-641	B-64
			12-6
			B-64
			FE907
			42-12394
PH-LUE	Reims/Cessna FA.150L Aerobat	0120	(LN-BEK)
PH-LUU	Reims/Cessna F.172L	0861	
PH-LVS	Jabiru SK	121	
PH-LWD	Piper PA-18-150 Super Cub	18-3931	OO-LWD
			EI-234
			I-EIQF
			MM542531
			54-2531
PH-LXG	Fokker F.28-0100	11420	XA-SHH
			PH-LXG
PH-LXW	Fokker F.27-050	20266	
PH-MBK	Fuji FA-200-160 Aero Subaru	226	
PH-MBM	Fuji FA-200-160 Aero Subaru	260	(PH-NAM)
PH-MBR	Beech C23 Sundowner 180	M-1977	
PH-MBS	Beech C23 Sundowner 180	M-1968	
PH-MBV	Reims/Cessna F.172N Skyhawk	1849	PH-AYO(2)
PH-MBW	Fuji FA-200-160 Aero Subaru	286	G-BEYU
PH-MCE	Boeing 747-21AC Combi	23652	N6038E
PH-MCF	Boeing 747-21AC Combi	24134	N6009F
PH-MCG	Boeing 767-31AER	24428	
PH-MCH	Boeing 767-31AER	24429	
PH-MCI	Boeing 767-31AER	25312	
PH-MCL	Boeing 767-31AER	26469	
PH-MCM	Boeing 767-31AER	26470	
PH-MCN	Boeing 747-228F	25266	(F-GCBN)
PH-MCP	McDonnell-Douglas MD-11F	48616	N90187
PH-MCR	McDonnell-Douglas MD-11F	48617	
PH-MCS	McDonnell-Douglas MD-11F	48618	
PH-MCT	McDonnell-Douglas MD-11F	48629	
PH-MCU	McDonnell-Douglas MD-11F	48757	
PH-MCV	Boeing 767-31AER	27619	
PH-MCW	McDonnell-Douglas MD-11F	48788	
PH-MDC	Cessna 560 Citation V Ultra	0280	N1298G
PH-MDE	Schweizer 269C	S-1777	N69A
PH-MDF	Reims/Cessna F.172N	1842	(PH-MFD)
PH-MDW	Piper PA-32RT-300 Lance II	32R-7885186	N36388
PH-MEC	Piper PA-38-112 Tomahawk	38-79A0764	" PH-MEG"
			(PH-MEC)
			G-BVFD
			N2551L
PH-MEG	American AG-5B Tiger	10171	N1001A
PH-MEX	Cessna 650 Citation VI	0217	N217CM
PH-MEY	Beech F33A Bonanza	CE-1434	N5534Y
PH-MFX	Cessna 650 Citation VI	0240	N51143
PH-MGJ	Piper PA-28RT-201T Turbo Arrow IV	28R-7931139	N2077Y
PH-MGT	Cessna 525 CitationJet	0042	N96GD
			(N3230M)
PH-MHE	Piper PA-32R-301 Saratoga SP	32R-8013089	D-EGIF(2)
			N8188S
PH-MIJ	Rand-Robinson KR-2S (Reservation 9.99)	63	
PH-MJB	Piper PA-28R-201 Arrow III	28R-7837227	N30028
PH-MJM	Reims/Cessna F.406 Caravan	0037	5Y-BIS
			D-ICAS
			F-WZDT
PH-MJS	Beech A23A Musketeer Custom III	M-1077	VH-MJS
			N2824B
PH-MKH	Fokker F.28-0100	11242	(PH-KRK)
			(PH-KLM)
PH-MLA	American AG-5B Tiger	10140	
PH-MLB	American AG-5B Tiger	10141	
PH-MLD	American AG-5B Tiger	10143	
PH-MLE	American AG-5B Tiger	10157	N1198B
PH-MLF	Cessna R.172K Hawk XP	2578	N736KB
PH-MLG	American AG-5B Tiger	10160	YL-CAH
PH-MLH	Piper PA-44-180 Seminole	4496013	N9281X
PH-MLM	Noorduyn/ N.American AT-16ND Harvard	14A-1444	B-71
			FT404
			43-13145
PH-MMA	Cessna 182Q Skylane	66579	(PH-GAC)
			(PH-MAD)
			(PH-ZAP)
			N95613
			N684WB
			N95613
PH-MMM	Cessna 177B Cardinal	2528	N18114
PH-MNZ	Dornier 228-212	8206	D-CDIV
			D-CDOQ
PH-MOE	Reims/Cessna F.150M Commuter	1406	(D-EFKW)
PH-MOP	Beech F33A Bonanza	CE-1169	(PH-MPO)
			N3084A
PH-MOT	Scintex CP.1315-C3 Super Emeraude	915	F-BJMP
PH-MRA	Cessna 172M Skyhawk	66964	C-GASV
			(N1269U)
PH-MRB	General Avia F.22B Pinguino	014	
PH-MRC	General Avia F.22C Pinguino Sprint	008	
PH-MRD	Cessna P.210N Pressurized Centurion II	0388	G-HRIS
			N4972K
PH-MRE	Piper PA-31-350 Navajo Chieftain	31-7652083	SE-GNI
PH-MRK	CASA I-131E Jungmann	" 2000/419"	(PH-MRN)
	(Possibly CASA c/n 2000)		D-EDWC
			E3B-419
PH-MRM	Piper PA-34-200T Seneca II	34-8070086	D-GIGF
			N99GN
			C-FJRN
			N35717
PH-MSE	Mooney M.20J Model 205	24-3359	
PH-MSI	Cessna 172P Skyhawk	75726	D-EGRP(2)
			N65309
PH-MVT	Cessna U.206F Stationair	1705	N9505G
PH-MXJ	Fokker F.27-050	20288	
PH-MXS	Fokker F.27-050	20299	(PH-MXT)
PH-MXT	Fokker F.27-050	20300	
PH-MXZ	Fokker F.27-050	20301	
PH-MYF	Neico Lancair 360	244	
PH-NCE	Erco 415D Ercoupe	4765	
PH-NDL	Fairchild F.24R-46A Argus III	961	HB723
	(Reservation)		43-14997
PH-NEH	Auster J/5B Autocar	2932	
PH-NEN	Cessna 195	7496	D-EVLA
			N9817A
PH-NET	Auster 5	1416	G-AIPE
			TJ347
PH-NGK	Auster III	344	8A-11
			R-18
			MZ231
PH-NLZ	Fairchild-Swearingen SA.226TC Metro II	TC-277	(PH-TST)
			N5651M
PH-NOD	Reims/Cessna F.150M Commuter	1165	
PH-NPT	Reims/Cessna F.172N Skyhawk	1641	PH-AXF(1)

Regn.	Type	C/n	Prev.Id.
PH-NRA	Piper PA-38-112 Tomahawk	38-80A0092	(PH-ARN)
			(PH-GEC)
			OO-HKH
			N9684N
PH-NSW	SE.3130 Alouette II (Crashed, 26.6.99)	1185	(PH-THC)
			G-BUIV
			XN132
			F-WIPG
PH-NVF	Fokker F.27 Friendship 100	10102	D-BAKI
			PH-NVF
PH-NVK	Cessna 340A	1018	N24CP
			N340GB
			(N4614N)
PH-NWG	Gyroflug SC-01B-160 Speed Canard	S-40	D-ENWG
PH-NZG	Sikorsky S-61N Mk.II	61753	
PH-NZK	Sikorsky S-61N Mk.II	61773	LN-OMO
			PH-NZK
PH-NZS	Sikorsky S-76B	760325	G-UKLS
			PH-NZS
PH-NZT	Sikorsky S-76B	760326	G-UKLT
			PH-NZT
PH-NZU	Sikorsky S-76B	760329	G-UKLU
			PH-NZU
PH-NZV	Sikorsky S-76B	760336	G-UKLM
			PH-NZV
PH-NZW	Sikorsky S-76B	760381	G-OKLE
			PH-NZW
PH-NZZ	Sikorsky S-76B	760316	N373G
			N363G
			N34RP
			N5AZ
PH-OAL	Piper PA-31-310 Navajo	31-7812037	D-ICAT
			N27595
PH-OEI	Piper J-3C-65 Cub	17360	N4210W
			N21922
			CF-JVX
			N70376
			NC70376
PH-OII	Cessna 182P Skylane	62722	D-EJXU
			N52625
PH-OKE	Hughes 269C	93-0241	D-HNAH
			F-GALG
			G-BCHI
PH-OLD	Cessna 414A Chancellor	0104	D-IJYC
			D-IAWB
			(N5346C)
PH-OLL	SOCATA TB-20 Trinidad	1244	F-GKVD
PH-OMC	Dassault Falcon 20F	239	I-AGEC
			N134CJ
			C-GBFL
			N10MT
			N4417F
			F-WPXM
PH-OOY	Brändli BX-2 Cherry	15/ NVAV-92	
PH-OPA	Stampe & Renard/ Stampe SV.4B	1202	(PH-PTB)
			(PH-SLZ)
			OO-SVC
			V-60
PH-OPC	Piper PA-28RT-201T Turbo Arrow IV	28R-8331031	N42978
			(PH-MMM)
			(PH-JJJ)
			N42978
PH-OTH	Piper PA-31-350 Navajo Chieftain	31-7552075	G-BXUV
			PH-OTH
			G-BXUV
			PH-OTH
			N59979
PH-OTJ	Cessna T.207A Turbo Stationair 8 II	0590	N37443
			OE-DNU
			(N73432)
PH-OTK	Reims/Cessna F.172N Skyhawk	1963	PH-AXY(3)
PH-OUQ	Supermarine VS.361 Spitfire LF.IXc (Reservation)	CBAF.IX.732	G-HVDM
			3W-17
			H-25
			MK732

Regn.	Type	C/n	Prev.Id.
PH-OZB	Boeing 737-3Y0	23921	5B-CIO
			F-GLTT
			EI-BTT
PH-PAC	Reims/Cessna F.182Q Skylane	0118	
PH-PAD	Piper PA-28-181 Archer II	28-8090316	N8218Q
PH-PAU	Stoddard-Hamilton Glasair IIRG	1065	(PH-IPA)
PH-PAW	Piper PA-25-260 Pawnee	25-2203	N6695Z
			N10F
PH-PBA	Douglas DC-3C	19434	(PH-TCB)
			PH-PBA
			(PH-RLD)
			PH-PBA
			42-100971
PH-PBB	Stinson L-5B-VW Sentinel	76-3401	OO-PBB
			PH-PBB
			44-17113
PH-PBL	Cessna 172M Skyhawk	67417	N73384
PH-PBY	Consolidated 28-5ACF Catalina (PBY-5A)	300	N27311
			C-FHHR
			CF-HHR
			N18446
			NC18446
			RCAF11022
			BuA.2459
PH-PCE	Cessna U.206B Super Skywagon	0705	(PH-VTE/-UCK)
			N376TS
PH-PCF	Cessna U.206G Stationair 6 /Soloy	5691	HB-CKM
			N5375X
PH-PCT	Cessna U.206F Stationair	2337	N2092U
PH-PCV	Fuji FA-200-180AO Aero Subaru	271	
PH-PDL	Piper PA-18-150 Super Cub	18-8276	N5509Y
PH-PDZ	Fuji FA-200-180AO Aero Subaru	249	
PH-PEB	Cessna 210J Centurion	59085	D-EAST(2)
			OE-DRW
			N6185F
PH-PEI	Brändli BX-2 Cherry	130	
PH-PEJ	Cessna 172P Skyhawk	75401	LN-SJK
			OY-JRG
			N63187
PH-PEP	Aviat Pitts S-2B	5251	G-CDEE
			N17IJH
PH-PGH	Zenair CH-601HDS Zodiac	6-3459	(PH-PGW/ -PGO/ -PCM/ -PCG/ -KIS)
PH-PGP	Aerotek Pitts S.2A	2186	
PH-PHE	Piper PA-28RT-201T Turbo Arrow IV	28R-8331022	N42921
PH-PHY	Schweizer 269C	S-1668	N69A
PH-PHZ	Schweizer 269C	S-1384	OO-COM
			D-HGUS
PH-PIE	Piper PA-28RT-201T Turbo Arrow IV	28R-8031165	D-EBHN
			N8253Y
PH-PIG	SOCATA TB-20 Trinidad	1053	(PH-PGI)
			SE-KBM
PH-PIM	Cessna R.172K Hawk XP	2376	N736AQ
PH-PIT	Mooney M.20J Model 201	24-1159	(PH-LIT)
			N1140M
PH-PJB	Piper PA-28-235 Cherokee E	28-7110004	D-EHBW
			N8583N
PH-PJL	Cessna 172N Skyhawk	75586	N64578
PH-PJT	SOCATA TB-10 Tobago	1462	
PH-PKA	American AG-5B Tiger	10145	N5000J
PH-PLA	Aérospatiale AS.350B2 Ecureuil	2878	F-WQDL(2)
			F-WQDC(2)
PH-PLB	Aérospatiale AS.350B2 Ecureuil	2884	
PH-PLF	SOCATA TB-20 Trinidad	971	F-GGPK
PH-PLG	Piper PA-28-181 Archer II	28-8190138	G-HUKT
			N8321P
PH-PLK	Gardan GY-80 Horizon 180	239	
PH-PME	SOCATA TB-10 Tobago	188	F-GHXO
			OO-TBT
			(OO-AJD)
PH-PNA	Partenavia P.68B	038	N777EW
			9Q-CMQ
			N777EW
PH-POP	Europa Aviation Europa	157	

Regn.	Type	C/n	Prev.Id.
PH-PPP	Piper PA-28RT-201T Turbo Arrow IV	28R-7931020	N2101J
PH-PPW	Piper PA-18-135 Super Cub	18-3812	(PH-JZM)
			(PH-GAP)
			R-122
			54-2412
PH-PRG	Fokker F.27-050	20155	
PH-PRH	Fokker F.27-050	20200	
PH-PRI	Fokker F.27-050	20201	
PH-PRJ	Fokker F.27-050	20212	
PH-PRM	Piper PA-44-180 Seminole	44-7995279	OO-HCV
			N2203X
PH-PRO	Reims/Cessna F.172M Skyhawk II	1039	
PH-PSC	Piper PA-18-135 Super Cub	18-3827	R-137
			54-2427
PH-PTC	Piper PA-31-350 Navajo Chieftain	31-7852052	G-CLAN
			N27549
PH-PTD	Piper PA-31-350 Navajo Chieftain	31-7852066	G-BRGV
			N27583
PH-PUL	Aero Designs Pulsar XP	252/NVAV-111	
PH-PUP	Aerotek Pitts S-1S	1-0045	N3KZ
			N9TH
PH-PVG	Reims/Cessna F.172M Skyhawk	1473	
PH-PWZ	Neico Lancair 360	300	
PH-PYL	Neico Lancair 360	609	
PH-RAA	Piper PA-28-161 Cadet	2841145	D-EDCC
			N9509N
PH-RAN	Mooney M.20J Model 201	24-0939	D-EAAB(2)
			N3788H
PH-RAP	Neico Lancair 360	266	N420BA
PH-RAX	Fairchild-Swearingen SA.227AT Merlin IVC	AT-493	F-GGLG
			N121FA
			F-GGLG
			OY-CHC
			N3075A
			CP-....
			N3075A
PH-RAY	Denney Kitfox IV	1411	
PH-RAZ	Fairchild-Swearingen SA.226TC Metro II	TC-252	OY-AZW
			D-IBCF
			OY-AZW
			N5456M
PH-RBC	Eurocopter EC.120B Colibri	1069	
PH-RCF	Reims/Cessna F.172N Skyhawk	2034	PH-AYO(3)
PH-RCM	SOCATA TB-20 Trinidad	1451	F-GLFO
PH-RCV	SOCATA TB-10 Tobago	1318	
PH-RDM	Piper PA-18-150 Super Cub	18-3532	R-104
	(Officially regd.with f/n 18-3639)		54-2332
PH-RER	Piper PA-28-181 Archer III	2843255	N41478
			(PH-RER)
			N9514N
PH-RES	Reims/Cessna F.172N Skyhawk II	1597	PH-AXN(1)
PH-RHC	Revolution Mini-500	0035	N500ZZ
PH-RIN	Reims/Cessna F.150M	1365	PH-AYD(1)
PH-RJB	SAAB S.91B Safir	91309	D-EBUC
			SE-XAU
PH-RJH	Brändli BX-2 Cherry	NVAV-127	
PH-RLA	SAAB S.91D Safir	91367	
PH-RLB	SAAB S.91D Safir	91368	
PH-RLD	SAAB S.91DSafir	91370	
PH-RMA	Cessna S550 Citation S/II	0145	(PH-HMA)
			(PH-HMC)
PH-RNB	SOCATA Rallye 150ST	3176	N900SW
			N29973
			PH-RNB
PH-RNC	SOCATA Rallye 150ST	3177	
PH-ROB	Piper PA-18-150 Super Cub	18-7910	N3974Z
PH-ROL	Robin R.2112 Alpha	180	F-GCAF
PH-ROX	Cessna 150M	76064	N66462
PH-RPB	Reims/Cessna F.172H	0568	
PH-RPH	Cessna 182R Skylane	67808	(PH-HCP)
			N6243N
PH-RPI	Cessna 182R Skylane	67809	(PH-HDP)
			N6245N

Regn.	Type	C/n	Prev.Id.
PH-RPJ	Cessna 182R Skylane	67833	N6390N
			(PH-AXQ (4))
			N6390N
PH-RPM	Pilatus Britten-Norman BN-2T Turbine Islander	2190	G-BLNK
			PH-RPM
			G-BLNK
PH-RPN	Pilatus Britten-Norman BN-2T Turbine Islander	2191	G-BLNL
			PH-RPN
			G-BLNL
PH-RPR	Bölkow BO.105C	S-356	D-HDGS
PH-RPS	Bölkow BO.105C	S-355	D-HDGR
PH-RPV	Bölkow BO.105CB	S-249	D-HDHI
PH-RPW	Bölkow BO.105CB	S-250	D-HDHJ
PH-RRR	Piper PA-28-181 Archer II	28-8290156	N8244X
PH-RUD	Reims/Cessna F.150M Commuter	1163	
PH-RVA	Bensen B-8M Gyrocopter (Reservation)	unkn	
PH-RVG	Piper PA-28-181 Archer II	28-8390024	N8316W
PH-RVH	Piel CP.328A Super Emeraude	NVAV-75	
PH-RVS	Partenavia P.68B	98	
PH-RWL	SOCATA TB-9 Tampico	1268	F-GKVC
PH-RWM	Rockwell Commander 112TCA	13150	(PH-PPP)
			N4619W
PH-RXA	Embraer EMB.145 (Reservation 11.99)	145-216	
PH-RYF	Hughes 269C	105-0444	(PH-HAH)
			PH-RYF
			OY-HCE
			D-HKEP
PH-SAV	Piper PA-31-350 Navajo Chieftain	31-7652056	N59818
PH-SBD	Piper PA-28-161 Cadet	2841057	N9627N
PH-SBE	Piper PA-28-161 Cadet	2841058	N9628N
PH-SBG	Piper PA-28-161 Warrior II	28-8616028	N9196M
PH-SBJ	Piper PA-28-161 Warrior II	28-8616032	N9260A
PH-SBK	Beech 200 Super King Air	BB-180	G-BHVX
			PH-SBK
			G-BHVX
			5N-AKR
PH-SBM	Reims/Cessna F.172N	1637	D-EECW
			(SU-...)
PH-SBU	Piper PA-28-161 Warrior II	28-7916392	N2249Z
PH-SBX	Piper PA-28-161 Warrior II	28-7916005	N39745
PH-SBY	Piper PA-28-161 Warrior II	28-7916006	N39746
PH-SBZ	Piper PA-28-161 Warrior II	28-7916007	N39768
PH-SCX	Cessna 152	82148	N68146
			(PH-SCX)
			N68146
PH-SCY	Aeritalia/SNIAS ATR-72-201	147	EC-GQS
			EI-CBC
			(N974NA)
			F-WWET
PH-SCZ	Aeritalia/SNIAS ATR-72-201	150	EC-GUL
			EI-CBD
			(N975NA)
			F-WWEI
PH-SDB	Piper PA-28-161 Warrior II	28-8016322	OO-HLX
			N82000
PH-SDH	DHC-8 Series 102	222	C-GFUM
PH-SDK	DHC-8 Series 311	254	C-GFYI
PH-SDM	DHC-8 Series 311	298	N511SK
			C-GETI
PH-SDN	Piper PA-28R-200 Cherokee Arrow II	28R-7535192	N33773
			PH-SDN
			N33773
PH-SDP	DHC-8 Series 311	300	N501DC
			N501CS
			C-GFRP
PH-SDR	DHC-8 Series 311	283	PH-SDE)
			EI-CED
			C-GFUM
PH-SDT	DHC-8 Series 311	276	C-FZBL
			PT-OKC
			C-GFRP
PH-SDU	DHC-8 Series 311	232	(YR-GPZ)
			C-FXXU
			HS-SKJ
			C-GFBW

Regn.	Type	C/n	Prev.Id.
PH-SEL	Cessna 172P	74194	(PH-SCW)
			N6409K
PH-SFL	Airbus A.300B4-203F	220	N860PA
			SE-DSF
			N74989
			N231EA
			F-GBNY
PH-SFM	Airbus A.300B4-203F	274	(N59274)
			N227KW
			N14977
			N235EA
			F-GDVC
PH-SGA	Slingsby T-67C-3 Firefly	2074	(PH-SBA)
			G-7-137
PH-SGB	Slingsby T-67C-3 Firefly	2077	(PH-SBB)
			G-7-136
PH-SGC	Slingsby T-67C-3 Firefly	2081	(PH-SBC)
			G-7-138
PH-SGE	Slingsby T-67C-3 Firefly	2083	G-7-146
			PH-SGE
			G-7-140
PH-SGF	Slingsby T-67C-3 Firefly	2087	G-7-141
PH-SGG	Slingsby T-67C-3 Firefly	2099	
PH-SGH	Slingsby T-67C-3 Firefly	2100	G-7-142
PH-SIG	Cessna 182P Skylane	63129	D-EDJX
			N7345N
PH-SII	Fokker S.11-1 Instructor	6215	E-24
PH-SIL	Piper PA-28RT-201T Turbo Arrow IV	28R-8231053	(PH-STI)
			N8392A
			(HB-PGY)
PH-SIR	Reims/Cessna F.172M Skyhawk	1263	D-ELEX
PH-SKB	Reims/Cessna F.172N Skyhawk	1549	PH-AXM(1)
PH-SKC	Reims/Cessna F.172N Skyhawk II	1673	PH-AXH(2)
			F-BNGR
			(SX-...)
PH-SKE	Cessna 172P Skyhawk	74730	N53364
PH-SKF	Cessna 150M	78927	N704WG
PH-SKG	Cessna 152	85168	N6145Q
PH-SKJ	Cessna 172M Skyhawk	66607	N80474
			C-GXBB
			N80474
PH-SKN	Cessna 172M	65655	N6939H
PH-SKP	Beech 200C Super King Air	BL-11	F-GIMD
	(Reserved as 5B-CJM .99)		N41JK
			(5H-...)
			I- MADY
			D- INEF
PH-SLA	Cessna 180J	52637	G-BDSI
			N9982N
PH-SLO	Fokker S.11.1 Instructor	6281	(PH-HOH)
			MLD:198
			E-38
PH-SLR	Cessna 172N Skyhawk	71965	N5930E
			(N5830E)
PH-SLW	McDonnell-Douglas MD-902 (Reservation)	unkn	
PH-SMA	Reims/Cessna F.172H	0506	D-EDDF
PH-SMD	Piper PA-32-300 Cherokee Six	32-7840196	N30156
PH-SNB	Piper PA-34-220T Seneca III	34-8133131	N8399D
PH-SNE	Piper PA-28-180 Cherokee Archer	28-7505181	N33794
PH-SNJ	Piper PA-34-220T Seneca III	34-8233119	N82115
			(TG-BUH)
			N9649N
PH-SOK	Partenavia P.68C	218	G-BJCR
			OO-EEC
PH-SPA	Grob G.115A	8043	(D-EGVV)
PH-SPC	Grob G.115A	8044	(D-EGVV)
PH-SPD	Grob G.115A	8078	(D-EGVV)
PH-SPE	Robin R.3000/140	137	
PH-SPF	Piper PA-28RT-201T Turbo Arrow IV	28R-8531006	N4388U
PH-SPH	Grob G.115	8024	G-BOUD
PH-SPI	Cessna 182S Skylane	80065	N9882F
PH-SPX	Grob G.115C	82041/C	D-EWAN
PH-SRN	Piper PA-28-151 Cherokee Warrior	28-7615053	(PH-GMA)
			N9644N

Regn.	Type	C/n	Prev.Id.
PH-SRP	Piper PA-28-151 Cherokee Warrior	28-7715209	(PH-SRO)
			OO-HCA
			N9539N
PH-SRU	Piper PA-28-161 Cherokee Warrior II	28-7816485	OO-HCN
			N9500C
PH-SRX	Robin DR.400/140B Major	1401	
PH-SSK	Aérospatiale SA.365C2 Dauphin 2	5010	5N-BAO
			PH-SSK
			EC-800
			PH-SSK
			RP-C1248
			PH-SSK
			F-GFAP
			PH-SSK
			5N-ALZ
			PH-SSK
			N9006N
			F-WZAY
PH-SST	Aérospatiale SA.365N Dauphin 2	6077	EC-EEP
			PH-SST
			F-WYME
PH-SSU	Aérospatiale SA.365N Dauphin 2	6074	5N-ATX
	(Reservation 12.99)		PH-SSU
			(G-BLDR)
			G-TRAF
			G-BLDR
PH-SSW	Aérospatiale SA.365N Dauphin 2	6103	V8-UDW
PH-SSX	Aérospatiale SA.365N Dauphin 2	6030	5N-BAR
			F-GCPH
PH-SSY	Aérospatiale SA.365C2 Dauphin 2 (Reservation.)	5055	EC-GVU
			PH-SSY
			EC-FOY
			EC-137
			CC-CJA
PH-STL	Cessna U.206G Stationair II Soloy	4266	HB-CKZ
			N756QF
PH-STV	Mudry CAP.10B	89	F-BXHW
PH-SVA	Robin R.2112 Alpha	188	
PH-SVE	Robin DR.400/120 Dauphin 80	1499	
PH-SVF	Piper PA-28-161 Warrior II	28-8316044	N4305D
			N4293C
PH-SVG	Piper PA-28-161 Warrior II	28-8616055	(F-GHLY)
			N9085V
PH-SVH	Piper PA-28-161 Cadet	2841300	(PH-VCR)
			N9528N
PH-SVI	Piper PA-28-161 Warrior II	28-8416075	N4352P
PH-SVJ	Piper PA-28-161 Warrior II	28-8316018	N83085
PH-SVL	Robin DR.400/120 Petit Prince	2379	
PH-SVM	Robin DR.400/120 Petit Prince	2388	
PH-SVW	Stoddard-Hamilton Glasair IIS RG	2037	
PH-SWD	Piper PA-28-180 Cherokee Archer	28-7405005	OE-DML
			N9558N
PH-SXA	SOCATA TB-20 Trinidad	1856	F-OIGH
PH-SXB	SOCATA TB-20 Trinidad	1857	F-OIGI
PH-SXC	SOCATA TB-20 Trinidad	1858	F-OIGJ
PH-SXD	SOCATA TB-20 Trinidad	1859	F-OIGK
PH-SXE	SOCATA TB-20 Trinidad	1860	F-OIGL
PH-SYA	Piper PA-32RT-300 Lance II	32R-7885212	(PH-PLW)
			(OO-HCQ)
			N36807
PH-SYD	Piper PA-28RT-201 Arrow IV	28R-8018094	N8246S
PH-SYR	Mooney M.20M TLS	27-0110	
PH-SZW	Cessna 172S Skyhawk	172S8056	N649SP
PH-TAJ	Pottier P.220S Koala	166	
PH-TAT	Slepcev Storch Mk.4	0049	
PH-TBD	SOCATA TBM-700	85	N300PW
PH-TBR(2)	Noorduyn/ N.American AT-16ND Harvard IIB	14A-808	B-182
			FS668
			43-12509
PH-TBT	SOCATA TB-9 Tampico	56	
PH-TDR	Tecnam P.92J Echo	012	
PH-TEB	SOCATA TB-10 Tobago	393	D-EJPF
PH-TED	Piper PA-28-161 Cadet	2841102	C-FDYA
PH-TEJ	Pottier P.180S	107/NVAV-80	(PH-TEI)
			(PH-JET)

Regn.	Type	C/n	Prev.Id.
PH-TET	Rotorway Executive 162F	6110	
PH-TEX	Reims/Cessna F.172M	1010	F-BUMX
PH-TEY(2)	Gyroflug SC-01B-160 Speed Canard	S-25	D-EOSC
PH-TGA	Reims/Cessna F.150M Commuter	1394	PH-AYH(1)
PH-TGB	Reims/Cessna F.152-II	1742	PH-AYC(3)
PH-TGC	Cessna 182R Skylane	68401	PH-AXS(4)
			N9352E
PH-TGD	Cessna 152-II	85960	(PH-TDG)
			N95705
PH-TGF(2)	Piper PA-28-181 Archer II	28-8590011	(PH-TGV)
			N147AV
PH-TGH	Cessna 172P	75457	OY-CPA
			N63625
PH-TGK	Piper PA-28-181 Archer II	2890012	N9107Z
PH-TGM	Reims/Cessna F.172N Skyhawk	1887	PH-AXV(3)
			(D-EEOR)
PH-TGV	Reims/Cessna F.172N Skyhawk	1640	
PH-THC	Robinson R-22B2 Beta	2756	
PH-THE	Colomban MC-15 Cri-Cri	2/ NVAV-131	
PH-THS	Cessna 172N Skyhawk	72193	N8374E
PH-TIM	Robin DR.400/180 Régent	2311	
PH-TKA	Boeing 757-2K2	26633	
PH-TKB	Boeing 757-2K2	26634	
PH-TKC	Boeing 757-2K2	26635	
PH-TKD	Boeing 757-2K2	26330	XA-TMU
			PH-TKD
			C-GTSR
			PH-TKD
PH-TLC	Neico Lancair 360	001	N360LA
PH-TMH	Piper PA-38-112 Tomahawk	38-79A0261	N2314D
PH-TOC	Cessna 172M Skyhawk	63689	N1597V
PH-TOF	Piper PA-25-260 Pawnee D	25-7405573	N54000
PH-TOG	Ayres S.2R Turbo Thrush Commander	2441R	EC-DES
	(Marsh conversion)		N8923Q
PH-TOK	Piper PA-18-135 Super Cub	18-3604	R-114
			54-2404
PH-TOL	Cessna 172M Skyhawk	63133	N4383R
PH-TOO	Cessna U.206G Stationair II	6258	N6376Z
PH-TOP	Piper PA-18-150 Super Cub	18-8257	
PH-TOR	Piper PA-25-260 Pawnee C	25-4960	N8539L
PH-TOW	Morane-Saulnier MS.885 Super Rallye	5254	(PH-FOW)
			D-EHQA
			OH-MRD
PH-TOY	Ayres S.2R Turbo Thrush Commander	2410R	N5632X
	(Marsh conversion)		
PH-TRT	Piper PA-22-160 Tri-Pacer	22-5933	D-ELPE
			N8750D
PH-TSW	Boeing 737-3L9	24219	OY-MMO
			G-BOZB
			(PH-OZB)
			G-BOZB
			(OY-MMO)
			N1786B
PH-TSX	Boeing 737-3K2	26318	
PH-TSY	Boeing 737-3K2	28085	
PH-TSZ	Boeing 737-3K2	27635	
PH-TTA	DHC-8 Series 102	237	G-BRYG
			C-GEOA
PH-TTB	DHC-8 Series 102A	241	G-BRYH
			C-GESR
PH-TVB	Piper PA-31-310 Navajo	31-408	N6453L
PH-TWB	Reims/Cessna F.172N Skyhawk	1572	D-EBJG
PH-TWF	Reims/Cessna F.152	1746	D-ENAX
PH-TWG	Piper PA-28-181 Archer II	28-8190256	N84001
PH-TWM	Cessna 172P	75859	N73ER
			N65755
PH-TWP	Piper PA-28RT-201 Arrow IV	28R-7918215	N2910W
			(PH-TWP)
			N2910W
			(PH-NDE)
			N2910W
PH-TWR	Ken Brock KB-2 Gyroplane	1006	
PH-TWS	Reims/Cessna F.172M Skyhawk	1402	OY-BUL
PH-TWT	SOCATA TB-20 Trinidad	459	D-EDEJ
PH-TWY	Reims/Cessna F.172M Skyhawk	1513	

Regn.	Type	C/n	Prev.Id.
PH-TWZ	Christen A-1 Husky	1110	
PH-TXD	Cessna 150M	79342	(PH-USB)
			N714QC
PH-TXL	Cessna 172P Skyhawk	75067	N54850
PH-TYG	de Havilland DH.82A Tiger Moth	82535	(PH-TGR)
			G-APCU
			(PH-TGR)
			G-APCU
			N9508
PH-TZC	Piper PA-18-135 Super Cub	18-3839	(PH-KNK)
			R-149
			54-2439
PH-UBG	SOCATA TB-21 Trinidad TC	1012	F-GLAA
PH-UCI	Piper J-3C-65 Cub	13351	45-4611
PH-UCS	Piper J-3C-65 Cub (L-4J)	13228/ NVAV-50	45-4488
PH-UEG	SAAB S.91A Safir (Reservation)	91143	SE-BNS
	(Rebuilt using parts of PH-UEA c/n 91125)		
PH-UGS	Piper PA-28-161 Warrior II	28-7916340	(PH-WWG)
			N2133X
			N9629N
PH-ULN	Tecnam P.92J Echo	006	
PH-URK	Piper PA-31-310 Navajo	31-478	N8504G
			N686DC
			N904AR
			N6562L
PH-USA	Cessna 172P Skyhawk II	74718	N53297
PH-USC	Cessna 172P Skyhawk	73517	N4970G
PH-USH	HOAC DV-20 Katana	20024	
PH-USI	HOAC DV-20 Katana	20072	
PH-USJ	HOAC DV-20 Katana	20139	
PH-UUB	Robinson R-44 Astro (Reservation 11.99)	0739	
PH-UUU	SOCATA TB-9 Tampico Club	919	D-ENDU
PH-UWA	Reims/Cessna F.150M	1274	LX-AVI
			LX-AIN
PH-UWL	Cessna 421C Golden Eagle	1234	(PH-UWG)
			N2722U
PH-VAR	SOCATA Rallye 150ST	3173	
PH-VBC	Piper PA-25-260 Pawnee	25-2264	(PH-VCW)
			G-ASLJ
			ST-ADS
			G-ASLJ
			ST-ACH
			G-ASLJ
			N6694Z
PH-VBI	Reims/Cessna FRA.150L Aerobat	0232	OO-KMM
			(OO-HMM)
			(OO-WMM)
			N199ER
			PH-VBI
			OO-WAG
PH-VCF	SOCATA TB-10 Tobago	784	F-GFQZ
PH-VCM	Cessna 421C Golden Eagle II	1212	(PH-ASA)
			N26610
PH-VCX	Piper PA-18 Super Cub 125	18-851	(PH-VCH)
	(Officially regd. with t/n 18-939)		R-205
			51-15686
PH-VCY	Piper PA-18 Super Cub 95	18-3601	R-111
	(Officially regd. with t/n 18-3785)		54-2401
PH-VDC	Cessna T.210M Turbo Centurion	0008/62368	(PH-AXZ(2))
	(Reims-assembled)		N761MR
PH-VDM	Cessna 172R Skyhawk	80187	N9939F
PH-VDN	Cessna 150M	76820	C-GWNY
			(N45277)
PH-VDS	Mooney M.20K Model 252	25-1001	N252JS
			(N251JS)
PH-VES	Reims/Cessna F.172P Skyhawk	2063	D-ECCA
PH-VFA	Piper PA-28-161 Cadet	2841360	D-ETPZ
			N9248Z
			(N137ND)
PH-VFB	Piper PA-28-161 Cadet	2841361	D-ETPV
			N92482
			(N9233Z)
PH-VFC	Piper PA-28-161 Cadet	2841314	D-EJTS
			N9271N
			N9210P

Regn.	Type	C/n	Prev.Id.
PH-VGA	Cessna T.303 Crusader	0157	N6503C
PH-VGB	Piper PA-28-161 Warrior II	28-8616003	N2427Q
PH-VGC	Cessna 172N	71277	N2426E
PH-VHB	Robin DR.400/180R Remorqueur	1552	D-ECDC
PH-VKA	Piper PA-44-180 Seminole	44-8095027	N8230Z
PH-VKB	Reims/Cessna F.150J	0451	D-EEBA
PH-VLG	Cessna 560 Citation V Ultra	0271	
PH-VLK	Piper PA-28-181 Cherokee Archer II	28-7890268	N2803M
PH-VLM	Fokker F.27-050	20135	OO-VLM
			LN-BBD
			(LN-AKH)
			PH-EXI
PH-VLN	Fokker F.27-050	20145	OO-VLN
			LN-BBE
			(LN-AKI)
			PH-EXT
PH-VLS	Reims/Cessna F.172N Skyhawk	1631	PH-AXZ(1)
PH-VMA	Piper PA-32R-301T Turbo Saratoga SP	32R-8129098	N8430F
PH-VMP	Beech B200 Super King Air	BB-1538	N3268L
PH-VMV	SOCATA TB-20 Trinidad (Reservation 8.99)	unkn	
PH-VOS	Reims/Cessna F.150L	1092	(PH-WAC)
PH-VPA	Piper PA-34-200 Seneca	34-7250182	D-GKZW
			N2873T
PH-VPI	Evans VP-1 Volksplane	V.2567/ NVAV-27	(PH-VDK)
PH-VRW	Reims/Cessna F.150K Commuter	0071	
PH-VSF	Reims/Cessna F.172L Skyhawk	0877	
PH-VSG	Reims/Cessna F.150L	1031	
PH-VSN	Reims/Cessna F.152-II	1714	PH-AXW(3)
PH-VSP	Reims/Cessna F.172N Skyhawk II	1951	(PH-AXN(3))
PH-VSR	Reims/Cessna F.172P Skyhawk II	2041	F-GCYG
PH-VSS	Reims/Cessna F.172P Skyhawk II	2199	D-EBDA
PH-VSU	Robin DR.400/100	1932	
PH-VSX	Piper PA-28-181 Archer III	2890231	LX-ABZ
PH-VSY	Piper PA-28-161 Warrior III	2842018	N9273N
PH-VTW	Piper PA-32RT-301T Turbo Saratoga SP	32R-8129089	N8415J
			(PH-VTW)
			N8415J
PH-VVB	Commander Aircraft 114B	14622	N77HQ
			N77HK
			N500JR
PH-VVD	Reims/Cessna F.150M	1372	PH-AYE(1)
PH-WAA	Reims/Cessna F.172L	0818	
PH-WAI	Reims/Cessna F.172M	0961	(OO-WAP)
PH-WAN	Piper PA-18-150 Super Cub	18-2063	(PH-VBF)
	(Officially regd.with f/n 18-2076)		(OO-WAN)
			PH-WAN
			R-77
			54-2463
PH-WAT	Piper PA-25-235 Pawnee	25-2380	G-ASLA
	(Rebuilt with frame c/n 25-5544 in 1974)		N6802Z
PH-WBR	Cessna 175C Skylark	57033	D-EHZE
			N8333T
PH-WCU	Piper PA-28R-201T Cherokee Arrow III	28R-7703094	N3156Q
PH-WDR	Piper PA-18-135 Super Cub	18-3852	R-162
			54-2452
PH-WDS	Cessna 172M Skyhawk	63719	N1707V
PH-WEE	Cessna 152	80083	G-BMNN
			N757XJ
PH-WEN	Hughes 269C	47-0591	
PH-WES	Cessna 421B Golden Eagle	0523	HB-LHG
			OE-FST
			HB-LHG
			N69886
PH-WGW	Mooney M.20R Ovation (W/o 7.9.99)	29-0150	
PH-WIL	Rand-Robinson KR-2	6371/60/ NVAV-68	
PH-WIM	Piper PA-38-112 Tomahawk	38-78A0592	C-GHPH
PH-WKA	SOCATA TB-10 Tobago	1027	D-EABE
PH-WLS	Piper PA-28-161 Warrior II	28-8016345	N8226X
PH-WMA	Reims/Cessna F.172P Skyhawk II	2064	D-EODP
			(D-EJIM)
PH-WOL	BAe.125-800B (Reservation 9.99, possibly 258235 ex D-CWOL)		
PH-WOW	Cessna A.185F Skywagon Amphibian	04186	P4-WET
			C-GKOS
			N61434
PH-WSD	Cessna 172M	66598	N80459

Regn.	Type	C/n	Prev.Id.
PH-WSF	Piper PA-28-140 Cherokee Cruiser	28-7325019	HB-OKM
			N11C
PH-WWG	Piper PA-28-161 Warrior II	28-8016235	N8141R
PH-WWL	Rans S-10 Sakota (Reservation)	1192150	
PH-WWO	Cessna 172P Skyhawk	74784	N53598
PH-WWR	Mooney M.20K Model 231	25-0688	N1167G
			(PH-WWR)
			N1167G
PH-WWS	Revolution Mini-500	339	
PH-WWW	Commander Aircraft 114B (Reservation .99)	14564	D-EWAT
PH-WXA	Fokker F.28-0070	11570	(PH-WWA)
			I- REJO
			PH-EZZ
PH-WXC	Fokker F.28-0070	11574	I-REJI
			PH-EZY
PH-WYN	Cessna 177B Cardinal	2310	N35291
PH-XLA	Embraer EMB.120RT Brasilia	120-081	G-BRAZ
			F-GFTC
			G-BRAZ
			PT-SKY
PH-XLB	Embraer EMB.120RT Brasilia	120-091	F-GFTB
			(F-GFTC)
			PT-SMI
PH-XLC	Aeritalia/SNIAS ATR-42-320	060	F-WQBX
			N47801
			F-WWEN
PH-XLD	Aeritalia/SNIAS ATR-42-320	075	F-WQBS
			N27806
			F-WWEA
PH-XLE	Aeritalia/SNIAS ATR-42-320	090	F-WQBR
			N18809
			F-WWEP
PH-XLF	Embraer EMB.120RT Brasilia	120-082	(PH-XLS)
			OO-DTF
			PT-SKZ
PH-XLG	Embraer EMB.120ER Brasilia	120-121	OO-DTI
			PT-SNN
PH-XLH	Aeritalia/SNIAS ATR-72-201	195	F-WQGO
			B-22701
			F-WWEI
PH-XLI	Aeritalia/SNIAS ATR-42-320	066	F-WQBO
			TG-AFA
			TG-MWG
			F-WQBO
			N76803
			F-WWEU
PH-XLK	Aeritalia/SNIAS ATR-42-320	093	(PH-ZLJ)
			TG-AGA
			TG-MWA
			F-WQCZ
			N17810
			F-WWES
PH-XPI	Piper PA-31-350 Navajo Chieftain	31-7752187	G-BFFR
			N27388
PH-XXV	North American B-25NMitchell	108-33832	N320SQ
	(Reservation 4.99)		N3698G
			44-29507
PH-YEB	Cessna 177RG Cardinal RG	0464	D-ELKB
			N2064Q
PH-ZCR	Piper PA-18-135 Super Cub	18-3865	(PH-KNS)
			R-175
			54-2465
PH-ZCT	Piper PA-18-135 Super Cub	18-3859	R-169
			54-2459
PH-ZLA	Reims/Cessna FA.150K Aerobat	0007	OO-SKD
PH-ZSM	Skystar Kitfox V Speedster	S9411-0064	
PH-ZSS	Reims/Cessna F.172M Skyhawk	1377	D-EMAO
PH-ZVC	Piper PA-18-135 Super Cub	18-3855	(PH-KNP)
			R-165
			54-2455
PH-ZZF	Cessna T207A Skywagon Soloy (Res)	00747	(PH-GEA/ -HOO/ -MMB/ -SEX)
			HB-CLM
			N9896M

Regn.	Type	C/n	Prev.Id.
PH-ZZM	HOAC DV-20 Katana	20058	
PH-ZZY	SOCATA MS.893E Rallye 180GT Gaillard	12704	OO-AON
			F-GACN

BALLOONS AND AIRSHIPS

Regn.	Type	C/n	Prev.Id.
PH-AAN	Cameron HAFB (Reservation 12.99)	unkn	
PH-ABH	Cameron N-120 HAFB	4088	
PH-ABP	Lindstrand LBL-77A HAFB	087	VH-SPB
			G-BVNZ
PH-ABS	Colt 90A HAFB	2383	
PH-ACK	Lindstrand LBL-260A HAFB	496	
PH-ADV	Schroeder Fire Balloons G HAFB	405	
PH-AFN	Cameron A-180 HAFB	4344	
PH-AGT	Cameron A-415 HAFB (Reservation .00)	4726	
PH-AHA	Cameron O-105 HAFB	3362	
PH-AHW	Colt 90A HAFB	1494	
PH-AIM	Schroeder Fire Balloons G HAFB	102	
PH-AIR	Thunder AX7-65 Bolt HAFB	236	
PH-AIX	Thunder AX10-180 SII HAFB	3909	
PH-AMS	Lindstrand LBL-105A HAFB	328	
PH-AMV	Colt 69A HAFB	1332	G-BPGI
PH-ANS	Thunder AX6-56 Bolt HAFB	205	
PH-ARN	Cameron N-133 HAFB	3458	
PH-ASK(2)	UltraMagic M-130 HAFB	130/22	
PH-ATH	Lindstrand LBL-69A HAFB	351	
PH-ATZ	Cameron N-105 HAFB	2992	
PH-AUS	Cameron N-90 HAFB	1029	
PH-AUW	Cameron Peacock-90 SS HAFB	3054	
PH-AVC	Thunder AX8-105 HAFB	331	
PH-AXO(4)	Cameron N-133 HAFB	4112	
PH-AYF(4)	UltraMagic M-145 HAFB	145/02	
PH-BAL	Cameron Bunch-100 HAFB	2898	
PH-BAM	Schroeder Fire Balloons G HAFB	129	
PH-BAU	Colt 90A HAFB	1191	
PH-BAV	Colt Beer Glass SS HAFB	2007	
PH-BBG	Cameron O-77 HAFB	1304	
PH-BBW	Cameron N-105 HAFB	3612	
PH-BCJ	Raven Europe RX-8 HAFB	E-209	
PH-BED	Cameron V-56 HAFB	1494	
PH-BEL	Colt 77A HAFB	1502	
PH-BEN	Cameron O-56 HAFB	15	
PH-BEO	Colt 90A HAFB	2038	
PH-BHK	Cameron N-105 HAFB	2691	
PH-BIO	Cameron A-180 HAFB	3274	
PH-BJA	Lindstrand LBL-180A HAFB	579	
PH-BKB	Colt 21A Cloudhopper HAFB	1251	(PH-HAS)
			G-TPII
PH-BKN	Colt 90A HAFB	613	
PH-BOE	Thunder AX7-77SI HAFB	1969	
PH-BOL	Cameron N-120 HAFB	3219	
PH-BPN	Colt 77A HAFB	1503	
PH-BSB	Cameron O-84 HAFB	1233	
PH-BSY	Cameron N-105 HAFB	3001	
PH-BTW	Schroeder Fire Balloons G HAFB	113	
PH-CAP	Cameron N-133 HAFB	4018	
PH-CBP	Cameron N-120 HAFB	2911	
PH-CCC	Colt 90A HAFB	982	
PH-CDJ	Cameron N-133 HAFB	3596	
PH-CIR	Cameron N-65 HAFB	2135	
PH-CLC	Cameron A-140 HAFB	4322	
PH-CMB	Cameron A-120 HAFB	4017	
PH-CML	Colt 120A HAFB	2277	
PH-CMP	Thunder AX8-105 SII HAFB	2298	G-BURA
PH-CMV	Cameron N-90 HAFB	2488	
PH-CRT	Lindstrand LBL-120A HAFB	442	
PH-CZG	Cameron N-133 HAFB	3843	
PH-DBV	Thunder AX9-120 SII HAFB	2209	
PH-DCX	Cameron N-133 HAFB	4649	(PH-IDC)
PH-DDM	Cameron N-90 Nail SS HAFB	2233	
PH-DHM	Cameron N-133 HAFB	3892	

Regn.	Type	C/n	Prev.Id.
PH-DHT	Sky 120-24 HAFB	155	
PH-DIJ	Cameron A-105 HAFM	1665	D-OEDA
			D-OFAT(1)
			D-Hellenstein I
PH-DJO	Thunder AX6-56Z HAFB	398	
PH-DLY	Cameron N-120 HAFB	4603	
PH-DOL	Schroeder Fire Balloons G HAFB	238	(PH-GEK/FUN)
			(PH-MOP)
			D-ORMB
PH-DOS	Thunder AX7-77Z HAFB	449	
PH-DPV	Raven Europe S-71A HAFB	E-213	
PH-DRP	Lindstrand LBL-150A HAFB	580	
PH-DTZ	Cameron A-210 HAFB	2993	
PH-DUE	Cameron N-120 HAFB	2769	
PH-DVA	Lindstrand LBL-105A HAFB	343	
PH-DVB	Cameron A-140 HAFB	4354	
PH-DVM	Colt 120A HAFB	2296	
PH-DWB	Cameron A-105 HAFB	2134	
PH-EAR	Cameron C-80 HAFB	3600	
PH-ECU	Colt 120A HAFB	2055	
PH-EEP	Colt 140A HAFB	2576	
PH-EGO	Cameron A-140 HAFB	4325	
PH-EGW	Cameron A-105 HAFB	3198	
PH-EJM	Cameron O-105 HAFB	3723	
PH-EKM	Cameron A-105 HAFB	4687	
PH-ELD	Schroeder Fire Balloons G HAFB	358	(PH-LDE)
PH-ELS	Cameron V-77 HAFB	3085	
	(New envelope, formerly c/n 538 and officially still regd as such)		
PH-EMR	Cameron A-105 HAFB (Reservation .00)	4784	
PH-ENS	Colt 105A HAFB	1435	
PH-EPI	Cameron A-210 HAFB	3787	
PH-ERS	Cameron O-105 HAFB	2971	
PH-EUR	Schroeder Fire Balloons G HAFB	168	
PH-EVE	Cameron N-120SV HAFB	3903	
PH-EVH	Cameron N-90 HAFB	1385	
PH-EVN	Colt 17A Cloudhopper HAFB	516	
PH-FRJ	Schroeder Fire Balloons G HAFB	396	
PH-FVL	Cameron N-180 HAFB	1350	
PH-FYN	Cameron N-120 HAFB	3721	
PH-GBB	Cameron N-105 HAFB	2133	
PH-GBF	Cameron Grolsch 105SS HAFB	3977	
PH-GBN	Cameron N-133 HAFB	2988	
PH-GET	Cameron A-210 HAFB	3181	G-TRAV
PH-GHB	Cameron N-120 HAFB	2987	
PH-GHJ	Cameron O-105 HAFB	3777	
PH-GJA	Lindstrand LBL-25A HAFB	342	
PH-GOK	Lindstrand LBL-120A HAFB	164	
PH-GPA	Thunder AX9-120 SII HAFB	2521	
PH-GPJ	Lindstrand LBL-240A HAFB	324	G-BXMK
PH-GPM	Lindstrand LBL-150A HAFB	563	
PH-GPR	Cameron N-133 HAFB	3698	
PH-GPU	Cameron N-90 HAFB	3934	
PH-GRF	Lindstrand LBL-105A HAFB	639	
PH-GST	Cameron N-120 HAFB	2550	
PH-GVM	Colt 120A HAFB	2046	
PH-GWJ	Colt 105A HAFB	2210	G-NIMO
PH-GWK	Cameron N-105 HAFB	3652	
PH-HAR	Colt 56B HAFB	2573	
PH-HAS	Colt 77 HAFB	1250	(PH-BKB)
			G-TRIV
PH-HBC	Augsburg K630/1-RI Gas Balloon	9886	(PH-BAL)
PH-HBE	Cameron A-250 HAFB	4010	
PH-HCB	Colt 120A HAFB	2531	
PH-HCV	Lindstrand LBL-120A HAFB	507	
PH-HDB	Cameron N-105 HAFB	4610	
PH-HGA	Cameron A-105 HAFB	3275	
PH-HHI	Cameron Inverted Balloon SS-78 HAFB	4454	
PH-HII	Cameron HAFB (Reservation)	unkn	
PH-HIO	Cameron N-133 HAFB	4456	
	(New envelope 1998, formerly c/n 3484)		
PH-HIP	Lindstrand LBL-180A HAFB	345	
PH-HIT	Sky-120-24 HAFB	090	(PH-VOT)
PH-HKC	Schroeder Fire Balloons G HAFB	134	D-OCOE
			D-Fuchs
PH-HKJ	Thunder AX7-77 HAFB	951	

Regn.	Type	C/n	Prev.Id.
PH-HOH	Colt 105A HAFB	760	(PH-HHV)
PH-HOO	Cameron HAFB (Reservation)	unkn	
PH-HOR	Thunder AX6-56Z HAFB	444	G-BKGP
PH-HOS	Cameron Nissan Micra SS HAFB	2883	
PH-HOV	Thunder AX7-77 SI HAFB	1768	
PH-HPC	Colt 69A HAFB	2567	
PH-HSL	Cameron V-77 HAFB	2495	
PH-HTD	Cameron A-140 HAFB	3190	
PH-HUL	Cameron O-77 HAFB	1664	
PH-HUR	Thunder AX10-180A SIII HAFB	2058	F-GHUR
PH-HYM	Cameron N-105 HAFB	4341	
PH-HYP	Thunder AX7-77 HAFB	405	
PH-IAB	Cameron N-180 HAFB	3981	
PH-IAC	Cameron N-145 HAFB	3979	
PH-IAD	Cameron N-210 HAFB	4059	
PH-IAE	Cameron C-80 HAFB	4032	
PH-ICR	Colt 120A HAFB	2309	
PH-IDR	Cameron HAFB (Reservation)	unkn	
PH-IHI	Cameron N-133 HAFB	4233	
PH-IHO	Cameron N-133 HAFB	4080	
PH-IJF	Monica Calafiore Hassa u Wolf MW77 HAFB	01	D-OGGI
PH-IMN	UltraMagic M-130 HAFB	130/13	
PH-INK	Cameron N-77 HAFB	399	G-PINK
PH-INT	Cameron N-77 HAFB	1386	
PH-IOI	Cameron HAFB (Reservation 6.99)	unkn	
PH-IRE	Cameron O-120 HAFB	4336	
PH-ISU	Colt 90A HAFB	932	
PH-ITR	Lindstrand LBL-150A HAFB	497	
PH-ITT	Thunder AX7-77 SI HAFB	1077	
PH-IVO	Schroeder Fire Balloons G HAFB	73	
PH-JAB	Cameron N-133 HAFB	4079	
PH-JAG	Raven Europe S-60A HAFB	E-130	
PH-JBL	Cameron N-120 HAFB	2256	
PH-JEF	Cameron N-56 HAFB	397	D-Bruijn II
			SE-ZYH
PH-JEL	Cameron N-77 HAFB	2199	
PH-JEM	Raven S-49A HAFB	3064	
PH-JEW	Cameron Film Can-90 SS HAFB	2986	
PH-JGG	Cameron N-105 HAFB	1949	
PH-JHW	Lindstrand LBL-180A HAFB	578	
PH-JJH	Cameron N-133 HAFB	4548	
PH-JKJ	Cameron O-105 HAFB	4397	
PH-JLW	Cameron N-105 HAFB	2252	(PH-ABB)
PH-JNJ	Lindstrand LBL-180A HAFB	128	G-BVPG
PH-JOU	Colt 77A HAFB	1089	
PH-JOY	Thunder AX7-77 HAFB	922	
PH-JPH	Raven Europe RX-8 HAFB	E-401	
PH-JRZ	Lindstrand LBL-105B HAFB	341	
PH-JSH	Cameron N-105 HAFB	4383	
PH-JUT	Cameron N-120 HAFB	2398	
PH-JVJ	Cameron A-105 HAFB	3396	
PH-JVK	Colt 120A HAFB	1618	D-OBPZ
			HB-BPZ
PH-JVR	Cameron N-120 HAFB	2989	
PH-JWM	Thunder AX8-105 SII HAFB	4179	
PH-KBE	Cameron N-105 HAFB	4066	
PH-KEI	Thunder AX8-90 HAFB	2500	
PH-KIM	Schroeder Fire Balloons G HAFB	60	
PH-KIP	Cameron Chicken-105 SS HAFB	2796	
PH-KIT	Colt 90A HAFB	2283	
PH-KKK	Cameron N-56 HAFB	1268	
PH-KMK	Cameron A-375 HAFB	3481	
PH-KNP	Thunder AX8-90 SII HAFB	1234	
PH-KNY	Lindstrand LBL-150A HAFB	479	
PH-KRE	Colt 120A HAFB	3746	G-BWJS
PH-KRH	Cameron A-180 HAFB	4388	
PH-KTS	Wörner NL-1000/STU Gas Balloon	1046	
PH-KUS	Schroeder Fire Balloons G HAFB	723	
PH-KWB	Cameron A-140 HAFB	3687	
PH-KWC	Lindstrand LBL-150A HAFB	625	
PH-LAK	Lindstrand LBL-150A HAFB	611	
PH-LBL	Lindstrand LBL-69A HAFB	315	G-BWMT
PH-LED	Schroeder AX9-205G HAFB	358	
PH-LEK	Colt 120A HAFB	1817	
PH-LEP	Cameron A-210 HAFB	1272	

Regn.	Type	C/n	Prev.Id.
PH-LEV	Colt Football SS HAFB	2174	(PH-BAL)
			G-OALS
PH-LFF	Lindstrand LBL-180A HAFB	319	
PH-LIV	Lindstrand LBL-150A HAFB	607	
PH-LJP	Colt 105A HAFB	1866	(PH-BDH)
PH-LOL	Colt 105A HAFB	846	
PH-LON	Cameron Andrélon Bottle SS HAFB	4213	
PH-LOR	Cameron A-300 HAFB	3862	
PH-LOU	Colt 120A HAFB	2015	
PH-LOX	Colt 105A HAFB	2341	
PH-LTI	Cameron Liptonice Can 120 SSHAFB	4534	
PH-LUV	Cameron Heart 120 SS HAFB	4639	
PH-MAJ	Colt Flying Windmill SS HAFB	1625	
PH-MDR	Cameron N-105 HAFB	2868	
PH-MEB	Cameron N-77 HAFB	865	
PH-MGZ	Lindstrand LBL-105A HAFB	591	
PH-MJV	Lindstrand LBL-120A HAFB	435	
PH-MKV	Cameron D-96 Hot Air Airship	1445	
PH-MMF	Schroeder Fire Balloons G HAFB	514	
PH-MMG	Schroeder Fire Balloons GHAFB	780	
PH-MMH	Schroeder Fire Balloons GHAFB (Res.12.99)	unkn	
PH-MMJ	Schroeder Fire Balloons G HAFB	236	(PH-MYB/
			-RHG/ -WKK)
PH-MOI	Cameron Concept C-80 HAFB	4469	
PH-MOS	Lindstrand LBL-105A HAFB	075	
PH-MPB	Sky 120-24 HAFB	139	
PH-MSH	Cameron O-77 HAFB	853	
PH-MTD	Cameron N-133 HAFB	3837	
PH-NKN	Cameron V-77 HAFB	672	
PH-NLM	Cameron A-160 HAFB	4652	
PH-NOB	Cameron A-120 HAFB	2770	
PH-NON	Cameron O-105 HAFB	3435	
PH-NYM	Cameron N-133 HAFB	3581	
PH-NYN	Colt 77A HAFB	4674	
PH-OAG	Cameron A-105 HAFB	3624	
PH-OBB	Thunder AX8-105 S-II HAFB	1423	
PH-OCE	Cameron A-105 HAFB	2862	G-BVIY
			PH-OCE
PH-OEK	Cameron N-100 HAFB	4339	
PH-OET(2)	Colt 120A HAFB	1321	(PH-OEN)
PH-OHE	Cameron A-210 HAFB	4425	
PH-OHI	Cameron Inverted 78 SS HAFB	4078	
PH-OHO	Cameron DP-70 Hot Air Airship	1683	
PH-OIH	Cameron Inverted 78 SS HAFB	4455	
	(New envelope 1999, originally c/n 3485)		
PH-OIL	Cameron N-105 HAFB	3177	
PH-OIN	Cameron N-100 HAFB	4261	
PH-OJE	Schroeder Fire Balloons G HAFB	366	
PH-OJO	Cameron C-80 HAFB	3921	
PH-OME	Colt 77A HAFB	1354	
PH-OOK	Thunder AX7-77Z HAFB	463	
PH-OOR	Cameron N-105 HAFB	2972	
PH-OOT	Cameron N-105 HAFB	1965	
PH-OVU	Cameron N-145 HAFB	2159	
PH-OWA	Lindstrand LBL-180A HAFB	569	
PH-PAK	Cameron A-140 HAFB	1116	
PH-PAM	Cameron N-133 HAFB	4291	
PH-PBN	Cameron A-180 HAFB	4234	
PH-PCI	Cameron N-120 HAFB	3606	
PH-PER	Schroeder Fire Balloons G HAFB	144	
PH-PIN	Colt 120A HAFB	2326	
PH-PJH	Raven Europe FS-83A HAFB	E-198B	HB-BRR
PH-PKB	Cameron A-140 HAFB (Reservation 1.00)	4775	
PH-PMS	Cameron N-105 HAFB	3168	
PH-PNR	Cameron N-133 HAFB	3732	
PH-POM	Colt 90A HAFB	1932	
PH-PPM	Cameron N-120 HAFB	4636	
PH-PPN	Colt 105A HAFB	1203	
PH-PRT	Cameron N-133 HAFB	3978	
PH-PRX	Cameron A-105 HAFB	4321	
PH-PUC	Cameron N-133 Face SS HAFB	4602	
PH-PUK	Colt 31A HAFB	1254	
PH-PVB	Cameron O-120 HAFB	3314	
PH-PVL	Thunder AX7-77 SI HAFB	892	
PH-PVO	Cameron N-120 HAFB	3883	

Regn.	Type	C/n	Prev.Id.
PH-PZG	Cameron N-90 HAFB	1347	
PH-RAD	Rigid Airship Design RA-180 Holland Navigator (Reservation)	unkn	
PH-RAF	Colt 90A HAFB	2554	
PH-RBN	Cameron N-105 HAFB	1950	
PH-RDA	Cameron V-77 HAFB	2358	
PH-RDD	Cameron A-300 HAFB	3710	D-ORED(1)
PH-RDE	Colt 77A HAFB	1076	G-BNNM
PH-RDF	Cameron N-120 HAFB	3567	
PH-RDR	Cameron N-105 HAFB	4060	
PH-REE	Cameron N-133 HAFB	4353	
PH-RET	Cameron A-120 HAFB	2249	D-OKIS G-BSAP
PH-RFA	Cameron A-105 HAFB	3382	
PH-RGM	Cameron A-210 HAFB	3150	
PH-RHV	Cameron A-180 HAFB	3155	G-BVHJ
PH-RIK	Thunder AX8-90 HAFB	2502	
PH-RJP	Cameron V-77 HAFB	2352	
PH-RNW	Cameron V-90 HAFB	2909	
PH-ROC	Cameron Frog 90 SS HAFB	4101	
PH-ROK	Cameron A-120 HAFB	4113	
PH-ROM	Cameron A-140 HAFB	3645	
PH-ROY	Cameron A-180 HAFB	3980	
PH-ROZ	Thunder AX7-77 HAFB	2509	
PH-RTV	Schroeder Fire Balloons G HAFB	591	
PH-RUN	Sky 160-24 HAFB	119	
PH-RUT	Lindstrand LBL-150A HAFB	344	
PH-RWB	Cameron N-90 HAFB	920	
PH-RWW	Cameron O-105 HAFB	1447	
PH-RYM	Cameron A-140 HAFB	3705	
PH-RYO	Cameron A-140 HAFB	2942	
PH-SGN	Cameron O-105 HAFB	3273	
PH-SIB	Cameron N-105 HAFB	2939	
PH-SIM	Thunder AX7-77Z HAFB	884	
PH-SMF	Schroeder Fire Balloons G HAFB	452	(PH-SUS)
PH-SMG	Cameron O-140 HAFB (Reservation 11.99)	4648	
PH-SML	Schroeder Fire Balloons G HAFB	310	D-OSUS
PH-SNS	Cameron O-105 HAFB	2635	
PH-SOD	Thunder AX7-77Z HAFB	1112	
PH-STO	Cameron V-77 HAFB	3029	
PH-SUP	Lindstrand Stove SS HAFB	302	
PH-SUS	Schroeder Fire Balloons G HAFB	476	
PH-SVW	Cameron N-120 HAFB	3039	
PH-SYP	Cameron N-120 HAFB	2431	
PH-TIB	Colt 105A HAFB	2223	
PH-TIJ	Cameron N-105 HAFB	3206	
PH-TJB	Cameron N-133 HAFB	3771	
PH-TLB	Raven Europe S-60A HAFB	E-323	
PH-TNC	Colt 120A HAFB	1523	
PH-TPG	Cameron HAFB (Reservation)	unkn	
PH-TUT	Lindstrand LBL-150A HAFB	040	
PH-TYR	Cameron N-77 HAFB	2267	
PH-UHC	Cameron N-105 HAFB	1980	
PH-UNI	Colt 90A HAFB	1375	
PH-UNX	Cameron Unox Hat 110SS HAFB	4323	(PH-NOX)
PH-UTS	Schroeder Fire Balloons G HAFB	413	
PH-UVI	Colt 210A HAFB	2375	G-BUVI
PH-UVO	Cameron Spaceship 110 SS HAFB	4041	G-BWZO
PH-VBH	Lindstrand LBL-240A HAFB	525	
PH-VBO	Cameron O-105 HAFB	4310	
PH-VBV	Cameron V-90 HAFB	3028	
PH-VBW	Cameron A-140 HAFB	4396	
PH-VCB	Cameron A-105 HAFB	2968	
PH-VDB	Schroeder Fire Balloons G HAFB	72	
PH-VEN	Cameron A-105SV HAFB	3639	
PH-VGO	Cameron A-140 HAFB	4525	
PH-VHG	Cameron Z-105 HAFB (Reservation 11.99)	4752	
PH-VNU	Cameron A-105 HAFB	1889	
PH-VRD	Cameron N-105 HAFB	2005	
PH-VTF	Cameron N-105 HAFB	4314	
PH-VUT	Thunder AX10-180 SI HAFB	3646	G-BWUY
PH-VYF	Cameron C-100 HAFB	4357	
PH-VZS	Colt 105A HAFB	1888	
PH-WAD	Cameron N-105 HAFB	1663	
PH-WAV	Cameron N-120 HAFB	2967	

Regn.	Type	C/n	Prev.Id.
PH-WBA	Cameron A-250 HAFB	2932	
PH-WBB	Cameron N-105 HAFB	2004	
PH-WBC	Cameron N-120 HAFB	2783	
PH-WBD	UltraMagic F15 Box SS HAFB	15/01	EC-028
PH-WBE	Cameron N-105 HAFB	2035	
PH-WBF	Cameron N-120 HAFB	3820	
PH-WBG	Cameron A-300 HAFB	3437	
PH-WBH	Cameron O-160 HAFB	2583	
PH-WBK	Cameron N-105 HAFB	3218	
PH-WBM	UltraMagic N-250 HAFB	250/08	
PH-WBN	Cameron N-120 HAFB	4604	
PH-WBS	Cameron A-180 HAFB	2400	G-BSXF
PH-WBT	UltraMagic M-130 HAFB	130/11	
PH-WBV	Cameron N-105 HAFB	2045	
PH-WEO	Cameron O-77 HAFB	3093	
PH-WFG	Cameron N-90 HAFB	2389	D-ORIT D-Westfalen
PH-WGN	Cameron N-105 HAFB	4492	
PH-WIE	Cameron C-80 HAFB	3265	
PH-WIN	Cameron N-77 HAFB	2885	
PH-WJB	UltraMagic M-105 HAFB	105/29	
PH-WLC	Cameron A-120 HAFB	3722	
PH-WLD	Cameron A-105 HAFB (Reservation 1.00)	4776	
PH-WPS	Colt 77A HAFB	2045	
PH-WPV	Colt 77A HAFB	2273	
PH-WRS	Cameron N-90 HAFB	4394	
PH-WSE	Cameron V-77 HAFB	1359	
PH-WVM	Colt 105A HAFB	1516	
PH-WWT	Cameron N-133 HAFB	3623	
PH-XXL	Cameron O-105 HAFB	2187	
PH-YTS	Raven Europe S-55A HAFB	E-124	
PH-YYY	Cameron N-105 HAFB	2838	
PH-YZR	Lindstrand LBL-310A HAFB	570	
PH-ZES	Cameron N-133 HAFB	4402	
PH-ZOT	Sky 140-24 HAFB	154	
PH-ZOZ	Thunder AX7-77Z HAFB	794	
PH-. . .	Thunder AX10-180 HAFB	3646	G-BWUY

GLIDERS AND MOTOR-GLIDERS

Regn.	Type	C/n	Prev.Id.
PH-102	Grunau Baby IIA	8	OO-ZUN PH-102
PH-103	Kranich II	49	D-9019
PH-104	Schleicher Rhönlerche II	706	(PH-1003) D-5433
PH-105	Schleicher Ka.2B Rhönschwalbe	44	BGA2909/ESF I-BGMR HB-570 D-5350
PH-106	Breguet 904S Nymphale	13	F-CCFX
PH-107	Scheibe Bergfalke IV/55	363	D-7102
PH-108	Schleicher K7 Rhönadler	7048	D-1923
PH-109	Bölkow Phoebus A-1	703	D-1180
PH-118	Schneider ESG	6006	
PH-167	Grunau Baby IIb	6049	BGA3972/HJB PH-167
PH-176	DFS Meise Olympia	6058	OO-ZJB PH-176
PH-192	Slingsby T-30A Prefect	735	
PH-194	Slingsby T-30A Prefect	737	
PH-196	Slingsby T-30A Prefect	739	
PH-198	Slingsby T-30A Prefect	741	
PH-206	Wolf Hirth Govier 4 III	416	
PH-207	Wolf Hirth Govier 4 III	417	
PH-210	Wolf Hirth Govier 4 III	420	
PH-212	Schleicher Grunau Baby IIb	91	
PH-213	Schleicher Grunau Baby IIb	92	
PH-214	Schleicher Grunau Baby IIb	93	
PH-226	Slingsby T-41 Skylark II	1004	
PH-236	Schleicher Rhönlerche II	154	
PH-239	Schleicher Rhönlerche II	157	

Regn.	Type	C/n	Prev.Id.
PH-240	Schleicher Rhönlerche II	158	
PH-241	Schleicher Rhönlerche II	159	
PH-246	Schleicher Rhönlerche II	164	
PH-247	Schleicher Rhönlerche II	165	
PH-260	Schleicher Ka.6CR Rhönsegler	663	
PH-261	Schleicher Ka.6CR Rhönsegler	664	
PH-262-MD	Schleicher Ka.6CR Rhönsegler	661	
PH-264	Schleicher K.7 Rhönadler	868	
PH-268	Schleicher K.7 Rhönadler	870	
PH-270	Schleicher K.7 Rhönadler	1078	
PH-271	Schleicher K.7 Rhönadler	1079	
PH-272	Schleicher K.7 Rhönadler	1080	
PH-273	Schleicher K.7 Rhönadler	1081	
PH-274-ZM	Schleicher K.7 Rhönadler	1082	
PH-275	Schleicher K.7 Rhönadler	1083	
PH-276-54	Schleicher K.7 Rhönadler	7006	
PH-278-VP	Schleicher K.7 Rhönadler	7008	
PH-279	Schleicher Rhönlerche II	1023	
PH-283	Schleicher K.7 Rhönadler	7055	
PH-284	Schleicher K.7 Rhönadler	7058	
PH-285	Schleicher K.8B	8073	
PH-286	Schleicher K.8B	8078	
PH-287	Schleicher K.8B	8076	
PH-288-49	Schleicher K.8B	8074	
PH-291	Schleicher K.8B	8118	
PH-294	Schleicher K.8B	8121	
PH-295	Schleicher K.8B	8122	
PH-300	Schleicher K.8B	8127	
PH-303	Schleicher K.8B	8128	
PH-311	Schleicher K.8B	8143	
PH-312-A2	Schleicher K.8B	8264	
PH-314-AD	Schleicher K.7 Rhönadler	7094	
PH-315	Schleicher K.7 Rhönadler	7095	
PH-316-50	Schleicher Ka.6CR Rhönsegler	6214	
PH-318-HI	Schleicher Ka.6CR Rhönsegler	6216	
PH-321-V3	Schleicher Ka.6CR Rhönsegler	6332	
PH-322-6	Schleicher Ka.6CR Rhönsegler	6333	
PH-324-89	Schleicher Ka.6CR Rhönsegler	6334	
PH-326	Schleicher K.8B	8208	
PH-327-RH	Schleicher Ka.6CR Rhönsegler	6223	D-5093
PH-328	Schleicher K.8B	8406	
PH-333	Schleicher K.8B	8404	
PH-334-91	Schleicher K.8B	8405	
PH-335-63	Schleicher Ka.6CR Rhönsegler	6335	
PH-337-F0	Schleicher Ka.6CR Rhönsegler	6337	
PH-338-T1	Schleicher Ka.6CR Rhönsegler	6342	
PH-339-VM	Schleicher Ka.6CR Rhönsegler	6354	
PH-340-5	Schleicher Ka.6CR Rhönsegler	6471	
PH-342-10	Schleicher Ka.6CR Rhönsegler	6473	
PH-343	Schleicher Ka.6CR Rhönsegler	6474	
PH-345	Schleicher K.8B	8533	
PH-348-17	Schleicher K.8B	8536	
PH-351	Schleicher K.7 Rhönadler	7245	
PH-353	Schleicher K.8B	8552	
PH-354	Brockmeier/Schleicher Rhönlerche II	3061/Br	
PH-355	Brockmeier/Schleicher Rhönlerche II	3068/Br	
PH-356	Schleicher K.8B	8553	
PH-357-4	Schleicher Ka.6CR Rhönsegler	6455	
PH-359	Schleicher K.8B	8656	
PH-360-82	Schleicher K.8B	8657	
PH-361	Schleicher K.8B	8658	
PH-362	Schleicher K.8B	8659	
PH-363	Schleicher K.8B	8660	
PH-364	Schleicher Ka.6E Rhönsegler	4171	
PH-365-SE	Schleicher Ka.6E Rhönsegler	4172	
PH-367	Schleicher ASK-13	13063	
PH-370	Schleicher K.8B	8678	
PH-371	Schleicher K.8B	8679	
PH-372-3	Schleicher K.8B	8680	
PH-374-PA	Schleicher Ka.6CR Rhönsegler	6568	
PH-375-KR	Brockmeier/Schleicher Rhönlerche II	30/8/Br	
PH-378-61	Schleicher Ka.6E Rhönsegler	4067	
PH-379-SL	Schleicher Ka.6CR Rhönsegler	6569	
PH-380-KB	Schleicher K.8B	8600/A	
PH-381-KZ	Schleicher Ka.6CR Rhönsegler	6511/A	

Regn.	Type	C/n	Prev.Id.
PH-383	Schleicher ASK-13	13136	
PH-384-C1	NV Vliegtuigbouw Sagitta 013	005	
PH-385-22	Schleicher Ka.6E Rhönsegler	4242	
PH-386-ND	Schleicher ASK-13	13137	
PH-387-L2	Pilatus B4-PC11	208	
PH-388	Schleicher K.7 Rhönadler	171/60	
PH-389	Schleicher K.8B	8767	
PH-391	Schleicher ASK-13	13065	
PH-393	Schleicher K.8B	8768	
PH-395-83	Schleicher Ka.6E Rhönsegler	4241	
PH-396-MN	Schleicher Ka.6E Rhönsegler	4251	
PH-397-NE	Schleicher Ka.6E Rhönsegler	4234	
PH-398	SZD-24 Foka 4A	W-379	
PH-399	SZD-24 Foka 4A	W-349	
PH-401	Schleicher Ka.6E Rhönsegler	4179	
PH-402	Schleicher K.8B	8946	
PH-403-HW	NV Vliegtuigbouw Sagitta 013	21	
PH-404-30	Schleicher Ka.6E Rhönsegler	4236	
PH-405	Schleicher ASK-13	13199	
PH-406	Schleicher ASK-13	13414	
PH-407-79	Glasflügel H.205 Club Libelle	143	
PH-408-JV	Schleicher K.8B	8943	
PH-409	Schleicher ASK-13	13200	
PH-411	Schleicher ASK-13	13202	
PH-412-16	Schleicher Ka.6E Rhönsegler	4315	
PH-413-VE	Schleicher K.8B	8808	
PH-414	Schleicher K.8B	8809	
PH-415	Schleicher K.8B	8810	
PH-416	Schleicher K.8B	8818	
PH-419	Schleicher ASK-13	13283	
PH-421	Schleicher K.8B	8838	
PH-423	Schleicher ASK-13	13284	
PH-425	Grob G.102 Astir CS Jeans	1154	
PH-429	Schleicher K.8B	8947	
PH-430-WP	SZD-30 Pirat	B-455	
PH-431	Schleicher ASK-13	13529	(PH-511)
PH-434-FE	Schleicher Ka.6E Rhönsegler	4387	
PH-435	Schleicher K.8B	8888	OO-ZNJ PH-435
PH-436	Schleicher ASK-13	13378	
PH-439-A7	Glasflügel H.206 Hornet	62	(PH-511) (PH-439)
PH-440-15	Glasflügel H.201B Standard Libelle	335	D-1089
PH-441-A3	Glasflügel H.206 Hornet	54	
PH-442-HC	Schempp-Hirth CS.II Standard Cirrus	190	
PH-443	SZD-36A Cobra 15	W-568	
PH-444	Schleicher K.8B	8894	
PH-446	Schleicher ASK-13	13379	
PH-447	SZD-30 Pirat	B-466	
PH-448-92	Pilatus B4-PC11	025	
PH-449	Schleicher ASK-13	13413	
PH-450	SZD-36A Cobra 15	W-567	
PH-453	Schleicher ASK-13	13530	
PH-454-L4	Schleicher ASK-13	13442	
PH-455	Schleicher K.8B	8948	
PH-457	Schleicher ASK-13	13439	
PH-458-51	Schempp-Hirth CS.II Standard Cirrus	282	
PH-461	Siebert SIE-3	3014	D-0390
PH-462	Schleicher ASK-13	13441	
PH-463	Schleicher ASK-13	13440	
PH-465-E1	Grob/Schempp-Hirth CS.II Standard Cirrus	156G	D-1100
PH-466-E2	Schleicher ASK-13	13460	
PH-468-31	Glasflügel H.201B Standard Libelle	522	
PH-470-96	Glasflügel H.201B Standard Libelle	524	
PH-472-94	Schempp-Hirth CS.II Standard Cirrus	506	
PH-473	Schempp-Hirth CS.II Standard Cirrus	524	
PH-474-43	Schleicher K.8B	8942	
PH-480-80	Schempp-Hirth CS.II Standard Cirrus	391	
PH-481-33	Glasflügel H.201B Standard Libelle	502	
PH-482-34	Glasflügel H.201B Standard Libelle	504	
PH-483-VT	Glasflügel H.201B Standard Libelle	526	
PH-484-H1	Glasflügel H.201B Standard Libelle	527	
PH-485-00	Glasflügel H.201B Standard Libelle	366	
PH-486-57	Schempp-Hirth CS.II Standard Cirrus	392	
PH-488-23	Pilatus B4-PC11	101	

Regn.	Type	C/n	Prev.Id.		Regn.	Type	C/n	Prev.Id.
PH-489	Pilatus B4-PC11	102			PH-612-JP	Eiri PIK-20D	20613	
PH-490	Pilatus B4-PC11AF	124			PH-613-MC	Rolladen-Schneider LS-3A	3178	
PH-492-55	Schleicher ASK-13	13467			PH-615-BY	Rolladen-Schneider LS-3	3085	(PH-605)
PH-493-66	Glasflügel H.201B Standard Libelle	503						D-2823
PH-494-S2	Schempp-Hirth CS.II Standard Cirrus	199	D-0883		PH-616-44	Schempp-Hirth Janus B	68	
PH-495-88	Schempp-Hirth CS.II Standard Cirrus	394			PH-618-E3	Grob G.102 Astir CS 77	1728	
PH-497	Schleicher ASK-13	13474			PH-619-56	Grob G.102 Astir CS Jeans	2138	
PH-498-36	Siebert SIE 3	3025			PH-620	Eiri PIK-20D	20625	
PH-499-13	Schempp-Hirth CS.II Standard Cirrus	430			PH-621-V4	Eiri PIK-20D	20626	
PH-500-60	Schempp-Hirth CS.II Standard Cirrus	450			PH-622-BK	Eiri PIK-20D	20629	
PH-501-T5	Schempp-Hirth CS.II Standard Cirrus	458			PH-626	Sportavia-Pützer RF-5B Sperber	51072	(D-KMPH)
PH-502-WW	Grob/Schempp-Hirth CS.II Standard Cirrus	424G			PH-628-R6	Glasflügel H.303 Mosquito B	130	
PH-503-72	Glasflügel H.201B Standard Libelle	560			PH-630-LB	Eiri PIK-20E	20211	
PH-510-AG	Schleicher ASW-15B	15371			PH-631-RS	Rolladen-Schneider LS-3A	3180	D-6944
PH-512	Siebert SIE 3	3026			PH-632-PF	Grob G.102 Astir CS 77	1749	
PH-513-B2	Schleicher K.8B	8975			PH-633	Eiri PIK-20D	20636	
PH-514-TX	Pilatus B4-PC11	178			PH-636-AL	Schleicher ASW-20	20111	
PH-515	Schleicher ASW-15B	15391			PH-637-KL	Schleicher ASW-20	20122	
PH-516	Schleicher ASK-13	13499			PH-639	Grob G.102 Astir CS 77	1751	
PH-517	Schleicher K.8C	81003			PH-641	Scheibe SF-25C Falke	44122	PH-ART
PH-519-87	Schempp-Hirth CS.II Standard Cirrus	601						D-KACJ
PH-520-EE	Glaser-Dirks DG-100	18			PH-642	Eiri PIK-20D	20642	
PH-521	Schleicher ASK-13	13498			PH-643-B6	Glasflügel H.303 Mosquito B	146	
PH-522-52	Siebert SIE 3	3027			PH-646	Grob G.102 Astir CS 77	1798	
PH-523	Pilatus B4-PC11A	126			PH-647-A9	Glasflügel H.303 Mosquito B	150	
PH-526-ME	Glasflügel H.205 Club Libelle	110			PH-649-VA	Rolladen-Schneider LS-3A	3235	D-2483
PH-527-RA	Glasflügel H.205 Club Libelle	109			PH-650-HM	Rolladen-Schneider LS-3A	3234	D-3919
PH-528-68	Schleicher ASW-15B	15442			PH-652-DE	Rolladen-Schneider LS-3A	3167	D-5902
PH-529	Siebert SIE 3	3024			PH-653	Eiri PIK-20D	20656	
PH-530-12	Schleicher ASW-15B	15443			PH-654-CM	Rolladen-Schneider LS-3A	3140	D-2842
PH-531	Pilatus B4-PC11	207			PH-656-KT	Eiri PIK-20D	20658	
PH-534-EK	Glasflügel H.205 Club Libelle	133			PH-657-C7	Grob G.102 Astir CS 77	1800	
PH-536-A1	Schempp-Hirth CS.II Standard Cirrus	655			PH-660-E6	Schleicher ASK-21	21017	
PH-538-JA	Schleicher ASW-19	19089	(PH-567)		PH-661-SV	Eiri PIK-20D	20655	
PH-539-DL	Glaser-Dirks DG-100 Elan	58			PH-662	Sportavia-Pützer RF-5B Sperber	51059	(D-KKOB)
PH-543-39	Glaser-Dirks DG-100 Elan	63						EC-CUQ
PH-544-FL	Grob G.102 Astir CS	1192						D-KKOB
PH-547	Grob G.102 Astir CS	1267			PH-664	Schleicher ASK-13	1582	
PH-548	Grob G.102 Astir CS	1354			*(Rebuiltd of PH-376 with fuselage no.1582)*			
PH-549-T2	Grob G.102 Astir CS	1376			PH-666-PK	Eiri PIK-20D	20659	(PH-656)
PH-550-LS	Rolladen-Schneider LS-3	3023	(PH-600)		PH-668-PG	Rolladen-Schneider LS-3A	3310	D-4285
			D-7913		PH-669	Grob G.102 Astir CS Jeans	2198	
PH-552-AS	Grob G.102 Astir CS	1430			PH-670-W5	Eiri PIK-20D	20660	
PH-554-MK	Grob G.102 Astir CS	1442			PH-673-GP	Rolladen-Schneider LS-3A	3382	D-3188
PH-556-E5	Grob G.102 Astir CS	1386			PH-676	Scheibe SF-25E Super Falke	4352	(D-KDGQ)
PH-557-R1	Grob G .102 Astir CS	1431			PH-678	Scheibe SF-25C Falke	44291	D-KDGT
PH-558-R2	Schleicher ASK-18	18045	(PH-533)		PH-679-NR	Rolladen-Schneider LS-3A	3390	D-6941
PH-561-FB	Grob G.102 Astir CS	1451			PH-681-R7	Schleicher ASW-20	20251	
PH-563-KK	Grob G.102 Astir CS	1407			PH-682	Schleicher ASK-21	21003	
PH-564-KP	Rolladen-Schneider LS-3	3139			PH-683	Sportavia-Pützer RF-5B Sperber	51054	D-KITT
PH-565-KN	Schleicher ASW-19	19094			PH-685-VB	Rolladen-Schneider LS-3-17	3387	
PH-567-TP	Grob G.102 Astir CS	1462			PH-686	Schleicher ASK-21	21019	
PH-568-K1	Grob G.102 Astir CS	1491			PH-687	Schleicher ASK-21	21052	
PH-569-AA	Grob G.102 Astir CS 77	1613			PH-688-VL	Schleicher ASK-21	21020	
PH-577-NC	Rolladen-Schneider LS-3	3138			PH-689	Grob G.103 Twin Astir	3233 II	PH-659
PH-579-EZ	Schleicher ASW-19	19144			*(Rebuild, using fuselage of PH-659 c/n 3233)*			
PH-580-D1	Schleicher ASW-19	19129			PH-690-W9	Rolladen-Schneider LS-3-17	3388	D-3546
PH-581-HF	Grob G.102 Astir CS 77	1668			PH-691	Rolladen-Schneider LS-3A	3389	D-6940
PH-582-78	Schleicher ASW-19	19135			PH-692-ML	Schleicher ASW-20	20328	
PH-583-WB	Schleicher ASW-19	19142			PH-693-DR	Eiri PIK-20E	20271	(PH-694)
PH-585-BS	Rolladen-Schneider LS-3	3159			PH-697	Grob G.103 Twin Astir II	3577	
PH-586-MA	Rolladen-Schneider LS-3	3141			PH-698-HA	Rolladen-Schneider LS-4	4004	D6577
PH-588-BU	Schempp-Hirth HS.7 Mini-Nimbus	39	(PH-585)		PH-699-DK	Glaser-Dirks DG-200/17C	2-138/CL10	D-7267
PH-589-D2	Grob G.102 Astir CS Jeans	2056			PH-700	Schleicher ASW-19B	19336	
PH-592-BL	Grob G.102 Astir CS Jeans	2051			PH-701-ZT	Glaser-Dirks DG-100G Elan	E46-G25	
PH-594	Schempp-Hirth HS.7 Mini-Nimbus	49			PH-702-NA	Rolladen-Schneider LS-3	3320	D-2639
PH-595-HV	Schempp-Hirth Janus B	60	D-7352		PH-704-HC	Schempp-Hirth Ventus b	28	
PH-597	Schleicher ASW-20	20068	OY-XTM		PH-708-MB	Grob G.103 Twin Astir II	3646	
			PH-597		PH-710	Grob G.109	6045	D-KGRO
PH-598	Rolladen-Schneider LS-3	3231			PH-712-T4	Schleicher ASK-21	21087	
PH-605-PR	Glasflügel H.206 Hornet C	98			PH-713	Schleicher ASK-21	21075	
PH-607-38	Schempp-Hirth HS.7 Mini-Nimbus B	63	(PH-606)		PH-714-YY	Schleicher ASK-21	21093	
PH-608-HD	Grob G.102 Astir CS Jeans	2126			PH-715-KM	Rolladen-Schneider LS-4	4114	D-0245
PH-609-VC	Grob G.102 Astir CS Jeans	2131			PH-718	Grob G.103 Twin Astir II	3696	
PH-611-BR	Rolladen-Schneider LS-3A	3177			PH-721-E4	Schleicher ASK-21	21109	

Regn.	Type	C/n	Prev.Id.
PH-723-NV	Glaser-Dirks DG-400	4-33	
PH-725	Scheibe SF-25C Falke	44334	D-KOOZ
PH-726	Grob G.102 Club Astir CS	5588 CB	D-6192
PH-727-SA	Centrair 101A Pégase	101-061	
PH-728	Sportavia-Pützer RF-5B Sperber	51014	OO-PIL
			D-KCIM
PH-729	Valentin Taifun 17E	1005	D-KELZ
PH-730	Grob G.102 Club Astir IIIb	5609 CB	BGA3226/FFM
			PH-730
PH-731-WY	Centrair 101A Pégase	101-074	
PH-733-NF	Schleicher ASK-21	21185	
PH-734	DFS-49 Olympia Meise 51	16	D-5444
			OE-0455
PH-735-TH	Schleicher ASW-19B	19314	D-7615
PH-737-FF	Schleicher ASW-20CL	20741	
PH-738-VW	Centrair 101A Pégase	101-102	
PH-739-RR	Schempp-Hirth Ventus b	186	
PH-740	Rolladen-Schneider LS-4	4380	D-6924
PH-742-FJ	Glaser-Dirks DG-400	4-84	(D-KLRS)
PH-743-FT	Glaser-Dirks DG-300 Elan	3E-35	
PH-745	Grob G.109B	6299	
PH-746	Grob G.109B	6315	
PH-751-FK	Grob G.103 Twin II Acro	33941K-K-174	
PH-752-MT	Glaser-Dirks DG-300 Elan	3E-80	
PH-753	Schleicher ASK-21	21255	
PH-754-YX	Schleicher ASW-19B	19118	D-7556
PH-755-RC	Schleicher ASK-23B	23024	
PH-756-DT	Schempp-Hirth Discus b	29	
PH-757-JH	Rolladen-Schneider LS-3A	3249	D-2850
PH-758-AM	Rolladen-Schneider LS-6	6017	
PH-759-V5	Schleicher ASK-21	21261	
PH-760-CF	Schleicher ASK-23B	23032	
PH-762	Schleicher K.8B	547	D-1590
PH-764-T7	Schleicher ASK-23B	23035	
PH-765-HS	Schleicher ASK-23B	23039	
PH-766-ZE	Schleicher ASK-23B	23030	
PH-767-EA	Schleicher ASK-23B	23043	
PH-768-DG	Glaser-Dirks DG-300 Elan	3E-110	
PH-769	Schleicher ASK-23B	23041	
PH-770-E7	Schleicher ASK-23B	23042	
PH-773-C	Schempp-Hirth Ventus b	262	
PH-774-74	Schleicher ASK-23B	23048	
PH-775-75	Schleicher ASK-23B	23049	
PH-776-AH	Glaser-Dirks DG-300 Elan	3E-130	
PH-778-YD	Rolladen-Schneider LS-4	4532	D-3483
PH-779-R5	Glaser-Dirks DG-300 Elan	3E-167	
PH-781	Scheibe SFS-31 Milan	6609	OE-9041
			(D-KAGT)
PH-782-NK	Schleicher ASK-23B	23052	
PH-783-LT	Glaser-Dirks DG-300 Elan	3E-140	(PH-779)
PH-784	Glaser-Dirks DG-300 Elan	3E-160	
PH-785-WF	Rolladen-Schneider LS-6	6068	D-1505
PH-786-AV	Rolladen-Schneider LS-4	4569	D-3539
PH-790-HG	Rolladen-Schneider LS-4	4579	(PH-786)
			D-3613
PH-791	Schleicher ASK-13	13238	OH-395
			OH-KKR
PH-794	Rolladen-Schneider LS-4	4177	D-3503
PH-795-SP	Centrair 101A Pégase	101A-0260	
PH-798	Schleicher ASK-23B	23077	
PH-799	Slingsby T-21B Sedbergh	613	WB946
PH-800-LL	Schempp-Hirth Ventus c	304	
PH-801	Grunau Baby IIB	003	OE-0059
PH-802	Rolladen-Schneider LS-4	4599	D-5265
PH-803	Schleicher ASW-20L	20392	D-8833
PH-804	Centrair 101A Pégase	101A-0274	
PH-805	Scheibe L-Spatz 55	673	D-8324
PH-806-AX	Schempp-Hirth Discus b	86	D-5242
PH-807	Caudron C.800	10008/348	F-CAAK
PH-808	Grob G.103A Twin II Acro	34043-K-274	D-6405
PH-809-E8	Schleicher ASK-23B	23094	
PH-810	Schleicher ASK-23B	23093	
PH-812	Grob G.103 Twin Astir	3003	D-7476
PH-813	Schleicher ASK-23B	23095	
PH-814	Raab Doppelraab V	1	D-1177
PH-816	Valentin Taifun 17E	1098	D-KHVA(28)
PH-817	Schleicher ASK-23B	23096	
PH-818	Scheibe SF-25B Falke	4629	D-KIMO
			(D-KIMG)
			(D-KIMA)
PH-819	Grob G.103T Twin Astir Trainer	3190	F-CFBY
PH-820	Grob G.102 Astir CS	1518	D-7454
PH-821	Schleicher K7 Rhönadler	864	D-5804
PH-822	Schleicher K7 Rhönadler	7150	D-5397
PH-823	Schempp-Hirth Ventus b	70	D-3048
PH-824	Glaser-Dirks DG-300 Elan	3E-258	
PH-825	Scheibe L-Spatz 55	688	D-1690
PH-826	Scheibe SF-25B Falke	4812	D-KBAU
PH-827	Slingsby T-43 Skylark 3	1027	BGA739/AXH
PH-828	Schleicher ASW-20L	20149	D-6860
			BGA2492/DYV
PH-829	Schleicher ASK-23B	23103	
PH-830	Glaser-Dirks DG-300 Elan	3E-275	
PH-831	Glaser-Dirks DG-400	4-222	(D-KIDG)
PH-832	Grob G.103 Twin Astir	3160	BGA2399/DUV
PH-834-DG	Glaser-Dirks DG-600/18	6-15	
PH-835	Grob G.109	6035	OO-PRZ
			D-KGRO
PH-836	SZD-36A Cobra 15	W-569	D-0929
PH-837	Glaser-Dirks DG-600/18	6-19	
PH-838	Scheibe L-Spatz 55	763	D-5922
PH-839	Schleicher ASK-21	21370	
PH-840	Grob G.103 Twin Astir	3195	D-5955
PH-842	Schleicher K.7 Rhönadler	1085	D-5133
PH-843	Schleicher ASK-23B	23107	
PH-844	Schleicher ASK-21	21382	
PH-845	Schleicher ASW-15	15149	D-0797
PH-846	Schempp-Hirth Janus C	138	N19WK
PH-847	Rolladen-Schneider LS-4a	4161	D-3571
PH-848	Schempp-Hirth Gö-III Minimoa	701	N37JK
			BGA1738/CRC
PH-849	Rolladen-Schneider LS-3	3040	D-2806
PH-850-AM	Rolladen-Schneider LS-7 WL	7005	D-1257
PH-851	Schleicher Ka.6BR Rhönsegler	307	D-5484
PH-852	Schleicher ASW-19B	19226	D-2690
PH-853	Scheibe SF-25C Falke	44229	D-KDCA
PH-855	Schempp-Hirth Mini-Nimbus	30	D-4985
PH-856	Schleicher Ka.6CR Rhönsegler	6130/Si	D-1899
PH-857	Glasflügel H303 Mosquito B	186	D-2558
PH-858	Schempp-Hirth Ventus cM	44/484	
PH-859	Rolladen-Schneider LS-4A	4736	D-1361
PH-860	Schleicher ASK-23B	23112	
PH-861	Rolladen-Schneider LS-7.WL	7007	D-1264
PH-862-KO	Rolladen-Schneider LS-7	7043	D-5157
PH-864	Glaser-Dirks DG-600	6-29	
PH-865	Schleicher ASK-21	21419	
PH-867-TE	Schleicher ASK-21	21420	
PH-868	Rolladen-Schneider LS-6a	6066	D-1497
PH-869	Glaser-Dirks DG-100G Elan	E70G45	OO-ZZE
PH-870	Schleicher Ka.6CR Rhönsegler	6172	D-7041
PH-871	Rolladen-Schneider LS-3A	3379	D-5899
PH-872	Schempp-Hirth Ventus cT	140/430	
PH-874	Schleicher Ka.6BR-PE Rhönsegler	341	D-3226
PH-875	Schempp-Hirth Discus bT	13/296	
PH-876	SZD-51-1 Junior	B-1845	(PH-874)
PH-877	Schleicher ASW-15	15014	D-0341
PH-878	Rolladen-Schneider LS-4	4769	D-9031
PH-879	Rolladen-Schneider LS-3-17	3402	D-6775
PH-880	Schleicher Ka.2B Rhönschwalbe	171	D-5457
PH-881-MH	Schleicher ASK-21	21436	
PH-882	Schleicher ASK-23B	23113	
PH-884	Glaser-Dirks DG-200/17	2-132/1731	D-6544
PH-885	Slingsby T-38 Grasshopper T.Mk.1	754	WZ758
PH-887	Rolladen-Schneider LS-4A	4776	D-1597
PH-888	Rolladen-Schneider LS-4A	4771	D-9033
PH-889	Rolladen-Schneider LS-6B	6105	D-1179
PH-890	Hoffmann H-36 Dimona	3517	TF-SKI
PH-891	Schempp-Hirth Ventus cM	23/454	
PH-892	Glaser-Dirks DG-300 Elan	3E-371	
PH-893	Glaser-Dirks DG-300 Elan	3E-370	

Regn.	Type	C/n	Prev.Id.
PH-894	Schempp-Hirth Mini-Nimbus	60	D-6444
			(PH-606)
PH-895	Technoflug Piccolo	045	D-KGTA
PH-896	Hoffmann H-36 Dimona II	36235	F-WGAO
PH-897	Scheibe SF-25CFalke	4405	D-KAAN
PH-898	Glaser-Dirks DG-600	6-46	
PH-899	Schleicher Ka.2B Rhönschwalbe	242	(PH-900)
			D-8562
PH-900(2)	Schempp-Hirth Ventus cM	71/536	
PH-901	Rolladen-Schneider LS-4A	4801	D-0579
PH-902-FI	Rolladen-Schneider LS-7	7110	D-1509
PH-903	Grob G.102 Astir CS Jeans	2074	D-7587
PH-904	Grob G.103 Twin III Acro	34155	
PH-905	Rolladen-Schneider LS-4	4795	D-0564
PH-907	Schleicher ASW-20CL	20806	D-3547
PH-908	Schleicher ASK-18	18037	D-4539
PH-909	Rolladen-Schneider LS-6C	6203	
PH-910	Brditschka HB-23/2400SP	23043	OE-9329
PH-911	Slingsby T-21B Sedbergh	1207	BGA1705/CPT
			RAFGSA251
			BGA878
PH-912	Sportavia RF-5B Sperber	51078	D-KECE(2)
PH-914-BY	Rolladen-Schneider LS-6C	6210	(PH-913)
			(PH-838)
PH-915	Rolladen-Schneider LS-7 WL	7123	
PH-916	SZD-48-3 Jantar Standard 3	B-1958	
PH-919	Schleicher Ka.2B Rhönschwalbe	186	OO-ZWO
			D-5460
PH-920	SZD-51-1 Junior	B-1934	
PH-921	Eiri PIK-20D	20582	D-6694
PH-922	Schleicher Ka.6CR Rhönsegler	6558Si	D-5830
PH-923-R9	Glaser-Dirks DG-300 Elan	3E-392	
PH-924	Rolladen-Schneider LS-6C/17.5	6211	
PH-925	Schempp-Hirth Ventus bT	6/126	(BGA2981)
			D-KMTL
PH-927	Rolladen-Schneider LS-7 WL	7144	
PH-928	Rolladen-Schneider LS-4A	4827	D-3529
PH-929	Schleicher ASK-23B	23127	
PH-931	Rolladen-Schneider LS-6C/17.5	6231	
PH-932-AY	Rolladen-Schneider LS-6C/17.5	6212	D-6420
PH-933	SZD-51-1 Junior	B-1995	
PH-934	SZD-51-1 Junior	B-1994	
PH-935	Grob G.103 Twin Astir	3087	D-3948
PH-936	Rolladen-Schneider LS-4A	4843	D-3587
PH-937	Glaser-Dirks DG-400	4-200	D-KCDG
PH-938	SZD-22B Mucha Standard	521	OO-ZSR
	(Also believed used parts from OO-ZSL c/n 524)		
PH-939(2)	Glaser-Dirks DG-500 Elan Trainer	5E-46T16	D-KILE
PH-940	Slingsby T-61F Venture	1872	XZ552
PH-941	Rolladen-Schneider LS-4A	4845	D-3599
PH-942	Schempp-Hirth Discus bT	73/401	N43573
PH-944	Scheibe SF-25C Falke	44520	D-KIOJ(4)
PH-945	Sportavia-Pützer RF-5B Sperber	51038	D-KFAG
			(D-KEAU)
PH-946-XX	Rolladen-Schneider LS-6C	6247	D-2527
PH-947	Brditschka HB-21	21013	D-KIDU(2)
			HB-2046
			(PH-900)
PH-949	Bölkow Phönix T	403	OO-ZQD
			D-0738
			HB-746
			D-8354
PH-950	Scheibe Specht	N4	D-1383
PH-951	Rolladen-Schneider LS-4B	4861	
PH-952	Schleicher ASK-21	21529	
PH-953	Schleicher ASH-25E	25037	D-4904
PH-954	Grob G.103 Twin IIISL	35009	D-KOIC(2)
PH-955	Rolladen-Schneider LS-6A	6053	D-8991
PH-956	Schleicher ASW-20BL	20643	D-5342
			OE-5342
PH-957	SZD-51-1 Junior	B-2005	(PH-953)
PH-958	Schleicher K7 Rhönadler	499	D-8309
PH-959	Schempp-Hirth Ventus cT	167/545	
PH-960	Grob G.103 Twin IIISL	35016	
PH-961	Schempp-Hirth Discus CS	074CS	
PH-962	Rolladen-Schneider LS-6C	6259	D-2572
PH-963	Glasflügel H303 Mosquito B	160	D-6463
PH-964	Glaser-Dirks DG-600/18	6-102S57	D-3120
PH-965	Centrair 101A Pégase	101A-0437	
PH-966	Schleicher K7 Rhönadler	7190	D-3626
PH-967	Schleicher Ka.6E	4175/A37	D-4735
PH-968	Glaser-Dirks DG-300 Elan	3E-215	D-4594
PH-969	Schleicher ASH-25E	25087	D-KIQU
PH-970	Grob G.109	6021	OO-GRB
			F-CFOA
			D-KGRO
PH-971	Scheibe SF-24B Motorspatz I	4028	OE-9005
			(D-KECO)
PH-972	Rolladen-Schneider LS-6C	6273	
PH-973-T6	Glaser-Dirks DG-500T Elan Trainer	5E-75T31	
PH-974	Rolladen-Schneider LS-4B	4894	
PH-975	Schleicher ASK-21	21565	
PH-976	SZD-51-1 Junior	B-2015	
PH-977	Rolladen-Schneider LS-4B	4897	
PH-979	Scheibe Zugvogel IIIB	1100	D-0037
PH-980	SZD-51-1 Junior	B-2017	
PH-982-KE	Rolladen-Schneider LS-4	4529	D-3486
PH-983	Glaser-Dirks DG-500M	5E-85M36	
PH-984	Schempp-Hirth Janus C	242	BGA3333/FKY
PH-985	Scheibe SF-25B Falke	4649D	(PH-984)
			D-KDVL
			(D-KEBH)
PH-986	Schleicher ASK-13	13183	D-0274
PH-987	Rolladen-Schneider LS-4A	4612	D-0205
PH-988	Rolladen-Schneider LS-6C/18	6223	D-4199
PH-989	Rolladen-Schneider LS-4B	4919	
PH-990	Schempp-Hirth Ventus b /16.6	175	D-5326
PH-991	Schleicher ASK-21	21563	
PH-992	SZD-36A Cobra 15	W-660	OY-VXL
PH-994	Glaser-Dirks DG-400	4-16	D-KAIC(2)
PH-995	Scheibe SF-25D Falke	4640D	D-KOHH
			(D-KEDC)
PH-996	Grob G.109B	6342	F-CAQK
			F-WAQK
PH-997	Schleicher ASW-24	24019	BGA3966/HHV
			RAFGSA-R19
PH-998	Schleicher ASW-19B	19390	(PH-1001)
			(PH-998)
			D-8710
PH-999	Bölkow FS.24 Phenix T	408	D-8411
PH-1000	Schempp-Hirth Discus CS	134CS	
PH-1001	Grob G.103C Twin III Acro	34187	
PH-1002	Schleicher Ka.2B Rhönschwalbe	79/55	OO-ZQC
			PL-12
PH-1003	Glaser-Dirks DG-400	4-11	D-KLAA
PH-1004	Grob G.103 Twin Astir	3067	D-4853
PH-1005	Schleicher K7 Rhönadler	5	D-1942
PH-1006	SZD-51-1 Junior	B-2129	
PH-1007	Schleicher K7 Rhönadler	7037A	D-6029
PH-1009	Rolladen-Schneider LS-4B	4923	
PH-1010	Glaser-Dirks DG-500M	5E-105M48	
PH-1011-FR	Schempp-Hirth Discus bT	133/506	
PH-1013	Schleicher ASK-13	13366	BGA3987/HJS
PH-1014	Schempp-Hirth HS.4 Standard Cirrus	269	OO-ZVW
			D-1982
PH-1015	SZD-51-1 Junior	B-2131	
PH-1016	Rolladen-Schneider LS-4B	4927	
PH-1017	Rolladen-Schneider LS-3	3094	HB-1360
PH-1018	Schleicher ASK-21	21605	
PH-1019	Schleicher ASW-24	24206	D-7217
PH-1020	Rolladen-Schneider LS-6C	6215	D-5458
			OH-793
PH-1021	Schleicher K7 Rhönadler	648	OO-ZYI
			D-5730
PH-1022	Scheibe Bergfalke II/55	355	D-9066
PH-1023	SZD-51-1 Junior	B-2134	
PH-1024	SZD-50-3 Puchacz	B-2089	(SP-4147)
PH-1025	Schempp-Hirth Discus CS	165CS	
PH-1027	Rolladen-Schneider LS-4	4575	D-3604
PH-1028	Rolladen-Schneider LS-4B	4939	

Regn.	Type	C/n	Prev.Id.
PH-1029	Schempp-Hirth Discus bT	145/523	
PH-1031	Rolladen-Schneider LS-6C	6242	(PH-1013)
			BGA3813/HBN
			D-6116
PH-1032	Brditschka HB-23/2400SP Hobbyliner	23046	OE-9332
			D-KSCV
PH-1033	Glaser-Dirks DG-300 Elan	3E-38	HB-1734
PH-1034	Hoffmann H-36 Dimona	3684	D-KERI
PH-1035-MS	Schempp-Hirth Duo Discus	023	
PH-1036	Schleicher Ka.6CR Rhönsegler	1004	D-4080
PH-1037	Glaser-Dirks DG-800S	8-44S13	D-0037
PH-1038	Grob G.102 Astir CS Jeans	2193	D-3816
PH-1039	Schleicher K.7 Rhönadler	503	D-6247
PH-1040	LET L-13SEH Vivat	900401	D-KIIP
			OK-0104
			D-KPPP
			OK-0104
PH-1041	PZL PW-5 Smyk	17.02.005	
PH-1042	PZL PW-5 Smyk	17.02.003	
PH-1043	Schempp-Hirth Discus CS	186CS	
PH-1044	Schempp-Hirth Ventus cM	51/495	D-KBFL
PH-1045	Slingsby T.21B Sedbergh	1214	BGA884/BDK
PH-1046	Glaser-Dirks DG-500M	5E-141M55	(PH-1045)
PH-1047	Rolladen-Schneider LS-8A	8022	D-2285
PH-1048	Rolladen-Schneider LS-8A	8023	D-2598
PH-1049	Schleicher ASK-14	14001	D-KIKY
PH-1050	Schleicher ASW-24	24041	D-6252
PH-1051	SZD-51-1 Junior	B-2146	
PH-1052	SZD-51-1 Junior	B-2147	
PH-1053	Rolladen-Schneider LS-4B	4984	
PH-1055	Stemme S-10V	14-012	(PH-1053)
			D-KGDE(1)
PH-1056	Schleicher ASW-19B	19105	D-3859
PH-1057-DX	Schempp-Hirth Duo-Discus	47	
PH-1058	Schempp-Hirth Discus CS	061CS	D-4111
PH-1059	Schleicher Ka.6CR Rhönsegler	328	D-8951
			HB-801
PH-1060	Schleicher ASH-26E	26064	(PH-1111)
			D-KBEB(2)
PH-1061	Rolladen-Schneider LS-4A	4825	D-0048
PH-1063	PW-5 Smyk	17.03.009	
PH-1064	Grob G.102 Astir CS	1307	D-7349
PH-1065	Grob G.109B	6289	SE-UAA
PH-1066	Grob G.102 Astir CS	1439	D-7429
PH-1067	Schempp-Hirth Duo Discus	60	
PH-1068	Grob G.103 Twin Astir	3028	D-2555
PH-1069	Standard Austria SH	49	D-2696
			OE-0696
PH-1070	Schleicher K7 Rhönadler	7156	D-5492
PH-1071-XB	Schempp-Hirth Janus CM	12/177	XB-EJP
PH-1072	Glaser-Dirks DG-500 Elan Orion	5E-153X10	D-1491
PH-1073	Scheibe SF-25C Falke	44602	D-KTIW
PH-1074	Rolladen-Schneider LS-8A	8050	D-3693
PH-1075	Schempp-Hirth Ventus 2a	28	
PH-1076	Schempp-Hirth Discus CS	141CS	D-4295
PH-1077	Schempp-Hirth Ventus 2a	21	
PH-1078	Schempp-Hirth Janus C	188	D-7719
PH-1079	Rolladen-Schneider LS-4A	4426	D-4542
PH-1080	Rolladen-Schneider LS-8A	8065	
PH-1082	Glaser-Dirks DG-500/22	5E-35S7	D-5219
PH-1083	Rolladen-Schneider LS-4A	4291	D-8190
PH-1084	Schleicher ASK-13	13363	D-0857
PH-1085	Schleicher Ka.6CR Rhönsegler	1038	OO-ZFJ
			D-9151
PH-1086	Grob G.102 Astir CS Jeans	2173	D-7755
PH-1088	Rolladen-Schneider LS-3A-17	3348	OO-ZZH
			HB-1509
PH-1091	Marganski MDM-1 Fox	213	
PH-1092	Grob G.103 Twin II	3547	D-2921
PH-1093	Schempp-Hirth Discus CS	230CS	
PH-1094	Schleicher ASW-27	27032	
PH-1095	Grob G.103 Twin Astir	3056	D-4846
PH-1096	Rolladen-Schneider LS-8A	8105	
PH-1097	Schleicher ASK-21	21648	
PH-1098	Glaser-Dirks DG-400	4-29	D-KDAU
PH-1099	Schempp-Hirth Duo Discus	119	
PH-1100	Glaser-Dirks DG-800B	8-81B18	(PH-1097)
			D-KDIL
PH-1101	HOAC HK-36TS Super Dimona	36520	
PH-1102	Schleicher Ka.6E	4366	D-7337
			OH-400
			OH-REE
PH-1103	Schempp-Hirth Ventus cT	134/414	D-KCMB
PH-1105	SZD-50-3 Puchacz	B-2107	
PH-1106	Grob G.109B	6429	D-KHGJ
PH-1107	Schempp-Hirth Ventus 2cM	30/53	D-KTLL
PH-1108	Glaser-Dirks DG-505/20 Elan	5E-170W8	
PH-1109	Glaser-Dirks DG-800B	8-97B32	D-KMAF
PH-1110	Schempp-Hirth Ventus 2cM	41/73	D-KBBF
PH-1111	Schempp-Hirth Ventus 2cT	17	
PH-1112	Schempp-Hirth Janus CT	9/264	D-KEAR(3)
PH-1113	Schleicher ASW-24	24079	D-9021
PH-1114	HOAC HK-36TC Super Dimona	36527	
PH-1115	Grob G.103 Twin Astir	3006	D-7479
PH-1116	SZD-50-3 Puchacz	B-2113	
PH-1117	Rolladen-Schneider LS-3A	3295	D-4583
PH-1118	Schempp-Hirth Ventus cT	180/596	LX-CCC
PH-1119	Schempp-Hirth Duo Discus	157	
PH-1120	Schempp-Hirth Nimbus 4 DM	28/42	
PH-1121	Slingsby T.31B Cadet III	PFA/42-11827/ 712	G-BSHM
	(Converted to Motor Cadet)		BGA3289/FJC
			WT917
PH-1122	Schleicher ASK-13	13445	D-2991
PH-1123	Rolladen-Schneider LS-8A	8179	
PH-1124	Schleicher ASK-23B	23148	
PH-1125	Scheibe Bergfalke II/55 (Reservation)	342	D-8870
PH-1126	Caproni-Vizzola A.21s Calif	250	I-IVCA
PH-1127	Glaser-Dirks DG-400	4-123	D-KCEM
PH-1128	Grob G.104 Speed Astir IIB	4085	D-2593
			N166SS
			D-2593
PH-1130	Schleicher Ka.6E	4014	D-5204
PH-1131-LR	Schleicher ASW-27	27081	
PH-1132	Grob G.102 Club Astir IIIB	5513CB	D-8848
PH-1133	HOAC HK-36TC Super Dimona	36528	
PH-1134	Grob G.103C Twin III Acro	34146	D-5531
PH-1135	Hoffman HK-36R Super Dimona	36394	HB-2259
PH-1136	Rolladen-Schneider LS-6C-18	6252	D-6436
			SE-UKO
PH-1137	Schempp-Hirth Janus CM	4	D-KKDR
			(D-KJMC)
PH-1138	HOAC HK-36TTC Super Dimona	36592	
PH-1139	Siren C.30S Edelweiss	36	F-CDAQ
PH-1140	Schleicher ASW-15B	15136	D-0763
PH-1141	Schempp-Hirth Duo Discus	193	
PH-1142	Glasflügel H303 Mosquito	38	D-4452
PH-1143	Glasflügel H303B Mosquito	149	HB-1454
PH-1144	HOAC HK-36TC Super Dimona	36530	
PH-1145	Schleicher ASW-20	20495	D-6393
PH-1146	Schleicher ASW-27	27092	
PH-1147	PZL PW-5 Smyk	17.12.001	
PH-1148	Schempp-Hirth Ventus cT (Reservation)	unkn	
PH-1149	Schempp-Hirth Janus CM	11	D-KHID
PH-1150	Rolladen-Schneider LS-8-18 (Reservation)	unkn	
PH-1151	Grob G.103C Twin III Acro	34157	D-0659
PH-1152	Schempp-Hirth Ventus 2cM	62/123	
PH-1153	Schempp-Hirth Nimbus 4 DM	11/19	D-KWMA
PH-1154	Schempp-Hirth Ventus 2b	85	
PH-1155	Schleicher Ka.2B Rhönschwalbe	894/60	OO-ABC
PH-1156	Schleicher ASH-26	26146	
PH-1157	HOAC HK-36TC Super Dimona	36647	
PH-1158	HOAC HK-36TC Super Dimona	36608	
PH-1159	Grob G.102 Club Astir IIIB	5646CB	D-3625
PH-1160	Schempp-Hirth Discus 2b	23	
PH-1161	Grob G.102 Club Astir IIIB	5591CB	D-4726
			D-6306
			ZK-GNF
PH-1162	Schempp-Hirth Discus CS	090CS	D-0279
PH-1163	Slingsby T.31B Cadet TX.III	678	WT868
	(Converted to Motor Cadet) (C/n quoted as FF1383)		

Regn.	Type	C/n	Prev.Id.
PH-1164	Schempp-Hirth Ventus 2b	89	D-4207
PH-1165	Glaser-Dirks DG-300 Elan	3E-157	D-4718
PH-1166	Schempp-Hirth Ventus 2cM *(Reservation)*	unkn	
PH-1167	Schempp-Hirth Discus bT WL	67/393	D-KSKI
PH-1168	SZD-50-3 Puchacz	B-2207	
PH-1169	Glaser-Dirks DG-800B	8-163B87	
PH-1170	Schempp-Hirth SHK-1	3	BGA1592/CJZ
			D-9349
PH-1171	Schempp-Hirth Duo Discus	219	
PH-1172	Rolladen-Schneider LS-8A-18 *(Reservation 9.97)*	unkn	
PH-1173	Rolladen-Schneider LS-8A *(Reservation 2.99)*	8266	
PH-1174	Rolladen-Schneider LS-4B	4892	D-2398
PH-1175	Schempp-Hirth Ventus 2cM	74/155	
PH-1176	Glasflügel H401 Kestrel	77	D-1047
			HB-1047
PH-1177	SZD-9 bis Bocian 1E *(Reservation 5.99)*	P-463	OY-FVX
PH-1178	Schleicher ASW-27B	27110	
PH-1179	Glaser-Dirks DG.400 *(Reservation 8.99)*	4-177	I-KILF
			D-KILF
PH-1180	Schempp-Hirth Ventus 2cM *(Reservation 9.99)*	unkn	
PH-1181	Grob G.103C Twin III Acro	34103	D-6868
PH-1182	Schempp-Hirth Ventus cT *(Reservation 10.99)*	114/385	D-KHAB
PH-1183	HOACHK-36TTC Super Dimona *(Res.12.99)*	36658	
PH-1184	Schempp-Hirth Discus bT	68/395	D-KKAX
PH-1185	Scheibe Sperber *(Reservation 12.99)*	820	
PH-1186	Scheibe SF-25C Falke *(Reservation .00)*	44181	D-KDEM

MICROLIGHTS

Regn.	Type	C/n	Prev.Id.
PH-1A8	Solar Wings Typhoon Buggy	T781208	
PH-1G9	Eipper Quicksilver MXQ-II	1090	G-MMOS
			PH-1G9
			G-MMOS
PH-1J2	American Aerolights Eagle XL	E5444	
PH-1J3	Solar Wing Sunfighter I	RFD-11	
PH-1J8	Behlen Lloyd Ladas	RFD-8301	
PH-1J9	Behlen Solar Stunter	RFD-8302	
PH-1K1	Continental Aerolights Eagle XL	300357	
PH-1K8	Skyin Sherpa II	141282/1036	
PH-1L8	Firebird Tri CX	025	
PH-1L9	Firebird Tri CX	039-83	
PH-1M1	Skyin Sherpa II	8311/1049	
PH-1M4	Firebird Sierra	333	
PH-1M5	Continental Aerolights Eagle CA	831102	
PH-1M8	Comco Ikarus Fox-D	84/0010	
PH-1M9	Skyin Sherpa II	8403/1053	
PH-1N2	UltraSport Panther XL	RFD-84101	
PH-1N5	Behlen Vampir II 14.2	RFD-84102	
PH-1P1	Firebird Sierra	252	
PH-1P2	Continental Aerolights Eagle XL	84083102	
PH-1P3	Continental Aerolights Eagle XL	84083103	
PH-1P4	Behlen Vampir IIM 14.2	84020	
PH-1P5	Comco Ikarus Sherpa II	84 . .-1065	
PH-1P6	Comco Ikarus Sherpa II	8412-1086	
PH-1P8	Comco Ikarus Fox-D	8504-FD25	
PH-1R1	Ultrasport Panther XL	870117	
PH-1R3	Continental Aerolights Eagle XL	85081015	
PH-1R4	Behlen Vampir IIM 14.2	1161951	
PH-1R5	Behlen Vampir II 18M	85/030	
PH-1R7	Comco Ikarus Sherpa II	8602/1113	
PH-1S2	Comco Ikarus Sherpa II	8604/1116	
PH-1S4	Comco Ikarus Sherpa II	8601/1115	
PH-1S6	Behlen Vampir II 18M	86/166	
PH-1S7	Aériane Sirocco	129	
PH-1T1	Sky-Walker 1+1	26152	
PH-1T2	Comco Ikarus Fox-C22	8703-3061	
PH-1T4	Comco Ikarus Fox-D	8710-FD42	
PH-1T5	Comco Ikarus Fox-C22	8802-3118	
PH-1T6	Sky-Walker 1+1	038-153	
PH-1T7	NST Minimum Saphir 17M	M207/102355	
PH-1T9	UPM Funplane 1	870022	

Regn.	Type	C/n	Prev.Id.
PH-1U1	Comco Ikarus Fox-C22	8705-3070	
PH-1U2	Sky Walker II	177	
PH-1U3	Aviasud Mistral	143	
PH-1U4	UPM Funplane 1	860016	
PH-1U5	Sky Walker II	178	
PH-1U6	Sky Walker II	175	
PH-1U7	Sky Walker II	183	
PH-1U8	Sky Walker II	187	
PH-1U9	Sky Walker II	188	
PH-1V1	Fisher FP.202 Koala	NVAV-97	
PH-1V2	Comco Ikarus Fox-C22	8803-3123	
PH-1V4	Sky Walker II	204	
PH-1V5	Sky Walker II	206	
PH-1V6	UPM Omega/Lotus 18	880052	
PH-1V7	HFL Stratos 300	003	
PH-1V9	Comco Ikarus Fox-D	8811-FD45	
PH-1W1	Sky-Walker II	210	
PH-1W2	Comco Ikarus Fox-D	8901-FD46	
PH-1W3	HFL Stratos 300	008	
PH-1W4	Sky-Walker II	217	
PH-1W5	Comco Ikarus Fox-C22	8903-3192	
PH-1W7	Behlen Vampir II 14.2	89017	
PH-1X1	Behlen Vampir II 14.2	EA 89-03	
PH-1X2	Behlen Vampir II 14.2	EA 89-04	
PH-1X3	Behlen Vampir II 14.2	EA 89-05	
PH-1X5	Behlen Vampir II 14.2	EA 89-07	
PH-1X6	Sky-Walker II	239	
PH-1Y2	Comco Ikarus Fox-C22	8908-3214	
PH-1Y3	Behlen Vampir IIM 14.2	S-88	
PH-1Y5	Behlen Vampir IIM 14.2	10/071/88/06	
PH-1Y6	Air Création Racer SX-12	952911	
PH-1Y7	Comco Ikarus Fox-C22	8910-3241	
PH-1Y9	Comco Ikarus Fox-C22	8910-3255	
PH-1Z1	Aériane Sirocco	89-103	
PH-1Z2	Aériane Sirocco	89-101	
PH-1Z3	Aériane Sirocco	89-102	
PH-1Z4	UPM Omega Lotus 18	900086	
PH-1Z5	Murphy Renegade Spirit	214/PFA/188-11423	G-MVSF
PH-1Z6	Air Création Racer SX-12	240004	
PH-1Z7	Sky-Walker II	273	
PH-1Z8	Aériane Sirocco	890043	
PH-1Z9	NST Minimum Magic IV-177	NQ-I	
PH-2A1	Solar Wings Pegasus Quasar [MAT"4"]		
		SW-WQQ-0373/SW-TQ-0036	
PH-2A2	Solar Wings Pegasus Quasar [MAT"2"]		
		SW-WQQ-0376/SW-TQ-0039	
PH-2A3	Solar Wings Pegasus Quasar [MAT"3"]		
		SW-WQQ-0375/SW-TQ-0038	
PH-2A8	Solar Wings Pegasus Quasar		
		SW-WQQ-0380/SW-TQ-0041	
	(c/n officially quoted as 0034)		
PH-2B1	Aviasud Mistral	119	
PH-2B2	Aviasud Mistral	120	
PH-2B3	Comco Ikarus Fox-C22	9007-3273	
PH-2B4	Comco Ikarus Fox-C22	9007-3274	
PH-2B5	Comco Ikarus Fox-C22	9007-3275	
PH-2B6	Air Création Racer SX-12	262561	
PH-2B5	Aériane Sirocco	90061	
PH-2B8	Cosmos BI 90	521	
PH-2C1	Behlen Vampir IIM 14.2	90029	
PH-2C2	Konsuprod Moskito 1b	90008	
PH-2C3	Air Création Racer SX 12	262562	
PH-2C4	NST Minimum Magic IV-177	M409	
PH-2C5	NST Minimum Magic IV-177	LF90-01	
PH-2C6	NST Minimum Magic IV-177	LF90-02	
PH-2C7	NST Minimum Saphir 17M	LF90-03	D-MHOF
PH-2C8	Sky-Walker II	313	
PH-2C9	Sky-Walker II	315	
PH-2D1	Sky-Walker II	320	
PH-2D2	Comco Ikarus Fox C-22	9009-3286	
PH-2D7	Platzer Kiebitz B	58	D-MHRM
PH-2D8	Cosmos BI 90	576	
PH-2D9	Cosmos BI 90	577	
PH-2E2	Solar Wings Pegasus XL-Q		
		SW-WQ-0417/SW-TE-0311	

Regn.	Type	C/n	Prev.Id.
PH-2E4	NST Minimum Magic IV-177	LF91-01	
PH-2E5	Cosmos BI 90	604	
PH-2E6	Light Aero Avid Flyer	442	D-MIPS
PH-2E8	Light Aero Avid Flyer	942	
PH-2E9	Solar Wings Pegasus XL-Q	SW-WQ-0441/SW-TE-0320	
PH-2F2	Cosmos BI 90	638	
PH-2F3	Comco Ikarus Fox-C22	9108-3366	
PH-2F4	Comco Ikarus Fox-C22	9108-3367	
PH-2F5	Comco Ikarus Fox-C22	9109-3368	
PH-2F6	Aviasud Mistral	152	
PH-2F7	Aviasud Mistral	154	
PH-2F8	Cosmos BI 90	669	
PH-2G1	Comco Ikarus Fox-C22	9110-3371	
PH-2G2	Bison Profil 19M	136707	
PH-2G3	Solar Wings Pegasus Quasar II	SW-WQT-0466/SW-TQC-0072	
PH-2G4	Tandem Air Sunny	28-92	
PH-2G5	Sky-Walker II	324	
PH-2G6	Rans S-12 Airaile	0691099	
PH-2G7	NST Minimum Magic IV-177	LF39-28	
PH-2H1	Comco Ikarus Fox-C22	9207-3439	
PH-2H3	Comco Ikarus Fox-C22	9206-3435	
PH-2H6	UPM-Cobra/Raven 15	920118	
PH-2H7	Light Aero Avid Flyer	1137D	
PH-2H8	Cosmos BI 90	797	
PH-2H9	Cosmos BI 90	785	
PH-2J2	Rans S-12 Airaile	0692234	
PH-2J3	Rans S-12 Airaile	0692231	
PH-2J6	Solar Wings Pegasus XL-Q /Quasar	SW-WQT-0555/SW-TE-0412	
PH-2J7	Solar Wings Pegasus XL-Q /Quasar	SW-WQT-0559/SW-TE-0424	
PH-2J9	Solar Wings Pegasus XL-Q /Quasar	SW-WQT-0561/SW-TE-0426	
PH-2K1	Solar Wings Pegasus XL-Q /Quasar	SW-WQT-0562/SW-TE-0427	
PH-2K2	Comco Ikarus Fox-C22	9302-3490	
PH-2K3	Comco Ikarus Fox-C22	9303-3502	
PH-2K4	Cosmos BI 90	0380	
PH-2K5	Solar Wings Pegasus Quasar IITC	SW-WX-0019/SW-TQ-0061	G-65-7
	(Rotax 582/40) prototype [MAT"5"]		
PH-2K6	Comco Ikarus Fox-C22	9303-3503	
PH-2K7	Sky-Walker II	201	D-MOBO
PH-2K8	Fisher FP.202 Koala	400	
PH-2K9	Light Aero Avid Flyer	1275D	
PH-2L1	Solar Wings Pegasus XL-Q / Quasar	SW-WQT-0578/SW-TE-0435	
PH-2L5	Aviasud AE-209 Albatros	30	
PH-2L6	Aviasud AE-209 Albatros	34	
PH-2L7	Comco Ikarus Fox-C22	9306-3527	
PH-2L8	Rodaro Storch	ST11004304	
PH-2L9	Aviasud AE-209 Albatros	03	
PH-2M1	Solar Wings Pegasus Q-462	6563	
PH-2M2	Pioneer Flightstar	680	D-MAUR
PH-2M3	Aviasud Mistral	153	
PH-2M4	Aviasud AE-209 Albatros	44	
PH-2M6	Aviasud AE-209 Albatros	45	
PH-2M9	Take Off Merlin G	20793	
PH-2N2	Cosmos BI 90	959	
PH-2N3	Solar Wings Pegasus Quantum 15	6609	G-65-10
	(This c/n quoted for G-MYLE, reference also made to c/n 6669 and to SW WX 0021. The pi was allocated to a Chaser export)		
PH-2N4	UPM-Cobra/Raven 15	930125	
PH-2N7	Air Création Mild GT-582ES	N4171753	
PH-2N8	Comco Ikarus Fox-C22 (Cr. 2.5.99)	9402-3569	
PH-2N9	Comco Ikarus Fox-C22	9406-3570	
PH-2P1	Aviasud AE-209 Albatros	64	
PH-2P2	Aviasud AE-209 Albatros	66	
PH-2P3	Aviasud AE-209 Albatros	62	
PH-2P4	Aviasud AE-209 Albatros	65	
PH-2P5	Aviasud AE-209 Albatros	63	
PH-2P6	Cosmos Chronos BI 90	21034	
PH-2P7	Comco Ikarus Fox-C22	9404-3580	
PH-2P9	Comco Ikarus Fox-C22	9405-3591	
PH-2R1	Light Aero Avid Flyer IV	1428D	
PH-2R2	Aviasud AE-209 Albatros	9	(F-)WAE-09
PH-2R4	Aviasud Mistral	144	
PH-2R5	TL Ultralight TL-32 Typhoon	"M503945"	
	(C/n incorrect, possibly could be 94.05)		
PH-2R6	TL Ultralight TL-2 Eso	E494H2735	
PH-2R8	Aviasud Mistral BRD	181	D-MNOS
PH-2S2	Comco Ikarus Fox-C22	9501-3641	
PH-2S3	Fisher FP-202 Koala	0253	
PH-2S4	Aviasud Mistral BRD	084	D-MKHV
PH-2S5	CFM Shadow Series CD	K232	
PH-2S6	Aviasud Mistral BRD	179	D-MONF
PH-2S7	III Sky Arrow 450TH	19	
PH-2S9	Interplane Skyboy	NO-SBS-011/95AS	
PH-2T1	Rans S-6S Super Coyote II	0194.717	
PH-2T2	SMAN Petrel	0-55	
PH-2T4	Kolb Twinstar Mk III	M3-203	
	(Possibly sold, c/n also quoted for N279FC)		
PH-2T5	Aviasud Mistral BRD	112	D-MHUH
PH-2T6	TL UltralightTL-132 Condor	95C15	
PH-2T8	Take Off Merlin	23545	
PH-2T9	Letov LK-2M Sluka	829409X12	
PH-2U1	Ultralair Weedhopper AX-3	C3123183	
PH-2U2	Pegasus Quasar II.TC [MAT"1"]	SW-QT-7071	
PH-2U3	TL Ultralight TL-22 Duo/ESO (?)	"E95CZ3"	
	(Not a TL-22 c/n, maybe 95G23; TL-2 c/n 95T23 is SE-YRM; or may be TL-132 Condor with c/n 95C23 ?)		
PH-2U4	Funk FK-9TG	048	
PH-2U5	Toresi Mini Straton D-7	033	
PH-2U6	Microlight AK-3 Kolibri	003	
PH-2U7	Aviasud Mistral BRD	086	D-MACS
PH-2U9	Tecnam P.92 Echo	136	
PH-2V1	TL Ultralight TL-132 Condor	95C18	
PH-2V2	Fisher FP.303	3220	
PH-2V3	Interplane Griffon	1195B	
PH-2V4	TL Ultralight TL-132 Condor	96C03	
PH-2V5	Tecnam P.92 Echo	154	
PH-2V6	Tecnam P.92 Echo	153	
PH-2V7	Kolb Twinstar III	003	
PH-2V8	Take Off Merlin Trike	25926	
PH-2V9	Comco Ikarus Fox-C22	9210-3446	D-MKRO
PH-2W1	Aviasud Mistral BRD	126	D-MJJJ
PH-2W2	TLUltralight TL-232 Condor	96C05	
PH-2W3	Comco Ikarus Fox-C22	9603-3706	
PH-2W4	Aviasud Mistral BRD	122	D-MOOO
PH-2W5	Aviasud Mistral BRD	176	D-MMOO
PH-2W6	Microlight AK-4 Kolibri	007	
PH-2W8	Comco Ikarus Fox-C22	9606-3709	
PH-2W9	III Sky Arrow 450 TH	28	
PH-2X1	Rans S-6 Super Coyote II	1095885	
PH-2X2	Microlight AK-4 Kolibri	005	
PH-2X3	TLUltralight TL-232 Condor	96C12	
PH-2X4	NST Minimum Saphir 17M	04589-01NST	
PH-2X5	NST Minimum Magic IV-177	04589	
PH-2X6	Letov ST-4 Aztek	402	
PH-2X7	TLUltralight TL-22 Duo/ESO	95G11	(PH-2X6)
PH-2X8	Air Création Mild GT 582ES	0113	
PH-2X9	Tecnam P.92 Echo	196	
PH-2Y1	Tecnam P.92 Echo	195	
PH-2Y2	Tecnam P.92J Echo	206	
PH-2Y3	Comco Ikarus Fox-C22	9612-3721	
PH-2Y4	Take Off Merlin	26508	
PH-2Y5	Comco Ikarus C-42 Cyclone	9701-6022	
PH-2Y6	JORA Jora	4795776	
PH-2Y7	Tecnam P.92 Echo	219	
PH-2Y8	Solar Wings Pegasus Quantum 15	7314	
PH-2Y9	Aviasud AE-209 Albatros	123	OE-7014
PH-2Z1	Air Création Mild GTE-503S	118	
PH-2Z2	JORA Jora	4837805	
PH-2Z3	Interplane Skyboy	9B9019-97C8	
PH-2Z4	Aviasud Mistral BRD	076	D-MDAR
PH-2Z5	Cosmos BI Phase II	21234	
PH-2Z7	Tecnam P.92 Echo	249	
PH-2Z8	Microlight AK-4 Kolibri	009	

Regn.	Type	C/n	Prev.Id.
PH-2Z9	Rans S-6S Super Coyote II	02971098	
PH-3A2	Aviasud Mistral BRD	113	D-MBGK
PH-3A3	Comco Ikarus C-42 Cyclone	9710-6076	
PH-3A5	Flight Design CT	97-11-03-15	
PH-3A6	Quad City Challenger II	CH2-0196-1436	
PH-3A7	Air Création Mild GT-582ES	T98005/4890750	
PH-3A8	TL Ultralight TL-232 Condor	98C02	
PH-3A9	Flight Design CT	98-01-01-18	
PH-3B1	HFL Stratos 300K	300/009K	
PH-3B2	TL Ultralight TL-232 Condor	98C06	
PH-3B4	Air Création Mild GT582ES	E101510	
PH-3B5	Quad City Challenger (Reservn 6.98)	CH2-0198-Y-1707	
PH-3B6	Tecnam P.92 Echo	302	
PH-3B7	Tecnam P.96 Golf	014	
PH-3B8	Air Création Clipper 582XP	4559554	59-SP
PH-3B9	Remos G-3 Mirage	043	
PH-3C1	Behlen Vampir IIM 14.2	10/0031	D-MHJR
PH-3C3	Murphy Renegade Spirit	606	
PH-3C4	Cosmos BI Phase II	21271	
PH-3C7	Zenair CH-601UL Zodiac	6-9024	
PH-3C8	Kappa KP-2UR Sova	05/98	
PH-3C9	TL Ultralight TL-96 Star	98S20	
PH-3D1	Dyn'Aero MCR-01 UL Banbi	76	
PH-3D2	Zenair CH.601UL Zodiac	6-9029	
PH-3D3	Comco Ikarus C-42 Cyclone	9810-6141	
PH-3D4	Solar Wings Pegasus Quantum 15-912	74.77	G-69-41
PH-3D5	Kappa KP-2UR Sova	06/98	
PH-3D6	TL Ultralight TL-22 Duo/Eso	5235830	
PH-3D7	Kappa KP-2UR Sova	01039802	
PH-3D8	Kappa KP-2UR Sova	08/98	
PH-3D9	Comco Ikarus Fox C-22B	9307-3475	D-MKOH
PH-3E1	Rams S-6S Super Coyote II	01981200	
PH-3E2	Mitchell Wing B10 (Reservation)	P.1444	
	(Also recorded as NVAV-77 / RLD No.A84-0045)		
PH-3E3	Tecnam P.96 Golf	043	
PH-3E4	JORA SRO Jora	C94-1999	
PH-3E5	WDFL D4BFascination	051	
PH-3E6	Cosmos BI Phase II	21325	
PH-3E7	Zenair CH-601UL Zodiac	6-9051	
PH-3E8	Tecnam P.96 Golf	55	
PH-3E9	Kappa KP-2URSova	0103/98	OK-DUU-31
PH-3F2	Remos G-3 Mirage	056	
PH-3F3	Comco Ikarus C-42 Cyclone	9904-6147	
PH-3F4	Zenair CH-601UL Zodiac	6-9050	
PH-3F5	Zenair CH-601UL Zodiac	6-9045	
PH-3F6	Comco Ikarus C-42 Cyclone	9907-6192	
PH-3F8	Comco Ikarus C-42 Cyclone	9907-6200	
PH-3F9	Comco Ikarus C-42 Cyclone	9908-6201	
PH-3G1	ATECZephyr	Z 100699 A	
PH-3G2	TL Ultralight TL-96 Star	99-S-29	
PH-3G3	TL Ultralight TL-96 Star	99-S-34	
PH-3G4	Air Création Clipper 582XP	5305983	
PH-3G5	Aeropro Fox	050698	
PH-3G6	Comco Ikarus Fox C-22	3182	
PH-3G7	Cosmos Samba	90	
PH-3G8	Comco Ikarus C-42 Cyclone	9911-6218	
PH-3G9	Comco Ikarus C-42 Cyclone	9910-6216	
PH-3H1	Rans S-6S Super Coyote II	06981239	
PH-3H3	Zenair CH-701 STOL (Reservation 11.99)	unkn	
PH-3H4	Urbanair UMF13 Lambada (Reservation .00)	unkn	
PH-3H5	Aeropro Fox	81099	
PH-3H6	Comco Ikarus C-42 Cyclone (Reservation 12.99)	unkn	
PH-3H7	Comco Ikarus C-42 Cyclone (Reservation 12.99)	unkn	

SE - SWEDEN

Many aircraft are still officially listed although long since destroyed or unairworthy.

Regn.	Type	C/n	Prev.Id.
SE-ADF	de Havilland DH.82A Tiger Moth	3113	SE-ATI
			Fv568
			Fv5568
			SE-ADF
SE-AGE	de Havilland DH.87B Hornet Moth	8136	
SE-AGO	Piper J-2 Cub (W/o 1.5.66)	993	
SE-AHG	Götaverken GV-38	8	
SE-AIC	Piper J-3C-65 Cub	2486	
SE-ALM	de Havilland DH.82A Tiger Moth	172	RNoAF:163
SE-AMA	S.A.I. KZ-III U-2	EAA No.111/81	OY-DVU
SE-AMB	Piper J-3C-65 Cub	12802	D-ENAC
	(Dbf 5-6.2.88)		SL-AAX
			F-BFQB
			44-80506
SE-AMC	Auster Mk.5	1159	D-EGAT
			I-METE
			HB-EON
			G-AKSI
			RT497
SE-AMD	CASA I.131E Jungmann	2141	G-OBLE
			E3B-541
SE-AME	S.A.I. KZ-III U-2	93	OY-DEA
SE-AMG	de Havilland DH.82A Tiger Moth	84589	OY-DET
			D-EKUR
			G-ANTV
			T6122
SE-AMH	de Havilland DH.82A Tiger Moth	84959	G-AIIZ
	(W/o 4.8.99)		T6645
SE-AMI	de Havilland DH.82A Tiger Moth	86526	G-AYVY
	(W/o 17.7.95)		F-BGCZ
			PG617
SE-AMK	Piper J-3C-65 Cub	12438	LN-KAT
			LN-RAD
			44-80142
SE-AML	Cessna C-34 Airmaster	302	N15463
			NC15463
SE-AMM	de Havilland DH.82A Tiger Moth	83226	G-ANEF
	(W/o 7.9.99)		T5493
SE-AMN	Auster J/2 Arrow	2387	OY-ALY
			D-EMYG
			OO-AXG
			OO-AXC
SE-AMO	de Havilland DH.60G-III Moth Major replica	unkn	(SE-BBT)
	(Under construction using wings of Fox Moth SE-AFL		
	and Hermes engine)		
SE-AMR	de Havilland DH.82A Tiger Moth	ASJA.49	Fv517
SE-AMT	Boeing Stearman A75N1 (PT-13D)	75-5659	G-BAVN
	((Reserved as D-EQHB, 6.99)		4X-AMT
			42-17496
SE-AMY	de Havilland DH.82A Tiger Moth	82720	N81DH
			G-ASSC
			R4776
SE-A..	de Havilland DH.82A Tiger Moth	85427	G-APMM
			DE419
SE-ARG	Auster J/1 Autocrat	1882	
SE-ARK	Auster J/1 Autocrat	1953	
SE-ARR	Auster J/2 Arrow	2358	
SE-ASP	Piper J-3C-65 Cub	11928	44-79632
SE-ASR	Piper J-3C-65 Cub	10486	D-EDOZ
			SE-ASR
			43-29195
SE-ASS	Piper J-3C-65 Cub	11994	44-79698
SE-ASU	Piper J-3C-65 Cub	11708	43-30417
SE-ASX	Piper J-3C-65 Cub	11711	43-30420
SE-ATE	Piper J-3C-65 Cub	11965	44-79669
SE-ATG	Piper J-3C-65 Cub	12043	OH-CPH
			SE-ATG
			44-79747
SE-ATL	Piper J-3C-65 Cub	11243	43-29952
SE-ATO	Piper J-3C-65 Cub	12517	44-80221
SE-ATT	Piper J-3C-65 Cub	11979	44-79683

Regn.	Type	C/n	Prev.Id.
SE-ATU	Piper J-3C-65 Cub	12146	44-79850
SE-ATZ	Piper J-3C-65 Cub	12319	44-80023
SE-AUE	Piper J-3C-65 Cub	9460	43-599
SE-AUF	Piper J-3C-65 Cub (Permit)	12387	44-80091
SE-AUH	Piper J-3C-65 Cub	12685	44-80389
SE-AUK	Piper J-3C-65 Cub	11697	43-30406
SE-AUL	Piper J-3C-65 Cub	12066	(LN-BDB)
			SE-AUL
			44-79770
SE-AUM	Piper J-3C-65 Cub	10875	D-ELOL
			SE-AUM
			43-29584
SE-AUR	SAAB S.91A Safir	91103	
SE-AUT	Piper J-3C-65 Cub	11615	43-30324
SE-AUU	Piper J-3C-65 Cub (W/o 7.7.82)	11661	43-30370
SE-AUW	Piper J-3C-65 Cub	11686	43-30395
SE-AWK	Piper J-3C-65 Cub	12418	44-80122
SE-AWL	Piper J-3C-65 Cub	12044	44-79748
SE-AWP	Piper J-3C-65 Cub	10123	SE-AWD
	(Officially quoted with f/n 9923)		43-1262
SE-AWW	Piper J-3C-65 Cub	16352	
SE-AXB	Republic RC-3 Seabee	268	
SE-AXG	Republic RC-3 Seabee	399	
SE-AXM	Republic RC-3 Seabee	467	
SE-AXX	Republic RC-3 Seabee	829	LN-TVV
			SE-AXX
SE-AXY	Republic RC-3 Seabee	830	(NC6560K)
SE-AYI	Fairchild F.24W Argus 2	572	43-14608
SE-AYM	Miles M.65 Gemini 1A	6296	G-AKDA
SE-AYZ	Piper J-3C-65 Cub	13264	45-4524
SE-AZU	Luscombe 8A Silvaire	4865	(NC2138K)
SE-AZY	S.A.I. KZ-III U-2	102	OY-DYB
SE-BCC	Stinson 108 Voyager	543	(NC97543)
SE-BCD	Globe GC-1B Swift	1065	OY-ADP
			SE-BCD
			(NC80660)
SE-BCL	Stinson 108-1 Voyager	2103	LN-BEJ
			SE-BCL
			N9103K
			NC9103K
SE-BCM	Stinson 108-1 Voyager	2113	N9113K
			NC9113K
SE-BCS	Piper PA-12 Super Cruiser	12-1257	
SE-BCW	Piper J-3C-85 Cub	16354	
SE-BCX	Piper J-3C-65 Cub	12672	LN-RAT
			44-80659(2)
			44-80376
SE-BCZ	Piper PA-18 Super Cub 95	18-370	
SE-BEA	Stinson 108-3 Voyager	4874	OY-AVE
			D-EKES
			N8674M
SE-BEB	Jodel D.112 Club	02	OY-ALE
			PH-VRG
			F-BBBG
			F-WBBG
SE-BEC	Piper J-3C-65 Cub	12904	OY-AVP
			LN-RAL
			(LN-RAK)
			44-80608
SE-BEE	Erco 415C Ercoupe	2614	N99991
			NC99991
SE-BEG	Piper J-3C-65 Cub	13384	D-EDYR
	(Officially quoted with f/n 13214)		(D-EDET)
			45-4644
SE-BEH	Piper J-3C-65 Cub	8535	D-ELAT
	(Officially quoted with f/n 8644 - repaired		HB-OWD
	using c/n 12281 in 6.50)		44-79985
SE-BEI	Piper J-3C-65 Cub	15500	N87882
			NC87882
SE-BEK	Piper PA-12 Super Cruiser	12-558	HB-OOD
			OO-SCD
SE-BEL	Piper J-3C-65 Cub	10951	G-AITP
			OO-AAO
			43-29660

Regn.	Type	C/n	Prev.Id.
SE-BEM	SNCAN/ Stampe SV.4C	33	D-EEMQ
			F-BCUU
SE-BEN	Piper J-3C-65 Cub	11968	OY-ALI
			D-EMAC
			OO-AAF
			44-79672
SE-BEO	Piper J-3C-65 Cub	13707	N68199
			NC68199
			45-4967
SE-BEP	Beech 35 Bonanza	D-718	N3270V
			NC3270V
SE-BER	Erco 415C Ercoupe	3283	(SE-XNL)
			N2658H
			NC2658H
SE-BES	Piper J-3C-65 Cub	12025	LN-HOL
	(Rebuilt using fuselage from SE-AST c/n 12007)		LN-HHF
			44-79729
SE-BET	Piper J-3C-65 Cub	17017	LN-AET
			D-EGEF
			N92648
			NC92648
SE-BEV	Piper J-3C-65 Cub	18658	9Q-CET
			5Y-KIM
			VP-KIM
			VR-TAL
			ZS-AZX
SE-BEW	Focke-Wulf FW.44J Stieglitz	2780	OH-SZG
			SZ-32
SE-BFD	Piper J-3C-65 Cub (Permit)	12535	44-80239
SE-BFK	Piper J-3C-65 Cub	11821	43-30530
SE-BFM	Cessna 140	12503	NC2111V
SE-BFX	Erco 415D Ercoupe	4413	(NC3788H)
SE-BFY	Erco 415D Ercoupe	4409	(NC3784H)
SE-BIO	DHC-2 Beaver Mk 1	1056	C-FMAV
			CF-MAV
SE-BIS	S.A.I. KZ-III U-2 (on rebuild)	84	OY-DVE
SE-BIW	SOCATA Rallye 110ST Galopin	3225	LN-BIW
			F-GBKX
SE-BKA	Aeronca 7AC Champion	6340	(SE-KSR)
			C-FDVT
			CF-DVT
SE-BKB	Aeronca 65C-A	CA14141	N33886
			NC33886
SE-BKG	North American P-51D Mustang	122-31590	4X-AIM
			IDFAF-38
			Fv.26158
			44-63864
SE-BKH	Percival P.66 Pembroke	P66/82	G-BNPG
	(Regd with c/n "K66/045")		XK884
SE-BNI	Piper J-3C-65 Cub	12608	LN-IKH
			SE-BNI
			44-80312
SE-BNK	Bücker Bu.181 Bestmann	108/"Lfs-1-1949"	CR+YU
SE-BNL	SAAB S.91A Safir	91128	SE-BNZ
			SE-BNL
			SE-BNZ
			SE-BNL
SE-BNN	SAAB S.91A Safir	91130	OY-DBT
			OO-MUG
			OO-HUG
			PH-UEB
			SE-BNN
SE-BOA	Boeing Stearman E75	75-1410	N59732
			N4988G
			BuA03633
SE-BOB	Boeing Stearman B75N1	75-6428	N75101
			BuA05254
SE-BOE	Boeing Stearman A75N1	75-294	N4988G
	(painted as '498')		N56402
			40-1737
SE-BOF	Boeing Stearman A75N1	75-862	N56561
	(painted as '561')		41-802
SE-BOG	Boeing Stearman B75N1	75-7128	N59085
			BuA07524
SE-BOZ	Boeing Stearman A75N1	unkn	

Regn.	Type	C/n	Prev.Id.
SE-BPT	Klemm Kl.35D	1922	Fv5033
	(Painted as Fv5033)		
SE-BRY	Beech D-17S	4920	G-BDGK
			HB-UIH
			SE-BRY
			OO-VIT
			FZ430
			43-10872
SE-BSZ	Focke-Wulf FW.44J Stieglitz	2775	SZ-12
	(Officially quoted with c/n 2778 but this is currently		
	restored and awaiting sale in Finland)		
SE-BUU	Lockheed 18-56 Lodestar	2076	VP-KFA
	(Scrapped in 1966)		G-AGBT
SE-BWM	Focke-Wulf FW.44J Stieglitz	655	Fv655
SE-BWU	Focke-Wulf FW.44J Stieglitz	39	OY-DVW
			D-ENYF
			SE-BWU
			Fv.657
SE-BXB	Republic RC-3 Seabee	953	LN-MAL
SE-BXC	Republic RC-3 Seabee	203	CS-AHA
SE-BXX	Andreasson BA-6	1	
SE-BYH	SAAB B17A	139	Fv.17239
SE-BYL	de Havilland DH.82A Tiger Moth (W/o 14.9.97)	ASJA.73	Fv.553
SE-BYR	Piper PA-18-150 Super Cub	18-2928	
SE-BYT	Auster J/5G Autocar (W/o 26.8.64)	3083	
SE-BYU	Auster J/1 Autocrat	1886	G-AHAO
SE-BZM	de Havilland DH.85 Leopard Moth	7061	LN-TVT
			G-ACRW
			AX783
			G-ACRW
SE-BZP	Stinson V-77 Reliant	6375	OO-NUT
			FB536
SE-BZT	Piper PA-20-150 Pacer	20-1078	
SE-CAB	SAAB S.91B-2 Safir	91334	RNo.AF:334
			57334/'UA-O'
SE-CAE	SAAB S.91B Safir	91306	SE-XAR
SE-CAL	Piper J-3C-65 Cub	9994	LN-SAT
			43-1133
SE-CAN	Piper J-3C-65 Cub	12645	44-80349
	(officially quoted with f/n 12475)		
SE-CBL	Piper PA-23-150 Apache	23-549	
SE-CBN	Piper PA-18-150 Super Cub	18-4846	LN-NAT
SE-CBS	Auster J/5G Autocar (W/o 12.4.63)	3082	LN-BDA
SE-CDA	Piper PA-22-135 Tri-Pacer	22-1556	N8977C
SE-CDF	Stinson 108-1 Voyager	1846	OY-EFK
	(W/o 16.6.95)		LN-BEK
			SE-CDF
			N8846K
SE-CDG	Cessna 170B (W/o 27.5.88)	26988	N3445D
SE-CDW	Beech A-35 Bonanza	D-1866	ET-P-12
			N8448A
SE-CEB	Piper PA-18A-150 Super Cub	18-5533	
SE-CEE	Piper PA-18-150 Super Cub	18-5700	
SE-CEF	Piper J-3C-65 Cub	19580	N6402H
SE-CEH	Piper PA-18-150 Super Cub	18-5821	
SE-CER	Piper PA-22-135 Tri-Pacer	22-1089	LN-AEK
			SE-CER
			N1847A
SE-CES	Piper PA-22-135 Tri-Pacer	22-1163	N1406C
SE-CET	Piper J-3C-65 Cub	11304	LN-MAE
			43-30013
SE-CEZ	Piper PA-18A-150 Super Cub	18-4748	N3988P
	(W/o 24.11.68)		
SE-CFP	Douglas C-47A	13883	Fv79006
			SE-CFP
			LN-IAF
			43-30732
SE-CFZ	SAAB S.91D Safir	91308	G-AVGS
			SE-CFZ
			SE-XAT
SE-CGM	Noorduyn UC-64A/S Norseman IV	780	LN-TSN
			R.NoAF:'RA-F'
			44-70515
SE-CHD	Piper PA-22-150 Tri-Pacer	22-3901	OY-DUW
			LN-BDU

Regn.	Type	C/n	Prev.Id.
SE-CHF	Republic RC-3 Seabee	646	LN-PAF
SE-CHG	de Havilland DH.82A Tiger Moth	85867	G-APOU
			DF118
SE-CHP	North American AT-6A Texan (Sk.16B)	77-4524	Fv16269
			41-16443
SE-CIA	Jodel D.126	861	
SE-CIB	Jodel D.113	789	
SE-CIC	Jodel D.126	787	
SE-CID	Jodel D.119	958	
SE-CIE	Jodel D.119	784	
SE-CIF	Jodel D.126	527	
SE-CIH	Jodel D.112 Club	785	OY-TRL
			SE-CIH
SE-CII	Jodel D.112 Club	783	
SE-CIK	Jodel D.112/113	unkn	
SE-CIM	Jodel D.119	959	
SE-CIN	Bowers Fly Baby 1A	SE-01	
SE-CIS	SOCATA MS.880B Rallye Club	1211	OY-DTU
SE-CKB	Piper PA-18A-150 Super Cub	18-6455	Army:51260
			SE-CKB
SE-CKC	Piper PA-18A-150 Super Cub	18-6458	Army:51261
			SE-CKC
SE-CKD	Piper PA-18A-150 Super Cub	18-6521	Army:51258
			SE-CKD
SE-CKE	Piper PA-18A-150 Super Cub	18-6520	Army:51257
			SE-CKE
SE-CKO	Piper PA-22-160 Tri-Pacer	22-5976	N7180D
	(W/o 14.5.61)		
SE-CKR	Piper PA-22S-150 Caribbean	22-6611	
SE-CKU	Piper PA-22-150 Tri-Pacer	22-6346	
	(CofA exp 6.75)		
SE-CKY	Piper PA-18 Super Cub 95	18-7149	
	(W/o 28.7.95)		
SE-CKZ	Piper PA-22S-150 Tri-Pacer	22-6250	N8103D
	(W/o 5.9.71)		
SE-CLA	Piper PA-22-150 Tri-Pacer (Permit)	22-3064	N2757P
SE-CLD	Piper PA-20-150 Pacer	22-100	N697A
	(Believed to be a PA-22 converted to PA-20 standard)		
SE-CLF	Piper PA-18S-95 Super Cub	18-3109	LN-BEE
			OL-L35
			53-4709
SE-CLI	Piper PA-18 Super Cub 95	18-5725	D-EJAQ
			SE-CLI
			N7363D
SE-CLK	Piper PA-22-150 Tri-Pacer	22-4710	N6057D
SE-CLM	Aeronca 7AC Champion	392	N81769
			NC81769
SE-CLN	Stinson SR-10J Reliant	5-5820	N21101
SE-CLP	Cessna 172	46518	N6418E
SE-CLR	Piper J-3C-65 Cub	11794	LN-BWN
			SE-CLR
			43-30503
SE-CLT	Cessna 172	36840	N3940F
SE-CLY	Cessna 150	17030	(EI-AKH)
			N5530E
SE-CLZ	Noorduyn UC-64A/S Norseman IV (Tp 78)	492	Fv78001
	(Displayed at Flygvapenmuseum at Linkoping		SE-ASC
	painted as Fv78001)		43-35418
SE-CMC	Auster 5	1603	D-EERK
			D-ELIR
			D-EFIR
			G-AMNU
			TJ587
SE-CME	Auster 5 Alpha	3410	G-APNN
SE-CMF	Auster 5D	1376	OY-ADY
			VR-RCC
			TJ295
SE-CMO	Cessna 175A (CofA exp 4.87)	56367	N6867E
SE-CMP	Cessna 150	17777	OY-AEG
SE-CMR	Morane-Saulnier MS.885 Super Rallye	14	LN-BWW
SE-CMU	Mooney M.20B Mark 21 (CofA exp 2.81)	1860	
SE-CMY	Cessna 140	11721	OY-BAI
			SE-CMY
			LN-TSK
			N77259

Regn.	Type	C/n	Prev.Id.
SE-CMZ	Cessna 185	0053	LN-TSR
			N9853X
SE-CNA	Champion 7EC Traveler	704	
SE-CNB	Champion 7EC Traveler	705	
SE-CND	Champion 7EC Traveler	719	
SE-CNR	Cessna 210 (W/o 27.11.96)	57331	N9531T
SE-CNS	Cessna 180B (W/o 4.8.82)	50658	N9158T
SE-CNW	Cessna 172A	47137	N7537T
SE-CNY	Cessna 180B	50629	N9129T
SE-COG	de Havilland DH.82A Tiger Moth	85593	G-APLI
			DE639
SE-COO	de Havilland DH.82A Tiger Moth	86372	G-ANKJ
	(W/o 26.9.81)		NL929
SE-CPB	Noorduyn UC-64 Norseman IV	89	(LN-AEN)
	(Preserved in Arlanda Museum)		R.NoAF:'RA-Y'
			42-5050
			RCAF 3538
SE-CPG	Malmö MFI-9 Junior	02	
SE-CPI	Malmö MFI-10B Vipan	03	Fv.54382
	(Displayed at Flygvapenmuseum		Fv.54002
	painted as Fv.54382)		SE-CPI
SE-CPL	Ryan Navion A	4-1786	(D-ELMI)
			N9828F
			N4786K
SE-CPT	Piper PA-18 Super Cub 95	18-6749	N9497D
SE-CPY	Cessna 172	28022	OY-AER
			LN-TSE
			N5022A
SE-CPZ	Piper PA-18 Super Cub 95	18-5883	N7587D
SE-CRC	Piper PA-18 Super Cub 95	18-6998	N9942D
SE-CRE	Piper PA-22-108 Colt	22-8743	
SE-CRF	Piper PA-22-108 Colt	22-8795	
SE-CRI	Piper PA-22-108 Colt	22-9120	
SE-CRU	Piper PA-22-108 Colt (W/o 12.10.70)	22-9113	
SE-CRW	Piper PA-22-108/150 Colt	22-9114	
SE-CSB	Piper PA-18-150 Super Cub	18-7280	
SE-CSD	Piper PA-18-150 Super Cub	18-7287	
SE-CSF	Piper PA-22-150 Caribbean	22-7133	
	(W/o 26.9.61)		
SE-CSG	Piper PA-22-150 Caribbean	22-7136	
	(W/o 6.1.70)		
SE-CSH	Piper PA-22-150 Caribbean	22-7137	
	(W/o 4.3.73)		
SE-CSM	Piper PA-22-150 Caribbean	22-7380	
SE-CSN	Piper PA-22S-150 Caribbean	22-7375	
SE-CSO	Piper PA-22-150 Caribbean	22-7245	
	(Sold to Norway in 1975)		
SE-CSP	Piper PA-22-150 Caribbean	22-7306	
SE-CSR	Piper PA-22-150 Caribbean	22-6942	
SE-CST	Piper PA-20-150 Pacer	20-616	N7789K
SE-CSU	Piper PA-20 Pacer 125	20-489	N7668K
SE-CSW	Piper PA-28-160 Cherokee B	28-1260	
	(W/o 7.11.85)		
SE-CSZ	Piper PA-22-150 Caribbean	22-7350	N3435Z
SE-CTD	Piper PA-24-180 Comanche	24-976	N5891P
SE-CTE	Piper J-4A Cub	4-612	OH-CPB
			G-AFWS
			ES923
			G-AFWS
SE-CTG	Piper PA-18A-150 Super Cub	18-6832	N9472D
SE-CTM	Cessna 185A	0381	N4181Y
SE-CTO	Cessna 175A	56767	N8067T
SE-CUG	Piper PA-18 Super Cub 95	18-7482	
SE-CUR	Piper PA-22-150 Caribbean	22-7453	OH-CPR
	(W/o 12.7.96)		SE-CUR
			N3544Z
SE-CUT	Piper PA-22-108 Colt (W/o 19.4.75)	22-8455	
SE-CUZ	Piper PA-22-108 Colt	22-8628	
SE-CWF	Binder CP.301S Smaragd	120	D-EDRI
SE-CWG	de Havilland DH.82A Tiger Moth	3364	G-AORA
			BB750
			G-ADLV
SE-CWL	Maule M-4-210 Rocket	1034	LN-HHI
	(W/o 26.6.77)		N15B
SE-CXB	Cessna 172A (W/o 25.2.68)	47518	N9718T

Regn.	Type	C/n	Prev.Id.
SE-CXD	Cessna 172A	47193	N7593T
SE-CXE	Cessna 172A (Modified)	47500	N9700T
SE-CXF	Cessna 180C (W/o 27.6.65)	50895	N9395T
SE-CXI	Cessna 150C	59871	N2071Z
SE-CXK	Cessna 175B	56888	N8188T
SE-CXL	Cessna 172B	48199	N7699X
SE-CXM	Cessna 180D	50968	LN-AEM
			SE-CXM
			N6468X
SE-CXN	Cessna 180D	50969	LN-TVW
			(LN-AEL)
			SE-CXN
			N6469X
SE-CXO	Cessna 175C	57099	
SE-CXW	Cessna 172B	48223	N7723X
SE-CYA	Cessna 182D	53322	N8922X
SE-CYH	Cessna 150B	59461	LN-DBK
			SE-CYH
			N7361X
SE-CYI	Cessna 172C (CofA exp 2.80)	48883	N8383X
SE-CYL	Cessna 182E	53680	N9280X
SE-CYO	Cessna 150	59166	OY-DGB
			SE-CXR
			N7066X
SE-CYZ	Cessna 210B (W/o 19.1.72)	58078	OY-EGC
			SE-CYZ
			N9778X
SE-CZA	Piper PA-22-108 Colt	22-9121	
SE-CZC	Piper PA-22-108 Colt	22-9123	
SE-CZE	Piper PA-22-108/150 Colt	22-9125	
SE-CZF	Piper PA-22-108 Colt	22-9126	
SE-CZG	Piper PA-22-108/150 Colt (W/o 23.8.75)	22-9127	
SE-CZH	Piper PA-28-150 Cherokee B	28-1188	
	(Instructional airframe at FTC Vasteras)		
SE-CZI	Piper PA-22-108 Colt	22-9129	
SE-CZK	Piper PA-22-108/150 Colt	22-9130	
SE-CZL	Piper PA-22-108 Colt	22-9131	
SE-CZM	Piper PA-22-108/150 Colt	22-9132	
SE-CZN	Piper PA-28-180 Cherokee B (W/o 2.9.67)	28-1356	N7227W
SE-CZO	Piper PA-22-108/150 Colt	22-8953	LN-BDB
SE-CZR	Piper PA-22-108 Colt	22-9136	
SE-CZT	Piper PA-22-108 Colt	22-9109	
SE-CZU	Piper PA-22-108 Colt	22-9110	
SE-CZZ	Piper PA-18-150 Super Cub	18-7046	OY-ACL
	(W/o 12.7.90)		
SE-DAS	McDonnell-Douglas DC-9-41	47610	
SE-DAU	McDonnell-Douglas DC-9-41	47627	
SE-DAW	McDonnell-Douglas DC-9-41	47629	
SE-DDP	McDonnell-Douglas DC-9-41	47747	
SE-DDR	McDonnell-Douglas DC-9-41	47750	
SE-DDS	McDonnell-Douglas DC-9-41	47777	
SE-DDT	McDonnell-Douglas DC-9-41	47779	N1002L
SE-DDY	Cessna 550 Citation II	0115	OY-CCU
			SE-DDY
			N127SC
			N2745L
SE-DEB	SE.210 Caravelle 10R	247	EC-CIZ
			D-ANYL
			F-WJAM
SE-DEC	SE.210 Caravelle 10R	263	(LN-TEC)
	(W/o at Arlanda 6.1.87 - used for		EC-CYI
	fire practice)		F-WJAK
			F-OCKH
			D-ABAF
			F-WJAN
			OY-SAZ
			F-WJAN
SE-DEG	Cessna 500 Citation	0276	N473LR
			N473LP
			N100CM
			N276CC
			(N5276J)
SE-DEY	Cessna 500 Citation	0370	N36897

Regn.	Type	C/n	Prev.Id.
SE-DEZ	Cessna 501 Citation 1/SP	0279	N43BG
	(Convtd from c/n 500-0371)		N371GP
			(N371GA)
			(N371GP)
			SE-DEZ
			N36919
SE-DGE	Fokker F.28 Fellowship 4000	11112	PH-EXK
SE-DGI	Fokker F.28 Fellowship 4000	11122	PH-EXP
SE-DGL	Fokker F.28 Fellowship 4000	11126	PH-EXV
SE-DGM	Fokker F.28 Fellowship 4000	11128	PH-EXR
SE-DGN	Fokker F.28 Fellowship 4000	11130	PH-JPV
			PH-EXU
SE-DGO	Fokker F.28 Fellowship 4000	11190	PH-EXU
SE-DGP	Fokker F.28 Fellowship 4000	11191	PH-EXZ
SE-DGR	Fokker F.28 Fellowship 4000	11204	PH-EXR
SE-DGS	Fokker F.28 Fellowship 4000	11236	PH-EZA
SE-DGT	Fokker F.28 Fellowship 4000	11239	PH-EZL
SE-DGU	Fokker F.28 Fellowship 4000	11241	PH-EZT
SE-DGX	Fokker F.28 Fellowship 4000	11225	PH-EZX
SE-DHL	Cessna 650 Citation III	0030	N650SC
SE-DHO	Gates Learjet 35A	35A-195	N555JE
			D-CONY
			N1471B
SE-DHP	Gates Learjet 35A	35A-075	N30FN
			N48RW
			(N117DA)
			N3503F
			JY-AFE
			HB-VEV
			N3503F
SE-DIB	McDonnell-Douglas DC-9-87	49605	N19B
SE-DIC	McDonnell-Douglas DC-9-87	49607	
SE-DIF	McDonnell-Douglas DC-9-87	49606	
SE-DII	McDonnell-Douglas DC-9-81	49909	
SE-DIK	McDonnell-Douglas DC-9-82	49728	(SE-DIE)
SE-DIL	McDonnell-Douglas DC-9-81	49913	
SE-DIN	McDonnell-Douglas DC-9-81	49999	
SE-DIP	McDonnell-Douglas DC-9-87	53010	
SE-DIR	McDonnell-Douglas DC-9-81	53004	
SE-DIS	McDonnell-Douglas DC-9-81	53006	
SE-DIU	McDonnell-Douglas DC-9-87	53011	
SE-DIX	McDonnell-Douglas DC-9-81	49998	
SE-DIZ	McDonnell-Douglas DC-9-82	53294	
SE-DKZ	Boeing 767-3Y0ER	24952	N249WP
			EI-CAL
			XA-RWW
			EI-CAL
SE-DLB	Dassault Falcon 10	183	N183SR
			N82CR
			N249FJ
			F-WZGO
SE-DLY	Cessna 550 Citation II	0286	N306SC
			N68631
SE-DLZ	Cessna 500 Citation	0411	G-NCMT
			G-BIZZ
			N6784Y
SE-DMA	McDonnell-Douglas DC-9-87	53009	
SE-DMB	McDonnell-Douglas DC-9-81	53314	
SE-DMF	McDonnell-Douglas MD-90-30	53457	
SE-DMG	McDonnell-Douglas MD-90-30	53461	
SE-DMH	McDonnell-Douglas MD-90-30	53543	
SE-DMT	McDonnell-Douglas DC-9-81	48003	HB-IND
			N19B
SE-DMU	McDonnell-Douglas DC-9-81	48005	HB-INF
SE-DMX	McDonnell-Douglas DC-9-81	48002	HB-INC
SE-DMZ	McDonnell-Douglas DC-9-81	48009	HB-INK
SE-DNM	Boeing 737-683	28288	
SE-DNP	Boeing 737-683	28295	
SE-DNR	Boeing 737-683	28296	
SE-DNS	Boeing 737-683	28297	N35135
SE-DNT	Boeing 737-683	28302	
SE-DNU	Boeing 737-683	28303	
SE-DNV	Boeing 737-683	28304	
SE-DNY	Boeing 737-683	28308	N1787B
SE-DNZ	Boeing 737-683	30190	N1786B
SE-DOI	McDonnell-Douglas DC-9-41	47599	LN-RLA
SE-DOK	McDonnell-Douglas DC-9-41	47626	LN-RLT
SE-DOL	McDonnell-Douglas DC-9-41	47630	LN-RLN
SE-DOM	McDonnell-Douglas DC-9-41	47634	LN-RLZ
SE-DON	McDonnell-Douglas DC-9-41	47748	LN-RLH
SE-DOO	McDonnell-Douglas DC-9-41	47778	LN-RLP
SE-DPA	Boeing 737-33A	25401	
SE-DPB	Boeing 737-33A	25402	N33AW
SE-DPC	Boeing 737-33A	25426	N34AW
SE-DPI	McDonnell-Douglas DC-9-83	49557	LN-RMB
			(LN-RLV)
SE-DPX	Lockheed L-1011-385-1 Tristar	1091	N31024
SE-DRA	BAe.146 Series 200	E-2115	G-BRXT
			C-GRNY
			G-5-115
			G-11-115
SE-DRB	BAe.146 Series 200	E-2057	N698AA
			N146AC
			G-5-057
			N146AC
SE-DRC	BAe.146 Series 200	E-2053	N695AA
			N142AC
			G-5-053
SE-DRD	BAe.146 Series 200	E-2094	G-CSJH
			G-5-094
SE-DRE	BAe.146 Series 200	E-2051	N694AA
			N141AC
			G-5-003
SE-DRF	BAe.146 Series 200	E-2055	N697AA
			N145AC
			G-5-055
			N145AC
			G-5-055
SE-DRG	BAe.146 Series 200	E-2054	N696AA
			N144AC
			G-5-054
SE-DRI	BAe.146 Series 200	E-2058	N699AA
			(D-ALOA)
			N699AA
			CP-2254
			N699AA
			N148AC
			G-5-058
			G-ECAL
			G-5-058
			N148AC
SE-DRK	BAe.146 Series 200	E-2108	N295UE
			G-5-108
SE-DRL	BAe.146 Series 200	E-2138	N138JV
			C-FHAA
			N138TR
			(N719TA)
			N883DV
			G-5-138
SE-DRS	Beech 400A Beechjet	RK-37	N8014Q
			(F-GLOR)
			N8014Q
			(F-GLPD)
SE-DSB	Lockheed L-1011-385-1 Tristar	1059	N31015
SE-DSO	Avro 146-RJ100A (Reservation 11.99)	E-3221	N504MM
			G-OIII
SE-DSP	Avro 146-RJ100A (Reservation 11.99)	E-3242	N505MM
			G-6-242
SE-DSR	Avro 146-RJ100A (Reservation 11.99)	E-3244	N506MM
			G-6-244
SE-DSS	Avro 146-RJ100A (Reservation 11.99)	E-3245	N507MM
			G-6-245
SE-DST	Avro 146-RJ100A (Reservation 11.99)	E-3247	N508MM
			G-6-247
SE-DSU	Avro 146-RJ100A (Reservation 11.99)	E-3248	N509MM
			G-6-248
SE-DSV	Avro 146-RJ100A (Reservation 11.99)	E-3250	N510MM
			G-6-250
SE-DSX	Avro 146-RJ100A (Reservation 11.99)	E-3255	N511MM
			G-6-255

Regn.	Type	C/n	Prev.Id.
SE-DSY	Avro 146-RJ100A *(Reservation 11.99)*	E-3263	N512MM / G-6-263
SE-DTF	Boeing 737-683	28309	N1787B
SE-DTG	Boeing 737-783	30191	N1786B
SE-DTH	Boeing 737-683	28313	
SE-DTI	Boeing 737-683	28314	N1786B
SE-DTJ to SE-DTT *Reserved for Boeing 737-683's for SAS*			
SE-DTU	Boeing 737-683	28311	N1786B
SE-DUC	Fokker F.28-0100	11324	PH-CFB / (PH-LNR) / PH-EZG / (G-FIOU) / PH-EZG
SE-DUD	Fokker F.28-0100	11325	PH-CFC / (PH-LNT) / PH-EZI / (G-FIOV) / PH-EZI
SE-DUE	Fokker F.28-0100	11326	PH-CFD / (PH-LNU) / PH-EZJ / (G-FIOW) / PH-EZJ
SE-DUK	Boeing 757-236	25054	N100FS / EI-CMA / XA-MMX / N3502P / (EC-668) / (G-BSNB)
SE-DUL	Boeing 757-2Y0	26151	SX-BBY / XA-KWK / XA-SCB
SE-DUO	Boeing 757-236	24792	G-BRJI / SX-BBZ / G-BRJI / SX-BBZ / G-BRJI / EC-FMQ / EC-786 / EC-EVC / EC-446 / G-BRJI
SE-DUP	Boeing 757-236	24793	G-OOOT / G-BRJJ / EC-490 / (G-BRJJ)
SE-DUR	Fokker F.28-0100	11332	PH-FZK / F-GKLY / PH-EZH
SE-DUS	Boeing 737-3Y0	24255	HB-IID / EI-CFQ / OO-IID / XA-RJP / G-MONL
SE-DUT	Boeing 737-548	25165	EI-CDT / PT-MNC / EI-CDT
SE-DUZ	Cessna 500 Citation	0143	N787BA / N14T / N14JZ / N3W / XB-CXF / XC-GUQ / N143CC
SE-DVA	Cessna 500 Citation	0397	OY-FFC / OH-CIT / N6563C / (N1958E)
SE-DVB	Cessna 500 Citation	0294	N924AS / (N501LG) / HL7226 / N5294J
SE-DVD	Hawker 800XP	258339	N23395
SE-DVE	Dassault Falcon 900EX	23	F-WWFS
SE-DVF	Lockheed L-1011-385-3 Tristar	1241	CS-TEC

Regn.	Type	C/n	Prev.Id.
SE-DVH	Airbus A.320-212	190	PH-DVR / G-UKLJ / G-BWKN / N484GX / F-WWDD
SE-DVI	Lockheed L-1011-500 Tristar	1248	V2-LEK / CS-TEG / JY-AGJ / N64959
SE-DVK	Dassault Falcon 50	249	N663MN / (XA-DMS) / N248FJ / F-WWHN
SE-DVL	Dassault Falcon 50	238	N238DL / N796A / XA-LRA / N50FJ, / N238FJ / F-WWHF
SE-DVN	Lockheed L-1101-385-3 Tristar	1196	N596AH / JY-AGF / D-AERL
SE-DVO	Boeing 737-85F	28822	
SE-DVP	Dassault Falcon 10	224	N135FJ / C-FREE / N128FJ / F-WZGM
SE-DVR	Boeing 737-85F	28826	
SE-DVT	Cessna 550 Citation II	0634	N550SB / PH-MDX / (N1258B)
SE-DVU	Boeing 737-85F	28825	N501GX
SE-DVX	Lockheed L-1011-500 Tristar	1183	N501GB / SE-DVM / N501GB / D-AERT
SE-DVY	Cessna 650 Citation VII	7011	N700VP / (N6111) / N5111 / N1260N
SE-DVZ	Cessna 550 Citation II	0808	N1299B / N5216A
SE-DXA	Hawker Hunter F.Mk.58	41H-697456	(OY-SKB) / J-4089
SE-DXB	SAAB J-29F	29670	Fv29670
SE-DXC	Hawker Hunter F.Mk.58A	41H-679995	J-4101 / G-9-294 / XG127
SE-DXD	Hawker Hunter F.Mk.58	41H-697390	J-4023
SE-DXE	Hawker Hunter F.Mk.58	XE-64/41H-697443	G-HONE / J-4076
SE-DXF	Hawker Hunter F.Mk.58	XE-75/41H-697454	G-HTWO / J-4087
SE-DXH	Hawker Hunter T. Mk 7A *(Previously given as 41H-695336)*	41H-695448	G-BWME / 9223M / XL616
SE-DXL	SAAB J32B Lansen	unkn	Fv.32605/26
SE-DXS	de Havilland DH.100 Vampire FB.6	705	J-1196
SE-DXT	de Havilland DH.115 Vampire T.55	972	U-1212
SE-DXU	de Havilland DH.115 Vampire T.55	40279	U-1238 / XD440
SE-DXV	de Havilland DH.115 Vampire T.55	981	U-1221
SE-DXX	de Havilland DH.115 Vampire T.55	40303	U-1236
SE-DXY	de Havilland DH.100 Vampire FB.6	693	J-1184
SE-DXZ	de Havilland DH.100 Vampire FB.6 *(W/o 6.7.93)*	630	HB-RVD / J-1121
SE-DYA, -DYC, -DYD *Reserved for Boeing 737 for SAS*			
SE-DYB	Dassault Falcon 100	216	N999WJ / 9M-ATM / VH-JDW / N100H / N276FJ / F-WZGZ
SE-DYE	Hawker 800XP	258382	N23451
SE-DYF	*Reserved for Boeing 737 for Nova*		

Regn.	Type	C/n	Prev.Id.
SE-DYG, DYH	Reserved for Boeing 737s for SAS		
SE-DYI	Airbus A.330 (Reservation for Nova)	unkn	
SE-DYK	Airbus A.330 (Reservation for Nova)	unkn	
SE-DYL	Boeing 737-36E (Reservation)	25264	EC-FLG
			EC-706
SE-DYM, DYN	Reserved for Boeing 737s for SAS		
SE-DYO	Cessna S550 Citation SII	0134	D-CFAI
			N134QS
			N1294M
SE-DYP	Reserved for Boeing 737 for SAS		
SE-DYR	Cessna 551 Citation II	0132	N78GA
			C-GTBR
			(C-FCFP)
			N2663J
SE-DYT, DYU	Reserved for Boeing 737s for SAS		
SE-DYV	Hawker 800XP	258385	N23466
SE-DYX	Cessna 560XL Citation Excel	5029	N5203S
SE-DYY	Cessna 550 Citation II (Reservation)	0707	N707EA
			RP-C4654
			N1202T
SE-DYZ	Cessna 560 Citation V	0153	N1SN
			(N153VP)
			N502F
			N502T
			N6804Y
SE-DZA	Embraer EMB.145	145-070	PT-SAO
SE-DZB	Embraer EMB.145	145-113	
SE-DZC	Embraer EMB.145	145-169	
SE-DZD	Embraer EMB.145	145-185	
SE-DZE	Reserved for Embraer EMB.145 for West Air Sweden		
SE-DZF	Boeing 767-3S1ER	25221	PH-AAM
			G-BXOP
			N770TA
			(N688EV)
			B-16688
			(YS-...)
SE-DZG	Reserved for Boeing 767 for Britannia AB		
SE-DZH	Boeing 737-804	28227	N1786B
SE-DZI	Boeing 737-804	28229	
SE-DZK	Boeing 737-804 (Reservation)	28231	
SE-DZL to DZO	Reserved for Britannia AB		
SE-DZP/R/S/T/U	Reserved for Embraer EMB-145s for Skyways AB		
SE-EAC	Cessna 172C	49209	N1509Y
SE-EAE	Cessna 172C	49354	N1654Y
SE-EAF	Cessna 172C	49259	N1559Y
SE-EAL	Cessna 172F	52008	N8108U
SE-EAN	Cessna 150B	59581	N1181Y
SE-EAP	Cessna 172D	49678	N2178Y
SE-EAR	Cessna 210-5 (205)	0101	N8101Z
SE-EAS	Reims/Cessna F.172F	0157	
SE-EAT	Cessna 172F	52107	N8207U
SE-EAU	Reims/Cessna F.172F	0163	
SE-EAW	Reims/Cessna F.172F	0150	
SE-EBS	SAAB MFI-9 Junior	07	LN-BFA
			SE-EBS
SE-ECC	Piper PA-25-235/260 Pawnee	25-2166	N6613Z
SE-ECD	Piper PA-28-180 Cherokee B (W/o 18.8.68)	28-995	
SE-ECE	Piper PA-23-235 Apache (W/o 26.9.75)	27-505	N4915P
SE-ECG	Piper PA-25-235 Pawnee	25-2230	
SE-ECM	Piper PA-23-250 Aztec B (W/o 4.3.75)	27-2281	(G-ASDX)
SE-ECN	Piper PA-18-150 Super Cub	18-7902	
SE-ECR	Piper PA-28-180 Cherokee B (W/o 11.7.73)	28-1351	
SE-ECS	Piper PA-30-160 Twin Comanche (CofA exp 6.87)	30-57	
SE-ECT	Piper PA-28-180 Cherokee B	28-1320	
SE-ECZ	Piper PA-18-150 Super Cub	18-8076	
SE-EDD	SAAB S.91C Safir	91318	OE-DSA
			(EI-AGY)
			SE-XBE
SE-EDO	Piper PA-22-108 Colt	22-8689	OH-CPL
			(G-AROM)
SE-EDY	Aero Commander 680E	335-28	N6828S
	(Scrapped after CofA expiry 4.88)		
SE-EEC	Cessna 180D (W/o 12.8.65)	51029	OY-AEP
			LN-DBA
			N8629X
SE-EEE	Binder CP.301S Smaragd	119	(D-EDFO)
SE-EEM	Cessna 185A	0439	N1639Z
SE-EES	Beech D95A Travel Air	TD-539	
	(Scrapped after wheels-up landing in 1984)		
SE-EET	Piper PA-18 Super Cub 95	18-6331	OH-CPK
			SE-CEP
	(W/o 21.11.91)		
SE-EEU	Beech D95A Travel Air	TD-540	OY-DPV
			SE-EEU
SE-EFC	SAAB MFI-9 Junior (W/o 29.12.88)	16	
SE-EFF	SAAB MFI-9 Junior	19	OH-MFC
			SE-EFF
SE-EFH	SAAB MFI-9 Junior	21	
SE-EFM	SAAB MFI-9B Trainer	025	SE-202
SE-EFO	SAAB MFI-9B Trainer	027	LN-DAA
			SE-EFO
SE-EFR	SAAB MFI-9B Trainer	029	
SE-EFS	SAAB MFI-9B Trainer	030	
SE-EFW	SAAB MFI-9B Trainer	033	
SE-EGD	Morane-Saulnier MS.880B Rallye Club	73	EL-ADM
SE-EGE	Lake LA-4 Skimmer (W/o 24.7.84)	303	N1141L
SE-EGK	Gardan GY-80 Horizon 160 (CofA expired 4.79)	52	
SE-EGL	Gardan GY-80 Horizon 160	26	OY-ATH
			SE-EGL
			F-BLVA
SE-EGN	Gardan GY-80 Horizon 160 (W/o 8.9.76)	106	(F-WLSE)
SE-EGO	Gardan GY-80 Horizon 160	113	
SE-EGT	Focke-Wulf FW.44J Stieglitz	081	D-EOIL
			OH-SZS
			SE-EGT
			Fv629
SE-EGU	Gardan GY-80 Horizon 180	143	F-BNQE
SE-EGY	Aero Commander 680FL	1410-61	(D-IBEZ)
			N6374U
	(Scrapped after CofA expiry 4.89)		
SE-EHA	Cessna 185B	0559	N2559Z
SE-EHD	Cessna 185C	0702	N5802T
SE-EHF	Reims/Cessna F.172E	50606/0030	
SE-EHI	Reims/Cessna F.172E	50769/0039	
SE-EHK	Reims/Cessna F.172F	0091	OY-TRM
SE-EHO	Cessna 206	0114	N5114U
SE-EHT	Cessna 172E	51653	N5753T
SE-EHU	Reims/Cessna F.172F (W/o 8.3.65)	0096	
SE-EHW	Reims/Cessna F.172F	0106	
SE-EHX	Reims/Cessna F.172F	0102	OY-BAH
SE-EIC	Piper PA-25-235 Pawnee	25-2591	D-EEIO
			SE-EIC
SE-EIH	Piper PA-18A-150 Super Cub	18-6875	OY-AIO
			N9798D
SE-EIM	Piper PA-28-180 Cherokee B (W/o 24.6.86)	28-1610	
SE-EIN	Piper PA-30-160 Twin Comanche	30-348	
SE-EIO	Piper PA-28-180 Cherokee B	28-1368	N7465W
SE-EIX	Piper PA-28-180 Cherokee B	28-1684	
SE-EKE	Beech 95-B55 Baron	TC-653	
SE-EKG	Beech A23 Musketeer (W/o 5.6.71)	M-638	
SE-EKL	Beech A23 Musketeer (W/o 22.6.66)	M-721	
SE-EKR	Beech 95-B55 Baron	TC-944	
	(Instructional airframe)		
SE-EKW	Beech D-95A Travel Air	TD-648	
SE-ELA	Beagle-Auster 6A Tugmaster	3724	G-ASHY
			VX110
	(W/o 21.8.71)		
SE-ELB	Beagle-Auster 6A Tugmaster	3732	TW538
SE-ELD	Beagle A.61 Terrier 1 (W/o 6.2.82)	3733	WE553
SE-ELF	Beagle-Auster 6A Tugmaster	3735	TW571
SE-ELG	Beagle-Auster 6A Tugmaster	3736	VF600
SE-ELK	Beagle A.61 Terrier 1 (W/o 16.7.76)	3739	VX935
SE-ELS	Cessna 182K Skylane	58259	OY-AHA
			N2559R
SE-ELY	Reims/Cessna F.172H	0490	OH-CNE
SE-ELZ	Cessna 185B	0578	LN-MAE
			SE-ELZ
			LN-DBH
			N2578Z
SE-EMB	Piper PA-28-140 Cherokee	28-20064	
SE-EMD	Piper PA-28-140 Cherokee	28-20053	
SE-EMH	Piper PA-28-180 Cherokee B	28-1746	N7738W
SE-EMI	Piper PA-18-150 Super Cub (W/o 30.6.72)	18-8149	

Regn.	Type	C/n	Prev.Id.
SE-EML	Piper PA-18-150 Super Cub	18-8294	OH-PDK
	(W/o 14.2.82)		SE-EML
SE-EMN	Piper PA-28-140 Cherokee	28-20361	
SE-EMR	Piper PA-28-150 Cherokee C	28-2081	
SE-EMW	Piper PA-28-180 Cherokee C	28-2192	
SE-EMX	Piper PA-25-235 Pawnee B	25-3125	
SE-END	SAAB MFI-9B Trainer	039	
SE-ENE	SAAB MFI-9B Trainer	040	
SE-ENG	SAAB MFI-9B Trainer	054	LN-LJA
			SE-ENG
SE-ENH	SAAB MFI-9B Trainer	055	
SE-EOB	Piper PA-28-150 Cherokee C	28-2234	
	(CofA expired 9.85)		
SE-EOC	Piper PA-28-150 Cherokee C	28-2220	
SE-EOD	Piper PA-28-180 Cherokee C	28-2481	
	(W/o 8.7.73, remains sold to Norway)		
SE-EOE	Piper PA-28-180 Cherokee C	28-3086	
SE-EOF	Piper PA-28-140 Cherokee (W/o 11.11.67)	28-21151	
SE-EOH	Piper PA-25-235 Pawnee B	25-3199	
SE-EOK	Piper PA-30-160 Twin Comanche	30-157	N7135Y
SE-EOL	Piper PA-28-140 Cherokee	28-20699	
SE-EOM	Piper PA-28-150 Cherokee C	28-2384	
	(Cr.8.10.72 - wreck sold to Norway)		
SE-EOO	Piper PA-28-180 Cherokee C	28-2185	
SE-EOP	Piper PA-28-140 Cherokee	28-20814	
SE-EOR	Piper PA-28-180 Cherokee C	28-2416	
SE-EOS	Piper PA-28-180 Cherokee C	28-2533	
SE-EOT	Piper PA-28-180 Cherokee C	28-2461	
SE-EOU	Piper PA-24-250 Comanche (W/o 10.99)	24-3506	OH-CPV
			N8202P
SE-EOZ	Piper PA-28-150 Cherokee C	28-2477	
SE-EPB	Piper PA-25-235 Pawnee B (W/o 12.7.82)	25-3264	
SE-EPF	Piper PA-18-150 Super Cub	18-8249	
SE-EPG	Piper PA-22-160 Tri-Pacer	22-7629	LN-BWS
SE-EPI	Piper PA-28-140 Cherokee	28-20976	
SE-EPK	Piper PA-28-140 Cherokee	28-20981	
SE-EPL	Piper PA-28-140 Cherokee	28-22422	
SE-EPM	Piper PA-18-150 Super Cub	18-8297	
SE-EPO	Piper PA-28-235 Cherokee	28-10614	N9038W
SE-EPR	Piper PA-23-250 Aztec C	27-3126	
SE-EPY	Piper PA-28-180 Cherokee C	28-2768	
SE-ERT	Republic RC-3 Seabee	846	N6573K
SE-ERU	SOCATA MS.880B Rallye Club	1267	
	(Converted to Rallye 150ST)		
SE-ERW	SOCATA MS.892A Rallye Commodore 150	11407	
SE-ERX	SOCATA MS.892A Rallye Commodore 150	11426	
SE-ERZ	SOCATA MS.892A Rallye Commodore 150	11442	OY-DJR
SE-ESA	Cessna 337 Skymaster (W/o 2.1.72)	0097	N2197X
SE-ESB	Cessna 150E	61007	OH-CEC
			N2507J
SE-ESC	Cessna 140	13284	OH-CSZ
			N3036N
SE-ESD	Reims/Cessna F.172F	0125	OH-CED
			SE-ESD
SE-ESF	Cessna 182H Skylane (W/o 4.5.67)	56211	N2311X
SE-ESG	Cessna P.206 Super Skylane (Dbf 27.4.67)	0138	N2638X
SE-ESM	Cessna 182H Skylane (Sold to UK 9.99)	56480	N8380S
SE-ESO	Cessna 150F	62142	N8842S
SE-ESS	Reims/Cessna F.172H	0341	
SE-EST	Cessna 210-5 (205)	0364	N8364Z
SE-ESU	Reims/Cessna F.172G	0248	
SE-ESX	Reims/Cessna F.172G (W/o 14.7.74)	0280	
SE-ETA	Cessna 150F	61882	N8282S
SE-ETB	Reims/Cessna F.172G (W/o 20.1.81)	0228	
SE-ETC	Reims/Cessna F.172G	0242	
SE-ETD	Reims/Cessna F.150F	62874/0021	
SE-ETE	Cessna 182J Skylane	57122	N3022F
SE-ETF	Reims/Cessna F.172H (W/o 16.6.75)	0374	
SE-ETL	Cessna 180H	51468	LN-BIG(1)
			N4768U
SE-ETN	Reims/Cessna F.150G	0193	
SE-ETO	Reims/Cessna F.150G	0196	
SE-ETP	Cessna 172H	55282	N3787F
SE-ETR	Cessna 150F	62718	N11B
			N8618G

Regn.	Type	C/n	Prev.Id.
SE-ETT	Cessna 150E (W/o 22.8.86)	60848	OY-TRO
			N6148T
SE-ETX	Cessna 150D	60105	LN-BFS
			N4105U
SE-ETZ	Cessna 336 Skymaster	0063	OY-TRH
	(CofA exp 12.81)		(HB-LCZ)
			N1763Z
SE-EUC	SAAB MFI-9B Trainer (W/o 27.4.75)	057	
SE-EUD	SAAB MFI-9B Trainer	058	
SE-EUF	SAAB MFI-9B Trainer	060	
SE-EUM	SAAB MFI-9B Trainer	043	Fv:801-43
			(SE-ENH)
SE-EUO	SAAB MFI-9B Trainer	045	Fv:801-45
			(SE-EUC)
SE-EUR	de Havilland DH.104 Dove 6A	04496	G-ATAP
			HB-LAP
SE-EUX	Beech A23-24 Musketeer Super	MA-131	
	(Sold to Germany after CofA expiry 12.74)		
SE-EWC	SAAB MFI-9B Trainer	048	Fv:801-48
			(SE-EUF)
SE-EWD	SAAB MFI-9B Trainer	049	Fv:801-49
			(SE-EUG)
SE-EWN	Beech A23-24 Musketeer Super (W/o 3.6.95)	MA-174	
SE-EWP	Beech 95-C55 Baron (W/o 9.93)	TE-403	
SE-EWW	Beech A23-24 Musketeer Super	MA-191	
	(W/o 11.10.84)		
SE-EWY	Beech A23-19 Musketeer Sport	MB-192	
SE-EXA	Cessna 182K Skylane	57739	(OY-EGR)
			N2539Q
SE-EXC	Reims/Cessna F.150H	0254	LN-FAI
SE-EXD	Reims/Cessna F.150J	0463	
SE-EXF	Cessna 185D Skywagon (W/o 5.6.81)	0902	N1544F
SE-EXL	Beech 95-B55 Baron	TC-1287	
SE-EXW	Beech 95-B55 Baron	TC-1073	
SE-EYA	Piper PA-25-235 Pawnee B	25-3676	
SE-EYB	Piper PA-25-235 Pawnee B	25-3680	
SE-EYC	Piper PA-28-180 Cherokee C	28-3114	
SE-EYG	Piper PA-28-140 Cherokee	28-21661	
SE-EYI	Piper PA-28-180 Cherokee C	28-3163	
SE-EYL	Piper PA-18-150 Super Cub	18-8347	N4166Z
SE-EYO	Piper PA-28-180 Cherokee C	28-3198	
SE-EYT	Piper PA-25-235 Pawnee B (W/o 6.7.70)	25-4076	
SE-EYU	Piper PA-28-140 Cherokee (W/o 7.10.89)	28-21794	
SE-EYX	Piper PA-25-235 Pawnee B	25-3898	
SE-EYY	Piper PA-28-140 Cherokee	28-21843	
SE-EZC	Piper PA-28-180 Cherokee C	28-3543	
SE-EZD	Piper PA-28-180 Cherokee C	28-3583	
SE-EZE	Piper PA-18S-150 Super Cub	18-8444	
SE-EZF	Piper PA-32-260 Cherokee Six	32-768	
SE-EZO	Piper PA-28-140 Cherokee	28-24361	
SE-EZT	Piper PA-28-140 Cherokee	28-22967	
SE-EZU	Piper PA-28-180 Cherokee C	28-3679	
SE-EZX	Piper PA-18-150 Super Cub	18-8610	
SE-EZY	Piper PA-31-310 Navajo (W/o 26.11.79)	31-22	N9016Y
SE-EZZ	Piper PA-18-150 Super Cub	18-8484	
SE-FAA	Piper PA-28-140 Cherokee	28-23338	
SE-FAC	Piper PA-28-180 Cherokee C (Stored)	28-4287	
SE-FAD	Piper PA-28-180 Cherokee C	28-4319	
SE-FAG	Piper PA-28-140 Cherokee (W/o 16.10.89)	28-23173	N9700W
SE-FAH	Piper PA-18-150 Super Cub	18-8618	
SE-FAI	Piper PA-28-140 Cherokee	28-22647	
SE-FAK	Piper PA-18-150 Super Cub	18-8479	N4299Y
SE-FAL	Piper PA-28-180 Cherokee D	28-4383	
SE-FAO	Piper PA-28-140 Cherokee	28-23298	
SE-FAX	Piper PA-28-140 Cherokee	28-22687	
SE-FAZ	Piper PA-18-150 Super Cub (W/o 2.7.95)	18-8495	N4281Z
SE-FBE	Reims/Cessna F.172H	0478	
SE-FBF	Reims/Cessna F.150H	0262	
SE-FBG	Reims/Cessna F.150H (W/o 10.5.80)	0272	
SE-FBL	Reims/Cessna F.150H	0260	
SE-FBM	Reims/Cessna FR.172E Rocket	0012	F-WLIL
	(W/o 10.7.87)		
SE-FBP	Reims/Cessna FR.172E Rocket	0029	
SE-FBT	Reims/Cessna FR.172E Rocket	0034	
SE-FCA	Piper PA-28-140 Cherokee	28-23548	N3419K

Regn.	Type	C/n	Prev.Id.
SE-FCB	Piper PA-28-140 Cherokee	28-23488	N9944W
SE-FCD	Piper PA-28-140 Cherokee	28-23455	N9931W
SE-FCG	Piper PA-28R-180 Cherokee Arrow	28R-30504	
SE-FCH	Piper PA-28-140 Cherokee	28-23905	
SE-FCI	Piper PA-28-140 Cherokee	28-23920	
SE-FCK	Piper PA-32-260 Cherokee Six	32-943	
SE-FCM	Piper PA-28-180 Cherokee D	28-4766	
SE-FCN	Piper PA-28-140 Cherokee	28-23556	N11C
			N3437K
SE-FCO	Piper PA-28-140 Cherokee	28-23504	N11C
			N9957W
SE-FCP	Piper PA-28-140 Cherokee	28-23533	N11C
	(W/o 8.8.89)		N9985W
SE-FDA	Piper PA-28-140 Cherokee	28-24386	
SE-FDB	Piper PA-28-140 Cherokee	28-24416	
SE-FDC	Piper PA-28-140 Cherokee	28-24451	
SE-FDD	Piper PA-28-140 Cherokee	28-24422	
SE-FDE	Piper PA-28-140 Cherokee	28-24433	
SE-FDG	Piper PA-28R-180 Cherokee Arrow	28R-30458	N4587J
SE-FDH	Piper PA-28R-180 Cherokee Arrow	28R-30664	
	(W/o 22.2.75)		
SE-FDI	Piper PA-28-140 Cherokee	28-24391	
SE-FDL	Piper PA-28-180 Cherokee D	28-4758	
SE-FDN	Piper PA-28-180 Cherokee D	28-4838	
SE-FDP	Piper PA-28R-180 Cherokee Arrow	28R-30837	
	(W/o 5.9.71)		
SE-FDT	Piper PA-28R-180 Cherokee Arrow	28R-30687	
	(accident 6.5.95)		
SE-FDV	Piper PA-28R-180 Cherokee Arrow	28R-30729	
SE-FDY	Piper PA-18-150 Super Cub	18-6279	LN-HHA
			SE-CTA
			N8675D
SE-FDZ	Piper PA-28R-180 Cherokee Arrow	28R-30873	
SE-FEL	Reims/Cessna F.150J	0412	
SE-FEP	Cessna 182M Skylane	59395	N70854
SE-FER	Cessna 207 Skywagon	00042	LN-BIP
			SE-FER
			N91055
SE-FES	Cessna 177A Cardinal *(W/o 2.10.79)*	01315	N30543
SE-FET	Reims/Cessna F.150J	0450	
SE-FEZ	Reims/Cessna FR.172F Rocket	0086	
SE-FFC	Piper PA-28-140 Cherokee B	28-25013	
SE-FFD	Piper PA-28-140 Cherokee B	28-25017	
SE-FFF	Piper PA-28-180 Cherokee D	28-4524	N5230L
SE-FFG	Piper PA-24-250 Comanche	24-2748	G-ARXI
			N7542P
SE-FFH	Piper PA-28-180 Cherokee D	28-5080	
SE-FFI	Piper PA-28-180 Cherokee D	28-5096	
SE-FFM	Piper PA-28-140 Cherokee B *(W/o 14.8.70)*	28-25092	
SE-FFR	Piper PA-28-140 Cherokee B	28-25446	
SE-FFU	Piper PA-28R-200 Cherokee Arrow	28R-35242	
	(CofA exp 9.86. Instructional airframe at Nykoping)		
SE-FFV	Piper PA-28-140 Cherokee B *(W/o 4.7.82)*	28-26152	
SE-FFX	Piper PA-28-140 Cherokee C	28-26842	
SE-FFY	Piper PA-22-135 Tri-Pacer	22-656	ZS-DHB
SE-FFZ	Piper PA-28-140 Cherokee B	28-25440	
SE-FGD	Maule M-4-220C Strata Rocket	2054C	N2061U
SE-FGI	Bellanca 7GCBC Citabria	309-71	
SE-FGK	Maule M-4-220C Strata Rocket	2063C	N2075U
SE-FGM	Champion 7GCAA Citabria	200	
SE-FGN	Fuji FA-200-180 Aero Subaru	3	JA3336
SE-FGO	Mitsubishi MU.2B-20	102	HB-LED
SE-FGR	Beagle B.121 Pup 100	047	G-35-047
SE-FGU	Beagle B.121 Pup 150	068	G-35-068
SE-FGV	Beagle B.121 Pup 100	079	G-35-079
SE-FGY	Beagle B.121 Pup 100	100	G-35-100
SE-FGZ	Beagle B.121 Pup 100	102	G-35-102
SE-FHC	Piper PA-28-140 Cherokee B	28-26160	N98305
SE-FHG	Piper PA-28-140 Cherokee B	28-25716	
SE-FHH	Piper PA-28-140 Cherokee B *(W/o 9.5.71)*	28-26140	(OH-PCD)
SE-FHI	Piper PA-28-140 Cherokee C	28-26844	
SE-FHN	Piper PA-28-140 Cherokee C	28-26721	
SE-FHO	Piper PA-28-180 Cherokee E	28-5614	
SE-FHT	Piper PA-31-310 Navajo	31-488	N6566L
	(Instructional airframe at Linkoping)		

Regn.	Type	C/n	Prev.Id.
SE-FHU	Piper PA-28-140 Cherokee B	28-26068	
	(Cr.9.8.80 - instructional airframe at Vasteras)		
SE-FHV	Piper PA-32S-300 Cherokee Six C	32-40919	
SE-FHY	Piper PA-28-140 Cherokee B *(W/o 15.3.72)*	28-26255	N5534U
SE-FHZ	Piper PA-28-140 Cherokee B	28-26250	N5533U
SE-FIA	SAAB MFI-9B Trainer	063	
SE-FIB	SAAB MFI-9B Trainer	064	
SE-FID	SAAB MFI-9B Trainer	066	OY-DRF
SE-FIG	SAAB MFI-9B-130 Trainer	069	
SE-FIM	SAAB MFI-15-200 Safari	006	
SE-FIO	SAAB MFI-15-200 Safari	15-901	ET-AGC
			SE-FIO
SE-FIP	SAAB MFI-15-200 Safari	15-902	ET-AGD
			SE-FIP
SE-FIS	Bölkow BO.208C Junior	617	OY-POK
			G-ATYP
			(D-EHUW)
SE-FIT	SAAB MFI-15-200A Safari	15-832	N24AF
			SE-FIT
SE-FKA	Reims/Cessna FR.172F Rocket	0110	
SE-FKD	Reims/Cessna F.150J	0453	
SE-FKF	Reims/Cessna F.150J	0525	
SE-FKH	Reims/Cessna FR.172F Rocket *(W/o 30.10.70)*	0114	
SE-FKL	Reims/Cessna FR.172F Rocket	0132	
SE-FKO	Cessna 177A Cardinal	01340	(LN-FAK)
			(OY-AGM)
			N30579
SE-FKS	Cessna 182M Skylane	59572	N71310
SE-FKX	Reims/Cessna F.150K	0595	
SE-FKY	Cessna A.185E *(W/o 22.11.79)*	01672	N1958U
SE-FLA	Piper PA-25-260 Pawnee C	25-4487	LN-VYM
SE-FLD	Piper PA-32-260 Cherokee Six	32-7200015	N4295T
SE-FLG	Piper PA-31-310 Navajo	31-361	LN-LMU
	(Instructional airframe at Vasteras)		
SE-FLI	Piper PA-31-310 Navajo	31-343	(OY-BKE)
	(Instructional airframe at Nykoping)		N9258Y
SE-FLR	Rockwell Commander 112A	328	(N1328J)
SE-FLS	Rockwell Commander 112A	350	(N1350J)
SE-FLV	Rockwell Commander 112A *(Sold to Germany)*	416	(N1416J)
SE-FLY	Rockwell Commander 114	14010	
SE-FMA	Cessna 172K *(W/o 5.8.87)*	58872	(LN-VYC)
			N7172G
SE-FMC	Cessna 150K	71529	LN-VYL
			(LN-VYS)
			(N6029G)
SE-FMK	Reims/Cessna F.172M	1237	D-EORE
			N94724
SE-FML	Reims/Cessna FR.172F Rocket	0136	
SE-FMO	Cessna 150H	68537	N22816
SE-FMU	Cessna U.206E Stationair	01478	N1478M
SE-FMX	Cessna A.185E Skywagon	01740	N1986U
SE-FMY	Reims/Cessna F.172M *(W/o 28.6.94)*	0907	
SE-FMZ	Cessna 182P Skylane	61431	N21126
SE-FNA	de Havilland DH.82A Tiger Moth	82003	D-EMWT
			D-EMVE
			N6730
SE-FNB	Beech A24R Sierra	MC-86	
SE-FNC	Robin HR.100-210 Safari	180	LN-BIW
			SE-FNC
			(G-BAYM)
SE-FNE	Piper PA-31-350 Navajo Chieftain	31-7405434	N54306
SE-FNK	Beech 95-B55 Baron *(W/o 15.6.84)*	TC-1373	
SE-FNN	DHC-1 Chipmunk 22	C1/0252	G-BCBF
	(Dbf 13.4.76)		WD309
SE-FNO	Cessna U.206A Stationair	0561	LN-DBS
			N4861F
SE-FNP	DHC-1 Chipmunk 22	C1/0756	G-BCYA
			WP867
SE-FNY	Beech 60 Duke *(W/o 6.10.90)*	P-10	D-ILVY
			N7204D
			D-ILVY
			N7204D
SE-FNZ	Beech 95-B55 Baron	TC-933	OH-BBZ
			SE-FNZ
			N354RJ

Regn.	Type	C/n	Prev.Id.
SE-FOG	Beagle B.121 Pup 150 (W/o 13.12.79)	045	G-AXCW / G-35-045
SE-FOK	Beagle B.121 Pup 150	086	G-AXID
SE-FOO	DHC-1 Chipmunk 22	C1/0676	G-BBWM / WP785
SE-FPC	Piper PA-28-140 Cherokee C	28-26723	OY-ANR / SE-FPC
SE-FPD	Piper PA-28-140 Cherokee C	28-26511	
SE-FPI	Piper PA-28-140 Cherokee C	28-26838	
SE-FPK	Piper PA-25-260 Pawnee C (W/o 3.7.77)	25-5199	N8753L
SE-FPL	Piper PA-23-250 Aztec D	27-4552	
SE-FPM	Piper PA-28-140 Cherokee D (W/o 10.2.79)	28-7125046	
SE-FPO	Piper PA-28R-180 Cherokee Arrow	28R-31263	N3292R
SE-FPP	Piper PA-28-140 Cherokee F (W/o 2.1.79)	28-7325017	
SE-FPR	Piper PA-25-260 Pawnee C (W/o 26.10.71)	25-5280	(CC-PGM) / N8793L
SE-FPS	Piper PA-18-150 Super Cub (W/o 31.7.95)	18-8733	LN-LMS
SE-FPT	Piper PA-28-140 Cherokee D	28-712172	
SE-FPV	Piper PA-28-140 Cherokee D	28-7125156	
SE-FRC	Cessna 310Q (Instructional airframe)	0119	OY-BFG / SE-FRC / N7619Q
SE-FRD	Cessna 414	0085	N8181Q
SE-FRE	Reims/Cessna FA.150K Aerobat	0067	
SE-FRF	Cessna 185D Skywagon	0909	LN-HHS / N1548F
SE-FRG	Cessna U.206D Stationair	01254	N72016
SE-FRM	Cessna U.206E Stationair (W/o 1.8.81)	01453	LN-BEV / N1453M
SE-FRN	Reims/Cessna F.150J	0414	LN-AEC
SE-FRP	Cessna U.206F Stationair	01970	(N51012)
SE-FRR	Cessna A.185F Skywagon (W/o 9.8.97)	02160	(N70416)
SE-FRV	Reims/Cessna F.172F	0101	OY-TRN
SE-FRY	Cessna 185C Skywagon	0661	OH-CSS / N2661Z
SE-FRZ	Cessna A.185E Skywagon (W/o 23.876.)	01772	LN-AED / (LN-BEA) / N5803J
SE-FSA	SOCATA MS.893A Rallye Commodore 180	10719	OY-DKR
SE-FSD	SOCATA MS.880B Rallye Club	1698	
SE-FSE	SOCATA MS.880B Rallye Club	1732	
SE-FSF	SOCATA MS.893A Rallye Commodore 180	11819	
SE-FSG	SOCATA MS.880B Rallye Club	1864	
SE-FSM	SOCATA MS.880B Rallye Club	1916	
SE-FSN	SOCATA MS.893A Rallye Commodore 180	11926	
SE-FSO	SOCATA MS.892A Rallye Commodore 150	11944	
SE-FSP	SOCATA MS.892A Rallye Commodore 150	11945	
SE-FSR	SOCATA MS.892A Rallye Commodore 150	12035	
SE-FSU	SOCATA MS.894A Minerva 220	12076	
SE-FSY	SOCATA MS.893A Rallye Commodore 180	12103	
SE-FSZ	SOCATA MS.880B Rallye Club	2409	F-BUZJ
SE-FTP	Aero Commander 680E (W/o 25.7.90)	623-1	HB-GOR / D-IBUC / N6235B
SE-FTT	American-Aviation AA-1A Trainer	0195	OY-AYJ / N9295L
SE-FTV	American-Aviation AA-5 Traveler	0422	N7122L
SE-FTY	Aerotek Pitts S-2A (W/o 20.5.95)	2049	G-BAPU
SE-FTZ	Gardan GY-80 Horizon 180	173	OY-DDG
SE-FUO	Maule M-4-210C Rocket (W/o 4.10.82)	1086C	
SE-FUR	Ryan Navion 4	4-1818	HB-ESF / N4818K
SE-FUT	Tipsy T.66 Nipper II	53	HB-SVI
SE-FUU	Bellanca 7ECA Citabria	809-71	
SE-FUV	Maule M-4-220C Strata Rocket	2122C	
SE-FUX	Mooney M.20B Mark 21	1780	D-ELER
SE-FUZ	North American AT-6A Harvard	14-526	Fv16144 / FE792 / 42-12279
SE-FVP	BAe. Jetstream Series 3102	719	G-BTXG / OK-RFJ / G-BTXG / OY-EEC / G-BTXG, N418MX, G-31-719
SE-FXB	Cessna 182N Skylane	60529	N8989G
SE-FXC	Reims/Cessna F.172F	0103	OH-CSJ
SE-FXP	Cessna U.206F Stationair (sold to Norway .97)	01779	N9579G
SE-FXR	Reims/Cessna F.172L	0830	
SE-FXT	Reims/Cessna F.172L	0856	
SE-FXV	Cessna 182P Skylane	61259	N20853
SE-FYC	Piper PA-28-140 Cherokee D	28-7125167	
SE-FYF	Piper PA-28-140 Cherokee E (W/o 11.10.78)	28-7225144	
SE-FYG	Piper PA-25-260 Pawnee C	25-5328	N8907L
SE-FYH	Piper PA-25-260 Pawnee C (W/o 8.6.72)	25-5351	N8840L
SE-FYK	Piper PA-18-150 Super Cub	18-8777	LN-BNY
SE-FYL	Piper PA-28-140 Cherokee E	28-7225145	
SE-FYN	Piper PA-28-180 Cherokee F	28-7105152	
SE-FYO	Piper PA-28-140 Cherokee E	28-7225196	
SE-FYS	Piper PA-28-180 Cherokee Challenger	28-7305009	
SE-FYT	Piper PA-28-140 Cherokee E	28-7225178	
SE-FYZ	Piper PA-28-140 Cherokee F (W/o 18.2.79)	28-7325006	
SE-FZE	Cessna 182P Skylane (W/o 21.11.89)	61597	N21379
SE-FZK	Cessna 402A (W/o 8.5.82)	0057	OY-AGN / N4557Q
SE-FZL	Cessna 414	0382	G-BARE / N1602T
SE-FZO	Reims/Cessna F.172M	1145	
SE-FZS	Reims/Cessna F.172M	1132	
SE-FZU	Reims/Cessna F.172M	1036	
SE-FZY	Reims/Cessna F.172M	1024	(D-EJXU)
SE-FZZ	Reims/Cessna F.177RG Cardinal RG	0099	
SE-GAD	Piper PA-34-200 Seneca	34-7350211	(SE-LCA) / OH-PNE / SE-GAD
SE-GAF	Piper PA-28-140 Cherokee E (W/o 30.7.82)	28-7225292	
SE-GAL	Piper PA-28-180 Cherokee G	28-7205256	
SE-GAN	Piper PA-28-180 Cherokee G	28-7205251	
SE-GAO	Piper PA-34-200 Seneca	34-7250224	LN-AED / SE-GAO
SE-GAT	Piper PA-28-180 Cherokee Challenger	28-7305420	
SE-GAU	Piper PA-28-180 Cherokee Archer	28-7405015	
SE-GAV	Piper PA-28-180 Cherokee Archer	28-7405203	
SE-GAZ	Piper PA-28-140 Cherokee F	28-7325216	
SE-GBB	Piper PA-28-180 Cherokee Challenger	28-7305486	(OY-BGH)
SE-GBE	Piper PA-28-151 Cherokee Warrior	28-7415071	
SE-GBF	Piper PA-25-235/260C Pawnee	25-7305529	N8925L
SE-GBG	Piper PA-31-310 Navajo	31-7401234	
SE-GBH	Piper PA-28-151 Cherokee Warrior	28-7415307	
SE-GBK	Piper PA-32-260 Cherokee Six E (accident 18.8.95)	32-7400027	
SE-GBL	Piper PA-34-200 Seneca	34-7450147	
SE-GBM	Piper PA-28-151 Cherokee Warrior	28-7415339	
SE-GBO	Piper PA-31-310 Navajo	31-7400983	
SE-GBP	Piper PA-28-151 Cherokee Warrior	28-7415582	
SE-GBR	Piper PA-28-151 Cherokee Warrior	28-7415587	
SE-GBV	Piper PA-28-151 Cherokee Warrior	28-7415650	
SE-GBY	Piper PA-28-151 Cherokee Warrior	28-7515027	
SE-GBZ	Piper PA-32-260 Cherokee Six D	32-7200006	N8668N
SE-GCB	Piper PA-18-150 Super Cub	18-8542	Army:51235
SE-GCC	Piper PA-18-150 Super Cub	18-8544	Army:51236
SE-GCD	Piper PA-18-150 Super Cub	18-8545	Army:51237
SE-GCF	Piper PA-18-150 Super Cub	18-8600	Army:51239
SE-GCG	Piper PA-18-150 Super Cub	18-8441	Army:51241
SE-GCH	Piper PA-18-150 Super Cub	18-8361	Army:51242
SE-GCI	Piper PA-18-150 Super Cub	18-8363	Army:51244
SE-GCK	Piper PA-18-150 Super Cub	18-7918	Army:51245
SE-GCL	Piper PA-18-150 Super Cub	18-7919	Army:51246
SE-GCM	Piper PA-18-150 Super Cub	18-7920	Army:51247
SE-GCN	Piper PA-18-150 Super Cub (W/o 16.3.75)	18-7921	Army:51248
SE-GCR	Piper PA-18-150 Super Cub	18-6806	Army:51254 / SE-CKL
SE-GCV	Reims/Cessna F.337G Skymaster	0068/01583	OH-CGN
SE-GCY	Cessna 150M	76410	N3179V
SE-CDB	Piper PA-28-180 Cherokee Challenger	28-7305304	
SE-GDD	Piper PA-28-140 Cherokee Cruiser (W/o 29.8.82)	28-7425411	
SE-GDE	Piper PA-28R-200 Cherokee Arrow	28R-7335160	
SE-GDG	Piper PA-28-140 Cherokee F	28-7325205	

Regn.	Type	C/n	Prev.Id.
SE-GDL	Piper PA-28-151 Cherokee Warrior	28-7415303	
SE-GDM	Piper PA-28-180 Cherokee Challenger	28-7305529	
SE-GDN	Piper PA-31-310 Navajo (W/o 12.99)	31-7300947	
SE-GDV	Piper PA-32-260 Cherokee Six E	32-7400029	
SE-GEE	DHC-6 Twin Otter 300	364	F-GFAH / SE-GEE / D-IDOT
SE-GEH	Cessna 402B (W/o 28.11.88)	1351	N6388X
SE-GEI	Grumman-American AA-5A Cheetah	0604	LN-KLE
SE-GEL	Cessna R.172K Hawk XP (W/o)	2879	N736XW
SE-GEM	Cessna 185D (W/o 26.5.79)	0827	LN-BIE / N10F / N4087F
SE-GEN	Cessna 180B	50510	LN-TSH / N5210E
SE-GES	Cessna A.185E Skywagon	1467	LN-RTN / N2717J
SE-GET	Cessna U.206F Stationair	01959	LN-BFI / N50950
SE-GEV	Bellanca 8GCBC Scout (W/o 25.6.83)	199-76	LN-HOA
SE-GFA	SOCATA MS.894A Minerva 220	12004	(D-ENML)
SE-GFB	SOCATA MS.893A Rallye Commodore 180	10944	OY-DJH / SE-CIY
SE-GFE	SOCATA Rallye 180T Galérien	3243	
SE-GFF	SOCATA Rallye 180T Galérien	3244	
SE-GFH	SOCATA TB-10 Tobago	45	F-ODMH
SE-GFI	SOCATA TB-9 Tampico	81	OH-TBB / SE-GFI
SE-GFN	Partenavia P.68B (W/o 20.4.87)	56	
SE-GFO	SOCATA TB-10 Tobago	79	
SE-GFP	SOCATA TB-10 Tobago (W/o 1.7.95)	159	
SE-GFR	SOCATA TB-10 Tobago (W/o 8.7.91)	160	
SE-GFT	SOCATA TB-9 Tampico	180	
SE-GFX	SOCATA TB-10 Tobago (Under rebuild)	264	F-OGLR
SE-GGB	Reims/Cessna F.172M	1046	
SE-GGK	Cessna A.185F	02456	N1736R
SE-GGO	Reims/Cessna F.172M	1171	OY-BFT
SE-GGP	Reims/Cessna F.150L	1128	(D-EOQC)
SE-GGU	Cessna 402B	0109	D-IDAL / N7859Q
SE-GGX	Reims/Cessna F.172M	1326	
SE-GHA	Mitsubishi MU.2B-20	283	N327MA
SE-GHB	Mitsubishi MU.2B-20	287	N331MA
SE-GHC	Mitsubishi MU.2B-20	289	N334MA
SE-GHD	Mitsubishi MU.2B-20	293	N453MA
SE-GHE	Mitsubishi MU.2B-20	294	N454MA
SE-GHF	Mitsubishi MU.2B-20	299	N459MA
SE-GHH	Mitsubishi MU.2B-20	222	N5PN / N4PN / N188MA
SE-GHI	Bellanca 8KCAB Decathlon (W/o 18.2.80)	486-79	
SE-GHL	Robin R.2100A	172	
SE-GHO	Cessna R.182 Skylane RG (W/o 27.8.87)	00287	N3630C
SE-GHR	Maule M-5-235C Lunar Rocket (W/o 24.6.83)	7257C	
SE-GIC	Piper PA-34-200T Seneca II	34-7570028	LN-KLK / (LN-KLS) / SE-GIC
SE-GIE	Piper PA-28-151 Cherokee Warrior	28-7515107	
SE-GII	Piper PA-28-151 Cherokee Warrior	28-7515216	
SE-GIK	Piper PA-28-180 Cherokee Archer	28-7505095	(N . . . . .) / SE-GIK
SE-GIL	Piper PA-28-140 Cherokee Cruiser	28-7525116	
SE-GIN	Piper PA-31-310 Navajo	31-7512039	
SE-GIO	Piper PA-28-180 Cherokee Archer	28-7505131	
SE-GIP	Piper PA-34-200T Seneca II	34-7570210	
SE-GIR	Piper PA-28R-200 Cherokee Arrow	28R-7535140	
SE-GIS	Piper PA-31-310 Navajo (W/o 30.6.83)	31-7512028	
SE-GIT	Piper PA-31-310 Navajo	31-7512041	
SE-GIX	Piper PA-28R-200 Cherokee Arrow (W/o 25.7.96)	28R-7435106	N54448
SE-GIZ	Piper PA-28-180 Cherokee Archer	28-7505015	N32009
SE-GKC	Reims/Cessna F.150M	1216	
SE-GKD	Reims/Cessna F.172M	1228	
SE-GKE	Reims/Cessna F.172M	1230	
SE-GKF	Reims/Cessna F.172M	1231	
SE-GKO	Reims/Cessna F.172M	1223	
SE-GKR	Cessna 337A Skymaster	0365	D-GIPY / (N6365F)
SE-GKT	Reims/Cessna F.172M	1329	
SE-GKY	Reims/Cessna F.172M	1215	OY-BID
SE-GKZ	Reims/Cessna F.172M	1332	OY-BIF
SE-GLC	Piper PA-28-180 Cherokee Archer	28-7505241	
SE-GLE	Piper PA-31-310 Navajo	31-7512056	
SE-GLH	Piper PA-28-181 Cherokee Archer II	28-7790159	
SE-GLR	Piper PA-28-181 Cherokee Archer II (W/o 12.7.84)	28-7690040	
SE-GLS	Piper PA-28-181 Cherokee Archer II (W/o 11.2.93)	28-7690076	
SE-GLU	Piper PA-28-151 Cherokee Warrior	28-7615031	
SE-GMA	Reims/Cessna F.172M	1463	
SE-GMC	Reims/Cessna F.172M	1456	
SE-GMD	Reims/Cessna F.172M	1430	
SE-GME	Reims/Cessna F.177RG Cardinal RG	0143	
SE-GMF	Reims/Cessna F.150M (W/o 25.9.87)	1288	
SE-GMI	Cessna A.185F Skywagon	02583	N4638C
SE-GMK	Cessna U.206F Stationair	03256	(N8395Q)
SE-GMM	Reims/Cessna F.337G Super Skymaster	01676/0077	
SE-GMN	Reims/Cessna FRA.150M Aerobat	0286	
SE-GMO	Cessna 402B (Current status unknown)	0809	LN-AED / N3817C
SE-GMS	Reims/Cessna F.150M	1315	
SE-GMT	Reims/Cessna F.150M	1320	
SE-GMU	Reims/Cessna F.172M	1481	
SE-GNA	Piper PA-31-310 Navajo	31-7612034	N9721N
SE-GNE	Piper PA-28-181 Cherokee Archer II	28-7690148	
SE-GNF	Piper PA-28-181 Cherokee Archer II	28-7690149	
SE-GNG	Piper PA-28-151 Cherokee Warrior	28-7615216	
SE-GNH	Piper PA-28-181 Cherokee Archer II (W/o 22.5.79)	28-7690226	
SE-GNL	Piper PA-28-151 Cherokee Warrior	28-7615280	
SE-GNN	Piper PA-28-181 Cherokee Archer II (W/o 1.2.96)	28-7690347	
SE-GNR	Piper PA-32R-300 Lance	32R-7680252	N75053
SE-GNS	Piper PA-28-151 Cherokee Warrior	28-7615340	
SE-GNU	Piper PA-28-181 Cherokee Archer II (W/o 28.1.95)	28-7690466	
SE-GNV	Piper PA-32R-300 Lance	32R-7680221	N9430K
SE-GOA	Cessna A.185F Skywagon	02603	N4853C
SE-GOB	Reims/Cessna F.172M	1175	D-EDJQ
SE-GOH	Cessna A.185F Skywagon	03079	N29070
SE-GOL	Cessna A.185F (W/o 19.9.83)	02900	N8712Z
SE-GON	Cessna 172M	67511	N73501
SE-GOO	Cessna U.206F Stationair (W/o 23.5.84)	03491	N8738Q
SE-GOP	Cessna U.206G Stationair II	03528	(N8776Q)
SE-GOR	Reims/Cessna F.172M	1050	G-BBKH
SE-GOY	Cessna A.185F Skywagon	03170	N93040
SE-GOZ	Cessna A.185F Skywagon	02994	N5065R
SE-GPC	Piper PA-28-151 Cherokee Warrior	28-7715241	
SE-GPD	Piper PA-28-151 Cherokee Warrior	28-7715242	
SE-GPE	Piper PA-28-181 Cherokee Archer II	28-7790232	
SE-GPF	Piper PA-18-150 Super Cub	18-7709057	
SE-GPG	Piper PA-18-150 Super Cub	18-7709068	
SE-GPH	Piper PA-28-161 Cherokee Warrior II	28-7716116	
SE-GPL	Piper PA-28-181 Cherokee Archer II	28-7790291	
SE-GPN	Piper PA-28-161 Cherokee Warrior II	28-7716051	N9602N
SE-GPO	Piper PA-28-181 Cherokee Archer II	28-7790373	
SE-GPR	Piper PA-28-161 Cherokee Warrior II	28-7716120	N9630N
SE-GPT	Piper PA-28R-201 Cherokee Arrow	28R-7737014	
SE-GPU	Piper PA-28-161 Cherokee Warrior II	28-7716200	
SE-GPX	Piper PA-34-200T Seneca II	34-7770290	N9538N
SE-GRA	de Havilland DH.104 Dove 6	04437	G-AMZN
SE-GRD	Lake LA-4-200 Buccaneer	499	OH-AKA / N5042L
SE-GRE	Beech A23-24 Musketeer Super	MA-164	OH-BMF
SE-GRG	Maule M-5-210C Strata Rocket	6166C	
SE-GRK	DHC-1 Chipmunk 22	C1/0104	RDAF: P-125
SE-GRL	Lake LA-4-200 Buccaneer	837	N6184V
SE-GRN	Lake LA-4-200 Buccaneer	778	N6025V

Regn.	Type	C/n	Prev.Id.
SE-GRO	Maule M-5-235C Lunar Rocket (Damaged 16.8.97)	7069C	
SE-GRS	Lake LA-4-200 Buccaneer	826	TF-GRS (SE-GRS) N6173V
SE-GRV	Maule M-5-235C Lunar Rocket	7080C	
SE-GRZ	Piper PA-32R-300 Lance	32R-7680231	N9586K
SE-GSE	Rockwell Commander 112B	508	
SE-GSF	Rockwell Commander 112B	537	
SE-GSH	Rockwell Commander 112B	544	
SE-GSS	Rockwell Commander 690C	11613	D-IBOB (N5865K)
SE-GST	Thrush Commander S2R-T34 (W/o 3.6.82)	1723R	OH-VKY N5523X
SE-GSV	Robin R.2100A	157	
SE-GSY	Robin HR.200/100 Club	107	
SE-GTD	SOCATA Rallye 100ST	2908	
SE-GTG	SOCATA MS.892E Rallye 150T	2969	
SE-GTI	SOCATA MS.893E Rallye 180GT Gaillard	12846	
SE-GTL	Cessna 172N	69254	N734ZW
SE-GTM	Cessna U.206G Stationair II	03731	N9930N
SE-GTN	SOCATA MS.892E Rallye 180T	3133	
SE-GTO	Thurston TSC-1A2 Teal II	31	N2031T
SE-GTP	SOCATA MS.892E Rallye 180T	3092	
SE-GTZ	Piper PA-18-150 Super Cub (f/n 18-494 quoted officially - rebuilt using parts of PH-NGU c/n 18-5538)	18-559	PH-LUD PH-GAV(1) R-208 51-15673 N7188K
SE-GUA	Piper PA-23-250 Aztec D	27-4523	D-IETT N13887
SE-GUD	Reims/Cessna F.172H	0491	OY-AGE
SE-GUF	Cessna U.206G Stationair II	03596	N7272N
SE-GUN	Cessna A.185E (W/o 28.8.83)	1461	LN-BFU (N2711J)
SE-GUO	Aero Commander 680 (W/o 7.7.94)	535-204	C-FFAC CF-FAC N1333
SE-GUP	Reims/Cessna F.172H	0672	OH-CBS
SE-GUS	Bellanca 7GCBC Citabria	1029-78	
SE-GUT	Reims/Cessna FR.172J Rocket	0373	OH-CFR
SE-GUV	Bellanca 8KCAB Decathlon	409-78	
SE-GUY	Bellanca 8GCBC Scout	228-76	N7833S
SE-GUZ	Grumman-American AA-5B Tiger	0831	
SE-GVA	Piper PA-28R-201 Arrow	28R-7837027	
SE-GVB	Piper PA-28-161 Cherokee Warrior II	28-7816195	
SE-GVD	Piper PA-28-161 Cherokee Warrior II	28-7816196	
SE-GVE	Piper PA-28-161 Cherokee Warrior II	28-7816164	
SE-GVG	Piper PA-28-181 Cherokee Archer II (W/o 11.3.92)	28-7890202	
SE-GVH	Piper PA-38-112 Tomahawk (CofA exp 5.81 - parts to G-BLNN/38-78A0505)	38-78A0053	
SE-GVI	Piper PA-32RT-300 Lance	32R-7885129	
SE-GVR	Piper PA-28R-200 Cherokee Arrow	28R-7535014	OH-PAA
SE-GVS	Piper PA-28-161 Cherokee Warrior II	28-7816436	
SE-GVT	Piper PA-28-161 Cherokee Warrior II	28-7816435	
SE-GVU	Piper PA-28-181 Cherokee Archer II	28-7890467	
SE-GVV	Piper PA-28R-201 Arrow	28R-7837213	
SE-GVX	Piper PA-28-181 Cherokee Archer II	28-7890524	
SE-GVY	Piper PA-28-181 Cherokee Archer II	28-7890427	
SE-GVZ	Piper PA-31-310 Navajo	31-7812079	
SE-GXB	Cessna U.206G Stationair II	04497	N756ZX
SE-GXI	Mooney M.20J Model 201	24-0844	
SE-GXU	Maule M-5-235C Lunar Rocket	7324C	
SE-GXY	Cessna 182P Skylane	63554	OY-ANT N5820J
SE-GYB	Reims/Cessna F.172N	1552	
SE-GYE	Reims/Cessna F.172N	1687	
SE-GYH	Reims/Cessna F.172N	1700	
SE-GYI	Reims/Cessna F.182Q Skylane	0072	
SE-GYO	Reims/Cessna F.172N	1740	
SE-GYR	Cessna U.206G Stationair II	04218	N756NF
SE-GYT	Reims/Cessna F.172N	1780	
SE-GYV	Reims/Cessna F.152	1586	(OE-CFC)
SE-GYX	Reims/Cessna F.172N	1794	
SE-GYY	Reims/Cessna F.172N	1820	
SE-GYZ	Reims/Cessna F.172N	1791	
SE-GZM	Reims/Cessna FR.172K Rocket	0600	
SE-GZO	Cessna 210M Centurion (W/o 18.4.86)	61767	N732TS
SE-GZP	Reims/Cessna F.150M	1287	(F-BXQY) (F-BXQO)
SE-GZR	Reims/Cessna F.182P Skylane	0018	
SE-GZS	Cessna 150J	70373	OH-CBD N60523
SE-GZT	Reims/Cessna FA.150K Aerobat	0027	OH-CBT
SE-GZU	Reims/Cessna FR.172G Rocket	0178	OH-CDZ
SE-GZV	Reims/Cessna FR.172E Rocket	0005	OH-CCM F-WLIO
SE-HAL	Agusta-Bell 47G-2	016	(LN-OTS) OH-HIG SE-HAL
SE-HBP	Bell 47G-5 (W/o 30.9.74)	7954	
SE-HCA	Bell 47G-2	1492	N2819B
SE-HCB	Agusta-Bell 47J-2	1026	(LN-OQF) (LN-OPL) SE-HCB
SE-HCM	Hughes 269B	98-0388	
SE-HCN	Hughes 269B	98-0389	LN-OSL SE-HCN
SE-HCW	Hughes 269B (W/o 25.7.75)	116-0276	N9480F
SE-HDD	Sud SE.3130 Alouette II (HKP-2)	1177	Fv84002
SE-HDL	Hughes 269C (CofA exp 11.87)	11-0084	
SE-HEE	Agusta-Bell 206A Jet Ranger II	8285	
SE-HEH	Bell 206B JetRanger II	734	N2915W
SE-HEI	Agusta-Bell 206B Jet Ranger II	8348	
SE-HEL	Agusta-Bell 206B Jet Ranger II	8332	
SE-HEM	Agusta-Bell 206B Jet Ranger II	8329	
SE-HEO	Bell 47G-2 (H-13E)	600	LN-OQE D-HIFI 51-13959
SE-HEV	Enstrom F-28A	085	
SE-HEX	Enstrom F-28A	084	
SE-HFL	Hughes 369HS (W/o 15.9.82)	74-0618S	
SE-HFN	Hughes 269C (Dbr 13.8.79)	75-0420	
SE-HFT	Hughes 369HS	15-0692S	LN-OTT SE-HFT
SE-HFU	Enstrom F-28A	310	OY-HBO
SE-HFV	Enstrom F-28A (W/o 8.8.81)	296	OY-HBN
SE-HFZ	Enstrom F-28A	108	
SE-HGC	Bell 47G-4	3346	OH-HIZ SE-HGC OH-HIZ SE-HGC G-BCCM N1193W
SE-HGY	Aérospatiale SA.315B Lama	2443	
SE-HGZ	Sikorsky S-55T (W/o 9.6.81)	55-1252	N62540 MM575981 57-5981
SE-HHF	Hughes 369D (W/o 24.8.91)	116-0049D	
SE-HHN	Enstrom F-28A (W/o 17.8.78)	295	OY-HBL
SE-HHO	Enstrom F-28A	379	
SE-HHT	Enstrom F-28C (W/o 23.7.79)	429	
SE-HHX	Hughes 269C	127-0654	
SE-HIC	Air & Space 18A (W/o 1.7.87)	18-73	N6161S
SE-HII	Agusta-Bell 206B Jet Ranger II	8290	D-HEPY
SE-HIK	Hiller UH-12B	676	OH-HHE N8504 Neth: O-17 54-863
SE-HIM	Bell 206B Jet Ranger II	2544	
SE-HIN	Hughes 269C	128-0749	
SE-HIO	Enstrom F-28C (W/o 19.8.89)	425	N51754
SE-HIT	Bell 205A-1	30286	N5015F
SE-HIU	Agusta-Bell 206B Jet Ranger II (W/o 25.6.86)	8537	G-BFGT
SE-HIZ	Enstrom F-28A	225	N9250
SE-HKA	Enstrom 280C Shark	1184	
SE-HKC	Bell 206L-1 Long Ranger II	45321	
SE-HKF	Hughes 269C	89-0821	

Regn.	Type	C/n	Prev.Id.
SE-HKI	Hiller UH-12B *(W/o 11.6.90)*	743	OH-HHD / N8507 / Neth: O-15 / 54-2949
SE-HKK	Agusta-Bell 206B Jet Ranger III (HKP-6A)	8603	Army: 06283/804 / SE-HKK
SE-HKL	Enstrom 280C Shark	1134	OH-HLK
SE-HKM	Hughes 269C *(W/o 3.11.84)*	129-0873	
SE-HKP	Bell 206B Jet Ranger II	2987	LN-OSM / SE-HKP
SE-HKR	Bell 206L-1 Long Ranger II	45444	
SE-HLA	Hughes 369D	50-0718D	OH-HLA / SE-HLA / OY-HSA / SE-HLA
SE-HLE	Bell 214B-1	28054	LN-ORM / SE-HLE
SE-HLI	Hughes 369D	120-0879D	
SE-HLK	Agusta-Bell 206A Jet Ranger	8047	LN-ORY
SE-HLP	Hughes 369D	61-0986D	
SE-HLR	Hughes 369D	51-0987D	LN-OSR / SE-HLR
SE-HLS	Aérospatiale SA.360C Dauphin	1016	F-BZAQ / F-WZAQ / F-WXFB / C-GLJQ
SE-HMK	Hughes 269C	46-0490	D-HHEI
SE-HMM	Aérospatiale AS.350B Ecureuil	1693	
SE-HMO	Bell 206L-1 Long Ranger II	46605	G-JAMI / N18090
SE-HMS	Bell 205A-1	30256	N16750
SE-HMT	Bell 205A-1	30180	N68HJ / PK-... / AMDB-111
SE-HMY	Hughes 269C *(W/o 16.12.88)*	1154	
SE-HNB	Hughes 269C	80-0036	PH-HEH / D-HKIS / OO-JJS
SE-HND	Hughes 269C *(W/o 25.1.87)*	1155	
SE-HNL	Hughes 369D *(W/o 5.12.86)*	89-0557D	EC-DIX
SE-HNR	Enstrom F-28F	739	
SE-HNT	Hughes 369E	0146E	LN-OTU / SE-HNT / LN-OMY / SE-HNT
SE-HNU	Hiller UH-12B	510	G-ASVH / XB474 / BuA134724
SE-HNZ	Hughes 369E *(W/o 8.7.91)*	0157E	LN-OMV
SE-HOK	Bell 206B Jet Ranger II	1693	N73DH / N13SG
SE-HOM	Bell 206B Jet Ranger II	2394	N48EA / N119AL
SE-HOO	Enstrom 280C Shark	1056	G-MEAD / N581H
SE-HOT	Agusta-Bell 206B Jet Ranger II	8094	LN-OQA / SE-HEP / G-AWOY / G-HOVA / G-BEYR
SE-HOY	Enstrom 280C Shark	1064	A40-AR / N49644
SE-HOZ	Bell 206B Jet Ranger II	1827	
SE-HPA	Agusta-Bell 47G-4	2511	
SE-HPG	Bell 47G-5A	25081	
SE-HPH	Bell 206B Jet Ranger II	1005	
SE-HPK	Bell 206B Jet Ranger II	1091	
SE-HPL	Bell 206L-1 Long Ranger II	45212	
SE-HPM	Bell 206L-1 Long Ranger II	45425	
SE-HPN	Bell 206L-1 Long Ranger II	45320	
SE-HPO	Bell 206L-1 Long Ranger II	45533	
SE-HPP	Bell 206L-1 Long Ranger II	45745	
SE-HRA	SE.3130 Alouette II (HKP-2)	1268	Navy 02038
SE-HRC	SE.3130 Alouette II (HKP-2)	1128	Navy 02039 / N7808B / YV-E-FPJ / F-WIEK
SE-HRE	Bell 206B Jet Ranger II	642	N7905J
SE-HRF	Hughes 269C	36-0479	N7438F
SE-HRH	Schweizer 269C	S-1227	LN-OTW / SE-HRH / (SE-HRN) / N41S
SE-HRK	Hughes 369D	1187D	LN-OPM / SE-HRK / LN-OMT / SE-HMN
SE-HRM	Bell 206B Jet Ranger II	2323	N21CK / N16936
SE-HRO	Aérospatiale AS.350B Ecureuil	1533	D-HHSB
SE-HRP	Schweizer 269C	S-1237	N41S
SE-HSB	Schweizer 269C	S-1262	N69A
SE-HSC	Schweizer 269C	S-1263	LN-OTW / SE-HSC / N41S
SE-HSG	MBB-Bölkow BO.105C (HKP-9A)	S-439	Army-09077 / D-HDMM
SE-HSI	Hughes 369D	81-1041D	D-HAFE(2) / SE-HSI / N50867
SE-HSN	Hughes 369E	0181E	OY-HEW
SE-HSP	Aérospatiale SA.315B Lama	2604	LN-OTB
SE-HST	Schweizer 269C	S-1290	N41S
SE-HSU	Schweizer 269C	S-1293	LN-OTM / SE-HSU / N69A
SE-HSY	Enstrom 280C Shark	2020	
SE-HTC	Bell 206B Jet Ranger II	3153	D-HBAD / N5759Q
SE-HTP	Bell 206B Jet Ranger II	1717	N49592
SE-HTR	Bell 206L Long Ranger	45395	C-GLMO
SE-HTU	Schweizer 269C	S-1353	N69A
SE-HTV	Bell 206B Jet Ranger II	4049	
SE-HUB	Bell 206L-3 Long Ranger III	51304	C-FGDY
SE-HUC	Bell 206L-3 Long Ranger III	51310	
SE-HUE	Bell 206L Long Ranger	45009	OH-HKR / SE-HUE / D-HAFV / F-BXPH / N49682
SE-HUF	Bell 206L-3 Long Ranger III	51348	N80EA / G-BVIB / SE-HUF / C-FHZY
SE-HUI	Enstrom 280C Shark	1033	N999NJ
SE-HUK	Enstrom F-28C	459	N4953M / C-GAIK / N5687J
SE-HUM	Aérospatiale SA.318C Alouette Astazou	2189	N8264
SE-HUO	Aérospatiale AS.350B Ecureuil	1867	D-HHLL
SE-HUP	Schweizer 269C	S-1356	N69A
SE-HUU	Hughes 369D *(W/o 11.4.94)*	109-0594D	OY-HCJ
SE-HVA	Hughes 369HS *(W/o 27.8.96)*	61-0323S	OY-HSE / N1040Z / RP-C1146 / PI-C1146
SE-HVE	Bell 206B Jet Ranger II	2949	G-OFAB / N22AB / N5734X
SE-HVI	Bell 206L-3 Long Ranger III	51407	
SE-HVM	Agusta-Bell AB.204B	3211	OH-HAK / LN-ORZ
SE-HVN	Aérospatiale AS.350B1 Ecureuil	2157	HB-XSA
SE-HVS	Schweizer 269C	S-1418	N426MS
SE-HVU	Schweizer 269C	S-1446	N41S
SE-HVY	Hughes 369D	97-0188D	VR-HPC / VR-HHM(2) / N9550F

615

Regn.	Type	C/n	Prev.Id.
SE-HVZ	Robinson R-22 Mariner	0436M	N85351
SE-HXA	Humlan Autogyro	001	
SE-HXB	Humlan Autogyro *(Reservation)*	unkn	
SE-HXE	Humlan Autogyro	003	
SE-HXH	Humlan Autogyro	05	
SE-HXI	Humlan Autogyro	12	
SE-HXK	Hollmann HA-2M Sportster *(Permit)*	65	
SE-HXL	Humlan Autogyro	31	
SE-HXN	Hollmann HA-2M Sportster	121	
SE-HXO	Humlan Autogyro	14-56	
SE-HXP	Tervamaki JT-5 *(Reservation)*	61	
SE-HXR	Humlan Autogyro *(Reservation)*	37	
SE-HXT	Humlan Autogyro *(Reservation)*	unkn	
SE-HXU	Humlan Autogyro *(Reservation)*	unkn	
SE-HXV	Humlan Autogyro *(Reservation)*	24	
SE-HXX	Humlan Autogyro *(Reservation)*	48	
SE-HXY	Humlan Autogyro *(Reservation)*	26	
SE-HXZ	Humlan Autogyro *(Reservation)*	unkn	
SE-HYA	Humlan Autogyro *(Reservation)*	unkn	
SE-HYB	Humlan Autogyro	112-419	
SE-HYC	Humlan Autogyro *(Reservation)*	unkn	
SE-HYD	Humlan Autogyro *(Reservation)*	unkn	
SE-HYE	Humlan Autogyro *(Reservation)*	unkn	
SE-HYF	Humlan Autogyro *(Reservation)*	unkn	
SE-HYG	Humlan Autogyro *(Permit)*	123	
SE-HYH	McCulloch J-2 *(W/o 2.7.95)*	012	N4302G
SE-HYI	Humlan Autogyro	104	
SE-HYK	Humlan Autogyro *(Permit)*	202	
SE-HYL	Barnett J-4B Gyroplane *(Reservation)*	02 N	
SE-HYM	Humlan Autogyro	55	
SE-HYN	Canadian Home Rotors Safari *(Permit)*	172	
SE-HYO	Rotorway Exec 90 *(Permit)*	5021	N4258S
SE-IAA	Piper PA-31-350 Navajo Chieftain *(W/o 23.1.90)*	31-7952113	LN-PAA (SE-ICP)
SE-IAC	Piper PA-31-310 Navajo	31-7812095	
SE-IAD	Piper PA-28-161 Cherokee Warrior II	28-7816599	
SE-IAE	Piper PA-32RT-300T Turbo Lance *(W/o 20.5.91)*	32R-7887183	
SE-IAH	Piper PA-38-112 Tomahawk	38-78A0694	
SE-IAI	Piper PA-38-112 Tomahawk *(W/o 21.7.95)*	38-78A0690	
SE-IAL	Piper PA-28-161 Cherokee Warrior II	28-7816652	
SE-IAM	Piper PA-28-161 Cherokee Warrior II	28-7816651	
SE-IAN	Piper PA-38-112 Tomahawk	38-78A0400	
SE-IAP	Piper PA-28-181 Archer II	28-7990094	
SE-IAR	Piper PA-38-112 Tomahawk	38-79A0265	
SE-IAS	Piper PA-31-310 Navajo	31-7912028	
SE-IAU	Piper PA-28R-201T Turbo Arrow IV	28R-7931046	
SE-IAX	Piper PA-28-161 Warrior II	28-7916200	
SE-IAY	Piper PA-28RT-201 Arrow IV	28R-7918101	
SE-IBC	Reims/Cessna FR.182 Skylane RG	0039	(LN-...) SE-IBC
SE-IBD	Reims/Cessna F.172N	1695	(LN-ALI)
SE-IBG	Reims/Cessna F.172N	1862	(OY-BNJ)
SE-IBK	Reims/Cessna F.182Q Skylane *(W/o 28.12.81)*	0147	
SE-IBO	Cessna 340A	0613	N8674K
SE-IBR	Reims/Cessna F.152	1756	
SE-IBT	Reims/Cessna F.152 *(W/o 29.7.84)*	1761	
SE-IBU	Reims/Cessna F.172N	1923	
SE-IBV	Reims/Cessna F.172N *(Accident 22.7.97)*	1948	
SE-IBX	Reims/Cessna F.172N	1964	
SE-ICA	Piper PA-18-150 Super Cub	18-7909083	
SE-ICE	Piper PA-38-112 Tomahawk	38-79A0744	
SE-ICF	Piper PA-38-112 Tomahawk	38-79A0745	
SE-ICG	Piper PA-38-112 Tomahawk	38-79A0746	
SE-ICL	Piper PA-28-181 Archer II	28-7990371	
SE-ICM	Piper PA-28-181 Archer II	28-7990372	
SE-ICT	Piper PA-28-161 Warrior II	28-7916470	
SE-ICV	Piper PA-28-181 Archer II	28-7990482	
SE-ICZ	Piper PA-18-150 Super Cub	18-8009016	
SE-IDA	Piper PA-18-150 Super Cub	18-8009015	
SE-IDF	Piper PA-28-151 Cherokee Warrior	28-7415243	OH-PDR
SE-IDG	Piper PA-28-161 Warrior II	28-8016259	
SE-IDK	Piper PA-28-181 Archer II	28-8190161	

Regn.	Type	C/n	Prev.Id.
SE-IDR	Piper PA-31-310 Navajo	31-7712085	LN-DAB SE-IDR LN-RAO (LN-RAG) LN-PAG
SE-IDS	Piper PA-28-181 Archer II *(W/o 28.4.89 in mid-air collision with OY-XOR)*	28-8190090	
SE-IDT	Piper PA-32R-301 Saratoga SP	32R-8129026	
SE-IDY	Piper PA-28-161 Warrior II	28-8116220	
SE-IEC	Cessna 172N	70709	LN-HHE N739PZ
SE-IED	Cessna A.185F Amphibian	03320	OH-COW (SE-IED) N124JD (N5075H)
SE-IEE	Gulfstream American AA-5B Tiger *(W/o 27.9.81)*	1140	LN-KLJ
SE-IER	Piper J-3C-65 Cub	19861	OY-DRJ D-EHEC N6657H
SE-IEU	Bellanca 8KCAB Decathlon	563-79	
SE-IEV	Maule M-5-235C Lunar Rocket *(W/o 20.2.83)*	7330C	
SE-IEX	Maule M-5-235C Lunar Rocket *(W/o 7.8.81)*	7332C	
SE-IFB	Reims/Cessna F.172N	2005	
SE-IFC	Cessna 172RG Cutlass	0397	N4837V
SE-IFD	Reims/Cessna F.172N	1864	(LX-SOS)
SE-IFF	Reims/Cessna F.172N	1969	
SE-IFL	Reims/Cessna F.172P	2074	
SE-IFR	Reims/Cessna FR.182 Skylane RG	0047	
SE-IFT	Reims/Cessna F.337H Super Skymaster	0086	N2270G
SE-IFX	Reims/Cessna F.152	1802	
SE-IFZ	Reims/Cessna F.152	1805	
SE-IGB	Piper PA-31P-425 Pressurized Navajo	31P-7300167	OY-CBM D-IGWZ N66805
SE-IGC	Cessna 172N	72979	N1228F
SE-IGE	Reims/Cessna FR.172F Rocket *(W/o in 1986)*	0098	OH-CNT
SE-IGG	Bellanca 8KCAB Decathlon *(W/o 15.5.82)*	605-80	
SE-IGK	SAAB S.91B Safir	91227	Fv50025
SE-IGL	SAAB S.91B Safir	91262	Fv50053
SE-IGM	SAAB S.91B Safir	91256	Fv50044
SE-IGO	SAAB S.91B Safir	91228	Fv50026
SE-IGR	SAAB S.91B Safir	91208	Fv50008
SE-IGT	Cessna TU.206G Turbo Stationair II *(W/o 1.8.89)*	05593	N5204X
SE-IGU	Reims/Cessna F.150H	0294	OH-CND
SE-IHC	Cessna 172RG Cutlass	0802	(N9352B)
SE-IHF	Cessna 172RG Cutlass *(Accident 11.7.95)*	0413	LN-HOU (N4899V)
SE-IHG	Reims/Cessna F.152	1920	
SE-IHI	Reims/Cessna F.172P	2167	
SE-IHR	Piper PA-23-250 Aztec E	27-7554033	LN-VIL SE-IHR HB-LIU N54239
SE-IHV	Cessna R.182 Skylane RG	01867	N5446T
SE-IIA	Britten-Norman BN-2A-26 Islander	48	G-AWVY N48BN G-AWVY
SE-IIB	Beech 65-C90 King Air	LJ-723	OY-ASI
SE-IID	Piper J-3C-65 Cub	23175	OY-AVS D-EGOZ N78434 NC78434
SE-IIK	Aerotek Pitts S-2A *(W/o 15.8.86)*	2118	N39CB
SE-IIL	SAAB S.91B Safir	91211	Fv50011
SE-IIN	Cessna 172N	70712	N739QC
SE-IIO	Republic RC-3 Seabee *(Under restoration)*	120	N14R N87558
SE-IIP	Beech 77 Skipper	WA-263	N3833L
SE-IIR	Beech 77 Skipper	WA-264	N3833P
SE-IIT	Cessna 172M *(W/o 7.6.83)*	67175	N1583U

Regn.	Type	C/n	Prev.Id.
SE-IIX	Cessna U.206A Stationair	0591	LN-NPD
			LN-HHE
			N4891F
SE-IKB	Cessna 140	9624	OY-EFT
			D-EBAP
			N72459
SE-IKE	SAAB S.91B-2 Safir	91339	LN-SAV
			57339
			339/'UA-T'
SE-IKF	Piper PA-24-250 Comanche	24-3591	OY-BAW
			N8399P
SE-IKI	SAAB S.91D Safir *(W/o 2.6.85)*	91359	SF-13
SE-IKK	SAAB S.91D Safir	91363	SF-17
SE-IKN	Robin R.2160D	161	D-EFSJ
			F-ODIL
SE-IKO	Piper PA-18 Super Cub 95	18-2038	LN-KCP
			R-46
			52-2438
SE-IKR	SAAB S.91D Safir	91417	OH-SFG
			SF-29
SE-IKV	Piper PA-31-350 Navajo Chieftain	31-7405148	G-BDFN
			EI-BKI
			G-BDFN
			5Y-ASI
SE-IKX	Cessna A.185E Skywagon	1530	LN-BDQ
			(N2780J)
SE-IKZ	Fairchild-Swearingen SA.226TC Metro II	TC-383	D-IBAN
	(Rebuilt using wings from SA226AT OY-AUI c/n AT-015)		
SE-ILB	SAAB MFI-15-200A Safari	808	
	(Sold to Germany, D-E . . . ?)		
SE-ILD	Piper PA-28-161 Warrior II	28-8116293	
SE-ILE	Piper PA-28-181 Archer II	28-8190294	
SE-ILG	Piper PA-28-161 Warrior II	28-8216224	N9619N
SE-ILL	Piper PA-31-350 Navajo Chieftain	31-7305117	4X-CCH
			N676GL
			N676LL
			N6767L
SE-ILN	Piper PA-38-112 Tomahawk	38-82A0100	
	(W/o 27.6.88)		
SE-ILO	Piper PA-28-140 Cherokee	28-21703	OY-BBF
SE-ILP	Piper PA46-350P Malibu Mirage	4636258	
SE-ILY	Piper PA-31-350 Navajo Chieftain	31-7852051	G-FTTA
			N27535
SE-IMA	Reims/Cessna F.152	1720	OY-BNO
SE-IMB	Reims/Cessna F.150M	1425	OY-AZS
			D-EOKY
SE-IME	SAAB MFI-9B Trainer	038	OY-DUJ
			SE-ENC
SE-IMF	Piper PA-18 Super Cub 95	18-1994	OY-ANW
			I-EIBA
			MM522394
			52-2394
SE-IMG	Piper PA-18 Super Cub 95	18-2006	OY-DVV
			I-EIFI
			MM522406
			52-2406
SE-IMH	Piper J-3C-65 Cub	12308	OY-AVD
			D-EFQK
			F-BFQK
			OO-ZOU
			44-80012
SE-IMP	SOCATA TB-10 Tobago *(W/o 28.9.97)*	368	F-BNGQ
SE-IMT	SOCATA TB-20 Trinidad	522	
SE-IMX	SOCATA MS.893A Rallye Commodore 180	10638	F-BODB
SE-IMY	SOCATA TB-10 Tobago	656	N20HN
SE-INI	Beech 200 Super King Air	BB-687	EI-BIP
	('003' of SOS Flygambulans, c/s SAG003)		
SE-INL	Cessna T.210N Turbo Centurion II	64692	N1403U
	(W/o 26.12.92)		
SE-INM	Britten-Norman BN-2A Islander	84	D-IAWD
SE-INN	Reims/Cessna F.172H	0556	PH-KAR
SE-INT	Cessna U.206D Stationair	1333	LN-LJR
			(LN-LJR)
			LN-LJR
			N95411

Regn.	Type	C/n	Prev.Id.
SE-INY	Cessna A.185E Skywagon	02030	LN-BNF
			(N70164)
SE-IOC	SAAB S.91D Safir	91441	OH-SFK
			SF-32
SE-IOD	Reims/Cessna F.150H	0238	G-AVTM
SE-IOI	SAAB S.91B-2 Safir *(W/o 5.7.85)*	91331	LN-BEE
			57331
			331/'UA-L'
SE-IOV	Mitsubishi MU-2B-26	337	N522MA
SE-IOZ	Mitsubishi MU-2B-26	320	N641KE
			N30EM
			N641KE
			N14645
			N508MA
SE-IPA	Reims/Cessna F.152	1949	
SE-IPF	Reims/Cessna F.152	1961	
SE-IPG	Reims/Cessna F.172P *(W/o 7.11.90)*	2234	
SE-IPI	Reims/Cessna F.172P	2240	
SE-IPL	Cessna TU.206G Turbo Stationair II	04046	N756FB
SE-IPP	Cessna 152	83490	N49653
SE-IPR	Cessna R.182 Skylane RG	00704	N9410R
SE-IPS	Cessna 172P	75462	OY-CPY
			N63658
SE-IPT	Cessna 340A	1816	N202MM
			PH-PSM
			N6603Q
			C-GJAV
			N1232P
SE-IPZ	Cessna 210R Centurion II *(W/o 20.4.90)*	64956	N6490U
SE-IRC	Reims/Cessna F.172P	2173	LN-NFP
			D-EAPY
SE-IRD	Reims/Cessna F.172N	1976	LN-NFJ
			D-EOOY
SE-IRI	Cessna A.185F Skywagon	03177	N93094
SE-IRK	Piper PA-28R-200 Cherokee Arrow	28R-7535091	LN-NFK
			D-EFFL
			N32795
SE-IRN	SAAB S.91D Safir	91369	PH-RLC
SE-IRS	Cessna A.185F Skywagon	02409	LN-BGN
			(N1686R)
SE-IRT	American AA-1 Yankee	0416	OY-AYE
SE-IRV	Cessna A.185E Skywagon	1161	LN-KAL
			N4707Q
SE-IRX	Christen Pitts S-2B	5039	N53234
SE-IRY	SAAB S.91D Safir	91360	OH-SFS
			SF-14
SE-IRZ	Piper PA-23-250 Aztec D	27-4257	LN-AEZ
SE-ISD	SAAB-Scania SF.340A	145	ZK-FXQ
			SE-ISD
			SE-F45
SE-ISE	SAAB-Scania SF.340A	156	YL-BAP
			ZK-NLF
			SE-ISE
			SE-F56
SE-ISG	SAAB-Scania SF.340A	162	SE-F62
SE-ISL	SAAB-Scania SF.340A	130	LN-SAA
			(SE-ISL)
			SE-F30
SE-ISP	SAAB-Scania SF.340A	015	SE-E15
SE-ISR	SAAB-Scania SF.340A	017	SE-E17
SE-IST	SAAB-Scania SF.340A	035	SE-E35
SE-ISV	SAAB-Scania SF.340A	045	SE-E45
SE-ISY	SAAB-Scania SF.340A	080	SE-E80
SE-ITA	Piper PA-31-310 Navajo	31-8012028	D-ICAS
			N3552U
SE-ITB	Piper PA-31-310 Navajo	31-8012059	N3585G
SE-ITC	Piper PA-31-310 Navajo	31-8012048	C-GBJE
SE-ITD	Piper PA-31-310 Navajo	31-8012035	N3553E
SE-ITE	Piper PA-31-310 Navajo	31-8012010	N3545C
SE-ITR	Beech 95-E55 Baron	TE-1021	N7253R
SE-ITS	Piper PA-31-310 Navajo	31-8212018	N4097P
SE-ITT	Piper PA-31-310 Navajo	31-8112065	N40943
SE-ITU	Piper PA-31-310 Navajo	31-8012085	N325EC
SE-ITY	Piper PA-25-235 Pawnee	25-2657	G-ASOV
SE-ITZ	Reims/Cessna F.172M	1197	LN-ASG

Regn.	Type	C/n	Prev.Id.
SE-IUA	Mitsubishi MU-2B-26	345	N730MP N730MA
SE-IUC	Piper PA-34-220T Seneca IV	3447013	
SE-IUD	Piper PA-28-181 Archer II	2890065	
SE-IUF	Piper PA-28-181 Archer II	2890069	
SE-IUH	Piper PA-34-220T Seneca III	3433102	
SE-IUI	Piper PA-28-161 Warrior II	2816043	
SE-IUO	Beech 95-B55 Baron *(Crashed in 1990)*	TC-1716	OY-POC N35BW
SE-IUS	Cessna A.185E Skywagon	1471	LN-VIQ (N2721J)
SE-IUU	PZL-104 Wilga 35	62165	OE-DRS SP-WDC
SE-IUX	Beech 200 Super King Air *('004' of SOS Flygambulans, c/s SAG004)*	BB-675	N26AD N26SD N6747T
SE-IVA	Mitsubishi MU-2B-36	666	N826RC
SE-IVE	CASA C.212CE Aviocar	343	
SE-IVF	CASA C.212CE Aviocar	346	
SE-IVK	Taylorcraft F21B	1512	N4417R
SE-IVL	Taylorcraft F21B	1513	N44177
SE-IVM	Piper PA-25-235 Pawnee B	25-3577	N7533Z
SE-IVO	Piper PA-18-150 Super Cub	18-2054	LN-KCV R-69 52-2454
SE-IVY	Vickers V.815 Viscount *(Scrapped at Malmö -Sturup in 1992)*	375	G-AVJB (LX-LGD) G-AVJB AP-AJF
SE-IXC	Beech B200 Super King Air *('005' of SOS Flygambulans, c/s SAG005)*	BB-1210	N7213J
SE-IXD	Piper PA-28RT-201T Turbo Arrow IV	28R-7931179	N20950
SE-IXE	Short SD.3-60	SH.3705	G-BNBA
SE-IXF	Cessna P210N Pressurized Centurion II	00377	N4944K
SE-IXH	Maule M-6-235C Super Rocket	7473C	N5662T
SE-IXI	Piper PA-25-235 Pawnee	25-2900	G-ASWG ST-ADM G-ASWG N7113Z
SE-IXK	Cessna U.206F Stationair	03341	LN-ALM OY-BUT N8483Q
SE-IXN	Reims/Cessna FR.172G Rocket	0196	OH-CDG
SE-IXP	Cessna A.185F Skywagon *(W/o 13.7.88)*	03727	LN-ALI N8533Q
SE-IXR	SAAB S.91D Safir	91-352	OH-SFI SF-6
SE-IXS	Piper PA-34-220T Seneca III *(W/o 3.8.93)*	34-8133008	N8329L
SE-IXT	Reims/Cessna F.150M	1199	OY-AZJ PH-VST
SE-IXV	Cessna 172P	74575	N52646
SE-IXY	Cessna 172P	75597	N64643
SE-IYC	DHC-2 Turbo Beaver III	1638/TB-21	N1638 C-FMAB CF-MAB
SE-IYD	Cessna 172P *(Accident 2.3.95)*	75052	N54788
SE-IYE	Piper PA-25-235 Pawnee D	25-7756005	G-BEXL N82428
SE-IYF	Cessna 172M	62765	OY-CPJ N13455
SE-IYG	Cessna P210N Pressurized Centurion II *(W/o 29.7.89)*	00527	(SE-IPN) N99WA
SE-IYI	Cessna 172P	74976	N54451
SE-IYL	Piper PA-30-160 Twin Comanche C	30-1923	D-GATI I-KATI N8767Y
SE-IYN	Cessna 172N	73424	N4877G
SE-IYT	PZL-104 Wilga 35A	18840776	SP-WDD
SE-IYY	Piper PA-28RT-201 Turbo Arrow IV	28R-7918214	N2910P
SE-IYZ	Embraer EMB.110P1 Bandeirante	110-288	G-BIBE N193PB G-BIBE PT-SBX
SE-IZG	Piper PA-28-161 Warrior II	28-7916103	N3003A
SE-IZH	Piper PA-28-161 Warrior II	28-8216075	N80021
SE-IZI	Piper PA-28-161 Warrior II	28-8016081	N8092D
SE-IZM	Piper PA-32R-301T Turbo Saratoga SP	32R-8129093	N8424B
SE-IZN	Cessna 172N	73647	OY-CPT N2770J
SE-IZO	Beech 99 *(W/o 8.5.89)*	U-48	N299ME N7699N
SE-IZP	Piper PA-25-235 Pawnee	25-2235	N6640Z
SE-IZS	Piper PA-22-108 Colt	22-8548	LN-AEW SE-CUX
SE-IZT	Piper PA-32R-300 Lance	32R-7780538	N701JB N44850
SE-IZY	Rockwell Commander 112TC	13100	LN-RAF N4610W
SE-IZZ	Piper PA-28-161 Warrior II	28-8416058	OY-CEB SE-ILP
SE-JAD	Hughes 369E	0458E	
SE-JAH	Schweizer 269C	S-1528	OY-HEB SE-JAH
SE-JAI	Schweizer 269C	S-1529	LN-OMF SE-JAI N69A
SE-JAJ	Aérospatiale SA.315B Lama	2401	N62339
SE-JAN	Aérospatiale AS.350B2 Ecureuil *(W/o 10.2.92)*	2348	N502AL
SE-JAP	Schweizer 269C	S-1333	HB-XSZ
SE-JAU	Hughes 369E *(Reservation)*	unkn	
SE-JAV	Schweizer 269C	S-1579	N41S
SE-JAX	Aérospatiale AS.350B2 Ecureuil	2618	F-WYMH
SE-JAY	Schweizer 269C	S-1204	LN-OTS OY-HDW N41S
SE-JBB	Schweizer 269C	S-1463	G-WISK N41S
SE-JBD	Schweizer 269C	S-1580	N69A
SE-JBJ	Schweizer 269D	0005	
SE-JBZ	MBB-Kawasaki BK.117A-4 *(Reservation)*	1023	B-77008 ZK-HKA JA9921
SE-JCA	Aérospatiale AS.350B2 Ecureuil	2619	F-WYMG
SE-JCH	Hughes 369D	120-0892D	LN-OQV N48AW
SE-JCI	Hughes 269C	96-0537	OY-HBW
SE-JCK	Aérospatiale SA.365N Dauphin 2	6090	G-BKXE
SE-JCV	Aérospatiale AS.350B3 Ecureuil	3064	F-WQDY
SE-JCX	Aérospatiale AS.350B2 Ecureuil	2930	
SE-JCY	Robinson R-22 Beta	1080	D-HOLZ N8048W
SE-JDA	Enstrom 480	5016	
SE-JDB	Agusta A.109A	7287	TC-HMK D-HOOB N109BH
SE-JDC	Hughes 269C	1077	LN-OTF (SE-HMG)
SE-JDH	Robinson R-44 Astro	0273	
SE-JDI	Hughes 369HS	74-0620S	LN-OMV OH-HOP N377ST
SE-JDK	Aérospatiale AS.355F1 Ecureuil 2	5096	N8794Y PT-HTW N813DB N5785T
SE-JDL	Hughes 369E	0018E	N501TS N189MD G-OFHS
SE-JDM	Aérospatiale AS.355F1 Ecureuil 2	5172	N302PS N57973
SE-JDO	Eurocopter EC.120B Colibri	1014	
SE-JDP	Eurocopter EC.120B Colibri	1019	
SF-JDR	Aérospatiale AS.350B3 Ecureuil *(Reservn)*	3175	
SE-JDS	Eurocopter EC.120B Colibri	1025	
SE-JDT	*Reservation for Eurocopter EC.120B Colibri 2.00*		
SE-JDV	Robinson R-44 Astro	0574	
SE-JDX	Aérospatiale AS.350B3 Ecureuil	3063	F-WQDX
SE-JDZ	Aérospatiale AS.350B Ecureuil	2227	F-GGGU

Regn.	Type	C/n	Prev.Id.
SE-JEB	Bell 407	53006	(N62828)
			C-FXDK
SE-JEC	Eurocopter EC-135T1 *(Reservation)*	unkn	
SE-JEH	SE.3160 Alouette III	1542	NethAF: A-542
SE-JEK	SE.3160 Alouette III	1494	NethAF: A-494
SE-JEL	SE.3160 Alouette III	1500	NethAF: A-500
SE-JEO	Aérospatiale AS.350B3	3225	
SE-JEP	Eurocopter EC.120B Colibri	1018	
SE-JER	Bell 206BJet Ranger II	2492	LN-OHR
			OY-HDJ
			HB-XBE
			D-HEPE
			(YV-O-PTJ-4)
SE-JEU	Eurocopter EC-135T1 *(Reservation)*	unkn	
SE-JEX	Bell 407	53145	N72243
SE-JEY	Aérospatiale AS.350B2 Ecureuil	1883	LN-ORT
	(Reservation 2.00)		N48CD
SE-JEZ	Sikorsky S-76A	760215	N72WW
			N5423V
SE-JFA	Sikorsky S-76+	760466	
SE-JFB	Sikorsky S-76+	760468	
SE-JFC	Sikorsky S-76C	760481	
SE-JFE	Aérospatiale AS.355F1 Ecureuil 2	5289	9M-DPK
			9V-BNI
			9M-AYW
			F-ODVY
			F-WZFQ
SE-JFF	Robinson R-44 Astro	0260	
SE-JFG	IRMA/SE.316B Alouette III	5377	F-GJGS
			F-OHGS
			CS-HBH
			F-GBDU
SE-JFJ	Bell 407 *(Reservation 1.00)*	53418	
SE-JFK	Aérospatiale AS.350B1 Ecureuil	1983	F-GPAT
SE-JFM	Robinson R-22 Beta	2009	OY-HFT
SE-JFP	Eurocopter EC.135T1	0105	
SE-JFV	Robinson R-22 Mariner	2008M	OY-HFO
SE-JFX	Aérospatiale AS.350B3 Ecureuil	3077	
SE-JFZ	Eurocopter EC.120B Colibri	1011	
SE-JGA	Robinson R-44 Clipper	0673	
SE-JGG	Robinson R-44 Astro	0084	D-HIBB
SE-JGK	Aérospatiale AS.350B2 Ecureuil	2930	RP-C8888
			F-OHNQ
SE-JGN	Robinson R-22 Mariner	2198M	N8337X
SE-JGP	Eurocopter EC.120B Colibri	1056	
SE-JGT	Aérospatiale AS.355F1 Ecureuil 2	5087	N1CG
SE-JLP	Bell 212	31146	HL . . . .
			N5756W
SE-JMP	Eurocopter EC.120B Colibri	1008	
SE-JUL	MBB-Kawasaki BK.117B-1	7186	D-HIMC
			JY-ACD
			D-HIMC
SE-JUP	Eurocopter EC.135T1	0005	D-HQQQ
SE-JUS	Sikorsky S-76A	760288	PT-YBG
			N770AM
SE-JUZ	Sikorsky S-76A +	760282	N92RR
			N92RP
			N63VW
SE-J . .	Bell 206L-3 Long Ranger III	51348	N80EA
SE-KBA	SOCATA TB-20 Trinidad	789	
SE-KBF	SOCATA TB-10 Tobago	662	F-GFEK
			N20JU
SE-KBH	SOCATA TB-9 Tampico	887	
SE-KBL	SOCATA TB-9 Tampico	1048	
SE-KBN	Piper PA-28RT-201 Arrow IV	28R-7918113	N2161Z
SE-KBO	Piper PA-18-150 Super Cub	18-7338	LN-BEB
			SE-EIK
			OY-ADD
SE-KBS	Piper PA-25-235 Pawnee D	28-7856033	OY-BRF
SE-KBT	Christen A-1 Husky	1036	
SE-KBU	Christen A-1 Husky	038	
SE-KBX	Mitsubishi MU-2B-35 *(W/o 3.1.89)*	247	N5TQ
			N5TC
SE-KBZ	Cessna R.172K Hawk XP	2637	N736MQ
SE-KCA	Cessna 340A	0541	D-ICBB
			N1MT
			(N4403A)
SE-KCB	Cessna 172P	74854	N54040
SE-KCC	Cessna 172P	76631	N9839L
SE-KCD	Piper PA-32R-300 Cherokee Lance	32R-7780533	OH-PAS
SE-KCE	Antonov AN-2	1G189-59	ES-CAE
			CCCP84592
SE-KCI	Short SD.3-60	SH.3648	G-OASS
			G-BLIL
			OY-MMB
			G-BLIL
			G-14-3648
SE-KCK	DHC-2 Beaver	119	C-FGQQ
			CF-GQQ
SE-KCL	Cessna U206G Stationair II	04270	LN-ALJ
			(N756QK)
SE-KCM	Cessna 150L	75261	OH-CTV
			C-FGWA
SE-KCN	Piper PA-46-350P Malibu	4636028	LN-ENE
			N350PM
			N92646
SE-KCO	Maule M-4-210C Rocket *(Reservation)*	1035C	LN-VYB
			N15B
SE-KCP	Fairchild-Swearingen SA.226TC Metro II	TC-330	N7217N
			ZS-LJC
			N30TR
			(F-GEJX)
			N30TR
			ZS-LJC
			HB-LLC
			N1007Y
SE-KCR	SAAB-Scania 340A	065	OH-FAA
			SE-E65
SE-KCS	SAAB-Scania 340A	066	OH-FAB
			SE-E66
SE-KCT	SAAB-Scania 340A *(Reservation)*	070	OH-FAC
			SE-E70
SE-KCV	SAAB-Scania SF.340B	310	F-GHVU
			SE-C10
SE-KCX	SAAB-Scania SF.340B *(Reservation)*	163	OM-UGU
			OK-UGU
			OO-RXL
			(F-GGZM)
			HB-AXZ
			(OO-RXL)
			SE-F63
SE-KCY	SAAB-Scania SF.340B *(Reservation)*	171	OM-UGT
			OK-UGT
			OO-RXM
			HB-AHY
			SE-F71
SE-KDB	Piper PA-31-350 Chieftain	31-8052098	OY-CGT
			N7PN
			N35817
SE-KDD	Yakovlev YAK-52	801003	UR-BNP
			DOSAAF-21
SE-KDE	Cessna 177RG Cardinal RG	1166	N836CW
			(N52090)
SE-KDF	Reims/Cessna F.182P Skylane	0014	OH-CGY
SE-KDH	Piper PA-25-235 Pawnee D	25-7856030	G-BGFN
			N9176T
SE-KDK	Beech 200 Super King Air	BB-909	N171M
			N36784
SE-KDL	Piper PA-38-112 Tomahawk	38-78A0748	OY-BRP
SE-KDM	Grob G.115A	8034	(D-EGVV)
SE-KDN	Piper PA-38-112 Tomahawk	38-79A0758	N2545L
SE-KDO	Piper PA-38-112 Tomahawk	38-79A0273	N2322D
SE-KDP	Cessna 172N	69731	N737WL
SE-KDS	Cessna 180H	52175	N123BD
			N9075M
SE-KDT	Piper PA-38-112 Tomahawk	38-79A0985	N2416P
SE-KDU	Piper PA-38-112 Tomahawk	38-79A0965	N2367P
SE-KDV	Cessna T.210N Turbo Centurion II	63855	N6288C
SE-KDX	Piper PA-38-112 Tomahawk	38-79A0945	N2321P

Regn.	Type	C/n	Prev.Id.
SE-KDZ	Piper PA-28-161 Warrior II	28-8416056	N4345A
SE-KEA	Cessna 180A	32470	LN-TSD
			N6573A
SE-KEC	Piper PA-31-350 Navajo Chieftain	31-7952098	LN-FAM
			G-TROT
			N35176
SE-KEE	Beech B36TC Bonanza	EA-484	
SE-KEF	Cessna R.172K Hawk XP	3002	N758DA
SE-KEG	Piper PA-18-150 Super Cub	18-1415	D-ELWK
			51-15415
SE-KEI	Piper PA-28-161 Warrior II	2816072	
SE-KEK	Piper PA-28-161 Cadet	2841309	N9266N
			N9208Q
SE-KEM	Embraer EMB.110P1 Bandeirante	110-340	N820AC
			N305EB
			N4268K
			PT-SDP
SE-KEN	Piper PA-28-161 Cadet	2841310	N9267N
			N9208Z
SE-KET	Cessna R.172K Hawk XP	2838	(SE-KDS)
			N736WD
SE-KEV	Cessna 172N	70165	N738QX
SE-KEZ	Piper PA-25-235 Pawnee	25-3701	N6955Z
SE-KFB	Cessna 172P	74993	N54506
SE-KFD	SAAB S.91D Safir	91442	OH-SFM
			SF-33
SE-KFE	Piper PA-34-220T Seneca III	34-8133015	N100LA
	(sold to Norway 6.97, operated as SE-KFE)		N9519N
SE-KFF	Cessna U.206F Stationair	01942	LN-HAO
			OH-CKA
			LN-HOM
			(LN-RTA)
			N50590
SE-KFH	Maule M-6-235C Super Rocket	7496C	
SE-KFK	Cessna 210L Centurion *(Reservation)*	unkn	
SE-KFL	Piper PA-28-151 Cherokee Warrior	28-7715160	N5962F
SE-KFM	Piper PA-28-181 Archer II	28-8190196	N8361P
SE-KFN	Mooney M.20J Model 201	24-1082	N8651M
SE-KFP	Beech B200C Super King Air	BL-132	
	('006' of SOS Flygambulans, c/s SAG006)		
SE-KFR	Piper PA-34-200T Seneca II	34-7870170	N9224C
	(Accident 18.8.95)		
SE-KFT	Boeing Stearman E75	75-5844	N1723B
			41-17681
SE-KFU	Cessna 180F	51258	LN-BDR
			N2158Z
SE-KFV	FFV Aerotec MFI-BA14	unkn	
SE-KFX	Cessna 172M	63417	N5200R
SE-KFY	Cessna 172N	73654	OY-CPF
			N6412J
SE-KFZ	Piper PA-28-181 Archer II	28-8090183	N3561A
SE-KGD	Christen A-1 Husky	1075	
SE-KGE	Christen A-1 Husky	1076	
SE-KGG	SOCATA MS.893A Rallye Commodore 180	10699	OY-DTI
SE-KGH	Piper PA-31-350 Navajo Chieftain	31-7305007	OY-BYF
			LN-MTK
			N7677L
SE-KGM	Bölkow BO.208C Junior	531	D-EGPU
SE-KGN	Piper PA-28-161 Cherokee Warrior II	28-7816521	N9716C
SE-KGP	Reims/Cessna F.172M	0957	OY-RYR
SE-KGR	Piper PA-28RT-201T Turbo Arrow IV	28R-8031020	OY-PEI
			N8117G
SE-KGS	Piper PA-28-161 Cherokee Warrior II	28-7816666	N789DT
			N9624N
SE-KGU	Maule M-7-235 Super Rocket	4067C	
SE-KGV	Short SD.3-60	SH.3670	HR-IAT
			N108PS
			B-3603
			G-BLWJ
			G-14-3670
SE-KGY	Piper PA-25-235 Pawnee D	25-7856007	I-TOZU
			G-BFPR
			N82591
SE-KGZ	SAAB S.91B Safir	91259	FV50047
SE-KHD	Yakovlev YAK-55	870209	RA-02183
SE-KHF	Piper PA-25-235 Pawnee D	25-7756019	G-BFBW
			N82452
SE-KHI	Piper PA-28-151 Cherokee Warrior	28-7615165	LN-NAJ
SE-KHK	Piper PA-25-235 Pawnee D	25-8056007	D-EIAG
			N2383Q
SE-KHL	Dornier 228-100	7003	LN-HPA
			D-IDNI
SE-KHN	Reims/Cessna F.172E	50659/0034	LN-BIN
SE-KHP	Piper PA-28-181 Archer II	28-8390029	N8332T
SE-KHS	Piper PA-28RT-201T Turbo Arrow IV	28R-7931065	N2193P
SE-KHT	Beech B24R Sierra	MC-253	N2546W
SE-KHU	Piper PA-28-181 Archer II	28-7990285	D-EFSB
			N3020Q
			N9589N
SE-KHX	Cessna 172N	72604	N6109D
SE-KHY	Cessna 172K	69989	N738HL
SE-KIB	Piper PA-28-161 Cadet	2841089	
SE-KIE	Piper PA-28-181 Archer II	2890110	
SE-KIF	Piper PA-28-181 Archer II *(W/o 8.1.91)*	2890111	
SE-KII	Piper PA-28-161 Cadet	2841155	(F-GHBA)
SE-KIK	Piper PA-28-161 Cadet	2841139	N9241G
SE-KIL	Piper PA-28-161 Cadet	2841138	N9240 F
SE-KIM	Piper PA-28-161 Cadet	2841088	
SE-KIN	Piper PA-28-181 Archer II	2890115	
SE-KIR	Piper PA-28-161 Cadet	2841157	
SE-KIT	Piper PA-28-181 Archer II	2890106	
SE-KIU	Piper PA-28-181 Archer II	2890133	
SE-KIX	Piper PA-28-181 Archer II	2890135	
SE-KKA	Gyroflug SC-01B Speed Canard *(Reservation)*	unkn	
SE-KKB	Gyroflug SC-01B Speed Canard *(Reservation)*	unkn	
SE-KKC	Piper PA-25-235 Pawnee D	25-7756014	G-BEOT
SE-KKD	DHC-2 Turbo Beaver	1629/TB-17	N4482
			CF-YOD
			TI-407L
SE-KKE	Cessna 140	13250	OY-EFH
			D-ENAM
			NC2992M
SE-KKF	Cessna TU.206G Turbo Stationair II	06386	N9315Z
	(Accident 30.7.95)		
SE-KKI	Cessna 172P	76017	N89929
SE-KKK	Beech B60 Duke	P-330	N6033S
SE-KKR	DHC-2 Beaver	1551	N5595N
			KAF-101
			N8340V
SE-KKU	Piper PA-34-220T Seneca III	34-8133018	
SE-KKV	Piper PA-28RT-201T Turbo Arrow IV	28R-8131208	N410FC
			N8441P
SE-KKX	Dornier 228-100	7004	LN-HPE
			D-ICGO
SE-KKY	Beech 60 Duke	P-94	G-DOOK
			D-ICAV
			G-AXEN
SE-KLA	Piper PA-28-140 Cherokee D	28-7125043	OY-BDJ
	(W/o 3.1.91)		(SE-FPK)
SE-KLB	Piper PA-25-235 Pawnee D	25-7656089	G-BFKV
			N82343
SE-KLG	Bellanca 8KCAB Decathlon	393-78	LN-HOB
SE-KLH	Cessna TU.206F Turbo Stationair	02857	N1176Q
SE-KLI	Piper PA-28-181 Archer II	28-8390026	N83222
SE-KLO	Short SD.3-60	SH.3609	N343MV
			(G-BKMY)
			G-14-3609
SE-KLR	Cessna 172N	71522	N3373E
SE-KLU	SOCATA MS.880B Rallye Club	1557	OY-DJN
SE-KLV	Piper PA-28-181 Archer II	28-8190139	OY-CEK
			G-BMKL
			ZS-KWL
			N8323L
SE-KLZ	Piper PA-28-161 Cadet	2841098	OY-JEB
SE-KMA	Piper PA-28-181 Archer II	2890142	
SE-KMB	Piper PA-18-150 Super Cub *(On rebuild)*	1809055	
SE-KMD	Piper PA-28-181 Archer II	28-8490020	N4329K
SE-KMG	Piper PA-28-161 Cadet	2841276	
SE-KMH	Piper PA-28-161 Cadet	2841277	
SE-KMI	Piper PA-28-161 Cadet	2841278	
SE-KML	Piper PA-28-161 Cadet	2841279	

Regn.	Type	C/n	Prev.Id.
SE-KMM(2)	Piper PA-28R-201T Cherokee Arrow III	28R-7703102	N3337Q
SE-KMN	Zlin Z.242L	0652	
SE-KMO	Piper PA-28-181 Archer II	2890147	
SE-KMR	Piper PA-28-181 Archer II	28-8490023	N4329V
SE-KMU	Piper PA-28-181 Archer II	2890160	
SE-KMZ	Piper PA-28R-201 Arrow IV	2837056	N9235Q
SE-KNA	Robin HR.200/160	106	OY-AJP
SE-KNB	Cessna 172P	74112	LN-MTD / N5445K
SE-KNC	Piper PA-28-140 Cherokee	28-25302	LN-BNC
SE-KNE	Christen A-I Husky	1123	
SE-KNF	Christen A-I Husky	1125	
SE-KNG(2)	Mooney M.20K Model 231	25-0169	OY-CBC / LN-DBW / OY-CBC
SE-KNH	Piper PA-28-181 Archer II	28-8390071	TF-GBG / N4309M
SE-KNL	SOCATA Rallye 235C	13074	
SE-KNR	SOCATA TB-200 Tobago XL	1382	
SE-KNS	SOCATA Rallye 235F	12105	F-GAFE / F-ZWRT
SE-KNV	SOCATA Rallye 235F	13394	
SE-KNX	SOCATA TB-20 Trinidad	1762	D-ETAT(2)
SE-KNY	SOCATA Rallye 235F	13395	
SE-KNZ	SOCATA TB-10 Tobago	1049	F-GRBC / EC-FMM / EC-962 / F-GHZZ
SE-KOA	Piper PA-28-181 Archer II	28-8490085	N4365V
SE-KOC	Cessna A.185F Skywagon	04367	N96DS / N9903N
SE-KOE	Piper PA-28-181 Archer II	28-8490104	OH-PKR / N135AV
SE-KOI	Beech F33A Bonanza	CE-1002	N6368X
SE-KOL	Beech 300LW Super King Air	FA-189	N2808B / N7241V
SE-KOO	Cessna 172M	61981	OY-DLG / N12436
SE-KOR	Piper PA-28-181 Archer II	28-8090043	N2417U
SE-KOV	Piper PA-32RT-300 Lance	32R-7985099	N2240V
SE-KOX	DHC-3T Otter	406	4657 / UB-657
SE-KOY	Piper PA-34-200T Seneca II	34-7870423	N39949
SE-KOZ	Cessna 207 Skywagon	00784	N1721Q
SE-KPD	SAAB-Scania SF.340A	037	PH-KJL / LN-NVD / SE-E37
SE-KPE	SAAB-Scania SF.340A	055	PH-KJH / LN-NVE / SE-E55
SE-KPF	Cessna 337G Super Skymaster	01806	N701AD
SE-KPK	Cessna 172RG Cutlass	0254	LN-NFA / N5138U
SE-KPL	Cessna 210M Centurion	62280	LN-BEC / N761HX
SE-KPM	Cessna 185B	0558	LN-DBO / (N2558Z)
SE-KPN	SAAB S.91D Safir	91435	LN-MAA / (LN-MAY) / G-BCFT / PH-RLX
SE-KPP	Cessna A.185F Skywagon	03661	OH-CKS / N8339Q
SE-KPR	Cessna TU.206D Turbo Stationair	01287	LN-BEU / N93411
SE-KPS	Piper PA-18 Super Cub 95	18-1423	LN-TEI / D-EOCB / ALAT / 51-15423
SE-KPU	Piper PA-22-150 Tri-Pacer	22-3017	OY-DDD / N2711P
SE-KPV	Piper PA-28R-201 Arrow III	28R-7837120	N3535M
SE-KPX	Maule M-5-235C Lunar Rocket	7138C	N9228E
SE-KPY	Bellanca 7ECA Citabria (on rebuild)	1344-80	N5069R
SE-KPZ	Cessna TU.206G Turbo Stationair II	06818	D-EDES(4) / F-GEDS / N6382R
SE-KRC	Cessna 180K	52799	N61790
SE-KRD	Cessna U.206G Stationair II	05771	N5457X
SE-KRE	SAAB S.91B Safir	91257	Fv.50045
SE-KRF	SAAB S.91B Safir	91283	Fv.50073
SE-KRG	Piper PA-28-181 Archer II	28-8090060	N8074N
SE-KRH	Piper PA-28-140 Cherokee	28-24351	LN-DAD / SE-FCZ
SE-KRI	Bellanca 7ECA Citabria	1349-80	
SE-KRK	Robin R.2160 Acrobin	159	LN-RAC
SE-KRL	Piper PA-23-250 Aztec E	27-7305173	OY-DZZ / N40457
SE-KRM	Cessna 172P	74481	N52285
SE-KRN	SAAB-Scania SF.340A	159	D-CHBC / (SE-ISI) / SE-F59
SE-KRR	Republic RC-3 Seabee (on rebuild)	653	N1CD / N6409K
SE-KSB	Cessna A.185E Skywagon	01794	OH-CFH / SE-FXG / N5825J
SE-KSC	SOCATA TB-9 Tampico	191	LN-KLJ
SE-KSD	Piper PA-28RT-201T Turbo Arrow IV	28R-7931027	N2166K
SE-KSF	Piper PA-28-181 Archer II	28-7990534	N2894A
SE-KSL	Piper PA-25-235 Pawnee C	25-4557	N4786Y
SE-KSM	Piper PA-28-181 Cherokee Archer II	28-7790421	OY-BTG
SE-KSN	SOCATA MS.880B Rallye Club	860	OY-DGG
SE-KSO	Cessna 172B	48484	N444CY / N444CW / N7984X
SE-KSP	Mooney M.20E Super 21	1199	OY-DDS / G-BHPC / OY-DDS / N9250M
SE-KSS	Beech A23-19 Musketeer	MB-250	OY-DKS
SE-KST	Piper PA-28-151 Cherokee Warrior	28-7415281	N41582
SE-KSZ	American AG-5B Tiger (Accident 6.7.95)	10086	N1194Y
SE-KTB	Reims/Cessna F.172K	0755	OH-CFD
SE-KTC	Fokker F.27-050	20124	OY-MMG / PH-EXI
SE-KTD	Fokker F.27-050	20125	OY-MMH / PH-EXJ
SE-KTF	Piper PA-31-350 Navajo Chieftain	31-7852119	LN-TSC(2) / N27720
SE-KTG	Piper PA-18-150 Super Cub (Reservation 2.00)	18-8336	9Q-CEL / N4168Z
SE-KTH	Cessna 208B Grand Caravan (Reservation 2.00)	0245	N751FE
SE-KTK	SAAB-Scania SF.340B	276	F-GHVT / SE-G76
SE-KTM	Dornier 228-100	7022	OY-CHG / SE-KTM / LN-HPG / D-IBLD
SE-KTP	SOCATA TB-21 Trinidad TC	715	HB-KDE / F-GLAD / D-EIBP
SE-KTR	Piper PA-28R-200 Cherokee Arrow	28R-7435046	N56812
SE-KTS	Piper PA-28-181 Archer II (Reservation)	unkn	
SE-KTT	Piper PA-28-161 Warrior II	28-8216097	N8064Z
SE-KTU	Piper PA-28-181 Archer II	28-8290066	N84698
SE-KTY	Bellanca 7ECA Citabria	1261-78	N5503M
SE-KTZ	Cessna 172N	72290	N9927E
SE-KUA	SAAB S.91B Safir	91254	Fv50042
SE-KUB	SAAB S.91B Safir	91275	Fv50066
SE-KUC	SAAB S.91C Safir	91408	Fv50093
SE-KUD	Cessna 172P	74397	OH-CMQ / N52024
SE-KUE	Piper PA-32-300 Cherokee Six	32-7340158	OY-POI / CS-AON / N56102
SE-KUF	Robin DR.400/180R Remorqueur	2118	
SE-KUI	Bellanca 7KCAB Decathlon	543-75	N5378S

Regn.	Type	C/n	Prev.Id.
SE-KUS	Cessna 414 Chancellor (RAM-conversion)	0482	OY-CYB / N7812Q
SE-KUT	SAAB-Scania SF.340A	087	LN-NVF / OK-SGY / SE-KUT / N110TA / LN-NVF / SE-E87
SE-KUV	Piper PA-28-181 Cherokee Archer II	28-7790183	N7111F
SE-KUX	Piper PA-25-235 Pawnee C	25-4920	G-BEAE / PH-CLM / N8505L
SE-KUY	Piper PA-28-235 Cherokee C	28-11135	N9410W
SE-KUZ	Cessna 150M	77894	N6419K
SE-KVB	SAAB S.91B Safir	91215	Fv50015
SE-KVD	SAAB S.91B Safir	91248	Fv50050
SE-KVE	Piper PA-32R-301 Saratoga	32R-8613004	N9289Y
SE-KVG	CASA C.212-CE	229	EC-502 / T-534 / CX-BPK / FAU-534
SE-KVI	Piper PA-18 Super Cub 95	18-1448	LN-RTF / ALAT / 51-15448
SE-KVK	Piper PA-28-161 Cherokee Warrior II	28-7816384	N3895M
SE-KVM	Reims/Cessna F.177RG Cardinal RG	0115	LN-NFV / D-EFST
SE-KVP	Piper PA-28-161 Cherokee Warrior II	28-7816650	OH-PMM / N36685
SE-KVR	Cessna U.206D Skywagon	1277	LN-RTP / N72084
SE-KVS	SAAB S.91B Safir	91221	Fv50019
SE-KVT	Piper PA-28-161 Warrior II	28-8116137	OH-PWA / N83291
SE-KVU	SAAB S.91B Safir	91218	Fv50018
SE-KVX	SAAB S.91B Safir	91269	Fv50060
SE-KVY	SAAB S.91C Safir	91397	Fv50082
SE-KVZ	SAAB S.91C Safir	91403	Fv50088
SE-KXM	Zlin Z.143L	0002	OK-ZOB
SE-KXR	Grumman G.164A Agcat	1120	N5085
SE-KXS	Piper PA-28-140 Cherokee	28-22792	LN-SAS / G-AVGF / N11C
SE-KXT	Cessna 152	81671	N66935
SE-KXX(2)	Beech 1900C-1	UC-44	N31261 / (N144GP) / N31261 / JA8864 / N31261
SE-KXY(2)	Beech 1900D	UE-236	
SE-KYA	SAAB S.91C Safir	91395	Fv50080
SE-KYD	SAAB S.91D Safir	91280	Fv50070
SE-KYF	SAAB S.91D Safir	91249	Fv50037
SE-KYG	SAAB S.91D Safir	91396	Fv50081
SE-KYH	Cessna 208B Grand Caravan (Reservation 1.00)	0817	
SE-KYI	Cessna 208B Grand Caravan	0629	
SE-KYK	Piper PA-31-350 Chieftain Panther	31-8252028	OY-ELK / N803DM / N4105K
SE-KYM	Robin R.3000/160	163	
SE-KYN	Robin HR.200/120B	282	
SE-KYP(2)	ARV Super 2 (ASL Opus 280)	033	G-BNVJ
SE-KYU	Antonov AN-2	1G138-50	ES-CAI / CCCP70232
SE-KYV	Antonov AN-2	1G77-12	ES-CAL / CCCP29329
SE-KYX	Cessna 172 (Permit) (Rebuilt with Volvo B5254 engine)	28379	G-AYOD / F-OARV / N5779A
SE-KYZ	Antonov AN-2	1G233-23	SP-FAI
SE-KZA	Piper PA-31-310 Navajo	31-7612088	PH-TUR / D-IBRU / N62859
SE-KZB	SAAB S.91B Safir	91255	Fv50043
SE-KZC	SAAB S.91B Safir	91399	Fv50084
SE-KZD	Fokker F.27 Friendship 100	10245	LN-SUE / PH-FFL
SE-KZE	Fokker F.27 Friendship 100	10248	LN-SUL / PH-SAF / LN-SUL / PH-FFO
SE-KZF	Fokker F.27 Friendship 100	10266	LN-NPI / VH-EWG / PH-FGH
SE-KZG	Fokker F.27 Friendship 100	10287	LN-NPM / VH-EWJ / PH-FIE
SE-KZH	Fokker F.27 Friendship 100	10319	LN-NPD / PH-FKO / VH-EWK / PH-FKO
SE-KZL	Piper PA-28-140 Cherokee	28-22852	LN-NPU
SE-KZM	SAAB S.91B Safir	91237	Fv50035
SE-KZN	SAAB S.91B Safir	91...	Fv500..
SE-KZO	SAAB S.91B Safir	91...	Fv500..
SE-KZP	Reims/Cessna F.172P	2238	LN-AFE / G-BLZO
SE-KZR	PZL-150 Koliber	0389048	OY-CRY / SP-WGE
SE-KZS	Piper PA-44-180 Seminole	44-8095018	9Q-CJR / OO-HLR / N8147H
SE-KZT	Piper PA-32R-301 Saratoga	32R-8213012	G-ROYI / G-BMEY / N8005Y / ZS-LCN / N8005Y
SE-KZV	Antonov AN-2	1G233-20	SP-FAG
SE-KZX	Antonov AN-2	1G233-24	SP-FAK
SE-KZY	Antonov AN-2	1G234-01	SP-FAN
SE-KZZ	SAAB S.91C Safir (W/o 1.3.97)	91406	Fv50091
SE-LAA	Piper PA-28-181 Archer II	28-8490112	(SE-KDD) / N134AV / N9638N
SE-LAE	SOCATA TB-10 Tobago	636	OH-TBE / F-GFQT / N20FF
SE-LAF	Piper PA-32R-300 Lance	32R-7680509	N9830F
SE-LAG	LET L-200 Morava	171404	SP-TNB
SE-LAH	PZL-104 Wilga 35 (W/o 29.7.91)	62172	SP-FVA / SP-WDA
SE-LAI	Piper PA-28RT-201 Arrow IV	28R-7918021	N3022K
SE-LAK	SAAB S.91B Safir	91271	Fv50062
SE-LAL	SAAB S.91B-2 Safir	91335	OO-NOR / RNoAF57335/'UA-P'
SE-LAM	Rockwell Commander 114A	14512	N5899N
SE-LAO	SAAB S.91B Safir	91253	Fv50041
SE-LAP	SAAB S.91C Safir	91400	Fv50085
SE-LAR	SAAB S.91B Safir	91270	Fv50061
SE-LAS	SAAB S.91B Safir	91285	Fv50075
SE-LAT	Cessna U.206G Stationair II	04466	LN-FAZ / N756YQ
SE-LAU	Sukhoi SU-26M	011	RA-02166
SE-LAV	Piper PA-34-200T Seneca II	34-7970424	OH-PBK / N2965Q
SE-LAX	Britten-Norman BN-2A-21 Islander	431	LN-MAC / G-BCWO
SE-LAY	SAAB S.91B Safir (Reservation)	912..	Fv500..
SE-LAZ	SAAB S.91C Safir	91407	Fv50092
SE-LBB	Slingsby T-67M Firefly	2046	LN-TFB / G-7-122
SE-LBD	Slingsby T-67M Firefly	2049	LN-TFD / G-7-124
SE-LBE	Slingsby T-67M Firefly	2050	LN-TFE / G-7-125
SE-LBG(2)	SAAB S.91B-2 Safir	91252	LN-HHW / RNoAF040 / Fv50040

Regn.	Type	C/n	Prev.Id.
SE-LBH	Cessna T.210N Turbo Centurion II	64541	(SE-LBG)
			LN-TFH
			N9536Y
SE-LBI	Maule M-7-235 Super Rocket	4029C	OY-JRM
			N5664M
SE-LBK	Reims/Cessna FA.152 Aerobat	0423	OH-NEW
SE-LBL	Mooney M.20R Ovation	29-0044	
SE-LBM	Mooney M.20R Ovation	29-0057	
SE-LBN	Piper PA-28-140 Cherokee	28-25668	LN-BNZ
SE-LBO	Mooney M.20M TLS	27-0057	N50LD
SE-LBR	Yakovlev YAK-50	791602	DOSAAF
SE-LBS	Yakovlev YAK-52	800504	DOSAAF
SE-LBT	Piper PA-28R-200 Cherokee Arrow II	28R-7535006	9H-ABK
			G-BCSZ
			N9584N
SE-LBU	Piper PA-38-112 Tomahawk	38-79A0606	N2382K
SE-LBV	Mooney M.20J Model 205	24-3365	
SE-LBY	Robin R.2160 Acrobin	287	
SE-LBZ	Partenavia P.68C	221	EC-FPZ
			N2200R
			(N13PK)
			N2200R
			D-GEME
SE-LCB	Beech B200C Super King Air	BL-139	N82431
	('001' of SOS Flygambulans, c/s SAG001)		
SE-LCD	SAAB S.91C Safir	91401	Fv50086
SE-LCE	Beech B200 Super King Air	BB-1355	N404SK
			N5595U
SE-LCF	ASL Opus 280	040	(G-BNVR)
SE-LCG	Antonov AN-2	1G238-11	SP-FBG
SE-LCH	Antonov AN-2	1G238-12	SP-FBH
SE-LCI	Antonov AN-2	1G238-13	SP-FBI
SE-LCK	Piper PA-28-180 Cherokee D	28-5241	OH-PCG
			SE-FFV
SE-LCL	Mooney M.20J Model 201	24-1522	N5785X
SE-LCN	Rockwell 500S Shrike Commander	3177	CS-APZ
			N57078
SE-LCO	Cessna A.185E Skywagon	1466	LN-BFZ
			(N2716J)
SE-LCP	Cessna 421C Golden Eagle II	0261	N421JK
			5Y-TRI
			G-DEDE
			N6148G
SE-LCR	Cessna 152	80685	OH-NAA
			N25481
SE-LCS	Yakovlev YAK-52	867304	ES-FYI
			DOSAAF
SE-LCT	Beech 300LW Super King Air	FA-25	N147CA
			N147CC
			N7CR
			N7225B
SE-LCU	American Champion 8KCAB (Reservation)	832-99	
	(Crashed on delivery ferry, under rebuild)		
SE-LCV	Sukhoi SU-29 (Reservation)	81-02	RA-01606
SE-LCX	Beech 1900D	UE-275	N11189
SE-LCY	Piper PA-46-310P Malibu	4608016	N9101V
SE-LCZ	Cessna A.185F Skywagon	02444	LN-ASE
			N1723R
SE-LDA	Short SD.3-60	SH.3688	G-BMLC
			G-14-3688
SE-LDB	CASA C.212-CB	154	N125JM
SE-LDC	CASA C.212-200	193	VH-ICJ
SE-LDD	SAAB S-91B Safir	91250	Fv50038
SE-LDG	CASA C.212-CC	192	N192MA
			LV-WEU
			N437CA
SE-LDH	BAe. Jetstream Series 3102	772	OY-SVK
			C-FAMJ
			G-31-772
SE-LDI	BAe. Jetstream Series 3112	785	C-FHOE
			G-31-785
SE-LDK	Short SC.7 Skyvan Mk.III	SH.1870	SX-BBO
			G-AXLC
			G-14-42
SE-LDL	Beech A100 King Air	B-213	F-GFEV
			N660CB
			N7243R
SE-LDN	Reims/Cessna F.182Q Skylane	0141	D-EFNQ
SE-LDT(2)	Robin R.2160 Acrobin	271	F-GMXT
SE-LDU	Piper PA-28-181 Archer III	2843237	OY-JAF
			N41352
			OK-NEW
			N9516N
SE-LDY	Piper PA-28RT-201T Turbo Arrow IV	28R-7931198	OY-CSA
	(Reservation 2.00)		N29333
SE-LDZ	Piper PA-18-150 Super Cub	18-7686	LN-HHQ
	(Officially quoted as c/n 18-1984)		D-EDPA
SE-LEA	Fokker F.27-050	20116	PH-GHK
			D-AFKX
			PH-GHK
			OE-LFY
			(VH-FNK)
			PH-EXJ
SE-LEB	Fokker F.27-050	20120	PH-JHD
			D-AFKZ
			PH-JHD
			(VH-FNO)
			PH-EXE
SE-LEC	Fokker F.27-050	20112	VH-FNG
			OE-LFX
			VH-FNG
			PH-EXW
SE-LED	Fokker F.27-050	20111	VH-FNF
			VT-RAB
			VH-FNF
			PH-EXV
SE-LEF	Fairchild-Swearingen SA.227AC Metro III	AC-451B	VH-NEM
			N211CA
SE-LEG	HS.748 Series 2A	1723	D-AFSF
SE-LEH	Fokker F.27-050	20108	VH-FNC
			PH-EXP
SE-LEI	Cessna A.185E Skywagon	1176	(SE-LEM)
			LN-NPF
			N4722Q
SE-LEK	HS.748 Series 2A	1725	D-AFSH
SE-LEL	Fokker F.27-050	20110	VH-FNE
			VT-RAA
			VH-FNE
			PH-EXL
SE-LEO	HS.748 Series 2A	1726	D-AFSI
SE-LEP	SAAB-Scania SF.340A	127	B-12200
			SE-F27
SE-LER	Cessna 208 Caravan	00112	D-FILM
			N9649F
SE-LES	SAAB-Scania SF.340A	129	B-12299
			SE-F29
SE-LEU	Fokker F.27-050	20115	9M-MGZ
			VH-FNJ
			OE-LFW
			VH-FNJ
			PH-EXD
SE-LEX	HS.748 Series 2A	1727	D-AFSJ
SE-LEY	HS.748 Series 2A	1631	LN-FOM
			PP-VDT
SE-LEZ	Fokker F.27-050	20128	PH-PRA
SE-LFA	Fokker F.27-050	20165	PH-EXG
SE-LFB	Fokker F.27-050	20169	PH-EXI
SE-LFC	Fokker F.27-050	20187	PH-EXN
SE-LFK	Fokker F.27-050	20188	PH-EXB
SE-LFN	Fokker F.27-050	20193	PH-EXP
SE-LFO	Fokker F.27-050	20198	PH-EXG
SE-LFP	Fokker F.27-050	20199	PH-EXH
SE-LFR	Fokker F.27-050	20215	PH-EXG
SE-LFS	Fokker F.27-050	20216	PH-EXO
SE-LGA	BAe. Jetstream Series 3101	636	N636JX
			G-BVDK
			N407MX
			G-31-636

Regn.	Type	C/n	Prev.Id.
SE-LGB	BAe. Jetstream Series 3101	639	N639JX
			N409MX
			G-31-639
SE-LGC	BAe. Jetstream Series 3108	645	G-BXLM
			N645JD
			PH-KJA
			G-31-645
SE-LGD	Cessna 172R	80359	
SE-LGE	Short SD.3-60	SH.3686	G-BMHX
			G-14-3686
SE-LGF	Reims/Cessna F.172L	0828	LN-BWC
SE-LGG	Piper PA-34-200T Seneca II	34-8070021	N8111H
SE-LGH	BAe. Jetstream Series 3112	773	OY-SVO
			C-FAMK
			G-31-773
SE-LGI	Cessna 172R	80381	LN-PWE
			N9519P
SE-LGK	Reims/Cessna F.172H	0647	OY-AGM
SE-LGL	Cessna 172R	80059	LN-PWB
			N376ES
SE-LGM	BAe. Jetstream Series 3112	781	OY-SVY
			C-FASJ
			G-31-781
SE-LGN	Britten-Norman BN-2A-8 Islander	377	D-IHUR
			G-BBUA
			G-51-377
			5T-TJV
			F-BUTN
			G-BBUA
SE-LGO	Grumman AA-5A Cheetah	0462	OY-GAO
SE-LGP	Piper PA-28-161 Warrior II	28-8016372	HB-PFH
	(Reservation 1.00)		N82469
			N8244V
SE-LGR	Piper PA-28-161 Warrior II (Res. 1.00)	28-8116137	HB-PGW
SE-LGT	Piper PA-32-260 Cherokee Six	32-7600017	N6155J
SE-LGU to -LGZ Reserved for BAe. ATPs for West Air 1.00			
SE-LHA	BAe. Jetstream Series 3201	842	N842JX
			N842AE
			G-31-842
SE-LHB	BAe. Jetstream Series 3201	844	N844JX
			N844AE
			G-31-844
SE-LHC	BAe. Jetstream Series 3201	846	N846JX
			N846AE
			G-31-846
SE-LHD	Dornier 228-201	8108	G-CAYN
			D-IABE
			D-CBDO(2)
			G-MLNR
			D-IOHI
			D-COHI
SE-LHE	BAe. Jetstream Series 3201	854	N854JX
			N854AE
			G-31-854
SE-LHF	BAe. Jetstream Series 3201	855	N855JX
			N855AE
			G-31-855
SE-LHG	BAe. Jetstream Series 3201	857	N857JX
			N857AE
			G-BREV
			G-31-857
SE-LHH	BAe. Jetstream Series 3201	848	N848JX
			N848AE
			N332QP
			G-31-848
SE-LHI	BAe. Jetstream Series 3201	841	N841JX
			N841AE
			G-BPZL
			N338AE
			G-31-841
SE-LHP	BAe. Jetstream Series 3102	638	G-BUFL
			OH-JAC
			G-BUFL
			N408MX
			G-31-638

Regn.	Type	C/n	Prev.Id.
SE-LHR	Reims/Cessna F.177RG Cardinal RG	0168	HB-CXU
SE-LHS	SOCATA TB-9 Tampico (Reservation 2.00)	692	LN-KLO
SE-LHU	Rockwell Commander 114	14359	OY-FIN
			N5775N
SE-LHV	BAe. Jetstream Series 3109	720	G-BRGL
			OK-SEK
			G-OEDC
			G-LOGU
			G-BRGL
			I-BLUA
			G-31-720
			G-BRGL
			G-31-720
SE-LHY	Short SD.3-60	SH.3755	G-BVMY
			G-OEEC
			G-BPKY
SE-LIA	HS.748 Series 2A	1717	F-GFYM
			ZS-JAY
			F-BUTR
			G-BASZ
			G-11-9
SE-LIB	HS.748 Series 2B	1776	FAC-1108
			G-11-14
SE-LIC	HS.748 Series 2B	1778	C-FKTL
			5U-BAS
			G-11-20
SE-LID	HS.748 Series 2A	1760	J5-GAT
			G-BFVR
			G-11-9
SE-LIE	HS.748 Series 2	1595	A10-595
SE-LIF	HS.748 Series 2	1596	A10-596
SE-LII	Yakovlev YAK-52	867015	ES-FYD
			DOSAAF-106
SE-LIL	Fairchild-Swearingen SA.227AC Metro III	AC-432B	F-GLPE
			N33042
			TC-FAB
			N1014T
SE-LIN	Fokker F.27-050	20138	PH-PRB
SE-LIO	Fokker F.27-050	20146	PH-PRC
SE-LIP	Fokker F.27-050	20147	PH-PRD
SE-LIR	Fokker F.27-050	20151	PH-PRE
SE-LIS	Fokker F.27-050	20152	PH-PRF
SE-LIZ	Opus 280	041	(PH-....)
			SE-V01
SE-LKA	Beech 76 Duchess	ME-295	(SE-LLL)
			F-GESU
			N6705Y
SE-LKB	EMB.120RBrasilia	120-016	(SE-LIZ)
			N124AM
			PT-SIL
SE-LKC	EMB.120RBrasilia	120-046	N273UE
			PT-SJP
SE-LKD	EMB.120RBrasilia (Reservation)	unkn	
SE-LKE	EMB.120RBrasilia (Reservation)	unkn	
SE-LKF	EMB.120RBrasilia (Reservation)	unkn	
SE-LKI	Partenavia P.68C	366	G-JACT
			G-NVIA
SE-LKK	Piper PA-22-108 Colt	22-9064	LN-BDK
			LV-PQV
			N10F
SE-LKM	Cessna 182R Skylane	67785	OY-CKM
			OH-CIU
			N5551N
SE-LKN	Cessna 172RG	0532	N5438V
SE-LKO	Cessna 172RG	0682	N6421V
SE-LKP	Cessna 172RG	0055	N5353R
SE-LKR	Cessna 172RG (Reservation)	0718	N6466V
SE-LKS	Cessna 172RG	0135	N5273R
SE-LKT	Cessna 172RG (Reservation)	0491	N5263V
SE-LKU	Cessna 172RG (Reservation)	0915	N9605B
SE-LKZ	Reims/Cessna FR.172ERocket (Reservation 11.99)	0039	OH-CNF
			(SE-FBU)
SE-LLA	Scottish Avn SAL-125 Bulldog (Res. 12.99)	BH100-148	Fv61038
			G-AZMS
SE-LMA	Mooney M.20J Model 201	24-3202	D-EMON

Regn.	Type	C/n	Prev.Id.
SE-LMM	Beech B200 Super King Air	BB-920	N83TJ
			PK-YPS
			N83TJ
			C-GSCM
SE-LMN	Beech B200 Super King Air	BB-1255	PK-HTI
			N125CU
			N2652M
SE-LMU	Yakovlev YAK-55 (Reservation)	unkn	
SE-LNK	Mooney M.20K Model 252	25-1016	OY-BHB
SE-LRA to LRZ	Reserved for DHC-8-400s for SAS		
SE-LSA	SAAB-Scania 2000	042	SE-042
SE-LSB	SAAB-Scania 2000	043	SE-043
SE-LSC	SAAB-Scania 2000	044	SE-044
SE-LSE	SAAB-Scania 2000	046	SE-046
SE-LSF	SAAB-Scania 2000	053	SE-053
SE-LSG	SAAB-Scania 2000	055	SE-055
SE-LSH	SAAB-Scania 2000	052	SE-052
SE-LSI	SAAB-Scania 2000	050	OM-DGA
			SE-050
SE-LTT	Piper PA-31-325 Navajo	31-8012041	N125TT
			OO-DFC
			C-GZVV
			N69XX
SE-RAA	Embraer EMB.135ER	145-210	

SE-RAA to -RAF Were reserved for Dornier 328-200s for Jet 2000 AB
SE-RAG to -RAZ Reserved for Airbuses for SAS
(SE-RAA to -RAS originally reserved for Boeing 737-505s of Braathens ASA to be re-registered from Norway but as yet no marks have been changed)

EXPERIMENTAL AND HOMEBUILT AIRCRAFT

Regn.	Type	C/n	Prev.Id.
SE-XCA	Andreasson BA-4B	2	
SE-XCC	Andreasson BA-4B	3	
SE-XCD	Andreasson BA-4B	4	
SE-XCE	Andreasson BA-4B	5	
SE-XCF	SAAB MFI-15 (W/o 17.12.88)	02	
SE-XCG	Bede BD-4	SE-01	
SE-XCH	Druine D.31 Turbulent	352	OY-CMA
SE-XCI	Jodel D.119-100	786	
SE-XCK	Andreasson Stil BA-11	1	
SE-XCL	Cassutt Racer IIIM	SE-75-01	
SE-XCO	Bede BD-4	unkn	
SE-XCP	Brügger MB-2 Colibri	05	
SE-XCR	Brügger MB-2 Colibri	09	
SE-XCS	Brügger MB-2 Colibri	10	
SE-XCT	Wittman Tailwind	206	SE-XFI
SE-XCU	Pazmany PL-2 (W/o 28.6.92)	SE-01	
SE-XCV	Brügger MB-2 Colibri	SE-03	
SE-XCX	Evans VP-2	V2 1269-15	
SE-XCY	Stewart Headwind	unkn	
SE-XCZ	Coot-A	001	
SE-XDA	Jodel D.113	526	
SE-XDB	Brügger MB-2 Colibri	19	
SE-XDC	Brügger MB-2 Colibri	11	
SE-XDD	Zenith CH-200	A.242/1979	
SE-XDE	Jodel D.113-3	1431	OY-BMF
SE-XDF	CEA Jodel DR.1050 Ambassadeur	222	OY-DHF
			F-BKGD
SE-XDG	Jodel D.113-3	030	
SE-XDH	Jodel D.112 Club	1420	OY-BMV
SE-XDI	JC-24A Weedhopper	0291	
SE-XDK	MFI-9HB Trainer	P1-827	
	(MFI-11 standard, built from MFI-9 c/n 08)		
SE-XDL	Cassutt IIIM	589	
SE-XDM	MFI-9HB Trainer	07	
SE-XDN	Brügger MB-2 Colibri	unkn	
SE-XDO	Jodel D.113-3	36	
SE-XDP	Christen Eagle II	0020	
SE-XDR	Jungster 1	7207	
SE-XDS	Aerosport Scamp-A	01	
SE-XDT	Druine D.31 Turbulent (CofA exp 8.89)	266	OY-AMC

Regn.	Type	C/n	Prev.Id.
SE-XDU	Brügger MB-2 Colibri	158	
SE-XDV	Druine D.31 Turbulent	232	OY-AMZ
SE-XDX	Jodel D.113	1460	OY-BMZ
SE-XDY	Jodel D.112 Club	830	OY-BMD
SE-XDZ	Jodel D.113	1151	OY-BMA
SE-XEA	Brügger MB-2 Colibri	12	
SE-XEB	Wassmer Jodel D.120 Paris-Nice	160	D-EDAW
SE-XEC	Rutan Vari-eze	1707	
SE-XED	Jodel D.119	1400	OY-AMT
SE-XEE	Stolp Starduster	1840	
SE-XEG	Druine D.31 Turbulent	298	OY-AMK
SE-XEH	Jodel D.113-3	S-64	
SE-XEI	Piel CP.301A Emeraude	102-53	D-EFKO
SE-XEK	Jodel D.119	1483	OY-CMC
SE-XEL	Evans VP-1 Volksplane	01	
SE-XEN	Druine D.31 Turbulent (W/o 20.8.88)	327	OY-BME
SE-XEO	Pitts S-1S-E	7-0419	SE-XEM
SE-XEP	Rutan Vari-eze	2091	
SE-XER	Piaggio P.149D-A4	317	D-EBQP
			96+20
			AC+468
			AS+468
SE-XES	Brügger MB-2 Colibri	173	
SE-XET	Andreasson MFI-9HB	031	LN-BFL
SE-XEU	SAN Jodel D.117 Grand Tourisme (W/o 25.12.94)	910	D-EMBI
			HB-SVY
			OE-AFA
SE-XEV	Jodel D.112 Club	1153	OY-AMU
SE-XEX	Jodel D.112/108	1395	OY-AMD
SE-XEY	Rand-Robinson KR-2	034	
SE-XEZ	Rutan LongEz	360	
SE-XFB	Fike-D	219	
SE-XFC	J-1B Don Quixote	085	
SE-XFD	Piel CP.301A Emeraude	181	OY-AOU
			F-BHMN
SE-XFF	Jurca MJ.2D Tempête	81	OY-AMV
SE-XFH	Jodel D.113-3	1436	OY-BMK
SE-XFK	Stoddard-Hamilton Glasair SH-2	404	
SE-XFL	SAN Jodel DR.100 Ambassadeur	83	OY-DIJ
			OE-ADA
SE-XFM	Rutan LongEz	746	
SE-XFO	DHC-1 Chipmunk T.20	C1/0695	RDAF P-131
SE-XFP	Zlin Z.226T Trenér 6	365	LN-MAX
			D-EDEW
			OH-TZD
			OK-M..
SE-XFR	Viking Dragonfly Mk.II	517	
SE-XFS	Rand-Robinson KR-2	AWW-28	
SE-XFT	Binder CP.301S Smaragd	114	OY-EAG
SE-XFU	Stoddard-Hamilton SH-2 Glasair	158	
SE-XFV	Rutan Vari-Viggen	517	
SE-XFX	Brügger MB-2 Colibri	189	
SE-XFY	Nitz-1/Zlin Z.326 Trenér Master	839	D-ENGA
			OK-SNB
SE-XFZ	Wassmer Jodel D.120L Paris-Nice	153L	D-EKIK
SE-XGA	Thorp T-18	1308	
SE-XGB	Rand-Robinson KR-2	4065	
SE-XGC	CEA Jodel DR.1050 Ambassadeur	36	D-EJRB
			F-BJRB
SE-XGD	Mraz M.1D Sokol	339	(OY-DNV)
			D-EMUP
			OE-AAY
			OK-D..
SE-XGE	Rutan Vari-eze	935	
SE-XGF	Stoddard-Hamilton SH-2 Glasair RG	476R	
SE-XGG	SAN Jodel DR.1050 Ambassadeur	286	D-EFJR
SE-XGH	Jodel D.113-3	1448	OY-CME
SE-XGI	Van's RV-3A	726	
SE-XGK	Wassmer Jodel D.120 Paris-Nice	49	D-EAFD
			F-BHYS
SE-XGL	Super Baby Great Lakes	8410K	
SE-XGM	Tipsy T.66 Nipper Mk.II	23	(D-EJAB)
	(Restoration project)		OY-ABO
SE-XGN	EAA Biplane	101	G-BJNW
			N67279

Regn.	Type	C/n	Prev.Id.
SE-XGO	SAN Jodel DR.1050 Ambassadeur	272	D-ELME
SE-XGP	Monnet Sonerai IILT	1180	
SE-XGS	Le Gare Sea Hawker	70	
SE-XGT	Rutan LongEz	607	
SE-XGU	Pitts S-1S Special	370-H/ PFA/1526	G-AYLU
	(c/n officially quoted as K-064)		
SE-XGV	Extra EA.230 Ultimate (W/o 1.8.91)	011	D-EMIN(3)
SE-XGX	Bölkow BO.207	250	D-EJFY
SE-XGZ	Rutan Cozy	unkn	
SE-XHA	Viking Dragonfly (W/o 19.6.94)	476	
SE-XHB	Laser 200	01	
SE-XHC	Scintex Piel CP.301C Emeraude	524	OY-AAW
SE-XHD	Andreasson MFI-9HB	43	
SE-XHE	Light Aero Avid Flyer	208	
SE-XHG	Andreasson MFI-9HB	50	
SE-XHH	Druine D.31 Turbulent (W/o 21.7.96)	373	OY-CMK
SE-XHI	Aviamilano P.19 Scricciolo	337	I-PIND
SE-XHK	Beagle A.61 Tugmaster 6A	3744	LN-AEV
SE-XHM	Wassmer Jodel D.120A Paris-Nice	178	F-BJIV
SE-XHN	Rand-Robinson KR-2	3405	
SE-XHO	Stolp SA.700 Acroduster 1	151	
SE-XHP	Andreasson BA-6B	3	
SE-XHR	Aerotek Pitts S-2A (W/o 21.6.91)	2163	N84PS
SE-XHS	Viking Dragonfly Mk.II	588	
SE-XHU	Wassmer WA.41 Baladou	112	F-BNHR
SE-XHV	Evans VP-1 Volksplane	V-2302	
SE-XHX	Pitts S-1C Special	JC-1	
SE-XHY	Monnet Sonerai IIL	01626L	
SE-XIA	Piper PA-18-150 Super Cub	18-5990	OY-AZI D-EMUC
SE-XIC	Neico Lancair 235	101	
SE-XID	Bölkow BO.208C Junior	700	PH-CEP D-EABN
SE-XIE	Light Aero Avid Amphibian	11	
SE-XIF	Light Aero Avid Flyer	325	
SE-XIH	Stoll Starlite	206	
SE-XII	Quickie	unkn	
SE-XIK	Pitts S-1C Special	1021	N2900V
SE-XIL	CVM 01 Tummelisa	362	
SE-XIM	WagAero Super CUBy	1465	
SE-XIN	Stoddard-Hamilton Glasair SH-2	159	
SE-XIO	Van's RV-4	432	
SE-XIP	Thorp T.18	548	
SE-XIR	Wassmer WA.40A Super IV	65	HB-DCC
SE-XIS	Andreasson MFI-9HB	062	
SE-XIT	CEA Jodel DR.1050-M1 Sicile Record	593	F-BMPD
SE-XIU	Rans S-10 Sakota	0588016	
SE-XIV	Zlin Z.526F Trenér Master	1318	
SE-XIX	Rutan LongEz	2031L	
SE-XIY	Orlican L-40 Meta-Sokol	150406	OH-SMA
SE-XIZ	Extra EA.300	006	
SE-XKA	Druine D.31 Turbulent	330	OY-CMF
SE-XKB	Piper PA-22-160 Tri-Pacer	22-6521	LN-TVL N9611D
SE-XKC	Binder CP.301S Smaragd	111	OY-EAF
SE-XKD	Light Aero Avid Flyer	390	
SE-XKE	Janowski J1 Don Quixote	unkn	
SE-XKF	Neico Lancair 235	188	
SE-XKG	Rand-Robinson KR-2 Turbo	84	
SE-XKH	Rutan LongEz	1939L	
SE-XKI	Spezio DAL-1	7	N1334
SE-XKK	Kukulka	T-026382	SP-PHN
SE-XKL	Pottier P.180S	147	
SE-XKM	Piaggio FWP.149D	133	OY-CPV D-EFRB(2) 91+12 D-EBDO KB+110
SE-XKN	Viking Dragonfly	127	
SE-XKO	Pottier P.180S	190	
SE-XKP	Light Aero Avid Amphibian	28	SE-YSP
SE-XKR	Druine D.31 Turbulent	303	OY-CMG
SE-XKT	Pottier P.180S	189	
SE-XKU	DHC-1 Chipmunk	C1/0102	OY-ATG P-123 12-123
SE-XKV	Pitts S-1C Special (W/o 2.7.94)	203H	N139
SE-XKX	Denney Kitfox II	524	
SE-XKY	Neico Lancair 235	102	
SE-XKZ	Aero Designs Pulsar	166	
SE-XLA	Zlin Z.526F Trenér Master	1150	SP-CDL
SE-XLB	Zlin Z.526F Trenér Master	1114	SP-CDH
SE-XLC	Zlin Z.526F Trenér Master	1248	SP-CPG
SE-XLD	Van's RV-6	20273	
SE-XLE	Rutan LongEz	9753	
SE-XLG	Murphy Renegade Spirit 912	0290	
SE-XLH	Binder CP.301S Smaragd	110	HB-SEM D-EGAZ
SE-XLI	Light Aero Avid Amphibian	22	
SE-XLK	Rans S-10 Sakota	0989061	
SE-XLL	Stoddard-Hamilton SH-2 Glasair RG	358	N100DE
SE-XLM	WagAero Super CUBy	562	
SE-XLN	Neico Lancair 235	165	
SE-XLO	Murphy Renegade Spirit EXP	0342	
SE-XLP	CEA Jodel DR.1050 Ambassadeur	569	PH-XAN
SE-XLR	Andreasson BA-4B	unkn	
SE-XLU	Light Aero Avid Amphibian	35	
SE-XLV	Corby CJ-1 Starlet	181	
SE-XLX	Stoddard-Hamilton SH-2 Glasair RG	1142	
SE-XLY	Light Aero Avid Amphibian	34	
SE-XLZ	Rutan LongEz	1868	
SE-XMA	Light Aero Avid Flyer Aerobat	781	
SE-XMB	Light Aero Avid Flyer Aerobat	737	
SE-XMC	Blériot XI (painted as 'A14')	82	
SE-XMD	Piper PA-18 Super Cub 95	18-1576	LN-TSO OO-HMR ALAT 51-15576
SE-XME	Light Aero Avid Flyer	391	
SE-XMF	Jodel D.18	274	
SE-XMG	Light Aero Avid Flyer	322	
SE-XMH	SAAB MFI-15-200A	847	
SE-XMI	Van's RV-6	20285	
SE-XMK	Light Aero Avid Flyer	549	
SE-XML	Light Aero Avid Flyer	326	
SE-XMM	Light Aero Avid Amphibian	043	
SE-XMN	Light Aero Avid Amphibian	83A	
SE-XMO	Light Aero Avid Amphibian	92A	
SE-XMP	Bushby Mustang II	1259	
SE-XMR	Brügger MB-2 Colibri	03	
SE-XMS	Nord 3400	39	ALAT
SE-XMT	Jodel D.18 (W/o 3.5.95)	273	
SE-XMV	Jodel D.113	523	
SE-XMX	Light Aero Avid Flyer	1035	
SE-XMY	SAN Jodel DR.1050 Ambassadeur	363A	D-ENJE D-EAHW LN-BNO G-BAUL N202IT
SE-XNA	Schweizer TSC-1A1 Teal	21	
SE-XNB	SAN Jodel D.140C Mousquetaire III	90	F-BKSI F-BKSE
SE-XNC	Neico Lancair 320	457	
SE-XND	Piel CP.301A Emeraude	003	D-EBUW
SE-XNE	Light Aero Avid Amphibian (W/o 24.9.95)	82A	
SE-XNF	Nord 3400	68	ALAT
SE-XNG	Steen Skybolt	JSG-1	N101JG
SE-XNH	Murphy Renegade Spirit EXP	0338	
SE-XNI	SOCATA ST-10 Diplomate	138	F-BJCT
SE-XNK	Smith Miniplane DSA-1	7337	N5093D
SE-XNM	Van's RV-6	20934	
SE-XNN	Denney Kitfox IV	1519	
SE-XNO	Denney Kitfox III	1067	
SE-XNP	SAAB MFI-15-200A	15-848	
SE-XNR	Hummelbirg Wandwagon	625	
SE-XNS	Steen Skybolt	1	OH-XTS
SE-XNT	Steen Skybolt	SE-1	
SE-XNU	Midget Mustang VJ-1	VJ129	N3151
SE-XNV(2)	Nord 3400	121	ALAT

Regn.	Type	C/n	Prev.Id.
SE-XNX	Rans S-10 Sakota	0989062	(SE-XNV)
			(SE-XNX)
SE-XNY	Stoddard-Hamilton Glasair II-FT	1108	
SE-XNZ	Pober Pixie	PP001	
SE-XOA	Pottier P.180S	193	
SE-XOB	CASA I-131E Jungmann	2075	EC-332
	(Painted as "781-60")		E3B-475
SE-XOC	Rand-Robinson KR-2	19	N1352A
SE-XOD	Smith Sidewinder	17	
SE-XOF	Denney Kitfox IV	1518	
SE-XOG	Yakovlev YAK-50	760806	LY-AKZ
			DOSAAF-08
SE-XOH	Kaminski Jungster 1 Super 150	8509	
SE-XOI	Van's RV-6	20898	
SE-XOK	Light Aero Avid Amphibian	84A	
SE-XOL	Van's RV-4 (Permit)	420	
SE-XOM	Van's RV-6	21717	
SE-XON	Jodel D.18	2731	
SE-XOO	Steen Skybolt	001	N619JS
SE-XOP	Neico Lancair 320	493	
SE-XOR	Murphy Renegade Spirit	327	
SE-XOT	Neico Lancair 320	53	
SE-XOU	Rand-Robinson KR-2	8493	
SE-XOV	Light Aero Avid Amphibian	12	
SE-XOX	GP3 Osprey II	1228	
SE-XOY	Jodel D.18	262	
SE-XOZ	GP3 Osprey II	87	
SE-XPA	Jodel D.112 Club	62	
SE-XPB	Piper PA-22-108 Colt	22-9134	LN-IKW
			SE-CZO
SE-XPC	Jodel D.18	384	
SE-XPD	WagAero Super CUBy Sport Trainer	600	
SE-XPE	Pitts S-1S Special	03	OH-XPE
SE-XPF	Tipsy T.66H Nipper II	26	OO-HAL
			(OY-AEL)
SE-XPG	Light Aero Avid Mk IV	1432A	
SE-XPH	Ultravia Aero Pelican PL	TP101-41	
SE-XPI	Van's RV-6 (Permit)	21371	
SE-XPK	Van's RV-4	3610	
SE-XPL	T-131 Jungmann	01	SP-FPF
SE-XPM	Denney Kitfox	678	
SE-XPN	Light Aero Avid Catalina EXP 912	128A	
SE-XPO	Murphy Rebel	468REB	
	(Believed sold in USA as N797R in 2.97)		
SE-XPP	CSS-13	0430	SP-FZP
SE-XPR	Murphy Rebel	238	
SE-XPS	T-131 Jungmann	04	SP-FBF
SE-XPT	SAN Jodel D.117 Grand Tourisme	647	D-EJDO
			F-BIBX
SE-XPU	Reynolds Wildcat Special	001	N7XS
SE-XPV	Aeronca 11AC Chief	1773	G-RONC
			G-BULV
			N3493E
			NC3493E
SE-XPX	Neico Lancair 360	635	
SE-XPY	Piper PA-18-135 Super Cub (Permit 11.99)	18-2588	Turkish AF/
	(F/n 18-2416 was quoted as c/n but aircraft is now		52-6270
	designated as replica with c/n 1 due to lack of paperwork)		
SE-XPZ	Ridder Silent Two	1	
SE-XRA	SAN Jodel DR.1050 Ambassadeur	460	D-ELFB
SE-XRB	Christen Eagle II	0438	5Y-FUN
SE-XRC	Christensen OPUS-3	002	
SE-XRD	Rutan Cozy III	124	
SE-XRE	Jodel D.112 Club (Reservation)	1408	
SE-XRF	Europa Aviation Europa (Permit)	304	
SE-XRG	Rans S-7 Courier (Permit)	0297212	
SE-XRH	Neico Lancair 360 (Permit)	921	
SE-XRI	Piaggio FWP.149D	122	D-EIOH
			91+02
			SB+216
			SB+422
			D-ELHY
			AS+413
SE-XRK	Van's RV-4 (Reservation)	2572	
SE-XRL	Andreasson MFI-9HB (Permit)	105	

Regn.	Type	C/n	Prev.Id.
SE-XRM	Jodel D.18 (Reservation)	324	
SE-XRN	Piper PA-18-150 Super Cub (Reservation)	18-5330	D-EEKL
	(On rebuild)		ALAT
SE-XRO	Rans S-6SCoyote II	11971187	
SE-XRP	Neico Lancair 320 (Reservation)	536-320-283	N3073Q
SE-XRR	Seawind Europe Seawind 3000 (Reservation)	136	
SE-XRS	Rutan LongEz (Reservation .99)	746	
SE-XRT	Europa Aviation Europa (Reservation)	318	
SE-XRU	Neico Lancair IVP (Permit)	LIV-284	N205AF
SE-XRV	Van's RV-6 (Reservation)	23793	
SE-XRX	Europa Aviation Europa (Reservation)	300	
SE-XRY	Fisher Celebrity (Reservation)	AV1086	
SE-XRZ	Rutan Vari-eze (Reservation)	1405	N529SK
SE-XSA	Monnet Monerai	unkn	
SE-XSB	Monnet Monerai	unkn	
SE-XSC	Monnet Monerai	unkn	
SE-XSD	Windex 1100	001	
SE-XSE	Schleicher Rhönlerche II	321	D-8234
SE-XSF	Monnet Monerai	335	
SE-XSH	Windex 1200	001	
SE-XSI	Monnet Monerai	309	
SE-XSK	Fournier RF-4D	4104	SE-TGX
SE-XSL	Fauvel AV-222	11	
SE-XSM	Windex 1200	unkn	
SE-XSN	Windex 1200	016	
SE-XSO	Windex 1200C	005	
SE-XSP	Windex 1200C	006	
SE-XUE	EAA Acro Sport II	2047	
SE-XVA	Van's RV-3A	663	
SE-XVD	Stoddard-Hamil;ton SH-2 Glasair II (Res. 1.00)	3182	
SE-XVI	Stoddard-Hamilton SH-2 Glasair III	3156	
SE-XVV	Rans S-7 Courier (Reservation)	1297/235	
SE-XVZ	Aero Designs Pulsar XP	515	
SE-XYZ	Ridder Silent Two (same c/n as SE-XPZ)	1	

BALLOONS

Regn.	Type	C/n	Prev.Id.
SE-ZAA	Cameron DS-140 Hot Air Airship	200	G-BEHI
SE-ZAE	Colt AS-56 Hot Air Airship	624	G-BLVJ
SE-ZAG	Colt AS-105 Hot Air Airship	815	
SE-ZAM	Colt AS-56 Hot Air Airship	687	OH-AIR
SE-ZBB	Colt 69A HAFB	552	
SE-ZBD	Colt 69A HAFB	638	
SE-ZBF	Cameron N-77 HAFB	1142	
SE-ZBG	Cameron N-56 HAFB	1158	
SE-ZBH	Thunder/Colt AX6-56A HAFB	685	
SE-ZBI	Colt 105A HAFB	467	G-BKLX
SE-ZBK	Colt 160A HAFB	681	
SE-ZBL	Cameron A-210 HAFB	1160	
SE-ZBM	Colt 77A HAFB	713	
SE-ZBN	Colt 77A HAFB	706	
SE-ZBP	Cameron N-77 HAFB	1236	
SE-ZBR	Colt 69A HAFB	785	
SE-ZBS	Balloon Works Firefly 6 HAFB	F6-008	
SE-ZBT	Colt 56A HAFB	807	
SE-ZBU	Colt 105A HAFB	828	
SE-ZBV	Colt 77A HAFB	798	
SE-ZBY	Colt 105A HAFB	534	G-BKZU
SE-ZBZ	Colt 14A Cloudhopper HAFB	340	G-BKDS
SE-ZCA	Cameron N-77 HAFB	1338	
SE-ZCB	SLB 56A HAFB	SLB-001	
SE-ZCC	Colt 105A HAFB	861	
SE-ZCD	Colt 120A HAFB	854	
SE-ZCE	Colt 69A HAFB	885	
SE-ZCF	Colt 17A HAFB	697	G-BMDA
SE-ZCG	Colt 90A HAFB	911	
SE-ZCH	Balloon Works Firefly 8-24 HAFB	F8-097	
SE-ZCI	Colt 77A HAFB	978	
SE-ZCK	Cameron N-105 HAFB	1082	G-BLOZ
SE-ZCL	Colt 69A HAFB	1062	

Regn.	Type	C/n	Prev.Id.
SE-ZCM	Colt 180A HAFB	1048	
SE-ZCN	Colt 180A HAFB	1061	
SE-ZCP	Cameron A-210 HAFB	1479	
SE-ZCR	Cameron A-105 HAFB	1522	
SE-ZCS	Cameron O-77 HAFB	1545	
SE-ZCT	Colt 105A HAFB	1155	
SE-ZCU	Cameron N-77 HAFB	1617	
SE-ZCV	Colt 240A HAFB	1160	
SE-ZCX	Thunder AX9-140 HAFB	1177	
SE-ZCY	Cameron A-210 HAFB	1687	
SE-ZCZ	Cameron A-210 HAFB	1912	
SE-ZDA	SLB Viking 77A SL HAFB	SLB-003	
SE-ZDB	SLB Viking 77A SL HAFB	SLB-004	
SE-ZDC	SLB Viking 180A HAFB	SLB-006	
SE-ZDE	Colt 77A HAFB	1225	
SE-ZDF	SLB Viking 120A HAFB	SLB-008	
SE-ZDG	SLB Viking 77A SL HAFB	SLB-OO9	
SE-ZDH	Colt 69A HAFB	1317	
SE-ZDI	Colt 90A HAFB	1347	
SE-ZDK	Cameron V-77 HAFB	1381	
SE-ZDL	Colt 77A HAFB	1410	
SE-ZDM	Cameron A-120 HAFB	1860	
SE-ZDN	Colt 105A HAFB	1216	
SE-ZDO	Cameron N-90 HAFB	1927	
SE-ZDP	Colt 120A HAFB	1390	
SE-ZDR	Cameron A-210 HAFB	1942	
SE-ZDS	Cameron N-77 HAFB	1136	G-BLWO
SE-ZDT	Colt 240A HAFB	1404	
SE-ZDU	Cameron A-120 HAFB	1943	
SE-ZDV	Colt 240A HAFB	1408	
SE-ZDX	SLB Viking 77A HAFB	SLB-015	
SE-ZDZ	SLB Viking 120A HAFB	SLB-011	
SE-ZEB	SLB Viking 69A HAFB	SLB-013	
SE-ZEC	Colt 77A HAFB	1566	
SE-ZED	SLB Viking 105A HAFB	SLB-017	
SE-ZEE	Colt 180A HAFB	1666	
SE-ZEF	SLB Viking 180A HAFB	SLB-016	
SE-ZEG	Colt 105A HAFB	1619	
SE-ZEH	Colt 90A HAFB	1406	
SE-ZEI	Colt 105A HAFB	1684	
SE-ZEK	Cameron N-105 HAFB	2204	
SE-ZEL	Cameron N-105 HAFB	2203	
SE-ZEM	Cameron N-77 HAFB	2152	
SE-ZEN	Cameron A-180 HAFB	2250	
SE-ZEO	Cameron A-180 HAFB	2251	
SE-ZEP	Cameron A-105 HAFB	1859	
SE-ZER	Thunder AX-77Z HAFB	1612	G-BRDK
SE-ZES	Colt 180A HAFB	1636	
SE-ZET	Cameron N-180 HAFB	2257	
SE-ZEU	SLB Viking 120A HAFB	SLB-018	
SE-ZEV	SLB Viking 77A HAFB	SLB-019	
SE-ZEX	Cameron N-105 HAFB	2386	
SE-ZEY	SLB Viking 56A HAFB	SLB-023	
SE-ZEZ	SLB Viking 105A HAFB	SLB-025	
SE-ZFA	Cameron N-56 HAFB	1471	G-BNZN
SE-ZFB	Cameron A-105 HAFB	2494	
SE-ZFC	Thunder AX10-160 SII HAFB	1921	
SE-ZFD	Colt 240A HAFB	1887	
SE-ZFE	Cameron V-90 HAFB	2582	
SE-ZFF	Thunder AX7-77 HAFB	1499	
SE-ZFG	SLB Viking 84A HAFB	SLB-028	
SE-ZFH	Colt 240A HAFB	2079	
SE-ZFI	Cameron V-90 HAFB	2701	
SE-ZFL	Cameron A-250 HAFB	2711	
SE-ZFM	Cameron A-210 HAFB	2633	
SE-ZFN	SLB Viking 105A HAFB	SLB-029	
SE-ZFO	SLB Viking 84A HAFB	031	
SE-ZFP	Colt 240A HAFB	2175	
SE-ZFR	Colt 240A HAFB	2180	
SE-ZFS	SLB Viking 105A HAFB	032	
SE-ZFT	SLB Viking 120A HAFB	SLB-033	
SE-ZFU	Colt 120A HAFB	2114	
SE-ZFV	Cameron N-77 HAFB	2882	
SE-ZFX	SLB Viking 120A HAFB	034	
SE-ZFY	Cameron A-210 HAFB	3220	

Regn.	Type	C/n	Prev.Id.
SE-ZFZ	SLB Viking 69A HAFB	SLB-030	
SE-ZGA	Lindstrand LBL-77A HAFB	107	
SE-ZGB	Lindstrand LBL-310A HAFB	100	
SE-ZGC	Lindstrand LBL-77A HAFB	084	
SE-ZGD	Lindstrand LBL-77A HAFB	166	
SE-ZGE	Lindstrand LBL-310A HAFB	086	
SE-ZGF	Colt 105A HAFB	944	G-BNEU
SE-ZGG	Lindstrand LBL-400A HAFB	200	
SE-ZGH	Lindstrand LBL-240A HAFB	199	
SE-ZGI	Cameron N-90 HAFB	3438	
SE-ZGK	Lindstrand LBL-240A HAFB	197	
SE-ZGL	Lindstrand LBL-9OA HAFB	201	
SE-ZGM	Lindstrand LBL-240A HAFB	258	
SE-ZGN	Lindstrand LBL-77A HAFB	284	
SE-ZGO	Cameron A-250 HAFB	3822	
SE-ZGP	Cameron A-250 HAFB	3823	
SE-ZGR	UltraMagic N-250 HAFB	250/3	
SE-ZGS	Lindstrand LBL-180A HAFB	350	
SE-ZGT	Cameron A-250 HAFB	3877	
SE-ZGU	Cameron Clown SS HAFB	2857	
SE-ZGV	Lindstrand LBL-9OA HAFB	426	
SE-ZGY	Cameron Flying Beer Can 77SS HAFB	3239	G-BVLB
SE-ZGZ	Colt 90A HAFB	863	G-IZMO
SE-ZHA	UltraMagic N-250 HAFB	250/06	
SE-ZHB	Lindstrand LBL-77A HAFB	209	
	(also regd as Colt 120A HAFB c/n 4197, 10.97)		
SE-ZHC	Lindstrand LBL Flying Newspaper SS HAFB	059	G-BVGK
SE-ZHD	Lindstrand LBL-240A HAFB	018	
SE-ZHE	Colt 56SS Flying Head HAFB	309	G-HEAD
SE-ZHF	Brita Balloon	001	
SE-ZHG	Lindstrand LBL-400A HAFB	300	
SE-ZHH	Lindstrand LBL-240A HAFB	377	
SE-ZHI	Lindstrand LBL-240A HAFB	378	
SE-ZHK	Lindstrand LBL-105A HAFB	461	
SE-ZHM	ZHM Kubicek BB-PNEU HAFB	053	OM-6002
SE-ZHN	Sky 400-28 HAFB	121	
SE-ZHO	Cameron SS Cabin HAFB	2820	G-ODIS
SE-ZHP	Lindstrand LBL-77A HAFB	209	
SE-ZHR	Lindstrand LBL-77A HAFB	034	G-BUYA
SE-ZHS	Colt Jeans SS HAFB	1747	G-JCJC
SE-ZHT	UltraMagic M-77 HAFB	77/151	
SE-ZHU	UltraMagic M-65C HAFB	65/79	
SE-ZHV	Sky 500 HAFB (Reservation)	151	
SE-ZHX	Sky 500 HAFB (Reservation)	157	
SE-ZHY	Sky 77-24 HAFB (Reservation 12.99)	176	
SE-ZIA	UltraMagic N-355 HAFB	355/01	
SE-ZIH	Colt 90A HAFB	4496	
SE-ZII	UltraMagic M-130 HAFB	130/14	
SE-ZIL	Cameron A-250 HAFB (Reservation 2.00)	unkn	
SE-ZIP	Lindstrand LBL-210AHAFB	613	
SE-ZKA	Cameron A-250 HAFB	4409	
SE-ZKF	Lindstrand LBL Drinks Can SS HAFB (Res 10.99)	642	
SE-ZKG	Cameron A-340HL HAFB	4377	
SE-ZSB	Larsson SLB Balloon	unkn	
SE-ZVA	Colt 56A HAFB	008	
SE-ZVD	Colt 77A HAFB	018	
SE-ZVE	Colt 56A HAFB	029	
SE-ZVF	Colt 56A HAFB	031	
SE-ZVG	Colt 77A HAFB	036	
SE-ZVH	Colt 56A HAFB	042	
SE-ZVI	Thunder AX6-56Z HAFB	198	
SE-ZVK	Colt 56A HAFB	046	
SE-ZVL	Colt 56A HAFB	044	
SE-ZVM	Colt 56A HAFB	051	
SE-ZVN	Colt 56A HAFB	043	
SE-ZVO	Colt 77A HAFB	052	
SE-ZVS	Colt 77B HAFB	063	
SE-ZVT	Colt 56A HAFB	058	
SE-ZVU	Colt 56A HAFB	059	
SE-ZVV	Colt 56A HAFB	083	
SE-ZVZ	Cameron O-84 HAFB	174	N65BB
SE-ZXB	Colt 56A HAFB	090	
SE-ZXC	Colt 56A HAFB	092	
SE-ZXE	Colt 21A Cloudhopper HAFB	096	
SE-ZXF	Thunder-Colt 69A HAFB	300	

Regn.	Type	C/n	Prev.Id.
SE-ZXG	Thunder AX7-77A HAFB	302	
SE-ZXH	Cameron CB-183 HAFB	600	
SE-ZXK	Colt 77B HAFB	084	G-BHRZ
SE-ZXL	Colt 77B HAFB	362	
SE-ZXM	Colt 56B HAFB	400	
SE-ZXN	Colt 69A HAFB	412	
SE-ZXO	Colt 56A HAFB	421	
SE-ZXR	Colt 77A HAFB	482	
SE-ZXS	Colt 77A HAFB	015	G-BHBD
SE-ZXT(2)	Cameron N-77 HAFB	893	
SE-ZXU	Colt 56A HAFB	500	
SE-ZXV	Colt 56A HAFB	511	
SE-ZXX	Colt 77A HAFB	515	
SE-ZXZ	SLB Viking 84A HAFB	SLB-026	
SE-ZYB	Thunder AX7-77A HAFB	090	
SE-ZYC	Thunder AX8-90 HAFB	092	
SE-ZYD	Cameron V-56 HAFB	368	
SE-ZYF	Colt 56A HAFB	004	
SE-ZYG	Colt 77A HAFB	006	G-BFRG
			EI-BDJ
SE-ZYI	Colt 56A HAFB	006	
SE-ZYL	Colt 56A HAFB	005	
SE-ZYN	Colt 56A HAFB (ex c/n 001)	321	
SE-ZYO	Colt 56A HAFB	002	
SE-ZYP	Colt 77A HAFB	009	
SE-ZYR	Colt 77A HAFB	001	
SE-ZYU	Colt 77A HAFB	005	
SE-ZYX	Colt 77A HAFB	002	
SE-ZZA	Piccard AX6-56 HAFB	102	
SE-ZZB	Piccard AX6-56 HAFB	114	
SE-ZZD	Cameron O-56 HAFB	103	
SE-ZZF	Thunder AX7-77A HAFB	040	
SE-ZZG	Cameron V-56 HAFB	214	
SE-ZZH	Thunder AX7-77A HAFB	066	
SE-ZZL	Thunder AX7-77A HAFB	072	
SE-ZZM	Cameron O-84 HAFB	160	
SE-ZZN	Thunder AX7-77A HAFB	034	
SE-ZZO	Thunder AX8-105A HAFB	129	
	(c/n still officially quoted as 026 - now G-THOR)		
SE-ZZP	Cameron O-84 HAFB	112	
SE-ZZR	Cameron O-84 HAFB	122	
SE-ZZS	Cameron O-84 HAFB	99	
SE-ZZT	Cameron O-84 HAFB	22	G-AZAA
SE-ZZU	Cameron O-56 HAFB	78	
SE-ZZV	Cameron O-84 HAFB	77	
SE-ZZY	Cameron O-84 HAFB	44	
SE-ZZZ(2)	Cameron O-84 HAFB	363	
	(Formerly c/n 53 ex G-BAGH)		
SE-Z..	Colt 180A HAFB	1172	
SE-Z..	Colt Chips Bag SS HAFB	1430	G-BREC

GLIDERS AND MOTOR-GLIDERS

Regn.	Type	C/n	Prev.Id.
SE-SFE	Grunau Baby IIB-2	113	
SE-SHG	DFS Olympia	1	
SE-SMB	Slingsby T-31B Cadet	699	WT904
SE-SMD	Slingsby T-21B Sedbergh	609	WB942
SE-SME	Slingsby T-21B Sedbergh	663	BGA3309/FJY
			BGA3242/FGD
			WG496
SE-SMF	Schulgleiter SG-38	162	
SE-SMG	Anfanger I	20	
SE-SMH	EoN Olympia 2B	EON/0/147	BGA1422/CBX
SE-SMI	Anfanger II	1	
SE-SMK	Slingsby T-21B Sedbergh	621	WB960
SE-SML	Grunau Baby IIb	8/125	
SE-SMM	Schweizer SGU-2-22E	194	C-FWTY
			CF-WTY
			N2745Z
SE-SMN	MHL/Slingsby T.21B Sedbergh	nil	WB979

Regn.	Type	C/n	Prev.Id.
SE-SUC	Scheibe Bergfalke II/55	211	
SE-SUF	Scheibe Bergfalke II/55	215	
SE-SUI	Scheibe Bergfalke II/55	217	
SE-SUL	Scheibe Bergfalke II/55	218	
SE-SUM	Scheibe Bergfalke II/55	219	
SE-SUR	Scheibe Bergfalke II/55	223	
SE-SUT	Scheibe Bergfalke II/55	231	
SE-SUU	Scheibe Bergfalke II/55	232	
SE-SUW	Scheibe Bergfalke II/55	233	
SE-SUX	Scheibe Bergfalke II/55	234	
SE-SUY	Scheibe Bergfalke II/55	236	
SE-SWA	Scheibe L-Spatz 55	576	
SE-SWB	Scheibe L-Spatz 55	577	
SE-SWF	Scheibe L-Spatz 55	643	
SE-SWT	Schleicher K.8B	845	
SE-SWU	Schleicher Ka.6CR Rhönsegler	962	
SE-SWX	Schleicher K.8B	917	
SE-SXA	Scheibe Bergfalke II/55	235	
SE-SXB	Scheibe Bergfalke II/55	261	
SE-SXD	Scheibe Bergfalke II/55	263	
SE-SXF	Scheibe Bergfalke II/55	265	
SE-SXI	Scheibe Bergfalke II/55	267	
SE-SXK	Scheibe Bergfalke II/55	269	
SE-SXL	Scheibe Bergfalke II/55	270	
SE-SXN	Scheibe Bergfalke II/55	281	
SE-SXO	Scheibe Bergfalke II/55	282	
SE-SXP	Scheibe Bergfalke II/55	283	
SE-SXU	Scheibe Bergfalke II/55	286	
SE-SXW	Scheibe Bergfalke II/55	287	
SE-SXY	Scheibe Bergfalke II/55	289	
SE-SXZ	Scheibe Bergfalke II/55	291	
SE-SYB	Scheibe Zugvogel IV	1029	
SE-SYC	Scheibe Zugvogel IV	1030	
SE-SYG	Scheibe Zugvogel IVA	1514	
SE-SYH	Schleicher Ka.6CR Rhönsegler	6231	
SE-SYI	Schleicher Ka.6 Rhönsegler	6246	
SE-SYK	Schleicher K.8B	8304	
SE-SYL	Schleicher K.8B	8305	
SE-SYM	Scheibe SF-26A	5023	D-4341
SE-SYN	Scheibe Bergfalke II/55	292	
SE-SYO	Scheibe Bergfalke II/55	293	
SE-SYR	Scheibe Bergfalke II/55	295	
SE-SYT	Scheibe Bergfalke II/55	296	
SE-SYW	Scheibe Bergfalke II/55	298	
SE-SYX	Scheibe Bergfalke II/55	299	
SE-SYY	Scheibe Bergfalke II/55	300	
SE-SZC	Schleicher Ka.6CR Rhönsegler	963	
SE-SZE	Schleicher K.8B	8005	
SE-SZH	SZD-25A Lis	F-764	
SE-SZI	SZD-22C Mucha Standard	768	SP-2235
SE-SZK	SZD-24C Foka	W-165	SP-2234
SE-SZ0	Schleicher Ka.6CR Rhönsegler	6140	
SE-SZP	Schleicher K.8B	8202	
SE-SZR	Schleicher K.8B	8156	
SE-SZU	Schleicher K.8B	8201	
SE-SZY	PIK-16C Vasama	14	
SE-SZZ	PIK-16C Vasama	20	
SE-TAA	Scheibe Bergfalke II/55	311	
SE-TAB	Scheibe Bergfalke II/55	312	
SE-TAC	Scheibe Bergfalke II/55	313	
SE-TAE	Scheibe Bergfalke II/55	316	
SE-TAF	Scheibe Bergfalke II/55	317	
SE-TAG	Scheibe Bergfalke II/55	318	
SE-TAI	Scheibe Bergfalke II/55	325	
SE-TAK	Scheibe Bergfalke II/55	327	
SE-TAM	Scheibe Bergfalke II/55	329	
SE-TAN	Scheibe Bergfalke II/55	331	
SE-TAO	Scheibe Bergfalke II/55	334	
SE-TAR	Scheibe Bergfalke II/55	336	
SE-TAT	Scheibe Bergfalke II/55	332	
SE-TAU	Scheibe Bergfalke II/55	345	
SE-TAX	Scheibe Bergfalke II/55	354	
SE-TAY	Scheibe Bergfalke II/55	356	
SE-TAZ	Scheibe Bergfalke II/55	360	
SE-TBA	Scheibe Bergfalke II/55	361	

Regn.	Type	C/n	Prev.Id.
SE-TBB	Scheibe Bergfalke II/55	365	
SE-TBD	Scheibe Bergfalke II/55	367	
SE-TBE	Scheibe Bergfalke II/55	368	
SE-TBG	Scheibe Bergfalke II/55	377	
SE-TBI	Scheibe Bergfalke II/55	381	
SE-TBL	Scheibe Bergfalke II/55	384	
SE-TBP	Scheibe Bergfalke III	5504	
SE-TBR	Scheibe Bergfalke III	5505	
SE-TBS	Scheibe Bergfalke III	5506	
SE-TBT	Scheibe Bergfalke III	5512	
SE-TBU	Scheibe Bergfalke III	5513	
SE-TBW	Scheibe Bergfalke III	5514	
SE-TBX	Scheibe Bergfalke III	5518	
SE-TBZ	Scheibe Bergfalke III	5532	
SE-TCA	PIK-16C Vasama	15	
SE-TCF	Scheibe L-Spatz 55	513	OY-DXU
SE-TCG	Scheibe Zugvogel IIIB	1091	
SE-TCK	Schleicher K.8B	8579	
SE-TCN	Schleicher Ka.6CR Rhönsegler	6385	
SE-TCR	Schleicher Ka.6CR Rhönsegler	6388	
SE-TCU	Schleicher K.8B	8308	
SE-TCX	Schleicher K.8B	8441	
SE-TCY	Schleicher K.8B	8442	
SE-TCZ	Schleicher K.8B	8330	
SE-TDA	SZD-22C Mucha Standard	602	OH-MSC
SE-TDC	SZD-22C Mucha Standard	590	SP-2168
SE-TDF	SZD-22C Mucha Standard	591	SP-2169
SE-TDG	SZD-22C Mucha Standard	638	SP-2253
SE-TDM	SZD-22C Mucha Standard	568	SP-2148
SE-TDP	Scheibe SF-27A	6044	
SE-TDU	Scheibe SF-27	6014	D-1771
SE-TDX	Scheibe SF-26 Standard	5041	
SE-TEB	Scheibe Bergfalke III	5536	
SE-TEC	Scheibe Bergfalke III	5540	
SE-TED	Scheibe Bergfalke III	5541	
SE-TEE	Scheibe Bergfalke III	5551	
SE-TEF	Scheibe Bergfalke III	5552	
SE-TEG	Scheibe Bergfalke III	5572	
SE-TEH	Scheibe Bergfalke III	5573	
SE-TEI	Scheibe Bergfalke III	5574	
SE-TEK	Scheibe Bergfalke III	5576	
SE-TEN	Scheibe Bergfalke III	5579	
SE-TEO	Scheibe Bergfalke III	5589	
SE-TEP	Scheibe Bergfalke III	5590	
SE-TEW	Scheibe Bergfalke III	5600	
SE-TEX	Scheibe Bergfalke III	5602	
SE-TEY	Scheibe Bergfalke III	5604	
SE-TFD	Schleicher Ka.6CR Rhönsegler	6463/Si	
SE-TFF	Bölkow Phoebus A-1	773	D-9130
SE-TFG	Schleicher K.8B	20	
SE-TFK	SZD-30 Pirat	W-328	
SE-TFL	Bölkow Phoebus A-1	798	
SE-TFO	Schleicher K.8B	8738	
SE-TFS	Glasflügel H301 Libelle	85	
SE-TFX	Schleicher Ka.6CR Rhönsegler	6647	
SE-TGA	Bölkow Phoebus C	828	
SE-TGD	Schleicher Ka.6CR Rhönsegler	6501	D-8903
SE-TGF	Schleicher K.8B	18	
SE-TGL	Schleicher Ka.6CR Rhönsegler	6653	
SE-TGX	Fournier RF-4D	4104	
SE-THA	Scheibe Bergfalke III	5613	
SE-THB	Scheibe Bergfalke III	5616	
SE-THC	Scheibe Bergfalke III	5621	
SE-THD	Scheibe Bergfalke III	5622	
SE-THE	Scheibe Bergfalke III	5623	
SE-THF	Scheibe Bergfalke III	5632	
SE-THG	Scheibe Bergfalke III	5633	
SE-THH	Scheibe Bergfalke III	5636	
SE-THI	Scheibe Bergfalke III	5638	
SE-THK	Scheibe Bergfalke III	5637	
SE-THL	Scheibe Bergfalke III	5642	
SE-THN	Scheibe Bergfalke III	5045	
SE-THO	Scheibe Bergfalke III	5646	
SE-THP	Grob G.102 Astir CS	1090	
SE-THR	Grob G.102 Astir CS	1141	
SE-THS	Grob G.102 Astir CS	1165	
SE-THT	Grob G.102 Astir CS	1475	
SE-THU	Grob G.102 Astir CS	1227	
SE-THV	Grob G.102 Astir CS	1308	
SE-THX	Grob G.102 Astir CS	1247	
SE-THY	Grob G.102 Astir CS	1408	
SE-THZ	Grob G.102 Astir CS	1416	
SE-TIB	Glasflügel H301B Libelle	111	
SE-TIF	Glasflügel H201B Standard Libelle	66	
SE-TIG	Schleicher K.8B	21	
SE-TIH	Bölkow Phoebus C	895	
SE-TIL	Schleicher K.8B	25	
SE-TIV	Schleicher ASW-15	15011	
SE-TIX	Schempp-Hirth Standard Cirrus	31	D-0528
SE-TKD	SZD-30 Pirat	B-537	
SE-TKE	SZD-30 Pirat	B-536	
SE-TKH	Scheibe L-Spatz	528	D-1185
SE-TKM	Schleicher K.8B	609	D-5693
SE-TKN	Schleicher K.8B	8866	
SE-TKP	Schleicher Ka.6CR Rhönsegler	6616	D-7609
SE-TKT	Schempp-Hirth Standard Cirrus	215	
SE-TKY	SZD-30 Pirat	B-473	
SE-TKZ	SZD-36A Cobra 15	W-622	SP-2658
SE-TLA	Scheibe Bergfalke IV	5808	
SE-TLB	Scheibe Bergfalke IV	5809	
SE-TLC	Scheibe Bergfalke IV	5810	
SE-TLD	Scheibe Bergfalke IV	5801	
SE-TLG	Scheibe Bergfalke IV	5821	
SE-TLH	Scheibe Bergfalke IV	5830	
SE-TLI	Scheibe Bergfalke IV	5833	
SE-TLL	Scheibe Bergfalke IV	5839	
SE-TLM	Scheibe Bergfalke IV	5848	
SE-TLO	Scheibe Bergfalke IV	5849	
SE-TLP	Scheibe Bergfalke IV	5850	
SE-TLS	Scheibe Bergfalke IV	5858	
SE-TLT	Scheibe Bergfalke IV	5859	
SE-TLZ	Scheibe SF-25B Falke	4643	D-KHEO
SE-TMA	Scheibe SF-25A Motorfalke	4519	D-KAJA
SE-TMB	Scheibe SF-25B Falke	46102	D-KECP
SE-TMC	Scheibe SF-25A Motorfalke	4532	D-KAMY
SE-TMD	Slingsby T-61A Falke	1733	G-AYYJ
SE-TME	Scheibe SF-28A Tandem-Falke	5764	D-KACQ
SE-TMF	Scheibe SF-26A	5046	OE-0734
SE-TMK	SZD-30 Pirat	S-02.05	
SE-TML	SZD-30 Pirat	S-02.04	
SE-TMN	SZD-30 Pirat	S-02.22	
SE-TMR	Scheibe L-Spatz 55	5	D-1425
SE-TMS	SZD-30 Pirat	B-553	SP-2657
SE-TMV	Schempp-Hirth Standard Cirrus	340	
SE-TMZ	Schempp-Hirth Standard Cirrus	256	
SE-TNB	Glasflügel H401 Kestrel 17	103	
SE-TND	Grob Standard Cirrus	439G	
SE-TNE	SZD-30 Pirat	S-02.19	
SE-TNG	Rolladen-Schneider LS-1D	290	
SE-TNM	Schleicher Ka.6CR Rhönsegler	6151	
SE-TNN	SZD-41A Jantar Standard	X-123	
SE-TNO	SZD-30 Pirat	S-02.26	
SE-TNP	SZD-30 Pirat	S-02.23	
SE-TNR	SZD-22C Mucha	797	OH-308 / OH-MSG
SE-TNU	Pilatus B4/PC-11	160	
SE-TNV	SZD-41A Jantar Standard	X-124	
SE-TNX	Eiri PIK-20	20009	
SE-TNY	Scheibe L-Spatz 55	768	D-8472
SE-TNZ	Scheibe L-Spatz 55	774	OY-MJX / D-5354
SE-TOA	SZD-24 Foka 4A	W-226	D-9391
SE-TOC	SZD-41A Jantar Standard	B-633	
SE-TOE	SZD-36A Cobra	W-716	
SE-TOF	SZD-41A Jantar Standard	B-632	
SE-TOG	Standard Cirrus	559G	
SE-TOI	SZD-41A Jantar Standard	B.631	
SE-TOK	SZD-30 Pirat	S-05.11	
SE-TOL	Eiri PIK-20	20048	
SE-TOM	Eiri PIK-20	20049	

Regn.	Type	C/n	Prev.Id.
SE-TOP	Glasflügel H101 Salto	53	
SE-TOR	SZD-36A Cobra 15	W-724	SP-2895
SE-TOV	Scheibe SF-25C Falke	44138	D-KDAL (D-KDDM)
SE-TOZ	Glasflügel H205 Club Libelle	88	
SE-TPA	SZD-41A Jantar Standard	B-695	
SE-TPB	SZD-30 Pirat	S-06.40	
SE-TPC	SZD-30 Pirat	S-07.10	
SE-TPD	SZD-30 Pirat	S-08.06	
SE-TPF	SZD-41A Jantar Standard	B-722	
SE-TPG	SZD-41A Jantar Standard	B-705	LN-GHJ SE-TPG
SE-TPH	SZD-41A Jantar Standard	B-711	
SE-TPI	SZD-42-1 Jantar 2	B-781	
SE-TPK	SZD-30 Pirat	S-06.44	
SE-TPL	Glasflügel H206 Hornet	39	
SE-TPN	Schleicher K.8B	95	D-5683
SE-TPP	Rolladen-Schneider LS-1F	382	
SE-TPS	Schempp-Hirth Standard Cirrus B	647	
SE-TPT	LET L-13 Blanik	026355	
SE-TPU	Schleicher ASW-19B	19016	
SE-TPV	Pilatus B4-PC11	192	
SE-TPY	Eiri PIK-20B	20118C	
SE-TPZ	Schempp-Hirth Standard Cirrus	690	
SE-TRA	Rolladen-Schneider LS-3	3055	
SE-TRB	Rolladen-Schneider LS-3	3062	
SE-TRC	Rolladen-Schneider LS-3	3072	
SE-TRD	Rolladen-Schneider LS-3A	3071	
SE-TRE	Rolladen-Schneider LS-3	3009	
SE-TRF	Rolladen-Schneider LS-1F	385	
SE-TRG	Rolladen-Schneider LS-1F	464	
SE-TRH	Rolladen-Schneider LS-1F	465	
SE-TRI	Rolladen-Schneider LS-1F	466	
SE-TRK	Rolladen-Schneider LS-1F	467	
SE-TRM	Rolladen-Schneider LS-3	3129	
SE-TRN	SZD-41A Jantar Standard	B-804	
SE-TRP	SZD-30 Pirat	S-09.30	
SE-TRS	SZD-41A Jantar Standard	B-844	
SE-TRT	SZD-48 Jantar Standard 2	W-880	
SE-TRU	SZD-48 Jantar Standard 2	W-882	
SE-TRV	SZD-48 Jantar Standard 2	W-898	
SE-TRY	SZD-48 Jantar Standard 2	W-865	
SE-TRZ	Schleicher K.8B	667	LN-GGM OY-XAV
SE-TSA	Schempp-Hirth Standard Cirrus B	683	
SE-TSB	Scheibe SF-25C Falke	4407	D-KAAX
SE-TSC	Scheibe SF-25B Falke	4624	D-KIMF
SE-TSD	Scheibe Bergfalke IV	5864	
SE-TSF	Scheibe SF-25B Falke	46138	D-KCAE
SE-TSG	SZD-24C Foka	W-203	OY-BXM
SE-TSH	Scheibe SF-25B Falke	4610	D-KOGU
SE-TSI	Scheibe Bergfalke IV	5866	
SE-TSL	Pilatus B4-PC11	100	OY-XBV
SE-TSM	Eiri PIK-20B	20006	OH-451
SE-TSO	Grob G.102 Speed Astir IIB	4041	
SE-TSP	Schempp-Hirth Mini-Nimbus HS.7	59	
SE-TSR	Schempp-Hirth Mini-Nimbus HS.7	34	
SE-TSS	Grob G.102 Astir CS	1440	
SE-TSU	Grob G.102 Astir CS 77	1607	
SE-TSX	Grob G.102 Astir CS 77	1709	
SE-TSY	Grob G.102 Astir CS 77	1712	
SE-TSZ	Grob G.102 Astir CS Jeans	2117	
SE-TTB	Eiri PIK-20D	20594	
SE-TTC	Grob G.102 Standard Astir III	5527S	
SE-TTH	Valentin Mistral C	MC 013/78	
SE-TTI	Eiri PIK-20	20019	OH-449
SE-TTL	Rolladen-Schneider LS-3A	3360	
SE-TTM	Rolladen-Schneider LS-3-17	3362	
SE-TTN	Rolladen-Schneider LS-3A	3361	
SE-TTO	IAR IS-28.M2	034	
SE-TTP	Rolladen-Schneider LS-3-17	3364	
SE-TTR	Rolladen-Schneider LS-4	4063	
SE-TTS	Rolladen-Schneider LS-4	4065	
SE-TTT	Schleicher ASW-19B	19083	
SE-TTX	Schleicher ASW-19B	19120	
SE-TTZ	Schleicher ASW-20	20323	
SE-TUA	Scheibe SF-25C Falke	44152	D-KEFB
SE-TUB	Eiri PIK-20E	20273	
SE-TUC	IAR IS-28.M2	035	
SE-TUD	Fournier RF-5	5055	D-KINC
SE-TUF	Scheibe SF-25B Falke	46201	D-KASP
SE-TUG	Scheibe SF-25B Falke	4627	D-KIMM
SE-TUH	Scheibe SF-25C Falke	4224	OY-XKY D-KEAE
SE-TUI	Hoffmann H-36 Dimona	3611	
SE-TUK	Scheibe SF-25B Falke	46256C	D-KLAP
SE-TUL	Scheibe SF-25D Falke	"4670-1D"	
	(C/n 4670D is also quoted for OE-9103)		
SE-TUN	Scheibe SF-24B Motorspatz	4039	D-KICO
SE-TUO	Hoffmann H-36 Dimona	3505	
SE-TUP	Scheibe SF-25B Falke	46119	D-KABR
SE-TUR	Scheibe SF-28A Tandem-Falke	5728	OY-XEE D-KAUN (D-KOAQ)
SE-TUU	Scheibe SF-25C Falke	44238	D-KDCL
SE-TUX	Scheibe SF-25B Falke	4603	D-K... SE-TUX D-KODA
SE-TUY	Hoffmann H-36 Dimona	3685	
SE-TVA	Schempp-Hirth Mini-Nimbus C	121	
SE-TVC	Schempp-Hirth Mini-Nimbus C	124	
SE-TVE	Pilatus B4-PC11	128	OH-544
SE-TVF	Eiri PIK-20B	20128C	OH-487
SE-TVG	Grob G.102 Astir CS	1189	D-7306
SE-TVH	Schleicher ASK-21	21024	
SE-TVI	Scheibe Bergfalke II/55	355	D-1417
SE-TVK	Scheibe SF-30A Club-Spatz	6804	
SE-TVL	Pilatus B4-PC11AF	116	LN-GGX HB-1145
SE-TVM	Scheibe Bergfalke II/55	369	D-1817
SE-TVP	Schempp-Hirth Ventus A	20	
SE-TVR	Pilatus B4-PC11AF	312	
SE-TVS	Schleicher ASW-19B	19329	
SE-TVT	Eiri PIK-20B	20136C	OH-485
SE-TVU	Pilatus B4-PC11A	198	OH-525
SE-TVV	Glaser-Dirks DG-100G Elan	E54-G31	
SE-TVX	Schleicher ASW-20	20436	
SE-TVY	Scheibe Bergfalke III	5659	
SE-TVZ	Scheibe Bergfalke III	5658	
SE-TXC	Rolladen-Schneider LS-4	4181	
SE-TXD	Rolladen-Schneider LS-4	4182	
SE-TXE	Rolladen-Schneider LS-4	4410	
SE-TXH	Rolladen-Schneider LS-4	4467	
SE-TXM	Scheibe Bergfalke II/55	290	LN-GBA
SE-TXO	Eiri PIK-20B	20138	OH-483
SE-TXP	SZD-50-3 Puchacz	B-968	SP-3237
SE-TXR	Grob G.103A Twin II Acro	3692-K-43	
SE-TXS	Schleicher ASW-20	20566	
SE-TXT	Pilatus B4-PC11	010	OH-424
SE-TXU	Grob G.102 Astir CS	1054	OH-553 D-7238
SE-TXV	Glaser-Dirks DG-100G Elan	E97-G67	
SE-TXX	Eiri PIK-20	20015	OH-457
SE-TXY	Pilatus B4-PC11AF	246	D-7843
SE-TXZ	Schleicher K.8B	756	LN-GAQ OY-VUX
SE-TYA-YA	Rolladen-Schneider LS-6	6069	
SE-TYB	Rolladen-Schneider LS-6	6013	
SE-TYC	Rolladen-Schneider LS-6	6086	
SE-TYD	Rolladen-Schneider LS-6	6136	
SE-TYL	Glaser-Dirks DG-100G Elan	E103-G73	
SE-TYM	Scheibe Bergfalke III	5526	
SE-TYN	Schleicher ASW-15B	15196	OH-409
SE-TYP	Schempp-Hirth Ventus b	114	
SE-TYR	Jastreb Standard Cirrus G/81	251	
SE-TYS	Scheibe Bergfalke IV	5868	D-6930
SE-TYT	Scheibe Bergfalke III	5511	
SE-TYU	Schempp-Hirth Janus B	172	
SE-TYV	Jastreb Standard Cirrus G/81	258	
SE-TYZ	Grob G.102 Astir CS	1225	D-4199

Regn.	Type	C/n	Prev.Id.
SE-TZA	Grob G.103 Twin Astir Trainer	3169-T-16	D-7806
SE-TZB	Siren C.30S Edelweiss	17	F-CCUO
SE-TZE	Centrair 101AP Pégase	101AP-100	
SE-TZF	Schleicher ASW-20B	20644	
SE-TZG	Jastreb Standard Cirrus G/81	306	
SE-TZL	Grob G.103 Twin Astir	3173	D-7809
SE-TZI	Glaser-Dirks DG-300 Elan	3E-27	LN-GHZ
			SE-TZI
SE-TZN	Grob G.103A Twin II Acro	34048-K-279	
SE-TZO	Schempp-Hirth Discus b	93	
SE-TZP	Grob G.103 Twin II	3612	OH-725
SE-TZR	Eiri PIK-20	20020	OH-467
SE-TZU	Centrair 101A Pégase	101A-0209	
SE-TZV	Glaser-Dirks DG-300 Elan	3E-101	
SE-TZX	Schempp-Hirth Discus b	28	
SE-TZY	Schleicher ASK-21	21251	
SE-TZZ	Schleicher ASW-20C	20739	
SE-UAB	Grob G.109B	6290	
SE-UAC	Scheibe SF-25B Falke	46238	OY-XEY
			(D-KAID)
SE-UAD	Scheibe SF-25B Falke	4620	D-KEGE
SE-UAE	Grob G.109B	6293	
SE-UAH	Scheibe SF-28A Tandem-Falke	5745	OY-XNI
			D-KOEW
SE-UAK	Scheibe SF-25B Falke	46152	D-KCAR
SE-UAL	Grob G.109B	6348	
SE-UAN	Scheibe SF-25C Falke	4247	D-KMPB
SE-UAO	Grob G.109B	6349	
SE-UAP	Scheibe SF-25B Falke	46122	D-KABV
SE-UAR	Scheibe SF-25B Falke	4678	D-KBAD
SE-UAS	Scheibe SF-25C Falke	44212	D-KDFH
SE-UAT	Scheibe SF-25C Falke	44112	D-KIPB
SE-UAU	Scheibe SF-25D Falke	46193D	D-KASH
SE-UAV	Scheibe SF-25C Falke	44392	(D-KNIG(1))
SE-UAX	Fournier RF-5	5005	D-KIGO
SE-UAY	Scheibe SF-25C Falke	4201	D-KAOF
SE-UAZ	Scheibe SF-25C Falke	44198	D-KDEX
SE-UBG	Scheibe SF-25C Falke	4430	D-KHON
SE-UBH	Scheibe SF-25B Falke	46154	D-KCAT
SE-UBI	Scheibe SF-25C Falke	44155	D-KEFE
SE-UBK	Scheibe SF-25C Falke	44227	OE-9150
			(D-KDFY(2))
SE-UBL	Scheibe SF-25C Falke	44414	D-KNIO(1)
SE-UBN	Scheibe SF-25B Falke	46235	OY-MVX
			(D-KAEO(1))
SE-UBP	Scheibe SF-25C Falke	44160	D-KEFM
SE-UBS	Scheibe SF-25C Falke	46217C	LN-GMJ
			D-KAAS
SE-UBT	Scheibe SF-25C Falke	4214	D-KAWC
SE-UBU	Scheibe SF-25C Falke	44203	D-KDFK
SE-UBV	Scheibe SF-25C Falke	44325	D-KOON
SE-UBX	Scheibe SF-25C Falke	44173	D-KEFV
SE-UBZ	Scheibe SF-25C Falke	4482	D-KEIB
SE-UCA	Valentin Taifun 17E-II	1131	(D-KHVA)
SE-UCB	Valentin Taifun 17E-II	1133	(D-KHVA)
SE-UCC	Scheibe SF-25C Falke	44241	D-KDCQ
SE-UCD	Grob G.109B	6248	
SE-UCF	Slingsby T.61F Venture	1983	ZA664
SE-UCG	Eiri PIK-20E	20282	OH-620
SE-UCH	Scheibe SF-25B Falke	46110	OH-560
			D-KMAE
SE-UCI	LET L-13SW Vivat	880216	
SE-UCL	Scheibe SF-25B Falke	4636	OY-XNA
			D-KETI
SE-UCM	Scheibe SF-25C Falke	4233	D-KAOT
SE-UCO	Scheibe SF-25CFalke	4452	OH-581
			D-KDAE
SE-UCP	Scheibe SF-25C Falke	44393	D-KNIE(3)
SE-UCR	Hoffman H-36 Dimona (Reservation 12.99)	unkn	
SE-UCT	IAR IS.28M-2	77	
SE-UCU	Scheibe SF-25C Falke	44251	D-KDBF
SE-UCV	Grob G.109	6036	(SE-UMI)
			D-KDMF
SE-UDE	HOACHK-36TTC Super Dimona	36655	OE-9419
SE-UEC	Glaser-Dirks DG-300 Elan	3E-155	
SE-UED	Glaser-Dirks DG-300 Elan	3E-156	
SE-UEE	Schleicher ASW-20C	20845	
SE-UEF	Schempp-Hirth Discus b	98	
SE-UEG	Grob G.103 Twin Astir Trainer	3089	D-3950
SE-UEH	Grob G.103 Twin Astir	3127	D-7789
SE-UEI	Grob G.102 Astir CS	1460	
SE-UEK	Scheibe Bergfalke IV	5802	LN-GBP
			D-0374
SE-UEL	Grob G.102 Astir CS Jeans	2034	D-3880
SE-UEM	Pilatus B4-PC11AF	23	D-1185
			HB-1115
SE-UEN	Molino PIK-16C	25	OH-297
			OH-VAL
SE-UEO	Scheibe Bergfalke III	5519	D-8625
SE-UEP	Rolladen-Schneider LS-4A	4398	OH-714
SE-UER	Schleicher ASK-21	21307	
SE-UES	Grob G.103 Twin Astir Trainer	3284-T-44	OH-673
			(SE-....)
			OH-673
			F-CFHL
SE-UET	Glasflügel H304	227	OH-613
SE-UEU	Rolladen-Schneider LS-4	4601	
SE-UEV	Rolladen-Schneider LS-4A	4613	
SE-UEY	Schempp-Hirth Discus b	157	
SE-UEZ	Schempp-Hirth Discus b	158	
SE-UFA	Rolladen-Schneider LS-4A	4615	
SE-UFC	Schempp-Hirth Ventus b/16.6	335	
SE-UFD	Grob G.103 Twin Astir	3157	BGA2409/DVF
SE-UFG	Schempp-Hirth Discus b	170	
SE-UFH	Schempp-Hirth Discus b	171	
SE-UFI	Rolladen-Schneider LS-6B	6139	
SE-UFK	Grob G.103 Twin Astir	3102	D-3959
SE-UFL	Eiri PIK-20D	20530	OH-555
			PH-555
SE-UFM	Scheibe SF-34	5111	BGA2786/EMC
SE-UFN	Grob G.102 Astir CS	1467	OY-XLR
			D-7438
SE-UFP	Grob G.103 Twin Astir Trainer	3005-T	OH-612
SE-UFR	Schleicher ASK-21	21357	
SE-UFS	Glaser-Dirks DG-300 Elan	3E-187	D-3343
SE-UFT	Glasflügel H304	226	OH-616
SE-UFU	Grob G.103 Twin Astir	3079	D-3943
SE-UFV	Schempp-Hirth Discus b	221	
SE-UFX	Pilatus B4-PC11	177	OH-455
SE-UFY	Schleicher ASK-21	21375	
SE-UFZ	Grob G.103 Twin II	3833	OH-682
SE-UGA	Grob G.103 Twin II Acro	3802-K-69	OE-5326
SE-UGB	Glasflügel H304	205	OH-564
SE-UGC	Schleicher ASH-25	25043	
SE-UGD	Grob G.102 Speed Astir IIB	4031	OH-656
			F-WFKA(1)
SE-UGE	Grob G.102 Astir C	2026	HB-1572
SE-UGF	Schleicher ASK-21	21373	
SE-UGG	Glaser-Dirks DG-600	6-20	
SE-UGI	Schempp-Hirth Discus b	230	
SE-UGK	Centrair 201B Marianne	201B-072	
SE-UGL	Schempp-Hirth Ventus c	383	
SE-UGN	Glasflügel H304B	325	OH-722
SE-UGP	Centrair 201B Marianne	201B-074	
SE-UGR	Glasflügel H304B	348	OH-718
SE-UGT	Grob G.103 Twin Astir	3189-T-20	D-7814
SE-UGU	Schleicher ASW-20C	20745	F-CBDJ
			F-WBDJ
SE-UGV	Rolladen-Schneider LS-7	7013	D-4680
SE-UGY	Rolladen-Schneider LS-7	7060	
SE-UHA-HA	Schleicher ASW-24	24037	
SE-UHB	Schempp-Hirth Janus C	254	
SE-UHD	Rolladen-Schneider LS-7	7052	D-1714
SE-UHE	Rolladen-Schneider LS-7	7017	D-4638
SF-UHF	Schempp-Hirth HS-7 Mini-Nimbus	158	D-2797
SE-UHG	Grob G.103 Twin Astir Trainer	3265-T-32	D-2394
SE-UHI	Scheibe SF-34	5121	D-7746
SE-UHL	Grob G.102 Astir CS	1122	D-1100
SE-UHM-6V	Rolladen-Schneider LS-6B	6174	D-0299
SE-UHN	Rolladen-Schneider LS-6B	6122	D-3711

Regn.	Type	C/n	Prev.Id.
SE-UHP	SZD-48-3 Jantar Standard 3	B-1896	
SE-UHR	SZD-24-4A Foka 4A	W-385	SP-2522
SE-UHS	SZD-50-3 Puchacz	B-1879	
SE-UHT	Grob G.103 Twin II	34135	
SE-UHU	SZD-50-3 Puchacz	B-1880	
SE-UHV	Grob G.103 Twin Astir	3113	OH-809
SE-UHX	Schleicher ASK-21	21434	
SE-UHY	Grob G.103 Twin Astir	3118	D-7785
SE-UIA	Rolladen-Schneider LS-4A	4780	
SE-UIB	SZD-41A Jantar Standard	B-701	SP-3049
SE-UIE	Schleicher ASW-24	24092	
SE-UIF	Glaser-Dirks DG-500 Elan Trainer	5E-38T12	
SE-UIG	Glaser-Dirks DG-500 Elan Trainer	5E-23T5	
SE-UIH	Schleicher Ka.6CR Rhönsegler	6041	OH-274
			OH-RSN
SE-UII	Eiri PIK-20D	20601	OH-533
SE-UIL	Glaser-Dirks DG-500 Elan Trainer	5E-28-T8	
SE-UIM	Schleicher K.8B	8760	D-5005
SE-UIN	Schleicher K7 Rhönadler	1029	OH-253
			OH-KKG
SE-UIO	SZD-48-4 Jantar Standard 4	X-143	SP-3378
			SP-P378
SE-UIP	Schempp-Hirth Janus C	266	
SE-UIR	SZD-24C Foka	W-159	SP-2377
SE-UIS	Eiri PIK-20D	20540	OH-517
SE-UIU	Rolladen-Schneider LS-7	"153-7"	
SE-UIV	Schempp-Hirth Discus b	361	
SE-UIX	SZD-48-3 Jantar Standard 3	W-903	SP-3171
SE-UIY	Pilatus B4-PC11	141	OY-VXO
SE-UIZ	Rolladen-Schneider LS-6C	6245	
SE-UKA	Schleicher ASW-24	24090	
SE-UKB	Schempp-Hirth Discus CS	021CS	
SE-UKC	LET L-23 Super Blanik	917813	
SE-UKD	Scheibe SF-34B	5134	
SE-UKE	Rolladen-Schneider LS-4B	unkn	
SE-UKF	SZD-24C Foka	W-138	SP-2366
SE-UKG	Schempp-Hirth Discus b	413	
SE-UKH	Schleicher ASK-21	21545	
SE-UKN	Rolladen-Schneider LS-6C	6253	
SE-UKP	Glaser-Dirks DG-600	6-101S56	
SE-UKR	SZD-55-1	551191014	SP-3521
SE-UKS	SZD-48-1 Jantar Standard	B-1015	OH-633
SE-UKT	LET L-13 Blanik	172127	DOSAAF
SE-UKU	Glaser-Dirks DG-300 Elan Trainer	3E-433A3	
SE-UKV	Schempp-Hirth Discus b	unkn	
SE-UKX	Rolladen-Schneider LS-6C	6314	
SE-UKY	Eiri PIK-20	20040	OH-481
SE-ULB	Rolladen-Schneider LS-6C	6332	
SE-ULC	Grob G.103 Twin Astir Trainer	3253-T-30	OH-541
SE-ULD	SZD-48-1 Jantar Standard	1014	LN-GIQ
			OH-617
SE-ULE	Schleicher ASK-21	21520	
SE-ULF	Schleicher Ka.6CR Rhönsegler	6030/Si	D-5209
SE-ULG	ICA-Brasov IS.28B2	359	
SE-ULH	Glaser-Dirks DG-100G Elan	E137-G105	OH-690
SE-ULI	Glaser-Dirks DG-500 Elan Trainer	5E-133T58	D-9050
SE-ULK	Glaser-Dirks DG-500	5E-37T11	
SE-ULL	SZD-55-1	551190001	
SE-ULM	SZD-50-3 Puchacz	B-2101	
SE-ULN	Standard Cirrus B	574	LN-GAW
SE-ULO	Schleicher ASK-21	21644	
SE-ULP	Schempp-Hirth Duo Discus	116	
SE-ULR	SZD-50-3 Puchacz	B-2105	
SE-ULU	PZL PW-5 Smyk	17.07.010	
SE-ULV	SZD-55-1	551190004	
SE-ULX	Rolladen-Schneider LS-8A	8167	
SE-ULY	Grob G.103 Twin Astir	3538	D-8731
SE-ULZ	Rolladen-Schneider LS-7	7055	D-1490
SE-UMA	Glaser-Dirks DG-500 Elan Trainer	5E-66T27	
SE-UMB	Glaser-Dirks DG-800B	8-144B68	
SE-UMC	Schempp-Hirth Janus	45	N468F
SE-UMD	Grob G.103C Twin IIISL Acro	36005	OH-841
SE-UME	Pilatus B4-PC11	174	D-7400
SE-UMF	Schempp-Hirth Discus b	68	OH-826
SE-UMG	Glasflügel H303 Mosquito	26	OH-567

Regn.	Type	C/n	Prev.Id.
SE-UMH	Grob G.102 Astir CS77	1753	LN-GHW
			OY-XNW
			LN-GLC
			D-4566
SE-UMK	Grob G.103 Twin Astir	3021	LN-GLY
			OY-XLJ
			OE-5154
SE-UML	Schempp-Hirth Ventus cM (Reservation 11.99)	105/602	HB-2246
SE-UMN	Schleicher ASK-21	21129	OY-XMN
SE-UMV	Schempp-Hirth Ventus cM	49/492	D-KICC(2)
SE-UMZ	Schleicher ASK-21	21660	
SE-UNG	Rolladen-Schneider LS-8A	8248	
SE-UNI	Schempp-Hirth Ventus 2cM	6/23	D-KRKR
			D-2945
SE-UNO	Rolladen-Schneider LS-8A	8145	
SE-UNZ	Schempp-Hirth Discus 2b (Reservation)	21	
SE-UPA	Schempp-Hirth Discus CS	018CS	(SE-ULX)
			BGA4028/HLL
			OH-833
SE-UPC	Schempp-Hirth Ventus 2b	42	
SE-UPD	Schleicher ASW-24	24089	
SE-UPE	Rolladen-Schneider LS-6A	6012	D-8866
SE-UPF	Rolladen-Schneider LS-8A	8166	
SE-UPK	Schempp-Hirth Ventus c	558	
SE-UPM	Rolladen-Schneider LS-8A (Reservation)	8116	D-4920
SE-UPN	Glaser-Dirks DG-505	5E-181X32	
SE-UPP	Rolladen-Schneider LS-7	7083	
SE-UPR	SZD-48-3 Jantar Standard 3 (Reservation)	B-1662	OH-761
SE-UPV	PZL PW-5 Smyk	17.04.021	
SE-URB	Rolladen-Schneider LS-4	4415	D-1676
SE-URH	Marganski MDM-1 Fox	226	
SE-URI	Schempp-Hirth Duo Discus	16	
SE-URK	Schleicher ASW-24	24166	
SE-URX	Schempp-Hirth Janus B	80	D-1216
SE-URZ	Schleicher ASW-20	20147	BGA3499/FSW
			ZS-GRF
			D-3329
SE-USA	Rolladen-Schneider LS-8A	8102	
SE-USD	Rolladen-Schneider LS-8A	8243	
SE-USE	Rolladen-Schneider LS-8A	8128	
SE-USF	Rolladen-Schneider LS-8A	8131	
SE-USS	ICA-Brasov IS.28B2	358	YR-1992
SE-UTC	Schleicher ASW-27	27003	
SE-UTD	Schleicher ASW-27	27020	
SE-UTE	Schempp-Hirth Ventus 2a	15	
SE-UTF	Slingsby T-59F Kestrel 19	1762	BGA1515/CFU
SE-UTI	Glasflügel H303 Mosquito	25	OY-XHF
SE-UTL	Schleicher ASK-21	21655	
SE-UTO	Schleicher ASW-27 (Reservation)	270 . .	
SE-UTT	Schempp-Hirth Discus 2b (Reservation)	40	
SE-UTZ	Schempp-Hirth Ventus cT	77/314	(SE-UTY)
			D-KAMH

MICROLIGHTS

Regn.	Type	C/n	Prev.Id.
SE-VAA	Fisher FP-202 Super Koala	SK-081	
SE-VAB	TL Ultralight TL-32 Typhoon	93A028	
SE-VAC	Denney Kitfox III	PFA/172-11921	G-BTRA
SE-VAD	Denney Kitfox III	1064	
SE-VAE	TL Ultralight TL-32 Typhoon	98A030	
SE-VAF	TL Ultralight TL-132 Condor	98C01	
SE-VAI	Brügger MB-2 Colibri (Reservation 1.00)	211	
SE-VAT	Jabiru ST3 UL	0171/UL0018	(LN-YMP)
SE-VBA	TL Ultralight TL-22 Duo ESO 2	96G10	
SE-VBB	Mainair Gemini/Flash IIA	897-0492-7-W692	G-MWYX
SE-VBC	TL Ultralight TL-22 Duo ESO-2	95C09	
SE-VBD	TL Ultralight TL-2 ESO-2	95C10	
SE-VBE	TL Ultralight TL-22 Duo ESO-2	96G11	
SE-VBF	TL Ultralight TL-2 ESO-2	96G13	
SE-VBG	TL Ultralight TL-2 ESO-2	96G14	

Regn.	Type	C/n	Prev.Id.
SE-VBH	Solar Wings Pegasus XL-R/Se		
		SW-WA-1176/SW-TB-1175	G-MTHL
SE-VBI	GTE Clipper/XP GTE	0396048	
SE-VBK	Mainair Gemini/Flash IIA	891-0392-7-W686	G-MWYK
SE-VBL	Polaris FIB 582	96A4189/963631	
SE-VBM	Air Création GTE XP-15	1G026	
SE-VBN	FIB Polaris 582	96A-4187/963632	
SE-VBO	Mayes Mosquito XS-155	1566/A10-207	
SE-VBP	TL Ultralight TL-2 ESO-2	97T001	
SE-VBR	Pegasus Quantum	7283	
SE-VBS	Pegasus Quantum	7282	
SE-VBT	FIB Polaris	96A4193/963636	
SE-VBU	FIB Polaris	96A4188/963630	
SE-VBX	TL Ultralight TL-2 ESO-2	97T002	
SE-VCA	FIB Polaris	99A4353/993779	
SE-VCB	FIBPolaris	99A4360/993789	
SE-VCC	FIBPolaris	99A4354/993780	
SE-VCD	FIB Polaris	99A4355/993781	
SE-VCE	FIB Polaris	99A4359/993788	
SE-VCF	Polaris/ESO-2	993782/990501	
SE-VCR	Air Création XP-Clipper 912	T99028	
SE-VPH	Rans S-7 Courier (Reservation 4.99)	889056	
SE-YAD	Eipper Quicksilver MX	3017	
SE-YAI	Eipper Quicksilver MX	3019	
SE-YAK	Eipper Quicksilver MX	3020	
SE-YAL	Eipper Quicksilver MX	3022	
SE-YAM	Eipper Quicksilver MX	3023	
SE-YAN	Eipper Quicksilver MX	3024	
SE-YAO	Eipper Quicksilver MX	3025	
SE-YAS	Weedhopper JC-24B	1417	
SE-YAU	Weedhopper JC-24B	1348	
SE-YAV	Eipper Quicksilver MX	3080	
SE-YAX	Eipper Quicksilver MX-II	3099	
SE-YAY	Eipper Quicksilver MX-II	3098	
SE-YAZ	Eipper Quicksilver MX-I	3093	
SE-YBA	Weedhopper JC-24B	1414	
SE-YBB	Weedhopper JC-24B	1511	
SE-YBC	Weedhopper JC-24B	1513	
SE-YBD	Weedhopper JC-24B	1506	
SE-YBE	Mitchell P-38	unkn	
SE-YBG	Weedhopper JC-24B	1507	
SE-YBI	Weedhopper JC-24C	1940	
SE-YBK	Weedhopper JC-24B	1508	
SE-YBL	Mitchell U-2	unkn	
SE-YBM	Weedhopper JC-24C	1942	
SE-YBN	Weedhopper JC-24B	1505	
SE-YBO	Weedhopper JC-24C	1941	
SE-YBU	Weedhopper JC-24C	1939	
SE-YBZ	Eipper Quicksilver MX	2082	
SE-YCC	Weedhopper JC-24C	2077	
SE-YCD	Weedhopper JC-24C	2075	
SE-YCH	Mitchell P-38	unkn	
SE-YCI	Wizard J-3	S-01	
SE-YCR	Eipper Quicksilver MX	1216	
SE-YCS	Eipper Quicksilver MX-I	3087	
SE-YCT	Weedhopper JC-24C	2079	
SE-YCU	Weedhopper JC-24C	2081	
SE-YCV	Weedhopper JC-24C	2186	
SE-YCX	Weedhopper JC-24C	2187	
SE-YCY	Weedhopper JC-24C	2188	
SE-YCZ	Weedhopper JC-24C	2189	
SE-YDA	Weedhopper JC-24C	2190	
SE-YDB	Weedhopper JC-24C	2080	
SE-YDC	Weedhopper JC-24C	2083	
SE-YDD	Weedhopper JC-24C	2082	
SE-YDE	Weedhopper JC-24B	1515	
SE-YDF	Eipper Quicksilver MX	3086	
SE-YDG	Eipper Quicksilver MX	3097	
SE-YDH	Eipper Quicksilver MX-II	3702	
SE-YDI	Eipper Quicksilver MX-I	3089	
SE-YDK	Eipper Quicksilver MX	3081	
SE-YDM	Eipper Quicksilver MX	3739	
SE-YDP	Eipper Quicksilver MX	3189	
SE-YDT	Weedhopper JC-24C	2193	
SE-YDU	Weedhopper JC-24C	2194	
SE-YDY	Weedhopper JC-24C	2197	
SE-YEA	Weedhopper JC-24C	2199	
SE-YEC	Eipper Quicksilver MX-II	unkn	
SE-YED	Lazair	A-477	
SE-YEG	Eipper Quicksilver MX-II	3986	
SE-YEK	Eipper Quicksilver	3974	
SE-YEL	Eipper Quicksilver MX-II	3983	
SE-YEM	Eipper Quicksilver MX	3737	
SE-YEO	Eipper Quicksilver MX-II	3976	
SE-YEP	Eipper Quicksilver MX-I	3738	
SE-YER	Eipper Quicksilver MX-II	3977	
SE-YES	Aerodyne Vector 610	1291	
SE-YEU	Eipper Quicksilver MX	3991	
SE-YEY	Eipper Quicksilver MX-II	3987	
SE-YEZ	Eipper Quicksil ver MX-II	3979	
SE-YFB	Eipper Quicksilver MX-II	3972	
SE-YFC	Eipper Quicksilver MX-I	3095	
SE-YFE	Lazair	A-479	
SE-YFF	Lazair	A-481	
SE-YFH	Eipper Quicksilver MX-II	3984	
SE-YFK	Eipper Quicksilver MX-II	3987	
SE-YFL	Lazair	unkn	
SE-YFM	Dragon 150	0012	
SE-YFN	Teman Monofly	unkn	
SE-YFP	Aerodyne Vector 610	1388	
SE-YFR	Eipper Quicksilver MX	3995	
SE-YFT	Lazair	unkn	
SE-YFX	Dragon 150	0052	
SE-YFY	Akka (Tierra 2)	unkn	
SE-YFZ	BJ Enduro	215	
SE-YGA	Dragon 150	0053	
SE-YGB	Eurowing Goldwing	unkn	
SE-YGC	Tiger Cub 440	unkn	
SE-YGF	Aériane Sirocco/KFM	37	
SE-YGG	MFI BA-12	BA12.01	
SE-YGI	Dragon 150	0060	
SE-YGL	Teratorn Tierra II	40002	
SE-YGN	Aériane Sirocco	64	
SE-YGS	Mitchell B-10	unkn	
SE-YGU	Dragon 150	0075	
SE-YGV	Mitchell P-38	317	
SE-YGX	Mitchell P-38	unkn	
SE-YGY	Lazair II	B027	
SE-YGZ	Dragon 150	0061	G-MMDL
SE-YHA	Aériane Sirocco	78	
SE-YHB	Aériane Sirocco	76	
SE-YHC	Eipper Quicksilver MX-II	1753	
SE-YHD	Mitchell P-38	06	
SE-YHF	Fisher FP-212 Koala	unkn	
SE-YHG	Teratorn Tierra II	40007	
SE-YHH	Teratorn Tierra II	40006	
SE-YHK	Teratorn Tierra II	40017	
SE-YHL	Teratorn Tierra II	40003	
SE-YHM	Teratorn Tierra II	40013	
SE-YHN	Teratorn Tierra II	40008	
SE-YHO	Teratorn Tierra II	40004	
SE-YHP	Teratorn Tierra II	40015	
SE-YHR	Teratorn Tierra II	40016	
SE-YHS	Teratorn Tierra II	40011	
SE-YHT	Teratorn Tierra II	40014	
SE-YHV	Teratorn Tierra II	40018	
SE-YHX	Teratorn Tierra II	40021	
SE-YHY	Teratorn Tierra II	40019	
SE-YHZ	Teratorn Tierra II	40010	
SE-YIA	Teratorn Tierra II	40025	
SE-YIB	Teratorn Tierra II	40024	
SE-YIC	Teratorn Tierra II	40022	
SE-YID(2)	Filcoa J-6 Karatoo	529/9/267	
SE-YIE	Sonaca-Falcon	SM-OO9	
SE-YIF	Mitchell P-38	JS-07	
SE-YIH	Fisher FP-202 Koala	2195	
SE-YII	Fisher Super Koala	unkn	
SE-YIK	J-3 Kitten	24861	
SE-YIL	MFI BA-12	002	
SE-YIM	Fisher Super Koala	unkn	

Regn.	Type	C/n	Prev.Id.
SE-YIN	Birdman Chinook WT-IIS	752	
SE-YIO	Mitchell U-2	unkn	
SE-YIP	Akka Flyg Akka	40027	
SE-YIR	Sonaca Falcon	SM-005	
SE-YIS	Baker Bobcat	218	
SE-YIT	Mitchell P-38	40	
SE-YIU	Birdman Chinook WT-IIS	01082	
SE-YIV	Akka Flyg Akka	40023	
SE-YIX	Eipper Quicksilver GT400	GT2801-1231	
SE-YKA	MFI-BA12 Rotax	004	
SE-YKB	MFI-BA12 Rotax	005	
SE-YKD	TEAM Hi-Max	617	
SE-YKE	Mitchell Wing B-10	P1313-6	
SE-YKF	Rans S-7 Courier (Permit)	1087.022	
SE-YKG	Rans S-9 Chaos	1187.032	
SE-YKI	Filcoa J-3 Kitten	2901858	
SE-YKK	Fisher FP-202 Super Koala	SK-40	
SE-YKL	Rans S-9 Chaos	1187.029	
SE-YKN	Fisher FP.202 Super Koala	0001	N4549B
SE-YKO	Comco Ikarus Fox-C22	8905-3199	
SE-YKP	Lazair	A-524	
SE-YKS	Rans S-6 Coyote II	0789.043	
SE-YKU	Murphy Renegade Spirit 532	249	
SE-YKV	Fisher Super Koala	SK039	
SE-YKX	Fisher FP-202 Super Koala	SK026	
SE-YKY	J-6 Karatoo	1881-5101	
SE-YLA	Lazair II	A526	
SE-YLB	First Strike Bobcat	513	
SE-YLC	Murphy Renegade Spirit	0272	
SE-YLD	Lidholm WLC-2	2	
SE-YLE	Rans S-6 Coyote II	1289.104	
SE-YLF	Murphy Renegade Spirit UL	248	
SE-YLG	Fisher FP-202 Super Koala	SKO-15	
SE-YLH	Murphy Renegade Spirit 532UL	273	
SE-YLI	Mitchell Wing B-10	P1276	
SE-YLK	Fisher FP-202 Super Koala	SKO-25	
SE-YLL	Fisher FP-202 Super Koala	73	
SE-YLM	Aces High Cuby II	LC 2091012 L1	
SE-YLN	ELAN Cuby II	AAH002	
SE-YLO	ELAN Cuby II	AAH003	
SE-YLP	ELAN Cuby II	AAH004	
SE-YLR	ELAN Cuby II	AAH005	
SE-YLS	ELAN Cuby II	AAH006	
SE-YLU	ELAN Cuby II 912	AAH010	
SE-YLX	Fischer FP-202 Koala	2197	
SE-YLZ	Eipper Quicksilver MX-II	339	
SE-YMT	Fisher FP-404 Classic	4045	
SE-YMU	Filcoa J-6 Karatoo	264	
SE-YMV	Aviasud Mistral 532	114/90	
SE-YMX	Rans S-7 Courier	0290067	
SE-YMY	Fisher Super Koala	SKO-45	
SE-YNA	Solar Wings Pegasus XL-Q	SW-WQ-0234/SW-TE-0219	
SE-YNB	Solar Wings Pegasus XL-Q	SW-WQ-0235/SW-TE-0220	
SE-YNC	Solar Wings Pegasus XL-Q	SW-WQ-0259/SW-TE-0235	
SE-YND	Solar Wings Pegasus XL-Q	SW-WQ-0277/SW-TE-0253	
SE-YNF	Air Création Safari GT B1 16SX	S-100-028	
SE-YNH	Air Ceation Racer ESO2	S-101-030	
SE-YNI	Slater Skytrike/Chronos 14	S-103	
SE-YNK	Air Création Safari GT B1	S-102	
SE-YNN	Mosquito	A10	
SE-YNO	Solar Wings Pegasus Quasar	SW-WQQ-0356/SW-TQ-0027	
SE-YNP	Solar Wings Pegasus Quasar	SW-WQQ-0359/SW-TQ-0028	
SE-YNR	Solar Wings Pegasus Quasar	SW-WQQ-0355/SW-TQ-0026	
SE-YNS	Solar Wings Pegasus Quasar	SW-WQQ-0354/SW-TQ-0025	
SE-YNU	Mosquito/Bauter Zephir	A10-106/1470	
SE-YNV	Solar Wings Pegasus XL-Q	SW-WQ-0237/SW-TE-0222	
SE-YNX	Mosquito/Rumour 14.5	A10-215/008	
SE-YNY	Cosmos Bidulum/Chronos 14	652	
SE-YNZ	Cosmos Bidulum/Chronos 14	655	
SE-YOA	Bautek/NST Saphir	47565/M	
SE-YOB	Behlen Trike Vampir II	2702R03/571	
SE-YOC	Behlen Trike/La Mouette PR.19	369	
SE-YOD	Solar Wings Pegasus XL-R	SW-WA-1251/SW-TB-1246	
SE-YOE	Behlen Trike/La Mouette PR	895	
SE-YOF	Behlen Trike/Hermes 16M LA M	601	
SE-YOG	Behlen Trike/La Mouette PR.19	493	
SE-YOH	Mainair TriFlyer 440/Flexiform Dual Striker	176-0783-1	
SE-YOI	Behlen Trike/La Mouette	612	
SE-YOK	Solar Wings Pegasus XL-R	SW-WA-1330/SW-TB-1318	G-MTWB(1)
SE-YOL	Behlen Trike/Hermes 16M LA	633	
SE-YOM	Magic 177 Minimum	M-315	
SE-YON	Solar Wings Pegasus XL-R	SW-WA-1376/SW-TB-1368	
SE-YOO	Solar Wings Pegasus XL-Q	SW-WQ-0139/SW-TE-0130	
SE-YOP	Solar Wings Pegasus XL-Q	SW-WQ-0115/SW-TE-0102	
SE-YOR	Mainair Gemini/Flash II A	712-1188-6-W502	
SE-YOV	Solar Wings Pegasus XL-Q	SW-WQ-0160/SW-TE-0146	
	(Same c/n as SE-YOZ - re-registered as such?)		
SE-YOX	Mainair Scorcher 503	769-989-2-W562	
SE-YOY	Behlen Trike/Hermes 16M	2120-021	
SE-YOZ	Solar Wings Pegasus XL-Q (Same c/n as SE-YOV)	SW-WQ-0160/SW-TE-0146	SE-YOV ?
SE-YPA	Cosmos Bidulum/Chronos 14	617	
SE-YPC	Cosmos Bidulum/Chronos 14	722	
SE-YPD	Cosmos Bidulum/La Mouette PR19	N-286	
SE-YPF	Cosmos Bidulum/Chronos 14	T-798/V92-39-05	
SE-YPG	Cosmos Bidulum/Chronos 14	777-68	
SE-YPH	Solar Wings Pegasus XL-R	SW-WA-1151/SW-TB-1153	
SE-YPI	Solar Wings Pegasus Quasar II.TC	SW-WQT-0549/SW-TQD-0110	
SE-YPK	Mainair Gemini/Flash IIA	919-0992-/-W717	
SE-YPL	Air Création Racer SX 12	S-105	LN-YFW
SE-YPP	Mainair Gemini/Flash IIA	898-0492-7-W693	G-MWYW
SE-YPR	Pegasus Quasar 2TL	SW-TQD-0107/SW-WQT-0545	
SE-YPS	Mainair Mercury	9261192-7-W725	
SE-YPT	Mainair Gemini/Flash IIA	949-0693-7-W744	
SE-YPU	Mainair Gemini/Flash IIA	956-0793-7-W751	
SE-YPV	Solar Wings Pegasus XL-R	6597	
SE-YPY	Mainair Gemini/Flash IIA	965-0993-7-W760	
SE-YPZ	Cosmos Chronos 16	938	
SE-YRA	Solar Wings Pegasus Quasar 2TC	6653	
SE-YRB	Pegasus Quantum 15	6670	
SE-YRC	Solar Wings Pegasus XL-Q	SW-TB-0023/SW-WQ-24	LN-YKR
	(Correct c/n may be SW-WQ-0023/SW-TE-0044)		
SE-YRD	Pegasus Quantum 15	6696	
SE-YRE	NST Pamir Minimum	M595/020511	
SE-YRF	Chronos 9 Bidulum	0030/3786881	LN-YJH
SE-YRG	Mainair Mercury	992-0694-7-W789-0694-5	
SE-YRH	TL Ultralight TL-2 ESO-2	94E018	
SE-YRI	Solar Wings TSR-85 Typhoon	T585-1403-SW-TC-1002	
SE-YRK	Air Création XP-GTE Clipper	0595084	
SE-YRL	TL Ultralight TL-2 ESO-2	95T22	
SE-YRM	TL Ultralight TL-2 ESO-2	95T23	
SE-YRN	Mainair Blade	1023-0295-7-W821	
SE-YRO	Air Création XP-GTE Clipper	0695097	
SE-YRP	TL Ultralight TL-22 Duo ESO-2	95E034	
SE-YRR	Mainair Blade	1113-0297-7-W916	
SE-YRS	Mainair Blade	1038-0595-7-W836	
SE-YRT	Mainair Blade	1026-0295-7-W824	
SE-YRU	Mainair Blade	1032-0495-7-W830	
SE-YRV	FIB Polaris	0411	
SE-YRX	Solar Wings Pegasus XL-Q-LC	SW-WQ-0017/SW-TB-1302	G-MTUO
SE-YRY	Solar Wings Pegasus XL-Q-LC	SW-WQ-0192/SW-TE-0183	G-MVSA

Regn.	Type	C/n	Prev.Id.
SE-YRZ	Solar Wings Pegasus XL-R		
		SW-WA-1180/SW-TE-0018	G-MTHP
SE-YSA	TL Ultralight TL-32 Typhoon	93A036	
	(Correct c/n may be 95A036)		
SE-YSB	Rans S-12 Airaile	0291057	
SE-YSC	Fisher FP-202 Super Koala	723	
SE-YSD	Light Aero Avid Catalina UL-582	138AB	
SE-YSE	Lamco EuroCUB 912UL	BAH001-1015	
SE-YSF	Lamco EuroCUB 912UL	BAH002-1016	
	(Sold as OH-U347, given as c/n CAH002 ?)		
SE-YSG	Lamco EuroCUB 912UL *(W/o 12.3.97)*	CAH-005	
SE-YSH	Jodel D.18	404	
SE-YSI	Kolb Twin Star Mk II	78811891	OH-U149
SE-YSK	Light Aero Avid Flyer	B.324	SE-XHT
SE-YSL	Lamco EuroCUB Mk 1	CAH-006	
SE-YSM	Light Aero Avid Flyer	389	SE-XLF
SE-YSN	Fisher FP.202 Super Koala	SK-074	
SE-YSO	TL Ultralight TL-32 Typhoon	9501	
SE-YSR	TL Ultralight TL-132 Condor	95C06	
SE-YSS	Denney Kitfox III	PFA/172-11918	G-RMGW
SE-YST	CFM Streak Shadow	K261SA	
SE-YSU	Fisher FP-303	3028	
SE-YSV	Comco Ikarus Fox-C22	8809-3156	OH-U102
SE-YSX	Jodel D.9 Bébé	834	
SE-YSY	Rans S-6E Coyote II	0689034	9-89
SE-YSZ	Light Aero Avid Catalina UL912	136AB	
SE-YTC	Fisher FP.202 Super Koala	SK0-61	
SE-YTD	Lidholm WLC-2	1	
SE-YTE	Comco Ikarus Fox-C22	8903-3195	
SE-YTF	Light Aero Avid Amphibian	127	(SE-XOE)
SE-YTG	TEAM Minimax *(Permit)*	1250-P	
SE-YTH	EuroCUB Mk I *(W/o 9.99?)*	CAH-012	
SE-YTI	Fisher FP.202 Super Koala	SKO-14	
SE-YTK	Tomi 3 Delphin	3/2127	
SE-YTL	Rans S-6S Coyote II	0196927	
SE-YTN	Light Aero Avid Amphibian	83A	SE-XMN
SE-YTO	Pelican Club GS	PFA/165-11214	G-PELI
SE-YTR	Denney Kitfox IV	172	N53PA
SE-YTS	EuroCUB Mk I	CAH-14	
SE-YTT	Jodel D.18	427	
SE-YTV	Diehl XTC	445	
SE-YTX	TL Ultralight TL-132 Condor	95C11	
SE-YTY	Fisher FP.202 Super Koala	SKO-84	
SE-YTZ	Denney Kitfox Classic IV *(Permit)*	C174	
SE-YUA	Rans S-6S Coyote II	1193562	N5290H
SE-YUB	TL Ultralight TL-132 Condor	99C05	
(	*Reservation, but reported W/o)*		
SE-YUC	Light Aero Avid Amphibian	119A	SE-XMZ
SE-YUD	Light Aero Avid Amphibian	33	SE-XKS
SE-YUE	Comco Ikarus Fox C22	8804-3128	OH-U085
SE-YUF	Rans S-12XL Airaile	04970795	
SE-YUG	Rans S-12XL Airaile *(Reservation)*	04970794	
SE-YUH	Rans S-6S Coyote II	10961056	
SE-YUI	Light Aero Avid Amphibian	21	SE-XIB
SE-YUK	Comco Ikarus C-42 Cyclone	9806/6102	
SE-YUL	Lamco EuroCUB Mk.1 912UL *(Reservation)*	CAH-019	
SE-YUM	Comco Ikarus C-42 Cyclone	9807/6108	
SE-YUN	Rans S-12X2 Airaile	04970796	
SE-YUO	CFM Shadow CD	K.146	G-MYCD
SE-YUP	TL Ultralight TL-322 Condor	99C01	
SE-YUR	Rans S-6 Coyote II *(Permit)*	7981251	
SE-YUS	Lamco EuroCUB Mk.1 912UL	CAH-016	
	(Reserved earlier for Rans S-7 Courier a/n 0889056)		
SE-YUT	Rans S-6SCoyote II *(Reservation)*	10971705	
SE-YUU	Jabiru ST-3 UL *(Reservation)*	0178	
SE-YUV	Ultraflight Lazair III *(Reservation)*	A523	
SE-YUX	Anglin J-6 Karatoo UL *(Permit)*	573196	
SE-YUY	Rans S-7L Courier *(Reservation)*	1189061	
SE-YUZ	Jodel D.18UL *(Reservation)*	408	
SE-YVA	Rans S-6S Coyote II *(Reservation)*	10971176	
SE-YVB	Jodel D.18UL *(Reservation)*	438	
SE-YVD	Filcoa J-6 Karatoo *(Reservation)*	529/9/269	
SE-YVE	Filcoa J-6 Karatoo *(Reservation)*	529/9/267	
SE-YVF	Rans S-6 Coyote II *(Reservation)*	0795853XL	
SE-YVI	Comco Ikarus C-42 Cyclone	9910-6217	

Regn.	Type	C/n	Prev.Id.
SE-YVK	Anglin J-6 Karatoo UL *(Permit)*	573198	
SE-YXA	Medway Raven X	MRB-139-120	
SE-YXB	Medway Raven X	MRB-141-123	
SE-YXC	FIB Polaris	97A4214/973655	
SE-YXD	Medway Raven X	MRB140/122	
SE-YXE	Medway Raven X	MRB142/124	
SE-YXF	TL Ultralight TL-2 ESO-2	"TL2G23/97E077"	
	(Not a TL Ultralight TL-2 c/n, correct c/n may be 97G23)		
SE-YXG	Medway Puma Sprint	"M515/126"	
	(Corrupt c/n. If 126 is the wing this could be Raven X c/n MRB126/108 previously G-MYVU cancelled 10.95)		
SE-YXH	TL Ultralight TL-2	unkn	
SE-YXI	Solar Wings Pegasus Flash	SW-WF-0005	G-MNJI
SE-YXK	FIB Polaris	95A5162/954038	
SE-YXL	TL Ultralight TL-2 ESO-2	97TL020	
SE-YXM	TL Ultralight TL-2 ESO-2	97TL021	
SE-YXN	FIB Polaris *(Reservation)*	96A4207/963628	
SE-YXO	Tomi 3 Delfin	31239/1124	OK-BZG-06
SE-YXP	FIB Polaris	98A4264/973690	
SE-YXT	Airborne Edge X	E304/E317	
SE-YXU	Airborne Edge X	E293/E321	
SE-YXV	FIB Polaris	98A4277/983708	
SE-YXX	FIB Polaris	98A4276/983707	
SE-YXY	FIB Polaris	98A4282/983714	
SE-YXZ	FIB Polaris	98A4286/983721	
SE-YYY	Lamco EuroCUB Mk 1 912UL	CAH-OO9	
SE-YZA	FIB Polaris ESO-2	98A4279/97G21	
SE-YZB	Mainair Blade 912	1159-0698-7-W962	
SE-YZC	Mosquito A10/Zephir	25070	
SE-YZE	Raven X	MRB153/132	
SE-YZF	TL Ultralight TL-2 ESO-2	TL-2/98-06	
SE-YZG	TL Ultralight TL-2 ESO-2	TL-2/98-07	
SE-YZH	Mainair Blade 912	1181-1098-7-W984	
SE-YZI	Tomi Cross 5.1/MW155	S/2107	OK-DZG-8
SE-YZK	Pegasus Quantum 15	7485	
SE-YZL	TL Ultralight TL-2 ESO-2	940201/TL-2-01	
SE-YZM	FIBPolaris *(Reservation)*	99A4336	
SE-YZN	TL Ultralight TL-2 ESO-2	980902/990202	
SE-YZO	Pegasus Quantum 15	7542	
SE-YZP	TL Ultralight TL-2 ESO-2	TL-2/980901	
SE-YZR	FIBPolaris *(Reservation)*	92A4498/890003709	
SE-YZS	FIBPolaris *(Reservation)*	99A4376/99A3802	
SE-YZT	FIBPolaris *(Reservation)*	99A4373/99A3801	
SE-YZU	NST Minimum *(Reservation)*	M735	
SE-YZV	Cosmos Bidulm/La Mouette	KSAKT0001-V001	
	(Reservation 10.99)		
SE-YZX	TL Ultralight TL-2/ESO-2 *(Reservation 2.00)*	99T03	
SE-YZZ	Pegasus Quantum 15	7581	

NON-CURRENT AIRCRAFT (For possible Restoration)

Regn.	Type	C/n	Prev.Id.
SE-ACR	Albatros B.II	unkn	SE-94
			SwNavy 5
SE-AHP	Piper J-3C-50S Cub	2371	
SE-AHU	Götaverken GV-38	12	
SE-ANX	BHT-1 Beauty *(Due to fly, 2000)*	1	LN-JHC
			SE-ANX
SE-ARB	Auster J/1 Autocrat	1847	
SE-ARD	Auster J/1 Autocrat	1867	
SE-ATH	Piper J-3C-65 Cub	12444	44-80148
SE-ATP	Piper J-3C-65 Cub	12057	44-79761
SE-AWR	Fairchild F.24W-41A Argus II	805	HB578
			43-14841
SE-AWS	Fairchild F.24W-41A Argus II	804	HB577
			43-14840
SE-BFH	de Havilland DH 60T Moth Trainer	1720	Fv.5600
SE-BGA	Klemm Kl.35D	1983	Fv.5054
SE-BPU	Klemm Kl.35D *(Under restoration)*	2009	Fv.5060
SE-BXI	Focke-Wulf FW.44J Stieglitz	34	Fv.652
SE-CAP	Auster 5	922	MT277
			G-ANHV

Regn.	Type	C/n	Prev.Id.
SE-CHY	Stinson 108-2 Voyager	1792	N8792K
SE-CIG	Jodel D.11	788	
SE-CNC	Champion 7EC Traveler	718	
SE-CRK	Piper PA-22 V-6 STOL	22-9081	
SE-EGC	Tipsy T.66 Nipper	22	OY-ABP
SE-EUH	SAAB MFI-9B/S Trainer	50	
SE-FXK	Reims/Cessna FRA.150L (Tailwheel)	0133	
SE-IET	Piper PA-22-150 Caribbean	22-6947	LN-HAI (2)
			N2973Z
SE-SAH	Grunau Baby II A	1752	
SE-STH	Grunau Baby II B	026	OY-BMX
			SE-STH
			Fv.8113
SE-...	de Havilland DH.82A Tiger Moth	85427	G-APMM
			DE419
SE-...	North American Harvard IIB	14-566	Fv.16106
			FE832
SE-...	Piper J-3C-65 Cub	12847	LN-KLT
			(SE-...)
			OY-ALP
			(D-EFBP)
			LX-ABO
			OE-ABO
			HB-OAB
			44-80551
SE-...	Piper PA-14 Family Cruiser	14-201	OO-JAK
SE-...	Piper PA-18 Super Cub	18-2506	CF-NIO
			N1294C
SE-...	Piper PA-22-108 Colt	22-9391	(SE-KYI)
			LN-IKN

SP - POLAND

Regn.	Type	C/n	Prev.Id.
SP-AAB(3)	Yakovlev YAK-12M	112602	PLW-602 ?
SP-AAC(3)	Yakovlev YAK-12M	112604	PLW-604 ?
SP-AAE(3)	Yakovlev YAK-12M	312619	PLW-619 ?
SP-AAF(3)	Yakovlev YAK-12M	03531	PLW-...
SP-AAG(3)	Yakovlev YAK-12M	312626	PLW-626 ?
			SP-CAA
SP-AAH(3)	Yakovlev YAK-12M	128408	PLW-408 ?
SP-AAI (3)	Yakovlev YAK-12M	7127147	PLW-...
SP-AAK(3)	Yakovlev YAK-12M	7127148	PLW-...
SP-AAL(3)	Yakovlev YAK-12M	158569	PLW-569 ?
SP-AAM(3)	Yakovlev YAK-12M	189774	PLW-774 ?
SP-AAN(3)	Yakovlev YAK-12M	169664	PLW-664 ?
SP-AAO(3)	Yakovlev YAK-12A	30113	PLW-113 ?
SP-AAP(3)	Yakovlev YAK-12A	200972	PLW-972 ?
SP-AAS(3)	Yakovlev YAK-12A	39109	SP-CXY
			PLW-...
SP-AAU(2)	Yakovlev YAK-12M	169661	PLW-661 ?
SP-AAY(2)	Antonov AN-2T	1G26-15	SP-FAY
			PLW-2615
SP-AAZ(3)	Antonov AN-2T	1G15-28	SP-FAZ
			PLW-1528
SP-ABA(3)	Yakovlev YAK-12A	30125	PLW-125 ?
SP-ABB(3)	Yakovlev YAK-12A	30114	PLW-114 ?
SP-ABC(3)	Yakovlev YAK-12A	30115	PLW-115 ?
SP-ABD(3)	Yakovlev YAK-12A	30132	PLW-132 ?
SP-ABE(3)	Yakovlev YAK-12M	200971	PLW-971 ?
SP-ABX(3)	Yakovlev YAK-12A	30121	PLW-121 ?
SP-ACB(3)	Yakovlev YAK-12M	2101000	PLW-...
SP-ACC(3)	Yakovlev YAK-12M	169655	PLW-...
			SP-RAF
			PLW-...
SP-ACD(3)	Yakovlev YAK-12M	200991	PLW-...
SP-ACE(3)	Yakovlev YAK-12A *(Reservation)*	19007	SP-FKE
			SP-CXO
			PLW-...
SP-ACM(3)	Extra EA.300/L	048	D-ETQ .?
SP-ADA(2)	Zlin Z.42M	0070	
SP-ADB(3)	Zlin Z.42M	0071	
SP-ADC(3)	Zlin Z.42M	0072	
SP-ADD(3)	Zlin Z.42M	0073	
SP-ADE(3)	Zlin Z.42M	0074	
SP-ADF(4)	Zlin Z.42M	0075	
SP-ADG(3)	Zlin Z.42M	0076	
SP-ADH(3)	Zlin Z.42M	0077	
SP-ADI (2)	Zlin Z.42M	0078	
SP-ADM(3)	Zlin Z.42M	0081	
SP-ADO(3)	Zlin Z.42M	0091	
SP-ADP(3)	Zlin Z.42M	0092	
SP-ADR(3)	Zlin Z.42M	0093	
SP-ADS(3)	Zlin Z.42M	0094	
SP-ADU(3)	Zlin Z.42M	0096	
SP-ADW(3)	Zlin Z.42M	0097	
SP-ADY(3)	Zlin Z.42M	0098	
SP-ADZ(3)	Zlin Z.42M	0099	
SP-AEA(3)	Zlin Z.42M	0101	
SP-AEC(3)	Zlin Z.42M	0103	
SP-AEF(3)	Zlin Z.42M	0106	
SP-AEG(3)	Zlin Z.42M	0107	
SP-AEH(3)	Zlin Z.42M	0108	
SP-AEI (2)	Zlin Z.42M	0109	
SP-AEL(3)	Zlin Z.42M	0116	
SP-AEM(3)	Zlin Z.42M	0117	
SP-AEN(3)	Zlin Z.42M	0118	
SP-AE0(4)	Zlin Z.42M	0122	
SP-AEP(3)	Zlin Z.42M	0120	
SP-AER(3)	Zlin Z.42M	0121	
SP-AES(3)	Zlin Z.42M	0124	
SP-AET(4)	Zlin Z.42M	0125	
SP-AEU(3)	Zlin Z.42M	0126	
SP-AEX(3)	Zlin Z.42M	0129	
SP-AEZ(3)	Zlin Z.42M	0128	
SP-AFA(3)	PZL-104 Wilga 35A	140538	
SP-AFB(3)	PZL-104 Wilga 35A	140539	

Regn.	Type	C/n	Prev.Id.
SP-AFC(3)	PZL-104 Wilga 35A	140540	
SP-AFE(3)	PZL-104 Wilga 35A	96318	SP-WFH
			SP-WHM
SP-AFK(3)	PZL-104 Wilga 80	CF15810602	
SP-AFL(3)	PZL-104 Wilga 35A	16820629	
SP-AFM(3)	PZL-104 Wilga 35A	16820630	
SP-AFR(2)	PZL-104 Wilga 35A	16820641	
SP-AFT(3)	PZL-104 Wilga 35A	16820643	
SP-AFU(3)	PZL-104 Wilga 35A (W/o 20.8.95)	17820685	
SP-AFV	PZL-104 Wilga 35A	17830704	
SP-AFW(3)	PZL-104 Wilga 35A	17820686	
SP-AFY	Piper L-4 Cub (Reservation 1.99)	12185	SP-FPA
			SP-AMH
			SP-AFY
			44-79889
SP-AFZ(3)	PZL-104 Wilga 35A	17830691	
SP-AGA(3)	PZL-104 Wilga 35A	17830711	
SP-AGC(3)	PZL-104 Wilga 35A	17830713	
SP-AGD(2)	PZL-104 Wilga 35A	17830714	
SP-AGE(3)	PZL-104 Wilga 35A	17830715	
SP-AGF(3)	PZL-104 Wilga 35A	17830733	
SP-AGG(3)	PZL-104 Wilga 35A	18840762	
SP-AGH(3)	PZL-104 Wilga 35A	18840763	
SP-AGI(3)	PZL-104 Wilga 35A	18840764	
SP-AGK(3)	PZL-104 Wilga 35A	18840765	
SP-AGN(3)	PZL-104 Wilga 35A	18840768	
SP-AGO(3)	PZL-104 Wilga 35A	18840769	
SP-AGP(3)	PZL-104 Wilga 35A	18840770	
SP-AGR(3)	PZL-104 Wilga 35A	18840771	
SP-AGS(3)	PZL-104 Wilga 35A	18840777	
SP-AGT(3)	PZL-104 Wilga 35A	18840814	
SP-AGU(2)	PZL-104 Wilga 35A	19850822	
SP-AGV	PZL-104 Wilga 35A	19860849	
SP-AGW(3)	PZL-104 Wilga 35A	19850823	
SP-AGX(3)	PZL-104 Wilga 35A	19860848	
SP-AGY(2)	PZL-104 Wilga 35A	19860847	
SP-AGZ(3)	PZL-104 Wilga 35A	19850824	
SP-AHA(3)	PZL-104 Wilga 35A	19870853	
SP-AHB(2)	PZL-104 Wilga 35A	118402	
SP-AHC(3)	PZL-104 Wilga 35A (Dismantled)	118405	
SP-AHD(4)	PZL-104 Wilga 35A	19870854	
SP-AHF(3)	PZL-104 Wilga 35A	129442	
SP-AHG(3)	PZL-104 Wilga 35A	19870855	
SP-AHH(3)	PZL-104 Wilga 35A	19870856	
SP-AHI(3)	PZL-104 Wilga 35A	19870857	
SP-AHK(3)	PZL-104 Wilga 35A	129452	D-EDDU
SP-AHL(3)	PZL-104 Wilga 35A	19880871	
SP-AHM(3)	PZL-104 Wilga 35A	19880872	
SP-AHR(3)	PZL-104 Wilga 35A	129443	SP-TWO
SP-AHS(3)	PZL-104 Wilga 35A	74206	PLW-206
SP-AHT(3)	PZL-104 Wilga 35A	74207	PLW-207
SP-AHU(4)	PZL-104 Wilga 35A	74200	PLW-200
SP-AHV	PZL-104M Wilga 2000	00970002	
SP-AHW(3)	PZL-104 Wilga 35A	74204	PLW-204
SP-AHX(3)	PZL-104 Wilga 35A	74198	PLW-198
SP-AHY(3)	PZL-104 Wilga 35A	20890877	SP-FWF
SP-AHZ(3)	PZL-104 Wilga 35A	74201	PLW-201
SP-AKC(2)	Zlin Z.42M	0163	
SP-AKD(3)	Zlin Z.42M	0164	
SP-AKE(3)	Zlin Z.42M	0170	
SP-AKG(3)	Zlin Z.42M	0172	
SP-AKH(3)	Zlin Z.42M	0173	
SP-ALD(2)	Zlin Z.42M	0145	
SP-ALE(3)	Zlin Z.42M	0146	
SP-ALF(3)	Zlin Z.42M	0147	
SP-ALH(3)	Zlin Z.42M	0149	
SP-ALK(3)	Zlin Z.42M	0151	
SP-ALL(3)	Zlin Z.42M	0152	
SP-ALN(3)	Zlin Z.42M	0154	
SP-ALO(3)	Zlin Z.42M	0155	
SP-ALP(3)	Zlin Z.42M	0156	
SP-AMB	Piper J-3C-65 Cub (L-4H)	10707	43-29416
SP-AML(3)	Antonov AN-2TD	1G168-05	
SP-AMM(3)	Antonov AN-2P	1G151-65	SP-KNE
SP-AMN(2)	Antonov AN-2P	1G174-41	SP-DRA

Regn.	Type	C/n	Prev.Id.
SP-AMO(3)	Antonov AN-2T	1G52-17	PLW-5217
SP-ANA(3)	Antonov AN-2T	1G29-21	PLW-2921
SP-ANC(3)	Antonov AN-2TD	1G52-14	PLW-5214
SP-AND(3)	Antonov AN-2TD	1G15-26	PLW-1526
SP-ANG(3)	Antonov AN-2TD	1G26-17	PLW-2617
SP-ANH(4)	Antonov AN-2TD	1G29-20	PLW-2920
SP-ANI(3)	Antonov AN-2TD	1G85-56	
SP-ANK(3)	Antonov AN-2TD	1G52-13	PLW-5213
SP-ANL(5)	Antonov AN-2TD	1G147-16	
SP-ANM(3)	Antonov AN-2P	1G149-08	
SP-ANN(3)	Antonov AN-2TD	1G142-31	
SP-ANO(4)	Antonov AN-2TD	1G25-01	PLW-2501
SP-ANP(4)	Antonov AN-2TD	1G185-07	
SP-ANR(4)	Antonov AN-2TD	1G15-27	PLW-1527
SP-ANS(3)	Antonov AN-2TD	1G157-10	
SP-ANT(5)	Antonov AN-2TD	1G98-64	PLW-9864
SP-ANU(4)	Antonov AN-2TD	1G119-66	PLW-1966
SP-ANV	Antonov AN-2TD	1G137-60	PLW-3760
SP-ANW(3)	Antonov AN-2TD	1G180-46	
SP-AOA(3)	Antonov AN-2TP	1G233-21	
SP-AOB(3)	Antonov AN-2TD	1G73-51	PLW-7351
SP-AOC(3)	Antonov AN-2TP	1G108-66	PLW-0866
SP-AOD(3)	Antonov AN-2T	1G108-64	PLW-0864
SP-AOF(3)	Antonov AN-2T	1G98-67	PLW-9867
SP-AOG(3)	Antonov AN-2TP	1G148-07	SP-WLS
SP-AOH(3)	Antonov AN-2T	1G73-57	PLW-7357
SP-AOI(3)	Antonov AN-2P	1G141-83	PLW-4183
SP-AOL(2)	CSS-13	0342	PLW-...
SP-AOM(3)	Antonov AN-2P	1G159-27	PLW-5927
SP-AON	Antonov AN-2P	1G151-55	PLW-5155
SP-AOO(3)	Antonov AN-2T (Reservation)	1G108-65	PLW-0865
SP-AOP(3)	Antonov AN-2P	1G159-26	PLW-5926
SP-AOR(3)	Antonov AN-2T	1G157-09	PLW-5709
SP-AOS(2)	Antonov AN-2TP (Reservation)	unkn	
SP-APA(2)	CSS-13	42076	SP-AIM(2)
			PLW-...
SP-APD(2)	CSS-13	42085	PLW-...
SP-ARI(2)	PZL-110 Koliber	24021	
SP-ARL(3)	PZL-110 Koliber	25026	
SP-ARM(2)	PZL-110 Koliber	25027	
SP-ARN(2)	PZL-110 Koliber	25028	
SP-ARO(2)	PZL-110 Koliber	038529	
	(Ex c/n 25029 and still referred to as such in a/c documents)		
SP-ARP(3)	PZL-110 Koliber	25030	
SP-ARR(2)	PZL-110 Koliber	038531	
SP-ARS(2)	PZL-110 Koliber	038532	
SP-ARU(2)	PZL-110 Koliber	038635	
SP-ASA(2)	Zlin Z.142	0347	
SP-ASB(2)	Zlin Z.142 (Wfu)	0353	
SP-ASC(4)	Zlin Z.142	0354	
SP-ASE(2)	Zlin Z.142	0356	
SP-ASF(3)	Zlin Z.142	0364	
SP-ASG(2)	Zlin Z.142	0365	
SP-ASH(2)	Zlin Z.142	0366	
SP-ASK(2)	Zlin Z.142	0369	
SP-ASL(3)	Zlin Z.142	0491	
SP-ASM(2)	Zlin Z.142	0492	
SP-ASN(2)	Zlin Z.142	0493	
SP-ASO(2)	Zlin Z.142	0494	
SP-ASW(2)	Mil Mi-2	5311106040	SP-FSG
			SP-FSE
SP-ASY(2)	Mil Mi-2 (W/o 2.98)	5211044129	SP-FDC
SP-ATA(2)	Zlin Z.142	0268	
SP-ATC	Zlin Z.142	0270	
SP-ATD	Zlin Z.142	0271	
SP-ATE	Zlin Z.142	0276	
SP-ATF	Zlin Z.142	0277	
SP-ATG	Zlin Z.142	0278	
SP-ATH	Zlin Z.142	0292	
SP-ATI	Zlin Z.142	0293	
SP-ATK	Zlin Z.142	0294	
SP-ATL	Zlin Z.142	0297	
SP-ATM	Zlin Z.142	0298	
SP-ATO	Zlin Z.142 (Crashed 9.99)	0300	
SP-ATP	Zlin Z.142	0316	

Regn.	Type	C/n	Prev.Id.
SP-ATS	Zlin Z.142	0318	
SP-ATU	Zlin Z.142	0322	
SP-ATV	Zlin Z.142	0333	
SP-ATW	Zlin Z.142	0323	
SP-ATX	Zlin Z.142	0332	
SP-ATZ	Zlin Z.142	0326	
SP-AUA	Zlin Z.50L	0008	OK-090
SP-AUB	Zlin Z.50L	0009	OK-092
SP-AUC	Zlin Z.50LS	0032	
SP-AUD	Zlin Z.50LS	0035	
SP-AWA	Yakovlev YAK-12A	30128	PLW-...
SP-AWB	Yakovlev YAK-12M	138488	PLW-...
SP-AWC	Yakovlev YAK-12M	189776	PLW-...
SP-AWD	Yakovlev YAK-12M	179728	PLW-...
SP-AWE	Yakovlev YAK-12M	138458	PLW-...
SP-AWF	Yakovlev YAK-12M	179727	PLW-...
SP-AWG	Yakovlev YAK-12M	169663	PLW-...
SP-AWI	Yakovlev YAK-12M	158568	PLW-...
SP-AWK	Yakovlev YAK-12M	169665	PLW-...
SP-AWL	Yakovlev YAK-12M	179729	PLW-...
SP-AWM	Yakovlev YAK-12M	2101003	PLW-003 ?
SP-AWO	Funk FK-9	027	
SP-AWZ	Yakovlev YAK-12A	30123	PLW-123 ?
SP-AZB	Zlin Z.142	0208	
SP-AZC(2)	Zlin Z.142	0209	
SP-AZE(2)	Zlin Z.142	0211	
SP-AZF(2)	Zlin Z.142	0212	
SP-AZG(2)	Zlin Z.142	0213	
SP-AZH(2)	Zlin Z.142	0214	
SP-AZI	Zlin Z.142	0215	
SP-AZK	Zlin Z.142	0216	
SP-AZL	Zlin Z.142	0227	
SP-AZM	Zlin Z.142	0230	
SP-AZN	Zlin Z.142	0244	
SP-AZO	Zlin Z.142	0245	
SP-AZP	Zlin Z.142	0246	
SP-AZR	Zlin Z.142	0257	
SP-AZT	Zlin Z.142	0458	
SP-CAG	Yakovlev YAK-12A	30133	SP-CXG
SP-CAZ	Yakovlev YAK-12A	30130	SP-CXZ
			PWL-130 ?
SP-CDE	Zlin Z.526F Trenér Master	1107	
SP-CDF	Zlin Z.526F Trenér Master	1108	
SP-CDN	Zlin Z.526F Trenér Master	1152	
SP-CDS	Zlin Z.526F Trenér Master	1165	
SP-CDW	Zlin Z.526F Trenér Master	1168	
SP-CEA(2)	PZL-101A Gawron	119301	SP-RXI
SP-CER	PZL-101A Gawron	96176	
SP-CET	PZL-101A Gawron	96177	
SP-CEY	PZL-101A Gawron	96179	
SP-CFC(2)	PZL-101A Gawron	96180	
SP-CFK(2)	PZL-101A Gawron	96181	
SP-CFR	PZL-101 Gawron	63079	
SP-CFZ	PZL-101A Gawron	96183	
SP-CGC(2)	PZL-101A Gawron	96184	
SP-CGE	PZL-101A Gawron	96185	
SP-CGF	PZL-101A Gawron	96186	
SP-CGK	PZL-101A Gawron (W/o 10.5.97)	96190	
SP-CHC	PZL-101A Gawron	63118	
SP-CHF	PZL-101A Gawron	74136	
SP-CHG	PZL-101 Gawron (Reservation 11.99)	63111	
SP-CHO	PZL-101A Gawron	85165	
SP-CKC	PZL-101A Gawron	107203	
SP-CKD	PZL-101A Gawron	107204	
SP-CKE	PZL-101A Gawron	107205	
SP-CKF	PZL-101A Gawron	107206	
SP-CKG	PZL-101A Gawron	107207	
SP-CKH	PZL-101A Gawron	107208	
SP-CKK	PZL-101A Gawron	107210	
SP-CKL	PZL-101A Gawron	107211	
SP-CKM	PZL-101A Gawron	107212	
SP-CKN	PZL-101A Gawron	107213	
SP-CKO	PZL-101A Gawron	107214	
SP-CKR	PZL-101A Gawron	119300	
SP-CNF	Antonov AN-2TD	1G98-53	
SP-CPH	Zlin Z.526F Trenér Master	1247	
SP-CPI	Zlin Z.526F Trenér Master (Crashed 8.99)	1249	
SP-CRL	PZL-104 Wilga 35A	59060	
SP-CRP	PZL-104 Wilga 35A	59084	
SP-CRW	PZL-104 Wilga 35A	59050	
SP-CRX	PZL-104 Wilga 35A	59059	
SP-CRZ	PZL-104 Wilga 35A	59058	
SP-CSA	Zlin Z.526AFS Akrobat	1201	
SP-CSE	PZL-104 Wilga 35A	61098	
SP-CSU	Zlin Z.526AFS Akrobat	1226	
SP-CSW	Zlin Z.526AFS Akrobat	1227	
SP-CSY	Zlin Z.526AFS Akrobat	1228	
SP-CTA	Zlin Z.526F Trenér Master	1250	
SP-CTB	Zlin Z.526F Trenér Master	1252	
SP-CTC	Zlin Z.526F Trenér Master	1253	
SP-CXU	Yakovlev YAK-12A	30118	PLW-...
SP-DDF(2)	PZL M-28 Skytruck	AJEP1-01	SP-PDF
SP-DDN	PZL M-18B Dromader	1Z015-07	D-FOHR
			DDR-TKR
SP-DEM	PZL M-18BDromader (Reservation 6.99)	1Z027-19	
SP-DEN	PZL M-18BDromader (Reservation 6.99)	1Z027-20	
SP-DFA(2)	Antonov AN-28	1AJ010-19	C5-GAD
			SP-DDF(1)
SP-DFC	PZL M-28 Skytruck	AJE001-10	
SP-DFM	PZL M-28 Skytruck	AJE001-15	
SP-DFN(2)	PZL M-28 Skytruck	AJE001-16	
SP-DFO	PZL M-28 Skytruck	AJE001-17	
SP-DFP	PZL M-28 Skytruck (Reservation 6.99)	AJE001-18	
SP-DFR	PZL M-28-02 Skytruck	AJE001-19	
SP-DFS	PZL M-28-02 Skytruck	AJE001-20	
SP-DLA(2)	Antonov AN-2P	1G178-08	SP-OLA
SP-DMA(3)	PZL M-20 Mewa	1AHP01-01	SP-PKA(1)
SP-DNH	Antonov AN-2R	1G86-10	
SP-DNL	Antonov AN-2TD	1G86-47	
SP-DWA(2)	PZL-104 Wilga 35A	19850829	
SP-EAA	PZL-104 Wilga 35A	48031	
SP-EAB	PZL-104 Wilga 35A	48032	
SP-EAF	PZL-104 Wilga 35A	48036	
SP-EAG	PZL-104 Wilga 35A	48037	
SP-EAH	PZL-104 Wilga 35A	48038	
SP-EAI	PZL-104 Wilga 35A (Crashed 3.99)	48039	
SP-EAN	PZL-104 Wilga 35A	59069	
SP-EAO	PZL-104 Wilga 35A	59070	
SP-EAP	PZL-104 Wilga 35A	59071	
SP-EAU	PZL-104 Wilga 35A	59075	
SP-EAZ	PZL-104 Wilga 35A	59078	
SP-EBA	PZL-104 Wilga 35A	59080	
SP-EBF	PZL-104 Wilga 35A	59085	
SP-EBI	PZL-104 Wilga 35A	61122	
SP-EBK	PZL-104 Wilga 35A	61123	
SP-EBL	PZL-104 Wilga 35A	61132	
SP-EBT	PZL-104 Wilga 80	CF1480558	
SP-ECA	PZL-104 Wilga 35A	62154	
SP-ECB	PZL-104 Wilga 35A	62155	
SP-ECC	PZL-104 Wilga 35A	62156	
SP-ECF	PZL-104 Wilga 35A	62159	
SP-ECH	PZL-104 Wilga 35A	62160	(DM-WBV)
SP-ECK	PZL-104 Wilga 35A	61125	PLW-125
SP-ECL	PZL-104 Wilga 35A	61126	PLW-126
SP-ECN	PZL-104 Wilga 35A	61136	
SP-ECO	PZL-104 Wilga 35A	61137	
SP-ECU	PZL-104 Wilga 35A	62173	
SP-EEA(2)	Aeritalia/SNIAS ATR-42-300	011	F-WQGF
			D-BAAA
			F-ODSA
			F-WWEQ
SP-EEB(2)	Aeritalia/SNIAS ATR-42-300	055	F-WQGI
			D-BBBB
			F-ODSB
			F-WWEJ
SP-EEC(2)	Aeritalia/SNIAS ATR-42-300	080	F-WQID
			D-BCCC
			F-WWEF

Regn.	Type	C/n	Prev.Id.
SP-EED(2)	Aeritalia/SNIAS ATR-42-300	031	F-OHLA(2)
			5R-MVU
			F-WHQR
			3B-NAH
			F-WWEM
SP-EEE(2)	Aeritalia/SNIAS ATR-42-310	024	F-WQJL
			OY-CIC
			F-WWEC
SP-EFA	PZL-102B Kos (Reservation)	209	SP-GLO
			(VH-CGC)
			SP-GLO
SP-EGA	Antonov AN-2TD	1G168-06	
SP-EGB	Antonov AN-2TD	1G168-07	
SP-EGC	Antonov AN-2TD	1G168-08	
SP-EHA	Zlin Z.526F Trenér Master	1317	
SP-EHD	Zlin Z.526F Trenér Master	1320	
SP-EHE	Zlin Z.526F Trenér Master	1321	
SP-EHF	Zlin Z.526F Trenér Master	1322	
SP-EHG	Zlin Z.526F Trenér Master	1323	
SP-ELA	Zlin Z.526AFS Akrobat	1326	
SP-ELB	Zlin Z.526AFS Akrobat	1327	
SP-ELD	Zlin Z.526AFS Akrobat	1310	
SP-ELE	Zlin Z.526AFS Akrobat	1329	
SP-EMB	Zlin Z.526F Trenér Master	1269	
SP-EMC	Zlin Z.526F Trenér Master	1270	
SP-EME	Zlin Z.526F Trenér Master	1272	
SP-EMF	Zlin Z.526F Trenér Master	1273	
SP-EMG	Zlin Z.526F Trenér Master	1274	
SP-EML	Zlin Z.526F Trenér Master	1279	
SP-EMN	Zlin Z.526F Trenér Master	1281	
SP-EMO	Zlin Z.526F Trenér Master	1282	
SP-EMR	Zlin Z.526F Trenér Master	1284	
SP-EMS	Zlin Z.526F Trenér Master	1285	
SP-EMT	Zlin Z.526ML Trenér Master	921	OK-WRR
			F-BORR
SP-ENA	Zlin Z.526AFS Akrobat	1301	
SP-ERH	PZL-110 Koliber	23015	SP-FRH
			SP-ARE(2)
SP-ERP	PZL-110 Koliber	24019	SP-FRP
			SP-ARG(3)
SP-ERS	PZL-110 Koliber	038637	SP-FRS
			SP-WGD
			SP-ARZ(3)
SP-FAF	Antonov AN-2T	1G240-33	(F-GROM)
			SP-FAF
SP-FAP	Antonov AN-2TD	1G27-02	SP-ANE(2)
SP-FAR	Antonov AN-2T	1G187-06	SP-TCF
			SP-TTA
			SP-DTA
SP-FAS	PZL-104 Wilga 35A	19860846	
SP-FAV	Antonov AN-2TP	1G214-06	SP-UXH
SP-FBA(2)	TS-8 Bies	1E04-26	SP-EFM
			PLW-0426
SP-FBC	Christen A-1 Husky (Reservation 5.99)	1193	
SE-FBE	Cessna 150D	60455	N4455U
SP-FBO(2)	Antonov AN-2T	1G108-55	PLW-0855
SP-FBT(2)	PZL M-18A Dromader	1Z023-10	
SP-FBU	PZL M-18A Dromader	1Z023-11	
SP-FCD(2)	Reims/Cessna F.172P	2247	D-EFCD(2)
SP-FCE(2)	Reims/Cessna F.150K (Reservation 10.99)	0613	D-ECEP(2)
SP-FCN(2)	CSS-13	420-102	SP-BHB
SP-FCU	Zlin Z.142	0518	
SP-FCV	SOCATA TB-20 Trinidad (Reservation 10.99)	1899	F-OIGU
SP-FCW	Zlin Z.142	0519	
SP-FCX	Zlin Z.142	0522	
SP-FCY	Zlin Z.142	0521	
SP-FCZ	Zlin Z.142	0520	
SP-FDA	PZL-104 Wilga 35A	62161	(DM-WBW)
SP-FDB	Cessna 172C (Reservation 1.00)	unkn	D-E . . .
SP-FDK	Bell 206B Jet Ranger II	2972	N209AA
			VT-ETH
			G-BOZL
			N701BG
			(N48EA),
			N70ED, N1084H

Regn.	Type	C/n	Prev.Id.
SP-FDM	Mil Mi-2	525141027	SP-SBE
SP-FDN(2)	Bell 407	53051	N1119J
SP-FDO	Antonov AN-26B	10503	RA-26031
			CCCP26031
SP-FDP	Antonov AN-26B	11903	RA-26098
			CCCP26098
SP-FDR	Antonov AN-26B	11305	RA-26067
			CCCP26067
SP-FDU	Antonov AN-2	1G195-01	SP-TWN
SP-FDV	Antonov AN-2TP	1G237-35	
SP-FDW	Antonov AN-2P	1G114-62	PWL-1462
SP-FDZ	Antonov AN-2T	1G74-43	PWL-7443
SP-FEA	Funk FK-9 (Reservation 5.99)	126	
SP-FEC	KO-8 For You	001	SP-PEC
SP-FED	KO-9 Delfin (Reservation)	002	
SP-FEL(2)	Piper PA-28R-201 Arrow	2844016	N4132U
			(SP-FEL)
			N9529N
SP-FEM	Schweizer 269C	S-1678	D-HUFR
			N69A
SP-FEN	Reims/Cessna F.172M	1138	D-EENN
SP-FEP	Reims/Cessna F.172N	1658	D-EFNM
SP-FES	Mil Mi-8	99150472	UR-25603
			CCCP25603
SP-FET	Reims/Cessna FA.150K Aerobat	0059	OO-WIB
SP-FEU	Reims/Cessna F.150M	1148	D-EOQB
SP-FEV	Cessna 421B Golden Eagle	0273	OY-BNY
			N4032L
SP-FEW	Reims/Cessna FR.172F Rocket	0125	D-EJZA
SP-FEX	Piper PA-28-181 Archer II	2890183	D-ETCG
			N9172N
SP-FEY	Reims/Cessna F.172L	0845	(SP-FLR)
			D-ECSV
SP-FEZ	Cessna 150M	77212	D-EWAC
			N63261
SP-FFC	PZL M-18B Dromader	1Z023-25	
SP-FFD	PZL M-18B Dromader	1Z023-26	
SP-FFH	PZL M-18B Dromader	1Z023-30	SP-DDO
			SP-PDM
SP-FFN	Antonov AN-28	1AJ006-08	TC-FEB
			SP-DDD
SP-FFS	PZL M-18B Dromader	1Z023-19	
SP-FFT	PZL M-18B Dromader	1Z023-17	
SP-FFU	PZL M-18B Dromader	1Z023-18	
SP-FFV	PZL M-18B Dromader	1Z023-24	
SP-FFW	PZL M-18B Dromader	1Z023-20	(SP-FWW)
			SP-PBE(2)
SP-FFX	PZL M-18B Dromader	1Z023-23	
SP-FFY	PZL M-18B Dromader	1Z023-21	
SP-FFZ	PZL M-18B Dromader	1Z023-22	
SP-FGA	Croses EC-3 Pouplume	SAK-01	(SP-AMA(3))
			SP-0023
SP-FGB(2)	Piper PA-32R-301 Saratoga II HP	3246143	N41734
SP-FGC	CSS-13	0431	SP-AIA(2)
SP-FGD	PZL-101A Gawron	107220	SP-RXF
SP-FGF	Robinson R-22 Beta (Reservation 7.99)	unkn	
SP-FGN	Grumman-American AA-1B Trainer	0618	SP-WGN
SP-FGO	PZL-101A Gawron	107215	SP-RXA
SP-FGP	PZL-101A Gawron	63119	SP-KZG
			SP-KXG
SP-FGS	Maule M-7-235C Super Rocket	25011C	
SP-FGV	Cessna 152-II	83584	N1368F
SP-FGW	Beech A23-19 Musketeer Sport III	MB-32	HB-ENO
SP-FGX	Cessna 152-II	84441	N6571L
SP-FGY	Cessna 152-II	82746	N89437
SP-FGZ	Cessna 152-II	82477	N69082
SP-FHK	Mil Mi-2	525933019	SP-SBU
SP-FHL	Mil Mi-2	568826104	PLW-8826
SP-FHM	Mil Mi-2	514520115	SP-SPE
SP-FHO	Mil Mi-2	533003063	PLW-3003
SP-FHP	Antonov AN-28	1AJ008-04	RA-28918
			CCCP28918
SP-FHR	Antonov AN-28	1AJ006-11	RA-28700
			CCCP28700

Regn.	Type	C/n	Prev.Id.
SP-FHS	Antonov AN-28	1AJ007-10	RA-28725
			CCCP28725
SP-FHT	Antonov AN-28	1AJ007-17	RA-28732
			CCCP28732
SP-FHU	Antonov AN-28	1AJ007-18	RA-28733
			CCCP28733
SP-FHW	Antonov AN-28	1AJ008-05	RA-28919
			CCCP28919
SP-FIA	Antonov AN-2R	1G161-02	SP-WOM
SP-FIC	Antonov AN-2TP	1G113-18	PLW-1318
SP-FIE	Antonov AN-2TP	1G185-02	SP-TWH
SP-FIF	Antonov AN-2R	1G153-25	EW-05712
			CCCP05712
SP-FIG	PZL-106BR Kruk	09870204	(D-FODA)
			DDR-TDA
SP-FII	PZL-106BR Kruk	10890234	D-FOEP
			DDR-TEP
SP-FIN	Antonov AN-2T	1G98-57	PLW-9857
SP-FIO	PZL M-18A Dromader	1Z015-17	D-FOLB
			DDR-TLB
SP-FIP	PZL M-18A Dromader	1Z015-19	D-FOLD
			DDR-TLD
SP-FIR	PZL M-18A Dromader	1Z021-12	D-FOMF
			DDR-TMF
SP-FIS	PZL M-18A Dromader	1Z018-03	D-FOLI
			DDR-TLI
SP-FIT	Antonov AN-2P	1G159-45	PLW-5945
SP-FIV	Antonov AN-2T	1G108-59	PLW-0859
SP-FIW	Antonov AN-2S *(Reservation 9.99)*	1G185-05	SP-UXC
SP-FIZ	Antonov AN-2T	1G73-53	PLW-7353
SP-FKB	OKA-5 Pelikan	01	
SP-FKE	Yakovlev YAK-12A	19007	SP-CXO
	(Reservation as SP-ACE, 12.99)		PLW-...
SP-FKH	Yakovlev YAK-12A	39108	SP-CXR(2)
			PLW-108 ?
SP-FKP	Yakovlev YAK-12A	19003	SP-CXM
			PLW-...
SP-FKR	Yakovlev YAK-12M	7127123	PLW-...
			SP-CFN (1)
			PLW-...
SP-FKT	Radwan KR-2PM3 *(Reservation)*	YL-002-SVL	SP-PKT
SP-FKU	Kukulka *(Reservation)*	"T-026382"	SE-XKK
	(C/n quoted may be engine number)		SP-PHN
SP-FKW	Yakovlev YAK-12A	30131	SP-CXX
			PLW-...
SP-FKX	Yakovlev YAK-12A	19001	SP-CXP(2)
			PLW-001
SP-FKY	Yakovlev YAK-12A	30127	SP-CXS(2)
			PWL-127
SP-FLA(2)	TL Ultralight TL-32 Typhoon	9502	
SP-FLB	TL Ultralight TL-32 Typhoon	93A031	OK-YUU-58
SP-FLF	Cessna 177RG Cardinal RG	0522	N2122Q
SP-FLG	Reims/Cessna F.177RG Cardinal RG	0128/0014	OH-CFX
			SE-FXH
SP-FLI	Reims/Cessna FR.172J Rocket	0493	D-EECD
SP-FLK	Cessna 172P	75030	N546CF
			N54664
SP-FLL	Reims/Cessna F.152	1975	D-EIFD(3)
SP-FLM	Reims/Cessna FR.172J Rocket	0479	OY-BFO
SP-FLN	Cessna 172P	75314	D-EDGJ
			N62626
SP-FLO	Reims/Cessna F.152	1711	D-EDND(3)
			HB-CNR
SP-FLP	Reims/Cessna F.172P	2170	D-EOWD
SP-FLR	Reims/Cessna FR.172H Rocket	0307	D-ECSP
SP-FLS	Cessna 172M	61292	D-EHHH
			N20444
SP-FLT	Reims/Cessna F.172H	0322	D-EGMI (2)
SP-FLX	Antonov AN-2R	1G178-27	LY-AEM
			CCCP62635
SP-FLY	Antonov AN-2R	1G170-45	SP-UXA
SP-FLZ	Antonov AN-2R	1G204-47	EW-17846
			CCCP17846
SP-FMA	Antonov AN-2P	1G163-35	
SP-FMC	AT-1	001	SP-PMC
SP-FMD	PZL M-20 Mewa	1AH001-03	SP-KMA
			SP-PKC
SP-FME	PZL M-20 Mewa	1AH002-07	SL-BPK
			(YU-BPK)
SP-FMF	PZL M-20 Mewa	1AH002-10	SP-DMC
SP-FMG	Cessna 150M	77716	D-EMSR
			N6464K
SP-FMH	Antonov AN-2 *(Reservation 9.99)*	1G98-61	PLW-9861
SP-FMK	Cessna T210M Centurion	62669	D-ETKK
			N887MM
			N888MM
			(N6045B)
SP-FML	Antonov AN-2R *(Reservation 12.99)*	1G187-08	SP-WZM
	(Previously reserved for c/n 1G173-02 ex SP-TCC)		
SP-FMM	Antonov AN-2R *(Reservation)*	1G187-07	SP-TCE
			SP-TTB
			SP-DTB
SP-FMN	Antonov AN-2P	1G177-21	SP-TWE
			SP-DFN
SP-FMP	Antonov AN-2T	1G147-23	PWL-4723
SP-FMR	Antonov AN-2P	1G163-34	SP-GFA
SP-FMS	Antonov AN-2 *(Reservation 2.99)*	1G178-16	LY-AFT
			LY-ACT
			CCCP62624
SP-FMT	Antonov AN-2	1G85-51	PWL-8551
SP-FMV	Cessna 150J	70996	N1016M
SP-FMW	LET L-200D Morava	171001	SP-FAU
			SP-MNK
			CCCP34500
SP-FMX	Cessna 150M *(Reservation 3.99)*	78490	N704BV
SP-FMY	Cessna 150M *(Reservation 3.99)*	74312	N19294
SP-FMZ	Cessna 150M *(Reservation 3.99)*	76386	N3109V
SP-FND	SOCATA TB-20 Trinidad	1381	SE-KNP
SP-FNE	SOCATA TB-9 Tampico	1089	SE-KNM
SP-FNF	Fokker F.27 Friendship 600	10179	D-BAKD
			F-GKJC
			PH-FCT
			TG-AEA
			P2-ANE
			P2-MNE
			JA8603
			(JA8303)
			PH-FCT
SP-FNH	Beech 300LW Super King Air *(Reservn)*	FA-227	D-ICBC
			N81418
SP-FNI	TL Ultralight TL-32 Typhoon	9601	OK-BUU-40
SP-FNK(2)	Beech A36 Bonanza	E-3014	N3263W
SP-FNL	SOCATA TB-9 Tampico *(Crashed 9.98)*	469	D-EGUF(2)
SP-FNN	TL Ultralight TL-32 Typhoon	9402	
SP-FNP	Birdman Chinook 2 Plus	02123	
SP-FNR	Light Aero AvidSpeedwing	YL-004	SP-PNR
SP-FNS	Beech B300 Super King Air	FL-134	N3252V
SP-FNT	Cessna 182Q	67479	D-ETRB
			N6664X
			YV-1883P
			(N4955N)
SP-FNU	Reims/Cessna F.172L	0835	OY-RYM
SP-FNV	Cessna 421C Golden Eagle	0805	D-INAS(2)
			N1206N
			JRV ....
			OE-FBI
			N26565
SP-FNX	Chinook Plus *(Reservation 3.99)*	unkn	
SP-FOF	PZL M-18B Dromader	1Z024-05	
SP-FOG(2)	PZL M-18B Dromader	1Z024-06	
SP-FOH	PZL M-18B Dromader	1Z024-07	
SP-FOI	PZL M-18B Dromader	1Z024-08	
SP-FOK	PZL M-18B Dromader	1Z024-09	
SP-FOL	PZL M-18B Dromader	1Z025-13	
SP-FOM	PZL M-18B Dromader	1Z025-14	
SP-FON	PZL M-18B Dromader	1Z025-15	
SP-FOO	PZL M-18B Dromader	1Z025-16	
SP-FOP	Cessna 182P *(Possibly SP-FUP)*	63561	OY-BII
			N5833J

Regn.	Type	C/n	Prev.Id.
SP-FOR	Cessna 172M	62639	D-EOFD
			C-FCFD
			LHR-11
			CF-CFD
			N1528S
SP-FOS	Cessna 182N	60235	HB-CUX
			N92503
SP-FOT	Piper PA-28R-200 Cherokee Arrow II	28R-7635273	N75181
	(Reservation 5.99, identity not yet confirmed)		
SP-FOU	Reims/Cessna F.172H *(Reservation 5.99)*	0439	D-ELBG
SP-FOW	Let-Mont Tulak *(Reservation)*	unkn	
SP-FOX	Reims/Cessna F.150L	1102	D-EDJB
SP-FOY	Reims/Cessna F.150L	0806	D-EEYF
SP-FOZ	Let-Mont Tulak *(Reservation 1.99)*	unkn	
SP-FPC	Piper PA-28-140 Cherokee	28-24606	N7261J
SP-FPD	Piper PA-28R-200 Cherokee Arrow	28R-7235180	N5033T
SP-FPE	TL Ultralight TL-232 Condor	97C02	
SP-FPN	Reims/Cessna F.182Q Skylane	0084	G-BPPN
			(G-BFFN)
			(G-BLHN)
SP-FPO	SOCATA Rallye 100T	2890	F-GAKF
SP-FPP	Piper PA-34-200T Seneca	34-7870066	D-GARA
			D-IARA
			N2127M
SP-FPR	SOCATA MS.880B Rallye Club	2893	F-GAKN
SP-FPS	Piper PA-60-601P Aerostar	61P-0710-7963342	N6075U
			(N311DS)
			N6075U
SP-FPT	Cessna 172M	64137	N30373
SP-FPU	Cessna 172P	73151	N6118F
SP-FPV	SOCATA MS.887 Rallye 125	2163F-BUJA	
SP-FPW	Cessna 172N	71715	D-EHMG(2)
			N5109E
SP-FPX	Bücker T-131PA Jungmann	102	
SP-FPZ	Bücker T-131P Jungmann	03	
SP-FRA	SOCATA Rallye 150T	2661	D-EBWK
			F-ODDG
SP-FRC	SOCATA/PZL-110 Rallye 110ST Galopin	2743	SP-WGA
			F-ODDF
SP-FRE	PZL-110 Koliber	23011	SP-ARA(2)
SP-FRG	SOCATA Rallye 110ST Galopin	2854	SP-WGB
			F-ODER
SP-FRI	PZL-110 Koliber	24020	SP-ARH(3)
SP-FRK	PZL-110 Koliber 150	24022	SP-ARK(2)
SP-FRL	PZL-110 Koliber 150	19003	SP-ZKA
SP-FRM	PZL-110 Koliber 150	19006	SP-ZKD
SP-FRN	PZL-110 Koliber	23013	SP-ARC(2)
SP-FRO	PZL-110 Koliber	23014	SP-ARD(2)
SP-FRR	PZL-110 Koliber	24018	SP-ARF(2)
SP-FRT	PZL-110A Koliber 150A	04940061	(D-ESDP)
SP-FRU	PZL-110A Koliber 150A	04950075	SP-WCF
			(N150AX)
SP-FRV	Morane-Saulnier MS.885 Super Rallye	252	D-EIAD
	(Reservation 11.99)		F-BKUF
SP-FRW	SOCATA MS.893E Rallye 180GT Gaillard	12753	OO-MIP
SP-FRX	SOCATA MS.893A Rallye Commodore `180	11497	D-ECCX
	(Reservation 11.99)		
SP-FRY	SOCATA MS.880B Rallye Club	2504	F-BVHE
SP-FRZ	SOCATA MS.893E Rallye 180GTGaillard	12535	D-EKLI
			F-BVZR
SP-FSC	Mil Mi-2	5311105129	
SP-FSD	Mil Mi-2	530603127	PLW-0603
SP-FSK	Mil Mi-2	510549127	PLW-0549
SP-FSL	Rotorway Executive 90 *(W/o 15.8.96)*	5150	
SP-FSM(2)	Mil Mi-2	530605127	PLW-0605
SP-FSN	Mil Mi-2	563622084	PLW-3622
SP-FSO(2)	PZL W-3A Sokol	370515	PLW-0515
	(Reservation. possibly ntu, flew as '0515')		(SP-FSO)
SP-FSR	Mil Mi-2	533602054	PLW-3602
SP-FSS	Mil Mi-2	524912086	SP-SNA
SP-FST	Mil Mi-2	529042100	SP-SUB
SP-FSV	Mil Mi-2	5210539038	SP-STC
SP-FSW	Mil Mi-2	532816023	
SP-FSX	Mil Mi-2	535401107	SP-SKM
SP-FSY	Mil Mi-2	5210401097	SP-STA(2)
SP-FTA	Cessna 172N	68002	G-BGIC
			N75854
SP-FTB	Cessna 172N	70230	N738TS
SP-FTC	Cessna 172M	63858	N160SH
			N20861
SP-FTD	Cessna 402B	0417	N678AC
			N69295
SP-FTE	Reims/Cessna F.172N	1977	G-BHNU
SP-FTF	Cessna 402 *(Reservation)*	unkn	
SP-FTG	BAe.Jetstream Series 3102	655	G-ENIS
			G-LOGR
			G-BRGR
			PH-KJD
			G-31-655
SP-FTH(2)	BAe.Jetstream Series 3102	649	G-SWAD
			G-LOGP
			VH-LJR
			G-BPZJ
			PH-KJC
			G-31-649
SP-FTN(2)	LET L-410UVP-E10	902515	SP-FGI
			(SP-TAE)
SP-FTS(2)	Piper PA-34-220T Seneca V	3449040	N321TS
SP-FTU	KR-02A *(Reservation 5.99)*	unkn	
SP-FTV	LET L-410UVP-E10	882038	SP-TAA
SP-FTW	SOCATA MS.892A Rallye Commodore 150	11874	D-EESW
			F-BTJA
SP-FTX	LET L-410UVP-E10	892301	SP-TAB
SP-FTY	LET L-410UVP-E10	892317	SP-TAC
SP-FUA	Kraska *(Reservation 9.99)*	unkn	
SP-FUB	Aeropro Fox 912/2A	023096	OM-CXAJ
SP-FUC	EOL-2BMW	E01.1	SP-PUC
SP-FUF	EOL-2	E04.5	SP-PUF
SP-FUH	EOL-2M	EK01.2	
SP-FUK	Fly Synthesis Storch	39R	
SP-FUL	Pottier P.220S-AT2 Koala	001	SP-PUL
SP-FUM	EOL-2	E16.17	SP-PUM
SP-FUO	EOL-2	EK04.05	SP-PUO
SP-FUP(2)	T-131PA Jungmann *(Reservation)*	105	
SP-FUR	T-131PA Jungmann *(Reservation)*	106	
SP-FUS	T-131PA Jungmann *(Reservation, see SP-GOS)*	107	
SP-FUT	EOL-2	EK05.6	
SP-FUW	Typhoon *(Reservation)*	unkn	
SP-FUX	T-131PA Jungmann	104	
SP-FUY	T-131PA Jungmann	103	
SP-FUZ	Tulak	TUL-06	
SP-FVC	PZL-104 Wilga 35A *(W/o 9.7.95)*	74193	PLW-193
SP-FVV	Cessna 421B Golden Eagle	0525	D-ILPD
			N421YS
			N69889
SP-FWB	Cessna 182S *(Reservation 9.99)*	80194	N2638A
SP-FWH	PZL-104 Wilga 35A	20890887	
SP-FWK(2)	Cessna T.210L Turbo Centurion	61152	N103AG
			D-EAWO
			N2191S
SP-FWL	Cessna 182P	61803	D-ECYB
SP-FWN	PZL-104 Wilga 80	CF15810599	SP-AFG(3)
SP-FWO	PZL-104 Wilga 35A	139501	SP-ZOC
SP-FWT	PZL-104 Wilga 35A	61104	SP-WHE
			PLW-104
SP-FWU	PZL-104 Wilga 35A	18840773	SP-ZOG
SP-FWW	PZL-104 Wilga 35A	19840812	SP-ZOE
SP-FWY	PZL-104 Wilga 35A	19850827	SP-ZOH
SP-FYA	PZL-104 Wilga 35A	74197	PLW-197
SP-FYB	Aviat Pitts S-2S *(No CofR issued)*	3018	
SP-FYD	Piper PA-28R-201T Turbo Cherokee Arrow III	28R-7703021	N1296H
SP-FYF	Antonov AN-2P	1G181-53	SP-TWK
SP-FYL	Antonov AN-2foto	1G185-57	SP-TDL
SP-FYM	Antonov AN-2TP	1G137-58	SP-TBM
			G-BTOV
			N2AN
			SP-KNA
SP-FYN	Bell 206B Jet Ranger III	4208	C-FNSV
			N206BF

Regn.	Type	C/n	Prev.id.
SP-FYO	Antonov AN-2P	1G185-56	SP-TBK
SP-FYP	Rotorway Exec 162F (Reservation 3.97)	unkn	
SP-FYR	Antonov AN-2T	1G174-43	SP-TWB
SP-FYT	Yakovlev YAK-40	9641851	LY-AAZ
			CCCP88245
SP-FYU	Yakovlev YAK-40	9211821	UR-87566
			CCCP87566
SP-FYV	PZL M-28 Skytruck	AJE001-01	
SP-FZC	PZL-104 Wilga 80	CF21930940	SP-WDH
SP-FZD	PZL-104 Wilga 35A	74203	SP-FWX
			PLW-203
SP-FZE	PZL-104 Wilga 80	CF21950961	
SP-FZF	PZL-104 Wilga 35A	20890889	SP-FWK
SP-FZG	PZL-104 Wilga 35A	16820635	SP-TWY
SP-FZL	PZL-104 Wilga 80	CF15810601	(SP-FWB)
			SP-AFI (2)
SP-FZN	CSS-13	42037	SP-AHT(2)
			PLW-...
SP-FZR	Funk FK-9	80	
SP-FZS	Bell 427 (Reservation 8.99)	56014	(SP-FJS)
SP-FZT	Piper PA-31-350 Chieftain (Reservn 1.00)	unkn	
SP-GBW	Cessna 182S	80194	N2638A
SP-GCA	Antonov AN-28	1AJ004-06	
SP-GHD	Zlin Z.42M	0119	
SP-GHE	Zlin Z.42M	0123	
SP-GHF	Zlin Z.42M	0140	
SP-GHK	Zlin Z.42M	0144	
SP-GKA	Piper PA-34-200T Seneca II	34-7670279	(HB-L...)
			N6299J
SP-GOS	T-131PAJungmann (Reservation 6.99)	107	(SP-FUS)
SP-GSC	Robinson R-44 Astro	0272	
SP-GSD	Robinson R-44 Astro	0322	
SP-GSE	Robinson R-44 Astro	0346	
SP-GSF	Robinson R-44 Astro	0355	
SP-GSG	Robinson R-22B2 Beta	2897	
SP-GSH	Robinson R-22B2 Beta	2983	
SP-GSM	PZL-104M Wilga 2000	00970003	
SP-GUH	Pottier P.220S AT-3 Koala	001	SP-PUH
SP-GWB	PZL-104 Wilga 35A	19870858	
SP-GWH	Mil Mi-2	535019116	
SP-HKL	Yakovlev YAK-12M	179714	SP-FKL
			SP-RAB
SP-HKM	PZL-104 Wilga 35A	74191	SP-FKM
			PLW-191
SP-HKN	PZL-104 Wilga 35A	74199	SP-FKN
			PLW-199
SP-HKO	Cessna 175B Skylark (Reservation 9.99)	56898	SP-KYM
			D-EFWH(2)
			N8198T
SP-KAA	Antonov AN-2TD	1G117-69	
SP-KAS	PZL M-20 Mewa	AH002-16	
SP-KAT	PZL-101A Gawron	96169	SP-KXT
SP-KBA	Antonov AN-2TD	1G185-06	
SP-KEA	PZL-104 Wilga 35A	59048	
SP-KFA	Zlin Z.43	0080	
SP-KFC	PZL-110 Koliber	19002	
SP-KFE	PZL M-20 Mewa	1AH002-13	
SP-KLA	Yakovlev YAK-12A	30126	PLW-...
SP-KLC	Yakovlev YAK-12M	158567	PLW-...
SP-KLD	PZL-104 Wilga 35A	19850821	
SP-KRC	Yakovlev YAK-12M	169653	PLW-...
			SP-RAE
			PLW-...
SP-KSA	Antonov AN-2TP	1G214-10	
SP-KYK	Extra EA.300/S	029	(SP-FEM)
			D-ETYU
SP-KYM	Cessna 175B Skylark	56898	D-EFWH(2)
	(Reserved as SP-HKO 9.99)		N8198T
SP-KZB	PZL-101A Gawron	96173	SP-KXZ
SP-KZD	PZL-101A Gawron	52073	SP-KXD
SP-KZF	PZL-101A Gawron	96167	SP-KXF
SP-KZI	PZL-104 Wilga 35A	74209	
SP-KZO	PZL-101A Gawron	96168	SP-KXO
SP-KZS	PZL-101A Gawron	63117	SP-KXS
SP-KZU	PZL-101A Gawron	85164	SP-KXU

Regn.	Type	C/n	Prev.id.
SP-LFA(2)	Aeritalia/SNIAS ATR-72-201	246	F-WWEM
SP-LFB(2)	Aeritalia/SNIAS ATR-72-201	265	F-WWEJ
SP-LFC(2)	Aeritalia/SNIAS ATR-72-201	272	F-WWEN
SP-LFD(2)	Aeritalia/SNIAS ATR-72-201	279	F-WWLD
SP-LFE(2)	Aeritalia/SNIAS ATR-72-201	328	F-WWLJ
SP-LFF(2)	Aeritalia/SNIAS ATR-72-201	402	F-WWLM
SP-LFG	Aeritalia/SNIAS ATR-72-201	411	F-WWEO
SP-LFH	Aeritalia/SNIAS ATR-72-202	478	F-WWEK
SP-LGA(2)	Embraer EMB-145EU	145-155	PT-SEJ
SP-LGB(2)	Embraer EMB-145EU	145-165	PT-SEK
SP-LGC	Embraer EMB.145EU	145-227	PT-SHM
SP-LKA(2)	Boeing 737-55D	27416	
SP-LKB(2)	Boeing 737-55D	27417	
SP-LKC(2)	Boeing 737-55D	27418	
SP-LKD(2)	Boeing 737-55D	27419	
SP-LKE(2)	Boeing 737-55D	27130	
SP-LKF(2)	Boeing 737-55D	27368	
SP-LLA(2)	Boeing 737-45D	27131	
SP-LLB(2)	Boeing 737-45D	27156	
SP-LLC(2)	Boeing 737-45D	27157	
SP-LLD	Boeing 737-45D	27256	
SP-LLE	Boeing 737-45D	27914	
SP-LLF	Boeing 737-45D	28752	
SP-LLG	Boeing 737-45D	28753	
SP-LLH	Boeing 737-4S3	25594	N2423N
			TC-AVA
			9M-MLJ
SP-LMC	Boeing 737-36N	28668	
SP-LMD	Boeing 737-36N	28669	
SP-LOA	Boeing 767-25DER	24733	N6046P
SP-LOB	Boeing 767-25DER	24734	
SP-LPA(2)	Boeing 767-35DER	24865	
SP-LPB(2)	Boeing 767-35DER	27902	
SP-LPC(2)	Boeing 767-35DER	28656	
SP-MBA	LET L.410UVP-E2	861803	
SP-MMT	Antonov AN-2TD	1G167-13	
SP-MRA	PZL M-20 Mewa	1AH002-03	SP-PRA
			SP-MRA
SP-MXA(2)	PZL M-20 Mewa	1AH002-08	SP-DMB(2)
SP-MXB(2)	PZL M-20 Mewa	1AH002-12	
SP-MXC(2)	PZL M-20 Mewa	1AH002-14	
SP-MXD	PZL M-20 Mewa	1AH002-09	SP-FMI
SP-NEA	PZL M-20 Mewa	1AH002-05	SP-PUE
SP-NEH	Antonov AN-2TD	1G188-34	
SP-NFA	Yakovlev YAK-12M	210997	PLW-...
SP-NSK	Antonov AN-2TD	1G167-12	
SP-NWA	PZL-104 Wilga 35A (Dismantled)	62176	
SP-NXA(4)	LET L.200D Morava	171408	HA-LDF
SP-NXK(2)	LET L.200D Morava	170908	SP-NRH
			CCCP34477
SP-NXL	LET L.200D Morava	171014	CCCP34513
SP-NXN(2)	LET L.200D Morava	171401	HB-LCU
SP-NXT	LET L.200D Morava	171327	SP-NPB
			CCCP02111
SP-NXX(2)	LET L.200D Morava	171206	HA-LDA
SP-NXY	LET L.200D Morava	171402	SP-NAC
SP-NXZ	LET L.200D Morava	171203	SP-NAB
SP-OSA	Antonov AN-2TD	1G187-27	
SP-PAM	Tulak (Reservation 3.99)	05	
SP-PBN(2)	YALO GM-01 Gniady		YL-003SH
SP-PBW(2)	PZL-106BT34 Turbo Kruk	11980254	
SP-PCM	DEKO-9 Magic (Reservation 3.99)	DK9.00.01	
SP-PEE	Aircab K-01 (Reservation)	unkn	
SP-PEF	HM.293 Pou du Ciel (Built, but still reservn)	unkn	
SP-PEG	E &K SBM-03 (Reservation)	unkn	
SP-PFL	KO-9 (Reservation)	unkn	
SP-PGU	Taifun TL-32 TOP (Reservation 1.00)	unkn	
SP-PHB	PZL-110 Koliber 160A	04980083	
SP-PIL	PZL I-23	002	
SP-PKO	KO-11 Gorka (Reservation 3.99)	unkn	
SP-PKT	Radwan Swift Mk.II		YL-002-SVL
SP-PLZ	KO-10 Amfibia (Reservation)	unkn	
SP-PMB	PZL-126P Mrowka (Reservation)	00980001	
SP-PNG	Funk FK-9S/TG	038A	
SP-PSE(2)	PZL W-3 Sokol	300106	

Regn.	Type	C/n	Prev.Id.
SP-PSL	PZL W-3A2 Sokol	370508	(SP-SYO)
SP-PSW	PZL SW-4	600103	
SP-PSZ	PZL SW-4	600104	
SP-PUH	Pottier P.220S-AT3 Koala *(formerly c/n 003)*	001	
SP-PUK	Pottier P.220S-AT3 Koala *(Reservation)*	002	
	(Ntu, used for static tests only)		
SP-PUP	EOL-VLA	E19	
SP-PUS	EOL-VL-X	E10	
SP-PUV	Bü.233P Jungmeister *(Reservation)*	101	
SP-PVX	RAF-2000 GTX-SE *(Reservation 12.99)*	"616521"	
SP-PVVI	PZL I-22 Iryda M93K	ANA003-01	PWL-0301
SP-PZD	JK-03 Junior *(Reservation 10.99)*	unkn	
SP-RAC(2)	PZL-101A Gawron	107217	SP-RXC
SP-RCB	PZL-101A Gawron	107216	SP-RXB
SP-RCL	PZL-101A Gawron	119303	SP-RXL
SP-RCM	PZL-101A Gawron	119304	SP-RXM
SP-SAB(2)	Mil Mi-2	536348119	SU-BHW
			SP-SAB(2)
SP-SAG	Mil Mi-2	512614102	Soviet AF
SP-SAK(2)	Mil Mi-2	512624102	Soviet AF
SP-SAM(2)	Mil Mi-2	512623102	Soviet AF
SP-SAO	Mil Mi-2	525522028	
SP-SAP(2)	Mil Mi-2	525523038	
SP-SAR(3)	Mil Mi-2	512617092	Soviet AF
SP-SAS	Mil Mi-2	525612048	
SP-SBA(3)	Mil Mi-2	529541125	
SP-SBC	Mil Mi-2	524740046	
SP-SBL	Mil Mi-2	525147037	
SP-SBN	Mil Mi-2	525149037	SU-BHY
			SP-SBN
SP-SBS	Mil Mi-2	525932128	
SP-SBZ	Mil Mi-2	525936128	
SP-SCA(3)	Mil Mi-2	529605016	
SP-SCC	Mil Mi-2	529607016	
SP-SCI	Mil Mi-2	529612016	
SP-SCO	Mil Mi-2	529626026	
SP-SCU	Mil Mi-2	529631026	
SP-SCV	Mil Mi-2	529636026	
SP-SCX	Mil Mi-2	529635026	
SP-SCZ	Mil Mi-2	529633026	
SP-SDC	Mil Mi-2	543908124	
SP-SDD	Mil Mi-2	543910015	
SP-SDH	Mil Mi-2	524004025	
SP-SDI	Mil Mi-2	524005025	
SP-SDM	Mil Mi-2	530322047	SP-PSC(1)
SP-SDS	Mil Mi-2	544529125	
SP-SEA	Mil Mi-2	542229012	
SP-SEF	Mil Mi-2	525227067	
SP-SEN	Mil Mi-2 *(Stored)*	534537125	
SP-SEO	Mil Mi-2	525517028	
SP-SEP	Mil Mi-2	525518028	
SP-SER	Mil Mi-2	544535125	
SP-SES(2)	Mil Mi-2	5210018116	
SP-SET(2)	Mil Mi-2	5210019116	
SP-SFC	Mil Mi-2	526506010	
SP-SFD	Mil Mi-2	526507010	
SP-SFF	Mil Mi-2	5210008106	
SP-SFG	Mil Mi-2	5210009106	
SP-SFL	Mil Mi-2	5210013116	
SP-SFN	Mil Mi-2	5210015116	
SP-SFP	Mil Mi-2	5210017116	
SP-SFW	Mil Mi-2	5311149 . . .	
SP-SFX	Mil Mi-2	5210308087	
SP-SFY	Mil Mi-2	5210307067	
SP-SFZ	Mil Mi-2	5210306067	
SP-SGA(2)	Mil Mi-2	5210415107	
SP-SGB	Mil Mi-2	5210416107	
SP-SGC	Mil Mi-2	5210417107	
SP-SGD	Mil Mi-2	5210418107	
SP-SGG	Mil Mi-2	5210421107	
SP-SGH	Mil Mi-2	5210540038	
SP-SGI	Mil Mi-2	5210432029	
SP-SGL	Mil Mi-2	5210434049	
SP-SGN	Mil Mi-2	5210436069	
SP-SGO	Mil Mi-2	5210437089	

Regn.	Type	C/n	Prev.Id.
SP-SGR	Mil Mi-2	5210439069	
SP-SGS	Mil Mi-2	5210440099	
SP-SGT	Mil Mi-2	5210441099	
SP-SGZ	Mil Mi-2	510621028	SP-ASZ(2)
			SP-FDD
			PLW-0621
SP-SHO	Mil Mi-2	515039017	
SP-SLI	Mil Mi-2	525645068	
SP-SLM	Mil Mi-2	525837108	
SP-SOA	Mil Mi-2	544409095	
SP-SPR	Mil Mi-2	535744098	
SP-SPU	Mil Mi-2	535747098	
SP-SRA	Mil Mi-2	529651056	
SP-SSH	Schweizer 269C *(Reservation 1.00)*	S-	
SP-STD	Mil Mi-2	5311230 . . .	
SP-SUA	PZL W-3 Sokol	310208	
SP-SUB	PZL W-3 Sokol	310412	
SP-SUC	PZL W-3 Sokol	300201	SP-PSF
SP-SUF	PZL W-3A Sokol	310308	CCCP04111
SP-SUG	PZL W-3A Sokol	310313	CCCP04116
SP-SUH	PZL W-3A Sokol	310205	CCCP04103
			SP-PSI
SP-SUI	PZL W-3 Sokol	310301	SP-PUI
SP-SUK	PZL W-3 Sokol	310302	CCCP04106
SP-SUL	PZL W-3 Sokol	310303	CCCP04107
SP-SUM	PZL W-3 Sokol	310305	CCCP04108
SP-SUN	PZL W-3 Sokol	310306	CCCP04109
SP-SUO	PZL W-3 Sokol	310314	CCCP04117
SP-SUP	PZL W-3 Sokol	310319	CCCP04118
SP-SUR	PZL W-3 Sokol	310320	CCCP04396
SP-SUS	PZL W-3 Sokol	310321	CCCP04397
SP-SUT	PZL W-3 Sokol	310307	CCCP04110
SP-SUW	PZL W-3W Sokol	360318	ZU-AGU
			SP-SUW
SP-SUY	PZL W-3A Sokol	310206	CCCP04104
SP-SUZ	PZL W-3A Sokol	310207	RA-04105
			CCCP04105
SP-SWB	Mil Mi-2	544534125	
SP-SWH	Mil Mi-2	535041126	
SP-SWM	Mil Mi-2	526510010	
SP-SWZ	Mil Mi-8 *(Reservation)*	10650	SP-SWW
SP-SXA(2)	Mil Mi-2 *(Stored)*	517002011	
SP-SXB(2)	Mil Mi-2	517301081	
SP-SXD(2)	Mil Mi-2	512619102	Soviet AF
SP-SXF	Mil Mi-2	519845076	
SP-SXG	Mil Mi-2	519943106	
SP-SXH	Mil Mi-2	5110007106	
SP-SXU	PZL W-3 Sokol	320210	SP-SUE
			SP-FXA
			SP-SZS
SP-SXZ(2)	PZL W-3 Sokol	370507	SP-SYE
SP-SYA	PZL W-3A Sokol	310204	CCCP04102
SP-SYB	PZL W-3A Sokol	310310	CCCP04113
SP-SYC	PZL W-3A Sokol	310311	CCCP04114
SP-SYD	PZL W-3A Sokol	310312	CCCP04115
SP-SYG	PZL W-3 Sokol	390411	PLW-0411
SP-SYI	PZL W-3AM Sokol	370705	
SP-TCC	Antonov AN-2R	1G173-02	(SP-FML)
			SP-TCC
SP-TKA	PZL-110 Koliber	19007	
SP-TKB	PZL-110 Koliber	19008	
SP-TKC	PZL-110 Koliber	19009	
SP-TKD	PZL-110 Koliber	19010	
SP-TKE	PZL-110 Koliber	24016	
SP-TKF	PZL-110 Koliber	24017	
SP-TKG	PZL-110 Koliber	24023	
SP-TKH	PZL-110 Koliber	24024	
SP-TKI	PZL-110 Koliber	25025	
SP-TKK	PZL-110 Koliber	38633	
SP-TKL	PZL-110 Koliber	38634	
SP-TPA	LET L-410UVP-E15 Turbolet	892318	
SP-TPB	LET L-410UVP-E15 Turbolet	892329	
SP-TSA	Mil Mi-2	544001025	SP-SDE
SP-TUA	PZL M-20 Mewa	1AHP01-02	SP-PKB
SP-TUB	PZL M-20 Mewa	1AHP01-04	SP-PKD

Regn.	Type	C/n	Prev.Id.
SP-TUC	PZL M-20 Mewa	1AH002-02	SP-PKE
SP-TUD	PZL M-20 Mewa	1AH002-04	
SP-TUK	SOCATA TB-9 Tampico Club	1635	F-OHDO
SP-TUL	SOCATA TB-9 Tampico Club	1722	F-OHDS
SP-TUM	SOCATA TB-9 Tampico Club	1787	F-OHTZ
SP-TWI	Antonov AN-2TP	1G185-03	
SP-TXA	LET L-410UVP-E16 Turbolet	892319	
SP-TXB	LET L-410UVP-E16A Turbolet	902414	
SP-TZB	PZL-104 Wilga 35A	18830759	
SP-UXB	Antonov AN-2S *(Cof A expired)*	1G185-04	
SP-UXE	Antonov AN-2S	1G211-01	
SP-UXF	Antonov AN-2S	1G211-02	
SP-UXI	Antonov AN-2S	1G214-07	
SP-WCG	Antonov AN-2R	1G126-22	
SP-WDB	PZL-104 Wilga 35A	62164	
SP-WDO	PZL-104 Wilga 80 *(Crashed 9.99)*	CF21990954	
SP-WDP	PZL-104M Wilga 2000 *(Reservation 11.99)*	00990009	
SP-WEB	PZL-101A Gawron	119324	
SP-WEC	PZL-104 Wilga 35A	61134	
SP-WEF(2)	PZL-104 Wilga 35A	21960962	(TC-ECZ)
SP-WEW	PZL-104 Wilga 35A	62169	DOSAAF SP-WER
SP-WHF	PZL-104 Wilga 35A	61131	PLW-131
SP-WHI	PZL-111 Koliber 235A Senior	00950001	SP-PHI
SP-WIA	Zlin Z.42M	0165	
SP-WIB	Zlin Z.42M	0166	
SP-WID	Zlin Z.42M	0168	
SP-WKB	Antonov AN-2TD	1G135-47	
SP-WKE	Antonov AN-2TD	1G135-50	
SP-WKF(2)	Antonov AN-2R	1G148-03	SP-WLN
SP-WKH	Antonov AN-2R	1G144-26	
SP-WKP	Antonov AN-2R	1G144-33	
SP-WKR	Antonov AN-2R	1G144-34	
SP-WKS	Antonov AN-2R	1G144-35	
SP-WKT	Antonov AN-2R	1G144-36	
SP-WLA	Antonov AN-2R	1G144-41	
SP-WLB	Antonov AN-2R	1G144-42	
SP-WLC	Antonov AN-2TD	1G144-43	
SP-WLD	Antonov AN-2R	1G144-44	
SP-WLF	Antonov AN-2R	1G144-46	
SP-WLI	Antonov AN-2R *(Crashed 5.99)*	1G144-49	
SP-WLP	Antonov AN-2R	1G148-05	
SP-WLR	Antonov AN-2R	1G148-06	
SP-WMA	Antonov AN-2R	1G156-16	
SP-WME	Antonov AN-2R	1G156-20	
SP-WMH	Antonov AN-2R	1G156-23	
SP-WMI	Antonov AN-2R	1G156-24	
SP-WMK	Antonov AN-2R	1G156-25	
SP-WMM	Antonov AN-2R	1G156-27	
SP-WMO	Antonov AN-2R	1G156-29	
SP-WMW	Antonov AN-2R	1G156-35	
SP-WMX	Antonov AN-2R	1G156-38	
SP-WND	Antonov AN-2R	1G156-41	
SP-WNF	Antonov AN-2R *(Crashed 6.98)*	1G156-43	
SP-WNI	Antonov AN-2R	1G155-16	
SP-WNM	Antonov AN-2R	1G155-19	
SP-WNN	Antonov AN-2R	1G155-20	
SP-WNS	Antonov AN-2R	1G155-24	
SP-WNW	Antonov AN-2R	1G155-27	
SP-WOA	Antonov AN-2R	1G160-14	
SP-WOC	Antonov AN-2R	1G160-16	
SP-WOG	Antonov AN-2R	1G161-14	
SP-WOH	Antonov AN-2R	1G160-21	
SP-WOP	Antonov AN-2R	1G161-05	
SP-WOS	Antonov AN-2R	1G161-13	
SP-WOW	Antonov AN-2R	1G163-03	
SP-WPA	Antonov AN-2R	1G163-07	
SP-WPC	Antonov AN-2R	1G163-09	
SP-WPD	Antonov AN-2R	1G163-10	
SP-WPE	Antonov AN-2R	1G163-11	
SP-WPG	Antonov AN-2R	1G163-13	
SP-WPL	Antonov AN-2R	1G163-17	
SP-WPN	Antonov AN-2R	1G167-22	
SP-WPZ	Antonov AN-2R	1G167-31	
SP-WSA	Antonov AN-2R	1G167-33	
SP-WSC	Antonov AN-2R	1G167-35	
SP-WSG	Antonov AN-2R	1G167-39	
SP-WSI	Antonov AN-2R	1G167-41	
SP-WSK	Antonov AN-2R	1G167-42	
SP-WSL	Antonov AN-2R	1G167-43	
SP-WSN	Antonov AN-2R	1G167-45	
SP-WSU	Antonov AN-2R	1G168-37	
SP-WSX	Antonov AN-2R	1G168-20	
SP-WSY	Antonov AN-2R	1G168-21	
SP-WTO	PZL-106B T-601 Turbo Kruk	11980260	
SP-WTU(2)	PZL-106B T-601 Turbo Kruk	11990261	(LV-...)
SP-WWB	Antonov AN-2R	1G173-53	
SP-WWC	Antonov AN-2R	1G173-54	
SP-WWL	Antonov AN-2R	1G177-02	
SP-WWY	Antonov AN-2R	1G180-02	
SP-WWZ	Antonov AN-2R	1G180-03	
SP-WXB	Mil Mi-2	542449072	
SP-WXD	Mil Mi-2	512723122	
SP-WXG	Mil Mi-2 *(Stored)*	513306123	
SP-WXI	Mil Mi-2	513311123	
SP-WXK	Mil Mi-2	513407044	
SP-WXL	Mil Mi-2	513901124	
SP-WXM	Mil Mi-2	513904015	
SP-WXN	Mil Mi-2	513902015	
SP-WXS	Mil Mi-2	513906015	
SP-WXT	Mil Mi-2	513925015	
SP-WXU	Mil Mi-2	514045035	
SP-WXZ	Mil Mi-2	543911015	
SP-WZA	Antonov AN-2R	1G180-05	
SP-WZG	Antonov AN-2R	1G182-27	
SP-WZM	Antonov AN-2R *(Reserved as SP-FML 12.99)*	1G187-08	
SP-ZCI	PZL-106BR Kruk	08850166	
SP-ZCK	PZL-106BR Kruk	08850167	
SP-ZCN	PZL-106BR Kruk	08850170	
SP-ZCP	PZL-106BR Kruk	08850172	
SP-ZCR	PZL-106BR Kruk	08850173	
SP-ZCV	PZL-106BR Kruk	09870201	
SP-ZCY	PZL-106BR Kruk	08860177	DDR-TDA
SP-ZDB	PZL-106BR Kruk	09870203	
SP-ZEG	Antonov AN-2R	1G187-42	
SP-ZFC	Antonov AN-2R	1G229-49	
SP-ZFE	Antonov AN-2R	1G229-51	
SP-ZFU	Antonov AN-2TP	1G233-54	SP-FAM
SP-ZOI	PZL-104 Wilga 35A	19850826	
SP-ZOK	PZL-104 Wilga 35A	74192	PLW-192
SP-ZOM	PZL-104 Wilga 35A	20890886	SP-FWL
SP-ZOO	PZL-104 Wilga 35A	20900900	
SP-ZOP	PZL-104 Wilga 35A	140543	SP-ART(2)
SP-ZPB	PZL-106B T-601 Turbo Kruk	10880218	
SP-ZPC	PZL-106B T-601 Turbo Kruk	10880221	
SP-ZPD	PZL-106B T-601 Turbo Kruk	10880220	
SP-ZPF	PZL-106B T-601 Turbo Kruk	10880219	SP-WAA(2)
SP-ZUA	PZL M-18B Dromader	1Z002-05	
SP-ZUB	PZL M-18 Dromader	1Z003-01	
SP-ZUC	PZL M-18 Dromader	1Z004-06	SP-DIC
SP-ZUD	PZL M-18 Dromader	1Z012-34	SP-DAV
SP-ZUF	PZL M-18B Dromader	1Z013-37	SP-DBB(2)
SP-ZUG	PZL M-18B Dromader	1Z003-08	SP-DWA(I)
SP-ZUL	PZL M-18A Dromader	1Z014-11	
SP-ZUM	PZL M-18B Dromader	1Z012-16	SP-DAY
SP-ZUN	PZL M-18B Dromader	1Z013-49	SP-DBF
SP-ZUO	PZL M-18B Dromader	1Z012-40	SP-DAA(3)
SP-ZUP	PZL M-18B Dromader	1Z013-01	SP-DAT(2)
SP-ZUS	PZL M-18B Dromader	1Z016-28	
SP-ZUT	PZL M-18B Dromader	1Z016-29	
SP-ZUU	PZL M-18B Dromader	1Z016-30	
SP-ZUV	PZL M-18A Dromader	1Z017-06	
SP-ZUW	PZL M-18BS Dromader	1Z017-02	
SP-ZUZ	PZL M-18B Dromader	1Z017-03	
SP-ZWA	PZL M-18 Dromader	1Z010-12	HA-MUO
SP-ZWB	PZL M-18 Dromader	1Z010-13	HA-MUP
SP-ZWC	PZL M-18B Dromader	1Z011-11	HA-MUS
SP-ZWE	PZL M-18B Dromader	1Z006-02	HA-MTH
SP-ZWF	PZL M-18B Dromader	1Z007-12	HA-MTV
SP-ZWG	PZL M-18B Dromader	1Z009-14	HA-MTY

Regn.	Type	C/n	Prev.Id.
SP-ZWI	PZL M-18B Dromader	1Z018-23	
SP-ZWK	PZL M-18B Dromader	1Z018-24	
SP-ZWL	PZL M-18A Dromader	1Z020-13	
SP-ZWM	PZL M-18A Dromader	1Z020-14	
SP-ZWN	PZL M-18A Dromader	1Z020-15	
SP-ZWO	PZL M-18B Dromader	1Z005-10	HA-MTF
SP-ZWP	PZL M-18B Dromader	1Z006-04	HA-MTJ
SP-ZWR	PZL M-18B Dromader	1Z009-16	HA-MUB
SP-ZWS	PZL M-18B Dromader	1Z010-21	SP-TDA
SP-ZWT	PZL M-18B Dromader	1Z011-20	SP-TDB
			SP-DAH
SP-ZWU	PZL M-18B Dromader	1Z001-01	SP-BBU(2)
			SP-PBU
SP-ZWW	PZL M-18 Dromader	1Z001-05	SP-BBT(2)
SP-ZWY	PZL M-18 Dromader	1Z014-17	SP-DBC
SP-ZWZ	PZL M-18B Dromader	1Z012-15	SP-DAZ
SP-ZXA	Mil Mi-2	514207065	
SP-ZXC	Mil Mi-2	514408105	
SP-ZXE	Mil Mi-2	544304085	
SP-ZXH	Mil Mi-2	514539125	
SP-ZXN	Mil Mi-2	515038126	
SP-ZXO	Mil Mi-2	515032126	
SP-ZXP	Mil Mi-2	515020116	
SP-ZXR	Mil Mi-2	515040017	
SP-ZXU	Mil Mi-2	515832108	
SP-ZXY	Mil Mi-2	516531030	
SP-ZXZ	Mil Mi-2	535643068	
SP-...	Cessna 150J	70339	N5230R
SP-...	Cessna 150L	73128	N5228Q
SP-...	Cessna 150L	74167	N19097
SP-...	Cessna 150M	76386	N3109V
SP-...	Cessna 150M	78490	N704BV
SP-...	Piper PA-28-181 Archer III	2843271	N4147V
SP-...	SOCATA TB-20 Trinidad	1899	F-OIGU

BALLOONS

Regn.	Type	C/n	Prev.Id.
SP-BIA(2)	Kubicek BB-30 HAFB	77	
SP-BIB(2)	Sekpol N-22 HAFB	00198	
SP-BIC	Kubicek BB-22 HAFB	86	
SP-BID	Cameron N-77 HAFB	4309	
SP-BIE	Cameron EB-90 SS HAFB	4120	
SP-BIF	Balloon Works Firefly F-7B-15 HAFB	381	
SP-BIG	Cameron Coldrex Mug 90SS HAFB	4405	
SP-BIH	Balloon Works Firefly F7-15 HAFB	F7-1043	
SP-BII	UltraMagic M-65 HAFB	65/83	
SP-BIK	Schroeder Fire Balloons G HAFB	706	
SP-BIL	Balloon Works Firefly F-7B-15 HAFB *(Reservation)*	382	
SP-BIM	Kubicek BB-30 HAFB	110	
SP-BIN	Aerotechnik AB-2 HAFB	910545	"SP-BVN"
			(SP-BTA)
			OK-1023
SP-BIO	Cameron C-70 Concept HAFB	4632	
SP-BIP	Cameron C-70 Concept HAFB	4614	
SP-BIR	Colt 69A HAFB	2447	D-OPUY
			N712TC
SP-BIS	Sekpol N-22 HAFB	unkn	
SP-BSC	Colt AS.105 Mk.II Hot Air Airship	4619	
SP-BVA	Cirkon Moskwa ATP-2401 HAFB	6240119304C	SP-PVA
SP-BVB	Interavia Moskwa AX-8 Balloon	0650393	
SP-BVC	Kubicek BB-22 HAFB	51	
SP-BVD	Cameron N-90 HAFB	3628	
SP-BVE	AX-6 HAFB *(Reservation)*	unkn	
SP-BVF	Balloon Works Firefly F-8B HAFB	F8B-301	N9032K
SP-BVG	Aerotechnik AB-8 HAFB	910530	OK-1010
SP-BVH	Cameron N-90 HAFB	3906	
SP-BVI	Kubicek BB-30 HAFB	58	
SP-BVK	UltraMagic M-77 HAFB	77/32	OO-BWD
SP-BVL	Kubicek BB-22 HAFB	069	

Regn.	Type	C/n	Prev.Id.
SP-BVM	Balloon Works Firefly F-8B HAFB	F8B-528	
SP-BVN	UltraMagic V-77 HAFB	77/131	
SP-BVO(2)	Sky 105-24 HAFB	087	G-BXFO
SP-BVP	Cameron V-65 HAFB	4116	
SP-BVR	Cameron C-80 HAFB	4138	
SP-BVS	Cameron O-65 HAFB *(Reservation .00)*	4780	
SP-BVT	Cameron V-65 HAFB	4184	
SP-BVU	MOS-1 1050m Gas Balloon *(Reservation)*	4/90	
SP-BVV	Cameron C-80 HAFB	4139	
SP-BVW	Cameron N-77 HAFB	4155	
SP-BVZ	Balloon Works Firefly F7B-15 HAFB	376	
SP-BWA	Aerotechnik AB2a HAFB	870207	
SP-BWB	Tomi AX-7 HAFB	BAV061/1989	
SP-BWC	Tomi AX-7 HAFB	BAV075/1989	
SP-BWD	RSZ-05 HAFB	1990/04	
SP-BWE	Tomi AX-7 HAFB	BAV074/1989	
SP-BWF	RSZ-03/1 HAFB	1989/002	
SP-BWG	Aerotechnik AB-8 HAFB	920550	
SP-BWI	Interavia Moskwa HAFB	0670793	
SP-BWK	Dirizablestroj AT-8 Balloon	059204012	
SP-BWL	Cameron N-65 HAFB	4374	
	(Envelope c/n 3311 replaced 1998)		
SP-BWM	Aerotechnik AB-2C HAFB	890418	
SP-BWN	Cameron C-60 HAFB	3847	
SP-BWO	Cameron V-77 HAFB	3466	
SP-BWP	Cameron O-65 HAFB	3004	
SP-BWR	Cameron V-65 HAFB	2709	
SP-BWS	Interavia Moskwa ZSRR AX-8 HAFB	037/442920457	
SP-BWT	Cameron C-80 HAFB	3334	
SP-BWU	Cameron N-77 HAFB	2457	G-BTBO
SP-BWV	Cirkon Moskwa ATP-2401 HAFB	70GA	
SP-BWW	Raven-Europe S-55A HAFB	E-248	
SP-BWX	Thunder AX8-90 HAFB	1709	D-Kitekat
SP-BWY	Thunder AX8-90 HAFB	1714	D-Cesar
SP-BWZ	Thunder AX8-90 HAFB	1717	D-Chappi
SP-BYA	ZSTIT BC-1 HAFB	001	
SP-BYB	Tomi AX-7 HAFB	029/1986	
SP-BYD	Tomi AX-7 HAFB	028/1986	
SP-BYE	Tomi AX-7 HAFB	027/1986	
SP-BYF	Tomi AX-7 HAFB	025/1986	
SP-BYH	Tomi AX-7 HAFB	BAV038/1987	
SP-BYI	Tomi AX-7 HAFB	BAV036/1987	
SP-BYK	Tomi AX-7 HAFB	BAV037/1987	
SP-BYL	Tomi AX-7 HAFB	BAV035/1987	
SP-BYM	Tomi AX-7 HAFB	BAV033/1987	
SP-BYN	Tomi AX-7 HAFB	BAV040/1987	
SP-BYO	Tomi AX-7 HAFB	BAV043/1988	
SP-BYP	Tomi AX-7 HAFB	BAV042/1988	
SP-BYR	Tomi AX-7 HAFB	BAV041/1988	
SP-BYS	Tomi AX-7 HAFB	BAV046/1988	
SP-BYT	Tomi AX-7 HAFB	BAV044/1988	
SP-BYU	Tomi AX-7 HAFB	BAV045/1988	
SP-BYV	Tomi AX-7 HAFB	BAV053/1988	
SP-BYW	Tomi AX-7 HAFB	BAV055/1988	
SP-BYX	Tomi AX-7 HAFB	BAV054/1988	
SP-BYY	RSZ-05/1 HAFB	1989/003	
SP-BYZ	Thunder AX7/77SI HAFB	1315	
SP-BZI	Cameron N-90 HAFB	1106	
SP-BZO	ZSTIT Gas Balloon	1	
SP-BZS	RSZ-05 HAFB	1984/002	
SP-BZU	RSZ-05 HAFB	1985/B/01	
SP-BZV	Tomi AX-7 HAFB	017/1986	
SP-BZW	ZSTIT Gas Balloon	004	
SP-BZX	Tomi AX-7 HAFB	015/1986	
SP-BZY	Tomi AX-7 HAFB	016/1986	
SP-BZZ	Aviotex Gas Balloon	03	
SP-B..	Cameron N-77 HAFB	2457	G-BTBO

Regn.	Type	C/n	Prev.Id.

MICROLIGHTS

Regn.	Type	C/n	Prev.Id.
PL-AAW	Libre II		
PL-APB	Type unknown		
PL-APG	Aero APT		
PL-APH	Aero APT		
PL-BAA	Plywajac		
PL-BAE	Plywajac		
PL-BAF	Plywajac		
PL-BAG	Plywajac		
PL-BAI	Plywajac		
PL-BAK	Plywajac		
PL-BAL	Plywajac		
PL-BAM	Plywajac		
PL-BAN	Plywajac		
PL-BAO	Plywajac		
PL-BAP	Libre II M2		
PL-BAR	Libre II M2		
PL-BAS	Stratus 2		
PL-BAT	Plywajac		
PL-BAU	Plywajac		
PL-BAW	Plywajac		
PL-BAZ	Plywajac		
PL-BBA	Libre II		
PL-BBB	Balans		
PL-BBC	Stratus E-2		
PL-BBD	Demon		
PL-BBE	Kanion-G		
PL-BBH	Kanion-K		
PL-BBI	Express		
PL-BBJ	'UP'		
PL-BBK	Kanion-G		
PL-BBL	Vega MX		
PL-BBN	Type unknown		
PL-BBO	Kanion-B		
PL-BBP	Demon		
PL-BBR	Balans		
PL-BBS	Aero		
PL-BBT	Libre I		
PL-BBU	Kanion-H		
PL-BBV	Kanion-K		
PL-BBW	Demon		
PL-BBX	Balans		
PL-BBY	Weekend		
PL-BBZ	Sensor		
PL-BCA	Kanion-B		
PL-BCB(1)	Kanion-I *(Built 1985. Still in use?)*		
PL-BCB(2)	Air Création Racer SX-II (Rotax 462) (Also noted as AC Apollo SX-II)		
PL-BCB(3)	Racer (Rotax 447)		
	(Note: All three a/c have different CofR nos, but (2) and (3) , both of 1994, may be the same aircraft re-engined)		
PL-BCC	Demon		
PL-BCD	Kanion-H		
PL-BCE	Libre II		
PL-BCF	Stratus R-15		
PL-BCG	Balans		
PL-BCH	Kanion-K		
PL-BCI	Demon		
PL-BCJ	R-Z		
PL-BCK	Demon		
PL-BCL(1)	Demon *(Out of use?)*		
PL-BCL(2)	Horizont		
PL-BCM	Demon		
PL-BCN	Kanion-B		
PL-BCO	Kanion-H		
PL-BCP	Demon		
PL-BCR	Kanion-B		
PL-BCS	Kanion-B		
PL-BCT	Magic		
PL-BCU	Magic		
PL-BCV	Magic Kiss		
PL-BCX	Magic Kiss		
PL-BCY	Moyes GTR		
PL-BCZ	Moyes GTR		
PL-BXD	Libre II		
PL-BXH	Kanion-B		
PL-BXU	Libre II		
PL-BYJ	Libre II		
PL-BYS	Stratus P-2		
PL-BYW	XP-15		
PL-GDC	Type unknown		
PL-GDG	Type unknown		
PL-GDL	Stratus P2 *(Cancelled?)*		
PL-GDP	"Aska" *(Cancelled?)*		
PL-GDW	"Goosia"*(Cancelled?)*		
PL-GWG ?	Aero 21 *(Reported as SP-GWG in 7.94)*		
PL-INA	Libre II		
PL-INO	Kannion-BM		
PL-INZ	Libre II		
PL-KIC	Moyes XS142		
PL-KID	Fecske		
PL-KIE	Moyes XS155		
PL-KIG	Moyes XS155		
PL-KIL	Moyes GTR162		
PL-KIR	Vega MX-2		
PL-KVA	Type unknown		
PL-LDA	Anla		
PL-LDB	Cross Rush		
PL-LDD	Libre II		
PL-LDF	Z-80B		
PL-LDH	Libre II		
PL-LDI	Libre II		
PL-LDN	Libre II *(Regn possibly used by another a/c 1996?)*		
PL-LDR	Vega		
PL-LDS	Sokol		
PL-LDT	Vega		
PL-LDW	Ohar		
PL-LDX	Ohar		
PL-LDY	Ohar		
PL-LEG	Libre II M		
PL-LEL	Sierra		
PL-LEM	Kanion-B		
PL-LER	Libre IIM2		
PL-LET	Libre IIM2		
PL-LEW	Ohar		
PL-MIA	Libre IIPL *(Szaman trike noted 8.97)*		
PL-MID	Libre II		
PL-MIE	Stratus R-IIc		
PL-MIF	Stratus R-IIc		
PL-MII	Stratus R-IIc		
PL-MIK	Stratus E-2		
PL-MIL	Libre IIM2		
PL-MIP	FL-33		
PL-MIT	Stratus E-3		
PL-NSA	Libre IIPL		
PL-NSC	Stranger		
PL-NSJ	Horyzont M2		
PL-OLA	Libre II		
PL-OLL	Demon		
PL-OPA	Balans		
PL-OPB	Libre II		
PL-OPC	Moyes		
PL-OPD	Vega		
PL-OPE	Kanion-B		
PL-OPF	Libre II		
PL-OPG	Sawa		
PL-OPH	Kanion-B		
PL-OPI	Kanion-B		
PL-OPJ	Kanion-B		
PL-OPK	Libre II		
PL-OPL	Z-80		
PL-OPM	LibreII		
PL-OPN	Kanion-B		
PL-OPO	Kosmos		
PL-OPP	Kanion-B		
PL-OPR	Kanion		
PL-OPS	Aero		
PL-OPT	Z-80		
PL-OPU	Kanion-B		
PL-OPV	Horyzont M-2		

Regn.	Type	C/n	Prev.Id.
PL-OPW	Balans		
PL-OPX	Kanion-B		
PL-OPY	Kanion-B		
PL-OPZ	Balans		
PL-OVE	Demon		
PL-PIE	Stranger		
PL-PIG	Lilienthal		
PL-PIJ	Libre II M		
PL-PIK	La Moet		
PL-PIS	Racer		
PL-PIT	Magic IV		
PL-PKA	Kanion-B		
PL-PKB	Libre II		
PL-PKC	Libre II		
PL-PKD	Libre II		
PL-PKI	Libre II		
PL-PKJ	Kanion-B		
PL-PKL	Libre II		
PL-PNX	Type unknown		
PL-PTE	Ohar		
PL-RAB	Libre II		
PL-RAC	Kanion		
PL-RAD	Super		
PL-RAE	Libre II		
PL-RAF	Super		
PL-RAG	Atlas 21		
PL-RAH	Libre II		
PL-RAI	Hazard		
PL-RAJ	Racer SX-II		
PL-RAK	Atlas 21		
PL-RAL	Hazard		
PL-ROL	Kanion-B		
PL-ROW	Kanion-B		
PL-ROZ	Kanion-B		
PL-RWA	Libre II (Second trike noted with this regn 1996)		
PL-RWB	Libre I		
PL-RWC	Kanion-G		
PL-RWD	Magic IV		
PL-RWE	Demon		
PL-RWF	Kanion-K 160M		
PL-RWG	Libre II		
PL-RWH	Flaming		
PL-RWI	Libre II		
PL-RWJ	Kanion-G		
PL-RWK	Stratus E-2s		
PL-SAA	Kanion-K 160		
PL-SAB	Libre II		
PL-SAD	C 14 Radziecka		
PL-SAE	Demon		
PL-SAF	Demon		
PL-SAG(1)	Libre II		
PL-SAG(2)	Stranger		
PL-SAG(3)	LAK-16M (motorised LAK-16 glider)	296	
PL-SAH	Demon		
PL-SAI	Kanion-K 120		
PL-SAK	Expres		
PL-SAO	Libre II		
PL-SAP	Demon		
PL-SAR	Libre II		
PL-SIA	Aero		
PL-SII	Kanion Tornado		
PL-SIJ	Demon		
PL-SIK	Kanion-B		
PL-SIL	Demon		
PL-SIP	Libre II		
PL-SIS	Demon		
PL-SIT	Magic		
PL-SIU	Libre II		
PL-SIV	Libre II		
PL-SIX	Stratus R150		
PL-SIY	JKanion-K 160		
PL-SIZ	Kanion-B		
PL-SUA	Slawuticz		
PL-SUB	Type unknown		
PL-SUC(1)	Libre II (VW-engined, re-engined as -SUC(3)?)		
PL-SUC(2)	Plywajac		
PL-SUC(3)	Libre II (Buran-engined, ex -SUC(1) ?)		
PL-SUD	Stranger		
PL-SUE	Stranger		
PL-SWA	Vega		
PL-SWB	Magic		
PL-SWC	Magic		
PL-SWD	Balans (Also reported as type 'ML-1')		
PL-SWE	Stratus R-16		
PL-SWF	Slawuticz		
PL-SWG	Kanion-B		
PL-SWH	Stranger		
PL-SWI	Slawuticz		
PL-SZA	Libre II		
PL-SZB	Balans		
PL-SZC	Kanion-B		
PL-SZD	Stranger		
PL-SZE	Un-named type, WSK engine		
PL-SZF	Slawuticz		
PL-SZG	Stranger		
PL-SZI	Stranger		
PL-SZJ	Libre IIM		
PL-SZK	Stranger		
PL-SZL	Stranger		
PL-TAI	Magic		
PL-TAW	Libre II		
PL-TOA	UFO		
PL-TOC	UFO		
PL-TOF	UFO		
PL-TOG	UFO		
PL-TOH	Stratus P-2		
PL-TOJ	Libre II		
PL-TOK	UFO		
PL-TOL	Antonow (Reported as Chibis KHDZ-29 c/n 0105 - same a/c?)		
PL-TOM	UFO		
PL-TON	UFO		
PL-TOO	Antonow		
PL-TOR	Libre II		
PL-TOU	Stranger		
PL-TOW	UFO		
PL-TOZ	Libre II		
PL-TRG	Libre II		
PL-TRJ	Stratus P-2		
PL-TRK	Libre II		
PL-WAE	Hazard 15		
PL-WAF	Hazard 15		
PL-WAJ	Stratus E-3		
PL-WAO	Type unknown		
PL-WAR	Stratus E-3		
PL-WBH	Stratus P-2		
PL-WBI	Stratus P-2		
PL-WBL	Stratus P-2		
PL-WBO	Hazard 13		
PL-WBS	Hazard		
PL-WBT	Hazard		
PL-WBU	Stratus P-2		
PL-WBV	Stratus P-2 (Two photos show different trike type 1996, 1997)		
PL-WBW	Type unknown		
PL-WBY	Stratus P-2		
PL-WBZ	Z-80/96		
PL-WDF	Moyes GTR		
PL-WDG	Moyes GTR		
PL-WDI	Eros 175		
PL-WRA	Libre II		
PL-WRB	Zefir		
PL-WRC	Libre II		
PL-WRD	Libre II		
PL-WRE	Libre II		
PL-WRF	Un-named type, Trabant engine		
PL-WRH	Libre II		
PL-WRI	Libre II		
PL-WRJ	Libre II		
PL-WRK	Un-named type, Trabant engine		
PL-WRM	Libre II		
PL-WRO	Libre II		

649

Regn.	Type	C/n	Prev.Id.
PL-WRR	Libre II		
PL-WRS	Racher		
PL-WRT	Racher		
PL-ZOA	Stratus P-2		

MOTOR-GLIDERS

Regn.	Type	C/n	Prev.Id.
SP-0001	SZD-45 Ogar	X-107	
SP-0003	SZD-45A Ogar	B-598	
SP-0005	SZD-45A Ogar	B-599	
SP-0006	SZD-45A Ogar	B-602	
SP-0008	SZD-45A Ogar	B-603	
SP-0010	SZD-45A Ogar	B-605	
SP-0012	SZD-45A Ogar	B-643	
SP-0015	SZD-45A Ogar	B-646	
SP-0017	SZD-45A Ogar	B-651	
SP-0021	SZD-45A Ogar	B-654	SE-TLY SP-0018
SP-0024	SZD-45A Ogar	B-757	
SP-0025	SZD-45A Ogar	B-770	
SP-0026	SZD-45A Ogar	B-756	
SP-0028	SZD-45A Ogar	B-822	
SP-0029	SZD-45A Ogar	B-759	
SP-0031	SZD-45A Ogar	B-821	SP-0020
SP-0032	SZD-45A Ogar (Reservation)	B-823	SP-0030
SP-P041	Delphin	unkn	
SP-P044	J-2a Polonez	unkn	
SP-0045	SZD-9bis Bocian M	YL-001/P-344	SP-P045 SP-2048
SP-0046	Janowski J-6 Fregate	001	SP-P046
SP-0047	SZD-45A Ogar	B-644	SP-0013
SP-P048	Janowski J-2B Polonez	unkn	
SP-0049	Janowski J-6 Fregate	002	SP-P049
SP-0050	PW-4	S-02	SP-P050
SP-0052	LET L-13SDM Vivat	950608	D-KULT
SP-P053	Malgosia (Motorized Marganski MDM-1 Fox)	P-17	(SP-3607)
SP-P054	Bocian M2000 (Built from SZD-9bis Bocian c/n 809)	YL-005	SP-2398

GLIDERS

Regn.	Type	C/n	Prev.Id.
SP-1433	SZD-12 Mucha 100	59	
SP-1742	SZD-12 Mucha 100	W-5	
SP-1745	SZD-12 Mucha 100	W-13	
SP-1790	SZD-12A Mucha 100A	340	
SP-1797	SZD-12A Mucha 100A	347	
SP-1801	SZD-12A Mucha 100A	351	
SP-1813	SZD-12A Mucha 100A	363	
SP-1814	SZD-12A Mucha 100A	364	
SP-1823	SZD-12A Mucha 100A	373	
SP-1824	SZD-12A Mucha 100A (Motorised)	374	
SP-1833	SZD-12A Mucha 100A	383	
SP-1844	SZD-12 Mucha 100	W-16	
SP-1846	SZD-12A Mucha 100A	W-20	
SP-1847	SZD-10bis Czapla	W-21	
SP-1858	SZD-10bis Czapla	W-34	
SP-1936	SZD-12A Mucha 100A	397	
SP-1937	SZD-12A Mucha 100A	398	
SP-1942	SZD-12A Mucha 100A	403	
SP-1960	SZD-12A Mucha 100A	F-421	
SP-1962	SZD-12A Mucha 100A	F-423	
SP-1969	SZD-12A Mucha 100A	F-430	
SP-1975	SZD-12A Mucha 100A	F-436	
SP-1979	Fauvel AV-36C	200/04	OE-0414
SP-1992	SZD-12A Mucha 100A	F-453	

Regn.	Type	C/n	Prev.Id.
SP-1998	SZD-12A Mucha 100A (Motorised)	F-459	
SP-1999	SZD-12A Mucha 100A	F-460	
SP-2003	SZD-12A Mucha 100A	F-464	
SP-2007	SZD-12A Mucha 100A	F-468	
SP-2017	SZD-12A Mucha 100A (Modified to SZD-22C Mucha Standard)	F-483	
SP-2018	SZD-12A Mucha 100A	F-479	
SP-2019	SZD-12A Mucha 100A	F-480	
SP-2021	SZD-12A Mucha 100A	F-482	
SP-2026	SZD-12A Mucha 100A	F-488	
SP-2033	SZD-9bis Bocian 1D	P-390	
SP-2105	SZD-22A Mucha Standard	271	
SP-2107	SZD-22B Mucha Standard	F-497	
SP-2124	SZD-22C Mucha Standard	F-542	
SP-2136	SZD-22C Mucha Standard	F-554	
SP-2139	SZD-22C Mucha Standard	F-559	
SP-2151	SZD-22C Mucha Standard	F-572	
SP-2159	SZD-22C Mucha Standard	F-581	
SP-2160	SZD-22C Mucha Standard	F-582	
SP-2163	SZD-22C Mucha Standard	F-585	
SP-2173	SZD-22C Mucha Standard	F-595	
SP-2239	SZD-22A Mucha Standard	269	
SP-2245	SZD-22C Mucha Standard	F-630	
SP-2250	SZD-22C Mucha Standard	F-635	
SP-2258	SZD-22C Mucha Standard	F-642	
SP-2259	SZD-22C Mucha Standard	F-643	
SP-2261	SZD-22C Mucha Standard	F-645	
SP-2263	SZD-22C Mucha Standard	F-647	
SP-2268	SZD-22C Mucha Standard	F-652	
SP-2278	SZD-22C Mucha Standard	F-664	
SP-2279	SZD-22C Mucha Standard	F-665	
SP-2284	SZD-22C Mucha Standard	F-670	
SP-2286	SZD-22C Mucha Standard	F-656	
SP-2287	SZD-22C Mucha Standard	F-662	
SP-2288	SZD-22C Mucha Standard	F-603	
SP-2295	SZD-22C Mucha Standard	F-681	
SP-2296	SZD-22C Mucha Standard	F-682	
SP-2299	SZD-22C Mucha Standard	F-685	
SP-2301	SZD-22C Mucha Standard	F-677	
SP-2303	SZD-22C Mucha Standard	F-679	
SP-2304	SZD-22C Mucha Standard	F-690	
SP-2310	SZD-22C Mucha Standard	F-696	
SP-2312	SZD-22C Mucha Standard	F-698	
SP-2314	SZD-22C Mucha Standard	F-615	
SP-2315	SZD-22C Mucha Standard	F-701	
SP-2316	SZD-22C Mucha Standard	F-702	
SP-2328	SZD-22C Mucha Standard	F-715	
SP-2330	SZD-22C Mucha Standard	F-717	
SP-2331	SZD-22C Mucha Standard	F-718	
SP-2334	SZD-22C Mucha Standard	F-721	
SP-2336	SZD-22C Mucha Standard	F-723	
SP-2338	SZD-22C Mucha Standard	F-725	
SP-2339	SZD-22C Mucha Standard	F-746	
SP-2361	SZD-25ALis (Reservation 11.99)	F-745	
SP-2363	SZD-24 Foka 4	284	
SP-2375	SZD-24C Foka	W-157	
SP-2379	SZD-24C Foka	W-161	
SP-2380-PP	SZD-24C Foka	W-162	
SP-2381	SZD-24C Foka	W-163	
SP-2383	SZD-24C Foka	W-168	
SP-2384	SZD-24C Foka	W-179	
SP-2386	SZD-24C Foka	W-171	
SP-2390	SZD-24C Foka	W-185	
SP-2395	SZD-24C Foka	W-186	
SP-2396	SZD-24C Foka	W-187	
SP-2400	SZD-9bis Bocian 1D	F-811	
SP-2405	SZD-22C Mucha Standard	F-782	
SP-2406	SZD-22C Mucha Standard	F-793	
SP-2407	SZD-22C Mucha Standard	F-794	
SP-2409	SZD-30 Pirat	B-369	
SP-2410	SZD-30 Pirat	B-370	
SP-2415	SZD-24 Foka 4A	W-236	
SP-2417	SZD-24 Foka 4A	W-229	
SP-2419	SZD-24 Foka 4A	W-238	
SP-2421	SZD-24 Foka 4A	W-243	

Regn.	Type	C/n	Prev.Id.
SP-2423	SZD-24 Foka 4M	W-247	
SP-2440	SZD-9bis Bocian 1D	F-849	
SP-2444	SZD-9bis Bocian 1D	F-853	
SP-2446	SZD-9bis Bocian 1D	F-855	
SP-2449	SZD-9bis Bocian 1D	F-858	
SP-2451	SZD-24 Foka 4A	W-234	
SP-2452(2)	SZD-30 Pirat	B-372	
SP-2454	SZD-24C Foka	W-217	
SP-2456	SZD-24C Foka	W-219	
SP-2457	SZD-24C Foka	W-220	
SP-2458	SZD-24C Foka	W-221	
SP-2459 -O	SZD-24C Foka	W-222	
SP-2460	SZD-24C Foka	W-223	
SP-2464	SZD-24C Foka	W-202	
SP-2482	SZD-21-2B Kobuz 3	W-270	
SP-2503	SZD-30 Pirat	W-290	
SP-2504-XI	SZD-32A Foka 5	W-291	
SP-2509	SZD-30 Pirat	W-317	
SP-2512	SZD-24C Foka	W-210	
SP-2514	SZD-30 Pirat	B-374	
SP-2516(2)	SZD-30 Pirat	B-376	
SP-2519	SZD-31 Zefir 4	293	
SP-2524-F	SZD-24 Foka 4A	W-387	
SP-2527	SZD-32A Foka 5	W-431	
SP-2530	SZD-32A Foka 5	W-434	
SP-2536	SZD-22C Mucha Standard	F-657	SP-2272
SP-2537	SZD-36 Cobra	W-474	
SP-2539	SZD-39 Cobra 17	W-476	
SP-2540	SZD-39 Cobra 17	W-477	
SP-2541	SZD-22C Mucha Standard	F-565	SP-2145
SP-2542	SZD-9bis Bocian 1E	P-504	
SP-2543	SZD-9bis Bocian 1E	P-505	
SP-2545	SZD-30 Pirat	B-346	
SP-2547	SZD-30 Pirat	B-348	
SP-2548	SZD-30 Pirat	B-349	
SP-2549	SZD-30 Pirat	B-350	
SP-2551-Y	SZD-30 Pirat	B-377	
SP-2553	SZD-35 Bekas	X-100	
SP-2554	SZD-30 Pirat	B-378	
SP-2555-EI	SZD-30 Pirat	B-379	
SP-2556	SZD-30 Pirat	B-380	
SP-2557	SZD-35 Bekas	X-101	
SP-2558	SZD-30 Pirat	B-355	
SP-2559	SZD-30 Pirat	B-381	
SP-2565	SZD-30 Pirat	B-387	
SP-2566	SZD-30 Pirat	B-388	
SP-2568	SZD-30 Pirat	B-390	
SP-2569-MR	SZD-30 Pirat	B-391	
SP-2570	SZD-30 Pirat	B-392	
SP-2572	SZD-30 Pirat	B-416	
SP-2573-C	SZD-30 Pirat	B-417	
SP-2574-AL	SZD-30 Pirat	B-418	
SP-2575-M	SZD-30 Pirat	B-419	
SP-2576-F1	SZD-30 Pirat	B-420	
SP-2578	SZD-30 Pirat	B-422	
SP-2579	SZD-36 Cobra 15	W-556	
SP-2582	SZD-36 Cobra 15	W-560	
SP-2583-PW	SZD-48 Jantar Standard 2	X-134	
SP-2585	SZD-42-2 Jantar 2B	B-858	
SP-2586	SZD-42-2 Jantar 2B	B-859	
SP-2587	SZD-9bis Bocian 1E	P-555	
SP-2588	SZD-9bis Bocian 1E	P-556	
SP-2589	SZD-9bis Bocian 1E	P-557	
SP-2590	SZD-9bis Bocian 1E	P-586	
SP-2591	SZD-9bis Bocian 1E	P-587	
SP-2593	SZD-30 Pirat	B-450	
SP-2594-JB	SZD-30 Pirat	B-451	
SP-2595	SZD-30 Pirat	B-452	
SP-2596	SZD-30 Pirat	B-453	
SP-2598	SZD-30 Pirat	B-456	
SP-2600-IT	SZD-30 Pirat	B-458	
SP-2601	SZD-30 Pirat	B-423	(SP-2581)
SP-2602-M	SZD-30 Pirat	B-482	
SP-2605-PS	SZD-30 Pirat	B-487	
SP-2606-ZX	SZD-30 Pirat	B-488	
SP-2608-OO	SZD-30 Pirat	B-484	
SP-2610	SZD-30 Pirat	B-511	
SP-2611	SZD-30 Pirat	B-521	
SP-2612-A	SZD-30 Pirat	B-522	
SP-2615	SZD-30 Pirat	B-525	
SP-2616	SZD-30 Pirat	B-526	
SP-2617-T	SZD-32A Foka 5	W-531	
SP-2618-J	SZD-32A Foka 5	W-532	
SP-2621	SZD-32A Foka 5	W-536	
SP-2622	SZD-32A Foka 5	W-537	
SP-2623-X4	SZD-32A Foka 5	W-538	
SP-2624	SZD-32A Foka 5	W-539	
SP-2626-M	SZD-32A Foka 5	W-541	
SP-2627	SZD-32A Foka 5	W-542	
SP-2628-55	SZD-32A Foka 5	W-543	
SP-2629	SZD-30 Pirat	B-425	
SP-2630-H	SZD-30 Pirat	B-426	
SP-2631-Y	SZD-30 Pirat	B-448	
SP-2632	SZD-9bis Bocian 1E	P-552	
SP-2633	SZD-32A Foka 5	W-544	
SP-2637	SZD-37 Jantar	X-105	
SP-2639	SZD-9bis Bocian 1E	P-592	
SP-2640	SZD-9bis Bocian 1E	P-593	
SP-2641	SZD-9bis Bocian 1E	P-594	
SP-2643	SZD-22C Mucha Standard	F-576	SP-2155
SP-2645	SZD-40X Halny	X-106	
SP-2646	SZD-30 Pirat	B-554	
SP-2647	SZD-30 Pirat	B-555	
SP-2648-M	SZD-30 Pirat	B-556	
SP-2649-ER	SZD-30 Pirat	B-557	
SP-2655	SZD-30 Pirat	B-589	
SP-2662	SZD-9bis Bocian 1E	P-621	
SP-2663	SZD-9bis Bocian 1E	P-622	
SP-2664	SZD-9bis Bocian 1E	P-623	
SP-2666	SZD-9bis Bocian 1E	P-630	
SP-2667	SZD-9bis Bocian 1E	P-631	
SP-2668	SZD-9bis Bocian 1E	P-632	
SP-2672-7	SZD-36A Cobra 15	W-653	
SP-2673	SZD-36A Cobra 15 (Reservation)	W-654	
SP-2674	SZD-30 Pirat	B-590	
SP-2675-V	SZD-30 Pirat	B-591	
SP-2676	SZD-30 Pirat	B-592	
SP-2677	SZD-30 Pirat	B-593	
SP-2680	SZD-30 Pirat	B-571	
SP-2684-2K	SZD-36A Cobra 15	W-606	
SP-2685-PK	SZD-41 Jantar Standard	X-110	
SP-2686-W	SZD-41 Jantar Standard	X-111	
SP-2687	SZD-9bis Bocian 1E	P-643	
SP-2689	SZD-36A Cobra 15	W-663	
SP-2692-IL	SZD-36A Cobra 15	W-675	
SP-2694-69	SZD-36A Cobra 15	W-679	
SP-2695	SZD-36A Cobra 15	W-681	
SP-2697	SZD-36A Cobra 15	W-706	
SP-2698	SZD-36A Cobra 15	W-707	
SP-2700	SZD-30 Pirat	S-01.01	
SP-2704	SZD-30 Pirat	S-03.03	
SP-2705	SZD-30 Pirat	S-03.17	
SP-2708	SZD-30 Pirat	S-02.24	
SP-2709-09	SZD-30 Pirat	S-02.25	
SP-2711-ET	SZD-30 Pirat	S-01.37	
SP-2714	SZD-30 Pirat	S-02.10	
SP-2715	SZD-30 Pirat	S-02.11	
SP-2716	SZD-30 Pirat	S-02.12	
SP-2717-KW	SZD-30 Pirat	S-02.13	
SP-2719	SZD-30 Pirat	S-02.16	
SP-2720	SZD-30 Pirat	S-02.29	
SP-2721	SZD-30 Pirat	S-02.30	
SP-2722	SZD-30 Pirat	S-02.31	
SP-2723	SZD-30 Pirat	S-02.32	
SP-2724-JS	SZD-30 Pirat	S-02.35	
SP-2725-S	SZD-30 Pirat	S-03.50	
SP-2727-9	SZD-30 Pirat	S-03.31	
SP-2728	SZD-30 Pirat	S-03.35	
SP-2732-J	SZD-30 Pirat	S-02.45	
SP-2734	SZD-30 Pirat	S-04.06	

Regn.	Type	C/n	Prev.Id.	Regn.	Type	C/n	Prev.Id.
SP-2735	SZD-30 Pirat	S-04.13		SP-2832	SZD-30 Pirat	S-04.04	
SP-2736	SZD-30 Pirat	S-04.14		SP-2834	SZD-30 Pirat	S-04.38	
SP-2737	SZD-30 Pirat	S-04.15		SP-2835	SZD-30 Pirat	S-04.39	
SP-2738	SZD-30 Pirat	S-04.16		SP-2836	SZD-30 Pirat	S-04.40	
SP-2741	SZD-30 Pirat	S-04.22		SP-2837	SZD-30 Pirat	S-04.41	
SP-2743	SZD-9bis Bocian 1E	P-710		SP-2838	SZD-30 Pirat	S-04.42	
SP-2744	SZD-9bis Bocian 1E	P-711		SP-2839	SZD-30 Pirat	S-04.43	
SP-2746	SZD-9bis Bocian 1E	P-772		SP-2841	SZD-30 Pirat	S-04.45	
SP-2747	SZD-9bis Bocian 1E	P-773		SP-2842-01	SZD-30 Pirat	S-04.46	
SP-2749	SZD-9bis Bocian 1E	P-776		SP-2843	SZD-30 Pirat	S-04.47	
SP-2751	SZD-9bis Bocian 1E	P-645		SP-2844	SZD-30 Pirat	S-04.48	
SP-2753	SZD-9bis Bocian 1E	P-647		SP-2845-ES	SZD-30 Pirat	S-05.27	
SP-2754	SZD-9bis Bocian 1E	P-648		SP-2846	SZD-30 Pirat	S-05.28	
SP-2755	SZD-9bis Bocian 1E	P-649		SP-2848	SZD-30 Pirat	S-05.02	
SP-2756	SZD-9bis Bocian 1E	P-650		SP-2849	SZD-30 Pirat	S-05.03	
SP-2757	SZD-9bis Bocian 1E	P-651		SP-2850	SZD-30 Pirat	S-05.04	
SP-2758	SZD-9bis Bocian 1E	P-652		SP-2851	SZD-30 Pirat	S-05.05	
SP-2759	SZD-9bis Bocian 1E	P-653		SP-2852	SZD-30 Pirat	S-05.06	
SP-2760	SZD-9bis Bocian 1E	P-654		SP-2853	SZD-30 Pirat	S-05.07	
SP-2761	SZD-9bis Bocian 1E	P-655		SP-2854	SZD-30 Pirat	S-05.08	
SP-2762	SZD-9bis Bocian 1E	P-656		SP-2855	SZD-30 Pirat	S-05.09	
SP-2763	SZD-9bis Bocian 1E	P-657		SP-2856-V	SZD-30 Pirat	S-05.10	
SP-2764	SZD-9bis Bocian 1E	P-658		SP-2858	SZD-30 Pirat	S-05.12	
SP-2765	SZD-9bis Bocian 1E	P-659		SP-2859	SZD-30 Pirat	S-05.13	
SP-2766	SZD-9bis Bocian 1E	P-660		SP-2860	SZD-30 Pirat	S-05.14	
SP-2767	SZD-9bis Bocian 1E	P-661		SP-2861	SZD-30 Pirat	S-05.15	
SP-2768	SZD-9bis Bocian 1E	P-662		SP-2863	SZD-30 Pirat	S-05.24	
SP-2769	SZD-9bis Bocian 1E	P-663		SP-2867	SZD-30 Pirat	S-04.36	
SP-2772	SZD-9bis Bocian 1E	P-666		SP-2868	SZD-30 Pirat	S-05.29	
SP-2774-IW	SZD-38A Jantar 1	B-621		SP-2869	SZD-30 Pirat	S-05.21	
SP-2776	SZD-9bis Bocian 1E	P-667		SP-2871	SZD-30 Pirat	S-05.32	
SP-2778	SZD-9bis Bocian 1E	P-669		SP-2872	SZD-30 Pirat	S-05.33	
SP-2779	SZD-9bis Bocian 1E	P-672		SP-2874	SZD-30 Pirat	S-05.35	
SP-2780	SZD-9bis Bocian 1E	P-673		SP-2875	SZD-30 Pirat	S-05.36	
SP-2781	SZD-9bis Bocian 1E	P-674		SP-2876	SZD-30 Pirat	S-05.47	
SP-2782	SZD-9bis Bocian 1E	P-675		SP-2877	SZD-30 Pirat	S-05.48	
SP-2784	SZD-38A Jantar 1	B-619		SP-2878-Z	SZD-30 Pirat	S-05.49	
SP-2788-EM	SZD-38A Jantar 1	B-625		SP-2879	SZD-30 Pirat	S-05.50	
SP-2789	SZD-38A Jantar 1	B-626		SP-2880-NB	SZD-30 Pirat	S-06.01	
SP-2790	SZD-38A Jantar 1	B-627		SP-2881	SZD-30 Pirat	S-06.02	
SP-2792-G/I	SZD-38A Jantar 1	B-636		SP-2882	SZD-30 Pirat	S-06.03	
SP-2793-WA	SZD-38A Jantar 1	B-637		SP-2883-K	SZD-30 Pirat	S-06.04	
SP-2796	SZD-9bis Bocian 1E	P-677		SP-2886	SZD-30 Pirat	S-06.50	
SP-2797	SZD-9bis Bocian 1E	P-678		SP-2887	SZD-30 Pirat	S-07.17	
SP-2798	SZD-9bis Bocian 1E	P-679		SP-2888-88	SZD-30 Pirat	S-07.18	
SP-2799	SZD-9bis Bocian 1E	P-680		SP-2890	SZD-30 Pirat	S-07.37	
SP-2800	SZD-9bis Bocian 1E	P-681		SP-2891	SZD-38A Jantar 1	B-616	
SP-2801	SZD-9bis Bocian 1E	P-682		SP-2892	SZD-38A Jantar 1	B-671	
SP-2802	SZD-9bis Bocian 1E	P-683		SP-2893	SZD-38A Jantar 1	B-675	
SP-2803	SZD-9bis Bocian 1E	P-684		SP-2894	SZD-38A Jantar 1	B-666	
SP-2804	SZD-9bis Bocian 1E	P-685		SP-2896	SZD-30 Pirat	S-04.35	
SP-2805	SZD-9bis Bocian 1E	P-686		SP-2900	SZD-38A Jantar 1	B-678	
SP-2806	SZD-9bis Bocian 1E	P-688		SP-2902	SZD-36A Cobra 15	W-735	
SP-2808	SZD-9bis Bocian 1E	P-690		SP-2903	SZD-36A Cobra 15	W-736	
SP-2809	SZD-9bis Bocian 1E	P-691		SP-2904	SZD-36A Cobra 15	W-741	
SP-2810	SZD-9bis Bocian 1E	P-692		SP-2905	SZD-36A Cobra 15	W-742	
SP-2811	SZD-9bis Bocian 1E	P-693		SP-2906	SZD-36A Cobra 15	W-743	
SP-2812	SZD-9bis Bocian 1E	P-695		SP-2907-X	SZD-36A Cobra 15	W-744	
SP-2813	SZD-9bis Bocian 1E	P-671		SP-2908	SZD-36A Cobra 15	W-745	
SP-2815	SZD-9bis Bocian 1E	P-697		SP-2909	SZD-36A Cobra 15	W-746	
SP-2816	SZD-9bis Bocian 1E	P-698		SP-2911	SZD-36A Cobra 15	W-748	
SP-2817	SZD-9bis Bocian 1E	P-699		SP-2912	SZD-36A Cobra 15	W-749	
SP-2818	SZD-9bis Bocian 1E	P-700		SP-2913-AG	SZD-38A Jantar 1	B-683	
SP-2820	SZD-9bis Bocian 1E	P-702		SP-2914-JW	SZD-38A Jantar 1	B-689	
SP-2821	SZD-9bis Bocian 1E	P-703		SP-2918-L4	SZD-36A Cobra 15	W-751	
SP-2822	SZD-9bis Bocian 1E	P-704		SP-2919-VV	SZD-36A Cobra 15	W-752	
SP-2823	SZD-9bis Bocian 1E	P-707		SP-2920	SZD-36A Cobra 15	W-753	
SP-2824	SZD-9bis Bocian 1E	P-708		SP-2921-Q	SZD-36A Cobra 15	W-754	
SP-2825	SZD-9bis Bocian 1E	P-709		SP-2922-I	SZD-36A Cobra 15	W-755	
SP-2826-Z	SZD-30 Pirat	S-04.25		SP-2923-L4	SZD-36A Cobra 15	W-756	
SP-2827	SZD-30 Pirat	S-04.09		SP-2924	SZD-36A Cobra 15	W-757	
SP-2828	SZD-30 Pirat	S-04.37		SP-2925-S	SZD-36A Cobra 15	W-758	
SP-2829	SZD-30 Pirat	S-04.28		SP-2931	SZD-30 Pirat	S-06.07	
SP-2830	SZD-30 Pirat	S-04.29		SP-2932	SZD-30 Pirat	S-06.08	
SP-2831-Y	SZD-30 Pirat	S-04.30		SP-2933	SZD-30 Pirat	S-06.09	

652

Regn.	Type	C/n	Prev.Id.
SP-2935	SZD-30 Pirat	S-06.11	
SP-2936	SZD-30 Pirat	S-06.12	
SP-2938	SZD-30 Pirat	S-06.14	
SP-2939	SZD-30 Pirat	S-06.15	
SP-2940	SZD-30 Pirat	S-06.16	
SP-2941-TR	SZD-30 Pirat	S-06.17	
SP-2942	SZD-30 Pirat	S-06.18	
SP-2943-AC	SZD-30 Pirat	S-06.19	
SP-2944-T	SZD-30 Pirat	S-06.20	
SP-2945-9D	SZD-30 Pirat	S-06.21	
SP-2946	SZD-30 Pirat	S-06.22	
SP-2947	SZD-30 Pirat	S-06.23	
SP-2948	SZD-30 Pirat	S-06.24	
SP-2949	SZD-30 Pirat	S-06.25	
SP-2950-71	SZD-30 Pirat	S-06.26	
SP-2951	SZD-30 Pirat	S-06.27	
SP-2954	SZD-30 Pirat	S-07.38	
SP-2955	SZD-30 Pirat	S-06.31	
SP-2959-MA	SZD-41A Jantar Standard	B-700	
SP-2961	SZD-42-1 Jantar 2	X-120	
SP-2962	SZD-36A Cobra 15	W-762	
SP-2963	SZD-36A Cobra 15	W-763	
SP-2964	SZD-36A Cobra 15	W-764	
SP-2965-16	SZD-36A Cobra 15	W-671	
SP-2966	SZD-36A Cobra 15	W-789	
SP-2967	SZD-36A Cobra 15	W-801	
SP-2968	SZD-36A Cobra 15	W-802	
SP-2969-W	SZD-36A Cobra 15	W-803	
SP-2970	SZD-36A Cobra 15	W-804	
SP-2971	SZD-36A Cobra 15	W-805	
SP-2972	SZD-30 Pirat	S-07.42	
SP-2973	SZD-30 Pirat	S-07.43	
SP-2974	SZD-30 Pirat	S-07.44	
SP-2975	SZD-30 Pirat	S-07.45	
SP-2976	SZD-30 Pirat	S-07.46	
SP-2978	SZD-30 Pirat	S-07.34	
SP-2983	SZD-30 Pirat	S-07.49	
SP-2985	SZD-30 Pirat	S-08.01	
SP-2986	SZD-30 Pirat	S-08.02	
SP-2987	SZD-30 Pirat	S-08.03	
SP-2989-V	SZD-30 Pirat	S-08.05	
SP-2990	SZD-30 Pirat	S-08.11	
SP-2991	SZD-30 Pirat	S-08.12	
SP-2992-TP	SZD-30 Pirat	S-08.08	
SP-2993-TN	SZD-30 Pirat	S-08.09	
SP-2994	SZD-30 Pirat *(Crashed 8.99)*	S-08.10	
SP-2996	SZD-30 Pirat	S-08.14	
SP-2997	SZD-30 Pirat	S-08.15	
SP-3001	SZD-30 Pirat	S-08.49	
SP-3004	SZD-30 Pirat	S-09.02	
SP-3006	SZD-30 Pirat	S-09.04	
SP-3007	SZD-30 Pirat	S-09.05	
SP-3008	SZD-30 Pirat	S-09.06	
SP-3009	SZD-30 Pirat	S-09.07	
SP-3011	SZD-30 Pirat	S-09.09	
SP-3012	SZD-30 Pirat	S-09.10	
SP-3014	SZD-30 Pirat	S-09.12	
SP-3015	SZD-30 Pirat	S-09.13	
SP-3016-LI	SZD-30 Pirat	S-09.14	
SP-3020-3K	SZD-30 Pirat	S-09.18	
SP-3021	SZD-30 Pirat	S-09.19	
SP-3022	SZD-30 Pirat	S-09.21	
SP-3023	SZD-30 Pirat	S-09.22	
SP-3024-J	SZD-30 Pirat	S-09.23	
SP-3025	SZD-30 Pirat	S-09.24	
SP-3026-EB	SZD-30 Pirat	S-09.25	
SP-3029	SZD-9bis Bocian 1E	P-729	
SP-3030	SZD-9bis Bocian 1E	P-730	
SP-3031	SZD-9bis Bocian 1E	P-731	
SP-3032	SZD-9bis Bocian 1E	P-732	
SP-3033	SZD-9bis Bocian 1E	P-735	
SP-3034	SZD-9bis Bocian 1E	P-736	
SP-3035	SZD-9bis Bocian 1E	P-737	
SP-3036	SZD-9bis Bocian 1E	P-738	
SP-3037	SZD-9bis Bocian 1E	P-743	
SP-3038	SZD-9bis Bocian 1E	P-742	
SP-3039	SZD-9bis Bocian 1E	P-741	
SP-3040	SZD-9bis Bocian 1E	P-744	
SP-3042	SZD-9bis Bocian 1E	P-749	
SP-3043	SZD-9bis Bocian 1E	P-751	
SP-3044	SZD-9bis Bocian 1E	P-752	
SP-3046	SZD-9bis Bocian 1E	P-759	
SP-3047	SZD-9bis Bocian 1E	P-760	
SP-3048	SZD-9bis Bocian 1E	P-761	
SP-3050	SZD-41A Jantar Standard	B-702	
SP-3051-LZ	SZD-41A Jantar Standard	B-703	
SP-3052	SZD-41A Jantar Standard	B-728	
SP-3053	SZD-41A Jantar Standard	B-730	
SP-3054	SZD-41A Jantar Standard	B-731	
SP-3056-ZS	SZD-41A Jantar Standard	B-729	
SP-3059-MF	SZD-41B Jantar Standard	X-125	
SP-3061-AO	SZD-42-2 Jantar 2B	B-869	
SP-3062-AW	SZD-42-2 Jantar 2B	B-864	
SP-3063	SZD-9bis Bocian 1E	P-745	
SP-3065	SZD-36A Cobra 15	W-806	
SP-3066	SZD-41A Jantar Standard	B-723	
SP-3067-C	SZD-41A Jantar Standard	B-725	
SP-3068	SZD-36A Cobra 15	W-580	
SP-3069	SZD-50-1M	X-127	SP-P069 SP-3069
SP-3070-ZM	SZD-41A Jantar Standard	B-732	
SP-3071-AP	SZD-41A Jantar Standard	B-733	
SP-3074-MR	SZD-41A Jantar Standard	B-736	
SP-3075	SZD-36A Cobra 15	W-775	
SP-3076-T	SZD-36A Cobra 15	W-794	
SP-3078	SZD-36A Cobra 15	W-808	
SP-3079	SZD-41A Jantar Standard	B-738	
SP-3080-M	SZD-48 Jantar Standard 2	W-848	
SP-3085	SZD-36A Cobra 15	W-814	
SP-3087-V	SZD-36A Cobra 15	W-818	
SP-3088	SZD-36A Cobra 15	W-819	
SP-3090	SZD-36A Cobra 15	W-823	
SP-3091	SZD-36A Cobra 15	W-824	
SP-3092	SZD-36A Cobra 15	W-826	
SP-3093	SZD-36A Cobra 15	W-827	
SP-3094	SZD-36A Cobra 15	W-828	
SP-3095	SZD-36A Cobra 15	W-829	
SP-3096	SZD-36A Cobra 15	W-830	
SP-3097	SZD-36A Cobra 15	W-831	
SP-3098	SZD-36A Cobra 15	W-832	
SP-3099	SZD-9bis Bocian 1E	P-767	
SP-3100	SZD-9bis Bocian 1E	P-768	
SP-3101	SZD-9bis Bocian 1E	P-769	
SP-3102	SZD-9bis Bocian 1E	P-770	
SP-3103	SZD-9bis Bocian 1E	P-771	
SP-3104-TM	SZD-42-1 Jantar 2A	B-782	
SP-3105	SZD-9bis Bocian 1E	P-777	
SP-3106	SZD-9bis Bocian 1E	P-778	
SP-3107	SZD-9bis Bocian 1E	P-779	
SP-3109	SZD-9bis Bocian 1E	P-781	
SP-3110	SZD-9bis Bocian 1E	P-782	
SP-3111	SZD-38A Jantar 1	B-677	
SP-3112	SZD-30 Pirat	S-09.27	
SP-3113	SZD-30 Pirat	S-09.28	
SP-3115	SZD-50-2 Puchacz	X-129	
SP-3116-TK	SZD-42-2 Jantar 2B	X-131	
SP-3117-KA	SZD-48 Jantar Standard 2	W-846	
SP-3121	SZD-30C Pirat	P-791	
SP-3123	SZD-30C Pirat	P-793	
SP-3125	SZD-30C Pirat	P-795	
SP-3129	SZD-30C Pirat	P-799	
SP-3131	SZD-30C Pirat	P-822	
SP-3134	SZD-30C Pirat	P-805	
SP-3135	SZD-30C Pirat	P-806	
SP-3136-21	SZD-30C Pirat	P-807	
SP-3137	SZD-30C Pirat	P-810	
SP-3138	SZD-30C Pirat	P-811	
SP-3140	SZD-30C Pirat	P-813	
SP-3141	SZD-30C Pirat	P-814	
SP-3145	SZD-30C Pirat	P-818	

Regn.	Type	C/n	Prev.Id.
SP-3146	SZD-30C Pirat	P-819	
SP-3147	SZD-30C Pirat	P-820	
SP-3149	SZD-30C Pirat	P-823	
SP-3150-VT	SZD-48 Jantar Standard 2	W-852	
SP-3151	SZD-48 Jantar Standard 2	W-849	
SP-3152-DG	SZD-48 Jantar Standard 2	W-878	
SP-3154	SZD-50-3 Puchacz	B-903	(SP-3081)
SP-3155	SZD-50-3 Puchacz	B-904	
SP-3157	SZD-50-3 Puchacz	B-906	
SP-3160	SZD-30C Pirat	P-825	
SP-3161	SZD-30C Pirat	P-826	
SP-3162	SZD-30C Pirat	P-827	
SP-3163	SZD-30C Pirat	P-828	
SP-3167	SZD-48-1 Jantar Standard 2	B-1102	
SP-3168-S	SZD-42-2 Jantar 2B	B-944	
SP-3170-MB	SZD-48-1 Jantar Standard 2	W-912	
SP-3172-LZ	SZD-48-1 Jantar Standard 2	B-999	
SP-3173-IF	SZD-48-1 Jantar Standard 2	B-1001	
SP-3174	SZD-48-1 Jantar Standard 2	B-1002	
SP-3177	SZD-48-1 Jantar Standard 2	B-1005	
SP-3178	SZD-48-1 Jantar Standard 2	B-1006	
SP-3179	SZD-48-1 Jantar Standard 2	B-1007	
SP-3181	SZD-50-3 Puchacz	B-959	
SP-3182-T	SZD-48-1 Jantar Standard 2	B-1103	
SP-3183	SZD-48-1 Jantar Standard 2	B-1106	
SP-3184-UT	SZD-48-1 Jantar Standard 2	B-1113	
SP-3185	SZD-48-1 Jantar Standard 2	B-1116	
SP-3186-HY	SZD-48-1 Jantar Standard 2	B-1117	
SP-3187-O	SZD-48-1 Jantar Standard 2	B-1121	
SP-3189-AB	SZD-48-1 Jantar Standard 2	B-1123	
SP-3190-MC	SZD-48-1 Jantar Standard 2	B-1124	
SP-3191-T	SZD-48-1 Jantar Standard 2	B-1146	
SP-3193	SZD-48-1 Jantar Standard 2	B-1148	
SP-3194-KL	SZD-48-1 Jantar Standard 2	B-1149	
SP-3195	SZD-48-1 Jantar Standard 2	B-1150	
SP-3196-MK	SZD-42-2 Jantar 2B	B-948	
SP-3197-RS	SZD-42-2 Jantar 2B	B-1069	
SP-3198-KS	SZD-42-2 Jantar 2B	B-1071	
SP-3199-MH	SZD-42-2 Jantar 2B	B-1072	
SP-3200	ULS PW	664/798	
SP-3201	SZD-50-3 Puchacz	B-957	
SP-3202	SZD-50-3 Puchacz	B-965	
SP-3203	SZD-50-3 Puchacz	B-960	
SP-3204	SZD-50-3 Puchacz	B-961	
SP-3205	SZD-50-3 Puchacz	B-962	
SP-3206	SZD-50-3 Puchacz	B-963	
SP-3208	SZD-50-3 Puchacz	B-1080	
SP-3209	SZD-50-3 Puchacz	B-966	
SP-3210	SZD-50-3 Puchacz	B-969	
SP-3211-PJ	SZD-51-1 Junior	X-115	
SP-3212	SZD-48-1 Jantar Standard 2	B-1157	
SP-3213-ER	SZD-48-1 Jantar Standard 2	B-1158	
SP-3214-YY	SZD-52-0 Jantar 15	X-136	
SP-3215-VI	SZD-52-0 Jantar 15	X-137	
SP-3216-YY	SZD-42-2 Jantar 2B	B-1311	
SP-3217-AK	SZD-42-2 Jantar 2B (Crashed 5.99)	B-1312	
SP-3218	SZD-48-1 Jantar Standard 2	B-1199	
SP-3219	SZD-48-1 Jantar Standard 2	B-1200	
SP-3220-I	SZD-48-1 Jantar Standard 2	B-1201	
SP-3221-LX	SZD-48-1 Jantar Standard 2	B-1202	
SP-3223-FL	SZD-48-1 Jantar Standard 2	B-1204	
SP-3224	SZD-48-1 Jantar Standard 2	B-1260	
SP-3225-TT	SZD-48-3 Jantar Standard 3	B-1298	
SP-3226	SZD-48-3 Jantar Standard 3	B-1300	
SP-3227-BK	SZD-48-3 Jantar Standard 3	B-1301	
SP-3228-BC	SZD-48-3 Jantar Standard 3	B-1302	
SP-3230	SZD-48-3 Jantar Standard 3	B-1304	
SP-3231-Σ	SZD-48-3 Jantar Standard 3	B-1345	
SP-3233	SZD-50-3 Puchacz	B-981	
SP-3234-NI	SZD-50-3 Puchacz	B-982	
SP-3235	SZD-50-3 Puchacz	B-983	
SP-3236	SZD-50-3 Puchacz	B-984	
SP-3238-FK	SZD-52-1 Jantar 15S	X-135	
SP-3240	SZD-52-3 Krokus S	X-138	
SP-3241	SZD-52-4 Krokus S	X-140	
SP-3244	SZD-52-3 Krokus S	X-139	
SP-3245-KM	SZD-52-4 Krokus	X-142	
SP-3246-TE	SZD-51-1 Junior (Crashed 8.99)	X-116	
SP-3247-KP	SZD-48-3 Jantar Standard 3	B-1347	
SP-3248-7	SZD-48-3 Jantar Standard 3	B-1348	
SP-3251-IM	SZD-48-3 Jantar Standard 3	B-1351	
SP-3252-LK	SZD-48-3 Jantar Standard 3	B-1352	
SP-3253-BM	SZD-48-3 Jantar Standard 3	B-1353	
SP-3254-I	SZD-42-2 Jantar 2B	B-1320	
SP-3255-SZ	SZD-42-2 Jantar 2B	B-1321	
SP-3256	SZD-50-3 Puchacz	B-1338	
SP-3257	SZD-50-3 Puchacz	B-1339	
SP-3258	SZD-48-1 Jantar Standard 2	B-1178	
SP-3260-MI	SZD-48-3 Jantar Standard 3	B-1355	
SP-3261-KG	SZD-48-3 Jantar Standard 3	B-1356	
SP-3262-D	SZD-48-3 Jantar Standard 3	B-1357	
SP-3263-TC	SZD-48-3 Jantar Standard 3	B-1359	
SP-3264	SZD-48-3 Jantar Standard 3	B-1360	
SP-3265-T7	SZD-48-3 Jantar Standard 3	B-1361	
SP-3267	SZD-48-3 Jantar Standard 3	B-1365	
SP-3268	SZD-48-3 Jantar Standard 3	B-1366	
SP-3269-DW	SZD-48-3 Jantar Standard 3	B-1367	
SP-3270-JR	SZD-48-3 Jantar Standard 3	B-1358	
SP-3271-RA	SZD-48-3 Jantar Standard 3	B-1362	
SP-3272-KA	SZD-48-3 Jantar Standard 3	B-1368	
SP-3274	SZD-48-3 Jantar Standard 3	B-1370	
SP-3275	SZD-48-3 Jantar Standard 3	B-1371	
SP-3276	SZD-48-3 Jantar Standard 3	B-1374	
SP-3277-C1	SZD-42-2 Jantar 2B	B-1323	
SP-3278-HR	SZD-42-2 Jantar 2B	B-1375	
SP-3279-C3	SZD-42-2 Jantar 2B	B-1380	
SP-3280-C2	SZD-42-2 Jantar 2B	B-1382	
SP-3281	SZD-42-2 Jantar 2B	B-1485	
SP-3282	SZD-50-3 Puchacz	B-1385	
SP-3286	SZD-50-3 Puchacz	B-1393	
SP-3287	SZD-50-3 Puchacz	B-1468	
SP-3288	SZD-50-3 Puchacz	B-1469	
SP-3289	SZD-50-3 Puchacz (Crashed 5.99)	B-1476	
SP-3290	SZD-50-3 Puchacz	B-1477	
SP-3291	SZD-50-3 Puchacz	B-1484	
SP-3292	SZD-48-3 Jantar Standard 3	B-1373	
SP-3293-ZK	SZD-48-3 Jantar Standard 3	B-1418	
SP-3294	SZD-48-3 Jantar Standard 3	B-1464	
SP-3295	SZD-48-3 Jantar Standard 3	B-1415	
SP-3296-AF	SZD-48-3 Jantar Standard 3	B-1431	
SP-3297-ET	SZD-48-3 Jantar Standard 3	B-1432	
SP-3298-LN	SZD-51-1 Junior	B-1495	
SP-3300	SZD-51-1 Junior	B-1497	
SP-3301	SZD-51-1 Junior	B-1498	
SP-3302-J	SZD-51-1 Junior	B-1499	
SP-3303-LK	SZD-51-1 Junior (Crashed 8.99)	B-1501	
SP-3304	SZD-51-1 Junior	B-1502	
SP-3305-BA	SZD-51-1 Junior	B-1615	
SP-3306-L	SZD-51-1 Junior	W-927	
SP-3307	SZD-51-1 Junior	W-928	
SP-3308	SZD-51-1 Junior	W-929	
SP-3309-YY	SZD-51-1 Junior	W-931	
SP-3310-DC	SZD-51-1 Junior	W-932	
SP-3311	SZD-51-1 Junior	W-933	
SP-3312-E	SZD-51-1 Junior	W-934	
SP-3313-P	SZD-51-1 Junior	W-935	
SP-3314	SZD-51-1 Junior	W-936	
SP-3315	SZD-51-1 Junior	W-937	
SP-3316	SZD-51-1 Junior	W-941	
SP-3317	SZD-51-1 Junior	W-943	
SP-3318	SZD-50-3 Puchacz	B-1544	
SP-3319	SZD-50-3 Puchacz	B-1545	
SP-3320	SZD-50-3 Puchacz	B-1546	
SP-3321	SZD-50-3 Puchacz	B-1547	
SP-3322	SZD-50-3 Puchacz	B-1548	
SP-3323	SZD-50-3 Puchacz	B-1549	
SP-3324	SZD-50-3 Puchacz	B-1550	
SP-3327-BB	SZD-42-2 Jantar 2B	B-1493	
SP-3328-HC	SZD-42-2 Jantar 2B	B-1556	
SP-3329	SZD-48-3 Jantar Standard 3	B-1504	

Regn.	Type	C/n	Prev.Id.
SP-3330-VI	SZD-48-3 Jantar Standard 3	B-1505	
SP-3331	SZD-48-3 Jantar Standard 3	B-1512	
SP-3332-CU	SZD-48-3 Jantar Standard 3	B-1507	
SP-3333-BZ	SZD-48-3M Brawo	B-1508	
SP-3335	SZD-48-3M Brawo	B-1510	
SP-3339	PW-2 Gapa	U-02	SP-P339
SP-3342	SZD-51-1 Junior	W-944	
SP-3343-P	SZD-51-1 Junior	W-945	
SP-3344-Y7	SZD-51-1 Junior	W-946	
SP-3345-L	SZD-51-1 Junior	W-947	
SP-3346	SZD-51-1 Junior	W-953	
SP-3347-IH	SZD-51-1 Junior	W-954	
SP-3348-Cx	SZD-51-1 Junior	W-955	
SP-3349-ZG	SZD-51-1 Junior	W-956	
SP-3350	SZD-50-3 Puchacz	B-1553	
SP-3351	SZD-50-3 Puchacz	B-1594	
SP-3352	SZD-50-3 Puchacz	B-1595	
SP-3353	SZD-50-3 Puchacz	B-1596	
SP-3354	SZD-50-3 Puchacz	B-1597	
SP-3355	SZD-50-3 Puchacz	B-1598	
SP-3356	SZD-50-3 Puchacz	B-1599	
SP-3357	SZD-50-3 Puchacz	B-1600	
SP-3358	SZD-50-3 Puchacz	B-1602	
SP-3359	SZD-50-3 Puchacz	B-1603	
SP-3360	SZD-50-3 Puchacz	B-1611	
SP-3361	SZD-50-3 Puchacz	B-1612	
SP-3362	SZD-50-3 Puchacz *(Crashed 5.99)*	B-1613	
SP-3363	SZD-50-3 Puchacz	B-1604	
SP-3364	SZD-50-3 Puchacz	B-1605	
SP-3365	SZD-50-3 Puchacz	B-1606	
SP-3366	SZD-50-3 Puchacz	B-1609	
SP-3367	SZD-50-3 Puchacz	B-1610	
SP-3368-SW	SZD-42-2 Jantar 2B	B-1557	
SP-3369-JJ	SZD-42-2 Jantar 2B	B-1558	
SP-3370-C4	SZD-42-2 Jantar 2B	B-1559	
SP-3371-C5	SZD-42-2 Jantar 2B	B-1560	
SP-3372-ZO	SZD-42-2 Jantar 2B	B-1562	
SP-3373	SZD-48-3 Jantar Standard 3	B-1589	
SP-3374-FK	SZD-48-3 Jantar Standard 3	B-1590	
SP-3375-H2O	SZD-48-3 Jantar Standard 3	B-1591	
SP-3377	SZD-48-3 Jantar Standard 3	B-1640	
SP-3379-F	SZD-51-1 Junior	W-964	
SP-3381	SZD-27 Kormoran	286	SP-2468
SP-3382-DH	SZD-48-3 Jantar Standard 3	B-1687	
SP-3383	SZD-48-3 Jantar Standard 3	B-1688	
SP-3384-Y3	SZD-48-3 Jantar Standard 3	B-1690	
SP-3387-EI	SZD-48-3 Jantar Standard 3	B-1705	
SP-3388-XT	SZD-42-2 Jantar 2B	B-1670	
SP-3389-ST	SZD-42-2 Jantar 2B	B-1671	
SP-3390-IV	SZD-42-2 Jantar 2B	B-1672	
SP-3391-C7	SZD-42-2 Jantar 2B	B-1673	
SP-3392	SZD-50-3 Puchacz	B-1621	
SP-3394	SZD-50-3 Puchacz	B-1623	
SP-3395	SZD-50-3 Puchacz	B-1624	
SP-3396	SZD-50-3 Puchacz	B-1625	
SP-3397	SZD-50-3 Puchacz	B-1628	
SP-3398	SZD-50-3 Puchacz *(Crashed 29.2.00)*	B-1630	
SP-3399	SZD-50-3 Puchacz	B-1631	
SP-3400	SZD-50-3 Puchacz	B-1632	
SP-3401	SZD-50-3 Puchacz	B-1633	
SP-3403	SZD-50-3 Puchacz	B-1635	
SP-3404	SZD-50-3 Puchacz	B-1636	
SP-3405	SZD-50-3 Puchacz	B-1717	
SP-3406	SZD-50-3 Puchacz	B-1718	
SP-3407	SZD-50-3 Puchacz	B-1719	
SP-3408	SZD-50-3 Puchacz	B-1728	
SP-3409	SZD-50-3 Puchacz	B-1730	
SP-3410	SZD-50-3 Puchacz	B-1731	
SP-3411	SZD-50-3 Puchacz	B-1732	
SP-3412	SZD-51-1 Junior	B-1767	
SP-3413	SZD-51-1 Junior	B-1771	
SP-3414-Y	SZD-51-1 Junior	B-1772	
SP-3415-M	SZD-51-1 Junior	B-1773	
SP-3416	SZD-51-1 Junior *(Crashed 8.99)*	B-1774	
SP-3417-RF	SZD-51-1 Junior	B-1777	
SP-3418-BA	SZD-51-1 Junior	B-1778	
SP-3419	SZD-51-1 Junior	B-1779	
SP-3420-K	SZD-51-1 Junior	B-1780	
SP-3421-KVolt	SZD-51-1 Junior	B-1782	
SP-3422	SZD-51-1 Junior	B-1783	
SP-3423-EZ	SZD-51-1 Junior	B-1784	
SP-3424	SZD-51-1 Junior	B-1786	
SP-3425-V2	SZD-51-1 Junior	B-1787	
SP-3426-i	SZD-51-1 Junior *(Crashed 5.99)*	B-1789	
SP-3427	SZD-51-1 Junior	B-1792	
SP-3428	SZD-51-1 Junior	B-1793	
SP-3429	SZD-51-1 Junior	B-1794	
SP-3430-AC	SZD-51-1 Junior	B-1795	
SP-3431-R	SZD-51-1 Junior	B-1796	
SP-3432	SZD-51-1 Junior	B-1797	
SP-3433-FI	SZD-51-1 Junior	B-1798	
SP-3435	SZD-51-1 Junior	B-1800	
SP-3436-X	SZD-51-1 Junior	B-1801	
SP-3437-ME	SZD-51-1 Junior	B-1802	
SP-3438	SZD-51-1 Junior	B-1803	
SP-3439	SZD-51-1 Junior	B-1804	
SP-3440	SZD-51-1 Junior	B-1805	
SP-3441	SZD-51-1 Junior	B-1806	
SP-3443	SZD-51-1 Junior	B-1808	
SP-3444-TH	SZD-48-3 Jantar Standard 3	B-1708	
SP-3445-HI	SZD-48-3 Jantar Standard 3	B-1709	
SP-3446-GT	SZD-48-3 Jantar Standard 3	B-1710	
SP-3447-LC	SZD-48-3 Jantar Standard 3	B-1711	
SP-3448-JW	SZD-48-3 Jantar Standard 3	B-1712	
SP-3449	SZD-48-3 Jantar Standard 3	B-1714	
SP-3451	SZD-48-3 Jantar Standard 3	B-1739	
SP-3452-DL	SZD-48-3 Jantar Standard 3	B-1885	
SP-3453	SZD-48-3 Jantar Standard 3	B-1886	
SP-3454-ZT	SZD-42-2 Jantar 2B	B-1675	
SP-3455-PC	SZD-42-2 Jantar 2B	B-1676	
SP-3456	SZD-42-2 Jantar 2B	B-1678	
SP-3457-P7	SZD-42-2 Jantar 2B	B-1679	
SP-3458	SZD-51-1 Junior	B-1809	
SP-3459	SZD-51-1 Junior	B-1810	
SP-3460-RS	SZD-51-1 Junior	B-1811	
SP-3461	SZD-51-1 Junior	B-1812	
SP-3462	SZD-51-1 Junior	B-1813	
SP-3463	SZD-51-1 Junior	B-1837	
SP-3464-E	SZD-51-1 Junior	B-1838	
SP-3465-QM	SZD-51-1 Junior	B-1817	
SP-3466	SZD-51-1 Junior	B-1820	
SP-3467-Z	SZD-51-1 Junior	B-1823	
SP-3468	SZD-51-1 Junior	B-1824	
SP-3469	SZD-51-1 Junior	B-1825	
SP-3470	SZD-51-1 Junior	B-1826	
SP-3471	SZD-51-1 Junior	B-1828	
SP-3472	SZD-51-1 Junior	B-1829	
SP-3473	SZD-51-1 Junior	B-1832	
SP-3474-TJ	SZD-51-1 Junior	B-1833	
SP-3475-TH	SZD-51-1 Junior	B-1834	
SP-3476	SZD-51-1 Junior	B-1835	
SP-3477	SZD-51-1 Junior	B-1836	
SP-3478-SC	SZD-51-1 Junior	B-1839	
SP-3479	SZD-51-1 Junior	B-1842	
SP-3480	SZD-50-3 Puchacz	B-1734	
SP-3481-F	SZD-50-3 Puchacz	B-1736	
SP-3482	SZD-50-3 Puchacz	B-1862	
SP-3483	SZD-50-3 Puchacz	B-1863	
SP-3484-UT	SZD-50-3 Puchacz	B-1864	
SP-3485	SZD-50-3 Puchacz	B-1865	
SP-3486	SZD-50-3 Puchacz	B-1866	
SP-3487	SZD-50-3 Puchacz	B-1867	
SP-3488	SZD-50-3 Puchacz	B-1868	
SP-3489	SZD-50-3 Puchacz	B-1871	
SP-3490	SZD-50-3 Puchacz	B-1872	
SP-3491	SZD-50-3 Puchacz	B-1873	
SP-3492	SZD-50-3 Puchacz	B-1874	
SP-3493	KR-03A Puchatek	01-01	
SP-3494	KR-03A Puchatek	01-02	
SP-3495	KR-03A Puchatek	01-03	SP-P495

Regn.	Type	C/n	Prev.Id.
SP-3496	KR-03A Puchatek	01-04	
SP-3497	KR-03A Puchatek	01-05	
SP-3498	KR-03A Puchatek	01-06	
SP-3499	Swift S1 *(Current, but in Kracow Museum)*	P-03/XP	SP-P600
SP-3500	PW-3 Bakcyl	L-01	SP-P500
SP-3503	SZD-51-1 Junior	B-1847	
SP-3504-EI	SZD-51-1 Junior	B-1848	
SP-3505-I	SZD-51-1 Junior	B-1855	
SP-3506	SZD-51-1 Junior	B-1856	
SP-3507	SZD-51-1 Junior	B-1857	
SP-3508-MM	SZD-51-1 Junior	B-1854	
SP-3509	SZD-51-1 Junior	B-1858	
SP-3510-AN	SZD-51-1 Junior	B-1914	
SP-3514	SZD-22C Mucha Standard	F-651	SP-2267
SP-3515	PW-2D Gapa	U-04	SP-P515
SP-3517	SZD-12A Mucha	435	SP-1974
SP-3518	SZD-22B Mucha Standard	F-503	SP-2113
SP-P519	SZD-54 Perkoz	X-148	
SP-3520	PW-2D Gapa	U-07	
SP-3523	SZD-50-3 Puchacz	B-1973	
SP-3524	SZD-50-3 Puchacz	B-1980	
SP-3525	SZD-9bis Bocian 1D	F-812	SP-2401
SP-3526-BD	SZD-55-1	551191018	
SP-3527-AC	SZD-55-1	551191017	
SP-3529	Swift S1	P-05/P2	SP-P601
SP-3530	PW-2D Gapa	U-08	
SP-3531	PW-2D Gapa	U-O9	
SP-3532	Swift S1	P-08/P-03	
SP-3534	SZD-25A *(Reservation)*	F-730	SP-2346
SP-3538	SZD-48-3 Jantar Standard 3	B-1887	
SP-3539-SO2	SZD-48-3 Jantar Standard 3	B-1888	
SP-3540-VL	SZD-48-3 Jantar Standard 3	B-1889	
SP-3542-X1	SZD-48-3 Jantar Standard 3	B-1894	
SP-3543	SZD-48-3 Jantar Standard 3	B-1897	
SP-3544	KR-03A Puchatek	02-01	
SP-3545	KR-03A Puchatek	02-02	
SP-3546	KR-03A Puchatek	02-03	
SP-3547-S	KR-03A Puchatek	02-04	
SP-3548	KR-03A Puchatek	02-05	
SP-3549	SZD-12 Mucha 100A	F-463	SP-2002
SP-3550	KR-03A Puchatek	02-06	
SP-3551	KR-03A Puchatek	02-07	
SP-3552	KR-03A Puchatek	02-08	
SP-3553	KR-03A Puchatek	02-09	
SP-3554	KR-03A Puchatek	02-10	
SP-3555	KR-03A Puchatek	02-11	
SP-3556	KR-03A Puchatek	02-12	
SP-3557	KR-03A Puchatek	02-13	
SP-3558	KR-03A Puchatek	02-14	
SP-3559	KR-03A Puchatek	02-15	
SP-3561	SZD-22C Mucha Standard	F-639	SP-2254
SP-3563	SZD-22C Mucha Standard	F-555	SP-2137
SP-3564-PV	SZD-56 (Prototype)	X-147	SP-P564
SP-3572-J	SZD-50-3 Puchacz	B-1622	SP-3393
SP-3575	PW-5 Smyk	K-01	SP-P575
SP-3577	SZD-22C Mucha Standard	F-507	SP-2117
SP-3578-LOT	Schleicher ASH-25	25081	
SP-3581-JT	SZD-56 Di ana	X-151	
SP-3585	SZD-36A Cobra 15	W-759	SP-2926
SP-3587-Q	Marganski MDM-1 Fox	P-11	SP-P587
SP-3588	LAK-12 Lietuva	6204	
SP-3590	PW-5 Smyk	17.02.002	SP-P590
SP-3595-A	Schleicher ASW-22	22063	D-4651
SP-3596	PZL PW-2Dbis Gapa	U-19	
SP-3601	PW-2D Gapa	U-18	SP-P601
SP-3603-TS	PW-5 Smyk	17.03.003	(ZK-GWW)
SP-3605	SZD-12A Mucha 100A	344	SP-1794
SP-3611	SZD-9bis Bocian 1D	P-371	SP-2061
SP-3616	SZD-9bis Bocian 1D	F-835	SP-2425
SP-3617	SZD-55-1	551196084	
SP-3618	PW-5 Smyk	17.04.006	
SP-3620	SZD-24C Foka *(Reservation)*	W-183	SP-2388
SP-3621	PW-5 Smyk (Code 'LOT')	17.07.014	
SP-3622-F1	PW-5 Smyk	17.07.015	
SP-3623	Marganski MDM-1 Fox *(Crashed 7.98)*	215	SP-P619

Regn.	Type	C/n	Prev.Id.
SP-3624	SZD-9 Bocian *(Reservation)*	unkn	
SP-3625	SZD-41A Jantar Standard 1	B-897	DOSAAF-92
SP-3626	SZD-9bis Bocian 1D	F-846	(SP-0051)
			SP-2437
SP-3627	SZD-24 Foka 4A	W-388	SP-2525
SP-3628	SZD-22C Mucha	F-506	SP-2116
SP-3630	SZD-24C Foka	W-137	SP-2365
SP-P631	PZL PW-6 *(Reservation)*	780000	
SP-3633	PZL PW-5 Smyk	17.12.002	
SP-3634	SZD-24CFoka	W-188	SP-2092
SP-3636	SZD-48-1 Jantar Standard 2	B-1056	DOSAAF
SP-3637	SZD-55-1	551198107	
SP-3650	PZL PW-5 Smyk *(Reservation 10.99)*	17.12.008	SP-3644
SP-3651	PZL PW-5 Smyk *(Reservatiion 1.00)*	unkn	
SP-3652	SZD-30 Pirat *(Reservation .00)*	B-363	D-3759
			DDR-1759
			DM-1759

SX - GREECE

Regn.	Type	C/n	Prev.Id.
SX-AAL(2)	Piper PA-32-301T Turbo Saratoga	32-8124004	HB-PFY
			N83166
SX-AAM	Snow Commander S.2D-600	1396D	4X-ASD
	(Identity officially quoted as "9905")		N1796S
SX-AAO	Air Tractor AT-301	301-0362	N2316T
SX-AAP	Air Tractor AT-301	301-0339	N653JC
SX-AAR	Cessna A.188B Agtruck	01929T	C-GDHH
			N70482
			C-GDHH
			N70482
SX-AAS	Cessna A.188B Agtruck	02123T	C-GIVA
			N2200F
			C-GIVA
			N9116R
SX-AAV	Piper PA-18-150 Super Cub	18-8271	N55WF
			N7155Z
SX-AAW	Cessna 172N	71024	N1497E
SX-AAX	Cessna A.188B Agtruck	01851T	C-GYDL
			N70150
SX-AAY	Cessna A.188B Agtruck	02559T	C-GDTO
			N4822Q
SX-AAZ	Piper PA-31-310 Navajo	31-604	OY-BDK
			N6718L
SX-ABF	SOCATA TB-10 Tobago	1111	F-GKUA
SX-ABH	Glaser-Dirks DG-400	4-155	G-WRMN
SX-ABI	Reims/Cessna F.182Q Skylane	0028	G-BEZM
			G-WALK
			G-BEZM
			F-WZDX
SX-ABJ	Piper PA-34-200T Seneca II	34-7670012	C-GGJA
SX-ABK	Piper PA-28R-180 Arrow	28R-30319	N3971T
SX-ABL	Piper PA-46-350P Malibu	4636020	N9264X
SX-ABM	Air Tractor AT-502	502-0165	N1532A
SX-ABN	Grumman-American AA-5A Cheetah	0142	N9742U
SX-ABR	Cessna 320E Skyknight	0004	N6ER
SX-ABS	Piper PA-28-181 Cherokee Archer II	28-7890456	N30682
SX-ABW	Mooney M.20	1155A	C-GJBD
SX-ABZ	Piper PA-28-151 Cherokee Warrior	28-7615333	N211SA
			N6215J
SX-ACJ	Robin R.2160 Acrobin	164	TU-TJC
			F-ODJC
SX-ACK	Cessna TP.206D Super Skylane	0522	D-EETG
			N8722Z
SX-ACL	Cessna 150H	68330	N22516
SX-ACT	Piper PA-28R-200 Cherokee Arrow II	28R-7435103	N54425
SX-ADA	Auster Mk.5 *(CofA expired)*	1453	G-ANIP
			TJ394
SX-ADC	Beech 35 Bonanza *(CofA expired)*	D-1049	SX-EAC
			HB-ECO
SX-ADD	Piper PA-11 Cub Special *(CofA expired)*	11-1313	49-2838
SX-ADE	SOCATA TB-9 Tampico	1424	F-GLFE
SX-ADF	Piper PA-11 Cub Special *(CofA expired)*	11-1298	49-2823
	(Also quoted as 18-3744 and as 11-1638)		
SX-ADL	SOCATA MS.892A Rallye Commodore 150	10928	
SX-ADN	Cessna 180H	51672	N2472F
SX-ADQ	Piper PA-18 Super Cub 95 *(CofA expired)*	18-1012	RHAF115315
	(Officially quoted with f/n 18-1084)		51-15315
SX-ADW	Piper PA-18-135 Super Cub	18-458	RHAF
			50-1802
SX-ADX	Piper PA-18-135 Super Cub	18-451	RHAF
	(Officially quoted with f/n 18-460)		50-1795
SX-ADZ	Cessna A.188B Agtruck	02734T	C-GQDK
			N731AA
SX-AEC	SOCATA TB-9 Tampico	1435	F-GLFH
SX-AED	SOCATA TB-9 Tampico	1540	F-GLFQ
SX-AEK	SOCATA TB-9 Tampico	1289	F-GRBE
			EC-FFM
			F-GKVJ
SX-AEL	Cessna 172N	72266	C-GLGR
			N9446E
SX-AEM	Mooney M.20J Model 201	24-1545	N3KN
			N2KN

Regn.	Type	C/n	Prev.Id.
SX-AER	SOCATA TB-9 Tampico	1443	F-GIRN
			F-OGSZ
SX-AEV	SOCATA TB-9 Tampico	1016	F-GLAM
SX-AFD	SOCATA MS.892A Rallye Commodore 150	11443	
SX-AFG	Reims/Cessna F.150G *(CofA expired)*	0147	
SX-AFH	Piper PA-18 Super Cub (ex.PA-11)	18-3743	
	(CofA expired)		
SX-AFL	SOCATA MS.893A Rallye Commodore 180	11774	
SX-AFM	SOCATA MS.880B Rallye Club	1860	
SX-AFN	SOCATA MS.880B Rallye Club *(CofA expired)*	1861	
SX-AFO	SOCATA MS.894A Minerva 220 *(CofA expired)*	11830	F-BSML
SX-AFQ	Bölkow BO.209 Monsun	165	D-EAAE
SX-AFR	Bölkow BO.209 Monsun	166	D-EAAF
SX-AFS	North American Navion 4 *(CofA expired)*	4-658	CS-ACP
			N8658H
SX-AFT	SOCATA MS.893E Rallye 180GT Gaillard	12181	
SX-AFU	Fuji FA-200-180 Aero Subaru	187	
SX-AFV	SOCATA MS.880B Rallye Club	2245	
SX-AFW	SOCATA MS.880B Rallye Club	2225	
SX-AFZ	Cessna A.1888 Agtruck	01085T	G-BBCV
			N21865
SX-AGA	Piper PA-28-140 Cherokee	28-23768	N3895K
SX-AGC	Piper PA-36-285 Pawnee Brave	36-7360040	N56349
SX-AGD	Piper PA-28-140 Cherokee	28-7425131	N54434
SX-AGE	SOCATA TB-9 Tampico	1434	F-GRBF
			EC-FLV
			EC-952
			F-GLFG
SX-AGH	SOCATA MS.880B Rallye Club	2478	
SX-AGI	Boeing Stearman PT-17 (N2S-5)	75-8499	SX-EAZ
			BuA43405
SX-AGJ	SOCATA MS.880B Rallye Club	2517	
SX-AGK	Piper PA-34-200 Seneca	34-7350113	G-BATO
			N15964
SX-AGM	SOCATA Rallye 150ST	2615	
SX-AGN	Piper PA-18-135 Super Cub	unkn	SX-ADY
	(Officially quoted with spare f/n 18-5000)		RHAF
SX-AGO	SOCATA MS.893E Rallye 180GT Gaillard	12637	
SX-AGR	SOCATA MS.892E Rallye 150ST *(Wfu)*	2694	
SX-AGT	SOCATA MS.892E Rallye 150ST	2665	
SX-AGU	Piper PA-18-135 Super Cub	unkn	SX-ADS
	(Officially quoted with spare f/n 18-5066)		RHAF
SX-AGV	Piper PA-25-235 Pawnee	25-2635	SE-FPZ
			OY-DDB
			SE-EIF
SX-AGX	SOCATA MS.892E Rallye 150ST	2749	(SX-AGS)
SX-AHA	Piper PA-18-135 Super Cub	18-3585	EI-195
			I-EIYO
			MM542385
			54-2385
SX-AHH	Brantly B-2	112	N5970X
SX-AHV	Cessna A.188B Agtruck (Reims assembled)	03132T	N731TA
SX-AHW	Cessna A.188B Agtruck (Reims assembled)	03129T	N731SX
SX-AHZ	Grumman-American AA-5A Cheetah	0481	N26374
SX-AIA	Reims/Cessna F.150J	0475	HB-CTT
SX-AIB	Reims/Cessna F.152-II	1505	F-BRQH
SX-AIG	Cessna A.188B Agtruck	01829T	5B-CCG
			N70068
SX-AIJ	Piper PA-25-235 Pawnee	25-2039	4X-APW
	(c/n is suspect as N6511Z is still current)		N6511Z
SX-AIK	Piper PA-25-235 Pawnee	25-4210	(SU-...)
			4X-APO
SX-AIO	Cessna A.188B Agwagon	01442	5B-CBY
			(5A-DEH)
			N9262G
SX-AIR	Reims/Cessna A.188B Agtruck	0021/03301T	N1957J
SX-AIX	Cessna A.188B Agtruck	03322T	N1987J
SX-AJP	Pitts S-1S Special	IF-1	ZS-UHZ
SX-AJQ	Cessna 310Q	0533	N7565Q
SX-AJT	Reims/Cessna FR.172K Hawk XP	0617	D-EJDP
			(F-GAQK)
SX-AJV	SOCATA TB-20 Trinidad	1665	F-OHDP
SX-AJW	Cessna 210	57007	G-ARDC
			N7307E
SX-AJX	Cessna 172L	52874	N2874Q

Regn.	Type	C/n	Prev.Id.
SX-AJY	Piper PA-18-150 Super Cub	18-7609116	PH-NKI
SX-AKH	Reims/Cessna F.150L	0749	D-EKOD / PH-LUO
SX-AKJ	Piper PA-28-161 Warrior II	28-7916367	5B-CEF / N2228Y
SX-AKK	Reims/Cessna F.172N	1844	
SX-AKL	Reims/Cessna F.152-II	1631	
SX-AKP	Reims/Cessna F.172M	1400	5B-CCU / (SX-...) / F-BSGY
SX-AKR	Reims/Cessna F.172N	1876	F-WZIB
SX-AKU	Reims/Cessna F.150H	0295	D-ECXE
SX-AKV	Reims/Cessna F.152-II	1689	N1661C / F-WZIF
SX-AKW	Reims/Cessna F.172N	2025	(D-EHPP) / F-WZIT
SX-AKX	Pitts S-1S Special	100	
SX-AKY	Cessna 172RG Cutlass	0462	D-EIRF / (N5189V)
SX-ALB	Reims/Cessna F.172N	1936	F-WZIN
SX-ALD	Cessna 152-II	82672	D-EOWL / N89203
SX-ALE	Piper PA-38-112 Tomahawk	38-80A0117	G-BHZD / N25381
SX-ALF	SOCATA MS.892E Rallye 150ST	2666	
SX-ALG	Cessna A.188B Agtruck	03580T	5B-CEJ / N2954J
SX-ALH	Cessna A.188B Agtruck	03578T	5B-CEI / N2915J
SX-ALI	Piper PA-25-235 Pawnee	25-2040	5B-CDZ / 4X-APG / D-EEVI
SX-ALM	Reims/Cessna F.150M	1205	
SX-ALO	Piper PA-18-135 Super Cub (L-21B)	18-3544	E-... / 54-2344
SX-ALQ	Piper PA-18-135 Super Cub (L-21B) *(Officially quoted with spare f/n 18-4924)*	unkn	E-...
SX-ALT	Piper PA-18-135 Super Cub (L-21B) *(Officially quoted with f/n 18-5096)*	unkn	E-...
SX-ALV	Gardan GY-80 Horizon 180	214	F-BNYZ
SX-ALY	Reims/Cessna F.152	1964	F-WZIB
SX-ALZ	SOCATA TB-9 Tampico	178	F-GCOT
SX-AME	Piper PA-18-150 Super Cub	18-7709063	PH-NKJ / N83539
SX-AMF	Reims/Cessna F.152	1962	F-WZIA
SX-AMG	Piper PA-28-181 Cherokee Archer II	28-7790517	HB-PCL / N5963V
SX-AMI	SOCATA TB-9 Tampico	356	F-GDBQ
SX-AML	Beech F33A Bonanza	CE-1106	N3021U
SX-AMM	Cessna 152-II	80216	C-GZKY / (N24325)
SX-AMR	Snow Commander S.2D-600	1332D	4X-ASY / SE-ENK / (N1732S)
SX-AMS	Snow Commander S.2D-600	1375D	4X-AWI / F-OGDE / N1775S
SX-AMT	Snow Commander S.2D-600	1319D	4X-AWJ / ZK-CPK / (N1719S)
SX-AMU	Snow Commander S.2D-600	"9702"	4X-AUM
SX-AMV	Snow Commander S.2D-600	1402D	4X-ASB / N1787S
SX-AMX	Cessna 172M	61361	N20523
SX-ANB	Cessna A.188B Agtruck	02554T	C-GZPY / N4817Q
SX-AND	Air Tractor AT-301	301-0531	PH-CPR
SX-ANE	SOCATA TB-10 Tobago	935	F-ODVB
SX-ANF	Piper PA-32 Cherokee Six	32-7740060	N3162Q / (D-EIRF) / N3162Q
SX-ANG	Cessna 150L	74838	N10315
SX-ANH	Snow Commander S.2D-600	1333D	4X-AUS / SE-ENL / (N1733S)
SX-ANI	Snow Commander S.2D-600	1415D	4X-ASG / N1768S
SX-ANL	SOCATA TB-20 Trinidad	984	F-ODVX
SX-ANM	Cessna A.188B Agtruck	02705T	N4971Q
SX-ANR	Cessna 150E	60801	N6101T
SX-ANS	Cessna 150H	67984	N7284S
SX-ANT	Cessna 172M	64001	N21746
SX-ANU	Piper PA-32-300 Cherokee Six	32-7840022	N47989
SX-ANV	Cessna 172N	67702	C-GDGW / N73824
SX-ANW	Cessna 172N	69164	C-GIXY / N734WC
SX-ANX	Piper PA-28-236 Dakota	28-8511014	G-BMFK / N2407Q
SX-ANY	SOCATA TB-9 Tampico	1075	F-ODTH(2)
SX-ANZ	Rockwell S.2D Snow Commander	1382D	4X-AWE / C-GMAD / N1766S
SX-AOA	Rockwell S.2D Snow Commander	1318D	4X-AWK / (4X-AWF) / N1720S / YS-... / N1720S
SX-AOB	Rockwell S.2D Snow Commander	1358D	4X-AWW / ZK-CPQ / (ZK-CTK) / (N1758S)
SX-AOC	Rockwell S.2D Snow Commander	1354D	4X-AWC / CF-UNR
SX-AOD	Rockwell Commander 112A	427	N1427J
SX-AOE	Rockwell S.2D Snow Commander	1313D	4X-AWN / ZK-CPH / (N1713S)
SX-AOG	Cessna A.188B Agtruck	02608T	N6500L / C-GWWX / (N4872Q)
SX-AOI	Piper PA-18-150 Super Cub	18-7964	N4014Z
SX-AOJ	Cessna A.188B Agtruck	03124T	N731SS
SX-AOK	Cessna A.188B Agtruck	03330T	N1995J
SX-AOL	Cessna A.188B Agtruck	02907T	SU-BHZ / SX-AMA / 5B-CDE / N731HK
SX-AOM	Cessna A.188B Agtruck	03312T	SU-IAB / SX-AJC / N1975J
SX-AOR	Air Tractor AT-301A	301-0375	N23310
SX-AOS	Cessna 421B Golden Eagle	0570	N224DR / N80F / N41033
SX-AOT	Piper PA-23-150 Apache	23-585	9J-RGC / ZS-CRD / VP-YOO / N2013P
SX-AOU	Piper PA-32-260 Cherokee Six	32-1294	N4853S
SX-AOV	Cessna 172N	71185	
SX-AOY	Piper PA-28-161 Cherokee Warrior II	28-7716228	N38156
SX-AOZ	SOCATA TB-9 Tampico	1026	F-ODRV / SX-... / F-ODTO
SX-APA	Cessna 172M	61849	N12154
SX-APB	Cessna 150H	68580	N22873
SX-APC	Piper PA-23-250 Aztec B	27-2310	N5251Y
SX-APD	Cessna 402	0055	N3255Q
SX-APE	Cessna 172P	75547	F-GJCE / N64338
SX-APG	Cessna A.188B Agtruck	01313T	N8812G
SX-APH	Cessna A.188B Agtruck	02750T	N731AT
SX-API	Beech 58 Baron	TH-970	N2034K
SX-APJ	Beech 200 Super King Air	BB-401	OY-JAO / F-GBLG
SX-APK	Cessna 182E	53630	N371VU / N9230X
SX-APL	Cessna 172M	65367	C-GSJL / N5190H

Regn.	Type	C/n	Prev.Id.
SX-APM	Rand-Robinson KR.2	273	
SX-APN	Cessna P.172D	57154	HB-CMF
			N7454E
SX-APO	Piper PA-28-140 Cherokee E	28-7225584	N15078
SX-APP	Piper PA-31-350 Chieftain	31-8152171	TF-ORF
			N4093G
SX-APQ	Cessna 182P	61087	N7447Q
SX-APT	Piper PA-28-140 Cherokee E	28-7225257	N2865T
SX-APU	Cessna 411	0159	N4959T
SX-ARA	Piper PA-28-161 Warrior II	28-8316053	N4294Y
SX-ARB	Piper PA-28-161 Warrior II	28-8316078	N8238Q
SX-ARC	Piper PA-28-181 Archer III	2843188	N4130Q
			N41300
			(SX-ARC)
			N9508N
SX-ARK	Piper PA-32R-301 Saratoga SP	3213012	G-HIHI
SX-ART	Cessna 182F	54663	F-BKQX
			N3263U
SX-ARV	Van's RV-6A (Officially c/n 20874)	20844	
SX-ATB	SOCATA TB-20 Trinidad	1209	F-GNHC
			F-ODSQ
SX-ATC	Reims/Cessna F.172M	1491	G-BEUR
			EI-BGE
			G-BEUR
SX-ATG	SOCATA TB-20 Trinidad	1799	F-OHUR
SX-ATL	SOCATA TB-10 Tobago	1269	F-GKVG
SX-ATN	Cessna 172M	65290	C-GNRL
			N64534
SX-ATQ	SOCATA TB-20 Trinidad	1800	F-OHUS
			F-WWRB
SX-ATS	SOCATA TB-20 Trinidad	1014	F-OHUV
			EC-FCE
			F-GHZN
SX-ATT	SOCATA TB-20 Trinidad	1814	
SX-...	Beech 58 Baron	TH-1341	N6342U
SX-...	Beech B200 Super King Air	BB-1493	N3015Q
SX-...	Canadair CL-215-6B11	2039	C-GELJ
SX-...	Cessna 182S	80426	N2357D
SX-...	Normand Dubé Aerocruiser	AND912-62	C-FQZR
SX-...	SOCATA TB-20 Trinidad	1315	F-GNHF
			F-OGSE
SX-BAO	Aeritalia/SNIAS ATR-72-202	326	F-GKOG
			F-WWLI
SX-BAP	Aeritalia/SNIAS ATR-72-202	330	F-GKOH
			F-WWLL
SX-BAR	BAC One-Eleven 215AU	096	N1130J
			N11181
SX-BBT	Boeing 737-33A	25011	F-GRSA
			OO-LTO
			VH-OAN
			OO-LTO
			N227AW
			PP-SOF
SX-BBU	Boeing 737-33A	25743	EC-FMP
			EC-970
			N3519L
SX-BBX(2)	Fairchild-Swearingen SA.227AC Metro III	AC-657	N26902
SX-BCA	Boeing 737-284	21224	
SX-BCB	Boeing 737-284	21225	
SX-BCC	Boeing 737-284	21301	
SX-BCD	Boeing 737-284	21302	N40112
SX-BCE	Boeing 737-284	22300	
SX-BCF	Boeing 737-284	22301	
SX-BCG	Boeing 737-284	22338	N8292V
SX-BCH	Boeing 737-284	22339	
SX-BCI	Boeing 737-284	22343	
SX-BCK	Boeing 737-284	22400	
SX-BCL	Boeing 737-284	22401	
SX-BDI	Piper PA-28-140 Cherokee E	28-7225175	N4608T
			N4502T
SX-BDK	Piper PA-28-140 Cherokee E	28-7325010	N15466
SX-BDL	Piper PA-23-250 Aztec E (Wfu)	27-7305081	N40268
SX-BDM	Piper PA-28-140 Cherokee E	28-7325007	N15149

Regn.	Type	C/n	Prev.Id.
SX-BDO	Reims/Cessna F.152	unkn	
SX-BDP	Reims/Cessna F.152 (Wfu)	1634	F-WZID
			N1646Q
SX-BDQ	Reims/Cessna FA.152 Aerobat	0360	
SX-BDR	Reims/Cessna F.152	1747	F-WZIH
SX-BDZ	Piper PA-44-180 Seminole	4496024	N4134R
			(SX-BDZ)
			N9526N
SX-BED	Airbus A.300B4-102	058	F-WZEH
SX-BEE	Airbus A.300B4-102	103	F-WZEC
SX-BEK	Airbus A.300B4-605R	632	F-WWAG
SX-BEL	Airbus A.300B4-605R	696	F-WWAK
SX-BFH	Short SD.3-60	SH.3738	4X-CSL
			G-ZAPF
			G-OLTN
			G-BOFH
			G-14-3738
SX-BFK	Aeritalia/SNIAS ATR-72-202	313	F-GKOD
			F-WWEI
SX-BFL	Piper PA-31-350 Navajo Chieftain	31-7952171	N64TT
			(N701RM)
			N64TT
			PH-SHA
			(PH-DAH)
			(N300SF)
			N300SM
			N27909
SX-BFM	Piper PA-31-350 Chieftain	31-8052204	N4504J
SX-BFN	Short SD.3-60	SH.3738	4X-CSL
			G-ZAPF
			G-OLTN
			G-BOFH
			G-14-3738
SX-BFP	Boeing 737-5K5	25062	D-AHLN(2)
SX-BFT	Boeing 737-3Q8	24470	N470KB
			PK-GWD
SX-BFU	Piper PA-31P Pressurized Navajo	31P-7530002	G-EHJM
			N54934
			OE-FHT
			N54934
SX-BFV	Boeing 737-430	27004	EI-CPU
			D-ABKF
			(D-ABKK)
			(D-ABKE)
SX-BFW	Short SD.3-60	SH.3769	EI-COR
			G-ZAPG
			G-CPTL
			G-BOFI
			G-14-3739
SX-BFY	Boeing 737-35B	24238	D-AGEE
SX-BGA	Short SD.3-30	SH.3043	G-BHJM
SX-BGB	Short SD.3-30	SH.3048	G-BHVL
SX-BGC	Short SD.3-30	SH.3065	G-BIOG
			G-14-3065
SX-BGD	Short SD.3-30	SH.3066	G-BITU
			G-14-3066
SX-BGF	Short SD.3-30	SH.3084	G-BJWA
SX-BGH	Boeing 737-4Y0	23866	N4360W
			B-2969
			EI-CMO
			VT-EWL
			TC-ADA
SX-BGI	Boeing 737-3L9	27061	D-ADBD
			OY-MAN
SX-BGJ	Boeing 737-4S3	25595	N280CD
			TC-APA
SX-BGK	Boeing 737-3Y0	24679	9V-TRA
SX-BGL	Fokker F.28-0100	11387	F-WQJK
	(C/h as quoted officially)		HL7207
			PH-KXB
SX-BGM	Fokker F.28-0100	11476	F-WQJJ
	(C/h as quoted officially)		HL7212
			PH-EZY
SX-BHC	Dornier 228-200	8030	D-IDBB
SX-BHD	Dornier 228-200	8034	D-IDBE

Regn.	Type	C/n	Prev.Id.
SX-BHE	Dornier 228-201	8050	D-IDBR(1)
SX-BHF	Dornier 228-201	8057	D-CAPO
SX-BHH	Dornier 228-201	8079	D-CLEC
SX-BHI	Dornier 228-201	8080	D-COLE
SX-BIA	Aeritalia/SNIAS ATR-42-300	169	F-WWEW
SX-BIB	Aeritalia/SNIAS ATR-42-300	182	F-WWER
SX-BIC	Aeritalia/SNIAS ATR-42-300	197	F-WWEE
SX-BID	Aeritalia/SNIAS ATR-42-300	219	F-WWEG
SX-BIE	Aeritalia/SNIAS ATR-72-202	239	F-WWED
SX-BIF	Aeritalia/SNIAS ATR-72-202	241	F-WWEA
SX-BIG	Aeritalia/SNIAS ATR-72-202	290	F-WWLQ
SX-BIH	Aeritalia/SNIAS ATR-72-202	305	F-WWLC
SX-BII	Aeritalia/SNIAS ATR-72-202	353	F-WWEK
SX-BIK	Aeritalia/SNIAS ATR-72-202	350	F-WWEG
SX-BIL	Aeritalia/SNIAS ATR-72-202	437	F-WWLC
SX-BKA	Boeing 737-484	25313	
SX-BKB	Boeing 737-484	25314	
SX-BKC	Boeing 737-484	25361	
SX-BKD	Boeing 737-484	25362	
SX-BKE	Boeing 737-484	25417	
SX-BKF	Boeing 737-484	25430	
SX-BKG	Boeing 737-484	27149	
SX-BKH	Boeing 737-4Q8	24703	N407KW
			LN-BUB
			9M-MJA
SX-BKI	Boeing 737-4Q8	24704	N405KW
			9M-MJB
SX-BKK	Boeing 737-4Q8	25371	N404KW
			VR-CAA
SX-BKL	Boeing 737-4Y0	24915	9M-MJT
			OO-VDO
			9M-MJP
SX-BKM	Boeing 737-4Q8	24709	N406KW
			9M-MJG
SX-BKN	Boeing 737-4Q8	26281	N401KW
SX-BLA	Boeing 737-33R	28869	N964WP
SX-BLT	Boeing 737-7K9	28090	N73712
SX-BLU	Boeing 737-7K9	28091	N73713
SX-BMA	Boeing 737-46J	27171	D-ABAE
SX-BMB	Boeing 737-46J	27273	D-ABAG
SX-BMM	Fairchild-Swearingen SA.227BC Metro III	BC-774B	N774MW
			XA-RXH
			N27617
SX-BNA	DHC-7 Series 102	90	C-GELW
			S5-ACA
			SL-ACA
			YU-AIE
			C-GFRP
SX-BNB	Piper PA-31P Pressurized Navajo	31P-48	N91884
			OO-WNG
			(OO-RBR)
			(OO-UTP)
			F-BUTP
			HB-LGG
			N6844L
SX-BNI	Piper PA-31P Pressurized Navajo	31P-7400209	N7330L
SX-BNK	Piper PA-32-301 Saratoga	32-8306005	N8301J
SX-BNL	Embraer EMB.110P2 Bandeirante	110-224	N614KC
			PT-GMQ
SX-BNN	Fairchild-Swearingen SA.227BC Metro III	BC-771B	N771MW
			XA-RVR
			N71NE
SX-BNS	Gates Learjet 55	55-072	N72ET
			PT-MSM
			N55AQ
			N55AS
			N58AS
SX-BNV	Piper PA-31-350 Navajo Chieftain	31-7952088	N112GD
			C-FYZF
			N35161
SX-BOA	Boeing 717-200 (Reservation)	55056	
SX-BOB	Boeing 717-200 (Reservation)	55053	
SX-BOG	Reims/Cessna FA.150K Aerobat	0063	SX-BDG
SX-BSA	Piper PA-34-200T Seneca II	34-7870044	N5151S
			C-GQYF

Regn.	Type	C/n	Prev.Id.
SX-BSB	Piper PA-34-200T Seneca II	34-7970282	N2851A
SX-BSI	SOCATA TB-10 Tobago	101	G-EWBJ
SX-BSK	Piper PA-23-250 Aztec C	27-3473	C-FUSD
			CF-USD
SX-BSM	SOCATA TB-200 Tobago XL	1425	F-GLFF
SX-BSP	Piper PA-18-150 Super Cub	18-7667	N3899Z
SX-BSR	BAe. Jetstream Series 3102	718	G-OAKI
			N417MX
			G-31-718
SX-BSS	HS. 125-3A	25116	N726CC
			N345CT
			(N90SR)
			N345DA
			N136LK
			N93TC
			G-ATZN
SX-BSZ	SOCATA TB-20 Trinidad	466	F-OHDM
			F-GENE
SX-BTV	Gates Learjet 55	55-124	N58CQ
			N58CG
			N39391
SX-...	BAe. Jetstream Series 3112	829	C-GMDJ
			G-BSIW
			G-OEDL
			G-OAKK
			G-BSIW
			HB-AED
			G-31-829
			C-FCPG
			G-31-829
SX-CBA	Boeing 727-284	20003	
SX-CBB	Boeing 727-284	20004	
SX-CBE	Boeing 727-284	20201	
SX-CBF	Boeing 727-284	19536	N3182B
			N7270L
SX-CBG	Boeing 727-230	20918	(N397PA)
			D-ABKJ
SX-CBH	Boeing 727-230	20790	N852SY
			D-ABTI
			N1787B
SX-CVM	Britten-Norman BN-2-III-2 Trislander	1054	Z-AIR
			A2-AGX
			Bots.DF: OE-1
			G-BEPJ
SX-DCI	Cessna 560 Citation V	0366	N52352
SX-DCM	Cessna 560XLCitation Excel	5051	N1324B
SX-DFA	Airbus A.340-313X	235	F-WWJN
SX-DFB	Airbus A.340-313X	239	F-WWJC
SX-DFC	Airbus A.340-313X	280	F-WWJJ
SX-DFD	Airbus A.340-313X	292	F-WWJB
SX-DKB	Britten-Norman BN-2A-36 Islander	2004	G-BESO
SX-DVA	Avro 146-RJ100	E-3341	(TC-RJA)
			G-6-341
SX-DVB	Avro 146-RJ100	E-3343	G-6-343
SX-DVC	Avro 146-RJ100	E-3358	G-6-358
SX-DVD	Avro 146-RJ100	E-3362	G-6-362
SX-ECG	Beech 200 Super King Air	BB-372	N4937M
SX-ECH	Dassault Falcon 900	26	HB-IAC
			F-WWFM
SX-GEO	Technoflug Piccolo B	065	D-KIMY
SX-HAQ	Bell 47G-4	3165	N1145W
SX-HAS	Enstrom 280C Shark	1044	
SX-HAY	MBB Bölkow BO.105S	S-389	D-HDLY
SX-HBA	Bell 47G-4	2861	SX-HAU
			G-BDRA
			N73944
SX-HBF	Bell 206B Jet Ranger II	3003	
SX-HBR	Hiller UH-12E	5128	5B-CEH
SX-HBT	Aérospatiale AS.355F Ecureuil 2	5296	F-WZFL
SX-HBU	Bell 47G-4A	7682	G-AYAE
			N1489W
SX-HBW	Bell 47G-4A	7543	N1385X

Regn.	Type	C/n	Prev.id.
SX-HBZ	Bell 47G-5	7930	N710KC
			N1452W
SX-HCB	Bell 47G-5A	25088	N14838
SX-HCC	Westland-Bell 47G3B1	WA/713	G-BHKW
			XW193
SX-HCD	Hiller UH-12E	2292	G-BDYY
			EI-BCA
			G-BDYY
			XS705
SX-HCE	Hiller UH-12E	2025	G-BFLR
			N706WA
			XB-NOS
			XA-TUF
			XB-XIU
			XC-CEC
SX-HCF	Agusta A.109A-II	7207	N71PT
			N4263A
SX-HCH	Bell 47G-4	3330	N1157W
SX-HCI	Hiller UH-12E	2007	N5339V
SX-HCJ	Hiller UH-12E	5150	N4030C
SX-HCK	MBB-Bölkow BO.105S	S-593	D-HDQP(2)
			Sweden "73"
			D-HDQP(2)
SX-HCL	Soloy-Hiller UH-12J3	HA3021	N121HA
SX-HCM	Hughes 369HS	109-0204S	5B-CGY
			SU-BKJ
			JA9041
SX-HCP	Robinson R-22 Mariner	1620M	
SX-HCQ	Robinson R-22 Beta	1761	N40761
SX-HCR	Bell 206L-3 Long Ranger III	51559	SX-HOR ?
			N4048G
			C-FMTE
SX-HCS	Bell 47G-4	3145	JA ....
			VH-KHR
			C-FPVV
			CF-PVV
SX-HCT	Hiller UH-12E	5142	N32062
			JA7669
SX-HCU	Hiller UH-12E	5121	N32064
			JA7667
SX-HCW	Robinson R-22 Beta	1875	
SX-HCX	Bell 47G-5A	25079	N14808
SX-HCY	Bell 206B Jet Ranger II	3943	N3209V
SX-HCZ	Bell 206B Jet Ranger II	4233	C-FNYU
SX-HDA	Agusta A.109A-II	7422	
SX-HDC	Aérospatiale SA.341G Gazelle	1205	YU-HBG
SX-HDD	Agusta A.109A-II +	7431	D-HPLE
			JA9948
SX-HDH	Aérospatiale AS.355F1 Ecureuil 2	5305	OE-FXI
			F-ODOQ
			F-WYMC
SX-HDI	Bell 206B Jet Ranger II	976	N823C
			N823H
			N83130
SX-HDJ	Bell 206B Jet Ranger II	3228	N824C
			N824H
			N3902L
SX-HDL	Aérospatiale SA.341G Gazelle	1566	N7448Y
			9Y-TGU
SX-HDM	Bell 47J-2	2837	N73949
SX-HDN	Bell 407	53017	
SX-HDO	Aérospatiale AS.350BA Ecureuil	1191	F-GIPN
			N3599X
SX-HDP	Robinson R-22M2 Mariner	2724M	
SX-HED	Hiller UH-12E	2164	G-BBLC
			N31702
			CAF112275
			RCAF10275
SX-HEE	Hiller UH-12E	2177	G-BBLE
			N31705
			(N31706)
			CAF112280
			RCAF10280
SX-HEF	Robinson R-22 Beta	1876	
SX-HEG	Hiller UH-12E	5030	N530HA

Regn.	Type	C/n	Prev.id.
SX-HEH	Bell 47G-5	25021	(SX-HBX)
			SU-BGS
			5B-CET
			SX-HAV
			OY-HAZ
			SE-HEC
SX-HEI	Westland-Bell 47G-3B1	unkn	
	(Identity quoted as "WAB185" - possibly c/n WA-566 ex 5B-CGI, G-BDVJ, 8430M, XV312, G-17-14)		
SX-HEK	Bell 47G-4	3331	N1158W
SX-HER	MBB-Bölkow BO.105S	S-879	D-HTKH
			D-HMBV
			D-HFNK
SX-HET	MBB-Bölkow BO.105CBS-4	S-864	D-HFHV
SX-HEW	Robinson R-22 Mariner	2516M	N83291
SX-HEX	Aérospatiale AS.355F2 Ecureuil 2	5394	F-WQIG
SX-HFA	Aérospatiale AS.355F2 Ecureuil 2	5563	F-WYMO
SX-HFB	Aérospatiale AS.355F2 Ecureuil 2	unkn	F-WY ..
SX-HIK	Bell 206B Jet Ranger II	4384	N9199C
SX-HIN	Aérospatiale AS.355F2 Ecureuil 2	5406	F-WQEE
SX-HJB	Robinson R-44 Astro	0556	
SX-HJP	McDonnell-Douglas MD.900	00013	N9213P
SX-HJS	Aérospatiale AS.355F2 Ecureuil 2	5484	N909GS
			N838M
			9M-TAS
SX-HKA	Robinson R-44 Astro	0550	
SX-HMA	Schweizer 269C	S-1749	N41S
SX-HMR	Robinson R-22M2 Mariner	2710M	
SX-HNA	Schweizer 269C-1	S-1691	N61460
			(N61376)
			(VT-. . .)
			N61376
SX-HNB	Schweizer 269C	S-1728	N41S
SX-HNT	Robinson R-22 Beta	0517	N2297X
SX-HPA	Bölkow BO.105CBS-5	S-897	D-HSMA
SX-HPB	Bölkow BO.105CBS-5	S-899	D-HSMB
SX-HPC	Bölkow BO.105CBS-5	S-909	D-HSTR
SX-HRA	Robinson R-44 Astro	0494	
SX-HRB	Robinson R-22M2 Mariner	2848M	
SX-HTJ	Bell 206B Jet Ranger II	unkn	
SX-H ..	Aérospatiale AS.350BEcureuil	1911	F-GIAN
			3A-MMD
			HB-XPZ
SX-H ..	Agusta A.109A-II	7431	D-HPLE
			JA9948
SX-H ..	Bell 206B Jet Ranger II	4320	N317CA
SX-H ..	Hiller UH-12E	2270	G-BEFY
			XS169
SX-H ..	Sikorsky S-76	760136	N1548U
SX-KOS	Cessna 150M	75897	G-BPMO
			N66177
SX-NAI	ERCO Ercoupe 415C	1477	N94154
			NC94154
SX-NAT	Piper PA-34-200T Seneca II	34-7970264	N2827U
SX-OAB	Boeing 747-284B	20825	
SX-OAC	Boeing 747-212B	21683	9V-SQH
SX-OAD	Boeing 747-212B	21684	9V-SQI
SX-OAE	Boeing 747-212B	21935	9V-SQJ
SX-ROB	Robin R.3000/160	156	F-WWZE
			F-WWZU?
SX-...	Solar Wings Pegasus XL-R	SW-WA-1177/SW-TB-	G-MTHM
SX-LS2	Aero Designs Pulsar	unkn	

Regn.	Type	C/n	Prev.Id.

BALLOONS

Regn.	Type	C/n	Prev.Id.
SX-MAA	Cameron O-77 HAFB	145	
SX-MAB	Cameron D-50 Hot Air Airship	756	
SX-MAC	*Reservation for Balloon*		
SX-MAL	Cameron C-80 HAFB	4335	
SX-MAN	Cameron N-77 HAFB	3295	G-BVOF
SX-MOA	Sky 120-24 HAFB	60	
SX-M..	Cameron Demestica SS HAFB	836	G-BLMO
SX-M..	Thunder AX10-180 HAFB	1962	G-BUOZ

GLIDERS AND MOTOR-GLIDERS

Regn.	Type	C/n	Prev.Id.
SX-106	Roda	unkn	YU-5180
SX-107	Chavka	unkn	YU-2149
SX-108	Roda	unkn	
SX-109	Focke Wulf Weihe	unkn	YU-4082
SX-110	Roda	unkn	YU-5219
SX-111	Chavka	unkn	YU-2235
SX-112	Chavka	unkn	
SX-113	Chavka	unkn	
SX-114	Chavka	unkn	
SX-116	Chavka	unkn	
SX-117	SZD-9bis Bocian 1D	P-378	
SX-118	SZD-9bis Bocian 1D	P-367	
SX-120	Schleicher ASK-13	13451	
SX-123	Glasflügel H303 Mosquito	95	
SX-125	Glaser-Dirks DG-100	100	N64790
SX-127	SZD-48-1 Jantar Standard 2	B-1114	
SX-128	SZD-48-1 Jantar Standard 2	B-1115	
SX-130	Schleicher ASK-21	21231	
SX-132	Schleicher K7 Rhönadler	AB-02	D-8571
SX-133	ICA-Brasov IS-28M2A	60	G-BLWS
SX-134	Scheibe Bergfalke II/55	228	D-9085
SX-135	Schleicher Ka.6CR Rhönsegler	6516	D-0045
SX-136	Scheibe SF-25A Motorfalke	4510	D-KLOU
			(D-KAGO)
SX-137	LET L-13 Blanik	173448	YR-211
SX-138	LET L-13 Blanik	173419	YR-203
SX-140	LET L-23 Super Blanik	958220	
SX-141	Schleicher Ka.6CR Rhönsegler	6252A	D-4629
SX-142	Schleicher Ka.6CR Rhönsegler	6469	D-6372

GOVERNMENT-OWNED AIRCRAFT

Regn.	Type	C/n	Prev.Id.
AC-1	Cessna 172RG Cutlass	0849	N9518B
AC-2	Cessna 172RG Cutlass	0860	N9532B
AC-3	SOCATA TB-20 Trinidad	814	F-ODVT
AC-4	SOCATA TB-20 Trinidad	815	F-ODVU
P-9	Grumman G-159 Gulfstream 1	120	
1067	Canadair CL.215-1A10	1067	YU-BRE
			JRV72202
			JRV74226
			C-GKDE
1069	Canadair CL.215-1A10	1069	YU-BRF
			JRV72203
			JRV74227
			C-GKDH
1070	Canadair CL.215-1A10	1070	YU-BRG
			JRV72204
			JRV74228
			C-GKDL
1110	Canadair CL.215-1A10	1110	YU-BRH
			JRV72205
			C-GDAT
1221	Grumman G.164A Agcat	1221	

Regn.	Type	C/n	Prev.Id.
1223	Grumman G.164A Agcat	1223	
1240	Grumman G.164A Agcat	1240	
1242	Grumman G.164A Agcat	1242	
1258	Grumman G.164A Agcat	1258	
1260	Grumman G.164A Agcat	1260	
1265	Grumman G.164A Agcat	1265	
1269	Grumman G.164A Agcat	1269	
1279	Grumman G.164A Agcat	1279	
1280	Grumman G.164A Agcat	1280	
1534	Grumman G.164A Agcat	1534	N8806H
1547	Grumman G.164A Agcat	1547	N8857H
1548	Grumman G.164A Agcat	1548	N8859H
1549	Grumman G.164A Agcat	1549	N8861H
1568	Grumman G.164A Agcat	1568	N8924H
1569	Grumman G.164A Agcat	1569	
1570	Grumman G.164A Agcat	1570	N8931H
1585	Grumman G.164A Agcat	1585	
1586	Grumman G.164A Agcat	1586	
1587	Grumman G.164A Agcat	1587	
1602	Grumman G.164A Agcat	1602	N8978H
1604	Grumman G.164A Agcat	1604	
1605	Grumman G.164A Agcat	1605	
1606	Grumman G.164A Agcat	1606	
1648	Grumman G.164A Agcat	1648	N48467
026	PZL M-18 Dromader	1Z010-26	
028	PZL M-18 Dromader	1Z010-28	
029	PZL M-18 Dromader	1Z010-29	
030	PZL M-18 Dromader	1Z010-30	
101	PZL M-18 Dromader	1Z011-01	
102	PZL M-18 Dromader	1Z011-02	
103	PZL M-18 Dromader	1Z011-03	
116	PZL M-18 Dromader	1Z011-16	
117	PZL M-18 Dromader	1Z011-17	
119	PZL M-18 Dromader	1Z011-19	
122	PZL M-18 Dromader	1Z011-22	
123	PZL M-18 Dromader	1Z011-23	
125	PZL M-18 Dromader	1Z011-25	
127	PZL M-18 Dromader	1Z011-27	
128	PZL M-18 Dromader	1Z011-28	
201	PZL M-18 Dromader	1Z012-01	
202	PZL M-18 Dromader	1Z012-02	
204	PZL M-18 Dromader	1Z012-04	
205	PZL M-18 Dromader	1Z012-05	
212	PZL M-18 Dromader	1Z012-12	
213	PZL M-18 Dromader	1Z012-13	

S5 - SLOVENIA

Regn.	Type	C/n	Prev.Id.
S5-AAA	Airbus A.320-231	043	SX-BAS
			S5-AAA
			SL-AAA
			YU-AOA
			F-WWDO
S5-AAB	Airbus A.320-231	113	SX-BAT
			S5-AAB
			SL-AAB
			YU-AOD
			F-WWIH
S5-AAC	Airbus A.320-231	114	SX-BAU
			SL-AAC
			YU-AOE
			F-WWII
S5-AAD	Canadair CL.600-2B19 Regional Jet	7166	C-FZWS
S5-AAE	Canadair CL.600-2B19 Regional Jet	7170	C-GAIK
S5-AAF	Canadair CL.600-2B19 Regional Jet	7272	C-FMND
S5-BAA	Gates Learjet 35A	35A-618	SL-BAA
			YU-BOL
			N10871
S5-BAE	LET L-410UVP-E	902503	UR-67650
			RA-67650
			CCCP67650
S5-BAG	LET L-410AB Turbolet	750409	OK-FDE
S5-CAA	Piper PA-34-220T Seneca III	34-8233058	SL-CAA
			YU-BPI
			N8042M
S5-CAE	Cessna 441 Conquest	0150	SL-CAE
			YU-BMG
			(N2628B)
S5-CAF	Cessna 310F	0149	SL-CAF
			YU-BAJ
			(HB-LBN)
			(N5849X)
S5-CAG	Piper PA-34-200 Seneca	34-7250356	N15052
S5-CAI	Rockwell Commander 690A	11121	D-IGAF
			(N57121)
S5-CAL	Antonov AN-2	1G178-53	CCCP62661
S5-CAN	Cessna 208B Grand Caravan	0810	N1223A
S5-CAP	Antonov AN-2P	1G132-54	HA-ANH
S5-CAR	Antonov AN-2	1G186-51	CCCP54903
S5-CEJ	Piper PA-31T1 Cheyenne IA	31T-1104015	D-IIAH
			N9168T
S5-CGB	Cessna 421A	0157	S5-CAB
			SL-CAB
			YU-BGE
			N3357Q
S5-CGC	Piper PA-31-350 Navajo Chieftain	31-7952153	S5-CAC
			SL-CAC
			YU-BMC
			(D-ILEE)
			N3529B
S5-CMO	Beech C90A King Air	LJ-1360	N1560U
S5-DAA	Piper PA-38-112 Tomahawk	38-78A0476	SL-DAA
			YU-DEO
			D-EHSU
			N9702N
S5-DAB	Piper PA-28R-201T Arrow IV	2803011	
S5-DAC	Piper PA-28R-201T Arrow IV	2803012	
S5-DAD	Maule MX.7-180 Star Rocket	11017C	SL-DAD
			N5658T
			- ? -
			N5658T
S5-DAE	Cessna U.206B	0851	SL-DAE
			YU-BDL
			(N3851G)
S5-DAF	Reims/Cessna F.172N	1781	SL-DAF
			YU-DDE
S5-DAG	Reims/Cessna F.152	1529	SL-DAG
			YU-DFI
			N4996U
S5-DAH	Champion 7GCBC Citabria	289-70	SL-DAH
			YU-CAO

Regn.	Type	C/n	Prev.Id.
S5-DAI	Piper PA-18-150 Super Cub	18-7809103	SL-DAI
			YU-DDV
			N9754N
S5-DAJ	Super Aero 145	19-11	SL-DAJ
			YU-BBL
S5-DAK	Piper PA-28-161 Warrior II	28-7816379	SL-DAK
			YU-DEV
			D-ELAO
			N9538N
S5-DAN	Reims/Cessna F.172M	0985	SL-DAN
			YU-DBF
			(D-EGBT)
S5-DAO	Piper PA-38-112 Tomahawk	38-78A0615	SL-DAO
			YU-DDP
			N9674N
S5-DAP	Champion 7GCBC Citabria	288-70	SL-DAP
			YU-CAN
S5-DAR	Piper PA-18-150 Super Cub	18-7809173	SL-DAR
			YU-DCG
			N84222
S5-DAS	Piper PA-38-112 Tomahawk	38-79A0446	SL-DAS
			YU-DDR
			N9683N
S5-DAT	Reims/Cessna F.172H	0678	SL-DAT
			YU-BHI
S5-DAU	Piper PA-18-150 Super Cub	18-7909093	SL-DAU
			YU-DDU
			N9753N
S5-DAV	Piper PA-18-150 Super Cub	18-8475	SL-DAV
			YU-DBG
			OE-APT
			N4246Z
S5-DAW	Reims/Cessna F.150L	0940	SL-DAW
			YU-DBE
			OE-ATK
S5-DAX	Reims/Cessna F.172G	0264	SL-DAX
			YU-BDS(2)
			OE-DLF
S5-DAY	Piper PA-18-150 Super Cub	18-611	SL-DAY
			YU-DMG
			D-EFGE
			XB-PEF
			N1039A
S5-DAZ	Piper PA-38-112 Tomahawk	38-79A0258	SL-DAZ
			SL-DDM
			YU-DDM
			N9712N
S5-DBA	Cessna U.206G Stationair *(Identity unconfirmed)*	03821	N9672G
S5-DBB	Bellanca 7KCAB Scout	507-75	SL-DBB
			YU-DME
			OE-AOR
S5-DBC	Champion 7GCBC Citabria	291-70	SL-DBC
			YU-CAT
S5-DBD	SOCATA MS.893A Rallye Commodore 180	11773	SL-DBD
			YU-DLB
			D-EAHI
S5-DBG	Piper PA-18-150 Super Cub	18-8493	SL-DBG
			YU-CXH
			N4263Z
S5-DBH	Piper PA-38-112 Tomahawk	38-78A0423	SL-DBH
			G-KING
S5-DBI	Piper PA-18-150 Super Cub	18-7809160	SL-DBI
			YU-DCE
			N82091
S5-DBJ	Cessna 172N	72625	SL-DBJ
			YU-DEJ
			N6193D
S5-DBK	Piper PA-28-161 Warrior II	28-7916174	SL-DBK
			YU-DDS
			N9557N
S5-DBL	Piper PA-38-112 Tomahawk	38-78A0618	SL-DBL
			YU-DDI
			N9675N

Regn.	Type	C/n	Prev.Id.
S5-DBM	Piper PA-38-112 Tomahawk	38-79A0742	SL-DBM / YU-DDN / N9677N
S5-DBN	Piper PA-18-150 Super Cub	18-7909104	SL-DBN / YU-DDW / N9759N
S5-DBO	Zlin Z.526F Trenér Master	1316	SL-DBO / YU-CDK / OK-GRH
S5-DBP	Zlin Z.726K Universal	1360-24	SL-DBP / YU-CDJ
S5-DBR	Piper PA-25-235 Pawnee	25-2424	SL-DBR / YU-BBB / N6815Z
S5-DBS	Cessna TU.206G Turbo Stationair II	0009/04717	SL-DBS / YU-DIJ / OE-DVT / N732TB
S5-DBT	Piper PA-38-112 Tomahawk	38-78A0482	SL-DBT / YU-DDL / N9701N
S5-DBU	Piper PA-38-112 Tomahawk	38-79A0743	SL-DBU / YU-DDK / N9678N
S5-DBV	Piper PA-18-150 Super Cub	18-7809161	SL-DBV / YU-DCD / N82096
S5-DBW	Piper PA-32-300 Cherokee Six D	32-7140066	SL-DBW / YU-BHM / N4897S
S5-DBX	Reims/Cessna F.172N	2021	SL-DBX / YU-DFV
S5-DBY	Reims/Cessna F.172N	1782	SL-DBY / YU-DDG
S5-DBZ	Reims/Cessna F.172H	0710	SL-DBZ / YU-BHA / OE-DLN
S5-DCA	UTVA-75	unkn	SL-DCA / YU-DEE / JRV53108
S5-DCB	UTVA-75	unkn	SL-DCB / YU-DFA / JRV53117
S5-DCC	UTVA-75	unkn	SL-DCC / YU-DIV / JRV53207
S5-DCE	UTVA-75	unkn	SL-DCE / YU-DHM / RV53198
S5-DCG	UTVA-75	unkn	SL-DCG / YU-DFS / JRV53165
S5-DCH	UTVA-75	unkn	SL-DCH / YU-DIU / JRV53210
S5-DCI	UTVA-75	unkn	SL-DCI / YU-DGF / JRV53171
S5-DCJ	UTVA-75	unkn	SL-DCJ / YU-DHC / JRV53188
S5-DCK	UTVA-75	unkn	SL-DCK / YU-DHE / JRV53
S5-DCM	UTVA-75	unkn	SL-DCM / YU-DHP / JRV53201
S5-DCN	UTVA-75	unkn	SL-DCN / YU-DJH / JRV53223
S5-DCP	UTVA-66	unkn	SL-DCP / YU-DLK / JRV51114
S5-DCR	SOCATA MS.893A Rallye Commodore 180	11670	D-EAHE
S5-DCS	Piper PA-28-140 Cherokee D	28-7125203	YU-DAZ / N1821T
S5-DCT	Piper PA-38-112 Tomahawk	38-78A0479	YU-DDO / N9732N
S5-DCU	Piper PA-18-150 Super Cub	18-7809167	YU-DCF / N82188
S5-DCV	Piper PA-18-150 Super Cub	18-7909094	YU-DDT / N9756N
S5-DCW	Piper PA-28-161 Warrior II	28-7916052	SL-DCW / YU-DCW / N21796
S5-DCZ	Piper PA-32-300 Cherokee Six	32-7540038	9H-AAI / N32406
S5-DDA	Piper PA-18-150 Super Cub	18-8637	SL-DDA / SL -CYV / YU-CYV / N4334Z
S5-DDC	Cessna 172N	72614	SL-DDC / YU-DEI / N6151D
S5-DDD	Christen Pitts S-2B	5268	
S5-DDE	Piper PA-18-150 Super Cub	18-7809174	YU-DCH / N82448
S5-DDF	Cessna 150L	73255	SE-IRA / OY-RPI / N5355Q
S5-DDG	Cessna 172N	72582	N5480D
S5-DDH	Cessna 150M	76204	N66678
S5-DDI	Cessna 172N	72307	N9982E
S5-DDJ	Piper PA-38-112 Tomahawk	38-78A0611	SL-DDJ / YU-DDJ / N9677N
S5-DDK	Maule MX.7-180 Star Rocket	11035C	D-ECQM(2) / N61076
S5-DDM	Cessna 150M	76219	N66701
S5-DDN	Beech C23 Sundowner	M-1797	N923JS / F-OGNA / N923JS / F-OGHJ
S5-DDO	Maule MX-7-180 Star Rocket	11020C	D-ESHH / PH-TZK / (PH-ZCT) / N56633
S5-DDP	Reims/Cessna F.172E	0042	OE-DCP
S5-DDR	Cessna 172N	68943	
S5-DDS	Bellanca 8GCBC Citabria	658-74	D-EBER(2)
S5-DDU	Cessna 172N	70516	N739FV
S5-DDV	Piper PA-28R-201T Arrow	28R-8031051	N74KG
S5-DDX	Cessna 172N	71918	N5683E
S5-DDY	Cessna 172N	70664	N739NB
S5-DDZ	Piper PA-38-112 Tomahawk	38-78A0382	N2137A / C-GIYI
S5-DEA	Champion 7GCBC Citabria	290-70	YU-CAP(2)
S5-DEC	Mooney M.20J Model 201	24-0345	OO-NEC / N29784 / C-GXUH
S5-DEG	Reims/Cessna F.172N	2014	SE-IFA
S5-DEH	Cessna 152	84451	N6589L
S5-DEI	Cessna 172N	70322	N738XR
S5-DEJ	Zlin Z.242L	0665	
S5-DEK	Zlin Z.242L	0666	
S5-DEL	Zlin Z.242L	0667	
S5-DEM	Piper PA-25-235 Pawnee C	25-7305526	9A-BIS / RC-BIS / YU-BIS / N6784L
S5-DEN	Cessna 150M	75919	N66207
S5-DEO	Piper PA-25-235 Pawnee C	25-7305547	9A-BIU / RC-BIU / YU-BIU / N6826L
S5-DER	Zlin Z.142	0529	OK-WNI
S5-DES	Piper PA-28-161 Warrior II	28-7816048	C-GQXS

Regn.	Type	C/n	Prev.Id.
S5-DET	Zlin Z.50M	0079	OK-...
			ZS-NEJ
			OK-WRP
S5-DEW	Robin DR.400/180R Remorqueur	1695	HB-KAV
S5-DEX	Cessna 172P	75550	N64366
S5-DEY	Cessna 150M	78573	C-GRXM
			N704FH
S5-DEZ	Cessna 172P	75803	N65657
S5-DGA	Rockwell Commander 112A	256	C-GNUY
S5-DGB	SOCATA MS.893E Rallye 180GTGaillard	12129	I-SUDT
S5-DGC	Zlin Z.242L	704	
S5-DGD	Zlin Z.242L	705	
S5-DGE	Zlin Z.242L	706	
S5-DGF	Zlin Z.242L	707	
S5-DGG	Zlin Z.242L	708	
S5-DGH	Zlin Z.143	8	
S5-DGI	Zlin Z.143	10	
S5-DGR	Robin HR.200/120B	302	D-EBPR
S5-DGY	SOCATA Rallye 150ST	3140	S5-DCY
			9H-AAY
			F-GBKP
S5-DHD	Cessna 172P	75414	N63289
S5-DHH	Cessna 150L	72668	N814DA
			N1368Q
S5-DHL	Cessna 172N	71491	C-FJHA
			N3280E
S5-DHT	Cessna 172N	73706	N5112J
S5-DIC	Reims/Cessna F.172N	1767	D-EFUH(2)
S5-DIO	Piper PA-28-181 Archer II	28-7790024	C-GDIO
			N4382F
S5-DKB	Cessna P.206 Super Skylane	0113	C-GJMQ
			N2613X
S5-DKK	Cessna 182P	61659	D-ECWW
			N21480
S5-DMA	Cessna 182S	80001	N182NU
S5-DMC	Reims/Cessna F.150L	0983	D-EJXG
S5-DMD	Zlin Z.242L	0657	
S5-DML	Reims/Cessna F.172N	1533	G-BEIB
S5-DMM	Cessna 172N	70502	S5-DEE
S5-DMR	Piper PA-28-140 Cherokee E	28-7225071	C-GMMC
			N2398T
S5-DMS	Cessna 182G	55279	D-EFQY
			N2079R
S5-DMT	Piper PA-28-140 Cherokee Cruiser	28-7725191	D-EAYZ
			N9620N
S5-DMV	Piper PA-36-300 Pawnee Brave	36-7860087	9A-BLS
			RC-BLS
			YU-BLS
			N9697N
S5-DNU	Cessna 172SP	unkn	
S5-DON	Yakovlev Yak-52	9010612	HA-JAN
			DOSAAF-54
S5-DSA	Cessna 172R	80505	
S5-DST	Cessna 210	57472	N9672T
S5-DSZ	SOCATA TB-200 Tobago XL	1810	F-OIDO
S5-DTT	Cessna 150G	64767	N4717X
S5-D..	UTVA-66	unkn	YU-DLE
			JRV51108
S5-D..	Cessna 172P	76339	N98723
S5-D..	Cessna 172S	172S8015	N23338
S5-D..	Partenavia P.68C	231	G-BJRZ
			G-OAKP
			G-BJRZ
S5-D..	Piper PA-28-181 Archer III	2843114	N41211
S5-HCB	MBB-Bölkow BO.105C	S-440	D-HDJB(3)
S5-HCF	Enstrom F-28C	385	N663H
S5-HCM	Enstrom F-28C	516-2	
S5-HCO	Enstrom F-28C	448	N51775
S5-HCP	Enstrom 280C Shark	1147	N51762
S5-HCW	Robinson R-22 Beta	1933	OE-XYY
			G-BTUP
S5-HGC	Bell 412EP	36093	N22909
S5-HKM	Bell 206B Jet Ranger II	4311	N2292E

Regn.	Type	C/n	Prev.Id.
S5-HPA	Agusta-Bell AB.412	25546	SL-HPA
			YU-HCX
S5-HPB	Agusta-Bell AB.212	5714	SL-HPB
			YU-HCJ
S5-HPC	Agusta A.109A	7129	SL-HPC
			YU-HBN
S5-HPD	Agusta-Bell 206B Jet Ranger III	8646	SL-HPD
			YU-HCV
			(G-BIZD)
S5-HPE	Agusta-Bell 206B Jet Ranger III	8643	SL-HPE
			YU-HCW
			(G-BIZC)
S5-HPK	Bell 206B Jet Ranger II	4403	N6276G
S5-HZJ	Bell 206B Jet Ranger II	4313	N2292J
S5-H..	Agusta-Bell 206B Jet Ranger	8255	D-HAFW(3)
			OE-BXO(1)
S5-JAA	RAF-2000GTX	H2-94-5-151	C-FWIU
S5-KAM-SI	Schleicher ASH-25M	25209	

HOMEBUILT AND KIT AIRCRAFT

Regn.	Type	C/n	Prev.Id.
S5-MAA	K1-Pajo	1	YU-ZAB
S5-MAB	Rand-Robinson KR-2	7531	YU-ZAM
S5-MAK	Rand-Robinson KR-2	unkn	
S5-MAM	Zenair CH-701 STOL	7-1280	
S5-MAZ	Light Aero Avid Flyer STOL	1360	
S5-MBA	LIBIS/LET L.200 Morava	170717	YU-BAM
S5-MBB	Aero-3	unkn	YU-CPX
			JRV40199
S5-MBC	LET L-13M Blanik	026235	YU-5354
S5-MBF	Murphy Renegade Spirit (See S5-NBA)	434	
S5-MBL	Piper PA-18 Super Cub	18-2034	OE-COR
			D-EMOR
			R-37
			52-2434
S5-NAA	Light Aero Avid Flyer	592	YU-ZAL
S5-NAC	Light Aero Avid Flyer	598	YU-ZAK
S5-NAD	Light Aero Avid Flyer	891	
S5-NAE	Light Aero Avid Flyer	786	
S5-NAG	Light Aero Avid Flyer	319	
S5-NAH	Light Aero Avid Flyer	890	
S5-NAI	Light Aero Avid Flyer	882	YU-ZAR
S5-NAJ	Light Aero Avid Flyer	788	
S5-NAK	Light Aero Avid Flyer	595	YU-ZAJ
S5-NAL	Light Aero Avid Flyer	784	
S5-NAM	Light Aero Avid Flyer	669	
S5-NAO	Light Aero Avid Flyer	unkn	
S5-NAP	Light Aero Avid Flyer	unkn	
S5-NAT	Light Aero Avid Flyer	unkn	
S5-NAU	Light Aero Avid Flyer STOL	unkn	
S5-NAV	Light Aero Avid Flyer	791	
S5-NAX	Light Aero Avid Flyer STOL	unkn	
S5-NAZ	Light Aero Avid Mk IV STOL	unkn	
S5-NBA	Murphy Renegade Spirit	434	
	(C/h quoted is same as S5-MBF - re-registered?)		
S5-NBB	F.Works FW2C65 Capella	1105791	
S5-NBE	Kolb Twinstar Mk III	unkn	
S5-NBF	Fisher FP.404 Classic	unkn	
S5-NBI	Bagalini	unkn	
S5-NBJ	Funk FK-9	95	
S5-NBP	Flight Team Sinus	unkn	
S5-NHA	Rotorway Exec-90	unkn	
S5-NHB	Rotorway Exec-90	unkn	
S5-NHC	Rotorway Exec-90	unkn	
S5-NKA	Albastar Apis (ultralight glider)	unkn	
S5-NKC	Albastar Apis	unkn	
S5-NKB	Lastovka	unkn	

BALLOONS

Regn.	Type	C/n	Prev.Id.
S5-OAA	Cameron O-105 HAFB	2847	SL-OAA
S5-OAB	Cameron V-77 HAFB	2827	SL-OAB
S5-OAE	Cameron N-90 HAFB	1109	G-BPZT
S5-OAF	Cameron V-77 HAFB	2325	SL-OAF
			YU-OAF
S5-OAI	Cameron V-77 HAFB	2943	SL-OAI
S5-OAJ	Cameron N-90 HAFB	3152	
S5-OAK	Tomi AX8 HAFB	14/1994	
S5-OAL	Cameron V-77 HAFB	3319	
S5-OAM	Cameron C-80 HAFB	3417	
S5-OAN	Cameron V-77 HAFB	3469	
S5-OAQ	Tomi AX-8 HAFB	34/1966	
S5-OAR	Cameron O-77 HAFB	3538	
S5-OAS	Cameron V-77 HAFB	3539	
S5-OAT	Cameron O-77 HAFB	3599	
S5-OAU	Tomi AX-7 HAFB	21/1995	
S5-OAV	Cameron N-77 HAFB	1222	LX-INT
S5-OAW	Cameron V-77 HAFB	1524	
S5-OAY	Cameron N-77 HAFB	1726	LX-BUL
S5-OAZ	Cameron N-90 HAFB	3874	
S5-OBA	Cameron C-80 HAFB	3967	
S5-OBB	Head Balloons AX9-118 HAFB	252	
S5-OBC	Kubicek BB-22 HAFB	102	
S5-OBD	Kubicek BB-45 HAFB	114	
S5-OBE	Kubicek BB-22 HAFB	99	
S5-OBF	Cameron A-105 HAFB	4671	
S5-OBH	Kubicek BB-22 HAFB	125	OK-0125
S5-OBO	Kubicek BB-22 HAFB	113	(OO-BHK)
S5-OBT	Balloon Works Firefly F-9B HAFB	F9-068	
S5-OHA	Cameron N-90 HAFB	3115	
S5-OHB(2)	Cameron O-77 HAFB	3540	
S5-OLZ	Cameron DP-70 Hot Air Airship	1703	G-BOPZ
S5-OPA	Balloon Works Firefly 7-15 HAFB	F7-112	
S5-OPJ	Kubicek Jägermeister SSHAFB	107	OK-8037
S5-OPR	SCB AX-7 SS HAFB	SCB 108/94	
S5-OSA	Balloon Works Firefly F8B-15 HAFB	F8B-536	
S5-OSL	Cameron N-90 HAFB	2946	SL-OSL
S5-OSP	Balloon Works Firefly 7-15 HAFB	F7-1010	
S5-OST	Balloon Works Firefly 7-15 HAFB	F7-782	N25621
S5-O..	Cameron O-77 HAFB	3541	
S5-O..	Cameron O-77 HAFB	3542	
S5-O..	Cameron C-80 Concept HAFB	3418	
S5-O..	Colt Bullet 56 HAFB	3550	
S5-O..	Colt 56A HAFB	484	G-BKND

MICROLIGHTS

Regn.	Type	C/n
S5-PAA	Rodaro Storch	110
S5-PAB	Rodaro Storch	13
S5-PAC	Ferrari Tucano S	5
S5-PAD	Eurofly Fire Fox	unkn
S5-PAE	Rodaro Storch II	unkn
S5-PAF	Rodaro Kangaroo	unkn
S5-PAH	Bagalini	unkn
S5-PAI	Bagalini	unkn
S5-PAJ	Rodaro Storch II	36
S5-PAK	Ikarus-Comco Fox-C22	9005-3265
S5-PAM	Rodaro Storch	57
S5-PAN	Rodaro Storch II	unkn
S5-PAP	Fisher FP.404 Classic	C069
S5-PAR	Type unknown	
S5-PAS	Euro Fly Fire Fox	1090
S5-PAV	Ferrari Tucano S	unkn
S5-PAW	Rodaro Storch	34
S5-PAX	Type unknown	
S5-PAZ	Type unknown	
S5-PBA	Ferrari Tucano	unkn

Regn.	Type	C/n	Prev.Id.
S5-PBB	Ferrari Tucano	003	
S5-PBC	Rodaro Wallaby	unkn	
S5-PBI	Rodaro Storch	unkn	
S5-PBJ	Rodaro Storch I	unkn	
S5-PBM	Ultralight Challenger II	unkn	
S5-PBP	Fly Synthesis Storch HS 582	050798	
S5-PBZ	Bagalini	unkn	
S5-PCD	Eurofly Fire Fox	unkn	
S5-PHA	Lisport CH-7 Angel	unkn	
S5-PKA	Type unknown		YU-8040
S5-PKB	MZ Pipistrel	unkn	YU-8039
S5-PKC	Type unknown		
S5-PKD	Type unknown		
S5-PKE	Type unknown		
S5-PKF	Type unknown		
S5-PKG	MZ Pipistrel Hazard	unkn	
S5-PKH	Type unknown		
S5-PKI	Type unknown		
S5-PKJ	Type unknown		
S5-PKK	Type unknown		
S5-PKL	Type unknown		
S5-PKM	Type unknown		
S5-PKN	Cosmos Chronos 14	unkn	
S5-PKO	MZ Pipistrel Hazard	unkn	
S5-PKP	MZ Pipistrel	unkn	
S5-PLC	MZ Pipistrel Hazard	unkn	
S5-PLM	Type unknown		
S5-PLS	MZ Pipistrel Hazard	unkn	
S5-PMH	MZ Pipistrel Hazard	unkn	
S5-PMR	MZ Pipistrel Hazard 15	unkn	
S5-PMX	Type unknown		
S5-PNA	MZ Pipistrel	unkn	
S5-POB	MZ Pipistrel Hazard	unkn	
S5-POL	MZ Pipistrel Hazard	unkn	
S5-POP	Firefly	unkn	
S5-PPR	MZ Pipistrel Hazard	unkn	

GLIDERS

Regn.	Type	C/n	Prev.Id.
S5-1000	SZD-12 Mucha	unkn	YU-4147
S5-1053	Libis Jastreb-54	248	YU-3053
S5-1135	VTC Delfin 3 (C/n officially '8/2')	F.BR.042	YU-4135
S5-1183	UTVA Cavka	unkn	YU-2183
S5-2000	L-Spatz 55	537/2	D-5634
S5-3000-MT	Glaser-Dirks DG-600	6-23	SL-3000
			YU-4458
S5-3001-AT	Glaser-Dirks DG-300 Elan	3E-56	SL-3001
			YU-4387
S5-3002-UK	SZD-48-3 Jantar Standard 3	B-1957	SL-3002
			YU-4461
S5-3004-PW	Glaser-Dirks DG-300 Elan	3E-204	SL-3004
			YU-4424
S5-3005	Glaser-Dirks DG-100G Elan	E57-G33	SL-3005
			YU-4289
S5-3006	SZD-41A Jantar Standard	B-849	SL-3006
			YU-4271
S5-3007	SZD-41A Jantar Standard	B-799	SL-3007
			YU-4240
S5-3009	Glaser-Dirks DG-100G Elan	E105-G74	SL-3009
			YU-4338
S5-3010	SZD-41A Jantar Standard	B-800	SL-3010
			YU-4241
S5-3011	Glaser-Dirks DG-100G Elan	E210-G176	SL-3011
			YU-4440
S5-3012	Glaser-Dirks DG-100G Elan	E207-G173	SL-3012
			YU-4439
S5-3013-G1	Glaser-Dirks DG-100G Elan	E153-G120	SL-3013
			YU-4350
S5-3014	Pilatus B4-PC11AF	299	SL-3014
			YU-4259

Regn.	Type	C/n	Prev.Id.
S5-3016	VTC-75 Standard Cirrus	201	SL-3016 YU-4297
S5-3017	Glaser-Dirks DG-300 Elan	3E-89	SL-3017 YU-4410
S5-3018	Bölkow Phoebus A	847	SL-3018 YU-4197
S5-3019	Glaser-Dirks DG-100G Elan	E27-G14	SL-3019 YU-4314
S5-3020-B5	Glaser-Dirks DG-100G Elan	E214-G180	SL-3020 YU-4441
S5-3022	Glaser-Dirks DG-100G Elan	E127-G95	SL-3022 YU-4343
S5-3023	Glaser-Dirks DG-100G Elan	E59-G35	SL-3023 YU-4290
S5-3026	Glaser-Dirks DG-100 Elan	E-1	SL-3026 YU-4298
S5-3027	Pilatus B4-PC11AF	112	SL-3027 YU-4217
S5-3028	Glaser-Dirks DG-100G Elan	E140-G108	SL-3028 YU-4348
S5-3029	Glaser-Dirks DG-300 Elan	3E-13	SL-3029 YU-4456
S5-3030	Glaser-Dirks DG-100G Elan	E107-G76	SL-3030 YU-4339
S5-3031	VTC-75 Standard Cirrus	223	SL-3031 YU-4315
S5-3032	Glaser-Dirks DG-101G Elan	E112-G81	SL-3032 YU-4341
S5-3033	Glasflügel H303 Mosquito	108	SL-3033 YU-4275
S5-3034	Pilatus B4-PC11AF	186	SL-3034 YU-42..
S5-3035	Pilatus B4-PC11AF	301	SL-3035 YU-4261
S5-3036	Glaser-Dirks DG-300 Elan	3E-266	SL-3036 YU-4444
S5-3037	Glaser-Dirks DG-101G Elan	E155-G122	SL-3037 YU-4362
S5-3038	Glaser-Dirks DG-101G Elan	E77-G52	SL-3038 YU-4337
S5-3039	Glaser-Dirks DG-101G Elan	E154-G121	SL-3039 YU-4349
S5-3041	VTC-75 Standard Cirrus	202	SL-3041 YU-4294
S5-3042	VTC-75 Standard Cirrus	206	SL-3042 YU-4296
S5-3043	SZD-41A Jantar Standard	B-741	SL-3043 YU-4238
S5-3045	Pilatus B4-PC11AF	171	SL-3045 YU-4222
S5-3046	Glaser-Dirks DG-300 Elan	3E-291	SL-3046 YU-4450
S5-3047	Glaser-Dirks DG-100 Elan	E-18	SL-3047 YU-4311
S5-3048	Grob G.102 Astir CS	1266	SL-3048 YU-4235
S5-3049	SZD-41A Jantar Standard	B-850	SL-3049 YU-4272
S5-3051	Glaser-Dirks DG-101G Elan	E129-G97	SL-3051 YU-4344
S5-3052	Glaser-Dirks DG-100G Elan	E157-G124	SL-3052 YU-4385
S5-3053	Glasflugel H205 Libelle	134	SL-3053 YU-4231
S5-3054	Glasflugel H205 Libelle	171	SL-3054 YU-4237
S5-3056	Schempp-Hirth Cirrus	222	SL-3056 YU-4209
S5-3057	VTC-75 Standard Cirrus	199	SL-3057 YU-4293
S5-3058	VTC-75 Standard Cirrus	203	SL-3058 YU-4295
S5-3059	VTC-75 Cirrus 17A	108	SL-3059 YU-4200
S5-3060	Glaser-Dirks DG-101G Elan	E76-G51	SL-3060 YU-4336
S5-3061	Glaser-Dirks DG-100 Elan	E-49	SL-3061 YU-4286
S5-3062	Pilatus B4-PC11AF	296	SL-3062 YU-4256
S5-3063	VTC-75 Cirrus 17A	141	SL-3063 YU-4211
S5-3064	Pilatus B4-PC11AF	297	SL-3064 YU-4258
S5-3065	Pilatus B4-PC11AF	298	SL-3065 YU-4257
S5-3067	Glaser-Dirks DG-300 Elan	3E-434	
S5-3068	Schempp-Hirth Nimbus 3	2	BGA2759/EKZ D-2148
S5-3069	Glaser-Dirks DG-303 Elan	3E-443	
S5-3070	VTC-76 Vuk-T	291	YU-4378
S5-3071	VTC-76 Vuk-T	302	YU-4373
S5-3072	VTC-76 Vuk-T	287	YU-4366
S5-3073	VTC-76 Vuk-T	317	YU-4395
S5-3074	VTC-76 Vuk-T	384	YU-4438
S5-3075	VTC-76 Vuk-T	338	YU-4414
S5-3076	VTC-76 Vuk-T	263	YU-4352
S5-3077	VTC-76 Vuk-T	344	YU-4420
S5-3085	Glaser-Dirks DG-303 Elan	3E-449	
S5-3086	Glaser-Dirks DG-303 Elan Acro	3E-456A14	
S5-3087	Glaser-Dirks DG-303 Elan	3E-459	
S5-3088	Glaser-Dirks DG-303 Club Elan	3E-442C76	
S5-3089	LET L-33 Solo	960407	
S5-3090	SZD-49-3 Jantar Standard 3	B-1902	DOSAAF
S5-3093	Glaser-Dirks DG-100 Elan (Reservation)	E-41	YU-4320
S5-3095	Glaser-Dirks DG-300 Elan (Reservation)	3E-203	YU-4423
S5-3099	Glasflügel H303 Mosquito	97	D-6797
S5-3100	SZD-48 Jantar Standard 2	W-887	OE-5196
S5-3101	Glaser-Dirks DG-101G Elan	E-221R	SL-3101 YU-4454
S5-3105	VTC-75 Standard Cirrus	238	YU-4329
S5-3106	Rolladen-Schneider LS-6	6318	D-4790
S5-3107-BP/PW	Glaser-Dirks DG-600	6-26	SL-3107 YU-4459
S5-3112	LAK-12 Lietuva	6149	CCCP6149
S5-3125	Pilatus B4-PC11	182	YU-4223
S5-3133	LET L-35 Solo	950320	
S5-3300-E3	Glaser-Dirks DG-300 Elan	3E-34	SL-3300 YU-4363
S5-3303	Glaser-Dirks DG-303 Elan	E-448	
S5-3335	Glaser-Dirks DG-300 Elan Acro	3E-483A25	
S5-7100	LET L-23 Super Blanik	907704	SL-7100 OK-....
S5-7101	LET L-13 Blanik	026922	SL-7101 YU-5374
S5-7102	LET L-13 Blanik	174902	SL-7102 YU-5330
S5-7103	LET L-23 Super Blanik	917920	SL-7103
S5-7104	LET L-23 Super Blanik	917919	SL-7104
S5-7105	LET L-13 Blanik	174822	SL-7105 YU-5325
S5-7106	LET L-13A Blanik	026238	SL-7106 YU-5353
S5-7107	LET L-13A Blanik	026237	SL-7107 YU-5352
S5-7109	LET L-13 Blanik	174424	SL-7109 YU-5313
S5-7110	LET L-13 Blanik	026923	SL-7110 YU-5376
S5-7111	LET L-13 N-10 Blanik	174101	SL-7111 YU-5314
S5-7112	LET L-13 N-10 Blanik	174414	SL-7112 YU-5312
S5-7113	LET L-13 Blanik	026719	SL-7113 YU-5369
S5-7114	LET L-13 N-10 Blanik	027046	SL-7114 YU-5381
S5-7115	LET L-13A Blanik	026241	SL-7115 YU-5357

Regn.	Type	C/n	Prev.Id.
S5-7116	LET L-13 Blanik	174103	SL-7116
			YU-5310
S5-7117	LET L-13 Blanik	174901	SL-7117
			YU-5329
S5-7118	LET L-13 Blanik	025309	SL-7118
			YU-5386
			I-PUFF
S5-7119	LET L-13 Blanik	175004	SL-7119
			YU-5338
S5-7120	LET L-13 Blanik	027014	SL-7120
			YU-5379
S5-7122	LET L-13 Blanik	174425	SL-7122
			YU-5311
S5-7123	LET L-13 Blanik	174829	SL-7123
			YU-5323
S5-7124	LET L-13 Blanik	027045	SL-7124
			YU-5380
S5-7125	LET L-13 Blanik	026801	SL-7125
			YU-5370
S5-7126	LET L-13 Blanik	174929	SL-7126
			YU-5337
S5-7127	LET L-23 Super Blanik	917820	SL-7127
S5-7128	LET L-23 Super Blanik	917821	SL-7128
S5-7129	LET L-13 Blanik	026637	SL-7129
			YU-5362
S5-7130	LET L-13 Blanik	026252	SL-7130
			YU-5363
S5-7131	LET L-13 Blanik	027023	SL-7131
			YU-5383
S5-7132	LET L-13 Blanik	026850	SL-7132
			YU-5373
S5-7133	LET L-23 Super Blanik	917925	
S5-7135	LET L-13 Blanik	027024	YU-5385
S5-7136	LET L-13 Blanik	174532	S5-7121
			YU-5316
S5-7137	LET L-13 Blanik	026540	CCCP6540
S5-7138	LET L-13A Blanik	827419	OK-2726
S5-7139	LET L-13 Blanik	172606	OK-3804
S5-5515	Glaser-Dirks DG-500 Elan Orion	5E-177X29	
S5-7520-E6	Glaser-Dirks DG-500/20 Elan	5E-132W4	
S5-7777	Marganski MDM-1 Fox	203	OE-5575
S5-9050	Glaser-Dirks DG-500 Elan Orion	5E-133T58	SE-ULI
			D-9050

The following YU- registered aircraft are known to be in Slovenia, either in store or awaiting registry :-

YU-BBF	LIBIS/ LET L-200D Morava	302-02	
YU-BCY	Macchi AL.60B-2	49/6229	
YU-CMY	Polikarpov Po-2	unkn	JRV0076
YU-DLE	UTVA-66	unkn	JRV51108
YU-4260	Pilatus B4-PC11	300 ?	
YU-4310	Glaser-Dirks DG-100 Elan	E-...	
YU-4391	VTC-76 Vuk-T	313 ?	
YU-4406	VTC-76 Vuk-T	333	
YU-4421	VTC-76 Vuk-T	345 ?	
YU-5043	DFS-108-30 Kranich II	211	
YU-5355	LET L-13 Blanik	026236	

TC - TURKEY

Regn.	Type	C/n	Prev.Id.
TC-AAC	Piper PA-18-150 Super Cub	18-2598	Turkish AF
	(Officially quoted with f/n 18-2422)		52-6280
TC-ABB	Airbus A.321-131	597	TC-ONI
			D-AVZY
TC-ABD	Airbus A.300B-622R	613	VH-HGF
			HL7520
TC-ABE	**Airbus A.300B-622R**	**611**	**VH-IWD**
			HL7519
TC-ABI	Cessna 172N	67601	N73665
TC-ACA	Boeing 737-4Y0	24519	VR-CAB
TC-ACN	Beech 200 Super King Air	BB-791	TC-DBY(1)
			N54LG
			F-GHNV
			N81TT
TC-ACS	Antonov AN-26	9709	UR-.....
TC-ADI	Cessna 172N	67601	
TC-AEZ	Cessna 172N	73362	PH-DBR
			N4814G
TC-AFA	Boeing 737-4Q8	26306	
TC-AFJ	Boeing 737-4Y0	23979	OO-SBN
			XA-SCA
			EI-CEV
			EC-EMI
			EC-239
TC-AFK	Boeing 737-4Y0	24684	
TC-AFM	Boeing 737-4Q8	26279	
TC-AFT	Boeing 727-230	21618	D-ABKN
TC-AFU	Boeing 737-4Y0	26081	D-ABAF(3)
TC-AFZ	Boeing 737-4Y0	23981	EI-CEW
			F-GNFS
			SU-BLL
			EI-CEW
			EC-EMY
			EC-251
TC-AGA	Boeing 737-4Y0	24512	VR-CAL
			(PT-TEN)
TC-AHU(2)	Cessna 172R	80027	N9719F
TC-AIO	Robinson Starduster Too	124	
TC-AIR	SOCATA TB-9 Tampico	1022	F-GHZT
TC-AKK	Dassault Falcon 900B	171	F-WWFW
TC-ALL	Airbus A.321-131	604	9Y-BWA
			D-AVZB
TC-ALN	Airbus A.300B4-2C	065	OO-MKO
			V2-LDY
			(OO-MKO)
			HS-TAY
			N404UA
			N205EA
			F-GBNA
			F-WZEN
TC-ALO(2)	Airbus A.321-131	614	9Y-BWB
			D-AVZD
TC-ALS	Airbus A.300B4-103	066	OO-ING
			HS-TAZ
			N405UA
			N206EA
			F-GBNB
			F-WZEO
TC-ANC	BAe.125 Series 800B	258208	G-BUID
			(TC-ANC)
			G-5-700
			G-BUID
TC-ANL	Boeing 737-4Q8	25374	TC-JEG
TC-ANT	Cessna 650 Citation III	0229	N1302X
TC-APB	Boeing 737-4YO	26290	TC-JEE
TC-APD	Boeing 737-42R	29107	
TC-APG	Boeing 737-82R	29329	N1786B
TC-APL	Boeing 737-86N *(Reservation .99)*	30231	N1787B
TC-APP	Boeing 737-4Q8	28202	
TC-APS	Cessna 340A	0247	N3964G
TC-ARC	Bombardier Learjet 60	60-094	N93BA
			A6-SMS
			N60LR

Regn.	Type	C/n	Prev.Id.
TC-ARE	Fletcher FU-24-950	247	ZK-EGY
TC-ART(2)	Cessna 340A	0478	N340LM
			N340BS
			(N340HL)
			N340BS
			N6307X
TC-ARZ(2)	Beech A36 Bonanza	E-2722	TC-ARI (2)
			N80225
TC-ATA(3)	Grumman G.1159C Gulfstream IV	1043	TC-ANA(2)
			N1761B
TC-ATC	Cessna 650 Citation III	7043	N78DL
			N78D
			N1265P
TC-ATV	Cessna 750 Citation X	0001	N751CX
TC-AUB	Antonov AN-2R	1G234-11	
TC-AUC	SOCATA TB-20 Trinidad	958	F-ODXS
TC-AUD	SOCATA TB-20 Trinidad	964	F-ODXT
TC-AUE	SOCATA TB-20 Trinidad	1223	F-ODXU
TC-AUF	SOCATA TB-20 Trinidad	1224	F-ODXV
TC-AUG	SOCATA TB-20 Trinidad	1225	F-ODXX
TC-AUH	SOCATA TB-20 Trinidad	1226	F-ODXY
TC-AUI	Piper PA-18-150 Super Cub	18-4227	Turkish AF
			54-2827
TC-AUM	American AG-5B Tiger	10098	N1195Z
TC-AUN	American AG-5B Tiger	10129	
TC-AUO	American AG-5B Tiger	10130	
TC-AUT	Beech C90 King Air	LJ-622	N104TT
			F-BUYS
TC-AUV	Beech C90 King Air	LJ-587	N61KA
			(N110PS)
			N61KA
TC-AUY	Beech 200 Super King Air	BB-333	F-GHLH
			C-FANG
			N3207
			N308F
TC-AYA	Boeing 737-4Y0	24683	9M-MJR
			PP-SOH
			HR-SHL
TC-AYH	Cessna R.172K Hawk XP	3203	TC-ASH ?
			N758MK
TC-AYL	Auster Mk.5	1375	TC-AYLA
			G-AKWK
			TJ299
TC-AZA	Boeing 737-4Y0	24691	9M-MJS
			PP-SOI
			HR-SHK
TC-AZE	Cessna 172N	71875	PH-DBC
			N5471E
TC-AZK	Mooney M.20J Model 205	24-3314	N1082Z
TC-BAF	Bellanca 7GCBC Citabria	"10121"	
TC-BAS	Cessna 421B Golden Eagle	0331	N77MH
			(N5991M)
TC-BBJ	Mil Mi-2	5210231057	RA-23230
			CCCP23230
TC-BBS	Beech B24R Sierra	MC-266	N2179W
TC-BHD	Hawker 800XP	258415	N31016
TC-BHO	Dassault Falcon 50	271	F-WWHV
TC-BIL	Piper PA-34-220T Seneca II	3448005	
TC-BLL	Piper PA-28-140 Cherokee	28-23704	N3726K
TC-BYD	Beech 400A Beechjet	RK-254	N3254P
TC-CAC(2)	Piper PA-31P Pressurized Navajo	31P-57	F-BTQB
			F-BTDV
			N7304L
TC-CAE	Cessna U.206B Super Skywagon	0884	N11B
TC-CAF	Cessna U.206B Super Skywagon	0885	N11B
TC-CAM	Cessna 207 Skywagon	00241	(N1641U)
TC-CAN	Cessna U.206G Stationair II	06181	N6185Z
TC-CAP	Cessna U.206G Stationair II	06074	N5163Z
TC-CAR	Cessna U.206G Stationair II	06128	N5517Z
TC-CAT	Cessna U.206G Stationair II	06230	N6314Z
TC-CAU	Cessna 208 Caravan	00248	N1123X
TC-CAV	Cessna 208 Caravan	00256	N1249T
TC-CAY	Cessna 402B Utililiner	1073	T.Army:10007
			N1552G

Regn.	Type	C/n	Prev.Id.
TC-CAZ	Cessna 421C Golden Eagle	0089	T.Army:10006
			N98783
TC-CBC	Slingsby T-67M-200 Firefly	2032	G-BMBL
TC-CBD	Slingsby T-67M-200 Firefly	2033	G-BMBM
TC-CBF	Slingsby T-67M-200 Firefly	2055	G-BOFP
TC-CBG	Slingsby T-67M-200 Firefly	2056	G-BOFR
TC-CBH	Slingsby T-67M-200 Firefly	2057	G-BOFS
TC-CBK	Slingsby T-67M-200 Firefly	2059	G-BOFU
TC-CBL	Slingsby T-67M-200 Firefly	2066	G-BOXL
TC-CBM	Slingsby T-67M-200 Firefly	2067	G-BOXM
TC-CBN	Slingsby T-67M-200 Firefly	2068	G-BPET
TC-CBP	Slingsby T-67M-200 Firefly	2069	G-BPEU
TC-CBR	Slingsby T-67M-200 Firefly	2075	G-BPEV
TC-CBT	Slingsby T-67M-200 Firefly	2078	G-BPMZ
TC-CCA	CCF/Beech T-34A Mentor	34-9	TAF: OK-06/
			54-5206
			(RCAF24206)
TC-CCB	CCF/Beech T-34A Mentor	34-10	TAF: OK-07/
			54-5207
			(RCAF24207)
TC-CCC	CCF/Beech T-34A Mentor	34-14	TAF: OK-11/
			54-5211
			(RCAF24211)
TC-CCD	CCF/Beech T-34A Mentor	34-15	TAF: OK-12/
			54-5212
			(RCAF24212)
TC-CCE	CCF/Beech T-34A Mentor	34-17	TAF: OK-14/
			54-5214
			(RCAF24214)
TC-CCF	CCF/Beech T-34A Mentor	34-27	TAF: OK-23/
			54-5223
			(RCAF24223)
TC-CCG	CCF/Beech T-34A Mentor	34-18	TAF: OK-15/
			54-5215
			(RCAF24215)
TC-CCH	CCF/Beech T-34A Mentor	34-19	TAF: OK-16/
			54-5216
			(RCAF24216)
TC-CCI	CCF/Beech T-34A Mentor	34-20	TAF: OK-17/
			54-5217
			(RCAF24217)
TC-CCO	Piper PA-18 Super Cub	18-426	Turkish AF
			50-1770
TC-CDA	Cessna 185D/U-17A	0838	T.Army:13154
			64-17927
TC-CDB	Cessna 185D/U-17A	0840	T.Army:......
			64-17928
TC-CDC	Cessna 185D/U-17A	0841	T.Army:14050
			64-17929
TC-CDD	Cessna 185D/U-17A	0843	T.Army:11059
			64-17931
TC-CDE	Cessna 185D/U-17A	0845	T.Army:12251
			64-17932
TC-CDF	Cessna 185D/U-17A	0846	T.Army:11061
			64-17933
TC-CDG	Cessna 185D/U-17A	0847	T.Army:13155
			64-17934
TC-CDH	Cessna 185D/U-17A	0851	T.Army:14055
			64-17937
TC-CDI	Cessna 185D/U-17A	0853	T.Army:11158
			64-17939
TC-CDJ	Cessna 185D/U-17A	0855	T.Army:......
			64-17940
TC-CDK	Cessna 185D/U-17A	0856	T.Army:13052
			64-17941
TC-CDL	Cessna 185D/U-17A	0860	T.Army:11164
			64-17944
TC-CEN	Dassault Falcon 20E	326/521	PH-ILY
			F-WRQQ
TC-CHA	Piper PA-18 Super Cub (L-21)	"7203-L-21"	
TC-CIN	Dassault Falcon 2000	26	F-WQFL
			N2000A
			N2046
			F-WWMN

Regn.	Type	C/n	Prev.Id.
TC-CMY	Cessna 650 Citation III	0141	N110TM / N1325E
TC-COG	Piper PA-18-150 Super Cub	18-7585	TC-KPC
TC-COS	HS.125 Series 600B	256048	N6567G / YU-BME / G-BHIE / HB-VDS / G-5-15
TC-CRO	Cessna 525 CitationJet	0102	N202CJ / N52038
TC-CSS	Piper PA-18-150 Super Cub	18-7626	TC-KPI
	(Officially quoted with f/n 18-7813 - identity not confirmed)		
TC-CUP	Piper PA-18-150 Super Cub	18-7909145	N2402S
TC-CYA	Piper PA-18-135 Super Cub	18-3884	Turkish AF 54-2484
	(Officially quoted with f/n 18-3905)		
TC-CYC	Piper PA-18-135 Super Cub	18-3969	Turkish AF 54-2569
TC-CYL	Dassault Falcon 2000	56	F-WWMO
TC-DAN	Cessna 172N	72691	N6284D
TC-DAT	Rockwell Commander 112B	538	N1475J
TC-DAZ	Beech C90 King Air *(Identity unconfirmed)*	LJ-587	N61KA
TC-DBA	Cessna 172RG Cutlass	1070	D-EGLC(2) / N9889B
TC-DBB	Cessna 340/RAM	0018	D-IFJB / N340HP / N5064Q
TC-DBC	Cessna 172N	72286	D-EFZL(2) / N9907E
TC-DBD	Reims/Cessna F.150H	0310	D-ENBX
TC-DBE	Reims/Cessna F.150K	0578	D-ECBI
TC-DBF	Cessna 172N	74103	D-EFZD / N5420K
TC-DBG	Reims/Cessna F.150M	1313	D-EIBT / (D-EIFY)
TC-DBI	Cessna 210L Centurion	60984	N2016S / (D-EDCT) / N2016S
TC-DBJ	Cessna 172N	73773	(D-EUCD) / N5383J
TC-DBK	Cessna 172N	71413	N3042E
TC-DBL	Cessna 172N	71807	(D-EUCB) / N5270E
TC-DBM	Cessna 172N	72170	(D-EUCC) / N8284E
TC-DBN	Cessna 172N	72731	(D-EUCE) / N6345D
TC-DBO	Cessna 172P	75288	N62509
TC-DBP	Cessna 172N	67788	N416CA / N75533
TC-DBS	Cessna 172P	75167	N55356
TC-DBT	Cessna 172N	73107	N4950F
TC-DBU	Cessna 172P	75887	G-BRNL / N5017J / C-GRNU / N65787
TC-DBV	Cessna R.172K Hawk XP	3327	N758SQ
TC-DBZ	Beech 65-C90 King Air	LJ-703	N793MA / N300CK
TC-DCK	Piper PA-28-140 Cherokee Cruiser	28-7725273	N38278
TC-DEL	Boeing 727-225	22439	N808EA
TC-DHB	Canadair CL.600-2B16 Challenger	5094	TC-OVA / C-FKNN / C-GLWT
TC-DHD	Piper PA-32R-301 Saratoga SP	3213090	
TC-DHE	Canadair CL.600-2B16 Challenger	5358	C-GBRQ
TC-DKU	Reims/Cessna F.172M	0957	SE-KGP / OY-RYR / F-GBHC
TC-DLA	SOCATA TB-10 Tobago	7	
TC-DME	Cessna 150K	71718	N6218G
TC-DPT(2)	Piper PA-31P-425 Pressurized Navajo	31P-7300127	PT-DPT
	(Identity not confirmed, PT-DPT was a PA-28)		XA-ROU / N88E
TC-DVK(2)	Cessna 402	unkn	
	(Possible error for DVK(1), Cessna 340 c/n 0241 exN7828Q ?)		
TC-DYC	Rockwell Commander 114	14013	N514CA
TC-EAP	Piper PA-18-150 Super Cub	18-?	Turkish AF 50-1715 ?
TC-EAV	Piper PA-18 Super Cub	18-430	Turkish AF 50-1774
TC-EAY	Piper PA-18 Super Cub	18-431	Turkish AF 50-1775
TC-EAZ	Piper PA-18-150 Super Cub	18-433	Turkish AF 50-1777
TC-EBD	Piper PA-18 Super Cub	18-981	Turkish AF 51-15284
TC-EBR	Piper PA-18-150 Super Cub	18-3072	Turkish AF 53-4672
TC-EBT(2)	Piper PA-18-150 Super Cub	18-4228	Turkish AF 54-2828
TC-EBV	Piper PA-18A-135 Super Cub	18-?	Turkish AF
	(Officially quoted with f/n 18-2414)		
TC-ECB	Piper PA-18-135 Super Cub	18-3895	Turkish AF 52-2495
	(Officially quoted with f/n 18-3908)		
TC-ECH	Piper PA-18-150 Super Cub	18-4232	Turkish AF 54-2832
TC-ECI	Piper PA-18A Super Cub	18-3973	Turkish AF 54-2573
	(Officially quoted with f/n 18-4551)		
TC-ECJ	Piper PA-18A Super Cub	18-3979	Turkish AF 54-2579
	(Officially quoted with f/n 18-4560)		
TC-ECK	Piper PA-18-135 Super Cub	18-5481	Turkish AF 55-4581
TC-ECL	PZL-104 Wilga 35A	140545	SP-WAA
TC-ECM	PZL-104 Wilga 35A	140546	SP-WAB
TC-ECS	PZL-104 Wilga 80	CF21950952	
TC-ECU	PZL-104 Wilga 35A	19870851	
TC-ECY	PZL-104 Wilga 35A	19870861	
TC-ECZ	PZL-104 Wilga 80	CF21950959	
TC-EDA	Piper PA-18-135 Super Cub	18-3996	TC-ECF / Turkish AF 54-2596
TC-EDB	Piper PA-18-150 Super Cub	18-465	TC-EBI / Turkish AF 50-1809
	(Officially quoted with f/n 18-469)		
TC-EDR	Siray 1-TX Experimental	1	
TC-EGE(2)	Mil Mi-2	5210725098	RA-14106 / CCCP14106
TC-EHA	Light Aero Avid Amphibian	A-46	
TC-ELL	Bombardier Learjet 60	60-030	N164PA / N4030W
TC-EMR	Cessna 340A	0269	EC-EVR / N4075G
TC-FAD	Piper PA-31P-425 Pressurized Navajo	31P-7400225	N7341L
TC-FAE	Cessna U.206G Stationair II	06614	N9701Z
TC-FAF	Robin DR.400/180 Régent	1698	
TC-FAH	Piper PA-42 Cheyenne III	42-5501033	
TC-FAI	Maule MX.7-235 Star Rocket	10059C	
TC-FAJ	Cessna U.206G Stationair II	05368	N6182U
TC-FAM	Robin DR.400/180 Régent	1719	
TC-FAN	Piper PA-30-160 Twin Comanche B	30-1521	I-TJTJ / N8449Y
TC-FAP	Cessna 421C Golden Eagle	0513	N67Q / N88536
TC-FAV	Piper PA-34-200T Seneca II	34-7970113	N3979S / (4X-CAS) / SE-ILZ / N2211N
TC-FAY	Maule MX.7-235 Star Rocket	10052C	
TC-FBC	Dornier Do.28D-2 Skyservant	4331	D-IDWM(2) / CN-... / D-IDWM(2)
TC-FCA	Maule MX.7-235 Star Rocket	10061C	N6109C
TC-FCK	Cessna 172RG Cutlass	0408	N4879V
TC-FET	SOCATA TB-20 Trinidad	1052	F-GHZY
TC-FHA	Reims/Cessna FR.172K Hawk XP	0625	G-KERR / PH-AXB
TC-FHT	Cessna 172RG Cutlass	0226	N5092U
TC-FIR	Beech 200 Super King Air	BB-1082	N801BC / N971BE / N6354X

Regn.	Type	C/n	Prev.Id.
TC-FLY	Piper PA-18-150 Super Cub	18-2608	Turkish AF 52-6300
TC-FSA	Cessna 172RG Cutlass	0350	N4658V
TC-FSM	Cessna 172N	73532	N5083G
TC-FYT	Piper PA-31P-425 Pressurized Navajo	31P-7400200	N38353 / D-IHWT / LN-MTF / N7316L
TC-GAP(2)	Grumman G-1159B Gulfstream IV	1027	N416GA
TC-GHB(2)	Boeing 737-33A	24791	VT-JAB / N222AW / PP-SOD
TC-GHC	Boeing 737-7L9	28004	OY-MRA / N35153
TC-GIZ	Piper PA-32R-301 Saratoga	32R-8013064	N8160X
TC-GPS	Cessna 421B Golden Eagle	0221	N5978M
TC-GTA	Airbus A.300B4-103	054	HS-THL / HS-TGL / F-WZED
TC-GTB	Airbus A.300B4-203	127	6Y-JMJ / G-BIMA / F-WZED
TC-GTC	Airbus A.300B2-202	48	F-BUAO / F-ODRF / D-AIAD / F-WNDB
TC-HAA	Aérospatiale AS.355F2 Ecureuil 2	5362	
TC-HAB	Aérospatiale AS.355F2 Ecureuil 2	5363	
TC-HAC	Bell 206L-3 Long Ranger III	51598	N5130B / C-FOKJ
TC-HAF	Rotorway Executive	F73415	
TC-HAG	Mil Mi-8MTV-1	95588	
TC-HAK(2)	Mil Mi-8P	8027	TC-HER
TC-HAL	Mil Mi-8P	5966	UR-25583 / CCCP25583
TC-HAT(2)	Agusta A.109A	7191	D-HXXH / N605FM / N4210T / I-CVMO
TC-HBD	Enstrom F-28C	368	
TC-HBE	Bell 206B Jet Ranger III	3827	
TC-HBF	Agusta-Bell 206B Jet Ranger III	8702	
TC-HBH(2)	Bell 222UT	47525	C-FVVA / JA9962 / N8171P / VH-HIA
TC-HBK	Bell 206B Jet Ranger III	3950	
TC-HBL	Bell 206B Jet Ranger III	3948	
TC-HBM	Bell 206B Jet Ranger III	3083	N30DM / N5747V
TC-HBS	Hughes 369D	41-0943D	N1106U
TC-HBT	Bell 206B Jet Ranger II	2299	D-HKWF / (D-HAHH)
TC-HCA	Agusta A.109C	7632	N61453 / (N109AP) / N61453 / JA6611
TC-HCC	Bell 206B Jet Ranger II	4024	C-FCYG
TC-HCD	Aérospatiale SA.365N1 Dauphin 2	6303	F-WYMQ
TC-HCF	Aérospatiale SA.365N1 Dauphin 2	6302	F-WYMP
TC-HCG	Aérospatiale AS.355F2 Ecureuil 2	5354	F-WYML
TC-HCH	Aérospatiale AS.355F2 Ecureuil 2	5369	F-WYMN
TC-HCJ	Aérospatiale AS.355F2 Ecureuil 2	5357	F-WYMM
TC-HCK	Aérospatiale AS.365N2 Dauphin 2	6434	F-WYMN
TC-HCM(2)	Bell 430	49032	N5254W
TC-HDA	Mil Mi-8PS	8561	TC-HEM / UR-..... / CCCP .....
TC-HDB	Mil Mi-8MTV-1	95479	UR-25170 / CCCP25170
TC-HDC	Mil Mi-8	98730815	UR-24231 / CCCP24231
TC-HDD	Mil Mi-8MTV-1	95528	CCCP25418
TC-HDE	Mil Mi-8MTV-1	95529	CCCP25419
TC-HDF	Mil Mi-8MTV-1	95740	RA-25124 / CCCP25124
TC-HDG	Mil Mi-8MTV-1	95866	RA-27032 / CCCP27032
TC-HDH	Mil Mi-8MTV-1	95895	RA-27061 / CCCP27061
TC-HDK	Mil Mi-8PS	8562	CCCP .....
TC-HDO	Aérospatiale AS.365N2 Dauphin 2	6497	F-WWOF / F-WQDC(3)
TC-HEA	Bell 206B Jet Ranger III	4108	N7138Z
TC-HID	McDonnell-Douglas MD.520N	LN-066	N5209Z
TC-HIK	Agusta A.109A-II	7413	D-HAAY / JA9906
TC-HIS	Mil Mi-8MTV-1	95486	CCCP .....
TC-HIT	Robinson R-44 Astro	0057	G-INNS
TC-HKJ(2)	Aérospatiale SA.365 Dauphin 2 *(Reservation)*	unkn	
TC-HKN	Sikorsky S-76B	760339	N22QP / N22CP
TC-HKS	Robinson R-22 Beta	1233	G-OJAK
TC-HLK	Robinson R-22 Beta	1705	
TC-HLS	Bell 222U	47570	N35GH / N356H / JA9915 / N3208N
TC-HMC(2)	Hughes 369D	50-0696D	EI-BYV / G-ITUP / G-KSBF / G-BMJH
TC-HMD	Bell 430	49010	N62839
TC-HMH	Bell 222	47014	ZK-HFQ / N1072F
TC-HMS	Mil Mi-8	22400	
TC-HNA	Mil Mi-8	8702	RA-.....
TC-HNH(2)	Bell 430	49033	N8060J
TC-HNS	Bell 206B Jet Ranger II	1965	N922DR / N9522K
TC-HRM	Bell 430	49018	
TC-HSA	Mil Mi-8	24299	CCCP24299
TC-HTS	Bell 230	23021	N5292L
TC-HUS	Mil Mi-8	5806	EZ-25960 / CCCP25960
TC-HYS	Bell 206L-1 Long Ranger II	45296	N77AR / N71BH / N71BR
TC-HZA	Bell 230	23031	N54387
TC-HZH	Bell 230	23038	N23890
TC-IAC	Boeing 737-382	24450	CS-TIE
TC-IAF	Boeing 737-4Y0 *(Reservation)*	unkn	
TC-IAG	Boeing 737-43Q *(Reservation)*	unkn	
TC-IAH	Boeing 737-86N	28591	
TC-IHK	CCF/Beech T-34A Mentor	34-24	TAF: OK-21/ 54-5221 (RCAF24221)
TC-IHL	CCF/Beech T-34A Mentor	34-25	TAF: OK-22/ 54-5222 (RCAF24222)
TC-IHS	Lockheed L.1329 Jetstar 2	5225	N42KR / N990CH / N746UT / N4021M
TC-ILC	Piper PA-18A-150 Super Cub *(Rebuilt 1966 using spare fuselage 18-8620)*	18-4737	TC-IL3
TC-ILS	Cessna 172N	69863	N738CC
TC-IYA	Boeing 727-2F2	22999	TC-JCE
TC-IYB	Boeing 727-243	21664	TC-JCK / (N581PE) / I-DIRL
TC-IYC	Boeing 727-2F2	21260	TC-JBM
TC-JBF	Boeing 727-2F2	20980	
TC-JBG	Boeing 727-2F2	20981	
TC-JBJ	Boeing 727-2F2	20983	
TC-JCA	Boeing 727-2F2 Cargo	22992	
TC-JCD	Boeing 727-2F2 Cargo	22998	
TC-JCL	Airbus A.310-203	338	F-WZET
TC-JCM	Airbus A.310-203	375	F-WWBA

Regn.	Type	C/n	Prev.Id.
TC-JCN	Airbus A.310-203	379	F-WWBB
TC-JCO	Airbus A.310-203	386	F-WWBC
TC-JCR	Airbus A.310-203	370	F-WZLH
TC-JCS	Airbus A.310-203	389	F-WWBG
TC-JCU	Airbus A.310-203	390	F-WWBH
TC-JCV	Airbus A.310-304	476	F-WWCT
TC-JCY	Airbus A.310-304	478	F-WWCX
TC-JCZ	Airbus A.310-304	480	F-WWCZ
TC-JDA	Airbus A.310-304	496	F-WWCV
TC-JDB	Airbus A.310-304	497	F-WWCH
TC-JDC	Airbus A.310-304	537	F-WWCO
TC-JDD	Airbus A.310-304	586	F-WWCK
TC-JDE	Boeing 737-4Y0	24904	
TC-JDF	Boeing 737-4Y0	24917	
TC-JDG	Boeing 737-4Y0	25181	
TC-JDH	Boeing 737-4Y0	25184	
TC-JDI	Boeing 737-4Q8	25372	
TC-JDJ	Airbus A.340-311	023	F-WWJN
TC-JDK	Airbus A.340-311	025	F-WWJP
TC-JDL	Airbus A.340-311	057	F-WWJF
TC-JDM	Airbus A.340-311	115	F-WWJN
TC-JDN	Airbus A.340-313X	180	F-WWJU
TC-JDT	Boeing 737-4Y0	25261	
TC-JDU	Boeing 737-5Y0	25288	(EI-CFT)
TC-JDV	Boeing 737-5Y0	25289	(EI-CFU)
TC-JDY	Boeing 737-4Y0	26065	(EI-CFS)
TC-JDZ	Boeing 737-4Y0	26066	
TC-JEC	Boeing 727-228	22287	F-GCDF
TC-JEI	Boeing 737-4Q8	26298	
TC-JEJ	Boeing 737-4Q8	25375	
TC-JEK	Boeing 737-4Q8	26299	
TC-JEM	Boeing 737-4Q8	26302	
TC-JEN	Boeing 737-4Q8	25376	
TC-JEO	Boeing 737-4Q8	25377	
TC-JER	Boeing 737-4Y0	26073	
TC-JET	Boeing 737-4Y0	26077	
TC-JEU	Boeing 737-4Y0	26078	
TC-JEV	Boeing 737-4Y0	26085	
TC-JEY	Boeing 737-4Y0	26086	
TC-JEZ	Boeing 737-4Y0	26088	
TC-JFC	Boeing 737-8F2	29765	N1786B
TC-JFD	Boeing 737-8F2	29766	
TC-JFE	Boeing 737-8F2	29767	
TC-JFF	Boeing 737-8F2	29768	
TC-JFG	Boeing 737-8F2	29769	
TC-JFH	Boeing 737-8F2	29770	
TC-JFI	Boeing 737-8F2	29771	
TC-JFJ	Boeing 737-8F2	29772	
TC-JFK	Boeing 737-8F2	29773	N1786B
TC-JFL	Boeing 737-8F2	29774	
TC-JFM	Boeing 737-8F2	29775	
TC-JFN	Boeing 737-8F2	29776	
TC-JFO(2)	Boeing 737-8F2	29777	
TC-JFP	Boeing 737-8F2	29778	
TC-JFR	Boeing 737-8F2	29779	
TC-JFT	Boeing 737-8F2 (Reservation .99)	29780	N1787B
TC-JFU	Boeing 737-8F2 (Reservation .99)	29781	N1795B
TC-JFV	Boeing 737-8F2 (Reservation .00)	29782	
TC-JFY	Boeing 737-8F2 (Reservation .00)	29783	
TC-JFZ	Boeing 737-8F2 (Reservation .00)	29784	
TC-JGA	Boeing 737-8F2 (Reservation .00)	29785	
TC-JGB	Boeing 737-8F2 (Reservation .00)	29786	
TC-JGC	Boeing 737-8F2 (Reservation .00)	29787	
TC-JGD	Boeing 737-8F2 (Reservation .00)	29788	
TC-JGE	Boeing 737-8F2 (Reservation .00)	29789	
TC-JGF	Boeing 737-8F2 (Reservation .00)	29790	
TC-JGG	Boeing 737-8F2 (Reservation .00)	29791	
TC-JIH	Airbus A.340-311	270	F-WWJF
TC-JYK	Airbus A.310-203	172	F-GEMF
			F-WZLI
TC-KAR(2)	Antonov AN-24 (Wfu, stored)	47309603	RA-46671 ?
			CCCP46671 ?
TC-KBN	Delta Kanat	386	
TC-KET(2)	Antonov AN-12BP (Wfu, stored)	402808	RA-11366
			CCCP11366

Regn.	Type	C/n	Prev.Id.
TC-KEU	Cessna 208 Caravan	unkn	
TC-KOC(3)	Cessna 650 Citation III	7006	N966K
			(N706VP)
			N966K
			N966H
			(N1259Y)
TC-KON(2)	Cessna 650 Citation VII	7084	N1127G
			TC-KON(2)
			N5094D
TC-KPE	Piper PA-18-150 Super Cub	18-7558	N3819Z
TC-KPS	Piper PA-18-150 Super Cub	18-8538	
TC-KUR	Britten-Norman BN-2A-3 Islander	290	G-51-290
			(N20JL)
TC-LAA	Cessna 560 Citation V	0212	N1284X
TC-LAB	Cessna 560 Citation V	0216	N1285N
TC-LEY(2)	HFB-320 Hansa	1043	TC-KHE
			16+03
			D-CIRI
TC-LIM	Cessna 525 CitationJet	0226	N1216N
			N5214J
TC-LMK	Beech C90A King Air	LJ-1080	N6931W
TC-MAE	Dornier Do.27Q-5	2141	
TC-MAZ	Beech C90A King Air	LJ-1412	N3106Y
TC-MCK(2)	Beech C90 King Air	LJ-962	N1213P
			N18299
TC-MDB	Beech 400A Beechjet	RK-164	N2164Z
TC-MDC	Hawker 800XP	258384	N23455
TC-MDE	Beech B200 Super King Air	BB-1539	N1089S
TC-MDJ	Beech 400A Beechjet	RK-120	N3261Y
TC-MED	Mil Mi-2	5210126027	RA-23205
			CCCP23205
TC-MEK(3)	Bombardier Learjet 60	60-016	N50163
TC-MET	Cessna 560 Citation V	0497	N5161J
TC-MGM	Beech F33A Bonanza	CE-562	TC-MVK
			N4125S
TC-MHK	Cessna 152	84971	N5538P
TC-MIA	Cessna R.172K Hawk XP	2818	N736VH
TC-MNA	Airbus A.300C4-203F	019	N742SC
			F-BVGG
TC-MNG	Airbus A.300C4-203F	083	EI-BZB
			RP-C3007
			EI-BZB
			D-AHLB
			F-WZES
TC-MSA	Beech 400A Beechjet	RK-124	N1124Z
TC-MSB(2)	Beech 400A Beechjet	RK-170	TC-MCX
			N2289B
TC-MSO	Boeing 737-8S3	29246	
TC-MSS	Beech C90A King Air	LJ-1276	N8065R
TC-MST	Cessna 310Q	0065	D-ILFS
			OY-AKS
			(N7565Q)
TC-MTR	Cessna 182R Skylane II	67968	G-BKKP
			N9600H
TC-MZZ	Boeing 737-8S3	29247	N1786B
TC-NAG	Callair B-1A	10021	N7274V
			N29A
TC-NAK	Rockwell A-9B Quail Commander	1450	
TC-NEO	Beech 400A Beechjet	RK-130	N1130B
TC-NMC	Cessna S550 Citation II	0072	N686MC
	(Reserved as N62NS, 2.00)		N186MT
			N1273A
			(N572CC)
			(N1273A)
TC-NSK	Cessna R.172K Hawk XP	2790	N736UC
TC-NUR	Cessna 172N	69384	N737FM
TC-OKN	BAe.125 Series 800XP	258388	N23488
TC-OMR(2)	Lockheed L.1329 Jetstar 731	5082/36	N82SR
			N917J
			N320S
TC-ONJ	Airbus A.321-131	385	D-AVZG
			F-WWIB

Regn.	Type	C/n	Prev.Id.
TC-ONK	Airbus A.300B4-103	086	TC-TKA, N14980, (N980C), N209EA, F-GBNE
TC-ONL	Airbus A.300B4-103	087	TC-TKB, N29981, (N981C), N210EA, F-GBNF
TC-ONM	McDonnell-Douglas DC-9-88	53546	
TC-ONN	McDonnell-Douglas DC-9 88	53547	
TC-ONO	McDonnell-Douglas DC-9 88	53548	
TC-ONP	McDonnell-Douglas DC-9 88	53549	
TC-ONR	McDonnell-Douglas DC-9-88	53550	
TC-ONS	Airbus A.321-131	364	D-AVZD
TC-ONV	Airbus A.300B4-2C	057	F-BUAQ, D-AIBB, F-WZEG, (D-AIAF)
TC-OZD	Beech B200 Super King Air	BB-1496	N3047L
TC-OZY	Beech B200 Super King Air	BB-1545	N1070E
TC-ROT	Cessna 560 Citation V	0454	N1216Z
TC-RTO	Mooney M.20J Model 205	24-3311	N1081W
TC-SAN(2)	Canadair CL.601-3A Challenger	5114	VP-BOA, VR-BOA, C-FOSK, C-GLYA
TC-SAT	Piper PA-18-135 Super Cub *(Officially quoted with f/n 18-395)*	18-413	TC-EAS, Turkish AF 50-1757
TC-SER	Piper PA-34-200T Seneca II	34-7970340	F-GCJJ, OO-HLK, N2908U
TC-SES(2)	Cessna 550 Citation II	0717	N600GH, XA-TCM, (N1205M)
TC-SGD(2)	Piper PA-18-135 Super Cub *(Officially quoted with f/n 18-2440)*	18-2597	Turkish AF 52-6279
TC-SHK	Piper PA-18-150 Super Cub *(Officially quoted with f/n 18-3011)*	18-3074	Turkish AF 53-4674
TC-SIS	Cessna 650 Citation III	0077	TC-EES, VR-BGB, N701AG, N677CC, (N1315Y)
TC-SKO	Beech B200 Super King Air	BB-1334	N5545B
TC-SKY	Piper PA-18-150 Super Cub *(Officially quoted with f/n 18-5506)*	18-4055	Turkish AF 54-2655
TC-SMA	Grumman G.159 Gulfstream 1	172	N172ED, N11Y, N44MC, N700DB
TC-SMB	Beech 400A Beechjet	RK-148	N1108T
TC-SMN	Piper PA-18-150 Super Cub *(Officially quoted with f/n 18-5501)*	18-4054	Turkish AF 54-2654
TC-SMS	Beech A36 Bonanza	E-2731	N80287
TC-SUA	Boeing 737-86N *(Reservation .99)*	28612	N1786B
TC-SUB	Boeing 737-86N *(Reservation .00)*	28614	N1786B
TC-SUC	Boeing 737-86N *(Reservation .00)*	28616	N1786B
TC-SUD	Boeing 737-86N *(Reservation .00)*	28620	
TC-SUP	Boeing 737-3Y0	24908	
TC-SUR	Boeing 737-3Y0	24910	
TC-SUS	Boeing 737-430	27007	D-ABKL
TC-SUT	Boeing 737-4Y0	25190	OY-MBL, EC-FMJ, EC-991
TC-TAC	HOAC DV-20 Katana	unkn	
TC-TAD	HOAC DV-20 Katana	unkn	
TC-TAE	HOAC DV-20 Katana	unkn	
TC-TAF	HOAC DV-20 Katana	unkn	
TC-TAY(2)	Piper PA-28-236 Dakota	2811032	
TC-TBA	Cessna 210M Centurion	62303	N761JX
TC-TEK(3)	BAe.125 Series 800A	258229	N229RY, PT-OTH
			N683BA, G-5-748
TC-THA	Avro 146-RJ100	E-3232	G-6-232
TC-THB	Avro 146-RJ100	E-3234	G-6-234
TC-THC	Avro 146-RJ100	E-3236	G-6-236
TC-THD	Avro 146-RJ100	E-3237	G-6-237
TC-THE	Avro 146-RJ100	E-3238	G-6-238
TC-THG	Avro 146-RJ100	E-3241	G-6-241
TC-THH	Avro 146-RJ100	E-3243	G-6-243
TC-THI	Avro 146-RJ70	E-1229	G-BUFI
TC-THJ	Avro 146-RJ70	E-1230	G-6-230, (N835BE)
TC-THK	Piper PA-42 Cheyenne III	42-5501031	TC-FAG
TC-THL	Avro 146-RJ70	E-1249	G-6-249
TC-THM	Avro 146-RJ100	E-3264	G-6-264, (N836BE)
TC-THN	Avro 146-RJ70	E-1252	G-6-252, (N837BE)
TC-THO	Avro 146-RJ100	E-3265	G-6-265
TC-TIP	Mil Mi-2	5210624058	RA-14080, CCCP14080
TC-TKG	Pilatus Britten-Norman BN-2T Turbine Islander	2231	G-BSAD
TC-TLS	Beech 60 Duke	P-117	YU-BGF, HB-GDX
TC-TMT	Airbus A.310-304	418	F-OGQN, F-GHUC, (F-OGQN), C-FSWD, F-WWCL
TC-TOM	Piper PA-38-112 Tomahawk	38-78A0683	N2427A
TC-TON(2)	Beech 1900D	UE-294	N21334
TC-TOP	Cessna 650 Citation III	0083	N944CA, N944H, N13166
TC-TOR	Antonov AN-24 *(Wfu, stored)*	67310507	
TC-TRI	Dornier Do.28D Skyservant	4003	Turkish Army, D-IBYL
TC-TRK	Dornier Do.28D Skyservant	4002	Turkish Army, D-IBYK
TC-TRL	Dornier Do.28D-2 Skyservant	4119	T.Army:10024, 58+44
TC-TRM	Dornier Do.28D-2 Skyservant	4122	T.Army:10031, 58+47
TC-TRO	Dornier Do.28D-2 Skyservant	4035	Turkish Army, D-IEMB
TC-TRP	Thorp T.211	007	N89DB
TC-UPS	Fairchild-Swearingen SA.226AT Merlin IV	AT-044	TC-BPS, C-GGPT, N544F, N5441F
TC-VIN	Beech 400A Beechjet	RK-188	N2298W
TC-VOR	Cessna 172N	69704	N737VG, (D-EUSW), N737VG
TC-YBB	Grumman AA-5B Tiger *(See TC-YSF)*	0654	N28613
TC-YBD	Grumman AA-5B Tiger	0632	N80JL, N28609
TC-YBE	Grumman AA-5B Tiger	1288	N4537L
TC-YPI	Beech 200 Super King Air	BB-883	N883BB
TC-YRT	Beech 400A Beechjet	RK-190	N2290F
TC-YSB	Piper PA-18 Super Cub 95	"10-10371"	TC-...
TC-YSF	Grumman AA-5B Tiger *(C/n quoted is same as TC-YBB, error or re-regd?)*	0654	N28613
TC-YSR	Dassault Falcon 50	246	N246FJ, F-WWHF
TC-YYB	Piper PA-18 Super Cub 95	18-449	TC-EAR, 50-1793
TC-ZAA	PZL M-18A Dromader	1Z015-28	
TC-ZAB	PZL M-18A Dromader	1Z015-29	
TC-ZAF	PZL M-18A Dromader	1Z017-08	
TC-ZAG	Antonov AN-2R	1G230-23	SP-ZZG
TC-ZAH	Antonov AN-2R	1G230-24	SP-ZZH
TC-ZAJ	Antonov AN-2R	1G230-25	SP-ZZI
TC-ZAK	Antonov AN-2R	1G230-26	SP-ZZK
TC-ZAN	PZL M-18A Dromader	1Z020-18	SP-DBT

Regn.	Type	C/n	Prev.Id.
TC-ZAP	PZL M-18A Dromader	1Z020-19	SP-DBU
TC-ZAR	PZL M-18B Dromader	1Z025-27	SP-DDR
TC-ZAT	PZL M-18B Dromader	1Z025-29	SP-DDT
TC-ZAU	PZL M-18B Dromader	1Z025-30	SP-DDU
TC-ZAV	PZL M-18B Dromader	1Z026-11	SP-DEK
TC-ZAY	PZL M-18B Dromader	1Z026-12	SP-DEL
TC-ZBC	Norman NAC-6 Fieldmaster 34	6002	G-NACM
TC-ZBD	Norman NAC-6 Firemaster 65	6003	G-NACN
			Z-NACN
			G-NACN
TC-ZKE	Ayres S.2R-T34 Turbo Thrush	2449R	N8941Q
TC-ZPD	Piper PA-25-235 Pawnee C	25-4250	N4664Y
TC-ZPE	Piper PA-25-235 Pawnee C	25-4257	N4666Y
TC-ZPH	Piper PA-25-235 Pawnee C	25-4319	N4638Y
TC-ZPK	Piper PA-25-260 Pawnee C	25-4658	N4945Y
TC-ZPL	Piper PA-25-260 Pawnee C	25-4638	N4948Y
TC-ZPM	Piper PA-25-260 Pawnee C	25-4513	N4755Y
TC-ZPP	Piper PA-25-260 Pawnee C	25-4420	N4689Y
TC-ZPV	Piper PA-25-235 Pawnee C	25-4876	N4373Y
TC-ZPY	Piper PA-25-235 Pawnee C	25-4882	N4380Y
TC-ZRC	Piper PA-25-260 Pawnee C	25-4812	N4355Y
TC-ZRD	Piper PA-25-260 Pawnee C	25-4963	N8542L
TC-ZRH	Piper PA-25-260 Pawnee C	25-4942	N4380Y
TC-ZRR	Piper PA-25-260 Pawnee C	25-5045	N8616L
TC-ZRV	Piper PA-25-235 Pawnee C	25-5146	N8694L
TC-ZSA	Piper PA-25-260 Pawnee C	25-5193	N8751L
TC-ZSB	Piper PA-25-235 Pawnee C	25-5085	N8646L
TC-ZSC	Piper PA-25-260 Pawnee C	25-5322	N8817L
TC-ZSF	Cessna A.188B Agwagon	00929	N21643
TC-ZSJ	Cessna A.188B Agwagon	00959	TC-ZTI
			TC-ZSJ
			N21668
TC-ZSK	Cessna A.188B Agwagon	00961	N21690
TC-ZSL	Cessna A.188B Agwagon	00966	N21699
TC-ZSM	Cessna A.188B Agwagon	00857	N4457Q
TC-ZSP	Piper PA-25-260 Pawnee C	25-5437	N8743L
TC-ZSR	Piper PA-25-260 Pawnee C	25-5438	N8744L
TC-ZSV	Piper PA-25-260 Pawnee C	25-5435	N8712L
TC-ZSZ	Piper PA-25-260 Pawnee C	25-5443	N8746L
TC-ZTA	Rockwell S.2R Thrush Commander	1660R	
TC-ZTD	Cessna A.188B Agtruck	01126T	N5637G
TC-ZTE	Cessna A.188B Agwagon	01141	
TC-ZTG	Cessna A.188B Agwagon	01146	N5755G
TC-ZTH	Cessna A.188B Agtruck	01151T	N5838G
TC-ZTK	Cessna A.188B Agwagon	01104	N1697C
			N21893
TC-ZTL	Cessna A.188B Agwagon	01160	N5886G
TC-ZTN	Cessna A.188B Agtruck	01250T	N1668C
TC-ZTP	Cessna 402B	0412	N69289
TC-ZTS	Ayres S.2R-T34 Turbo Thrush	1717R	TC-TZS
			TC-ZTS
			N5517X
TC-ZTT	Piper PA-36-285 Pawnee Brave	36-7360012	N55858
TC-ZUA	Piper PA-36-285 Pawnee Brave	36-7360008	N55350
TC-ZUB	Piper PA-36-285 Pawnee Brave	36-7360006	N15690
TC-ZUC	Grumman G.164A Agcat	1067	N4760
TC-ZUD	Grumman G.164A Agcat	1024	N5411
TC-ZUF	Rockwell S.2R Thrush Commander	1685R	N5585X
TC-ZUG	Piper PA-36-285 Pawnee Brave	36-7360024	N9526N
TC-ZUH	Piper PA-36-285 Pawnee Brave	36-7360026	N9527N
TC-ZUJ	Piper PA-36-285 Pawnee Brave	36-7360030	N9532N
TC-ZUK	Piper PA-36-285 Pawnee Brave	36-7360034	N9533N
TC-ZUN	Piper PA-25-235 Pawnee D	25-7405566	N6833L
TC-ZUP	Piper PA-25-235 Pawnee D	25-7405567	N6834L
TC-ZUR	Piper PA-25-260 Pawnee D	25-7405568	N6832L
TC-ZUS	Piper PA-36-285 Pawnee Brave	36-7360064	N56643
TC-ZUT	Piper PA-25-235 Pawnee D	25-7405562	N6830L
TC-ZUU	Piper PA-36-285 Pawnee Brave	36-7360042	N56369
TC-ZUY	Rockwell S.2R Thrush Commander	2001R	N4233X
TC-ZVA	Rockwell S.2R Thrush Commander	1899R	N4898X
TC-ZVE	Piper PA-25-235 Pawnee D	25-7556131	N9832P
TC-ZVG	Piper PA-25-235 Pawnee D	25-7556124	N9825P
TC-ZVH	Bellanca 8GCBC Scout	106-74	OE-AOW
TC-ZVJ	Cessna 402B	1073	N1552G
TC-ZVK	Piper PA-25-260 Pawnee D	25-7405612	N9527P

Regn.	Type	C/n	Prev.Id.
TC-ZVL	Piper PA-25-260 Pawnee D	25-7656118	N82402
TC-ZVM	Piper PA-25-235 Pawnee D	25-7756006	N82430
TC-ZVR	Ayres S.2R Thrush Commander	2487R	
TC-ZVT	Ayres S.2R Thrush Commander	2495R	
TC-ZVU	Piper PA-25-235 Pawnee D	25-7756008	N82437
TC-ZVV	Piper PA-25-235 Pawnee D	25-7756007	N82432
TC-ZVY	Piper PA-25-235 Pawnee D	25-7756031	N82488
TC-ZVZ	Piper PA-25-260 Pawnee D	25-7656061	N82306
TC-ZYA	Piper PA-25-260 Pawnee D	25-7656071	N82307
TC-ZYC	Piper PA-25-235 Pawnee D	25-7856017	N9165T
TC-ZYE	Piper PA-25-235 Pawnee D	25-7756028	N82461
TC-ZYF	Antonov AN-2R	1G185-58/1	SP-DMA
TC-ZYG	Antonov AN-2R	1G185-59	TC-ZIG ?
			TC-ZYG
			SP-DMB
TC-ZYH	Antonov AN-2R	1G191-01	(YV-382A)
			SP-DBA
TC-ZYI	Antonov AN-2R	1G191-02	(YV-384A)
			SP-DBB
TC-ZYJ	PZL M-18 Dromader	1Z006-07	SP-DAA
TC-ZYN	Cessna A.188B Agtruck	03910T	(N9981J)
TC-ZYP	Cessna A.188B Agtruck	03864T	(N9925J)
TC-ZYR	Cessna A.188B Agtruck	03890T	(N9961J)
TC-ZYS	Antonov AN-2-35	1G206-35	SP-ZYS
TC-ZYT	Antonov AN-2T	1G208-03	SP-ZYT
TC-ZYU	Antonov AN-2T	1G208-04	SP-ZYU
TC-ZYV	Antonov AN-2R	1G208-01	SP-ZYV
TC-ZYY	Antonov AN-2R	1G208-02	SP-ZYY
TC-ZYZ	Antonov AN-2R	1G199-04	SP-ZYZ
TC-...	Ayres S.2R-600 Thrush Commander	2502R	N40055
TC-...	Beech 400A Beechjet	RK-211	N3028U
	(Believed to TC-NNK, unconfirmed)		
TC-H...	Bell 206L-3 Long Ranger III	51547	D-HMKB(2)
			F-GHYO
			C-FMEI
TC-H ...	Bell 222U	47572	N32GH
			(N326H)
			JA9935
			N3209D
TC-H ..	Bell 230	23036	N67354
TC-H ..	Bell 407	53085	
TC-H ..	Bell 407	53263	N407BE
TC-H ..	Bell 430	49043	N8151Y
TC-...	Cessna 150M	78330	N9381U
TC-...	Cessna 152	81589	N65499
TC-...	Cessna 152	81854	N67475
TC-...	Cessna 152	85300	N67513
TC-...	Cessna 152	85384	D-ECCF(3)
			N93045
TC-...	Cessna 172G	54812	N1317F
TC-...	Cessna 172M	64020	N21790
TC-...	Cessna 172R	80287	N9524P
TC-...	Cessna 172R	80368	N9505V
TC-...	Cessna R.172K Hawk XP	2577	N736KA
TC-...	Cessna 182A Skylane	51400	N2100G
TC-...	Cessna 182S	80110	N9506W
TC-...	Cessna A.188B Agwagon	00998	N21744
TC-...	Cessna A.188B Agtruck	01755T	N53314
TC-...	Cessna A.188B Agwagon	01984	N84470
TC-...	Cessna A.188B Agtruck	02137T	N9169R
TC-...	Cessna A.188B Agtruck	02789T	N731CK
TC-...	Cessna A.188B Agtruck	03017T	N731ND
TC-...	Cessna A.188BAgtruck	03027T	N731NP
TC-...	Cessna 207A Stationair 8	00658	D-EDDJ(2)
			N75954
TC-...	Cessna 421	0109	YU-BEJ
			N3128K
TC-...	Fisher FP.404 Super Koala	SK002	N200SK
TC-...	Grumman G.164A Agcat	1033	N5418
TC-...	Grumman G.164A Agcat	534	N5254
TC-...	Grumman G.164B Agcat	665B	N8367K
TC-H ..	Hughes 369HS	54-0595S	N9191F

Regn.	Type	C/n	Prev.Id.
TC-...	Maule M-5-235C Lunar Rocket	7329C	D-EJYY
			N5639Y
			N30MD
			N5639Y
TC-...	Maule M-7-235 Super Rocket	4121C	N360FS
TC-...	Piper PA-25-260 Pawnee C	25-4678	N4875Y
TC-...	Piper PA-25-260 Pawnee D	25-7556205	N9895P
TC-...	Piper PA-28-140 Cherokee	28-7425044	N56818
TC-...	Piper PA-28R-200 Cherokee Arrow II	28R-7335006	D-EJES(3)
			HB-OIY
			N15056
TC-...	Piper PA-36-300 Pawnee Brave	36-7760068	N59657
TC-...	Rockwell S.2R Thrush Commander	1913R	N4062X
TC-...	Rockwell S.2R Thrush Commander	2341R	N8854Q
TC-...	Rockwell S.2R Thrush Commander	2392R	N5691X
TC-H..	Rotorway Executive 90	5075	G-BUIS
TC-H..	Schweizer 269C	S-1291	
TC-H..	Schweizer 269C	S-1292	
TC-H..	Sikorsky S-70A	70-1882	N50056
TC-...	SOCATA TB-10 Tobago	1307	N5555N
TC-...	SOCATA TB-20 Trinidad	1712	F-OHIT
TC-...	SOCATA TB-20 Trinidad	1713	F-OHIU
TC-...	SOCATA TB-20 Trinidad	1714	F-OHIV
TC-...	SOCATA TB-9 Tampico	1851	F-OIDP
TC-...	SOCATA TB-9 Tampico	1852	F-OIDQ
TC-...	SOCATA TB-9 Tampico	1853	F-OIDR

Regn.	Type	C/n	Prev.Id.
TC-PEA	SZD-50-3 Puchacz	B-971	
TC-PEF	SZD-50-3 Puchacz	B-974	
TC-PEG	SZD-50-3 Puchacz	B-977	
TC-PEH	SZD-50-3 Puchacz	B-978	
TC-PEI	SZD-50-3 Puchacz	B-979	
TC-PEJ	SZD-50-3 Puchacz	B-1398	
TC-PEK	SZD-50-3 Puchacz	B-1399	
TC-PEL	ICA Brasov IS.29D2	185	
TC-PEM	ICA Brasov IS.29D2	186	
TC-PEN	ICA Brasov IS.29D2	187	
TC-PEP	ICA Brasov IS.29D2	191	
TC-PER(2)	SZD-50-3 Puchacz	B-1466	
TC-PET	SZD-50-3 Puchacz	B-1467	
TC-PFA	SZD-50-3 Puchacz	B-1727	
TC-PFB	SZD-50-3 Puchacz	B-1726	
TC-PFC	SZD-50-3 Puchacz	B-1733	
TC-PFD	SZD-50-3 Puchacz	B-1735	
TC-PFE	SZD-50-3 Puchacz	B-1869	
TC-PFF	SZD-50-3 Puchacz	B-1870	
TC-PFG	PZL PW-5 Smyk	17.08.008	
TC-PFH	PZL PW-5 Smyk	17.08.009	
TC-PFM	Schempp-Hirth Discus b	276	
TC-PFN	Schempp-Hirth Discus b	277	
TC-PFP	Schempp-Hirth Ventus c	428	
TC-PFR	Schempp-Hirth Ventus c	429	

BALLOONS AND AIRSHIPS

Regn.	Type	C/n	Prev.Id.
TC-AVK	American Blimp Corporation A150	3	N153LG
TC-BAA	Cameron V-77 HAFB	935	
TC-BAB	Raven S-55A HAFB	1026	
TC-BAC(2)	Colt 69A HAFB	528	
TC-BAD	Cameron V-77 HAFB	2078	
TC-BAE	Colt 105A HAFB	1267	
TC-BAL	Cameron N-77 HAFB	2384	
TC-BAT	Cameron V-90 HAFB	3677	
TC-BBP	Cameron O-120 HAFB	3678	
TC-BDG	Cameron N-105 HAFB	3017	
TC-BIK	Cameron V-77 HAFB	3676	
TC-BIS	Colt 105A HAFB (Reservation)	4644	
TC-BRO	Colt 105A HAFB	1898	
TC-BRP	Colt 240A HAFB	2121	
TC-B..	Colt 300A HAFB	2096	G-RAVI
TC-B..	Head AX7-77B HAFB	250	N8303F

GLIDERS

Regn.	Type	C/n	Prev.Id.
TC-PCU	SZD-22C Mucha Standard	F-755	
TC-PCV	SZD-22C Mucha Standard	F-601	
TC-PCY	SZD-10bis Czapla	W-134	
TC-PCZ	SZD-10bis Czapla	W-135	
TC-PDA	SZD-9bis Bocian 1D	P-398	
TC-PDD	SZD-10bis Czapla	W-131	
TC-PDI	Scheibe Bergfalke II/55	5823	
TC-PDJ	Scheibe Bergfalke II/55	5824	
TC-PDK	Sportavia-Pützer RF-5BSperber	51049	D-KATM(1)
TC-PDL	Sportavia-Pützer RF-5BSperber	51052	D-KILO
TC-PDO	SZD-48-1 Jantar Standard 2	B-1154	
TC-PDP	SZD-48-1 Jantar Standard 2	B-1156	
TC-PDR	SZD-48-1 Jantar Standard 2	B-1167	
TC-PDS	SZD-48-1 Jantar Standard 2	B-1073	
TC-PDT	SZD-48-1 Jantar Standard 2	B-1180	
TC-PDU	SZD 48-1 Jantar Standard 2	B-1181	
TC-PDV	SZD-48-1 Jantar Standard 2	B-1125	
TC-PDY	SZD-42-2 Jantar 2B	B-1126	
TC-PDZ	SZD-50-3 Puchacz	B-967	

MICROLIGHTS

Regn.	Type	C/n	Prev.Id.
TC-UAB	Phantom MCHU Microlight	2071	
TC-UAC	Type unknown (Phantom?)	2010	
TC-UAD	Comco Ikarus Fox II	8604-1118	
TC-UAF	Comco Ikarus Fox II	8601-1114	
TC-UAH	Type unknown (Phantom?)	2003	
TC-UAI	Type unknown (Phantom?)	2022	
TC-UAJ	Type unknown (Phantom?)	2017	
TC-UAK	Rotec Panther 2 Plus	3563247	
TC-UAL	Rotec Panther 2 Plus	unkn	
TC-UAM	Rotec Panther 2 Plus	unkn	
TC-UAN	Rotec Panther 2 Plus	2538676	
TC-UAP	Type unknown	unkn	
TC-UAR	Type unknown (Phantom?)	2019 ?	
TC-UAS	Type unknown (Phantom?)	2019 ?	
TC-UAT	Comco Ikarus Fox II	8604-1121	
TC-UAU	Comco Ikarus Fox II	8604-1117	
TC-UAY	Type unknown	11110	
TC-UCA	SMAN Pétrel UL	034	
TC-UCB	Air Command 532	unkn	
TC-UFO	Type unknown	431	
TC-UYK	YUKA Ultralight	1	
TC-U..	Solar Wings Pegasus XL-Q	SW-WQ-0038/SW-TE-0048	G-MTYNB

TF - ICELAND

Regn.	Type	C/n	Prev.Id.
TF-ABA	Boeing 747-267B	22530	B-HID VR-HID
TF-ABB	Cessna 172N	69176	TF-USA(3) N734WQ
TF-ABC(2)	Zlin Z.326 Trenér Master	908	
TF-ABE(2)	Lockheed L-1011-385-1 Tristar *(Wfu, stored Marana 1.00)*	1022	VR-HOA N314EA
TF-ABF(2)	Boeing 737-230C	20258	D-ABHE
TF-ABG(3)	Boeing 747-128 *(Scrapped, Marana .99)*	20377	F-BPVG
TF-ABI(2)	Boeing 747-246B *(Scrapped, Marana .99)*	20924	N550SW JA8122
TF-ABJ(3)	Groves Pitts S-1J Special	02	C-GSMP
TF-ABM(2)	Lockheed L-1011-385-1 Tristar	1072	SE-DPP (SE-DPN) N41020
TF-ABP(2)	Boeing 747-267B	22429	B-HIC VR-HIC
TF-ABQ(2)	Boeing 747-246B	20529	N554SW JA8113
TF-ABR	Boeing 747-133 *(Wfu and broken up, Marana .99)*	20014	N874UM (C-GLUS) N874UM TF-ABR C-FTOB N621FE C-FTOB EI-BRR EC-DXE C-FTOB CF-TOB
TF-ABT(2)	Lockheed L-1011-385-1 Tristar	1231	N7035T SE-DPR N7035T
TF-ABU(2)	Lockheed L-1011-385-1 Tristar	1051	VR-HHY N325EA
TF-ABX	Boeing 737-230C	20257	D-ABGE
TF-AFI	Piper PA-18A-150 Super Cub	18-6968	TF-KAZ
TF-AGN(2)	Light Aero Avid Flyer	240	
TF-AIB	Cessna 140	13825	N1653V (NC1653V)
TF-AKK	Piper PA-12 Super Cruiser	12-3340	N4400M NC4400M
TF-ALK	Piper PA-18 Super Cub 105 *(Also quoted with f/n 18-419)*	18-468	OY-ALK D-EGLG (D-EHFV) Greek AF 50-1812
TF-ALP	Piper PA-12 Super Cruiser	12-2223	D-EJEZ N3374M NC3374M
TF-APE	Denney Kitfox	197	
TF-API	Cessna 152	80923	N48637
TF-ARC	Alon A-2 Aircoupe	A-164	N5664F
TF-AST	Cessna 140	9359	TF-JET N72186 (NC72186)
TF-ATA	Boeing 747-230B	20527	N78019 G-BJXN (C-....) G-BJXN N611BN D-ABYG
TF-ATB	Boeing 747-246B	19824	N558SW JA8105
TF-ATC	Boeing 747-267B	22149	B-HIB VR-HIB
TF-ATD	Boeing 747-267B	21966	B-HIA VR-HIA
TF-ATE	Boeing 747-146A	20531	N557SW JA8115
TF-ATF	Boeing 747-246B	19825	N556SW (TF-...) N556SW JA8106
TF-ATH	Boeing 747-341	24106	PP-VOA N6046P
TF-ATI	Boeing 747-341	24107	PP-VOB N6018N
TF-ATJ	Boeing 747-341	24108	PP-VOC N6005C
TF-AVA(2)	Cessna 152-II	81871	TF-KGL N67501
TF-AZX(2)	Stinson SR-7B *(Preserved, not airworthy)*	9685	N16123 NC16123
TF-BAA	Piper PA-23-150 Apache	23-606	N2031P
TF-BAB	Cessna 140A	15720	N1157D
TF-BEB	Beech 77 Skipper	WA-237	TF-BED OY-BEV N3833R
TF-BEH	Beech K35 Bonanza	D-5817	N5344E
TF-BEZ	Beech 77 Skipper	WA-238	OY-BEZ N3833U
TF-BGH	Piper PA-22-160 Tri-Pacer	22-6306	N9246D
TF-BKB	Cessna 177 Cardinal	01163	OY-AHU N30268
TF-BKG	Piper PA-28-235 Cherokee	28-10291	N8751W
TF-BMC	Beech C23 Sundowner	M-1083	N6937Q
TF-BMW	Partenavia P.68 Observer	389-02-OB2	N8082Y I-DOLF
TF-BMX	Cessna 337G Super Skymaster	01701	N53559
TF-BOJ	Cessna 152	79935	TF-FTK N757RC
TF-BOR	Piper PA-22-160 Tri-Pacer	22-6578	N9662D
TF-BOY	Piper PA-28-161 Cherokee Warrior II	28-7816404	N6282C
TF-BRO	SOCATA TB-9 Tampico	263	OY-CDA LN-KLL
TF-BTH	Pitts S-2S Special	BTH-1	
TF-BUY	Cessna 172M	61621	N92801
TF-CCB	Yakovlev YAK-55	870309	HA-JAI DOSAAF-177 DOSAAF-22
TF-CUB(2)	Piper J-3C-65 Cub (L-4H)	10606	TF-JMF(1) N51550 43-29315
TF-CUP	Piper J-3C-65 Cub *(Officially quoted as c/n 12990 but f/n is 11663 which results in c/n above)*	11837	TF-GEV G-BCYS F-BFYH HB-ZAH 43-30546
TF-DAB	Piper PA-16 Clipper	16-238	(TF-DUF) (TF-SPO) N5627H
TF-DGA(2)	Cessna 182P Skylane	63610	N6033J
TF-DGB	Cessna 150F	63171	N6571F
TF-DHC	DHC-1 Chipmunk 22	C1/0744	OY-AVI RDAF: P-137 RDAF: 12-137
TF-DOV(2)	Dornier Do.28B-1	3091	TF-CWE SE-CWP
TF-DUA	Cessna 172C	48915	TF-DGA(1) N8415X
TF-DUF	Piper PA-16 Clipper *(Reservation)*	16-238	(TF-SPO) N5627H
TF-DUK	CEA DR.220	5	TF-LAK G-BLAK F-BNVH
TF-DUO	Cessna 152	82146	N68143
TF-DYR	Piper J-3C-65 Cub	14578	TF-JMA(1) N42328
TF-EFF(2)	Cessna 150M	75896	TF-FTC N66176
TF-EGD	Piper PA-38-112 Tomahawk	38-79A0059	N2433B
TF-EGO	SOCATA TB-20 Trinidad	1463	
TF-EGU	Piper PA-31-350 Navajo Chieftain	31-7952033	N27895

Regn.	Type	C/n	Prev.Id.
TF-EHA	Erco 415C Ercoupe	2105	N99482
			(NC99482)
TF-EJG	Cessna R.172K Hawk XP	3035	N758EK
TF-ELA	Dornier 228-202K	8156	TC-FBN
			D-CORN(2)
TF-ELF	Dornier 228-201	8046	LN-NVC
			D-IDBN
TF-ELH	Dornier 228-201	8070	SE-KVV
			TF-ELH
			SE-KVV
			LN-NVG
			D-CLIC
TF-ELI	Beech 200 Super King Air	BB-468	TF-ELT(4)
			N204KA
			N2KH
			N6056T
TF-ELJ	Aeritalia/SNIAS ATR-42-300	118	C-FIQN
			F-WWEO
TF-ELK	Aeritalia/SNIAS ATR-42-300	059	F-OGNS
TF-ELL(2)	Boeing 737-210C	20138	N41026
			F-GGFI
			N4906
TF-ELM	Boeing 737-2M8	21736	F-GLXG
			G-IBTX
			G-BTEB
			OO-TEL
			TC-ATU
			OO-TEL
			PH-RAL
			OO-TEL
			4X-ABL
			OO-TEL
TF-ELN	Boeing 737-3Q8	23766	OO-ILK
			VH-NJE
			N101GU
			N188LF
			EC-EHM
			EC-153
			N315SC
			G-BNCT
			N1716B
TF-ELT(6)	Beech E90 King Air	LW-116	F-BVRS
TF-ELX	Cessna A.185F	03214	N93296
TF-EMM	Cessna 150K	71523	N6023G
TF-EOS	Piper PA-28-151 Cherokee Warrior	28-7715027	N4377F
TF-ESI	Cessna 150M	77405	(SE-KPG)
			TF-ESI
			N63576
TF-ETT	Piper PA-23-250 Aztec D	27-4445	N13797
TF-EXP	Cessna R.172K Hawk XP	2189	N1426V
TF-FAR	Aero Commander 100	243	(TF-AFI)
			TF-JEG(1)
TF-FBA	Piper PA-28R-200 Cherokee Arrow	28R-35666	TF-FHA
			SE-FPA
			N3097R
TF-FBI	Cessna R.172K Hawk XP	2664	N736NT
TF-FET	Piper PA-28-180 Cherokee Challenger	28-7305182	N15907
TF-FFB	Beech 77 Skipper	WA-83	N6720Z
TF-FFC	Beech 77 Skipper	WA-10	C-GJPL
TF-FFD(2)	Cessna 172N	70582	TF-FTS(1)
			N739JP
TF-FFE	Beech 77 Skipper	WA-50	C-GTJR
TF-FFH(3)	Piper PA-28R-201T Turbo Arrow III	28R-7803202	N3929M
TF-FFL	Cessna 172N	72816	N6465D
TF-FFU	Cessna 172N	68799	TF-FFH(2)
			TF-UPP
			N734DS
TF-FHB	Cessna 150G	63872	N4822X
TF-FHE(2)	Cessna 152-II	83998	TF-BMW
			N4887H
TF-FHI (2)	Cessna 152-II	83911	N6443B
TF-FHR	Cessna R.172K Hawk XP	2054	TF-SJS
			N7317K
TF-FIA(3)	Boeing 737-408	24352	
TF-FIB	Boeing 737-408	24353	

Regn.	Type	C/n	Prev.Id.
TF-FID(2)	Boeing 737-408	25063	
TF-FIE(2)	Boeing 737-3S3F	23811	D-ABWS
			N841LF
			G-DIAR
			G-BNPA
			C-FGHQ
			G-BNPA
TF-FIF	Cessna 172N	67963	TF-GOD
			N75804
TF-FIH	Boeing 757-208	24739	
TF-FII	Boeing 757-208	24760	
TF-FIJ(2)	Boeing 757-208	25085	G-BTEJ
			(TF-FIJ)
TF-FIK	Boeing 757-28A	26276	
TF-FIM(4)	Piper PA-18-150 Super Cub	18-5621	SE-CEC
TF-FIN(2)	Boeing 757-208	28989	N1790B
TF-FIO(2)	Boeing 757-208 (Reservation)	unkn	
TF-FIR	Fokker F.27-050	20243	PH-EXM
TF-FIS(2)	Fokker F.27-050	20244	PH-EXN
TF-FIT	Fokker F.27-050	20250	PH-EXT
TF-FIU	Fokker F.27-050	20251	PH-EXU
	(Reserved as PH-WXH 7.97)		
TF-FKR	Cessna P.206C Super Skylane	0481	N8681Z
TF-FLY(2)	Light Aero Avid Flyer	225	
TF-FMS	Beech B200 Super King Air	BB-1221	(TF-UUU)
			D-IUUU
			F-GKGH
			N7230U
TF-FOX(2)	Cessna 177RG Cardinal RG	0751	N177CB
			(N1577H)
TF-FRK	Cessna 172N (STOL)	70553	N739HJ
TF-FRU(5)	Dornier Do.27B-1	186	TF-EHO
			TF-FHG
			F-BUOP
			D-EBAK
			55+54
			GD+158
			LB+158
			BD+192
			AC+912
			AS+912
TF-FTB	Cessna 150L	72885	N1585Q
TF-FTD	Cessna 150M	76466	N3340V
TF-FTE	Cessna 152-II	83646	N4805B
TF-FTF	Cessna 152-II	80838	N25893
TF-FTG(2)	Cessna A.152 Aerobat	0890	TF-TPB(1)
			N4781A
TF-FTI	Cessna 172N	69376	TF-HUS
			N737FC
TF-FTJ	Cessna 152	80591	TF-OFS
			N25318
TF-FTL(2)	Cessna 152	79824	N757LL
TF-FTN	Piper PA-44-180 Seminole	44-7995239	N2288C
	(Officially quoted incorrectly as 44-7995379)		OO-SEM
			(OO-TIM)
			N66515
			YV-1507P
			N9600N
TF-FTS(2)	Cessna 152	85540	TF-FFD(1)
			N93707
TF-FTV	Reims/Cessna F.172M	1060	TF-POP
			SE-FZP
TF-GAG	Piper PA-22-150 Tri-Pacer	22-4093	D-EFOT
TF-GIN	Piper PA-12 Super Cruiser	12-1098	TF-CAB
			TF-CUB(1)
TF-GJA	Cessna 172N	72240	C-GJPS
			N9364E
TF-GMG	Cessna 170B (Reservation)	26715	N4371B
TF-GMT(2)	Cessna 182P Skylane (Robertson STOL)	61197	TF-SIJ
			TF-OHM
			TF-FRJ
			TF-FRU(4)
			TF-KOT
			N20779

Regn.	Type	C/n	Prev.Id.
TF-GRL	Boeing 757-236	25620	G-CSVS
			G-IEAC
	(To be OY-GRL in 1999)		
TF-GTC	Cessna 402C	0355	SE-IFH
			(N2663J)
TF-GTM(2)	Partenavia P.68B	79	OY-PRW
TF-GTO	Cessna 310Q	0735	TF-LFA
			(TF-LTA)
			TF-GTS
			N5093Q
TF-GTR	Cessna 172RG	1143	N9378D
TF-HAL	Cessna 172N	67906	N75727
TF-HER	Piper PA-28-140 Cherokee	28-20682	N6593W
TF-HFN	Cessna R.172K Hawk XP	2515	N736GL
TF-HHG	Bell 206L-1 Long Ranger II	45677	F-GHHH
			N87BF
			N2088V
TF-HHX	Hughes 269C	S-1587	D-HSSB
			(D-HINS)
			N41S
TF-HIS	Cessna 180	30310	N1610C
TF-HOF	Piper PA-23-160 Apache	23-1487	N4012P
TF-HRB	Aeronca 7AC Champion	5208	N1643E
			NC1643E
TF-IBK	Cessna 182Q Skylane	65988	N759GS
TF-IBM	Piper PA-20 Pacer *(Current but CofA exp 4.87)*	20-148	
TF-ICE	Cessna 150M	76111	N66542
TF-ICI	Cessna 152-II	83438	N49222
TF-ICY	Cessna 152	83677	N4858B
TF-IFR	Cessna 182P Skylane	63801	N6691M
TF-IOI	Reims/Cessna F.172L	0815	TF-IOO (1)
TF-IOO(5)	Cessna 180	31603	TF-GVG
			TF-DVD
			N4705B
TF-ISC(3)	Cessna 172N	70782	N739TA
TF-ISE(2)	Cessna 172N	70142	N738PY
TF-ISL(2)	Beech C23 Sundowner	M-1784	TF-OLI
			N9171S
TF-IVR	Aeronca 7DC Champion	109	N4492E
			NC4492E
TF-JEC	Cessna 150M	75901	TF-JEG(2)
			N803AA
TF-JEG(3)	Cessna 172N	72954	N1088F
TF-JFA	Beech C-45H	AF-602	TF-JMP
			TF-JME(1)
			52-10672
TF-JMB(4)	Piper PA-38-112 Tomahawk	38-78A0361	TF-SKA
TF-JMC(2)	DHC-6 Twin Otter 300	413	C-GIZR
			SE-GRX
			D-IDLT
TF-JMD(3)	DHC-6 Twin Otter 300	475	C-GDAA
TF-JMF(2)	Piper PA-38-112 Tomahawk	38-78A0370	
TF-JME(4)	Fairchild-Swearingen SA.227DC Metro 23	DC-880B	N3002K
TF-JMG	Piper PA-31-350 Navajo Chieftain	31-7652093	G-BWAL
			SU-BBY
			G-BWAL
			A6-ABA
			N59861
TF-JMH	Piper PA-23-150 Apache	23-1027	N3107P
TF-JMI (2)	Piper PA-31-350 Navajo Chieftain	31-7652133	N62849
TF-JMK	Fairchild-Swearingen SA.227AC Metro III	AC-467	N3046L
TF-JML	Fairchild-Swearingen SA.227DC Metro 23	DC-881B	N3004D
TF-JPP	Cessna 172M	64798	TF-FTK(2)
			TF-VIV
			(SE-KRB)
			TF-VIV
			N61784
TF-JSO	Cessna 172N	64972	N64026
TF-JVB	Cessna 402B	0875	TF-SUD
			OY-BIR
			SE-GKV
			OY-BIR
			N5788J
TF-JVC	Cessna 402B	0884	OH-CGS
			CB-51
			(OH-CGS)
			(N5197J)
TF-JVD	Piper PA-23-250 Aztec D	27-4146	TF-JMA(2)
			N6808Y
TF-JVE	Macchi AL.60B2	57/6237	I-GROS
TF-KAB	Cessna 150L	73801	TF-TWO
			N18122
TF-KAD(2)	Cessna 150D	60518	TF-BAD
			(TF-BAC)
			N4518U
TF-KAF(2)	Cessna 170B	20525	N2373D
TF-KAH(2)	Cessna 180	31997	N370G
			N3199D
TF-KAI	Piper PA-22-108 Colt	22-8663	TF-KAX
			(G-AROL)
TF-KAJ(2)	Piper PA-18-150 Super Cub	18-7609019	N9669P
TF-KAK	Piper J-3C-65 Cub	15271	
TF-KAN	Fleet 16B Finch II	651	RCAF4772
TF-KAO(2)	Piper J-3C-65 Cub	19694	TF-GUL
			N6507H
			NC6507H
TF-KAP	Piper J-3C-65 Cub (L-4H)	12328	G-ALGH
			44-80545(2)
			44-80032
TF-KAS	Piper J-3C-65 Cub	22596	
TF-KAT(2)	Piper J-3C-85 Cub	16863	(N103CT)
			N92401
			NC92401
TF-KEA	H.S.Evans VP-1 Volksplane	2341	
TF-KEM	Cessna 152-II	81898	(SE-KPH)
			TF-KEM
			TF-KLM(1)
			N67536
TF-KFX	Denney Kitfox	155	
TF-KGK	Reims/Cessna F.150H	0277	TF-TOB
			TF-FHI
			OY-AHJ
TF-KIK	Piper PA-22-108 Colt	22-8098	N4589Z
TF-KJO	Piper PA-20 Pacer	20-764	N1561A
TF-KLG	Reims/Cessna F.152-II	1527	OY-BNA
			(D-EFEO)
TF-KLM(2)	Cessna 172N	73004	N1464F
TF-KLO	Cessna 172N	71646	TF-MUS
			N4781E
TF-KNM	Piper PA-22-160 Tri-Pacer	22-6363	N9341D
TF-KOK	Cessna 172N	69422	N737HD
TF-KOT(3)	HS.44 Aerokot	101	
TF-KOZ	Bellanca 7GCBC Citabria	1021-78	N2949Z
TF-KRA(2)	Cessna 172N	68349	N733KH
TF-KZA	S.A.I. KZ-III U-2	86	
TF-LAX(2)	Denney Kitfox	220	
TF-LBP	Auster 5 *(Reservation, on rebuild)*	1577	TJ592
TF-LEO	Piper PA-18-150 Super Cub	18-7509074	N7479L
TF-LDS	Dornier Do.27A-4	443	OO-LVH
	(C/n given as 27-1003-433 incorrectly)		D-ENAT
			57+15
			PX+222
			PP+108
TF-LIF	Aérospatiale AS.332L Super Puma	2210	F-WQDA
			F-WKAZ
			F-WYMX
TF-LIZ	Piper PA-22-150 Tri-Pacer	22-5168	N7407D
TF-LOA	Aeronca 11AC Chief	1283	N9642E
			NC9642E
TF-LRL	Cessna 150M	76216	TF-FLY(1)
			N66694
TF-MAY	Cessna 172N	67700	TF-LAX
			N73821
TF-MBF	Bellanca 7KCAB Citabria	505-75	TF-MBL
			N8623V
TF-MED(2)	Piper PA-28-161 Cherokee Warrior II	28-7816194	N9781K

Regn.	Type	C/n	Prev.Id.
TF-MEL	Piper PA-25-235 Pawnee	25-3271	N4238C
			C-GIBA
			N7323Z
TF-MEY	Piper PA-28-180 Cherokee C	28-3355	TF-MEN
			TF-MED(1)
			TF-MEY
			N9276J
TF-MID	Cessna 152-II	82328	N68712
TF-MIN	Piper PA-28-161 Cherokee Warrior II	28-7716275	
TF-MLP	Cessna 172M	61109	N20224
TF-MRS	Cessna 140	10553	N76156
			NC76156
TF-MYA	Cessna 152	83296	N48178
TF-MYF	Piper PA-31-310 Navajo	31-779	9H-ACF
			SE-KFG
			N7402L
TF-MYV	Piper PA-31-350 Navajo Chieftain	31-7852139	TF-OOJ
			N355SB
			N355SS
TF-MYY(2)	Cessna U.206F Stationair	02831	N35960
TF-NDB	Piper PA-22-135 Tri-Pacer	22-2165	N3360B
TF-NEI	Cessna 182P Skylane	62864	N52810
TF-NES	Cessna 172N	66122	N9371H
TF-NEW	Cessna 172M	64560	N124JV
			N9927V
TF-NPK	Douglas C-47A-60-DL	13861	TF-ISH
	(Also quoted as c/n 13861/23506		43-30710
	ex.TF-ISH, KG762, 43-48045)		
TF-ODO	Piper PA-22-150 Tri-Pacer	22-4561	N5900D
TF-OIA	Cessna A.185F Skywagon	02508	N1792R
TF-OII	Reims/Cessna F.150L	0945	
TF-OIL	Cessna A.185E Skywagon	01815	N42LS
TF-OLA	Piper PA-28-151 Cherokee Warrior	28-7615061	N7706C
TF-OLB	SEEMS MS.892A Rallye Commodore 150	10487	(TF-OBL)
			F-BMVQ
TF-OMI	Piper PA-38-112 Tomahawk	38-79A0128	N2573B
TF-OND	Cessna 152-II	79862	N757NA
TF-ONE	Cessna 172M	62726	N13395
TF-ORN	Cessna A.185F Skywagon	02355	TF-IOD
			N53068
TF-OSK(3)	SOCATA MS.894A Minerva 220	12088	G-BBAB
TF-OWL	Denney Kitfox III	1115	
TF-OXO	Piper PA-22-150 Tri-Pacer	22-4656	N6005D
TF-PAC	Piper PA-18 Super Cub 95	18-3442	D-EDCM
	(Composite rebuilt aircraft)		96+19
			QW+901
			QZ+001
			AC+507
			AS+506
			54-742
TF-PAM	Piper PA-28-161 Cherokee Warrior II	28-7716134	N3072Q
TF-PEP	Cessna 152	81326	TF-SKM
			N49803
TF-PIA	Piper PA-28-161 Warrior II	28-8016294	SE-IDI
TF-PJE	Cessna 172M	64323	N8967V
TF-POL	Reims/Cessna FR.172J Rocket	0454	TF-PQL
			F-BURG
TF-POU	Piper PA-28-140 Cherokee Cruiser	28-7425038	OY-POU
			N56797
TF-REF(2)	SAN Jodel D.140C Mousquetaire III	16	TF-JDL
			F-BJQR
			F-OBLF
TF-REK	Rockwell Lark Commander 100/180	5188	N4088X
TF-RJC	Piper PA-28-181 Archer II	28-7990231	N3069H
TF-RJR	CEA DR.250/160 Capitaine	94	F-BOCD
TF-RLR	Cessna R.172K Hawk XP	3156	N758KL
TF-ROB	CEA DR.221 Dauphin	118	F-BPKT
TF-RPM(2)	Cessna 150H	68273	N22428
TFRSH	Piper PA-28-180 Cherokee B	28-1566	TF-NFJ
			TF-SPG
			TF-FFH
			TF-FHE
			OY-DTH
			LN-HAF
			N7607W
TF-RUT	Cessna 172N	72066	C-GCJH
			N6788E
TF-RVK(2)	Cessna R.172K Hawk XP	3155	N758KK
TF-RVM(2)	Piper PA-28-181 Cherokee Archer II	28-7890367	N6380C
TF-SEX	Cessna 172M	65398	N5303H
TF-SGA	SOCATA MS.893E Rallye 180GT Gaillard	12679	TF-SOE
			TF-SGA
TF-SIF(3)	Aérospatiale SA.365N Dauphin 2	6136	F-WYMM
TF-SIR	Piper PA-28-140 Cherokee	28-22799	TF-ROM(1)
			N4405J
TF-SIX	Cessna 172M	65258	N64478
TF-SJM	Reims/Cessna F.172L	0809	N5196
TF-SJO	Lake LA-4-200 Buccaneer	550	N39786
TF-SKA(2)	Cessna 150J	70966	LX-MVE
			N61326
TF-SKN	Cessna 172N	69445	TF-LUX
			N737JD
TF-SKO	Cessna 172N	67822	N75578
TF-SKY	Cessna 337A Super Skymaster	0397	G-ATPU
			F-OCLP
			(G-ATPU)
			N6397F
TF-SMA	Quickie Quickie 2	74	
TF-SMS	Rans S-10 Sakota	100-SMS	
TF-SNF	Denney Kitfox III	1198	
TF-SPA	Piper PA-28-151 Cherokee Warrior	28-7615257	TF-KRA
			N75135
TF-SPY	Cessna 172N	69581	TF ONO
			N737QA
TF-STR	Cessna 172M	64692	TF-HFL(1)
			N61638
TF-SUE	Piper PA-22-150 Tri-Pacer	22-5571	N8046D
TF-SUL	Stinson 108-2 Voyager *(Reservation)*	2156	TF-SRM
			N9156K
			NC9156K
TF-SUX	Klemm L.25E	847	D-ESUX
	(Preserved at Vestmannaeyjar)		
TF-SVO	SOCATA TB-10 Tobago	44	F-GBHP
TF-SWP	Piper PA-22-160 Tri-Pacer	22-6442	N9526D
TF-SYN	Fokker F.27 Friendship 200	10545	(PH-EXC)
TF-SYR	Aérospatiale AS.350BEcureuil	1322	TF-GRO(3)
			D-HKHL
TF-TAL	Cessna P.206 Super Skylane	0141	PH-KFF
			OO-DRJ
			PH-KFF
			N2641X
TF-TBX	SOCATA TB-10 Tobago	723	HB-KIX
			D-ENGU(2)
TF-TOA	Piper PA-28R-200 Cherokee Arrow	28R-7635029	TF-GLK
			SE-GLK
TF-TOB	Piper PA-28-180 Cherokee C	28-2830	TF-HRE
			TF-HRL
			N8866J
TF-TOC	Piper PA-23-160 Apache G	23-2044	TF-EGG
			G-ASDG
			N10F
TF-TOD	Piper PA-28-140 Cherokee B	28-25647	TF-ENN
			N8802N
TF-TOE	Piper PA-28-140 Cherokee	28-20257	TF-AIT
			N6299W
TF-TOG	Cessna 305A Bird Dog (L-19)	22615	N5270G
			51-12301
TF-TPB(2)	Cessna 172M	64839	TF-MYY(1)
			TF-FRU(3)
			N61847
TF-TUG	Piper PA-25-235 Pawnee B	25-4037	TF-TUN(1)
			N4418Y
TF-TWA	Bellanca 7GCAA Citabria	225-70	N9084L
TF-UFO(2)	Mudry CAP.10B	86	
TF-UGL	Cessna 172N	70823	N739UT
TF-ULF(2)	SAN Jodel D.140C Mousquetaire III	132	F-BMBO
TF-ULV	SAN Jodel DR.1050 Ambassadeur	119	OY-ACJ
TF-UNA(2)	Cessna 172M	65801	N9857Q
TF-UPS	Piper PA-28-161 Cherokee Warrior II	28-7816056	N47234

Regn.	Type	C/n	Prev.Id.
TF-UTA	Cessna 172M	65561	TF-MWL
			N6742H
TF-VEJ	Partenavia P.68C	290	N714G
			N4496M
TF-VEL(2)	SOCATA TB-10 Tobago	381	TF-EGO
			F-GDGN
TF-VEV	Piper PA-31-350 Chieftain	31-8152007	N4051Q
TF-VEY	Partenavia P.68B	109	G-JVMR
			G-JCTI
			G-OJOE
			SE-GUI
TF-VHH	Cessna A.185F Skywagon	02092	N70283
TF-VIP	Cessna T.337H Turbo Skymaster	01928	N1496S
TF-VOT	Gislason Aventura II	AP2A0036	N8199G
TF-YRD	Jodel D.9 Bébé	PFA/928A/940 / SAS/001/	G-AXKI
TF-ZZZ	Erco 415C Ercoupe	82	N37115
			NC37115
TF-...	Boeing 737-3S3	23811	D-ABWS
			N841LF
			G-DIAR
			G-BNPA
			C-FGHQ
			G-BNPA

GLIDERS AND MOTOR-GLIDERS

Regn.	Type	C/n	Prev.Id.
TF-SAA(2)	Scheibe SF-28A Tandem-Falke	5767	(D-KACT)
TF-SAB(2)	Schleicher K.7 Rhönadler	7052/A	D-5309
TF-SAC	Schleicher ASK-21	21617	
TF-SAE(2)	Schleicher Ka.6E	4264	D-0152
TF-SAF	Schweizer TG-3A	unkn	42-53117
TF-SAG(2)	Schleicher ASW-19	19034	N19EM
TF-SAJ	Grunau Baby	37/54	
TF-SAL	Rolladen-Schneider LS-4	4498	HB-1761
TF-SAP	LET L-13 Blanik	173323	
TF-SAR	Schleicher K.8B	8701	
TF-SAS	Schleicher Ka.6CR Rhönsegler	6554	D-1947
TF-SAT	Schleicher Rhönlerche II	524	OY-BZX
			D-5051
			D-6188
TF-SAV	Schleicher K.8B	159/59	D-5286
TF-SBA	Schweizer TG-3A	unkn	42-53120
TF-SBE	Schleicher Rhönlerche II	3006	
TF-SBF	Schleicher K.8B	8592	
TF-SBJ	LAK-12 Lietuva	6184	LY-GLA
	(Cancelled?)		DOSAAF
TF-SBK	Schleicher K.7 Rhönadler	1	D-0202
TF-SBN	PZL PW-5 Smyk	17.07.011	
TF-SDA	Grunau Baby IIb	43/54	
TF-SDF	LAK-12 Lietuva	6207	LY-GJO
TF-SIA	Schreder HP-16 (Kit)	1341	
TF-SIG	Schleicher K.8B	8044	TF-SAM(2)
			D-6332
TF-SIK	Eiri PIK-16C Vasama	42	OY-XCO
			OO-ZAD
TF-SIP	Grob G.102 Speed Astir IIB	4087	
TF-SIS(2)	LAK-12 Lietuva	6189	DOSAAF
TF-SKG	LAK-12 Lietuva	6141	LY-GKG
TF-SLS	Rolladen-Schneider LS-3-17	3428	
TF-SOL(2)	Grob G.102 Standard Astir CS 77	1829	
TF-SON	Breglieb BG-12/16 (Kit)	HP-01	
TF-SPO	Eiri PIK-20B	20132C	OH-490
TF-STE	Centrair 101A Pégase	101A-0132	N40KG
TF-SZD	SZD-36A Cobra	W-697	DOSAAF
TF-UTU	Fibera KK-1e Utu	14	(TF-SBJ)
			OY-FKX
TF-S..	PZL PW-5 Smyk	17.07.011	

T7 - SAN MARINO

Regn.	Type	C/n	Prev.Id.

No recent reports of further allocations have been received.

T7-035	Tecnam P.92 Echo	unkn	
T7-036	Tecnam P.92 Echo	unkn	
T7-038	SG Aviation Storm 280	51	

T9 - BOSNIA-HERZEGOVINA

Regn.	Type	C/n	Prev.Id.
T9-ABA	CASA C.212-CD	302	F-GHOX
			TT-LAL
			F-ODTT
T9-ABB	Ilyushin IL-18D	184007405	EL-ADY
			LZ-AZO
			RA-75553
			D-AOAO
			DDR-STF
			DM-STF
			CCCP75553
T9-ABC(1)	Douglas C-47B	16187/32935	3C-JJN
	(Cancelled, but still extant in Malta)		N48ME
			F-GILV
			F-ODQL
			(D-CDST)
			F-ODQL
			ZS-EYO
			7Q-YKM
			VP-YKM
			G-AMPT
			KN462
			44-76603
T9-ABC(2)	Yakovlev Yak-42	unkn	
T9-ABD	Yakovlev YAK-42D	unkn	UR-42 . . .
T9-ABE	Antonov AN-74	3654709732	
T9-BIH	Cessna S550 Citation II	0045	BH-BIH
			YU-BOE
			N1269Y
T9-BSA	Piper PA-34-200 Seneca	unkn	
T9-CAB	Ilyushin IL-76TD	1023408265	
T9-CAC	Ilyushin IL-76TD		
T9-CLM	UTVA-75	unkn	YU-DHB
			JRV53187
T9-CLO	Piper PA-18-150 Super Cub	18-7809162	YU-DCB
			N82168
T9-DCA	Piper PA-18-150 Super Cub	unkn	
T9-HAA	Mil Mi-8	unkn	
T9-HAB	Mil Mi-8	unkn	
T9-HAF	Mil Mi-8	unkn	
T9-HAI	Mil Mi-8	unkn	
T9-HAL	Mil Mi-8	unkn	
T9- . . .	Antonov AN-2	1G158-14	9A-DBZ
			CCCP07694
T9- . . .	Bell 206BJet Ranger II	3435	9A-HAF
			TC-HNO
			N411SB
			N20879
T9- . . .	Zlin 526F Trenér Master	1262	YR-ZAJ

Regn.	Type	C/n	Prev.Id.
YU-DHI	UTVA-75	unkn	JRV53194
YU-DLH	UTVA-66	unkn	JRV51 . . .
YU-4268	Pilatus B4-PC11	unkn	
YU-4321	VTC-75 Standard Cirrus	unkn	
YU-4324	VTC-75 Standard Cirrus	unkn	
YU-4386	Glaser-Dirks DG-300 Elan	unkn	
YU-5334	LET L-13 Blanik	174917	
YU-5348	LET L-13 Blanik	unkn	

The following YU- aircraft are known to have been active in Bosnia or reported to have been sold there - their current status is unknown :-

YU-BKG	Antonov AN-2T	1G167-28	
YU-BKZ	Cessna 500 Citation	415/0373	N98449
YU-BML	Cessna 500 Citation	0399	N2069A
YU-CAK	Champion 7GCBC Citabria	282-70	
YU-CDM	Piper PA-18-150 Super Cub	18-7809031	D-EKDC
			N82947
YU-CDN	Piper PA-18-150 Super Cub	18-7809032	D-ELRI
			N82949
YU-DBJ	Reims/Cessna FR.172J Rocket	0435	(D-EJXV)
YU-DBK	Reims/Cessna FR.172J Rocket	0436	(D-EJXW)
YU-DBL	Reims/Cessna FR.172J Rocket	0439	(D-EJXZ)
YU-DBX	Piper PA-18-150 Super Cub	18-7809156	N82076
YU-DBY	Piper PA-18-150 Super Cub	18-7809157	N82081
YU-DBZ	Piper PA-18-150 Super Cub	18-7809158	N82084
YU-DCA	Piper PA-18-150 Super Cub	18-7809159	N82086
YU-DCC	Piper PA-18-150 Super Cub	18-7809163	N82169
YU-DDF	Champion 7GCBC Citabria	unkn	
YU-DEP	UTVA-75	unkn	JRV53109

YL - LATVIA

Regn.	Type	C/n	Prev.Id.
YL-BAA(2)	Boeing 737-236	22028	G-BGJG
			(RA-71430)
			G-BGJG
YL-BAB	Boeing 737-236	22032	G-BGJK
YL-BAC	Boeing 737-236	22034	YL-LAC
			G-BGJM
			LY-GBA
			G-BGJM
			(YL-LAC)
			G-BGJM
YL-BAG	SAAB-Scania SF.340A	007	SE-LBP
			HB-AHB
			SE-E07
YL-BAK	BAe.146 Series RJ70	E-1223	N832BE
			G-6-223
YL-BAL	BAe.146 Series RJ70	E-1224	N833BE
			G-6-224
YL-BAN	BAe.146 Series RJ70	E-1225	N834BE
			G-6-225
YL-BAR	Fokker F.27-050	20149	PH-LVL
			OY-MMT
			PH-EXV
YL-BAS	Fokker F.27-050	20162	OY-KAE
			PH-EXE
YL-BAT	Fokker F.27-050	20163	OY-KAF
			PH-EXF
YL-CAB	Sport Nika (Homebuilt)	0001	
YL-CAC	Antonov AN-2T	1G85-22	DOSAAF
YL-CAF	American AG-5B Tiger	10153	
YL-CAJ	American AG-5B Tiger	10109	N1196F
YL-CAK	PZL-104 Wilga 35A	107340	DOSAAF
YL-CAL	PZL-104 Wilga 35A	96303	DOSAAF
YL-CAM	PZL-104 Wilga 35A	16820662	DOSAAF
YL-CAN	PZL-104 Wilga 35A	178307	DOSAAF
YL-CAO	Antonov AN-2T	1G98-48	DOSAAF
YL-CAP	Antonov AN-2T	1G162-03	DOSAAF
YL-CAR	Antonov AN-2T	1G73-26	DOSAAF-40
YL-CAS	PZL-104 Wilga 35A	15800569	DOSAAF
YL-CAT	PZL-104 Wilga 35A	128421	DOSAAF
	(Also quoted as c/n 139495)		
YL-CAU	PZL-104 Wilga 35A	139477	DOSAAF
YL-CAV	PZL-104 Wilga 35A	139479	DOSAAF
YL-CBA	PZL-104 Wilga 35A	15800575	DOSAAF
YL-CBB	PZL-104 Wilga 35A	15800571	DOSAAF
YL-CBH	Yakovlev YAK-50	832507	DOSAAF-05
YL-CBI	Yakovlev YAK-52	811202	DOSAAF-09
YL-CBJ	Yakovlev YAK-52	790404	DOSAAF-20
YL-CBK	Yakovlev YAK-18T	17-31	
YL-CBL	Yakovlev YAK-18T	17-32	
YL-CBM	Grumman AA-5A Cheetah	0136	N9736U
YL-CBN	Cessna 150L *(Identity unconfirmed)*	72614	N1314Q
YL-CBP	Air Command 582 Gyrocopter	unkn	
YL-CBR	Grumman AA-5A Cheetah	0466	C-GXSJ
YL-CBZ	Cessna 152	81070	N48955
YL-CDA	Cessna 172N	68704	D-EKRL
			N734AN
YL-DCU	Yakovlev YAK-52	unkn	
YL-KAA	Antonov AN-28	1AJ009-14	CCCP28948
YL-KAB	Antonov AN-28	1AJ009-15	CCCP28949
YL-KAC	LET L-410UVP	851531	CCCP67559
YL-KAD	Antonov AN-28	1AJ004-02	CCCP47747
YL-KAE	LET L-410UVP	790209	RA-67173
			CCCP67173
YL-KAF	Antonov AN-28	1AJ009-09	RA-28943
			CCCP28943
YL-KAG	Cessna 421 *(Identity not yet confirmed)*	0075	N40JL
YL-LAA	Tupolev TU-154B	76A-133	CCCP85133
YL-LAB	Tupolev TU-154B-1	81A-515	CCCP-85515
YL-LAJ	Ilyushin IL-76	083414432	RA-76510
			CCCP76510
YL-LAK	Ilyushin IL-76	0003424707	RA-76522
			CCCP76522

Regn.	Type	C/n	Prev.Id.
YL-LAL	Ilyushin IL-76T	0013433984	RA-76755
			CCCP76755
			YI-ALL
			IAF-4600
YL-LAO	Ilyushin IL-18D	2964017102	CCCP75916
YL-LBD	Tupolev TU-134B-3	63235	CCCP65694
YL-LBE	Tupolev TU-134B-3	63385	CCCP65695
YL-LBF	Tupolev TU-134B-3	63295	CCCP65696
YL-LBG	Tupolev TU-134B-3	63333	CCCP65699
YL-LBH	Tupolev TU-134B-3	63340	CCCP65700
YL-LBI	Tupolev TU-134B-3	63365	CCCP65701
YL-LBJ	Tupolev TU-134B-3	63410	CCCP65704
YL-LBK	Tupolev TU-134B-3	63425	CCCP65706
YL-LBL	Tupolev TU-134B-3	63515	CCCP65712
YL-LBN	Tupolev TU-134B-3	63187	CCCP65799
YL-LCA	Antonov AN-24	77303106	CCCP46226
YL-LCC	Antonov AN-24V	07305908	CCCP46367
YL-LCD	Antonov AN-24V	77303902	CCCP46400
YL-LCE	Antonov AN-24V	87304205	CCCP46427
YL-LCG	Antonov AN-24V	47309507	CCCP46666
YL-LCI	Antonov AN-24RV	67310510	CCCP47351
YL-LCJ	Antonov AN-24V	37304404	CCCP46443
YL-LCK	Antonov AN-24V	79901110	YL-LCN
			CCCP47747
YL-LCL	Antonov AN-24V	79901202	CCCP47749
YL-LDB	Antonov AN-26	10810	CCCP26047
YL-LDC	Antonov AN-26	12010	CCCP26109
YL-LEB	Antonov AN-2	1G41-16	CCCP62446
YL-LEU	Antonov AN-2R	1G165-45	CCCP19731
			SP-ZFP
			CCCP19731
YL-LEV	Antonov AN-2R	1G148-29	CCCP07268
YL-LEW	Antonov AN-2R	1G182-28	CCCP56471
YL-LEX	Antonov AN-2R	1G187-58	CCCP54949
YL-LEY	Antonov AN-2R	1G173-11	CCCP40784
YL-LEZ	Antonov AN-2R	1G165-47	CCCP19733
YL-LFA	Antonov AN-2R	1G172-20	CCCP40748
YL-LFB	Antonov AN-2R	1G173-12	CCCP40785
YL-LFC	Antonov AN-2R	1G206-44	CCCP17939
YL-LFD	Antonov AN-2R	1G172-21	CCCP40749
YL-LHA	Mil Mi-2	545524028	CCCP14390
YL-LHC	Mil Mi-2	527541032	CCCP20724
YL-LHE	Mil Mi-2	529222055	CCCP23333
YL-LHG	Mil Mi-2	549326065	CCCP23346
YL-LHH	Mil Mi-2	549329075	CCCP23349
YL-LHJ	Mil Mi-2	534637026	CCCP20566
YL-LHK	Mil Mi-2	543719094	CCCP23951
YL-LHL	Mil Mi-2	548149053	Soviet AF
			DOSAAF
YL-LHM	Mil Mi-2	548944114	Soviet AF
			DOSAAF
YL-LHN	Mil Mi-2	524006025	CCCP20320
YL-LHO	Mil Mi-2	535025126	CCCP20619
YL-LHR(2)	Robinson R-44 Astro	0445	
YL-LHS	Mil Mi-2	unkn	
YL-LHT	Mil Mi-2	525803088	YL-LHB
			CCCP15201
YL-PAA	Aero L-29S Delfin	491119	37 (Red)
YL-PAE	Aero L-29S Delfin	591636	06 (Red)
YL-PAF	Aero L-29S Delfin	591771	18 (Red)
YL-PAG	Aero L-29S Delfin	491273	51 (Red)
YL-RAA	Antonov AN-26	06210	CCCP29107
YL-RAB	Antonov AN-26	01701	CCCP26009
			CCCP58643
			S3-ABA
			BangAF:0001
YL-RAC	Antonov AN-26	09903	CCCP79169
YL-RAD	Antonov AN-26B	13909	RA-26589
			CCCP26589
YL-TRA	Yakovlev YAK-40	9510939	RA-87340
			CCCP87340
YL-TRB	Yakovlev YAK-40	9721353	RA-88275
			CCCP88275

682

Regn.	Type	C/n	Prev.Id.
YL-VIP	HS.125-700B	257103	VR-BOJ
			G-LTEC
			G-BHSU
			G-5-12
YL-...	Cessna 172N	69293	N737BP
YL-...	Lake LA-4-200 Buccaneer	478	N5021L

The following Russian/Soviet-registered aircraft are also known to be based or stored in Latvia, some wearing only numerical markings:-

CCCP19734	Antonov AN-2	1G165-48
CCCP33308	Antonov AN-2	1G225-25
CCCP35143	Antonov AN-2	1G112-25
CCCP54948	Antonov AN-2	1G187-57
CCCP56509	Antonov AN-2	1G183-07
CCCP62646	Antonov AN-2	1G178-38
CCCP62649	Antonov AN-2	1G178-41
CCCP71303	Antonov AN-2	1G201-31
CCCP71304	Antonov AN-2	1G201-32
CCCP20184	Mil Mi-2	533546054
CCCP25948	Mil Mi-8	4886
CCCP25949	Mil Mi-8	4887

BALLOONS

Regn.	Type	C/n	Prev.Id.
YL-001	Interavia 90 Balloon	6231291	
YL-002	Dirigible Moscow Balloon	0792-04-014	
YL-003	Interavia 77 Balloon	0640393	
YL-004	Interavia 90 Balloon	unkn	
YL-005	Interavia 90 Balloon	unkn	
YL-006	Cameron V-77	2276	G-BSGM

MICROLIGHTS

Regn.	Type	C/n	Prev.Id.
YL-MIG	Aviatika MAI-890 Baby MIG	037	

GLIDERS

Regn.	Type	C/n	Prev.Id.
YL-DAA	LAK-12 Lietuva	692	DOSAAF
YL-DAB	LAK-12 Lietuva	6146	DOSAAF
YL-DAC	LAK-12 Lietuva	6150	DOSAAF
YL-DAD	SZD-41A Jantar Standard	B-887	DOSAAF
YL-DAE	SZD-41A Jantar Standard	B-745	CCCP6745
			DOSAAF
YL-DAF	SZD-48-1 Jantar Standard 2	"B-1055"	DOSAAF
	(Quoted c/n is also YL-DAG, believed correctly)		
YL-DAG	SZD-48-1 Jantar Standard 2	B-1055	DOSAAF
YL-DAH	SZD-48-1 Jantar Standard 2	B-1270	DOSAAF
YL-DAI - 91	SZD-48-3 Jantar Standard 3	B-1511	DOSAAF
YL-DAK	LET L-13 Blanik	172227	DOSAAF
YL-DAL	LET L-13 Blanik	174636	DOSAAF
YL-DAM	LET L-13 Blanik (Believed now N61TB)	026434	DOSAAF
YL-DAN	LET L-13 Blanik (Believed now N106SS)	027029	DOSAAF
YL-DAO	LET L-13 Blanik	027030	DOSAAF
YL-DBA	LET L-13 Blanik	027154	DOSAAF
YL-DBB	LET L-13 Blanik (Believed now N98KK)	027155	DOSAAF
YL-DBC	LET L-13 Blanik (Believed now N2271W)	173624	DOSAAF
YL-DBD	LET L-13 Blanik (C/n not possible)	"027263"	DOSAAF

Regn.	Type	C/n	Prev.Id.
YL-DBE	LET L-13 Blanik	172414	DOSAAF
YL-DBF	LET L-13 Blanik	027322	DOSAAF
YL-DBH	LET L-13 Blanik	173474	DOSAAF
YL-DBI	LET L-13 Blanik	174515	DOSAAF
YL-DBJ	LET L-13 Blanik	174315	DOSAAF
YL-DBK	LET L-13 Blanik	174617	DOSAAF
YL-DBL	LET L-13 Blanik	026432	DOSAAF
YL-DBM	LET L-13 Blanik	026659	DOSAAF
YL-DBN	LET L-13 Blanik	026701	DOSAAF
YL-DBO	LET L-13 Blanik	026702	DOSAAF
YL-DBP	LET L-13 Blanik	027160	DOSAAF
YL-DBR	LET L-13 Blanik	027032	DOSAAF
YL-DBS	LET L-13 Blanik	027027	DOSAAF
YL-DBT	SZD-48-1 Jantar Standard 2	B-1047	DOSAAF
YL-DBU	SZD-48-3 Jantar Standard 3	B-1586	DOSAAF
YL-DBV	SZD-48-3 Jantar Standard 3	B-1281	DOSAAF
YL-DBZ	LAK-12 Lietuva	6124	DOSAAF
YL-DCA	LAK-12 Lietuva	676	DOSAAF
YL-655	LAK-12 Lietuva	unkn	
YL-670	LAK-12 Lietuva	unkn	

YR - ROMANIA

Regn.	Type	C/n	Prev.Id.
YR-AAP	Antonov AN-2	1G199-34	HA-MAP
			RA-31525
			CCCP31525
YR-ABA	Boeing 707-3K1C	20803	
YR-ABB	Boeing 707-3K1C	20804	
YR-ABC	Boeing 707-3K1C	20805	
YR-AER	Antonov AN-2	1G154-45	UR-05805 ?
			CCCP05805
YR-AMX	Antonov AN-24V *(Wfu)*	57302107	
YR-AMZ	Antonov AN-24V *(CofA expired)*	57301702	ST-AWC
			YR-AMZ
			CCCP46784
YR-ANT	Antonov AN-2R *(CofA expired)*	1G108-67	
YR-AOA	Antonov AN-2	1G197-38	UR-31415 ?
			CCCP31415
YR-AOB	Antonov AN-2R	1G176-09	UR-62546?
			CCCP62546
YR-AOR	Antonov AN-2	1G145-03	HA-MBX
			CCCP70527
YR-APB	Antonov AN-2R *(CofA expired)*	1G116-43	
YR-APD	Antonov AN-2R *(CofA expired)*	1G116-45	
YR-APG	Antonov AN-2R	1G124-27	
YR-API	Antonov AN-2R *(CofA expired)*	1G124-29	
YR-APL	Antonov AN-2R *(CofA expired)*	1G124-33	
YR-APO	Antonov AN-2R	1G124-36	
YR-APR	Antonov AN-2	1G124-37	Rom.AF 37
			YR-APR
YR-APX	Antonov AN-2R *(CofA expired)*	1G124-44	
YR-APY	Antonov AN-2R	1G124-45	
YR-ARA	Antonov AN-24RV	57310105	YR-BMA
YR-ARB	Antonov AN-24RV	57310405	YR-RRB
			YR-BMG
YR-ATA	Aeritalia/SNIAS ATR-42-512	566	F-WWLF
YR-ATB	Aeritalia/SNIAS ATR-42-512	569	F-WWLH
YR-ATC	Aeritalia/SNIAS ATR-42-512	589	F-WW..
YR-ATD	Aeritalia/SNIAS ATR-42-512	591	F-WW..
YR-ATE	Aeritalia/SNIAS ATR-42-512	596	F-WWLY
YR-ATF	Aeritalia/SNIAS ATR-42-512	599	F-WWEB
YR-ATY	Aeritalia/SNIAS ATR-42-320	083	F-WQBV
			N4207G
			F-WWEI
YR-BCI	BAC One-Eleven 525FT	252	
YR-BCJ	BAC One-Eleven 525FT	253	TC-AKB
			TC-ARI)
			(TC-JCP)
			YR-BCJ
YR-BCK	BAC One-Eleven 525FT	254	TC-JCP
			YR-BCK
YR-BCM	BAC One-Eleven 525FT *(Wfu)*	256	EI-BVI
			YR-BCM
			OE-ILD
			YR-BCM
YR-BCN	BAC One-Eleven 525FT	266	EI-BSY
			YR-BCN
			YU-AKN
			YR-BCN
			YU-ANM
			YR-BCN
YR-BEA	Bell 206B Jet Ranger II	unkn	
YR-BEL	Bell 206L-1 Long Ranger II	45375	N573W
			N5735P
YR-BGA	Boeing 737-38J	27179	
YR-BGB	Boeing 737-38J	27180	
YR-BGC	Boeing 737-38J	27181	
YR-BGD	Boeing 737-38J	27182	
YR-BGE	Boeing 737-38J	27395	
YR-BGX	IAR Ag-6	unkn	
YR-BGY	Boeing 737-36M	28332	OO-VEA
			(OO-EBA)
YR-BGZ	Boeing 737-548	24878	EI-CDA
			EI-BXE
YR-BMB	Antonov AN-24RV *(CofA expired)*	57310106	
YR-BME	Antonov AN-24RV *(CofA expired)*	57310310	

Regn.	Type	C/n	Prev.Id.
YR-BMH	Antonov AN-24RV *(CofA expired)*	57310407	
YR-BMI	Antonov AN-24RV	57310408	
YR-BML	Antonov AN-24RV	77310805	
YR-BMM	Antonov AN-24RV	77310807	
YR-BMN	Antonov AN-24RV	77310808	
YR-BMO	Antonov AN-24RV	77310710	TC-FPB
			YR-BMO
YR-BNB	Britten-Norman BN-2A Islander *(Wfu)*	97	G-51-32
			(G-AXKC)
YR-BNH	Britten-Norman BN-2A-27 Islander *(Wfu)*	775	G-BDMX
			YR-BNH
			G-BDMX
YR-BNK	Britten-Norman BN-2A-27 Islander *(Wfu)*	778	G-BDNA
			YR-BNK
			G-BDNA
YR-BNL	Britten-Norman BN-2A-27 Islander *(Wfu)*	790	G-BDRX
			YR-BNL
			G-BDRX
YR-BNM	Britten-Norman BN-2A-27 Islander *(Wfu)*	808	G-BDYV
YR-BNN	Britten-Norman BN-2A-27 Islander *(Wfu)*	804	G-BDYR
YR-BNO	Britten-Norman BN-2A-27 Islander *(Wfu)*	821	G-BELD
YR-BNP	Britten-Norman BN-2A-27 Islander *(Wfu)*	822	G-BELE
YR-BNR	Britten-Norman BN-2A-27 Islander *(Wfu)*	824	G-BELG
YR-BNT	Britten-Norman BN-2A-27 Islander *(Wfu)*	816	G-BEGP
YR-BNV	Britten-Norman BN-2A-27 Islander *(Wfu)*	840	G-BEMS
YR-BNW	Britten-Norman BN-2A-27 Islander *(Wfu)*	853	G-BEWB
YR-BOR	Antonov AN-2	1G192-13	HA-MAN
			CCCP84695
YR-BRB	ROMBAC One-Eleven 561RC	269/402	EI-BSS
			YR-BRB
			EI-BSS
			YR-BRB
			EI-BSS
			YR-BRB
			EI-BSS
			YR-BRB
YR-BRC	ROMBAC One-Eleven 561RC	403	YU-ANS
			YR-BRC
YR-BRE	ROMBAC One-Eleven 561RC	405	
YR-BRI	ROMBAC One-Eleven 561RC	409	
YR-CCF	Antonov AN-2	1G141-15	UR-70361
			CCCP-70361
YR-COR	Antonov AN-2R	1G225-14	HA-MAK
			UR-40497?
			CCCP40497
YR-CXA	Kamov Ka.26	7203003	
YR-CXB	Kamov Ka.26	7203106	
YR-CXC	Kamov Ka.26	7202606	
YR-CXD	Kamov Ka.26	7202706	
YR-CXG	Kamov Ka.26	7303206	
YR-CZF	Kamov Ka.26	7404317	ER-.....
			YR-CZF
YR-DAV	Antonov AN-2	1G183-17	UR-56519 ?
			CCCP56519
YR-EAA	Kamov Ka.26	7706203	
YR-EAD	Kamov Ka.26	7806412	
YR-EAF	Kamov Ka.26	7806414	
YR-EAJ	Kamov Ka.26	7806418	
YR-EAM	Kamov Ka.26	7806501	
YR-EAN	Kamov Ka.26	7303505	CCCP19339
YR-EAO	Kamov Ka.26	7705912	CCCP24395
YR-ECM	IAR/SA.316B Alouette III	1960/07	YR-ELH
YR-EKE	Kamov Ka.26	7000803	
YR-EKL	Kamov Ka.26	7202806	
YR-EKN	Kamov Ka.26	7202808	
YR-EKO	Kamov Ka.26	7202809	
YR-EKT	Kamov Ka.26	7706102	
YR-EKV	Kamov Ka.26	7706202	
YR-EKY	Kamov Ka.26	7706103	
YR-ELC	SA.316B Alouette III	1909	
YR-ELL	IAR/SA.316B Alouette III *(Wfu)*	26	
YR-ELR	IAR/SA.316B Alouette III	50	
YR-ELS	IAR/SA.316B Alouette III	93	
YR-ELT	IAR/SA.316B Alouette III *(Wfu)*	94	
YR-ELU	IAR/SA.316B Alouette III	95	

Regn.	Type	C/n	Prev.Id.
YR-EWA	Extra 300/L (Reservation)	096	
YR-EWB	Extra 300/L (Reservation)	097	
YR-EWC	Extra 300/L (Reservation, w/o on delivery 2.00)	unkn	
YR-EWD	Extra 300/L (Reservation)	unkn	
YR-FLA	Antonov AN-2	1G238-37	UR-02260
			CCCP02260
YR-FLB	Antonov AN-2	1G190-57	UR-84625
			CCCP84625
YR-FLC	Antonov AN-2	1G238-36	UR-02259
			CCCP02259
YR-GRP	Bell 206BJet Ranger II	4483	
YR-IMM	Ilyushin IL-18D	187009904	
YR-IMZ(2)	Ilyushin IL-18GRM	187009802	
YR-ION	Antonov AN-2	1G210-04	HA-MAO
			RA-17980
			CCCP17980
YR-ITA	Antonov AN-26	6407	LZ-MNH
			UR-26504
			CCCP-26504
YR-IVA	Antonov AN-2R (CofA expired)	1G190-01	OK-KIG
YR-JBA	BAC One-Eleven 528FL	234	G-BJRT
			D-ALFA
YR-JBB	BAC One-Eleven 528FL (CofA expired)	238	G-BJRU
			D-ANUE
YR-JCA	Boeing 707-327C (CofA expired)	19530	CC-CYA
			N707ME
			B-2424
			N707ME
			9V-BDC
			N7103
YR-JCB	Boeing 707-321B (Wfu)	20022	CC-CYB
			N730Q
			N883PA
YR-LCA	Airbus A.310-325	636	F-WWCG
YR-LCB	Airbus A.310-325	644	F-WWCO
YR-MAC	Antonov AN-2	1G209-53	HA-MAI
			RA-17969
			CCCP17969
YR-MCR	Kamov Ka-26	7203007	UR-19311
			CCCP19311
YR-MLA	Mil Mi-8PS (CofA expired)	10731	
YR-MLB	Mil Mi-8PS	10735	
YR-NOR	Robinson R-44 Astro	0308	D-HIGG
YR-PAA	Antonov AN-2R (CofA expired)	1G124-46	
YR-PAB	Antonov AN-2R	1G124-47	
YR-PAD	Antonov AN-2R	1G164-32	
YR-PAE	Antonov AN-2R (CofA expired)	1G164-33	
YR-PAF	Antonov AN-2R (CofA expired)	1G137-06	
YR-PAH	Antonov AN-2R	1G164-35	
YR-PAI	Antonov AN-2R (CofA expired)	1G164-36	
YR-PAJ	Antonov AN-2R (CofA expired)	1G164-37	
YR-PAK	Antonov AN-2R	1G164-38	
YR-PAL	Antonov AN-2R (CofA expired)	1G164-39	
YR-PAM	Antonov AN-2R	1G164-40	
YR-PAO	Antonov AN-2R	1G164-51	
YR-PAP	Antonov AN-2R (CofA expired)	1G164-52	
YR-PAS	Antonov AN-2R	1G164-53	
YR-PAT	Antonov AN-2R	1G164-54	
YR-PAV	Antonov AN-2R (CofA expired)	1G164-56	
YR-PAW	Antonov AN-2R	1G164-57	
YR-PAX	Antonov AN-2R	1G164-58	
YR-PAY	Antonov AN-2R (CofA expired)	1G164-59	
YR-PAZ	Antonov AN-2R (CofA expired)	1G164-60	
YR-PBA	Antonov AN-2R	1G166-36	
YR-PBB	Antonov AN-2R	1G166-37	
YR-PBC	Antonov AN-2R	1G177-26	
YR-PBD	Antonov AN-2R	1G177-27	
YR-PBG	Antonov AN-2R	1G180-43	
YR-PBI	Antonov AN-2R	1G185-41	
YR-PBJ	Antonov AN-2R	1G185-42	
YR-PBK	Antonov AN-2R (CofA expired)	1G196-35	
YR-PBL	Antonov AN-2R	1G196-36	
YR-PBM	Antonov AN-2R	1G196-51	
YR-PBN	Antonov AN-2R (CofA expired)	1G196-52	
YR-PBO	Antonov AN-2R	1G202-21	
YR-PBP	Antonov AN-2R	1G202-22	
YR-PBR	Antonov AN-2R	1G202-23	
YR-PBT	Antonov AN-2R	1G215-21	
YR-PBU	Antonov AN-2R	1G215-22	
YR-PBW	Antonov AN-2R (CofA expired)	1G224-07	
YR-PBX	Antonov AN-2R (CofA expired)	1G224-08	
YR-PMA	Antonov AN-2R (CofA expired)	1G227-11	
YR-PMB	Antonov AN-2R	1G227-12	
YR-PMC	Antonov AN-2R	1G227-13	
YR-PMD	Antonov AN-2R	1G227-14	
YR-PME	Antonov AN-2R	1G227-15	
YR-PMF	Antonov AN-2R (CofA expired)	1G227-16	
YR-PMH	Antonov AN-2R	1G231-34	
YR-PMI	Antonov AN-2R	1G231-35	
YR-PMJ	Antonov AN-2R (CofA expired)	1G231-36	
YR-PMK	Antonov AN-2R	1G231-37	
YR-PML	Antonov AN-2R	1G231-38	
YR-PMM	Antonov AN-2R	1G231-39	
YR-PMN	Antonov AN-2R	1G231-40	
YR-PMO	Antonov AN-2R	1G233-01	
YR-PMR	Antonov AN-2R	1G233-03	
YR-PMS	Antonov AN-2R	1G233-04	
YR-PMT	Antonov AN-2R	1G233-05	
YR-PMU	Antonov AN-2R	1G233-06	
YR-PMV	Antonov AN-2R	1G233-07	
YR-PMX	Antonov AN-2R	1G233-09	
YR-PRA	IAR/SA.316B Alouette III	201	
YR-PSA	Antonov AN-2R	1G177-22	
YR-PSB	Antonov AN-2R (CofA expired)	1G177-23	
YR-PSD	Antonov AN-2R	1G177-25	
YR-PVA	Antonov AN-2R (CofA expired)	1G175-01	
YR-PVB	Antonov AN-2R	1G175-02	
YR-PVC	Antonov AN-2R	1G175-03	
YR-PVD	Antonov AN-2R	1G175-04	
YR-PVF	Antonov AN-2R	1G174-37	
YR-PVG	Antonov AN-2R	1G175-06	
YR-PVH	Antonov AN-2R	1G175-07	
YR-PVI	Antonov AN-2R	1G175-08	
YR-PVK	Antonov AN-2R (CofA expired)	1G175-11	
YR-PVL	Antonov AN-2R (CofA expired)	1G175-10	
YR-PVM	Antonov AN-2R	1G175-12	
YR-PVN	Antonov AN-2R	1G175-13	
YR-PVO	Antonov AN-2R	1G175-14	
YR-PVP	Antonov AN-2R	1G175-15	
YR-PVR	Antonov AN-2R	1G175-16	
YR-PVU(2)	Antonov AN-2R	870901	
YR-RAG	Robinson R-44 Astro (CofA expired)	0085	
YR-RAP	Bell 206LT Twin Ranger	52170	N6275S
YR-RCO	Robinson R-44 Astro	0181	D-HGPT
YR-RCP	Robinson R-44 Astro	0181	
YR-RDA	Robinson R-22 Beta (CofA expired)	2549	
YR-RDV	Robinson R-44 Astro (CofA expired)	0164	
YR-REE	Robinson R-22 Beta	2356	OE-XPB
			N8013Q
YR-RNA	Robinson R-22	0251	D-HBRB
YR-RRA	Antonov AN-2	1G216-16	LZ-1229
YR-SAN	Antonov AN-2	1G182-24	UR-56467
			CCCP56467
YR-STF	Gemini Ultra	unkn	
YR-TPB	Tupolev TU-154B (CofA expired)	76A-161	
YR-TPD	Tupolev TU-154B (Wfu)	77A-224	
YR-TPE	Tupolev TU-154B-1 (Wfu)	77A-225	
YR-TPF	Tupolev TU-154B-1 (Wfu)	77A-239	
YR-TPG	Tupolev TU-154B-1 (CofA expired)	78A-262	
YR-TPK	Tupolev TU-154B-2 (Wfu)	80A-415	
YR-TPL	Tupolev TU-154B-2 (Wfu)	80A-428	
YR-VGA	Yakovlev YAK-40	9810757	ER-JGE
			RA-87210
			CCCP87210
YR-VIB	PZL-104 Wilga 35 (Wfu)	25026	
YR-VIC	PZL-104 Wilga 35 (Inactive)	25020	SP-CRK
YR-VIF	PZL-104 Wilga 35 (Inactive)	25022	
YR-VIG	PZL-104 Wilga 35 (Wfu)	48044	
YR-VIJ	PZL-104 Wilga 35 (Inactive)	59053	
YR-VIK	PZL-104 Wilga 35 (Wfu)	59054	

Regn.	Type	C/n	Prev.Id.
YR-VIM	PZL-104 Wilga 35 (Inactive)	59056	
YR-VIN	PZL-104 Wilga 35 (Inactive)	59057	
YR-VIO	PZL-104 Wilga 35A (Wfu)	118379	
YR-VIP	PZL-104 Wilga 35A (Wfu)	118380	
YR-VIR	PZL-104 Wilga 35A	118381	
YR-VIS	PZL-104 Wilga 35A	118382	
YR-VIT	PZL-104 Wilga 35A	118383	
YR-VIU	PZL-104 Wilga 35A	118384	
YR-VIV	PZL-104 Wilga 35A	118385	
YR-VIW	PZL-104 Wilga 35A (CofA expired)	118386	
YR-VIX	PZL-104 Wilga 35A	118387	
YR-VIY	PZL-104 Wilga 35A	118390	
YR-VIZ	PZL-104 Wilga 3 A	118388	
YR-VLA	PZL-104 Wilga 35A	118389	
YR-VLB	PZL-104 Wilga 35A	129445	
YR-VLC	PZL-104 Wilga 35A	129446	
YR-VLD	PZL-104 Wilga 35A (CofA expired)	129447	
YR-VLE	PZL-104 Wilga 35A	139502	
YR-VLF	PZL-104 Wilga 35A	139503	
YR-VLG	PZL-104 Wilga 35A	139504	
YR-VLH	PZL-104 Wilga 35A	139509	
YR-VLI	PZL-104 Wilga 35A (Wfu)	149514	
YR-VLK	PZL-104 Wilga 35A (Wfu)	149516	
YR-VLL	PZL-104 Wilga 35A	149517	
YR-VLN	PZL-104 Wilga 35A	149519	
YR-YAV	Antonov AN-2	1G124-47	RusAF:47 YR-PAB
YR-ZAV	Zlin Z.50LA (Inactive)	0015	
YR-ZAX	Zlin Z.50LS (Inactive)	0034	
YR-ZAY	Zlin Z.50LS (CofA expired)	0036	
YR-ZBA	Zlin Z.726	1336	
YR-ZBB	Zlin Z.726	1337	
YR-ZBC	Zlin Z.726	1338	
YR-ZBD	Zlin Z.726	1339	
YR-ZBF	Zlin Z.726	1341	
YR-ZBG	Zlin Z.726	1342	
YR-ZBH	Zlin Z.726	1343	
YR-ZBI	Zlin Z.726	1344	
YR-ZBJ	Zlin Z.726	1345	
YR-ZBK	Zlin Z.726	1346	
YR-ZBL	Zlin Z.726	1347	
YR-ZBM	Zlin Z.726	1348	
YR-ZBN	Zlin Z.726	1349	
YR-ZBP	Zlin Z.726	1351	
YR-ZBR	Zlin Z.726	1352	
YR-ZCA	Zlin Z.142	0396	
YR-ZCB	Zlin Z.142	0397	
YR-ZCD	Zlin Z.142 (CofA expired)	0391	
YR-ZCF	Zlin Z.142	0423	
YR-ZCG	Zlin Z.142 (Wfu)	0424	
YR-ZCI	Zlin Z.142	0461	
YR-ZCJ	Zlin Z.142 (Wfu)	0462	
YR-ZCK	Zlin Z.142 (Wfu)	0463	
YR-ZCL	Zlin Z.142	0464	
YR-ZCM	Zlin Z.142	0465	
YR-ZCN	Zlin Z.142 (Wfu)	0468	
YR-ZCO	Zlin Z.142	0469	
YR-ZCP	Zlin Z.142 (CofA expired)	0470	
YR-ZLJ	Zlin 526F Trenér Master	1092	
YR-ZNA	Zlin Z.50LS (CofA expired)	0039	
YR-ZNB	Zlin Z.50LS (Inactive)	0043	
YR-...	Beech B300 Super King Air	FL-73	N8270R
YR-...	Bell 206L-1 Long Ranger II	45362	N333DZ
YR-...	Bell 412EP	36154	N7233Z C-GFNM
YR-...	Reims/Cessna F.150G	0185	D-EBZO

GLIDERS AND MOTOR-GLIDERS

Regn.	Type	C/n	Prev.Id.
YR-101(2)	SZD-48 Jantar Standard 2 (Dism.)	W-859	
YR-102(2)	SZD-48 Jantar Standard 2 (Dism.)	W-867	
YR-103	SZD-41A Jantar Standard	B-909	
YR-105	SZD-48 Jantar Standard 2 (Dism.)	W-873	SP-3153
YR-106	SZD-48-1 Jantar Standard 2 (Dism.)	B-987	
YR-107-RF	SZD-48-1 Jantar Standard 2 (Dism.)	B-1099	
YR-108	SZD-48-1 Jantar Standard 2	B-1100	
YR-109-RT	SZD-48-1 Jantar Standard 2	B-1250	
YR-110-RC	SZD-48-1 Jantar Standard 2	B-1252	
YR-131-VT	SZD-42-2 Jantar 2B	B-863	
YR-132	SZD-42-2 Jantar 2B	B-870	
YR-133-RN	SZD-42-2 Jantar 2B	B-908	
YR-134	SZD-42-2 Jantar 2B	B-1065	
YR-135-RL	SZD-42-2 Jantar 2B	B-1313	
YR-156	SZD-24-4A Foka	W-303	
YR-157	SZD-24-4A Foka (Dism.)	W-309	
YR-158	SZD-24-4A Foka	W-339	
YR-159	SZD-24-4A Foka	W-362	
YR-160	SZD-24-4A Foka	W-363	
YR-162	SZD-24-4A Foka	W-333	
YR-163	SZD-24-4A Foka	W-331	
YR-164	SZD-24-4A Foka (Dism.)	W-355	
YR-165	SZD-24-4A Foka (Dism.)	W-356	
YR-166	SZD-24-4A Foka (Dism.)	W-357	
YR-167	SZD-24-4A Foka	W-358	
YR-168	SZD-24-4A Foka	W-369	
YR-169	SZD-24-4A Foka	W-375	
YR-170	SZD-24-4A Foka	W-376	
YR-171	SZD-24-4A Foka	W-377	
YR-172	SZD-24-4A Foka	W-381	
YR-173	SZD-24-4A Foka	W-382	
YR-174	SZD-32A Foka 5	W-435	
YR-175	SZD-32A Foka 5	W-436	
YR-176	SZD-32A Foka 5	W-437	
YR-178	SZD-32A Foka 5	W-439	
YR-179	SZD-32A Foka 5 (Dism.)	W-446	
YR-180	SZD-32A Foka 5	W-447	
YR-181	SZD-32A Foka 5	W-463	
YR-184	SZD-32A Foka 5	W-466	
YR-188	IAR IS.29D	26	
YR-193	IAR IS.29D	48	
YR-194	IAR IS.29D2 (Dism.)	55	
YR-196	IAR IS.29D2	57	
YR-205	LET L-13 Blanik (Dism.)	173421 ?	
YR-212	LET L-13 Blanik (Dism.)	173449 ?	
YR-213	LET L-13 Blanik (Dism.)	173458 ?	
YR-281	IAR IS.28B2	06	
YR-283	IAR IS.28B2 (Dism.)	141	
YR-286	IAR IS.28B2	30	
YR-291	IAR IS.29D2	65	
YR-292	IAR IS.29D2 (Dism.)	75	
YR-295	IAR IS.28B2	107	
YR-296	IAR IS.28B2	131	
YR-298	IAR IS.28B2 (Dism.)	unkn	
YR-300	IAR IS.28B2	135	
YR-301	IAR IS.28B2	136	
YR-302	IAR IS.28B2	137	
YR-304	IAR IS.28B2	139	
YR-307	IAR IS.28B2	162	
YR-310	IAR IS.28M2	140	
YR-311	IAR IS.28M2	161	
YR-312	IAR IS.28B2 (Dism.)	165	
YR-315	IAR IS.28B2	168	
YR-317	IAR IS.28B2 (Dism.)	142	
YR-319	IAR IS.28B2	unkn	
YR-323	IAR IS.28B2 (Derelict)	unkn	
YR-326	IAR IS.28B2 (Dism.)	unkn	
YR-327	IAR IS.28B2 (Dism.)	unkn	
YR-328	IAR IS.28B2 (Dism.)	183	
YR-329	IAR IS.28B2	184	
YR-331	IAR IS.28B2	186	
YR-332	IAR IS.28B2	unkn	
YR-333	IAR IS.28B2	188	

686

Regn.	Type	C/n	Prev.Id.
YR-334	IAR IS.28B2	144	
YR-337	IAR IS.28B2	210	
YR-343	IAR IS.28B2	223	
YR-345	IAR IS.28B2	225	
YR-346	IAR IS.28B2	unkn	
YR-347	IAR IS.28B2	155	
YR-348	IAR IS.28B2	158	
YR-351	IAR IS.28B2	226	
YR-353	IAR IS.28B2	255	
YR-356	IAR IS.28B2	146	
YR-357	IAR IS.28B2 (Dism.)	256	
YR-358	IAR IS.28B2	261	
YR-360	IAR IS.28B2	231	
YR-364	IAR IS.28B2	257	
YR-366	IAR IS.28B2	unkn	
YR-369	IAR IS.28B2 (Dism.)	264	
YR-370	IAR IS.28B2 (Dism.)	284	
YR-371	IAR IS.28B2	unkn	
YR-372	IAR IS.28B2	283	
YR-373	IAR IS.28B2	233	
YR-375	IAR IS.28B2	265	
YR-376	IAR IS.28B2	285	
YR-377	IAR IS.28B2	267	
YR-378	IAR IS.28B2	unkn	
YR-383	IAR IS.28B2 (Dism.)	268	
YR-384	IAR IS.28B2	unkn	
YR-385	IAR IS.28B2	276	
YR-388	IAR IS.28B2	307	
YR-390	IAR IS.28B2 (Dism.)	305	
YR-391	IAR IS.28B2	316	
YR-393	IAR IS.28B2	313	
YR-394	IAR IS.28B2	314	
YR-395	IAR IS.28B2	325	
YR-502	IAT IS.29D2 (Dism.)	89	
YR-503-E	IAR IS.29D2 (Dism.)	74	
YR-504	IAR IS.28B2	unkn	
YR-508	IAT IS.29D2 (Dism.)	unkn	
YR-511-C	IAT IS.29D2 (Dism.)	101	
YR-513	IAT IS.29D2 (Dism.)	103	
YR-514-J	IAT IS.29B1 (Dism.)	108	
YR-516	IAT IS.29D2	111	
YR-518	IAT IS.29D2	114	
YR-520	IAT IS.28B2 (Dism.)	unkn	
YR-524	IAT IS.29D2	120	
YR-529	IAT IS.29D2 (Dism.)	128	
YR-531	IAR IS.28D2	122	
YR-532	IAT IS.29D2 (Dism.)	123	
YR-537	IAR IS.28D2	140	
YR-539	IAR IS.28D2	134	
YR-540	IAT IS.29D2	135	
YR-541	IAR IS.28D2	136	
YR-543	IAR IS.28D2	143	
YR-546	IAT IS.29D2	146	
YR-548	IAT IS.29D2	148	
YR-550	IAR IS.28D2	152	
YR-551	IAR IS.28B2	unkn	
YR-555	IAT IS.29D2	195	
YR-557-W	IAT IS.29D2 (Dism.)	198	
YR-558	IAT IS.29D2	162	
YR-560	IAT IS.29D2 (Dism.)	204	
YR-602	IAR IS.28D2 (?)	12	
YR-603	IAR IS.28/29 (Dism.)	14	
YR-605	IAR IS.32A	07	
YR-803	IAR IS.28M2	06	
YR-809	IAT IS.29M2	47	
YR-811	IAT IS.29M2	49	
YR-812	IAT IS.29M2 (Dism.)	66	
YR-904	IAR IS.3D (Stored)	unkn	
YR-909	IAR IS.3D (Dism.)	unkn	
YR-910	IAR IS.3D (Dism.)	unkn	
YR-911	IAR IS.3D (Stored)	unkn	
YR-1006	IAR IS.29C	unkn	
YR-1007	IAR IS.28B	01	
YR-1012	IAR IS.29D 2	unkn	
YR-1013	IAR IS.28B - M2	01	

Regn.	Type	C/n	Prev.Id.
YR-1015	IAR IS.28M (Dism.)	02	
YR-1017	IAR IS.32	01	
YR-1018	IAR IS.28M-1	01	
YR-1020	IAR IS.30 Metallique	01	
YR-1023	IAR IS.34	02	
YR-1026	IAR IS.28M-A	01	
YR-1028	IAR IS.29D2	93	
YR-1033	IAR IS.35 Acro	01	
YR-1036	IAR-35 Acro	01	
YR-1037	IAR-46	01	
YR-1926	IAR IS.28M-2	unkn	
YR-1976	IAR IS.28M-2	56	

MICROLIGHTS

Regn.	Type	C/n	Prev.Id.
YR-1500	Quicksilver GT-500	unkn	
YR-5000	AK-22	unkn	
YR-6106 ?	Servoplant Aerocraft	unkn	
YR-6117	Servoplant Aerocraft	02	
YR-6118	Type unknown	unkn	
YR-6119	Apollo	unkn	
YR-6120	Servoplant Aerocraft	03	
YR-6121	Eipper Quicksilver GT-500	unkn	

YU - YUGOSLAVIA
(SERBIA & MONTENEGRO)

The status of many aircraft on the Register is unknown

Regn.	Type	C/n	Prev.Id.
YU-AHN	McDonnell-Douglas DC-9-32	47470	
YU-AHU	McDonnell-Douglas DC-9-32	47532	
YU-AHV	McDonnell-Douglas DC-9-32	47460	
YU-AJH	McDonnell-Douglas DC-9-32	47562	N1345U
YU-AJI	McDonnell-Douglas DC-9-32	47563	N1346U
YU-AJK	McDonnell-Douglas DC-9-32	47568	
YU-AJM	McDonnell-Douglas DC-9-32	47582	
YU-AKB	Boeing 727-2H9 *(Wfu ?)*	20931	
YU-AKD	Boeing 727-2H9 *(Lsd. to Air Gabon)*	21040	OY-SBJ
			YU-AKD
			JRV74302
			JRV14302
			YU-AKD
YU-AKE	Boeing 727-2H9 *(Wfu ?)*	21037	
YU-AKF	Boeing 727-2H9 *(Wfu ?)*	21038	
YU-AKG	Boeing 727-2H9 *(Wfu ?)*	21039	
YU-AKH	Boeing 727-2L8	21080	OY-SBP
			YU-AKH
			JRV74301
			JRV14301
			(YU-AKH)
YU-AKI	Boeing 727-2H9	22393	
YU-AKJ	Boeing 727-2H9	22394	N8281V
YU-AKK	Boeing 727-2H9	22665	TS-JEA
			YU-AKK
			N1780B
YU-AKL	Boeing 727-2H9	22666	TS-JEB
			YU-AKL
YU-AKM	Boeing 727-243 *(Wfu ?)*	22702	HK-3618X
			YU-AKM
			I-DIRT
YU-AKP	Yakovlev Yak-40 *(to Serbian AF?)*	9120707	JRV71501
YU-AKT	Yakovlev Yak-40	9222020	JRV71503
YU-AKV	Yakovlev Yak-40	9630849	JRV71505
YU-ALN	Aeritalia/SNIAS ATR-72-201	180	F-WWEP
YU-ALO	Aeritalia/SNIAS ATR-72-201	186	F-WWEW
YU-ALP	Aeritalia/SNIAS ATR-72-201	189	F-WWED
YU-AMB	McDonnell-Douglas DC-10-30 *(Stored)*	46988	
YU-AND	Boeing 737-3H9	23329	
YU-ANF	Boeing 737-3H9	23330	
YU-ANH	Boeing 737-3H9	23415	TC-CYO
	(Wfu, stored ?)		YU-ANH
			PP-SNY
			YU-ANH
YU-ANI	Boeing 737-3H9	23416	
YU-ANK	Boeing 737-3H9	23715	
YU-ANP	Boeing 737-2K3	23912	
YU-ANV	Boeing 737-3H9	24140	
YU-ANW	Boeing 737-3H9	24141	TS-IED
			YU-ANW
YU-AOH	Fokker F.28 Fellowship 4000	11184	OO-DJB
			TY-BBN
			PH-ZCE
			(N524)
			PH-EXO
YU-AOI	Fokker F.28 Fellowship 4000	11176	PH-CHN
			PK-MSX
			PH-CHN
			OK-MEO
			PH-CHN
			(N522)
			PH-EXU
YU-BCB	Piper PA-25-235 Pawnee B	25-....	
	(c/n 25-3065 quoted, but this is confirmed as EC-AYV)		
YU-BCC	Antonov AN-2M	600310	
YU-BCJ	Antonov AN-2M	600407	
YU-BCL	Antonov AN-2M	600406	
YU-BCM	Antonov AN-2M	600408	

Regn.	Type	C/n	Prev.Id.
YU-BCW	Piper PA-25-235 Pawnee B	25-3848	N7691Z
YU-BCZ	Macchi AL.60B-2	73/6253	
YU-BDW	LET Z-37 Cmelák	02-06	
YU-BEI	Antonov AN-2M	701725	
YU-BEK	Antonov AN-2M *(Cld ?)*	701726	
YU-BEV	Grumman G.164 Agcat *(Cld ?)*	499	
YU-BFX	Piper PA-25-235 Pawnee	25-2590	SE-EIB
YU-BGB	Piper PA-30-160 Twin Comanche C	30-1903	N8750Y
YU-BGW(3)	PZL-104 Wilga 35A	140547	(SP-WDD)
	(Possible error for YU-DGW ?)		
YU-BGX	Grumman G.164A Agcat *(Cld ?)*	671	
YU-BHK(2)	Beech A60 Duke	P-164	N4232A
YU-BHL	Beech A60 Duke	P-176	N9325Q
YU-BIB	UTVA-66	0841	
YU-BII	Cessna 402B	0352	N5088Q
YU-BIW	Cessna 340	0345	N6950B
YU-BIX	Cessna 402B	0593	N3735C
YU-BJF	Antonov AN-2R	1G160-03	
YU-BJG	Gates Learjet 25B	25B-187	
YU-BJI	Grumman G.164A Agcat *(Cld ?)*	1422	
YU-BJK	Grumman G.164A Agcat *(Cld ?)*	1466	
YU-BJN	Grumman G.164A Agcat *(Cld ?)*	1420	
YU-BJT	Grumman G.164A Agcat *(Cld ?)*	1484	
YU-BJX	Piper PA-25-235 Pawnee	25-2592	YU-BFY
			SE-EID
YU-BJZ	Antonov AN-2R *(To Z3- ?)*	1G167-04	
YU-BKG	Antonov AN-2T *(To T9- ?)*	1G167-28	
YU-BKK	Antonov AN-2R	1G167-08	
YU-BKL	Antonov AN-2R	1G167-11	
YU-BKM	Antonov AN-2R	1G172-49	
YU-BKO	Antonov AN-2R *(Cld ?)*	1G172-51	
YU-BKR	Gates Learjet 25D	25D-221	N3819G
YU-BKU	Grumman G.164B Agcat	210B	N6696Q
YU-BKV	Grumman G.164B Agcat	228B	N6712Q
YU-BKW	Grumman G.164B Agcat	235B	N6724Q
YU-BKX	Grumman G.164B Agcat	246B	N6732Q
YU-BLE	PA-25-235 Pawnee	25-37756	YU-BDI
			N7789Z
YU-BLG	Grumman G.164B Agcat *(Cld ?)*	329B	N6871Q
YU-BLH	Grumman G.164B Agcat *(Cld ?)*	330B	N6872Q
YU-BLJ	Piper PA-25-260 Pawnee D	25-7856035	N9180T
YU-BLK	Cessna T.310R	1431	D-IBEK(2)
			YU-BLK
			N5287C
YU-BLM	Cessna T.310R	1433	N5290C
YU-BLN	Cessna T.310R	1434	N5292C
YU-BLX	PZL M-18 Dromader	1Z001-03	SP-PBY
YU-BLZ	PZL M-18 Dromader	1Z001-04	SP-PBX
YU-BMJ	Grumman G.164B Agcat *(Wfu)*	379B	N6583K
YU-BMM	Piper PA-31T-620 Cheyenne	31T-8020021	"YU-IIOO"
			(D-IIOO)
			N2382W
YU-BMY	PZL M-18A Dromader	1Z010-02	
YU-BMZ	PZL M-18A Dromader	1Z010-03	
YU-BNA	Dassault Falcon 50	43	JRV72102
			F-WZHO
YU-BNB	PZL M-18A Dromader	1Z010-04	
YU-BNC	PZL M-18A Dromader	1Z010-05	
YU-BND	PZL M-18A Dromader	1Z010-06	
YU-BNG	PZL M-18A Dromader	1Z010-14	
YU-BNH	PZL M-18A Dromader	1Z010-15	
YU-BNJ	Cessna 310	unkn	
YU-BNK	PZL M-18A Dromader	1Z010-18	
YU-BNL	PZL M-18A Dromader	1Z010-19	
YU-BNM	PZL M-18A Dromader	1Z010-20	
YU-BNT	PZL M-18A Dromader	1Z013-11	
YU-BNU	PZL M-18A Dromader	1Z013-12	
YU-BNV	PZL M-18A Dromader	1Z013-13	
YU-BNY	PZL M-18A Dromader	1Z013-41	
YU-BOA	Antonov AN-2R	1G216-02	
YU-BOB	Antonov AN-2R	1G216-01	
YU-BON	Antonov AN-2R	1G221-60	
YU-BOT	Antonov AN-2R	1G223-11	
YU-BOU	Antonov AN-2R	1G223-12	
YU-BOV	PZL M-18A Dromader	1Z016-13	

Regn.	Type	C/n	Prev.Id.
YU-BOX	Antonov AN-2R	1G223-39	
YU-BPA	Antonov AN-2R	1G225-31	
YU-BPB	PZL M-18A Dromader	1Z016-11	SP-DBO
YU-BPC	Antonov AN-2R	1G228-45	SP-BPC
YU-BPD	PZL M-18A Dromader	1Z017-01	SP-DBN
YU-BPE	Antonov AN-2R	1G228-25	
YU-BPF	Piper PA-31T Cheyenne II	31T-8020006	N801CM
YU-BPG	Piper PA-31T Cheyenne II	31T-8020012	N2328W
YU-BPH	Piper PA-31T Cheyenne II	31T-8020063	N2389V
YU-BPO	Antonov AN-2R	1G231-56	SP-DNC
YU-BPY	Gates Learjet 35A	35A-173	N116EL
			(N83DM)
			N116EL
			N100GU
			(HZ-NCI)
			N750GL
			HZ-MIB
			N750GL
YU-BPZ	Dassault Falcon 50	25	JRV72101
			F-WZHI
YU-BRA	Gates Learjet 25	25-202	JRV70401
			JRV10401
			N3807G
YU-BRB	Gates Learjet 25B	25B-203	JRV70402
			JRV10402
			N3811G
YU-BRD	Piper PA-32-300 Cherokee Six	32-40209	N4141W
YU-BRL	Antonov AN-2R	1G218-52	SP-FLD
			RA-33065
			CCCP33065
YU-BRM	Cessna 421C (Identity unconfirmed)	0893	N282PT
YU-BRN	Antonov AN-2R	1G229-06	SP-FLE
			RA-33514
			CCCP33514
YU-CAK	Champion 7GCBC Citabria (To T9- ?)	282-70	
YU-CAW	Champion 7GCBC Citabria	unkn	
YU-CBK	Reims/Cessna FRA.150L Aerobat	0166	
YU-CCI	Reims/Cessna F.150L	1056	(I-NOLQ)
YU-CCK	Reims/Cessna F.172M	1148	
YU-CCM	Reims/Cessna F.172M	1073	
YU-CCN	Reims/Cessna F.172M	1074	
YU-CCO	Reims/Cessna F.172M	1077	
YU-CCP	Reims/Cessna F.172M	1078	
YU-CCS	Reims/Cessna F.172M	1154	
YU-CCT	Reims/Cessna F.172M	1155	
YU-CCU	Reims/Cessna F.172M	1160	
YU-CCV	Reims/Cessna F.172M	1167	
YU-CCW	Reims/Cessna F.172M	1172	
YU-CCX	Reims/Cessna F.172M	1173	
YU-CCY	Reims/Cessna F.172M	1177	
YU-CCZ	Reims/Cessna F.172M	1183	
YU-DAY	Piper PA-28-140 Cherokee D	28-7125609	N11C
YU-DBW	Piper PA-18-150 Super Cub	18-7809055	N4077E
YU-DCC	Piper PA-18-150 Super Cub	18-7809163	N82169
YU-DCK	Piper PA-18-150 Super Cub	18-7809165	N82177
YU-DCL	Piper PA-18-150 Super Cub	18-7809166	N82182
YU-DCM	Piper PA-18-150 Super Cub	18-7809154	N82071
YU-DCN	Reims/Cessna F.172N	1738	
YU-DCO	Reims/Cessna F.172N	1741	
YU-DCP	Reims/Cessna F.172N	1742	
YU-DCR	Reims/Cessna F.172N	1745	
YU-DCS	Reims/Cessna F.172N	1746	
YU-DCT	Reims/Cessna F.172N	1747	
YU-DCU	Reims/Cessna F.172N	1748	
YU-DCV	Piper PA-28-161 Warrior II	28-7916051	N21714
YU-DCX	Piper PA-28-161 Warrior II	28-7916053	N21797
YU-DCZ	Piper PA-28-161 Warrior II	28-7916055	N21865
YU-DDB	Piper PA-28-161 Warrior II	28-7916057	N21963
YU-DDF	Champion 7GCBC Citabria (To T9- ?)	unkn	
YU-DEP	UTVA-75 (To T9- ?)	unkn	JRV53109
YU-DER	UTVA 75	unkn	JRV53110
YU-DET	UTVA 75	unkn	JRV53 . . .
YU-DEZ	UTVA-75	unkn	JRV53116
YU-DFC	PZL-104 Wilga 35A	139505	
YU-DFD	PZL-104 Wilga 35A	139506	
YU-DFE	PZL-104 Wilga 35A	139507	
YU-DFF	PZL-104 Wilga 35A	139508	
YU-DGG	UTVA-75	unkn	JRV53172
YU-DGM	UTVA-75	unkn	JRV53178
YU-DHA	UTVA-75	unkn	JRV53186 ?
YU-DHD	UTVA-75	unkn	Z3-DCG
			YU-DHD
			JRV53189
YU-DHH	UTVA-75	unkn	JRV53193 ?
YU-DHJ	UTVA-75	unkn	JRV53195
YU-DHK	UTVA-75	unkn	JRV53196
YU-DHO	UTVA-75	unkn	JRV53200
YU-DHS	PZL-104 Wilga 80	CF15810604	
YU-DHV	PZL-104 Wilga 80	CF15810607	
YU-DHX	PZL-104 Wilga 80	CF15810611	
YU-DHY	PZL-104 Wilga 80	CF15810612	
YU-DIA	Reims/Cessna F.172P	2157	
YU-DIB	Reims/Cessna F.172P	2158	
YU-DIC	Reims/Cessna F.172P	2159	
YU-DID	UTVA-75	unkn	JRV53 . . .
YU-DIE	UTVA-75	unkn	JRV53 . . .
YU-DIL	UTVA-75	unkn	JRV53208
YU-DIS	Reims/Cessna F.172P	2192	F-WZNE
YU-DIT	Reims/Cessna F.172P	2193	F-WZNF
YU-DIX	UTVA-75	unkn	JRV53 . . .
YU-DIY	UTVA-75	unkn	JRV53 . . .
YU-DJF	UTVA-75	unkn	JRV53 . . .
YU-DJK	UTVA-75	unkn	JRV53 . . .
YU-DJU	UTVA-75	unkn	JRV53234
YU-DJV	UTVA-75	unkn	JRV53235
YU-DJW	UTVA-75	unkn	JRV53236
YU-DJY	Reims/Cessna FA.152	0383	F-WZNG
YU-DJZ	Reims/Cessna FA.152	0386	F-WZNH
YU-DKA	Reims/Cessna FA.152	0387	F-WZNI
YU-DKB	UTVA-75	unkn	JRV53240
YU-DKC	UTVA-75	unkn	JRV53241
YU-DKL	UTVA-75	unkn	JRV53124
YU-DKM	UTVA-75	unkn	JRV53250
YU-DKO	UTVA-75	unkn	JRV53136
YU-DLH	UTVA-66 (To T9- ?)	unkn	JRV51 . . .
YU-DMH	Zlin Z.142 (Wfu ?)	0531	
YU-DMI (2)	Cessna 172	unkn	
YU-DML(2)	Piper PA-28-161 Warrior II	28-8116319	N8436H
YU-DMM(2)	UTVA-75	unkn	JRV53247
YU-DMN	UTVA-66	unkn	JRV51182
YU-DMP	Piper PA-28-	unkn	
YU-DMR	UTVA-66	unkn	JRV51 . . .
YU-DMT	UTVA-66	unkn	JRV51 . . .
YU-DMV	Cessna 172	unkn	
YU-HAS	Agusta-Bell 206A Jet Ranger II	8311	
YU-HAT	Agusta-Bell 206A Jet Ranger II	8317	
YU-HAU	Agusta-Bell 206A Jet Ranger II	8316	
YU-HAW	Agusta-Bell 206A Jet Ranger II	8314	
YU-HAY	Agusta-Bell 206A Jet Ranger II	8318	
YU-HAZ	Agusta-Bell 206A Jet Ranger II	8319	
YU-HBB	Aérospatiale SA.341G Gazelle (Cld ?)	1020	
YU-HBH	Aérospatiale SA.341G Gazelle	1292	
YU-HBJ	Aérospatiale SA.341G Gazelle	1304	
YU-HBK	Aérospatiale SA.341G Gazelle	1348	
YU-HBS	Bell 206L-1 Long Ranger II	45274	N2769C
YU-HBU	Bell 206B Jet Ranger II	2731	N2769P
YU-HBV	Bell 206B Jet Ranger II	2735	N2770D
YU-HBW	Bell 206B Jet Ranger II	2739	N2770H
YU-HBX	Bell 206B Jet Ranger II	2747	N2770N
YU-HBY	Bell 206B Jet Ranger II	2749	N2769X
YU-HCA	Agusta-Bell 212	5709	
YU-HCB	Agusta-Bell 212	5710	
YU-HCC	Agusta-Bell 212	5712	
YU-HCE	Agusta-Bell 212 (Crashed)	5713	
YU-HCL	Bell 206B Jet Ranger II	2897	
YU-HCN	Bell 206L-1 Long Ranger II	45399	N1082A
YU-HCO	Bell 206B Jet Ranger II	2978	N1086S
YU-HCU	Aérospatiale SA.365N Dauphin 2	6112	
YU-HDD	Mil Mi-2 (Stored, France)	541108069	
YU-HDE	Mil Mi-2 (Stored, France)	541129069	

Regn.	Type	C/n	Prev.Id.
YU-HDN	Soko 341G Gazelle	unkn	JRV126 ..
YU-HDP	Soko 341G Gazelle	27	JRV12659
YU-HDR	Mil Mi-2	unkn	
YU-HDY	Soko 341G Gazelle	unkn	JRV126 ..
YU-HEE	Soko 341G Gazelle	unkn	JRV12622
YU-HEF	Soko 341G Gazelle	009	JRV12617
YU-HEH	Soko 341G Gazelle	011	JRV12619
YU-HEI	Soko 341G Gazelle	unkn	JRV126 ..
YU-HEJ	Mil Mi-2	unkn	
YU-HEK	Soko 341G Gazelle	012 ?	JRV12620
YU-HEL	Mil Mi-2	511109059	JRV12511
YU-SEB	Sikorsky S-76B	760444	
YU-XAF	UTVA-75 AG-II	unkn	JRV53265
YU-YAB	Soko Galeb G-2A	unkn	JRV23170
YU-ZBI	Zmo *(Destroyed in crash)*	unkn	
YU-ZBJ	Aero Poni V *(Destroyed in crash)*	unkn	
YU-ZBK	Rans S-6 Coyote II (Kojot)	unkn	
YU-ZBM	Rans S-6 Coyote II (Kojot)	unkn	
YU-. . .	Reims/Cessna F.152	1572	D-EABN(2)

BALLOONS AND AIRSHIPS

YU-O........	Colt 69A HAFB	916	
YU-O........	Colt 77A HAFB	917	
YU-O........	Colt 69A HAFB	918	
YU-O........	Colt AS-56 Hot Air Airship	919	
YU-OAE	Cameron V-77 HAFB	8909	
	(Correct c/n possibly 1909, not connected with S5-OAE)		

GLIDERS

The following gliders include those known to have been active in Serbia in 1990/1 prior to hostilities, together with recent reports of current aircraft. The current status of many cannot be confirmed.

YU-4207-VS	VTC Cirrus	unkn
YU-4208-08	Schempp-Hirth Standard Cirrus	unkn
YU-4215	VTC-75 Standard Cirrus	unkn
YU-4221-21	VTC Cirrus 17	unkn
YU-4227-27	VTC-75 Standard Cirrus	unkn
YU-4229-29	VTC-75 Standard Cirrus	unkn
YU-4265	VTC-75 Standard Cirrus	unkn
YU-4268	Pilatus B4-PC11 *(To T9- ?)*	unkn
YU-4276	VTC-75 Standard Cirrus	unkn
YU-4277-77	VTC-75 Standard Cirrus	unkn
YU-4284	VTC-75 Standard Cirrus	unkn
YU-4299	VTC-75 Standard Cirrus	unkn
YU-4303-03	VTC-75 Standard Cirrus	unkn
YU-4305-05	VTC-75 Standard Cirrus	unkn
YU-4310	Glaser-Dirks DG-100 Elan *(To S5- ?)*	unkn
YU-4332-32	VTC-75 Standard Cirrus	unkn
YU-4333	VTC Cirrus 17A	unkn
YU-4334	VTC Cirrus 17A	unkn
YU-4335	VTC-76 VUK-T	unkn
YU-4347-FI	Glaser-Dirks DG-100G Elan	unkn
YU-4355	VTC-76 VUK-T	266
YU-4356	VTC-76 VUK-T	267
YU-4357	VTC-76 VUK-T	268
YU-4359	VTC-76 VUK-T	270
YU-4360	VTC-76 VUK-T *(W/o ?)*	271
YU-4361	VTC-76 VUK-T	272
YU-4364	VTC-76 VUK-T	285
YU-4371	VTC-76 VUK-T	unkn

Regn.	Type	C/n	Prev.Id.
YU-4375	VTC-76 VUK-T	298	
YU-4376	VTC-76 VUK-T	299 ?	
YU-4380	VTC-76 VUK-T	301	
YU-4381	VTC-76 VUK-T	304	
YU-4383	VTC-76 VUK-T	308	
YU-4389	VTC-76 VUK-T	311	
YU-4392	VTC-76 VUK-T	314	
YU-4394	VTC-76 VUK-T	316	
YU-4400	VTC-76 VUK-T	322 ?	
YU-4401	VTC-76 VUK-T	323	
YU-4402	VTC-76 VUK-T	324	
YU-4415	VTC-76 VUK-T	339	
YU-4422	VTC-76 VUK-T *(Belgrade Museum)*	346	
YU-4425-AM	Glaser-Dirks DG-300 Elan	unkn	
YU-4426	VTC-76 VUK-T	347 ?	
YU-4428	VTC-76 VUK-T	349	
YU-4429	VTC-76 VUK-T	350	
YU-4430	VTC-76 VUK-T	376	
YU-4431	VTC-76 VUK-T	377	
YU-4432	VTC-76 VUK-T	378 ?	
YU-4434	VTC-76 VUK-T	380	
YU-4436	VTC-76 VUK-T	382	
YU-4457	Glaser-Dirks DG-300 Elan	unkn	
YU-5322	LET L-13 Blanik	unkn	
YU-5331	LET L-13 Blanik	174915 ?	
YU-5332-33	LET L-13 Blanik	174905	
YU-5333	LET L-13 Blanik	174916	
YU-5356	LET L-13 Blanik	unkn	
YU-5366	LET L-13 Blanik	unkn	
YU-5367	LET L-13 Blanik	unkn	
YU-5371	LET L-13 Blanik	026721	
YU-5375	LET L-13 Blanik	026921	
YU-5377	LET L-13 Blanik	unkn	
YU-5393	KR-03A Puchatek	03-02	
YU-6012	Grob G.109	unkn	

ZA - ALBANIA

Regn.	Type	C/n	Prev.Id.
ZA-ADA	Embraer EMB.110P1 Bandeirante	110-303	F-GCMQ
			PT-SCK
ZA-HOV	Bell 222UT	47555	AL-HOV
			SE-HOV
ZA-HTB	Aérospatiale AS.350B Ecureuil	1851	
ZA-HTD	Aérospatiale AS.350B Ecureuil	1852	
ZA-H..	Aérospatiale AS.350B Ecureuil	1853	

Former Yugoslav Republic of
Z3 - MACEDONIA

Regn.	Type	C/n	Prev.Id.
Z3-AAA	Boeing 737-	unkn	
Z3-AAB	McDonnell-Douglas DC-9-32	47571	YU-AJL
Z3-AAC	McDonnell-Douglas DC-9-83	49442	EI-CBO
			HB-IUL
			SE-DRU
			TC-TRU
			EI-CBO
			EC-ECO
			N6203D
Z3-ARA	McDonnell-Douglas DC-9-33RC	47530	S5-ABG
			SL-ABG
			YU-AHW
Z3-ARB	McDonnell-Douglas DC-9-81	48046	N801VV
			S5-ABE
			SL-ABE
			YU-AJZ
Z3-ARC	McDonnell-Douglas DC-9-41	47613	OH-LNC
	(Cancelled ?)		EC-DQT
			OH-LNC
			N54641
			JA8429
Z3-ARD	McDonnell-Douglas DC-9-41	47606	OH-LND
	(Cancelled ?)		JA8426
Z3-ARE	McDonnell-Douglas DC-9-32	47567	YU-AJJ
			N1347U
Z3-ARF	Boeing 737-3H9	23716	YU-ANL
			TS-IEC
			YU-ANL
Z3-BAA	Gates Learjet 25B	25B-205	YU-BKJ
			N1468B
Z3-BAB	Beech 200 Super King Air	BB-652	YU-BMF
			(N88DA)
			YU-BMF
			N6727C
Z3-BGA	Antonov AN-2R	1G167-01	YU-BJV
Z3-BGB	Antonov AN-2R	1G160-15	YU-BLD
			SP-WOB
Z3-BGC	Antonov AN-2R	1G167-03	YU-BJY
Z3-BGD	Antonov AN-2R	1G111-15	YU-BGK
Z3-BGF	Antonov AN-2R	1G231-55	YU-BPJ
Z3-BGG	Antonov AN-2R	1G115-15	YU-BGZ
Z3-BGH	Antonov AN-2R	1G111-12	YU-BGH
Z3-BGJ	Antonov AN-2	1G166-04	LZ-1502
			RA-19750
			CCCP19750
Z3-BGL(2)	Antonov AN-2R	1G206-19	LZ-1202
Z3-DCA	Antonov AN-2	unkn	
Z3-DCB	UTVA-66	unkn	YU-DLN
			JRV.....
Z3-DCC	UTVA-75	unkn	YU-DFB
			JRV53118
Z3-DCD	UTVA-75	unkn	YU-DKR
			JRV53159
Z3-DCF	UTVA-75	unkn	YU-DGX
			JRV53183
Z3-DCH	UTVA-75	unkn	YU-DLX
			JRV53...
Z3-DCL	Reims/Cessna F.172M	1062	D-ELON(3)
Z3-DCM	Zlin Z.242L	0700	OK-BNE
Z3-DCN	Zlin Z.242L	0701	OK-BNF
Z3-DCO	Zlin Z.242L	0702	OK-BNG
Z3-DCP	Zlin Z.242L	0703	OK-BNH
Z3-DCR	Antonov AN-2	unkn	LZ- ?
Z3-HAA	Agusta-Bell 206B Jet Ranger II	8365	YU-HBD
Z3-HAB	Agusta-Bell 212	5626	YU-HBP
Z3-HHC	Mil Mi-17 (Reservation)	unkn	
Z3-HHD	Mil Mi-17 (Reservation)	unkn	
Z3-HHE	Mil Mi-17 (Reservation)	unkn	
Z3-HHF	Mil Mi-17 (Reservation)	unkn	

Regn.	Type	C/n	Prev.Id.
Z3-...	Antonov AN-2R	1G167-04	YU-BJZ
Z3-...	Cessna 210K Centurion	59422	D-EOCV
			N8122G
Z3-...	Piper PA-28-181 Archer II	28-8490030	N4332B

BALLOONS

Z3-OOA	Cameron V-65 HAFB	657	G-BHOU

GLIDERS

Z3-4001	Pilatus B4-PC11AF	303	YU-4266
Z3-4002	Pilatus B4-PC11AF	304	YU-4267
Z3-4003	VTC-75 Standard Cirrus	193 ?	YU-4279 ?
Z3-4004	Glaser-Dirks DG-100 Elan	E-37	YU-4318
Z3-4005	VTC-76 VUK-T	343	YU-4419
Z3-4006	VTC-76 VUK-T	297	YU-4382
Z3-4007	VTC-76 VUK-T	319	YU-4397
Z3-4008	VTC-76 VUK-T	379	YU-4433
Z3-4009	VTC-76 VUK-T	269	YU-4358
Z3-4010	VTC-76 VUK-T	303	YU-4374
Z3-4011	VTC-76 VUK-T	337	YU-4413
Z3-4012	VTC-76 VUK-T	286	YU-4365
Z3-4013	VTC-76 VUK-T	334	YU-4407
Z3-5001	LET L-13 Blanik	174903	YU-5327
Z3-5002	LET L-13 Blanik	174904	YU-5328
Z3-5003	LET L-23 Super Blanik	897515	YU-....
Z3-5004	LET L-23 Super Blanik	968301	
Z3-5005	LET L-23 Super Blanik	968302	
Z3-5006	LET L-23 Super Blanik	988318	

3A - MONACO

Regn.	Type	C/n	Prev.Id.
3A-MAC(2)	Aérospatiale AS.350B Ecureuil	1673	HB-XBC
			F-WZKS
3A-MBF	SIAI-Marchetti SF.260D	789	
3A-MBG	Cessna R.182 Skylane RG	01979	N6322T
3A-MBT	Piper PA-31T Cheyenne	31T-7920039	HB-LOZ
			N32745
			C-GVON
			(N610MW)
			N9739N
3A-MCH	Cessna 310R	0128	F-BFOD
			N5004J
3A-MEC	Aérospatiale AS.355F1 Ecureuil 2	5271	I-LIEM
			PH-SLB
			EC-DTO
			CC-CJH
			EC-DTO
			PH-SLB
			(PH-VDL)
			F-WZKD
3A-MGG	Agusta-Bell 47J-3	2114	MM80496
3A-MGR	Dassault Falcon 20F	473	F-GEJR
			F-WRQT
3A-MIK	Aérospatiale AS.350BAEcureuil	1091	I-ELIL
			3A-MMB
			HB-XGW
3A-MIO	Piper PA-31T Cheyenne	31T-7920001	I- NANE
			N123HK
			N333P
3A-MJP	Aérospatiale SA.365C3 Dauphin 2	5015	F-WYMC
			N90049
3A-MKC	Aérospatiale AS.350B Ecureuil	1760	
3A-MKQ	Robin DR.400/120	2185	
3A-MLD	Aérospatiale AS.350B Ecureuil	1357	F-GCQD
3A-MLE	Robinson R-22M2 Mariner	2787M	
3A-MLG	Aérospatiale SA.315B Lama	2641	F-GEPU
			G-BNHZ
			N5803H
3A-MLM	SOCATA TB-20 Trinidad	720	F-GHGA
			D-EKHC
3A-MLS	Bell 206B Jet Ranger II	3661	C-GWPI
			ZK-HSP
3A-MNB	Aérospatiale AS.350B Ecureuil	1043	I- ARIT
3A-MOI	Partenavia P.68B	19	F-GDRY
			I-VICV
			G-BCFM
3A-MON(3)	Beech C90 King Air	LJ-710	D- IAFH
3A-MPR	Aérospatiale SA.341G Gazelle	1225	F-GHGO
			C-FBRM
			N895SC
			N31PA
			(N7605B)
			N31PA
3A-MRL	Beech C90A King Air	LJ-1391	HB-GJE
3A-MSB	Piper PA-31T Cheyenne	31T-7820010	G-GGAT
			D-IFPD
			N333PD
			N82211
3A-MSY	Aérospatiale AS.365N2 Dauphin 2	6467	F-WQDP
			F-WYMH
			F-GJGD
			(F-GJRF)
			F-WYMH
3A-MTP	Aérospatiale AS.350B2 Ecureuil	1996	I-LOLO
3A-MTT	Aérospatiale AS.350B2 Ecureuil	1967	I-LUPJ
3A-MTV	Aérospatiale AS.365N Dauphin 2	6096	F-OHNZ
			RP-C1304
			9V-BOW
			F-WYMX
			G-PDES
			G-BKXK
3A-MVB	Cessna 152	80070	F-GHKC
			N757VW
3A-MYO	Eurocopter EC.120B Colibri	1036	

Regn.	Type	C/n	Prev.Id.

GLIDERS

Regn.	Type	C/n	Prev.Id.
3A-MCD(2)	Rolladen-Schneider LS-7	7135	
3A-MPV	Caproni Vizzola A.21S Calif	202	F-CGPV
			I- CCPV
3A-MTO	Siren C.30S Edelweiss	22	F-CCUT

BALLOONS

Regn.	Type	C/n	Prev.Id.
3A-MAS	Cameron C-80 HAFB	3205	

5B - CYPRUS

Regn.	Type	C/n	Prev.Id.
5B-CAR	Reims/Cessna F.172H	0461	
5B-CAS	Piper PA-25-235 Pawnee C	25-4247	N4579Y
5B-CBE	MBB Bölkow BO.105S	S-579	D-HDQB(2)
5B-CBP	Reims/Cessna F.150L	0744	N4798
5B-CBW(2)	Reims/Cessna F.172M	0999	(D-EGBX)
5B-CDM	Piper PA-31-310 Navajo	31-263	5B-CHO
			N9196Y
5B-CDP	Piper PA-28-140 Cherokee B	28-25790	G-AXIP
			N11C
5B-CDR	Cessna 152	82172	G-BGIA
			G-SACC
			G-BGIA
			N68187
5B-CDU	Cessna 182P Skylane	60868	G-AZLD
			N9328G
5B-CDV	Piper PA-38-112 Tomahawk	38-78A0523	HB-PCT
			N4413E
5B-CDW	Piper PA-25-260 Pawnee C	25-5377	5B-CBM
			N8914L
5B-CEE	Cessna 152-II	80522	N25059
5B-CEK	Reims/Cessna F.152-II	1643	N1662Q
			N8812L
5B-CEL(2)	Piper PA-31-350 Navajo Chieftain	31-7305083	N4NP
			N1NP
5B-CEM	Reims/Cessna F.172P	1445	G-BEMC
5B-CEN	Cessna 172M	61918	N8064H
			OD-PAI
			(N12296)
5B-CFC	Bell 47G-5	7868	4X-BBB
5B-CFM	Piper PA-23-250 Aztec B	27-2311	G-ASFG
5B-CFO	Piper PA-28-140 Cherokee B	28-26253	G-AXTG
			N11C
5B-CFQ	Westland-Bell 47G-3B1	WA/372	G-BFLS
			XT213
5B-CFR	Agusta-Bell 47G-3B1	1590	G-BFFV
	(CofA exp 8.6.89)		XT124
5B-CFU	Agusta-Bell 47G-3B1	1577	G-BIEB
	(CofA exp 8.6.89)		HB-XHS
			XT111
5B-CFV	Bell 47G-2A1	3173	G-BJFI
			TF-HUG
			63-13673
5B-CFX	Bell 47G-5A	25084	G-AZVW
			N14811
5B-CFY	Bell 47G-5A	25085	G-AZVX
			N14812
5B-CFZ	Piper PA-28-140 Cherokee D Fliteliner	28-7125287	N481FL
5B-CGA	Piper PA-28-140 Cherokee E Fliteliner	28-7225317	N709FL
5B-CGC(2)	Piper PA-23-250 Aztec D	27-4570	G-AYZC
	(Derelict at Lakatamia 1996)		N13955
5B-CGD(2)	Piper PA-24-180 Comanche	24-1344	G-NUNN
			G-AWKW
			N6239P
5B-CGE	Piper PA-23-250 Aztec C	27-2546	G-BAJU
			N5459Y
5B-CGI	Westland-Bell 47G-3B1	WA/566	G-BDVJ
			843OM
			XV312
			G-17-14
5B-CGL	Cessna E310K	0068	G-ATLD
	(Wfu 1996)		N6968L
5B-CGS	Cessna 340A	0076	C-GAWM
			N1377G
5B-CGU	Piper PA-31-310 Navajo	31-681	G-TISH
			G-BFKJ
			N506V
5B-CHC	Cessna 150F	62319	N3519L
5B-CHD	Britten-Norman BN-2A-26 Islander	166	(OD-...)
			G-BJWL
			4X-AYC
			G-51-166

Regn.	Type	C/n	Prev.Id.
5B-CHE	Lockheed L-1329 Jetstar 731	5114/18	N26GL
			N111GU
			N94K
			N930M
			N930MT
			N7959S
5B-CHG	Britten-Norman BN-2A-26 Islander	870	G-BFCX
5B-CHJ	Cessna 150M	77421	N63603
5B-CHM	Piper PA-28-181 Cherokee Archer II	28-7790178	N7050F
5B-CHP	Cessna 172N	72480	N5263D
5B-CHQ	Cessna 150M	79143	N714FN
5B-CHS	Cessna 150K	71827	N6327G
5B-CHU	Piper PA-44-180 Seminole	44-7995028	N39726
5B-CHV	Britten-Norman BN-2A-26 Islander	878	G-PASZ
			G-BPCD
			G-BFNV
5B-CHW	Grob G.115A	8101	
5B-CHY	Grob G.115A	8097	D-EGVV
			F-GGOK
			(A6-...)
5B-CIA	Piper PA-28R-201 Arrow III	28R-7837131	N3705M
5B-CIB	Reims/Cessna F.152	1611	G-BGVI
5B-CIC	Reims/Cessna FA.152 Aerobat	0362	G-STAP
			EI-BIE
5B-CIH	Helio H-700 Stallion Amphibian	H-7	N961RD
			N40353
5B-CII	Piper PA-38-112 Tomahawk	38-82A0082	N91591
5B-CIK	Piper PA-31-350 Navajo Chieftain	31-7305111	N66549
			C-GNIR
			N74962
5B-CIR	Reims/Cessna F.172H	0482	5B-CCC
			G-AWGW
5B-CIT	Cessna 152	85310	N67794
5B-CIV	Rockwell Commander 112B	500	N1162J
5B-CIW	Cessna 150E	61383	G-ATEG
			N3983U
5B-CIX	Piper PA-34-200 Seneca	34-7350250	OH-PNH
			(SE-IRO)
			OH-PNH
5B-CIY	Reims/Cessna F.172H	0448	G-AVUL
5B-CIZ	Slingsby T-61D Falke	1723	NEJSGSA-9
			G-AYPY
5B-CJA	Piper PA-38-112 Tomahawk	38-82A0018	N91373
5B-CJB	Cessna 150M	78205	G-BRLW
			N9255U
5B-CJF	Republic RC-3 Seabee	894	N6621K
5B-CJG	IAI 1125 Astra SPX	099	N987A
5B-CJH	Hughes 269C	100-0050	N9633F
5B-CJI	Piper PA-34-220T Seneca III	34-8233134	G-MRPP
			N8202P
5B-CJJ	Republic RC-3 Seabee (Reservation)	unkn	
5B-CJK	Cessna 310R	0252	SX-CRY
			(SX-AAT)
			N44HB
5B-CJL	Beech 65 Queen Air (Reservation)	unkn	
5B-CJM	Beech 200CSuper King Air	BL-11	PH-SKP
			F-GIMD
			N41JK
			(5H-...)
			I-MADY
			D-INEF
5B-CJN	DHC-6 Twin Otter Srs 310	572	5N-AKY
			PH-SAK
			C-GSXW
5B-CJO	Robinson R-44 Clipper	0632	
5B-CJP	Cessna T337GP Pressurized Skymaster	P3370185	D-ICSK
			HB-LHX
			N87S
5B-C..	Dassault MD.312 Flamant	250	F-AZEN
			Fr.AF
5B-C...	Piper PA-28-140 Cherokee	28-7425268	N41656
5B-C..	Republic RC-3 Seabee	441	C-GGXD
	(Possibly intended as 5B-CJJ)		N6238K

Regn.	Type	C/n	Prev.Id.
5B-DAQ	Airbus A.310-203	300	F-WZEG
5B-DAR	Airbus A.310-203	309	F-WZEM
5B-DAS	Airbus A.310-203	352	F-WZEO
5B-DAT	Airbus A.320-231	0028	YU-AOB
			5B-DAT
			F-WWDE
5B-DAU	Airbus A.320-231	0035	F-WWDX
5B-DAV	Airbus A.320-231	0037	F-WWDN
5B-DAW	Airbus A.320-231	0038	F-WWDZ
5B-DAX	Airbus A.310-204	486	F-WWBN
5B-DBA	Airbus A.320-231	180	F-WWIT
5B-DBB	Airbus A.320-231	256	F-WWBH
5B-DBC	Airbus A.320-231	295	F-WWIE
5B-DBD	Airbus A.320-231	316	F-WWBC
5B-DBE	Boeing 727-30	18371	9M-SAS
			V8-BG2
			V8-BG1
			V8-UHM
			N727CH
			VS-UHM
			VR-UHM
			VR-BHP
			N727CH
			D-ABIQ
5B-HAA	Bensen B-80 Gyrocopter	2513	
5B-HAC	Rutan RA-40 Defiant	162	
5B-HAD			
5B-HAE	Reservation for Homebuilt for D.Charalantas		
5B-HAF	Murphy Rebel	"12174"	
	(Not a Murphy c/n, possibly PFA232-12174 ?)		
5B-HAG	Bede BD-5B (Reservation)	5156	(5B-CBR(2))
5B-HAH	FIB Polaris	unkn	
5B-HAI	FIB Polaris	unkn	
5B-HAJ	Mainair Gemini/Flash IIA (Reservation)		
5B-HAK	Mainair Gemini/Flash IIA (Reservation)		
5B-HAL	Bill Parsons Gyrocopter (Reservation)		
5B-PBY	Canadian Vickers PBY-5A Catalina	CV-333	C-FPQF
			CF-PQF
			RCAF11042

Aircraft operated by Cyprus Police:

CP-1	Pilatus Britten-Norman BN-2T Islander	2207	5B-CPA
	(Still officially registered 5B-CPA)		G-CYPP
			G-BPLO
CP-2	Bell 412SP	33202	(5B-CPB)
			N3216P
CP-4	Bell 412SP	unkn	
CP-?	Bell 412EP	36155	N72335

NORTHERN CYPRUS

No ICAO prefix has been allocated to the Turkish-backed breakaway region of Northern Cyprus. The following are the only aircraft known to be operating under the unofficial prefix of KKH.

KKH-001	Mil Mi-17		unkn
KKH-002	Mil Mi-17		unkn

Services between Turkey and Northern Cyprus are operated by Kibris Türk Hava Yollari (Cyprus Tutkish Airlines) which is 50% owned by THY.
KTHY currently operate ex-THY Boeing 727s TC-JBF, -JBG, -JBJ and -JEC, together with Airbus A.310s TC-JCO, -JYK and -TMT, full details of which will be found in the Turkish section. Occasional short-term leases are also made.

9A - CROATIA

Regn.	Type	C/n	Prev.Id.
9A-BAA(2)	Antonov AN-2	1G110-36	(9A-BTT)
			UR-35070
			CCCP35070
9A-BAE	Reims/Cessna F.150K	0559	(9A-DTT)
			I-ALAP
			(HB-CUC)
9A-BAG	Piper PA-23-250 Aztec	27-334	RC-BAG
			YU-BAG
			N6830Z
9A-BAN	LET L-410UVP	851407	UR-67503
			CCCP67503
9A-BDJ	Piper PA-25-235 Pawnee B	25-3260	RC-BDJ
			YU-BDJ
			N7314Z
9A-BDM	Reims/Cessna F.172H	0351	YU-BDM
9A-BDR	Reims/Cessna F.172H	0412	RC-BDR
	(new fuselage c/n 2062 fitted?)		YU-BDR
9A-BFT	Antonov AN-2R	1G99-16	YU-BFT
9A-BHT	Antonov AN-2R	1G135-43	Croatia AF
			YU-BHT
9A-BHV	Antonov AN-2R	1G135-45	YU-BHV
9A-BIE	Cessna A.188B Agwagon	01073	RC-BIE
			YU-BIE
			N21847
9A-BKA	Antonov AN-2	1G167-05	Croatia AF
			YU-BKA
9A-BKC	Antonov AN-2R	1G167-07	YU-BKC
9A-BKK	Antonov AN-2	1G185-28	UR-54868
			CCCP54868
9A-BKP	Cessna A.188B Agtruck	02875T	YU-BKP
			N731GB
9A-BKS	Cessna A.185F Skywagon	03325	RC-BKS
			YU-BKS
			N5152H
9A-BLA	Cessna A.188B Agwagon	02943	RC-BLA
			YU-BLA
			N731KA
9A-BLF	Piper PA-25-235 Pawnee C	25-7305527	RC-BLF
			YU-BLF
			YU-BIT
			N6785L
9A-BLP	Piper PA-36-300 Pawnee Brave	36-7860075	RC-BLP
			YU-BLP
			N9702N
9A-BLT	Piper PA-36-300 Pawnee Brave	36-7860088	RC-BLT
			YU-BLT
			N9686N
9A-BMA	Antonov AN-2R	1G181-46	RC-BMA
			YU-BMA
			SP-DEK
9A-BMH	Piper PA-28R-201T Arrow IV	28R-7803313	N36192
9A-BMN	Piper PA-25-260 Pawnee D	25-8056006	RC-BMN
			YU-BMN
			N9777N
9A-BNA	LET L-410UVP	851518	CCCP67554
9A-BOF	Antonov AN-2R	1G223-56	RC-BOF
			YU-BOF
9A-BOG	Antonov AN-2	1G214-08	CroatiaAF
			YU-BOG
9A-BOL	Cessna 172N	69410	N174LG
			N737GQ
9A-BOW	Antonov AN-2R	1G223-57	RC-BOW
			CroatAF"BOW"
			YU-BOW
9A-BPR	Reims/Cessna FR.172J Rocket	0578	RC-BPR
			YU-BPR
			PH-DIK
			D-EDBF
9A-BTT	Reims/Cessna F.172M	0972	(9A-BAF)
			D-EDEI
			F-WLIL

Regn.	Type	C/n	Prev.Id.
9A-BTA	LET L-410UVP-E	912538	OK-WDO
			J2-KBE
			OK-WDD
			CCCP67670
9A-BZB	Antonov AN-2	1G225-40	RA-33321
			CCCP33321
9A-CAB	Canadair CL.215-IA10	1004	C-FYWQ
			CF-YWQ
			CF-PQH
9A-CAC	Canadair CL.215-IA10	1012	C-FTXE
			CF-TXE
			CF-PQQ
9A-CAF	Champion 7GCBC Citabria	255-70	YU-CAF
9A-CAG	Canadair CL.215-6B11	2027	C-FZQZ
9A-CAH	Canadair CL.215-6B11 (Code "55")	2041	C-GEUN
9A-CBW	Reims/Cessna FRA.150L Aerobat	0203	RC-CBW
			YU-CBW
9A-CCE	Cessna 207 Skywagon	00232	RC-CCE
			YU-CCE
			N1632U
9A-CCG	Reims/Cessna F.150L	1044	RC-CCG
			YU-CCG
9A-CCH	Reims/Cessna F.150L	1040	RC-CCH
			YU-CCH
9A-CDH	Reims/Cessna F.150M	1368	RC-CDH
			YU-CDH
9A-CDZ	Reims/Cessna F.172H	0427	YU-CDZ
			D-EBUF
9A-CGZ	SOCATA MS.893E Rallye 180GT Gaillard	12269	OE-KTL
			D-EEOG
			F-BUJG
9A-CRO(2)	Canadair CL.600-2B16 Challenger	5322	N604CL
			C-GLXY
9A-CRT	Canadair CL.600-2B16 Challenger	5067	9A-CRO(1)
			N603CC
			C-GLXF
9A-CTF	Airbus A.320-211	258	F-OKAI
			F-GMAI
			(F-GHQN)
			F-WWBJ
9A-CTG	Airbus A.319-112	767	F-WWDF
			D-AVYA
9A-CTH	Airbus A.319-112	833	D-AVYJ
9A-CTI	Airbus A.319-112	1029	D-AVYC
9A-CTJ	Airbus A.320-214	1009	F-WWDN
9A-CTS	Aeritalia/SNIAS ATR-42-300	312	F-WWEK
9A-CTT	Aeritalia/SNIAS ATR-42-300	317	F-WWEO
9A-CTU	Aeritalia/SNIAS ATR-42-300	394	F-WWLJ
9A-DAA	Cessna 152	80199	SE-KEB
			LN-MTG
			N24293
9A-DAB	Cessna T.210N Turbo Centurion II	64104	(9A-CBA)
			SL-CBA
			(YU-BPT)
			N5168Y
9A-DAD	Cessna 172R	80174	N9362F
9A-DAE	Aero Commander 560F	1279-55	D-IACT
			(SE-EDX)
9A-DAF	Reims/Cessna FR.172J Rocket	0390	D-ECZP
9A-DAH	Reims/Cessna F.150K	0631	RC-DAH
			YU-DAH
			F-BRXV
9A-DAJ	Reims/Cessna F.150L	0814	D-EEYS
9A-DAL	Cessna 175A/Horton STOL	56586	C-FCZV
			CF-CZV
			N7086E
9A-DAM	Antonov AN-2	1G212-53	CCCP32748
9A-DAP	Cessna 172R	80690	N2285P
9A-DAS	Cessna 172N	69567	N737PL
9A-DAT	Piper PA-23-250 Aztec E	27-7554060	OY-BLK
9A-DAV	Antonov AN-2	1G199-09	CCCP31500
9A-DAX	Piper PA-23-250 Aztec F	27-7854135	N611WW
9A-DAZ	UTVA-66	unkn	JRV51...?
9A-DBB	Cessna 152	80886	N25968

Regn.	Type	C/n	Prev.Id.
9A-DBD	Piper PA-31-325 Navajo	31-7512008	D-INJA
			N61508
9A-DBR	Piper PA-18-150 Super Cub	18-7809172	RC-DBR
			YU-DBR
			N82405
9A-DBS	Piper PA-18-150 Super Cub	18-7809170	RC-DBS
			YU-DBS
			N82370
9A-DBU	Piper PA-18-150 Super Cub	18-7809169	RC-DBU
			YU-DBU
			N82196
9A-DBW	Cessna 172M	67560	N73587
9A-DCC	Cessna 152	83429	N49133
9A-DCI	Piper PA-18-150 Super Cub	18-7809155	YU-DCI
			N82073
9A-DDA	Piper PA-28-161 Warrior II	28-7916056	RC-DDA
			YU-DDA
			N21952
9A-DDD	Cessna 172N	73541	N5092G
9A-DDH	Reims/Cessna F.172N	1783	RC-DDH
			YU-DDH
9A-DEF	Cessna 172N	72636	RC-DEF
			YU-DEF
			N6209D
9A-DEG	Cessna 172N	72640	RC-DEG
			YU-DEG
			N6216D
9A-DEM	Reims/Cessna F.182Q Skylane	0095	RC-DEM
			YU-DEM
			N90114
9A-DEN	Cessna TU.206G Turbo Stationair II	0010/04656	RC-DEN
	(Reims-assembled)		YU-DEN
			N732BZ
9A-DFH	Reims/Cessna F.172N	1880	RC-DFH
			YU-DFH
			N1661Q
9A-DFK	Reims/Cessna F.172N	1978	RC-DFK
			YU-DFK
9A-DFO	Cessna 310R-II	1537	RC-DFO
			YU-DFO
			N5296C
9A-DGZ	Scheibe SF-25B Falke	4815	D-KBAX
9A-DIH	UTVA-75	unkn	RC-DIH
			YU-DIH
			JRV53206
9A-DIP	Beech A36TC Bonanza	EA-104	N36787
9A-DIT	Cessna A.150K Texas Taildragger	0046	N8346M
9A-DJI	UTVA-75	unkn	RC-DJI
			JRV53224
9A-DJZ	Piper PA-28-140 Cherokee Cruiser	28-7425212	N4998C
			N170SU
			N41259
9A-DKG	Air Tractor AT-400	400-0353	OE-ERP
9A-DKH	Piper PA-28-161 Warrior II	28-8216100	N8268D
9A-DKJ	Air Tractor AT-400	400-0372	YU-DLR
			OE-ETP
			N10126
9A-DLC	Cessna TU.206G Turbo Stationair II	07001	YU-DLC
			N9960R
9A-DLR	Beech A60 Duke	P-233	N71DG
	(Stored, for sale)		N711MP
			(N510NE)
			N710DL
			N711AA
9A-DMB	Cessna 172N	69959	YV-1919P
			N738GD
9A-DMI	Cessna 150M	76522	RC-DMI
			YU-DMI (1)
9A-DMJ	Reims/Cessna FR.172F Rocket	0078	RC-DMJ
			YU-DMJ
			D-EBMJ
9A-DML	Cessna 150M	76479	RC-DML
			YU-DML(1)
			N3373V

Regn.	Type	C/n	Prev.Id.
9A-DMM	Cessna 150M	79061	RC-DMM
			YU-DMM
			N714BY
9A-DMT	Cessna R.172K Hawk XP	2991	N758CP
9A-DMZ	Piper PA-28-201T Turbo Dakota	28-7921087	N2890G
9A-DNA	Cessna 177B Cardinal	01713	N34220
9A-DSB	Piper PA-25-235 Pawnee B	25-3876	Croatia AF
			YU-BDH
			N7713Z
9A-DSD	Piper PA-31P-425 Pressurized Navajo	31P-7630014	OE-FDE
			N321RL
			N57550
9A-DVJ	Cessna 172K	58601	N87452
9A-DVT	Cessna 172M	63632	(D-E . . .)
			OH-CMB
			C-GWMO
			N1503V
9A-DZB	Piper PA-23-250 Aztec E	27-7305143	OE-FKM
			D-IBRM
			N40379
9A-DZD	Reims/Cessna F.172M	1143	S5-DDB
			SL-DDB
			YU-CCJ
			(D-EIQW)
9A-DZP	Cessna 210L Centurion	60163	N127S
			N59212
9A-EMZ	Robin R.1180TD Aiglon	271	D-EOUP
			F-GCUP
9A-HAC	Mil Mi-8MTV-1	95978	RA-27155
			CCCP-27155
9A-HAD	Mil Mi-8MTV-1	95988	RA-27138
			CCCP-27138
9A-HAE	Mil Mi-8	10662	SP-SZR
			PLW-662
9A-HAF	Bell 206B Jet Ranger II	3435	TC-HNO
	(To be registered T9- . . .)		N411SB
			N20879
9A-HAG	Robinson R-22 Beta	2541	N595HS
9A-HBC	Agusta-Bell 206A Jet Ranger II	8333	RC-HBC
			YU-HBC
9A-HBD	Rotorway Exec 90	unkn	
9A-HBM	Agusta-Bell AB.212	5569	RC-HBM
			YU-HBM
9A-HBZ	Bell 206B Jet Ranger II	2762	RC-HBZ
			YU-HBZ
			N27697
9A-HCG	Bell 206B Jet Ranger II	2754	RC-HCG
			YU-HCG
			N27731
9A-HDB	Bell 206B Jet Ranger II	4152	RC-HDB
			YU-HDB
9A-HIH	Mil Mi-8T	99254272	RA-25774
			CCCP25774
9A-HIT	Bell 407	53013	
9A-HMF	Bell 206B Jet Ranger II	4290	N289CA
9A-HRH	Mil Mi-8MTV-1	95876	RA-27042
			CCCP27042
9A-H . .	Bell 206B Jet Ranger II	4444	N1209W
9A-H . .	Mil Mi-8T	99254291	RA-25775
			CCCP25775
9A-ISC	Dornier Do.28D-2 Skyservant	4171	(9A-NDH)
			Turkish AF
			58+96

The following aircraft are known to be in Croatia - either in storage or awaiting registry :-

YU-BIR	Piper PA-25-235C	25-7305525	N6766L
YU-CAR	Champion 7GCBC Citabria	2 . . -70	
YU-CNI	Polikarpov Po-2	unkn	JRV0027
YU-CPE	Aero-3	unkn	JRV40173
YU-CWE	Aero-3	unkn	JRV40105
YU-DBD	UTVA-60	unkn	JRV50503

Regn.	Type	C/n	Prev.Id.

BALLOONS

Regn.	Type	C/n	Prev.Id.
9A-OAA	Thunder AX7-77 HAFB	1372	"YU-Zagreb 01" YU-OAA
9A-OAB	Cameron O-56 HAFB	1739	YU-OAB
9A-OAC	Colt 77B HAFB	4296	
9A-OAD	Thunder AX7-77 HAFB	1632	RC-OAD YU-OAD
9A-OAE	Cameron V-77 HAFB	1524	
	(Identity now quoted for S5-OAW)		
9A-OAF	Tomi AX-7 HAFB	38/1997	HA-...
9A-OAG	Cameron N-77 HAFB	2345	S5-OAG YU-OAG
9A-OAR	Thunder AX8-90 HAFB	2634	
9A-OAS	Kubicek BB-33 HAFB	84	
9A-OA .	Colt 77A HAFB	1864	G-BTEH
9A-OOO	Colt 56 Bullet HAFB	3550	

MICROLIGHTS

Regn.	Type	C/n	Prev.Id.
9A-UAA	Apollo CX-19	unkn	
9A-UAB	Apollo CX-19	09/90	RC-UAB
9A-UAC	Apollo CX-19	51/90	RC-UAC
9A-UAE	Apollo CX-19	43/89	
9A-UAG	Lomac Trick	I P 0495	
9A-UAH	Polaris Lomac	unkn	
9A-UAI	Stratos II UL	001	
9A-UAJ	Spider	212	
9A-UAL	Polaris Lomac	unkn	
9A-UAN	Polaris Lomac	unkn	
9A-UAP	Pipistrel-15	unkn	
9A-UAR	Apollo CX Tandem	unkn	
9A-UAS	Apollo CX RGT	47/89	
9A-UAT	Struc TR 600	unkn	
9A-UAU	Rodaro Storch (Damaged 16.8.98)	67	
9A-UAV	Apollo CXM Racer GT	MZ 40/92	
9A-UBA	Apollo CX	0165-94	
9A-UBC	Apollo C4M	74/90	
9A-UBE	Apollo CX	MZE 049/89	
9A-UBF	Cross Country 503	0079-95	
9A-UBG	Apollo CX 19	01014390	
9A-UBH	Euro III Eurotrike	unkn	
9A-UBI	Apollo CX	67/90	
9A-UBJ	Pipistrel 15	15560150291	
9A-UBK	Apollo CXM	51/89	
9A-UBL	Apollo CX GYEV	02-017	
9A-UBM	Apollo C15	220	
9A-UBR	Pipistrel-15	01045	
9A-UBT	Lomac Trick	983716	
9A-UCV	Rodaro Storch	020	9A-UVC
9A-UDB	Apollo CX	MZE 047/89	
9A-UDD	Tucanov	104	RC-UDD
9A-UDK	Europa Aviation Europa II	B11 2984	
9A-UDN	Cosmos 50	unkn	
9A-UDR	Apollo CX-15	950104	
9A-UDZ	Rodaro Wallaby	unkn	
9A-UEI	Apollo CX	890605	
9A-UER	Hazzard-15	090/90-8	
9A-UEZ	Apollo CX	MZ 09/91	
9A-UFM	Apollo CX-M	960226	
9A-UFO	Rodaro Storch HS	190	
9A-UFS	Genesis	065	
9A-UGV	Apollo CX-M	960220	
9A-UHC	Pipistrel Spider	191	
9A-UHS	Apollo C4M	125/90	
9A-UJZ	Apollo C4M 1500	73/90	
9A-UKB	Firefly	unkn	
9A-UKC	Apollo CX-19	02368	
9A-UKZ	Apollo C4M	9017	
9A-ULI	Apollo CX-19	unkn	
9A-UMA	UL Plus 7	1511190494	

Regn.	Type	C/n	Prev.Id.
9A-UMN	Pipistrel 15	370070990	
9A-UNK	Apollo CX-14	unkn	
9A-UNM	Apollo CX Hazar	unkn	
9A-UPZ	Rand-Robinson KR-1	nil	RC-ZAD YU-ZAD
9A-URI	Rand-Robinson KR-2	nil	RC-ZAA YU-Z ..
	(ditched, 1.6.98)		
9A-URK	Pipistrel 15+4	1461140294	
9A-USB	Apollo CX	960248	
9A-USD	Pipistrel Basic	606-90	
9A-UTE	Pipistrel 5	unkn	
9A-UTM	Teenie Two	15/2029	(YU-XAE)
9A-UTZ	Pipistrel 15	560240191	
9A-UVC(2)	Pipistrel Basic	0231/96	
9A-UVG	Apollo CX-14	unkn	
9A-UVI	Pipistrel 15	unkn	
9A-UVL	Pipistrel 15	unkn	
9A-UVS	Pipistrel Plus 7	MZ150061190	
9A-UZD	Light Aero Avid Amphibian	AA-066	9A-XZD
9A-UZG	Rand-Robinson KR-1	002	9A-XZG

EXPERIMENTAL REGISTER

Regn.	Type	C/n	Prev.Id.
9A-XAC	Light Aero Avid Amphibian Catalina	140AB	
9A-XHS	VTC-3 Delfin	012	YU-4125
9A-XPC	UTVA Aero-3	unkn	YU-CPC JRV 40154
9A-XZV	Homebuilt	0001	RC-XZV

GLIDERS

Regn.	Type	C/n	Prev.Id.
9A-GAA	VTC-76 Vuk-T	310	YU-4388
9A-GAB	VTC-76 Vuk-T	383	YU-4437
9A-GAJ	SZD-51-1 Junior	B-1932	YU-4460
9A-GBA	LET L-13 Blanik	027048	(9A-GAA) 9A-5378 RC-5378 YU-5378
9A-GBB	LET L-13 Blanik (Wfu ?)	174102	(9A-GAB) 9A-5309 RC-5309 YU-5309
9A-GBC	LET L-13 Blanik	174918	(9A-GAF) 9A-5339 RC-5339 YU-5339
9A-GBD	LET L-13 Blanik	026720	(9A-GAG) 9A-5368 RC-5368 YU-5368
9A-GBE	LET L-13 Blanik	026641	(9A-GAM) 9A-5365 RC-5365 YU-5365
9A-GBF	LET L-13 Blanik	174809	(9A-GAO) 9A-5321 RC-5321 YU-5321
9A-GBG	LET L-13 Blanik	173059	OK-4824
9A-GBH	LET L-13 Blanik	026149	YU-5349
9A-GBK	LET L-13 Blanik	174530	(9A-GAU) 9A-5318 RC-5318 YU-5318
9A-GBM	LET L-13 Blanik	174529	YU-5317
9A-GBR	Glaser-Dirks DG-100 Elan	E-45	YU-4325
9A-GBS	VTC Standard Cirrus 75	213	YU-4304

Regn.	Type	C/n	Prev.Id.
9A-GCA	VTC-75 Standard Cirrus *(Crashed 9.99)*	198	(9A-GAE)
			9A-4285
			RC-4285
			YU-4285
9A-GCB	VTC-75 Standard Cirrus	214	(9A-GAH)
			9A-4308
			RC-4308
			YU-4308
9A-GCD	VTC-75 Standard Cirrus	212	(9A-GAT)
			9A-4306
			RC-4306
			YU-4306
9A-GJA	SZD-41A Jantar Standard	B-801	(9A-GAJ)
			9A-4263
			RC-4263
			YU-4263
9A-GKC	LET L-13 Blanik	174928	OK-1858
9A-GPA	Pilatus B4-PC11AF	291	(9A-GAC)
			9A-4251
			RC-4251
			YU-4251
9A-GPB	Pilatus B4-PC11AF	293	(9A-GAL)
			9A-4253
			RC-4253
			YU-4253
9A-GPC	Pilatus B4-PC11AF	285	(9A-GAN)
			9A-4245
			RC-4245
			YU-4245
9A-GPD	Pilatus B4-PC11AF	287	(9A-GAP)
			9A-4247
			RC-4247
			YU-4247
9A-GPE	Pilatus B4-PC11AF	295	(9A-GAR)
			9A-4255
			RC-4255
			YU-4255
9A-GPF	Pilatus B4-PC11AF	294	(9A-GAV)
			9A-4254
			RC-4254
			YU-4254
9A-GPI	Pilatus B4-PC11AF	292	YU-4252
9A-GP .	Pilatus B4-PC11AF	283	YU-4243
9A-GRA	SZD-30 Pirat	B-393	(9A-GAD)
			9A-4199
			RC-4199
			YU-4199
9A-GSB	LET L-13 Blanik	174821	YU-5324
9A-GSO	Meteor 57	unkn	RC-4111
			YU-4111

The following gliders are in Croatia awaiting registration or restoration:

9A-G ..	Libis-18	279-03	YU-5057
9A-G ..	Libis-18	unkn	YU-50 ..
9A-G ..	Pilatus B4 PC11	292	YU-4252
9A-G ..	UTVA Vrabac	unkn	YU-2 ...
9A-G ..	VTC-76 Vuk-T	262	YU-4351
9A-G ..	VTC-76 Vuk-T	265	YU-4354
9A-G ..	VTC-76 Vuk-T	unkn	YU-4368
9A-G ..	VTC-76 Vuk-T	unkn	YU-4372
9A-G ..	VTC-76 Vuk-T	292	YU-4379
9A-G ..	VTC-76 Vuk-T	unkn	YU-4393
9A-G ..	VTC-76 Vuk-T	320	YU-4398
9A-G ..	VTC-76 Vuk-T	unkn	YU-4403
9A-G ..	VTC-76 Vuk-T	unkn	YU-4404
9A-G ..	VTC-76 Vuk-T	335	YU-4405
9A-G ..	VTC-76 Vuk-T	unkn	YU-4409
9A-G ..	VTC-76 Vuk-T	unkn	YU-4418

9H - MALTA

Regn.	Type	C/n	Prev.Id.
9H-AAE	Agusta-Bell 47G-2	225	74+02
	(Reported dismantled 1997)		AS+392
9H-AAH	Bell 47G-2	1991	74+35
	(Dismantled for restoration 1997)		AS+394
9H-AAP	CASA C.212-100 Aviocar	009	EC-CRV
9H-AAQ	CASA C.212-100 Aviocar	119	(N505TF)
			9H-AAQ
			ECT-105
9H-AAR	CASA C.212-200 Aviocar	161	
9H-AAS	CASA C.212-200 Aviocar	162	
9H-AAV	SA.316B Alouette III	2288	LC2288
9H-AAW	SA.316B Alouette III *(Stored)*	2295	LC2295
9H-AAX	SA.316B Alouette III	2315	LC2315
9H-ABE	Boeing 737-2Y5	23847	
9H-ABF	Boeing 737-2Y5	23848	
9H-ABP	Airbus A.320-211	112	F-WWIF
9H-ABQ	Airbus A.320-211	293	F-WWDZ
9H-ABR	Boeing 737-3Y5	25613	
9H-ABS	Boeing 737-3Y5	25614	
9H-ABT	Boeing 737-3Y5	25615	
9H-ABW	Piper PA-28-160 Cherokee	28-586	HB-OVK
			N5500W
9H-ABY	Hughes 369HM (Floats)	62-0220M	MM80848
9H-ABZ	Bredanardi NH-500M *(Wfu 1997)*	122-0227M	MM80854
9H-ACA	Cessna 305M (O-1E) Bird Dog	0018	EI-34/
	(Wfu 1997)		MM612972
			61-2972
9H-ACC	Cessna 305M (O-1E) Bird Dog	0032	EI-25/
			MM612986
			61-2986
9H-ACD	Cessna 305M (O-1E) Bird Dog	0038	EI-26/
	(Target tug)		MM612990
			61-2990
9H-ACE	Cessna 305M (O-1E) Bird Dog	0035	EI-12/
			MM6212281
			62-12281
9H-ACG	Reims/Cessna F.177RG Cardinal RG	0056	G-AZUO
9H-ACJ(2)	Mooney M.20J Model 205	24-3084	SE-KYB
			N5272N
9H-ACL	Cessna 172M	60955	N20042
9H-ACR	Cessna 550 Citation II	0025	N78PR
			N78PH
			N664J
			N664JB
			N9014S
			EP-KIC
			(EP-KID)
			N3239M
9H-ACU	Pilatus Britten-Norman BN-2B-26 Islander	2159	9M-TAD
			G-TWOB
			G-BKJJ
9H-ACW	Cessna 152	85176	N6159Q
9H-ADA	SE.3160 Alouette III	1209	NethAF:A-209
9H-ADB	SE.3160 Alouette III	1399	NethAF:A-399
9H-ADD	Piper PA-42-720 Cheyenne III	42-8001101	N30MA
			F-GEHR
			N41139
9H-ADF	Pilatus Britten-Norman BN-2B-26 Islander	2156	G-LIPP
			G-BKJG
9H-ADH	Boeing 737-33A	27459	
9H-ADI	Boeing 737-33A	27460	N1787B
9H-ADJ	Boeing 737-4H6	27353	9M-MQI
9H-ADK	Boeing 737-4H6	27673	9M-MQN
			9H-ADK
			9M-MQN
9H-ADL	Boeing 737-4H6	27674	9M-MQO
			9H-ADL
			9M-MQO
9H-ADM	Boeing 737-382	24365	CS-TIB
9H-ADN	Boeing 737-382	25161	CS-TIK
9H-ADO	Boeing 737-430	27003	EI-COK
	(Reserved as D-ABKD 10.99)		D-ABKD(2)

698

Regn.	Type	C/n	Prev.Id.
9H-ADQ	Scottish Aviation Bulldog T.1	337	XX691
9H-ADR	Scottish Aviation Bulldog T.1	345	XX696
9H-ADS	Scottish Aviation Bulldog T.1	358	XX709
9H-ADT	Scottish Aviation Bulldog T.1	363	XX714
9H-UMA	Polaris Cross Microlight	4159717	
9H-UMB	Polaris FIB Amphibian	4297130	
9H-...	Piper PA-28-140 Cherokee Cruiser	28-7325009	D-EEGV
			OO-TGB
			N15167

Regn.	Type	C/n	Prev.Id.

LATE ADDITIONS:

Regn.	Type	C/n	Prev.Id.

ADDITIONS:

Regn.	Type	C/n	Prev.Id.
CS-T..	BAe. ATP	2025	G-BRLY / TC-THP / G-BRLY
D-AGYC	Boeing 767-304ER	28041	G-OBYC / D-AGYC / G-OBYC
D-CFLY	Cessna 560 Citation V	0145	N57ML / (N6877L)
D-O...	Cameron A-210 HAFB	3045	G-BUYH
ES-NOV	Antonov AN-28	1AJ003-3	RA-28814 / CCCP28814
F-G...	Robinson R-22M Mariner	2101M	3A-MJM
HB-Z..	Aérospatiale AS.350B1 Ecureuil	2174	G-MSDJ / G-BPOH
LN-G..	Rolladen-Schneider LS-8A	8010	SE-UTP / D-1646
LN-O..	Schweizer 269C-1	0071	N27HT / (HL....) / N69A
OH-PPI	Cessna 750 (for 5.00 delivery)	0115	
PH-...	Lindstrand LBL-180A HAFB	150	G-BWCL
TC-...	Beech 76 Duchess	ME-192	G-BXSK / EI-CMX / N60450
9A-...	Cessna T.303	00186	D-IHDM / N303CE / (N9558C)

DELETIONS:

Regn.	Type	Prev.Id.
D-AHLM	Exported as JA8930, 2.00	
D-KEBG(3)	Exported as OE-9423, 1.00	
D-4081	Exported as OO-YRV, 2.00	
EC-GFU	Exported as F-GNFU, 2.00	
OO-HFS	Exported as G-BIOA, 2.00	
PH-HJM	Cancelled	
SE-DYL	NTU, to N316FL, 2.00	
9H-ADO	Exported as F-GRNZ, 3.00	

Regn.	Type	C/n	Prev.Id.	Regn.	Type	C/n	Prev.Id.

AIR-BRITAIN SALES

Companion publications to European Registers Handbook 2000 are also available by post-free mail order from

Air-Britain Sales Department (Dept ERH00)
19 Kent Road, Grays,
Essex RM17 6DE

Orders may be sent by e-mail via our website or to mike@absales.demon.co.uk
Visa / Mastercard / Delta / Switch accepted - please give full details of card number and expiry date.

UNITED KINGDOM & IRELAND CIVIL AIRCRAFT REGISTERS 2000 £15.00 (Members) £18.50 (Non-members)

Acknowledged to be the leading publication of its type, now over 600 pages, with all current UK and Irish registered civil aircraft, including gliders, microlights and non-British aircraft based in the UK, airfield frequencies and many other features.

AIRLINE FLEETS 2000 £16.00 (Members) £19.50 (Non-members)

Over 2000 fleets listed by country plus numerous appendices including airliners in non-airline service, IATA and ICAO airline and base codes, operator index.

BUSINESS JETS INTERNATIONAL 2000   Hardback: £13.00 (Members) £16.00 (Non-members)
Softback: £12.00 (Members) £15.00 (Non-members)

Complete production lists of all purpose-built business jets with full 20,000+ registration and c/n cross-reference.

TURBOPROP AIRLINERS AND MILITARY TRANSPORTS OF THE WORLD 2000 £ To be announced

Detailed production lists of 80 turboprop airliner types including Eastern European and military transports with full cross-reference index.

JET AIRLINERS OF THE WORLD 1949-2000 £ To be announced

Including military transport, reconnaissance and surveillance types and variants. Detailed production lists of nearly 100 jet airliner types with expanded coverage of Russian-built types and purely military jet transports. Full cross-reference index containing over 45,000 registrations and serials.

THE BRITISH CIVIL AIRCRAFT REGISTERS 1919-1999 £30.00 (Members) £37.50 (Non-members)

Contains details of all known UK and Ireland registrations allotted, with information on type/model, c/ns, previous identities, original registration date and subsequent identity or fate for each entry. Covers K100 - K175, G-EAAA - G-EBZZ, G-AAAA - G-ZZZZ and EI- series including microlight registrations, plus 1919-29 colonial usage of G-AU, G-CA, G-CY, G-IA, G-NZ and G-UA batches. Some 49,000 entries, 912 pages.

BOEING 707/720/C-135 £30.00 (Members) £37.50 (Non-members)

Full production histories, airline and air force operators, registration index, almost 500 A4 pages, 200 colour and nearly 100 black & white photos.

MILITARY TITLES

Air-Britain also publishes a comprehensive range of military titles -
RAF Serial Registers
Detailed RAF aircraft type " Files "
Squadron Histories
Royal Navy Aircraft Histories

**IMPORTANT NOTE - Members receive substantial discounts on prices of all the above Air-Britain publications.
For details of membership - see overleaf or visit our website at http://www.air-britain.com**

AIR-BRITAIN MEMBERSHIP

If you are not already a member of Air-Britain, why not join now?

Members can receive -

Discounts on **Air-Britain Monographs**

Quarterly **Air-Britain Digest**
A4 size magazine containing articles of current and historical aviation interest with comprehensive black & white and colour photographic coverage.

Monthly **Air-Britain News**
A5 size magazine, normally with 140 pages, includes full coverage of UK civil and military aviation scene; comprehensive updates on virtually all overseas registers, including USA; sections on bizjets, bizprops and jet, turbine & piston-engined commercial aircraft; full coverage of air displays, UK and overseas. Illustrated in black & white and colour.

Quarterly - **Archive** and **Aeromilitaria.**
Historical A4 magazines packed with previously unpublished civil or military information and photos.

Access to our **Information Services, Black and White Photo and Colour Slide Libraries, Air-Britain Travel** to overseas airfields, museums and displays.

Access to our expanding **Branch Network.**

Basic Membership fee for 2000 is £33.00
(to include four Air-Britain Digests and twelve Air-Britain News).

Visa / Mastercard / Delta / Switch accepted - please give full card details including number and expiry date.

Full details of Membership and all our services are available on the Air-Britain website at
http://www.air-britain.com

Alternatively, to join or for more information please write to:-
Air-Britain Membership Department (Dept ERH00)
1 Rose Cottages
179 Penn Road
Hazlemere
Bucks HP15 7NE
United Kingdom

For samples of Air-Britain Digest and News, please enclose £1.00; with samples of Aeromilitaria and Archive please forward £2.00.